The *Papers* *of*
HENRY CLAY

Mary W. M. Hargreaves *and*

James F. Hopkins, *Editors*

VOLUME 6

SECRETARY OF STATE

1827

THE UNIVERSITY PRESS OF KENTUCKY

*"My ambition is that we may enter a new
and larger era of service to humanity."*

Dedicated to the memory of
JOSIAH KIRBY LILLY
1861–1948
President of Eli Lilly and Company
Founder of Lilly Endowment, Inc.

Whose wisdom and foresight were
devoted to the service of
education, religion, and
public welfare

ISBN: 0–8131–0056–9
Library of Congress Catalog Card Number: 59–13605

Copyright © 1981 by The University Press of Kentucky

Scholarly publisher for the Commonwealth,
serving Berea College, Centre College of Kentucky,
Eastern Kentucky University, The Filson Club,
Georgetown College, Kentucky Historical Society,
Kentucky State University, Morehead State University,
Murray State University, Northern Kentucky University,
Transylvania University, University of Kentucky,
University of Louisville, and Western Kentucky University.

Editorial and Sales Offices: Lexington, Kentucky 40506

PREFACE

With this volume James F. Hopkins and I retire as editors and successive directors of the Clay Papers Project, marking the termination of a happy working relationship which began with the inception of the program in 1952. Lewis Burton Milward, senior research assistant over the past fifteen years, also leaves at this time. E. Wayne Cutler, senior research associate when this volume was begun, has since become editor and project director of the Polk *Papers*; his place through most of the preparation of this volume was assumed by Richard Bland. Lynwood M. Dent, Jr., as a fellow, 1974–1975, under the editorial training program of the National Historical Publications and Records Commission, Catherine A. Dreier, typist and research assistant, 1975–1978, and Sheila Breeding, typist through the fall of 1978, also contributed to this effort. To all these people sincere thanks are due—and particularly to Dr. Hopkins, who not only remained with the project five years beyond his formal retirement but also joined me over yet another year in donating our time to see this work through the press so that forward progress might be uninterrupted. We welcome as the new project director Robert Seager II, who came to us in the fall of 1977 and becomes editor of the remaining volumes.

So momentous a transition in personnel at this midway stage in the program justifies a brief review of our goals and criteria. We began with an assumption that our work served the interests of a wide audience, both scholarly and nonprofessional in interest, concerned about identification and explanation of Clay's role in the local setting as well as on the national and international scenes. As a politician who held a leadership position for half a century, the Kentucky statesman provided a reflection of, and a directing force for, a significant segment of the society of that period. We aimed to illuminate that history, not merely the life of the individual. Such an approach provides, we believe, an across-the-board purview which monographic scholarship cannot readily attain, a background of correlative events which may shed light, both directly and indirectly, to the specialized concerns of other researchers.

The directions which those interests may take are not for us to delimit. We sought to cover as broad a gamut as the material and our understanding of it encompassed. We ruled out only the most routine official papers and the briefs of Clay's law practice, the latter being a highly specialized category which more professionally trained scholars might better explore. In administration of the estates of Thomas Hart and James Morrison, however, Clay was so personally involved, and in the Morrison executorship so politically implicated, that his role has been developed, usually by summary of the available documents. The close friendship (and familial ties in the case of James Brown) between Clay and several of the diplomatic emissaries during his service as Secretary of State led to such overlapping of official and personal correspondence that, again, blanket exclusion of professional documents was impracticable. From the standpoint of shedding light upon Clay's public activities, moreover, such exclusion was undesirable—as it was in relation to his long legislative career. But numerous categories of material clearly identifiable with the office rather than with Clay have been excluded; these categories are listed in the preface to Volume 4 and in the note to the "Circular" of June 8, 1826 (V, 420).

Letters strongly personal in content, whether incoming or outgoing, have been published in complete text. Clay's diplomatic role, generally neglected in historical literature, seemed to us to warrant full reproduction, also, of his outgoing instructions. In a few cases lengthy passages of official, routine, or repetitive comment have been summarized, within brackets, as parts of these major documents. More commonly, official correspondence has been provided in summary form, under subordinate headings, and in reduced type.

Letters of recommendation and application for office proved to include immensely valuable information on political organization with which Clay was intimately involved. In Volumes 4 and 5 and the first quarter of the present volume these documents were briefly noted and politically significant passages quoted. In Volume 6, however, space limitations have compelled us, with great regret, to omit "Applications and Recommendations" after March, 1827. We have provided, under the heading "Miscellaneous Letters," excerpts of the direct political content of this correspondence. The same space constraints made it necessary to summarize one lengthy Clay document, his *Address to the Public* of December 29, 1827, the text of which should be readily available through the designated sources.

Few standards of transcription had been established when our work was begun. Clarence Carter's pamphlet *Historical Editing* (National Archives Bulletin no. 7, 1952) became our guide, and we have adhered to it so far as practicable in our situation. We have not collected original manuscripts, although we have had access to material in that form through the extensive holdings of several local repositories—notably the Henry Clay Memorial Foundation, Transylvania University, the Filson Club, the Kentucky Historical Society, and the Margaret I. King Library of the University of Kentucky. A great many privately held letters have also been put into our hands for direct transcription.

For the most part, however, we have worked from photographic copies —never, unless specifically so noted, from intermediary transcripts. We are aware that filmed reproduction can occasion some errors, most commonly in punctuation or obscured words along margins. We have checked most of our uncertainties by consulting original texts in the Library of Congress and the National Archives, and we have bracketed insertions where we know that something was written which we could not fully see. Incidentally, we have found that occasionally the photographic process clarifies faded letters scarcely visible to the naked eye.

For the generous cooperation of several hundred library and private owners who have supplied us with reproductions of documents from their collections, we are most appreciative. Few have imposed restrictions upon our making this material available either by publication or through use of our typescripts. We have, however, insisted that the owners of the originals be cited, and consulted if access is desired to the original form of the documents. Transcription inherently introduces the possibility of error, a circumstance which retains for the manuscript primary value.

We have, nevertheless, attempted to reproduce texts as exactly as press limitations permit duplication of script. Our typescripts retain the author's interlineations and deletions until the copy is set in type. At that stage the former are incorporated in the main text and the latter are omitted, with notation only when the emendations have seemed to us significant. Public papers written during Clay's incumbency as Secretary of State sometimes exist in several preliminary forms; because the process of policy development may hold importance for scholars, such variations have been carefully collated and noted. The document in final form or the letter as it was viewed by the recipient constitutes our preferred text. While State Department letterbook copies have been officially accepted as texts, where personal or legation files of the recipients provide the document in the form it was received, we have substituted that version.

We do not interject editorial changes in documents fully transcribed. Our bracketed insertions are generally limited to material obliterated at margin or by seal and signify that the writer produced the text as supplied. In rare instances bracketed words have been italicized, indicating some degree of doubt. If words are indecipherable, however, we customarily enclose ellipses in brackets and note the extent of the omission. We do not "correct" capitalization, spelling, or paragraphing. If the completion of a parenthesis or quotation marks has been omitted, we do not attempt to amend the error. Use of the bracketed word *"sic"* has been limited to the first occasion of misspelling of a given word in the document and to situations which might reasonably be attributed to mistranscription or printing error. We have assumed that the reader's judgment is as good as ours in interpreting textual irregularities.

Clarity and economy do, however, necessitate a few formal alterations. Letters in superscript, denoting abbreviations, have been lowered; where this appears to occasion confusion, the abbreviation is annotated. The common manuscript use of a single or double period, ditto marks, a colon, a hyphen, or a dash under such elevated letters has been consolidated in the form of a single period following the abbreviation. Circumflex or linkage lines over abbreviations have been dropped. Brackets appearing in the text have been changed to braces. Words run together have been divided. When a date appears at the end of a document, it has been shifted to the heading. Salutations and complimentary closings have been realigned.

A project of this scope quickly demanded efforts greater than the capacities of the editors who initiated it, and with growth in organizational structure came a need for funding. From the first we have had the assistance of the University of Kentucky Research Foundation. In 1957 the Lilly Endowment, Inc., provided the basic grant under which a research staff was established and publication of the papers was begun. Since 1964 the National Historical Publications (and Records) Commission has joined in support. For all this aid we are immensely grateful. We relinquish our work now with regret that it is unfinished but with confidence that Clay's *Papers* will continue to generate for others the excitement that has so long held us enthralled.

M. W. M. H.

SYMBOLS

The following symbols are used to describe the nature of the originals of documents copied from manuscript sources.

AD	Autograph Document
AD draft	Autograph Document, draft
ADI	Autograph Document Initialed
ADS	Autograph Document Signed
AE	Autograph Endorsement
AEI	Autograph Endorsement Initialed
AES	Autograph Endorsement Signed
AL	Autograph Letter
AL draft	Autograph Letter, draft
ALI	Autograph Letter Initialed
ALI copy	Autograph Letter Initialed, copy
ALI draft	Autograph Letter Initaled, draft
ALS	Autograph Letter Signed
ALS draft	Autograph Letter Signed, draft
AN	Autograph Note
AN draft	Autograph Note, draft
ANI draft	Autograph Note Initialed, draft
ANS	Autograph Note Signed
Copy	Copy not by writer (indicated "true" if so certified)
D	Document
DS	Document Signed
L	Letter
L draft	Letter, draft
LI draft	Letter Initialed, draft
LS	Letter Signed
N	Note
N draft	Note, draft
NS	Note Signed

The following, from the *Symbols Used in the National Union Catalog of the Library of Congress* (9th ed., rev.; Washington, 1965), indicate the location of the original documents in institutional libraries of the United States.

CSmH	Henry E. Huntington Library and Museum, San Marino, California

CtY	Yale University, New Haven, Connecticut
DLC	Library of Congress, Washington, D. C.
DLC-HC	Library of Congress, Henry Clay Collection
DLC-TJC	Library of Congress, Thomas J. Clay Collection
DNA	United States National Archives Library, Washington, D. C. Following the symbol for this depository the letters A. and R. mean Applications and Recommendations; M, Microcopy; P. and D. of L., Publication and Distribution of the Laws; R, Reel; and RG, Record Group.
IHi	Illinois State Historical Society, Springfield, Illinois
InHi	Indiana Historical Society, Indianapolis, Indiana
InU	Indiana University, Bloomington, Indiana
KyHi	Kentucky Historical Society, Frankfort, Kentucky
KyLoF	Filson Club, Louisville, Kentucky
KyLxT	Transylvania University, Lexington, Kentucky
KyU	University of Kentucky, Lexington, Kentucky
MB	Boston Public Library, Boston, Massachusetts
MH	Harvard University, Cambridge, Massachusetts
MHi	Massachusetts Historical Society, Boston, Massachusetts
MoSHi	Missouri Historical Society, St. Louis, Missouri
NBuHi	Buffalo Historical Society, Buffalo, New York
NcD	Duke University, Durham, North Carolina
NcU	University of North Carolina, Chapel Hill, North Carolina
NHi	New York Historical Society, New York City
NjP	Princeton University, Princeton, New Jersey
NN	New York Public Library, New York City
NNPM	Pierpont Morgan Library, New York City
OClWHi	Western Reserve Historical Society, Cleveland, Ohio
OCX	Xavier University, Cincinnati, Ohio
OMC	Marietta College, Marietta, Ohio
PHC	Haverford College, Haverford, Pennsylvania
PHi	Historical Society of Pennsylvania, Philadelphia, Pennsylvania
THi	Tennessee Historical Society, Nashville, Tennessee
ViU	University of Virginia, Charlottesville, Virginia

The Papers of HENRY CLAY

To Thomas I. Wharton

Dear Sir   Washington 1st. January 1827

With the Compliments of the Season, I transmit you inclosed the proposals which were made in Kentucky for the publication of my Speeches.[1] And I send by the same mail which carries this letter all the speeches mentioned in the proposals except those against which a cross is marked. The others are intended to be forwarded hereafter as soon as they can be got, together with my speech made at Lewisburg,[2] my Circular to my Constituents on the Presidential election[3] and some other petit choses. What is now transmitted may be about half. I should think that the whole matter would make an Octavo of from three to four hundred pages.

I repeat, that Mr Smith[4] may be perfectly relied on for the fulfillment of the contract. I am greatly obliged for your kind and friendly offer to superintend the publication. An author yourself you have a just conception of the feelings which one has who, for the first time, is about to appear in the perilous form of a book.

Your recommendation[5] of a director of the B. of the U. States did not reach this place until after the President had made his nomination of the directors for the ensuing year. It would otherwise have been duly weighed and considered. I am with high regard Cordially & faithfy. Yrs.

T.I. Wharton Esq   H Clay

ALS. KyLoF.   [1] Cf. below, Sparks to Clay, April 9, 1827, and note.
[2] Above, *ca.* August 30, 1826.   [3] Above, March 26, 1825.   [4] Thomas Smith.
[5] Not found.

From James Harper

H. Clay Esqr   Office B. U States
Dear Sir   Lexington Jany. 1. 1826 [*i.e.,* 1827]

I have the Satisfaction of informing you, that an arrangement was made by the Bank with the heirs of Doctr W. Warfield on the 27. Ulto. which Secures the payment of your $2400 debt in which he was Security for Major Parker[1]

The terms of the arrangement are that the Mortgage of Parker (on his Store House) which is now in Suit shall proceed to foreclosure and a Sale[2] be made under the decree at which the Bank guarantees the bid of a certain Sum agreed on (say $7000) and the heirs of Warfield on their part have paid in Cash and assigned Dr Richardsons Notes for the balance of the debts of Parker—and they are to have the benefit of the excess, if any, that may be bid for the property over the Sum we guarantee. It is desired that this Sum should not be publickly known as it might have an influence in fixing a price for the property when it would otherwise possibly sell for more than the $7000

Our doubts as to the intentions of the heirs & the difficulty we were likely to encounter in arresting them in any unfair course, had such been their object (which however it is but justice to them to say I am *now* satisfied they never intended) induced us to make the guarantee of a larger bid, than will probably be made by any individual & it is therefore probable the Bank will have to purchase the property.

After deducting the proportion of T T Crittendens Note (which is Secured in the Same Mortgage) from the $7000 there remains about $6000 to apply to Parkers Bank debt of $9500 and leaves the heirs of Warfield to pay & secure about $6.700 including your $2400 debt

Considering that they have also to pay Doctr Boswell[3] about $3000 for Parker, I think the arrangement may be viewed nearly as favourable to us as it may be esteemed hard on them

Doctr Warfields own proper debts remain to be Settled by his Admr and I understand from Col Quarles that the doubts he had about making the assignments will probably be removed—

With my wishes that the New year may in all respects be a happy & successful one to you— I remain with great regard Yr Ob Sevt

J HARPER CASHR

ALS. DLC-TJC (DNA, M212, R13). Addressed as "Private." Endorsed on verso by Clay: ". . . Answd. 13 Jan."; answer not found. Cf. above, Clay to Harper, December 6, 1826. [1] Cf. above, III, 519, 525, 549–50n.   [2] No record found.   [3] Joseph Boswell.

INSTRUCTIONS AND DISPATCHES   January 1, 1827

From G[EORGE] THEODORE LADICO, Port Mahon. Reports that tonnage duty in Spain on American ships is as high as one dollar per ton and that the Spanish King (Ferdinand VII) intends to take the duty off if Spanish ships in the United States are so exempted. ALS. DNA, RG59, Cons. Disp., Port Mahon, vol. 1 (M-T422, R1). Received August 2, 1827.

Ladico, of Port Mahon, was consul at that port, on the Island of Minorca, from 1820 to 1834.

From A[BRAHAM] B. NONES, Maracaibo. Announces plans to visit Bogotá and appointment of Joseph S. Marks as vice-consul in his absence. Notes that Marks is his secretary and a citizen of the United States. LS. *Ibid.*, Maracaibo, vol. 1 (M-T62, R1). Enclosed in Marks to Clay, January 8, 1827.

MISCELLANEOUS LETTERS   January 1, 1827

From A[uguste] P. Chouteau, "Cantonment, Gibson, Arks. Ty." States that he has "long delayed" his reply to Clay's "very acceptable letter of the summer of 1825" (above, Chouteau and De Mun to Clay, May 3, 1825, note) and observes that probably because of "the press of business" the government has not acted on his spoliation claim against Spain. Requests Clay's assistance in seeing the matter to "a speedy conclusion." ALS. DNA, RG176, Mexican Claims Commissions.

From J[ohn] Holmes, Senate. Requests a list of claims for "captures or injuries" from French spoliations for the period 1793 to 1800. Asks for details of the capture, destruction, and disposition of the property; for the amount of the seizures and detentions; whether the State Department has any additional evidence pertinent to these claims; and how additional evidence may be obtained. ALS. DNA, RG59, Misc. Letters (M179, R65). Holmes was acting as Chairman of the Senate's Select Committee on French Spoliations. For Clay's reply, see below, Clay to Holmes, January 22, 1827.

From William Wirt, Baltimore. Reports that he has assisted in prosecuting John Gooding for slave trading, as Clay requested "last Spring" (see above, May 16, 1826). Explains that he will be unable to complete the action because the session of the Supreme Court opening "next Monday" will require his presence in Washington. Suggests that Clay call on "Mr. Purviance" (probably John Purviance) to take his place, since Purviance has heard most of the evidence and "legal discussion." ALS. DNA, RG59, Misc. Letters (M179, R65). See below, Clay to Wirt, January 2, 1827.

From L[ewis] Wood, Huntsville (Alabama). Notes that he has been informed that the State Department will transmit the enclosed correspondence to Consul (Thomas) Aspinwall. Comments that Clay's conduct "on this matter will add another motive" for continuance as his "admirer." ALS. DNA, RG59, Misc. Letters (M179, R65).

On January 17, Daniel Brent informed Wood (not identified) that the papers had been forwarded as requested. Copy, in DNA, RG59, Dom. Letters, vol. 21, p. 458 (M40, R19).

APPLICATIONS, RECOMMENDATIONS   January 1, 1827

William L[ittle] Brown, Nashville, recommends Oliver B. Hayes for the office of United States attorney for the District of West Tennessee; mentions also Francis B. Fogg and William Thompson as "unexceptionable" and standing "very high in their profession"; and adds: "You are perhaps as well or better acquainted with Mr. Thompson than I am, as he studied law I believe with you—" ALS. DNA, RG59, A. and R. (M531, R4). Cf. above, Yeatman to Clay, December 29, 1826, note.

Francis Brinley Fogg, born and educated in Connecticut, had moved to Columbia, Tennessee, in 1818 and subsequently settled in Nashville, where he practiced law as a partner of Brown. Fogg served as a trustee of the University of Nashville for 57 years (1823–1880) and was elected as a Whig to the State Senate in 1851.

Formerly of Mercer County, Kentucky, William Thompson had practiced law in Glasgow, Kentucky, for twelve years before removing to Tennessee. For further reference to his study under Clay, see below, Thompson to Clay, January 3, 1827.

To Albert Gallatin

Dear Sir   Washington 2. Jan. 1827.
The Honble Mr. Hemphill,[1] late a distinguished member of the
House of Representatives, being about to visit Europe, I take much
pleasure in availing myself of the occasion to introduce him to your
acquaintance, as a gentleman enjoying deservedly high consideration
in this Country and especially in the State of Pennsylvania, of which
he is a Citizen. I am with great respect Faithfully Your ob. Servant
Albert Gallatin Esqr.   H. CLAY

ALS. NHi-Gallatin Papers (MR14).
[1] Joseph Hemphill visited porcelain factories in Europe and upon his return became
associated in business with William Ellis Tucker, of Philadelphia, the first porcelain
manufacturer in the United States.

From Nicholas G. Boss

Honble. Henry Clay.
Sir,   Newport January 2nd. 1827.
Understanding that Benjamin W. Case[1] is at Washington, and presuming that he will assume a character to which he is not entitled, I
take the liberty of enclosing a circular from the W. Grand Lodge of
this State, in order that you may fully understand his Masonic character. *The difficulty still exists*, and it may be of great service to the
regular masons here, if the enclosed should be perused by the Masons
of distinguished standing in Washington.[2] I am, Sir, with great respect
Your obedt. Servant   NICHOLAS G BOSS
Secretary of St. Johns Lodge No. 1

ALS. DNA, RG59, Misc. Letters (M179, R65). Boss had been a notary public and justice
of the peace for Newport County, Rhode Island, in 1824; from 1827 to 1831 he served as
a militia officer.
[1] Surgeon of the Rhode Island militia, 1812–1815.   [2] The enclosed circular states
that in 1818 the Worthy Grand Lodge of the Masonic Order in Rhode Island had ruled
that Case and his faction had been elected illegally to their offices in St. Johns' Lodge
No. 1 of Newport. Before a new election could be held, Case and his supporters had
"robbed" the Masonic Hall of its jewels, record books, by-laws, Masonic charter, and the
State charter by which the Lodge held its property. The Grand Lodge had responded on
November 30, 1818, by expelling Case and his associates from the Masonic Order.

MISCELLANEOUS LETTERS   January 2, 1827

To WILLIAM WIRT. Reports consultation with the President and relays instructions to ask "Mr. Purviance" (probably John Purviance) to assume Wirt's duties
in assisting the United States district attorney at Baltimore (Nathaniel Williams)
in the prosecution of John Gooding for slave trading. LS. DNA, RG60, Letters
Recd. from the State Department. See above, Wirt to Clay, January 1, 1827.
Gooding had been indicted before the United States Circuit Court for Maryland on a charge of fitting out and employing the vessel *General Winder* in the
slave trade. On a certificate of division the case was subsequently appealed to the
United States Supreme Court, where Associate Justice Joseph Story delivered an

opinion on March 16, 1827, resolving the procedural questions and remanding the case to the lower court for further adjudication. 25 *U. S.* (12 Wheaton) 460–78. As late as December, 1827, President Adams was receiving, and rejecting, appeals on Gooding's behalf that the prosecution be dropped. Adams, *Memoirs,* VII, 377. Further action has not been found.

From S[AMUEL] L. S[OUTHARD], Navy Department (1). Acknowledges receipt of "Mr. Bradfords letter of the 14th. ulto. referred . . . to this Department" and notes that it has been placed on file. Copy. DNA, RG45, Exec. Letterbook, 1821–1831, p. 232. The Bradford letter and Clay's note of transmittal have not been found. Cf. above, Southard to Clay, January 13, 1826.

From S[AMUEL] L. S[OUTHARD], Navy Department (2). Acknowledges receipt of "Mr. Starks letter of the 25th. ulto. referred . . . to this Department" and comments: "There is no vacancy in the Marine Corps at this time, nor is one expected to occur—" Copy. DNA, RG45, Exec. Letterbook, 1821–1831, p. 232. The Stark letter and Clay's note of transmittal have not been found; Stark has not been identified.

APPLICATIONS, RECOMMENDATIONS   January 2, 1827

WILLIAM THOMPSON, Nashville, noting the appointment of (Henry) Crabb to the (Tennessee) Supreme Court, wants his "pretensions to the office lately held by . . . [Crabb] to be weighed with those of other gentlemen." Comments that he will write again (see below, Thompson to Clay, January 3, 1827). ALS. DNA, RG59, A. and R. (M531, R8). Unaddressed. On the appointment, cf. above, Yeatman to Clay, December 29, 1826, note.

JOSEPH M. WHITE, Washington, recommends William Allison McRea to succeed Adam Gordon, whose resignation, as district attorney of Middle Florida, is enclosed. Urges an early appointment "as there is business . . . almost daily." Also recommends reappointment of the two marshals of East and West Florida (Waters Smith and William Sebree). ALS. DNA, RG59, A. and R. (M531, R5).

McRea, a Virginian, who had practiced law in Florida for the past year, was nominated to the recommended post on January 18 and confirmed on January 22, 1827. On May 26, 1828, he was appointed attorney for the newly created District of Southern Florida and held the latter office until his removal in 1829. On the marshals' reappointment, see below, Clay to Sebree, February 12, 1827; Clay to Smith, February 13, 1827.

From Charles Hammond

My Dear Sir   Cincinnati Jany 3d. 1827

   I received this morning your letter of the 23d of December— The application of Major Eaton was undoubedly [*sic*] a curious one. Suppose you had furnished me the documents alluded to, what right had Gen. Jackson to complain? He keeps no terms with you— Why should you not communicate *facts* that affected him? You were perfectly correct in the reply you made— I have addressed a letter to Major Eaton on this affair, a copy of which I enclose for your perusal[1]— This appeared to me the proper course— It was necessary that you should apprise me of the call upon you, and its objects— He could expect nothing less, and I thought it due to you and to myself to make a plain statement of facts to Major Eaton, for the reasons stated in my letter to him—

I have no doubt but that it is upon the difficulties that have arisen in respect to the colonial trade with the British West Indies that the opposition will break ground, if at all, during this Session— From that ground of attack they can, in my opinion, derive no advantage—

With respect to the Vice Presidency, my present opinion is that you should be the candidate. I have not leisure now to enter into the reasons upon which I found this opinion. But I shall take an occasion to do it before the congress rises.[2] Yours Sincerely

H. Clay Esqr   C. HAMMOND

ALS. DLC-HC (DNA, M212, R2).
[1] See above, Clay to Hammond, December 23, 1826, note.   [2] See below, Hammond to Clay, March 20, 1827.

From Peter B. Porter

Dear Sir,   (Private)   Albany January 3rd. 1827.

I arrived here, on monday last, from Black Rock, and the Legislature commenced its session on tuesday. I have no doubt but that there is a considerable majority of the members returned, opposed to the administration, and the general conviction of the truth of this fact, is calculated to make that majority still larger. I have not come to this conclusion, however, in consequence of any thing I have seen or heard since my arrival—for great reserve, & even coyness has [sic] been observed by a great proportion of the members in regard to the presidential question thus far. I am glad of this, for I was fearfull [sic] that the opposition would be disposed to push their presumed advantage and draw lines which could not, afterwards, be easily altered. However much the politicians at this place friendly to the Admn may have heretofore erred—and they unquestionably did err—in not availing themselves of their former superiority of force, it is, now, their obvious policy to avoid a direct encounter. The violent Jacksonians had selected a new man for speaker of the Assembly, but, finding that we should give Gen. Root a strong support, they made a merit of necessity & fell in with us.[1]

A new (daily) Administration paper will make its appearance in this city, next week, to be edited by a man of talents;[2] and I cannot but hope that it will produce the most favourable results. I shall take occasion to write to you frequently on the state of things at this place.

I forwarded some days since my seperate [sic] report under the 7th. article of the Treaty of Ghent, to Maj. Delafield,[3] for exchange. I received a letter from him, this day, saying that he had made the exchange; but that, Mr. Barclay[4] having furnished but one copy of *his* report, I must wait several days before he can send it to me. He informs me that Mr Barclay has taken great latitude (which I was prepared from my knowledge of him to expect) in the representation of facts, as coming within his personal knowledge, & which he has assumed as the basis of his arguments. But he informes [*sic*] me, moreover (what I was not prepared to hear) that Mr. Barclay has accompanied his report by affidavits of third persons which were never permited [*sic*] in evidence before the Board,[5] & which Maj. Delafield is satisfied contain statements not supported by fact; but which, if substantiated, might have a very important bearing on the points at issue. Is this course of proceeding to be tolerated? and shall I not be permitted to controvert this *ex parte* evidence?

My report is accompanied by only three special documents—one, a copy of Mr Fergusons affidavit[6] taken from the files of the Board; and the two others, statements & certificates, which do not pretend to impart any new facts, but are mere calculations & deductions from the maps & surveys on the files of the commission; and prepared by them at my request, for the mere purpose of a more ready explanation of my argument which is founded on the official documents.

After reading Mr Barclay's report I will write you again & make such remarks as its contents may suggest. In the meantime I should be pleased to know whether the President & yourself are satisfied with the views which I have taken of the subject. Very respectfully & truly yours
Hon H Clay.   P. B. PORTER

ALS. DLC-HC (DNA, M212, R2).
[1] David W. Bucklin, of Jefferson County, New York, had received a plurality of the votes on the first two ballots at the Democratic caucus, January 1, 1827, but on the third ballot Erastus Root had won the party's nomination. Hammond, *History of Political Parties in the State of New York. . .* , II, 242.   [2] The new administration organ, the Albany *Morning Chronicle*, was not established until a year later, the daily edition first appearing on January 19, 1828. It terminated in early December, shortly after the election. The editor to whom Porter probably referred was Isaac Q. Leake (cf. below, Hammond to Clay, April 11, 1827); but the editor who brought out the paper was Samuel B. Beach, a native of Connecticut, who had published a novel, *Escala, an American Tale*, at Utica in 1824. Beach was appointed to a clerkship in the Post Office Department in 1841.   [3] Joseph Delafield.   [4] Anthony Barclay.   [5] The Commissioners under Article VII of the Ghent Treaty, relative to the northern boundary of the United States.   [6] Dated September 20, 1826, relative to the channels of the St. Mary's River. *House Docs.*, 25 Cong., 2 Sess., no. 45, p. 32. James Ferguson, born in Scotland, had come to the United States as a child and, still a young man, had been attached since 1819 as a surveyor to the boundary commission under the Treaty of Ghent. From 1827 to 1832 he served as a civil engineer for the State of Pennsylvania; from 1833 to 1847, as first assistant in the United States Coast Survey; and from 1847 to 1867, as assistant astronomer of the United States Naval Observatory.

From Luther F. Thompson

Honble. H. Clay—
Dr Sir   Richmond (Va) Jany 3rd. 1827
Will you have the goodness to answer Soon as your convenience will

admit, Some questions relative to the utility of the "Ohio hemp Machine," established by a Mr. Smeeds[1] on your plantation, in the fall (If I mistake not) of 1824[2]— The operation of Said machine has been much Spoken of, and the quantity and quality it produced unexampled— Many of the planters near this city, are desirous of raising hemp, for *Summer clothing* Of their negroes and for various other plantation uses &c, and are disposed to manufacture it unrotted after the aforesaid process &c— The aforesaid planters as well as myself, not knowing from any other Source where we could get a correct information, as your having a machine of the aforesaid character once established on your plantation, and no doubt Often inspected by you, the many points of its Utility &c, therefore, beg leave to ask the following questions, viz—

1st. After the hemp being cut & dried— What quantity will 100 pounds of the unrotted stem, or [. . .] hemp make run through said machine— how much fibre (dressed similar to that of the Russian, as to cleanliness, [. . .] offered in market) will that 100 lbs of stem yield in wt. [. . .] per. cent?

2nd. Will Said machine brake, or Dress (like the Russian [. . .] 600 to 800 lbs with four horses In 12 hours?

3rd. What will 100 lbs of stem, or straw hemp, *laid out* and Dewrotted make, after taken up, and dressed in the ordinary way, how many pounds of fibre &c?

If you will have the goodness to answer the few questions above, Soon as convenient you will confer a Singular favor on the Said planters, as well as on the one who now addresses you— With Sentiments of high respect your Devoted Servt—   LUTHER F. THOMPSON

P.S. I have understood, the Legislatu[re] of Ohio, in the Winter of 1824, reported on a simi[lar] machine,[3] to the one established on your plantation— Have you th[e] report, or have you been informed of its content &c, &c If so please Inform us—

ALS. DNA, RG59, Misc. Letters (M179, R65) . Margin obscured. Thompson not further identified.
[1] Abraham K. Smedes.   [2] See above, III, 735n.   [3] Ohio H. of Reps, *Journal*, 22 Assy., 1 Sess. (1823–1824), 392–94.

MISCELLANEOUS LETTERS   January 3, 1827

To EDWARD EVERETT, Chairman of the Committee of the House of Representatives on the Library. Transmits copies of correspondence requested (above) December 28, (1826). Copy. DNA, RG59, Report Books, vol. 4, pp. 190–91. Published, with the accompanying correspondence, in U. S. H. of Reps., *Reports*, 19 Cong., 2 Sess., no. 91. pp. 2–16.

From THOMAS H. BENTON, "Senate chamber." States that he is "requested by the parties interested to present the enclosed papers to the Executive government of the U. S. and to ask its interposition with the government of Mexico to obtain

compensation for the losses of which the proof is now given." Cites the precedent
of the United States indemnity to Mexican citizens, as "in the case of Don
Manuel de Escudero, robbed by the Osages on the left bank of the Arkansas river."
ALS. DNA, RG76, Mexican Claims Commissions. Endorsed: "Thos Eaton Dudley
& Others . . . Claims upon Mexico." See below, Clay to Poinsett, January 5, 1827.

Manuel Simón de Escudéro, a merchant of Chihuahua and member of the provincial assembly of that State, has been identified as "the first Mexican to take
a caravan over the [Santa Fé] trail." Ralph Emerson Twitchell, *The Leading Facts
of New Mexican History* (2 vols.; Albuquerque, 1963), II, 118. He had visited the
United States in the fall of 1825 as an emissary from the Governor of New Mexico,
Bartolomé Baca, seeking official assurances of better protection for the overland
traders. Escudéro's recent losses from robbery by the Osages were then reported.
Niles' Weekly Register, XXIX (October 8, 1825), 85. Record of his compensation
has not been found. Baca, a sheep rancher and retired militia officer, was himself
engaged in prairie commerce. He had been provincial governor from August,
1823, to September, 1825.

From DAVID DICKSON, Jackson, Mississippi. States that he has been unable to
execute his consular bond and that he cannot go to his post (San Antonio) immediately because of the "continued Indisposition of a Son" (not further identified). Reports that Anthony Butler, just returned from Texas, has informed him
"of the revocation of [Hayden] Edwards' grant by the Mexican Government" and,
in consequence, the assemblage of "several hundreds, of all colours . . . at Nacogdoches with a determination to march against San Antonio Saltillo and other places."
Predicts that although the insurgents will fail, "the Country will be a scene of
Indian barbarity for months." Comments: "Benj. Edwards who seems to be the
leader, . . . you may perhaps recollect . . . as a merchant, (some years ago) at Rus-
selville [sic] Ky." Promises to depart for his post this month but laments that "it
will be with some doubts and fears as to . . . safety." Notes that Butler gives a
horrible description of the people of the Country. ALS. DNA, RG59, Cons. Disp.,
Texas vol. 1 (M-T153, R1). Received March 25.

The so-called "Fredonian Rebellion" had broken out November 22, 1826, when
Benjamin W. Edwards and his forces seized Nacogdoches. Edwards' brother
Hayden was at the time in the United States seeking financial assistance. The
revolutionaries proclaimed the "Fredonian Republic" on December 16 but retreated into Louisiana when Mexican armed forces approached on January 31,
1827. Walter P. Webb and H. Bailey Carroll, eds., *The Handbook of Texas* (2
vols.; Austin, 1952), I, 546, 547, 643.

Benjamin W. Edwards, born in Kentucky, had resided in Jackson, Mississippi,
prior to his removal to Texas in 1825. He later returned to Mississippi, where
he raised funds and military support for the Texas independence movement.

APPLICATIONS, RECOMMENDATIONS   January 3, 1827

ALFRED BALCH, Nashville, recommends William Thompson for appointment as
United States attorney in West Tennessee. ALS. DNA, RG59, A. and R. (M531,
R8). Cf. above, Yeatman to Clay, December 29, 1826, note.

THE[ODORICK] F. BRADFORD, Bedford County, Tennessee, recommends Thomas H.
Fletcher for appointment as United States attorney for West Tennessee. ALS.
DNA, RG59, A. and R. (M531, R3). Dated January 3, 1826.

G[EORGE] W[ASHINGTON] CAMPBELL, Nashville, recommends Oliver B. Hayes for
appointment as United States attorney in West Tennessee. ALS. *Ibid.* (R4).

WILLIAM CARROLL, Nashville, recommends Thomas Washington for appointment as United States attorney in West Tennessee. LS. *Ibid.* (R8).

ANDREW ERWIN, "Pleasant Retreat," Tennessee, recommends Thomas H. Fletcher for appointment as United States attorney for the District of West Tennessee. States that he has been "intimately acquainted with Mr Fletcher the last nineteen years" and that he (Erwin) expects "Some would be great men of this State both in & out of Congress" will oppose Fletcher's appointment. ALS. *Ibid.* (R3). Dated "Jany 3d 1826."

J[AMES] ERWIN, Bedford County, Tennessee, recommends Thomas H. Fletcher for appointment as United States attorney for the District of West Tennessee. Expresses belief that (John Henry) Eaton, (Hugh Lawson) White, and other leading Jacksonians "will be arrayed against him because he on a late occasion (in the election of Eaton) opposed the mandate of Genl Jackson." Contends that, although Fletcher gave some "speeches which were made for home Consumption," he "is now and always has been . . . [Clay's] friend and has the power to be an efficient one." ALS. *Ibid.*

G[EORGE] W. GIBBS, Nashville, recommends that Thomas H. Fletcher, Thomas A. Duncan, and Oliver B. Hayes be considered for the position as United States attorney for the District of West Tennessee. ALS. *Ibid.*

A[DAM] G[IBBS] GOODLET, Nashville, recommends William Thompson for appointment as United States attorney for the District of West Tennessee. Expresses "most respecfull [*sic*] compliments" to Clay and his family and concludes: "I cannot deny myself the pleasure which this occasion affords me of expressing to you the unshaken confidence in your honour integrity and patriotism which I always entertained; and I assure you Sir I admired that lofty and highminded Sentiment in you that induced you to forego that Ephemiral [*sic*] popularity for the more Substantial and lasting benifits [*sic*] which you purchased for your country. by the course you pursued—" ALS. *Ibid.* (R8).

Born in Orange County, Virginia, and educated for medicine in Lexington, Kentucky, and Philadelphia, Goodlet had begun practice in Lexington prior to the War of 1812. After serving as a surgeon in that conflict, he settled in Nashville and continued medical practice there until his death in 1848.

DANIEL GRAHAM, Nashville, recommends Thomas Washington for appointment as United States attorney for the District of West Tennessee. ALS. *Ibid.* Graham had served as clerk of the Tennessee Senate (1817–1819) and as Tennessee secretary of state (1819–1831).

M[ICAH] TAUL, Winchester, Tennessee, applies for the position of United States attorney for the District of West Tennessee. Comments: "From our long and intimate acquaintance, I apprehend it is unnecessary to furnish any evidence in addition to what you know of your own knowledge of my qualifications." Notes that he will write to (James) Clark and other friends at Washington but that he does not know many Tennessee Congressmen. Expresses belief that the Nashville bar is supporting someone else. ALS. *Ibid.*

WILLIAM THOMPSON, Nashville, solicits the position of United States attorney for the District of West Tennessee. Comments: "If . . . you should think proper to favour my wishes, this testimonial of your regard and friendship in my more advanced years will redouble the obligation of my youth to you for your kind instruction and patronage." ALS. *Ibid.* Cover endorsed: "private."

From John P. Erwin

Dear Sir—   Nashville 4 Jany 1826 [*i.e.*, 1827]
  I sometimes apprehend, that I may be considered as officious in my correspondence, & that the information contain'd will not repay you for the trouble & time of reading— But on the other hand, I take it for granted you consider my object as being a good one, & can make the requisite allowance for occasional indiscretion of suggestion—or superfluity of communication— It is only by a continued influx from the minor Streams, that the large fountain of intelligence can be supplied with all kind [*sic*] of information—   This is probably prelude enough!—
  I together with many others have addressed you on the Subject of the appointment of District Atto. here[1]— It is apparently a Small matter, yet seems to create some degree of interest—not enough perhaps to draw out Genl Houston & Maj Eaton, with another Protest.[2]— There are about 8. applicants as I understand— Mr. *Duncan*, brother of Genl D— of *Ills*[3] has called on me this evening for my signature together with others, to a general recommendation[4]— The statement contained in that recommendation is strictly true— He is qualified, & not unacceptible [*sic*] to the public— In fact none of the gentlemen who are applicants are particularly objectionable— Were I to say who had the slighest [*sic*] pretensions on account of legal acquirements &c, it would be Mr Overton[5]— Those having the highest *legal* pretensions, & *talents*, are *Fletcher, Duncan, Thompson, Hayes, Washington* & *Fogg*[6]—among whom there is no great disparity— *Hayes, Washington* & *Thompson* are the oldest Lawyers— *Fogg* is a man of good acquirements— Fletcher is a man of superior talents to any of them— *Thompson* is the brother of your Ky. friend[7] and is a very reputable, and amiable man— *Duncan* is connected by marriage with the Mc. Nairy family[8] here, and is Considered a sprightly intelligent young Lawyer— *Washington* is a very respectable Lawyer, has no family— *Hayes* is the oldest lawyer among them.   Motives, & reasons will be attached by your revilers here, to the appointment of any one— If *Duncan* is appointed, they will say a reference was had to the politics of *Ills*.— If *Thompson*, it will be said it is in consideration of the vote given by his brother when in Congress[9]— If *Fletcher*, they will attribute it to yr friends here, who are known to be his—vz. *Carroll*[10] &c— Those considerations will of course have as little weight with you as they deserve— I merely name them, as minor intelligence— A majority of the applicants are, & have been either openly, or privately friendly to yourself & Mr. As.[11]— Mr *Duncan* has always avowed his preference to you, over all others— *Fletcher*, has of late come out very warmly in behalf of the Admn— *Washington* & *Hayes*, have been silent friends

of the Admn.— *Thompson* has not interfered in politics since he came among us— Fogg is a Yankee but has been claimed as a Jacksonite—his partner Foster[12] is one of your most open mouthed and foul tongued slanderers—*Overton* like all of the name, is a furious Jacksonite, altho they do not abuse you—

I presume you will Consider this enough to say about so small a matter—.

James[13] & family are expected here from Duck River in a day or two to take passage for New Orls.— I am very Sincerely.   J. P. ERWIN

I fear I acted amiss in sending some enclosures[14] to you, rel to the U. S. Bank— I hope you have, if you deemed them not such as should go further, committed them to the fire—

I had previously written to Mr Biddle, a mere letter of information, & enquiry &c, not by any means confidential—& today recd. a very satisfactory reply—from which I learn that nothing will be done hastily on the subject[15]—   Our Govr.[16] will probably see you in W— during the winter— You have no friend who is more sincere.— Yrs &
                                                                      J. P. E

ALS. DNA, RG59, A. and R. (M531, R2). Addressed to Clay.
[1] Above, December 30, 1826.   [2] Samuel Houston and John Henry Eaton. Cf. above, Williams to Clay, September 20, 1826, note.   [3] Thomas A. Duncan; Joseph Duncan.   [4] Addressed to the President, January 4, 1827. DNA, RG59, A. and R. (M531, R2).   [5] John W. Overton.   [6] Thomas H. Fletcher; William Thompson; Oliver B. Hayes; Thomas Washington; Francis B. Fogg. On the appointment see above, Yeatman to Clay, December 29, 1826, note.   [7] Philip Thompson.   [8] Reference is made probably to the John McNairy family; the marriage connection has not been found.   [9] Cf. above, Kendall to Clay, February 20, 1825, note.   [10] William Carroll.   [11] John Quincy Adams.   [12] Ephraim H., son of Robert C., Foster had been born near Bardstown, Kentucky, but reared near Nashville, graduated from Cumberland College (now George Peabody College), and in 1820 admitted to the Nashville bar. A veteran of the Creek War, he had served as private secretary to Andrew Jackson (1813–1815). From 1829 to 1831 and 1835 to 1837 he was a member of the State legislature and from September, 1838, to March, 1839, and October, 1843, to March, 1845, a United States Senator. He was Fogg's law partner for twenty-five years.   [13] James Erwin.   [14] Not found.   [15] Erwin's correspondence with Nicholas Biddle, not found, probably referred to the establishment of a Nashville Branch of the Bank of the United States, which occurred later in the year.   [16] William Carroll.

DIPLOMATIC NOTES   January 4, 1827

To COUNT FERDINANDO LUCCHESI-PALLI DI CAMPOFRANCO. Acknowledges receipt of the Count's letter of December 22 and undertakes to correct "one or two misconceptions which the Count appears to entertain" relative to customs and tonnage duties of the United States. Explains: "The Government of the United States has always reserved to itself, exclusively, the right of fixing the amount of both those descriptions of duties; and it does not negotiate with any foreign nation on the basis of reducing them, in both Countries, to the same exact standard. Such an equalization of duties could only be justifiable between two Countries whose circumstances, external and internal, and whose policy were precisely alike. If the principle were extended to all Nations it would be destructive of every thing like uniformity in the amount of duties levied in the ports of the same nation. As to duties on Merchandize, the Government of the United States, is willing to admit that of any Nation on the footing of the most favored nation, provided the principle is reciprocated. Such a basis would ensure to the parties acceding to it the reception of their respective produce upon the most favourable terms at the same time that it would leave to each party the freedom of judging, according to his actual condition, what ought to be the rate of duties. The produce and merchandize of the two Sicilies pay no higher duties in the ports of the United States, when imported in American Vessels, than similar produce and merchandize of any other Country.

"In respect to duties on tonnage, the United States have offered to all maritime nations the liberal proposal of placing their vessels in our ports upon the same footing as our own, provided the principle is reciprocated in their ports. Whatever may be the rate of duties, it is evident, that by adopting this principle of equality between the National and the foreign vessel, fair competition in their respective marines is secured."

Refers to the act of Congress of January 7, 1824 (4 *U. S. Stat.*, 2–3) and, specifically, to section 4 of that act and states that the President offers assurance "that he would, with satisfaction, issue the proclamation which he is empowered by the above section to put forth, whenever the previous condition which it requires shall be fulfilled by His Majesty the King of the two Sicilies [Francis I]."

Comments that the difference between the amount of duties collected in the port of Messina and that in other Sicilian ports "is evidently a pecularity [*sic*] which could have no analogous circumstances in any port of the United States." Concludes by expressing hope that Count Lucchesi will see in the above proposal evidence of the "strong desire, on the part of the Government of the United States to cultivate the most friendly relations with that of the two Sicilies." Copy. DNA, RG59, Notes to Foreign Legations, vol. 3, pp. 319–21 (M38, R3). AL draft, in CSmH.

INSTRUCTIONS AND DISPATCHES   January 4, 1827

From J[OHN] M. FORBES, Buenos Aires, no. 44–1. Requests permission to return to the United States for a few months in order to recover his health. Encloses a copy of the proposed constitution (of the Argentine Republic). L, written and signed at dictation by J. Dickinson Mendenhall. DNA, RG59, Dip. Disp., Argentina, vol. 3 (M69, R4). Published, under date of January 5, in Espil (comp.), *Once Años en Buenos Aires*, 454–56. Received April 3.

From ALBERT GALLATIN, London, no. 49. Encloses a copy of a note to (George) Canning (dated January 3, 1827) regarding lighthouses and "other contemplated improvements" on the British side of the Florida straits. States that he does not have the map (showing location of lighthouses) mentioned in his instructions (above, Brent to Gallatin, June 27, 1826), since American ministers leave behind correspondence relating only to unfinished business. Notes that he has left a full record of his service in France and suggests that all ministers should be instructed to leave copies of public correspondence. Reports that he has employed an assistant (probably Richard H. Richards), as he was authorized to do. ALS. DNA, RG59, Dip. Disp., Great Britain, vol. 33 (M30, R29). Extract published in *American State Papers, Foreign Relations*, VI, 755. Received March 8.

From ROBERT MONROE HARRISON, Antigua. Reports increased British defense preparations in the West Indies, particularly construction of permanent barracks, hospitals, and docks. Notes that Antigua's new dockyard is capable of accommodating the largest ships of the line and that the speed of construction suggests that the barracks are to be occupied very soon. States that British officers report heavy expenditure on Bermuda fortification, warns that those islands will serve as a base of British naval operations off the United States Atlantic Coast, and expresses astonishment at the rapid strengthening of Britain's fleet. Refers to the view of many of the inhabitants that "something like a State of hostility may grow out of the difficulties, which may be experienced in adjusting" the current disputes and urges that Congress pass legislation for improving the discipline of the American militia.

Cites his "expectation" of hearing soon concerning his application for appointment to St. Bartholomew "or elsewhere." ALS. DNA, RG59, Cons. Disp., Antigua. vol. 1 (M-T327, R1). Received "12 feby."

From DAVID OFFLEY, Smyrna. Transmits his reports on shipping, distressed seamen, and "wages retained." Notes that there are about seventy distressed seamen, "discharged in Greece from on board the Frigate [*Hellas*] brought from New York" and expresses hope that "Captain [John B.] Nicolson [*sic*]" will provide a "public vessell" to transport them to a port where they can take passage to the United States, inasmuch as captains of American merchantmen sailing from here to Boston "refuse to receive any number on board beyond what the law directs even at fifty dolls. cash for their passage." Comments that this country continues to manifest a friendly disposition toward the United States although the Pacha (Hassan) requested information about "the arrival of a Frigate in Greece under the American flag which was then tranfered [*sic*] to the Greeks. . . ." Mentions that "Some weeks past" two American vessels were plundered by Greek cruisers and their crews badly treated; urges that two American warships remain "on this station" for protection of commerce. LS. *Ibid.* Smyrna, vol. 1 (M-T238, R-T1). Received May 4.

Under the terms of the distressed seamen's act (2 *U.S. Stat.*, 204) masters were not required to carry more than two such men per 100 tons of vessel weight.

MISCELLANEOUS LETTERS   January 4, 1827

To SAMUEL R. BETTS, Newburgh, New York. Transmits commission as judge of the United States for the Southern District of New York. Copy. DNA, RG59, Dom. Letters, vol. 21 (M40, R19). Betts acknowledged receipt of the commission on January 11, 1827, ALS, in DNA, RG59, Acceptances and Orders for Commissions (M-T645, R2).

From BENJ[AMIN] ESTILL, House of Representatives. Complains that no compensation was given him for surrendering title to about 12,000 acres of Yazoo lands; requests that the State Department supply him evidence of his titles, which were not returned by the Claims Commission. AN. DNA, RG59, Misc. Letters (M179, R65).

Estill, born in Hansonville, Virginia, had attended Washington Academy (now Washington and Lee University), practiced law in Abingdon, and served as prosecuting attorney for Washington County and as member of the State House of Delegates (1814–1817). A member of Congress for only one term (1825–1827), he was named in 1831 as a judge of the Virginia circuit courts and remained on the bench until 1852, when he retired to a farm in Oldham County, Kentucky.

On January 10, 1827, Daniel Brent informed Estill "that all persons interested in claims to Yazoo lands were required by Law to relinquish their titles to the United States, in consideration of the indemnification which might be awarded to them by the Board of Commissioners. . . ." He notes that several acts had been passed by Congress "from time to time . . . authorising [*sic*] this Department to deliver back papers, thus circumstanced, in particular cases. . . ." Copy, in DNA, RG59, Dom. Letters, vol. 21, pp. 453–54 (M40, R19).

From J[OSIAH] S[TODDARD] JOHNSTON, Senate. On behalf of the Committee on Commerce, requests information concerning (Henry) Perrine, who has been nominated as consul at Campeche. ALS. DNA, RG59, Misc. Letters (M179, R65). See above, Clay to Southard, November 17, 1826, note.

From JOSEPH KARRICK, Philadelphia. States that he plans to sail for Cartagena about the middle of the month and would like to have, before that time, a reply to his letter of November 29 (1826). ALS. DNA, RG76, Misc. Claims, Colombia, env. 13, claim no. 176.

From JOB PALMER, 17 Maiden Lane, New York. Requests payment of Clay's subscription to the *American Monthly Magazine*; mentions that he wrote "some time since" on this matter. ALS. DNA, RG59, Accounting Records, Misc. Letters. Cf. above, Palmer to Clay, December 18, 1826.

APPLICATIONS, RECOMMENDATIONS   January 4, 1827

WILLIAM L. BROWN, Nashville, who has learned since his letter of January 1 that (William) Thompson "is an applicant for the office of [Federal] district attorney of West Tennessee," comments that no appointment "would be *more* generally acceptable. . . ." Attributes this support to Thompson's "great intrinsic worth . . . & his high standing as a lawyer" but notes, too: "His politics . . . are friendly to the administration, or perhaps more properly speaking to you." ALS. DNA, RG59, A. and R. (M531, R8). Misdated as "1828." Cf. above, Yeatman to Clay, December 29, 1826, note.

G[EORGE] W[ASHINGTON] CAMPBELL, Nashville, recommends Thomas Washington for appointment as United States attorney "for this district." ALS. DNA, RG59, A. and R. (M531, R8).

FELIX GRUNDY, Nashville, recommends Leonard P. Cheatham for appointment as Federal district attorney in West Tennessee; comments that "some regard should be paid to the descendants of old Genl James Robertson. . . ." ALS. *Ibid.* (R2).
    Leonard Cheatham had married Elizabeth Robertson, granddaughter of James Robertson, member of the North Carolina legislature in 1785 and pioneer leader in the settlement of the Cumberland Basin.

JACOB PECK, Nashville, recommends Thomas Washington to be United States attorney for the District of West Tennessee. ALS. *Ibid.* (R8). Incorrectly dated, "1826."
    Born in Virginia, Peck had been admitted to the bar in 1808 and, having removed to Tennessee, had been elected to the State Senate, from Jefferson County, in 1821. He was a judge of the Tennessee Supreme Court from 1822 to 1835 and published a volume of the decisions of that court.

J[AMES] B. REYNOLDS, Clarksville, Tennessee, recommends Leonard P. Cheatham for appointment as Federal attorney in Tennessee. Mentions that the Cheatham family supported him notably in his last election, "while a thousand lies were in circulation" about Clay and himself; argues that Cheatham's appointment "would certainly have a powerful effect, and particularly when it would be known or said that it possibly resulted" from Clay's "great partiality" for Reynolds; and comments: "Mr. Cheatham belongs to the most powerful Connexion in this State. It pervades both East and West Tennessee. He is nearly related by marriage with Genl. Robertson's family [see above, Grundy to Clay, this date]; and it need not be conceal'd from you, that Genl. Jackson out of the question, they are all your friends." Notes also: "The people who reflect in this State, are well Satisfied with the Course of the administration. And I know Mr. Cheatham has frequently observed, that the appointments already made have been with a view to merit alone, regardless to your own aid hereafter." Concedes that Cheatham, "because such is the ancient friendship of Genl. Jackson for this family, . . . *is oblig'd to be for him*, and . . . will so declare himself." Mentions that Cheatham's cousin, Richard, now in the legislature, *"has a warm side"* for Clay. ALS. DNA, RG59, A. and R. (M531, R2).

Reynolds, a supporter of Andrew Jackson, one who had voted for him in preference to John Quincy Adams in the House election of February, 1825, was, nevertheless, an admirer of Clay, and an advocate of internal improvements. On Reynolds' defeat in the "last election," cf. above, Carroll to Clay, October 4, 1825.

Richard Cheatham, born in Springfield, Tennessee, in 1799, was a merchant, stock-raiser, and cotton ginner. He returned to the State legislature in 1833 and served in Congress, as a Whig, from 1837 to 1839.

R[OBERT] WEAKLEY, Nashville, recommends Thomas A. Duncan for appointment as Federal attorney for the District of West Tennessee. Notes that Duncan has informed him that Clay is "well acquainted with his Father [Joseph Duncan]", that the younger Duncan "was raised near . . . [Clay] and professes to be one of . . . [his] warm friends," and that a brother of the young man "is the Member elect. from Illinois" to Congress (Joseph Duncan—see above, Edwards to Clay, September 21, 1826, and note). ALS. DNA, RG59, A. and R. (M531, R2).

The father, a veteran of the Revolutionary War, had settled in Kentucky in 1788 and built the residence later known as Duncan Tavern in Paris. He had died in 1803.

T[HOMAS] I. WHARTON, Philadelphia, recommends (Clement C.) Biddle for appointment as naval officer of the port of Philadelphia. ALS. *Ibid.* (R1). See above, Peters to Clay, October 24, 1826, note.

From John J. Marshall

Honble Henry Clay   Frankfort Jany 5th. 1827
    Altho' I am not a citizen, at present, of Kentucky,[1] yet my early attachment & the knowledge I have of the conspicuous characters of the State, must be my sole excuse for obtruding this letter. Mr Bibb[2] you will have seen from the public prints has been nominated as the "Chief Justice of Kentucky." Last night after a most violent and angry debate in which Mr. Wickliffe[3] Mr. Chilton Allan and Mr John Pope were the most conspicuous parties and we would suppose a permanent breach was produced Mr Bibb was confirmed by a vote of 21: to 17: D. Given James Crutcher, Locker from Chistian [sic] and Mr. B's brother in law Mr. T. Slaughter from Logan of the old Court and Mr. Pope of no Court voting with all the New Court members for the confirmation.[4] It is not known whether Mr. Bibb will accept, but

beleiving [sic] that he may be so inconsistent as to do so, I take the liberty of stating that J. J. Crittenden would accept of the office of District attorney now held by Mr. Bibb, should there be a vacancy or should it be determined not to renew Mr. Bibb's commission.[5]

[Testifies to Crittenden's high standing, even among his opponents, and comments: "The administration will gratify its friends and conciliate it's [sic] enemies by the appointment."] With respect

J J MARSHALL

ALS. DNA, RG59, A. and R. (M531, R2).
[1] Cf. below, Marshall to Clay, January 15, 1827.   [2] George M. Bibb.   [3] Robert Wickliffe.   [4] Ky. Sen., *Journal, 1826–1827*, p. 182. Dickson Given, of Livingston County, had served in the Kentucky House of Representatives from 1814 to 1816 and in the Kentucky Senate from 1817 to 1822; he had returned to the latter body in 1825 and retained the seat until 1829. George L. Locker, born and reared in Fairfax County, Virginia, had established a mercantile business in Christian County, Kentucky, which he represented in the Kentucky Senate during the session of 1826–1827. Thomas S. Slaughter, a brother of James and cousin of Gabriel Slaughter, had been born in Culpeper County, Virginia, settled in Nelson County, Kentucky, shortly before the turn of the century, and removed to Logan County in 1805. He was a merchant at Russellville and State Senator (1818–1822, 1826–1829). In 1801 he had married Bibb's sister, Lucy.
[5] On January 24, 1827, President Adams nominated John Jordan Crittenden as Federal attorney for Kentucky; the appointment was approved on February 8. U. S. Sen., *Executive Journal*, III, 564, 566.

From Henry R. Warfield

My dear Sir   Fredericktown January 5th. 1827
    I indulge the hope because I cannot think it a delusive one, that you will freely withdraw your attention for a few moments from more important concerns to bestow a little attention on one whom I think you know is cordially your friend, and became so at a time, when few things were more foreign to his Expectations, than asking a favour in any form or under any circumstances[1]— Such however are the rugged Events, almost inseperably [sic] interwoven with our Journey through this life of turmoil, that things least to be Expected do Sometimes occur which no foresight or prudence, cou'd Either anticipate or avert
    More than twelve months have passed away my Dear Sir since I communicated to you in the language of unreserved confidence the serious shock which my private affairs had sustained from liberality to others[2] — I knew from the feelings of my own heart I was *your* Friend, and you had told me under peculiar circumstances, and in Impressive terms you were *mine*— I believed you— nor has that belief been shaken, nor will it, untill [sic] facts shall occur as indisputable in their character, as the tenets of our Holy Creed— I have thought and do still think that if you have not Evinced those feelings in the manner I cou'd have wished you were influenced by considerations more imperative than the indulgence of private friendship— For tis surely nothing but Poetic fiction when we are told

> That Friendship is but a *name*
> a charm that lulls to sleep
> a thing that follows wealth and fame
> and leaves the wretch to weep[3]—

I have not the writer by me and am not sure the quotation is correct—

I do not wish under any possible condition of things to be importunate, and I sincerely hope I do not ask for any thing unreasonable or Improper

To be the constant solicitor for *all or any* appointment, a *Hackneyed candidate for office,* is what I despise and abhor— But in Every Government which the wisdom, or the busy Brain of man has yet devised there must be persons to discharge the duties of public Stations, and placing personal regard altogether out of View, the important points for consideration are "Is he honest is he capable is he faithful to his country"—

On the score of Family respectability it must be universally conceeded [sic], there is no one in Maryland on a fairer footing than myself, Either with regard to present connections, or my ancestors, whose zealous and active Exertions Essentially, contributed at considerable sacrafice [sic], to the Establishment of "Independence"— which we now all prize as a Jewel of inestimable value[4]— For the last thirty years it has been my pride and my pleasure to be in Intimate association with men both within and without the limits of the State, preeminent for virtue and talents—

Of my qualifications I say nothing— We do not see ourselves as others see us[5]—

That there is a malignant opposition to the administration Ever ready to ascribe the worst of motives to the purest of actions is notorious to the world, but they are neither formidable in numbers, nor powerful in talents— Opposition, Ever has Existed; Ever will Exist in popular Governments— We see it in the pages of antiquity—and we have seen it in all its Endless varieties from the period Our Government went into operation to the present moment,— Indeed it requires no Extraordinary Effort of mental vision to see it for years *"in futuro"* hower [sic] abortive it may [sic]

That there are restless, dicontented [sic] disappointed beings prepared to condemn the appointment of any one to office, who from a Fortuitous concurrance [sic] of Circumstances, had been prominent in the Election of a President is most true[6]— The Existence of those beings, and their incorrigible propensities to Deeds of Darkness has been seen in numberless instances   But who regards them?— The "Integer Vite" of which Horrace [sic] so beautifully speaks, wholly disregards them— Conscious rectitude is so powerful a consolation, such a perfect shield, that it Cannot be peirced [sic] by arrows of malevolence— The instances you enumorated [sic] in your address at the

white Sulphur Springs of appointments made by Messrs. Jefferson
Madison and Monroe of many Gentlemen who were prominent actors
in Elevating them to the Presidency shews that the measure has been
sanctioned by long and Established Usage[7]

If Mr. Adams had been turned from his purpose by the malignant
fulminations of adventurous malcontents, this country wou'd not now
be benefited by your talents and services, which if not Universally
acknowledged are most certainly gaining daily influence with the
virtuous and the wise— I certainly cou'd not count on a very conspicuous situation in the outset— Judge Duvall[8] of the United States
Court who was one of the most conspicuous supporters of Mr. Jefferson in this state, was appointed by that Gentleman in 1802 Comptroller of the treasury and was Elevated to the high office he now holds
by the Friendship of Mr Madison— The present secretary of the treasury[9] was also raised from that appointment to the Exalted station he
now holds— If Congress shou'd during the present session Establish
a Home department,[10] which it is certainly their imperative duty to
Do, there might be some situation in which I cou'd be useful— For I
speak the language of my heart when I say it wou'd be one of the first
pleasure[s] of my life to be near you, and at the same time to be in a
situation, to which my talents and services wou'd be fully Equal—
after compleating my collegiate Education at St. Johns, and passing
through a regular course of legal studies in the office of Chancellor
Hanson[11] at annapolis and being admited [sic] in all the superior
courts in the this [sic] state, I commenced, and continued the practice of Law for more than fifteen years   I derived great gratification
from being Engaged at the Bar with men of first rate abilities and
many of them of inestimable worth of character— I became independent, nay rich— I left the Bar and settled on a most valuable Estate—
I represented my District in congress— I Extended my acts of friendship to several of my Friends,—The late unlooked for Earthquake in
the pecuniary concerns of this country & indeed of the world, has
swallowed up my property— such is the mutability of all terrestial
[sic] things that we are Sometimes withered by the lightning [sic] of
adversity before we perceive the flash—

I have resumed the practice of the Law in this place, and am Engaged in most of the trial causes, but the business is greatly Diminished
and the profits small— moreover the lapse of Six and Twenty years has
produced [sic] to total revolution amoung the members of the Bar—
R. B. Taney who now resides in Baltimore, is the only survivor
amoung the list of those who were at this Bar when I commenced the
practice here— I may almost say in the language of the celebrated
Roman General "Marius," that in my latter days it seems to be my
unlucky fate to be a wrestler with boys[12]—

Puting [sic] aside the good Deeds done by my ancestors, and their high standing in the community—I think I am *Entitled* to an Honbl. situation in the Government of my country from *my own Qualifications, and rank in society*— There are numbers of the first men in Maryland who concur with me in this opinion— But You Sir are the appellate court, and can Easily reverse or confirm their opinions—

I may say as Othello did— "I have none[13] the state some service; but no more of that"

Of Mr. Adams' reElection and of your succeeding him to the Presidency I no more doubt than that I am writing this letter— If I offended him by voting Maryland to him at the last Election I can truly say it was not my intention to do so— and *If he requests it* I will ask pardon and promise "pon Honor" not to do so again— He ought not to be angry, for I can truly say it was not my intention in the outset of the business to vote for him at all— I had a great deal more to say, but I concur in the opinion You are about to Express that I have already said Enough to weary the patience of any one— Most truly yours—   HENRY R. WARFIELD

ALS. DLC-HC (DNA, M212, R2).
[1] See above, II, 861n; III, 147–50, 210–14, 335–38.   [2] See above, Warfield to Clay, January 23, 1826.   [3] Oliver Goldsmith, "The Hermit," *Poems and Plays* (New York, n.d.), stanza 19, p. 48.   [4] Charles Alexander Warfield, father of Henry R., had been a militia officer and member of the Whig Club of Anne Arundel County at the outset of the Revolutionary War. He had been the leader of a party which compelled Anthony Stewart, Annapolis merchant, to destroy his own brig, the *Peggy Stewart*, when it arrived in port loaded with tea. Joshua Dorsey Warfield, *The Founders of Anne Arundel and Howard Counties, Maryland, a Genealogical and Biographical Review* . . . (Baltimore, 1905), 444–45.   [5] Robert Burns, "To a Louse, on Seeing One on a Lady's Bonnet at Church," *Poems and Songs*, ed. by James Kinsley (London, 1969), lines 43–44, pp. 156–57.   [6] Cf. above, III, 815. On Warfield's critical role in the political arrangements which aligned Maryland in support of John Quincy Adams, see Livermore, *Twilight of Federalism*, 174–77, 182.   [7] See above, V, 658.   [8] Gabriel Duvall.   [9] Richard Rush.   [10] See above, Clay to Webster, February 16, 1826, note.   [11] Alexander Contee Hanson, also a graduate of St. John's College (founded as King William's School at Annapolis in 1696 and chartered under the modern name in 1784), had been a member of the Maryland House of Delegates (1811–1815), the United States Congress (1813–1816), and the United States Senate (1816–1819). A practicing lawyer at Annapolis and editor of newspapers at Baltimore and Georgetown, he had been an ardent Federalist, strongly opposed to United States involvement in the War of 1812.   [12] Though past the age of 65, Caius Marius, seven times a consul of Rome, had daily exercised with the young men and "showed himself still nimble in his armour, and expert in riding; though he was undoubtedly grown bulky in his old age, and inclining to excessive faintness and corpulency." Plutarch, *The Lives of the Noble Grecians and Romans*, trans. by John Dryden and rev. by Arthur Hugh Clough New York, [1932], 515.   [13] That is, "done"; the quotation here omits, after the word "service," the clause, "and they know't." The lines are taken from Shakespeare, *Othello* (Horace Howard Furness [ed.], *A New Variorum Edition* . . . [27 vols. . , Philadelphia, 1871–1956], VI [2nd edn., c. 1886]), Act V, sc. 2, lines 412–13.

INSTRUCTIONS AND DISPATCHES   January 5, 1827

To J[OEL] R. POINSETT, Mexico, no. 18. Instructs Poinsett to request from the Mexican Government indemnity for losses sustained by Thomas Eaton Dudley and Jacob C. Wilson in a Comanche raid upon their party while returning to Missouri from a trading expedition to the adjoining Mexican province (New Mexico) in the spring of 1824. Encloses affidavits of Dudley and Wilson deposing the circumstances of the assault. Observes that diplomatic appeals for satisfaction are better than direct action against the Indians, for the President wishes "to preserve and strengthen" the harmonious relations between the two nations. Suggests that the indemnity paid to Manuel (Simón) de Escudéro (see above, Benton to Clay, January 3, 1827) establishes the precedent that the United States accepts responsibility for Indian depredations committed within its territorial limits and comments: "It is expected by the President that this just example will be followed by Mexico." LS. DNA, RG84, Mexico (MR17, frames 49–50). Copy, in DNA, RG59, Dip. Instr., vol. 11, pp. 227–28 (M77, R6); ALI draft, in DLC-HC (DNA, M212, R8). Cf. below, Poinsett to Clay, April 13, 1827. Dudley and Wilson not further identified.

From J[OHN] M. FORBES, Buenos Aires, no. 44-2, "Private." Reports that he is too ill to go into details of the controversy between himself and (George W.) Slacum; transmits a copy of a statement which he has prepared "for a very limited and confidential circulation, principally among . . . Congressional friends"; mentions that on two occasions he and Slacum suspended all intercourse "except that of a strictly official character"; and complains that Slacum chose "his most devoted sycophant and . . . [Forbes'] decided enemy, Doctr. [Robert] Kortright," to serve as acting consul (cf. above, Slacum to Clay, August 6, 1826). L, written and signed at dictation by J. Dickinson Mendenhall. DNA, RG59, Dip. Disp., Argentina, vol. 3 (M69, R4). Published in Espil (comp.), *Once Años en Buenos Aires*, 456–57. Received April 3. Forbes' statement, a printed letter addressed to his "friends" and dated "10th Nov. 1826," includes copies of his correspondence with Slacum relating to Kortright's appointment.

MISCELLANEOUS LETTERS   January 5, 1827

From GEORGE H. RICHARDS, London, "Private." Notes that he has requested (Gideon) Tomlinson to present to the (United States) Government his (Richards') "new modes of Subterranean and Submarine warfare" and requests Clay's support. Refers to "former proofs" of Clay's assistance (cf. above, Clay to Brown, March 23, 1826), comments that he is currently "writing for the Legation here" (cf. above, Gallatin to Clay, January 4, 1827), and adds that he hopes soon to complete successfully his European business venture. ALS. DNA, RG59, Misc. Letters (M179, R65).

APPLICATIONS, RECOMMENDATIONS   January 5, 1827

P[ARRY] W[AYNE] HUMPHREYS, Tennessee, recommends Leonard P. Cheatham as United States attorney for the District of West Tennessee. ALS. DNA, RG59, A. and R. (M531, R2). Cf. above, Yeatman to Clay, December 29, 1826, note.

DUDLEY MARVIN transmits letters from (Elisha B.) Strong and (Daniel Dewey) Barnard, urging appointment of Elisha Ely, of Monroe County, New York, "as Consul at some of the South American Ports." Notes that Barnard is the newly elected member of Congress for the district now represented by Moses Hayden. Adds personal testimony in support of Ely and comments: "The Western part of New York has at all times shared but very sparingly in the favors of Government, and it is for this reason as well as my personal friendship for Mr. Ely, that induces with me a strong hope he may receive an *elligible* [sic] appointment of the kind asked for—" ALS. DNA, RG59, A. and R. (M531, R3). Undated—enclosures, addressed to Marvin, dated December 26 and 27, 1826, respectively, and the latter postmarked from Rochester December 29; Marvin letter filed before January 5.

Strong, a prominent banker and land developer, had been the first judge of the Monroe County court of common pleas.

Barnard, born in Sheffield, Massachusetts, and graduated from Williams College, had begun the practice of law in Rochester in 1821. He was prosecuting attorney for Monroe County when elected to Congress for the term 1827–1829. He removed to Albany in 1832, became a member of the State Assembly in 1838, and returned to Congress from 1839 to 1845. From 1850 to 1853 he was United States Minister to Prussia.

Ely, also a native of Massachusetts, was now a Rochester miller. He was nominated and the appointment confirmed on March 3, 1827, as consul to Santa Marta; but on March 22, Daniel Brent wrote Ely, at President Adams' request, to explain that the commission could not be issued because William Sever had already been named to the consulate earlier in this Congressional Session. Copy, in DNA, RG59, Dom. Letters, vol. 21, pp. 500–501 (M40, R1). Cf. above, Sever to Clay, August 5, 1826, note.

THOMAS NEWTON [JR.], Washington, recommends Reuben Harvey of the firm of Harvey, Son, and Deaver of Cork for appointment as consul at Cork. He is "not personally acquainted" with Harvey but recommends him upon the advice of a friend. ALS. DNA, RG59, A. and R. (M531, R4). Cf. above, Cropper, Benson, and Company to Clay, November 7, 1826, note.

ELISHA I. WINTER, Lexington, notes his understanding "that G. M. Bibb was yesterday appointed chief Justice of the State of Ky." and recommends Richard H. Chinn to replace him as United States attorney. ALS. DNA, RG59, A. and R. (M531, R2). Dated: "Jany 5-1826—"

INSTRUCTIONS AND DISPATCHES   January 6, 1827

From W[ILLIAM] R. HIGINBOTHAM, Bermuda. Notes that two American vessels will be condemned as unseaworthy; requests permission that their cargoes be carried in British vessels and protected against seizure by American (customs) collectors, inasmuch as the British Order in Council (see above, Gallatin to Clay, August 19, 1826) prevents transfer of the goods to American bottoms. LS. DNA, RG59, Cons. Disp., Bermuda, vol. 1 (M-T232, R1). Received February 10.

From W[ILLIAM] TUDOR, Lima, no. 55, "Duplicate." Transmits copies of correspondence with the Minister of Foreign Affairs (José María Pando) and discusses its import. Notes that the government by decree, newspaper publication of which is also enclosed, has ruled that whaleships may "sell a sufficent quantity of oil, & also naval stores, to obtain their supplies, without paying the tonnage duties exacted from merchant vessels." Comments that, while the government has declined lessening import duties, it has established the same rate on all "plain, foreign cottons." Expresses view that the tariff was adopted principally for revenue purposes, since foreign cotton goods will still undersell that of the native weavers. ALS. *Ibid.*, Lima, vol. 1 (M154, R1). Received May 30.

MISCELLANEOUS LETTERS   January 6, 1827

To DANIEL LeROY, Detroit. Transmits his commission as attorney of the United States for the Territory of Michigan. Copy. DNA, RG59, Dom. Letters, vol. 21, p. 452 (M40, R19).

To WILLIAM ROSSELL, Burlington, New Jersey. Transmits his commission as judge of the United States for the District of New Jersey. Copy. *Ibid.*, p. 451. Erroneously dated as "1826." Cf. above, Clay to Rossell, November 12, 1826.

Rossell's recess appointment had been reported to the Senate with his formal nomination on December 13; the appointment had been confirmed December 19. U. S. Sen., *Executive Journal*, III, 544, 545. On January 26 Rossell acknowledged receipt of Clay's letter of "January 5 [*sic*]" and requested information on how to obtain "the laws of the U. S. touching the duties of the District Courts." ALS. DNA, RG59, Misc. Letters (M179, R65).

To HARRY I. THORNTON, Huntsville, Alabama. Forwards his commission as attorney of the United States for the Northern District of Alabama. Copy. DNA, RG59, Dom. Letters, vol. 21, p. 452 (M40, R19).

On February 3, 1827, Thornton acknowledged receipt of the commission and accepted the appointment. ALS, in DNA, RG59, Misc. Letters (M179, R65).

From N[ICHOLAS] BIDDLE, Bank of the United States, Philadelphia. Informs Clay of the conclusion of the Bank's negotiations with (Charles R.) Vaughan. ALS. *Ibid.* See above, Biddle to Clay, December 22, 1826; Clay to Vaughan, December 27, 1826.

From ROBERT LITTLE, Washington. Recalls that the Secretary assured him that he would "not be forgotten" in any future reorganization of the Patent Office and that the Secretary terminated his employment as a temporary clerk until Congress appropriated money for additional personnel in that office (cf. above, Clay to McLane, January 14, 1826, note). Observes that for the past six months he has continued to record patents and requests that remuneration for said service "be included in those arrangements recommended to Congress" (below, Clay to House of Representatives, January 11, 1827). ALS. DNA, RG59, Misc. Letters (M179, R65).

Robert Little, an Englishman, had come to Washington around 1820 and opened a store on Pennsylvania Avenue. Having formerly held a Unitarian pastorate in Lincolnshire, he had begun conducting such services in Washington in 1821 and had become the pastor of the First Unitarian Church there when it was organized that autumn. Little had also edited the *Washington Quarterly Magazine of Arts, Science, and Literature* in 1823 and 1824, which published notice of patent issues. He had been employed recording patents from March through June, 1826, and was paid subsequently $630 from the contingency fund of the State Department, for services dating from June 30, 1826, to March 3, 1827. *House Reports*, 20 Cong., 1 Sess., no. 226, p. 64. On the appointment subsequently authorized (cf. above, Clay to McLane, January 14, 1826, note), see below, Thornton to Clay, March 6, 1827.

APPLICATIONS, RECOMMENDATIONS   January 6, 1827

LEONARD P. CHEATHAM, Nashville, solicits appointment to the (Federal attorney's) office vacated by (Henry) Crabb. ALS. DNA, RG59, A. and R. (M531, R2). Unaddressed; enclosed in Cheatham to Adams, this date. *Ibid.* On the appointment, see above, Yeatman to Clay, December 29, 1826, note.

James B. Reynolds had previously advised Cheatham that in applying for this office, deference should be shown the President: "For you must observe, that he and Mr. Clay must converse freely on the subject of this appointment & all others. In doing so Mr. C will state the information he has, and from what sources. Now the President may become jealous & fancy that We believe Mr. C the president in fact, as it relates to the affairs of the West, (which by the bye he is,) and then *he might kick up*. To guard against this I have come out candidly to him, and referred him to my letter to Mr. C" (above, January 4, 1827). Reynolds to Cheatham, January 5, 1827, in DNA, RG59, A. and R. (M531, R2). Reynolds to Adams, January 5, 1827, was received on January 31 and placed in file 16; letter not found. MHi-Adams Papers (MR254).

JAMES HARPER, Lexington, recommends R (ichard) H. Chinn to succeed (George M.) Bibb as United States district attorney for Kentucky. ALS. DNA, RG59, A. and R. (M531, R2). Cf. above, Marshall to Clay, January 5, 1827, note.

From Squire Turner

Dr sir   Frankfort Kentucky Jany. 7h 1827
Before this reaches you, the nomination of G M Bibb as chief Justice of our state & his confirmation will be known to you through other channels[1]— It is now beleived [sic] he will accept the office and of course vacate that of U S district attorney

Our freind [sic] J J Crittendon [sic] will with alacrity accept the latter office. indeed he desires it— He will not directly apply for it because much has of late been said about him in the newspapers[2]— I have conversed with him and speak advisedly—

Our legislature is now in session and there is no doubt a large majority prefer [sic] Mr Critendon [sic] to any other individual who desires this office— His tallents [sic] and attainments as well as his standing are well known to you & the president—

I presum [sic] you have had frequent information from him of the state of things— more may still interest you— There are about twenty of a majority on a Joint ballot of the two houses in favour of the re-election of Mr. Adams— About two thirds or more approve the measures of the present administration—

Our local struggle will cease I think but much exertion is making to rally a strong interest against the admn—

The Jackson men are trying to make the impression that late events in New York are against Mr Adams   Pamphlets are circulating giving an explanation of the politics of that state favourable to Jackson

C A Wickliffe lately wrote to R Wickliffe not to take a stand in favour of the admn that New york was certainly for Jackson & new Jersey also—probably Maryland[3]— Now the freinds of the administration write us nothing   indeed the newspapers and every thing else of late are silent—

The letter to R Wickliffe had no influence on him— he came out in the senate the other day & since he recd the letter openly against Mr Pope & the Jacksonians[4]— He reveiwed [sic] Popes whole life and excluded him finally from the old court ranks

Pope replied, abused the old court men, spoke well of Adams—

but said in Europe the clergy Governed & in the U S the lawyers ruled   that their rule was a bad one and no person could break them down save a Military chieftain—and Jackson was the man   he proceeded to eulogise [*sic*] him very high— He finally said he wished [to] be neutral— But sir his neutrality consists in stimulating every possible opposition— In his opposition consists the surest prospect of our success— He is now down never never to rise again in Kentucky—

In Madison County where I live there are twenty three hundred voters and eighteen hundred at least of those are for Adams [*sic*] reelection—

The proposed amendment of the Constitution has not been acted on[5]

Before this reaches you—you will have seen the report of the committee in the H R. If after two trials no election is made then lots are to be cast for the presidency

Now these very constitution tinkers who wish to Gamble off the presidency are the very men who are attempting to excite so much prejudice against the president for having billiard tables & chess men[6]

Govr Desha & his faction are the tinkers & nothing could render the project more unpopular— They have disregarded all constitutional law and now ask to take that instrument into their own keeping—

In your letter to me last spring[7] you cautioned me against publishing any thing in the papers from you that would of course not have been done without your request to do so—

Your speech at Louisburgh[8] has silenced your enemies— Health and success   Yours   SQUIRE TURNER

ALS. DNA, RG59, A. and R. (M531, R2). Unaddressed.
[1] See above, Marshall to Clay, January 5, 1827.   [2] Cf. above, Clay to Force, October 9, 1826, note; Crittenden to Clay, November 25, 1825, note.   [3] Cf. above, Clay to Hammond, October 7, 1826, note; Clay to Everett, October 19, 1826; Goldsborough to Clay, November 1, 1826; Crittenden to Clay, November 25, 1826; Porter to Clay, December 24, 1826; and below, Degrand to Clay, February 8, 1827; Van Rensselaer to Clay, March 17, 1827; Clay to Brown, March 27, 1827, notes.   [4] Robert Wickliffe had attacked John Pope, and the latter had replied at length, in the course of the debate on George M. Bibb's nomination as Chief Justice. Frankfort *Argus of Western America*, January 17, February 21, 1827.   [5] Governor Joseph Desha, in his message to the General Assembly on December 4, had recommended action to procure a Constitutional amendment to take the Presidential election out of Congress and rest it in the people. Ky. Sen., *Journal, 1826–1827*, pp. 15–16; cf. above, Clay to Hammond, November 1, 1825, note. The House committee appointed to consider the proposal had reported on December 15, but the report had been tabled. For the report, see Frankfort *Argus of Western America*, December 27, 1826. The Senate, however, took up the subject on January 11 and adopted resolutions consonant with Desha's proposal. When this proposal was amended, by House action on January 18, to stipulate that the voting of the State's Congressional representatives was correct if in accordance with the will of their constituents, the Senate on January 24 decided to table the resolutions and the amendment. Ky. Sen., *Journal, 1826–1827*, pp. 15–16, 214–18, 310–11; Ky. H. of R., *Journal, 1826–1827*, pp. 24, 99, 276–80, 285–87, 331–33.   [6] John Adams, Jr., in reporting to Congress on February 8, 1826, the expenditures for "Furniture of the President's House," had listed a billiard table at $50.00; billiard balls, $6.00; and chessmen, $23.50. *House Reports*, 19 Cong., 1 Sess., no. 122, pp. 14, 15. On May 17 Samuel Price Carson, Representative from North Carolina (1825–1833), had questioned whether Congress intended "that the public money should be applied to the purchase of gaming tables and gambling furniture?"

Register of Debates, 19 Cong., 1 Sess., 2655. Despite President Adams' subsequent explanation that those expenditures had been paid for personally and had been erroneously reported on the account, the subject became a topic of partisan attack. See, for example, Washington *United States Telegraph,* January 1, 1827; *Niles' Weekly Register,* XXXII (April 28, 1827), 149–50.   7 Not found.   8 Above, August 30, 1826.

DIPLOMATIC NOTES   January 7, 1827

From P[EDRO] GONZALEZ, Washington. Relates details concerning "the events which have lately taken place in Central America." Discusses the discovery in "March last" that the newly appointed Commandant Inspector General of Artillery, N (icholas) Raoul, was involved in a revolutionary movement supported by the government of the State of Guatemala. Notes that the (Federal) government "proceeded to the arrest of the Chief of the State [Juan Barrundia] by order of the 5th. of September of last year," that the assembly and executive power of that State, "the exercise of which had devolved upon the Vice Chief" (Cirilo Flores), then removed to the City of Quezaltenango, that mob rising, in the course of which the Vice Chief was killed, was precipitated there by the military impositions of the State authorities, and that President (Manuel José) Arce thereupon intervened. On November 3 the Secretary of State (Juan Francisco de Sosa) informed Gonzalez that the people had "pronounced in favour of the national Government and of order." ALS, in Spanish with trans. in State Department file. DNA, RG59, Notes from Central American Legation, vol. 1 (M-T34, R1).

Raoul, a recent arrival from Colombia, was a French mercenary. Barrundia, a native of Guatemala and a member of the Liberal Party, had been named Chief of State in October, 1824. After removing him from office, Arce failed to prosecute the case against him; he was released on bonds and thereupon emigrated to Mexico. Flores had presided over the Assembly of Guatemala in 1823 and the following year had been elected Vice Chief.

INSTRUCTIONS AND DISPATCHES   January 7, 1827

From A[LEXANDER] H. EVERETT, Madrid, no. 64, "Duplicate." Reports that (Luiz António de Abreu e) Lima was presented at Court on (January) 5, as Chargé d'Affaires from Portugal, that the Count de Casa Florez was received at Lisbon on (December) 25 to resume his function as Spanish Ambassador, but that (Frederick James) Lamb has not attended Court since October 14. Mentions (Manuel Gonzáles) Salmón's letter to Lamb of December 15, acknowledging the Portuguese Constitution; the general belief that Britain with the support of France "and the other Powers" has also demanded the removal of the Minister of Justice, (Francisco Tadeo) Calomarde, and the military commanders responsible for supplying the Portuguese refugees; and the refusal of the King (Ferdinand VII) to yield to these latter exactions. Notes the appointment of Count Ofalia as Spain's Minister at London, "as well qualified to make fair weather in that quarter as any one who could have been selected." Discusses at length the military preparations of the Spanish and Portuguese Royalist volunteers moving on Portugal and the arrival and strength of the British forces under Sir W(illiam) H. Clinton. States that the two Swiss Regiments under French orders in Madrid (see above, III, 313n) have been alerted to prepare for withdrawal from the country, that there is "general impression among judicious and well informed persons . . . that Spain will give way," but that the Apostolic Party anticipates that the struggle in Portugal will subside "into a guerilla [*sic*] war" which will weary the British and gain time for "some favorable accident, especially a change of Ministry in France," which might aid the Anti-Constitutional Party. Comments that (George) Canning's speeches in Parliament engendered "a mixed feeling of disgust and rage" in Spain and offended the French.

Observes that he has "lately heard with surprise and regret the proceedings of [Simón] Bolivar at Lima" and expresses view that they not only "change very considerably the situation in Spanish America" but "must produce . . . an effect upon . . . [United States] policy in regard to those countries." Comments that the United States cannot "encourage the establishment of a military despotism in Columbia [*sic*] and Peru the first operation of which would be to place an advanced post on the Island of Cuba," that such a project would be dependent upon "the aid of the coloured casts [*sic*]," and that "A military despot of talent and experience at the head of a black army is certainly not the sort of neighbour whom we should naturally wish, if we had the choice, to place upon our Southern frontier." Concludes that if the moment were "favourable for resuming the negotiation at this place upon American affairs (as it evidently is not) . . . [he] should hesitate about the propriety of insisting any longer upon the recognition of the republic of Columbia as a thing agreeable to the United States."

Reports that little progress has been made on the question of indemnities but that he will see Salmón this day on the subject (see below, Everett to Clay, February 13, 1827). Encloses copy of a proposed contract "to farm the royal monopoly of Tobacco" for an annual rent double the present receipts.

Adds in a postscript, dated January 12, that the Swiss troops have begun their withdrawal and that the King has circulated a letter to the Captains General of the different provinces indicating that he will not yield to the demands for a change of ministry and punishment of the border commanders. LS; postscript, AE. DNA, RG59, Dip. Disp., Spain, vol. 26 (M31, R28). Extract published in Manning (arr.), *Diplomatic Correspondence . . . Latin American Nations*, III, 2139–40. Received March 11.

Calomarde, born in Aragon, had studied at Saragossa and had attained distinction for his writings in economics. With the re-establishment of absolutism under Ferdinand VII, in 1823, Calomarde had been named secretary to the Council of Castile and, in January, 1824, Minister of Grace and Justice. He remained in power until 1832 and exercised under Ferdinand a preponderant influence for absolutism and in support of the Apostolic Party. When the King fell gravely ill in 1832, Calomarde transferred his loyalty to Don Carlos and was, accordingly, driven into exile under the regency of Queen Christine. He died in Toulouse in 1842.

Narciso de Heredia, Count of Ofalia, was a brother of José de Heredia and had been Secretary of Legation in the United States before assuming ministries over the Departments of Ecclesiastical Affairs and Justice in 1823 and State in 1825. He moved from the embassy at London to Paris in 1829.

Sir William Clinton, who had risen rapidly in military rank during the Napoleonic Wars, had served in 1812 as commander-in-chief of the British troops on the east coast of Spain and now commanded the forces sent to Portugal from December, 1826, until their withdrawal in April, 1828. He had been a member of Parliament from 1794 to 1796 and continuously since 1806.

APPLICATIONS, RECOMMENDATIONS   January 7, 1827

N[OTLEY] M[ADDOX] FLOURNOY, Georgetown (Kentucky), recommends Richard H. Chinn for appointment as United States attorney for Kentucky. ALS. DNA, RG59, A. and R. (M531, R2). Cf. above, Marshall to Clay, January 5, 1827.

ELIJAH HUNT MILLS encloses recommendations from Boston merchants in behalf of Thomas Backus as consul (commercial agent) at St. Iago de Cuba. Notes that he has been assured by (Churchill C.) Cambreleng that (James J.) Wright has resigned and that "the friends of Mr. Wright were anxious for the appointment of Mr. Backus." ALS. DNA, RG59, A. and R. (M531, R1). Unaddressed. Enclosure is dated January 1, 1827, and signed by Robert G. Shaw and three others. On January 6, 1827, Daniel Brent had advised Cambreleng that the Department had received Wright's resignation (above, August 10, 1826) and that the vacancy had not been filled. DNA, RG59, Dom. Letters, vol. 21, p. 450 (M40, R19). For Backus' appointment, see below, Clay to Backus, March 7, 1827.

Robert Gould Shaw, born in Maine, had settled in Boston, where he had been apprenticed to a commercial house. He subsequently amassed a fortune as a merchant and, beginning in 1807, speculator in Maine lands.

J[AMES] F[ISHER] ROBINSON and others, Georgetown, Kentucky, recommend Richard H. Chinn for appointment as district attorney for Kentucky. ALS. DNA, RG59, A. and R. (M531, R2). Signed by Robinson and twelve others.

THOMAS L. WILLIAMS, Knoxville, Tennessee, recommends Thomas H. Fletcher for appointment as United States attorney for West Tennessee. ALS. *Ibid.* (R3).

Thomas L. Williams, brother of John and Lewis, was a Knox County lawyer. He had served as a State Senator (1819–1825) and, briefly in 1826, as a member of the State Supreme Court. On the recommended appointment, cf. above, Yeatman to Clay, December 29, 1826, note.

From Porter Clay

Dr Brother   Frankfort 8th January 1827

The Political aspect of affairs has considerably changed within these few days, and whether for the better or wors [sic] I cannot tell. Strange as it may seem to you George M Bibb takes his seat upon the old court bench to day as Chief Justice   his nomination was approved by the Senate 21–17 after a most boistrous [sic] discussion in which Messes [sic] Wickliff [sic] Allan of Clark &C on one side and Messrs Pope Davies [sic] Dudley &C &C on the other side[1] in which great Personal abuse was indulged in to the disgrace I was going to say to both sides of the question but I will not go so farr [sic] for I only heard Mr Pope who spoke in terms of great disrespect of Mr Allan and indeed pronounced him beneath his notice   he came over his usual slang about you & you [sic] bull Dogs—and stated that he had not yet taken a stand for nor against the administration[2]

What will be the effect of Bibb's exceptance [sic] I cannot foursee [sic]   it is thougt [sic] by a good number here that it will give the go by to our local disputes   If so we should rejoice, but great fears are entertained by others that some deep designes [sic] are at the bottom of all this for the purpose of involving us in another three or four years quarrell [sic], from which God in his mercy protect us[3]

The office of attorney for the U. U. S [sic] will necessarily be vacant and for the first time in my life I am compelled to act with some litte

[sic] duplcity [sic]   Crittenden[4] wants it and indeed ought to have it. but I am told he will not apply for it— I wish Mr Adams could be prevailed upon to tender it him   he is poor and you know he has made great sacrifices for his country and is ready to do more,   he has never once named the thing to me but I know his resouces [sic] are limited and his family large

Before I knew what was going on I was called upon the other day by Mr John Trimble and was prevailed upon to say that I would join in a recommendation for him in the event of Bibbs resigning and taking his seat with the old court for the fact is I did beleive [sic] at that time that he could act [sic] so inconsistent as to take a seat with men he had abused and traduced as being unworthy of the conf [sic] and respect of any Honest man— I shall however fulfill [sic] my promise and consequently you will either receive a letter from me recommending John Trimble or I shall joine [sic] with others in it[5]

We are all well God bless & preserve you many years
                                                              Yours PORTER CLAY

ALS. DNA, RG59, A. and R. (M531, R2).
1 Robert Wickliffe, Chilton Allan, John Pope, Samuel Daveiss, and Jephthah Dudley. Daveiss, a younger brother of Joseph Hamilton Daveiss, had been born in Bedford County, Virginia, and brought to the vicinity of Danville, Kentucky, in 1779 as a child. A lawyer, he had represented Mercer County in the Kentucky House of Representatives from 1822 to 1825 and in the Kentucky Senate thereafter. He remained in the latter body until 1829 and returned there from 1833 to 1835.   2 See above, Turner to Clay, January 7, 1827.   3 See above, Kendall to Clay, December 22, 1824, note.   4 John Jordan Crittenden. See above, Marshall to Clay, January 5, 1827, note.   5 Not found.

From William Gibbes Hunt

Sir,   Nashville January 8. 1827
    You will, I trust, excuse the liberty I take in addressing you on a subject, about which, I have no doubt, you will be pleased to receive suggestions from persons at this place, whose ideas you can compare and give such weight as on reflection you may think them entitled to.

    [Refers to the vacancy in "the office of District Attorney for the U. States in West Tennessee," cites his own preference for the appointment of Leonard P. Cheatham, and discusses the relative merits of alternative candidates. He explains that all who have been named for the position "are respectable in standing and worthy of confidence as men and as lawyers"; but he finds objections to several of them: to Thomas H. Fletcher, because of his "pecuniary embarrassments" carried over from an earlier mercantile business and because of his current residence "so far from Nashville," where, if he returned, the presence of his principal creditors "might furnish difficulties and embarrassments alike perplexing to him and hazardous to the faithful, prompt and strict discharge of duty"—to William Thompson, Thomas A. Duncan, and himself because of the recency of their settlement in Tennessee—and to Thomas Washington, because he is "rather slow in his mental operations and wanting in confidence in his own judgment" and because "he is still a bachelor, and seems little disposed to obey one of the first and greatest commands of omnipotence, or to do the duty of a good citizen by rearing a family for the benefit of succeeding generations." He describes Oliver B. Hayes briefly as a "neat fluent speaker, and a respectable lawyer," whose political views are "*suspected* of being on the side of the administration."]

I have made free to express my sentiments on this subject thus fully, believing that it might be a satisfaction to those whose opinions would have peculiar weight in the selection, as well as to the president himself, to learn from every practicable source the state of public sentiment and the respective claims of the candidates presented for consideration. You are, no doubt, aware of the situation in which I myself stand with relation to the politics of Tennessee. I came here as a professional man, determined to keep aloof from all the political excitement which I saw prevailing around me. I have, however, been drawn by a succession of peculiar circumstances into a situation imposing a political responsibility, and which may ultimately involve me, in a manner which I would gladly have avoided, in the political controversies, which, in this quarter, threaten a considerable violence. As the editor of a public print,[1] I shall not, when occasion shall seem to require, shrink from any responsibility, however unpleasant the faithful performance of duty may be. I wish however to acquire an influence before I attempt to exercise it and I am resolved, at no time, to lend the paper which I conduct and which has a very extensive circulation, to any violent or intemperate course. That the people of Tennessee should be generally attached to the man, who, more than any other, has given importance to the state by his military fame,[2] is naturally to be expected, nor would a moderate and temperate support of him, as a candidate for the presidency, by a native and uniform resident of this state, when attended by candor and respect towards his competitors, be considered, I presume, as furnishing an objection to any appointment, which would otherwise be deemed expedient and proper.

The appointment of postmaster[3] in this town has been made the theme of much violent and intemperate abuse, but, so far as I can learn, the manner in which Mr Erwin discharged the duties of the office, gives the most thorough and universal satisfaction.

Permit me, in conclusion, again to ask your indulgence for the freedom I have used, and to suggest that having spoken with a frankness which the occasion seemed to require, respecting the characters of some of my most esteemed personal friends, I trust this communication will be regarded as strictly confidential, except so far as it may be thought proper to submit its contents to the president of the United States. I am, Sir Very Respectfully Your humble servant

W. G. Hunt

ALS. DNA, RG59, A. and R. (M531, R2). Unaddressed.
1 *Nashville Banner and Whig.*   2 Andrew Jackson.   3 John P. Erwin. On the controversy concerning his appointment, see above, Williams to Clay, September 20, 1826, note.

From Barton Warren Stone

Dr Sir.   Georgetown. Ky. Jany. 8th. 1827
You may be surprized at receiving a letter from a person with whom you have so slight an acquaintance. Do not, sir, consider it an intrusion. I have applied in vain to get the constitution of the colonization society.¹ Many of us in this country, and in Tennessee, are highly pleased with the object, as far as we have information respecting it; we wish to form into societies to co-operate with that in Washington. Do, sir, be so obliging as to send me the constitution, with whatever information you may deem necessary on this subject. We are conducting a religious periodical work in Georgetown,² which is extensively circulated through the western & southern states. We should be very glad to give cheering intelligence on this momentous subject. With due respects your sincere friend   Barton W. Stone

ALS. DNA, RG59, Misc. Letters (M179, R65). Addressed to Clay. Stone, born in Maryland and reared in Pittsylvania County, Virginia, had entered Guilford Academy, in North Carolina, in 1790, to study law. Instead he had become a candidate for the ministry in Orange Presbytery in 1793, had received his license in 1796, and had been ordained while in charge of churches at Cane Ridge and Concord, Bourbon County, Kentucky, in 1798. His questioning of religious orthodoxy had led him to withdraw from the Synod of Kentucky and to organize the Springfield Presbytery in 1803. A year later he and his followers had dissolved the latter body and denominated themselves simply as Christian, with only the Bible as their creed. He had moved to Lexington in 1813 and taught school there and at Georgetown, Kentucky, in addition to carrying on evangelical work in Kentucky and Ohio. He removed to Jacksonville, Illinois, in 1834 and resided there until his death, while visiting relatives at Hannibal, Missouri, in 1844.
1 The American Colonization Society   2 *The Christian Messenger*, established by Stone in 1826. He continued to edit the journal at Georgetown until 1832 and at Jacksonville, somewhat intermittently, until his death.

From Thomas P. Taul

Dear Sir.   Winchester Ten. Jan. 8th. 1827.
[Recommends his father¹ as United States attorney for the District of West Tennessee.]
In every appointment to be made by the government, the political creed of the applicants Should at least constitute an item for consideration. What the political Sentiments of my Father *are* and *have been, you need* not to be informed. Either by accident, or from the

great respect he had ever entertained for your opinions, he has at least concured [sic] with you on every question of Politics. In reference to the present Administration I beleive [sic] his opinion has been expressed somewhat distinctly. That *he* has not been among those who have *"cried aloud and Spared not,"* has not as yet, I am well satisfied, been forgotten by you. But my Father would not wish an appointment (and certainly I Should desire [sic] it for him) predicated alone on his friendship for the administration. But presented as he is with *at least* equal claims and qualifications, with any one before the Executive; he would f[ai]n hope that the government would select its officers rather from the Ranks of its friends than its enemies—and when from the Ranks of its friends rather from among those who direct [sic] and avowed, than from those who are equivical [sic] and oscillating. *For or against the adminis*tration? Should not be made the Sole test, in appointments, But other things being equal, it is not only matter of policy, but there is a Species of obligation resting on the Administration, to advance *those* who are for *it*—for by such it was called into existence, and by such its measures are advocated and Sustained.

Mr. Fletcher[2] of this place is among the applicants for this office,   personally I Should have no objections to his getting the appointment, if my Father was not before the President. As to his politics, to be Sure, they are Somewhat wavering. He is almost to be ranked among that class of Politicians who scarcely "Stay long enough on any one Side to be counted." He was in the original Presidential election favorable to the elevation of Mr. Crawford, as is manifested in a production of some note written by him during the canvass, known by the name of the *"Political Horse Race."*[3] After the choice had devolved upon Mr Adams—he avowed for Jackson in a Speech delivered in the Legislature of this State; upon the nomination of the Genl. by that body for the term commencing upon the expiration of that for which Mr. Adams had been elected. He was perhaps the mover, he certainly, was the warm advocate of the Resolutions on that Subject. Mr. Fletcher cannot however be looked upon as one of the General's most Zealous friends *"at heart"* however decided he may be *in terms*; for I beleive he would worship at any Shrine from which *propitious Oracles are delivered.*

The friends of the administration constitute the minority in this State, its avowed friends are not greatly numerous,   among them my Father is not the least of the open & direct. My Father, Mr. Clay, has been *at all times with you,* he is now *before you.* and we do most earnestly hope that he will not be forgotten in the appointment which is to be made. Your friendship is solicited not without a confident expectation, that it will be exerted for my Father— He could not apply to those who are against the administration, for office— if they had office to give his being the Known and undeviating friend of Mr Clay would exclude expectation. If then the liberal statesman, *with whom,* and *for whom,* he has been during his whole life—at the swelling tide of whose prosperity he has ever gladdened should forget him, I know not to whom he could apply with expectations of success. Respectfully your Obdt Servt.   THOS. P. TAUL

P.S. This letter can be submitted to the executive if usual & proper

ALS. DNA, RG59, A. and R. (M531, R8). Addressed to Clay. Cf. above, Yeatman to Clay, December 9, 1826, note.
[1] Micah Taul.   [2] Thomas H. Fletcher.   [3] See above, Carroll to Clay, November 25, 1825.

INSTRUCTIONS AND DISPATCHES   January 8, 1827

To BEAUFORT T. WATTS, no. 1. Notes that part of the evidence is not at hand to indicate whether the claim of Joseph Karrick against Colombia merits governmental interposition. Instructs Watts to examine the evidence when it is presented to him and, if it warrants action, to afford such aid as seems best calculated to render him satisfaction. Copy. DNA, RG59, Dip. Instr., vol. 11, p. 229 (M77, R6). AL draft, in DLC-HC (DNA, M212, R8). See Karrick to Clay, above, September 22, 1826; below, January 26, 1827.

From JOSEPH S. MARKS, Maracaibo. Transmits a letter from A. B. Nones (above, January 1, 1827) nominating Marks as vice consul. Reports that President Bolívar reached Puerto Cabello safely and arranged "a general reconciliation" with dissidents, thus avoiding civil war. Notes that General (José Antonio) Páez has been restored to former honors and that "all things bear the aspect of a general amnesty." Encloses copies of the President's proclamation and decrees. LS. DNA, RG59, Cons. Disp., Maracaibo, vol. 1 (M-T62, R1). Received March 7.

From W[ILLIAM] TUDOR, Lima, no. 56, "*Confidential.*" Discusses the political state of the country during (Simón) Bolívar's return to Bogotá. Notes that General (Francisco de Paula) Santander has written General (Juan Jacinto) Lara that the meeting with Bolívar would be "the most trying day of his life" and cites Santander's opinion that, if Bolívar's opponents can resist for a few days, they may be able to salvage the present constitution. Reports that discontent among the Colombian troops, "both here & in Upper Peru," is rising and that some may have to be sent home. Reviews possibilities that General (Andrés) Santa Cruz or General (José de) La Mar might assume the presidency of (an independent) Peru.

Comments on the ability shown by the Minister of Foreign Affairs, (José María) Pando, in rejecting the French Agent (Jean Baptiste Chaumette des Fossés), because he was not properly accredited, and states that the five French ships of war assembled in Callao "are about leaving."

Mentions publication of a decree permitting liberty of the press, questions how it will be applied, but terms it "an opening to something like the expression of opinion, which ever since the domination of the libertador has been annihilated." ALS. *Ibid.*, Lima, vol. 1 (M154, R1). Extract published in Manning, *Diplomatic Correspondence . . . Latin-American Nations,* III, 1814–15. Received April 26.

Lara, born in Venezuela, had made a fortune as a rancher but had suffered severe financial reverses during the struggle against Spanish rule. Having held important military commands in that conflict, he had been sent to Peru in 1822 as one of the commanders of the Colombian forces and since 1824 had been intendant and general commander of Arequipa, Cuzco, and Ayacucho.

MISCELLANEOUS LETTERS January 8, 1827

To NICHOLAS BIDDLE, Philadelphia. Transmits his commission as director of the Bank of the United States. Encloses commissions of the other directors appointed by the government: John McKim, Jr.; Victor DuPont; Campbell P. White; and Benjamin Hatcher. Copy. DNA, RG59, Dom. Letters, vol. 21, pp. 452–53 (M40, R19).

Hatcher, a Virginian, had formerly been president of the State-chartered Farmers' Bank of Richmond, and had been forced to resign from that office in 1819 because of political differences with the Richmond Junto. Harry Ammon, "The Richmond Junto, 1800–1824," *Virginia Magazine of History*, LXI (1953), 401. President Adams on December 26, 1826, had nominated Hatcher, with the other Federal appointees, as a director of the Bank of the United States. The appointments had been confirmed on January 3, and Hatcher continued as a director throughout the Adams administration.

To JOHN MCKIM, JR., VICTOR DUPONT, CAMPBELL P. WHITE, and BENJAMIN HATCHER, "Circular." Informs them of their appointment and confirmation as directors of the Bank of the United States. Copy. DNA, RG59, Dom. Letters, vol. 21, p. 453 (M40, R19). White accepted the appointment by letter of January 14, 1827. ALS, in DNA, RG59, Acceptances and Orders for Commissions (M-T645, R2).

From BENJ[AMI]N GRUT, Maracaibo. Encloses proclamations by the President (Simón Bolívar) extending peace terms to General (José Antonio) Páez and his troops. Comments that such action is Bolívar's "favorite means of enslaving the hearts of his foes to the interests of his country," that he "possesses the art of popularity in an eminent degree," and that he invited Grut to dine, "which gave . . . an opportunity to appreciate his personal attractions, during an hour's conversation. . . ." Reports local opinion that a (constitutional) convention will be called in five months. ALS. DNA, RG59, Misc. Letters (M179, R65).

APPLICATIONS AND RECOMMENDATIONS January 8, 1827

NICHOLAS CALLAN, JR., Washington, solicits appointment as a messenger or assistant messenger (in the State Department). Notes that he has been a life-long resident of Washington. ALS. DNA, RG59, A. and R. (M531, R2). Callan not further identified.

N[EWTON] CANNON, Harpeth, Tennessee, recommends Thomas Washington for appointment as (Federal) attorney (for the District of West Tennessee). ALS. *Ibid.* (R8). On the recommended appointment, cf. above, Yeatman to Clay, December 29, 1826, note.

JOHN T. DRAKE "of Cincinnati," writing from Nashville, recommends William Thompson for appointment as United States attorney for "this district" (West Tennessee). ALS. DNA, RG59, A. and R. (M531, R8). Drake was a "bookseller and Stationer." *The Cincinnati Directory for 1825* . . . (Cincinnati, 1825), 33.

J[OHN] H. EATON, JOHN H. MARABLE, and ADAM R[ANKIN] ALEXANDER recommend Leonard Cheatham for appointment as (United States) district attorney for West Tennessee. ALS by Marable, signed also by Eaton and Alexander. DNA, RG59, A. and R. (M531, R2). Undated; filed between letters of January 6 and 8, 1827.

Alexander, a native of Virginia, who had moved to Tennessee in 1801, had served in the State Senate in 1817 and was now a member of Congress (1823–1827). He later held a seat in the Tennessee House of Representatives, 1841 and 1843.

J[OHN] T. JOHNSON, Georgetown (Kentucky), recommends appointment of (Richard H.) Chinn as district attorney (for the District of Kentucky) should (George M.) Bibb be appointed "Chief Justice of Ky." ALS. *Ibid.* Unaddressed; erroneously dated, "1826." Cf. above, Marshall to Clay, January 5, 1827, note.

WILL[IAM] MORTON and others, Lexington, recommend appointment of Richard H. Chinn as (United States) attorney *vice* George M. Bibb, resigned to accept the appointment of Chief Justice of the (Kentucky) Court of Appeals. LS by Morton and 21 others. DNA, RG59, A. and R. (M531 R2).

To Benjamin G. Leonard

9h Jan. 1827.

Mr. and Mrs. Clay
request the favor of
Mr. Leonard's
Company on Wednesday evening
the 10h inst and on every
alternate Wednesday evening during the
Session of Congress.

N, partially engraved; name inserted in Clay's hand. OMC. Addressed to Leonard "at Brown's Hotel." Leonard, born in Connecticut and reared in Lewiston, New York, was now a Columbus, Ohio, lawyer. Identification of him as Clay's correspondent is indicated by letters from Leonard to his brother, Abiel, December 20, 1826, and February 6, 1827, referring to Benjamin's presence at this time in Washington. MoHi-Abiel Leonard Collection.

DIPLOMATIC NOTES   January 9, 1827

To JOSÉ MARÍA SALAZAR. Transmits extracts of dispatches from the United States ministers in Russia (Henry Middleton) and Spain (Alexander H. Everett), with enclosures, and copies of Clay's correspondence with the Russian Chargé (Baron Maltitz) in reference to "Peace or an Armistice between the New American Republics and Spain." Comments that this correspondence justifies "a strong hope" that peace "can not be much longer delayed," testifies to the "enlightened views" of "the reigning Emperor of Russia" (Nicholas I), and substantiates the "friendly interest" of the United States. Copy. DNA, RG59, Notes to Foreign Legations, vol. 3, pp. 321–22 (M38, R3). ALI draft, in CSmH. Published in Manning (arr.), *Diplomatic Correspondence . . . Latin-American Nations*, I, 279–80.

From CHARLES R. VAUGHAN, Washington. Informs Clay that he will comply with the third article of the convention of November 13, 1826, between Great Britain and the United States, which requires Great Britain to pay to the United States the sum of $602,480 for partial (one half) payment of claims arising under the Convention of St. Petersburg of July 12, 1822, and indicates that he will make payment on or before January 15, 1827. LS. DNA, RG59, Notes from British Legation, vol. 14 (M50, R15). Received January 10, 1827. See above, Clay to Biddle, December 20, 1826; Clay to Vaughan, December 27, 1826.

On January 11 Clay acknowledged receipt of Vaughan's note and agreed to accept payment of the money on January 15. Copy, in DNA, RG59, Notes to Foreign Legations, vol. 3, pp. 322–23 (M38, R3). ALS draft, in CSmH. By *procés verbale* dated January 15, 1827, Clay and Vaughan acknowledged transfer of the stipulated sum. Copy, in DNA, RG59, Notes to Foreign Legations, vol. 3, p. 323. AD draft, in CSmH.

INSTRUCTIONS AND DISPATCHES   January 9, 1827

From JOHN CUTHBERT, Hamburg. Reports that he is sending (Lewis Anthony) Humbert and (Charles) Cowan to the United States aboard the brig *Omega*, "of and bound for Philadelphia," and that he has directed a copy of "the evidence" to the clerk of Circuit Court (at that place) and another copy to the State Department, as Clay instructed (above, September 26, 1826.) ALS. DNA, RG59, Cons. Disp., Hamburg, vol. 3 (M-T211, R3). Received June 30.

On January 15, 1827, Cuthbert informed Clay that he had drawn on him for $230 as transportation expense for Humbert and Cowan. ALS, *ibid.* Cowan, a seaman, had been witness to the murder.

From CONDY RAGUET, Rio de Janeiro, no. 23. Acknowledges receipt of Clay's letter of October 22 and offers an explanation concerning the proposed treaty negotiation. Notes that, in accordance with his instructions of April 14, 1825, he informed the Minister of Foreign Affairs (Luiz Joze de Carvalho e Mello) on November 2, 1825, of "the willingness of The United States to conclude . . . 'a treaty of Peace, amity, navigation and Commerce' " and stated that, if Brazil preferred to negotiate at Rio de Janeiro, instead of Washington, "the requisite powers would be transmitted. . . ." Comments that, since this official replied on November 5, informing him that the Brazilian Minister in Washington (José Silvestre Rebello) had been directed to notify the American Government that the proposed negotiation should be conducted in Rio de Janeiro, and copies of this correspondence had been transmitted to the State Department in Raguet's dispatch of November 12, 1825, he had been awaiting receipt of the requisite powers. Comments: "The instructions with which I am now furnished under date of 22d October, seem to me to have been drawn up without a due reference to the existing state of the question between this government and me, at least so far as I have understood it, and were I now to complain of the injustice of Brasil, in giving advantages to the productions of Great Britain and France which are not accorded to those of The United States, I should most certainly be answered, that I had no right to complain, seeing that more than a year ago, it had been made known, that this Government had consented to treat with ours, as she had with those of the Nations, which enjoy these advantages."

Referring to his instructions to propose a negotiation at Tacubaya, Raguet protests that he cannot "see, how, without an apology for the non-fulfilment[*sic*] of the existing engagement, or without the assigning of some reasons for departing from a proposal of our own," he can now urge a change of treaty site. Furthermore, he argues, since the Brazilian Government has no Minister at Tacubaya, "nor is there just now any probability, that any will go," a proposal to negotiate at that place would merely afford an excuse for procrastination. Encloses a copy of his answer of January 3 to the Foreign Minister's rejection of the doctrine of previous warning (Inhambupé to Raguet, December 10, 1826, enclosed in Raguet to Clay, December 22, 1826). ALS. DNA, RG59, Dip. Disp., Brazil, vol. 5 (M121, R7). Extracts, including enclosure, published in *American State Papers, Foreign Relations*, VI, 1051–54. Received March 6, 1827.

While Raguet's dispatch of November 12, 1825, and the enclosed correspondence, had mentioned the desire that treaty negotiations be conducted in Rio de Janeiro, it had emphasized that the proposal for trade reciprocity was declined.

APPLICATIONS, RECOMMENDATIONS   January 9, 1827

S[AMUEL] M. BROWN, Lexington, recommends appointment of Richard H. Chinn as (Federal) attorney (for Kentucky). ALS. DNA, RG59, A. and R. (M531, R2). Unaddressed. Cf. above, Marshall to Clay, January 5, 1827, note.

JAMES COWAN, Lexington, recommends appointment of Richard H. Chinn as United States attorney for the Kentucky District. ALS. DNA, RG59, A. and R. (M531, R2).

G[EORGE] E. DYSON, Washington, solicits appointment to "any vacany or additional clerkship which may be created in the Department of State." ALS. *Ibid*. In an undated note addressed to Clay, Dyson explained that for seven years he had been engaged in commerce at New Orleans, that he had recently come north and opened a "Wine and Liquor Store," but that heavy losses "in the winding up of several Speculations in Cotton and Tobacco to Europe" had taken his capital and now compelled him to seek other employment. ALS, *ibid*. On the legislation establishing additional clerkships, see above, Clay to McLane, January 14, 1826, note; on the desired appointment, cf. below, Barnard to Clay, January 10, 1827, note.

M[ATTHEW] T. SCOTT, Lexington, recommends appointment of Richard H. Chinn as United States attorney for the Kentucky District. ALS. DNA, RG59, A. and R. (M531, R2).

To George Ticknor

Dear Sir   Washington 10h January 18[27]
    Mr. Alfred Shelby[1] of Kentucky, a [son of the] late governor Shelby, being about to visit the North[ern] Cities, I take great pleasure in introducing him to you as a young gentleman of much worth & respectability—a relation of Mrs. Clay,[2] and one in whose behalf [we] feel the strongest interest. I am with great respect Your Ob. Servant
Mr. Tichenor [*sic*]   H. CLAY

    ALS. KyU-Shelby Papers. On the same date Clay sent a letter of the same text to George Blake. ALS, in KyLoF.
    [1] The youngest son of Isaac and Susanna Hart Shelby, Alfred had attended Transylvania University and had inherited the Lincoln County farm of his father, deceased in July, 1826.   [2] Lucretia Hart Clay was a cousin of Susanna Hart Shelby.

From J[ohn] Harvie

My Dear Sir   Frankfort Kentucky Jany. 10. 1827.
    You have no doubt learned ere this that Mr Bibb[1] has been appointed to the Chief Justiceship of the Court of Appeals of this State,

which appointment it is now understood. has been accepted by him. As he cannot hold a State and an United States Office at the same time. I presume he has or means to resign that of Federal attorney for the district of Kentucky. In that contingency I would beg leave to suggest as his successor Mr J J Crittenden[2] of this place. [Discusses at length the qualities of Crittenden, refers to "The local divisions" of Kentucky which make "the exercise of the appointing power somewhat delicate and embarrasing [sic] to the administration," and stresses "that none [other] stand [sic] so favourably with his own party nor less offensively to the minority."]

It is the universal wish of the party to which he is attached that he should become at the approaching election a candidate for the Executive seat. Indeed many consider the success of the party as somewhat dependant [sic] on his doing so. I think other wise. But you know his situation,   A large family, accustomed from birth to the comforts and elegancies of life, dependant almost entirely upon his professional exertions & success for their enjoyments. Under such circumstances the sacrafice [sic] would be great for him to yield to the wishes of his friends. Greater I think than the occasion demands. He is not himself seeking this office But his friends and well wishers think it would be of service to him, and that it could not be as well or as acceptabley [sic] to the citizens generally bestowed on any other.

[. . . . Continues in praise of Crittenden.]

It is many a day since I received a line from you. I have attributed, perhaps with more of vanity than of truth the silence to the numerous and momentous avocations of the department of State   We are in a queer way here. Your devotion to correct & fundamental principles, and your wish to see the [sic] state government administered on principles of justice and honesty has raised up some opposition to you. But I think and most sincerely hope, it is diminishing and weakening hourly. The new Court party or their leaders have been endeavouring to excite prejudice and to proscribe you.[3] But they are beginning to find that the people are not to be duped. The acts of the administration as heretofore devolloped [sic] are too correct and unexceptionable in themselves to answer their purposes— They therefore resort to extraneous subjects, and puff among the great body of the people the exploits & prowess of Jackson   It will not answer, Kentucky if I am not egregiously deceived is most decisively with the administration maugre all the intrigues & machinations of some of our great or rather would be great men— Truly   J HARVIE

LS. DNA, RG59, A. and R. (M531, R2). Addressed to Clay.
[1] George M. Bibb.   [2] John J. Crittenden. Cf. above, Marshall to Clay, January 5, 1827, note.   [3] On the old court-new court controversy, see above, III, 902n. On the emerging political re-alignment, see above, Worsley to Clay, November 3, 1826; Crittenden to Clay, November 25, 1826.

DIPLOMATIC NOTES   January 10, 1827

From JOSÉ MARÍA SALAZAR, Washington. Reports the capture of the *Zulmé* (see above, Rodney to Clay, June 24, 1826, note) by Spanish vessels operating in the territorial waters of the United States. Calls upon the American government to press the claim "that said Privateer and her crew be set at liberty in the same state and condition in which they were captured." LS, in Spanish, with trans. in State Dept. file. DNA, RG59, Notes from Colombian Legation (M51, R2).

INSTRUCTIONS AND DISPATCHES   January 10, 1827

From WILLIAM TAYLOR, Veracruz. Reports that United States trade at Veracruz has declined greatly in the past two years and that the amount of capital employed, exclusive of shipping, is comparatively small. Suggests that this decline may have been offset by increases at Tampico and Refugio, attributed to the better facilities afforded at the latter ports "to merchants generally, facilities not enjoyed here [at Veracruz] to any extent except by the Spanish merchants, who, retaining all their wonted influence with the Officers of the Customs, do pretty much as they please." Notes that cottons are about the only production of the United States permitted to be imported, that under an order of last November the tariff on cottons has nearly doubled, and that the protests of United States Minister (Joel) Poinsett and local merchants have been unsuccessful. Comments, however, that holders of English goods pay the same duty.

Postscript requests permission for Taylor to visit the United States in May. Notes that the Mexican squadron under Captain David Porter put to sea on December 5 (1826).

ALS. DNA, RG59, Cons. Disp., Veracruz, vol. 1 (M183, R1). Received February 23. On March 9, 1827, Clay notified Taylor that the President had granted his request for a leave of absence. Copy, in DNA, RG59, Cons. Instr., vol 2, p. 414 (M78, R2).

APPLICATIONS, RECOMMENDATIONS   January 10, 1827

I[SAAC] D. BARNARD, Harrisburg (Pennsylvania), recommends William S. Derrick of Washington for appointment as a clerk in the Department of State. States that Derrick "resided in the same town" as he for many years and that Congressman (Charles) Miner, from Chester County, knows him well. ALS. DNA, RG59, A. and R. (M531, R2).

Derrick was appointed a clerk in the Department of State on March 3, 1827, and remained in that employment until his death in 1852. He served as chief clerk of the Department from 1843 to 1844 and from 1849 to 1852. The other two appointees under the legislation of 1827 (cf. above, Clay to McLane, January 14, 1826, note) were Philip R. Fendall and Aaron Vail, also dating from March 3.

P[ETER] BARRETT AND OTHERS, members of the Kentucky Senate, "recommend to the president John Trimble Esquire as a proper person to fill the Office of District Attorney for the State of Kentucky." DS by Barrett and 19 others. DNA, RG59, A. and R. (M531, R8). Not addressed. Endorsed on wrapper in Clay's hand: "Recd. 25 Jan. 1827." For the appointment to fill this post, cf. above, Marshall to Clay, January 5, 1827.

Barrett, of Harrison County, had been a member of the Kentucky House of

Representatives during the Session of 1819–1820 and of the State Senate since 1822. He remained in the latter body through the Session of 1829–1830.

V[ICTOR] DU PONT, Brandywine (Delaware), recommends (Henry) Wilson "from Pensacola," whom he has known "a long time," for an "appointment . . . far below his merits—but also very necessary to his comfort." ALS. DNA, RG59, A. and R. (M531, R8).

Wilson, who had been in Pensacola with Jackson's forces as early as 1818, had been seeking governmental appointments there under both the Navy and Treasury Departments during 1826. At about the date of the present letter he was in Washington to press for the post of naval storekeeper at Pensacola. For his appointment as Federal marshal of West Florida, see below, Clay to Wilson, November 27, 1827. The following May he was transferred as marshal to the Southern District of Florida and held that office until July, 1829.

MADISON "CLAY [i.e., CONYERS]" JOHNSON, Lexington, Kentucky, recommends appointment of Richard H. Chinn as (United States) attorney (for the Kentucky District). ALS. DNA, RG59, A. and R. (M531, R2).

R[ICHARD] M[ENTOR] JOHNSON recommends appointment of John Gardiner as a "temporary clerk . . . to bring up the business of the Patent office." States that he has known Gardiner for fifteen years, ten of them as a clerk in the Treasury Department. ALS. Ibid. (R3). Addressed to Clay. Letter endorsed (AES) by James Noble with remark that he concurs "in the foregoing statements. . . ."

Gardiner, a native of England, had resigned as chief clerk of the General Land Office on March 15, 1821. On the recommended appointment, cf. below, Thornton to Clay, March 6, 1827.

B[ENJAMIN] MILLS, Frankfort, Kentucky, recommends George "Robinson [i.e., Robertson]," former member of Congress and current Speaker of the Kentucky House of Representatives, for appointment as United States attorney for the (Kentucky) District. Recommends as alternatives Daniel Mayes, "of this place", or Richard H. Chinn, "in the order in which they are named." ALS. DNA, RG59, A. and R. (M531, R7).

WILLIAM OWSLEY, Frankfort, Kentucky, recommends appointment of George Robertson as United States attorney for the Kentucky District. Mentions that G(eorge) M. Bibb "this morning took his Seat upon the bench of the old court with Judge Mills" and himself. ALS. Ibid. Addressed to Clay.

HUMPHREY PEAKE and others, Alexandria (District of Columbia), recommend William Cowing, "of this city," for appointment as bearer of dispatches to Europe. ALS by Peake, signed also by R(obert) I. Taylor, John Roberts, Edmund J(ennings) Lee, Christopher Neale, and Thomas Swann. Ibid. (R2). Endorsed (AES) on verso of cover, January 14, 1827, by W(alter) Jones, supporting Cowing's candidacy.

Cowing and Taylor not further identified. Lee, a brother of Henry ("Light-Horse" Harry) Lee, had been mayor of Alexandria from 1814 to 1818. Swann had been Federal attorney of the District of Columbia since 1821 and from 1825 to 1827 president of the Washington Office, Bank of the United States.

HENLEY ROBERTS AND OTHERS, members of the Kentucky House of Representatives, recommend "John Trimble esquire to the President as a fit person to fill the office of district Attorney for the United States in Kentucky"; refer to his having been "repeatedly honored with Judicial Appointments in the State government"; and note that he is currently a member of the House. DS by Roberts and 52 others.

Ibid. (R8). Not addressed. Endorsed on wrapper in Clay's hand: "Rec'd 25 Jan. 1827."

Roberts, of Nicholas County, an Army officer during the War of 1812, had been a member of the Kentucky Legislature during the Sessions of 1820 and 1826–1827.

E[LISHA] WARFIELD, Lexington, recommends appointment of Richard H. Chinn as United States attorney (for the Kentucky District). ALS. *Ibid.*

R[OBERT] WICKLIFFE, Lexington, recommends appointment of Richard H. Chinn as (United States) attorney for the (Kentucky) District. ALS. *Ibid.*

To the House of Representatives

Department of State, 11. January 1827.

The Secretary of State, in obedience to a resolution of the House of Representatives of the 19th. Ulto.[1] by which he is directed to inform the House, "whether there has been any neglect or omission to record the Patents which have issued from the Patent Office, and for how long a time this neglect has existed, whether any additional number of Clerks is necessary, in order to bring up the business of that Office, which is now in arrears: and what further organization of that Office is necessary for the due execution of the Law in future, for the issuing and recording Patents" has the honour now to report in conformity with all of the above Resolution except the requirement contained in the last paragraph.[2]

That the Patents issued from the Patent Office since the year 1802 have not been recorded as required by Law, with the exception of some few which were recorded since the 4h. March 1825: That on enquiry into the general condition of the Patent Office, the Secretary ascertained that the Patents had not been recorded, owing to the want of the requisite assistance of Clerks in that Office: That he therefore directed an Extra Clerk to be employed on the business of recording the Patents, until the pleasure of Congress could be known; and the state of the Patent Office, in this particular, was communicated to the Committee of Ways and Means by a letter addressed to their Chairman,[3] under date the 14th. day of January 1826 and was adverted to, in another letter, from this department, under date the 16. February 1826. addressed to the Chairman[4] of the Committee raised by the House of Representatives on an enquiry into the expediency of establishing an additional Executive Department, to both of which Letters the Secretary begs leave to refer: That Congress having adjourned without making provision at the last Session for the employment of any other Clerk, the Extra-Clerk[5] was dismissed, it not being deemed proper to continue them,[6] without such provision, after the state of the Patent Office was known to Congress.

That in order to bring up the business at the Patent Office which is in arrear and to despatch the current business the Superintendent deems it necessary that there should be three additional Clerks authorized:[7] and the Secretary would respectfully suggest the propriety of an authority to employ permanently one additional Clerk, and for a limited time (say three years) two other additional Clerks. at the end of which period it could be ascertained whether their services would be longer needed or might thereafter be dispensed with.

In answer to the enquiry "what further organization of the Patent Office is necessary for the due execution of the Law, in future, for the issuing and recording Patents" it is respectfully stated that, in the event of the Establishment of a Home Department,[8] it is believed that the publick interest would be promoted by placing the Patent Office under its direction: that, at present, the business of the Patent Office is transacted in a different building and in a distant part of the City, from that in which the other business of the Department of State is executed; and owing to the press of other duties, the attention of the Secretary of State is only occasionally and generally directed to the Affairs of the Patent Office: That the business of that Office has greatly augmented: That the number of patents issued the last year amounted to 321. more than six times the number which were issued about twenty years ago: That with this increase of business is a proportionate increase of labour and of responsibility on the part of the Superintendent; and it is respectfully, therefore, recommended that his Salary, now below that of many of the Clerks employed in the different Departments, should be augmented so as to correspond better with the present extent and responsibility of his duties: That the fact of his long and faithful service may be supposed to furnish an additional motive for such increase.[9]

That the income considerably exceeds the disbursements of the Patent Office: That the receipts of the last year were $9420 and the expenditures were $6198 67/100: That if three additional Clerks should be authorized and the Salary of the Superintendent should be encreased in any reasonable amount, the expences of the Office would still be below its income.

With respect to the Enquiry of the House as to "what inconveniencies or hardships, if any, have been shewn by experience to result from the provisions of the several laws now regulating Patents and Copy rights" it is necessary to examine the various decisions of the Judiciary on those Laws as well as to collect much other information, not now in the possession of this Department: That to afford the requisite time to make such an examination and collection of information, the Secretary of State asks permission to report to the House of Representatives at some future Session of Congress.[10]

He requests that the Papers hereto annexed marked A. B. & C. may be taken as Parts of this Report. The first being a letter from the

Superintendent presenting his views of the wants of the Patent Office. The Second exhibiting the number of Patents issued and the receipts of the Office including the period of the last twenty six years. And the third, the amount of expences of the Office during the last year. All which is respectfully submitted.   H. CLAY.

Copy. DNA, RG59, Report Books, vol. 4, pp. 192–94. Published with covering letter of same date and accompanying papers in *House Docs.*, 19 Cong., 2 Sess., no. 47 (January 13, 1827).
   1 Introduced by Samuel Lathrop of Massachusetts on December 18, 1826. U. S. H. of Reps., *Journal*, 20 Cong., 2 Sess., p. 68. Cf. also above, Thornton to Clay, December 21, 1826.   2 An amendment offered by Gulian C. Verplanck, of New York, on December 19, 1826. *Ibid.*, 74–75. The printed version of the report includes Verplanck's amendment and reads as follows: "And, also, what inconveniences or hardships, if any, have been shewn by experience to result from the provisions of the several laws now regulating patents and copy rights."   3 Louis McLane.   4 Daniel Webster.   5 Robert Little. See above, Little to Clay, January 6, 1827, and note.   6 Printed copy reads "him" for "them".   7 See above, Thornton to Clay, December 21, 1826.   8 Cf. above, Brown to Clay, January 30, 1826, note.   9 Thornton, who served as Superintendent of the Patent Office from 1802 until his death in 1828, received a salary of $1500 per annum, which sum was not increased.   10 No further report on the subject found. For reference to Congressional action evolving from the current report, cf. above, Clay to McLane, January 14, 1826, note; and below, Thornton to Clay, March 6, 1827.

From James B. Reynolds

My dear Sir,   Clarksville Janry. 11, 1827.
   I am shock'd at the information received from France respecting the conduct of our citizens towards La-Fayette.[1] Should it be true, that there are those, who borrows [*sic*] money from him, without any hopes of ever paying it, I would hang them, as soon, as a traitors [*sic*] to their Country. And if I was in Congress, I would consider, whither [*sic*] it would not be proper to make enquiry on certain information, and if it turned out to be well founded, I should follow the subject up, by resolution, expressing the deep concern of the American Congress, and its detestation of such conduct &c. We made him the boon,[2] and would it not be the meanest of all traffics, in our citizens to take it from him? I hope for the honour of our Country it is not true, but if it is, I equally trust, that you, and the President will, through, Congress Shew to the World, that the American people view with indignation, any attempt to take from that good man, one Sous, that was given to him.
   Letters are yet flying from Nashville, about the attorny [*sic*], that is to be appointed for the U States in this State. I wrote you very hastily on this Subject, and I am afraid, that I have urged the claims of my friend rather too boldly.[3] But I know you will be dispos'd to excuse me, as it flows from the heart. I am certain, that the appointment of Mr. Cheatham will do more, in restoring to you, your former high Standing in this State, than any event, during the present administration, and am quite certain it will be of great service to me. I

am just informed, that Mr. Thompson[4] of Nashville is also before you for the appointment. He is a worthy man, and am told, he is an old acquaintance of yours. I know your strong attachments, and sorry I should be to disturb them, for a moment, but my dear Sir, he is only a little time in the state, & appears to take no part in politicks, the other is a native, surrounded by numerous friends and acquaintances, bold & open, in whatever he undertakes. It is true Mr. Thompson is the brother-in-law of Judge Brown[5] who is now a candidate for a seat on the Supreme bench of the Union. Now, to say the least of it, they are manifesting a considerable spirit for monopoly, which I detest, and which does not go down well, in any Country. There is a degree of delicacy wanting, I did not think Mr. Thompson would be guilty of. I had a letter from a nother [sic] brother-in-law (Mr. Hays)[6] saying to me that he was an applicant for the office of attorney, and requesting me, to write to you in his behalf, but I suppose on consulting with the judge, he was laid aside for a more fortunate candidate. The fact is, this same judge Brown is one of the most selfish, cautious men, in the world. He is of little service to any friend, unless his own views are promoted at the same time. He is rapt [sic] up in the misterious [sic] mantle of his own greatness, and the storm may pelt and be ready to over whelm you, and there is no helping hand from him if his own interest or fame is to be danger [sic]. I should not have said this much about this gentleman, having written to you in his behalf,[7] but since that period, and perhaps before, he has been endeavouring to bring out a *nother brother in law* a Mr. Huling[8] (who has been flourishing in the legislature of this State) against me for Congress. Now, I do not think this is fair play, and this is the thanks I get for entering warmly into the recommendation of him to you. In One word, I find him uncertain in his friendship, and very ambitious. In the present Case, however, I have nothing to fear on the ground of ingratitude. The Cheatham family are noble, bold, independent and grateful. I know them well, I have experienced their uniform & warm friendship for twenty years, without the least diminution or disguise &c— I hope my dear Sir I shall have my Spirits cheer'd up Once more, by your bestowing this office upon my friend Cheatham— I remain Ever yours most Sincerely   J. B. REYNOLDS
Hon Henry Clay
Secretary of State

I forgot to say, that I am highly pleas'd with your State paper, your letter to Gallatin,[9] but I am afraid Canning[10] will do nothing.— Do drop me a line Should you be pleas'd to give the office to Mr. Cheatham &c &c

ALS. DNA, RG59, A. and R. (M531, R2).
[1] Cf. above, Lafayette to Clay, December 29, 1826.   [2] See above, III, 900n.
[3] Reynolds to Clay, January 4, 1827, recommending Leonard P. Cheatham.

4 William Thompson.   5 William L. Brown.   6 Oliver B. Hayes.   7 Not found.   8 Frederick W. Huling, of Montgomery County, Tennessee, a lawyer and large landowner, served in the Tennessee House of Representatives from 1825 to 1835, and was Speaker the last four years.   9 Above, November 11, 1826.   10 George Canning.

From Joseph M. Street

Sir,   Vandalia Ill. Jany. 11. 1827.

Your former friendship, in kindly passing over the extraordinary events of 1806–7 & 8 in Ky, and the part I acted at that time in relation to yourself, has induced me to beleive [sic] the liberality of your mind, in consideration of my youth, will not permit you to remember against me, any objectionable portion of my conduct.[1] In 1820, I received from you at Washington, that polite & friendly attention to myself and interests, that I could not ask or reasonably expect, from one whose political standing I had attempted to injure.[2] But in Justice you ought to know, that I conscintiously [sic] believed the course I was pursuing was correct. So soon as maturer years and the developement [sic] of facts, began to clear the intentionally clouded horison [sic] in which I had moved, and the dawnings of a pureer [sic] light shone around me;— I ought to have done an act of Justice to the innocent. It was due to patriotism & high worth, to rend the veil of mistery [sic] and present to an admiring people, uncontaminated worth,—doubly consigning the guilty to a deserved fate.—This I could have wished; but human nature is frail—and this is one of the errors of my early life. I retired in deep disgust to the quiet scenes of private life— I declined the troubled field of politicks—and availed myself of every oppertunity [sic] to do justice by correcting any errors into which I had been lead [sic] by misinformation.

A different course from the one adopted against me might have enabled me earlier to retire—unfortunately I never could be driven. This much is said in Justice. Why should the forgotten times rise in review?—I might not have troubled you with the reading (tho' I have frequently avowed the entire misconception arrising [sic] from misinformation, of the course you then persued [sic]) if I had not an occasion to ask the extension of your kindness towards me.

The office to which you (with other friends) recommended me in 1820, from domestic considerations, I declined, and authorised our representation to inform Mr. Monroe & the Department of my declining the office. I did not wish to remove my family against the desire of my wife.[3] Subsequently I have suffered very deeply as the securety [sic] of a Mr. Laffarty[4] who leased a part of of [sic] the Wabash Saline and died greatly in debt. This has compelled me to sell out and remove. I contemplate a removeal [sic] to the N. West part of this State, or the N. W. Territory hoping in that newly settling country to make some provision for a large family.— I have six Sons and two

Daughers [sic], promising & sprightly—this from the Father you will account words of course. I think not. Two of the oldest—(Sons) are at College.—Thomas Posey, and Joseph.[5] As the grand children of a highly respected officer of the Revolution, who died poor,—these would to some, seem to claim the good feelings of the patriot.—

I am in mind, prepared to go wherever any imployment [sic] may call, that my friends should in their partiality think me capable of performing with usefulness to the Government. And I would desire no appointment that I was not considered of sufficint [sic] Capacity to fill with credit to those who recommended, and benifit [sic] to the Administration that confered [sic] it.

I expect Mr. Cook[6] will particularly propose me for some appointment (should any occur) which I have every reason to believe will be aided by the united voice of the representation from this State, and friends elsewhere. You will greatly oblige me, if you can feel at liberty to help me in this moment of *extraordinary need*.[7] I wd. generally refer you to Mr. Cook, on the subject.

You will doubtless have earlier information than this scrawl from this quarter—but in a word I will give you peep at the West of the Ohio & Mississippi.— Benton[8] is elected in Missou. Jackson Resolutions were offered in the H. of R. here some time early in the Session— Two unavailing attempts have been made to pass them & I presume they will never more be heard of[9]— The party is evidently on the decline— the Administration friends in the Senate are a majority of near 2 for 1. The law for electing electors for P. by *general ticket* passed 2 days ago.[10]— It is now considered certain that the whole vote of Ill. will be for Mr. Adams. It is clearly understood here that Mr. Cook does not owe his defeat to his Presidential vote, *or* the strength of Jackson;—but to the advantage that was taken of his Father-in-law[11] & himself both coming before the people at the same time. A cry of *Family influnce* [sic], and for an equal *division of officers*, made a deeper impression that you are aware of. However the inaugural address of Gov. Edwards has made a deep impression in his favour with the people—and friends & foes agree that he will be the most popular man in the state in less than 2 years if he gains upon the people as fast as he has the last 2 months. His enemies say he stoops to the people & is courting popularity— his course is certainly popular; but evidently the dictation of an able and experienced politician, and if perservered [sic] in, must eventual[ly] increase the prosperity and happiness of the people over whose interests he has been called to preside.

Should you find leisure to write me, which I trust you will—dire[ct] to Shawanee [sic] town— I am here attending the Legislature & return hom[e] in 10 or 12 days— Excuse this long letter— Whn [sic] I commenced I did no[t] expct [sic] to be able to fill one page. With high rispict [sic] devotedly your frien[d]   JOS. M. STREET

ALS. DLC-HC (DNA, M212, R2). Addressed to Clay.
[1] See above, I, 244–46, 329–43, 649n.   [2] Reference not found but cf. above, II, 214–15.   [3] Eliza Maria Posey Street, daughter of Thomas and Mary Alexander Thornton Posey.   [4] Probably Cornelius Lafferty, appointed justice of the peace for Gallatin County, Illinois, in 1818, who with Street and others had petitioned in 1816 for relief from payment of debts for land purchased at Shawneetown, near the Saline. Carter (ed.), *Territorial Papers*, XVII, 457–59.   [5] Street wrote Ninian Edwards on May 30, 1826, that he planned to move to the Springfield area. Washburne (ed.), *The Edwards Papers*, 272–77. Thomas Posey and Joseph Hamilton Daveiss Street were natives of Henderson County, Kentucky, and residents of Wisconsin from 1827 until the early 1840's, when the elder son died and J. H. D. Street moved to Iowa. In 1848 the latter was one of the founders of the Ottumwa, Iowa, *Des Moines Courier*; he died in 1875 in Montana. Both sons pursued careers in the legal profession. The location of their collegiate education has not been found.   The other Street children were Thornton Montfort (1814–1833), Mary (1816–1877), Lucy Frances (born in 1817), William B. (born, 1819), Alexander (1821–1877), and Washington P. (1825–1852). Another child, Sarah A., born in 1823 had died the following year.   [6] Daniel Pope Cook.   [7] Street was named as Indian Agent at Prairie du Chien on August 8, 1827, and his appointment to that office was confirmed by the Senate on February 15, 1828.   [8] Thomas Hart Benton.   [9] On December 9, 1826, partisans of Andrew Jackson in the Illinois House of Representatives had introduced a resolution endorsing the General for the Presidency and charging corruption in the House election of John Q. Adams in 1825. Subsequently an amendment merely expressing confidence in Jackson had lost by a tie vote, and another amendment limited to a nomination of Jackson had been defeated by two votes. On January 8 the original proposal had failed, again by a tie vote, on the question of bringing the measure to action. But on the last day of the legislative session, when five administration supporters were absent, a resolution endorsing Jackson's candidacy passed the House by a vote of 19 to 11. Pease, *The Frontier State*, 116–17.   [10] Illinois, *Revised Code of Laws . . . Enacted by the Fifth General Assembly . . .* (Vandalia, 1827), 188–89. Presidential electors had previously been chosen by district.   [11] Ninian Edwards. See above, Clay to Adams, July 25, 1826, note.

INSTRUCTIONS AND DISPATCHES   January 11, 1827

To ALBERT GALLATIN, London, no. 17. Requests him to procure information regarding British patent regulation and practice. LS. NHi-Gallatin Papers (MR14). Copy, in DNA, RG59, Dip. Instr., vol. 11, p. 230 (M77, R6); ALI draft, in DLC-HC (DNA, M212, R8). A letter of similar content, inquiring about French practice, was addressed to James Brown, instruction no. 9, the same date. LS, in KyU-William H. Fishback Papers.

From ALBERT GALLATIN, London, no. 50. Requests instruction regarding cash advances to consuls for seamen's relief and office expenses. Notes that most ministers of the British Government will not return to London until Parliament meets. Encloses a copy of (George) Canning's note "on the subject of the light houses." ALS. DNA, RG59, Dip. Disp., Great Britain, vol. 33 (M30, R29). Copy, in NHi-Gallatin Papers (MR14). Received March 2. In the enclosure dated January 11, 1827, Canning informed Gallatin that the latter's note of January 3 (see above, Gallatin to Clay, January 4, 1827) had been transmitted to the Admiralty.

From BENJAMIN GARDNER, Palermo. Acknowledges receipt of his commission (see above, Clay to Gardner, April 6, 1826) and files his annual report. Notes that the quarantine on United States shipping has not been lifted and will not be until the Neapolitan Consul General to the United States (Count Lucchesi-Palli di Campofranco) files information on the health at American ports; comments that "Commerce between the two Countries . . . is now most unjustly cramped." Reports the death of John Broadbent, American consul at Messina. ALS. DNA, RG59, Cons. Disp., Palermo, vol. 1 (M-T420, R1). Received March 29, 1827.

APPLICATIONS, RECOMMENDATIONS   January 11, 1827

R[ICHARD] PINDELL, Lexington, recommends Richard H. Chinn to replace George
M. Bibb as (Federal) attorney for the District of Kentucky. ALS. DNA, RG59, A.
and R. (M531, R2). Cf. above, Marshall to Clay, January 5, 1827, note.

C[LIFTON] R[ODES] THOMSON, Lexington (Kentucky), recommends R(ichard) H.
Chinn for appointment as United States attorney for the District of Kentucky;
requests that Thomson's respects be presented to Clay's son Theodore. ALS. DNA,
RG59, A. and R. (M531, R2). Erroneously dated "1826."
    Thomson, a lawyer, had been graduated from Transylvania University with the
Bachelor of Arts degree, in 1822. Theodore Wythe Clay had received the same
degree at the institution in 1821 and a Bachelor of Laws degree there in 1823.

To John James Appleton

No 2. J. J. Appleton
Chargé d'Affaires at Stockholm.   Department of State
Sir.   Washington 12th Jany 1827.
    Having just indirectly heard of your arrival at Stockholm, I am
directed by the President to call your immediate attention to the
subject of the Treaty which was concluded in that Capital and signed
on the 4th. day of September 1816.[1] The Treaty expired on the 25th
of last September.[2] It had been the President's wish, by a new negotiation, and by engrafting some further regulations upon it, to prevent
the event which has occurred. The illness and subsequent death of
your predecessor,[3] and your engagement on another public service,[4]
together with the incidental delay in your arrival at Stockholm, have
prevented, on our part, the opening of the negociation there. We had
moreover, some reason to believe that the Baron de Stackelberg would
have been provided with instructions to negociate on that subject
here. It was not until about the time of the expiration of the Treaty
that we were disappointed in the fulfilment of these expectations. On
the 26th day of September last, a note was received from the Baron,
of which a copy, together with a copy of the answer[5] which was returned to it, is herewith transmitted.
    As he announced in that note the determination of the Government
of Sweden to continue to observe the rule of the treaty notwithstanding it should expire without being renewed, he was informed that the
President would recommend to Congress to provide by law for its
observance on our part, until the issue should be known of the intended negociation. He has, accordingly, in his message to Congress
on the opening of its present session[6] (a copy of which accompanies
this despatch) recommended to that body, the enactment of the necessary law, to secure to the navigation and commerce of Sweden the
benefit of the treaty, until the result of the negociation is known. A

bill has been introduced into the H. of R. (of which a copy is herewith sent) to admit the vessels of Sweden upon the terms stipulated in the treaty, and making provision to refund any discriminating duties, should any such have been collected from Swedish vessels or their cargoes, between the 25th of September last, and the date of the law. No doubt is entertained of the passage of the bill,[7] prior to the adjournment of Congress, nor is any inconvenience anticipated, before the renewal of the treaty, from the limitation of the law to the single object of the discriminating duties. The bill would have been shaped so as to comprehend all the regulations of the treaty, but for doubts which were felt by some members of Congress as to the competency of the legislative power to extend to some of the stipulations which were believed to appertain strictly to the treaty-making power. As it is hoped that the interval will not be long before the treaty is renewed, and that no intermediate prejudice will arise to Sweden, it was not considered important to press a decision on those doubts. Your knowledge of our Constitution will enable you to explain the reasons of the President's being unable, without the concurrence of Congress or of the Senate, to direct the enforcement of the provisions of the treaty in the same summary manner as has been done in the ports of Sweden. By the Act of the 7th day of January 1824[8] the vessels of Norway will continue, without interruption, to enjoy an exemption in our ports from the payment of the discriminating duties.

You are now authorized to propose the renewal of all the articles of the treaty, with the exception of the third, fourth and sixth, to which the Senate, when it was submitted to them for their advice and consent to its ratification, objected, and with which exceptions it was ultimately ratified by both parties. The third and fourth articles related to the reciprocal introduction into the ports of the two Powers of the produce of the Baltic and the West Indies in the vessels of each, and providing a discrimination of ten per cent. more on the duties when paid by the foreign than the national vessels. The sixth specified the evidence which should be taken as conclusive of the fact of origin of the produce of the two countries. The same considerations which formerly induced the Senate to object to those three articles, would, probably still prevail, if they should be again inserted in a new treaty. In lieu, and as entirely superseding the necessity of them, you will propose a stipulation of a more liberal and comprehensive character; that is, that whatever can by law be imported from, or exported to any foreign country, place or possession, including the colonies of either party, in the vessels of one party, may be in those of the other, the foreign vessel and her cargo paying no higher or other duties or charges of any kind than the national vessel. A model of an article to that effect, which may serve as your guide, you will find in the fourth article of a treaty which was concluded at Washington on the 5th day of Decr. 1825, between the United States and the Federation of central America,[9] of which a copy is now transmitted. If this article be agreed to, the vessels of the United States will be entitled to navigate between the ports of Sweden and Norway, and the Swedish Colony of St. Bartholomew as well as between those ports, and all other foreign countries and places; but the vessels of neither party will be entitled to share in the coasting trade of the other. It is possible that it will be insisted that the intercourse between Sweden and Norway and that colony should be reserved exclusively to the parent country. The President being very anxious to secure the adoption of the general principle without qualification, and that it should ultimately be extended to all the colonial powers, you will oppose the reservation as long as there is any prospect of your prevailing on the Swedish Government to yield the point. You may urge that the inconsiderable trade of the colony can render the monopoly of no importance to Sweden; that she is equally with the United States interested in the universal adoption of the general principle without any exception; that the uncertainty of her continuing to hold the Island, in events of such frequent occurrence in Europe, should induce her to concur in the introduction of a liberal rule of permanent duration, not likely to be affected by those events, rather than adhere to a monopoly which might be lost upon the first occurrence of any one of them; that she will gain more, by her example, in her intercourse with other colonial Powers, as well as those which are without colonies, than by contending for the retention of a worthless monopoly; and, finally, that considering the relative amount of the Commerce and Navigation of the two countries, the United States manifest a liberality, in the offer of this proposal, which ought to be reciprocated.

Should your efforts, to induce a waiver of the monopoly be unsuccessful, you are then authorized to agree to an article similar to the before mentioned fourth Article in the treaty with the federation of the centre of America, with an exception like that which is contained in the sixth article of a treaty lately concluded between the United States and Denmark[10] (of which a copy is herewith transmitted) to the following effect: "But it is further agreed that this treaty is not to extend to the direct trade, between Sweden and Norway and the island of St. Bartholomew, but in the intercourse with that colony, it is agreed that whatever can be lawfully imported into, or exported from the said Colony in vessels of one party, from or to ports of the United States or from or to the ports of any other foreign country, may in like manner, and with the same duties and charges, applicable to vessel and cargo, be imported into, or exported from the said Colony, in vessels of the other party."

According to one so framed, Sweden will retain the monopoly, but the vessels of the United States will be allowed to trade between the Island and any other country or place, Sweden and Norway only excepted.

If the Swedish government should decline agreeing to an article in either of the two forms suggested, you are then at liberty to agree to a simple renewal of the treaty of 1816, with the exception of the third, fourth and sixth articles before mentioned. (The duration of any treaty on which you may finally agree, according to the preceding instructions, may be fixed to any term of between eight and fifteen years, to which you will propose a clause to guard against the event of its expiration, of similar import with the 11th article of our treaty with Denmark.[)]

A power[11] authorizing you to open and conclude the negociation is now also transmitted.

As the law which is at present before Congress, will probably be limited to the end of the next session, it is advisable that you should transmit the treaty which it is expected you will be able to conclude, in time to be laid before the Senate at the next session of Congress.[12]

I am, Sir, respectfully, Your Obt. Servant   H. CLAY

P.S.   20th. Jany. 1827.

Since the preceding letter was written, your despatch, under date the 1st. Novr. has been received with its accompanyments. Considering the tenor of the treaty which you state to have been lately concluded between Denmark & Sweden, no difficulty is anticipated in your prevailing upon the Swedish Governt to accede to the broad principle of our treaty with the Republic of the federation of the centre of America, by which Swedish vessels and those of the United States would be reciprocally allowed to import into, or export from the ports of the respective countries, whatever national vessels could import or export from or to any foreign country. To that rule, as we understand you, there is but one exception which is confined to the article of salt, the importation of which is as it respects Sweden and Denmark, limited to national vessels. But this limitation does not apply to Denmark and Norway. If the Government of Sweden should insist upon making the same exception of the article of Salt, you are authorized to agree to it, taking care that the stipulation be mutual.

Perhaps it may be urged that the 10th article of the treaty lately concluded between Sweden and Great Britain,[13] disables the former from agreeing to the above mentioned principle, that article providing that "Salt, Hemp, Flax, Oil of all kinds, Grain of all kinds, Wine, tobacco, Salt or dried fish, wool and stuffs of all kinds," shall be imported into Sweden only in vessels of Sweden and Norway, or in vessels of the country of which such articles were the produce. But if it formed no obstacle to the subsequent conclusion of the above mentioned stipulation between Denmark and Sweden, it is presumed it can form none to the proposed stipulation with the United States. We suppose also that the stipulation in that tenth article was not intended to abridge the liberty of Sweden to contract whatever engagements it might deem proper with any other Foreign Power, upon proper equivalents; but was designed to limit the right of British vessels to import the specified articles into the ports of Sweden.

Information has been received at this Department that there are certain advantages enjoyed by swedish, and now by british vessels (under the late treaty concluded between Great Britain and Sweden) as regards vessels arriving under distress on the coasts of Norway and Sweden, as also in pilotage and harbor dues which are not enjoyed by vessels of the United States. You will enquire and ascertain if that information be correct, in which case you will propose an article securing to our vessels the same advantages.

In order to prevent any evasion of the principle of equality between the vessels of the two countries, which forms the basis on which the Government of the United States offers to treat with that of Sweden, you will propose the following article: "No priority or preference shall be given, directly, or indirectly by the government of either country, or by any corporation, company or agent acting in its behalf or under its authority, in the purchase of any article, imported into the other, on account of, or in reference to, the character of the vessel in which such article was imported; it being the true intent and meaning of the contracting parties that no distinction or difference whatever shall be made in this respect."

Should you be unable to prevail on the Government of Sweden to agree to the principle of our Guatemala treaty, with, or without the exception of the article of Salt, as above mentioned, or to that of our treaty with Denmark, you will understand that your authority extends to a renewal of the expired treaty.

Copy. DNA, RG59, Dip. Instr., vol. 11, pp. 231–37 (M77, R6). ALI draft, in DLC-HC (DNA, M212, R8); published in *American State Papers, Foreign Relations*, VI, 717–19.
1 See above, II, 427–28n.   2 See above, Stackelberg to Clay, September 26, 1826.
3 William C. Somerville.   4 See above, Clay to Appleton, May 12, 1825.   5 Clay to Stackelberg, October 31, 1826.   6 December 5, 1826. Richardson (comp.), *A Compilation of the Messages and Papers of the Presidents*, II, 353.   7 Introduced January 5, 1827, and approved February 22, 1827. U. S. H. of Reps., *Journal*, 19 Cong. 2 Sess., 126; 4 *U.S. Stat.*, 206.   8 See above, Lorich to Clay, March 16, 1825, note.   9 See above, December 5, 1825.   10 See above, April 26, 1826.   11 Dated January 23, 1827. Copy, in DNA, RG59, Ceremonial Communications, II, 57.   12 The Treaty of Commerce and Navigation, with separate article, was signed at Stockholm July 4, 1827, submitted to the Senate December 12, 1827, approved by the Senate January 7, 1828, ratified by the United States January 17, 1828, exchanged at Washington January 18, 1828, and proclaimed January 19, 1828. Miller (ed.), *Treaties*, III, 283–301. For a collation of the instructions and treaty, see below, Appleton to Clay, July 11, 1827.
13 See above, Appleton to Clay, November 1, 1826.

From John J. Crittenden

Hon: H. Clay,

Dr Sir,   Frankfort Jany: 12th 1827

Our local differences & difficulties[1] seem to be rapidly approaching to a termination— Mr. Bibb[2] has accepted the office of Chief Justice—recognizes his brethren Mills & Owsley,[3] & is now cordially co-operating with them in court. And so ends that chapter of our ills— On yesterday the bill which had been sent from the Senate making appropriations for rebuilding the capitol at Frankfort, passed the House of representatives by a vote of 60 to 38[4]— Our constitution is repaired— Our capitol will be rebuilt, & Kentucky will be herself again— All these settlements & reconciliations will, I think, have a happy effect for you, & upon our national politics— They will extinguish in a great degree those local distinctions, & those passions, which oponents [sic] & the opponents of the administration, have endeavoured to avail themselves of, & to turn against the general government— It is the design of your friends in the Legislature to obtain some expression of its approbation of the administration— You may calculate with confidence, I think, that it will be done.[5]

I thank you for the documents you sent me— Your letter to Mr. Gallatin[6] is very fine— The subject to which it relates will, I fear, prove a very vexatious one— And if it should prove to be the seed of some future war, it would be no matter matter [sic] of surprise—

There is a subject which the administration has been acting upon, & to which it has given a very prominent attitude. I mean the Militia[7] — I fear this subject— I fear the consequences of your attempting at this time to exercise the power of organising & dicipling [sic] the Militia. Such a measure extends its practical effects through all society— it supersedes all local regulations upon the same subject, & interferes with the habits & usages of the people— I would not be understood as giving any opinion against the intrinsic propriety & policy of the measure, but I do not want to see the experiment now made— Your trained Militia would be assimilated to John Adams provisional army, & the misrepresentations that would most certainly be made, might prove as fatal to the present administration, as was the standing army to the administration of the late Mr. Adams.[8] I am not the only one of your friends here, that entertains these apprehensions— The motive that dictates, must excuse these suggestions— They are probably altogether unnecessary,— In that event they can do no harm, & they may serve to call your particular attention to a subject, which in the multiplicity & perplexity of your affairs, may not have received all the consideration it merits. When you shall have considered it in all its bearings, you will best know what to do.

I have wandered far from the subject on which I intended to write you in behalf of my very particular friend Wm. Thompson, now of Tennessee, & whom I wish to recommend to your good graces— I had best, perhaps, make it the subject of another letter to accompany this[9]—

As executor of Morrison you have a suit now in the Court of Appeals with Hubbard Taylor Esqr.[10]— He is your very good friend & mine, and is anxious that I should appear as his counsel in the case, & makes indeed some claim to my services on the grounds of some former conversations about the suit, which I do not remember— I told him my engagements with you, made it my duty to appear against him— But that I would write to you, & that under all the circumstances of the case, I thought you would consent to my appearing for him— Let me know as soon as your convenience will permit, whether you will so consent or not— Wickliffe & C— Allen[11] are both attending for you. Yr Friend   J J CRITTENDEN

ALS. NcD. Copy, in DLC-Crittenden Papers.
[1] The old court-new court controversy. See above, III, 902n.   [2] George M. Bibb.
[3] Benjamin Mills; William Owsley.   [4] Ky. Sen., *Journal, 1826–1827*, p. 117; Ky. H. of Reps., *Journal, 1826–1827*, p. 230.   [5] No measure specifically referring to the conduct of the Adams administration was introduced in this session of the assembly. Cf. above, Turner to Clay, January 7, 1827, note.   [6] See above, Clay to Gallatin, November 11, 1826.   [7] By authority of a joint resolution of Congress, dated May 17, 1826, the War Department had investigated the subject of militia reform and prepared a report based on the findings of a special board of officers appointed to study the question. In his annual message of December 5, 1826, President Adams had noted that he was enclosing a report on the militia. The report and accompanying documents were published as part of "Documents from the War Department Accompanying the President's Message to Congress," *House Docs.*, 19 Cong., 2 Sess., no. 2, part III, pp. 269–506. On January 31, 1827, John Chandler of the Senate Committee on Militia reported a bill based largely on the report of the War Department; on February 28 the Senate read the bill a second time and laid it on the table. No further action was taken at that Session of Congress. U. S. Sen., *Journal*, 19 Cong., 2 Sess., pp. 133, 252. See also below, Clay to Crittenden, January 25, 1827.   [8] After reporting on the deterioration of the relations of the United States with France, John Adams on May 16, 1797, had recommended that Congress form "a provisional army." Richardson (comp.), *A Compilation of the Messages and Papers of the Presidents*, I, 238. By act of May 28, 1798 (1 *U. S. Stat.*, 558–61), Congress had reluctantly authorized an army of 10,000 men. During the following year, when no use for the army had developed, public resentment had mounted against the taxation necessary for military support and the political rivalries manifest in appointment of the commanding officers. The army had been quickly disbanded when the French convention was negotiated in 1800 (see above, Clay to Adams, May 20, 1826, note).   [9] See below, this date.   [10] The suit, *Morrison's Exor. vs. H. Taylor*, on appeal from Clark Circuit Court, concerned the applicability of a power of attorney under which a note had been assigned to James Morrison. Robert Wickliffe represented the appellant, and Crittenden was among the counsellors for the appellee (cf. below, Clay to Crittenden, January 25, 1827). The decision of the lower court was sustained at the October Term, 1827. 22 *Ky. Repts.* (6 Monroe), 82–90.   [11] Probably Chilton Allan.

From Charles S. Morehead

Hon. Henry Clay,
Dear Sir,   Hopkinsville Jan'y 12th 1827.
    The notes placed in my hands [...][1] Mr. Crockett[2] for collection, by you, were sent to Nashville [wh]ere he then resided to get him to

confess judgment upon them, but before any court came on, he removed to his mills in another county in that State, and the notes were sent back to me. Since that time I saw Mr Crockett in this place and concluded I would bring suit on the notes and obtain judgment. He seemed perfectly willing to confess judment [sic], but no court was in session at the time. At the next term of the court judgment will be rendered agst him.

He suggested to me that you probably had from some collateral source obtained a part of the money due to you and desired me to write to you, to ascertain the fact, and if so, how much, that it may be allowed as a credit on his notes before judgment rendered agst him.

In consequence of the elevation of Col. Crabb[3] to the bench of of [sic] the Supreme Court of Tennessee, the office of Attorney for the District of West Tennessee has become vacant, and I take the liberty of inviting your attention to the claims of Mr William Thompson of Nashville to fill the vacancy. [Writes of the high regard held "in this section of the state" concerning Thompson's integrity and of the gratification which would attend his appointment.]

You are no doubt aware of the great and growing popularity of the present administration of the General Government in this quarter of your almost native land. Among all the candidates to supply the vacancy in Congress occasion[ed] by the death of Maj. Henry,[4] not one was bold enough to hoist the flag of opposition. They indeed seemed to vie with each other in commendation of the measures, which during your whole political life, you have boldly and strenuously advocated.

I feel proud of the part of the state in which I live. Bei[ng a] Kentuckian by birth I cherish all the feelings of one.

Mrs Morehead joins me in respectful compliments to Mrs Clay and Mrs Smith.[5] I am, dear sir, most sincerely Yr friend

CHS. S. MOREHEAD.

ALS. DLC-TJC (DNA, M212, R10). Endorsed by Clay: "Answd."; answer not found. [1] MS. torn; one or two words missing. [2] Probably Robert Crockett. See above, Memorandum of Assets, December 26, 1822. [3] Henry Crabb. See above, Yeatman to Clay, December 29, 1826. [4] Robert P. Henry. See above, Crittenden to Clay, November 25, 1826. All the candidates had been considered friendly to the administration; but Chittenden Lyon, one of the principal contenders had been claimed by both parties. Niles' Weekly Register, XXXI, 67, 210, 241. Lyon, son of Matthew Lyon, had been born in Vermont and brought to Kentucky as a child, in 1801. Now a merchant in Eddyville, he had been a member of the State House of Representatives (1822–1824) and from 1827 to 1835 served in the United States Congress, where he was identified as a Jacksonian. [5] Nanette Price (Mrs. Thomas) Smith.

MISCELLANEOUS LETTERS   January 12, 1827

To [JOHN QUINCY ADAMS]. Reports, in reference to the House Resolution of May 20, 1826 (U. S. H. of Reps., *Journal*, 19 Cong., 1 Sess., p. 611), requesting information "touching the impressment of Seamen from on board American vessels . . .

by the Commanders of British or other foreign Vessels . . . since the 18h. of February 1815," that on last May 8 a correspondence was begun with the British Minister, (Charles R.) Vaughan, concerning an incident which involved "the taking of two seamen from on board the Brig Pharos," that further details on the matter are being sought by both the American and the British officials, and that the only other instance of impressment, "falling within the scope of the Resolution," is one cited by (Condy) Raguet in a recent dispatch (Raguet to Clay, October 31, 1826). Transmits copies of the relevant correspondence. Copy. DNA, RG59, Report Books, vol. 4, pp. 194–95. ANI draft, in DLC-HC (DNA, M212, R2); published with accompanying papers in *American State Papers, Foreign Relations*, VI, 368–72. See above, Hodges to Clay, March 16, 1826; Clay to Hodges, June 20, 1826; Clay to Vaughan, May 8, June 15, 1826; Vaughan to Clay, May 10, 22, June 22, 1826.

From S[AMUEL] L. S[OUTHARD], Navy Department. Notes that he has received "Mr. Mc. Narrs letter of the 8th. ulto.," referred by Clay to this Department and "will converse . . . on the subject of it" when he and Clay next meet. Copy. DNA, RG45, Exec. Letterbook, 1821–1831, p. 229. Cited letters not found; McNarr (possibly John McNair, Jr., who resided on a farm adjoining "Ashland") not identified.

From MARTIN VAN BUREN, W(ashington). Notes that the nomination of Andrew Scott as Judge of Arkansas Territory has been referred to the (Senate) Committee on the Judiciary, "& its attention directed to certain papers said to be on file in the Department of State implicating his conduct & furnishing grounds on which application was made for his removal in 1824." Requests that these papers and a copy of the Arkansas dueling law be provided to the Committee. ALS. DNA, RG59, Misc. Letters (M179, R65). Published in Carter (ed.), *Territorial Papers*, XX, 366–67.

Scott, brother of Congressman John Scott of Missouri, had been born in Virginia and, when first named to the bench of the Superior Court of Arkansas Territory, on March 3, 1819, had resided in Potosi, Missouri. He had been reappointed in 1822 to a four-year term ending March 3, 1827; and on December 26, 1826, President Adams had nominated him for reappointment again. U. S. Sen., *Executive Journal*, III, 184, 312, 314, 552.

Scott had killed Joseph Selden on May 26, 1824, in a duel fought in Mississippi, across the border from Montgomery's Landing. A native of Henrico County, Virginia, Selden had served as a major in the War of 1812 and had continued in Army service until 1820, when he had resigned to accept appointment to the Superior Court of Arkansas Territory. Van Buren reported on January 30, 1827, that the Judiciary Committee had investigated the charges of improper conduct by Scott and found that the Territorial laws then in force declared the taking of life in a duel to be murder, imposed severe penalties for extending or accepting a challenge to duel within the Territory, and rendered offenders ineligible to hold office; that in 1824 a challenge had been given and accepted within the Territory, although the duel had been fought beyond its jurisdiction; that Selden had been killed in the duel. The committee had agreed that, apart from the Selden duel, Scott's appointment would be "unexceptionable." The Senate, by vote of 23 to 14, rejected Scott's nomination and on February 26 declined reconsidering its decision. *Ibid.*, 564–65, 572.

APPLICATIONS, RECOMMENDATIONS   January 12, 1827

ROBERT [JEFFERSON] BRECKINRIDGE, "Representative Hall of Kentucky, Frankfort," recommends appointment of Richard H. Chinn as United States attorney for

Kentucky. ALS. DNA, RG59, A. and R. (M531, R2). Cf. above, Marshall to Clay, January 5, 1827, note.

ROBERT H. BUNCH, Cartagena, solicits appointment as consul at this port, inasmuch as he has heard that John M. MacPherson plans to resign. States that MacPherson has been gone from the post for the past two months and that his deputy, after designating a successor, has also left. Stresses the need for a permanent consul. Mentions that he (Bunch) was introduced to the President (Adams) by (Richard C.) Anderson (Jr.) at Quincy in 1825; cites as references LeRoy, Bayard, and Company, G. G. and S. Howlands, and Ebenezer Stevens and Sons of New York; and asserts that his own establishment "receives fully three-fourths of the American Business at this Port." ALS. DNA, RG59, A. and R. (M531, R1). Bunch, not further identified, received no appointment. Cf. above, MacNeal to Clay, July 1, 1825, note.

Ebenezer Stevens, a major-general in the American Revolution, had later become a prosperous merchant, head of a firm which was active for some eighty years.

J[OHN] J. CRITTENDEN, Frankfort, recommends William Thompson to replace (Henry) Crabb as United States attorney for West Tennessee. Writes enthusiastically of Thompson's character and legal qualifications and concludes: "For God's sake, give him the attorneyship, if you can." ALS. DNA, RG59, A. and R. (M531, R8). Cf. above, Yeatman to Clay, December 29, 1826, note.

JACOB HARVEY recommends his uncle Reuben Harvey as consul at Cork. Transmits Reuben's letter of application (above, Harvey to Clay, November 25, 1826) and supplementary recommendations. AN. DNA RG59, A. and R. (M531, R2). Among the enclosures were, above, Cropper, Benson, and Company and others to Clay, November 7, 1826; Thomas Wilson and Company and others to Clay, November 7, 1826.

FRANCIS G. MACY, New York, recommends his nephew, Henry G. Macy, for appointment to the military academy at West Point; encloses letter (not found) from Henry Shaw "requesting . . . [Clay's] friendly interference. . . ." States that young Macy is the grandson of Gideon Gardner of Nantucket, who was a member of the Eleventh Congres. ALS. DNA, RG94, Cadet Applications, 1826-114 (M688, R43). Endorsed in Clay's hand: "Refered [sic] to the Honble Sec of War [James Barbour]. H. C." Cf. above, Shaw to Clay, August 10, 1826.

Francis G. Macy of Nantucket had served in the Massachusetts General Court, 1824–1825. Gideon Gardner, also of Nantucket, was a shipmaster and merchant; he had served in Congress from 1809 to 1811.

ALFRED H. POWELL, Washington, recommends Thomas Cramer for a clerkship "in one of the departments." ALS. DNA, RG59, A. and R. (M531, R2) Cramer, not identified, received no appointment.

JOHN TALIAFERRO, Washington, recommends S. A. M. Leland of Northumberland County, Virginia, for a clerkship in the State Department. Mentions that the young man has been a deputy in the county clerk's office for the past five years. ALS. *Ibid.* (R5). Leland not further identified. On the recommended appointment, cf. above, Barnard to Clay, January 10, 1827, note.

From James Brown

Dr. Sir,   (Private)   Paris Jany. 13. 1827.

When I last wrote you[1] the prevailing opinion was that the peace of Europe would not shortly experience any interruption. The unanimity and promptitude with which the succors to Portugal were voted and sent, the decided manner in which Ministers here condemned the ensurrection [sic], approved the conduct of Great Britain, and threatened to withold [sic] from Spain any assistance in case of her involving herself in a war by intermedling [sic] in the affairs of the Regency, all tended to create a belief that Ferdinand would observe a strict neutrality, and that the insurgents would speedily submit to the constitutional Government. The British Ambassador at Madrid[2] demanded that Spain should immediately recognize the Government of the Regency, dismiss the obnoxious Minister Calomarde, and punish those Commandants by whose assistance or connivance the refugees had invaded Portugal. No answer to this demand has yet been communicated to the public in an official form. The Quotidienn [sic][3] an Ultra paper notoriously in the interests of the apostolical party has stated that the demand was refused, and we now are informed from a less questionable quarter, that whilst Spain has consented to receive a Minister from the Regency and to send one to Lisbon, she has ordered a large army amounting, as some accounts state, to twenty thousand men, under the command of General Rodil,[4] to proceed to the Portuguese frontier, for the ostensible purpose of preventing the malcontents of Portugal from entering the Spanish Territory. The composition of this army, the character and political opinions of its commander, and the influence under which it is supposed to act, have given rise to the opinion that it is intended to encourage if not to assist the insurrectionary movements in Portugal. This apprehension is strengthened by the violence of the Apostolical party here and the encouragement which their friends in Spain will derive from the representations they will no doubt make of their numbers and of their influence with persons of elevated rank in the Government.

The Marquis de Moustiers[5] late French Ambassador at Madrid returned some time ago and was, it is said, not very well received by Ministers. He was however received by the King, and in a manner, as he states, not calculated to impress him with the opinion that he was disgraced. Some Spaniards suspected of intriguing in favor of the Apostolical party and of furnishing matter for the Quotidienne, have been ordered to leave Paris. It is said that they still remain in the City and boast that they have powerful protection. These circumstances are mentioned in the political circles as reasons for apprehending that the troubles in Portugal may be more serious and of longer duration than we had at first imagined. The accounts we receive of the strength and progress of the disaffected party in Portugal, are confused and contradictory. The dislike to the new order of things is however more general than it was at first believed to be, and at the last accounts the invading armies were advancing [tow]ards Oporto and Lisbon. As the

Ministers of all the great powers are doing every thing they can to prevent War I cannot think that the Spaniards will be so rash and inconsiderate as to provoke it. Orders have actually been sent to the Swiss Regiments at Madrid to return to France and attempts are making to replace them by voluntary enlistments from the body of Royalist Volunteers. As these however have entered into service more for the purpose of plundering and insulting the Constitutionalists than of defending the interests and honor of their Country, they are unwilling to engage action for any definite period. If we may we [sic] believe the latest accounts from Madrid a great portion of the troops ordered to the frontiers of Portugal had already deserted, and indeed it is suspected that the portugueze [sic] insurgents will be reenforced by desertions from the Spanish army.

The Chambers have been in Sessions several weeks and the and the [sic] projects of Laws proposed by Ministers have been under discussion in the Committees. The one on the liberty of the press seems to encounter the most violent opposition.[6] It is somewhat singular that whilst it has been attacked with an unusual degree of asperity by the opposition Journals, the Ministerial papers have not said a word in support of it. It is true that after bearing the attacks during eight or ten days, an article supposed to be written by one of the Ministers appeared in the *Moniteur*,[7] but this was not inserted in any other paper until a formal order requiring its insertion was addressed to the several Editors by the Prefect of Police.[8] It then appeared accompanied by editorial strictures calculated to render its insertion more injurious to Ministers than would have been a suppression of it. If an opinion as to the fate of this bold attempt to destroy the Press might be formed from present appearances, we would be inclined to think that both Branches are prepared to reject it. As the influence in support of that law is believed to flow from an elevated source, the public mind is greatly agitated and will continue to be restless until it shall be either rejected or amended in many important respects.

The Swiss Regiments in French service have been ordered back from Madrid.

We have nothing new from Greece.

The Queen Mab being a bad sailer, I shall write you more particularly by the Lewis which will sail in a few days.[9] I am Dear Sir with great regard Your very faithful Servt.   JAMES BROWN
Hon Henry Clay

ALS. DLC-HC (DNA, M212, R2). Cf. above, Everett to Clay, January 7, 1827.
[1] Above, Brown to Clay, December 29, 1826.   [2] Frederick James Lamb.
[3] Paris *Quotidienne, ou la Feuille du jour.*   [4] José Ramón Rodil y Gallo.
[5] Clément-Edouard, Marquis de Moustier.   [6] See above, Brown to Clay, December 13, 1826, note.   [7] Paris *Moniteur Universel.*   [8] Guy Delavau, noted for his ultra Catholic and royalist sympathies and his repressive policies toward liberals.   [9] The *Queen Mab*, a 270 ton packet built in 1824, originally for coastal trade, sailed between New York and Havre from 1824 to 1828 and required 40 days for the westward crossing.

The *Lewis*, a packet of 412 tons, had been built in 1822 for New York to Havre service and required only 37 days for the return voyage; but the *Lewis* was wrecked off Barnegat Inlet on March 6, 1827, in attempting to enter New York Harbor. William Armstrong Fairburn, *Merchant Sail* (Ethel M. Ritchie, ed.; 6 vols., Center Lovell, Maine, 1945–1955), II, 1106–7, 1234, 1297.

From Felix Grundy

Dear Sir,   Nashville, January 13th 1827—
    I am at last able to furnish something like a satisfactory account of the whole matter relating to the money due you as Extr of Thos Hart Senior—and I assure you it has given me more uneasiness than any pecuniary matter of my whole life— You had my receipts for the notes[1]— I was unable to shew what payments I had made & knew you would not exact from me money you had already receivd— But the misfortune was neither of us could shew what was right— I was confident of the main fact, that I had paid over the money receivd—but had no means in my power to shew it— I always beleived [sic], you did not know how the matter stood— My inability was produced by the fact of my having transferred in the Bank $2400 receivd by me in Octr 1817 to Mr R McGavock[2] my brother in law to enable him to take up any draft, you might draw on me to that amount, should it be presented in my absence,   accordingly your draft[3] for that sum was taken up by him, as appears by the books of the Bank— The whole subject passed from my memory, hence my so often insisting that you should furnish a statement of the monies receivd. by you— Altho, this matter had given me so much concern, that to prevent all controversy, I actually offered a few days ago, to give my note payable in twelve months—for any sum, which Mr Erwin[4] yr son in law should make due by a calculation, without then knowing or claiming any credit for the $2400, receivd by me in the fall 1817,— I never for a moment beleived, or suspected that you would do me an act of injustice—or claim one Cent more than you beleivd to be Justly due—and altho I have always used this language when I spoke of it.—It would be well to preserve this declaration of mine on this subject— For I should regret very much, that any man should be affected by a private transaction with me, in which he was not culpable— In a statement furnished Mr Erwin, I claimed a credit for $1300, merely on the ground of my perfect conviction that as that sum was credited on the small bond, it might have been transmitted—& might enable you to ascertain how the matter was— In the note I offered I claimed no such credit— My son in law[5] is now engaged in making a statement to inclose in this letter, therefore remarkes [sic] or explanations are all that is necessary— You placed in my hands two notes, one for $25,000 [sic], due 12th [sic] May 1812, this bond or note was lost in the Clerks office—& the decln filed on it— This rendered a settlement between Colo Sand-

ford[6] & myself impracticable, unless the payments made to you could be ascertaind as he had not receipts for some payments, except on the bond—and I was suspicious enough to do him great injustice in supposing he had not made any thing near the payments, actually receivd by me— On this note as appears by my receipt to you, $200 was paid to you in Octr 1811, also $200 in Octr 1814—$630 paid Mr Tilford[7] in Febry 1816,— thus indorsed the note was placed in my hands— As a further credit Colo Sandford has Colo Benton's receipt for $481, with an order or authority from you in favor of Colo Benton,[8]— I know this ought to be allowed as I am acquainted with the handwriting of both Mr Clay & Mr Benton, the date I cannot state, but it is about the time the note became due— The other note for $2170 came into my hands without any indorsal & was due 1st April 1813— Immediately after the reception of the notes, $220 was placed in Saml, Filfords [sic] hands, who sent you a draft for it, as by yr letter to him,[9] now in Mr Tilfords hands— In Octr 1817 a large payt. was made to me, & the money deposited in the Nashville Bank[10] & checked for by me in favor of R McGavock in order to meet Mr Clay's draft, whenever it should be presented, in my absence; In Febry 1818 Mr Clay sold a draft on me payable at sight for $2400 to the Office of Discount & Deposit at Washington City, as appears by his letter of 16th of Febry 1818,[11] this was paid at Nashville Bank on presentation— In Nover 1818, the money collected on the Judgt. for the ballance [sic] due on the small note was paid over to me,—(the note had been credited by me for a part of the $2400)   This money I had no mode of transmitting to Mr Clay so as to meet Mr Clay's wishes   In March 1819, I deposited $950 in the Nashville Bank to the credit of Henry Clay Extr &c.   this Mr Clay checkd for,[12]— In June 1819 I sent by Judge Todd,[13] a check for $450 on the Farmers & Mechanics Bank of Nashville— This money I beleive was drawn out by Mr Levy[14]—I recollect that Mr Levy after I had sent the check applied to me to exchange it, & I refused, alledging [sic] that I had receivd the same money & had neither used it nor exchanged it. My Commissions on the sums collected at 5 pr Cent which is usual will be about $200 or 201—

Colo Sandford claims $60 for his lawyers fee in the suit in Equity to procure the title to the land. I have refusd to allow it— you might say whether I shall give a credit for it or not? I never agreed to allow it nor is it right— My Commissions would not be charged so high but for the trouble I had with the Equity suit—

There is as you will see but a small ballance due from Colo Sandford—so soon as you say whether the $60 shall be allowed or not I shall close the business— You must direct what shall be done with Colo Bentons receipt—

You will perceive that precise accuracy, as to dates is not attended to— I could not attain it without seeing Colo Sandford— I have hastily, at the first moment it was in my power proceeded [*sic*] to give you this statement, which is substantially correct—& will I hope satisfactorily account to you for a delay, which is acknowledged to have been unreasonable & which unaccounted for might Justly subject its author to censure— I intend to be at Washington next winter, & will bring with me an accurate statement— If that will be satisfactory & If any ballance be due from Colo Sandford or myself, it will then be paid— My coming to Washington does not depend on my being elected[15]— I have some business in the Supreme Court—& elected or not shall be there— write to me on receipt of this— yrs respectfully,

FELIX GRUNDY

preserve the inclosed statement also
[Enclosure][16]

Note due first of May 1812 for	$2500
Amount paid before due	207
	2293
" " " " to Benton	481
	1812
Int. from 1st May 1812 to 1st. April 1813	99 66
	1911 66
Another note of	2170
	4081. 66
Int. from 1st. April 1813 to 1st Oct 1814	367 34
	4449 00
Deduct payment made	200
	4249 00
Int. from 1st. Oct 1814 to first Feby 1816	339 44
	4588 44
Deduct payment by Tilford	630
	3958 44
Deduct payment by Tilford	220
	3738 44
" paid costs of suit in Equity	45 50
	3692 94
Int. from first Feby 1816 to 1st Oct. 1817	370 20
	4063 14
Deduct payment	2400
	1663 14
Int. from 1st Oct 1817 till 15„. Nov 1818	112 26
	1775 40
Deduct payment	950
	825 40

do   do   450
                                                                                  ─────────
                                                                                    375 40
Deduct for commissions of 5 pr cent on $4020   ....   201 00
                                                                                  ─────────
                                                                                    174 40

Statement made by F Grundy to Henry Clay Extr &c 14th January
1827   F. Gr.

ALS. DLC-HC (DNA, M212, R2). Addressed to Clay; enclosed in Grundy to Clay,
January 14, 1827.
   1 Not found. Cf. above, I, 781.   2 Randal McGavock had married Sarah Dougherty
Rodgers, a sister of Grundy's wife, Ann Phillips Rodgers. Born in Rockbridge County,
Virginia, and educated at Carlisle Academy, Pennsylvania, McGavock had moved to
Nashville in 1796 and had been clerk of the Old Supreme Court of Mero District and,
from 1810 to 1834, of the Davidson County circuit court and the State Court of Errors
and Appeals. In 1824–1825 he had served as mayor of Nashville. He later removed to a
farm near Franklin, in Williamson County, Tennessee, where he died in 1854. The
Rodgers girls, residents of Kentucky at the time of their marriage, came from a family
which had moved west out of Lunenburg County, Virginia. Mrs. Grundy had founded
the first Sunday School in Nashville, in 1820.   3 Not found.   4 James Erwin.
   5 Jacob McGavock, nephew of Randal, had married Louisa Caroline Grundy in 1819.
Jacob, born in Virginia, had joined his uncle in Nashville in 1807, where he had assisted the latter in his clerical duties. Jacob was himself commissioned clerk of the
Davidson County circuit court from 1834 to 1836.   6 James T. Sandford.
   7 Probably Samuel Tilford, in 1812 a resident of Lexington, Kentucky; a cousin of
John and Robert Tilford.   8 Thomas Hart Benton; the order not found. Cf. above,
I, 819–20.   9 Draft and letter not found.   10 The Nashville Bank, founded in
1807, had suspended specie payments in 1819 and closed in 1827.   11 Draft and letter
not found.   12 Not found.   13 Thomas Todd. The check not found.
   14 William Leavy.   15 See above, Carroll to Clay, November 25, 1825, note.
   16 AD by Jacob McGavock, in DLC-TJC (DNA, M212, R16).

From Robert Scott

Dear Sir,   Lexington, 13th. Jany 1827
    Please receive herewith, your Accounts with Colo. Morrison's Estate
and with me down to the first of the present month[1]—
    By your Account with me, you will perceive the expence of repairs
of the Stable &c. have been considerable, but Mr. Kennedy and T. W.
Clay[2] and my self have done what we beleived [sic] most to your interest in making these repairs and hope it will meet your approbation— Hereafter or rather from the 1st. inst. Mc.Cracken[3] is to pay
specie rent at the same rate as before—150$ per anm.—
    Herewith also, is a statement of Pork slaughtered at Ashland, by
which you will perceive it has been but a poor business this last season— Doctrs. Pindell and Satterwhite[4] have not paid for what they
got of it—they say they have a medical account against you—
    Mr. Kerr[5] informs me he has put down all your hemp, and has
nearly a ton broke out— We have sold it all @ 7$50 per Cwt. deliver-
able at any time between this and first of August next— Our weather
has been so severe that Mr. Kerr has been unable to break up any
ground as yet— The hemp is to be paid for as delivered—
    By the accounts of the estate, you will perceive that I have not any

specie funds on hand— But an excellent house servant and carriage driver being offered to Mrs. Morrison[6] and feeling desirous to accommodate and gratify her, I purchased him at the high price of 600$ on credit, with interest until paid— I informed her that I had no funds on hand and that I very much doubted whether you would consent to pay interest, particularly as the price was so high, when she agreed that if you refused to pay the interest she would— I hope however that it will not amount to much, as I am in daily expectation of the arrival of W. Morgan[7] and payment of his debt and if not disappointed will pay for the servant— I hope too, to receive some money soon on Acct of Leathers's debt[8]—

I have failed in getting from Pike and Warner[9] any part of their protested Bill and have given it to Mr. Chinn[10] for suit—

Aunt Morrison says she is determined to set out about the first of April on a visit for Baltimore &c.   She and all the family are well— Very respectfully Your Hble Servt   ROBT. SCOTT
The Honble Henry Clay
[Enclosure][11]

Statement of Pork killed at Ashland in
Novr. and December 1826 viz

15	Hogs sold Doctr. Pindell	2394 lb @ 1 3/4	$41″89 1/2
13	Ditto „ Satterwhite	2083 „ „ „	36″45 1/4
6	Ditto „ Mrs. Morrison	863 „ „ „	15″10 1/4 pd
1	Ditto „ Mrs. Hart[12]	100 „ „ „	1″75 pd
35		5440 lb	$95″20
44	Salted up-not weighed		
79			

ALS. KyLxT.
[1] The quarterly accounts of Clay with James Morrison's estate and with Scott are located in KyLxT and incorporated in the annual statements summarized below, July 16, 1827.   [2] Matthew Kennedy; Theodore Wythe Clay.   [3] John McCracken.   [4] Richard Pindell; Thomas P. Satterwhite.   [5] John H. Kerr.   [6] Esther Montgomery Morrison   [7] Willis Morgan, of the Pond River district of Muhlenberg County, Kentucky, was one of the proprietors of a grist mill and a heavy investor in lands. His debt of $665.76 to the Morrison estate, due June 11, 1821, was listed as "Good." Cf. above, Debt Account, ca. August 12, 1826.   [8] John Leathers, who had filed a land entry for 1000 acres in Fayette County in 1782, had been appointed justice of the peace of Campbell County in 1798 and resided there as late as 1825. His debt for $1950 to the Morrison estate, due October 25, 1825, was listed as "Good" and currently in suit in Campbell County. Ibid.   [9] James M. Pike; Elijah Warner. Pike at this time had expanded his Lexington business activities as lottery agent, auctioneer, and commission merchant.   [10] Richard H. Chinn.   [11] AD by Scott.   [12] Susannah Gray Hart (Mrs. Thomas, Sr.).

INSTRUCTIONS AND DISPATCHES   January 13, 1827

From THOMAS L. L. BRENT, Lisbon, no. 37. Reports that he attended "the royal sitting of the ordinary Cortes" on January 2, encloses a copy of the speech of the Infanta Regent (Isabel María), and quotes passages praising the British for aiding Portugal. Notes that about five thousand British troops have arrived and that ten

British war vessels are off the Portuguese coast (see above, Gallatin to Clay, December 13, 1826, note). Comments that quartering of British troops in private homes has produced difficulties but that reports of the complaints are exaggerated and explains that differences of religious habit account for most of the anti-British sentiment. States that the Portuguese Government has been considering whether Lord Beresford should be appointed to command the combined armies but that the belief is prevalent that he will soon return to England. Traces the movements of the government and rebel armies and warns that peaceful resolution of Portuguese-Spanish difficulties is not likely, for the passions of the ultra-royalists "in Spain and in Europe" are too excited. LS. DNA, RG59, Dip, Disp., Portugal, vol. 7 (M43, R-T6). Received March 8, 1827.

MISCELLANEOUS LETTERS   January 13, 1827

From L[OUIS] McLANE, House of Representatives. On behalf of the Ways and Means Committee requests explanation of current "estimates of appropriations for the intercourse with Foreign Nations." Inquires why an outfit is needed for a Chargé d'Affaires in Guatemala, when the current Chargé (John Williams) is expected to return to the United States, and whether appointments for Chargé to Guatemala and Minister to Colombia will be proposed at this Session of Congress; why the estimated salaries for commissioner and arbitrator under Article 1 of the Treaty of Ghent (and Convention of St. Petersburg) exceed those for the previous year by $1,663 and whether the recent convention (with Great Britain of November 13, 1826) will not dissolve the present commission and render appropriations for that object unnecessary; and what is the present state of surveys made under Articles 6 and 7 of the Treaty of Ghent and when expenditures for that object may cease. Asks, finally, whether or not it would be in the public interest to reduce diplomatic expenditures, "especially by reducing the number or grade of missions to the Governments of S. A. or any of them?" ALS. DNA, RG59, Misc. Letters (M179, R65). For the estimates, see above, Clay to Nourse, November 16, 1826, note. For Clay's answer, see below, Clay to McLane, January 15, 1827.

APPLICATIONS, RECOMMENDATIONS   January 13, 1827

JOHN BOYLE recommends George Robertson for appointment as United States attorney for the District of Kentucky. Comments that (John J.) Crittenden "is the only man who stands upon an equality" with Robertson and that, if Crittenden wishes the appointment, it should go to the one "most desirous of obtaining" it. ALS. DNA, RG59, A. and R. (M531, R7). Cf. above, Marshall to Clay, January 5, 1827, note.

M[ATTHEWS] FLOURNOY, Frankfort, recommends appointment of Richard (H.) Chinn as United States attorney for the Kentucky District. ALS. DNA, RG59, A. and R. (M531, R2). Addressed on cover filmed for Henry Clay Papers Project; cover not supplied in source cited.

JESSE MOORE, District of Columbia, solicits reappointment as justice of the peace (for Washington County, D.C.). ALS. Ibid. (R5).
    Moore, of Georgetown, possibly the Revolutionary War veteran of that name, had been first appointed justice of the peace on December 21, 1821. Adams had renominated him to the position on December 26, 1826; but on February 8, 1827,

the Senate rejected the appointment. U. S. Sen., *Executive Journal*, III, 257, 260, 553, 557, 566.

CHRISTOPHER TOMPKINS, Glasgow, Kentucky, recommends appointment of William Thompson as United States attorney for the West Tennessee District. Notes that Thompson resided in Glasgow for twelve years before removing to Nashville and that for most of that period he was engaged in "successful practice of the law. . . ." ALS. DNA, RG59, A. and R. (M531, R8). Cf. above, Yeatman to Clay, December 29, 1826, note.

Tompkins, reared in the home of John Breckinridge, under whom he had studied law, had begun practice at Henderson, Kentucky, and in 1805 had represented Henderson and Muhlenberg Counties in the State legislature. Shortly thereafter he had removed to Glasgow, where for a number of years prior to 1824 he had served as judge of circuit court. Defeated in the gubernatorial campaign of that year, he was subsequently elected to the United States Congress for two terms, from 1831 to 1835, and returned to the State legislature in 1835 and 1836.

WILLIAM WHITE, Nashville, recommends appointment of Thomas A. Duncan as United States attorney for the Western District of Tennessee. ALS. DNA, RG59, A. and R. (M531, R2). Misdated as "1826."

From Felix Grundy

Dear Sir,   January 14th 1827—
    In looking over the inclosed[1]—I discover that I have not named the fact, that your letter of the 16th Febry 1818[2] had been filed away in an old bundle of papers, in which nothing but political letters &c were kept & this letter is principally on political subjects— there is only one paragraph on the subject of the money or draft— Mr McGavock,[3] whose check appears by the Bank books to have paid the draft, I suppose kept the draft; I have never seen it—& he never named the subject to me, so far as I recollect— he is not here at this time, having removed about 20 miles off—but you can by calling at the Office of Discount & Deposit in Washington,[4] ascertain that all is right— You know If your Draft on me for $2400 had not been promptly met, both of us would have remembered it— yrs respectfully   FELIX GRUNDY

ALS. DLC-HC (DNA, M212, R2). Addressed to Clay.
[1] Above, Grundy to Clay, January 13, 1827.   [2] Not found.   [3] Randal McGavock.   [4] The Washington Branch of the Bank of the United States.

APPLICATIONS, RECOMMENDATIONS   January 14, 1827

JOHN L. BRIDGES, Frankfort, applies for the office of United States attorney for the Kentucky District. Refers to his "long acquaintance" with Clay and "the indications of friendship manifested in the Course of that acquaintance" as encouragement for this approach. ALS. DNA, RG59, A. and R. (M531, R1).
    Bridges, a son-in-law of Governor John Adair (Bridges had married Nancy Adair in 1803), had served in the Kentucky House of Representatives from 1801 to 1805 and in the State Senate from 1817 to 1820. In the last-named year he had

been appointed judge of circuit court. On the result of his current application, cf. above, Marshall to Clay, January 5, 1827, note.

To Louis McLane

To: L. Mc. Lane, Esqre.
Chairman of the Committee of Ways and Means
Department of State. Washington, 15. January 1827.
In answer to your Note of the 13th. instant, I have the honour to state that the estimate of an Outfit for a Charge des Affaires to Guatemala is founded on the expected return of Col. Williams[1] who is supposed to be now on his voyage home; The bad state of his health at Guatemala is believed to be the principal reason which has induced him to return. The President will nominate to the Senate, prior to the adjournment of Congress, a Minister to Colombia and a successor of Col. Williams, unless intervening events should render it inexpedient.[2]

The Estimate of the salaries of the Commissioner and Arbitrator under the St. Petersburg Convention was made prior to any knowledge in this Department of the Conclusion of the late Convention with Great Britain. According to that Convention the mixed Commission is to be dissolved from the date of the Exchange of the ratifications of the Convention. The exchange is to be made in London, but at what time it will take place can only be matter of conjecture. The ratification of the Convention has been made by the Government of the United States and that of Great Britain may be confidently anticipated. Should the improbable event occur of a refusal of the British Government to ratify it, the appropriation, according to the estimate, will be wanted; and on the contrary event, only so much of it will be requisite as to meet the expences of the mixed Commission up to the time of the exchange of the ratifications. It is probable that Congress may deem it proper to create a new Commission to execute the Convention upon the contingency of the British Ratification.[3] And in that case, the unexpended balance of the Appropriation may be assigned to the new Commission. The Estimate was founded upon an estimate presented to this Department by the Secretary of the mixed Commission,[4] and, is for the same amount as the estimate of the preceding year. The Appropriation of last year was $1663. less than the estimate of that year; and hence the difference between the present estimate and that appropriation.

With respect to the time when the expenditure will cease in regard to the Commission under the 6. & 7. Articles of the Treaty of Ghent, it cannot at present be definitely stated. It is yet in progress, but some disagreement has lately arisen between the American and British

Commissioner [sic],[5] which has induced the latter to refer the matter to his Government. And a correspondence has recently taken place between the British Minister and this Department, on the subject of that difference.[6] The delay is chiefly to be ascribed to the great extent, difficulty and precision with which the part of the work executed has been attended. None, which he could avoid is believed to be imputable to the American Commissioner. Nor is it intended to ascribe any to his Colleague. If it be desired by the Committee the whole correspondence with this Department will be submitted confidentially to their inspection.

It is not believed that any reduction of the amount of appropriation for the diplomatic service other than that which has been proposed in the Estimates can be made compatibly with the public interest. Nor that, at this time, with reference to the same object, the number of Missions to the Governments of South America can be lessened. It is contemplated, on the return from Chili, of Mr. Allen, to whom Instructions have, for that purpose, been transmitted[7] to reduce the grade of the Mission to that Republic to that of a Chargé des Affaires. But he is not expected to arrive in the United States until towards the next autumn.

I have the honor to be with great respect Your Obedient Servant.

H. CLAY.

Copy. DNA, RG59, Report Books, vol. 4, pp. 195–96. ALI draft, in DLC-HC (DNA, M212, R2).
    [1] John Williams; see above, Williams to Clay, November 24, 1826.   [2] See below, Clay to Watts, March 8, 1827; Clay to Rochester, March 11, 1827.   [3] Cf. above, Clay to Gallatin, December 28, 1826 (no. 15), note. Funds for the new commission were provided in the organic act. By another act of March 2, 1827 (4 *U. S. Stat.*, 208–14), Congress appropriated $12,000 for the salaries of the commissioner, arbitrator, and staff of the earlier commission.   [4] James Baker.   [5] Peter B. Porter and Thomas Barclay. See above, Delafield to Clay, November 15, 1826.   [6] See above, Vaughan to Clay, October 23, 1826; Clay to Vaughan, November 15, 1826.   [7] See above, Clay to Allen, November 1, 1826; Clay to Larned, November 4, 1826.

To Martin Van Buren

Martin Van Buren, Esqre., Chairman of Committee
on the Judiciary of the Senate.
Sir,   Department of State.   Washington, 15 January 1827.
I have the honour to transmit you herewith, in compliance with your request,[1] all the letters which appear to have been on file in this Office,[2] recommending Andrew Scott as Governor or Judge in Arkansas— With respect to the Papers to which you also refer and with which you request to be likewise furnished, implicating the conduct of Mr. Scott, and submitted for the purpose of procuring his removal from office in 1824, I have the honour to state, that sundry papers of

that description, as I am told, chiefly or altogether Publications in Newspapers were lodged in this Office, in that year, but that they were immediately withdrawn by the Gentleman[3] who had so lodged them. I am, Sir, with great Respect, Your obedt. Servt.   H. CLAY.

Copy. DNA, RG59, Report Books, vol. 4, p. 191.
[1] See above, Van Buren to Clay, January 12, 1827.   [2] None now found there.
[3] Not identified.

From James Erwin

My dear Sir   Nashville Jany 15th. 1827
    I have for the last few days been endeavoring to settle with Mr Grundy.[1] The Claim that you have against him as Executor of Col. T Hart—on which suit was sometime since ordered and the papers placed in the hands of Mr H Crabb for that purpose,   his late appointment to the Supreme Bench of the State[2] has rendered it necessary to transfer them to Mr Thos. Washington who has instituted Suit[3]— Mr Grundy begged more delay which I refused having already indulged him too long. The face of the papers even after admitting Some credits which he claims but has no vouchers Shew a Balance against him of $5229.87.   he offered me his note at 12 months for Such Balance as I claimed before he ascertained what that Balance would be, altho he said one of Sanfords notes had been lost & that he had never collected one cent theron [sic], which Bond itself with the int that would be due amounts to $3952.   this amt of course from his own Statement must be due   But when I made outt [sic] my Statement Claming [sic] So large a Balance—his recollection was wonderfully invigorated or renewed—and he can now recollect, that he has collected part of both Bonds & remitted you the greater part of the Money. of which you have no account nor he any receipts or vouchers of any Kind.
    Inclos[e]d you have an exact Copy of Statement rendered by him acknowledging a Balance when the int is added of upwards of $2000 for this I presume he would be willing to execute his note,   you will perceive he claims first a credit of $1300—paid or remitted you in Oct 1817.   he acknowledges that he has no recollection or evidence of having paid you this amt. But infers that he did so from the fact of the records here shewing you that he had at that time collected that amt from Sanford & supposes that as in duty bound he had remitted it—a conclusion not likely to be drawn by those who know him best— The fact is Mr Grundy has no money on hand, and he wishes to gain time by equivocation & hopes to impose on you by his own statements—   he also claims a credit of $481— Which was paid by Sanford to Thos. H Benton on your order—prior to the claim coming into his hands, but which ct. was not entered on it—   this may be correct.   if

so Benton instead of Grundy will account to you for that amount—
he also claims $450 paid Wm Levy [sic]. on your order. which he
can not prove but which I suppose is correct—

Mr Grundy will write you on the subject of this claim   one object
will be to prevail on you to dismiss this suit another to instruct me to
settle with him agreeably to his Statemt   in doing which I feel confident from his own acknowledgmts. to me, you will do yourself great
injustice   You will bear in mind that in matters touching his pecuniary interests very little reliance can be placed in any Statemts. made
by him   But Such orders as you may give either to Me or to Mr Washington will be Shortly attended to,

We are Still detained here by low Waters, its now raining & we hope
to leave in a few days. Anne will Write her Mother[4] by this or the next
mail, to whom you will Remember me Kindly   Very Truly

                                                               J ERWIN

ALS. DLC-TJC (DNA, M212, R10)
[1] Felix Grundy. See above, Grundy to Clay, January 14, 15, 1827.   [2] Henry Crabb.
Cf. above, Yeatman to Clay, December 29, 1826, note.   [3] Cf. below, Washington to
Clay, December 7, 1827.   [4] Anne Brown Clay Erwin (Mrs. James Erwin); Lucretia
Hart Clay (Mrs. Henry Clay)

DIPLOMATIC NOTES   January 15, 1827

To JOSÉ MARÍA SALAZAR. Acknowledges receipt of Salazar's note of January 10.
States that on the basis of this communication (Alexander H.) Everett has been
instructed to demand from Spain restoration of the privateer *Zulmé* and her crew
but warns that proof of the charges "resting . . . upon the ex-parte statement of
the Captain [Denis Thomas] . . . will not be deemed sufficient to make out the
case." Requests Salazar to furnish "authentic and complete evidence verifying the
illegality of the Capture." Copy. DNA, RG59, Notes to Foreign Legations, vol. 3,
p. 324 (M38, R3). ALI draft, in CSmH. Published in Manning (arr.), *Diplomatic
Correspondence . . . Latin-American Nations*, I, 280. See below, Clay to Everett,
January 15, 1827.

INSTRUCTIONS AND DISPATCHES   January 15, 1827

To ALEXANDER H. EVERETT, no. 7. States that he has received a note (above, January 10) from the Colombian Minister (José María Salazar) complaining of capture
of the Colombian privateer *Zulmé* in United States waters. Notes that the crew is
confined at Havana and that the *Zulmé* is probably there. Directs that Everett
demand from the Spanish Government release of the ship and crew and payment
of damages in compensation for "the violated authority of the United States."
Copy. DNA, RG59, Dip. Instr., vol. 11, pp. 237–38 (M77, R6), ALI draft, in DLC-
HC (DNA, M212, R8).

From CHARLES BARNET, Antwerp. Requests instructions on how to handle almost
daily cases of Negro crewmen on American ships bound for South Carolina, where
State law provides severe punishment for such crewmen entering port. Notes that
they beg to be discharged in Antwerp but that captains are reluctant to lose them
or to supply the three months wages required when terminating employment in a

foreign port. ALS. DNA, RG59, Cons. Disp., Antwerp, vol. 1 (M-T181, R-T1). See above, Gallatin to Clay, December 21, 1826, note.

From W[ILLIAM] TUDOR, Lima, no. 57. Transmits his semi-annual report on American shipping and comments that a decline in such shipping to Callao, which will be reflected more accurately in the next report, is attributable to the renewed production of wheat in Chile, the restoration of the estates in Peru, and the increase in tariff duties on American produce. Observes that British trade has also declined but that of the French has increased. Reports that he has named Samuel B. Harrison, of Philadelphia, newly arrived as a merchant at Bolívar (Trujillo), to be vice-consul for that port and that he informed the new agent that he ought to solicit a regular appointment from the President. Communicates a new decree by the government, requiring ship masters to file two copies of their manifests within twenty-four hours of their arrival "on penalty of being excluded from discharging." Estimates that the Peruvian mint coined two million dollars worth of gold and silver in 1826 and that the amount will be doubled. Encloses an issue of *El Peruano* containing some notes, which he attributes to Foreign Minister (José María de) Pando, on the political situation in South America. ALS. DNA, RG59, Cons. Disp., Lima, vol. 1 (M154,R1). Received May 30. Endorsed by Clay: "This is to be submitted to the President."

When William Radcliff was appointed Tudor's successor as consul at Lima (see below, Clay to Radcliff, August 10, 1827), Daniel Brent, on October 1, 1827, transmitted to him copies of this Tudor letter and its enclosures, with the comment that they might "be useful and interesting." Copy, in DNA, RG59, Cons. Instr., vol. 2, p. 444 (M78, R2).

Harrison, not further identified, received no formal appointment.

MISCELLANEOUS LETTERS   January 15, 1827

To [JOHN QUINCY ADAMS]. Reports payment made this day by the British Minister (Charles R. Vaughan) of $602,480 "agreeably to the third Article of the Convention with Great Britain signed on the 13th. day of November last." Copy. DNA, RG59, Report Books, vol. 4, pp. 191–92. Published in *American State Papers, Foreign Relations*, VI, 372. See above, Vaughan to Clay, January 9, 1827.

From THOMAS H[ART] BENTON, Senate Chamber. Transmits a letter from the Mexican Minister (Pablo Obregón) requesting information about depredations committed on American citizens by Indians in Mexico. States that Obregón has been referred to Clay. ALS. DNA, RG59, Notes from Mexican Legation, vol. 1 (M54, R1). In the enclosure Obregón commented that, in his opinion, "no Government is obliged in justice to make similar indemnifications, even when those who commit the robberies are their Citizens," but conceded that the example cited by Benton of the action of the United States in indemnifying Mexican citizens would give reason for reciprocal action. Accordingly, he inquired whether the indemnification was authorized by act of Congress, how many such indemnifications had been made, and what amount had been paid to (Manuel) Simón (de) Escudéro. ALS in Spanish, with trans. in State Department file. See above, Benton to Clay, January 3, 1827.

From HENRY R. STORRS, Chairman of the (House) Committee on Naval Affairs. Requests information on the enclosed petition (not found) of W[illiam] C. Parke regarding his claim on the Danish Government for prize money. ALS. DNA, RG59, Misc. Letters (M179, R65).

Parke, not further identified, was the son and heir of Matthew Parke, captain

of Marines on the frigate *Alliance*, which claimed one of three prizes taken while
in service with the squadron of Captain John Paul Jones in 1779 and subsequently
seized and surrendered to the British by the Danes. On March 21, 1848, Congress
finally passed legislation to compensate the legal representatives of Jones, "and
the officers, seamen, and marines of the squadron under his command," for the
loss of the prizes. 9 *U. S. Stat.*, 214.

APPLICATIONS, RECOMMENDATIONS   January 15, 1827

H[ENRY] ATKINSON, St. Louis, "Private," recommends Beverly Allen for appointment as United States attorney for the District of Missouri. Ranks him "among
the first men in the state for talent, integrity & popularity." States that Allen is
Clay's friend and that he "drew up and introduced the resolutions in the Legislature of this state, at the recent session, approbatory of the measures of the general government." ALS. DNA, RG59, A. and R. (M531, R1).
   Atkinson, a native of North Carolina, had entered the Army in 1808, advanced
to the rank of colonel in 1814, headed the Yellowstone Expedition in 1819 (cf.
above, II, 599n), and returned to St. Louis in 1820, with the rank of brigadier
general in command of the right wing of the Western Department of the Army.
   Beverley Allen of Ste. Genevieve, Missouri, was nominated for the recommended
office and the appointment confirmed on March 3, 1827; he served until his removal in 1829. A native of Virginia and a graduate of Princeton, Allen had moved
to Missouri Territory and opened a Latin school at Jackson in 1820. Shortly
thereafter he had moved to Ste. Genevieve, where he shared a law practice with
John Scott. Following his removal from office in 1829, he resided in St. Louis and
represented St. Louis County in the State legislature. His resolutions commending the Administration have not been found.

LESLIE COMBS, Washington, recommends appointment of (Richard H.) Chinn as
United States attorney for the Kentucky District. Observes that, if he were to
consult his own interest, he might desire the position for himself but that he will
pursue his past rule of conduct and not solicit appointment. Comments: "I now
feel *independent* & when, hereafter, I may advocate the great leading measures of
the present administration, it Shall not be charged to me, that I have been a
Seeker of office under it—" ALS. DNA, RG59, A. and R. (M531, R2). Cf. above,
Marshall to Clay, January 5, 1827, note.

WILLIAM COWING, Alexandria (Virginia), submits "In Obedience to your instructions of the 6th. inst." a letter from Humphrey Peake and others (above, January
10, 1827). Postscript refers also to James Barbour and Roger Jones as sources of
information. ALS. DNA, RG59, A. and R. (M531, R2).
   Jones, born in Virginia, had entered the Marine Corps in 1809, had served with
gallantry through the War of 1812, and in 1825 had been appointed adjutant
general of the Army, a position he held until his death in 1852.

JOHN F[LOURNOY] HENRY, Washington, recommends appointment of Daniel Mayes
as United States attorney for the Kentucky District. Requests that the office be left
open until Mayes' application is received. ALS. *Ibid.* (R5). Addressed to Clay.

J[OHN] J. MARSHALL, Cincinnati, recommends appointment of his brother (Thomas A.) as United States attorney for the Kentucky District. Explains that he did
not know of his brother's candidacy when he recommended (John J.) Crittenden
for the post (above, Marshall to Clay, January 5, 1827). ALS. *Ibid.*

J[OSEPH] R[ODGERS] UNDERWOOD, Frankfort, recommends appointment of William Thompson of Nashville as United States attorney for the West Tennessee District. ALS. *Ibid.* (R8). Unaddressed. Cf. above, Yeatman to Clay, December 29, 1826, note.

From James W. Denny

Dr. Sir   Frankfort 16. Jany. 1827
[Recommends John J. Crittenden as United States attorney for the Kentucky District.[1]]
I have no boubt [sic] but that our unfortunate disputes on the subject of New & old Court are now ended; the appointment of Mr Bibb seems to satisfy us *reorganizers* & the other party seem satisfied with Owsly [sic] & Mills.[2]
I suppose you have various accounts at the City as to the course to be persued [sic] by Kentucky in regard to the presidential Election. I think I hazard nothing in asserting that at least two thirds of Kentucky are decidedly for the administration
In the Louisville Dist. Dotr. Burr Harrison will beat Wickliffe,[3] I have no doubt— Harrison is decidedly in favor of the administration.
If I could obtain from the Federal Gov an appointment to suit me & which I could with propriety accept I would be pleased. I think I could discharge the duties of a Secretary of legation or Secretary to a Territory & if such an appointment were to be disposed of I believe I should be a candidate[4]—
If you think there would be any chance of my success, I would procure the necessary recommendations. I am very respy Yr. friend
                                                        J W. DENNY

ALS. DNA, RG59, A. and R. (M531, R2). Unaddressed in this source; cover supplied with letter as originally filmed for Clay Papers Project.
1 Cf. above, Marshall to Clay, January 5, 1827, note.   2 William Owsley and Benjamin Mills. Cf. above, Kendall to Clay, December 22, 1824, note.   3 Charles A. Wickliffe. See above, Worsley to Clay, November 3, 1826, note.   4 Denny received no Federal appointment.

DIPLOMATIC NOTES   January 16, 1827

From CHARLES R. VAUGHAN, Washington. Complains that agents of the States of Maine and Massachusetts are "surveying and laying out Townships in the disputed Territory" along the northeastern boundary under the Treaty of Ghent. Warns that such action may lead to a "collision of a most disagreable [sic] nature between the Settlers in that Territory" and expresses hope that the intervention of the Government of the United States will be "effectually exerted" in "so conciliatory a spirit" as was evidenced in connection with his correspondence a year previously. LS. DNA, RG59, Notes from British Legation, vol. 14 (M50, R15). Published in Manning (arr.), *Diplomatic Correspondence . . . Canadian Relations,*

II, 575–76. Cf. above, Vaughan to Clay, November 15, 1825; Clay to Vaughan, January 18, 1826.

INSTRUCTIONS AND DISPATCHES   January 16, 1827

From ANDREW ARMSTRONG, Port au Prince (Haiti). Transmits documents relating to a protest which he has filed with the local authorities over an incident representative of his ambiguous position (as an unaccredited commercial agent) in the country. Explains that feelings toward the United States are not friendly but that, under a recent act France has lost "all real advantage she possessed" over the United States; "from the 1st inst vessels of All Nations Are to pay the Same export duty." Continues: "And, as those vessels trading under Haitian Colors, Are mostly owned by Americans, man'd & commanded by Americans, And sailed for American Account, it is in reallity [sic] opening a door by which our Merchants can introduce Our own and European Manufactures into the country, on better terms than can be done by the most favoured Nations—" Notes that the British, recognizing the possible role of this country in the event of maritime war, have sent a consul general (Charles MacKenzie) and keep a warship "constantly in the roads." Urges that American naval vessels be instructed to "look in" occasionally. ALS. DNA, RG59, Cons. Disp., Cap Haitien, vol. 6 (M9, R6). Received February 15.

The enclosed documents relate to the case of an American seaman, Henry B. Pullen, who deserted his ship for service on a British naval vessel and, imprisoned on charges by the American skipper, Captain W. Hoodless, was surrended to the British by local authorities. On the Haitian export duties, cf. above, Armstrong to Clay, June 1, 1826; below, Armstrong to Clay, February 22, 28, 1827. MacKenzie served as British consul in Haiti from 1826 to 1833.

MISCELLANEOUS LETTERS   January 16, 1827

From SAMUEL L. SOUTHARD, Navy Department (1). Transmits an extract of a letter "dated Rio 27 Novemr. 1826" from (James) Biddle. LS. DNA, RG59, Misc. Letters (M179, R65). In the enclosure Biddle reported that the Brazilian Government refused to exempt from customs inspection and duty stores for United States naval vessels unless the United States would agree to a reciprocal exemption on supplies which might be sent to the latter country for use of Brazilian warships. States that Condy Raguet, while refusing to commit the United States to the arrangement, did assume personal liability for the duties if his government rejected it. Urges that the United States accept the Brazilian proposal and free Raguet from his commitment. Notes that the supplies for his ships have now been released but that he has been delayed in sailing to the River Plate. LS, *ibid.* Cf. above, Raguet to Clay, November 27, 1826.

From S[AMUEL] L. S[OUTHARD], Navy Department (2). Acknowledges receipt of "Mr. Sebree's letter of the 14th. ulto. referred by you to this Department" and replies that the appointment went to another applicant. Copy. DNA, RG45, Exec. Letterbook, 1821–1831, p. 229. The letter not found; Sebree not identified.

APPLICATIONS, RECOMMENDATIONS   January 16, 1827

SAMUEL APPLETON and others, Boston, recommend John Larkin Payson to succeed [John] Broadbent, deceased, as consul at Messina. LS, signed also by seven others. DNA, RG59, A. and R. (M531, R6). Enclosed in Webster to Clay, below, January 25, 1827. Cf. above, Celigioli to Clay, November 6, 1826, and below, Everett to Clay, January 21, 1827.

D[AVID] BARTON, Senate Chamber, transmits a letter by (Spencer) Jarnagin recommending (Thomas H.) Fletcher for appointment as United States attorney for the West Tennessee District. Observes that Fletcher is a member of the (Tennessee) Assembly from (Jacob C.) Isacks' district (Winchester) and that Fletcher is "one of the few *quasi* friends of the existing administration, in Tennessee." ALS. DNA, RG59, A. and R. (M531, R3). Jarnagin's letter, dated December 30, 1826, and addressed to Barton, is in Fletcher's file, *ibid*. Cf. above, Yeatman to Clay, December 29, 1826, note.

Spencer Jarnagin, born in Grainger County, Tennessee, had been graduated from Greenville College in 1813 and admitted to the bar four years later. He had begun practice in Knoxville, served in the State Senate (1833–1835), and subsequently (1837) moved to Athens, Tennessee. Jarnagin was elected as a Whig to the United States Senate in 1843 but was defeated in his bid for re-election in 1847. He later removed to Memphis and practiced law there until his death in 1853.

DANIEL P. COOK, Washington, recommends appointment of Sidney Breese, of Kaskaskia, Illinois, as United States attorney. ALS. DNA, RG59, A. and R. (M531, R1).

Breese, born in Whitesboro, New York, graduated from Union College, Schenectady, in 1818. Admitted to the Illinois bar in 1820, he had commenced practice in Kaskaskia and served as State prosecuting attorney from 1822 to 1826. He was nominated Federal attorney for the Illinois District on January 18, 1827, and the nomination was confirmed on February 12. Removed from office in 1829, he compiled and published the first volume of Illinois Supreme Court reports in 1831, served as a judge of State circuit courts (1835–1841) and of the State Supreme Court (1841–1842), and was elected as a Democrat to one term in the United States Senate (1843–1849). He returned to the Illinois Supreme Court in 1857, where he remained on the bench until his death in 1878.

ANN CLIFTON PATTON, Spring Bank (Pennsylvania), solicits a clerical position for her son Robert. AN. DNA, RG59, Misc. Letters (M179, R65). Month omitted in date, but document filed with January letters.

Mrs. Patton was the daughter of Benjamin Reeder. She and her son have not been further identified. The young man was hired as a copyist in the State Department later in the year and received $52.50 for copying 52,500 words. *House Reports*, 20 Cong., 1 Sess., no. 226, p. 88.

JAMES H[AYS] PIPER, Wythe C[ourt] H[ouse], Virginia, identifies himself as a native Virginian, one who has "ever been in favor of those principles of government, and that construction of the Federal Constitution, which long have characterized the policy of" that state, and admits that he "was among those who proposed another candidate to the *distinguished individual* [John Quincy Adams] who now presides. . . ." With "these circumstance, thus openly and candidly avowed," he solicits Federal appointment. ALS. DNA, RG59, A. and R. (M531, R6).

Piper, a graduate of Washington (later Washington and Lee) College, in 1830 received the M. A. degree from East Tennessee College and in 1833 entered the Presbyterian ministry. He did not receive Federal appointment.

R[OMULUS] M[ITCHELL] SAUNDERS, "Repres Hall," recommends Archibald Murphy for a "diplomatic mission." Notes that Murphy is convalescent and "his physician advises his going to a Southern climate." ALS. *Ibid.* (R5). Cf. above, Yancy to Clay, December 13, 1826.

HUGH L[AWSON] WHITE, Washington, encloses letters recommending appointment of (Thomas) Washington as (United States) district attorney for West Tennessee. States that he, himself, does not wish "to be understood as making any recommendation," although he is willing to say, at Washington's request, that the applicant "is intitled [*sic*] to all the character given him by the writers of those letters." ALS. DNA, RG59, A. and R. (M531, R8). Addressed to the Secretary of State. The enclosures, addressed to White, are from Thomas Stuart, J(oseph) Philips, and R(obert) Whyte. Cf. above, Yeatman to Clay, December 29, 1826, note.

Stuart, admitted in 1796 to the bar of Davidson County, Tennessee, and commissioned in 1803 as Federal attorney for the District of West Tennessee, had been judge of the fourth judicial circuit and the Supreme Court of Errors and Appeals of that State since 1809. He retired in 1836 to his farm near Franklin in Williamson County, Tennessee.

Robert Whyte (White), born in Scotland and educated at the University of Glasgow, had come to America about 1784 and studied law, probably at William and Mary College, had begun practice at Tarboro, North Carolina, around 1789, and had represented Green County in the North Carolina House of Commons from 1797 to 1802. Licensed to practice law in Tennessee in 1802, he had been appointed a judge of the State Supreme Court in 1816 and held that office until 1834. Enoch L. Mitchell, "Robert Whyte, Agrarian, Lawyer, Jurist," *Tennessee Historical Quarterly*, X (1951), 4–6.

Philips probably had moved to Tennessee from Edgecombe County, North Carolina, in 1792, had been a justice of the Davidson County Court in 1796, and was a practicing lawyer there.

To James Taylor

My Dear Sir   Washn. 17 Jan. 1827

I recd. your very friendly letter under date at Columbus the 26h. Decr.[1] and thank you for the kind interest which you took in behalf of my son[2] at Worthington. Retaining, I assure you most sincerely, my friendly feelings towards you in their full and unabated force, I receive and peruse always your letters with much pleasure. If I do not regularly acknowledge them, you must attribute it to the press of business.

Nothing has been yet decisively done in respect to a Successor of Col. Anderson.[3] An act of Congress is necessary, and the subject is now before that body.

I perceive that a great effort is to be made in K. to overthrow the present Administration. I am assured however that it will not prevail.[4] On that question, as you may naturally suppose, I feel much solicitude. The attempt which is there making to separate the case of Mr. Adams and my own deserves no countenance. We are both guilty or both innocent of the calumnies which have been propagated against both, 'though chiefly directed out of K. against me. And after all that has

occurred, I should be compelled to regard a decision of K. against Mr. A. as amounting to a condemnation of me, painful as the conclusion would be. And so after such an event it would be interpreted by some of the very men who, before its occurrence, are protesting against the inference. I pray you to make my best respects to your lady and family. Your friend   H CLAY
Genl. James Taylor

ALS. KyHi.   1 Not found.
2 James B. Clay. See above, Clay to Brown, March 22, 1826.   3 Richard C. Anderson, Sr. See above, Taylor to Clay, November 6, 1826. In December, 1826, Ohio legislators had called for action to replace Anderson and to recover his papers, but the Public Lands Committee of the House of Representatives did not introduce a bill on the subject until January 31, 1827. No action was then taken on it during that term of Congress. On January 4, 1828, another bill to appoint a surveyor of the Virginia military lands in Ohio was presented by the Public Lands Committee. This measure passed the House at the end of the First Session of the Twentieth Congress and the Senate late in the Second Session. It was approved on February 24, 1829. U. S. H. of Reps., Journal, 19 Cong., 2 Sess., pp. 51, 92, 225; 20 Cong., 1 Sess., pp. 119, 790; U. S. Sen., Journal, 20 Cong., 2 Sess., pp. 137, 139, 153; 4 U. S. Stat., 335–36.   4 See above, Crittenden to Clay, November 25, 1826; Worsley to Clay, December 11, 1826.

DIPLOMATIC NOTES   January 17, 1827

From JOAQUIM BARROZO PEREIRA, Philadelphia. States that he has sent to the Portuguese Minister of Foreign Affairs (Francisco de Almeida Portugal) a copy of his note to Clay of December 30 (1826); requests that a copy of Clay's reply be sent to Lisbon. ALS. DNA, RG59, Notes from Portuguese Legation, vol. 2 (M57, R2).

INSTRUCTIONS AND DISPATCHES   January 17, 1827

From J[OEL] R. POINSETT, Mexico, no. 68. Transmits translation of a message of the President (Guadalupe Victoria) delivered at the opening of the Mexican Congress. LS. DNA, RG59, Dip. Disp., Mexico, vol. 2 (M97, R3). Received February 24, 1827. Enclosure filed with dispatch.

From JOHN SERGEANT, Mexico, "Private" (1). Reports his arrival at Veracruz on December 24 and at Mexico (City) on January 9. Notes that he has found there only three of the Ministers to the Tacubaya Congress, (José) Dominguez, (José Mariano) Michelena, and (Antonio) Larrazábal; that none of the treaties drafted at the Congress has been ratified; and that (Joel R.) Poinsett thinks the Mexican Congress will not act on them until "the treaty with the United States has been disposed of." Observes that the Dutch Commissioner (Jan Verveer) is "very anxious to go home" and that the British have no commissioner (see above, Gray to Clay, September 15, 1826). Comments that he is waiting "further instruction . . . in consequence of the communication from Mr. [José María] Salazar" (see above, Salazar to Clay, November 20, 1826). Encloses a copy of his note announcing his arrival to the other Ministers. ALS. DNA, RG43, Records re Panama Congress (M662, R1). Received February 23, 1827.

Dr. Larrazábal had received degrees in philosophy, theology, and law (1789–1797), taken holy orders (1794), and served as secretary of the Archdiocese of Guatemala. In 1810 he had been elected Guatemala's delegate to the Cortes de Cádiz, and from 1814 to 1820 he had been under house arrest because of his po-

78   SECRETARY OF STATE

litical activities in that body. Upon his release he had become rector of the University of Guatemala and had served in that post until his appointment in 1826 as Minister to the Panama Congress. *Anales de la Sociedad de Geografía e Historia de Guatemala,* XXVII (Marzo, 1953), 58–71.

From JOHN SERGEANT, Mexico, "Private" (2). Explains that, "Since writing this morning," he has seen a letter dated November 24 (1826), from (William) Tudor to (Joel R.) Poinsett, noting that since (Simón) Bolívar's departure and that "of the persons who were exiled on account of their opposition (either actual or apprehended) to his views, political discussion is at an end." Quotes, further: "His constitution has been now accepted throughout Peru, as well as Bolivia, and he chosen President for life. If he can bring Columbia [*sic*] to take the same course, his projects will be in an advanced state—the Consulate for life may then be considered settled, and the Empire will follow of course with such additions and revisions as the limits of South America offer to his vast ambition." ALS. DNA, RG43, Records re Panama Congress (M662, R1). Received February 23.

MISCELLANEOUS LETTERS   January 17, 1827

To [JOHN QUINCY ADAMS]. Reports regarding a resolution of the House of Representatives dated January 6 (1827), requesting "if compatible with the public interest," the correspondence with the Netherlands Government related to discriminating duties. States that some of the letters were supplied in a State Department communication of February 10, 1825, and that copies of relevant subsequent correspondence are herewith enclosed. Copy. DNA, RG59, Report Books, vol. 4, p. 197. Published, with the accompanying papers, in *American State Papers, Foreign Relations,* VI, 374–81. For the earlier communication on this subject, see *ibid,* V, 590–98.

From ELISHA WHITTLESEY, Washington. Recalls that Clay "was so obliging last winter as to direct a communication to our Consul at Porto Cabello . . . calling his attention to the estate of the late William A. Schofield" (see above, Clay to Whittlesey, January 10, 1826; cf. also, above, Clay to Litchfield, January 12, 1826), and asks whether any information has been received that would enable him to answer an inquiry by Schofield's "surviving connections." ALS. DNA, RG59, Misc. Letters (M179, R65).
    Daniel Brent replied to Whittlesey, January 18, 1827, informing him that Litchfield had enclosed, in his dispatch of July 20, 1826, a letter containing the desired information, which letter Brent had forwarded to Chester Bailey.

APPLICATIONS, RECOMMENDATIONS   January 17, 1827

HUGH L[AWSON] WHITE, Washington, states that it is not his intention to make a recommendation but transmits a letter supporting the candidacy of (Leonard P.) Cheatham as attorney for the West Tennessee District. ALS. DNA, RG59, A. and R. (M531, R2). Addressed to the Secretary of State. Enclosure is a letter from Felix Robertson to White, dated January 5, 1827.
    Robertson, son of the Tennessee pioneer, James Robertson, was a prominent Nashville physician and in 1830 a founding member of the Tennessee State Medical Society.

To Samuel L. Southard

Dear Sir   Thursday morning [January 18, 1827]
Mr. Mifflin,[1] who will call on you respecting his son,[2] is a particular
friend of mine, for whom I have long entertained a high regard; and
I should be much pleased if his wishes in respect to his Son could be
gratified. Yr's faithfully   H CLAY

ALS. NjP-Samuel L. Southard Papers. Addressed on wrapper and endorsed: "recd. 18
Jany. No ans."
    [1] Probably Samuel Mifflin, president of the Union Canal Company of Pennsylvania and
active in the Pennsylvania Society for the Promotion of Internal Improvements. The
Union Canal Company, merging the earlier projected Delaware and Susquehanna Canal
with the Schuylkill River development, had been organized around 1821; the Canal was
opened by 1830.   [2] Henry Mifflin, of Pennsylvania, had been appointed midshipman
in the United States Navy on December 1, 1824, and had been assigned duty in the
frigate *Brandywine*. He was not listed in the "Naval Register" for 1827, but his name
does appear in that for 1828, when he was assigned to rendezvous at Philadelphia.
American State Papers, Naval Affairs, II, 453, 458; III, 110, 262, 273, 423, 811.

DIPLOMATIC NOTES   January 18, 1827

To CHARLES R. VAUGHAN. Acknowledges receipt of Vaughan's note of January 16
and declares that the State Department has no information on the acts complained of, that the President's views remain the same as those expressed in the
earlier correspondence, and that copies of Vaughan's note will be sent to the
Governors of Maine (Enoch Lincoln) and Massachusetts (Levi Lincoln), together
with a request for "forbearance and moderation," which it would "be expedient
for both Governments to observe." Copy. DNA, RG59, Notes to Foreign Legations,
vol. 3, pp. 324–25. ALI draft, in CSmH; published in Manning (arr.), *Diplomatic
Correspondence . . . Canadian Relations*, II, 129.

INSTRUCTIONS AND DISPATCHES   January 18, 1827

From THOMAS L. L. BRENT, Lisbon. Reports successful operations of the united
armies of the Portuguese Government, led by the Count of Vila Flor, in forcing a precipitous retreat towards Spain by the Portuguese insurgents under
the Marquis of Chaves. Notes that Sir William Clinton has been selected to command the allied forces of Portugal (and Britain) and has begun a march into the
interior with 1500 troops. Transmits a private letter received from (Alexander H.)
Everett, who contends that, while Spain talks of peace, she is preparing for hostilities. Postscript dated January 19 mentions enclosure of an official report by
Vila Flor. ALS. DNA, RG59, Dip. Disp., vol. 7 (M43, R-T6). Received March 19,
1827. Cf. above, Brent to Clay, January 13, 1827.
    António José de Sousa Manuel e Meneses Severim de Noronha, 1st Marquis,
7th Count de Vila Flor, and 1st Duke da Terceira, born in Lisbon, had begun his
military career under the Duke of Wellington in the Peninsular wars, had accompanied King John to Brazil from 1816 to 1821, and, upon his return to Portugal, had risen in 1823 to the rank of general. He was at this time governor of the
Province of Alemtejo. As a supporter of the Constitutional forces he was exiled
by Miguel I in 1829 but named at that time Duke da Terceira by Maria de Gloria.
Following her return to power, he was named First Minister in 1836. He held this

position only briefly, served as Minister of War in the cabal of 1846, tried without success to form a government in 1851, and again rose to power in 1859, shortly before his death.

Manuel da Silveira Pinto da Fonseca, 2d Count d'Amarante, 1st Marquis da Chaves, had also fought in the Peninsular wars and, as a supporter of King John, had been created Marquis da Chaves and promoted to the rank of "tenente-general" in 1823. But he was a vigorous opponent of the Constitutionalists and had fled to Spain in 1826. He was decorated by Miguel in 1828 for support of the cause of absolutism. Chaves died in 1830.

From FRANCISCO XAVIER DE EALO, Bilbao. Reports that imports consist chiefly of sugar, tobacco, whale oil, rice, hides, and pepper; exports, Spanish flour for Havana, wool, and iron. ALS. DNA, RG59, Cons. Disp., Bilbao, vol. 1 (M-T183, R1). Addressed to "Secretary of State"; received March 17.

A native of Bilbao, Francisco Xavier de Ealo served as United States consul at that port from December, 1818, until his resignation in 1833.

From A[LEXANDER] H. EVERETT, no. 65. Transmits an application to the President and a letter to Clay from (William) Stirling, acting consul at Barcelona, who seeks appointment to that consulship, vacated "some time since" by the resignation of (Richard) McCall. Recommends Stirling for the position and comments that, although McCall is supporting the appointment of Andrew Thorndike, a son of Israel Thorndike of Boston and McCall's "partner in trade," Everett's investigation does not support the latter recommendation. Explains that the younger Thorndike has been engaged in lengthy litigation with his former partner, (John) Leonard, and that Thorndike left the country "somewhat abruptly" when the final decision of the courts required that he pay Leonard about $50,000. LS. DNA, RG59, Dip. Disp., Spain, vol. 26 (M31, R28). Received March 22.

On Stirling's later appointment to the office, cf, above, King to Clay, June 22, 1825, note; Stirling to Clay, July 20, 1826; below, Douglas to Clay, May 26, 1827. Leonard, consul at Barcelona from 1803 to 1811, had been removed from office because his consular activities had become involved in the business dispute which culminated in dissolution of the partnership of Thorndike, Leonard, and Company. From 1832 to 1835 he held appointment as consul at St. Iago de Cuba.

McCall, a Philadelphian, had been consul at Barcelona since 1815 and Navy agent at Gibraltar since at least as early as 1820. He retained the latter post until 1830 and died the following year in Philadelphia, leaving a large fortune accumulated from mercantile activities.

MISCELLANEOUS LETTERS   January 18, 1827

From JOSEPH BAILY, Wilmington, Delaware. Inquires whether the claim he and others have for restitution for British seizure of flour at Alexandria during the War of 1812 will be encompassed in the settlement under the recent indemnity convention (see above, Clay to Gallatin, December 28, 1826, no. 15). ALS. DNA, RG59, Misc. Letters (M179, R65).

On January 23, Daniel Brent, as "directed by the Secretary," acknowledged receipt of Baily's letter and replied that the validity and amount of all claims would be determined by a board for which Congress had been asked to provide in carrying the Convention into effect (cf. above, Clay to Gallatin, December 28, 1826 [no. 15], note). Copy, in DNA, RG59, Dom. Letters, vol. 21, p. 461 (M40, R19).

Baily had long been president of the Bank of Delaware and of an apothecary firm. His claim had not been included in the "definitive list" submitted to the mixed commission for indemnities under Article I of the Treaty of Ghent. No record of an award to him has been found.

From MICHAEL TIERNAN, Baltimore. Inquires about payment of his claim for the schooner *Caroline* and cargo taken by the British in Chesapeake Bay in January, 1815. ALS. DNA, RG59, Misc. Letters (M179, R65).

On January 19, Daniel Brent, as "directed by the Secretary," acknowledged receipt of Tiernan's letter and replied that "copies of the late Convention with England, to which it relates," had been submitted to Congress for action in establishing a claims commission "to decide upon the validity and amount of claims of individuals" (see above, Clay to Gallatin, December 28, 1826). Copy, in DNA, RG59, Dom. Letters, vol. 21, p. 459 (M40, R19).

Tiernan's claim amounted to $3,217.37, as carried on the "definitive list" submitted to the mixed commission under Article I of the Treaty of Ghent. *American State Papers, Foreign Relations*, V, 807. Record of the disposition of the claim has not been found. The *Caroline*, a vessel of 129 tons, had sailed as a highly successful privateer under Captain Joseph Almeda (Almeida, Almeyda) during the War of 1812. Fairburn, *Merchant Sail*, II, 845, 894.

APPLICATIONS, RECOMMENDATIONS   January 18, 1827

LEWIS WILLIAMS, Washington, recommends (Thomas H.) Fletcher for appointment as United States attorney for the West Tennessee District. Observes: "My friends in Tennessee are particularly anxious that he should succeed. . . ." ALS. DNA, RG59, A. and R. (M531, R3). Cf. above, Yeatman to Clay, December 29, 1826, note.

J[OHN] W[ATKINS] WOOLDRIDGE, Hopkinsville (Kentucky), recommends appointment of Hector West, of "this County" (Christian), a youth of eighteen or nineteen years, to "the millitary [*sic*] school at West Point." Elaborates upon his request in a former letter (not found) for appointment of himself to some position "under the federal government" that would "nett . . . [him] as an individual $4 or $500 a year. . . ." ALS. DNA, RG94, Military Academy Applications, File 1827/72. Addressed to Clay; endorsed, not by Clay: "refd. to Secy of War" (James Barbour).

Neither Wooldridge nor West received the appointments desired. Young West not further identified.

INSTRUCTIONS AND DISPATCHES   January 19, 1827

From HEMAN ALLEN, Valparaiso, no. 48. Explains that he expected to have received letters of recall carried by the *Brandywine* and that he hopes he and his wife will be permitted to return aboard "a publick ship," which would afford accommodations and medical aid for passengers. Since he has received no orders, he concludes that the Government wants his residence there "prolonged." Postscript notes that word "has just arrived that Genl. [Antonio José de] Sucre has been elected President of Bolivia for life;—and that a constitution very similar to hers was adopted in Peru, on the 9. ultimo, under which, Bolivar has been declared President for life also." ALS. DNA, RG59, Dip. Disp., Chile, vol. 2 (M-T2, R2). Received April 26.

Sucre, who had assumed office in December, 1826, retained the Presidency only until July, 1828, when he was forced to resign. He was assassinated in 1830.

From JOHN SERGEANT, Mexico, no. 1. (Repeats in large part information given in his private dispatch of January 17, 1827.) Notes the reported arrival of (Pedro) Gual, the Colombian Minister. Mentions that the Minister from Peru (Manuel Pérez de Tudela) "embarked at Panama for this Country, but the vessel put back in distress. . . ." Notes rumor "that Lord Orford is coming out as Envoy Extraordinary [from Great Britain] to Mexico, and that Mr. [Henry George] Ward, the present Chargé, is to be appointed to Tacubaya." States that (José Mariano) Michelena, one of the two Ministers from Mexico, thinks the Congress (at Tacubaya) will not convene within the next three months. Encloses translations of replies received from (Antonio) Larrazábal and (José) Domínguez in response to his notes of January 16, 1827, announcing his arrival. ALS. DNA, RG43, Panama Congress (M662, R1). Received February 23, 1827.

Horatio Walpole, who had succeeded to honors as the 3rd Earl of Orford in 1822, did not serve as Minister to Mexico.

From F[REDERICK] J[ACOB] WICKELHAUSEN, Bremen. Encloses semi-annual report; notes that trade "goes its regular course"; advocates that the United States expand its West India and South American trade by negotiating preferential commercial treaties; says that the Regency of Bremen has formed a trade mission to Brazil; adds in postscript that the Bremen delegation, led by J(ean) C(harles) F(rédéric) Gildemeister, a Senator, will seek to reduce the Brazilian duties from 24 to 15 percent, the rate paid by Great Britain and France; also states that it appears Bremen and Hamburg have agreed to send a joint mission to Brazil. ALS. DNA, RG59, Cons. Disp., Bremen, vol. 2 (M-T184, R2). Original and duplicate sent with Wickelhausen's dispatch of March 7; received May 11.

On November 17, 1827, a treaty of commerce and navigation, including a reciprocal "most-favored-nation" clause, was signed in Rio de Janeiro between Brazil and the Hanseatic towns of Lübeck, Bremen, and Hamburg; ratifications were exchanged in London on March 18, 1828. *British and Foreign State Papers, 1826–1827*, pp. 715–23.

APPLICATIONS, RECOMMENDATIONS   January 19, 1827

ROBERT TRIMBLE, at Washington, transmits a letter "received this morning" from his son-in-law, (Garrett) Davis, in reference to appointment of (Thomas A.) Marshall as (United States) attorney for the Kentucky District. Expresses his own concurrence with the sentiments voiced in Davis' letter but notes that he had previously received a letter from Richard H. Chinn stating a desire for the appointment and that he believes Chinn would "fill the place well." Requests that the Davis letter and his own be laid before the President. ALS. DNA, RG59 A. and R. (M531, R5). The Davis letter is dated January 7 and addressed to Trimble. On the appointment, cf. above, Marshall to Clay, January 5, 1827, note.

Davis, born in Mt. Sterling, Kentucky, had been admitted to the bar in 1823 and had begun practice at Paris, Kentucky. He later served in the Kentucky Legislature (1833–1835), the United States House of Representatives (1839–1847). and the United States Senate (1861–1872). Long prominent as a Whig, he was nominated by the American Party for the Presidency in 1856, but declined the nomination, and in 1867 campaigned as a Democrat. He had married Trimble's daughter, Rebecca, in 1825.

Speech before American Colonization Society

[January 20, 1827]

I cannot . . . withhold the expression of my congratulations to the Society on account of the very valuable acquisition which we have obtained in the eloquent gentleman from Boston, (Mr. Knapp,)[1] who has just before favoured us with an address. He has told us of his original impressions, unfavourable to the object of the Society, and of his subsequent conversion. If the same industry, investigation and unbiassed [sic] judgment, which he and another gentleman, (Mr. Powell,) who avowed at the last meeting of the Society, a similar change wrought in his mind, were carried, by the public at large, into the consideration of the plan of the Society, the conviction in its favour would be universal.[2]

I have risen to submit a resolution, in behalf of which I would bespeak the favour of the Society. But before I offer any observations in its support, I must say that, whatever part I shall take in the proceedings of this Society, whatever opinions or sentiments I may utter, they are exclusively my own. Whether they are worth any thing or not, no one but myself is at all responsible for them. I have consulted with no person out of this Society; and I have especially abstained from all communication or consultation with any one to whom I stand in any official relation. My judgment on the object of this Society has been long since deliberately formed. The conclusions to which, after much and anxious consideration, my mind has been brought, have been neither produced nor refuted by the official station the duties of which have been confided to me.

From the origin of this Society, every member of it has, I believe, looked forward to the arrival of a period, when it would become necessary to invoke the public aid in the execution of the great scheme which it was instituted to promote. Considering itself as the mere pioneer in the cause which it had undertaken, it was well aware that it could do no more than remove preliminary difficulties and point out a sure road to ultimate success; and that the public only could supply that regular, steady, and efficient support, to which the gratuitous means of benevolent individuals would be found incompetent. My surprise has been that the Society has been able so long to sustain itself, and to do so much upon the charitable contributions of good and pious and enlightened men, whom it has happily found in all parts of our country. But our work has so prospered, and grown under our hands, that the appeal to the power and resources of the public should be no longer deferred. The resolution which I have risen to propose contemplates this appeal. It is in the following words:—

"*Resolved*, That the Board of Managers be empowered and directed, at such time or times as may seem to them expedient, to make respectful application to the Congress of the United States, and to the Legislatures of the different States, for such pecuniary aid, in further-ance of the object of this Society, as they may respectively be pleased to grant."[3]

In soliciting the countenance and support of the Legislatures of the Union and the States, it is incumbent on the Society, in making out its case, to show, 1st. That it offers to their consideration a scheme which is practicable.— And 2nd. That the execution of the practicable scheme, partial or entire, will be fraught with such beneficial conse-quences as to merit the support which is solicited. I believe both points to be maintainable. 1st. It is now a little upwards of ten years since a religious, amiable and benevolent resident* of this City, first conceived the idea of planting a Colony, from the United States, of free people of colour, on the Western shores of Africa. He is no more, and the noblest eulogy which could be pronounced on him would be to inscribe upon his tomb, the merited epitaph, "Here lies the projec-tor of the American Colonization Society." Amongst others, to whom he communicated the project, was the person who now has the honour of addressing you. My first impressions, like those of all who have not fully investigated the subject, were against it. They yielded to his earnest persuasions and my own reflections, and I finally agreed with him that the experiment was worthy of a fair trial. A meeting of its friends was called—organized as a deliberative body, and a Constitu-tion was formed.[6] The Society went into operation. He lived to see the most encouraging progress in its exertions, and died in full confidence of its complete success. The Society was scarcely formed before it was exposed to the derision of the unthinking; pronounced to be visionary and chimerical by those who were capable of adopting wiser opinions, and the most confident predictions of its entire failure were put forth. It found itself equally assailed by the two extremes of public sentiment in regard to our African population. According to one, (that rash class which, without a due estimate of the fatal consequence, would forth-with issue a decree of general, immediate, and indiscriminate emanci-pation,) it was a scheme of the slaveholder to perpetuate slavery. The other (that class which believes slavery a blessing, and which trembles with aspen sensibility at the appearance of the most distant and ideal danger to the tenure by which that description of property is held,) declared it a contrivance to let loose on society all the slaves of the

---

* It has been, since the delivery of the Speech, suggested that the Rev. Robert Finley,[4] of New Jersey, (who is also unfortunately dead,) contemplated the formation of a Society, with a view to the establishment of a Colony in Africa, and probably first commenced the project. It is quite likely that he did; and Mr. C. recollects seeing Mr. Finley and consulting with him on the subject, about the period of the formation of the Society. But the allusion to Mr. Caldwell[5] was founded on the facts well known to Mr. Clay of his active agency in the organization of the Society, and his unremitted subsequent labours, which were not confined to the District of Columbia, in promoting the cause.

country, ignorant, uneducated, and incapable of appreciating the value, or enjoying the privileges of freedom.† The Society saw itself surrounded by every sort of embarrassment.[7] What great human enterprise was ever undertaken without difficulty? Whatever failed, within the compass of human power, when pursued with perseverance and blessed by the smiles of Providence? The Society prosecuted undismayed its great work, appealing for succour to the moderate, the reasonable, the virtuous, and religious portions of the public. It protested, from the commencement, and throughout all its progress, and it now protests, that it entertains no purpose, on its own authority or by its own means, to attempt emancipation partial or general; that it knows the General Government has no Constitutional power to achieve such an object; that it believes that the States, and the States only, which tolerate slavery, can accomplish the work of emancipation; and that it ought to be left to them, exclusively, absolutely, and voluntarily, to decide the question.

The object of the Society was the colonization of the free coloured people, not the slaves, of the country. Voluntary in its institution, voluntary in its continuance, voluntary in all its ramifications, all its means, purposes, and instruments are also voluntary. But it was said that no free coloured persons could be prevailed upon to abandon the comforts of civilized life and expose themselves to all the perils of a settlement in a distant, inhospitable and savage country; that, if they could be induced to go on such a quixotic expedition, no territory could be procured for their establishment as a Colony; that the plan was altogether incompetent to effectuate its professed object; and that it ought to be rejected as the idle dream of visionary enthusiasts. The Society has outlived, thank God, all these disastrous predictions. It has survived to swell the list of false prophets. It is no longer a question of speculation whether a Colony can or cannot be planted from the United States of free persons of colour on the shores of Africa. It is a matter demonstrated; such a Colony, in fact, exists, prospers, has made successful war, and honourable peace, and transacts all the multiplied business of a civilized and Christian community.[8] It now has about five hundred souls, disciplined troops, forts, and other means of defence, sovereignty over an extensive territory, and exerts a powerful and salutary influence over the neighbouring clans.[9]

Numbers of the free African race among us are willing to go to Africa. The Society has never experienced any difficulty on that subject, except that its means of comfortable transportation have been inadequate to accommodate all who have been anxious to migrate. Why

† A Society of a few individuals, without power, without other resources than those which are supplied by spontaneous benevolence, to emancipate all the slaves of the Country!

should they not go? Here they are in the lowest state of social grada-
tion—aliens—political—moral—social aliens, strangers, though natives.
There, they would be in the midst of their friends and their kindred,
at home, though born in a foreign land, and elevated above the natives
of the country, as much as they are degraded here below the other
classes of the community. But on this matter, I am happy to have it in
my power to furnish indisputable evidence from the most authentic
source, that of large numbers of free persons of colour themselves.
Numerous meetings have been held in several churches in Baltimore,
of the free people of colour, in which, after being organized as deliberative assemblies, by the appointment of a Chairman (if not of the same
complexion) presiding as you, Mr. Vice President,[10] do, and Secretaries, they have voted memorials addressed to the white people, in
which they have argued the question with an ability, moderation, and
temper, surpassing any that I can command, and emphatically recommended the Colony of Liberia to favourable consideration, as the
most desirable and practicable scheme ever yet presented on this interesting subject. I ask permission of the Society to read this highly
creditable document.

[Here Mr. C. read the Memorial referred to.][11]

The Society has experienced no difficulty in the acquisition of a
territory, upon reasonable terms, abundantly sufficient for a most extensive Colony. And land in ample quantities, it has ascertained, can
be procured in Africa, together with all rights of sovereignty, upon
conditions as favourable as those on which the United States extinguish the Indian title to territory within their own limits.

In respect to the alleged incompetency of the scheme to accomplish
its professed object, the Society asks that that object should be taken
to be, not what the imaginations of its enemies represent it to be, but
what it really proposes. They represent that the purpose of the Society
is to export the whole African population of the United States, bond
and free; and they pronounce this design to be unattainable. They
declare that the means of the whole country are insufficient to effect
the transportation to Africa of a mass of population approximating
to two millions of souls. Agreed; but that is not what the Society contemplates. They have substituted their own notion for that of the
Society. What is the true nature of the evil of the existence of a portion
of the African race in our population? It is not that there are *some*,
but that there are so *many* among us of a different caste, of a different
physical, if not moral, constitution, who never can amalgamate with
the great body of our population. In every country persons are to be
found varying in their colour, origin, and character, from the native
mass. But this anomaly creates no inquietude or apprehension, because the exotics, from the smallness of their number, are known to
be utterly incapable of disturbing the general tranquillity. Here, on

the contrary, the African part of our population bears so large a proportion to the residue, of European origin, as to create the most lively apprehension, especially in some quarters of the Union. Any project, therefore, by which, in a material degree, the dangerous element in the general mass, can be diminished or rendered stationary, deserves deliberate consideration.

The Colonization Society has never imagined it to be practicable, or within the reach of any means which the several Governments of the Union could bring to bear on the subject, to transport the whole of the African race within the limits of the United States. Nor is that necessary to accomplish the desirable objects of domestic tranquillity, and render us one homogeneous people. The population of the United States has been supposed to duplicate in periods of twenty-five years. That may have been the case heretofore, but the terms of duplication will be more and more protracted as we advance in national age; and I do not believe that it will be found, in any period to come, that our numbers will be doubled in a less term than one of about thirty-three and a third years.[12] I have not time to enter now into details in support of this opinion. They would consist of those checks which experience has shown to obstruct the progress of population, arising out of its actual augmentation and density, the settlement of waste lands, &c. Assuming the period of thirty-three and a third, or any other number of years, to be that in which our population will hereafter be doubled, if, during that whole term, the capital of the African stock could be kept down, or stationary, whilst that of European origin should be left to an unobstructed increase, the result, at the end of the term, would be most propitious.— Let us suppose, for example, that the whole population at present of the United States, is twelve millions, of which ten may be estimated of the Anglo-Saxon, and two of the African race. If there could be annually transported from the United States an amount of the African portion equal to the annual increase of the whole of that caste, whilst the European race should be left to multiply, we should find at the termination of the period of duplication, whatever it may be, that the relative proportions would be as twenty to two. And if the process were continued, during a second term of duplication, the proportion would be as forty to two—one which would eradicate every cause of alarm or solicitude from the breasts of the most timid. But the transportation of Africans, by creating, to the extent to which it might be carried, a vacuum in society, would tend to accelerate the duplication of the European race, who, by all the laws of population, would fill up the void space.

This Society is well aware, I repeat, that they cannot touch the subject of slavery. But it is no objection to their scheme, limited as it is exclusively to those free people of colour who are willing to migrate, that it admits of indefinite extension and application, by those who alone, having the competent authority, may choose to adopt and apply it. Our object has been to point out the way, to show that colonization is practicable, and to leave it to those States or individuals, who may be pleased to engage in the object, to prosecute it. We have demonstrated that a Colony may be planted in Africa, by the fact that an American Colony there exists. The problem which has so long and so deeply interested the thoughts of good and patriotic men, is solved— a country and a home have been found, to which the African race may be sent, to the promotion of their happiness and our own.

But, Mr. Vice President, I shall not rest contented with the fact of the establishment of the Colony, conclusive as it ought to be deemed, of the practicability of our purpose. I shall proceed to show, by reference to indisputable statistical details and calculations, that it is within the compass of reasonable human means. I am sensible of the tediousness of all arithmetical data, but I will endeavour to simplify them as much as possible.— It will be borne in mind that the aim of the Society is to establish in Africa a Colony of the free African population of the United States; to an extent which shall be beneficial both to Africa and America. The whole free coloured population of the United States amounted in 1790, to 59,481; in 1800, to 110,072; in 1810, to 186, 446; and in 1820, to 233,530. The ratio of annual increase during the first term of ten years, was about eight and a half per cent. per annum; during the second, about seven per cent. per annum; and during the third, a little more than two and a half. The very great difference in the rate of annual increase, during those several terms, may probably be accounted for by the effect of the number of voluntary emancipations operating with more influence upon the total smaller amount of free coloured persons at the first of those periods, and by the facts of the insurrection in St. Domingo, and the acquisition of Louisiana,[13] both of which, occurring during the first and second terms, added considerably to the number of our free coloured population.

Of all descriptions of our population, that of the free coloured, taken in the aggregate, is the least prolific, because of the checks arising from vice and want. During the ten years between 1810 and 1820, when no extraneous causes existed to prevent a fair competition in the increase between the slave and the free African race, the former increased at the rate of nearly three per cent. per annum, whilst the latter did not much exceed two and a half. Hereafter it may be safely assumed, and I venture to predict will not be contradicted by the return of the next census, that the increase of the free black population will not surpass two and a half per cent. per annum. Their amount at the last census, being 233,530, for the sake of round numbers, their annual increase may be assumed to be 6000, at the present time. Now if this number could be annually transported from the United States during a term of years, it is evident that, at the end of that term, the parent capital will not have increased, but will have been kept down at least to what it was at the commencement of the term. Is it practicable then to colonize annually six thousand persons from the United States, without materially impairing or affecting any of the great interests of the United States? This is the question presented to the judgments of the Legislative authorities of our country. This is the whole scheme of the Society. From its actual experience, derived from the expenses which have been incurred in transporting the persons already sent to Africa, the entire average expense of each Colonist, young and old, including passage money and subsistence, may be stated at twenty dollars per head. There is reason to believe that it may be reduced considerably below that sum. Estimating that to be the expense, the total cost of transporting 6000 souls, annually to Africa, would be $120,000. The tonnage requisite to effect the object, calculating two persons to every five tons (which is the provision of existing law) would be 15,000 tons.[14] But as each vessel could probably make two voyages in the year, it may be reduced to 7500. And as both our mercantile and military marine might be occasionally employed on this collateral service, without injury to the main object of the voyage, a further abatement might be safely made in the aggregate amount of the necessary tonnage. The navigation concerned in the commerce between the Colony and the United States, (and it already begins to supply subjects of an interesting trade,) might be incidentally employed to the same end.

Is the annual expenditure of a sum no larger than $120,000, and the annual employment of 7500 tons of shipping, too much for reasonable exertion, considering the magnitude of the object in view? Are they not, on the contrary, within the compass of moderate efforts?

Here is the whole scheme of the Society—a project which has been pronounced visionary by those who have never given themselves the trouble to examine it, but to which I believe most unbiassed men will yield their cordial assent, after they have investigated it.

Limited as the project is, by the Society, to a Colony to be formed by the free and unconstrained consent of free persons of colour, it is no objection, but on the contrary a great recommendation of the plan, that it admits of being taken up and applied on a scale of much more comprehensive utility. The Society knows, and it affords just cause of felicitation, that all or any one of the States which tolerate slavery may carry the scheme of colonization into effect, in regard to the slaves within their respective limits, and thus ultimately rid themselves of an universally acknowledged curse.— A reference to the results of the several enumerations of the population of the United States will incontestably prove the practicability of its application on the more extensive scale. The slave population of the United States amounted in 1790, to 697,697; in 1800, to 896,849; in 1810, to 1191,364; and in 1820, to 1538,128. The rate of annual increase, (rejecting fractions and taking the integer to which they make the nearest approach,) during the first term of ten years was not quite three per cent. per annum, during the second, a little more than three per cent. per annum, and during the third, a little less than three per cent. The mean ratio of increase for the whole period of thirty years was very little more than three per cent. per annum. During the first two periods, the native stock was augmented by importations from Africa in those States which continued to tolerate them, and by the acquisition of Louisiana. Virginia, to her eternal honour, abolished the abominable traffic among the earliest acts of her self-government. The last term alone presents the natural increase of the capital unaffected by any extraneous causes. That authorizes, as a safe assumption, that the future increase will not exceed three per cent. per annum. As our population increases the value of slave labour will diminish, in consequence of the superiour advantages in the employment of free labour. And when the value of slave labour shall be materially lessened either by the multiplication of the supply of slaves beyond the demand, or by the competition between slave and free labour, the annual increase of slaves will be reduced, in consequence of the abatement of the motives to provide for and rear the offspring.

Assuming the future increase to be at the rate of three per cent. per annum, the annual addition to the number of slaves in the United States, calculated upon the return of the last census (1,538,128) is 46,000. Applying the data which have been already stated and explained, in relation to the colonization of free persons of colour from the United States to Africa, to the aggregate annual increase both bond and free of the African race, and the result will be found most encouraging. The total number of the annual increase of both descriptions is 52,000. The total expense of transporting that number to Africa, (supposing no reduction of present prices) would be one million and forty thousand dollars, and the requisite amount of tonnage would be only 130,000 tons of shipping, about one-ninth part of the mercantile marine of the United States. Upon the supposition of a vessel's making two voyages in the year, it would be reduced to one half, 65,000. And this quantity would be still further reduced, by embracing opportunities of incidental employment of vessels belonging both to the mercantile and military marines.

But, is the annual application of $1,040,000; and the employment of 65 or even 130,000 tons of shipping, considering the magnitude of the object, beyond the ability of this country? Is there a patriot, looking forward to its domestic quiet, its happiness and its glory, that would not cheerfully contribute his proportion of the burthen to ac-

complish a purpose so great and so humane? During the general continuance of the African slave trade, hundreds of thousands of slaves
have been, in a single year, imported into the several countries whose
laws authorized their admission. Notwithstanding the vigilance of the
powers now engaged to suppress the slave trade, I have received information, that in a single year, in the single island of Cuba, slaves
equal in amount to one-half of the above number of 52,000, have been
illicitly introduced.[15] Is it possible that those who are concerned in
an infamous traffic can effect more than the States of this Union, if
they were seriously to engage in the good work? Is it credible—is it
not a libel upon human nature to suppose, that the triumphs of fraud
and violence and iniquity, can surpass those of virtue and benevolence
and humanity?

The population of the United States being, at this time, estimated
at about ten millions of the European race, and two of the African, on
the supposition of the annual colonization of a number of the latter
equal to the annual increase, of both of its classes, during the whole
period necessary to the process of duplication of our numbers, they
would, at the end of that period, relatively stand twenty millions for
the white and two for the black portion. But an annual exportation
of a number equal to the annual increase, at the beginning of the
term, and persevered in to the end of it, would accomplish more than
to keep the parent stock standing. The Colonists would comprehend
more than an equal proportion of those of the prolific ages. Few of
those who had passed that age would migrate. So that the annual increase of those left behind would continue gradually, but, at first,
insensibly, to diminish; and by the expiration of the period of duplication it would be found to have materially abated. But it is not
merely the greater relative safety and happiness which would, at the
termination of that period, be the condition of the whites. Their
ability to give further stimulus to the cause of colonization will have
been doubled, whilst the subject on which it would have to operate
will have decreased or remained stationary. If the business of colonization should be regularly continued during two periods of duplication,
at the end of the second, the whites would stand to the blacks, as forty
millions to not more than two, whilst the same ability will have been
quadrupled. Even if colonization should then altogether cease, the
proportion of the African to the European race will be so small that
the most timid may then, for ever, dismiss all ideas of danger from
within or without, on account of that incongruous and perilous element in our population.

Further; by the annual withdrawal of 52,000 persons of colour,
there would be annual space created for an equal number of the white
race. The period, therefore, of duplication of the whites, by the laws
which govern population, would be accelerated.

Such, Mr. Vice President, is the project of the Society; and such is the extension and use which may be made of the principle of colonization, in application to our slave population, by those States which are alone competent to undertake and execute it. All, or any one, of the States which tolerate slavery may adopt and execute it, by co-operation or separate exertion. If I could be instrumental in eradicating this deepest stain upon the character of our country, and removing all cause of reproach on account of it, by foreign nations—if I could only be instrumental in ridding of this foul blot that revered State that gave me birth, or that not less beloved State which kindly adopted me as her son,[16] I would not exchange the proud satisfaction which I should enjoy for the honour of all the triumphs ever decreed to the most successful conqueror.

Having I hope shown that the plan of the Society is not visionary, but rational and practicable; that a Colony does in fact exist, planted under its auspices; that free people are willing and anxious to go; and that the right of soil as well as of Sovereignty may be acquired in vast tracts of country in Africa, abundantly sufficient for all the purposes of the most ample Colony, and at prices almost only nominal, the task which remains to me of shewing the beneficial consequences which would attend the execution of the scheme, is comparatively easy.

Of the utility of a total separation of the two incongruous portions of our population, supposing it to be practicable, none have ever doubted. The mode of accomplishing that most desirable object, has alone divided public opinion. Colonization in Hayti, for a time, had its partisans.[17] Without throwing any impediments in the way of executing that scheme, the American Colonization Society has steadily adhered to its own. The Haytien project has passed away. Colonization beyond the Stony Mountains has sometimes been proposed;[18] but it would be attended with an expense and difficulties far surpassing the African project whilst it would not unite the same animating motives. There is a moral fitness in the idea of returning to Africa her children, whose ancestors have been torn from her by the ruthless hand of fraud and violence. Transplanted in a foreign land, they will carry back to their native soil the rich fruits of religion, civilization, law and liberty. May it not be one of the great designs of the Ruler of the Universe, (whose ways are often inscrutable by short sighted mortals,) thus to transform an original crime into a signal blessing, to that most unfortunate portion of the Globe. Of all classes of our population, the most vicious is that of the free coloured. It is the inevitable result of their moral, political and civil degradation. Contaminated themselves, they extend their vices to all around them, to the slaves and to the whites.[19] If the principle of colonization should be confined to them; if a colony can be firmly established and successfully continued in Africa which should draw off annually an amount of that portion of our population equal to its annual increase, much good will be done. If the principle be adopted and applied by the States, whose laws sanction the existence of slavery, to an extent equal to the annual increase of slaves, still greater good will be done. This good will be felt by the Africans who go, by the Africans who remain, by the white population of our country, by Africa and by America. It is a project which recommends itself to favour in all the aspects in which it can be contemplated. It will do good in every and any extent in which it may be executed. It is a circle of philanthrophy, every segment of which tells and testifies to the beneficence of the whole.

Every emigrant to Africa is a missionary carrying with him credentials in the holy cause of civilization, religion, and free institutions. Why is it that the degree of success of missionary exertions is so limited, and so discouraging to those whose piety and benevolence prompt them? Is it not because the missionary is generally an alien and a stranger, perhaps of a different colour, and from a different tribe? There is a sort of instinctive feeling of jealousy and distrust towards foreigners which repels and rejects them in all countries; and this feeling is in proportion to the degree of ignorance and barbarism which prevail. But the African Colonists, whom we send to convert the heathen, are of the same colour, the same family, the same physical constitution. When the purposes of the Colony shall be fully understood, they will be received as long lost brethren restored to the embraces of their friends and their kindred by the dispensations of a wise Providence.[20]

The Society is reproached for agitating this question. It should be recollected that the existence of free people of colour is not limited to the States only which tolerate slavery. The evil extends itself to all the States, and some of those which do not allow of slavery, (their cities especially,) experience the evil in an extent even greater than it exists in the slave States.[21] A common evil confers a right to consider and apply a common remedy. Nor is it a valid objection that this remedy is partial in its operation or distant in its efficacy. A patient, writhing under the tortures of excruciating disease, asks of his physician to cure him if he can, and, if he cannot, to mitigate his sufferings. But the remedy proposed, if generally adopted and perseveringly applied, for a sufficient length of time, should it not entirely eradicate the disease, will enable the body politic to bear it without danger and without suffering.

We are reproached with doing mischief by the agitation of this question. The Society goes into no household to disturb its domestic tranquillity; it addresses itself to no slaves to weaken their obligations of obedience. It seeks to affect no man's property. It neither has the power nor the will to affect the property of any one contrary to his consent. The execution of its scheme would augment instead of diminishing the value of the property left behind. The Society, composed of free men, concerns itself only with the free. Collateral consequences we are not responsible for. It is not this Society which has produced the great moral revolution which the age exhibits. What would they, who thus reproach us, have done? If they would repress all tendencies towards Liberty and ultimate emancipation, they must do more than put down the benevolent efforts of this Society. They must go back to the era of our Liberty and independence, and muzzle the cannon which thunders its annual joyous return.[22] They must revive the slave trade, with all its train of atrocities. They must suppress the workings of British philanthropy, seeking to meliorate the condition of the unfortunate West Indian slaves. They must arrest the career of South American deliverance from thraldom. They must blow out the moral lights around us, and extinguish that greatest torch of all which America presents to a benighted world, pointing the way to their rights, their liberties, and their happiness. And when they have achieved all these purposes, their work will be yet incomplete. They must penetrate the human soul, and eradicate the light of reason and the love of liberty. Then, and not till then, when universal darkness and despair prevail, can you perpetuate slavery, and repress all sympathies, and all humane and benevolent efforts among freemen, in behalf of the unhappy portion of our race who are doomed to bondage.[23]

Our friends, who are cursed with this greatest of human evils, deserve the kindest attention and consideration. Their property and their safety are both involved. But the liberal and candid among them will not, cannot, expect that every project to deliver our country from it is to be crushed because of a possible and ideal danger.

Animated by the encouragement of the past, let us proceed under the cheering prospects which lie before us. Let us continue to appeal to the pious, the liberal and the wise. Let us bear in mind the condition of our forefathers, when, collected on the beach of England, they embarked, amidst the scoffings and the false predictions of the assembled multitude, for this distant land; and here, in spite of all the perils of forest and ocean, which they encountered, successfully laid the foundations of this glorious Republic. Undismayed by the prophecies of the presumptuous, let us supplicate the aid of the American Representatives of the people, and redoubling our labours, and invoking the blessings of an all-wise Providence, I boldly and confidently anticipate success. I hope the resolution which I offer will be unanimously adopted.

Henry Clay's Speech before the American Colonization Society. Washington, 1827. Variant reported versions published in Washington *Daily National Intelligencer,* January 22, 1827; Washington *Daily National Journal,* January 22, 1827. Significant differences in content are noted below.
1 Samuel Lorenzo Knapp, born in Massachusetts and graduated from Dartmouth

College, had been a member of the Massachusetts General Court (1812–1816), practiced law, and edited the *Boston Gazette* (1824–1826) and the *Boston Monthly Magazine* (1825–1826). After further short-lived editorial experience, for some time as editor of the Washington *National Journal*, he removed to New York, where he resumed legal practice and worked on the *Commercial Advertiser*. In 1835 he returned to Boston, where he died three years later. His most distinguished work was in biographical writing, of which one volume, *Biographical Sketches of Eminent Lawyers, Statesmen, and Men of Letters*, had already been published, in 1821. A colorful orator, he had delivered a lengthy speech to the January 20 meeting of the Colonization Society, seconding a resolution expressing the thanks of the body to a number of Masonic Lodges which had contributed funds to the organization. For this speech, see Washington *Daily National Journal*, January 22, 1827.　　[2] Alfred H. Powell, at the meeting of January 13, 1827, had testified that while "he had at first looked upon it as calculated to produce evil instead of good," he was now "convinced that this Society promised to be the instrument of great and beneficent results." Washington *Daily National Intelligencer*, January 15, 1827.　　[3] On March 3, 1827, a select committee of the House of Representatives, reporting in answer to "sundry memorials of the American Colonization Society, of citizens of various portions of the United States, together with the resolutions of the Legislatures of the States of Delaware and Kentucky, inviting the aid of the Federal Government to colonize in Africa, with their own consent, the free people of color of the United States," expressed some questioning on the desirability of the Government's undertaking to provide power and protection for Liberia but agreed that "pecuniary resources" might very properly be applied. The committee concluded, however, that the scarcity of time remaining to the current Congress precluded action on the proposal and recommended it to the attention of the next. *House Reports*, 21 Cong., 1 Sess., no. 348, pp. 233–39. Repeatedly such proposals were offered to Congress, but that body persistently refused to take action. Fox, *American Colonization Society*, 54–55.　　[4] Finley, born at Princeton, New Jersey, had studied at Nassau Hall, Princeton College, and had been ordained in the Presbyterian ministry in 1795. He had served a church at Basking Ridge, New Jersey for 22 years and also operated a small academy there before coming to Washington in December, 1816, to promote the Colonization program. He had then removed to Georgia, to assume the presidency of the University at Athens, where he had died in October, 1817. P. J. Staudenraus, *The African Colonization Movement, 1816–1865* (New York, 1961), 15–16, 23, 33.　　[5] Elias Boudinot Caldwell, who had died in June, 1825, was a brother-in-law of Finley. Elected secretary of the Society at its organizational meeting, Caldwell had held that position until his death.　　[6] The reported versions of this speech refer to the first organizational meeting "in a tavern in this city" but omit reference to the formation of a deliberative body with a constitution. Clay apparently referred to the meeting at Davis' Hotel, which he had addressed December 21, 1816 (above, II, 263–64). For the constitution of the Society, adopted at another meeting, on December 28, 1816, see American Colonization Society, *A View of Exertions Lately Made for the Purpose of Colonizing the Free People of Colour in the United States, in Africa, or Elsewhere* (Washington, D. C., 1817), 11–12.　　[7] The text through the remainder of this paragraph and the first sentence of the next is here considerably expanded over reported versions. The *National Journal* summation included a sentence not incorporated here: "Everyone opposed to promiscuous association, opposed the scheme because they considered it a scheme of the slave holders intended to rivet the chains of these [*sic*] slaves."　　[8] After several unsuccessful early attempts to found a colony (cf. above, Address, January 18, 1821, note), an agreement had been made with local chiefs, in December, 1821, for purchase of a tract at the mouth of the Mesurado River. During the succeeding months the few survivors of earlier settlement efforts had been brought to this area and supplemented by 55 colonists led by Jehudi Ashmun, a young teacher, born in New York and educated at the University of Vermont and Middlebury College, who had been interested in the colonization movement and hoped to develop commercial ties. Ashmun had assumed leadership in preparing the colonists for defense against hostile tribesmen and leading them through two major attacks during November and December, 1822. With assistance from the officers and crew of the British sloop *Driver* peace had been established, but the next two years had been discordant. In the summer of 1824 Ashmun had been restored to authority under a formal constitution. The name *Liberia*, chosen by Robert Goodloe Harper, had been approved by the Colonization Society at its annual meeting in 1824 and promptly adopted by the colonists. By 1827 a printing press, a school, and a public library of 1200 volumes had been established; over a hundred farms were in operation; and commerce was flourishing. Natives were sending their children to live with colonists so that they might become educated. Ashmun, gravely ill, returned to the United States in the spring of 1828 and died the following August. C. Abayomi Cassell, *Liberia: History of the First African Republic* . . . (New York, [c. 1970]), 31, 65–89 passim.　　[9] In the reported versions this sentence was omitted, and the material of the next two paragraphs given after the statistical data. 10 Richard Rush, one of the vice presidents, who had assumed the chair while Clay, presiding officer on the occasion, stepped down to speak. 11 Meetings at the Bethel Church on December 7, 1826, and the African Church, Sharp Street, on December 11, had adopted the same memorial, published in *House Reports*, 21 Cong., 1 Sess., no. 348, pp. 240–42. Reported versions of Clay's address note that he read only a part of the memorial, "the length of which, and the lateness of the hour, caused him to desist before having finished it, recommending its perusal to every person interested in the Society." Washington *Daily National Intelligencer*, January 22, 1827. 12 Clay's projection was inaccurate for the period prior to 1890. Population doubling in 25 years was more nearly the prevalent rate. U. S. Bureau of the Census, *Historical Statistics of the United States, Colonial Times to 1957* (Washington, D.C., 1960), Series A 1–3. 13 These last two explanations supplied in published version, not in the reports. 14 Reported as 130,000 tons in Washington *Daily National Journal*, January 22, 1827, which apparently confused the figures pertaining to colonization of free blacks with those Clay cites below in reference to colonization of both free blacks and slaves. A law limiting the number of passengers that might be carried in a vessel, as Clay indicated, had been enacted March 2, 1819 (3 *U.S. Stat.*, 488–89). Under section one a charge of $150 was levied for each passenger over the limit of two passengers per five tons of ship-weight. Under the second section the vessel was liable to forfeiture if the number of excess passengers was 20 or more. 15 This estimate not included in reported versions. 16 Virginia; Kentucky. This sentence not included in reported versions, which vary considerably in concluding text. Generally the argument is extended in the published form, but both reported versions include a reference not here found, relating to British support of slavery during the American colonial experience: "He knew we had much, as these eloquent Africans have told us, to reproach our ancestors with; and much to cast upon that government, by whose misrule this curse has been entailed upon us. But, we ought not, therefore, to sit down and say: this has been brought upon us by the tyranny of another government. Let us show we are not willing accomplices in this crime of that government. If we do not, we may still continue to reproach that government; but we may be assured, that posterity will include us in the same reproach. There is also a higher tribunal, to which, unless we do every thing in our power to reduce the evil, we shall be made responsible for its continuance." Washington *Daily National Journal*, January 22, 1827. 17 Proposals for emigration of free Negroes to Haiti had circulated since the founding of the American Colonization Society; but in 1824 the idea had been actively promoted by Loring Dewey, New York agent for the Society, who had contacted Jean Pierre Boyer on the matter. Boyer, in response, had named a special agent to cooperate with Americans interested in such emigration and had provided funds for chartering emigrant ships. A Society for Promoting the Emigration of Free Persons of Colour to Hayti had been organized in New York and had drawn heavily in its membership from the ranks of New York and Philadelphia colonization societies, but the leadership of the American Colonization Society had repudiated Dewey's overtures to Boyer, and the latter had withdrawn his assistance when the Haitian agents absconded with transportation funds. In 1825 some 200 disillusioned emigrants, complaining of poverty and mistreatment in Haiti, had returned to the United States. Staudenraus, *The African Colonization Movement*, 82–85. 18 In 1806 John Parrish, a Philadelphia Quaker, had urged that Congress distribute homesteads in the "Western wildness" to each Negro family. A decade later Charles Fenton Mercer won support of the Virginia House of Delegates for resolutions urging Federal colonization of free Negroes, "an asylum, beyond the limits of the United States," on the coast of Africa or the shore of the North Pacific. Shortly thereafter the North Carolina legislature had also called for Negro colonization on the Pacific coast. *Ibid.*, 4, 31. 19 The last two sentences in this version are much stronger than the passage in the reported versions, which observes merely that the lot of those proposing to emigrate will be bettered in Africa: "Here they are in a state of the lowest degradation: there they will feel themselves elevated to the level of human beings; there their scale of happiness will be far superior to that of their race in this country." Washington *Daily National Journal*, January 22, 1827. 20 In one reported version the passage relating to missionary effort reveals something of the contemporary expansion of this activity: "Those who wish to circulate the best of books are sending to all parts of the globe to diffuse the truths of the gospel by this means; but here is the noblest work which can employ mankind; every colonist is in himself a missionary, carrying with him an acquaintance with those truths, coupled with a knowledge and unconquerable love of those principles of freedom in which he has been bred." *Ibid.* 21 None of this paragraph, and notably nothing of this thought, appears in the reported versions.

To Condy Raguet

Condy Raguet, Chargé d'Affaires to Brazil.

Sir   Department of State. Washington 20th. Jany. 1827.

Your despatches from No 14 to No. 19 inclusive[1] have been received and submitted to the President— He regrets the personal difficulties in which you have been placed in respect to the exemption to which you are entitled, in virtue of your public character, from the payment of duties on objects intended for your own consumption, and in regard to the house which you had hired for your residence— In relation to the first subject, I have nothing to add to my letter No. 5, under date, the 22d. day of Octr. last— Foreign ministers accredited by this Government (including the Brazilian) are allowed the full benefit of the prevailing usage in its most liberal extent, according to which, duties are not levied upon articles bona fide imported for the consumption of their families— The President hopes the case will not arise in which it may be necessary to consider the propriety of withholding the benefits of that usage from the foreign Minister, of any nation, in consequence of its not being reciprocated in behalf of our representative at such nation.

With respect to the embarrassments to which you have been exposed, on account of the house which you had hired for your use, lively sympathy is felt on account of them; and, if any assistance could be afforded from here, to enable you to extricate yourself from them, it would be cheerfully rendered— Controversies of that description, when they unfortunately arise, must be determined, if the minister chooses to waive his privilege, by the local tribunals designated for that purpose, unless they can be otherwise arranged— Our own constitution, you are aware, contemplates the existence of similar disputes, and particularizes the tribunal to whose cognizance they are to be submitted.[2]

From the long residence of the President abroad he is fully sensible, from his own experience and observation of these personal inconveniences, and justly appreciates the feelings which their occurrence naturally excites— In the general, it is best to avoid, as much as possible, a written correspondence with the Government where a minister is placed, on these topics— This remark, indeed, may be applied to many of the minor public duties of a Minister— It is often much easier to effect an object by a personal interview, and oral explanations, conducted with courtesy and kindness, than by an exchange of notes.

The perusal of other parts of your despatches has occasioned the President the most lively regret— He sees that there has unfortuately arisen a state of relation between yourself and the Brazilian Government which may possibly affect the public interests committed to your charge— Our commerce and navigation have undoubtedly, during the present war respecting the Banda Oriental, been some times subject to aggravating perplexities, especially on the part of the Brazilian squadrons and cruizers— Redress for these injuries and others of a similar character which we may experience, in the future progress of the war, ought to be sought by you in language firm and decisive, but at the same time temperate and respectful— No cause is ever benefited by the manifestation of passion, or by the use of harsh and uncourteous language— If the remonstrances and reclamations which you have been called on, during your mission, to present have not always been attended with immediate success, several of them appear to have accomplished their purpose, although the measure of redress may some times have fallen short of just expectations— It is the fate of all maritime nations, neutral in maritime wars, to find their commerce and navigation often exposed to serious vexations— The existing Brazilian war forms no exception to their general character— But the United States do not appear to be the only injured power— On the contrary, the commerce and navigation of England, France and Spain have all suffered, and some of them to a greater extent than ours— War is the ultimate and last resort, and much ought to be borne before a nation, one especially whose interests, generally, are so obviously on the side of peace as are those of the United States, should appeal to arms— If we had declared war upon the occasion of causes of complaint of no greater amount than those which we have had against the South American belligerents (and there is no disposition to underrate them) the United States would have enjoyed scarcely a year of repose, since the establishment of their present constitution.

The case of the Ruth which is described in your despatch under date the first of September was one, undoubtedly, deserving all your zeal, and of a nature to excite all your energies, in behalf of her outraged crew. Still the President believes that it would have been better, in the pursuit of your object, to have abstained from the use of some of the language which you employed in your interview with Mr. Lisboa, chief Clerk of the Department of Foreign Affairs— No nation, claiming to be civilized and christian, can patiently hear itself threatened to be characterized as an uncivilized people— It must be also recollected that one of the topics on which you animadverted (that of the personal outrage inflicted by the commander of the Brig Emprehendedor on the Supercargo of the Spanish vessel Escudera [sic]) did not appertain to your official functions but belonged to those of the Representative of Spain,[3] to whose judgement and discretion, exclusively, it would have been most proper to have left the conduct of it, according to his own sense of his duty.

The degree of service which a foreign Minister is able to render his country, depends much upon the respect and deference which he observes, in his intercourse, with the ministers and Government where he is accredited; and this is more especially the case in governments constituted and administered like that of the Brazils. The President makes great allowances for the feelings which you naturally entertain as a free Citizen of the United States, and as a friend of liberal institutions, as well as on account of the strong character of some of those injuries, sustained by our commerce and Countrymen, for which it has been your official duty to demand redress. But he would have been better satisfied if you had never allowed yourself to employ, in your intercourse and correspondence with the Brazilian Government, provoking or irritating expressions. These, he thinks ought always to be avoided. The effect produced on that Government by the character of your correspondence, is noticed in your despatch No. 17, and you appear to have anticipated, as a possible consequence of it, that the Brazilian Government might decline all further intercourse with you. The President hopes that such will not be the termination of your mission; and he is desirous that you should, in future, whilst you assert with dignity decision and promptitude, all our rights, carefully avoid giving any just dissatisfaction in the particular which it has been my painful duty to call to your attention.

With respect to the nature of instructions which may be sent to you, and of orders to the Commanders of our public vessels, that must rest with the President, where the Constitution has placed it. If those instructions or orders do not correspond in all respects with your wishes or expectations, you must recollect that he is enabled, at this distance, to take a calmer view of things than you are; that we have relations with other nations besides those which exist with the Brazils, and that, even if we had not, war or threats of war ought not to be employed as instruments of redress, until after the failure of every peaceful experiment. It is the more incumbent on the President to be guarded in throwing out warlike menaces, because the constitution having wisely confided to Congress alone the power of declaring war, it cannot be known, in all cases before hand, that the denunciation will be certainly followed by the commencement of hostilities.

You will make to the Brazilian Government suitable acknowledgements for the accommodation afforded to our squadron in admitting, free of duties, the supplies, destined for its use, imported in the Draco and Georgiana[4]— It is believed to be according to usage to exempt from duties supplies belonging to the Public, imported under such circumstances and not intended to enter into the consumption of the country, but designed for the use of public ships— You may, therefore assure the Brazilian Government that if hereafter any of their public vessels should be placed in our ports in an analogous condition, the like exemption from duties shall be extended to their supplies, according to what we understand to be the prevailing usage; or if, contrary to our belief, any defect of law should exist in that respect, the President will recommend to Congress to reciprocate the accommodation which has been extended to our public vessels.

A particular hardship appears to exist at Monte Video in the cognizance which is there exercised over admiralty cases. The tribunal appears to be unwilling to decide, or incapable of deciding, any question, but refers all cases to Rio. The delay, expence [sic] and uncertainty incident to this mode of proceeding, are grievous— You will remonstrate against it, and insist upon the prompt decision of all American cases that may be brought before it.

You will continue your exertions in behalf of such of our citizens as shall experience injuries, in violation of the public law; and you will not fail to manifest the sensibility of this Government to any and every instance of impressment which may occur of any of our seamen.

Should the Government of Brazils decline all further official intercourse with you, it is the President's wish that you should immediately return to the United States.[5]

I am, with great respect, Your obedient Servant.   H. CLAY.

Copy. DNA, RG59, Dip. Instr., vol. 11, pp. 238–42 (M77, R6).
[1] September 1, 23, October 2, 31, November 18, 27, 1826.   [2] Art. III, Sec. 2.
[3] I. B. Ardison, the consul-general, was Spain's representative pending resumption of formal diplomatic relations. The incident involving the *Escuderia* had been cited by Raguet as one comparable to that involving the *Ruth* in the barbarity of the treatment accorded the crew. The commander of the Brazilian Navy vessel *Emprehendedor* was a Frenchman, Luiz Clemente Poitiers. For the full report of Raguet's protest, see text in *American State Papers, Foreign Relations*, VI, 1031.   [4] The *Georgiana*, originally a British schooner of 16 guns, had been seized as an American prize in November, 1813, and sold at Boston. The *Draco* has not been identified.   [5] Cf. below, Raguet to Clay, March 12, 1827.

To Chauncey Whittelsey

Dear Sir   Washington 20h. Jan. 1827
I recd. today under date the 22d. Ulto. your letter informing me of the settlement of my demand, as Exor of the late Col. Morrison, against Cox &c. The gentlemen of the Bar make very large charges in N. Orleans for their professional services.

I find that you state the bonds of Mathers to be payable in 1832, and to bear an interest in the mean time at 10 per Cent. Is payment of the interest as it annually accrues coercible? How? When the principal becomes due can payment of it be then coerced, or has the obligor a right upon any and what conditions to defer still longer the payment?

You will oblige me by answering these enquiries, which you will

do more promptly than Mr. Duralde. Yr's respectfy.   H Clay
Genl Whittelsey.

ALS. KyU.

INSTRUCTIONS AND DISPATCHES   January 20, 1827

From Albert Gallatin, London, no. 51. Transmits packets from (Henry) Middleton and (Thomas L. L.) Brent and notes that the latter was left open for his perusal. Reports the loss of any papers sent by the American packet *Panthea*, wrecked near Holyhead (Wales) after sailing from New York on December 26 for Liverpool. Encloses also a newspaper describing the disposition of British forces; comments that, in the event of war, Britain "could hardly, on account of Ireland & of her fortresses in the Mediterranean, collect more than ten or twelve thousand men in Portugal"; but notes that because of her naval superiority, "placing her own colonies out of danger," she "might dispose of five or six thousand men in the West Indies for offensive operations." Concludes that the British might blockade but not directly attack Havana, "in the case of actual war between this Country and Spain." ALS. DNA, RG59, Dip. Disp., Great Britain, vol. 33 (M30, R29). Received March 9.

From William B. Hodgson, Algiers [no. 87]. Explains that in November the consul-general (William Shaler) had given him leave of absence to visit Paris, that Shaler had at that time prepared a dispatch referring to this matter, but that Shaler's illness since then has precluded both the visit and revision of the enclosed dispatch. Transmits a transcript of the journal of the consulate since December 1, the date of the consul-general's dispatch, and copies of correspondence by which Shaler sought from Commodore John Rodgers at Port Mahon a national vessel for conveyance to Italy, where he seeks restoration of his health at "the baths of Abano in the Venetian State." Notes that he (Hodgson) will be left as Chargé d' Affaires in Shaler's absence. Expresses continuing hope that he will receive "the books necessary to prosecute . . . Oriental Studies; and notwithstanding present difficulties, . . . accomplish the object of . . . [his] mission in the course of this year." Comments that the journal of the consulate will give information on the peace recently concluded between Algiers and Spain. ALS. DNA, RG59, Cons. Disp., Algiers, vol. 11 (M23, R-T13). Received April 14. Shaler's and Hodgson's dispatches of December 1, 1826, above, also enclosed.
    Daniel Brent informed Hodgson, on July 12, 1827, after acknowledging receipt of his two letters, that the President had disapproved his request for a leave of absence and had expressed a wish that he remain at his post. Copy, in DNA, RG59, Dom. Letters, vol. 21, p. 574 (M40, R19).

From Joel R. Poinsett, Mexico (City), no. 69. Reports that the General Congress has declared unconstitutional the act of the legislature of the State of Mexico voiding the elections of their successors and explains that the Mexican Constitution vests the general government with such power "in relation to the acts of the State Legislatures." States that he has obtained information about two articles of the Treaty of Panama, "which are intended to restrain the ambitious projects of General Bolivar": first, a provision " 'that if any one of the States now constituted a Member, of the Confederation by this Treaty, shall essentially alter its form of government, it shall be *ipso facto* excluded from the Confederation, nor shall it be again admitted a member of it without the unanimous consent of all the other contracting parties' "; and second, " 'that in the event of an auxiliary army from one State entering the territory of either of the other States, it may be recruited therein; but that the Citizens of the country to which the assistance has been rendered, shall be discharged from the service on the withdrawal of that army, if they think proper.' " Comments that the Peruvian deputies "sought refuge in the Congress of Panamá against Bolivar" and expresses belief that Bolívar's "vast schemes of ambition" will fail for lack of "pecuniary resources." Notes that the expenses of the civil and military establishments in Bolivia, Peru, and Colombia "have always far exceeded . . . revenue." Forecasts that Bolívar's "madness" will result in better relations between Mexico and the United States and that the proposed treaty (cf. above, Poinsett to Clay, July 12, 1826, note) will be ratified by the Mexican Congress, which at present "is exceedingly well disposed towards the United States." LS. DNA, RG59, Dip. Disp., Mexico, vol. 2 (M97, R3). Received January 23.

MISCELLANEOUS LETTERS　　　　　　　　January 20, 1827

From [THOMAS] LIPPINCOTT and [JEREMIAH] ABBOT, Edwardsville, Illinois. Assign to Hooper Warren their rights to publish the public laws. ALS. DNA, RG59, P. and D. of L. Cf. above, Clay to Editor of *Edwardsville Spectator*, December 7, 1826.

From CLIFTON WHARTON, St. Louis. Notes that his claim for loss of baggage during shipwreck (see above, Wharton to Clay, June 29, 1826) has been rejected with comment (not found) by Clay that "the Government could not insure"; argues that special circumstances entitle his claim to consideration by "the Government exercising Chancery powers"; and explains that his baggage was pilfered because, during the peril of the wreck, his trunk was unlocked to retrieve "the public property" and there was not time to relock it. Requests $450, a sum which "may appear large, but it is accounted for by the fact that much of . . . [his] clothing was new, particularly . . . [his] uniform, which was expensive." ALS. DNA, RG59, Misc. Letters (M179, R65).

APPLICATIONS, RECOMMENDATIONS　　　　　January 20, 1827

JOHN COCKE, Washington, encloses letters addressed to him relating to the appointment of a United States attorney for the West Tennessee District. Observes that he has "but a limited acquaintance with the persons recommended." Singles out Judge (Thomas L.) Williams' recommendation of (Thomas H.) Fletcher and says he will not be dissatisfied if Fletcher is appointed, although he feels "but little anxiety" over the matter. Identifies Judge Williams as "the brother of our friend Col [sic] John & Lewis Williams." ALS. DNA, RG59, A. and R. (M531, R3). Williams' letter to Cocke, dated January 7, 1826 (*i.e.*, 1827), and one from Fletcher to Cocke, dated December 31, 1826, are in Fletcher's file, *ibid*. A letter from Thomas Washington to Cocke, dated January 3, 1827, soliciting the appointment, is found in Washington's file, *ibid*. (M531, R8). On the appointment, cf. above, Yeatman to Clay, December 29, 1826, note.

JOHN CONARD, Philadelphia, encloses an application to the President for continuance as marshal of the Eastern District of Pennsylvania and solicits Clay's "good offices in the request." ALS. DNA, RG59, Misc. Letters (M179, R65). See below, Clay to Conard, February 6, 1827.

R[UFUS] EASTON, St. Louis, encloses a copy of "a paper . . . to be laid before the President." Refers Clay to the (Missouri) delegation in Congress and to (Jesse B.)

Thomas, (Daniel P.) Cook, and (Elias Kent) Kane of Illinois "for the standing and character of the persons who have signed it." ALS. DNA, RG59, A. and R. (M531, R3). The enclosure, dated January 6, is addressed to the President, and signed by nine citizens of Missouri who anticipate creation of a new judicial circuit and recommend appointment of Easton (as judge) in that eventuality.

On January 11, 1827, Representative Daniel Webster for the Judiciary Committee had reported "A Bill further to amend the Judicial System of the United States"; the House read the bill twice, but took no further action. U. S. House of Reps., *Journal*, 19 Cong. 2 Sess., pp. 144, 406. Cf. above, III, 551n.

JOHN F. HENRY and others recommend William Thompson for appointment as United States attorney for the West Tennessee District. LS by Henry, T(homas) P. Moore, Fr(ancis) Johnson, C(harles) A. Wickliffe, W(illiam) S. Young, Thomas Metcalfe, Robert P. Letcher, and Richard A. Buckner. DNA, RG59, A. and R. (M531, R8).

SAMUEL HOUSTON transmits "the names of several Gentlemen . . . who are applicants, for the appointment of United States District Atto. for west Tennessee," together with letters of recommendation forwarded to him in support of some of the applications. Comments that he will not designate "any *one*, in particular," although he has "a decided preference." Explains: ". . . did I believe the expression of it, wou'd secure the appointment to the individual, I wou'd most cheerfully unite with my Colleagues, in recommending him for the situation. But inasmuch as I believe, it wou'd be entirely unavailing: from facts, and circumstances well known to all; I will forbear the expression of any preference, and leave the Department alone: to make the selection." ALS. *Ibid.* (R2). Houston's letter is filed with recommendations in behalf of Leonard P. Cheatham.

J[ACOB] C. ISACKS, Washington, recommends Thomas (H.) Fletcher, Francis B. Fogg, and Thomas Washington as candidates for the position of United States attorney for the West Tennessee District. Notes that he favors the appointment of Fletcher because of the latter's financial distress. Encloses a letter from James Rucks giving information on other candidates, with whom he (Isacks) is not "sufficiently acquainted" to make a recommendation, and letters from N(athan) Green and James Campbell (in Fletcher's behalf), along with one from Fletcher describing his financial situation. ALS. *Ibid.* (R3). In his letter to Isacks of December 4, 1826 (postmarked January 4) Rucks mentions the candidacies of (George W.) Gibbs, (Thomas) Washington, (Francis B.) Fogg, (William) Thompson, (Thomas A.) Duncan, and John W. Overton. Green's and Campbell's letters to Isacks are dated January 5, 1827; Fletcher's, December 31, 1826. These enclosures are located in Fletcher's file, *ibid.*

Rucks, a North Carolinian who as a youth had moved with his parents to Tennessee, had studied law and opened practice at Carthage. He had subsequently removed to Lebanon and in 1828 settled in Nashville, where he entered into partnership with George W. Gibbs and Felix Grundy. The following year he moved to Jackson, Mississippi, but he returned to Tennessee sometime before 1838, when he was commissioned a judge of circuit court in Davidson County.

Green, a son of Willis Green, was a Virginian by birth, and had begun legal practice at Winchester, Tennessee, shortly after the War of 1812. He had been elected to the State Senate in 1826 and was named chancellor of the eastern district of Tennessee in 1828. From 1831 to 1852 he served as a judge on the State Supreme Court. Campbell, now a farmer of Winchester, in Franklin County, Tennessee, had been cashier of the Knoxville branch of the Bank of the State of Tennessee at its founding in 1820.

FRANCIS JOHNSON, Washington, recommends appointment of William Thompson of Nashville as United States attorney for the West Tennessee District. ALS. *Ibid.* (R8).

JOHN H. MARABLE, Washington, encloses letters recommending two candidates (unnamed) for the position of United States attorney for the West Tennessee District. Expresses no preference. ALS. *Ibid.* (R2). A letter dated December 30, 1826, from J(oseph) Philips to Marable supports the candidacy of Thomas Washington (*ibid.*, R8); other candidate not identified.

J[OHN] MARSHALL, Washington, transmits a letter requesting him "to apply to the President in favour of . . . Thomas A. Marshall who is a candidate for the office of District Attorney in Kentucky." Expresses repugnance "to solicit for . . . friends, especially where the office is in a different state. . . ." States that he will not apply to the President but that if Clay thinks communication of the enclosure will aid the candidate and if Clay himself supports his pretensions, he will "oblige . . . by laying it before him." ALS. *Ibid.* (R5). The enclosure, dated January 7, 1827, is from H(umphrey) Marshall. On the appointment, cf. above, Marshall to Clay, January 15, 1827, note.

D[ANIEL] SPRIGG, Hagerstown, recommends John Harry for "a clerkship in any one of the Departments whenever a vacancy may happen." ALS. DNA, RG59, A. and R. (M531, R4).

Sprigg, a native of Washington County, Maryland, served for a number of years as cashier of the Hagerstown Bank. He later moved to Buffalo, New York, where he was cashier of the office of the Bank of the United States in that city from 1831 to 1835, when he became cashier of the Merchants Bank of Baltimore. He retained the last position until his death in 1871.

Harry, of Hagerstown, Maryland, had been engaged in mercantile business since 1803 and had been justice of the Washington County, Maryland, Levy Court from 1813 to 1819. Although known to be a friend of the Adams administration, he did not receive the desired appointment.

JOHN YOUNG, St. Louis, recommends appointment of Rufus Easton as judge of the new district which Congress may create. ALS. *Ibid.* (R3). Unaddressed. Cf. above, Easton to Clay, January 20, 1827. Young was a land developer, merchant, and civic promoter in east-central Missouri.

From Christopher Hughes

My dear Sir,   Brussels; Jany 21st. 1827: (*private.*)
    [Acknowledges receipt of papers and dispatches brought this day by "Mr. Huygens."[1] Regarding instruction no. 4,[2] expresses disbelief that the Dutch "have any idea, *whatever*, of making any change, *whatever*, in their 10 per Ct. allowance, to their own traders; or in their system, as it now exists." Quotes views of an Amsterdam merchant "deeply interested in our trade," whose letter of January 18, 1827, reads in part as follows: " 'I fear the Dutch Government look upon the advantages, which the americans unrestrainedly offer, too much as a nominal thing; they are not in a way of profiting of them; for I really believe, that not three Dutch Vessels have frequented the United States during the last year: the bonification, which is observed

here, to Dutch vessels, is indeed of no importance, in comparing the
benefits the Americans are reaping, from the Trade with the Netherlands; and I should under existing circumstances, consider it highly,
unprofitable (or impracticable) if *your* Government was to enforce
measures, against the Dutch, by which, the advantages *now* enjoyed
by americans might become curtailed! —you will still say, that the
principle of reciprocity can only exist wholly, and not in part! and I
will add, that it would be much better, and more honourable, *if they*
had played open cards with you!' "

[Reports conversation with Baron (J. G.) Verstolk, (Dutch) Minister of Foreign Affairs, who expressed interest in buying the American
property at the Hague;[3] comments that the Baron may be an agent for
the King of the Netherlands,[4] who "would not scruple much, at getting at it circuitously and cheap!"

[Requests that his diplomatic credit be transferred to London, as
he does not believe Willinks (& Van Staphorst) allow enough for the
United States dollars; estimates that the difference in exchange rates
would have amounted to 2,000 francs in his favor during the past year.

[Predicts that Britain and France will go to war within twelve
months and will involve, "in a general conflagration," all of Europe,
except Russia, "who will not soon again march her hordes south, &
near the sources of light, free principles & constitutions!"[5] Contends
that (George) Canning's "insolence has sunk deep in the hearts of
frenchmen," that "the sacerdotal party is all powerful in the Peninsula
and in *France*"; and that two-thirds of the Portuguese "neither understand, nor want, Don Pedro's Constitution."[6]] So much the worse for
them, ignorant devils, but it is not the less true!— In a word, I look to
war as inevitable, in the course of a 12 month. Sir C. Bagot dont agree
with me; that dont shake my *instinct* on the matter.

I have written with more rapidity, than reflection; I fear you may
find my letter loose & illegible; but I do not want to lose a post, to
acknowledge receipt of dispatches of Mr. Huygens; I hear very often
from Mr. Brown;[7] his health is quite good; He was deeply afflicted at
the shocking death of his excellent Brother.[8]

This has been a heavy winter on me; we are but just now *fixed* in
our House; on a smaller, modest scale; but the expenses of fitting &
furnishing it, have fallen very heavily on me.   and the expense of
living here, is very much greater, than when you were at Ghent in
1814! I shall go on economically & thriftly [*sic*]; and I may add,
hopefully!—

I pray to offer my most respectful compliments to the President; I
read your *reply*, instructions, giving a full view of the whole West
Indian topic, to Mr. Gallatin,[9] with pride, pleasure & profit.— May we
beg our best wishes to Mrs. Clay; Send me one of your Boys! I'll take
care of him; my Son is at the *best* school I ever met [*sic*], & making

good progress! Remember, *Send* me one of your Boys. He Shall be received by me & treated by Both my wife & Self, as if he were a Son of our own! You risk nothing, believe me.

I had a late & most affectionate letter from Genl. Lafayette.— He mauls Canning[10] about his *"I:"* I have also a letter from my friend de Cabre;[11] I have a great mind to send it; it will amuse Mr. Adams. I am sure; yet I fear it *wont* do; but I cannot resist; & I enclose it! (*Rumbo* is Count Rumigny, French Minister at Dresden[12]) May I ask you to recal [*sic*] me to Mr. & Mrs. Johnson![13] I shall never forget either, though *he* forgot my *promised* Louisiana snuff! With True devotion & respect I am &c   C. HUGHES
To Mr. Clay Washington.

N.B.   I fear it is rather flippant & free to send Cabre's letter; but it will amaze you, as a specimen of english writing by a frenchman, & amuse you, as a witty production! The *Caudine* is Madame de Rumigny, daughter of Marshal Mortier (Duc de Trevise:)[14] and as tall as Genl. Scott;[15] Rumigny had promised Cabre a call, on his return from a visit to Paris, where he had been to try for the mission here; there will be no change; when there is, it will be between R. & Geo. Caraman![16] The Elector of Hesse has *taken up* with a loose Countess,[17] his son[18] remonstrated; the old man *drew* on him; the Son fled & found refuge with his Uncle K. of Prussia:[19] The Electress[20] has found an asylum here, with his sister, the Queen![21] I had written on this topic to Cabre & recounted a running fight, on which I was the *parthian* when about 18 years old, with —! I dont remember, if I ever shewd you, a little diary kept by me, in London, during 23 days, in 1823! I was offered one thousand pounds Sterling for it a few days ago, by an eminent literary friend of mine, by the authority of a Great London Bookseller; with a promise to subdue some passages, so as not to compromise *me*! Of course I refused but it is pleasant to be able to live on ones wit (not wits:) Everett's Book[22] sticks still in the throats of the great men & of the society of this country! He left me *up-hill work*!

ALS. DNA, RG59, Dip. Disp., Netherlands, vol. 8 (M42, R-T12). Received March 19.
[1] Roger Bangeman Huygens, son of C. D. E. J. Bangeman Huygens. Young Huygens himself served as Secretary and interim Chargé of the Netherlands Legation in the United States for a year and a half in 1832–1833. A formal note, from Hughes to Clay on this date, also acknowledged receipt of these documents. ALS, *ibid.*   [2] Above, Clay to Hughes, December 12, 1826.   [3] Cf. below, Hughes to Clay, March 2, 1827.
[4] William I.   [5] Cf. above, Middleton to Clay, January 7, 1826.   [6] See above, Raguet to Clay, May 6, 1826.   [7] James Brown.   [8] Preston W. Brown.
[9] Above, Clay to Gallatin, November 11, 1826.   [10] George Canning.
[11] Probably Jean Antoine de Cabre, French Secretary of Legation in the United States (1808), Chargé d'Affaires in Denmark (1811–1814), and Minister to Hesse-Cassel (1821–1839).   [12] Until September, 1827. Rumigny, not further identified. The enclosure, unsigned, from Cassel, January 2, 1827, filed with Hughes' letter, is omitted by editors.
[13] Josiah Stoddard Johnston; Eliza Sibley Johnston.   [14] Edouard-Adolphe-Casimir-Joseph Mortier, Duke de Trévise, had begun his military career in 1791 and had been named a general in 1799, marshal in 1804, and Commander of Saint-Louis in 1820. He had been given title as Duke de Trévise in 1807 and Chevalier of the Order of the King

in 1825. From December, 1830, to September, 1831, he served as Ambassador to Russia and, from November, 1834, to February, 1835, as Minister of War and President of the Council of State.   15 Winfield Scott, who at age 19 was six feet, five inches tall. William A. Ganoe, in *Dictionary of American Biography*, VIII, pt. 2, p. 505.   16 There was no imminent change in the French Ministry at the Hague. Georges-Joseph-Victor de Riquet, Count de Caraman, had been Secretary of Legation in Washington from 1812 to 1814 and then Chargé at the Hague until 1816, when Clay and Hughes would have known him. He had subsequently served as Secretary of Legation at London and since 1822 as Minister at Stuttgart. From September, 1827, until 1830 he was Minister to Saxony.   17 William II of Hesse-Cassel was Elector from 1821 to 1847, although in 1831 he retired from public affairs and committed them to his son, as regent. The Elector's paramour was Emilie Ortlöpp, whom he created Countess of Reichenbach.   18 Frederick William, who became regent in 1831 and, after the death of his father in 1847, Elector. He ruled until Hesse-Cassel was annexed to Prussia in 1866.   19 Frederick William III.   20 Frederica Catherine Augusta, daughter of Frederic William II of Prussia.   21 Frederica Louise Wilhelmina, who in 1791 had married the Grand Duke of Luxembourg, later William I of the Netherlands.   22 See above, Hughes to Clay, December 28, 1826.

MISCELLANEOUS LETTERS   January 21, 1827

From JOHN FORSYTH, Georgetown, "Informal." Requests on behalf of the Committee on Foreign Affairs "a list of the claims proposed to be inserted in the bill for the Execution of the late Convention with Great Britain," together with information showing the grounds upon which (Langdon) Cheves deemed them "to be considered as [of] the definitive list." Explains that the papers, including "the correspondence with Gt. B. on the subject of the mixed commission," transmitted to him "at the beginning of the Session have not been seen by the Comee. in consequence of the unexpected call for the Correspondence by the Dept." Notes that it "would be satisfactory" to him and the Committee "if those papers could be sent . . . again, before the bill on the subject of the Convention, is acted upon." Promises that they would be "considered confidentially communicated as before." ALS. DNA, RG59, Misc. Letters (M179, R65).

The House accepted the Senate's version of the bill establishing the claims commission (see above, Clay to Gallatin, December 28, 1826 no. 15, note). Section 12, which listed no specific claims, added all those "which were deposited in the Department of State, and by mistake omitted . . ." from the definitive list. 4 *U. S. Stat.*, 221. Inability to resolve the particular question of adding the omissions had raised the prolonged debate on whether the arbitration process should be applied to disagreements over the meaning of the Convention itself. See extracts of the journal of the mixed commission, December 20, 1824, enclosed in Cheves to Adams, December 28, 1824; extracts of the Journal, December 29, 1824, to January 14, 1825, enclosed in Cheves to Adams, January 17, 1825 (DNA, RG76, Indemnity for Slaves); and above, Clay to King, May 10, 1825; Clay to Vaughan, October 12, 1826. For Clay's reply to Forsyth's request, see below, January 22, 1827. No communications relative to the Committee's previous confidential review of this subject have been found.

APPLICATIONS, RECOMMENDATIONS   January 21, 1827

WILLIAM EATON, New York, solicits a position as consul or commercial agent in France or Ireland; notes that the linguistic, religious, and political connections of his daughter, son-in-law, and son, the last being Charles James Madison Eaton, educated as a merchant in New York, all now resident in France, will aid him should he receive appointment; and cites as references the Reverend (William)

Matthews, the Reverend Daniel Baker, (Joseph) Watson, (Stephen) Van Rensselaer, and (John W.) Taylor. States, in a postscript, that "it is well known to the President and *others* at Washington" that he was "in some degree (*not small*) instrumental, both at Washington, and in this State, and *active* to promote, the Election of the present Administration of the Genl, Gover ment [*sic*]—" ALS. DNA, RG59, A. and R. (M531, R3). Eaton and his relatives not identified. He did not receive an appointment at this time.

The Reverend Daniel Baker, born in Georgia and educated at Hampden-Sydney College and Princeton University, had been ordained into the Presbyterian clergy in Virginia in 1818. In the early 1820's he had removed to Washington, where he was pastor of the Second Presbyterian Church until 1828. He subsequently served churches in Savannah and Tuscaloosa and became a missionary in Texas, where he helped establish Austin College at Huntsville in 1849.

The Reverend William Matthews, born in Maryland and educated for the Roman Catholic priesthood at St. Mary's Seminary, Baltimore, had been ordained in 1800 and had assumed the pastorate of St. Patrick's Church at Washington in 1804. Although continuing in that position, he had been named president of Georgetown College in 1809 and, as co-founder in 1811 of the Washington Public Library, president of the latter institution from 1821 to 1834.

EDWARD EVERETT, Washington, "Private," recommends appointment of John Larkin Payson as United States consul at Messina. States that Payson, of Charlestown, Massachusetts, received a liberal education, trained in one of "the first mercantile houses in Boston," and has operated a business at Messina the past seven years. Comments: "His appointment, besides Conducing to the public Service, will Confer a favor *on his Numerous & respectable connexions in Charlestown, the largest town in my district; & not less distinguished for its support of the present Administration, than for having ever been the Head quarters of the Republicanism of Massachusetts.*—" Solicits the appointment "as a personal favor." ALS. *Ibid.* (R6).

Payson was nominated for the position on February 27 and the appointment approved on March 3, 1827. He served until his recall in 1846.

MISCELLANEOUS LETTERS   January 22, 1827

To JOHN FORSYTH, Chairman of the Committee on Foreign Affairs, House of Representatives. Upon request (above, Forsyth to Clay, January 21, 1827) sends correspondence on the Mixed Commission authorized by the St. Petersburg Convention, including the letter from the Department of State to the Commission of December 10, 1824 (*i. e.*, December 8, 1824), the protocol of the Commission's proceedings thereupon, and copies of letters and documents to which that letter referred. Copy. DNA, RG59, Report Books, vol. 4, p. 197.

On December 8, 1824, Adams had transmitted to the Commission a definitive list of claims and several packets of documents which were thought to be evidentiary material for claims already listed but which were in fact new claims. Adams to the Mixed Commission, December 8, 1824. DNA, RG59, Dom. Letters, vol. 20, pp. 485–86 (M40, R18).

To JOHN HOLMES, Senate. Transmits at his request, by letter of [January] 1, "a list of spoliations and other injuries on the property of American citizens by the French," from 1793 to 1800. States that the list is incomplete, because of the "deficiency of the materials on which it is founded"; that without further examination of the files it cannot be determined whether all evidence to support the claims is in the Department; that some information may be in the office of the agent of claims in Paris; and that the list is "essentially and greatly deficient" as to the actual number of claims. Copy. DNA, RG59, Report Books, vol. 4, p. 198. Published, with the list, in *American State Papers, Foreign Relations*, VI, 563–77. Cf. below, Cowper to Clay, July 31, 1827, note.

To D[UDLEY] MARVIN, House of Representatives. In answer to his request (not found) for information on the reduction of duty on wool imported to England since passage of the current tariff law of the United States (see above, III, 756n) transmits a volume containing the latest British statutes known to the (State) Department on the subject. Reports that the duty on wool imported from any place other than a British possession was 6 d. in January, 1823; that it was reduced to 3 d. from September 10 to December 11, 1824; and that it was then lowered to 1 d. Suggests that (Matthew St. Clair) Clarke, clerk of the House, may have a subsequent volume of the British statutes which could provide further information. Copy. DNA, RG59, Dom. Letters, vol. 21, pp. 459–60 (M40, R19).

The British tariff was ½ d. per pound if the wool was valued at a shilling or less and 1 d. if more than a shilling; British colonial wool was admitted free. After 1825, British wool growers could not meet native processors' demands. Mark A. Smith, *The Tariff on Wool* (New York, 1926), 101; George B. Curtiss, *The Industrial Development of Nations . . .* (3 vols.; Binghamton, N.Y., 1912), I, 108.

From S[AMUEL] SMITH, Senate Chamber. Transmits, on behalf of the Committee on Finance, a petition from William Smith, of Kentucky, with a request for "any information or document relative to the claim." LS. DNA, RG59, Misc. Letters (M179, R65). Cf. above, Smith to Clay, June 22, 1826; below, Smith to Clay, February 13, 1827.

APPLICATIONS, RECOMMENDATIONS   January 22, 1827

E[DWARD] BATES, St. Louis, transmits a "paper" regarding Rufus Easton. States that, since he is uninformed "of the views of the Executive, and of the relative fitness of the various expectants . . . of the office indicated," he does not intend "to take any part in the affair. . . ." ALS. DNA, RG59, A. and R. (M531, R3). Enclosure, dated January 6, 1827, and addressed to the President, carries twenty-four signatures endorsing Easton for appointment as judge of the proposed new judicial circuit (see above, Easton to Clay, January 20, 1827, note).

JOHN F. HENRY, Washington, transmits a letter from Thomas A. Duncan. ALS. DNA, RG59, A. and R. (M531, R2). Enclosure, addressed to Henry and dated January 7, 1827, is Duncan's application for office as United States attorney in West Tennessee. He cites his "relationship to the Judge of the district, in which the vacancy has occured [sic—John McNairy], and . . . [his] stil [sic] closer connection with the member elect from Illinois [Joseph Duncan] . . . both of whom have ever been warm admirers of Mr. C.," as factors conducive to his appointment. Cf. above, Yeatman to Clay, December 29, 1826, note; Erwin to Clay, January 4, 1827.

J[AMES] C. MITCHELL, Washington City, encloses letters of Thomas H. Fletcher and Thomas Washington, applying for the position of United States attorney for West Tennessee. States that they "are both respected Lawyers in point of *Letters*— and will discharge the duties well." Also forwards letter of (James) Campbell recommending Fletcher. ALS. DNA, RG59, A. and R. (M531, R3). Enclosures are addressed to Mitchell—those from Fletcher, dated December 31, 1826, and Campbell, dated January 3, 1827, in Fletcher's file, *ibid.*; that from Washington, dated January 8, 1827, in Washington's file, *ibid.* (R8).

DUTEE J. PEARCE, Washington, recommends Francis Fogg for appointment as United States attorney for West Tennessee. Explains that he rarely offers remarks concerning applicants for office who are not residents of his own State but that no one "in this City" knows Fogg better than he. States that Fogg and he were students in the same law office at Newport, Rhode Island, and began practice there at about the same time. ALS. *Ibid.* (R3).

To William Jones

My Dear Sir (Private and Confidential) Washington 23d. Jan. 1827.

When I was in Philada. in Novr.[1] I gave you a hint of the appointment which has been since made of you as Collr. of Philada. I need not say to you that in all the consideration of the matter whilst it was before the Cabinet I was your firm friend. I will add that Mr. Rush[2] was also your friend. Besides the estimate which we both made of your qualifications and your merits, I confess to you candidly that I did anticipate from you a direction of the office which would render it less inimical to the Administration than it had been in the hands of your predecessor[3]— I have heard therefore, I must say with some regret, that you are disposed to leave all things just as you have found them.[4] Certainly I would be the last person to recommend a harsh and persecuting course; but without pursuing that a few examples might be made of those who have shewn the least decency in the temper of their Opposition to an Administration, whose patronage they are at the same time enjoying. It was expected here particularly that Mr. Binns, who, whatever faults he may have, has rendered more service to the cause of the Administration than any other editor in Pennsa, would obtain the printing of your office if he would execute it on as favorable terms to the public as others. And much disappointment will be felt if he does not get it.

I trust to our mutual friendship for your just appreciation of the motives which dictate this letter. I am truly Your friend   H CLAY
Capt. William Jones

ALS. PHi.   [1] See above, Wetherill and others to Clay, November 24, 1826.
[2] Richard Rush.   [3] John Steele. Cf. above, Binns to Clay, May 10, 1826.
[4] Clay's source of information not identified. Cf. below, Jones to Clay, January 25, 1827.

To Jared Sparks

Jan: 23rd 1827

Mr. and Mrs. Clay request the favor of Mr J. Sparks'[1] Company on Wednesday evening the 24th inst

Partially engraved, specific details in Clay's hand. MH. Addressed: "Mr. J. Sparks At Mrs. [Eliza] Clarke's [*i.e.,* Clark's]."
[1] Cf. below, Sparks to Clay, January 31, 1827.

From James Brown (1)

Dear Sir   Paris Jany 23. 1827
Inclosed you have a letter for Mrs. Clay from her sister[1] which will give you all the news of the family. I delayed writing to you until the last moment in the hope that we should have had some thing more worthy of being communicated than what you will find in my despatch[2] which goes by this ship. Many here believe that Spain will feel herself bound to put down the Portuguese Constitution *malgre* the English and that she will obtain funds from the Clergy every where to aid her in this undertaking. If the French troops were withdrawn,[3] I should not be astonished if this Government would be much pleased to see England engaged in an unprofitable guerrilla war in the Mountains of Spain, and would receive as much amusement in seeing Great Britain born [*sic*] down by the load of Portugal as Mr Canning was with finding France groaning under the burthen of Spain. In truth England is in a very perilous Situation and she knows it. If the Ministry here would unite the people by honestly administering the Government agreeably to the Constitution, and would not give up the reins to the Jesuits this would be the strongest Nation in Europe. The portuguese do not generally wish a Constitution, and it is no easy matter to force one down upon them, more especially when the insurgents are encouraged by Spain and by the Clergy in this Country.

I have not heard from you since October[4] but this is easily accounted for by the numerous matters which at this season claim your whole attention. I wish the Session was over. I am afraid it will be more stormy than the last. Tell Johnston[5] to write to me.

I have sent in my account[6] and wish it settled to the first of the year. My postage account grows in consequence of the passage of Mr Everetts and sometime[s] Middletons and Appletons[7] correspondence through this place.

My health has become very good and I hope another Summer at the Waters will entirely restore it   I am Dear Sir Yours truly
Hon Henry Clay.   James Brown.

ALS. DLC-HC (DNA, M212, R2).   1 Ann Hart Brown.
2 Below, this date.   3 Cf. above, Everett to Clay, January 7, 1827.   4 Above, October 8, 1826.   5 Josiah Stoddard Johnston.   6 Brown's account, numbered as dispatch 63 and dated January 17, 1827, has been omitted by the editors as routine. LS, in DNA, RG59, Dip. Disp., France, vol. 23 (M34, R26).   7 Alexander H. Everett; Henry Middleton; John J. Appleton.

From Robert Scott

Dear Sir,   Lexington 23rd. Jany 1827
On the 13th. inst. I forwarded Accounts down to the 1st. inst. which I hope you will receive in a day or two—

You will recollect that at the last May Term of the U S. C.K.D.[1] John Bruce as surviving partner of Morrison & Bruce, obtained a Judgement against John McKinley, and that he proposed giving his Notes payable in one and two years for the amount with interest— And it was agreed to receive his Notes as proposed, provided he would give security residing in Lexington, but he declined doing so and the business has laid over[2]— I see Mr. McKinley is now in Washington and if you think it advisable to close the business by taking his Notes without security please have it done— I presume from your various and important avocations it will be inconvenient for you to attend to it personally,— in that case Mr. T W. Clay I apprehend will under your instructions do it— Herewith are Mr. McKinleys letters on the subject and a statement of the amount due[3]—

The year for which the house occupied by Mrs. Morrison,[4] was insured against fire, is I beleive about expiring, or perhaps has expired— Should you think it advisable to continue the insurance, it would be well to write to Messrs. Gratz s[5] on the subject—and in case you do, it will be necessary to have a new policy as the one we had has been lost or mislaid— Or if you prefer it I can have the house insured here upon as good terms as in Philada., as there are resident agents here of several insurance companies— Perhaps the latter would be most convenient as it will save the trouble of remitting to Phila.

Our weather has been excessively severe for our climate since a little before Christmas, with the exception of two or three days, so that hands could not do full work— It is now however mild and hope it may continue until the frost is out of the ground so that Mr Kerr[6] can get to ploughing— He says he will in a day or two have all the Hemp that is up broke out—upward of a ton—and will be taking up some of that which is down rotting— Respectfully Yr. obt. Servt.

The Honble Henry Clay   ROBT. SCOTT

ALS. DLC-TJC (DNA, M212, R13).   [1] United States Court for the District of Kentucky.
[2] On May 11, 1826, a jury had awarded Bruce $1,028.50 in damages, plus his costs of suit; but on May 15, on motion of the defendant and for sundry reasons, including the introduction of new evidence, the judgment had been set aside and a new trial ordered. Both parties had agreed to the latter action, and the absence of further record suggests that an out-of-court settlement was reached. U. S. Circuit Court, Seventh Circuit, Order Book L, 133, 150–51.   [3] Enclosures not found.   [4] Mrs. Esther Montgomery Morrison.   [5] Simon Gratz and Brothers.   [6] John H. Kerr.

INSTRUCTIONS AND DISPATCHES   January 23, 1827

From JAMES BROWN, Paris, "Private" (2). Reports that the removal of the Swiss troops from Madrid (see above, Everett to Clay, January 7, 1827) has been welcomed by the absolutist and constitutional parties of Spain, "each feeling an equal confidence in its capacity to crush the other in the absence of foreign assistance." Notes that "the organisation of corps for the frontier of Portugal is going on with great zeal," despite the announced determination of the Spanish

Cabinet to maintain a neutral position between the contending parties. Notes the existence of "Strong suspicions" regarding such professions and the belief of "well informed individuals" that the absolutists will, if encouraged, urge Spain "to support the Portuguese malcontents at the hazard of provoking a war with England." Expresses doubt that the continent will be drawn into war, because nine-tenths of the French people want peace and are preoccupied with issues "of great delicacy and difficulty," and cites specifically the problems of the return of the Jesuits, the projected law on the press (see above, Brown to Clay, January 13, 1827), and a proposed measure "for the more effectual suppression of the slave trade." Comments in reference to the last: "It will, if passed, be wholly inefficient, and I am not sure that the chambers would be disposed to sanction one of a more efficient character." LS. DNA, RG59, Dip. Disp., France, vol. 23 (M34, R26). Received March 11, 1827.

France, by legislation of April 15, 1818, had provided penalties against those engaged in the slave trade, and this effort had been re-enforced by Royal ordinance of August 13, 1823. Proposals further to strengthen the law had been presented in the parliament in 1826 and, after heated discussion, passed both Chambers on April 25, 1827. *British and Foreign State Papers, 1817–1818*, p. 1025; *1822–1823*, pp. 769–70; *1826–1827*, pp. 646–47; *Annual Register, 1826*, p. 241; *1827*, pp. 205–206.

MISCELLANEOUS LETTERS   January 23, 1827

To DUDLEY MARVIN, Committee of Ways and Means, House of Representatives. In reply to Marvin's letter of December 30, 1826, states that William Maclure was one of the claims commissioners appointed under authority of Article VI of the Convention of April 30, 1803, with France. Encloses a statement (not found) from the Register of the Treasury (Joseph Nourse) of the settlements accorded Maclure's fellow commissioners, John Mercer and Isaac Cox Barnet, and comments that there appears no reason why Maclure's account should not be settled on the same basis. Copy. DNA, RG59, Report Books, vol. 4, pp. 198–99.

Marvin, in the cited letter, omitted by the editors, had requested, on behalf of the Committee, information pertinent to "determining whether or not the whole or any part of the alledged [*sic*] claim [of Maclure] should be paid." ALS, in DNA, RG59, Misc. Letters (M179, R65).

Two conventions relating to financial arrangements had accompanied the treaty for the cession of Louisiana, all signed on April 30, 1803. Under the convention to which Clay here refers, the United States had assumed the obligation of paying its citizens for various types of claims which they held against France. Article VI provided for appointment by the American negotiators (Robert Livingston and James Monroe) of three commissioners to investigate and certify the validity of the claims as defined. Miller (ed.), *Treaties. . .* , II, 516–23.

Mercer, who had traveled to Paris with Monroe and recorded some of the proceedings, has not been further identified. Maclure, a native of Ayr, Scotland, had been trained in commerce and had become a partner in a London mercantile firm. He had visited the United States in 1796 and may then have initiated steps toward American citizenship; by 1803 he had been naturalized but maintained extensive business connections in Europe. Having acquired a fortune early in life, he subsequently turned to scientific and philanthropic pursuits that led him to geological studies of the United States, membership in and presidency of the Academy of Natural Sciences of Philadelphia and the American Geological So-

ciety, introduction into the United States of the Pestalozzian method of education,
financial backing of Robert Owen's New Harmony colony, and founding of the
New Harmony Working Man's Institute. George P. Merrill, in *Dictionary of
American Biography*, VI, pt. 2, pp. 135–37.

Maclure's claim was not brought out of committee during the current Congressional Session, but it was favorably reported during the following term. By act of
May 19, 1828, Congress appropriated $7,037.03 in settlement to Maclure. U. S.
H. of Reps., *Journal*, 20 Cong., 1 Sess. (December 12, 1827; January 14, 1828), pp.
44, 163; *House Reports*, 20 Cong., 1 Sess., no. 94; 6 *U. S. Stat.*, 379.

From DAVID DICKSON, "Homesville [*sic*]," Mississippi. Reports that the "continued
indisposition" of his small son has delayed his departure for San Antonio but that
he expects to leave in ten days. Notes that "recent and authentic accounts from
there leaves [*sic*] no longer any doubt of the province of Texas being in a complete State of Revolution." Adds: "The Insurgent party is Composed of such materials as to Induce a belief that neither myself or property would be safe there
at this time— The *Head Men* are respectable . . . Hayden Edwards Benj. Edwards.
Wm. B. Ligon & Col. Palmer [*sic*] are said to be the principal leaders." ALS. DNA,
RG59, Cons. Disp., Texas, vol. 1 (M-T153, R1). Postmarked at Holmesville, Mississippi, January 28; received February 24.

See above, Dickson to Clay, January 3, 1827, note. Both Ligon and Martin
Parmer had signed the Fredonian treaty with local Indians on December 23, 1826,
allying the two groups against the Mexicans. Parmer had emigrated to Texas in
1825 after residence in Virginia, Tennessee, and Missouri. He had served in the
Missouri House of Representatives from 1820 to 1821 and in the Senate of that
State from 1824 to 1825. A colonel of Missouri militia, he now commanded the
Fredonian military forces.

APPLICATIONS, RECOMMENDATIONS   January 23, 1827

ADAM R. ALEXANDER, House of Representatives, states that he has received letters
recommending Thomas H. Fletcher, Thomas Washington, and Leonard (P.)
Cheatham for the position of United States attorney in (West) Tennessee; forwards only one favoring Cheatham, as "all other letters embrace various other
subjects which prevent their being enclosed." ALS. DNA, RG59, A. and R. (M531,
R2). Enclosure is from J(ames) B. Reynolds. Cf. above, Yeatman to Clay, December 29, 1826, note.

THOMAS A. DUNCAN, Nashville, solicits appointment as United States attorney for
West Tennessee; promises that any interest Clay may find warranted in his behalf
"will be thankfully remembered." Postscript notes: "I saw your daughter Mrs.
[Ann Brown Clay] Erwin, last evening She was well." ALS. DNA, RG59, A. and
R. (M531, R2).

DAVID IRVINE, Richmond (Kentucky), recommends J(ohn) Speed Smith for appointment as United States attorney for the Kentucky District. ALS. *Ibid.* (R7).
Irvine, son of William and a cousin of David C. Irvine, had succeeded his father
as clerk of Madison County Court upon the latter's death in 1819 and subsequently
(1846) represented Madison County in the Kentucky Legislature. On the recommended appointment, cf. above, Marshall to Clay, January 5, 1827, and below,
Clay to Smith, March 11, 1827, and note. Smith held the position as Federal attorney briefly in 1829 and 1830. U. S. Sen., *Executive Journal*, IV, 42, 72, 127.

JACOB [C.] ISACKS, Washington, transmits a letter from Micah Taul announcing that he is an applicant for the position of (United States) attorney of West Tennessee, refers to his (Isacks') earlier "communication on this subject" (above, January 20, 1827). ALS. DNA, RG59, A. and R. (M531, R8). Cf. above, Yeatman to Clay, December 29, 1826, note.

C[HARLES] F[ENTON] MERCER, House of Representatives, notes that, although he has previously recommended Byrd Willis for the position as secretary to the Territorial Government of Florida, he hopes he will not be deemed "inconsistent" in now submitting a recommendation to the President, signed by 13 delegates of Virginia, in behalf of (William Mason) McCarty. Adds that he has mislaid another letter "of the same purport" from the "entire body of Senators present at Richmond" (cf. below, Mercer to Clay, ca. January 24, 1827). Encloses also a letter from McCarty for Clay's eye only. ALS. DNA, RG59, A. and R. (M531, R5).

The recommendation from the Virginia delegation has not been found. McCarty's letter to Mercer, dated January 17, 1827, mentions that (Joseph M.) White has informed the writer of the pending vacancy but notes that White, to satisfy his Florida constituents, must recommend a citizen of that Territory. McCarty consequently asks his own "friends in Washington" to present his recommendations. He expresses hope for support from William Wirt and George Graham and suggests that Mercer might ask "Judge [Francis T.] Brooke" to send a letter of recommendation (cf. below, Brooke to Clay, February 4, 1827). The remainder of the letter, most of it not included in the file, apparently concerns Virginia politics.

Byrd C. Willis, a native of Virginia, had been an Army officer during the War of 1812 and in 1821 had been appointed county clerk of St. Johns, Florida. No recommendation of Willis by Mercer for the secretaryship has been found. Mercer had signed with numerous others, including many of the Virginia congressional delegation, a letter dated January 8, 1827, recommending Willis to the Secretary of the Navy (Samuel L. Southard) as naval storekeeper at Pensacola. On the transmittal of the latter communication to Clay, cf. below, Southard to Clay, January 24, 1827. Willis was named Navy agent at Pensacola in 1832.

McCarty, born in Fairfax County, Virginia, had attended William and Mary College, practiced law, and served in the Virginia Senate, from 1823 to 1827. He was appointed secretary of the Territory of Florida on March 3, 1827, and moved to Tallahassee. Returning to his native State in 1830, he resumed the practice of law and again served in the Virginia Senate, 1830–1839. In 1840 he was elected as a Whig to complete the congressional term of Charles Fenton Mercer, who resigned.

On July 15, 1827, McCarty, from Tallahassee, reported to Clay that he had arrived on July 5 and immediately entered upon the duties of his office. ALS, in DNA, RG59, Misc. Letters (M179, R65).

HUGH L[AWSON] WHITE, Washington, transmits a letter from Samuel Anderson, "a lawyer of respectable standing," recommending (Thomas) Washington for district attorney in West Tennessee. ALS. DNA, RG59, A. and R. (M531, R8). For White's earlier transmittal of Washington recommendations, see above, January 16, 1827.

Anderson, of Scotch-Irish parentage, had been born in Virginia and in 1810 licenced there to practice law. He had begun practice in Knoxville, Tennessee, but after about a year had removed to Murfreesboro, where he resided the rest of his life. He had been a member of the Tennessee Legislature in 1817 and 1819 and from 1835 to 1851 served as a State circuit court judge.

From Saterlee Clark

[D]ear Sir,   Washington 24th Jany 1827.
Did you [read] my memorial, or letter, [addressed] *to the President*,[1] and did you observe anything *in it which* was disrespectful to him? In a [very] short time after I presented it, an order [was sent by] the Secretary, to the Agent of the *Treasury to instruct* the District attorney[2] to move *for a new trial*, in the case of the united States *against me. in what* ever may have been the motive [of] Mr. Adams for this act, he will have good reason [. . .] "could have better spared a better man."[3] [An] *act of justice* it is not, and he has not done it in *the conscientious* discharge of his official duty.

If it is a political manouvre [*sic*] to catch popularity, he is *mistake*n *in his view*s, and is ignorant of human na*ture*.When I *apply to Congress*, as I shall do immediately, *the best drilled soldier in* in [*sic*] his ranks will not dare *to open his mouth or even* to vote against a bill for *my relie*f. *I will presen*t such a case, as will leave *no grounds for opposition.*

I would have you work not for any good which you have [. . .] *in-dividua*lly, but for the services which *I have rendered to my* country, which I love more [. . .] *my childre*n, my wife, or myself. I would [prefer]ably *travel the same* road with you, if I could *without sacrificing my* principles; but I am not. *You* agreed to [. . .] *with one* who is so like his father, [. . .] my father, ("Old Rifle")[4] was [. . .] that I must leave you, *and pursue a differe*nt path.

If hereafter you find me in the ranks of the opposi*tion*,[5] *do me the justice* to believe that the only reason *why I was not origina*lly there, was, that *you* were *a part of the administr*ation. I am Your Friend
                                                            SAT. CLARKE

ALS. DLC-HC (DNA, M212, R2). Left half of MS partially illegible—water-stained, torn, and somewhat obscured by interpolations in different hand. Cover endorsed: "Cannot make much of it L. H. C.," probably Lucretia Hart Clay, one of Henry Clay's grand-daughters. Interpolated wording italicized by editors; faded wording indicated by brackets.

1 Cf. above, Clark to Clay, September 10, 1825. On February 16, 1826, Clark had written to President Adams a letter, explaining the status of his case, as an endorsement on a printed copy of the ruling in his favor for $27,569.14, certified by arbiters appointed by the Federal Court for the Southern District of New York. Clark had concluded his statement with reference to his application for a government appointment and had identified himself after his signature as "late a Paymaster in the U. S. army, dismissed without a trial, upon a Report which is rather a compliment than a censure, after having served . . . [his] country 20 years without reproach, to give place to the Son in law of Genl. [Jacob J.] Brown." ALS, in MHi-Adams Papers, Letters Received (MR474).

Edmund Kirby, a native of Litchfield, Connecticut, had entered the Army in 1812, served in 1819 as aide to General Brown, and in 1824 succeeded Clark as paymaster. The following year Kirby had married Brown's daughter, Eliza. He subsequently served with distinction as a staff officer in the Mexican War.   2 Richard Rush; Stephen Pleasonton; Robert Tillotson.   3 Shakespeare (Furness [ed.], *A New Variorum Edition*), *King Henry IV, Part One*, Act V, sc. 4, line 104.   4 Possibly Isaac Clark, for many years a chief judge of county court, an officer in the American Revolution and the War of 1812, and a member of the Constitutional Convention.   5 Cf. Adams, *Memoirs*, VII, 396.

APPLICATIONS, RECOMMENDATIONS   January 24, 1827

LANGDON CHEVES, Washington, recommends appointment of John S. Ellis as secretary of the new commission to be established under the terms of the recent Convention with Great Britain (cf. above, Clay to McLane, January 15, 1827, note). Notes that Ellis was de facto secretary to the American side of the Mixed Commission created by the Convention of St. Petersburg. LS. DNA, RG59, A. and R. (MR2). On the recommended appointment, cf. below, Clay to Ogden, March 23, 1827.

WILLIAM COOLIDGE, JR., Georgetown, solicits a position in the Patent Office or the Home Department, should Congress create one. States that he is a native of Boston but has resided in the District of Columbia for the past two years. ALS. DNA, RG59, A. and R. (M531, R2).
    Coolidge, who had been occasionally employed as a transcriber in the Navy Department, did not receive appointment in the State Department. Cf. above, Barnard to Clay, January 10, 1827, note; below, Thornton to Clay, March 6, 1827.

FRANCIS JOHNSON, Washington, recommends appointment of (John J.) Crittenden as United States attorney for the Kentucky District. Encloses several letters regarding the attorneyship. ALS. DNA, RG59, A. and R. (M531, R2). Enclosures not found. Cf. above, Marshall to Clay, January 5, 1827.

C[HARLES] F[ENTON] MERCER (Washington) states that he has "this morning sent to the President the certificate, by the Senators present in Richmond, of Mr. McCarty's worth and capacity to fill the office of Secretary of the territorial government of Florida" (cf. above, Mercer to Clay, January 23, 1827). Encloses a letter (dated January 19, 1827) received from McCarty proving that the applicant did not himself solicit the Senators' "strong recommendation." Explains that, while silent on McCarty's application, (Territorial Delegate Joseph M.) White privately prefers McCarty over any other candidate; observes that the emergence of "a rival candidate [Byrd C. Willis], in his own district or territory" has compelled White, "with Mr McCarty's approbation," to withhold "that ostensible support of Mr. M., in his application for this appointment, which he would, under other circumstances, afford him." Requests that his letter "may not extend beyond . . . [Clay's] own knowledge." Adds that by his support of McCarty, he does not intend to detract from the merits of Willis, whom he recommended "for an office in Florida" of an undisclosed denomination without reading the testimonial, but concedes the "unquestionable superiority of Mr McCarty, to him, in every quality, but honesty, for the office of Secretary of the Territory of Florida." ALS. DNA, RG59, A. and R. (M531, R5). Letter not dated but written subsequent to and in connection with Mercer to Clay, January 23, 1827.

SAMUEL L. SOUTHARD transmits, on behalf of Byrd C. Willis, "certain recommendations" filed in the (Navy) Department "when the Office of Naval Store-Keeper at Pensacola was vacant." Notes that he is himself "well acquainted" with Willis and would "feel sincere gratification" if he were appointed secretary of Florida Territory. LS. DNA, RG59, A. and R. (M531, R8). The only enclosure found in the file is the recommendation dated January 8, 1827, which includes the signature of C(harles) F(enton) Mercer, cited above, Mercer to Clay, January 23, 1827.

T[ENCH] TILGHMAN, Rockland (Maryland), recommends John Harry for "a station in one of the offices." Notes that Harry is "a warm friend to the present administration." ALS. DNA, RG59, A. and R. (MR2).
    Tilghman (1782–1827), the father of Tench Tilghman (1810–1874), cited above,

Goldsborough to Clay, February 26, 1826, was a farmer and leader in agricultural improvement in Talbot County, Maryland. On the recommended appointment, see above, Sprigg to Clay, January 20, 1827, note.

To Cornelius Comegys

Sir   Washington 25 Jan. 1827.
I have recd. your letter of the 11 instant.[1] The land which Mr. Bradford conveyed to me I believe not valuable and it lies in the Green river Country.[2] It was conveyed in Security for the debt. I have either here or at home the title papers and would deliver them to your order. Bradford died in the Arkansas territory, and I believe was possessed of some estate, but I am unable to say whether the balance due to you or any part of it could be recovered of him. Any money which he paid to me, if I did not account for it to you, must have been applied in payment of fees and expences incidental to the Suits against him.

Possibly the delegate from that territory[3] might buy your claim. What is the amt. of it, and what is the lowest sum you would take for it?

I regret very much that I have it not in my power to assist your son[4] in obtaining some official situation for him. It would afford me pleasure to do so, if I could.   Yr. ob. Servant   H. CLAY
Mr. Cornelius Comegys

ALS. NcD.   [1] Not found
[2] William Bradford. Cf. above, III, 465–66.   [3] Henry W. Conway.   [4] William
H. J. Comegys. Cf. above, Comegys to Clay, May 5, 1826.

To John J. Crittenden

My Dear Sir   Washn. 25 Jan. 1827.
I recd. today your favor of the 12h. instant. A nomination was made yesterday to the Senate of yourself as Atto. for the Kentucky District, and of Mr. Tho. H. Fletcher for West Tennessee.[1] I should have been happy if circumstances had admitted of the appointment of Mr. Thompson,[2] whom I know well, and whose merits I know are not inconsiderable. In making the selection which was made by the President he yielded to a most preponderating weight of recommendation.

I yield my assent to Mr. Taylor's employing you, in the suit between him and myself as exor. of Col. Morrison, upon the condition that you will not try the cause in the absence of Mr. Wickliffe, to whom I request you will communicate the reliance I place on his services.

I hope the resolution of approbation which you anticipate from the General Assembly will pass. It will do much good.

I do not think it very probable that any thing will be done at this session with the militia. I remain Cordially Your friend

John J Crittenden Esq   H Clay.

ALS. DLC-John J. Crittenden Papers (DNA, M212, R 20).
[1] Cf. above, Yeatman to Clay, December 29, 1826, note; Marshall to Clay, January 5, 1827, note.   [2] William Thompson.

From William Jones

My dear Sir,   Philada. 25h. Jany 1827

I have received your letter of the 23d Inst. and thank you for the friendly interest you have taken in my behalf of which I have never doubted the existence. You say, you had anticipated that my direction of the Collectors Office would render it less inimical to the administration than it had been in the hands of my predecessor, and express your regret at having heard that I was disposed to leave all things just as I have found them: This is not true, I have never declared any such intention, and here I beg leave to guard you against interested & exaggerated accounts from this quarter. I have been most unreasonable [*sic*] and indecorously pressed by Mr. Binns from the time my nomination was first informally announced although he was informed that nothing would be wanting in the printing line during the first quarter as it had been the practice to provide in the last quarter of the year a sufficiency for the ensuing quarter. I have been but *two days in office* and your ample experience will enable you to determine what are the objects which for some time must necessarily engross my undivided attention in an office of such high responsibility and complicated concerns. My duty to the U S to myself and my sureties require [*sic*] that all minor objects should give place to these considerations. Investigation and arrangement according to the order and importance of the several objects are indispensable, and first in the accounting department. I have heard much of virulent and clamorous opposition on the part of some of the officers but within doors I have never witnessed the least indecorum or even discussion   In the outdoor Depmt there probably are some indecorous opponents whom I may have occasion to restrain or remove, when I have an opportunity between this and the opening of the Spring to ascertain the actual deportment of its members. I am sure it is not intended (and if it was I am not a fit instrument) to proscribe any officer for the decent expression of his opinions and exercise of his rights. The policy is as unwise as the practice is reprehensible. When the removal for any just cause shall be necessary I shall not be wanting in decision. During the late War many of the Clerks in the public offices at Washington were notoriously hostile to the Administration and openly triumphed in its reverses. My office[1] alone was cleared though I had to encounter the labour and inconvenience incident to the introduction of an entire new set of Clerks. When last I had the pleasure of a personal intercourse you observed that the policy of the Cabinet was forbearance, which to a reasonable extent is certainly a wise policy—and I presume it is not expected that subordinate officers shall practice what the administration condemns

Discerning men who are not blinded by their zeal or self interest distinctly perceive the tranquil amelioration of sentiment in this quarter toward the administration. This I know to be the case of some of you [sic] personal firends who were ative [sic] in opposition to the administration but are now passive or rather amicably disposed

There are however among its professed friends some whose interest and business it is to produce the greatest possible excitement in order to enhance their own services. My confidence in and respect for the administration is entire and is not of the new birth.[2] All that I can justly do either officially or individually to promote its honnor [sic] and interest will be cheerfully and fearlessly done.

I have written by this mail to Mr Rush[3] on the subject of the printing and shall await his answer. I beg leave to refer you to that letter and remain   Dear Sir Very sincerely Your friend   WJ.
The Hon Henry Clay

AD draft. PHi.   [1] See above, I, 811n.
[2] Cf. above, Sergeant to Clay, October 2, 1826.   [3] Richard Rush; the letter, not found.

DIPLOMATIC NOTES   January 25, 1827

ELIE BEATTY AND OTHERS, citizens of Washington County, Maryland, recommend despatch by which . . . [his] Government urged the claim which was made to that of the United States respecting the Privateer of the Republic, the Zulmé," and notes that the extract includes reference to the claim of the proprietor, the formal complaint of the *Zulmé's* captain (Denis Thomas), and the deposition of Levy James (a witness), whose testimony has been certified by (John M.) McPherson, United States Consul at Cartagena. Inquires whether, without prejudice to the instructions to the United States Minister at Madrid (above, Clay to Everett, January 15, 1827), mentioned in Clay's note (above, Clay to Salazar, January 15, 1827), the United States could not "interpose its respectable mediation" with the Captain General of Havana (Francisco Dionisio Vives). Complains that the slowness of Spanish answers and decisions in such matters makes it more difficult for his government to observe conciliatory relations. LS, in Spanish, with trans. in State Dept. file. DNA, RG59, Notes from Colombian Legation, vol. 1, pt. 2 (M51, R2). Received January 25, 1827.

Levy James, a resident of Key West, Florida, has not been further identified.

INSTRUCTIONS AND DISPATCHES   January 25, 1827

From R[EUBEN] G. BEASLEY, Havre. Notes that he has learned of the "extraordinary construction" the French have put on the convention (of 1822—see above,

III, 53n), "confining us so rigidly to the direct voyage, as not even to permit the calling for orders," and comments that notices in French newspapers indicate that French vessels bound for the United States have been habitually touching and "trading at some of the Islands." ALS. DNA, RG59, Cons. Disp., Havre, vol. 1 (M212, R1). Received March 22. Cf. above, Beasley to Clay, August 16, September 15, 1826; Brown to Clay, September 11, 1826.

From J[OEL] R. POINSETT, Mexico, no. 70. Acknowledges receipt of Clay's instructions no. 17 (above, December 7, 1826) and enclosure. Recalls his successful representations to the Mexican Government in behalf of Taylor and Sicard (cf. above, Poinsett to Clay, July 18, 1825) and encloses a copy of his letter (to Lucas Alamán) of July 18, 1825, requesting rebate of duties. Observes that upon learning of other similar claims, he addressed a second note (to Camacho, December 1, 1825), a copy of which is also enclosed (cf. above, Poinsett to Clay, December 1, 1825). Notes that English goods have also been charged the increases and that the objections of their merchants have been urged without satisfaction. Mentions his dispatch (above, December 27, 1826) wherein he notices that the Government has again increased the duties without prior warning. Encloses translations of two circulars from the Mexican Secretary of the Treasury (José Ignacio Esteva) to the customs officials and comments that the circulars demonstrate "the obscurity in which this subject is involved." LS. DNA, RG59, Dip. Disp., Mexico, vol. 2 (M97, R3). Received February 24. Because of misinterpretations of his circular of October 14, 1826, Esteva had written a second circular, dated November 18, 1826, reviewing the Government's regulations on cotton imports.

APPLICATIONS, RECOMMENDATIONS   January 25, 1827

ELIE BEATTY AND OTHERS, citizens of Washington County, Maryland, recommend John Harry for "some Vacancy, which may occur, in some one of the departments." LS, by Beatty and twelve others. DNA, RG59, A and R. (M531, R4). Undated but filed in State Department with other documents of this date delivered personally by Harry. On the recommended appointment, see above, Sprigg to Clay, January 20, 1827, note.

Elie, a brother of Adam Beatty and brother-in-law of Nathaniel Rochester, was cashier of the Hagerstown Bank from 1807 until his death in 1859, except for the years from 1831 to 1833, when he served as president of the bank.

FRE[DERICK] DORSEY, Hagerstown, introduces John Harry, a merchant and miller, who seeks appointment as "clerk in some of the Public offices"; declares that the appointment would be a personal favor to himself; and asks to be recalled to Mrs. Clay and family and to Margaret Ross. ALS. DNA, RG59, A. and R. (M531, R4).

WILLIAM PRICE, Hagerstown, recommends John Harry, who seeks "some situation" with the government; suggests a clerical appointment; advises that assistance to Harry would be "highly gratifying" to many of Clay's friends. ALS. Ibid.

Price, born in Washington County, Maryland, and educated at Dickinson College, was a lawyer and had been in 1825 a member of the State Senate. He later moved to Baltimore, represented that district in the State legislature in 1862, and from 1862 to 1865 served as Federal attorney for Maryland.

DANIEL WEBSTER, House of Representatives, transmits a recommendation for appointment of John Larkin Payson as consul at Messina and endorses the candidacy. ALS. Ibid. (R6). Dated "January 25." For enclosure, see above, Appleton and others to Clay, January 16, 1827; for disposition of the office, see above, Everett to Clay, January 21, 1827, note.

Hugh L[awson] White, Washington, transmits a recommendation from (John C.) McLemore for appointment of Thomas A. Duncan as United States district attorney for West Tennessee; explains that he does not have sufficient personal knowledge to judge Duncan's abilities but has confidence in McLemore's judgment. ALS. DNA, RG59, A. and R. (M531, R2). Received January 26. McLemore was a West Tennessee land developer. On the appointment, cf. above, Yeatman to Clay, December 29, 1826, note.

O[tho] H[olland] Williams, Hagerstown, recommends John Harry for "a situation in one of the public Offices"; notes that Harry has been retired from mercantile business "for some time" and intends to move to Georgetown, his wife's birthplace. ALS. DNA, RG59, A. and R. (M531, R4).
    Mrs. Harry has not been further identified.

To Francis T. Brooke

My Dear Sir   Washington 26 Jan. 1827
    I duly recd. your favor of the 24h instant.[1] You will have since seen the late Convention with England which has been communicated to Congress and published.[2] A great and somewhat general mistake has prevailed in respect to the extent of the claim which existed on G. Britain on account of slaves and other property taken away or destroyed. The claim, on the part of American Citizens, arises out of the first article of the treaty of Ghent, which stipulates "All territory, places and possessions whatsoever, taken by either party from the other, during the War, or which may be taken after signing this treaty, excepting only the islands herein after mentioned, shall be restored without delay, and without causing any destruction, or carrying away any of the artillery, or other public property originally captured in the said forts or places, and which *shall remain therein upon the exchange of* the ratifications *of this treaty, or any slaves or other private property.*"[3] The parties differed about the meaning of this clause, and refered [sic] their dispute to the Emperor Alexander.[4] He decided it in favor of the U. States, and a tripartite convention was concluded at St. Petersburg to give effect to this decision. The mixed Commission (composed of Messrs. Jackson and Cheves)[5] was created to execute that Commission. But they could not agree, and the late Convention, by which the U. States agree to accept, in behalf of the claimants, a gross sum, was substituted to the Commission.
    Now it is evident, from this narrative, that the new Convention could only provide for that class of claimants who were comprehended in the first article of the treaty of Ghent Government, in fact, was only an Agent or trustee for that class. If you go back beyond the treaty of Ghent, perhaps one class of persons who had their property taken away or destroyed, during the late War, has as much equity as

another. But the treaty did not provide for any but one class. To that limited extent, G. Britain has always been dissatisfied with the stipulation and the interpretation put upon it. Government now can do no more than see that the class provided for shall have the benefit of a most fortunate provision made for them in the treaty. It can not undertake to divide a fund, intended exclusively for that class, among those who are unfortunately not comprehended in the treaty of Ghent. If it were to go out of the treaty, where would be the stopping place?

A board will probably be created by Congress during the present session, but its duty will be restricted to a fair execution of the treaty of Ghent, the Imperial decision and the late Convention.[6] The average value fixed by the mixed Commission, and the definitive list sent to it from the Dept. of State, in pursuance of the Convention of St. Petersburg, will govern the new Board.[7] And it will belong to that to decide, under the limitations stated, upon all cases thus presented to it, and upon the sufficiency of the evidence by which they are made out.

Should there by a surplus in the fund, Congress alone possesses the power to dispose of it. I am with great regard Your's faithfy

The Honble F Brooke.   H. CLAY

ALS. DLC-TJC (DNA, M212, R10).   [1] Not found.
[2] The text of the Convention of November 13, 1826 (see above, Gallatin to Clay, November 13, 1826), had been published in the Washington *Daily National Intelligencer*, January 17, 1827.   [3] Cf. Miller (ed.), *Treaties*, II, 574–75.   [4] Alexander I of Russia.   [5] George Jackson and Langdon Cheves.   [6] See above, Clay to Gallatin, December 28, 1826 (no. 15), note.   [7] For the average values and the list of claims, see *House Docs.*, 19 Cong., 1 Sess., no. 122.

From Joseph Kent

My Dear Sir   Annapolis 26th. Jany 1827

I have received your valued favour of the 18th. Inst.[1]

No doubt shou'd your friends determine to run you for the V. Presidency, that it wou'd give considerable strength to the next election, when I fear we shall want all the aid we can obtain—Does Govr. Clinton[2] design to be a Candidate for that office?—His singular & contradictory opinions communicated in his message, upon the subject of Internal improvement looks as if he intended to furnish Van buren[3] with a lever by which he might wield the Southern interest in his favor, in the event of his being proposed for that office—

You have ardent & influential friends throughout the U. States, all of whom wou'd be pleased to see you associated with Mr. Adams at the next election and those in Maryland I have conversed with appear to consider it highly important— It is unnecessary for me to add that whatever you may determine on in the matter will receive my hearty concurrence

What will grow out of the rupture between G. Britain & Spain?[4] Will not the latter disavow her offensive measures towards Portugal and thereby terminate the affair—You must try & keep old S.[5] straight— *Dorsey*[6] *has vouched for him every way*— Against that contemptible wretch (D) you shou'd be always guarded— There is no act of duplicity or treachery that he is not capable of.

He represents me I understand as being in a minority here— I never had half the strength in the State I have at this time—

On yesterday I received a letter from Robt. H. Goldsborough formerly of the U. S. Senate, who informs me that Mr. Martin of the H. of R. had applied to you for a Clerkship for a Son of his (Wm. Goldsborough)[7] who is a fine young man, well educated, possessing very genteel manners and interesting appearance— I shou'd be pleased to hear that you had been able to provide for this young gentleman— His Father is entirely with us & possesses considerable influence— Very sincerely your frien[d] and Obt. Sert.   JOS: KENT
Honble. H. Clay Secty. State Washington

ALS. DLC-HC (DNA, M212, R2).   1 Not found.
2 DeWitt Clinton.   3 Martin Van Buren. Clinton's message to the New York Legislature, which had convened on January 2, had strongly opposed, as unconstitutional, Federal aid for internal improvements. Washington *Daily National Intelligencer*, January 8, 1827; *Niles' Weekly Register*, XXXI (January 13, 1827), 309.   4 See above, Gallatin to Clay, December 13, 1826.   5 Probably Samuel Smith.   6 Clement Dorsey.   7 Cf. above, Martin and others to Clay, March 23, 1826.

From John Sergeant

Dear Sir,   (Private)   Mexico, Jan: 26th. 1827.
Herewith you will receive the duplicate of my dispatch of the 19th. inst. to which I have nothing now to add of a nature to require a public letter. The matter of the Congress remains as it was, except that we have an account from Bogota of the reception of the foreign ministers by Genl. Bolivar upon his return to that capital, and copies of the speeches made upon the occasion, in the course of which the Congress is mentioned and a compliment paid to the President. You will probably have seen them in our newspapers, and if not, you will find them in the paper I have enclosed.[1]

In Mexico, there has occurred nothing new but the apprehension of a friar charged with an attempt to corrupt the military commandant and to engage him in a conspiracy to overthrow the present government and restore the power of Ferdinand.[2] It is treated as a serious matter. The investigation is going on, and rumor is even more busy than the public authorities. The person apprehended is worthless and insignificant, and on that account it is difficult to believe that he can have been entrusted with the secrets of a conspiracy or employed as its instrument. This affair has given rise to a motion in both houses of Congress to expel from the Country all European friars, unless they can give evidence of their adherence to the cause of independence.[3] Such a measure, I am told, would work a dissolution of several establishments possessing large and valuable estates in almost every part of Mexico, which would then become the property of the Government.

There has been no disturbance, and no agitation but of the tongue and the press. The latter throws off daily handbills, which are hawked about the streets and pressed upon one with as much importunity as the supplications of the beggars. This description of persons abounds in Mexico and exhibits a variety of disgusting deformity and disease far exceeding what I have witnessed any where else.

The last arrival from the United States brought us Philada. papers to the 11th. Decr., containing among other things the message of the Governor of Pennsylvania.[4] He has come out more decidedly than I expected. It was well understood that he was favorably disposed to the administration of the Genl. Government, but I did not believe he would venture to shew his leaning so clearly as I think he has done in the Message. It will have a great effect.

We look with anxiety for the next arrival, which we hope will bring us intelligence to near the end of December, and of course give us some glimpse of what is going on in Congress. My impression has been that the fury of opposition was exhausted last winter. The moment the powerful passion which was the only common feature in its character, is abated, I think it must be broken to pieces by the repulsive force of its materials. There is no tie, to keep them together. The support of Genl. Jackson is certainly not a common object, and the support of Mr. Calhoun seems from the election of Judge Smith to have failed even in Carolina.[5] In truth, the Country is well satisfied with the measures of the administration, and, when that is the case, an opposition of leaders (if it be not to use too much levity) is like people dancing without music. There is nothing to connect them with the byestanders [sic]—no sympathy between them—and their movements appear ridiculous or insane, as they are sure to be out of time. Still, some become so enamoured of their own performance that they keep on in spite of every thing, as a recent dinner at Philada. may serve to exemplify.[6]

When I last had the pleasure of seeing you, you supposed a further instruction might be necessary in consequence of the last communication from Mr. Salazar.[7] I hope to receive it soon. I would be glad if you would also consider, and instruct me, what course will be proper to be taken in case the Congress should decline to exhibit its former proceedings.

Let me beg the favor of you, further, to direct my salary, as it becomes due, to be placed to my credit in the Bank of the U. States.

I believe it was only mentioned in conversation, and it may have escaped your recollection, Very respectfully & truly Yrs.

The Honble Henry Clay.   JOHN SERGEANT.

(P.T.O.)

P.S.   I have now received the answer of Mr. Michelena and will send you a translation.[8] It is certainly not more satisfactory than the others—In the Corres enclosed herewith,[9] you will find part of a debate in the Mexican Senate upon the allowance to their ministers. They are at present upon the old establishment, $10,000 a year. This debate seems to consider the Congress as a permanent body.

ALS. InU.

[1] Enclosure not found. In response to remarks by Beaufort T. Watts greatly praising Bolívar, the latter had praised the United States as the first state to send a Minister to Colombia and as the "first to point out . . . the path that led to independence." Requesting that Watts convey these sentiments to his Government, Bolívar had urged Watts also "to express the desire of Colombia to cultivate with it [the United States] relations of the strictest and most sincere friendship; as well as . . . [his] personal admiration and respect for its illustrious President, whose opinions with respect to the American Congress, give it a solemnity which it had no right to look for." Washington *Daily National Journal*, January 15, 1827.   [2] Father Joaquín Arenas and other alleged conspirators had been seized on January 19, with papers purportedly incriminating them in an attempt to restore rule by Ferdinand VII of Spain. While in prison Arenas confessed to having been commissioned by Ferdinand to lead a revolt in conjunction with Commodore (Angel) Laborde and the Spanish fleet off Cuba. Arenas was convicted of treason and shot on June 2. *Annual Register, 1827*, [342–43].   [3] The Mexican State of Jalisco passed legislation banishing all Spanish natives except the physically infirm, men who had living American wives, or men who, as widowers, had families by American mothers. A committee of the Mexican Congress subsequently declared that the State action was invalid, but the Congress itself then passed legislation excluding Spaniards from public employment until Spain recognized the independence of the Republic. *Ibid.* See also, below, Taylor to Clay, November 2, 1827, note.   [4] John A. Shulze. Cf. above, Clay to Brooke, December 11, 1826, note.   [5] Andrew Jackson; John C. Calhoun; William Smith (cf. above, Clay to Brown, December 14, 1826).   [6] Cf. above, Sergeant to Clay, September 28, 1826, note; October 2, 1826.   [7] Above, November 20, 1826.

[8] Sergeant's numbered dispatch no. 2, also dated January 26, transmits a duplicate of his letter of January 19 and a translation of the answer of José Mariano Michelina to Sergeant's note of January 16, announcing his arrival. ALS. DNA, RG43, Records re Panama Congress (M662, R1). Received February 23. According to the enclosure Michelena had stated, on January 25: "the reunion of the Congress depending upon circumstances either very uncertain or to be determined by the respective Governments, all that is positively fixed is, that the time allowed for the exchange of ratifications will expire in less than two months, at the end of which time it will be necessary to enter into a correspondence (contestaciones) for the purpose either of receiving such exchanges, or of prolonging the time allowed."   [9] No enclosures found.

MISCELLANEOUS LETTERS   January 26, 1827

To J[OHN QUINCY ADAMS]. In response to a Senate resolution of January 23, requesting that the President communicate a copy of the commission and credentials of John Sergeant as Envoy Extraordinary and Minister Plenipotentiary to the assembly transferred from Panama to Tacubaya and any information "tending to show what are the objects proposed to be accomplished by the said assembly," whether the United States was invited to send a Minister, "and, if so, for what purposes," Clay transmits a copy of the desired commission and letter of credence and "also, copies of certain documents which have been communicated to the House, during its present Session, relating to the Congress of Panama . . ." (see above, Clay to Adams, December 21, 1826). Explains that these documents and those previously communicated to Congress (see above, Clay to Adams, December 20, 1825; January 9, March 14, April 3, 1826), together with the instructions to the Ministers (see above, Clay to Anderson and Sergeant, May 8, 1826), provide all the information in this Department on the objects of the Congress and that the instructions as prepared for the meeting at Panama "are equally applicable to the Congress at Tacubaya." Copy. DNA, RG59, Report Books, vol. 4, p. 199. Published, with the cited enclosures, in *American State Papers, Foreign Relations*, VI, 383–84.

The resolution had been introduced by Littleton W. Tazewell on January 15, tabled on January 16, and passed on revival by Nathan Sanford, on January 23. This inquiry was an aspect of the Senate debate on President Adams' nomination, January 3, of Joel R. Poinsett "to be Envoy Extraordinary and Minister Plenipotentiary of the United States to the Assembly of American Ministers transferred from Panama to Tacubaya. . . ." On February 12, the Senate resumed consideration of the nomination. A resolution, offered by Thomas Hart Benton, declaring it "not expedient" to replace Richard C. Anderson as a Minister to the Congress was defeated by vote of 25 to 22. A second resolution, offered by Benton, noted that, since there had been no formal invitation to send plenipotentiaries to Tacubaya, the Senate advised "that no farther steps ought to be taken in that mission, or any further expense incurred." This resolution was also defeated, by 26 to 22. Poinsett's appointment was then approved. U. S. Sen., *Journal*, 19 Cong., 2 Sess., Appendix, pp. 321–24.

From JOSEPH KARRICK, New York. Acknowledges receipt of the dispatch that Clay has addressed to the Chargé at Bogotá (above, Clay to Watts, January 8, 1827), for which he expresses "sincere thanks." States his willingness to convey additional communications Clay may wish to make to Colombia. ALS. DNA, RG76, Misc. Claims, Colombia, env. 13, claim no. 176.

From S[AMUEL] L. S[OUTHARD], Navy Department. Believing it important that "this Department should be accurately informed of the existing state of the Military Marine of other Nations" and that "the political Agents" of the United States Government residing abroad are the best source for "obtaining safe and authentic information on the subject," requests that they be forwarded the enclosed letters. ALS. DNA, RG59, Misc. Letters (M179, R65). Enclosures not found.

APPLICATIONS, RECOMMENDATIONS   January 26, 1827

E[DWARD] BATES, St. Louis, resigns his office as United States attorney for Missouri, effective February 20; asks that Hamilton R. Gamble, recently resigned as secretary of state of Missouri, be considered as his replacement. ALS. DNA, RG59, A. and R. (M531, R3). Cf. above, Atkinson to Clay, January 15, 1827; Bates to Clay, November 25, 1826.

THOMAS HART BENTON, "Senate Chamber," transmits a recommendation. AN. DNA, RG59, A. and R. (M531, R8.) The enclosure, addressed to the President, is a petition from 34 members of the Missouri General Assembly, endorsing Robert W. Wells, currently attorney general of Missouri, for appointment as United States attorney for the State. Cf. above, Atkinson to Clay, January 15, 1827, note.

Wells, born in Virginia, had moved to Missouri around 1816 and practiced law in St. Charles. He had been a member of the State legislature from 1822 to 1826, had then been named attorney general, a position he retained until 1836, and became a Federal district judge from 1836 until his death in 1864.

JAMES R[ICHARD] MILLER, "six Buildings, Washington City," solicits an office. Claims no merit, "but should it become a quality indispensably necessary for a candidate for office to possess," points to his military record. Cites his loss of property as a Virginian "by the late war" but praises Clay's efforts "touching the affairs under that head. . . ." Extends his "best respects" to Andrew Erwin, who, he is informed, is at Clay's home and requests that this be considered "a private note." ALS. DNA, RG59, A. and R. (M531, R5).

Miller, who had served as a lieutenant of infantry in the War of 1812, held a claim for one slave for which he sought indemnity under Article I of the Treaty of Ghent (cf. above, Gallatin to Clay, November 13, 1826). *House Docs.*, 19 Cong., 1 Sess., no. 122.

The Six Buildings, at the northwest corner of 21st Street and Pennsylvania Avenue, had housed the first Washington offices of the Navy and State Departments and residences of several leading political figures.

HAYM M. SALOMON, New York, asks whether the place of [Cortland] Parker, deceased, formerly consul at Curaçao, has been filled; notes that local merchants would welcome appointment of an individual, currently visiting in New York, "whose house does the principal business for . . . [American] Merchants there." LS. DNA, RG59, Misc. Letters (M179, R65).

Haym, younger brother of Ezekiel Salomon, was a New York merchant.

Philip Robinson was not formally appointed to the consulate until March 3, (cf. above, V, 136n); he had resigned by the following December. U. S. Sen., *Executive Journal*, III, 576, 583.

INSTRUCTIONS AND DISPATCHES   January 27, 1827

From THOMAS L. L. BRENT, Lisbon. Encloses a letter addressed to himself by (Alexander H.) Everett. Notes that, notwithstanding the resistance of the King of Spain (Ferdinand VII) to the English demands, as reported by Everett, the Spanish Ambassador (Count de Casa Flórez) has been informed that his government will remove and bring to trial all public officers who have given aid to the Portuguese rebels. Reports that Lord Beresford has sailed for England, that the forces of the Marquis de Chaves have re-entered Portugal, and that some additional "partial desertions" of (Portuguese) forces into Spain have occurred. ALS. DNA, RG59, Dip. Disp., Portugal, vol. 7 (M43, R-T6). Received April 3.

Everett's letter, dated January 20, reports the withdrawal of French troops from Spain, an action which he interprets as evidence that the King has determined "not to yield any thing more." Everett also comments that he thinks hostilities probable.

From A[LEXANDER] H. EVERETT, Madrid, no. 66. Reports that "The Convention on Indemnities" (cf. above, Everett to Clay, December 18, 1826) is before the Council of State but that he has had no opportunity to press issues of United States-Spanish relations, given the present crisis in which "warlike preparations" continue. Notes that the President's message to Congress (see above, Pleasants to Clay, December 9, 1826, note) is well received in Europe. LS. DNA, RG59, Dip. Disp., Spain, vol. 26 (M31, R28). Received March 24. Enclosed is a translation of a lengthy "Editorial Article from the Madrid Gazette" of January 18. Although unfriendly in tone towards Portugal, it disclaims any Spanish intention of interfering in that country or antagonizing her friends (cf. above, Brent to Clay, January 27, 1827).

From JOSEPH PULIS, JR., Malta. Reports the arrival of "the United States Ship North Carolina . . . from Tunis where the Consul [Samuel Heap] was landed" after boarding at Toulon; notes the illness of about one hundred men of Commodore John Rodgers' crew and comments upon the hospitality accorded them by the Government of Malta. ALS. DNA, RG59, Cons. Disp., Malta, vol. 1 (M-T218, R-T1). Received May 10.

MISCELLANEOUS LETTERS　　　　　　January 27, 1827

From JOHN HOLLINS, Baltimore. States that Richard R(eynal) Keene has suggested that authentic transcripts be made of documents sent to Madrid in reference to his (Hollins') pending claim against the Spanish Government. Requests that the copies be sent to the United States Minister at Madrid (Alexander H. Everett) with the earliest dispatches, "to be there subject to Mr. Keene's order." LS. DNA, RG59, Misc. Letters (M179, R65). Cf. above, Mayer to Clay, April 11, 1825.

On January 30, Daniel Brent acknowledged receipt of Hollins' letter, inquired whether he wanted authenticated or "informal" copies of the requested documents, and explained that authenticated copies were more expensive and would require longer to prepare. Copy, in DNA, RG59, Dom. Letters, vol. 21, p. 465 (M40, R19).

Richard Reynal Keene, Baltimore lawyer, went to Spain later in the year "as agent for the recovery of certain claims of citizens of the United States, on Spanish subjects, as well as on the Government of Spain. . . ." In 1829 he petitioned Congress praying "that such measures may be adopted as shall cause Spain to render him speedy and full justice" for financial injuries sustained as a result of his allegedly illegal deportation from that country. The petition was referred to the House Committee on Foreign Affairs, but no recorded action was taken. U. S. H. of Reps., *Journal*, 20 Cong., 2 Sess. (February 16, 1829), pp. 289–90. Cf. below, Little and Barney to Clay, January 30, 1827.

APPLICATIONS, RECOMMENDATIONS　　　January 27, 1827

JOHN TALIAFERRO, ALFRED H. POWELL, GEORGE HOLCOMBE, H[ENRY] H. GURLEY, and WILLIAM BRENT, Washington, recommend appointment of John D. Simms as secretary of the Florida Territory. ALS in Taliaferro's hand, signed also by the others. DNA, RG59, A. and R. (M531, R7). Simms was appointed a clerk in the Navy Department in April, 1827, became chief clerk in 1839, and continued in that office until 1843. Cf. above, Mercer to Clay, January 23, 1827.

From Jabez D. Hammond

Sir,　　　　　　(Private)　　　　　　New York Jany. 28. . 1827

You will have heard before this reaches you that Genl. Van Rens-sellaer [*sic*] has been nominated at Albany as a Candidate for the office of U. S. Senate by a portion of the Friends of the National Administration in the Legislature[1]— I left Albany more than a week ago but I labored much to bring about this result before I left there—

—I know well that an immense majority of those who supported Mr. Clinton[2] at the last election were honest & zealous in their determination to support the National Administration but it is not to be disguised that Mr. Clinton has been looking in another direction— This circumstance produced difficulty but happily it has been overcome—

—It is now in the power of *two Individuals only*, both of them *your Friends* to defeat the re-election of Mr. V. Buren— I mean Gen. P. B. Porter & Col. Young[3]— If their Friends Caucus with the opponents of the Administration they will be beaten— But if the Bucktail Friends of Administration take the ground that they will support Gen. V. R. and to which in principle there can be no objection (and personally there surely can be none) his election is certain— Or, if they take the ground that they will not support any man who is opposed to the Administration, and proceed to nominate and vote for a Bucktail who concurs with them in opinion, in that case there will be three Candidates voted for and of course no election this year—

—But why not support Gen V. R.?— The effect would be that Genl. V. R. & his Clintonian Friends would be separated from Mr. Clinton and Gen. Porter & Col. Young and their Friends would be separated from Mr. V. B. and his Friends— Mr. V: B could not induce his Friends to coalesce with Gov. C.—and the result would be that one if not both of these Gentlemen would be left "scuding under bare poles"—

Heed not the Friends of Gen Porter & Col. Young *at Washington* but urge upon them the course which it seems to me both duty & policy demand— *NOW* is the time to form a strong administration Party in this state— If the present moment is neglected the opportunity may not again occur— I shall return in a few days to Albany— I am with great respect Your Obedt. Servant

The Hon. H. Clay—   JABEZ D. HAMMOND

N.B.   On recollection you will find I have at no time been mistaken as to political results in this State except in the opinion I formed in 1826. that the Crawford party in this State would eventually support another & more worthy Candidate— I am *certain* I am right now[4]

ALS. DLC-HC (DNA, M212, R2).
[1] Stephen Van Rensselaer had been nominated January 26. Hammond, *History of Political Parties in the State of New York*, II, 246.   [2] DeWitt Clinton. On the political maneuvering in New York during this period, cf. above, Shaw to Clay, September 10, 1826; Clay to Porter, December 12, 1826; below, Rochester to Clay, January 30, 1827; Moore to Clay, February 10, 1827; Porter to Clay, February 27, 1827; Mallory to Clay, April 4, 1827; Van Buren, *Autobiography*, 196–200; Remini, *Election of Andrew Jackson*, 47–49, 53–57.   [3] Martin Van Buren; Peter B. Porter; Samuel Young.   [4] On Van Buren's re-election, see above, Clay to Porter, June 22, 1826, note. Cf. also, above, Porter to Clay, December 24, 1826. On Hammond's views in 1826, cf. above, Hammond to Clay, March 16, 1826.

From ALBERT GALLATIN, London, no. 52. Encloses a copy of (George) Canning's note of January 27, 1827, in reply to his own note of December 28 (see above, Gallatin to Clay, December 28, 1826, enclosure). Comments in reference to Canning's note: first, that Clay's letter to (Churchill C.) Cambreleng (of December 25, 1825) was intended to show Clay's interpretation of the act of Parliament (of July 5, 1825); second, that the vote of the House of Representatives on the Baltimore petition (see above, Gallatin to Clay, August 19, 1826, note) demonstrated that the House concurred with the Executive's understanding of the British legislation; third, that the British Government "was so clearly and early informed of the passing & of the true intent of the Act of Congress of 1st March 1825 [_i.e._, 1823]," that on March 27 Stratford Canning wrote the Secretary of State (John Q. Adams) on that subject and, indeed, while the bill was under discussion in the Senate, Stratford Canning had presented written remarks upon it; and, fourth, that although the acts of Parliament of July 5, 1825, did not apply to any specific country, the British Government should have communicated them to the United States because of their importance to the negotiations, which at the time were merely suspended, not terminated. Indicates that he will not answer Canning's note unless instructed to do so. Expresses belief that Canning will not negotiate further the question of the West India trade, although the "general temper and tone of the Note are so different from those manifested in that of the 11th of September" (see above, Gallatin to Clay, September 13, 14, 1826). Acknowledges receipt of Clay's instruction of December 28, 1826, and expresses agreement with the opinion that "the British Government would be well satisfied with such a state of legislation, as would give the commerce between her colonies and the United States to Danish or any other vessels, to the exclusion of our navigation." Requests instructions authorizing him "to avail himself of any new circumstances that may occur and induce this Government to alter their opinion." States that if there should be a change in the British position, it will be effected "rather by mutual legislation than by Convention." ALS. DNA, RG59, Dip. Disp., Great Britain, vol. 33 (M30, R29). Published without enclosure, in Adams (ed.), _Writings of Albert Gallatin_, II, 354–56. Received March 8.

In his note to Gallatin of January 27, 1827, Canning rejected Gallatin's complaint that the act of Parliament of July 5, 1825, had not been communicated to the United States and contended, in reply, that the British Government had not been officially informed of the act of Congress of (March 1) 1823 and that the King's Minister to the United States (Stratford Canning) had been forced to make "repeated and pressing enquiries" to obtain a true interpretation of the "or elsewhere" clause. He explained, however, that the British had not withheld communication of the act of Parliament of 1825 from any sense of retaliation but from regard for propriety in relation to foreign governments, who might have mistaken such a communication as an imposition of the legislation upon them. Noting that the stipulations of the act of 1825 had been accepted and acted upon by some governments and that the United States had not found it expedient so to act, he asserted that consideration of legislation on the subject by Congress indicated that the intent of the Parliamentary action had been understood; and, with an apology for the reference to a private correspondence, he stated that "the continuance of the benefits of the then existing state of things to the United States for nearly a twelve month longer than they would otherwise have enjoyed it" (cited in Clay to Cambreleng, December 25, 1825) had been permitted in consideration of the pending legislation. Canning asserted, too, that, while Congress had been considering the Baltimore petition (see above, Gallatin to Clay, August

19, 1826, note), Charles R. Vaughan had been instructed, "upon receiving an assurance from the American Government that the restrictions and charges on British Shipping and British Colonial Produce would be withdrawn," to give notification that "the discriminating duties imposed upon American Ships and their Cargoes in the West Indies should immediately cease." When Congress rejected the proposed action, Canning argued, any communication of such intention "might, perhaps have been considered as an improper appeal against the formal decision of the American Legislature"; accordingly Vaughan had then been directed to announce "the intention of His Majesty's Government to pass the order in Council of July. . . ." Canning concluded with the statement that he would "not allow himself to be drawn again into a discussion of topicks already more than sufficiently debated" but qualified "such refusal with the declaration that it . . . [was] not in any degree dictated by sentiments, either unfriendly or disrespectful to the United States, or by indifference to the amicable settlement of all other Questions . . . pending between them and Great Britain."

For the exchange of correspondence between Stratford Canning and John Q. Adams regarding the act of Congress of March 1, 1823, see Canning to Adams, March 27, April 10, May 17, 1823, and Adams to Canning, April 8, May 14, 1823, printed in *American State Papers, Foreign Relations*, VI, 231–33.

From D[ANIEL] W. SMITH, Matamoros. Notes that he has not received replies to several letters sent to the (State) Department since receiving his commission. Questions whether his reports, specifically that of July 24, 1826 (above), are reaching their destination ALS. DNA. RG59, Cons. Disp., Matamoros, vol. 1 (M-T18, R1).

MISCELLANEOUS LETTERS   January 28, 1827

From SAMUEL L. SOUTHARD, "Navy Department." Encloses a copy of a report from Captain B(eekman) V. Hoffman, of the United States sloop *Boston*, for Clay's consideration. ALS. DNA, RG59, Misc. Letters (M179, R65).

In the enclosure, dated November 8, "off the Harbor of Rio de Janeiro," Hoffmann reported the capture of the American brigs *Ruth*, *Pioneer*, and *Sarah George* and the removal of their crews, "turned on shore to shift for themselves." He noted that the brig *Flora*, "from Philadelphia, bound to Buenos Ayres, with Lumber," had also been taken, but released and her cargo disposed of prior to his sailing. He added that he had taken the crew of the *Pioneer* to Buenos Aires and offered support to the others who sought it at Montevideo. See above, Raguet to Clay, September 1, October 2, December 4, 1826; Bond to Clay, October 28, 1826.

INSTRUCTIONS AND DISPATCHES   January 29, 1827

To HENRY MIDDLETON, St. Petersburg, no. 5. Encloses a narrative by Prince Demetrius Augustine Gallitzin relating "the circumstances of his case and . . . his present condition" and instructs Middleton to employ unofficially "friendly offices with the Imperial Government in such a manner as may appear . . . to be most conducive to the ends of justice which the Prince seeks." States that the President directs such instructions not only from his sense "of the merits of the Prince's claims" but also "upon the strength of the accompanying letters of introduction from the venerable sole survivor of the Signers of our Declaration of Independence [Charles Carroll], from the Archbishop of Baltimore [Ambrose Marechal] and from Mr

R[obert] Oliver. . . ." Copy. DNA, RG59, Dip. Instr., vol. 11 (M77, R6), p. 243. ALI draft, in DLC-HC (DNA, M212, R8). Enclosures not found.

Gallitzin, converted to Roman Catholicism at age 17, had migrated to Baltimore in 1792, at age 22. Three years later he had been ordained a priest and in 1799 had founded a mission at Loretto, Pennsylvania. Because of his faith and his profession, he had been disinherited by Emperor Alexander I in 1808. Naturalized as Augustine Smith in 1802, the Prince had resumed his family name in 1809 and pressed for restoration of his rights to family estates. He was heavily indebted, in large part to Charles Carroll, on behalf of the Loretto mission and in 1827 issued a public appeal for its support. By the close of his life Gallitzin had repaid his creditors, largely through charitable contributions, but his elevation to bishoprics throughout the West had been repeatedly denied, on objections, first by Carroll and later by Maréchal, citing his indebtednes. He died at Loretto in 1840.

Ambrose Maréchal, born near Orléans, France, in 1764, had entered the Sulpician Community in 1782 and had been ordained and sent to America in 1792. Recalled to France in 1803, he had returned to Baltimore in 1812 and taught at St. Mary's Seminary until his consecration as Archbishop of Baltimore in 1817. He died in 1828.

From J[OHN] J. APPLETON, Stockholm, no. 9. Reports that the King (Charles XIV) has left unexpectedly for Norway to attend the opening of the Storthing, on February 5, with hope of favorably influencing the discussion on the Crown's propositions, among them the "conversion of the *suspension* into the *absolute* Veto" (cf. below, Appleton to Clay, March 25, 1827). Notes that under the constitution this is the last time he may present this proposal and that general opinion in Norway opposes giving him additional powers, "less from any distrust of his intentions than from a fear of becoming instrumental in drawing closer the bond of Union with Sweden. . . ." States that the Prussian-Swedish commercial negotiations have opened, that there is "good prospect of . . . a Treaty founded on the most liberal principles," and that new commercial arrangements with France are also "probable" (cf. above, Appleton to Clay, November 1, 1826, note). Encloses a translation of an ordinance reducing duties under the tariff of March (16), 1826; comments that only one or two articles affected by it are profitably carried here by Americans, notably coffee. ALS. DNA, RG59, Dip. Disp., Sweden and Norway, vol. 5 (M45, R6). Received March 24. Ordinance dated December 13, 1826, enclosed.

From THOMAS L. L. BRENT, Lisbon. Transmits a translation of an article appearing in the Lisbon *Gazette*. ALS. DNA, RG59, Dip. Disp., Portugal, vol. 7 (M43, R6). Received April 2. The enclosure is an extract of a dispatch from the Portuguese Chargé d' Affaires at Madrid (Luis António de Abreu e Lima) to the Portuguese Minister of Foreign Affairs (Francisco de Almeida), dated January 22, 1827, which stated that all commandants of the Spanish Army who failed to take action against Portuguese rebels passing through their jurisdiction have been suspended from the command and ordered to appear before court martial. The dispatch noted specifically the removal of General (Francisco) Longa, Captain General of Old Castile, and of Field Marshal (Manuel) Freire, Governor of Ciudad Rodrigo, and the renewal of orders for the capture and deportation of the Marquis of Chaves and Viscount Canelas.

Longa and Freire had achieved distinction as nationalist leaders during the Peninsular War. António da Silveira, Count de Amarante and first Viscount Canelas, also a veteran of that conflict, had been raised to the nobility in 1823.

From ALBERT GALLATIN, London, no. 53. Reports receipt of the "ratified convention" and Clay's no. 15 of December 28; encloses a copy of his note of January 26 to Canning and states that he accompanied it with a private note urging an "immediate exchange of ratifications." Notes that Canning, in reply to the latter document on January 27, explained that his confinement by a cold would necessitate some delay; expresses doubt that (Edward) Wyer will be able to return before the packet of February 8.

Comments that he has "waded through the tedious arguments, reports &c. of the Commission on the North East boundary" and, despite his lack of copies of the maps, concludes: "I am now prepared to make a preliminary statement of the case, to be substituted on our part to all those under the Commission; and indeed, if I was authorized, I would have no hesitation that it should be considered as conclusive so as to bar any further arguments on the subject, provided that the statement which the British Plenipotentiaries may prepare should also be considered as conclusive so as to bar any further argument or reply on their part." ALS. DNA, RG59, Dip. Disp., Great Britain, vol. 33 (M30, R29). Extract published in Manning (arr.), *Diplomatic Correspondence . . . Canadian Relations*, II, 576. Received March 8.

Gallatin's note of January 26 had given formal notification of the ratification of the Convention of November 13, 1826, on the part of the United States, and of Gallatin's readiness to exchange ratifications "in the usual manner." Gallatin had also expressed the President's satisfaction with the arrangement of the dispute and "his hope that the same spirit of mutual conciliation" might govern "the discussions and the issues of all other subjects of difference between the two Governments." *Ibid.*

From T[HOMAS] M. RODNEY, Havana. States that he has been informed that Admiral [Angel] LaBorde has sailed to capture the Mexican naval forces led by Commodore (David) Porter, now taking refuge in Key West, where they are under blockade, and that the Spanish plan embraces the risks involved in entering the harbor of Key West to seize the Mexican ships. ALS. DNA, RG59, Cons. Disp, Havana (M-T20, R5).

Porter had left Veracruz in December to attack Spanish shipping off Cuba. LaBorde had chased him into Key West and stood offshore. But whether Porter was under legal blockade is questionable, for he was not prevented from using Key West until spring as a base of attacks on Spanish merchantmen nor from then making a round trip to Mexico. David F. Long, *Nothing Too Daring, a Biography of Commodore David Porter, 1780–1843* (Annapolis, 1970), 265–68. Cf. below, Rochester to Clay, January 31, 1827, note.

MISCELLANEOUS LETTERS   January 29, 1827

To THE GOVERNORS OF MAINE [ENOCH LINCOLN] AND MASSACHUSETTS [LEVI LINCOLN]. Transmits the complaint of the British Minister (Charles R. Vaughan) of January 16 and expresses belief that the governors will act to restrain the activities of their citizens insofar as they are "repugnant to the conciliatory course recommended by the President. . . ." Copy. DNA, RG59, Dom. Letters, vol. 21, pp. 462–63. Cf. above, Clay to Vaughan, January 18, 1827; Clay to Lincoln, December 15, 1825; Clay to Parris, January 4, 1826.

From J[OSIAH] S. JOHNSTON, on behalf of the Senate Commerce Committee. Requests information on (Charles B.) Allen, who has been nominated as consul at (Pará) Brazil. ALS. DNA, RG59, A. and R. (M531, R1). Cf. above, Corning to Clay, April 8, 1826, note.

From GEORGE W. SLACUM, Annapolis. Reports his arrival by way of Buenos Aires, Montevideo, and Rio de Janeiro, states that he had hoped to leave Buenos Aires soon after writing to Clay on June 19 (letter not found; cf. above, Slacum to Clay, August 6, 1826) but could not depart until November because of (John M.) Forbes' opposition. Presuming that Forbes may have made unfavorable references to him in letters to Clay, pledges to present evidence that the Minister has been jealous of him and that he has been the victim of "official and private Slander." Notes that he will visit Clay when recovered from his voyage. ALS. DNA, RG59, Cons. Disp., Buenos Aires, vol. 3 (M70, R4). Cf. above, Slacum to Clay, April 18, 1826; Forbes to Clay, January 5, 1827; below, Slacum to Clay, February 14, March 14, 1827; Clay to Forbes, February 16, 1827.

From THOMAS WHIPPLE [JR.], Public Lands Committee, House of Representatives. Asks, on behalf of the committee, "to what officers of the Government the Laws of the United States have been . . . distributed. . . ." ALS. DNA, RG59, Misc. Letters (M179, R65).

APPLICATIONS, RECOMMENDATIONS   January 29, 1827

THOMAS NEWTON [JR.], Washington, recommends "Col. William Lambert," of Virginia, "to fill the station for which he is recommended" (secretary of the commission proposed by the Convention of November 13, 1826, with Great Britain). Encloses recommendation (by William McCoy and 19 other members of the Virginia delegation to Congress). ALS. DNA, RG59, A. and R. (M531, R5). Cf. above, Clay to McLane, January 15, 1827; below, Clay to Ogden, March 23, 1827.
    Lambert, who signed his application for this appointment as William Lambert, Jr., was not the mathematician identified above, Bill from Columbian Institute, November, 1826, but a native of Richmond, trained in law, who had served for a number of years prior to 1812 as a clerk in the Federal District Court at Richmond. Cf. also, below, Lambert to Clay, February 13, 1827.

From Christopher Hughes

My dear Sir,   *Private!*   Brussels 30th. January; 1827.
    I wrote to you, a few days ago, via Havre, a short letter &, via Liverpool, *its* duplicate, together with a long letter;[1] since then, I have written a long Letter, via. L.pool, to General Smith;[2] with a request that he would send it to you; you may find a good deal of loose & flippant stuff in it; and vote me to be a most egotistical & vain *Sub*, to connect, even in the most attenuated association, the idea of my name, & fitness for affairs, with that of Mr. Gallatin; you will be right, without doubt! yet, I wont admit, *in extenso* (as one of your predecessors, a near Relation (common folks say, *Relative*, which Dr. Johnson[3] says is bad:) to my wife,[4] was in the trick of saying, at every turn. There was one *turn*, that put an end, *"in extenso,"* to all his public labours; and that was a *turn* out; which he fully justified, by, what Mr. Canning calls in his [. . .][5] "My Pocket Book" or "a postliminious preface" —a pamphlet;[6] for which, neither his country, nor I, has, or should ever forgive him. And yet, the fault of this should rest on other's shoulders; for he, "good-easy man," allowed himself to be led, as the General, his Brother, in after-years, allowed himself to be ruined, by

the same baleful charlatan, not to say, vile Rogue, James A. Buchanan, of Bank Stock memory![7] Neanmoins. Robert Smith is an amiable, though not an able man; & of most agreeable & gentlemanlike commerce!)

I was going to say, before I conceived two pregnant parentheses, that I would *not* admit the allegation of *thorough* ineptitude! for there is a tact, as well as "a *tide* in the affairs, of men;"[8] Besides, accident & incidents sometimes create usefulness, as effectually as great talent & knowledge. However, I pray you to pardon my presumption; as also, this new page that amplifies the former treatize [*sic*], upon the most noxious egotism.

I have nothing new, or additional, to add to my late letters;   My opinion as to a war being inevitable, remains unweakened;   a great many of the political cognoscents dont agree with me; or, say they dont;   for example, I met the Minister of foreign-affairs[9] yesterday, in the park;   we walked & talked for an hour or more;   he is a very amiable, agreeable & able man; (as all such officers should be; & I am willing to believe are & have been; saving the *able* in the case of meus avunculus Robertus, vel, mei avunculi Roberti:) but if I have any *tact* in character, His Excellency Baron Verstolk de Soelen, will never subscribe to any arrangements having, for their object, a liquidation of claims either on public or private account, *if* he can possibly *avoid*, or *evade*! I said the same thing of old Ct. Engeström, with whom Mr. Russell[10] wrote & *graphied*, to make a word, papers enough to cover half the Pensylvania-Avenue [*sic*]; and I was, *not* wrong. 'Well,' H. E. Baron Verstolk, remarked, among other things in our walk & talk, "that he did *not* believe, there would grow-up a war, out of the present state of things." To believe him or not, is the question? i.e. did he *speak* as he *thought*? I give what he said; for it is only fair, to say that very many differ from me; though I here iterate, that my opinion is the same, as formerly written!—

Do you ever see Cobbett?[11] I hope you do! We know what to think of him & his principles & character; yet he wields a ponderous sledge; *his character* cannot change that of truth & reason; & there is a vast deal, in some of his late papers, where he treats of *U. S.* (as:) "The Devil can quote scripture," is a proverb; we may doubt the devil's motives—but, still it is *scripture*; which we *may not* doubt!   it is, in this sense, that I read Cobbett! His last No.[12] in which he devotes the last branch of his letter "to the nobles, on the good things Mr. Canning & Mr. Huskisson[13] have in store for them," to us, to the President & to his message, & in which he gives a List of American Books, with a summary notice of them, ought to be read by all Johns & all Jonathans.—

Here, at the risk of being called a Croaker, (not a John Wilson Croker,[14] the greatest foe our country has, & the greatest scoundrel in the world; I have it from the Duke of Sussex;[15]   H. R. H. said to me, in 1823, "Mr. Hughes, there is one of the d——est (his very words) rascals breathing, in this same Kensington Palace." I looked aghast! it was before dinner in the Duke's Library;   I did not know, whom he meant;   I felt sure he did not mean *me*; & I could not suspect him of meditating moral Suicide, & meaning his Royal Self;   at last, out he bolted, "*I mean John Wilson Croker*, Secy. to the admiralty." I was refreshed. (called a *croaker*;–) Let me implore you to have my Washington Newspapers sent by some other route, than *N.York & Holland*; if they may not be sent, via Havre, care of Beasley,[16] it will be a thousand times better, to have them sent to the *Collector at Baltimore*, with instructions to forward them, by some of the Tobacco ships to Rotterdam or Amsterdam! *Maryland* carries on an immense trade with Holland! There are constantly ships sailing, from *Baltimore*. I shall then get the papers, in six or 7 weeks; whereas, I have no dates, fresher than 3 months or more! I am really wretched for want of news. from home; especially, now Congress is in Session! I beseech you to say a word to Mr. Brent,[17] to have the papers sent, via Baltimore & Holland to be given to the Consuls, who have already my request to forward them by Diligence here; May I also beg you to send me 2 copies of the Calendar for 1827,[18] by some route! & any pamphlet, or late work, touching home affairs or politics! Do not think me importunate or greedy, but it is really grievous to me, to be without all manner of home public tidings!—

Mr. Huygens Jr.[19] is a very gentlemanlike, intelligent, young man; I have received him with all the kindness in my power;   he told me, & I heard it with much pleasure, that you had communicated to his father,[20] the favourable terms, in which I had written (as I think) of the King[21] & Government of the Netherlands;   I am to dine with him, to day, at the Minister of foreign affairs, & on Sunday, at Sir C. Bagots! To night, I am to go, from *official duty*, to a Ball, at the Prince of Orange's. Mrs. Hughes will *not go*! We went to the Fete, at the Queen's[22] birth-day: the *first time*. Mrs. Hughes had been at Court, excepting her presentations. Etiquette forbids Chargé d'affaires, & *their wives*, from sitting at the Royal table; but hospitality & decency require that *a Lady*, a stranger, & the wife of certainly *somebody*, & a *representative* of his country too, ought to have a seat at *some* table! So without being such an ass as to quarrel with Etiquette, on our not finding a seat, for my wife, in any one of two or three rooms, where there were supper tables, we very calmly & quietly, called a Hackney Coach, & went home; without shawls or Clokes [*sic*] which gave my wife a violent cold, that lasted 10 days! Of course, she feels under *no sort* of *obligation* to expose herself to a similar fate;   the subject has been very much talked of in Society & in Town, & it is unpleasant I admit; but Pilled Garlic Chargé d'affaires must know how to smile

over a little humiliation; it is *tough* work, I acknowledge; mais, Que faire? If some of our very thrifty Representatives, of our 24 Sovereignties, knew & *understood* this, they might, perhaps, have less unprofitable thrift & economy & more regard for the dignity & comfort of their representatives! I say all this, I assure, you not complainingly! —I should be most gratified to receive a line, or a word, now & then, from you; but I know yr. occupations & do not now, hint this complainingly! I can say nothing yet, about Mr. Huygens return;   I shall have an official talk with Min. of Foreign affs. in a day or two, & report its Substance to you! Mrs. Hughes begs to be respectfully mentioned to Mrs. Clay;   the best message I can send her, is to say, that the news of her husband's improved health, has given real joy, to his friend & Servt   C: HUGHES
Mr. Clay. Washington

N.B.   respectful compliments to Mr. Adams. — —

ALS. DNA, RG59, Dip. Disp., Netherlands, vol. 8 (M42, R-T12).
1 See above, Hughes to Clay, January 21, 1827.   2 Samuel Smith.   3 Samuel Johnson appears to define the words interchangeably in his *Dictionary of the English Language* (London, 1755; 2d. edn., London, 1784).   4 Laura Sophia Smith Hughes, niece of Robert Smith, Secretary of State from 1809 to 1811.   5 Word illegible.
6 *Robert Smith's Address to the People of the United States* had been first published as a pamphlet at Baltimore in 1811 and republished in the Washington *National Intelligencer*, July 2, 1811. It precipitated hostile criticism and proved an unsuccessful attempt to defend Smith's administration as Secretary of State. The quoted phrases of George Canning have not been found.   7 Cf. above, II, 698. How Buchanan was directly involved in the incident is not clear. Robert Smith's conduct, while Secretary of the Navy in the summer of 1809, had been subjected to Congressional investigation on charges that he had cashed bills of exchange drawn by S. Smith and Buchanan on the firm of (C.) Degen, (William Young) Purviance, and Company, naval supply agents at Leghorn, Italy, for the Mediterranean Squadron, when the Baltimore firm had not shipped sufficient bullion to meet the bills. Degen shortly thereafter had been declared insolvent. Frank A. Cassell, *Merchant Congressman in the Young Republic, Samuel Smith of Maryland, 1752–1839* (Madison, Milwaukee, and London, 1971), 148. In response to a House resolution of December 24, 1810, Secretary of the Treasury Albert Gallatin on February 22, 1811, had presented a report showing the extent of the deficiency in the accounts of Degen, Purviance, and Company. This report had been published in the Washington *Daily National Intelligencer* on March 12, 1811. Robert Smith's forced resignation as Secretary of State has been dated as March 12 or 13. Cassell, *op. cit.*, 171. His ties with the firm of S. Smith and Buchanan were also cited in an editorial attack, attributed to Joel Barlow, on July 6, which charged that Secretary Smith's opposition to the first Macon Bill (see above, I, 452n) had been motivated by consideration of the effect it would have upon the commercial concerns of that business house. Washington *Daily National Intelligencer*, July 6, 1811; Adams, *History of the United States* . . . V, 187.   8 Shakespeare (Furness [ed.], *A New Variorum Edition*), *Julius Caesar* (2nd edn.). Act IV, Sc. iii, line 248.   9 Baron J. G. Verstolk Van Soelen.
10 Count Laurent d'Engeström; Jonathan Russell.   11 William Cobbett.
12 "To the Nobility of England, on the Blessings which Messrs. Canning and Huskisson Have in Store for Them," *Cobbett's Weekly Register*, vol. 61, no. 4 (January 20, 1827), cols. 193–226.   13 George Canning; William Huskisson.   14 Croker, born in Ireland and graduated from Trinity College, Dublin, had studied law at Lincoln's Inn and practiced that profession for some years in Ireland. He had been acting chief secretary for Ireland in 1808 and was a member of Parliament, from 1806 to 1832, and Secretary of the Admiralty, from 1809 to 1830. Greatly interested in literary endeavors, he had been one of the founders of the *Quarterly Review*, in 1809.   15 Charles Frederick, Duke of Sussex, Earl of Inverness, and Baron Arklow, the sixth son of George III. He was known for his liberal political views and scholarly interests and from 1830 to 1838 served as president of the Royal Society. Hughes had stopped a few days in London, en route to

the United States, in April, 1823.   16 Reuben G. Beasley.   17 Daniel Brent.
    18 Probably the *Calendar of the United States House of Representatives and History of Legislation,* a report of the status of all bills introduced into the House.   19 Roger Bangeman Huygens.   20 The Chevalier C. D. E. J. Bangeman Huygens.
    21 William I.   22 Frederica Louise Wilhelmina.

From John W. Overton

My Dear Sir;   Nashville January 30th 1827.
    At the Commencement of this new year, I presumed to address a letter to you, and several members of Congress from this State and Kentucky. On the Subject of the Appointment of District Attorney for the United States, at this place.[1] Having been born & raised within three miles of you, and having known you from the earliest period of my recollection, and also knowing your liberality of mind, in Some measure emboldens me, again to write to you. The Solicitude I feel in procuring this Office, and the great advantage it would be to me, as I am very poor, also urge me to trouble you again with the Contents of this letter— Any thing I would Say in my Own behalf, might be considered fulsome & egotistical, and therefore, I shall leave it with my friends— I have not written many letters myself, nor taxed my friends much in this way; knowing that you were acquainted with me and all my family in Kentucky,[2] & this therefore, would be unnecessary. I have rested my hopes of success upon your liberality and inteligence [*sic*], & shall be more than happy to find your exertions in my favor.
    [Cites his war service and poverty as considerations for the appointment.]
    Col Johnston of Kentucky,[3] will inform you, that this Office was promised to me, Some years back when it was expected that Col. Crabb[4] would then resign— If this promise will avail me aught, let me now have the benefit of it—
    I saw your daughter Mrs. James Erwin last Evening,   She appeared to be in good health, and will set Out in a few days for Orleans[5]— Mr. Erwin told me that your son Thomas was living in Woodville Mississippi and was about Commencing the practice of law at that place[6]—
    I hope my Dear Sir You will not consider my Communications to you, On the Subject of this letter, as troublesome— My anxiety to know my fate, has urged me to it, this is my Only apology
    I hope you will accept my best wishes for your health & happiness and a long life of peace and prosperity. Your friend Sincerely
Honble. Henry Clay Secretary of State   JNO: W. OVERTON

ALS. DNA, RG59, A. and R. (M531, R6).
    1 Cf. above, Overton to Clay, December 30, 1826; additional letters have not been found.   2 Cf. above, III, 157n.   3 Richard Mentor Johnson.   4 Henry Crabb.

5 Cf. above, Erwin to Clay, January 4, 1827.   6 Cf. above, Poindexter to Clay,
December 1, 1826.

From Nathaniel Rochester

Dear Sir,   Rochester 30h. January 1827.
You as well as others at the seat of Government, and in every other
part of the Union, except within this State, must be at a loss to account for the political course pursued in this State, not only at the
event of our last general election,[1] but at the movements in our State
Legislature now in session. You have been informed I presume that
Mr Clinton got his election by a tour he made last Summer through
the southern tier of Counties in this State, where the inhabitants are
desirous of geting [sic] a Turnpike road from the Hudson river to
Buffalo, (a distance of about 650 miles) at the expence of the State of
not less than two million of dollars.[2]
On my return from the South I was in New York early in October
where I spent four days, and where I saw most of the leading republicans of that City, who uniformly approved of the Herkimer nominations[3] and said the City of New York would give those nominations a
very large majority, even the Editor of the Enquirer[4] came out in
favor, but previous to the election Mr. Clinton went to New York;
and either he, or his friends there prevailed with Noah to shift sides
and come out in favor of Clinton, and ascribing my son Williams [sic]
nomination to the influence of the Administration of the Genl. Government, this coming out at the eve of the election and too late to be
answered had the effect intended by Clinton and his friends, and gave
him a majority there of about 120[0] altho the republican members
of Congress and assembly had large major[ity.]   if this defection had
not taken place in New York William would have been elected, notwithstanding the effect of Mr. Clintons tour through the Southern
Counties which probably gave him 5000 Votes more than he would
otherwise have got. You must have seen that out of ten new senators in
this State, eight Anti-Clintonians were elected, and more than two
thirds of the assemblymen.   had not those two sections been worked
on by decep[tion] (if not corruption) William would have been elected
by a majority of 10,000 at least. I think however it has been best for
him that he was not elected. I think the main object in opposing Mr.
Clintons election has been gained by his lean majority.   it will satisfy
the people of other [states] that he is not so popular in this as they
have been taught to believe from the presses under his and his friends
controul.   it is well unders[tood] in this State, and has been for a
long time that Mr. Clintons object [is] the Presidency two years
hence,   his, or rather his friends declaration that he was friendly to

the Administration of the Genl. Government was [not] believed. The late movement at Washington goes to strengthen the op[inion] I have long had, that Genl. Jackson is to be dropt and Mr. Clinton taken up by his Jacksons friends as a more prominent opponent to Mr. A[dams.]

You may suppose the appointment of Genl. Root[5] speaker of the Assembly by the republicans indicates hostility to the Administration, but this does not follow, as the presidential question was not mixed with that appointment. I do not think Mr. Van Buerens election to the Senate for six years more, improbable,[6] as I know many Republicans and friends to the Administration who will vote for him.   this will be no indication of hostility to Mr. Adams, as they do not believe he will be in the opposition.   he is considered a man of talents and devoted republican and took a very active and decided part at our last election in favor of the Herkimer nominations, and did say he was not opposed to the Administration of the Genl. Government, altho he opposed the Panama mission for the reasons he gave in his speech in the Senate on that subject[7]   The Clintonians are making great exertions to prejudice the republicans against him, with a view to divide and conquer   You will have seen that the Clintonians in the Legislature of our State have had a Caucus where about 30 members met, and adjourned for the purpose of geting a larger meeting, but at their second meeting they mustered but 18 who would agree to nominate a Senator. which eventuated in 9 votes for Genl. Van Renselear [sic], 7 for Mr. Tracy and two for Speaker Taylor.[8]

It is believed here, and I have no doubt of the fact, that the caucus was got up by Mr. Clinton for the purpose of injur[ing] the prospect of Mr. Adams's re election, by inducing the people [of] other States to think that those 18 compose his strength in our Legislature. They are known to be Mr. Clintons warmest friends   that Mr. Clinton will be a candidate for the presidency two years hence there can be no doubt, and he will get a part of the electoral Votes in this State as our elections hereafter is [sic] to be by Districts, but he has no chance of geting a Majority in the State. Should Gen. Jackson [be a] candidate I do not believe he will get one electoral Vote [in the] State.

You will please forward the enclosed to my son William, with [my] respects to Mrs. Clay, and with very high respect & esteem I am DSir, Your Mo. Ob. Servt.   N. ROCHESTER

ALS. DNA, RG59, Misc. Letters (M179, R65). Addressed to Clay. Margins partially obscured.

1 See above, Rochester to Clay, November 18, 1826.   2 Cf. above, Rochester to Clay, August 30, 1826.   3 Cf. above, Rochester to Clay, May 9, 1826, note.   4 Mordecai M. Noah, editor of the *New York Enquirer*.   5 Erastus Root.   6 See above, Clay to Porter, June 22, 1826, note.   7 In March, 1826. *Register of Debates*, 19 Cong., 1 Sess., pp. 234–63.   8 Stephen Van Rensselaer; Albert H. Tracey; John W. Taylor. On the political maneuvering of this nomination, cf. above, Hammond to Clay, January 28, 1827.

INSTRUCTIONS AND DISPATCHES   January 30, 1827

From ROBERT CAMPBELL, Genoa. Encloses shipping report; notes an increase in tonnage and value of goods imported; a decrease in exports; the advantage held by the French, owing to a bounty granted by that Government on codfish; and the extension of most-favored-nation treatment to American vessels. ALS. DNA, RG59, Cons. Disp., Genoa, vol. 1 (M-T64, R1). Received May 6.

From ALBERT GALLATIN, London, no. 54. Transmits a copy of (George) Canning's reply to his note of January 26 and a letter, received under open seal, from (Thomas L. L.) Brent. Advises that the report of (Cornelius) Van Ness and his own projected statement "will be sufficient to make . . . [Clay] master of the subject" of the northeastern boundary, except that Van Ness gave no opinion on "the boundary along the 45th parallel of latitude" and that the arguments of (William C.) Bradley also had "great merit" but were "less condensed and . . . encumbered with matter which may now be considered as unnecessary for a complete understanding of the subject." Asserts that the position of the United States regarding the Maine boundary is correct and "the irksome pleadings of the British agent [Ward Chipman] are a tissue of unfounded assertions and glaring sophistry; . . . the British Commissioner's [Thomas Barclay's] decision on that point . . . scandalous." Concedes that "the British have at least plausible ground" for their argument on the northwestern source of the Connecticut River and that the United States have no more than "a decent objection with respect to the boundary from Connecticut to the St. Lawrence (not the geocentric latitude). . . ." ALS. DNA, RG59, Dip. Disp., Great Britain, vol. 33 (M30, R29). Published in Adams (ed.), *Writings of Albert Gallatin*, II, 356–57; extract published in Manning (arr.), *Diplomatic Correspondence . . . Canadian Relations*, II, 576–77. Received March 8. The enclosure from Canning, dated January 29, stated that British ratifications would be ready for exchange February 6. Cf. above, Gallatin to Clay, January 29, 1827, and Moore, *History and Digest of the International Arbitrations*, I, 81–82.

Chipman, born at Marblehead, Massachusetts, and graduated in 1770 with an M. A. degree from Harvard University, had been a Loyalist during the American Revolution and had served after that conflict as secretary to a commission at New York to receive claims for supplies furnished to the British Government. In 1784 he had been appointed solicitor general of New Brunswick and had moved to that Province. He had there served in several Sessions of the Provincial Assembly and had been appointed a member of the Provincial Council in 1806 and a judge of the Supreme Court in 1809. He had acted as the British agent under the British-American treaty of 1794 (Jay's Treaty) to locate the St. Croix River and again under the Treaty of Ghent to determine the northeastern boundary of the United States. In 1823 he had been appointed "president and commander-in-chief of the province of New Brunswick." He had died a few months later, in February, 1824. Isabel M. Calder, in *Dictionary of American Biography*, IV, 74.

From JOHN RAINALS, Copenhagen. Acknowledges receipt of Clay's letter of October 31; expresses regret at the omission from the treaty (of April 26, 1826); but notes that Count (Ernst Heinrich) Schimmelman, the Danish Foreign Minister, has given assurance that the omission was "entirely accidental, and can in no shape effect [sic] the Treaty." Transmits his consular reports, a copy of the treaty between Denmark and Sweden signed "in November last" (see above, Appleton to Clay, November 1, 1826), and a copy of the edict by the King (Frederick VI) freeing Americans from the tax on property removed from Danish dominions (cf. above, Ritchie to Clay, November 13, 1826). Comments that trade regulations affecting the United States remain the same and that the last grain harvest "fell short," leaving little available for export. ALS. DNA, RG59, Cons. Disp., Copenhagen, vol. 3 (M-T195, R3). Received June 8.

MISCELLANEOUS LETTERS   January 30, 1827

To [EDWARD] EVERETT. States that he "will cause an examination immediately to be made in the negotiations [not further identified] to which he refers and apprize him of the result." AN. MHi. Endorsed in strange hand: "Jan. 30, 1827.?"

To TENCH RINGGOLD. Notifies him that his commission as United States marshal for the District of Columbia has been forwarded to William Cranch. Copy. DNA, RG59, Dom. Letters, vol. 21, p. 464 (M40, R19).
    On the same date Cranch was instructed to deliver the commission upon receipt of the required bond. Copy, in *ibid.* On February 7, Cranch notified Clay that Ringgold had fulfilled the prescribed requirements for the office. ALS, in DNA, RG59, Misc. Letters (M179, R65). Ringgold acknowledged receipt of the appointment on the latter date. *Ibid.*

To [JOHN W. TAYLOR, Speaker of the House of Representatives]. Transmits a report prepared "In Obedience to a resolution of the House of Representatives of the 19. May 1826. . . ," calling for a schedule of the claims of Americans upon "the Governments of France, Naples, Holland, and Denmark, for illegal captures, spoliations, Confiscations or any other illegal Acts, since the year 1805. . . ." Explains that the report has been delayed "by the inattention of Claimants to the punctual transmission of their Claims" and that the list may not include "all the claims comprehended in the terms of the Resolution." Copy. DNA, RG59, Report Books, vol. 4, pp. 200–201. Published, with the accompanying list of claims, in *American State Papers, Foreign Relations* VI, 384–553. Cf. above, Circular Request, June 8, 1826, and note.

From PETER LITTLE and JOHN BARNEY, House of Representatives. Enclose a letter received from Robert S. Hollins, David Hoffman, Benjamin C(hew) Howard, and Charles F. Mayer; also a copy of "a letter addressed to the Hon. John Q. Adams secretary of State" from the same correspondents. ALS by Little, signed also by Barney. DNA, RG59, Misc. Letters (M179, R65). Endorsed as follows: "Respecting a passport &c. to R[ichard] R[eynal] Keene. 5 feb: Returned to Mr Little at his request as verified in his letter of the 1st Inst the Enclosures [not found] of this." Cf. above, Hollins to Clay, January 27, 1827; below, Little to Clay, February 1, 1827.
    Robert S. Hollins of Baltimore, a son of John and Janet Smith Hollins, was, with Hoffman, Howard and Mayer, acting in reference to his father's financial affairs. Janet Smith Hollins was the sister of General Samuel Smith.
    David Hoffman, a native of Baltimore, had attended St. John's College and was a prominent member of the Maryland Bar. He had published a *Course of Legal Studies* in 1817 and lectured in the law school of the University of Maryland from 1823 to 1843. Subsequently he moved to Philadelphia where he practiced law and pursued private literary interests.
    Benjamin Chew Howard, a native of Belvedere, Maryland, had been graduated from the College of New Jersey (Princeton University) in 1809; admitted to the Maryland bar in 1816; commissioned a brigadier general in the Maryland militia; and elected to various local and state offices, 1820–1824. He represented Baltimore in Congress from 1829 to 1833 and from 1835 to 1839 and was reporter to the United States Supreme Court from 1843 to 1861.

From Francis T. Brooke

My Dear Sir   Richmd January 31st 1826 [*i.e.*, 1827]

I received your favour on the Slave Subject[1]— I believe it will be Satisfactory to those interested, though Mr Cabell[2] of the Senate remarked to me that you were one of Jobs comforters— he is very friendly in his feelings and did not mean I am Sure that he was dissatisfied with your reasons— I Should not have troubled you with a letter on that Subject of itself— but to Say to you that Governor Tyler is denounced here by the enthusiasts for having written you a letter[3] approving of your vote for Mr Adams and acceptance of the Situation you hold   from what Source they got that fact I do not know,   he Said to me two or three days ago that he was so denounced —without admitting that he wrote the letter, though he by no means denied it— he Said that as the friend of Mr Crawford you would have been the Secretary of State in the event of his election,   I told him I had a Similar assurance from Mr Forsyth,[4]   he then went on to Say— he had no doubt that in the event of Genl. Jacksons election that department would have been offered you— Mr Giles was to have called up his resolutions[5] to day but has not come to the house   I think he is playing a game that must increase the friends of the admn. if he goes no further that [*sic*] to ask an expression of the opinion of the assembly, disapproving of the tariff and internal improvements, he will get a large vote,   if the first only almost an unanimous vote, but if he asks it to adopt a countervailing tariff upon American manufacturers he will get a very Small vote,   on the Subject of the Tariff he will be ably opposed by Genl Taylor[6] and the Subject will be better understood by the people of Virginia than it has been,   in every point of view Mr Giles is doing the work of those opposed to his projects— With great respect & Esteem your friend   FRANCIS T. BROOKE.

ALS. DLC-HC (DNA, M212, R2). Addressed to Clay.

[1] Probably the Speech, above, January 20, 1827.   [2] Joseph Carrington Cabell, of Amherst (now Nelson) County, Virginia, a graduate of William and Mary College in 1798 and a lawyer, had served in the Virginia House of Delegates (1808–1810) and, since 1810, in the State Senate. He continued in the latter body until 1829 and returned to the House of Delegates from 1831 to 1835. He was distinguished for his active support of internal improvements, agricultural reform, and popular education.   [3] Above, March 27, 1825.   [4] John Forsyth.   [5] On January 29, William Branch Giles had introduced resolutions in the Virginia House of Delegates calling for appointment of a committee to "enquire into and report upon 'certain unauthorized assumptions of power on the part of the Government of the United States' " and "to report such measures for the adoption of the General Assembly, as they shall think, will most effectually tend to arrest these usurpations; to stay the hand of avarice and despotism; to reinstate the good people of the Commonwealth in all their essential rights and liberties; and the Government thereof in all the rights granted and secured to it by the fundamental laws." Giles called up his resolutions on February 1, and on the following day they were adopted and the committee appointed.   Reporting for the committee on February 13, Giles elaborated the resolutions into a strong statement of the State's "exclusive jurisdiction over all the territory, persons and things within the limits of this Commonwealth"; a concession that concurrent jurisdiction was shared with the Federal Government for the conduct of "certain specified powers"; but an insistence that exclusive jurisdiction was granted to that Government only over the District of Columbia and tracts "purchased by the

consent of the Legislature of the State in which the same shall be, for the erection of forts, magazines, arsenals, dock-yards, and other needful buildings." The report also proposed resolutions protesting "the claim or exercise of any power whatever, on the part of the general government, to make internal improvements within the limits of the state of Virginia . . ."; "any claim or exercise of power, whatever on the part of the general government, which serves to draw money from the inhabitants of this state, into the treasury of the United States, so as to disburse it for any object, whatever, except for carrying into effect the grants of power to the general government, contained in the constitution of the United States"; and ". . . the claim or exercise of any power, whatever, on the part of the general government to protect domestic manufactures . . ." and, specifically, "the operation of the act of congress, passed May 22d, 1824 . . . generally called the tariff law, which vary [*sic*] the distributions of the proceeds of the labor of the community, in such a manner as to transfer the property from one portion of the United States to another; and to take private property from the owner for the benefit of another person, not rendering public service,—as unconstitutional, unwise, unjust, unequal and oppressive." Concluding that the time remaining in the legislative session was too limited to permit further action, the committee called for adoption of these resolutions as a "solemn protest against the . . . usurpations of the federal government." After extended debate, the report and the resolutions were adopted by the House of Delegates on March 2 and by the Senate on March 5. Richmond *Enquirer*, January 30, February 3, 15, 17, 24, 27, March 1, 3, 1827; Virginia House of Delegates, *Journal, 1826–1827*, pp. 116, 134–36, 185–92; Virginia Senate, *Journal, 1826–1827*, pp. 127–37, 138.   6 Robert Barrand Taylor opened his remarks on February 23, continued them on February 24 and 27, and on March 1 offered a substitute for the proposal. The Taylor measure was defeated, on March 2, by vote of 131 to 48. Richmond *Enquirer*, February 24, 27, March 1, 3, 1827.

From William B. Rochester

Hon. H. Clay Washngtn.

My Dr. Sir   City of Mexico 31. Jany. 1827.

I sit down for the purpose of redeeming my pledge to write you from this Country— I addressed a short letter to our friend Genl. V. Renssllaer [*sic*] pr. Mr. Mason[1] from V:cruz in which I begged to be remembered to all friends in Washington City— the latter gentl. has probably apprized you, that we passed safely thro' that hot-bed of yellow fever & blk vomit diseases with which a few strangers were afflicted at the time of our landing, and which, we learn, have since proved fatal in almost every case— The President's Message[2] overtk. us at Jalapa 31st. Ultmo. We have Washington News-papers as late as 14th. decb. The atmosphere of this valley is of a remarkably soft and uniform temperature, although at such a height above the level of the Sea as to be included within what is distinguished from the less elevated regions as part of the *tierras frias*: the breathing of it connected with the sea voyage, has been of essential benefit to me— the barometer [*sic*] generally ranges at this season from 58.° to 62°— the objection to it, is, that the air being extremely rarified, evaporation goes on too rapidly; the effect of which is that, on the arid plains surrounding this capital & entirely destitute of forest trees, there is very little verdure, consequently besides being exposed to much dust, we sensibly experience a difficulty of respiration, after taking moderately active exercise— this complaint is common to all foreigners— the barometrical pressure is put at from 22 to 23 inches—

Doubtless you will have been apprized (ere this reaches you) from a more responsible source, of the probability or rather improbability of an early meeting of the Congress at Tacubaya[3]— this beautiful village is situated about four miles from this city at the base of one of the porphyritick mountains which surround the Valley of Mexico— the selection of it for the sessions of the Congress in preference to the Capital, was certainly judicious—

Besides Mr. Sergeant & the two Deputies of this Republick, there are now here but two others viz. Larizabal [sic] from Central America & Doctr. Gual[4] of Columbia [sic], who arrivd. about the 19h. or 20h. inst.— It has been asserted and is believed that one of the Mex: Deps. (Michelina) is on the point of resigning, not on account of any aversion to the service, but for causes wholly unconnected with it, but which have not sufficiently transpired to justify a direct allusion to them— Of the political state of this Country, I can scarcely venture, on account of my brief residence in it, to indulge even in conjectures— Every thing appears tranquil upon the surface, but it is a tranquility apparently maintained by the universal presence of a strong military force— there has been some excitement within a few days, produced by the arrest of a miserable friar—Arenas,[5] who is charged with having submitted to the Captain-General[6] some seditious propositions: four other friars are inculpated with him and also in confinement— if tried, as they probably will be (by a Court *Martial*) it is thought they will be shot, yet the master spirit is generally looked upon as more fool than fanatic, hardly deserving the serious notice of Government and on that account, they may only be banished by the mere fiat of the Executive, a mode of getting rid of suspected individuals, for which they are not without abundance of precedents—

What gives importance to the affair, is the fact, that the Congress is now seriously discussing a proposition to banish all friars, who shall not be enabled, within a given period, to lay before the proper Tribunal, indubitable evidence of their devotion to the cause of the Revolution, at the period when the contest with the Mother Country was at its crisis— This proposition is calculated to spread consternation among that numerous Body of individuals, particularly in Puebla de los Angeles, which city has alway [sic] been deemed the focus of clerical loyalty to Ferdinand &. of attachment to the old order of things, and whose Bishop,[7] an highly talented man is now watched with a very jealous and vigilant eye by the existing government— There is in this Country, vastly more of the *penchant* towards a monarchical form of Govt. than I had imagined previously to my arrival— it is however chiefly confined to the clergy and to the Gatchupines[8]— Next to this Capital, Puebla & Vera Cruz are the cities in which this leaven mostly abounds—

There is a Strong opposition among the Laymen to the Administration, at the head of which is Genl. Guerrero,[9] whose title, name and bias, all indicate that his fort [sic] consists more in the *fortiter* than in the *suaviter*— he is a flaming Republican, deadly hostile to Gatchupines of Old Spain, popular with the mixed blood & a prominent candidate for the Presidential chair in succession to Victoria;[10] the opposing candidate will probably be Gomez Pedrasa [sic], who has just abandoned the post of Secy. of War & Navy[11]— By the bye, speaking of resignations, Estêva,[12] late Secy. of the *Hacienda* (which is in some degree analogous to our Treasry. Dept.) has also sent in his resignation within the last fortnight— in fact, resignations have become quite frequent of late[13]— the incumbents in their high and responsible stations find themselves in thankless Situations and do not seem to be endowed with sufficient moral courage to encounter calmly the constant senseless clamours of a querulous and noisy Editor[14] in this Metropolis, of whom it may be said that he at least enjoys a quant: suf: of freedom in his line— Garcia[15] has been nominated to succeed Estêva, but it is thought, he will decline accepting— no successor to Pedrasa has been named— You are probably aware of Mr. Obregon's contemplated resignation of his office of Minstr. plenipy. near the U.S.   it is here said that the vacancy will be supplied by the appt. of Zavala,[16] a Senator from Yucatan, who is almost the only individual in office here who reads and speaks English—

We called pretty Soon after our arrival to pay our respects to the President, whose residence is in the *palace*! We found him a modest, unassuming man, sufficiently tinged to denote his origin—a batcheler [sic] of about forty—grave, steady & reserved, indicating by his manners that he had spent most of his life among Soldiers, who still constitute his hobby— in the course of conversation he discovered none of the traces of a well-stored & cultivated mind— I take him to be a sound Patriot, but credulous and liable to be easily imposed on by designing men—

The palace is an immense building, covering an entire large square, constantly guarded at each angle & every avenue by armed men and containing within its walls, besides the spacious apartments for the Presidents residence, the office[s] of the four Cabinet Ministers, the mint, two Quartets [sic] capacious enough for a regiment, three Court rooms with contiguous prisons, a Senate chamber, a Reps. hall, a botanical garden &c &c indeed when ranging through this immense pile & surveying its numerous courts, its open passages and private communications, its splendid galleries, its massive columns, its magnificent arches and its stupendous domes united by a species of cement which time seems to have improved and which has for years "derided the solstitial rains" I have vividly brought to my recollection the description of the palace of the Abyssinian Prince[s][17]

In my h'ble view, this Government is as yet, a military one practically— Liberty is, (with the mass of the people) more a national than an individual matter—   the poorer and vastly most numerous class are despised, degraded and oppressed— thievish & cowardly— so true it is that "oppression never fails to corrupt morals."[18]— they are of every variety of caste but exhibiting nothing of that marked diversity of features, which mental discipline and freedom of opinion & of action produce— if it be true that the people are happiest and most free under that Government where the machinery of power operates, as it were, invisibly and where the wand of authority is least felt & most seldom seen, then have the citizens of this Republick not yet arrived at that desirable point in the March of civil liberty— We hear of banishments, without previous trials—arbitrary imposition of duties without legislative enactments and of grave Senators denying in debate that Congress have the power of controuling the Militar[y] &c— In every city, town and village, nay in every road, you are are [sic] met by the badged minions of power, nor can you emerge in any direction without having at your heels at each pass a swarm of officers prying into your baggage and demanding your passports   Besides, the hand of power is constantly felt by the citizens through the medium of a priveleged [sic] ecclesiastical corps, whose numbers give them the faculty of ubiquity and who firmly hold both the mind and purse in subjection—

This tirade, you will naturally infer, brings me to the conclusion, that however much of energy, there is but little moral force either in the Country or among its Rulers—

The importance of official responsibility seems not to be duly appreciated or attended to— the fault lies in the absence of that great lever *public opinion*, which in our happy country is sooner or later always correct and to a certain extent supposed to bear upon all departments, and which, however it may be obscured, in times of excitement, by the mists of faction, never fails, under the influence of free popular institutions, ultimately to break out purely and in proper direction— if there be such a thing as public sentiment prevailing here among that class which is not ecclesiastical or directly under the banns of fanaticism, it is at best somewhat diverted from its legitimate objects and centers at last in a deep-rooted hatred of Spain & of Natives of Spain— it is the policy of those who are in and of those who want to be in power, to keep alive this prejudice— It is to be hoped however that most of the evils to which I have alluded, will be mitigated, if not removed, by time, a State of peace, more toleration upon questions of conscience and above all by the diffusion of education & its invariable con-comitant [sic], liberality of sentiment.

Strange as it may appear, some of the leading politicians, (especially those who feel securely entrenched upon the seats of power) do not seem to desire peace—   they profess to deprecate the possible recognition of their independence, on the part of Spain, as a calamity— Such an event would leave them without a pretext for keeping up so large a military force and besides then would the "occupation" of many an Othello be "gone"— Again, believing, as they do, that theirs is the most favoured land of Heaven, they are unwilling to afford any additional facilities to foreigners, particularly to Spaniards, for immigrating amongst them and participating in those bounties designed by Providence for themselves alone— it is really amusing at times to hear them felicitating themselves upon their happy destiny— Our great Country! how rich in silver & gold &c &c!— In many points of view they undoubtedly have abundant cause for congratulation, not to mention the varieties of their production, soil & climate &c

It is conceded however that they never can become a great naval power, yet the same cause (the want of sea ports and of navigable rivers) which denies to them such a pre-eminence, must alway [sic] prove to them a strong pillar of defence— indeed, if they be united, any attempt at invasion must invariably prove abortive— the descent from the interior (where the wealth & physical strength of the country lye [sic]) to the coast is so short and rapid, that, combined with the fevers & rocks & shallows of the Sea-board & the ocean currents, they must ever be secure from attack by water, whilst to the North they present a barrier of warlike Indian tribes, and when that barrier shall be removed, they have on that side, kind, just and generous neighbours— From present appearances, they have most to dread from a numerous, ill-appointed and idle army at home— want of employment, perhaps a want of funds, and, if it prevail, the genius of Republicanism, must eventually invite to and compel its reduction— when that day arrives I apprehend that, as the military makes them every day more unfit for civil life, a momentary convulsion may be anticipated,   at least the State of Society will be, for a season, troubled and uncertain— the privates and officers too (for with few exceptions there is little difference) are a dissolute and reckless band— Even at this time the Govt. find it expedient to keep under pay many officers of rank, whom they dare not intrust with the performance of any duty or with the command of a single man— I confess I know not what safe disposition may be made of them, unless it be (as they now sometimes do with convicts) to station them on the coast, where the black vomit will soon render them harmless by thinning their ranks—

Como. Porter's success[19] has not, apparently, attracted much attention here— indeed I have hardly heard his name mentioned since I left Vera Cruz— he had much trouble in prevailing upon the Government to allow him to fit and man his little fleet for immediate service— he was not invited into the service, it would seem, with a view to active duty at Sea   this did not "jump with" the Commodore's "humour"— their main object was, as I understand, to secure the services of a naval precepter [sic] in port— they, of course, yielded a reluctant compliance with his desire for a cruise—

In travelling from Vera Cruz to Mexico nothing strikes a citizen of the U. S. more obviously than the remarkable scarcity of forest trees and of water-courses— for a greater part of the way, particularly along the extensive plains between Jalapa & Puebla, I was constantly reminded of our wide and flat Western priaries [sic], as the latter appeared to me in the months of Jany. & Feby. when deprived of their tall grass— with this difference however, in favour of the former,—they are occasionally intersected by ditches of many miles length, made for irrigating, and shepherds are now & then to be seen in the dark heath tending large flock[s] of sheep & goats, in the vicinity of little clusters of dwarf pines and oaks— besides, after stretching your eyes for immense distances all around, they repose at last upon the grandeur of Mountain wildness— upon stupendous active & extinguished volcanoes covered with eterna[l] snow— the whole irresistibly impressive of the omnipotence of Nature and producing the effect describe[d] by a living author "of imposing an idea of Solitude even upon those who travel in great numbers, so much is the imagination affected by the disproportion between the vast wild around and our own insignificance." [20]

We have unfavourable accounts from Guatemala & Cola.[21] but trust the infection will not reach this Republick, & that she may be strong and sound enough to resist the external pressure— You may well conceive, from the length of this letter, that I have much leisure on hand   I am very truly & respectfully yr. hble Serv

WM B ROCHESTER

P.S.   in a letter to a friend in the State of N.Y. I have incorporated *in haec verba,* some of the foregoing reflections— he will have too much discretion to give them publicity—   W B R—

ALS. DLC-HC (DNA, M212, R2).   [1] Stephen Van Rensselaer; John Mason, Jr.
[2] Adams' annual message, of December 5, 1826.   [3] See above, Sergeant to Clay, January 26, 1827, note.   [4] John Sergeant; José Domínguez and José Mariano Michelena; Antonio Larrazábal; Pedro Gual.   [5] Joaquín Arenas. See above, Sergeant to Clay, January 26, 1827.   [6] Francisco Dionisio Vives.   [7] Joaquín Antonio Pérez y Martínez Robles, a native of Puebla, had been elected a deputy to the Spanish Cortes in 1810 and bishop of Puebla, the oldest diocese in New Spain, in 1814. Sympathetic to the revolution, he had been named a member of the provisional Junta and the regency of 1821, following the declaration of Mexico's independence from Spain.
[8] *Gachupines,* a Mexican vulgarism for European Spaniards.   [9] Vicente Guerrero, President of Mexico from 1829 to 1831, shot in the course of a revolt against his government in the latter year.   [10] Guadalupe Victoria.   [11] Manuel Gómez Pedraza relinquished the office only briefly, from February 10 to March 3, 1827, when he resumed the post until his election to the Presidency, January 12, 1829. When revolt broke out at the announcement of his election, Guerrero assumed the Presidency instead.
[12] José Ignacio Esteva.   [13] Cf. below, Poinsett to Clay, February 21, 1827.
[14] Manuel Lorenzo Justiniano de Závala, founder in November, 1826, of *El Correo de la Federación,* organ of the Yorkinos, had published on January 1, 1827, a strong attack on the ministry under President Guadalupe Victoria. Závala, born in Yucatan and a leader in the revolutionary movement in that province in 1812, had been a deputy to the Spanish Cortes in 1820 and a delegate in the first Mexican Congress, of 1822. He had

been elected to the Mexican Senate in 1825 and in 1827 became Governor of the State of Mexico. He served briefly in 1829 as Minister of the Hacienda, lived in European exile from 1829 to 1832, returned the latter year as Governor of the State of Mexico, and in 1833 became Mexican Minister to France. He resigned from that post to join in the Texas revolt in 1835 and was one of those who declared the independence of Texas on March 2, 1836. Elected *ad interim* vice president of the Republic of Texas, he died the following November. Závala was also the author of a very popular history of the Mexican revolution.   15 General Francisco García Salinas had been a deputy to the first Congress after Mexican independence. He did not succeed Esteva immediately and later held the Presidency for only one month, in November, 1827. From 1829 to 1834 García was governor of the State of Zacatecas.   16 Pablo Obregón remained the Mexican Minister in Washington until his suicide "by suspending himself from the lamp iron in the passage of his dwelling house in this City," Washington *Daily National Journal*, September 11, 1828.   17 Reference not found.   18 Quotation not found.
    19 Commodore David Porter's fleet had been reported earlier in the month to have captured a Spanish vessel with a valuable cargo of quicksilver off the port of Havana. Though supposedly blockaded in the harbor at Key West, his small vessels slipped freely between the reefs; and, it was said, one brig alone had captured nine Spanish vessels during the last two or three weeks of January. *Niles' Weekly Register*, XXXI (January 20, 1827), 328; XXXII (March 31, 1827), 83.   20 Quotation not found.
    21 See above, Litchfield to Clay, May 22, 1826; Gonzalez to Clay, January 7, 1827.

INSTRUCTIONS AND DISPATCHES   January 31, 1827

From ROBERT MONROE HARRISON, Antigua. Notifies Clay that customs officials in Barbadoes have prohibited "the entry of American produce from any of the foreign colonies." Reports that local plantation interests expect the (British) Government to make the prohibition general, notwithstanding the distress it will cause the country, and Ireland in particular. Evaluates the order's effect on various British possessions in the West Indies. Relates in a postscript that he has received confidential information contending that in case of war with Spain, Britain will take possession of Puerto Rico and that the island would be restricted to raising corn, rice, and other foodstuffs essential to the war effort. ALS. DNA, RG59, Cons. Disp., Antigua, vol. 1 (M-T327, R1). Received March 9. On the indirect American trade with British colonies through non-British colonial ports in the West Indies, see below, Harrison to Clay, May 3, 27, 1827.

From WILLIAM TAYLOR, Veracruz. Reports that the Government has taken measures to put down a possible conspiracy in the metropolis (Mexico City). Describes troop movements in Veracruz and its environs. Observes that there have been no arrests except that of Friar (Joaquín) Arenas (see above, Sergeant to Clay, January 26, 1827, note). Suggests that the plot may have had its origin with the Government itself in order to justify further consolidation. ALS. DNA, RG59, Cons. Disp., Veracruz, vol. 1 (M183, R1). Received February 24.

MISCELLANEOUS LETTERS   January 31, 1827

To THE PRESIDENT [JOHN QUINCY ADAMS]. Reports in answer to the House resolution "of the 9th. instant," inquiring "Whether any and if any, what number of Chargés des Affaires have been appointed since the 4th. day of March 1789 without the advice and consent of the Senate; and whether, in any case, such appointment has been made after notice had been given of the intention of a Minister abroad to return, and after his successor had been appointed; if so, by what authority, and what length of time did said temporary appointment continue, what the general duties to be discharged, and what the compensation paid— And that the President also inform this House from what period the person [*sic*] appointed Minister and Secretary of Legation to Panama, received their Commissions and from what period they have been paid their Salaries."

After nearly two pages recording the appointments, as required on the first point, prior to his assumption of the Secretaryship, Clay continues:

"John A. King, left Charge des Affaires at London by Rufus King, 1. July 1826 with the approbation of the President [see above, Clay to King, May 2, 1826]. Mr. [Albert] Gallatin was appointed Minister, 10 May 1826.

"He was again left in charge x x x x x x x x of our Affairs by Mr. Gallatin, during a short excursion which he made to Paris in the fall 1826 [cf. above, Brown to Clay, October 22, 1826, note].

"Beaufort T. Watts left Charge des Affaires at Bogota by Mr. [Richard C.] Anderson [Jr.] 26. March 1825 till 20 Jan. 1826, during the return of that Minister on leave to the United States [cf. above, Anderson to Clay, May 17, 1825; January 26, 1826]. He was again left and yet remains in charge of our Affairs on Mr. Anderson's leaving Bogota, 12 June 1826 to proceeds [sic] on the Mission to Panama [see above, Anderson to Clay, June 7, 1826].

"2. Most of the preceding appointments of Chargés des Affaires were made whilst we had Ministers appointed to reside near the same Governments.— . . . . [A page of illustrative references associated with the period before Clay's administration is here omitted by editors.]

"Mr. Watts was left at Bogota in charge of our Affairs in the year 1825, during Mr. Anderson's absence on a visit to the United States. And, lastly, Mr. John A King was left by Mr. Rufus King in charge of our Affairs after the appointment, but before the arrival of Mr. Gallatin at London. The necessity of confiding temporarily to a chargé the Affairs of a Government which is ordinarily represented by a Minister Plenipotentiary, arises out of the absence of the Minister, no matter from what cause. It is supposed not to be affected by the fact of a Minister's having his intention to return [sic] and the appointment of his Successor.

"3. The authority under which the above appointments were made, is believed to be furnished by the Constitution of the United States and the public law [2 U. S. Stat., 608, May 1, 1810] and usage of Nations. So important is it regarded to preserve without interruption the diplomatic intercourse between Nations who are mutually represented by Ministers, that upon the death of a Minister, the Secretary of Legation becomes, by established usage, ipso facto, Chargé des Affaires until his Government is advised and provides for the event. The period during which they respectively continued to act in the character of Chargé des Affaires will be seen by an inspection of the annexed Abstract [omitted by editors] from the books of the Treasury, marked A. to which a reference is respectfully requested.

"4. The duties to be performed by a Chargé des Affaires so appointed are to be found in the same public Law and usage and may be stated, in the general to be the same as those of the Minister whose place he supplies— He transacts the ordinary business of the Legation; keeps its archives and an Office; corresponds with the Government where he is accredited and with his own; and sustains an expence [sic] and maintains an intercourse with the diplomatic Corps, corresponding with the new station to which he is elevated.

"5. The compensation received by the several persons so appointed . . . may be seen in the above abstract from the Treasury. From that abstract, it appears first, that the allowance of salary in the character of Chargé, in the cases there stated has been uniform. 2dly. That the allowance of an Outfit has been most usually but not always made. 3rdly. That in some instances the temporary appointment has been continued after the intervention of the Session of a Senate . . . and in two cases . . . [illustrative references omitted by editors] after the intervention of several Sessions of the Senate. And 4thly. that in the case of Mr. John A King, the allowance made to him was a medium between the highest and lowest allowances that had been previously made. The highest was made in the cases of Mr. [Jonathan] Russell and Mr. [Henry] Jackson to each of whom, besides the Outfit and salary of a Chargé, a quarters [sic] return salary was allowed. Mr. King was not allowed Salary as a Chargé during the absence of Mr. Gallatin on his visit to Paris last fall; nor was he allowed a quarters return salary as Chargé. He was moreover the bearer of a Convention [see above, Gallatin to Clay, November 14, 1826], the first intelligence of the conclusion of which reached the department by his delivery of the Instrument itself. Such a service is always regarded in the transactions of Government as one of peculiar interest.

"He might have been, but was not, allowed the usual compensation made to Bearers of Dispatches. An Extract from a Letter addressed by the late Secretary of State [John Quincy Adams] to the Chairman of the Committee of Ways and Means [Louis McLane]. marked B. accompanies this Report [document omitted by editors].

"6. The Commissions of the Ministers to Panama and Secretary of Legation, bear date the 14. day of March 1826. Mr. Anderson's Salary as one of these Ministers commenced, and his Salary as Minister to Colombia ceased, on the 12th. June 1826. when he left Bogota to proceed to Panama. Mr. [John] Sergeants commenced on the 24th. October 1826 when he was notified to prepare to proceed on the Mission. Mr. [William B.] Rochester [sic] salary as Secretary of the Legation, commenced with the date of his Commission [see above, Clay to Rochester, November 15, 1826]. The considerations which induced the fixation of its commencement at that period were these: He resided in the interior of New York, remote from the Sea Board and was required shortly after the confirmation of his appointment to repair to the City of New York, where he accordingly came to proceed on the Mission which it was then expected would depart in the course of the last Spring. Subsequent events not chargeable to him prevented his departure. He moreover resigned about the period of his nomination to the Senate a judicial station which he held under the State of New York to enable him to accept this new appointment; and held himself in readiness to depart on the mission from the date of his appointment to the period when he actually sailed from the United States." Copy. DNA, RG59, Report Books, IV, 201–208. Published with accompanying documents in *American State Papers, Foreign Relations*, VI, 554–58.

This resolution constituted another of the many efforts by Jackson supporters to embarrass the administration. John Blair of Tennessee had introduced the measure on January 8 as a call for information on the appointment of Chargés since January 1, 1826, a date designed to focus on the elevation of John A. King. The more generalized request for information dating from 1789 represented an amendment "by consent of the mover." U. S. H. of Reps., *Journal*, 19 Cong., 2 Sess., pp. 136–37, 139. As treated by the Jackson press, the payment of an "outfit" for King's brief service represented an "illegal fee . . . given to purchase the KINGS of New York." Clay received particular censure for having instituted an "inquisition" among the governmental clerks under threat of dismissal for the one "who had disclosed the fact. . . ." Washington *United States Telegraph and Commercial Herald*, January 25, 1827.

From JOHN REED, House of Representatives. Requests for his friend (Rufus) Bacon "a signed certificate from the Secretary of State shewing the amount & particular items of the claims allowed by the Colombian Government to the owners & freighters of the Schooner Minerva of Troy. . . ." ALS. DNA, RG59, Misc. Letters (M179, R65). Cf. above, Bacon to Clay, September 4, 1826; see also, Anderson to the

Secretary of State, March 18, 1825. Copies of Clay's certification and of a letter of transmittal by Daniel Brent, both dated February 6, 1827, in DNA, RG59, Dom. Letters, vol. 21, pp. 472, 473 (M40, R19).

From JARED SPARKS, Baltimore. Encloses a copy of a letter he has sent to the President and requests Clay's support for the project therein proposed. ALS. DNA, RG59, Misc. Letters (M179, R65). In the letter to President Adams, Sparks proposed to edit the foreign correspondence from "the revolutionary papers in the office of the Secretary of State" and sought copyright privileges in exchange for his services. Quoting a Congressional resolution providing for publication of the documents, he expressed belief that the resolution was still operative and would sanction his project. For the joint resolution of March 27, 1818, see 3 *U.S. Stat.*, 475.

The work was published as *The Diplomatic Correspondence of the American Revolution, Being the Letters of Benjamin Franklin, Silas Deane, John Adams, John Jay, Arthur Lee, William Lee, Ralph Izard, Francis Dana, William Carmichael, Henry Laurens, John Laurens, M. Dumas, and Others Concerning the Foreign Relations of the United States during the Whole Revolution. . . ,* edited by Jared Sparks (12 vols., Boston and New York, 1829–1830). A new edition, in six volumes, was published at Washington in 1857. An appropriation act of March 18, 1830 (4 *U. S. Stat.*, 382) provided $31,300, "For enabling the Secretary of State [Martin Van Buren] to execute a contract with Jared Sparks, of Boston, made by Henry Clay . . . for printing and publishing the foreign correspondence of the Congress . . . from the first meeting thereof to the ratification of the definitive treaty of peace . . ." in 1783. See below, Sparks to Clay, March 13, 1827.

APPLICATIONS, RECOMMENDATIONS   January 31, 1827

DANIEL P. COOK, House of Representatives, recommends the (Springfield, Illinois) *Sangamo Spectator*, edited by Hooper Warren, to publish the laws. States that this paper was formerly the *Edwardsville Spectator*. ALS. DNA, RG59, P. and D. of L. See above, Clay to Editor, December 7, 1826, note.

On February 3, William Browne informed Cook that the firm of (Thomas) Lippincott and (Jeremiah) Abbott had been awarded the contract to publish the laws for the current Session of Congress and noted that (Hooper) Warren had not requested the appointment in his new location. Copy, in DNA, RG59, Dom. Letters, vol. 21, p. 468 (M40, R19).

EDWARD EVERETT AND FOURTEEN OTHERS recommend William Coolidge, Jr., for a clerkship in the Patent Office or "elsewhere," if additional clerkships are authorized. Copy. DNA, RG59, A. and R. (M531, R2). Cf. above, Coolidge to Clay, January 24, 1827.

JOSEPH M. WHITE states that he has received numerous recommendations supporting the candidacies of Samuel R. Overton, James Webb, and David B. Macomb, all of Florida, for the position of Territorial Secretary. Notes that Overton's service on the (Florida) Land Commission received "the highest commendation of Congress" (cf. above, White to Clay, July 5, 1825, note), that Webb "was unanimously recommended by all the Legislature of Georgia, & all the Judges of that State," when he applied some years earlier for an office in Florida, and that Macomb, formerly of Ohio, is "much esteemed in Florida. . . ." Comments that the people of that Territory "would be greatly obliged" if the appointment were made to a local resident but that they know "they have been indulged in the few appointments made in the last year. . . ." Observes that if the appointment is given to some one out of the Territory, William M. McCarty of Virginia, who "has already purchased lands & removed his negroes to the Country" would be "a very acceptable appointment to the Territory." Pointing out that McCarty "is a friend to Internal improvement," White concludes: "The only argument I have heard against his appointment is that he is independent— The late defalcation of the Secretary of the Territory, who was appointed on account of his *necessity* having spent a fortune of two hundred thousand dollars, & being the *son* of one of the signers of the declaration of independence, induce [*sic*] us to hope, we shall never have *one* again whose necessities, or bankrupcy [*sic*] constitutes his claim, and avoids responsibility—" ALS. DNA, RG59, A. and R. (M531, R8-Webb file). Cf. above, Mercer to Clay, January 23, 1827.

Webb, born in Georgia and educated at William and Mary College, had practiced law in his native State and sat on the State Supreme Court. He was appointed in 1828 judge of the Southern Judicial District for the Territory of Florida and retained that office until 1839, when he moved to Texas. He served as attorney general, secretary of state, and Senator under the Texas Republic and later as secretary of state and judge of the State of Texas.

For the resignation of George Walton as secretary of Florida Territory, see above, Walton to Clay, December 14, 1826. He was the son of George Walton, a native of Virginia, who had practiced law in Savannah, Georgia, represented that State in the Constitutional Convention, and served as Governor of Georgia from 1779 to 1780, Chief Justice of that State from 1783 to 1789, and Governor again from 1789 to 1790. The elder Walton had also been a United States Senator from 1795 to 1799.

The charge of "defalcation" here mentioned in reference to the son was refuted in a letter from the Second Auditor of the United States Treasury to Governor William P. Duval, January 27, 1827, published in part in Carter (ed.), *Territorial Papers. . . ,* XXIII, 688n.

To James Erwin

Dear Sir   Washn. 1 Feb. 1827.

I have recd. your favor of the 14h. Ulto.[1] together with a letter and statement from Mr. Grundy to whom I have written.[2] I have consented that the final adjustment of my business with him shall abide his coming here next fall. I think there is more due than he presents. However, I speak from memory entirely. The bal. will be increased by calculations of interest founded on corrections of dates; and I thinks [*sic*] he claims one or two inadmissible credits.

You may let the business remain as it is until I see him, or until I again write you.

I addressed my last to you at N. O.[3] Nothing very important has since occurred. My health is not as good as it was.

We are very anxious that you and Anne[4] should join us here. My love to her. Yr's affectionately   H CLAY

ALS. THi. Addressed to James Erwin on attached sheet.
[1] Probably above, Erwin to Clay, January 15, 1827.   [2] See above, Grundy to Clay, January 13 and 14, 1827; Clay's reply not found.   [3] No letter found since Clay to Erwin, April 28, 1826.   [4] Anne Brown Clay Erwin.

From Cornelius Comegys

Sir,   *private*   Philadelphia February 1. 1827

Honored with your letter of the 25 Ulto, allow me in the first place to offer an apology for intruding so much on your time and patience, but as it is a duty I owe to myself to enquire into affairs committed to your charge as a Lawyer, I trust on that score you will neither think me officious or troublesome. In the next place I thank you for the interest taken in regard to my son and regret that it is not in your power to obtain, or give him, a situation in your department, and I regret it the more because I am persuaded from his Education, knowledge of business and facility of writing, he would fill a subordinate situation in any of the public offices to advantage & I have felt more than anxious, having served myself several years in the Treasury department, as Mr Nourse[1] the Register of the Treasury will testify, and where I gained much useful information. If I could command half what is due to me in the State of Kentucky only, I could at once establish him in Trade— of this however there is no prospect, but as regards him I pray you will accept my thanks and give yourself no further trouble.

From the tenor of your letter as regards my claim on Bradford and the suggestion made in its conclusion, I now inclose a Statement,[2] with Copies of the Correspondence between Bradford[3] and my late firm at Baltimore— I have never recd. directly or indirectly, one cent on accot. of that claim, nor have I any evidence of your having recd. any, further than what Bradford state[d] in his letter, copy of which was inclosed in my last letter to you which is dated "Fort Strother March 6th. 1814"— If it is a fact that he paid you that sum in March 1814, or any time previous, money was then equal to specie and surely the fees and expences of the Suit being prosecuted but a short time could not have amounted to one third of Three hundred and fifty dollars, and it is rather hard that I should no[t] participate in what little was recd— To share its operation I make a statement to prove its effect which I submit to yourself to do as justice would appear to dictate— I wa[s] informed by a gentleman who travelled near to Bradford['s] late residence and heard that he Bradford was reputed to be worth *Thirty thousand dollars* and as you say, "possibly the Delegate from that Territory might buy the claim, and what is the lowest sum I will take for it"— The statement of the claim including interest you will find to be $2652 60/100, and I will take $1000 and assign over all my right to the claim, as well as the land spoken of, and as you no doubt often see the said Delagate [*sic*] I shall esteem it a faver [*sic*] if you will converse with him on the subject and give him the necessary explanations— In short I will agree to any terms you can make,[4] so anxious am I to bring all my affairs to a close. Very respectfully your friend & Obt. Servt   CORNS. COMEGYS

ALS. DLC-HC (DNA, M212, R2). Addressed to Clay.
1 Joseph Nourse. Comegys had been a Federal collector of internal revenue in Maryland in 1801.   2 Enclosures not found.   3 William Bradford.   4 Cf. below, Agreement with Henry W. Conway, March 9, 1827.

MISCELLANEOUS LETTERS   February 1, 1827

From HENRY GRAY, Boston. Summarizes the case of the brig *Otter*, owned by him, which, on a voyage from Boston to La Guaira, was captured on June 22, 1823, by a privateer from Puerto Rico, taken to that island, and condemned. An appeal to "the Superior Court in Cuba" resulted in a judgment for restitution and damages; but, by that time, the vessel was "in a dilapidated state" and "neither the Goods nor Captors Could be found." Encloses an estimate of the loss. LS. DNA, RG76, Misc. Claims, Spain, env. 10.

Henry Gray, second son of William Gray, was a merchant. The case of the *Otter*, built at Somerset, Massachusetts, in 1821, had been referred to the State Department upon recommendation of the Senate Committee on Naval Affairs in December, 1823. *American State Papers, Foreign Relations*, V, 251.

APPLICATIONS, RECOMMENDATIONS   February 1, 1827

ALEXANDER G. McRAE, Clarksburg (West Virginia), states that he has been informed that a (Robert I.) Curtis, editor of the *Wheeling Gazette*, has applied for the public printing and has wrongly informed the State Department that McRae stopped printing. Notes that he discontinued for only three weeks, "for the purpose of arranging some business and making improvements in the Office," and that he hopes his application for renewal of the printing contract will be approved. ALS. DNA, RG59, P. and D. of L. Cf. above, McRae to Clay, December 8, 1826, note.

S. WHITEHEAD, Norfolk, recommends "Mr. [Nathaniel] Wolf," a "late townsman," for an office in the Marine Corps. ALS. DLC-Gideon Wells Papers. Addressed to Clay and endorsed (AES) on cover: "Mr. Whitehead is a gentleman of the highest respectability, and his recommendation deserves great consideration. H. Clay." The correspondent may have been Swepson Whitehead, a plantation owner in Princess Anne County. Wolf, given name supplied by clerical endorsement, has not been further identified. He received no appointment.

Invitation to Mr. and Mrs. John Agg

Feb: 2nd 1827

Mr. and Mrs. Clay request the favor of Mr & Mrs Agg's Company on Wednesday evening the 7 inst and on every alternate Wednesday evening during the Session of Congress

N, partially printed. DLC-Riggs Family Papers. Agg, English by birth, was a writer and editor of the Washington *Daily National Journal*. He later published the first volume of a projected *History of Congress . . .* (Philadelphia, 1834).

MISCELLANEOUS LETTERS   February 2, 1827

From JON[ATHAN] H. LAURENCE, president of the Pacific Insurance Company. Relates that the case of the *Spermo* was "decided by the court at Pernambuco against the Captors in April 1826," that the issue has been suspended by an appeal to the Superior Court at Rio de Janeiro, that the agent, John Bayard Kirkpatrick, has pressed unsuccessfully for a final decision, and that (Condy) Raguet has asserted that he can do nothing "unless by some express Order of Government." Notes that the suit has been defended in the name of the original owners but that the Pacific Insurance Company, having "paid the loss on abandonment, are principally interested in the result. . . ." Requests that measures be taken "to afford relief." LS. DNA, RG76, Misc. Claims, Brazil. Laurence, of New York, has not been further identified.

On February 5, Daniel Brent informed Laurence that Raguet had been instructed to "pursue such measures as might be best calculated to obtain . . . the indemnity" and that these instructions had been "repeated and enforced by subsequent and recent letters. . . ." Copy, in DNA, RG59, Dom. Letters, vol. 21, pp. 471–72 (M40, R19).

From THO[MAS] B. REED, Washington. States that shortly before leaving home two letters were entrusted to him, the first, "the production of an old slave . . . belonging to a Mr. Foster," is directed to the slave's "relations in the Kingdom of Morocco"; the other, "from Col. Marschalk, a respectable citizen of Natchez," explains the circumstances of the case. Comments that he has long known "this unfortunate old Slave," that he claims to be related to the Royal Family of Morocco, that he was taken captive in war as a youth, and that he "is still anxious to revisit the land of his nativity." Requests Clay's "humane offices" to transmit his letter to the American consul (John Mullowny) at Tangier. ALS. DNA, RG59, Misc. Letters (M179, R65). See below, Mullowny to Clay, March 24, 1827. The slave, Prince, or Abduhl Rahahman, was the property of Thomas Foster, a planter near Natchez, Mississippi. For an account of the case, see Charles S. Sydnor, "The Biography of a Slave," *The South Atlantic Quarterly*, XXXVI (1937), 59–73.

Andrew Marschalk, as an officer in the United States Army, had been sent to Natchez in 1797, taking with him a small printing press, on which he had printed in 1799 the first laws of the Mississippi Territory. Leaving the Army in 1802, he had begun publication of a newspaper in Natchez. After the village of Washington had been made the territorial capital, he had begun there, in 1813, the *Washington Republican*, which, removed to Natchez, had evolved into the *Natchez Gazette* and, later, the *Mississippi State Gazette*. In September, 1825, he had been appointed surveyor and inspector of revenue for the port of Natchez; he was subsequently reappointed and retained the office until his removal in 1834.

APPLICATIONS, RECOMMENDATIONS   February 2, 1827

J[OHN] H[ENRY] EATON and HU[GH] L[AWSON] WHITE, Washington, note that (John) Williams has returned from Guatemala and recommend William Carroll as his replacement. ALS by Eaton, signed also by White. DNA, RG59, A. and R. (M531, R2). Cf. above, Clay to McLane, January 15, 1827.

INSTRUCTIONS AND DISPATCHES   February 3, 1827

To BERNARD HENRY, Gibraltar, recommends to his attention Representative (Edward F.) Tattnall, of Georgia, who plans to go to southern Europe for his health. Copy. DNA, RG59, Cons. Instr., vol. 2, p. 412 (M78, R2). Henry, a Pennsylvanian, was consul at Gibraltar from 1816 to 1832.

Similar letters were also addressed on this date to William Shaler at Algiers, Joshua Dodge at Marseilles, and Thomas Appleton at Leghorn.

From ANDREW ARMSTRONG, Port au Prince. Transmits copies of further correspondence relating to the incident discussed (above) in his dispatch of January 16, reports that the Secretary General (Joseph-Balthasar Inginac) has replied by a "most unsatisfactory private" note in respect to the episode and, when questioned concerning the protection to be accorded Armstrong in the discharge of his duties, again by a mere private note. Inquires whether he "should remain in this place." Notes rumors that a commercial treaty was negotiated by the British consul general, (Charles) MacKenzie, and the Haitian Government but "so little satisfactory to the Consul General, that he had refused it his signature." ALS. DNA, RG59, Cons. Disp., Cap Haitien, vol. 6 (M9, R6). Received February 25. On Armstrong's recall, see below, Clay to Armstrong, March 1, 1827.

Inginac, a general, had earned distinction for his service as Secretary General under both Alexandre Pétion and Jean Pierre Boyer. He was driven from the country with the fall of the latter in 1843, returned the following year, but lived thereafter in retirement until his death in 1847.

From THOMAS L. L. BRENT, Lisbon. Reports threatened attack by the refugee army, under the Marquis de Chaves, upon the city of Oporto; notes that British troops are moving into the interior. ALS. DNA, RG59, Dip. Disp., Portugal, vol. 7 (M43, R6).

From WILLIAM PHILLIPS, Guatemala (City). Notes that, since (John) Williams left on December 2, the other four states of the (Central American) Federation have contemplated measures "to counteract the plans of the Executive" (cf. above, Gonzalez to Clay, January 7, 1827); encloses related documents (not found); and observes that "as procrastination is the order of the day, perhaps something decisive may take place in the course of this or next year." Reports that he has received his exequatur as consul *pro tempore* for the Federation and that Robert Parker's exequatur for the San Salvador district is being forwarded to him. Encloses a copy of his protest to the Federation's State Department (regarding the John Marshall incident—see above, Williams to Clay, November 24, 1826), notes that he has not received an answer, and cites evasions by government authorities in giving satisfaction for the insult. Says that he plans to leave Central America as soon as he adjusts his personal affairs, which were nearly ruined by his "unfortunate Agency in the Nicaragua *Canal Bubble*," not so much because of his loss of the money and time invested as from the withdrawal of confidence and support by his friends "& the Merchants in Philadelphia . . . [his] Voyage here being to obtain information and for commercial purposes—" Adds that an agent "named Yrisarri has arrived here from a Mr. Curtis Bolton of New York, with a new Canal *Project*." Comments that because of the "complete political Chaos" of the country "nothing can be done. . . ." Observes that the British "have made no movements, and the Government will give [Aaron H.] Palmer time to do his utmost towards complying with the Contract." Explains that he has written thus extensively on the subject, "Knowing the interest our Government takes that this splendid enterprize should not fall into the hands of any European Powers. . . ." ALS. DNA, RG59, Cons. Disp., Guatemala, vol. 1 (M-T337, R1). Received May 23. Enclosed copy of Phillips' protest, dated January 19, 1827, and addressed to (Juan Francisco de) Sosa, requests that government officials responsible for the Marshall incident "be suspended from their functions until a full investigation takes place." Accompanying Phillips' letter is a copy of a certified deposition taken from Mariano Montenegro, a resident of Guatemala City, who recounts his version of the altercation between Marshall and the customs officials at Gualan.

Aaron H. Palmer of New York was general agent for the Central American and United States Atlantic and Pacific Canal Company. On June 14, 1826, Palmer had obtained a charter from the Federation Government to construct a canal across Central America through Nicaragua. Hoping to raise a capital of $5,000,000, he associated himself with DeWitt Clinton and others of New York and went to London to obtain additional backing. Lack of investment interest and chaotic political conditions in Central America led to the project's failure. See *House Repts.*, 30 Cong., 2 Sess., no. 145, pp. 360–403; cf. below, Phillips to Clay, March 2, August 8, 1827.

António José de Yrisarri (Irisarri), born in Santiago, Chile, had been educated in Europe but returned in 1806, to his native land, where he participated in the revolution against Spanish rule. He had served as Secretary of State in 1818 and as envoy to the United States (1818–1819) and to Britain (1819). He had founded newspapers in Chile (1813) and London (1820) and subsequently continued his publishing career with journals at Guatemala City (1828), Guayaquil (1839–1843), Quito (1844), Bogotá (1846–1847), and Curaçao and New York (1849–1850). From 1855 until his death in 1868, he was Minister to the United States from Guatemala; he performed similar duties in this country for El Salvador from 1855 to 1863 and for Nicaragua from 1856 to 1859.

Bolton was affiliated with the Havre "Old Line" packet service, founded in 1822, which he himself headed after 1830. He had visited Nicaragua in 1825 with backing from other New York merchants interested in canal development but found that the Palmer contract had been previously awarded. *House Repts.*, 25 Cong., 3 Sess., no. 322, pp. 159–60. No venture matured through the agency of Yrisarri. Phillips' "Agency" in these projects has not been identified; it may have been related only to mercantile concerns.

From WILLIAM TUDOR, Lima, no. 58, "*Confidential.*" Recounts events of "the 26th ulto.," when "a majority of the [Colombian] officers, the senior of whom, & present commander of the troops, is Lt Colonel [José] Bustamante, . . . arrested their two Generals [Juan Jacinto] Lara & [Arthur] Sands [*sic*], & five Colonels. . . ." Notes that Bustamante recalled General (Andrés) Santa Cruz from his vacation to "take care of the public security" and assured him "that the steps they had taken concerned only themselves & their country: that they had been obliged by their officers to swear to the Bolivian Constitution which they abjured; & that they had been compelled by their duty to their country, & fidelity to its constitution to arrest their cheifs [*sic*], who would be immediately sent home, & that they should wait the orders of their government: that they would not be made the instruments of enslaving Peru, that they declined absolutely all interference with its government, but they would lend their aid at all times, to preserve the public tranquility." Observes that Santa Cruz and his Ministers were "confounded" and "excessively alarmed" by this action. Relates that on the following day the Cabildo (of Lima), which had been suppressed by the Constitution of Bolívar, reassembled and resolved to invite Santa Cruz to become "President *interino* . . . till a constituent Congress with full powers could be called," to abolish the (newly instituted) constitution, to re-establish the former one, to proclaim a call for a congress, and to appoint new ministers replacing the present ones. Says that Santa Cruz "tacitly accepted these conditions" and appointed (Manuel Lorenzo de) Vidaurre as Minister (of Foreign Affairs) in place of (José María de) Pando and (Manuel) Salazar (y Baquijano) in place of (Tomás de) Heres as Minister of War.

Summarizes contents of Lara's correspondence from Bolívar and (Antonio

José) Sucre and conjectures that the "very considerable light on the designs of the former" thus revealed will greatly strengthen (Francisco de Paula) Santander in preserving the Colombian Constitution. Notes that this correspondence also reveals Sucre's position (in Bolivia) to be "nearly desperate." States that the (Colombian) officers (in Lima) hope to capture other documents, reported to be en route from Bogotá, that will reveal the discrepancies between Bolívar's public and private orders and "umask [sic]" him "beyond the possibility of further deception. . . ." Sketches a general outline of Bolívar's imperial plan, as revealed "partly from him, & partly from his Secretary, Gen. [José Gabriel] Pérez [Pagola] to one of the Ministers in Panama. . . . North America to be occupied by two great republics, the U. S. & Mexico: & South America by two great empires, for which Guatimala [sic], Colombia, the two Peru's, Chile & Buenos Ayres would constitute one for Bolivar, the other formed by the Brazils." Concludes that the recent events "will·shatter this extravagant project to pieces."

Reports that a call has been issued "for assembling a Congress the first of May" and that he has forwarded to Dr. (Francisco Javier) Luna Pizarro letters inviting his return. States that (José de) Lamar (y Cortázar) will probably be elected President and that he with Luna Pizarro would provide leadership under which "Peru may hope for prosperity & happiness, & the adjoining States for honest neighbours." Expresses his "hope that Bolivar's schemes are now effectually destroyed," an outcome which relieves South America "from a military despotism" but also the United States "from a future dangerous enemy." Cites Bolívar's "proscription of slavery" as "his cheif reliance to redeem himself with the liberal party in the world. . . ."

Mentions that he called upon Santa Cruz "today" and, "Wishing to have him act fully with the patriot party," assured him that, under his obligation "to maintain the public tranquillity," he was compelled to follow "the wishes of the nation," as evidenced now that force was removed. Adds that Santa Cruz, like Bolívar himself and others of his adherents, protested that Bolívar wanted only to be rid of command and to retire to his estate. Postscript, dated February 6, reports that "a similar revolution" has taken place in Upper Peru (Bolivia). ALS. DNA, RG59, Cons. Disp., Lima, vol. 1 (M154, R1). Published in Manning (arr.), *Diplomatic Correspondence, Latin-American Nations*, III, 1815–23. Received June 8.

Bustamante, a native of Socorro, Colombia, headed the Third Colombian Division, stationed at Lima. Sandes (Sanders), born in Valencia, Venezuela, of British parentage, had been active in the movement for Latin-American independence since 1810. He had fought with distinction in most of Bolívar's campaigns; and, after escaping to Colombia from the revolt here discussed, he ended his career as one of the leaders who brought about the overthrow of the Peruvians under José de Lamar, at the battle of Tarqui, in Upper Peru, in February, 1829.

Salazar y Baquijano, who had held rank as a militia colonel during the revolution, had been a member of the first Constituent Congress of Peru, a member of the junta and president of the Congress that sat in October-November, 1823, and prefect of Lima in 1825. He was Vice President of Peru from 1827 to 1829 and President of the Council of State in 1834. He held the last office for brief periods on three different occasions and was president of the Senate from 1845 to 1849.

Pérez Pagola, a Venezuelan active in the independent movement from its beginning, had been Bolívar's secretary until the summer of 1825, when he had been released so that he might assume a more active governmental role in Peru without appearing merely as Bolívar's agent. Bolívar to Santander, June 28, 1825, in Lecuna and Bierck (eds.), *Selected Writings*, II, 511. He was Supreme Commander of Bolívar's forces in the South during the spring of 1827, when he was taken prisoner at Guayaquil by the forces opposing the Liberator. He shortly afterward escaped to Quito but was repudiated by the leaders there. He died before the end of the year.

Luna Pizarro, born in Arequipa, had received a doctorate in theology at the University of Cuzco and had been ordained in 1806. Having gone to Spain in 1809, he had supported the cause of Spanish liberalism at Cádiz and, upon his return to Peru, continued such efforts as a delegate to the metropolitan assembly of Lima in 1812 and deputy to the first Constituent Congress of Peru. He was appointed dean of Arequipa Cathedral in 1831, titular bishop of Alalia in 1838, and archbishop of Lima in 1845.

MISCELLANEOUS LETTERS   February 3, 1827

From PETER LITTLE, House of Representatives. States that (Charles F.) Mayer has asked him to return "the copy of the letter to Mr. Adams in the case of [John] Hollins," which was enclosed in his letter (above, Little and Barney to Clay, January 30, 1827) requesting that (Richard) Reynal Keene be named bearer of dispatches. Says that he wishes Clay to return the other enclosure as well. ALS. DNA, RG59, Misc. Letters (M179, R65).

On February 5 Brent returned the correspondence as requested. Copy, in DNA, RG59, Dom. Letters, vol. 21, p. 471 (M40, R19).

From WILLIAM NEILSON AND OTHERS. Enclose copies of two letters from George Slacum, consul at Buenos Aires, to owners of the brig *Merope*, lost with cargo off Patagonia. Note that some of her cargo appears to have been saved and that the State Department has documents related to its salvage. Request, as underwriters and representatives of the owners of the vessel, copies of these papers and solicit the assistance of the Executive, if necessary, in pursuing their claim with the Buenos Aires Government. ALS by J. R. Hurd, president of the Neptune Insurance Company, signed also by Neilson, president of the American Insurance Company of New York, Richard M. Lawrence, president of the Union Insurance Company; Jon[athan] H. Laurence, president of the Pacific Insurance Company; Abraham Ogden, president of the Ocean Insurance Company; and Walter R. Jones, "Assistant of the Atlantic Inse. Coy. of New York." DNA, RG59, Misc. Letters (M179, R65). Copies of Letters from Slacum to G. G. and (S.) Howland, New York, enclosed, indicate that property "to the amount of 30-40,000$ had been saved from the wreck. . . ." In the first, dated October 27, 1826, Slacum explained that the Buenos Aires Government had cooperated cordially in assisting his agent, John H. Duffy, to recover the property but that the latter had been found concealing part of the goods, principally wax. Slacum asserted further, that Duffy had been "so counseled and protected by . . . charge d'affaires J M Forbes" that as consul he had had recourse to legal action "in defence of the interests of the absent owners. . . ." He had recovered some $17,278 by auction of the property but expected to obtain an additional sum as the result of court proceedings. The second letter, dated from Annapolis January 29, reported that there had been delay of the court proceedings but expressed confidence that the issue would be resolved shortly. Slacum again alluded to his contentious relationship with Forbes.

Neilson had been a junior partner in the New York shipping firm of William Neilson and Company since 1797 and president of the American Insurance Company since its founding in 1815. He remained head of the latter company until it was terminated, with expiration of its charter, in 1842.

Duffy, an Irishman who had served on a Buenos Aires privateer during the latter years of the Argentine revolt from Spain, was for some four years private secretary to John M. Forbes. For testimony that his activities had ranged beyond privateering to outright piracy, see William R. Manning (arr.), *Diplomatic Correspondence of the United States, Inter-American Affairs, 1831–1860* (12 vols., Washington, 1932–1939), I, 167–75.

Hurd, formerly of Boston, and Ogden, uncle and father-in-law of David B. Ogden, both combined mercantile and insurance operations. Abraham Ogden was also distinquished as a lawyer.

Jones was "easily the outstanding figure in New York marine insurance circles in his day." He later, in 1849, organized the Life Saving Benevolent Association and established stations for this service along the shores of Long Island. Albion, *New York Port*, 240, 273.

Lawrence has not been further identified.

From P[ELEG] SPRAGUE, House of Representatives. States that Ashur Ware, United States District Judge for Maine, has not received the last volume of (Wheaton's) *Reports* (above, II, 915n) and would like to know whether one has been mailed. Requests that Clay answer Ware's inquiry. ALS. DNA, RG59, Misc. Letters (M179, R65).

Ware, born in Sherborn, Massachusetts, and educated at Harvard, had studied law and in 1817 settled at Portland, Maine. There he edited the *Eastern Argus* and was active in Democratic party affairs. He became secretary of state for Maine in 1820 and in 1822 was named Federal district judge, a position he retained for 49 years.

On February 5 (misdated as 1826), Daniel Brent informed Sprague that the State Department had not received volume 11 of Wheaton's *Reports* and noted that Congress had made no provision for paying the reporter. Copy, in DNA, RG59, Dom. Letters, vol. 21, p. 470 (M40, R19).

APPLICATIONS, RECOMMENDATIONS   February 3, 1827

DANIEL P. COOK notes receipt of a letter from (William) Browne (dated February 3) in reply to his letter to Clay of January 31 and states that Browne's letter reflects misunderstanding. Explains that the *Edwardsville Spectator* (Illinois) edited by (Thomas) Lippincott and (Jeremiah) Abbott, has been transferred to (Hooper) Warren and the latter has moved the journal to Sangamon County and renamed it the (Springfield, Illinois) *Sangamo Spectator*. Notes that the firm of Lippincott and Abbott no longer exists and that he has been urging appointment of Warren (to publish the laws). ALS. DNA, RG59, P. and D. of L.

DUTEE J. PEARCE, Washington, encloses a memorial from "some of the most respectable citizens in R. Island, all friends to the present administration." Comments: "I approve the policy of appointing those who are friendly to *us*, and the act of which you are now accused [cf. below, McGiffin to Clay, February 19, 1827, note] is one of the best acts of your life, if in ex extenso [*sic*] true, as has been represented, and I wish this policy had been more generally adopted." ALS. DNA, RG59, P. and D. and L. Enclosure from James Maxwell and 29 others, addressed to Clay and dated January 18, 1827, requests that the *Northern Star and Warren and Bristol Gazette* be commissioned to print the public laws.

The *Northern Star* received no commission during the Adams administration. Maxwell had served as justice of the peace of the court of common pleas and general sessions of Bristol County from 1802 to 1810.

WILLIAM B. QUARRIER, Norfolk, acknowledges receipt of Clay's letter of November 11 (not found; apparently not the letter of November 14, cited above, Quarrier to Clay, November 6, 1826, note), in which he has spoken in a "flattering manner" concerning Quarrier's father, and comments: "Volumes could not be more gratifying." Notes that Clay also offered to consider the younger man's wishes "if any specific object should present itself" and asks that he be appointed a bearer of dispatches should Congress authorize the reported proposal to build two schooners to facilitate intercourse with the Pacific. ALS. DNA, RG59, A. and R. (M531, R6).

Alexander Quarrier, father of William B., had been born in Scotland, had come to America in 1774, and had served as an officer in the Revolution. He had subsequently been a coach-maker at Philadelphia and in 1786 had moved his shop to Richmond. At the turn of the century his establishment had been used for storing machinery for the manufacture of arms, and during the next decade he had been inspector of the arsenal and captain of the capitol guard in Richmond. He died later in the year 1827.

Young Quarrier received no appointment under the Adams administration. For reference to the abortive proposal for improving communication with the Pacific, see Washington *Daily National Journal*, January 25, 1827.

J. I. STULL, Georgetown (District of Columbia), transmits a letter relating to the postmastership at Hagerstown. ALS. DNA, RG59, A. and R. (M531, R7). In the enclosure, from W(illiam) Ross to Otho Stull, dated January 16, 1827, Ross noted that he had been approached to support the latter's candidacy for the postmastership, expressed regret that despite a connection by marriage with the President, he did not know him well enough to warrant correspondence, but remarked that he was "certainly the warm friend of the Administration" and that Stull's opponent for the appointment, (Thomas) Kennedy, was at best "an equivocal friend, for at the last Congressional Hustings in Frederick, when called upon to declare whether he were the friend or not of the Administration, he declined to answer. . . ."

William Ross of Frederick, Maryland, was a prominent lawyer and long-time president of the Frederick branch of the Farmer's Bank of Maryland; his wife, Kitty Johnson Ross, and Louisa Johnson Adams were first cousins. John Thomas Scharf, *History of Western Maryland* . . . (2 vols., Philadelphia, 1882), I, 453–54, 474, 539.

Otho Stull of Hagerstown, Maryland, was proprietor of the Washington Hotel, one of the founders (in 1813) and part-owner of the newspaper, *Torch-Light*, and postmaster from July 8, 1827, to November 17, 1829, *Ibid.*, II, 1044, 1066, 1143.

Kennedy, a justice of the peace from 1806 to 1812 and member of the Maryland House of Delegates from 1817 to 1820, 1822, 1825, and 1832, had served as Hagerstown postmaster since October 23, 1826.

From Francis T. Brooke

My Dear Sir   Richmd Feb 4h 1827

The inclosed letter[1] was only handed to me a few days ago though of older date, I concur with the Subscribers to it, in the high Character which I am Sure Colol McCarty merits—and if he can be gratified know that it will be very agreeable to a wide circle of relations and friends— You will See by the papers that the resolutions moved by Mr Giles have been referred,[2]   the report of the committee will disclose his plan— his friends are fearful it will be too Strong for public feeling and if rejected will do more harm than good—Your friend   FRANCIS BROOKE

ALS. DNA, RG59, A. and R. (M531, R5). Addressed to Clay.
[1] William B[yrd] Page and Edward Colston to [Brooke], January 18, 1827. The writers speak of William Mason McCarty's move to Florida, of efforts to obtain for him the appointment as secretary of that Territory (cf. above, Mercer to Clay, January 23, 1827), and of the wish that Brooke would write to Clay in McCarty's behalf. They note that McCarty is a grandson of George Mason, member of the Federal Constitutional Convention and chief proponent of the movement for a Bill of Rights which culminated in the first ten Amendments. Page, of Winchester, Frederick County, Virginia, had been a member of the House of Delegates from 1820 to 1823 and of the State Senate from 1823 to 1826.   [2] See above, Brooke to Clay, January 31, 1827.

APPLICATIONS, RECOMMENDATIONS   February 4, 1827

FREDERICK DORSEY, Hagerstown, recommends William Fitzhugh, his brother-in-law, also of Hagerstown, for appointment as postmaster of that town; notes that (Thomas) Kennedy is reportedly being favored only because Fitzhugh is believed to be wealthy; and explains that Fitzhugh bears heavy financial commitments on behalf of relatives. ALS. DNA, RG59, A. and R. (M531, R3). On the appointment, cf. above, Stull to Clay, February 3, 1827, note.

JAMES S[TRUDWICK] SMITH, Hillsborough, North Carolina, solicits appointment as Commissioner for settling claims under Article V of the Treaty of Ghent. States that he believes he could "at any time" again represent his district (in Congress) but that he "cannot make the sacrifice." Observes that the desired appointment would permit him "to go into the legislature next winter...," since Judge (Henry) Seawell's combining of the roles as Arbitrator and State Senator indicates that the duties are not incompatible. Concludes: "This Situation would enable me to aid my friends which heretofore I haved [sic] had the inclination to do But which I could not effect to much purpose from my limited sphere of action—" ALS. DNA, RG59, A. and R. (M531, R7).
    Smith probably sought appointment as Commissioner under Article I, not V, of the Treaty of Ghent. This supposition would better accord with the allusion to Seawell and with the fact that discussion of the northeastern boundary question at this time was stalemated. See above, Gallatin to Clay, June 29, 1826.
    A graduate of Jefferson Medical College, Philadelphia, Smith had resumed medical practice at Hillsborough after leaving Congress in March, 1821. He had been elected to the State legislature that year and the next. He did not receive the desired Federal appointment and did not return to the legislature.

INSTRUCTIONS AND DISPATCHES   February 5, 1827

From ALBERT GALLATIN, London, no. 55. Reports that (William) Huskisson's illness prevents immediate resumption of negotiations. Transmits a letter, which he received unsealed, from Thomas L. L. Brent and a copy of a letter that he (Gallatin) has written to James Brown. Comments that accounts to the British Government from Lisbon and Madrid indicate peace will be maintained but no word has been received on disarming of the Portuguese insurgents. Advocates a "positive agreement with Great Britain which should secure the United States against the danger of her attempting under any circumstances to occupy Cuba" (cf. above, Gallatin to Clay, December 30, 1826). ALS. DNA, RG59, Dip. Disp., Great Britain, vol. 33 (M30, R29). Copy, in NHi-Gallatin Papers, Letterbook vol. 14, pp. 72–73 (MR20); extracts published in Manning (arr.), *Diplomatic Correspondence ... Canadian Relations*, II, 577, 578; *ibid.*, *Latin-American Relations*, 1587–89. Received March 19.

Gallatin's letter to Brown, dated February 2, concerned his desire for clarification of the intentions of the British and French with respect to Cuba, his ignorance of what had transpired in relation to (George) Canning's proposal for a tri-partite agreement on the subject, "which Mr. Clay appears to have declined" (see above, King to Clay, August 9, 11, 24, 1825; Clay to King, October 17, 26, 1825), and a suggestion that, by reference to the danger of British action against Cuba in the event of war, Brown might induce France to press more earnestly "in her efforts to induce Spain to cease giving just causes of offence and to pursue a course calculated to preserve peace." Gallatin also informed Brown of the conclusion of the Convention on slave indemnities (see above, Gallatin to Clay, November 13, 1826) but concluded: "In other respects our negotiations will not produce any important results."

MISCELLANEOUS LETTERS   February 5, 1827

To ROBERT CRITTENDEN, Secretary, Arkansas Territory, Little Rock. Notifies him of his (re)appointment, forwards his commission, and requests a receipt. Copy. DNA, RG59, Dom. Letters, vol. 21, pp. 469–70 (M40, R19). See above, Conway to Clay, December 13, 1826.

To WILLIAM WOODBRIDGE, Detroit. Forwards his commission as secretary for the Michigan Territory. LS. MiD-B. Copy, in DNA, RG59, Dom. Letters, vol. 21, p. 469 (M40, R19); published in Carter (ed.), *Territorial Papers*, XI, 1052. The Senate had confirmed Woodbridge's appointment on January 12, 1827. On March 2, 1827, Woodbridge wrote Clay acknowledging receipt of the commission. ALS, in DNA, RG59, Acceptances and Orders for Comns. (M-T645, R2).

From HENRY BANKS, Frankfort (Kentucky). Encloses a memorial defending his brother John's (army supply) services during the Revolutionary War. LS, body of letter printed. DNA, RG59, Misc. Letters (M179, R65). Addressed to the Secretary of State. No memorial is filed with this document, but one addressed to Congress and dated March 25, 1826, on behalf of John Banks, was included in Henry Banks, *The Vindication of John Banks of Virginia . . .* (Frankfort, Ky., 1826), 5–8.

For a detailed account of Henry and John Banks' contracting difficulties, see Alexander Hamilton's report on the Nathanael Greene claim, December 26, 1791, in *American State Papers, Claims*, 33–49. Although Henry Banks repeatedly pressed claims against the United States for losses allegedly sustained in behalf of the Confederation Government, he and his heirs were unsuccessful in their efforts. See *Sen. Docs.*, 27 Cong., 2 Sess., no. 150.

John Banks, born in Stafford County, Virginia, and educated in Fredericksburg, had begun his business career in the latter town, later moved to Norfolk, and subsequently entered the tobacco trade at Richmond. Unsuccessful in his army contracting ventures, he had died in 1784.

From SAMUEL McKEAN, House of Representatives. Requests information, for a "friend," concerning the duty "on white pine boards at Lisbon." ALS. DNA, RG59, Misc. Letters (M179, R65).

On February 9, Daniel Brent replied that the State Department had no data by which to answer McKean's inquiry. Copy, in DNA, RG59, Dom. Letters, vol. 21, p. 484 (M40, R19).

APPLICATIONS, RECOMMENDATIONS   February 5, 1827

JOHN WILLIAMS, Knoxville, encloses a letter addressed to him by (Thomas) Washington and supports the latter's application (for the district attorneyship of West Tennessee). States that he will leave "in four or five days for Washington." Congratulates Clay on his "restoration to good health" and comments that its "importance . . . to this nation is plainly increasing—" ALS. DNA, RG59, A. and R. (M531, R8).

DIPLOMATIC NOTES   February 6, 1827

From JOAQUIM B[ARROZO] PEREIRA, Philadelphia. Requests answers to his communications of "the 17th ultimo" and "30th December last." ALS. DNA, RG59, Notes from Portuguese Legation, vol. 2 (M57, R2). Cf. below, Clay to Southard, this date; Southard to Clay, February 13, 1827.

INSTRUCTIONS AND DISPATCHES   February 6, 1827

From THOMAS L. L. BRENT, Lisbon, no. 38. Reports that, according to the official *Gazette*, Spain is moving to bring to courts-martial Spanish officers who did not comply with governmental orders in reference to the Portuguese rebels, to disarm the rebels in Spain, and to capture and deport the Marquis of Chaves and the Count of Canelos. Notes that the Spanish Ambassador (Count de Casa Flórez) received this information "on the 26th. instant [*sic*]," that he has been given a leave of absence, but that he will probably not depart for a month. Comments that Lord Beresford has returned to England and recounts details of recent military events, including the reinforcement of Oporto by Government forces. LS. DNA, RG59, Dip. Disp., Portugal, vol. 7 (M43, R6). Received April 3. Encloses a translation of an extract from the dispatch dated (January) 22 by the Portuguese Chargé in Madrid (Luiz António de Abreu e Lima) to the Minister of Foreign Affairs (Francisco de Almeida), reiterating the Spanish orders cited above. Cf. above, Brent to Clay, January 27, 29, 1827.

From ALBERT GALLATIN, London, no. 56. States that in the afternoon he and (Henry U.) Addington will exchange ratifications of the Convention of November 13, 1826. Explains that (George) Canning is "indisposed" and unable to attend the ceremony. Adds in an initialed postscript of same date that the exchange did take place, and that (Edward) Wyer will embark by packet from Liverpool for Philadelphia with this dispatch and the exchange documents. ALS. DNA, RG59, Dip. Disp., Great Britain, vol. 33 (M30, R29). Received March 19.
    Canning had caught cold in early January. During the first two weeks of February he was "quite incapacitated," and for nearly two months, until February 27, he remained at Brighton, recuperating. He never fully recovered. Temperley, *The Foreign Policy of Canning*, 417–18, 443–44. On Canning's death, cf. below, Gallatin to Clay, August 9, 1827.

MISCELLANEOUS LETTERS   February 6, 1827

To JOHN CONARD, Philadelphia. Informs him that his commission as United States marshal for the Eastern Pennsylvania District has been sent to (Richard) Peters, (United States) district judge, and that his commission may be obtained from Peters after completing the usual requirements; requests acknowledgment of receipt of the commission. Copy. DNA, RG59, Dom. Letters, vol. 21, p. 474 (M40, R19). A copy of Clay's letter of transmittal, of same date, to Peters, *ibid.* Conard's acknowledgment of compliance was sent to Clay on February 20, 1827. ALS, in DNA, RG59, Acceptances and Orders for Comns. (M-T645, R2).

To OLIVER WAYNE OGDEN, New Germantown, New Jersey. States that his commission as United States marshal for New Jersey has been sent to (United States) District Judge (William) Rossell and that the commission will be delivered by Rossell after the usual requirements have been fulfilled; requests acknowledgment of its receipt. Copy. DNA, RG59, Dom. Letters, vol. 21, p. 473 (M40, R19). A copy of Daniel Brent's letter of transmittal, of same date, to Rossell, *ibid.*, 472. Ogden served as marshal in New Jersey from 1807 to 1830, when he was removed by Andrew Jackson. On February 28, 1827, Ogden acknowledges receipt of Clay's letter and assures the Secretary that he will deliver the necessary bond and take the required oaths of office. ALS, in DNA, RG59, Misc. Letters (M179, R65).

To SAMUEL SOUTHARD. Transmits a copy of a letter from the Portuguese Chargé (Joaquim Barrozo Pereira) concerning the suit of (Richard W.) Habersham against "certain Africans, the Cargo of the General Ramirez," together with that letter's enclosures; requests information to enable him to answer Pereira. LS. DNA, RG45, Misc. Letters Recd. Pereira to Clay, December 30, 1826 (cf. above), and copies of two enclosures included. Cf. above, Pereira to Clay, January 17 and February 6, 1827; and below, Southard to Clay, February 13, 1827.

APPLICATIONS, RECOMMENDATIONS   February 6, 1827

THOMAS COLQUHOUN, Petersburg (Virginia), refers to his "acquaintance" with Clay in London, renewed "in Richmond about three years ago"; solicits Clay's interest in behalf of Robert Emmet Robinson, who is seeking admission to the United States Military Academy; and notes that the young man is "the Grand Son of a Revolutionary Officer," Captain William Murray of Amelia, with whose family Clay is "no doubt" familiar. Extends Mrs. Colquhoun's regards to Clay. ALS. DNA, RG94, U. S. Military Academy Application Papers, 1827/111.
  Colquhoun, born in Scotland, had come to the United States before 1795 and established a mercantile business in Richmond. Mrs. Colquhoun has not been further identified. Young Robinson was admitted to the Military Academy in July, 1827, but did not graduate; he has not been further identified.

From John Sergeant

Dear Sir,   (Private)   Mexico, Feb. 7. 1827.
  [Notes that plans for the (Tacubaya) Congress remain uncertain and that no word has been received concerning ratification of the (Panama) treaties.]
  We are without advices from the United States later than the 10th.

December, except a National Intelligencer of the 13th. and one of the 14th., which came to Mr. Poinsett. . . .[1]

The two papers mentioned, are full of interest, containing the correspondence with England,[2] and the Annual Treasury Report. The publication of the correspondence cannot fail to do good. We have the advantage in every point, in temper, in manners, and in the argument. Mr. Canning has done an ungracious thing, in a most ungracious way, and taken a false position for its support. The notion of a *boon* in trade, granted by England, without an equivalent; and granted, too, to her most powerful commercial rival, is quite ridiculous, as is the notion also of injury (in his sense of the term) inflicted by our regulation. But Mr. Canning could not resist the antithesis.

Mr. Rush seems to have put the Committee of Ways and Means of last session entirely in the wrong, and of course to have placed himself in the right.[3] He will be a gainer by the conflict.

If I rightly understand, the character of the Senate's Committees; there is cause of congratulation in the operation of the rule that has been adopted.[4] The elections appear to indicate a decided approbation in that body of the conduct of the Executive.[5] Very respectfully & truly. Yr. most obt. servt.   JOHN SERGEANT.

P.S. It occurs to me to say that you will probably have accounts in the U. States of movements in Mexico portending disturbances.[6] Genl. Barragan[7] went down to Vera Cruz in a great hurry, reinforced the garrison of the castle; and, it was said, laid in four months provisions. There was a talk at the same time of an embargo. Some additional troops were also brought in to this City— But there is perfect tranquility at present, and no appearance of danger of any sort.
The Honble Henry Clay.

ALS. DNA, RG43, Records re First Panama Congress (M662, R1).
[1] Washington *Daily National Intelligencer*; Joel R. Poinsett.   [2] Cf. above, Clay to Gallatin, November 11, 1826, note 26.   [3] Cf. below, Rush to Clay, May 10, 1827; *House Repts.*, 19 Cong., 1 Sess., no. 64.   [4] The Senate on December 8, 1826, had approved a resolution providing that "in the appointment of the standing committees, the Senate will proceed by severally appointing the chairman of each committee; and then, by one ballot, for the other members necessary to complete the same; and a majority of the whole number of votes given shall be necessary to the choice of a chairman." U. S. Sen., *Journal*, 19 Cong., 2 Sess., p. 27.   [5] Cf. above, Clay to Crittenden, December 12, 1826.   [6] Cf. above, Sergeant to Clay, January 26, 1827; Taylor to Clay, January 31, 1827.   [7] Miguel Barragán, born in the Province of San Luis Potosí, in 1789, had been named military commander of the State of Veracruz in 1824 and had forced the surrender of the Spanish at the Castle of San Juan de Ulloa (cf. above, Poinsett to Clay, November 23, 1825). He was deposed during the political disturbances of the next few years but was recalled in 1832 and served intermittently as acting President of Mexico until his death in 1835.

INSTRUCTIONS AND DISPATCHES   February 7, 1827

From S[AMUEL] D. HEAP, Tunis. States that his letter of (January) 15 (not found) explained his late arrival in Tunis, on December 27. Notes that his consular present was well received by the Bey (Hassein), that there are yet a number of "expectants," to whom he will give small articles as will "most conduce to the interest of the Consulate," that he has used part of his second year's contingency allowance on such presents, but that he believes he has stayed within the law of 1810 (2 *U. S. Stat.*, 609) on the matter. Explains that the Bey was "highly incensed" against his predecessor (Charles D. Coxe), because the latter had presented "articles which were not only of little or no value, but had not even the merit of being new. . . ." Transmits "a statement of the Naval force of this Regency, and its present disposition." ALS. DNA, RG59, Cons. Disp., Tunis, vol. 5 (M-T303, R5). Received July 7.

From J[OEL] R. POINSETT, Mexico, no. 71. Transmits an abstract of "the Report of the Secretary of the Treasury [José Ignacio Esteva] of this Republic, presented to Congress on the first of January of this year." LS. DNA, RG59, Dip. Disp., Mexico, vol. 2 (M97, R3). Received March 22.

From J[OEL] R. POINSETT, Mexico, no. 72. Transmits a translation of a note from the Mexican Secretary of State (Juan José Espinosa de los Monteros) "complaining of an aggression committed by some persons, residing within the territory of the United States, upon the civil authorities of the Mexican town of Nacogdoches, . . . together with a copy of . . . [his] reply. . . ." LS. *Ibid.* Received March 22. Espinosa's note was dated February 2, 1827, and Poinsett's answer, February 4, 1827. Poinsett promised to forward the complaint to his Government and gave assurance that all legal measures would be taken to punish "the aggressors in this case" and prevent "a recurrence of similar outrages. . . ."

From CONDY RAGUET, Rio de Janeiro, no. 24. States that he now believes "affairs with this government are in a train of adjustment," that he will soon "be enabled to advise . . . of the restoration of all the captured vessels belonging to citizens of The United States, with adequate damages for their detention," and that the change of ministry last month will produce a new and more favorable policy toward the United States. Reviews correspondence regarding Brazilian violations of neutral rights. Encloses a copy of his note, dated January 17, to the Minister of Foreign Affairs (Viscount Inhambupé), claiming restoration of the American brig *Matilda* and the American-owned cargo of the Swedish brig *Anders* (see above, Raguet to Clay, December 22, 1826); also sends copies of three notes, dated January 18, from the Marquis of Queluz, the new Foreign Minister, and summarizes their contents. Expresses surprise that in the midst of these negotiations the Superior Court rendered an adverse decision in the case of the American ship *Spermo* (see above, Raguet to Secretary of State, March 11, 1825) and encloses a copy of his protest of January 24, urging that the Emperor affirm the decision of the inferior court, "which had restored the Ship and condemned the captors in costs and damages. . . ." Sends also a copy of Queluz' answer of January 25, which asserts the power and duty of the Executive to review judicial decisions and expresses the opinion that the revision will end complaints. States that he has not had further communication with the government, but has heard that it "is now occupied in maturing arrangements for the termination . . . of our difficulties." Reports evidence that Admiral (Rodrigo) Pinto (Guedes) put his new orders into operation last December (cf. above, Raguet to Clay, December 5, 1826). Observes that the President's (Adams') remarks on the Brazilian blockade in his message of December 5 have created great excitement and that the diplomatic community has applauded United States' efforts to protect neutral rights. Comments that this language "went very far to convince this government, that the Executive Power has a right to interfere with the Judiciary. . . ." Adds: ". . . the previous symptoms of a disposition to conciliate, were the result of the little power, with which I felt myself armed by your letter of 22d October."

Notes that (José Leandro) Palacios arrived in the (United States) brig *Spark* on January 27 to take up his duties as Minister Plenipotentiary and Envoy Extraordinary for the Republic of Colombia and that he delivered to Raguet an introductory letter (not found) from Clay; comments: "Your letter to me in favour of Col. Palacio [*sic*], will be of service to him, as well in his relations with the Government, as with society." States that (Juan Maria) Gómez has also arrived as secretary of the Colombian Legation, (Joze Dominguez) Caceres (not further identified), as Chargé d'Affaires of Peru, and (Ignacio Federico) d'Olfers, as Chargé of Prussia, and suggests that the excellence of their reception by the Emperor (Peter I) stems from his disposition "to turn these republican missions to account by announcing them as evidence of his amicable relations with the American States, and proofs that the Buenos Ayreans will not be aided in 'the present unjust war, which they are waging with Brazil,' by neighbouring republics."

Relates recent news from Buenos Aires that there is no disposition "to give up the contest, nor has any been here yet openly manifested." Cites exchange rates and concludes that "financial concerns begin to pinch." Comments that reports of troubles in Portugal and of the arrival of British troops there do not "excite much interest here." ALS. DNA, RG59, Dip. Disp., Brazil, vol. 5 (M121, R7). Extracts published in *American State Papers: Foreign Relations*, VI, 1054–55. Received March 6, 1827.

Joao Severiano Maciel da Costa, Viscount and Marquis of Queluz, became Minister of Foreign Affairs on January 17, 1827, and served until November of that year.

The first of the enclosed copies of Queluz' correspondence is a cover letter to the second, which answers Raguet's note of January 3, on the doctrine of previous warning; the third acknowledges receipt of Raguet's note of January 17 and promises an early answer.

Ignacio Federico Olfers, born in Münster, had studied medicine in Berlin and had been sent to Rio de Janeiro first in 1818 as physician for the Prussian Legation. He remained in Brazil until 1830, when he returned to Münster.

MISCELLANEOUS LETTERS   February 7, 1827

To CHAPMAN COLEMAN, Lexington. Notifies him that his commission (for reappointment) as United States marshal for Kentucky has been sent to [John] Boyle, United States district judge and may be obtained from him upon completing the usual requirements; asks for notification of receipt of the commission. Copy. DNA, RG59, Dom. Letters, vol. 21, p. 475 (M40, R19). Clay's letter of transmittal to Boyle is located *ibid.*, p. 476. The commission, dated January 12, 1827, and signed by John Quincy Adams and Clay (DS) is filed in KyHi. On March 1, 1827, Coleman acknowledged receipt of the commission. ALS, in DNA, RG59, Acceptances and Orders for Comns. (M-T645, R2).

To [the SENATE AND HOUSE OF REPRESENTATIVES]. Presents, in accordance with "an act of the 25th [*sic*] of April, 1818" (*i.e.*, April 20, 1818– 3 *U. S. Stat.*, 445, 447), the annual report of the names and salary of the clerks employed in the Department of State. Notes that George E. Ironside received, additionally during the last year, $350 "out of the contingent fund of this Office for his services as Translator" and that $150 was also paid "for making an Alphabetical Index to the Laws of the last Session of Congress. . . ." Concludes: "It is likewise proper to state that the sum of six thousand seven hundred and twenty three dollars & forty six cents was paid to other persons, not belonging to the Office, out of the same contingent fund for assistance rendered this Department, including the Patent Office, in transcribing and translating numerous documents during the last year requiring despatch which could not seasonably have been accomplished without this aid, and for arranging and putting in order the various books and papers of the old confederation, which, from their frequent removals with this Office, had been thrown into a state of great confusion and disorder." Copy. DNA, RG59, Report Books, vol. 4, pp. 210–11. Published in *House Docs.*, 19 Cong., 2 Sess., no. 89, p. 3.

To HENRY R. STORRS, Chairman Committee on Naval Affairs, H(ouse of) Representatives. Replies to his letter of January 15 and states that no arrangement has been made on the claim of William C. Parke; returns Parke's petition and encloses a copy of the recent Danish Convention (see above, Convention, April 26, 1826) with relevant correspondence which declares that the omission of an indemnities provision in the Convention is not to be considered a relinquishment of claims against Denmark (see above, Clay to Pedersen, April 25, 1826). Copy. DNA, RG59, Report Books, vol. 4, p. 212.

From TENCH RINGGOLD, "Marshals off D Ca." Transmits a letter "from Major [Joseph H.] Hook of the United States Army complaining of the servants of some of the foreign ministers, in their conduct towards the orderlies, who by his kindness have been for the last six years detailed from his command to assist . . . in preserving order at the Presidents House on all public occasions." Observes that he believes the statement of Sergeant Rainey (not further identified) and that he himself was subjected to insolent language "on Wednesday last" by the coachman (not identified) of (Pedro) Gonzales, Baron Stackelberg, and (George) Jackson. Stresses that, although the "duty out of doors on all these public assemblages at the Presidential Mansion is arduous and disagreeable," it will "always be discharged with pleasure" but warns that it will require "resort to force" unless measures which Clay may take shall prove effective. ALS. DNA, RG59, Misc. Letters (M179, R65).

Enclosures include a letter from Hook to Ringgold, February 3, 1827, transmitting one from Rainey to Hook, February 1, 1827. *Ibid.*, filed as February 30, 1827. Hook requested that some means be adopted to avoid incidents such as the one described by Rainey, who noted that on the previous evening the coachman (not identified) of the Colombian Minister (José María Salazar), when asked to move off for another carriage, had threatened bodily injury to any of the orderlies he might subsequently encounter individually. Rainey added that several others, "all Ministers' drivers," had then joined in abusive epithets against the orderlies, the marshal, and the President, and a hackdriver had seized an orderly "by the neck and threatened [him] with immediate destruction. . . ."

For Clay's response, see below, Circular, February 18, 1827.

Hook, of Maryland, was a career officer in the United States Army and had received the rank of brevet major in 1823.

From PETER W. SPROAT, Philadelphia. Acknowledges receipt of (Daniel) Brent's letter of March 19, 1825, relative to the case of the *Morning Star*; requests further information on the question of indemnity for losses sustained by detention of the vessel; cites his letter of March 15, 1825, for particulars in the case. ALS. DNA, RG59, Misc. Letters (M179, R65). Cf. above, Raguet to Clay, March 20, 1826.

From ISRAEL THORNDIKE, Boston. Notes the failure of previous efforts to secure indemnity from the Russian Government for loss of the brig *Hector* and cargo (cf. above, Thorndike to Clay, March 13, 1825). Advises that he has retained an agent, Jacob T. Slade, to go to St. Petersburg and "to make one more pointed effort in this unfortuate business." Requests in Slade's behalf "a *particular* Letter of Introduction" to the American Minister (see below, Clay to Middleton, February 12, 1827), "through whom he might gain an introduction to the Minister of Foreign Affairs in St. Petersburg [Count Karl Robert Nesselrode]." LS. DNA, RG76, Misc. Claims, Russia, env. 1, folder 4. On Slade, see below, Webster to Clay, February 11, 1827, with which Thorndike's letter was enclosed.

APPLICATIONS, RECOMMENDATIONS   February 7, 1827

J[OHN] McKINLEY, Washington, recommends appointment of Alexander Adair of Alabama as marshal for the Middle District of Florida Territory. ALS. DNA, RG59, A. and R. (M531, R1).
  Adair, a lawyer and, formerly, a bank cashier in Alabama, was appointed to the recommended post on February 27, 1827, and held it until his death in 1831.

JAMES P. PRESTON, Richmond, recommends appointment of William M. McCarty as secretary of Florida Territory. ALS. *Ibid.* (R5). Unaddressed. Cf. above, Mercer to Clay, January 23, 1827, note.
  Preston, born in Montgomery County, Virginia, graduated in 1790 from William and Mary College, and, seriously crippled as an officer in the War of 1812, had been Governor of Virginia from 1816 to 1819 and subsequently served several terms in the State Senate. He was at this time (1827), and for several years thereabout, postmaster of Richmond.

To Francis T. Brooke

My dear Sir   Washington 8 Feb. 1827.
  I send by this Mail the Copies of the British acts of Parliament desired.[1]
  It is a subject of deep regret with me (and I beg you to say so to Govr. Tyler) that his friendly letter to me, on the occasion of my vote in the H. of R. on the late P. election should have been used to assail or annoy him.[2] In any casual allusion which I ever made to that letter, it was far from my intention that it should have been made instrumental to his prejudice. The truth is that it is one of a hundred similar letters which I recd. about the period of its date from all quarters of the Union, and from some of the most distinguished men in it. I have heard that the letter was inadvertently (and certainly with no unfriendly purpose towards the Govr) spoken of by a Mr. Clarke, a lawyer of Winchester,[3] who had been a few days before with me, and to whom I expressed, what I certainly felt, much gratification with his election,[4] and stated that I had the satisfaction to believe that Govr. Tyler did justice to the motives which had influenced me on the above memorable occasion, as he had addressed to me at the time a letter couched in the most friendly terms. I understand that Mr. Clarke incidentally spoke of this conversation, not recollecting that

a printer was by who felt himself at liberty to make the matter a topic in his next paper[5]—

Whether it was in this way or not that it got out I cannot tell. It may have been in some other manner; for there is an espionage prevailing which spares no privacy and which unless checked must destroy all confidence.

Tell the Govr. that he must not take the matter much at heart; to recollect how much I have borne, and with what philosophy and fortitude. Tell him moreover that we shall certainly prevail; and that I do not even despair of our native State. When he comes here, no one entertains the idea that he will renounce any of the great principles of his public action, and least of all that by which he judges of men and things as they are and not as passion, party or prejudice may represent them. I am truly Your friend   H CLAY
The Honble F. Brooke—

ALS. DLC-TJC (DNA, M212, R13).
[1] Documents not identified. Cf. below, Clay to Brooke, February 16, 1827.   [2] Cf. above, Brooke to Clay, January 31, 1827.   [3] Probably William L. Clark, of Winchester, Virginia.   [4] Tyler's election as Governor of Virginia, in 1825.   [5] Tyler's recent election to the United States Senate (see above, Pleasants to Clay, December 24, 1826, note) had stimulated comment concerning his congratulatory letter to Clay of March 27, 1825. Samuel H. Davis, editor of the Virginia *Winchester Republican,* had apparently first publicized the matter. One of the editors of the *Richmond Enquirer* had reportedly stated that Tyler, upon being informed of the Winchester account exclaimed: *"Mr. Clay has betrayed me."* Robert Douthat, in a letter dated February 14, and Tyler in an accompanying statement to Douthat, both published in the *Enquirer* of February 15, denied that the Virginia Governor had been embarrassed by revelation of the letter. Tyler, in his statement, confessed that he had probably protested to (Claiborne W.) Gooch that the letter did not commit him to support of the Adams administration but reaffirmed that he had approved Clay's course during the presidential election in the spring of 1825, that he (Tyler) had "esteemed Mr. Adams as decidedly better qualified for the Presidency than Gen. Jackson," and that he "had no right to complain of Mr. Clay, and in fact no possible motive to do so, merely because he had spoken of a letter not confidential, and the sentiments of which . . . [Tyler] had over and over again avowed. . . ." *Richmond Enquirer,* February 13, 15, 1827. See, also, Robert Seager II, *And Tyler Too: a Biography of John and Julia Gardner Tyler* (New York, 1963), 76, 79–81. Douthat, who during the 1790's had been the first postmaster at Staunton, Virginia, owned the old Byrd family plantation "Westover" on the James River.

From Nicholas Biddle

Dear Sir;   (Private)   Phila. Feby. 8. 1827.
On returning my [sic] duties to day I found letters from Paris & London containing some expressions which I thought might interest you, as coming from very intelligent men of business, and I therefore extract a few passages   These may perhaps add something to your stock of information from other quarters.

Messrs Baring Brothers & Co write on the 30th of Decr.   "There is not yet any official account of the landing of our troops in Portugal, but every days intelligence from the continent strengthens our first opinion, that there is no probability of this Country & France being brought into war."[1]

Messrs Hottinguer & Co[2] of Paris write on the 23d of Decr. "Since the date of the annexed[3] we have had great fluctuation in our funds, arising from the warlike appearance of England. The 3% fell rapidly to 65, but confidence being restored & peace likely to last, they got up again to 68.50, at which rate they are now."

A postscript to the same letter by the branch of the house of Hottinguer & Co at Havre dated the 26th of December says "The same warlike appearances combined with some improvement in our manufacturing districts & in those of England produced a vigorous demand for Cotton & about 10,000 bales were bought up last week by trade at an advance of 1 to 1½ and in some instances even 2 on preceding prices. We have however again relapsed into a profound calm. Our rates have not retroceded, but are almost nominal at &c &c &c.

As these gentlemen write for the Bank alone, & I do not wish them quoted, you will have the goodness to regard this as for your private perusal. With great respect Very truly Yrs   N. BIDDLE
Honble. Henry Clay Washington

Copy. DLC-Nicholas Biddle Papers (DNA, M212, R20).
[1] Cf. above, Brent to Clay, January 13, 1827.   [2] Hottinguer & Companie of Paris became a correspondent of the Bank of the United States in 1826. The French merchant bankers were long "identified with the cotton market as well as with banking." Walter Buckingham Smith, *Economic Aspects of the Second Bank of the United States* (Cambridge, Mass., 1953), 44, 145.   [3] Probably a price quotation; not found.

From Peter Paul Francis Degrand

Hon Henry Clay Washington
Dear Sir   Private & Confidential   Philada. 8 Feby 1827
    Your esteemed favor 4 Instt is recd.[1] You state that "what is desired will, you presume, *ultimately* be done, in regard to the Pr'nting."[2]— Allow me, again, to state that I deem it of the highest importance that this shd. be done *at once*;—& that, *at once, Mr. Binns shd. receive assurance, from Mr Jones, that it shall be so.*— I clearly perceive, by your letter, that you have the most unreserved confidence, in me.— I therefore speak to you just as I think:—& you will naturally imagine that when, for shortness sake, I say *I* think so, it is the result of the best opinions I can get at.— *I think I have the key of the Politics of Pensylva.*— All we want is that the Admn. shd. be true to itself.— It is truly out of all reason, to require our friends, to fight your Battles, when they find all your officers, arrayed agt them.

    I repeat it.— I see no difficulty in obtaining the state, if you will only follow the hints, which I can give you.— Govr. Shultz[3] is true to the Administration:— & he has, in each County, at least three im-

portant appointments,[4] wholly dependent, on his will & pleasure.—
The Genl. Govt. have C. House Officers & Post Masters, in every part
of the State.— *Let their course demonstrate that they look to their
open & avowed friends, to fill the Places*:— Govr. Shultz will follow
suit.— & I will answer, for the result.— —we shall, at least, show so
much fire, as to make Pensylv appear doubtful:— But we shall do
more: we will get the Electoral Vote of the State, if I am not very much
mistaken.— I have, indeed, no doubt we will get it, if you follow these
hints.[5]

Mark one point particularly. *Let the Administration not be afraid
of producing excitement in the State.*— If no excitement is produced,
it is taken for granted that the State is Jackson;— Our true force lays
dormant;— the timid & wavering do nothing or go agt. us;— & we lose
the Battle.— & we lose it, ingloriously, like cowards, without a fight.

If, on the contrary, an excitement is produced, it brings out a force,
to public view, in favor of the Administration;— it animates our
friends to exertion;— it appalls the timid & wavering;— it thus gives
us a fair chance of availing ourselves of whatever force public sentiment does, in good faith, say belongs to us.— This is all I ask to winn
[*sic*] the Battle

If any appointment, by the Genl. Govt., in Pensylva., is attacked,
on the ground that the admn. made it *"because the person named was
their partisan"*,— it is all the better.— It animates all to become "partisans".— & it is but fair we shd. meet "Partisans" of Jackson, by "Partisans" of Adams.

If I do not write you often, it is because I am busy, very busy:— But
I am not the less watchful of what may promote our view nor will I
neglect placing, under your eye, such hints as I may deem necessary:—
But remember, we have a great deal to do.— "& if you call upon Her-
cules, why not put your own shoulder to the wheel[6]

In regard to the State of New-York I have, for many years, taken
much pains to get at the key of their Politics.— I never have been able
to succeed.— I never cd. find an individual that knew any thing about
it.— All I have been able to do has been to guess.— I guess we shall
have the State.[7]— In favor of this, will be the force of public sentiment
which approves of the measures of the admn.;— the friends of Clay &
of Adams;— some of the friends of Crawford;[8]— the Northern feeling— the non-slave holding feeling;— the opposite Ticket being composed of *two* men from slave-holding States;— states extreme South;—
both natives of the same State;[9]— & all the folly of Randolph, Calhoun
&c— Is it possible that intrigue, Machinery of Party & apathy will bear
down these great Barriers of the Republic, in the Great State of New-
York?— No.— I will not believe it, I would not believe it, if it were
told me, as to Masss, by a Politician, in Masss, whose fore-cast was well

known to me;— much less will I believe it, on the authority of any one from the ever-confused forecast of the New-York Politicians.

In regard to the Vice Presy, I consider the reasons you gave to me, as entirely conclusive.— There are also other reasons, wholly conclusive.— We know, by the Elections, the result of our present mode of fighting, keeping you as Secty of State.— All has been said agt. it that will ever be said.— Yet, we have beat in Louisiana, New-Jesey [sic], Maryland, Ohio & Kenty— & certainly we have gained ground in Pensylv.[10]— But who has a sufficient forecast to tell us all the new combinations & difficulties that will arrise [sic], from changing our Battle ground, our armor, our discipline, our weapons?— who can tell us what new jealousies may arrise out of an appt. for Secty of State? Yours faithfully   D

As regards New-York, I beg you to observe another leading fact, conclusive of itself.— Jackson had no strength there, during the last Campaign, neither in the People, nor in the Legislature.— The Jackson party has gained no where in the US since, as is clearly shown, by the Elections which have taken place, by the People— There has been no *local* cause to let Jackson gain, with the People, in the State of New-York.— Hence it follows, with the irresistible force of a deduction, almost Mathematical, that Jackson can have *no strength* with the People of New-York.

& I don't care who it is, who in the State of New-York, has any fears.— Whoever he is, he is a New-York Politician & surrounded by a New-York atmosphere & of course accustomed as often, *at least*, to profecy *wrong*, as to profecy right

The facts I rely on are such as never deceive.— They are such as will controul all leaders, in despite of all they think, of all they wish, of all they can do.

The following is only for yourself & J. Q. A.— "Measures are taking to organize in every County in the State, the friends of the Administration, by establishing Corresponding societies, collecting & communicating information, & encouraging each other, to an active & a persevering zeal:— The contest will become bitter; but our friends are determined to enter into it, as soon as possible."

[Marginal note:]
Along side of these suggestions, bear in mind the fact, that Jackson's friends have, until very lately *put down* our friends, by *intimidation*.— Is it not fair to meet this?

ALS. DLC-HC (DNA, M212, R2). Endorsed on verso by Clay: "Mr. Degrand."
1 Not found.   2 Cf. above, Clay to Jones, January 23, 1827; Jones to Clay, January 25, 1827.   3 John Andrew Shulze.   4 Judges of the courts of common pleas, sheriffs, and coroners.   5 Cf. below, Clay to Brown, March 27, 1827 note.
6 Reference not found.   7 Cf. below, Clay to Brown, March 27, 1827, note.
8 William H. Crawford.   9 Jackson, of Tennessee, and John C. Calhoun, of South

Carolina; both born in South Carolina.   10 Cf. above, Binns to Clay, May 10, 1826, and note; Gurley to Clay, August 20, 1826; Clay to Hammond, October 7, 1826, note; Sloane to Clay, October 16, 1826; Clay to Brooke, December 11, 1826.

MISCELLANEOUS LETTERS   February 8, 1827

To the HOUSE OF REPRESENTATIVES, Washington. Reports, with James Barbour and William Wirt, on findings of the board of inspection authorized by a House resolution of May 19, 1826, which called for "devising a plan for improving the Hall, so far as to render it better suited to the purposes of a deliberative assembly . . ." (cf. above, Bulfinch to Clay, November 1, 1826, note). Encloses copies of correspondence between the House clerk (Matthew St. Clair Clarke) and William Strickland; also attaches copies of architectural recommendations by Strickland and Charles Bulfinch (cf. above, Strickland to Clay, October 21, 1826. and Bulfinch to Clay, November 1, 1826). Explains that because there was insufficient time between Sessions of Congress to execute any of the alterations proposed, the board of inspection declined "to give their sanction to either of the two suggested plans." States that the board "suggested to the architects the propriety of testing the efficacy of the suspended ceiling, by stretching a covering of silk over the space which it was intended to occupy; but it was stated that the absorbent qualities of that, or of any cloth, are such as would prevent its being a fair experiment; and that it was also mentioned, that, in the year 1814, such a test, (though not with silken cloth,) was applied, and that the inconveniences which it occasioned induced the House quickly to direct its removal." Copy. *House Docs.*, 19 Cong., 2 Sess., no. 93, pp. 5–6. Transmitted under cover of Clay to John W. Taylor, February 9, 1827 (*ibid.*, 3). For subsequent action on the acoustical problem, see Mills to Clay, October 14, 1826, note.

To JOHN NICHOLSON, New Orleans. Notifies him that his commision as United States marshal for Eastern Louisiana has been sent to District Judge (Thomas B.) Robertson, who will deliver it when the usual requirements are met. Copy. DNA, RG59, Dom. Letters, vol. 21, pp. 476–77 (M40, R19). Copy of Clay's letter of transmittal and instruction to Robertson, of the same date, is in *ibid.*, 477. On March 15, 1827, Nicholson accepted reappointment to his post and forwarded his bond to the Department. ALS, in DNA, RG59, Misc. Letters (M179, R65).

APPLICATIONS, RECOMMENDATIONS   February 8, 1827

JOSEPH S. BAKER solicits any "honorable employment"; states that he has temporary employment under (Joseph) Nourse; and lists references, including his brother, the Reverend D(aniel) Baker. ALS. DNA, RG59, A. and R. (M531, R1). Joseph Stevens Baker, at this time age 28, became a Baptist preacher and editor. William Mumford Baker, *Life and Labours of the Rev. Daniel Baker, D. D.* (Philadelphia, 1858), 22.

ROBERT BOWMAR, Tuscaloosa (Alabama), refers to his "former slight personal acquaintance" with Clay and seeks his aid in obtaining a cadet appointment at the West Point Military Academy for Curatius Tindall, eldest son of Dr. (John Lewis) Tindall of Tuscaloosa, formerly of Kentucky. ALS. DNA, RG94, U. S. Military Academy, Cadet Applications, 1827/166. Endorsed on cover (AEI): "Submitted to the Secy. of War [James Barbour]. HC."
    Bowmar, born in Woodford County, Kentucky, resided in Tuscaloosa from about 1823 to 1829 and then returned to Kentucky. Young Tindall appears to

have been nominated to the Military Academy but either failed to report or was rejected for admission. *House Docs.*, 21 Cong., 1 Sess., no. 79, p. 67. His father, a native of Columbia, Georgia, had begun there the practice of medicine, had moved to Kentucky in 1806, and had removed to Tuscaloosa in 1816. He continued medical practice, was president of the State Bank, and served in the Alabama Legislature from 1823 to 1836. In 1837 he moved on to Aberdeen, Mississippi, where he farmed for the remainder of his life.

JAMES H. PECK, St. Louis, recommends Spencer Pettis, Josiah Spalding, Hamilton R. Gamble, or Beverley Allen for United States attorney in the Missouri District. ALS. DNA, RG59, A. and R. (M531, R1). Cf. above, Atkinson to Clay, January 15, 1827, note.

DIPLOMATIC NOTES   February 9, 1827

To JOAQUIM BARROZO PEREIRA, Washington. Acknowledges receipt of Pereira's letter of "the 6th instant," soliciting a reply to his earlier notes; promises an answer to the note of December 30 last, as soon as the necessary information may be obtained. Copy. DNA, RG59, Notes to Foreign Legations, vol. 3, p. 325 (M38, R3). L draft, in hand of Daniel Brent, in CSmH.

APPLICATIONS, RECOMMENDATIONS   February 9, 1827

JOSEPH BELLINGER, Charleston (South Carolina), seeks an appointment at the West Point Military Academy for Lucius (Bellinger) Northrop, the eldest son of Bellinger's cousin (not further identified) and Amos B. Northrop, deceased. Notes that young Northrop's father studied law under Langdon Cheves and left a lucrative practice, to which (Robert Y.) Hayne succeeded. Comments: "Mrs. Northop, thinking she had some claim on Colo Hayne, has written to him on this subject more than a year ago, but so far her application has proved abortive. I have written to Judge [William] Smith, and the Secretary of War, on this subject with no better success. I could not write to Colo. Hayne as we are opponents in Politicks; and I fear Judge Smith has not fulfilled the expectation of the Republicans here, in the Course he has taken— We who are friendly to the Administration, have no organ to speak for us at Washington." Postscript adds that "Mrs. Northrop is a Planter of Barnwell District where few or no favours of this kind has [*sic*] been confered [*sic*]." ALS. DNA, RG94, U. S. Military Academy, Cadet Applications, 1823/29. Endorsed (AES): "Refered [*sic*] to the Secy. of War [James Barbour] with the particular recommendation of H Clay."

Young Northrop was admitted to the United States Military Academy July 1, 1827, and graduated in 1831. After a 30-year Army career at various Western posts, he joined the Confederate forces in 1861, as commissary general with the rank of colonel. He gained notoriety for his refusal to provide adequate food for prisoners of war and was imprisoned by the Federal authorities for some months in 1865. Upon his release he retired to a farm near Charlottesville, Virginia.

T[HOMAS] CLAYTON recommends William H. J. Comegys for a clerkship in the State Department or some other office of government. States that he has a "deep interest" in the appointment of Comegys, whose father (Cornelius) is "one of the most respectable men in the State of Delaware." Adds that the father "has more political influence than any other single individual in the State; and . . . is decidedly friendly to the powers that be." ALS. DNA, RG59, A. and R. (M531, R2). Cf. above, Clay to Comegys, January 25, 1827.

JAMES H. McCULLOCH, Baltimore, recommends attention to the wishes of the gentleman (Robert Monroe Harrison) whose letter is enclosed. ALS. DNA, RG59, A. and R. (M531, R4). Enclosure addressed to McCulloch and dated January 11, 1827, discusses Harrison's reasons for wanting a new assignment. Cf. above, Harrison to Clay, September 20, 1826.

JOHN MORTON, Washington, solicits a clerkship in the State Department. States that he served as a captain in the Ordnance Department in Washington from 1812 to 1821 and as first clerk in that Department from 1821 to 1825; that he left his employment because of poor health; and that now he is recovered and seeking reinstatement in public service. ALS. DNA, RG59, A. and R. (M531, R5). Morton, a native of New York, received no appointment in the State Department.

JOHN O'FALLON, St. Louis (Missouri), writes that Clay's "friend Mr. Richd. Lane of Union Town Pa. at present a resident of this State," wants "an Indn appointment, and would accept the Sub Agency for the Ioway Indians. . . ." ALS. *Ibid.* Lane, not further indentified, received no appointment under the Adams administration.

DANIEL SMITH, Harrisonburg, Virginia, recommends Joseph Fawcett for appointment as a commissioner of claims under the Treaty of Ghent (Article I). States that Fawcett's mercantile business of 20 years in Harrisonburg failed. ALS. *Ibid.* (R3). Cf. above, Clay to McLane, January 15, 1827; below, Clay to Cheves, March 23, 1827. Fawcett has not been further identified.

To Nicholas Biddle

Dear Sir   Private   Washn 10 Feb 27.
    I thank you for the information contained in your letter of the 8h. inst. The information recd. at this departmt. by the late arrivals,[1] from several points of Europe authorizes the confident belief that the affair of Portugal will not disturb the general peace. I am with great regard Yrs faithfy.   H CLAY
N. Biddle Esq.

ALS. KyU.
[1] Cf. above, Everett to Clay, December 3, 1826; Brown to Clay, December 13, 1826; Gallatin to Clay, December 13, 1826.

To John Bradford

Dear Sir   Washington 10 Feb. 1827.
    I recd. your favor of the 24th. Ulto.[1] communicating the resignation of Mr. Holley as President of Transylvania,[2] and the wish of the Board of Trustees that I would aid them in looking out for a suitable successor. I shall take great pleasure in complying with their wish. It appears to me, considering the state of the funds of the institution, that it would be advisable not to hasten the appointment of a President, but to employ (at least during the remainder of the present Session) an additional tutor, if necessary. The advantage of this mode

will be to nurse the finances, and to give ample time for a judicious selection.

I see nothing in the condition of Transylvania to occasion despair. Many other Colleges have experienced at this period a diminution of the ordinary number of students.[3] It is to [be a]ttributed to scarcity, to the recent establishment of the Virginia University,[4] in short, to those re-actions from which no bodies are exempt. But its present state ought to stimulate to new efforts, and above all should teach us to prevent if possible those feuds which have too often afflicted the College. I am, with great respect, Your ob Servt.   H CLAY
John Bradford Esq
   &c. &c. &c.

ALS. KyLxT.   [1] Not found.
[2] Horace Holley resigned on January 10, 1827, effective March 5 of the same year. Rebecca [Smith] Lee, *Mary Austin Holley: A Biography* (Austin, 1962), 171–72. Cf. above, Clay to Holley, February 21, 1826.   [3] Enrollment had decreased from a high of 419 in 1826 to 286 in January, 1827; by the end of the latter year the figure stood at 184. Jennings, *Transylvania*, 122.   [4] See above, Clay to Jefferson, May 13, 1826, note.

From Robert Moore

D Sir   Beaver 10th. Feby 1827
Our Editor of the Beaver Argus[1] has come out in favour of the Administration decidedly   he has a Large subscription for a Country paper say 600,   there is a manifest change in favour of the Administration   we will do well in Beaver County,   we are in favour of internal improvements and the Tariff, which protects our manufacturers,   the people are beginning to see their true interests. Our Citizens are much opposed to the Course pursued by the Penna. Legislature,[2]   every Step the Legislature takes produces reaction against Genl Jackson and his cause;   the Sober men of our State are coming round fast, the Crawfordites are all most [*sic*] to a man Administration men. You may rest assured that any resolution that the Legislature may pass will injure the cause of Jackson   his friends heretofore were great Brawlers against Caucuses, and caucussing,   the people see their inconsistency;   the Jackson leaders evince a disposition to force Jackson on the people   in fact they are working their own ruin faster than their opposers could effect it, by their arbitrary indiscreet conduct,— if it could be so managed to have Govr. Shultz[3] taken for vice President at the ensuing election it would secure Penna. but this must be approached cautiously,   what think you of it,   Genl Eatons concern with Simpson[4] has had good effect in this section of Country,   the charges made against others are recoiling on their own heads,— any data that could be furnished that would aid the administration communicated through me would get publicity in our paper—,   a docu-

ment shewing the amount of capital invested in the united states in Manufactures particularly in Penna. would be very useful and any evidence founded on facts to shew Genl Jacksons Hostility to manufactures and internal improvements would have a powerful effect,—

The friends of the Administration in this County are taking decided and I trust prudent measures to frustrate Jacksonism— they are seriously alarmed at the anticipated consequences from his rashness of character and the violence of his active friends—in case of his election   The Jacksonites here count on New York for him[5]   how is this from the best information you possess— is Clinton Hostile, and will he and Van-beauron [sic] form a Coalition in favour of Jackson, and if so what would be the probable result,—

if convenient and you should think proper I would like to hear from you, and you can impose any condition you may think proper. With Sentiments of high regard I remain your friend   ROBERT MOORE
Hon H Clay Esqr

ALS. DLC-HC (DNA, M212, R2). Moore, born near Washington, Pennsylvania, had attended Washington (now Washington and Jefferson) College, studied law, and in 1802 opened legal practice at Beaver, Pennsylvania. He had served as treasurer of Beaver County from 1805 to 1811, a State militiaman during the War of 1812, and a member of Congress from 1817 to 1821. He was later, in 1830 and 1831, a member of the Pennsylvania Legislature.
   [1] Thomas Henry, a native of Ireland, who had fled British rule and settled in Beaver in 1798. He had held local office as a justice of the peace (1809) and county commissioner (elected in 1810), prothonotary and clerk of courts (1816–1821), and sheriff (elected in 1821), had served in the War of 1812, and had been a member of the State legislature (1815). He later became county treasurer (1828–1829) and a member of Congress for three terms (1837–1843). He was editor of the Beaver *Argus* from 1821 to 1831.   [2] Several attempts had been made in the Pennsylvania Senate in January, 1827, to win passage of a resolution endorsing the presidential candidacy of Andrew Jackson. When a considerably weaker proposal was finally adopted, administration supporters protested that the Senate had become overly partisan. Klein, *Pennsylvania Politics*, 210–11.   [3] John A. Shulze.   [4] John Eaton had lent $1500 to support Stephen Simpson's Philadelphia *Columbian Observer* as a Jackson organ. The funding had been revealed in Simpson's schedule of debts "when he applied for the benefit of the insolvent law." *Register of Debates*, 19 Cong., 2 Sess., pp. 1343–44; Washington *Daily National Journal*, March 21, 1827, reprinting Trenton *True American*.   [5] See above, Degrand to Clay, February 8, 1827, note. For references to the political maneuvering in New York during this period, see above, Hammond to Clay, January 28, 1827, note.

From George F. Strother

Sir   St Louis February 10h 1827
   I was last evening much mortified to see my name in the Telegraph connectd [sic] with a charge against you[1]— it is an outrage upon my feelings totally unauthorised

The conversation I had in washington with Mr Crawford in the spring of 1825 I communicated the next day to you— For Mr Crawford I had the highest respect; and on my return home in [. . .][2] repeated the conversation in the presence of Green;[3] and perhaps on his inquiry said he was at liberty to mention the conversation not deeming it confdntial [*sic*] or wiṣhing to give it mysterious importance but certainly I never authorised or expected this man to drag me from my retirement[4] before the publick in connexion with this matter—

I have reflected with painfull ánxiety upon the line of duty dictated by this painfull outrage upon my feelings. My high respect for Mr Crawford; my professed personal friendship for you; my invinceable repugnance at this moment to appear in the newspapers give a sting and a perplexity to this matter keener & deper [*sic*] than it deserves. at one time I had determined to make an explanation in the papers but was fearfull to give trifles in a political and material point of view the appearance of importance but could not in justice do otherwise than give you this explanation— the conversation is highly colored by Green— I repeated to him what I told you verbatim   Yours respectfully   GEORGE F STROTHER

ALS. DLC-HC (DNA, M212, R2).
[1] The Washington *United States Telegraph*, on January 20, 1827, had reported a conversation between Strother and William H. Crawford wherein the latter claimed that Adams had offered him "a *carte blanche* to choose his station under him, in case he (Mr. A.) was elected." The article suggested that if "Mr. Adams would, at such a time, attempt to purchase Mr. Crawford, would he not when necessary, bargain with Mr. Clay?" The comment had preceded the text of a recent speech in the Virginia legislature by (William) Smyth, who had therein disclosed the contents of Crawford's conversation with Strother. According to Smyth's account, Crawford had stated that (Tobias) Watkins conveyed Adams' offer. On March 16 Adams noted that Watkins had drafted a lengthy letter in reply, which Adams thought might better be abbreviated to a distinct denial. Cf. Adams, *Memoirs*, VII, 242.   [2] Word illegible.   [3] Duff Green.
[4] Strother had resigned from Congress in 1820 to accept appointment as receiver of public moneys. He had resigned the latter post some time during the congressional recess in 1824, probably before his race for re-election (cf. above, III, 843n). He did not again return to public life.

INSTRUCTIONS AND DISPATCHES   February 10, 1827

From J[OHN] J. APPLETON, Stockholm, no. 10. Reports that he called the attention of the Count of Wetterstedt to the portion of the President's (annual) message regarding Sweden (see above, Clay to Appleton, January 12, 1827); that the Count expressed satisfaction "with the tenor of it"; and that, in response to the Count's inquiry, he gave assurances that he expected instructions on the matter, probably of a "character" like "the two treaties . . . recently concluded with Denmark & Central America" (above, Treaty, December 5, 1825; Treaty, April 26, 1826). Notes that the Count also inquired about United States relations with the Latin American states, that he (Appleton) referred to the section of the President's message indicating hope that the steps taken by this country "to promote a general recognition of their independence would eir [*sic*] long be successful," and that the Count commented that "the Emperor Nicholas . . . look'd much more calmly on questions of this nature than his predecessor [Alexander I], and whatever might be his own conduct towards the new states, he would not certainly do much to prevent other Governments from acting in the case as they chose." Adds that he mentioned his understanding that a number of states, including in August, 1825, Sweden, had pledged "not to act upon the question of recognition but in concert with" Russia and that Wetterstedt, while admitting that such an engagement had been considered, explained that the arrangement had been "defeated" when the King (Charles XIV) refused to make such a pledge without "a precise knowledge of the line of conduct which the Emperor meant to pursue towards the new states. . . ." Recounts Wetterstedt's further comment that Sweden had failed to open diplomatic negotiations with the new American states "because she had no interest to promote in that quarter which could justify the expense of a Mission" but that she would receive "the Vessels of any of those Republics" and treat them as friends.

Mentions that in the negotiations underway between Sweden and Prussia there is agreement upon the principle of reciprocity, "this equality being applicable to the *indirect* as well as the direct trade, and made to embrace the importation of Salt, which had been excepted in the Treaty with Denmark . . ." (see above, Appleton to Clay, November 1, 1826; December 20, 1826).

States that the proposed negotiation with the Netherlands has broken down because the latter Government "proposed as a basis a mutual fixation of the duties upon articles in exchange between the two countries. . . ." ALS. DNA, RG59, Dip. Disp., Sweden and Norway, vol. 5 (M45, R-T6). Received April 24.

MISCELLANEOUS LETTERS   February 10, 1827

From JOSEPH NATHAN, New York. Notes that, in 1823 or 1824, he wrote to Clay's "predecessor in the Department of State" (John Quincy Adams), concerning "a claim . . . on the French Government for supplies furnished to the said Government in St. Domingo" but does not know whether the letter was received. Transmits now the amount of the claim, for which he holds "authentic, and undisputable vouchers. . . ." LS. DNA, RG76, Misc. Claims, France, env. N. The enclosure reveals that the supplies were furnished by Nathan Brothers, of whom Joseph is "surviving Partner."

Nathan (not further identified) was probably a brother of Jacob Nathan, who had come to America from Santo Domingo in 1792 but after a brief residence in Virginia had left. Joseph R. Rosenbloom, *A Biographical Dictionary of Early American Jews, Colonial Times through 1800* ([Lexington, Ky, c. 1960]), 132. Nathan Brothers had been included in an earlier settlement of a very similar claim, over which some disagreement had arisen regarding division of the remuneration. A congressional committee, reporting through Albert Gallatin in 1808, had recommended that the issue be referred to adjudication. Poore, *Descriptive Catalogue of Government Publications*, 74.

APPLICATIONS, RECOMMENDATIONS   February 10, 1827

S[AMUEL] SMITH, "Capitol Hill," notes that the Senate has passed "the Bill allowing more Clerks for the Dept" (see above, Clay to McLane, January 14, 1826, note) and recommends appointment of William, son of Robert H. Goldsborough, "formerly of Senate [*sic*], a Consistent federalist, and a leader among the friends of the Administration. . . ." ALS. DNA, RG59, A. and R. (M531, R3). Cf. above, Martin and others to Clay, March 23, 1826, note; Barnard to Clay, January 10, 1827, note.

ROBERT SWARTWOUT recommends his eldest son (Henry) "for a Cadetship at West Point." Concludes: "The application backed by Your influence I have reason to think will be Successfull, and will be forever most gratefully rembered [*sic*]." ALS. DNA, RG94, Application Papers, U. S. Military Academy, 1824/142. Endorsed (AEI) on cover: "Referred with the favorable recommendation of H C. to the Secy of War [James Barbour]. HC."

Henry Swartwout was appointed to the United States Military Academy July 1, 1827, and graduated in 1832. He remained in the Army throughout his life and died, in the rank of captain, at Fort Meade, Florida, in 1852.

To Joseph M. Street

WASHINGTON, 11 FEB., 1827.

DEAR SIR: I rec'd your letter of the 11 ult communicating your wish to obtain some public employment. I assure you most sincerely that I have all the disposition to serve you which you could desire. With respect to past transactions to which you advert, I look upon them as matters long since gone by, and I have already given you evidence that they have left no unfriendly impression on my mind.

There is but little patronage in my Department, much less than in any other, and not I presume of a kind which you would expect or desire. With respect to the other departments, from obvious reasons of delicacy and propriety, I but seldom interfere. But if you will at any time indicate any particular mode in which you suppose I can be useful to you, I will give it the most friendly consideration, and do anything I can with propriety. I am Y'rs respctfy   H. CLAY.
GEN. STREET.

Copy. *Annals of Iowa*, 3d. Series, V (April, 1901), 71.

From Francis T. Brooke

My Dear Sir   Richmd Feb 11 1827

I received your letter last night and the documents,[1] but Genl Taylor[2] has just left me and though he was pleased to get what you Sent, Seemed disappointed in not getting what he wanted—   I therefore enclose you a memorandum[3] which if you see fit, you can attend to— the opposition has been much divided by the result of the election of governer [*sic*],[4]   Some of Floyd's friends blame Gen Smyth for reading Floyds letter to the house, in which he Spoke of the combination being so perfect and Complete, as to ensure its Success against the admn— I imagine you will See a very particular account in the next Whig as I Saw Pleasants there,[5]   there are now three distinct parties, the Patent gentlemen or anticorruptionists as Some of them call themselves— the antiadministration men who will not take the whole creed, and thirdly the administration men,   Mr Giles I understand has given up his excise or counterreacting tariff, but will make a report very Strong, his friends Say against internal improvements &c[6]   you See wha[t] Ritchie Says in the last inquirer [*sic*] on the Georgia Subject,[7]   I dined yesterday at Ch[apman] Johnsons with a large party, and was Surprised to hear Leigh[8] Justify Mr Adams message— I think a majority of the Richmd party as it is called will be against Ritchie Giles Drumgol [sic]⁹ on that Subject,   The Georgia resolutions¹⁰ were before a committee and before the arrival of the message I understand it had concluded, merely to express a regret that the collision had taken pla[ce] and its pleasure that the events had passed away— whereby it was unnecess[ary] to express any opinion on the merits of the controversy— but Since the arrival of the message some of the committee are now for going in to the whole Subject,¹¹   Genl Taylor is a member of that committee— I shall take an opportunity to Say what you request to G Tyler¹² he is completely outlawed by the patent party— I think it probable that most of the west has deserted this party— I write in haste and conclude myself your friend

FRANCIS BROOKE

ALS. DNA, RG59, Misc. Letters (M179, R65).
1 Cf. above, Clay to Brooke, February 8, 1827.   2 Robert Barrand Taylor.
3 Not found.   4 On February 10, William B. Giles was elected, with a total of 107 votes, over Hugh Nelson (62) and John Floyd (37). *Niles' Weekly Register*, XXXII, (April 14, 1827), 114–15.   5 Alexander Smyth had read to the Virginia House of Delegates extracts from letters by John Floyd and various unidentified members of Congress asserting that Floyd could more usefully serve the interests of Virginia by remaining in Congress than by becoming Governor. John H. Pleasants, editor of the Richmond *Constitutional Whig*, protested in his issue of February 16 that only extracts of the correspondence had been read and that still briefer extracts had been released for publication. The editor noted as particularly "curious" that General Smyth had "suppressed" from publication a passage, read to the House of Delegates, in which Floyd had written: ". . . the *COMBINATIONS* for effecting the elevation of gen. Jackson, were nearly complete, and that he wished to remain in congress until they were complete." Quoted in *ibid.*, 115.   6 Cf. above, Brooke to Clay, January 31, 1827, note.   7 On February 10 the *Richmond Enquirer*, edited by Thomas Ritchie, had criticized President Adams for threatening to use force against the State of Georgia, for retaining an Indian agent there who was unsympathetic to Georgia's interests, and for failing to buy the disputed lands from the Indians (cf. above, Clay to Southard, July 3, 1825). On February 5, 1827, Adams had submitted to Congress a letter from John Crowell, agent to the Creek Indians, presenting their plea for Federal protection against the incursions on their lands by surveyors from the State of Georgia. Adams reported that he had given instructions for the offenders to be brought to justice under civil process but noted that he had abstained from use of his authorized military powers because he recognized that the surveyors were acting "as agents of a sovereign State. . . ." While commenting that perseverance in such "acts of encroachment upon the territories secured by a solemn treaty to the Indians" would compel him "to enforce the laws and fulfill the duties of the nation by all the force committed for that purpose to his charge," he had emphasized that military force would be applied "only in the event of the failure of all other expedients provided by the laws. . . ." Richardson (comp.), *Messages and Papers of the Presidents*, II, 370–73.   8 Benjamin Watkins Leigh.   9 William B. Giles; George C. Dromgoole. Dromgoole, born and educated in Virginia, had practiced law, served, from 1823 to 1826, in the House of Delegates, and in 1826 entered the State Senate. He remained in the latter body until 1835, and then, from 1835 to 1841 and again from 1843 to 1847, was a member of Congress. On the Richmond party, cf. above, Sloane to Clay, December 19, 1822, note.   10 In December, 1826, a committee of the Georgia Legislature had drawn up a lengthy report and accompanying resolutions relating to the Creek treaties and the State's "differences with the General Government. . . ." The resolutions included an assertion of Georgia's sovereignty over "all the territory within her present chartered and conventional limits" and her "right to exercise over any people, white or red, within those limits, the authority of her laws . . ."; a protest against the "threatening" of a State with armed force; and condemnation of the refusal "to arrest and punish a military officer of the General Government [Edmund Pendleton Gaines—see above, Clay to Hammond, September 23, 1825] who had grossly violated a law of the land, in abusing and insulting the highest authorities of a State," and of "the retention of a civil officer in power [John Crowell], after earnest and repeated solicitations for his removal. . . ." Under the terms of the resolutions the report and accompanying

supportive documents were to be presented to Congress and to the Governors of the several States with a request that the latter officials lay the material before the State legislatures. *House Docs.*, 19 Cong., 2 Sess., no. 59.   11 No action specifically identified with the above-cited Georgia resolutions was taken by the Virginia Legislature, but the subject was probably encompassed under the general topic of conflicting Federal and State jurisdiction as treated in the report on the Giles resolution.   12 Governor John Tyler.

From Henry R. Warfield

My Dear Sir—   Frederick Town 11th. February 1827.
   I observe by the public prints that Commissioners are to be appointed to carry into Effect the provisions of the treaty of Ghent[1]— Maryland I believe is as deeply interested on that Subject as almost any State in the union—
   The appointment of Commissioner wou'd be Very agreeable to me— Upon this point I will only remark shou'd it be thought necessary, the fullest recommendations can be had from any man of character and talents in Maryland—
   The late proceedings in Congress have Excited considerable feeling in this part of the Country— I would say much on those and other Subjects, but our Court is now in Session and my Engagements are infinitely more Extensive than I had any Expectation of from the length of time I have been from the bar[2]— It is more than probable the Court may continue two weeks longer, making a Session of a month,— But if it shou'd adjourn in time to give me the opportunity of spending a few days in Washington before Congress rises I intend to be there— For there are many men in that body for whom I feel great personal regard and know the feeling to be reciprocated— Your affectionate friend   Henry R. Warfield

ALS. DNA, RG59, A. and R. (M531, R8).
   1 Cf. above, Clay to McLane, January 15, 1827; below, Clay to Cheves, March 23, 1827.
   2 Cf. above, Warfield to Clay, January 23, 1826.

MISCELLANEOUS LETTERS   February 11, 1827

From Daniel Webster. Encloses a "communication [received] by the Mail of today" (above, Thorndike to Clay, February 7, 1827) and states that, as "the case seems to require dispatch," he sends the letter by a servant. Notes that "Mr [Jacob T.] Slade is a respectable man, a merchant; & has resided . . . several years at St. Petersburg." ALS. DNA, RG76, Misc. Claims, Russia, env. 1, folder 5. Letter dated "Sunday Eve."

APPLICATIONS, RECOMMENDATIONS   February 11, 1827

James P. Preston, Richmond (Virginia), recommends James H. Piper, son-in-law of General Alexander Smyth, "for a government job." ALS. DNA, RG59, A. and R. (M531, R6). Cf. above, Piper to Clay, January 16, 1827.

From Tobias Watkins, Daniel Brent, and William Brent

WASHINGTON,
To the HON. the SECRETARY OF STATE: 12*th February*, 1827

SIR: Having, in compliance with your request, verbally communicated to us by Thomas Law, Esq., perused, and attentively considered, certain papers put into our hands by that gentleman, proposing and developing a new and advantageous scheme of public finance, to which he was solicitous of attracting your notice and sanction, we have the honor to submit the following report:

Our philanthropic fellow-citizen, the author of this fiscal proposition, seems to have taken it for granted, that, if the *means* could once be devised, the National Legislature would not be slow in showing the *inclination*, to patronise and promote, by pecuniary aid, the great work of Internal Improvement; and, upon this assumption, the whole energies of a mind, not less remarkable for the unabated vigor of its conceptions, than for its persevering devotion to the general service of the human family, have been directed to the discovery of this *desideratum*—to the invention of a moneyed capacity, which shall be available, without imposing a burden upon the Treasury, and which may become efficient in promoting the great end in view, without drawing upon the public revenue, or materially diminishing the sources from which it is derived.

[Note that "The first and principal object . . . seems to be the creation of means for" construction of the Chesapeake and Ohio Canal, although "the plan" could "be applied . . . to the accomplishment of every other scheme of Internal Improvement" that the United States wished "to encourage and promote."]

The proposition is of the simplest character, and may be explained in a few words. It is this: That the Government be authorized, by an act of Congress, to issue *Treasury Notes*, not bearing interest, of various convenient denominations, from *five* to a *thousand* dollars, to the amount of *five millions*, which is the estimated cost of the canal; to be made receivable at the Treasury and different Land Offices, in payment for public lands. That the Government be further authorized to *loan* these *Treasury Notes*, or *scrip*, to any individual or corporation, who shall subscribe for shares in the canal, to the amount of such loan, at an interest of three per cent, per annum; that the payment of the principal so loaned as well as of the interest accruing on it, be secured to the United States, in the first place, by the pledge of the shares for which the borrower shall have subscribed; and, secondly, by some additional and different quantity, which shall be deemed equivalent in value to *one-fourth* of the loan; that, at the expiration of five years from the date of the loan, at which time it is reasonable to suppose the contemplated canal, or other work undertaken, will have been completed, and that the revenue from it will be already sufficient to divide a considerable profit to its stockholders, the borrower be called upon to repay to the United States, *five per cent.* of the principal loan, and the same annually thereafter; or more or less, at the discretion of the Government, until the whole sum borrowed, be repaid; and that, upon the failure of the borrower, at any time, to pay the interest, or any portion of the principal, at the periods when the same shall become due, the shares which shall have been pledged, shall be forfeited, and the additional security of one-fourth, shall, in like manner, be made available to the use of the United States.

But, as it is believed that the sum of a million of dollars will be as much as can be conveniently or advantageously expended, in any one year, it is proposed, that no more than that sum of Treasury Notes shall be annually issued, until the whole amount of five millions, shall have been demanded.

It forms a part of the proposition of Mr. Law, however, though it does not constitute an essential feature of his plan, that the Government itself shall be authorized to subscribe *one-third* of the notes or scrip issued. The advantages that would be derived to the public from a participation by the Government in the shares of the Canal, or any other public improvement, are so obvious that it can scarcely be necessary to recite them. It would communicate a more directly national character to the work, would inspire a general confidence in its ultimate success, and would induce moneyed individuals to embark in its prosecution.

It may be observed, too, that the proposition to *limit* the direct interest of the Government to *one-third* of the stock, is not without its attendant advantages. Were the Government to become concerned to an extent of shares, which, by the established usages of such Companies, would give it a preponderating influence in the appointment of Directors, Contractors, and Agents; there is good reason to believe, that less economy, both of time and money, would be observed, and less attention paid to all the great interests at stake, than if the chief management were entrusted to individuals, or Corporations, by allowing them to subscribe a majority of the Stock.

[Present, in the next ten paragraphs, "some of the arguments by which both the practicability and expediency of the measure proposed may be supported." Observe, in the latter connection, that "The objection which has been, on many occasions, and with some show of justice, urged against the policy of making the whole nation tributary to schemes of improvement, which must, in the nature of things, be local and partial in their benefits, is entirely removed by the plan here suggested of creating the means."]

In conclusion, we cannot forbear to remark, that whether the author of the suggestion here made, be right or wrong in the ground assumed as to the disposition of Congress, he must indeed be a fastidious stickler for the bare and rigorous letter of the Constitution who can find, in any fair construction of that instrument, a valid objection to the adoption of a scheme which promises such extensive benefits to his country at large, without encroaching upon the rights, or curtailing the peculiar advantages of any portion of it; which promises to ameliorate and improve the general condition of all the great classes of the community, without sacrificing or diminishing the particular interests of any; which promises, in short, to augment the resources of the nation, without subtracting from those of a single individual.

We beg to be understood, however, as making this remark, not upon the presumption that the plan, if adopted, must necessarily accomplish all that it promises, but upon the consideration that, as its failure could bring with it no serious evil, its application, if successful at all, must be successful to an extent which may well justify the experiment.

We have the honor to be, Sir, very respectfully, your obedient servants

> T. WATKINS,
> DANIEL BRENT,
> WM. BRENT.

Washington *Daily National Intelligencer*, April 24, 1827. The document is introduced by the following statement: "Mr. LAW submitted a financial plan to Mr. Clay whose acuteness and discernment, and whose political firmness he admired, and knowing that his multiplication of business would prevent his attention thereto, at Mr. L's particular desire, three gentlemen were named by Mr. C. to investigate the same, and to give their sentiments." Thomas Law's communication to Clay has not been found. Law, a native of England, had begun his career in the employ of the East India Company, amassed a fortune farming taxes in India, left the British civil service in 1791, and migrated to the United States. He speculated in Washington real estate, was one of the founders of the Columbian Institute, and, as lecturer before that body and correspondent in the local press, won distinction as an advocate of a national paper currency.

DIPLOMATIC NOTES   February 12, 1827

To FRANCISCO DIONISIO VIVES, Governor and Captain General of Cuba. Details complaints of the Minister from Colombia accredited to the United States (José María Salazar) in reference to the Colombian schooner *Zulmé* (cf. above, Salazar to Clay, January 25, 1827). States that, desiring to maintain "perfect impartiality" between the belligerents, the United States must vindicate its violated territorial rights and "cause full reparation to be made, should the facts as stated turn out to be true." Observes that (Alexander H.) Everett "has been accordingly instructed [Clay to Everett, January 15, 1827] to make the proper representations at Madrid." Suggests that delays may be avoided if Vives "should see fit to interpose . . . [his] authority to cause the restoration and indemnity due to the occasion to be at once made." Copy. DNA, RG59, Notes to Foreign Ministers and Consuls, vol. 3, pp. 326–27 (M38, R3). ALI draft, in CSmH, dated February 5, 1827; published in Manning (arr.), *Diplomatic Correspondence . . . Latin-American Nations*, I, 281.

INSTRUCTIONS AND DISPATCHES   February 12, 1827

To HENRY MIDDLETON, no. 6. Instructs Middleton to give official aid to William (*i.e.*, Jacob) T. Slade, agent for Israel Thorndike in the case of the brig *Hector*. Copy. DNA, RG59, Dip. Instr., Russia, vol. 11, 243–44 (M77, R6). LI draft, in DLC-HC (DNA, M212, R8). Cf. above, Thorndike to Clay, March 13, 1825, February 7, 1827.

From JAMES BROWN, Paris, no. 64. States that he has shipped all the books he has been requested to purchase for the State Department, except those for which he has not received further directions as requested in his dispatch of August 12 last. Encloses a statement of items sent and their cost. ALS. DNA, RG59, Dip. Disp., France (M34, R26). Received March 24.

MISCELLANEOUS LETTERS   February 12, 1827

To WILLIAM SEBREE, Pensacola. Advises him that his commission as United States marshal for the West Florida District has been sent to Henry M. Brackenridge, who will deliver it upon receipt of the required bond and forms. Copy. DNA, RG59, Dom. Letters, vol. 21, p. 478. Clay forwarded Sebree's commission to Brackenridge by letter of the same date. Copy, *ibid.*

From S[AMUEL] SMITH, Senate Chamber. Encloses a letter from (David) Winchester and inquires "whether the State Department will furnish copies free of cost." ALS. DNA, RG59, Misc. Letters (M179, R65). The enclosure, a letter from Winchester to Smith, dated February 11, 1827, argues that claimants whose cases were disallowed by the commissioners under the (Adams-Onís) Treaty (cf. above, II, 678n) are entitled to have their documents returned or at least copied free of charge by the State Department (cf. above, Hollins to Clay, January 27, 1827, note). Winchester maintains that the Government should not have agreed to the provision (in Article XI) of the treaty, wherein the documents are to be deposited permanently with the State Department, for denial of access to the originals may prejudice the interests of those claimants who appeal their cases to Madrid.

APPLICATIONS, RECOMMENDATIONS   February 12, 1827

ATHANASIUS FORD, Washington, solicits one of the new State Department clerkships to be created by Congress (cf. above, Clay to McLane, January 14, 1826, note). ALS. DNA, RG59, A. and R. (M531, R3). Cf. above, Ford to Clay, December 7, 1825, note.

MORITZ FURST, Philadelphia, expresses hope that he has not lost Clay's "valuable esteem"; seeks Clay's "interference" to get him employment, since he is "deserted from means and business." LS. DNA, RG59, A. and R. (M531, R3). On December 9, 1826, John Quincy Adams had noted that Furst was soliciting employment in the War and Navy Departments as a medallist. Adams had also reported that he had then requested Furst's bill for 10 silver medals struck to commemorate Adams' inauguration as President. Adams, *Memoirs*, VII, 203. Cf. below, Furst to Clay, April 6, 1827.

JOSEPH KENT, Annapolis, recommends Robert Brooke for a clerkship in the State Department. ALS. DNA, RG59, A. and R. (M531, R1). On Robert Brooke, who received no appointment under the Adams administration, cf. below, Brooke to Clay, March 3, 1827.

B[ENJAMIN] F. POWERS, Cincinnati, recommends Major Charles Larrabee, a veteran of "the last war, in which he lost an arm," for appointment as an officer should contemplated legislation designate Cincinnati as a port of entry. Concludes: "Nothing here of a political nature to interest you— The vote in the senate on the Bankrupt bill [see above, Shaw to Clay, August 27, 1826, note] has created great surprise [*sic*]." ALS. DNA, RG59, A. and R. (M531, R5).

Born in Connecticut, Larrabee had served as an officer in the Army from 1808 until 1825. He held appointment as surveyor of the port of Cincinnati from 1831 to 1835.

A bill to establish customs collection districts in Kentucky, Ohio, Indiana, Illinois, and Missouri, rejected at the First Session of the Nineteenth Congress, had been re-introduced by William Henry Harrison in the Senate on January 4, 1827. It was tabled on February 28. Similar proposals passed the Senate both Sessions of the Twentieth Congress, in 1828, but failed to come to vote in the House. An act of March 2, 1831, finally provided that duties on foreign merchandise could be secured and paid at Cincinnati, Pittsburgh, Wheeling, St. Louis, Nashville, or Natchez. Duty estimates were to be made by surveyors assigned to those cities, but the collector of customs at New Orleans retained responsibility for entry. *Register of Debates*, 19 Cong., 2 Sess., 29; U. S. Sen., *Journal*, 19 Cong., 2 Sess., 77, 256; 20 Cong., 1 Sess., 195, 271–72; 20 Cong., 2 Sess., 20, 52; 4 *U. S. Stat.*, 480–82.

S[AMUEL] L. S[OUTHARD] refers an accompanying letter to the Secretary of State. AEI. DNA, RG59, A. and R. (M531, R4). The letter dated January 31, 1827, from Richard W. Habersham to Southard, recommends appointment of Charles Harris, of Savannah, as a commissioner to settle claims for slaves carried away by the British "during the late war . . ." (cf. above, Clay to Gallatin, December 28, 1826, no. 15, note).

Harris, born in England and educated in France, had settled in Georgia in 1788, had studied law and practiced that profession in Savannah, and from 1813 to 1816 had served as Federal attorney for the District of Georgia. He had repeatedly declined election as circuit judge and nomination to the United States Senate. He died March 17, 1827. On the requested appointment, cf. below, Clay to Cheves, March 23, 1827.

From Elisha Smith

D Sir   Mt. Vernon[1] Feb. 13, 1827

[Notes that (Richard M.) Johnson has introduced "a Bill before the Senate" for the benefit of William Smith "as deputy Marshal,"[2] reminds Clay that "better than a year" ago[3] he (Elisha Smith) requested that "the necessary dockuements" be given to (Robert P.) Letcher, and states that "the old man" now requests that the papers be handed to Johnson "if they have been . . . found."]

P.S.   A few days since I rec[eived] a letter from an Uncle of mine in Texas,[4] dated in Octr. last, which states th[at] people of that province were consirting [*sic*] measures to declare them independent of the

Govt. of Mexico— I discover in the prints (which you have seen before this) that a revolt took place in Decr.[5]— I rejoice at it— If the War in Europe should be serious, England will want Cuba as an indemnity.[6] This Govt. should not suffer her to take possession of that Island. Indeed I doubt the policy of permiting [sic] any of the S. A. Governments to revolutionize it, tho' they are at War with Spain.[7] There is some expectations [sic] that Colo. Smith of Madison[8] will be a Candidate agst Letcher— he has no chance— I much respect him, but I am sorry to say he is disposed (as I think and do not doubt his honesty) to straddle [the] rail between the two parties[—] I mean Jackson & Adams— these remarks are for yourself. Hastily. Yr. sincere friend
H. Clay Esqr.   E. SMITH

ALS. DNA, RG59, Misc. Letters (M179, R65).
[1] Kentucky.   [2] A petition on behalf of William Smith had been filed by Johnson on January 19, 1827. It had been referred to committee and was not thereafter reported. Johnson again presented petitions for Smith in both Sessions of the Twentieth Congress, and on both occasions they were reported adversely and rejected. U. S. Sen., *Journal*, 19 Cong., 2 Sess., p. 107; 20 Cong., 1 Sess., pp. 59, 89, 93; 20 Cong., 2 Sess., pp. 29, 60, 64.   [3] Cf. above, Clay to Smith, June 22, 1826.   [4] Not identified.   [5] See above, Dickson to Clay, January 3, 1827, note.   [6] Cf. above, Gallatin to Clay, December 13, 16, 22, 30, 1826; February 5, 1827; below, Brown to Clay, this date.   [7] Cf. above, Clay to Salazar, December 20, 1825; Clay to Anderson, December 30, 1825.   [8] John Speed Smith. Cf. below, Clay to Sergeant and Poinsett, March 16, 1827. Letcher's Congressional service remained unbroken until March 3, 1833.

INSTRUCTIONS AND DISPATCHES   February 13, 1827

From JAMES BROWN, Paris. Reasserts his view that a general European war may now be avoided but predicts that a "trial of strength" between the forces of representative government and absolutism is "not far distant"; comments that a free press and representative government in Portugal and France would result in the overthrow of the Spanish Government and "most of the Monkish and bigotted institutions which have reduced that fine portion of Europe to its present state of [w]eakness and degradation"; forecasts that agitation against Portugal will continue, "either in the way of open force or secret intrigues," but that despotic intervention against Portugal will be restrained by England; and comments that war financing would be difficult for European nations, including France, where confidence in the Government has been shaken by "the law converting five per cent into three per cent stock" (see above, Brown to Clay, April 1, October 29, 1825). Warns that the strongest motive for the United States "to wish for peace will be found in the precarious situation of the important island of Cuba." Notes that the French Ministry has "this year been very unfortunate" in its legislative proposals—those regarding slave trade and juries have been amended and the measure on the press "made almost an entirely new law," which may still not pass (see above, Brown to Clay, December 13, 1826, note).

Transmits a letter from (Charles Peter) Stephen Wante to (Stephen Hus) Desforges, of Lexington (Kentucky), on the latter's claim for indemnity as an "Antient Colonist of St. Domingo" (see above, Brown to Clay, May 27, 1826), and requests that Clay forward it. Concludes: "Mrs. Brown is well and joins me in respects to Mrs. Clay. I hope you have both borne with patience the fatigues and dissipation [sic] of the Winters Campaign." ALS. DNA, RG59, Dip. Disp., France, vol. 23 (M34, R26). Received March 25.

France was bound by treaty with Great Britain to abolish the slave trade in her

West Indian colonies, but her laws were weak and poorly enforced. The Ministry had proposed legislation which, though still weaker than that of the United States and Britain, would carry fines "equal to the value of the ship and cargo," condemnation of the vessel, and banishment for "all the principals in the voyage," including the underwriters. The measure passed both chambers and was signed by Charles X on April 25, 1827. *Annual Register, 1827*, pp. 205–207; *British and Foreign State Papers, 1826–1827*, pp. 646–47.

A proposal to expand the jury lists, to "deprive the prefects of the power . . . to be partial," introduced early in the current Session of the Chambers, had been strongly criticized because it yet permitted the prefects to make the final selection from the basic list, rather than to draw the names by lot. Although the proposal passed the Chamber of Peers, it was nullified when extensive amendment in the Chamber of Deputies proved unacceptable to the Ministry. Instead, the matter was referred "to the consideration of the bureaus." *Annual Register, 1827*, pp. 197, 202–204.

Desforges had come to Lexington as early as 1807 and resided there until his death in 1834. In 1818 he was proprietor of a grocery store at the corner of Short and Main Cross (Broadway) Streets.

From A[LEXANDER] H. EVERETT, Madrid, no. 67. Encloses a copy of a note (dated February 11, 1827) which he has sent to (Manuel González) Salmón regarding the indemnity question (cf. above, Clay to Everett, April 27, 1825, note); explains that Salmón urged him to send such a note so that it might be used to bring the matter to the attention of the Council of State. Notes that the committee of the Council (cf. above, Everett to Clay, December 18, 1826) has not reported on the matter but that three members of the four-man committee have reviewed the papers and are believed to be favorably disposed to making a settlement; estimates that, if nothing extraordinary intervenes, he will be able "to terminate the arrangement in the course of the next month." Mentions that Salmón "appears pretty well disposed" to negotiate a commercial treaty with the United States but that he (Everett) has not taken up the project in a serious manner because he wished to make "each in its time the exclusive object of attention." Transmits copies of correspondence with Salmón on the seizure last October, by Customs House officers at Miranda del Etro, of some dispatches brought for Everett by (Obadiah) Rich from the Legations at London and Paris. Comments on the dismissal of the Captain General of Castille (Francisco Longa—see below, Everett to Clay, February 27, 1827), recent troop movements of the Portuguese refugees, the powerful influence of the Apostolic party over Cabinet policy, and the potential for revolution among the ill-paid Spanish Army, "whenever it may suit the policy of England to use it in that way." LS. DNA, RG59, Dip. Disp., Spain, vol. 27 (M31, R28). Received April 23. The enclosed copies of correspondence on the Miranda del Etro affair reveal that Everett and Salmón disagreed on the question whether customs officers might notice the nature of the materials sealed as diplomatic dispatches. The packages in question had contained books. Settlement of the indemnity question was not effected until the treaty of February 17, 1834. Miller (ed.), *Treaties. . .* , III, 811–14; Moore, *History and Digest of the International Arbitrations. . .* , V, 4533–47.

From ALBERT GALLATIN, London, no. 57. Reports that (William) Huskisson's continued illness has prevented the renewal of negotiations and that (George) Canning's absence (see above, Gallatin to Clay, February 6, 1827, note) and "some other causes" may result in further delay. Encloses a statement of the Naval estimates debated in Parliament the previous day; observes that the United States was mentioned "more than once" in the debates; and calls attention to the appropriations for Kingston, Halifax, and Bermuda—that for the last "intended for the great naval station" (cf. above, Harrison to Clay, January 4, 1827). Transmits copies of private correspondence (with Viscount Melville). Comments that no news has been received regarding disarmament of the Portuguese insurgents by Spain. ALS. DNA, RG59, Dip. Disp., Great Britain, vol. 33 (M30, R29). Received March 24. The enclosures include Melville to Gallatin, February 10, 1827, covering transmittal of a letter dated February 5, 1827, from William King, Captain of H. M. S. *Astrioea*, reporting that Joseph Morris, a gunner deserted from His Majesty's brig *Frolic*, now believed to be serving as a quartermaster on an American warship, carried with him "3 or 400 dollars of the Commander's. . . ." Melville disclaimed any wish "that the person mentioned in the inclosed letter should be delivered up" but commented that his present officer ought to be "made aware of the circumstances. . . ." Gallatin, replying on February 12, expressed thanks for the information and hope that an agreement might "be concluded for the mutual surrender of deserters." In the same letter Gallatin recalled to Melville "the subject of the light houses on Abaco and the Bahama Banks," on which the United States Government sought British action. Cf. above, Gallatin to Clay, December 9, 1826; January 11, 1827.

From ROBERT MONROE HARRISON, Antigua. Reports that St. Bartholomew "is at the moment full of *Privateers* waiting the expectation [*sic*] of *War* between *Gt Britain Spain* and *Portugal*"; comments that since the United States has many "Merchant vessels in that place the probability is, that those *cruisers* will be Manned entirely by the *Seamen* of the *U S*, seduced from their duty; and which the Government of that Island will *connive* at, there being no one there to whom the Masters . . . can apply to for address [*sic*]." Cites examples of atrocities committed at sea by Colombian naval vessels and privateers. Explains that he has entered into particulars "to shew the harmful effects that result from them, not only as regards the decrease in the number of our Seamen, but the immorality of allowing them to engage in such enterprises, if it could in any way be prevented." ALS. DNA, RG59, Cons. Disp., Antigua, vol. 1 (M-T327, R1). Received March 14.

MISCELLANEOUS LETTERS   February 13, 1827

To ADRIEN DUMARTRAIT, St. Martinsville, Louisiana. Notifies him that his commission as United States marshal for the Western Louisiana District has been sent to Judge (Thomas B.) Robertson and that the commission will be delivered after completion of the usual requirements. Copy. DNA, RG59, Dom. Letters, vol. 21, p. 481 (M40, R19). Letter of transmittal to Robertson of the same date, *ibid.*, pp. 481–82. Dumartrait wrote, September 8, 1827, that he had filed his bond and his "commission . . . lately received." ALS, in DNA, RG59, Acceptances and Orders for Comns. (M-T645, R2). He had been appointed in 1823 and was now reappointed for another four-year term. He was removed from office under the Jackson administration in 1829.

To JOSEPH EDSON, Randolph (Vermont). States that his commission as United States marshal for Vermont has been sent to (Elijah) Paine, United States District Judge for Vermont, and may be obtained upon completion of the usual requirements. Copy. DNA, RG59, Dom. Letters, vol. 21, p. 480 (M40, R19). Letter of transmittal to Paine of the same date, *ibid*, p. 481. Edson, originally appointed marshal in 1823, was now reappointed for a second four-year term. Paine, a native of Connecticut, Revolutionary War veteran, and graduate of Harvard University, had opened legal practice in Vermont and had been a member of the State

House of Representatives from 1787 to 1791, a judge of the State Supreme Court from 1791 to 1795, and a United States Senator from 1795 to 1801. He had been named Federal District Judge in 1801 and remained on the bench until his death in 1842.

Edson acknowledged, on March 19, 1827, receipt of both Clay's letter and the commission. ALS, in DNA, RG59, Acceptances and Orders for Comns. (M-T645, R2).

To WATERS SMITH, St. Augustine. Advises him that his commission as United States marshal for the East Florida District has been sent to (Joseph L.) Smith, Federal District Judge, who will deliver it upon receipt of the required bond and established forms. Copy. DNA, RG59, Dom. Letters, vol. 21, p. 479 (M40, R19). Clay forwarded the commission to Judge Smith by letter of the same date. Copy, in *ibid.* On March 7, 1827, Judge Smith acknowledged receipt of the commission. ALS, in DNA, RG59, Misc. Letters (M179, R65). On March 13, 1827, Waters Smith acknowledged receipt of Clay's letter and of the commission. ALS, *ibid.*

From BENJAMIN GRUT, Maracaibo. Notes the instability "in the public mind" and states that it is "extremely difficult to form an opinion as to what may occur." Comments that the President (Simón Bolívar), seems to oppose both a congress and a constitutional convention but that he may favor adoption of the Bolivian Constitution (cf. above, MacPherson to Clay, October 2, 1826, note). Encloses a copy of Bolívar's letter to General (José Antonio) Páez (of August 8, 1826). Observes that if the President intends to unite the Republics, "a title differing from that of Pres[ident] is considered indispensably necessary"; and notes that "some Europeans and a few military men" favor a monarchy. ALS. DNA, RG59, Misc. Letters (M179, R65). Received February 23. Enclosure in Spanish accompanied by translation.

In the communication, published in Lecuna (comp.) and Bierck (ed.), *Selected Writings of Bolívar*, II, 627–30, Bolívar discussed the current threat of anarchy in Colombia and suggested that, with some alteration, the Bolivian code might be adapted to serve a confederation government. Appealing to Páez for understanding, Bolívar concluded: "In my mind, the ruin of Colombia was consummated from the very day you were called to congress" (see above, Litchfield to Clay, May 22, 1826, note).

From SAMUEL L. SOUTHARD, Navy Department. Acknowledges receipt of Clay's letter of February 6. Explains that while the Africans were in the possession of the Portuguese vice consul at Savannah (Francis Sorrel) "he hired them to individuals and received considerable sums of money, amount unknown, for their services"; that when the Supreme Court dismissed the Portuguese claim (see above, Pereira to Clay, December 30, 1826, note), "the District Attorney [Richard W. Habersham] was instructed by this Department to demand of the Vice Consul the moneys received by him for hire" and to take the steps " 'necessary to enforce payment,' " on the presumption "that as the Vice Consul had no right to the Africans themselves, he had none to their labor, or to the money received therefor"; and that the question of his liability is now under appeal to the Supreme Court (cf. below, Southard to Clay, March 7, 1827, note). Concedes that the Supreme Court, in reversing the Circuit Court on the issue of restitution, made no reference to the payment of court costs and that the latter court, on review of the Supreme Court decree, "determined that as no restitution took place, no costs could be charged to the party" but argues that fairness requires "that when one party commences a suit and urges a claim which cannot be sustained . . . the one whose claim is dismissed should bear a proportion of the costs of which he has been the cause." Adds that the district attorney objected to the bill of the marshal (John H. Morel) for maintenance of the Africans as excessive— "not with the intention of shifting the payment from the United States to the Portuguese Consul, but to obtain a reduction of the amount"— and states that he (Southard) will ascertain from the district attorney "the nature and object of the suit now complained of," since he had no instructions "from this Department" to recover maintenance expenses for the Africans while in the custody of the marshal. LS. DNA, RG59, Misc. Letters (M179, R65).

APPLICATIONS, RECOMMENDATIONS   February 13, 1827

JOHN COCKE, Washington, recommends Robert A. Thruston for a clerkship in the Department of State. ALS. DNA, RG59, A. and R. (M531, R8). Robert A. Thruston was a son of Buckner and brother of Thomas L. Thruston. On the recommended appointment, cf. above, Barnard to Clay, January 10, 1827, note.

JEROMUS JOHNSON and JOSHUA SANDS, Washington, recommend "Augt." W. Radcliffe of New York for appointment as bearer of dispatches to Mexico. ALS. DNA, RG59, A. and R. (M531, R7). Sands, a veteran of the Revolutionary War and a merchant, had been a member of the New York Senate (1792–1799), collector of customs at the port of New York (1797), and member of Congress (1803–1805, 1825–1827). Radcliffe, not further identified, received no appointment.

WILLIAM LAMBERT, JR., Washington, solicits the position as secretary to the Commission for settling claims under the Treaty of Ghent; cites his services as acting consul in Lisbon during the War of 1812. ALS. *Ibid.* (R5). Cf. below, Clay to Ogden, March 23, 1827.

ALFRED H. POWELL, Washington, recommends Robert A. Thruston for a State Department clerkship. ALS. DNA, RG59, A. and R. (M531, R8).

THOMAS B. REED, Senate Chamber, recommends Robert A. Thruston for appointment as a clerk in the State Department. LS. *Ibid.*

B[UCKNER] THRUSTON recommends Francis (S.) Taylor for clerk of the claims commission under the "British Treaty" (of November 13, 1826—cf. above, Clay to McLane, January 15, 1827). Cites the fact that Taylor's father (Edmund) and nine uncles (James, Jonathan, Francis, Richard, John, William, Charles, Reuben, and Benjamin) had served in the Revolution, "If hereditary revolutionary claims are entitled to any consideration. . . ." ALS. *Ibid.* Undated and unaddressed; filed between documents dated February 13 and 15.

On the applicant's career, see below, Watkins to Clay, this date, enclosure. On the recommended appointment, cf. below, Clay to Ogden, March 23, 1827. Charles has not been further identified. Born in Virginia, the others had all settled in Kentucky, where Benjamin served three terms (1808–1811) in the legislature. Richard, the naval captain, was commonly known as "Commodore" and was the father of Richard ("Hopping Dick") Taylor, the Frankfort tavern keeper.

T[OBIAS] WATKINS, Washington, transmits and supports a recommendation for appointment of Francis S. Taylor of Norfolk (Virginia) as secretary or clerk "of the Commission about to be instituted . . ." (see above, Clay to McLane, January 15, 1827). ALS. DNA, RG59, A. and R. (M531, R8). According to the enclosed petition, dated February 9, 1827, and signed by William B. Lamb, president, and nine other officers and directors of the Branch Bank of Virginia at Norfolk, Taylor had served that institution as an officer for nearly twenty years prior to his resignation in 1823. On the recommended appointment, cf. below, Clay to Ogden, March 23, 1827.

Check to Thomas B. Reed

14h. Feb. 1827.

Pay to Thomas B. Reed or order Two hundred dollars.
Cashr. of the Off. of B. U States Washn.[1]   H CLAY

ANS. DLC-TJC (DNA, M212, R16).   [1] Richard Smith.

From George Dawson and Others

Honle Henry Clay
Dear Sir   Brownsville Pa Feby 14th 1827
    It is probable that an appropriation will be made at the present session of Congress for the repair of the Cumberland road[1]—and in anticipation of that event many applications have already been made for the superintendance or rather expenditure of the money thus applied. Amongst the number of applicants we have understood that Mr Solomon G Krepps[2] of Bridgeport is one— That gentleman, probably aware of his own inadequacy, or probably from a compunction of conscience to present a petition aking [sic] an appointment from an administration which he had so vehemently abused did not seek for recommendatory letters in his own neighborhood, but secretely [sic] repaired at an early period of the last session, when an appropriation was expected, to your city and through the relationship by marriage with Messrs Wickliff & Beecher,[3] interested those gentlemen & through them, some others until it is said a respectable recommendation has been obtained.[4] But we are well persuaded had those gentlemen been sufficiently acquainted or known his inadequacy they would not be so will[ing] to urge his claims
    It will not be denied that a person superintending a road ought to possess a knowledge of some of the branches of Mathematicks and to have turned his attention to and sought out the most approved manner of making and repairing artificial roads. Neither of these has Mr Krepps acquired and although practice has afforded him an opportunity of becoming a pretty good mechanical handler of the quill we nevertheless consider him incompetant [sic] of his own exertions to draw up and make out a report of his Proceedings—
    You will probably have some personal recollection of this man yourself. He is the same Mr Krepps who crossed the Monongahela river at this place and travelled a short distance in your company when on your way to Kentucky the last summer, and also the associate and

friend of the persons who were engaged in that disgraceful transaction which took place at the Glass works at that time[5]—

We would not have thus troubled you but we are well assured of the deep interest which you have always taken in this National work and feeling a very great interest ourselves we are extremely desirous that a competant person may be appointed and whatever appropriation may be made may be judiciously and advantageously applied, which we are persuaded cannot be done under the management of so superficial a man as Mr Krepps. With great Respect we have the honor to be your obt Sts

GEO DAWSON
JACOB BOWMAN
GEO. HOGG
BASIL BRASHEAR

ALS by Dawson, signed also by Jacob Bowman, George Hogg, and Basil Brashear. DNA, RG59, A. and R. (M531, R4). Dawson had studied medicine in Ireland and operated a drug store in Pittsburgh prior to settling in Brownsville. Bowman, a native of Maryland, had built the first nail factory west of the Alleghenies, around 1795, and had served as postmaster of Brownsville for the past 30 years. Born in England, Hogg pioneered in developing a chain of dry goods and grocery stores in western Pennsylvania and Ohio, owned a glass factory in Brownsville, and built a toll bridge over the Monongahela River. Brashear was a saddler.
[1] See above, Tarr to Clay, May 1, 1826, note.   [2] Krepps, who had settled in Bridgeport (West Brownsville) in 1813 was prominent as a merchant and local politician. He was several times a burgess of Bridgeport, held a seat in the borough council, and served one term in the State legislature. Boyd Crumrine (ed.), *History of Washington County, Pennsylvania* . . . (Philadelphia, 1882), 783.   [3] Krepps' family ties with Philemon Beecher have not been identified. Charles A. Wickliffe had married Margaret Crepps, probably a cousin of Solomon Krepps, in Bullitt County, Kentucky, in 1813.
[4] Not found.   [5] Incident not further identified.

From John H. Pleasants

D Sir.   Richmond 14th. Feby 1827.

You have no doubt seen the row (or rather heard of it) kicked up by Tyler's letter, to you in 1825,[1] and which I saw on my way to *South America*.[2] I really was sorry, when I observed that you had spoken of its existence. I was very well persuaded that it was mentioned with your usual frankness and without any reference to consequences. It has however, exposed him to a most unpleasant persecution. It was largely seized on by the rank gentlemen here, and among others by Ritchie & Gooch.[3] *They* would not move in it, but *they* & others, stimulated, or rather *enabled* the wretch[4] who conducts the Jackson Republican, and who is really morally and mentally, one of the most despicable of the species—they instructed him how to proceed. He has bored Tyler accordingly, & with so much the more effect, that his contemptible standing has been in some degree imparted to Tyler by the collision. Tyler is himself coming out in the Enquirer[5] of tomorrow—against my advice I confess. The thing is subsiding and will in a short time subside entirely if let alone. I am afraid his moving in it will give it renewed consequence. May I ask the circumstances under which you spoke of the letter for my *private* gratification?

Giles reported yesterday,[6] though it will be some days before the Report is acted upon. I have not yet determined what course it will be prudent to observe towards it. I wish he had been permitted to come out with his reinstating scheme but he was overruled by the more prudent— The resolutions are merely declaratory. He could not have coined any *projet* which looked towards resistance— The elementes [*sic*] are not *quite* so hot here as is supposed at a distance—at least there are so many *quite* cool, that the whole mass will be kept at a moderate temperature. Nothing has given me so much pain of late, as the passage of the Manufacturers' Bill[7] *at this time*. It gives new energy to Giles & his party, and new materials for popular reclamation. I hope it may be rejected in the Senate, both on *principle*, and for the consideration I have stated. Had there been no measures of this kind I should really have had hope that this State would go against Jackson.

You have seen the Governor's election[8] & the proceedings thereon. A certain *Dr* Floyd has doctored himself to some purpose. As Jack Baker says, he is a dead corpse.[9] He has sealed his fate with the whole Western Country in his letters to Smyth,[10] which that *fool* (for he is destitute of common sense) read to the House. The members from his District, all I believe but three, are violent against him, and they say that there is some prospect of turning him out. This would make his attitude after his letters, supremely ridiculous. God accomplish it! for I abhor the man. Hoping to hear from you ere long, I remain   With great Respect,   JNO H PLEASANTS

ALS. DLC-HC (DNA, M212, R2). Addressed to Clay.
[1] Cf. above, Brooke to Clay, January 31, 1827.   [2] Cf. above, Pleasants to Clay, July 7, 1825.   [3] Thomas Ritchie; Claiborne W. Gooch.   [4] Samuel H. Davis.
[5] See above, Clay to Brooke, February 8, 1827, note.   [6] See above, Brooke to Clay, January 31, 1827, note.   [7] Proposed tariff revision in 1827, known as the woolens bill, through a series of minimum valuations applicable to both raw and manufactured wool, was more protectionist than the existing tariff. The bill had passed the House on February 10 but was tabled in the Senate on February 28 by the tie-breaking vote of Vice President John C. Calhoun. *Register of Debates,* 19 Cong., 2 Sess., pp. 496, 1098–99.
[8] The election of Giles as Governor of Virginia (see above, Brooke to Clay, February 11, 1827, note).   [9] John Floyd; Baker allusion not found.   [10] Alexander Smyth.

INSTRUCTIONS AND DISPATCHES   February 14, 1827

From ANDREW ARMSTRONG, Port au Prince. States that the national legislature met yesterday in this city and that in his message to that body the President (Jean Pierre Boyer) reported that the King of France (Charles X) has warned that any violation of the Ordinance (cf. above, Holden to Clay, July 16, 1825) would constitute "a just cause for a rupture." Notes that this news "together with the information that a large fleet was fitting out in France, has caused a great deal of commotion among the people," a "state of uneasiness" such as he has "never before witnessed in this country." Advises that there is yet considerable American property here that would be lost "in case of any thing serious taking place," unless protection were provided by American warships. ALS. DNA, RG59, Cons. Disp., Cap Haitien, vol. 6 (M9, R6). Received March 7.

From J[OEL] R. POINSETT, Mexico, no. 73. Encloses a letter from American ship masters at San Blas recommending appointment of John Hall as consul at that port. Notes that he previously forwarded a recommendation in behalf of Alexander Forbes (cf. above, Poinsett to Clay, December 13, 1826) and explains that, while it would be "preferable to have the post filled by a Citizen of the United States, still it is so important it should be filled speedily" that he hopes one of these two men will be named to the position on a provisional basis. Observes that "not one of the individuals appointed Consuls for the ports of the Pacific in Mexico, is at his post, nor has presented his commission to this government." LS. DNA, RG59, Dip. Disp., Mexico, vol. 2 (M97, R3). Received March 28. Enclosure from Seriah Eldridge and others to Poinsett, January 20, 1827, in DNA, RG59, A. and R. (M531, R4), states that Hall had engaged in commercial pursuits for several years during his residence in Mexico. He did not receive an appointment in the consular service.

Hall and Eldridge have not been further identified.

From JOHN RODGERS, "U. S. Ship N. Carolina," Malta. Expresses surprise at the neglect of "the Capudan Pacha of the Ottoman fleet" (Khosref Mehemet) to send a promised communication (cf. above, Rodgers to Clay, July 19, 1826). Suggests that this failure may "be attributed to the unfriendly reports which have lately been circulated by the Agents of certain European powers in relation to the Frigate Hope," in which they have informed the Porte that the vessel carried military supplies for the Greeks, "with the . . . sanction of . . . [the United States] Government" (cf. above, Clay to Brown, May 22, 1826, note). Notes that, "ten or fifteen days before the arrival of the Hope," the Pasha sent him "a splendid portrait of the Sultan" (Mahmud II), painted especially for Rodgers and regarded by him as "a proof of the friendly feelings entertained by the Sultan" and the Pasha toward the United States, whose "neutral character" had until then been acknowledged. Comments: "Other nations, and particularly England, . . . is [sic] becoming jealous of our increasing commerce in the Archipelago, and her agents will leave nothing undone that lying and dissimulation can effect to prevent our participating in the trade of a section of the Globe of which she had not long since almost the exclusive monopoly."

Reports that "The Capudan Pasha [sic] since his return to Constantinople is reported to be more popular than ever" and may "be appointed Grand Vizier," while the "Pacha of Smyrna [Hassan Pacha] is to be appointed Capudan Pacha." Copy. DNA, RG59. Dip. Instr., Turkey, vol. 1, pp. 36–37 (M77, R162).

From JOHN SERGEANT, Mexico, "Private." Transmits a translation of the debate in the Mexican House of Deputies concerning the salaries for their Ministers to Tacubaya, notes that the Deputies "seem to put the meeting of the Congress very much upon the pleasure of Colombia," and concludes that the opinion which rests the resumption of the (Panama) Congress upon the will of (Simón) Bolívar is "correct enough." Notes that Dr. (Pedro) Gual has expressed the view that the Congress "could not proceed effectively in less than six or seven months," although he was confident that Colombia would ratify the treaties (see above, Salazar to Clay, November 20, 1826) and return them shortly. Comments that the role of the United States in the Congress has been treated "here with little regard"

and that his own "arrival in Mexico has never been noticed in the papers. . . ."
Expresses his personal observation that, "while there is no positively unfriendly
feeling, it is equally true that there is no warm regard or respect" in the "disposition of the Mexican government towards the U. States." ALS. DNA, RG43,
Panama Congress (M662, R1). Received March 27.

MISCELLANEOUS LETTERS   February 14, 1827

From GEORGE W. SLACUM, Washington. Discusses the hostility toward himself
shown by Chargé J(ohn) M. Forbes; notes Forbes' refusal to arrange for acceptance
of (Robert) Kortright by the Buenos Aires Government as acting consul; and requests formal appointment of Kortright to that position (cf. above, Forbes to
Clay, January 5, 1827). Explains that his own return to the United States was
necessary so that he might deal with a lawsuit brought by the underwriters of
the *Merope* (cf. above, Neilson and others to Clay, February 3, 1827, note) and
settle some intestate accounts. ALS. DNA, RG59, Cons. Disp., vol. 3 (M70, R4).
Copy of Slacum's authorization for Kortright to act as consul enclosed.

From S[AMUEL] L. S[OUTHARD], Navy Department. Transmits an extract (not
found) of a letter from Robert M(onroe) Harrison, concerning the slave trade and
impressment of American seamen. LS. DNA, RG59, Misc. Letters (M179, R65).

APPLICATIONS, RECOMMENDATIONS   February 14, 1827

JOHN GEDDES, Charleston (South Carolina), apologizes for taking the liberty of
recommending Thomas Hunt, of Charleston, for "a Situation under the Government"; explains that he could not without offense withhold writing. Adds that he
solicits Clay's "friendly aid' in obtaining an appointment for himself, but not if
it would "in the remotest degree lessen . . . [the administration's] weight and influence in the *Nation*." Concludes: "I am now satisfied that the view taken by
you of our Senator Judge [William] Smith is a correct one, & that the administration has not much to expect from him, but at the same time it must be recollected
that he is to be preferred to his competitor Mr. [Daniel E.] Huger." ALS. DNA,
RG59, A. and R. (M531, R4). Marked, "private." No enclosures and no record
that either Hunt or Geddes received appointment have been found.

JOHN TALIAFERRO, Washington, recommends appointment of Henry Jackson as
secretary or clerk of the claims commission to be created to settle claims under the
Treaty of Ghent. ALS. *Ibid.* Cf. below, Clay to Ogden, March 23, 1827.

INSTRUCTIONS AND DISPATCHES   February 15, 1827

From A[LEXANDER] H. EVERETT, Madrid, no. 68. Transmits a translation of a
decree on trade which appeared in the official *Gazette*. Comments that, although
the edict is to apply to "America," only Cuba and Puerto Rico are affected and
notes that foreigners generally may now trade under the same conditions which
for years have been allowed only under special license. Suggests that the translation be published in United States newspapers "as the trade in question is
principally in the hands of our countrymen." LS. DNA, RG59, Dip. Disp., Spain,
vol. 27 (M31, R28). Received April 24.

MISCELLANEOUS LETTERS   February 15, 1827

From EDWARD BARRY, Philadelphia. Requests postponement of suit against him until he hears from the Colombian Government. ALS. DNA, RG59, Misc. Letters (M179, R65). Cf. above, Barry to Clay, May 4, 1826, and note; below, Clay to Ingersoll, February 20, 1827.

APPLICATIONS, RECOMMENDATIONS   February 15, 1827

DAVID BARTON, Washington, recommends Hamilton R. Gamble for appointment as United States attorney for the Missouri District but comments that Abiel Leonard of Franklin is "the best appointment that can be made." ALS. DNA, RG59, A. and R. (M531, R3). Cf. above, Atkinson to Clay, January 15, 1827, note. Leonard, born in Vermont and educated at Dartmouth College, had moved to Missouri and opened the practice of law in 1818. He had been appointed State prosecuting attorney in 1824 but had been removed later that year upon conviction of dueling, an offense for which he had been pardoned by private legislative act in December. He enjoyed a successful legal career and served on the State Supreme Court from 1855 to 1857.

THOMAS NEWTON [JR.], Washington, recommends appointment of Francis S. Taylor of Norfolk as clerk of "the Commission to be raised for settling claims for deported Slaves." ALS. DNA, RG59, A. and R. (M531, R8). Cf. above, Clay to McLane, January 15, 1827; below, Clay to Ogden, March 23, 1827.

JAMES H. PECK, St. Louis, recommends appointment of John Simonds, Jr., as United States marshal for the Missouri District; relates that Simonds has been serving simultaneously as deputy marshal and deputy sheriff of St. Louis County. ALS. DNA, RG59, A. and R. (M531, R7). Simonds was nominated and confirmed as marshal in December, 1827. He had previously served under a temporary appointment in place of Henry Dodge, resigned.

SPENCER PETTIS, St. Louis, recommends appointment of John Simonds, Jr., as United States marshal for the Missouri District. ALS. *Ibid.*

JOSEPH M. WHITE, Washington, recommends appointment of Henry Younge, of Quincy, Florida, as United States marshal for the Middle District of Florida and encloses the resignation of the incumbent (John M. Hanson). Urges that an appointment be made quickly "in consequence of the approaching term of that court. . . ." ALS. *Ibid.* (R8). For Hanson's resignation, see below, Hanson to Clay, February 28, 1827. On the recommended appointment, cf. above, McKinley to Clay, February 7, 1827, note. Henry Younge had been appointed to the Florida Legislative Council in 1823.

To Francis T. Brooke

My Dear Sir,   Washn. 16 Feb. 1827.
    The volume of the British acts of Parliament containing those which Genl. Taylor[1] desires is in possession of the Clerk of the H. of R.[2] We have not been able to get it back and I fear may not in time

for the use of the General. But if I can regain it, I will send it by Mail for his use.

I do not wish you to write to Govr. Tyler. It will do to speak to him when you see him. I should regret very much if he feels hurt about the letter.[3] I can only repeat that any allusion which I made to it in conversation was far from any design to prejudice him or any expectation that it shd. get into the public prints. I hope, on the other hand, that he has not permitted himself to attribute to me the violation of any confidential correspondence. His letter had nothing confidential in it. It was public in its nature, public topics were treated of, and it was addressed to a public man. It was spontaneous; and therefore more prized by me.

We have no news. Faithfully I am Yr friend   H CLAY

ALS. DLC-TJC (DNA, M212, R13). Addressed to Brooke.
[1] Robert Barrand Taylor—cf. above, Brooke to Clay, February 11, 1827.
[2] Matthew St. Clair Clarke.   [3] See above, Tyler to Clay, March 27, 1825; Clay to Brooke, February 8, 1827.

INSTRUCTIONS AND DISPATCHES   February 16, 1827

To JOHN M. FORBES, Buenos Aires. Requests that he will "make known to the Government of Buenos Ayres that the Act of Mr. Slacum in the designation which he made of Mr. Kortright to supply his place during his absence is approved by this Government, and that it would be agreeable to it, if the accustomed facilities and indulgence should be extended to him." Comments that "as soon as circumstances permit, this Department will take into consideration and decide upon the various complaints and charges which have, from time to time, been preferred" by George W. Slacum and Forbes concerning their performance of duties "as the Functionaries at the same place, of this Government. . . ." Acknowledges receipt of Forbes' dispatches through no. 42. LS, "duplicate." DNA, RG84, Argentina (MR13). L draft, in DLC-HC (DNA, M212, R8); copy, in DNA, RG59, Dip. Instr. (M77, R6). Cf. above, Slacum to Clay, February 14, 1827.

APPLICATIONS, RECOMMENDATIONS   February 16, 1827

W[ILLIAM] R. DICKINSON, Washington, recommends Francis S. Taylor, who, he has heard, is "about to ask of the Government an Office of some trust and confidence. . . ." ALS. DNA, RG59, A. and R. (M531, R8). Cf. above, Thruston to Clay, February 13, 1827; below, Clay to Ogden, March 23, 1827.

PETER LITTLE, Washington, recommends Francis S. Taylor for appointment as "secretary to the board of Commissioners about to be appointed regulating the distribution of the fund for satisfying claimants for Slaves and other property taken . . . during the late War." ALS. DNA, RG59, A. and R. (M531, R8). Cf. above, Clay to McLane, January 15, 1827; below, Clay to Ogden, March 23, 1827.

GEORGE PETER AND OTHERS recommend George Price of Frederick County, Maryland, for appointment as a clerk in the State Department. LS, signed also by Peter Little, John C. Weems, John Barney, and George E. Mitchell. DNA, RG59, A. and R. (M531, R6). Endorsement (AES) by T(homas) C(ontee) Worthington supports the recommendation. Cf. above, Clay to McLane, January 14, 1826, note; Barnard to Clay, January 10, 1827, note.

Price was a Maryland businessman.

ALFRED H. POWELL, Washington, recommends appointment of Francis S. Taylor as clerk of the slave indemnity commission. ALS. DNA, RG59, A. and R. (M531, R8).

ROBERT TAYLOR, Washington, recommends Francis S. Taylor for clerk of the projected "commission expected to be established for the distribution of the money granted under the Ghent Treaty for indemnifying those who lost slaves. . . ." ALS. *Ibid.*

R[OBERT] WASH, St. Louis, recommends appointment of John Simonds, Jr., as United States marshal for the Missouri District. ALS. *Ibid.* (R7). Cf. above, Peck to Clay, February 15, 1827, note.

Check to William R. Dickinson

17 Feb 1827

Pay to W. R. Dickinson or order Twenty four dollars.
Cashr. of the Off. of B. U. S. Washington[1]   H CLAY

ADS. DLC-TJC (DNA, M212, R16).   [1] Richard Smith.

INSTRUCTIONS AND DISPATCHES   February 17, 1827

From HEMAN ALLEN, Valparaiso, no. 49. Reports "another revolutionary Attempt, and attended with great violence," at Santiago, when Colonel (Enrique) Campino, brother of the former Minister of Foreign Relations (Joaquín Campino) entered the Hall of Congress on horseback and "demanded the dissolution of that body. . . ." States that the Congress elected General (Ramón de) Freire temporary President, with "extraordinary powers," and then "merely suspended their sessions," that the rebels were suppressed and their leaders imprisoned, and that the Congress then reconvened. Notes reports that the Congress will retain Freire as President, select General (Francisco Antonio) Pinto (Diaz) Vice President, appoint a Senate, and adjourn *sine die* without drafting a constitution. Cites the leniency of treatment accorded the leaders, who "have all been pardoned by the Congress, of any capital offence and since banished the country by the executive!" Attributes to such a policy the fact that "frequent revolutionary movements have become a sort of *common law* in Chile. . . ." Expresses doubt that Chile will send a delegate to the Panama Congress. Comments that the Chilean Congress has postponed ratification of a treaty with Buenos Aires until the provinces of the latter state have accepted the proposed constitution to establish the "Argentine Nation" (cf. above, Forbes to Clay, December 4, 1826), that "The war in the South against Pincheira has assumed of late a more favourable aspect," and that the French commercial officials (Charles A. L. de La Forest; Jean Baptiste Chaumette des Fossés) have arrived in Chile and Peru. Explains that "in consequence of some alledged [*sic*] informality in his papers," the latter agent was not received and has returned to Valparaiso "to await the orders of his government. . . ." Postscript confirms the information that Freire has been appointed President and Pinto (Diaz), Vice President and notes that the former has accepted the office. ALS. DNA, RG59, Dip. Disp., Chile, vol. 2 (M-T2, R2). Received May 30.

Pinto Diaz, born in Santiago, had begun legal practice in 1806 but had joined the Chilean movement for independence in 1810 and for the next seven years had served the revolutionary forces as a diplomatic agent, at first in Buenos Aires and from 1813 to 1817 in England. Subsequently he had fought the Spanish in Peru until 1824, when he had been appointed Chilean Minister of the Interior and Foreign Relations. Retiring from these offices, he had served briefly as Intendant of Coquimbo. He accepted the Vice Presidency in 1827 and succeeded Freire as President later that year. Re-elected in 1829, he resigned shortly thereafter under revolutionary pressures.

For the projected treaty of commerce and friendship between Chile and the United Provinces of the Rio de La Plata, signed in Santiago on November 20, 1826, see *British and Foreign State Papers, 1826–1827*, pp. 968–73. It was never ratified.

The "war in the South" concerned operations to terminate the activities of the brothers Pablo and José Antonio Pincheira, who mingled banditry with a pretense of continued support for Spain. Their raiding was centered in the Provinces of Concepción and Maule but by February, 1828, had been pushed into the Andes and Argentina. Their activities were not terminated, however, until 1832, when Pablo was killed and his brother surrendered. *British and Foreign State Papers, 1827–1828*, p. 1256; Luis Galdames, *A History of Chile*, trans. and ed. by Isaac Joslin Cox (Chapel Hill, 1941), 505.

From THOMAS L. L. BRENT, Lisbon. Reports that reinforcements sent to Oporto (cf. above, Brent to Clay, February 3, 6, 1827) have forced the Marquis of Chaves to retreat "precipitately into Spain with the loss of his artillery and about six or eight hundred men. . . ." Adds that (Sir William) Clinton and his corps of artillery and lancers have marched for Coimbra, "where most of the british [*sic*] troops had already arrived." ALS. DNA, RG59, Dip. Disp., Portugal, vol. 7 (M43, R6). Received April 23.

MISCELLANEOUS LETTERS   February 17, 1827

From JOSEPH GONSOLVE AND OTHERS, Havana. State that they, American citizens, "masters [an]d Super cargoes of vessels and residents at this place," desire the appointment of an American consul or accredited agent to Havana; express a belief that American trade with "this place" is "Second only to Liverpool"; assert that, when approached for aid in redressing grievances, "our Commercial Agent [Thomas M. Rodney] has uniformly disclaimed interference on the ground that his official capa[city] had not been recognised by this Government"; note that France and the Netherlands have consuls (Sant Iago María Angeluce; Lobe) in that port (cf. above, Wright to Clay, July 31, 1825; Everett to Clay, June 2, 1826; Gray to Clay, August 8, September 30, 1826; Rodney to Clay, August 29, 1826); and solicit the attention of the Government to their grievances. LS, signed by Gonsolve, of the ship *Anne*, and 37 others. DNA, RG59, Misc. Letters (M179, R65). Enclosed in Evans to Clay, below, March 20, 1827. Gonsolve has not been further identified.

APPLICATIONS, RECOMMENDATIONS   February 17, 1827

WILLIAM L. BRENT, House of Representatives, recommends Francis S. Taylor "as a Clerk or accountant. . . ." ALS. DNA, RG59, A. and R. (M531, R8). Unaddressed. Cf. above, Thruston to Clay, February 13, 1827; below, Clay to Ogden, March 23, 1827.

JOHN MORTON, Washington, encloses papers supporting his application for a clerkship in the State Department. ALS. DNA, RG59, A. and R. (M531, R5). Enclosures, variously dated and not addressed, include testimonials from George Bomford, W(illiam) Wade, Richard M. Johnson, Richard Cutts, James Eakin, William Lee, Tobias Watkins, Stephen Van Rensselaer, Edward Livingston, and Joshua Sands. Cf. above, Morton to Clay, February 9, 1827.

Wade, a native of New Jersey, was an officer in the Army Artillery, breveted major in 1825. Eakins, also born in New Jersey, was chief clerk of the Second Auditor's Office and served in that post until 1845.

M[ARTHA WOOD SOUTHALL (MRS. GEORGE FREDERICK)] STRAS recommends her son, Henry, a graduate of Georgetown College, as a translator for the State Department. ALS. DNA, RG59, A. and R. (M531, R7).

Mrs. Stras, born in Goochland County, Virginia, was a widow now residing in Washington. On her marriages, cf. below, McArthur to Clay, April 18, 1827. The only son identified as born of her marriage to Stras was Joseph, born in 1808 and also graduated from Georgetown College. He was admitted to the bar of Tazewell County, Virginia, in 1830. John N. Harman, *Annals of Tazewell County, Virginia* (2 vols., Richmond, 1922–1925), II, 531–32. Henry, not otherwise identified, did not receive the desired appointment.

JOHN TALIAFERRO, Washington, recommends Francis S. Taylor for appointment as secretary or clerk "to the Board which is to be organized to execute the late Convention with G. Britain." ALS. DNA, RG59, A. and R. (M531, R8). Unaddressed. Cf. above, Clay to McLane, January 15, 1827; below, Clay to Ogden, March 23, 1827.

To Foreign Ministers in the United States

To: [Circular]   Feb 18. 1827.

I have the honor to transmit herewith a copy of a letter which I have received from the Marshall [*sic*] of the District of Columbia,[1] who is charged with the duty on public occasions of preserving order in the Court yard and grounds attached to the Presidents House, accompanied by Copies of statements from persons associated with the Marshall in the performance of that duty. It appears that the Coachmen and other attendants of several of the gentlemen of the Foreign diplomatic Corps have committed acts of irregularity, and allowed themselves to address abusive language to the officers of the police, whilst engaged in the line of that duty. Being entirely sure that your servants derive no countenance, in such Misconduct, from you, I have nevertheless thought it expedient to apprise you of it, in the persuasion that you would adopt the necessary measures to prevent the recurrence of any such excesses, on the part of any of your servants.

I request that you will accept assurances of my distinguished consideration

AD draft. DNA, RG59, Misc. Letters (M179, R65). Clay had discussed the proposed circular with President Adams on February 9, 1827. Adams, *Memoirs*, VII, 223.
[1] Cf. above, Ringgold to Clay, February 7, 1827.

From Ephraim Pentland

Dr Sir,   Pittsburgh, February 18th 1827.

It is the anxious desire of a number of your friends in this city and its neighbourhood, personal as well as political, that you should visit us, in the course of the coming season, on your way to Kentucky. The excitement[1] which existed at the commencement of Mr. Adams' presidential term has almost entirely passed away—indeed, it never, at any time, extended to the more respectable part of our population. Since your last visit to this place, the population has almost doubled its numbers;[2] we have got over the terrible prostration of '17 & '18; and our manufactures have increased, and are increasing, as fast as our best friends could reasonably expect or desire: whilst our improvements in roads, bridges and canals have progressed beyond our most sanguine expectations. Our interests, public and private, are identified with those of the friends of *"domestic manufactures and internal improvement"* throughout the Union—and the next battle to be fought in good old Pennsylvania, will be between the friends of those measures and their opponents. I am glad to perceive that the opposition are willing to risk their cause and candidate upon such principles. I never did despair of Pennsylvania, notwithstanding the wild-fire which overrun [*sic*] us in '24–5.[3] Mr. A. has gained strength every day since his election; and the administration are daily improving in the affections of the people. Presuming that you will make a journey next spring or summer to Kentucky, it will do us a great deal of good, and yourself no harm, I assure you, if you would make it convenient to pass thro' here on your way; the friends of domestic manufactures & internal improvement would be glad of the opportunity at once to wipe out a foul blot from our history, and to suitably reward one of their earliest, ablest, and most consistent advocates. May we not expect you?[4] In sending you this communication, I gratify a large number of my fellow citizens, and none more than Your humle Sert. &c. with much respect, &c.   E PENTLAND.

Hon. H. Clay, Washington City.

ALS. DLC-HC (DNA, M212, R2). Pentland had learned the newspaper trade while working on the Philadelphia *Aurora* and in 1805 had started the Pittsburgh *Commonwealth*. From 1807 to 1821 he served as prothonotary of Allegheny County, and from 1821 until his death in 1839 he was employed as recorder of the mayor's court of Pittsburgh.
[1] Cf. above, Address, March 26, 1825, note.   [2] Clay had visited Pittsburgh in March, 1819; see above, II, 681–82. The population of Pittsburgh at that time was 7,248; in 1830 it totaled 12,568.   [3] Andrew Jackson had polled 35,929 votes; John Q. Adams, 5,436; William H. Crawford, 4,182; and Clay, 1,705. Klein, *Pennsylvania Politics*, 175.   [4] Reply not found. Cf. below, Clay to Shaler and Mountain, June 19, 1827.

APPLICATIONS, RECOMMENDATIONS   February 18, 1827

LETITIA (PRESTON BRECKINRIDGE GRAYSON) PORTER, Black Rock (New York), recommends her friend Mrs. Larned's son Charles for admission (to the United States

Military Academy). ALS. DNA, RG94, USMA, Cadet Application Papers, 1826/ 218. Enclosed in Clay to Barbour, February 27, 1827. Mrs. Larned was probably the wife of Charles Larned. Charles H. Larned, who later changed his name to Larnard, had been born in Rhode Island and was admitted to the Military Academy from that State on July 1, 1827. He was graduated in 1831 and remained in the Army until his death in 1854. He served in the Mexican War, when he attained the brevet rank of major for gallantry in the battles of Palo Alto and Resaca de la Palma.

GEORGE PRICE, Washington, solicits appointment as a clerk in the State Department. ALS. DNA, RG59, A. and R. (M531, R6). Misdated "1826." Cf. above, Clay to McLane, January 14, 1826, note; Barnard to Clay, January 10, 1827, note.

To Pablo Obregón

Don Pablo Obregon,
Envoy Extraordinary & Minister Plenipotentiary from Mexico.
Sir,   Department of State, Washington, 19th. Feby. 1827.
     Information having reached this City of disturbances in the Province of Texas,[1] adjoining the territory of the United States, which appears to threaten the peace of the United Mexican States, I hasten by the direction of the President to express to you the very great regret which he feels on account of the existence of those disturbances. The frankness which has ever characterized the Government of the United States, in all its intercourse with foreign powers, and the friendly feelings which it cherishes for the welfare of the Republic of the United Mexican States supersede altogether any necessity for the assurances, which nevertheless I take pleasure in making, that, the Government of the United States has not given the smallest countenance or encouragement to those disturbances. The President has directed orders to be conveyed to that portion of the Military force of the United States which is stationed on the Mexican frontier to give no aid or succor of any kind to those who have taken arms against or may oppose the authority of the Government of the United Mexican States. And he will see the restoration of tranquility with much satisfaction.
     I pray you to accept assurances of my high consideration.
                                                                H. CLAY.

Copy. DNA, RG59, Notes to Foreign Legations, vol. 3, p. 327 (M38, R3). ALI draft, in CSmH.
[1] Cf. above, Dickson to Clay, January 3, 1827, note. The Washington *Daily National Journal*, February 8, 1827, had reprinted news of the revolt in Texas as originally reported in New Orleans papers under date of January 13.

From Thomas McGiffin

My Dear Sir.   Washington[1] February 19. 1827
     The most bitter violent and unrelenting portion of the Opposition

party at Brownsville are making a desperate effort to obtain the removal of the Post Master at Brownsville who is and all his friends are, administration supporters— Jacob Bowman Esq the present incumbent and who has held the Office for thirty years without reproach or complaint, so far as regards the discharge of the duties, and who is as respectable for integrity wealth and connections as any man in our Country is to give place to a man of yesterday, whose character is not established merely because it is thought politic that the Jackson people should have the controul of the post Office— The effort is making by Stewart and Krepps[2] (a member of the Penna Legislature)— The man to whom Stewart wrote that *inflamatory* [sic] letter immediately after the Presidential Election (of which a copy was sent to you)[3] and in consequence of which letter a town meeting was held, at which this same Soln. Krepps moved the resolution approving the conduct of George Kremer[4]   These people have an abusive printing establishment under their controul[5] and finding that the friends of the Adn. are about establishing a paper, they think it all important to get hold of the Mail— The *ostensible* ground is that he lives off the Turnpike Street and that it is inconvenient and dangerous to go by his office for the mail— None of the stage owners complain— they are all as I am informed his friends— (they have all said so) and I am not aware that passengers complain— I frequently pass in the stage and the idea of *danger* never occurred to me— *It is a mere pretext*— The real disgrace is to remove a *friend* of the Adn. & get in a *Creature* of the opposition— This would be *suicidal* in any adn. and of course it is confidently believed will not be tolerated in this— "A *house* divided against itself cannot stand"[6] and if your Post Master General[7] is permitted to wield the whole force of that Department in opposition to the adn. the chance of sustaining that adn. is much lessened, if not jeopardized   On this subject I know I need not dilate it is much better understood by you than I can explain   This fact of the Post Master Genl. being some what *tinctured* with (at least Calhounism—which by the bye contains *per se* all the other *isms* is not doubted any where so far as I know and altho, it is presumed, he has long since been apprized that it is necessary that all the *party* should harmoniously act in concert, yet it is believed, he acts differently, whenever he can, without avowedly coming in *collision*— Feeling the most timely interest in the success (of at least the right arm) of the present adn. and having been permitted heretofore to speak my sentiments freely, I hope I shall be pardoned on the present occasion— I know well the delicacy of your position in regard to any interference with the discharge of duties entrusted to other departments but in regard to these matters I believe there is a law of *necessity*, of self-preservation which supersedes all laws of Courtesy and altho, it might be worse than impolitic to intermeddle directly with the Head of that Department, yet assuredly there is a *Head* over all with whom your opinions and advice will be controuling, especially as regards the *West*— As you may have observed by the proceedings of a meeting forwarded you in a news-paper,[8] we are *breaking ground* in this quarter, feebly to be sure, but I trust in such manner as will have much effect in due time— Our fundamental positions of "measures and not men" and Internal Improvements and Protection of Domestic Manufactures are received without cavil or dissint [*sic*]— all concur here & will throughout Penna.— The only difference will be as to the fact and in due time I trust this will be equally apparent to all. But if in addition to the *swell tide* of the *Huzza boys* we have to contend with the power & consequences resulting from official stations and those too conferred by the Adn. non-support, our chance of success is much impaired. This man Krepps who is so busy in controuling the Post-Office is also an applicant himself for Superintendant [*sic*] of repairs of the Cumberland Road[9]— It is most probably premature to speak on this subject as unaccountably, so far this measure has been permitted to slumber[10]— As however it may still be passed in some shape, I will take this occasion to say one word— Independant [*sic*] of all the other objections to this man— He is unqualified. He has no experience—and has not otherwise one solitary qualification which would entitle him to it— The best appointment in my sincere, deliberate judgment which could be made would be that of William Ewing Esq[11] of the neighbourhood of Brownsville— This man has experience in road making— He is a man of business—of property—of unquestioned and unquestionable integrity and honor and a firm dicided [*sic*] supporter of the Government. He is the father of the Ewing whom you saw here and also Nathl Ewing Esq. of Union Town[12]—both of whom are as repectable as any young men of their age any where   This man has been my personal and intimate friend for near twenty years and I can pledge whatever of character I have for candor and sincerity in the averment of his preeminent competency & efficiency— And I hoped [*sic*] to be pardoned when I go farther [*sic*] & say that no appointment whatever would give me as much personal gratification and none I am well convinced would ensure more public and general satisfaction—

By the introduction of those general resolutions at our meeting, I think I have obtained a position behind our principle battering-ram— The Editor[13] is with us—seconded the resolutions by previous agreement and is I think so far committed, that he cannot preserve his neutrality— This paper—the Reporter, has a controuling influence on the Politics of this County especially and has had it so long that I have no fears of the result here provided we can *get* him & *keep* him out— I have heard but one opinion expressed as to the character and import of the "ad hominem" reso[lu]tion of Saunders— And it is a matter of astonishment that they have not long since been disposed of— Our majority men have not sufficient organization and efficiency or they would not permit the minority to controul their proceedings and prevent them from doing anything for the good of the Country— It would seem to me that an efficent [sic] Leader is wanting in the house[14]— Webster[15] has no doubt many qualifications for that station—perhaps superior to any, but he does not seem to take his *Position*.

Like a good Presbyterian—after sinning, with much de[li]beration— I ask pardon and hope to be accepted as such, when I remember myself sincerely your friend   THOMAS McGIFFIN

ALS. DLC-HC (DNA, M212, R2). Addressed to Clay; endorsed on cover (AEI): "Refered [sic] to the Secy of War [James Barbour] with a request that it may be returned. H C."
[1] Pennsylvania.   [2] Andrew Stewart; Solomon G. Krepps. Bowman, a native of Maryland, retained the postmastership at Brownsville, Pennsylvania, through 1827 but had been replaced by 1829. U. S. State Dept., *Biennial Register, 1827*, p. 12; *1829*, p. 14.
[3] Not found.   [4] Cf. above, Clay to Gales and Seaton, January 30, 1825; Kremer to Clay, *ca.* February 3, 1825. Further reference to the town meeting and the Krepps resolution has not been found.   [5] Probably the Washington *Examiner*, established in 1817. See Philadelphia *Democratic Press*, July 3, 1827.   [6] Mark 3:25.   [7] John McLean.   [8] Not found.   [9] Cf. above, Dawson and others to Clay, February 14, 1827.   [10] Cf. above, Tarr to Clay, May 1, 1826, note.   [11] Ewing had moved from York County to Fayette County, Pennsylvania, as a surveyor about 1790. He had shared the contract for laying the roadbed from Brownsville to Hillsborough on the National Road.   [12] Nathaniel Ewing and, probably, John Hoge Ewing, both of whom had been graduated from Washington College in Pennsylvania and had studied law under McGiffin. Nathaniel had been admitted to the bar in 1816; his brother, in 1818. Nathaniel settled in Uniontown, Pennsylvania, in 1817, practiced law, and from 1838 to 1848 was president judge of the court of common pleas. John H. remained in Washington as McGiffin's partner for a year or two and until 1820 shared with his father the contract for laying the National Road. He became a member of the Pennsylvania House of Representatives in 1835 and 1836, the State Senate from 1838 to 1842, and the United States Congress from 1845 to 1847. Both were ardent Whigs in politics.   [13] William Sample was one of the founders and editor of the *Washington Reporter* (Pennsylvania) from 1808 to 1833, excepting the period 1819 to 1821. He sold the journal in 1833 and moved ultimately to Lee County, Iowa.   [14] On January 31, 1827, Romulus Mitchell Saunders had introduced in the House of Representatives a resolution calling upon the Secretary of State to communicate to that body lists of the newspapers designated to publish the laws of Congress in 1825, 1826, and 1827 and to state the reasons for any changes in such appointments. In the course of the ensuing debate Saunders specifically accused Clay of selecting the journals "for political and personal objects." The discussion, which continued with interruptions until February 28 and terminated without a vote on the resolution, ranged broadly, with great partisan bitterness, over the issue of control of the press. *Register of Debates*, 19 Cong., 2 Sess., pp. 895–1414 *passim* (quoted phrase on p. 896, February 1, 1827).   [15] Daniel Webster.

MISCELLANEOUS LETTERS   February 19, 1827

From GEORGE WATTERSTON. States that he and (Nicholas B.) Van Zandt are preparing "a compendious statistical view of the U. S." and plan to send a circular to "such persons in the different states as may furnish the information" required. Asks Clay's authorization "to allow the communications to be sent under cover to . . . [him], that the heavy expense of postage . . . may be avoided." Adds in postscript that Van Zandt will show Clay "the form of the circular." ALS. DNA, RG59, Misc. Letters (M179, R65).
    Clay's reply has not been found. A native of New York, Watterston served as Librarian of Congress from 1815 to 1829 and thereafter edited the Washington *National Journal*. Author of numerous literary works, including novels and poetry,

he and Van Zandt in 1828 published *Tabular Statistical Views . . . of the United States* and in 1833 supplemented their earlier work with *Continuation of the Tabular Statistical Views of the United States.* Both compilations were published under the patronage of Congress. 4 *U. S. Stat.,* 260, 321, 613.

APPLICATIONS, RECOMMENDATIONS   February 19, 1827

DAVID KIZER, Baltimore, notes that he was an unsuccessful candidate for United States marshal in Maryland (cf. above, Williams to Clay, October 22, 1825, note) and now solicits the consulship in Liverpool. Argues that one who is young, poor, and a veteran should replace James Maury, who is old, rich, and not a former soldier. Cites letters of recommendation in his behalf from "Genl." (Jacob) Brown and S(amuel) L. Southard written about December 12, (1826—not found). ALS. DNA, RG59, A. and R. (M531, R4). Kizer, a Pennsylvanian who had served as a lieutenant during the War of 1812, received no appointment during the Adams administration.

C[HARLES] F[ENTON] MERCER, Washington, introduces (Richard H.) Love, born in his district (Loudon County, Virginia) but long a resident of Culpeper County; identifies him also as a son-in-law of Ludwell Lee of "Belmont," in Loudon County. Notes that Love is a candidate for any vacancy in Clay's Department, alludes to the probable passage of legislation authorizing an additional number of clerks (cf. above, Clay to McLane, January 14, 1826, note; Smith to Clay, February 10, 1827), and asserts that, while this development has prompted the present application, Love's "pretensions have been before submitted to the President. . . ." ALS. *Ibid.* (R5). Enclosed in Love to [Clay], March 1, 1827.

Love's file includes letters, dated in 1825 and addressed to Adams, recommending the Virginian as register of the land office in East Florida. He had married Eliza Matilda Lee, his first cousin, in 1811. On the recommended appointment to a clerkship, cf. above, Barnard to Clay, January 10, 1827, note.

JAMES NOBLE AND OTHERS, Washington, recommend appointment of Davis Floyd as secretary of Florida Territory. ALS by William Hendricks, signed also by Noble, John Test, R(atliff) Boon, and Jonathan Jennings. DNA, RG59, A. and R. (M531, R3). Enclosed in Hendricks to Clay, February 20, 1827. On the requested appointment, cf. above, Mercer to Clay, January 23, 1827, note.

JAMES ORD, Washington, solicits appointment to one of the additional clerkships expected to be created during the present Session of Congress. States that he is from Allegany County, Maryland, that he moved his family to Washington in 1819, and that on occasion he has been employed temporarily in the State Department. ALS. DNA, RG59, A. and R. (M531, R6). On the requested appointment cf. above, Barnard to Clay, January 10, 1827, note; below, Clay to Ogden, March 23, 1827, note. Ord, an officer in the War of 1812, had been appointed justice of the peace for Washington County, Maryland, in 1822 and reappointed on February 8, 1827. The magisterial appointment was renewed again in 1832 and 1837.

Check to Tobias Watkins

20h. Feb. 1827.

Pay to Dr. T. Watkins or order Two hundred dollars.
Cashr. of the Off. of B. U. S. Washington.[1]   H. CLAY

ANS. DLC-TJC (DNA, M212, R16). The payment may have been made in behalf of John Martin Baker. On February 9 Daniel Brent had written to Watkins in reply to a communication of February 8 (not found). Brent stated that Clay declined acceptance of Baker's bill and refused to give an order to collect it from his salary. Copy, in DNA, RG59, Dom. Letters, vol. 21, p. 478 (M40, R19).

1 Richard Smith.

DIPLOMATIC NOTES   February 20, 1827

From PABLO OBREGÓN, Mexican Legation, Washington. Acknowledges receipt of Clay's letter (above, February 19, 1827) respecting "the seditious commotion in Texas." States that he will forward the communication to his Government. LS, in Spanish with trans. in State Dept. file. DNA, RG59, Notes from Foreign Legations, Mexico, vol. 1 (M54, R1).

INSTRUCTIONS AND DISPATCHES   February 20, 1827

From ALEXANDER BURTON, Cádiz. Encloses a copy of a royal order issued "on the 9th instant, allowing foreign vessels to carry on the commerce between Spain and her American possessions, without the necessity of a special Licence for each vessel, as has heretofore been the case." ALS. DNA, RG59, Cons. Disp., Cádiz, vol. 4 (M-T186, R4). Received April 14. Cf. above, Everett to Clay, February 15, 1827.

MISCELLANEOUS LETTERS   February 20, 1827

To CHARLES J[ARED] INGERSOLL, Philadelphia. States the wish of the President (John Quincy Adams) that, should Ingersoll obtain a judgment against Edward Barry, surety for (Juan Gualberto de) Ortega, he "forbear to enforce its execution, 'till further directions from this Department." Copy. DNA, RG59, Dom. Letters, vol. 21, p. 484 (M40, R19). Cf. above, Barry to Clay, February 15, 1827. On February 20, also, Daniel Brent transmitted to Barry a copy of Clay's letter to Ingersoll. Copy, in DNA, RG59, Dom. Letters, vol. 21, p. 485 (M40, R19).

From SAMUEL ALLINSON, Gibraltar. Complains about the conduct of B(ernard) Henry, United States consul at this port. Charges that Henry has damaged the credit and business operations of the firm of Scotto and Allinson, American merchants at Gibraltar; that he has neglected the interests of American seamen and travelers, including "the amiable relict & family of the late Excellent C[aesar]. A. Rodney" and the widow of Major (Townshend) Stith, while displaying marked deference to Britons; and that he has disregarded the interests of the United States in performing his official duties as consul and, during the frequent absences of (Richard) McCall, as Naval agent, specifically by supplying spoiled butter to a warship and by selling American bills of exchange at unnecessarily heavy discounts. Presents notarized documents relating to the origin of the quarrel with Henry and cites John Mullowny as one who can testify "that Mr. Henry did, even in writing, endeavour to degrade the Character, & blacken the reputation" of Mrs. Stith. ALS. DNA, RG59, A. and R. (M531, R4—Bernard Henry file). Received April 18 and endorsed by Clay: "To be submitted to the President." No reply found; cf. below, Allinson to Clay, December 24, 1827. The accompanying documents, two depositions by Bartholomew Scotto and a third by Emanuel Gonzales de Estrada, all dated March 2, 1827, with a certification of the signatures of the notary, by Bernard Henry, dated March 6, 1827, are filed in DNA, RG59, Cons. Disp., Gibraltar, vol. 3 (M-T206, R-T3).

Allinson, of Burlington, New Jersey, was a merchant and brewer. He served as consul at Lyons, France, from 1831 to 1835 and from 1839 to 1843. Bartholomew Scotto, Allinson's mercantile partner since 1824, was a native of Gibraltar and had been Allinson's consignee there since 1820.

Mrs. Rodney, née Susan Hunn of Philadelphia, had been with her husband in Buenos Aires at his death in June, 1824. She and the family had arrived at New Castle, Delaware, in the brig *America*, from Buenos Aires, in early September of that year. *Niles' Weekly Register*, XXVII (September 11, 1824), 32. Apparently the sailing route had touched at Gibraltar.

Townshend Stith, of Virginia, an officer in the War of 1812, had served as United States consul at Tunis from 1819 to 1823. In failing health he had left his post for Mahón in August, 1823, and died before the end of the year. His wife was the former Katharine Potter of Philadelphia.

APPLICATIONS, RECOMMENDATIONS   February 20, 1827

N[ICHOLAS] BRICE AND OTHERS recommend (William) Fromentin Winder, "Son of the late General [William H.] Winder," for a clerkship in the State Department, "or in any of the departments of the government wherein his services may be useful. . . ." LS, signed also by 13 other residents of Baltimore. DNA, RG59, A. and R. (M531, R8). Undated; probably enclosed in Webster to Clay, below this date.

Brice, educated as a lawyer, was long prominent in Baltimore civil affairs, one of the founders in 1796 of the Library Company, active in the 1820's in the work of the Baltimore Bible Society and in formation (in 1829) of a Temperance Society. With the formation of the Baltimore city court in 1816, he had been named chief judge; he remained on the bench for more than 30 years.

On the identification of young Winder, cf. above, Breckinridge to Clay, October 20, 1826; below, Winder to Clay, [*ca.* February 20, 1827]. On the recommended appointment, cf. above, Clay to McLane, January 14, 1826, note; Barnard to Clay, January 10, 1827, note.

WILLIAM HENDRICKS, Senate Chamber, encloses a letter recommending Davis Floyd for appointment as secretary of Florida Territory; comments that according to (Joseph M.) White the choice has been made; but adds that if the recommendation "should do no good it can do no harm." ALS. DNA, RG59, A. and R. (M531, R3). See above, Noble and others to Clay, February 19, 1827.

JOHN O'FALLON, St. Louis, recommends appointment of John Simonds (Jr.) as United States marshal for the Missouri District. Praises Simonds' qualifications and concludes: "What is to me of the first importance, he is a uniformly devoted and active friend of the administration of the General Govt." ALS. DNA, RG59, A. and R. (M531, R7). Cf. above, Peck to Clay, February 15, 1827, note.

DANIEL WEBSTER notes that some Baltimore friends have asked that he support the application of "Genl. [William H.] Winder's son [William Fromentin Winder]" and that he has confidence in their recommendation. ALS. DNA, RG59, A. and R. (M531, R8). Year undated. Cf. above, Brice and others to Clay, this date; Winder to Clay, this date.

WILLIAM F[ROMENTIN] WINDER makes application "In the event of a vacancy, or in the Contemplation of an increase of clerks in . . . [Clay's] Department. . . ." ALS. DNA, RG59, A. and R. (M531, R8). Undated. On the dating, cf. above, Webster to Clay, this date.

From Spencer D. Pettis

Dr. Sir   St. Louis. Feby. 21. 1827.

In consequence of my absence and that of Colo. Sullivan[1] from this place I have not until to day, had an opportunity of settling with him the business between us. arising out of your claim against Majr. Graham[2]

I readily acceded to your proposition to leave the question of my fee to honorable men   It was left to Messrs E. Bates & J Spalding[3] (gentlemen chosen by Col. S.) and they decided that the fee should be $150 instead of $200. I acquiesce, altho my opinion is not changed, and I suppose you will do the same notwithstanding yours may not be altered   I still think my charge was right

I have therefore corrected the error you pointed out and paid Col. S. the sum coming to you which is $50:98. You will see by the annexed statement that I have charged you with 2/3. of all costs. It appears by a paper you sent to Col S. that in the case of Bledsoe vs. Graham,[4] the credit should have been $110 instead of $150. I followed your instructions in this business and Bledsoes letter of 1811. mentioned $150. By that I was governed

The receipts given by me were for the sums paid only; and the judgments yet stand for the balance   Graham says he will not pay more unless compelled   Your instructions will be followed.

The letter from Bledsoe I have no doubt was genuine and indeed was proved by Walker Reid esq. of Maysville   I therefore supposed that all was right— Be pleased to acknowledge the recipt [*sic*] of this.

I have the Honor to be Sir respectfully Your Obdt Servt

                                          SPENCER PETTIS

[Enclosure]

Statement

Amt of H Clays. judgt vs. Graham		$499.14
Do. Bledsoe Do .. Do.		199.64
(after deducting credits)		698 78

Costs of former suit	$9.69		
Pltffs pt of costs of present suit.	22.20		
My fee as *fixed by referees*	150 00		
2/3 of this sum	$181.89–	is–	121.26
		leaves–	577 52
	7h July. 1826–pd Col. Sul.		526-54
	pd. Col. Sullivan this day–		$ 50 98
			50.98

ALS. DLC-TJC (DNA, M212, R13). Addressed to Clay; cover endorsed by Clay: "Answd. 21st. March 1827." The answer has not been found.

1 John C. Sullivan.   2 Richard Graham. Cf. above, Clay to Sullivan, June 12, 1826.   3 Edward Bates and Josiah Spalding.   4 Not found, probably involving Jesse Bledsoe.

DIPLOMATIC NOTES   February 21, 1827

From José SILVESTRE REBELLO, Washington. States that Captain (James) Biddle of the United States frigate *Macedonian* removed two seamen from the (French brig) *La Junon,* which had been captured and brought to Rio de Janeiro. Admits that the two seamen may be American citizens but protests that Biddle violated "the Laws of Nations" by taking such action without first applying to competent authorities of the Brazilian Government. Suggests that his case is analogous to the incident in the West Indies in which the United States satisfied Spanish complaints by court martialing the offending officer (David Porter—cf. above, Nelson to Clay, April 6, 1825, note). Says he will entrust "the quality of the satisfaction" to the United States. ALS, in Portuguese with trans. in State Department files. DNA, RG59, Notes from Foreign Legations, Brazil, vol. 1 (M49, R1). For Clay's reply, see below, Clay to Rebello, March 22, 1827.

INSTRUCTIONS AND DISPATCHES   February 21, 1827

From A[LEXANDER] H. EVERETT, Madrid, no. 69. Relates that he has been informed by the Saxon minister here (Julius Traugotte de Koenneritz) that (Frederick Augustus) Mensch has been appointed his country's consul at New York and (Charles Augustus) Davis has been designated its consul general for the United States; declares that this arrangement is satisfactory to him and will probably be so to Davis (cf. above, Everett to Clay, December 17, 1826); states that the matter should no longer affect recognition. Postscript notes enclosure of a translation of a Spanish decree, just issued, which calls for conscription of 25,000 men, a measure which has been interpreted "as an indication of the spirit of the Govt.," since it is "equivalent to the raising of an army . . . entirely de novo"; reports renewed negotiations between (Frederick James) Lamb and (Manuel Gonzáles) Salmón on the British and Portuguese demand for removal of the captain-general of Castille (Francisco Longa), new promises of a change in command, but no word that it has been effected; comments that the abundance of money available here "creates some doubt of the good faith of France towards England"; notes that the (Portuguese) refugees have retreated for a third time into Spain and may not "be as cordially received and as amply supplied as before"; but concludes that the British may "have reason to regret that they committed themselves so far in this business," since "The Constitution is said to be unpopular in Portugal & the British still more so." LS, postscript in Everett's hand. DNA, RG59, Dip. Disp., Spain, vol. 27 (M31, R28).

From J[OEL] R. POINSETT, Mexico, no. 74. Reports changes in the Mexican cabinet: (Manuel) Rincon replaces (Manuel) Gomez Pedraza as War Minister; (Tomás) Salgado probably will take (José Ignacio) Esteva's position as Treasury Minister; and (José Miguel) Ramos Arizpe, Minister of Grace and Justice, is under pressure from Congress to resign. Expresses confidence in Salgado, who has served as "Juez of Hacienda—an office answering to that of our Comptroller. . . ." Observes that Congress has taken up the conspiracy "of some monks and European Spaniards to overturn the existing order of things" and comments that the plot had little chance of success (cf. above, Sergeant to Clay, January 26, 1827, note). Reviews late news from Texas: (Richard) Fields, (Benjamin) Edwards, and John (Dunn) Hunter are said to be the leaders of the insurrection; they have made Nacogdoches their head-quarters; the movement claims independence for Texas as far west as the Rio Bravo del Norte and involves about 50 whites and 1,000 Indians (cf. above, Dickson to Clay, January 3, 1827, note). Notes that the (Mexican) House of Representatives voted $500,000 "to defray the expenses of quelling this insurrec-tion, and in debate in secret session, some of the ignorant members did not hesi-tate to express their opinion that the Government of the United States was privy to this movement—if, indeed, it had not encouraged it." Expresses his belief that "the true cause of discontent . . . [is], the fear entertained by these people that the Mexican Government is about to liberate all the slaves in the Commonwealth." States that (Vicente) Rocafuerte arrived at Veracruz on "the 16th instant" with a commercial treaty concluded in London between Great Britain and Mexico (cf. above, Gallatin to Clay, December 16, 1826, note). LS. DNA, RG59, Dip. Disp., Mexico, vol. 2 (M97, R3). Received April 2.

Manuel Rincon served as War Minister from February 10 to March 3, 1827 (cf. above, Rochester to Clay, January 31, 1827, note); Tomás Salgado succeeded Esteva, who resigned on March 4, 1827; Ramos Arizpe did not relinquish the Ministry of Justice until March 8, 1828. Bancroft, *Works*, XIII, 36n.

Richard Fields, half-breed chief of the Cherokee tribe in east Texas, had sought to establish a separate nation under Mexican sovereignty. Failing to receive a tribal land grant, he plotted with Anglo-American settlers to overthrow Mexican authority and partition Texas between the Indian and white races. His tribe, how-ever, refused to support the Americans in the Fredonian revolt (see above, Dick-son to Clay, January 3, 1827, note) and on May 8, 1827, executed Fields and his chief adviser, John Dunn Hunter.

From W[ILLIAM] TUDOR, Lima, no. 59. Reviews public reaction in various parts of Peru to the revolt of January 26 (see above, Tudor to Clay, February 3, 1827) and finds widespread support for the rejection of the Bolivian Constitution; ex-presses belief that Colombian troops in Bolivia will follow the lead of their coun-terparts in Lima; describes Bolívar's public abjurance of seizing power as "almost ludicrous" in the light of his ambitious plans. Reports that he has learned from a Colombian officer (unnamed) that the Government of Colombia has concluded that no measure short of armed resistance will prevent usurpation (by Bolívar) and "has agreed to the adjournment of Congress till the year 1828, then to take up the subject of amendments [to the Constitution]." ALS. DNA, RG59, Cons. Disp., Lima, vol. 1 (M154, R1). Extract published in Manning (arr.), *Diplomatic Correspondence . . . Latin-American Nations*, III, 1823–25. Received June 21.

MISCELLANEOUS LETTERS   February 21, 1827

From MICHAEL WITHERS, Baltimore. Complains of "An unprecedented hostility, long continued, and insatiable," directed against himself by (William) Thornton, Superintendent of the Patent Office. Explains that he obtained a patent on August 24, 1813, "for an improvement in the Winged Gudgeon," which he patented originally April 13, 1804, and for which he is prepared to establish a claim as in-ventor "even many years earlier"; that shortly after he received the later patent, Thornton issued numerous statements to the effect that he (Withers) was an imposter; that consequently users of the invention have "very generally refused to pay the premiums" owed to him; that, although he won a suit in the Federal District Court at Baltimore challenging the validity of his rights, Thornton has continued to publish notices identifying him as an imposter; and that, since his patent has less than six months to run, he (Withers) is taking steps to defend his reputation, by judicial decision and by appeal for Clay's "interference" to shield him "from the weight and influence" of Thornton's office. Notes that judicial process would be so slow that such action would entail "a total loss of . . . patent right, by expiration; while his [Thornton's] inability forbids all hope of indemnity in damages." Suggests "that a formal disclaimer by the superintendent, with . . . [Clay's] disavowal of his authority and competency, would be most satisfactory" and that, in such an event, he would "have no inclination to urge an action against him [Thornton]." Requests six certified copies "of the patent under the proper seal which the superintendent has refused to grant" and for which "the customary fees" are enclosed. ALS. DNA, RG59, Misc. Letters (M179, R65). Copy, in MHi-Adams Papers, Letters Recd. (MR479); published in Washington *Daily National Journal*, April 24, 1827. Endorsed on cover, AE in hand of Daniel Brent: "Mr Clay wishes the Doctor to read the within Charges against him, and to offer what he has to say, in justification of the course he has taken— Mr. Clay is of opinion that Withers is entitled to copies of his Patent, upon paying for them: and he sends ten dolls now for that purpose." Endorsed on cover, AES by William Elliot: "When Mr. Withers was shown the drawing in Mr. Oliver Evans book of the Mill Gudgeon, he did not make any remarks that there was any difference between that and his." In a supplementary endorsement, AEI by Elliot, it was noted that Withers had claimed the invention antedated Evans'. The reference was probably to Oliver Evans, *The Young Mill-Wright Miller's Guide, in Five Parts—Embellished with Twenty-five Plates . . .* (Philadelphia, 1795).

Further endorsements, AEI by W(illiam) T(hornton), refer Clay to a "Decision of the Court in Virginia [not found], where the Patentee proved himself the Inventor of the Tobacco Boats on the Potomak & James River [*sic*]. . . ," and note that the Secretary of War (James Barbour) "complains of the injuries suffered by this Fellow & his agents in Virga."

Withers, formerly of Stroudsburg, Pennsylvania, claimed to be the inventor of an improvement in the gudgeon mill. His patent, dated April 30 (not 13), 1804, was issued for a device used in "hulling clover seed." Edmund Burke (comp.), *List of Patents for Inventions and Designs . . .* (Washington, 1847), 13, 254. In a sworn deposition printed in the Washington *Daily National Journal*, April 24, 1827, Withers claimed that he had invented the "Winged Gudgeon" in the 1780's.

The Federal suit, to which Withers referred, had been brought by Caleb Kirk, to vacate Withers' patent. Heard in the District Court of Maryland on June 5, 1817, the action had been dismissed. *Niles' Weekly Register*, XII (June 28, 1817), 282–84; transcript of the case included in documents accompanying Withers to Clay, below, March 22, 1827. Withers also enclosed in the latter communication a clipping from the *Baltimore Patriot* of February 21, 1827, reprinted from the *Lancaster Gazette*, Pennsylvania, a letter by Thornton, dated December 15, 1826, warning the public against Withers as an imposter.

For related correspondence, see below, Causten to Clay, March 1, 1827; Withers to Clay, March 5, 22, April 16, 1827; Thornton to Clay, March 8, 1827; Clay to Withers, March 9, 1827.

APPLICATIONS, RECOMMENDATIONS   February 21, 1827.

J[OHN] S[TRODE] BARBOUR, House of Representatives, encloses a letter from (Sidney F.) Chapman of Fauquier (County, Virginia); reminds Clay of Chapman's desire for an executive appointment, particularly in Clay's service. ALS. DNA, RG59, A. and R. (M531, R2). Enclosure not found.

Barbour, born in Culpeper County, Virginia, and graduated from the College of William and Mary, had been admitted to the bar in 1811 and served in the War of 1812. He had been a member of the State legislature from 1813 to 1816 and from 1820 to 1823, was a member of Congress from 1823 to 1833, and returned to the State legislature in 1833 and 1834. He was a cousin of James and Philip Pendleton Barbour.

On Chapman's appointment, see below, Clay to Cutts, *ca.* March 31, 1827.

THOMAS BIDDLE, St. Louis, recommends appointment of John C. Sullivan as (Federal) marshal for Missouri. Notes that the latter has "advantageously filled" office as "A member of the [State Constitutional] Convention, a member of the Legislature, Colonel of Militia & Judge of the [St. Louis] County. . . ." Comments: "The want of integrity in so many of the public Agents employed in this Country is a matter of much regret to all of its best friends   The loss sustained by the Government from the unfaithfulness of public Agents is, in amount, enormous: and I am extremely sorry to add that delinquents have not been pursued, with that energy & vigour which the interest & reputation of the Country appear to require, or have flagrant wrongs to the public Treasury been followed by a withdrawal of confidence or discontinuance of employment." ALS. DNA, RG59, A. and R. (M531, R7).

A native of Philadelphia and an officer in the War of 1812, Biddle had moved to St. Louis in 1820, where he became paymaster of troops in that place. He died in 1831 from a wound received in a duel with Spencer Pettis, who was also killed in the fight. Biddle was a brother of Nicholas Biddle. On the recommended appointment, cf. above, Peck to Clay, February 15, 1827, note.

JOHN BUCHANAN, Frederick (Maryland), recommends George Price "of this county" for one of the projected additional clerkships in the State Department. ALS. DNA, RG59, A. and R. (M531, R6). Cf. above, Clay to McLane, January 14, 1826, note; Barnard to Clay, January 10, 1827, note.

From Marquis Barnett

Nelson Cty Ky 22d Feby 1827

Dear Sir—I have made free to write you a line on the subject of the presidential election— I hope you will excuse me in making thus free when I inform you that I was born & raised in and about Lexington and learned the art of printing with W. W. Worsley[1]— The presidential question is much discussed by our back woods politicians at this time and I have been compelled owing to this to think a great deal about the matter. I find that the illiterate or unthinking part of mankind are easily led away by sounding names; the brave warrior the hero of N. Orleans, &c[2] pass very current with that class of mankind; & Mr. Adams[3] being from a nonslave holding state is talked of by some as a kind of raw head and bloody bones; a western president has its charm too; all this added together with unremitted exertions on the part of the Jacksonites sending to and fro their United states Telegraph Duff Green editor. I know of men who have received this paper who could not read nor write "please hand this to your neighbors" on the margin. The printer at Elizabethtown[4] in this state at first came out an administration man; a Mr. Shelton[5] who offered his services some time past as a candidate for congress (a Jackson man) in opposition to Dr Wm. Young[6] has been at work with him for some time; at length Mr. Shelton wrote a letter to Gen. Jackson & received another packed full of something, no one knows what, and the next day out came our editor a Jackson man— I have been warmly solicited by several of the citizens of the place to establish an opposition paper in favor of the administration at that place but I have not the capital or I would immediately accede to their proposition.— there is no doubt at this time a majority in that district in favor of the administration   at all events the most influential part are,   they are working industriously on the ignorant; this Shelton is a powerful man on the stump, having once been a baptist preacher but finding it a slow way of getting along has become a lawyer— In the district represented by C. A. Wickliff [sic][7] Esq the leading prints are for Jackson but the people are for the administration

Whilst Mr. Adams is assiduously engaged in public business at Washington Jackson and his friends are straining every nerve to put him out and place themselves in office   This I have seen for some time and is more and more apparent in our section every day and I declare to you sir that want of funds is the only barrier that prevents me at this time from marching out in the cause of my country for I believe that should such a man as Gen Jackson get to be president he might almost revolutionize the government and I have no doubt he would make the experiment; look at the Washington of South America as he has been styled (Boliver [sic])[8] and that is enough to make N. Americans fear military men   when power is placed in their hands; there is some exceptions it is true, but the conduct of Jackson in the case of Arbuthnot and Ambrister[9] and many others is enough to convince any rational being that he would be a dangerous man to trust with much power. Mr. Adams was not my first choice for president   I prefered [sic] yourself or Mr. Crawford[10] to him; general Jackson was the last man whom I would have chosen on the ticket—

Excuse the disconnected manner in which I have written as I assure you it was done in haste   the reason which induced me to write was to give you an idea of the unfair manner in which they are carrying on the electioneering campaign in this section of Kentucky   I assure you sir that I am your warm friend and have always exerted my feeble talent in your behalf and hope I shall never have occasion to do otherwise. I feel proud to think a Kentuckian fills so high a station and with such honor to himself   Yours truly   M. BARNETT

ALS. DNA, RG59, Misc. Letters (M179, R65). Postmarked at Bardstown, Kentucky; addressed to Clay. Barnett had formerly edited the *Bardstown Repository*.
1 William W. Worsley.   2 Andrew Jackson.   3 John Quincy Adams.
4 Charles W. Hutchen, editor of the Elizabethtown, Kentucky, *Western Intelligencer*.
5 Thomas Chilton.   6 William S. Young, of Elizabethtown.   7 Charles A. Wickliffe, of Bardstown.   8 Simón Bolívar.   9 Alexander Arbuthnot; Robert C. Ambrister. See above, II, 612n, 664–46, 648–51, 660n–61n.   10 William H. Crawford.

From Porter Clay

Dr Brother   Frankfort 22 February 1827

Your favour of the 3rd inst[1] come to hand in due time and I heartily
thank you for the valuable inclosures particularly your speach before
the Colonization society,[2]   your views upon that subject have my
most hearty concurance and I pray almighty God may bless the institution with his approbation and make it the means of Extending
the light of this glorious Gospell [sic] into that benighted land, that
Etheopia may streach out her hand to God and the Isles of the see be
made to rejoice in the fullness of his free salvation   you are right whe
[sic] you say "that God may convert that which has been our great
sinn [sic] into an extencive blessing to that people"— not that we
shoud [sic] be incouraged to do evil that Grace may abound, God forbid—for how then should God judge the wourld—but that he through
his all wise providence should get to himself a revenue of Glory by
that which in us was originally wicked. But I think in your arguments
in relation to the Practicability of the scheeme you have omited [sic]
one very strong point in which that subject might be viewed which is
this: when the colony shall have increased so much as to make it an
object of the merchantile and commercial portion of our community,
to have traiding establishments there, the natural increase of wealth
amongst the colonist [sic] themselves will enable them to participate
very greatly in the expence of transporting there own connexions,
this Idea probably would have but little wait in the present estimate
of Expence but by a recurance to the history of our own country it
will be found that the natural ties of kindred, brougt [sic] from the
shores of europe to our own country the largest portion of emigrants,
and that increased as fast as the wealth and population of our country
increased and indeed it is yet a stimuluus [sic] that excites to vigorous
effort most of the emigants [sic] that are pressing into our beloved
country from all parts of the wourld.

I have watched with some little attention here lately, the movements of our political men and I never was more at a loss to make up
an opinion as to the point to which they are stearing in my life,   Indeed my Brother there is more corruption in our country at this time
than ever was at any former period of our history. The fact is that
the examples of base depravity have been so frequent and advocated
so openly that even those whose integrity was unshaken before are
furnished with excuses now to gratify either their ambition or vanity
in any way howevr [sic] inconsistant and then plead the example of
others in there Justification   F.P.B.[3] whome you thought was unshaken in his attachments to the administration as any man living
and in a particular manner to you personally is now the avowed
enemy not only of administration but of yourself   C.H. Allen[4] after

making a strong speach in the senate on one day in favour of the Admn. the next he is the avowed enemy and indeed two or three of the senators from Green river came up here friends to the adm and went away hostile to it,   I believe that the great body of the People are with the administration and were they let alone would remain so, but you know the excitability of the people of Kentucky and how easy they can be inflaimed upon political subject [*sic*], and when the Demegogus [*sic*] can once get them arroused you might as well attempt to control the currant of the Mississippi— It is confidently asserted here that Fayette will give a majoriety for Jackson and as changes are so frequent I do not know what to think   B Harrison[5] has declined a poll for congress in the Jefferson district   he appeard very zelous dureing the Session in favour of the admn.   it is possible that he may have changed about,   the fact is I never had much confidence in him as a politition in my life and you know we were Boys togeather about the time you came to Key   There is another consideration to be taken into the estimate— the friends of Jackson are desperat [*sic*] and clamerous and consequently active while the friends of the admn. are inactive and luke warm and with out any concert   you must certainly come out early this year and spend as much time with us as you can spair and if an organized effort can be made I shall not fear the result

I forwarded a coppy of Haggans bill in my last[6] which you must have received before now and you will give what instructions you think best— I have received $19 in Commonwealth money for nearly two months hire for Aaron[7]   he asked me for a pass to go to Lexington about the first of this month and I have not heard from him since— I wrote to Mr. Scott[8] to hire him out in that place if he could, but have not learnt whether he has gotten a place for him or not

we are all well and desire to be remembered affectionately to Lucretia & family   yours sincerely   P. CLAY

ALS. DLC-TJC (DNA, M212, R10). Addressed to Henry Clay.   [1] Not found.
[2] Above, January 20, 1827.   [3] Francis Preston Blair.   [4] Charles H. Allen.
[5] Burr Harrison. Cf. above, Denny to Clay, January 16, 1827.   [6] Probably James Haggin. Porter Clay's letter of January 8, 1827, mentions no enclosure; no intervening correspondence has been found.   [7] Aaron Dupuy.   [8] Robert Scott.

Bill from John Gadsby

[*ca.* February 22, 1827]
NATIONAL HOTEL WASHINGTON CITY
Honble. H. Clay To John Gadsby Dr.
February 1827
22nd. To Subscription to the Birth-Night ball $5.00

[Endorsed][1] Recd. payt. for J. Gadsby   P. Brady

AD, in hand of Peter Brady. DLC-TJC (DNA, M212, R16).   [1] AES.

INSTRUCTIONS AND DISPATCHES   February 22, 1827

From J[OHN] J. APPLETON, Stockholm, no. 11. Encloses a copy of the speech delivered by the King (Charles XIV) upon opening the Norwegian Storthing. Notes that "the changes in the Constitution formerly proposed by the King are alluded to in a tone of sufficient earnestness, tho' it bespeaks no great confidence in the disposition of the Storthing to adopt them" (cf. Appleton to Clay, above, January 29, 1827; below, March 25, 1827). Points out that references to relations with Prussia confirm the information transmitted in his last dispatch (February 10, 1827). Observes that the King mentions his desire to continue in operation the expired treaty with the United States (cf. above, Clay to Appleton, January 12, 1827, note). States that the speech alludes to current negotiations for commercial treaties with the new American states but that he is not aware "that any thing of the Kind is in treaty here" (cf. below, Appleton to Clay, March 25, 1827). ALS. DNA, RG59, Dip. Disp., Sweden and Norway, vol. 5 (M45, R-T6). Received May 6. Enclosed is a printed copy of *Discours du Roi, à l'ouverture du Storthing du Royaume de Norvège, à Christiania, le 12 Fébrier 1827.*

From ANDREW ARMSTRONG, Port au Prince. Refers to his dispatch of (January) 16 (1827) in which he reported that French shipping had been placed on equal footing with that of other nations regarding export duties; relates that the French Chargé has declared this a violation of the "Ordonnance" (cf. above, Holden to Clay, July 16, 1825, and note); and expresses belief that the export duties will be abolished. Comments that French trade does not interfere with American interests, that the French advantage is merely nominal. ALS. DNA, RG59, Cons. Disp., Cap Haitien, vol. 6 (M9, R6). Received March 21.

J. B. Maler had been appointed Chargé d'Affaires and consul general for France in Haiti in the autumn of 1825. From 1815 to 1822 he had served as French Chargé in Rio de Janeiro.

From ALBERT GALLATIN, London, no. 58. Reports that he wrote a private note to (Henry U.) Addington, asking that their conferences be resumed, and encloses a copy of a letter from (William) Huskisson to Addington by which the latter replied. Comments that, while Huskisson "is still indisposed," other factors may explain the delay—the fact that Huskisson's "measures are strongly attacked by the shipping interest and from other quarters" and the revelation in the tonnage reports for 1826, of which a statement is enclosed, "that it is not in the intercourse with the United States alone that, when placed on a footing of equality, the British cannot stand the competition of foreign shipping," but that, excluding "countries that have no navigation (Russia, Spain, Portugal, and Turkey) and the British colonies," in trade "with the rest of the world, the ratio of British to Foreign tonnage employed is about two to three."

Notes that (George) Canning "is recovering from a serious indisposition" (see above, Gallatin to Clay, February 6, 1827, note); that Lord Liverpool, "the principal bond of Union of the present Cabinet," may "survive and linger" but that his political life is ended; that the King (George IV) is averse to change; that each party in the Cabinet is opposed "to the introduction of a new member not of their own colour"; and concludes that (Frederick John) Robinson will be "transferred to the House of Lords, or that some man of high rank and considered as of no party & of no importance will be made the nominal Premier." Predicts that "there cannot be any important progress" in the negotiations until these Cabinet difficulties are resolved and that American affairs "are not likely to be affected by the result whatever it may be," because the Cabinet dissension relates "to internal objects, (the Catholic question, Corn laws &c) and not to the foreign policy of the Country." LS. DNA, RG59, Dip. Disp., Great Britain, vol. 33 (M30, R29). Copy, in NHi-Gallatin Papers (MR14). Received April 13. In his letter to Addington, dated February 16, 1827, Huskisson had cited ill health as the explanation for postponement of the conferences. The enclosed tonnage report was "A Comparative Statement of the British and Foreign Tonnage Which Have Entered the Several Ports of Great Britain up to 10th October 1826. . . ," G. B. *Sess. Papers, 1826–1827* (no. 52) XVIII, 367–70.

Lord Liverpool had suffered a stroke on February 17. The Cabinet crisis thus precipitated centered primarily upon the fact that Canning was an ardent advocate of Catholic emancipation, one of a minority of four holding such views in the 12-man Cabinet. When Liverpool, a Protestant, had to be replaced, most of the Cabinet refused to serve under Canning. The King's request on April 10 that Canning undertake organization of a government led to a split in the Tory Party, and Canning rested his support upon a coalition with the Whigs. Temperley, *The Foreign Policy of Canning*, 413–34.

On April 28, 1827, Robinson, also an advocate of Catholic emancipation, was elevated to the peerage as Viscount Goderich and named Secretary of State for War and Colonies and Commissioner for India. He served as leader of the House of Lords until August, 1827, when, on Canning's death, he headed the new government. Embroiled in controversy, Goderich resigned the following January. He subsequently held Cabinet posts in 1830, from 1833 to 1834, and from 1841 to 1843. In 1833 he was created first Earl of Ripon, the borough which he had represented in the House of Commons from 1807 to 1827.

From WILLIAM WHEELWRIGHT, Guayaquil. States that he has received accounts of a revolution in Peru against (Símon) Bolívar's regime and in favor of "the *Constitution Peruana*" (cf. above, Tudor to Clay, February 3, 1827). Reports that General (Andrés) Santa Cruz has retained command at Lima, that the revolt began with the mutiny of Colombian troops against General (Juan Jacinto) Lara, who with his principal officers has been sent under guard to Bogotá, and that "a Capt [José] Bustamente remained in commd of the [Colombian] Troops." Adds that he has heard reports of a revolt in Chile (cf. above, Allen to Clay, February 17, 1827). Says that he finds the public mind in Guayaquil greatly agitated and fears the country will suffer both revolution and anarchy (cf. below, Wheelwright to Clay, April 19, 1827). ALS. DNA, RG59, Cons. Disp., Guayaquil, vol. 1 (M-T209, R1). Published in Manning (arr.), *Diplomatic Correspondence . . . Latin-American Nations*, II, 1308. Received May 21.

APPLICATIONS, RECOMMENDATIONS   February 22, 1827

P[HILEMON] BEECHER, Washington, states that he, "General" (James) Findlay and "Mr." (probably William L.) Brent, recommend appointment of James Ombrosi as consul at Florence if one is needed there; mentions that he is enclosing a letter (not found) relating to this subject, and adds that Bishop Fenwick's "recommendation may be credited without danger." Postscript notes that the Bishop "has lately returned from Rome. . . ." ALS. DNA, RG59, A. and R. (M531, R6). On the recommended appointment, cf. above, Ombrosi to Clay, March 29, 1825, note. Benedict Joseph Fenwick had been student, teacher, and administrator at Georgetown College, Washington. From 1827 until his death in 1846 he was Bishop of Boston.

On February 23 Daniel Brent returned to Beecher Bishop Fenwick's letter and noted that Ombrosi had already received the recommended appointment. Copy, in DNA, RG59, Dom. Letters, vol. 21, p. 486 (M40, R19).

JOHN TRAVERS, Paterson, New Jersey, encloses a letter (dated October 30, 1826) from a friend (James J. Cummins) and recommends him for appointment as consul at Cork. ALS. DNA, RG59, A. and R. (M531, R2). Unaddressed. Cf. above, Cummins to Clay, November 6, 1826.

From James Brown

My dear Sir   Paris Feby 23. 1827

The troubles in Portugal are on a scale so diminutive and the incidents accompanying them are of so little importance, that I shall not add a despatch on that subject to those you will receive from our diplomatic agents at Lisbon and Madrid.[1] You may form a just opinion as to what is thought of the probability of a war here and at London by examining the prices of the *Stocks* which you are to bear in mind are so sensitive as to have been depressed by the law on the Press[2] here and by the indisposition of Mr Canning[3] at London whilst the news from Portugal has had little or no influence upon them. The insurgents are few in numbers and desperate in future and character and they have been beaten wherever they have shown themselves to the constitutional troops, although these are neither very well disciplined nor heartily attached to the constitution. The ranks of the rebels are daily becoming thin by the desertion of the divided regiments who joined them— The apostolical purse from which all the ways and means have been obtained is nearly exhausted and the partizans of disorder have become discouraged by finding that all the Cabinets in Europe have frowned on their cause. England has trouble enough with her corn laws, Catholic question, and the growing distresses among the poorer order. France is prosperous but not satisfied or happy. Ministers have excited alarm and discontent by the protection of the Jesuits, the encouragement given to the Congregations, by the laws on the Juries[4] and the Press and in a word by a supposed attempt to fritter down the Charter and restore the ancient regime. Russia and Austria and even Prussia have strongly recommended a peaceful policy to Spain. With such an influence on the side of peace I have little apprehension that hostilities will commence at least for some time. I hope our merchants have not speculated on the prospect of War.

The Chambers have been in Session ever since the 14 Decr. and have not passed a single law of any importance   The project on the press has undergone many amendments in the Committee and may probably pass as amended— It is even now very unpopular and indeed I think it may be considered as deserving all the odium it has excited.

I have not had any letters or papers from Washington of a later date than the 1st. Jany. The last Packet from N york has now been out 40 days the longest passage from the United States which has been made

in the last three years. The Winter here has been universally severe—
I have however had no return of my rheumatism   Mrs. Brown enjoys
her usual good health— I am very anxious to hear how you got through
the Session— I shall [*sic*] you on the 5⁵   Yours truly
Hon. Henry Clay   JAMES BROWN

ALS. DLC-HC (DNA, M212, R2).   ¹ Thomas L. L. Brent; Alexander H. Everett.
² See above, Brown to Clay, December 13, 1826, note.   ³ George Canning. See
above, Gallatin to Clay, February 6, 1827, note.   ⁴ Cf. above, Brown to Clay, August
23, 1826; February 13, 1827.   ⁵ Figure is not clearly legible. Brown's next letter was
written on March 3, 1827.

From George Thompson

Dear Sir   Pleasant fields 23th. Feby. 1827
    I am this day Seventy Eight years old   its about Sun up and I began
to write to a man that no one Can rival in my Esteem. I recd. Some
time past your friendly letter,¹ in which you inform me that the president is an Early riser. May he live fifty years & have good health, and
may you have all the blessing[s] this world can afford untill you are a
hundred years old and then be Eternarly [*sic*] happy in heaven. I am
a Very old man and am Still fond of hunting have a fine pack of
hounds can ride Very Well   I Expect as well as the Prest. or the
Secretary, but I do hope and believe that they will ride on their
Enemies. I do declare I beleave the people of Virginia are run mad.
I have for many years taken the Enquirer² printed in Richmond. Yesterday, I wrote to the Editors³ incloseing the balance I owed them and
directed them to Send Me No more of their papers. I have inclosed
you a copy of the letter I wrote,⁴ Ritchie & Gooch,   at this time I have
a young Gentelman [*sic*] liveing with me teaching my two grand
Sons   this young man by the Name of Taylor⁵ is a friend of Thos. P.
Moor who is our Member in Congress (and Moor writes by almost
Every Mail to Taylor and encloses Every news paper that abuses the
administration. I Expect T. P. Moor writes By Every Mail to More
than 50. persons in this district, but I do Believe, the Prest. & Secry.
are like pure gold get briter [*sic*] Every time it is put in the fire,
when I began to write only Expected to Say a few words to my friend
and tell him how old I was this being my birth day. I now put my
Self in mind of a Man by the Name of Hopkins.⁶   when he began to
dance he did Not know when to Stop. So am I, when I write to you.
I wish to Say a great deal but So Many things comes [*sic*] in My Mind
at once that I am at a loss which to Set down first   I believe the present
Congress are doing more harm than good,   what is the matter,   has
that body John Randolph who never did any good in his life, Joined
him Self to T. H. Benton⁷ John Rowan &c. &c. in order destroy [*sic*]
the peace of our beloved Country   if he has I hope he will be mistaken— I never could write or Spell well, but I can write a great deal in

a day. and I do write to many of my friends in Virginia & Else Where & ask them to Say to me if Mr. Jefferson did act when he was prest. in Such a Manner as to please them and did not Mr. Madison do the Same as Mr. Jefferson did or Nearly So. and is not Mr. Adams doing as Well as Either J. or M. they all Know he is doing as well or better. I have Named to you on the other Side that I have enclosed you a copy of my letter to Ritchie & Gooch it is a true Copy I am Not shure wheather you can read this Scrawl or the Copy to the printers: if you can the only wish I have is that you & the president will be So good as to remember that this letter Comes from a man that would not axcept any office in the u:S. Nor has he any friend to recomend [sic]. I Know I am a firm freind [sic] to you & the president. because I believe Each of you to be firm friends [sic] to my beloved Country— I never Expect to See Mr. Adams I beleave him to be an honest man be pleased to give my respects to him. I hope to See you many times. when you come to Kentucky I hope you will come & See me & if you'l bring the president I will give him an Elk I have No fear as to the Next Election for president, Jackson can Not go it as the watermen Say— Mr. Adamss [sic] & your Enemies dont care for Jackson they dont love him but they hate you two, but for what I am Not able to tell, Nor can they tell, they can Say take care & cry out Mad dog. I believe I have Said Enough I Could tell all about Lewis Robards he was my aversara [sic] I was a Member of the assembly in Virginia when Robards got a divorce & I was in Richmond when Robards got two hundred pounds from Peyton Short for crim con[8] I will lay down my pen as soon as I tell you that I am Dear Sir yr. friend & mo. Ob   G. THOMPSON

PS. My Son his fine wife[9] and Seven fine Children are all well & doing well and I am Sure were they present they would Send their respects together with mine to you Mrs. Clay & family—

ALS. DLC-HC (DNA, M212, R2). Addressed to Clay.
[1] See above, Clay to Thompson, September 23, 1826.   [2] The *Richmond Enquirer*.
[3] Thomas Ritchie and Claiborne W. Gooch.   [4] The enclosure, addressed to Ritchie and Gooch and dated February 7, 1827, enclosed payment closing Thompson's account and terminated his subscription until the editors returned to their political views of "three or four years past." Thompson noted that he did not know Ritchie, though he believed him to be a Virginian, the State of Thompson's birth and love; but he recognized Gooch as a "blooded relation" and invited him to visit. Of Clay, Thompson wrote: ". . . if I did not convince him [Gooch] that Mr. Clay was an ornament to the U. S. I would give him a tract of land. I have been well acquainted with H. Clay from his boyhood. I believe him to be one of the greatest and best Statemen [sic] I have Ever known and I believe him to be as honest a man as any in the U. S. I was not friendly to Mr. Adams's late Election. But he has acted so Extremely well Since he has been president as far as I know or believe that I am now in favr. of his Second Election in preference to any man that Can be named. I believe we have at this time as able and & [sic] as virtuous a Cabinet as we have Ever had all this I believe. although I loved Mr. Jefferson as Much as a brother and the Virtuous Madison is my Relation—" ALS, in DLC-HC (DNA, M212, R2). Thompson's relationship to Gooch and James Madison has not been found.   [5] Not identified. Two of George Thompson's grandsons were George Madison Thompson, who died in 1829, and William

Thompson.   6 Not identified.   7 Thomas Hart Benton.   8 Short paid Ro-
bards $1000 as satisfaction for supposed excessive attentions to Mrs. Robards, later Mrs.
Andrew Jackson. James, *Andrew Jackson*, 855–56.   9 George C. Thompson; Sarah S.
Thompson, who had married Thompson after the death in 1818 of his first wife, Mary.

APPLICATIONS, RECOMMENDATIONS   February 23, 1827

RICHARD B. DORSEY, Washington, solicits employment in the State Department
because "the great decline in the price of agricultural products" has caused him
to change his vocation. Mentions that correspondence should be addressed to him
at Brookville, Montgomery County, Maryland. ALS. DNA, RG59, A. and R.
(M531, R2). Enclosed in Dorsey to Clay, March 2, 1827. Richard B. Dorsey had
married his cousin Anne Eliza, daughter of Clement Dorsey; he did not receive
an appointment in the State Department.

EDWARD LLOYD, Annapolis, recommends Thomas E. Waggaman, the bearer of this
letter, for a clerkship. Comments: "his connections are highly respectable, his
friends are numerous—and politically he has heretofore *done some service*." ALS.
DNA, RG59, A. and R. (M531, R8). Waggaman, born in Maryland and married
to Martha Jefferson Tyler, sister of (Senator) John Tyler, had formerly been a
merchant in Nashville. Cf. below, Waggaman to Clay, March 29, 1828.

To Albert Gallatin

No. 18. Albert Gallatin, Envoy Extraordinary and Minister
Plenipotentiary U. S. London.
Sir.   Department of State, Washington, 24 Feby. 1827.
    Your dispatches from No. 26 to 48, inclusive,[1] have been received,
together with the accompanying documents, and have been all laid
before the President. And I shall now, under his direction, communicate to you such instructions as appear to be called for by the state of
the pending negotiations between the United States and Great Britain, with which you are charged. In doing this, I shall take up the
several subjects, which require notice, in the order in which they
have been considered in the conferences which you have had with the
British Plenipotentiaries, beginning with
    1st. The North Western Boundary. As there seems to be no prospect
of an agreement, at this time, upon a permanent boundary which shall
separate the territories of the two powers beyond the Stony Mountains, and as no utility is perceived in prolonging the discussions which
have arisen on that subject, I shall abstain from any particular notice
of the written statement, annexed by the British Plenipotentiaries[2]
to the protocol of the sixth Conference, of the claims and views of
Great Britain relative to that Country. New and extraordinary as
those claims and views strike us, they will nevertheless receive all the
consideration which is due to the high respect which is sincerely felt
for the Government of Great Britain, and to the official and deliberate
exhibition which has been made of them. They certainly have not yet

produced any conviction in the mind of the President of the validity of the pretensions brought forward, nor raised any doubts of
the strength and solidity of our own title: I repeat what has been already stated in your general Instructions,[3] that the offer of a boundary on the parallel of 49° was made in a spirit of liberal concession,
and notwithstanding our belief that our title might be satisfactorily
made out much further North. Supposing Great Britain to have any
well founded claim, if there be, as there are believed to be, no other
powers than the United States and Great Britain who can assert rights
of territorial sovereignty between 42°. and 54°. 40′, there can be no
equitable division of the intermediate space, but an equal partition.
Such an equal partition would assign about the parallel of 49° as the
common boundary. The President regrets that the British Plenipotentiaries have thought proper to decline the proposal which you
made of that line. And I am charged by him to direct you to communicate the expression of this regret, and to declare that the American
Government does not hold itself bound hereafter, in consequence of
any proposal which it has heretofore made, to agree to the line which
has been so proposed and rejected, but will consider itself at liberty
to contend for the full extent of our just claims, which declaration
you will have recorded in the protocol of one of your conferences.
Such a protest you have already made and had recorded in the protocol
of the third conference;[4] but it will give more weight to it to have it
stated that it has been done by the express direction of the President.

As you have not been able to conclude any agreement fixing a
permanent boundary, it is preferred that there should be a simple
renewal of the third article in the Convention of 1818, without any
other alteration than that which you proposed of the omission of the
clause respecting the claims of other powers,[5] and on that modification
you will not insist, if it be objected to.

The second article in the projet presented by the British Plenipotentiaries is inadmissible. So far as its tendency would be to prevent
the United States from exercising acts of exclusive Sovereignty at the
mouth of the Columbia, it would be contrary to their rights as acknowledged both in the treaty of Ghent, and by the surrender of that
place[6] made by the British Government in consequence of that treaty.
It is also objectionable because it does not define, but leaves open to
disputation, the acts which might be deemed the exercise of an exclusive Sovereignty. And it has been properly observed by you that,
from the nature of our institutions, our rights in that quarter must be
protected, and our Citizens secured in their lawful pursuits, by some
species of Government, different from which it has been or may be
the pleasure of the British Government to establish. The Form of
Territorial Government is that which is most approved by our experience; but such a Government might be considered incompatible

with the second article, if it were agreed to. If there be a simple renewal of the third article of the Convention of 1818,[7] Great Britain will have abundant security in the good faith of the United States for the Fulfilment of all its stipulations. And you will therefore resist the adoption of the second article in the British projet, if it should even render you unable to come to any agreement for the renewal of the provision in the Convention of 1818.

With respect to the assignment of certain portions of the territory to each power, over which they may respectively exercise acts of exclusive Sovereignty, leaving intermediate debateable [sic] space, it does not appear probable that such an arrangement as would be satisfactory to both parties can be made. If, for example, we were to agree that such exclusive Sovereignty might be exerted by the United States over all the territory from the mouth of the Columbia South to the 42d. parallel, and by Great Britain over all the territory from 49° and would give us less territory on the Pacific than if we were at once to agree to 50°. 40'. the intermediate space between the Columbia and 49° being common to both parties, a larger extent of territory would be assigned to Great Britain than to the United States, and, in the end that which was thus held in common would probably be equally divided between the two parties, as the only equitable mode of separating it. Such a division would place the common boundary line South of the parallel of 49° to an equal division of the entire space between 42° and 54°. 40'.[8] If, which is not likely, Great Britain would consent to the exercise of exclusive Sovereignty, on the part of the United States, over the whole space from the mouth of Columbia South to the 42°, leaving the residue from the mouth of the Columbia to 54°. 40' in common, as is provided for in the third article of the Convention of 1818, we should be willing to agree to such a stipulation.

In respect to the duration of the renewed provision, the President prefers that it should be fixed for the same term of ten years which is limited in the Convention of 1818. But if the article in regard to this subject should not be thrown into the shape of a separate Convention, but should be inserted in the same Convention which regulates our commercial intercourse with the British European possessions, you are then authorized to agree that the whole Convention shall continue in force, after the expiration of the term of ten years and until one party shall have given to the other six months written notice of his desire to put an end to the Convention.[9]

2. Further renewal of the Convention of 1815.[10] As the British Plenipotentaries decline agreeing to the proposal of the general provision to allow the ships of both Countries the same privileges, in exportation and importation, as national vessels enjoy, without limitation on account of the origin of the cargo, the modification of that principle which you anticipate will be offered[11] has been considered.

In regard to a liberty to be allowed to vessels of the United States to import directly from the United States into Great Britain any produce or manufacture, wherever originating, which British vessels might import into Great Britain, in consideration of a similar liberty to be extended to British vessels coming directly from Great Britain to the United States, the President does not think that we should receive, in such an arrangement, a fair equivalent. At present, American vessels are authorized by law to import into the United States from Great Britain the produce or manufactures of any Country whatever. The proposed stipulation, therefore, would not enlarge the privileges of American vessels in respect to importations from Great Britain. British vessels are prohibited to introduce into the United States from Great Britain any other than British produce, whilst American vessels are under a similar interdict as to importations into Great Britain. And the question is, whether we should find in the privilege of carrying any foreign produce from the United States into Great Britain—a privilege which British vessels now exclusively enjoy, an equivalent for a grant of the privilege to British vessels to bring any foreign produce to the United States—a privilege which American vessels now exclusively enjoy? A solution of this question depends upon the probable amount of foreign produce which would find its way into the ports of the one Country through those of the other. When we take into view the superiority in extent of British Capital, and the advantages of the position and the means[12] of the British isles for concentrating foreign European produce, the proposed arrangement, it appears to us, would be manifestly more beneficial to Great Britain than to the United States. Very little, if any,[13] produce of foreign origin would pass to Great Britain through the ports of the United States, whilst, in consequence of the circumstances adverted to, a great amount of foreign produce would come to the United States through the British ports. The British merchant and the British Ship owner would be both interested in importations into Great Britain of foreign produce for the supply of American consumption. These importations would be made exclusive of American vessels,[14] and our navigation would divide with a foreign navigation that subsequent transportation of the foreign produce from British ports,[15] which it now exclusively enjoys. The advantage gained by Great Britain would be further increased, if she should finally accede to the proposal of this Government in relation to the Colonial trade. According to that proposal Great Britain is to monopolize the circuitous trade through her Colonies. Supposing both arrangements to be made, British vessels could bring to the United States British produce, foreign produce, and Colonial produce, without any reciprocal liberty on the part of our vessels.[16] How would American navigation, which can sustain any just competition, support itself against such great inequalities?

But the British proposition which you anticipate is more disadvantageous to the United States than that which I have been considering. According to your dispatch No. 41,[17] you state Mr. Huskisson to say, that the proposition "he might make, in its utmost latitude, would be, that vessels of the United States, coming from the United States, should be permitted to bring into Great Britain on the same terms with British vessels, articles not the produce or manufacture of the United States, excepting always the produce and manufacture of the British Colonies and possessions abroad, (East Indies &c) of China, and perhaps of all Countries beyond the Cape of Good Hope." With such a sweeping exception as this, what foreign produce would remain to be taken from the ports of the United States to those of Great Britain, by way of equivalent for the produce foreign to Great Britain brought from British ports to those of the United States? There might be some inconsiderable articles from South America; but the produce of the Countries of Europe would not bear the expenses of two voyages across the Atlantic to go back to Great Britain, so near the place of its origin.

Should the anticipated proposition therefore, be made, you will decline accepting it; and agree only to a further renewal, without alteration, of the Convention of 1815. And if such renewal should be refused, without an agreement on our part to any of the modifications which have been suggested to you, by the British Plenipotentiaries, you will decline its renewal altogether. You appear to think that they will not insist on any new provision to secure admission of their vessels into our Southern ports, when navigated by crews, a part of which happens to be persons of colour. You have properly stated that the regulation complained of in South Carolina is not confined to British vessels but equally extends to those of the United States. It may be added, that it is a regulation of police only, not affecting the right of navigation, but the conduct of the crew whilst the vessel is lying in port. And further, that the Courts of justice are alike open to British subjects and to American Citizens to try the validity of the regulation, with the advantage of the former that if it be contrary to the stipulations of the Convention it is null by the express provision of the Constitution of the United States. The complaint respecting the difference of duty between rolled and hammered bar iron has been heretofore examined and shewn to have no foundation. If, in point of fact, rolled bar iron is manufactured alone in Great Britain, she does not possess any exclusive right to the manufacture. And surely the true interpretation of the treaty cannot depend upon the fact whether the industry of any other nation is or is not applied to the production of a similar article. You are not, therefore, authorized to agree to any clause providing "that the same articles shall not be liable to a higher rate of duty on account of a difference in the manner in which they have been manufactured or prepared for market," Such a clause might itself become the source of different opinions and of new controversy. The candour and patience with which each party will listen to the complaints of the other, and the good faith with which both are believed to be animated must form an adequate security for the faithful execution of the Convention. Doubtful points will arise under any form of language that can be employed, and those which occur on the one side, in the general, will be found to be neutralized by others arising to the disadvantage of the opposite party.

3. The North Eastern boundary.[18] The second and fourth articles of the projet offered by the British Plenipotentiaries, providing for a reference of the question,[19] cannot be agreed to for the reasons stated in your dispatch No. 43.[20] The President would be satisfied with a Convention for that purpose of which the sketch furnished in your dispatch No. 47.[21] should be the basis. To which it might be advisable to add a clause stipulating that the Arbitrator may direct, at the common expense of the parties, such surveys explorations and observations in the disputed territory as he may deem necessary, to inform his judgment, and that he may also designate the Commissioner or Commissioners to be charged with the execution of them.

Should you be able to agree neither upon a transfer of the negotiation to Washington, nor upon the conditions under which the difference shall be referred to the Arbitrator, you are then authorized to stipulate for a simple reference of the question to the Arbitrator, and to provide that he shall, in the course of the arbitration, settle all questions of evidence, as well as those on the mode of conducting the discussions which may arise between the parties. The analogy between the Arbitrator and an ordinary tribunal of Justice will be then complete. Such a simple submission of the question will increase both the labour and the responsibility of the arbitrator to an extent which we should be extremely unwilling to devolve on him but from necessity. It is better, with all its inconveniences, than doing nothing, since it would at least hold out a prospect of a decision of this long contested matter. Whether you agree upon a submission in general terms, or with a particular statement of the conditions under which it is made, it will be advisable to annex a clause, providing that the decision of the Arbitrator shall not be delayed beyond a limited period, (say of about two years)[22] in consequence of the failure of the parties, or of either of them, to exhibit the testimony or to offer the arguments which they might wish to adduce. Without such a stipulation the decision might be indefinitely postponed. It is not intended by it to hasten the Arbitrator to make a premature decision, if for his own satisfaction and at his own instance the final decision should be postponed beyond the specified period.[23]

4. Impressment. From all that we can observe, at this distance, there

does not appear to be a likelihood of any disturbance of the general peace of Europe, in consequence of the state of affairs in Portugal;[24] and of course there is not the same urgency for the settlement of the question of impressment, as when you wrote under prospects of an immediate war. It is, nevertheless, extremely desirable to have the question finally put at rest. War may suddenly break out; and we have seen that even a season of peace does not afford always and at all places a perfect security against the practice. I transmit you herewith, in support of this latter observation, a copy of all the correspondence (a part of which you have been heretofore put in possession of) respecting the case of impressment which occurred on the Western Coast of Africa, made by Captain Clavering[25] of the Redwing. We have not yet received the decision of the British Government in regard to that case; and you will remind it, on some suitable occasion, that it is expected.

But however desirable it may be to settle this question, all the considerations which operated, when your general instructions were prepared, to prevent the renewal of the negotiation, on this subject, at our instance, continue to have their full force. We have exhausted all the propositions which we can make. We must henceforward abide by our incontestible rights, in full confidence that the revival of the practice of impressment will not be attempted by Great Britain. According to your general instructions you are authorized to receive any proposals which may come from Great Britain, and to agree to them. provided they conform to the instructions which were given to Mr. Rush,[26] and which, on this subject, you will consider as governing you.

5. Fugitive Slaves. The General Assembly of Kentucky, one of the States which is most affected by the escape of slaves into Upper Canada, has again, at their Session which has just terminated, invoked the interposition of the General Government.[27] In the treaty, which has been recently concluded with the United Mexican States, and which is now under the consideration of the Senate, provision is made for the restoration of fugitive slaves.[28] As it appears from your statement of what passed on that subject with the British Plenipotentiaries,[29] that they admitted the correctness of the principle of restoration, it is hoped that you will be able to succeed in making a satisfactory arrangement. I am, with great respect, Your obedient Servant,

H. CLAY

LS. NHi-Gallatin Papers (MR14). Copy, in DNA, RG59, Dip. Instr., vol. 11 (M77, R6); AL draft, dated February 19, and LI draft, dated February 24, in DLC-HC (DNA, M212, R8).
1 November 16–December 30, 1826. Brief summaries of these dispatches and of the protocols of the seven negotiating conferences in which Gallatin had participated during the period, in Clay's hand, apparently written in preparation for the drafting of this document, may be found in DNA, RG59, Dip. Disp., Great Britain, vol. 33 (M30, R29). Summaries of Gallatin's subsequent dispatches through that of November 22, 1827, were added in the writing of various State Department clerks.   2 William Huskisson: Henry U. Addington. For the Protocol and the appended statement, see *American State Papers, Foreign Relations*, VI, 661–66.   3 Above, June 19, 1826.   4 *American*

State Papers, Foreign Relations, VI, 660.   5 See Protocol of the fourth conference, *ibid.*   6 Astoria. See above, Clay to King, May 10, 1825, note.   7 See above, II, 611n.   8 This sentence inserted as marginal note, in Clay's hand, on draft copy.
    9 On February 14 Adams wrote: "Mr. Clay spoke of the instructions to be given to Mr. Gallatin. I agreed that he should be authorized to renew the Convention of October, 1818, without alteration, for ten years, preferring that term to the one proposed by the British Government, of twenty or fifteen years. I would leave the Northwestern boundary 'in statu quo' rather than accept anything proposed by the British, or concede anything to them." *Memoirs*, VII, 226.   10 See above, II, 57–59, 611n.   11 See above, Gallatin to Clay, September 20, 1826. The phrase, "in exportation and importation," interlined by Clay in first draft copy.   12 Last three words interlined by Clay in first draft copy.   13 Last two words interlined by Clay in first draft copy.   14 Last nine words interlined by Clay in first draft copy.   15 The word "subsequent" and the last seven words interlined by Clay in first draft copy.   16 Last sentence interlined by Clay in first draft copy.   17 Above, December 21, 1826.   18 On February 7 Adams reported that Clay "said it would be impossible for him to prepare the instructions [for Gallatin] concerning the Eastern boundary. . . ." Clay had proposed employing E(dward) Livingston; Adams suggested (John) Holmes. Adams, *Memoirs*, VII, 222. No Clay correspondence indicates that either assisted in preparing the instructions.
    19 Last seven words interlined by Clay in first draft copy.   20 Above, December 22, 1826.   21 Above, December 30, 1826. For the proposal, see *American State Papers, Foreign Relations*, VI, 673.   22 Last five words interlined by Clay in first draft copy.
    23 Adams concluded his entry of February 14 concerning his discussions with Clay as follows: "A statement must be made to present to the *umpire* in relation to the Northeastern boundary. The prospects of our relations with Great Britain are dark." *Memoirs*, VII, 226.   24 See above, Everett to Clay, December 3, 1826; Gallatin to Clay, December 13, 1826; Brown to Clay, December 13, 23, 1826.   25 D. C. Clavering. Cf. above, Clay to Adams, January 12, 1827.   26 Richard Rush. See above, Clay to Gallatin, June 19, 1826.   27 Ky. Gen. Assy., *Acts, 1826–1827*, pp. 197–98, a resolution approved January 24, 1827.   28 Cf. above, Poinsett to Clay, July 12, 1826, note.
    29 See above, Gallatin to Clay, December 21, 1826.

To Albert Gallatin

No 19. Albert Gallatin, Envoy Extraordinary and Minister Plenipotentiary U. S to Great Britain.

Sir,   Department of State, Washington, 24 feby 1827.

The President has given full Consideration to your desire to return to the United States, as expressed in your Letter of the 30th December last; and you cannot doubt his disposition to authorize, on that Subject, every thing that could contribute to your Convenience or Comfort, consistently with the public interests— With respect to the Understanding about your return, to which you refer, it is proper, however, to say, that The President is not, nor am I, aware of any Understanding, according to which any precise time was fixed for your return— All that is recollected in regard to it is, that you were told, it would not be insisted that you should remain in England, if you wished to come home, after the Conclusion of the several negociations with which you are charged— No Estimate was, or could be made of the time which they would consume: but it was certainly not anticipated by me, that they would be brought to a termination until towards the end of the present year. I advert to the Subject of this alleged Understanding with some regret, because you had not left the

United States before it was made one of News-paper Commentary.[1] I feel myself also called upon, in consequence of a statement which is understood to have been recently made in debate in the Senate by General Smith,[2] of Maryland, as he averred, with your authority, that a Carte blanche had been offered you in the conduct of the Negociations, to say, that I know of Nothing which warranted any such statement: and I cannot but be persuaded, that, in referring to your name, as a Source of Authority for it, he has proceeded upon an entire misconception.

Every facility has been, and will continue to be given, compatible with full deliberation on the various important matters confided to your direction, to enable you to bring the Negociations to a Close. The Instructions[3] which accompany this Letter, when in conjunction with previous Instructions in your Possession, are believed to cover all the Aspects of the Negociations, as presented at the Period of your latest Despatch[4]— And, whilst it is expected, that they will not be hurried in a manner detrimental to the Public Interests, I have to express The President's Consent, that you may return Home, if you desire it, at the Conclusion of the Negociation on the several Subjects committed to your Charge.[5] I am, with great Respect, Your Obedient Servant,   H. CLAY

LS, in Daniel Brent's hand. NHi-Gallatin Papers (MR14). ALI draft, in DLC-HC (DNA, M212, R8); copy, in DNA, RG59, Dip. Instr., vol. 11, pp. 254–55 (M77, R6). Cf. below, Gallatin to Clay, April 7, 1827.
    [1] Not found.   [2] Addressing the Senate on February 21, 1827, Samuel Smith had argued that the British "act of Parliament of July, 1825" had been "plain . . . to the meanest understanding" on the point about whether American vessels might carry the produce of the British West Indies to foreign countries, other than the British dominions, "in like manner with British vessels." Smith wondered why Vaughan had been questioned about the meaning of that legislation (see above, Clay to Vaughan, October 19, 1826). Smith had then commented that Gallatin "had better have had a *carte blanche*" in conducting the negotiations, "for he understood the subject as well at least as any of us," *Register of Debates*, 19 Cong., 2 Sess., p. 413.   [3] See above, Clay to Gallatin, no. 18, this date.   [4] December 30, 1827.   [5] Gallatin and his family landed in New York on November 29, 1827. *Niles' Weekly Register*, XXXIII (December 8, 1827), 228.

From James Burnham

Sir,   Newbury Port[1] Febry 24. 1827
    Permit me to ask you, if, in your opinion, an instructor of the French Language, English Grammar, reading, writing, arithmetic & geography, would probably meet with respectable encouragement, in any part of your extensive acquaintance in the State of Kentucky? With sentiments of respect, I am, Sir, your obedient Sert
Hon Henry Clay.   JAMES BURNHAM—

ALS. DNA, RG59, Misc. Letters (M179, R65). Enclosed under cover from John Anderson, Washington, to Clay, March 1, 1827 (omitted by editors). Burnham has not been further identified; no reply by Clay has been found.
    [1] Massachusetts.

INSTRUCTIONS AND DISPATCHES   February 24, 1827

From THOMAS L. L. BRENT, Lisbon. Reports that the Marquis of Chaves, having been asked to leave Spain, has entered Tras os Montes; that he is recruiting there; and that an army led by Correa de Mello (not further identified) is being sent against him. ALS. DNA, RG59, Dip. Disp., Portugal, vol. 7 (M43, R6). Received April 23.

From C[HARLES] D. COXE, Tunis. Acknowledges receipt of dispatches dated in April, 1826 (see above, Clay to Coxe, April 21, 1826), including his commission as consul to Tripoli, on December 27, by the hand of Dr. S(amuel) D. Heap; complains of the long delay in their delivery and of the neglect by the Department of State to answer his communications. Notes that the "only event of any consequence" since his last report "was the refusal of the Bey [Hassein] and his Ministers to receive the Consular present . . . prepared for them." Explains that their "expectations had been raised very high" by the treaty entered into with Dr. Heap, that they offered "several frivolous pretexts for not accepting the present, such as its slight value in comparison with the grants by France and Sardinia, and that (William) Shaler has expressed approval of his stand. Notes that some time later he was informed that the Bey "was sorry for what had happen'd with respect to the present and that he would receive it and be good friends," that he replied that he no longer had the power "to offer the present after it had been refused" and that Dr. Heap who was coming as his successor "would no doubt be prepared with a present for the Bey and Ministers." Adds that he will dispose of the "agricultural instruments intended for the Bey of Tunis" and purchase "other articles in France more congenial to the taste of the Bashaw of Tripoly [Yusuf Karamanli]." LS. DNA, RG59, Cons. Disp., Tripoli, vol. 5 (M-T40, R-T5). Received July 28. Cf. above, Heap to Clay, February 7, 1827.

On February 24, 1824, Heap had signed a convention with Tunis, revising four articles of the treaty of 1797 so as to provide for opening Tunisian ports to vessels of the United States on more lenient terms. The treaty had been ratified by the United States some time between January 13 and 21, 1825. Cf. Miller (comp.), *Treaties. . . ,* II, 402–26; III, 141–49.

From JOHN SERGEANT, Mexico, "Private." Notes that he has heard nothing from Colombia, Guatemala, or Peru, nor of Mexican action concerning ratification of the Panama treaties. Comments: "For the present, I am sorry to be obliged to say to you, that the symptoms in regard to the Congress [at Tacubaya] continue to be extremely unfavorable, and such as to warrant me in suggesting for your consideration the possibility of its total failure." ALS. DNA, RG43, First Panama Congress, vol. 1 (M662, R1, frames 130–31). Received April 26.

MISCELLANEOUS LETTERS   February 24, 1827

From EPHRAIM BATEMAN, "Senate Chamber." States that during a recent call at the State Department he was told by a clerk in Clay's absence that if (Robert) Johnston, editor of the Bridgeton, New Jersey, (Washington) *Whig and Observer,* would "re-certify his relinquishment" in favor of (Hugh R.) Merseilles, payment would be made to the latter; encloses such a certificate, which he hopes with a letter left at Clay's office will be satisfactory; expresses view that Merseilles should be paid; and adds that he will call upon Clay again for his decision. ALS. DNA, RG59, Accounting Records, Misc. Letters. Cf. above, Merseilles to Clay, June 27, 1826; November 27, 1826; Southard to Clay, November 6, 1826, note.

To Peter Force

Dear Sir   Sunday. [February 25, 1827]
I wish you would publishe [*sic*] the inclosed, as an Editorial para-
graph, in your paper tomorrow   Yrs.   H. CLAY.
[Enclosure] [1]

The Colonial Trade

Our readers will perceive that the subject of the British Colonial
trade is before one branch, as in a few days it must be considered by
the other branch of Congress.[2] They will also remark that there is
great diversity of opinion in regard to it. This was to have been expected from the extraordinary course pursued by the British Government, and from the complexity of the British legislation in regard to
their Colonies. In a very able speech delivered a few days ago by Mr.
Johnston of Louisiana in the Senate, displaying great diligence and a
thorough knowledge of the subject, on the part of that Senator, he
stated, that the confusion and uncertainty of the British statutes was
such that a learned Judge (no other than Sir William Scott) had
recently decided in the case of the Jubilee a question of salvage without being aware that the Statute on which he placed his opinion was
repealed by the act of Parliament of 1825![3] And yet it was required by
G. Britain that, without any official communication of that act, or
any official explanations of its provisions, the American Government
should comprehend the import of a British Law which the first Judge
in England did not understand. Independent of all other considerations, this state of uncertainty of the British laws demonstrates the
propriety of the opinion of the Executive that it was better that the
Colonial Intercourse should be regulated by treaty than legislation.[4]
Indeed we understand Mr. Tazewell, who was one of the most urgent
members for the passage of an act of Congress at the last Session, as
now admitting that any act which may be passed will only be the basis
of *negotiation*.[5] Such is undoubtedly the case. Now, if we are to end
was it not wise to have begun with negotiation? Previous legislation is
attended with the disadvantage of exposing to the other party, in the
first instance, the ultimatum, and thus losing the chance of obtaining
better terms.

We hope however that the different views which may be taken of
this matter, by the members of Congress, will not prevent the passage
of a law which shall take care of the interests, the character, and the
dignity of this Country. What is briefly the true state of the question?
During a suspended negotiation between the two Countries, on this
very subject, as well as others, after (as late as March 1826) we were
assured by the B. Government that they were preparing to resume the
negotiation, and at the moment of Mr. Gallatin's arrival in England
to enter upon it, G. Britain suddenly determined that she will not

treat with us about it. She interdicts our vessels from entering her Colonial ports, tauntingly tells us that our participation in the trade is a *boon*, and that if we do not make up our minds to accept the terms which *she* has presented without deigning to consult us, by the first of Decr. last, she does not know that she will let us into the trade at all, after that period! In the mean time, the American government, acting with its accustomed moderation, continued to admit B. vessels coming from Colonial ports shut against ours, on the sole condition of paying the alien duties which are exacted from the vessels of all Foreign nations, with which we have no commercial arrangement.   In this state of things so disadvantageous to us, an act of Congress is proposed, which leaves the British vessels in the enjoyment of the monopoly of the navigation until the 30h. Sept. next, and only provides that if, by that day, the Colonial ports are not opened to our vessels, on equitable terms, our ports shall be closed agt. B. vessels coming from Colonial ports. A proposition so moderate might have been expected to conciliate general support. But it appears that some gentlemen of the Senate seem to think that it would be wrong to adopt it; and Genl. Smith proposes to meet the British interdict of American vessels by granting further privileges to British vessels, that is to repeal the alien duties to which British vessels are now liable, and to allow a free and unrestricted trade to G. Britain, which has prohibited altogether our navigation. We hope that a majority of Congress will take a different view of the matter, and consider that it is not the wisest course when one cheek is struck to present the other to the blow of the assailant.

ALS. DLC-HC (DNA, M212, R2). Addressed to Force
1 AD. *Ibid.* Published in Washington *Daily National Journal,* February 26, 1827.
2 On January 23, Josiah Stoddard Johnston for the Senate Committee on Commerce had reported a bill recommending "absolute and rigid non-intercourse" with the British colonies in the West Indies and North America after September 30 "next." In Committee of the Whole Samuel Smith had proposed an amendment to substitute a bill which in section one provided that, after December 31, British vessels would be admitted from ports in those colonies under no higher duties than United States vessels paid on entering from those ports. A second section of Smith's bill called for suspension of the trade legislation of 1818, 1820, and 1823 (see above, II, 565–66n; III, 729n), except for the "discriminating duties on the tonnage of foreign vessels and their cargoes," until December 31, when as he noted, Congress would be in Session and could act as the situation required. Smith's substitute bill passed the Senate on February 28. The House of Representatives on March 2, by motion of Gideon Tomlinson, amended the Senate bill to provide that the non-intercourse provisions of the acts of 1818 and 1820 would be activated and the legislation of 1823 and the first sections of the new measure annulled if the British did not remove their restrictions by December 31. On the same day the Senate, by vote of 25 to 20, adhered to its bill; and still later on that date the House, by vote of 75 to 65, insisted upon its amendment. The Congress adjourned on March 3 without further action. U. S. Sen., *Journal,* 19 Cong., 2 Sess., pp. 109, 211–12, 239–44, 280–83, 298–300; U. S. H. of Reps., *Journal,* 19 Cong., 2 Sess., pp. 366, 384–86; *Sen. Docs.,* 19 Cong., 2 Sess., no. 27, p. 15; *Register of Debates,* 19 Cong., 2 Sess., pp. 397–454, 456– 86, 491–98, 501–506, 1501–1507, 1514–31.   3 Cf. above, Gallatin to Clay, December 28, 1826, note. Johnston's speech had been delivered on February 23. The passage cited is in *Register of Debates,* 19 Cong., 2 Sess., pp. 437–38.   4 See above, Gallatin to Clay, August 19, 1826, note; Clay to Lloyd, November 8, 1826.   5 Littleton W. Tazewell. See *Register of Debates,* 19 Cong., 2 Sess., p. 429.

From Theodore Lyman, Jr.

Sir.   Philadelphia. Feb. 25. 1827

I met yesterday in this town with Mr. Harris,[1] who was formerly a consul of the United States at St. Petersburg. He informed me, that he had in his possession a copy of the correspondence, which he held with the Russian government, while he was consul, and which was in some degree diplomatic, as, also, a copy of the correspondence of the commission of Messrs. Adams, Bayard and Gallitin [sic].[2] He appeared very desirous of communicating the correspondence to me, as he thought I should find it exceedingly useful for my work;— and he, also, expressed an opinion at the same time, that there was no part of it, which, the government could be at all unwilling, should be published. But as Mr. Harris has been for some time a private citizen, and has never had any communication with the Government respecting this correspondence, he intimated a wish to me, (as I thought with great propriety and a very becoming delicacy) that I should, before enjoying the benefits of an examination of it, obtain the permission of your Department to that effect.

I could possibly have no other unwillingness to take that step than the extreme reluctance I feel to give you farther [sic] trouble in a matter, which is, I believe, after all, of little importance to any one but myself. It is, however, just and proper for me to say, that I am truly anxious to see this correspondence, as my work is at present very meagre on the head of Russia,[3] though I obtained many valuable materials at Washington. Mr. Harris is a gentleman, with whom I had only a slight acquaintance, but I understood him to say, that he was the first American agent officially recognized by the Russian Government. I was well aware that Mr. Dana's mission in 81. & 82, which the President accompanied, as I found stated in the correspondence in your office, was not attended with success.[4] Having extracted a full account of that mission, access to Mr. Harris' papers would enable me to complete in detail the History of our relations with Russia to the treaty of Ghent.

I hope, Sir, you will pardon me for the trouble of this letter. I have been all along concerned to have been compelled to solicit any portion of your attention at a period when, I well know, you have such a number and variety of important engagements.

Whenever you happen to have a moment of leizure [sic], may I beg you to do me the favor to address a letter to me to the care of Mrs Henderson[5] No. 67 Greenwich Street, New York. Have the goodness, also, to accept my most sincere and particular acknowledgments for your very obliging and valuable attentions to me at Washington, wh[ich] I shall, ever, remember with the greatest satis[fac]tion. I am,

Sir, ever with great respect your most obedient and very faithful
Servant.   THEODORE LYMAN. JR.

ALS. DLC-HC (DNA M212, R2). Addressed to Clay. Lyman, born in Massachusetts and
educated at Harvard College, had served in the State legislature from 1820 to 1825. A
staunch Federalist, he had published in 1823 *A Short Account of the Hartford Convention.* In 1826 he had also published *The Diplomacy of the United States . . . from
the First Treaty with France, in 1778, to the Treaty of Ghent, in 1814, with Great Britain.*
This latter work was revised and extended to the current period, in two volumes published in 1828. Opposed to the election of John Q. Adams in 1824, Lyman supported
Andrew Jackson in 1828. After a brief affiliation with anti-Jackson forces in 1831, he was
elected mayor of Boston in 1833 and 1834 with Jacksonian support. He devoted his remaining years to philanthropic endeavors.
  1 Levett Harris.   2 John Quincy Adams; James A. Bayard; Albert Gallatin. Cf.
above, I, 799n.   3 Lyman's treatment of the diplomatic relations with Russia was
expanded by nearly six pages in the revised edition, in elaboration of the record on
Dana's mission.   4 Francis Dana, of Massachusetts, a graduate of Harvard College
and a lawyer before entering politics, had served in the Continental Congress and had
gone to France in 1779 as John Adams' Secretary of Legation. At the behest of the Congress he had undertaken a mission to St. Petersburg in 1781 to solicit Russian recognition
of American independence. Although he had withheld public announcement of his
ministerial character until after receipt of news of the signing of the Treaty of Paris in
1783, he had been denied accreditation. Returning home, he had resumed his legal
practice and from 1791 to 1806 presided over the Massachusetts Supreme Court. John
Quincy Adams had served as Dana's secretary from 1781 to 1782.   5 Mrs. Henderson
was probably the mother of Lyman's wife, née Mary Elizabeth Henderson.

MISCELLANEOUS LETTERS   February 25, 1827

From RICHARD W. HABERSHAM, Savannah. Notes that he has been instructed by
the Secretary of War (James Barbour) "to place in the hands of the Marshal [John
H. Morel] of this District, a warrant for the arrest of certain persons charged with
being engaged in Surveying the lands of the Creek Indians . . ." (cf. above, Brooke
to Clay, February 11, 1827, note). States that he has taken steps to obtain
the necessary witnesses and has assured the Secretary of War that, as soon as the
warrant could be obtained, he would deliver the requisite instructions to the
marshal; explains that he has so acted from a sense of duty that "the interests of
the United States" should be represented; but, now that there is an interval in
the proceedings, communicates through Clay "to the President, that neither . . .
feelings, nor convictions will permit . . . [him], to prosecute the case in behalf of
the United States." Citing the higher duties "which he owes to his native State,"
concludes: "If therefore it becomes necessary that further proceedings should be
had in this matter, I have no alternative, but to tender back to the President the
Trust which has been confided to me. . . ." ALS. DNA, RG59, Letters of Resignation and Declination.
  Clay replied, April 27, 1827, that this letter had been submitted to the President,
who directed him to inform Habersham that the resignation was accepted. Copy,
DNA, RG59, Dom. Letters, vol. 21, p. 526 (M40, R19). Habersham subsequently
became attorney general for the State of Georgia.

Draft by Thomas Hart Clay

$300   New York Feb. 26th 1827
H Clay Washington City
      At sight Pay J. J. Astor or order three hundred dollars & place the
same to acct of yours   T H CLAY

[Endorsements on verso][1]
John Jacob Astor

. . .

Recd. payment Wm. Ratree Jr[2]
Accepted H. Clay
5 March 1827.

ADS. DLC-TJC (DNA, M212, R16).
[1] Three intervening cashier endorsements have been deleted, where indicated, by editors.   [2] Not identified.

From Forsythe, Dobbin and Company

Henry Clay Esqr.   Wheeling 26th. Feb 1827
   Above we hand you receipt[1] for 1 Box recd. from Maysville in December last—which should have been forwd. earlier, had an Opportunity offerd.
   it is but seldom we can forward small Packages direct to your City   Yours Respectfully   Forsyth & Dobbin
                                                          By H. D. BROWN[2]

ADS. DNA, RG59, Misc. Letters (M179, R65).
[1] Duplicate receipt to "Forsyth & Dobbin," dated February 22, 1827, and signed by Levi Waddle, acknowledges acceptance, at Wheeling of a box weighing 45 pounds and promises "to deliver in Similar good order in 18 days to Mr Henry Clay Washington City DC & he paying . . . $1.00 carriage for Same." Waddle, not further identified, signed his name with a mark of "X"; text and identification of signature in Brown's hand.
   [2] Not further identified.

MISCELLANEOUS LETTERS   February 26, 1827

From PETER LITTLE, Washington. Encloses a letter from (Thomas) Kell, attorney general of Maryland, and requests information with which to answer Kell's inquiries. ALS. DNA, RG5, Misc. Letters (M179, R65).
   Kell had served for 20 years as deputy prosecutor of Annapolis. He held the post of attorney general from 1824 to 1827 and subsequently became a judge of the Baltimore County Court.
   Daniel Brent answered Little's letter on February 26, 1827, and returned its enclosure with an explanation that the Slave Indemnity Commission (cf. above, Clay to McLane, January 15, 1827, note) would "decide upon the claims of individuals without reference to the opinion of this Department." He added that the claims mentioned by Kell probably would be excluded because the Convention with Great Britain (of November 13, 1826) limited "the adjudication of this new commission to cases in the definitive list of this Department, furnished the Board under the St. Petersburg Convention. . . , especially if they should not be comprehended in the law . . . now on its passage thro' the House of Representatives for the establishment of that commission." DNA, in RG59, Dom. Letters, vol. 21 (M40, R19), 488. For the abovementioned claims list, see above, Clay to Adams, March 7, 1826.

From SAMUEL L. SOUTHARD, Washington. Requests that Clay return "a letter of recommendation in favor of Mr. R. Stockton for the office of District Judge in N.

Jersey." AN. DNA, RG59, Misc. Letters (M179, R65). Letter not found. Cf. above, Parsons to Clay, September 25, 1826.

APPLICATIONS, RECOMMENDATIONS   February 26, 1827

DAVID BARTON, Washington, notes that the bearer, Garret Anderson, wishes to be a State Department clerk, that he has an excellent record as a land office clerk, and that his appointment would be "gratifying" to Barton. ALS. DNA, RG59, Misc. Letters (M179, R65).

Anderson, who had been employed in connection with the Yellowstone expedition in 1819 (cf. above, II, 599n), had been residing in St. Louis. He now came to Washington as a permanent resident but did not receive the desired State Department appointment. Cf. above, Barnard to Clay, January 10, 1827, note.

HENRY W. CONWAY, "Congress Hall" (1), encloses a recommendation for appointment of Thomas P. Eskridge as judge of the Superior Court of the Arkansas Territory and seeks Clay's support. ALS. DNA, RG59, A. and R. (M531, R3). Published in Carter (ed.), *Territorial Papers. . . ,* XX, 400–401. Recommendation by Conway and 17 others, addressed to the President and dated February 13, enclosed.

Eskridge, a native of Virginia and a resident of Arkansas Territory since 1820, had been a circuit judge for the past five years. He was appointed to the recommended position in March, 1827, and reappointed in 1831.

HENRY W. CONWAY, "Congress Hall" (2), states that Samuel C. Roane and William Quarles, of Arkansas Territory, are respectable members of the bar and applicants for appointment as judge of the Superior Court of the Territory. ALS. DNA, RG59, A. and R. (M531, R7). Published in Carter (ed.), *Territorial Papers. . . ,* XX, 401.

Roane, a pioneer lawyer and planter in Arkansas, served as United States attorney for the Territory from 1821 to 1836. He was also attorney for the Third Judicial Circuit of the Territory from 1825 to April 17, 1827, when he was appointed as judge of the First Judicial Circuit of the Territory. He resigned the last post in October, 1827, but in October, 1831, became judge of the Jefferson County court in Arkansas. He was president of the first State Senate, in 1836. Quarles has not been further identified.

WILLIAM JOHNSON (of South Carolina) recommends appointment of Charles Harris as a member of the Slave Indemnity Commission. ALS. DNA, RG59, A. and R. (M531, R4). Cf. below, Clay to Cheves, March 23, 1827.

ALFRED H. POWELL, Washington, notes that J(ames) H. Bennett "has business connected with department of State" and solicits Clay's aid for him. ALS. DNA, RG59, A. and R. (M531, R1). Cf. below, Bennett to Clay, March 22, 1827.

To Thomas Swann and Others

Gentlemen   27 Feb. 1827.

A balance stands in your books against me on my a/c as late Speaker of the H. of R. of $136, of which $100 are in consequence of an erroneous payment of a check at the Bank, which was drawn by me, but never indosed [*sic*] by the person[1] to whom it was payable. As the payment was not valid against him, it could not be in respect to me; and in point of fact I never could be credited with it at the Treasury. It is a clear case of a loss which must fall on the Bank, or the officer who made the payment erroneously. I shall be much obliged to the Board if they will look into the transaction, and have my account corrected by striking from it the $100. With respect to the residue of the above bal: it consists of errors on the part of the late Sergeant at Arms,[2] for which I am responsible, and which shall be paid. I am respectfully Your ob. Servt.   H. CLAY

President & Directors of the Off. of B. U. States Washington

ALS. PHi-Etting Collection.   [1] Not identified
[2] Thomas Dunn had served as Sergeant at Arms of the House from December, 1823, until his death the following year; his son, John Oswald Dunn, who had been serving as assistant doorkeeper under his father, had then been named Sergeant at Arms. The latter retained the post until June, 1832, when he resigned because of irregularities in his accounts.

From Peter B. Porter

Dear Sir,   (Confidential)   Black Rock Feby 27th. 1827.

I have not written to you since sometime before the election of Mr Van Buren,[1] which I believe formed the principal topic of my last letter.[2] This election has resulted as I then anticipated, and, indeed (knowing that his election was unavoidable, without the utter destruction of our party) *as I wished.*

The Republican party in this State, as you are well aware, was prostrated by their divisions on the subject of the late presidential election.[3] An effort (& I hope it will yet prove an auspicious one) was made last year, to reunite them by mutual concessions on this subject. Rochester, the known & avowed friend of the administration, was nominated for Governor, & zealously & efficiently supported by Van Buren & his friends.[4] When Van Buren's term expired it would have been bad faith in Rochesters friends to discard him on the ground of his presidential preferences—the very cause of difference which they had agreed to bury & forget; and they could assign no other plausible reason for dropping him.

There were other considerations connected with this election. Clinton & Van Buren, as I have often told you, & of the truth of which even Mr. Adams must be, by this time convinced, are equally hostile to the administration. They attempted a coalition[5] more than a year ago, which was broken off only by the disgust which they saw it created among their friends. They are ready to unite again whenever they think it will advance their interests. If a bare majority of the republicans in the Legislature (and this was the most that under existing circumstances could have been calculated on) had taken up any other candidate than V. Buren, his (V.B's) friends would have denounced this majority as treacherous, & would have been joined by the friends of Clinton, & in this way, his election probably secured. And this would have given to the proceeding the character (of which it is now divested) of an administration vote. I received letters from my friends in the Legislature, in January, offering to make me a candidate. I, however, not only declined this proposition altogether, but earnestly recommended for the reasons I have suggested to give the undivided vote of the party to Van Buren, and am gratified that this course has been taken. It is a strong evidence of the fidelity of the friends of the administration in the execution of the mutual arrangement entered into last year.

That both Van Buren & Clinton are using all their efforts to destroy the influence of the administration, and support the interests of Genl. Jackson, in this State, is not to be questioned; and, if I know any thing of the sentiments and feelings of our citizens, it is equally certain that they will both be disappointed & disgraced. I shall be at Albany before the adjournment of our Legislature, & will write you again from that place. In haste yours respectfully & truly.

P. B. PORTER

ALS. DLC-HC (DNA, M212, R2). Addressed to Clay.
[1] Martin Van Buren's re-election to the United States Senate had occurred on February 6, 1827.   [2] Cf. above, Porter to Clay, January 3, 1827. Van Buren's senatorial prospects were discussed in Porter to Clay, above, December 24, 1826.   [3] Cf. above, III, 859–61.   [4] Cf. above, Rochester to Clay, May 9, 1826, note; Stuart to Clay, October 7, 1826; Porter to Clay, October 8, 1826.   [5] Cf. above, Shaw to Clay, September 10, 1826, note.

INSTRUCTIONS AND DISPATCHES   February 27, 1827

From ALEXANDER H. EVERETT, Madrid, no. 70. Reports having learned that "the Board of duties would be disposed to revoke without difficulty the extraordinary tonnage duty which was laid upon our vessels by the decree of Octr. 20. 1817 upon being assured that our discriminatory duties on Spanish vessels were or would be also repealed" (cf. above, Clay to Everett, April 27, 1825, note 11). Notes that, mindful of the act of Congress of January 7, 1824 (cf. above, Lorich to Clay, March 16, 1825, note), he wrote (Manuel González) Salmón, the Minister of State, proposing such an arrangement, and encloses a copy of that letter (dated February 19). Observes that an informal agreement to repeal discriminating duties "may afterwards be made permanent by a treaty which may also provide for such other matters as require adjustment" (cf. above, Everett to Clay, February 13, 1827, note). Mentions that the Captain General of Castille (Francisco Longa) has given his command to (probably Francisco de Paula) Escudero and that the Portuguese refugees aided by the Captain General "in their second invasion of Portugal were compelled again to retreat and attempted for the third time to take refuge in Spain." Adds that, while some of the refugees were disarmed, others have refused to give up their weapons and have returned to Portugal. ALS. DNA, RG59, Dip. Disp., Spain, vol. 27 (M31, R28). Received May 12.

Escudero, a naval officer, had been named Minister of Marine upon the accession of Ferdinand VII. He had retained that post under the constitutional regime until 1822 but had been removed from office with the overthrow of the constitutionalists.

MISCELLANEOUS LETTERS   February 27, 1827

To JAMES BARBOUR. Requests information with which to answer the enclosed letter (above, Porter to Clay, February 18, 1827). AN. DNA, RG94, USMA, Cadet Application Papers, 1826/218.

From PETER B. PORTER, Black Rock (New York) (2). Proposes that, upon learning of final passage of appropriations for the expenses of the (Northern) Boundary Commission, he will instruct Major (Joseph) Delafield to prepare for a survey "to ascertain and establish the 49th parallel of Latitude at the Lake of the Woods, and the Red River as proposed last fall," unless in the meantime he or (Thomas) Barclay should receive instructions from Great Britain "to suspend the execution of that service" (cf. above, Porter to Clay, October 18, 1826). States that he and Barclay will meet in New York on the first of March, or later if Barclay has not received by that date an answer to his request of last fall for instructions. LS. DNA, RG76, Northern Boundary: Treaty of Ghent, 1814, Arts. VI and VII, env. 1, folder 1, item 78.

APPLICATIONS, RECOMMENDATIONS   February 27, 1827

THOMAS CULBRETH, Annapolis, recommends Edward Dubois for a clerkship. ALS. DNA, RG59, A. and R. (M531, R2). Enclosed in Dubois to [Clay], below, March 1, 1827. Cf. above, Culbreth to Clay, August 9, 1826.

THOMAS Y[OUNG] SPICER, Washington, solicits appointment as consul or commercial agent. ALS. DNA, RG59, A. and R. (M531, R7). Enclosed in Cambreleng to Clay, February 28, 1827.
   Spicer, a lieutenant of infantry in the War of 1812, was a New York merchant. He received no appointment.

F[REDERICK] W. SYMMES, Pendleton, South Carolina, inquires concerning continuation of his contract to publish the laws and asks whether, if his contract be not extended, compensation will be allowed him for publishing the treaties with Denmark and Guatemala. ALS. DNA, RG59, P. and D. of L. Cf. above, Mitchell to Clay, November 10, 1826, note.
   On March 12, 1827, William Browne, answering on behalf of the State Department, replied that the amount due for publishing the treaties would be paid. Copy, in DNA, RG59, Dom. Letters, vol. 21, p. 496 (M40, R19).

JOHN TALIAFERRO AND OTHERS, Washington, recommend appointment of Edward T. Tayloe as Secretary of Legation in Mexico, state that Tayloe resides in Mexico and is "one of the family" of the United States Minister (Joel R. Poinsett). ALS by Taliaferro, signed also by J(ohn) S(trode) Barbour, James Strong, S(tephen) Van Rensselaer, and William L. Brent. DNA, RG59, A. and R. (M531, R8). Cf. above, Taliaferro to Clay, December 22, 1825, note; Poinsett to Clay, December 29, 1826.

H[ENRY] S[CHUYLER] THIBODAUX, New Orleans, recommends L[awrence] de Cruise for appointment as Chargé "to any of the Italian States, Greece, or any other part of Europe. . . ." ALS. DNA, RG59, A. and R. (M531, R2). Cf. above, De Cruise to [Clay], October 9, 1825.

INSTRUCTIONS AND DISPATCHES   February 28, 1827

To JOEL POINSETT, Mexico, no. 19. Notifies him of his appointment as Minister to the Congress of Tacubaya (see above, Poinsett to Clay, August 20, 1826, note) and encloses his commission and letter of credence. States that his instructions are the same as those prepared for (Richard C.) Anderson and (John) Sergeant (above, May 8, 1826) and that the instructions are "in the hands of Mr Sergeant or Mr [William B.] Rochester, the Secretary of the Mission, and will be there accessible. . . ." Notes that the House of Representatives limited the outfit to the sum of $4,500, that the Senate "has since stricken out the provision altogether," and that, under these circumstances, "the president has no authority to make . . . any allowance in the form of outfit." LS. DNA, RG84, Great Britain and Mexico (MR17). Copy, in DNA, RG59, Dip. Instr., vol. 11, p. 256 (M77, R6). In a draft of this instruction Clay stated that the House of Representatives had allowed but $4,500 for Poinsett's outfit, that probably the Senate would agree to that sum, but that if the Congress of Tacubaya did not assemble, the President would not make any allowance for an outfit. ALI draft, dated "21 Feb. 1827," in DLC-HC (DNA, M212, R8). The commission and letter of credence, both dated February 12, 1827, are in DNA, RG59, Ceremonial Communications, II, 58–59. For Congressional deliberations on Poinsett's outfit, in the House of Representatives on February 14–15 and in the Senate on February 26, see *Register of Debates*, 19 Cong., 2 Sess., pp. 486, 1161–76, 1187–1213, 1214. Cf., also, above, Clay to Adams, January 26, 1827, note.

From ANDREW ARMSTRONG, Port au Prince. Encloses a copy of the law (dated February 22, 1827) repealing export duties (on domestic products). ALS. DNA, RG59, Cons. Disp., Cap Haitien, vol. 6 (M9, R6). Received March 21.

MISCELLANEOUS LETTERS   February 28, 1827

To SAMUEL BEARDSLEY, Blenheim. Forwards his commission as attorney for the Northern District of New York. Copy. DNA, RG59, Dom. Letters, vol. 21, p. 491 (M40, R19). Beardsley accepted the office by letter from Utica, April 7, 1827. ALS. DNA, RG59, Acceptances and Orders for Comns. (M-T645, R2).

To JOSEPH S. BENHAM, Cincinnati. Forwards his commission as attorney for the District of Ohio. Copy. DNA, RG59, Dom. Letters, vol. 21, p. 489 (M40, R19).

To SIDNEY BREESE, Kaskaskia. Forwards his commission as attorney for the District of Illinois. Copy. *Ibid.*, p. 490. On April 20 Breese acknowledged receipt of this letter. ALS. DNA, RG59, Acceptances and Orders for Comns. (M-T645, R2).

To JOHN BROWNSON, St. Martinville. Forwards his commission as attorney for the Western District of Louisiana. Copy. DNA, RG59, Dom. Letters, vol. 21, p. 490 (M40, R19). Brownson, a native of Vermont and an infantry officer from 1804 to 1815, served as United States attorney for the Western District of Louisiana from 1823 until his removal from that office in 1829. He acknowledged on April 26, 1827, receipt of the commission. ALS, in DNA, RG59, Acceptances and Orders for Comns. (M-T645, R2).

To WILLIAM ALLISON MCREA, Tallahassee. Forwards his commission as United States attorney for the Middle District of Florida. Copy. DNA, RG59, Dom. Letters, vol. 21, p. 490 (M40, R19). McRae acknowledged receipt of this letter and enclosure on April 10, 1827. *Ibid.*, Acceptances and Orders for Comns. (M-T645, R2).

From H[ENRY] and D[AVID] COTHEAL, New York. State that "When Mr.   [sic] left this on his embassy [sic] to Spain," they "put into his hands all" their "papers relating to" their claim against Spain in the case of the *Mosquito* but have "heard nothing about the business." Ask "whether any thing has been done, or whether there is any prospect of . . . ever recovering any thing from that quarter." ALS. DNA, RG76, Misc. Claims, Spain, env. 9, folder 3. See above, Cotheals and Hallett to Clay, April 28, 1825, and note.

From J[OHN] M. HANSON, St. Augustine, Florida. Submits his resignation as marshal of the Middle District of Florida. LS. DNA, RG59, Letters of Resignation and Declination. Postdated and enclosed in White to Clay, February 15, 1827; received (February) 17.

APPLICATIONS, RECOMMENDATIONS   February 28, 1827

D[AVID] BARTON encloses a recommendation (in favor of Rufus Easton). ANS. DNA, RG59, A. and R. (M531, R3). Enclosure is a copy of a petition addressed to the President, dated January 6, 1827, and signed by 18 citizens of Missouri. Cf. above, Easton to Clay, January 20, 1827.

JOHN BOONE, Washington, solicits one of the additional clerkships which may be created by Congress. ALS. DNA, RG59, A. and R. (M531, R1). cf. above, Clay to McLane, January 14, 1826, note; Barnard to Clay, January 10, 1827.
    Boone, the son of Ignatius Boone, a clerk in the Treasury Department until his death in 1826, received a clerkship in the office of the Post Master General in 1828.

C[HURCHILL] C. CAMBRELENG, Washington, encloses an application (of Thomas Young Spicer) and supports it. ALS. DNA, RG59, A. and R. (M531, R7). See above, Spicer to Clay, February 27, 1827.

WILLIAM HEBB reminds Clay of his offer to render him "a service in any appointment other than those immediately in . . . [his] department" and seeks his "friendly interposition" in support of Hebb's "application for the appointment of Commissioner (or event [sic] Clerk) to Board to be appointed to distribute the fund awarded the United States by the Emperor of Russia [Alexander I] under the Ghent Treaty." ALS. DNA, RG59, A. and R. (M531, R4). Cf. below, Clay to Cheves, March 23, 1827; Clay to Ogden, March 23, 1827.

THOMAS MUNROE recommends John Boone for appointment as a clerk in some Department of the Government. ALS. DNA, RG59, A. and R. (M531, R1). Unaddressed. Cf. above, Boone to Clay, February 28, 1827.

PETER B. PORTER introduces (Chauncey) Goodrich, who has a recommendation from (William B.) Rochester (above, November 22, 1826) and who wishes to "obtain the employment of a Bearer of dispatches . . . to the commission of which the Judge [Rochester] is Secretary" (cf. above, Clay to Rochester, November 30, 1825; Sergeant to Clay, November 17, 1826, note); expresses his hope that this arrangement can be made. AL draft. NBuHi. Not dated; endorsed on verso: "Letter to Mr Clay in fav. of C. Goodrich Feby 1827."

INSTRUCTIONS AND DISPATCHES   March 1, 1827

To ANDREW ARMSTRONG, Port au Prince. Acknowledges receipt of Armstrong's letter "of the third ultimo" and states that it has been reviewed by the President, who directs Armstrong to return to the United States. Instructs him to inform the Government of Haiti that "in taking this step, it is not . . . [the United States'] purpose otherwise to disturb the relations of Commerce and amity now subsisting between the people of the two Countries." Copy. DNA, RG59, Cons. Instr., vol. 2, p. 413 (M78, R2).

From W[ILLIAM] TUDOR, Lima, no. 60. Reports "universal" approval in Peru of the recent revolt (cf. above, Tudor to Clay, February 3, 1827). Relates that General (Andrés) Santa Cruz has offered General (Antonio José de) Sucre assistance in removing his Colombian troops (from Bolivia) via "the ports of the Intermedios" but has warned him not to enter Peru from any other direction. Notes that the custom house is about to be returned from Callao to Lima. Mentions that he writes "by this occasion" to the Secretary of the Navy (Samuel L. Southard), urging measures to increase commercial intercourse with Peru, Chile, Guatemala, Mexico; argues that a packet service "on both seas" would have "the most important influence on . . . commercial relations w[ith] these countries"; and comments that present communications are irregular and slow, as is proven by the fact that his "latest letters from the U. S. are only to Sept. 1st." ALS. DNA, RG59, Cons. Disp., Lima, vol. 1 (M154, R1). Received June 25.

From BEAUFORT T. WATTS, Bogotá, no. 24. Encloses copies of his correspondence with the Colombian Foreign Minister (José M. Restrepo) on implementation of a law authorizing the government to declare Guayaquil, Cartagena, and Puerto Cabello ports of deposit. ALS. DNA, RG59, Dip. Disp., Colombia, vol. 4 (M-T33, R4). Received April 7.

From BEAUFORT T. WATTS, Bogotá, no. 25. Recalls that he previously made inquiry concerning his right to an allowance of an outfit (cf. above, Watts to Clay, July 9, 1826). States that (Stephen) Pleasonton has expressed his opinion that Watts is entitled to one, in which case the Government will owe him "nearly one thousand dollars after the payment of the Bills . . . drawn up to this date." ALS. *Ibid.* Received April 7. In the same source are three notices of drafts, ALS by Watts, on Clay, each dated "March 1st", for $421, $500, and $1,063, respectively. Cf. below, Clay to Watts, March 8, 1827.

MISCELLANEOUS LETTERS   March 1, 1827

From NOYES BARBER, House of Representatives, Washington. Encloses a letter from a constituent (Jedediah Huntington) and requests that Clay "enquire of the Mexican Minister [Pablo Obregón] whither [sic] there can be anything done for the benefit of Col. Younges [sic] family." ALS. DNA, RG59, Misc. Letters (M179, R65). In his letter to Barber, dated "Norwich Jany 24, 1827," Huntington stated that Guilford (Dudley) Young served in the War (of 1812), joined (Francisco Xavier) Mina's expedition to Mexico (cf. above, II, 511n), was "either slain in battle or shot . . . by the Spaniards," and left a wife and six children "destitute of even a dollar to support them." Huntington further noted that he had petitioned the Mexican Government (for relief) of Young's widow, but that he has been unable to learn whether anything was granted. He asked Barber to enquire whether any aid could be obtained for Mrs. Young.

Huntington was a prosperous merchant of Norwich, Connecticut. Young, also a native of that State, had attained the rank of lieutenant colonel in the War of 1812, had been honorably discharged in 1815, and had been killed in 1817, while in Mina's service. Mrs. Young filed a claim against the Mexican Government for her husband's back pay, amounting to $8,913.89; the claim was eventually rejected by the claims commission appointed under the Treaty of Guadalupe Hidalgo. *Sen. Docs.*, 35 Cong., 2 Sess., no. 18, p. 57.

From JAMES H. CAUSTEN, Washington. States that, at the request of Michael Withers, he visited the Navy Yard and found "in the entire works five pair of Winged Gudgeons only" and that workmen employed there, "prior as well as subsequent to the destruction of the Yard, in 1814," assert that "there was at no former period a greater number in use than at the present time." Notes that (William) Thornton has published a statement that there were 4,000. Comments that Clay's answer (below, March 9, 1827) to Withers' letter (above, February 21, 1827) "is looked for with intense anxiety," since Withers' patent "has nearly expired by limitation, and the publication by the Superintendent of the Patent Office has as effectually repealed his patent as an act of Congress could have done," and Withers cannot proceed "to vindicate his character or sustain his right" until Clay's decision is known. ALS. DNA, RG59, A. and R. (M531, R8). Copy, in MHi-Adams Papers, Letters Recd. (MR479); published in Washington *Daily National Journal*, April 24, 1827. Thornton's attack on Withers' claim had been published as a letter to an unnamed correspondent in the *Baltimore Patriot and Mercantile Advertiser*, February 21, 1827, reprinted from the *Lancaster Gazette* (Pennsylvania).

The Navy Yard had been burned, August 24, 1814, on orders of Navy Secretary William Jones, to avoid its capture by invading British troops during the War of 1812.

From JOHN H. HOWLAND AND COMPANY, New York. Request instructions from the State Department for (Albert) Gallatin to present a claim on their behalf to the British Lords of the Treasury. State that in September, 1825, a company vessel, the *Byron*, was stranded on the coast of Scotland; that the "sails, rigging, and sundry other appendages of the vessel" were placed at auction; and that Benjamin Lord, captain of the *Byron*, "bid them in, under the impression that he would not, as he took them home . . . be subjected to the payment of duty." Explains that Captain Lord paid £300 in duties, that he solicited a refund upon returning the salvage items to the United States, and that the Lords of the Treasury rejected his petition. ALS. DNA, RG76, Misc. Claims, Great Britain, env. 2, folder 9. See below, Clay to Gallatin, March 29, 1827; Lawrence to Clay, December 4, 1827, and note.

John H. Howland was a New York shipping specialist and manager of 16 vessels, the owners of which were, for the most part, from the New Bedford region of Massachusetts. Howland was the sole owner of but two of the ships, although he held a part interest in several of them. Benjamin Lord has not been further identified.

From JOSEPH M. WHITE, House of Representatives. Requests that Alexander Adair's commission as marshal of the Middle District of Florida be sent to Tallahassee. ALS. DNA, RG59, A. and R. (M531, R1). Misdated "Feb 29th."

APPLICATIONS, RECOMMENDATIONS   March 1, 1827

LEWIS CONDICT, House of Representatives, recommends William P. Elliot for appointment as a bearer of dispatches. States that Elliot is a student of architecture and wants to go to London. ALS. DNA, RG59, A. and R. (M531, R3). Endorsed (AES) at the bottom of the page: "I cheerfully acquiesce in the above representation. *Eph. Bateman* March 1st 1827." Recommendations misfiled in folder of "William Elliott."

Cf. below, Clay to Gallatin, April 16, 1827.

During the year young Elliot received $100 for expenses as bearer of dispatches to London.

WILLIAM COOLIDGE, JR., Georgetown, submits "testimonials" in his favor (cf. above, Coolidge to Clay, January 24, 1827). ALS. DNA, RG59, A. and R. (M531, R2). Annexed at the end of his letter is a copy of Everett and others to Clay, above, January 31, 1827.

EDWARD DUBOIS, Washington, encloses recommendations in his favor. ALS. DNA, RG59, A. and R. (M531, R2). Letter unaddressed. Enclosures are Culbreth to Clay, February 27, 1827, and Joseph Kent to William Thornton, February 27, 1827.

THOMAS KITTERA recommends (Athanasius) Ford for a clerkship in the State Department. States that the applicant is thought to be the son-in-law of General (William) Duncan. ALS. DNA, RG59, A. and R. (M531, R3). Cf. above, Ford to Clay, February 12, 1827.

Ford's wife has not been identified. William Duncan of Pennsylvania, a collector of direct taxes under the administration of James Madison, superintendent of United States military stores at Philadelphia during the War of 1812, and a brigadier general of militia from 1811 to 1813, was a prosperous merchant of Philadelphia and a member of the Pennsylvania Legislature from 1825 to 1829. In 1829 he became surveyor of customs for the Philadelphia district.

RICHARD H. LOVE, Washington, transmits "a letter from Mr [Charles Fenton] Mercer [above, February 19, 1827] with copies of those" to which he refers and requests that Clay "give them" his "kind consideration." ALS. DNA, RG59, A. and R. (M531, R5). Unaddressed.

WILLIAM M. THOMPSON, "Thompsonville, Culpeper Co. Va," encloses a letter (above, Strother to Clay, October 28, 1826). Comments that he does not know Clay personally, although he has been "several times introduced. . . ." Notes that he was born in Hanover County, Virginia, whence he removed to Culpeper, where he was a merchant until recently, that he has "sustained great vicissitudes in pecuniary matters by securityship & the changes in the value of property," and that he would like employment in one of the Departments of Government. Cites Strother and James Barbour as references. ALS. DNA, RG59, A. and R. (M531, R8).

Check to Robert P. Letcher

2 March 1827

Pay to Robert P. Letcher or order Five hundred dollars.
Cashr. of the Off. of Dt. & Dt. Washington[1]   H CLAY

ADS. DLC-TJC (DNA, M212, R16). Endorsed on verso by Letcher and Thomas Metcalfe.
[1] Richard Smith.

From Meshech Frost

Honl. Sir,   Frostburg (Md.) March 2nd. 1827

In the perusal of the Washington city papers I observe the passing of a bill in the House of Representatives for the repairing of the Cumberland road, to Wheeling (Va.) $375. pr mile is the appropriation contemplated in the bill.[1] I would be willing to undertake eight miles, say 4 east of Frostburg and 4 west, which takes in Savage Mountain, which no doubt you are well aware is a portion of the worst road on the above mentioned route.

The terms upon which I would be willing to engage upon are these. viz: I would repair at the present time, and keep in *good repair* the eight miles aforesaid, from the time I undertake untill [*sic*] the expiration of *five years*, The United States, paying me the sum appropriated at the time the contract may be made. You will understand Sir, that I will not only keep the road in good repair, but will also leave it in good repair; any security (in reason) which may be required for the faithful fulfillment on my part, will be given. The road now spoken of, is (no doubt you are acquainted) considerably out of repair; and the heavy rains which are common in the mountains here lay it liable to be kept out repair by washes. You will at a moment's glance then, I presume, see the necessity of employing residents on the road, in whom confidence may be placed and I make no doubt that such men may be found. Perhaps it will be necessary for me to add, previous to my closing, that I would be understood that the above contract that I would enter into, will be exempt from tollgates or any Superintendant.

Not more than 3 or 4 years since, Government appropriated *twenty five thousand dollars* which was expendend [*sic*] for the repairing of this road,[2] & in *twelve months* after it was nearly as much out of repair, as it was previous to the repairing, and the cause is obvious; for unless a person be immediately on the spot after a heavy continued rain, in order to immediately repair such places as require, (which may some times be accomplished in 3 or 4 days) it will cost the labour of 4 or 5 weeks. I know from actual observation for I generally keep a portion of the road immediately on my premises in repair, and am certain it requires instant attention upon the slightest rupture.

From the slight acquaintance you have perhaps of my character, (although you have been pleased at times in your travels from the Westward to honor me with your company) I have thought well to refer you to Chauncy Forward,[3] a member from Pennsylvania now in your city or to Michael C. Sprigg Esqr. with whom (I believe) you are acquainted. You will have the goodness to address me on the subject,[4] and should the contract be entered into, I shall use my best exer-

tions to keep the road in such good repair, that there will be no room left for either Government or Travellers to censure. With high Respect I am Sir, Yrs etc.   MESHECH FROST
Hon. Henry Clay Washington City D. C.

ALS. DNA, RG59, A. and R. (M531, R3). Meshech Frost, founder of Frostburg, Maryland, was proprietor of a tavern which had become a popular stopping place for Congressmen, including Clay, when travelling the Cumberland Road. He subsequently entered the coal mining business and in 1845 organized the Frostburg Coal Company.
1 See above, Tarr to Clay, May 1, 1826, note.   2 By act of February 28, 1823, Congress had appropriated $25,000 for repairing the public road from Cumberland, Maryland, to Wheeling, Virginia. 3 *U. S. Stat.*, 728. Cf. above, III, 190n.   3 Chauncey Forward, brother of Walter Forward, practiced law in Somerset, Pennsylvania, and served in Congress from 1826 to 1831.   4 No reply found.

INSTRUCTIONS AND DISPATCHES   March 2, 1827

From CHRISTOPHER HUGHES, Brussels. Acknowledges receipt of Clay's instructions of December 12, 1826. Encloses copies of correspondence with Willinks and Van Staphorst and with Delpratt (Molière) relating to plans for selling the American Hotel at The Hague. Observes that Delpratt's appraisal of the property at $1,200 demonstrates "the expediency of effecting a sale without further delay," that he has decided "to expose the House & Lot at public auction, about the middle of next April," that he declined an offer by the Minister of Foreign Affairs (Baron Verstolk) on behalf of his Government (cf. above, Hughes to Clay, January 21, 1827), and that he (Hughes) thinks individuals may bid for the property, "speculating on the known wish of the Government to make the purchase." ALS. DNA, RG59, Dip. Disp., Netherlands, vol. 8 (M42, R-T12). Received April 23. Delpratt-Molière, who acted as Hughes' agent in this matter, has not been further identified.

From WILLIAM PHILLIPS, Guatemala. Refers to his letter of "the 3d inst" (*i.e.*, February) and now adds to that information. Encloses a copy of his "last note to this Government respecting the new Tariff [see above, Williams to Clay, August 4, 1826], and pressing an answer upon the Subject of the Gualan outrage [*i.e.*, the incident involving John Marshall, at Gualan—see above, Williams to Clay, August 29, 1826]—" Notes the present "complete state of anarchy," with "the Supreme Court of the State of Guatemala denying the legality of the State Assembly," "a decree from Sn Salvador anulling [*sic*] the new elections to the Federal Congress," a decree by the President (Manuel José Arce) "for a constituent assembly to reorganize the Constitution," "another decree from the Provinces calling the old members of the last Congress to meet . . . on the 15th. of March to impeach the President, and try the merits of the case between him & the late Chief of the State" (see above, Gonzalez to Clay, January 7, 1827), and "the President declared an Outlaw and his wife & children ordered out of Sn. Salvador—" States that (Antonio José) Cañaz and (Fernando) Valero have arrived, that they are keeping "aloof from Party Strife," that the former has declined appointment to the Treasury Department (cf. above, Williams to Clay, November 24, 1826), and that they are appreciative of "the kind reception" accorded them in the United States. Adds that (Juan Manuel) Rodriguez, who "was one of the Commissioners with [Manuel José] D'Arce to the United States" (see above, Clay to Miller, April 22, 1825, note), and now is Director of the Public Credit, is "also friendly disposed." Comments that "This Augean Stable wants cleaning out, for it is the head quarters of Ferdinandism and as much of a Spanish Colony as Porto Rico—" Reports his arrangements for care of the Legation books, seals, and cypher and expresses regret at leaving his post before his successor arrives but explains that such action is necessary because of his "heavy losses by that infamous *Canal bubble*, and the support of . . . friends being withdrawn in consequence of it. . . ." Continues: "The failure of the Canal contract, and the consequent disappointment of the receipt of the $200,000 as Stipulated, $8,000 of which was appropriated for the expenses of the Legation of this Government near the U States, has had an unfavorable influence here." Mentions rumors of contemplated military action in the provinces against Guatemala. Promises to send a detailed report on "the mining department in the 5 Provinces. . . ." LS. DNA, RG59, Cons. Disp., Guatemala, vol. 1 (M-T337, R1). Misdated as February 30. Brief extract published in Manning (arr.), *Diplomatic Correspondence . . . Latin-American Nations*, II, 884. Received May 23.

From BEAUFORT T. WATTS, Bogotá. no. 26. Reports that (Simón) Bolívar's presence in Venezuela has quelled "civil commotions" there which had become more serious than previously imagined (cf. above, Litchfield to Clay, May 22, 1826). Comments that it is strange "how this revolution has been brought about; and how the insurgents have imposed upon the people; triumphed with impunity against the government; and accomplished their purposes." States that, although Dr. (Miguel) Peña, President of the (Colombian) High Court of Justice, was suspended from office for one year on grounds of having committed a misdemeanor, he was entrusted to deliver $200,000 in doubloons on loan by the Congress to the agriculturalists of Caracas and that now the Congress "were resolved to impeach him again" for exchanging the specie for depreciated Caracas currency and pocketing the exchange premium. Notes that at the same time General (José Antonio) Páez was accused by the municipality of Caracas with "forcing the militia to military obedience contrary to law." Observes that, in order "to save themselves from the odium which would eventually follow the investigation of their acts [Páez and Peña] have set the government at defiance, stopped the operation of the laws—destroyed the national Credit. . . ." Adds that the people "had shown no disapprobation to the existing government. . . ." Attributes restoration of order to Bolívar's presence, complains that "the ungrateful and the invidious . . . impeach him with aspiring to monarchy," and expresses mortification that he has seen "perhaps too current in our prints, such ungenerous allusions." Argues that if Bolívar's critics "knew the materials upon which his theories had to act, they would accord him, at least, magnanimity and disinterestedness." ALS. DNA, RG59, Dip. Disp., Colombia, vol. 4 (M-T33, R4). Received April 7.

On March 4, 1827, Watts sent Clay a duplicate of the present dispatch and added at the end several observations on the causes of Colombian political instability. This he attributed to the prevailing "spirit of innovation," the dispersion of a small population "over an immense tract of land," and the lack of wealth, education, and industry. ALS, in *ibid.* Received April 18.

MISCELLANEOUS LETTERS   March 2, 1827

From PETER LITTLE, House of Representatives. Requests that the State Department supply information with which to answer the enclosed letter from "Capt. Rothrock." ALS. DNA, RG59, Misc. Letters (M179, R65).

On March 5, 1827, Daniel Brent returned Rothrock's letter with the explanation that the French Minister (Baron Durand de Mareuil) did not know any one by the name of "King" as agent of his government at Baltimore. Copy, in DNA, RG59, Dom. Letters, vol. 21, p. 492 (M40, R19). Rothrock has not been further identified.

APPLICATIONS, RECOMMENDATIONS   March 2, 1827

WILLIAM CRANCH, Washington, recommends his son, William G. Cranch, for a clerkship in the Patent Office, should Congress pass "the bill respecting the patent office." ALS. DNA, RG59, A. and R. (M531, R2). Cf. above, Cranch to Clay, December 15, 1826; Thornton to Clay, March 6, 1827.

C[LEMENT] DORSEY (no. 1) recommends his son-in-law (Richard B. Dorsey) for an appointment in the State Department and encloses his application (above, Dorsey to Clay, February 23, 1827). Notes that "his appointment would be very flattering to very many of . . . [Clay's] best friends." ALS. DNA, RG59, A. and R. (M531, R2).

C[LEMENT] DORSEY (no. 2) recommends (Athanasius) Ford for a clerkship in the State Department. ALS. Ibid. (R3). Cf. above, Ford to Clay, December 7, 1825, note; February 12, 1827, note.

WILLIAM MARKS, Washington City, recommends James Wilson, son of the late Thomas Wilson, for a clerkship in the State Department. Encloses a recommendation "from a number of very respectable characters in Pittsburgh." ALS. DNA, RG59, A. and R. (M531, R8). The enclosure, an unaddressed and undated petition, signed by E[phraim] Pentland and six others, states that James Wilson resided in Pittsburgh and served as prothonotary of Allegheny County.

Young Wilson did not receive the desired appointment. His father had been a long-time resident of Erie, Pennsylvania, had held various local offices before serving in Congress (1813–1817), and subsequently had filled the post of prothonotary of Erie County until his death in 1824.

JOHN MORTON, Washington, renews his application (cf. above, Morton to Clay, February 9, 1827) for a clerkship in the Patent Office and states that, while he would accept any position that might be offered, he would prefer to be placed under the Secretary's "immediate notice and employment." ALS. DNA, RG59, A. and R. (M531, R5).

S[AMUEL] SMITH, Capitol Hill, recommends George Brent for employment. ALS. Ibid. (R1). Unaddressed; enclosed in Brent to Clay, March 3, 1827.

JOHN B. THORP, New York, recommends appointment of Jacob Radcliff as Chargé d'Affaires in Denmark. ALS. DNA, RG59, A. and R. (M531, R7).

Thorp not further identified. Radcliff, a native of New York, had been graduated from the College of New Jersey (Princeton University) in 1783, admitted to the New York bar in 1786, and elected New York Assemblyman (1794–1795), assistant attorney general (1796–1798), justice of the New York Supreme Court (1798–1804), and mayor of New York (1810 and 1815). From 1805 to 1817 he had also served as a trustee of Columbia College. He did not receive the recommended appointment.

From Mathew Carey

Hon Henry Clay, Esqr Secretary of State
Dear Sir,   Philada. March 3. 1827
By direction of the Greek Comee.[1] I address you for information, whether the vessel or vessels from this port with Supplies for the Greeks, could be in any way provided with protection from the pirates,

after her [*sic*] arrival at Gibraltar. I am well aware that regular convoy cannot be afforded without an infringement of our neutrality. But the business might be managed in some what of a covert way, so as to Secure the Precious cargo from depredation. Very respectfully Your obt hble servt   Mathew Carey

ALS. DNA, RG45, Misc. Letters 1827/2. Endorsed by Daniel Brent, on cover: "Referred to Secy Navy." See below, Clay to Southard, March 8, 1827.
[1] The Philadelphia Greek Committee had been organized at a meeting in Masonic Hall on December 11, 1823. Carey was the secretary. Besides adopting resolutions calling upon Congress to consider "the expediency of recognizing the independence of the Greeks" (cf. above, III, 598–99n), the meeting had undertaken to collect funds "by voluntary contributions" in aid of the Greeks. Such a grant from the Philadelphia committee had been acknowledged by the Greeks in June, 1824, but with a plea for additional support. Further solicitation in 1827 brought funds amounting to nearly $20,000. *Niles' Weekly Register*, XXV (December 20, 1823), 246–47; XXVII (September 4, 1824), 11–12; XXXIII (November 24, 1827), 197; Philadelphia *United States Gazette*, April 28, 1827.

From Philander Chase

My Dr. Friend.   New York 3. Mar. 1827.
    The letter of instruction to Mr. Wiggin[1] was duly red. and forwarded.
    Is Transylvania University supplied with a President?[2] If not, will you permit me to name to you the Rev. Mr. Mc Ilvaine[3] now at West Point?— He is decidedly the most eloquent man in our section of the Community. He is much of a Gentleman and a most excellent scholar. On trial I am confident he would suit all good men of all parties— The choice of him I know would redound to the honour of Kentucky[4]—
    The Subscription[5] goes on well. We have now rising of $6,000. Please address me after this, & until advised otherwise in Boston.
    With most affectionate regards to Mrs. Clay and love to little John I am Your faithful & obliged Friend   Philander Chase
Hon. H. Clay.

ALS. DNA, RG59, Misc. Letters (M179, R65).
[1] Timothy Wiggin, of Manchester, England, an old college friend of Philander Chase, and a brother-in-law of Philander's older brother, Baruch. On the letter of instruction, cf. below, Wiggin to Clay, March 26, 1827.   [2] Cf. above, Clay to Bradford, February 10, 1827.   [3] Charles Pettit McIlvaine, of New Jersey, graduated from the College of New Jersey (Princeton University) in 1816. Ordained a priest in the Protestant Episcopal Church in 1823, he had served as Chaplain of the United States Senate during the Session of 1821–1822 and as chaplain and professor of geography, history, and ethics at the United States Military Academy from 1825 to 1827. In 1831 he was named Bishop of Ohio.   [4] Cf. below, Chase to Clay, April 19, 1827, note.   [5] For Kenyon College.

From John Jordan Crittenden

Dear Sir   Frankfort March 3rd 1827
    Your favours of the 14 & 16th of Feby:[1] have been received, & shall be attended.
    From what I heard about the close of the last session of the legisla-

ture, Mr. M. Flournoy, of Fayette, had some fancy to become a competitor of Clarke's at the next election for Congress.[2] I have heard nothing very lately as coming from him on the subject, and I trust that a more calm consideration of the matter has induced him to abandon all idea of becoming a candidate— Ben: Taylor Esqr.,[3] of Woodford, is already announced as a candidate— He is opposed to the administration. Under such circumstances the friends of the administration can not be insensible of the flagrant impolicy of permitting themselves to be divided by a plurality of candidates on their side— I should extremely regret to witness any competition between between [sic] Clarke & Flournoy, & shall not fail to do all I can to avert it.

In this District I think my brother's election[4] may be safely counted upon. And his success is rendered more certain by the embarrassments in which the opponents of the administration have involved themselves by their artifices. They are caught in the cunning of their devices— After having negotiated & wheedled that poor creature Allen[5] into a desertion of his avowed sentiments by promising that Mr. Lecompte[6] should decline & that he should be sent to Congress, it is said that they have found out that they had reckoned without their host, & that the said Mr. Lecompte is most perversely disinclined to ratify this compact. A few weeks will disclose what is to be the course of things. If Lecompte & Allen are both candidates they & their friends will contend with all the rage of civil warfare, & the petty little confederacies which have produced all this confusion will be exposed to the full flow of the derision & contempt with which it already begins to be regarded.

I am looking with curiosity & interest to the conduct of Mr. Senator Tyler[7] of Va:— Is he to be intimidated by the editors of a newspaper or two? I fear that he is a little tremulous, & that he may take refuge in some unbecoming evasion. It is a critical moment with him, & requires all his prudence & firmness. And my only wish is that he may acquit himself like an honorable & independent man.

I wish you success with all my heart, but I am if possible still more anxious for the discomfiture of that clamorous band of political fanatics, mountebanks & pretended patriots, by which you are assailed. I certainly do not intend to apply this description to all those who are in opposition to the administration. I mean it emphatically for the leaders of that opposition in Congress. There seems to be a vulgar emulation among them to surpass each other in indiscriminate opposition to, & in the coarsest abuse of the administration.

Mr. Calhoun seems to be almost overwhelmed by the ponderous acquital [sic] which he has received from his Committee.[8] Take this proceeding altogether & it is as genuine a "fanfaronade" as ever was witnessed. What is to become of the subordinates in this Drama? I mean Mr. Vandeventer & the other officials[9] who are implicated in the peculations that have practised upon the Treasury. I do not see how the administration can retain them in office after the report of the Committee— If that report has done them injustice it is greatly to be deplored, but politically it must be regarded as conclusive— It is a verdict by the representatives of the people, which you can't set aside, & according to which you must therefore pronounce judgment.

The pro-di-gi-ous importance given in Congress to your selection of public printers, has exploded the affair,[10] & made it a common subject of ridicule. Yr Friend   J J CRITTENDEN
Hon: H Clay, Secty: &c

ALS. NcD.   [1] Not found.
[2] Matthews Flournoy did not run for Congress in 1827; James Clark won re-election.
[3] Benjamin Taylor ran for Congress unsuccessfully in 1827.   [4] Henry Crittenden.
See above, Crittenden to Clay, November 25, 1826.   [5] Charles H. Allen.
[6] Joseph Lecompte.   [7] John Tyler—see above, Pleasants to Clay, February 14, 1827.   [8] On December 29, 1826, Vice President John C. Calhoun had requested that the House of Representatives investigate charges that he had been an interested party in the so-called "Rip-Rap" contract, awarded by the War Department while he was Secretary of War. Such allegations had appeared in the Alexandria, Virginia, *Phoenix Gazette* of December 28. The House had appointed a select committee to conduct the inquiry; and on February 13, 1827, the committee had reported that Calhoun was not financially involved. The controversy stemmed from an agreement in 1818 under which Elijah Mix was to supply stone at the Rip Rap Shoals, near Old Point Comfort, site of Fort Monroe. Mix, a resident of New York City, was a brother-in-law of Christopher Van de Venter, chief clerk of the War Department. In 1822 Congress had investigated the arrangement and found that Van de Venter had acquired half interest in the contract shortly after its signature. Testimony had further revealed that Calhoun had advised Van de Venter that, although there was no legal impediment to the clerk's investment, such involvement might lead to undesirable criticism. Van de Venter had denied that he had exerted any influence in the granting of the contract. Mix and Van de Venter had subsequently quarreled over the accounts, and in 1825 Mix had stated in a letter to "Hancock" of the New York *National Advocate* (Saterlee Clark) that Calhoun as well as Van de Venter had participated in the profits. Clark, a known political opponent of Calhoun, had held the letter confidential until late 1826, when he had discovered that Mix was to be awarded another government contract. His revelation of the letter had provided the documentation for the account in the *Phoenix Gazette*. The House committee had rejected Mix's testimony on grounds that he was not a reliable witness. For the reports and documents of the two House investigations, see *House Reports*, 17 Cong., 1 Sess., no. 109; 19 Cong., 2 Sess., no. 79.   [9] Van de Venter had testified that (Richard) Forrest of the State Department had contracted with the Ordnance Department while James Monroe was Secretary of War and that (George) Boyd, formerly of the War Department, had had similar dealings while William H. Crawford was head of that Department. *House Reports*, 19 Cong., 2 Sess., no. 79, pp. 51–52.   [10] See above, McGiffin to Clay, February 19, 1827.

INSTRUCTIONS AND DISPATCHES   March 3, 1827

From JAMES BROWN, Paris, no. 65. Acknowledges receipt of "dispatch No. 9" (see above, Clay to Gallatin, January 11, 1827, note) and states that he will obtain the information "with as little delay as possible." LS. DNA, RG59, Dip. Disp., France, vol. 23 (M34, R26). Received April 24.

APPLICATIONS, RECOMMENDATIONS

WILLIAM L. BRENT, House of Representatives, recommends his brother, George, "for an appointment in the Dist. of Columbia," and encloses supporting statements. ALS. DNA, RG59, A. and R. (M531, R1). The enclosures include Sprigg to Clay, December 8, 1826, and Smith to Clay, March 2, 1827, both above; and letters to the President from Edmund Key and 13 others, November 23, 1826, and from Joseph Kent, December 10, 1826.

CLEMENT BROOKE, "Perrywood near Upper Marlborough Md.," recommends his son (Robert Brooke) for a clerkship in the State Department; offers to supply, if required, testimonials other than that of (Joseph) Kent (above, Kent to Clay, February 12, 1827). ALS. DNA, RG59, A. and R. (M531, R1).

DANIEL DRAKE, Lexington, presents the application of Dr. (Gerard) Troost for an object "fully set forth in his letter to the President. . . ." Notes that Troost is a German who has been in the United States for several years and has during this period been associated with the "first Scientific men," who have held him "in the highest estimation." Alludes to the President's desire to "encourage such methods of inquiry into our National Resources," as evidenced in "his enlightened message to Congress when entering upon the duties of his office" (see above, Clay to Stuart, December 1, 1825, note). ALS. *Ibid.* (R3). Misfiled under "Froost."

Troost, a native of Holland, had received his education in pharmacy and medicine at the Universities of Amsterdam and Leyden, specializing in the study of chemistry, natural history, and geology. In 1810 he had travelled to the United States en route to Java, where he planned to pursue scientific studies, but he had remained in Philadelphia and in 1812 established a pharmaceutical laboratory. He was one of the founders and the first president of the Academy of Natural Sciences of Philadelphia, in 1812. In 1825 he had joined Robert Owen's community at New Harmony, Indiana, and two years later he moved to Nashville, Tennessee. In 1828, he was elected to the faculty of the University of Nashville (Peabody College), where he taught geology for 22 years. He served as State geologist of Tennessee from 1831 to 1849. His letter to Adams has not been found. According to the Register of Letters Received, Troost had written Adams on February 8, 1827; the subject of the letter is described as a request "For himself, mineralog. surveys." MHi-Adams Papers (MR254), p. 149.

RICHARD HINES, "Dowsons No. 1," urges appointment of John Singletary "to a suitable office." Notes that he is "considered as one of the best scholars (a graduate of Yale) and best writers in the district in which he resides . . ."; adds that his personal friends "are both numerous and Respectable"; and comments: "Both Mr. Singletary and Dr. Williams (the father in law of Mr. Singletary) is now and always have been the decided and sincere friends of the present administration and in the County of Pitt where Dr. Williams resides so great is his influence that out of 1100 votes which it gives at least 1000 would be for the reelection of Mr. Adams—" Postscript presents the claims of North Carolina for an appointment: "There is at present (I believe) but three of her native citizens in all the different Departments of the government at Washington   no minister no charge des affairs and but very *few* in any office under the governmen[t] of the U. States." ALS. DNA, RG59, A. and R. (M531, R7).

Singletary, born in Washington, North Carolina, and in 1814 graduated from Yale, practiced law in Beaufort County. He later studied for the Episcopal ministry, was ordained a deacon in 1834, served as a missionary for several years near Tarboro, and held rectorships at Washington and in the western part of the State. His wife, Eliza, was a daughter of Dr. Robert Williams, a native of North Carolina, educated in medicine at Richmond and Philadelphia, and a surgeon in the Continental Army of the Revolution. Dr. Williams had served in the North Carolina Assembly in 1786–1787, 1791, 1793–1795, 1802–1806, 1808, and 1813–1814. His continuing political prominence was evident in his election to the State constitutional convention of 1835.

MISCELLANEOUS LETTERS   March 4, 1827

From JOHN McDONELL, Detroit. Inquires whether his recess appointment to the Michigan Legislative Council (above, Clay to Woodbridge, October 25, 1826) has been confirmed by action of the Senate. ALS. DNA, RG59, A. and R. (M531, R5). Published in.Carter (ed.), *Territorial Papers*, XI, 1057.

Adams had submitted McDonell's name on December 14, 1826; and the Senate had approved the nomination on January 4, 1827. Cf. below, Clay to McDonell, March 20, 1827.

APPLICATIONS, RECOMMENDATIONS   March 4, 1827

GEORGE McCULLOH, Frostburg (Maryland), refers to the congressional appropriation for repairs on the Cumberland Road (cf. above, Frost to Clay, March 2, 1827) and solicits aid in procuring for himself "the Managment [*sic*] of all that part of the Road laying between Cumberland [Maryland] and Union Town [Pennsylvania]"; expresses belief "that the result of the Next Presidential Election in this District will very much depend on this County [Allegany]"; and states a wish that his application be kept confidential: "If I am disappointe[d] it would give the Jacksonites of this County a degree of pleasure that I should be excessivly [*sic*] mortified at." ALS. DLC-HC (DNA, M212, R2).

McCulloh had settled at Frostburg around the turn of the century and had served in the Maryland House of Delegates in 1812 and 1813. On the appointment, cf. above, Tarr to Clay, May 1, 1826, note.

To Peter Force

Dear Sir   Monday morning [March 5, 1827]
My servant[1] tells me that the note which I sent by him to you yesterday,[2] he, by mistake, understood to be addressed to Mr. Poor, the Auctioneer[3] to whom he delivered it, and who opened it but did not read it, as he instantly discovered the error. It was then returned to the Servant, who put it into your box in the state in which you received it. Yr's faithfully   H CLAY

ALS. DLC-HC (DNA, M212, R2). Addressed to Force. Dated on cover in strange hand: "March.5. 1827."
[1] Possibly Charles Dupuy.   [2] Not found.   [3] Moses Poor.

Check to William Ratree, Jr.

                                                    5 March 1827.
Pay to W. Ratree Junr. or order Three hundred dollars.
Cashr. of the Off. of B. U. States.[1]   H. CLAY

ADS. DLC-TJC (DNA, M212, R16). Endorsed on verso: "Wm. Ratree Jr." Cf. above, Draft by Thomas Hart Clay, February 26, 1827.
[1] Probably Richard Smith, of the Washington branch.

INSTRUCTIONS AND DISPATCHES   March 5, 1827

From JOHN SERGEANT, Mexico, "Private." Reports no change in the prospects of
the Congress of Tacubaya (see above, Sergeant to Clay, February 14, 1827). States
that (Simón) Bolívar and (José Antonio) Paéz have reached "a good understanding" (see above, Marks to Clay, January 8, 1827); that in Peru there is "great dissatisfaction, and appearances of approaching disturbance" (cf. above, Tudor to
Clay, February 3, 1827); that the constitutional government of Guatemala seems
"to be regaining its authority" (cf. above, Phillips to Clay, March 2, 1827); and
that in Mexico "there is nothing new, unless it be the preparation of an expedition to subdue the independents in Texas . . ." (see above, Dickson to Clay, January 3, 1827). Observes that the last matter may "prove a very serious one to Mexico,
draining its resources . . . and increasing the disorders and difficulties, of which
it has more than enough already to contend with" (see above, Sergeant to Clay,
January 26, 1827; Taylor to Clay, January 31, 1827). Comments that "this little
incident, insignificant as it appears at present, may become the source of very
important consequences." Adds: "If, indeed, we were inclined to be extremely
selfish, and disregard the troubles of our neighbors, we might perhaps find cause
to rejoice that the fountain of disturbance to Mexico being thus distinctly placed
to the South of our borders, could not hereafter be traced to the U. States. At
present, the Mexicans are much disposed to hold us accountable for whatever occurs in that quarter, as well as to impute to us a violent desire to possess ourselves
of their country." Notes the existence in Mexico of a party violently opposed to
the United States and strongly pro-British; attributes the feeling toward England
to her employment of power and money but finds the attitude toward the United
States more difficult to understand. Suggests that, if the pro-British party should
attain "a great influence with the Government, England will be introduced into
a very intimate union with American affairs, and be furnished with pretexts for
quarrelling" with the United States. Concludes: "A barrier between us and Mexico, would remove one great cause of irritation." ALS. DNA, RG43, First Panama
Congress, 1825–1827 (M662, R1). Received June 9.

MISCELLANEOUS LETTERS   March 5, 1827

To BEVERLEY ALLEN. Forwards his commission as United States attorney for the
Missouri District. LS. MoSHi. Copy, in DNA, RG59, Dom. Letters, vol. 21, p. 492
(M40, R19). Allen, writing from "Ste. Genevieve, Mii.," on March 30, 1827, acknowledged receipt of the commission, accepted the appointment, and stated his
intention of removing to St. Louis. ALS, in DNA, RG59, Acceptances and Orders
for Comns. (M-T645, R2).

From ROBERT LITTLE, Washington. With the "permission & advice" of (David)
Trimble encloses a copy of the latter's committee report to the House of Representatives "on the affairs of the Patent Office." States: "Though the direct object
of this report was not obtained at the late Session, yet it is presumed that enough
was elicited by it to induce you to order payment for my past services, and to
continue them by the aid of the Contingent fund of the Department, until provision can be obtained from Congress more effectually to fulfill the Law." ALS.
DNA, RG59, Misc. Letters (M179, R65). Enclosure not found; for a copy of the
Trimble report, see *House Reports*, 19 Cong., 2 Sess., no. 99, pp. 1–3. For payment
of Little's compensation, see Little to Clay, January 6, 1827, note.

From MICHAEL WITHERS, Baltimore. Refers to his letter of February 21; notes that he "this morning" received the requested certified copies of his patent but that he still awaits an answer to his inquiry. Complains of the injury to which he may be subjected by the delay and continues: "It has become of the more importance, as, in the event of your declining to express a decision upon the point submitted, I shall have no alternative but institute [sic] an action at law against the Superintendent himself [William Thornton]: You will at once perceive, however, that in the event of your assuming or sustaining his acts, which by no means ought to be anticipated, I cannot with propriety look to him for redress.

"As the injuries complained of arises [sic] out of the acts performed by an officer of the Government, it seems to follow, that I ought to appeal to the Government for protection; and it was with that view my former as well as the present letter is dictated. I flatter myself that I have not mistaken the proper channel to convey my complaints; but if in this I am in error, your suggestion of a different course will be promptly adopted." Suggests that the Attorney General (William Wirt) be consulted "upon the question, whether the Patent laws justifies [sic] the Superintendent in the course he has pursued. . . ." ALS. DNA, RG59, Misc. Letters (M179, R65). Copies, in DNA, RG60, Letters Recd. from the State Department (MR14), and in MHi-Adams Papers, Letters Recd. (MR479); published in Washington *Daily National Journal*, April 24, 1827. For Clay's reply, see below, March 9, 1827. James H. Causten requested in Withers' behalf a ruling by Wirt and forwarded him copies of Withers' and Clay's correspondence. See below, Withers to Clay, March 22, 1827, enclosure. Wirt gave no official opinion in the matter, but he had previously advised Withers of his legal rights. See Wirt to Withers, February 4, 1827, in Washington *Daily National Journal*, April 24, 1827.

APPLICATIONS, RECOMMENDATIONS   March 5, 1827

CHARLES A. BEATTY, Georgetown (District of Columbia), notes that, although he is a stranger to Clay, he may have been mentioned favorably by his friends, "Judge [Adam] Beatty, and the Rochester family." Recommends Mead Fitzhugh for a clerkship in the State Department; states that Fitzhugh was formerly an employee of (John) Mason (in the office of the Superintendent of Indian Trade) and more recently of George Graham in the General Land Office. ALS. DNA, RG59, A. and R. (M531, R3).

Beatty had practised medicine in Georgetown since 1782; his relationship to Adam Beatty has not been found. Fitzhugh had served as clerk and assistant packer in the office of the Superintendent of the Indian Trade for 14 or 15 years, until the office was abolished in 1822–1823. In 1836 he was named to an interim appointment as principal clerk of private land claims, in the General Land Office, but he served only briefly and resigned before the appointment was presented for Senate confirmation. U. S. Sen., *Executive Journal*, IV, 577, 579.

D[ANIEL] G. GARNSEY recommends Orris Crosby of Chautauqua County, New York, as a bearer of dispatches to South America; reminds Clay of their conversation last spring in which the Secretary extended him the privilege of naming someone from that State, should circumstances permit such an appointment. ALS. DNA, RG59, A. and R. (M531, R2).

Crosby, a physician, had been studying medicine in Canada at the outbreak of the War of 1812, impressed aboard a British warship, and severely wounded when he refused to fight. He had subsequently served in the American forces as a volunteer surgeon's mate. In 1846, when he was pensioned for his war-time wound, he was a resident of Boone County, Illinois. *House Reports*, 29 Cong., 1 Sess., no. 154; 32 Cong., 1 Sess., no. 161; 9 *U. S. Stat.*, 661. He does not appear to have received a Federal appointment.

DANIEL WEBSTER, transmitting a letter written by "a very respectable man," states that he has been told that "Mr Kingman" (the subject of the letter), whom he has just met, "is the Reporter of the Senate proceedings for the Journal." ALS. DNA, RG59, A. and R. (M531, R4). Undated; received "5 March 1827." In the enclosure, unaddressed, dated "Boston Dec. 18 1826," Bradford Sumner recommends "Eliab Kingman Esq. formerly of R. Island but now resident in Washington," who wishes "to obtain employment, in one of the public offices, under the government."

Kingman had at one time been employed by the Washington *National Intelligencer*. Allen C. Clark, "Joseph Gales, Junior Editor and Mayor," in Columbia Historical Society, *Records* 1920, pp. 113, 115. Webster apparently understood him to be at this time a reporter for the Washington *Journal*. Sumner was a member of the Suffolk County, Massachusetts bar.

From John Taliaferro

My dear Sir,   Hagley 6th. of March 1827—
    Will you do me the favor to see the Secrety of War[1] and do all you can to prevent the dismissal of Cadet Thos: M: Lewis[2] from West Point— This youth is the Son of my friend & *your* friend Samuel Lewis[3] now of Kentucky— He has sustained you most zealously in the unholy war that has been waged against you— He is a fine fellow & well dserves [*sic*] the efforts of his friends to sustain him in affair [*sic*] of such serious import to him— I know your feelings on all such occasions, & feel assured that you will exert yourself in this case as far as you can with propriety— I am dear Sir most respectfully and truly yours   JOHN TALIAFERRO

ALS. DNA, RG77, Letters Recd., 1826–1837, serial no. T-275. Addressed to Clay. Endorsed on cover (AEI): "Respectfy referred to the Secy of War. H C."
    [1] James Barbour.   [2] Thomas Miller Lewis of Morganfield, Kentucky, had entered the United States Military Academy in 1824. Because of his involvement in the "eggnog riot," Christmas, 1826, he was expelled, with 18 other cadets, after court martial proceedings which extended from late in January to March 15, 1827. Young Lewis was formally dismissed the following May. For reference to the nature of the riot, the participants in it, and some of the proceedings of the Court of Inquiry and General Courts Martial, see Haskell M. Monroe, Jr., and James T. McIntosh (eds.), *The Papers of Jefferson Davis*, I, *1808–1840* (Baton Rouge, 1971), 55–80, 82, 83–85.   [3] Not further identified.

INSTRUCTIONS AND DISPATCHES   March 6, 1827

From J[OHN] J. APPLETON, Stockholm, no. 12. Encloses "a french [*sic*] translation of the report of the King [Charles XIV] upon the situation and administration of Norway during the years 1824–25. & 26," an elaboration of the King's address at the opening of the Storthing (see above, Appleton to Clay, February 22, 1827). States that the report derives "its greatest interest from the view it presents of the internal position of that Country, where, under the influence of free institutions and a liberal Government, all the elements of public prosperity are acquiring daily more life and expansion." ALS. DNA, RG59, Dip. Disp., Sweden and Norway, vol. 5 (M45, R-T6). The King's report was dated January 22, 1827.

From ALEXANDER H. EVERETT, Madrid, no. 71. Transmits a translation of a reply (dated February 25, 1827) from the Foreign Minister (Manuel Gonzáles Salmón) to his protest of November 24, 1825 (see above, Everett to Clay, December 2, 1825, note), regarding "the proceedings of the Spanish Consul [Ramundo Chacon] at Boston in the case of Mr John Coffin Jones. . . ." Also forwards a copy of his answer (dated February 28, 1827). Expresses belief that "the proceedings of the Consul have been disapproved and some measures adopted to prevent a repetition of them" and comments that the President "will decide whether the satisfaction that is offered ought to be considered sufficient." Encloses also a "translation of an advertisement that appeared lately in the Diario of this place and which it may be well to publish in the newspapers as a notice to the person concerned." ALS. DNA, RG59, Dip. Disp., Spain, vol. 27 (M31, R28). Received May 10.

The *Diario* of February 25, 1827, carried an official notice that Juan Carisomo of Philadelphia would be allowed a six months' period in which to file a claim against Felipe de los Heros, an "inhabitant and broker of the City of Cadiz," who owed Carisomo 21,000 reals and was petitioning the Royal Council of Castile for a "postponement" of his debts.

From ALBERT GALLATIN, London, no. 59. Reports that (William) Huskisson is still "seriously indisposed" and that nothing will "call him out but such a close vote on the Catholic question as may render his, an object of importance." Notes belief that, "if the question is carried at this time, some change will take place in the ministry, and the newly modified cabinet will henceforth be considered as pledged for the measure" (cf. above, Gallatin to Clay, February 22, 1827, note). Attributes much of the opposition to the fear that passage "would probably bring in the administration some person or persons belonging to the old Whig party . . ." but observes that (George) Canning has "not made its success a sine quo non, and intends to remain in office, whether with new or with his present colleagues. . . ." States that such "internal concerns have for a while diverted the public attention from the affairs of Portugal" (see above, Brent to Clay, January 13, 1827). Adds that "the consequences of a war with Spain are better understood . . . and this Government will be disposed to shut their eyes to some part of the conduct of the Spanish authorities. . . , provided nothing too intolerable is done. . . ." Relates that he and (Henry U.) Addington have held two "informal conversations" about details of the northeast boundary question and that he has found the latter "extremely unmanageable . . . because he has imbibed all the prejudices and zeal of the British agents and provincial authorities on that question." Comments that Commissioner (Cornelius P.) Van Ness was correct in his view "that it was not the nature of the ground but the *position* of the highlands, respectively contended for, which was alone to be taken into consideration." Points out that this interpretation "admits that the two contending lines may both be considered as being generally highlands, leaving as the only question at issue, which are *the* highlands meant by the treaty [of Paris, 1783]." Asserts that, if the matter is decided on any other basis, the arbitrator, should one be named, will insist that new surveys be made, for those made by the boundary commission are "merely conjectural," the distances having been "guessed at by walking over the ground," and the hills or ridges "not even walked over. . . ." Says that he has proposed that the plenipotentiaries direct the drawing of "a general map on the plan stated in the enclosed paper"; adds that while the British have acceded to this proposal in general, they continue to throw up "difficulties and cavils at every step . . ."; and notes that he hopes to manage the negotiations in such fashion as to prevent the necessity for further surveys. Acknowledges receipt of Clay's instruction no. 17 (January 11, 1827) and has taken measures to secure the information requested. Complains, in an initialed postscript, that the British Government receives from its Minister in Washington (Charles R. Vaughan) printed copies of all of the congressional documents, while he must depend on newspapers for this information. ALS. DNA, RG59, Dip. Disp., Great Britain, vol. 33 (M30, R29). Published in Adams (ed.), *The Writings of Albert Gallatin*, II, 361–64; extract published in Manning (arr.), *Diplomatic Correspondence. . . , Canadian Relations*, II, 578–80. Received April 26. The enclosure consists of a three-point proposal: (1) that the plenipotentiaries make a map showing "the *actual* surveys of both parties"; (2) that, if necessary, two maps be made, noting on each "the points of difference" between the two parties; (3) that the map or maps be "laid before the Arbiter, in lieu of all the general maps, surveys, plans and reports of the several surveyors . . . under the late Commissioners."

On March 6, the British House of Commons by a four-vote margin declined to consider the question of removing certain civil disabilities imposed on Roman Catholics. Huskisson did not attend the House on this occasion, but his vote in favor of relief was paired with that of a member opposing the proposal. No further legislation expanding the rights of Catholics was adopted until April 13, 1829, when they were authorized to sit in Parliament and hold all civil offices, excepting the Lord Lieutenancy of Ireland and the Lord Chancelorships of Great Britain and Ireland; they were prohibited, however, from influencing the patronage of the established Church. *Hansard*, XVII (New Series), 1009–13; 10 *Geo. IV*, 693–98.

MISCELLANEOUS LETTERS   March 6, 1827

From AMOS LAY, New York. States that he is "compiling and publishing a Map of the United States" and requests permission "to take such sketches from the government maps in the hands of Major [Joseph] Delafield" as will enable him to determine "with accuracy the boundary Line between the United States and the Canadas." ALS. DNA, RG59, Misc. Letters (M179, R65). Endorsed by Clay on cover: "Permission given as asked."

Lay had published in 1812 a map of northern New York and around 1815 a map of the "Seat of War in Lower Canada." His map of the United States was not issued until 1833.

APPLICATIONS, RECOMMENDATIONS   March 6, 1827

JACOB HARVEY, New York, expresses his "sincere thanks" for the appointment of Reuben Harvey (above, Cropper, Benson & Company and others to Clay, November 7, 1826, note), his uncle, as consul at Cork. ALS. DNA, RG59, A. and R. (M531, R4).

WILLIAM THORNTON, Patent Office, recommends Alexander McIntire for a clerkship in the Patent Office. States that while writing this letter he has learned of McIntire's appointment and expresses his approval of the selection. ALS. *Ibid.* (R5).

On the congressional action authorizing the appointment, cf. above, Clay to McLane, January 14, 1826, note; Clay to House of Representatives, January 11, 1827. McIntire, long a resident of Washington, had performed as an extra copyist in the Patent Office during 1825 and 1826 and as a clerk from July, 1826, until his formal appointment. He retained the latter office until June, 1834.

INSTRUCTIONS AND DISPATCHES   March 7, 1827

To THOMAS BACKUS, "Consular Commercial Agent of the United States at St. Iago de Cuba." Transmits "the evidence of" his appointment and "a copy of the printed Circular Instructions to Consuls." Copy. DNA, RG59, Cons. Instr., vol. 2, pp. 413–14 (M78, R2). Cf. below, Adams to Clay, March 11, 1827.
  In a letter to Clay, July 4, 1827, Backus acknowledged receipt of his appointment. ALS, in DNA, RG59, Cons. Disp., Santiago de Cuba,-vol. 1 (M-T55, R1).

From PROSPER FROBERVILLE, "Port Louis Isle of france." Refers to his letter of December 31, 1826; reports that he has appointed Paul Froberville as acting consular agent until further orders are received from Clay. LS. DNA, RG59, Cons. Disp., Port Louis, vol. 1 (M-T118, R-T1). Received September 5.
  Paul Froberville, not further identified, received permanent appointment to the post during the Jackson administration.

From J[OEL] R. POINSETT, Mexico, no. 75. Acknowledges receipt of Clay's instructions of December 21, 1826; states that before writing the Department (above, November 23, 1826), Messrs. (Gardiner Greene and Samuel) Howland knew of his efforts to recover their shipment of wax seized at Alvarado by customs officials; forwards copies of his correspondence with the Minister of Foreign Relations (Juan José Espinosa de los Monteros) regarding the Howland case; reports that he has also conferred with the Secretary of the Treasury (José Ignacio Esteva) and that the Secretary declared he had no power to intervene, "as the case was before the legal tribunals of the country"; adds that "the suit is now pending before the Circuit Court at Tehuacan" and that he has had his friends write "to obtain for the claimants a favorable decision, as in strict justice they are entitled to." LS. DNA, RG59, Dip. Disp., Mexico, vol. 2 (M97, R3). Received May 10.

From J[OEL] R. POINSETT, Mexico, no. 76. Transmits copies of correspondence with the Mexican Ministers to the Congress of Panama (José Dominguez and José Mariano Michelena). States: "They were blamed by their government for making . . . disclosures to me, and were compelled to address me on the subject." Observes that his reply "was dictated by a regard for their feelings." Adds that his information was "substantially correct" and that "it was derived from the sources there alluded to." LS. Ibid. Received May 10.
  In their notes of February 17, 1827, Dominguez and Michelena state that the United States Government has transmitted to Congress two of Poinsett's dispatches (above, September 6 and 23, 1826) attributing news of the Panama proceedings to the Ministers of that assembly; the Mexican Plenipotentiaries recall that they spoke to Poinsett only on two topics, the probable delay in reconvening the Congress and the absence of the United States Minister (Richard C. Anderson) at the Panama meeting. In his reply of February 20, 1827, Poinsett says that as he spoke to several persons about the Congress and as those conversations were six months past, he cannot remember what particular information he gathered from each individual.

From FREDERICK JACOB WICKELHAUSEN, Bremen. Explains that, since a severe winter delayed the departure of his dispatch of January 19, he is adding "a few lines." States that the Bremen delegation to Brazil left on February 28 and that Hamburg's deputies, Syndic (Karl S.) Sieveking and "Secretary Schram" (the lat-

ter, not further identified), "passed this city on the 2nd March for the same destination." Notes reports that the Brazilian Emperor (Peter I) is prepared to grant
Bremen and Hamburg the same duty reductions allowed Great Britain and France
(see above, Wickelhausen to Clay, January 19, 1827, and note). Observes that the
reports are probably accurate, for as the Emperor is "very desirous to attrack [sic]
a great number of new Settlers from this country. . . , it is a wise and judicious
politic [sic] of this Monarch to keep on friendly terms with the Governments of
Hamburg & Bremen, as these cities, in a great way influence the resolutions of the
german people, by favouring or impeding such emigrations, which in general are
looked upon, as proving very prejudicial to such Individuals, as are following and
relying on the flattering promises of the Brazil agents." ALS. DNA, RG59, Cons.
Disp., Bremen, vol. 2 (M-T184, R2). Received May 11.

Sieveking, a native of Hamburg, had received a degree in law from the University of Göttingen in 1810, had served as Minister to St. Petersburg from 1819 to
1821, and in 1820 had been elected a Syndic of Hamburg. He held a seat in the
Bundestag at Frankfurt from 1830 until his death in 1847.

MISCELLANEOUS LETTERS   March 7, 1827

To THOMAS P. ESKRIDGE, Little Rock. Transmits his commission as judge for
Arkansas Territory. Copy. DNA, RG59, Dom. Letters, vol. 21, p. 493 (M40, R19).
Eskridge acknowledged receipt of his commission and indicated, April 8, his ac-
ceptance of the appointment. ALS, in DNA, RG59, Acceptances and Orders for
Comns. (M-T645, R2).

From JEPHTHAH HARDIN, Shawneetown (Illinois). Acknowledges receipt of Clay's
letter of February 12 and that of D(aniel) P. Cook "on the subject of the case The
United States against William Skinner in the District Court of this State." Relates
that he was informed by the register of the land office at Edwardsville (William P.
McKee) that Skinner "was in the daily habit of cuting [sic] wood on Government
land lying in the vicinity of Edwardsville for the purpose of selling to the Citizens
of the Town." Says that he brought suit against Skinner in the district court, that
he proved his case, and that the jury "found him [Skinner] guilty and assessed the
damage to twelve dollars." Adds that "an example seems absolutely necessary to
prevent Trespasses." ALS. DNA, RG59, Misc. Letters (M179, R65). Endorsed on
verso (AEI): "Mr. fenall [Philip Ricard Fendall] will please to see the Letter which
was written by this Dept and to which this is an answer— I presume that the
Petition of Skinner to The President for the Remission was sent to the Dist Atto.
& ought to have been returned by him. D B [Daniel Brent]."

Brent had written to Hardin on February 12, noting that Skinner had applied
through Representative Cook, "for the remission of a fine and costs" and that the
President had requested that the case be referred for a report. Brent also had
transmitted by order of the Secretary of State "the letter of Mr. Cook, to the
President, in behalf of Mr. Skinner. . . ." Copy, in DNA, RG59, Dom. Letters,
vol. 21, p. 480 (M40, R19). Cook's letter to Adams, dated December 27, 1826, and
received the following day, not found but listed in MHi-Adams Papers, Register
of Letters Recd. (MR 254).

Jephthah Hardin, brother of Benjamin Hardin of Kentucky, had been appointed United States attorney for Illinois in 1819 and was reappointed to that
post in 1823. His nomination for reappointment in 1827 had been rejected by
the Senate on January 12. U. S. Sen., *Exec. Journal*, III, 184, 312, 314, 552, 558.
William P. McKee, a native of Kentucky, served as register of the Edwardsville
land office from 1822 to 1835. William Skinner has not been further identified.

From SAMUEL L. SOUTHARD, Navy Department. Refers to his letter of February 13, 1827 (above), and transmits a copy of the reply by (Richard W.) Habersham to his (Southard's) inquiry. Comments that Habersham's views "seem . . . so correct" that he "cannot but concur in them." LS. DNA, RG59, Misc. Letters (M179, R65).

Habersham, on February 22, 1827, wrote that "two different proceedings" were pending against Francis Sorrel, one to recover the money he had received for the labor of the Africans formerly in his custody and the other to compel him "to pay costs and expenses . . . in part incurred, in consequence of his insisting upon a portion of these Negroes being Portuguese property. . . ."

On March 15, 1827, the Supreme Court upheld the circuit court ruling that the Portuguese vice consul was not liable for maintenance expenses, that the marshal (John H. Morel) had no lien upon the Africans for those expenses, and that his bill was chargeable to the Government, although not as an interested party in the claims litigation. The Supreme Court also observed that the litigants had paid the court costs and that the order assessing those charges was not under appeal. 25 *U. S.* (12 Wheaton) 546–54.

APPLICATIONS, RECOMMENDATIONS   March 7, 1827

DAVID BARTON AND DANIEL P. COOK, Washington, "concur in the recommendation of John Simonds, Jr. [for appointment as United States marshal in Missouri], for the reasons assigned by Mr. [Edward] Bates." NS. DNA, RG59, A. and R. (M531, R7). Unaddressed; noted at bottom of Bates to Cook, February 12, 1827. Bates advised Cook that for several years Simonds had served as deputy marshal and deputy sheriff of St. Louis (County, Missouri), that most of the business of the marshal's office had been left to him, and that General (Henry) Dodge favored the appointment. See above, Peck to Clay, February 15, 1827, note.

E[LIAS] K[ENT] KANE, Kaskaskia, transmits a recommendation, in which he concurs, based on the supposition "that the present marshal [Henry Conner] intends to resign"; asserts that "Genl. [Thomas] James has been intensively . . . engaged in trade with the Northern & Western provinces of Mexico and is more perfectly acquainted with the geography of that region of country than any man amongst us"; credits James with "much intelligence a sound head and an honest heart"; and adds: "In the event of a treaty with Mexico providing for running the divisional line between the two jurisdictions I have been requested to name him to You as a candidate for the Appt. of Commissioner on the part of the U S[.]" ALS. DNA, RG59, A. and R. (M531, R4). The enclosure, neither addressed nor dated, recommending James "as a person eminently well qualified to fill the office of marshall [*sic*] for the State of Illinois," is signed by William Kinney and seven others.

Henry Conner had been appointed marshal for the Illinois District in 1820 and remained in that office until his removal in 1829.

Thomas James, a native of Maryland, who had moved to Illinois in 1803 and to Missouri in 1807, had been engaged in the fur trade and in 1821 led one of the earliest trading expeditions to Santa Fé. He served in the Illinois Legislature from 1825 to 1828.

William Kinney, a native of Kentucky, had settled in St. Clair County, Illinois, and served as Lieutenant Governor of that State from 1826 to 1830. He lost his bid for the governorship in 1834 but in 1838 was elected by the legislature to the Illinois Board of Public Works.

The second additional article to the proposed treaty of July 10, 1826 (see above, Poinsett to Clay, July 12, 1826, note), provided that the United States and

Mexico would undertake "as early as possible" negotiations for a treaty of limits; in addition, the two parties pledged to assist each other in exploring their common borderlands. *American State Papers, Foreign Relations,* VI, 613.

Theodorick Lee, Washington, recommends "Mr. Page" for temporary clerical employment in the Department; notes that Page "has wrote in a clerks office" and that he "aided Mr. [Philip Ricard] Fendall, in the case of French spoliation"; and adds that he "is something deaf and enough so, to deprive him of some of the pleasure of social conversation," but that this impediment "induces more thoughtful consideration and increases, attention, to business, assuring more service and utility." ALS. DNA, RG59, A. and R. (M531, R6).

Lee was a brother of "Light-Horse Harry" Lee and uncle of young Henry Lee.

Fendall had been paid $650 on February 3, 1827, for "preparing schedule of claims of American citizens against the Governments of France, Naples, Holland, and Denmark" (cf. above, Clay to Taylor, January 30, 1827). W. B. Page was paid $120.96 for copying, "at 10 cents per hundred [words]," in 1827. *House Repts.,* 20 Cong., 1 Sess., no. 226, pp. 59, 88.

John Scott, Washington City, recommends John Simonds, Jr., as United States marshal for Missouri. ALS. DNA, RG59, A. and R. (M531, R7). See above, Peck to Clay, February 15, 1827, note.

To Samuel L. Southard

Dep: of State, Wasn 8 March 1827.

The Secretary of State presents his Respects to Mr. Southard and asks the favor of his perusal of the enclosed Letter,[1] and whether its object is attainable.

N, in Daniel Brent's hand. DNA, RG45, Misc. Letters, 1827/2. Endorsed: "Answd 9th March."
[1] Above, Carey to Clay, March 3, 1827.

INSTRUCTIONS AND DISPATCHES   March 8, 1827

To Beaufort T. Watts, Bogotá, no. 2. Sends notice of Watts' appointment as Chargé des Affaires to the Republic of Colombia (see above, Watts to Clay, November 15, 1826, note) and encloses his commission; instructs Watts to inform the Colombian Government that the United States does not intend "to make any permanent change in the rank" of its diplomatic representatives; states that the President has decided to allow him an outfit of $4,500 and a salary at the annual rate of $4,500 and that the President also has given permission for him to return to the United States for the reason stated in Watts' letter of December 27, 1826; and asks that before leaving his post he have corrected "the error which was committed in the amount of indemnity due in the case of the Josephine," previously noticed in the Secretary's instruction (to Richard C. Anderson) of September 16, 1825. LS. DNA, RG84, Colombia (MR14). Copy, in DNA, RG59, Dip. Instr., vol. 11, pp. 257–58 (M77, R6). A copy of Watts' commission, dated March 3, is located in DNA, RG59, Ceremonial Communications, vol. 2, p. 63.

From J[ohn] M. Forbes, Buenos Aires, no. 45. Reports that "the attempt to conciliate the disaffected provinces and to obtain the adoption of the Constitution (cf. above, Forbes to Clay, December 4, 1826) has entirely failed." Observes that

the "gloom of this failure is somewhat lighted up by the success against the foreign
enemy (cf. above, Raguet to Clay, December 23, 1825) by the navy in this neighborhood, and recently by the national army." Details (William) Brown's victories
over Brazilian naval forces on the Uruguay (River) and on the Río de la Plata.
Describes General (Carlos Antonio José de) Alvear's "most glorious victory over
the enemy" (at Ituzaingó on February 20, 1827). Continues the dispatch on March
9 and again on March 12; mentions a report that "the basis of a peace is already
settled, chiefly through the negotiation of Sir William [*i.e.*, Robert] Gordon with
the Brazilian Government at Rio de Janeiro"; and encloses a copy (not found)
of newspaper accounts of recent military operations. L, written and signed at
dictation by J. Dickinson Mendenhall. DNA, RG59, Dip. Disp., Argentina, vol.
3 (M69, R4). Published in Espil (comp.), *Once Años en Buenos Aires*, 457–60;
extract, in Manning (arr.), *Diplomatic Correspondence . . . Latin-American Nations*, I, 660. Received June 3.

Brazil and Buenos Aires did not agree upon peace terms until 1828; cf. below,
Forbes to Clay, June 29, August 20, 1827; Wright to Clay, August 10, 1827.

From J[OEL] R. POINSETT, Mexico, no. 77. States that General (Manuel) Rincon
has departed for Veracruz, where he will take command of the expedition organized to quell the Texas revolt (see above, Dickson to Clay, January 3, 1827,
note); that the 1,000-man force will land at Matagorda and rendezvous with about
10,000 troops gathered from the interior; and that the Mexican Congress has
voted $500,000 for expenses and has declared "that the President [Guadalupe
Victoria] should be furnished with whatever amount might be necessary." Explains: "A desire was manifested to evince on this occasion great promptness and
energy, so as to prevent similar attempts being made elsewhere." Reports that
although the President does not believe the United States Government encouraged
the insurrection, he does desire "that the President of the United States would
give some public manifestation of his disapprobation of this insurrection in a
frontier province, and take steps to prevent the Indians of . . . [United States]
territory from passing over in a hostile attitude into Texas" or citizens of the
United States from "joining the insurgents." LS. DNA, RG59, Dip. Disp., Mexico,
vol. 2 (M97, R3). Received May 10. Endorsed (AEI) on separate sheet: "To be
submitted to the President   H C."

From J[OEL] R. POINSETT, Mexico, no. 78. Transmits "a description of the revolv-
ing light recently erected on the castle of San Juan de Ulua in the port of Vera
Cruz." LS. *Ibid.* Received May 10. Enclosure is a translation of a letter, dated
February 28, 1827, from (José Ignacio) Esteva to Poinsett.

MISCELLANEOUS LETTERS   March 8, 1827

From WILLIAM THORNTON, Patent Office. States that he feels "bound to give an
answer" in response to "a Letter of complaint from Michael Withers" (above,
Withers to Clay, February 21, 1827). Says that he considers Withers an "Imposter,
who has been robbing the Public from one end of the Continent to the other, by
demanding payment for an Invention that was in use before he was born . . .";
that the "winged Gudgeon was published in Oliver Evans's Miller's Guide, twenty
years ago . . ."; and that the decision in Virginia "relative to the Head Steering
Oar [not found], would set aside the Patent, even if he had been the Inventor."
Explains that his office "never refused Copies of the Patent, for by the 11th Section
of the Patent Law of 1793 [1 *U. S. Stat.*, 318–24] . . . copies may be demanded by
paying the legal fees . . ." but that he has "refused to subject the Secy. of State

to subserve the Tricks of Patentees, by refusing authenticated Copies, except [as] demanded by Courts of Justice, as in the provision of the 3d. Section of the same law; & this has been the practice of the Patent Office under every Administration." ALS. DNA, RG59, Misc. Letters (M179, R65).

APPLICATIONS, RECOMMENDATIONS   March 8, 1827

THOMAS LAW, Washington, recommends "Mr. Henshaw," his accountant, for a clerkship in the Patent Office. LS. DNA, RG59, A. and R. (M531, R4). Henshaw not further identified; on the recommended appointment, cf. above, Thornton to Clay, March 6, 1827.

To Michael Withers

Mr. Michael Withers, Baltimore.

Sir,   Dept. of State, Washington 9 March 1827.

   Your letters under date the 21st. ulto, and 5th. instant have been received. You are right in your supposition stated in the letter, that the press of official business had prevented my answering the former.—

   The perusal of your letter of the 21st. February gave me the first information of the relations between Doctr. Thornton[1] & yourself. I regret them very much.— So far as the Doctor's official conduct is concerned, it is under my control; but I have no power to interfere with the exercise of the common rights of every citizen. These entitle him to judge of the utility of inventions, and to express freely his opinions, being responsible to the Laws. If he has formed erroneous con- conceptions [sic] of the origin, or merit of the Winged Gudgeon, that would not, I think, justify animadversion from me. I must, therefore, abstain from any interposition in the affair between you and Doctor Thornton, further than as respects his discharge of official duty—

   It is not usual to authenticate Copies taken from the Patent Office, under the official seal of this Department, unless they are intended to be used in some suit actually pending   still, as I think you have a strict right to have the six Copies of your patent so authenticated, it shall be done according to your request[2]— I am respectfully, Sir, Your Obedt. Servant,   H. CLAY.—

   Copy. DNA, RG59, Dom. Letters, vol. 21, pp. 493–94 (M40, R19). Copy, in MHi-Adams Papers, Letters Recd. (MR479).
   [1] William Thornton.   [2] Cf. above, Withers to Clay, March 5, 1827; Thornton to Clay, March 8, 1827.

Agreement with Henry W. Conway

[March 9, 1827]

An agreement between H. Clay and H.W. Conway.

The said Clay has contracted to purchase from Cornelius Comegys surviving partner of C. and John Comegys a Judgment recovered by them at the May term of the U States Circuit Court for the District of Kentucky, in May 1811,[1] for the sum of Twelve hundred and thirty four dollars and 85 Cents, with interest thereon at the rate of six per Cent per annum from the 27h. day of February 1808, and $39"61 Costs. Upon which judgment the defendants are entitled to a credit of about three hundred and fifty dollars as per receipts which are held by them or one of them.

The contract above mentioned with Cornelius Comegys is not yet completed, but is expected to be executed in a few days.[2]

For the above Judgment the said Clay has agreed to pay one thousand dollars.

It is agreed between the said Clay and Conway that the said Conway shall have one half of what is due on the said Judgment, for which he agrees to pay the said Clay the sum of five hundred dollars at the City of Washington within six months from this day.

The said Clay is to procure a power of Attorney to the said Conway from the said Comegys authorizing him to collect the sum due, and the said Conway is to pay over to the said Clay one half of any sum so collected, retaining to himself the other half.

Witness the hands and seals of the parties this 9h day of March 1827.

H. CLAY Ls
H.W. CONWAY Ls

ADS, by Clay, signed also by Conway. KyLxT. Endorsed on verso in Clay's hand: "Agreemt about debt of [William] Bradfords."
[1] Cf. above, Comegys to Clay, February 1, 1827.   [2] Not found.

From Christopher Hughes

My dear Sir   *Private*   Brussels; 9 March; 1827.

[States that the American Hotel at the Hague will be sold at public auction "about the middle of April." Reports that he has spoken with Baron Verstolk about "the discrimination made in the Ports of the Netherlands, in behalf of [the] Dutch, to the disadvantage" of American vessels[1] and that the Minister rejects the complaint "in *so many words*." Notes that Huygens[2] will remain in Holland "yet some time, to visit his family connections"; that Anduaga,[3] the new envoy from Spain, has arrived in the city; and that Rumpff,[4] "Son in law of Mr. Astor & at present, the Hanseatic Chargé d'affaires at Paris," is reported to come to Washington as the Hanseatic envoy, "with instructions and power to make a Treaty of Commerce, on the basis of the Guatamala Convention." Mentions that he has had separate conversations with Gildemeister and Sieveking,[5] who recently passed through the city en route to Rio de Janeiro, that he gave them letters of introduction to Brown and Gallatin, and they may return to Europe through the United States, "concerning which there seems to be no bounds to the curiosity and speculation of the different European nations!"]

I have here been interrupted by a visit from Mr. Geo. S. Bourne, son of the late Consul of Amsterdam;[6] from which place he came to this, with the object of asking my responsibility for advances, to be made by Messr. Crommelyns,[7] for his maintenance; until he could hear of Mr. Meredith's[8] of Balto. having paid his draft, for advances already made. On my saying, that it was impossible for me to do so, & advising him to return to Amsterdam, (where he is known, & not to remain here, where he knows no one & would be most certainly imprisoned. if he had not means to pay his way;) he said, he could not return; for he had but 10 florins in his pocket."— So here was an unavoidable necessity put on me, to pay his expenses back. I really was pained at heart to see him, a clever, & most gentlemanlike young man, in such straits, but the advance, or *gift*, being the 3rd or 4th time that I have been *compelled* to lend several pounds Sterling, to Americans or to see them sent to jail, (added to the enormous expenses of this country compared to what they were, when you were here:) incommoded me very severely; but was it *possible* to leave him, in the condition?—

You must not suspect me of making a poor mouth, to use a very vulgar phrase, but I assure you, that with all the economy possible, it is hardly practicable to get on, especially this first year! My house rent, payable in advance, is 3000 franks, the inevitable expenses of papering, painting & repairing (all which were thrown on me by the Landlord.) have exceeded 3000 franks; I have taken the house, as is the rule, for 3, 6, & 9 years; so that my rent is 4,000 francs. or 800, dolls. and yet I have not a room much wider than your passage—that is, wider than 12 or 13 feet! There were dozens of English ready to take the house; & it was a sort of favour to get it, such is the extraordinary demand for houses from the influx of English! There are upwards of 7,000 of all classes—200 of them, *invitable* persons (to coin a word) at their Ambassadors—[9]& from 40 to 50 English families—spending from £1.500 to £5,000 Sterling a year, besides multitudes, living in Lodgings & hotels & spending an enormous amount of money in this place! New Quarters of the Town are building up, & every thing bears marks of the most astonishing prosperity! My house formerly rented for 1,400 francs! All these causes make living extremely dear; and yet, we go to court in a Hackney coach; do not attempt to see company; & in fact have not given a cup of tea to a human being this winter, except when Charles Bonaparte[10] was here; he dined with me one day with my intimate friend Chevr. d'Ohsson,[11] Swedish Minister, & an eminent French Naturalist, an old friend of Charles'; & the two other days of his stay, he dined en famille, with Mrs. Hughes & my children![12] The expenses of furnishing, though made barely to consuld [*sic*] rigid decorum, have quite overpowered me; and during this *first* year, I shall be quite embarrassed, but having got through, or not, these expenses, which *once* made, are not to be repeated, and by persevering in this rigid observance of economy; and being merely so as to keep up a decent appearance, I hope to be more easy, in the next & succeeding year! So completely unconcerned was the Landlord, whether I took his house, or *not*, that I am not even allowed to under let, if I chose [*sic*] to pass the summer, for economy, in the country!—not that I could ever consent to *underlet*; for in my public situation, it would be looked on as *indecent*.

I have gone thus into a detail, from a conviction, that you take a sincere & friendly interest in my concerns & welfare, & that you will not disbelieve me when I say, how heartily, how *inconceivably* welcome would be to me, the news of the President's having adopted the opinion, that the public interests would be promoted, by raising this mission, to its former rank. The Government here look with discontent, (for the King[13] is *high*, & this country commends the eulogies & admiration of all Europe) at their Minister not being reciprocated; I know this; I see it; I *feel* it & I hear it! Still the King is personally kind to me; I never go to court, without his addressing some civil and amiable speech to me; & he was particularly gracious to Mrs. Hughes, a few Evenings ago, in consequence of His Majesty's having learnt, that the stiff etiquette, which excludes *Charges* from the Royal Table, had apparently *shocked* us a little, the first time we were at Court![14] Mrs. Hughes accepts merely when decorum requires that she should attend; that is, for every two or three invitations, she makes her appearance *once*! This is *indispensable*; she must go, *occasionally*; but we can neither afford the dressing expense, nor *swallow* the meats of a 2d. or 3d. table!—

I think I *may* say, that I stand pretty well, *dans l'esprit* of the Minister of foreign affairs, of the dignitaries of the Country, and of my colleagues; I have got over *some* of the first difficulties; but those of my subaltern rank are incurable, and there is no success, without, now & then, giving these diplomatic gentry a good dinner & having the air & appearance of keeping a gentlemanlike house! it is astonishing, how far this goes, & how much depends on hospitality & digestion!

The King has lately established a system of public lectures on all the branches of science, & named professors; I attended the inauguration ceremony, by invitation from the Bourgemaitre;[15] and it was with no little pride & comfort, that I heard the very eloquent Professor of Literature lay down this proposition, "that the President of the U.S. had made himself the *Interprête du Siècle*, when he had lately said, before the world, that science was the most efficacious instrument in all social amelioration";[16] (or to this effect; but I shall send a copy of the discourse) the sentiment was received with rapturous applause & I was felicitated and complimented, in the Evening, at the Prince d'Arenberg's,[17] by several of the first men of this country, on the subject.

The world seems to have glided quietly back again into the habits and persuasion that *War* is quite an impossibility; a few weeks ago, & the very reverse was the doctrine. The death of the Empress of Brazil,[18] as it is supposed to destroy all the influence of the Emperor of Austria at that Court, & to cut the last *tie* that bound Don Pedro to the Union of European Monarchs, is regarded as an event of great political importance.

a very valued friend of mine, an officer in the British army, & a respectable *author*, has written to me for some letters; as he means to visit the U.S. & Mexico. I shall take the liberty of introducing Captain de Capel Brooke[19] to you, and you will gratify me by being kind & useful to him; he is a most honourable & amiable man, the eldest Son of a very respectable English Baronet! I am very desirous, that he should be in *good hands,* for I know he means to *write!* I shall feel, therefore, a public as well as private interest, in Captain Brooke's being well received; if I did not *know* him to of [sic] the right class, & a perfectly well bred man, I should not present him to you; for I by no means approve of the *letter* so freely dealt out, in U.S. to vagrant *Bulls.*

Sir C. Bagot enquires, very often, & always most affectionately about you; he requests to be particularly recalled to you. I am, my dear Sir, very respectfully & truly Your frd. & Servt.   C HUGHES ·

N.B.   I am overjoyed at John Randolph's defeat! The Legislature of Virginia have done wisely and *decently!*[20]   C. H.
To Honble. Henry Clay; Secretary of State; Washington.

ALS. DNA, RG59, Dip. Disp., Netherlands, vol. 8 (M42, R-T12). Received May 3.
    [1] Baron J. G. Verstolk Van Soelen—cf. above, Clay to Huygens, December 10, 24, 1825; October 25, 1826; Hughes to Clay, July 16, 1826; January 21, 1827; Clay to Hughes, December 12, 1826; Huygens to Clay, September 15, November 11, 1826; below, Hughes to Clay, April 15, 1827.   [2] Roger Bangeman Huygens.   [3] Le Chevalier Joaquin d'Anduaga, appointed as Spanish Minister to the Netherlands in the fall of 1826, had represented Spain as Minister to the United States from 1821 to 1823.   [4] Eliza, the youngest daughter of John Jacob Astor, had been married to Viscount Vincent Rumpff in December, 1825. Swiss by birth, Rumpff represented the German Free Cities of Hamburg, Lübeck, and Bremen at Paris. He arrived in New York on September 9 and was presented to President Adams on November 5 as Minister Plenipotentiary to conduct the proposed negotiations. See below, Convention, December 20, 1827.   [5] Jean Charles Frédéric Gildemeister and Karl S. Sieveking. Cf. above, Wickelhausen to Clay, January 19, March 7, 1827.   [6] Young Bourne, not further identified, was the son of Sylvanus Bourne.   [7] Crommelin and Sons, of Amsterdam.   [8] Probably Jonathan Meredith, a native of Philadelphia, who was at this time a prominent member of the Baltimore bar and a regular practitioner before the Supreme Court.   [9] Sir Charles Bagot.
    [10] Charles Lucien Jules Laurent Bonaparte, 2d Prince of Canino, was a nephew of Napoleon I and in 1822 had married Zénaïde, daughter of Joseph and Julie Clary Bonaparte, the Count and Countess of Survilliers. The young couple had subsequently resided with her parents near Philadelphia, and Charles had travelled extensively in the United States as a student of ornithology. In 1825 he had begun publication of *American*

Ornithology, or History of the Birds of the United States (4 vols., Philadelphia, 1825–1833), designed as a supplement to the work of Alexander Wilson. He removed in 1828 to Italy, was active in the revolution of 1848 in Rome, and in 1850 was permitted to return to Paris, where four years later he assumed the directorship of the Jardin des Plantes. He published extensively on European as well as American birds and fauna.
    [11] Abraham Constantin Mouradgea d'Ohsson.   [12] Laura Sophia Smith Hughes; Charles John and Margaret S. Hughes.   [13] William I.   [14] See above, Hughes to Clay, January 30, 1827.   [15] Not identified.   [16] The professor not identified. On Adams' remark, cf. above, Stuart to Clay, December 1, 1825, note.   [17] Auguste-Marie-Raymond, Prince d'Arenberg, had fought in the American Revolution and in the service of Austria beginning in 1793. He had returned to residence in Brussels in 1815 and held rank as a lieutenant general.   [18] Maria Leopoldina Joseph Carolina, daughter of Francis I of Austria.   [19] Arthur de Capell Brooke, son of Sir Richard de Capell Brooke, had been graduated from Oxford, with an M. A. degree in 1816, had entered the Army, but had spent much of his life in foreign travel. In 1823 he had published *Travels through Sweden, Norway, and Finmark to the North Pole in the Summer of 1820*, and in 1827 he brought out *A Winter in Lapland and Sweden. . .*, together with a companion volume of illustrative plates, *Winter Sketches in Lapland. . . .* A decade later he published a two-volume work, *Sketches in Spain and Morocco*, but he appears never to have prepared a volume on travels in the United States. He succeeded to his father's estates in 1829 and in 1846 attained the military rank of major.   [20] See above, Pleasants to Clay, December 24, 1826, note.

MISCELLANEOUS LETTERS   March 9, 1827

From BRYANT AND STURGIS, Boston. State that their agent in Russia (not identified) has advised them that he has received indemnity payment on the brig *Pearl*, as arranged between Clay and the Russian Minister (Baron de Tuyll); express their appreciation "for the prompt interference of the Government" in their behalf. LS. DNA, RG59, Misc. Letters (M179, R65). Copy, in MH-BA. See above, Clay to Tuyll, April 19 (2), 1825; Tuyll to Clay, April 22, 1825.

From SAMUEL L. SOUTHARD, Navy Department. States that he has read Mathew Carey's letter enclosed in Clay's note of the previous day and that he does not perceive "that the object he has in view can be attained, further than by the general orders" under which all officers act. Adds: "There is no doubt that ample protection will be afforded to the Vessels containing the supplies, if they fall in with any of our Ships of War." LS. DNA, RG59, Misc. Letters (M179, R65).

From BENJAMIN D. WRIGHT, Pensacola. Acknowledges receipt of a letter from the Department (not found) with an accompanying petition (not found) which he now returns. Notes that the instructions require him to investigate and report on charges made by Maria Machado (not further identified) in her petition against (Joseph E.) Caro, Keeper of the Public Archives, in West Florida. States that the application to the President "must have originated in misconception." Observes that "Madame Machado" was no longer liable for Caro's surety bond, which "expired by the operation of the act of Congress passed 3d March 1825 [4 *U. S. Stat.*, 126]. . . ." Expresses belief that "a family feud existed between Mr Caro and one of his brother[s] which . . . must have been the occas[ion] of the application in question." ALS. DNA, RG59, Misc. Letters (M179, R65). Published in Carter (ed.) *Territorial Papers*, XXIII, 788–89. Cf. below, Caro to Clay, March 10, 1827.

Promissory Note from John Scott

Washington City March 10th. 1827

For Value Received I promise to pay Henry Clay or order four hundred and twelve dollars ninety one Cents. with Interest from date till paid. Witness my hand and seal the day and date above.

JOHN SCOTT [seal]

ADS. DLC-TJC (DNA, M212, R16). Endorsed in pencil on verso: "Enclosed in 1842, May 26, John Scott to H Clay."

INSTRUCTIONS, DISPATCHES   March 10, 1827

From ANDREW ARMSTRONG, Port au Prince. Transmits trade report for 1826. Notes that United States trade has declined at this port but that there is no longer doubt it "must hold a preponderance"; observes that the present difficulties arise from recent crop failures and from over-trading by the French, who have been forced to sacrifice their prices. States that the abolition of export duties (see above, Armstrong to Clay, February 28, 1827) appears to have been accepted without objections and that it has given "a fresh impulse to trade." Expresses belief that internal disorders are to be feared more than external attack, though "the former would be the certain consequence of the latter." ALS. DNA, RG59, Cons. Disp., Cap Haitien, vol. 6 (M9, R6). Received March 30.

From THOMAS L. L. BRENT, Lisbon. Reports that the refugees under the Marquis de Chaves retreated as General (Correa de) Mello and his army approached, that Mello expected "to enter Braganza about the 3rd instant," and that the Count of Vila Flor should now be in Miranda. Observes that the refugees are thought to be "much discouraged and full of disunion and insubordination." Notes that Russia is said to have exhorted Spain "not to mix directly or indirectly in the affairs of Portugal" and that France "has made fresh representations" of a similar kind. ALS. DNA, RG59, Dip. Disp., Portugal, vol. 7 (M43, R6). Received May 9.

MISCELLANEOUS LETTERS   March 10, 1827

To MATHEW CAREY, Philadelphia. States that he received Carey's letter and referred it to the Secretary of the Navy (cf. above, Clay to Southard, March 8, 1827, note); transmits the Secretary's reply; and adds: "I regret that public considerations, which, I hope, the Committee will justly appreciate, prevent the Government from affording a more effectual protection than that which is indicated in the Secretary's Answer." Copy. DNA, RG59, Dom. Letters, vol. 21, p. 495 (M40, R19).

To DUDLEY MARVIN. States that upon examination of Department records from 1817 to 1820, "it does not appear that Noah Webster deposited a spelling book at any time during that period, for the purpose of securing the copyright." Copy. Ibid., p. 494.

From N[ICHOLAS] B[IDDLE], Philadelphia. Sends an extract (not found) of a letter from Messrs. Hottinguer (and Company), dated Paris, January 23, 1827; indicates that the extract begins "Nous ne doutons" and ends "soit portugais." Copy, initialed. DLC-Nicholas Biddle Papers, President's Letter Book, 251 (DNA, M212, R20). Dated: "March 9. 10. 1827."

From JOSEPH E. CARO, Pensacola. States that, "as Keeper of the Public Archives," he has not forwarded his bond and requests instruction as to which department it should be sent; adds that his bond "has been executed according to Law since 7th May 1825, but has not been forwarded for want of the information above requested." ALS. DNA, RG59, Misc. Letters (M179, R65). Endorsement (AEI): "Examine the law and ansr this letter. H C"

On the relevant legislation, cf. above, Caro to Clay, September 23, 1825. On April 2, 1827, Clay replied to Caro that the bond should be sent to Joseph Anderson, First Comptroller of the Treasury. Copy, in DNA, RG59, Dom. Letters, vol. 21, p. 511 (M40, R19).

From WILLIAM PRINCE, Linnaean Botanic Garden, New York. Requests a list of United States consular and diplomatic personnel; states that he would not ask for assistance but for his wish "to extend this establishment & to render it more worthy [o]f our Republic, whose rapid march in [th]e path of greatness seems to impart . . . enthusiasm to the bosom of every American." ALS. DNA, RG59, Misc. Letters (M179, R65).

William Prince of Flushing, New York, had founded the Linnaean Botanic Garden and Nurseries in 1793. He issued an annual nursery catalogue, published several essays, including *A Short Treatise on Horticulture* (1828), and held membership in the horticultural societies of New York, London, and Paris. On March 22, 1827, Daniel Brent sent Prince the requested list. Copy, in DNA, RG59, Dom. Letters, vol. 21, p. 501 (M40, R19).

From [THOMAS] WATSON and [— —] MACHEN, office of the *Carolina Sentinel*, New Bern. State that (John I.) Pasteur has transferred "his interest in the establishment to Mr. Machen." LS. DNA, RG59, P. and D. of L.

Pasteur had published the journal since 1818. Watson, a native of England, had been engaged in publishing at New Bern since 1807 and had been admitted to partnership in the *Sentinel* in March, 1820. Machen, not further identified, appears to have retained an interest in the journal for only a few months; while Watson continued active at least through the Adams administration.

APPLICATIONS, RECOMMENDATIONS   March 10, 1827

EDMUND F. BROWN, Washington City, solicits a clerkship in the State Department and encloses letters of recommendation (not found). States that his father (Daniel Brown) "was yesterday dismissed from the Genl. Land Office, in consequence of the order of Congress to reduce the number of clerks" (4 *U. S. Stat.*, 233–34). Adds, following his signature, "a native of New Jersey." ALS. DNA, RG59, A. and R. (M531, R1).

Daniel Brown, also of New Jersey, had been employed in the General Land Office for over a decade when he and five others were released because the "arrearages" of the work in the office had been caught up and the number of land claims "much diminished." *Sen. Docs.*, 19 Cong., 2 Sess., no. 1, pt. 4, pp. 138–39. Cf. also below, Edwards to Clay, May 2, 1827, note.

Edmund F. Brown was not employed in the Government during the Adams administration but was hired as a clerk in the Post Office Department from 1829 to 1837. He also served briefly by interim appointment in 1843 as a justice of the peace for Washington, D. C., but his nomination was not confirmed. U. S. Sen., *Executive Journal*, IV, 465; VI, 199, 240.

JOHN W. SCOTT, Vicksburg, Mississippi, states that the Jackson *State Journal* "has been suspended in consequence of Mr. [Peter] Isler's being engaged in printing the laws of the state." Requests that the (Vicksburg) *Eagle* be given the *Journal's* contract to publish the (Federal) laws. ALS. DNA, RG59, P. and D. of L.

The *State Journal* retained the contract through the Adams administration.

Scott, perhaps earlier an editor in Wiscasset, Maine, and Philadelphia, has not been further identified.

To William B. Rochester

William B. Rochester, Appointed Chargé d'Affaires
to the Government of Central America
Sir   Department of State. Washington 11th March 1827.
    The President having, by and with the advice and consent of the Senate, appointed you Chargé des Affaires of the United States to the Republic of Central America,[1] I transmit herewith your Commission together with a letter of credence to be presented in the event of your acceptance of the appointment to the Minister of Foreign Affairs[2] of that Republic in your first interview with him. Should you accept the appointment, the President leaves it at your option tò proceed from Mexico at once to Guatemala, without returning to the United States, or to return, and after making at home such arrangements of your private affairs as you wish, preparatory to your absence, then to proceed on your mission.[3] In the first contingency, your salary at $4500. per annum will be considered as commencing with the date of your Commission, and you may draw from Mexico on this Department for your outfit of $4,500, and for a half year's salary in advance. In the second contingency, your salary will not commence, nor your outfit be payable, until you shall be ready to proceed from the United States to Guatemala.

    The first object which should claim your attention will be that of seeing that the treaty[4] between the Central Republic and the United States is faithfully executed in all its stipulations on the part of that Republic.

    And it should be your constant endeavor to impress the Government of that Republic with the desire of the President of the United States to strengthen the amicable relations, and to extend the commercial intercourse between the two republics. If in the prosecution of that intercourse by citizens of the United States, they should, at any time, experience vexations or embarrassments, you will afford your official interposition in their behalf, in such manner as may appear to you most likely to obtain redress.

    It should be a leading and constant object of your attention to obtain and communicate to this Department by every opportunity of conveyance that may occur, information as well respecting the physical condition of the country, as the political and moral character of its institutions and inhabitants— The geographical boundaries of the republic, its connections with Mexico, Colombia and Peru, the present state of its Government, revenue, Army and Navy, its prospect of forming a permanent republican constitution, the present and former produce of its mines, and the state of its relations with European Powers or Asiatic countries, will all form important matters of inquiry and investigation. You will especially observe the country with reference to its present and future capabilities of a commerce mutually advantageous to the United States and to that republic, and communicate the result of your observations.

We should like, also, to possess accurate information as to the actual condition of the Aborigines within the limits of the Central Republic. Have they made any, and what, advances in civilization? are they governed by their own laws, or those of Spain formerly and the Republic now? or partly by one code and partly by the other? Have they any civil rights or privileges secured to them, and do they take any, and what, part in the government of the Republic? Have they a taste for, and a sense of the value of, property? Has any progress been made in their conversion to the christian religion? What have been, and are now the means employed to civilize them?

You will answer in the most frank and full manner all inquiries touching the practical operations of our confederacy, or any of our institutions, and you should cautiously abstain from treating with disrespect whatever you may remark to be peculiar in the habits or usages of the people of the Central Republic civil or religious. Respectfully &c   H. CLAY

Copy. DNA, RG59, Dip. Instr., vol. 11, pp. 258–60 (M77, R6). L draft, first page in Clay's hand, in DLC-HC (DNA, M212, R8).
[1] The appointment had been made and confirmed on March 3. Copies of Rochester's commission, dated March 3, and his letter of credence, dated March 10, are in DNA, RG59, Ceremonial Communications, II, 61, 62.   [2] Juan Francisco de Sosa.   [3] See below, Rochester to Clay, May 12, 1827.   [4] See above, Convention, December 5, 1825.

From Edward Ingersoll

Dear Sir   Philada March 11. 1827.
I owe you thanks for your kind and early reply to the letter with which I troubled you at a very hurried period, the last week of the Session,[1] and I pray your further indulgence to listen to another communication touching the same subject, which I obtrude with reluctance on your attention, or at least with fear of being found troublesome beyond excuse.

I should not have been so inconsistent as to avow my desires for an appointment and then, when the appointment was about to be made, to withhold my application[2] if I had not been misled by our friend Miner[3] who with the best disposition is I fear somewhat heedless, at least I have reason to think him so in this instance.

He promised with alacrity to watch the appropriation bill and let me know if it comprised any provision for the agency at Copenhagen.
He wrote to me repeatedly without telling me and at last wrote that

he was 'sorry to say it did *not*.'[4] This was in answer to a specific request that he would *ascertain*.

Now I very likely may overlook considerations of weight and importance but I cannot help fancying that if I had been rightly informed by Miner and had gone before the President with such recommendations as I might have had there would have been a reasonable chance of his thinking fit to appoint me.

I venture to say further to you in the frankness encouraged by the kindness of your friendship, that such an appointment would have made me very happy and the duties implied in it would have been not disreputably performed, nor would the administration have incurred any reproach or disparagement in consequence of its being given to me.

Mr. Wheaton[5] it seems considers the favour, altogether on the other side, done by him *to* the administration; just as my brother[6] does in respect to his holding the District-Attorney-ship;—and I confess I do not like to hear gentlemen that *hold* good offices which others would gladly execute and be grateful for speaking of their acceptance of such favours as a condescension towards the cabinet. He did not want it nor expect it and does not know whether he can indulge the Administration so far as to accept it, Mr Wheaton says. At all events he does not wish to be "exported without benefit of drawback" {the figure is his own} and must have an understanding as to some ulterior arrangement before he goes into such an exile.[7]

In truth Mr Wheaton would be quite right to decline it   his present office is profitable and safe, and improves in value— By going to Copenhagen he cannot augment his fortune and would exchange a certainty for an uncertainty.

With me it would have been somewhat different and I do not think there would have been a much more contented man, as to his own situation, in the United States than myself—if I had this very appointment which Mr W. thinks so burdensome.

If he should happen to be visited by Minerva and listening to the suggestions of prudence should decline, may I ask the President to think of me, or would it be quite absurd? I do not, dare not, ask you to do or say more than may be comprised in a friendly hint to me.

Markley's appointment has not raised the storm that the disturbed imaginations of some of our friends predicted. I am convinced more people in Philadelphia, to say nothing of Pennsylvania, are gratified by it than would have been by Mr Biddle's appointment.[8]

The decided indications of the policy of the opposition that have lately appeared give us a new opportunity to awake the reason of our fellow citizens of this State. The anti-American, anti-improvement, anti-manufacturing principles of South Carolina are now fixed upon the Jackson party;[9] I have stronger hopes of Pennsylvania than hereto-

fore. And wishing to aid a good cause I am meditating some further
HINTS which if they are received as kindly as those I published last
autumn[10] may not be without their utility.

Judge Clark[11] left us today, Mr Smith's book is nearly completed
but he wants to decorate it with a picture, and cannot find one *handsome* enough—he says.[12] Very truly Your devoted but troublesome
friend   EDWARD INGERSOLL

ALS. DLC-HC (DNA, M212, R2).   [1] Neither letter has been found.
[2] No letter of application found.   [3] Charles Miner.   [4] The appropriation bill enacted March 2, 1827, had included the $9000 sum requested above, Clay to Nourse, No-
vember 16, 1826, covering a year's salary and outfit for a Chargé to Denmark. 4 *U. S. Stat.*,
214.   [5] Henry Wheaton.   [6] Charles J. Ingersoll.   [7] Comment not found.
Wheaton's friends are known to have been unenthusiastic about the appointment because they considered him worthy of a more important assignment. He had hoped to
succeed Thomas Todd on the United States Supreme Court (cf. above, Scott to Clay,
April 28, 1826). Wheaton informed James Monroe that he had accepted the Danish Mission for reasons of health and from a hope to aid the country. Wheaton to Monroe, April
16, 1827, quoted in Elizabeth Feaster Baker, *Henry Wheaton, 1785–1848* (1st ed., 1937;
reprinted, New York, 1971), 75, 77.   [8] Philip S. Markley; Clement C. Biddle. Cf.
above, Peters to Clay, October 24, 1826, note.   [9] Apparently a reference to Senator
William B. Giles' attack upon the role of the Federal Government in support of internal
improvements and a protective tariff. Cf. above, Brooke to Clay, January 31, 1827, note.
[10] Cf. above, Ingersoll to Clay, September 22, 1826. No further publication found.
[11] Probably James Clark.   [12] Samuel Harrison Smith published in 1827 a *Memoir
of the Life, Character, and Writings of Thomas Jefferson, Delivered in the Capitol, before the Columbian Institute, on the Sixth of January, 1827.*

From Philip S. Markley

Dear Sir   Norristown March 11th 1827
    I reached home on Thurday [*sic*] evening[1]—I remained in Phila
but three or four hours during which time I had the pleasure of seeing
a number of our friends—who expressed them selves highly gratified
that I was coming to reside among them[2]— Since my return home I
have been visited by an unusual number of my constituents amongst
whom were many of my old & well tried republican german friends—
They are beginning to be seriously alarmed at the violence of the opposition— The vote on the woollen bill and the conduct of the State
of Georgia against the general government[3] has satisfied them pretty
well that it is not the interest of Pennsylvania or of the Union to
elevate Genl Jackson to the Presidency— Thus far they approve of the
measures of the administration and although Mr Adams was not originally their choice, but whilst his administration adheres to republican
principles and the general policy it has pursued, they have determined
not alone to sustain his administration but fearlessly to support his re-
election— I assure you there are many who I have seen, since my return
that were formerly the warm advocates of Genl Jackson are now & will
continue to be the warm & ardent supporters of the reelection of Mr
Adams—and when the proper period arrives the votes not alone of my
District but the State at large will shew herself triumphant on the side

of measures & not of men— all that is necessary is concert & exertion—
They have recently had a Jackson meeting in Berks County— The
meeting was a small one and its political complexion was a complete
amalgation [*sic*] of *Federalist* [*sic*] & *quids*[4]— all the prominent men
who composed the meeting were the enemies of Governor Shulze[5] at
his last & first election— such meetings will have the desired effect of
bringing about the Democracy of the State in support of Mr Adams—
I shall visit Harrisburg after I get fairly located in the City—for the
purpose of forming some concert of union & understanding throughout the state— You shall however hear from me during the intermediate time

Give my best respects to Mrs Clay—and believe me very truly your
friend   PHP. S. MARKLEY
Hon H. Clay

ALS. DLC-HC (DNA, M212, R2).
[1] From Washington, after the adjournment of Congress.   [2] Cf. above, Peters to
Clay, October 24, 1826, note.   [3] Cf. above, Pleasants to Clay, February 14, 1827; Clay
to Southard, July 3, 1825, note.   [4] The term "quids" had a meaning in Pennsylvania
politics dating from 1804 as a third party of moderates, combining "Constitutional Republicans" and middle-of-the-road Federalists. Noble E. Cunningham, Jr., "Who Were
the Quids?" *Mississippi Valley Historical Review*, L (September, 1963), 254. More
recently the term had referred to Samuel D. Ingham and the Pennsylvania followers of
John C. Calhoun, Klein, *Pennsylvania Politics*, 126.   [5] John A. Shulze. For the
political machinations which had incurred for him the hostility of the "Independent
Republicans," see Klein, *op. cit*, 135–50, 209–14, 220–23.

INSTRUCTIONS AND DISPATCHES   March 11, 1827

To JOHN SPEED SMITH. Informs Smith of his appointment and confirmation as
Secretary to the Tacubaya Mission. Encloses commission and requests Smith to
indicate whether or not he accepts the position. Copy. DNA, RG59, Dip. Instr.,
vol. 11, pp. 260–61 (M77, R6). ALI draft, in DLC–HC (DNA, M212, R8). A copy
of Smith's commission, dated March 3, 1827, is in DNA, RG59, Ceremonial Communications, II, 60.

Stating that family and business concerns prevented his acceptance, Smith on
March 29, 1827, declined the appointment. ALS, in DNA, RG43, First Panama
Congress (M662, R1). No alternative appointee was named.

MISCELLANEOUS LETTERS   March 11, 1827

From ROBERT ADAMS, Philadelphia. States that Richard W. Meade handed him a
State Department packet "containing Thos. Backus commission, the letter of advice thereof, and the Pamphlet prescribing the duties &c, *but the two blank Bonds*
noticed did not accompany." Continues: "thinking this an oversight, and an op-
ortunity [*sic*] shortly expected for St. Iago, I have presumed to ask most respectfully regarding the Blank Bonds, that I may forward them to Mr. Backus
with the other documents." Mentions that he is "engaged considerably in the trade
to St. Iago. . . ." ALS. DNA, RG59, A. and R. (M531, R1).

Clerical endorsement on cover reads: "Respecting Thos. Backus' Appointment
as Consular Commercial Agent at St. Iago de Cuba. Why was the *packet* addressed
to Mr. Backus, under Seal of State *broken open*, it was particularly addressed to

the Care of Mr. Mead? There was no omission on the part of the person sending blank bonds,—Commercial Agents give no bonds." On March 19, Daniel Brent advised Robert Adams that no error of omission had been committed by the Department. Copy, in DNA, RG59, Dom. Letters, vol. 21, p. 498 (M40, R19). Adams has not been further identified.

APPLICATIONS, RECOMMENDATIONS   March 11, 1827

GEORGE C[ORBIN] WASHINGTON, Georgetown, recommends William Beall for appointment as clerk or translator in the State Department. States that Beall is the son of Lloyd Beall, an officer in the Revolutionary War, whose family is in "reduced circumstances." ALS. DNA, RG59, A. and R. (M531, R1).

William Beall, not further identified, received no appointment. His father had entered the Revolutionary forces in 1777 as a lieutenant in the Seventh Maryland Regiment, had been wounded in the Battle of Germantown and taken prisoner at Camden, and, after escaping custody, had risen to the rank of captain in 1781 and served through the end of the war.

To Joel R. Poinsett

No. 20.   Joel R. Poinsett, Envoy Extraordinary and
Minister Plenipotentiary U. S.   Mexico
Sir,   Department of State, Washington, 12 March 1827.
    The eight months, within which the exchange of the ratifications of the treaty which you lately concluded with Mexico[1] was to take place in this City, expired on the 10th. instant, without our receiving the Mexican ratification. This was not to have been anticipated. As the treaty was negotiated under the immediate eyes of the Mexican Government, which must have been well informed, at every stage, of the whole progress, and of every incident, of the negotiation, there was less occasion on the part of that Government than on that of ours for time to deliberate on the question of the ratification of the treaty. The period was not short which was fixed for the exchange of the ratifications; but long as it was we are yet ignorant of the final pleasure of the Mexican Government. You will communicate the surprize [*sic*] which the President has felt at this incomprehensible delay. All Governments are entitled to ample time for full deliberation on the pacts and treaties which they may conclude with foreign nations. But when a period, after mature consideration, has been definitively settled for the interchange of their mutual decisions, it is not usual to allow it to pass away, without communicating what are those decisions. Had Mexico been designated as the place where the exchange of ratifications was to be made, this Government would not, without most solid and satisfactory reasons, have failed to announce to that of Mexico, within the prescribed period, its ultimate determination, whether it was to ratify the treaty, with or without modifications, or not. The effect of the lapse of the limited period, without consummating the

treaty, is to absolve the United States from all sort of obligation, in consequence of the conclusion of the treaty, and to leave them free to conclude a new one with similar or other stipulations. If the Senate of the United States had, before the 10th. instant, given its consent and advice to the unconditional ratification of the treaty on our part, it would have been notwithstanding necessary again to submit the instrument to that body, if the Mexican ratification had arrived here after that day.[2]

As the late[3] Session of the Senate was rapidly expiring, when Mr. Mason[4] brought the treaty, the President determined, without waiting for, but in confident anticipation of, the Mexican[5] ratification of it, to lay the counterpart[6] which you had transmitted, before the Senate for its advice and consent. The advantage of this course consisted in the saving of time. If the Senate advised the ratification of the treaty, the President would be prepared to ratify it, and to authorize the exchange of ratifications, whenever the Mexican ratification should be received within the period limited for that ceremony, although the Senate might not be in Session.[7] If the Senate proposed amendments or alterations, these could be offered with less scruple when it was not known whether the Mexican Congress had given their consent to the treaty with or without conditions. And any such modifications could be forthwith transmitted to you to re-open the negotiation, without the delay of waiting to receive the ratification of the Mexican Government.

Accordingly the President on the 12th. day of last[8] month communicated the treaty to the Senate for consideration. It was referred to the Committee of Foreign Relations, and has been maturely considered both there and in the Senate. The result of these deliberations will be found in the resolutions of the Senate adopted on the 26th. Ulto.,[9] of which I herewith forward you a copy. You will perceive from a perusal of them that the Senate advise and consent to most of the provisions of the treaty, but that there are certain parts of it which have not obtained the approbation of the Senate. It is my purpose, now, to call your attention to those parts.

The first resolution of the Senate expresses its objection to the first additional article of the Treaty. According to the terms of that article it comprehends as well persons "born in the European dominions of His Catholic Majesty, the King of Spain," established in the United States, who may have been regularly naturalized according to our Laws, as those who remain aliens. Of the first mentioned class, that is, native Spanish subjects naturalized in the United States, there are very few. With the exception of those in Louisiana, who are presumed to be generally favourable to the cause of the Mexican revolution, there are believed to be not a hundred in the United States. It was not therefore on account of the extent of the operation, but to preserve inviolate an important *principle*, that the Senate is supposed to have objected to that article. Under our Institutions, the native and the naturalized Citizen are invested, with few exceptions applicable to ourselves alone, with the same rights; and the Government would be extremely reluctant to admit of any invidious distinction. That which is embraced in the provision of the first additional article can be of no importance to the Mexican Government. Of the few naturalized Citizens who were born in the Spanish dominions, and who are established in the United States, a very small number, if any, would probably engage in the commerce with Mexico. Those, as well as any native citizens of the United States, whilst within the Mexican territories, would be amenable to the laws of the Mexican Government. And, if they should so far forget their duty as Citizens of the United States, and their obligations of temporary allegiance to the Government of Mexico, as to attempt any thing injurious to the safety of the United Mexican States, those laws would be competent to vindicate their authority. The importance of the first additional article, to the security of the Mexican Republic, its professed object, is still further diminished by the alteration which is proposed by the Senate in its second resolution.

According to that resolution the word "Citizens" is proposed to be substituted for that of "Inhabitants." The effect of this amendment, if adopted, will be to limit the privileges secured by the third article of the Treaty[10] to Citizens of the respective Republics, to the exclusion of Inhabitants who are not Citizens. It would follow that any native born Spanish subject, established but not in fact naturalized in the United States, would not be entitled to those privileges; and the Mexican Government would, consequently, be free to adopt any measures of precaution, with respect to such persons not naturalized, that expediency or policy might recommend. Restricted as the third article would be, with this modification, there would remain scarcely any persons on whom the first additional article could operate. This change of phraseology in the third article was probably suggested by the Senate to obviate any repugnancy which the Mexican Government might feel to the omission of the first additional article, and it is hoped that it will, accordingly, have that effect.

By the third resolution of the Senate, its consent and advice to the sixteenth and seventeenth articles,[11] are made to depend upon the condition of the annexation to the sixteenth article, of the following proviso,[12] "Provided, however, and it is hereby agreed, that the stipulations in this article contained, declaring that the flag shall cover the property, shall be understood as applying to those Powers only who recognize this principle; but if either of the two contracting parties shall be at war with a third, and the other neutral, the flag of the neutral shall cover the property of the enemies whose Governments acknowledge this principle, and not of others."

The effect of this proviso would be to limit the benefit of the liberal principle that free ships shall make free goods to those powers who agree to it. You are aware that such is the limitation of the principle in our treaty with Colombia.[13] It would seem difficult to resist the force of those considerations which unite in refusing to any power the benefit of a principle to which such power will not subscribe. The reason assigned by the Mexican Plenipotentiaries, in the twelfth conference which you had with them, as appears from the protocol, that is, that they had pending negotiations with Great Britain which might be injuriously affected by their agreement to that limitation of the principle,[14] never was entitled to any weight; but if it ever ought to have influenced their decision, it can no longer operate, as, according to our information, the treaty between the Mexican and British Governments has been concluded.[15]

The last amendment desired by the Senate is to the duration of the treaty which is proposed to be fixed at six years, to be computed from the day of the exchange of the ratifications, instead of twelve years. To this modification no objection is anticipated. From the recent establishment of the Mexican Government, it must be in want of experience as to the operation of Commercial regulations, whether made by treaty or by law. Any arrangement, therefore, by which a Commercial treaty will be speedier subjected to revisal and amendments, if from its practical operation it should be[16] found necessary, must be conformable to the interests of that Government. As we have more commercial experience than Mexico, in consequence of our longer existence as an independent Nation, the abridgement of the period of the treaty cannot be so important to us as to the Republic of Mexico. Among the considerations, which are supposed to have influenced the Senate, that probably had most weight arising out of the fact of the existing war,[17] and the probability, before the expiration of the six years, of peace, between Spain and Mexico. The state of peace, being common to both Republics, will be more favourable to a fair and impartial consideration of the conditions by which their mutual Navigation and Commerce should be regulated, than when one is at war, and the other at peace.

You will communicate, in a friendly and conciliatory manner, to the Mexican Government the conditions on which the Senate consents to and advises the ratification of the treaty; and you will endeavour, by a renewal of the negotiation, to get it modified in conformity to the views of the Senate.

If the alterations proposed shall be agreed to by the Mexican Government, and the treaty shall be duly ratified, when so modified, by that Government, the exchange of the ratifications may then be made at Washington, but not without again submitting the treaty to the Senate of the United States.[18]

The two amendments, to which the Senate may be supposed to attach the most consequence, are probably the first and third. It is believed that without these[19] the Senate would never advise the ratification of the treaty. You will use your best exertions to prevail on the Mexican Government to consent to all the proposed[20] amendments;[21] and you are authorized to propose an additional article similar to that in our late Convention with France, and in our treaty with the Central Republic, stipulating that the treaty shall remain in force beyond the six years until one of the parties shall give to the other six months written notice of his desire to terminate it, at the end of which time it shall accordingly cease.[22] Such an article may reconcile the Mexican Government to the abridgement of the duration of the treaty proposed by the Senate.[23]

If the Mexican Government will[24] not agree to the amendments proposed by the Senate, no alternative will then remain but to terminate the negotiation. I am, with great respect, Your obedient Servant,

H. CLAY

LS. DNA, RG84, Mexico (MR17, frames 141–45). Copy, in DNA, RG59, Dip. Instr., vol. 11, pp. 261–67 (M77, R6); AL draft and L draft with Clay interlineations and amendments, both originally dated February 27, 1827, in DLC-HC (DNA, M212, R8). The AL version was written first, but the copyist's version with Clay's interlineations and amendments is identified in Clay's hand as "1t. Draft." The latter version also bears the date "27 Feby" crossed out and "12 March" written above in Clay's hand. Other significant differences in the draft versions are indicated in the notes below.
  1 See above, Poinsett to Clay, July 12, 1826.   2 The whole first paragraph was added in Clay's hand in the L draft.   3 The word "present" appeared in the AL draft; the change to "late" was made by Clay in the L draft.   4 John Mason, Jr.
  5 Last seven words inserted in Clay's hand in the L draft.   6 This word substituted by Clay for "treaty" in L draft.   7 Last 15 words interlined by Clay in L draft.
  8 This word substituted by Clay for "this" in L draft. Adams' letter of transmittal was dated February 8, 1827. U. S. Sen., *Executive Journal*, III, 568–69.   9 *Ibid.*, 570–72. Clay supplied the date in lieu of "yesterday" in L draft.   10 This substitution was made in the final version of Article III, which provided mutual freedom of access by the "inhabitants of the two countries" to the respective marine facilities of both nations. The right of merchants freely to reside at these places, warehouse their cargoes there, and trade their merchandise was also provided in this article, as was a standard "most favored nations" clause with respect to various duties, imports, and harbor fees. Both nations, however, reserved their coastal trade "only to national vessels." *American State Papers, Foreign Relations*, VI, 608.   11 Article 16 prescribed, in case of war between either of the contracting parties and a third party, application of the principle that "free ships shall also give freedom to goods, and that everything shall be deemed free and exempt which shall be found on board the vessels belonging to the citizens of either of the contracting parties, although the whole lading, or any part thereof, should appertain to the enemies of either; contraband goods being always excepted." In addition, persons "on board a free vessel. . . , although they be enemies to either party, . . . shall not be made prisoners, or taken out of that free vessel, unless they are soldiers, and in actual service of the enemy." Article 17 provided that, "where the neutral flag of one of the contracting parties shall protect the property of the enemies of the other, by virtue of the above stipulation, . . . the neutral property found on board such enemy's vessel shall be held and considered as enemy's property" and subject to seizure unless it had been "put on board . . . before the declaration of war, or even afterwards, if it were done without the knowledge of it"; but after two months following a declaration of war "their citizens shall not plead ignorance thereof." If, on the other hand, "the flag

of the neutral does not protect the enemy's property, . . . the goods and merchandise of the neutral embarked in such enemy's ships shall be free." *Ibid.*, 610.   [12] Clay's AL draft had directed the copyist to supply the quotation.   [13] Cf. above, IV, 127–28. For this provision of the treaty, see Miller (ed.), *Treaties. . .* , III, 171–72.   [14] Although this limitation had been discussed in earlier conferences, including the twelfth, this particular reason for objecting to it was apparently not brought out until the thirteenth conference. See *American State Papers, Foreign Relations*, VI, 596, 598.   [15] See above, Gallatin to Clay, December 16, 1826, note.   [16] Last seven words interlined by Clay in L draft.   [17] Last five words are a revision by Clay in L draft from the original statement: "existing state of the War."   [18] Clay had originally continued the paragraph with a sentence marked for deletion in L draft, as follows: "But, if a part of those alterations should be agreed to and another part declined, or if any new stipulations, not now in the treaty, should be introduced, it would be in either of those contingencies, necessary again to lay the treaty before the Senate for its advice and consent."   [19] Clay had originally continued with a phrase marked for deletion in L draft: "even if the others should be agreed to."   [20] Word inserted by Clay in L draft.   [21] Clay had here written a lengthy passage, which he deleted in L draft, as follows: "but if they will not yield it, you may agree to strike out the 16h. and 17h. articles from the treaty. Anxious as the President is to get the principle of free ships making free goods adopted by as many nations, and especially American nations, as possible, it will be better that the treaty should be silent altogether on that subject, than that the principle should be presented in an exceptionable form. On the other hand, it would not be proper to deprive ourselves of the benefit of other provisions of the treaty because we may be unable to get incorporated in it that principle with the necessary modification. Should you be brought to the alternative of agreeing to the omission of those articles, as the treaty must in that case be again presented to the Senate, ..." The next word, "and," was supplied by Clay in L draft.   [22] See above, III, 53n; IV, 879. The Convention of June 24, 1822, with France, did include provision for termination after six-months prior notification; no such clause was incorporated in the treaty of December 5, 1825, with the Central American Federation. Cf. Miller (ed.), *Treaties. . .* , III, 81, 231.   [23] This sentence supplied by Clay in L draft.   [24] Clay's original draft, amended in the revised draft, had substituted for the next nine words the phrase: "neither agree to all the amendments proposed by the Senate, nor to the omission of the 16h. and 17h. articles as hereinbefore stated, and the adoption of the other amendments. . . ."

Bill from Daniel Brent

Mr Clay to Daniel Brent Dr.   Washington, 12 March 1827.
To the wintering of an horse from 24 October 1826 to 12 March 1827,
19 weeks and 6 days at Dolls 2 87/100 per week   }   Dolls 57:08½.

ADS. DLC-TJC (DNA, M212, R16).

From Francis Johnson

Dear Sir   Steam Boat Wm. Tell   12 Mar 1827
We travelled[1] on the Mail Stage to Wheeling & of course with great rapidity, we arrived at Wheeling About 4 and put off at 7 on this (Evening) boat, consequently but little opportunity was afforded me of questioning public sentiment.   at Fredericktown,[2] John Nelson has come out a violent Jackson man, this is what we expected— at Hagerstown, we had but a moment. & saw but few— I am induced to believe however that the most part of Maryland will be safe— Court was sitting at Union Town, I met with Mr McKennan of Washington

Pena. [sic] Mr McGilpin, Judge Beard & some others[3]— I travelled with some Jackson men part of the road to Brownsville— the friends of this admn affirm & the enemies admit, that great change has taken place, and the Genls. friends admit his cause is much impaired, by a meeting held at Union Town and the discussion which took place there,[4]   There is unquestionably great excitement in Pena. upon the Woolen Bill & the subject of internal improvement,[5]   I met with Majr Jno Tilford of Lexington who is now aboard of this boat, on his way home from Phila. He was in Gettisburg [sic], he tells me, that he was informed then, that City had at the last Election given Genl J. a majority of 2,000 votes and that at this time it would give Mr Adams a majority of 1500. I find that some of the Jackson men in Stewarts district[6] complain that Stewart has become an Administration man, that now seems to be the understanding and if he has only firmness to stick, the District will go with him, I venture 3 to 1. if not more[7]— Calhoun[8] is the most unpopular man in the Nation— and they cannot now separate his fate from the Genls.— I was told, there were but two Jackson men in Wheeling— I have met with a gentleman from Winchester distributing pamphlets & a memorial, to urge the people to a convention in Virginia. I have little doubt, all west Virginia will be moved on that subject and I find that most of the convention men are inclined to the support of Mr Adams, and it is natural they should be, as tis the Richmond party, who have defeated them and who too are opposed to the conv[9]— I advised this Gentleman in a Jocular way, to get the Conventionists to head their publications, For adams & a Convention and put at once to the test, the strength of the East & West ends of the State—

I have met with some individuals from our State, the accounts they give are favorable— I shall probably write you again from Louisville— Mr Brown the Contractor of Ohio,[10] is on board and a violent anti admn man— He cannot now cheat the Govt. I should suppose was one cause— I find my humble remarks[11] are sought for in Pena. and I left some in the East— there is great enthusiasm displayed by the frinds [sic] of the admn.

The Mr McKennan mentd. is the same Gent. who was in the Canal Convention[12] & is I hear decidedly for the admn. Yr friend

Fr. Johnson

P.S.   Your son Thomas is on board & quite steady[13]—

ALS. DLC-HC (DNA, M212, R2). Addressed to Clay and endorsed "private." Endorsed on verso by Clay: "Answered." Answer not found.
   1 From Washington.   2 Maryland.   3 Thomas McKean Thompson McKennan; Thomas McGiffin; Thomas H. Baird.   4 At a public meeting held in Fayette County on March 6 resolutions favoring governmental aid for internal improvements and a "judicious Tariff" had been introduced but, because of opposition from Jackson's friends, had not been acted upon. Philadelphia United States Gazette, March 23, 1827.

5 Cf. above, Ingersoll to Clay, March 11, 1827; Markley to Clay, March 11, 1827.
6 The Fourteenth Congressional District, including Andrew Stewart's residence, Union-town.   7 Stewart was defeated by Thomas Irwin, of Uniontown, in the race for Congress in 1828. *Niles' Weekly Register*, XXXV (November 1, 1828), 147. Born in Phila-delphia, Irwin had attended Franklin (now Franklin and Marshall) College, had studied law, and in 1808 had been admitted to the bar. He had been an editor of the *Philadel-phia Repository* in 1804, had served as Indian Agent at Natchitoches, Louisiana, from 1808 to 1810, and had practiced law at the latter place and, since 1811, at Uniontown. He was a member of the State legislature from 1824 to 1828 and of Congress from 1829 to 1831. From 1831 to 1859 he sat as Federal judge for the Western District of Penn-sylvania.   8 John C. Calhoun.   9 The Virginia House of Delegates on January 26, 1827, had defeated a bill calling for a convention to revise the State constitution, a measure backed by western Virginians, who wanted revisions to expand the suffrage on the basis of manhood rather than a freehold qualification and to limit the basis of representation to white voters. Opposition to the proposal had been centered in eastern Virginia for more than a decade. *Richmond Enquirer*, January 27, 1827; Jacob Neff Brenaman, *A History of Virginia Conventions* . . . (Richmond, 1902), 43.   10 No contractor named Brown has been found.   11 Johnson's *Speech . . . on the Resolu-tion, That the Secretary of State Communicate . . . a List of Each Newspaper, in Each of the States, in Which the Laws of Congress Were Directed to Be Published in the years 1825 and 1826* (see above, McGiffin to Clay, February 19, 1827, note) had been published as a 32-page pamphlet.   12 A convention had met in Harrisburg from August 4 to 6, 1825, to press for construction of a "mainline communication" between Pittsburgh and Philadelphia. Though, to allow for alternatives as to the form of the development, the body avoided use of the word "canal," the assembly was popularly identified as a "Canal Convention." Julius Rubin, "On Imitative Public Improvement; the Pennsyl-vania Mainline," in Carter Goodrich (ed.), *Canals and American Economic Development* (New York, 1961), 82; Washington *Daily National Intelligencer*, August 9, 1825.
13 Cf. below, Clay to Henry Clay, Jr., April 2, 1827.

From William Neill

Sir,   Dickinson College Carlisle, Pa. 12th March, 1827
    Your note of the 8th inst. covering a line from a person callinging [sic] himself Wm. H. Richardson & a student of this College,[1] came to hand yesterday, & has been carefully attended to. The design of the appeal to your generosity is manifestly fraudulent. We have no stu-dent of the name, in our institution; nor do I know any person of the name of Richardson, in this borough. We shall take pains to detect the rogue; &, should he be found to be a member of the College, he will be promptly disciplined. I am fully persuaded, however, that none of our students have [sic] had any thing to do with this base & vexatious deed. I am happy to think that the villain has not suceeded [sic] in his attempt to impose upon you.
    With sentiments of great respect, I am, Sir, yours &c
H. Clay.   WILLIAM NEILL, President
                                                     of Dick. College

ALS. DNA, RG59, Misc. Letters (M179, R65). Neill, a native of Pennsylvania, gradu-ate of the College of New Jersey (1803), and a prominent Presbyterian minister, had served pastorates in Cooperstown and Albany, New York, and in Philadelphia. He was president of Dickinson College from 1824 to 1828, after which he returned to pastoral duties, at Germantown, and, later, to volunteer church work in Philadelphia. He was a founder of the American Bible Society, a director of the Princeton Theological Semi-nary, and the author of two books and several shorter works.
1 Neither document has been found; Richardson has not been identified.

From George C. Smoot

Dear Sir,   Columbian Office[1] Washington, March 12th 1827

It was my intention, at the commencement of the last Session of Congress, to have addressed you upon the subject of employment in your Department; but when I communicated my intention to my friends, I was informed that my prospect of success would probably be better in the Post Office Department. My arrangements were made accordingly, but with no other success than that of having my name placed among the list of applicants, preceded by something like Five hundred. My prospect of success, therefore, in that Department, if at all possible, is at least very improbable— I have, therefore withdrawn my papers, & enclosed them to you,[2] for your inspection, in the hope that you might probably feel disposed to aid a native of your own State.

My family residence, is Jefferson County near Louisville, Kentucky;[3]— I served an apprenticeship to to [sic] the printing business with William Hunter of Frankfort; and was in his office during the great contest between yourself & Felix Grundy Esqr on the subject of the Old Kentucky Insurance Company.[4] A short time after the termination of my apprenticeship, I became engaged in the publication of a newspaper in Vincennes, Indiana Territory,[5] at the time Genl. Harrison[6] was its Govr. which I was compelled to relinquish for want of a support sufficient for two persons. From thence I returned to Kentucky, where I remained until after the close of the last War.[7] But being too poor to enter fully into the printing business, & the wages being to [sic] low to give me a genteel support as a journey man, I shortly after left the New, for the Old States; & have, since that period supported myself entirely by what I could earn as a Journey man printer. I have been engaged in severall [sic] of the Cities & Towns of the Middle & Atlantic States, but principally in this City & Baltimore; and have scarcely, if ever during the whole period of 12 or 13 years been idle either from sickness or want of employment, and have not been able to do any thing more, in a pecuniary point of view, than barely to support myself; and the only satisfaction I have enjoyed during this period of painful dependence, was the approbation of of [sic] my employers, & of being enabled, without a solitary exception, to add them to the list of my friends. The persons by whom I have been engged [sic] in this City are Gales & Seaton for about 4 years Way & Gideon, about 18 months, and at present in the Star Office, where I have been superintendent for about a year.— My family Connexions, are numerous, have ever been your friends & warm supporters, and though to [sic] poor to extend pecuniary relief, and too humble to procure it for me by their influence: the person, who could, & would do so, would Certainly receive their thanks;— and I venture to assert, that the sin of ingratitude will never be numbered in the list of their transgressions in a Coming day. My father is a farmer of Kentucky— has a raised [sic] a large family of sons & daughters,[8] who are all married & settled within ten around [sic] him; and are as independent as persons can be, who possess the Conveniences of life without its luxuries, and who have it not in their power to procure a market for the surplus produce of their farms

I should offer an apology for the trouble which the perusal of this hasty scroll will occasion you; if I did not believe that your goodness of heard [sic] would excuse an effort, prompted by the first principles of nature. I have the honour to be, with high consideration   Yours Very obediently   GEO C SMOOT
Hon H. Clay

ALS. DNA, RG59, A. and R. (M531, R7).

[1] The Washington *Columbian Star*. One volume, running from 1822 to 1825, is located in the Library of Congress; this journal is not listed in Winifred Gregory (ed.), *American Newspapers, 1821–1936; a Union List of Files Available in the United States and Canada . . . (New York, 1937)*.   [2] An accompanying memorandum (ANI) notes that, besides the enclosed correspondence, letters in Smoot's behalf were addressed to (John) McLean by (William Henry) Harrison, F(rancis) Johnson, John F. Henry, (Charles A.) Wickliffe, (William C.) Rives, and R(oger) C. Weightman, but that, since these letters were addressed to McLean, "he has thought proper to retain" them. The note also refers Clay to Weightman, (William W.) Seaton, and (Andrew) Way (Jr.). An undated note from Smoot to Clay (ALS) explains that after he had sent his memorandum, the letters from the members of Congress "there in mentioned" were supplied by McLean and are enclosed herewith. Smoot's file also includes a letter addressed to him from Baron Stow, of Washington, dated February 20, 1827, probably the enclosed correspondence mentioned in the accompanying memorandum.   Baron Stow, born in New Hampshire and graduated from Columbian College, Georgetown, D. C., in 1825, was ordained to the Baptist ministry at Portsmouth, New Hampshire, later in 1827. After holding a pastorate some five years at Portsmouth, he moved to Boston, where he continued a distinguished career in the ministry until 1867.   [3] On the "Big road leading to Salt River." Katharine G. Healy (comp.), "Calendar of Early Jefferson County, Kentucky, Wills, Will Book No. 2; June, 1813–December, 1833," in *Filson Club History Quarterly*, VI, 306.   [4] See above I, 166–67, 168, 171–72, 180, 212n, 214–15.   [5] The *Western Sun*, in August and September, 1807. Brigham, *History and Bibliography of American Newspapers*, I, 144.   [6] William Henry Harrison.   [7] Smoot had been editor of the *Louisville Gazette* in 1811, of the *Louisville Correspondent* from January, 1813, to May 1814, of the Shelbyville *Kentuckian* from 1814 to 1815, of the Lexington *Western Monitor*, apparently very briefly, in 1815, and of the *Bardstown Repository* in March and April, 1815. Brigham, *op. cit.*, I, 146–47, 169–71, 178; II, 484.   [8] Four sons (including George C.) and three daughters were listed in Alexander Smoot's will. Healy, "Calendar. . . ," *Filson Club History Quarterly*, VI, 306.

DIPLOMATIC NOTES   March 12, 1827

From CHRISTIAN MAYER, "H. M. the King of Wurttemberg's Consul General," Baltimore. Applies, by direction of "the Minister of foreign relations [Count de Beroldingen, not further identified] of H. M. the King of Wurttemberg [William I]" for certain documents, "concerning various interests of natives of Wurttemberg, some of whom have emigrated to these United States," which were delivered to (Albert) Gallatin in 1822 and 1823 and by him transmitted to the State Department. Adds, by instruction: "As so long a time has elapsed since these papers were transmitted, . . . the wished for delivery of them . . . may be dispensed with, if the search for them should be difficult or laborious." ALS. DNA, RG59, Notes from Foreign Consuls. Cf. below, Mayer to Clay, May 29, 1827.

INSTRUCTIONS AND DISPATCHES   March 12, 1827

From HEMAN ALLEN, Valparaiso, no. 50. Reports news from Peru "of a recent change in the political affairs of the country . . ." (cf. above, Tudor to Clay, February 3, 1827; Wheelwright to Clay, February 22, 1827). Expresses belief that (Ramón de) Freire and (Francisco Antonio) Pinto (Diaz) will enter the (Chilean) Government again (cf. above, Allen to Clay, February 17, 1827). Notes that Chileans "have long since lost all confidence in [Simón] Bolívar, and have regarded with much apprehension, his late movements in Bolivia and Peru." Says that because his mission may be prolonged, he has taken quarters in Santiago and will leave with his family for that place on March 15. ALS. DNA, RG59, Dip. Disp., Chile, vol. 2 (M-T2, R2). Extract published in Manning (arr.), *Diplomatic Correspondence . . . Latin-American Nations*, II, 1116. Received July 3.

From CONDY RAGUET, Rio de Janeiro, no. 25. Announces that "one of the most deliberate and high-handed insults against our flag and national honour, has recently been committed by the express orders of this government" in the seizure (on March 4), search, and detention of "The Brig Spark of New York, formerly a ship of war in the service of the United States. . . ." Gives details of the affair (cf. below, Raguet to Clay, March 17, 1827). Recalls other outrages against the flag, citizens, and property of citizens of the United States, in no instance of which has redress been given, and cites specifically the cases of the *Spermo*, the *Exchange*, and the *Ruth*. Reports that his note requesting information about the grounds for the detention (of the *Spark*) was answered by an attempt to place him "in the position of the party complained of" and that the demand of the United States consul (William H. D. C.) Wright for release of two seamen, who had been detained, brought no satisfactory reply. Advises that, in consequence of these matters, he determined to terminate his mission and has demanded his passports. Promises to send copies of his correspondence "upon these subjects." ALS. DNA, RG59, Dip. Disp., Brazil, vol. 5 (M212, R7). Published in *American State Papers, Foreign Relations*, VI, 1061–63. Received May 10. Cf. above, Raguet to Clay, October 31, 1826; Clay to Raguet, January 20, 1827.

From W[ILLIAM] H. D. C. WRIGHT, Rio de Janeiro. Reports the discharge and disposition of 168 crewmen, United States citizens, of the frigates *Amazon* and *Baltimore*, which have been sold to the Brazilian Government. Expresses regret that continued instances of insult to the American flag have induced (Condy) Raguet to ask for his passports. ALS. DNA, RG59, Cons. Disp., Rio de Janeiro, vol. 2 (M-T172, R3). Received May 10.

The *Amazon*, not further identified; the other vessel, built in Baltimore "for the Brazilian government," had been on public display at Baltimore in October, 1826, prior to sailing. Washington *Daily National Intelligencer*, October 17, 1826; *Niles' Weekly Register*, XXXII (May 19, 1827), 201.

MISCELLANEOUS LETTERS   March 12, 1827

To DANIEL P[OPE] COOK, "Confidential Agent to Cuba." Appoints him to this post. The wording of the greater part of the document is virtually the same as that found above, Clay to Roberts, December 7, 1825. The third sentence differs: "Having determined to accept it, you will be pleased to proceed without unnecessary delay, to the Havana, from such port of the United States as may appear to you most convenient and agreeable." To the four "objects" listed in the earlier document, another is added:

"5th. What are the Spanish means of resistance, naval and military, if war should be the issue of her present relations with Great Britain; and the latter should attack Havana? And what are the dispositions of the inhabitants towards a colonial connexion with Great Britain?

The last paragraph of the earlier document is replaced here by two paragraphs, stipulating an allowance of $4,500 a year, to begin with Cook's departure from Washington "to proceed to a port of embarkation" and to continue "until the occasion which has suggested it shall cease," together with travel allowances. Copy. DNA, RG59, Dip. Instr., vol. 11, pp. 267–70 (M77, R6). L draft, without the two last paragraphs in DLC-HC (DNA, M212, R2); copy, together with a copy of Cook's certificate of appointment, also dated March 12, 1827, in MHi-Adams Papers, Letters Recd. (MR479). Published in Manning (arr.), *Diplomatic Correspondence . . . Latin-American Nations,* I, 282–83.

On this same day Clay reported to the President that "he had seen Mr. D. P. Cook and offered him the secret Agency at the Havanna, which the circumstances of the present time render peculiarly expedient [cf. above, Gallatin to Clay, December 13, 22, 30, 1826; February 5, 1827; Brown to Clay, February 13, 1827], and which he has accepted. He proposes to embark immediately. Mr. [Samuel L.] Southard and Mr. [John] McLean, the Postmaster-General, had earnestly urged this appointment." Adams, *Memoirs,* VII, 238. For the previous appointee's declination of the post, see above, Robertson to Clay, January 19, 1826.

From DANIEL P[OPE] COOK, Washington. States that, after consulting a physician regarding his health, he has decided "to proceed with the least possible delay to sea, and thence to Havannah [*sic*]." Requests that instructions "be prepared this day" and says that he would "be glad to be on the road tomorrow. . . ." Adds that before his departure he will call on Clay and the President. ALS. DNA, RG59, Dip. Disp., Special Agents, vol. 9 (M37, R9).

From STEPHEN H. DESFORGES, Lexington. Encloses documents respecting his Haitian indemnity claim; requests that they be forwarded to France and that (James) Brown be charged with selecting an attorney to handle the claim and any subsequent remission of funds. Attributes to Clay's "love of justice" and "tender solicitude" the removal of "the exclusion" to which the emigrants had been condemned. ALS, in French with trans. in State Department files. DNA, RG59, Cons. Disp., Cap Haitien, vol. 6 (M9, R6). Cf. above, Clay to Brown, October 25, 1825, no. 2; Brown to Clay, December 28, 1825; January 9, February 13, 1826, "Private."

From HENRY PERRINE, "81 Sullivan St. New York." States that he has "anxiously waited" permission to proceed to Campeche to take up his consular duties and suggests that "much additional inconvenience, personal and pecuniary, will be prevented by his being enabled to sail . . . on or about the 1st of April." ALS. DNA, RG59, A. and R. (M531, R6). On the appointment, approved January 10, 1827, cf. below, Clay to Perrine, March 22, 1827.

From JOSEPH REED, Philadelphia. Inquires "whether any appointment of Secty of Legation to the Mission [to the Panama Congress] has been made to succeed Judge [William B.] Rochester." ALS. DNA, RG59, Misc. Letters (M179, R65).

Reed, father of William B. Reed, was a native Philadelphian, a graduate of Princeton, and a lawyer. He had held office as prothonotary of the Supreme Court of Pennsylvania (1800–1809), State attorney-general (1810–1811), and since 1810 as a recorder of the city of Philadelphia. He also published *The Laws of Pennsylvania* (5 vols., Philadelphia, 1822–1824). On the desired appointment, cf. above, Clay to Smith, March 11, 1827, and note.

APPLICATIONS, RECOMMENDATIONS   March 12, 1827

WILLIAM P. ELLIOT, Washington, solicits appointment as a dispatch bearer to London, where he wishes to study architecture. Explains that his father (William Elliot) "is unable to pay the whole of the expense. . . ." ALS. DNA, RG59, A. and R. (M531, R3). Cf. below, Clay to Gallatin, April 16, 1827.

H[ENRY]. C. MARTINDALE, Washington, recommends (Chauncey) Goodrich of New York for appointment "as a governmental agent to the Mexican Republic or to South America." ALS. DNA, RG59, A. and R. (M531, R3). Cf. above, Tracy to Clay, October 3, 1826, note.

From Jared Sparks

Sir,   Washington, March, 13th. 1827
I have examined anew, and with a good deal of care, the mass of papers constituting the Diplomatic Correspondence during the Revolution, which was authorized to be published by a joint resolution of Congress on the 27th. of March, 1818. I find it impossible to judge with much accuracy what amount of labor will be requisite to prepare them for the press. It is very evident, however, that they require a rigid and patient examination, and that great discretion must be used in selecting such parts only, as are suited to be brought before the public. There are twenty two volumes of manuscripts copied into books, five of which are chiefly in the French language. It is to be presumed that there are other papers, which come under the resolution, that have never been copied, but of this I am not certain, as I have not looked over the originals.

Unfortunately our early ministers abroad soon fell into personal differences, and these appear more or less in a large portion of their correspondence, and sometimes with a heat, that would now seem discreditable to the parties. Such evidences of passion and excited feeling I conceive would be of little service to the cause of hitory [*sic*]; and none to the character of the country, or of individuals, yet so intimately are they blended with the most important topics, that it will often be a task of much labor and delicacy to separate one from the other, and at the same time preserve such a sequence of causes & events, as to exhibit in a proper light the opinions, motives, and conduct of the actors. In this point of view I feel the undertaking to be a responsible one.

There are many letters, also, which may be termed incidental, either treating of subjects remote from the public station of the writer, or written to subordinate agents, or which are of a private nature. These should seldom be printed in detail, but they often contain parts, which have an important bearing, and which should be selected with care and discrimination.

The heaviest part of the labor will be in translating and preparing the French papers. In addition to the five volumes of correspondence with the French Ministers in this country, which are almost wholly in French, letters in this language, received by our ministers abroad, are interspersed throughout all the volumes. These must be translated with more than usual accuracy.

Moreover, the original letters, and not merely the copies bound in volumes, must in all cases be consulted, and compared with the manuscripts sent to the press.

These remarks I have made, that you may have, in as few words as possible, my views of the undertaking. It is not easy for any person, who has not some experience in these matters, to realize the kind and extent of labor necessary for its accomplishment. To finish the work, as it ought to be done, will require, I think, not much less time than three years; and I should supposed [sic] it would be embraced in six, or perhaps eight volumes. These estimates are formed on data so imperfect, however, that they may prove erroneous. The Correspondence should be preceded by a historical Introduction, exhibiting a connected series of events in our early Diplomatic Relations; brief notes should also be occasionally appended both for explanation, and for introducing collateral facts of history; and the whole should be followed by a copious Index. Thus constructed the work would be useful, not merely as a repository of antiquated papers, but as containing materials set forth in a form to give them a permanent interest and value among the historical records of the country.

After the investigation, which has brought me to the above results, I now make a proposal, which, from the tenor of your remarks, when we conversed on the subject, I think will meet your views;

1st.—That I will prepare the Correspondence for publication, according to the Resolution of Congress above referred to, and the general plan here indicated, and translate, or procure to be translated at my own charge, all the French papers;—

2dly.—That I will cause the work to be printed in volumes of the octavo form, averaging about five hundred pages each, and in a similar style of printing and paper to that of the Secret Journal of the Old Congress recently published;[1]— and,

3dly.—That I will supply Congress with one thousand copies of the work thus printed.

These terms of the contract I agree to fulfil [sic], on the consideration;—

1st.—That I shall receive (blank) hundred dollars a volume for preparing the manuscript, the amount for each volume to be paid when it is ready for the press, it being understood that all the copying shall be done by clerks in the office at the expense of the Government;

2dly.—That I shall receive for the one thousand copies furnished to Congress the sum of two dollars & fifty cents for each volume well put up in boards, or if bound in any other manner, the customary price for such binding shall be added; the whole to be paid when the work is delivered in Washington;— and,

3dly—That I shall be allowed the privilege of circulating the work in the market in the usual manner adopted by booksellers, and have the entire benefit of such circulation; but without any reservation of a copyright, except on such conditions as may be agreed on at some future time, and with reference to this contract.

This last provision, in regard to circulation I deem of some consequence, because, disconnected from any pecuniary views of the subject, it is desirable for the interests of knowledge, that the work should go into as many hands as possible, and the method here suggested is the only one by which it can be made accessible to the community.

I have left the blank for further consideration. I wish a fair compensation, and nothing more. The President is probably better acquainted than any other person with the condition of the papers, and what is to be done to prepare them for the press. He can doubtless suggest to you such hints, as will enable you to form a pretty accurate opinion respecting the value of the labor. My own impression is, that five hundred dollars a volume will be no more than reasonable pay. I shall be obliged to leave my business at home, and reside in Washington at different periods, during the whole time that I shall be engaged in the work. Should the above sum be thought too high, however, I doubt not that we shall agree on the proper amount, for I want no more than what is just & reasonable

At my request Mr Webster[2] has been kind enough to examine the papers with me. He takes a good deal of interest in the subject. I have read to him the preceding proposals, and he allows me to say that they are such as approve themselves in all respects to his judgment.

I shall go to Mount Vernon to day, and as soon as you come to a decision, you will do me a favor to send me a line directed to the post office at Alexandria.[3] Should the contract be closed, I shall wish to prepare some of the papers for copying, before I return to Boston, which will be about the first of June. I have the honor to be, Sir, with high consideration[s] of respect & sincere regards, your most obt. Servt

Honble. Henry Clay, Secretary of State.   JARED SPARKS

ALS. DNA, RG59, Misc. Letters (M179, R65). Cf. above, Sparks to Clay, January 31, 1827.
1 See above, Clay to Nourse, November 11, 1825, note.   2 Probably Daniel Webster.

[3] On April 5, 1827, Daniel Brent replied that Clay would like to discuss the project as soon as convenient to Sparks. Copy, in DNA, RG59, Dom. Letters, vol. 21, p. 515 (M40, R19).

From Elisha Whittlesey

Dear Sir   Canfield March 13th 1827
   I reached home Yesterday morning[1] and found my family in health. I had the pleasure of seeing several Gentlemen in Pittsburgh who called on me, among whom were Gen Lacock, Mr Pentland and Judge Shaler.[2] In the course of the conversation, we held, and towards the close of the evening, Mr Pentland asked me whether you proposed to cross the Mountains during the present summer. I informed him that I had understood from you that you would visit Kentucky, and your son[3] in Ohio. He said in that event, he hoped you would make it convenient to pass through Pittsburgh and on the subject expressed much anxiety. I understood the Gentlemen present to concur with him in the sentiments he advanced. Mr. Trimble[4] was present, and I requested him as I was to leave the City early the next morning, to see Judge Shaler with whom I had made him acquainted, and to hold with him another conversation, and apprise you of the result. I found the Gentlemen present much more decided in favor of the administration than I had expected, and in fact unless they were capable of practising a duplicity with which I would not suspect any honorable men, they are, its warm friends. If you could pass through Pittsburgh without too much inconvenience, I can but hope you will do it. I had a few moments conversation with several gentlemen at Beavertown, and learned from them that the changes in the public sentiment there, for the last few weeks had been very great, arising from the general belief that the friends of Gen Jackson were opposed to the American policy—and to internal improvements. I saw at Petersburgh,[5] a well informed plain man, who resided in the upper part of Beaver County, who said, the disclosures made, that, Gen Jacksons friends (alluding to the affairs of Eaton, and Donaldson) were purchasing up presses, and controlling the publication of the News Papers,[6] had proved deeply injurious to the General's prospects in that quarter. I was told at Beavertown, that Mr Stevenson could not, in consequence of the course he pursued on the tariff bill,[7] now obtain, 100 Votes in the County. I trust that things are doing very well. Be pleased to present my respects to Mrs Clay and believe me most sincerely and respectfully Yours
Hon Henry Clay   E WHITTLESEY

   ALS. DLC-HC (DNA, M212, R2).   [1] After the adjournment of Congress.
[2] Abner Lacock, Ephraim Pentland, and Charles Shaler.   [3] James Brown Clay.
   [4] David Trimble.   [5] The context of the letter indicates that Whittlesey is referring to the town of Beaver, in Beaver County, Pennsylvania, and Petersburg in Mahoning County, Ohio, close to the Pennsylvania border, rather than to Beavertown, in Snyder County, and Petersburg, in Huntington County, both in central Pennsylvania.   [6] The

Washington *Daily National Intelligencer*, March 20, 1827, carried an unsigned letter dated March 16, 1827, from a Harrisburg, Pennsylvania, correspondent, who reported that Jackson agents were attempting to buy a journal there for $2,000. The same news item quoted the Trenton *True American* of March 17 in a report that "an opposition gentleman" had recently boasted of having a $50,000 fund for acquiring press support in several States. Cf. also, above, Moore to Clay, February 10, 1827.   [7] James S. Stevenson had voted against the proposed woolens bill (see above, Pleasants to Clay, February 14, 1827). Speaking on the subject, February 8, he had explained that he favored protection for the manufacturers and sheepraisers of the West but that he was opposed to the prohibitive levels which, by curtailing imports of manufactured woolens, would contribute to the accumulation of raw wool surpluses abroad and so reduce the price levels generally for that commodity—an aid for New England industrialists to the detriment of "interior and Western manufactories" and wool growers. *Register of Debates*, 19 Cong., 2 Sess., pp. 1020–25, 1099.

DIPLOMATIC NOTES   March 13, 1827

From BARON DE MAREUIL, Washington. Protests the exactment of discriminating duties on three French vessels, *La Ville du Havre*, the *Sully*, and the *Eugénie*, which with partial shipments loaded in France had sailed from Martinique and arrived in Savannah in December last. States that the demand of the French vice consul (Thomasson, not further identified) for a refund of the charges was refused. Admits that the Convention of 1822 (cf. above, III, 53n) does not speak specifically of the colonies but questions the discrimination against vessels which merely enter port in a colony and maintains that a distinction should be made between those that make use of a colonial port and those that enter but do not unload. Asserts that, if for the prevention of fraud it was thought necessary to restrict the privileges of the Convention to direct navigation between the two countries, the exclusion for the same reason of vessels that have touched at a foreign territory does not necessarily apply to the vessel that has made port in a colony of its own nation, without touching at a foreign port. Comments that the royal order of February, 1826, which admitted United States vessels to Martinique and Guadeloupe on the same basis as French vessels coming from the United States (see above, Brown to Clay, February 13, 1826), affords him the right to invoke a claim for reciprocity regarding French vessels coming (to the United States) from the said colonies. Requests that by Clay's interposition the United States Government refrain from imposing any duty of that nature again. Adds that he has not yet informed his government of this protest, as he wishes to transmit at the same time Clay's answer, "qui influera nécessairement sur la maniere ultérieure dont les rapports de navigation entre des deux Pays devront être considerés." LS, in French. DNA, RG59, Notes from French Legation, vol. 10 (M53, R-T9). Translation published in *American State Papers, Foreign Relations*, VI, 828–29.

On March 14 Clay acknowledged receipt of this note and promised a reply as soon as information was received from "the proper Offices." Copy, in DNA, RG59, Notes to Foreign Legations, vol. 3, pp. 329–30 (M38, R3). For Clay's answer, see below, March 20, 1827.

INSTRUCTIONS AND DISPATCHES   March 13, 1827

From ROBERT MONROE HARRISON, Antigua. Reports that the British Government has set aside the ruling that prohibited the entry to Barbados of American produce through the "Neutral colonies" (cf. above, Harrison to Clay, January 31, 1827). Concludes that the British ministers realize the necessity of accepting supplies from the United States, either directly or indirectly, for United States produce is cheaper, of higher quality, and more accessible than that from the Baltic. Notes that the Germans will not allow credit to the West Indians and observes that American traders soon learn of the West Indian indifference toward debt payment. Discusses the "deplorable" conditions imposed by the Government on the planters, who are "goaded on to desperation, and only want the power [to] plunge at once into open rebellion." ALS. DNA, RG59, Cons. Disp., Antigua, vol. 1 (M-T327, R1). Received April 2.

MISCELLANEOUS LETTERS   March 13, 1827

To NICHOLAS BIDDLE. Thanks him for the enclosure in his letter of March 10; adds that, though he thinks "peace will be preserved between Spain and England," late news from Europe indicates that war between them is not "so improbable as it appeared to be by previous intelligence." Notes that "Spain has not complied with all the demands of England [see above, Everett to Clay, January 7, 1827], and has certainly exhibited more vigor in preparations for any exigency than could have been anticipated." ALS. DLC-Nicholas Biddle Papers (DNA, M212, R20).

APPLICATIONS, RECOMMENDATIONS   March 13, 1827

NATHANIEL P. CAUSIN, Washington, solicits "the situation lately held by R. B. Lee Esq." States that he previously served as a judge of the (Charles County, Maryland) orphan's court, that he mistakenly sent his application to the President, and that he can secure additional letters from (Joseph) Kent and (Clement) Dorsey. ALS. DNA, RG59, A. and R. (M531, R2). Richard Bland Lee, judge of the orphan's court in the District of Columbia since 1819, had died March 12, 1827. Causin, a Washington physician, received no appointment at this time but was named to the desired post in 1838 and held it for 10 years.

To William Jones

Dear Sir: Washington, 14th March, 1827.
The bearer hereof, the Honorable Mr. Reed[1] a Senator of the United States from the State of Mississippi, intending to visit the North, and to pass some days in your city, I take much pleasure in introducing him to your acquaintance, as a gentleman of great worth and merit, whom I have long and intimately known. I am, with great respect, Your obedient servant,   H. CLAY

LS. PHi-Uselma Clark Smith Collection. Recipient identified doubtfully, on the basis of the letter's inclusion in this collection.
[1] Thomas B. Reed.

To Francisco Dionisio Vives

To His Excellency Don Francisco Dionisio Vives,
Governor & Captain General of Cuba.   Department of State,
Sir,   (Confidential)   Washington, 14th. March 1827.
The Honble Daniel P. Cook, late a member of the House of Representatives of the United States from the State of Illinois who will

deliver you this Letter, being advised by his Physicians to try the effect of a sea voyage and the climate of Cuba upon the very delicate state of his health, I beg leave to recommend him to your kindness and hospitality during his abode on the island of Cuba. The President has thought it expedient, to avail himself of the opportunity of Mr. Cook's visit to the Havannah [sic] to charge him confidentially with a commission,[1] in the execution of which I have also to request such aid as Your Excellency may think proper to give. Your Excellency need not now be told of the frankness and impartiality which have constantly characterized the Government of the United States, during the whole of the war between Spain and her late Colonies; nor is it necessary to remind you of the explicit and repeated declarations of the wishes of the Executive of the United States that the actual posture of things in regard to Cuba should not be disturbed. The solicitude which the United States naturally feel in the preservation of the present condition of that island is greatly increased by the doubtful aspect of the relations between Spain and Great Britain.[2] And it would tend to quiet our apprehensions if we were assured that the means of defense which the island of Cuba possesses are adequate to repel any attack that may possibly be made either by any European power or by the new States of America. The object therefore of the commission with which Mr. Cook is charged is to ascertain as far as it may be deemed proper the capabilities of the island to resist any such attack, and also information on any collateral points which may assist us in forming an accurate judgment on the degree of safety and security which the island actually enjoys. Your Excellency will fully appreciate the motives which influence the President in instituting this enquiry, and I hope will feel yourself authorized to cause any facilities in your power to be afforded to Mr. Cook in the accomplishment of the above commission.

I seize with pleasure, this occasion to tender to Your Excellency assurances of my high consideration. H. CLAY.

Copy. DNA, RG59, Notes to Foreign Legations, vol. 3, pp. 330–31 (M38, R3). ALI draft, in CSmH; published in Manning (arr.), *Diplomatic Correspondence . . . Latin-American Nations*, I, 284.
[1] See above, Clay to Cook, March 12, 1827. [2] Cf. above, Clay to Biddle, March 13, 1827.

From Benjamin W. Crowninshield

Dear Sir, *Private.—* Philaa. March 14th. 1827—

I am now here, detained by sickness, was first attacked at Baltimore, by much trouble got as far as this, & I can expect to tarry a week or ten days more.— Since I have been here, the politicians favorable to our Side have called to see me, among them, our friend PPF. Degrand, who bro't with him a judge Barnes,[1] I think that is the right name, a man who appears to be well versed in the Affairs of this State, he says our party are well organized, from one, to the other end of the State, he says, the Quakers are all with us, the sober & discreet men throughout the state are with us, the Federts. too, all but the *Ultras* ones [*sic*], & they are against us,   a vast majority of all, are with the Administn.;[2] but the germann population, are against us. Four upon whom they rely for information, *their leaders*, are with us.[3] The Govr. of the State[4] is with us. The Senator Bernard[5] is with us, & it is said their [*sic*] is now actually a *majority* of the members in both Branches of the State Lege. who are decided friends to the administration, but the difficulty seems to be, that no one is hardy or strong enough to come out & take the field,   each thinks the Jacksonians so strong, that they are be [*sic*] overwhemled [*sic*] if any one comes out to oppose. When then shall they come out? they say the Govr. expected them to have seconded him in his attempt, when his message was delivered,[6]   it was delayed & that chance went by,   the Govr was a *little hurt at it.* now they say the spring elections are to come on, & they must take the field, & they speak confidently of success; but they want help   they say to me that *Binns*,[7] is the mainmast of their power in the interior, that to keep up a regular communication with the country & German people, it is *time & money* & he must have the printing— all that can be given to him, from the *post Office*, & from the Custom House dept.,   he lately gets a part for [*sic*] Mr *Jones*[8] *given with great reluctance* but none whatever from the Post Office,   can this be otherwise? I write this to give you an idea, of what they want, & they add it is of the greatest importance. *be wise & consider.* Jones & Markley[9] will do no good here, they will be both a sleep, in a week after they take the chair.—

From all that I can learn, the state of things are [*sic*] well in this State, & with proper *support* & management, this state may be gained to the administration.   a *trip for ones health*, at the proper time, might happen just right. —&c. &c.— my respects to your family— burn this letter & believe me to be respectfully your friend—
Hone. Henry Clay Washington.   B W CROWNINSHIELD—

[1] Peter Paul Francis Degrand; probably Joseph Barnes, educated at Williams College and the Litchfield Law School, formerly registrar of wills and judge of the "old district court of Philadelphia." *Pennsylvania Magazine of History and Biography,* LXV, 373.
[2] Cf. above, Markley to Clay, March 11, 1827.   [3] German leaders at this time supporting the administration included Joseph Ritner, Amos Ellmaker, Simon Cameron, and, perhaps, William Marks. On Ritner and Cameron, see Klein, *Pennsylvania Politics,* 222, 225; on Marks, cf. *ibid.,* 190; Adams, *Memoirs,* VII, 536. For Ritner's repudiation of this stand, cf. below, Sergeant to Clay, September 11, 1827, note; on Cameron's change of position, see below, Sergeant to Clay, October 30, 1827, note.   Ritner, born in Berks County, Pennsylvania, and settled as a young man on a farm in Washington County of that State, had served in the War of 1812 and, from 1821 to 1826, as a member of the Pennsylvania Legislature, where he had been speaker of the House in 1825 and 1826. Later prominent as an anti-Masonic gubernatorial candidate (1829, 1832, 1835, 1838), he was elected Governor in 1835, primarily on the basis of his opposition to Jackson.   Ellmaker, born in Lancaster County, Pennsylvania, and educated at Yale and the Litchfield Law School, had been admitted to the bar at Harrisburg in 1808, had been a member of

the State legislature from 1812 to 1814, president-judge of district court from 1815 to 1816, and State attorney general from 1816 to 1819. In 1821 he had settled in Lancaster, where he practiced law for another 30 years. He became the anti-Masonic candidate for Vice President in 1832.   4 John A. Shulze.   5 Isaac D. Barnard.   6 Cf. above, Clay to Brooke, December 11, 1826, and note.   7 John Binns.   8 Cf. above, Clay to Jones, January 23, 1827; Jones to Clay, January 25, 1827; Degrand to Clay, February 8, 1827; below, Clay to Crowninshield, March 18, 1827.   9 Philip S. Markley.

DIPLOMATIC NOTES   March 14, 1827

From the BARON DE MAREUIL, Washington. States that he has not received an answer to his letter (above, April 16, 1826) regarding the *Calypso* and *La Revanche*, in which he enclosed documents "which might on this subject [rescue and salvage] occasion a mutual arrangement between France and the United States." Requests a reply. LS, in French with trans. in State Department file. DNA, RG59, Notes from French Legation, vol. 10 (M53, R-T9).

INSTRUCTIONS AND DISPATCHES   March 14, 1827

From ALBERT GALLATIN, London, no. 60. Reports the "general results" of his inquiries on British patent regulations (cf. above, Clay to Gallatin, January 11, 1827): (1) patents are routinely granted through the offices of the attorney and solicitor general; (2) patent disputes are contested in courts of equity, there being "no statute on that subject"; (3) "patents for discoveries are granted by virtue of the prerogative of the crown" for a term of 14 years, renewable only by a private act of Parliament; (4) the expense of obtaining distinct patents in England, Scotland, and Ireland exceeds £300 and constitutes "the best security against the otherwise innumerable applications"; and (5) patents are issued "to subjects or aliens, as well for imported inventions or improvements as for original discoveries." Transmits (Richard) Godson's treatise, which "is said to have superseded preceding works and to contain all the necessary information." Says he will make additional inquiries on the subject.

States that he and (Henry U.) Addington may resume their talks in the coming week, that (William) Huskisson "is slowly recovering," that (George) Canning has suffered a relapse (cf. above, Gallatin to Clay, March 6, 1827), that ministerial arrangements are uncertain, and that the King (George IV) "is expected tomorrow in town, probably for the purpose of coming to a final determination." ALS. DNA, RG59, Dip. Disp., Great Britain, vol. 33 (M30, R29).

Godson's work, *A Practical Treatise on the Law of Patents for Inventions and of Copyright. . .*, had been published in London in 1823.

From JOHN SERGEANT, Mexico, "Private." Reports that he has nothing to add to his dispatches of February 24 and March 5. Expresses belief that the Mexican Congress will not consider the Panama treaties before the ratification deadline (March 15, 1827). Says that the Government (of Mexico) has learned of the dissolution of the (Colombian) Congress at Bogotá, the pending departure of General (Francisco de Paula) Santander, and the probable assumption of power by (Simón) Bolívar, until "the Bolivian constitution shall be introduced by the Convention about to assemble" (cf. above, Tudor to Clay, February 21, 1827; below, Watts to Clay, March 14, 1827). Observes that "accounts from New Orleans respecting Texas are not very clear" (cf. above, Poinsett to Clay, March 8, 1827). Concludes "that there will be no Congress at present" and inquires concerning the President's views "as to the line of conduct" he ought to follow, given the uncertain future of the Congress. ALS. DNA, RG43, First Panama Congress (M662, R1). Received May 10.

From JOHN SHILLABER, Batavia. Reports a decline in trade with the United States. Notes, in relation to the worsening state of affairs in Java, that the anticipated addition of European troops probably will be insufficient to crush the rebellion and that the Government is financially distressed. Repeats his suggestion that an American naval vessel be stationed "in these seas" and observes that there has been a "great increase of Pirates" and that the English have prohibited their traders from carrying war material to Siam or "to any Island north of the Equator after Dec. 1st. 1827." States that he has received word of an insurrection in Cochin China, where each party fears Siamese intervention. Adds that the Siamese are fortifying their coastal towns and keeping watch "at the entrance of the river leading to Bankok [sic]." Expresses hope that he can leave for the United States in May or June. ALS. DNA, RG59, Cons. Disp., Batavia, vol. 1 (M-T95, R1). Forwarded with dispatch of April 23; received August 10.

On the rebellion in Java, cf. above, Shillaber to Clay, September 18, 1825; February 27, 1826. The Cochin China insurrection, which spread throughout the Red River delta in 1826 and 1827, was led by N. Guyen Hanh, a leader in an earlier revolt who had been living in exile in China since 1802. Helen B. Lamb, *Vietnam's Will to Live: Resistance to Foreign Aggression from Early Times through the Nineteenth Century* (New York, 1972), 71.

From BEAUFORT T. WATTS, Bogotá, no. 27. Emphasizes the "fluctuating state of affairs from Peru to Venezuela": information of the adoption in Peru of (Simón) Bolívar's constitution and of his election as President for life was followed shortly by news of a revolution there, where the earlier actions were now considered precipitate and where "The Council of Government recommend" the convocation of delegates to frame a new constitution and choose a new President and Vice President; meanwhile, Bolívar, in Venezuela to allay discontent, was so mortified by events that he has resigned as President of Colombia. Expresses hope that the Colombian Congress will not accept the resignation and fear that lamentable consequences will follow Bolívar's retirement. Declares: "there is an intrinsick [sic] moral force in the man, that awes the disaffected and inspires courage in the patriot." Encloses a translation of Bolívar's resignation. ALS. DNA, RG59, Dip. Disp., Colombia, vol. 4 (M-T33, R4). Published in Manning (arr.), *Diplomatic Correspondence . . . Latin-American Nations*, II, 1309. Received June 25. Cf. above, Tudor to Clay, February 3, 1827.

On July 6, 1827, Daniel Brent acknowledged, "In the absence of the Secretary" (cf. below, Clay to Erwin, June 3, 1827), receipt of Watts' "Despatches to No. 27, of the 19 [sic] March, inclusively. . . ." LS, in DNA, RG84, Colombia (MR 14).

MISCELLANEOUS LETTERS   March 14, 1827

To [RICHARD RUSH], Washington. Transmits a "copy of a note received from the French Minister" (above, Mareuil to Clay, March 13, 1827); requests "information as to the Treasury construction" of the French convention and "the practice under it in cases of French vessels bound from French ports, and touching at French Colonial ports. . . ." Copy. DNA, RG59, Dom. Letters, vol. 21, pp. 496–97 (M40, R19). Addressed to "the Secretary of the Treasury."

From GEORGE W. SLACUM, Alexandria. States that he is "in receipt of letters from Buenos Ayres" which relate to (John M.) Forbes' activities and which he (Slacum) wishes placed on file in the State Department. Claims that the letters confirm the motives he attributed to Forbes both in the case of the *Merope* and with reference to the appointment of an acting consul. ALS. DNA, RG59, Cons. Disp., Buenos Aires (M70, R4). Cf. above, Slacum to Clay, February 14, 1827.

To Theodore W. Clay

Theodore H. [*sic*] Clay Esqre Bearer of Despatches
Department of State Washington March 15th. 1827.

Having occasion to employ a special messenger as bearer of despatches from this Department to the Minister of the United States at Mexico, and to their Commissioners at the Congress of American Ministers at Tacubaya, I have selected you for that service with the understanding that you are now prepared to enter upon it. You will accordingly forthwith repair with the despatches which are committed to your care, to some convenient port in the United States to procure a passage there in the first vessel bound to La Vera Cruz; and after landing, proceed thence with all practicable expedition to the City of Mexico, where you will deliver to Mr. Poinsett and Mr. Sergeant[1] the several despatches addressed to them.

Your compensation for this service will be, for the voyage out and home, one hundred and fifty Dollars each, a per diem allowance at the rate of six dollars, from the time of your departure hence, till your return, and a reimbursement of your travelling expenses to the port of embarkation, and from the port of your landing to the City of Mexico, back again from Mexico to the port of your embarkation, and from the port of your landing in the United States to this city.

You will not protract your visit to Mexico beyond a period of two weeks, unless Mr. Poinsett, or the joint Ministers of the United States at the Congress of Tacubaya should require you to remain longer for the purpose of sending despatches by you to this Government.

The sum of One thousand Dollars is advanced to you on account. I am &c &c   H. CLAY.

Copy. DNA, RG59, Dip. Instr., vol. 11, pp. 273–74 (M77, R6). L draft, in Daniel Brent's hand, in DLC-HC (DNA, M212, R8).
1 Joel R. Poinsett; John Sergeant.

Check to Richard Forrest

15h. March 1827.

Pay to Richard Forrest or order one hundred and twenty five dollars.   H. CLAY
Cashr. of the Off. of Dt. & Dt. Washn.[1]

ADS. DLC-TJC (DNA, M212, R16). Cf. above, Rental Agreement, October 11, 1825.
1 Richard Smith.

To Joel R. Poinsett

Joel R Poinsett, Envoy Extraordinary and Minister
Plenipotentiary to Mexico.   Department of State,
Sir   Washington 15th. March 1827.

The great extent, and the facility which appears to have attended
the procurement, of grants from the Government of the United Mexican States, for large tracts of country, to citizens of the United States,
in the province of Texas[1] authorize the belief that but little value is
placed upon the possession of the province by that Government.[2] These
grants seem to have been made without any sort of equivalent, judging according to our opinions of the value of lands. They have been
made to, and, apparently, in contemplation of being settled by, citizens
from the United States. These emigrants will carry with them our
principles of law, liberty, and religion, and, however much it may be
hoped they might be disposed to amalgamate with the ancient inhabitants of Mexico, so far as political freedom is concerned, it would
be almost too much to expect that all collisions would be avoided on
other subjects. Already some of these collisions have manifested themselves,[3] and others, in the progress of time, may be anticipated with
confidence. These collisions may insensibly enlist the sympathies and
feelings of the two Republics, and lead to misunderstandings.

The fixation of a line of boundary of the United States on the side
of Mexico should be such as to secure, not merely certainty, and apparent safety in the respective limits of the two countries, but the
consciousness of freedom from all danger of attack on either side, and
the removal of all motives for such attack. That of the Sabine brings
Mexico nearer our great western commercial capital[4] than is desirable
and although we now are, and, for a long time, may remain perfectly
satisfied with the justice and moderation of our neighbor, still it would
be better for both parties, that neither should feel that he is in any
condition of exposure on the remote contingency of an alteration in
existing friendly sentiments.

Impressed with these views, the President has thought the present
might be an auspicious period for urging a negotiation, at Mexico, to
settle the boundary between the territories of the two Republics[5]—
The success of the negotiation will probably be promoted by throwing
into it other motives than those which strictly belong to the subject
itself[6]— If we would obtain such a boundary as we desire, the Government of the United States might be disposed to pay a reasonable pecuniary consideration[7]— The boundary which we prefer, is that which,
beginning at the mouth of the Rio del Norte[8] in the sea, shall ascend
that river to the mouth of the Rio Puerco, thence ascending this river
to its source, and from its source, by a line due North to strike the
Arkansas, thence, following the course of the southern bank of the

Arkansas to its source, in Latitude. 42°, North.; and thence by that parallel of latitude to the South Sea.[9] The boundary thus described would, according to the H. S. Tanner's map, published in the United States, leave Sta. Fé within the limits of Mexico, and the whole of Red River, or Rio Rojo, and the Arkansas, as far up as it is probably navigable, within the limits assigned to the United States. If that boundary be unattainable, we would, as the next most desirable, agree to that of the Colorado, beginning at its mouth, in the Bay of Bernardo,[10] and, ascending the river to its source, and thence by a line due North, to the Arkansas, and thence, as above traced, to the South Sea. This latter boundary would, probably also give us the whole of the Red River, would throw us somewhat farther from Santa Fé, but it would strike Arkansas, possibly at a navigable point. To obtain the first described boundary, the President authorizes you to offer[11] to the Government of Mexico, a sum not exceeding one million of dollars— If you find it impracticable to procure that line, you are then authorized to offer for the above line of the Colorado[12] the sum of five hundred thousand dollars— If either of the above offers should be accepted, you may stipulate for the[13] payment of the sum of money, as you may happen to agree within[14] any period not less than three months after the exchange, at the City of Washington, of the ratifications of the Treaty.

Should you be able to conclude a treaty, it will be necessary that it should contain a stipulation for the mutual right of navigation of the Rio del Norte, or the Colorado as the one or the other of them may be agreed on, and for the exercise of a common jurisdiction over the river itself. The treaty may also provide for the confirmation of all bona fide grants for lands made prior to *its date*, with the conditions of which there shall have been a compliance. And it may contain a provision similar to that in the Louisiana and Florida Treaties for the incorporation of the inhabitants into the Union as soon as it can be done consistently with the principles of the Federal Constitution, and for their enjoyment of their liberty, property and religion.[15]

There should also be a provision made for the delivery of the country to the United States simultaneously, or as nearly so as practicable, with the payment of the consideration.[16] We should be satisfied with a surrender of possession at that time, as far as the river line extends (the Del Norte, or the Colorado) and to receive the residue as soon as the line to the Arkansas can be traced, which the Treaty ought to provide should be done without unnecessary delay; and, at all events, before a future day to be specified.[17]

Immediately after intelligence reached us of the revolt in Texas, I addressed a note to Mr. Obregon to which I received an answer on that subject[18]— I herewith transmit copies of both, in order to put you in possession of what has occurred here, and to enable you to efface any impression, if any impression should exist at Mexico, that the United States have given countenance to the insurrection. I am, with great respect, Your Obt. Servant   H. CLAY

Copy. DNA, RG59, Dip. Instr., vol. 11, pp. 270–273. AL draft and L draft with inter-lineations and a supplementary paragraph in Clay's hand, both originally dated February 26, 1827, in DLC-HC (DNA, M212, R8). The second draft has a correction of the date and other emendations as indicated in the notes below. Another copy of the letter is found in DLC-Jackson Papers (DNA, M212, R21).
   1 Cf. above, Poinsett to Clay, July 27, 1825.   2 Cf. above, Poinsett to Clay, July 22, 1825; Clay to Stuart, December 1, 1825.   3 Cf. above, Dickson to Clay, January 23, 1827; Poinsett to Clay, February 7, 21, March 8, 1827; Sergeant to Clay, March 5, 1827.
   4 New Orleans.   5 Cf. above, Kane to Clay, March 7, 1827, note.   6 At this point in the second draft Clay deleted a sentence: "Mexico is laboring, at this time, with great activity, to construct a marine, of which she stands much in need both for pur-poses of offense and attack."   7 The last five words substituted by Clay, in L draft, replacing the phrase: "aid in the accomplishment of that object." Adams had "advised" Clay "to leave out the offer of ships of war, and offer only money." Adams, Memoirs, VII, 240.   8 The Rio Grande.   9 The Pacific Ocean.   10 Matagorda Bay.
   11 Clay had originally written the following passage in lieu of the next four words, which he inserted in L draft: "a ship of the line, mounting not less than ninety guns, including all the guns and other equipment necessary for immediate service, exclusive of seamen, or at the option of the Government of Mexico. . . ." The sum "one million" later in the line was inserted in Clay's hand in L draft.   12 Clay had originally written the following words at this point in AL draft, deleted in L draft: "a sixty gun Ship, including the guns and other equipment for immediate service, or at a similar option with that above mentioned. . . ." The figure of $500,000 later in the sentence was added by Clay in L draft. Two sentences written by Clay following the one here under consideration were deleted in L draft: "Of the two modes of payment we should prefer that in money. Both are suggested that you may offer them successively, or in such manner as shall appear to you best calculated to effectuate the object in view."
   13 The following words were deleted at this point in L draft: "delivery of the Ship at La Vera Cruz or in a port of the United States, or the. . . ."   14 The following six words inserted by Clay in L draft.   15 For the pertinent article in each of these treaties, see Miller (ed.), Treaties. . . , II, 501; III, 8.   16 This word substituted by Clay in L draft for the word "equivalent."   17 The following paragraph was added in Clay's hand in L draft.   18 Above, February 19, 20, 1827.

From Joseph Haines

Honl. H. Clay,   Logan County, Ohio, March 15th, 1827.
   On account of an open line between your survey and one of General McArthurs on waters of Mill Creek, I find myself on your survey in-stead of Mc.Arthur's. It is they [sic] survey you bought of him.¹ Thus circumstanced, I have endeavoured to observe that justice to you that has restricted me from any abuse of timber, &c., on the lands without my improvements. These as yet are limited to but between 10 and 12 or 14 acres. I have thought, sir, it best to thus let you know my situ-ation in these respects, and to ask your permission of a lease of 100 acres of the survey for seven years from this time at the accustomed rates in this country. I am situated on the S.E. Corner; and though it is, perhaps, inferiour in timber and land to perhaps any other corner I would, haveing [sic] made the before mentioned improvements, to-gether with a small dwelling house and a few other necessary out-houses, remain and obligate myself to leave Thirty acres under a good fence and in a state for cultivation at the end of that time, if I did not

choose then to pay for it, at a reasonable price per acre, should you now be pleased to set that price, if disposed to sell. Be pleased, sir, to let me know whether these propositions will meet your sanction by a letter to me to the postoffice from which this shall have been sent in this county.[2] The land I can inform you, is timbered by Beech of small size, with sugar tree scattered through most of it. It is a springy or wet soil of course, but it has no living water on it through the ordinary summer, and I have been obliged to dig a well to remdy [*sic*] the difficulty. If I should purchase, I would take the land to its south and eastern lines pretty much in a square form. And land of a better quality can be had on Mc.Arthur's survey adjoining it at $1.50 unimproved. Should you sell, however you will, I hope, give me a preference over other purchasers. I am, dear Sir, Your most obt Sert.

JOSEPH HAINES.

ALS. DLC-TJC (DNA, M212, R13). Haines has not been further identified.
[1] For the transaction by which Clay had obtained this land from Duncan McArthur, see above, III, 7–9, 16.   [2] The letter is postmarked, by hand: "April 4th. 1827. Garwoods Mills. 0.   free"

APPLICATIONS, RECOMMENDATIONS   March 15, 1827

JOSEPH CAREY, Hyattstown, Maryland, solicits a clerkship in the government. Recalls that he was recommended previously (above, May 8, 1826) but that he has received no word from the State Department. ALS. DNA, RG59, A. and R. (M531, R2).

To John Sergeant and Joel R. Poinsett

Messrs. John Sergeant ⎱
and Joel R Poinsett   ⎰
Envoys Extraordinary and Ministers Plenipotentiary to Tacubaya.

Department of State Washington 16th. March 1827.

By the appointment of Mr. Poinsett, made by and with the advice and consent of the Senate, as one of the Ministers of the United States to the Congress of America Nations expected to assemble at Tacubaya, you have become associated in that mission.[1] Mr. Poinsett, it is therefore anticipated, will be disposed cordially to co-operate in the performance of those duties which have been enjoined by the instructions heretofore addressed to Mr. Anderson and Mr. Sergeant, or to either of them,[2] so far as they remain to be executed. And the President relies with great confidence on the zeal and ability of both of you to promote, in this important service, the interests of our country.

The instructions addressed to Messrs. Anderson and Sergeant have been sufficiently explicit as to the nature of the assembly. According to our views, it is to be considered as entirely diplomatic. No one of the represented nations is to be finally bound by any treaty convention or compact to which it does not freely consent, according to all the forms of its own particular government. With that indispensible [*sic*] qualification, the mode of conducting the conferences and deliberations of the Ministers is left to your sound discretion, keeping in view the observations which have been made in your general instructions— I am induced again to advert to this topic, in consequence of a letter from the Colombian Minister, under date of the 20th November last[3] (a copy of which is herewith transmitted) from the tenor of which it might probably be inferred as his opinion, that a majority of voices in the Assembly, on any given proposition, is to be decisive— We have not yet obtained copies of the treaties concluded at Panama, which are mentioned in that note. To these we have a right and we shall continue to expect them.

We have no later information than that contained in Mr. Sergeants despatch No 1. under date the 19th. January last and its accompanyments, as to the probable time of the convention of the ministers of the several Powers. The course which he had adopted of announcing himself to such of them as had arrived at Mexico is approved. From the anwers he received to his note, it appears that eight months from the 15th. of July last were specified as the period within which the treaties concluded at Panama were to be ratified, and when it was expected the Congress would again meet. That term expired on the 15th. Instant— It is probable, therefore, that about this time the ministers of the various Powers will assemble at Tacubaya. But if they should not meet before the 1st. of June next, Mr. Sergeant may, after that day, return to the United States, without further detention— In the event of his return, Mr. Poinsett will consider the duties of the joint mission as devolving on him alone, and should the Congress assemble subsequent to that period and Mr. Sergeant should avail himself of the permission now given him to leave Mexico, Mr Poinsett will attend the Congress in behalf of the United States.

The intelligence which has reached us from many points as to the ambitious projects and views of Bolivar,[4] has abated very much the strong hopes which we once entertained of the favorable results of the Congress of American Nations— If that intelligence is well founded (as there is much reason to apprehend) it is probable that he does not look upon the Congress in the same interesting light that he formerly did. Still the objects, which are contemplated by your instructions, are so highly important, that the President thinks their accomplishments ought not to be abandoned whilst any hope remains. Their value does not entirely depend upon the form of the Governments which may concur in their establishments, but exists at all times, and under every form of Government.

You will, in all your conversations and intercourse with the other ministers, endeavor to strengthen them in the faith of free institutions, and to guard them against any ambitious schemes and plans from whatever quarter they may proceed, tending to subvert liberal systems.

Mr. Rochester having been appointed Charge des Affairs to Guatemala, Mr. John Speed Smith of Kentucky formerly a member of the House of Representatives, is appointed Secretary to your mission[5]— In the event of his acceptance (of which advice has not yet reached the department) he is expected to proceed from Kentucky by the way of New Orleans, to join you.

You are at liberty to detain the bearer of this letter[6] a reasonable time to convey any despatches you may wish to forward to this Government. If you should not wish him to remain at Mexico for that purpose, after stopping about two weeks to recover from the fatigues of the journey and voyage, he will return to the United States with such despatches as you may confide to him.— I am with great respect, Your obedt. Servant   H. CLAY.

Copy. DNA, RG59, Dip. Instr., vol. 11, pp. 274–77 (M77, R6).
[1] See above, Clay to Poinsett, February 28, 1827.   [2] Above, Clay to Anderson and Sergeant, May 8, 1826; Clay to Sergeant, November 14, 1826.   [3] Above, Salazar to Clay.   [4] For examples, see above, Tudor to Clay, August 24, November 21, December 13, 1826; February 3, 1827; Allen to Clay, November 15, 1826; Forbes to Clay, September 5, 1826; Poinsett to Clay, September 6, November 15, 1826; MacPherson to Clay, October 2, 1826; Watts to Clay, October 14, 1826; Hughes to Clay, October 16, 1826; Gallatin to Clay, December 16, 1826; Brown to Clay, December 29, 1826; Everett to Clay, January 7, 1827; Sergeant to Clay, January 17, 1827.   [5] See above, Clay to Rochester, March 11, 1827; Clay to Smith, same date.   [6] See above, Clay to Theodore Wythe Clay, March 15, 1827.

DIPLOMATIC NOTES   March 16, 1827

To BARON DE STACKELBERG. Transmits a copy of a recent act providing for temporary suspension of discriminating duties on Swedish and Norwegian vessels and cargoes (cf. above, Clay to Tomlinson, December 25, 1826). States that the "duration of the Act is limited to the end of the next Session of Congress, not with any intention of reviving those duties at that period. . . , but under the hope that, in the mean time a more permanent arrangement, by treaty will be made." Notes that this legislation provides for refunding any discriminating duties collected "during the interval between the date of the expiration of the treaty and that of the passage of the Act." Copy. DNA, RG59, Notes to Foreign Legations, vol. 3, pp. 331–32 (M38, R3). L draft, in clerk's hand, in CSmH. Cf. above, Clay to Stackelberg, October 31, 1826.

From HILARIO DE RIVAS Y SALMON, Philadelphia. States that he has received no answer to his notes relative to Juan Miguel Losada's protest (see above, Salmon to Clay, October 25, 1826) and that he has been directed to inquire again into the matter. ALS. DNA, RG59, Notes from Spanish Legation, vol. 9 (M59, R-T12).

INSTRUCTIONS AND DISPATCHES   March 16, 1827

From THOMAS L. L. BRENT, Lisbon, no. 39. Reports having learned that the (Spanish) order for suspension and trial of certain army officers, mentioned in his last dispatch (above, February 6, 1827), has been implemented in a "lame and dilatory" fashion and only "upon the continued and pressing demands of England and the advice of the other powers"; that "the most earnest exhortations" have been made by Russia to Spain "not to mix directly or indirectly in the affairs of Portugal . . ."; and "that France has made fresh representations in the same sense." Notes a change in the attitude of some members of the diplomatic corps toward the Portuguese Government. Conjectures that Dom Miguel, financially independent and under the influence of Austria, probably will not go to Brazil. States that he (Brent) rejected a request from (Frederico) Torlade (de Azambuja) to "endeavor in conversation with the Minister of Foreign Affairs [Francisco de Almeida] to accelerate his departure" for the United States; that he suggested to Torlade, however, that, if "a corresponding appointment" were not made (by Portugal), the United States might choose "not to keep a regularly appointed chargé d'affaires at this Court"; and that "the Minister" (Almeida) subsequently informed him that Torlade would soon depart. Advises that he has called Almeida's attention to the incident on the Isle of Mayo (see above, Hodges to Clay, May 19, 1826; Brent to Clay, July 27, August 2, 1826) and the cases of the brig *Osprey* (above, Brent to Clay, July 11, 1825; May 1, June 30, 1826) and the American schooner *Napoleon* (see above, Brent to Clay, May 1, 1826). Encloses "copies of the correspondence on the last Subject not heretofore communicated." Adds a postscript (AEI) asking that the unmarked documents enclosed be added to his dispatch no. 36 (see above, December 29, 1826). LS, with autographed complimentary close. DNA, RG59, Dip. Disp., Portugal, vol. 7 (M43, R6). Received May 12. Enclosures include translations of correspondence leading to the renewal of diplomatic relations between Spain and Portugal and documents relating to the incident aboard the *Napoleon* (see above, Brent to Clay, May 1, 1826).

From THOMAS L. L. BRENT, Lisbon, no. 40. Notes that he has not alluded, heretofore, in discussions with the Minister of Foreign Affairs (Francisco de Almeida) since the death of the King (John VI), "to any commercial arrangements," but has "occasionally in other quarters spoken of the commercial relations of the United States and Portugal. . . ." Summarizes conversation, concerning pending legislation, with "the chairman of the committee of commerce of the house of deputies" (not identified), who holds "quite a liberal feeling on these questions." Reports that, soon afterward, the Minister of Foreign Affairs adverted to the same subject, whereupon a frank discussion ensued relative to "the languor existing in the trade" with the United States, the preferential treatment accorded by Portugal to British trade, and the possibility of placing the commerce of the United States and Portugal "on the footing of the most favored Nation. . . ." Notes that the House of Deputies has passed laws "equalizing the duties on all articles the produce or manufacture of the foreign Country when imported direct in Vessels of the same or in those of Portugal" and "allowing the deposit and re-exportation of all articles the produce and manufacture of foreign Countries with the exception of corn and some few other articles, on the payment of a very small duty. . . ," but expresses doubt that the Upper House will approve these measures. Comments that, while the Deputies rejected "the project of a law . . . to allow the admission of foreign corn for consumption at an advanced price and its deposit and re-exportation at a trifling duty. . . ," the vote was close and he has "every reasonable expectation that at the next meeting it will pass that house. . . ." Encloses copies of correspondence exchanged with the United States consul in Lisbon (Israel P. Hutchinson). ALS. DNA, RG59, Dip. Disp., Portugal, vol. 7 (M43, R6). Received May 10. Enclosures include Brent's requests for information on Portuguese commerce and Hutchinson's replies.

From THOMAS L. L. BRENT, Lisbon. Forwards "translation of an official article" in the Lisbon *Gazette* of this date, containing a "Communication by Spain to the foreign Envoys at Madrid of the fact that the Spanish [*sic*] refugees had on entering Spain been disarmed to the amount of 3,000 men." ALS. *Ibid*. Received May 10. The enclosure refers to "Portuguese troops."

MISCELLANEOUS LETTERS   March 16, 1827

From DANIEL P. COOK, Baltimore. Acknowledges receipt of a "packet . . . with enclosures to Judge [David] Barton" and himself. States that to avoid delay he and the Judge will go to Philadelphia to embark and that the journey "thus far has not proved prejudicial." ALS. DNA, RG59, Dip. Disp., Special Agents, vol. 9 (M37, R9). No letter of transmittal or other reference to the packet and its enclosures has been found. On Cook's journey, see above, Clay to Cook, March 12, 1827; Cook to Clay, same date.

From WILLIAM GIBSON, St. Marys, Georgia. States that as "one of the Justices of the Inferior Court" of Camden County in 1815, he submitted numerous claims of local inhabitants against the British Government; lists 25 claims that do not appear in Clay's report (above, Clay to Adams, March 7, 1826); and specifies instances in which ownership of particular slaves is subject to question. Adds that he has resided at St. Marys since 1790. ALS. DNA, RG76, Misc. Claims, Treaty of Ghent, G. B. 4, folder 3. Endorsed on cover: "Submitted to Board of Commissioners under the Law of Congress passed at its late session" (cf. above, Clay to McLane, January 15, 1827). Gibson not further identified.
    On March 30 Daniel Brent acknowledged receipt of Gibson's letter and conveyed the information noted on the endorsement. Copy, in DNA, RG59, Dom. Letters, vol. 21, p. 509 (M40, R19).

From Stephen Van Rensselaer

Dear Sir   New York March 17, 1827
    Since my arrival here[1] I have associated with many influential Character [*sic*] and have pleasure in assuring you that our prospects are not so gloomy as we have been led to believe at Washington   I have also seen Gent from Albany who encourage me that if the friends of Mr. Adams will shew themselves number [*sic*] will flock to the standard— it is proposed to hire an Editor for Albany to counteract the influence of the Jackson presses[2]— it shall be done[3]— now for office a friend of mine reduced by misfortunes—of respectable standing & connections is desirous of obtaining an [*sic*] Clkship in one of the Offices[4]   he is highly recommended by Judge Platt[5] & could forward testimonials if necessary— he cannot obtain a place here at the Custom House as he & his friends are in favor of the administration—
Yours sincerely   S V RENSSELAER

ALS. DLC-TJC (DNA, M212, R10). Addressed to Clay.
[1] Following the adjournment of Congress.   [2] For example, the *Albany Argus*.
[3] Cf. above, Porter to Clay, January 3, 1827, note; below, Hammond to Clay, April 11,

1827.   4 Francis W. Taylor, not further identified. Cf. below, Taylor to Clay, November 19, 1827; April 8, 1828. He did not receive the desired appointment.   5 Jonas Platt.

DIPLOMATIC NOTES   March 17, 1827

To [CHARLES R.] VAUGHAN. Transmits, for communication to the British Government, "a Copy of a Proclamation issued by the President of the United States on this day, in pursuance of an Act of Congress of the 1st. March 1823, by the effect of which the Acts of Congress of the 18th. day of April 1818, and of the 15th. day of May 1820, Copies of which accompany the Proclamation, are revived." States that, while the President would have preferred announcing "a measure of a directly opposite tendency," existing laws required the course of action he has taken, that the President will "seize with pleasure any fit occasion that may hereafter arise for his concurrence in measures to put an end to a state of things which is believed to be prejudicial to the interests both of the United Kingdom and the United States by opening the trade and intercourse with the British Colonies upon just and reciprocal terms." Sends a copy of Treasury Department instructions to customs officials on implementation of the laws revived by the proclamation. Observes that the "Government of His Britannic Majesty cannot fail to recognize in these orders a strong evidence of the friendly disposition of that of the United States . . . to mitigate the effects of that measure as much as possible in its operation upon individual cases." Copy. DNA, RG59, Notes to Foreign Legations, vol. 3, pp. 332–33 (M38, R3). AN draft, in CSmH; published in *American State Papers, Foreign Relations*, VI, 985.

   On the acts here cited, see above, II, 564–66; III, 729n. For the proclamation, which prohibited, after December 1, 1826, trade "between the United States and the British colonial ports enumerated in the . . . act . . . of the 1st of March, 1823," see *American State Papers, Foreign Relations*, VI, 638. On March 12, Adams had requested Clay "to Prepare a draft of the proclamation"; the draft was slightly altered "and abridged by one-half" by Adams; and "Some further alterations were made" at a cabinet meeting on March 14, when a decision was reached to issue it "to-morrow or the next day." In a conference with Clay on March 17, Adams had "suggested some softening alterations of the draft [of the letter to Vaughan], which he adopted." Vaughan acknowledged, on March 18, receipt of Clay's note. NS, in DNA, RG59, Notes from Foreign Legations, Great Britain, vol. 14 (M50, R15); published in *American State Papers, Foreign Relations*, VI, 985.

From FRANCISCO DIONISIO VIVES, Havana. Acknowledges receipt of Clay's letter relative to the capture of the *Zulmé* (above, February 12, 1827); states that "este negocio es del resorte del Sor. Comandante General de este Apostadero [probably Angel Laborde]" and that, even if it fell within his own jurisdiction, he has no authority to undertake discussions with Clay's Government concerning the legality of the capture. LS. DNA, RG76, Records re French Spoliations, 1791–1829. Received April 17.

INSTRUCTIONS AND DISPATCHES   March 17, 1827

From FELIX CICOGNANI, Rome. Reports that the Papal Government has informed him of "its full adhesion to the system of reciprocity as it is established by the Act of Congress . . . of the 3d. of March 1815" (cf. above, Clay to Forbes, April 14, 1825, note) and wishes him "to sollicit [*sic*] in favour of the Papal vessels the abolition of the discriminating duties now in force in the United States. . . ." Observes that he expects a Presidential proclamation in favor of Papal vessels and instructions from Clay to enable him to answer the communication he has received. Notes that the Papal Government has informed its consul at Washington (Count Lucchesi) of its decision. ALS. DNA, RG59, Cons. Disp., Rome, vol. 1 (M-T231, R1). No received date; the cover bears a New York postmark, May 4; the duplicate of this dispatch was received June 29.

Cicognani, an Italian, was United States consul for Rome from 1823 to 1836. For reference to his original suggestion to the Papal Government that it take the action here indicated, see below, Supplement, Cicognani to Clay, July 15, 1825.

From JOSEPH S. MARKS, Maracaibo. Notes a rumor that the President (Simón Bolívar) has resigned (cf. above, Watts to Clay, March 14, 1827). Encloses correspondence relative to the imprisonment of G(eorge) W. Johnston, a citizen of the United States, and the confiscation of his property; notes that Johnston has since settled "the business with the Administration and been released. . . ." ALS. DNA, RG59, Cons. Disp., Maracaibo, vol. 1 (M-T62, R1). Received April 30, 1827.

Johnston was a member of an American mercantile firm operating in Maracaibo. His debt for customs duties, which occasioned the controversy here reported, amounted to less than half the sum due the company from the Colombian Government on contracts for provisioning Colombian troops. The latter claim was presented by the United States Government in negotiations in 1858, but no action was taken on it. *Sen. Docs.*, 35 Cong., 2 Sess., no. 18, p. 126; Moore, *History and Digest of the International Arbitrations. . .* , II, 1361 ff.

The episode was the outgrowth of protest by foreign merchants operating in Colombia who held large amounts of government bonds, notes, and drafts which were supposed to be redeemable at the customs houses but upon which payment had recently been suspended. The merchants had agreed that no payments would be made to the customs houses unless the suspension was removed, but Bolívar had retaliated early in February by ordering a settling of customs house accounts and imprisonment of those who refused payment of sums due. The difficulty was aggravated by the disorder prevailing in customs house records as an accompaniment of changes incurred during the Páez revolt (see above, Litchfield to Clay, May 22, 1826; Foster to Clay, August 2, 1826). Washington *Daily National Journal*, March 27, 1827.

From J[OEL] R. POINSETT, Mexico, no. 79. Transmits a translation of the treaty between Great Britain and Mexico (see above, Gallatin to Clay, December 16, 1826, note), "which has lately been ratified by the House of Representatives here, and will probably pass the Senate in a few days." Notes that this copy includes but 12 of the treaty's 15 (*i.e.*, 19) articles. Adds that the United States' treaty with Mexico "has at length been presented to the House with a favorable report by the Committee on Foreign Relations. . . ." LS. DNA, RG59, Dip. Disp., Mexico, vol. 2 (M97, R3). Received April 30. Poinsett's translation of the British-Mexican treaty omitted articles 1, 9–13, and 15. *British and Foreign State Papers, 1826–1827*, pp. 614–29.

From CONDY RAGUET, Rio de Janeiro, no. 26. States that he has received his passports from the Foreign Office. Supplies additional information to that in his dispatch of March 12, 1827, with regard to the seizure and detention of the *Spark*: the vessel arrived at Rio de Janeiro on January 27 with a cargo and passengers and was offered for sale to the Brazilian Government; the Minister of Marine (Viscount de Paranagua) wished, however, to buy only the brig's guns, "which the Captain [Clark, not further identified] refused to sell alone"; since ten guns were mounted, while only four were shown on the clearance, Brazilian authorities insisted that the extra six be landed before the vessel should be permitted to sail; on Raguet's recommendation Captain Clark complied and, later, "attempted to proceed on his voyage to Montevideo," with the result reported earlier. Charges that the Brazilian Government was interfering with United States "municipal regulations" to its own advantage, "by declaring how many guns and men, an American vessel shall carry." Notes that the Minister of Marine "notified on 15th Inst. the Consignees of the Spark, Mess J. Birckhead & Co. that she should not leave the port with more men than she brought"; and that the Captain, foreseeing "nothing but ruin, in an endless delay at this expensive port," has abandoned his vessel and left "her in the entire possession of the Government. . . ." Explains that the restriction against adding seamen in Brazilian ports will force stranded Americans into service in the Brazilian Navy, while American vessels sailing short-handed will be unable to fill their crews.

Encloses the correspondence between himself and the Government relative to the *Spark*. Declares his understanding of the seriousness of the step he has taken and his willingness "to meet all the consequences, even though one of them should be, [his] . . . being offered up as a sacrifice on the altar of publick good—" ALS. DNA, RG59, Dip. Disp., Brazil, vol. 5 (M121, R7). Received May 10. Published in *American State Papers, Foreign Relations*, VI, 1063–64.

From JOHN SERGEANT, Mexico, "Private." Reports that (Pedro) Gual expects to receive "extensive communications" from Colombia, including confirmation of the ratification of the Panama treaties. Notes that prospects for resumption of the (Panama) Congress are better than suggested in his letter of March 14. States that Gual is "justly dissatisfied with the Mexican Government and the Mexican Ministers, for failure to approve the Panama treaties, and is evidently considering what he is to do, in case the treaties are not ratified." Comments that the British proclamation denying the United States "the trade of the bay of Honduras" (cf. above, Duane to Clay, December 21, 1826) is "a most audacious thing", considering that the "country belongs to Guatemala, and the British are there only by sufferance." ALS. DNA, RG43, First Panama Congress (M662, R1). Received April 30.

Under the Treaty of Paris of 1763 the Spanish had accorded British subjects operating in the Bay of Honduras the privilege "of cutting, loading, and carrying away logwood" and of constructing and occupying "the houses and magazines necessary for them, for their families, and for their effects. . . ." Clive Parry (ed.), *The Consolidated Treaty Series* (80 vols.—; New York, 1969–), XLII, 329–30. This clause had been renewed by the British and Spanish in the Treaty of Versailles of September 3, 1783, the Convention signed at London July 14, 1786, and the Additional Articles to the Treaty of Friendship and Alliance signed at Madrid July 5, 1814. *Ibid.*, XLVIII, 484; L, 47; LXIII, 264. But the British had as yet signed no treaty with the Federation of Central America ratifying the arrangement.

MISCELLANEOUS LETTERS   March 17, 1827

To SAMUEL CHASE. Transmits a commission as "Judge of the Orphan's Court for the County of Washington in the District of Columbia." Copy. DNA, RG59, Dom. Letters, vol. 21, p. 497 (M40, R19). Chase, son of Judge Samuel Chase, was, until receiving this appointment, "a messenger in the Navy Commissioners' Office." Adams, *Memoirs*, VII, 239–40. On March 19 the younger Chase acknowledged receipt of Clay's letter and the commission and accepted the appointment. ALS, in DNA, RG59, Acceptances and Orders for Comns. (M-T645, R2).

From RICHARD RUSH, Treasury Department. Responds to Clay's letter of March 14 by transmitting a communication from the Comptroller of the Treasury, to whom the letter was referred. LS. DNA, RG59, Misc. Letters (M179, R65). In the enclosure, dated March 16, Joseph Anderson stated that the question of defining "a continuous voyage," under the convention with France, had never been submitted to the Treasury Department but that, after the Convention with Great Britain (see above, II, 57–59) went into effect, a rule was adopted providing that the voyage of a British vessel loaded in a British European port with part of her cargo unloaded at a British colonial port and the remainder brought to the United States, would not be considered broken. He cited the quarterly report of the collector at Savannah as showing that duties were "exacted . . . *on the Cargoes* of the three French Vessels in question, in the same manner as if they were foreign Vessels not entitled to any exclusive privileges by a special law of Congress, or by Treaty Stipulation." Cf. below, Clay to Mareuil, March 20, 1827.

APPLICATIONS, RECOMMENDATIONS   March 17, 1827

From JOHN ALLEN, Baltimore. Solicits employment as translator of French or Spanish. States that he has taught French for 25 years and mentions Dr. (Tobias) Watkins as a reference. ALS. DNA, RG59, A. and R. (M531, R1). Endorsed (AEI) on cover: "Inform him that there is now no vacancy. HC." No answer found.

Allen may have been the author of an anonymous tract on the work of the American Colonization Society, *An Essay on the Policy of Appropriations Being Made by the Government of the United States, for Purchasing, Liberating and Colonizing without the Territory of the Said States, the Slaves Thereof. . .* By a citizen of Maryland (Baltimore, 1826). Cf. Sabin, *Bibliotheca Americana. . .*, I, 103.

To Steen A. Bille

Dear Sir,   Washington, 18 March, 1827.

I take pleasure in introducing to your acquaintance, Mr Wheaton, lately appointed Chargé des Affaires to Denmark,[1] who will present you this Letter. He has not yet finally decided to accept the appointment, but I hope will ultimately conclude to allow the Public to avail itself of his Services. At all events, he will be happy to know you, as I am persuaded you will be to make his acquaintance. I am, with great respect, Your ob: Servant   H. CLAY.
Mr Billé [*sic*]

Copy, in Henry Wheaton's hand, on Clay to Wheaton, below, this date in NNPM.
[1] Cf. above, Clay to Nourse, November 16, 1826, note; below, Clay to Wheaton, May 31, 1827.

To Benjamin W. Crowninshield

(Private.)   WASHINGTON, 18 Mar., 1827.

My dear Sir,—I was sorry to learn from your favor of the 14th inst. that you are indisposed; and I hope your health will be soon restored.

If you will go to my friend Chapman,[1] he will cure by no other remedy than that of agreeable conversation.

I regret that Mr. Binns is not given all the public printing in Philada. But I have done all that I could.[2] With the P. Off. department I cannot interfere, for reasons that must at once strike you.[3] You must address your efforts to the President, to whom I have said all that was proper for me.

I am glad to hear so favorably of Penna. My own information from other quarters corresponds with it. Still, that which has been so long wanted is still wanted,—firmness and boldness to avow opinions which are entertained. That want creates our only danger. I have sketched a plan of co-operation,[4] which I enclose for your consideration. Be pleased to copy it in a fair hand. If the first movement takes place in Philada, no pains should be spared to make it numerous, reputable, and imposing. Let all persons (friends of D. M. I. I.[5] and the Admin.), without regard to party denominations heretofore existing, be brought out. Let Ch. Justice Tilghman or Judge Barnes[6] preside. Get M. Carey[7] to attend. Let the meeting publish an address,[8] well drawn, temperate in language, but firm in purpose, and eloquent and animated in composition. This meeting will form a nucleus.

I do not think that Mr. Binns makes the most of the proceedings in the Virginia legislature agt the American system.[9] These shd form a prominent topic in the address and in all friendly papers in Penna. You know, if the present mongrel opposition gets into power, there is an end, at least a suspension, of that system for a long time.

The state of my health, which is not good, will oblige me to travel some this spring and summer. I shall be in Penna, but in what parts and at what times I cannot now say. Let me hear from you. Your friend,   H. CLAY.

MR. CROWNINSHIELD.

The Quarterly Journal of Economics, II (July, 1888), 490–91.
    [1] Dr. Nathaniel Chapman.   [2] Cf. above, Clay to Jones, January 23, 1827; Jones to Clay, January 25, 1827; Degrand to Clay, February 8, 1827.   [3] Cf. above, Binns to Clay, April 21, May 10, 1826.   [4] Not found. Cf. below, Clay to Henry, September 27, 1827, enclosure.   [5] Domestic manufactures; internal improvements.   [6] William Tilghman; Joseph Barnes. Tilghman had been born in Maryland in 1756, had graduated from the College of Philadelphia, had been a Loyalist during the Revolution, had begun the practice of law in 1783, and had served successively in the Maryland Assembly and Senate. In 1793 he had moved to Philadelphia, where he had practiced law and held judicial appointments before being made Chief Justice of the Pennsylvania Supreme Court, in 1806. He died April 29, 1827.   [7] Mathew Carey.   [8] From May 14 to 19, 1827, a meeting was held in Philadelphia by the Pennsylvania Society for the Promotion of Manufactures and the Mechanic Arts. This was one of numerous meetings over the State which culminated in a State Convention at Harrisburg on June 27 and a national convention, also at Harrisburg, from July 30 to August 3, 1827, designed similarly to promote manufactures. The three meetings here specifically noted all published addresses. Philadelphia United States Gazette, May 25, July 11, August 8, 1827. Organized by Alexander Hamilton as the Philadelphia Society for the Promotion of National Industry, the Pennsylvania Society for the Promotion of Manufactures and Mechanic Arts had been renamed in 1820 and during the ensuing decade actively pro-

moted tariffs for protection of domestic industry. Mathew Carey was a leading member, and Charles Jared Ingersoll was vice president.   9 Cf. above, Brooke to Clay, January 31, 1827, note.

To Henry Wheaton

[ca. March 18, 1827]

With Mr. Clay's Compliments.

AN. NNPM. Addressed: "Mr. Wheaton at Miss Polks." Cf. above, Clay to Bille, this date. Ann Polk's boarding house was located on Pennsylvania Avenue, in Washington.

From Thomas Law

Dear Sir—   March 18th 1827—

If the report of the gentlemen selected for the Committee who investigated my land note plan;[1] & the publication on this subject[2] have met with your approbation, I have a *"ne plus ultra"* one to submit to you for the President.

With this I shall close my career, & as the successful aged pugilist laying down his gauntlet exclaimed *"hic cæstus artemque repono"*[3] so shall I throw aside my pen, before I betray imbecility[4]—

I mean not to publish this plan, but I wish the President or you, to desire some intelligent persons to examine it & give their sentiments upon it, before it claims your attention; I also indulge the belief that it will, be recommended in the next Presidential address to Congress[5]— I am sure that it will be an agreeable surprise to a distracted & I may add distressed people to paralyse intrigues silence disorganizers & subdue party spirit— Then also will members of Congress fear to thwart the measures of an Executive who is immoveable in the esteem affection & confidence of their constituents of all throughout the Union—

It may be said why not submit this to Mr Rush?[6] I intended to be his pioneer & with sincere regard was anxious to devote my labors for him to benefit his Country—but a plan which cost my Son Edmund[7] & me much thought; & much writing was mislaid, & I have not even a Copy to write upon the back of it *atque* [sic] *hæc olim neminisse juvabit.*[8]

This opus maximum [sic] will be more pleasing to the people than even the victory of New Orleans & Mr Adams may adopt this triumphant motto—

  Cedant arma togæ.[9]

as I thus prize my last work, of course I am apprehensive lest it should be neglected, & though Mr Rush is enlightened & indefatigable, he might not have leisure to attend to it.

Not having been indifferent to passing scenes, nor a negligent observer of influences on the human mind, I expect much immediate effect & permanent good from my proposition— If those who are to sit in judgement, upon it, should condemn it, I shall not have caused much trouble to the President & to you, who are burthened with much important business, but if deemed worthy of your serious attention it may afford you a satisfaction to justify this intrusion, & cheer my few remaining days— With esteem respect & regard yr mt obt St

THOMAS LAW

ALS draft. DLC-Thomas Law Papers. This letter may never have been sent. Although he tells Clay, in it, that he has a new plan "to submit to you for the President," on March 26 Law, in person, "announced to . . . [Adams] that he had prepared a plan of finance such as never was presented to any nation, which would place at the command of the Government many annual millions to be applied to internal improvement and to strike all opposition dumb." He requested that Adams submit "copies of it to two or three . . . friends, and, if they should approve it, . . . recommend it . . . to Congress." Adams replied that if, after examining the paper, he "should determine to refer" the paper to anyone, "it would be to" members of the administration, "as they were responsible for their advice. . . ." Law then, the President noted: "hesitated whether he should send me his paper at all; but I rather cheered him to send it, and he left me expecting to receive it." Adams, *Memoirs*, VII, 247–48.
   1 See above, Watkins, Daniel Brent, and William Brent to Clay, February 12, 1827.
   2 No earlier publication on this subject has been found. The Committee's report and Law's replies to their criticism were published together later, in the Washington *Daily National Intelligencer*, of April 24, 1827. A broadside, without place or date of issue but using the type of the *Intelligencer* publication, appeared under the title *Financial Plan . . . Proposing and Developing a New and Advantageous Scheme of Public Finance . . . the Object . . . to Be Accomplished . . . to Be the Creation of Means for Immediately Commencing and Prosecuting to Its Completion, the Contemplated Canal to Unite the Waters of the Ohio and the Chesapeake.*   3 Law omitted the second word, "*victor,*" of the quotation from Virgil's *Aeneid*, V, line 484—"Victorious I lay down my gloves and skill"—spoken by the boxing champion, Entellus.   4 Law continued to publish elaborations of his proposal for a national paper currency until 1833, the year prior to his death.   5 His hope was disappointed.   6 Richard Rush.   7 Edmund Law, born in India in 1790, had been one of the organizers of the Bank of the Metropolis, established in Washington in 1814; an officer of the Columbian Institute; and a member of the Washington City Council (1812–1814, 1825, 1828). He had been appointed in 1821 one of the commissioners to take possession of the Spanish Archives and to adjust land claims in Florida. During the next two years he had held a variety of minor civil offices in East Florida, including the judgeship of St. John's County court, and in May, 1822, had been appointed to the Territorial Legislative Council, over which he presided later that year. Needed to assist in handling his father's Washington business, he had left Florida in the autumn of 1822 but in 1825 accompanied Commodore David Porter to Mexico. Law returned to Washington in 1828 and died there the following summer. Allen C. Clark, *Greenleaf and Law in the Federal City* (Washington, 1901), 311–12. Cf. also, above, III, 69n.   8 The first words, misquoted, should be "*forsan et,*" with the line translating as: "Perhaps some day even these things will be a joy to recall." Virgil *Aeneid*, I, line 203.   9 "Let arms to toga yield." Cicero *De Officiis*, I, line 77.

DIPLOMATIC NOTES   March 18, 1827

From CHARLES R. VAUGHAN, Washington. Refers to his note of March 9, 1827, and Clay's reply (March 12); notes that the President's proclamation of March 17 (cf. above, Clay to Vaughan, March 17, 1827) revives "the Act of Congress of 1820, in which . . . it is expressly stated, that British Vessels arriving in a Port of the United States, from the Islands of Bermuda, is [*sic*] liable to forfeiture." Asks whether a British mail packet is exempt from "that liability." NS. DNA, RG59, Notes from British Legation, vol. 14 (M50, R15).

MISCELLANEOUS LETTERS   March 18, 1827

From H[ENRY] W[HEATON], Washington. Lists selected papers, largely from (George W.) Erving's correspondence while Minister to Denmark, which he wishes copied *"in a bound Book"*; suggests "that a Clerk should commence the task at once"; argues that no "part of what he has noted can be dispensed with, as we have no regular mission in Copenhagen, & consequently there are no Archives there"; surmises that "Papers relating to the Claims, & the Claimants' letters were left by Erving at Copenhagen in Mr [John M.] Forbes' hands (cf. above, Clay to Hughes, March 24, 1825) & . . . must have been left by Mr F. in the Consulate"; and concludes: "But the whole subject is submitted to Mr Clay's superior judgment." ADI. DNA, RG59, Dip. Disp., Denmark, vol. 1B (M41, R3).

To John Brockenbrough

John Brockenbrough Esqr. Cashier of the
Bank of Virginia, Richmond.   Dept. of State,
Sir,   Washington 19 March 1827.
　　Your letter of the 30th. of November last, was duly received by me, and I owe you many apologies for its having remained so long unnoticed. The truth is, that it was put away with a number of other letters and papers requiring attention, to be considered and answered, and was not brought to my recollection 'till a day or two ago, at the very moment for the first time, since its receipt, when the occasions of this Department have required a remittance of any considerable amount, to be made to England. The usage of this Department, upon such occasions, is to request the Secretary of the Treasury[1] to cause a remittance of the sums which it requires, from time to time, to be made to our Bankers, Baring, Brothers and Company, of London, and to leave to this Department exclusively the care of procuring Bills, upon such terms and responsibilities as may be satisfactory to it. In the present case, in reference to the remittance which this Department wishes now to be made, the sum of 30,000 Dlls., an intimation will be given to the Secretary of the Treasury, that it would be very agreeable to it, if the preference should be given to the Bank of Virginia to supply the Bills required in the usual way.[2]— Yours &c
                                                        H. CLAY.

　　Copy. DNA, RG59, Dom. Letters, vol. 21, p. 497 (M40, R19).　　[1] Richard Rush.
[2] On April 4, 1827, Daniel Brent wrote Brockenbrough, stating that no reply to this letter had been received and asking him to inform the Secretary of the Treasury whether he can supply the bills.

DIPLOMATIC NOTES   March 19, 1827

To [CHARLES R.] VAUGHAN. Acknowledges receipt of Vaughan's note of March 18 and states "that the interdict . . . does not apply to vessels owned by or in the *actual employment* of the British Government, engaged in the service of transporting the mail, and that, consequently, it will not apply to the British Packets which may arrive at Annapolis." Copy. DNA, RG59, Notes to Foreign Legations, vol. 3, p. 334 (M38, R3). LI draft, in CSmH.

INSTRUCTIONS AND DISPATCHES   March 19, 1827

From HEMAN ALLEN, Santiago de Chile, no. 51. Notes that the account in his last dispatch (March 12, 1827) "of the late revolution in Peru" was incorrect and now gives a later version: soon after (Simón) Bolívar's departure, Colombian troops in Peru revolted "and applied to General Santa Cruz . . . who . . . took the lead in these movements, which have resulted in the complete subversion of the constitution and of the election of Bolívar as President for life." Adds that "the electoral College of the district of Lima has reassembled and declared that the election of Bolívar as President, was altogether a compulsory act, that the proceedings on that occasion are henceforth void, and recommended to the electoral Colleges in all the other districts to do the same." States that "the Colombian troops have supported these measures throughout"; that "The odious tyranny of Bolívar in Peru, has been the cause of this important change"; that "as his confidential troops have deserted him," he cannot be reinstated; and that new Ministers have been appointed to replace those who resigned. ALS. DNA, RG59, Dip. Disp., Chile, vol. 2 (M-T2, R2). Extract published in Manning (arr.), *Diplomatic Correspondence . . . Latin-American Nations*, II, 1116–17. Received June 21.

From A[LEXANDER] H. EVERETT, Madrid, no. 72. Acknowledges receipt of dispatches of December 9, 1826, and January 17 (*i.e.*, 15), 1827. States that he has presented to the Spanish Government one of the claims of Robert Oliver; but, pending a closer examination, he is inclined to think that the other, relative to the ship and cargo seized in 1808, "is precluded by the 9th article of the Florida Treaty" (regarding renunciation of claims, see above II, 678n). Expresses belief that the case of the *Zulmé* "will be attended with little or no difficulty, as well from the clear justice of the demand as from the effect of the late example set by the United States in the affair of the invasion of Puerto Rico by Commodore [David] Porter" (see above, IV, 224n–25n). Adds that he anticipates delay in settling the matter because of lack of official information about it. Encloses a copy of a note he has written in protest against "the Sanitary system . . . applied to our Commerce in the ports" of Spain, although he has little hope of better treatment, especially in ports controlled by French garrisons, where American trade "is in fact almost wholly ruined by these restrictions." Reports tranquillity in "Political affairs," the disarmament of "The last corps of Portuguese that entered" Spain, the imminent departure of Count Ofalia "as Envoy Extraordinary to London for the purpose of completing the pacific arrangements and probably of endeavouring to persuade Great Britain to withdraw her troops from Portugal" (cf. below, Gallatin to Clay, April 14, 1827; Brown to Clay, April 27, 1827; Hughes to Clay, September 16, 1827, note), that the Portuguese Constitution is so unpopular "in that country that it would not subsist a week without the presence of the British army," and that "The Spanish Ambassador at Paris Duke de Villa Hermosa is just recalled" in a "change . . . occasioned by the late recall of the

French Ambassador at this Court [Marquis de Moustier] but is not supposed to be of any political importance." ALS. DNA, RG59, Dip. Disp., Spain, vol. 27 (M31, R28). Received May 6.

From ALBERT GALLATIN, London, no. 61. Reports information, derived from the United States consul at Fayal (Charles W. Dabney), concerning the rescue at sea, in September, 1826, of the crews of two American vessels by Lieutenant (Joseph) Rawlins Thomas, of the British Navy, who was at that time captain of a merchant vessel. Characterizes Thomas as "a very worthy man with a family, in reduced circumstances, a good officer . . . and long . . . in service," who, however, "having no interest, has very little chance of promotion." Notes that Thomas and his friends hope his "meritorious act should have some effect towards advancing him." Encloses copies of an exchange of letters with Lord Melville concerning the matter and transmits a copy of an "application" to be submitted to the President. ALS. *Ibid.*, Great Britain, vol. 33 (M30, R29). Received May 8.

The "application," from "Merchants of London trading to the United States," requests Gallatin to lay before the President "the noble conduct of this officer. . . , under the hope that His Excellency may condescend to recommend Lieutenant Thomas to the favourable consideration of his Majesty's Government for promotion in the Royal Navy in which he has served with unqualified credit for nearly twenty four years." Cf. below, Clay to Gallatin, May 12, 1827.

From WILLIAM TAYLOR, Veracruz. Reports that the Arenas affair (see above, Sergeant to Clay, January 26, 1827) is "no longer food for conversation" but "Another subject. . . , infinitely more important to an American is, the insurrection in Texas [see above, Dickson to Clay, January 3, 1827, note], which evil minded persons attribute to the United States." Charges that the Mexican Government exaggerates the affair, which "is said to be confined to but a small part of Texas and to consist of only fifty Whites with some Indians *their Allies.*" Describes the movement of troops to Texas for suppression of the rebellion. Cites information, brought by "a Mexican vessel of War" from Key West, that Commodore (David) Porter is still "there blockaded by Como. [Angel] LaBorde" (cf. above, Rodney to Clay, January 29, 1827). ALS. DNA, RG59, Cons. Disp., Veracruz, vol. 1. Received April 26.

MISCELLANEOUS LETTERS   March 19, 1827

From CHARLES AUGUSTUS DAVIS, New York. Expresses a wish "to do away any impediment to the recognition of Mr [Frederick Augustus] Mench [*sic*] . . . which may have been created on my account by the suggestions of Mr. [Alexander H.] Everett." ALS. DNA, RG59, A. and R. (M531, R5). Cf. above, Everett to Clay, December 17, 1826; February 21, 1827.

From BENJAMIN GRUT, Maracaibo. Expresses regret that he cannot "write favorably on the state of this country" but comments that fears are justly entertained of future evils, while the taxes are encreased [*sic*], the revenue is lessened, & yet the same establishments are kept up as formerly." Asserts that "The president's [Simón Bolívar's] resignation [see above, Watts to Clay, March 14, 1827] is considered an act of political prudery"; that, before tendering it, he made promotions beyond constitutional limits to high ranks in the army; that, instead of reducing the army as promised, he has levied taxes to support it; and that "more than all, he has impaired the obli-[*sic*] of contracts . . . for supplying the army with provisions from the U. S. . . . ." Reports the imprisonment of two Dutchmen for non-payment of duties, although the Government is indebted to them, and notes that the Dutch consul (not identified) after remonstrating in vain, has sent "an express to Curaçao for instructions. . . ." Adds that the British consul (Robert Sutherland) has sent for "a light Brig" and "a sloop of war," and that the United States "were also mortified by an act of oppression similar to that practised on the dutchmen," in the case of (George W.) Johnston, "a citizen of the U. S." (above, Marks to Clay, March 17, 1827). States that the Congress faces "The invidious task of reducing the the army," which may "rise in opposition & offer [a] crown to one who publicly confesses the fears he entertains of ambition." Notes the increasing popularity of the Vice President (Francisco de Paula Santander). ALS. DNA, RG59, Misc. Letters (M179, R65). Received April 30. Endorsed on cover sheet by Clay: "To be laid before the President."

Robert Sutherland served as British consul at Maracaibo from 1825 into the early 1830's.

From HUGH MERCER, Fredericksburg. Asks, if the Secretary of War (James Barbour) is in Washington, that Clay "hand him this communication, & . . . beg him to consider it as addressed to him also—" States that he has just learned that his son (Hugh Weedon Mercer), a cadet at the United States Military Academy, was involved "in some Riot—about Christmas [see above, Taliaferro to Clay, March 6, 1827, note]—a Court martial has acted upon their Case, & he is under arrest, awaiting the decision of the President & the final Sentence—" Makes the following appeal: "May I trust that your friendship & that of the Secy of War, & of my friend Mr [Samuel] Southard, will be exerted as far as propriety & duty will authorise, in behalf of my Son, with the President, to save him from the *disgrace* of a Dismissal from the academy—" Admits that "Some punishment" is deserved but notes that this is "the first error he [young Mercer] has committed" in "nearly 3 years" at West Point. Asks, "In anxious conclusion," if he "may . . . not fondly trust that his [the son's] good conduct heretofore, & his *very high standing* in his classes, will plead with the President in his favor—" and adds, "he is the grandson too, of one [General Hugh Mercer], who gave up his life to secure our liberties & the great blessings we enjoy as a Nation." ALS. DNA, RG77, Letters Recd., 1826–37, Serial no. M-222). Addressed to Clay, with the notation on cover: "If Mr Clay should be absent, for Mr. Barbour or Mr. [Samuel L.] Southard to open." Endorsed (AEI) by Clay on cover: "Refd. to the Secy of War. H C."

Young Mercer was graduated from West Point in 1828, ranked third in his class. Resigning his commission in 1835, he became a banker in Savannah, Georgia. After serving as a Confederate officer during the Civil War, he returned to Savannah as a banker and commission merchant. He later moved to Baltimore and died abroad in 1877.

APPLICATIONS, RECOMMENDATIONS   March 19, 1827

DUDLEY MARVIN, Baltimore, expresses a strong wish that "Col. [Chauncey] Goodrich" be appointed "as bearer of Despatches to some of the South American Republics"; notes that Goodrich "visited Colombia some years since, and is now anxious again to see that country, and with a view of making a more permanent residence in it." Comments: "It must be every way important to our own political interests, to have in those states, enterprising young men from among ourselves, who must feel identified with the substantial interests of their native Country while adopting a new." Suggests that, "Should a bearer of Despatches not be wanted, some vacant Consulship or other office" would be acceptable. Notes that he (Marvin) is on his way home. ALS. DNA, RG59, A. and R. (M531, R3). Cf. above, Tracy to Clay, October 3, 1826.

To the Baron de Mareuil

The Baron de Mareuil,
Envoy Extraordinary and Minis.
Plenipotentiary from France.   Department of State,
Sir,   Washington, 20 March 1827.

Having submitted to the President of the United States your letter of the 13th. instant, in relation to the French vessels, the Ville du Havre, the Sully, and the Eugenie, which arrived at Savannah in December last, from the port of St. Pierre, Martinique, with remnants of cargoes of French produce, taken on board in France, and which were subjected to the payment of the discriminating duty, I have the satisfaction now to inform you that the Presidents decision is, that neither those vessels nor their cargoes, were, under the circumstances stated, legally chargeable with the discriminating duty.[1] Orders will be issued, from the Treasury Department, to refund it, and to prevent, in future, the collection of the duty from French vessels similarly situated.

The President entirely concurs with you in opinion, that, since the Convention of 1822 makes no specific allusion to Colonies, French vessels coming from France, and laden with the produce of France, are, by virtue of the stipulations of that instrument, exempt from all duties but those for which it provides; and that this right of exemption is not lost by the fact of such vessels touching, in the course of their voyage, at the Colonial dependencies of France.

To entitle the Vessels of the two countries reciprocally to the rate of duties which the Convention stipulates, all that is necessary is, that their cargoes shall consist of "articles of the growth, produce, or manufacture" of those Countries respectively. The Convention is equally silent both as to Colonies and Foreign Countries. And, in the opinion, of the President, its privileges are not forfeited, because, in the course of the voyage a French or American vessel, (as the case may be,) shall happen to touch at the Colonial port, or the port of a third power, provided the vessel, on her arrival at her destination, imports only the produce of the Country to which she belongs. It has been seen with regret, that a different interpretation has been put upon the Convention in France; and that an American vessel has been deemed to have lost the benefits of the Convention, because, during her voyage, she touched at a British port, merely for information, without discharging any part of her cargo, or taking in a single article whatever.[2] This interpretation cannot be considered as authorized. Nor is there any justification of it in the desire to repress fraud, which you assign as its motive. The same reason, if it were well founded, would apply equally to vessels touching at Colonial ports, and at the ports of third powers, both description of those ports being alike excluded from the terms of the Convention, which, however, does not forbid a vessel touching at either. It is certainly practicable to devise some other mode of preventing fraudulent importations of produce, not authorized by the Convention to be made into the two Countries in their respective vessels, than that of either prohibiting the importation of that which the Convention does authorize, or subjecting it to a higher rate of duty.

The hope is therefore indulged, that, on a reconsideration of this question in France, a different construction will be adopted; and that the duties which have been illegally exacted, will be refunded, and proper orders given to prevent the collection of similar illegal duties in future.

I pray you to accept assurances of my distinguished consideration.

H. CLAY.

Copy. DNA, RG59, Notes to Foreign Legations, vol. 3, pp. 336–37 (M38, R3). ALI draft, without significant change, in CSmH.
[1] Cf. above, Rush to Clay, March 17, 1827.   [2] See above, Beasley to Clay, August 16, September 15, 1826; January 25, 1827; Brown to Clay, August 23, September 11, October 22, 1826; Gray to Clay, December 2, 1826.

To Richard Riker

Sir   Washington 20h. March 1827

I received, in due course of the Mail, your letter of the 26h. Ulto.[1] and I have since received the copy of Mr. Colden's Memoir, on the New York Canals,[2] which the Common Council of the City of New York has done me the honor to present to me, through you. Those great and interesting works form a distinguished epoch in the annals of our Country. And the celebration of their completion has been commemorated in a manner worthy of them and honorable to the City of New York. I am greatly obliged by the Common Council thinking so kindly of me as to transmit me a copy of the memoir, which I shall carefully preserve with the most grateful recollection. I pray you to make my suitable acknowledgments on the occasion, and to accept yourself assurances of the high respect of Your obedient Servant
R. Riker Esqr. &c. &c. &c.   H. CLAY

ALS. KyU. Riker, born on Long Island, had been trained as a lawyer and admitted to the New York bar in 1795. He had been district attorney of New York from 1802 to 1804 and was distinguished for long service as recorder there, from 1815 to 1819, 1821 to 1823, and 1824 to 1838.
[1] Not found.   [2] Cadwallader D. Colden, *Memoirs, Prepared at the Request of a Committee of the Common Council of the City of New York, and Presented to the Mayor of the City, at the Celebration of the New York Canals* (New York: Printed by Order of the Corporation of New York, 1825).

From Enoch Lincoln

State of Maine.
Executive Department,
Sir;   Portland, 20th March, 1827.

Having had the honor to receive your letter of January 29th last, I transmit, in reply, the accompanying Report and Resolves, relative to the North eastern boundary of the State of Maine.[1]

The attention which you have heretofore paid to the adjustment of the United States' boundary, especially in another part of the Union,[2] assures me that you will receive the documents, I have mentioned, with that interest to which they are entitled

With the confidence which belongs to the patriotic and paternal character of the government of the Union, and without complaining of it, in any particular, I may be permitted to say that the growing importance of the Country claimed against the United States and Maine, carries along an increasing desire to have an open or confidential developement [sic] of the material facts.—

The Report and Resolves contain the evidence of the present disposition and purposes of the State which will receive my official cooperation with the same zeal and fidelity that will cheerfully be applied, if requisite, in aiding to carry into effect any federal measure applicable to the protection of the rights in question.

The anxiety of a Sovereign State to possess the documents, (or copies of them,) which contain the evidence of a title to soil and of a jurisdictional authority which it will, under the United States, maintain, if it shall discharge its duty either to those States or to itself, will be duly appreciated by yourself and by the President. While that anxiety is here entertained by all the Citizens, it is not only with reference to an important local concern, but is connected with their inclination to a harmonious action with all who consent to admit of it.

In pursuance, therefore, of the Resolve of the Legislature of Maine, I have the honor to solicit such information, relative to the North-eastern boundary of that State, as the President may deem proper to consent to have communicated.

It is also my duty to add, that great benefit will be derived from an early determination of a claim harassing to the State, interrupting its best pursuits, threatning [sic] to some of its best hopes, and beleived [sic] to be unfounded. I am, with great respect, Your Obedient Servant,
Hon: Henry Clay Secy of State,   ENOCH LINCOLN
of the United States, Washington.

LS. DNA, RG76, Northeast Boundary: Misc. Papers, env. 4, item 12.
[1] The report, dated February 16, 1827, made by "a Joint Select Committee" of the Maine Legislature, traced the history of the dispute and asserted the validity of the State's title to the territory in question; the joint resolution, of February 23, requested the Governor "to take all such measures, both in acquiring information and in procur-

ing a speedy adjustment of the dispute according to the treaty of seventeen hundred and eighty three, as he may deem expedient and for the interest of the State." D, in DNA, RG76, Records of Boundary and Claims Commissions and Arbitrations, U. S.-Canadian Border.   2 A reference to Clay's protest over the surrender, in the Adams-Onís Treaty, of claim to territory west of the Sabine River. See above, II, 800, 810–15. Clay's correspondence and instructions in reference to the Oregon and northern boundaries (see above, Clay to Gallatin, August 8, 1826; Clay to Vaughan, November 15, 1826) had not yet been published.

DIPLOMATIC NOTES   March 20, 1827

To José María Salazar. Transmits, in reply to Salazar's note, "under date the 5th. [*i.e.*, 25] of January last," concerning the *Zulmé*, a copy of his (Clay's) letter of February 12 to (Francisco Dionisio) Vives. Requests him "to excuse the accidental delay which has occurred in answering . . . [his] note." Copy. DNA, RG59, Notes to Foreign Legations, vol. 3, p. 335 (M38, R3). LI draft, in CSmH; published in Manning (arr.), *Diplomatic Correspondence . . . Latin-American Nations*, I, 285. Salazar acknowledged, on March 26, 1827, receipt of this note. LS, in Spanish with trans. in State Department file. DNA, RG59, Notes from Colombian Legation, vol. 1, pt. 2 (M51, R2).

INSTRUCTIONS AND DISPATCHES   March 20, 1827

To Alexander H. Everett, Madrid, no. 8. Transmits translations of (José María Salazar's) notes of January 10 and 25, relative to the capture of the *Zulmé*. Instructs him to "lose no time in laying before the Spanish Government the representation which has been thus made to this, and in requiring the redress which properly belongs to the case, namely the despatch of orders to the Havanna [*sic*] for the immediate restoration of the captured vessel and crew, with such damages as are rightfully due, if the facts set forth in Mr. Salazar's communications should appear to be well founded." Copy. DNA, RG59, Dip. Instr., vol. 11, pp. 278–79 (M77, R6). L draft, in Daniel Brent's hand, in DLC-HC (DNA, M212, R8).

To Albert Gallatin, no. 20. Notes the arrival, "yesterday," of (Edward) Wyer "with the British ratification of the Treaty of indemnity" (cf. above, Gallatin to Clay, November 13, 1826; February 6, 1827; Clay to Gallatin, December 28, 1826), which was promulgated this day (*i.e.*, March 19—*American State Papers, Foreign Relations*, VI, 638) by Presidential proclamation. States that "Congress having adjourned without" new legislation "on the subject of the intercourse with the British Colonies, the President" issued his proclamation of March 17 "in conformity with the act of 1st. March 1823." Transmits copies of the latter proclamation, of the acts of 1818 and 1820, and "of the Circular addressed to the Collectors from the Treasury Department, relative to their enforcement" (cf. above, Clay to Vaughan, March 17, 1827). Transmits also exchanges of notes with (Charles R.) Vaughan with regard to the proclamation and to "the British packets which are to arrive at Annapolis" (above, March 9, 12, 18, 19, 1827).

Declares his intention soon to send "an instruction in relation to the Colonial question, in which some notice will be taken of the two last notes addressed [to Gallatin] by Mr. Canning . . . on that subject" (cf. above, Gallatin to Clay, November 20, 1826; January 28, 1827). Expresses doubt that the British Government will make any overture soon "for the arrangement of this difference by Convention" but authorizes him, "should such an overture be made, . . . to conclude a Convention upon the basis of either of the alternatives contained in the fifth section of two bills (copies of which are herewith transmitted) reported to the House of Representatives and to the Senate, respectively, by Committees of those bodies, during the last Session of Congress." Adds: "According to the first of those alternatives the circuitous trade between Great Britain and the United States, through the Colonies, will be left in the exclusive possession of Great Britain. By the second alternative the trade will be limited to the direct intercourse with the Colonies." Points out that Gallatin is, until instructions are sent him, not to "make any proposal for the regulation of this trade"—Clay's "purpose only now is to" prepare him "for meeting any that may be made from the other side." LS. NHi-Gallatin Papers (R14). Copy in DNA, RG59, Dip. Instr., vol. 11, pp. 277-78 (M77, R6).

On the history of the congressional proposals concerning the British West Indian trade, cf. above, Clay to Force, February 25, 1827, note. The bills as presented by the respective Committees on Commerce were almost identical. They included, as section five, two provisos for suspending application of the proposed legislation if by the stipulated September 30 the President received "satisfactory evidence" that either of two alternatives had been met. Under the first, vessels of the United States coming from the United States were to be admitted to stipulated British colonies and possessions, including the West Indies, subject to no "other or higher duties or charges than British vessels, and their cargoes, arriving from the United States"; the vessels of the United States might "import into said Colonies and possessions, from the United States, any article or articles which a British vessel could, by law, import from the United States into the said Colonies or possessions"; and the vessels of the United States might "export, to any country whatever, other than to the dominions or possessions of Great Britain, any article or articles, from the said Colonies or possessions, which vessels of Great Britain . . . [might] export therefrom." Under the second proviso, the stipulated British colonies or possessions were merely to be "open to the admission of vessels of the United States, coming from the . . . United States" and carrying articles "the produce or manufacture of the United States," subject to no other or higher duties than were exacted from "British vessels and their cargoes, arriving from the United States, in the said Colonies and possessions." *Register of Debates,* 19 Cong., 2 Sess., pp. 222-23; Washington *Daily National Journal,* January 23, 1827.

From GEORGE G. BARRELL, Malaga. Notes that American productions are, in Malaga, "either altogether prohibited" or subjected to "such a very high duty . . . as almost to amount to a prohibition." Expresses despair that conditions in "This Country" will ever improve "without the dreadful alternative of a civil War, which is at all times to be deprecated in every Country, and among these wretched, half civilised & half Barbarian People more particularly." ALS. DNA, RG59, Cons. Disp., Malaga, vol. 2 (M-T217, R-T2). Received May 20.

MISCELLANEOUS LETTERS   March 20, 1827

To HEZEKIAH HUNTINGTON, "Atty. U. S. for the District of Connecticut." Transmits, by direction of the President, "a report of the Judiciary Committee of the House of Representatives, made to that House during its last Session, upon the subject of sundry charges" against him "for taking illegal fees from certain defendants in suits of the United States against them"; informs him that he is allowed "a reasonable time" to vindicate himself; and states that "This Department will accordingly submit to the President any communications" Huntington wishes to make. Copy. DNA, RG59, Dom. Letters, vol. 21, p. 499 (M40, R19).

On January 18, 1826, the House Judiciary Committee had been directed: "to inquire whether any cases have occurred in which attorneys of the United States have received compensation from defendants, in causes under their care, in which the United States are plaintiffs, for services rendered in such causes for defendants. . . ." U. S. H. of Reps., *Journal*, 19 Cong., 1 Sess., p. 163. On December 12, 1826, the House had ordered that the file on the conduct of Huntington as presented before the Committee of the Judiciary in consequence of the above-mentioned resolution should again be referred to the Committee "and that the said committee have power to send for persons and papers." On March 3, John C. Wright, for the committee, presented a report indicating belief that Huntington had collected from defendants on two occasions payments greatly in excess of services rendered to them, in relation to prosecutions which he brought on behalf of the United States. Concluding that impeachment of an officer holding a position "of inferior grade," on a term appointment, should be resorted to only "in cases of the most urgent necessity" and only when proof of the charges should "have been first submitted to the President," the committee recommended that a copy of their report and "the evidence returned with it" should be sent to the Executive. The House accepted their recommendation. The report was subsequently incorporated in Huntington's personnel file, but he remained in office until the expiration of his four-year term, in January, 1829. *Ibid.*, 19 Cong., 2 Sess., pp. 44, 392; DNA, RG59, A. and R. (M531, R4). Cf. below, Huntington to Clay, March 31, April 30, 1827; and above, Lockwood to Clay, May 5, 1826, note.

To "JOHN MC.DOWELL [*i.e.*, MCDONELL]." Transmits his commission as "a member of the Legislative Council of the Michigan Territory. . . ." Copy. DNA, RG59, Dom. Letters, vol. 21, p. 449 (M40, R19). Published in Carter (ed.), *Territorial Papers. . .*, XI, 1061–62.

From BENJAMIN EVANS, "Supr [*sic*] Cargo of Ship Atlantic of Philada.," Havana. Transmits a memorial from captains and supercargoes of American vessels at Havana (above, Gonsolve and others to Clay, February 17, 1827). Calls attention to an exchange of letters with Francisco D(ionisio) Vives, published in the Philadelphia *National Gazette*. Explains that the concern of Americans in Havana results from the beating of Captain John Mott, of the *Canton*, at the hands of a soldier, and from insults to other Americans, who have no one to seek redress for them. ALS. DNA, RG59, Misc. Letters (M179, R65). Evans not further identified.

Mott had been captain of the *Robert Fulton* when in 1820 it made the first voyage by steam from New York to New Orleans. He later became a partner in a New York shipping firm. Fairburn, *Merchant Sail*, II, 315; V, 3315. The incident at Havana had occurred when Mott attempted to have some cordage removed from the wharf. Some soldiers barred removal of the cargo pending payment of their claim "for services officiously [*sic*] rendered"; and, when Mott persisted in his effort, he had been severely beaten. The next day Americans in the port had sought redress from General Vives, who was reported to have ordered the arrest of all men in the offending guard detail and to have issued assurances "that any aggression from abuse of military or civil power . . . [would], at all times, be promptly redressed." *Niles' Weekly Register*, XXXII (March 3, 1827), pp. 8–9.

From WILLIAM ALLISON MCREA. Tallahassee. Notes having learned, "through the medium of private letters," of his appointment as district attorney, although he "cannot act, until officially notified thereof." ALS. DNA, RG59, Misc. Letters (M179, R65). Cf. above, Clay to McRea, February 28, 1827.

APPLICATIONS, RECOMMENDATIONS   March 20, 1827

J[OSIAH] S. JOHNSTON endorses "The Bearer of this Letter" for "the place he solicits" and refers "to the Recommendations which he holds." ALS. DNA, RG59,

A. and R. (M531, R4). Unaddressed; filed in Richard Houghton's file in State Department. Recommendations not found. Houghton, not identified, received no appointment.

To James Brown

No. 10 James Brown. Envoy Extraordinary,
and Minister Plenipotentiary to France.   Department of State
Sir,   Washington 21st. March 1827.

I transmit you herewith copies of two notes which have been enterchanged between the French Minister and myself, respecting discriminating duties in the case of importation of French produces [sic] in French vessels, which happen, in the course of their voyage to touch at the ports of any of the French Colonies.[1] From a perusal of that correspondence, you will perceive that the President has decided that the discriminating duties are not chargeable in cases of such importations; and that orders will be issued from the Treasury Department to refund those which had been collected from the three French vessels mentioned by Baron de Mareuil.

This decision will furnish you with a fit occasion to ask a reconsideration of that which was given in France, and by which American vessels were held to have lost the benefits of the Convention of 1822 by the mere fact of touching at the port of a third Power, without discharging any portion of her [sic] cargo, or taking in any additional articles.[2] This decision we consider as manifestly contrary to the Convention. There is no difference between a touching at a colonial port, or one of a third Power. Neither is forbidden, nor expressly authorized by the convention, which is silent as to the point of a circuitous, or direct voyage. The national character of the vessel and of her cargo is the only circumstance necessary to found a right to the privileges of the convention.

You will therefore urge the good faith with which, on our part, the convention has been executed, as a ground independent of other just considerations, on which it is expected that the duties which have been illegally exacted will be restored, and orders given to prevent the collection of any others under similar circumstances. I am respectfully Your Obt. Servt.   H CLAY.

Copy. DNA, RG59, Dip. Instr., vol. 11, pp. 279–80 (M77, R6). ALI copy, in DLC-HC (DNA, M212, R8).
[1] See above, Mareuil to Clay, March 13, 1827; Clay to Mareuil, March 20, 1827.
[2] See above, Beasley to Clay, August 16, 1826; Brown to Clay, August 23 (1), September 11, 1826.

To Stephen Van Rensselaer

My Dear General   Washington 21st. March 1827.

I am glad to hear by your obliging favor of the 17h. inst. from New

York that political prospects appear brighter there than they did from this distant point. All that is wanted in New York to ensure success is confidence and concert. There is nothing discouraging but the apathy among our friends. Every where to the West and in Pennsa. things look well.

I need not assure you how much real pleasure it would give me to gratify your friend by his appointment to a clerkship, if I could do it; but there is now no vacancy.[1] I filled the appointments authorized in my department at the last Session of Congress immediately on its adjournment, and it was necessary to fill them with persons possessing particular attainments, of which one was of a knowledge of Foreign languages.

I hope you will let me hear from you occasionally I pray you to make my best respects to Madame and Miss V. R.[2] Yr's faithfully S. V Rensselaer.   H CLAY

ALS. NcD.
[1] Cf. above, Clay to McLane, January 14, 1826, note; Barnard to Clay, January 10, 1827, note.   [2] Cornelia Paterson (Mrs. Stephen) Van Rensselaer and her oldest daughter, Catherine, born in 1803. Miss Van Rennsselaer was married in 1830 to Gouverneur Morris Wilkins, later identified as of Castle Hill Farm, Westchester County, New York, the author of several literary tracts.

INSTRUCTIONS AND DISPATCHES   March 21, 1827

From ALBERT GALLATIN, London, no. 62. Notes that (George) Canning has recovered to the extent that he is "able to give audiences to most of the foreign ministers." Reports Canning's regret that the negotiations have been delayed and hope that they can be resumed "week after next." States that he (Gallatin) and (Henry U.) Addington, with (William) Huskisson's approval, have agreed to have "a general map prepared of the . . . explorations, made by order, of the late commission under the 5th article of the treaty of Ghent" (cf. above, IV, 182n; Clay to Gallatin, June 19, 1826) to replace the contradictory maps presented by each side in the controversy. Foresees no difficulty with regard to water courses, but predicts further disagreement concerning the highlands. Suggests that it is to Britain's interest "to continue to perplex the subject, by still insisting that there are no highlands along our assumed line." Adds that "On that subject" Addington cannot be moved and that he (Gallatin) will "press earnestly" to convince Huskisson and, if necessary, Canning of "the propriety of reducing the question to one on which a foreign Sovereign can decide. . . ." ALS. DNA, RG59, Dip. Disp., Great Britian, vol. 33 (M30, R29). Published in Manning (arr.), *Diplomatic Correspondence . . . Canadian Relations*, II, 580–81. Received May 8.

From JOHN SERGEANT, Mexico, "Private." Encloses copies of notes he wrote March 19 "to the Mexican Plenipotentiaries" (José Mariano Michelena; José Dominguez; cf. above, Sergeant to Clay, January 17, 1827); promises to send copies of the answers, when received, to Clay and to (Pedro) Gual and (Antonio Larrazábal) in an effort "to relieve the business of the [Tacubaya] Congress from its present state." Asserts that neither "the Mexican plenipotentiaries . . . nor their Government seem to be duly impressed with a sense of what they owe to the stipulations of the treaties [cf. above, Salazar to Clay, November 20, 1826] or to the obligations of hospitality." Reports that "The [Mexican] Congress has now been in session between five and six months," part of the time in special session, without action on the Panama treaties, "tho' the time fixed for the exchange of ratifications has expired." Notes that "The treaty with the United States has shared the same fate," although "The British treaty . . . has . . . received immediate attention, has passed the house of Deputies, and is now before the Senate whose sanction it will soon receive." Adds: "The neglect would be more offensive if it were confined to us. But it extends to the States who were parties to the treaties, and especially must be provoking to those who have Ministers here (Colombia, and Guatemala). . . ." Advises patience and good temper but, "at the same time," the use of every "opportunity to quicken these very slow paced people, when it can be done without offense." ALS. DNA, RG43, First Panama Congress (M662, R1).

MISCELLANEOUS LETTERS   March 21, 1827

To WILLIAM J[AMES] SEVER, "Consul of the United States for the Port of Santa Martha in the Republic of Colombia." Transmits his commission, printed circular instructions, and a blank consular bond. Copy. DNA, RG59, Cons. Instr., vol. 2, pp. 415–16 (M78, R2). Cf. above, Sever to Clay, August 5, 1826, note; Marvin to Clay, *ca.* January 5, 1827, note.

From [SAMUEL L.] SOUTHARD. Requests "such information as will enable him to answer the enclosed Letter—which is from a most estimable & worthy man." N. DNA, RG59, Misc. Letters (M179, R65). Endorsed by Clay (AEI) on attached sheet: "Mr. [Stephen] Pleasonton will furnish me with the information desired. HC." Enclosure not found; cf. below, Clay to Southard, March 22, 1827.

To José Silvestre Rebello

The Chevalier Rebello,
Chargé d'Affaires from Brazil,   Department of State,
Sir,   Washington 22d. March 1827.
    [Acknowledges receipt of Rebello's note of February 21, 1827, which has been submitted to the President.]
    The circumstances of the case as reported by Mr. Raguet[1] are these: In the month of June last, the Brig Leonidas, of Boston, bound from China to Buenos Ayres, was captured by the Brazilian Squadron, in the River Plate, and sent into Monte Video.[2] At that port five of her seamen, in violation of the immunity of the flag of her Country, were forcibly taken out of the Vessel and conveyed on board the Imperial frigate Piranga, where they were required to perform duty, and, in consequence of refusing so to do, were put upon short allowance, and threatened [*sic*] as prisoners of war. After a detention of about a month, they were placed on board different prize vessels, of nations other than their own, for the purpose of assisting to navigate them to Rio de Janeiro. Two of them were placed on board the French ship Juno, when one named Watson Farris,[3] in consequence of refusing to perform duty, which the prize master had no right to require of him, was severely beaten. In that vessel they arrived at the port of Rio, in

company with the American Brig Ruth, captured by, and then under Convoy of the Imperial Brig of War Independencia ou Morte, on the 29th. of August.[4] On the following day the Master of the Leonidas,[5] who had previously arrived, and had obtained possession of his Vessel under bonds, hearing of the situation of his two seamen, whose services he needed, went on board the Juno, and requested their release, which was refused by the Prize Master. The matter then being represented by him to Captain Biddle,[6] who had just heard that the Supercargo, Master and Crew of the Ruth, after a long confinement as prisoners on board the Independencia ou Morte, had been sent, like a gang of convicts, from that Vessel, the common depôt of criminals, the Preziganga, and having understood that the two men in question were fearful that they would be, that night, impressed on board the said brig of war, immediately sent an officer, in a boat, to demand their discharge, the time happening to be eight o'clock in the evening. This demand was not accompanied by the employment of force, or the threat that any would be employed for its enforcement. It is altogether unlikely that any was contemplated, as the demand was made in a harbor protected by the forts and ships of war of his Imperial Majesty. With this demand there was a compliance.

Upon this state of the case, I think you must agree that the injuries requiring redress were altogether on our side. And the expectation is confidently indulged that the justice of the Government of Brazil will be exercised in causing adequate indemnity to be made to the parties aggrieved, and taking precautionary measures to prevent the like aggressions in future.

Whilst indulging this expectation, the President is at all times ready to animadvert upon the conduct of any of our naval commanders, who may commit any irregularities towards foreign Powers. This disposition was manifested in the case referred to by you. But without adverting to the statement which has been just detailed, and confining his consideration to the circumstances of Captain Biddle's conduct, as brought forward by you, he cannot perceive any just ground for his interposition. According to your statement, Captain Biddle, in the port of Rio de Janeiro, claimed from the Commander of the Brazilian prize, the Junon [sic] at anchor in the same port, two American seamen that were on board as sailors, without applying to the competent authorities. If Captain Biddle had resorted to the employment of force, to coerce their surrender, it would have been very irregular; but that is neither alleged, nor would its allegation be warranted by facts. If the demand had been refused, it would have been Captain Biddles duty, then, to have invoked the aid of the Civil authorities. The employment of force is justifiable in resisting aggressions, before they are complete. But when they are consummated, the intervention of the authority of Government becomes necessary, if redress is refused by the aggressor. There would appear to be a peculiar fitness in making application, as was done, to the injuring party, and if, as was also done, his sense of his own injustice prompted a compliance with the application, there would be no necessity to incur the expense, and to submit to delay incident to an application to the Civil Magistrate.

The case is altogether unlike that which occurred at Porto Rico, in which the Government of the United States caused satisfaction to be made to that of Spain. In that case force was employed and the local authorities were coerced by its use. The disavowal of the conduct of Captain Porter,[7] and the prompt redress afforded to Spain, on the part of the Government of the United States, afford ample proof of the respect which is here entertained for the rights and feelings of other nations.

I pray you to accept assurances of my high consideration.

H. CLAY.

Copy. DNA, RG59, Notes to Foreign Legations, vol. 3, pp. 338–40 (M38, R3). L draft, mostly in Clay's hand, dated March 19, but without significant change, in CSmH.
[1] In his dispatches, above, October 2 and 31, 1826, and to a great extent in enclosures forwarded with them.   [2] Cf. above, Bond to Clay, June 20, 1826; Raguet to Clay, July 17, September 1, November 27, 1826.   [3] Neither Farris nor the other seaman here referred to, Christian Brehen, has been further identified.   [4] Cf. above, Raguet to Clay, September 1, 23, October 2, 31, November 27, December 4, 5, 1826; Wright to Clay, Sptember 2, 1826; Southard to Clay, November 17, 1826.   [5] — — Bartlett.
[6] James Biddle.   [7] David Porter.

From Jabez D. Hammond

Dear Sir,   Albany March 22, 1827

In my last[1] I suggested that in case Mr. Wheaton did not accept his Appointment to Denmark I was desirous that the vacancy should not be immediately supplied— It is now understood here that Mr. W. *will* accept the appointment,[2] but I will nevertheless take the liberty of acquainting you with my reasons for making that request—

You may possibly recollect that in a communication I made to you about a year ago[3] I reminded you of the fact that there are about three hundred Civil Officers at Washington exclusive of the officers for the District of Columbia held by appointment from the U. S. Government— That only about six of the three hundred Civil Officers had been taken from the State of New York— That there is not even a bureau at Washington under the direction of a New Yorker the highest office held by a Citizen of this State being that of Chief Clerk in the Treasury Department.[4] And that independent of these facts in my judgment it was necessary for the Administration to have some person *constantly* at the seat of Government from this State who might give information as *to matters of fact* and who of course should be well acquainted with the principal men and with the various *political combinations here—*

I have not changed my opinion on this subject. Indeed the experience of the last year has served to confirm me in its correctness— In the present state of things the Administration altho' influenced by the best possible motives will commit errors— If therefore Mr. Wheaton had declined the appointment of Charge d'Affaires, it was my intention to have suggested the propriety of appointing one of the Auditors to that station and of giving the office of such Auditor to one of the Citizens of this State— May not some such arrangement be effected if Wheaton accepts the Appointment?— I may misjudge but I do consider the project deeply important— If such a measure should be deemed proper I did intend to offer myself as a Candidate for the appointment—but not with any anxious wish for the office if another person could be found who would accept it and whose acquaintance in this State is as extensive as mine—

Considering the public stations I have held in my Judgment I could not with propriety accept a Clerkship in any of the public offices— but I would take any other appointment not calculated to draw towards me the attention of the public (which I wish to avoid) and not derogatory to my time of life & standing in Society— Will you allow me to solicit your candid and *frank* opinion on the subject?—

If in your Judgment I am not fited [sic] for a station of the kind I have mentioned, if you differ from me in opinion as to the necessity of bringing to the Seat of Government a Citizen of this State perfectly well acquainted the [sic] characters and political combinations of its Citizens or if any other person can be named whose appointment you shall be of opinion will be more judicious, I solemnly assure you it will never produce one unkind impression upon my mind—

Altho I am not rich I have (by my own industry) procured a competent stock of wealth to enable me to educate my little family in a style frugal indeed; but at the same time one that is suited to my taste. My professional business affords me sufficient employment to render me contented— I do not therefore want office for its emoluments much less do I desire it for the distinction it may confer— I therefore repeat that I am not anxious for office, but I do feel a very deep solicitude that the prostration of the political influence of the eastern and and [sic] western States should be prevented— The apprehension that this disastrous event may be produced by the desertion by New York of her Eastern & western neighbors renders that solicitude more intense—

I beg you to state to me your opinion with the most perfect frankness— I shall regard your communication as sacredly confidential—

I do not wish an appointment and indeed I woul[d] not accept one if offered me unless it should receive the approbation of & be recommended by, not only the political Friends with whom I have acted in the local politics of this State but of such leaders of the Party *to whom I have heretofo[re] been opposed* as are friendly to the National Ad-

ministration— I mean such men as Col. Young, Gen. Porter[5] &c— I am with great respect Your Obedt. Servt.   JABEZ D. HAMMOND
The Hon. H. Clay—

I have just seen Col. Young who expresses his determination of taking a bold and decided stand in favor of the Administration and against Mr. V. B.[6]

ALS. DLC-HC (DNA, M212, R2). MS. somewhat defaced by over-writing. On March 27 Clay took this letter to President Adams and suggested that a vacancy be created for Hammond. Adams, *Memoirs*, VII, 349–50.
[1] Not found. This is probably the letter Clay had read to the President on March 23. *Ibid.*, VII, 246.   [2] Cf. below, Wheaton to Clay, April 2, 1827.   [3] Not found.
[4] Edward Jones of New York, who had held this post since 1816 and continued in office until March 31, 1829.   [5] Samuel Young; Peter B. Porter.   [6] Martin Van Buren.

From William R. McCall

Honbl. H. Clay   Vincennes March 22d. 27
Sir I recvd [*sic*] yesterday a letter from Hon J Jennings dated 1st March informing me he had failed in making the deposit of $30. in the U States Treasury, Which I spoke of in my letter to you enclosing the necessary papers for a Patent of the Family Spinner—
I must respectfully Solicit your attention, to patronize and aid me in this usefull machine,   Enclosed you have a blank deed for the district of Columbia and Myrland [*sic*][1] Which any Gent. or comp Can own on the payment of the above sum in the U States Treasury
I chalenge [*sic*] the best artists or mechanics to show a Well grounded objection to this Spinner,, I am well assured this Machine will be introduced in the differen[t] Woolen factories. If this scheme Should fail to raise the Money, please to let me know,   I have sold Conditionally—If its patentd. 3 of the Southern states for $1000— I have directed My Brother, Ross[2] to exhibit this Machine to the Lexington agricultural society[3]—
Your goodness to this will be amply reciprocated by your frend [*sic*] & Humb Sevt.   WM R MCCALL
Hon H Clay

ALS. DNA, RG59, Accounting Records, Misc. Letters. McCall, of Vincennes, Indiana, received in May, 1828, a patent for an invention for "spinning wool and cotton from the roll." Burke, *List of Patents*, 94. By 1833 he had removed to Calhoun County, Michigan Territory.
[1] For exclusive rights "of making, & vending to others to make & use" the machine in these two areas "for the term of fourteen years. . . ."   [2] Not further identified.
[3] Probably the Kentucky Society for Promoting Agriculture. Cf. above, II, 703n, 712.

From Samuel Mifflin

Dr Sir,   Harrisburg March 22. 1827
Thro' our mutual friend,[1] you no doubt have been made acquainted,

with the result of my enquiries since I had the pleasure of seeing you at Washington, in relation to the Presidential movements, in this State, & which I have strong reason to believe, are rapidly tending, to a correct view, of the course of the General Administration, & disgust, at the violent & intemperate zeal of the opposition; indeed to use an expression, which yesterday, fell from a *reputed* Jackson man "I harr [*sic*] of *many*, who are going over to the Ad. but I know of *none*, who are falling off."— The truth is the Jackson interest, is supposed to be the popular one, because, there has not as yet, been any event, to rouse the attention of the great body of the people, to reflect upon the subject *but*, should such a measure, as a Caucus of our Legislature, in favor of Jackson, take place & the opinion of the Members have been sounded, on this point, you may be assured, there will be expression, in favor, of the Ad. which will not a little, surprise the friends of the General—

You may recollect, my remarking to you, that if, an Individual could be found, of talent & influence, who would boldly, expose the views of the Opposition, much would be done, to to [*sic*] bring out the timid, & those, who perhaps, have not yet formed their opinions; such a person, I think will be found, in the Speaker of the H.R.,[2] with whom, I have had a *free* communication. I find him, decidedly in favor of the Ad. & strongly attatched [*sic*] to your personal character, which, he has on all occasions, defended with zeal & ability—

You no doubt know, that Mr. R. looks forward, to political promotion & I would therefore suggest, the propriety, of being authorised to say, that whatever can be done, consistently with the interests of the Country, will be done, by his friends at Washington, to promote his views. I am induced to say this much, because our friend desired me, to address myself to you & I beg you to be assured whatever confidence you may think proper to place in me, on this delicate subject, will be used with all due caution.—

I have just read a very severe piece, in the Upland Union, of Chester, on the course pursued by Mr. Buchannan [*sic*], in relation to the Wool bill.[3] Gentlemen from that quarter, say, that his vote will be fatal to his next election & I find, that there [*sic*] papers, have come out against Stevenson on the same ground.[4]

I shall remain here a sufficient lenght [*sic*] of time, to hear from you in reply.— I beg you to be assured of my esteem   SAML. MIFFLIN
The Honorable Henry Clay Washington

ALS. DLC-HC (DNA, M212, R2).   [1] Not identified.
[2] Joseph Ritner.   [3] The Chester *Upland Union* had been established as the *Post Boy* in 1819; the name had been changed in 1826. On the woolens bill, see above, Pleasants to Clay, February 14, 1827. James Buchanan, discussing the proposal on February 7, 1827, had urged protection for Pennsylvania's grain farmers and had moved to recommit the measure for such amendment. In the final voting he had opposed passage of the

bill. *Register of Debates*, 19 Cong., 2 Sess., pp. 995–1000, 1099.   [4] For James S. Stevenson's action on the bill, see above, Whittlesey to Clay, March 13, 1827, note. Buchanan was re-elected to Congress in 1828, but Stevenson was defeated.

INSTRUCTIONS AND DISPATCHES   March 22, 1827

From ROBERT MONROE HARRISON, Antigua. Reports that the alien laws and transient tax "are in full operation in the [British West India] Colonies"; that no American may undertake any mercantile business "or follow trade of any Kind"; and that the tax varies in the different islands, from 2 to 5 percent on consigned shipments and from 8 to 10 percent on goods not consigned. Warns that the colonial legislatures, if allowed to tax foreign trade, could contravene treaty concessions granted by the mother country. Points out that American shipmasters cannot reclaim deserters because the colonial laws make no provision for legal action by aliens. Expresses hope that Anglo-American trade may soon take a more certain pattern, for he is doing no business and his family suffers in the United States. If a new commercial arrangement should soon be made, he would prefer to remain in Antigua, where he is well-liked but now accorded little attention by the colonial authorities. ALS. DNA, RG59, Cons. Disp., Antigua (M-T327, R1). Received May 11.

From WILLIAM PHILLIPS, Guatemala. Reports that the city has for two days been invested by troops from San Salvador and that "a scene of alarm & confusion" results. Observes "that any change in this Government must be for the better and that "Sn [*sic*] Salvador wants to reestablish the federal system of Government. . . ." Notes that he had been "upon the eve of . . . departure for the United States" but is remaining at his post because "American property to the amount of at least 150,000 Dolls. is in jeopardy here. . . ." ALS. DNA, RG59, Dip. Disp., Central America, vol. 1 (M219, R2). Received June 27. Cf. above, Gonzalez to Clay, January 7, 1827; Phillips to Clay, February 3, March 2, 1827.

MISCELLANEOUS LETTERS   March 22, 1827

To JOHN BOYLE, "Judge of the U. S. for the District of Kentucky, Harrodsburg." Transmits his commission. Copy. DNA, RG59, Dom. Letters, vol. 21, p. 499 (M40, R19). Cf. above, Clay to Boyle, October 20, 1826, note.

To JOHN J. CRITTENDEN, "Attorney for the U. S. for the District of Kentucky Frankft." Transmits his commission. Copy. DNA, RG59, Dom. Letters, vol. 21, p. 500 (M40, R19). Cf. above, Marshall to Clay, January 5, 1827, note.

To E[LEUTHÈRE] IRENÉE DU PONT, "Director of the Bank U. S., Wilmington [Delaware]." Transmits his commission. Copy. DNA, RG59, Dom. Letters, vol. 21, p. 501 (M40, R19). Du Pont, who had been a director of the Bank from 1823 through 1825, had been replaced by his brother, Victor, for the years 1826 and 1827 (see above, Clay to Du Pont, December 28, 1825); but following the latter's death, Adams on February 27, 1827, had nominated E. Irenée to complete the term. He was subsequently reappointed until 1830.

To HENRY PERRINE, "Consul of the United States at Campeche, in the United Mexican States." Transmits his commission, printed circular instructions, and a blank consular bond. Copy. DNA, RG59, Cons. Instr., vol. 2, p. 416 (M78, R2). Perrine acknowledged, on April 20, receipt of these materials and returned the bond. ALS, in *ibid.*, Cons. Disp., Campeche, Mexico, vol. 1 (M286, R1).

To the SECRETARY OF THE TREASURY [RICHARD RUSH]. Transmits a copy of a letter to the French Minister (Clay to Mareuil, March 20, 1827), "informing him that Orders will be issued from the Treasury, for refunding certain duties which were levied upon three French vessels . . . at Savannah, and for preventing in future the Collection of the Duty under Analogous Circumstances"; requests that "these Orders . . . be given." N, in Daniel Brent's hand. DNA, RG217, 1st Comptroller, Letters Received from Secretary of State, 1826–56.

From JOSEPH DELAFIELD, New York. Reports "that the meeting of the Boundary line commission" scheduled for March 1 (cf. above, Delafield to Clay, November 15, 1826; Porter to Clay, February 27, 1827) did not occur because the British Commissioner (Anthony Barclay) had not received the instructions he expected. Conjectures that the instructions have arrived and that the board will meet as soon as the British Commissioner "can repair from Savannah (where he now is) to New York. . . ." States that (Peter B.) Porter has directed him to arrange for "the proposed operations of the coming season, viz the true determination of the parrallel [sic] of latitude 49°. N. where it intersects the Lake of the Woods, and the Red river, taking care to avoid" unnecessary expense. Promises that the surveyor will proceed "as soon as the Ice leaves the Lakes." ALS. DNA, RG76, Northern Boundary: Treaty of Ghent, 1814, Arts. VI & VII, env. 1, folder 2.

From MICHAEL WITHERS, Baltimore. Notes that he has decided to place his case "before Congress at the next ensuing session with such a reservation of . . . [his] rights, and such proof of the wrongs extended to . . . [him], as will induce Congress to grant an extension of . . . patent"; explains that he has accordingly "prepared the enclosed protest"; and requests that it "be filed in the Department of State." LS. DNA, RG59, Misc. Letters (M179, R65). Published in Washington *Daily National Journal*, April 24, 1827. The enclosed documents include a notarized statement of the history of his patent claims; a copy of his patent certificate of August 24, 1813; a transcript of the Federal District Court, Maryland District, record in the case of *Caleb Kirk vs. Michael Withers*; a copy of the report of the case as presented in *Niles' Weekly Register*, XII (June 28, 1817), 283; a clipping from the *Baltimore Patriot*, February 21, 1827; and copies of correspondence from Withers to Clay, February 21, March 5, 1827; Causten to Clay, March 1, 1827; Clay to Withers, March 9, 1827—the preceding letters all noted above; and Causten to Wirt, March 7, 1827; Withers to John Q. Adams, March 10, 1827.

   Withers' petition was presented to Congress on January 28, 1828; but three days later leave was given for its withdrawal. U. S. H. of Reps., *Journal*, 20 Cong., 1 Sess., pp. 225, 238.

APPLICATIONS AND RECOMMENDATIONS March 22, 1827

JAMES H. BENNETT, Washington, solicits appointment as consul "at Rio Grande South, or any other desireable [sic] vacancy." States that he wishes "to convince the Government, that great injustice was done" him at Pernambuco. ALS. DNA, RG59, A. and R. (M531, R1). Cf. above, Bennett to Clay, November 19, 1826. Bennett received no further appointment.

From James Brown (1)

Dear Sir,   (private & cf.)   Paris March 23. 1827
   The state of things in Europe has been so extraordinary for some

time and the uncertainty as to what would be the future condition of Europe so great that I have forborn [sic] to trouble you with the loose speculations which we hear every day but which are generally destroyed by the events of the morrow. Since writing my despatch[1] which will go by this vessel the news of the 13 has been received from Madrid. It is stated in private letters that General Sarsfield[2] who commanded the army on the frontier of Portugal finding it disposed to revolt and to join the Constitutionalists, immediately left it, proceeded to Madrid, obtained an audience of the King,[3] communicated the discovery he had made, and advised, that war should, by all means be avoided if the King did not wish a revolution. In consequence of these intimations Ferdinand it is said issued orders to the Officer commanding at Zamora[4] to disarm the Rebel Portuguese and march them into the interior. It is now said that their number amounts to four thousand including Chaves, Montaliagre [sic], Telles Jordao[5] and other officers of distinction. It is fortunate for Great Britain if this news is true for if the Spanish army had felt equal zeal with the Government in the cause of despotism the British troops could not have remained three months in Portugal.[6]

I shall by the next Packet send you all the information you wish on the French law for granting patents.[7] I presume you mean to make it the subject of a report to next Session and you shall have it in time.

The rumors that we were preparing for war with England on account of Boundaries and with France respecting our Claims[8] have made some little stir here but were not generally credited   I am afraid the Administration will find much trouble from Congress on the subject of our Claims with France should that question come before on [sic] the eve of a Presidential election. The discussion of our foreign relations in Congress unless unless conducted with great prudence may do much harm to the negociations. The opposition eager to find fault with the administration will in their angry criticisms furnish arguments to foreign nations which they will not fail to use against us. I am well convinced that France will never recede from the ground she has taken unless she shall by some political events be placed in a situation which will make it her interest rather to do us justice than to find our weight thrown into the scale against her. A renewed demand for the third or fourth time will meet the same answer and can do no good to our cause.

Count de Menoue [sic] has been very anxious to be appointed Minister[9] but has not succeeded— I do not know that he sollicited [sic] it but I know he had friends who wished it for him— I do not know who will be appointed   Count Krudener[10] the Minister for Russia is expected here soon on his way to Washington— He is represented as a man of excellent talents and amiable manners but unfortunately hearing imperfectly.

The winter has been unusually gay and although Lent has commenced yet we have parties almost every evening. My health has been very good and we have made this winter a very large circle of acquaintances. I have sent home my accounts for the last year and I pray my good friend Mr Pleasonton[11] to close them for me again to the first of Decr   You know how much I am afraid of being behind in the Government books. If he finds my postage account increased you can account for it. Letters and Packages pass through Paris to Holland Spanish & Russian Legations, and you know that many letters are sent through the Department of State some of which require the payment of postage here. But still he will perhaps find this Legation not more expensive than some others.

Mrs. Brown enjoys her usual good health & joins me in love to Mrs Clay   I am Dear Sir very sincerely Your friend   JAMES BROWN
Honle. Henry Clay

ALS. DLC-HC (DNA, M212, R2).   1 Below, this date.
2 Pedro Sarsfield (Saarfield), born in Corunna of Irish parentage, had fought in the Spanish forces against Napoleon and later earned distinction as captain-general of Navarre, supporting Isabella in the Carlist war (see above, Brown to Clay, August 26, 1825, note).   3 Ferdinand VII.   4 Probably General Minet (not further identified), who was commanding at Zamora the following August, when he was transferred to Catalonia. *Annual Register, 1827*, p. [239].   5 The Marquis of Chaves; the Viscount Montalegre; Joaquim Teles Jordão. Luís Vaz Pereira Pinto Guedes, the second Viscount Montalegre, a veteran of the Peninsular War against Napoleon, had been commander in Trás-os-Montes from 1823 to 1826, when he rebelled against the regime under the new constitutional Charter. He subsequently became a leader of the forces supporting Dom Miguel and was dismissed from the Army with the latter's defeat in 1834. Teles Jordão had also risen rapidly in the Army during the Peninsular War. His opposition to constitutional government had led to his dismissal from the Army in 1822. Reinstated the following year, he became one of the leaders in repudiating the Charter of 1826. As Governor of the State of Torre de S. Julião da Barra during the ascendancy of Miguel in 1828, Teles Jordão acquired notoriety for the severity of his punishments. He was killed in combat in 1833 as leader of a force defeated in the overthrow of Miguel.
6 Cf. above, Everett to Clay, January 7, 1827, note.   7 See above, Clay to Brown, January 11, 1827.   8 Rumors not found. Cf. above, Clay to Brown, November 14, 1825, note; Brown to Clay, November 28, 1825; January 30, April 13, 1826; Clay to Lincoln, May 13, 1826; Gallatin to Clay, November 5, 1826, note.   9 Rather than Chargé d'Affaires. Cf. above, Brown to Clay, November 29, 1826. A new minister was not appointed until 1830, at which time the Baron de Mareuil was formally recalled.
10 Paul de Krüdener. See above, Middleton to Clay, July 30, 1826.   11 Stephen Pleasonton. On the accounts, see above, Brown to Clay, January 23, 1827, note.

DIPLOMATIC NOTES   March 23, 1827

From CHARLES R. VAUGHAN, Washington (1). Transmits "a Copy of a despatch which was addressed to" (Charles) Mackenzie, Consul General in Haiti, "upon the receipt by His Majesty's Government of the Representation made by Mr. Clay" (above, Clay to Vaughan, November 13, 1826). Calls "attention . . . to the expression of disapprobation of the proceedings of Mr. Mackenzie, contained in the . . . despatch." NS. DNA, RG59, Notes from British Legation, vol. 14 (M50, R15). The enclosure, written by John Bidwell, contains, at the direction of (George) Canning, the following: ". . . if the statement [in Clay's note] as to the citation . . . be correct, there can be no doubt that such a proceeding on your part was an unjustifiable exercise of Authority over the Master of the American Vessel in a Foreign Port, and one in which you cannot be supported by your Government."

Bidwell had served in the British Foreign Office since 1798 and had become superintendent of the Consular Service in 1825.

From CHARLES R. VAUGHAN, Washington (2). Transmits an extract, received from his Government, "from a Letter addressed by Captain [D. C.] Clavering . . . to the Commander of His Majesty's Naval Forces on the Coast of Africa, explaining the alleged impressment of two American Seamen" (cf. above, Clay to Vaughan, May 8, 1826). Asserts that "it removes at once all imputation of that Officer having committed any Act of violence amounting to the Impressment of American Seamen." NS. *Ibid.* The enclosure, from a letter addressed by Clavering to "Commodore [Charles] Bullen," September 19, 1826, states that two men from the *Pharos* came on board his vessel in December, 1825, "desiring to enter"; one, an Englishman named Edward Palmer, and the other, a Dane, who, proving unfit for the duty he requested, "was dismissed, and . . . [Clavering believes] returned to his original vessel."

Captain Bullen, who had entered the British Navy in 1779, had attained his first command in 1798, had served as a flag captain in the battle of Trafalgar, and from 1824 to 1827 had been commodore of the fleet off the west coast of Africa. He became superintendent of the Pembroke dockyard in 1830, captain of the Royal Yacht from 1830 to 1837, a rear admiral in 1837, vice admiral in 1846, and admiral in 1852. The seaman, Palmer, has not been further identified.

INSTRUCTIONS AND DISPATCHES   March 23, 1827

From JAMES BROWN, Paris, "Private" (2). States that, according to "intelligence from Madrid down to the 12th instant," Spain has disarmed "A body of about two thousand Portuguese rebels," has sent them into the interior, and will return their arms to "the Portuguese constitutionalists" (cf. above, Everett to Clay, March 19, 1827). Reports that the French Ministry "consider this measure, the first of a friendly character on the part of Spain," as the first step toward ending "the hopes of the insurgents" and preventing war. Notes the existence of a different opinion but remarks that "neither Great Britain nor France are [*sic*] ready for war" and that the former will consult with the latter in regard to a policy toward Spain. Adds that reports from Greece are "very gloomy," that efforts of England and Russia "to effect the pacification of Greece, have been ineffectual [cf. above, Brown to Clay, April 13, 1826; Middleton to Clay, June 13, 1826]," and that he would "not be surprised if the Emperor [Nicholas I] shall e'er long address stronger arguments to the Ottoman power. . . ." LS. DNA, RG59, Dip. Disp., France, vol. 23 (M34, R26). Published in Padgett (ed.), "Letters of James Brown to Henry Clay," *Louisiana Historical Quarterly*, XXIV (October, 1941), 1033–34. Received May 10. Endorsed by Clay (AEI) on verso of last page: "To be submitted to the President   HC."

From W[ILLIAM] TUDOR, Lima, no. 61, "*Confidential.*" Acknowledges, with "the greatest relief & satisfaction," Clay's letter of October 27 (1826). Reports the sailing, from Callao, of 2,000 Colombian troops, whom General (Andrés) Santa Cruz says he "had never expected to get rid of . . . without a battle" (cf. above, Tudor to Clay, March 1, 1827). Discusses the intrigues of (Simón) Bolívar's agents in Peru and identifies the most dangerous of them as "Doña Manuela Saens (the wife of a Doctor Thorn [*sic*] an Englishman) the enthusiastic friend of Gen. Bolívar,

& of whom he is passionately fond, & to whom he allows 500$ a month. . . ." Describes the activities of "This lady familiarly known here under the name of the Libertadora," whose counter-revolutionary efforts led to her being arrested and placed in a convent, from whence she was freed after the troops departed. Claims that the troops are being sent to various areas still under Bolívar's control and predicts that "Quito & Guayaquil will return to the support of the Constitution of Colombia [cf. above, Watts to Clay, October 21, 1826; March 14, 1827; Wheelwright to Clay, February 22, 1827; below, Wheelwright to Clay, April 5, 19, 1827; Tudor to Clay, April 25, May 15, 1827], when these troops arrive, if they should not have done so before. . . ." Refers to this expedition as "truly to be called liberators"; notes that (José) Bustamante is the senior officer of one division, while "Col. Elisalde," a member of "one of the most respectable" families in Guayaquil heads the other as a volunteer. Interprets "The whole of these events" (cf. above, Tudor to Clay, February 3, 1827) as showing "the very fragile nature of arbitrary power, especially when it is a usurpation, unless sustained by a greater force than Bolivar had at his disposal" and, at the same time, marvels at the success of the revolutionaries, "enthusiastic & honorable young men . . . almost without organization and system. . . ." Notes the existence of "Much anxiety . . . to know what course will be followed by the government of Bogota, when this revolution became [sic] known to it." Comments on "several confidential letters," including one written by Bolívar, which "have fallen into hands for which they were not intended." Explains why he thinks Bolívar will not be able to return to Peru; asserts that "The feeling in favour of the late change appears universal throughout the country," that elections are being held, that they are being won by persons opposed to Bolívar, and that the largest vote went to General (José de) Lamar, who "will be elected President of Peru by a unanimous vote. . . ." Recommends that two of Lamar's nephews " (he has no children)," being sent "to be educated in St Mark's [sic] College Baltimore," be offered appointments to "the [United States] Military Academy." States that he is without information from Upper Peru (Bolivia) "as to the course that may be finally pursued by General [Antonio José de] Sucre," who, "seeing Bolivar's system ruined, [may] determine to act for himself." Characterizes Sucre as able, "extremely popular," and a wise administrator. Comments on other prominent men, including General Santa Cruz and [Manuel Lorenzo de] Vidaurre. Cites a change in the tariff, which he thinks will be "of very uncertain duration." Mentions his "day to day" anticipation of the arrival of (James) Cooley (cf. above, Clay to Cooley, June 6, 1826). Adds, in a postscript dated March 25, that he has received a letter from Lamar, who "appears equally delighted & surprized at the fortunate revolution that had occurred here, by which he says they have escaped from a yoke more infamous & oppressive than that from which they had been finally liberated by the battle of Ayacucho . . ." (cf. above, IV, 105n). Appends a second postscript, March 26, stating that letters received by various persons from Sucre indicate "that he was still ignorant of the state of feeling in Peru. . . ." ALS. DNA, RG59, Cons. Disp., Lima, vol. 1 (M154, R1). Extracts published in Manning (arr.), *Diplomatic Correspondence . . . Latin-American Nations*, III, 1825–31. Received August 9.

Manuela Sáenz de Thorne, born in Quito in 1797, had been married in 1817 to James Thorne, a middle-aged English merchant (not a doctor), who traded along the west coast of South America. In 1822 she had met Bolívar, an affair had developed, and in 1823 she had deserted her husband to become Bolívar's mistress. Because of their Roman Catholicism, she and her husband were never divorced, but she remained one of Bolívar's favorites until his exile in 1830. She also was exiled from Bogotá in 1834 and spent the remainder of her life until 1856, as a confectioner in Paita, Peru. Thorne was murdered in Pativilca, Peru, in 1847.

Juan Francisco Elizalde was a veteran of the campaigns for independence of Colombia and Peru, including the great victory at Ayacucho. He was expelled from Ecuador in 1830 and spent the remainder of his life in Lima.

Lamar's nephews, not identified, do not appear to have entered the United States Military Academy. Tudor probably erred in referring to St. Mary's College, Baltimore.

MISCELLANEOUS LETTERS   March 23, 1827

To LANGDON CHEVES (1). Transmits "the President's Commission, appointing . . . [Cheves], James Pleasants, & Henry Seawell, Commissioners" to put into effect the convention of November 13, 1826, with Great Britain, "agreeably to the provisions of the Law" providing for adjustment of claims under Article I of the Treaty of Ghent and for distribution to the claimants of sums paid by Great Britain for that purpose. Copy. DNA, RG59, Dom. Letters, vol. 21, p. 502. Cf. above, Clay to Gallatin, December 28, 1826 (no. 15), note; Clay to McLane, January 15, 1827. On March 27, 1827, Cheves acknowledged receipt of this letter and accepted the appointment. ALS, in DNA, RG59, Acceptances and Orders for Comns. (M-T645, R2).

To LANGDON CHEVES, Washington (2). Notes that "The fifth Article of the late Convention with England stipulated" dissolution of "the joint Commission appointed under the Convention of St. Petersburg of the 12th July 1822" and the delivery, to a person or persons named by the United States, of documents in possession of the Commission and of the British Commissioner (George Jackson) relating to claims under that convention. States that ratifications of the convention were exchanged in London February 6. Requests, "by the direction of the President," that Cheves receive the documents mentioned above and "pass them over to the Commission, the appointment of which is authorized by the Act of Congress passed at the last session." Copy. DNA, RG59, Dom. Letters, vol. 21, pp. 503–504 (M40, R19). Cf. above, Clay to Gallatin, December 28, 1826 (no. 15), note; Clay to Gallatin, March 20, 1827.

To AARON OGDEN, "New Jersey." Transmits "a commission appointing" him "Clerk to the Board of Commissioners, established by the Act of Congress, a Copy of which is" enclosed. Copy. DNA, RG59, Dom. Letters, vol. 21, p. 503. Cf. above, Clay to Gallatin, December 28, 1826 (no. 15), note; Clay to McLane, January 15, 1827. Writing from "Elizabeth Town New Jersey" on April 3, 1827, Ogden acknowledged receipt of his commission. ALS, in DNA, RG59, Acceptances and Orders for Comns. (M-T645, R2).

Ogden was officially identified as "Clerk" when the Commissioners first met on July 10 but shortly thereafter he appears to have been denominated "secretary" and James Ord assumed the duties of "clerk." Cf. below, Williamson to Clay, March 27, 1827, note; *Biennial Register, 1827*, p. 16.

To JAMES PLEASANTS, Richmond, Virginia. States that the commission appointing Langdon Cheves, Pleasants, and Henry Seawell "Commissioners for carrying into effect, the law of the last Session of Congress, a copy of which is" enclosed, has been forwarded to Cheves (see above, Clay to Cheves, this date). Copy. DNA, RG59, Dom. Letters, vol. 21, pp. 502–503. Endorsed: "The same to Henry Seawell."

From B. AYMAR AND COMPANY, New York. Encloses a memorial "which after perusal" they request Clay to lay before the President. State that they address Clay because they think this the proper procedure and because he "so well" understands "[th]e merits of the case" and has "ever been ready [to] attend to the Commercial interest of the [Co]untry." LS. DNA, RG59, Misc. Letters (M179, R65). Endorsed on separate sheet (AEI) by Clay: "To be submitted to the President. H.C."

The memorial, addressed to the President and signed by "B. Aymar & Co." and six other New York mercantile firms, requests modification of the Treasury circular issued in accordance with the President's proclamation of March 17, 1827 (cf. above, Clay to Vaughan, March 17, 1827), to permit vessels (from the West Indies) "which may arrive in the United States by the first day of July next and which may have sailed before the existence of the prohibition was known at the Port from which they last sailed bound to the United States . . . to enter and to unlade their Cargoes."

The circular issued on March 17 by Secretary of the Treasury Richard Rush and addressed to the collectors as an accompaniment to the President's proclamation closing the trade with certain enumerated British colonies had been published in the Washington *Daily National Journal*, March 19, 1827. It provided that vessels arriving prior to July first should be given notice of the prohibition, "accompanied by orders for their departure within twenty-four hours, without unlading"; otherwise the provisions of the relevant legislation were to be enforced.

The firm of B(enjamin) Aymar and Company had been organized in 1821 as an outgrowth of shifting partnerships in a business dating back to 1784. Benjamin Aymar, who had begun as a clerk in the parent company, had been admitted to partnership in 1809 and remained active in the business until 1845.

From HUGH MERCER, Fredericksburg (Virginia). Thanks Clay for his "kind letter" (not found—cf. above, Mercer to Clay, March 19, 1827) in the morning mail; continues: "I trust that the great distress of mind I am under, because of the *possibility* of my Son's dismissal from the Academy, will induce you to bear with me on account of the *great solicitude* I have expressed on the occasion— You judge me most correctly in supposing, that I would not desire him to be tried by any other principle than that you have mentioned—" States that he continues "most humbly to hope, that his [son's] *fault* has not been of that *serious cast*, as that the good of the institution shall require his *Dismissal.* . . ." Professes "great astonishment . . . as well as . . . deep regret, that he [the son] was drawn into any conduct disorderly in its character. . . ." Requests that the President not decide the case until the return to Washington of the Secretary of War (James Barbour), who knows the young man. Expresses a wish, not to "have any interview with the President," but to see Clay and Barbour before his "Son's *Dismissal*, should that *probably* be the issue of the Deliberations on his case." ALS. DNA, RG77, Letters Received, 1826–1837, serial no. M-223. Endorsed (AEI) by Clay on cover: "Submitted to the Secy of War   HC."

From ROBERT SPEIR, New York. Requests Clay's intercession with the President, for a special permit to allow discharging and reloading of a cargo of pork, flour, corn, bread, and tobacco carried by a British vessel chartered under contract "with Messrs. William & Henry Thomas of St. Johns Newfoundland," prior to knowledge of the proclamation of March 17 (cf. above, Clay to Vaughan, March 17, 1827). LS. DNA, RG59, Misc. Letters (M179, R65). Certified copies of related documents accompany the letter. Wrapper endorsed by Clay: "To be submitted to the President   HC." Cf. below, Clay to Speir, March 30, 1827. Speir has not been further identified.

JOHN THAW, Washington City, mentions that he has recently left college and solicits employment. ALS. DNA, RG59, A. and R. (M531, R8). Thaw, not further identified, received no appointment.

Check to Daniel Brent

24 March 1827.

Pay to D. Brent or order Fifty seven dollars & 8 Cents.
Cashr. of the Off. of B. U. S Washn.[1]   H CLAY

    ADS. DLC-TJC (DNA, M212, R16). See above, Bill, March 12, 1827.
    [1] Richard Smith.

To Elisha Whittlesey

Dear Sir: Washington, 24th March, 1827.
    I am glad to perceive, by your letter of the 13th instant, that you have safely reached home. When I go to Kentucky this Spring,[1] it will be quite convenient for me to pass by Pittsburg [sic]; and if I should become satisfied that my visit to that place will not be unacceptable to any considerable portion of the inhabitants, I shall very probably stop there.[2]
    I am very glad to be able to tell you that late accounts, which I have received from Albany, assure me that our friends in New York, have resolved, at length, to bestir themselves on the Presidential question, and that no doubt is entertained of a favorable result.[3]
    I am, with great regard, faithfully, Your obedient servant,
Hon. E. Whittlesey.   H CLAY

    LS. OClWHi.   [1] See below, Clay to Erwin, June 3, 1827.
[2] Cf. above, Pentland to Clay, February 18, 1827; below, Clay to Shaler and Mountain, June 19, 1827; Speech, June 20, 1827.   [3] Cf. above, Van Rensselaer to Clay, March 17, 1827; Clay to Van Rensselaer, March 20, 1827.

From James Madison

Dear Sir   Montpellier [sic] Mar. 24. 1827
    After your kind offer,[1] I make no apology for inclosing another letter which I wish to have the advantage of a conveyance from the Department of State. Its object is to obtain from Mr. Gallatin a small service for our University,[2] and that with as little delay as may be.
    Whilst I was charged with the Department of State, the British doctrine against a neutral trade with belligerent ports shut in peace and opened in war, was examined at some length, and the examination published in a stout pamphlet.[3] I have been applied to by several

friends for a copy, which I could not furnish; nor do I know that they are attainable, unless obsolete copies should remain in the Department. If this be the case, I should be thankful for the means of complying with the applications.

Mrs. Madison joins in offering to Mrs. Clay & yourself assurances of cordial regards & best wishes.   JAMES MADISON
Mr. Clay

ALS. DLC-HC (DNA, M212, R2). Endorsed on verso (AEI) by Daniel Brent: "to be attended to by Mr [Philip R.] fendall. I have given directions for procuring copies of the pamphlet of which we have none in the Office. D B."
¹ Not found. Cf. above, Clay to Brooke, August 28, 1826; Clay to Southard, September 26, 1826.   ² Albert Gallatin; the University of Virginia. Cf. below, Clay to Madison, April 4, 1827. Letter of transmittal not found.   ³ [James Madison], *An Examination of the British Doctrine Which Subjects to Capture a Neutral Trade Not Open in Time of Peace, Containing a Letter from the Minister Plenipotentiary of the United States, to Lord Mulgrave* . . . [n. p.], 1806), 204 pages. A second edition appeared in the United States and London later in this same year. In 1807 Madison published in Philadelphia *An Examination of the Conduct of Great Britain, Respecting Neutrals*, 72 pages, which also appeared in a second edition in 1808.

From Sylvester S. Southworth

My Dr Sir   Providence R. I. March 24. 1827
In the last note,¹ I had the honor of addressing to you, I took the Liberty to say, when adverting to the thus anticipated political supper, that you would perceive by the papers of the day,² that the supper was one, rather devoted to Mr Clay than to the administration generally, or language to that effect. My opinion thus formed, was based on the assurances of a gentleman who was foremost in the getting up of the supper, and I wrote you accordingly. The papers of the day did not fully sanction my assertion, and hence I deem it necessary to make an explanation. It is true, that from the toasts prepared, the supper, would have appeared, as one got up to promote the interests of the Secretary of State, but as it was afterwards considered inexpedient, to make any distinction between the friends of the administration generally and Mr Clay, they were, upon after consideration, supplied   In consequence of there being persons present at the feast, with whom I hold no intercourse, I did not attend.

It is my intention to visit Philadelphia and Baltimore early in May, and it is probable that I shall visit the city of Washington, when I hope, by my personal appearance to assure you that I am not altogether unworthy of the notice, you have been pleased to take of me. My Visit to Washington, will however depend upon your being there, and may I ask, if it is probable, that I shall at that time find you in the city? Your very faithful Servant and humble friend
                                        SYLVESTER S SOUTHWORTH
                                        Ed. Lit Cadet

ALS. DNA, RG59, Misc. Letters (M179, R65). Addressed to Clay.   [1] Not found.
[2] No reference found.

INSTRUCTIONS AND DISPATCHES   March 24, 1827

To ALBERT GALLATIN, no. 21 States Clay's understanding "that the British Government have been engaged in revising their Commercial [*i.e.*, "criminal"; see Clay's draft and State Department copy] Code, and have proceeded so far as to cause some important documents to be printed at the Government press, explanatory of a proposed Codification of their penal Law, and containing a draught of a new Code"; and that these papers are not for sale, "but for private distribution under the control of Mr. [Robert] Peel." Requests Gallatin to "procure two Copies of these printed papers" for the use of the [State] Department. Adds, in a postscript: "We have the Transactions of the Royal Society complete from the beginning to 1826 inclusive, except 1st. part of volume published for 1821" (cf. above, Lawrence to Clay, December 5, 1826). LS. NHi- Gallatin Papers (MR14). Copy, in DNA, RG59, Dip. Instr., vol. 6, p. 280; ALI draft, in DLC-HC (DNA, M212, R8).

Peel, educated at Christ Church, Oxford, had become a member of the House of Commons in 1809, had been Chief Secretary for Ireland, 1812–1818, and had served as Home Secretary since 1822. He resigned his office briefly in the spring of 1827 but again held the post from the summer of that year until 1830. He was First Lord of the Treasury and Chancellor of the Exchequer from 1834 to 1835 and became Prime Minister from 1841 to 1846.

From J[OHN] M. MACPHERSON, Cartagena. Encloses a published copy of a letter in which (Simón) Bolívar announced "his determination to retire from public life" (cf. above, Watts to Clay, March 14, 1827). States that Bolívar, since returning "from the South," has issued several "extremely oppressive decrees," two of which levy "excessively obnoxious" taxes (cf. below, Bousquet to Clay, May 15, 1827; Nones to Clay, December 31, 1827). Notes, further, that orders have been issued "to lay up all the Ships of War, except two Corvettes," and it has been announced that no money exists to pay arrears of wages or to provide "foreigners in the service . . . with means to leave the Country." Predicts a blockade of the coast "so soon as the news reaches . . . Havana." Informs Clay that Manuel Peoli (Pioli), a Colombian agent, "has been in New York for some time past inlisting [*sic*] Seamen" (cf. above, MacPherson to Clay, June 19, July 3, August 7, 1826), of whom he has sent 39 on one vessel and 48 on another. Adds that "these unfortunate men will now be thrown on shore, without the means of supporting themselves." ALS. DNA, RG59, Cons. Disp., Cartagena, vol. 1 (M-T192, R1). Received April 18.

From JOHN MULLOWNY, Tangier, no. 47. Transmits a translation of "a letter written in arabic," which, with an accompanying letter (a copy of which is also enclosed), was "received through the department of State" (cf. above, Reed to Clay, February 2, 1827). Expresses belief that the purpose of the first-mentioned letter is "to prove" that the writer "is a moor, as the whole is taken from the Koran to excite an exertion for his relief." Urges that this man be freed and sent home. Notes that the Bashaw offers reimbursement for expenses attending transfer of the man to Tangier; advises against accepting this offer; and points out that generosity in this case will be beneficial to the United States and "to unfortunate persons who may fall" into the hands "of subjects belonging to this Empire." Cites the average "price of a young healthy male slave in this empire" as "about $60, male is rather less than female." Requests that "this man" (the subject of this letter) be sent to him, "that he may be restored to his King and family. . . ." Reports that "Our affairs continue on a . . . good understanding with the King [Abd-er-Rahman II]" but complains: "the funds I am allowed I regret to say, will for ever check, and never produce a generous respect from men in general." ALS. *Ibid.*, Tangier, vol. 4 (M-T61, R4). Received June 5. Endorsed (AEI) on verso by Clay: "To be submitted to the President.

"☞The propriety of a purchase of the Slave & of sending him home is respectfully recommended. HC."

The second enclosure mentioned above is a copy of a letter written by An(drew) Marschalk to Thomas B. Reed, at Natchez, October 3, 1826, as follows:

"The inclosed letter in Arabic was written in my presence by a venerable old Slave named Prince, belonging to Mr. Thomas Foster of this County. I have known him about fifteen years, and can bear full testimony to his very correct deportment, he claims to belong to the royal Family of Morocco, and the object of his letter, as he states to me is to make enquiry after his relations and with a hope of rejoining them. I have undertaken to endeavor to forward his letter for him, and therefore beg leave to commit it to your care, with a request that you will lend your aid to the old man's wishes."

In a letter to Marschalk, July 12, 1827, Daniel Brent requested, at the direction of the President, "information . . . on the following points—Viz:

"1st. Would Mr. Foster be willing to sell the Slave, with a view to his return to his native Country? 2d. If so what price would be demanded for him?"

Brent added: "It would be agreeable to the President to receive, also, in connection with the information now asked, any additional information on the subject which you may possess.—" Copy, in DNA, RG59, Dom. Letters, vol. 21, p. 273 (M40, R19).

From J[OEL] R. POINSETT, Mexico (City), no. 80. Reports an insurrection in the State of Durango, which the "General Government" is taking steps to suppress, although "it is scarcely able to bear" the expenses that will be incurred. Notes that "The expedition to Texas is ordered to proceed, although the Government has received information of the insurrection being checked" (see above, Dickson to Clay, January 3, 1827). Comments also on an insurrection in Sonora, where the Yaquis, "agriculturists and an industrious people," have been goaded to resistance by harsh treatment. Observes that "The plans discovered by the folly of Friar Arenas [see above, Sergeant to Clay, January 26, 1827], are now found to have been more extensive than was at first supposed," but that "any attempt in favor of Spain must have proven vain. . . ." LS. DNA, RG59, Dip. Disp., Mexico, vol. 2 (M97, R3). Received April 30.

The Durango insurrection was occasioned by the efforts of an Army unit to force a new election of the provincial assembly a year earlier than the stipulated two-year term. The troops, led by their officers, dissolved the legislature and obliged the governor to convoke a new assembly for the following August; but with the backing of the general Government the regularly constituted authorities restored order. *Annual Register, 1827*, pp. [342]–[344].

MISCELLANEOUS LETTERS   March 24, 1827

To GEORGE JACKSON, "Commissioner on the part of G B under the Conventn. of St. Petg." Informs him of the appointment of Langdon Cheves "to receive . . . the papers and documents" as stipulated in Article 5 of the Convention of November, 1826. Copy. DNA, RG59, Dom. Letters, vol. 21, p. 504 (M40, R19). Cf. above, Clay to Cheves, March 23, 1827.

From NICHOLAS BIDDLE, Philadelphia. Quotes from a letter, of February 14, from Baring Brothers and Company: "The money market is very easy, and all idea of war having ceased English and other European Stocks have resumed their previous position." Notes that "Judge [Jacob] Burnet for the pleasure of whose acquaintance" he is indebted to Clay "left Philada. yesterday having succeeded in the purpose of his visit as there was no difficulty in rectifying the misapprehension of the Agent." Copy. DLC-Nicholas Biddle Papers, Letterbook, p. 252 (DNA, M212, R20). Burnet's mission has not been identified.

From HENRY H. WILLIAMS. Complains of "wrongs and grievances . . . inflicted by authorities of Colombia in the case of brig [sic] Morris and her cargo, this vessel owned by Mr Richard, [sic] H. Douglass of Baltimore and" himself "and registered in May, 1824 at that port . . ." (cf. above, Watts to Clay, January 6, 1826; Anderson to Clay, February 18, April 9, 1826). States that the vessel, carrying cargo owned by Douglass and himself as well as freight transported for Thomas Backus of New York and goods consigned to "Wm. Cosens & Co of Gibraltar" (not further identified), was captured off Cape Trafalgar, May 12, 1825, by a Colombian privateer and brought to Porto Cabello for trial; comments bitterly and in detail on the injustice inflicted by the court, which caused vessel and cargo to be sold for about half their value; and charges that the proceeds of the sale were confiscated by General (José Antonio) Páez. Encloses "notarial copies of the sentences of the courts"; solicits "the interposition of" the United States Government "to obtain indemnification for the value of the brig Morris, . . . and for the decidedly neutral part of her cargo"; and, in a postscript, itemizes the claim for $53,901.00. ALS. DNA, RG84, Venezuela (MR23). Undated; on the approximation of the dating, cf. below, Clay to Watts, March 26, 1827.

APPLICATIONS, RECOMMENDATIONS   March 24, 1827

GEORGE GRAHAM, Washington, recommends the appointment of Fleet Smith, "for many years" a Virginia lawyer, as "Judge of the Orphans Court for this County." ALS. DNA, RG59, A. and R. (M531, R7). Smith, at this time resident and practicing in Washington, received no appointment under the Adams administration but was named a justice of the peace for Washington County in 1834.

CHARLES WHITMAN, Waterford, Maine, solicits appointment as a clerk. ALS. Ibid. (R8). Endorsed on cover by Clay: "Ans—that there is no vacancy." Daniel Brent replied to Whitman (not further identified) on April 2, 1827, in accordance with these instructions. Copy, in DNA, RG59, Dom. Letters, vol. 21, p. 511 (M40, R19).

To Peter Force

[March 25, 1827]

With Mr. Clays Compliments, he sends an article for tomorrows Journal.

[Enclosure][1]

A report having found its way into several papers that an arrangement of the difference on the Colonial question with G. Britain had been made by Mr. Gallatin,[2] we have taken some pains to enquire into the truth of it. We learn that there is no ground whatever for the report, but that, on the contrary, G. Britain perseveres in altogether refusing to treat on that question.[3] There is therefore no prospect whatever of any adjustment of it by Convention—

It is now more than ever a matter of regret that Congress should have adjourned, without passing any new law. The bill which was simultaneously reported by the Committees of the two houses specified the conditions on which this Government was willing to place the trade.[4] They were reasonable and moderate; and contained the smallest amount of privilege with which this Country, with any regard to its interests, could be satisfied. Had that bill passed it would have substantially met the terms of the British act of Parliament of 1825,[5] and been a Legislative proposition to the British Government, which could not have been declined without its being manifest to the whole world that G. Britain is unwilling to place the trade with this Country on the same footing as she has put it with all other nations. It may be asked why cannot the same conditions be thrown into the form of a Convention? The answer is because G. Britain *will not treat*. The Senate by putting aside the bill of its own Committee, and substituting that of Genl. Smith, and then refusing an amendment of the House, which was necessary to give effect to his bill, and called for by the honor and character of this Country, has left the question in a most embarressing [sic] state. Nothing can be done now until Congress at the next Session shall supply the defect of Legislation at the last   The consequence is that one year if not more is lost by the course which the Senate pursued—

AN. DLC-HC (DNA, M212, R2). Addressed by Clay on verso: "Peter Force Esq."
   [1] AD. *Ibid.* Published in Wahington *Daily National Journal*, March 26, 1827.
   [2] The Washington *Daily National Intelligencer*, March 21, 1827, had reported the arrival of Edward Wyer, as bearer of dispatches from Albert Gallatin, supposedly including the ratification of the treaty on the "Ghent Commission" (see above, Clay to Gallatin, March 20, 1827), and noted: "A sensation seems to have been produced in Baltimore and elsewhere, by a rumor that Mr. W. was the bearer of a Treaty negotiated by Mr. Gallatin concerning Colonial intercourse. For this report we believe, there is no foundation."   [3] Cf. above, Gallatin to Clay, January 28, 1827.   [4] Cf. above, Clay to Force, February 25, 1827, and note; Clay to Gallatin, March 20, 1827.   [5] See above, Rush to Secretary of State, March 26, 1825, note; Gallatin to Clay, August 19, 1826.

From Daniel Webster

My Dear Sir   Private & confidential   Philadelphia Mar: 25. '27

I staid [sic] a day in Baltimore, mainly for the purpose of seeing some of our friends; & had the good fortune to fall in with many of them. Indeed some pains were taken to bring them together.

The general state of feeling, there, seems entirely satisfactory. Nobody complains of the measures of Government, & Genl Smith, even, has few or no followers in his crooked path.[1] Still, the state of the *Press*, in that City, is not quite so favorable as might be wished. The Proprietors & Editors of the Public Journals are, generally, well disposed; but they are not willing to *take a side*, & to make their papers political papers. In the mean time, injuries from another quarter begin to act vigorously on the public mind. This requires counteraction; for unremitted efforts, to produce whatever convictions, will, in time, prevail if totally unresisted. You know the grievance of the *Patriot*, about the public printing.[2] That has *neutralized* its Editor,[3] & all the rest were *neutral* before. I have felt it to be necessary to change this *neutrality* of the Patriot into active support; & by the aid of friends measures are in train, which, I hope, may have that result:[4] It is not necessary now to trouble you farther [*sic*], on that head. I think what has been done will be satisfactory & efficient.

I wish I felt as well satisfied with the state of things here. I have now been here three days, & have heard nothing but one continued din of complaint; not at the general measures of Government, but at the disposition of the *offices* which have been recently in the gift of the Executive. I suppose there must be some, of course, who are gratified at the late Custom House appointments here,[5] but upon my honor I have not found one such. Enemies laugh, & friends hang down their heads, whenever the subject is mentioned. Our friend Markley is, I dare say, entirely well qualified for his office, & was probably recommended by a great Country interest: but I doubt whether those recommendations came from any deeper source than mere good nature & good wishes. I doubt whether the recommenders themselves are *gratified*, still more whether any of them are *attached*, by his appointment; while it is too evident that warm & zealous friends here are, some disappointed, & others disgusted. The truth is, that there seems to be a feeling prevalent here, that to be active & prominent in support of the Administration, *is the way to throw one's self out of the chance of promotion, & the sphere of regard.* Those who wish for office, think the policy for them is to hold back, in the ranks of opposition until they shall be offered their price. All gratuitous support of Government, they seem to think a foolish abandonment of their own interes[ts.]

Then, again, as to the state of the Press. I cannot learn that there is any *one* paper in the City, except the Democratic Press, which may fairly be called an Administration Paper. There are many neutrals—many *candid* papers—many whose devotion to good Government carries them so far, that they will, occasionally, admit peices [*sic*] which others have taken the pains to write;—& many others, I suppose possibly, waiting, either for *terms*, or for tokens of what is to ensue, in political affairs.

At the same time, I am persuaded, that a distinct majority of the City is with the administration, and that if there could be a proper spirit infused, and a just degree of *confidence* excited, not only might the City return us a favorable member,[6] but it might act also, *efficiently*, on the State.

In short things here seem to me to be precisely in that state, in which there is every thing to encourage effort, & nothing to be hoped for, without effort.

This I think the truth; tho' I should be glad to write a more cheering letter.

I said something to you about the West point Visitors. Since I came here, I have heard, tho probably it is without foundation, that they have been already appointed, & that the persons, or many of them, are *opposition men*;—so that it would seem our friends cannot even have *feathers*.[7] Do inquire about this. In short, all protection, all proof of regard, all patronage, which can justly be afforded by the Executive Government, must be given to friends; or otherwise it is impossible to give any general or cordial support to the Administration before the people. I speak freely, because you know I speak disinterestedly. I have neither relation, friend, or connexion, for whom I ask any thing. I go solely on the grounds of the common interest of us all.

I have conversed with Gentlemen here about *a public meeting*. They think it hardly practicable, just now. Time must mollify the feeling produced by recent events, before such a meeting would be attended. I have not, however, seen Mr Wharton,[8] but shall meet him today, & learn what he thinks of it.

We had great difficulty, as you know, last year, to prevent the District Atty from being disgraced. He must have gone, *& would have gone*, but for the President's kindness towards him.[9] Yet, I do not believe he would now walk round one square of the City to prevent Genl Jackson from turing [sic] the President out of Office. In the meantime his 700 *ridiculous* Indictments, not only brig [sic] great expense to the Government; but what is much worse, expose it to censure & reproach.[10] Add to this, that the whole influence of the Custom house *has been*, & that much the greater part of it *is likely still to be opposed* to the friends of the Administration, & then we see what the prospect is. In my poor judgment, the general interest of the Country, & the interest of the Administration, alike required that that custom house should be thoroughly reformed. And I think, moreover, that even now, room should be found or *made*, to place there three or four competent, & faithful men. After what the Judges of the Supreme Court felt it their duty to say, on the conduct of the Officers of that Custom house, in the late *Tea case*, I think public opinion would justify, & indeed that it will peremptorily require, some efficient change in the subordinate branches of the establishment.[11]

But I will not weary you further. In hopes of being able to make a

less dolorous Epistle, the next time I write I remain   My Dear Sir,
with true regard Your's   DANL. WEBSTER
Hon Mr Clay

Mar. 26. P.S.   The rumour about the West point appointment[s]
is not, I am told, well founded. Col Prevost[12] is said to be one of the
Board, which is as it ought to be.

I do not know that it would now be important to ask Mr *Walsh*[13] to
be of the number. Mr. Walsh leaves here for Washington tomorrow—
You will of course see him, & I hope will converse with him freely.
Perhaps I may venture to write you again, on this point, before I leave
the City.

ALS. DLC-HC (DNA, M212, R2).
[1] On Samuel Smith's criticism of the administration's response to the closing of the
British West Indies trade, cf. above, Clay to Force, February 25, and note; March 25,
1827.   [2] See above, Williams to Clay, January 3, 1826; Mitchell to Clay, January 16,
1826; Clay to Mitchell, January 17, 1826. The Baltimore *American and Commercial
Daily Advertiser* retained the public printing throughout the Adams administration.
[3] Isaac Munroe.   [4] The *Baltimore Patriot and Mercantile Advertiser* received no
public printing contracts during the Adams administration; but on March 23 Webster
had written to President Adams urging that he personally subscribe to the journal.
"The giving of such a direction," he commented, "would, I think, be a useful thing, and
have a healing tendency." Webster, *Writings and Speeches*, XVI, 149.   [5] Of William
Jones and Philip S. Markley. Cf. above, Peters to Clay, October 24, 1826, note; Clay to
Jones, January 23, 1827; Jones to Clay, January 25, 1827.   [6] On the contest for
representative from the Philadelphia district, see above, Sergeant to Clay, September 28,
1826, note.   [7] As Webster indicates later in this document, his alarm was unjusti-
fied. The West Point Visitors for 1827 included a large majority of administration supporters. Cf. *Senate Docs.*, 20 Cong., 1 Sess., no. 132, pp. 7–10; below, Clay to Webster,
April 14, 1827. The list was publicly announced in Washington *Daily National Intelligencer*, June 16, 1827, when the Board met.   [8] Thomas I. Wharton.   [9] Charles
J. Ingersoll's reappointment as United States attorney for the Eastern District of Pennsylvania had been delayed for several weeks in 1822 pending consideration of adverse
reports. When renewal of the appointment had again been under consideration in 1826,
the Committee on the Judiciary had noted that fresh evidence placed "the chief transaction, . . . [earlier] referred to, in a light more favorable to Mr. Ingersoll," that they accordingly concurred in the report which earlier had supported his appointment, but that
they now found a new charge placed against him, stating that he had received payments
from Conrad Hester (not identified) "for indulgence granted him," when he was under
prosecution as surety for a Philadelphia partnership. After consideration on two separate days, the Senate by vote of 28 to 7 had consented to the reappointment. U. S. Sen.,
Executive Journal, III, 258, 264, 281, 285, 286, 448, 523, 524–25.   [10] Litigation related to the "Tea Cases" carried through the Federal courts to three Supreme Court
decisions in the years 1826 to 1830 and resulted in a loss to the United States of nearly
a million dollars for duties, over a quarter million dollars for the value of the disputed
goods and damages, and attendant legal fees. The Government's concern in the matter
stemmed from the business failure of Edward Thomson, a Philadelphian engaged in
the China trade and father of John R. Thomson, then United States consul at Canton.
Edward Thomson owed heavily for import duties, including those on five ships of tea
which the collector at Philadelphia (John Steele) had certified for entry on Thomson's
general bond, with only the tea as security. The Government's seizure of the tea occasioned suits involving both New York distributors of the merchandise and an insurance
company which claimed prior lien on part of the shipment. *United States vs. 350 Chests
of Tea: Lippincott and others, Claimants*, 25 *U. S. Reports* (12 Wheaton) 486–97; *John
Conard vs. The Atlantic Insurance Company of New York*, 26 *U. S. Reports* (1 Peters)
386–453; *John Conard, Marshal of the Eastern District of Pennsylvania vs. Francis H.
Nicoll*, 29 *U. S. Reports* (4 Peters) 291–310. In April, 1827, following the Government's
defeat in the first of these Supreme Court rulings, the United States attorney (Ingersoll)
ordered *nolle prosequi* actions on each of his indictments for seizure of individual tea
chests. Washington *Daily National Journal*, April 17, 1827. Webster had argued this

case for the claimants before the Supreme Court on March 8, and the decision had been rendered March 15.　　　[11] Commenting upon the fact that the tea chests had been taken from the Government warehouse without a surety bond, purportedly through use of the customs inspector's key delivered up "for another purpose," Justice Bushrod Washington had observed: ". . . that they should be so removed, with the fraudulent connivance, or in consequence of the culpable carelessness of the inspector, or of any other officer of the customs, was a risk which probably did not enter in the contemplation of the legislature [in framing the security requirements]." 25 *U. S. Reports* (12 Wheaton) 491.　　Judge William P. Van Ness, in his decision on the case in the Federal District Court, had been still more caustic: he had asserted that the duty of issuing certificates of importation, under which documentation the tea chests had been transshipped from the port of entry, Philadelphia, to New York, was not understood by all collectors, "for collectors are not always men of sense, as we know by experience." Continuing, he had commented: "For the certificates are evidence of nothing but what is stated on the face of them, and how it could have ever entered the mind of a collector, or any other man, that they had the most remote connection with payment of duties, I am utterly unable to comprehend." *Niles' Weekly Register,* XXX (June 24, 1826), 311, reporting the case of *U. S. of America vs. 350 Chests of Hyson Tea, Marked E. T. Joshua Lippincott & William Lippincott, Claimants.*　　[12] Andrew M. Prevost, a Pennsylvania militia officer who had risen rapidly in rank as a member of a Philadelphia division during the War of 1812.　　[13] Robert Walsh, Jr., who was not included among the Visitors for 1827. He called upon President Adams in Washington on March 31 and discussed "political subjects," including Walsh's advice that "the Government make some federal appointments in Pennsylvania" and specifically his "very urgent" recommendation of Joseph Hopkinson. Adams, *Memoirs,* VII, 251–52.

INSTRUCTIONS AND DISPATCHES　　　　　　　March 25, 1827

From J[OHN] J. APPLETON, Stockholm, no. 13. Comments that the King (Charles XIV) returned from Norway disappointed at his failure to obtain the Storthing's approval for his suggested revisions of the Constitution (cf. above, Appleton to Clay, January 29, February 22, 1827). Encloses a copy of the message by which the King withdrew his proposed changes and a copy of the Storthing's reply to him. Reports the signing, on March 14, of the commercial treaty between Sweden and Prussia (cf. above, Appleton to Clay, November 1, 1826; February 10, 1827); notes that the reference, in the King's speech to the Storthing, to trade with South America (cf. above, Appleton to Clay, February 22, 1827) "induced the Russian Cabinet to demand explanations here, which proved satisfactory." ALS. DNA, RG59, Dip. Disp., Sweden and Norway, vol. 5 (M45, R6).

From Timothy Wiggin

To the Honourable Henry Clay　　Washington
Sir　　　　　　　　　　　　　　　　London March 26 1827
I have just received a letter from our excellent friend Bishop Chase enclosing an order to me,[1] Signed by the Committee of the Trustees of the Ohio Convention,[2] to place in the hands of Messrs. Baring Bros & Co,— to the credit of the Bank of the United States, the proceeds of funds raised here for the Theological Seminary in Ohio.[3] I should have acted upon this order, without delay, if I had not have acted previously, upon advice from the Bishop, (which he informed me would be confirmed by Said Committee) which caused me to instruct my Agent in Philadelphia[4] to pay to the Bank of the United States for the use of the aforesd Committee the full proceeds of drafts on me for

£3500 Sterling. I instructed Said Agent to advise you that he had paid the same as directed and of the amount. Acting under the same advice I purchased United States Bank Shares, which I have Sent to Messrs. Prime Ward King & Co[5] to be transfered [sic] as directed here after. I purchased more shares than the balance due to the seminary will require, and nothing further can be done till I have sold the Stock and have made up the account. As our funds are rising I thought it best to postpone the Sale for a Short time, as I could do so without exposing the Committee to any disappointment by taking the course I did. I trust what I have done and am doing in this matter will be benificial [sic] to the Charity, and as I do the business without charge, economical, also. The Bishop's friends here, many of whom are of the first respectability, are much gratified by a knowledge of the fact that you have rendered important Services to the good cause. I assure you that the friends of the cause here neither diminish in number or [sic] in kind wishes— I take the liberty of inclosing a letter for the Bishop, at whose request I also take the liberty of writing thus to you, and beg you will excuse both, believing me to be most respectfully your faithful & Obt Servt   TIMOTHY WIGGIN.

ALS. DNA, RG59, Accounting Records, Misc. Letters.
[1] Cf. above, Chase to Clay, March 3, 1827.   [2] Of the Protestant Episcopal Church of Ohio.   [3] Kenyon College.   [4] Not identified.   [5] The New York merchant banking firm founded by Nathaniel Prime included as partners, after 1808, Samuel Ward, a native of Rhode Island, reared in New York and trained in the banking house, and after 1824, James Gore King, the third son of Rufus King. Prime retired in 1832, but Ward remained active in the firm until his death in 1839 and King, until the firm failed in 1847. King was also president of the Erie Railroad in 1835, active in the New York Chamber of Commerce (1817–1853), and a member of Congress from 1849 to 1851.

DIPLOMATIC NOTES   March 26, 1827

To CHARLES R. VAUGHAN (1). Acknowledges receipt of Vaughan's note of March 23 (1) and adds: "The President sees, with satisfaction the expression of disapprobation of the proceedings of Mr. Mc.Kenzie, and hopes it will have the effect, of preventing similar irregularities in future." Copy. DNA, RG59, Notes to Foreign Legations, vol. 3, p. 341 (M38, R3). N draft, in CSmH.

To CHARLES R. VAUGHAN (2). Acknowledges receipt of Vaughan's note of March 23 (2). Notes that he has "not yet been able to procure, from the Captain [Ephraim Merchant] of the Pharos, his statement of the transaction." Copy. DNA, RG59, Notes to Foreign Legations, vol. 3, pp. 341–42 (M38, R3). N draft, in CSmH. Cf. above, Vaughan to Clay, May 22, 1826; Blake to Clay, June 7, 1826; Clay to Vaughan, June 15, 1826; Clay to Hodges, June 20, 1826.

INSTRUCTIONS AND DISPATCHES   March 26, 1827

To BEAUFORT T. WATTS, "Chargé d'Affaires to Colombia." Directs him to aid Captain Henry H. Williams, who is going to Colombia to present a claim against that Government (cf. above, Williams to Clay, ca. March 24, 1827). Adds: "I have examined into the justice of his claim, and satisfied myself it cannot be well resisted. Indeed it appears to have been marked by peculiar hardship—" Copy. DNA, RG59, Dip. Instr., vol. 11, p. 281 (M77, R6). Clay wrote also on this date to John G. A. Williamson at La Guaira presenting a similar request concerning this claim. Copy, in DNA, RG59, Cons. Instr., vol. 2, p. 416 (M78, R2).

MISCELLANEOUS LETTERS   March 26, 1827

From LANGDON CHEVES, Washington. Reports dissolution of the joint commission under the St. Petersburg Convention (cf. above, III, 318n, 736n), in accordance with Article 5 of "the Convention of London of the 13th. November 1826" (cf. above, Gallatin to Clay, November 13, 1826); receipt, under authority of Clay's letter of March 23, of documents from the British commissioner (George Jackson), which are listed on "the accompanying Memorandum and Schedule" and "herewith delivered at the Office of State"; and, "in pursuance of . . . Verbal instructions" from Clay, the transfer, "for the use of the new Commission, the Furniture of the late joint Board. . . ." Copy. DNA, RG76, Treaty of Ghent, G. B. 8, folder 4.

From GEORGE JACKSON, Washington. Acknowledges receipt of Clay's letter of March 24 and states that he has, under instructions from his Government, "this day made over to" Langdon Cheves "the papers and documents contained in the annexed schedule." LS. *Ibid.*, G. B. 9, folder 8.

From ROBERT RALSTON, Philadelphia. Transmits a memorial (not found) from "the Philadelphia Chamber of Commerce" to the President "on the subject of establishing a communication from a port or place in the United States across the Isthmus of Panama to the Pacific Ocean." ALS. DNA, RG59, Misc. Letters (M179, R65). Cf. below, Radcliff to Clay, July 16, 1827, note.

APPLICATIONS, RECOMMENDATIONS   March 26, 1827

JOHN ROBERTS, Alexandria, noting that the charter "of this City gives the mayor 'All the powers of a Justice of Peace within the said town' " but that he has no authority to "send an officer, or his warrant one inch over the [city] limits;" requests that the President "send a Commission of Justice of the Peace, for the *County* of Alexandria, to our new Mayor, Thompson [*sic*] F. Mason"; adds that his own experience, just ended, as mayor (of Alexandria) leads him to make this request, of which Mason is uninformed. ALS. DNA, RG59, A. and R. (MR3—not included in M531 series). Endorsed by Clay on cover: "To be submitted to the President   H C."
   Thomson F. Mason, of the old Fairfax County family, was given the recommended appointment as justice of the peace of Alexandria County by recess commission and retained the office until his death, in December, 1838. He was mayor for several terms during that period and at the time of his death was also judge of the criminal court of the District of Columbia.

To James Brown

My Dear Sir   Washington 27h. March 1827
   I receive regularly your obliging favors which I hope you will continue to write, notwithstanding my failure regularly to acknowledge

them. The oppressive extent of my correspondence, public and private, is the cause of my omission, and you can appreciate that and I hope will consider it as forming a sufficient excuse.

A stormy Session of Congress has just close [sic] which like the preceding one was characterized less by attention to the public interests than by arrangements in reference to the coming Presidential election. In the House, the majority of friends to the Administration remained firm. In the Senate towards the close of the Session (owing to a change of a Senator from Delaware[1] and to the perfidy of Saml Smith[2] who was elected and only could have been elected upon the pledge to support the Administration[3]) the majority was less certain. Should McLane of Delaware (as is conjectured) and Bernard and Tyler newly elected Senators from Pennsa and Virginia,[4] all be opposed to the Admon, we shall at the next Session be in the minority in the Senate. But if as is believed Bernard should support us[5] we shall have a small majority. Should we be in the minority in that branch, our situation will be the same in regard to that body as was that of several previous Administrations. In the H. of R. we do not expect to lose the Majority.[6]

Notwithstanding this state of things in the Senate, I entertain no doubts of Mr. Adams's re-election. I think he will obtain the votes of the electoral Colleges of every Western State that supported him in the H. and R. and also that of Indiana.[7] He will also take from Jackson the vote of New Jersey.[8] New York he will *certainly* obtain, possibly with the loss of three or four electoral votes, if the law be not altered.[9] A powerful reaction has taken place in Pennsa. and it is now believed that his prospects of getting the vote of that State are good.[10] Virginia is uncertain, 'though I shall not be surprized if Jackson should obtain the votes of the four Atlantic Southern States.[11] We shall have a warm contest in Kentucky, owing to many of the Relief party (now happily defeated and put down, by a restoration of the Constitution and the old Court) going over to Jackson; but I think we shall succeed in every part of the State.[12] The elections in August next will test the strength of parties.

The Nat. Intellr discloses the machinations of a secret Caucus held here last winter. The developements [sic] of that paper have produced great effect.[13]

The duties of my office continue to be very laborious. I obtained some assistance in additional Clerks at the last Session which will tend to relieve me.[14] Mr. Poinsett negotiated a treaty with Mexico which has been sent back with some modifications proposed by the Senate.[15] That minister has not fulfilled the expectations of his friends. Mr. Gallatin will do nothing in England, except the Slave Convention, which he has negotiated.[16] The Colonial question is unadjusted, and I apprehend is not likely to be shortly settled. The President has issued a proclamation reviving the Laws of 1818 and 1820.[17]

We find that we are able to live on our Salary, leaving the income of my property in Kentucky to operate as a sinking fund of my remaining debt.[18] The beneficial effect of this arrangement has been already sensibly felt. If I should live a few years more, I will be entirely out of debt, not only without parting with any of my property, but with considerable additions to it, since the commencement of my private troubles.[19]

My own health, though not good, has been rather better during the last winter, than it was the preceding. I hope to be able to visit Kentucky in May, and to derive from the journey the customary benefit. Mrs. Clay will not accompany me, but remain here. Her health is not so good, but like her mother[20] she eats heartily and complains of indigestion.

I write to Mrs. Brown[21] to purchase some articles for her Sister for the amount of which I will thank you to draw on me.

I ought to have mentioned that the increased violence of party has produced one of its too usual effects, a certain degree of non-intercourse. Our kinsman Col. Benton[22] no longer visits—nay does not speak to us. With great regard I am Yr's truly   H CLAY
James Brown Esqr.

P.S.   This letter is sent by Sontag, the son of the first wife of Baron de Mareuil,[23] whom I recommend to your kindness, and who will be able to add much that you may wish to hear.   H.C.

ALS. DLC-HC (DNA, M212, R2).
 1 Daniel Rodney, former Governor of Delaware (1814–1817) and Congressman (1822–1823), had filled only briefly the vacancy in the Senate occasioned by the death of Nicholas Van Dyke, May 21, 1826. Rodney, a second cousin of Caesar A. Rodney, had been succeeded on January 23, 1827, by Henry M. Ridgely.   2 See above, Clay to Force, February 25, March 25, 1827.   3 Cf. above, Smith to Clay, June 7, 1826.
 4 Louis McLane; Isaac D. Barnard; John Tyler. McLane had been elected to the United States Senate on January 12 and had resigned from the House of Representatives.
 5 Cf. above, Crowninshield to Clay, March 14, 1827.   6 After the new Congress had assembled, President Adams wrote, December 3, 1827 (Memoirs, VII, 367): "There is a decided majority of both Houses of Congress in opposition to the Administration—a state of things which has never before occurred under the Government of the United States."   7 Adams had carried the votes of Kentucky, Louisiana, Ohio, Illinois, and Missouri in the House of Representatives election of February 9, 1825 (see above, Clay to Brooke, February 10, 1825, note; Washington Daily National Journal, February 10, 1825). In the election of 1828, Jackson carried all these States: Kentucky's 14 electoral votes, by a popular majority of 39,397 to 31,460; Louisiana's 5 votes, by 4,603 to 4,076; Ohio's 16 votes, by 67,597 to 63,396; Illinois' 3 votes, by 9,560 to 4,662; and Missouri's 3 votes, by 8,272 to 3,400. Indiana, which had supported Jackson in 1825, gave 5 votes to him in 1828, by a popular majority of 22,257 to 17,052. Schlesinger, Israel and Hansen (eds.), History of American Presidential Elections, I, [492].   8 New Jersey, which had supported Jackson in 1825, gave Adams 8 electoral votes in 1828, by a popular majority of 23,764 to 21,951.   9 See above, Clay to Brooke, December 11, 1826, note. Cf. also, above, Degrand to Clay, February 8, 1827; Van Rensselaer to Clay, March 17, 1827. Adams had obtained 26 electoral votes in 1824 as opposed to 10 for his three opponents. In 1828 Jackson received 20 to Adams' 16, with a popular majority of 140,763 to 135,413.   10 Cf. above, Degrand to Clay, February 8, 1827; Moore to Clay, February 10, 1827; Pentland to Clay, February 18, 1827; Ingersoll to Clay, March 11, 1827; Markley to Clay, March 11, 1827; Johnson to Clay, March 12, 1827; Crowninshield to Clay, March 14, 1827; Mifflin to Clay, March 22, 1827; below, Lacock to Clay, March 27, 1827; Webster to Clay, April 14, 1827; Sergeant to Clay, April 17, 1827; Mifflin to Clay, April 22, 1827;

Markley to Clay, April 28, 1827; Clay to Adams, June 23, 1827; Cameron to Clay, *ca.*
July 26, 1827; Wharton to Clay, August 3, 1827; Ingersoll to Clay, August 11, 1827;
Sergeant to Clay, September 11, 1827; Johnston to Clay, September 14, 1827; but cf. also,
below, Binns to Clay, April 28, 1827; Carroll to Clay, May 3, 1827; Learned to Clay,
September 27, 1827. Pennsylvania in 1828 gave all 28 electoral votes to Jackson, by a
popular vote of 101,652 to 50,848.   [11] Cf. below, Pleasants to Clay, April 2, 1827;
Caldwell to Clay, August 8, 1827, note. Virginia, the Carolinas, and Georgia gave all their
electors to Jackson in 1828.   [12] Cf. above, III, 902n; Clay to Brown, October 8, 1826.
Kentucky's 14 electoral votes went to Jackson in 1828, by a popular majority of 39,397
to 31,460.   [13] The Washington *Daily National Intelligencer*, as one of a series of
editorials on the subject, carried on March 12, 1827, a long piece denouncing the caucusing of opponents of the administration. While disclaiming in an accompanying footnote any personal knowledge supporting the rumor, the journal asserted: ". . . we state
it as a common report, that a regular weekly Caucus was held, during the last session,
and particularly during the latter part of it, composed of members of the Opposition,
at which time some one of the number presided and another acted as Secretary; that,
when thus formally organized, public questions were there discussed, with reference to
their political expediency, and their bearing on the Presidential election; and that
regular votes were taken, the whole body considering itself bound by the decisions of
the major part of it." Cf. also, editorial in *ibid.*, June 23, 1827; below, Sergeant to Clay,
April 17, 1827, note.   [14] See above, Clay to McLane, January 14, 1826, note.
   [15] On the treaty, see above, Clay to Poinsett, March 12, 1827.   [16] On the convention with Great Britain, see above, Gallatin to Clay, November 13, 1826.   [17] See
above, Clay to Vaughan, March 17, 1827.   [18] Cf. above, Clay to Brown, May 22,
1826.   [19] See above, II, 795, and note.   [20] Susannah Gray (Mrs. Thomas) Hart
(Sr.).   [21] No letter found.   [22] Thomas Hart Benton.   [23] Fortuné de Sontag,
who had arrived in the United States with Mareuil in 1824, in the capacity of an attaché of legation. Mareuil's first wife has not been identified.

To Enoch Lincoln

To His Excellency, Enoch Lincoln,
Governor of Maine, Portland &c.
Sir,   Dept. of State Washington 27 March 1827.
   I have to acknowledge the receipt of the letter, which your Excel-
lency did me the honor to address to me on the 20th. instant, with a
copy of the Report of the joint select Committee of the Senate and
House of Representatives of the State of Maine, enclosed, both of
which I have submitted to the President. The deep interest which is
taken by the State of Maine, in the settlement of our North Eastern
Boundary with Great Britain, is very natural.— And I assure you that
it is a subject, on which the President feels the most lively solicitude.
Mr. Gallatin is charged with, and has actually entered on, a Negotiation concerning it, but which was not brought to a close at the last
dates from him, nor is it probably yet terminated.— At that period,
the prospect was, that there would be no other alternative than that
of referring the difference between the two Governments to arbitration, according to the provisions of the Treaty of Ghent. Much difficulty was experienced even in adjusting certain preliminary points
necessarily connected with the reference, and they have not yet been
finally arranged[1]— When an application was made, during the session
of Congress prior to the last by the Senators of Maine, for Copies of
all the papers in this Department, respecting the disputed boundary,

it was not deemed expedient to furnish Copies of the Reports and Arguments of the Commissioners, the publication of which, it was believed, would be prejudicial. Copies of any surveys, Maps or documentary evidence were offered.[2] The same considerations which then existed, are still believed to be opposed to letting Copies go from this Department, of those reports and arguments. With that exception, copies of any of the other papers returned by the Commissioners will be furnished whenever application is made for them.—

It is stated in the report of the joint select Committee, that "we cannot view the Acts complained of by the British Government as encroachments upon the rights of New Brunswick,[3] or Great Britain, for they relate, and were only intended to relate to the territory within the description of the Treaty"[4]— Although the President might be disposed entirely to coincide in this opinion with the State of Maine, it must not be forgotten that an opposite opinion is entertained by Great Britain with whom we are now treating. If whilst the controversy is unsettled, and, during the progress of a negotiation, each party proceeds to take possession of what he claims to belong to him, as both assert title to the same territory, an immediate collision is unavoidable. The British Government has abstained, according to the assurances given through their Minister here, from the performance of any new Acts which might be construed into an exercise of the rights of Sovereignty, or soil over the disputed territory; and they so abstained, on our representations, and at our instance.[5] Under these circumstances, the President continues to think that it is most advisable that we should practise the like forbearance, as recommended in the letters which I had the honor of addressing to your Excellency on the 4th. January of the last, and the 29th. of January of the present year.[6] This mutual forbearance is believed to be essential to the harmony between the two countries, and may have a favorable tendency in the amicable adjustment of the difference between them.—

It is worthy, also, of consideration that although Maine is most, she is not the only State interested in the settlement of this question.—

Your Excellency may be perfectly persuaded that every effort will be employed to obtain a satisfactory, and as speedy a decision of this matter, as may be practicable. And that not less attention will be paid to it, than has been shewn, on the part of the Executive of the United States in the adjustment of their Boundary in another part of the Union to which you refer, whilst, it is hoped that some unpleasant incidents, which occurred there,[7] may be avoided in the North East.—

I transmit herewith for the consideration of your Excellency an Extract from a despatch of Mr. Gallatin, under date the 30th. October last.[8]— I am with great respect, Yr. Excellency's obedt. Servt.

H CLAY.—

Copy. DNA, RG59, Dom. Letters, vol. 21, pp. 505–506 (M40, R19).
  1 Cf. above, Gallatin to Clay, January 29, 30, 1827; Clay to Gallatin, February 24, 1827.
  2 See above, Holmes and Chandler to Clay, February 1, 1826; Clay to Holmes and Chandler, March 6, 1826.   3 See above, Vaughan to Clay, January 16, 1827.
  4 Of Paris, of 1783.   5 Cf. above, Clay to Addington, March 27, 1825; Addington to Clay, May 23, 1825.   6 The letter of January 4, 1826, was addressed to Albion K. Parris, then Governor of Maine.   7 Cf. above, Lincoln to Clay, March 20, 1827, note; Clay to Poinsett, March 26, 1825; March 15, 1827. Clay apparently alluded to the numerous filibustering incidents on the Louisiana-Texas frontier. See, e.g., Harris Gaylord Warren, *The Sword Was Their Passport, a History of American Filibustering in the Mexican Revolution* (Baton Rouge, La., 1943).   8 Gallatin had written in his letter of October 30, 1826: "Agents had been appointed by the States of Massachusetts and Maine [George W. Coffin and James Irish, respectively], whose operations have since been suspended at the request of the general Government, for purposes connected with the rights of sovereignty and soil of those States to the disputed territory. It would seem, from certain proceedings of the Legislature of New Brunswick, that some of those agents . . . suggested that an amicable arrangement of the boundary might take place, by making the River St. John's the line of division. This suggestion appears to me incautious, and I think that the States ought to be put on their guard on that subject. It must not be forgotten that the chance of an arrangement by compromise is extremely uncertain, and the necessity of resorting to the arbitration very probable. An Umpire, whether he be a King or a Farmer, rarely decides on strict principles of law: he has always a bias to try if possible to split the difference; and, with that bias, he is very apt to consider any previous proposal from either party as a concession that his title was defective, and as justifying a decision on his part that will not displease too much either party, instead of one founded on a strict investigation of the title. It seems indeed that, in any negotiation which may take place for a compromise, any proposition on our part inconsistent with our construction of the treaty, and which would not secure to us all the waters that empty into the St. John's west of the line running North from the source of the St. Croix, would be dangerous. If such proposal, deemed on the whole better than to run the chance of an arbitration, comes from Great Britain, it may then, but, I think, not till then, be taken into consideration." ALS extract, in DNA, RG59, Dip. Disp., Great Britain, vol. 33 (M30, R29).

From Henry Clay, Jr.

Dear father   West Point.[1] March 27th. 1827.

Since I last heard from you[2] Mr & Mrs Smith, with Margaret Ross,[3] have been here: they remained but a day or two, and seemed delighted with the place.   from them I learned that you were well, and that Theodore is going as a bearer of despatches to the Congress of Panama[4]   likewise that it is your intention to visit Kentucky some time in May,[5] but they do not inform me, whether my mother goes with you or not: should you come to the determination of leaving Washington, I should be extremely happy to you see you here; the lakes will then be open, and will afford you a speedy and pleasant route: Worthington will be very little out of your way and by calling, you will gratify James.[6]

I learned from Mr Holley[7] that he goes to Europe in a few months where he will superintend the education of 8 or 10 young men, who will accompagny [sic] him from this country: Were it at my option to go with him, or not I should embrace this occasion of perfecting my education under so learned a man, as he is; with the greatest pleasure; but as it is, I shall remain at West Point, and endeavour to graduate, and enter the army, should there be a prospect of my being able to get a furlough for a year: Although I know very well that the fame of the warrior is far inferior to that of the Statesman; he only acting the secondary execution; still I put down all feelings of ambition, when they are not in accordance with wishes long formed, and upon which I may say with great truth, I have lived.

You will oblige me, by telling me where I may find an explanation of the principles of the banking systems of England and of this country

Give my respects to our friends at Washington and tell my mother that I recieved [sic] her present, which came very opportunely, Y'r affte Son   H. CLAY j'r.

P.S.   I am requested by Mr Carr,[8] a cadet who wishes to travel for the benefit of his health, to inform you that should you have any despatches to send to Caraccas, he will consider it as a favour, if you will permit him, to carry them; but his relation Mr Secretary Barbour must have spoken to you on the subject; and this notice will therefore be unnecessary. H Clay j'r.

ALS. Henry Clay Memorial Foundation, Lexington, Kentucky.
[1] Cf. above, Clay to Porter, October 11, 1826, note.   [2] No letter found.   [3] Mr. and Mrs. Thomas Smith; Margaretta Ross.   [4] Cf. above, Clay to Theodore Wythe Clay, March 15, 1827.   [5] Cf. above, Clay to Whittlesey, March 24, 1827.   [6] Cf. above, Clay to Brown, March 22, 1826.   [7] Horace Holley. Cf. above, Clay to Bradford, February 10, 1827.   [8] Dabney Overton Carr, born in 1802, a nephew of Dabney Carr, had entered the Military Academy from Charlottesville, Virginia, in 1823. He resigned, effective May 31, 1827, without being graduated, after having been involved in the "egg-nog" riots (cf. above, Taliaferro to Clay, March 6, 1827). His relationship to James Barbour has not been found.

From Abner Lacock

Canal line, Spring-dale postoffice Allegheny county
Dear Sir—   27 March 1827

I have spent some months at Harrisburgh [sic] our seat of Government, the past winter, beside visiting the cities of Phia. & Lancaster, and from the observations I have been able to make, I do not believe Penna. should be counted upon as lost at the next Presidential election. The most intelligent & respectable men of all parties are with us; The Governor[1] and every Member of the Penna. administration (except Genl. Bernard[2] lately elected an U S Senator, & with him I did not converse) are decidedly with us. It is true there is a want of political or moral courage among them, a fearfulness of taking responsibility, this curse and bane of *Republics*, that must & I think will be overcome.[3] And recent events that have taken place at Washington will, or I mistake, do much to set us right,— The question of "who shall be our next President?" has assumed a different shape,   It is no longer a question of personal prefference [sic] as to men, but involves the support or overthrow of principles of primary and vital importance to the republic.[4]— This will be the fulcrum upon which the next Election will turn. and I will not believe Penna. will sacrifice her best interests in such a struggle.

Penna. will be the battle ground, the Flanders of the union. Without Penna. Jacksons chance is hopeless, with it very uncertain and doubtful; Thus situated it becomes the advocates of correct principles, with us to exert themselves, & we shall not fail to do it,   It is here we have dificulties [sic] & prejudices to overcome, but I think they are not insuperable.— To many of the Democrats of Penna. the name of Adams is very obnoxious,   the measures however by him adopted & the course of his policy since Pret.[5] has done much to remove those unfriendly feelings.— As it relates to myself, although I thought it a triumph to get Adams in place of Jackson, I had not much confidence in him, more especially as I knew he had prostituted his talents, perhaps to please the Executive, in his celebrated *Don Onis* letter, in which he vindicated & Justified the most flaggrant [sic] violations of the Constitution, &C &C.   and by which he furnish'd a Cudgel to break his own head.[6]— In short without doubting the honesty or talents of the man, I had strong doubts of his prudence, as well as the correctness of his veiws [sic] as to our national policy,   But my doubts are removed as it regards both,   the course of his policy has been essentially republican & truly American, nor has he in a single instance betrayd [sic] the frailties of his temper.— Let us then forget the past, & provide for the future— In Penna. we must have a new political organization,   The basis of which must be the support of Domestic Manufactures, & internal improvements,   To advance this policy the aid of the general Government is indispensable, and we have the administration pledged to this effect. And this in strict accordance with the state administration, & the course of Penna. policy. recommended & pursued.[7]

The object of this letter was not to present these loose hints, but to state my wish that on your Journey to the west you should pass through Pittsh.[8] I ask you to visit that place because I think it will be serviceable in a public point of view,— If I mistake not it has been some years since you were in the place, and its increasing importance as a Manufacturing City will be gratifying, and you will obtain information necessary and useful to the Nation, and not subject to errour & deception like every thing secured second handed. Some will misinterpet [sic] & misconstrue your motives and so they would were you to turn an anchorite & spend the ballance [sic] of your days in the Mammouth cave,[9]— You will meet a friendly and cordial reception in Pittsburgh, you will gratify many friends & I think make some new ones, and soften others.

Should I be so fortunate as to hear of the time of your arrival I shall

have the pleasure of greeting you personally, in the Mean time believe
me Yours &C   A LACOCK
Henry Clay Esqr

ALS. DLC-HC (DNA, M212, R2). Endorsed by Clay (AES) on cover: "{Ansd. 5 Apl.
1827}." Answer not found.
    ¹ John A. Shulze.   ² Isaac D. Barnard.   ³ Cf. above, Crowninshield to Clay,
March 14, 1827.   ⁴ Cf. above, Markley to Clay, March 11, 1827; Johnson to Clay,
March 12, 1827.   ⁵ President.   ⁶ Reference to the exchange of correspondence,
Adams to Luis de Onís, July 23, 1818, and Onís to Adams, August 5, 1818, relating to Jack-
son's invasion of Florida (see above, II, 612n), published in *American State Papers, Foreign
Relations*, IV, 497–99, 504–506. In actuality, President James Monroe had sketched the
argument for Adams' note, but in so doing he had considerably moderated Adams' stand.
Cf. J. M. to [Adams], July 20, 1818 [MHi-Adams Papers, Letters Recd. (MR443)]; Adams,
Memoirs, IV, 108, 111–14.   ⁷ In his inaugural address, upon beginning his second
term, Governor John Andrew Shulze on December 19, 1826, had pointed to Pennsylvania's
mineral resources and commented: "It will be the business of the government to promote these important interests by improving the means of transportation, and opening
a market to the remotest parts of the state." He had also pointed to the "wise and
judicious tariff," which had "given increased activity to . . . infant manufactures, which
already begin to rival, the fabrics of the old world." Reed (ed.), *Pennsylvania Archives*,
Fourth Series, V, 686–87. In his annual message of December 6, 1826 (cf. above, Clay to
Brooke, December 11, 1826, note), Shulze had spoken in greater detail and with enthusiasm of the transportation development underway in Pennsylvania. Reed (ed.),
Pennsylvania Archives, Fourth Series, V, 655–58. For the steps taken to initiate construction of the Pennsylvania Canal, cf. above, Sutherland to Clay, February 13, 1826.
Lacock, himself, as an acting commissioner, had put under contract a segment of the
canal along the Allegheny River, in the western division. See his reports, dated September 14, December 9, 1826, with accompanying documents, in Penna. H. of Reps., *Journal,
1826–1827*, pp. 201–207, 210.   ⁸ See above, Pentland to Clay, February 18, 1827,
notes.   ⁹ Edmonson County, Kentucky, natural phenomenon.

INSTRUCTIONS AND DISPATCHES   March 27, 1827

From JOHN SERGEANT, Mexico, no. 3. Encloses translations of replies received in
response to his notes to (José Mariano) Michelena and (José) Dominguez (cf.
above, Sergeant to Clay, March 21, 1827). Concludes that "the whole matter [of
a meeting of the Congress at Tacubaya] is as much at large as" when he last wrote
Clay. Notes a belief that the Mexican Congress has not considered the treaties;
the presence still of only two Ministers (from other nations—Pedro Gual; Antonio
Larrazábal); the lack of information on the matter from other States; and the
expectation of the Colombian Minister that dispatches from his Government
would reach him soon. Reports hearing of a revolution in Peru against (Simón)
Bolívar and of the expectation of one in Bolivia (cf. above, Tudor to Clay, February 3, 1827). Expresses a wish to know the President's opinion as to what he
should do under existing circumstances. ALS. DNA, RG43, First Panama Congress (M662, R1). Received April 30.
    In reply to Sergeant's inquiry, Michelena stated his understanding that the
meeting at Tacubaya would "take place as soon as the Plenipotentiaries who assembled at the Isthmus . . . [should] arrive here with the treaties ratified by their
respective Governments." Dominguez concurred in this view.

MISCELLANEOUS LETTERS   March 27, 1827

To JOHN W. SMITH, "Atty. of the U. S. for the Eastern District of Louisiana."
Transmits a copy of a letter, forwarded by (Joel R.) Poinsett (above, February 7,
1827), "complaining of the conduct of citizens of the United States," and states

that the President directs him to "investigate the complaint brought forward in that letter; and, if any citizens of the United States shall be found . . . to have committed any infractions of the public law, or of the particular laws of the United States by entering the territories of the Mexican Republic, and then committing the irregularities complained of, or others, . . . to institute the proper prosecution to bring the offenders to justice." Copy. DNA, RG59, Dom. Letters, vol. 21, pp. 504–505 (M40, R19).

Smith, appointed clerk of Orleans in 1805 and of the First Superior Court District of Louisiana Territory in 1807, was a Federal attorney in the State from 1811 to 1829.

From JAMES WILLIAMSON, Frederick, Maryland. States that British forces in 1813 took from his house property valued at $155.68 and that he has learned that "the British have or are about to remerate [sic] those," who suffered losses in this manner. Requests Clay to tell him "how to proceed in the above business. . . ." ALS. DNA, RG76, Misc. Claims, Great Britain, 1814–1866, env. I, folder 25.

Daniel Brent acknowledged, on April 4, 1827, by direction of "the Secretary," receipt of Williamson's letter of the "24th. [sic] of March," stated that the Department was "entirely uninformed of the course" that he "should adopt," and that the Board of Commissioners (under the Convention of November 13, 1826) to assemble in July, would determine the validity of his claim. Copy, in DNA, RG59, Dom. Letters, vol. 21, p. 512 (M40, R19).

Letters from Williamson to Clay, dated April 28, May 21, August 6, 24, and October 24, 1827, located in the same documentary source and here omitted by the editors, present routine inquiries on the progress of the claim. On August 28, 1827, Brent informed Williamson that his correspondence had been referred to James Ord, clerk of the Board of Commissioners, for answer. Copy, in DNA, RG59, Dom. Letters, vol. 22, pp. 39–40 (M40, R20).

During the early years of the century, at least as late as 1809, Williamson had resided at Annapolis. He was living in 1827 at Woodvale Academy, not further identified, near Frederick.

From Charles Hammond

My Dear Sir.   Cincinnati March 28. 1827

I had thought that in political affairs I could be surprised at nothing. But the events of the last four months have filled me with both surprise and sorrow— The combination which has been formed against the administration, the parties that compose it, its principle of action, and the men who seem prepared to unite with it, taken all together, present an Extraordinary spectacle— And one well calculated to excite alarm for our future destiny as a people—

Certainly nothing is more obvious than that the principle, upon which this opposition array themselves is one, which must always be in operation— If the Supporters of one or more disappointed candidates for the Presidency may rightfully regard the defeat of their favorite, an injury, to be avenged upon the successful candidate as the perpetrator of that injury, we may bid farewell to all considerations of the public good— And whether Jackson or Calhoun, Crawford or Van Buren[1] be the offended party, or whether all have their greiveances [sic], the result must be the Same: an organization to perplex degrade and demolish. The discordent [*sic*] materials which it has been found practicable to combine and unite, in this instance, were assuredly as uncongenial as any that may hereafter exist. Success now, gives good hopes of success at any future time.

The means too are of easy access— It is but to resolve, as Burke said, that no circle shall be drawn around us by our morals,[2] and we are prepared for the work— This is common ground, upon which Duff Green can meet Martin Van Buren as an equal—. Kremer[3] can shake hands with Louis McLane, and Penn and Rowan again act in concert.[4] The basest and the best are upon equal terms, and may be equally useful in a society where it is a maxim with all, that the end justifies the means.

To me it is not the least ground of sorrow that this description of organization should have originated amongst the Senators of the Union; and that most of my old federal friends are parties in it. When Mr Ridgely of Delaware[5] can assort himself with Duff Green, God help us— I begin to distrust even myself and am almost ready to despair. not only of the Republic, but of every thing

I do not perceive that any strong impression is made in this quarter by the events of the last Congress— The adherents of Jackson here, are most of them possessed with the spirit of the antient Jews, on the subject of the Messiah. They would cling to Jackson, though warned against it, by one who arose from the dead— So far as any impression is visible it is against the opposition— But the warfare of the press is so incessant and so heated that should changes take place they would not be loudly expressed— Great confidence in the success of Gen. Jackson is asserted and reiterated, and by men too whose opinions are calculated to deceive— For instance Gen Cadwallader,[6] with strong expressions of personal regard for yourself, and an avowed confidence in the administration, yet travelling from Philadelphia to Nashville & back, speaks confidently that Jackson is certain—

The efforts made, in the West, to misrepresent the woollen bill[7] show how many are ready to abandon their former professions of principle, in favour of the Hero— This is a ticklish subject in Ohio, and is touched only by those whose violence prostrates all discretion— We see however, that in Kentucky it is boldly laid hold of by Kendal [*sic*] and by Penn, as well as by Moore & Wickliffe[8]— And there it is that the battle must be fought— Every thing depends upon the result, and no means should be left unessayed to secure a successful issue— I fear too much confidence more than any thing else. Nothing should be considered safe—indeed nothing is safe where men like those to be encountered have so much at stake— If your presence can do good you should be there; The denunciations already uttered in reference to such an event show how the opposition feel[9]— They are intended to intimidate, and will be continued and encreased, whether you remain at Washington or visit Kentucky— You can do nothing to encrease, nothing to abate the virulence against you. It is uttered not because it is believed but because it is deemed indispensible [*sic*] to success—

I was to say something to you on the subject of the Vice Presidency[10]— My opinion is that you should be the candidate— With me, one strong reason for this is a reference to future contingencies— I do not like the succession from the State department to the Presidency[11] and I wish it broken— I feel now, as strong as heretofore, the objections to looking to the heads of departments, for persons to fill the two principal offices— Heretofore we agreed upon the many inconveniences dangers and mischiefs resulting from such a state of things[12]— In my mind they are as numerous as Ever. We have no other Western man, whom we can run for Vice President, either with reputation or advantage— Whatever may be objected against you may be more strongly objected against others, I speak in reference to public measures— Much can be urged in your favour, that can be truly said of no one else—general knowledge of public affairs, capacity to preside— and qualification to discharge the duties of the first office, if cast upon the second officer. Intrepidity and perseverance— once these were but common virtues— Now they are rare— And for this reason— We have no political barometer of unerring certainty— It is difficult to decide which side is strongest, and politicians are politic—seeking to scud with the wind, and veering to obtain sea room should a tack be necessary, to their own success—

It comports with those traits of character I have just hinted at, to cast yourself upon the people, before whom you have been so vilely accused— It is asking a trial by those who are most concerned, directly in your own case—not indirectly in the character of the whole administration— It is the President and Secretary that are denounced, for their unholy and corrupt coalition—the President and Secretary Mr Adams and Mr Clay put themselves and their conduct upon the good sense and just interpretation of the people, ask their candid judgment, and avow their readiness to acquesce [*sic*] in the decision.

Combination in the South & South West must be met by concert and combination between the East and the West. Confidence must be encreased between them— No room should be left for jealousy, that either would abandon the other. What mean of confidence or bond of union so strong, as the connection of the two principal men in the near relation of candidates before the people for the first and second offices. Theologians admit, nay teach that omnipotence acts by appropriate means   Men, no matter what their stations or pretensions, must do the same thing— And their means must be adapted to the exigencies that surround them.

I am not to be asked, who, in the event of your success, is to take the station you occupy?— The occasion cannot fail to call forth the man— My opinion is that we could get along very well if Mr. Adams and Mr. Clay & Gen. Jackson, Mr Calhoun & Mat. Van Buren to boot, were all in heaven— It is one thing to determine who should be run for Vice President, the organization of a cabinet is quite another affair and belongs to another period time [sic],

I send this by Dr Drake,[13] who, excepting that in one thing he is much like yourself, a little too sanguine, can give you general information of matters and things. I shall therefore say nothing of weather or trade or business, steam boats or canals— But I have a few words to say upon another subject which I had almost forgotten—.

Does the administration consider that its continuance depends upon so frail a tenure, as retaining a covert enemy in its vitals? Does the concealment of a cancer render its corrodings less fatal? or do you really believe that the great engine of the Post office is no worse than neutral, where the associates and bosom friends of its head[14] have declared there shall be no neutrals? I have not been a successful politician myself, and therefore, it is a fair subject of debate, how far my notions of policy may be worth any thing— It is my opinion that the time has come when the head of the Post-office should possess the cordial confidence of the administration, and should cooperate with them— That throughout the country, the tribe of deputies should be made understand that it was no part of their duty to denounce the chief officers of the Executive government, and that if such were their propensities and they indulged them, they should be indulged in another service— I may be wrong, but I think it would be in the performance of duty, for the President to say to the P. M general, as your opinions and feelings are not with us, but with those who have proclaimed us the enemies of the country, and have combined to put us down, you could pursue the bent of your inclinations more honorably, and without distrust or suspicion in private pursuits— You are suspected, and this is grieveous [sic] to an honorable man— But I need not enlarge— Remember I want no office and will have none— Vacancies therefore concern me not—

I am glad Mr Dunlevy[15] was appointed to examine land offices— He is a faithful and a decided man—more concerned for the public than for himself— His son, the Editor at Lebanon,[16] tho a little more cautious is equally unyielding—.

Make my affectionate respects to Mrs. Clay— My acquaintance with her is slight, but I always think of her as a friend— Sincerely Yours
C. HAMMOND

ALS. DLC-HC (DNA, M212, R2).
1 Andrew Jackson; John C. Calhoun; William H. Crawford; Martin Van Buren.
2 "Man acts from adequate motives relative to his interest; and not on metaphysical speculations. Aristotle, the great master of reasoning, cautions us, and with great weight and propriety, against this species of delusive geometrical accuracy in moral arguments,

as the most fallacious of all sophistry." Edmund Burke, *Speech . . . on Moving His Reso-lutions for Conciliation with the Colonies, March 22, 1775* (2d. edn.; London, 1775), 86.
    [3] George Kremer.   [4] Shadrach Penn and John Rowan, both former Federalists, had divided in their views on the old Court-new Court controversy (see above, III, 902n.).
    [5] Henry M. Ridgely. Probably Hammond alludes to the voting in the Senate on March 2, 1827, when Duff Green had received a plurality endorsement as printer for the Senate the following Congress; but the only roll call published in this connection was on the question of terminating further balloting, when Green had failed to attain the required majority. Ridgely had then voted with the Jacksonites to close the balloting. When the next Congress met, on December 4, 1827, a resolution was adopted that restored the requirement for election to the one having "the greatest number of votes" and designated Green as the winner. Ridgely again voted with the Jacksonite majority. *Register of Debates,* 19 Cong., 2 Sess., pp. 498–99; 20 Cong., 1 Sess., p. 3.   [6] Thomas Cadwalader.
    [7] See above, Pleasants to Clay, February 14, 1827.   [8] On March 14, 1827, the Frankfort *Argus of Western America,* edited by Amos Kendall, had defended Jacksonian opposition to the bill on the ground that the tariff would protect the manufacture of woolen cloth but not the production of wool. Three days later, Penn's journal, the *Louisville Weekly Public Advertiser,* expressed satisfaction at the defeat of the bill, which it described as designed "to make nabobs of the persons concerned in a few northern manufacturing associations, at the expense of all other classes of society. . . ." The latter journal on the same date, March 17, 1827, had published letters by T. P. Moore, "To the Citizens of the Seventh Congressional District," dated February 16, 1827, and by C(harles) A. Wickliffe, "To the Citizens of Nelson, Bullitt, Jefferson, and Oldham Counties," dated February 27, 1827. Both the latter documents had attacked the woolens bill.   [9] Another article in the *Louisville Weekly Public Advertiser* of March 17, 1827, had dismissed the idea that Clay could change the political views of the Kentucky electorate and advised him "to remain at Washington, and attend more strictly to the duties of his station." The journalist had attributed the loss of the British West India trade to Clay's failure "to furnish Mr. Rufus King with the necessary instructions to open a negotiation on that subject, on his arrival at London." Cf. above, Clay to King, May 10, 1825; King to Clay, February 13, March 29, April 11, 1826.   [10] Cf. above, Clay to Hammond, December 23, 1826; Hammond to Clay, January 3, 1827.   [11] Each President since 1809 had served as Secretary of State under his predecessor.   [12] No statement found.   [13] Daniel Drake. Cf. below, Clay to Everett, April 13, 1827.
    [14] John McLean. Criticisms of McLean's role in the administration had been mounting since the episode involving the appointment of Henry Lee (see above, Allen to Clay, September 18, 1825, note; Jabez Hammond to Clay, March 16, 1826; Binns to Clay, April 21, 1826; McGiffin to Clay, February 19, 1827). In May, 1827, Adams noted the currency of an "opinion" that McLean was hostile to the administration but that the latter "very earnestly" repudiated it. As Adams viewed the problem: "His [McLean's] conduct is ambiguous, and he is much devoted to Mr. Calhoun, bearing also no friendship to Mr. Clay. This position and these feelings have prompted him to acts adverse in their effects to the Administration, and give countenance to the prevailing opinion of his hostility to it. As he is an able and efficient officer, I have made every allowance for the peculiarity of his situation, and have not believed him wilfully treacherous." *Memoirs,* VII, 275. By October, 1827, Adams recognized that McLean's use of the immense patronage of his office had been "so managed as to conciliate to himself all the opposition party, while every other member of the Administration . . . [had] been the object of the most violent and outrageous abuse." Such "exemption from persecution," many believed, had been won for McLean "by a system of duplicity in his conduct, and by favoring so far as has been in his power, the views of the opposition." While Adams remained "slow to believe this," he concluded: "His [McLean's] friendship is suspicious; his war is in disguise." *Memoirs,* VII, 343.   [15] Francis Dunlavy. Cf. above, Hammond to Clay, November 26, 1826, note.   [16] Anthony Howard Dunlevy.

From Hezekiah Niles

Sir,   Baltimore March 28. 1827.

    I enclose the bill & bill of lading for the last volume of the Register,[1] sent to the Department. Please to direct that the usual check be forwarded to me.

    It is with great pleasure I believe that the "American system" will

be sustained by new acquisitions of strength, against the recent converts in opposition.[2] Delaware, I think, will be fully with us, on the great question, and I have much hope of Pennsylvania.[3] Yours very respectfully
                                                                          H NILES

ALS. DNA, RG59, Accounting Records, Misc. Letters. Addressed to Clay.
[1] Volume 31, September 2, 1826–February 24, 1827.   [2] Cf. above, Brooke to Clay, January 31, 1827; Hammond to Clay, March 28, 1827.   [3] The new Senators from Delaware, Henry Moore Ridgely and Louis McLane, were both Federalists and known to hold like views; but their support went to Jackson rather than the administration. See above, Clay to Brown, March 27, 1827; Hammond to Clay, March 28, 1827; Clay to Webster, April 14, 1827; Clay to Everett, May 2, 1827. For reference to the political situation in Pennsylvania, see above, Clay to Brown, March 27, 1827, note.

DIPLOMATIC NOTES   March 28, 1827

To the BARON DE MAREUIL. Acknowledges receipt of Mareuil's note of March 14, "referring to that" of April 16, 1826. States that "After the most respectful and deliberate consideration of the contents of . . . [the] Note last mentioned, the President cannot feel himself authorized to vary the decision" announced to Mareuil in Clay's note of November 9, 1825. Explains that "The general rule is that foreigners are bound to apply to the" courts, if open, for redress of grievances before appealing "to the Government of those tribunals"; that the courts of the United States are open to foreigners and citizens alike; and that, "during the existence of the Florida Law, now repealed [see above, Henry to Clay, April 6, 1825], instances of as great apparent hardship to Citizens of the United States occurred as that which is alleged" in the cases of the *Calypso* and *Revenge*. Notes that owners of these vessels have not exhausted all legal means to obtain redress; that "the degree of actual peril encountered" by these ships would now be difficult to assess; and that the rules applied to the French coasts might not be proper for the "peculiarly perilous" Florida coast. Concludes by stating that the President is willing to receive favorably "the overture made in" Mareuil's note of April 16, 1826. Copy. DNA, RG59, Notes to Foreign Legations, vol. 3, pp. 342–44 (M38, R3). AL draft, in CSmH.

INSTRUCTIONS AND DISPATCHES   March 28, 1827

From J[OEL] R. POINSETT, Mexico (City), no. 81. Transmits "despatches received from Lima," containing "details of the revolution lately effected there by the Colombian troops" (cf. above, Tudor to Clay, February 3, 1827), and "a translation of a declaration published by the Officers of that division of the Colombian Army." Expresses a belief "that [Francisco de Paula] Santander and a large majority of both Houses of Congress [of Colombia]" will object to (Simón) Bolívar's plans and "most probably openly oppose the adoption of the Bolivian Constitution" (cf. above, MacPherson to Clay, October 2, 1826). Notes that Colombia "appears . . . to be preparing a Separation into three parts . . ." (cf. above, Litchfield to Clay, May 22, 1826). States that "There is reason to . . . believe, that the disturbances in Guatemala will soon be . . . terminated" (cf. above, Gonzales to Clay, January 7, 1827; Sergeant to Clay, March 5, 1827; Phillips to Clay, March 22, 1827) and that he has only recently learned of (John) Williams' departure from that country. Encloses "a translation of the Act of Congress [of Mexico] respecting the valuation of cotton goods," which valuation he expects "will be adopted in the new Tariff." Suggests "that the law ought to be published." ALS. DNA, RG59,

Dip. Disp., Mexico, vol. 2 (M97, R3). Extract published in Manning (arr.), *Diplomatic Correspondence . . . Latin-American Nations*, III, 1659. Received June 8. Endorsed by Clay on verso of last page: "To be submitted to the President."

In the enclosed declaration, the officers of the Colombian Army declare their determination "to support at all hazards the Constitution" (of their Republic) and express a feeling of alarm at "the criminal proceedings . . . of General [José Antonio] Paez and of the municipalities of Guayaquil, Quito, Cuenca, Cartagena and others . . ." (cf. above, Litchfield to Clay, May 23, 1826; McPherson to Clay, October 2, 1826; Watts to Clay, October 21, 1826; Tudor to Clay, March 23, 1827; below, Wheelwright to Clay, April 5, 19, 1827; Tudor to Clay, April 25, May 5, 1827).

The enclosed Mexican law, of March 10, 1827, fixed the valuation of cotton goods "at the rate of two reals (25 cents) for the narrow cloths, and three reals (37½ cents) for the wide ones, until the subject shall be definitively settled in the Tariff now before Congress. . . ." This enclosure was endorsed on verso by Clay: "To be published in the Journal & Intellr." Publication not found.

From JOHN SERGEANT, Mexico, "Private." Notes that occurrences in Peru "may have the effect of checking Genl. [Simón] Bolivar in Colombia" but "will not advance the matter of the Congress, nor will it quicken this inconsiderate Government, which suffers the treaties to remain undecided in defiance of the clear obligation to act upon them." Adds that "whatever is calculated to lesson the power of Bolivar, is felt here as a relief." Expresses "despair as to the Congress." ALS. DNA, RG43, First Panama Congress (M662, R1). Received April 30. Cf. above, Sergeant to Clay, March 27, 1827.

MISCELLANEOUS LETTERS   March 28, 1827

To CHRISTOPHER NEALE. Transmits his commission as "Judge of the Orphans Court for the County of Alexandria in the District of Columbia." Copy. DNA, RG59, Dom. Letters, vol. 21, pp. 506–507 (M40, R19). Cf. above, Clay to Neale, September 20, 1826.

Neale acknowledged, March 30, 1827, receipt of the commission. ALS, in DNA, RG59, Acceptances and Order for Comns. (M-T645, R2).

APPLICATIONS, RECOMMENDATIONS   March 28, 1827

WILLIAM L. REANEY, Boston, having learned through Edward Everett of the appointment of (William) Simmons (Jr.) to "the Consulship of Porto Rico" (cf. above, Clay to Simmons, January 24, 1826), solicits some other appointment for himself. ALS. DNA, RG59, A. and R. (M531, R7).

DIPLOMATIC NOTES   March 29, 1827

From JOSÉ SILVESTRE REBELLO. Acknowledges receipt of Clay's note of March 22; declares that the purpose of the exchange of correspondence is not "to ascertain how the seamen in question came on board the . . . Juno"; argues that (James) Biddle transcended his orders, failed to apply to local authorities, and, "by sending his boat twice in the night to demand" the two seamen from the *Juno*, committed "an act clearly forbidden by the Law of Nations"; characterizes the act in this instance "more violent" than that earlier at Puerto Rico, "although at Porto Rico, it appears to have been more scandalous"; and concludes that the satisfaction given by the United States to Spain in the one case leads to hope that "the satisfaction demanded" by Brazil will be forthcoming. ALS, in Portuguese, with AL trans. in State Department file. DNA, RG59, Notes from Brazilian Legation, vol. 1 (M49, R1).

INSTRUCTIONS AND DISPATCHES   March 29, 1827

To ALBERT GALLATIN, no. 23. Refers to Gallatin's "No. 50" (above, January 11, 1827); authorizes him, by authority of the President, to continue to advance funds to (Thomas) Aspinwall, "as far as they may be required for the Relief and Protection of destitute American Seamen, but not for salary, clerk-hire or Office-rent," which are to be paid at the end of the quarter. Encloses "an Extract from the personal instructions to Mr. [Richard] Rush, which were accidentally omitted in those to . . . [Gallatin], upon the subject of Consular accounts. . . ." LS. NHi-Gallatin Papers (MR14). Copy, in DNA, RG59, Dip. Instr., vol. 11, p. 282 (M77, R6); L draft, in DLC-HC (DNA, M212, R8).

The personal instructions (Instructions no. 12) to Gallatin, omitted from these volumes, were dated June 20, 1826. Rush had been Gallatin's predecessor as Minister to Britain.

To ALBERT GALLATIN, no. 24. Encloses a copy of "a letter from John H. Howland and Company" to Clay (above, March 1, 1827) and states with "pleasure . . . that, as far as . . . [Gallatin's] agency may be properly and usefully employed in the case, it would be very agreeable to this Department, that it should be so employed." LS. NHi-Gallatin Papers (MR14). Copy, in DNA, RG59, Dip. Instr., vol. 11, p. 283 (M77, R6); L draft, in DLC-HC (DNA, M212, R8).

On March 30, 1827, Daniel Brent informed Howland of Clay's action and transmitted to him the instructions to Gallatin "under a flying seal." Copy, in DNA, RG59, Dom. Letters, vol. 21, p. 509 (M40, R19). Cf. below, Lawrence to Clay, December 4, 1827, and note.

To JOEL R. POINSETT, Mexico (City), no. 22. Transmits a copy of the letter sent to the attorney of the United States for the Eastern District of Louisiana (above, to Smith, March 27, 1827) and directs Poinsett "to lay before the Mexican Government this new proof of the desire of the United States to maintain unimpaired the friendship and good neighbourhood of the people of the two countries, and to repress any infraction of the public Law—or of the laws of the United States, by irregular and unauthorized incursions into the territories of the Mexican Republic from those of the United States. . . ." LS. DNA, RG84, Mexico (MR17, frames 150–51). Copy, in DNA, RG59, Instr. and Disp., vol. 11, pp. 283–84 (M77, R6); L draft, in DLC-HC (DNA, M212, R8).

From ALBERT GALLATIN, London, no. 63. Acknowledges receipt of Clay's "despatches of 24th ulto. Nos 18 & 19," which he does not have time to answer "by the packet of the 1st of April." Requests "a copy of the draft of a convention respecting maritime rights, which accompanied Mr [John Quincy] Adams's instruction to Mr [Richard] Rush of 28th July 1823, but which is not printed in the *confidential* pamphlet" (cf. above, Clay to Gallatin, June 19, 1826). States that, although (George) Canning has intimated that he would confer with him (Gallatin) "as soon as the ministerial arrangements were completed" (cf. above, Gallatin to Clay, February 22, 1827), there appears to be little reason to expect any change in the feeling of hostility "to the just rights of the United States." Observes: "You will see by the news papers that Mr Canning, has communicated to

Parliament his correspondence with me on the colonial intercourse." Adds that Canning was reported in the papers to have said, "in answer to a question of Mr Hume, that he considered the correspondence as final since he had the last word." Interprets a private note from Canning, claiming not to have been quoted "quite correctly," as not intended to raise expectations of negotiations on colonial trade "but only to intimate that he had not treated it with unbecoming levity." ALS. DNA, RG59, Dip. Disp., Great Britain, vol. 33 (M30, R29). Published in Adams (ed.), *Writings of Gallatin*, II, 370–71.

The correspondence communicated to Parliament had included letters between Gallatin and Canning as cited above, Gallatin to Clay, August 28, September 14, 20, 22, October 27, November 14, 20, December 28, 1826; January 28, 1827. Great Britain, House of Commons, *Sessional Papers, 1826–27*, XXV, [25]–[51].

Joseph Hume, trained as a surgeon, had begun his career in the service of the East India Company. After a decade in various capacities with that firm, he had resigned and begun a political career. He had served a brief term in Parliament as a Tory in 1812, lost his seat, but returned in 1818 under liberal auspices. He remained in the House of Commons as an active leader of reform causes until his death in 1855.

From NATHAN LEVY, St. Thomas. Refers again (cf. above, Levy to Clay, June 14, October 1, 1826) to the difficulties occasioned by the failure to deposit ships papers with this consulate, citing it as a factor increasing his expenses for care of sick seamen, "left behind by their respective Captains, who enters [*sic*] them on their log Book (sometimes) as runaways and . . . when they get to the U S. have other means to account with the Collector for their not being forthcoming according to law"; notes his discovery, by inadvertence, of a schooner "traversing the seas without any legal Pass, Register, or paper whatever as an American under its flag." LS. DNA, RG59, Cons. Disp., St. Thomas, vol. 2 (M-T350, R2). Received April 30.

From J[OHN] M. MACPHERSON, Cartagena. Transmits a copy of a complaint by George Woodbine of the Island of San Andrés, against "Mr. Bossier [J. S. Boissiere] Master of the Schr Argunot belonging to Baltimore." Asserts that, if the statement is correct, Boissierre's conduct "cannot fail to be injurious to our trade on the Indian Coast." ALS. *Ibid.*, Cartagena, vol. 1 (M-T192, R1). Received April 30.

The enclosure describes an incident in which Boissierre participated, with Torquit Bowie, a local judge who had been "legally suspended" from his office, to break up with armed force a called "Meeting of the Inhabitants" of the island. Woodbine and Bowie not further identified.

MISCELLANEOUS LETTERS   March 29, 1827

To ALEXANDER ADAIR. Informs him that his commission as "Marshal of the United States for the Middle District of Florida, has just been forwarded" to Judge (Augustus B.) Woodward of that district, pending filing of the official bond. Copy. DNA, RG59, Dom. Letters, vol. 21, p. 507 (M40, R19). A copy of Clay's letter of transmittal to Judge Woodward, on the same date, is located *ibid*. Cf. above, McKinley To Clay, February 7, 1827, note.

On May 29 Adair replied that he had given bond and had received his commission. ALS, in DNA, RG59, Misc. Letters (M179, R65).

To B. AYMAR AND COMPANY, New York. Acknowledges receipt of their letter of March 23. Replies that the President "is perfectly sensible of the inconvenience resulting from a sudden interruption of an existing trade, without sufficient notice to the persons engaged in it to enable them to accommodate their enterprizes to the new state of the law," but that he "could not direct the modification which is desired, without a violation of the law of the land. . . ." Copy. DNA, RG59, Dom. Letters, vol. 21, pp. 508–09 (M40, R19).

To THOMAS H. FLETCHER, Nashville. Forwards his commission as "Attorney for the United States for the District of West Tennessee." Copy. *Ibid.*, 208 (M40, R19).
    Fletcher's acceptance is dated at Nashville, April 24, 1827. ALS, in DNA, RG59, Acceptances and Orders for Comns. (M-T645, R2).

From JOHN McLEAN. States that "Sometime last spring before the laws were ready for distribution," he informed Clay that the mail had become so bulky and heavy "that to distribute the laws through it, as had been the practice some years past, would be extremely inconvenient and injurious to the public" and "suggested the propriety of his adopting some other plan of distributing them." Notes that Clay later stated "that he should forward in the mail only a few copies of the laws to the United States' officers in each state, and should make arrangements to distribute the balance of them through his own department." ADS. DNA, RG59, Misc. Letters (M179, R65). Endorsed by clerk on cover: ". . . certificate in relation to distribution of Laws."

From SAMUEL L. SOUTHARD, Navy Department. Returns "Copy of the correspondence between Lord Melville and Mr. Gallatin, respecting Joseph Morris, a deserter from the British Brig of War Frolic." LS. *Ibid.* Cf. above, Gallatin to Clay, February 13, 1827.

From James Tallmadge

Sir,   Poughkeepsie March 30th, 1827.
    I have had the honour to receive your kind favour of the 22th. [*sic*] accompanied with your excellent & eloquent address before the Colonization Society[2]—and also four volumes of "The Secret Journals of Congress."[3] I beg you will accept my respectful acknowledgements for this renewed indication of your kindness & good will— The discourse, is a readable paper, containing much useful information; and matter for deep reflection— Such discourses, are of immense benefit to the subject upon which they treat, so vitally important to our country— The Secret Journals form an interesting & curious addition to my library— where both will be preserved, not more for their innate worth, than as a remembrance of him from whom I received them—
    It is with deep solicitude I learn that you feel your public labours, press so heavily upon your constitution— I have some time past feared the pressure of your duties might impare your health, But latterly had believed—& still hope your health will sustain your toils—
    It is appreciated, that great burthens are heaped upon you—while your friends & admirers have been gratifie[d] to discover that the

Principal spoke in an important wheel, has proved adequate to the load— It may be observed however that a little present sacrafie [*sic*], for recreation, will invigorate & promise continued usefulness—

I am with sentiments of respect most Truly yours &c.

Hon:ble. H. Clay—   JAMES TALLMADGE

ALS. DLC-HC (DNA, M212, R2)   [1] Not found.
[2] See above, Speech, January 20, 1827.   [3] Cf. above, Sparks to Clay, March 13, 1827, note.

From Joseph Watson

Sir,   U S Ship Boston Rio de Janeiro 30th March 1827

I trust that the nature of the case herein stated will prove some apology for obtruding affairs of a private nature on your notice, nor should I now presume to encroach upon your valuable time did I know where else to apply.

A young gentleman acting as Midshipman on board this Ship, by the name of John S. Hart who represented himself as being in possession of considerable property and a near relation of yours, imprudently contracted a number of small debts on shore, which could not be left unpaid without affecting the honor and standing of the United States Naval Officers on a foreign station. He exhibited to me a letter from his brother Thos. P. Hart, by which he was authorized to draw upon him for such sums as he might from time to time require. I was induced in consequence to advance him Three hundred Dollars taking his Bill on his brother, which you will perceive by the enclosed notice of protest just received that the Bill has been returned for non payment

Midn. Hart returned to the United States in the Corvette Cyane, which circumstance precludes all explanation from him on the subject. Since our arrival here several persons have called upon me with bills against him which remain to be discharged.

I beg Sir, that you will have the goodness to give me any information in your possession that may lead to a developement [*sic*] of the facts in relation to the Messieurs Harts or their responsibility[1]

Allow me to reiterate my sincere regret that the circumstances of the case have made it necessary for the obtrusion of this affair in the midst of the high and important duties of your Station   I have the honor to be most respectfully Sir, Your Obedt. Servt.

Honble. Henry Clay &c &c &c   JOSEPH WATSON
                                                        Purser U. S. [N.]

ALS. DNA, RG59, Misc. Letters (M179, R65). Watson, born in Massachusetts, had entered the Navy from New York, as acting purser, in 1821. He had been commissioned as purser in 1824 and remained in this service until his death in 1831.
[1] On the consequences to young Hart, cf. below, Key to Clay, August 2, 1827; Clay to Meade, August 4, 1827. Hart was dismissed from the naval service December 31, 1828.

INSTRUCTIONS AND DISPATCHES   March 30, 1827

From J[OHN] M. MACPHERSON, Cartagena. Refers to his "letter of the 28th Inst."
(not found; cf. above, MacPherson to Clay, March 24, 1827); states that he has
learned that General (Simón) Bolívar has no intention of retiring from public
life, despite his proclamation to that effect. Reports that the people of Cartagena
oppose the party led by the Vice President (Francisco de Paula Santander). Names
General (Mariano) Montilla, "a man of accomplished manners," and Admiral
(José) Padilla, "a man of Colour (a sambo) uneducated, but said to possess daring
courage," as men of the most power and influence in Cartagena. Notes that these
leaders "were, at one time, on unfriendly terms" but are "now reconciled and
both devoted to Bolivar." Cites recent rumors that "the public feeling will be
taken on the subject of separation from the general government, and to invite
Bolivar to take the reins into his own hands." Expresses belief that "The union
of Bolivar with [José Antonio] Paez in Venezuella [sic—cf. above, Marks to Clay,
January 8, 1827; Sergeant to Clay, March 5, 1827] has tended to widen the breach
between the Libertador and the Vice-President. . . ." Observes that, in the Colombian Army, "the whole body of privates and Non Commissioned Officers, are
Negroes, Mulates and Indians, and that the Officers, with very very few exceptions,
are also of these different Colours." ALS. DNA, RG59, Cons. Disp., Cartagena,
vol. 1 (M-T192, R1). Received April 30.
    Montilla, born and educated in Caracas, had fought with the Spanish Royal
Guards in Portugal in 1799 but joined in the movement for Venezuelan independence as early as 1810. In 1824 he had been promoted to general of a division. His
differences with Padilla were revived in 1828, when Montilla quelled a popular
uprising by Padilla's supporters in Cartagena. Montilla was finally driven from
Cartagena in 1831 and went into exile at Jamaica. He had spent some time in the
United States during the early years of the Venezuelan revolt from Spain and in
later life represented his homeland as diplomatic representative in various European capitals.

MISCELLANEOUS LETTERS   March 30, 1827

To ROBERT SPEIR, New York. Acknowledges receipt of his letter of March 23 and
adds: "I have presented your application to the President, who regrets very much
his incompetency to comply with it. The sudden stoppage of the direct intercourse with the British West Colonies, in the vessels of the two Countries, by the
operation of the laws which are revived in consequence of the issuing of the
proclamation [cf. above, Clay to Vaughan, March 17, 1827], is productive of inconvenience to those engaged in the trade, which the President would gladly
prevent, if he had the power. But he has no power to dispense with the enforcement of the laws—and is, therefore, compelled to decline giving the permission
requested.—" Copy. DNA, RG59, Dom. Letters, vol. 21, p. 510 (M40, R19). Cf.
above, Clay to B. Aymar and Company, March 29, 1827.

To Richard Cutts

Saturday morning [*ca.* March 31, 1827]
Mr. Clay's Compliments to Mr. Cutts and presents to him Mr.
Chapman, who will deliver this note. Mr. Chapman is the gentleman

whom Mr Clay wishes Mr. Cutts to appoint as a Clerk in his office,[1] and he calls for the purpose of conversation.

Copy, by Ralph L. Ketcham from the original (AN) owned by Charles M. Storey.
[1] Sidney F. Chapman was appointed a clerk in the Second Comptroller's Office of the Treasury Department and held the position from April 1, 1827, through September 30, 1829.

From Thomas Metcalfe

The Honbl. H. Clay
Sir   Forest Retreat[1] 31st March 1827
I herewith inclose Mr. Stewarts letter[2] in behalf of Littleberry Hawkins of Lexington—for the appointment of Indian Agent in the room of Jno H Morton who declines accepting that appt.[3]

I have also received a letter from a particular friend & connexion of mine who has just seated himself in Lexington requesting me to drop you a line in his behalf for the same appointment. He is a worthy man, much oppressed in his pecuniary affairs with a large & interesting family as he travels the down-hill of life. Wm. Shackleford[4] is his name   he is a man of good mind, and considerable reading—though he is not as I suppose a well quallified [sic] accountant— he thinks of relying on his son in law James Hickman[5] for assistance. I could not do otherwise than drop you a line at Mr. Shacklefords request;   If he is thought to be sufficiently quallified, his appointment will give me sincere pleasure—if not, I am contented

As I came through Mason County[6] I was warmly & cordially received by the citizens generally   In Nicholas & Bourbon—or rather in the Millersburg neighborhood—the most extraordinary activity had been used to prejudice the public mind against the Administration. The *Amos*[7] affair &c &c is taken as proof positive, of the hostility of the Administration to the *reorganizers*[8]   They have been actively casting about, for some one to run against me. Judge *John* Trimble—late of the New Court of Appeals has been, as he declares, warmly & earnestly *solicited* to move into this district for my special benefit—he has not yet determined the point; but talks of settling in Millersburg or Carlisle.[9] The oppositionists are much at a loss how to proceed. They complain that the strong men are on my side—even the strongest, or most popular, of the Jackson Men &c   As I expect to be off for Natchez in the course of a week it may be, that by the time of my return some one will be out. If not, it will be because of a conviction on their parts that I can not be beaten—for some of those who are opposed to me are nevertheless good enough to declare publicly, that no man lives, who can beat me. But in making this declaration they honor me over much, for they swear, that a decided majority of the district are for Jackson—and yet they say that if Jackson was in the district, he could himself [*sic*] succeed against me &c— There are others who say that I can & shall be left out.[10] I have visited Millersburg—*eat dinner* —and attended Court at Carlisle; and I am in good spirits, both as it respects the *cause*, and my individual prospects   But I am much at a loss about candidates for the Legislature, in this County

I shall attend the Bourbon County Court next Monday, and endeavor to drop you a line before my departure for Natchez   Yours sincerely & truly   THOS. METCALFE

ALS. DLC-HC (DNA, M212, R2).
[1] Metcalfe's home, built 1817–1820, in Nicholas County, Kentucky.   [2] Not found. Stewart has not been identified.   [3] Neither Hawkins nor Morton received formal appointment.   [4] Shackelford (or Shackleford), of Lincoln County, Kentucky, had married Sabina Metcalf(e), of Bourbon County, in that State, in 1799. The relationship of Sabina to Thomas Metcalfe has not been found. Shackelford did not receive the desired appointment.   [5] Maria Shackelford, the eldest daughter of William, had married James Lewis Hickman, of Frankfort, in September, 1818, at which time her family was residing in Fleming County, Kentucky. Young Hickman, a nephew of Richard Hickman, had fought in the War of 1812 and was from 1825 until around 1847 a merchant and justice of the peace in Lexington, Kentucky. He served briefly in August, 1847, as sheriff of Fayette County but resigned to accept appointment the next month as commissioner for settling estate accounts. Not long thereafter he removed to Todd County, Kentucky, where he died in 1855.   [6] Kentucky.   [7] Cf. above, Clay to Crittenden, December 12, 1826. Amos Kendall had commented bitterly during the early months of 1827 concerning his loss of printing contracts under both the State and Federal governments because of "Mr. Clay's displeasure." See, *e.g.*, Frankfort *Argus of Western America*, January 10, February 21, 1827.   [8] The new Court, or relief, party in Kentucky. Cf. above, Crittenden to Clay, November 25, 1826; Harvie to Clay, January 10, 1827; Clay to Brown, March 27, 1827.   [9] Cf. below, Metcalfe to Clay, April 11, 1827. Trimble had resigned from the "new Court" December 20, 1826.   [10] Metcalfe was re-elected.

INSTRUCTIONS AND DISPATCHES   March 31, 1827

From A[LEXANDER] H. EVERETT, Madrid, no. 73. Transmits a copy of his note of the preceding day to (Manuel Gonzales) Salmón "on the subject of the convention of Indemnities" (cf. above, Everett to Clay, February 13, 1827). Explains that "The matter is still pending in the Council of State" and the delay results from "the universal sluggishness and torpor that pervade all branches of the administration" and from "the neglect of Mr. Salmon. . . ." Reports that rumors of the impending retirement of Salmón are again current and that "The Duke of San Carlos," now on his way home from Paris, will become "Secretary of State" (cf. above, Everett to Clay, September 1, 1826). Suggests that this appointment may "exercise a favorable influence on the question of the acknowledgement of the independence of the [Latin American] Colonies." Notes that, according to information received from "the Bishop of Cervia, Secretary of the [Papal] Embassy here," the "conclusion of Concordats" between Rome and the new American states is imminent but that the matter is being kept secret until negotiations are completed. Adds: "The first effect of these arrangements in America will be to fill the vacant sees through the whole vast extent of the new States", an event that "will be . . . highly favorable to the good order and tranquillity of those countries," though, perhaps, not to the republican form of government. Attributes "the somewhat sudden termination of these negotiations to the influence of [Simón] Bolívar, who probably conceived that an established church will serve to consolidate the new constitution, which it appears to be his intention to introduce in Colombia and Peru." LS. DNA, RG59, Dip. Disp., Spain, vol. 27 (M31, R28). Extract published in Manning (arr.), *Diplomatic Correspondence . . . Latin-American Nations*, III, 2140–41. Received May 18.

The Bishop of Cervia was Ignazio Giovanni Cadolini. Since 1821 the Latin American republics had been endeavoring to establish diplomatic relations with the Vatican. Colombian independence was not formally recognized by the Church until 1835, but Leo XII in 1827 agreed to preconize archbishops for Bogotá and Caracas and four bishops. Jesús María Henao and Gerardo Arrubla, *History of Colombia*, tr. and ed. by J. Fred Rippy (Chapel Hill, 1938), 416–17.

Leo XII, born Annibale della Genga, near Spoleto, Italy, had had a long career as a Papal diplomat before his elevation to the College of Cardinals in 1816 and to the Papacy in September, 1823. His pontificate continued until February 10, 1829.

From ROBERT MONROE HARRISON, Antigua. Expresses disappointment upon learning that Congress adjourned "without passing the bill introduced in both Houses, to regulate our future intercourse with the British Colonies [see above, Clay to Force, February 25, 1827; Clay to Gallatin, March 20, 1827]—leaving the responsibility on the President of either interdicting or permitting the entry of their vessels into our Ports." Notes that he will "be very uncomfortably situated" unless his request "for a temporary appointment to St Barts. should be granted . . ." (cf. above, Harrison to Clay, January 5, September 20, 25, November 23, 1826; January 4, 1827). Requests information concerning the negotiations with Great Britain. ALS. DNA, RG59, Cons. Disp., Antigua vol. 1 (M-T327, R1). Received May 11.

From SAMUEL HODGES, JR., "Cape de Verd. Islands   Villa da Praya, St. Iago." Requests permission to return to the United States on leave of absence. ALS. *Ibid.*, Santiago, vol. 1 (M-T434, R1). Received May 24.

Daniel Brent replied, on May 24, "that the Secretary" grants the permission requested, on condition that leave "not be extended beyond a reasonable length of time. . . ." Copy, in DNA, RG59, Cons. Instr., vol. 2, p. 427 (M78, R2).

MISCELLANEOUS LETTERS   March 31, 1827

To [GEORGE H. HART and JOSEPH R. CHANDLER]. On instructions from Clay, Daniel Brent requests that the State Department be listed as a subscriber to the (Philadelphia) *United States Gazette*. Copy. DNA, RG59, Dom. Letters, vol. 21, p. 510 (M40, R19).

Chandler, born in Kingston, Massachusetts, had moved to Philadelphia about 1815. There he conducted a school until 1826, when he and Hart acquired ownership of the *United States Gazette*. They remained proprietors of that journal, prominent as an organ of Whig views, until 1847. Chandler was also a member of the Philadelphia city council from 1832 to 1848 and of the United States Congress from 1849 to 1855. From 1858 to 1860 he was Minister to the Kingdom of the Two Sicilies. Hart has not been further identified.

From J[OSEPH] BLUNT, New York. States that, having received no answer to a request, of "About the first of January last," for certain documents "to be inserted in the American Annual Register," which is "now in press," he wishes a list of "names of the prominent public officers of the government. . . ." Adds that, "as the Register formerly published by Davis & Force is no longer continued" (cf. above, IV, 671n), he wishes to obtain a copy of the "blue book published by order of the government." ALS. DNA, RG59, Misc. Letters (M179, R65). Endorsed by clerk: "Last Biennial Register."

In reply to this letter Daniel Brent stated, April 3, 1827, that Clay had no recollection of the earlier request and that a copy of the publication was being forwarded. Copy, in DNA, RG59, Dom. Letters, vol. 21, p. 511 (M40, R19).

The *Biennial Register,* issued by the State Department from 1816 to 1859, was commonly known as the "Blue Book." U.S. Supt. of Docs. (comp.), *Checklist of United States Public Documents, 1789–1909* . . . (3d. edn., rev.), 908.

From HEZEKIAH HUNTINGTON, "Attorney's Office, Hartford." Acknowledges receipt of Clay's letter of March 20, with its enclosure; discusses his communications with (John C.) Wright of the House Judiciary Committee; explains that ill health has prevented earlier preparation of his defense; declares the charges against him "utterly *False.* & . . . *Supported only by Perjury*"; gives "assurance that a further Communication will be made, with as little delay as Possible." ALS. DNA, RG59, Misc. Letters (M179, R65).

From CHARLES F. MAYER, Baltimore. Writing "as Counsel for Captain [Henry H.] Williams in relation to the Brig Morris and her Cargo" (cf. above, Williams to Clay, *ca.* March 24, 1827), and "at Capt. William's [*sic*] instance," censures in harsh terms "the tribunals of Colombia" for their treatment of the case; remarks that Clay's "letter commending Capt. William's affairs to Mr. Watt's care [above, March 26, 1827] indicates his "strong feeling in accordance with the sentiments" here "expressed"; informs him, however, that Williams wishes him (Clay) "to specify more pointedly the business which is to engage the attention of Mr. Watts," since in his instruction he does "not particularize the matter as the concern of the Morris & her cargo"; notes that Williams wishes Watts' attention called to "the question whether at the arrival of the vessel in Colombia, . . . after the ratification of the Treaty of the United States with Colombia, tho' before the exchange of Ratifications [cf. above, Clay to Salazar, March 21, 1825], The Treaty did not shield that portion of the Cargo which was condemned as Spanish"; cites "that article of it which applies the principle of 'free ships and free goods' to the property of all nations on board of our vessels who recognize that abstract principle." Argues that Spain acknowledged "that principle as to us . . . by the Treaty of 1795" (the Pinckney Treaty) and solicits Clay's views "on this subject. . . ." Requests Clay's "earliest notice of this communication." ALS. DNA, RG76, Misc. Claims, Colombia.

On April 4, 1827, Daniel Brent replied, that he was directed to say that Clay believed no further instructions to Watts necessary; that in Clay's opinion the treaty with Colombia went into effect upon the exchange of ratifications at Washington; that the Department normally gave "only general Instructions to the Agents of the United States abroad, and . . . [left] very much to their discretion, the selection and choice of arguments." Added that a copy of Mayer's letter was being forwarded to Watts. Copy, in DNA, RG76, Dom. Letters, vol. 21 (M40, R19).

On the same day, sending Watts a copy of the Mayer letter, Brent wrote: "It is the Secretary's wish that you should avail yourself of the observations and suggestions of Mr. Mayer, as far as you may deem useful to procure for Captain Williams the justice which he seeks." Copy, in DNA, RG59, Dip. Instr., vol. 11, p. 284 (M77, R6).

From NATHANIEL WILLIAMS, "Dist. Atty. D. M.," Baltimore. States that John Gooding intends seeing Clay, in Washington, concerning his trial (cf. above, Williams to Clay, May 15, 1826) and "wishes . . . to go to the W. Indies for testimony." ALS. DNA, RG59, Misc. Letters (M179, R65).

From J[OHN] J. CRITTENDEN, Frankfort (Kentucky). Quotes the "postscript to a letter [not found] just received from" Clay: "Have you not forgotten to inform us of your acceptance of the office of Dt. Atty.?" Denies having "received any commission or official notice of . . . appointment" (cf. above, Clay to Crittenden, March 22, 1827); surmises that Clay's "communications on this subject have no doubt miscarried"; and advises that "it should be remedied as soon as possible." Concludes: "The public business requires it, if I may judge from the number of applications that have been made to me as atty." ALS. DNA, RG59, Misc. Letters (M179, R65). Endorsed on cover: "Mr. [Daniel] Brent will see if the Commission is sent to Mr. Crittenden. H C."

To Henry Clay, Jr.

My Dear Son   Washn. 2d. Apl. 1827.

I recd. your letter of the 27h. March and was glad to hear from that, as well as from Mr. Smith, that his party had visited West point. He informed me, and I was rejoiced to hear, that you were contented and happy. My desire is strengthened rather than weakened that you should continue at the point, and prosecute your studies there with assiduity and perseverance. When they are completed, the choice of professions will be before you. You may enter the army if you please, or study the law. Whatever course you pursue, your studies will have been of the greatest advantage and, my life on it, you will when they are completed never regret it. You *hint* at something about joining Mr Holley. My dear Son, I think Mr. Holleys project most quixotic. You will find it will so turn out. It is a scheme to enable Mr. Holley, at other people's expence, to gratify his inclination to pass a few years in Europe. Mr. Holley is not the man that I would commit, in such an enterprize, the care of my son to. But if his plan were good, and if he were the fit person to execute it, I have not the means to enable you to join him. I have promised you, and if I live I will perform it, to let you go to France, after you have remained at West point, to stay some months. It will be at a season of life when you can profit more by the voyage.

I am the more anxious about you, because I have not much hope left about my two older sons.[1] Poor Thomas! he brought tears from me to behold him.[2] He begins to shew, at his early age, the effects of a dissipated life—swollen face &c &c. He *promises*, but there I fear the matter will end. If you too disappoint my anxious hopes a Constitution, never good, and now almost exhausted, would sink beneath the pressure. You bear my name. You are my son, and the hopes of all of us are turned with anxiety upon you.

I expect to go to Kentucky towards the last of next month.[3] Your mother will not accompany me, but remain here. I shall send you some money before I go. It is my wish and present expectation to return by West point, and perhaps bring James with me.

We are about to go into Mrs. Decaturs house,[4] which we have rented. The change will be very agreeable. There is great accommodation in it, and a fine garden.

I should be glad to gratify the wishes of Cadet Carr, but I do not think it likely that we shall have despatches to send to Caraccas [sic].

John[5] is very well, and we all send you our love and best wishes.

H. Clay Junr.   H CLAY

ALS. Henry Clay Memorial Foundation, Lexington, Kentucky.
[1] Theodore Wythe and Thomas Hart Clay.   [2] Cf. above, Johnson to Clay, March 12, 1827.   [3] Cf. below, Clay to Erwin, June 3, 1827.   [4] The rental agreement has not been found. Cf. above, Rental Agreement, October 11, 1825; Mrs. Decatur to Clay, March 30, 1826.   [5] John Morrison Clay.

To Jabez D. Hammond

Dear Sir   (Private & Confidential)   Washn. 2d. Apl. 1827.

I duly recd. your favor of the 22d. Ulto. It is one of the greatest wants of the Administration to have some person conversant in the affairs of N. Y. residing here. We all *know* and *feel* it. And I assure you that it would give me much satisfaction (and I will add the President too, with whom I have freely conversed about you) if the public could be availed of your services in some suitable station at this place. I do not think that you aspire at all too high when you say that you ought not to accept a less important place than that of Auditor. At this time however there are no vacancies. All the Auditors have families, and they either do not possess the inclination or the qualifications for foreign service, with the exception perhaps of one. But the thing shall be borne in mind, and I shall be rejoiced if circumstances at no distant day should admit (as I hope they may) of an arrangement that would bring you to reside here with us. I will give you the first intelligence of any such occurrence. Long before the receipt of your letter I had thought much of you in relation to such an arrangement. And since the receipt of your letter the President has expressed his hope that it may be found practicable to make it.

I have not heard of Porter's arrival at Albany.[1] Nor have I recd. the Muster Roll[2] which you promised. Expecting soon to hear from you I am Cordially Your friend   H. CLAY

J. D. Hammond Esqr

ALS. NjP.
[1] Cf. above, Porter to Clay, February 27, 1827; below, Porter to Clay, April 6, 1827.
[2] Cf. below, Hammond to Clay, April 11, 1827.

To Josiah Stoddard Johnston

Dear Sir   Washn. 2d. Apl. 1827.

I was glad to learn from your letter[1] dated at Wheeling that you had safely advanced so far on your journey. I will attend to your wish about the note to your Speech[2] so far as it is practicable. Since you left us, the City has been very quiet. From Albany our friends write us in a tone of confidence, as to ultimate success, about which I think they can hardly be mistaken.[3] The developements [sic] of the Intellr. have produced great effect in that quarter.[4] And from other parts of Pennsa. than those which you visited our information still runs in a favorable current. They tell this anecdote of Buckhanan [sic]:[5] At a tavern in Harrisburg, where he was electioneering, he remarked that he had heard much of changes from Jackson to Adams, but could see no body that had changed. A member of the Legislature from Mead-ville[6] who was present replied Yes, Sir, here are eleven members of the Legislature, all of whom were the friends of Genl. Jackson and now are the friends of Mr. Adams. And I will tell you why; because the Administration is right and the Opposition has been defeating the best measures. They will nevertheless attempt a Caucus at Harrisburg, and may possibly get up one, to recommend Genl. Jackson,[7] but if they do it will be attended by such circumstances as to deprive it of much effect. A very respectable man from Delaware[8] was with me to-day, who assures me that he entertains no doubt about that State being friendly to the administration.

We frequently see Mrs. Johnston. Her health appears pretty much as usual, but she seems to bear your absence badly. You should return to her as soon as you can.

We have taken Mrs. Decatur's house and move to it next week. I am Cordially Yr's   H. CLAY
The honble J. S. Johnston.

ALS. PHi.
1 Not found. Johnston was apparently en route home after the adjournment of Congress.   2 Probably a reference to Clay's editorial remarks (see above, Clay to Force, February 25, 1827) on Johnston's speech of February 23.   3 Cf. above, Van Rensselaer to Clay, March 17, 1827.   4 Cf. above, Clay to Brown, March 27, 1827, and note; below, Sergeant to Clay, April 17, 1827, note.   5 James Buchanan.
6 Thomas Atkinson, founder and from 1805 to 1831 editor of the Meadville *Crawford Weekly Messenger*. That journal, which since 1822 had been identified as a Jackson organ, was supporting Clay in the spring of 1829. Klein, *Pennsylvania Politics*, 259. The remark here reported by Clay suggests an earlier change of sentiment and apparently different causation for it than is indicated by Klein.   7 Cf. below, Mifflin to Clay, April 4, 1827.   8 Not identified. Cf. above, Niles to Clay, March 28, 1827, note; below, Clay to Webster, May 14, 1827, note.

From Silvius Hoard

Sir   Black Rock Erie County N. Y. April 2d. 1827.
I have, in connection with many others a desire to form a Respect-able Settlement on the Columbia River in our north west Territory, upon condition that the Government will grant such facilities as to render it encouraging to the Settler, and with the view to ascertain what such a settlement might expect from the Government, I have as well on their behalf, as my own, taken the liberty to ask of you the in-

formation whether, there is already any settlement of Americans there, and about how much, if so—whether there is any Military force there to protect them—whether there are any or many Spaniards Settled on that River—whether any Land is given by the Government to Settlers, if so, how much and upon terms [*sic*], and what is the price of Government Land when purchased, and whether individuals are limited as to quantity in their purchase?[1] I have the honor to be Sir Your most obt & very Humble Servant   SILVIUS HOARD
Honorable Henry Clay Secr'y of State Washington City

LS. DNA, RG59, Misc. Letters (M179, R65). Enclosed in a letter of the same date to Jacob [J.] Brown, in which Hoard (not further identified) wrote: "Some years ago I recollect the subject was before Congress, but what was done in relation to it I do not remember, if I ever knew, nor am I certain to what Department I should apply for information, or whether any attention will be paid to an application from one who is wholly unknown at the Department." He asked Brown to deliver to Clay the enclosed letter and added: "An enterprize of this kind would suit me extremely well, and my talent, if I possess any, is peculiarly adapted to such an undertaking." *Ibid.*
   President Monroe in December, 1824, and President Adams in December, 1825, had recommended to Congress that a military post be established "at the mouth of Columbia River, or at some other point in that quarter within our acknowledged limits. . . ." The latter had urged, also, "the equipment of a public ship for the exploration of the whole northwest coast of this continent." Richardson (comp.), *A Compilation of the Messages and Papers of the Presidents,* II, 262, 313. A bill to effect Monroe's recommendation, introduced in the House of Representatives by John Floyd, of Virginia, had passed that body overwhelmingly in December, 1824, and had won considerable support in the Senate, where the bill had been tabled on March 1, 1825, by vote of 25 to 14. Two reports by a select committee of the House, headed by Francis Baylies (cf. above, Gallatin to Clay, November 5, 1826, note) had vigorously supported Adams' proposal in 1826, but no action had resulted. U. S. H. of Reps., *Journal,* 18 Cong., 2 Sess., 78–79; U. S. Sen., *Journal,* 18 Cong., 2 Sess., 222–23; *House Reports,* 19 Cong., 1 Sess., no. 35, p. 213.
   [1] On the fate of Astoria as a trading operation, see above, Clay to King, May 10, 1825, note. Floyd's proposed bill had included sections providing for a land bounty to encourage settlement and for extension of territorial government to the region, without definition of its northern boundary; but both these sections had been rejected by amendment before the measure for establishment of a military post had been adopted in the House of Representatives. *Register of Debates,* 18 Cong., 2 Sess., 38, 44. The limits to Spanish occupation of the area had been defined by the Adams-Onis Treaty (above, Speech, April 3, 1820, note 19).

From James Pleasants

Dear Sir   Goochland 2d April 1827
   I owe you probably an apology for not having written to you earlier on the subject of the appointment conferred on me by the president & Senate of commissioner for settling claims under the late convention with G. Britain.[1] Though long a member of Congress I do not possess much information as to the forms of the offices, and had supposed some notification of the appointment would have been forwarded to me, but think it probable I have been mistaken, & have determined to address this letter to you on the subject. Mr. Barbour[2] had informed a friend of mine in Richmond of the appointment, & I also saw it in a newspaper,[3] & should have written on directly to you announcing my acceptance but for the circumstance above mentioned. Be pleased to present my respects to the president & tell him I accept the office

with pleasure & shall endeavour to be present on the day of meeting prepared to give as close an attendance till we get through with it as circumstances will admit.

The political tempest is raging in this quarter with much violence. If I have not mistaken the characters of the president and yourself, no two men in the Union are better calculated to meet it without fear. There would be no apprehensions I think but for the military feeling in favour of the old General; how far that may operate I cannot tell but I am always afraid where that is in the way. With great respect & friendship Yr. Obt.   JAMES PLEASANTS

ALS. DNA, RG59, Misc. Letters (M179, R65).
1 See above, Clay to Pleasants, March 23, 1827.   2 James Barbour.   3 Possibly the Washington *Daily National Intelligencer*, March 5, 1827.

DIPLOMATIC NOTES   April 2, 1827

From C. D. E. J. BANGEMAN HUYGENS, Washington. Transmits additional information just received from his Government, concerning the *Celia* and her master, as requested by Clay's note of September 8, 1825. ALS, in French with trans. in State Dept. file. DNA, RG59, Notes from Netherlands Legation, vol. 1 (M56, R1). The enclosure describes the vessel—of "153 tons English measurement" built at Bonang, as a brig first named *Bonang*, then altered to a ship named *Betsy*, and in 1821 renamed *Celia*—and her commander, Lloyd, by birth an American.

INSTRUCTIONS AND DISPATCHES   April 2, 1827

From ROBERT MONROE HARRISON, Antigua. Gives further explanation of the transient tax (cf. above, Harrison to Clay, March 22, 1827). ALS. DNA, RG59, Cons. Disp., Antigua, vol. 1 (M-T327, R1).

MISCELLANEOUS LETTERS   April 2, 1827

From NATHAN SARGENT, Cleveland, Ohio. Requests the return to him of letters recommending him "for the appointment of Clerk to the board of Comrs. lately appointed [cf. above, Clay to Cheves, March 23, 1827] to carry into effect the award of the Emperor of Russia. . . ." ALS. DNA, RG59, A. and R. (M531, R7). Endorsed by Clay on cover: "Let the letters be retd. H C." Further endorsed, in strange hand: "Returned 15h. May 1827."

Sargent, born in Putney, Vermont, educated in law, and in 1818 admitted to the New York bar, had practiced in Cahaba, Alabama, from 1818 to 1826, when he had returned to New York. In 1830 he abandoned law and founded the Philadelphia *Commercial Herald* as a National Republican organ. He later was a political journalist for the Philadelphia *United States Gazette* and in 1844 published a campaign biography, *Brief Outline of the Life of Henry Clay.*

From HENRY WHEATON, New York, "Private." Cites his absence, at Albany, as the reason for not informing Clay earlier of his acceptance of the mission to Denmark (cf. above, Clay to Bille, March 18, 1827). Notes that the chief of the "public & private concerns" that detain him from assuming his post immediately "is the preparation of the Reports of the Decisions [of the United States Supreme Court] of the last Term." Expresses a wish to have certain "portions of the correspondence relating to Danish affairs . . . copied into a Book" for his use. Reports conversations with "Mr [Steen Andersen] Billé," who "has put in a plea of *poverty* as to our claims on his Government," adding "that they are living upon borrowed money, of which resource there *must be an end*." Promises to write "an official letter [not found; cf. below, Wheaton to Clay, April 12, 1827] accepting the appointment." ALS. DNA, RG59, Dip. Disp., Denmark, vol. 1B (M41, R3).

Wheaton's last volume of *Reports* covered the term which had ended March 16.

Court Settlement and Memorandum

Fayette Circuit Court Clerks [*sic*]   April 3d. 1827
     [Detailed accounting of the legal costs, amounting to $522.51 ½, in the cases of Henry Clay against Elijah Warner and James M. Pike, attested by Thomas Bodley, clerk of Fayette Circuit Court.]
       Interest on 500$ from 3 Apl. to 12 July 1827 is 3 ms. 7 ds.   7.07
                                             529.57 [*sic*]

[Endorsement] [1]
500. pd. by Warner to Clay 15 July 1827   Cost & interest to this date relinquished and suit vs Pike to be prosecuted by Warner at his expense & for his benefit—   Robt. Scott

     ADS by Bodley, except interest entry in Scott's hand. DLC-TJC (DNA, M212, R16). Cf. above, Scott to Clay, November 21, December 25, 1826 (1), January 13, 1827; Chinn to Clay, December 31, 1826.
     [1] AES by Scott.

From Philander Chase

To The Honle H. Clay
Very Dear Sir.   Boston April 3. 1827.
     you doubtless recollect that the Secy. at War, thro' the papers which was [*sic*] laid before him, promised me the privilege of remuneration ($100 each per ann) for Six Indian Youths of promise should I find such take and educate them in our School in Ohio.[1] I was able to find only four of the partially civilized tribe in which I was providentially interested and accordingly drew on the Secretary for their support as directed.
     As I never came up to the extent of privilege allowed me viz $600 per ann: I was sorry to find as the inclosed will shew my privilege reduced to 200 per ann.[2] This arrangement prevents me (except at my own expense which however I shall not hesitate to suffer) from fulfilling my engagements with the Chiefs of this Tribe The Oneidas[3] who now look to me for this small yet to them most inestimable boon.
     If the Secy. at War knew how this business is situated—how seriously this failure in the expectations justly excited by his kind letter to me will affect these my poor Indian pupils, he would, I am confident grant

me the privilege of retaining the present number (*Four*) this year; and of increasing them to the orinal [*sic*] number promis[ed] at the expiration of the time mentioned in Mr. McKenney [*sic*] Note.

Have the goodness still to address me at Boston. Your Sincere & Faithful Frien[d]   PHIR. CHASE

P.S.   Will you not have the goodness to present the inclosed Acct.[4] & receive & send the avails to my Dear Wife who is in want of money?
                                                                PHIR. CHASE

ALS. DNA, RG59, Misc. Letters (M179, R65).
1 Kenyon College. Cf. above, Barbour to Clay, November 1, 1825.   2 In the enclosed letter to Chase, Thomas L. McKenney, "Department of War, Off: Ind: Affairs 9 Feby. 1827," explained that only $7,000 remained of the annual allocation of $10,000 "for the civilization of the Indians," thus necessitating "a new apportionment," of which Chase's share for the year was $200.   3 Chase had met the chiefs of the scattered remnants of the tribe at Oneida Castle, New York, in September, 1826. He had shortly thereafter also visited a branch of the tribe on the Sandusky River, in Ohio. Chase, *Reminiscences*, II, 524.   4 Not found.

From Samuel Mifflin

Dr Sir   Harrisburg April 3d 1827

I beg a reference, to the enclosed[1]— You no doubt have heard, that Judge Trimble, dismissed the Louisville case, upon the ground, that the proceedings, in the Kentucky State Court, were conclusive[2]— An appeal has been entered, to the Court, at Washington,[3] & I am very desirous of obtaining the papers, from the Office, for the purpose, of submitting them to the inspection of my Counsel, in Phila[4]—

Would it be too much, to ask you, how I can get the papers, out of the office, without paying for the Copy. I have already, expended a large sum, in this matter & if it is consistant [*sic*] with rule I should like to avoid any further disbursement   Very truly your friend & obt. servt   SAML. MIFFLIN
Honorable Henry Clay

ALS. DLC-TJC (DNA, M212, R10).   1 Enclosure not found.
2 A suit had been brought in the Federal Circuit Court, Kentucky District, in February, 1818, by Thomas, James, and Margaret Connolly (Connelly; Conolly), David David, Francis Bodley (or Badley), and Samuel Mifflin against Richard Taylor, Fortunatus Cosby, William Lytle, and Henry Clay, associated with the land transactions presented above, I, 261–62, 306–307, 348–49, 478–79, 495–96, 628, 829. The court in chancery proceedings signed by Robert Trimble on May 29, 1826, had dismissed the complaint but granted an appeal to the United States Supreme Court. U. S. Seventh Circuit Court, Order Book L, 214.   Probably the Richard Taylor here named was a cousin of "Commodore" Richard Taylor and an uncle of "Hopping Dick" Taylor. He was also the father of Zachary Taylor, the twelfth President of the United States. Under act of the Virginia Legislature on October 10, 1785, Richard Taylor had been designated one of the trustees to lay out a town on land seized from the Loyalist John Campbell. Hening (comp.), *Statutes at Large*, XII, ch. 108. As a resident of Jefferson County, Taylor had been a member of the Kentucky constitutional conventions of 1792 and 1799 and of the Kentucky Legislature in 1792.   3 The United States Supreme Court, at the January Term, 1829, accepted jurisdiction of the case and, by divided opinion, affirmed the decree of the Federal Circuit Court. The issue had concerned whether the defendants, in purchasing the lands, were chargeable "with the equity which was attached to it, while in pos-

session of [John] Campbell and his heirs. . . ." More attention was attached to the question of jurisdiction than to the matter in dispute, for Mifflin, a Pennsylvanian, had been joined with aliens against William Lytle, of Ohio, and the Kentuckians in the District Court action. To correct this error violating the terms of section 11 of the Judiciary Act of 1789 (1 *U. S. Stat.*, 78–79) the bill of complaint had been amended in 1821 to drop Mifflin as complainant and add him as defendant. U. S. Seventh Circuit Court, Order Book H, 130. Chief Justice John Marshall, in ruling on the case, elaborated upon the principles by which the jurisdiction was sustained. 27 *U. S.* (2 Peters) 556–65.

⁴ Probably John Sergeant, who was one of the attorneys for the defendants.

From Jonathan Thompson

Sir,   Custom House New York. Collector's Office April 3rd. 1827.—

Enclosed is a bill of lading¹ for two embaled cases by the Schr. Prompt for Washington. The case directed to yourself was received from the wreck of the Ship Lewis from Havre, stranded on the Jersey shore,² and the other marked MC or HC. No. 1. by the Ship Cadmus from Havre—having been forwarded by our Minister Mr. Brown for your Department.³ I am respectfully Your Obt. Servt.

JONATHAN THOMPSON
Collector

Hone. Henry Clay Secretary of State. Washington.

LS. DNA, RG59, Misc. Letters (M179, R65). Endorsed by Clay on cover: "Mr. B[rent]. will please acknowledge the receipt of this letter."
¹ DS by H. Rodbert for John Hennell, also dated April 3, 1827. *Ibid.* Neither Rodbert nor Hennell has been identified.   ² See above, Brown to Clay, January 13, 1827, note.   ³ Cf. above, Brown to Clay, February 12, 1827.

INSTRUCTIONS AND DISPATCHES   April 3, 1827

From J[OHN] J. APPLETON, Stockholm, no. 14. As a postscript to an explanation of his accounts, acknowledges receipt of Clay's letter of January 12 and expresses gratification for "the new proof of confidence which it contains." ALS. DNA, RG59, Dip. Disp., Sweden and Norway, vol. 5 (M45, R6).

From ISAAC ENGLISH, Dublin. States that Thomas Wilson, "having been Gazetted as Consul to [*sic*] the U. States for Dublin, . . . is now acting in that capacity" and that, in closing his own "labours in behalf of the U. States," he has "endeavoured to uphold their interests, faithfully." ALS. DNA, RG59, Cons. Disp., Dublin, vol. 1 (M-T199, R-T1). Cf. above, Maury to Clay, March 29, 1825, note.

From ALBERT GALLATIN, London, no. 64. Reports that [Karl] Sieveking of Hamburg and [Jean Charles Frédéric] Gildemeister of Bremen, on their way to Brazil (cf. above, Wickelhausen to Clay, January 19, 1827), expressed to him "the wish of the Hanse towns to be placed, by treaty or by the acts of Congress, on the same footing as Denmark . . . [see above, Treaty, April 26, 1826], in their intercourse with the United States." Notes that he advised "a direct negotiation at Washington"; that they replied that (Vincent) Rumpff was to be appointed for the purpose; and that they requested transmittal to Clay of "the enclosed verbal notes." Comments "that Mr Sieveking . . . was particularly desirous that the navigation of Denmark should not be more favoured in our ports than that of Hamburg." ALS. DNA, RG59, Dip. Disp., Great Britain, vol. 33 (M30, R29). Received May 13.

From ALBERT GALLATIN, London, no. 65. Reports receipt of a request from Robert Oliver "to call on the British Government for indemnity on account of three schooners and cargoes captured by the British and definitively condemned in the year 1809." Notes that an earlier application by Oliver "to the Treasury" was rejected; that Oliver states that (Rufus) King "had been instructed to support his application [Daniel Brent to King, June 24, 1825, in DNA, RG59, Dip. Instr., vol. 10, p. 372 (M77, R5)], but was not called on for that purpose"; and that he (Gallatin) knows nothing of such instructions. Points out that "this is one of the numerous cases of vessels condemned by the British courts either under illegal decrees or under false pretences, and for which no indemnity was obtained by the treaty of peace" (the Treaty of Ghent). Recalls "that at Ghent, we made a kind of protest for the purpose of preserving the rights of the United States and of their citizens notwithstanding that omission" but expresses doubt that Britain will entertain the claim. Suggests that the administration must "determine whether there are any sufficient reasons to make the demand at this time. . . ." ALS. DNA, RG59, Dip. Disp., Great Britain, vol. 33 (M30, R29).

While accepting changes in their *projet* of a treaty, the American Commissioners at Ghent, in a letter to their British counterparts on November 30, 1814 (cf. above, I, 959, 1001–1002), had specified understanding "that the rights of both Powers on the subject of seamen, and the claims of the citizens and subjects of the two contracting parties to indemnities for losses and damages sustained prior to the commencement of the war, shall not be affected or impaired, by the omission in the treaty of any specific provision with respect to those two subjects." *American State Papers, Foreign Relations*, III, 741.

The claim concerned the schooners *Rapid*, *Fox*, and *Fly* of Baltimore, captured by the British in 1806–1807 en route from Veracruz to Baltimore.

From HENRICH JANSON, "Consul of the United States of America for the Port of Christiansand [Kristiansand] residing at Bergen [Norway]." Transmits, with his annual report on vessels entering the port from the United States, a table of duties on imports. LS. DNA, RG59, Cons. Disp., Bergen, vol. 1 (M-T369, R1). Received May 29.

Janson, a resident of Norway, was United States consul at this port from January, 1822, until December, 1828.

From J[OHN] G. A. WILLIAMSON, La Guaira. Reports more political order and more "security of person & property" in Venezuela since he wrote last. Notes the brief appearance of two American naval vessels at this port; states that there is now "no particular necessity of a vessel of war" there, but repeats that there is need for frequent visits by such vessels; and predicts that the death of (Simón) Bolívar would end the existing quietness and "rouse the sleeping factions." Complains of the practice of ship captains evading the law in discharging seamen, by mistreating them "to induce them to abscond," whereupon they become vagrants or privateers, "or call upon the Consul for support & to be sent home." Expresses a wish for advice on this subject. ALS. DNA, RG59, Cons. Disp., La Guaira, vol. 1 (M84, R1). Extract published in Manning (arr.), *Diplomatic Correspondence . . . Latin-American Nations*, II, 1310–11. Endorsed on cover by Clay: "To be submitted to the President—"

For the basic legislation on "distressed seamen," cf. above, Clay to Quarrier, May 12, 1825. An act of March 3, 1825 (4 *U.S. Stat.*, 117) had provided, further: "That if, any master or commander of any ship or vessel, belonging, in whole, or in part, to any citizen or citizens of the United States, shall, during his being abroad, maliciously, and without justifiable cause, force any officer, or mariner of such ship or vessel, on shore, or leave him behind, in any foreign port or place, or refuse to bring home again, all such of the officers and mariners of such ship or vessel, whom he carried out with him, as are in a condition to return, and willing to return, when he shall be ready to proceed in his homeward voyage, every master or commander, so offending, shall, on conviction thereof, be punished by fine, not exceeding five hundred dollars, or by imprisonment, not exceeding six months. . . ."

MISCELLANEOUS LETTERS   April 3, 1827

From [JOHN GOODING], Baltimore. Notes having been informed by N[athaniel] Williams of the latter's communication to Clay (above, March 31, 1827); contends that, since he agreed to Williams' taking "depositions of two seafaring persons. . . , who were about going beyond Seas," the Government should not object to his (Gooding's) "taking a Commission to the West Indies. . . ." Refers to his interest "in a claim filed in the Department of State by Mr. Cary Seldon [sic] for John Donnell for the value of the Ship Countess of Harcourt, alias Sabine" (claim not found); states that Selden informs him "that the claim was not preferred in time under the Treaty of Ghent"; inquires whether "there will be a Surplus or has not the Commissioners [sic] lately appointed [cf. above, Clay to Cheves, March 23, 1827] the power to admit this claim." ALS. DNA, RG59, Misc. Letters (M179, R65). Signature destroyed; endorsed by clerk on cover: "J. Goodwin [sic]."

Selden, of Virginia, had served for several years as agent employed by his State to settle accounts with the United States.

To James Madison

Mr. Madison
Dear Sir,   Washington 4 April 1827.
I duly received your letter of the 24th. ultimo, transmitting one for Mr. Gallatin, which I have taken pleasure in causing to be forwarded according to your request.—

I have delayed answering your letter for the purpose of endeavoring to procure the Copies you desired of the pamphlet, of which, unfortunately, none remained in the office. Mr. Brent[1] has, however, been able to obtain some, and I now forward, by the same Mail that carries this letter, half a dozen which, I hope, will reach you in safety.—

With the best respects of Mrs. Clay and myself to Mrs. Madison.—
I am faithfully Your Obedt. Servt.   H. CLAY.

Copy. DNA, RG59, Unofficial Letter Book of Henry Clay, 1825–29, p. 12.
[1] Daniel Brent.

To John W. Taylor

Dear Sir   Washn. 4h. Apl. 1827.
I thank you for your obliging favor of the 26h. Ulto.[1] The account you give of the causes which led to Mr. Van Buren's re-election is confirmed by that which I receive from Porter and others.[2] Several friends have written me highly encouraging letters from Albany and

other parts of New York.[3] Col. Young,[4] I understand, is resolved to take a very decided part in support of Mr. Adams.

My information from Western Pennsa.[5] and from Kentucky[6] is very favorable. I shall be disappointed if K. does not return a larger number of friends to the administration in the next Congress than we had in the last.[7] I intend visiting it towards the last of May.[8] I should be glad to see you here, in the mean time, if convenient and you should come as far South as Philadelphia. Could you not write a letter to Judge Clarke[9] (Winchester.K.) giving as encouraging an account of matters in New York as truth warrants? Such letters to different parts of K. between this and August, and which might be published, without names, would have good effect.

I hope this letter will find your health restored. I am with great regard faithfully Yrs   H. CLAY
The Honble John W. Taylor.

ALS. NHi.   [1] Not found.
[2] See above, Porter to Clay, February 27, 1827; Rochester to Clay, January 30, 1827.
   [3] Cf. above, Van Rensselaer to Clay, March 17, 1827.   [4] Samuel Young. Cf. above, Hammond to Clay, March 22, 1827.   [5] Cf. above, Clay to Brown, March 27, 1827, note.   [6] Cf. above, Johnson to Clay, March 12, 1827; below, Clay to Johnston, April 17, 1827.   [7] Almost all the Kentucky delegation to the House of Representatives had supported the administration in the Nineteenth Congress on such a test vote as that for the Panama Mission—the exceptions being Charles A. Wickliffe (not voting) and Joseph Lecompte (opposed). U. S. H. of Reps., *Journal*, 19 Cong., 1 Sess., 462-63. James Johnson had, however, been replaced in 1826 by Robert L. McHatton, a Jackson Democrat. In the Twentieth Congress, besides Lecompte, Wickliffe (now identified with the Jackson forces), and McHatton, there were at least four other Jackson Democrats—Henry Daniel, Chittenden Lyon, Thomas P. Moore, and Joel Yancey. The Senators, Richard M. Johnson and John Rowan, were Jackson supporters in both Congresses.   [8] Cf. below, Clay to Erwin, June 3, 1827.   [9] James Clark.

To John C. Wright

Dear Sir   Washn. 4h. Apl. 1827.
I recd. your favor of the 29h. Ulto.[1] One of the Districts will be retained for Col. Collier[2] for the distribution of the Laws. It will be time enough if he is here by the 20h. or 25h. instant.

I do not think Barbour and myself can conveniently travel together Westwardly. He leaves the City tomorrow for his residence and will not return for about a month, after which I shall begin to think of moving, which will then be too soon for him.[3] I have not yet concluded to go by Pittsburg [sic]. Our news from Albany is good.[4]

I am glad to hear that your health is improving, and sincerely hope it may be completely re-established. Yr's faithfully   H. CLAY
The Honble J.C. Wright.

ALS. DLC-John C. Wright Papers (DNA, M212, R22). Endorsed: ". . . An'd 18 April 1827." Answer not found.
   [1] Not found.   [2] James Collier.   [3] James Barbour left Washington for his home in Virginia on April 5 and was back in Washington by May 1. Clay left for Kentucky on June 11. Barbour spent July 4 at Bedford Springs but again returned a few

days later to Washington. Washington *Daily National Intelligencer*, April 7, 1827;
Adams, *Memoirs*, VII, 265; Washington *Daily National Journal*, June 14, 1827; *Niles'
Weekly Register*, XXXII (July 28, 1827), 358, 366.   4 Cf. above, Van Rensselaer to
Clay, March 17, 1827.

From Mrs. Anne Izard Deas

Sir   Philadelphia April 4th. 1827.
   It is not without some fears of being thought troublesome, & intrusive that I venture to address you. When however, you recollect My
recent misfortune, & that it is now My duty to exert Myself to the utmost, for the benefit of My Children, I hope you will excuse the
liberty I take in soliciting your aid, in a matter of great importance to
me at present.
   My second Son Edward (now in his 16th year) has for near 2 years,
been a candidate for admission at West Point, but in the usual course,
I fear his appointment May yet be long delayed. Several of My friends
have told me, that if you would interest yourself in the matter, there
is no doubt that his Warrant might be obtained immediately.[1] As he
is prepared to enter in June, May I Sir flatter myself that you will have
the goodness to do so, & add one more to the many favors I received
from you, & your family when we were in Kentucky.
   I beg to present My best Compliments to Mrs. Clay, & have the
honor to be Sir with great respect Your obedt. Sert.   A. I. DEAS

   ALS. DNA, RG94, U. S. Military Academy, Cadet Applications, 1827/7. Endorsed by
Clay (AEI) on cover: "Mrs. A I Deas of So. Carolina residing in Philadelphia—Refered
[*sic*] to the favorable consideration of the Secy of War. H. C." Mrs. Deas (cf. above,
Southard to Clay, January 25, 1826), daughter of Ralph Izard, American commissioner
to Tuscany (1776–1779), member of the Continental Congress (1782 and 1783), and
United States Senator (1789–1795), had married William Allen Deas in Charleston,
South Carolina, in 1798. Her husband, who had been secretary to Thomas Pinckney and
acting Chargé d'Affaires in London in 1794 and 1795, had resided in "the western country" in 1821. Adams, *Memoirs*, V, 235. He was in Philadelphia in December, 1826, but
appears from the text of this document to have died shortly thereafter. Cf. John Hammond Moore, "The Deas-Thomson Papers in Australia," *South Carolina Magazine*, LXXI
(1970), 192.
   1 Young Deas was admitted to the United States Military Academy in July, 1828, and
graduated in 1832. He was commissioned a second lieutenant in 1833, first lieutenant in
1836 and captain in 1848. He was a disbursing agent in the removal of the Creek and
Cherokee Indians (1835–1839) and fought in the Mexican War (1846–1848). While in
service in Texas in 1849, he was drowned.

From Daniel Mallory

D Sir,   New york, April 4h. 1827.
   You have been so long the subject of abuse from the disappointed
adherents of Genl Jackson that any thing new on the occasion can
hardly surprize you. I have sent by this mail a pamphlet[1] replete with
vituperation, said to be the production of Genl Saml. Swartout [*sic*].
Ordinarily, it is better not to notice anonymous attacks, but in the

present instance I am of opinion that such disgraceful language and such debaseing [*sic*] falshoods [*sic*] should be made to redound on the writer & his cause. I should judge from the silence maintained by the opposition as to this work that, they think S——— has gone too far; and that the less notice taken of it, the better for their cause. The pamphlet is not for sale that I can learn. I want your authority altho, I know it to be destitute of truth, for denying the paragraph on the 36 Page, as mkd in pencil— if I make any use of it at present, it will be done with the approbation of judicious friends[2]— In this state there is a singular jumble of conflicting interest & feeling—not easily seen through; and more difficult to understand.[3] Some of your warmest friends (Worth,[4] for instance) and the friends of Clinton & Van Beauren [*sic*], of course, personally opposed to Mr Adams— It is scarcely possible, I should think, that Mr Clinton will connect himself with Mr. Van Beaurens projects of uniting the interest of this State with the South.[5] It is too unnatural to last, if formed. Pardon me for my crude notions. Sincerely & respectfully Yours,   D MALLORY
Honl. H Clay

ALS. DLC-HC (DNA, M212, R2).   [1] Not found.
[2] No identifiable reply found.   [3] Cf. above, Hammond to Clay, January 28, 1827; Degrand to Clay, February 8, 1827.   [4] Gorham A. Worth.   [5] Cf. above, Kent to Clay, January 26, 1827; below, Clay to Porter, May 13, 1827, note.

From Samuel Mifflin

Dr Sir   Harrisburg April 4, 1827
I duly received your favor of the 27. Ult.,[1]   The idea you suggest, of meetings, in relation to manufactures &c., is certainly worthy of reflection & I think, before the great question is decided, may be carried into operation, with great & decisive effect, altho', I am inclined to doubt the propriety of the measure, at this moment. I have conversed with some of our leading friends, on this subject & we all agree, in opinion, that altho' the indications of a rapid change, in favor of the Ad., are strong, yet, it may not at this moment be so decided, as to justify a measure, the failure of which, might do injury.

It is very evident, that the anxiety of the friends of the Gen,[2] to preoccupy public opinion, is doing him much harm & indeed, that it is the principal cause, which is now operating, upon the public mind, of this state & we think it better, as they appear to hurry from one step, to another, to leave them to be entrapped, in their own net—

These views, were fully explained, to your friend Mr Smith, of Lexington,[3] who spent yesterday with us. He left this, in the Morning Stage (having previously, written you hasty [*sic*] letter,[4] in relation to a caucus which was held last evening, by a number of the General's friends— It was got up, by Doctor Sutherland, aided, by Doctor Burden, from the County of Phila. & Mr Krepps, from Fayette[5]— General Ogle,[6] openly declared his disapprobation, of the measure, as calculated to injure their Candidate, altho' he was compelled to join in it, having been named, as Chairman. There were 32 members present; a Committee was appointed, to prepare resolutions, (which had been ready then three weeks.) & report on friday[7]— The plan no doubt originated with General McKean,[8] who passed about that time thro' this, from Washington, to Bradford. as he was heard to say, that "unless, some thing was done, the party would be lost—" It will be proposed, to recommend an organization of the party, to trust in the magic 8th of Jany next, & declare their adhesion to their leader, & place him in power.— That they will not succeed, I was led to believe, from a combination of circumstances, which cannot however be detailed, in a letter— One may however be worth communicating— A few nights ago Judge Huston, of the Supreme Bench,[9] was in company with Eleven Members, of the Legislature, & I think, some Genl.[10] from Baltimore who were here, in relation to a rail road, from that City, to the west, when Mr. B—— of Lancaster[11] entered & remarked, that he had heard much, of changes said to have taken place in Penn: but, that he had never been able, to discover a single case, where it had occurred— To this remark, nine of the 11 declared, in succession, that altho, original friends of General Jackson, disgusted by the course pursued by his friends, they were now favorable, to the Ad. & we may be assured, of the truth of this statement, as I have it from a Gentleman of veracity, who was present & if confirmation, were necessary it could be obtained thro' other channels—

Altho' I have expressed an opinion, adverse to meetings, at this moment, yet I beg you to believe, that I will keep the matter in view & urge it, upon our friends— Their present plan, is, to call a pure democratic meeting, on the 4th March, 1828, as the day, which by the common consent of the party, has been used, to make their nominations[12]— None, but their party, will be permitted to participate & having appointed a Committee, of Established Democratic Citizens, a review will be taken [of] the course, which has been pursued by the Ad., & the opposition, & thus the matter will be fairly brought before the public.—

The necessity of assuming an independent attitude, on the main point of difference, of policy, between Penn: & Virginia, wil[l] be a powerful argument, with us here.— We have been long, under an impression, that Virginia, considered us, as a Satellite, ever ready, to obey her mandate.[13]— With great respect I remain Your friend & Obt. Sert   SAML. MIFFLIN

ALS. DLC-HC (DNA, M212, R2).   1 Not found.   2 Andrew Jackson.   3 Thomas Smith.   4 Not found.   5 Joel B. Sutherland; Jesse R. Burden; and Solomon G. Krepps. Burden had been a member of the Pennsylvania House of Representatives, 1825–1826; sat, during the 1830's, in the State Senate, from which he retired as Speaker in 1838; and, subsequently, was prominent as a lecturer at the Philadelphia College of Medicine.   6 Alexander Ogle, born in Frederick, Maryland, had settled in Somerset, Pennsylvania, in 1795. He held the rank of major general in the Pennsylvania militia, had served in the State Legislature repeatedly in the period from 1803 to 1823, had been prothonotary and clerk of courts from 1812 to 1817, and had been a member of Congress from 1817 to 1819. In 1827 and 1828 he sat in the Pennsylvania Senate.   7 A caucus of Jackson supporters was to have been held in Harrisburg on March 26 but had been postponed until April 3. Thirty-five of the 132 members of the Pennsylvania Legislature attended, and the principal action was adoption of a resolution to hold a convention at Harrisburg the next January 8, "to nominate a candidate for the Presidency of the United States." Washington *Daily National Intelligencer*, March 31, April 9, 1827; Washington *Daily National Journal*, April 11, 1827. The designated date, marking the anniversary of the Battle of New Orleans, testified to their endorsement of Jackson.   8 Samuel McKean.   9 Charles Huston, born in Bucks County, Pennsylvania, in 1771, graduated from Dickinson College in 1789, and admitted to the bar of Lycoming County in 1795, had developed an outstanding reputation as a specialist in land law and court-room argument. He had been named president judge of district court in 1818 and an associate justice of the State Supreme Court in 1826. After retiring from the bench in 1845, he published a classic study on land law, *An Essay on the History and Nature of Original Titles to Land in the Province and State of Pennsylvania* (Philadelphia, 1849).   10 Probably an abbreviation of "Gentlemen." The Pennsylvania Legislature took no action in 1827 concerning the proposed railroad from Baltimore to the Ohio River, for which a company had been chartered by the State of Maryland on February 28. The State of Virginia had confirmed the charter on March 8; Pennsylvania so acted on February 22, 1828. The preliminary surveys had not yet been undertaken in the spring of 1827, and there was uncertainty whether the route should be linked to the river at Wheeling or Pittsburgh. Edward Hungerford, *The Story of the Baltimore & Ohio Railroad, 1827–1927* (New York, 1928), 27, 31, 33.   11 James Buchanan. See above, Clay to Johnston, April 2, 1827.   12 Cf. above, III, 668–69, and note.   13 See Klein, *Pennsylvania Politics*, 48, 77.

From Letitia Porter

Dear Sir   Black Rock N. Y. April 4th. 1827.
    I cannot express my gratitude to you for the interest you have taking [*sic*] in behalf of the son of my friend Mr Larned.[1] I believe Charles Larned will do credit to his friends & the institution he is going to enter for he was when I last saw him the most promising boy I ever saw. I presume his Mother has heard the glad tidings before this time; his father (if at home) is an inefficient man & has been very unfortunate & on the Mother depends the future advancement of the children. *You will have her prayers* & you know they are efficacious. Gen Porter[2] left home 4 days since for New York. please present my best regards to Mrs Clay & accept for yourself dear Sir the friendship & gratitude of your obliged friend   LETITIA PORTER
Hone. Henry Clay.

ALS. DLC-HC (DNA, M212, R2).
    1 Probably Mrs. Charles Larned. Cf. above, Mrs. Porter to Clay, February 18, 1827; Clay to Barbour, February 27, 1827.   2 Peter B. Porter.

DIPLOMATIC NOTES   April 4, 1827

To [C. D. E. J. BANGEMAN] HUYGENS. Refers to Huygens' notes of September 2, 1825, and April 2, 1827 (both above), concerning "the case of the Ship Celia, Captain Lloyd," and assures him "that orders will be given by the proper Department for affording the assistance promised" in Clay's note of September 8, 1825 (above). Copy, DNA, RG59, Notes to Foreign Legations, vol. 3, p. 344 (M38, R3). L draft, in CSmH.

MISCELLANEOUS LETTERS   April 4, 1827

To JOHN GOODING, Baltimore. States, in answer to Gooding's application (above, April 3, 1827), "that the President does not feel that he can with propriety interfere in the conduct of the prosecution"; advises him to appeal "to the Court, or . . . to the U. States Attorney" (Nathaniel Williams); and writes: "I need not add that no desire is felt by the President that unnecessary rigor should be exercised in the conduct of the prosecution." Informs him that the claim referred to in his letter "is not provided for by the late convention with England, unless it was filed in time, according to the provisions of that of St. Petersburg" (cf. above, Clay to Brooke, January 26, 1827). Notes that "Should there be any surplus of the Sum which G. B. has agreed to pay, its disposition will rest with Congress." Copy. DNA, RG59, Dom. Letters, vol. 21, p. 513 (M40, R19).

On the same date Daniel Brent, at Clay's direction, transmitted a copy of this letter to Nathaniel Williams. Copy, in *Ibid.*, p. 515.

To [RICHARD RUSH]. Transmits to the Secretary of the Treasury "translations and copies of a correspondence between the Chevalier Huygens . . . and this Department, concerning the Ship Celia, Captain Lloyd" and requests "that orders may be given by the Department of the Treasury for affording the assistance promised, under the Instructions of the President, in the event of the Captain coming within our jurisdiction." Copy. *Ibid.*, p. 514. Cf. above, Clay to Huygens, this date.

From J[AMES] L. E[DWARDS], "War Department, Pension Office." States that Samuel McGee's claim "to a pension on account of revolutionary service has been" disallowed because "Colonel Kingston, under whom he states to have served did not belong to the continental establishment," as required by the act of March 18, 1818. Copy. DNA, RG15, Letter Books, General, vol. 19, pp. 438–39.

McGee, of Woodford County, Kentucky, and at this time 81 years of age, had been a private in the Virginia militia during the Revolutionary War. Kingston has not been identified. On the pension act, see above, II, 681n.

From STEPHEN KINGSTON, Philadelphia. Refers to his request (not found) of November 18 and December 13, 1826; expresses a hope that his "case has been transmitted to Mr. [Albert] Gallatin with a recommendation to his Special attention"; and asks for information. ALS. DNA, RG59, Misc. Letters (M179, R65). Cf. above, Brown to Clay, September 12, 1826; Kittera to Clay, February 3, 1827. No communication to Gallatin on this subject has been found.

To Edward Everett

My Dear Sir   Washington 5h. Apl. 1827.
This letter I presume, from your unsubscribed letter dated in Philadelphia on the 28h. March,[1] will find you safely at home. I was glad to perceive that you saw things in that City in a more favorable light than that under which some other friends viewed them. I believe you saw them correctly.

You will have seen that the press has exhibited more activity and spirit in this City since the adjournment of Congress. It has been well and ably supplied.[2] And I think it will continue to manifest the same industry and zeal.

From Pennsa. the information I receive continues to be highly encouraging. I think we shall get the State. My information from Kentucky is also as I would have it.[3] We must not however be too confident but be "up and doing."

Can you not find time to prepare such a pamphlet (for that wd. be the best form of circulation) as I suggested on I. Improvements and D. M. intended for the meridian of Pennsa.? It should be clear, strong, bold and energetic. And it shd. take Mr. Giles's resolution which lately passed the Virga. Assembly as the *text*.[4] The developements [*sic*] every day shew that those are the two great subjects which divide the parties, and we ought not to desire better ground. With the advantage of position which that ground gives us if we do not beat we must be a poor set.

It is possible that the precaution of a Cypher may some times be necessary; but I have not been aware of any violation of a very extensive correspondence in which I have been engaged for several years.

You appear to have divisions in Massachusetts.[5] What do they imply?

I think the New England press and people would do well to exhibit a little more activity. Delusion is one of the devices of the enemy, and they will assert that their favorite will get votes even in New England.

We have no Foreign news, of which you are not I suppose possessed. Mr. Gallatin had not resumed his negotiations at his last dates.[6] I have prepared, and shall send off in a few days, new instructions on the Colonial question[7] which must have the effect either of leading to an adjustment of it or of giving us still firmer ground to stand on.

Mrs. Clay joins me in respectful Compliments to Mrs. E. And I add assurances of my esteem and regard for yourself.					H CLAY
Mr. Everett.

ALS. MHi.		[1] Not found.
[2] See above, Clay to Brown, March 27, 1827, note; below, Clay to Watterston, this date; Sergeant to Clay, April 17, 1827, note.		[3] On Pennsylvania, see above, Clay to Brown, March 27, 1827, note; on Kentucky, above, Johnson to Clay, March 12, 1827; below, Clay to Johnston, April 17, 1827.		[4] Cf. above, Brooke to Clay, January 31, 1827; Pleasants to Clay, February 14, 1827. Everett wrote such a pamphlet, not found, on May 1 and on May 17 noted that his "pamphlet Addressed to the citizens of Penn. had been Copied off & had gone on to Penn. with Money to print in English & German." Edward Everett, Diary, in MHi-Everett Papers, vol. 139, pp. 124, 132.		[5] The Massachusetts General Court was divided on the election of United States Senator—the House on January 16 supporting re-election of the incumbent, Elijah H. Mills; the Senate the following day selecting John Mills and, a month later, Levi Lincoln. As the House persisted in its original choice, the body on February 16 voted to postpone the election indefinitely, leaving the matter for the incoming legislature in May. Lincoln, in response to the Senate election, declined the honor, requested that his name not be considered by the House, and in April was re-elected to the Governorship. When the General Court reconvened in June, Daniel Webster was named to the Senate seat, in place of Mills, "whose delicate health induced his friends to withdraw him." *Niles' Weekly Register*, XXXI (February 3, 17, 1827), 353, 387; XXXII (March 17, April 21,

June 16, 1827), 43, 130, 260; Claude Moore Fuess, *Daniel Webster* (2 vols.; Boston, 1930), I, 335–7. That the divisions also permeated local partisan activity is indicated below, Webster to Clay, May 18, 1827, and note.   John Mills, of Springfield, Massachusetts, was a lawyer and from 1836 until 1841 United States attorney for that State. He was active in the Free Soil Party of 1848.   6 Above, February 5, 6, 13, 1827.   7 See below, Clay to Gallatin, April 11, 1827.

To George Watterston

Dear Sir   Washn— 5h. Apl. 27.

I read the article[1] to which, in your obliging note of today,[2] you refer, although I was not aware before I recd. your note to whom I was indebted for the friendly and flattering allusion to my name. I thank you, most cordially for it. And I hope you will never have occasion to regret that you have persevered in your attachment to one, who has always felt grateful for your kind proofs, not few nor unimportant, of that attachment.

I have observed, with satisfaction, that the Journal[3] has been recently edited with more spirit and ability. Indeed the remark may be applied to several other respectable prints which have espoused the cause of the Administration. My confidence in the final success of that cause, never shaken, is strengthened by recent intelligence. I am truly & faithfly Your friend   H. CLAY

Geo. Watterston Esq

ALS. KyU-Wilson Collection.
    1 The Washington *Daily National Journal* of April 2 and 3, 1827, had contained a long unsigned editorial article captioned, *"Parties which have existed, and which do now exist in this country."* There was reference in the second instalment to an unnamed presidential candidate of 1824, clearly described as Clay, who was praised for his firmness in casting his support for Adams as opposed to the *"Military leader."* Later in the paragraph Clay was acclaimed by name for putting his talents "in requisition to sustain the Administration which he had joined with others to form."   2 Not found.
    3 The editorial cited above was one among numerous such pieces which appeared in the Washington *Daily National Journal* beginning March 29. The articles were highly complimentary to the administration and sharply critical of the opposition to it, particularly that by Martin Van Buren, Andrew Jackson, and the principal journalistic proponents of the latter's candidacy—the Washington *United States Telegraph*, the New York *National Advocate*, and the *Richmond Enquirer*.

Receipt from Ann Bressie Lewis

Portsmouth Va. April 5th, 1827.

Receiv'd of the Hon Henry Clay two Hundred and fifty Dollars being the Ballance [*sic*] in full of the money collected by Him of Rowlands Estate[1] in Kentucky for me as Administratrix of Bressie Lewis Decd.

ANN LEWIS

Test
John Cocke[2]
[Endorsement][3]
Sir,   Portsmouth April 5th. 1827
    Above I hand you a receipt in full for two Hundred and fifty dol-

lars for money Collected for me of Rowlands Estate and according to the direction contained in yours of the 27 Ultmo,[4] I have this day drawn on you for that Sum say $250 which you will please Honour Whith [sic] great Respect your Obt. Servt.   Ann Lewis

N.B.   I think that I am entiled [sic] to three years interest for 250 dollars

ADS. DLC-TJC (DNA, M212, R16). Addressed to Clay and endorsed by him: "Mrs. Anne Lewis {With a receipt in full for Rowlands debt} Paid the amt. in a check on the Off. at Washington." See below, draft, this date, endorsement.
1 Not identified.   2 Possibly John Hartwell Cocke, of "Bremo," an estate on the James River west of Richmond. Having attended William and Mary College and risen to the rank of brigadier-general in the Virginia militia during the War of 1812, Cocke spent the remainder of his life as a planter, with estates in Virginia and Alabama. He was active in the founding and direction of the University of Virginia, a vigorous proponent of agricultural reform, a vice president of the American Colonization Society, and nationally prominent in the temperance movement (president of the American Temperance Union at its founding in 1836). For a lengthy sketch on his qualities as a Southern "liberal," see Clement Eaton, *The Mind of the Old South* (revd. edn., [Baton Rouge], 1967), 23–43.   3 AES.   4 Not found.

Draft by Ann Bressie Lewis

$250—   Portsmouth Va Aprl 5th 1827
    At Sight please pay to the order of John Cocke Two Hundred & fifty Dollars and charge to the act of your obt. St
                                                             Ann Lewis
To the Honle. Henry Clay Washington City D C.
[Endorsement on verso][1]   10 Apl. 1827
    Pay the within mentd. sum of Two hundred and fifty dollars to R. Smith or order   H Clay
Cashr. of the Off. of B. U. States   Washn[2]—

DS. DLC-TJC (DNA, M212, R16).
1 AES. Three other endorsements, as banking transactions, precede Clay's.
2 Richard Smith.

INSTRUCTIONS AND DISPATCHES   April 5, 1827

To Alexander H. Everett, Madrid, no. 9. Transmits a copy of a letter from B(enjamin) Evans (above, March 20, 1827) and its enclosed memorial (from Gonsolve and others, above, February 17, 1827). Comments: "Considering the extent of our commerce with that port [Havana], which is greater than that of all other Foreign nations together, and which is alike beneficial to Spain and to the United States, it is very difficult to perceive why, upon that sole ground, Spain should not be willing to admit and recognize an American Consul. But when to that consideration is added that we are entitled, by the express provisions of the Treaty of 1795 (Spain having admitted the Consuls of France and the Netherlands [Sant Iago María Angeluce; Lobe]) to demand that our Consul should be received, longer declining to receive one is postive injustice, and a violation of the most solemn obligation." Instructs Everett "to express in strong terms" the President's

(Adams') "just expectation that a decision will be promptly given in conformity with the right of the United States and the interests of both Governments." Copy. DNA, RG59, Dip. Instr., vol. 11, pp. 284–85 (M77, R6). ALI draft, in DLC-HC (DNA, M212, R8). Cf. above, Clay to Everett, April 27, 1825; Everett to Clay, September 25, October 16, November 21, December 2, 12, 1825.

From WILLIAM WHEELWRIGHT, Guayaquil. Notes preparations by the local government for defense against an attack by 2800 troops, who left Lima March 19 for the purpose of taking the city and defending "the lawful Constitution of the country agt. the inroads of Genl. Bolivar." ALS. DNA, RG59, Cons. Disp., Guayaquil, vol. 1 (M-T209, R1). Published in Manning (arr.), *Diplomatic Correspondence . . . Latin-American Nations*, II, 1311. Cf. above, Tudor to Clay, March 23, 1827; below, Wheelwright to Clay, April 19, 1827; Tudor to Clay, April 25, May 5, 15, 1827.

MISCELLANEOUS LETTERS   April 5, 1827

From SAMUEL M[ILLS] HOPKINS, Albany. Writes on behalf of William G. Ver Planck and his brother, P. A. Ver Planck, who "have succeeded to some property in the island of St. Croix . . . which they wish wholly to withdraw; but on which the local authorities continue to demand, as they have heretofore done, the duties of 6th's and 10th's on exportation" (cf. above, Claxton to Clay, September 30, 1826; Ritchie to Clay, November 13, 1826). Requests information on the treaty with Denmark (above, April 26, 1826), which, he has learned, the local government "seem unwilling to promulgate. . . ." LS. DNA, RG59, Misc. Letters (M179, R65). Endorsed by Clay on cover: "Mr. B[rent]. will prepare an ansr. Send a Copy of the treaty, and Copy of the correspondence with Mr. Bille [above, November 10, 11, 1826]—HC." A copy of Brent's letter to Hopkins, dated April 11, is located in DNA, RG59, Dom. Letters, vol. 21, p. 518 (M40, R19).

Hopkins, born in Connecticut and graduated in 1791 from Yale University had conducted a successful legal practice in New York City, from whence he had removed to Albany in 1821. He had been a member of Congress from 1813 to 1815 and of the New York House of Representatives from 1820 to 1827. He published a volume of *Chancery Reports* (New York, 1827), was granted an LL. D. degree by Yale University in 1828, and served as judge of New York circuit court from 1832 to 1836. The Ver Plancks have not been identified.

From Peter B. Porter

Dear Sir,   Albany April 6th 1827.

I arrived at this place last evening, where I shall spend four or five days in making the necessary preparations for the departure of our Surveyors to the northwest,[1] and shall then proceed to New York, in the expectation of meeting Mr. Barclay,[2] who ought to have been there several weeks ago, but had not arrived on wednesday last. I shall be under the necessity, of making a draft on you in the course of this day in favour of the Mechanics & Farmers Bank[3] for say, about $5000, toward defraying our expenses for the current year.

Living, as I do, on the extreme borders of the State I have had no adequate means of understanding the political intrigues going on at this place, or of judging of the success which has attended, or is likely hereafter to attend, the joint labors of Mr Van Buren & Mr. Clinton on the subject of the presidency; and I have not had time since my arrival to make the necessary inquiries. I will however write to you the moment I arrive at New York, by which time I shall have gathered a much better stock of information than I now possess. In the mean time I can only say that I do not myself, augur, from this unnatural and corrupt combination (of the existence of which I apprised you more than a year ago)[4] imposing as it appears to be, any ultimate disadvantage to the interests of Mr Adams in this State. I received your private letter of the —— of March,[5] before I left home. Should you write on the receipt of this, a letter addressed to me *at N York*, will find me. very respectfully yours P. B. PORTER.
Hon. H. Clay

ALS. DLC-HC (DNA, M212, R2).   [1] Cf. above, Delafield to Clay, this date.
[2] Anthony Barclay.   [3] Of Albany.   [4] See above, Porter to Clay, March 4, 1826.
[5] Not found.

DIPLOMATIC NOTES   April 6, 1827

To BARON DE MALTITZ. Informs him of the signing, on November 13, 1826, of the Convention with Great Britain (cf. above, Gallatin to Clay, November 13, 1826), "subsequently ratified by both parties, by which His Britannic Majesty's Government agreed to pay to that of the United States the sum of $1,204,960. in full satisfaction of the indemnities due to the Citizens of the United States from Great Britain, in virtue of the decision of His Imperial Majesty, the late Emperor of Russia [Alexander I], and the Convention of St. Petersburg." Expresses "grateful acknowledgments for the friendly and effectual agency of Russia in bringing about that desirable event." Copy. DNA, RG59, Notes to Foreign Legations, vol. 3, p. 345 (M38, R3). ALI draft, dated April 3, in CSmH.

On April 8, Maltitz formally acknowledged receipt of Clay's note and observed that the Emperor (Nicholas I) would be pleased that the mediation of Russia had led to "un arrangement avantageux pour le Gouvernement Americain." ALS, in DNA, RG59, Notes from Russian Legation, vol. 2 (M39, R2).

To PABLO OBREGÓN (1). Asks that he excuse the delay in answering his note of September 25, 1826 (with regard to the case of the *Eagle*). Confesses: "I had been under an impression that an answer to the same complaint, received through the Minister of the United States near the Republic of Mexico, had been forwarded to him; but I find, on a review of my Correspondence with him, that I was mistaken."

Assures him, by direction of the President, that "if any of our Citizens, led by commercial or other pursuits to the Republic of Mexico, shall violate, in any respect, its laws, they will act contrary to their duty towards both Countries, and the President would see the offenders brought to justice, in the tribunals of Mexico, without dissatisfaction." Continues: "Neither, however, our own Laws, nor as is believed, those of any foreign Country, make provision for the enforcement of the penal Laws of another Country, the general rule being, that the Laws of every nation are competent to vendicate [*sic*] their own authority."

Declares that the Mexicans alleged to have been brought on the *Eagle* to New Orleans "would not have been legally detained one moment after their arrival at that Port, and must have been instantly liberated." Adds: "We have no information whatever of their having been detained in confinement, but if you should be otherwise informed, on communicating the fact to this Department, the necessary orders will be promptly given for their immediate enlargement, or at your option, for their delivery over to you." Copy. DNA, RG59, Notes to Foreign Legations, vol. 3, pp. 345–47 (M38, R3). L draft, in CSmH.

Clay had given instructions to Poinsett concerning a response on the case of the *Eagle*, above, June 23, 1826. There is no indication that Clay enclosed a formal note of reply, and Poinsett failed to acknowledge receipt of the instruction.

To PABLO OBREGÓN (2). Asks to be excused for the delay, which "has arisen from the press of business, and from an impression that an answer had been returned," in replying to his note of September 25, 1826 (relating to the case of the *Nile*).

States that he is charged by the President "to say, that, assuming the statement of Captain Newells conduct to be correct, he has acted in a manner highly unworthy the character of an American Citizen." Continues: "But whilst the Government of the United States always sees with regret and disapprobation, any misconduct of Citizens of the United States in Foreign Countries, it does not hold itself responsible for such misconduct." Points out that "the Tribunals of the United States are open to the Government of the United Mexican States, in like manner as they are to the Government and Citizens of this Republic."

Adds that a United States consul has been appointed for Mazatlan (cf. above, Clay to Kennedy, November 1, 1826). Copy. DNA, RG59, Notes to Foreign Legations, vol. 3, pp. 347–49 (M38, R3). L draft, partially in Clay's hand, in CSmH.

INSTRUCTIONS AND DISPATCHES   April 6, 1827

To JAMES BROWN, no. 11. Transmits a "copy of a Resolution of the House of Representatives, passed at the last session of Congress requesting the President . . . to ascertain, and report to that house, at the next session of Congress, whether the Governments of Great Britain and France will furnish facilities to the landing and safe passage, through their respective possessions on the Coast of Africa, of such Africans as may have come into the possession of the United States by captures and condemnations under the slave trade laws, which Africans this Government may desire to restore to the countries to which they respectively belong—" Instructs him "to bring this subject to the notice of the French Government. . . ." Copy. DNA, RG59, Dip. Instr., vol. 11, pp. 286–87 (M77, R6). The same letter was addressed to Albert Gallatin, as no. 25, on this date. LS, in NHi-Gallatin Papers (MR14); copy, in DNA, RG59, Dip. Instr., vol. 11, pp. 285–86 (M77, R6). L drafts of both letters, in DLC-HC (DNA, M212, R8).

For the resolution, passed on March 3, 1827, see U. S. H. of Reps., *Journal*, 19 Cong., 2 Sess., 364, 391. Congress on March 3, 1819, had approved legislation providing that the President might order armed vessels of the United States to seize slave ships along the coasts of the United States and Africa and that he might appoint agents on the African coast to receive "negroes, mulattoes, or persons of colour, delivered from on board vessels, seized in the prosecution of the slave trade, by commanders of the United States armed vessels." 3 *U. S. Stat.*, 532–34. For references to other legislation related to the slave trade, see above, Clay to Addington, April 6, 1825, note; Clay to Raguet, April 14, 1825, note.

MISCELLANEOUS LETTERS April 6, 1827

From JOSEPH DELAFIELD, New York. Refers to his letter of March 22 and states that "The approach of the season when our surveyor should commence his expedition, and the long distance from this place to the residence of the British commissioner" (Anthony Barclay) impelled him to seek information from Barclay's father, "Col: [Thomas] Barclay of this city," who said "that dispatches had been received; that they were addressed to him; and that he perused them before transmitting them to his Son." Reports having learned "that it appeared from these instructions that the British Government were unwilling to carry into effect the proposed observations at the Lake of the Woods and the Red River; and that they would confine themselves exclusively to the provisions of the Ghent Treaty." Notes that Barclay "also made a casual remark, that it was Mr [George] Canning's wish to refer the subject to a friendly power," and suggests the probability "that the instructions are not calculated to produce an agreement upon the question in dispute under the 7th article of the Treaty" (cf. above, Porter to Clay, October 16, 1826; Vaughan to Clay, October 23, 1826; Clay to Vaughan, November 15, 1826). Adds: ". . . as Genl [Peter B.] Porter had anticipated such contingency in ordering the necessary outfit, I have suspended all arrangements requiring all expense, in accordance as I believe with his Views." ALS. DNA, RG76, Northern Boundary: Treaty of Ghent, 1814, Arts. VI & VII, env. 1, folder 2.

From MORITZ FURST, Philadelphia. Notes his understanding "that the Great Seal of the U. States for the treaty of Ghent is not to . . . [Clay's] satisfaction and the Government wish to have one engraved better executed in a more Masterly Style"; states his willingness to undertake the task "on reasonable terms"; states that he has written "the President on the Same Subject" (letter not found); and offers to sell to the Government 200 medals which he has on hand. LS. DNA, RG59, Misc. Letters (M179, R65).

The great seal of the United States had been adopted by Congress in 1782, on the basis of a design by William Barton, of Philadelphia, and Charles Thomson, the secretary of Congress. Made for impression on wax, it occasioned dissatisfaction until 1841, when Daniel Webster, without congressional authority, had a double-faced die cast that would give an impression directly on paper. [Gaillard Hunt], *The History of the Seal of the United States* (Washington, 1909), 41.

To Albert Gallatin

Dear Sir:— Washington, 7th April, 1827.

The Revd H. Holley, late President of Transylvania University, and his lady,[1] being about to visit and for some time to sojourn in Europe, I take pleasure in introducing them to you as friends whom we have long and intimately known, and highly esteemed. They have resided the last eight or ten years in Lexington, where they greatly endeared themselves to a large acquaintance, and the Society of the place, including my family. I shall be obliged by any attention you may find it convenient to shew them. I am, respectfully, Your obedient servant,

[. . .] Gallatin Esq. H. CLAY

LS. KyLxT. A letter of the same content was also addressed on this date to (James) Maury, United States consul at Liverpool. Copy. KyU-Wilson Papers.
[1] Mary Austin Holley.

To Josiah Stoddard Johnston

My Dear Sir   Washington 7h. Apl. 1827.
The account of the abortive attempt at a Caucus contained in the inclosed letter[1] is corroborated by a similar a/c in a letter I recd. from Mr. Mifflin.[2] Meetings are beginning in Pennsa. to take place declaring their determination to adhere to the policy of that State as to Intl. Imp. & D. M.[3]

I have not seen Mrs. Johnston for a day or two but I understand she is well. Your youngest child[4] was quite ill some days ago, but Dr. Hunt[5] told me that he had got perfectly well again.

I begin seriously to feel the necessity of relaxation, which I shall take, I hope, next month. Cordially Your friend   H CLAY
The Honble J. S. Johnston.

ALS. PHi. The cover, probably bearing an address, is missing, but cf. above, Clay to Johnston, April 2, 1827.
[1] Not found.   [2] Above, Mifflin to Clay, April 4, 1827.   [3] Internal improvements and domestic manufactures. See above, Clay to Crowninshield, March 18, 1827, note. Other meetings of this nature were held in Fayette, Greene, and Washington Counties. *Niles' Weekly Register*, XXXII (April 7, 1827), 103.   [4] See above, Clay to Everett, October 19, 1826.   [5] Henry Huntt, socially prominent physician, resident on 14th Street between Pennsylvania Avenue and F Street.

From David A. Hall

Sir,   Washington 7th. April 1827.
It may be thought an unwarrantable liberty I am taking, in putting into your possession the enclosed letter[1] which I have just recd. It is from William Hall Esq. of Vermont,[2] whose standing and political experience enable him to judge candidly of the state of the public feelings on the subject which is treated of, in the latter part of the letter. And as it tends to show that in the estimate of an intelligent man, the violent and unprovoked attack which Gov. Van Ness has thought fit to make upon the administration of the general government,[3] is not likely to be sustained by the responsive voice of the people, I have thought that it might be gratifying to those upon whom the attack is made, to know from an unsuspected source, how it is received by those upon whom it was first intended to operate. I am Respectfully Sir, Your Obt.   D. A. HALL.

ALS. DLC-HC (DNA, M212, R2). Addressed to Clay; endorsed on verso by Clay: ". . . {With a letter from his brother abt. Vermont}."
[1] Not found.   [2] A half brother of David A. Hall, William had begun business in Grafton, Vermont, but had moved as a young man to Rockingham Center, where he had prospered. He was a trustee of Middlebury College, had served as State Treasurer, and was active in promoting improvement of navigation on the Connecticut River. In 1830 he became one of the charter subscribers to the Connecticut River Steamboat Company.
[3] The Burlington *Northern Sentinel*, March 16, 1827, reprinted in Washington *Daily National Journal*, April 5, 1827, had published an address delivered by Cornelius P. Van Ness on March 15, 1827, announcing his support for Jackson's candidacy and charging that the administration had aided (Horatio) Seymour in attaining victory over Van Ness

in the recent senatorial election. One basis of the complaint centered on the activities of William Slade (Jr.), during a visit to Vermont in August, 1826, under appointment to distribute the laws. For correspondence detailing the charges and countercharges, see Slade to Van Ness, April 3, June 8, 1827; Van Ness to Slade, May 8, 1827—all published in Washington *Daily National Journal*, April 4, June 8, 9, 1827. Cf. also below, Keith to Clay, April 12, 1827, note. A copy of the letter of appointment written by Daniel Brent to Slade, July 31, 1826, is located in DNA, RG59, Dom. Letters, vol. 21, pp. 360–61 (M40, R19).

From Gideon Morgan, Jr.

Sir   Calhoun. April. 7. 1827—

I have Lately been informd. that a number of Letters comprising a part of the communication between Jackson and Burr remains Still in the federal court at Richmond, V, A, undecyphered.[1] If this is the fact it is doubtless known to Mr. Wirt.[2] some months since c [*sic*] accident threw into my possession the Key to this Treasounous [*sic*] & Villianous [*sic*] Transaction. The Key however is Lost but with Some trouble I think—I can procure it   to me at that time it was of no use nor did I believe it would be to My friends. Should these Letters remain there in their original obscurity possibly, Barbour[3] may Know something of them   I have referd [*sic*] him to you. Could this correspondence be unraveled, it would be some satisfaction—to myself & I hope a benefit to my Country and thuss [*sic*] bring to Light the Secret Drawer and unfold to our country transactions of which the actors were full willing to sacrifice its Best intrests [*sic*] uppon [*sic*] the the [*sic*] altar of popularity, ambition & wealth—in thus addressing you I am fully aware of the awful vastnes [*sic*] in which I should be ingulpht [*sic*]— therefore silen[ce] except to your particular friends. I never must be known its author   I cannot now Give the key entire for the reasons before Stated   I think I recollect the outlines and will Give them to you without attempting the alphabetical order. possibly the characters themselves. will Shew wheth[er] the Key when complete will decypher the correspondence or not. I am Sir Sincerely your Friend   GIDEON MORGAN JR

I have no Dictionary   you may if you Can unravel or decypher this

X

ALS. DLC-HC (DNA, M212, R2). Addressed to Clay; postmarked: "Calhoun T 13 April Free"; and endorsed on cover by Clay: "Calhoun (Tennessee). . . ." Morgan, who had moved to Tennessee from Virginia, in 1806, was a partner in a family-operated mercantile house in Knoxville.

[1] No other reference to such letters has been found. Ciphered correspondence of Jonathan Dayton and Aaron Burr with James Wilkinson, cited in connection with the Burr trial, does not utilize the code provided by Morgan to Clay, below, April 27, 1827. *American State Papers, Miscellaneous*, I, 558–59; see also, *ibid.*, 551. When the relationship of Jackson to the Burr conspiracy was raised as a political issue, in the spring of

1828, it centered on Jackson's correspondence with Nathaniel W. Williams. See Bassett (ed.), *Correspondence of Andrew Jackson*, III, 391–93. Dayton, for whom the city of Dayton, Ohio, was named, had served in the American Revolution, the Federal Constitutional Convention, the Continental Congress (1787–1789), the United States House of Representatives (1791–1799), and the United States Senate (1799–1805). His political career then was terminated by his involvement in the Burr conspiracy. Williams, who testified that he had been recruited by Jackson for the Burr forces, had been appointed a judge of the Tennessee circuit courts in 1810. He continued on the bench and was acquitted of impeachment charges in 1829.   2 William Wirt. Cf. above, II, 398n.
    3 James Barbour.

INSTRUCTIONS AND DISPATCHES   April 7, 1827

From J[OHN] J. APPLETON, Stockholm, no. 15. Cites his letter of April 3 and reports further that he has informed Count Wetterstedt of the receipt of authorization to begin negotiations for a treaty, has provided him a copy of the House bill, and has given him the explanations suggested in Clay's letter of January 12. Explains that the advantages, mentioned by Clay, enjoyed by Swedish and British vessels over others, "as regards arrivals in distress on the coast of Norway and Sweden," result from the requirement (abolished by the treaty between Britain and Sweden) that foreign vessels, "during the first sixty hours after stranding," may apply only to the "Diving and Saving Company" for aid. Encloses documents that "shew . . . where and to what extent" the difference exists "between the pilotage and harbour dues collected upon Swedish and American vessels." Promises to try during the impending negotiation to obtain equality for American vessels. Asks how to send the treaty, when completed, to the United States and states that he will, if without directions, forward it by his "friend and inmate [sic], Mr. Cucheval. . . ." ALS. DNA, RG59, Dip. Disp., Sweden and Norway, vol. 5 (M45, R-T6). Published in *American State Papers, Foreign Relations*, VI, 719–20. Received June 5.
    James Cucheval (Coucheval), not further identified, was paid as a bearer of dispatches and for services as a transcriber in the American Legation at Stockholm in 1827. *House Reports*, 20 Cong., 1 Sess., no. 226, p. 87.

From ANDREW ARMSTRONG, "United States Agency Port au Prince." Transmits a copy of a note in which he undertook to make General (Joseph-Balthasar) Inginac "Sensible of the wrong course of policy they were pursuing towards us; And . . . Acquainted with the motives by which Our govt is Actuated, and the basis on which our diplomatic relations are founded." Surmises that the communication "was not much relished by the General," who has not replied. Notes that "matters Slipped Along very Smoothly, without any interference in our concerns on their part, untill [sic] a few days Since, when they recommenced their vexacious [sic] measures by forcing a Captain to discharge a coloured Seamen and to pay him his wages—"
    Reports that "Mr. Maller [J. B. Maler] the French Consul Genl." and "Mr. McKensey [Charles MacKenzie] the british Consul Genl." will depart soon, leaving in their places a consul and a vice-consul, respectively. Adds that "A Consul [not identified] from Sweden and Norway has just arrived" and probably will be accredited.
    States that the legislature is discussing the tariff behind closed doors, that the country is quiet, that the crop has been good, and, "though our trade is not so great As it was a few years Since, Yet the business is better, the consumption of our produce is Steady at prices that leave a fair profit to the merchant." ALS. DNA, RG59, Cons. Disp., Cap Haitien, vol. 6 (M9, R6).

From THOMAS L. L. BRENT, Lisbon. Transmits "a translation of the speech of the

Princess Regent [Isabel Maria] on the occasion of the rising of the Cortes" and notes "the many reports in circulation respecting" the mission of "the Physician Abrantes," who has just returned from Rio de Janeiro. Reports that the Spanish Ambassador (Casa Flórez) has begun a leave of absence. Surmises that (Alexander H.) Everett has previously sent information "of the Count of Ofalia's mission from Spain to England and the order of the King of Spain [Ferdinand VII] for an additional levy of 24,000 men" (see above, Everett to Clay, February 21, March 19, 1827). Credits that monarch, however, with "greater fidelity" in executing "the demands of England and Portugal since the last defeat of the refugees and since the late representations of France and Russia . . ." (cf. above, Brown to Clay, February 13, March 23, 1827; Brent to Clay, March 10, 16, 1827). ALS. DNA, RG59, Dip. Disp., Portugal, vol. 7 (M43, R6). Received June 5. Endorsed by Clay on verso of one sheet: "To be submitted to the President. HC." No comment by Adams has been found.

Bernardo José de Abrantes e Castro, born in Santa Marinha and educated in medicine at the University of Coimbra, was physician of the Royal House and a Counselor of State. Because of his close relationship to Isabel Maria, his journey to Brazil in a Portuguese brig of war in the fall of 1826 had occasioned speculation that he carried some important communication to Dom Pedro. During the subsequent ascendancy of Dom Miguel as ruler of Portugal, Abrantes was forced into exile in England, from which he did not return until shortly before his death, at Lisbon, in 1833.

From A[LEXANDER] H. EVERETT, Madrid, no. 74. Reports that, having failed in earlier efforts to obtain the release of "several citizens of the United States who have been taken by the Spaniards in the service of the new American Governments" and who "are liable to be treated as rebels, and to suffer the punishment of death," he obtained "a personal audience" with the King (Ferdinand VII) at which he pleaded "the motives of humanity" in behalf of the prisoners. Notes that "the King received the application very civilly" and "promised to take the matter into consideration. . . ." Expresses concern for "John Lyon, formerly a Lieutenant in the Navy," held "at the Canary Islands, and several individuals . . . imprisoned at Ceuta. . . ." Encloses copies of a memorandum, listing the names of the prisoners, that he submitted to the King; "another short memorandum on the subject of the Indemnities" (cf. above, Everett to Clay, March 31, 1827), also sent to the King; a note he addressed "to the Minister [Manuel Gonzales Salmon] demanding the restoration of the Colombian Privateer [Zulmé] captured within our jurisdiction"; and "a second note upon the Quarantine Laws," sent the previous week "in consequence of further advices from Cadiz" (cf. above, Everett to Clay, March 19, 1827). States that "the report that the Duke of San Carlos will be appointed Secretary of State seems" to be losing ground. LS. DNA, RG59, Dip. Disp., Spain, vol. 27 (M31, R28). Extract published in Manning (arr.), Diplomatic Correspondence . . . Latin-American Nations, III, 2141–42. Received August 2.

A John Lyon was listed as midshipman in the Navy in 1805 and purser in 1807 but has not been found subsequently in the records of the Department. Edward William Callahan (ed.), List of Officers of the Navy of the United States and of the Marine Corps from 1775 to 1900 . . . (New York, 1969; repr. from 1901), 343.

The Americans confined at Ceuta were survivors of the crew of the Colombian privateer General Soublette, which had run aground on the Spanish coast. Reporting Everett's success in obtaining their release, Hezekiah Niles questioned whether those who had violated the neutrality law of the United States should "be permitted to shelter themselves under its eagle-banner in the day of their need. . . ." Niles' Weekly Register, XXXII (June 9, 1827), 244.

From ALBERT GALLATIN, London, no. 66. Acknowledges receipt of Clay's "despatch No. 19 of 24th. February last"; states that Clay's "recollection of the understanding alluded to in . . . [Gallatin's] letter of 30th Decer. 1826 [no. 48], is very correct"; and asserts: "I am confident that, on reading again that letter, you will be satisfied that it is not susceptible of the construction you seem to have put on it." Quotes, with regard to the "understanding" concerning the length of his mission, from Clay's communications of May 3, 5, 11, 1826, and from his own letters of May 7 and December 30, 1826 (no. 48). States that he "was perfectly aware that there was no understanding [and] . . . did not suggest that there was any, fixing any precise time for . . . [his] return, other than the termination of the negociations." Adds: "I need hardly say that you never offered me carte blanche, and that it was neither wished or expected. I can not say that the instructions gave me, as to details and subordinate points, the discretionary power I had anticipated. The personal inconvenience is a very inferior consideration. But such limited discretion, so far as I have known, has been usual, and might, as I thought perhaps erroneously, have been safely and advantageously entrusted to me." ALS. DNA, RG59, Dip. Disp., Great Britain, vol. 33 (M30, R29). Received May 18. Gallatin kept a copy of this letter in his personal papers (NHi-Gallatin Papers, Letterbook, vol. 15, pp. 141–44 [MR21]), but the Foreign Service Post records state merely: "Note. Dispatch No. 66 to the Secretary of State is not recorded." DNA, RG84, Great Britain (MR16, frame 128).

MISCELLANEOUS LETTERS   April 7, 1827

From J[OHN] J. APPLETON, Stockholm, *"private."* Expresses a wish to convey to the United States "the Treaty about to be negociated," in order to give him an opportunity to visit his "aged parents." ALS. DLC-HC (DNA, M212, R2). A "Duplicate" of this letter is located in DNA, RG59, Dip. Disp., Sweden and Norway, vol. 5 (M45, R6).
    Appleton's father, John, had been the United States consul at Calais during Jefferson's administration; his mother has not been further identified.

From WILLIAM GREENE, Cincinnati. States that he has had no reply to a letter he wrote Clay, on October 31, 1826 (not found), "enclosing a draught of a Power of Attorney," which he wished authenticated in order to "give it effect in . . . Europe"; requests the "return of the paper referred to, whether authenticated or not." ALS. DNA, RG59, Misc. Letters (M179, R65). In response to this letter Daniel Brent, on April 13, transmitted the requested authentication and stated that it had been prepared earlier but had not been sent because Greene's first letter had been lost. Conveys Clay's apology for the delay. Copy, in DNA, RG59, Dom. Letters, vol. 21, p. 520 (M40, R19).
    Greene, born in Rhode Island, graduated from Brown University in 1817, and trained in law at Litchfield, Connecticut, had moved to Columbus, Ohio, and from there to Cincinnati, where he practiced law until 1862. He was active in politics, first as a Whig and later as a Republican. Returning to Rhode Island in 1862, he became lieutenant governor from 1866 to 1867.

From Francis Johnson

Dear Sir   (Private)   Bowling Green[1] 8 April 1827
    I retd last night from [. . .][2] to Monroe County, to the Circuit Court —the most decided Jackson County in the district— My opponent[3]

had been riding in the County 12 days before—reading, Amos & the Telegraph[4] and estimates for divers things not approved nor adopted—&c &c The labors of the campaign are painful in anticipation— The Billiard Table[5] has more effect than I could have immagined [sic]— Mr John Adams[6] promised to send me a Certificate from the Auditor when the account is settled— Mr Yancey has he says letters & certificates to prove the fact beyond doubt of its being paid for out of the public Money— every thing else is Swept from under them, with those who are willing to be convinced— the twice Charged expences from St Petersburg, is endeavored to be handled, and also the expence of the presidents family[7]— If I could get Genl Jacksons account in Florida I could balance it—for he charges for the expence of his family & other expences some thousands—but how to come at it I dont know— the auditors could not give it to me, without your direction— I had rather not have it than you should appear in it[8]— His accounts that I have got, shuts them up pretty much[9]— my friends are warm & ardent, so are the Jackson men— my friend E. M. Ewing Esqe. of Russellville,[10] has just informed that letters have gone to the Frankfort junto,[11] to request they will order Yancey off the track—that they may bring Breathitt[12] on— they believe it seems, that Yancey will be beaten and they now wish to get rid of him— But it was necessary first to array him and his forces against me— he certainly can carry over more of the New Court party[13] than any Other— had Yancey remained for me— Breathitt could not have come within 1500 of me, but if they succeed in getting Yancey off and Breathitt on—I cant answer for the result now, after putting so many of the New Courts agst. me— and Breathitt too will come out under the feigned pretence of supporting the Admn & prefering [sic] the Genl. at the next Election— The Jackson men up the Country have sworn I shall beaten [sic]— I am told by a respectable man of this town—that he was told in Louisville the other, [sic] supposing him to be a Jackson man, that $1000 could be raised in 20 minutes, to have me beaten— I am not of opinion yet that they will be able to beat me, if I have my health— Yr friend   FR. JOHNSON
Hon H Clay.

ALS. DLC-HC (DNA, M212, R2).   1 Kentucky.
2 Two words illegible.   3 Joel Yancey.   4 Amos Kendall; Washington *United States Telegraph*.   5 Cf. above, Turner to Clay, January 7, 1827, and note.
6 John Adams (Jr.).   7 John Quincy Adams had been paid the regular salary as Minister to Russia while he had also been reimbursed for travel and living expenses on the Ghent Mission. His application for reimbursement to cover the charges for moving his family from Russia to France had been rejected. MHi-Adams Papers, J. Q. A. Miscellany, Accounts with the U. S., 1809–1822 (MR206). Jacksonian critics charged that, in lieu of charges for moving Adams' family, the accounting officers had permitted him to restate the account to cover "his own travelling expenses from Ghent to St. Petersburg, a journey which he never performed." Frankfort *Argus of Western America*, April 25, 1827. This restatement, if filed, does not appear in Adams' record of the transaction.
8 Cf. below, Clay to Hammond, June 1, 1827, and note.   9 On March 16, 1827, the *Liberty Hall and Cincinnati Gazette* had countered the Jacksonians' criticism of Adams' accounts by noting that the General's accounts for quarters, fuel, servants' rations and

clothing, forage, and military pay, amounted to $4,510, annually, over the period from April 1, 1815, to June 1, 1821, during which period he had been residing at home excepting only the approximately eight months of his involvement in the Seminole War. For continuation of this criticism, see also *ibid.*, April 10, 1827.   [10] Ephraim McLean Ewing.   [11] Reference to the movement in support of Jackson's candidacy led by Amos Kendall and Francis P. Blair.   [12] Probably John Breathitt.   [13] See above, III, 902n.

INSTRUCTIONS AND DISPATCHES   April 8, 1827

From A[EXANDER] H. EVERETT, Madrid, no. 75. Notes that he has just been informed "that the King has consented to the release of the persons" for whom Everett had interceded (see above Everett to Clay, April 7, 1827). LS. DNA, RG59, Dip. Disp., Spain, vol. 27 (M31, R28). Received August 2.

From T[HOMAS] M. RODNEY, Havana. Reports that three crew members "of the Schooner Mark Time of New York," Robert W. Dayton, master, brought in by a Spanish warship, were delivered to him (Rodney) and placed with all available evidence, on the American ship *Lexington*, Captain (William B.) Shubrick, for delivery "to the proper authorities in the United States." Adds that "the Schooner was given up to the former Consigner...." ALS. DNA, RG59, Cons. Disp., Havana, vol. 5 (M-T20, R5). Received April 24.

Neither the *Mark Time* nor her master has been further identified; additional reference to the incident has not been found.

From Jared Sparks

Dear Sir,   (Private)   Mount Vernon, Apl. 9th. 1827
    In compliance with your request, communicated in Mr Brent's favor of the 2d. inst,[1] I shall be happy to have further conversation with you, on the subject of publishing the Diplomatic correspondence of the Revolution. I expect to be in Washington on the 17th. of the present month, and hope then to have the pleasure of waiting on you.
    Meantime will you do me the favor to desire Mr Brent to look back in the books, & ascertain on what terms the contract was made with Mr Wait[2] for supplying Congress with the volumes of the Secret Journals? In fixing on the amount proposed by me, I did not consult a printer, but took the price at which books of that size and quality usually sell, presuming there would be little risk in going upon that calculation. It may, however, be too high or too low, and as Mr. Wait is a printer I think I shall be safe in contracting on the same terms as he did, since the mechanical execution of the volumes is intended to be similar, and this part of the business after all will be a printer's job.
    You will be glad to learn, that the historical materials in the archives of Mount Vernon are extensive and valuable. No man ever lived perhaps, who was more careful to preserve copies of all he wrote than Gen. Washington. There are *seventy* large folio volumes of his own letters, besides many that have not been recorded. About forty of these pertain to the Revolution; but by far the most interesting letters are those written after that period to many of the first men of the age, both

in this country and Europe. Of the letters received by Gen. Washington, there are more than *twenty thousand* on file. Among these is a long very curious letter by Mr Jefferson, on the origin of his difficulties with Hamilton.[3] He uses plain language, and charges Hamilton with constantly interfering in his department using improper means to influence the members of Congress to accomplish his designs, and writing anonymous and inflammatory articl[es] in the newspapers. Whereas Mr Jefferson affirms that he had carefully avoided all such offe[n]ces, and makes the extraordinary declaration, that he had never in his life to that day writte[n] anything in any newspaper to which he had not affixed his name.[4]

But I will not intrude upon you with these matters, yet I trust the above facts will not be without interest to you. My purpose is to publish a series of volumes, containing the most important parts of Washington's papers, with suitable notes and illustrations; and from the imperfect examination which I have as yet been enabled to make, I am well convinced they will fully answer all reasonable anticipations.[5]

More than a year ago the papers announced, that an edition of your Speeches, selected & revised by yourself, might soon be expected from the press, but the work has not yet appeared in the bookstores. Permit me to hope, that the project has not been relinquished.[6] A work, exhibiting in a light so favorable the eloquence of our national legislature, elucidating so clearly, and defending so ably and successfully, many of the fundamental principles of our Constitution, could not fail at all times to meet, from every liberal mind, the reception it deserves, and, at the present crisis I cannot but think it would render an essential public service.

Excuse the freedom with which I have written this letter, and accept the assurances of the very high respect & Sincere regards of your most obt. Servt.   JARED SPARKS

Hon. Henry Clay.

ALS. DNA, RG59, Misc. Letters (M179, R65).
[1] See above, Sparks to Clay, March 13, 1827, note.   [2] Thomas B. Wait.
[3] Thomas Jefferson; Alexander Hamilton.   [4] The letter, dated September 9, 1792, is published in Lipscomb (ed.), *Writings of Thomas Jefferson*, VIII, 394–408.   [5] The work subsequently appeared as Sparks (ed.), *The Writings of George Washington; Being His Correspondence, Addresses, Messages, and Other Papers, Official and Private, Selected and Published from the Original Manuscripts; with a Life of the Author, Notes and Illustrations* (12 vols., Boston, 1834–1837).   [6] An advertisement in the Lexington *Kentucky Reporter*, February 27, 1826, had announced such a proposal, and the Lexington project had been reported in *Niles' Weekly Register*, XXX (March 18, 1826), 35. No compilation published in Lexington at this time has been found; but Sabin states that one was issued in 1826 at Philadelphia, under the title: *The Speeches of Henry Clay, Delivered in the Congress of the United States: To Which is Prefixed a Biographical Memoir, with an Appendix. Bibliotheca Americana*, IV, 140. The following year Carey and Lea, of Philadelphia, published a collection under the same title extended, after the word "Appendix," as follows: *Containing His Speeches at Lexington and Lewisburgh, and before the Colonization Society at Washington; together with His Address to His Constituents, on the Subject of the Late Presidential Election. . . .* A volume under the latter title was also published in 1827 at Cincinnati. Cf. above, Clay to Wharton, January 1, 1827.

From Ferdinand Valero

To the Honore. Henry Clay Secretary of State—Washington
Sir   Guatemala April 9th 1827.

As I have not had any opportunity after I left the United States[1] to reiterate you [sic] my respects and to show you my most friendly recollection of your honorable person, permit me now, Sir, the satisfaction of sending to you the expressions of my sincere affection towards you.

I arrived in this city the 30th of December last— I had not the pleasure of seing here Mr. John Williams of whom I entertained a high idea: he departed from this city some days before my arrival.[2] I met here with Mr. W. Phillips consul pro tempore of the U. S. to this country: This Gentleman is about to leave us.[3] I regreat very much his departure, for he is a worthy american estimed in this country and well adapted for the service of the U.S. here in any consular or diplomatic capacity as he is very well acquainted with the language, caracter, customs, & circumstances of this people.

We have had here some domestic differences of rivality betwen the States; but nothing of a serious consequence: all is geting well now & I hope that we shall be alltogether tranquil as far as our political infancy permits.[4] I am, Sir, with the highest consideration Your most humble and obt. Servant   FERDINAND VALERO
Sir   Be so kind as to excuse the bad english of this letter.

ALS. DLC-HC (DNA, M212, R2).   [1] See above, Valero to Clay, October 29, 1826.
[2] Cf. above, Phillips to Clay, February 3, 1827.   [3] Cf. above, Phillips to Clay, March 2, 22, 1827.   [4] Cf. above, Gonzales to Clay, January 7, 1827; Rochester to Clay, January 31, 1827; Phillips to Clay, March 2, 22, 1827; Poinsett to Clay, March 28, 1827.

MISCELLANEOUS LETTERS   April 9, 1827

To CHARLES BARTLETT ALLEN, "Consul of the United States for the Port and Province of Para, in Brazil." Transmits his commission, printed circular instructions, and a blank consular bond. Copy. DNA, RG59, Cons. Instr., vol. 2, p. 421 (M78, R2). Similar letters were addressed on this date to Charles W. Dabney, consul "for the Azores, or Western Islands"; Charles Douglas(s), consul at Barcelona; Robert Monroe Harrison, consul at St. Bartholomew's Island; Reuben Harvey, consul at Cork, Ireland; James Lenox Kennedy, consul at Mazatlan, Mexico; John Larkin Payson, consul at Messina, Sicily; Philip Robinson, consul at Curacao; and Charles W. Webber, consul at Chihuahua, Mexico. *Ibid.*, 417–20.

In the case of Dabney and Kennedy, this action represented confirmation of interim appointments (see above, Clay to Kennedy, November 1, 1826; Clay to Dabney, November 3, 1826), which the former had accepted with thanks on March 29, 1827. ALS. in DNA, RG59, Cons. Disp., Fayal (M-T103, R-T1).

Allen acknowledged receipt of the documents in a letter to Clay on August 30, 1827. ALS, in *ibid.*, Maranham, vol. 1 (M-T398, R1).

From JONATHAN ELLIOT, Washington. Encloses "a specimen of the minion type," in which he proposes printing the *Biennial Register*, should he be selected for the job. Notes that "The letter, herewith, is quite new and beautiful; and would produce a more handsome volume than any that has been offered to the Department under . . . [Clay's] predecessors." ALS. DNA, RG59, Misc. Letters (M179, R65).

On Elliot's relinquishment of editorship of the *Washington City Gazette*, cf. above, Hammond to Clay, April 7, 1826, note.

From J[ACOB] C. ISACKS, Winchester, Tennessee. States that Thomas H. Fletcher has not received "any *Official* notice of his Appointment of District Attorney for West Tennessee"; requests that the commission, if not yet forwarded, be addressed to Fletcher at Nashville. ALS. DNA, RG59, Misc. Letters (M179, R65). Cf. above, Clay to Fletcher, March 29, 1827, note.

From CHARLES SAVAGE, Barnstable, Massachusetts. Reports his inability to return to Guatemala before next autumn because of the state of his health. ALS. DNA, RG59, Cons. Disp., Guatemala, vol. 1 (M-T337, R1). Addressed to the Secretary of State.

INSTRUCTIONS AND DISPATCHES   April 10, 1827

From JAMES BROWN, Paris, no. 66. Presents in considerable detail the information requested in Clay's "dispatch No. 9" (above, January 11, 1827) and states that he is forwarding "an excellent work by Theodore Regnault, advocate in the royal court, in which the legislation and jurisprudence of France on patent rights, are treated in a very comprehensive and masterly manner." LS. DNA, RG59, Dip. Disp., France, vol. 23 (M34, R26).

The volume was apparently Regnault's *De la Législation et de la Jurisprudence Concernant les Brevets d'Invention* . . . (Paris, 1825).

From J[OEL] R. POINSETT, Mexico (City), no. 82. Transmits "a translation of the Report of the Committee of the House of Deputies on the Treaty concluded here on the 10th. of July last" (cf. above, Poinsett to Clay, July 12, 1826). States that the report, discussed in secret session of the House, has been "sent back to the Committee with instructions"; that the House disapproved some parts of the document "and moreover, desired to have inserted in the Treaty an additional Article, declaring the Treaty of Limits concluded at Washington between the United States of America and Spain [the Adams-Onís Treaty (for the boundary, see above, II, 816, note 19)] to be valid and binding upon the high contracting parties"; and that "The argument for this declaration . . . is the propriety of considering this Republic as having inherited all the rights of Spain." Explains that the establishment of this principle, "hitherto urged effectively in all the disputes between the civil and ecclesiastical authorities, . . . is of the utmost importance to this government. . . ." Adds that "The Committee has not yet reported."

Notes ratification of the British Treaty (see above, Gallatin to Clay, December 16, 1826, note). LS. DNA, RG59, Dip. Disp., Mexico, vol. 2 (M97, R3).

MISCELLANEOUS LETTERS   April 10, 1827

To the SECRETARY OF WAR [JAMES BARBOUR], "Circular." Transmits "a copy of a joint Resolution of the two Houses of Congress, approved on the 27th. of April 1816. which makes it the duty of this Department to compile a Biennial Register" (3 *U. S. Stat.*, 342); requests the information needed for the task; and "earnestly" asks "that the lists be furnished in time to meet the demand of the Resolution, that each member of the Senate and House of Representatives may be supplied with the copy to which he is entitled, on the first Monday in January next—" Adds: "This request is induced by the dissatisfaction which was evinced in the House of Representatives at the first Session of the 18th. Congress, upon the circumstances of the Register's not having been so prepared." LS. DNA, RG107, Letters Received, Reg. vol. 22, C-82.

Responses to this circular have been omitted by the editors as routine.

From JAMES MADISON, "Montp[elie]r." Acknowledges receipt of the pamphlets sent with Clay's letter of (April) 4 and offers to reimburse (Daniel) Brent for their cost. Encloses "an addition" to his "last letter to Mr. Gallatin. . . ." ALI draft. DLC-James Madison Papers (DNA, M212, R22).

From ROBERT SCOTT, Lexington. Transmits "the Accounts of the [James Morrison] estate &c." ALS. KyLxT. See below, Accounts, July 16, 1827.

To Albert Gallatin

No. 26. Albert Gallatin, Envoy Extraordinary
and Minister Plenipotentiary U.S. to G. Britain.
Sir,   Department of State, Washington 11 April 1827.

In the letter which I addressed to you on the 20th. ultimo, I stated that it was my intention, in a few days, to prepare and transmit to you some instructions on the subject of the Colonial Trade. I shall now execute that intention; but before I proceed to the specific directions required by the present state of it, some few observations appear to be called for, on the two notes of Mr. Canning, under date the 13th. November of the last, and the 27th January of the present year.[1] In submitting these, it is not desired to subdue the repugnance which Mr. Canning expresses against being "drawn again into a discussion of topics already more than sufficiently debated." But whilst the diplomatic relations between the two countries remain open, and sentiments of amity are professed on both sides, it would seem more consistent with that profession, and more in that spirit of candour, as well as courtesy, which ought to animate the councils of friendly nations, to be willing both to give and to receive the correction of any misapprehension under which either may be labouring, than to permit such misapprehension to continue, perhaps, to the prejudice of both. The United States, at least, whose whole course, on this subject, has ever been sincere, direct and open, who have never sought to arrogate to themselves any right, or claim, to question[2] the power of Great Britain to give the law to her own Colonies, nor advanced any other claim, on their part, than the right to regulate their own commerce with Foreign nations on fair and equal terms, owe it to themselves to disavow those peculiar and exorbitant pretensions which are intimated, in no very obscure terms, in the two notes of Mr. Canning, and to deny, in the most explicit manner, the rejection of any friendly overture from Great Britain, founded on equality, with regard to this trade, which has ever been distinctly and intelligibly offered to their choice. To impute a contrary course of action to the Government of the United States, and to express, in the same paper, a determination not to be drawn again into the further discussion of these topics, would seem to be closing the door, studiously, against all explanation, and not to harmonize very happily either with professions of friendship, or with that natural respect and forbearance which have usually characterized the intercourse of equal nations in modern times. The United States, however, disposed rather to heal than to inflict wounds, and taking more pleasure in removing than in creating causes of dissatisfaction and complaint, are desirous that the Court of Great Britain shall be set right, as to certain matters of fact, and certain principles of policy, maintained on our part, with regard to which that Court is manifestly yet in error, and which seem to have had a material influence on their own decisions. Until those errors shall have been removed by a full and candid explanation, we shall not be satisfied that we have done all we ought to do to extirpate this germ of misunderstanding, and to restore those commercial relations between the two countries, which we are not less convinced than Mr. Canning that it is equally the interest of both to maintain.

The general proposition laid down by Mr. Canning, that there is a right, in a mother country, (universally admitted among nations,) to interdict to Foreign nations a trade with her Colonies,[3] never has been controverted by this Government. But that is a very different proposition from the question which has been under discussion between the two Governments; which is, whether, when the parent country, relaxing its colonial monopoly, chooses to open the trade of its Colonies to Foreign nations, these nations have not a right to examine, for themselves, the terms on which it is so opened, and to treat of such modifications of them as will secure reciprocity in the mutual intercourse. To contend that the parent country, in the case of such open trade, may exclusively prescribe the conditions on which it shall be carried on with Foreign powers, to which conditions, without regard for their interests, they must submit, would be, in effect, to assume a right of legislation, not for the Colonies only, but for such Foreign powers.

It is alleged by Mr. Canning that "no other nation than the United States has ever complained of the interdiction of the trade to the Colonies; because, in all ages, all nations, having Colonies, have maintained such an interdiction." If Great Britain had maintained the most rigorous prohibition of all intercourse between her colonies and this country, we should have had no right to complain, and we never should have complained. Our rights begin at that precise point when she chooses to allow a trade between her Colonies and the United States. At that moment, she departs from the principle of her colonial monopoly— At that moment, a new party (the United States,) is brought forward, and what before was under the exclusive controul of one, becomes now a matter of consideration and arrangement between two. It is not at all extraordinary, that if, as is alleged by Mr. Canning, prior to the passage of the Act of Parliament of July, 1825,[4] no other Foreign nation than the United States had any trade with the British Colonies, there should have been no complaints in regard to the terms of intercourse permitted by the British Government, put forward by other Foreign nations. Where there is no commerce in fact, there can be no cause of objection as to the abstract conditions on which it is proposed. Besides, most of the commercial nations of Europe are, at the same time, Colonial powers: and it may be quite as convenient to them as to Great Britain to assume the right to prescribe, exclusively, the terms on which the intercourse between their Colonies and Foreign States shall be allowed. We have seen, too, in the act of 1825, more favourable conditions offered by Great Britain to the Colonial powers than to other nations. It would have been very remarkable if any of those powers had refused to accept such conditions. But the fact of acceptance implies the right of deliberation, and the consequent power of rejection.

So far as Mr. Canning places the right to trade between the United States and the British Colonies, in British vessels alone, on the ground of usage, neither the principle nor the fact can be admitted to be with him. As to the first: a nation may find its interest in tolerating, even for a long time, a trade which is prosecuted on unequal or unjust terms. It may not be its policy to foster its navigation. It may find compensation in some branch of its foreign trade with other nations. But, from whatever cause it may choose to submit to the injustice, no length of time can so far sanction it as to confer a right on the power, which puts forth unequal regulations, to insist upon their uninterrupted continuance. And it indisputably belongs to the party suffering under such injustice to put an end to the unequal state of things whenever he thinks proper. As to the fact of this alleged usage: neither power can fairly go back to any period beyond the 4th. of July 1776. The usage on which Mr. Canning rests the British monopoly of the Colonial trade, as it existed anterior to that epoch, would tend as much to sustain our side of the argument as the British. But as Great Britain then gave law to the Thirteen Colonies, afterwards forming the United States, as well as to the British West India Colonies, no argument can be rightfully drawn from the state of the usage prior to that period. During the war which succeeded, all commerce, between the United States and the West India Colonies, was interrupted. Peace was restored on the 30th. day of November 1782.[5] Now, if the usage contended for had existed, without disturbance, from that day down to

1818, the duration of time would have hardly been sufficient, in the affairs of nations, to create any right by prescription.

But how stands the fact? From the date of the peace up to that of the formation, in 1789, of the present Constitution of the United States, the history of the two[6] countries presents frequent struggles on[7] the subject of this very Colonial trade. Several of the States sought, by their own separate legislation, to secure for themselves a participation in it. The powers of the old Congress, under the articles of Confederation, were incompetent to the adoption and enforcement of a system of regulations for the trade, which should countervail those of Great Britain; and this incompetency was one of the most operative inducements which led to the establishment of our present Constitution. From that time down to the close of the European war, the trade had been, generally, open to the navigation of the United States, by repeated acts of British authority. Since the establishment of our present Constitution—further, since the peace of 1782, the trade has been open to us a longer period of time than it has been shut. And if the right were to be decided by the mere[8] fact of the greater[9] duration of the usage, one way or the other, the right would be with us.[10]

Mr. Canning states that these relaxations did nothing more than permit British vessels to bring certain articles into the Colonial ports directly from the place of their production, instead of circuitously through the United Kingdom; and that it was a mere municipal concern, which did not vary the exclusive character of the Colonial system. But they did something more. Whilst the supplies for the Colonies and their exports were drawn through the mother country, the commerce of that mother country being open to the United States, their navigation could fairly participate in the trade. But when British vessels were allowed a direct trade between the Colonies and the United States, to the exclusion of American shipping, it put an end to the circuitous trade, and the navigation of the United States, if they submitted to the British monopoly of this direct trade, would be deprived of their fair proportion of the transportation of the subjects of Colonial commerce which they would have enjoyed through the parent country.

Whatever may be the abstract rights of Great Britain and the United States, in respect to the regulations of an intercourse between the British West India Colonies and the United States, Great Britain did, in fact, consent to negotiate on that subject. She might have taken and adhered to the ground that she would not treat, but she did not. By consenting to treat, and by inviting the American Government to renew the negotiation, as late as March, 1826,[11] more than eight months after the date of the[12] Act of Parliament in July, 1825, we were forbidden to anticipate that, without any sort of intimation, the door of negotiation was to be suddenly closed. If we had no right to assume "that there would be at all times an unabated disposition, on the part of the British Government, to make the trade of the West India Colonies the subject of diplomatic arrangement," it must be admitted that our surprise was quite natural that you, who were sent to England among other reasons, in consequence of that very invitation, in March, should upon your arrival there, in the succeeding July,[13] and before the presentation of your credentials, be unexpectedly met by the annunciation of a measure arresting, at the threshold, all negotiation on the Colonial trade.[14]

When two nations undertake to arrange a matter of common interest between them, in a given mode, if one of them, not only without, but in opposition to, notice to the other, should itself proceed, exclusively, to regulate, by a different and less friendly mode, that interest, it cannot be denied that there is just ground of complaint. Undoubtedly, it is within the competence of a nation to refuse after agreeing to negotiate, or to break a negotiation in any stage of its progress, without ascertaining the practicability of an amicable adjustment, but this is not according to prevailing usage among friendly States.

We must think that the frankness of friendly correspondence required of the[15] British Government[16] to communicate[17] the change of its resolution as to the manner of regulating the Colonial trade, and at the same time an official communication of[18] the act of Parliament of July, 1825. Had such communications been made, the American Government would have been prepared to consider, during the succeeding Session of Congress, the conditions offered in that act. And upon receiving from the British Government those explanations which the ambiguity of the act rendered necessary, Congress could have passed an act which might have proved satisfactory to both parties. By the forbearance to make those communications, we remained in entire ignorance of the altered purposes of the British Government, and in full confidence that it was their desire, as it was our expectation, to arrange the intercourse by Convention.

Although, as is alleged by Mr. Canning, it is not the habit of the two Governments reciprocally to communicate to each other all[19] the acts of their respective legislatures, when a particular act is passed, which is intended to put aside a negotiation contemplated by both parties, there is an evident fitness, if not obligation, in point of frankness, to communicate it. And there is believed to be no example in which, under such circumstances, any Government has failed to communicate its act.

But, if it has not been the practice of the two Governments to interchange the whole body of their res- respective [sic] statutes, it has been usual, at least on the part of this Government, to communicate those which are the objections of negotiation. Repeated instances of such communications of acts of Congress imposing commercial restrictions, occurred, during the late European war; and the Convention of 1815 with Great Britain was made in pursuance of an act of Congress which was officially communicated to the British Government.[20]

So far from being accurate is the statement that[21] the act of Congress of March, 1823, was[22] not[23] communicated to the British Minister at Washington, that the bill, during its progress in Congress,[24] and in the form in which[25] it passed, was communicated to him by the Secretary of State, and it became a topic of official conference and correspondence while on its passage, and of official[26] correspondence between them in less than a month[27] after its enactment.[28]

We do not mean now to allege that the omission to communicate the British act was an intentional discourtesy towards the American Government; but we do mean to aver that the[29] omission, and the neglect to inform us that the act was to supersede all negotiation, combined with the explicit invitation of Mr. Vaughan to renew the negotiation given as late as March 1826,[30] had the effect of misleading us in regard to the views of the British Government. It was to this end only that reference was made in your instructions of the 11th. of November, last, to the letter which had been addressed from the Department of State to a member of Congress.[31] That letter, which was never private, acquired[32] by being published in the gazettes of the day, and a copy of it having been, at the time, furnished to Mr. Vaughan, and transmitted by him, to his Government,[33] a public, if not diplomatic character, which fairly entitled it to be cited as evidencing the known views taken, at Washington, of the British Act. The opinion expressed in that letter, that negotiation, and not legislation, was the instrument, in the contemplation of both Governments, by which they intended to regulate the Colonial intercourse, was subsequently confirmed by the forbearance of the British Government to enforce the act of Parliament towards the United States. And yet that very forbearance, which had the effect of deceiving us, though certainly not so intended, is now brought forward as a reason for declining to treat, and for[34] closing the Colonial ports. It is alleged by Mr. Canning to have been in consideration of the pendency of the proposition before Congress for conforming to the conditions of the act of 1825. If that had been stated at the time, we should not have been deceived.

Although that act did not relate specially to the United States, but addressed itself to all the Foreign Powers, the United States were the only Power with which Great Britain was negotiating on its subject matter. And as it now appears that[35] it was intended to be a substitute for the negotiation, it is difficult to resist a conviction of the obvious propriety of its being communicated to the American Government, even admitting such a communication to have been unnecessary to other Powers.

Whilst the Government of the United States must ever insist that, so long as there is an intercourse between them and the British Colonies, they have a clear right to participate in the regulation of that intercourse, their attachment to any specific mode of regulation has never been so strong as to exclude the accomplishment of that object in any other mode. They have preferred that it should be effected by Convention, because, in that way, it would be more certain, binding and durable, and, moreover, conformable to what they had just reason to suppose were the wishes of the British Government. Had they been apprized that it was the choice[36] of that Government to regulate the trade by mutual acts of separate legislation, they could have had no difficulty in adapting their measures,[37] in that respect, to those of[38] of the British Government.

Mr. Canning states, "that the act of 1825 offered like terms to all nations who were willing to purchase the right to trade with the Colonies. Some have acceded to the terms. The United States *would not*. They cannot feel it unkind or unjust that having, upon a free, and (as is known from the public proceedings of their legislature,) deliberate consideration declined to subscribe to the terms on which exception from Colonial prohibition was impartially tendered to all nations, they should find themselves, in common with such of those nations as have decided like themselves, liable to the exclusion which is, and always has been, the general principle of Colonial trade."

No exception need now be taken to the regularity of a foreign Government in[39] referring to the proceedings of the Legislature of another nation which have terminated in no affirmative act; although the practice of a Foreign Government looking any where but to the established organ of international intercourse for the acts and resolutions of Government, might have a most mischievous tendency.[40] Independent[41] of all other considerations, the danger is, if a Foreign Government undertakes to enter the halls of domestic legislation, in order to comprehend the votes and resolutions on measures which have not been matured into the form of any legislative act, that such Foreign Government may misconceive the motives and bearing of those votes and resolutions. Native Citizens often find it difficult clearly to comprehend all the causes, in numerous as- assemblies [sic], which may have occasioned the failure or passage of any given measure, or to assign, with certainty, the specific reason which may have led to either of those results.

We are quite sure that Mr. Canning had no wish to misconceive the proceedings which took place in Congress in the Session of 1825–6, in relation to the Colonial question, and yet he has greatly misconceived them. He is even mistaken as to the branch of Congress in which those proceedings were had. There was no resolution proposed in the House of Representatives, and, consequently, no debate and decision upon it, such as he describes. For the purpose of correcting the errors into which he has[42] been unintentionally drawn, I will now take some notice of those proceedings.

It is perfectly true that although the British Government made no official communication of the act of Parliament of July, 1825, the American Government, nevertheless, obtained possession of a copy of it.

It is also true that such a petition from Baltimore,[43] as Mr. Canning describes, was presented to Congress.[44]

But it should be remarked that the petitioners were uniformed [sic] of the negotiations of 1824, or of the correspondence which subsequently passed between the two Governments on the Colonial subject.[45] And, it is not, therefore, improbable that if they had been aware that the American Government expected and were desirous to arrange the intercourse by treaty, they would have abstained from petitioning Congress.

The petition was referred in both Houses to the regular Committees. That of the House of Representatives[46] made no report. The Senate's Committee reported, (a copy of their report is now transmitted to you,) that[47] "From this view of the subject and a cursory reference to the numerous acts which have been passed in relation to it, during the last ten years, both by the United States and by Great Britain,[48] evidence will at once be furnished of the complexity of the interests connected with it, of the difficulty satisfactorily to arrange them, and especially of the inefficacy of isolated legislation for the attainment of this international object; and also affording, as the Committee cannot but believe, a strong ground of preference, for an arrangement being effected, if practicable, by a Convention between the two Governments, on a just and liberal basis, which when agreed to, would be permanent and unalterable for the term of its duration." Again "From the Committee having reason to believe that an adjustment of the Commercial intercourse between the United States and the British Colonial possessions forms one of the special and prominent objects which have been committed to the Minister of the United States at the Court of London—that a corresponding desire to arrange it on a satisfactory footing appears to exist on the part of the British Government, and that the negotiations respecting it are expected to come to a definitive issue, before the next Session of Congress, the Committee, although fully agreeing with the Memorialists in the wish to cultivate and extend the trade in question, which they trust may be done to the mutual advantage of the parties concerned in it, are still unanimously of opinion that it is not expedient, at this time, to legislate on the subject; and therefore ask to be discharged

from the further consideration of the memorial." This report, it
should be borne in mind, was made to the Senate on the 31st. day of
March 1826, only nine days after Mr. Vaughan had invited the American Government to renew the negotiation.

This report was recommitted, with an understanding on the part
of the Senate that the Committee of Finance should[49] report a bill
repealing the discriminating duties. A bill was accordingly reported
on a subsequent day, (a copy of which is herewith transmitted,) containing a repeal, and nothing but a simple repeal of those duties.

This bill was reported[50] near the close of the Session, and amidst
the pressure of other business was laid upon the table; a parliamentary
disposal of it which, far from implying its rejection, admitted of its
being again taken into consideration, during any hour of any remaining day of the Session. There was then no decision on the merits of
the bill; and there was no refusal in either branch of Congress to
accede to the terms of the British act of 1825.

That there was no direct and final decision on it has been alleged,
by the member of the Senate who was most zealous in its support, to
have been owing to the want of time.[51] It is probable that that consideration had some influence; but it is most likely that the chief
cause which prevented its passage was the belief, generally entertained, that the Colonial subject was in a course of negotiation, and
would be satisfactorily arranged by treaty.[52]

Had the bill passed it would not have been in conformity with the
expectations of the British Government, as they have been since
communicated.

The first official information to this Government of the instructions
transmitted to Mr. Vaughan, by which he was authorized, in the contingency of the passage of an act of Congress to deliver a note declaring that the discriminating duties imposed upon American ships and
their cargoes, in the West Indies, should immediately cease, is contained in Mr. Canning's note of the 27th. January, 1827. No such
infor- information [sic] was communicated by Mr. Vaughan during
the Session of Congress of 1825–6.[53] If the bill which was before the
Senate had passed into a law, it would not have been such a measure
as was contemplated by the British Government; because it did not
contain a repeal of the restrictions on[54] British shipping, as to the
circuitous voyage, which is now understood to be an indispensable
requisite. We are altogether unable to comprehend why he was not
instructed to communicate the offer of the British Government during the Session of Congress. Or for what purpose an allusion is now
made to instructions which were not disclosed to the American Government, and which, having been locked up in the port-feuille of the
Minister,[55] might, for all practical purposes, as well have never been
given.

It cannot, therefore, be alleged, with any sort of propriety, that the American Government refused to accede to the terms of the act of Parliament, of 1825, nor that, upon a free and deliberate consideration, they have declined to subscribe to terms on which exception to Colonial prohibition was impartially tendered to all nations. The American Congress has never had fairly before it, and therefore has never freely and deliberately considered, the conditions of the act of 1825. And, consequently, it could not have, and has not, pro- pronounnced [sic] any decision on those conditions. Up to this day, we are far from being sure that we understand the terms on which that act tenders to Foreign nations a participation in the Colonial intercourse. Although Mr. Vaughan might not have been authorized to enter into any discussion of the provisions of the act, after the termination of the Session of Congress, it was not unreasonable to expect that he was at all times prepared by instructions to explain the purport of its provisions.

The preceding review has been taken, not for the purpose of conveying reproach, but with the hope of satisfying the Government of His Britannic Majesty, that the Government of the United States, ever animated by an anxious desire to preserve, extend, and strengthen amicable relations between the two countries, and always frank and open[56] in its correspondence and intercourse with Foreign nations, has not, in regard to the Colonial trade, deviated from its established character for good faith and fair dealing. From a careful and dispassionate consideration of all that has passed between the two Governments, on that subject, supposing, which cannot be doubted, that each has been actuated by a sincere wish to effect a satisfactory arrangement of the terms of the intercourse, it is manifest that there has been a misconception of each others' views, as to the mode of accomplishing that desirable object. Whether the Ame- American [sic] Government ought, or ought not, to have confided in their belief that it was the intention of the British Government, in the contemplated negotiation, to concur in the adjustment, by Convention, of the conditions of the trade, the American Government did, in point of fact, so confide. Whether the British Government ought, or ought not, to have expected the passage of an act of Congress acceding to the conditions of an act of Parliament of 1825, it did, in point of fact, so expect it. We have been disappointed in the negotiation which was anticipated. The British Government has been disappointed in the legislation which it anticipated. Both travelling to the same place, we have each failed to reach the point of destination, by misconception of the course of the other.[57] It is now useless and unavailing to dwell upon the past, which cannot be recalled. It will be more profitable and consistent with a friendly understanding between the two countries to survey our present mutual position, and to ascertain if it be now practicable, in any mode, to reconcile their respective interests in regard to the Colonial trade. It would not be very creditable to the councils of two great and enlightened nations, if they are substantially agreed as to the terms of that intercourse, and willing that it should be opened on these terms, that they should, nevertheless, put an entire stop to it, because they had [58] differed on the point whether those terms [59] should be inserted in the form of a Convention, or in that of reciprocal acts of legislation,[60] or because they may not be able to agree on the abstract questions of *Right, Claim* and *Usage* which Mr. Canning has discussed. To persist in closing the trade on those grounds might create doubts whether they were ever sincere in their mutual professions that it should be open.

It has been already stated that we preferred, for reasons which appeared to us to be solid, an arrangement by Convention, rather than one by law; but that, at the same time, we were not so wedded to that mode of effectuating the object as to prevent our surrender of it, in a spirit of compromise and conciliation, to the preference of Great Britain for a regulation of the intercourse by respective acts of legislative authority. We should have promptly yielded our preference, if we had been made acquainted with that [61] of the British Government. There is one advantage in a legislative regulation which an arrangement by treaty does not possess; and that is, that [62] if the amount of concession made in the law to a foreign nation, is found, upon experiment, to be injurious to the domestic interests, the law can be at any time repealed. Whereas the treaty must be allowed to have its operation, whatever that may be, during the whole term to which it is limited. From this difference in the effect of the two modes of regulation, a Government may be induced to grant commercial privileges by law, which it would not consent to throw into the more permanent and obligatory shape of conventional stipulations. On the point, for example, of the circuitous trade between the United States and the United Kingdom, through the British Colonies, the President would consent with much reluctance to a stipulation in a treaty by which British navigation should be allowed the enjoyment of that trade, to the exclusion of the shipping of the United States, whilst he would be willing that the experiment should be made, under reciprocal acts of the two Governments, revocable at the pleasure of either.

Under the influence of these considerations, the Government of the United States acquiesces in the decision which has been taken by the British Government, that the Colonial trade shall be regulated only by law.

You will avail yourself of some fit occasion to communicate to the British Government the substance of this despatch and the President's acquiescence in that decision. And you will, at the same or some other more suitable time, ascertain the disposition of that Government to open the trade by separate acts of the two Governments.

The President is willing to recommend to Congress, at its next Session, 1st. to suspend, as to the British Government, the alien duties, on vessel and cargo, and to allow the entry into our ports of British vessels, laden with the same kinds of British produce, or British colonial produce, as American vessels can lawfully import, the British vessel paying no higher charges of any kind than American vessels are, under the same circumstances, bound to pay: and, 2ly. to abolish the restriction contained in the act of the 1st. March, 1823, confining the trade to a direct intercourse between the Colonies and the United States: The effect of which will be to leave Great Britain in the exclusive possession of the circuitous trade between the United Kingdom and the United States, through the British Colonies. You will enquire, whether,[63] if Congress should pass a law to the above effect, the Order in Council of July last will be revoked, the discriminating duties operating to the disadvantage of our vessels in the British Colonial ports will be abolished, and our vessels[64] suffered to enjoy the privileges of trade and intercourse according to the enactments of the act of Parliament of the 5th. July, 1825.

Should the intercourse be opened on the above conditions, the American Government will have waived the demand heretofore made, that our produce should be received into the British Colonial ports, paying no higher duties than similar produce pays in those ports when imported from other ports of the British possessions. We should have regarded the above inquiry altogether unnecessary, and that, as a matter of course, the privileges of the act of Parliament would be extended to our navigation upon the passage of such an act of Congress as the President now offers to recommend, but for the declaration contained in Mr. Canning's note of the 11th. September last.[65] According to that declaration the British Government announced that "after having been *compelled* to apply to any country the interdict prescribed by the act of 1825, it cannot hold itself bound to remove the interdict, as a matter of course, whenever it may happen to suit the convenience of the Foreign Government to reconsider the measures by which the application of that interdict was occasioned."

If this Government had, upon full consideration, with a clear knowledge of the intention of Great Britain to regulate the Colonial trade, by law, and not by treaty, rejected the terms of the act of Parliament, after fully comprehending the import of those terms, and thereby *compelled* Great Britain to apply to the navigation of the United States the interdict of the act of Parliament, the determination of the British Government, communicated in that declaration, would not furnish any just occasion of complaint. But the Government of the

United States has never decided to reject those terms; and, from a candid and impartial consideration[66] of all that has passed, on the subject, between the two Governments, it is manifest that we have all along been looking to a different mode of arrangement from that which now appears to have been in the contemplation of the British Government. We think that we were authorized so to look, by the official correspondence which passed between them; but whether that justified us or not, we did, in point of *fact*, depend exclusively upon an arrangement by[67] Convention.[68] We can hardly suppose, under these circumstances, that the British Government, after the passage of such an act of Congress as you are now authorized to state that the President is willing to recommend, would refuse to remove the interdict which has been applied only to the navigation of the United States. A denial to them alone of the privileges of the act of Parliament of 1825, offered to all nations, would not be easily reconcileable [*sic*][69] with those friendly relations which it is the interest of both nations, as it is the anxious endeavour of the Government of the United States to cultivate and maintain.

The time and manner of executing the instructions contained in this despatch are confided to your judgment and discretion. You may have the advantage of local lights which, at this distance, do not reach us. Judging, with the aid of such as we possess, it would probably be best for you, in the first instance, to deliver an official note, limited to a presentation of such of the preceding observations as are intended to refute some of the arguments and facts brought forward by Mr. Canning in his two notes of November and January last, and there leave the subject, without making the enquiry as to the practicability of an arrangement by mutual acts of legislation. In the correspondence to which that note may possibly lead, the British Government may disclose their purposes and intentions, without formally making that enquiry, which it would be better to avoid, if those purposes can be otherwise ascertained. The powers of the President are incompetent to open the trade now, without the concurrence of Congress. It will, therefore, be sufficient to obtain a knowledge of the disposition of the British Government, in the event of the passage of such an act of Congress as has been intimated, in season for the next Session. If the British Government should not, itself, spontaneously manifest that disposition, you will then make the enquiry herein directed. Some time in the approaching autumn, when, if there shall have been any feeling of dissatisfaction produced in the British Government by the late proclamation,[70] that feeling will have abated, may prove to be a suitable time to present the enquiry. But, I repeat, you will exercise, on this matter, your own judgment. I am, with great respect, Sir, Your obedient Servant, H. CLAY

LS. NHi-Gallatin Papers (MR14). Copy, in DNA, RG59, Dip. Instr., vol. 11, pp. 288–305 (M77, R6); LI draft, with emendations in Clay's hand (noted below), in DLC-HC (DNA, M212, R8). Minor differences in capitalization, spelling, and punctuation, between the draft and the received version, have not been noted.   On April 3 President Adams observed that Clay had read him a draft of his "instruction to Mr. Gallatin, containing a reply to Mr. [George] Canning's last note on the Colonial Trade." Adams continued: "He apologized for its length, and also for the more than moderation of its tone. It answers and refutes all that has a show of reason in Canning's note, and points out its departures from matters of fact. . . . Mr. [Richard] Rush had already seen this draft, and Mr. Clay wished that Governor [James] Barbour before he leaves the city, and Mr. [Samuel L.] Southard, should examine it. Southard said he thought there was rather too much of concession in it. I inclined to the same opinion myself."   On April 11 Adams recorded that he had had "a final conversation" with Clay upon these instructions and commented: "He [Clay] said he had adopted all my suggestions minuted on the draft of his dispatch, excepting an objection to the closing paragraph, which I thought too direct a threat of hostility, and which he finally promised to soften. He also proposed to leave it discretionary whether to make any overtures for particular reciprocal legislation or not. My inclination was against it." *Memoirs*, VII, 254, 257. Comparison of the original draft with the final version is annotated below.

   1 See above, Gallatin to Clay, November 14, 20, 1826; January 28, 1827. Both notes, as well as Gallatin's reply to the first, are published in full in *American State Papers, Foreign Relations*, VI, 963–70.   2 The last four words replace others, crossed out and now indecipherable, in the draft version.   3 Following this statement, in the draft, the words, "is incontestible [*sic*], and," were crossed out.   4 Cf. above, Rush to Secretary of State, March 26, 1825, note.   5 By the preliminary treaty between the United States and Great Britain.   6 This word interlined on both the draft and the received versions.   7 This word replaces "of," crossed out, in the draft.   8 This word interlined in the draft.   9 This word replaces "more," crossed out, in the draft.   10 At this point in the draft version the following paragraph was crossed out: "It is said that it was occasionally opened; but these occasions were of [this word inserted in the line] so frequent recurrence [this word interlined] as to throw it generally open. It is admitted that the United States might, if they had thought proper, when it was first [this word interlined] so opened, have refused to admit into their ports British vessels, unless those of the United States were allowed to participate in the trade. If they had this right when the trade was first opened, they must have been equally possessed of it whenever, by any new act of the British Government, it was subsequently again opened."   11 See above, Vaughan to Clay, March 22, 1826.   12 The last three words interlined in draft.   13 The last four words interlined in draft.

   14 See above, Gallatin to Clay, August 19, 1826.   15 The last seven words interlined in draft.   16 The next word, "ought," in the draft version was crossed out.

   17 This word substituted for "have communicated," crossed out, in the draft.

   18 The last eight words substituted for "ought to have officially communicated to the American Government," as written in the draft.   19 This word underscored in the draft.   20 See above, II, 31, 37n.   21 This word substituted for "of," crossed out, in the draft.   22 This word interlined in the draft.   23 The next word, "being," crossed out in the draft.   24 The last four words replace "its passage," crossed out, in the draft.   25 The last five words replace "as," crossed out, in the draft.

   26 The last ten words interlined in the draft.   27 The last four words ("less" on the line, and the others interlined) replace "   days," the latter word crossed out, in the draft.   28 See the correspondence between John Quincy Adams and Stratford Canning, published in *American State Papers, Foreign Relations*, VI, 220–22, 231.

   29 This word is "that" in the draft.   30 The last 18 words interlined in the draft.
   31 Above, V, 905. For the letter, see above, Clay to Cambreleng, December 25, 1825.
   32 This word interlined in the draft.   33 The letter had been published in the Washington *Daily National Intelligencer*, January 10, 1826. For Clay's information that Canning had received a copy of the letter, cf. above, Gallatin to Clay, January 28, 1827.

   The word "acquired" was crossed out at this point in the draft.   34 This word interlined in the draft.   35 This word interlined in the draft.   36 This word replaces "desire," crossed out, in the draft.   37 The last three words replace "complying," crossed out, in the draft.   38 The last three words replace "with the pleasure of," crossed out, in the draft.   39 This word interlined in draft version.   40 At this point in the draft the following sentence was crossed out: "If, for example, we were to scrutinize the proceedings of the British Parliament, we might [this word replaces "should," crossed out] there sometimes find, in the speeches of His Majestys Ministers, opinions and doctrines advanced not of the most friendly character in relation to this country."   [41] In the draft, this word begins a new paragraph.   [42] The words "no doubt" have been crossed out in the draft.   [43] The last two words interlined by a clerk in the draft.   [44] Cf. above, Lloyd to Clay, February 20, 1826; Gallatin to Clay, August 19, 1826, and note.   [45] Cf. above, Clay to Gallatin, June 19, 1826, note 9.   [46] The last two words interlined in the draft.   [47] The remainder of this paragraph was added by Clay in the draft, the greater part in space apparently left for it and the rest in the right-hand margin, lengthwise on the page.   [48] Clay originally wrote, "by G. Britain and the U. States" and changed the phrase to "by the U. States and by G. Britain."   [49] The last 14 words replace "directions to the Committee to," crossed out, in the draft.   [50] This word interlined in the draft.   [51] See remarks by Samuel Smith to the Senate, February 21, 1827. *Register of Debates*, 19 Cong., 2 Sess., 407–408.   [52] Cf. above, Clay to Lloyd, November 8, 1826.   [53] Vaughan's first communication on the subject was that, above, of September 28, 1826.   [54] This word replaces "of," crossed out, in the draft.   [55] At this point in the draft the words "for all practical purposes" were crossed out and, instead, interlined after the word "might."   [56] This word replaces "straightforward," crossed out, in the draft.   [57] The last seven words replace "both having taken the wrong road," crossed out, in the draft.   [58] This word interlined in the draft.   [59] The last two words interlined by a clerk in the draft.   [60] Clay attached the remainder of the paragraph to the draft.   [61] This word replaces "the wishes," crossed out, in the draft.   [62] This word interlined in the draft.   [63] This word interlined in the draft at this point and crossed out after the word "effect," at the end of the conditional clause.   [64] The last two words replace "they," crossed out.   [65] Cf. above, Gallatin to Clay, September 13 (no. 8), 14, 20, 1826.   [66] This word interlined, apparently by copyist, in the draft.   [67] In the draft the next word "the" was crossed out.   [68] From this point the original conclusion of the draft, except for the formal closing, was crossed out. The deleted portion reads as follows: "Under those circumstances, if the British Government were, after the passage of such an act of Congress as you are now authorized to state that the President would recommend, to refuse extending to the navigation of the United States the privileges offered to all Foreign Nations by the act of Parliament, however disposed we may be to give to the acts of that Government the most friendly interpretation, we should be reluctantly constrained to form a very different judgment, on such refusal, from that which we should entertain upon the supposition of a deliberate rejection, at Washington, of the conditions of the Act of Parliament." The revised conclusion was copied, in a hand (not Adams') different from that in which the earlier part of the document is written, from two sheets of manuscript in Clay's hand. On these sheets, which are filed with the draft, Clay made several minor changes, apparently as he wrote. He also used a few abbreviations, which were copied into the draft.   [69] This word was spelled correctly by Clay and was copied correctly on the draft.   [70] Of March 17, 1827 (cf. above, Clay to Vaughan, March 17, 1827).

To David A. Hall

Wednesday morning [11th. April 1827.]

Mr. Clay's respects to Mr. Hall and he returns the letter from his brother,[1] with many thanks for the opportunity obligingly afforded to Mr. C. to peruse it. The clumsy attempt of Govr. Van Ness to injure the Administration appears to be justly estimated in Vermont. It is perfectly evident that he has been all along a secret enemy and a pretending friend. It is better that he should throw off the mask without a seat in the Senate than with one, which there can be no doubt from his own showing he would have done, had he been elected.

AN. NcD. Dated, in a strange hand, as an endorsement; addressed to Hall.
[1] Above, Hall to Clay, April 7, 1827.

To Thomas I. Wharton

My Dear Sir   Washington 11h. April 1827.

I recd. your favor of the 7h. instant.[1] I wish the Miniature painting, from which Mr. Long Acre made the engraving,[2] put in an Oval frame, so that it may be used as a pendant. I am no judge of the likeness which he has produced. Some parts of the face I think are correct.

Mr. Rush promised me to write a strong letter to the Collector on Mr Binns' affair,[3] and I have no doubt did. I hope it has produced the desired effect. Yr's Cordially   H CLAY
T. I. Wharton Esqr

ALS. KyU.   [1] Not found.
[2] James Barton Longacre, born in Delaware County, Pennsylvania, in 1794, had set up his own business as an engraver in 1819 and had prepared the portraits of George Washington, John Hancock, and Thomas Jefferson for a facsimile of the Declaration of Independence, published by John Binns the following year. His most famous work was in collaboration with James Herring, a native of London, who had emigrated to New York in 1804, and had established a portrait studio in Philadelphia in 1822. Longacre and Herring published *The National Portrait Gallery of Distinguished Americans*, in four volumes, 1834–1839. The latter publication included a Longacre engraving of Clay, but the reference here alludes to another Longacre engraving from an original miniature for *The Casket and Philadelphia Monthly Magazine*, where it was published in April, 1828.   [3] Richard Rush; William Jones; John Binns. Cf. above, Binns to Clay, May 10, 1826; Crowninshield to Clay, March 14, 1827, and note.

From Jabez D. Hammond

Dear Sir,   Albany April 11. 1827
It is now ascertained *beyond a doubt* that there is a Majority of the Senate & a large majority of the Assembly of this State friendly to the Administration— There are many who hold themselves in reserve so that the exact result can not be given— In the Assembly which consists of 128 Members only 22 can be found who avow themselves for Genl. Jackson!— This result has been obtained by the most cautious & careful inquiry & can be relied upon— I think there is a Majority of the Bucktails[1] and about two to one of the Clintonians in the Legislature who *are determined* to give the administration a fair & honest support *under any circumstances*— The people & middling class of Politicians are right but many of the Leaders of both parties are against them— On the side of the administration however is Genl. Porter, Col. Young, Mr. Sanford Gen. Van Renssellaer, Judge Spencer and I think in a few days you may reckon Ch. Justice Savage[2]—Who you probably remember as one of the best & most amiable of men—

—We are about to establish a paper in this City which will probably be managed by I. Q. Leake a former Co. Editor of the Argus[3]— It will support the Administration and denounce the combination between Gov. C. & Mr. V. B[4]— This measure is indispensable—

In short if the Administration is fortunate in the distribution of its Patronage in this State for the year to come (and I lament to say there is no portion of the Union who are so much influenced by the distribution of Patronage as New York) there cannot be a doubt of the most splendid triumph—

Gen. Porter has done much good here— Peter Sharpe of N. York will be here in a day or two— If Mr. Sanford would act with decission [*sic*] and energy he would effect much—but he is timid & over cautious— Strange delusion! If the Jackson Party succeed his political annihilation is as certain as it is that the sun will rise on the 4th March 1829—

I feel most gratefully the kind and very friendly expressions contained in your last letter[5]— I leave the subject of that letter and of my last letter on the same subject[6] entirely to you with this suggestion. That if anything shall be thought best to be done I wish to have notice of it before it is done, that I may ascertain positively that it will [me]et the approbation of *all* the prom[in]ent Friends of the Administration here before a step is taken which can not be retraced. And to again entreat you to be governed not by any desire to gratify my wishes but to act solely with reference to the success of the Administration in this State—

I am with great respect Your Obedt. Servt.

The Hon. H. Clay—   JABEZ D. HAMMOND

Allow me to say confidentially that altho' Gen. Brown is beyond question sincere in his attachment to the Administration he frequently judges very erroneously in relation to men & things in this State—

—It is fifteen years since he was a Politician here[7]— Since that time a new generation has grown up— Would it not be wise to hint this to the President?—   J.D.H.

ALS. DLC-HC (DNA, M212, R2).   [1] See above, III, 150n.
[2] Peter B. Porter; Samuel Young; Nathan Sanford; probably Stephen Van Rensselaer; Ambrose Spencer; John Savage.   [3] Cf. above, Porter to Clay, January 3, 1827, note.
[4] DeWitt Clinton; Martin Van Buren. Cf. above, Porter to Clay, April 6, 1827.
[5] Above, April 2, 1827.   [6] Above, March 22, 1827.   [7] Jacob J. Brown had been a county judge in northern New York prior to his appointment as a colonel of militia, in 1809; thereafter his career had been principally military.

From George McClure

Dear Sir   New York City 11th. April 1827

I have been in this City several days and have quietly observed the movements of the political parties,   a desperate attempt will be made to break down the present Administration, in order to pave the way for General Jackson, or rather the grand attack will be aimed against you, because it is well understood that Mr. Adams stands or falls with you,   therefore you must be prepared to meet the enemy. I have just seen a Jackson pamphlet, wherein your name is used in such a way as should call forth the indignation of every honorable man in community [*sic*],   I have procured the pamplet [*sic*] and will as soon as I return take the liberty of laying something before the public on the subject,[1]—

The question was not agitated this winter at Albany,   The Election of Van buren was no test of the strength of parties on the Presidential question,   opposition would have been useless, although were it to take place now he could hardly be elected, on account of his opposition to the Woollen bill,[2]   I barely write you these few lines at present to apprise you of approaching danger, and will immediately on my return write you more fully,   I cannot as yet go for Jackson, — —

Accept assurances of my regard and believe me yours sincerely—
Honble. H. Clay   GEO, MCCLURE

ALS. DLC-HC (DNA, M212, R2) .
[1] Cf. above, Mallory to Clay, April 4, 1827. No response by McClure has been found.
[2] See above, Pleasants to Clay, February 14, 1827, note. Van Buren, who himself had some $20,000 invested in sheep, had sought in the Senate to amend the woolens bill to provide duties on raw wool comparable to those on manufactured woolens. This amendment had been defeated. Although he had spoken on another measure shortly before the motion to table the woolens bill, he had not voted on the latter proposal. He subsequently explained that he had left the Senate Chamber "to accompany a friend on a visit to the Congressional Cemetery. . . ." Professor Remini notes Van Buren's embarrassment during this debate, as he recognized the popularity of the bill with his New York constituency and the hostility to the measure among the Virginians with whom he was seeking to build a political alliance. Remini, *Van Buren and the Making of the Democratic Party*, 134–36; Van Buren, *Autobiography*, 169; *Register of Debates*, 19 Cong., 2 Sess., 495, 496.

From Thomas Metcalfe

Dear Sir   Maysville Ky 11th Apl. 1827
I duly received your letter of the 25th Ult.[1] respecting the written opinion of Genl. Jessup &c, and I thank you for the interest you take in giving it publicity.[2] Though the doctrine established by that opinion is hardly contetested [sic] here, it may be differently viewed elsewhere

I came here yesterday and am waiting the arrival and departure of a descending Boat, for Natchez— I hope to return from that place in about five weeks. I must not delay. Judge Jno. Trimble has rented a House in *Carlisle*, and is actually coming from Cynthiana to run on the Jackson hobby[3]—he is "warmly solicited from various quarters of the district"   I am told that Desha[4] lately met with this Judge in Cynthiana and in reality did urge him to come on & run me out. It is expected that he will not only ride the Jackson hobby, but that he will come out the advocate of *state rights*, without regard to the *rights of the States*!!   They have already charged me as being the friend of *consolidation* &c   The attack will most probably be made before my return: and I shall not be backward in meeting & repeling [sic] it. My friends have advised me not to make the attack but to fight on the defensive and not to spare. Hitherto I have been very backward in taking the stump: and generally not a little embarrassed. But on this occasion

I shall neither be backward or embarrassed. I will throw dart for dart at those who throw at me and at least two for one at him that throws at my friends. Hickory shall not be spared if God spares me   There shall be no temporising now.— I will go gallantly down, or put down for a long time to come the tools & leaders of the b . . . e force by which we are to be assailed. I am not afraid of the result. A boat is in sight, and I must prepare to be off— My best respects to Mrs. Clay   Your friend &c   THOS. METCALFE

Honb. H. Clay

ALS. DLC-HC (DNA, M212, R2).   1 Not found.
2 The Washington *United States Telegraph* had published a letter, dated March 20, 1827, from Thomas S. Jesup, denying that, as president of a Court of Honor acting in reference to an earlier duel, he had delivered an opinion "that the PISTOL is the weapon sanctioned by custom on such occasions." The editor of the *Telegraph* (Duff Green), suggesting that Jesup was quibbling, had then called upon him to state his connection with the "Court." Four days later Jesup had replied by supplying a formal statement of the decision originally delivered in 1821. The ruling indicated that, as a matter of "right" from "*uniform usage*," the challenged party might name the weapons; but as a matter of opinion, "derived from the correspondence as . . . exhibited," the referees concluded that the proposition of the challenger should be accepted. The statement concluded: "This opinion is predicated upon the conviction that affairs of this kind, between honorable men, should be settled upon terms of the most perfect equality."
In referring to the matter Green had alluded to the controversy revealed in recently published correspondence between James Clarke and James Hamilton, Jr., as seconds in a proposed encounter between Metcalfe and George McDuffie. Clarke, pleading Metcalfe's inexperience with pistols, had requested rifles; Hamilton had explained that McDuffie's physical infirmity inhibited his use of a rifle and cited the "approved grounds of the sentiment and usage which have assigned the pistol, as the appropriate weapon for the decision of controversies of this character. . . ." When Clarke, as spokesman for the challenged party had insisted upon the right to name the weapons, Hamilton had refused to continue the arrangements. The *Telegraph*, commenting upon the episode, had suggested that Metcalfe so managed it as "to provoke" McDuffie to issue the challenge, so that the Kentuckian "might claim the right of the challenged party to fight with rifles, and thereby obtain an advantage. . . ."   3 Cf. above, Metcalfe to Clay, March 31, 1827. Trimble was not Metcalfe's opponent in 1827. He appears to have continued residence in Cynthiana until his death in 1852.   4 Joseph Desha.

From Hyde de Neuville

Dear Sir   Paris ce 11 avril 1827.

cette lettre vous sera remisse Par monsieur le Cte de Villers[1] qui voyage aux états unis Pour Son plaisir et Son instruction— il compte Se rendre de la au méxique et à la havanne permettez moi de reclamer pour lui toute votre obligeance,   Mr. de Villers appartient à une famille fort respectable, et Par lui même il est digne de tout votre interêt. quant à moi j'ai de Plaisir à mettre en rapport l'un de mes compatriotes avec l'un des hommes les plus distingués de ce bon Pays, que je nomme, à juste titre, ma Seconde patrie— je me Plais aussi à vous le recommander, car vous m'avez appris depuis longtems [sic] à compter Sur votre obligeance. je vous prie de vouloir bien donner ou faire donner à Mr. de Villers des lettres Pour le Méxique—

Veuillez nous rappeler Madame de Neuville et moi au Souvenir de

Madame Clay et agréer Pour vous l'assurance de ma haute considera-
tion et de mon attachement devoué.   J Hyde de Neuville
Veuillez nous rappeler aux Personnes qui Gardent de nous Souvenir.
                                                              J:
Hble. Henry Clay Secretary of State: Washington

ALS. DLC-HC (DNA, M212, R2).   1 Not identified.

INSTRUCTIONS AND DISPATCHES   April 11, 1827

To John J. Appleton, no. 3. Transmits a copy of his note of March 16, 1827, to
Baron Stackelberg and a copy of the act enclosed with it; directs Appleton to "take
some fit occasion to make known to the Government of Sweden and Norway, and
turning [*sic*] to the best account, in . . . negotiations for a permanent arrangement,
the provisions of this act. . . ." Copy. DNA, RG59, Dip. Instr., vol. 11, pp. 287–88
(M77, R6). L draft, in Daniel Brent's hand, in DLC-HC (DNA, M212, R8). Published in *American State Papers, Foreign Relations*, VI, 719.

From Albert Gallatin, London, no. 67. Transmits "the bill respecting the Corn
trade, . . . as it will probably pass the House of Commons"; notes that "It will
not be taken up in the House of Lords till after the Easter recess." States that he
has "received no communication on the subject, and . . . had no opportunity of
asking explanations in reference to the Corn and Flour, the produce of the United
States which may be imported here from Canada, and for which no provision
seems to have been made by the Bill." Cites a new restriction, in the measure,
against continuing the practice of importing "such corn and flour . . . as the
produce of Canada. . . ."
    Declares that one clause, added to the bill in committee, requires "immediate
attention" because it makes acceptance by foreign nations of provisions of the
act of Parliament of July 5, 1825 (see above, Rush to Secretary of State, March 26,
1825, note; Gallatin to Clay, August 19, 1826) "an indispensable condition of the
admission of foreign corn and flour in Great Britain," that is, "such countries
shall place, not only the commerce and navigation of Great Britain itself, but of
all her dominions abroad, on the same footing with the National Commerce and
navigation." Expresses his concern: "It was hardly credible that" Britain intends
"to apply these provisions to the United States either in violation of the Convention of 1815 [above, II, 57–59], or in order to prevent its renewal. Yet, after
all that has passed relating to the continuation of Acts of Parliament, it appears
to me necessary to obtain an explicit and immediate explanation of what was intended on that subject." Encloses an exchange of correspondence with (George)
Canning on the matter. LS. DNA, RG59, Dip. Disp., Great Britain, vol. 33 (M30,
R29). Received May 18.
    In reply to Gallatin's query, Canning explained, on April 10, that the clause in
question "goes no farther than to vest, in the Crown, a power purely discretionary,
and that the exercise of such discretionary power must, of course, be measured and
controlled in each instance, by antecedent positive obligations."
    The proposed measure had been introduced in the House of Commons on
March 29 and the committee amendment adopted on April 6; the bill passed that
body on April 12. It was taken up by the House of Lords on May 25 but was there
so amended that Canning withdrew it on June 13. Great Britain, *Sessional Papers,
House of Commons, 1826–1827*, I, 413–28; Hansard, *Parliamentary Debates*, New
Series, XVII, 292, 392, 1258; *Annual Register, 1827*, pp. 146–61.

From James Brown

My dear Sir   Paris April 12. 1827
    It was my intention to have written you a despatch by this vessel
on the subject of which you hear so much through the letters of Mr
Everett[1] which pass through this Legation, but when I reflect that the
state of things has undergone no essential change since my last and
that the future is envelloped [sic] in such obscurity that the best informed Politicians in Europe are altogether in doubt whether we shall
have peace, or war I feel some repugnance to giving a grave and official form to speculations in which I have myself no great confidence
and which may be proved by the events of to morrow to be visionary
and unfounded.
    [Comments on the surprise occasioned by announcement of the de-
cision of "the King of Spain[2] to disarm the Portuguese refugees and to
restore their equipments" and speculates that the change of policy
"arose from the complete defeat of the rebels and from an apprehension of treachery among the Spanish troops."[3] Notes that the friends
of the rebels state "that Ferdinand only wished to gain time"; "that
he will very shortly unite his force to that of the Insurgents, march
into Portugal, and put down the Constitution"; and that "Don Miguel
is the Legitimate sovereign of Portugal," who will soon "pass through
Spain to Lisbon and assume the reins of Government." Cites, in support of "this allegation," that Miguel "has declined the invitation
sent to him to visit Rio Janeiro"[4] and that "accounts from Zamora"
indicate that about 500 refugees there refuse "to give up their horses
arms and accoutrements. . . ." Weighs the influences making for war
and peace and warns of the possibility "that the offensive, and boasting speech of Mr Canning, delivered at the time of sending out the
troops to Lisbon,[5] followed as it has been, by a wavering and timid
policy, and connected with a knowledge of the embarrassments produced by the Condition of Ireland,[6] and the diminished fruits of the
revenue, may encourage the Continental enemies of Great Britain to
force her into a War. . . ."
    [Predicts that amendments to the proposed law (in France) "to re-
strict the liberty of the Press" will render the measure harmless.[7]]
    It is thought that our friend General Lafayette will be presented
as a Candidate for a Department in which the Deputy who fills the
place is not expected to survive many days.[8] Many of his friends here
think that he would consult his own happiness and the best interests
of his family in declining the honor, and I confess I am inclined to
unite with them in that opinion. He can do no good and may involve
himself in unprofitable disputes and enmities. He has passed the winter in Paris and now enjoys very excellent health.

I find you have had a stormy Session and we have every reason to expect that the next will not assume a milder character. I hope the President bears the storm with courage and I am happy to hear that your health has greatly improved.

I have learned that the Packet ship Lewis Captain Macey [*sic*] has been stranded on the Jersey short on the 8 Ulto.[9] I sent home in that vessel my last years accounts and vouchers and should feel some uneasiness had I not learned that the letter bags had been saved.[10] I hope you have received my despatches by that Vessel and that you will request Mr Pleasonton[11] to close my account[s] to the first of Jany. The very idea of having any thing sai[d] about my money matters as a Public servant is painful to me and as my accounts are exceedingly simple so I wish to have them regularly closed at the expiration of every year.

It will give my friends some pleasure to hear that my health ever since my return from the waters of Savoy has been very good, and I have every reason to hope for an exemption from my troublesome complaint. Mrs. Brown enjoys excellent health and spirits and begs me to remember her to her sister[12] to whom be pleased to present the affectionate regards of Dear Sir Your friend & faithful servt.

Honb. Henry Clay Secretary of State   JAMES BROWN

ALS. DLC-HC (DNA, M212, R2). Published in Padgett (comp.), "Letters of James Brown to Henry Clay," *Louisiana Historical Quarterly*, XXIV (October, 1941), 1034–37.
    [1] Alexander H. Everett.   [2] Ferdinand VII.   [3] Cf. above, Brown to Clay, March 23, 1827; Brent to Clay, April 7, 1827.   [4] Cf. above, Brent to Clay, March 16, 1826.
    [5] Cf. above, Gallatin to Clay, December 13, 1826; Brown to Clay, December 23, 1826; Everett to Clay, January 7, 1827; Hughes to Clay, January 21, 1827.   [6] In Ireland the issue of Catholic emancipation (see above, Gallatin to Clay, February 22, March 6, 1827) complicated the general problem of economic unrest noted above, King to Clay, December 21, 1825; February 4, April 28, 1826; Brown to Clay, March 22, May 10, 1826. The *Edinburgh Review* of December, 1826 (LXXXIX, 49–74), had published the "Report from, and Minutes of Evidence Taken before, the Select Committee of the House of Commons, on Emigration from the United Kingdom," ordered for printing on May 26, 1826, recommending public support for emigration to relieve the acute pauperism in Ireland. The article was reprinted in the Washington *Daily National Intelligencer*, April 13 and 14, 1827.   [7] Cf. above, Brown to Clay, December 13, 1826, note; January 13, February 13, 1827.   [8] The Baron François de Pinteville de Cernon, Deputy for Meaux, died, and Lafayette was elected his successor on June 23, 1827. When Charles X called for new elections on November 5, Lafayette was re-elected; and after the dissolution of the Chambers on May 16, 1830, he was again re-elected. The dissolution of the Chambers before they convened on August 1 led to the revolution of 1830, in which Lafayette assumed a leading role.   [9] See above, Brown to Clay, January 13, 1827, note. Robert J. Macy, born at Hudson, New York, commanded vessels on the Havre line from 1823 to 1831 and on the Liverpool Black Ball Line from 1831 to 1834.   [10] Cf. above, Brown to Clay, January 23, 1827, note; Thompson to Clay, April 3, 1827.
    [11] Stephen Pleasonton.   [12] Mrs. Clay.

DIPLOMATIC NOTES   April 12, 1827

To J[OAQUIN] B[ARROZO] PEREIRA, Philadelphia. Expresses regret for "the unavoidable delay" in replying to his letter of December 30, 1826; points out that the district attorney (Richard W. Habersham) "did no more than exercise" his right in making the appeal of which Pereira complains; and refers to the recent decision of the Supreme Court (cf. above, Southard to Clay, March 7, 1827, note), which he hopes "may prove entirely satisfactory" to Pereira. Copy. DNA, RG59, Notes to Foreign Legations, vol. 3, pp. 349–50 (M38, R3). ALI draft, in CSmH.

INSTRUCTIONS AND DISPATCHES   April 12, 1827

From J[OHN] M. FORBES, Buenos Aires, no. 46. Acknowledges receipt of (Daniel) Brent's letter of December 21 (cf. above, Verplanck to Clay, December 7, 1826, note), "accompanying sundry documents in support of the claim against this Government for the illegal Capture of the ship *Hope* by the English, in the outer Roadstead of this Port, during our war with Great Britain." Notes having learned, from this communication, of "a previous instruction on the same subject which never reached" him (cf. above, Mercein to Clay, April 21, 1826, note). Transmits "copies of some of" the communications that passed between W(illiam) G. Miller and the Government of Buenos Aires "at the time of the Hope's capture, . . . which will shew . . . the pretexts set up for this Government's refusing its intervention on the just demand of Mr. Miller." Expresses regret "that this claim, so just in its principles, should present itself at such an unpropitious moment," when "The situation of this Country has never been more dark and desperate. . . ." Exclaims: ". . . how ungracious would be the necessity of presenting a large pecuniary claim! and how hopeless would be its result!" States that it would "be expedient to limit" himself "in the first instance to a formal notification of the existence of the claim . . . , accompanied by conciliatory personal explanations," and that he will probably adopt this course. LS. DNA, RG59, Dip. Disp., Argentina, vol. 3 (M69, R4). Published in Espil (comp.), *Once Años en Buenos Aires*, 461–63. Received September 6. Endorsed by Clay on verso: "To be submitted to the President. HC."

Miller, a resident of Philadelphia, had been recognized as vice consul at Buenos Aires in 1811, "the first foreign representative" accredited by the republican government. Charles Lyon Chandler, "The Life of Joel Roberts Poinsett," *Pennsylvania Magazine of History and Biography*, LIX (1935), 29n. In June, 1812, he had been appointed consul at Montevideo, but he appears to have remained at Buenos Aires until March, 1821, when for some six months he corresponded as consul at Montevideo. U. S. Sen., *Executive Journal*, II, 227; Manning (arr.), *Diplomatic Correspondence . . . Latin-American Nations*, I, 322–33 *passim*, 355–56, 537–40, 570; II, 680, 897; III, 2175–86.

From J[OHN] M. FORBES, Buenos Aires, no. 47. Acknowledges receipt of Clay's letter of October 23, 1826. Reports that "In consequence of the admission on the part of the Brazilian Government of the necessity of previous notice of the existence of blockade to justify capture of vessels attempting to elude it [cf. above, Raguet to Clay, December 5, 1826; February 7, 1827], our flag acquired great favor in the eyes of the . . . almost desperate adventurers." States a belief "that, in more than one case, enterprizes have been formed between three or four English merchants, who have purchased our fast sailing vessels at Montevideo, covering the purchase by the flimsy veil of a pretended Charter party," and by use of such vessels successfully evading the blockade. Notes that "In two or three cases," he "had no proofs or even suspicions until" the vessels had been transferred (their papers surrendered to him) and commissioned as privateers, but that in a later case, that of the *La Fayette*, of Baltimore, he expects to confiscate her papers. Requests, in view of threats of prosecutions against himself, an opinion from "the Attorney General [William Wirt] as to the validity of simulated Charter-parties to cover illegal sales." Adds, in a postscript dated April 20, 1827, that Manuel José García has departed for England, via Rio de Janeiro, where he is authorized to negotiate a peace treaty should the Emperor (Peter I) be "disposed to listen to fair and reasonable terms" (cf. above, Forbes to Clay, September 25, 1826), although García's "ultimate diplomatic destination is London, at which place he has powers to promote peace or to seek the means of continuing the war. . . ." Points out that "The humiliating necessity which has dictated the mission of Mr. García, the active but secret enemy of the present Ministry and the devoted Agent of the British and Brazilian factions, augurs but poor hopes of the basis which he may be empowered to propose." Defines that basis as "The mutual evacuation of the disputed territory [the Banda Oriental], leaving its inhabitants to the election of their future lot and character" and possibly leading to an appeal to "some European Government" for aid.

Observes that "The projected Congress at San Juan is fast organizing" and expresses fear, that, in the face of a growing "opposition party," the Government may make "some more important National sacrifices to the foreign foe, rather than such concessions as may be necessary to conciliate their domestic rivals. . . ." L, written and signed at dictation by J. Dickinson Mendenhall. DNA, RG59, Dip. Disp., Argentina, vol. 3 (M69, R4). Published in Espil (comp.), *Once Años en Buenos Aires*, 463–66; extract published in Manning (arr.), *Diplomatic Correspondence . . . Latin-American Nations*, I, 660–61. Received September 6.

Opposition to the unitarian constitution, approved by the Congress at Buenos Aires in December, 1826 (see above, Forbes to Clay, December 4, 1826), had been earlier marked in the hostility of General Juan Bautista Bustos and the withdrawal of the Province of Cordoba from the union (see above, Forbes to Clay, September 25, October 25, 1826).

Bustos had communicated his views to numerous leaders of the interior provinces, notably Manuel Gregorio Quiroga Carril, who had become Governor of San Juan Province in January, 1827. Under the latter's stimulus, plans had been developed for an agreement joining these provinces nominally as a federal republic, cemented by pacts of friendship signed by the provinces of San Luis and Mendoza on March 27 and by these provinces with San Juan on April 1. On March 28 San Luis Province had formally rejected the Buenos Aires Constitution, and on April 5 San Juan had repudiated the authority of President Rivadavia and the national Congress. Antonio Zinny, *Historia de los Gobernadores de las Provincias Argentinas* (rev. edn., 4 vols.; Buenos Aires, 1920), III, 451–53, IV, 142–43.

From NATHAN LEVY, St. Thomas. Reports his efforts to restrain the American shipmaster from "discharging and leaving behind his seamen" and the crews from "running away from their support." Again notes the difficulties encountered from withholding ships' registers from the consulate (cf. above, Levy to Clay, June 14, October 1, 1826; March 29, 1827). Comments: "If, Sir, an opinion was permitted me to express without possessing proof sufficient to substantiate the fact, I should say, The nefarious proceedings allowed and carried on here, under the American flag with or without papers to designate a nationality, makes it a solicitous policy with the Authorities to keep your Consul hoodwinked. . . ." Transmits copies of correspondence showing his "intention to guard if possible, the trust placed" with him. Cites his actions to block departure under American flag of another vessel, the schooner *La Paulita*, sailed "by a person named Andrew Wallace, . . . who calls himself a native American," after purchasing the vessel in January under condemnation "at Sierra Leone under Spanish colors for being engaged in the illicit trafic [*sic*] in Slaves." LS. DNA, RG59, Cons. Disp., St. Thomas, vol. 2 (M-T350, R2). Received May 15. The enclosed correspondence presents his request, and its rejection by Governor J. Söbötker, that an order be issued requiring that, prior to departure from port, captains of American vessels be required to present the lists of their crews to the United State consul.

Wallace, *La Paulita*, and Söbötker have not been further identified. Söbötker was apparently serving in a temporary capacity, for since 1823 the titular Governor of St. Thomas had been Peter Carl Frederick Scholten, who was at this time on leave in Denmark. Cf. below, Levy to Clay, July 29, 1827.

From J[OEL] R. POINSETT, Mexico (City), no. 83. Transmits copies of his correspondence with the Mexican Government "on the subject of deserters from our merchantmen in the ports of this Republic, being received and employed on board the Mexican vessels of war." LS. DNA, RG59, Dip. Disp., Mexico, vol. 2 (M97, R3). Received June 8.

From J[OEL] R. POINSETT, Mexico (City), no. 84. Transmits copies of a translation of a note from the Mexican Secretary of Foreign Affairs (Juan José Espinosa de los Monteros), "complaining of the conduct of a party of . . . [United States] citizens, who have entered the territory of Mexico, contrary to the laws of the country, to hunt the nutria (otter)," and of his reply, in which he "did not think proper to say, that . . . [the United States] could not prevent these incursions, and that this government ought to exercise its own police within its own territory, because such an expression of . . . opinion would have been immediately followed by violent measures against the hunting party." Suggests that Mexican "regulations . . . respecting passports . . . be published, especially in the Western States." Notes that one law applies to foreigners who enter Mexico by sea and another, adopted later, forbids entry "by land without passports countersigned by a Mexican Vice-Consul." LS. *Ibid.* Received June 8.

MISCELLANEOUS LETTERS   April 12, 1827

From CALVIN J. KEITH, "Librarian to the State," Montpelier, Vermont. States that "The Laws & State Papers of the 2d. Session of the 18th. Congress are now in this place, charged with $8.   or 10.   freight, Storage &c—"; and that "They have come once before, charged in the same manner." Inquires whether the United States Government intends to deliver them free, or whether the "Executive of each State" is expected to "pay the expense of transportation &c." ALS. DNA, RG59, Misc. Letters (M179, R65).

Daniel Brent replied, on April 20, that the State Department would, upon receipt of a statement, make reimbursement for the expense of transporting these documents. Copy, in DNA, RG59, Dom. Letters, vol. 21, p. 524 (M40, R19).

Keith's inquiry was an outgrowth of the complaint over the role of William Slade (Jr.) in delivering the laws to Vermont (see above, Hall to Clay, April 7, 1827, note). Among the charges brought against Slade's activities was the claim that he had not personally delivered the boxes as commissioned. Slade asserted that he had forwarded the laws for Vermont from his home in Middlebury to Burlington. Slade to Van Ness, June 6, 1827, published in Washington *Daily National Journal*, June 9, 1827.

From HENRY WHEATON, New York, *"Private."* Refers to his earlier letter (above, April 2, 1827); expresses a wish to receive at once his outfit; states that he does "not expect to be detained longer than the 1st July"; and asks that Clay "suggest the manner of" writing "an official letter," accepting the appointment, so as to provide a basis for remitting the outfit. ALS. DNA, RG59, Dip. Disp., Denmark, vol. 1B (M41, R3).

INSTRUCTIONS AND DISPATCHES   April 13, 1827

From J[OEL] R. POINSETT, "Private." States that, before presenting the claim of Thomas Eaton Dudley and Jacob C. Wilson (cf. above, Clay to Poinsett, January 5, 1827), he thinks "it proper to give . . . some information" that he "cannot well make the subject of an official despatch. . . ." Explains that the Mexican Government, regarding Indians "as a component part of the population," attempts, feebly, "to restrain them from committing depredations upon Mexicans and foreigners"; that "The Comanchy [sic] Indians" are regarded as "lawless Banditti," who attack all who come within their reach; that they may even respect United States citizens more than Mexicans; and that consideration of the validity of a claim for "losses sustained by a foreigner . . . may be questionable." Notes that the Mexican "government entertains an unfounded jealousy of the United States, and does not view with a favorable eye the internal commerce carried on . . . from Missouri"; that he has received repeated "Verbal complaints . . . against those traders for selling arms to the Indians, and for acting with violence and arrogance towards the local authorities of the Country"; that in the recent negotiations Mexico wished to prevent American trade with the Indians in her territory; and that he has "reason to know that this government is disposed to discourage the trade from the United States over land to New Mexico and Texas." Warns of the danger of giving Mexican authorities "additional motives" for obstructing that trade.

Adds "another reason why such a precedent ought to be established with great caution, and which arises from the character of these people": American "Traders are . . . honorable men, who respect the sanctity of an oath" and "would never prefer fictitious claims," but "Not so these people, they would make a business of it, and . . . [the United States] government would be continually pressed for claims, which had not a shadow of right. . . ." Cites the probability of deception in the claim of Manuel de Escudero, whose "Countrymen do not believe a word of his having been plundered by the Osage Indians," and who is "a man in other respects so utterly worthless" that Poinsett doubts "his story altogether."

Reports continued trouble "in the State of Durango" (cf. above, Poinsett to Clay, March 24, 1827); the financial problems of the (Mexican) government, which "instead of reducing the expences [sic] seeks to anticipate the revenues"; and the current belief "that if their resources can only be eked out for two or three years, the mines will afford them an ample revenue thereafter." Observes that "Their extreme vanity in this respect, as in every other, would be diverting, if it were not likely to be attended with such injurious effects."

Promises to press the claim if instructed to do so, although Mexico is in no condition to pay. LS. DNA, RG59, Dip. Disp., Mexico, vol. 2 (M97, R3). Received June 6.

President Guadalupe Victoria, addressing the Mexican Congress in January, 1827, had commented: ". . . the majority of the mining undertakings after having recourse to works which must precede the extraction of the metals, begin to obtain the fruits of their toils." Trans. enclosed with Poinsett to Clay, above, January 17, 1827. Foreign investment had brought increased activity in Mexican gold and silver mining; some old mines had been reopened. H[enry] G[eorge] Ward, *Mexico in 1827* (2 vols., London, 1828), II, 373ff.

MISCELLANEOUS LETTERS   April 13, 1827

To E[DWARD] EVERETT. Introduces "Doctor D[aniel] Drake" of Cincinnati, who intends to visit Boston, as a "highly esteemed friend" well known in the "Western Country" for his "scientific and professional attainments. . . ." LS. MHi.

To ALBERT GALLATIN. Introduces "Messrs. Joseph S. and John P. Smith, sons of the late Mr. James Smith, one of the most respectable merchants and citizens of Philadelphia. . . ." Explains that he has received recommendations "in their behalf." LS. NHi-Gallatin Papers (MR14).

James Smith may have been the merchant cited above, I, 50n; he was apparently not the James Smith, Jr., mentioned frequently above. Joseph S. Smith has not been identified; the other son may have been John Pancoast Smith, of Philadelphia, who died in Paris in 1844 at age 41.

From JOSEPH DELAFIELD, New York. Reports that he has "this morning" received from (Anthony) Barclay "a letter dated Savannah April 3d.," which concerns "the proposed expedition to the Lake of the Woods and the Red River." Subjoins an extract. ALS. DNA, RG76, Northern Boundary: Treaty of Ghent, 1814, Arts. VI and VII, env. 1, folder 2. Endorsed by Clay on wrapper: "To be submitted to the President." Cf. above, Delafield to Clay, March 22, April 6, 1827.

The enclosed extract reports Barclay's instructions "by His Majesty's Government, under the existing state of things, to relinquish all farther operations upon the Boundary, beyond that portion of it which is embraced by the 7th article of the Treaty of Ghent."

From LEANDRO PALACIO[s], Rio de Janeiro. Expresses thanks for Clay's letter (not found) of introduction to Condy Raguet, by whom this letter is being sent. Adds: "El interes publico ha hecho qui el Señor Raguet nos leje; y yo espero que el gobierno de los Estados Unidos havá justicia a su celo patriotia." ALS, in Portuguese, with trans. in State Department file. DNA, RG59, Notes from Brazilian Legation, vol. 1 (M49, R1). Cf. above, Raguet to Clay, February 7, 1827.

To Daniel Webster

My Dear Sir   (Private and Confidential)   Washn. 14h. Apl. 1827

As I observe, from the public prints, that you have reached Boston, I will no longer postpone the acknowledgment of your obliging favor of the 25h. Ulto. under date at Philada.

The state of things you found in that City was not very encouraging; but there was some misrepresentation to you. In the City, I fear, our friends are not all the most disinterested. On the contrary, there are some whose sole object is the aggrandizement of themselves or their immediate connexions. These it is extremely difficult to satisfy. From other parts of Pennsa. the information which reaches me (and it is not a little) is of the most satisfactory kind.[1] The abortive movement at Harrisburg (in which only 35 members of the Legislature could be got to recommend Jackson)[2] is very significant.

Henceforward, I think the principle ought to be steadily adhered to of appointing only friends to the Administration in public offices. Such I believe is the general conviction in the Cabinet. It appears to me to be important that we should, on all occasions, inculcate the incontestible [sic] truth that now there are but two parties in the Union, the friends and the enemies of the administration, and that all reference to obsolete denominations is for the purpose of fraud and deception. In this way, the efforts in particular places to revive old names may be counteracted. It is curious to see McLean and Van Buren[3] (the former endeavoring to keep alive the Federal party in Delaware, and the latter to crush it in New York) co-operating in the cause of Jackson.

I mentioned to Mr. Everett[4] that some of you who have leisure and talent ought to prepare a series of pieces, calculated for the region of and to be first published in Pennsa., in which a solemn appeal should be made to her patriotism and intelligence to stand by the great principles of National policy which she has hitherto so uniformly favored. The text ought to be Mr Giles's late resolutions in the Legislature of Va. Such a production, well executed, would have great effect in and out of Pennsa. We ought not too hastily to conclude that the state of any portion of the American population is such as to render it inaccessible to reason. Such a conclusion would strike at the foundation of all our institutions.

Powell[5] has lost his election in Va. by a small majority. I regret that event very much. In other respects, and as far as we have yet heard the elections in that State have resulted more favorably than could have been anticipated.

From the West the information continues good.

Walsh[6] has been here; and left the City more favorably impressed than when he came. He says that some prominent appointment must be given to a Philada. federalist, and that that Federalist must be Hopkinson;[7] and he also says that you concur with him in both particulars. Towards Mr. H. I have friendly feelings; but I really fear that any other Federalist in Pennsa. (not excepting James Ross) may be appointed with less injury to the Admon than Mr. H.

You were misinformed about the West P. visitors. I believ[e] very good selections (and generally friends) have been made. I mentioned Walsh and I think he is to be one. The Secy of War[8] is at present absent.

I transmit you a letter recd. this morning from Mr. Smith (Editor of the Lexn. Reporter)[9] who has just passed from Philada. to Pittsburg [sic] through Harrisburg. His opportunities of collecting information were not bad.

D. Webster Esq.

AL, signature removed. DLC-Daniel Webster Papers (DNA, M212, R22).
[1] See above, Clay to Brown, March 27, 1827.   [2] Cf. above, Clay to Johnston, April 2, 1827; Mifflin to Clay, April 4, 1827.   [3] Louis McLane; Martin Van Buren.
[4] Above, April 5, 1827   [5] Alfred H. Powell.   [6] Robert Walsh, Jr.
[7] Joseph Hopkinson.   [8] James Barbour.   [9] The letter, from Thomas Smith, has not been found. Cf. above, Mifflin to Clay, April 4, 1827.

From Daniel Webster

My Dear Sir   Private & Confidential   Boston April 14. 1827.
    I wrote you last from Philadelphia.[1] Before leaving that City I did

what little I could towards allaying feelings of partial dissatisfaction, & inspiring confidence & zeal among friends. What I learned there, & what I have heard since, make me *almost* confident that Pennsylvania will go right, in the autumn of next year. New York presented a better state of things than I expected. I saw many people in the City, & some members of the Legislature direct from Albany. All concurred in saying that the Administration not only stood well, but was gaining ground daily. It is difficult to conceive of such credulity, yet the truth seems to be that Mr Clinton[2] believes, & his friends believe, that it is possible *& probable* that Genl. Jackson's friends may take *him* up, & abandon the Genl. A New Yorker naturally attaches great importance to New York; & supposes that whoever can secure that State in his favor must necessarily prescribe his own terms; & Mr C. I believe, is as confident as Mr. *V. Buren is*, that *he*, too, can control the votes of the great state. Both will be disappointed. If we can continue to create a little more activity & exertion among our friends, a large majority of the New York votes will be certain for Mr. Adams. The recent appointments, Stagg, Rochester & Wheaton,[3] are thought to be very judicious & acceptable. I doubt whether any thing but a good judge was obtained by the appointment of Mr Betts.[4]

In this quarter, there is nothing very interesting. Our Legislature meets the end of next month, & will have to make a Senator. There will be some difficulty in finding a suitable man for the exigency of the case.[5]

I have persuaded myself to think that it would be well for the New England Legislatures, or some of them, in their summer sessions, to take occasion to express their opinions, respecting Mr. Adams' election, the merits of his Administration, and the conduct of the opposition. It seems to me high time to let our opinions be known. My wish would be to bring this matter forward in that State, in which, (of the N. E. States) there is most show of opposition; I mean New Hampshire.[6]

I could wish that some competent member of the popular branch should bring forward Resolutions, expressing distinct opinions, on the topics above mentioned, & support them by an able discussion. They would pass, by a large majority; & friends would then be known from foes. If you concur in these opinions, I wish you would take occasion to suggest them to Mr *Bell*. His opinion would have much weight with the good people in the New Hampshire Legislature.[7]

I have some communications from beyond the mountains, which are agreeable & encouraging; but your information from that quarter must be much more correct than mine, & I shall be glad to learn what you hear. At what time do you expect to leave W. for Kentucky?

The Newspapers, I observe, repeat the report that Mr Gallatin is to return in the summer.[8] I trust it is not true. He ought to stay at least till the matters now pending are all disposed of; —I mean such as are subjects of pending negotiation. Yours, with most true regard, Hon H. Clay Sec. State   DANL. WEBSTER

ALS. DLC-HC (DNA, M212, R2) .   1 Above, March 25, 1827.
2 DeWitt Clinton.   3 Peter Stagg; William B. Rochester (see above, Clay to Rochester, March 11, 1827); Henry Wheaton (see above, Clay to Nourse, November 16, 1826, note). Stagg, prominent in New York banking and commercial circles, had been nominated on January 18, 1827, as surveyor and inspector of revenue for the port of New York, to succeed Joseph G. Swift, whose commission had expired.   4 Samuel R. Betts.   5 See above, Webster to Clay, June 8, 1826, and note.   6 Cf. above, Morril to Clay, March 8, September 18, 1826; Webster to Clay, June 8, 1826; below, Webster to Clay, May 18, 1827.   7 Samuel Bell, a leading Adams supporter, acted (Clay letter not found) to promote a meeting of the "Republican friends of the Administration," designed to prepare resolutions in support of Adams, to be presented to the New Hampshire Legislature when it convened in June. But instead of joining all the friends of the administration, including the one-third of the legislature which was Federalist, the gathering under Republican delineation alienated a large body of Federalist support. The proposed resolutions were tabled in the legislature by a vote of 137–70, through combined action of the Federalists and Jacksonians in opposition to the administration. A meeting which joined Federalists and Republicans in support of Adams finally took place at Portsmouth in December, 1827, but many Federalists had by then turned to Jackson. Livermore, *Twilight of Federalism*, 226–27; Donald B. Cole, *Jacksonian Democracy in New Hampshire, 1800–1851* (Cambridge, 1970), 64–65.   8 Newspaper reports have not been found. Cf. above, Gallatin to Clay, December 30, 1826; Clay to Gallatin, February 24, 1827.

INSTRUCTIONS AND DISPATCHES   April 14, 1827

From ALBERT GALLATIN, London, no. 68. Comments that Clay probably knows of the Spanish request that French troops evacuate Spain, "it being understood that Portugal should at the same time be evacuated by the British troops." States that he has been informed that France favors the proposal and that the Spanish Minister to London, Count d'Alcudia, "has made a formal corresponding application to" the British Government. Notes that the arrangement, "on general grounds, would be acceptable" and may be embarrassing to (George) Canning, but the objective of Spain—to isolate Portugal—"is so evident" that the (British) Cabinet will reject it. Reports having learned that de Villèle "connects the recognition of the new American States with the question of the evacuation of the [Iberian] Peninsula" and has assured "the Mexican . . . agent, (Mr [Sebastián] Camacho) that he will be ready to make a treaty of commerce with Mexico, in October next, if . . . the evacuation takes place at that time"; but, "Should this event be . . . delayed, he gives only vague hopes" of negotiations. ALS. DNA, RG59, Dip. Disp., Great Britain, vol. 33 (M30, R29). Received June 5. Endorsed on verso of last page by Clay: "To be submitted to the President."

On the British and French troop withdrawals, cf. above, Brown to Clay, January 13, 1827; Everett to Clay, March 19, 1827; below, Brown to Clay, April 27, 1827; Hughes to Clay, September 16, 1827, note. The Count d'Alcudia was probably Fernando de Aguilera Contreras, Marquis de Cerralbo and Count d'Alcudia, who in 1819 had served as Ambassador of Ferdinand VII to Saxony. Despite the announced appointment of Count Ofalia (see above, Everett to Clay, January 7, March 19, 1827; below, Everett to Clay, April 19, 1827; Brown to Clay, April 27, 1827) as Minister to Great Britain, Count d'Alcudia was still holding the post into June, 1827 (cf. below, Everett to Clay, August 17, 1827).

From ALBERT GALLATIN, London, no. 69. Notes expectations "that Mr [George] Canning would be prime Minister," but adds that "the secession of a majority of the Cabinet had not been anticipated" (cf. above, Gallatin to Clay, February 22, 1827). Names "Amongst the seceders" (Robert) Peel and Lord Melville, and states that "Not the least extraordinary circumstance is that the King [George IV] . . . should have decided as he has." Predicts difficulty for Canning in forming "an administration, which will be opposed by the high Church and Tory party, without the assistance and co-operation of the Whigs." Speculates that "Our relations and negotiations with this Country" will not be "materially affected by the definitive result, whatever this may be," but that the negotiations will be delayed. ALS. DNA, RG59, Dip. Disp., Great Britain, vol. 33 (M30, R29). Received May 18.

From CHRISTOPHER HUGHES, Brussels. Expresses a hope that Clay has received his letter of March 2 "and the copies of the letters concerning the proposed sale of the House at the Hague" (cf. above, also, Hughes to Clay, March 9, 1827). Reports that he has advertised the property but has had an expression of interest from only one person, "the Minister of Foreign affairs [Baron Verstolk Van Soelen] for account of the Government" and expects a bid of "not more than 3000 Florins. . . ." Adds that he has "countermanded the Sale" and awaits the President's orders. Ascribes "the depreciation . . . to the ruinous condition of the House, which has been uninhabited and neglected for more than 20 years" and to the depressed value of "real property in Holland. . . ." Contrasts conditions in Holland with "the prosperity of Belgium. . . ." ALS. DNA, RG59, Dip. Disp., Netherlands, vol. 8 (M42, R12). Received June 5. Endorsed by Clay on verso of last page: "To be submitted to the President— Shall peremptory orders to Sell be given?"

From W[ILLIAM] TUDOR, Lima, no. 63. Predicts that (James) Cooley, whom he expects in May, "w[ill] find great difficulty in living in this city on his salary." States that he expects to leave (for the United States) in February and that he hopes soon to learn that some one has been appointed to the consulate (cf. above, Radcliff to Clay, January 23, 1826, note). ALS. DNA, RG59, Cons. Disp., Lima, vol. 1 (M154, R1). Received August 31.

Report of Interview

[ca. April 15, 1827]

After reading this extraordinary declaration of General Jackson *"before all his company,"* I called on Mr. Clay and inquired if he knew any thing about it. He replied without hesitation and with his accustomed frankness "that the statement that his friends had made such a proposition as the letter[1] describes, to the friends of General Jackson was, as far as he knew or believed, *utterly* destitute of foundation;— that he was unwilling to believe that General Jackson had made any such statement; but that no matter with whom it had originated, he was fully persuaded it was a gross fabrication, of the same calumnious character with the *Kremer* story,[2] put forth for the double purpose of injuring his public character, and propping the cause of General Jackson;—and that *for himself and for his friends* he DEFIED the substantiation of the charge before any fair tribunal whatever."

Extract from letter to John Binns, April 18, 1827, unsigned as published in Philadelphia *Democratic Press*, April 23, 1827.
[1] In a letter to Edward J. Hale, editor (1825–1865) of the Fayetteville, North Carolina, *Carolina Observer*, March 8, 1827, Carter Beverley reported that he had "just returned from General Jackson's," where he had found a crowd of company with him," including

"seven Virginians," and that *"before all his company"* Jackson had made the following statement in reference to "the election of J. Q. Adams to the Presidency": ". . . Mr. Clay's friends made a proposition to his friends, that if they would promise *for him, not* to put Mr. Adams into the seat of Secretary of State, Clay and his friends would in *one hour,* make *him,* Jackson, the President. He most indignantly rejected the proposition, and declared he would not compromit himself; and unless most *openly and fairly* made the President by Congress, he would never receive it. He declared," Beverley continued, "that he said to them, he would see the whole earth sink under him, before he would *bargain* or intrigue for it." Beverley, born at Blandfield, Virginia, in 1774, had served as a justice of the peace of Culpeper County in 1799, and had subsequently moved to Staunton, in Augusta County, where he had suffered severe financial reverses about 1810. Little is known of his later career. He died at Fredericksburg in 1844.   2 See above, Clay to Gales and Seaton, January 30, 1825, note; Kremer to Clay, *ca.*, February 3, 1825; Appeal to the House, February 3, 1825, and note.

INSTRUCTIONS AND DISPATCHES   April 15, 1827

From C[HRISTOPHER] HUGHES, Brussels, "PRIVATE." Refers to his dispatch of the previous day; discusses the condition and value of "the House & Lot at the Hague"; and strongly advises that the property be sold. Explains that he countermanded sale of the property pending further instructions for his own justification, since "it will appear almost incredible, on reading the description of the property, and on referring to the price paid for it some years ago, (whatever that may have been:) and on reflecting on the general happiness & prosperity of this Kingdom, that such a property will not sell for more than 1200 dollars; and yet . . . [he feels] assured that such will turn out to be the fact. . . ."

Acknowledges receipt of Clay's "private" letter of December 11, 1826 (not found), which "arrived at New York after Mr. [Roger Bangeman] Huygens' departure"; states that, "had it come *by* Mr Huygens," it would have saved him (Hughes) "the *sickness* 'of hope deferred. . . .'" Admits having "received, from home, much encouragement to expect a promotion. . . ." Continues: "Edwd. Livingston spoke on the subject, on his journey through Baltimore, to several of my friends, & he & others of my congress: friends seemed to think, that it would have *gone through!* However, I have read the *Poynsett Debates* [see above, Clay to Adams, January 26, 1827, note], with great attention; and I am too well assured of your & of the Presidents better judgement, & I may add, of your concern about me, connected as it happily & certainly is, with the public importance of raising this mission, to have the least doubt of your having judged wisely." Declares, however, that "the rank of our mission is a matter of surprise & discontent to the public here & to this Government" and that he is "assailed, every day & by all classes, noble & commercial and . . . exposed to no unfrequent [*sic*] moments of mortification at the *mesquine* manner, in which . . . [he is] obliged to live, & to the comparatively shabby appearance, inseparable from an inevitable participation in all the fêtes & entertainments, on the part of a public man, . . . who never makes any, the smallest return! and returns are out of the question for . . . the expenses of this country are so incredibly augmented, that . . . [he finds necessary] the closest, almost a mean economy, in every item of unavoidable household expense." Adds that "all this has depressed & dejected . . . [him] during the last two or three months," rendering him "seriously unhappy & almost good for nothing"; but promises "to rally & . . . not plague . . . [Clay] further with this painful, & . . . [he fears Clay] will say, endless topic."

Quotes a statement from Clay's letter, concerning relations between the United States and the Netherlands— "Congress will, in all probability, legislate on the subject" (cf. above, Clay to Hughes, December 12, 1826)—and warns "that any legislation on our part, *will not* be met by an abrogation of the 10 pr. Ct. bounty (for they will not allow it to be a *discrimination*; though whatever may be its name, such is undoubtedly its effect:) but will be met by some countervailing measure, on the part of this country!" Recounts, in substantiation, the details of a recent conversation with the Minister of Foreign Affairs (Baron Verstolk Van Soelen), as well as the views of the local merchants. Emphasizes "the difficulty & delicacy of the subject" and cites "the universal eagerness & malicious watchfulness, with which the European Commercial world has seemed to anticipate & look forward to some *break up*, some commercial quarrel, some misunderstanding between the two nations!"

Quotes unnamed Dutch merchants to have said: ". . . the duties upon your [United States] produce are merely nominal . . . & look at our ports; look, for example, at Antwerp; there are Forests of American masts; we are almost driven off the seas by you." Comments: "The number of our ships arrived at Antwerp, since the opening of the navigation, far exceeds the experience of all former years. The Consul, Mr. [Charles] Barnet, was here yesterday. . . ; and he said, it was astonishing! almost all of the Maryland & Virginia ships go to Rotterdam; the trade of Amsterdam dwindles away."

Summarizes information, on the Cabinet crisis in England, gained from a conversation with Sir C (harles) Bagot, with whom Hughes is on friendly terms. Concludes with a lengthy recital of a scandal involving the Prussian Minister, the Count de Schladen, "who is charged with *cheating at cards!*" and who "avers the charge to be the work of a diabolical conspiracy. . . ." ALS. DNA, RG59, Dip. Disp., Netherlands, vol. 8 (M42, R-T12).

Born in Berlin and reared in Nürnberg, Friedrich Heinrich Leopold von Schladen had studied law and government at Erlangen and Göttingen before entering upon a diplomatic career in 1790. He had held assignments as Secretary of Legation to Vienna and Lisbon and as Minister to St. Petersburg, Vienna, and Constantinople, when in January, 1824, he had been named to the post in the Netherlands. The scandal mentioned by Hughes forced his retirement in 1827.

INSTRUCTIONS AND DISPATCHES   April 16, 1827

To ALBERT GALLATIN, no. 27. Transmits, "through the hands of Mr. William P. Elliot. . . , who goes to London for the purpose of prosecuting his studies in Architecture in the Royal Academy, transcripts of all the maps referred to in the arguments, copies of which have been already sent [above, Clay to Gallatin, October 12, 1826] . . . , of the American and British Agents under the 5th. Article of the Treaty of Ghent. . . ." Notes that these copies are being sent in response to a suggestion in Gallatin's "No. 43" (above, December 22, 1826) and that a list of the documents is also being transmitted. LS. NHi-Gallatin Papers (MR14). Copy, in DNA, RG59, Dip. Instr., vol. 11, pp. 306–309 (M77, R6). Published in Manning (arr.), *Diplomatic Correspondence . . . Canadian Relations*, II, 134.

MISCELLANEOUS LETTERS   April 16, 1827

To HENRY WHEATON. Informs him that, in conformity with his request of April 12 "and by the permission of the President," his outfit, $4,500, will "forthwith" be remitted to him in New York, although his salary will not begin until "about the time of" his departure. Copy. DNA, RG59, Dip. Instr., vol. 11, pp. 305–306 (M77, R6).

From MICHAEL WITHERS, Baltimore. Calls attention to "a further denunciatory publication" against himself and his patent by (William) Thornton in "the

National Intelligencer of the 12th. Ins."; assumes that Clay will agree that he (Withers) should "meet this unbridled maniac, not only in a Court of Justice . . . but also in the public prints"; states that he will publish on "Monday next . . . a justificatory exposition." Encloses "the last number of Niles' Weekly Register" (XXXII [April 14, 1827], 113) in order to show "that the Doctor's statements are not regarded as *private* acts"; encloses also a copy of his "contemplated answer to Doctor Thornton's late publication. . . ." ALS. DNA, RG59, Misc. Letters (M179, R65). Published in Washington *Daily National Journal*, April 24, 1827. See above, Withers to Clay, February 21, March 5, 22, 1827; Thornton to Clay, March 8, 1827; Clay to Withers, March 9, 1827.

To Josiah S. Johnston

My Dear Sir   Washn. 17h. Apl. 1827.
    I received your obliging message[1] about the state of things in Kentucky through Mrs. Johnston. Other accounts which have reached me concur with yours.
    In a letter which I have this day recd. from Hammond at Albany, under date the 11h. inst. he writes "It is now ascertained *beyond a doubt* that there is a majority of the Senate and a large majority of the Assembly of this State friendly to the administration". . . . "In the Assembly which consists of 128 members only 22 can be found who avow themselves for Genl. Jackson". . . . "I think there is a majority of the Bucktails and about two to one of the Clintonians in the Legislature who are determined to give the Administration a fair and honest support, under any circumstances. The people and middling Class of politicians are right but many of the leaders of both parties are against them.". . . . He adds "In short if the Administration is fortunate in the distribution of its patronage in this State for the year to come (and I lament to say that there is no portion of the Union who are so much influenced by the distribution of patronage as New York) there cannot be a doubt of the most splendid triumph." Other accounts from N. York concur with Mr. Hammond.
    I send you a letter recd. today from Maryland.[2] Our friends are getting into motion there.
    Powell[3] has unfortunately from local causes lost his election, which is greatly to be regretted. The other elections in Virginia, as far as we have heard from them, are more favorable to the Administration than could have been expected.
    In Pennsa. the current which you observed increases in depth and strength in favor of the Administration. A meeting of the people has just been held at Chambersburg, the largest it is stated that ever convened in that place, and strong resolutions were adopted in behalf of the Administration.[4]
    We have moved from F. street to Mrs. Decatur's house.[5] The change is agreeable in all respects, except that of separating us a little farther

from some friends. I saw Mr. [sic] Johnston last evening. She and your
sons[6] were all well. I am Cordially Your friend   H. CLAY
The Honble J. S. Johnston.

ALS. PHi. Addressed to Johnston, at New Orleans, via "Steam Boat. Cavalier."
[1] Not found.   [2] Not found.   [3] Alfred H. Powell.   [4] The Chambersburg
meeting, held on April 10, had condemned the "factious & mischievous" opposition to
the administration, proclaimed "full confidence in the ability and integrity of John Q.
Adams," applauded his selection of Clay as Secretary of State, praised Clay for his support of the tariff and for his administration of the State Department, and denounced
the corrupt bargain charges as "the base and unfounded calumnies of malicious and ungenerous enemies." The body had also expressed support for protection of domestic
manufactures, opposition to the defeat of the woolens bill (see above, Pleasants to Clay,
February 14, 1827), and regret at the failure of the last Congress to pass a colonial trade
bill (see above, Clay to Force, February 25, 1827, enclosure). Washington *Daily National
Journal*, April 16, 20, 1827, the latter account quoting the resolutions as published in
the Chambersburg *Franklin Repository*.   [5] Cf. above, Rental Agreement, October
11, 1825; Clay to Henry Clay, Jr., April 2, 1827; Clay to Johnston, April 2, 1827.
[6] Cf. above, Clay to Everett, October 19, 1826, note.

From William W. Worsley

Dear Sir,   Baltimore, 17 Apl. 1827
    I regret very sincerely that it will be out of my power to take Wash-
ington City in my route home. I had all along intended doing so; but I
fell in with Mr. James Anderson, of Louisville, who will accompany
me the whole way, and the importance of having a friend and old acquaintance as a travelling companion, has induced me to forego the
pleasure of paying you a visit. I presume you have 'ere this received the
pamphlets which I forwarded to you from Philadelphia.[1]
    Whilst addressing you, I hope you will pardon me for mentioning
a subject which I consider of immense importance to the administration. I mean the giving of its patronage to its *decided* friends in place
of its enemies or its lukewarm friends. A contrary course has in no instance within my knowledge conciliated an enemy, but has, I am apprehensive, in many cases made friends who would otherwise have
been ardent and enegertic [sic], a good deal cold in the cause. For myself I have nothing to ask. I wish nothing. It is the success of the cause
which I think so important to our common country, that induces me to
throw out these suggestions.— The late advertisement of Mr. Rush on
the subject of paying off the National Debt, and one from your department on the subject of Slaves taken by the British during the late war,[2]
should, I think, have been published in the active and conspicuous
administration papers, whether publishers of the laws or otherwise. I
regret that they were not ordered for publication in the Patriot of this
place, the editor of which is a man of talents, and a warm and decided
friend to the administration.[3] Instead of which they were inserted in
the American, which is, to say the least, entirely neutral. Pardon me,
my dear Sir, if my zeal should have induced me to o'erstep the bounds
of propriety in throwing out these hints.

Present me respectfully to Mrs. Clay, and believ[e] me most sincerely
your friend,   W. W. WORSLEY

ALS. DLC-HC (DNA, M212, R2). Addressed to Clay and endorsed by him on verso:
"Answd. 20. Apl 1827." Answer not found.
    1 The "pamphlets" have not been identified.   2 The advertisements had begun
in the Washington *Daily National Intelligencer* on October 16, 1826, and March 9, 1827,
respectively. The first notified holders of unredeemed six percent Government stock,
issued under act of Congress of February 8, 1813 (2 *U. S. Stat.*, 798–99), that certificates
as listed, amounting to $2,002,306.71, were to be paid on January 1, 1827, and that no
interest would accrue thereafter. The second announced that the commissioners to adjust claims under the first article of the Treaty of Ghent (see above, Clay to Cheves,
March 23, 1827) were to convene in Washington on July 10, 1827, to begin their duties.
The latter statement concluded with a request that specified newspapers, including the
Baltimore *American*, publish the notice weekly for four weeks.   3 Isaac Munroe. Cf.
above, Webster to Clay, March 25, 1827.

INSTRUCTIONS AND DISPATCHES   April 17, 1827

From JOHN SERGEANT, Mexico, "Private." Reports that "There is nothing yet to
add to what is contained in" his earlier letters. Comments on the inaction of
Colombia in regard to the (Panama) treaties, on the increasingly "disastrous"
situation of Central America, and on the lack of information from Peru. Charges
that "Mexico continues to trifle with her obligations" and that (José Mariano)
Michelena and (José) Dominguez "are afraid to take a step of any sort lest they
should give an advantage to their enemies." Comments: ". . . some explanation
will be due to the U. States from the Nations who invited, [sic] for this extraordinary neglect, especially if it should continue much longer. The causes, it is true,
are very obvious. But it is rather an awkward thing for us to be obliged to make
their apology. If Colombia, Central America, and Peru, would handsomely acknowledge their sense of the prompt and liberal conduct of the U. States, and
their regret that unexpected occurrences had prevented the fulfilment [sic] of
their wishes, it would go far, even in the event of a total failure, to relieve the
case from some of its unpleasant incidents." Notes that (Joel R.) Poinsett received his commission by yesterday's mail, which also brought letters from home.
Concludes from the latter that "The late session [of Congress] has been marked by
more indiscriminate violence than the former one." Continues: "It has spared
neither friend nor foe, as appears in the instances of Mr. Poinsett [see above,
Hughes to Clay, April 15, 1827] and of Gales & Seaton. Mr. Van Buren's project
for 'improving the press' is worthy of the Arch Bishop of Toledo, and argues the
existence of an 'Apostolic Junto' in the U. States. The Senators who joined with
him seem to me to be true 'Apostolicals,' at least as far as the spirit is concerned.
Gales's article appears to me to be an able one, and likely to have effect. Accounts
from Pennsylvania are highly encouraging." Adds, in a postscript: "Mr. Larriza-
bal [Antonio Larrazábal], from Central America, is understood to have sent home
his resignation." ALS. DNA, RG43, First Panama Congress (M662, R1). Received
June 6. Endorsed by Clay on cover: "To be submitted to the President."
    Joseph Gales, Jr., and William W. Seaton, as editors of the Washington *Daily
National Intelligencer*, which had held the contracts as congressional printers
since 1819, had been the focus of the attack by which Jacksonians had attempted
to divert the printing of the Senate to Duff Green (cf. above, Hammond to Clay,
March 28, 1827, note). Resentment at the partisan derivation of the assault had
generated the *Intelligencer's* editorial criticism of political "caucusing" during
the Second Session of the Nineteenth Congress (see above, Clay to Brown, March
27, 1827) and accounted for that newspaper's more vigorous support of the Adams

administration, although it had endorsed William H. Crawford's candidacy in the election of 1824 (see above, III, 316, 808, 818). In the course of the Senate debate, Martin Van Buren had stated that "he had long been of opinion that the public interest might be promoted, the condition of the press, as well here as throughout the country, improved, and respect for the Senate, and accuracy in the publication of the proceedings of the Senate, better secured, by a judicious revision of the laws relative to the public printing at large. . . ." He noted that he hoped for legislation to this effect "At a more convenient season. . . ." *Register of Debates*, 19 Cong., 2 Sess., 498–99. The editor of the *Intelligencer* interpreted the comment as a threat to revive "the odious principle of the old Sedition Law, viz: the right of a party to protect itself by or from the Press through the agency of legislation by Congress." He found it "somewhat an extraordinary coincidence, that, whilst in the other House, the conduct of the Secretary of State was arraigned for changing some of the Publishers of the Laws [see above, McGiffin to Clay, February 19, 1827, note] . . . , it should be gravely proposed, as a *desideratum*, in the Senate, that the Press, not only here, but throughout the country, should be regulated by the distribution of the Public Printing. . . ." Washington *Daily National Intelligencer*, March 7, 1827.

The archbishops of Toledo, who presided over the principal see of Spain, were wealthy, politically powerful, and usually served as inquisitors-general. The Inquisition, suppressed in Spain in 1820, had gained renewed countenance as a religious office with the restoration of Ferdinand VII to power in 1823. Cf. below, Brown to Clay, September 29, 1827, and note.

To Peter B. Porter

Dear Sir:—   Washington, 18th April, 1827.

The Baron de Mareuil, the French Minister, prior to his return to France, being about to visit the Niagara frontier, I avail myself of the occasion to introduce him to your acquaintance. During the Baron's residence in this City, for about three years, he has by his dignity, intelligence, and uniform endeavor to preserve amicable relations between France and the United States, inspired all who have the satisfaction to know him here, with the highest respect. I beg you to receive him as one who has my most sincere esteem, and from whom I part with the greatest regret. I am, with great regard, Your friend and obdt. servt.   H. CLAY
Gen. Peter B. Porter.

LS. NBuHi. Delivered by Baron Mareuil.

From Duncan McArthur

Dear sir,   Chillicothe April 18th. 1827

I received a proposition, through Mrs. M. Stras, to purchas [sic] the interest of her daughter & son-in-law Mrs. & Mr. Cutts in a land warrant obtained for the services of her first husband, Stephen Southall.[1]

At her request I enclose to your care, a Deed to be executed by Mr. & Mrs. Cutts, to my son,[2] for their interest in said land warrant. He will forward fifty dollars to you, to be paid, upon the receipt of the Said Deed, duely executed, acknowledged and authenticated agreeably to the laws of the state of Maine.

I also enclose a note to Mrs. Stras which you will have the goodness to forward to her with the Deed.

I suceeded [sic] in two suits for the lands between the lines of Ludlow & Roberts,[3] the first was upon a Bill in Chancery, brought by Dun & Galloway[4] for a small tract of land which they purchased in the county of Clark, for the purpose, as they said, of testing my titles between the said lines. At the last t[erm] the Court of Common pleas dismissed their Bill with costs— They gave notice of an appeal as a [ma]tter of course, to keep up appearances.[5] The other was the suit of Ejectment brought vs. John Reynolds in the County of Champaign,[6] merely, in the first place, for the purpose of procuring legal testimony with respect to the sources of the Little Miami & Scioto rivers, to be laid before Congress, to counteract the erroneous statements, of the interested Dun, Wallace and Galloway.[7] This suit coccupied [sic] the Court [. . .] days, examining witnesses, reading depositions and arguing the case; but the Jury were not ten minutes, in making up, and returning their verdict. In this suit they also gave notice of an appeal.

I am notified by Mr. Wallace, the U.S. agent, as he styles himself, to attend on the 25th. inst. at the Northerly end of Roberts' line farther to executes [sic] surveys in those suits. There is now no doubt in the mind of any person, I believe, who heard the evidence in the Reynolds suit, but the lands claimed by me, are within or East of a direct line from the source of the Little Miami to that of the Scioto. Mr. Wallace himself, appears to have given up that point. And his only hope now appears to be, that he may be able to find a jury who may be pursua[de]d, that all the lands on the waters of the Big Miami, East of a direct line from the source of the one river to that of the other, ought to be excluded from the Va. reservation. And with that view Mr. Wallace is now about to have a survey executed of the dividing ridge or ground between the waters of the Scioto and great Miami. This will be a useless expense, of several hundred of dollars. It is really strange, and so thought by every thinking man in this country, that Mr. Rush[8] does not employ some honest disinterested person to attend to this business—so that the government would not be involved in such unnecessary expenses. The facts continually misrepresented, and the secretary and Comr. of the Genl. Land Office[9] kept ignorant of those facts.

Had an honest disinterested person been appointd [sic], instead of

Mr. Wallace, by the secretary of the Treasury, this business would long since have been settled, perhaps as much to the honor and interest of the U S. as it ever will be.

It is here well understood, that the opposition press, which prints "the Chillicothean," (owned by Messrs. Wallace & Co.) [10] the Echo of the Telegraph of your City, [11] is kept up, to slander the administration and its friends, by way of compensating the opposition in Congress to the passage, of what is called, my Bill. And it is believed, that Mr. Rush would not knowingly thus arm a party in opposition to the Administration and the interest of the country. I am Dear sir, very respectfully yours   DUNCAN MC.ARTHUR
Hon. Henry Clay

ALS. DLC-TJC (DNA, M212, R13). MS. tear obliterates words as bracketed.
[1] Martha Wood Southall (Mrs. George Frederick) Stras, had married, first, in 1784, Stephen Southall, who had served as an officer in the Virginia forces in the Revolutionary War. Following his death, at Richmond in 1799, she had married George Frederick Stras, a native of Strasburg, France, who had emigrated to the United States during the French Revolution. Stras had also died in Richmond, in 1811. Mrs. Cutts, née Lucy Henry Southall, had been born in 1785. Her husband was Charles Cutts.   [2] Allan C. McArthur, educated at Dickinson College.   [3] See above, III, 8n–9n.   [4] Walter Dun; James Galloway. The latter, born in Gettysburg, Pennsylvania, had settled in Bourbon County, Kentucky, around 1776, had participated with Kentucky forces in the Indian fighting of 1782, and had removed from Lexington, Kentucky, to the vicinity of present-day Xenia, Ohio, in 1797. He had been treasurer of Greene County, Ohio, from 1803 to 1819.   [5] State court cases not found. The suit was finally carried into the Federal Courts as Duncan McArthur's Heirs vs. Walter Dun's Heirs, originally filed on a bill of complaint on the equity side of the Circuit Court of the United States for the District of Ohio, which reached the United States Supreme Court at the January Term, 1842. It was then remanded to the Circuit Court for correction of a clerical error and was not finally decided until the January Term, 1849, when McArthur's patent was upheld. 48 U. S. (7 Howard) 262–72.   [6] This suit was also carried, on appeal from the Supreme Court of Ohio, to the United States Supreme Court, as John Reynolds, Tenant, the United States, vs. Duncan McArthur. McArthur's action of ejectment was upheld at the January Term, 1829. 27 U. S. (2 Peters) 417–41. Reynolds may have been the Illinois Congressman, 1834–1837, 1839–1843, who had been born in Philadelphia in 1789, had settled with his parents near Kaskaskia in 1800, and had begun the practice of law at Cahokia in 1812. He had been elected to the Illinois Supreme Court in 1818, was a member of the State House of Representatives from 1827 to 1829, was Governor of Illinois from 1830 to 1834, and, following his congressional career, returned to the State House of Representatives in 1846 and 1852.   [7] By act of May 26, 1824 (4 U. S. Stat., 70), Congress had authorized the President to enter into negotiations to quiet the claims of those holding lands under Virginia military warrants between Ludlow's and Roberts' lines in Ohio. During succeeding Sessions of Congress a number of bills were introduced to authorize the President to purchase the disputed claims. On December 13, 1824, Walter Dun, Cadwallader Wallace, and James Galloway, with others, had addressed a memorial to the Senate and House of Representatives, noting that they had respected the boundary line and "made no entries to interfere with the lands surveyed or sold by the government west of it" while McArthur's entries had been made at a date when they were "illegal and void" because the lands had already been sold by agents of the Federal Government. They stated, too, that Ludlow's line had been run upon advice from MacArthur and Lucas Sullivant, "the two military surveyors who had the best knowledge of the northerly part of the Virginia military district. . . ." Wallace on January 9, 1825, and Dun, representing also Galloway, on February 9, 1825, had filed statements further explaining their opposition to MacArthur's claims. American State Papers, Public Lands, IV, 71–81. Legislation was finally approved, May 26, 1830, allotting $62,515.25, with interest at 6 percent per annum from March 4, 1825, as an overall indemnity to the Virginia claimants. 4 U. S. Stat., 405.   [8] Richard Rush.   [9] George Graham.   [10] Established July 28, 1826.   [11] Washington United States Telegraph.

From Peter B. Porter

Dear Sir,   (Confidential)   New York April 18th 1827

I arrived here yesterday morning from Albany where I spent ten days waiting for information from Mr Barclay.[1] It would be difficult for me to discribe [sic] the political state of things at that place, for in truth I do not well understand it myself. I found that the personal friends of Mr Van Buren, comprising most of the State officers who are stationed at the seat of Government, & such members of the Legislature as are his devoted partizans, secretly but most actively engaged in making converts to the cause of Genl. Jackson, and, at the same time, openly inculcating neutrality & the dangers of premature committals on the Presidential question—while the friends of the Admn. were standing aloof, or acting without system or concert. I made some efforts to rouse them to exertion, but with what effect is yet to be determined.

The Albany Argus, which is a political paper & has more general circulation through the State than any other, is owned, and of course controuled by Mr V.B. & his friends. The course which it is to take (altho' against the private opinions of Croswell[2]—its Editor) has been clearly indicated for several months past. The Daily Advertiser is a Clintonian paper & will also go for Jackson. And the National Observer which alone favours the Admn. has a very limited circulation, and its editor,[3] altho' once powerfull, has, now, but little hold on the confidence of the community. The first & most obvious measure for the friends of the Admn was to establish a paper at Albany & we have succeeded in getting at Albany a partial subscription of friends for this purpose, & are now endeavouring to fill it up at this place. If we succeed, we have a clever man for an Editor,[4] who besides a good general knowledge of the politics of the day, is intimately acquainted with character & localities throughout the State. He will probably issue his *Prospectus* (if at all) within a fortnight from this time & commence publication in June or the first of July.

There is probably a majority of our present Legislature friendly to the Admn but it was not practicable to bring them out during the session. They will however hold an adjourned session in September. The belief of a coalition between Clinton & Van Buren,[5] has caused serious difficulties to the friends of the latter in bringing over proselytes & they are determined to drive him (Clinton) off the ground after having secured his partizans. He is at present very unpleasantly situated, & extremely mortified, and I am not sure that they will not eventually force him into the support of Mr Adams— I hope however that this may not happen very *soon*.

If we get up a paper at Albany I think it will have the effect to bring out those in the western parts of the State, most of which have been, thus far, entirely mute on the presidential question.

I am gratified to learn that you intend to visit this State during the Summer. If your business requires you to go to Kentucky, your journey out by the way of N.York, the Canal, & the lakes, would occupy but little additional time, & afford you an opportunity of seeing a very interesting country & its inhabitants. My advice as to your route would be that you spend a week in this City—another at Albany from which you might visit the neighboring towns of Troy, Waterford &c and their *manufactories*.— Spend a few days at the Springs[6]—take the canal at Schenectady—stop a day at Utica (without fail) & another at Syracuse— Leave the canal at Weed's basin,[7] & proceed by land through Auburn, Geneva, & Canandaigua, to Rochester, spending a day, if convenient, at each of them, but more particularly at Rochester. Take the canal again at Rochester & proceed to Black Rock.

I shall write you an official letter in the course of today or tomorrow on the Subject of our Commission.[8] Please burn this. Yours very truly & respectfully   P. B. PORTER

ALS. DLC-HC (DNA, M212, R2). Addressed to Clay, "*Private.*"
[1] Anthony Barclay. Cf. above, Delafield to Clay, April 13, 1827.   [2] Edwin Croswell.
[3] Solomon Southwick.   [4] Isaac Q. Leake.   [5] Cf. above, Hammond to Clay, January 28, April 11, 1827; Porter to Clay, February 27, April 6, 1827; Mallory to Clay, April 4, 1827.   [6] Saratoga Springs.   [7] Weedsport.   [8] See below, April 20, 1827.

INSTRUCTIONS AND DISPATCHES   April 18, 1827

From J[OEL] R. POINSETT, Mexico (City), no. 85. Acknowledges receipt of Clay's "despatch, No 19" (above, February 28, 1827); promises, "in consequence," to hold himself "in readiness to attend that Congress, jointly with Mr. Sergeant, whenever it shall assemble." Reports, with regret, the latest information from Guatemala—that 3,000 troops from San Salvador were approaching the capital (cf. above, Phillips to Clay, March 22, 1827; Valero to Clay, April 9, 1827); that "President [Manuel José] Arce was on the point of marching out against them"; and that wealthy Guatemalians were seeking "asylum in the Mexican States." States that late information from Durango indicates a "favorable termination of the differences there" (cf. above, Poinsett to Clay, March 24, April 13, 1827) when the insurrection collapsed and its leaders fled. Notes that (Henry G.) Ward, the British Chargé, is being succeeded by (Sir Richard) Packenham and that "It was announced, that on the Treaty [cf. above, Gallatin to Clay, December 16, 1826, note; Poinsett to Clay, March 17, 1827] reaching England, a Minister Plenipotentiary would be sent to represent His Britannic Majesty in Mexico." LS. DNA, RG59, Dip. Disp., Mexico, vol. 2 (M97, R3). Received June 8.

Sir Richard Packenham, born in Westmeath, Ireland, and educated at Trinity College, Dublin, had entered diplomatic service as an attaché at the Hague in 1817. He had been named Secretary of Legation in Switzerland in 1824 and held only that rank in his appointment to Mexico. He was raised to the rank of Minister Plenipotentiary in Mexico in 1835, where he remained until 1843. He served as Minister to the United States from 1843 to 1847 and, after brief retirement, as Minister to Portugal from 1851 to 1855.

From WILLIAM BLAGROVE, New York. Sends "a Sample of Superfine Sealing Wax, just made by Mr James Thomas of this city," who "is a poor, but very ingenious & good citizen," and who offers his product at one dollar per pound, "*half* price or thereabout, over the imported, of certainly not superior quality." ALS. DNA, RG59, Accounting Records, Misc. Letters. Endorsed by Clay on cover: "Try the Wax, and if good get some of it   H C." Cf. below, Thomas to Clay, May 24, 1827. Thomas has not been further identified.

From ENOCH LINCOLN, Portland, Maine. Responds to Clay's letter of March 27 (1827) on the northeast boundary question, which also contained (enclosure) excerpts from Gallatin's communication (above, Gallatin to Clay, October 30, 1826), and comments: This communication "being the foundation of some of your remarks, allow me to advert to a view of the subject, to which he [Gallatin] informs you he was led by procedures of the Legislature of New Brunswick. I now refer to what he has said as to propositions of compromise by Agents of Maine and Massachusetts relating to the boundary line. The danger of inferences under such circumstances, from the 'proceedings of the Legislature of New Brunswick,' is so evident that you will not be surprised by a denial of their correctness." Agrees with Gallatin's view of United States insistence on securing control of "all the waters which empty into the St John's west of the line running north from the source of the St. Croix" and asserts that "The Agents . . . had no authority to propose any compromise as to . . . [Maine's] boundary, and if any was offered it was officious and unwarrantable. . . ." Charges that the affair has been "misrepresented" to Gallatin.

Protests Clay's "denial [to the State] of the use of the Reports and Arguments of the Commissioners under the treaty of Ghent." Observes that, while "the State must be bound to believe in a mutual regard and to endeavor to avoid any embarrassing applications on her own part, . . . it may not be unsuitable for her to expect a degree of confidence in return." Promises "All that forbearance which the occasion requires" of the State "on the request of the General Government, until the imperious call of duty shall summon her to occupy her inheritance.—" Warns, however, that, "this State may probably claim the right to use her moral and physical energies as she may be directed by the future emergencies and. . . , if her good will shall impel her with power enough, to sustain her right to soil and jurisdiction wherever she may properly claim them, against any probable foreign and arrogant assumption: especially with the aid of the General Government."

Argues that Maine entered the Union "as a sovereign and independent State." Notes that she is particularly vulnerable to military invasion in the event of war between the United States and Great Britain. Raises question concerning "the extent of her municipal jurisdiction" and whether "she ought to be silent and passive" before a mandate of the executive of the United States, under an act of the treaty making Power. . . ." Maintains that her right to the "boundary in dispute" was established by treaty and "the difficulty has occurred only as to the application of the rule in those treaties contained. . . ." Comments: "No surrender was made, and there is not a moral or political, in other words, a govermental [*sic*] force sufficient to change the true, honest determination of the land mark."

Continues: "In regard to the sentence which you have extracted from the report of the joint select Committee as it contains a sentiment approved by the legislature and acquiesced in by the people, I shall trouble you with a brief comment in regard to it. It rests upon the idea before suggested that Maine with Massachusetts has a perfect title in the disputed territory and that the former State has a vested

indefeazible jurisdictional controul over it, the exercise of which it may irrespon-
sibly apply. It is a proposition which has been demonstrated by yourself so clearly
as to have commanded general respect that the abstraction of the territory of the
United States cannot be made by the treaty making or executive power [see above,
II, 800, 808–810]. Much more then must the domain of a State within its acknowledged limits be sacred, and much more and more is it evident that neither department of the federal government, nor all, can be the exclusive and final arbiter
as to the ascertainment of a boundary already established in description; because,
if one department, or all, have this power, they may ascertain the line falsely,
indirectly cede our State, converting it into a British dependency, and thus by
the arguments I had the invaluable satisfaction of hearing applied in another
case violate the Constitution. If, therefore, the Committee have fallen into error
it has not been in the principle of their judgment as to the rights of this State
abstractly considered; but in their view of the extent of our territory and of the
application of our authority over it."

Expresses "alarm" at Gallatin's suggestion that an umpire might be appointed
to settle the disputed boundary: "I cannot but hope that no arrangement will be
effected which will endanger the half, from the mere circumstance of a wrongful
claim to the whole, under the pitiful weakness which is liable to split the difference
between right and wrong." Warns "most respectfully, but solemnly, . . . that Maine
is bound to claim at the hands of the federal government the protection of the
integrity of her territory, the defense of her sovereignty, and the guardianship of
her State rights."

Requests for the Legislature "a schedule of those documents which may be communicated." LS. DNA, RG76, Northeast Boundary; Misc. Papers, env. 4, item 13.
Published in *American State Papers, Foreign Relations*, VI, 924–26.

From SETH SWEETSER, Jr., Baltimore. States that he forwarded "some time ago"
a packet addressed to William F. Taylor, containing a commission as consul for
Quilca and Arica (see above, Clay to Taylor, April 7, 1826), that did not reach its
destination, and that Taylor wishes him to request a duplicate, which Sweetser,
who plans to visit Peru, will deliver. ALS. DNA, RG59, A. and R. (M531, R8).

From Irah Chase

Dear Sir,   Newton, (near Boston) Mass. April 19, 1827.
    Through some unaccountable accident, your obliging letter of the
22nd ult.[1] was not received till the present week. I am happy in per-
ceiving the caution with which you would proceed in selecting a
gentleman for so elevated a station as the presidency of Transylvania
University. I am fully aware of the importance and the difficulties of
such a station; and, certainly, it can be no act of wisdom nor of real
kindness to elevate a man to an Office, till we have satisfactory evidence of his being capable of performing its duties with reputation
and usefulness.

    I feel greatly obliged, dear Sir, for the manner in which you have
stated the case, and opened the way for my communicating further
information; and I now have the happiness of sending some testimonials.

    Dr Fishback,[2] of Lexington, wrote to the Professors at Andover, (none of whom are Baptists) requesting them to state what they know of Mr. Woods.[3] They sent him their recommendation, and were pleased also to send me a copy, of which I send a transcript[4] to yourself, for your own satisfaction, and in order to secure the recommendations coming properly before the Trustees. In regard to the Professors at Andover I would just remark that Mr Stuart, in matters pertaining to his profession, is, doubtless, the most learned man in America; that Dr Porter is the senior officer and Professor of Rhetoric, and has more than once declined the presidency of a University; and that Dr Woods is universally regarded as one of the ablest theologians of the present age, and not merely a theologian, but a man whose practical wisdom and whose correct judgment of men and things, have given him more influence in the eastern states, than is possessed, probably, by any other man of his profession.[5]

The other recommendation is from Mr Henry J. Ripley, Professor of Biblical Literature and Pastoral Duties in the Newton Theological Institution, a gentleman who is himself a distinguished son of Harvard University.[6]

Mr Woods is very nearly or quite *thirty three* years of age; and the whole course of his life has been admirably adapted to fit him for such a station as the one which is to be filled at Lexington He is happily connected in marriage with a most amiable and accomplished lady.[7] I mention this fact; for you wish to know, and you have a right to know *all about Mr Woods*; and manifestly, a knowledge of this fact is of no small importance in enabling you to form an estimate of the probabity [*sic*] of his future usefulness.

In a few days, I hope to have the pleasure of sending you some additional certificates.[8]

Please to accept my cordial thanks for the copies of your Speech,[9] which you were so kind as to enclose. with great respect, your obedient servant,   IRAH CHASE

Hon. Henry Clay, &c. &c.

ALS. KyLxT. Chase, not related to Philander Chase, was a Baptist minister. Born in Stratton, Vermont, he had been educated at Middlebury College and Andover Theological Seminary and had been ordained in 1817. He had taught several years at the Columbian College (George Washington University) and from 1825 to 1845 was a member of the faculty at Newton Theological Institution. He was renowned for his emphasis upon linguistic study in interpretation of the Scriptures.
   [1] Not found. Cf. above, Clay to Bradford, February 10, 1827.   [2] James Fishback had practiced law and medicine before turning to the ministry and in the last capacity had shifted in 1816 from the Presbyterian to the Baptist faith. He ultimately embraced the views of Alexander Campbell, a founder of the Disciples of Christ, and became a Campbellite preacher in Lexington. Fishback had opposed Horace Holley's coming to Lexington as president of Transylvania, because of the latter's Unitarian views, and in 1822 had attempted to divest him from pulpit duties by urging his appointment to the professorship of "Belles Lettres, Criticism, and Elocution." When in 1825 Holley had publicly criticized one of Fihback's sermons, their alienation had become open enmity. Attacks upon Holley's religious views had left him and the university vulnerable to the social and political attacks which had induced his resignation. Sonne, *Liberal Kentucky*, 234-41.   [3] Born in Shoreham, Vermont, graduated with honors from Harvard University in 1817, and trained at Andover Theological Seminary, he had been ordained

a Baptist minister in 1821 and then appointed to a professorship in mathematics, natural philosophy, and ecclesiastical history at Columbian College. While abroad to collect equipment for the college, he had attended lectures at Oxford, Cambridge, Edinburgh, and Glasgow before returning in 1823. He had taught only one year at Columbian when he had been named to a professorship at Brown University and had served as interim president at the latter institution from December, 1826, until February, 1827. In February, 1828, he became president of Transylvania University and in 1831 removed from there to the presidency of the University of Alabama. There his views in opposition to slavery proved unpopular, and student rioting disrupted his tenure. In 1837 he returned to Providence, Rhode Island, and devoted the remainder of his life to a variety of philanthropic services. 4 Not found. 5 Moses Stuart, a graduate of Yale, had been admitted to the bar in 1802 but never practiced law. He had tutored briefly at Yale, had been licensed to preach in 1803, had been ordained to the ministry in 1806, and then had become pastor of a Congregational church in New Haven. In 1810 he had been named professor of sacred literature at Andover and held that chair until 1848.

Ebenezer Porter, also of Connecticut, had been graduated from Dartmouth College in 1792 and ordained a minister of the Congregational faith in 1796. He had preached for some 13 years and in 1812 had become professor of homiletics at Andover. In 1827 he became president of that institution. Leonard Woods, uncle of Alva Woods, had been born in Massachusetts, graduated in 1796 from Harvard, ordained pastor of a Congregational church in 1798, and named professor of theology at Andover at its founding in 1808. Prominent as a founder of the American Board of Commissioners for Foreign Missions (1810), the American Tract Society (1814), and the American Temperance Society (1826), he remained at the Andover Seminary until 1846. 6 Ripley, born in Boston, had been graduated from Harvard in 1816 and from the Andover Seminary in 1819. He was a Baptist and taught from 1826 to 1860 at Newton, founded in 1826 by the Massachusetts Baptist Education Society. 7 Woods had married Almira Marshal, of Boston, in 1823. 8 Cf. below, Bolles and Lincoln to Clay, May 2, 1827; Sharp to Clay, May 2, 1827; Ruggles and Caswell to Clay, May 3, 1827. 9 Cf. above, Sparks to Clay, April 9, 1827.

From Benedict Joseph Flaget

To his Excellency Henry Clay the Secretary of State
Dear Sir   April 19th. 1827

Once more I come to trespass on your patience & your time. Just now I receive a letter from a friend[1] of mine whom I Sent last year to Italy with letters of introduction to the various Courts of that Country.— He informs me he has been well received by all these Princes & that valuable presents to adorn my Cathedral Shall be Sent to me.[2] The King of Naples[3] in particular has promised to forward me a magnificent tabernacle with Six large Candle Sticks the whole of Brass Sumptuously gilt, & executed by the best Artists in his Kingdom. He Speaks also to Send fine paintings & many other vestments & ornaments for divine Service.— If the duties are to be paid for all these valuable articles which are not, and cannot be objects of commerce, I will be under the painful necessity to Send them back to my princely Benefactor; because at this moment, on account of a large building added to our college,[4] we have exhausted all our founds [sic] & we are involved in debts, & will be So for nearly two years. I Know that Congress alone who has enacted the law can dispense of it. But when the intention of Congress is manifested by the grant of a privilege of the Same nature & in behalf of the Same individual[5] who now Sollicits [sic]—

Has not the President the power of interpreting the law according to the precedent already established by Congress itself?— His Excellency the minister[6] of the King of Naples is to write to you upon the Same Subject. For God's Sake, give me another proof of your generous friendship, & in favour of a town where, I have been told, you have been partly trained up.[7]— My zeal for the Country which I have freely & deliberately adopted is unrelenting; & thanks be to God the good effects of it are Sensibly felt not only in Kentucky, but in all the Western Country— The Same friend I Sent into Italy tells me also that most probably he will bring along with him a Botanist & a Pharmacian [sic] of the first rate abilities, & also an excellent Drawing master. These two Learned men, if they come, will be a great acquisition for the Country, & will render important Services to the community at large— All these considerations, I trust in God, will make an impression upon our worthy President, & you on your Side you will do your best, I am Sure, in order to encourage my constant & arduous exertions for the good of Kentucky— Be So good, if you please, to inform me by your Secretary what I have to fear or to hope in the present circumstance, & with all the Sentiments of my Sincere gratitude & cordial affection I remain Of your Excellency The most obedt. & Devoted Servt. & friend

BENEDICT JOSEPH FLAGET Bishop of Bardstown

ALS. St. Maur's Library, South Union, Kentucky.
[1] Cf. above, Flaget to Clay, September 21, 1825. Flaget had sent, in his stead, Robert Abell, one of the first two native Kentuckians ordained to priesthood. Born in Washington County, Abell had entered the seminary of St. Joseph's College at Bardstown in 1812, had been given tonsure in 1814, and had been ordained in 1818. After service in the missions of western Kentucky, he was named pastor of St. Louis Church in Louisville in 1823 and returned to that parish, after a two-year European tour, in 1828.
[2] Construction of St. Joseph's Cathedral, at Bardstown, had been begun in 1816 under Flaget's ministry. By act of March 31, 1832 (6 U. S. Stat., 484) duties were remitted "on certain paintings, and other articles, for the use of the church, imported . . . into the port of New Orleans from Marseilles," by Flaget in 1827. The shipment included eight paintings, attributed to Van Eyck (probably Jan), "The Annunciation" and "Descent of the Holy Spirit"; Anthony Van Dyck, "St. Peter in Chains," "St. John Baptist," and "The Winged St. Mark"; Bartolomé Esteban Murillo, "The Coronation"; Peter Paul Rubens, "Flaying of St. Bartholomew"; and an unknown artist, "St. Aloysius Teaching."
[3] Francis I. Identification of Flaget's benefactor at this time is uncertain. The bill for the bishop's relief (see below, note 5) attributed the gifts to "the King of the French" (Louis Philippe). Robert Wickliffe, who presented the principal argument for it, described them as donated by "persons in Italy and France." Register of Debates, 22 Cong., 1 Sess., 2202. Louis Philippe, as Duke of Orleans, an emigré from France, had visited Bardstown, en route from Washington to New Orleans, in October, 1797, and had been delayed there some weeks by illness. He had met Flaget in Havana the following year. In 1809 the Duke of Orleans had married Marie Amélie, who was a sister of Francis I. Flaget, in petitioning for the relief, had attributed an earlier benefaction to "his Grace the Duke of Orleans. . . ." U. S. H. of Reps., Journal, 18 Cong., 2 Sess., 91.   [4] Flaget and his priests had been conducting St. Joseph's College, in association with the Cathedral, since 1819. When a small Catholic college at New Orleans had failed in 1824, a block of 70 students had transferred to St. Joseph's, crowding the existing facility. In 1825 a central building of two stories, joining two older wings, had been built for the college at an estimated cost of $7,000 to $8,000. In the spring of 1827 some $20,000 was owed to the college in unpaid tuition for the New Orleans students. Shaulinger, Cathedrals in the Wilderness, 225–26, 239.   [5] A bill to remit duties on "certain vestments, furniture, and paintings," sent to Flaget by Louis Philippe in 1824, had been passed by

Congress on May 20, 1826 (6 *U. S. Stat.*, 346).   6 Count Fernando Lucchesi-Palli di
Campofranco.   7 Cf. above, Clay to Harrison and others, July 25, 1826.

DIPLOMATIC NOTES   April 19, 1827

To the BARON DE MAREUIL. States that he (Clay) "lost no time," following Mareuil's "intimation that a Note, . . . addressed to this Department on the 15th.
November 1824, was still unanswered," in attempting to obtain information "concerning the claim to prize money of M. Petit, who had served as a mariner on
board the American Privateer, True Blooded Yankee, during the late war between
the United States and Great Britain." Reports that his "investigation has not yet
led to a satisfactory result" but expresses confidence "that upon a regular application at the proper place, Mr. Petit will be able to obtain his distributive share
of any money belonging to the Crew of that Vessel." Copy. DNA, RG59, Notes to
Foreign Legations, vol. 3, pp. 350–51 (M38, R3). L draft, in CSmH.

A memorandum accompanying Mareuil's earlier note in the State Department
file (DNA, RG59, Notes from Foreign Legations, France, vol. 9 [M53, R7]) comments that the United States Government had no interest in privateer awards,
other than the two percent payment due the pension fund, but that Petit might
contact one William Garrett, a disabled sailor from the vessel, now resident in
Suffolk County, Massachusetts, for the name of the prize agent.

The *True Blooded Yankee*, a French brig commissioned as an American privateer, had raided British Channel shipping with great success during 1813. In all
she had captured 27 vessels, one of them worth $400,000. Edgar Stanton Maclay,
A History of American Privateers (1st. edn., 1899; New York, 1924), 274–77. By
act of June 26, 1812 (2 *U. S. Stat.*, 759–64), prize money from captures made by
privateers was to go to the owners, officers, and crew, "to be distributed according
to any written engagement between them; and, if there be none, then one moiety
to the owners, and the other to the officers and crew." Two percent of the net
amount was to be paid to the Government as a fund for relief of those with disabilities resulting from such operations.

INSTRUCTIONS AND DISPATCHES   April 19, 1827

From A[LEXANDER] H. EVERETT, Madrid, no. 76. Encloses "a translation of the
note from Mr. [Manuel González] Salmon communicating" the decision, mentioned in Everett's last dispatch (above, April 8, 1827), of the King (Ferdinand
VII) relative to the Americans imprisoned at Ceuta and Santa Cruz (Canary
Islands). Encloses also a translation of Salmón's reply to Everett's "second note
on the subject of the seizure and detention of the public despatches borne by Mr
[Obadiah] Rich" (cf. above, Everett to Clay, February 13, 1827) and points out
that the only action taken was that "the Custom house officers who made the
seizure" were "reprimanded and directed to abstain from any similar proceedings
in future." Reports having been told by Salmón "that the King had spoken to
him on the subject of the Convention of Indemnities [cf. above, Everett to Clay,
April 7, 1827] and directed him to terminate the affair without delay." Expresses
a hope "that this business will now proceed a little more rapidly. . . ." Notes that
"The report of the appointment of the Duke of San Carlos to the place of Secretary
of State has . . . subsided, and the existing arrangement . . . seems likely to continue. . . ." Cites evidence showing the continued predominant influence of the
clergy on the King, despite concessions to the Portuguese and English. Expresses
a belief that Count Ofalia, on his way to London, will endeavor in Paris to restore

relations between the two Courts (of France and Spain) to "the usual footing." Discounts intimations by French newspapers that Ofalia has been instructed to inform France and England of Spain's intention "to fit out a new expedition against Mexico." Adds, however, that "the dominant party are less inclined than ever to an acknowledgment of the Independence of the Colonies" and attributes to "The late movements of Bolivar in Peru and Colombia and the disturbed state of some of the other Governments" (see above, Litchfield to Clay, May 22, 1826, and note; Tudor to Clay, February 3, 1827) the revival of "expectations which had been a good deal depressed by the constant ill success of the Royal arms on the Continent of America." Attributes little importance to brief "disturbances" in Catalonia, "conducted in the name of the apostolic party" and suppressed by "local authorities." ALS. DNA, RG59, Dip. Disp., Spain, vol. 27 (M31, R28). Extract published in Manning (arr.), *Diplomatic Correspondence . . . Latin-American Nations*, III, 2142–43. Received July 2.

From SAMUEL LARNED, Santiago de Chile. Acknowledges receipt, on April 14, of Clay's communication of November 4, 1826. States that "Mr. [Heman] Allen seems to think it will not be possible for him to leave this country for some two or three months to come. . . ." ALS. DNA, RG59, Dip. Disp., Chile, vol. 2 (M-T2, R2). Received September 28.

From F[RANKLIN] LITCHFIELD, Puerto Cabello. Reports a decline of commerce because of political unrest. Repeats his request for warships (cf. above, Litchfield to Clay, May 22, July 20, August 12, November 27, December 16, 1826); notes the influence of Admiral (Alexander) Cockburn, British Envoy Extraordinary at La Guaira; and, referring to the late revolution in Peru, comments on the growing unpopularity of (Simón) Bolívar, who, Litchfield thinks, will accede to the will of the people. ALS. DNA, RG59, Cons. Disp., Puerto Cabello, vol. 1 (M-T229, R1). Received May 17.

From JOSEPH S. MARKS, Maracaibo. Encloses, with his semiannual report, "the last paper recd. from Bogota, which contains the Acct of the insurrection of the Colombian Troops in Peru" (cf. above, Tudor to Clay, February 3, 1827). ALS. *Ibid.* Maracaibo, vol. 1 (M-T62, R1). Received May 16.

From WILLIAM WHEELWRIGHT, Guayaquil. Reports that "Genl. [José de] Lamar is now the chief: the command was enforced upon him." Encloses a newspaper giving "the particulars of events which occurred on the night of the 16th inst." (when the new government was established). ALS. *Ibid.*, Guayaquil, vol. 1 (M-T209, R1). Received July 11. Cf. above, Wheelwright to Clay, April 5, 1827; below, Tudor to Clay, May 5, 15, 1827.

MISCELLANEOUS LETTERS   April 19, 1827

To JAMES COLLIER. Instructs him to deliver "copies of the Laws of the last Session of Congress, and of the Congressional proceedings and Documents of the preceding Session, to the Executives of the States of Ohio, Indiana, Illinois, Missouri, Kentucky, Tennessee, Mississippi, Louisiana and Alabama. . . ." Informs him that the Department will pay his "personal expenses, and all other expenses actually incurred in the transportation and delivery of" these documents, that he will be paid five dollars a day for the service, that an advance is being made to him and that he is authorized to draw on the Department "for any further sum . . . indispensably necessary." Copy. DNA, RG59, Dom. Letters, vol. 21, pp. 520–22 (M40, R19).

A marginal notation indicates that this circular was also sent to Benjamin O. Tyler, relative to the deliveries for Pennsylvania, Delaware, Maryland, Virginia, North Carolina, South Carolina, and Georgia, and to John Davis concerning those for New Jersey, New York, Vermont, Rhode Island, Connecticut, New Hampshire, Massachusetts, and Maine. *Ibid.*, 520–21. Copies of letters by Clay to Tyler and to Davis, dated May 17, 1827, and June 9, 1827, respectively, conveying this information, are located in *ibid.*, pp. 539–40, 554–55 (M40, R19). Daniel Brent had written similar letters of appointment, concerning distribution of the laws of the previous Session of Congress, to Davis, on July 22, 1826, and to Tyler, on August 5, 1826. Copies, in *ibid.*, 355–56, 364–65.

Davis was probably the boarding-house proprietor of C Street, north, between 4½ and 6 Streets, west, in Washington.

To JARED SPARKS. Informs him, in response to his note (not found) of this date, "that Mr. [George W.] Slacum has not resigned the office of Consul at Buenos Ayres; but, on the contrary, intends to return to the duties of the station." ALS. MH.

From H[UTCHINS] G. BURTON, Raleigh (North Carolina). States that the North Carolina Legislature has commissioned him "to obtain from the British Government, information . . . relating to the history of the State"; requests Clay to forward "the accompanying papers" to (Albert) Gallatin. ALS. DNA, RG59, Misc. Letters (M179, R65). Endorsed by Clay on verso: "Mr. B. will inform Govr. B. that his letter shall be forwarded to Mr. Gallatin. HC." Daniel Brent's letter to Burton was dated April 25. Copy, in DNA, RG59, Dom. Letters, vol. 21, p. 526 (M40, R19). On this latter date Brent, "by direction of the Secretary," also forwarded Burton's letter to Gallatin. Copy, in DNA, RG59, Dip. Instr., vol. 11, p. 311 (M77, R6).

To Peter B. Porter

Dear Sir   Washington 20h. April 1827.
I should have earlier acknowledged the receipt of your favor dated on the 6h. instant at Albany, if I had not waited the arrival of that which you promised to address me from New York, and which has not yet come to hand.[1]

The draft of $5000 made by you was paid. What are we to understand from the B Govt. now declining to co-operate in the fixation of the boundary beyond the stipulation of the 7h. article?[2] After having through Mr. Barclay originally made the proposal?

The French Minister (the Baron of Mareuil) and his family are about to visit Niagara. I have taken the liberty to furnish the Baroness with a letter to Mrs. Porter,[3] and the Baron with one to you.[4] I hope you will find it convenient to pay them some attention, of which you will discover they are every way worthy. I am Yr's Cordially
Genl. Peter B. Porter   H. CLAY

ALS. NBuHi.   [1] See below, this date.
[2] See above, Delafield to Clay, April 13, 1827.   [3] Not found. The Baroness has not been further identified.   [4] Above, Clay to Porter, April 18, 1827.

To Daniel Webster

My Dear Sir   (Private and Confidential)   Washn. 20h. Apl. 1827.

I duly recd. your favor of the 14h. inst. Meetings are beginning to take place in Pennsa. of the friends of the Administration. One was held at Chambersburg a few days ago which is represented to have been the most numerous and respectable that ever assembled in that place. You will see an account of its proceedings in the Journal.[1] I think with you that there is much reason to hope of a good result in that State. Hammond gives me assurances, from Albany, that there is ascertained to be a majority in the Senate, and a large majority in the Assembly, favorable to the Administration. They have determined to establish a new and efficient paper there to expose both Clinton & V.B.[2] The delusion of the former which leads him yet to suppose that Jackson will be abandoned and he taken up is wonderful.

I have written to Mr. Bell of N. H. as you desired. I think the time has come when demonstrations should be made, and be made too in N. England, as well as elsewhere. You have no doubt heard that they had a preliminary meeting in Balto. of a most gratifying character as to the persons composing it, in which it was resolved to take the field in May, and organize the friends of Mr. Adams throughout the State.[3]

My information from the West continues good. I feel perfectly confident that there will be no loss in that quarter.

Information has just reached the City that the re-election of Newton[4] is placed beyond all doubt by the vote of Norfolk County at the beginning of this week in which he obtained about 390 to 90. Taliaferro and Mercer are or will be both re-elected.[5] I think we shall make up for the loss of Powell by the election of a friend in place of W. Smith.[6] So that the vote of Virginia will probably remain relative to the parties the same in the next that it was in the last Congress.

I have written to Mr. Gallatin that it is not expected that he will return until he shall have brought the negotiations with which he is charged to a conclusion. And I have given him a rebuke for the reports, traced to himself, of his intention to return this summer.[7] Unless therefore he comes away in violation of all rule, I do not think that he can get back this year, or, at any rate, until the last of the year— Huskissons illness prevented the renewal of the negotiation on the first of Feb, as was arranged; and, from the late accounts, it could not have recommenced as late as the 10h. March, if it indeed has by this time.[8] If there should be a change of Ministry (and I think a total change not improbable[9]—some must take place—it may be the fall before they get to work again— Your's with sincere esteem
D Webster Esq.   H Clay

P.S.   Say, when you have occasion again to write, what you hear from or about Oakley.[10]   H C

ALS. DLC-Daniel Webster Papers (DNA, M212, R22) .
¹ Cf. above, Clay to Johnston, April 17, 1827, and note.   ² See above, Porter to
Clay, January 3, 1827, note.   ³ Report of the "preliminary meeting" has not been
found. Cf. below, Clay to Everett, May 2, 1827.   ⁴ Thomas Newton, Jr. The vote in
Norfolk County, Virginia, was 393 to 92; the vote in his district, as a whole, was 623 to
121. *Niles' Weekly Register*, XXXII (May 5, 1827), 162.   ⁵ Both John Taliaferro
and Charles Fenton Mercer were re-elected.   ⁶ Alfred H. Powell; William Smith.
The latter's seat was filled by Lewis Maxwell of Weston, in present-day West Virginia.
Born in Chester County, Pennsylvania, but reared in Virginia from the age of 10, Maxwell was a lawyer and had served in the State legislature from 1821 to 1824. He held his
congressional seat as a National Republican until 1833, when he did not run for re-
election.   ⁷ Above, February 24, 1827.   ⁸ See above, Gallatin to Clay, February
5, 1827. The Washington *Daily National Intelligencer* and *Daily National Journal* on
April 20, 1827, reported arrival on April 16, of the packet ship *Columbia* from London,
carrying British newspapers to March 12, inclusive. They reported George Canning's
illness and possible resignation but nothing about resumption of the negotiations with
Huskisson.   ⁹ Cf. above, Gallatin to Clay, February 22, 1827, note.   ¹⁰Thomas
Jackson Oakley, New York lawyer, graduate of Yale, former member of Congress (1813–
1815) and of the State assembly, who was elected to the Twentieth Congress. He served
in that body from 1827 until his resignation May 8, 1828, when he became a judge (1828–
1857) in New York City. A Federalist and a Clintonian, Oakley joined the supporters of
Jackson in Congress.

From John Myers

Dear Sir,   Norfolk April 20h. 1827
Mr. Newton¹ not being in town, having gone to the E. City² election is my excuse for addressing you. That you may know who I am
personally, I enclose you a letter³ some time since recd. from my deceased friend R. C. Anderson, the object of which having been relinquished, it was not sent to you.

You will not consider that I have now any sinister design. I have
never asked my government for an office, and however desirable, or
entitled to one in common with my countrymen I might be, should
never seek it in person But a desperate & factious opposition are not
to be appeased by concession. We have just defeated in this district
the attempt to turn out Mr Newton, by a decisive though not yet
complete overthrow, in the vote of Norfolk Country [*sic*].⁴ His election
is safe. But opposition not dead. The part I have taken in this matter
entitles me I hope to speak the sentiments of his friends. The Collector
is dead,⁵ and two of the most decided opponents, who are officers of
the Customs here,⁶ have gone off for the office. As I presume there will
be other applicants, and these two are decidedly unpopular here, &
have no influence It is hoped that the President will not be hasty in
a selection.⁷

Mr. Adams knows me from meeting him last Summer. But why
should I make excuses? The proceedings in Shenandoah,⁸ as well as
here & elsewhere, prove that I only advocate the cause of order & good
government

You will see Mr. Tyler's address at the dinner in Charles City
County⁹— In haste very respectfully Your obed St
Henry Clay Esqr.   JNO. MYERS

ALS. DNA, RG59, A. and R. (M531, R5). Endorsed by Clay: "Submitted to the Secy of the Treasury. H C." Further endorsed: "Respectfully submitted to the President— R. Rush   April 26. 1827." Myers, a son of Moses Myers, had been an officer in the War of 1812 and, since 1809, a partner in the mercantile firm Moses Myers and Sons. His brothers, Frederick and Myer, were the other members of the firm.

1 Thomas Newton, Jr.   2 Elizabeth City County, one of eight Virginia shires established in 1634, now incorporated in the city of Hampton.   3 Not found.
4 Cf. above, Clay to Webster, this date.   5 Brazure W. Pryor had died on April 17. Washington *Daily National Intelligencer*, April 21, 1827.   6 Not identified.
7 On December 19, 1827, President Adams nominated Moses Myers, then about 75 years of age, collector of customs "for the district of Norfolk and Portsmouth, Virginia." The appointment was confirmed January 15, 1828. U. S. Sen., *Exec. Journal*, III, 580, 594. John Myers was shortly thereafter named deputy collector. Moses was removed from office by President Jackson in February, 1830, and John died the following November. For a confusing implication that the collectorship was in New York, cf. Adams, *Memoirs*, VII, 397.   8 The Washington *Daily National Journal* of April 16, 1827, had reprinted from the *Winchester Republican* (Virginia) an account of vote frauds in the town of Woodstock, Shenandoah County, when Jackson partisans had assaulted their opponents and permitted unqualified voters to cast ballots.   9 John Tyler had been honored at a public dinner in Richmond on March 3, on the occasion of "his retirement from the Chief Magistracy" of Virginia. He had there confirmed his preference for Adams over Jackson in the election of 1824 and his endorsement of Clay's choice of Adams (cf. above, Tyler to Clay, March 27, 1825), but he announced that from the moment he saw Adams' first annual message (see above, Clay to Stuart, December 1, 1825, note) he had "distinctly opposed . . . this administration." Basing his attack upon his commitment to "the federative principle of our government," he declared himself ready to make war for that principle "under any banner, and almost under any leader." "In such a cause," he continued, "I will consent to become a zealot." His accompanying toast saluted: "The Federative System— In its simplicity there is grandeur—in its preservation, liberty—in its destruction, tyranny." *Richmond Enquirer*, March 6, 1827.

From Peter B. Porter

Sir,   New York April 20th. 1827.

You may probably recollect, that in the course of last year, my Colleague, Mr. Barclay,[1] in compliance as he stated with instructions from his government, made a written proposition to me, that, after having ascertained the most north western point of the Lake of the Woods, where the boundary to be run under the 7th. article of the treaty of Ghent terminates, we should proceed to run, from this point of termination, a meridian line to the 49th. parallel of latitude which constitutes, by the treaty of 1818,[2] the boundary between the two countries to the west of the Lake of the Woods, and erect a monument at the point of intersection: and that this proposal was assented to by the President.[3]

As the execution of this new duty would require us again to send our Surveyors to the north west, it was subsequently suggested either by Mr. Barclay or myself and assented to by the other, that, with the consent of the two governments, the Surveyors should be instructed to trace while in that country, the parallel of 49. as far west as the red river, and there erect another monument, inasmuch as the settlements forming on that river rendered a knowledge of the boundary at that place desirable, and the ascertainment of it would add but little either to the expence or duration of the Commission. To this proposition also, the assent of the President was obtained[4]— But Mr. Barclay did not feel authorised to enter into an unqualified stipulation on this part of the subject until it should receive the sanction of his government, of which he did not then entertain any doubts.

To enable him to communicate with his government in regard to the last mentioned proposition as well as in relation to several more important points connected with our decisions under the 7th. article of the treaty, we adjourned—to meet again at New York on the 1st. of March, provided he should, in the mean time, receive answers from his government of which he was to give me the earliest notice—otherwise to meet as soon thereafter as these answers should arrive.[5]

After waiting at Black Rock until the first of April without receiving the expected information, I concluded that, as the season was approaching when it would be necessary to dispatch our Surveyors to the north west, I would repair to New York in the hope of meeting Mr. Barclay here.[6] On my arrival however Major Delafield[7] presented me with the following letter from Mr. Barclay dated at Savannah on the 3d. instant, and addressed to him.

"In a letter lately received by me from General Porter he requests me to communicate to you without delay the purport of such instructions as might be furnished me from England concerning the proposed expedition to the Lake of the Woods and the Red River. Last night the information so long desired reached me, and I avail myself of the earliest moment to impart it to you.

I am directed by his Majestys Government under the existing state of things, to relinquish all farther operations upon the Boundary, beyond that portion of it, which is embraced by the 7th. article of the Treaty of Ghent— I write in much haste and very truly I am &c."

"Anth: Barclay"

It thus appears that the British Government has thought proper not only to reject the modified proposition offered by Mr. Barclay and myself, but also to recall the original one submitted by its direction and assented to by the President.

In this state of the business nothing remains for us to do, but to complete the duties prescribed to us by the 7th. article of the Treaty, and I shall write to day to Mr. Barclay proposing to him to meet me as soon as his portion of the Maps and surveys (which are now in the hands of his Surveyors in an unfinished state) shall be completed, for the purpose of preparing and exchanging our final reports, and adjusting the expenses of the commission. I have the honor to be, very respectfully Your Obt. Servt.   PETER B. PORTER

Hon. Henry Clay Secretary of State

LS. DNA, RG76, Northern Boundary: Treaty of Ghent, 1814, Arts. VI and VII, env. 1, folder 1, item 79. Endorsed by Clay on verso: "To be submitted to the President."
[1] Anthony Barclay.   [2] Cf. above, II, 611n.   [3] Cf. above, Clay to Porter, September 25, 1826.   [4] Cf. above, Clay to Porter, October 22, 1826.   [5] Cf. above,

Porter to Clay, February 27, 1827.   6 Cf. above, Porter to Clay, April 6, 18, 1827.
   7 Joseph Delafield.

INSTRUCTIONS AND DISPATCHES   April 20, 1827

To JOHN M. FORBES, Buenos Aires, no. 5. Acknowledges receipt of his "despatch
No. 44, of 4 Jany last"; states that the President believes himself constrained by
"public considerations" to refuse the request; and adds that, "if private considerations should indispensably require" Forbes to come home, he should "take a
respectful leave of the Government of Buenos Ayres, and make known to it the
President's intention of forthwith appointing" a successor. LS. DNA, RG84,
Argentina (MR13). Endorsed by Forbes: "Recd. 25 April 1828 Answd." Extract
published in Espil (comp.), *Once Años en Buenos Aires*, 455n.

MISCELLANEOUS LETTERS   April 20, 1827

From [SAMUEL] H[EZEKIAH] HUNTINGTON, JR., Hartford, Connecticut. Encloses "a
letter of introduction [not found] from . . . Mr. [Timothy] Pitkin"; states his
(Huntington's) intention of sailing from New York on May 8; and concludes: "any
letters with which you may favour me, can be addressed to me at New York, to
the care of Anson Haydn Esq." ALS. DNA, RG59, Misc. Letters (M179, R65).
   Huntington has not been further identified. Haydn was a member of a firm of
New York commission merchants.

To James Erwin

My Dear Sir   Washington 21 April 1827.
   I recd. this morning your favor of the 22d. Ulto.[1] from which I am
sorry to learn that there is not so good a prospect as you had anticipated
of making the arrangement which I had desired about the bonds of
Mathers.[2] Should it finally fail, I do not wish any sacrifice to be made
of the bonds. I will not take less for them than their par value. Was
not there some interest payable and was it paid in February? When
can we *coerce* payment of the principal?
   I regret extremely that Anne[3] has not determined to precede you.
I think she might have trusted herself with Claiborne and your
brother[4] or either of them. We are now residing in the best house, I
think, in the City that of the late Commodore Decatur,[5] with the most
spacious apartments and extensive grounds attached to the dwelling.
Mrs. Clay has set apart a chamber with a dressing room attached to it,
next her own for Anne. We can accommodate your family, without
the least additional expence and we shall be much disappointed if you
do not come. I expect to leave here towards the last of next month,[6]
Mrs. Clay remaining behind, for K. where I shall not stay long. Mrs.
Clay will be very loansome I fear in my absence, unless Anne should
come. Give her our love and believe me Afftly Yrs   H CLAY
Mr. J Erwin

ALS. THi. Addressed to Erwin at New Orleans.   1 Not found.
2 Cf. above, Whittelsey to Clay, December 22, 1826; Clay to Whittelsey, January 20, 1827.
    3 Anne Brown Clay Erwin.   4 William C. C. Claiborne (cf. below, Erwin to Clay,
May 21, 1827); John P. Erwin. Cf. below, Clay to Brown, May 30, 1827.   5 Cf. above,
Clay to Henry Clay, Jr., April 2, 1827.   6 Cf. below, Clay to Erwin, June 3, 1827.

To Charles Hammond

My dear Sir (Private and Confidential) Washington 21st. April 1827

Dr. Drake delivered me your obliging favor of the 28h. Ulto. which I have read with great attention. I agree with you in most of your observations on the conduct & principles of the Opposition, and the consequences of *such* an Opposition upon our political systems. If the Opposition shall be defeated (as I trust they will be) in their present aim to elevate Genl. Jackson, the effect on the future may be salutary. If they succeed, undoubtedly an encouragement is held out to similar combinations hereafter.

You are right in supposing that the first battle to be fought is in Kentucky. I wish it may not be a harder one than my friends believe. They assure me, from various parts of the State, that if the number of the friends of the Admon in the H. of R. from K. in the next Congress is not increased (which they hope will be the case) it will certainly not be diminished.[1] If we do not lose ground in that election I think there will be no danger in the fall of the next year. I should be glad if your paper[2] would continue to lend a helping hand to our friends in Kentucky. The topics to be treated are the principles of the present Admon which are in conformity with those of that State, and (if you will not think me vain) myself. A plain practical explanation of the Woolen bill[3] would have good effect in K. Judge Clarke writes me from my old district that he feels entirely safe, though there is great exertion made on the Jackson side.[4] Some of the strongest relief or new Court men[5] are with him. And one of them (that I was extremely glad to hear entertained those opinions) declared that he would vote for no body who was against the Woolen bill or for Jackson.

I anticipate more violence in the next Session than we have had at either of the former Sessions; because parties will be more equally divided, and the eagerness will increase as the period of the election approaches.

Your reasons in favor of my being brought out as a Candidate for the V.P. have occurred to me, and undoubtedly have weight. On that subject, I have decided chearfully to submit to the decision of my friends, be it what it may, without interposing my judgment, or intimating any wish, one way or the other, which I may have. My opinion is clearly that the selection ought to be made of him who can bring the most aid to the main object (the election of President) to which every thing else should be made to yield. I believe there was an understanding among many friends of the Admon that the question should be adjourned from the last to the next Session of Congress and then finally considered.

Mr. Calhoun's[6] friends press him, I believe, with much tenacity; but my opinion is that they will ultimately be compelled to give him up.

I am mortified and chagrined with the state of feelings in which Genl. Harrison[7] left this City, of which I had but too much evidence. It is, I fear, mainly to be traced to his wishes in respect to the V.P. God knows, if he can be elected, with Mr. Adams, no man would more sincerely rejoice at it (and I so told him) than I should. He thinks, I fear, that I desire the place, and that I am unfriendly to his elevation. What can be done to remove such erroneous and (to me) distressing impressions?

The suspicions, which prevail as to the fidelity of the P.M.G. to the Administration, or rather the cause of them, is much to be regretted. The President is well apprized of the whole matter, 'though he thinks there is some exaggeration to the disadvantage of that officer. So I have been inclined also and wished to believe. I hardly think that a case exists strong enough to justify his removal; and, if it did, Mr. Adams's unwillingness to do any thing which, has even the appearance of harshness, would prevent his taking so decided a measure. I know that some time ago the strongest assurances were given by that officer to the President. They satisfied him at the time.[8]

The elections in Virginia have not eventuated more unfavorably than was to be anticipated from the extraordinary excitement which has been kept up there. Newton's re-election is now known to be uncertain [sic], with probably a larger majority than he obtained on the occasion of former contested elections. I regret extremely Powells defeat, which is attributable however more to local than political causes.[9]

You see much display of public meetings in Maryland. They are nothing but smoke. A few persons collect at a tavern or a small village, appoint a chairman, secy. &c and adopt resolutions. Out comes the Telegraph, with a *numerous* and respectable meeting &c.[10] In some instances the resolutions have been published although, in point of fact, no meeting was organized. I am Cordially Your friend & ob. Servt.
Charles Hammond Esqr.   H. CLAY

ALS. InU.   [1] Cf. above, Clay to Taylor, April 4, 1827, and note.
[2] Cincinnati *Liberty Hall and Cincinnati Gazette*. Cf. above, Clay to Hammond, November 10, 1826.   [3] Cf. above, Pleasants to Clay, February 14, 1827, note.   [4] Cf. above, Crittenden to Clay, March 3, 1827, note. Clarke's letter to Clay has not been found.
[5] See above, III, 902n.   [6] John C. Calhoun.   [7] On February 9, 1827, while William Henry Harrison was in attendance at Congress, Clay had proposed to Adams that the General be appointed Minister to Colombia. Adams does not record his answer at that time; but when the recommendation was renewed by Joseph Vance in May, 1828, Adams commented: "This person's [Harrison's] thirst for lucrative office is absolutely rabid. Vice-President, Major-General of the army, Minister to Colombia—for each of these places he has been this very session as hot in pursuit as a hound on the scent of a hare." Adams

described him as of "lively and active, but shallow mind, a political adventurer, not without talents, but self-sufficient, vain, and indiscreet." Adams had been advised as early as February 19, 1827, that Harrison was looking to the next Vice-Presidency "very earnestly." *Memoirs*, VII, 223, 229, 530.   8 Cf. above, Hammond to Clay, March 28, 1827, note.   9 Thomas Newton, Jr.; Alfred H. Powell.   10 The Washington *United States Telegraph* on April 5, 6, 13, 14, 16, 18, 1827, had reported a series of district and county meetings (cf. below, Kent to Clay, May 7, 1827) to elect delegates to a Baltimore Convention (cf. below, Goldsborough to Clay, August 9, 1827, note) in support of Jackson's candidacy.

From Spence Monroe Grayson

Honbl. Henry Clay, Sir,   Natchez April 21st. 1827

In November last, I wrote to you[1] on the Subject of the Suit pending in the Federal court of this State between J. Harper assignee of Morrison.s Exr. vs Anthony Butler.[2] I informed you *then*, that an objection had been taken to the jurisdiction of the court. and that I was apprehensive the objection would be sustained. On yesterday [*sic*] the court delivered an opinion against the plaintiff. You are already informed of the nature of the objection.

It was, that, Morrison.s Executor in the State of Kentucky could not vest his assignee with authority to sustain a suit in the District Court, unless he himself could maintain the suit—and it was contended that the executor could not sustain a suit until he had taken out letters testamentary within the State of Mississippi.

You have not answered my letter of November last. I desired you to inform me, what course you would have pursued in the event of a decision against the plaintiff. Not having heard from you, I am at a loss to know what step to take. However, I prayed a writ of error—which has been granted. I will not send up the cause until I hear from you.

You will therefore please inform me whether you desire the cause to be Sent up to the Supreme Court. Respectfully Yr. Obt. Sevt.
To The Honbe. H. Clay Washington City   S. M. GRAYSON

ALS. DLC-TJC (DNA, M212, R13). Grayson, born in Virginia, had been reared and educated near Natchez, Mississippi, where he had been licensed in 1825 or 1826 to practice law. In 1835 he moved to Yazoo County and purchased a large plantation near Benton. He represented Yazoo County in the State Senate in 1838, but his political career was cut short when he died the following year.
1 Letter not found.   2 On Butler's debt, see above, III, 628; Scott to Clay, January 3, March 9, 1825. The suit, which James Harper lost in the District Court, was carried to the United States Supreme Court in 1829. Chief Justice Marshall then delivered the opinion that, because the law of Mississippi permitted an assignee to institute an action in his own name, the decision should be reversed. 27 *U. S. Reports* (2 Peters) 239–40.

From F. M. S. Phelps

Hon. Henry Clay.
Dr. Sir   Canandaigua April 21st[1] 1827

In the character and apparel of a friend I assume the privilege of endeavouring to establish a correspondence. I am the individual of whom Genl. Marvin[2] Spoke in a private interview concerning a desire on my part to look into the records of the title respecting the old Yazoo question.[3] What recommendation he may have then given of me in point of character I know not, nor is it mater[ial] as I always rely upon prin[ciple] as the source of genuine character, & I leave it for my friends upon trial to say whether I have talents or not.   the next Presidential election is fast approaching as you sensibly know, individuals, communities & States are endeavouring to collect & collate the weight of popular favor concerning the issue as regards the candidates.   there must always be two, if not more parties, & each upon its own favorite grounds, will entertain their peculiar sentiments & opinions upon every subject.   it is unnecessary for me to allude to the antipathies growing out of the views of opponents to the conspicuous traits of character & dispositions of the members of the present administration or with regard to the floating Surmises concerning the bearing operation & extent of your views arising from the leading features or measures of the administration.   one connected chart (so to express myself) stretching from Maine to Georgia & spread back from our Maratime Coast to the full length of the region of the lakes, one connected chart of Newspaper discussion affords a mirror through which in the prospect the events, the actors & the machinery employed by the opponents of the administration may be Seen[4] but in the emphatic adage of the New England people, it all Seems & may be construed into more talk than cider.   as for my part a recent tour of a wide circuit embracing an extensive range and solid mass of individual sentiment among all classes independent of fire side estimate, has created within me an inclination to beleive [sic] the present administration not to be either in a reeling or a prostrated attitude.   indeed as in public, previous to the last election I was decidedly in favor of Henry Clay, so now I can not see any solid reason why I should not be & use my influence in favor of the present administration,   to this end, I could exert myself, & can now half predict the valuable consequences which may flow from the pursuit of a series of plan coinciding with the present principles & policy of the administration, to be digested & disclosed to me confidentially by correspondence. At Such a proposal you may Stare with extraordinary emotions of wonder and I have a distrust overcoming every hope of success when I reflect upon the various biases which your wonderfully discriminating views of human nature may array in your judment [sic] against the desired disclosure.   & yet if you knew me as also the opportunity I have to promote your popularity, you could repose in me with far more child like [conf]idence, than even Columbus ha[d], when he committed his memory in a cask to the waves of the atlantic.[5]   to obtain light relative to my unsullied character for honor & integrity, you may enquire of one & all of your acquaintances here.   say of Genl. Marvin.   but of the opportunity, as Emmet said of the epitaph upon his character, you can learn only of me.[6]   if you ask what is my motive for the poposed [*sic*] action. I answer, it is the extension by an experiment upon a small scale, of the political benefits of some of those questions advocated by yourself with all the powers of a transcendant genius inflamed by the most expansive & glowing patriotism.   if any thing is done let it be done quickly   With much consideration, candour & esteem I am sir Yours very respectfully.   F M S PHELPS

the favor I ask of you, if nothing should be done, if you wish to retain a friend is to suppress my name.

ALS. DLC-HC (DNA, M212, R2) . Phelps has not been further identified.
[1] Postmarked "APR 14" on the last page of MS.   [2] Dudley Marvin.   [3] Cf. above, I, 229n.   [4] Cf. Remini, *Election of Andrew Jackson*, 76–80, 128–29.
[5] Nearing the coast of Portugal on his return voyage, Columbus had encountered a storm so severe that he apparently feared loss of the *Niña* and of the record of his discovery. He summarized his journal, wrapped the account "in a waxed cloth, fastened this packet inside a wooden cask, and threw it overboard." Randolph G. Adams, *The Case of the Columbus Letter, An Address Prepared for the Washington Square College Book Club of New York University* . . . (New York, 1939), 6.   [6] Robert Emmet, of Dublin, a leader in Irish rebellion, had been captured and hanged in September, 1803, after an abortive uprising. He had directed: "let no man write my epitaph—no man can write my epitaph. . . . Let my character and my motives repose in obscurity and peace, till other times and other men can do them justice:—then shall my character be vindicated; then may my epitaph be written." Charles Phillips, *Recollections of Curran and Some of His Contemporaries* (New York, 1818), 216–17; Varina Anne Davis, *An Irish Knight of the 19th Century; Sketch of the Life of Robert Emmet* . . . (New York, c. 1888), 80.

INSTRUCTIONS AND DISPATCHES   April 21, 1827

From HEMAN ALLEN, Santiago de Chile, no. 52. Acknowledges receipt of Clay's "dispatch No. 4" (above, November 1, 1826); notes the absence of United States naval vessels from that station; promises that, as soon as he "can make any suitable arrangements for the departure of" himself and family, he will turn the Legation over to (Samuel) Larned; reports that "the Congress is still discussing the project of a federal constitution"; refers to "A recent arrival from Peru," who "brings intelligence of the very acceptable manner, in which, the overthrow of the late dynasty of Bolivar, has been received by the Provinces" (cf. above, Wheelwright to Clay, April 5, 1827; below, Tudor to Clay, April 25, May 15, 1827); and cites "letters, from that country," that "speak confidently of the ability of the existing government, to maintain the position, it has just assumed" (see above, Tudor to Clay, February 3, March 23, 1827). ALS. DNA, RG59, Dip. Disp., Chile, vol. 2 (M-T2, R2). Copy, in MHi-Adams Papers, Letters Recd. (MR480). Received August 11.

From ALBERT GALLATIN, London, no. 70. Observes that the recent resignations from the Cabinet (cf. above, Gallatin to Clay, February 22, 1827, note) were based more on personal feeling than on political principle and that, since "this has not been concealed, it has added to Mr Canning's strength." Notes that Canning's "master stroke . . . has been to place the heir presumptive [the Duke of Clarence] at the head of the admiralty," although there are many difficulties to be faced. Reports that (William) Huskisson is now well enough to attend to business (cf. above, Gallatin to Clay, February 5, 1827), although negotiations with him will not "be renewed until the administration is settled. . . ." States, without knowing what "steps the President may take respecting the colonial intercourse," that "These, or any act which Congress might have passed, cannot . . . alter the policy adopted by this [British] Government." Cites criticisms of Huskisson, "unjustly called a theorist"; the efforts of (Daniel) Sykes, a member of Parliament, to prevail on the Ministry to refuse "to come to any arrangement with the United States on the West India question"; and "the expectations held out by Mr Sykes that this exclusion [of the United States from the West Indies] would be sufficient to give occupation to all the unemployed British shipping." Encloses "an act of Parliament of 2d JUne [sic] 1821, respecting the North West territory, which may have escaped . . . [Clay's] notice," as it had his own. Discusses various features of the act and states that Huskisson "never alluded to it." ALS. DNA, RG59, Dip. Disp., Great Britain, vol. 33 (M30, R29). Copy, in NHi-Gallatin Papers, Letterbook, vol. 14, pp. 112–15 (MR20). Extracts published in *Sen. Docs.*, 22 Cong., 1 Sess., no. 132, p. 19; Manning (arr.), *Diplomatic Correspondence . . . Canadian Relations*, II, 582.

When Canning assumed leadership of the government, the office of Lord High Admiral was revived to replace the old Board of Admiralty and the Duke of Clarence was named to the post. Those members of the old board willing to serve under Canning were designated an advisory council to the Duke. The third son of George III, the Duke had entered the Navy as an "able seaman" in 1780 and had risen to the rank of captain in 1785, rear admiral in 1790, vice admiral in 1794, admiral in 1799, and admiral of the fleet in 1811. With the death of Frederick Augustus, Duke of York, in January, 1827, he became next in line to the throne and as William IV succeeded his eldest brother, George IV, in 1830.

Reference has not been found concerning the activities of Daniel Sykes, member of Parliament from Hull from 1820 to 1830 and from Beverley to 1831, in opposition to reopening the West India trade to the United States. He was, however, reported to have remarked to the House of Commons on May 15, 1827, that he supported the government's policies in opening that trade to other nations. Hansard (comp.), *Parliamentary Debates*, New Series, XVII, 835.

The Parliamentary act to which Gallatin apparently referred, was dated July 2, 1821 (1 & 2 *Geo. IV*, 422–24, "An Act for Regulating the Fur Trade, and Establishing a Criminal and Civil Jurisdiction within Certain Parts of North America"). It provided for licensing of the trade and extension of judicial process over the Indian lands, but it took cognizance of the agreement with the United States concerning joint occupation of "any country on the North West Coast of *America*, to the Westward of the *Stony Mountains*" (see above, II, 611n). The act disclaimed intent to grant exclusive trade to "any Body Corporate, Company or Person" within the limits of that agreement but stipulated "that no *British* Subject . . . [should] trade with the *Indians* within such Limits, without such Grant or Licence [sic] as . . . by the Act required."

From Samuel Mifflin

Dr Sir   Phila April 22. 1827

While at Harrisburg, I duly received your favor, of the 3d.[1] I thank you, for the information respecting the record, in Connolly's case.[2] I have now, a letter before me, from the Clerk of the Court, to which, I shall reply, in a day or two—

The Caucus at Harrisburg,[3] will I think, prove to be an abortion. Got up by men, almost unknown, even in this State, it was pushed thro', at the meeting, (composed in part, of men, led there by curiosity) without a single remark, from any of the friends of the Genl. & I doubt not, will turn out, but another step, calculated to injure his cause— Be assured, every attempt which has been made, to pledge the State, & engage the feelings of the people, in favor of the Chief, has produced, a result diametrically opposite, to that, look [sic] for. While the temperate course pursued by the Ad. & its friends, have [sic] operated powerfully, to convince the people, of the folly I may say danger of a change— Facts from all quarters convince me, that I am correct in this opinion. & I annex an extract of a communication which I have received, from a Gent who arrived at Lebanon, from Pitt. o[n] the 13 Inst.

"While in Pitt. I was informed by Col. Ramsay[4] & several other Gentlemen, of intelligence, that if the Election were to take place, at this time, there would be a decided majority, in favor of the present Ad. of the General Govern., whereas, in 1824 Mr. A., had but 13 votes, in the City of Pitt.[5] In a conversation with Mr. Moore,[6] of Beaver County, formerly a member of Congress, & now an Attorney, in that & the adjoining Counties, he stated that he had no doubt, but Beaver would give two to one, & that Mercer would give a majority, in favor of the Ad.—   his statement was confirmed by Mr. Thomas Henry, late Sheriff, of that County & present Editor, of the Beaver Argus.—

General Horry, of Armagh, of Indianna [sic] County,[7] told me, that there appeared to be great change, in the minds of the people, in favor of the Ad. & that the violence, of the professed friends, of Gen. Jackson, was doing him serious injury, if not, rendering his election, extremely doubtful. Mr. Brown a late member of Congress, from Mifflin County,[8] was a passenger in the Stage from Huntington, to Lewistown, he stated, that the people pretty generally, were becoming satisfied with Mr. Adams' Ad. & that Gen. Jackson, would not receive, any thing like the the [sic] support he did, at the last presidential election & by many, his receiving the vote of the State, was considered doubtful   Both going to & returning from Pitt., the Stage was full of passengers, & but one, of the whole number, appeared decidedly in favor of Genl. Jackson & he was a young man, from Somerset & near neighbour of Gen. Ogle[9]—"

I could, were it necessary, give you other details, upon which my opinion is founded & which have led me to a decided conclusion, that all will end right, altho the *public* demonstration, has not as yet been such, as to make it evident to our neighbours— All however in good time—

You may recollect, our speaking of a Genl.[10] (whom you formerly knew in Europe—) when I was at Washington— At that time, he certainly favored Genl. J., but he now declares, he should dread a revolution, should the Opposition succeed—

Never, having taken an active part, in public affairs, You may naturally ask, why all this zest, on the present occasion— I answer. a personall [*sic*] feeling towards, your good self, first turned my attention to the matter & that the serious danger which I apprehend to the institutions of our Country if the good sense of the people, does not put down the faction, now opposing the Ad. has determined me, to leave no stone unturned, to effect this object— My concerns lead me to mix a good deal with the Germans, who I think are following the course, which I have spoken of in other parts of the Country   if we can succeed, in one of the large G. C's[11] for insta[nce] in Berks, I should consider the question conclusively decided   My friend Mr Loring Ed. of the Lebanon Republican,[12] is earnest in his efforts. I gave yesterday, to our *friend* here,[13] one of the numbers. He will send it to the National Journal,[14] & if that paper would exchange with the L. R. it would gratify Mr. L & induce him to redouble his efforts—

I shall occasional [*sic*] communicate such matters, as I may pick up   I remain Most truly Your friend   SAML. MIFFLIN
The Honorable Henry Clay   Washington

ALS. DLC-HC (DNA, M212, R2). Margins obscured.   1 Not found.
2 Cf. above, Mifflin to Clay, April 3, 1827, note.   3 Cf. above, Mifflin to Clay, April 4, 1827.   4 Proprietor of a hotel at the corner of Third and Wood Streets, Pittsburgh.
5 The vote of Allegheny County for Adams was only 18. *Niles' Weekly Register*, XXVII (November 27, 1824), 194.   6 Robert Moore.   7 Possibly Peter Horry, born in South Carolina, a brigadier general in the American Revolution, who had collaborated with Mason Weems in *The Life of Gen. Francis Marion, a Celebrated Partizan Officer . . .* (Baltimore, 1809).   8 John Brown, of Lewistown, had been a member of the Pennsylvania House of Representatives from 1809 to 1813 and a United States Congressman from 1821 to 1825. Later in 1827 he removed to Buncombe County, North Carolina.
9 Alexander Ogle.   10 Not identified.   11 German Counties.   13 Possibly Nathaniel Loring, who in 1825 had been a spokesman for Lebanon County's opposition to canal development. The *Lebanon Republican* apparently ran for only a couple of years, terminating in the spring of 1828.   13 John Binns.   14 Washington *National Journal*.

DIPLOMATIC NOTES   April 23, 1827

To BARON DE STACKELBERG. Places in his hands a duplicate of the commission "appointing Robert Monroe Harrison Consul of the United States for the Island of St. Bartholomews [*sic*]" (cf. above, Clay to Harrison, April 9, 1827) and requests his "good offices" in obtaining from the King of Sweden and Norway (Charles XIV) "recognition . . . of the official character of Mr. Harrison . . . and an Exequatur in the usual form. . . ." Copy. DNA, RG59, Notes to Foreign Legations, vol. 3, p. 355 (M38, R3). L draft, in CSmH. Three days later Daniel Brent, "by direction of the Secretary," informed Harrison of this action. Copy, in DNA, RG59, Cons. Instr., vol. 2, pp. 421–22 (M78, R2).

Baron Stackelberg on April 28 acknowledged receipt of Clay's communication and promised to transmit the document to his Government. ALS, in DNA, RG59, Notes from Swedish Legation, vol. 3 (M60, R2).

INSTRUCTIONS AND DISPATCHES   April 23, 1827

From J[OHN] J. APPLETON, Stockholm, no. 16. Reports receipt of a note from Count Wetterstedt informing him that the Count has been authorized to negotiate "the new Treaty of Commerce." Encloses copies of the note and his reply. ALS. DNA, RG59, Dip. Disp., Sweden and Norway, vol. 5 (M45, R-T6). Published in *American State Papers, Foreign Relations*, VI, 721–22.

From JOHN SHILLABER, Batavia. Advises that, as mentioned in his accompanying dispatch of March 14, 1827, he will leave for the United States in May and that he has appointed as consular agent an American resident, Owen Mansits Roberts. ALS. DNA, RG59, Cons. Disp., Batavia, vol. 1 (M-T95, R1). Roberts was again serving as acting consular agent, from 1833 to 1835, when Jackson finally removed Shillaber as consul and named Roberts to the post. The latter remained consul until his death in 1845.

Check to John Burke

24h. Apl 1827

Pay to John Burke or order forty dollars and 18 Cents.
Cashr. of the Off. of Dt. & Dt. Washn.[1]   H CLAY

ADS. DLC-TJC (DNA, M212, R16). Endorsed on verso by Burke, who was a clerk in the office of the first comptroller.
[1] Richard Smith.

DIPLOMATIC NOTES   April 24, 1827

To HILARIO DE RIVAS Y SALMON. Presents the results of the President's "most attentive consideration" of Rivas y Salmon's "several letters of the 6th. January 1825 [cf. above, Rivas y Salmon to Clay, October 25, 1826], 25th. October 1826, and 16th. March 1827, together with the documents accompanying the first": no evidence is presented to support the charge that (Juan Miguel de) "Losada sustained any injury or losses" from the (American) occupation (of West Florida); the papers submitted in support of "the claim founded on the sale of Losada's property under the judgment of the Court of Escambia" give an incomplete "transcript of the record"; if the court "unjustly compelled" Losada "to pay a debt to [Joseph E.] Caro which the Spanish Government was bound to discharge, the appropriate resort for Losada's redress would seem to be that Government." Continues: "There is no such palpable error in the decision of the Court as could alone justify, in any case an appeal, at the instance of one foreign Government, in behalf of one of its Citizens, to another foreign Government." Argues that Losada's "defense . . . to the suit" was inadequate, that he made no appeal to higher courts, and that if "the Court of Escambia had no jurisdiction," as is claimed, "then its judgment is a nullity, and the sale of Losada's property is void, and he might consequently now retake and recover the possession." Reports the President's conclusion "that no just claim on the part of Losada can be recognized on the Government of the United States." Copy. DNA, RG59, Notes to Foreign Legations, vol. 3, pp. 351–55 (M38, R3). AL draft, dated April 16, 1827, in CSmH.

INSTRUCTIONS AND DISPATCHES   April 24, 1827

To JOEL R. POINSETT. Daniel Brent, "by direction of the Secretary," transmits a copy of a letter (to Brent, April 16, 1827) "just received from Mr. Henry R. Storrs

. . . concerning the detention of a sum of money in the hands of Mr. [James Smith] Wilcocks, our Consul at Mexico, belonging to the estate of Seth Hayden . . ." (cf. above, Storrs to Clay, June 20, 1826), and adds: "I am particularly instructed by Mr. Clay to state that he wishes you to inform Mr. Wilcocks the President expects he will pay over to you immediately, according to the desire of Mrs. Hayden, or remit, through this Department, the amount so received by him, for the benefit of the estate of her deceased husband." Copy. DNA, RG59, Dip. Instr., vol. 11, pp. 310–11 (M77, R6).

From Thomas L. L. Brent, Lisbon, no. 41. States that, since the defeat of the refugees (cf. above, Brent to Clay, January 13, 1827), Spain has become "more compliant with regard to the demands of England and Portugal," although her conduct "still continues to be evasive and unsatisfactory"; while "On the other hand Portugal . . . uses every exertion to give no umbrage" to Spain. Comments on the absence of "further revolutionary movements" in Portugal and on the recent proclamation of "amnesty and general pardon," from which there are exceptions. Observes that "The british forces continue in the same positions," that "they now harmonize much better with the inhabitants," and that they "find a disposition . . . more cordial than they had anticipated from their reception on their arrival." Refers to the return of (Bernardo José de) Abrantes (e Castro) from Rio de Janeiro (cf. above, Brent to Clay, April 7, 1827), where he was well received by the Emperor (Peter I), who sent him back to continue his anti-Spanish activities in Portugal; adds, however, that through the influence of the British Ambassador (William A'Court) Abrantes has been sent out of the Kingdom by an appointment as "Counsellor of Embassy" in England. Reiterates his disappointment that the proposed commercial legislation [discussed above, Brent to Clay, March 16, 1827 (no. 40)] has not passed and his expectation that "at the next meeting of the ordinary cortes" the Deputies will approve the measure "for the admission of foreign corn when the price in Portugal is at a great advance. . . ." Characterizes the news from England of the appointment of (George) Canning as Prime Minister as a blow to the hopes of "the Ultraroyalist party" in Portugal and of the Spanish Ambassador (the Count de Casa Flórez). Encloses copies "of the speech of the Regent [Isabel Maria] at the close of the second session of the Cortes" and of the answer, just received, to Brent's "note respecting the conduct of the military commandant at the Island of Maio . . ." (cf. above, Hodges to Clay, May 19, 1826; Brent to Clay, July 27, August 2, 1826). Promises to inform Clay "of whatever step" he "may follow in relation to this subject." LS. DNA, RG59, Dip. Disp., Portugal, vol. 7 (M43, R-T6). Received June 22.

In the enclosed note, Francisco de Almeida asserts that the complaint by "the American Vice Consul at the Island of Maio [Ferdinand Gardner, who had written the letter transmitted by Hodges] . . . is not exact" and that "the vexation incurred by . . . Price [i.e., William Prince] is almost entirely imputable to his caprice of refusing to buy the 4 moios of Salt of the Commandant [Pedro Paulo de Silveria] who according to privilege had a right to ship them in every vessel that went there to load. . . ." He adds, however, that "to avoid the repetition of similar disagreeable incidents," that privilege has been revoked.

From I[srael] Pemberton Hutchinson, Lisbon. Asks Clay to request for him from the President a six months' leave of absence; adds that "the intercourse between this & the U S is very limited. . . ." ALS. DNA, RG59, Cons. Disp., Lisbon, vol. 5 (M-T180, R5). Received August 6. Endorsed by Clay on verso: "A letter to be written giving the permission requested. H. C." Daniel Brent replied as directed, on August 7, 1827. Copy, in DNA, RG59, Cons. Instr., vol. 2, p. 437 (M78, R2).

From FRED[ERIC]K JACOB WICKELHAUSEN, Bremen. Transmits a prize-winning book on yellow fever, by Dr. (Carl Christian) Matthaei, who is sending copies to European Monarchs, as well as to the President. Suggests, since "the principle maintained therein" is that the disease can be transmitted by contact even to Northern Germany, which conclusion may adversely affect American trade, a refutation by "some learned and able Physicians of the U S, who are acquainted with the german [sic] language. . . ." ALS. DNA, RG59, Cons. Disp., Bremen, vol. 2 (M-T184, R2). Received July 11.

An enclosure identifies Matthaei as "Physician to the household of His British Majesty residing at Verden, Kingdom Hannover [sic]." Matthaei authored several medical treatises other than the *Untersuchung über das Gelbe Fieber* (2 vols.; Hanover, 1827).

MISCELLANEOUS LETTERS   April 24, 1827

From G[EORGE] W. OWEN, Claiborne (Alabama). States that Francis McGwin, an old man residing in Alabama, "formerly of New London," believes "that some award has been made him under the Florida Treaty, by the Board of Commissioners [cf. above, II, 678n], as being one of the crew of the Ship 'Miantinoma of Narrage [Norwick] and New London' belonging to Messrs. Coit & Tracy of New London"; asks an investigation of the matter. ALS. DNA, RG59, Misc. Letters (M179, R65).

An undated, unaddressed report, by Joseph Forrest, reveals that the vessel, "on a Sealing & Trading Voyage to the Pacific Ocean, in 1799. 1800," had been "seized by the Spaniards," that a claim had been "made by Messrs. Coit & Tracey [sic]," and that the Board (of Commissioners) had "allowed for the value of the *Outward Cargo*." Forrest concludes: "If the Seamen have any claim, it must be on the owners. . . ." ALS, *ibid*. Daniel Brent answered Owen's letter on May 15, 1827, using much of the information supplied by this report. Copy, in DNA, RG59, Dom. Letters, vol. 21, pp. 537–38 (M40, R19).

The vessel has been cited otherwise as *Miantonomah*. James Kirker, *Adventures to China; Americans in the Southern Oceans, 1792–1812* (New York, 1970), 79. McGwin, Coit, and Tracy (Tracey) have not been further identified.

DIPLOMATIC NOTES   April 25, 1827

From PABLO OBREGÓN. Sends "the *Sol* of Mexico of 21 January . . . and a translation of those parts of the same in which they treated of the occurrences happened [sic] at Texas [cf. above, Dickson to Clay, January 3, 1827, note], as he offered to Mr. Clay the last Sunday." N. DNA, RG59, Notes from Mexican Legation, vol. 1 (M54, R1). Dated April 25; endorsed by clerk: ". . . 25 April 1827."

The copy of the newspaper has not been found. The translation, of an account of proceedings in the Mexican legislature, includes, first, mention of "official letters received . . . from the state of coahuila and Texas," explaining that "what had happened in Nacodoches [sic], by no means was an invasion from the United States of America, but only a sublevation of some individuals," and, second, information from a report to the Secretary of War (Manuel Gómez Pedraza) "that Hadens Stward [Hayden Edwards] had attacked with 30 men the place of Nacodoches, and that the governor of coahuila and Texas [Victor Blanco] was marching against them. That Stward being a foreigner, who was by order of the government cast out of the country, he had threaned [sic] the inhabitants of Texas saying that he would come with 700 men to stablish [sic] a Colony there."

El Sol, established in the early 1820's, was the principal organ of the Escoses Party in Mexico, a conservative journal strongly supporting the central government.

Blanco, of Monclova, had been an alternate deputy for the province in the national Congress of 1823 and Governor from May 30, 1826, to January 27, 1827. He was elected first vice-governor the following July under the Coahuila-Texas Constitution of 1827 and was a Senator in the national legislature from 1833 to 1837.

From Joaquim Barrozo Pereira, Philadelphia. Acknowledges receipt of Clay's note of April 12; agrees, as a general principle, on the right of appeal but asks "could it, in justice or equity, be applicable to the case in question?" Dissents from Clay's opinion concerning its application to that case; presents at great length his own views, which are critical of the actions of the district attorney (Richard W. Habersham); and expresses satisfaction in the decision of the Supreme Court "affirming the decree of the Circuit Court which had exempted the Portuguese Vice Consul [Francis Sorrel] from the payment of any share of the costs and expenses incurred in the maintenance of the Africans." This decision, he thinks, proves that his "views of the case were perfectly correct" and his "complaint . . . well grounded." Concludes: "Although I failed in my endeavors to prevent further injury, by subjecting an innocent individual to trouble and expense, and which I sincerely regret, the Note I had the honour to address to you remonstrating upon this subject, as well as that final result of the appeal, will be the best evidence I can furnish the Government and the Nation I have the honour to represent, that I discharged my duty." ALS. DNA, RG59, Notes from Portuguese Legation, vol. 2 (M57, R2).

From José Maria Salazar, Baltimore. Transmits two documents—one, "una protesta . . . hecha en debida forma"; the other an estimate of damages—stipulated by the captain of the *Zulmé*, Denis Thomas, and the purser, Cornelius F. Gahne. LS, in Spanish. DNA, RG59, Notes from Colombian Legation, vol. 1, pt. 2 (M51, R2).

The first-mentioned enclosure was taken and notarized at Key West, Florida, February 26, 1827, and the other, "a further extension thereof," was made and notarized at Baltimore, April 16, 1827.

INSTRUCTIONS AND DISPATCHES   April 25, 1827

From David Dickson, San Antonio de Bexar, Texas. Reports his departure for this place from New Orleans on February 24; his inability to see "Col [Stephen F.] Austin" at San Felipe de Austin, where he arrived on March 13, because that gentleman "and the political chief [José Antonio Saucedo] had gone to the Eastward to settle the affairs of the Fredonian Republic" (cf. above, Dickson to Clay, January 3, 1827, note); and his own arrival at San Antonio on April 22, in bad health, under escort provided by General (Anastasio) Bustamente. Comments on the "civility" of that officer, his eager enquiry "after the manners Customs habits &&& of our Countrymen," and his efforts "to assemble an Army to operate against the Comanche Indians." Cites the depredations of this tribe and the terror in which they are viewed by the Mexican soldiers, while "five or six Americans travel where they please with their long rifles." Describes San Antonio as "a small village very meanly built and the Public works . . . all in a state of dilapidation," its "Political Chief" serving merely as an organ of communication with the administering authorities at Saltillo. Notes that the local commerce is so limited that his office "is not worth one farthing" unless his district be defined to include

Matagorda, Brazos, and Trinity. ALS. DNA, RG59, Cons. Disp., Texas, vol. 1 (M-T153, R1). Received June 21.

Anastasio Bustamente had fought with the Spanish against the Mexican revolutionaries during the early years of that movement but in 1821 had supported Agustin Itúrbide and the Republic. He was vice president of Mexico early in 1829 and, with the success of Santa Anna's revolt, became president from 1829 to 1832. He was, in turn, driven into exile by Santa Anna in 1832 but returned as president from 1837 to 1841. Again forced out of office, he remained in Europe until 1845, when upon coming back to Mexico, he was appointed president of the Congress.

Saucedo had been active in the local governmental assembly as early as 1806. He had served as president of the provincial deputies to the national Congress in 1824 and as chief political officer at Bexar from 1824 to 1827.

From WILLIAM TUDOR, Lima, no. 64, "Confidential." Sketches "political events" subsequent to the date of his letter of March 23, noting that "The expedition of the Colombian troops which sailed on the 19th ulto disembarked two batallions [sic]" at Paita to "march for Loxa [Loja] & Cuenca," while the remaining three battalions sailed for "the coast back of Guayaquil" for the purpose of marching on that city; that a small naval force was sent to intercept them; that the "liberating troops," it is expected, "will be every where received with open arms" (cf. above, Wheelwright to Clay, April 19, 1827; below, Tudor to Clay, May 15, 1827). Observes that "The next object of anxiety is the course that [Antonio José de] Sucre will follow"; that Sucre "fortunately . . . was in the dark a[s] to the nature of this revolution for a long period" and when he sent General (José Maria) Córdoba, "his best general," to Lima the latter arrived "about a fortnight" after the expedition had departed. Notes, further, that Córdoba was "accompanied by Dona Manuela S[áenz] the favorite of [Simón] Bolivar"; that Sucre has sent reinforcements to the garrison at Lima, "but of course they will not be allowed to land"; and that "Troubles are beginning to appear in Bolivia. . . ." Encloses a document (not found) which, he thinks, "should be made widely known in the U. S."; explains that it was an appeal presented to Bolívar, "on his arrival at Bogota in November last," not to consummate "the ruin of his country, & of his own reputation," but that he caused it to be suppressed. Expresses expectation that the newly elected "Congress at Peru" will meet in May. ALS. DNA, RG59, Cons. Disp., Lima, vol. 1 (M154, R1). Received August 31.

Córdoba, born in Colombia to wealthy parents, had espoused the republican cause as a youth. He had been made a general of brigade for his role in the victory of Pichincha, which led to the fall of Quito in 1822, and general of division for his heroism at Ayacucho in 1824. At the outbreak of war between Colombia and Peru early in 1828, he was directed to lead the Colombian forces; but, disaffected with Bolívar, he raised a revolt in 1829, received little support, and was captured and killed.

MISCELLANEOUS LETTERS   April 25, 1827

From JAMES H. McCULLOCH, "Custom House Baltimo." States that he has received "from the Department of State, a packet directed to Wm Taylor Consul of the U' States at Vera Cruz," which will be sent to the collector at Philadelphia or New York; remarks that he should have informed Clay earlier "that as our trade runs in a different track to that country" he has been sending "packets & letters under the same direction to Phila to be forwarded" and that henceforth "such dispatches" should be sent to Philadelphia or New York. ALS. DNA, RG59, A. and R. (M531, R5).

To John Bradford

Sir: Washington, 26th April, 1827.

I transmit, enclosed, some testimonials in behalf of Professor Alva Woods, who has been suggested to me as a fit person for the Presidency of Transylvania. If, as is probable, some of these documents shall have reached you, through another channel, I shall only have performed an unnecessary office in now forwarding them. The Revd Mr Chase, whose letter I also transmit, promises to furnish other testimonials in behalf of Mr. Woods, which, when received, shall be given the same direction. I am, Sir, with great respect, Your obedient servant,

John Bradford, Esqr &c. &c. &c.   H. CLAY

ALS. KyLxT. See above, Chase to Clay, April 19, 1827.

To George Thompson

My dear Sir: Washington, 26 April, 1827.

I was very much gratified by the perusal of your friendly letter of the 23d of February. I observe that you retain at the advanced age of seventy-eight your wonted bouyancy and cheerfulness. I hope you will have many more years added to your life, and that you will continue to be as happy hereafter as you have always been heretofore. I delivered your message to the President, who desires me to assure you of his best respects, and that it would give him particular satisfaction to see you at Pleasant Fields. I am not sure that it will be in my power, when I go to Kentucky this Summer, to cross the Kentucky river; but if I can command the time, you may be perfectly persuaded that I shall not want inclination to see you and your son[1] at your residence

Of political affairs, I will trouble you only by saying that I think they will all go well. There is a great deal of noise and smoke; but the virtue and intelligence of the people will be found, on the day of trial, competent to their complete evaporation.

I beg you to make my warm regards to your son, and believe me, faithfully, Your friend and obedient servant,   H. CLAY

Col. George Thompson.

LS. MoSHi.   [1] George C. Thompson.

From Samuel M. Brown

Dear Sir   Louisville Apl, 26h. 1827—

My object when I wrote you last week[1] was to start up the cuntry [sic] forthwith and endeavour to obtain Judges Trimble and Boyle[2] and J. J. Crittenden Esqr recommendation, under the beleif [sic] that they were so well known to the administration that nothing more

would be required, but being called off to the Oldham Circuit Court on Monday to oppose the Hon. Chs, A. Wickliff [sic] in a discussion before the people of that County, was prevented— In the mean time the Judges, Clerks and members of both Barr's, tendered me a certificate of my qualification, which will be seen on the other page,[3] all of whom are practiseing Lawyers, except Maj. Luckett[4] and he claims to belong to our order— Here then you have the united testimony of Old Court and new* Court,[5] Jackson and administration friends to bear you out in any thing, which may be done for me— True they have not requested an appointment, but this I could not look for, as Worden Pope and John Rowan Esqs, were among the foremost to offer me this mark of respect & they at the same time at the head of the opposition here— Tomorrow or next day I shall start to procure the first intended recommendation— in the mean time prepare for any result— Your friend.   S. M. BROWN
[Marginal note]
* H. Davdge [sic] & H. Pirtle are Circuit Judges and Worden Pope & I. R. Gwathmey Clerks[6]—

ALS. DNA, RG59, A. and R. (M531, R1). Endorsed by Clay on cover: "To be submitted to the President."
   [1] See above, April 21, 1827.   [2] John Trimble; John Boyle.   [3] The "certificate," not addressed, bears 27 signatures.   [4] Craven P. Luckett.   [5] See above, III, 902n.
   [6] Henry Davidge, who had been admitted to the bar in Ohio County in 1799 and had served several terms as representative of that district in the Kentucky Legislature during the period 1802 to 1807, had removed to Gallatin County, which he served as a State senator in the Session 1818–1819 and circuit court judge through the decade of the 1820's, until his death in 1831. Henry Pirtle, born in Washington County, Kentucky, in 1798, had also begun the practice of law in Ohio County but had shortly thereafter moved to Louisville, where he was a judge of the circuit and general courts from 1826 to 1832. He was a State senator from 1840 to 1843 and chancellor of the Louisville Chancery Court from 1850 to 1856 and again from 1863 to 1868. He taught in the Department of Law at the University of Louisville from 1846 to 1869 and in 1832 published a *Digest of the Decisions of the Court of Appeals.* Isaac Robertson Gwathmey, graduated from Transylvania University in 1811, resided in Oldham County.

INSTRUCTIONS AND DISPATCHES   April 26, 1827

From WILLIAM TAYLOR, Veracruz. Reports that "the disturbances in Texas" and Durango (cf. above, Dickson to Clay, January 3, 1827, note; Poinsett to Clay, March 24, 1827, note) have been put down and that "the expedition to Texas [cf. above, Poinsett to Clay, March 8, 24, 1827] has not yet sailed—and it is now expected to be abandoned." Notes that additional arrests have been made in connection with the Arenas conspiracy (cf. above, Sergeant to Clay, January 26, 1827) and that "A third party in opposition to the Yorkinos and Escoses [sic] has been organizing for the last several months." Adds that "the duty on Cotton Goods [cf. above, Poinsett to Clay, December 27, 1826] has . . . been reduced to the old aforo [valuation]." ALS. DNA, RG59, Cons. Disp., Veracruz, vol. 1 (M183, R1). Received May 24.
   The "third party" to which Taylor refers was probably composed of the followers of Manuel Gómez Pedraza, who, originally a member of the Escoceses, had "joined the Yorkinos when they came into existence, and then set to work to build up a personal machine of his own." George Lockhart Rives, *The United*

States and Mexico, 1821–1848; a History of the Relations between the Two Countries from the Independence of Mexico to the Close of the War with the United States . . . (2 vols.; New York, 1913), I, 171. Pedraza's candidacy for the presidency in 1828 drew support from a broad range of conservative interests, including the Escoceses, who sought a conciliatory policy within the government.

From W[ILLIAM] TUDOR, Lima, no. 65, *"Confidential."* Reports that "The present administration of this government, whose labours are fortunately drawing near a close [cf. above, Tudor to Clay, February 3, 1827], . . . have taken the humiliating step of writing to the French Inspector destined for this country [Jean Chaumette des Fossés—cf. above, Brown to Clay, January 11, 1826, note; Tudor to Clay, January 8, 1827], & who retired to Valparaiso, inviting him to return." Adds that "The effect therefore of Mr [José María de] Pando's very able correspondence & dignified conduct, will be wholly lost; & this government which had nothing to fear from that of France, will have the just reputation of being timid, irresolute, & wanting in self respect." Describes an instance of encouragement by France of trade "to this coast" but predicts that, though "The French comm[erce] has greatly increased here within the year, . . . [it] probably will not be sustained." Suggests that a Jesuit missionary group from France, en route to the Sandwich Islands, will, "If allowed to land there, . . . soon drive [out] our Calvinist missionaries, & perhaps prep[are] the way for some ulterior views of the Fre[nch] government on those islands." ALS. DNA, RG59, Cons. Disp., Lima, vol. 1 (M154, R1). Received August 31.

The group of French missionaries, priests of the Society of Picpus, of the Congregation of the Sacred Hearts of Jesus and Mary, founded on the Rue de Picpus, at Paris, in 1800, arrived with a few artisans in Honolulu in July, 1827. Designed as the nucleus for a French colony in the central Pacific, the venture met opposition from the American missionaries and the Hawaiian queen, Kaahumanu (regent from 1824 to 1832). Several of the colonists left the island within the first two years, and the remainder were expelled in 1831. Bradley, *The American Frontier in Hawaii,* 184–86.

MISCELLANEOUS LETTERS   April 26, 1827

To ALBERT GALLATIN. Introduces, at the request of (Timothy) Pitkin, "Mr. H. Huntington Junr. a native of Connecticut . . . about to visit England" on "some business there in which he may possibly have occasion for" Gallatin's "friendly assistance. . . ." ALS. NHi-Gallatin Papers (MR14). Cf. above, Huntington to Clay, April 20, 1827.

From C[HARLES] J[OSEPHUS] NOURSE, Department of War. Acknowledges receipt of "General [Peter B.] Porters letter [not found] to . . . [Clay], on the subject of the application of the proprietors of the pre-emption title to certain lands in the State of New York, and in compliance with" Clay's wish to know "what has been done, or is doing on the subject" encloses "a copy of a letter [not found] from the Office of Indian Affairs to Messrs. Troup, Ogden & Rogers, in relation to the subject." Copy. DNA, RG75, Letters Sent, vol. 4, p. 34.

Nourse, a son of Joseph Nourse, had been born in Brooklyn, New York, in 1786 and commissioned a lieutenant in the Army in 1809. He had served throughout the War of 1812 and had resigned, with the rank of captain, in February, 1827, to become chief clerk in the War Department. He was removed from office by President Jackson in 1829 and subsequently managed a flour mill in Georgetown, District of Columbia.

By a treaty signed at Buffalo Creek in 1826, Robert Troup, Thomas Ludlow

Ogden, and Benjamin W. Rogers had acquired 123,000 acres from the Senecas, for the sum of $48,216; but the firm was still attempting to gain possession of nearly 75,000 acres, for which they held a right of preemption acquired through transfer of such rights initially granted by the Senecas to Oliver Phelps and Nathaniel Gorham on July 8, 1788, and confirmed by the Massachusetts General Court, November 21, 1788. The claim to the tract had passed to Robert Morris in 1791, from him the following year to a group of Dutch bankers who shortly thereafter organized the Holland Land Company, and from that firm to David A. Ogden, attorney for the company and founder of the Ogden Land Company, in 1810. No further action to remove the Indians from the lands was taken until 1838, and the issue was not resolved until 1857. See George Dewey Harmon, *Sixty Years of Indian Affairs, Political, Economic, and Diplomatic, 1789–1850* (Chapel Hill [North Carolina], 1941; New York: Kraus Reprint Co., 1969), 24, 260–69; Neil Adams McNall, *An Agricultural History of the Genesee Valley, 1790–1860* (Philadelphia, 1952), 13–16.

Gorham and Phelps, Massachusetts merchants and legislators, had projected development of some 6,000,000 acres in western New York, for which they were to pay $300,000 within three years to the State of Massachusetts. Speculating upon payment in depreciated State currency, they had been able to meet only the first of three annual payments and so had acquired title to but the eastern third of the tract, an area roughly defined between the longitudes of Lake Seneca and the Genesee River. The remainder of their tract had reverted to the State of Massachusetts and had been sold to Morris. The Holland Land Company ultimately acquired over 4,000,000 acres in western New York and northwestern Pennsylvania.

Troup, born in New York City and graduated, in 1774, from Kings College (Columbia University), had fought in the Revolution, studied law, and for several years served as judge of the United States District Court of New York. He had subsequently become principal agent for the land development of Sir William Pulteney, an English investor who had acquired the Phelps and Gorham patents. Troup at this time resided in Geneva, New York. Thomas Ludlow Ogden was a brother of David A. Ogden, a son of Abraham Ogden, and a cousin of David B. Ogden. Rogers was a New York merchant, president of the New York South American Steam Boat Association (cf. below, Rogers and Van Winkle to Clay, June 14, 1827).

From ABRAHAM OGDEN AND OTHERS, New York. Request, "if the Case will admit of it, the interference of the Executive" in securing the protection and "restitution to the rightful Owners" of property saved from the *Merope* and detained at Buenos Aires (cf. above, Neilson and others to Clay, February 3, 1827; Slacum to Clay, February 14, 1827). ALS, by J. R. Hurd, signed also by Ogden; William Neilson; Jonathan Whetten, president of the Hope Insurance Company, New York; Richard M. Lawrence; and Jonathan H. Laurence. DNA, RG59, Cons. Disp., Buenos Aires, vol. 3 (M70, R4).

Whetten, who had sailed in the China trade as early as 1785, had commanded ships for John Jacob Astor and other leading New York merchants before entering himself into the shipping business around 1812.

From PHILIP YOST, JR., Baltimore. Transmits a "package" entrusted to him, upon his departure from Port au Prince, by Andrew Armstrong. Comments that the Haitian Government "would not Keep Sacred any treaty unless [it] was their Interest to do So" but that, nevertheless, "it would be much to our advantage to Keep [a] good understanding with them." ALS. DNA, RG59, Misc. Letters (M179, R65).

Yost had served in the Army during the War of 1812, rising from the level of sergeant to a commission as first lieutenant by September, 1814; but he had been from the level of sergeant to a commission as first lieutenant by September, 1814; but he had been "dropped 1 January 1815." Francis B. Heitman, *Historical Register and Dictionary of the United States Army . . .* (Washington, 1903; repr. Urbana: University of Illinois Press, 1965) , 1066.

To Peter B. Porter

Dear Sir   Washington 27h. April 1827.

I recd. your favor of the 18h. instant. The course which you describe, as pursued by Mr. V.B. & his friends, of publickly preaching against premature committals and secretly practising to produce them, I thought I discovered several months ago to be their plan of operation. I learn from Albany that your presence there has been attended with the best effect.[1] I hope you will succeed in the object of establishing a good paper at Albany. Apathy, or too great confidence, is the vice of our friends in New York. A large majority, originally, may, in the progress of things, lose a good cause, if it be inactive, whilst there is concert and co-operation on the other side.

I am obliged to visit Kentucky, and I wish much to be in N. York this summer; but if I should be able to realize this wish it must be *on* or *after* my return from K. Should I accomplish the object, I shall not fail to observe your kind suggestions, as far as practicable, in regard to places &c to be seen.

I recd. your letter[2] about the desired modification in the Indian treaty. The Secy. of War[3] is absent at this time, but a communication to the parties immediately interested has been sent from his Dept. Your's truly & cordially   H. Clay
Genl. P. B. Porter

ALS. NBuHi.   [1] See above, Hammond to Clay, April 11, 1827.
[2] Not found. Cf. above, Nourse to Clay, April 26, 1827.   [3] James Barbour.

From Gideon Morgan, Jr.

A B ·	C D ·	E F ·
G H ·	I K ·	L M ·
N O ·	P Q ·	R S ·

Sir   [April 27, 1827]

above you have the Key. as well as the alphabet. to the Correspondence between Burr Jackson and Blanerhaset.[1] I am indebted to Templin W. Ross[2] for it— he is known to John L. McKenney[3] &

Should it prove really advantageous to the administration he deserves. well of them and. I Should Expect the pledges made to me by. Mr. Calhoun in the Case of George Harlands reservation[4] adjusted as I. had a right to believe they would   the equivacol manner in which I have been treated on that Subject has Brought me nearly to the Brink of ruin   Barbour[5] & McKinnie knows [sic] the situation of the Claim if you Say I Shall Come on to Washington for its adjustment I certainl[y] will without delay. Should you write relative to the Scypher Let it be on a Separate piece of paper inclosed as a Letter from you would. create a universal anxiety. to know its contents   you Could write in your Letter Somethi[ng] relative to the Highwassee Canall [sic].[6] for which I have felt, & expressed a Strong desire to See established   God Bless you all   GIDEON MORGAN JR.

NB   you will discover two. Letters to Each figure. the Second being. distinguished by a dot.

ALS. DLC-HC (DNA, M212, R2). Not dated. Postmarked: "Calhoun [Tennessee] 27 April."

[1] Aaron Burr; Andrew Jackson; Harman Blennerhassett. Cf. above, Morgan to Clay, April 7, 1827.   [2] Not identified.   [3] That is, Thomas L. McKenney.   [4] George Harlin, apparently a Cherokee, had been granted a reservation of 640 acres, to be held in fee simple, under the Cherokee treaty of February 27, 1819. He had reputably been promised the tract for his services in promoting emigration of the Cherokee. Statement by Return J. Meigs, dated February 23, 1819, accompanying Gideon Morgan, Jr., to John C. Calhoun, February 23, [1819], in W. Edwin Hemphill (ed.), *The Papers of John C. Calhoun*, III (Columbia, [S.C.], 1967), 607; Charles J. Kappler (comp. and ed.), *Indian Affairs: Laws and Treaties* (Sen Docs., 57 Cong., 1 Sess., no 452; 2 vols., Washington, 1903), II, 125.   [5] James Barbour.   [6] The Hiwassee Canal proposal was designed to link the Hiwassee, one of the headwaters of the Tennessee River, to the Coosa River via a canal from a point on the Okou, a branch of the Hiwassee, to the Conesaugo, a branch of the Coosa, near the Georgia-Tennessee boundary. Under act of December 30, 1823, the Tennessee Legislature had incorporated the Coosa Navigation Company and authorized it to take subscriptions for the project. When the necessary funds were not raised, the legislature by act of January 11, 1827, had incorporated the Alabama and Tennessee Canal Company for the same purpose. The latter company was also unsuccessful, and the canal was never built. William Elejius Martin, *Internal Improvements in Alabama* (J.M. Vincent and others [eds.], *Johns Hopkins University Studies in Historical and Political Science*, XX, *Colonial and Economic History*, no. 4 [Baltimore, 1902]) , pp. 37–38.

INSTRUCTIONS AND DISPATCHES   April 27, 1827

From JAMES BROWN, Paris, "Private." Describes the popular demonstrations of joy following withdrawal by the King (Charles X) of the projected "law on the press" (cf. above, Brown to Clay, December 13, 1826; February 13, 23, April 12, 1827). Notes that "By some of those who witnessed what passed at the commencement of the revolution, these scenes are considered as indication of a state of popular opinion dangerous to the present dynasty." Takes issue with this point of view and maintains that "The present state of things in France is very different from that which existed in 1790." Adds that there is no "common centre around which the disaffected can rally"; that "The republicans, if there are any in France, are few in number"; and that "The family of the late Emperor [Napoleon Bonaparte] has now no avowed adherents, and is nearly forgotten." Expresses hope for France under "the present charter" but views with concern "the growing influence of the clergy, the increase in the number and wealth of religious foundations, the activity and intolerance of the missionaries and congregations, and the open encouragement given by Government to the jesuits . . ." (cf. above, Brown to Clay, August 12, 1826; April 12, 1827, note).

Reports that the "last accounts from the east are favorable to the Greeks," although "It is believed that the negotiations set on foot by Mr. [Stratford] Canning, and carried on in conjunction with the Russian Ambassador at Constantinople [Count Alexandre Ribeaupierre] for the pacification of Greece [cf. above, Brown to Clay, April 13, 1826, March 23, 1827 (2)], have been unsuccessful." Reports, also, that [Sebastián] Camacho has been well received in Paris and that "It is believed . . . that France has instructed her Agent of the Marine [Alexandre Martin], who has for some time resided as commercial agent at Mexico, to assume with the consent of the Mexican Government, the functions and character of Consul-General," after which the Mexican secret agent in Paris [Tomás Murphy] will be "acknowledged as Consul-General or Commercial Agent for France" (cf. above, Brown to Clay, June 12, 1826).

Predicts that Count Ofalia, now in Paris, will fail in the object of his mission if it be, as rumored, "that of inducing France and England to withdraw their troops from the peninsula and leave Portugal and Spain to settle their own matters in their own way" (cf. above, Everett to Clay, March 19, April 19, 1827; Gallatin to Clay, April 14, 1827 [no. 68]; below, Hughes to Clay, September 16, 1827, note). ALS. DNA, RG59, Dip. Disp., France, vol. 23 (M34, R26). Received June 19.

Ribeaupierre served as Ambassador from Russia to Turkey at this time, charged with negotiating a treaty for Greek independence. He was subsequently, from 1836 to 1839, Ambassador to Berlin and in 1846 was named Grand Chamberlain of the Russian Court.

From JOHN SERGEANT, Mexico, "Private". Disclaims any intention to trouble Clay with the "many vexations . . . chiefly of a personal nature" he has had since coming to Mexico, but has concluded he should report one that has occurred recently. Quotes from a letter received from (William) Taylor: "Mr. [Joel R.] Poinsett informs me you would like to pay a short visit to your family this season but for the fear of the Vomito [yellow fever] here." Encloses his reply to Taylor, written after calling upon Poinsett. Declares: "This interference is entirely unaccountable, and it is the more extraordinary, as it was not only unknown to me, but at a time when I was in correspondence with Mr. Taylor, and could have made the enquiry myself, if it had been at all necessary. But it was not. I know what my public duty is, and I know, too, what my duty is to the President and to you, and I do not mean to let any wishes or feelings of my own interfere with the fulfilment of my obligations." Notes that Taylor and Sicard have published "their opinion that the Congress [at Tacubaya] would never meet" and that they have fruitlessly attempted to obtain information in that regard from (William B.) Rochester. Adds: "What their ulterior views are, or whether they are acting a principal or only a secondary part, I do not know. *This is a very vile place.*" States that "The matter of the Congress remains exactly as it was when" he wrote last. ALS. DNA, RG43, First Panama Congress (M622, R1). Received June 7.

MISCELLANEOUS LETTERS   April 27, 1827

To WILLIAM JOHNSON, Charleston, South Carolina. Informs him that (Richard W.) Habersham has resigned the office of United States district attorney for Georgia (see above, Habersham to Clay, February 25, 1827); that "The President had been disposed to offer the appointment to Mr. [Charles] Harris," who has, however, died (see above, Southard to Clay, February 12, 1827, note); and that the President does not have sufficient knowledge "of the qualifications and attainments" of Georgia lawyers to enable him "to supply the place of Mr. Habersham." Transmits a "blank Commission" and, by direction of the President, requests Johnson to fill it "with the name of some competent member of the bar, and communicate to this Department information thereof. . . ." Copy. DNA, RG59, Dom. Letters, vol. 21, p. 527 (M40, R19). See below, Johnson to Clay, May 30, 1827.

From John Binns

My Dr. Sir,   Private & Confidential   Phila. April 28, 1827.
    Yours of the 26th.[1] is before me. I know the value of your time too well to enter upon discussions in relation to appointments which have have [sic] been made and I have every disposition never again to obtrude my opinions on any which shall hereafter be made. My sole and entire object, in the few lines I addressed to you,[2] was to set before you the real state of things that you should as far in [sic] you lies labor to effect that "confidence, co-operation and concert among the friends of the Ad. in Pena." It is indeed much wanted.
    I do not desire to bandy opinions as to the State of public opinion in Pena. I know what it is as well as any man can. I have in the last two weeks had forty four letters from individuals of both parties on the subject and I have written nearly as many besides the printed Circulars I have committed to the Post Office.[3] I am as sanguine and ardent as any man and I am well persuaded that, at this hour, if Pena. was polled Genl Jackson would have two thirds of all the votes. It would be more gratifying to me and more agreable [sic] to you to give a different and more flattering picture. I could do it but I desire you to know the truth. Our German population, and they move pretty much altogether, are generally opposed to us. The German counties, and they are very populous, Lancaster, Berks, Northptn, Lehigh, &c are for Jackson. The way to revolution[ize] them the most promptly & certainly is by inducing the Governor, if possible, to come out and take the use of his name from our enemies.[4] This shall be effected if it can be done. You know, as well as I do, that although the Adn. must stand or fall by its measures & rely upon the Intelligence & Patrotism [sic] of People, yet, that channels must be opened to communicate with the people; to do this active & liberal partisans, men who have personal interests involved are of great value, are indeed indispensible. Who are to furnish funds? I do not know an officer of the Genl Govt in the district upon whom we could confidently call for five dollars to print a pamphlet &c. This is plain language but the times require it. Trust me my Dr. Sir, I never laboured harder or with more ardent zeal than in this cause. I shall so continue to do. I have this week sent communications to six newspapers in different parts of the Union.[5] I am full of hope as to Pena. With perfect Esteem I am Yrs Respectfully
H Clay Esq   JOHN BINNS.

ALS. DLC-HC (DNA, M212, R2).   1 Not found.
2 Not found.   3 Possibly the editorial announcement of Binns' endorsement of Adams
as opposed to Jackson, for the Presidency in the election of 1828, published in Philadelphia *Democratic Press*, March 27, 1827. On April 26, John Quincy Adams noted that
Tobias Watkins had shown him "a letter from J. Binns, at Philadelphia, with a printed
circular." Adams criticized the letter for its complaint that the administration did "not
support its friends," but he made no comment on the content of the circular. It may
have been an early version of the "coffin handbill." Cf. Adams, *Memoirs*, VII, 262; and
below, Clay to Everett, August 19, 1827, note.   4 Cf. above, Clay to Brooke, December 11, 1826; Crowninshield to Clay, March 14, 1827; Lacock to Clay, March 27, 1827.
Professor Klein points out that Governor Shulze conducted himself "So discreetly . . .
that almost to the end both the Jackson and the Adams men were claiming him for their
own." He maintains that the Governor's preference for the administration finally became apparent in his annual message to the Assembly on December 3, 1827. *Pennsylvania
Politics*, 220–23.   5 Cf. Lexington *Kentucky Reporter*, April 25, 1827.

From Joseph Kent

My Dear Sir   Rose Mount 28th. April 1827
    Our friend Harry[1] as you will percieve [sic] from the inclosed letter[2]
is getting quite wroth— Do send him to the West Indies, although his
letter is such an one as he nor no other person shoud [sic] have written— Return it to me— I shall not neglect to write to Woodson[3]— as
yet my engagements have prevented it—
    Tomorrow week I go to Annapolis & if you will not join me there
& eat soft crabs, I will endeavour after my return to spend a night with
you before you to [sic] go to Kentucky— Yours very truly
Honble. H. Clay   JOS: KENT

ALS. DLC-HC (DNA, M212, R2). Postmarked, by hand: "Bladensburg Apl 29."
1 Possibly John Harry. Cf. above, Sprigg to Clay, January 20, 1827.   2 Not found.
3 Samuel H. Woodson. Cf. below, Clay to Woodson, July 4, 1827, note.

From Philip S. Markley

Dear Sir   Phila. April 28th 1827
    Although you have not heard from me for some time, be assured
I have not been an inactive labourer since by return home in the political operations of Pennsylvania in the cause of the administration
of the General Government— It was my intention to have visited
Harrisburg prior to the adjournment of the Legislature, but my private and official engagements prevented me— I shall however be in
Harrisburg on the 8th of May in the character of a *delegate* to the
Episcopal Convention of this state to elect an assistant Bishop— and
as Church & state very often go hand in hand a favourable opportunity
will be afforded to effect much political good— As to the recent caucus
held in Harrisburg by a number of the Members of the Legislature,[1]
will prove with the people to have a different bearing than was expected by its movers, as far as I can learn, it has met the decided disapprobation of the majority of the people and has not been acceptably
received by many who were formerly zealous supporters of Jackson—

a very respectable and intelligent member of our state Legislature called on me yesterday and in conversation on the subject of the caucus stated to me that he was one of the number who composed the Caucus —that many like himself attended out of mere curiosity and he assured me, not 50 who attended would have sanctioned the proceedings with the signature of their names and that he firmly believed a majority of the Democratic party of the state were now with the administration and that before the election Mr Adams would be considered and supported as the real & exclusive candidate of the Democratic party of Penna.— The great interest that the ultra Federalist [sic] in this and the adjoining state of Delaware are taking in favour of Jackson[2] must and will completely revolunize [sic] Penna in favour of the administration from whose policy they have every thing to expect and gain— and by taking an opposite course they unite themselves with a party whose policy & views are in direct opposition to the best interest of the state

I mean to avail myself in the visit to Harrisburg to have an interview with several of the German Editors in the Counties through which I shall necessarily pass, and get them to take a stand and also to urge the holding of meetings preparatory to the Fall elections— — On no consideration I hope you will give up the idea of visiting Penna. after your return from Kentucky— I have received several letters from New York two of which you may have seen in the Democratic press [sic] some time since[3]— the accounts from that state I am happy to say are very flattering

In Phila. I have every reason to believe the administration are gaining strength particularly with the republican party— I should be glad to hear from you before I go to Harrisburg   I contemplate starting on the 6th of May   Very truly your friend   PHP. S. MARKLEY
Hon H. Clay

ALS. DLC-HC (DNA, M212, R2).   [1] Cf. above, Mifflin to Clay, April 4, 1827.
[2] Cf. above, Crowninshield to Clay, March 14, 1827; Niles to Clay, March 28, 1827, note; Clay to Webster, April 14, 1827; below, Clay to Taylor, September 7, 1827, note. Cf. also, Livermore, *Twilight of Federalism*, 235–39; Klein, *Pennsylvania Politics*, 211–18; John A. Munroe, *Louis McLane, Federalist and Jacksonian* (New Brunswick, 1973), 208–11.
[3] Probably the letters from Albany, dated March 26, 1827, and from Utica, dated April 9, 1827, which appeared in Philadelphia *Democratic Press*, March 30, April 26, 1827, respectively. Both reported strong support for the Adams administration.

DIPLOMATIC NOTES   April 28, 1827

To CHARLES R. VAUGHAN. States that "The interposition of the President has been requested by a Citizen of the United States to ascertain the condition of his Son," James Ringgold Slemaker, a native of Annapolis, born in 1805, who sailed from New York in 1822 in a vessel commanded by "Capn. Cathel, a relation of Slemaker." Adds that "Information has reached the Father" that, "in consequence of severe treatment," his son ran away from this vessel and went on board the British frigate "Sybil, Captain Rowley, then lying at Carthagena, stating to the

Captain that he was a British Subject. . . ." Requests Vaughan "to institute . . . enquiries to ascertain whether the young man remains in the British service, and if not what has become of him?" Expresses a hope that, if still in that service, he may be discharged and "restored to his family." Copy. DNA, RG59, Notes to Foreign Ministers and Consuls, vol. 3, pp. 356–57 (M38, R3). AL draft, in CSmH.

On May 2 Vaughan acknowledged receipt of Clay's note and promised to send a copy of it to England at the "earliest opportunity." NS, in DNA, RG59, Notes from British Legation, vol. 14 (M50, R15).

The father of James Ringgold Slemaker, not further identified, was Jacob H. Slemaker of Annapolis. Captain "Cathel" may have been Clement Cathell, Baltimore merchant and sea captain, who had been highly successful as a privateer during the War of 1812 and continued in such operations down to at least 1819, presumably under Colombian commission. The British ship *Sybille* was active at this time in suppressing the slave trade in the Atlantic. "Captain Rowley," not further identified.

INSTRUCTIONS AND DISPATCHES   April 28, 1827

From ALBERT GALLATIN, London, no. 71. Acknowledges receipt of Clay's "Despatch No. 20 of 20th ulto., with . . . enclosures." States that "No overture can be expected from this Government on the subject of the Colonial Intercourse" and that it is improbable that the President can take any measures to affect "their policy and induce them to negotiate." Expresses belief that "the only question will be, whether it may be best to let the matter rest for the present, or to draw the British Cabinet into a more explicit avowal of their real object." Suggests that Clay's "expected instructions" and what Gallatin may learn of the Cabinet's "disposition will point out the proper course." Discusses [George] Canning's efforts to form a Cabinet (cf. above, Gallatin to Clay, February 22, 1827); notes that "Lord Dudley & Ward is considered as qualified for the foreign department"; and adds: "But when introduced to us as his successor by Mr. Canning, at a diplomatic dinner. . . , he (Mr. C.) said that he would come back to us within four months." Declares "it is almost certain that Mr. Canning has obtained a promise of being supported by the mass of the Whig party." Quotes Canning as saying: " 'You see that the opinion universally entertained abroad and very generally indeed in England, that this Government is an Aristocracy, is not true. It is, said he emphatically, *a Monarchy*. The Whigs had [*sic*] found it out in 1784 when they tried to oppose the King's prerogative of choosing his prime Minister. The Tories have now repeated the same experiment and with no greater success.' " Remarks on Canning's appearance of confidence. Predicts no change, "For the present," in policy toward the United States and conjectures that "any reaction, as relates to us, . . . must come from the West Indies, and perhaps at last from the manufacturing interest." Promises to "ascertain . . . whether it is intended that our negotiations should be resumed." Concludes: "Mr. Canning, on the 23rd, again expressed great regret that they should have been so long interrupted, and intimated his intention of having within a few days a special conversation with me." ALS. DNA, RG59, Dip. Disp., Great Britain, vol. 34 (M30, R30). Published in Adams (ed.), *Writings of Albert Gallatin*, II, 371–72. Received June 7.

John William Ward, 1st Earl of Dudley and 4th Viscount of Dudley and Ward, had entered the House of Commons in 1802 and served there most of the period until 1823, when he succeeded to the peerage. Offered the undersecretaryship of the Foreign Office in 1822, he had declined it; but he accepted the post of Foreign Minister under Canning on April 30, 1827. He was created Earl of Dudley the following September, continuing in office after Canning's death in August, 1827, until May, 1828. He was not again politically active, except briefly as a participant in debates in 1831.

In December, 1783, George III had dismissed the coalition under which Charles James Fox and Frederick North had shared duties as Foreign Secretary in a ministry headed by the Duke of Portland. Still supported by a majority in the House of Commons the governmental coalition had denounced the royal influence, but the King had, nevertheless, dissolved Parliament and called for new elections. Although Fox had been returned to Parliament, some 160 of his supporters had been defeated. Fox had returned as Foreign Secretary again in 1806 but held office then only a few months before his death.

Frederick North, 2d Earl of Guilford, had entered Parliament in 1754, served as First Lord of the Treasury and head of the ministry from 1770 to December, 1782, and returned to governmental prominence four months later when the coalition with Fox was effected. North had succeeded to the title Earl of Guilford in 1790, two years before his death.

William Henry Cavendish Bentinck, 3d Duke of Portland, had been Prime Minister on two occasions, in 1783 and from 1807 to 1809, but had achieved his greatest distinction as Secretary of State for the Home Department from 1794 to 1801.

From ROBERT MONROE HARRISON, Antigua. States that he has received letters announcing his "nomination to the Consulate of St Bartholomew." Expresses thanks to the President and "warmest gratitude" to Clay for his "promptitude and kindness in attending to . . . [his] request." Informs Clay that he will await the arrival of his commission before going to his new post and will "invest" R. B. Eldridge, a business associate for the past four years, "with powers to superintend and protect the interests of the Citizens of the U States who by stress of weather or otherwise may be constrained to put into this Colony to refit." Suggests, in a postscript, that his appointment of Eldridge be confirmed by letter. ALS. DNA, RG59, Cons. Disp., Antigua, vol. 1 (M-T327, R1). Received June 5.

On June 16, 1827, Daniel Brent acknowledged, "By direction of the President, and in the absence of the Secretary," receipt of this letter and communicated "the Presidents confirmation of" Harrison's appointment of Eldridge. Copy, in DNA, RG59, Cons. Instr., vol. 2, pp. 431–32 (M78, R2).

MISCELLANEOUS LETTERS   April 28, 1827

To R[OBERT] PORTER AND SON, Wilmington, Delaware. Daniel Brent, as "directed by the Secretary," requests that the (State) Department be considered "as a subscriber for the Delaware Journal, . . . edited by Mr. M. Bradford. . . ." Copy. DNA, RG59, Dom. Letters, vol. 21, p. 527 (M40, R19).

Robert Porter, a printer, with his son, John, publishers of two almanacs at this time, had founded the Wilmington *Delaware State Journal* with the issue of April 24, 1827. Moses Bradford, the editor, who had from 1814 to 1816 established and edited the Wilmington *Delaware Gazette*, continued with the *State Journal* until 1833. The journal was set up to promote Adams' candidacy. Bradford was later active as a local leader of the Whig Party.

From WILLIAM WOODBRIDGE, Detroit. Transmits "some printed pamphlets." Surmises that "the base attack" made on him "will have been, or will be communicated to the President," but professes pride in the knowledge that he has performed his "Duty in this as well as in other respects, openly—fearlessly—& with integrity." Requests Clay, if he "should think the matter worthy of the consideration of the President, . . . to refer the whole matter to him." Concludes: "The proceedings of the Board of Canvassers, to which allusion is made, will be found at large in my returns as Secretary of this Territory for the year 1825." ALS. DNA, RG59, A. and R. (M531, R8). Published in Carter (ed.), *Territorial Papers*, XI, 1072–73.

Woodbridge had been criticized for his role as one of the canvassers in the election for Michigan Territorial Delegate to Congress in 1825. Cf. above, Richard to Clay, October 17, 1825; Clark to Clay, February 2, 1826. He had recently published *A Letter to the Hon. Abraham Edwards, President of the Legislative Council of the Territory of Michigan* (Detroit, April 14, 1827). For "A Report of the Proceedings in Relation to the Contested Election for Delegate to the Nineteenth Congress, from the Territory of Michigan. . . ," signed by Woodbridge, as secretary, see Carter (ed.), *Territorial Papers*, XI, 711–69.

From Francis Johnson

Dear Sir.   Bowling Green[1] 29 April 1827

Yours of the 7 Inst[2] was duly recd. since which I have visited Edmondson [*sic*] County, where I happy [*sic*] to say my opponent[3] met with very poor encouragment [*sic*]— I yesterday attended a petty muster in the lower end of this county,[4] in the bounds of which Company it was asserted my opponent would not get a vote—   in this town which contains about 112 votes It is said he will not get two votes—
he passed through town this evening to Genl Covingtons,[5] where he has called several times before,   One of the Genl's sons & his eldest daughter[6] was here last evening & today— I understand the Genl nor none of his family will Support Yancy [*sic*] and that Genl Covington has told him so, yet he continues his visits;   I mention this to show, the pertinacity and persever[ence] of Mr Yancy—   from present prospects, my opinion is that I shall obtain a Majority of from 500 to 700 in this County, about the same in Logan— My opponents say 4 or 500 —my friends say 6 or 800— In Barren (Mr Y's county) about 2 or 300.
in Simpson my friend [*sic*] from 150 to 200.— Allen & Monroe about even—   and Edmondson which has only about 180 votes [*sic*] that vote in the district, I think my majority may be fairly set down at 100— And I feel persuaded the cause is gaining ground daily—   the Wollens [*sic*] Bill & my vote agt. an increased duty on foreign Spirits,[7] was attempted to be used agt. me; but it is abandoned—   the People as far as I learn are perfectly satisfied with my vote in both cases— It is a fatiguing campaign, but I have entered on it with determination if life & health last to go through with it— Many who were for the 'Hero' have left him and I hope many more will follow the example, until He will have so few left, that they can not raise a struggle—   last nights mail brought a package of hand Bills—from the Nashville Jackson committee[8]—signed by 'John Overton' in which Mr Buckner and myself are noticed—   what Mr Buckner has done I know not, but they represent me as having made a charge agt. the genl. which I have not made, and

498

then they undertake to answer it— so you see, the extent to which this committee is going— I Can but view it as having been got up to operate on the Elections in this state. But if I am not mistaken they will repent it— as soon as I can get one of their hand Bills, I will send it to you, unless it shall appear in the papers and then you will see it—

At the Edmondson Court—I met with Mr Calhoun [sic] & Doct. Young[9] the candidates in the adjoining District— Mr Chilton the Jackson man meeting but 4 friends at Grayson Court—returned home and declined—leaving the field to the two admn: Candidates— Calhoun is an advocate of the Woollens Bill, and wields it against Doct Young with some force[10]— Calhoun is a man of promise and a daring Spirit— Speaks well and in my opinion would be a considerable acquisition to the Ky Delegation and will I think be Elected. He has defended the admn & Mr Adams & yourself agt. the Jackson slang—which has given him great favor with the people, the Doctr. was incompetent to debate with Chilton—but Calhoun was his match, [If] it was not for the misfortune[11] which befel [sic] the Doctor and which excites [much] Sympathy with some Calhoun would beat him easily and even *that* [ma]y not enable the Doctr to beat him— Calhoun is a thorough going admn man— the Doctr. we know is timid as evinced on McLanes amendt to the *panama* mission[12] & the Wollens Bill— and had Buckner voted for the Wollens Bill,[13] I believe it would have helped him, But he is said to be safe— Colo. New holds on and is likely to do so and so will Henry and I fear it may result in Lyons Election[14]— the information I have is that many Contend Henry is strongest & has a claim on the people and New ought to give way— there is but one candidate in this district out for the State Legislature, that is known to be a Jackson man— and He is in Monroe and as yet without opposition— and if they will Start a strong man on the other side against him—I have hopes he will be beat[15]— John B Bibb Esqr the youngest brother of Judge Bibb[16]—the same that was at your House in the City is out in Logan, strong & decided for the admn— the probability is h[e] will have no Opposition— he was started by the New & Old Court men, being himself a decided but mild Old Court man— our friends look with anxiety to the Legislature as well as Congress— in this county two admn men are Skiles the late member, and Mr Grider a lawyer, who studied with me and is also the Brother in Law of Genl Covington— they are both warm, the latter makes a good *stump* speach—and comes out boldly for the admn— there may probably be other candidates[17]— In Allen the Jackson men threaten Thomas the late member, if he does not declare for Jackson, that he shall be opposed— the last I heard—he had remained Silent on the Subject— I do not think he will take part against me— if he does not I will shake the Jackson men in that County *terribly*[18]— The policy of the present admn, pleases the people well— And all that they have to Op-

pose it with is the Household furniture, the Billiard Table[19] &c. which
I hope to give a final blow to e're long— If I do get beat, I have resolved
it shall not be for want of exertions on my part— I last night recd. a
letter from Chs S Todd. of Shelby[20]— desiring me to state the policy of
the Administration—and the assailable points of the Opposition, to
use in that district— surely they cannot be at a loss on these points—
but I will write him the first leasure I have— he tells me if allen &
Lecompe both hold out Crittenden will be Elected with ease—but if
Allen gives way, which he thinks is probable—it will be a severe contest[21]— Abram Morton,[22] the younger brother of Jno H. Morton—was
here yesterday he lives in Oldham— he entertains great hopes that
White[23] will beat Wickliffe— Respectfuly [sic] Yr friend
Hon: H. Clay   FR: JOHNSON

ALS. DLC-HC (DNA, M212, R2). Addressed to Clay as *"Private."* MS. slightly defaced.
[1] Kentucky.   [2] Not found.   [3] Joel Yancey. Cf. above, Clay to Taylor, April 4,
1827, note.   [4] Warren County, of which Bowling Green is the county seat.
[5] Elijah M. Covington, a brother of Thomas A., had come to Kentucky from North
Carolina around 1795 and is thought to have held his military title in the North Carolina militia. Elijah acquired his first land in Warren County in 1798 and ultimately held
some 20,000 acres in that vicinity. He was the first sheriff of the county, organized in 1796,
and county surveyor from 1799 to 1833.   [6] Harriett, at this time age 16, was Covington's oldest daughter; he had four surviving sons. Harriett later married Richard Delafield, of New York.   [7] On the woolens bill, cf. above, Pleasants to Clay, February 14,
1827, note. Johnson had voted in the House of Representatives for passage of the measure. During the course of the debate, on February 10, 1827, James Buchanan had proposed that the bill be returned to committee with instructions to make changes, including an increase in duty on foreign spirits, "not less than ten cents per gallon. . . ."
The motion was defeated, with Johnson voting against it. U. S. H. of Reps., *Journal,* 19
Cong., 2 Sess., 278.   [8] Jackson's "Central Committee," formed "for the purpose,"
according to one of its leaders, "of corresponding with other Jackson committees in the
different sections of the union," was composed of 18 members, of whom John Overton
was one, its "activities . . . carefully superintended by Jackson himself." Remini, *Election
of Andrew Jackson,* 63–64. The handbill was a circular, dated at Nashville, April 23,
1827, announcing organization of the committee, citing charges against Jackson relative
to the execution of the six Tennessee militiamen (see above, Watkins to Clay, Sept. 30,
1826, note), and refuting those charges. The document concluded with a "Certificate" by
Colonel (Philip) Pipkin, commander of the regiment to which the militiamen were attached, exonerating Jackson from the allegations "erroneously charged" against him by
(Richard A.) Buckner and "Frank" Johnson in relation to the incident. The circular was
published in the Lexington *Kentucky Gazette,* May 4, 1827, and in the Frankfort *Argus
of Western America,* May 23, 1827.   [9] John Calhoon; William S. Young. The former,
a Hardinsburg lawyer, had been born in Henry County, Kentucky, in 1797, and had been
a member of the State legislature, from Ohio County, in 1820 and 1821. He was later
elected to that body, from Breckinridge County, in 1829, 1830, and 1840. He lost the current congressional race to Young, who died on September 19, 1827. A special election in
November to choose Young's successor resulted, after the returns from one county were
thrown out, in victory for Calhoon. He resigned, however, in order to avoid a contest,
and joined his opponent, Thomas Chilton, in petitioning for a new election, which the
latter won. Calhoon was from 1835 to 1839, a member of Congress. He afterward practiced
law for a short time in St. Louis and then returned to Kentucky, where he became a
district judge in 1842.   [10] Young had consistently opposed the bill in the voting of
the House of Representatives. U. S. H. of Reps., *Journal,* 19 Cong., 2 Sess., 197–98, 231–32,
253–54, 278–84.   [11] Newspaper reports on Young's death, "after a few days of painful illness," suggested that it had been hastened because "he was made to drink deep of
the cup of domestic affliction. . . ." His wife, according to one account, had been ab-
ducted and seduced by one of Young's political rivals, "while Young was at Washington,
who, on his return home, learnt for the first time, what had taken place during his
absence, in finding himself surrounded by his little children, abandoned by a mother
who had exiled herself with her seducer, to a foreign land, carrying with her all the

property or estate she could readily command or control." Washington *Daily National Journal*, October 25, 1827, reprinted from Newport *Rhode Island Republican*; *Albany Argus*, October 15, 1827.   [12] During debate in Committee of the Whole of the House of Representatives, on April 20, 1826, concerning the appropriations for the Panama Mission, Louis McLane had proposed an amendment: "The House, however, in expressing this opinion, do not intend to sanction any departure from the settled policy of this Government; that in extending our commercial relations with foreign nations, we shall have with them as little political connection as possible: and that we shall preserve peace, commerce, and friendship with all nations, and form entangling alliances with none. It is, therefore, the opinion of this House, that the Government of the United States ought not to be represented at the Congress of Panama, except in a diplomatic character, nor ought they to form any alliance, offensive or defensive, or negotiate respecting such an alliance with all or any of the Spanish American Republics; nor ought they to become parties with them, or either of them, to any joint declaration for the purpose of preventing the interference of any of the European Powers with their Independence or form of Government, or to any compact for the purpose of preventing colonization upon the Continent of America: but that the People of the United States should be left free to act, in any crisis, in such a manner as their feelings of friendship towards these Republics, and as their own honor and policy may, at the time, dictate."

Young had supported this amendment, but it had been defeated and the appropriation bill passed (see above, Clay to Anderson, March 15, 1826, note). U. S. H. of Reps., *Journal*, 19 Cong., 1 Sess., 451–59 *passim*.   [13] Buckner had joined with Young in voting against passage of the bill. *Ibid.*, 19 Cong., 2 Sess., 282–84.   [14] Richard B. New; John F. Henry; Chittenden Lyon. An effort was made to avoid the division between the administration supporters in the Twelfth Kentucky District, by a written agreement under which a committee of ten, five from each camp, were to conduct meetings in each county "to ascertain their relative strength, and pledging themselves that the one who shall be found weakest shall decline holding a poll." Nashville *Banner and Whig*, July 14, 1827. The arrangement failed. The combined vote of New and Henry was 315 less than the vote for Lyon. Frankfort *Argus of Western America*, September 12, 1827. New, of Todd County, had attended Transylvania University from 1806 to 1808 and was a member of the Kentucky House of Representatives in the Sessions from 1823 to 1827, 1830–31, and 1833–34. During the last of these he served as Speaker.   [15] James McMillan, a Jacksonite, of Monroe County, had served in the Kentucky Assembly since 1825 and was re-elected for the Session of 1827–1828 without contest.   [16] Bibb, a brother of George M. Bibb, was a veteran of the War of 1812 and represented Logan County in the Kentucky House of Representatives from 1827 to 1829 and in the State Senate from 1830 to 1834. He subsequently resided in Frankfort, Kentucky, for many years.   [17] James Rumsey Skiles and Henry Grider were both elected as Warren County representatives in the State legislature. Skiles had been brought to Kentucky as a child, in 1803, and trained in law at Nashville, Tennessee. Throughout his public career he was active in support of internal improvements; he was one of a group who in 1830 placed the first steamboat on the Green River and in 1836 organized the Portage Railroad to carry goods from the river to the town of Bowling Green. Skiles, first elected to the Kentucky House of Representatives in 1825, remained through the term ending in 1828 and was re-elected for the two terms extending from 1840 through 1842. He removed to Texas in 1855 and died there in 1866. Grider, born in Garrard County, Kentucky, was a veteran of the War of 1812 and practiced law in Bowling Green. He served in the Kentucky House of Representatives for the Sessions beginning in 1827 and 1831, in the Kentucky Senate from 1833 to 1838, and in the United States Congress from 1843 to 1847 and from 1861 until his death in 1866. He had married Rachel Covington.

[18] Walter Thomas, one of the first justices of the peace of Allen County, organized in 1815, was a member of the Kentucky House of Representatives from 1824 to 1828 and from 1831 to 1833. He was elected in 1827 as a Jacksonite. Johnson lost Allen County to Yancey by a vote of 561 to 249. Lexington *Kentucky Reporter*, August 29, September 1, 1827.   [19] Cf. above, Turner to Clay, January 7, 1827.   [20] Todd had acquired a farm in Shelby County shortly after his return from Colombia (cf. above, III, 811, 813n).

[21] For the outcome of the race involving Charles H. Allen, Joseph Lecompte, and Henry Crittenden, see above, John J. Crittenden to Clay, November 25, 1826, note.

[22] Abraham B. Morton had been living in Lexington as late as 1820. He was appointed by Andrew Jackson as register of the land office at Milwaukee, Wisconsin Territory, in 1836 and remained there until 1844, when he was shifted, in the same capacity to the land office at Clinton, Missouri. He was removed from the latter appointment in the fall of 1845.   [23] Charles A. Wickliffe defeated Lee White, the administration candidate in the congressional contest for the Ninth District, by nearly 2,000 votes. Lexington

Kentucky Reporter, August 18, 1827. White was elected to the Kentucky Legislature from Jefferson County in 1829.

DIPLOMATIC NOTES   April 30, 1827

To BARON DE STACKELBERG. Informs him "that the Law of the last Session of Congress, for the benefit of Swedish Navigation [cf. above, Clay to Stackelberg, March 16, 1827], was on the first of March, last, published in the National Journal; and further, that . . . orders were transmitted from the Treasury Department to the Collector of New York [Jonathan Thompson] to desist from collecting the Alien duties from Swedish Vessels and to refund any that had been improperly received." Copy. DNA, RG59, Notes to Foreign Ministers and Consuls, vol. 3, p. 357. L draft, in CSmH.

Writing to Clay on the same day, Stackelberg expressed thanks for this communication. ALS, in DNA, RG59, Notes from Swedish Legation, vol. 3 (M60, R2).

INSTRUCTIONS AND DISPATCHES   April 30, 1827

From HENRY MIDDLETON, St. Petersburg, "*Private.*" Explains the lapse of time since his last dispatch (no. 68, December 13, 1826, "duplicate," received September 7, 1827; omitted by editors as routine in nature) by adverting to the death of his daughter (Eleanor Isabella, January 26, 1827) and his subsequent "seclusion from society," which prevented his "collecting any articles of intelligence" to communicate. Notes a belief that negotiations concerning Greece have been conducted by Russia and England in London (cf. below, Brown to Clay, July 12, 1827), without known results. Presumes that Russia, since she does not wish to extend her empire southward, will end the war with Persia after "sufficiently" chastising "the Persian for his unadvised attack . . ." (cf. above, Middleton to Clay, September 17, 1826, note). Reports that on February 26 he "addressed a note to Count Nesselrode . . . upon the long standing claim of Mr. [Israel] Thorndike" (cf. above, Thorndike to Clay, March 13, 1825; Clay to Middleton, February 12, 1827) and is "informed that it has been taken into consideration. . . ." ALS. DNA, RG59, Dip. Disp., Russia, vol. 11 (M35, R11). Dated "30/18 April 1827"; received September 7.

From HENRY MIDDLETON, St. Petersburg, no. 69. States that "The opening of the navigation" enables him to forward two documents: an offical publication of the Russian tariff duties and "a printed form of the rules of Etiquette observed at the Imperial Court of Russia in the reception" of diplomatic personnel. ALS. DNA, RG59, Dip. Disp., Russia, vol. 11 (M35, R11). Dated "18/30 April, 1827"; received September 7.

MISCELLANEOUS LETTERS   April 30, 1827

From EDWARD EVERETT, Boston. Forwards a letter (above, the second from George Jarvis, November 18, 1826), which had reached him "this day". Characterizes the writer as "an honest worthy young man," devoted to the Greek cause, but comments on his "[ra]ther obscure" writing style and his failure to give as many facts as could be desired. States that he has also received "letters from Dr. [Samuel Gridley] Howe in Greece, which will [app]ear in the [Daily] Advertiser of tomorrow and the [next] day." Asks in a postscript that Clay have (Daniel) Brent send him G (eorge) W (illiam) Erving's address. ALS. DNA, RG59, Misc. Letters (M179, R65).

Samuel Gridley Howe, of Boston, had been graduated from Harvard University with the A.B. degree in 1821 and the M.D. in 1824. He had then joined the Greeks in their revolt from Turkey and remained in Greece as a guerrilla fighter and naval surgeon for six years. In 1831, he became head of a school for the blind, incorporated by the State of Massachusetts in 1829. During his 44 year administration the school developed into the Perkins Institute, a model for such work in the United States and abroad. He also pioneered in the use of oral rather than sign language for the deaf, agitated for reforms in penal care and the treatment of the insane, and became active, even to the point of running for Congress, in support of the antislavery campaign. He was defeated in his political ventures but worked assiduously to promote Negro education and suffrage until his death in 1876. His letters, published in the *Boston Daily Advertiser* on May 1, 2, 1827, and widely copied in other American newspapers, were dated from the steamship *Kateria* in the Aegean and eastern Mediterranean Seas, November 23, December 18, 1826.

From HEZEKIAH HUNTINGTON, "Attorneys Office Hartford." Discusses, in explanation of the delay in submitting the additional information promised in his letter of March 31, 1827, a number of cases under his care; acknowledges that he has "perhaps too minutely refered [*sic*] to some of the *causes*, which prevented a further explanation and *refutation*, of the Charges against" him; and promises "a further statement . . . without delay—" ALS. DNA, RG59, Misc. Letters (M179, R65).

From Peter B. Porter

Dear Sir,   (Confidential)   Black Rock May 1st. 1827

I intended to have written to you again, before I left N. York, but my departure was somewhat sudden & unpremeditated, & I pursued my journey night & day without stopping untill I reached home.

My late excursion afforded an opportunity to learn something of the state of public sentiment in regard to the next Presidency. The coalition between Clinton & Van Buren[1] (the prominent leaders of the two opposing parties) and carrying with them, as a matter of course, most of their partisan politicians, or body guards, and many of the party presses, could not fail to produce an effect, and exhibit the appearance at least of combining the whole strength of our state against the administration. When I reached Albany on my way down, and for some time previous, the Jackson Men were extremely clamorous & confident, while the friends of the Admn. astounded at this extraordinary state of things, were afraid not only to avow their own sentiments & predilections, but to inquire what were those of others. Some pains, however, were taken toward the close of the session, to produce an interchange of opinion & concert of action—and it resulted in a very general conviction that a decided majority of the two houses were friendly to the Administration.

The two political Journals at Albany (namely, the Daily Advertiser which is Clintonian, & the Argus which belongs to Van Buren & his friends) are for Jackson, & the first & most obvious measure to be adopted was the establishment of a new press at that place. Some funds, for the purpose, were obtained at Albany, & the remainder of the subscription was nearly or quite filled at N. York before I left there. The proposed Editor is Mr Leake,[2] who was Senior editor of the Argus for several years, but was driven from that establishment by V. B. & its other owners, in consequence of his support of you at the last election. The Kings[3] & their friends in N. York, were very zealous & liberal in their efforts to get up this paper, and, indeed, were disposed to take a more conspicuous part in it than was deemed advisable by many others. They were however given distinctly to understand that the new paper must not be a mere echo of the "American"[4]— That the polar star of its policy must be the encouragement of domestic manufactures & support of the tariff, which you know the American has opposed— that it must be purely democratic, & that, keeping the same common object in view, the oftener it crossed the path of the American in minor matters, the better. To this they assented, and I have reason to believe, from the situation in which the business stood when I left N. York, that this paper will soon appear.

I am persuaded that a large majority of the city of New York is hostile to the pretensions of Genl. Jackson, but not entirely agreed as to his opponent. I had an opportunity to converse not only with members of the two parties generally, but with individuals belonging to most of the sections or clans which compose the respective parties. Besides federalists of different complections, I saw, among the republicans, such as Judge Edwards, Maxwell, Gardner, Crolius,[5] & their friends, Eckford. Price[6] &c & their adherents, and several amongst the most influential, of the "Swamp"[7] a ultra democratic party. The reluctance to go for Jackson in any event, is very general & decided, but many of our democratic friends are disposed to take you up in place of Mr Adams. These difficulties, I trust, however will be reconciled.

The views of the "National Advocate" have, I think, been mistaken by Mr Gales.[8] It certainly did, some time since, make demonstrations in favor of Jackson & Van Buren. But its course that way is not yet decided; and I am inclined to think that it will eventually come out for Mr Adams, or, I more fear, for yourself—and that its "master spirit" will turn out to be you, instead of Van Buren. This paper is, or can be, controuled by Eckford, and his plan is, as he expresses it, "to check mate Van Buren by playing a game as deeply democratic as his own." I should feel entirely confident of the support of this paper, were it not for Eckford's embarrassments, which may induce him to adopt expedients at war with his better judgment & feelings.[9]

On the whole my opinion is, that after the temporary excitement which the zeal & authority of Genl. Jacksons friends have created, shall subside—and it is already evidently in the wane—there will be a most decided majority of the people of N. York found on the side of the Administration. Clinton carries with him only his violent political partisans, while the great body of his former supporters, who are the moderate federalists, will adhere to the administration. It remains to be seen how far V. B. will be successfull in carrying with him the democratic party.

Mr Marvin was at my house yesterday, and Mr Storrs[10] the day before. They have been attending the Circuits in some of our western counties, & speak most encouragingly of the state of public sentiment. Your favour of the 20th. ult. addressed to me at N. York, was received yesterday. Will you let me know when I may expect to see you & Mrs Clay at Black Rock?

Our pier has again been pretty bad[ly] handled, this spring near its upper end by the ice.[11] We intend, in repairing, to alter the direction & character of the work at that point, by which we hope to avoid similar accidents in future. With great respect & esteem Your Obt Sert
Hon. H. Clay.   P. B. Porter

Your friends, the French Minister & Lady,[12] will be received with great pleasure by Mrs Porter & myself. I have only regret that the peculiar condition of Mrs P's health, at this moment,[13] will not permit her to be very *active* in her attentions.

ALS. DLC-HC (DNA, M212, R2).
    1 Cf. above, Hammond to Clay, January 28, 1827; Porter to Clay, April 18, 1827.
    2 Isaac Q. Leake. On the proposed administration organ at Albany, see above, Porter to Clay, January 3, 1827, note.   3 Probably including Rufus King and sons Charles and John A. Cf. above, III, 357n. Rufus King had died April 29, 1827.   4 *New York American*.   5 Ogden Edwards; Hugh Maxwell; probably Charles Kitchel Gardner; Clarkson Crolius. Maxwell, born in Scotland, had graduated from Columbia College in 1808, had studied law and entered practice, had become assistant judge advocate general of the Army in 1814, and from 1819 to 1829 was district attorney for New York County. He later became a prominent Clay Whig and served as collector of the Port of New York from 1849 to 1852. Crolius, born and reared in New York, had inherited a pottery factory, had long been a member of the city council identified with the Tammany faction, and for a decade had been a member of the State legislature, of which he had been speaker in 1825.   6 Henry Eckford; possibly William M. Price. The latter, educated at Columbia College and prominent as a lawyer, had long been active as a Federalist but had now transferred his allegiance to Tammany Hall and Andrew Jackson. He was rewarded in 1834, when he was appointed Federal attorney for the Eastern District of New York. He resigned in 1838 in default as a receiver of the public moneys. Allan Nevins (ed.), *The Diary of Philip Hone, 1828–1851* (New York, 1970), 365–66.
    7 Possibly a reference to an area along Ferry Street near the East River, originally called "Beekman's Swamp." It had been laid out in lots in the mid-eighteenth century, sold for tanneries, and developed as the center of the leather trade. "More immense fortunes have been made about that region than any other of the same extent in the city." William L. Stone, *History of New York City from the Discovery to the Present Day* (New York, 1872), 90–91n.   8 Joseph Gales is here cited as editor of the Washington *Daily National Intelligencer*, which as recently as March 13, 1827, had identified the New York *National Advocate* as "flattering" Martin Van Buren's "projects". On April 17, however, the *Intelligencer* had remarked on the *Advocate*'s concern "that the name of Mr. Van Buren should not be connected with that of the Advocate" and commented: "For any thing we are certain of, such connexion may be unjustly imputed to them. . . ." The following day the *Intelligencer* noted: "The vane of the New York Advocate has veered

quite round to a point opposite to that which it marked on the 1st or 2d of March, and for a month afterwards." 9 On Mordecai Noah's removal as editor of the New York *National Advocate* in 1824, cf. above, Stuart to Clay, March 15, 1825, note. Thomas Snowden had then been named titular manager for a group of Tammany leaders, the most prominent of whom were Henry Eckford, Jacob Barker, and John Targee (a silversmith). Eckford, a former Crawfordite, in 1827 opposed the candidacy of Andrew Jackson and supported the Adams administration; Barker had long been an admirer of Clay. On April 7, refusing yet to endorse a candidate, the editor of the *National Advocate* had retorted to the Washington *National Journal*'s assertion that he was supporting Van Buren, by commenting: "Mr. Clay himself has just as much influence over its concerns as the New York Senator has." And on April 24, the editor had expressed his personal choice of Clay over any of the leading candidates but nevertheless committed the journal to support whomever the Republican Party nominated. On May 10 Snowden secretly agreed to back the Adams campaign; and on June 18, announcing that Samuel S. Conant had become a joint proprietor with Snowden, the *Advocate* predicted that New York would adhere to Adams and that the journal would concur in that support. The *National Advocate* remained the official Tammany organ until August and continued to receive the patronage of publishing the Society's notices until the autumn, but by October the growing strength of the Jacksonians had split the Tammany organization into two distinct camps. Jerome Mushkat, *Tammany, the Evolution of a Political Machine, 1789–1865* (Syracuse, 1971), 104–107. The *National Advocate* remained the organ of the Tammany Adamsites; but the Jacksonian New York *Morning Courier* founded May 3, 1827, spoke for the increasingly dominant segment of the Tammany movement. *Albany Argus,* August 7, 10, 1827. Eckford and Barker, meanwhile, sank into political oblivion. In September, 1826, with numerous others they had been indicted for fraud involving several million dollars in misappropriated investment funds. The first trial had ended in a divided jury. Two subsequent trials resulted in conviction. On appeal, the indictments were quashed in November, 1827, but civil actions continued the litigation for many years. Jacob Barker, *Incidents in the Life of. . . ; with Historical Facts, His Financial Transactions with the Government, and His Course on Important Political Questions, from 1800 to 1855* (Washington, 1855), 150–79, 194, 200–201 *passim*; Gustavus Myers, *The History of Tammany Hall* (New York, 1917), 70–71. Conant, of Vermont, assumed the editorial management of the *National Advocate* at this time and continued in that role after the journal's merger with the New York *Statesman* to form the New York *Morning Herald,* in 1829. 10 Dudley Marvin; Henry R. Storrs. 11 Cf. above, Clay to Porter, June 22, 1826. On April 21, 1827, the *Rochester Daily Advertiser* had referred to recent damage near Pendleton but reported that it would be repaired so as to re-open navigation by April 22. The journal noted, further, that the damage to Black Rock Harbor was not sufficiently serious to "impede the passage of boats to Buffalo." Quoted in the *Albany Argus and Daily City Gazette,* April 26, 1827. 12 The Baron and Mme. Mareuil. See above, Clay to Porter, April 18, 1827. 13 Cf. below, Porter to Clay, August 19, 1827.

MISCELLANEOUS LETTERS   May 1, 1827

From MATTHEW ST. CLAIR CLARKE, "Clerk Ho. Rep. U S." Notes that "An Indian Treaty contained in 6 Vol 684. made at Washington, with the Cherokees, contains in the last clause of Art. 2. a Proviso concerning the assent of South Carolina—" Asks: "Was this approval ever promulgated?—Or was it made known to the Department of State—?—" Explains that he does "not wish to omit any thing" from the "system of Land Laws" he is preparing. ALS. DNA, RG59, Misc. Letters (M179, R65). Endorsed by Clay (AEI) on cover: "Mr B. will examine into this enquiry. H C." Daniel Brent wrote Clarke, May 4, 1827, that the South Carolina Legislature had assented to the treaty by an act of December 19, 1816. Copy, in DNA, RG59, Dom. Letters, vol. 21, p. 528 (M40, R19).

Clarke was citing the Bioren and Duane edition of the United States statutes (see above, II, 560n). Cf. 7 *U. S. Stat.*, 139, art. 2, of the Cherokee treaty of March 22, 1816. Clarke's compilation, *Laws Relative to the Public Lands,* was published in two volumes by the Law Library of Congress in 1828. Poore, *Descriptive Catalogue of the Government Publications. . . ,* 194.

From FRANCIS HARRIS, Albany, New York. States that "Some time since" he sent to Clay's "department a Petition for the grant of a Patent in the improvement of Steam Engines &c. and with it thirty dollars, which was returned." Quotes a letter received from W (illiam) Browne, which explained that the money was not "receivable at the U. S. Br. Bk." in Washington and requested in its place "U. S. notes of Any Branch." Notes that he immediately complied with the request but has "had no returns," and asks Clay "to advise" him "as soon as possible on the Subject." ALS. DNA, RG59, Misc. Letters (M179, R65).

After first informing Harris, in a letter dated "May 1827," that "the money stated . . . to have been forwarded to this department," had apparently not been received, William Browne wrote Harris again, May 19, 1827, to tell him that his letter and money, having "been mislaid," had been found, the fee had been paid to the Treasury, and the patent would be forwarded. Each a copy, in DNA, RG59, Dom. Letters, vol. 21, pp. 533, 541 (M40, R19).

Harris, not further identified, received a patent for a rotary steam engine July 10, 1827.

To Pascal Paoli Enos

Sir: Washington, 2d May, 1827.

I have to thank you for your letter of the 12th ult.[1] transmitting the "Sangamo Spectator."[2] The interesting proceedings which it contains, demonstrate that the people of Sangamo County justly comprehend, and faithfully adhere to those principles of National policy which are best calculated to advance the welfare of Illinois.[3] The munificent grant made by Congress at its last Session, to aid in the execution of your canal, is only one, among many evidences of the anxious desire of the present Administration, to promote the prosperity of the Western as well as the other sections of our country. I hope that the trust which is implied in that grant will be executed by the Legislature of Illinois, in a manner entirely satisfactory to the people of that State. I am, respectfully, your obedient servt.   H. CLAY.
P. P. Enos, Esq.

LS. IHi. Addressed to Enos at "Sangamo Court House, Illinois." Enos, a native of Connecticut, had resided briefly in Ohio and Missouri before removing to Madison County, Illinois, in 1821. He held appointment as receiver of the land office at Springfield from 1823 to 1829 and became one of the founders of the city of Springfield, where he died in 1832. John Carroll Power, *History of the Early Settlers of Sangamon County, Illinois* . . . (Springfield, 1876), 288–89.
[1] Not found.   [2] Published at Springfield, Illinois.   [3] Following passage of the legislation for a public land grant to support construction of the Illinois and Michigan Canal (see above, Clay to Edwards, July 18, 1825, note), residents of Sangamon County early in April had urged a call for the Illinois Legislature to meet in special session to act on the proposal. George Forquer to Ninian Edwards, April 20, 1827, in Washburne (ed.), *Edwards Papers*, 278–80.

To Edward Everett

My Dear Sir   Washington 2d. May 1827.

I thank you for the satisfactory exposition[1] of the state of political parties in Massachusetts. I am glad to perceive from it that there is no danger to be apprehended, in that quarter, to the cause of the Administration.

Our friends in Maryland and Pennsa. are becoming aroused and have held some, and contemplate other, meetings of the people.[2] One is advertized for Balto. on saturday, respecting which the best anticipations are indulged. The progress of change, in our favor, continues in Pennsa. and our friends there are quite sanguine that the vote of that State will be right.

On the point whether Mr. Webster should be transfered [sic] from the House to the Senate, I think the pro's and con's are so nearly equal that he may fairly exercise his own predilection, if the option should be presented to him. He is wanted in the Senate, and it would be very elegible [sic] to retain him in the House, where his weight you know is very great.[3] There is one consideration which is worth some little attention, and that relates to McLane of Delaware. His principles and his true political interests should put him on the side of the Admon. If he has a prospect of being the leader of the friends of the Admon in the Senate, I am not sure that he will not take the attitude which he ought. Should that prospect be destroyed it may have an influence in confirming him in the attachment which is attributed to him for the cause of the Opposition.[4] Mr. Webster would shade him in the Senate. This speculation is without any other knowledge of Mr. McL.s actual views and purposes than such as you or any other public man may possess.

I know Shaw[5] well and correspond with him, though I have not received a letter from him for several months. He professes (I believe most sincerely) great regard for me. I think you will never find him intentionally contributing to the success of Genl. Jackson.

Mrs. Clay unites with me in assurances of sincere esteem for Mrs. E. and in best wishes for her health and happiness. I pray you to communicate mine to Miss B.[6]

We have made a most agreeable change of residence since you left this City, by getting into Mrs. Decatur's house, which is the best private dwelling in the City.[7] Believe me faithfully Your friend
E. Everett Esqr.   H. CLAY

P.S.   The elections in Virginia are not quite so unfavorable to us as might perhaps have been anticipated. If, as is probable, Mr. Lovell is elected in the South Western District, we shall have only lost one member in the H. of R.[8]   H. R. [sic]

ALS. MHi.   1 Not found.
2 Cf. above, Clay to Johnston, April 17, 1827. A meeting of administration partisans at Baltimore on May 5 adopted a preamble and resolutions which defended Adams' election and Clay's appointment to the Cabinet in 1825, praised the policies of the administration, specifically the support for internal improvements, set up a local campaign organization, and called for similar actions in all parts of the State as a prelude to a State convention to be held at Baltimore, July 23. Washington Daily National Journal, May 8, 1827, and below, Goldsborough to Clay, August 9, 1827, note. Reports of the Baltimore meeting

cited also the call for a similar gathering at Annapolis on May 12. *Ibid.*, May 3, 1827; and below, Kent to Clay, May 7, 1827.   [3] Cf. above, Clay to Everett, April 5, 1827, note.   [4] Cf. above, Clay to Brown, March 27, 1827; Hammond to Clay, March 28, 1827; Clay to Webster, April 14, 1827.   [5] Henry Shaw.   [6] Abigail Brown Brooks was a younger sister of Charlotte Gray Brooks Everett. Abigail had visited the Everetts in Washington and there met Charles Francis Adams, the third son of the President, who resided with his parents for three years after his graduation from Harvard University in 1825. Abigail and Charles Francis were married in September, 1829.   [7] Cf. above, Clay to Henry Clay, Jr., April 2, 1827; Clay to Johnston, April 2, 17, 1827.

[8] Joseph Lovell was defeated by Lewis Maxwell (cf. above, Clay to Webster, April 20, 1827, note). Both men were, however, identified as "friendly to the . . . Administration." Washington *Daily National Intelligencer*, May 10, 1827.

From Lucius Bolles and Heman Lincoln

To the Hon. Henry Clay—Secretary of State,
to the United States of America

Boston May 2. 1827

The interest we feel in the promotion of sound learning and the diffusion of correct principles, will, we trust constitute an apology for the present communication. It has been announced that the presidency of Transylvania University is vacant. That institution is highly important to our country, and destined to exert a powerful influence on the character, happiness and usefulness of many of her sons, and particularly those of the extensive State of Kentucky. It can not be concealed, however, that its utility may be either increased or diminished by circumstances. Very much may be supposed to depend on the character of its President. If a gentleman can be introduced there, whose literary qualifications are undisputed, and whose religious principles are in agreement with those of his supporters, he will naturally receive far more patronage, than where the latter are wanting. If our impressions are correct, a large majority of the inhabitants of Kentucky are Baptists.[1] The Presbyterians have a College[2] in the State, and will send their sons to it. Who, then, are to furnish the students for the University, if Baptists do not?[3] And if they furnish the students, why should they not be gratified in the principles and views of at least the presiding officer? Doubtless sound policy would sanction such an appointment, provided a suitable man can be found. We believe, that the Rev. Professor Woods, of Brown University, has already been recommended to your consideration with a view to the place.[4] Of him we can speak with confidence. His disposition is amiable; his manners chaste and dignified; his classical attainments of a high order, having sustained the usual courses at Cambridge and Andover,[5] and subsequently visited the principal Universities of Europe. His experience in the office he now sustains, has confirmed the opinion before entertained of him by his friends, and shown him to be worthy, in our esteem, of the high situation, to which we recommend him. It will be a gratification to us, should he receive your distinguished countenance and support.

Be assured, dear Sir, of our high respect for yourself, and of the pleasure we derive from the consideration of the elevated station you occupy. Long may you enjoy the confidence and support of the faithful friends of our Republic, and live to bless mankind by the soundness of your political maxims and example. With much regard, we are your Obt. Servts—   LUCIUS BOLLES
                                                           HEMAN LINCOLN

ALS. by Lincoln, signed also by Bolles. KyLxT. Bolles, born in Connecticut, had been ordained into the Baptist ministry in 1805, had served as pastor of a church at Salem, Massachusetts from 1805 to 1826, and from 1826 to 1842 was corresponding secretary of the Baptist General Convention for Foreign Missions. He had been a trustee of Brown University from 1807 to 1818 and was a fellow there from 1818 to 1844. He had also been named one of the original trustees of the Newton Theological Institution, in 1826.
   Lincoln was a Boston lumber merchant.
   1 Of those identified with a religious affiliation, the Baptists at this time held a plurality. Robert Bishop, *An Outline of the History of the Church in the State of Kentucky, during a Period of Forty Years* . . . (Lexington, 1824), 306–307; Alonzo Willard Fortune, *The Disciples in Kentucky* . . . [Lexington, Ky., c. 1932], 101–102. But less than a sixth of the population of the State was included in any compilation of church membership.   2 Centre College.   3 Georgetown College, the first Baptist college west of the Alleghenies, opened its doors to students on January 11, 1830.   4 See above, Chase to Clay, April 19, 1827; Clay to Bradford, April 26, 1827.   5 Harvard University; Andover Theological Seminary.

From Daniel Sharp

Dear Sir,   Boston, May 2. 1827.
   At the instance of Prof. Chase,[1] I take the liberty of addressing a few lines to you in relation to Rev. Alva Woods, who is now a Professor in Brown University, Providence, R. I.

   The testimony of Dr. Woods[2] you have probably seen. As he is a relative of the Gentleman in question, he may perhaps, be suspected of partiality in his statements. I therefore beg leave to assure you, from an intimate and personal acquaintance with Mr. W. for many years, that he is fully entitled to the character given him by his reverend Uncle.

   Were I to describe the character of Prof. W's mind I should say, he was remarkable for good common sense. His attainments as a scholar are truly respectable. His uniformly studious habits give promise of his future eminence. And his talents for maintaining order, and exciting a laudable emulation among the students, have been frequently mentioned by such of the Corporation of Brown University, as reside in Providence.

   In his personal demeanor Mr. W. is a gentleman. He has enjoyed frequent opportunities of mingling with good society, and has wisely improved them. Were it [sic] I might add that Mrs. W. is a lady of respectable connexions,[3] & would do honor to the sphere, in which as the wife of President of a College she would be destined to move.

Prof. W. is a baptist. But he is a liberal minded man. I am confident, from a long acquaintance with his views & feelings, that in all his official conduct, he would endeavour to deserve, & be so happy as to secure the approbation of all other denominations as much as his own. He is truly religious. But while there is nothing of that levity in his principles or conduct which degrades Christianity, neither is there any thing of that severity and unsociableness of manner which render it forbidding

Although I feel great respect for Prof. Woods, yet I would not have obtruded this communication on your notice, were I not persuaded that he is worthy of being considered a Candidate for the Presidency of Transylvania College. Should he be elected, I believe it will be found that his warmest friends have not over-rated his abilities, and that it will be an event highly auspicious to the interests of learning, morality & religion in the West.

Should you wish to know what reliance are [sic] due to my statements, I beg leave to refer you to Dr. Staughton—to Docr. James M. Staughton or to Docr. Sewall, all of your City.[4]

As a token of my respect for your talents, and for the services which you have rendered to our Country, permit me to request your acceptance of two sermons which were delivered before the Legislature of Massachusetts.[5] I Am, respectfully your Obedt. Servant
Hon. H. Clay Esqr. Sec. of State—   DANIEL SHARP.

ALS. KyLxT. Sharp, born in England, had come to the United States in 1805, at age 22, as the American agent of a Yorkshire mercantile firm. Shortly thereafter, he had decided to enter the Baptist ministry; he had been ordained in 1809; and in 1812 he had become pastor of the Third, or Charles Street, Baptist Church of Boston, where he remained the rest of his life. He was a leader in his denomination, for a time president of the American Baptist Foreign Mission Society, a member of the board of trustees of Newton Theological Institution, a fellow of Brown University, and a Harvard Overseer.
    [1] Irah Chase.   [2] See above, Chase to Clay, April 19, 1827; Clay to Bradford, April 26, 1827.   [3] Almira Marshall Woods was the daughter of Josiah and Priscilla Waterman Marshall, of Boston. Marshall was a wealthy merchant, engaged in the China and East India trade.   [4] William Staughton, born in England and educated as a Baptist clergyman, had come to the United States in 1793, had been ordained while head of an academy in Bordentown, New Jersey, in 1797, and subsequently had been awarded a degree of Doctor of Divinity from the College of New Jersey (Princeton). He had held pastorates in Philadelphia from 1805 until about 1823, when he had moved to Washington as president of the newly established Columbian College (George Washington University). He resigned the post in Washington in 1829 and shortly thereafter accepted the presidency of Georgetown College in Kentucky. He died December 12, en route to his new assignment. James M. Staughton, son of William, had been born in Bordentown, New Jersey, and educated in medicine at the University of Pennsylvania. He practiced in Washington and for one semester taught chemistry at the Columbian College. After two years of studying surgery in Europe, he had returned to assume the chair in surgery at Columbian College. He joined the faculty of the Medical College of Ohio in 1831 and served briefly as dean, but he died, at age 33, in the cholera epidemic of 1833. Thomas Sewall, a native of Maine, had been graduated in medicine from Harvard University in 1812. After further study at the University of Pennsylvania, he had opened practice in

Ipswich and Essex, Massachusetts. From 1821 until his death in 1845 he was professor of anatomy at Columbian College in Washington. He was renowned for his exposition of the errors of phrenology and his research on the pathology of drunkenness.

5 Probably his *Discourse, Pronounced before His Excellency William Eustis, Esq., Governor, the Honorable Council, and the Two Houses, Composing the Legislature of Massachusetts, May 26, 1824* . . . (Boston, 1824); and *Sermon, Preached at the Funeral of His Excellency William Eustis. . . , in Presence of the Constituted Authorities of the State, February 11, 1825* (Boston, 1825).

INSTRUCTIONS AND DISPATCHES   May 2, 1827

From WILLIAM B. HODGSON, Algiers, no. 88, "In duplicate." Reports the departure of (William) Shaler, on April 20, 1827, on "The U.S. Schooner Porpoise," sent by Commodore (John) Rodgers in response to Shaler's request, to convey him to Mahon. Notes that he sent "Copies of Mr. Shaler's letter to Commodore Rodgers, and of the medical reports accompanying it," to Clay "on the 25h of January, with dispatch No. 87, of the 1t of December ulto." (cf. above, Hodgson to Clay, January 20, 1827). States that Shaler appointed him "Chargé d'Affaires of this Consulate, during his [Shaler's] contemplated absence." Transmits "the claim and its vouchers, of Alexander Tulin Esq. against the late Major [Townshend] Stith, U. S. Consul at Tunis," for $120. Explains that the money had been borrowed from Tulin, at that time "British Pro-Consul at Tunis, . . . now, His Britannic Majesty's Vice-Consul at Algiers," and that "Mr. Shaler was of opinion, that the Government would, early, order its payment."

Reports Shaler's views in regard to "the Consular present," which, under "the Treaty of 1816, with Algiers" (see above, II, 80n), is never "to be required of the United States, yet Mr. Shaler, at that time, deemed it proper to make a present of $17,000." Adds: "In the opinion of Mr. Shaler, the next Consular present of the United States, should differ from the last, in the character, amount, and mode of presentation and distribution." ALS. DNA, RG59, Cons. Disp., Algiers, vol. 11 (M23, R-T13). Received July 20.

Hodgson enclosed a certified copy of Tulin's account. Documents supporting Tulin's claim, attached to Tulin to Coxe, September 20, 1825, located in *ibid.,* Tunis, vol. 5 (M-T303, R5), show that Stith had borrowed 800 piastres "to facilitate his departure," of which 540 piastres ($120) was not covered by assets left as security. The debt was to carry 1/2% a month interest dating from March 16, 1825.

From WILLIAM B. HODGSON, Algiers, no. 4, *"Duplicate."* Explains that he does not think his "report on the particular objects" of his mission "should be connected with the official dispatch from this Consulate" and that he makes, "therefore . . . this separate communication."

Notes that the "difficulties" mentioned in his "letter of January 25h [*i.e.,* 20th]" remain, although he expects to receive his "Oriental books . . . in a few weeks." Transmits a translation he has just made "of the Treaty of 1816, between the U. States and Algiers" (see above, II, 80n) and calls attention to differences he has discovered between the Turkish and English texts of that document. States that he hopes soon to furnish evidence of his progress in Arabic, that he speaks "the Lingua Franca with tolerable facility," that he has "compiled a Vocabulary and Dialogues in Lingua Franca, and Arabic," and that he intends "to add the corresponding Turkish." Notes that he has spent $250 for books and instructions. ALS. DNA, RG59, Cons. Disp., Algiers, vol. 11 (M23, R-T13).

From JOHN SERGEANT, Mexico, "Private." Reports the arrival of Clay's son (Theodore W.), bringing Clay's dispatch of March 16 and his "private letter [not found] of the same date." States that Clay's communications were "not unexpected" but expresses regret concerning "the untoward course of affairs in this part of the world, threatening to disappoint the hopes and expectations of a wise and liberal consultation upon the great principles to serve as the basis of future intercourse." Exclaims: "How much might be done for the welfare of mankind! How I should have delighted to take part in such deliberations!" Declares that the Congress is not likely to meet or to produce "much good' if it should assemble. Promises to "be guided by circumstances" but reveals his expectation that his "mission will terminate in June." Refers to (William) Taylor's letter (cf. above, Sergeant to Clay, April 27, 1827), which he considers "of less consequence now. . . ." Notes that Clay's son "will write . . . by the present opportunity" [no letter has been found]. Adds, in a postscript: ". . . one of the ministers from Peru has arrived at Acapulco with the treaties ratified. This may raise a question as to the power that has sent him" (cf. above, Tudor to Clay, February 3, 1827). ALS. DNA, RG43, Records re Panama Congress (M662, R1). Received June 14.

Sergeant's information appears to have been erroneous, for Peru "failed to ratify the treaties." Lockey, *Pan-Americanism*, 347.

MISCELLANEOUS LETTERS   May 2, 1827

From J[AMES] L. E[DWARDS], "War Department, Pension Office." Informs Clay that, "In answer to the enclosed letter [not found] from Mr. Samuel Smith, . . . an order was sent from the 2d. Comptroller's Office on the 20th. of March last, directing the Pension Agent in Philadelphia [Nicholas Biddle] to resume the payment of Captain Thomas Collins's pension." Adds that, though not the customary procedure, "to remove every difficulty . . . such an order has this day been transmitted from this Office to the Agent." Observes, however, "that the other objection mentioned in Mr. Brown's letter [not found] as to the Prothonotary's certificate; can only be obviated by making the amendment suggested by the Pension Agent." Copy. DNA, RG15, Letter Books, General, vol. 19, p. 487.

Samuel Smith was probably a resident of Uniontown, Pennsylvania, and may have been associate judge of Erie County, Pennsylvania, from 1803 to 1805 and member of Congress from 1805 to 1811.

Collins, a captain of the Pennsylvania Volunteer Militia, had been placed on the pension roll in October, 1823, with a grant of $120 annually dating from July 19, 1823. He died in November, 1827.

"Mr. Brown" was probably Daniel Brown, whose release as a clerk in the General Land Office was noted above, Brown to Clay, March 10, 1827. He remained on the payroll of the Treasury Department through June 30, 1827, and was not entered on the roll of the War Department until August 8, 1827. In the latter connection, however, he served as a clerk in the Pension Office, a position which he retained until his death in 1847. *House Docs.*, 20 Cong., 1 Sess., no. 54, p. 13; no. 184, p. 5; 30 Cong., 1 Sess., no. 31, p. 11; Washington *Daily National Intelligencer*, October 4, 1847.

From HEZEKIAH HUNTINGTON, Hartford. Refers to "the death of Gen. [Andrew] Hull [Jr.], Marshal of this district"; argues that, since "his efficient deputies" remain and can carry on the duties of the office, "neither the Public interest—nor individual Convenience, *require,*—the immediate appointment of a Successor"; and notes that friends of applicants for the position have requested that "this representation should be made." Urges that the office be kept in Hartford. ALS. DNA, RG59, A. and R. (M531, R4). Cf. above, Barber to Clay, April 30, 1827.

From R[ICHARD] H. MOSBY, Littleton, North Carolina. Notes that, "Some time since," he sent Clay a letter (not found), "inclosing several to the Secretary of War [James Barbour]" and soliciting Clay's good offices in favour of" an applicant for admission to "the Military school at West Point," but that he has received no reply. Conjectures that his letter did not reach Clay, or if it did, Clay could not comply with the request. Asks, if the latter possibility be the case, that the enclosures be returned to him. ALS. DNA, RG77, Letters Recd., 1826–37, serial no. M-240. Endorsed by clerk: "Refd. May 8th."
    On May 11 Alexander Macomb transmitted to Clay a copy (not found) of his answer to Mosby's letter of May 2. Copy of the letter of transmittal, in DNA, RG94, Military Academy Letters, vol. 2, p. 36.

From JOHN MOUNTZ, Georgetown (District of Columbia). States "that the Commission of the Levy Court of the County of Washington, District of Cola., will expire on Monday next, and that a vacancy occurred in the Board by the death of N———— Young esqr———" ALS. DNA, RG59, Misc. Letters (M179, R65).
    Mountz was clerk of the Corporation of Georgetown from 1789 to 1856. The levy court, or board of commissioners, was composed of the justices of the peace. Its duties included not only the fiscal functions of assessment, tax collection, and maintenance of public services but also the appointment of the constabulary. Nicholas Young had been first appointed a justice of the peace in 1807 and reappointed in 1812 and 1823. The vacancy noted by Mountz was filled by the appointment of David A. Hall on June 11, 1827.

From WILLIAM B. QUARRIER, Norfolk. Refers to E (ben) Babson's letter to Clay of March 29, 1826, to his own letter to Clay of November 6, 1826, and to Clay's (i.e., Daniel Brent's) reply to each. States that "the draft [a copy of which is enclosed] bearing date subsequent to the 1st June," he "considered it useless to send it." Notes that repeated letters to (William R.) Higinbotham have brought no reply; that, "at the special instance of the Messrs [William Z. and C. E.] Hall's [sic]," he requests advice as to "the best mode of proceeding"; and that he thinks Higinbotham "deserves censure." Asks that the enclosure be returned. ALS. DNA, RG59, Accounting Records, Misc. Letters. Endorsed on cover by Clay: "Ansr. the inclosed and say that I can give no other advice than that of a resort to the drawer— Return the paper   HC." Clay's instructions were carried out by William Browne, who wrote Quarrier on May 9, 1827. Copy, in DNA, RG59, Dom. Letters, vol. 21, pp. 533–34 (M40, R19).

Check to Tucker and Thompson

3 May 1827

No.   OFFICE OF DISCOUNT & DEPOSIT, Washington,
    PAY to Tucker and Thompson or order Two hundred and seventy four Dollars, 50/100   H CLAY
$274 DOLLARS, 50/100

    ADS, partially printed. DLC-TJC (DNA, M212, R16). Cf. below, Receipted Account, this date. Tucker (not further identified) and Richard Thompson were "merchant tailors," located on Pennsylvania Avenue, in Washington.

Receipted Account with Tucker and Thompson

Henry Clay Esq   To Tucker & Thompson   Dr   [May 3, 1827]
1825

Sepr	24th.	To Blk silke [*sic*] Stock	$3..00
Nov	24	‚‚ Making & Triming [*sic*] Coat & Pantas [*sic*]	13 .75
1826	28	‚‚ Blk Cassimere Gators [*sic*]	3 .50
Feby	28	‚‚ Repg Coat, pockets &c	1..25
Apl	18	‚‚ Repg Coat buttons & Sleevelings[1]	2..75
	28	‚‚ Repg Green frock	0..75
May	17	‚‚ 3 vests	14 —
	‚‚	‚‚ 3 pr of Pantaloons	18 .50
June	6	‚‚ Blue Habit Cloth Coat	28 —
	‚‚	‚‚ 2 Doublets	13 —
	‚‚	‚‚ Sufu[2] Blk Cloth Pantas	18 —
	‚‚	‚‚ gray Cloth Pantas	12 .50
Decr	15	‚‚ Blk cloth Coat. Son T. W. Clay	36 —
	‚‚	‚‚ Blk ‚‚ Pantaloons Do	16 —
	‚‚	‚‚ Blk florentine & White Marells[3] Vests do ..	11 —
	‚‚	‚‚ Corbeau[4] frock Coat .... do	34 —
1827	26	‚‚ Blue Cloth Coat Son	28 —
Jany	2	‚‚ Blk silk & blue Cloth Vests Son	12 —
May	12	gray lastings Pants. Son T W. Clay ...	8..50

$274..50

1827 May 3d.   Recd Payment—
Tucker & Thompson

DS. DLC-TJC (DNA, M212, R16). Cf. above, Clay to Tucker and Thompson, this date.
[1] Probably "sleeve linings."   [2] Not identified.   [3] Probably "marcella," a twilled cotton or linen cloth used for waistcoats.   [4] Very dark green or black, from the French word for raven.

From William Carroll

My dear Sir,   Nashville, May 3rd. 1827
In a letter[1] addressed to you, shortly before I set out on my late Journey to Pennsylvania, I stated that I should visit Washington before I returned to Tennessee. I c[on]ceive it proper to state the principal cause which prevented me from executing that intention.

A few days after my arrival in Philadelphia, a most unexpected demand was made of me for the payment of a bill of exchange which I had endorsed in the year 1819. The holder at the time of protest had taken colateral [*sic*] security from the drawer and given time for payment, which, as I conceived released me from all liability. But as the demand was made in the presence of an individual in whose integrity I had no confidence, I was fearful, in the event of a suit, that he might swear to a new acknowledgement of responsibility. In this dilema [sic], I thought it more prudent to leave the city, than to risk an arrest which would have abliged [sic] me to call upon gentlemen not previously known, to be my appearance bail. Had I gone to Baltimore and Washington, I should have remained three or four days at each of those places, and as the claim would certainly have followed me, I should have been liable to the same disagreeable consequences in either city as at Philadelphia. The circumstances were peculiarly mortifying and the cause which deprived me of the pleasure of paying my respects to the President and Heads of Departments.

The subject of the appoaching Presidential election seems to agitate every section of the Union. In this State where the great body of the people think alike, we are not free from strong excitement. The contest between Mr. Grundy and Colo. Bell[2] is carried on with the greatest vigor on both sides, and the result cannot be looked upon in any other light than as doubtful, though it is certain, that Bell has now a very decided advantage and will be elected unless the Jackson question is brought to bear with much more power than we have reason to anticipate. Calhoun, Ingham,[3] and others have written to Grundy, that it is of the utmost consiquence [sic] to the Jackson cause that he should be elected. Those letters have not produced any beneficial effect, and Felix finds that nothing short of a Waterloo fight will insure him victory.

To you, who have been so much the object of news paper abuse, it is scarcely necessary to say, that the statements of my having gone to Pennsylvania for political purposes, are wholly destitute of foundation. My object in going to the State was to visit my friends who are numerous of both parties, and it would have ill become me to have interrupted social intercourse by indeavouring [sic] to make political proselytes. In Pennsylvania the Administration has many warm and influential friends whose operations are not without effect; and altho a considerable majority is still for General Jackson, it is impossible to foresee, the result which the woolen bill,[4] Internal improvements, a division of his friends (which I look upon as almost certain through feelings of jealousy) and other causes may produce. I understood from your friends in Pittsburgh, that they intended inviting you to visit their city on your way to Kentucky.[5] I am confident that you would be received by them with great kindness and hospitality, and I am sure that your presence would tend to remove prejudices which exist against you.

I learn that your daughter, Mrs. Erwin will be here in a few days, and that her situation will not authorize her to meet you in Kentucky should you even be there.[6] Should that be the fact, may we not anticipate the pleasure of seeing you among us. I assure you that notwithstanding there are those who have never ceased to pour their abuse upon you, ever since the late Presidential contest, yet there are very many who would be gratified with the opportunity of paying you the respect and attention, whi[ch is] justly due to your exalted talents and numerous and valuable public services.

The information I received during my late journey satisfies me that Ohio, Indiana and Kentucky will go for the Administration,[7] though it will not be amiss for you to pay those state[s a] visit. The result in my Judgment depends greatly on the ultimate course taken by New York. Any information you may be pleased to communicate with regard to that State will be most thankfully received. ·

I was much gratified with the appointment of Thos. H. Fletcher as District Attorney for West Tennessee.[8] It was received here as I expected without a murmur, though Several hot partizans were greatly mortified.

I am aware that your public duties in a great degree preclude you from ingaging [sic] in private correspondance [sic]. Still if you can spare a moment, it will afford me infinite pleasure to hear from you. With assurances of my unalterable esteem I am, most Sincerely, Your friend,   Wm. CARROLL
Hon: Henry Clay, Secy. of State, Washington City.

ALS. DLC-HC (DNA, M212, R2).   1 Not found.
2 Felix Grundy; John Bell. See above, Carroll to Clay, November 25, 1825, note.
   3 John C. Calhoun; Samuel D. Ingham.   4 Cf. above, Pleasants to Clay, February 14, 1827.   5 Cf. above, Pentland to Clay, February 18, 1827; Whittlesey to Clay, March 13, 1827; Clay to Whittlesey, March 24, 1827; Lacock to Clay, March 27, 1827.   6 Cf. below, Clay to Brown, May 30, 1827.   7 Cf. above, Clay to Brown, March 27, 1827, note.   8 Cf. above, Clay to Crittenden, January 25, 1827; Clay to Fletcher, March 29, 1827.

From William Ruggles and Alexis Caswell

To The Hon Henry Clay,   College Hill D. C. May 3d 1827.
   Sir, Having learned, that the Presidency of Transylvania University is, at present, vacant; & that the Rev. Alva Woods Prof. of Math. & Nat. Phil. in Brown University R. I. has been presented as a candidate for the office, we beg leave to express to yourself and through you, to the other curators of the University, the high sense we entertain of of [sic] his qualifications for that important station.

After having received the honours of Harvard University and of the Theological Seminary at Andover Mass. he was elected to fill the Professorships of Math. & Nat. Phil.; & Ecclesiastical History and Christian Discipline in the Columbian College D. C.; &, subsequently, the Professorship which he now holds in Brown University.

From his acquaintance with the economy of Institutions for Public Education, both in this Country & in Europe, his character as a scholar, & his acknowledged moral worth, we have the utmost pleasure in stating that he would, in our judgment, fill the office for which he has been nominated, to the great advantage of Science & Religion; & with honour to himself & the distinguished governors of the University. With sentiments of Great Respect Your Obedient Servants

WM. RUGGLES

A. CASWELL

Late Profs in the Columbian College, D. C.

ALS, by Caswell, signed also by Ruggles. KyLxT.

Ruggles, born in Massachusetts, had graduated from Brown University in 1820, had been given a tutorial appointment at the Columbian College in 1822, and from 1827 until his death in 1877 taught courses in mathematics, natural philosophy, astronomy, political economy, or civil polity at the latter institution. He was acting president of the college from 1841 to 1843, 1854 to 1855, and 1858 to 1859. Caswell, also a native of Massachusetts, graduate of Brown University (1822), and tutor at the Columbian College (1823–1825), had been named professor of ancient languages at the Washington school in 1825. In 1827 he resigned to become pastor of a Baptist church at Halifax, Nova Scotia, and the following year moved to the First Baptist Church of Providence, Rhode Island. Shortly thereafter he was named professor of mathematics and natural philosophy at Brown University, where he remained until 1863. He was later called from retirement to assume the presidency of Brown from 1868 to 1872.

INSTRUCTIONS AND DISPATCHES   May 3, 1827

From JOHN M. FORBES, Buenos Aires, no. 48. Reports that, in obedience to Clay's "dispatch No. 4, 16th. February 1827," he informed the Minister of Foreign Affairs (Francisco de la Cruz) of Robert Kortright's appointment as acting consul, requested "the usual authority for him to perform the duties of his office," and "was promised an affirmative answer," which has not yet been received. Adverts, in a manner highly critical of his antagonist, to his quarrel with (George W.) Slacum. Concludes: "If the Government should find any thing worthy of Consideration in the charges preferred by Mr. Slacum against me, I hope that I shall be favored with an opportunity of full and early vindication." Copy. DNA, RG84, Argentina (MR13).

This document does not exist in DNA, RG59, Dip. Disp., Argentina, vol. 3 (M69, R4). Espil surmised that, through clerical error, the number 48 was not used for a Forbes dispatch. *Once Años en Buenos Aires*, 466n.

From ALBERT GALLATIN, London, no. 72. Reports that "Mr. [James] Colquhoun, the Agent of the Hanse towns in London," has informed him of their appointment of "Mr. [Vincent] Rumph [sic], their chargé d'affaires at Paris, special Minister to the United States, with powers to negotiate a treaty of commerce" and that Rumpff intends sailing for America in August. Adds that Colquhoun was also "charged by the City of Hamburg to obtain from" Gallatin the answer the latter "might receive" from his "Government to the note of Mr. [Karl S.] Sieveking" (cf. above, Gallatin to Clay, April 3, 1827, no. 64) and that he informed Colquhoun of his opinion that an answer would not be made. Notes his belief, derived "from the general tenor of the conversation . . . that not only are the Hanse towns anxious of concluding a treaty of commerce with the United States on account of its immediate advantages, but that they believe that it will have a tendency to encrease [sic] the consideration in which they are held and to strengthen the tenure on which they hold their situation of independent Republics." Warns "that they are very narrow and selfish, as regards merchants residing within their own precincts and that they may be unwilling to grant to citizens of the United States . . . the same privileges, which foreign merchants indiscriminately enjoy, in common with our own citizens, in the ports of the United States where they reside." ALS. DNA, RG59, Dip. Disp., Great Britain, vol. 34 (M30, R30). Received June 17.

James Colquhoun, son of Patrick Colquhoun, was Scotch by birth and had been educated at Cambridge. He had been named as the London representative of the Hanse towns in 1817 and in 1827 was appointed consul general for Saxony. In 1848 he became Chargé d'Affaires for Oldenburg in London and at that time was accorded the title Chevalier de Colquhoun.

From ROBERT MONROE HARRISON, Antigua. Informs Clay that, since the (British colonial) ports in the West Indies have been closed to United States shipping, American masters have gone to the neutral islands, chartered "small craft under English colors," and brought their cargoes in to be sold. Anticipates that the colonial authorities will stop such transshipments and promises to inform American citizens when the "contemplated measure is carried into effect." ALS. DNA, RG59, Cons. Disp., Antigua, vol. 1 (M-T327, R1). Received June 5.

From WILLIAM TAYLOR, Veracruz. Reports that the requirement, initiated by "Mr. [Pablo] Obregón's unlawful Consular regulations . . . in 1825," of "a Consular Certificate . . . for goods shipped from the U. S. to this Country [cf. above, Clay to Obregón, December 20, 1825; Obregón to Clay, January 4, 1826 (2)], has latterly become so oppressively vexatious. . . , altho' the subject has been all along before Mr. [Joel R.] Poinsett to whom it properly belongs," he (Taylor) "could no longer refrain from remonstrating with the authorities here against a course of proceedings the more unfriendly and offensive as levelled exclusively at the Commerce of the U.S." Encloses copies of his correspondence with those officials. Calls attention to the fact that "the Consular Certificates are required from Baltimore, Philadelphia & New York only," there being no (Mexican) consul at other United States ports, "so that the measure is at best, a very lame one." ALS. DNA, RG59, Cons. Disp., Veracruz, vol. 1 (M183, R1). Received June 6.

To Elisha I. Winter

Dear Sir: Washington, 4th May, 1827.

I received your letter of the 19th ultimo.[1] The condition of Transylvania University frequently occupies my thoughts, and engages much of my anxiety. I have made some, and am now prosecuting other inquiries, in relation to a suitable President for the Institution.[2] I know Dr Staughton[3] well. He is a very amiable and benevolent man: but, I am perfectly confident, will not answer our purposes. He has neither the scientific attainments nor the capacity for government, which are necessary to the President of Transylvania. You may rely upon it, he will not do, and all thoughts of him should be at once dismissed. I hope that, in the course of the Summer, we shall be able to find a suitable character; and, in the meantime, I should think it best to postpone, indefinitely, the procurement of a President of the Institution, rather than even run a hazard of getting an incompetent man.

I hope to hope [sic] to have the pleasure of seeing you, in the month of June, in Lexington, in the mean time, I am, faithfully, Your obedient servant,   H. CLAY.
Elisha I. Winter. Esqr.

LS. KyLxT.   1 Not found.
2 Cf above, Clay to Bradford, February 10, April 26, 1827; Chase to Clay, April 19, 1827.
3 William Staughton.

From John H. Pleasants

My dear Sir,   Richmond 4th. May 1827.
Enclosed is an A/c[1] vs. the Transylvania University, which if you
will forward to the heads of that Institution, you will greatly oblige us.
Will you consent to be run for the V. Presidency? Is it your wish or
that of your friends?[2] The question is beginning to excite some interest among us, & for one, I am anxious that some individual should be
selected and nominated for that office— I have thought that your name
had been mentioned by the opposition for insidious ends. If you do
not wish it, I have been thinking of Gov. Shulze.[3] Whoever he may be,
if any respectable man, the party will cheerfully support him against
Calhoun.[4] If you will be brought forward, I think the move ought to
be made in Pa. If Shulze I think it best to be made in Va. I do not think
that we can organize too soon. I know not what to say of Va. The
Admn. has a *powerful* party in the State avowedly—a much larger one
secretly. The organization of the other side, may be, and I fear *will be*,
stronger than all. I shall be happy to hear from you & remain Dr Sir
Yr frd Truly   JNO H PLEASANTS.

ALS. DLC-HC (DNA, M212, R2). Addressed to Clay.   1 Not found.
2 Cf. above, Clay to Hammond, December 23, 1826; April 21, 1827; Hammond to Clay,
January 3, March 28, 1827.   3 John A. Shulze.   4 John C. Calhoun.

DIPLOMATIC NOTES   May 4, 1827

From FRANCISCO DIONISIO VIVES, Havana, "*Confidential.*" States that Daniel P.
Cook has delivered Clay's letter of March 14; expresses a sincere desire to comply
with Clay's wishes. Observes that he has never doubted "la sinceridad de los deseos
manifestados por el Gobierno de U. S. con respecto a que esta Ysla se conserve en
su actual estado"; indicates his understanding of the injury to American commerce and agriculture that would result from a change in the status of the island
and his belief that the President (Adams) would use force to prevent an invasion
or a blockade of Cuba; professes to have "considerable sea and land forces," for
which he expects reinforcements, strong enough to repel "any aggression"; and
claims also to have the support of the great majority of the inhabitants of the
island. LS, in Spanish with trans. in State Dept. file. DNA, RG76, Records re
French Spoliations, 1791–1829. Copy, in MHi-Adams Papers, Letters Recd. (MR-
479). Endorsed in margin of first page: "15 feb. 1828   Rec'd from Govr. Ninian
Edwards."

INSTRUCTIONS AND DISPATCHES   May 4, 1827

From ALBERT GALLATIN, London, no. 73. Acknowledges receipt of Clay's dispatches
of March 24 and 28 (the latter, omitted by the editors as routine); states that he

has "taken steps to procure the information" relative to the penal code, "requested by the letter of the 24th," but that "There have been no steps taken towards an alteration of the Commercial laws, those contained in the acts concerning navigation, duties and warehousing only excepted." Reports a brief audience with Lord Dudley, who stated, in response to a hope expressed by Gallatin that the pending negotiations would not be further postponed, "that he had received a paper from Mr. [William] Huskisson on the subject, which he had not yet had time to examine," and "that he had also before him a report from the Admiralty on the case of impressment, with which one of his Majesty's officers (Capt. [D. C.] Clavering undoubtedly) was charged, . . . in justification of that officer's conduct" (cf. above, Hodges to Clay, March 16, 1826; Clay to Gallatin, February 24, 1827). Observes that, apparently, Clay has not yet "obtained the deposition of the Captain of the 'Pharos' [cf. above, Clay to Vaughan, March 26, 1827], which is necessary to the discussion of the case." Adds that "Lord Castlereagh's administration was more friendly disposed towards the United States than any that had preceded or than that which succeeded it." Encloses "a [published] correspondence relative to the petitions of the ship-owners" and calls attention to "the last paragraph of the letter of the Board of Trade of the 22d. of March last," which gives "additional evidence of the intentions of this Government on the question of Colonial Intercourse." LS. DNA, RG59, Dip. Disp., Great Britain, vol. 34 (M30, R30). Copy, in NHi-Gallatin Papers (MR14). Received June 17.

The shipowners' petitions and accompanying documents, published as *Sess. Paper, 1826–1827* (no. 278), XVIII, 221–53, protested the reciprocity provisions of the British trade policy as effected by act of July 18, 1823 (4 *Geo. IV*, c. 77–cf. above, Clay to Cambreleng, December 25, 1825, note) and William Huskisson's program in 1825 (see above, Rush to Secretary of State, March 26, 1825, note; Clay to Carey, June 6, 1825, note).

In the paragraph cited above, Thomas Lack, as secretary for the Lords of the Committee of Privy Council for Trade, informed "George Lyall, Esq. &c. &c. &c.," that "discussions . . . with the government of the United States, on the subject of the British Order in Council [of July 27, 1826–cf. above, Gallatin to Clay, August 19, 1826], as well as the provisions of the Bill now under the consideration of the American legislature [cf. above, Clay to Gallatin, December 28, 1826, note 4], have not only confirmed His Majesty's government in the grounds upon which they felt it their duty, in the course of the last year, to advise His Majesty to issue that order, but have also afforded additional proofs of the expediency, under present circumstances, of not relaxing in any of its regulations."

Lack had been clerk to the Board of Trade from 1786 to 1822 and was secretary from 1810 to 1836, when he retired. J. C. Saintly (comp.), *Office-Holders in Modern Britain*, III, *Officials of the Board of Trade, 1660–1870* ([London], 1974), 104. Lyall, who had inherited a mercantile business in 1805, was for several years chairman of the Shipowners' Society of London and in 1834 a member of the original committee which compiled *Lloyd's Register* of shipping. He promoted the organization of several marine insurance companies, in 1830 became a director of the East India Company, and from 1833 to 1835 and from 1841 to 1847 sat in Parliament.

MISCELLANEOUS LETTERS   May 4, 1827

To JOHN C. WEEMS, Waterloo, Maryland. States that his "letter . . . of the ——— [*sic*]" to the President, enclosing one from J. H. Slemaker to Weems, was referred to the State Department; encloses copies of the exchange of correspondence with the British Minister in this connection (above, Clay to Vaughan, April 28, 1827;

Vaughan to Clay, May 2, 1827); expresses hope that, if "young [James Ringgold] Slemeker [*sic*] is still in the British Service," he will be restored to his family. Copy. DNA, RG59, Dom. Letters, vol. 21, p. 529 (M40, R19).

On August 11, Daniel Brent wrote to Weems, stating that he was transmitting copies of the exchange of correspondence concerning Slemaker. Copy, *ibid.*, vol. 22, p. 25 (M40, R20).

From ALEXANDER MACOMB, "Engineer Department." This letter, erroneously dated by its author, May 4, 1826, was summarized above under that date. The "Mr. Harris" mentioned in it and identified as "probably . . . John Harris" was Benjamin James Harris. Cf. above, Benjamin James Harris to Clay, May 1, 1827; Kerr to Clay, May 1, 1827.

INSTRUCTIONS AND DISPATCHES   May 5, 1827

From THOMAS L. L. BRENT (Lisbon). States that he is sending "herewith a copy of" his last letter to Mr. [Alexander H.] Everett." AES, DNA, RG59, Dip. Disp., Portugal, vol. 7, (M43, R6). Undated; written on the last page of the copied letter, dated May 5, 1827; received June 29. In the communication to Everett, Brent states that "The Infanta Regent" (Isabel Maria) has "been delivered of a child" and is in critical condition; traces the line of succession to the Regency should she die; charges that "The ultraroyalist party, and apostolick Junta" have "in their machinations to upset the constitution" created "new disturbances"; remarks on the "great uneasiness among the friends to the constitution," the "general want of confidence in the stability of the government," and notes the arrival of over 1,000 British troops in this city. He cautions, in a marginal note, that, although the birth of the child "is very generally known, . . . it would be well to be prudent in speaking of it."

Through April and May the Princess Regent remained very ill, unable to attend to affairs of state, a situation which increased the danger of a Miguelite revolt. No other reference to the nature of her illness has been found. London *Times*, April 13, 1827; *Niles' Weekly Register*, XXXII (June 30, July 14, 1827), 294, 328; *Annual Register, 1827*, p. 265.

From JOHN CUTHBERT, Hamburg. States that he has been requested to advise his Government that "Hamburg . . . Lübeck, and Bremen had determined to send a Minister to Washington" to negotiate a commercial convention and that (Vincent) Rumpff has been selected for the mission. Cites instructions received from (John Q.) Adams in 1822, "to object to the tithe of 10 per cent, exacted on the property of persons removing from the Hanseatic Cities to the United States," and points out "that this hatefull imposition is still in force." ALS. DNA, RG59, Cons. Disp., Hamburg, vol. 3 (M-T211, R3).

From ALBERT GALLATIN, London, no. 74. Discusses in some detail the problems faced by (George) Canning in forming a Cabinet (cf. above, Gallatin to Clay, February 22, 1827, note), reviews possible appointees to that body, and notes that "the aid of the Whigs becomes more necessary, and they may obtain a still greater share in the Government." Concludes: "The great mass of them, indeed with very few exceptions, support Mr. Canning: and it is probable, that, with their aid, that of his personal friends & of the moderate tories, together with the influence of office, he will be able to stand his ground, notwithstanding the discordant opinions of his supporters, *provided the King* [George IV] *remains firm on his side*." ALS. DNA, Dip. Disp., Great Britain, vol. 34 (M30, R30). Copy, in NHi-Gallatin Papers (MR20). Received June 17.

From WILLIAM TUDOR, Lima, no. 66, "*Confidential.*" Summarizes information, received in a letter from "Col. [Juan Francisco] Elizalde who commanded the second division of the Colombian troops" (cf. above, Tudor to Clay, March 23, April 25, 1827), concerning the successful operations of that unit. Adds that Elizalde was preparing "to march on Guayaquil which he probably entered about the 15h ulto." Reviews the case of the *Chesapeake*, of Baltimore, seized for having on board tobacco from Cuba in violation of "the decree of Apl 17h. 1825," prohibiting the importation of Spanish goods (cf. above, Tudor to Clay, April 22, 1825, and note; Clay to Hull, December 20, 1825); expresses expectation that the vessel will be liberated; and asserts that, "should it be otherwise," he can "as soon as the Congress assembles . . . procure a formal repeal of this decree & restoration of all property seized under it." Notes that his "friend Dr. Luna Pizarro the leading member of Congress has just arrived at Callao, from Chile where he was banished by the Usurper [Simón Bolívar]" and that he (Tudor) has "reason to think" that "Gen. [José de] La Mar is also . . . on the way from Guayaquil to the Congress." Conjectures that General (Antonio José de) Sucre cannot "long sustain himself [in Bolivia], cut off as he is, from all succours." Describes, in a paragraph dated May 6, the welcome given Pizarro on his entry into Lima. ALS. DNA, RG59, Cons. Disp., Lima, vol. 1 (M154, R1). Received August 31.

MISCELLANEOUS LETTERS   May 5, 1827

From EDWARD LIVINGSTON, New York. States that, "Agreeably to the permission" (not found) granted him by Clay, he has requested (James) Brown to forward letters for him to the Department of State; requests such letters to be directed to him at New York. LS. DNA, RG59, Misc. Letters (M179, R65).

Daniel Brent replied on May 10, as "directed by the Secretary," that any letters for Livingston, "from Mr. Brown or any other person," would be forwarded. Copy, in DNA, RG59, Dom. Letters, vol. 21 (M40, R19). Cf. above, Clay, by Brent, to Woodward, December 12, 1825.

To Enoch Lincoln

To His Excellency E. Lincoln, Portland, Maine.
Sir,   Dept. of State, Washington 7 May 1827.
I have the honor to acknowledge the receipt of your Excellency's letter of the 18th. ultimo, and to inform you that I have submitted it to the President. The solicitude which is felt by your Excellency and the Legislature of Maine, in regard to the settlement of our North Eastern boundary, so interesting to that State, and so important to the whole Union is perfectly natural and justly appreciated by the President: And he is entirely disposed to communicate any information in the possession of the Executive of the U. S. on that subject which can in his opinion be communicated without the danger of public detriment. Accordingly, when, at the session of Congress before the last, an application was made at this Department, by the Senators from Maine, for copies of all the papers, maps, and other documents reported by the Commissioners who were appointed under the fifth Article of the treaty of Ghent, it was stated to those Gentlemen, that

the copies would be furnished whenever requested, with the exception of the arguments and statements of the Commissioners, transcripts from which, considering their peculiar character, in the then state of the question, the President did not think it expedient to allow to be taken. The Senators from Maine availed themselves of the permission, and obtained copies of some of the Maps.[1] Copies of all the papers reported by the Commissioners, which are very voluminous, would require the services of two or three copyists for many weeks; but the labour of preparing them would be cheerfully encountered for the accommodation of the State of Maine.

The negotiation with Great Britain is still pending; but there is reason to expect that it will soon be brought to some conclusion, perhaps in a shorter time than would be requisite to copy and transmit the papers reported by the Commissioners, to your Excellency. The President continues to think that the public interest requires that the communication of transcripts of the arguments and statements of the Commissioners, even under the limitation proposed by your Excellency, should be postponed, for the present, and until it can be made without the risk of any injurious effect upon the state of the negotiation— Your Excellency's experience in public affairs will enable you to make a just estimate of the reserve and delicacy which ought to be observed, in all negotiations with foreign powers, involving subjects of deep national interest. This consideration has such weight, that it is the uniform practice of Congress, as no one knows better than your Excellency, to annex a qualification to the calls which are, from time to time, made for papers relating to the foreign Negotiations of the Government. There would not be the smallest objection to an exhibition to the inspection of your Excellency, or confidentially to any person, that you might think proper to designate, of all the papers, without exception, reported by the Commissioners. I abstain from a particular notice of many of the topics of your Excellency's letter, not from the least want of respect, (on the contrary, I entertain the highest, personally and officially) for your Excellency, but from a persuasion that the discussion of them is without utility. It has been thought most profitable to limit my answer to the specific requests contained in your letter.—

I transmit, herewith, in conformity with your wish, a list[2] of the papers reported by the Commissioners, copies of any of which may be procured, for the use of the State of Maine, whenever desired, with the exception which has been Stated.— I am with great respect Your most obedt. Servt.,   H. CLAY.

Copy. DNA, RG59, Dom. Letters, vol. 21, pp. 529–31 (M40, R19).
[1] Cf. above, Holmes and Chandler to Clay, February 1, 1826; Clay to Holmes and Chandler, March 6, 1826. The latter document referred to the transmittal of papers as requested by the letter of February 1, but also according "to the particular designation of Mr. Holmes." The restriction to which Clay alludes may have been orally expressed;

no written statement of the limitation has been found.   [2] Omitted by the editors.
Published in *American State Papers, Foreign Relations,* VI, 926, entry no. 18.

To Thomas I. Wharton

My dear Sir   Washington 7h. May 1827
    I recd. your obliging favor of the 3d. instant[1] and thank you for your
kind attention to the miniature,[2] which I will be further obliged by
your having carefully enclosed and sent by Mail. I transmit you enclosed a check for $13[3] to reimburse the advance which you have had
the goodness, on that account, to make.
    I have not received any copy of the Speeches &c,[4] and should be glad
to receive one by mail. I am truly Your friend & ob. Servt
T. I. Wharton Esqr.   H. CLAY

    ALS. KyU.   [1] Not found.
[2] Cf. above, Clay to Wharton, April 11, 1827, note.   [3] Not found.   [4] Cf. above,
Sparks to Clay, April 9, 1827, and note.

From Henry Clay, Jr.

Dear father.   West Point May 7th 1827
    It is with the greatest concern and distress that I have to inform you
of a circumstance, which will distress you as much, at least, as it does
me, and which can only be palliated by my youth.
    I shall give you as well as I recollect it my whole conduct in this
affair, and the consequences resulting from it—
    Something more than a month ago, I went to the Post Office to take
out a letter which was unpaid for; but the clerk being unable to
change the note which I gave him I left the money at the Office as a
deposite. Sometime after this, I went there, for the purpose, as before,
of getting out a letter: but in the mean time another clerk had arrived here who it seemed knew nothing of the deposite having been
made, and therefore could not permit me to obtain the letter without
first paying for it with other money which I did; but at the same time,
requested him, to enquire into the transaction by the next time I
should come there; which he promised to do. Last Friday I went there,
but was again put off by him, and told the second time that he knew
nothing of the affair, and therefore could do nothing: I then told him,
that he should have enquired into it; that I could not be put off in this
manner; that the agreement was made with the post office, without
any regard to persons: upon which he told me that it was not his duty
to attend to it; that I must settle it with the person with whom the
arrangement was made: Finally he told me, and repeated it several
times, that I knew nothing about his duty, and should therefore say

nothing about it: which incensed me very much, and caused me to tell him that if he repeated it again, I should injure him; upon this he immediately ordered me out of the office, and repeated what he had said before; I struck him gently, or rather laid upon his shoulder, a small piece of iron, which was lying near me and he being a much stronger man than myself pushed me out of the door with great violence.

I came up to the barrack on the instant, and without reflection, armed myself, and went down there for the purpose of chastising him, but was prevented from doing that, which had I done, I should be forever miserable: My arms were taken from me by Cadets, and I was again left in the power of Burret[1] who again forced me out of the door.

The same evening upon which it happened I wrote a note to Col Thayer,[2] stating the circumstances in nearly the same words, that I now relate them to you: He sent for me & told me that he was very sorry the thing had taken place, but that he would see into it. Yesterday evening an order was read that I should leave the post; immediately after hearing this order I went to him, and requested an explanation of it: he gave it me [sic], and said that however much interested he was in my welfare, still his duty had forced him to act as he had done, he having received communications from the post master,[3] a short time after I left him, which represented my conduct to be unwarrantable.

However he expressed an interest in my welfare, and advised me if I did not prefer going to Washington, to go to Newburgh a town, but a short distance up the river from this place, where he has many friends to whom he proposed to give me letters of introduction; and according to his advice I shall remain at Newburgh untill [sic] I receive letters from you on the subject which will be anxiouly [sic] expected by me.

You must not understand by the order which I have received, that I am debarred from entering the Ac'my in June, it still depends upon you, whether I shall join or not.

I expect to be recalled in a very short time if I remain in the neighbourhood; and when I enter, I am inclined to think that I shall obtain a very excellent standing in my class.

Give my best respects to all our friends and tell my mother, that although her son has acted precipatately [sic] he has nevertheless acted honourably, and that now he suffers as severe a punishment as a person can do when he reflects upon his conduct and how much it will affect you all, for whom I entertain the greatest love and respect. Your Distressed though aff'te son   HENRY CLAY J'R

Col Thayer has undoubtedly written to you before this and has given you all the information on the subject which this does not contain, as well as the reasons for his acting as he has done[4]— your's
                                        H. CLAY. J'R

ALS. Henry Clay Memorial Foundation, Lexington, Kentucky.
1 Not further identified.   2 Sylvanus Thayer.   3 Roger Alden, born in Connecticut, had held the rank of major in the Revolutionary War and had left the Army to complete his education at Yale College, where he had been graduated in 1783. From 1795 to 1825 he had been employed as an agent for the Holland Land Company at Meadeville, Pennsylvania; and from January, 1825, until his death in 1836, he served as military storekeeper at the United States Military Academy. His duties by 1827 included those of the postmastership at West Point.   4 No letter found.

From Joseph Kent

My Dear Sir   Annapolis 7th. May 1827
Do me the favour to pass the inclosed to Mr. Brent[1] and aid him in furnishing the desired information— It is wanting for a meeting to take place on Saturday next, in favour of the Administration, in the low [sic] part of this County[2]—

I hope you were gratified with the Adams meeting in Bato. [sic] on Saturday evening last[3]—

In Calvert County I am assured the Jackson meeting consisted of 8 & in Harford of 11[4]— From every part of Maryland informat[ion] is of the most favourable char[ac]ter— — In haste—yours very truly--
Honble. H. Clay   Secty State   Jos: KENT

ALS. DNA, RG59, Misc. Letters (M179, R65).
1 Daniel Brent. The enclosure has not been found.   2 On May 12, a meeting was held in the first election district of Anne Arundel County. It adopted resolutions defending the administration's handling of the controversy with Governor George M. Troup (cf. above, Clay to Southard, July 3, 1825, note), asserting the right of the "General Government to make internal improvements," praising Clay for his role in President Adams' election, and pledging support to Adams' re-election. The meeting also named delegates to a convention to be held at Baltimore on July 23. Washington Daily National Journal, May 18, 1827; and below, Goldsborough to Clay, August 9, 1827, note.
3 Cf. above, Clay to Everett, May 2, 1827, note.   4 Cf. Washington Daily National Journal, May 8, 1827. Reference to the meeting in Harford County has not been found.

From Jared Sparks

Dear Sir,   Mount Vernon, May, 7. 1827
Enclosed you have the memoranda of our agreement,[1] which I believe embrace all the essential points, except the price of my own labor, which you must make as liberal as your judgment dictates. My views of the subject you fully understand. I will thank you to have the contract drawn up in form, as soon as the 15th. or 20th. of the month, by which time I shall be in Washington with a view to close the business.

Since I saw you I have made arrangements with Judge Washington[2] to remove all Gen. Washington's papers to Boston.[3] They are thus more particularly in my charge, & I shall have the pleasure to take

with me for your perusal the opinions of Hamilton & Jefferson, which I mentioned to you, respecting the treaty with France.[4] I have the honor to be, Sir, with the highest respect, & sincere regards, your most obt. sert.   JARED SPARKS
Hon. Henry Clay.

ALS. DNA, RG59, Misc. Letters (M179, R65).
[1] The terms are essentially those outlined above, Sparks to Clay, March 13, 1827.
[2] Bushrod Washington.   [3] Cf. above, Sparks to Clay, May 7, 1827.   [4] On April 18, 1793, President George Washington had submitted to his Cabinet a circular and 13 questions concerning the applicability of the United States treaty of alliance of 1778 with France under the circumstances of the war which had broken out between Great Britain and France. Secretary of State Thomas Jefferson believed that the Secretary of the Treasury, Alexander Hamilton, had composed the inquiries. The Cabinet on April 19 had considered some of the questions; subsequently Hamilton and Jefferson had submitted written responses concerning the remainder. For the circular and questions, see John C. Fitzpatrick (ed.), The Writings of George Washington from the Original Manuscript Sources . . . (39 vols.; Washington, [1939–1944]), XXXII, 419–21; for publication of the notes of the Cabinet meeting and of Jefferson's response to the inquiries, see Paul Leicester Ford (ed.), The Works of Thomas Jefferson . . . (12 vols.; New York, 1904–1905), VII, 280–81, 283–301; and for Hamilton's role and views, see Harold C. Syrett (ed.), The Papers of Alexander Hamilton . . . (15 vols. to date; New York, 1961–), XIV, 327n, 367–96.

From John W. Taylor

Dear Sir   Ballston Spa N.Y. May 7. 1827.
    You have my thanks for your letter of the 4h. April which came duly to hand. On the 30h. my friend L. B. Langworthy high Sheriff of this County[1] wrote to Judge Clarke[2] an account of our prospects in this State in my opinion as correct as encouraging. I enclosed the letter in one of my own informing him who the writer was & adding such other matters as appeared proper. Last week I spent several days in Albany & Troy. Gen. Van Rensselaer & Mr Dickinson[3] were in N. Y. Judge Spencer & Mr Hammond[4] in the Country, so I saw neither of them but I recd. information from several sources which satisfies me they all are not only sincerely with us, but that they embrace all proper opportunities of making known their opinions & exerting their influence. I conversed with Chief Justice Savage[5] who until recently has professed neutrality. The Jackson opposition to manufactures[6] has brought him out decidedly for administration. He says his brother Judges of the Supreme Court Woodworth & Southerland[7] are with us, also Judge Duer[8] of the Albany circuit. Judge Conklin[9] with whom I conversed fully has the success of administration much at heart. He is doing all he can to induce the Albany daily[10] to act with us. The proprietors of that paper hate Van Buren & have no love for Clinton.[11] They are in natural opposition to the Argus[12] which will follow in the steps of V. B.   Hunter however one of them is for Jackson & the other two are rather undecided. Clark the Editor[13] who is employed on a salary is

heartily with us, but is dependant [sic] on the proprietors. This statement accounts for the vacillating course of that paper. It has a very
large circulation & is profitable to the owners. Mr Clinton has no in
fluence over it. Measures are in a train, which promise success, to induce it to take firm stand with us. I conversed also with the old Lt.
Governor John Tayler[14] who long stood at the head of the republican
party in Albany, & with Gideon Hawley[15] late Superintendent of the
Common Schools of the State, they are decided friends of administration as is also George Merchant,[16] the old Chairman of the republican
meetings in Albany. These three gentlemen of late years have supported Mr Clinton. It is the opinion of Judge Conklin that throughout
the state nine tenths of those who at the two last elections supported
Gov. Clinton are friends of the Gen. Adm. & will vote for Adams
electors. Clinton himself is as hostile as his worst enemies could wish
him. I do not learn that he participates in any systematic opposition &
indeed on some occasions during the winter & spring he has spoken
with respect of the Adm. & its friends, but in all companies where he
thinks it will be tolerated he gratifies his spleen by indulging in gibes
& sarcasms against the President, the Secy. of State, & the delegation in
the late Congress from this State, particularly your humble servt. I
think Judge Conklin's estimate of nine tenths is too large but in my
opinion it might safely be put at $3/4$— I have endeavored without success to see Col. Young since my return. He has been absent from the
County all the winter & spring & recently came home with his bride,
a second wife married in the vicinity of N. Y.[17] We made on them a
family call & spent half an hour with his wife, but he was not at home.
I do not find that his opinions in reference to the administration are
known to any person in this quarter, but in Albany, Judge Conklin
said, he was understood to be friendly.

In Troy I saw Mr Van Schoonhoven Cashier of the Farmers Bank &
Mr Badger late one of the N. Y. Rep. in Congress from Onondaga[18]
who has business concerns which keep him much in Troy. They say
the People in Troy are generally for the administration, & that our
prospects through the state are brightening. Both these gentlemen are
heartily in the cause & will do all in their power to promote it. Gen.
Van Schoonhoven of Waterford in this County[19] is for Jackson, & was
active in getting up the Jackson meeting against me last autumn, but
he has no influence with his brother of Troy. Mr Dickinson[20] is Pres.
of the Bank of which Mr V. S. is Cashier. It will not be in my power to
be in Philadelphia until after the period of your intended visit to
Kentucky, as I shall be engaged here in my business as a Commissioner
of Loans until near the close of this month.[21] Command me in any
thing calculated to advance the common cause and believe me to be
Very Faithfully Your obliged friend   JOHN W. TAYLOR
The Honorable Henry Clay

. ALS. DLC-HC (DNA, M212, R2).

[1] Lyman Barker Langworthy, born at New Lebanon, New York, had been trained as a clock and watch maker and had opened such a business in Quebec; but with the beginning of the War of 1812, he had returned to the United States and set up a hardware establishment at Ballston Spa. He held office as sheriff of Saratoga County from shortly after his arrival until 1828, when he removed to Rochester. There he operated a foundry and hardware enterprise and was for a time superintendent of the Rochester-Tonawanda railroad.   [2] James Clarke.   [3] Stephen Van Rensselaer; John D. Dickinson.

[4] Ambrose Spencer; Jabez D. Hammond.   [5] John Savage.   [6] Cf. above, Ingersoll to Clay, March 11, 1827; Clay to Everett, April 5, 1827.   [7] John Woodworth; Jacob Sutherland. The latter, elected to a seat in the New York Senate in 1822, had resigned, before the legislature met, to accept appointment as an associate justice of the New York Supreme Court. He remained on the bench until his resignation in 1836.

[8] William A. Duer.   [9] Alfred Conkling.   [10] Albany Daily Advertiser, owned by James Hunter; other proprietors have not been identified. On the journal's endorsement of Adams' administration, see below, Southard to Clay, July 9, 1827.

[11] Martin Van Buren; DeWitt Clinton. Cf. above, Porter to Clay, April 18, May 1, 1827.   [12] Albany Argus.   [13] Israel W. Clark had earlier (1814–1817) edited the Cooperstown, New York, Watch Tower and, from 1817 to the early 1820's, the Albany Register. He had been identified as a supporter of DeWitt Clinton and as an advocate of internal improvements. Hammond, History of Political Parties in the State of New York, I, 472.   [14] Born in New York City, Tayler had settled near Lake George, where he had operated a provision business in support of the troops during the French and Indian War. He had subsequently removed to Oswego and served briefly in the Revolutionary War and as a member of the provincial assembly of 1776 and the council of safety in 1777. He had been Lieutenant Governor of New York from 1813 to 1822. He was 85 years old in 1827 and died two years later.   [15] Born in Huntington, Connecticut, Hawley had been taken as a youth, in 1794, to Ballston Spa and, in 1798, to Charlton, New York. He had graduated from Union College in 1809 and in 1812 had been admitted to the bar at Albany. He was master in chancery at Albany from 1812 to 1830, secretary of the Albany Insurance Company from 1819 to 1853, and active in promotion of railway development as an officer of several New York lines. His most important distinction, however, came through his service in development of public education in the State. He was the first superintendent of public education (1812–1821), secretary of the Board of Regents (1814–1841), and from 1842 until his death in 1870 a member of the Board of Regents of the University of the State of New York. He was also a member of the Board of Regents of the Smithsonian Institution from its establishment in 1846 until 1861.   [16] Merchant, reputedly a native of Holland, had graduated from Princeton, had operated a private school for several years, and had been one of the founders and first trustees of Union College, founded at Schenectady in 1795. He had served as an Army storekeeper in 1802 and district paymaster from 1812 to 1814, and had held office as mayor of Albany, treasurer of the State of New York, and county clerk, the last of which positions he yet held at his death in 1830.

[17] Samuel Young had been married to Mrs. Sarah Lasher, of New Hurley, Ulster County, New York, on March 28. Albany Argus, March 30, 1827.   [18] Probably James Van Schoonhoven; Luther Badger. The former, a political leader of the Dutch aristocracy, held militia rank as a colonel. In 1819 he had been appointed judge advocate of the Saratoga County infantry division, and the following year he had become judge of the Saratoga County court of common pleas. Badger, a native of Massachusetts who had been brought to New York as an infant, was a lawyer and had been a member of the Nineteenth Congress (1825–1827). He removed to Broome County, New York, in 1832, held various offices there, and in 1849, returned to the practice of law in Onondaga County, where he died in 1869.   [19] Guert Van Schoonhoven, who had served as a militia paymaster for Albany County as early as 1786, had risen in the Saratoga County militia to the rank of brigadier general in 1818 and major general the following year. He was a lawyer and proprietor of the Congress Hall, the most fashionable hotel at Saratoga Springs. He had held a number of public offices, including that of State Senator in 1815, and had been elected judge of the Saratoga County court of common pleas in 1823.   [20] John D. Dickinson.   [21] Taylor, a lawyer by profession, practiced in Ballston Spa and had been a county commissioner of State loans since about 1810. Such officers, elected from among the freeholders by the supervisor and judges of county courts, administered the county allotments of proceeds from the sale of public lands, sums which under various legislative provisions were to be lent to individuals on property security under mortgage. Don C[onger] Sowers, The Financial History of New York State from 1789 to 1912 (Columbia University Studies in History, Economics, and Public Law, LVII, no. 2; New York, 1914), 259–62.

From Daniel Webster

My dear Sir,   *Private & confidential*   Boston May 7. 1827

I have to thank you for your's of the 14. & 20th. of April. The general information they contain, respecting the state of things in the South & West, is encouraging, & confirms what I learn from other quarters. The means agreed on, at the close of the Session, & which have been partially applied,[1] have, evidently, tended to awaken a good spirit. We cannot I think too strongly feel the conviction that public opinion is very likely to take a decisive direction between this time & the next meeting of Congress. We are all ready & willing, here, to do our part, that that direction shall be the right one.

A principal part of my present purpose is to ask your attention to a matter personal to myself. The state of Mr. Mills' health puts his re-election to the Senate out of the question.[2] Of course, our friends here have to find a successor, & I see pretty significant signs of an intention to offer the place to me. A similar proposition was made to me last June, when Mr Lloyd[3] resigned; & repeated, with some urgency, afterwards, when an attempt was making to supply Mr Mills' place. On those occasions I was able *to get excused*, without great difficulty, & without giving offence. If the same thing should be proposed again, it will come under different circumstances, & it is necessary, therefore, to consider beforehand, what will be proper to be done. I need not trouble you with particular details of our politics: suffice it to say, that the opposition, (for there is a little knot of gentlemen, desiring that appellation) have seized on some local subjects,—especially a taking proposition for a *free-bridge*,[4] by means of which they hope to strengthen their ranks. The leader of the *free-bridge* party is Mr Jarvis,[5] now speaker of the H. R. & who was one of the candidates for Senator last winter. He will probably be so again. He *professes* friendship for Mr. Adams; but Mr. Adams' friends in the Legislature, when he is proposed for Senator, think of what happened in N. Hampshire, & *almost* happened in Vermont.[6] They do not incline to choose him. Mr. John Mills will, or may, also be thought of. I believe *he* is a very true man, but not one likely to take an active part in affairs. If Gov. Lincoln would take the appointment, it would be highly satisfactory; but I believe he is not willing, at this time, to go to the Senate, & his friends are, also, a great deal averse to his leaving the place he now fills. Beyond all these reasons, a considerable degree of new feeling is springing up, in the state, in favor of the administration; & this feeling will require that *something be done*. The Senate is looked upon as weak, & a strong desire is felt, to do all that can be done to give the Govt. aid *there*.

From these & other considerations, added to what I hear & see, I fear a strong disposition, to the effect I have intimated, may prevail, unless it be prevented, or diverted by seasonable means. I have made some attempts to this end, myself, but with no great success. I have stated my own *decided wish* to stay where I am; but am told that I have no right to my own preferences, but must be disposed of as others think best. I have hinted, that my appropriate place was in the House, that my habits were made up to it, that it was accustomed to the sound of my voice—& I could do more good there than elsewhere, &c. &c. The answer is, the House will provide for itself; it is a numerous body, & somebody will appear to supply my place, &c.— But the Senate is a small body—in whic[h] vacancies occur seldom, & which now, most woefully, requires amendment.—

I need not say to you, my dear Sir, that both my *feelings* & my *judgement* are *against* the transfer. It would be to me a great sacrifice to make the exchange. And yet, on the other hand, as I am situated here, it would be extremely unpleasant & perhaps impossible, for me, to meet the offer if it should be made, *with a flat refusal.* I have therefore taken the liberty to write to you on the subject, for the purpose of asking you to consider of it, a little, & then to suggest what occurs to you for the use of confidential friends here. The Legislature mee[ts] the last Wednesday of the present month; & one of their first acts will probably be the choice of Senator.

You will perhaps find occasion to mention the ma[t]ter to Mr Adams, & having done so, I will thank you to write a line to Mr Silsbee,[7] such as may be shewn to the Govr. & other confidential friends, expressing your opinion & feeling. If it be possible to persuade the Govr. to accept the place, all will be well; but if not, I greatly fear, I shall hardly escape. Upon the whole, having distinctly expressed my feeling, & my opinion, I must now leave the matter to the decision of others. A professional engagement will call me to New York, the 25. inst.; so that I shall not be at home, probably at the election.

I conclude by repeating that for the little time I may remain in Congress, I have a strong,—a very strong—personal wish to stay in the House; nevertheless, *if it is clearly better* that *I go elsewhere,* I must be disposed of as the common good requires.

On one or two other subjects I had intended to say something; but shall spare your patience till another post.

Have you anything new, as to Mr McLane's intended course?[8]— I fear he is gone, but have thought it *possible* that the public sentiment in Del. might keep him right. Yrs. always with mo true regard

Hon H Clay.   DANL. WEBSTER

ALS. DLC-HC (DNA, M212, R2).
[1] Cf. above, Crowninshield to Clay, March 14, 1827; Mifflin to Clay, April 4, 1827; Clay to Everett, April 5, 1827; Clay to Webster, April 14, 1827; April 20, 1827; below, Webster to Clay, May 18, 1827; Johnston to Clay, May 19, 1827; Clay to Sloane, May 20, 1827.   [2] Elijah H. Mills—cf. above, Webster to Clay, June 8, 1826, note.   [3] James Lloyd.   [4] An organization known as the Warren Bridge Company had won authorization from the Massachusetts Legislature to build a "free" bridge from Boston to

Charlestown, Massachusetts, but Governor Levi Lincoln had refused to sign the measure on the ground that it would destroy the business of the Charles River Bridge Company, chartered by the State in 1785 and the charter having been extended in 1792 to run for 70 years. The issue had occasioned such division among Lincoln's supporters that there had been some concern about his re-election (cf. above, Clay to Everett, April 5, 1827, note). In 1828 the Warren Bridge Company was granted a charter, which provided that the bridge should be turned over to the State after construction costs had been collected. Litigation pressed by the Charles River Bridge Company eventually brought the case to the United States Supreme Court, where the decision in 1837 (*The Proprietors of the Charles River Bridge vs. The Proprietors of the Warren Bridge et al.*, 36 *U. S.* [11 Peters] 420–649), rejecting the claim to vested rights as asserted by the older company, established an important precedent in interpretation of the contract clause of the United States Constitution. Ambiguities in the terms of a contract, the Court ruled, must be resolved in accordance with public interest (p. 549). Meanwhile, in April, 1827, opponents of the Warren Bridge Company proposal had organized a mass meeting at which Webster had delivered the principal address, promoting Adams' presidential candidacy. Arthur B. Darling, *Political Changes in Massachusetts, 1824–1848* (New Haven, 1925), 49–50, 52.

5 William C. Jarvis, of Charlestown, was prominent as a partisan for Levi Lincoln but also as a leader in the project for the Warren Bridge Company. He had declined to oppose Lincoln's gubernatorial re-election and had received enough personal support in Middlesex County to carry it. Shortly after the Governor's re-election, his followers had paid tribute to Jarvis' loyalty by selecting him Speaker of the Massachusetts House of Representatives. *Ibid.*, 50–52. 6 On the New Hampshire problem, evidenced in the election of Benjamin Pierce, cf. above, Morril to Clay, September 18, 1826; Webster to Clay, April 14, 1827; below, Webster to Clay, May 18, 1827. On the defeat of Governor Cornelius P. Van Ness in Vermont and his subsequent endorsement of Jackson, see above, Hall to Clay, April 7, 1827; Clay to Hall, April 11, 1827. 7 Nathaniel Silsbee—cf. above, Webster to Clay, June 8, 1826, note; Clay to Everett, April 5, 1827, note.

8 Cf. above, Clay to Brown, March 27, 1827, note; Hammond to Clay, March 28, 1827; Niles to Clay, March 28, 1827; Clay to Webster, April 14, 1827.

INSTRUCTIONS AND DISPATCHES   May 7, 1827

From J[OEL] R. POINSETT, Mexico, no. 86. Forwards a notice, signed by himself, publication of which he recommends "in some one paper of every state in the Union," informing Americans of Mexican passport laws; also transmits a list of American citizens who obtained passports at the American Legation between the date of his arrival and January 1, 1827. LS. DNA, RG59, Dip. Disp., Mexico, vol. 3 (M97, R4). Received July 2.

In the enclosure Poinsett warns "that every American citizen, who leaves the United States with the intention of visiting Mexico, is expected to furnish himself with properly authenticated certificates of citizenship, countersigned by an agent of the Republic. Passports issued by the Mexican Vice-Consuls in the ports of the United States, will not be considered as sufficient testimony of citizenship at this Office."

From W[ILLIAM] H. D. C. WRIGHT, Rio de Janeiro. Reports that, since the departure of (Condy) Raguet, on April 16, "some new aggressions upon our Flag, have led to a correspondence" with the Minister of Foreign Affairs (the Marquis of Queluz), who "has assumed a strange ground, to justify his Government, in shipping and protecting deserters from Our Vessels. . . ." Transmits copies of the correspondence (including rejection of Wright's request for the return of a deserter from "the American Brig Sylph," of Philadelphia). Observes that, after this response he did not demand, in a similar case, release of two deserters from "the Ship Charleston, of New York." Outlines the case of "The Brig Ontario of Philadelphia," which, on a charter voyage to bring Brazilian legislators from Bahia to Rio, "was Overhauled by a Buenos Ayrean Privateer" and the passengers robbed. The *Ontario* is not allowed to depart from Rio "until her Captain [Hugh McKenzie, not further identified], gives bond, to Abide the decision of a suit, brought against him upon the charge of his being an accomplice with said Privateer. . . ." Encloses copies of correspondence with the Minister of Foreign Affairs relative to this case and copies of correspondence with Admiral (Rodrigo Antonio de) Lamare concerning impressed seamen. States that the Emperor (Peter I) declared to the General Assembly, which began its Session May 3, "his intention to prosecute the War against Buenos Ayres. . . ." Notes that the war continues to become more unpopular as Brazilian forces suffer defeats, "commerce is much annoyed by Privateers," and the currency has suffered "a depreciation of 50 pr Cent. . . ." Encloses two newspapers.   ALS. DNA, RG59, Cons. Disp., Rio de Janeiro, vol. 2 (M-T172, R3). Received June 28, 1827.

The owners of the *Ontario* finally received settlement "in full by Brazilian government" for the "Detention and consequent demurrage and loss," to the extent of $1,742.31, arising from the incident here reported. *Sen. Docs.*, 35 Cong., 2 Sess., no. 18 (January 19, 1859), p. 113.

Lamare (or Lemare), who signs as "Chefe de Esquadra Commandante do Porto," has not been further identified.

Promissory Note to Daniel Brent

$1350   Washington, May 8th 1827
SIXTY *days after date*, I *promise to pay to the order of* Daniel Brent Thirteen hundred and fifty dollars *for value received, payable at the Office of the Bank of the United States, at Washington.*

H. CLAY

DS, partially printed. DLC-TJC (DNA, M212, R16).
On May 7, Daniel Brent, with William Brent as co-signer, had deeded to Richard Smith the slaves Ned, Fanny, Tom, George, Harriet with her infant child, and Bill, with the understanding that Brent would pay Smith the above note as drawn by Clay, who had "kindly undertaken [no agreement found] to lend his negotiable note" so that Brent might pay a balance owed to Robert LeRoy Livingston, secured by deed of trust for the slaves. Since the slaves were hereby assigned to Smith, Clay was to incur no liability in the transaction. ADS. DLC-TJC (DNA, M212, R16). Recorded in Montgomery County Court (Maryland), May 23, 1827. Clay re-issued notes to Brent dated July 10, 1827; October 22, 1827; November 13, 1827; January 15, 1828; May 20, 1828, all DS, in DLC-TJC (DNA, M212, R16), the last of which, endorsed by Daniel Brent and George Watkins, was protested for lack of funds on July 22, 1828. A document dated September 11, 1827, signed by Daniel Brent (*ibid.*) stipulated that he assumed responsibility as endorser "Of Henry Clay's note [not found] due this day, in the office of discount & Deposit, Washington, for $1.350. . . ." A note from Clay to Brent during March, 1828, if written, has also not been found. Cf. below, Deed from Brent, October 22, 1828. Robert LeRoy Livingston, born in Claverack, New York, and graduated in 1784 from Princeton College, had been a member of Congress from 1809 to 1812 and an Army officer during the War of 1812. His wife, Anna Maria Digges, was a niece of Daniel and William Brent.

From Nicholas Biddle

Dear Sir,   Phila. May 8th. 1827
To one who has made so many good speeches & been obliged to hear so many bad ones it must be wearisome to hear or to read more   I do not propose to inflict on you that suffering—but I wish merely to place the enclosed[1] on your table as an evidence of the respect & regard of Yrs very truly   NB
Honble H. Clay Esq.   Washington Ca.

ALI draft. From the Biddle Family Papers, by courtesy of James Biddle, Andalusia, Pennsylvania.
1 Nicholas Biddle, *An Eulogium on Thomas Jefferson Delivered before the American Philosophical Society, April 11, 1827* (Philadelphia, 1827), a 55-page pamphlet.

MISCELLANEOUS LETTERS   May 8, 1827

To JAMES MITCHEL, Groton, Connecticut. Informs him that a commission appointing him "Marshal of the United States for the District of Connecticut, has just been forwarded . . . to Mr. [William] Bristol, the District Judge," to be delivered after Mitchel gives bond and complies "with the established forms in similar cases." LS. DLC-HC (DNA, M212, R2).

A copy of Clay's letter of transmittal, addressed to Judge Bristol on the same date, is located in DNA, RG59, Dom. Letters, vol. 21, p. 532 (M40, R19). On June 4, 1827, Mitchel acknowledged receipt of his commission. ALS, in DNA, RG59, Misc. Letters (M179, R65).

From WILLIAM PRIESTMAN, Philadelphia. Asks, in a postscript to a letter enclosing a claim on France, whether he is "ever to get any more money from [Humphrey] Marshall." ALS. DNA, RG76, Misc. Claims, France, Spoliations by European Powers since 1801, env. W-loose papers. Cf. above, I, 587; II, 705, 911–12.

From HENRY WHEATON, New York. States his expectation of being "ready to leave the Country about the *middle of June*" and his hope that Clay will send his "instructions by the *first of the next month*." Reminds Clay "of the purport" of their conversation; expresses a hope that he "may be entrusted with as much discretion as to the *manner* of arranging the Claims as the President may think fit"; and notes that he has "heard nothing from the Treasury on the Subject to which" Clay's letter of April 16 refers. ALS. DNA, RG59, Dip. Disp., Denmark, vol. 1B (M41, R3).

Editorial Article

[May 9, 1827]

We present our readers today with an interesting note from Mr Secretary Canning to Mr. Gallatin, under date the 27h. Jan. last, which appears to have been recently laid before the British Parliament, with the correspondence which has passed between the two Govts. on the Colonial question.[1] From the tenor of this note it would seem that there is no prospect of a settlement of that question by negotiation. Whether it has closed the correspondence or not we are unable to say. Mr. Canning is reported to have said in the House of Commons, in allusion to this subject, and with some self complacency if not levity that he had had the *last* word; but we think it not unlikely that his note has formed the subject of some instructions from the Dept. of State to Mr. Gallatin, which may be submitted to Congress at the next Session.[2] For we presume that our Govt.[3] has not felt itself bound by the testiness of Mr. Canning, who "will *not allow* himself to be drawn again into a discussion of topics already more than sufficiently debated" to abstain from any observation which it may consider as being called for by the terms or tenor of that note

Mr. Canning states that "an instruction was sent to Mr. Vaughan[4] grounded on the belief of the British Govt. that Congress would not separate without adopting the resolution then under consideration. In that case, and upon receiving an assurance from the American Govt. that *the restrictions and charges* on British Shipping and British Colonial produce wd. be withdrawn by the U States, Mr. V. was authorized to deliver a note to the American Secy. of State declaring that the discriminating duties imposed on American ships and their Cargoes in the W. Indies should immediately cease." From this statement it is clear that something more was required than the simple repeal of the American discriminating duties, although the *restrictions and charges* are not specified. This instruction Mr. Vaughan never communicated to the American Govt., but in lieu of such communication, invited on the 22d. March 1826 (at the very moment when the undivulged instruction above mentd. was in his pocket)[5] the American Govt. by the direction of his own, to proceed in the negotiation embracing the Colonial question. Could any thing be better adapted than such an invitation to divert the attention of the American Govt. from legislation and direct it to negotiation? Whatever may have been the design the effect of the double & opposite instructions of the B. Govt. to their Minister at Washington must have been to mislead the Govt. of the U. States.

We do not think that Mr. Canning makes out any justification for the acknowledged omission to communicate officially to the Govt. of the U. States the British act of Parliament of July 1825.[6] Whatever may be the usage as to the interchange generally of reciprocal acts of the respective Legislatures of the two Countries, when a particular act passes, which is intended to supersede an existing or contemplated negotiation, the propriety of its being officially communicated with a notification that such is its intended operation is too evident to be contested.

We think it now quite apparent that the B. Govt. had altered its views with respect to the Col. intercourse and has availed itself of a mere pretext to occasion a rupture in the negotiation.[7] From some statements of the British & Foreign tonage [sic] recently laid before Parliament it would appear that B. Navigation is incapable of sustaining a competition on equal principles with Foreign shipping. With the exception of Spain Portugal & Russia, those statements present to the British Statesman the appalling fact that foreign tonnage is employed to an extent of near three fifths of the navigation concerned in the trade between G. B. and foreign Countries.[8] Hence the complaints of the British Shipping interest and the apprehension of an

increase of the disproportion; and hence probably the change of the
policy of the B Govt. in regard to the Colonial intercourse. We perceive that a circuitous trade between the U. S. and the B. W.[9] has been
substituted to[10] the direct intercourse which is interdicted by the laws
of the two Countries.[11] We shall[12] derive from this Circuitous trade
nearly all the advantages which could be obtained from the direct
intercourse.

AD. KyU. Published, with the changes noted below, and with minor revisions of
punctuation, capitalization, and abbreviation, in Washington *Daily National Intelligencer,* May 10, 1827. Cf. above, Clay to Force, March 25, 1827.
    [1] Cf. above, Gallatin to Clay, March 29, 1827.   [2] See above, Clay to Gallatin, April
11, 1827. In the newspaper the last clause of this sentence reads as follows: "but we
have very little doubt, from the spirit already evinced by our Government in this controversy, that his note now published, has hardly been suffered to pass without comment." Clay's instructions to Gallatin were submitted to Congress among the papers
communicated on April 28, 1828 (cf. below, Clay to Adams, on that date), and published
in *American State Papers, Foreign Relations,* VI, 370–75.   [3] The words "The Executive" are substituted for "our Govt." in the published version.   [4] Charles R.
Vaughan.   [5] After the word "communication" the published version reads: "on the
22d March 1826 (at the moment when the above mentioned undivulged instruction was
in his possession) he invited. . . ."   [6] Cf. above, Gallatin to Clay, August 19, 1826,
note.   [7] This sentence is changed, in the newspaper, as follows: "We think it is
now quite apparent that the British Government had *altered its views* with respect to
the Colonial Intercourse and has availed itself of one of those pretexts with which
diplomatists are familiar, to occasion a rupture in the negotiation."   [8] Cf. above,
Gallatin to Clay, February 22, May 4, 1827, note.   [9] These initials are changed to
"West Indies" in the published version, and the sentence begins a new paragraph.
    [10] Changed to "for" in the published version.   [11] Cf. above, Harrison to Clay,
March 13, May 3, 1827. An editorial in *Niles' Weekly Register,* XXXII (March 31, 1827),
31, had predicted such a development: ". . . articles desired of us will be obtained as
heretofore, and must be paid for as usual; they will, however, be obtained through new
channels, and an indirect trade will take the place of a direct one."   [12] The words
"will probably" are substituted in the published version.

To Edward Everett

My dear Sir   Washington 9h. May 1827.
    I thank you for the opportunity afforded me of perusing Mr. Far-
rands Letter, now returned.[1] I shall be happy to render him any service in my power in his project of introducing the Cashmere Goat,
and which he may indicate. There is much reason undoubtedly to
believe that among our various climates one may be found favorable
to the rearing of that valuable animal.
    Other accounts which I receive from Pennsa. concur with that of
Mr. F. as to political affairs, and they all present a state of things full
of hope and deserving the most strenuous exertions. I count much
upon your pamphlet,[2] which I am eager to see.
    The movement in Balto.[3] has been highly satisfactory, and cannot
fail to stimulate our friends in other parts of Maryland and extend its
influence to other States.
    We have just recd. intelligence of the important changes in the
British Ministry,[4] 'though we are not yet able fully to comprehend

them. The best solution which has presented itself is that the Catholic question has been the leading principle, the resigned ministers having been all opposed to Catholic emancipation. The change will not probably have any material effect on our interests. Mr. Huskisson's[5] state of health was not on the 31st. March such as to admit of his negotiating with Mr. Gallatin. Your's Cordially   H CLAY
E. Everett Esq.

ALS. MHi.
[1] Probably William P. Farrand, who in addition to publishing texts on Greek and Latin grammar and some legal studies, was a Philadelphia importer.   [2] Cf. above, Clay to Everett, April 5, 1827.   [3] Cf. above, Clay to Everett, May 2, 1827, note; Kent to Clay, May 7, 1827.   [4] Cf. above, Gallatin to Clay, February 22, 1827, note. The steamship *Pacific* had arrived at New York on May 6, with news from Liverpool as late as April 12, including reports of the Cabinet changes in Britain but lacking confirmation of Canning's rumored appointment as Prime Minister. Washington *Daily National Journal*, May 10, 1827.   [5] William Huskisson. Cf. below, Gallatin to Clay, May 22, 1827.

Bill from James Madison Cutts

Honble H. Clay.   [May 9, 1827]

1 Tea Urn		$ 15.50
4 Mahog. Waiters	3 50	,, 14 —
3½ doz. Candle Gs.	6.75	,, 23.62.
2 Pr. Plated Salts		,, 8 —
1 Fire Screen		,, 8 50
1 ,, ,, ...		,, 8 00
6 Chairs	3.50 —	,, 21. —
1 Small Night Table		,, 9.50
1 ,, Mahogy Table		,, 5 00
1 Arm Chair		,, 7.00
1 Screen		,, 7.50
1 Bureau		,, 41. —
1 Paper Stand		,, 14.50
2 Card Tables	21	,, 42 —[1]
1 Morocco Settee		,, 35 —
		$ 218 12

[Note on bottom of document:]
Colo Roberdeau[2] assures me that Mr. Clay had permit[ted] him to take the two card tables— & that he would bill Mr C— the rest are all sent— and as carefully as possible   J M CUTTS

ADS. DLC-HC (DNA, M212, R2). Date supplied subsequently by unidentified source. On the Clays' recent move to the Decatur house, cf. above, Clay to Johnston, April 2, 17, 1827.   Cutts, a son of Richard Cutts and nephew of Dolly Payne Madison, was a clerk in the Second Comptroller's Office of the United States Treasury. Appointed in 1821, he became chief clerk in 1849 and Second Comptroller in 1857. He died while still holding the latter office in 1863.
[1] Card-table item struck through on manuscript.   [2] Isaac Roberdeau, born in Philadelphia, had studied engineering in London. Returning to the United States in

1787, he had been employed in the laying out of the city of Washington, in 1791 and 1792. For the next 20 years he had been professionally active in Pennsylvania and in 1813 had been commissioned a major in a newly organized unit of topographical engineers in the United States Army. After the disbanding of the Army, he had been reinstated in his wartime rank to continue topographical work, first at the United States Military Academy, from 1816 to 1818, and subsequently in Washington, where he was chief of the topographical bureau from its establishment. In 1823 he had been brevetted lieutenant colonel. He died on January 15, 1829.

INSTRUCTIONS AND DISPATCHES   May 9, 1827

To FELIX CICOGNANI, "United States Consul at Rome." States, in response to Cicognani's letter of March 9 (*i.e.*, 17), that "The President views with satisfaction the determination of the Government of His Holiness, the Pope [Leo XII], to reciprocate the policy by which the United States had offered to be regulated in their Commercial intercourse abroad"; but that, until that determination, "however gratifying to the President," has been "officially announced to him by the Papal Government," he will withhold the expected proclamation. Transmits "a copy of the Act of Congress, of the 7th of January 1824," and calls attention to section 4, which states the "circumstances" under which "the President is authorised to issue his proclamation" (see above, Lorich to Clay, March 16, 1825). Copy. DNA, RG59, Cons. Instr., vol. 2, pp. 422–23 (M78, R2).

From JOHN SERGEANT and JOEL R. POINSETT, Mexico. Acknowledge receipt of documents brought by Theodore W. Clay. Report that "Since Mr. Sergeants dispatch of the 27th. March last, no change has taken place in the state of things" there and that the Panama treaties have not been ratified by Colombia. Cite disorders in Colombia, Peru, and Central America (cf. above, Litchfield to Clay, July 20, 1826; Tudor to Clay, February 3, 1827; Gonzalez to Clay, January 7, 1827) that have distracted attention from the treaties and given Mexico, though "enjoying tranquillity herself," "a motive and a justification for delaying the consideration of" them. State that, should the Congress of Tacubaya not meet before June 1, "and there should then be no greater probability than now appears of its meeting soon after," Sergeant will return home. Add that "Mr. [Theodore W.] Clay will leave Mexico on Tuesday the 11th. inst. . . ." LS. DNA, RG43, Records re Panama Congress, vol. 1 (M662, R1). Received July 2.

From JOHN G. A. WILLIAMSON, La Guaira. Transmits a newspaper which gives information on "a revolution in Peru, since the Liberator Presidents [Simón Bolívar's] departure for Colombia, founded on the adoption of the Bolivian Constitution" (cf. above, Tudor to Clay, February 3, 1827). States a general belief that Bolívar's efforts "have been directed since his arrival in Colombia & this department, to the same end" (*i.e.*, adoption of a governmental structure like that of the Bolivian Constitution—cf. above, MacPherson to Clay, October 2, 1826; Grut to Clay, February 13, 1827) but that "it will not go down but by force" and that "His warmest friends previous to his arrival are opposed to it. . . ." Reports the arrival of Alexander Cockburn, "minister plenry. to this Govt.," whose mission is understood to include an offer of British protection to Colombia and the conversion of its government "into a Constitutional Monarchy." Notes information of British activity, including the presence of ships of war, at Curaçao. Comments on the disposition felt by New Granada to separate from Venezuela (cf. above, Litchfield to Clay, May 22, 1826, note; Watts to Clay, December 27, 1826, no. 22). Urges, if the United States wishes to "maintain an influence in this Country," the assignment of a political "representative" in Caracas. Refers to the absence of common interests among the various provinces of the country, the difficulty of communication, and the unwillingness of this department to be governed by "laws or men" other than those of their own choosing. Adds, in an addendum on the same date, that "A Gentleman direct from Curacoa [*sic*]" brings information of improvement of that island's fortifications, allegedly "under the direction and with the su[pport] of England (tho a dutch Island.)—" ALS. DNA, RG59, Cons. Disp., La Guaira, vol. 1 (M84, R1). Received May 28. Endorsed on cover by Clay: "To be submitted to the P[resident]   HC"

To Jacob Bugg Hopkins

Dear Sir: Washington, 10th May, 1827.

I received your letter of the 21st of April,[1] with its enclosures; three dedimuses, and a notice to take my deposition, to be used as evidence in suits pending with Mr. Lyne.[2] My recollection of the transaction as to which you wish me to testify, is so general and indistinct that I am apprehensive it would not tend to the elucidation of the truth of the case. I had no motive for preserving in my memory the circumstances which attended it, and could now only speak from impressions which remain. I understood Mr. Lyne to attend at the sale,[3] and to have become the purchaser of the property which was sold, with two objects; one of which was his own personal security, and the other to prevent the sacrifice of the property. I conceived him to be acting as the friend of the heirs of General Hopkins, and, also, in his own right, in consequence of his connection with the family. I supposed his intention to be to acquire a legal title to the property, in order to render his security and indemnity perfect: But I believed, also, that whenever he was reimbursed the amount advanced, he would restore the property purchased to the family. Such are the impressions which remain on my mind from my intercourse with Mr Lyne, at the time, and from what passed at the period of the sale. I have no doubt that by applying to Mr. Morton,[4] you will be able to obtain from him a more full and correct statement of the affair. I will add that I should have made the sale with great reluctance, if I had not supposed Mr. Lyne to have been acting with the above intentions. From this imperfect recollection of the transaction, and doubting whether, if it were thrown into the form of a deposition it would be of any service in the suits, I shall not give my testimony, unless I again hear from you. If, contrary to my impressions, it should be deemed of any importance, I should be glad if this letter could be taken as its substitute. I am, with great regard, Your obedient servant,   H. CLAY
Jacob B. Hopkins, Esqr.

LS. Henderson County Historical Society, Kentucky. Addressed to Hopkins, a son and heir of General Samuel Hopkins, at Henderson.
[1] Not found.   [2] George Lyne.   [3] Cf. above, Horsley to Clay, April 17, 1825.
[4] John H. Morton. Cf. above, II, 236–37.

From Joel R. Poinsett

Dear Sir   (Private)   Mexico, 10th. 1827 May

As your Son[1] cannot remain here the whole summer, and as the danger attending his return will be increased by every day's delay, both Mr. Sergeant[2] and myself have thought it adviseable [sic], that he should set out at once, especially as he will now have the advantage of accompanying Mr. Rochester and Mr. Ogden.[3] This arrangement accords with his wishes.

The desicion [sic] of Senate with regard to the Treaty[4] was not un-expected by me. My only motive for consenting to insert the additiona[l] article, for I was aware of the main objection to it,[5] was a wish not to leave the field entirely open to the British negociators[6] by break-ing off the negociations here a second time.[7] You can form no idea of the difficulties of treating with these people. They want good faith themselves and are constantly afraid of being deceived.

I am much indebted to you for the interest you manifest in the af-fair of my outfit.[8] I fully understand the feeling, which led Congress to refuse it; but in fact am too much gratified with this renewed in-stance of the President's confidence to complain of the parsimony of Congress.

I send you herewith the treaties concluded by the confederate states at Panam[a][9] and beg you will permit me to observe[,] that neither the treaty nor the sou[rce] from whence it was obtained ought to b[e] divulged; as it might prevent me hereaft[er] from procuring copies of important state papers, which the Mexican government may desire to keep secret.

I cannot but regard the meeting of the Congress of Tacubaya as very remote[10]— The non existence of the ratifying power in some of the States, parties to the treaties of Panama, and the evident disinclination of this government to act upon them lead me to this conclusion. Mex-ico does not think it to be her interest at present to enter into this confederation. She considers the contingent assigned her as too great, and in fact her finances are not in a state that would allow her either to move troops for the defence of other States, or to furnish subsidies. The deficit increases[11] and by my latest information was not short of three millions of dollars.

I fear the sum offered for the Territory[12] is too small. The expenses of the governmt. are so great, that they dont regard so insignificant a sum as a Million, as of much use to them.

As the language used by Doctr. Gual in his reply to me[13] appeared to me to require explanation, I sought a conference with him. His principal objection to attend [sic] the Congress of Tacubaya arises from the non ratification of a convention which specifically provides for the protection and privileges of the Ministers from the american

States during their residence within the Mexican territory. He did not feel him [sic] at liberty to give us a copy of it; but permitted Mr. Sergeant and myself to read it. To the best of my recollection the following are the chief stipulations. It provides for the transfer of the congress from Panamá to the town of Tacubaya in the Valley of Mexico, or to any other place they may think it fit either in the territory of Mexico or elsewhere, where they can enjoy health and security. Their Sessions to be of three months duration, with liberty to prolong them two months beyond that term. On the arrival of the Ministers within the territory of the government where the assembly is to be held, they are to be considered as invested with all the rights, privileges and immunities which Ministers plenipotentiaries duly accredited to the government to which the territory may belong enjoy: and for this purpose they are to send in a list of the persons composing their suite in order that they may be invested with the same privileges and immunities as the families of Ambassadors are entitled to. The correspondence of the Ministers to be free from postage—   Tacubaya or any other place fixed upon to be free from any garrison of troops, unless at the desire and petition of the Congress. Nor any authority of this government to be allowed to enter the town without permission of the Congress, on any pretext whatever, except the civil and municipal authorities of the place.

This convention not having been acted upon by this government, in whose territory the Congress was expected to meet, Doctr. Gual regards the invitation give[n] by the Mexican Plenipotentiaries to the Congress of Panama to transfer their sessions to Tacubaya as not approved o[f] by their government: for the Congress mig[ht] have ratified separately that conventio[n,] if it thought it expedient to confirm the invitation. He says therefore that he will not attend the Congress if it shou[ld] meet at Tacubaya before this convention is ratified, because such an assemblage would not have the sanction of the Government in whose territory they are. I asked him if we were at liberty to mention the convention and his view[s] of it to our government; he replied[,] that we were so.

It appears to me a strong case. It would perhaps have been better to have made no such special Convention: but being at Panamá under the protection of Treaties it was not thought adviseable [sic] to remove to any other place without positive stipulations for the privileges of the members and the sanctity of the place of meeting.

Your son will give you an account of the state of things here. I presented him to the President[14] and to my friend General Guerrero[15]— and am sorry that I saw so little of him: but Mr. Sergeant monopolized him. I am with great respect Your obt. Servt.   J. R. POINSETT

LS. DNA, RG59, Dip. Disp., Mexico, vol. 3 (M97, R4). Received July 2. Margins obscured in binding.
1 Theodore W. Clay.   2 John Sergeant.   3 William B. Rochester; Francis Bar-

ber Ogden—both listed as passengers arriving at New Orleans from Veracruz on June 4, 1827. On young Clay's separate sailing for New York, cf. below, Sergeant to Clay, May 30, 1827. Ogden, born in New Jersey in 1783, had served through the War of 1812 and had been Jackson's aide-de-camp at New Orleans. In 1817 he had gone to England, where he won recognition as designer and builder of a low-pressure condensing engine for steamboat operation. He was United States consul at Liverpool from 1830 to 1840 and at Bristol from 1840 until his death in 1857.   4 See above, Clay to Poinsett, March 12, 1827.   5 See above, Poinsett to Clay, July 12, 1826, and note.   6 Cf. above, Poinsett to Clay, May 5, 1825, note; February 1, 1826.   7 Cf. above, Poinsett to Clay, September 28, 1825; February 18, April 30, 1826.   8 Cf. above, Clay to Poinsett, February 28, 1827.   9 Cf. above, Salazar to Clay, November 20, 1826.   10 Cf. above, Sergeant to Clay, May 2, 1827.   11 Cf. above, Sergeant to Clay, March 5, 1827; Poinsett to Clay, April 13, 1827.   12 See above, Clay to Poinsett, March 15, 1827.   13 Cf. below, Poinsett to Clay, this date, no. 87, and note.   14 Guadalupe Victoria.   15 Vicente Guerrero.

DIPLOMATIC NOTES   May 10, 1827

From HILARIO DE RIVAS Y SALMON, Spanish Legation, Philadelphia. Acknowledges receipt of Clay's note of April 24; undertakes in detail and at length to refute each of Clay's statements in regard to the suit between Juan Miguel de Losada and (Joseph E.) Caro; expresses a wish that his remarks be laid before the President. ALS, in Span. with ALS trans. in State Dept. file. DNA, RG59, Notes from Spanish Legation, vol. 9 (M59, R-T12).

INSTRUCTIONS AND DISPATCHES   May 10, 1827

From JAMES OMBROSI, Florence. Reports that "an American by the name of [John M.] Allen," supposedly a recruiter for Greece, has been banished from Tuscany for an abortive attempt to seize a Turkish war vessel in the port of Leghorn. Notes a threat of war by "The Bashaw of Tripoli" [Yusuf Karamanli] against the Grand Duke (Leopold II) in support of a demand for $4,000 "as a Consular present, which the G. D. has so far refused." ALS. DNA, RG59, Cons. Disp., Florence, vol. 1 (M-T204, R1). Received August 21.

From JOEL R. POINSETT, Mexico, no. 87. Transmits "copies and translations of . . . [his] correspondence with Ministers of the American States to the Congress to be assembled at Tacubaya, who are in this city." ALS. DNA, RG43, Records re Congress of Panama (M662, R1). Received July 2.
    The enclosures include Poinsett's letter to José Mariano Michelena, April 30, 1827 (presumably the same note was sent to the other Ministers), announcing his appointment to act with (John) Sergeant to represent the United States at the Tacubaya Congress, and the replies he received from Antonio Larrazábal, J[osé] Dominguez, Pedro Gual, and Michelena.

From JOEL R. POINSETT, Mexico, no. 88. Acknowledges receipt of Clay's "dispatches, Nos. 20 and 21 [March 12, 15, 1827], sent by Mr. Theodore Clay." States that he has "already signified to" the Mexican "government the resolutions of the Senate of the United States with regard to the Treaty, and proposed to renew the negociations." Adds: "The Treaty was still before the House, and will be withdrawn by the Executive." LS. DNA, RG59, Dip. Disp., Mexico, vol. 3 (M97, R4). Received July 2.

From JOHN SERGEANT, Mexico (Private). Reports that Clay's "son [Theodore W. Clay] will depart tomorrow evening" and that his own departure "will take place soon after the 1 June, as there is no probability of an early meeting at Tacubaya."

Regrets his lack of contact with the Mexican Ministers. Expresses, in a postscript, his esteem for Judge (William B.) Rochester. ALS. DNA, RG43, Records re Panama Congress (M662, R1). Received July 2.

MISCELLANEOUS LETTERS   May 10, 1827

To GEORGE JARVIS, Greece. Daniel Brent, in reply to Jarvis' letters to Clay of November 6 (i.e., 18), 1826, states that only the courts can grant naturalization and returns Clay's thanks for his "interesting letter . . . in relation to the affairs of Greece. . . ." Copy. DNA, RG59, Dom. Letters, vol. 21, p. 535 (M40, R19).

From RICHARD RUSH, Washington. Returns (Samuel) Mifflin's letter (not found) and transmits "for Mr M. the report of the committee of ways and means, of Feb: 1826, and the annual treasury report of last December, having marked in the margin, such parts of each document as relate to the subject of his inquiry." Notes that the House of Representatives acted on his (Rush's) renewed recommenda- tion of a loan, or exchange of stocks, by readily passing a bill to that effect," but that the Senate failed to act. Comments: "Our loss in consequence supposing the loan to have been obtained, (and in my mind there is not the least doubt that it would have been—the whole from the bank of the U. S. if in no other way) amounts to one hundred and sixty thousand dollars a year, being the sum that would have been saved the nation, in interest, by paying five instead of six per cent upon sixteen millions of dollars." ALS. DNA, RG59, Misc. Letters (M179, R65).

On February 6, 1826, the Committee of Ways and Means had reported "On the State of the Finances," opposing a proposal by Secretary Rush for refunding $9,000,000 of public debt in 1826 and $6,000,000 in 1827 to reduce the rate of in- terest from six to five percent on a part of the outstanding indebtedness. The committee argued that "the saving to the Government would scarcely justify any attempt, in the present embarrassed state of the money market, to change the stock to the prejudice of the stockholders." They proposed, instead, that the Treasury wait until it had sufficient funds to pay "the whole of any loan" or to pay off quarterly, out of Treasury surpluses, so much of the debt as could be "dis- charged by such surplus. . . ." House Repts., 19 Cong., 1 Sess., no. 64, pp. 4, 6.

For the House action on the proposed refunding bill, see U. S. H. of Reps., Journal, 19 Cong., 2 Sess., 406. Cf. also, above, Worsley to Clay, April 17, 1827, note.

From GEORGE W. SLACUM, Alexandria (District of Columbia). Transmits "the correspondence and other documents in relation to the affair of the american Brig Merope" (cf. above, Neilson and others to Clay, February 3, 1827; Slacum to Clay, February 14, March 14, 1827). States that, although these materials "carry with them intrinsic evidence of the character of the whole transaction, and par- ticularly of the course which our Chargé d'Affaires [John M. Forbes] has thought proper to pursue towards" him, he prosposes to draw Clay's "attention to the most prominent points of the case. . . ." Proceeds to develop the statement, charging his clerk, John H. Duffy, with fraud and Forbes with improper conduct. LS. DNA, RG59, Cons. Disp., Buenos Aires, vol. 3 (M70, R4).

MISCELLANEOUS LETTERS   May 11, 1827

To [WILLIAM WIRT]. Submits to the Attorney General "the question, whether Richard Sealy, the applicant, is entitled to a patent, or not, for his improvement as described in his schedules herewith sent. . . ." States that "Dr. [William]

Thornton has declined giving him the patent prayed for, upon the ground that his improvement consists in the substitution of glass for metal . . . and that the change only in the composition of the matter to be used is not such a discovery to entitle him to letters patent for it. . . ." Encloses "Two letters from Wm Blagrove, the first to Dr. Thornton, and the last to the Secretary [above, November 13, 1826]. . . ." N. DNA, RG60, Letters Recd. from State Dept. (MR14). Endorsed on verso: "Answered June 4, 1827"; no answer has been found.

From DUTEE J. PEARCE, Newport (Rhode Island). Solicits for Joseph Howard, of Providence, a passport and, "as a personal favor to" himself, a letter of introduction to (James) Brown. Adds: "Referring to general matters, I can only say the work goes bravely on, and every thing looks well." Requests, in a postscript, that Clay give Howard a letter of introduction to (Albert) Gallatin, "as Mr. H has one to Mr. Brown from the Hon Mr. [William] Hunter." ALS. DNA, RG59, Misc. Letters (M129, R65).

Howard, now age 24, was the son of Thomas Howard, Jr., a Providence merchant, and was apparently traveling in connection with the family business. He died on the island of Madeira a decade later.

From James Brown

My dear Sir,   Paris May 12. 1827

Your letter of the 27 March reached me yesterday and I perceive from it a confirmation of what I had already gathered from the papers, that you had passed through a stormy and rather unprofitable Session, and that the opposition had increased, if not in numbers at least in violence. It is but too much to be apprehended that the public mind will continue to be greatly diverted until the result of the next Presidential election shall have been proclaimed, and indeed I fear much longer. I had no idea however until I learned the fact from your letter, that party spirit was carried so far as to interrupt the harmony of society and loosen the bonds of Kindred associations. Colo Benton[1] has at every former session written me very long and friendly letters, and I have answered them in that spirit of Kindness which I really feel for him. I have no answer to my last and although I can hardly believe it, he may possibly have transferred to me a small portion of the unfriendly dispositions he feels to the Administration. Now all this is really very unjust, and I may say foolish also, because the next wind of party or accidental turn of affairs may approximate his opinions to those of the very persons from whom he thus gratuitously withdraws himself, and force him to one of those things which to me are very awkward and embarrassing, a reconciliation with those from whom we have no reason for estranging ourselves. As to V. B—[2] he is in his element when he is engaged in political intrigue and he is not disconcerted by changing friends and systems half a dozen of times in as many years. The next Session will be still more stormy than the last provided the question of who shall fill the second and other offices on the coming in of a New President can be harmoniously disposed of and the race be run by the President and Jackson only. This may [be] a matter of some difficulty but may be arranged by the combined Operations of a Mother Caucus with Branches in the several States. New York so long practised in this system may furnish information and a Model;[3] Pennsylvania has been initiated[4] and Virginia and the Northern States long as they have boasted of their open and frank manner of conducting elections and much as they have inveighed against the Caucus system may be modeled by the hand of the great political Juggler of the North.[5] I have had no letters from New Orleans but I have been told that the Jackson interest has increased there since the last election. I regret the loss of a majority in the Senate because I fear it will have an unfavorable influence on our foreign associations. The Colonial question has been a fortune to the opponents of the Administration. Without that their topics of complaint would have few [sic] and insignificant. It is hardly probable that the new Ministry in England will relax their policy on that question. Here we have nothing at the moment to expect. Our questions are not of very great magnitude but still they are such as touch the interests of an influential class whose combined clamors may have some weight in a moment of high party excitement. In many of our former negociations when the circumstances of the times favored our claims we succeeded beyond our own expectations. This has created a belief in the strength of our diplomacy which may disappoint those who do not attend to the different circumstances in which Europe and the United States now find themselves.

Mrs. B. has received your letter and will carefully execute her sisters commissions. To do this well, to get the best articles and at the most moderate prices will require some weeks. I am happy Mrs. Clays taste for dress is reviving as it implies an increase of health and spirits. You may assure her that the sum is large enough to supply her with many handsome things, and her sisters taste is approved even at Paris where they certainly dress in better style than in any other part of the world.

I have been mortified to learn from your letter that Mrs. Price[6] had only received ninety eight dollars out of the three hundred which I requested you to obtain for her annually by your drafts on my nephew John B Humphreys.[7] Mrs. Price wrote in Sept. to her sister[8] acknowledging the receipt of the ninety eight dollars and stated that Mr Smith[9] was about writing for the ballance [sic] of the three hundred which she expected to receive in a short time. If Humphreys has not yet paid I pray you to draw on him for the two hundred and two dollars, the ballance for last year and pay to Mrs. Price and her mother the four hundred and fifty which I expend for Mrs. Clay as an increased allowance for the present year commencing in March last. I have further to request my dear Sir, that with all that candor which I know belongs to your character, you will inform me, whether more is wanting to make the existence of these two relatives so dear to me comfortable, because if I know myself I can safely say that I could not spend a happy day if I thought they were subjected to any privations or wants which God has given me the means or power to relieve. I am told I have made a pretty large crop last year and although my Nephew by his skill, perseverance, and good management for the last fifteen years has become the proprietor of one third of it yet I have still something to aid any of my relatives, particularly my own and wifes sisters, to *spare* and it will giv[e] me a heartfelt gratification to make that application of it

We have still a great many Americans at Paris and I hope they are satisfied with the reception we give them. I do not know what report they make of us on returning but I know that if they are not satisfied it is not likely they will find in any one who may be sent to replace me more reasons to be pleased. It is acknowledged by my Colleagues and indeed by all Parisians who frequent our house that we keep up our rank in our mode of entertaining in House style of furniture and the number of entertainments. My standing at Court and with the King[10] & Ministers is I believe as good as that of any of my Predecessors and if we obtain nothing I have every reason to be assured that our failure arises from no dislike to the negociator. We have some imprudent *friends* with whom we must associate but we do all we can to prevent them from committing themselves and their friends. With all the dislike which the persons in power feel for *some persons* who they know equally dislike them, they do me the justice to say that whilst I openly defend my own Country and its interests I do not middle [sic] in the intrigues of *this*. I am surprized [sic] how some persons have got along here without a knowledge of the character of the people or even of the language. They have left behind them some impressions of no very favorable kind. My Predecessor[11] was generally very highly respected and I think he deserved it. Others with equally good intentions were not as well qualified for the place. I am told he is very anxious to leave England and indeed I am not surprized at it as living is very expensive and society on a very disagreeable footing for one accustomed to the free and easy style of our country.

Mr Hemphill and his brother in law Mr Coleman[12] have been with us for some days and will set out to morrow for Italy. We were as usual very attentive to him and he appears pleased with Paris. We expect Mrs & Mr Derby[13] (God help us to please them) and Mr & Mrs. Russell,[14] by the first arrivals, who are said to be discreet and easily satisfied. Mr Cooper[15] is here and I am much pleased with him. He goes into good society and enjoys the esteem of all who know him.

The National Guard has been disbanded some of them having when under arms at a review in presence of the King cried out à bas les Ministres! à bas les les [sic] Jesuites! [16]

I presume this letter will find you in Kentucky where you will wit-

ness the struggles of the approaching election. I hope you will preserve your sang froid because a calm state of mind is essential to the preservation of your health   Your friend & Obedt Servant   J. B.
Hon. Henry Clay.

ALS. DLC-HC (DNA, M212, R2).   [1] Thomas H. Benton.
[2] Martin Van Buren.   [3] Cf. above, Cocks to Clay, September 26, 1826; Porter to Clay, December 24, 1826; Hammond to Clay, January 28, 1827, and note.   [4] Cf. above, Moore to Clay, February 10, 1827; Mifflin to Clay, April 4, 1827.   [5] Cf. above, Shaw to Clay, September 10, 1826; Kent to Clay, January 26, 1827; Mallory to Clay, April 4, 1827.
[6] The comment in reference to Susannah Price presumably had been made in the letter to Mrs. Brown.   [7] Cf. above, Brown to Clay, April 1, 1825.   [8] Mrs. Brown.
[9] Thomas Smith. Cf. above, Scott to Clay, November 21, 1826, note.   [10] Charles X.
[11] Albert Gallatin.   [12] Joseph Hemphill; Edward Coleman. The latter, a wealthy and politically prominent resident of Lancaster, Pennsylvania, had served in the Pennsylvania Legislature as either Representative or Senator since 1818.   [13] Not identified.
[14] Possibly Mr. and Mrs. Jonathan Russell.   [15] James Fenimore Cooper.
[16] For the significance of the events on April 29 and 30, in the mounting French political crisis, see *Annual Register, 1827*, pp. 221–26.

From George Graham

Henry Clay Esqr. Secy. of State   12. May 1827
Sir,   Your Son[1] delivered to me the papers relative to your lands purchased at Vincennes,[2] & you have enclosed the copy of a letter addressed by me to the Register of the Land Office.[3]

You have also enclosed a Relinquishment for the tracts you propose to relinquish which you will sign & forward to the Register whenever you make the deposit, as pointed out in my letter[4]— I am &c.

G. G.

Copy. DNA, RG49, Misc. Letters Sent, vol. 19, p. 101.
[1] Probably Theodore Wythe Clay.   [2] Cf. above, III, 134; IV, 553.   [3] John Badollet, a native of Switzerland, had come to the United States around 1780 and settled near his friend Albert Gallatin in western Pennsylvania. Through the latter's influence Badollet had been appointed register of lands at Vincennes in 1804 and held the office until 1836.   [4] Neither the relinquishment nor the letter has been found.

INSTRUCTIONS AND DISPATCHES   May 12, 1827

To ALBERT GALLATIN, no. 28. States that his "despatch No. 61 [above, March 19, 1827] . . . together with the correspondence . . . [with] Lord Melville . . . have been received and submitted to the President." Adds: "He [the President] approves of the acknowledgments which you made to Lord Melville of the benevolent and meritorious conduct of Lieutenant [Joseph Rawlins] Thomas, and requests that you will, also, express to the British Government his sensibility, in behalf of the American Government to the important and perilous service rendered, on that trying occasion, by that officer, in whose future welfare this Government will ever feel a particular interest. It is by such signal and successful daring, both in its direct and collateral effect, that the cause of humanity is subserved, and men are made justly to appreciate the value of their being members of a common family, however they may happen to be divided into different nations." LS. NHi-Gallatin Papers (MR14). ALI draft, in DLC-HC (DNA, M212, R8).
Thomas' name does not appear on promotion lists for the ensuing decade.

From JAMES BROWN, Paris, no. 67. Reports that (Vincent) Rumpff has been appointed by the Hanse Towns "to proceed to the United States, for the purpose of negociating a treaty of commerce and navigation. . . ." Encloses copies of Rumpff's letter informing him "officially" of the appointment and of his reply to it. LS. DNA, RG59, Dip. Disp., France, vol. 23 (M34, R26). Received June 29. Cf. above, Hughes to Clay, March 9, 1827; Gallatin to Clay, April 3, May 3, 1827; Cuthbert to Clay, May 5, 1827.

From WILLIAM PHILLIPS, Omoa (Honduras). Summarizes the controversy over recognition by the Central American Government of his diplomatic and consular character; describes the adverse effects of a new Central American tariff upon trade with the United States; outlines his difficulties in obtaining passage from Omoa to return home; inventories the property of the Legation and describes his arrangements for storing and safeguarding it; and reports victory in March by Guatemala over the invaders from San Salvador (cf. above, Phillips to Clay, March [2], 22, 1827). ALS. DNA, RG59, Disp. Disp., Central America, vol. 1 (M219, R2). Received June 27.

From J[OEL] R. POINSETT, Mexico, no. 89. Transmits a translation of an act of the Mexican Congress, "depriving all native born Spaniards of their employments, military, civil, and ecclesiastical"; notes that it "is a consequence of the late conspiracy (cf. above, Sergeant to Clay, January 26, 1827, note). Reports reception by the Government of "advices" from Captain (David) Porter "that an expedition is fitting out in Colombia for the invasion of either Cuba or Puerto Rico; that an embargo is laid in all the Atlantic ports of that Republic; that the Captain General of Puerto Rico [Don Miguel de la Torre] has asked assistance of General [Francisco Dionisio] Vives, and that Admiral [Angel] Laborde, with all his squadron, has been called off to Havana." Observes that (Simón) Bolívar might attempt such an expedition, and, although "his means are certainly inadequate" to invade Cuba, "emigrants from that Island . . . may have prevailed upon him to make a rash attempt," in which case their only hope of success lies in "arming the negroes." Adds that Colombia has means "better suited" to invade Puerto Rico, and, while such an expedition should be "deprecated. . . . [it] is not of such importance to the United States." Concludes that Mexico "will view any such attempts on the part of Colombia with great jealousy." LS. DNA, RG59, Dip. Disp., Mexico, vol. 3 (M97, R4). Published in Manning (arr.), *Diplomatic Correspondence . . . Latin-American Nations*, III, 1659–60. Received July 2.

Torre, who had risen to the rank of brigadier general by 1816, had commanded the Spanish forces in Tierra Firme following the Spanish defeat at Carabobo in 1821 (see above, II, 505). In 1823 he was named civil and military governor of Puerto Rico and held that office until shortly before his death in 1837. He was accorded the title Count of Torrepando in 1836.

From WILLIAM B. ROCHESTER, Mexico City. Acknowledges receipt of Clay's dispatch of March 10, forwarding his instructions and commission as Chargé d'Affaires from the United States to the Republic of Central America; discusses his proposed route for travelling to Guatemala City; reports his intention to draw upon the State Department in favor of his brother, Thomas H. Rochester, for his outfit. LS. DNA, RG59, Dip. Disp., Central America, vol. 1 (M219, R2). Received July 2.

Thomas Hart Rochester, the sixth child of Nathaniel Rochester, had settled at the falls of the Genesee River in 1815, had removed for a brief sojourn in St. Louis, but had returned shortly. He became mayor of Rochester in 1838 and subsequently sat as a judge in that city.

MISCELLANEOUS LETTERS   May 12, 1827

From SPENCER PETTIS, "Department of State. City of Jefferson—Missouri." Recalls Clay's promise (dated October 9, 1826, but omitted by the editors as routine, in response to Pettis' letter of September 17, 1826 [not found]) to forward "such Laws, State Papers & Public Documents of the United States as could be obtained and which were not already placed in this Office"; suggests that the documents could be sent with "the Acts of the last session of Congress"; and asserts that this is a matter "of much moment" to the State and its officers. ALS. DNA, RG59, Misc. Letters (M179, R65).

To Peter B. Porter

My dear Sir   Washn. 13h. May 1827

I received your obliging favor of the first instant, and thank you for the very clear and comprehensive account which it conveys of political affairs in New York. It is a little remarkable that at the very time when, at Black Rock, you were predicting the course of the N. Advocate it should at New York have fulfilled your prediction. The use which it has been pleased to make of my name afforded me no particular satisfaction. I should certainly promptly repel any serious attempt to employ it as a Candidate for the presidency. Such an attempt could not fail to produce mischief. The conduct of the Jackson party has left me no wish but for Mr. Adams's re-election. By their calumnies they have completely identified us; and I hope every friend I have will see in Mr. Adams re-election my interests as much involved, as if by [*sic*] name were directly held up for the Presidency.

I have received a very encouraging letter within a day or two past from Mr. Speaker Taylor.[1] Among other interesting facts he states that Chief Justice Savage has avowed himself explicitly in favor of Mr. Adams.

I have not yet seen the prospectus for the new paper to be edited by Mr. Leake.[2]

V. Buren passed through the City from the South[3] yesterday. I saw him but had no political conversation with him. He invited me very civilly to visit New York, but said he hoped that he would be able to put all matters there right before I came.

I regretted to hear of the crevasse in your pier. I hope it is not of a nature to occasion very great expence [*sic*] or to oblige you to abandon your great enterprize.

I wish, if I can, to set out for K. in about a fortnight. Mrs. Clay does not accompany me, but remains in the City. Should I be able to visit Black rock, I will hereafter inform you of the time.

Mrs. Clay joins me in respectful compliments to Mrs. Porter. And I remain Cordially Your friend   H CLAY
Genl. P. B. Porter.

ALS. NBuHi.   1 Above, May 7, 1827.
2 Isaac Q. Leake. Cf. above, Porter to Clay, January 3, 1827, note; Hammond to Clay, April
11, 1827.   3 Van Buren had initiated his rapprochement with Southern political
leaders in December, 1826, when he had spent the Christmas holidays at "Ravensworth,"
the estate of William Henry Fitzhugh, in Fairfax County, Virginia, conferring there with
John C. Calhoun. To reassure the latter of the feasibility of bringing the former supporters of William H. Crawford into the alliance, Van Buren had written to Thomas
Ritchie, January 13, 1827, sketching his proposal for "*reorganization of the Old Republican Party.*" By April the Richmond editor had agreed to support Jackson's candidacy. Following the adjournment of Congress Van Buren had set out on a tour through
Virginia and the Carolinas to Georgia. His first major stop had been at Charleston, and
from there he had taken ship to Savannah for a visit with Crawford. He had returned
overland by way of Columbia, South Carolina. From Washington, he departed for Albany on April 13. Remini, *Martin Van Buren*, 129–46 *passim*. William Henry Fitzhugh,
born in Virginia in 1792 and graduated from Princeton in 1808, was a vice president of
the American Colonization Society and an essayist in its support. He died at Cambridge,
Maryland, in 1830.

From James Thomas

Dear Sir   New York 13. May 1827

Things continue to develope [*sic*] themselves favorably in relation to
the administration,   the sup. court of the State is now in session in
this City, which brings together many leading and intelligent men
from various parts,   with some of these I have held several political
conversations, the result of which is, and I have conversed with men of
all sides as well as *no side* that the state is not only with the adm. but
daily prepon[dera]ting in favor of it, and so will continue in support
of its measures until (although we may *choose* electors by Districts)
that, [*sic*] Jackson dont have a vote,   for myself I am very much inclined to the opinion that, when the time comes he won't have a vote
in the College,—   with regard to the Govr.¹ he would wish to be
thought as *standing alone* (and the time seems to be fast approximating
when he will) but his *body guard* are occasionally out for Jackson,
tho' his most influential and intelligent frds. are generally decidedly
and loudly for the adm. and many more [wo]uld be so, provided
*Charles King and the American*² [wou]ld give them a chance,   but it
would seem from his frequent and too often personal attacks that
no[ne] but a particular class of individuals should go, or belong to
the adm. party,   I wish he was more moderate,   I have a good deal
of trouble to answer questions touching the Course he pursues, and I
sometimes find myself under the necessity of speaking against him.³—
I was told since my return by one of the *High Minded*⁴ a term applicable here to 40. Gentlemen formerly *feds.* who came round some years
since to the support of Mr. Munro's⁵ adm. that, an adm. paper was in
the course of 8. days to be set up at Albany, I. Q. Leake the Ed.⁶— Mr.
Leake is a small fish and by some considered a poor creature it would
be much better to take an established press—and this I trust might be
done,— I saw Mr. Hammond⁷ the other day, formerly a member in
Congress from the Western part of this State, now resident at Albany,

many years a politician and the frd. of Mr. Clinton, but latterly he has been much inclined to like the *Strong* side best, he says it is perfectly clear to him that this State at the next election will go for Mr. Adams. I asked him what Mr. Clintons Course was to be, he shook his head and with a significant look, expressed himself to say, he did not know what the devil he was about, I have been many years acquainted with Hammond and he knows me [. . .][8] to speak as he thinks,— Judge Betts[9] has been holdi[ng] a term of the District Court, I can tell b[etter] what I think of him as a Lawyer after I hear the Jury Charged in *My Case*.[10]— Seth Hunt Esqr. now of Alabama left here a few days since for the North, I shall know some things when he returns that may be worth communicating, if so, and he returns in season I'll write you before you leave for the West— In the mean time I remain as always Yr frd. & Obedient Sevt.   JAMES THOMAS
Hon Henry Clay

ALS. DLC-HC (DNA, M212, R2). Addressed as *"Private"* on cover. MS stained and slightly torn.
    [1] DeWitt Clinton.   [2] *New York American.*   [3] Cf. below, Rochester to Clay, September 17, 1827, and note.   [4] Cf. above, III, 421.   [5] James Monroe.   [6] Cf. above, Porter to Clay, January 3, 1827, note; May 1, 1827.   [7] Jabez D. Hammond.
    [8] Probably two words obliterated.   [9] Samuel R. Betts.   [10] The verdict was rendered at the August Term of the United States District Court, when Thomas was cleared of charges that he owed the Government $5,202 on his accounts as an acting District Paymaster in the United States Army. Instead, the jury awarded him a certificate stating that the Government owed him, as defendant, $6,060. *New York American,* September 19, 1827. Cf. also, *House Docs.,* 17 Cong., 1 Sess., no. 32, p. 105. By act of March 3, 1831, Congress directed the accounting officers of the Treasury Department to allow Thomas credit for justified expenditures up to the amount for which he was held liable. 6 *U. S. Stat.,* 468. He later returned to Congress for relief according to the terms of the judicial decision, and by act of July 2, 1836 (6 *U. S. Stat.,* 679–80), Congress so stipulated.

INSTRUCTIONS AND DISPATCHES   May 13, 1827

From ALBERT GALLATIN, London, no. 75. Notes that he has "received no intimation on the subject of a renewal of . . . conferences" with (William) Huskisson, who "is now able to attend Parliament," and that he has "written . . . a private note to Mr. [George] Canning, to remind him of the desire he had expressed that no unnecessary delay should take place." Calls attention to Huskisson's view, expressed "in the parliamentary debate of Tuesday last, on the motion relative to the presumed distress of the shipping interest," that it was "a subject of congratulation, that the United States had not availed themselves of the offer of Great Britain, by which they might have participated in the Colonial trade." Expresses uncertainty whether Huskisson "alluded to the act of Parliament of 1822, or to that of 1825" (cf. above, III, 729n; Gallatin to Clay, August 19, 1826). Acknowledges receipt of Clay's "dispatches Nos 25 & 26, dated 6th. & 11th April," but adds that number 24 (above, March 29, 1827) has not arrived. ALS. DNA, RG59, Dip. Disp., Great Britain, vol. 34 (M30, R30). Copy, in NHi-Gallatin Papers, vol. 14, pp. 127–28 (MR20). Received June 22.
    On the distress of the British shipowners, cf. above, Gallatin to Clay, May 4, 1827; Editorial Article, May 9, 1827. The debate to which Gallatin refers had occurred on Monday, May 7, not Tuesday, and had concerned a resolution to appoint a "Committee of Inquiry into the state of the Shipping Interest." The pro-

posal had been rejected in action of May 8. In the course of his remarks, Huskisson had noted the failure of the United States to comply with the conditions for admission to the colonial trade and commented: "This was their choice in declining our terms; but, since they were declined, I cannot say that, with a view to the interests of our navigation, I regret the course which the policy of the American government has forced us to adopt." Hansard (comp.), *Parliamentary Debates,* New Series, XVII, col. 647; G. B. House of Commons, *Journal,* vol. 82 (1826–1827), p. 437.

To Robert Monroe Harrison

Robert Monroe Harrison Esq.

Sir,   Department of State Washington 14th May 1827.

The President is desirous to avail the public of your services on a tour of observation and inquiry, with a view to the collection of information which it may be important to the Government to possess. The confidence he has in your zeal, ability and experience acquired by a long residency in the West Indies, as well as his wish to afford you a proof of the *estimate he has* made of your former services, has induced him to designate you for this Agency, and to direct me to invite your acceptance of it.

The service to which I refer is that of visiting the respective British West India Islands, and by personal examination and inquiry ascertaining the effect upon them of the existing state of the Laws of the United States and Great Britain, by which all direct intercourse between those islands *and* the United States, in the Vessels of the two Countries, is interdicted.[1] The particular points to which your attention, if you enter on this Service, should be directed, are

1.   The kind of supplies which are required by the wants of the respective Islands from Foreign Countries.

2.   How far those supplies are or can be drawn from the United Kingdom, or from Continental Europe, from the British-North American possessions, or from portions of the American Continent other than the territories of the United States.

3.   Whether the Islands do now, or can produce, within themselves, any, and what, portion of those supplies which they have heretofore received, or might hereafter introduce, if there were an unrestrained intercourse with foreign countries from abroad.

4.   Whether the United States supply them with any objects of consumption cheaper and better than they can obtain from any other Country.

5.   Whether the United States supply them with any articles, and what, which they cannot procure from any other Country.

6.   What has been the effect of the Act of Parliament of July, 1825, upon the Trade between those Islands and the Continent of Europe?

7.   Is that trade carried on chiefly by British Navigation, or partly,

and in what degree by the navigation of the Continental Powers, and by British navigation?

8. What are the comparative advantages and disadvantages to the Islands in procuring their supplies from Europe and from the United States?

9. Supposing the continuation of such interdict, would the direct trade be carried on by the Vessels of Denmark or any, and what, third Power?

10. Supposing the direct intercourse between the Islands and the United States to remain interdicted to the Vessels of the two Countries, would the trade be carried on circuitously? and what are the disadvantages to the circuitous compared to the direct intercourse?

11. Are the Inhabitants of the Islands disposed to acquiesce in that interdict or are they likely to remonstrate against it?

12. Are there any taxes, duties, or charges, in the trade between the Islands and Continental Europe, to which Foreign vessels are subject, and from which British Vessels are exempt?

13. And, generally, any information to show the degree of dependence of the British West Indies on the United States for articles of necessary consumption; The ability of those Islands to find substitutes in other countries, or within themselves, for the objects of commerce obtained from the United States, and the probability of a continuation of the existing British interdict of the Vessels of the United States from the West India ports; and also, whether it is likely that the circuitous trade between the United States and the British West Indies, will be tolerated or prohibited.

Should you undertake the Agency thus offered to your acceptance, you will regard it as confidential and to be executed without noise or parade. There is nothing in its character contrary to public law. But to insure it the desired success it is deemed best that a knowledge of it should be confined to yourself and to this Government.

It is our wish that you should visit all the British West India Islands with which the United States have heretofore had any commercial intercourse. The order in which you shall do it is left to your knowledge of their positions and to your discretion.

I transmit you herewith, a copy of the Presidents Proclamation, issued on the 17th. day of March last, reviving the operation of the Acts of Congress of 1818, and 1820, of which copies are also transmitted. The precise time when you may set out on this tour of observation is left to your discretion, but it is expected to be in the course of the summer or Fall. As the effect of the Proclamation of the President has but recently commenced in the Islands, by delaying your departure for a month or two, you may be able more distinctly to understand what that effect is or likely may be. Perhaps it will be best for you to report your observations, and the result of your inquiries, from each

Island, as you visit them in succession, should you be able to avail yourself of opportunities for that purpose. We should be glad to acquire as much information as may be practicable during the next winter and Spring, so as to be used in the course of the next Session of Congress, which will be a long one.

The compensation which will be allowed you for this service will be at the rate of $4500. per annum, inclusive of all charges and expenses which are to be borne by yourself; and this compensation will commence from the day of your departure from your residence on the service, of which you will notify the Department. You may draw on this Department for the above compensation as it becomes due; and on your setting out on the voyage, you are authorized to draw in advance for $500, to be charged in account.

It is presumable that you may in a period of about eight months visit the different British Islands, at least the most important of them, and procure the desired information. During your absence from the Consulate you may commit the duties of it to such agent as you may designate. I am respectfully, Your most obedt. Servt.   H. CLAY.

Copy. DNA, RG59, Cons. Instr., vol. 2, pp. 423–27 (M78, R2).
[1] Cf. above, Gallatin to Clay, August 19, 1826, and note; Clay to Vaughan, March 17, 1827, and note.

To John W. Taylor

Dear Sir   Washn. 14h. May 1827.
I have duly recd. your favor of the 7h. instant. The prospect which it presents of political affairs in New York is very encouraging. Genl. Porter, since his return to Black rock, has written me a long and satisfactory letter on the same subject.[1] He tells me that the friends of the Administration had made effective arrangements for the establishment of a new press at Albany, to be conducted by Mr. Leake,[2] and designed to neutralize the efforts of the Argus. Such a measure, I should think, was judicious, and I hope it will not fail.

From Kentucky I learn, that, although there will be a warm struggle there in some districts, the result upon the whole will be favorable; and that we shall lose none of our strength, derived from that State, in the next H. of R.[3] The current is still running strongly with us in Pennsylvania.[4]

I will thank you to make my congratulations to Col. Young on the recent interesting event which has happened to him; and say that I shall be glad, after the Honey moon is over, to hear from him.

I am trying to get off to Kentucky in about two weeks. Yr's with great regard   H CLAY
The Honble John W. Taylor.

ALS. NHi   [1] Above, May 1, 1827.
[2] Cf. above, Porter to Clay, January 3, 1827, note.   [3] Cf. above, Clay to Taylor, April

4, 1827, and note; Johnson to Clay, April 8, 1827; Clay to Johnston, April 17, 1827; Clay to Hammond, April 21, 1827.   4 Cf. above, Clay to Brown, March 27, 1827, note.

To Daniel Webster

My dear Sir   (Private & Confidential)   Washington 14h. May 1827.

I duly received your favor of the 7h. instant and on the interesting subject of it I have conversed with the President.

I had previously written to Mr E.[1] that the pro's and con's on the question of your translation from the House to the Senate were so nearly balanced that I thought you might safely pursue the bent of your own inclination. The public interests require you in the House, and you are wanted in the Senate. So far as your personal interests are to be advanced, I incline to think you had better remain where you are. If your place could be supplied in the House, then I should say go to the Senate. Oakley or Sergeant might enable the Administration to get along in the popular branch, but the course of the one and the election of the other is uncertain.[2] If neither of them come to our aid, we *possibly* may do without them, should you be compelled to accept a place in the Senate. The administration loses much directly as well as morally for the want of such abilities as you would carry into that body—directly by the array of talents on the one side (which it must be owned the Opposition there exhibits) without an adequate counterpoise on the other; which has the effect of disheartening friendly Senators—morally by the extraneous effect on the Country of this unequal contest.

What the President would be glad to see is, that Mr Lincoln should come in place of Mr Mills,[3] as the state of this latter gentleman's health does not admit of his longer serving; and if, as is said to be probable, Mr. Silsbee[4] should resign, in consequence of his being elected Governor, or from any other cause, that you, after the ensuing Session, should take his place. But if Governor Lincoln cannot be prevailed upon to accept a seat in the Senate, then the President decidedly prefers your coming in at the next Session, as Mr. Mills's successor[5]—

From McLane I have heard directly nothing. I have hoped that, if Delaware should send to the House of R. next fall a friend to the Administration,[6] and no very adverse events should occur elsewhere, Mr. McL. might see that it was his interest to adhere to his principles, and disentangleate [sic] himself from his new associates; and I had thought that the probability of his adopting a correct course might be influenced by the consideration of his being the leader of one party, instead of being eclipsed in the ranks of the other. But all this is speculation; and, should you go into the Senate, he may still find that his future advancement lies rather on the side of working with than against you. Unless I am much deceived Delaware will send to the H. of R a friend to the administration.

The recent changes in the British Ministry are very great,[7] and they must have been the result of a radical difference of opinion on some important subject. We have no explanation of them from Mr. Gallatin, from whom I have received no letter subsequent to the resignations. The most obvious cause is that of the Irish Catholics. On the last day of March Mr. Huskisson[8] remained too unwell to resume the negotiation with Mr. Gallatin. He was trying to settle a preliminary point, respecting our North Eastern boundary with Mr. Addington,[9] but was able to make very little progress. I should think that the new ministerial arrangements would occasion some further delay. I see therefore but little prospect of Mr. Gallatin's speedily coming home.

I have very little late political news. The meeting in Balto. was all that we could have desired it to be.[10] The progress of correct thinking in Pennsa. continues to be encouraging. And in New York our friends are as confident of success as they need be. They are about to establish a new paper to be edited by Mr. Leake,[11] formerly senior editor of the Argus, and I hope they will not fail in that object. It is much wanted.

From K. my friends write me in good spirits. We shall have however warm work there growing out of our "Free bridge" question, alias the Relief system.[12]

I have written a short letter to Silsbee[13] communicating the preceding views in regard to the Senate.

I am making efforts to get off to Kentucky in about a fortnight. Unless there should be some unexpected occurrances [sic] I think I shall go about that time. I am Cordially Your friend & ob. Servt
D. Webster Esq.   H. CLAY

P.S.   Your late Speech at Faneuil Hall was all that it should have been.[14] It presented the true condition of the existing state of things, and pointed out clearly the only correct line of policy. In spite of all the carpers, it will have good effect—   H. C.

ALS. DLC-Daniel Webster Papers (DNA, M212, R22).
1 Edward Everett—see above, May 2, 1827.   2 On the political affiliations of Thomas Jackson Oakley, see above, Clay to Webster, April 20, 1827, note; on the election of John Sergeant, see above, Sergeant to Clay, September 28, 1826, note.   3 Levi Lincoln; Elijah Hunt Mills. Of Mills' "inability to take an active part in the debates of the Senate," Adams had written on February 10, 1827: "it is a great misfortune to me." Memoirs, VII, 224.   4 Nathaniel Silsbee.   5 Cf. above, Webster to Clay, June 8, 1826, note.   6 Kensey Johns, Jr., of New Castle, was elected Representative from Delaware following Louis McLane's resignation to enter the Senate (see above, Clay to Brown, March 27, 1827, note). Graduated from Princeton in 1810, Johns had begun the practice of law at New Castle in 1813. He served in Congress from 1827 to 1831 but did not seek re-election after the second term. From 1832 until his death in 1857 he held appointment as chancellor of Delaware. Politically he was identified as a Federalist; he was elected as a supporter of the Adams administration.   7 Cf. above, Gallatin to Clay, February 22, 1827, note.   8 William Huskisson. Cf. below, Gallatin to Clay, May 22, 1827.   9 Henry U. Addington. Cf. above, Gallatin to Clay, March 21, 1827.
10 Cf. above, Clay to Everett, May 2, 1827, note.   11 Isaac Q. Leake. Cf. above, Porter to Clay, January 3, 1827, note.   12 Cf. above, III, 902n; Webster to Clay, May 7, 1827, note.   13 Nathaniel Silsbee. The letter has not been found.   14 Addressing a public meeting at Faneuil Hall, Boston, on April 20, Webster had supported resolutions which called for unity among those who approved "the general course of the

government. . . , without reference to former party, in the election of members to the [Massachusetts] legislature, favourable to that government, and inclined to give it a sincere and hearty support." He noted that, since James Monroe had been "the last of the Revolutionary patriots" to hold the Presidency, it was natural that there might be division over his successor. But, he continued, the ultimate choice had been made in the House of Representatives; and, if the nation were not to sink into "perpetual strife and dissension," citizens should support "the will of the whole as constitutionally expressed. . . ." "Certainly he thought the present President was entitled to a somewhat kinder treatment than that which he had received." The President, Webster emphasized, was a citizen of Massachusetts, a State which "had manifested no exclusive regard to those who belonged to herself." While he "wished to speak with great respect of Virginia," he noted that she "had never once given her vote for the office of President, to any but a native of her own State." If, then, it was agreed that "the administration ought to be supported against personal or groundless opposition," Webster urged a union of the old parties, whose "sentiments and objects were now acknowledged to be the same." The issues of division had ended with the peace of 1815. The President had assumed office with a commitment to sacrifice "party feeling" and "party prejudice," a sentiment which, Webster acknowledged, would have been shared by either of the other candidates. The administration asked to be supported on its own principles. Those who had elected Adams to office must be united and firm if they were to sustain and maintain him "in all just measures." *Boston Daily Advertiser*, April 23, 1827. The address was published in Webster, *Writings and Speeches* (National edn.), XII, 21–34.

From Duncan McArthur

Fruit hill May 14th 1827

Dear Sir, Your favour of the 3rd. instant[1] was duly [re]cieved [sic]. I beg you to accept my thanks for your [ki]nd attention to the Cutts[2] business.— Enclosed you will receive a draft[3] from the Bank of Chillicothe on a Philadelphia Bank for fifty dollars, payable to your order. When the Deed of conveyance from Mr. & Mrs. Cutts to my son Allan C. McArthur, shall be returned to you, duly executed hav[e the good-] ness to endorse the Draft to them, and trans[mit] the Deed to me.

The Deed from Mr. Van Zandt & wife,[4] I return to them for correction. My son has written to them upon the subject.

I received a letter from Doctr. Watkins upon the subject of the Nashville letter, which was published in the Fayetteville Observer,[5] which I will answer,[6] but can only say, that I heard nothing of the alledged proposition, by your friends to those of Genl. Jackson.

When it was ascertained, that you would not be one of the three, which would be returned to the House,[7] it was well Known, that my next choice was Mr. Crawford.[8] Had it not been for his ill health, and there being no reasonable probility [sic] of his election, in his then situation, several of the Ohio delegation, besides my self, would have supported him. And it is with regret, that I now see his friends so much divided, and many of them uniting with a party, who, when he was a candidate for the presidency, persecuted him with such unge[ner]ous & unmerited violence.[9] It was then evident to all, that the election did then lie, between Mr. Adams & Genl. Jackson. The course which the latter gentleman and his f[rien]ds had pursued, with regard to Internal Improvements, and the Tariff, and indeed, their opposition to every measure which we thought of interest to the country generally and particularly to the West, put it out of the power of the Ohio delegation to support the [election] of Genl. Jackson. Upon the other hand, it was [e]vident, that for the support of those measures, our own reliance must be upon the friends of Mr. Adams and the liberallity [sic] of the East. Another and more serious consideration with us, was, the qualifications of those gentlemen who, were by the Constitution, placed upon an equal footing before the House.

So far as I was acquainted with the Sentiments of your friends, I do not believe, that they could have been prevailed upon to have supported the election of Genl. Jackson upon any conditions whatever, much less that of excluding Mr. Adams from the appointment of Secretary of State.

The language held by some of the friends of the Genl. before the election, *was*, "that the friends of Mr. Clay *dare not* vote for any man but General Jackson." This was so often repeated in a menacing manner, that it would seem, that they considered us not at liberty to think or act, according to our own judgment, upon any condition whatever.
your sincere friend   DUNCAN MC.ARTHUR
Honble. Henry Clay

ALS. DLC-HC (DNA, M212, R2). Endorsed on verso by Clay: "Privat[e bu]siness—Fayetteville letter of Gen. Jackson." MS. torn.
[1] Not found.   [2] Mr. and Mrs. Charles Cutts. Cf. above, McArthur to Clay, April 18, 1827.   [3] Not found.   [4] Possibly Elisha and Margaret Van Zandt, of Fleming County, Kentucky.   [5] See above, Report of Interview, *ca.* April 15, 1827, note. Tobias Watkins' letter has not been found. Its major point of inquiry was quoted in the reply of Francis Johnson, May 23, 1827: "If such a proposition were ever made by the friends of Mr. Clay to those of General Jackson, it may have been known to many persons, and the fact, therefore, may be ascertained. May I ask the favor of you to inform me whether you know or believe any such proposition was ever made? Or whether conditions, of any sort, were made by the friends of Mr. Clay to any person, on a compliance with which their vote was made to depend?" Published as supportive documentation with Clay's *Address . . . to the Public*, below, December 29, 1827, Appendix, 44–45.   [6] McArthur to Watkins, May 18, 1827, published *ibid.*, Appendix, 31–32.   [7] Cf. above, Clay to Easton, December 18, 1824.   [8] William H. Crawford.   [9] Cf. above, III, 427.

From Robert Troup

Dear Sir,   New York 14 May 1827
I acknowlege [sic] the receipt of your obliging letter of the 10th inst.[1]

The Trustees, for the proprietors of the Indian reservations, have received letters from the War department, couched in very civil terms, and fully complying with their wishes.[2]

For this favorable result, I am well persuaded the Trustees are much indebted to the exercise of your good offices with the President; and the debt is certainly increased by your condescending to exercise those offices out of the sphere of your particular department.

I pray you therefore to accept my grateful acknowlegemts for your

kindness together with my sincere wishes for your happiness in private, and for your prosperity in public life. With the most respectful consideration I remain Dear Sir, Your obliged Servt
The Honble Henry Clay Esqr   ROB: TROUP

ALS. DLC-HC (DNA, M212, R2).   1 Not found.
2 Cf. above, Nourse to Clay, April 26, 1827.

INSTRUCTIONS AND DISPATCHES   May 14, 1827

From HEMAN ALLEN, Santiago de Chile, no. 53. Notes that "the late President [Ramón de] Freire has again tendered his resignation" and Vice President (Francisco Antonio) Pinto (Diaz) has succeeded him; describes Pinto as one of Chile's "most liberal and enlightened sons," one who "has always manifested great respect and friendship for the government and people of the United States"; mentions Pinto's determination to send a Minister to the United States; and states that (José) Miguel del Solar has been appointed Minister of Foreign Relations. Reports that the southern Indians "have generally joined the standard of Chile, and that the war in that quarter is nearly at an end" (cf. above, Allen to Clay, February 17, 1827). Outlines his attempts to secure passage home and offers his services should "any situation . . . again" arise in which he could be useful. ALS. DNA, RG59, Dip. Disp., Chile, vol. 2 (M-T2, R2). Received October 25. Extract published in Manning (arr.), *Diplomatic Correspondence . . . Latin-American Nations*, II, 1117–18.
    Solar, born in Santiago and ordained a priest at the age of 20, had become a sympathizer of the Chilean revolt as early as 1810, while on his first charge. In 1823 he was president of the provincial Junta of Coquimbo, and in 1826 a deputy of the national Congress from that province. During Pinto's administration, Solar was offered portfolios as Minister of the Interior and of Foreign Affairs and later that of Justice, but he did not accept them. In 1829 he was named archbishop of Santiago, and for a time he was on the faculty of theology of the University of Chile. He served as a member of the Council of State in 1836 and as a Senator from 1837 until his death in 1847.

From WILLIAM SHALER, Port Mahon. Notes that "relations with the Regency of Algiers" have "continued upon the most friendly footing" and, "as the Algerines rise in arrogance toward other powers, they appear to increase their respect for the United States." Reports that, through the "kindness & humanity" of Commodore (John) Rodgers, who learned of "the dangerous state of" his (Shaler's) health, he has been brought to Port Mahon (cf. above, Hodgson to Clay, May 2, 1827), where he has received medical attention, and that he has left (William B.) Hodgson in charge of the consulate. Applies for "permission to return to the United States next year on the same terms on which leave to do so was before given. . . , leaving Mr. Hodgson in charge of the Consulate until it be otherwise disposed of." ALS. DNA, RG59, Cons. Disp., Algiers, vol. 11 (M23, R-T13). Received August 2; a duplicate, LS, was received July 20. Endorsed by Clay at botton of last page: "An ansr. to be prepared communicating the President's regret on account of the indisposition of Mr. Shaler and giving him the requested permission to return to the U. S. H C."
    The answer, dated August 13, 1827, and signed by Clay, conformed to the endorsement, with the stipulations that Shaler's return was to be made "without detriment to the public service" and that Shaler's agent "attend to the affairs of the Consulate without additional charge to the public." Copy, in DNA, RG59, Cons. Instr., vol. 2, pp. 439–40 (M78, R2).

Shaler had been given a year's leave of absence under similar stipulations by letter from John Quincy Adams, July 18, 1820. Copy, in *Ibid.*, pp. 210–11. In subsequently announcing his intention to leave his post for reasons of health (see above, Shaler to Clay, April 12, 1825), Shaler had referred to "the verbal permission" given him by Adams to do so whenever he "might have occasion. . . , provided that . . . the public service were not injured by it. . . ."

From BEAUFORT T. WATTS, Bogotá, no. 28. Acknowledges receipt of Clay's note of January 8; states that he has "carefully examined such of the evidence as" Joseph Karrick has submitted to him "in support of his claim" and has concluded "that our Government has nothing to do with it, and that it would be improper . . . to interpose with this government in its support." Explains the case and encloses a copy of a letter to Karrick presenting his views. ALS. DNA, RG59, Dip. Disp., Colombia, vol. 4 (M-T33, R4).

From BEAUFORT T. WATTS, Bogotá, no. 29. Reports that on May 12 the Congress took up "the subject of the President's [Simón Bolívar's] resignation" (cf. above, Watts to Clay, March 14, 1827); and, after sharp debate, "A motion . . . happily prevailed in both Houses" calling on "him to appear . . . and take the Oath of Office, for the next term, for which he has been elected." Blames confusion arising out of "the unsettled state of the Republic" for injustices to some United States citizens residing there. Transmits copies of his correspondence with the Minister of Foreign Affairs (José M. Restrepo) in the cases of George W. Johnston (cf. above, Marks to Clay, March 17, 1827), Robert K. Travers, and N(athaniel) B(rown) Palmer of the brig *Bogotá*. Observes "In justice to the Government . . . that at all times" he finds "it disposed to remedy the errors, and correct the defects which unavoidably befals [*sic*] it." ALS. DNA, RG59, Dip. Disp., Colombia, vol. 4 (M-T33, R4). Extract published in Manning (arr.), *Diplomatic Correspondence . . . Latin-American Nations*, II, 1312. Received July 11.

The enclosures reveal that, upon receipt of Watts' notes, Restrepo had recommended that "justice . . . be rendered to" Johnston; had requested from the Secretary of the Treasury [José María del Castillo y Rada] an explanation of two levies, of $50 each, imposed on Travers, a commission merchant (not further identified) at Mompós, who had been imprisoned for refusing to pay; and had requested "the Secretary of the Navy" (probably Felipe Estevez) to order payment to Palmer, who had brought 42 seamen "from New York to Carthagena for Capt. Pioli" and had been paid by a bill of exchange, later "protested for non acceptance."

Nathaniel Brown Palmer, born in Stonington, Connecticut, was renowned for South Sea explorations. He had discovered the mainland of Antarctica in 1820 and the South Orkney Islands in 1822. The areas known as Palmer Land and the Palmer Peninsula were named in his honor. He became a packet captain in 1834 on the New York to New Orleans run and subsequently on the line to Liverpool. Still later he commanded clipper ships between China and New York. He retired about 1850 and died in 1877.

Castillo y Rada, born in Cartagena and early identified with the revolt from Spain, had been named President of Colombia as a member of the triumvirate which ruled at the declaration of independence. Following the union of Colombia with Venezuela and the elevation of Bolívar to the Presidency, Castillo y Rada became Vice President. He served as Minister of the Treasury, under Bolívar, from 1823 to 1828. He also served as a mediator during the months of political instability which culminated in the death of Bolívar in 1830 but subsequently retired from politics.

Estevez, born in La Guaira and active in the revolt since 1811, had been associated with Bolívar as early as 1813. Estevez served as head of the Department of the Navy from 1821 to 1827 and held military rank as a major general.

The brig *Bogotá* has not been further identified.

From David B. Ogden

Dear Sir   [*ca.* May 15, 1827]

Among the most efficient Friends of the administration in this city, and perhaps the most useful one, I consider Mr. Henry Eckford. You know from the Public papers the proceedings which have been had against him, upon a charge of a conspiracy to defraud, which [c]harge all who know him believe to be wholly unfounded.[1] In consequence of the charge however having been made Mr. Eckford has of course considered himself as under a cloud and he has therefore in a great measure retired from public view and has taken very little part in public measures— The District Attorney[2] of the State who is conducting the prosecution against Mr. E. has I am credibly informed expressed an opinion within a few days that he is convinced that the charge against Mr. E. is unfounded. and I have no doubt is anxious to abandon it if he can— He is now afraid if he should discontinue the prosecution that he will be attacked for it in the News paper called the American.[3] and his fears prevent his doing what he wishes— This I have no doubt is the present state of the facts [as] to Mr. Maxwell the District attorney— I this morning had a casual conversation with Eckford, who thre[w] out an observation of this kind, that he thought the time had now arrived when you could be of great use to him, without explaining to me in what manner.

Now as he is a very important man in this city, it has suggested itself to me, whether it might not be useful for you to write him a short letter expressing your regard for him; and wishing to know whether it was in your power to render him any service[4]—

Such a letter will depend upon it, prove in future of no small consequence to you, and can possibly do no harm. He will then of course answer what he thinks you can do for him, an[d] you can then either comply with his wish, or if he wishes you to do any thing improper, you will of course decline it, in a manner not offensive to him—

Excuse me for this suggestion and believe me with great respect Your's &c   DAVID B OGDEN
The honbl. H. Clay

ALS. DLC-HC (DNA, M212, R3). Undated; on the dating, an approximation by the editors, cf. below, Eckford to Clay, May 29, 1827. Cover endorsed by Ogden: "*Private.*" Margins obscured.
[1] See above, Porter to Clay, May 1, 1827, note.   [2] Hugh Maxwell.   [3] *New York American.*   [4] Cf. below, Eckford to Clay, May 29, 1827.

INSTRUCTIONS AND DISPATCHES   May 15, 1827

To ALBERT GALLATIN, no. 29. Transmits a copy of the document requested by
Gallatin in his "Letter No. 63, of the 29th. of March last. . . ." Asks him to procure,
if possible, and transmit to the State Department "a copy of the Report of the
Lords of the Committee of the Privy Council of Trade and Plantations, dated
28th. of January, 1791; republished in 1807 by the Ship owners in London, with
an appendix; and which is particularly referred to in the Statistical Annals of the
United States, by Seybert, p. 294." LS. NHi-Gallatin Papers (MR14). Copy, in
DNA, RG59, Dip. Instr., vol. 11 (M77, R6); L draft, in Daniel Brent's hand, in
DLC-HC (DNA, M212, R8).

A few copies of the report had been published for members of the British
Cabinet, and subsequently recalled, under the title, *A Report of the Committee
of Privy Council, Appointed for All Matters Relating to Trade and Foreign Plan-
tations, on the Commerce and Navigation between His Majesty's Dominions, and
the Territories Belonging to the United States of America, 28th January, 1791*
([London], 1791). The printing by order of the Society of Ship-Owners of Great
Britain had been included in *Collection of Interesting and Important Reports and
Papers on the Navigation of Great Britain, Ireland, and the British Colonies in the
West Indies and America* . . . ([London], 1807).

Adam Seybert, born in Philadelphia and graduated in medicine from the University of Pennsylvania in 1793, had entered practice in 1797 and also operated
an apothecary shop. His extensive studies in chemistry and mineralogy had brought
him membership in the American Philosophical Society. He had been a member
of Congress from 1809 to 1815 and again from 1817 to 1819, where his interest in
public revenue led him to collect and publish the *Statistical Annals . . . of the
United States* (New York, 1818). Seybert had traveled in Europe from 1819 to
1824 and settled in Paris, where he had died in 1825.

From J[OHN] J[AMES] APPLETON, Stockholm, no. 17. Encloses a copy of a treaty of
commerce and navigation recently concluded between Sweden and Norway, on
the one hand, and Russia, on the other (cf. above, Appleton to Clay, January 29,
February 10, 1827); notes that, although an appointment with the Count de Wetterstedt on the following day will enable him (Appleton) to state the views of his
Government, he does not think progress can be made in negotiations until the
Count returns from a brief visit "he intends paying, in a few days, . . . to his estate
in the Country. . . ." ALS. DNA, RG59, Dip. Disp., Sweden and Norway, vol. 5
(M45, R-T6). Published in *American State Papers, Foreign Relations*, VI, 722–23.

From WILLIAM TUDOR, Lima, no. 67. Reports revolt at Guayaquil, "against the
insolent agents of the Dictatorship" (cf. above, Wheelwright to Clay, April 19,
1827) and the demand of the people that (José de) "LaMar . . . place himself at
the head of affairs," to which he consented while warning that "he must shortly
leave them." Notes receipt of a letter from Lamar, who expects soon to set out for
Lima to attend the Congress. States that, of 800 troops being sent by (Antonio
José de) Sucre from Arica to Panama, 520 on a Dutch ship mutinied and landed
at Guayaquil while the remainder, on a Peruvian vessel, were expected to "take
the same course" and that these men, plus 140 who sailed from Lima under (José
María) Cordoba, "will be a reinforcement to the *liberating* troops. . . ." Asserts
that "The whole scheme of Bolivar seems dissolving, like snow under a tropical
sun." Observes that "The Congress had their first preparatory meeting today"
and that "Gen. Santa Cruz aided by [Manuel Lorenzo de] Vidaurre is exerting
every kind of intrigu[e] & corruption" to become President, while his opponents
strive to prevent action until the arrival of Lamar. States that he has seen (James)
Cooley, just arrived from Callao. Quotes, in a postscript, from a letter received

from (Joel R.) Poinsett, "that the Congress of Tacubaya will open its session as soon as a Minister from Peru makes his appearance," and adds: "It will probably be some time before such Minister is named, & I should think he will hardly reach Tacubaya before the close of the year. . . ." ALS. DNA, RG59, Cons. Disp., Lima, vol. 1 (M154, R1). Received August 31.

MISCELLANEOUS LETTERS   May 15, 1827

From P[ETER] BOUSQUET, Philadelphia. Encloses "extracts of letters received" from an American merchant trading in Maracaibo, complaining of injuries inflicted upon American trading interests there by the "unjust and arbitrary acts of President [Simón] Bolivar and of the local authorities." ALS. DNA, RG59, Misc. Letters (M179, R65).

The enclosures complain that, because of a decree issued by Bolívar on December 20, 1826, the Government has suspended payments on all contracts made with it prior to that date, that the Government refuses to receive "their *vales*" as payment for duties, and that United States citizens in the area are not receiving adequate representation or protection. One unidentified correspondent requests that the United States send a vessel of war into the area to enhance the protection and influence of its citizens.

Bousquet was himself a Philadelphia merchant.

Bolívar's regulations in late December, 1826, and January, 1827, were issued at Caracas and applied only to Venezuela. For a discussion of their political import, see David Bushnell, *The Santander Regime in Gran Colombia* (Newark, Del., 1954), 345–46. The specific decree cited above has not been found. For the effect of the policy on American merchants, cf. above, Marks to Clay, March 17, 1827, note.

From MATHEW CAREY, Philadelphia. Transmits "three copies of a Set of papers, on the prevailing errors respecting British policy, in which" he thinks he has "proved that all the pretensions to a liberal System have been illusory, & intended to force [other] nations to relax those restrictions which threaten by Slow, but certain degrees, to reduce the exorbitant power & influence of that nation within limits better proportioned than at present to her extent & population." ALS. DNA, RG59, Misc. Letters (M179, R65).

Under the pseudonym "Colbert" three letters on the British trade laws, identified as "Third Series," no. 1, dated April 17; no. 2, "Second Edition," dated May 3; and no. 3, "Third Edition," dated May 23, were published in the Washington *Daily National Intelligencer*, April 23, May 8, 28, 1827, respectively. On Carey's identification with this series, cf. below, Clay to Carey, May 19, 1827. On the revision of British trade legislation and Carey's earlier publication on this subject, see above, Clay to Carey, June 6, 1825, note.

From P[ETER] P. F. DEGRAND, Philadelphia. Declares that all that his friend, Peter Bousquet, "may state deserves great consideration. . . ." ALS. DNA, RG59, Misc. Letters (M179, R65).

DIPLOMATIC NOTES   May 16, 1827

From the BARON DE MAREUIL, New York. Calls attention "de nouveau" (cf. above, Clay to Brown, May 9, 1825), before leaving for Europe (cf. above, Brown to Clay, November 29, 1826; Clay to Porter, April 18, 1827), to the increasing disadvantages suffered by the French flag in competition with the American in navigation and commerce under the Convention of 1822. Suggests that, in order to justify the French Government in continuing "indéfiniment un état de choses si évidement préjudiciable aux interets maritimes du Pays," advantages be given French commerce in the form of reduced duties on wine, brandy, and silks, while at the same time the tariff be increased on silks from countries beyond the Cape of Good Hope. Notes that his Government would be willing to reciprocate in some manner, as for example, by reducing the duty "sur les cotons longue Soie [sic] provenant de leur Territoire." ALS. DNA, RG59, Notes from French Legation, vol. 10 (M53, R-T9).

INSTRUCTIONS AND DISPATCHES   May 16, 1827

From JAMES OMBROSI, Florence. Reports intelligence received from Constantinople of successive conferences between the Reis Effendi (Saida) and Russian Minister (Alexander Ribeaupierre), the English Minister (Stratford Canning), and the French Minister (Armand-Charles, Count Guilleminot), although "a veil of mystery covers every thing"; adds that "The Turks do not think seriously of what is happening out of the Capital." ALS. DNA, RG59, Cons. Disp., Florence, vol. 1 (M-T204, R1). Received *ca.* September 10; "Duplicate" received August 21.

Saida, who was replaced as Minister of Foreign Affairs in 1828, has not been further identified.

From J[OEL] R. POINSETT, Mexico, no. 90. Reports intelligence from Guatemala that President (Manuel José) Arce has marched upon San Salvador, the center of rebellion, and is expected to enter the city without opposition; that several of the rebel chiefs have surrendered to the general government; and that the departments of Sonsonate and Santa Ana "have seceded from the self-erected government of San Salvador." Concludes that "there is some prospect of peace being restored and order re-established in Central-America." Forwards translation of an official note received by the Guatemalan Minister in Mexico (José María del Barrio), reporting the success of Arce's movements. LS. DNA, RG59, Dip. Disp., Mexico, vol. 31 (M97, R4). Received July 2.

Barrio, not further identified, retained his post in Mexico into the mid-1830's.

From Macdonald and Ridgely

Sir   Baltimore May 17th. 1827

We yesterday recd. from Messrs. Forsyth & Dobbin of Wheeling 2 boxes of Bacon which have been forwarded by Stinchcombs wagon[1] and we herewith transmit a Bill of Lading.[2] The charges paid here (as p mem: at foot) will be added by Stinchcomb to his bill of Freight.

very respy Sir yr ob Serts   MACDONALD & RIDGELY

[Endorsement]

Carriage from Wheeling 2 Boxes, Wt p Rect 1112.175c [sic]— 19″46
drayage to wag Off: 19¢—Coopge. 25c.   Postage—wag rct   63
                                  recd of Mr J Stinchcomb   20:09

ALS. DLC-TJC (DNA, M212, R13).
[1] John Stinchcomb was proprietor of a Baltimore wagon office.   [2] The enclosure, signed by E. Shahan (not further identified) for Stinchcomb, acknowledges receipt of the

boxes, weighing, respectively, 532 and 570 pounds (total, 1102 pounds), and agrees to deliver them "at the Wagon Offices   Washington, D C.," Clay to pay "carriage @ ¾ Per pound."

INSTRUCTIONS AND DISPATCHES   May 17, 1827

From ROBERT MONROE HARRISON, Antigua. Acknowledges receipt of Clay's "despatch of the 9th ult" and of his "commission as Consul for the Island of St. Bartholomew. . . ." Expresses fear, however, "that unless the President insists on the right of our Government to have a Consul" there, "his benificient [*sic*] view as regards" Harrison "will be frustrated through chicanery and fraudulent measures of Individuals at the head of the Provisional Government of that Island. . . ." Encloses a "letter from one of the members of the Royal Council" to show "the frivolous reasons which has [*sic*] been alledged [*sic*] for refusing to recognize" him. Refers to the difficulties he has experienced over the past seven years in trying to support his family and asserts that his "situation at present is the most uncomfortable immaginable [*sic*]. . . ." Repeats an earlier request (included in the letter above, January 5, 1826) that Clay "get the Baron Stackelberg to address a letter to the provisional Government of St. Barts" regarding his recognition. ALS. DNA, RG59, Cons. Disp., Antigua, vol. 1 (M-T327, R1). Received June 15.

On June 16, 1827, Daniel Brent informed Harrison that his letter had been received after Clay's departure (for Kentucky—see below, Clay to Erwin, June 3, 1827). Brent commented that the difficulties anticipated concerning Harrison's "recognition as Consul at St. Bartholomew's . . . would not probably be removed by the Letter" requested but that there was "every reason to expect" the problem would be resolved "through the intervention of Mr. [John J.] Appleton." Copy, in DNA, RG59, Cons. Instr., vol. 2, pp. 431–32 (M78, R2). Cf. above, Clay to Stackelberg, April 23, 1827.

MISCELLANEOUS LETTERS   May 17, 1827

From D[EBORAH] S. WARNIER, Edenton (North Carolina). Requests that "Enclosed letters" be forwarded to James Brown; states that "It relates to indemnity for Spoiliations [*sic*] committed on the property of . . . [her] Family during the revolution in St. Domingo . . ." (cf. above, Clay to Brown, June 13, 1826; Brown to Clay, August 10, 1826; Warnier to Clay, October 23, 1826; also Brown to Warnier, May 12, July 11, November 6, 1827, in DNA, RG84, France). ALS. DNA, RG59, Misc. Letters (M179, R65). Endorsed on cover by Clay: "Mr. B. will inform the Lady that her letter shall be sent." Daniel Brent wrote accordingly to Mrs. Warnier on May 25, 1827, in DNA, RG59, Dom. Letters, vol. 21, p. 544 (M40, R19).

From Daniel Webster

My Dear Sir   Private & confidential   Boston May 18. 1827
    Notwithstanding the insanity of some men, of all parties, & especially of some Federalists, by means of which this City will not be fully represented in the Legislature;[1] yet the returns shew that the House will be very strong, both in numbers & talents. No opposition man will be in either Branch, from Boston; nor hardly one from any

other parts of the State. All the large towns have acted on the Union principles; & the House will therefore be mainly composed of friends of the Administration, of both parties. The folly of a part of the Federalists, here, is mortifying enough; but perhaps has done no great mischief, on the general scale.

Since I wrote you last, I am strengthened in the conviction that I ought not to be a candidate for the Senate.[2] The more I think of it, the more fully I am persuaded of the propriety of remaining where I am. I hope an effort will be made, *from all quarters*, to persuade Govr. Lincoln[3] to take the situation.

A *pamphlet*, for the especial benefit of Pennsylvania, will make it's [*sic*] appearance from Philadelphia, soon. It will be printed in English & German, and circulated as widely as may be.[4] I think it will do good. It's leading object is to present, by way of contrast, the politics of the Administration, & those of the opposition. As manifestations of the leading principles of the former, the Presidents first message,[5] the doctrines of your Speech,[6] &c &c are fully exhibited; & as sure [g]uides to a knowledge of the latter, Mr Giles Resolutions[7] & other things equally authentic, are prominently put forth. I think the work will hit the sentiments of Pennsylvania, Ohio, & Western Va.

Copies will of course be sent to you.—

I have seen a good deal of the New Hampshire People, in the course of the Spring. A warm battle is to be fought, in that State; & the sooner our friends understand it so, the better. For two years, the attempt has been to put down Mr Hill,[8] by the *organization of the Republican party*. It has not been done, & cannot be done. Although four fifths of the people, in that party, are friends of Mr Adams, yet Hill, himself, & a few other cunning & indefatigable *Caucus* men, control the movements, & arrange the organization, of the *party*. Mr Hill himself would not, probably, have been elected Senator, if the *Journal*[9] would have consented to nominate *any other* candidate, Federal or Republican; but it would not, as I have understood; becau[se] Mr Hill was the *regular Caucus Candidate*.

The only way is to appeal directly to the *People*[.] The great popular current is with the Govt there, as well as elsewhere; but half the benefit is not derived, which ought to be derived, from this favorable course of opinion. However the Journal seems to be more in earnest, at last; & I think it likely the ensuing session of the Legislature may produce some new movements. The Federalists in the Legislatur[e] a third in number, or more, & three thirds in talents & ability, are entirely willing to do any thing they can do, without personal dishonor; but they will not, & cannot, & ought not, to act with Mr Adams' Republican friends, until these last will cease to keep any terms with Mr Hill, & his party. I believe Mr Bell[10] will see the state things are in, when he goes to Concord, I trust his fidelity & good sense to give them a proper direction.

I go to New York next week, where I shall see Mr Oakley.[11] Before leaving the City, will write you, unless I shall previously learn that you have gone west.—

I have today a very encouraging letter from Washington Co. Tenn.— Yours always truly & faithfully   DANL. WEBSTER
Hon H. Clay

ALS. DLC-HC (DNA, M212, R2).
   [1] Because Bostonians had supported five separate tickets at their election on May 10 for the General Court, where a majority vote was requisite, only eight candidates had received the necessary support. A second election, on May 24, was also unsuccessful. Consequently the city seated only eight of the 30 allotted representatives. Some Federalist partisans, resentful of the pleas for "Union" or coalition with administration supporters (see above, Clay to Webster, May 14, 1827, note), had met separately on May 8 to draw up their own list of candidates and, while asserting their friendship for the measures of the administration, "so far as they are just and wise," called for backing of the Federalist ticket by party members "not yet ready to be transferred, bargained, assigned, and sold by a few individuals. . . ." *Niles' Weekly Register*, XXXII (May 19, 26, 1827), 198–99, 210; Washington *Daily National Journal*, May 17, 30, 1827.   [2] Cf. above, Clay to Everett, April 5 (note), May 2, 1827; Webster to Clay, May 7, 1827; Clay to Webster, May 14, 1827.   [3] Levi Lincoln.   [4] Cf. above, Clay to Everett, April 5, 1827; Clay to Webster, April 14, 1827.   [5] Cf. above, Clay to Stuart, December 1, 1825, note.
   [6] Probably that at Lewisburg, Virginia (above, August 30, 1826).   [7] Cf. above, Brooke to Clay, January 31, 1827.   [8] Isaac Hill, who in March, 1827, had been elected to the State Senate. Washington *United States Telegraph*, March 24, 1827.   [9] Concord *New Hampshire Journal*. Cf. above, Morril to Clay, September 18, 1826; Bell to Clay, December 9, 1826. See also, Cole, *Jacksonian Democracy in New Hampshire*, 63–64.
   [10] Samuel Bell. Cf. above, Webster to Clay, April 14, 1827; Clay to Webster, April 20, 1827.   [11] Thomas Jackson Oakley.

MISCELLANEOUS LETTERS   May 18, 1827

From [ROBERT] POTTER, "Mrs. Myers's [Salome Myer], 7th. Street." States that he is in Washington, wishes an interview with Clay, and "has been disappointed in the expectation, of finding on his arrival here, a letter of introduction from a gentleman of distinction in No. Carolina, a friend of Mr. Clay, and is thus reduced to the awkward alternative of announcing himself. . . ." AN. DLC-HC (DNA, M212, R2).

To Nicholas Biddle

Washington 19h. May 1827.

I thank you, my dear Sir, for your highly interesting discourse on Jefferson. If you did not wish to seduce me from my official duties, you should not have placed on my "table" such a temptation   Faithfully & respectfy Yrs   H CLAY
Nicholas Biddle Esqr

ALS. The Biddle Family Papers, Andalusia, Pennsylvania. Cf. above, Biddle to Clay, May 8, 1827.

To Mathew Carey

[Washington, May 19, 1827]

I thank you for the numbers of "Colbert,"[1] which you did me the favour to send me. They tear off the veil of liberality, which Great Britain has recently assumed with so little grace.

Excerpt. Mathew Carey, *Autobiography* (*Research Classics*, no. 1; Brooklyn, New York, 1942), 130.
[1] Cf. above, Carey to Clay, May 15, 1827.

From Josiah S. Johnston

Dear Sir   May 19th. 1827.

I have remained about 40 days in N. orleans, where my time has been agreeably spent—amidst the society of my friends personal & political—indulging in the hospitalities & amusements of the place— My stay was unexpectedly prolonged by the necessary attention to my affairs,—in which I have been very fortunate— Two years ago I thought I was rich enough to devote myself to the public but the fall of Cotton,[1] the depreciation of property & the increased expenses had made an alarming change in my situation—& seemed to point out the necessity of retiring—to repair damages—but I believe I have replaced myself in such a manner as to enable me to remain where I am & avoid the loss of property which I anticipated.— It was painful to think of changing my Course of life—but it was a sacrifize [*sic*] I was prepared to make, if my Credit or Independence had required it—personal credit is intimately Connected with private character—& Independence is indispensable to the purity & dignity of public life— Pecuniary independence is essential to personal & political independence—which is only another name for personal & political integrity— I flatter myself I have restored my affairs, so as to pursue my public course— preserve my credit—& my Independence— I have avoided the humiliation of borrowing—& the mortification of being in debt—& my property is safe—

My residence here has enabled me to see all the principal men of the State & to ascertain the public Opinion with regard to the Presidential Election—& without descending to particulars I can assure you the state is perfectly safe.[2]

I have no doubt there is a great majority of both populations—of all the men of Talents & property—of all the men in office & of the professions favorable to the Admt.— I would instance the Governor,[3] a majority of the Legislature—the Supreme Court the District Judges —Parish Judges—Lawyers & most men of influence—

Thibideau [*sic*] is a Candidate for Governor[4] is good for one fourth of the votes of the State is favorable to the admt. & opposed to Genl.

J. Genl. Thomas in Florida[5] the same— Bouligny is making a Tour through the State & will be a Candidate[6]

I shall see most of the principal men in the State myself.— We shall form the Electoral Ticket—*reform* the press—& organize—before I leave the State— Genl. Jackson has accepted the invitation to visit N. orleans—but the invitation which was a foolish & weak Compliance on the part of the Legislature, is intended to distinguish between the military chief & the Statesman—

They were surprized into it— The proposition was was [*sic*] made to invite him to the Celebration of the 8th. Jany[7]— & although a majority of both Houses are opposed to his Election—they did not feel at liberty to vote against the invitation for this particular object— They did not wish to evince any mark of personal respect to the Hero— or gratitude for his service— But if they believe there is in this invitation any indication of public feeling towards him or that his presence will produce any effect they are greatly mistaken— No appropriation is or will be made for the expense—& his friends will incur the responsibility of providing for him   When that proposition is introduced into the Legislature they will find them prepared to resist.[8]— Davison[9] seems to be his principal Correspondent in this State—& it is said he is to spend the summer with him.

The friends of the Admt are Cool & moderate but firm & fixed in their purpose & Cannot be shaken— They Constitute the Talent, wealth & influence of the State— Public opinion is in every free Country the aggregate of property & Talent—

I have not received your Speeches[10]— They should be sent to this State. I have just read Cannings Electionering [*sic*] Speeches[11]— They are by no means worthy his fame.—& I think you will remark a great meagreness [*sic*] in them— His Sentences are long & loose—& without much point or force of thought— Now & then a splendid sentence—

In reading Everetts America[12]—I am exceedingly struck with his remarks on Religion—& the necessary Connection between church & State— I refer you to pages 195.6 &c— The opinions Expressed do not belong to this Country nor to this Government— They may suit the Ideas of the Legitimates & the meridian of madrid— They may Correspond with the views of the French Court—& the established doctrine at St. James—but they are at variance with all our opinions as well as the opinions of all the Liberals throughout the world— I am unable to account for his extraordinary opinions—or the necessity of bringing that subject into discussion   Such opinions will do no honor to the American Embassador [*sic*]—

I am on board the Planter[13] & shall reach Alexandria[14] tomorrow— I hope to be able to see Washington by the 10h. July— With great regard   J. S. JOHNSTON

[On verso]   I have been solicited to become a Candidate for the office of Governor—& have recd. assurances that some of the Candidates will withdraw— But so far I have resisted— I think I have a good excuse— & that I shall be able to get off— If my means enable me to live at Washington— I should esteem a place in the Senate as the highest in this or any Country to which I could aspire—One that is entirely equal to my ambition or my hopes—

    The Boat shakes so much that I find it difficult to write—

ALS. DLC-TJC (DNA, M212, R13).

1 After prolonged depression from 1819 to the spring of 1824, a flurry of speculative activity had sent cotton prices as high as 29.5 cents a pound in June, 1825. Production had accordingly expanded. The following autumn, at harvest season, the market collapsed. "For eleven weeks cotton buying in the New Orleans market was 'almost totally suspended.' Price quotations dropped steadily from 15 cents in November to 9.5 cents by the following July; and throughout the year 1826–27 declined steadily until they reached 8.8 cents." The market situation improved slightly in 1827, but cotton at New Orleans brought less than ten cents a pound for most of the remaining period until 1832. Lewis Cecil Gray, *History of Agriculture in the Southern United States to 1860* (2 vols., Washington, 1933) , II, 698. Cf. also, above, Maury to Clay, April 18, July 30, 1825; Clay to Erwin, August 30, 1825; Brown to Clay, January 30, 1826; Clay to Brown, February 21, 1826.   2 Cf. above, Clay to Brown, March 27, 1827, note.   3 Henry Johnson.

4 Henry S. Thibodaux died October 24, 1827. Johnson was succeeded by Pierre Auguste Charles Derbigny, who, as an Adams supporter polled 1592 votes to a combined vote of 930 for two Jacksonites. *Niles' Weekly Register*, XXXIV (August 2, 1828), 361.

5 Probably Philemon Thomas; but cf. above, Thomas to Clay, April 30, 1825, note.

6 Charles Joseph Dominique Bouligny's term in the United States Senate did not expire until March 4, 1829, when he was replaced by the Jacksonian, Edward Livingston.

7 Cf. above, Mifflin to Clay, April 4, 1827, note.   8 Hezekiah Niles reported "much discordance in the accounts of the reception and treatment of gen. Jackson, in his visit to New Orleans." *Niles' Weekly Register*, XXXIII (February 9, 1828), 92–93. The Louisiana Legislature by act of February 11, 1828, finally appropriated $10,000 "for the reception and entertainment of general Jackson" but accompanied the funding with a statement that Jackson had been invited *"solely* in compliment to the *military* services rendered" by the General "and not for *political* purposes, or in any way to express an opinion on the approaching election of president." *Ibid.*, XXXIV (March 7, 1828), 20.

9 Possibly Thomas Green Davidson, a lawyer of Greensburg, Louisiana, who was at this time only 22 years of age. Davidson had become actively involved in the Jackson movement the previous year. He was a member of the Louisiana House of Representatives from 1833 to 1846, of the United States Congress from 1855 to 1861, and again of the State legislature from 1874 to 1878, in 1880, and in 1883, when he died.   10 See above, Sparks to Clay, April 9, 1827, note.   11 George Canning's *Speeches . . . during the Election in Liverpool* had been published for elections in 1818, 1820, and some earlier campaigns. A much more comprehensive collection of his *Speeches . . . Delivered on Public Occasions in Liverpool . . .* had been published at Liverpool in 1825. To which volume Johnston refers is not clear; no American publication of Canning's speeches has been found.   12 Alexander H. Everett, *America: or, A General Survey of the Several Powers of the Western Continent, with Conjectures on Their Future Prospects . . . By a Citizen of the United States . . .* (Philadelphia, 1827). In the discussion to which Johnston refers, Everett argued that "the theory of the natural separation of church and state" had "no foundation whatever in truth," that both church and state were committed to upholding "Morality, or natural law, . . . the basis of all legislation," and that "The unity, or in other words the existence of government, requires that in every community the controlling power in religion should be held and exercised by the same persons who also hold and exercise the controlling power in politics." He strongly suggested that the Latin American states, which had a tradition of the "powerful intervention of the religious principle, in the machinery of government," ought to have preserved this force for stability "as the mainspring and principal basis of the new political institutions." He argued that in the United States only agreement that "the sovereign power in religion as well as politics resides in the people" preserved a unity of church and state in theory and avoided "the practical inconvenience of collision between the two lawgiving powers. . . ." (p. 199).   13 A sidewheel steam vessel built at Cincinnati in 1826. She continued in service out of her home port of New Orleans until 1835.   14 Louisiana.

From Philip S. Markley

Dear Sir   Phila May 19th 1827.

I returned from my excursion to Harrisburg, and some of the middle Counties on Tuesday last[1]— The result of my political efforts have [sic] exceeded my expectations, and I have every reason to feel assured that my visit will be attended with some good in support of the administration of the Genl Govt— That there is an evident change of public sentiment in Penna in favour of Mr Adams can no longer be doubted and if the changes should continue to increase as they have within the last two months, the "Key stone of the federal arch" will be among the most prominent of the States in the union sustaining the administration

The Governor[2] is decided and firm,—he openly avows himself the friend of the administration, and in conversation with the people that call on him he makes it a point to express himself decidedly friendly to the re-election of Mr Adams— The Penn-Intelligencer[3] will be out in a decisive tone in a few days, and also the German Democratic paper printed at Harrisburg[4] which will be followed by other German papers printed in the adjacent Counties— we have considered it most adviseable [sic] to defer the calling of public meetings until towards our Fall elections— The most important matter to be effected at this time is to get out the presses throughout the state in favour of the administration— we made arrangements at Harrisburg to have the administration toasted as far as practicable in the different counties on the 4th of July— all the movements in Penna in relation to the reelection of Mr Adams in order to produce the desired effect, must be identified with the Democracy of the state— to malgamate [sic] with the federalist [sic] in our Meetings would be fatal,[5] although I believe we shall receive a respectable support from the federal party— The friends of Jackson will fix their Electoral ticket on the 8th of Jany having in view the *hero* regardless of any devotion to principles or measures— The Democratic Republicans friendly to the administrations of the general & state Govts will fix their Electoral ticket on the 4th of March at Harrisburg being the usual time of holding of all our republican Conventions in the State

Our friends at Harrisburg expects [sic] a visit from you during the summer or Fall. When do you expect to leave Washington for Kentucky[6]— I should be glad to hear from you after your arrival at Lexington in relation to the political prospects of that state   very truly your friend   PHP. S. MARKLEY
Honble H Clay

ALS. DLC-HC (DNA, M212, R2).
[1] Cf. above, Markley to Clay, April 28, 1827.   [2] John A. Shulze.   [3] Harrisburg *Pennsylvania Intelligencer.*   [4] Probably the *Harrisburger Morgenröthe Zeitung,* a weekly established in 1799 and continued until 1840.   [5] Cf. Remini, *Election of*

Andrew Jackson, 144, which emphasizes the importance of fusion by administration supporters with the Federalists for success in Pennsylvania.   6 See below, Clay to Erwin,
June 3, 1827.

MISCELLANEOUS LETTERS   May 19, 1827

From JOHN C. WEEMS, Oakland Mills (Maryland). Acknowledges receipt of Clay's
letter of May 4 with enclosures and expresses thanks to him and through him to
the President, for the attention given to his request. ALS. DNA, RG59, Misc.
Letters (M179, R65).

To John Sloane

Dear Sir   Washn. 20 May 1827.
    I recd. this day your favor of the 10h. inst.[1] Dr. Watkins[2] has ad-
dressed a letter, similar to that which you have recd., to all the members of the Western delegation, and to one or two others, who voted
for Mr Adams. The intention is thus to collect a mass of evidence, to
be used or not hereafter, according to contingencies, and as may be
thought best. He has already received several answers to his circular,
and I hope he will get them from all the gentlemen he has addressed.
I think it was most proper that you should have limited, as you have
done, your response to a defense of the Fayetteville attack;[3] but I do
not know if it may not be advisable to give, in another letter to Dr.
Watkins, an account of the overtures made to you through the friends
of Genl. J. which of course would not be used but upon full consideration, nor without your permission.[4]
    I did not care much, on my own account, about the Fayetteville af-
fair; but (supposing the letter to be genuine) as the calumny is now
fixed upon the Genl, I thought it quite fair to press the matter; and
the idea of the agency of a friend, instead of appearing in it myself,
seemed most expedient. The Genl. will be silent, or will come out
with his proofs. In the former case, we may, at a suitable time, present
to the public the mass of negative proof which is proposed to be collected. In the latter, we shall be prepared with repulsive evidence.
    If the fact could be established that members of Congress own the
Telegraph,[5] I concur entirely with you in thinking that it should be
brought out; but I have no confidence in Elliott.[6] He has made advances to me of a renewal of friendly offices. I have recd. him civilly,
but that is all.
    I have decided to go by Pittsburg [*sic*], on my way to Kentucky. I
intend leaving here, if I can, in about a fortnight.[7]
    The complexion of the news I get from N. York, from Kentucky,
from Maryland, Delaware and N. Jersey is very good. That from Pennsylvania higly [*sic*] encouraging.
    We must oppose concert to concert, and not be outdone in activity.

Our cause is good. It is the cause of free institutions. It is whether America can resist with success the principle which has unhappily overturned all free Governments. With sincere friendship I am Cordially Yr's   H CLAY

The Honble J. Sloane.

ALS. MH-Houghton.   1 Not found.
2 Tobias Watkins.   3 Regarding "the Fayetteville attack," cf. above, Report of Interview, *ca.* April 15, 1827; McArthur to Clay, May 14, 1827. Sloane's letter, addressed to Watkins and dated May 9, was included as supportive documentation with Clay's *Address . . . to the Public,* below, December 29, 1827, Appendix, 33–34. In the letter Sloane asserted that he had "never heard the most distant insinuation" from Clay's "supporters and friends," with all of whom he thought himself "in the entire confidence," that they would have supported Andrew Jackson for the Presidency in 1825, "if there was any prospect of choosing either of the other candidates." He continued: "That any of the friends of Mr. Clay, in Congress, ever made any proposition of conditions on which their votes would depend, to the friends of General Jackson, or any other person, I do not believe. Had General Jackson been chosen, they would have felt no concern as to who he might have appointed members of his cabinet; and, as to Mr. Clay's accepting an appointment under him, they would, to a man, have most certainly opposed it. I judge of this from the opinion which I know they entertained to General Jackson's want of capacity, and the fact that it was not until some time after the choice of Mr. Adams that they agreed to advise Mr. Clay to accept of the office he now holds. His acceptance has always been regarded by them as a favor done to the country, and not as one conferred upon him."   4 Sloane produced no such letter, but his letter of May 9 to Watkins, referred to "the importunity of some of General Jackson's friends." Not until June 20, 1844, did Sloane issue a further statement about that "importunity," explaining that he had not heretofore elaborated upon the matter because he considered the issue as centering upon the question whether "Clay's friends had made propositions to Jackson for a bargain." He then finally reported a conversation of December, 1824, with Sam Houston, who had "evinced much solicitude" concerning the vote of the Ohio delegation in the House election for the Presidency and, at one point, had exclaimed: "What a splendid Administration it would make, with Old Hickory President, and Mr. Clay Secretary of State." Sloane also reported that Houston had concluded with the observation: "Well, I hope you from Ohio will aid us in electing General Jackson, and then your man (meaning Mr. Clay) can have any thing he pleases." Sloane's statement quoting Houston is printed, with the parenthetical explanation, in Colton (ed.), *Private Correspondence of Henry Clay,* 489–90.   5 On May 25, 1827, the Washington *United States Telegraph* noted that the New York *National Advocate* had charged that six Senators owned stock in the *Telegraph* and had lobbied that the journal be given the public printing. The editor of the latter journal, Duff Green, replied "that the entire property and control of the Telegraph, is solely and absolutely vested in the nominal Editor, who is the only and real Editor." That the ethical issue was, nevertheless, relevant appears by a statement dated May 20, 1826, indicating that John H. Eaton had endorsed a loan of $3,000 to Green and that Eaton's endorsement was supported by notes totaling $2,000 from J(ames) Hamilton, Jr., of South Carolina, George Kremer, George Peter, John S(trode) Barbour, James K. Polk, J(acob) C. Isacks, S(amuel) D. Ingham, D(aniel) H. Miller, John Branch, William (R. de Vane) King, and Samuel (Price) Carson, "to be demandable and to be made whenever any call is made that Mr. Green cannot meet." The "Memorandum of the object for which the enclosed Notes are drawn," signed by Eaton and Miller on the above-named date, carries an endorsement by Eaton on May 26, 1828, noting that Hamilton's note for $300 was "given to him to be drawn for, if contingency arise." Bassett (ed.), *Correspondence of Andrew Jackson,* III, 301–302. The annotation suggests that the agreement remained effective at the dates of this letter and of the *National Advocate's* inquiry. Eaton, Branch, and King were Senators; the others were members of the House of Representatives, in which Green had also been supported as a candidate for the public printing (*Register of Debates,* 19 Cong., 2 Sess., 1267).
    Miller, born in Philadelphia, served in Congress as a Representative from Pennsylvania for four terms, 1823 to 1831. Branch, born in Halifax, North Carolina, and graduated in 1801 from the University of North Carolina, had been admitted to the bar but practiced only briefly. He had been a member of the State Senate from 1811 to 1817 and again in 1822, Governor of North Carolina from 1817 to 1820, Federal judge for the Western District of Florida in 1822, and a United States Senator since 1823. He resigned from the

Senate in March, 1829, to become Secretary of the Navy and held that office until 1831, when he entered upon a term in the House of Representatives. Subsequently he served from 1844 to 1845 as Territorial Governor of Florida.   6 Jonathan Elliot.   7 Cf. below, Clay to Erwin, June 3, 1827.

DIPLOMATIC NOTES   May 20, 1827

From COUNT FERDINANDO LUCCHESI, New York. Announces his intended departure from the United States, to become Chargé d'Affaires in Brazil, and states that he will leave N. Edward Fowls, vice consul of the Two Sicilies for the District of Columbia, in charge of the consulate. Adds that Fowls will also be acting consul general for the "Court of Rome." LS, in French, with trans. in State Dept. file. DNA, RG59, Notes from Two Sicilies Legation, vol. 1 (M55, R1). Endorsed by Clay on verso of second page: "To be translated."

Fowls has not been further identified.

INSTRUCTIONS AND DISPATCHES   May 20, 1827

From JOHN RAINALS, Copenhagen. Reports the death of John Alexander Balfour, American vice consul, under appointment by Rainals, at Elsinore, and the appointment to that position of "James Marshall Ellah of the firm of Balfour, Ellah, Rainals & Co. Merchants in that Town"; expresses a hope that his action in this matter will be approved. States that John Cuthbert, United States consul at Hamburg, has expressed a wish "to be appointed vice Consul for the Duchy of Holstein," which "might be useful to" American trade up the Elbe; that Count Schimmelmann has no objection, provided Cuthbert will establish an office at Altona; and that Rainals is corresponding with him on the subject. Notes expectation of the arrival of a Russian fleet on its "way to the Mediterranean" (cf. below, Middleton to Clay, June 23, 1827). ALS. DNA, RG59, Cons. Disp., Copenhagen, vol. 3 (M-T195, R3). Received September 12.

Ellah has not been further identified.

MISCELLANEOUS LETTERS   May 20, 1827

From J[EHUDI] ASHMUN, "U. S. Agency for Recaptured Africans Cape Mesurado." Summarizes the manifold "duties of an Agent of the U. States at this secluded Station," which "has become a place of resort for the Marine Public & Civil, of all commercial Nations," and where "the Agent in the absence of a consul is daily called upon, As the only officer to whom recourse can be had in the contingencies incident to maritime & commercial transactions." States that "These services have . . . been rendered cheerfully, & gratuitously of course—and will be as cheerfully continued provided the necessary helps are furnished." Requests that the agency be furnished with "a Copy of the Laws of Congress." ALS. DNA, RG59, Misc. Letters (M179, R65).

On the public nature of Ashmun's role, cf. above, Speech, January 20, 1827, note. Ashmun's letter suggests that he had been named a commercial agent, an office which did not require senatorial approval. No notice of appointment has been found.

To Pablo Obregón

Dn. Pablo Obregon, Envoy Exty. & Minister Pleny. from Mexico.
Sir,   Department of State, Washington, 21st. May, 1827.
    Commodore Porter, in the service of the United Mexican States,

with the Mexican Squadron under his command, has been, as you are no doubt aware, some time in the Port of Key West, an appendage of East Florida.[1] From the remote situation of that port, and the almost uninhabited condition of the Island, the Government here has not been always regularly advised of the movements of Commodore Porters squadron. His entry into the port was supposed to be for the purpose of that hospitality, which the United States are ever ready to dispense alike to the Public Vessels of all friendly foreign Countries, and his subsequent detention in it was supposed to be in consequence of the presence of a superior Spanish force, which rendered his egress hazardous. But information has recently reached this Department, that Commodore Porter is availing himself of his position to increase his force, and to send out cruisers to annoy the Spanish Commerce.[2] Such a belligerent use of a port of the United States is contrary to that state of known neutrality in which they stand in respect to the existing war between Mexico and Spain. Whilst the Government of the United States is ever ready and anxious to fulfil all the obligations of the most liberal hospitality, they cannot allow any departure within their jurisdiction from the line of a strict and impartial neutrality.

I am directed therefore by the President to request that you will adopt such measures as may appear to you proper to prevent any act or proceeding on the part of Commodore Porter, in violation of the neutrality of the United States.

I pray you to accept assurances of my high consideration.

H. CLAY.

Copy. DNA, RG59, Notes to Foreign Legations, vol. 3, pp. 357–58 (M38, R3). AL draft, in CSmH.

[1] Cf. above, Rodney to Clay, January 29, 1827; Taylor to Clay, March 19, 1827.

[2] No communication of this information to the State Department has been found. On May 10, 1827, President Adams noted that (Samuel L.) Southard had read to him letters from several naval officers, including Captain (Melancthon Taylor) Woolsey, and added: "Woolsey, in a private letter, complains that Captain David Porter, now in the Mexican service, and having taken refuge in a frigate at Key West, is using that place as a station of annoyance to the Spanish commerce, and abusing its neutrality, obviously for the purpose of making misunderstanding between the United States and Spain." Adams, *Memoirs*, VII, 269. Porter's presence at Key West had already been the subject of discussion at a Cabinet meeting on February 19. *Ibid.*, 229. Woolsey, born in northern New York, had entered the Navy as a midshipman in 1800. He had served in the Barbary wars of 1802 to 1807, from which he emerged with the rank of lieutenant, and on the Great Lakes and Lake Champlain from 1808 to 1825, with promotion to captain in 1816. During 1826 he had commanded the *Constellation* in the campaign to suppress piracy in West Indian waters, and he was currently, until 1830, in charge of the Pensacola Navy Yard. From 1832 to 1834 he commanded the Brazil Squadron, in the rank of commodore. He died at Utica in 1838.

From James Erwin

Dear Sir   New Orleans May 21st. 1827.

I yesterday Recd. yours of the 21st. Apl. from Washington in which you inquire when the Notes of Mather will be due. I was under the impression that Genl. Whittlesy had sent you a copy of the annual Statement furnished by him to Mr Duralde & myself[1] from which you will see that payment of principal Can not be forced until 15th Feby 1832 more than four years hence, unless they should fail to pay the interest yearly in which case by the terms of the act the whole payment becomes due

I regret extremely that I was not able to make the disposition of those notes you desired. But it could not be done nor can they be cashed at anything near their par value.

Mr Claiborne[2] leaves here tomorrow with Duralde Jr.[3] for Washington. I expect to leave about ten days hence to join my family near Shelbyville Tennessee. Where we will be compelled to remain a few months—it has been to me a matter of great regret that Anne[4] could not visit Mrs. Clay at Washington this Summer— But it was perhaps most prudent as she started so late that she did not continue on— We have had the pleasure of Mr J S Johnstons society in the same house with us some weeks[5] & of hearing from you very often thro him,   we find him a most delightful acquaintance and I am induced to hope he may not have found me an unprofitable one to him, as I believe I have Enabled him to get the claim of Gov. V.[6] by raising the wind for him altho I did not at the time know for what purpose he wanted the money. My impression is however that he has purchased that claim, I have only expressed this opinion to you, & perhaps. he might think that improper.   you will therefore say nothing to him of the matter. But I fear you will think me stupid in not doing what he has done but it could only be effected in one way and that was different from the one pointed out. Mr Johnston is now in Rapids,[7] & expected here again in two weeks. I think he will not offer for Gov.—and unless he does I am inclined to think Marigny will be the man.[8] We shall be much pleased to hear from you at Shelbyville Ten—Where you may find repose as we are well aware of the labour & fatigue you will have to endure while in Kentucky   Very Truly   J ERWIN

ALS. DLC-HC (DNA, M212, R2).
[1] The statement, enclosed, is a copy of that sent by Chauncey Whittelsey to Clay, above, December 22, 1826. Cf. also above, Clay to Whittelsey, January 20, 1827.
[2] William C. C. Claiborne.   [3] Clay's grandson, Martin Duralde (III).   [4] Mrs. James Erwin. Cf. below, Clay to Brown, May 30, 1827.   [5] Cf. above, Johnston to Clay, May 19, 1827.   [6] Probably Jacques Philippe Villeré, who had filed a claim for indemnity, under the St. Petersburg Convention, for 53 slaves, valued at $580 each. *House Docs.*, 19 Cong., 1 Sess., no. 122, pp. 167–69; and cf. above, Forsyth to Clay, January 21, 1827, note. Villeré, born in Louisiana, had been educated in France, had returned to Louisiana in 1784, and had become a sugar planter near New Orleans. He had been a member of the Louisiana Constitutional Convention of 1812, had held a commission as major general of militia during the War of 1812, and had been the second Governor of his State, 1816–1820.   [7] Rapides Parish, Louisiana.   [8] Bernard Marigny was overwhelmingly defeated in the Louisiana gubernatorial election of 1828. Cf. above, Johnston to Clay, May 19, 1827, note.

INSTRUCTIONS AND DISPATCHES   May 21, 1827

To Albert Gallatin, no. 30. Acknowledges receipt of his "despatches from 49 [January 4, 1827] to 62 [March 21, 1827], inclusive"; adds that "several of a later date" have also arrived and "will, hereafter, be more particularly acknowledged." Expresses regret for the delay in negotiations, "on account both of the public interest and . . . [Gallatin's] personal wishes," and anxiety "to know the complexion of the new Ministry. . . ." LS. NHi-Gallatin Papers (MR14). ALI draft, in DLC-HC (DNA, M212, R8).

From Albert Gallatin, London, no. 76. Reports that [George] Canning promises, "in a private note," that Gallatin's "shall be the *first* foreign business taken in hand"; notes, however, that the affairs relating to Portugal and Greece "continue to engross daily the attention of the Ministry"; and expresses doubt that the negotiations will be resumed "before the adjournment of Parliament, which is expected to take place about the middle of June." States that nothing has occurred to alter his belief that the British are determined "in fact to exclude . . . [the United States] altogether from any participation in the [West Indies colonial] trade" and that "the measure is universally popular in England, and . . . the only chance of a change in this policy is the effect it may have on the West Indies colonies and the complaints these may address to Government."

Observes that he considers "it quite immaterial, as to the nature of the answer that will be given, whether the application is made now or in October, or whether the substance of . . . [Clay's] despatch of 11th April (No. 26) is communicated in one, or made the subject of two Notes." Emphasizes the importance of avoiding "any argument on abstract questions of right, and every statement of facts which may be controverted or indeed give rise to any cavil." Declares "Canning's object, from the first outset, [to have been] to divert the attention from the real intentions of the British Government and from the just reasons we had to complain of their proceedings." Notes that, but for the "necessity, to place the conduct and object of Great Britain in an uncontrovertible light at home," he would prefer "to let the subject rest altogether for the present, and to wait, as was done in 1818–1822, for the changes which very few years must produce . . ."; however, since an "explicit answer" must be obtained from Great Britain before the meeting of Congress, he has decided "to omit all the arguments contained in the first part of . . . [Clay's] despatch [of April 11] that relate to the colonial trade generally and to the questions of right and usage," and ". . . to modify in some degree the declarations respecting the proceedings in Congress, so as to run no risk of denial or of being drawn into a discussion on that subject." Points out that "The argument of Mr Canning was that the Baltimore petition [cf. above, Gallatin to Clay, January 28, 1827] brought fairly before Congress the question of complying with the terms of the Act of Parliament, and that this was rejected by a majority of two votes." Comments: "He has confounded the two houses and misconceived the vote which was not a rejection, nor on the acceptance of the terms of the British act." Adds his own observation "that, at no time, either during the session of Congress of 1825–1826, or during the last one, has any bill or proposition been brought from any quarter which was or could be considered as a simple and full compliance with the terms of the act of Parliament, that is to say, proposing, in the words of the act, 'to place the navigation of Great Britain and of its Possessions abroad upon the footing of the most favoured Nation.'" Concludes: "it is possible" that this Government, when urged on the subject [of renewing the negotiations], may, rather than absolutely refuse to raise the interdict, offer to do it provided an Act is passed by Congress, accepting the terms in the very words of the Act of Congress [*i.e.*, Parliament]." Adds, in a postscript, that the President's proclamation (cf. above, Clay to Vaughan, March 17, 1827) was expected but warns that the Government might "make it a pretense for refusing even an explanation." ALS, DNA, RG59, Dip. Disp., Great Britain, vol. 34 (M30, R30). Published in Adams (ed.), *Writings of Albert Gallatin*, II, 372–76. Received June 29.

From ROBERT MONROE HARRISON, Antigua. States that he is enclosing a copy of a letter (not found) "from the Island of St. Bartholomew on the subject of recognizing" him as consul. Expresses confidence that the President, in appointing him, "did not contemplate for a moment that it would be necessary to send to Stockholm and wait a year (which often happens) for His Majestys [Charles XIV's] pleasure to be had thereon. . . ." Charges that there would be no question of his recognition by the local authorities if he "were to relinquish the right of demanding *fees* which they are in the habit of receiving and on which the principal part of their income depends"; professes to have been told that "the old unprincipled" former Governor, now living there in retirement, his "two Sons in Law forming the provisional Government," is using his influence against him; prays that Clay will not let him "be sacrificed . . . to the *chicanery* of such an unprincipled set"; and characterizes "the modern Sweedes" as "the most immoral nation in the world." Cites "the nature of the Trade" to show the need for an experienced consul on St. Bartholomew: "The inhabitants of the British Colonies are making Mercantile establishments there daily and getting their small craft under Sweedish colours, so to have two *sets of papers*—" Declares his intention of going to the Island about June 1, "leaving R B Eldridge . . . [at Antigua] as a kind of Agent. . . ." Repeats his request (see above, Harrison to Clay, May 17, 1827) that Clay ask Baron Stackelberg to intercede with the authorities of St. Bartholomew in his behalf. ALS. DNA, RG59, Cons. Disp., Antigua, vol. 1 (M-T327, R1).

The former Governor was Johan Norderling, not further identified, with whom Harrison had quarreled on the issue of his recognition as consul in 1821. Major James H. Haasum was the "first member of the Provisional Government" of the island and Lars Gustaf Morsing, the "Justiciary," in 1827. The latter, while still "Justiciary," had succeeded Haasum as President of the Council of Government by 1832.

MISCELLANEOUS LETTERS   May 21, 1827

From JOHN W[ILLIAMS] QUINCY, Boston. Transmits extracts of a letter from "a near relative" who has lived in Buenos Aires "as a merchant over 20 years"; states that "Some parts of the Letter . . . may be" useful to Clay and others may amuse him; and adds that he leaves to Clay the decision on "what is proper to lay before the Public. . . ." ALS. DNA, RG59, Misc. Letters (M179, R65).

The author of the extracts, which are dated March 7, 1827, characterizes "the political State of the [cou]ntry" as "a labyrinth indeed" and his friend (Bernardíno) Rivadavia as just, as "the only man to bring things into order, & Consolidate the Government," and as facing "a wicked opposition to his measures. . . ." States that Rivadavia "has formed an Army of 8000 Cavalry," the "finest Horsemen in the world," which is achieving success against "the Enemy," and speculates that, if "these provinces" should unite and join forces, they could drive "the Emperor of Brazil [Peter I] . . . into the Atlantic." Contends that a speedy peace might be expected but for the partiality of Great Britain for the Emperor and that "Lord Ponsonby in this Country at this moment, while it is engaged in so important a war" is "as a Wolf amongst Sheep."

On May 26 Daniel Brent, as "directed by the Secretary," thanked Quincy for his communication and informed him that Clay "declines giving an opinion" on publishing the extracts but "can of course have no objection to that step on" Quincy's part. Copy, in DNA, RG59, Dom. Letters, vol. 21, p. 545 (M40, R19).

Quincy, of Boston, was himself a merchant and notary public.

To Edward Everett

My dear Sir   Washington 22d. May 1827.

Your obliging favor of the 18h. instant is just recd.[1] The same mail brought me a letter from Webster, who speaks in flattering terms of the pamphlet.[2] I am consoled for the delay which I shall experience in the opportunity of perusing it, by the reflection that it will sooner reach its particular destination. The idea of translating it into German was very good.

I have read the letters addressed to Geo. Canning Esqr., and I read them with particular satisfaction.[3] Shortly after the close of the last Session, I addressed a long despatch to Mr. Gallatin,[4] on the subject of Mr. C.s "last word," in which I employed the same train of reasoning as that which you have used, in your series. The fact you assert, that the Foreign ministers are furnished with the public documents printed by the order of Congress, is true. They receive them at once from the public printers, and under an order of the House. They are not however supplied with Copies of the Session acts, after they are printed for distribution. These are given only to our own Ministers abroad.[5] I believe you are mistaken in supposing that Foreign ministers at London are not supplied with the public domuments by G. Britain. Mr. Gallatin sends us lots of parliamentary papers which, I presume, he receives from that Government.

I regret Govr. Lincoln's[6] determination to decline a seat in the Senate. If he adhere to it, I am inclined to think that it will be well for Webster to go there. We can get along in the House with you and other friends to take care of the public interests. Should Oakley be friendly and should Sergeant[7] come to the house, you will find powerful auxiliaries in them, and in that contingency, there will be less occasion to regret Mr. W.s transfer. I have written to W. fully on this interesting subject.[8]

Intelligence from all quarters continues to run in the same favorable current. Our friends in Pennsa. are acquiring what they wanted, confidence in their strength and their cause. I am told that Shulze[9] suffers no body to leave him, without a good word for the administration; and that the Intellr at Harris'burg and a German paper are about to take a positive stand.[10] From K.[11] my friends assure me of success. We shall not lose, if we do not gain (as is probable) in the number of friends in the next H. of R.

You will have seen the Vindication from the Nashville Comee. of —(what shall I call it?)[12] The affair of shooting the six militia men is one of which much may be made, we think here. It is said that another, a Clergyman, was also shot.[13] Thus the poor fellows were hurried out of the world, without the benefit of Clergy. With great regard I am Cordially Your friend   H. CLAY

P.S.   Be pleased to communicate my thanks to your brother,[14] for his acceptable present of his late work.

Your message to Mrs. Johnston[15] shall be delivered.

My best regards to Mrs. E. and to Miss Brooks.[16] Tell the latter that I should have prized much higher her present through you, if I had not heard a whisper that she had given the same object to a gentleman in this City, who is somewhat my junior.   H C.

ALS. MHi.   1 Not found.
2 Cf. above, Webster to Clay, May 18, 1827; Clay to Everett, April 5, 1827, note.
    3 A series of nine letters addressed to George Canning and signed "An American Citizen" was published in the Washington *Daily National Journal*, May 18, 21, 29, 31, June 4, 6, 11, 19, 27, 1827, reprinted from the *Boston Patriot*. Written by Everett, they were designed to answer Canning's letter of January 27 addressed to Albert Gallatin (cf. above, Gallatin to Clay, January 28, 1827).   4 Above, March 20, 1827.   5 See above, Gallatin to Clay, March 6, 1827. Cf. 3 *U. S. Stat.*, 439–40 (April 20, 1818), which provides for distribution of the laws of each Session of Congress at the discretion of the Secretary of State to foreign ministers and consuls. Provision for such distribution of the public documents was not included in the legislation respecting distribution of T. B. Wait and Sons' *State Papers* (3 *U. S. Stat.*, 473—December 23, 1817), and no such provision with reference to the public documents has been found until an act of July 20, 1840 (5 *U. S. Stat.*, 409). However, the relevant concern in respect to the controversy over American knowledge of the British trade laws was the arrangement for distribution of statutes, not the public documents. Everett's statement on the matter had appeared in the letter reprinted in Washington *Daily National Journal*, May 18, 1827.   6 Levi Lincoln. Cf. above, Webster to Clay, June 8, 1826; May 7, 18, 1827; Clay to Webster, May 14, 1827.
    7 Thomas Jackson Oakley; John Sergeant.   8 Above, May 14, 1827.   9 John Andrew Shulze.   10 The Harrisburg *Pennsylvania Intelligencer* and *Die Harrisburger Morgenröthe Zeitung*. Cf. above, Markley to Clay, May 19, 1827.   11 Kentucky.
    12 On the Nashville Committee, cf. above, Johnson to Clay, April 29, 1827, and note. The Washington *United States Telegraph*, on May 14, 1827, had published a "Circular," dated April 25, in which the Committee refuted four charges which had been directed at Jackson: first, that he had been brutal in the execution of the six Tennessee militiamen (see above, Watkins to Clay, September 30, 1826, note) ; second, that he had charged the Government rent for his own use of his home; third, that he had secretly favored the Alien and Sedition Acts of 1798 (see above, II, 464n); and finally, that while a delegate to the Tennessee Constitutional Convention in 1796, he had advocated a property qualification for voting.   13 One of the six militiamen, John Harris, was a Baptist preacher. Charges that General Jackson had ordered the execution of a varying number of regular army personnel under his command were also circulating, but none has been identified as a clergyman.   14 Alexander H. Everett. See above, Johnson to Clay, May 19, 1827, note.   15 Mrs. Eliza Sibley Johnston, wife of Josiah Stoddard Johnston.   16 Charlotte Gray Brooks Everett; Abigail Brown Brooks.

Order to Washington Branch, Bank of United States

WASHINGTON, May 22 1827

Office of Discount and Deposit,

PAY to P. Doddridge[1] *or bearer, the nett proceeds of* his *note*[2] *of* One hundred & fifty dollars *discounted this day to my credit.*
$148 40/100   H. CLAY

ADS, partially printed. DLC-TJC (DNA, M212, R16).   1 Philip Doddridge.
2 Not found.

From Theodorick Lee

Sir   Washington May 22. 1827—

I believe you were among, if not the first statesman, who suggested and advised a real American policy, to be organised on a general principle, and on an unvariable basis, to sustain an undeviating friendly and beneficial intercourse with all foreign powers[1]— The determination of England to regulate, by legislation her colonial trade,[2] presents a happy opportunity to consummate, your own design, on which you must have seriously reflected— The political institutions of the united states and their, pecu[liar object]ives, connected with numerical strength, enterprise, extensive trade, an[d] abundant agricultural product, warrants the prudence to place their commercial intercourse with all nations on an equality, by legislation rather than by treaty agreement— If any portion or branch of commerce, can be regulated advantagious [sic] by legislation, there will be no difficulty, to apply it to commerce generally— The same rule, that will manage a part, will take care of the whole— Nor ought it to be doubted, but the commerce of this magnificent Country, fruitful, in whatever can be useful to man, or to the power of nations, will prosper as much, if not more by a uniformity of legislation than by any special treaties, aiming, but in vain, to effect the same desired object. A well adjusted law, offering to all nations, the same equal liberal privileges, asking from all, only a reciprocal equality, will terminate in more general good and of [sic] mutual friendship, than any that has been or ever will be the acquision [sic] by treaties, they being but seldom equal and generally of a short duration, circumstances distressing to industry, to enterprize and to profit—

[Continues to argue, at considerable length, the desirability that the United States regulate its commercial relations by general legislation rather than individual treaty arrangements.]

These incohate [sic] and desultory thoughts are with much diffidence are [sic] submitted to your perusal and reflection— so far they cannot injure, and may not be intrusive— They may however, find acceptance and may induce, perchance more attention, than even the writer, was he under a delusion of vanity, could hope— They mean only to express a hope, the great interest of this only representative republic may prosper and continue to be the seat of liberty, enjoying all [the benefits] of social intercourse, with all the nations of this globe, not by special engagements, but by a general engagement, offered to all mankind, and that by a permanent Law—not deviating because of casual circumstances or by the movements of nations— Like the sun, to remain stationary, and benignily [*sic*] shine on every object, that will not shun, its invigorating and animating rays. Accept the respects of yr vy ob St.   THEODORICK LEE

ALS. DLC-HC (DNA, M212, R2). Addressed to Clay. MS. torn.
1 Possibly a reference to Clay's substitution of reciprocity for the most-favored-nation principle in commercial negotiations—a policy pursued by Clay and Gallatin in their negotiations on the Commercial Convention with Great Britain in 1815, even before Adams' arrival in London (cf. above, II, 31–32, 41–42, 57–58), and in the instructions from Clay to Poinsett, March 26, 1825, as distinguished from those which Adams, as Secretary of State, had addressed to Richard C. Anderson (see above, IV, 168–70). In both the cited instances, recent congressional action had laid down the guidelines which were to be observed in treaty negotiations relating to commercial policy, but no reference to Clay's involvement in the legislative proceedings has been found. Clay's repeated argument for a protective tariff, which he defined as "a genuine American policy" (see, e.g., Speech, March 30–31, 1824, above, III, 692), expressed concern for foreign trade but emphasized the importance of creating a domestic market. For statements of the administration's preference for handling the specific issue of colonial trade regulation by negotiation rather than by legislation, see above, Clay to Gallatin, August 19, 1826, note; November 11, 1826.   2 See above, Rush to Secretary of State, March 26, 1825, note; Clay to Carey, June 6, 1825, note; Gallatin to Clay, September 13, 1826.

INSTRUCTIONS AND DISPATCHES   May 22, 1827

From JAMES COOLEY, Lima, no. 1. Reports his arrival in this city on May 15; encloses copies of his correspondence with Manuel del Rios, the acting Foreign Minister (not further identified), arranging an appointment to present his credentials to General (Andrés) Santa Cruz, the President of the Council; and notes the latter official's praise of the United States as "so great and magnanimous a nation. . . ." States that "The Congress which has been summoned [cf. above, Tudor to Clay, February 3, April 25, 1827] are now holding some preparatory meetings" to agree upon procedural rules before convening formally; describes the general opinions of those persons with whom he has conversed, to the effect "that should Gen. [José de] La Mar, Mr. [Francisco Javier Luna] Pizarro & their friends succeed to the Executive Departments of the Government, the best results may be anticipated: But should Santa Cruz & [Manuel Lorenzo] Vidaurre succeed, . . . but little good can be expected." Concludes: "I confess it seems to me that there are too many epauletted Gentlemen & too many bayonets bristling in the neighborhood of the hall, for that freedom of debate & of action so essential in a deliberative Assembly." ALS. DNA, RG59, Dip. Disp., Peru, vol. 1 (M-T52, R1). Received August 11.

From ALBERT GALLATIN, London, no. 77. Reports receiving an invitation to join (Henry U.) Addington and (William) Huskisson "on Thursday next, at the board of trade, for the purpose of resuming the interrupted conferences, on the Subjects of discussion between the two countries." ALS. DNA, RG59, Dip. Disp., Great Britain, vol. 34 (M30, R30). Published in Manning (arr.), *Diplomatic Correspondence . . . Canadian Relations*, II, 582–83. Received June 29. Cf. above, Gallatin to Clay, February 5, 13, 22, March 6, 14, April 21, 1827.

From ALBERT GALLATIN, London, no. 78. Reports "the arrest of . . . [his] coachman on a charge of assault"; notes that he "took every precaution to avoid giving more importance to the incident than it deserved"; and indicates that he expects "a notification, in the course of the day, from the foreign office, in conformity with the intimation given in Mr. [John] Backhouse's letter to Mr. [William Beach] Lawrence, copy of which is enclosed." Identifies Backhouse as "the new Under-

Secretary of State." States that "This will of course enable . . . [him] to dismiss the man against whom they may then proceed." ALS. DNA, RG59, Dip. Disp., Great Britain, vol. 34 (M30, R30). Received June 29.

The enclosure answered, in "unofficial form," the "questions of law arising out of the circumstances" of the arrest by pointing out that under "The Statute of the 7 Anne, ch. 16," which in all but its penal parts simply repeated the law of nations, diplomatic immunity did not extend "to protect the mere servants of Ambassadors from arrest upon Criminal Charges. . . ." However, the letter noted Lord Dudley's "regret" for any "personal inconvenience" caused Gallatin by the manner in which the warrant was executed by the police.

Backhouse, born in Liverpool, had been trained as a merchant and had begun his public career as an agent for Liverpool commercial interests in their dealings with the Government. After several years in this position he became George Canning's private secretary and continued in the latter capacity until Canning's death. Meanwhile, in 1824 he had been named a Commissioner of Excise and in 1827 became Receiver General of that office. He retained the post of Under Secretary of State for Foreign Affairs until 1842, retired then for reasons of health, and died in 1846. *Gentleman's Magazine*, 2d Series, XXV (January, 1846), 95–97.

From JOHN MULLOWNY, Tangier, no. 48. Transmits his accounts; explains "the charge for passage to & fro [sic] Gibraltar," as well as his absence at the time: "The sum limited at present [cf. above, Clay to Mullowny, October 22, 1825] requires more than common economy which led me to Gibraltar, personally to procure the most suitable articles wanted"; and states his expectation, with Clay's approval, of repeating the trip annually. Reports that all American visitors have, by necessity, lodged at his house; that the British consul has gone home on leave but, because of "his stubborn opposition to the authorities here" and "his refusal to comply with old established customs," he will not be received again; and that other consuls have experienced difficulties. Asserts: "If civilities were to be bought by value in presents, or by comparison, I should be in the rear." Notes that a Boston brig, at Mogador in February, "is all the commerce of the United States in this Empire since . . . [his] last report." States that the country is in good condition, that "the King [Abd-er-Rahman II] has . . . some opposition among the Sloughs, a numerous, warlike, and powerful people of this Empire," but that "the Bashaw [probably Mohamet Omemon] here is from that part, and is about going to head the King's troops. . . ." ALS. DNA, RG59, Cons. Disp., Tangier, vol. 4 (M-T61, R4). No date of receipt noted, but "Duplicate" received August 22.

The British consul at Morocco in 1826 was J. Douglas, not further identified, who had returned to his post by 1828.

The "sloughs," or Chleuhs, were Berbers of the Greater Atlas Mountains. Henri Terrasse, *Histoire du Maroc, des Origines à l'Etablissement du Protectorat Français* (Casablanca, 1930), 365.

No reference has been found concerning when Mohamet Omemon, not further identified, replaced Ali as Bashaw of Tangier. Cf. below, Mullowny to Clay, June 26, November 26, 1827.

From W[ILLIAM] TUDOR, Lima, no. 68. Encloses copies of his correspondence with the Peruvian Government relating to the seizure and condemnation of the American merchant vessel *Chesapeake* (see above, Tudor to Clay, May 5, 1827). States that he will turn the matter over to (James) Cooley; that the case is yet before the judicial tribunal; and that, if the Government's extraordinary measures should be upheld, the Congress will likely repeal the decrees because their provisions have proved offensive to neutral nations and "noxious" to Peru. ALS. DNA, RG59,

Cons. Disp., Lima, vol 1 (M154, R1). Received August 12. On the outcome of the case, see below, Tudor to Clay, June 15, 1827.

MISCELLANEOUS LETTERS   May 22, 1827

To JOHN SIMONDS, JR., St. Louis. Informs him that his commission as United States marshal for the District of Missouri has been forwarded to Judge James (H.) Peck, to be delivered when the required bond has been posted. Copy. DNA, RG59, Dom. Letters, vol. 21, p. 542 (M40, R19).

A copy of the letter of transmittal to Peck, on the same date is located *ibid.,* 541–42. Simonds acknowledged, on June 12, 1827, receipt of the letter and his commission. ALS, in DNA, RG59, Acceptances and Orders for Comns (M-T645, R2).

From JONAH DUNN, "Houlton Plantation, County of Washington, Maine." Complains of "a heavy duty" levied on products from Maine entering the Province of New Brunswick and requests information on the possible settlement of the boundary dispute (cf. above, Clay to Addington, March 27, 1825; Clay to Lincoln, May 13, 1826). ALS. DNA, RG59, Misc. Letters (M179, R62). Misfiled under date of March 22, 1825.

Dunn has not been further identified. Houlton is now located in Aroostook County, organized in 1839.

For the table of duties on foreign productions "imported or brought into any of the British Possessions in America. . . , by Sea of by Inland Carriage or Navigation," see 6 *Geo. IV,* c. 114, pp. 493–95 (July 5, 1825). It included charges of 5s. a barrel on wheat flour, 1s. a bushel on wheat, 14s. per 1000 shingles over 12 inches in length, 12 to 15s. per 1000 for oak staves, 1£/1s. to 1£/8s. per 1000 feet for various kinds of lumber, and 5s/3d. per 1000 for wood hoops. By act of 7 and 8 *Geo. IV,* c. 56, art. 33 (July 2, 1827) the British removed the duties on "Masts, Timber, Staves, Wood Hoops, Shingles, Lathwood, Cordwood for Fuel, raw Hides, Tallow, Ashes, fresh Meat, fresh Fish," and a few other items, "being brought by Land or Inland Navigation into the *British* Possessions in *America.* . . ." This action, which appealed to inland traders such as Dunn, was designed to promote British shipping to the West Indies.

From Nathaniel Silsbee

SALEM, *May* 23, 1827.

DEAR SIR: Absence from home has prevented an earlier acknowledgment of your letter of the 15th instant.[1]

It has long been proverbial here that "Boston folks are full of notions," and the Republicans of the other sections of the Commonwealth have too often found this to be the case with their political friends of the metropolis; but, independent of this natural propensity to pursue a course counter to that of their friends, the divisions which have been evinced in the recent elections may be attributed to other causes, and principally to the recent decisions of the State government upon the bridge and lottery questions,[2] which have caused some excitement throughout the Commonwealth, and much in the vicinity of Boston; and the opponents of the Administration are unwearied in their efforts to make these divisions subservient to their purposes, the effect of which will not be such as may be apprehended at a distance.[3]

It is yet quite uncertain who will be elected to the United States Senate in place of Mr. Mills.[4] It seems to be the wish of a large majority of our friends in this town that Governor Lincoln should be the man, but it is apprehended that he will not consent to be a candidate, and it is the opinion of some that he ought not to, while others yet entertain a hope that he may be prevailed on to consent to a nomination when he sees (as he will) that Mr. Mills declines. I have a letter now before me from Mr. Lincoln (in reply to one written to him on the subject), in which he says, "I know full well that the policy of a transfer from my present office, at this time, is much doubted by a large proportion of our Republican friends; and the circumstances which existed, and the manner in which I was sustained by the people of the Commonwealth, in the late election, impose on me the highest obligation to respect this expression of their sentiments.[5] I, therefore, beg leave to be permitted explicitly to repeat *my entire disinclination* to be considered a candidate for the place to which you refer. *It is an arrangement to which I cannot consent.* There are reasons, both of a public and private character, which I am sure might satisfy you of the propriety of this determination.

Notwithstanding this communication, I have promised some friends here that I will see the Governor the moment he arrives in Boston, and endeavor to remove his objections to a nomination, but really I see but little hope of success. If he persists in declining, Mr. Webster will, I think, be selected, though at this moment doubts are expressed of the expediency of removing him from the House to the Senate. So far as my own feelings are concerned, I should prefer seeing Mr. Webster in the Senate, at this time, to any individual that could be sent from the State; but fears are entertained by many that his removal may be productive of more injury than benefit, especially if Mr. Oakley,[6] from New York, should be found in the opposition. The "divisions and commotions" which now exist in Boston will, I am afraid, operate unfavorably to the removal of Mr. Webster, as many of his constituents are apprehensive that they may not be able, at this time, to elect a Representative with whom they should be satisfied, and some of them think a new election quite too hazardous to be attempted. As soon as the Legislature meets, efforts will be made toward a suitable nomination. No one *avowedly* unfriendly can succeed. The exertions of the opposition will, therefore, be directed toward one whom they may think most susceptible of conversion.

Anxious as I am to resign, and great as will be the sacrifice to me, both of interest and of inclination, by omitting to do it, yet I shall not

resign unless the result of the election about to take place is such as to show, satisfactorily, that it can be done without hazard. With the highest respect, your obedient servant,   NATHL. SILSBEE.
Hon. Henry Clay.

Copy. Published in George Ticknor Curtis, *Life of Daniel Webster* (2 vols.; New York, 1870), I, 298–99.
    1 Not found. Cf. above, Clay to Webster, May 14, 1827.   2 On the bridge issue, see above, Webster to Clay, May 7, 1827, and note. The Massachusetts General Court in 1826 had turned down a petition for a lottery to finance a canal from Boston to the Hudson River. During the early months of 1827 several religious groups were organized in Boston to rally public opinion against "raffles, liquor booths on the Boston Common on holidays, and steamboat riding to Nahant on Sundays." Lyman Beecher, the Presbyterian clergyman—born in New Haven, graduated in 1797 from Yale University, and ordained in 1799—conducted from 1826 to 1832 at the Hanover Street Church, Boston, a continuous revival which focused on the lottery among other issues of public morality. See John Samuel Ezell, *Fortune's Merry Wheel, The Lottery in America* (Cambridge, Mass., 1960), 123, 197–98.   3 Cf. above, Clay to Everett, April 5, 1827, note. While the Jackson forces carried the southern and western counties of Massachusetts in the election of 1828, President Adams received all the State's electoral votes and a popular vote of 29,876 to Jackson's 6,016. Remini, *The Election of Andrew Jackson*, 100; Arthur M. Schlesinger (ed.) and Fred L. Israel (assoc. ed.), *History of American Presidential Elections, 1789–1968* (4 vols.; New York, [1971]), I, 492.   4 Elijah H. Mills. Cf. above, Webster to Clay, June 8, 1826, note.   5 Levi Lincoln explained his views more fully to Webster in a letter dated May 24, 1827. He noted his obligation to the "public sentiment" which had returned him to the governorship and cited his specific announcement during the course of that campaign that he would "absolutely decline the place, if offered. . . ." He accordingly advised Webster to accept "the *transfer.*" Curtis, *Life of Daniel Webster*, I, 295.   6 Thomas Jackson Oakley.

INSTRUCTIONS AND DISPATCHES   May 23, 1827

From WILLIAM TUDOR, Lima, no. 69, "*Confidential.*" States that he will continue "to give . . . brief details of political occurrences" until (James) Cooley "shall have time to get acquainted with the new field he has come upon, & the characters who occupy it. . . ." Summarizes a letter from Colonel (Juan Francisco) Elizalde, who has sent "a column in the direction of Quito, to join the division under [José] Bustamante" and who has learned that General (Francisco de Paula) Santander is pleased with these developments. Declares that (Antonio José de) Sucre, despite his intrigues, finds his situation increasingly difficult, and he will probably have "to evacuate a country, which . . . he can no longer retain in submission." Predicts that "The whole of this melancholy Bolivar farce must . . . soon be every where at an end." Reports the failure of efforts by (Andrés) Santa Cruz and (Manuel Lorenzo de) Vidaurre "to hasten the opening of the session [of Congress], in the hope that the election of President might be made before the arrival of [José de] La Mar, & some other principal members who are known to be on the way." ALS. DNA, RG59, Cons. Disp., Lima, vol. 1 (M154, R1). Published in Manning (arr.), *Diplomatic Correspondence . . . Latin-American Nations*, III, 1831–33. Received August 12.

From Thomas H. Baird

Dear Sir.   Washington Penna. May 24. 1827

    I had been informed that you intended visiting this country about the last of the present month, but have understood lately that your journey will be deferred.[1] You have many personal and political friends here who are desirous of an opportunity of expressing by public manifestations their high respect for yourself individually, and their unshaken confidence in the administration.— Will you apprise us of the precise time when we may expect to see you, and in what manner it will but comport with your own wishes & convenience, and most advance the *good cause*, that we shall receive you?— My own opinion is that public dinners, to which some of the most popular leaders from the country would be invited, might produce a happy effect.— In the west we are much excited on the subjects of internal improvement & domestic manufactures.— These will form the turning point of Penna. politics.   If we can completely identify the present administration with these favorite measures, all will be well.— When occasions occur, calling upon you for a public expression of your sentiments & views of policy, a judicious reference to these popular topics would have in this part of the country an irresistible influence. I am with the most sincere & devoted regard Your Obt svt.

TH H BAIRD

[Note on margin]
Would it be at all convenient for you to ride into Greene County?— I have strong reasons to wish you to visit that section.— I believe an entire change can be effected there.— Perhaps on your return you can pass that way.

ALS. DLC-HC (DNA, M212, R2). Addressed to Clay.
[1] Cf. below, Clay to Erwin, June 3, 1827.

From Moses Dawson

Sir   Cincinnati. O. 24h. May 1827

The inclosed paper was received here by me from the mail of 23d instant— I do not exchange papers with the Editor of the national Journal[1] and from that as well as the circumstance that the paper appears directed to the "Register" and that direction scratched out with the pen I have no idea that it was sent directed to me by the Editor of the Journal or any of his clerks—but must have been forwarded from the "Register" office wherever that may be—

The paltry threat thrown out on its lower margin against my Press I despise—but as it must have emanated from some person who professes to be your friend I have taken the liberty to inclose it to you that you may, if you think proper, by enquiring at the office of the Journal find out who it is that takes such an unworthy way of shewing his friendship to you and your party— I have not the most distant idea that you would either authorise or approve of such conduct but considered it not improper to inform you of the manner in which some of your friends advocate your cause— I am sir your obedt servt

The Hon: H. Clay   MOSES DAWSON
                                              Editor Cincinnati Advertiser

[Copy of enclosure]

Now the fact is Mosey it is well known in this burgh that you cleared out from the emerald Isle not exactly for stealing emeralds but potatoes my dear! therefore Note Bene if you dont let let [sic] Charley[2] alone depend on it there will be an "improvement" made upon your Press[3] in short order. Send your answer to this to Henry Clay   Blag legs & co[4]—

ALS draft. OCX-Moses Dawson Collection. Endorsed on second page: "Copy to H. Clay   Sec: of State."
[1] Peter Force.   [2] Probably Charles Hammond.   [3] Cf. above, Sergeant to Clay, April 17, 1827.   [4] Last phrase not clear, apparently an allusion to the occasion for the Clay-Randolph duel of April, 1826 (cf. above, Clay to Randolph, March 31, 1826, note).

DIPLOMATIC NOTES   May 24, 1827

To COUNT FERDINAND LUCCHESI, "Consul Genl. of His Holiness, the Pope [Leo XII] and of the King of the two Sicilies [Francis I]." Acknowledges receipt of Lucchesi's note of May 20; announces "compliance with . . . [his] request to receive Mr. Fowls in the double character indicated"; testifies "to the satisfaction . . . experienced in . . . official intercourse" with him and "to the pleasure . . . derived from . . . [his] personal acquaintance"; and wishes him success in his new mission. Copy. DNA, RG59, Notes to Foreign Legations, vol. 3, p. 359 (M38, R3). ALI draft, in CSmH.

Fowls informed Clay, by letters dated at New York, June 25 and August 29, 1827, of receipt of official notice of his appointment. ALS, in DNA, RG59, Notes from Two Sicilies Legation, vol. 1 (M55, R1). Clay acknowledged, on September 5, 1827, receipt of Fowls' letter of June 25, apologized for the delay in replying to it, and assured its author that he would "be duly received and respected. . . ." Copy, *ibid.*, Notes to Foreign Legations, vol. 3, pp. 385–86 (M38, R3).

To CARDINAL JUL. [GIULIO] MAR[IA] DELLA SOMAGLIA, "Deacon of the Sacred College and Secretary of State to His Holiness Leo the 12th." States that he has signed and delivered to M (athew) Carey, R (ichard) W. Meade, and J (ohn) J. Borie, United States citizens, "a certificate [not found] of their respectability." Asserts that they, "belonging to the Roman Catholic Church, . . . intend to make some application to His Holiness, for the purpose of improving the condition of that portion of the Church to which they belong." Disclaims involvement in their concern, "it being a fundamental principle in the institutions of the United States not to mix together the affairs of State and Church," but testifies to the "high respect and Esteem" which these citizens enjoy. Copy. DNA, RG59, Notes to Foreign Legations, vol. 3, p. 360 (M38, R3). ALI draft, in CSmH.

Cardinal Somaglia, born in Piacenza, Italy, in 1744, had held a number of church administrative offices prior to his elevation to the cardinalate in 1795. He was named bishop of Frascati and secretary of Holy Office in 1814, bishop of Ostia and Velletri in 1820, and Secretary of State for the Holy See in 1823. He retired from the last post in 1828.

Carey, Meade, and Borie were an acting committee, named on behalf of a general committee of 30, designated to present the protest of the pewholders of St. Mary's Church at Philadelphia against the suspension of their pastor, the Reverend William Vincent Harold, by Bishop Henry Conwell, of Philadelphia. At a meeting of the pewholders, held at the United States Hotel, Philadelphia, on April 24, with Carey presiding, objections had been expressed against the "dangerous and re- volting example of arbitrary power" and a resolution adopted to seek from the Pope "a speedy and permanent remedy against the abuse. . . , by the establishment of the canonical rights of . . . clergy." In the view of the assembly, such a suspen- sion of the clergy "without regular process" reflected unfavorably upon Catholi- cism in the eyes of the American Protestants. Philadelphia *Gazette of the United States*, April 26, 1827; *Niles' Weekly Register*, XXXII (May 5, 1827), 163.

St. Mary's Church had opened in Philadelphia in 1763 as the parish church, with an earlier church, St. Joseph's attached as a chapel. The Reverend William Vincent Harold, a Dominican, had emigrated to the United States in 1808 from Ireland and around 1811 had been appointed vicar-general of the newly-estab- lished episcopal see of Philadelphia, in residence at St. Joseph's. He had during the next few years become involved in controversy with his church superiors and for a time returned to Europe. Bishop Henry Conwell, also a native of Ireland, had been appointed Bishop of Philadelphia in 1819 and had assumed his duties at St. Mary's in 1820. He had named the Reverend Father Harold again as vicar- general and on October 9, 1826, had yielded authority to the trustees of St. Mary's to determine salaries and veto his appointments. The Pope, displeased by these concessions and by the persistent dissension in the Church, called Bishop Conwell to Rome and removed him from the administrative functions of his see. The trustees, however, after prolonged dissension, were stripped of their power by the closing of the church and its cemeteries in April, 1831. The following month the trustees yielded their pretensions, and the church was reopened. *New Catholic Encyclopedia*, edited at the Catholic University of America (15 vols.; New York, [1967]), IV, 349–50; XI, 794.

From JOSÉ MARÍA SALAZAR, Baltimore. Introduces the bearer, Denis Thomas, captain of the *Zulmé*, who will answer any questions Clay may wish to ask. Denies any wish to violate the usual formalities in the negotiation. LS, in Spanish with trans. in State Dept. file. DNA, RG59, Notes from Colombian Legation, vol. 1, pt. 2 (M51, R2). Cf. above, Rodney to Clay, June 24, 1826; Salazar to Clay, Janu- ary 10, 1827.

INSTRUCTIONS AND DISPATCHES   May 24, 1827

To ALBERT GALLATIN, no. 31. Transmits "a copy of . . . resolutions adopted . . . by the general Assembly of Kentucky, in respect to fugitive slaves. . . ." States that Gallatin, "Already charged with such a negotiation, . . . may . . . make such use of" the resolutions as seems best. LS. NHi-Gallatin Papers (MR14). ALI draft, in DLC-HC (DNA, M212, R8); published in Manning (arr.), *Diplomatic Correspon- dence . . . Canadian Relations*, II, 135. Cf. above, Clay to Gallatin, February 24, 1827 (no. 18).

From J[OHN] M. FORBES, Buenos Aires, no. 49. Reports that as a consequence of his decision to confiscate the papers of the *La Fayette* (see above, Forbes to Clay, April 12, 1827), the owners resold the vessel, which "is now fitted out under the Flag of this Country as a privateer"; adds that he also refused papers to the brig *Independence* because she was owned by foreigners. Notes that no information has been received on (Manuel José) García's mission to Rio de Janeiro and that there is little hope for peace because reports from Rio de Janeiro indicate that "the Emperor [Peter I] . . . is determined to continue the war." States that he was told, at the time of García's departure, "by the Chief of the Department of Foreign Affairs [Francisco de la Cruz] that the Government would immediately occupy themselves about sending a Minister to Washington," but that he has "since learned, through the same channel, . . . that . . . the President [Bernardino Rivadavia] declared his opinion that, in the present extreme [sic] uncertain state of affairs in this Country, it was expedient to postpone it for the present." LS. DNA, RG59, Dip. Disp., Argentina, vol. 3 (M69, R4). Published in Espil (comp.), *Once Años en Buenos Aires*, 466–67. Received October 3, 1827.

The *Independence* was probably the brig *Independencia del Sud*, built at Baltimore. She was commanded from 1816 to 1818 by Americans, but operated as an Argentine privateer. Cf. Luis de Onís to Adams, March 26, April 19, 1817, June 9, 1818, in Manning (arr.), *Diplomatic Correspondence . . . Latin-American Nations*, III, 1923, 1935–42 and note, 1967–68.

MISCELLANEOUS LETTERS   May 24, 1827

From BEVERLEY ALLEN, "Office of U S: attorney District of Missouri. St. Louis." Requests "to be furnished with the copies of the Acts of Congress passed at the 1st. & 2d. sessions of the 17th: Congress & at the 2d session of the 19th. Congress." States that "The subject of claims to land, by virtue of incipient titles derived from the French & Spanish governments, remains involved in uncertainty & obscurity." Expresses a wish, "if practicable," for "a copy of every ordinance or regulation of the King of France or Spain relative to the granting of the King's domain in this country. . . ." ALS. DNA, RG59, Misc. Letters (M179, R65).

Writing again on the following day, Allen acknowledged receipt, "this day," of the acts of "the 2d. session of the 19th. Congress." ALS, in *ibid.*

From WILLIAM BLAGROVE, New York. Encloses duplicate bill of lading, signed by James Thomas of New York, for 15 pounds of red sealing wax; states that he has "taken the liberty of adding 5 lbs. to . . . [Clay's] order[,] the orders expected from Washington having been very deficient." ALS. DNA, RG59, Accounting Records, Misc. Letters. The bill of lading, addressed to Clay and dated May 24, receipted the anticipated $15 payment and indicated the wax was for State Department use. Cf. above, Blagrove to Clay, April 18, 1827.

From JOHN CONNELL, Philadelphia. Acknowledges receipt of Clay's letter of May 21 (not found); states that the cases on which he wishes (Henry) Wheaton's help "are the cargoes of the Ships Fair Trader & Minerva Smyth & Brig Ariel, detained at Kiel" in 1812. Adds, in a postscript: "NB. Your opinion upon another subject, perfectly agrees with my own." ALS. DNA, RG59, Misc. Letters (M179, R65).

The cases involving the three named vessels differed somewhat from the general pattern of Napoleonic seizures in Denmark. In 1810 Danish consular officials had issued public notice "that the ports . . . were open to American vessels, having regular consular documents"; but when the vessels arrived, "they and their cargoes bona fide, property of citizens of the United States, and furnished with the prescribed documents," they had been seized by a Danish privateer, detained two years, and finally released "after paying enormous duties equal to half the cargoes." Christopher Hughes to Count Schimmelmann, August 18, 1825.

After extended negotiations, Wheaton on March 28, 1830, signed a convention under which Denmark agreed to pay "650,000 Spanish milled dollars" for total claims, with the United States Government to assume responsibility for distributing the sum among the claimants. By act of February 25, 1831 (4 *U. S. Stat.*, 446),

Congress established a commission to effect the distribution, and on March 28, 1833, the latter body reported the completion of its work. Moore, *History and Digest of the International Arbitrations.* . . , V, 4553, 4563, 4569.

To Francis T. Brooke

My dear Sir,   Washington, May 25, 1827.

I took the liberty of sending you a few days ago, a copy of some speeches, etc., of mine, which have been recently published in Philadelphia,[1] and which I hope you will have safely received.

Have you read the accounts about the execution of the six militia-men at Mobile, early in 1814 [*sic*]? I think the Nashville Committee are entitled to the public thanks for bringing that matter to light.[2] I had a vague impression about it, but I had really put it in the large class of doubtful reports. The Committee have undeceived me; and I think if they favor the public with many more similar disclosures, they will serve most effectually the cause they have espoused. What has become of the eloquent pen of Algernon Sidney?[3] I think the case of these poor deluded militia-men furnishes a theme on which it might be employed with as much instruction and benefit as when it was formerly exercised with such powerful influence.

Colton (ed.), *The Private Correspondence of Henry Clay*, 162–63.
[1] Cf. above, Sparks to Clay, April 9, 1827, note.   [2] Cf. above, Watkins to Clay, September 30, 1826, note; Johnson to Clay, April 29, 1827, note.   [3] Cf. above, I, 367n. Under this pseudonym a series of letters had been published in the *Richmond Enquirer* in 1818–1819, in reference to Andrew Jackson's Seminole campaign, and again in May–June, 1821, "On the Lottery Decision." Both series were subsequently republished, the former as *The Letters of Algernon Sydney, in Defense of Civil Liberty and Against the Encroachments of Military Despotism* . . . (Richmond, 1830); the latter, under the above title, much later. Scholars have commonly cited these letters as the work of Spencer Roane. See Ambler, *Thomas Ritchie*, 70; Harry Ammon, *James Monroe, the Quest for National Identity* (New York, c. 1971), 430; Norman K. Risjord, *The Old Republicans, Southern Conservatives in the Age of Jefferson* (New York and London, 1965), 225–26. The later reprints, however, are attributed to Benjamin Watkins Leigh in Sabin, *Bibliotheca Americana*, vol. 14, p. 192; vol. 24, p. 389. Clay's letter and Brooke's correspondence, below, June 1, November 23, 1827, support the latter identification. Cf. also, Adams, *Memoirs*, IV, 227.

DIPLOMATIC NOTES   May 25, 1827

To the Baron de Mareuil. Acknowledges receipt of Mareuil's note of May 16, which has been "submitted to the President"; states that "The Government of the United States is sincerely desirous that the greatest degree of activity should prevail in the Commercial intercourse between the two Countries, and that every measure should be adopted, consistently with their mutual interests, to increase the consumption of their respective productions." Indicates that, while he is not prepared to admit that the Convention of 1822 (cf. above, III, 53n) operates to the disadvantage of France, he is "charged by the President to say that any overtures which the French Government may choose to make . . . will be received and considered in a friendly spirit and with an anxious desire to reconcile the interests of both Countries." Copy. DNA, RG59, Notes to Foreign Legations, vol. 3, pp. 360–61 (M38, R3). AN draft, in CSmH.

INSTRUCTIONS AND DISPATCHES   May 25, 1827

To JAMES BROWN, no. 12. Subjoins "a list of books . . . to be procured for, and sent to" the State "Department according to the suggestion and advice of the President." Copy. DNA, RG59, Dip. Instr., vol. 11, pp. 315–16 (M77, R6).

   The list comprises six works, on trees, the vine, and agriculture.

To ALBERT GALLATIN, London, no. 32. Subjoins "a list of books . . . to be procured for, and sent to," the State "Department, according to the suggestion and advice of the President." LS. NHi-Gallatin Papers (MR14). Copy, in DNA, RG59, Dip. Instr., vol. 11, p. 315 (M77, R6).

   The list includes "1. Millers Gardeners Dictionary,—ninth, or Professor Martyn's Ed. 2. Evelyns Silva, or a discourse of Forest Trees, last Edition, coloured plates 3. The works, complete, of Charles Butler   4. Transactions of the Royal Academy for 1821, part 1.—"

   Philip Miller's *The Gardener's and Florist's Dictionary* had been first published in 1724. The edition formally identified as the "ninth" did not appear until 1835, but that by Thomas Martyn, a Cambridge University botanist, had appeared in 2 vols., 1797 and 1804, after the eighth edition of 1768.

   John Evelyn, a landscape gardener, had published *Sylva, or a Discourse of Forest-Trees, and the Propagation of Timber . . . To Which Is Annexed Pomona, or, an Appendix Concerning Fruit-Trees. . .* , at London in 1664. The latest edition was the fourth (in 2 vols.) published at York in 1812.

   Charles Butler's writings do not appear to have been collected, but he had published *The Feminine Monarchie*, a treatise on bees, in 1609.

From W[ILLIAM] H. D. C. WRIGHT, Rio de Janeiro. Encloses correspondence with the Minister of Foreign Affairs (Marquis de Queluz), relative to the Brazilian Government's detention of a deserter from the American brig *Sylph*, to the case of the American brig *Ontario* (cf. above, Wright to Clay, May 7, 1827), and with Admiral (Rodrigo Antonio de) Lamare, regarding the detention of two seamen. Notes the arrival of (Manuel José) García as Minister from Buenos Aires but expresses the view that expectations for a peace treaty have declined since García arrived with authority to negotiate a settlement. Reports that the French Minister (probably Paul-Joseph-Alphonse-Marie-Ernest de Cadoine, later Marquis de Gabriac) has demanded indemnification for the capture of French vessels and threatened reprisals if his demands are not met; observes that the Minister of Foreign Affairs took the French demands to the House of Deputies but that the House declined jurisdiction and referred the matter of prize cases to the executive and the judicial tribunals. ALS. DNA, RG59, Cons. Disp., Rio de Janeiro, vol. 2 (M-T172, R3). Received July 16.

   Gabriac had been named Ambassador to Rio de Janeiro in 1825. When he arrived is uncertain. Count A. M. de Gestas, who had come to Brazil in 1823 as consul, had signed the Brazilian-French commercial treaty of January 8, 1826, and thereafter assumed the rank of Chargé d'Affaires. Robertson, *France and Latin-American Independence*, 434. Gestas was identified as the French representative by *Almanac de Gotha* in 1827, but still in the rank of Chargé, the title he retained in the listing for 1828. By the last year, Gabriac was also listed, as Minister.

   Gabriac, born in Heidelberg, had been named the French Secretary of Legation to Naples in 1811, first secretary to the embassy at Turin in 1814 and to that at

St. Petersburg in 1819, and Minister Plenipotentiary to Sweden in 1823. His success in pressing for the indemnification here demanded led to his appointment as Ambassador to Sweden from 1828 to 1830. He was raised to the peerage in 1841.

MISCELLANEOUS LETTERS   May 25, 1827

From SAMUEL L. SOUTHARD, Navy Department. Notes having "been informed that Thomas B. Tilden, . . . once a *Midshipman* in the Navy. . . , has . . . exhibited to the Brazilian Government a Commission as *Lieutenant* in our Navy." Requests Clay to inform "the Brazilian Government, that this man's resignation as a Midshipman was accepted . . . 27th. December 1824, and that he has never received from . . . [this] Government a Commission as Lieutenant in the Navy." ALS. DNA, RG59, Misc. Letters (M179, R65).

From Jefferson Dorsey

Henry Clay Esqr.   Harrisonburgh Louisiana [May 26, 1827]
    Sir. Although I am not personally acquainted with you. your Station in our Government. as one of the instruments. to carry into execution whatever has for its tendency the General Good: is a sufficient apology for addressing you.— But in the first place I would inform you that I am a native of Kentucky. who witnessed until the last year those political aberrations from justice[1] that has [*sic*] cast a Stigma on that unfortunate State that can be swept away only. by redoubled vigilance and energy on the part of those to whom is confided the administration of justice. I am too one who hears with mortification that the most able men in that State are advocating the cause of a man[2] whose political sentiments (if he have any) are prejudicial to the interests of the Union and more especially to the West. But whose fame has never been other than that of a mere military man.—
    As I believe that every man should do something in behalf of his country and as nothing can have a greater tendency to its advancement in prosperity than the correction of the abuses of public trust, I here would mention a small matter immediately concerning my own neighborhood. we have in this place a P. master whose name is T. A. King[3] who has so far violated the trust reposed in him as to waste about $100 dollars placed in his hands by his predecessor to be paid upon the draft of the P M General.[4] The draft was Sent back to Washington with a true statement of the case   I should be glad that the head of that department could be given a hint by some influential man to examine into the abuses of which his department is pregnant. I would not mention it to you but for the neglect on the part of the proper officer & my confidence in your devotion to the interests of our Country—   no matter how small a part we may be of the United States. still we compose a part of the great whole & have an equal right to a redress of grievances—

In addition I would mention to you the propriety of coming to Such an understanding. with the government of the Mexican Republic as to prevent much inconvenience under which many of the Southern citizens labour in obtaining property that has been carried into the provinces bordering on the U. S   property as under a mortgage is frequently conveyed into Taos clandestinely by emigrants from this Country to that. and so far as I have become acquainted with the laws of that Government there is no other remedy provided. than an application to the Mexican Republic through the Minister. There is one Case (a friend requests me to mention) it involving the value of—a considerable amount. The negroes mortgaged have been taken to the province of. Taos or Texas.— The instrument will have reached Washington[5] perhaps before your return from Kentucky.   with it you will receive a more Specific account of the matter. And whatever conference is necessary as one of the executive officers of the Union we call upon you to hold.

Possibly there may be some provisions made by treaty with Mexico. by which we may arrive at justice. with more facility than I anticipate—   Should there be I am unapprized of it at present. This I do know. That there ought to be a more speedy. mode than that of making application to. the diplomatists of the country. It certainly works a great injury to many. who are placed in situations similar to that of the individuals above alluded to. If the mode be as I judg[e] I think it would hereafter settle inquiry could Such a mode be adopted. as exists in the United States. where a mortgage or Hypothecation is made in one State and the property Hypothecated is carried into a Sister State.[6]

your attention to these hasty lines will confer a favour on the people of this section and your most Obedient Humble Servt

                                                        JEFFERSON DORSEY

ALS. DNA, RG59, Accounting Records, Misc. Letters. Postmarked: ". . . May 26th." Endorsed on cover by Clay: "Jefferson Dorsey {Ansd. in general terms from Lexn. 2 July 1827}." Answer not found. Dorsey was probably the dry-goods merchant, of Philadelphia, cited in a letter of February 14, 1789, by James Wilkinson to Esteban Miró, the Spanish governor of Louisiana, as seeking to engage in traffic from Kentucky to New Orleans. Published in Gayarré, *History of Louisiana*, III, 246.
  1 The relief and old court-new court controversies (see above, III, 902n).   2 Andrew Jackson.   3Thomas A. King, who apparently was removed before 1829.   4 John McLean.   5 No memorial has been found.   6 The Constitutional provision that "Full Faith and Credit shall be given in each State to the . . . judicial Proceedings of every other State" (Art. IV) had been upheld in numerous opinions—*Moore vs. Spackman*, 12 *Pa.* (Sergeant and Rowles) 287 (1825); *Kimmel vs. Schultz*, 4 *Ill.* (1 Breese) 169 (1826); *Holt vs. Alloway, Ind.* (2 Blackford) 108 (1827).

DIPLOMATIC NOTES   May 26, 1827

From PABLO OBREGÓN, Philadelphia. Acknowledges receipt of Clay's note of May 21; promises to take care that Captain (David) Porter and his command do not violate the neutrality of the United States. LS, in Span. with trans. in State Dept. file. DNA, RG59, Notes from Mexican Legation, vol. 1 (M54, R1).

MISCELLANEOUS LETTERS   May 26, 1827

From CHARLES DOUGLAS, Tuscumbia (Alabama). Acknowledges receipt of his commission as consul at Barcelona (cf. above, Clay to Douglas, April 9, 1827), but declines it. Expresses preference for appointment in the western hemisphere, such as the rumored vacancy at Lima, since he has a partiality for "the liberal political institutions of our sister republics. . . ." ALS. DNA, RG59, Cons. Disp., Barcelona, vol. 2 (M-T121, R2).

From VINCENT GRAY, Havana. States that, "under authority of the Secretary of State [James Monroe]," he drew on that official, on April 12, 1814, for expenses incurred in obtaining "the release of Benedict Pignon, and his associates, of New Orleans," from (Cuban) authorities; that his bill was returned, "under a belief, that it was for the relief of Hargrave and his associates, under the Charge of Doctor Flood"; and that he has "redrawn again upon" Clay for $2,098.32½, the amount of the original sum plus interest. Identifies Pignon as a New Orleans lawyer; explains his own role in effecting the release and providing for the support of both the Pignon and Hargrave parties; and opines that, if the Government had known of the extent of his help to his "unfortunate countrymen" in Havana and the service he "actually rendered in saving the City of New orleans from Conflagration and . . . [his] Country from the disgrace of a defeat at that all important crisis in 1814," it would not have rejected his bill. LS. DNA, RG76, Misc. Claims, Spain.

On June 20 Daniel Brent replied to Gray that he had presented the claim "to the consideration of the 5th. Auditor of the Treasury," (Stephen) Pleasonton, and that this officer requested more information to substantiate the claim. Brent added that he had "received no communication from General Jackson" for Gray. Copy, in DNA, RG59, Cons. Instr., vol. 2, pp. 432–34 (M78, R2).

Pignon has not been further identified. William H. Hargrave, a judge of quarterly court in Mississippi Territory, and six others, who had participated in the West Florida revolt of 1810, had been captured by the Spaniards and imprisoned for six years in Cuba. William Flood, Virginian by birth, had been one of the first Americans to settle in New Orleans, had served as a member of the Territorial Council and as physician of the ports of Louisiana. A close friend of Governor W. C. C. Claiborne, Dr. Flood had been sent to organize the parishes of Biloxi and Pascagoula in 1811, following the American annexation of West Florida.

Gray had addressed two letters to Andrew Jackson, on December 30, 1826, and February 14, 1827, recalling to him the fact that he (Gray) was the author of several letters to the general in the summer and fall of 1814 which had given warning of the intended attack on New Orleans and, particularly, of the feint on Mobile as merely a decoy to conceal the focus of the campaign. DLC-Jackson Papers, Series 1 (MR34).

INSTRUCTIONS AND DISPATCHES   May 27, 1827

From ROBERT MONROE HARRISON, off St. Thomas. Transmits duplicate of his dispatch of April 11 (not found), "containing many additional notes and remarks," together with "a *correct list from the Custom House* [of Jamaica], of the *Imports* from the North of Europe and the Mediterranean, since the Colonial Ports were closed to our flag." Comments relative to the latter: "This is a document of considerable importance in as much as it clearly shews what little *faith or dependence*, are to be placed on the *reports or Statements* of our *enemies,* or interested *persons.*" Notes that, while he had been "told that vessels were daily arriving in that Colony from various parts of Europe, laden with every thing which formerly came from the U States," the fact was that not a vessel arrived from Continental Europe during the month he was there and shipments were coming daily from St. Iago and St. Thomas—a long and expensive double portage, which merchants of Jamaica yet found "more to their interest . . . than to trade with the Baltic, notwithstanding all that may be said to the Contrary by *theorists,* and *enemies* of America in *England* and *elsewhere!*" ALS. DNA, RG59, Cons. Disp., St. Thomas, vol. 2 (M-T350, R2). Received June 16. Enclosures not found.

To James Brown

No. 13 James Brown Envoy Extraordinary and
Minister Plenipotentiary at Paris
Sir,   Department of State Washington, 28 May 1827

I transmit herewith, a report from this Department to the House of Representatives, made at the last Session of Congress, in pursuance of a Resolution of the House, containing a schedule of Claims of Citizens of the United States on Foreign Governments arising out of spoliations committed on our Commerce during the wars of the French Revolution.[1] The Schedule is as comprehensive as the materials in the possession of the Department would admit, but it is not to be taken as by any means exhibiting the full amount of the just claims of our Citizens. The common casualties incident to human nature have probably prevented the transmission to the Department of many claims. Some did not come in until after the expiration of the period fixed in the resolution of the House of Representatives for their being forwarded to the Department, and others were received subsequently to the presentation of the Schedule to the House. The claims which are excluded ought not to be considered as affected, in the least degree, by their omission. The design of the House of Representatives, in requiring a statement of the amount of Claims upon Foreign Governments, was to obtain a general and proximate view of their extent, without any purpose of impairing the validity of those which, from whatever cause, should not be forwarded.

Although, for the reasons just mentioned, the schedule ought to be received as an imperfect exhibit of the total number and amount of the Claims which it was intended to include, the aggregate sum which it, in fact, presents, is sufficient to enlist the best exertions of the Government to procure for the Claimants the indemnity to which they are justly entitled. Whether we regard the enormity of the aggressions out of which those claims spring, the numerous persons interested in the liquidation of them, or the vast amount at issue, the Government of the United States can never be indifferent to their satisfactory adjustment, and, however unpromising appearances may, from time to time, be, it will persevere to the last, until indemnity be obtained.

The Schedule was referred by the House of Representatives, to its Committee of Foreign Affairs, which, on the 23. February last, made a report,[2] of which a copy is herewith transmitted. The Committee conclude their report by observing that the confidence which they entertain "that the measures within the competence of the Executive will eventually prove successful is measured by the reliance which is felt in the justice and honour of Foreign Governments. 'Till those measures shall have been exhausted, and found inadequate, the time will not have arrived for legislative interference." It is the expectation of the Claimants, of Congress, and of the Country, that a renewed appeal shall be made, through the Executive, to the justice of France. The Committee properly remark in their report that "justice could not perhaps with propriety be enforced from the other Powers before, nor dispensed with after, it shall have been done to Our Citizens by this powerful, prosperous and magnanimous State, of whose elevated and liberal policy the people of the United States have had too many proofs to fear a final difference of sentiment on this subject." It should be added that France may be properly considered as the parent source of all the wrongs inflicted by the Continental Powers, during the Revolutionary wars, on the Commerce of the United States; and both for that reason, and on account of the greater magnitude of the Claims upon France, which, according to the schedule, is nearly double the amount of those upon all the other continental Governments together, there is an evident fitness in that Nation's taking the lead in equitable reparation, which took the lead in the original aggression.

It is, therefore, the President's wish that you should again bring the subject of the American Claims to the view of the French Government, and demand that satisfaction which has been so long unjustly withheld. In executing this duty, it may not be unprofitable, that you should present to its notice a brief review of the treatment which has been given by the present Government, since the final overthrow of Napoleon, to similar demands when urged by your predecessor[3] and Yourself.

[Summarizes at length, with citations to and quotations from numerous documents, the negotiations since 1816.]

Such is a faithful account derived from official correspondence, of the course of conduct which France has deemed proper to pursue in respect to the demands made by the American Government for satisfaction of just claims, amounting, according to the Schedule before mentioned, to a sum little short of ten Millions of dollars, and founded upon unexampled wrongs.— The American Government cannot contemplate it without unmixed regret and dissatisfaction. The argu-

ments offered to the consideration of the French Government, in support of those claims, by your predecessor, and by yourself, dispense
with the necessity of my renewing, at this time, the discussion. They
stand to this day unanswered, because they are unanswerable. I shall
content myself with a few observations only, upon some of the more
prominent features of the Correspondence.

The justice of the American Claims has never been controverted by
France, unless what has recently passed in the communications from
the Baron de Damas to yourself (and which will be hereafter more
particularly noticed) is to be regarded as controverting them. It
cannot be denied,[4] a large portion of those claims has been expressly
admitted to be just, by more than one French Secretary of Foreign
Affairs. A verbal offer was made, upwards of ten years ago, by the
Duke de Richelieu, then filling that Department, of indemnity for
vessels burnt at sea, and for those, the proceeds of which had been
only sequestered and deposited in the Caisse d'Amortissement, which
offer was promised to be put in writing,[5] but the promise was not fulfilled. In subsequently declining to commit the French Government
by a written proposal, as[6] was stated by the Duke that they were not
willing to reject, absolutely and definitively, our reclamations, but
that they could not admit them *at that time*. And he afterwards repeated that he wished it to be clearly understood that the postponement of our Claims was not a rejection.[7] More than five years ago, the
Viscount de Montmorency stated to Mr. Gallatin that he had read the
papers relative to the Antwerp Sequestrations and that he was struck
with the justice of the Claim.[8] On a subsequent occasion (the 18h May
1822) a prospect, unfortunately not afterwards realized, was presented,
of a satisfactory arrangement, by the payment of a stipulated sum, in
full discharge of the demands of the United States for spoliations, to
be distributed by the American Government, or the reference of the
whole case to a joint Commission.[9]

The causes which have hitherto delayed or obstructed the fulfilment [sic] of the well founded expectations of the American Government, are far from being satisfactory. When our Claims were first
presented by Mr. Gallatin, in 1816, and for some time afterwards, the
embarrassed state of France was urged by the French Government, as
a consideration for their postponement to a more auspicious period.[10]
This period at last comes, when France is again powerful and prosperous, and her finances flourishing. We are then told that our Claims
might have been more favorably received in 1816.[11] We have been
unfortunately too soon or too late.

The Commercial difficulties which afterwards arose between the
two Countries, and which originated with France, were made the
pretext of a further postponement until those difficulties should be

adjusted. They were happily terminated by the Convention at Washington, of 1822.[12] Then we had a right confidently to expect the long-deferred indemnity. But where the disposition to redress wrongs does not exist, the means of evasion[13] and procrastination will never be wanting. We can regard in no other light the claim brought forward by France under the eighth Article of the Louisiana Treaty.[14] That claim has been fully examined and elaborately discussed by the two Governments. Every argument has been exhausted, and the most respectful and patient consideration has been given to the pretensions of France. A clear conviction is felt by the American Government that they are without foundation.[15] Even if we could suppose France to entertain the opposite conviction, it would afford no just reason for withholding satisfaction of our claims. The two subjects are perfectly incongruous. One appertains to a contract, about the interpretation of which the parties may sincerely differ, the other arises out of wrongs, committed in notorious violation of the public law, the character of which admits of no difference of opinion. One is national, the other individual. Supposing the respective claims of the two Countries to be similar in their nature, the priority of injury gives us a right to prior satisfaction. Nor can there be perceived any adequate motive for withholding that satisfaction from the consideration of settling *all* matters of difference. The expediency of removing all causes of misunderstanding, if it be practicable, is readily admitted, but if that be not attainable, it does not follow that none should be removed, and especially it does not follow, that those should not be obviated which are attended with a deep sense of the aggressions from which they have had their origin.

It may be true, as alleged by Baron de Damas, that the King of France,[16] on reascending the throne, "could not take, nor has *taken*, the engagement to satisfy all the charges imposed on him as indemnity for the acts of violence, and for the depredations committed by the usurping Government."[17] And yet the obligation of France to redress those Acts and depredations may be perfect. It is not necessary to discuss the question of usurpation, which is put forward. It is sufficient for us that those acts and depredations proceeded from the actual Government of France; and that the responsibility of France to make reparation, for wrongs committed under the authority of any form of government which she may have adopted, or to which she may have submitted, from time to time, cannot be contested. The King of France, in reascending the throne of his ancestors, assumed the Government with all the obligations, rights and duties which appertained to the French Nation. He can justly claim absolution from none of those obligations or duties. And our complaint is precisely that he has not taken upon himself the engagement to make that indemnity to which American Citizens are entitled, in consequence of the wrongful acts committed under previous French Governments.

That engagement might have been voluntarily assumed, by the King of France, from a spontaneous sense of justice and the claims of American Citizens satisfied, without the interposition of the Government of the United States. It is because that has not been done, that this interposition became necessary, and for the last ten years has been constantly made.

The Government of the United States is ever ready to acknowledge any proofs of justice or benevolence which may be exhibited by Foreign Nations towards its Citizens. It regrets that it cannot concur with Baron de Damas in estimating, as among that number, any consent, which France has hitherto given to examine the American claims,[18] especially since that examination has been hitherto eluded, and the consent itself coupled with inadmissible conditions.

Nor can the President admit the propriety of associating in the same negotiation the disputed demand under the 8h. article of the Louisiana Treaty, and incontestible [sic] claims of American Citizens, a large portion of which, it has been seen, so far from being questioned, has been admitted by France to be just.

He sees therefore, with surprise and regret, the adherence of France to the principle of such an unnatural connexion. But whilst the American Government must constantly protest against it, and reiterate its strong conviction that the French pretension under the Louisiana Treaty has no just foundation, I am charged by the President to instruct you to afford a new and signal proof of the equitable disposition of this Government, by proposing to that of France, as a basis for the settlement of the question under that Treaty, that it be referred to arbitration. Should that basis be agreed to, it will then become necessary to specify the particular question to be submitted, and the details of the Arbitration. By the Commercial Convention between the two powers, concluded in 1822, there will be on the first day of October next, a perfect equalization of duties on the Vessels and their Cargoes, of the two Countries, employed in the trade between them. The complaint of France has been, that this equality did not exist, but that French vessels, and their Cargoes, have been liable in the Ports of Louisiana to pay the Alien duties imposed by the Laws of the United States, from which duties British vessels were exempt. And her claim is the reimbursement of those duties. Should the proposed basis, therefore, be acceded to, You are authorized to refer to arbitration the question, whether France be entitled, or not, to have refunded any of those alien duties collected from French Vessels, or their Cargoes, between the periods of the date of the Louisiana Treaty and the first day of October 1827. And, if the demand be sustained by the Arbitrators, that they shall then proceed to determine the Amount which is to be so refunded, which Amount shall be credited to France against the American Claims, and if it should exceed them, the excess shall be paid by the United States.

Two modes of constituting an Arbitration present themselves. One is to refer the question to a friendly Power; the other, to submit it to individuals, to be chosen by the Parties. If it were referred to a friendly power, some functionary of the Government of that Power would probably be designated to examine, and, in effect, decide the question. For that reason, and because no friendly power would perhaps be very willing to undertake the arbitration, it would be most expedient to submit the controversy, at once, to individuals, selected by the parties themselves. You are authorized, therefore, to propose that each Power shall appoint one or two Citizens or subjects, being natives of some other nation, and that the two or four so appointed, shall be authorized to appoint a third or fifth, also being a Citizen of some nation other than the United States or France, and that the three or five persons (as the case may be) thus appointed, shall be empowered to hear and decide the question, as above stated, arising under the 8h. Article of the Louisiana Treaty; and, if the decision be favorable to France, to fix the amount to which, in consequence of it, she may be entitled.

Should the arbitration be agreed to, other details will be necessary, as to the oath to be taken by the Arbitrators, their compensation, the time and place of their meeting, the duration of the Arbitration, and the right of the parties to be heard by their agents, to all of which you are authorized to agree. Models for the draft of articles comprehending similar details are furnished in several of our Treaties, particularly those with Great Britain, in 1794[19] and in 1814, at Ghent.

It will probably be most advisable to propose the basis of an Arbitration in general terms, and not to state the precise question as above defined, and the other details, until that basis shall have been agreed to.

Possibly the French Government may offer to refer the question upon the condition of submitting to the same arbitration the American Claims and those of France. You will oppose that condition on the ground of the difference in the character of the two subjects, and for the reasons which have been urged by this Government against their being comprehended in the same negotiation.[20]

Should France prefer a reference of the question to a Sovereign Power, instead of private persons, you may agree to such a reference. We are not prepared, nor is it necessary, in the present stage of the business, to designate the Sovereign Power, nor the persons to whom we should be willing to submit the matter. Ample time will probably be afforded, during the progress of the negotiation, to make such a nomination. Or should France promptly agree to the reference, and you should deem it inexpedient to wait for futher [*sic*] instructions from this Department as to the Arbitrators, a clause may be inserted in the Convention, providing that the two Governments shall within a period of (say) six months agree upon a nomination of them.[21]

Whatever may be the nature of the reception or the ultimate fate of the overture which you are now authorized to make, for the settlement of the question growing out of the Louisiana Treaty, you will earnestly press for satisfaction of our claims. The instructions heretofore given to your predecessor and to yourself indicate the modes, according to which the amount of them may be ascertained, and indemnity may be secured; and also authorize provision for any just claims of French subjects on the American Government. I am with great Respect Your Obedient Servant   H CLAY

P.S.[22]   The schedule of claims on Foreign Governments is in the hands of the printer, and a Copy cannot now be sent. It will be transmitted as soon as it shall be printed.   H. C.

LS. KyLxT-Haupt Collection. Copy, in DNA, RG59, Dip. Instr., vol. 11, pp. 316–39 (M77, R6). Two drafts, in DLC-HC (DNA, M212, R8)—most of the first is in Clay's hand; the second, a clerk's copy, includes on the last page marginal additions and a concluding paragraph by Clay and bears a notation that the record was to be made from it. Significant variations among these versions are noted below.
    [1] See above, Clay to Taylor, January 30, 1827.   [2] *House Repts.*, 19 Cong., 2 Sess., no. 87.   [3] Albert Gallatin.   [4] In the first and second drafts a period ends a sentence at this point.   [5] See Albert Gallatin to James Monroe, January 20, 1817, extract in *American State Papers, Foreign Relations*, V, 287. Cf. above, Brown to Clay, November 29, 1826.   [6] This word is "it" in the two drafts and the copy.   [7] See Gallatin to [John Quincy Adams,] April 23, July 12, 1817, extracts published in *American State Papers, Foreign Relations*, V, 288, 289.   [8] See Gallatin to Adams, January 28, 1822, extract published *ibid.*, 306. The "Antwerp sequestrations" encompassed the cargoes of seven vessels which had arrived at Antwerp early in 1807 and had been permitted to unload. Under an order of the French Government, dated May 4, 1810, the cargoes had been sequestered and sold without condemnation proceedings, and the receipts from the sale had been placed in the public treasury. Gallatin to Richelieu, November 9, 1816, *ibid.*, 286.   [9] See Gallatin to [Adams], June 13, 1822, *ibid.*, 309.   [10] See Gallatin to [Adams], April 23, 1817, *ibid.*, 288.   [11] According to the summary, and to the dispatch (Brown to Adams, January 20, 1825 [LS, in DNA, RG59, Dip. Disp., France, vol. 22 (M34, R25)]), this statement had been made to Brown by the Baron de Damas during an interview on January 17, 1825. Cf. above, Brown to Clay, September 24, 1825.   [12] Cf. above, III, 53n.   [13] This word was substituted by Clay, in the second draft, for "elusion."   [14] Cf. above, III, 382, 383n.   [15] Cf. above, Brown to Clay, March 23, 1825. See also, Adams, *Memoirs*, VII, 279.   [16] Louis XVIII.   [17] Cf. above, Brown to Clay, December 12, 1825; November 29, 1826.   [18] A statement of this nature had been made by Damas in a note to Brown, November 11, 1825, a copy of which had been transmitted with the latter's dispatch, above, no. 37, of November 28, 1825.   [19] Jay's Treaty.   [20] In the two drafts the paragraph continues: "But if you should be unable to prevail on the French Government to consent to the separation of the two subjects, you are then authorized to agree to a submission of both the American and French claims along with the Louisiana question to the same arbitration." During a discussion of these instructions in a meeting of the Cabinet, according to Adams, "Mr. [Richard] Rush objected to this reference of the claims, as did Governor [James] Barbour—I thought," Adams continued, "with good reason. I suggested that the claimants themselves might make it a ground of future claim against this Government. Mr. Clay thought the prospects of the claimants would be improved by submission to an arbitration, but agreed to modify his letter of instruction to Mr. Brown so that the proposal of

arbitration should be confined to the question upon the Louisiana Convention. I have little confidence in anything that we can now do for the attainment of indemnity for these claims, and believe that the only benefit to be expected from this instruction will be to show that they are not abandoned by the Government, and to serve as the foundation of a report concerning them to Congress at the next session." Adams, *Memoirs*, VII, 279. Because the entire paragraph, in the second draft, was crossed out, perhaps inadvertently, the following marginal notes in Clay's hand appear on the last page of that copy: "Memo: The clause stricken out it was thought by the President best to omit. 26 May 1827. H C. That part of the clause beginning with 'Possibly' on the other side and ending with negotiation in the third line on this side to be retained. H C"

[21] Clay's first draft ends at this point. The next paragraph was added, in his hand, to the second draft. [22] This addendum, none of which is in Clay's hand, was written in the right hand margin of the last page of the second draft. The opposite margin of the same page carries the following notation, in a clerk's hand: "18 July—The schedule is just recd from the Printers and a copy is now Sent. Noted in a Duplicate."

To Daniel Webster

Washington, 28th May, 1827.

MY DEAR SIR: I received your favor under date the 18th instant, from Boston. I regret the state of things there which defeated the election, but it will have no bad effect on the general scale.

Governor Lincoln,[1] I fear, will not be prevailed upon to run as Senator. I transmit you a letter this day received from Mr. Silsbee on that subject.[2] The Governor, I believe, is well apprised of the President's anxious desire that he should be in the Senate. I know not of any further exertions that can be made to induce him to alter his determination. Should he adhere to it, I have ventured to express the opinion that it would be expedient that you should be sent. Should Oakley[3] be friendly, that will abate the objections to your transfer, although, as it regards yourself personally, I do not think they will be entirely removed.

The condition of affairs in New Hampshire is to be regretted. But, if you are right in supposing four-fifths of the Republican party in that State to be favorable, Mr. Hill[4] cannot effect much. And sooner or later he must meet with the fate which he merits. I have always supposed that New England, in all its parts, was so friendly as not to leave any doubt of its final decision.[5] I have not a single regular correspondent in New Hampshire. I think Governor Bell[6] (with whom I have occasionally exchanged a letter) may be entirely confided in.

From the West, and from Pennsylvania and Maryland, the current of news continues to run in a good channel. They are getting very warm in Kentucky, but, unless I am entirely deceived, there is no uncertainty in the final issue.

I *wish* to leave here about the middle or last of next week. I shall go by Pittsburg [sic], where I anticipate a cordial reception.

I shall be glad to hear from you while you are in New York.

The affair of Rio is much less serious in fact than it is represented to be in the papers.[7] I think Mr. Raguet acted rather precipitately.

And I hope we shall be able to arrange it satisfactorily. I am always Cordially your friend, H. CLAY.

D. Webster, Esq.

Curtis, *Life of Daniel Webster*, 299–300. ¹ Levi Lincoln.
² Above, May 23, 1827. ³ Thomas Jackson Oakley. ⁴ Isaac Hill. ⁵ Adams carried New England decisively in 1828, by both popular and electoral vote. One vote of Maine's nine was all that Jackson received. Schlesinger and Israel (eds.), *History of American Presidential Elections*, I, [492]. ⁶ Samuel Bell. ⁷ Cf. above, Raguet to Clay, March 12, 17, 1827. The Washington *United States Telegraph*, May 17, 1827, had called "upon the government for protection and redress" in reaction to "The insult offered to the American flag, and the injury done to an American citizen by the Brazilian functionaries. . . ." The same journal had reprinted items from the *Philadelphia Gazette and Daily Advertiser* and the Baltimore *Gazette and Daily Advertiser*, Jacksonian organs, criticizing the administration's failure to require United States naval commanders to afford protection against the Brazilian seizures. The Washington *Daily National Intelligencer*, on May 18, 1827, had suggested that there might be two sides to the matter, that the Brazilian Government might "not be exclusively in fault in reference to it," and that Raguet might better have waited for instructions before taking action.

MISCELLANEOUS LETTERS May 28, 1827

From PETER CARE, JR., Philadelphia. Inquires respecting a claim he made, when (John Quincy) Adams was Secretary of State, against Spain "for robbery and detention of" himself "in the port of Manzanillo de Cuba, as Master & Owner of the Schooner Antelope. . . ." ALS. DNA, RG76, Misc. Claims, Spain, env. 2, folder 1. Endorsed by Clay on cover: "Mr. B. will ansr. this letter H C." No answer has been found. A document (unaddressed and undated, but endorsed as accompanying this MS. in the file "with C. F. Mayer's Letter of 23 Jany 1829") reveals that the incident had occurred in 1824. No record of a settlement has been found.

From James Brown

My dear Sir, Paris May 29. 1827

I have received your letter of the fifteenth of April¹ in which I was sorry to find that you speak of your health as requiring a journey to Kentucky. I am afraid the labor of your office and the unpleasant state of party feeling much of the acrimony of which seems to be directed at you have an unfavorable influence on your health and I regret to discover that there is little reason to look for a more mild state of the political atmosphere until after the next Presidential election. Until I received a letter from you and from another of my friends I had no idea that the question had excited so much feeling as to have interrupted the usual intercourse of society. I am sorry to find that Benton has thought it necessary to prove his friendship to Jackson by renouncing it for any of his old friends but more especially for you to whom I once thought him sincerely attached.² In truth our poor offices badly paid and of short tenure are dearly bought when obtained at the price of contests with those whom we have long cherished and esteemed.

I have been anxious to know whether the Dispatches I sent by the Lewis which vessel you may remember was lost on the Jersey shore,³ have arrived and whether like some other letters sent by that opportunity they have been rendered illegible by the sea. My accounts and vouchers for the last year were on board. I hope if they have arrived that Mr Pleasonton has done me the kindness to settle them to the first of this year.

The French have been for some time engaged in preparing some of their large Vessels for sea at Brest and Toulon, and conjectures have been afloat as to their destination   The Baron de Damas told me on the 28 that he was afraid he should have soon to inform me that France had quarrelled with the Algerines[4]   I have not heard the particulars of the dispute. The prevailing conjecture has been that France was going to carry a force to Haiti in consequence of some difficulty growing out of the Treaty with Boyer.[5] I can hardly believe this conjecture correct and yet if the Algerines are the enemy to be attacked it would seem more easy to employ the Fleet at Toulon— It is possible however that the increased strength of Algiers and the resistance they made when attacked by Lord Exmouth[6] may suggest the policy of attacking it with an overwhelming force—

Mrs Brown[7] is busy purchasing handsome things for Mrs. Clay and will have an opportunity of sending the Jewelry and small articles by Mrs. Rumpff[8] the daughter of Mr Astor[9] and wife of the Gentleman who goes in August to Washington to make a Commercial treaty with the United States[10]   I am Dear Sir truly Yours   J. B.
Hon. Henry Clay.

ALS. DLC-HC (DNA, M212, R2).   [1] Not found.
[2] Cf. above, Clay to Brown, March 27, 1827; Brown to Clay, May 12, 1827.   [3] Cf. above, Brown to Clay, January 13, 1827, note; April 12, 1827.   [4] The French and the Algerines had been quarreling since early in the decade over a claim by the latter for payment on a contract arranged under the French Republic. On April 30, 1827, the Dey (Husséin) had hit the French consul (Pierre Deval) in the face with a fly swatter when the latter complained that Barbary corsairs were pillaging French vessels. *Annual Register, 1827,* [226]; *1829,* [172]. Deval, who had entered the French consular service as a youth and served all his life in various Moslem states, had been consul general at Algiers since 1815. He had been involved in negotiations concerning the disputed debt in 1817 and 1818 and was himself charged with fraud by the contending parties in the controversy over its repayment. He was evacuated from Algiers with other French subjects by the French Navy on June 11, 1827, and died the following month.   [5] Jean Pierre Boyer. Cf. above, Brown to Clay, May 10, 1826.   [6] Edward Pellew, 1st Viscount Exmouth, born at Dover, had entered the British Navy in 1770, had acquired some distinction for service on Lake Champlain during the American Revolution, had been knighted for action against the French in 1793, and had been raised to a barony for gallantry in 1796. In service through the wars with France, he had been named commander in chief in the Mediterranean in 1811. He had been elevated to the peerage as Baron Exmouth in 1814, awarded the rank of admiral of the blue in 1815, and accorded titles as K.C.B. and G.C.B. in the latter year. In July, 1816, he had been sent to effect the release of British subjects held by the Barbary Powers. While this mission had been successfully accomplished, the Dey of Algiers, Ōmar Pacha (1815–1817), had rejected a further demand that he abolish the enslavement of Christians. Exmouth had been ordered to return to Algiers upon reports of further outrages and on August 27, 1817, had opened fire on the city. The attack had lasted nearly eight hours before the Algerines had finally yielded to all Exmouth's demands. He had returned to England as commander in chief at Plymouth from 1817 to 1821 and thereafter performed little active service.
    [7] Ann Hart Brown.   [8] Mrs. Vincent (Elizabeth Astor) Rumpff.   [9] John Jacob Astor.   [10] Vincent Rumpff. Cf. above, Hughes to Clay, March 9, 1827, note.

From Henry Eckford

Dear Sir   *Confidential*   New York 29 May 1827

I received your favours of the 20h & 23d[1] for the sentiments you have been pleased to express in your first, I tender you my thanks

Your views, as expressed in that of the 23d I have little doubt are in the main about as things really are

You do not however it seems to me give that consequence to Party, that it is entitled to in this State, I do not mean to argue its reasonableness, it is enough, that such is the State of things

Every office in this state is held by party men [no]t friends of Mr V. B,[2] generaly [sic]—, but friends [of th]emselves, and they will sustain party, and [no] one better understands that than Mr V.B— it [is] his Strong Hold.—

These office Holders cannot be made by Mr V. B. or any other man, to take courses that they think will endanger their offices, consequently some indication, and it must be publick is required before they will cast loose from their present anchorage—which I have no doubt they think is Mr Adams—, at least to the West

But the friends of the administration ought by no means to be idle, they can take count and unite, as well as the oposition [sic]—

In the City New York for instance no effort ought to be spared to unite the party in suport [sic] of the adminn. those men who supported Mr Crawford[3]— or as many as possible ought to be brought in if possible.—

Should you write a friendly letter to the Venerable Colonel Henry Rutgers,[4] expressing your Respect, and disposition to hear his opinions—it would go far to prom[ote] such a State of things,   Mess. Jefferson M[adison] & Monroe—used to do so occasionaly [sic]—with [him] and Colonel Willet,[5] and it tended great[ly] to keep union, Thompson. Targee. Bloodgoo[d.] Riker, Maxwell[6] &c &c, these concentrate around Rutgers, and should they find that through him they can [en]joy a reasonable share of influence that is [a]ll that is wanted—

Maxwell wants the U.S. atorneyship [sic] for this District, when Tillotson[7] retires—

He would consequently be anxious to promote such good feelling [sic]— I have named Maxwell fearfull [sic] that on account of the feellings [sic] which you can readily imagine I have towards him which to be sure are as bitter as my nature admits of[8] I mention him as the strongest case that can [. . .][9] with me and that I should feel more troubled still if I was to [a]llow myself for one moment to permit [any] private wrongs to interfere in any way [whic]h might mar the general object, which [is] polictical [sic] union,— My private affairs can be setled [sic] after that, let him be in what situation he may,—

Should you write Rutgers should [*sic*] like to know it,— I think it can be done to some advantage, without stating the fact publicly,[10]

I am the more desirous some course like this should be pursued—as one of the reasons for endeavouring to keep things quiet was a fear that those people might imagine, that, they migh[t] be circumvented by me, if we were on the same side, and in consequence of such idea, I did not think it prop[er] to be open—untill [*sic*] they were commited [*sic*] or at least, I was satisfyed, they wer[e] lost, which they need not be as I se[e] it— I am Sir With great Respect Your Most ob

H. Clay Esqr—   HENRY ECKFORD

ALS. DLC-HC (DNA, M212, R2). MS. torn.

[1] Not found. Cf. above, Ogden to Clay, *ca.* May 15, 1827.   [2] Martin Van Buren.

[3] William H. Crawford. On the divisions within the Tammany organization, cf. above, Porter to Clay, May 1, 1827, note.   [4] Rutgers, born in New York and, in 1766, graduated from King's College (Columbia University), had held rank as a captain in service during the American Revolution and subsequently commanded a New York militia regiment. In 1784 and for a number of subsequent terms he had been a member of the New York Legislature. Wealthy and philanthropically motivated, he served as regent or trustee of several academic institutions, including the University of the State of New York, Princeton, and Queen's College (renamed in 1825 in his honor) for extended periods. In 1811 he had raised $28,000 for construction of the Tammany Wigwam. He died in 1830.

[5] Marinus Willett, born at Jamaica, Long Island, and educated at King's College, had served as an officer in both the French and Indian and Revolutionary Wars, in the latter of which he had acquired the rank of lieutenant colonel. He had served as sheriff of the city and county of New York from 1784 to 1788 and again from 1792 to 1796 and as mayor of the city from 1807 to 1811.   [6] Probably Jonathan Thompson, John Targee, Abraham Bloodgood, Richard Riker, and Hugh Maxwell. Bloodgood, a ship carpenter, was a Tammany leader, prominent in 1832 as a Van Buren supporter.   [7] Robert Tillotson.   [8] Maxwell was the prosecuting attorney in the litigation currently involving Eckford, noted above, Porter to Clay, May 1, 1827.   [9] Word illegible.

[10] See below, Clay to Rutgers, June 4, 1827.

From William Marks

Dear Sir   Pittsburgh May 29th. 1827.

The Subject I mentioned to you before I left Washington, I now learne [*sic*] has been has been [*sic*] decided on by the chancey [*sic*] Court at Fredericksbg. Va. and the proceedings are to be transmited [*sic*] to you for examination[1]

[Gives details of the case, involving title to 1,000 acres of land in Brooke County, Virginia (now West Virginia), purchased by Marks in 1826 from the heirs of James Johnston, of Caroline County, Virginia, and which had been bound by a judgment secured by the heirs of Johnston's brother, John.]

When I was at Fredericksbg in March an arrangement had taken place between the Heirs of John & James Johnston, with the exception of one in Tennessee[2] who remained to be heard from. I am now informed by letter, that the Heirs of John Johnston have affirmed the Sale of the land in Brooke by the Heirs of James Johnston. and that the chancery Court have Decreed the sale to be valid and directed the money to be paid to the extinguishment of the Judgment— I H Williams Esqr³ of Frederick attends to the case in my behalf. and is to transmit the chancery Decree to you and the money I deposited in the branch bank at Washington to be paid over as the Court directs. the Craft for $1320—I have transmitted to the Cashier⁴ payable to your order. I am not advised to whome [*sic*] the Court has directed the money to be paid   the decree will explain that circumstance   I beleive [*sic*] Mr Williams to be a gentleman of integrity who will not advise an improper act.   still I wish you to be well satisfied with the proceedings before you direct the payment to be made

I have procured the conveyance from the Heirs of James Johnston   the lean [*sic*] on it removed compleats the title   I am with sentiments of respect your friend   WILLIAM MARKS
Hon Henry Clay

ALS. DLC-TJC (DNA, M212, R13).
¹ Neither the case report nor the documents have been found.   ² The Johnstons were probably the veterans of the Virginia Line who had also entered a number of military warrants for Kentucky lands; they have not been further identified.   ³ Isaac Hite Williams, who had been admitted to the Winchester bar in 1794, was a distinguished lawyer.   ⁴ Richard Smith.

DIPLOMATIC NOTES   May 29, 1827

From CHRISTIAN MAYER, Baltimore. States that he has not received an answer to his letter of March 12 and transmits a duplicate. ALS. DNA, RG59, Notes from Foreign Consuls, vol. 2. Duplicate endorsed: "Mr. B. will answer the enclosed. H.C." No answer has been found.

INSTRUCTIONS AND DISPATCHES   May 29, 1827

From JAMES BROWN, Paris, no. 68. Acknowledges receipt of Clay's instructions no. 10 (above, March 21, 1827). States that he had planned "to wait a few days for the adjournment of the Chambers" before acting on Clay's instruction but a case "has unexpectedly presented itself at Marseilles, which is in some degree connected with this affair and which . . . required . . . immediate interference." Recites details and notes that he has been promised an interview with the French Minister of Finance (the Comte de Villèle). Reports his arguments to the Baron de Damas, in an interview on May 28, regarding "the repeated vexations" experienced by American ships "from the rule established by the French Government requiring the direct voyage"; notes that he reminded Damas "of the decision of the President, in the instances mentioned in the correspondence of the Baron de Mareuil" (see above, Clay to Mareuil, March 20, 1827; Clay to Brown, March 21, 1827), and that the Baron, although "not prepared to decide on it," seemed to consider "that the decision of the President was more conformable to the words and designs of the treaty [of 1822], than that which had been given . . . [by the French Government]." LS. DNA, RG59, Dip. Disp., France, vol. 23 (M34, R26). Received July 13.

From ALBERT GALLATIN, London, no. 79. Reports that his eighth conference (with the British negotiators) occurred on May 24 but that agreement on the protocol has not yet been reached. Notes that he "made the declaration reserving to . . . [the United States] the right of contending for the full extent of the claims . . .

to the territory west of the Stoney Mountains" (cf. above, Clay to Gallatin, February 24, 1827, no. 18) and that (William) Huskisson replied that the British would "enter on the record a protest against those claims." Adds that he (Gallatin) stated "that the President [Adams] could not agree to the provisions of the second article of the Projet of Convention for a joint occupancy of the territories in question [cf. above, Gallatin to Clay, December 20, 1826], and that . . . he was still of opinion that a simple renewal of the former agreement [cf. above, II, 611n] for a limited term of years was sufficient and the most eligible course to be adopted for the present: it being of course understood that, during that period, the two Governments would . . . unite their endeavours to adjust their differences by the establishment of a permanent boundary. . . ." This statement "was taken ad referendum" by the British negotiators. Gallatin, in turn, for want of full documentation of the American justification for levying a higher duty on rolled than forged iron, suspended an informal discussion on the British proposal "respecting rolled iron" in connection with renewal of the commercial convention (cf. above, II, 57–59, 611n; Gallatin to Clay, December 21, 1826; Clay to Gallatin, February 24, 1827, no. 18). Comments that Huskisson "expressed himself very warmly" in reference to the latter controversy and said that if the Americans opposed the British proposal, "the intercourse between the two Countries might be left, like that with the Colonies, to be regulated by mutual legislation" (cf. above, Gallatin to Clay, August 19, 1826). Concludes that "when the subject is regularly taken up," he will rely on Clay's "observations on the merits of the case and avoid any altercations on questions of fact." Postscript notes that "in respect to the Western territory," Gallatin reminded "the British Plenipotentiaries of the act of Parliament by which Great Britain had actually extended her jurisdiction over it" (cf. above, Gallatin to Clay, April 21, 1827, and note) and expressed "surprize [sic] that any objection could have been made to the supposed intention of the United States to pursue the same course." Reports Huskisson's explanation that he objected "to the intention of establishing a custom house and exacting duties . . . as contrary to the third article of the Convention of 1818" and comments: "So far he may be right." ALS. DNA, RG59, Dip. Disp., Great Britain, vol. 34 (M30, R30). Published in *American State Papers, Foreign Relations*, VI, 673. Received July 16.

MISCELLANEOUS LETTERS   May 29, 1827

From ENOCH LINCOLN, Portland, Maine. Accepts Clay's offer (above, May 7, 1827) to supply "copies of all the papers in . . . [his] office, relative to the boundary between this State and New Brunswick, which the President may permit to be transmitted." Requests specifically the maps and transcripts of the arguments of (Ward) Chipman and (James) Sullivan, "as Agents under the commission for determining the true St. Croix; and . . . of Mr. [James Trecothick] Austin and Mr. Chipman, under the fourth Article of the Treaty of Ghent, together with the reports of the Commissioners in both cases." Refers to "the punctilio of expense," which he wishes "to see liquidated." Notes that he has addressed a letter directly to the President on the matter of the Northeastern Boundary. LS. DNA, RG76, Northeastern Boundary, env. 4, item 15. Published under date of April 29, 1827, in *American State Papers, Foreign Relations*, VI, 929.

Lincoln's letter to President Adams, May 19, 1827, also published, *ibid.*, 927–29, protests the proposed arbitration of the dispute on the Maine boundary: "It is not controverted that the control of our foreign relations belongs to the United States as to objects which have arisen under the Constitution or existing laws; but in regard to rights acquired by an independent party, and interests vested by acts anterior to the existence of that compact, the interposition by the Federal Executive, without an express grant of power, seems to be gratuitous."

Sullivan, born in Berwick, Maine, had been an active proponent of the American Revolution and throughout the war a member of the Massachusetts General Court. He had served also as a justice of the State supreme court from 1776 to 1782, a member of the Continental Congress in 1782, an advocate for the Federal Constitution in 1787, State attorney general, from 1790 to 1807, and Governor in 1807 and 1808. He had been a distinguished lawyer, particularly in the field of land titles, and had published volumes on that subject and on the history of Maine. He had been an agent to the commissioners meeting at Halifax on the Maine boundary in 1796.

Austin, born in Boston and educated at Harvard, had been admitted to the bar in 1805 and held office as Suffolk County attorney from 1807 to 1832. He had been named in 1816 as agent under the terms of the Treaty of Ghent and in 1828 was appointed a commissioner to settle a boundary dispute between Massachusetts and Connecticut east of the Connecticut River. From 1832 to 1843 he served as attorney general of Massachusetts and, subsequently returning to private practice, was recognized as one of the leading lawyers of the State.

The commissioners under the Halifax negotiations of 1796, named under Article V of Jay's Treaty to identify the St. Croix River, had been Egbert Benson, David Howell, and Thomas Barclay; those under Articles IV and V of the Treaty of Ghent, Cornelius Van Ness and Barclay. Benson, born in New York and graduated from King's College (Columbia University), had been attorney general of New York from 1777 to 1789, a member of the Continental Congress from 1784 to 1788 and of the Federal Congress from 1789 to 1793 and from 1813 to 1815, a judge of the State supreme court from 1794 to 1801, and a judge of the United States Circuit Court from 1801 to 1802.

From HENRY WHEATON, "Private." Acknowledges receipt of Clay's "note of the [2]2d." (not found). States that he intends leaving next month for Copenhagen, via England; that he will resign as United States Supreme Court reporter on June 1; and that he expects his salary as Chargé to begin on that date. Requests that "this note" not be placed in the files and promises to "write . . . an official Letter on the 1st prox: which may be filed." Adds, in a postscript: "I have sent you the sheets of the Reports, thinking you might wish to see, at least, the cases of Political Cav, which [y]ou will find very interesting.— I am [g]lad to see our friend Judge [Robert] Trimble appear so well." ALS. DNA, RG59, Dip. Disp., Denmark, vol. 1B (M41, R3). Dated May 29.

The reference to "Political Cav" has not been identified. Several cases of political significance had been decided during this term of the Court—e.g., *United States vs. 350 Chests of Tea* (see above, Webster to Clay, March 25, 1827) and *Ogden vs. Saunders* (see above, Boyle to Clay, January 10, 1825). In the latter Clay among others had argued on behalf of George M. Ogden against Wheaton and Daniel Webster, who represented Lewis Sanders. Judge Trimble, who had then sat for his first term on the Court, had handed down a large number of decisions and had supported Ogden's cause in an opinion concurring with the majority that State bankruptcy legislation was valid in so far as it did not conflict with any congressional act. On the outcome of the case of *Ogden vs. Saunders*, however, cf. below, Scott to Clay, September 27, 1827, note.

Editorial Article

[ca. May 30, 1827]

A learned U. States Senator is writing a series of dull pieces, under the signature of "Senex" on the Colonial question, which has been extended to the appalling length of the Nineteenth number.[1] Nobody reads them, no paper copies them, except the Enquirer, which in this respect shews its judgment, by placing them in the background. The Senator has gone back to the Trojan War, and has just come down in his last number to these modern times. He labors hard to prove that the British Government (that model of perfection with the Opposition) has been always right, and the American Government always wrong. By the Constitution this Senator has to express his opinion upon all treaties. If one should be made with G. Britain, he will be a most impartial and unprejudiced guardian of American interests.

A learned judge of the same Senate with the above Senator (the same who has recently found it necessary to write Three hundred and forty five pages to deliver *one* opinion in a cause decided by the Court of which he is a member) has also favored the public with a brief article, under the title of a Farmer, on the same Colonial subject.[2] And what does the reader suppose is the burden of his song? It is, that Mr. Adams deceived Congress, and attempted to cheat the British Government, in order to procure for the American people an acknowledged benefit, that of securing the introduction of their produce into the British Colonies on the same terms as British produce is there received.

If the learned judge mutilates the records on which he is to decide as much as he does the Colonial correspondence, suitors have not much chance for justice before his honor. For he has stated that Mr Vaughan's formal invitation, which was given in March *1826*,[3] to renew the negotiation was given in *1825*

It would be a most amusing & profitable course of reading for an American Student of Law and politics, to begin with Cokes chapter on Warranty,[4] then to read the above mentioned short[5] opinion of Three hundred and Forty five pages, and finally the essay signed "Farmer," and the erudite numbers of Senex.

AD. DLC-HC (DNA, M212, R2). Published, with minor alterations, in Washington *Daily National Journal*, May 31, 1827.
[1] Littleton W. Tazewell published a series of 20 articles, entitled "The Colonial Trade," which first appeared in the Norfolk *Herald* and were reprinted in the *Richmond Enquirer* between April 20 and June 26, 1827. The series was subsequently published as a pamphlet in London under Tazewell's authorship and with the title, *A Review of the Negociations between the United States of America and Great Britain, Respecting the Commerce between the Two Countries, and More Especially Concerning the Trade of the Former with the West Indies* (London, 1829). On the background of the journalistic controversy, cf. above, Clay to Force, February 25, March 25, 1827.　　[2] The judge has not been identified. The article on "The Colonial Trade," signed "A Farmer," had appeared in the *Richmond Enquirer*, March 30, 1827.　　[3] Above, March 22, 1826.
[4] Coke, Edward, *The First Part of the Institutes of the Laws of England . . .* (11th edn., London, 1719), chap. XIII.　　[5] This word was omitted in the printed version.

To James Brown

My Dear Sir　(Private & Confidential)　Washington 30h. May 1827.
I receive, from time to time, your letters which, though not regularly

acknowledged, afford me much gratification. I hope you will not be discouraged in continuing to address them to me, by any apparent neglect, or supposed insensibility to their value.

I shall send you in a few days, a long instruction on the subject of our claims,[1] which is now in the hands of the Copyist. It authorizes you to propose a reference of the question whether France, under the Louisiana treaty, is entitled to have *refunded* the alien duties collected between its date and the first of October next. Your attention shd. be directed to the *precise* question to be submitted, if an arbitration should be agreed to. We should not, for example, like to refer the broad question, whether the French interpretation of that treaty be correct, and to make the decision of the arbitrators obligatory; because, if it should be against us, France might contend hereafter that she would have, under such a decision, the right to introduce any goods whatever, without regard to the place of production, according to the principle of our Guatemala treaty;[2] and that might in effect make Louisiana, so far as navigation is concerned a mere colony of France. Hence, in the conduct of the negotiation, I have thought it best, that you should in general terms propose an arbitration as a basis, and if that be agreed to adjust the details afterwards. If when you come to these details the French Govt. should not be satisfied with a simple reference of the specific question above mentd. and should insist upon the submission of the broad question, you had better take the matter ad referendum. I anticipate a rejection of the proposal, which will place us on stronger ground, without any commitment on matters of detail.

If France should offer to accept the basis of an arbitration but should insist upon refering our claims also, and you should not be able to prevail on her to give up that condition, you had better refer to your Govt. that condition also.

On American politics, I will only now say that my confidence in Mr. Adams's re-election is very great; that we shall have a most embittered contest, uncomfortable in all respects; and that the struggle in Kentucky will be hot and sharp, but I think not doubtful.

I expect to set out in a few days to Kentucky.

Our affair at Rio Janeiro [*sic*], which you will see an account of in the papers,[3] is not likely to lead to any serious consequences. Mr. Raguet acted rashly and precipitately, although the Brazilian Govt. was in the wrong about the Spark.[4] There is a good prospect of a satisfactory arrangement here.

Our comforts are equally increased by our removal to Decatur's house.[5] So our expences are likely to be. We want more lights, and I have to request that Mrs. Brown will procure for us two more glass Chandeliers, exactly like the former one she was good enough to send us, and also six more wall brackets, and four bronze Candle sticks.[6]

I send two volumes of some of my Speeches recently published here.[7] They are published in the same crude state as they were uttered to the public in the prints of the day. One of them is intended for yourself, and I will thank you to get the other neatly bound and presented in my name to Genl. La Fayette.

My health is better than it was this time last year. That of Mrs. Clay is as usual.

We have been disappointed in having Anne[8] to spend the summer with us, in consequence of her being in a family way. I regret it the more as Mrs. Clay does not accompany me to Kentucky.

Be pleased to give our love to Mrs. Brown— I am faithfully your friend   H. CLAY
James Brown Esq.

ALS. ViU.   1 Above, May 28, 1827.   2 Above, Convention with Central American Federation, December 5, 1825.   3 Cf. above, Clay to Webster, May 28, 1827, note.   4 Cf. above, Raguet to Clay, March 12, 17, 1827.   5 Cf. above, Clay to Henry Clay, Jr., April 2, 1827.   6 No record of the purchase of a glass chandelier has been found. Cf. above, Clay to Brown, May 22, 1826.   7 Cf. above, Sparks to Clay, April 9, 1827, note.   8 Mrs. James Erwin. The Erwins' first son, Henry Clay Erwin, was born June 14, 1827. He died at Louisville, Kentucky, August 18, 1859.

From John Sergeant

Dear Sir,   (Private)   Mexico, May 30. 1827.

The U. S. Schooner Shark is at Tampico, to sail about the 10th June. I avail myself of the occasion to write you a line, tho' it is not improbable that I may be in the U. States before the arrival of that vessel. My present intention is to leave Mexico[1] on the 4th. June, and proceed directly to the coast, so that it is quite possible I may embark by the 15th, unless in the mean time, something should occur to detain me. Up to the present moment, no change whatever has taken place, except that the Congress of Mexico has adjourned without acting upon the Panama treaties.[2] An extraordinary session is talked of, in August. But it will do nothing— If I could perceive the least prospect of a meeting of the Congress of Tacubaya,[3] or even any thing upon which an argument could be founded, I should incline to stay. I feel, very sensibly, the awkwardness of going home as I came. All things considered, however, it appears to me that continuing longer here, under existing circumstances, would aggravate the evil. It seems hardly compatible with a due respect for the dig[ni]ty [of] the U. States.

Mr. Clay[4] sailed from Vera Cruz on the 23d for New York in the Brig Ranger, Com. Porter[5] being also a passenger. Mr. Rochester[6] sailed on the 22d in the Genl. Warren for N. Orleans. I am glad they are well off. It is very sickly at Vera Cruz, and has been more than usually so throughout the winter.

I received yesterday, via Tampico, letters and papers from home to the 21st. April. The aspect of affairs seems encouraging, but there is a

bad spirit abroad, incessantly active and desperately bold. I have been afraid that the good cause would be left (as a good cause is very apt to be) too much to itself. The movement in Chambersburg,[7] however, is a good beginning, and I am glad to see that my friends Chambers and McCulloh[8] took an active part in it. They are resolute men, and very persevering. The Green County proceedings, too, are judicious, and I am in hopes Fayette will do something.[9] Pennsylvania ought to be, to a man, on the side of the Administration. Very respectfully and truly yrs.   JOHN SERGEANT.
The Honble Henry Clay.

ALS. DLC-HC (DNA, M212, R2).   [1] City.
[2] Cf. above, Salazar to Clay, November 20, 1826.   [3] Cf. above, Poinsett to Clay, August 20, 1826, note.   [4] Theodore W. Clay.   [5] David Porter.   [6] William B. Rochester.   [7] Cf. above, Clay to Johnston, April 17, 1827.   [8] George Chambers; Thomas Grubb McCullough—both named to the committee of correspondence set up by the assembly. Chambers, born in Chambersburg, graduated in 1804 from Princeton College, and admitted to the bar in 1807, was elected to Congress as a Whig (1833–1837) and sat on the Pennsylvania Supreme Court briefly in 1851. McCullough, born in Greencastle, Franklin County, Pennsylvania, had been admitted to the bar in 1806, had served in the War of 1812, and from 1820 to 1821 had sat in Congress. He was for a time manager and editor of the Chambersburg *Franklin Repository* and from 1831 to 1835 a member of the Pennsylvania House of Representatives.   [9] Meetings in support of a protective tariff and internal improvements had already been held in Fayette, Greene, and Washington Counties of Pennsylvania. That at Waynesburg, Greene County, held on March 20, had adopted resolutions stressing that the authority "to make internal improvements is one of the most important and essential rights of the general government," that "the promotion of *internal improvements* and *domestic manufactures*, constitutes the grand 'American system,'" and that by this program the United States would "be elevated to . . . proud preeminence among the nations of the earth. . . ." *Niles' Weekly Register*, XXXII (April 7, 1827), 103.

DIPLOMATIC NOTES   May 30, 1827

From COUNT FERDINAND LUCCHESI, New York. States that, under a recent decision by Pope Leo XII, henceforth foreign vessels will be received in ports of the Papal States on payment of six "Bajocchi" per ton, "de droits maritime," except that vessels of nations which admit in their ports Roman vessels on the same conditions as their own will pay only three bajocchi—the same as paid by Roman vessels; that, as to customs duties, foreign vessels will be received in Papal ports on the same footing as Roman vessels; and that these decisions have been communicated to (Felix) Cicognani (cf. above, Cicognani to Clay, March 17, 1827). Notes his expectation that the President will now proclaim the opening of American ports to Roman vessels under the same conditions as American vessels (cf. above, Lorich to Clay, March 16, 1825, note). Adds, in a footnote: "Un *Bajocco* Romain est presqu' egal à un centîme des Etats Unis." LS, in French with trans. in State Dept. file. DNA, RG59, Notes from Foreign Consuls.
      Adams issued the expected proclamation on June 7, 1827. Richardson (comp.), . . . *Messages and Papers of the Presidents*, II, 376–77.

From JOSÉ SILVESTRE REBELLO, Washington. States that the Emperor of Brazil (Peter I) hopes the Government of the United States disapproves the action of Condy Raguet in demanding his passports (cf. above, Raguet to Clay, March 12, 17, 1827) and will appoint a replacement, who will find the Emperor's Government disposed to settle questions relating to the case of the *Spark* and, generally, to American vessels detained for attempting to enter the port of Buenos Aires (cf. above, Slacum to Clay, January 28, 1826; Copeland to Clay, May 18, 1826; Bond to Clay, June 30, October 28, 1826; Raguet to Clay, September 1, October 2, 31, 1826; February 7, 1827; Southard to Clay, January 28, 1827; Wright to Clay, May 7, 1827). Requests a written reply indicating disapproval of Raguet's conduct and the willingness of the United States to negotiate. ALS, in Portuguese with trans. in State Dept. file. DNA, RG59, Notes from Brazilian Legation, vol. 1 (M49, R1). Published in *American State Papers, Foreign Relations*, VI, 823–24.

Before composing this document, Rebello had stated to Clay "his willingness to write a note giving assurance of the friendly disposition of his Government, and their readiness, in the event of the appointment of a new Minister, to adjust all the matters of complaint which had been preferred against them conformably to the laws of nations." Clay "requested him," before sending "the note definitively, to let him see the draft of it; to which he [Rebello] agreed." Adams, *Memoirs*, VII, 281. On May 30, Clay took Adams "the note from Mr. Rebello, urging the appointment of a Minister to Brazil, and promising in that event a fair adjustment of . . . complaints." "I thought," Adams commented, "the note might be accepted, with some remarks upon two or three passages in it." *Ibid.*, 283.

INSTRUCTIONS AND DISPATCHES   May 30, 1827

From ALBERT GALLATIN, London, no. 80. Summarizes his course of action after learning of the arrest of his coachman (cf. above, Gallatin to Clay, May 22, 1827); states that he "wished to avoid making of the incident an important question, but thought it necessary to see that nothing was done that did not accord with the general practice of this Government towards foreign Ministers." Encloses copies of correspondence relating to the matter. ALS. DNA, RG59, Dip. Disp., Great Britain, vol. 34 (M30, R30). Received July 16.

From SAMUEL LARNED, Santiago de Chile. Transmits "some printed papers [not found] of interest, having relation to the affairs of Colombia, and the late revolution in Peru" (cf. above, Tudor to Clay, February 3, 1827). ALS. *Ibid.*, Chile, vol. 2 (M-T2, R2). Received August 11.

MISCELLANEOUS LETTERS   May 30, 1827

From H[ENRY] DODGE, St. Genevieve (Missouri). Resigns from the office of marshal of the Missouri District. ALS. "Duplicate." DNA, RG59, Letters of Resig. and Declin.

From WILLIAM JOHNSON, Charleston (South Carolina). Reports that "in Pursuance of . . . [Clay's] Communication" of April 27 "the Commission of District Attorney of the United States for the Dist[r]ict of Georgia has been transmitted to Mathew Hall McAllister Esq. of Savannah," who has accepted the appointment. ALS. DNA, RG59, Misc. Letters (M179, R65).

McAllister, born in Georgia, educated at Princeton, and around 1820 admitted to the bar, was practicing law in Savannah when he received this appointment. He continued as Federal Attorney until 1835, was active as a Democrat in politics, and later became mayor of Savannah for several years and a member of the Georgia House and Senate. In 1850 he moved to San Francisco, where he practiced law and from 1855 to 1862 held appointment as judge of the United States Circuit Court.

From WILLIAM JOHNSON, Charleston, "private." Transmits "The official Communication" (above, this date) concerning "the Dist. Atty of Georgia," as well as copies of his correspondence with McAllister. Reports that he has "not the least Reason to apprehend the Slightest Opposition to the regular Administration of the Laws in Georgia." Notes that purchasers of "Lots in the disputed Territory will now soon go into Possession of it & thus afford the most direct and simple means of trying the question of Right without coming into direct Collision with the Fanatics and the State." Renews his suggestion (earlier statement not found) that "the Boundary line . . . between the two States [be] run under the superintending Eye of the general Government." Contends that the United States has a right to intervene in that manner. ALS. *Ibid.*

The territorial dispute here mentioned concerned the boundary between Georgia and Alabama, on which commissioners of the two States had disagreed in September, 1826. *Niles' Weekly Register,* XXXI (September 23, 1826), 57. The issue was not resolved until 1839.

From S[AMUEL] L. S[OUTHARD], Navy Department. Transmits, for Clay's information, a "Copy of a letter from Commodore James Biddle, Commanding the Naval force of the United States off the Coast of Brazil and La Plata, dated off Monte Video 20th. March last.—" ALS. DNA, RG59, Misc. Letters (M179, R65).

In the enclosure, Biddle states that there had been no recent seizure of an American vessel by the (Brazilian) blockading squadron and that "Recent decisions at Rio de Janeiro, by which damages have been awarded against the Captors, cannot fail to render the Brazil Cruisers more circumspect in their future conduct towards neutral vessels." Reports that on February 20 the Brazilian army suffered, "according to the official despatch of General (Carlos Antonio José de) Alvear," a disastrous defeat and that "It is now manifestly his [Peter I's] interest to make peace without delay and for the sake of obtaining it, to relinquish his pretensions to the Banda Oriental." Suggests, further, that loss of her trade to Buenos Aires explains Great Britain's "anxiety for peace" and that additional "trade to Brazil, caused by the war, fully compensates . . . [Americans] for the *partial*" loss of their "trade to Buenos Ayres." Adds: "It seems probable too that not a single American vessel seized by the blockading Squadron will be confiscated finally. On the other hand, our Vessels occasionally succeed in eluding the Blockading Squadron . . . and get war prices for every thing at Buenos Ayres."

On February 21, General Alvear had reported to his Government, that "after two partial engagements" on February 13 and 16, a victory at Ituzaingo had left 1200 of the enemy dead, with losses to his own forces of less than 400 killed and wounded. Letter published in *Niles' Weekly Register,* XXXII (May 19, 1827), 201. The same news item reported also an Argentine naval victory with the capture of 18 vessels "in the river Uruguay." But Peter I, addressing the national assembly on May 3, had vowed to continue the war so long as the Argentinians claimed the Banda Oriental. *Ibid.* (June 30, 1827), 294.

To Henry Wheaton

No. 1. Henry Wheaton, Appointed Chargé d'Affaires of the
United States to Denmark.

Sir,   Department of State. Washington 31st. May, 1827.

The President having, by and with the advice and consent [*sic*],[1] appointed you Chargé D'Affaires to the King of Denmark,[2] and you having notified the Department of your acceptance of the appointment, and that you will be ready to depart on your mission by the middle of next month,[3] I transmit, herewith, your commission, together with a letter of credence,[4] to be presented by you to the Danish Minister of Foreign Affairs,[5] on your first interview with him. You will proceed to Denmark by such conveyance, at your own expense, as may be most agreeable to you.

On your arrival at your post, it will be your duty, generally, to take care of the interests of the United States, and of their citizens, in the discharge of which you will be governed by such instructions as may now, or hereafter, be given to you, and, where these are silent, by the public law applicable to the particular case calling for your interposition.

The extent and importance of the relations which exist between the United States and Denmark, perhaps required at an earlier period that we should have a representative at the court of his Danish Majesty; but considerations of economy had heretofore delayed the appointment. The treaty recently concluded at Washington between the United States and Denmark,[6] and the great value of the commercial intercourse between the two countries, which, it is hoped, that treaty may serve still further to strengthen and increase, did not appear to the President to admit of longer delay in instituting a permanent mission to Denmark. You will accompany these explanations with an assurance to the Danish government of his wish to see the amicable relations between the two countries long preserved and invigorated.

Among other means of effecting that desirable object, a satisfactory arrangement of the claims of American citizens, for injuries committed on their commerce during the late European war,[7] would have the happiest tendency. These aggressions were inflicted during the years 1808, '9, '10, & '11., on various pretexts. The amount of property, of which American citizens were thus unjustly deprived, was very great; and the interruptions to our lawful trade in the Baltic, were very numerous and highly vexatious.

Early in the year 1811, the President of the United States[8] determined on a special mission to Denmark, to arrest the progress of capture and condemnation of our vessels, then threatening the total destruction of our trade in the Baltic and adjacent seas, and to demand indemnity for the past. Mr. G. W. Erving was selected for the service, and proceeded to Copenhagen. His mission was attended with only partial success. He was able to prevail on the Danish Government to repress some irregularities, and to check the condemnation of most of our vessels whose cases were then pending, or which were captured and brought into port after his arrival; but he was not able to procure satisfaction in cases of erroneous and unjust condemnation by the Danish tribunals. At the close of his mission he was, however, assured by Mr. de Rosenkrantz,[9] Minister of Foreign Affairs of the King of

Denmark, in an official note under date the 8th. day of May. 1812, that "If his Majesty could be persuaded that in particular cases it should happen that appearances might have prevailed in the examination of some causes to the detriment of some American citizens, who might not have been able to demonstrate sufficiently that their enterprizes of commerce were legitimate, he would assuredly be led to redress just complaints, as he has, on several particular occasions, given proofs of his favourable dispositions towards the American vessels which circumstances have conducted to the ports of his kingdom. The king wishes, therefore, to give himself proofs to the government of the United States of the sentiments of justice with which he is animated. The undersigned flatters himself that the President of the United States will easily be persuaded that during so hard a contest as that which Denmark now sustains against the government who so evidently disavows the rights of nations engaged in navigation,[10] *the moment* is not favourable to bring anew under consideration the reclamations which the government of the United States may find it convenient to make, at that period, in relation to the objects in discussion."

Copies of the instructions which were given to Mr. Erving, together with his correspondence, during his mission, are now furnished you, and your attention is particularly directed to his note, addressed to Mr. de Rosenkrantz, under date the 4th. November 1811, with the statement accompanying it,[11] as exhibiting in detail most of the claims of American citizens upon the Danish government for indemnity, and the grounds on which they depended.

From the perusal of those instructions and correspondence, you will perceive the nature of our claims, and the objections which were urged against the allowance of them by the Danish Government. The discussions which occurred between Mr. Erving and Mr. de Rosenkrantz are so full as to render unnecessary any other than a few observations which I have to offer.

The allegations on which the seizure and condemnation of American vessels and their cargoes were made and attempted to be justified, were principally three.

1t.   The possession of false and simulated papers by which it was alleged an American character was stamped on British property.

2d.   Sailing under British convoy, whereby it was alleged our vessels lost the immunities of our flag, and subjected themselves to be treated as British property. And

3d.   The possession of French consular certificates of origin after the French consuls were forbidden to give them, except to vessels sailing direct to French ports.

With respect to the first ground, supposing a British vessel, by means of false and fraudulent papers, to have assumed the guise of an American vessel, there can be no doubt that she could not, in virtue of these same papers, justly escape condemnation on trial before a Danish tribunal. That there were instances of such fraudulent assumptions of the American flag, during the late wars in Europe, is undeniable. The American Government, far from affording them any favor or countenance, would have been the first to denounce and punish them. In cases of that sort, the question is not as to the principle of condemnation, but as to the *fact*. And as the cupidity of the Danish cruisers was stimulated to make out real American to be British vessels, covered by American papers; and as by means of the force which they commanded, they possessed themselves of vessel and cargo, and persons and papers on board, and were thereby enabled to shape the evidence to promote the interests of the captors, many condemnations, it is believed, took place, of genuine American vessels. Compensation is claimed by the government of the United States, in cases where the property of American citizens has been thus sacrificed.

The right of the Danish government to capture and condemn American vessels because they had been protected by a British convoy, cannot be admitted. It is denied, whe[12] the protection was, as to the protected vessels, voluntary or involuntary. In point of fact, in several instances, they were compelled by superior force to join the convoy. In cases of that description it is manifest that they did not subject themselves to lawful condemnation, when captured by Danish cruisers, unless the monstrous principle be[13] maintained, that the illegal application of superior force, by one belligerent, to the property of an innocent neutral, creates, in consequence thereof, a right in another belligerent to that property whenever he can violently seize it.

But supposing the convoy to have been voluntarily sought by the American vessel, the right of capture on the part of the Danish cruiser is still denied. Why should such a penalty be incurred for such an act? It is said that by placing themselves under British[14] protection, they took sides with the enemy of Denmark, and thereby entitled her to consider them as inimical: But for what purpose was this protection assumed? Surely in the ravages to which neutral commerce was exposed on every sea, and from every European nation, in that disastrous period, an innocent motive may be presumed on the part of a neutral who should endeavour under the cannon of one, to guard herself against the wrongs of all. In the case supposed, the American vessels did not join the British convoy to combat Denmark, or any other power, but for the justifiable purpose of innocently pursuing their lawful commerce, and avoiding all unjust assailants. They were unarmed, and in no condition to fight any one. By accepting the protection of the British convoy, they neither added to the strength of the British arms, nor increased the weakness of Denmark. The effect, in fact, of their joining the convoyed fleet, was to weaken, rather than strengthen the British force, since it expanded the sphere of its protecting duty. If a friend's goods, found on board an enemy's vessel, are not, (as undoubtedly they are not,) liable to condemnation, why should a friend's vessel, consorting with an enemy's fleet of merchantmen, which are under the protection of a public vessel, be deemed subject to seizure and condemnation? The property of the friend and the belligerent is much more intimately blended in the former case, than in that of of [sic]¹⁵ a ship of a friendly nation, accidentally taking refuge for a short time among a number of merchant vessels enjoying the protection of a public ship belonging to the enemy of another nation.

The third ground of capture and condemnation of American vessels assumed in Denmark, that of their being possessed of French consular certificates of origin after the French consuls were prohibited to issue them, except to vessels bound directly to French ports, was not true in point of fact. It seems that French consuls were accustomed to give these certificates to any American vessel applying for them, without regard to her port of destination, except that it was a port of France, or of a neutral, or an ally of France. The French government forbade the granting of these certificates to any other vessels than those bound directly to the ports of France, but the orders to that effect did not reach the French consuls in America until the 13h. November 1810., [sic] prior to which those certificates bore date which were made the pretext for the seizure of American vessels by the Danish cruizers. Even if the certificates had not been genuine, as was supposed, contrary to the fact, that would have been no justifiable cause for the capture and condemnation of a vessel, under Danish authority. It might have warranted the detention of the vessel, and possibly her condemnation, in a French tribunal. As to Denmark, a French certificate of origin, genuine or false, was a paper altogether unimportant and superfluous.

Upon these and other grounds a large amount of American property was condemned by the Danish tribunals, and in many instances of acquittal of American vessels, they were not only not indemnified for the detention and losses incident to their capture, but were sometimes obliged themselves to pay costs and damages.

It is due to the Danish government to state, (and the acknowledgement is made with satisfaction) that after the arrival of Mr. Erving an efficient interposition of its authority was made, in most instances, to prevent additional condemnations of our vessels, and to prevent further excesses of the Danish cruisers. I regret that the truth of the case does not authorize a similar testimony to the justice of his Danish Majesty in redressing, at that period, wrongs which had been perpetrated under his authority. Nor were the reasons assigned by his Minister for withholding satisfaction, such as could be deemed suf-

ficient, or could communicate any consolation to the American sufferers for the sacrifice of their property.

Those reasons were that the King of Denmark could not "permit a
revision of the sentences pronounced, terminating the causes arising
from captures made by the cruisers under the flag of the State.

"The principles which have formed the basis of the privateer regulations, and which have not been lost sight of in giving the instructions
to the tribunals charged to examine in matter of prizes, are the same
as those generally received, and according to which the Danish tribunals of the admiralty judge and decide on the captures of vessels
under other flags than that of the U. States.

"The special minister will be pleased to find in this assertion, which
is founded on the facts he may have made himself acquainted with,
since his residence here, that the American flag has, upon all occasions,
been treated, in the maratime [sic][16] tribunals, conformably to the
rules established, precisely in the same manner as the neutral flag [sic][17]
of Europe.

"The undersigned is, moreover, authorized to observe to Mr. Erving, Special Minister of the United States, that if permission were
given to the captured, who have pleaded before the tribunals which
have decided by a definitive sentence between the parties, to make in
their favour revision of the causes terminated, the same indulgence
shall be given to the captors, who might complain of the sentences
pronounced against them; and that, in that manner, the causes arising
from prizes would experience indefinite delays, as prejudical to the
captured as to the captors."[18]

The demand which Mr. Erving was instructed to make, and which
he did make, was not for a *revision* of the sentences of Danish tribunals, against which we had a right to protest as having been pronounced in derogation of the public law, but for the indemnity to
which American citizens were entitled, in consequence of those unjust decisions. The government of Denmark was and is of course free
to adopt any means it may deem proper to satisfy itself of their injustice, one of the most natural of which would be a discussion of the
cases complained of, conducted in a respectful and friendly spirit
under the sanction of the two governments. But if, in the arrangement
of the tribunals of Denmark, His Danish Majesty has not thought
proper to allow any further judicial examination of those decisions,
it does not follow that a foreign government is to regard them as in-
fallible, or must agree that Denmark may entrench herself behind
them from the responsibility which she lies under to the citizens of
each foreign Government, in consequence of the injustice sustained
by them under those decisions.

Even in the case of decisions by the ordinary tribunals of a country,
although the general presumption is that they are correct, this pre-

sumption does not always prevent a foreign citizen from making out the injustice of a particular decision, and invoking the aid of his own Government to obtain redress from the Government of the erring tribunal. But the ordinary tribunals of a country acquire a right to exercise their authority over the person or property of a foreign citizen, in consequence of his voluntary act in bringing himself or his property within its jurisdiction. Not so, when Courts of Admiralty exercise their powers on vessels captured at sea. There the property of foreigners is brought by force within the jurisdiction of those courts. It would, then, be strange if their decisions were to be more[19] binding and conclusive than those of the ordinary tribunals.

The tribunals of any country are but a part, and a subordinate part, of the Government of that country. But the right of redress against injurious acts of the whole Government—of the paramount authority —incontestibly exists in foreigners. Much more clearly, then, must it exist, when those acts proceed from persons, or from tribunals, responsible to their own government, but irresponsible to a foreign Government, otherwise than by its action on their Government.

The injustice of his Danish Majesty's considering the decisions of his high court of admiralty as absolutely binding and conclusive upon Foreign nations, without any examination, is manifest from a single consideration, growing out of the convoy cases. The American vessels which had been under a British convoy, were liable to condemnation only in virtue of the clause[20]   of the 11th. article of the royal in-instructions of 10th. March, 1810, declaring as a cause of condemnation, "the making use of English convoy."[21] These instructions were adopted and promulgated by the King of Denmark, and were the authority of his cruisers to capture, and the law of his tribunals to condemn American vessels in the specified contingency. When the American owner objects to the condemnation of his property, he is told by the Danish tribunal that it is the inevitable result of the royal instructions operating upon the fact of his having been under British convoy. Well; the injured American applies for redress to his Majesty, whose minister tells him that he cannot *permit a revision* of the sentences of his tribunals. Thus the Danish tribunals retreat behind the king, and the king behind his tribunals, and between both, the American citizen is unlawfully divested of his property.

It is said by M. de Rosenkrantz that if permission were given to the captured to have the decisions of the Danish tribunals revised, in cases of condemnation, a like permission must be given to captors in cases of acquittal.[22]

M. de Rosenkrantz appears erroneously to have treated Mr. Erving's application as one for a judicial examination of the judgements of the Danish tribunals, in the nature of an appeal, to be prosecuted according to all the forms of law. But I have already stated that that was not his application. It was for indemnity for wrongful captures, followed by wrongful condemnations of American property. But it may be said, that, if indemnity be made in such instances, it ought always[23] to be made in cases of rightful capture followed by wrongful acquittal of American property. No such cases are understood to have been presented to the Danish Government. If there be any, it belongs to the equity and wisdom of his Danish Majesty to consider whether he will not make redress commensurate with the wrongs which have proceeded from his tribunals, whether inflicted on his own subjects or upon foreigners. If he does not choose to do it; if it be impossible to give to his reparation a scope so comprehensive, we cannot agree that it therefore follows, that he ought to do nothing in behalf of American citizens. If the reason assigned were good, it would have the effect of preventing redress, in any case whatever, of an erroneous decision pronounced by the prejudice of a foreigner.

But the condition of the Danish subject and the American citizen— the captor and the captured—is widely different. The tribunal deciding is the tribunal of the *captor*, instituted, appointed, paid, controlled by *his* Government. The American citizen is forced, contrary to his will within the jurisdiction of this tribunal, in which he is not represented, and which cannot be supposed to have any sympathies with him. To a demand therefore, for redress, on the allegation of an erroneous acquittal to the prejudice of a Danish subject, and founded on the precedent of indemnity made to an American citizen, in consequence of an erroneous condemnation, the Dane may be satisfactorily told that his case had been tried by his own tribunal, with all the advantages resulting from that fact, and from the trial taking place at his own home, with his knowledge of the language of the country, the laws, and the habits and practices of the tribunal; and that therefore he has no cause to complain, nor right to redress.

Upon the termination of Mr. Erving's mission in the Spring of 1812, he left Mr. Forbes as an agent of American claims, in which character he was recognized by the Danish Government. His long residence at Copenhagen, was altogether unavailing in procuring satisfaction of our claims. A Copy of so much of his correspondence as it may be useful for you to possess, accompanies these instructions.[24]

In the Fall of 1818, Mr. Campbell,[25] appointed Minister of the United States to St. Petersburgh, on his way to that capital, stopt at Copenhagen, and, in an interview with M. de Rosenkrantz, stated, that although not instructed to review the discussion of our claims at that time, he had it in charge to state to him, "that my Government, entertaining the strongest conviction of their justice, had not, and could not, think it their duty to abandon them." A copy of Mr. Campbell's despatch, giving an account of that interview, is herewith.[26]

In August, 1825, Mr. Hughes,[27] on his way from Stockholm to the

Netherlands, to which he had been recently appointed Chargé d'Affaires of the United States, was directed to call at Copenhagen, and repeat the demand for satisfaction of the American claims. Accordingly, in execution of this duty, on the 5th. of that month, he presented a note to Count Schimmelman, the Danish Minister of Foreign Affairs, urging anew the indemnity which had been so long delayed. On the 17th. of the same month he received an answer, in which the ground is again taken of the irreversible character of the sentences of the High Court of Admirals. Mr. Hughes in a despatch addressed to me, under date the 19th. August, giving an account of his mission, says: "The general result of his observation during his short stay of eighteen days is, that there does exist a disposition to go into an examination of the claims, which the owners of them may perhaps, turn to a favourable account; a disposition produced by views and calculations of the importance of our trade, and of the benefits to be derived from a commercial convention. The owners of the claims must consent to forget, in a great measure, their justice, and to take up the subject on the most liberal principles of compromise. There is neither the will nor the ability to pay the whole sum." A copy of the correspondence incident to Mr. Hughes' mission is now furnished you.

Finally, at the moment of the signature, at Washington, on the 26th. day of April, 1826, of the General Convention of Friendship, Commerce, and Navigation between the United States of America and His Majesty the King of Denmark, I addressed a note to Mr. Pedersen, of which the following is a copy:[28]

Such has been the persevering pursuit of the American Government after a just indemnity to the injured citizens of the United States, for sacrifices of their property captured by the cruisers, and condemned by the tribunals of Denmark. Far from being discouraged by the ill success of past endeavours, the American Government is resolved to continue to demand satisfaction until it is finally obtained. This satisfaction it has a right to expect from the justice itself of the claims. It has a right, moreover, to expect it from the pledge given to Mr. Erving, in 1812, by M. de Rosenkrantz.

The President, therefore, indulges a confident hope that you will be able, from the views which are here presented, and from such additional lights as you may throw on the sub—[29] to make the Danish Government sensible of the injustice of longer persisting in withholding indemnity.

With respect to the mode in which the amount should be ascertained of what is due to American citizens, the President would prefer that it should be by a Board of Commissioners; in a similar manner to that which was organized in virtue of the seventh article of the Treaty of 1794. between the United States and Great Britain.[30] This

Board may be also authorized to decide on any claims of Danish subjects against the government of the United States.

But the mode of ascertaining the amount is less important than the object of procuring the indemnity itself. Attending to the suggestions of Mr. Hughes, that the affair should be taken up in the most liberal principles of compromise; and that there is neither the ability nor the will in the government of Denmark to make full satisfaction, if you should find your efforts unavailing to get a Board established, you are then authorized to say that the Government of the United States will agree to a basis formed on the principle of a compromise, and will[31] accept a gross sum as a complete discharge of all claims, arising from illegal or irregular captures or condemnations of American vessels and other property,[32] and you will invite the Danish Government to state the sum which it would be willing to pay, and communicate it to this Department. The President would yield with great reluctance to the principle of accepting, in any case, a less indemnity for wrongs done to American citizens, than what would amount to a full reparation; but there may be circumstances which would render it expedient to receive a present and imperfect satisfaction, rather than insist upon a full measure of reparation at a future, indefinite and remote time. Such circumstances are believed to exist in the present case. But we are not now prepared to fix a minimum, below which you would not be authorized to accept a gross sum; and therefore the President prefers that you would take ad referendum, any that may be offered. A copy of that part of A schedule, reported to the House of Representatives at the last session, of claims of American citizens on Foreign Governments, which relates to the Danish claims, is now placed in your hands.

As further evidence of the friendly disposition of the United States to accomodate [sic][33] the government of Denmark, you are also authorized[34] to propose receiving whatever sum may be awarded by the Board of Commissioners, or may be accepted by way of compromise, in Danish stock, bearing such interest, and reimbursable at such time, as may enable the holders of it to sell it at par[35] in the money market of either London, Paris, Amsterdam or Copenhagen.[36] The above arrangement, however, whether through a Board of Commissioners, or by compromise, is to be considered as distinct from and not comprehending the claim for the cargoes of the ships Fair Trader and Minerva Smyth and the brig Ariel, detained at Kiel, during the year 1812,[37] and if a compromise should be made,[38] it must also be understood as extinguishing any claims of Danish subjects upon this Government. The claim on account of those three vessels rests upon peculiar ground, that of the most manifest injustice in the application and the execution of the municipal laws of Denmark to the cargoes of those vessels. The circumstances of the case are stated in Mr. Hughes' letter to Count Schimmelman under date the 18th August, 1825,[39] of which a copy is herewith. Mr. John Connell, of Philadelphia, has been the Agent of the owners of those cargoes, and has been long endeavoring to get the injustice corrected, of a retrospective operation of the revenue laws of Denmark, under circumstances attending those three vessels of uncommon hardship. He was in the prosecution of that object in 1825, and obtained from Count Schimmelman assurances which authorize the belief that redress will be at last afforded. It is understood that Mr. Connell will shortly proceed to Denmark for the same purpose; and you are directed to afford to him such official aid and co-operation as may appear to you best adapted to the accomplishment of his agency.

Auxiliary considerations in favor of a satisfactory arrangement of our claims are desirable, from the late Commercial convention with Denmark. That convention marks the liberal spirit of the United States towards Denmark. It recognizes, what, at least on principle, was not free from doubt, the right of Denmark to duties on the passage of the Sound and the Belts: And it places the navigation of Denmark on an equal footing with our own. The Danish navigation, indeed, enjoys, under the stipulations of that convention, and in consequence of the present posture of our relations with the British Colonies,[40] advantages superior to our own, since it is authorized to import into the United States, directly from those colonies, their products, which the vessels of the United States cannot now directly introduce. And there is no immediate prospect of any change in this unequal state of things. I am, Sir, Respectfully Your obed: Sert.   H. CLAY

LS. DNA, RG84, Denmark (MR14, frames 318–31). Copy, in DNA, RG59, Dip. Instr., vol. 11, pp. 339–54 (M77, R6); three drafts in DLC-HC (DNA, M212, R8)–the first, except for three paragraphs from a document, copied by a clerk, is in Clay's hand; the second, is in a clerk's hand, with emendations by Clay; the third, is also in a clerk's hand, with a few minor textual changes by Clay, and is endorsed on the last page: "Recorded P. 339."

President Adams noted, on June 1, that Clay had sent him "the draft" of these instructions, which he had "read and sent back to the Department." Memoirs, VII, 284.

[1] The copy and drafts include the words, "of the Senate."   [2] Frederick VI.

[3] See above, Wheaton to Clay, April 2, May 29, 1827.   [4] The commission, dated March 3, and the letter of credence, dated May 21, 1827, are located in DNA, RG59, Ceremonial Communications, vol. 2, pp. 65, 66.   [5] Count Ernst Heinrich Schimmelmann.   [6] Above, April 26, 1826.   [7] Cf. above, Hughes to Clay, March 19, 1825; Clay to Hughes, March 24, 1825.   [8] James Madison.   [9] Niels Rosenkrantz.

[10] Great Britain.   [11] See State Papers and Publick Documents of the United States . . . (2d. edn., 10 vols.; Boston, 1817), IX, 119.   [12] The word comes at the end of a line; it appears as "whether" in the copy and drafts.   [13] In the copy and drafts, the words "is to" precede "be."   [14] In the copy and drafts, the word "the" precedes "British."   [15] The second "of" is not found in the copy and drafts.   [16] Spelled correctly in the copy and drafts.   [17] The word appears as "flags" in the drafts.

[18] See State Papers and Publick Documents of the United States . . . (2d. edn.), IX, 109.   [19] In the copy and drafts, the word "held" precedes "more".   [20] Identified as "clause d" in the first two drafts.   [21] See Erving to Rosenkrantz, June 6, 7, 1811, in American State Papers, Foreign Relations, III, 522, 524–25.   [22] Rosenkrantz to Erving, April 9, 1812, in State Papers and Publick Documents . . . (2d. edn.) , IX, 109.

[23] The word appears as "also" in the first draft.   [24] For copies of John M. Forbes' correspondence with Rosenkrantz and Secretaries of State James Monroe and John

Quincy Adams, over the period from May 31, 1811, to August 24, 1818, see DNA, RG59, Dip. Disp., Denmark, vol. 1B (M41, R3).   25 George Washington Campbell.

26 Campbell to John Quincy Adams, September 15, 1818, in DNA, RG59, Dip. Disp., Russia, vol. 7 (M35, R7).   27 Christopher Hughes.   28 The note, here omitted by the editors, to Peter Pedersen is summarized above, V, 270.   29 The end of a line; the word is "subject" in the copy and drafts.   30 Cf. above, Cheves to Clay, April 19, 1826, and note. The treaty had called for naming five commissioners, two by each of the contracting powers and the fifth by unanimous vote of the other four. If agreement could not be reached on the choice of the fifth commissioner, he was to be selected by lot. Three of the five commissioners, one named on each side together with the fifth, were to constitute a board to ascertain damages and losses. Miller (ed.), *Treaties. . .* , II, 250–52.   31 The first draft reads: ". . . authorized to accept . . ."; the additional wording was interlined by Clay in the second draft.   32 From this point, where a period follows the word "property," to the end of the paragraph, the first draft reads: "And, if, after after [*sic*] making all reasonable exertions to obtain a larger sum, you should find it impracticable, you are authorized to accept the sum of $ and to grant that discharge in consideration of it.(a) [Continued along the left margin:] (a) According to a schedule reported from this department to the H. of R. at the last Session of Congress exhibiting the claims of American Citizens on Foreign Governments [above, Clay to Taylor, January 30, 1827], the amount of them upon Denmark is stated to be $. This schedule, from several causes, is not perfect, and should not be taken as comprehending all claims. A copy of that part of it which relates to the Danish claims is now placed in your hands. From an inspection of it you will perceive that the sum which you are now authorized to accept falls far short of the aggregate amount there presented." This wording was copied into the second draft; there nearly all of it was crossed out; and the final version was interlined by Clay.   33 Spelled correctly in the copy and drafts.   34 The next 21 words were interlined by Clay in the second draft to replace the following: "to accept such an amount of."   35 The last two words were interlined by Clay in the second draft.   36 With no period after "Copenhagen," the next 13 words were interlined by Clay in the second draft to replace the following language from the first: "for the above mentd. sum of $. This sum however."

37 Cf. above, Connell to Clay, May 24, 1827.   38 The last six words were interlined by Clay in the second draft.   39 Cf. above, Hughes to Clay, August 19, 1825; Connell to Clay, May 24, 1827.   40 Cf. above, Gallatin to Clay, August 19, 1826..

To José Silvestre Rebello

The Chevalier Rebello, Chargé d'Affaires From Brazil.

Sir,   Department of State, Washington, 31st. May 1827.

I have received the note which you did me the honor on yesterday to address to me, and submitted it to the President.

He is aware that during the progress of a maritime war the commerce of Neutral Nations is liable to occasional interruption and vexation. That of the United States has been frequently subject to embarrassments and aggressions under color of Brazilian authority prior to and during the war unhappily existing between His Majesty the Emperor of Brazil and the Republic of Buenos Ayres. When these injuries are inflicted it is the just expectation of the Neutral that prompt and full redress will be made by the belligerent upon friendly representation. The President regrets that this expectation has not been fulfilled in frequent instances of well founded complaint on the part of Citizens of the United States, urged by Mr. Raguet, during his mission to the Court of the Brazils; and particularly that satisfaction was not promptly made for the illegal seizure and detention of the Spark, under circumstances of no ordinary aggravation. Mr. Raguets demand of his passports, in consequence of withholding that satisfaction was without orders, and[1] his personal act, for which he is accountable to his own Government and to that only. The President regrets an occurrence which in Mr. Raguets view of it has led to an interruption at Rio Janeiro[2] [sic] of the Diplomatic relations of the two Countries. But no such interruption exists at Washington, and it would have been agreeable to the President if you had been authorised and empowered to make here that indemnity due[3] to American Citizens, which has been unavailingly demanded at Rio Janeiro [sic].

The President however participating in the desire which the Government of Brazils professes,[4] to preserve and to extend still further, if possible the friendly relations between the two Countries, charges me to say; that, he is disposed to render a new and signal proof of that desire by nominating[5] a successor to Mr. Raguet;[6] without unnecessary delay, upon the assurance which you have given that he shall be received with the consideration due to his official character, and provided you are also authorised to give the assurance that in all cases in which injuries have been inflicted on the property or persons of American Citizens, contrary to the public Law, a prompt[7] arrangement will be made by the Government of Brazil, satisfactory to that of the United States.

I pray you to accept assurances of my distinguished Consideration.

H. CLAY.

Copy. DNA, RG59, Notes to Foreign Legations, vol. 3, pp. 362–64 (M38, R3). AL draft, in CSmH. Textual revisions which might have been inserted after consultation with President Adams are noted below. On the Brazilian interpretation of this letter, cf. below, Rebello to Clay, June 1, 1827, note.
[1] Last three words interlineated on draft copy, in Clay's hand.   [2] Last three words interlineated on draft copy, in Clay's hand.   [3] This word interlineated on draft copy, in Clay's hand.   [4] This word substituted for "entertains" on draft copy, in Clay's hand.   [5] Last 15 words interlineated on draft copy, in Clay's hand.   [6] At this point, words "shall be sent" were deleted on draft copy.   [7] Last two words substituted for "an" on draft copy, in Clay's hand.

DIPLOMATIC NOTES   May 31, 1827

From HILARIO DE RIVAS Y SALMON, Philadelphia. Quotes from (Emmerich de) Vattel on the duties of neutrals and from the treaty of 1795 (Pinckney's Treaty) between Spain and the United States to support charges of violations of the professed neutrality of the United States in the conflict between Spain and her rebellious colonies; cites his notes of September 22 and November 29, 1825, and complains of the depredations on Spanish commerce committed by the vessels named in those communications. Contends that the United States has violated the treaty of 1795, as well as principles expounded by Thomas Jefferson, in letters to Gouverneur Morris and Edmond Genêt, in 1793, by failing to prevent David Porter and other American citizens from accepting commissions in naval forces hostile to Spain; also assails the American Government for allowing, by its inaction, Porter to use Key West, where he received reinforcements of 160 men, sent from New York on March 17, and where he is safer than he would be in a Mexican port, as his base of operations against Spanish commerce. Transmits documents, sent him by General (Francisco Dionisio) Vives, that support the charges relative to Porter, who is being blockaded in Key West by (Commodore Angel) Laborde, and requests that the United States Government (1) demand forfeiture of the bonds exacted when the vessels complained of were permitted to sail and (2) punish its citizens, especially Porter, who have violated its neutrality and its treaties. ALS, in Spanish with trans. in State Dept. file. DNA, RG59, Notes from Spanish Legation, vol. 9 (M59, R-T12).

Among the enclosures is a deposition, given at Havana, April 5, 1827, by Alexander Thompson, twenty-nine years old, a native of New York, who had been commissioned a lieutenant in the Mexican Navy on June 12, 1826, had been under Porter's command, had been made a prisoner by an uprising of Spanish prisoners under his charge, on March 31, 1827, and had been brought by them to Havana.

Thompson had been commissioned a midshipman in the United States Navy in 1815 and had resigned effective August 8, 1826. He was paroled by Admiral Laborde, arrived back at Key West about June 1, 1827, and about a month later arrived at St. Augustine from Key West. Washington *Daily National Journal*, July 12, 1827; *Richmond Enquirer*, July 20, 1827. He apparently had not, however, left the Mexican Navy, for in 1829 Joel R. Poinsett complained to the Mexican Government about seizure of the American vessel *Two Friends* by the Mexican schooner *Louisiana* under Thompson's command. *House Docs.*, 25 Cong., 2 Sess., no. 351, pp. 304–305.

INSTRUCTIONS AND DISPATCHES   May 31, 1827

To JOEL R. POINSETT, no. 23. Transmits copies of correspondence with Pablo Obregón, concerning the use made by (David) Porter "of his position at Key West" (above, Clay to Obregón, May 21, 1827; Obregón to Clay, May 26, 1827). Instructs him "to bring this subject under the immediate notice of the Mexican Government, and to claim from its justice the adoption of such measures as will correct the irregularities complained of, and prevent any further act or proceeding on the part of Commodore Porter, in violation of the neutrality of the United States." Acknowledges receipt of Poinsett's "despatches to No. 80 [March 24, 1827], inclusive. . . ." Copy. DNA, RG59, Dip. Instr., vol. 11, p. 361 (M77, R6). L draft, in DLC-HC (DNA, M212, R8).

From CONDY RAGUET, New York, no. 27. Reports his arrival and his intention to come to Washington. States that no communication occurred between himself and any member of the Brazilian Government between the date of his last dispatch, March 17, and April 5, on which date he requested "an audience for the purpose of taking leave of The Emperour" (Peter I). Notes that after the audience, on April 7, he learned that Mr. (Izidoro da Costa) Oliveira had that day sailed on a secret mission to the United States and that "It was thought" that Oliveira's object "was to make such explanations and promises of indemnity to the American government as would avert any serious misunderstanding." Acknowledges receipt of Clay's instructions of January 20, part of which he "communicated to the Government." Reports lack of progress in the cases involving several American vessels and charges that a note, dated March 9, 1827, received by him from the Marquis of Queluz (a copy of which was enclosed in his dispatch of March 17) contained an incorrect statement regarding the time of a "judicial investigation . . . in the case of the Spark." Informs Clay that he reserves "for verbal communication" further information relative to his departure from Brazil and to "the potential situation of the Empire, which is sufficiently precarious—" ALS. DNA, RG59, Dip. Disp., Brazil, vol. 5 (M121, R7). Published in *American State Papers, Foreign Relations*, VI, 1068. Received June 3.

Oliveira, who had held the post of Secretary of Legation for Brazil, in the United States since January, 1825, had returned home in October, 1826. He arrived back in Washington on May 29, 1827. Cf. Washington *United States Telegraph*, May 23, 31, 1827. It is probable that the Rebello note, above, May 30, 1827, reflected instructions transmitted by Oliveira.

MISCELLANEOUS LETTERS   May 31, 1827

From ALEXANDER MACOMB, Engineer Department, Washington. States, with regard to the letter from "Mr. F. Crutchfield, of Virginia," to Clay, of May 20 (not found), "upon the subject of procuring a Cadet appointment for his son," that he cannot report the views of the Secretary of War, who is absent; that "appointments for this year have all been made"; and that the "application will be continued on file, should it be desired. . . ." Returns the Crutchfield letter to Clay and encloses "for Mr. Crutchfield's information a printed paper upon the subject of Cadet Matters. . . ." Copy. DNA, RG94, Records of the U. S. Mil. Academy, vol. 2, p. 40.

The father was Francis Crutchfield of Falling Spring Valley, Bath County, Virginia, a schoolmaster and a cousin of William W. Worsley. *Calendar of Virginia State Papers*, V, 16a; and below, Crutchfield to Clay, June 12, 1827. The son, not further identified, was not appointed to the United States Military Academy.

From J. R. MULLANY, "Good Stay, Bergen Point, New Jersey, near New York City." Cites his personal acquaintance with Clay; lists military officers and public officials who have known him "in public and private life"; traces his military career during the War of 1812 and as "Qr. Master General of the Northern Division of the Army" from 1816 to 1818; and notes that he has "experienced every difficulty in" attempting to settle his accounts. Explains that under a law of "last July" (6 *U. S. Stat.*, 345–May 18, 1826), calling for an audit of his accounts, a balance of "3 to four thousand dollars" was found in his favor, but that "the 2d. Comptroller by reversing the decisions of the 2d. Auditor, makes a balance of $3,709 against" him, while he claims $27,030. States that he has "proposed a reference of the items in dispute, to three impartial Citizens, or to the decision of Genl. [Thomas Sidney] Jessup Dr. [Tobias] Watkins and Mr. [Nathaniel] Frye, Officers of the Government," and appeals to Clay "to recommend the reference which . . . [he] respectfully and earnestly" claims. ALS. NBuHi-Peter B. Porter Papers (M226, R4).

In Clay's absence, Brent acknowledged, on June 11, 1827, receipt of Mullany's letter, which, he stated, had been referred to the Secretary of War [James Barbour]. Copy, in DNA, RG59, Dom. Letters, vol. 21, p. 555 (M40, R19).

Mullany, born in Ireland, had come to the United States as a boy and had been commissioned into the Army from New York in 1812. He had risen to the rank of lieutenant colonel in 1813 and colonel in 1814, had been honorably discharged in 1815, had re-enlisted in 1816, and had been again honorably discharged in 1818. His connection with Clay and the final ruling on his case have not been found.

Frye, a resident of Georgetown, District of Columbia, had been born in Maine but had been employed in the paymaster general's office since 1798. He had performed the duties of chief clerk since at least as early as 1816.

To Duncan Cameron

Sir   Washn. 1st June 1827
I regret extremely to learn, from your letter of the 22d. Ulto,[1] that
Mr. W. H. Caperton, of Richmond (K) has acted in a professional
affair committed by you to his care, in a manner so dishonorable; and
the more, since you state that, one of your inducements to entrust him,
was a letter of introduction given by me, in his behalf, addressed to
you.[2] I have not a perfect recollection of having given him that introduction, 'though I do not doubt it, from your statement. At the time,
Mr. Caperton enjoyed a good reputation, and was thought a very
promising young man. It must have been on the strength of that reputation, and some acquaintance that I I [sic] had with him, that I took
the liberty of addressing you.
I would most willingly, if it were in my power, prevail on him to
render you justice; but it does not occur to me that I can do more than
to transmit your letter to him, and express my mortification at the
perusal of its contents, and the hope that he will promptly make you
ample satisfaction.[3] I am Your ob. Servt.   H CLAY
Mr. D. Cameron

ALS. NcU-Southern Historical Collection.   [1] Not found.
[2] Above, III, 463–64.   [3] No such communication by Clay to Caperton has been found.

To Charles Hammond

My dear Sir   (Private & Confidential)   Washn. 1st. June 1827.
I shall send you to day a statement of the account of Genl. Jackson,
as Govr. of Florida,[1] made out by one of the Clerks in the Dept. of
State. Some of the items will surprize you. Mr. Monroe[2] was very
liberal in allowances, and the act for taking possession of Florida having placed $100.000. at his disposal for that purpose,[3] the extra al-
lowances to Genl. Jackson beyond his Salary (which was very liberal)
were made out of that fund. Genl. Jackson never resigned his Commission as Majr. Genl. in the army. He was discharged as a supernumerary
under the act of 2d. March 1821, and I think the account for his military services shews that he recd. the three months to which he was
entitled under that act, in consequence of his discharge from the 1st.
June 1821. Thus he recd. *double* pay Vizt. that three months' pay,
and during the *same* time Salary & allowances as Govr. of Florida.
After all, this scouting into accounts long since settled is a little affair, but it commenced with the opposition,[4] and in such a case *offsetts*
are fair.
As to my account, you will recollect that a transfer of the negotiation for peace took place from Gottenburg to Ghent.[5] I had taken a

house[6] at Gottenburgh [*sic*], under the impression that the negotiation was to be there. After the transfer, I gave up the house and had to pay rent for it during a time that I did not occupy it. I also lost a small sum upon a cheap carriage (the only mode of travelling in the Countries through which I passed) which I purchased for the journey from Gottenburg to Ghent. I charged Govt. with the rent which I had to pay for the house whilst I did not occupy it, with the loss on the carriage, and with my travelling expences [*sic*]. All these disbursements, which amount to a small sum, were the result of the change of the place of negotiation, which was made from public considerations, and by which the public in fact saved ultimately a good deal. For by going to Ghent we got much nearer London than Gottenburg, and as the British Commrs., upon every exchange of official notes, were in the habit of transmitting ours to the British Ministry for fresh instructions, if the negotiation had taken place at Gottenburg it would have been much longer protracted, in consequence of that habit.

Your paper is regularly recd. here and perused by the President and all of us with the greatest interest. It is estimated as one of the best that is published.

I do not know when I was so much mortified as I was by the letter of Mr. Edd. King. I know not what defence Wright can make, but I do most anxiously hope that he is able to give some satisfactory explanation.[7]

Prospects are bright every where North of Mason and Dixon's line. I should not be surprized if the Hero does not get a solitary vote North of that line. You may rest assured that Mr. Adams will get the vote of Jersey, Delaware, and at least 10 out of the 11 in Maryland; and that there is a deep, strong and increasing current in his favor in Pennsa.[8] I am Cordially Your friend   H CLAY
C. Hammond Esq.

P.S.   I need not suggest to your discretion the expediency of avoiding a reference to my name in any use you may think proper to make of the a/c. H C

ALS. InU.
[1] Cf. above, III, 54n. Jackson had been commissioned as Governor of East and West Florida on March 10, 1821. The Province of East Florida had been formally transferred to the United States on July 10 and West Florida, on July 17, 1821. Jackson's salary as Governor had begun as of June 1, 1821, the day after termination of his Army service under legislation of March 2, 1821 (3 *U. S. Stat.*, 615–16), "*to reduce and fix the military peace establishment of the United States.*" Carter (ed.) , *Territorial Papers*, XXII, 8–9, 111, 122.   The account as published by Hammond in the *Liberty Hall and Cincinnati Gazette*, June 22, 1827, included, besides charges for transportation and board for the General and his suite en route to Florida, $370.15 in unspecified "Incidental expenses"; $1,047.39, "bill of sundries, say wines, &c. &c. for the use of Gen. Jackson and his family"; and Jackson's salary "as Governor of the Floridas from 1st June, 1821, to 1st January, 1822," $2,921.19. For the answering statement, explaining that the wine was for ceremonial use in connection with the transfer of the government of the Floridas, see Frankfort *Argus of Western America*, August 8, 1827.   [2] President James Monroe.
[3] *U. S. Stat.*, 637–39, sec. 6.   [4] Cf. above, Turner to Clay, January 7, 1827, and

note; Johnson to Clay, April 8, 1827, and note.   5 Cf. above, I, 919, 928; II, 100–101.
6 Cf. above, I, 894.   7 Outraged at learning that John C. Wright had apparently both congratulated King on his election as speaker of the Ohio House of Representatives and, in other correspondence, criticized that appointment, King had retaliated by revealing that Wright in another letter, addressed to him on January 23, 1827, had advised that Jackson was to remain a Presidential candidate, "that Mr. Adams would never *affiliate* the interests of the *Western States*—that the politics of Mr. Adams and the *interests* of Ohio were *antipodes*—that Kentucky would like to keep Ohio drawing in the shafts, while she ate the sweetmeats herself—and that, under the . . . state of things, it was best for this State [Ohio] . . . to keep *aloof from the contest for the next Presidency.*" Wright to Duff Green, April 23, 1827; King to [Green], May 17, 1827—published in Washington *United States Telegraph*, May 1, 24, 1827, respectively.   8 On the vote of 1828 in New Jersey and Pennsylvania, cf. above, Clay to Brown, March 27, 1827, note. Adams received Delaware's 3 electoral votes but only 6 of Maryland's 11. Schlesinger and Israel (eds.), *History of American Presidential Elections*, I, [492].

From Peter Paul Francis Degrand

Hon Henry Clay Washington
Dear Sir   Philadelphia 1 June 1827

After perusal of the enclosed letter,[1] I will be obliged to you to have the goodness to return it to me.— Instead of putting the present letter in the Phila Post Office, I send it to you, via Balto. The enclosed is from one of our most valuable friends E. E.;[2] & if you cannot guess who that is, I dare say the Prest can.

I had penned, for the consideration of the Cabinet, letters for the Prest, Mr Rush[3] & yourself, setting forth facts, in relation to the use of your own Power, to oppress your friends here, as it is, actually exercised by the Jackson men holding office under [. . .] or rather under the present Administration. & to their baneful influence, even your friend Mr Wm. Jones gives his aid.— He is so thoroughly sorrounded [*sic*] by Jackson men that, it seems, he cannot escape even making indirect war, upon me;—whose friend he always was before & who was always his friend.— It is principally due to the influence of his Depy Collr.,[4] who dared to tell me "he hoped one of these days to ketch [*sic*] at fault, so as to fine me."

I shew my letters to a friend. He said "You must not send them *yet*; for they wd. lead inevitably to the *instantaneous* dismissal of the Depy Collr. & perhaps some others & we wd not, *just now*, know how to select a successor.— Let your letters go, by & bye."

I therefore have foreborne sending my letters for the present.

Don't be frightened when you see that Jacob Holgate[5] was Chairman of the Manufs. Meeting for the City & County of Phila.— That affair goes just exactly right.— The Delegation to Harrisburg is *all Adams*.[6] Yours faithfully   D

Have my letters[7] reached you?

                                    3 June 1827

Being exceedingly busy, I have not had time to send the above letter. I think Holgate is coming round.— He said to Redwood Fisher,[8]

coming back from the Manufs. Meeting: "why did you not put in a Resolve, censuring Ingham & others, who opposed the Measures in Congress?[9] If I was in Congress, I cd. not find it, in me, to oppose the present Admn., for they have done & are doing right in every thing."

I send you the Proceedings of the Manufs Meeting.— Jas. Ronaldson[10] is a Jackson man & I am told the only one & they think he will not go to Harrisburg— His being in arrises [sic] from there [sic] inexperienced hands—not knowing that he was a Jackson Man.— However, we have all but one & all will go right.— I am consulted at every step.

I pray you to Dismiss no body, from office, here, *for the moment.*— When the time has arrived, I will let you know.

Holgate was originally Adams & I am told will be Adams, as soon as he is brought to believe that Adams has the Majority

It is most excellent that Binns shd. have the furnishing of the Stationary [sic].[11]— you have done yourself much credit in that affair.

ALS. DLC-HC (DNA, M212, R2). Addressed: "Private"; endorsed by Clay on verso of cover: "Mr. P. P. F. Degrand." Word erased in second paragraph.
    [1] Not found.   [2] Probably Edward Everett.   [3] Richard Rush.   [4] John Kerne had been deputy collector at Philadelphia since 1825 and remained in office until his death in 1841.   [5] A veteran of the Revolution, Holgate was a carpenter by trade and a mill owner. He had long been active in local politics and supported the agitation for internal improvements, particularly the Pennsylvania Canal.   [6] Cf. above, Clay to Crowninshield, March 18, 1827, note.   [7] Above, April 14, May 15, 1827.
    [8] Redwood S. Fisher, Philadelphia merchant, who later moved to New York and edited a daily newspaper. He there acquired a reputation as a compiler and publisher of statistical data on the United States.   [9] Samuel D. Ingham had spoken at length in opposition to the woolens bill (above, Pleasants to Clay, February 14, 1827). *Register of Debates*, 19 Cong., 2 Sess., 1087–98.   [10] Scotch by birth, Ronaldson had settled in Philadelphia and had become proprietor of one of the largest type-foundries in the nation. He had been active in the organization of the Franklin Institute of the State of Pennsylvania for the Promotion of the Mechanic Arts and served as its first president, from 1824 to 1842. He also acquired prominence as a horticulturalist and in 1840 published *Observations on the Sugar Beet and Its Cultivation.*   [11] On May 18, Richard Rush had advised William Jones that when "from time to time," stationery supplies were needed for the Philadelphia custom-house, "on Mr. [John] Binns' undertaking to furnish them, on terms just and satisfactory to the public, in all respects," he should be given the orders. *House Docs.*, 20 Cong., 1 Sess., no. 105. Clay's agency in the arrangement was not documented when the House of Representatives, under a resolution introduced by George Kremer, on January 22, 1828, requested "copies of any correspondence which may have taken place between any of the officers of the customs at the port of Philadelphia and the Secretary of the Treasury; also, any correspondence between the said officers. . . , or the Secretary of the Treasury, and any other person, in relation to the supplying of printing and stationery . . . at the port aforesaid." U.S. H. of Reps., *Journal*, 20 Cong., 1 Sess., p. 205.

DIPLOMATIC NOTES   June 1, 1827

From JOSÉ SILVESTRE REBELLO, Washington. Acknowledges receipt of Clay's note of May 31; urges prompt appointment of a successor to (Condy) Raguet; and pledges that his government will provide indemnity for injury done "sob a bandeira de S. M. O. Imperador," to Americans or their property in violation of "direito publico." Expresses pleasure in the willingness of the United States Government to negotiate with him but notes that the necessary documents are in Rio de Janeiro. ALS, in Portuguese. DNA, RG59, Notes from Brazilian Legation, vol. 1 (M49, R1).

President Adams noted on this date (*Memoirs*, VII, 284) that Clay "had . . . a reply from Mr. Rebello translated by himself, and containing some exceptionable expressions, which are thought would make it necessary for Mr. Clay to see him again." The State Department files contain three translations of this letter. The first, presumably of Rebello's original note, bears the following endorsement near the top of its first page: "The original of this letter was taken back by Mr. Rebello, and a new one substituted with the omission of some passages." The second translation, which accompanies the revised version of Rebello's note, is endorsed: "with the original." The third, which differs only slightly in wording from the second, is published in *American State Papers, Foreign Relations*, VI, 824. The "exceptionable expressions" of the original letter appear to have occurred in a paragraph in which Rebello summarized Clay's note of May 31. This summation in the filed translation omitted reference to the American criticism of Brazilian "aggressions"; stated: ". . . the President considers the proceeding of Mr. Raguet at Rio de Janeiro, in suddenly demanding his passports, as a personal act for which he will answer to his Government, inasmuch as it was committed without a special order"; and concluded: "the President wishing, moreover, to give a proof of his desire to continue, and even to increase if possible, the friendly relations subsisting between the two nations, has directed your Excellency [*i.e.*, Clay] to inform the undersigned [Rebello], that, in order to give a proof of these pacific dispositions, he will appoint, without unnecessary delay, a successor to Mr. Raguet. . . ." The effect of this wording was to suggest that Raguet was to be chastised and that the Adams administration was somewhat desperately seeking to mend relations between the two countries.

INSTRUCTIONS AND DISPATCHES   June 1, 1827

From JOHN G. A. WILLIAMSON, La Guaira. Transmits his "semi annual return of the American Commerce" but declares that it is neither full nor correct. States that he trusts "the Govt." and Clay to "see the necessity, to obtain that full and correct statement of trade, to require a manifest of all Cargoes to be handed to every Consular office." Declares that merchants and others who appear to withhold such information in order to protect trade secrets should recall that it can be obtained, for a price, "from some officer of the Customs." Deplores the inadequacy of fees and authority provided for American consuls, who are unable to acquire the information needed to give an accurate accounting of American trade. Emphasizes "that many advantages ar[e] lost by the present system. . . ." ALS. DNA, RG59, Cons. Disp., La Guaira, vol. 1 (M84, R1). Received (June) 28.

MISCELLANEOUS LETTERS   June 1, 1827

From BETSEY HAWLEY, "No. 77 Laurens Street   New York." Quotes an item from "the Connecticut papers of Oct. A. D. 1825" concerning the death, "At Porto Cabello, in August last," of her brother, "Capt. Isaac P. Hawley, of the Marine Corps of Colombia, aged about 28 years," stating that "He was the son of Col. Hawley of Fairfield County [Connecticut]," and referring "His relatives who may wish for further information respecting his effects, &c. . . . to Capt. Caleb Brintnall   New Haven." Notes that she has been unable to obtain information from Brintnall and that her letters to the American consul at Puerto Cabello (Franklin

Litchfield) have elicited no reply. Appeals for help. ALS. DNA, RG59, Cons. Disp., Puerto Cabello, vol. 1 (M-T229, R1).

In compliance with this request, Daniel Brent by Clay's direction sent Miss Hawley on June 8 a letter, also dated June 8, under flying seal addressed to the United States consul at Puerto Cabello. Copy, in DNA, RG59, Dom. Letters, vol. 21, p. 552 (M40, R19).

Miss Hawley, as a resident of Norwalk, Connecticut, in 1840 and 1848 was still attempting to recover her brother's effects, and as late as 1856 filed a petition with a complaint against "certain clerks" in the State Department. U. S. H. of Reps., *Journal*, 26 Cong., 1 Sess., pp. 291, 292, 749; 30 Cong., 1 Sess., pp. 587, 698; 34 Cong., 1 Sess., pp. 952, 1170; U. S. Sen., *Journal*, 34 Cong., 1 Sess., p. 150. Neither the Hawleys nor Brintnall have been further identified.

From JOSEPH ROFFIGNAC, Mayor, New Orleans. Refers to Clay's interest in the prosperity of New Orleans and the interior states, of which that city is the depot, and explains the financial difficulties encountered by the city corporation in attempting to pave the business streets and quays. States that the difficulties could be solved if the city were allowed to sell the ground between the road and the houses facing the Mississippi River, a step the corporation was preparing to take when stopped in 1825 by an injunction obtained by the United States district attorney (John W. Smith), who maintains that the property is owned by the United States. Traces the history of ownership and use of this area; argues that the United States implicitly gave up its claim in 1818, when Congress authorized the sale of property acquired by the general government in the purchase of Louisiana; and cites French and Spanish law that considered the alluvion deposited on the banks of rivers as property of the owners of the banks. Requests that Clay urge the President to order dissolution of the injunction and encloses a plat of New Orleans showing the original plan and the increase of vacant space between the row of houses nearest the river and the river itself. ALS, in French with trans. in State Dept. file. DNA, RG59, Misc. Letters (M179, R65), filed with William Wirt's letter to Clay of August 25, 1827.

Count Louis Phillippe Joseph de Roffignac, born at Angoulême in France, had come to the United States in 1800 and had become an American citizen when the United States acquired Louisiana in 1803. He had served for ten years as a representative in the Territorial and State legislatures and since 1820 as mayor of New Orleans. In 1828 he resigned and returned to France.

By act of April 20, 1818, 3 *U. S. Stat.*, 465–66, the President of the United States had been authorized to abandon use of the Navy arsenal, military hospital, and barracks in New Orleans, to lay off the sites into lots and streets, and to have them sold.

From HENRY WHEATON, New York. Reports that he expects to embark by July 1 on his mission to Denmark. ALS. DNA, RG59, Dip. Disp., Denmark, vol. 1B (M41, R3).

From Francis T. Brooke

My Dear Sir   Richmd June 2d 1827

I have delayed writing you much longer than I intended,   your Book was an acceptable present and I Shall prise [*sic*] it very highly— I took the liberty to Shew your letter[1] to Leigh[2]   he was pleased I Saw at the compliment to Algernon Sidney— I could but remark his observation after he had read it— he Said he would be damned if he would write on either Side, that it was damned hard to be obliged to vote for either of the candidates, and he would not vote for either,   I have no doubt if Mr Randolph was to die, he would vote for the present incumbent,[3]   I think he has very good feelings for you after all,

I wish most Cordially you may not be too Sanguine though I think it impossible that the people of the U S, will elect the Hero[4]— there certainly is a pause of feeling on that Subject, and but for the exertions of those who have committed themselves I should promise myself Some effectual reaction,   Pleasants has Scored Ritchie[5] very Severely and has made Some impression—his attacks upon the Hero have also had Some effect upon the moral and religious part of the people, Leigh amused himself much with the notion in the west, that the Hero had expurgated himself by marrying his wife over again[6]—I think his committee at Nashville will do the State Some Service if they will gives [sic] us Some more facts and then vindicate them,[7]   the latter will be the most useful, there is a rumour here that you are going very Soon to Kentuckey[8] [sic] how is that can you [sic] be Spared,   Yours very Sincerely & truly   F Brooke

ALS. InU. Addressed to Clay.   [1] Above, May 29, 1827
[2] Benjamin Watkins Leigh.   [3] John Randolph; John Quincy Adams.   [4] Andrew Jackson.   [5] The Washington *Daily National Journal*, May 26, 1827, reprinted the comments of John H. Pleasants, editor of the Richmond *Constitutional Whig*, on the "somerset" of Thomas Ritchie, editor of the *Richmond Enquirer*, in his current support of Jackson after having strongly criticized the General for his actions in the Seminole campaign of 1818 (cf. above, II, 612–13n).   [6] Cf. above, Wilkinson to Clay, July 27, 1825, note.   [7] Cf. above, Clay to Everett, May 22, 1827, and note. The Jackson Committee of Nashville had published a letter explaining the misunderstanding under which Jackson and Rachel Robards had supposed the action of the Virginia Legislature in authorizing a judicial inquiry for a decree of divorce constituted the full divorce proceedings. *Albany Argus and Daily City Gazette*, July 3, 1827.   [8] See below, Clay to Erwin, June 3, 1827.

From John Murray St. Clair

Near Laughlins town Westmoreland County[1]
Honourd [sic] Sir   June 2nd. 1827
In the beliveef [sic] that the friend of the Father will allso [sic] befriend the son Causes me thus to address you in Consequence of The losses sustaind by my reverd and Decasd. [sic] Father from his Country For publick services rendered by the advanc [sic] of moneys for revolution Purposes to wich [sic] I belive [sic] you to be no stranger   as I always understood by him you ware [sic] his friend[2] and his friends knew well his Services you no doubt know well his being Indian agent in the year of 1786 and 1787 and of Conducting a treaty[3] under the Old Confederation for wich I always understood from him that the Government of the united States was Considerable [sic] indebtted [sic] to him for the nessary [sic] Supplys to Carry that Treaty into Effect

Now as I am pretty far advance [sic] in years and have a family to Suport [sic] and from being Concernd in the building of a Furnace[4] with my father which has been the Cause of reducing me to that degree that I am Scarcely able to live for thes [sic] som [sic] years back— Now Sir as I have a Claim or title to some land in the Illinoise [sic] Country   from local Surcumstance I have not been able to see after nor could I Procure Information in regard to what the Government of the united States has done with French and British rights in that Country[5]   my Claim is in the name of Col John Edgar[6] of Kaskaskies [sic] the land lying in the neighbourHood of a place calld Prairee [sic] du Rocher.   now my dear Sir as you are at the head of affairs and have access to the offices of Government will you so far serve the son of an Old servant of the Government as to Examine into the title of a large Survey in the name of John Edgar & John M. St Clair[7] & let me know by the mail what the title is and what it is worth and procure a purchaser or becom [sic] one yourself as I am anctious to Embarke [sic] in the Salt business and am not able unless I can procure some funds from my my [sic] Claim to these lands. I have had thoughts of aplying [sic] to Congress for them to take the land and give me a Certain value theirfor but Sir your advise [sic] will be thankfully received on the whole business and your procureing [sic] a draft from the General land office of this tract between the Villiages [sic] of Kaskakies [sic] and Prairee du Roch— I Conveyd the one half of my Claim to this tract of land to a Certain Rufus Easton then a member of Congress for his attention to the land and paying the taxes   the Survey as I had receivd the draft Containd 13986 Acres which I understood from a Mr Jones[8] of Kaskakies on a reSurvey was Considerable more   if you Sir will Examine the offices or cause an Examination in the business and give me an account of the matter and forward a bill of the Expence [sic] of the office fees and so on I Shall remit it by the member of the next Congress of this district Mr Caulter [sic][9]   I must Confess that I am trouble some but knowing you are a Father I now Suppose myself to be the son wanting advice which I presume you will not be backward in Communicating and beliveing [sic] as I do at this moment from the little I know about you that you are a kind and Indulgent parent. I once when at School in Philadelphia had a school mate of your name and have wondered if you could be the same[10]   Should you think this land worth your notice and your opinion as to price I will transfer my right to you for a small sum of a bout five or six hundred dollars   if I had five hundred dollars at this time I belive it would Enable me to prosecuet [sic] a Salt well so as to make a fortune thare by [sic] as having in my possession one of the best Salt licks west of the laurel hill[11] and from the want of so much finance as will procure the water I am not able to do anything with it and those that can are not willing as the saying is nowadays unless they can make a Speck which I am not

willing to give.   now if you can accomodate [sic] me with the sum of
of [sic] five hundred dollars and tak [sic] my Kaskaskies land in Security for that sum in Case of a failure of procuring water or as a
Security for the refunding the money is thankfully Submitted to your
Consideration and an answar [sic] Humbly saught [sic] for by Sir your
most Obedient and Humble Servant with affection and gratitude for
those services render [sic] to him whose worth his Country knew not
Except washington [sic] himself   JOHN M STCLAIR
the Honourable Henry Clay City of Washington

P S   I have had thoughts for these two last years of addressing you and
have still forborne but as it is becom [sic] so nessary for some Struggle
and Sacrifise [sic] to be made I know no one to apply to as to the [. . .]¹²
of feeling it is in evil¹³ to be compard with that of necsatiy [sic]
                                                                J M S

ALS. DLC-HC (DNA, M212, R2). Addressed as "Private"; endorsed by Clay on verso
of cover: ". . . {Ansd.—declined his requests}." The answer has not been found.   St.
Clair, son of Arthur St. Clair and now about 59 years of age, owned a 75-acre farm and
a hotel and storehouse on the stage road from Bedford to Pittsburgh.
   ¹ Pennsylvania.   ² Clay had aided in procuring a pension for the elder St. Clair
in 1818. *Annals of Cong.*, 15 Cong., 1 Sess., 852.   ³ As Governor of the Northwest
Territory from 1787 to 1802, Arthur St. Clair had administered Indian affairs and had
represented the United States in negotiating the Treaty of Fort Harmar, signed January
9, 1789. For the treaty, see Parry (ed.), *Consolidated Treaty Series*, L, 403–410.   ⁴ An
iron furnace, for the manufacture of stoves and castings.   ⁵ The Northwest Ordinance, of July 13, 1787, confirmed the laws of "descent conveyance of property" as existing among "french and canadian inhabitants & other settlers of the Kaskaskies, Saint
Vincents and the neighbouring villages who have heretofore professed themselves citizens
of Virginia. . . ." It specifically ordained, as "Article the Second," in protection of
property rights, "that no law . . . shall in any manner interfere with, or affect private
contracts or engagements, bona fide and without fraud previously formed."   ⁶ Edgar,
born in Belfast, Ireland, had served in the British Navy during the early years of the
American Revolution but had become sympathetic to the colonial cause, and in consequence had had much of his property seized and had been imprisoned by the British.
He had settled in the Illinois country about 1784, engaged in trade, salt manufacture,
and milling, and was one of the wealthiest men and one of the largest land owners in
the Northwest Territory, holding nearly 50,000 acres in southwestern Illinois. He had
been judge of the court of common pleas for nearly a quarter century, from 1790, and
had sat in the first Territorial legislature, 1799. Active in the militia, he had been appointed brigadier general in 1816.   ⁷ The patent for the tract, dated August 12,
1800, designated the size as 13,986 acres, although it was "said to contain more than
double that quantity." Secretary of the Treasury (Albert Gallatin) to Michael Jones and
Elijah Backus, May 23, 1810, in Carter (ed.), *Territorial Papers.* . . , XVI, 105. Jones,
formerly of Pennsylvania and Ohio, was register of the land office at Kaskaskia from
1804 until 1822; Backus, receiver of public moneys at the Marietta, Ohio, land office
from 1800 to 1804, had become receiver at the Kaskaskia office the latter year.
   ⁸ Probably Michael Jones.   ⁹ Richard Coulter.   ¹⁰ Neither the school nor the
schoolmate has been identified.   ¹¹ On the Cumberland Road, in Pennsylvania.
   ¹² One word illegible.   ¹³ Last two words unclear.

From Daniel Webster

My Dear Sir   Private & confidential   New York June 2. 1827
   I thank you for yours of the 28 May, which I recd. yesterday. My
fears are as great as yours, as to Govr. Lincoln's consenting to go into

the Senate. I enclose a copy of a letter which I have recd. from him since I left home.[1] My friends in Boston are instructed by me today, that if the Governor persists in declining the place, I may be disposed of, as the general opinion of what is useful & expedient may decide; preferring, however, on my part, not to be placed in the Senate, if any other satisfactory appointment can be made. I know not exactly what will be done; & having now the advantage of being *away* from the scene, I intend to retain that advantage till the affair shall be settld [sic].[2]

I have seen very many persons since I came here, & had much conversation about the politics of this State. The public attention seems to begin to be roused, at last; and as far as I can judge, the general feeling is good, very good. More union among friends is now manifested, & something like common understanding, & general system, prevails. The paper at Albany[3] is likely to commence under very good omen, & it is believed that the *Advocate*, which is supposed to have more weight & consequence in the *Country*, will, ere long, come out on the right side.[4] Mr Oakly [sic] is here, & I have had some conversation with him, I learned something also respecting him from other sources. I am satisfied of what his course will be, *so far as it may not be altered hereafter by events*. He will not be made a tool, in the hands of the Southern members of opposition. So far, I have no doubt. I have no doubt, also, that he will vote for Mr. Taylor to be speaker; that he will support the woolen bill, and, generally speaking, go with that interest on which the strength of the Administration rests.[5] But, then, there is another side of the account. He is *against* roads & canals, & internal improvements, except so far as the Tariff goes. This will be a considerable drawback from his usefulness. He is, too, an attached friend of Mr Clinton,[6] altho' I believe he now has very little intercourse or communication with him. This part of his character will cease to be hurtful, as events shall, or I suppose they probably will, more & more remove Mr Clinton from the theatre of political competition   I do not think that Mr. Oakly has any idea of a permanent connexion with the Government; at least, not in the Legislative Departments. His objects lie in the line of his profession.[7] His standing, too, in his District, is rather precarious, having recd a majority of 40 only, where 6 or 7 thousand votes were taken. Upon the whole, I am rather inclined to think, that we have little to fear, & something to hope, from Mr Oakley's course in Congress; & that that course will, probably, be rendered more favorable, rather than less so, by events. What I have stated, I have gathered from such sources, that I would not wish to have much said of it, even to friends. I believe it may be relied on, as presenting a true view of the case, as it at present stands.

Vance has been here, & is now gone to W. Point.[8] He says he left every thing well at home, & found Every thing well in the Western Districts of this State   Gen Van Rennslaer[9] I have met with also. He has become decided, & spirited in his efforts to sustain the Govt.— Depend on it, the "Universal Yankee Nation"[10] will give a good account of themselves from the bottom of Lake Erie to Penobscot River.

I am anxious to hear that you have departed for Kentucky. To that State, more than any other, at the present moment, I look with anxiety. If that be safe, all is safe. Pray when you get there make some of our lazy friends write to us, & inform us how things look.

I am yet to be here two or three days longer, & if I learn any thing interesting will write you again. Yours always truly

DANL. WEBSTER

ALS. DLC-HC (DNA, M212, R2). Addressed to Clay; designated on cover as "Private." [1] See above, Silsbee to Clay, May 23, 1827, note.   [2] Cf. above, Webster to Clay, June 8, 1826, note.   [3] Cf. above, Porter to Clay, January 3, 1827, note.   [4] Cf. above, Porter to Clay, May 1, 1827, note.   [5] Thomas Jackson Oakley did not arrive to take his seat in Congress until after the election for Speaker, when John W. Taylor was defeated (cf. below, Clay to Taylor, September 7, 1827, note). Oakley did not support the new tariff bill, which included a section on woolens; and, in his opposition, he voted with the southern delegation in Congress. U. S. H. of Reps., *Journal*, 20 Cong., 1 Sess., pp. 7, 56, 609; *Niles' Weekly Register*, XXXIII (January 5, 1828), 289, 317.   [6] DeWitt Clinton.   [7] Cf. above, Clay to Webster, April 20, 1827, note.   [8] Joseph Vance, of Ohio, was a member of the board of visitors for the United States Military Academy, which filed its report under date of June 21, 1827. *Sen. Docs.*, 20 Cong., 1 Sess., no. 1, pp. 68–75. Vance's son, Joseph C., a native of Ohio, entered the Academy in the class beginning July 1, 1827. The young man was graduated in 1832 and served in the artillery until 1835, when he resigned his commission. He was killed in an accident in Virginia in 1840.   [9] Stephen Van Rensselaer.   [10] Origin of the phrase has been attributed to Robert Walsh, Jr., in the Philadelphia *National Gazette*, November 6, 1822, when he answered an appeal to New England Republicans for support of William H. Crawford by identifying John Quincy Adams as "the candidate of *all New England*—of the universal Yankee nation wherever dispersed throughout the Union." Livermore, *Twilight of Federalism*, 95–97.

DIPLOMATIC NOTES   June 2, 1827

To JOSÉ SILVESTRE REBELLO. States that Rebello's note of June 1 has been submitted to the President, who has directed Clay to reply, for the information of Rebello's Government, "that relying upon the authorized assurance . . . that on the arrival at Rio Janeiro [*sic*] of a successor to Mr. [Condy] Raguet a full and adequate indemnity will be promptly made for any injuries which have been committed on the persons or property of Citizens of the United States in violation of the public Law, under color of authority derived from his Imperial Majesty, the Emperor of Brazil [Peter I], such a successor will be accordingly sent" without unnecessary delay. Adds: "Confidently anticipating a satisfactory arrangement of all just claims of Citizens of the United States, upon the Government of the Emperor of Brazil, according to the assurance which has been given, the President hopes that all past unfriendly impressions will be thus entirely effaced, and that fresh vigor will be given to the amicable intercourse which both Countries have so much reason to cultivate with each other." Copy. DNA, RG59, Notes to Foreign Legations, vol. 3, p. 364 (M38, R3). AL draft, in CSmH. Published (except for omission of 13 words from the phrase "committed on the . . . public Law") in *American State Papers, Foreign Relations*, VI, 825.

From JOSEPH BURNET, Hackensack, New Jersey. Inquires "whether the property taken from Alexandria [District of Columbia] by the British, during the late War, is to be paid for, out of the money receivd. from the British Goverment [*sic*—cf. above, Gallatin to Clay, November 13, 1826] or Whether it is only the Slaves that are to be paid for"; explains that he "had a Vessel there at the time," which the British seized. ALS. DNA, RG76, Misc. Claims, Great Britain (MR3).

Endorsed on cover by Clay: "Mr. B. will answer that the provision of the treaty of Ghent is not limited to slaves; but that the Commrs., under the late Convention with England must decide to what cases the provision extends. H C." Daniel Brent's reply, dated June 4, 1827, informed Burnet that his letter would be submitted to the Board of Commissioners, "at its first meeting in this City [Washington], . . . next month." LS, *ibid.* The letterbook copy of Brent's communication is dated June 12, 1827. DNA, RG59, Dom. Letters, vol. 21, p. 559.

Documents in the case file reveal that Burnet's vessel, "the Schooner William Eaton," had been carried off by a British squadron "on or about the first day of September in the year one thousand eight hundred and fourteen." Burnet has not been further identified. His petition to the next Session of Congress for relief was reported unfavorably; the report was then tabled. *House Repts.*, 20 Cong., 1 Sess., no. 198.

To James Erwin

Dear Sir   Washington 3d. June 1827.

We have been greatly mortified and disappointed that Anne[1] has not joined us. We had heard of her setting out with that intention from N. Orleans, and she would have now been here if she had not altered her mind. Our residence is the most agreeable in the City, large and commodious,[2] and there is no body in it but her mother,[3] myself and John.[4] In my absence from this place, she would have been a great comfort to her mother

I shall leave here for Lexington on the 10h. and expect to reach it about the 25h. I shall not remain there I think beyond a fortnight, being compelled to be here again on the first of August.

I should be glad to receive a letter from you at Lexington, informing me of the state of the health of Anne yourself and child,[5] or children.[6]

Be pleased also to inform me who has the possession of Mathers's bonds.[7] I have a thought of endeavoring to convert them into Cash in one of the Atlantic Cities. Give me your opinion of what they are worth in the market of N. Orleans, and particularly as to the adequacy of the security of their ultimate payment. Was not the interest paid on them and to whom last February?

Political prospects are good. Mr. Adams will be re-elected in my opinion, without doubt, and with great ease.

Lucretia joins me in love to Anne and yourself. Yr's affectionately
Mr. James Erwin   H. CLAY.

ALS. THi.   1 Anne Brown Clay Erwin.
2 Cf. above, Clay to Henry Clay, Jr., April 2, 1827.   3 Lucretia Hart Clay.   4 John
Morrison Clay.   5 Julia D. Erwin.   6 Cf. above, Carroll to Clay, May 3, 1827,
note.   7 Cf. above, Whittelsey to Clay, December 22, 1826; Erwin to Clay, May 21,
1827.

To Peter Force

For the Journal of tomorrow (4h)   [June 3, 1827]
[Attachment]¹

There have been lately frequent conferences between Mr. Clay,
and Mr. Rebello,² the Chargé of His Majesty the Emperor of Brazil,³
and several official notes have passed, in relation to a late unpleasant
incident at Rio. de Janeiro.⁴ We are told that such satisfactory assurances have been made as will preserve the friendly relations between the two Countries.

AN. DLC-HC (DNA, M212, R2). Addressed by Clay on cover: "Peter Force Esqr."
1 AD. *Ibid.* Published, with minor variations, in Washington *Daily National Journal*,
June 4, 1827.   2 José Silvestre Rebello.   3 Peter I.   4 Above, Rebello to
Clay, May 30, June 1, 1827; Clay to Rebello, May 31, June 2, 1827.

MISCELLANEOUS LETTERS   June 3, 1827

From WILLIAM B. ROCHESTER, New Orleans. Reports his arrival on the preceding
day (cf. above, Sergeant to Clay, May 30, 1827), his expectation of being "detained
. . . a week or ten days" awaiting the arrival of his servant and most of his baggage,
and his discovery "that an early conveyance to Omoa is not to be obtained without
chartering a vessel for that purpose exclusively." Notes his unwillingness to incur
"the expense of chartering a suitable" vessel, "since the public interests do not
seem to require an immediate departure." States that he will, "Consequently,"
send his "baggage to N. York by water"; that he intends to reach "that City in
good time, thro the interior"; and that, meanwhile, he will go directly to Lake
Erie, "with the view of remaining a few weeks or months with . . . [his] family."
Adds: "I have (by letter of this date) countermanded the order for my out-fit, in
hope that my Brother [Thomas H. Rochester; cf. above, Rochester to Clay, May
12, 1827] may receive it in due time—if he do not, I flatter myself that its payment
at an earlier day than was intended, will not be deemed a matter of much importance—" Concludes by citing letters and newspapers, received by him, by which
"it appears that the cause of the disaffected [in Central America] had become entirely hopeless"; that "President [Manuel José] Arce was near S. Salvador, with
his troops"; that the city, repentant, had invited him "to enter it with his army";
and that the rebel leaders had fled (cf. above, Phillips to Clay, March 2, 22, May
12, 1827; Poinsett to Clay, April 18, May 16, 1827; Valero to Clay, April 9, 1827).
ALS. DNA, RG59, Dip. Disp., Central America, vol. 1 (M219, R2).

To Francis T. Brooke

My dear Sir   Washington 4h. June 1827.
    I received your favor of the 2d. instant. You ask me if I am going
to Kentucky soon, and if I can be spared? I am compelled by my
private business and particularly by that of the Estate of my deceased

friend Col. Morrison,[1] of which I am the only acting executor, to go to Kentucky, and I shall leave this City for that purpose on the 10h. inst. It is my intention to return by the first of August. I shall leave the business of the Department in such condition that I do not believe that any prejudice to the public will arise from my absence. Yr's truly & Cordially   H. CLAY
The Honble F. Brooke.

ALS. DLC-TJC (DNA, M212, R10).   [1] James Morrison.

To Henry Rutgers

Dear Sir.   (*Private & Confidential*)   Washn. 4h. June 1827
    Long accustomed to regard you as one of the fathers of the Republican church, to which we both belong, I hope I shall be excused from that circumstance, if I am not authorized by our acquaintance, in taking the liberty of addressing this letter to you.
    You have felt too deep an interest and had too much agency in the public affairs of our Country to admit of your beholding with indifference what is now passing or to allow you to forbear from giving, whilst you are spared among us, the benefit of your matured counsels. And I am greatly mistaken in the estimate I have made of your judgment and character if you can approve the conduct of the Opposition to the General Administration, or the object, or the means which they are employing to accomplish that object, of supplanting Mr. Adams and electing Genl Jackson.
    During the administration of the father[1] of our present Chief Magistrate, I was too young and too poor to take any part in the public councils, but I nevertheless had very decided opinions to which I gave all the effect I could in private circles, against some of the prominent measures of that Administration and what I believed to be its tendency, if not the ultimate aim of some of its principal supporters. But I could not allow myself to transfer my dislike of the Administration of the father to the person and public character of the Son, who I firmly believe, after an acquaintance with him of more than 20 years, to be sincerely attached to our free institutions and to the general cause of Liberty. When, therefore, the only alternative presented on a late occasion to my choice in the H. of R. was between him and Genl. Jackson, who appeared to me to possess no other than military pretensions, I could not doubt the side on which duty and safety laid.[2] Far from regretting the choice which I then made, I should make it again, under similar circumstances, and I must ever think that the election of Genl. Jackson at that or at any time would be a most unfortunate event for this Country. I accepted a place in the Administration from a full conviction that it was a duty, I owed myself, after the flagitious

attacks made upon me, one object of which was to intimidate me, and under the unanimous advice of all my Congressional friends.[3]

If there be one characteristic which, more than any other, distinguishes the Republican party, and of which, more than any other, they may be justly proud, it is their devotion to Liberty and to the guarrantys [sic] for its preservation which experience and reason demonstrate to be necessary. Does not the history of all nations & of all times prove that the greatest danger to Freedom is from mere Military men? With this light before them, can the Republican party, if they are faithful to their own principles, and desirous to perpetuate in their posterity that liberty which they themselves enjoy, lend themselves to the election of a chief magistrate, who possesses no other qualification, than that of being a successful Military commander? I thought they could not, and yet believe that they cannot.

It would be a great satisfaction to me to find that the opinions which I have now expressed receive your approbation. But whether I am so fortunate or not, I hope you will do justice to my motives in communicating them, and in addressing you at the present period, and at the same time be fully persuaded that with the greatest respect and veneration for your character   I am, faithfully, Your obedient Servant   H. C.

ALI draft. DLC-TJC (DNA, M212, R10). Endorsed by Clay on attached sheet: "Draught of a Letter to Col. Rutgers." Published, without the reference to privacy and confidentiality, in Colton (ed.), *Private Correspondence of Henry Clay*, 163–64.

   1 John Adams.   2 Cf. above, Clay to McClure, December 28, 1824; to Featherstonhaugh, January 21, 1825; to Dun, January 22, 1825; to Brown, January 23, 1825; to Porter, January 23, 1825; to Brooke, January 28, February 4, 10, 1825; to Blair, January 29, 1825; Address, March 26, 1825.   3 Cf. above, Clay to Brooke, February 18, 1825; Creighton to Clay, February 19, 1825; Drake to Clay, February 20, 1825; Clay to Featherstonhaugh, February 26, 1825; Blair to Clay, March 7, 1825.

INSTRUCTIONS AND DISPATCHES   June 4, 1827

From ALEXANDER H. EVERETT, Madrid, no. 77. Expresses discouragement, following additional conversations with (Manuel Gonzáles) Salmón, in regard to "the subject of the pending negotiations" (cf. above, Everett to Clay, February 13, 1827, and note); describes his futile "effort to try the effect of a direct appeal to the King in person"; and encloses a copy of his letter to Salmón, in which he included "the proposed communication" to the King. Declares that, should this approach do no good, he will ask Clay "for fresh instructions." Notes that Salmón, whose "tone was as usual plausible and friendly," told him "that the Committee of the Council [of State] were fully prepared some time ago to make their report on the Indemnity question" (cf. above, Everett to Clay, December 18, 1826; March 31, April 7, 19, 1827); that further delay had been caused by a search for relevant documents "in the war department"; and "that he hoped and believed that the arrangement would be very soon completed." Comments: "The President will judge after the successive failures of the many former assurances of the same description what degree of confidence is due to this."

Transmits copies of correspondence with "the Minister" (Salmón) in a futile effort to bring about a correction of abuses in the application "of the Sanitary laws of the Kingdom" to American commerce (cf. above, Everett to Clay, March 19, 1827) and concludes that "Under such a system of management [as prevails in Spain] there is very little hope of obtaining the correction of any abuses." Charges "that the French Military authorities at Cadiz and Barcelona either from an honest apprehension of contagion . . . or from a disguised wish to encourage the French Commerce at the expence [sic] of ours, do in fact enforce the existing Sanitary laws, whatever they may be, in such a way as to make their operation (which is hardly felt at any other port) amount at these to a complete prohibition of intercourse for the greater part of the year." Indicates that he expects no improvement until the end of the French occupation, which, as "now understood," is to occur "in the course of the present year." Notes his pleasure at having been informed by Salmón "that he was prepared to lay before the Council of State a proposal for the admission of Consuls of all friendly foreign powers in the ports of the Islands of Cuba and Puerto Rico" and predicts that the "measure . . . after the intervening delay incident to the transaction of all business by that body, will probably be carried into effect." LS. DNA, RG59, Dip. Disp., Spain, vol. 27 (M31, R28). Received August 18.

From ALBERT GALLATIN, London, no. 81. Encloses "the copy of a letter addressed this day to Lord Dudley on the subject of the Colonial intercourse" (cf. above, Gallatin to Clay, August 19, September 14, 1826). Notes that "On general grounds, it might perhaps have been preferable to let the whole matter rest for a twelve-month, waiting with patience for such change in the policy of this Country, as a reaction from the West India British colonies, a more favorable disposition on the part of the Ministry, or other circumstances may produce," but that he is "fully aware of the necessity of obtaining, before the next session of Congress, an explicit declaration of the real object of this Government [cf. above, Gallatin to Clay, April 28, 1827; Editorial Article, ca. May 9, 1827], which alone can secure the necessary concert, on the part of the United States, in adopting the measures fitted for the occasion." Points out that he added to his communication "a general expression of the President's disposition to promote a restoration of the intercourse founded on mutual legislation" (cf. above, Clay to Gallatin, April 11, 1827) and explains that "It is simply proceeding one step farther than in the Note of 28th Decer. last to Mr [George] Canning [cf. above, Gallatin to Clay, December 28, 1826], which concluded by expressing the readiness of the United States to treat on the subject, whenever it should be the inclination of Great Britain to negotiate upon it." Cites "a former dispatch" (above, May 31, 1827) in which he gave his "reasons for omitting in the Note some of the arguments contained in . . . [Clay's] despatch No. 26 [above, April 11, 1827]. . . ." Adds, in a postscript, that he also encloses a copy of another note to Lord Dudley "on the subject of the Africans intended to be returned to their own Country" (cf. above, Clay to Gallatin, April 6, 1827). ALS. DNA, RG59, Dip. Disp., Great Britain, vol. 34 (M30, R30). Published in Adams, Writings of Gallatin, II, 376–77. Received July 20.

In his note of June 1, 1827, to Lord Dudley, Gallatin refers to efforts by the United States Government to return "to their native country" Africans taken from "vessels illegally engaged in the Slave trade"; notes difficulties experienced "in cases where they belonged to interior provinces of Africa"; and inquires whether the British Government "would be disposed to afford facilities to the landing and safe passage, through His Majesty's possessions on the coast of Africa, of such Africans" as the American Government may wish to restore to the interior.

From JOHN SERGEANT AND JOEL R. POINSETT, Mexico. Refer to their dispatch of May 9 and report "that the Congress of Mexico has terminated its session without acting upon the Panama treaties." Note that "In other respects no change whatever has taken place" and that, since their last dispatch, "nothing has occurred . . . to increase the probability of an early meeting [of the Congress at Tacubaya]." Add that Sergeant will soon leave for the United States. LS. DNA, RG43, Records re Panama Congress, vol. 1 (M662, R1). Received August 10.

MISCELLANEOUS LETTERS   June 4, 1827

To HENRY M. MORFIT, "Consular Commercial Agent of the United States, at Halifax." Transmits "the evidence of" his appointment and "a copy of the printed Circular Instructions to Consuls." Copy. DNA, RG59, Cons. Instr., vol. 2, p. 428 (M78, R2).

In a letter addressed to Daniel Brent on May 30, 1827, Morfit had inquired concerning establishment of the position, inasmuch as "the greater part" of the trade with the British West Indies would pass through Halifax under the existing trade restrictions (cf. above, Gallatin to Clay, August 19, 1826; Clay to Vaughan, March 17, 1827). ALS, in DNA, RG59, A. and R. (M531, R5). Brent had endorsed the cover of the letter (AE) as follows: "Mr. Morfit is a Lawyer of this Place, and a man of great Respectability of Character. If an agency should be determined upon, the appointment would be very acceptable to him." After the election of 1828 he was active as a member of Andrew Jackson's Central Committee and in 1832 was a delegate from Washington to the Democratic nominating convention at Baltimore.

From JOSHUA DODGE, New York. Notes that, his "leave of absence [cf. above, Dodge to Clay, September 7, 1825; November 8, 1826] . . . being nearly expired," he plans to embark on June 15 to return to his post at Marseilles. States that he would "be much gratified by hearing from the Department" before his departure. ALS. DNA, RG59, Cons. Disp., Marseilles, vol. 2 (M-T220, R-T2).

Writing to Clay from Paris, July 30, 1827, Dodge reported his arrival and his intention to continue to his "Consular residence at Marseilles . . . in a few days." ALS, *ibid.*

From NEHEMIAH FOSTER, Cambridge, Massachusetts. States that he "Shiped [*sic*] last November Some property to Porto Cabello, Columbia [*sic*]," with a consular certificate, signed by James Andrews of Boston, which has been protested by P. Meneses, the collector at Porto Cabello, and returned; that he thus learned "the Duties amount to nearly three times what they ought to have been." Notes that Andrews has given him no satisfaction and, conceiving "this an infringement of the Commeretial [*sic*] Treaty," asks how he is "to obtain restitution." ALS. DNA, RG76, Misc. Claims, Colombia.

Endorsed by Clay on cover: "Inform the writer that redress can only be obtained by an application to the Colombian Govt. by himself or his Agent or by this Govt. upon being furnished with evidence to establish the fact. H C." A letter, dated June 11, 1827, imparting this information was sent to Foster by Daniel Brent. Copy, in DNA, RG59, Dom. Letters, vol. 21, p. 557 (M40, R19). Foster wrote again, December 6, 1827, to acknowledge receipt of Brent's letter, request information as to the status of his claim, and ask whether his supporting documents had been sent to the Colombian Government. ALS, in DNA, RG76, Misc. Claims, Colombia (MR1).

Foster and Meneses have not been further identified; Andrews was a merchant. Reference to the outcome of the case has not been found; it apparently remained unsettled in 1859. Cf. *Sen. Docs.*, 35 Cong., 2 Sess., no. 18, p. 103.

To Charles Hammond

My dear Sir   Washn. 5h. June 1827.
    I received this morning your favor of the 25h. Ulto.[1] Col. Davis[2] is
here, and has I believe made some arrangement with Mr. Rush[3] (to
whom I introduced and recommended him) relative to Mr. Hunt's
business,[4] which, if it do not come up to his wishes, is deemed satisfactory for the moment. He will no doubt make the proper communication about it.
    You have seen the different versions of the Fayetteville story.[5] I stand
perfectly unassaible [sic] by them. Nor do I believe (if they stick to
truth) that they can bring forward any thing whatever to implicate my
friends. Means have been adopted, and are now in a progress of execution, to collect a mass of testimony of which at the proper time a
proper use will be made, if circumstances should appear to render it
necessary.[6]
    There is a tone of confidence among our friends on this side of the
Mountains, and in Kentucky, which bespeaks conscious strength and
certain success.
    Baldwin's course at Cincinnati[7] does not surprize me. Possessed of
some talents, I have been compelled to think for a long time unfavorably of the stability of his principles   If you have not already
formed the same opinion, you will finally adopt it.
    I shall set out for Kentucky on the 10h. instant via Pittsburg [sic],
and the Ohio river, if in a navigable state. I *may* possibly go to Louisville, but time will not admit of my stopping at Cincinnati. I shall
travel to Pittsburg in my own carriage, and do not expect to leave that
City before the 22d. or 23d.— Truly Your friend   H CLAY
C. Hammond Esq

ALS. InU.   1 Not found.
2 Samuel W. Davies, born in London, England, had come to the United States about
1799 and for a brief time had been a grocer in New York City. Around 1802 he had
settled at Williamsburg, in Clermont County, Ohio, where he had kept a general store,
had invested in land, and had become active in politics and the State militia. Removing
to Cincinnati about 1809, he had been from 1814 to 1819 cashier of the Farmers and
Mechanics Bank in that city and one of the proprietors of the Cincinnati Manufacturing
Company. In connection with the latter venture he had built in the years 1817 to 1819
a "hidraulic acqueduct," for which in 1826 he had obtained a State charter of incorporation as the Cincinnati Water Company. He continued politically active and from 1833
until his death in 1843 served five terms as mayor of Cincinnati.   3 Richard Rush.
    4 On Jesse Hunt's debt to the United States Government, cf. above, III, 389n; Benham
to Clay, January 30, 1826. A balance of $12,348.01 remained due from Hunt in the list
of "Unsettled Accounts . . . Office Third Auditor . . . 30th September [1826]," *House Docs.*,
19 Cong., 1 Sess, no. 141, sig. 39. Indulgence had been granted until June 1, 1826, whereupon the estate of the principal and sureties had been levied upon.   5 Cf. above,
Report of Interview, *ca.* April 15, 1827, note.   6 Cf. below, Address, December 29,
1827.   7 Probably Henry Baldwin, whose Cincinnati visit has not been traced. Although he had subsequently attended the dinner honoring Clay (above, Toasts, May 19,
1825), he had been one of the earliest proponents of the Presidential candidacy of
Andrew Jackson. See Klein, *Pennsylvania Politics*, 123–24.

To John F. Henry

Dear Sir: Washington, 5th June, 1827.
I shall leave this city for Lexington, via Pittsburg [*sic*], and the Ohio river, if it be navigable, on the 10th instant, but do not expect to reach Lexington before the 26th or 27th. I shall not be able to remain there longer than about a fortnight. As I shall be very desirous to know the prospects in your district,[1] you will greatly oblige me by communicating them to me at that place. I am, truly and cordially, Your friend,
The Honble Jno. F Henry   H CLAY

LS. DLC-Short Family Papers.   [1] See above, Johnson to Clay, April 29, 1827, note.

Order on Washington Office, Bank of the United States

WASHINGTON, June 5th. 1827
Office of Discount and Deposit,
PAY *to* Jos. Vance *or bearer, the nett proceeds of* his *note of* two thousand dollars *discounted this day to my credit.*   H CLAY
$1978 67/100

DS. DLC-TJC (DNA, M212, R16).

Receipt from Susan Decatur

George Town June 5th 1827
Reciv'd [*sic*] from the Honble Henry Clay two hundred dollars for one quarters House rent due on the 15th July 1827[1]—
SUSAN DECATUR

ADS. DLC-TJC (DNA, M212, R16).
[1] Cf. above, Clay to Henry Clay, Jr., April 2, 1827.

From John Lane Gardner

Sir   Quarter Master Generals Office 5 June 1827
The enclosed letter addressed to you,[1] was received under cover of a short note from the writer to myself, as his friend—and left open to put me in possession of the subject matter—
I feel awkward in being thus made (unavoidably[)] the medium of the communication—but my embarrassment proceeds less from the nature of the request it makes of you, than from its implicating in some degree the discretion of a young gentleman who claims to be your kinsman—which circumstance may therefore make it the cause of pain to you—

Permit me, however to observe that my knowledge of Mr Watson's character, justifies me in affirming that he has candidly stated his motives in loaning the amount to Mr Hart,[2] and in addressing you on the subject—and that in the latter particular he simply seeks *advice* from you, which may save him a sum he can ill afford to lose— I will do myself the honor to call on you, when I may find you at leisure— With great respect I am Sir Yr obed svt.

Hon: Henry Clay Secy of State   JNO L. GARDNER (Capt U S Army)

ALS. DNA, RG59, Misc. Letters (M179, R65). Gardner, born in Boston and a veteran of the War of 1812, had been assigned to Washington, in the office of the quartermaster general, since 1818. He returned to regimental duty in 1830, served in the Seminole and Mexican Wars, and attained rank as major in 1845, lieutenant colonel in 1852, and colonel in 1861.

[1] Above, Watson to Clay, March 30, 1827.   [2] John S. Hart.

INSTRUCTIONS AND DISPATCHES   June 5, 1827

From ALBERT GALLATIN, London, no. 82. States that no conference has been held "since that of the 24th ulto. [cf. above, Gallatin to Clay, May 29, 1827], the Protocol of which is not yet agreed on"; that the "long discussion on the North East boundary was, from the numerous points to be arranged, extremely desultory"; that "it would have been very desirable to settle" certain principles before attempting "to reduce the projet of Convention to the form of Articles"; and that "Finding it however necessary to bring the questions to some issue," he has followed the British example (cf. above, Gallatin to Clay, December 22, 1826, no. 43) by sending them "a Non Official Projet [a copy of which is enclosed] . . . as an informal paper," which puts "in a more definite shape all the points which had been the subject of verbal discussion." Adds that "It would be premature to attempt" to explain at this time "the provisions of the Projet." ALS. DNA, RG59, Dip. Disp., Great Britain, vol. 34 (M30, R30). Published, with enclosure, in *American State Papers, Foreign Relations*, VI, 673. Received July 20.

From ALBERT GALLATIN, London, no. 83. Encloses a copy of Lord Dudley's answer, dated June 2, to his note of May 25 (cf. above, Gallatin to Clay, May 30, 1827). States that Dudley's communication, "Being official, . . . gives an official character to Mr. [John] Backhouse's note of 18th ulto. to Mr. [William Beach] Lawrence" (cf. above, Gallatin to Clay, May 22, 1827) and that, "Together, they may now be considered as the avowed exposition of the construction put by Great Britain, on that branch of the law of Nations, which relates to the immunities of public ministers." Notes that "The most striking feature is the substitution, habitual to Great Britain, of her own laws and practice and of her own arbitrary construction of the law of Nations to that, which may prevail amongst other Nations, or which is supported by the best writers on the subject." Declares his belief that it would be best "not to pursue the discussion to which . . . Dudley's exposition might lead" and "to reserve . . . arguments and . . . strength for the discussion of those truly important questions. . . ." ALS. DNA, RG59, Dip. Disp., Great Britain, vol. 34 (M30, R30). Received July 20.

In addition to confirming the statement contained in Backhouse's note, the enclosure supplied "an Omission in that statement, with respect to the question of the supposed inviolability of the premises occupied by a Foreign Minister," by adding that, "since the abolition of Sanctuary in England," no place, including an Ambassador's residence, was "protected from the intervention of criminal process." Dudley added, "however," that he considered "it to be most agreeable to the Spirit of" the law of nations and "most consistent with the courtesy which the British Government . . . [was] always anxious to shew to the Ministers of Foreign States residing in this Country, that their houses should not be entered without their permission being first solicited, in cases where no urgent necessity . . . [pressed] for the immediate capture of an offender. . . ."

From J[OEL] R. POINSETT, Mexico, no. 91. Transmits translations of a message by the President (Guadalupe Victoria) "on closing the Session of Congress . . . and of a law admitting the importation of building timber free of duty for the term of two years." Suggests "that this law . . . be published throughout the United States as soon as possible." LS. *Ibid.*, Mexico, vol. 3 (M97, R4). Received July 29.

MISCELLANEOUS LETTERS   June 5, 1827

From JEDEDIAH BURCHARD, Philadelphia. Refers to an act, passed at the last Session of Congress, "for the relief of Butterfield and Kendall while engaged in sutling for the Army of the United States"; asks, "in behalf of . . . [his] sister, the widow of the late Mr. Butterfield . . . for information respecting the requisitions of the statute"; and notes that Butterfield was a lieutenant in the Army "during the last war" but resigned his commission to become a sutler. ALS. DNA, RG59, Misc. Letters (M179, R65).

Daniel Brent replied, in a letter dated "June 1827" (*i.e.*, June 10, 1827), that Clay had received this inquiry "some days before his departure yesterday . . . on a visit to Kentucky" and referred Burchard "to a Law of the last session of Congress, entitled an "Act for the relief of the assignees, or legal Representatives of Kendall and Butterfield, passed on the 3d. of March of the present year [6 *U. S. Stat.*, 365], and to the accounting officers of the Treasury Department, . . . authorized and required by that Act to settle the claims of the Assignees or legal Representatives of Kendall and Butterfield." Copy, in DNA, RG59, Dom. Letters, vol. 21, pp. 549–50 (M40, R19).

Burchard, born in Connecticut and reared in central New York, had failed in business at Albany and then studied for the ministry. Granted a probationary license from the Congregational Association at Adams in 1822, he had been ordained as an evangelist by the Watertown Presbytery in 1824. He led revivals in Jefferson County, western New York, over the next five years, held a pastorate briefly at Utica, then returned to evangelistic work in western New York from 1831 to 1833. He preached in western New England during the mid-thirties, in New York City in 1837, and by 1841 was back in western New York, at Rochester. His influence as an evangelist was extended through the work of Charles G. Finney and Orson Parker, whom he converted. Whitney R. Cross, *The Burned-Over District: the Social and Intellectual History of Enthusiastic Religion in Western New York, 1800–1850* (Ithaca, 1950), 188–89; Franklin B. Hough, *A History of Jefferson County in the State of New York . . .* (Albany, 1854), 76, 164, 391; John A. Haddock, *The Growth of a Century: as Illustrated in the History of Jefferson County, New York, from 1793 to 1894* (Albany, 1895), 384.

Shubael Butterfield, born in New Hampshire, had served as a lieutenant through the War of 1812, had re-enlisted, and had been serving as regimental paymaster when he resigned in 1816. He had died at Baltimore in October, 1824, when he was identified as "late of Sackett's Harbor, New York." Washington *Daily National Intelligencer*, October 23, 1824. His partner in the firm may have been William Kendall, who had also entered the Army from New Hampshire, resigned at about the same time in 1816, and resided in the vicinity of Watertown, New York, in 1817. Mrs. Butterfield has not been further identified.

From Henry Wheaton

My Dear Sir,   (Private)   New York, June 6, 1827.

I am much obliged by your kind letter of the 2d inst.,[1] marked "Private & Unofficial", which was received this day.—

The Instructions,[2] &c were received yesterday. I shall acknowledge their reception in an *official* letter[3]—

So far as I can judge by a single hasty reading, your Instructions are drawn up in a very satisfactory manner, & the commentary upon them will be fully supplied by the Correspondence to which I am referred. But will you allow me to ask a question, (which my inexperience in this sort of business probably alone renders necessary,) whether as I am only accredited to the Minister of foreign affairs,[4] & not to the Sovereign,[5] I ought not to be furnished with a "full power," in case it should become necessary to sign a Convention respecting any of the subjects mentioned in my Instructions? or whether my Letter of Credence and Instructions, when in connexion, imply such an authority?[6]—

I have no doubt all is right, & according to the usual course of office; but I should be glad of a *single word* of explanation, as I am sure the Dane will make every possible formal difficulty, & the only books on diplomatic lore which I have been able to consult since receiving your official Letter are very unsatisfactory on the subject.—

Will you be so kind as to have the *printed sheets* of th [sic] Reports of the S. Court which I sent you,[7] transmitted to my friend Judge Trimble[8] at *Paris, Kentucky*, as he is anxious to anticipate the regular transmission of the volume, & I have no equally sure means of sending the sheets to him.—

Mr Webster[9] left here yesterday for Boston.—

I feel very sensibly the kind expressions of good wishes contained in your letter, and beg leave most respectfully to reciprocate them. I am very truly your friend,   HENRY WHEATON

The hon. Mr Clay &c &c &c

ALS. DLC-HC (DNA, M212, R2).   [1] Not found.
[2] Above, May 31, 1827.   [3] Below, Wheaton to Clay, *ca.* June 7, 1827, note.
[4] Count Ernst Heinrich Schimmelmann.   [5] Frederick VI.   [6] On the letter of credence, see above, Wheaton to Clay, May 31, 1827, note. A general letter of accreditation as Chargé d'Affaires, specifically authorizing Wheaton to negotiate on the subject of claims, is dated June 8, 1827. Copy, in DNA, RG59, Ceremonial Communications and Credences, 66–67.   [7] Cf. above, May 29, 1827.   [8] Robert Trimble.   [9] Daniel Webster.

INSTRUCTIONS AND DISPATCHES   June 6, 1827

To JAMES BROWN, no. 14. Transmits "the copy of a correspondence, between Baron de Mareuil and . . . [the State] Department, upon the subject of the present state of the navigation and commerce, between the United States and France" (above, Mareuil to Clay, May 16, 1827; Clay to Mareuil, May 25, 1827), in order to inform

Brown of "the views of the President in relation to the matter." Copy. DNA, RG59, Dip. Instr., vol. 11, pp. 364–65 (M77, R6).

From JOHN CUTHBERT, Hamburg. Lists amounts exported during the last year from Hamburg to Newfoundland, for English accounts and in British vessels, of flour, pork, beef, butter, and " 'Brigs' Bread" and adds that, according to his information, contracts for the current year exceed those for the last. Notes that "This is a new branch of Trade for Hamburg"; expresses doubt that it "can be increased . . . so as to do serious injury to the trade of the United States"; but concludes that "the attempt will no doubt be made." ALS. DNA, RG59, Cons. Disp., Hamburg, vol. 3 (M-T211, R3). Received September 1.

MISCELLANEOUS LETTERS   June 6, 1827

From MATTHEW ST. CLAIR CLARKE, New York. States that he is forwarding "Samples of the best papers . . . [he] ever saw manufactured in this Country" and requests Clay's opinion of them. Adds that "Hudson, of Hartford," the manufacturer, "begs leave . . . to say, that . . . [Clay's] exertions while in the House of Rep [sic] in support of manufactures have greatly and mainly contributed to make the character of these Samples what they are. . . ." Notes that other manufacturers, of paper, "Wax-Pencils and quills" are forwarding samples and prices for consideration at Washington and that he hopes "to turn out articles which will shew what can be done *at home*." Appends a postscript stating that he has "sent Samples to Mr. [Richard] Rush." ALS. DNA, RG59, Misc. Letters (M179, R65). Endorsed by Clay on verso: "Mr. Brent will please Ansr. the inclosed. H C."

On June 11, Brent wrote to inform Clarke that the Department had on hand an adequate supply "of the very paper represented by the Samples." Copy, in DNA, RG59, Dom. Letters, vol. 21 (M40, R19).

At about this time Henry Hudson, one of the founders of the Hartford Fire Insurance Company in 1810 and mayor of Hartford from 1836 to 1840, established a paper mill at Oakland (Manchester), Connecticut, which was operated by his family for some thirty years. J. Hammond Trumbull (ed.), *The Memorial History of Hartford County, Connecticut, 1633–1884* (2 vols.; Boston, 1886), II, 251, dates the mill from 1832.

Check to Susan Decatur

No.   OFFICE OF DISCOUNT & DEPOSIT⎱
                                      Washington,⎰ 7 June 1827
    PAY to Mrs. S. Decatur or order on the third day of July next Two hundred Dollars, /100
$200 DOLLARS, /100   H. CLAY

DS, partially printed. DLC-TJC (DNA, M212, R10). Cf. above, Receipt from Susan Decatur, June 5, 1827.

To Daniel Webster

My dear Sir   (Private)   Washington 7h. June 1827
    I recd. yesterday your obliging letter of the 2d. inst. with a Copy of one from Govr. Lincoln.[1] Since he so positively declines, I sincerely

hope you may be elected. I have some fears however that Mr. Mills
will create some trouble and difficulty.[2]

The tone of confidence which the public prints of K.[3] & the letters
which I receive from my friends there assume, I think, is evidence of
their conscious strength and certain success. I am fully aware of the
very great importance of a favorable issue in the elections in that
State; and I am much deceived if the Administration does not maintain its relative strength, that is two thirds of the members to the
H. of R.[4]

I take my departure for Lexington on the 10h. via Pittsburg [sic].
I intend to return to the City by the first of August.

Oakley's[5] opinion about Internal improvements will do no harm.
What I am most anxious about, on that subject, is that they should be
supported in New England, and that the West and Pennsa. should be
made *sensible* of that support. After the next Census, we shall have a
great increase of strength to the cause from the West. You have some
difficulty to sustain it in New England, but I hope notwithstanding
your limited territory and its improved condition you will be able to
sustain it by prudence & discretion. You have your equivalents in
other forms, if not in that of I. Improvements. We must keep the two
interests of D. M. & I. I.[6] allied, and both tend to the support of that
other great & not less important interest of Navigation. Always Cordially Your friend   H CLAY
D. Webster Esq

ALS. DLC-Daniel Webster Papers (DNA, M212, R22).   1 Levi Lincoln.
2 On the difficulty with Elijah Hunt Mills, cf. below, Webster to Clay, June 22, 1827.
    3 Kentucky.   4 Cf. above, Clay to Taylor, April 4, 1827, and note.   5 Thomas
Jackson Oakley.   6 Domestic Manufactures and Internal Improvements.

MISCELLANEOUS LETTERS   June 7, 1827

From L[EMUEL] SAWYER, "Elizabeth, N. C." Transmits a letter to Clay from "A
fellow townsman, Matthew [sic] Cluff" (below, June 8, 1827), relating to a claim
against Great Britain. Notes that Cluff, who has heard nothing concerning a
petition submitted to the Lords of Admiralty over a year ago, wishes to obtain
information, through Clay, "of the state of his claim" as well as Clay's "interposition in favour of it." ALS. DNA, RG76, Misc. Claims, Great Britain (MR3).
Addressed to Clay at Washington.
    Identified as a resident of Norfolk, Virginia, in 1815, Cluff was active as a mer-
chant in Elizabeth City, North Carolina, into the 1830's. *House Docs.*, 21 Cong.,
2 Sess., no. 50, p. 379; U. S. H. of Reps., *Journal*, 22 Cong., 1 Sess., p. 868.

From HENRY WHEATON, "Private." Acknowledges receipt of *"General & Personal"*
instructions (cf. above, Wheaton to Clay, June 6, 1827) and promises to write an
official acknowledgment "as soon as the Books, &c." reach him. States the manner
in which he wishes his "Papers, &c" forwarded to Copenhagen, "taking all proper
precautions to avoid excessive [pos]tages to the public charge." Admits that he is
"probably speaking to one who knows much more about these things than" he,
and adds that his desire is to give "no ground for complaint," in his case, "as to

excessive charges for *Contingencies.*" Requests Clay, upon receipt of the Department's copies of the "Reports of the Decisions of the Supreme Court," to send the "necessary Certificate to *Mr* [Richard] *Harrison,* without delay," and ask him to forward Wheaton's salary. ALS. DNA, RG59, Dip. Disp., Denmark, vol. 1B (M41, R3). Not dated; endorsed on verso of last page: "Recd 10th June."

Wheaton's formal acknowledgment of his "*General & Personal* Instructions" and, on June 10, of "the two Trunks containing the Books and Documents mentioned" by Clay is dated June 11. ALS, in *ibid.*

INSTRUCTIONS AND DISPATCHES   June 8, 1827

From ALBERT GALLATIN, London, no. 84. Notes that, though informed by Lord Melville, "near three months ago [cf. above, Gallatin to Clay, December 9, 1826; February 13, 1827]," that the Admiralty had reported favorably "on the subject of the lights necessary for the safety of the Navigation of the Bahama Banks," he has received "no official communication . . . of the intention of this Government on the renewed application of the United States" (cf. above, Gallatin to Clay, January 4, 11, 1827). Reports that he has addressed to Lord Dudley two notes (copies of which are enclosed), one official and the other private, calling his attention to the matter. ALS. DNA, RG59, Dip. Disp., Great Britain, vol. 34 (M30, R30). Published in *American State Papers, Foreign Relations,* VI, 756. Received August 4.

MISCELLANEOUS LETTERS   June 8, 1827

To ENOCH LINCOLN, "Governor of the State of Maine." States, in reply to Lincoln's letter of May 29, that he has ordered the requested copies "prepared, without any avoidable delay, and transmitted. . . ." LS. MWA.

In a letter to Lincoln on June 15, Daniel Brent stated that he had been "directed by the Secretary . . . to have Copies prepared of the Books &c. requested" in the letter of May 29 "and to transmit them . . . with all possible dispatch"; noted that he had "collected together" fourteen manuscript books, "averaging each about 250 pages of close writing on foolscap paper," transcripts of which Lincoln wanted, as well as other materials which "embrace a mass of writing nearly as voluminous as that of the books"; referred to "the delay which must, of consequence, attend the execution of" the commission and to his reluctance "to venture upon making a selection for the Copyists, tho' . . . this might be advantageously done"; and proposed that the Senators from Maine, (John) Holmes and (John) Chandler, who "have seen the books, and . . . were furnished with copious extracts from them, . . . might favor this Department, through . . . [Lincoln] with some suggestions leading to a convenient curtailment" satisfactory to him. Copy, in DNA, RG59, Dom. Letters, vol. 21, p. 562 (M40, R19). Cf. below, Clay to Lincoln, October 30, 1827.

From MATHEW CLUFF, Elizabeth City, North Carolina. Relates the circumstances attending the seizure of his schooner, the *John Rodman,* on January 27, 1826, "near Ragged Island by the British Brig of War Ferret." Notes that the American consul at Nassau, (John) Storr, purchased the schooner (at the condemnation sale), for Cluff, for $173.00 and sent it to the United States with "fifteen American Seamen on board as Passengers"; that "after allowing for the Seamens Passage," Cluff owed Storr only $94.00; but that he lost "the expenses of the Voyage about 5,000 lbs. Coffee and 200 Bushels Corn." Solicits "the Interference of Government" in the case; admits the intention "to violate a [British] Regulation which only permits to American Vessels [*sic*] a Direct Intercourse with their Colonies—and Prohibits vessells from Saint Domingo Communicating with their Neighboring Islands —neither of which had previously been enforced at the Salt Islands"; and argues that "the Utmost Right . . . the British Authorities should Claim under such circumstances is the Right to Order off or Refuse entry—" Encloses a letter from Storr. ALS. DNA, RG76, Misc. Claims, Great Britain, env. II, folder 29 (MR3).

Cluff apparently had not heard of the closing of the West India trade. Cf. above, Gallatin to Clay, August 19, 1826. Storr, born on the Island of New Providence, in the Bahamas, was consul at Nassau from 1821 to 1833.

From S[AMUEL] L. S[OUTHARD], Navy Department. States that he has received and placed on file "Mr. Slaughters letter [not found] of the 18th. ulto, referred by" Clay to the Navy Department. Copy. DNA, RG45, Executive Letterbook, vol. 1821–1831, p. 257.

Slaughter, probably George H., of Culpeper, Virginia, has not been further identified.

To Enoch Lincoln

His Excellency Enoch Lincoln, Govr. of Maine, Portland.—
Sir,   Dept. of State, Washington 9 June 1827
The President has received the letter which your Excellency addressed to him under date, the 29th. Ulto.;[1] and I am charged by him[2] to convey to you his assurances that your observations on the interesting subject of our North Eastern boundary shall receive attentive and respectful consideration. I beg leave to add that, in no contingency is any arbitration of the difference between the U. S. and G. B. relative to that Boundary, contemplated but that for which provision has been solemnly made by Treaty.[3] It would afford great satisfaction to the President, if a resort to that alternative for quieting the dispute could be avoided by obtaining from G. Britain an explicit acknowledgment of the Territorial claims of Maine, in their whole extent. Candor, however, compels me to state that the prospects of such an acknowledgment, at the present time, are not encouraging.—

I avail myself of this occasion to renew to your Excellency assurances of the high respect and consideration of.— Your obedt. Servt.,

H. CLAY.

Copy. DNA, RG59, Dom. Letters, vol. 21, pp. 552–53 (M40, R19).
[1] Published in *American State Papers, Foreign Relations*, VI, 927–30.   [2] Adams noted, on June 7, 1827: "I requested Mr. Clay to answer a letter that I have received from Governor Enoch Lincoln, of Maine." *Memoirs*, VII, 290.   [3] Article V of the Treaty of Ghent. Cf. above, I, 1006; Clay to Addington, March 27, 1825, note; Clay to Gallatin, June 19, 1826.

To Hilario de Rivas y Salmon

Don Hilario de Rivas y Salmon, Chargé d'Affaires from Spain.
Sir,   Department of State, Washington, 9th. June 1827.
I have the honor to acknowledge the receipt of your Note of the

31st. ultimo, which I have submitted to the President of the United States.

Without entering into the general discussion of the principles which should regulate the conduct of a neutral Nation, during a state of war, which may unhappily exist between other nations—a discussion which does not appear to me to be necessary at this time, I will limit myself to a few general observations.

The United States have been most anxious, during the whole course of the war between Spain, and the Southern Republics, strictly to perform towards each party all the duties of an impartial neutrality. The Government of this Union has never willingly permitted a violation of any of those duties. If there has been any such violation, it has not been with the consent or knowledge of the Government. Should any instances have nevertheless happened, it ought to be recollected, on the other hand, that the United States have had much cause to complain of injuries inflicted by the Belligerents on their lawful commerce; and sometimes of violation of their territorial jurisdiction. A recent instance of want of respect to that jurisdiction occurred on the same Coast of Florida to which you refer, in the capture of the Colombian Schooner the Zulme by two armed vessels in the service of the King of Spain. And to this day we have no information that any punishment has been inflicted by Spain on the persons thus invading our territorial rights, or any indemnity awarded to the parties who suffered in consequence thereof.[1]

With respect to the vessels, built within the United States, which are referred to in your two notes of the 22d. September and 29th. November 1825, they did not leave our ports armed and equipt for hostile action. And it is remarkable that at the very moment when the precautionary measure was adopted in the United States of placing those vessels under bond,[2] that very measure was suggested by the Duke del Infantado the Spanish Minister of Foreign Affairs to the Minister of the United States at the Court of Madrid, as one that would be proper, and satisfactory to the Government of Spain.[3]

If vessels have been built in the United States and afterwards sold to one of the belligerants [sic] and converted into Vessels of War, our Citizens engaged in that species of manufacture have been equally ready to build and sell vessels to the other belligerent. In point of fact both belligerants have occasionally supplied themselves with vessels of war from Citizens of the United States. And the very singular case has occurred of the same ship builder having sold two vessels, one to the King of Spain, and the other to one of the Southern Republics, which vessels afterwards met and encountered each other at Sea.[4]

During the state of war between two Nations the Commercial industry and pursuits of a neutral Nation are often materially injured. If the neutral finds some compensation in a new species of industry which the necessities of the belligerents stimulate or bring into activity it cannot be deemed very unreasonable that he should avail himself of that compensation, provided he confines himself within the line of entire impartiality, and violates no rule of public law.

The article in the treaty of 1795,[5] between the United States and His Catholic Majesty cited by you does not apply to such a service as that in which Commodore David Porter has engaged under the Government of the United Mexican States. That article prohibits any Citizen Subject or inhabitant of the United States to apply for or take any Commission or Letters of Marque for arming any ship or ships to act as privateers against the subjects of His Catholic Majesty "or the property of any of them, from any Prince or State with which the said King shall be at War." Commodore Porter is not known to have applied for or taken any Commission or Letter of Marque from the Government of Mexico, for arming any ship or ships to act as privateers against the subjects of his Catholic Majesty, or their property. He is understood to have entered the public Naval Service of that Government, and that is not prohibited by the Treaty. But even if he had incurred the penalty of piracy, which is denounced by the same article of the treaty, it cannot be admitted that the United States are bound to seize and punish him. Should he be taken a captive by Spain, it will belong to her to consider whether he is comprehended or not in that provision of the treaty.

The refuge which Commodore Porter has taken in the port of Key West was not desired by the Government of the United States. He sought it to escape from the danger of a superior force, and to enjoy that hospitality which the United States dispense equally to all friends and which would be satisfactorily rendered to a squadron of his Catholic Majesty, under analogous circumstances. The fact of his long continuance there the Government of the United States supposed attributable to the presence of that superior force, which if it has as you state, proceded [sic] to Blockade the port of Key West, has under-undertaken [sic] what it had no right to do by the public law.

Key West as you well know is one of the remotest points of our Southern frontier. It is but thinly peopled. This Government has no force there. Information from it is not very regularly received. Reports having however reached Washington that some of the proceedings of Commodore Porter at Key West might not be considered as strictly compatible with the neutrality of the United States, prior to the receipt of your note, a representation to that effect was made from this Department to the Mexican Minister who, in answer, gave the strongest assurances that due respect should be paid to the neutrality of the United States.[6] I have the honor to transmit to you herewith a copy of a Letter from the Collector of that port[7] addressed to Commodore Laborde, from a perusal of which you will perceive that nothing has been done within the knowledge of that officer by Commodore Porter, contrary to our neutral obligations. And this statement of the Collector is corroberated [sic] by the testimony of Lieut. Thompson[8] furnished by yourself, in which he states that the authorities at Key West were ignorant of the expedition which was placed under his command.

If the force of Commodore Porter, while his Squadron has been at Key West, has been augmented, if he has availed himself of that position to send out Cruizers for the purpose of annoying the Spanish Commerce, and capturing Spanish Vessels, and returning into port with them, and if he has undertaken to sell his prizes in that port, he has abused the hospitality of the United States.

Assuming the accuracy of the documents transmitted by you to this Department, which we have no reason to doubt, Commodore Porter has made a belligerent use of that station, which he ought not to have done. This being the first authentic information which we have received of his illegal conduct, I have the satisfaction to inform you that prompt and efficient measures will be taken to cause the neutrality of the United States to be duly respected by Commodore Porters squadron in the port of Key West.[9]

We have no information whatever of 160 seamen having been sent from the port of New York to strengthen the force of Commodore Porter, other than that which is contained in your Note;[10] and we cannot but believe that there is some mistake, in that respect, on the part of the Spanish Consul who communicated the statement to you.

With respect to the demand which you make that the Bonds which have been taken from the owners of Vessels, that they should not employ them against any power with which the United States are at peace, the President would direct the necessary prosecutions to be instituted against the obligors, if we possessed any evidence of the breach, of their obligations, and if you will furnish such evidence, or inform us where it can be procured by reasonable efforts, the prosecutions will be accordingly ordered. But the mere fact of the employment of any such Vessels by the Enemies of Spain, in belligerent operations, would not of itself be sufficient to subject the obligors to a forfeiture of their bonds. They did not bind themselves that, at no future time indefinitely, after they had, by a bonafide transfer, of their vessels, lost all control over them, should they be empoloyed [sic], in the possession of others, against a friend of the United States. They were bound for their own good conduct, not for the acts of others.

I pray you to accept assurances of my high Consideration.

                                                        H. CLAY.

Copy. DNA, RG59, Notes to Foreign Legations vol. 3, pp. 365–69 (M38, R3). AL draft, in CSmH.
1 Cf. above, Rodney to Clay, June 24, 1826, note; Clay to Everett, January 15, March 20, 1827; Clay to Vives, February 12, 1827; Vives to Clay, March 17, 1827; Everett to

Clay, March 19, April 7, 1827.   2 Cf. above, Clay to Rivas y Salmon, December 15, 1825; Tillotson to Clay, same date.   3 With the "Duplicate" of Everett's dispatch no. 7, above, September 25, 1825, was a long statement, "Notes of a conversation with Mr. [Francisco de] Zea [Bermudez]," asserting "that he thought the American Government might prohibit the building of ships of a certain Size, which must necessarily be intended for warlike purposes, unless the persons interested would furnish a Satisfactory guarantee that they were not destined to act against a friendly power, and that in fact the same condition might easily be attached to the building and equipping of ships of any size. . . ." No similar statement has been found in reference to the Duke del Infantado, who succeeded Zea Bermudez as Foreign Minister within the next month.

4 Reference not found.   5 Pinckney's Treaty.   6 Cf. above, Clay to Obregón, May 21, 1827; Obregón to Clay, May 26, 1827.   7 William Pinkney, son of the diplomat and Congressman of that name, was a native of Baltimore and a veteran of the Battle of Bladensburg. He served as collector at Key West from 1824 to 1830, when he was removed by President Andrew Jackson.   8 Alexander Thompson.   9 At a Cabinet meeting, June 7, 1827, "The questions considered were, what should be done upon Mr. Salmon the Spanish Chargé d'Affaires' complaint of violations of neutrality by Commodore Porter. It was deemed important to prevent him from making use of his station at Key West for annoyance against Spain. But the questions of the precise authority of the Executive to restrain him by force, and of the mode in which it should be exercised, were much discussed. It was finally concluded that the Secretary of the Treasury [Richard Rush] should write to the Collector at Key West, directing him generally not to permit any violation of neutrality by the Commodore; particularly that he should not be allowed to fit out his prizes there as privateers and then order them to return there with their prizes; and that he should not be allowed to arm, and in any manner increase, his force there. Instructions are to be given by the Secretary of the Navy [Samuel L. Southard] to the Commander of our West India squadron [Charles Goodwin Ridgely] to touch occasionally at Key West and give to the Collector any aid that he may need to enforce his discharge of his duties. The instructions to the Collector, and those to the Commander of the squadron, are to be adapted to each other, and the answer by Mr. Clay to Mr. Salmon is to be conformable to them. Attention is, however, to be given to two important points: one, to authorize no act of force of doubtful legality; the other, not to endanger the life and health of the men in our public ships by requiring them to remain any length of time, at this and the approaching season of the year, at Key West." Adams, *Memoirs*, VII, 289–90. The instructions from Rush to Pinkney and from Southard to Ridgely were both dated June 14, 1827. T. Frederick Davis, "Pioneer Florida, Mexican Squadron Based at Key West, 1827," *Florida Historical Quarterly*, XXV (July, 1946), 71–72.   Born in Baltimore with the surname Goodwin, Ridgely (variously spelled as Ridgeley and Ridgley) had assumed the latter name under the terms of a legacy. He had entered the Navy in 1799, served in the Tripolitan War and the War of 1812, and attained the rank of captain in 1815. Thereafter he had served three years in the Mediterranean and several years as commander of the Baltimore Naval Station before assuming command of the West India Squadron in 1827. He remained there two years and subsequently commanded the New York Navy Yard from 1834 to 1839, the Brazil Squadron from 1840 to 1841, and the Baltimore Naval Station from 1843 until his death in 1848.   10 No documentation has been found.

From Greenberry W. Ridgely

My dear Sir   Philadelphia June 9th 1827

I thank you for the letter[1] which you were good enough to write to me, and for the friendly interest in my welfare which it expresses— It arrived just as I was on the point of starting to Harrisburg, where the Episcopal Convention of this state met a few weeks since for the purpose of electing a Bishop— The anticipation of this event kept us for some time in a continual excitement; and the consummation of it has at length restored a tranquility [sic] to our ecclesiastical affairs, which has been long a stranger to them[2]—

Since my return to Philadelphia I should have had the pleasure of acknowledging the receipt of your communication, if I had not have been in daily expectation of going on to Washington myself— As to the appointment, I really am in *want of* it;[3] and I am persuaded that a word from you will accomplish it at once, if it can with any degree of propriety, be done— The truth is that I am at present harrassed [*sic*] by a little pecuniary embarrassment, which although it would be nothing to any body else is yet extremely unpleasant to a Clergyman—; and the salary of such an office, would in a few months be sufficient to relieve me— Perhaps you will be surprized at this, when you remember that I have several wealthy relations[4] who could *blow away* my petty difficulties with a breath, if they were disposed to do so— But, although I am on very good terms with them, I am not sufficiently so to ask money of them— When I resolved to abandon my former profession and become a minister of the Gospel, they disapproved the step— I solicited aid from them, and was repulsed in a manner, which renders it a thing impossible for me to renew such a request— I struggled through my theological studies[5] witht. help from any, but *Him* who is a "present help in every time of need"— I am very happy in my humble labours—far more so than I ever was when my mind was dazzled with the dream of ambition—because this seems to me to be the path that Providence has appointed me to walk in— But if the Government, through your recommendation could be induced to give me the station which I asked from them it would at present very materially promote my comfort— I am told that the salary is something like 12.00$ [*sic*] pr. annum,[6] which would place me far above my present trivial embarrassments here—

I am much pleased with Philadelphia, and could spend my time in the work of the Ministry as agreeably amongst this people, as any that I have seen— The delicate state of my health however would be an objection to taking upon me the labours of a regular pastoral charge— The duties of a chaplaincy are much lighter—

—You intimate that there is at present a want for authority to make the appointment— I presume that this must refer to the pecuniary appropriation—   If from what you know you could say to me that it is your opinion that the appointment *will* be made within any limited time, say 6 or 8 months, I could make such temporary arrangements, as would keep me here until then— If not I fear I shall be obliged to leave the City—

I hope you will excuse me, my dear Sir for troubling you with so long a letter about myself— Your past kindness and recent assurances of regard must be my apology for doing so— I thought, [*when I*][7] had made the application my best plan was [*to tell*] you frankly and fully how matters stand with me—

It has been intimated to me that my old friend Charles McIvain [*sic*] thinks of resigning his situation at West point shortly[8]— They are anxious I believe (so says Mr. Benjn. Gratz who is at present here) to make him President of Transylvania.⁹ If this should take place, I should like to be his successor; in case that I can not secure a settlement in Philadelphia— My favorite studies have been those which the professorship of moral phylosophy would require—

I am no longer Editor of the magazine¹⁰ which I sent to Mrs. C.— It was only the arrangment of a few months— The society are too poor at present to support an Editor— In this I have been disappointed— My best respects to Mrs. Clay— If you could take some leisure moment to give me your *real opinion* as to the prospect of obtaining the Chaplaincy within the time specified above, it would regulate my movements and greatly oblige   Very sincerely and respectfully Your friend
H. Clay Esqr.   G. W. RIDGELY.

ALS. DNA, RG59, Accounting Records, Misc. Letters. Endorsed in strange hand on last page: "Ansd. by Mr. [Samuel] Southard at Mr. Clay's request, 20 June 1827.—"
    ¹ Not found.   ² The Protestant Episcopal Church in Pennsylvania had for some time been deeply divided between the Evangelical and the High Church adherents. William White, born in Philadelphia and educated at the College of Philadelphia (later University of Pennsylvania), had been trained for the priesthood in London, ordained there in 1772, and consecrated in 1787 by the English episcopal hierarchy as the first bishop for the diocese of Pennsylvania. Sympathetic with the High Church faction, he had precipitated sharp controversy at a special diocesan convention in 1826, when he had requested election of an assistant bishop. The matter had finally been deferred until the regular convention, which had met in Harrisburg on May 8–10 and elected the High Church candidate, Henry Ustick Onderdonk. The latter, born in New York and graduated from Columbia College in 1805, had attained an M. D. degree from the University of Edinburgh and for a time practiced medicine before turning to the Church. He had been ordained a priest in 1816 and since 1820 had been rector of a church in Brooklyn. He was consecrated as Bishop White's associate in October, 1827, and succeeded him, at his death in 1836, as the second bishop of Pennsylvania. For a detailed study of the controversial election, see David L. Holmes, "The Making of the Bishop of Pennsylvania, 1826–1827," *Historical Magazine of the Protestant Episcopal Church*, XLI (1972), 225–62; XLII (1973), 171–97. Ridgely was a leader of the Evangelical proponents.   ³ No earlier application from Ridgely has been found. He was commissioned chaplain in the United States Navy on April 14, 1828, entered service April 24, was stationed at the Philadelphia Navy Yard, and resigned, September 2, 1830.   ⁴ In Maryland, including his uncle, Nicholas Greenberry Ridgely.   ⁵ He had attended the Princeton Theological Seminary and had been graduated in 1823.   ⁶ The salary of a Navy chaplain in 1827 was $40 a month and two rations daily. *Biennial Register, 1827*, p. 140.
    ⁷ One or two words here and later in the sentence have been obliterated by the seal.
    ⁸ Charles Pettit McIlvaine resigned his chaplaincy at the United States Military Academy effective December 31, 1827.   ⁹ Cf. above, Chase to Clay, March 3, 1827.
    ¹⁰ The magazine has not been identified. Ridgely may be referring to the American Bible Society, founded in 1816 as an interdenominational organization to promote circulation and reading of the Bible. Ridgely was at this time a traveling agent for the Society. See Holmes, "The Making of the Bishop of Pennsylvania. . . ," *Historical Magazine of the Protestant Episcopal Church*, XLI, 249n.

INSTRUCTIONS AND DISPATCHES   June 9, 1827

To J[OEL] R. POINSETT, no. 24. States that "R[ichard] W. Meade, of Philadelphia, has a claim upon the Mexican Government . . . for which he has not been able to obtain satisfaction" and instructs Poinsett, should his assistance be requested, to "investigate the claim, and render . . . such official or informal aid as may seem to be called for by its nature. . . ." LS. DNA, RG76, Mexican Claims Commission,

Claimant File, entry 24, folder 38. ALI draft, in DLC-HC (DNA, M212, R8); copy, in DNA, RG59, Dip. Instr., vol. 11, p. 365 (M77, R6).

In the ultimate settlement of claims of American citizens upon the Mexican Government, Margaret Coates Butler Meade sought $45,703.12, "For damages on certain bills of exchange drawn by the Mexican government on the Barings, of London, in favor of her husband, R. W. Meade, in July, 1822." The umpire under the negotiations of 1839 returned the claim without decision; the commissioners under the treaty of 1848 awarded her $5,791.66. *House Reports*, 27 Cong., 2 Sess., no. 1096, p. 17; *Senate Docs.*, 35 Cong., 2 Sess., no. 18, p. 58.

Meade had married in 1801 the daughter of Anthony Butler, a Perth Amboy, New Jersey, merchant.

From JAMES BROWN, Paris, no. 69. Reports having been informed "that the Dey of Algiers [Husséin] having incurred the displeasure of . . . [the French] Government, a squadron has sailed from Toulon with orders to the commander to demand reparation, and in the event of its being witheld [*sic*], then to declare the place in a state of blockade and to capture Algerine vessels." Adds that "The Brest fleet" is also preparing to sail, although "It is generally believed . . . that the Dey . . . will avoid" a rupture with France "by making such reparations as may be asked." LS. DNA, RG59, Dip. Disp., France, vol. 23 (M34, R26). Received August 2. Cf. above, Brown to Clay, May 29, 1827 (private letter).

From A[LEXANDER] H. EVERETT, Madrid, no. 78. Reports that a "slight alarm," occasioned by the movement of some English troops in Portugal toward the Spanish border, and a counter movement toward the same frontier by "a detachment of the Spanish army of observation," and ended by the withdrawal of the latter after "Remonstrances" and "explanations" by British and Portuguese agents, "appears to have led to the idea of attempting by mutual arrangement to station the forces on both sides at a greater distance from the frontier," but that most of the British troops have since been concentrated at Lisbon, "on account of the interior situation of the country," and the matter has been dropped. Adds that orders have been issued for further withdrawal of the Spanish Army, for which "The principal motive is the great desertion into Portugal which goes on regularly and which it is found impossible to prevent. . . ."

Notes the failure of Count Ofalia to obtain "his principal object" at Paris (cf. above, Brown to Clay, April 27, 1827) and his decision to go "on to London to renew the negotiation there" and predicts that "the British Ministry is" not "likely to lend its countenance" to the Count's proposals (cf. above, Everett to Clay, March 19, 1827). Explains that "The object" of Spain and France "is to clear the Portuguese territory of British troops before the time when the Infante Don Miguel attains the legal age of majority (which is in the course of next October) and when by the existing Constitution he will have a right to claim the Regency." Cites a belief that Miguel, if "placed at the head of the Government and left to act independently . . . will pretty soon rid himself of the trammels of the Constitution" (cf. above, Raguet to Clay, May 6, 1826; Pereira to Clay, November 2, 1826), an event desired by "the leading Continental Powers" as well as by Spain. States that information on the mission of the Baron de Neumann, just returned from Brazil, where he had been sent by the Emperor of Austria (Francis I) to obtain Don Pedro's "assent . . . to this arrangement," has "been kept pretty secret," although "it is reported . . . that Don Pedro requires that his brother [Miguel] should present himself at Rio Janeiro [*sic*] before he assumes the Regency of Portugal" (cf. above, Brown to Clay, April 12, 1827). Observes that proposals leading to the overthrow of the Portuguese Constitution will not be acceptable to

England, "although it might be difficult to assign any sufficient motive in good policy why the British Government should employ the resources of their country in imposing upon Portugal a new Political system which is evidently unpopular and unsuited to the social state of the Kingdom." Dismisses as "baseless" rumors that Ofalia is authorized to offer, in his negotiation, "the acknowledgment by Spain of one or more of the new American States and of a part of the Loan contracted by the Cortes." Comments on reports concerning the success of (Sebastián) Camacho's visit to Paris (cf. above, Brown to Clay, April 27, 1827) and on the departure from Madrid of the Papal Nuncio (Giacomo Giustiniani) and his secretary, the Bishop of Cervia, leaving their "Embassy . . . for the moment entirely vacant." Gives details of the recall of General Loriga, who had been "lately appointed to command the second military division on the Island of Cuba" for the ultimate purpose, according to rumor, of directing "a new expedition against the Continent." Continues: "It was reported here that his recall was occasioned by a denunciation made by me of a plot for delivering the Island to the English in the event of actual hostilities in which Loriga was concerned." States that Spain has proposed sending the Duke of San Carlos as "Ambassador to France in place of the Duke de Villa Hermosa who has arrived here on his return [cf. above, Everett to Clay, March 19, 1827] provided the King of France [Charles X] would name an agent of the same rank to represent him at this Court." LS. DNA, RG59, Dip. Disp., Spain, vol. 27 (M31, R28). Extract published in Manning (arr.), *Diplomatic Correspondence . . . Latin-American Nations*, III, 2143–46. Received August 22.

Under Article 92 of the new Portuguese Constitution, the regency was to be held by the nearest relative over age 25 during the minority of the sovereign. H. V. Livermore, *A History of Portugal* (Cambridge, England, 1947), 416. Miguel had been born October 26, 1802.

Baron Philipp von Neumann had been secretary to the Austrian Legation in London in 1818 and somewhat of a protegé of Prince Metternich, but the Austrian chancellor roundly condemned his handling of the mission to Brazil in 1826–1827. "Neumann," wrote Metternich, "has only made 'des betises' at Rio. . . . Neumann, instead of imbuing himself in our decision never to allow the Infant to go to Brazil, has acted as if the contrary were the object of our wishes." Again, he commented: "Neumann's great fault was a want of obedience in circumstances where no latitude had been left to the negotiator. He was ordered to take *ad referendum* the expression of Don Pedro's wish that his brother should come to Brazil. Instead of confining himself to this, he said 'Yes,' when we said nothing; which brought about that the speaker found himself contradicted, which is neither desirable for a Court, nor agreeable for the person who undergoes the contradiction." Metternich to his son Victor, May 21, 31, 1827, in Metternich (ed.), *Memoirs*, IV, 349–50.

Monsignor Giustiniani, then Bishop of Imola, had been recalled on request of Ferdinand VII, who was irritated by the decision of Pope Leo XII to preconize bishops in Colombia (cf. above, Everett to Clay, March 31, 1827). Elevated to the archbishopric of Petra, Giustiniani was appointed Nuncio to the Court at Lisbon the next autumn. Cf. below, Everett to Clay, June 22, 1827.

Ignazio Giovanni Cadolini, born at Cremona in 1794 and educated in civil and canon law at Bologna, had accompanied Giustiniani to Madrid as secretary in 1815 and in 1818 had been ordained into priesthood. He had been designated Bishop of Cervia in 1826 but remained active in affairs at Madrid through the negotiations for the recognition of Tiberi. In 1831 he was named Bishop of Foligno, as well as of Cervia, and transferred to administration of the Umbrian bishopric until 1834. Meanwhile, he had been named Archbishop of Spoleto in 1832 and in 1838 was called to Rome as Archbishop of Edessa and secretary of the

Congregation for Propagation of the Faith. In 1843 he was elevated to cardinalcy and designated Archbishop of Ferrara.

General Loriga has not been identified. On Everett's concern about a plot for British capture of Cuba and the Canary Islands, cf. below, Everett to Clay, August 17, December 12, 1827.

From ROBERT MONROE HARRISON, Antigua. Encloses a copy of the rejection, by "the Provisional Government of Saint Bartholomews" of his "application to exercise the duties of . . . [his] office provisionally." Points out that, in this statement, "they have at length acknowledged the right of the U States to have a resident Consul, at St. Barts, yet are determined by chicanery to deprive us of the benefit that should grow out of the appointment." Attributes his difficulties "to the influence of the late Governor" (Johan Norderling—cf. above, Harrison to Clay, May 21, 1827, note); notes that R. B. Eldridge has been acknowledged by the Governor of Antigua (Patrick Ross) as agent for Harrison "and that of the U States"; and adds, with reference to his own "most disagreeable situation": "I once more intreat [sic] you to use your interest to cause me to be recognized, and to protect me so long as I deserve it." ALS. DNA, RG59, Cons. Disp., Antigua, vol. 1 (M-T327, R1). Received July 1.

Patrick Ross, born in County Perth, had entered the army in 1794, served in India nine years, in Portugal during the Napoleonic wars, and from 1816 until the mid 'twenties in the Ionian Islands. He had attained the rank of major general in 1821, had been appointed to the governmental staff of the Ionian Islands in 1824, and, shortly thereafter, had been named Governor of Antigua, Montserrat, and Barbuda.

MISCELLANEOUS LETTERS   June 9, 1827

From JOHN NORVELL, Philadelphia. Requests a letter of introduction to James Brown for Samuel Smith, a Philadelphia merchant who plans "to take a portion of his family to Paris" on a pleasure trip. Concludes: "I need not add because I am sure that the fact could have no influence in such cases, that Mr. Smith is a friend to the administration. . . ." ALS. DNA, RG59, Misc. Letters (M179, R65).

Daniel Brent replied on June 11, informing Norvell that his letter had arrived after Clay's departure for Kentucky and enclosing "a few lines" to serve as an introduction of Smith to Brown. Copy, in DNA, RG59, Dom. Letters, vol. 21, pp. 555–56 (M40, R19).

Smith has not been further identified.

MISCELLANEOUS LETTERS   ca. June 10, 1827

From CHARLES W. GOLDSBOROUGH. In a letter, dated June 9, 1827, addressed to Goldsborough at the Navy Department, John McNerhany, of Washington, requests help in obtaining a release for his fourteen-year old son, James, who has "enlisted . . . in a scotch Regiment. . . ." Explains that, when he emigrated from Ireland to the United States in 1817, his parents were left to care for the child, but that now the grandfather is dead and the grandmother is 70 years old. Adds that he has resided in the District of Columbia since 1818 and in Washington nearly four years; that he is a citizen of the United States, and that he is an ensign in the United States Army. ALS. DNA, RG59, Misc. Letters (M179, R65). Goldsborough's name, as addressee, at the bottom of the second (and last) page of the document, has been crossed out, presumably by himself, and the words "Henry Clay, Secy of State" substituted for it.

On June 13 Daniel Brent transmitted a copy of this letter to Thomas Wilson, Dublin. Brent admitted not knowing "what course to suggest or recommend" but stated that he was "entirely persuaded that the Secretary, who is now absent from the Seat of Government will fully approve of the step" he is taking. Copy, in DNA, RG59, Cons. Instr., vol. 2, pp. 430–31 (M78, R2).

The McNerhanys have not been further identified.

INSTRUCTIONS AND DISPATCHES   June 11, 1827

From JOHN MULLOWNY, Tangier, no. 49. Reports receipt of a "circular" giving "notice that the Emperor Muley Abdrahaman [sic], is to be here on the 6th. July next" after "having very lately completely defeated the party in rebellion against him [cf. above, Mullowny to Clay, May 22, 1827]. . . ." States that since "it is necessary to be prepared according to custom," his "credit being limited in London as pr. [Clay's] letter of 22 Oct 1825," he has drawn on Clay for $1600, to be expended in the purchase of presents for the Emperor. ALS. DNA, RG59, Cons. Disp., Tangier, vol. 4 (M-T61, R4).

From James Brown (1)

My dear Sir,   Paris June 12. 1827

I presume you will have returned from the West about the time when this letter will reach Washington and I hope will have found your health greatly improved by the Journey.[1] My only fear has been that you would be vexed and fatigued by the violence and activity of party spirit in the West amongst the relief men who beaten on the great questions of paper money and stop-laws have mounted the presidential question in hopes of again getting into power by the election of General Jackson.[2] I have some doubts whether these combined interests may not endanger the election in Kentucky and thus with a part of New York which may be carried over by Mr Van Buren turn the scale against Mr Adams.

You promised twelve months ago to give me some fresh instructions relative to French Claims.[3] I have never received any since I sent you the definitive answer of Baron de Damas refusing to treat on the claims apart from the 8 article of the Louisiana treaty.[4] I was apprehensive that the subject would be called up at the last Session of Congress and that it might be added to the other groundless causes of complaint against the Administration. It is not easy to perceive how we can treat or which is the same thing yield on the Treaty question and three distinct written refusals to treat in any other way[5] would render a fresh application on the same ground rather humiliating and would certainly, during the existence of the present Ministry be rejected.

The claimants will probably endeavor to press their claims at the next Session, and bring on a discussion as injurious to their success as has been that at the last and preceeding [sic] Session to questions in contestation with the British Government.[6] The present state of parties is unfavorable to the success of diplomatic questions it being known that whilst treaties are made under instructions from the President a majority of the Senate is disposed to thwart all his measures. I sincerely wish that the next election may be decided by the popular voice without an appeal to the house of Representatives. Perhaps the state of parties might in that case be less violent than it is now when artful men represent the peoples voice as having been disregarded by their Representatives.[7]

I consider the Greek war as being near its termination. The great powers have intimated to the Porte that he[8] must desist and in case of his proving refractory Naval means will be employed to prevent supplies of men and provisions from being sent into Greece.[9] What disposition it may please the rulers of Europe to make relative to that country whether it is to be a Republic or a Monarchy, and if the latter who is to ascend the throne are questions either undecided or concealed from the public. It seems to be the prevailing opinion that it will be erected into a monarchy and the eldest son of the Duke of Orleans, the Duke of Chartres is said to be the choice of France.[10] He is an intelligent interesting prince of about eighteen years of age, and I should pity him if I saw him mount a throne under such unfavorable appearances, as the present state of Greece presents.

The Legislature here has passed a Session of six months and has done about as much business as was transacted at the last Session of Congress. The law to restrain the liberty of the press was withdrawn[11] to the great joy of the great majority of the Nation, and yet it is not very certain that much has been gained by it except in the triumph of the opposition. It is supposed that ministers acting under a power conferred by a former law[12] will establish the censorship until the next meeting of the Chambers. The King[13] it is said is greatly opposed to frequent changes in the Ministry believing that to have been one of the causes of the misfortunes of Louis the 16.

As far as I can judge my standing at this Court is as good as I could wish. My conduct is such that I have no prejudices to combat as they relate to me personally. I have professed and practised a perfect system of neutrality in the party contests which divide the Country. It is in this way alone that I can have any influence in serving my Government.

It is probable we shall accept an invitation which we look for about the 20 Inst. to go to La Grange in order to be present at the marriage of one of the Generals grandaughters [sic].[14] My health is nearly as good as it has ever been. We shall remain during the summer in Paris.

Mrs. Brown sends her love to her sister[15] to whom present my affectionate remembrances   I am Dear Sir very truly Your friend
Hon Henry Clay.   JAMES BROWN

ALS. DLC-HC (DNA, M212, R2).   [1] Cf. below, Clay to Erwin, August 4, 1827.
[2] Cf. above, III, 902n; Clay to Brown, March 27, 1827.   [3] Cf. above, Clay to Brown,
May 22, October 8, December 14, 1826; May 28, 1827.   [4] Cf. above, Brown to Clay,
September 24, November 28, 1825.   [5] Villèle to Gallatin, November 6, 1822; Chateaubriand to Brown, May 7, 1824; Damas to Brown, November 11, 1825—all published, in
translation, in *American State Papers, Foreign Relations*, 311–12, 481. Cf. above, III,
313n, 382, 383n.   [6] Cf. above, Clay to Force, February 25, 1827.   [7] Cf. above,
Address, March 26, 1825 (IV, 155–56).   [8] Mahmud II.   [9] Cf. below, Brown to
Clay, July 12, 1827.   [10] Cf. above, Somerville to Clay, October 11, 1825, note; Lafayette to Clay, February 28, 1826. Born in Palermo in 1810, Ferdinand-Philippe-Louis-Charles-Henri, the elder brother of the Duke de Nemours, had succeeded to the title
Duke de Chartres in 1814. He became Duke d'Orleans in 1830, upon the accession of
Louis Philippe as King. The Duke had a distinguished military career during the decade
before his death in 1842, but he was not involved in the affairs of Greece.   [11] Cf.
above, Brown to Clay, December 13, 1826, and note; April 27, 1827.   [12] The existing
law gave the King authority to establish censorship during adjournments or prorogation
of the Chambers if he considered that circumstances warranted so serious an action.
Consequently, as soon as the budget was approved by the Chambers, their Session was
terminated; and two days later, on June 22, a royal ordinance established the censorship.
Annual Register, 1827, 221–22.   [13] Charles X.   [14] Louise, daughter of Anastasie-Louise-Pauline de Lafayette, Countess de la Tour-Maubourg, was married in July, 1827,
to Count Hector-Perrone di San Martino, born in the Piedmont of Italy but French in
citizenship. The groom was "Under Capital proscription in His Native Country for the
part He took in the Last Revolution." Lafayette to John Quincy Adams, August 12,
1827 (MHi-Adams Papers, Letters Recd. [MR482]). Louise, born in 1805, died in 1828.
[15] Lucretia Hart (Mrs. Henry) Clay.

From Francis Crutchfield

Dear Mr Clay,   Warm-Springs, Bath County,[1] 12th June, 1827.

Your very friendly Letter,[2] together with the Letter of the Inspector
of the military Academy, and a printed System of the Order and Rules
of that Institution, in Answer to mine of the 20th of last Month,[3] came
safely and quickly to Hand:—and the Design of this Letter, is not only
to return you my sincere Acknowledgements [*sic*], for the Part you
have taken in Behalf of my Son,[4] but also for your warm and kind
Wishes, in his Favor, as expressed in your Letter.

Although you did, at the Hot-Springs,[5] give me considerable Instruction, with Regard to the Order and Rules of the military Academy, yet I never *fully* understood all the parts of the Subject, until I
received your last Letter, together with the papers, which came with
it; neither did I conceive, that you, my Friend, would be placed in a
disagreeable Situation, by your kind Attentions, to my Son:— after
you explain the Subject, you "rely upon" my "Candor, for a just Appreciation of" your "Motives:"— my dear Mr Clay, please to be assured, that I do appreciate,—*I duly appreciate*,—not only your Motives,
as to this Subject, but also with Regard to the whole Tenor of your
passed, public Life; and I feel happy, under the Impression.

God grant you long Life, for the Sake of our *common* Country.

Your Speech, expressed before the American Colonization Society, on the 20th of last January, together with the Appendix, came to Hand, before I wrote you my last Letter of the 20th of last Month; but I was called to a Distance, from Home, immediately after receiving it, so that, when I returned and wrote to you, I had not found Time to read it, and seriously contemplate its Contents:— and this is the Reason why I did not pay my Respects, to you, in Consideration thereof. But I have since had Time and Opportunity, to read and deliberately consider the whole Subject Matter, in a public Company, to the entire Satisfaction of every Individual present.

I could now expatiate upon the Subject of the Speech,—I could say *much*, as to your Discussion and Arguments thereupon,—I could shew the Justness and Exactitude of all your Conclusions,—and more and better than all, I could speak abundantly about that philanthropic Spirit, which inspired your manly Soul,* throughout the whole Course of your arduous Investigation, for the Good, for the Comfort, for the eventual Happiness of your *Fellow-Man*;—but I shall only say, that I gratefully receive the Speech, as a Testimony of your Respect and Friendship, for me, and shall keep it, as long as I live.

It will afford me Matter sufficient to lecture my pupils† occasionally:—for every Principle, (religious, moral, civil, and political) is embraced therein, and may be easily deduced therefrom, to answer this valuable Purpose.

I have, for a Number of Years passed, been impressed with the same Sentiments, which you express in this Speech; but I never discovered the *Depth and Expansion* of the Subject, which it exhibits and unfolds, until I read and duly contemplated its Contents.

Permit me now to say, that my most respectful Compliments wait upon your Lady. I suppose you have your smaller Children, with you:[6]— I offer my Love to them.

Your Station is an exalted one,—and your Charge is great!—but God, who first raised you up, for the Support of those republican principles, which are *well pleasing to the divine Mind*, is able to sustain and keep you safely.

Into his holy keeping, I commit you, with my fervent Prayers, for his Glory and your Happiness, in Time and in Eternity.

FRANCIS CRUTCHFIELD

* Pray, excuse my Effusion:—for this is a private Letter, and I think, yea, *I know*, that you will not doubt my Integrity.

† I expect, on the 18th of the present Month, to be engaged again, in the Business of my Profession.

ALS. DLC-HC (DNA, M212, R2).   [1] Virginia.
[2] Not found.   [3] Cf. above, Macomb to Clay, May 31, 1827.   [4] Not identified.
[5] Presumably in the summer of 1826. Cf. above, Clay to Adams, July 25, August 12, September 20, 1826.   [6] Cf. above, Clay to Erwin, June 3, 1827.

From Christopher Hughes

My dear Sir,   Private.   Brussels, June 12th. 1827.

I have nothing of a novel or interesting nature to write; and I merely write, from a motive of duty:

The general politics of Europe seem to have resumed, completely, their quiet & peaceful aspect; such as it had been, before the english expedition to portugal:[1] and peace seems to have become as much the fixed habit of the old world, as war had been, for the 25 years ante-cedent to the Battle of Waterloo! The discussions on the formation, or reformation of the english ministry,[2] the sharp encounters, and spirited debates in the French H. of Deputies;[3] with now & then an allusion to Greek affairs, constitute the chief topics of political con-versation! As to the first, the general persuasion is, that Mr. Canning's[4] very great superiority, in talent, over his opponents, will carry the day, & that he will stand. His financial view is looked on as gloomy; & the deficit of more than 2 millions, however he may describe it "as spread over the operations & space of 5 years," is calculated to awaken alarm, (& has so done, among the English) for the future;[5] but *he* has the comfort of not being blamed; and he will profit by the clemency shown him, on all hands, on account of his newness in the Exchequer, & the consequent willingness to give him time, & a chance, to act in his new office.

As to french politics, Mr. Villelle[6] is considered as the firm & fixed Lord of the ascendant, & no sort of change in the present system is anticipated.   Hyde de Neuville & Genl. Sebastiani & Benjn. Constant certainly do speak out,[7] with a boldness & an eloquence worthy of the rights & privileges of representatives in the freest possible Govern-ment; but the Ministry are rather pleased, than vexed, at this; they adroitly turn this apparent *courage*, & safety of speech, to two purposes, or rather to *one*; it serves to occupy & to tantalize & partially to satisfy the discontented part, (which is by far the majority;) of the french nation; thro phantom of freedom gratifies, but deludes the people; while Mr. de Villelle and his friends are noting in the real joys, the *substance* of power! Nor does he care how long this shade may flit be-fore their eyes; indeed, he would be sorry to expel it from the stage; He & his priestly party[8] are enjoying all the good things, *behind* the curtain.   and apostolical stomachs are not often attacked by indiges-tion; and least of all are they liable to it, when the chief dish, or what the french call, la piece de résistance, is seasoned with that most pi-quante of all Sauces—*Power*! In a word, there will be no change in France, unless some violent popular commotion break out, & this is not impossible! In their relations with England, there would appear to be the most perfect harmony & good understanding.

As to greece, no one seems to know, or to care, any thing about it;

there would seem to be much more sympathy & enthusiasm for them, in the U. S. than there is in Europe! though let me say it, & I do so, with a *blush*, (to which, you know, I am prone:) that an indelible stain seems to be thrown upon us, by the vile & notorious frauds, committed at New York, in the frigate affair![9] any thing like a blight, or slur, that can be thrown on our fame, is most ardently and industriously seized on by our implacable enemies,—*the English*! (for I shall go to my grave, with the conviction, that they are & ever *will* be, implacable, in their jealousy, spite & enemity [*sic*] towards us! and I think that every american ought to have his mind fixed on this fact; and to observe a sleepless vigilance, ready to meet & to resist, all the efforts & consequences that may grow out of it; keeping down, however, in his own heart, as far as possible, sentiments of malice or revenge:) the English, I say, have vilified us, on the right & on the left, & in every quarter in Europe, for this most scandalous & lamentable Greek-frigate business; they have used it, as a foil; & have diverted the public attention from their tenfold more vile treason & robbery in the Greek stock—Greek Steam Boat—& Greek committee concerns in London;[10] Which, by the way, were operated by their Eminent men, their M. P.s; whereas, the N. York delinquents, were broken Brokers & Merchants.

I have nothing to communicate, as to our concerns & relations, commercial and political, with this government: there seems to be the most friendly and hearty dispositions, both in the Government & the Nation, to maintain the kindliest intercourse with us; but they *will not* give up their 10 Per Ct. return to their native ships, upon the amount of duties![11]   they say, we have no right to complain; that it is applied to all other nations;—that it is a mere fireside-domestic rule; of which, no one else complains; that in its amount and operation, as far as we are concerned, or rather as far as their 10 or 12 ships, (that go to us:) are concerned, it is a mere trifle; that we are favoured, in every way, in their ports, excepting in this bagatelle; in which *no* nation is favoured; that it makes an unalterable part of their system;—& is an essential condition in the treatment, commonly described, as "the most favoured," with which every body else is satisfied. That they should deeply lament our making it a ground, for altering the present footing of dutch trade, in our ports; for any such alteration would, without doubt, be retaliated here; "and after all," said the Secretary of State[12] to me the other day, "any such alteration, made *by you*, would act upon "only 12 or 14 of *our* ships; whereas, retaliation, *by us*, would act upon 200 or 300 of *yours*; this we should deplore; and we hope to be spared the necessity! Observe," added *His* Excellency, with his usual courtesy, "I do not tell you positively, that we should retaliate; I am not authorized to say so; nor did I anticipate, nor was I prepared for, this conversation; which you will please to regard, as casual & informal; but I have given you my general impressions; and

expressed to you my hopes, that yr. Govt. will cease to attach importance to this matter; which, we look on, as purely domestic, & not to
be changed by us; or objected to by you: and as to your numerous
ships that come to our ports, we are delighted to see them; and shall
be more so, to see the number doubled; but the very actual number
proves, that they are pretty well satisfied with our treatment of them;
we know very well what trade means;   if they were not satisfied,
they would not come; for they certainly dont come here for our amusement & advantage."— In reply to a question I put "whether, if they
relaxed their 10 pr. Ct. it might not affect, or offend, their engagements with England?"—H. E. answered, & with ardent earnestness—
and emphasis, "We have *no engagements* with *any* nation; we are *perfectly free.*" Now this looked as if they consider the footing, as it
exists, of our commercial intercourse with this country, as a matter,
quite within the right & controul of either power; & that may be
changed and modified, at any moment, & at the good pleasure of
either party, without giving to the other any cause of complaint; in a
word—that the respective regulations of the two powers, which profess
reciprocity, as their basis, and the loadstar [*sic*] of their commercial
policy, in their relations with each other, are not considered as having
the validity and virtue of a contract; or of an engagement, binding on
both, or either; but may be modified, or abrogated, at the will & caprice of either! To be sure—this gives us all the rights & freedom, that
they claim to themselves; but it certainly shocks the idea of fixedness,
which it is pleasing to associate, and to believe to exist, in the system,
that controuls objects & relations so important, as are those, involved
in our commerce with this country.

As I have said above, our conversation was casual & informal; but
it is in perfect consistency with all that has hitherto passed; and all,
that I am convinced to be, the determination of this Government, in
the affair in question! I have, therefore, not pressed the matter, by any
formal note, or demand for a categorical statement of their final resolution,   as to the 10 pr. Ct.   I am sure, that the answer will be in strict
accordance with what I have written in this, & in my former private
letters; & I have thought it advisable to waive official & irrevocable
measures, until I shall be further instructed by you. I hope I have done
well in this? The delay can, in-no-wise, do harm.

The diplomatic corps, here, have had two very uncomfortable affairs, on hand; you will have seen them both noticed, but imperfectly narrated, in the London Courier. One was the lamentable and
unmerited disgrace that has fallen on the ex-prussian Minister Count
Schladen, who has been the victim of a vile complot; I have not the
smallest doubt of his innocence; I mentioned this matter, in a former
letter.[13] The other affair was a sort of social, or unsocial *Row*, between
the Corps dipc. & the Hereditary Prince of Orange; the corps was

unanimous & led on by Bagot.[14] I shall write you the whole story; at present, I will not inflict it on you! All I will say is, that the Prince said to a very eminent nobleman, a friend of mine, "I should like to know what Hughes thinks of all this; I am sure he must think it a bundle of nonsense; but why the devil did he mix himself up in it? I should like to know."— I sent him a word, "that I really *did* look on it, as a bundle of nonsense & purely *European*; not at all *american*; that I was perfectly satisfied with H. R. H's conduct to me; that he had shown me all kinds of flattery, good humoured & friendly civility, & even *equality*, in his outer carriage & manner; & that I begged him to turn H. R. Eyes to the *real*-diplomatic malcontents; that I had not come from the other side of the atlantic to espouse other persons quarrels; or to appear to feel slights, that were never practised towards me; & which if ever practised at all, I knew were never meant *for me*; that any gentleman, or *Prince*, who met me gallantly & good-humouredly, & gave me *his hand*, as he does heartily & cheerfully, might feel assured, that I was not going to pout, because others found themselves miffed; in a word, that I had laughed at the whole business; but did not feel myself exactly warranted to stand alone & make bad blood, that could never be purged, if *once* made, between me & *all* my colleagues." The Prince sent me a good humoured message, "that he was sure that I had always looked on the whole affair, as one of downright nonsense; that he perfectly understood my feelings & position, & was quite pleased & satisfied with what had been said to him from, & about me." So we are very good friends; & indeed, so are the Corps,—generally; though the Secy. of State, by his Majesty's[15] orders, read us *all* a lesson; & then proposed that, the affair should be considered as *non avenue*! I replied to H. E. for myself, "that I was perfectly agreed & did not care one straw about the matter!" Having said so much, & you perhaps not having seen the Courier, I will add, that the cause of the war, was the unanimous refusal of the Corps. dipc. to accept an Invitation to a Ball, given by the Russian Minister,[16] at which the P. & Ps.[17] of Orange were known to be expected, on the ground, that they had *reason to believe*, that H. R. H. did not like their *company*, as well as their *room*.

The length of this letter, is worthy of the abbé de Pradtt; I am admonished by a knowledge of your occupation, to stop! But I am impelled, by my feelings, to say a word, on one other topic; a topic of the deepest interest to my country, & of course to my heart.

If I were to believe what *some* of my correspondents write to me, from U. S. I should suppose, that it was all *up* with the administration; and that Mr. Adams was in a hopeless way, as to the next election.

I happen to have other correspondents, whose reports are not founded on the incidents of a limited neighbourhood, or on the violent acts & declarations of a *rump* faction; composed of malcontents and hungry aspirants; and this very morning, I received letters from

America, giving me the most cheering accounts; and confirming my previous conviction, that the people are not to be led hoodwinked; and that the happiness of the country at home, and its reputation abroad, are not to be so deeply compromised, as the foes of the administration fondly anticipate. I know how valuable your time is;—but one moment and two lines, from you, on this subject, would be the most welcome favour you can accord me! The Administration receives the unbounded applause of all Europe! The financial wisdom and honour of the Government—and rapid extinction of the debts of the Nation, and this too, at a time when such vast appropriations have been applied to national works, to the augmentation of the navy, and the fortification of the country,[18]—these objects are looked on as phenomena, not merely unexampled in all previous history, but unhoped for, in the most promising projects and dreams of European statesmen. It is grateful to my heart & ear, to listen to the unqualified justice and praise, that are accorded to our Government by all here, without a dissentient voice! John Bull himself is forced to consent.—

The King of the Netherlands takes a deep interest in every thing concerning the U. S. I sent him, a few day's [sic] ago, a splendid copy of the New York Canal Memoir,[19] that the City of N. Y. had had the kindness to send to me; H.M: read it with attention and satisfaction. The Secy. of State, on sending home the Book wrote me! "Particulière! Monseiur; J ai l'honneur de vous renvoyer avec mes sincères remercimens, le Memoire sur le nouveau canal de N. York, avec la médaille[20] y rélative, que vous avez eu l'obligeance de me faire parvenir, il y a quelques jours. C'est avec beaucoup d'interêt, que le Roi, acquel j'ai communiqué le dit Mémoire, a pris connaissance d'une entreprize si honourable pour les auteurs. Permittez moi Mr. &c. &c. &c.   Signé Verstolk de Soelen.

His Majesty expressed a curiosity to see the portraits of the Mississippi Indians, (copies of which I have, by King:) that were made at Washington a few years ago;[21] I dont know whether they are exactly among the friends of Col. Troup:—but I believe they were among Mr. Forsythe's topics of vituperation.[22] I sent them to the Palace & his Majesty was highly delighted; and so was the queen;[23] especially with the headgear of one of our Countrymen, whose decoration might gain him the name of Front-le-Boeuf![24] I said that in this country of the fine arts & pictures, I heard often the boast, that the pictures of some great amateur were des originaux—but that I could boast, that mine were des aborigaux [sic].—

I think I have written now quite enough: I saw your old friend, Made. Greban,[25] yesterday; She desired to be particularly remembered to you & to Mr. Adams.— All of my Gent [sic] friends come to see me & invariably enquire after you & Mr. Adams & Mr. Gallatin;[26]   Even the old Dowager Countess d'Hane[27] came to see me, & brought scores of her offspring. Made. Pottlesburg, her daughter,[28] is living here & is very hospitable & kind to us.   Cornellessen[29] comes very often & on all great academic & fine arts committees he is called here. Mr. Van Huyfel,[30] Mr. Adams', *tête de Guide*, friend, President of the academy of Ghent came here a few days ago to decide the prize pictures at the annual Exhibition! He was so enthusiastic, that it made me quite nervous;   He praised us better than he could *paint* us; insisted on "my Excellency" accepting a most treasonable daub of Napoleon, when 1st. Consul, painted by him 24 years ago;[31] & made an attempt upon my *own person,* so far as I may so call a most flagitious proposition, to debauch me, into permitting him to *ebaucher* my fine face;   I was absolutely *forced* to take his Napoleon; a most monstrous caricature of poor Bonaparte; but my virtue held out against his soft persuasions;   if he sketch my Tom-Moore-nose,[32] he must shoot me flying! I am positively *afraid* to go to Ghent; I should be shown-up in every paper in Europe; for I am sure, that my arrival, my movements— the happiness of possessing my renowned person in "The City of the Congress," once more, would be blazoned in all the Ghent-news- papers, to my utter misery, confusion & ridicule. I had hard work to fight off the quizzing compliments of all my Colleagues of the Corps, at the brilliant paragraph announcing my unasked for, my annoying admission, into all their learned and classic societies last winter;[33]   I was exposed to many *botanical* enquiries & interrogatories:—& the only expedient I could devise to relieve myself, was, after a dinner at Sir C. Bagots, when Lady B. was showing, with great pride some deli- cate & beautiful exotic, my Botanical Worship was quietly & quizingly [*sic*] asked "What is the name of this plant, Mr. Hughes"—I roared out, I believe it is a *Holly Hock*! They then left me in peace; as you will thank me for leaving you!   & as I do with our best complts: to Mrs. Clay, & respects to Mr. Adams.   C. HUGHES

To Mr. Clay—Washington.

ALS. DNA, RG59, Dip. Disp., The Netherlands, vol. 8 (M42, R-T12). Received August 21.
   1 Cf. above, Gallatin to Clay, December 13, 15, 1826.   2 Cf. above, Gallatin to Clay, February 22, 1827.   3 Cf. above, Brown to Clay, December 13, 1826, note; February 13, 23, April 12, 27, 1827.   4 George Canning.   5 For a detailed summary of Canning's budget message of June 1, see *Annual Register, 1827,* 172–75.   6 The Count de Villèle.   7 On Neuville, cf. above, Brown to Clay, February 13, March 13, 30, 1826.   François-Horace-Bastien, Count Sebastiani, of Corsican birth, had had a distinguished career as soldier and diplomat under Napoleon. Following the return of the Bourbons, he had retired from the army and in 1819 had been elected a Deputy. His vigorous support of the opponents of the Ministry had led to his defeat for re- election in 1824, but in 1826 he had been named to replace Maximilian-Sébastien Foy. Following the revolution of 1830, Sebastiani held several cabinet posts, including from 1830 to 1832 the Ministry of Foreign Affairs. He served as Minister to London from 1835 to 1840 and returned to the Chamber of Deputies from 1840 to 1848. He had been given the title Count in 1808 and was named Marshal of France in 1840.   Henri-Benjamin Constant de Rebecque, born in Lausanne and educated at Oxford, Erlangen, and Edin- burgh Universities, had been active since 1796 as a liberal publicist and politician of

France. He also had been elected to the Chamber of Deputies in 1819, where he remained until his death in 1830, a voice in opposition to the tyranny of the Restoration government. Freedom of the press was one of his particular concerns.   [8] Cf. above, Brown to Clay, October 29, 1825; Brown to Clay, August 12, 23 (1), 1826.   [9] See above, Clay to Brown, May 22, 1826, note.   [10] Cf. above, Brown to Clay, September 12, 1826, and note.   [11] Cf. above, Clay to Huygens, December 10, 1825; October 25, 1826; Clay to Hughes, April 27, December 12, 1826; Hughes to Clay, July 11, August 12, 1826; January 21, April 15, 1827; Huygens to Clay, September 15, November 11, 1826.   [12] Johan Gijsbert Verstolk Van Soelen.   [13] Above, April 15, 1827.   [14] Sir Charles Bagot. Report of the incident has not been found.   [15] William I.   [16] Probably Count Alexander Gourieff, a general in the Napoleonic War and at this time Russian Chargé d'Affaires at The Hague.   [17] On February 21, 1816, the Prince of Orange had been married to the Grand Duchess Anna Pavlovna, sister of Alexander I of Russia.

[18] Cf. above, Worsley to Clay, April 17, 1827, note. Adams' second annual Message, December 5, 1826, had emphasized that during the past year his administration had reduced the principal of the public debt by $7,000,000 and that he expected to end the year with an increase of $1,200,000 in the Treasury balance. He had also pointed to the completion, over the past eight years, of a program for the "*gradual increase of the Navy*," which had brought that force to a total of 12 line-of-battle ships, 20 frigates, and war sloops in proportion, and construction during the same period of "a system of fortifications upon the shores themselves." Richardson (comp.), *A Compilation of the Messages and Papers of the Presidents*, II, 357, 361–62. The same report had cited pending plans for improving communication "between the tide waters of the Potomac, the Ohio, and Lake Erie." Legislation of the Nineteenth Congress had provided for maintenance of the Cumberland Road, for construction of roads in Florida, Michigan, and Ohio, and for Federal aid by means of land grants to the States of Illinois and Indiana for canal construction and by subscription to stock in the Louisville and Portland Canal Company (see above, Speech, January 17, 1825, note 19; Thom to Clay, November 29, 1826) and the Dismal Swamp Canal Company (cf. above, Allens to Clay, *ca.* December 4, 1826). 4 *U. S. Stat.*, 162, 169, 227–28, 231–32, 234, 236, 241–42.   [19] Possibly *Facts and Observations in Relation to the Origin and Completion of the Erie Canal* (New York, 1825), a 36-page brochure.   [20] Lead medals commemorative of completion of the Erie Canal had been distributed on October 26, 1825. On one side was a picture of Satyr seated on a cornucopia with his arm around Neptune's shoulders, and inscribed: "Union of Erie with the Atlantic." On the reverse was a shield bearing the sun, surmounted by a half globe and eagle, with the word "Excelsior" below the shield and at the bottom the artist's identification: "Thomason." Sir Edward Thomason, born in Birmingham, England, had been manufacturing artistic metal buttons and medals since 1793. Jacques Fischer, *Sculpture in Miniature* (Louisville, 1969), 11, 93.   [21] Thomas L. McKenney, as superintendent of the Indian trade, had begun an Indian Portrait Gallery in the winter of 1820–1821, when a group of Indians came to Washington to visit President James Monroe. The government paid Charles B. King as artist for 25 of the portraits of this first delegation. He subsequently painted other Indians, either from life or as copies of other portraits, to form the basis of the portfolio published by McKenney and James Hall as *History of the Indian Tribes of North America, with Biographical Sketches and Anecdotes of the Principal Chiefs, Embellished with One Hundred and Twenty Portraits from the Indian Gallery in the Department of War, at Washington* (3 vols., Philadelphia, 1836–1844).   [22] On George M. Troup, cf. above, Clay to Southard, July 3, 1825, and note. John Forsyth had written a protest, dated March 10, 1824, by which the Georgia Senators and Representatives had called upon President Monroe to order the removal of the Cherokees from Georgia lands. Forsyth had also served as chairman of a select committee of the House of Representatives which on April 15, 1824, had brought in resolutions of similar import. On the basis of this report Congress had appropriated the funds for conducting the Creek negotiations. Alvin Laroy Duckett, *John Forsyth, Political Tactician* (Athens: University of Georgia Press, 1962), 107–108.   [23] Frederica Louise Wilhelmina.   [24] Probably Shaumonekusse (Con-Mon-I-Case; L'Ietan), an Oto half-chief, who, wearing bison horns, had been painted by King in Washington in 1821. The Oto, however, were a Sioux tribe who resided on the Missouri and Platte rivers.   [25] Madame C. Greban.   [26] Albert Gallatin.

[27] Marie Madeleine Isabelle, Countess d'Hane de Steenhuyse, whose husband, Jean Baptiste Marie Joseph François Ghislain, Count d'Hane de Steenhuyse, of Flemish birth, had served as Intendant over the Southern Netherlands from February, 1814, to September, 1815. Count d'Hane had died in January, 1826.   [28] The Count and Countess d'Hane had but one daughter, not further identified. Her husband was probably Maurice-Henri-Ghislain, Viscount de Nieulant et de Pottelsberghe, Flemish by birth and a graduate in 1821 from the military school at Delft. The young man was promoted to

lieutenant in 1828 and as an officer in the Belgian Army after 1830 rose to the rank of major general before his retirement in 1859. He attained distinction as the founder of the Red Cross in Belgium and for his service in that organization during the Franco-Prussian War of 1870.   29 Egide-Norbert-Cornelissen, born at Antwerp and educated at the University of Louvain, had been in charge of the Ghent police when Clay and the other negotiators had met him there in 1814. Three years later he had been named adjunct-secretary to the University at Ghent and subsequently "secretaire-inspecteur," a post which he held until 1835. He had developed the idea of periodical art exhibitions in the city of Ghent and in 1808 had organized a society for horticultural expositions. He was a member of the Royal Academy of Belgium from its organization in 1816 and active throughout his life in promoting the intellectual life of Flanders.

    30 Pieter Van Huffel.   31 This portrait is in the Antwerp Museum. [Michael] Bryan's Dictionary of Painters and Engravers, revd. and enld. under the supervision of George C. Williamson (5 vols.; New York, 1903–1905), III, 83.   32 Thomas Moore, the Irish poet, who had visited the United States, including Washington and Baltimore, in 1804 and had been at the height of his lyrical powers during the decade 1807 to 1817, was a man of small stature with a somewhat large nose and flaring nostrils, "a little tilted upwards." Howard Mumford Jones, The Harp That Once—A Chronicle of the Life of Thomas Moore (New York, [c. 1937]), 50, 331n.   33 Cf. above, II, 7–8n. Reference to Hughes' election to these societies has not been found.

DIPLOMATIC NOTES   June 12, 1827

From HILARIO DE RIVAS Y SALMON, Philadelphia. Acknowledges receipt of Clay's note of June 9; corrects the statement in his own communication of May 31, that (Angel) Laborde was blockading (David) Porter at Key West, by declaring that the Spaniard was cruising about that port to prevent Porter's escape but was not imposing a blockade; cites the letter, enclosed by Clay, from the collector (William Pinkney) as testimony to the correctness of Laborde's conduct; and, finally, undertakes a lengthy, detailed, point by point refutation of the assertions made by Clay. LS, in Spanish with trans. in State Dept. file. DNA, RG59, Notes from Spanish Legation, vol. 9 (M59, R-T12).

INSTRUCTIONS AND DISPATCHES   June 12, 1827

From JAMES BROWN, Paris, "Private" (2). Reports that "It is a received opinion here that the five powers, Russia, England, France, Austria and Prussia, have united in requiring, of the Porte, that hostilities against Greece shall immediately cease, and in insisting that she shall be independent, paying only a small annual tribute to her former Sovereign" (cf. below, Brown to Clay, July 12, 1827). Notes reports of a strong remonstrance by the Reis Effendi [Saida], who "alluded to the principles of the Holy Alliance, . . . urged that all those principles would be subverted by the emancipation of his rebellious subjects," cited "the conduct of the allied Sovereigns in the late insurrections in Naples [cf. above, II, 863n] and Spain [cf. above, III, 313n], . . . inveighed against" their "inconsistency . . . in now insisting that an insurrection equally unprovoked and flagrant against the authority of a Sovereign equally legitimate with those of Spain and Naples, should be crowned with success by the intervention of the very same alliance by which those above alluded to had been suppressed," and declared "that to admit the claim of the Greeks would eventuate in the destruction of his empire by the encouragement it would hold out to rebellion in every part of it." Observes that "Strong as those arguments might have been if employed by a christian minister, it would seem that they have had no weight when used by an infidel. . . ." States that "the demand has been repeated" and, "it is believed," should the Turkish answer "prove unsatisfactory, the fleets of England and France in the Mediterranean, will immediately cut off all intercourse between Greece and Turkey. . . ."

Notes a recent victory by Greek forces, which was "sullied by the wanton massacre of the Turkish prisoners in spite of the authority and remonstrances of the Greek commanders." Conjectures that Greece will "be created into a monarchy" (cf. above, Brown to Clay, this date) and that the orders received by the fleet at Brest, "ostensibly for the purpose of aiding in an attack on Algiers [cf. above, Brown to Clay, June 9, 1827], . . . relate to the state of things in Greece and Constantinople." Refers to the Ofalia mission, now removed to London (cf. above, Everett to Clay, June 9, 1827), and to rumors that "the whole or the greater part" of foreign "troops will be recalled" from the (Iberian) Peninsula. Explains: "France has long ago seen her error in having intermeddled in the affairs of Spain, and England finding the Portuguese either lukewarm or opposed to the Constitution, would be pleased with an opportunity of extricating herself from the task of supporting it." Remarks on the ineffectiveness of the last Session of "The chambers" and on the unpopularity of the Ministers. Expresses doubt, however, "that any change of the ministry will take place in the course of this year." LS. DNA, RG59, Dip. Disp., France, vol. 23 (M34, R36). Received August 2.

The Turkish note protesting European interference in the Greek operations had been delivered on June 9. *Annual Register, 1827,* 308.

In an effort to relieve the siege of Athens, Lord Thomas Cochrane had landed Greek troops at Piraeus on April 25 and overrun a number of small redoubts. The Albanian defenders, Turkish forces, had taken refuge in the monastery of St. Spiridon. As the Greeks had prepared to storm it, the Church fathers had arranged a capitulation; but fighting had broken out during the evacuation. Accounts of the number of Albanians slaughtered vary from 120 to 200. Only 70 had escaped. Cf. George Finlay, *A History of Greece from the Conquest by the Romans to the Present Time* . . . (New edn., revd. by author and ed. by H. F. Tozer, 7 vols.; Oxford, 1877), VI, 425–28; Douglas Dakin, *The Greek Struggle for Independence, 1821–1833* (Berkeley: University of California Press, 1973), 210–11.

MISCELLANEOUS LETTERS   June 12, 1827

From PHILIP ROBINSON, Curaçao. States that he is honored by the appointment as consul (cf. above, Clay to Robinson, April 9, 1827) but that, having decided to leave Curaçao, he is returning his commission. ALS. DNA, RG59, Cons. Disp., Curaçao, vol. 1 (M-T197, R1).

From D[EBORAH] S. WARNIER, Edenton (North Carolina). Acknowledges receipt of (Daniel) Brent's letter of May 29 (cf. above, Mrs. Warnier to Clay, May 17, 1827, note). States that (James) Brown has advised her "to employ an agent in Paris to transact . . . [her] business"; forwards to Brown "a power to that effect"; and expresses a hope that Clay will transmit that paper and allow her as "heretofore . . . the privilege of corresponding" through his office with Brown and her agent. ALS. DNA, RG59, Misc. Letters (M179, R65).

From Joseph Lawrence and Others

To the Hon. H. CLAY: WASHINGTON, PA. JUNE 13, 1827.

Sir: Having been appointed a Committee on behalf of your personal and political friends in this county, to make the necessary arrangements for a dinner which is proposed to be given to you, in this place, demonstrative of their steady regard and unshaken confidence in your political integrity and private worth; we have the honor to tender, on behalf of our constituents, our sincere greetings upon your arrival in the Western country, and request that you will fix upon the time when it will be most convenient for you to favor us with your company for that purpose.[1] Your uniform and stedfast [sic] support of the great manufacturing and agricultural interests of our country; the fearless, eloquent, and efficient manner in which you have invariably advocated the great cause of internal improvement; the undeviating consistency of your political course; and, in one word, your attachment to the great *"American System,"* command our most unqualified regard and approbation. We feel it more particularly our duty and our privilege to make this expression of our views and feelings in consequence of the attempts that have been made, and are making, to detract from your public character, to weaken the efficiency of the present Administration, and to effect its downfal [sic].   Be pleased, sir, to accept assurance of our private and individual consideration and respect.

We have the honor to be, your most obedient servants,

JOSEPH LAWRENCE,   GEORGE WILSON,
F. JULIUS LE`MOYNE,   JAMES STEVENS,
JOSEPH HENDERSON,   W. BAIRD.[2]

Washington *Daily National Intelligencer,* July 2, 1827.

1 Clay's reply has not been found. Cf. below, Toast and Address, June 18, 1827.

2 Francis Julius Le Moyne, born at Washington and graduated in 1815 from Washington College, had received the M.D. degree from the University of Pennsylvania in 1823. He practiced medicine in Washington, was active in a variety of reform movements, including abolition, and in 1876 opened the first crematory in the United States.   Henderson, a Virginian by birth, had moved to Steubenville, Ohio, in 1815 but the following year had become a clerk in the office of the prothonotary of Washington County, Pennsylvania. From 1823 to 1828 he was clerk of courts in that county and from 1829 to 1832, sheriff. He was also postmaster of Washington during the Adams administration and later a member of the Pennsylvania Legislature. Upon the organization of the Washington Anti-Slavery Society in 1834, he became its first president. He was also active in transportation development.   Wilson has not been further identified.   Stevens, a native of Connecticut, had studied medicine in New York and opened practice in Washington, Pennsylvania, about 1816. He remained active in the profession there for some 42 years.   William Baird, educated at Washington College, had been admitted to the bar in Washington in 1812. He practiced law until his death in 1834 and from 1819 to 1824 had served as deputy attorney general.

INSTRUCTIONS AND DISPATCHES   June 13, 1827

From ALBERT GALLATIN, London, no. 85. Reports that (William) Huskisson and (Henry U.) Addington have invited him "to a conference for Saturday, 16th instant, at which it is probable that some of the subjects of negotiation may be definitively disposed of, as Mr Addington intimated that there would be a Cabinet Council to day on American affairs." Encloses a copy (not found) of a bill which "has been brought in the house of Commons, . . . which affects in various ways the commercial relations of the United States." Notes that "The tables of duties alluded to in the bill, which will be discussed in Committee of the Whole to morrow, have not yet been reported, or at least published," and that "the duty of 12/ pr cwt. on salted beef and pork imported for home consumption has been adopted by the House and ordered to be made part of the bill. . . ." Calls attention to various sections of the measure that affect the United States, including the following: removal of the ban on importing salt beef and pork, on payment of the duty; requirement that such meat "as is warehoused (duty free) may no longer be so exported as to be used as stores by vessels sailing from England"; provision that "Lumber generally (deals excepted) and ashes may be . . . imported duty free, local duties excepted. . ."; and designation of "Kingston and Montreal . . . [as] warehousing ports . . . and every other frontier post in Canada (including St. John's) . . . a receiving port, whence goods brought inland may be transported to one of the warehousing ports." Comments that, "Although . . . the duty of 5/ pr barrel on flour is not repealed, the flour may be warehoused duty-free. . ."; and ". . . sections 22 to 24 appear intended to prevent the importation of East India or British goods into any British Colony except in British vessels." Explains that the measure converts "into a legal provision of a general nature, Mr [George] Canning's declaration in his note of 11th Septer. last [cf. above, Gallatin to Clay, September 13, 14, 20, 1826], that the British Government was not bound to remove, as a matter of course, the interdict on the navigation of a Foreign Country, in case such Country should hereafter accede to the conditions proposed, by the Act of Parliament of 1825" (6 *Geo. IV*, c. 114); and notes that "The proviso of the 38th Section still leaves to the King the power, given by that Act, to grant the privileges contemplated by it, although its conditions should not in all respects be fulfilled by some foreign Country." Points out that, "although this [last mentioned provision] leaves a door opened for reconsideration hereafter, if the present experiment should fail, the enacting clauses are undoubtedly intended as the answer to any application which may at this time be made by the United States." Viewing them as affording "conclusive evidence of the intentions of this Government," expresses regret that he failed to include in his "note of the 4th. instant [cf. above, Gallatin to Clay, June 4, 1827], . . . the intended inquiry in that respect." States that he will "probably make the bill," after its enactment, "the foundation of the enquiry, the answer to which" may be anticipated. Observes that he had no intimation "of any of the provisions of the bill; and as it does not appear to infringe any right, . . . [he has] no pretence to ask for explanations, unless . . . [the] conference should offer an opportunity." Refers Clay to "the [London] 'Times' of to day" for "a short sketch of the debate on appropriating money for the Canada canals." Adds that "The vote on the Corn bill [cf. above, Gallatin to Clay, April 11, 1827, note] is an evidence of the strength of the opposition to the Ministry in the House of Lords." Adds, however, that "that Ministry is strong in talents & in the public opinion." ALS. DNA, RG59, Dip. Disp., Great Britain, vol. 34 (M30, R30). Extracts published in Manning (arr.), *Diplomatic Correspondence of the United States, Canadian Relations,* II, 588–89. Received August 4.

The contemplated legislation was enacted, July 2, 1827, as "An Act to amend the Laws relating to the Customs." 7 & 8 *Geo. IV*, c. 56. The section numbers cited by Gallatin do not correspond to those in the statute.

The London *Times*, June 13, 1827, carried a report of the debate in the House of Commons on the preceding day concerning a resolution authorizing a grant of £56,000 to defray the expense of improving water communication in Canada. Opposition was expressed on the ground that the colony should bear the expense; supporters of the measure argued that it would provide for defense against possible attacks by the United States. The grant was approved by vote of 78 to 11.

From A[BRAHAM] P. GIBSON, St. Petersburg, "Duplicate." Transmits "a certificate of protest made by Charles R. Lenartzen, . . . Consular Agent at Cronstadt, against Captain Asa H. Swift, master of the Ship Galaxy of New York, for his having unlawfully discharged one of his Seamen [cf. above, Williamson to Clay, April 3,

1827, note], Joseph Robinson, who was certified to be a Citizen of the United States, by Beverly Chew Esqre. the Collector of the port of New York." Notes that Swift's claim that the seaman was a British subject led "to several interviews between Sir Daniel Bailey [sic] H. B. M's Consul General in this City," and Gibson. Expresses hope that Swift will be punished as a warning to other masters of vessels. LS. DNA, RG59, Cons. Disp., St. Petersburg, vol. 2 (M81, R-T2). Dated "June 1/13, 1827." Received September 7.

On September 8, 1827, Daniel Brent transmitted to Robert Tillotson, "Atty. U. S. for the S. D. of New York," copies of Gibson's note and of Lenartzen's protest, with the instruction that "the Secretary" wanted him to "institute such legal proceedings against Captain Swift, or the owners of the Galaxy, or both, as . . . proper in the case. . . ." Copy, in DNA, RG59, Dom. Letters, vol. 22, p. 47 (M40, R20).

Gibson, a native of New York, was United States consul at St. Petersburg from 1819 to 1850. Lenartzen, Swift, and Robinson have not been further identified.

Bayley, born near Manchester, England, had been British consul general at St. Petersburg since about 1814 and for brief periods in 1820 and 1826 served as Chargé des Affaires there.

From VINCENT GRAY, Havana. States that (Thomas M.) Rodney, ill with "a fever," departed for the United States on June 5, leaving Gray "charged with the Commercial agency at this Port, till his return." Reports having learned that "Commodore [David] Porter" has sailed from Veracruz (cf. above, Sergeant to Clay, May 30, 1827), with a new brig and two other vessels, for Key West, and that "two of the best Frigates" at Havana are being sent, "under the Command of Commodore [Angel] Laborde, in search of him." Notes that "Lieut. [Alexander] Thompson of New York and Midshipman [possibly Charles F. M.] Spotswood of Richmond have been paroled and arrived at Key West—they were treated uncommonly well while here." Expresses his expectation of obtaining a reversal of the sentence of Commodore (Edward) Preble's nephew (Thomas Preble; cf. below, Gray to Clay, July 24, 1827), who in 1825 "was arrested and taken from" an American schooner "for having shot one of the crew by accident, and Condemned to serve on board a man of war for Eight years." LS. DNA, RG59, Cons. Disp., Havana, vol. 5 (M-T20, R5).

Charles F. M. Spotswood was not yet a midshipman in the United States Navy. He was a Virginian, commissioned a midshipman November 1, 1828. He qualified as passed midshipman in 1834, was promoted to lieutenant in 1841, and was dismissed in 1861. Callahan, *List of Officers*, 515.

Edward Preble, born at Falmouth (now Portland), Maine, in 1761, had gone to sea in a privateer in 1777 and joined the Massachusetts navy in 1779. At the end of the Revolutionary War he had engaged in merchant service until 1798, when he had entered the United States Navy. He had commanded the frigate *Essex* on its voyage around the Cape of Good Hope in 1799–1800 and had been commanding officer of the Mediterranean Squadron during the early months of the Tripolitan War (1803–1804). Recalled in 1804, he had died three years later.

From Samuel Finley Vinton

Dear Sir.   Gallipolis (Ohio) June 14th. 1827.

Your letter of the 1st. instant[1] requesting me to answer one addressed to me some time since by Doc. Watkins[2] came to hand last night.

Doc. W. has probably received my answer before now; my absence upon the Circuit attending the Courts, at the time of its arrival being the reason why the Doctor's communication was not sooner replied to— On the subject of Gen. Jacksons declaration,[3] it has been my opinion from the time I first saw a notice of it, and still is my opinion that all our endeavours to bring out the General (or his friends, who deal so liberally in general charges of bargain, corruption &c) to make any distinct and triable issue will prove unavailing.

If however it cannot be done now, we can hardly hope for a better opportunity— Should it become absolutely necessary to do so, it seems the foundation is already laid for a disavowal by giving out to the public the name of a Garrulous Itenerant [sic],[4] who could probably be sacrificed without injury to himself or the cause— But this course will no doubt be the dernier resort, and I look for a repetition of some thing like the Kremer affair, in a perfectly intangible shape, like that which the matter finally assumed,[5] if any body can be found subservient to answer such a purpose— Congress not being in Session, they cannot get up a creature and a plot without time and labor, and hence we may wrench out a reluctant disavowal or he may mantle himself in *dignified silence.* You make no inquiry how things stand in this quarter, Still I presume it would not be wholly uninteresting to you to know— On this side the Ohio (I speak now of my own District) the Administration is gradually and silently gaining a great and decisive accession of strength— The General's friends are not only decreasing in numbers, but what is perhaps the best omen of all, those here who still profess to adhere to him are become daily more and more torpid, and nothing is more evident than that the ardor of their first love is all burnt out— In all the Western Country, Mr. Giles resolutions[6] are more precious to the Administration than Millions of *Gold and patronage* could be— I have just been along on the Margin of Trimble's[7] District for forty or fifty Miles, and find that a pretty formidable and certainly very furious opposition has been got up against him— Great and unwearied exertions are made by the Jacksonians, and judging from their language they feel confident of success over him, in which, however, they are probably mistaken[8]— There seems to be a sort of Madness in the public Mind in Kentucky, which reason makes more mad, as is often the case with instances of the most hopeless and incurable mental alienation— There must, however, be a restoration to reason and health with the removal of the causes that have impaired them, and that process is evidently gradually and surely going on[9]— In fact, it seems to me, from the little peep I have got into the Politics of Kentucky, that even now there is little else than the lashing of the waves after the storm has subsided and which must weary themselves out with their own violence— I am, Sir, truly yours &c—

SAML. F. VINTON

ALS. DLC-HC (DNA, M212, R2). Addressed to Clay. Born in Massachusetts in 1792, Vinton had been graduated from Williams College in 1814 and had begun practicing law at Gallipolis about 1816. He was a member of Congress from his adopted State, 1823–1837, 1843–1851, and a presidential elector, 1840. He died in Washington, D. C., in 1862.
    ¹ Not found.   ² Tobias Watkins. Cf. above, McArthur to Clay, May 14, 1827; Clay to Sloane, May 20, 1827.   ³ Cf. above, Report of Interview, *ca.* April 15, 1827, and note.   ⁴ James Buchanan. Cf. below, Smith to Clay, August 1, 1827, note.
    ⁵ On the Congressional investigation of the charges of George Kremer, see above, Appeal to the House, February 3, 1825, note.   ⁶ Cf. above, Brooke to Clay, January 31, 1827.   ⁷ David Trimble.   ⁸ Cf. above, Clay to Adams, July 25, 1826, note.
    ⁹ See above, III, 902n.

INSTRUCTIONS AND DISPATCHES   June 14, 1827

From HEMAN ALLEN, Santiago de Chile, no. 54. Reports that the Congress of Chile, "though elected for the purpose of adopting a constitution," after an eleven month session has recessed, deciding "to submit to the Provincial Assemblies, and to the civil Authorities of the country, the proposition, as to the form of government, proper to be established." Complains that "it is obviously characteristic of this people, to do every thing in a wrong way." Notes new intelligence indicating that Guayaquil and Quito are renouncing the authority of Colombia in order "to form a separate, independent government" (cf. above, Tudor to Clay, May 15, 23, 1827) and that political disturbances have broken out in Bolivia (cf. above, Williamson to Clay, May 4, 1827; Tudor to Clay, May 5, 1827). Encloses copies of his correspondence with the United States Navy agent, (Michael) Hogan, regarding Hogan's claims against the Government of Chile for the repayment of "certain duties . . . unjustly exacted" upon "certain articles purchased for the consumption of the [U. S. Navy] Squadron" (cf. above, Allen to Clay, December 19, 1826), and lists the reasons why he cannot support Hogan's claims. ALS. DNA, RG59, Dip. Disp., Chile, vol. 2 (M-T2, R2). Extract published in Manning (arr.) *Diplomatic Correspondence . . . Latin-American Nations*, II, 1118. Received September 18.
    The renunciation of Colombian authority by Guayaquil and Quito, in turning to the leadership of General José de Lamar, tended to maintain a tie with Peru which was not broken until 1830, when the Republic of Ecuador was finally established as an independent entity.

From JAMES COOLEY, Lima, no. 2. States that the Peruvian "Congress was formally opened on the 4th Inst, when [Francisco Javier] Luna Pizarro was elected President of that Body" and that, on the same day, "Gen. [Andrés] Santa Cruz delivered his message, a copy of which is . . . enclosed." Reports that on June 9 the Congress elected General (José de) Lamar as President of the Republic and (Manuel) Salazar (y Baquijano), Vice-President, but that until Lamar arrives from Guayaquil (cf. above, Tudor to Clay, May 5, 1827), Salazar will discharge the executive duties; adds that the elections were moved ahead because Santa Cruz, who consented at the opening of Congress to administer provisionally the Executive Department, suddenly resigned. Expresses belief that "the party now in power appears very favorably inclined towards the United States."
    Transmits, relative to the *Chesapeake* seizure (cf. above, Tudor to Clay, May 5, 22, 1827), copies of his correspondence with the Department of Foreign Affairs; notes that a lower court decision rendered in favor of the owners of the *Chesapeake* has been upheld by the Supreme Court; and remarks that a "strong probability" exists that the Congress will repeal the decree under which the vessel was detained.
    States that he expressed the "willingness" of the United States "to enter into a treaty of Amity commerce & navigation with the Republick of Peru." Advises that

the claims of United States citizens against this government will not be formally presented until the office of Minister of Foreign Relations has been "permanently filled. . . ." ALS. DNA, RG59, Dip. Disp., Peru, vol. 1 (M-T52, R1). Received October 24.

From BEAUFORT T. WATTS, Bogotá, no. 30, "Duplicate." Notes the publication, in "a Caracas paper," of a letter he wrote on "the 15th. March last to President [Simón] Bolívar, requesting him to return to Bogota and assume the responsibility and government of the Republic." Explains that "The letter was written in consequence of the arrival of information of the disaffection and mutiny of the Colombian auxiliary army which Bolívar had left in Peru" (cf. above, Tudor to Clay, February 3, 1827). Gives his interpretation of events—including bribery of (José) Bustamante and his soldiers by Peru to induce them to leave (cf. above, Tudor to Clay, March 23, 1827); the return of Bolívar (to Venezuela), where, "as was expected," he "saved the nation from massacre and disaster" (cf. above, Watts to Clay, March 2, 1827); and, upon receipt in Bogotá of news of the mutiny in Lima, the assembling of a crowd, "at the instance, and the influence of the Vice President [Francisco de Paula Santander]," that shouted cheers both for that official and for Bustamante (cf. above, Tudor to Clay, May 23, 1827). Declares: "At this period of faction and disorder, of mistrust and want of confidence in the government—When it was rumored that the Province of Cundinamarca, of which Bogota is the Capital would separate from Venezuela, and Quito, and make the Vice President its chief [cf. above, Poinsett to Clay, March 28, 1827, no. 81; MacPherson to Clay, March 30, 1827].—When the whole country from Lima to Venezuela was divided and torn by intestine commotion.—When the President was in Caracas and the Vice President in Bogota, each of them exercising Executive Powers; issuing conflicting decrees, and paralysing the government—I looked to him who is the constitutional chief magistrate of the Republic, as the individual who unites popular opinion, an unimpeachable integrity, an elevated sentiment of Character, of talents and experience that have passed the trial of seventeen years, devoted to the emendation of the social compact."

Denies having intended in the letter, published by authority of Bolívar, to criticize the Vice President, who, however, "is highly incensed. . . ." Adds: ". . . I have rec'd a note from the Minister of Foreign Affairs [José Manuel Restrepo] informing me that he will ask an explanation of my Government."

Cites the cases of "Mr. [David Y.] Lanman a respectable citizen residing in Maracaibo as a merchant" and of George W. Johnston (cf. above, Marks to Clay, March 17, 1827; Grut to Clay, March 19, 1827; Watts to Clay, May 14, 1827) to illustrate the equivocation of the government at Bogotá, which stated that demands for payment of obligations to these men must be presented to the Liberator President.

Claims that if he has "unintentionally offended the Vice President" he has "pleased the President" and has "acted in unanimity with the sentiments and wishes of all the foreign representatives residing at this government," which "may have had some influence in bringing the President to a determination to assume the Executive Chair. . . ." Expresses pleasure that Bolívar's "resignation has not been accepted" (cf. above, Watts to Clay, May 14, 1827, no. 29) and that "by the 7th. of August he may be expected, and will take charge of the government" (cf. below, Watts to Clay, September 28, 1827).

Concludes: "In taking the step which I have, I ardently hope it may meet the President's approbation—And instead of an insult having been offered or indirectly intended by me—I have received the insult: The note of the minister of foreign Affairs of the 12th. Instant I have not answered as yet— When I do—It shall be with firmness, but respect.—" ALS. DNA, RG59, Dip. Disp., Colombia, vol. 4 (M-T33, R4). Copy, in MHi-Adams Papers, Letters Recd. (MR481). Extract published in Manning (arr.), *Diplomatic Correspondence . . . Latin-American Nations,* II, 1315–18. Received September 3.

In his letter of July 6, 1827 (cf. above, Watts to Clay, March 14, 1827, note), Daniel Brent informed Watts that the President "has seen with no little surprize the publication, in the Newspapers of this Country, of a Letter purporting to be from yourself, as the Representative of the United States, to General Bolivar, entreating General Bolivar to return forthwith to Colombia, to repress by his moral force the irritated passions of the discontented in Venezuela. A copy of that Letter is herewith transmitted to you, and although the President is willing to believe that it was not written by you, yet I am instructed by him to ask precise information of you upon this point, as I accordingly have the honor of doing. His suspicion concerning its genuineness, is in some measure increased, by its being unnoticed in your Despatch of the 19th. of March, already referred to, four or five days after the date which that communication bears in the Newspapers."

"It is unnecessary to add, after these observations," Brent continued, "that the President would be greatly dissatisfied in receiving authentic intelligence of the genuineness of the paper in question."

President Adams noted, on October 16, 1827, that [José María] Salazar, Colombian Minister to the United States, "spoke of a complaint which, by order of the Vice-President, Santander, he had addressed to Mr. Clay against Beaufort T. Watts . . . for a very strange letter which he wrote to the President, Bolivar, and which he published." Adams commented:

"I told Mr Salazar that that letter had been unauthorized, and was disapproved by me.

"He said Mr. Clay had given him the same information; and he wished as much as possible to soften the complaint against Mr. Watts, whose letter, he said, had been attributed to indiscretion rather than to any evil intention. He said that on the 4th of July last Mr. Watts had given a public dinner, at which the Vice-President, Santander, had attended, and he hoped the misunderstandings between them had been in a great measure healed." *Memoirs,* VII, 337–38.

MISCELLANEOUS LETTERS   June 14, 1827

From CHARLES KING, New York. Introduces "Mr. [Fulgence] Chegaray a French gentleman who has long been a resident of this City" and who "visits Washington on business Connected with the N York South American steam boat association." States that he knows nothing of Chegaray's "objects nor of those of the association he represents [cf. below, Rogers and Van Winkle to Clay, this date]. . . ." ALS. DNA, RG59, Letters of Introduction.

Chegaray has not been further identified.

From B[ENJAMIN] W. ROGERS AND J[OHN] S. VAN WINKLE, New York. State that in 1825 the New York South American Steam Boat Association, "having concerted a plan for the navigation of the river Amazon, and its tributary streams, by means of Steam vessels, . . . deemed it necessary previous to putting this plan in execution, to ascertain, whether it would meet the countenance and protection of the government of Brazil"; quote extracts from correspondence between the president of the company (William Bayard in 1825; Rogers in 1826) and José Sylvestre Rebello, in which the latter repeatedly gave encouragement to the project; note that the association built "a Steam vessel," named the *Amazon*, and sent "a confidential person, Mr. F[ulgence] Chegaray to Rio de Janeiro, to obtain there a grant of the privileges they were desirous of securing"; and cite the cost of the vessel and her cargo and the date of sailing ("the 29th. of March 1825 [*i.e.*, 1826]"). Provide a translation of a letter written by Rebello "to the President [not identified] of the province of Para," informing him of the venture, emphasizing its importance to the province and to Brazil, and soliciting his protection for the vessel. Charge that, although the latter official "courteously received" the *Amazon* on her arrival in May (1826), "his conduct suddenly changed," he professed to have received orders not to allow her to ascend the river, "and after 9 months being wasted," she "was obliged to sail from thence." Estimate the losses caused "by this breach of faith by the Government of Brazil"to be "at least" $150,000. Summarize the frustrations of Chegaray, who reached Rio de Janeiro in December, 1825, "was met by references from one minister of the Emperor of Brazil [Peter I] to another," and finally, after seven months, learned that the grant of privilege being sought could "not take place at present." Solicit Clay's attention to the case, asking "the intervention of the National Government to procure from that of Brazil, redress for the loss . . . sustained from the bad faith of the latter. . . ." LS, in Van Winkle's hand. Signed by Rogers as "President of the N York South American Steam Boat Association" and countersigned by Van Winkle, a New York merchant, as "Secy." DNA, RG76, Misc. Claims, Brazil (MR1).

Endorsed on verso of last page: "Mr. [William] Tudor should be instructed to sustain, so far as may be proper, the Representations of this Company to the Government of Brazil—But as matter of contract, between the Company and the Brazilian Government, that of the United States can interpose only by its good offices. J.Q.A.
5 July 1827."

Daniel Brent wrote Rogers, on June 19, acknowledging receipt of the letter and informing him that, in Clay's absence, it had been submitted to the President and that no action on it was likely to occur until Clay's return, when steps would be taken to fill the vacancy occasioned by the departure of Condy Raguet from Brazil (cf. above, Raguet to Clay, March 17, 1827). Copy, in DNA, RG59, Dom. Letters, vol. 21, p. 563 (M40, R19).

On June 1, 1827, Clay had recommended to Adams "W. Tudor to take C. Raguet's place, and that the appointment should be speedily made." The President had agreed. Adams, *Memoirs*, VII, 284. Daniel Brent wrote Tudor, on June 28, 1827, informing him, "by direction of the President and in the absence of the Secretary," of his appointment as "Chargé d'Affaires of the United States at Rio de Janeiro" and transmitting his commission "and a letter with the signature of the Secretary of State, addressed to the Minister of Foreign Affairs at Rio de Janeiro [the Marquis of Queluz]," introducing Tudor in his capacity as Chargé. Brent urged Tudor to proceed "with all possible despatch," if he agreed to accept the appointment, and advised him that the President wished him to say that his mission was "instituted especially" for the purpose of maintaining "the most friendly relations with that Government . . . and to obtain, by friendly explanations with its ministers, from the justice and liberality of the Emperor, the indemnities and reparations to which citizens of the United States, who may have sustained injuries from acts under color of his authority, . . . [should] be found to be fairly entitled. . . ." LS, in DNA, RG84, Brazil (MR14, frames 50–51, 58); copy, in DNA, RG59, Dip. Instr., vol. 11, pp. 366–68 (M77, R6). For copies of the commission, Adams and Clay to Tudor, dated June 26, 1827, and of the letter of introduction, Clay to the Minister of Foreign Affairs, on the same date, see DNA, RG59, Ceremonial Communications, II, 68, 69.

Toast at Uniontown Public Dinner

[June 15, 1827]

Our American System—Success to it against all opposition, foreign or domestic, open or insidious.

Philadelphia *Democratic Press*, July 5, 1827.   Clay reached Uniontown, Pennsylvania, on June 15 and was honored by a public dinner that afternoon. John Kennedy served as chairman of the assemblage, and other dignitaries included John M. Austin, James Todd, and Andrew Stewart. Clay's toast followed his brief speech, on protection, which was not reported.   Kennedy, born in Cumberland County and graduated in 1795 from Dickinson College, had been admitted to the bar in 1798 and thereupon opened practice in Uniontown. He was named to the Pennsylvania Supreme Court in 1830 and served on that bench until his death in 1846.   Austin and Todd had been active proponents of the woolens bill (cf. above, Pleasants to Clay, February 14, 1827) at a meeting in Uniontown on June 2. The former has not been otherwise identified; the latter was State attorney general in the late 1830's.

INSTRUCTIONS AND DISPATCHES   June 15, 1827

From JAMES OMBROSI, Florence. States that "The coincidence of names of individuals reprobated by the Austrian Police, as well by the absolute Princes of the different States of Italy, not seldom occasions inconvenience and trouble to the American travellers, which would be avoided if the United States had a Consul General in Italy." Refers to his communication of May 8, 1826 (addressed to Daniel Brent), in which he noted "that the King of Prussia [Frederick William III] has a Consul General [the Count Lucchesini] in Italy, who acts as Chargé d'Affaires in Florence, the Government here refusing to admit of the residence of an Agent with the title simply of Consul"; expresses willingness to serve the United States in a similar manner, without salary; explains that the title means nothing to him, but "with the Tuscan Government it is every thing." Recommends that the United States "name a Consul General in Upper Italy, who would be acknowledged by the Austrian Government. . . ." Cites two cases of American travelers whose names have caused them to be harassed by police. ALS. DNA, RG59, Cons. Disp., Florence, vol. 1 (M-T204, R1). Received August 17.

Count Lucchesini, not further identified, had recently been appointed to the combined functions and held them at least through 1828.

From WILLIAM SHALER, "Baths of Caldas near Barcelona." Reports on the state of his health; again requests a leave of absence (cf. above, Shaler to Clay, May 14, 1827, and note); expresses a hope that he will be able to return to his post for the winter; but notes that he "cannot remain there longer than the first of May . . ." without risk to his life. ALS. DNA, RG59, Cons. Disp., Algiers, vol. 11 (M23, R-T13). Received August 21.

Caldas de Montbuy, a town 14 miles north of Barcelona, was noted for its hot sulphur springs.

From WILLIAM TAYLOR, Veracruz. Cites the enclosures with his letter of May 3 to show that the Mexican Government, though it has consuls in Europe, requires "from no Country other than the United States, and from no place in the U. S. other than Baltimore, Philadelphia and New York . . . the Mexican Consular Certificate . . . at this Custom House." Rejects the "only reason assigned" for this partiality—that certificates from European ports cannot be required because the independence of Mexico has not been recognized in those countries and, in consequence, Mexican consuls there "have no authority, or are not permitted, to act"

—and declares that "the fact is they do Act," although in cases where they "have informed against those Merchants who had refused or neglected to take" the consular certificates the collector at Veracruz (Fausto Acedo, not further identified) ignores the complaints. Charges, therefore, "that the Nations of Europe by not acknowledging the independence of this Country have avoided those vexatious and offensive regulations to which we, who have acknowledged it, are daily Subject." Transmits copies of his correspondence with the collector. Reports the execution of "The friar [Joaquín] Arenas" (cf. above, Sergeant to Clay, January 26, 1827) on June 3; the abandonment, "about the Same time," of the proposed "expedition to Texas" (cf. above, Poinsett to Clay, March 8, 1827; Taylor to Clay, April 26, 1827); the unfavorable state of public finances and credit; and the existence of "a considerable degree of excitement, and no little alarm throughout this Country," for which, he thinks, "party spirit, which is very high," is partly responsible. ALS. DNA, RG59, Cons. Disp., Veracruz, vol. 1 (M183, R1). Received July 29.

From WILLIAM TUDOR, Lima, no. 70, "*Confidential.*" Reports that the "Superior Court" has ruled in favor of the *Chesapeake* (cf. above, Cooley to Clay, June 14, 1827), which has been released. Acknowledges giving "a brief of the argument" to a few members of Congress, "which should induce a repeal of the decree . . . against Spanish merchandize. . . ." Analyzes the composition of the Congress, which has "full powers to alter the Peruvian Constitution"; praises Luna Pizarro, the first president of that body; and notes that, although the Constitution provides for two houses, the Senate "was never organized, as the same day the constitution was finally accepted, it was suspended by conferring the Dictatorship on [Simón] Bolivar; & when . . . the period arrived for his resigning that power, he destroyed the Congress. . . ." States that "A committee of eight are named for the revision of the constitution"; that the departments favor a federal system, while residents of the capitals "in all parts of South America" are "adherents of a consolidated republic"; and that "sensible men . . . wish to proceed deliberately & without rashness. . . ." Encloses two numbers of the *Lima Chronicle* and calls attention to "a few general remarks relative to the federal system of government," which were "principally written by . . . [himself], with a few additions" by the editor, "Mr. [José María de] Pando late Minister of Foreign Affairs." Expresses pleasure in the selection by Congress of (José de) Lamar (y Cortázar) and (Manuel de) Salazar (y Baquijano) as President and Vice President, respectively, "of the republic" and notes that the latter, "in the absence of LaMar was immediately installed in his office." Surmises that (Andrés) Santa Cruz "will be called to preside over . . . [Upper Peru] under a new constitution; & the Peruvian government will aid his views in that respect to cultivate hereafter a close alliance & perhaps partial federation." Speculates that (Simón) Bolívar, in response to the recent revolutions, "will pass the Styx or the Atlantic before the end of the year." Reviews, disparagingly, Bolívar's military career. Mentions inquiries from (Joel R.) Poinsett and (John) Sergeant concerning the "probability . . . of Ministers being sent from . . . [Peru] to the Congress of Tacubaya" and expresses his opinion that "nothing will be done" and "that Congress will fall thro' for the present at least—" Refers to the "anxiety" with which Lamar's arrival is "looked for" and to the tasks which await him. ALS. DNA, RG59, Cons. Disp., Lima, vol. 1 (M154, R1). Extract published in Manning (arr.), *Diplomatic Correspondence . . . Latin-American Nations*, III, 1833–35. Received October 27.

MISCELLANEOUS LETTERS   June 15, 1827

From AUSTIN E. WING, Detroit. Solicits, in behalf of "two gentlemen, who are interested in the matter, information in relation to the boundary line run and established by the Commissioners under the Treaty of Ghent [cf. above, Vaughan to Clay, October 23, 1826; Porter to Clay, November 4, 1826; Clay to Vaughan, November 15, 1826], in the Detroit River"; notes that "their object is to ascertain to which government belongs an Island in the Detroit River, called *Fighting Island;* The original French name Gross [*sic*] Isle Aux Dinde [*sic*] (Eng) Turkey Island. . . ." ALS. DNA, RG59, Misc. Letters (M179, R65). Published in Carter (ed.), *Territorial Papers,* XI, 1086.

The line from 45° north on the Iroquois River west to Lake Superior, as determined by the commissioners under a decision of June 18, 1822, placed the boundary in the Detroit River west of "Fighting or Great Turkey island," thus awarding it to Canada. *American State Papers, Foreign Affairs,* VI, 859–60.

From Henry Clay, Jr.

Dr. Sir.   Washington 16h. June 1827.

According to your desire, I shall leave this place for W. Point on Monday the 18h. inst.; And shall probably arrive there on the wednesday following.

To day I receid. a letter from Bradford,[1] a cadet of whom I am particularly fond, and of whom, I fear, you entertain an opinion too low for his merits. As to his talents, his standing at the Academy is a sufficient recommendation—his conduct too has been generally good, perhaps better than that of most Kentuckians who have been there. You supposed, judging from your letters last winter,[2] that his advice to me tended rather to make me unpopular with the officers, and unfit to remain at the Academy— I assure you, if ever I had a sincere friend, Bradford has been one to me— My disposition, which is naturally wild, he has in many instances, curbed by timely advice, such as friend should render to friend.

In this same letter he says "Your letter contained nothing with which I was so much pleased as the expression of your determination to return to the Point, and your resolution to endeavour to graduate. I know you could do nothing which would gratify your father and the majority of your friends so much as to pas [*sic*] through with a respectable standing the several classes of the institution"— Yes frequently has Bradford spoken of the affair of last winter[3] with sorrow for he thinks that you have lost entirely your good opinion of him— I told him as often that you had not, that probably you had already forgotten it: as his letter contained excuses which to me at least, were amply sufficient to justify his conduct.

he intends visiting Kentucky soon, and if it is in your power to show him any politeness, by doing so you will oblige your affectionate son   HENRY CLAY JR.

P.S.   My mother requests me to remind you of some wool which you are to bring for her.

She and John[4] send their love to you

                                                                        H. CLAY JR.

Mr H. Clay.

June 18

Dear Sir, I have opened this letter to inform you of the arrival of William Claiborne and little Duralde,[5] who arrived here yesterday from New York after a voyage of 18 days by sea from New Orleans having started on the 22d. of last month.   your son

HENRY CLAY JR.

ALS. Henry Clay Memorial Foundation, Lexington, Kentucky. Addressed to Clay at Lexington.
[1] James Andrew Jackson Bradford, a son of Benjamin J. and grandson of John Bradford, had been born in Tennessee, had entered the United States Military Academy in 1823, and was graduated fourth in his class in 1827. He attained the rank of captain in 1832 and held that rank in 1861 when he resigned to accept a colonelcy in the Confederate Army.   [2] Not found.   [3] Incident not found.   [4] Lucretia Hart Clay and John Morrison Clay.   [5] William C. C. Claiborne (Jr.); Martin Duralde III. Cf. above, Erwin to Clay, May 21, 1827.

From Nathaniel Dike and Others

Steubenville,[1] June 16 [1827].

To the Hon. Henry Clay.—Sir. A number of the citizens of this town, warmly attached to the great cause of the American System, of which they justly regard you the father and advocate, and deeply impressed with a sense of the importance of maintaining what are called Western rights and western interests, of which you are known to be the tried and faithful friend, have assembled and appointed the undersigned a committee to invite you, in token of the respect they entertain for the distinguished services you have rendered your country, to partake of a public dinner, at such time as you shall designate.— We, sir, have long watched your political course, and witnessed a zeal and devotedness to the cause of our country which we cannot too much admire, or too highly appreciate.

The committee avail themselves, with pleasure, of this occasion to assure you of their highest esteem and confidence.

N. Dike,	*W. R. Dickinson,*[3]
A. Sutherland,	*J. Andrews,*
D. Stanton,	*Jas. R. Wells,*
M. Roberts,	*D. L. Collier,*
J. Henry,	*A. Wise,*
M. Lennox,[2]	*I. Jenkinson.*[4]

Lexington *Kentucky Reporter*, July 11, 1827. Dike, born in Massachusetts and graduated from Yale University, had settled in Steubenville in 1816. He had practiced law briefly but spent most of his life in mercantile pursuits. He was, for a time, a judge of common pleas and in 1842 served in the State legislature. He had been a Clay supporter in the election of 1824.
[1] Ohio.   [2] Alexander Sutherland, a Clay supporter in 1824, was a native of Ohio and a merchant. David Stanton, a Steubenville physician, had settled in that town in 1814. He died in January, 1828. Matthew Roberts, born in Pennsylvania, was a manufacturer and merchant in the Ohio town. James Henry and Lennox have not been further identified.   [3] William R. Dickinson.   [4] John Andrews, a physician and merchant, became in 1831 a charter member of the Ohio Historical Society and in 1848

one of the incorporators of the Steubenville and Indiana Railroad Company. James Ross
Wells had been a member of the Ohio Legislature in 1826. Daniel L. Collier, born in
New England, was a lawyer and, later, also an incorporator of the Steubenville and
Indiana Railroad Company. Adam Wise, born in Pennsylvania, was an engineer. Jenkin-
son, probably also a native of Pennsylvania, has not been further identified.

From Robert S. Rose

Dear Sir   Geneva[1] June 16. 1827
    I mentioned to you last winter my friend Daniel W. Lewis,[2] a Law-
yer of this place, who wishes to be appointed to the Bench in Michigan; and promised to draw your attention to the subject and to our
conversation by a written communication— Some time last Spring
Mr. L. wrote to an acquaintance of his, a man of high standing and
character in the territory of Michigan, and one whose judgement and
candour may be relied upon, communicating his wish to live at Detroit & to be employed in the Judiciary of the territory & requesting
such information on the subject as his correspondent should see fit to
give him. He has shown me the letter recd. in answer, which I think
should be inclosed to you: but he thinks himself not at liberty to do so
without the express permission of the writer. As I have no doubt of
the correctness of the Statement contained in the Letter, I send you
by way of extract from it, all it contains on the subject. "The Judges
of our Supreme Court are appointed by the President for four years—
their term expires I think next February, at which time unless for reasons appearing, they will probably expect a re-appointment. Judge
Hunt's[3] health is exceedingly bad, and it is thought very doubtful
whether he will survive the summer—his death would occasion a
vacancy which it would be well to provide against, as in the event of
any vacancy we shall have a host of applicants. We very much need a
presiding Judge here from abroad from some state of established laws
and established practice   Delays of justice are here intolerable not so
much from the defects of our laws as from any thing like uniformity
of decisions or practice. Judge Witherell[4] the President is an old
Soldier of the Revolution, who never was a Lawyer, bred I believe a
physician or perhaps rather a farmer, once of strong mind, good judgement & great integrity, but now doting through age. Sibley[5] possibly
a tolerable lawyer, though I do not think so & admitted on all hands
to be a very inferior Judge, owing to inconquerable prejudices and
other natural disqualifications   Hunt is generally esteemed the best
Judge of the three—though a superficial lawyer—either from long
commercial pursuits & inattention to Law, or from never having
possessed legal acquirements beyond the ordinary local practice of
Mass'tts.— From these and other causes, method is much wanted in
the transaction of business & our courts can hardly be said to have any
Such thing as practice; although abounding in rules they are generally

a dead letter; procrastination to a ruinous degree prevails, all is confusion throughout the term, and very little business effected. There being no certainty when the Court will compel a trial, a corresponding laxness in the Bar and Witnesses may well be expected. Thus I have endeavoured to give you a hasty yet just and humiliating view of the State of our Supreme tribunal—a tribunal embracing law equity, admiralty & all other jurisdiction known in our country. You will readily infer that we much need correction—we are sensible of this & as sensible that the present Bench will never remedy the evil— It will require what all disinterested men here seem to agree upon, a gentleman from a distance not contaminated by our evil habits, of legal acquirements of decision & a faculty for business and despatch."[6]

The administration is gaining friends in this quarter daily, and nothing in my opinion is necessary to insure it's [sic] complete success but a thorough investigation of the correctness of its measures, and of the motives and qualifications of the opposition. My friend Van Buren will find he has a much more difficult task to perform in this state than his southern friends seem to anticipate: to what extent he has pledged himself to them I know not; but even with the aid of Mr. Clinton I do not believe he can get one-fourth of the votes of this state for Jackson— Mr. Clinton's course last winter[7] has lost him a great majority of his former friends; and nothing could be more gratifying to me than to see him come out openly in the opposition—I am with great respect your friend   ROBT. S. ROSE

ALS. DNA, RG59, A. and R. (M531, R5).   1 New York.
2 Daniel Wadsworth Lewis, born in Connecticut and educated in law at Litchfield, had practiced for a time in that town and had been State attorney for Litchfield County. He had moved to Geneva, New York, in 1800. He later removed to Buffalo, where he died in 1837.   3 John Hunt.   4 James Witherell.   5 Solomon Sibley.   6 On the appointment, cf. below, Chipman to Clay, August 3, 1827, note.   7 See above, Shaw to Clay, September 10, 1826, note.

From Richard Rush

My dear Sir.   Washington June 16. 1827
    There are now grounds for supposing, not indeed from official returns as yet before me, but on information that I think can not greatly if at all mislead, that the revenue from imports will yield us about a *million* of dollars *more* this year than it yielded last year. I know what satisfaction it will give you to hear this,[1] though we are not yet sufficiently through our fiscal year to affirm the fact with *absolute confidence.*[2] I can say no more just now. We have no accounts of you since you left us. Always my dear Sir and very much yours
Mr Clay.   RICHARD RUSH.

ALS. DLC-HC (DNA, M212, R2).
    1 Cf. above, III, 707–709; Speech, January 17, 1825 (IV, 28) ; Martin to Clay, September, 1826 (V, 741).   2 Duties on imported merchandise had amounted to $26,083,448 in 1826; they totaled $27,951,372 for 1827. *House Docs.*, 21 Cong., 1 Sess., no. 29, p. 7.

INSTRUCTIONS AND DISPATCHES   June 16, 1827

From JOEL R. POINSETT, Mexico (City), no. 92. Reports the arrival of "a Messenger despatched by Mr [Sebastián] Camacho," who has concluded commercial agreements with Prussia and France. Charges that, "By this informal arrangement, which will probably place the commerce and shipping of France upon the footing of the most favored nation, the cabinet of the Tuilleries [*sic*] will silence the clamors of the merchants and manufacturers of that kingdom, who were loudly demanding the recognition of these Countries, and will secure all the advantages of a commercial treaty without committing the nation with Spain or the other members of the holy alliance." Observes that "This people [Mexico], by accepting such an agreement, will deprive themselves of the means now in their power of aiding the clamors of the liberal party in France, which might perhaps compel that court to treat with the Americas on the terms of independent nations." Conjectures that "the Executive" [Guadalupe Victoria] may "sanction the agreement," while the Congress may "insist upon Mexico being treated with by France on the footing of an independent nation." Notes that the legislature of "the State of Vera Cruz, where the army destined for Texas has been for some time assembled" (cf. above, Taylor to Clay, June 15, 1827), has enacted "decrees in direct violation of the Federal Constitution" and has "refused to permit" (José Ignacio) Esteva "to take possession of the employment of Commissary General of the Customs of Vera Cruz—an office purely executive and federal" (cf. below, Poinsett to Clay, July 8, 1827). Adds that "The government" has withdrawn the troops from Veracruz, that "the whole expedition destined for Texas will probably return to the capital," and that "order will be restored." Comments on the financial embarrassment of the country. LS. DNA, RG59, Dip. Disp., Mexico, vol. 3 (M97, R4). Extract published in Manning (arr.), *Diplomatic Correspondence . . . Latin-American Nations*, III, 1661. Received July 9.

A commercial treaty between Mexico and Prussia at this time has not been found. On the signing of an agreement with Hanover, cf. below, Poinsett to Clay, August 10, 1827. That with France, denominated a "declaration," rather than a formal treaty, was dated May 9, 1827, and provided reciprocal most-favored-nation treatment, excepting the coastal trade and that with Haiti under the ordinance of April 17, 1825 (cf. above, Holden to Clay, July 16, 1825; Brown to Clay, May 10, 1826, note). *Annual Register, 1827*, p. 227.

MISCELLANEOUS LETTERS   June 16, 1827

From JOHN DODGE, Boston. Explains, as executor of the estate of his dead brother, Unite Dodge, a "Native of Salem, Masstts.," who resided in "St. Domingo, Hayti," from 1799 to 1803, that property belonging to his brother's "children & heirs" was "sequestered by [Henri] Christophe in the year 1807" and that "It is presumed that we have a just claim on the Government of France for a portion of the St. Domingo Indemnity by the late Treaty, with Hayti" (cf. above, Holden to Clay, July 16, 1825; Brown to Clay, February 13, May 10, 1826, note). Requests information as to "what measures ought be adopted to obtain a portion of the Said Indemnity." Refers to "The friendly & humane Interest" Clay has "taken in favor of the French Emigrants in th[is] Country. . . ." ALS. DNA, RG59, Misc. Letters (M179, R65).

John Dodge, born in Boston, had resided and carried on a mercantile business in Haiti for some 20 years. In association with William Gray he had from 1822 to 1826 operated the firm Marple, Dodge, and Company, one of the largest American establishments operating on the island. His brother, Unite, has not been further identified.

To Nathaniel Dike and Others

Pittsburgh, June 18 [1827]

Gentlemen:—I have received the invitation[1] which, as a committee, in behalf of a number of the citizens of Steubenville, you did me the honor to address to me on this day. And I will have the honor to dine with them on Saturday next,[2] if that day will suit their convenience. The value of this distinguished proof of their confidence and esteem is not diminished, nor will a grateful recollection of it be less cherished, by the conviction which I feel, that in the support of the System, the rights and the interests to which you refer, my agency has been that only of zealous co-operation with others to whom the greater merit belongs.

Tendering to you, gentlemen, cordial assurances of my high personal regard, I pray you at the same time to believe that I am, with great respect, Your obedient servant,   H. CLAY.
Messrs. N. Dike, W. R. Dickinson, A. Sutherland, John Andrews, D. Stanton, M. Roberts, J. R. Wells, D. L. Collier, M. Lennox, A. Wise, I. Jenkinson, and Jas Henry.

Lexington *Kentucky Reporter,* July 11, 1827.   [1] Above, June 16, 1827.
[2] June 23, 1827.

INSTRUCTIONS AND DISPATCHES   June 18, 1827

From VINCENT GRAY, Havana. States that "Commodore [David] Porter returned to Key West on Saturday last [June 16], in an american Brig of, [*sic*] and bound to New York from VeraCruz [cf. above, Gray to Clay, June 13, 1827]. . . ." Notes that (Angel) Laborde attempted "to intercept him and his vessels of War, but they are now Cruizing on the Coast of Campeachy to intercept the privateers from this Port [Havana], who have destroyed their Campeachy Trade, except one, his Brigs [*sic*]; who also evaded Leborde [*sic*]." Comments on the severity of "the fever" in Havana. Adds, in a postscript, that Porter "carried with him to Key West p40000." ALS. DNA, RG59, Cons. Disp., Havana, vol. 5 (M-T20, R5). Received July 8.

Porter, in fact, went to New Orleans to recruit seamen and "spent at least some of the $10,000 in cash sent to him by Mexico on recruitment. . . ." Long, *Nothing Too Daring,* 270.

From ALEXANDER HAMMETT, Naples. Informs Clay of additional allowances granted by the King of Naples [Francis I], under certain conditions, on duties paid on "cargoes imported from the East and West Indies, in vessels over 200 tons burthen . . . under the flag of the Two Sicilies. . . ." Explains that the purpose of "this diminution" is "to encourage distant expeditions, and to countervail the extraordinary Tonnage Duties in these Countries." ALS. DNA, RG59, Cons. Disp., Naples, vol. 1 (M-T224, R-T1). Received October 14.

From JOSEPH S. MARKS, Maracaibo. Reviews, from accounts received from Bogotá, "the insurrection of the Colombian Troops in the South" and the expeditions to Guayaquil and Quito (cf. above, Tudor to Clay, February 3, March 23, April 25, May 5, 23, 1827); notes that "Some think" the movement to Guayaquil "a mere artifice to conceal the Views of Peru who wishes that part of Colombia to be incorporated with her." Reports that the (Colombian) Congress was to have "taken into Consideration," on June 6, "the resignation of the President [Simón Bolívar; cf. above, Watts to Clay, March 14, 1827] and Vice President [Francisco de Paula Santander]"; and adds that Bolívar was expected soon to leave Caracas for Cartagena. ALS. *Ibid.*, Maracaibo, vol. 1 (M-T62, R1). Received July 23.

MISCELLANEOUS LETTERS   June 18, 1827

From ANTHONY WOODWARD, New York. Transmits petitions and documents from "Consignees of the British Brig William," seeking relief "from certain penalties & forfeiture therein mentioned," and requests that the matter be presented to the President "for his decision." ALS. DNA, RG59, Series #690, Case of the British Brig William (unnumbered file).

Woodward and the claim have not been further identified; they appear to be concerned in a seizure under the proclamation of March 17, 1827 (cf. above, Clay to Vaughan, March 17, 1827).

Promissory Note to Daniel Brent

$6500   WASHINGTON, June 19. 1827

SIXTY days after date, I promise to pay to the order of Daniel Brent, Six thousand five hundred dollars—*for value received, payable at the Office of the Bank of the United States, at Washington.*

                                                                H. CLAY

DS, partially printed form. DLC-TJC (DNA, M212, R16).

To Charles Shaler and A. Sidney T. Mountain

                                                Pittsburgh, June 19, 1827.

GENTLEMEN: I accept with much pleasure the invitation[1] which, in behalf of a number of my fellow-citizens of Pittsburgh, you have done me the honor to give me, to a public entertainment to be furnished to-morrow at the Anchor Paper Mill.[2] And I pray you to make to them my respectful acknowledgements for their friendly consideration of me, and also suffer me to assure you of the personal esteem and regard entertained for yourselves by Your obedient servant,

To the Hon. Charles Shaler,   H. CLAY.
A. Sidney T. Mountain, Esq.

Washington *Daily National Journal*, June 28, 1827, reprinted from the *Pittsburgh Gazette*, June 22, 1827. Algernon Sidney Tannehill Mountain, born in Pittsburgh and admitted to the bar at the age of 17, in 1821, was a prominent young lawyer, one of the most active members of the Pittsburgh Thespian Society. He died suddenly on August 9, 1827.

[1] Below, this date. Clay had reached Pittsburgh on Sunday, June 17.   [2] The Anchor Steam Paper Mill, located between Water and Front Streets, east of Ross, had been built in 1814 and the following year put in operation by Henry Holdship as Pittsburgh's first paper mill. In 1826 the mill employed 88 workers and produced 40 reams weekly. Lois Mulkearn and Edwin V. Pugh, *A Traveler's Guide to Historic Western Pennsylvania* (Pittsburgh: University of Pittsburgh Press, 1954), 30. Besides his manufacturing operations, Holdship was proprietor of a bookstore and author and publisher of *The United States' Spelling Book* (Pittsburgh, 1826).

From "Obediah Penn"

Pittsburg [*sic*], 6th month, [*ca*. 19,] 1827.

Friend Henry—In behalf of the friends of good order, and the sober decencies of life, I am constrained to say to thee, and through thee to the Committee of Arrangements at the *Anchor Paper Mill*,[1] their invitations are painful to the meek and humble hearted, and verily they are compelled to decline the request to join thee at the feast and rejoicings of the day.

Although I have not the pleasure of thy close acquaintance, and perhaps, as intimates we may never meet, yet, from circumstances deeply connected with the quiet, decorum, and prosperity of Pittsburg, together with an unchanging wish for the re-election of our mutual friend, the man John Q. Adams, I feel it my duty to address thee; with this view alone, thou must bear with my remarks, though public opinion challenge the propriety of thy conduct.

True, man is made for society; to it he is impelled, by every dictate of his nature, every disposition of his heart, his hopes and his fears, his wants and his desires, all conspire to render him social; divest him of these, aed [*sic*] wretched indeed were the condition of man; a gloomy, insensate misanthrope, without affection for his fellow, and without reverence for his God!—a mere machine bearing the divine impress stamped upon the grosser attributes of the animal. But human impulses were given for noble purposes—to honor the Author of our being, to meliorate the condition of humanity here, and to prepare it for felicity hereafter. Now, friend Clay, what are the best means to effect this end? The fiddle and the flute, the dance and the song, and the toast and convivial cup, are surely not calculated for it; they but excite the baser passions of the soul, and tend directly to the follies and vanities of life. Verily, my friend, thy movements are productive of no moral, or political good, and like the deadly Sirocco of the desert, or like James Barbour's speech at Annapolis,[2] thy convivial protestations and professions, will finally poison the wholesome atmosphere of our hopes, and secure to our enemies the object of their presumptuous aspirations; besides, thou disturbest the tranquility of the place; the young men and maidens, the old men and matrons, are most unbecomingly stirred up with the prospect of the revel at the *Mill*, and all thought and action appear to be absorbed in the anticipation of its tumultuous pleasures. Truly it hath grieved me sore to find so many goodly people entirely given up to the faithless demonstration to the worldly minded.

.   .   .   .

[Discourses for a paragraph upon the elevation of man over "the lower order of beings," because "Reflection is a primary principle of his nature...."]

.   .   .   .

[Continues to philosophize on the "pageant of pleasure," the "folly and infatuation" which "mark the progress of society."] At no remote period, however, we may safely anticipate better things. When the countenance of our statesmen and heads of Departments shall be withdrawn from those thriftless and *deceitful* associations— when we can turn with confidence and satisfaction to men who are not only qualified for the duties of their exalted stations, but who may be willing to lend the solemn influence of their example in all things which may become an independent and a pious people. Such men, whose habits of meditation whose peculiar penetration into the human character, and above all, whose sovereign power over our language enable them to impart energy to every intellectual sensation, to add richness to the colorings, and spirit to the images of nature, must bear with them a charm to give efficacy to admonition, and sooner or later they must give a new direction to character, and put a new pulse in the hearts of those who are prone to giddiness and depravity as the sparks fly upward.

Among men of desperate station in life, without a disposition to amend their lot by industry, or to raise their reputation by virtuous actions, the spirit of slander is not to be wondered at: it is ever the subterfuge of paupers in character and intellect, and the bosom companions of desperate demagogues. But where reputation and talent are distinguished, and when fortune and friends conspire to sustain a man in public esteem, he can have no cause for wanton defamation, but that contraction of heart which never permits its owner's breast to beat with a free, manly, and honorable impulse: Friend Clay!! thou hast, therefore, no excuse for the ruffian-like attack upon the character of an unoffending, virtuous woman.[3] If it be true, that thy *creatures* in the West consulted thee before they published their dastardly falsehoods, thou art altogether responsible for their calumny, and the infamy and its consequences must rest on thee alone.[4]

I pity thee, Henry!—from my heart I pity thee! Thou, who wert destined by nature for the high places of the earth, and whose fame might have been commensurate with the glory of thy country, art now so degraded in the people's eyes as to have thy name identified with that of Binns, Hammond, and Arnold,[5] the convicted slanderers of a pious woman! Although these men profess to be governed by the injunctions of the Decalogue, and hold themselves honorable in community, yet they can coolly contemplate the destruction of a virtuous character, for the abandoned purposes of self-elevation.

Let me ask thee, friend Clay, wouldst thou, in any case, refuse to administer to the temporal wants of a fellow creature in distress? If so, my advice can never reach thee, and thy degenerate feelings have marred the purpose of their creation: But if thy nature do revolt at cruelty and unkindness, and thy sympathies prompt thee to relieve the unfortunate;—if thou deemst it a duty, at the hazard of thy life, to save a blind man from the horrors of a precipice, how infinitely more art thou obliged to light and lead his mind in the proper path of morality and reflection, and to rescue him from the downward path of ignorance and crime!

If thou must necessarily retain the man John Binns,[6] put him immediately to his purgation, under a system of moral discipline: for thou hast seen his friends dashed beneath the foot of this changeling, and hast heard his abjurations of consistency: The light of truth is extinguished, and the charities of nature are all chilled at his approach! The widow's moan, and the orphan's cry for bread, disturb not the reckless enjoyment of his plenteous board:—The wretched rest of exhausted misery, molesteth not the quiet of his stupid slumbers: nor doth the pitiless fury of the storm, pressing to the earth its homeless wandering victim, chill the pulsations of his insensate heart!— And thou hast accumulated upon him the patronage of the Government, to the exclusion of a destitute and worthy widow, Lydia Bailey,[7] whose only offence is her inability to promote the political crusade in which thou and thy friends have recently embarked.

With these remarks, I will conclude this note; barely adding, however, that if they have had a due weight with thee; and since thou, with Daniel Webster and a few of our friends in Philadelphia, hast thought proper to convoke an assemblage at Harrisburg for the purpose of deliberation upon the *American System*,[8] Simon B———, Ephraim S———,[9] and Obediah P. will cheerfully join thee in spirit for the promotion of the public good, and the security of the re-election of the son of John Adams of '98. Thy friend,

OBEDIAH PENN.

Washington *United States Telegraph*, July 7, 1827. The document is prefaced by the following note, from an unnamed source: "*To the Editor of the United States' Telegraph.* "SIR—The subjoined epistle to Henry Clay was received from the author himself, whom I know to be a man of honor and integrity, although he is an ultra-federalist and a fast friend of the present Administration." Obediah Penn, probably a pseudonym, has not been further identified.

[1] Cf. below, Shaler and Mountain to Clay, this date.   [2] While visiting Governor Joseph Kent at Annapolis, Barbour had been invited to a public dinner, on June 5. Toasts were drunk to the President and his heads of Departments, to which Barbour had responded by noting that "too many of our public journals" had "become mere vehicles of unfounded slander." "I thank God," he commented, "that I have not the faculty to conceive of any indemnity which earthly honors, or earthly wealth, can offer for an act of treachery to be committed by a man who has grown grey in the service of his country —the place of his nativity, and from which he has received nothing but kindness and honors—Suspicion of such a crime, without proof, can originate only in the dark recesses of wicked and malignant hearts in which are found the base originals of the characters given to others." Washington *Daily National Journal*, June 11, 1827, reprinted from Annapolis *Maryland Republican*.   [3] Rachel Donelson Robards Jackson.   [4] Cf. above, Clay to Hammond, December 23, 1826.   [5] John Binns; Charles Hammond; Thomas Dickens Arnold. Born in Virginia but reared in Knox County, Tennessee, Arnold had served in the War of 1812 as a drummer boy, at age 14. He had been horrified when Jackson ordered the execution of a young soldier found guilty of straggling on the march to Mobile. Admitted to the bar in 1820, Arnold was politically active and

bitterly hostile to Jackson. In the course of the campaign for election to Congress in 1827 Arnold published a pamphlet addressed *To The Freemen of the Counties of Cocke, Sevier, Blount, Jefferson, Grainger, Claiborne and Knox* (Knoxville, Tennessee, 1827), in which he attacked Jackson's public and private character, including purported quotation of a boast by "one of the General's prominent friends . . . that the General had 'driven Robards off like a dog, and had taken his wife'" (cf. above, Wilkinson to Clay, July 27, 1825, note) Washington *Daily National Journal*, March 26, 1827. Defeated in 1827 (cf. below, Erwin to Clay, August 12, 1827), Arnold served as a Whig Congressman from 1831 to 1833 and from 1841 to 1843. In 1836 he became a brigadier-general of the Tennessee Militia. Following his retirement from Congress, he returned to the practice of law.   6 See above, Binns to Clay, December 5, 1825; Clay to Crowninshield, March 18, 1827.   7 Lydia R. Bailey had been married at age 19 to Robert Bailey, a Philadelphia printer. When Bailey died a decade later, leaving her with four small children, she had taken over the business. Her specialty was book printing, but she had supplied the printing and stationery for the Philadelphia Customs House for many years until the contract was awarded Binns. Philadelphia *United States Gazette*, January 25, 1828. From 1830 to 1850 she held the contract as public printer for the city of Philadelphia.

   8 See above, Clay to Crowninshield, March 18, 1827, note.   9 B——— and S——— have not been identified.

From Charles Shaler and A. Sidney T. Mountain

Pittsburgh, June 19, 1827.

SIR: A number of your fellow citizens residing in this city, are desirous of paying to you a small tribute of respect, for your zealous and untiring exertions in the cause of Internal Improvement, Domestic Industry, of the humane and wise principles of Universal Emancipation, and of every measure which can add wealth or honor to our common country. We, therefore, Sir, for ourselves, and in behalf of a numerous portion of our fellow-citizens, invite you to a public entertainment, to be given at the "Anchor Paper Mill" of Mr. Holdship, to-morrow, at 2 o'clock, P.M. Respectfully, your friends and fellow-citizens,

CHARLES SHALER, Chairman of the Com. of Arrangements.

A. SIDNEY T. MOUNTAIN, Secretary of the Comm.

Washington *Daily National Journal*, June 28, 1827, reprinted from the *Pittsburgh Gazette*, June 22, 1827. Cf. above, Clay to Shaler and Mountain, June 19, 1827.

INSTRUCTIONS AND DISPATCHES   June 19, 1827

From WILLIAM TUDOR, Lima, no. 71. Transmits "the 3d No. of Mr. [José María de] Pando's journal [cf. above, Tudor to Clay, June 15, 1827]" and calls attention to an article in which Pando's "language serves to show that he always thought the plan [contained in "the treaty or Convention" emanating from the Panama Congress] illusory, & that the political changes which have since occurred in Peru & Colombia have destroyed all hopes of any useful result." Reports learning from Dr. (Francisco Javier) Luna Pizarro that (José de) Lamar's election (cf. above, Cooley to Clay, June 14, 1827) "will be well received in" Arequipa, where "An attempt of one or two petty officers to form a disturban[ce] among the troops . . . [has] been discovered & punished." ALS. DNA, RG59, Cons. Disp., Lima, vol. 1 (M154, R1). Received October 27.

Toasts and Response at Pittsburgh Public Dinner

[June 20, 1827]

11. *Our distinguished guest*—Let us not like the ungrateful butler of Pharaoh, "forget Joseph,"[1] but remember him who cheered us in the midst of gloom, and foretold, with prophetic spirit, our deliverance and prosperity.

.   .   .   .

Mr. President, and Fellow-Citizens:

I thank you for the very cordial reception with which I have been honoured, during my visit to this city. I thank you for the present distinguished proof of your confidence and esteem. I thank you for the sentiment which has been just drank [*sic*]. The approbation of our fellow-citizens is always gratifying. There are times, and places, and circumstances, which give an uncommon interest to the manifestations of their friendly feelings.

In foreseeing, as many years ago I thought I did, the success which would crown the exertions of the people of the United States, by the application of a portion of their industry to the arts,[2] I was gifted with no spirit of prophecy. I only studied the character and resources of our countrymen and our country. Of their enterprise, ingenuity, and perseverance, no doubt could be entertained. We produced all the essential raw materials, and we had the command of boundless power, natural and artificial. With these elements, physical and moral, why should we fail? Nor was the strength of my conviction abated by the discouraging predictions of the timid and the interested. These have not been wanting, in every stage of our national progress; and the failure of our arms, in both our wars, as well as of our arts, had been confidently foretold. Our march has nevertheless been onward, successful, triumphant and glorious.

If the friends of American industry had presented a system for its protection, based upon doubtful theory and visionary speculation—if they had offered to the consideration of their countrymen a scheme which experience in other nations had demonstrated to be impracticable and injurious, all the opposition which they encountered would have been patriotic and justifiable. But they came forward with no doubtful project. They were sustained by the experience of all countries, and especially of that from which we sprung [*sic*]. And now the very great success which has attended those branches of our manufactures which were adequately protected, enables us to add that of our own as a testimony to the wisdom of self-defence and protection.

Notwithstanding the new markets which have been created, the wants which have been supplied, and the animation which has been given to labor, the foes of the American System continue their opposition with a perseverance worthy of a better cause. Availing themselves of the irritations and divisions incident to a late contested election, and enlisting under the banners of a distinguished name,[3] they have taken fresh courage, and assail the further progress of our manufactures with renovated vigor. Prior to that event, they had contented themselves with controverting the policy of encouragement; and no statesman in Congress had been seen bold enough seriously to question the right of Congress to afford it. But now the Legislature of a distinguished state, after long deliberation and mature consideration, has solemnly resolved that Congress does not possess the power to counteract foreign legislation, by laws of self-protection.[4] From the very commencement of the government, and throughout all the stages of its existence, in peace and in war, the power has been asserted and exercised. It is delegated by more than one clause in the Constitution. Under the authority to regulate commerce with foreign nations,[5] we have seen the power exercised to suspend, for long and indefinite periods, commercial intercourse with all nations, and especially with Great Britain and France.[6] The power to regulate our foreign commerce is plenary, clear, and explicit; and, if the clause which conveys it is not adapted to the purpose, human language is incompetent to supply the appropriate terms. Under another clause, also full and explicit, the power is granted to lay imposts,[7] without limitation as to amount, and has been exercised to an extent far beyond the wishes of the friends of the American System to apply it.

I hope the vigour of this new attack upon the system will be met by corresponding vigour in its defence. Let us treat our antagonists with the greatest respect, and be tender even of their prejudices. But, faithful to measures, let us firmly meet concert and co-operation on the other side, by concert and co-operation on ours. Let us oppose mind to mind and exertion to exertion; and if we must fail—if the bright prospects which lie before us are to be dissipated and destroyed, let there be no occasion for reproaching ourselves. If our opponents can make themselves the majority, however much we may deplore the issue of the struggle, we will bow with submission and deference to the will of the majority. If, as I hope, our system is preserved and improved, I will now hazard the prediction, that, in less than 20 years, the value of our exported manufactures will exceed in amount that of all the exports of raw produce from our country.

To me it has been a source of the greatest satisfaction, that I have ever been an humble co-operator with the representation from Pennsylvania, in supporting the good cause. I only seconded the efficient and able exertions of her distinguished sons, some of whom represented this city. Indeed, throughout a public service in the national councils, which commenced more than twenty years ago, it has been my happiness never to differ with that state on any great measure of national policy. I will not make an exception of the Missouri question, because I agreed with her in the abstract on the subject of slavery, and on all practical and constitutional means of ridding the country of its evils,[8] and she ultimately hailed the amicable settlement of that threatening question, with patriotic joy.[9]

I have differed only once with Pennsylvania, and that was a difference in relation to men,[10] and not measures. It was not among the most inconsiderable reasons which induced me on that occasion to make the selection which I did, that I thought the measures which Pennsylvania approved would be safer under the Administration of our present Chief Magistrate. I knew his opinions, and I have not been disappointed. I did not certainly know the opinions of his great rival. I had my fears, and succeeding events have not been of a nature to quiet them.

I differed from you only about men. We did not disagree about the business of the national family. You wanted one foreman: I thought, under the guidance of another, our work would be better planned and executed, our accounts better kept and settled, and all parts of the concern would enjoy higher prosperity.

We differed only about men. You wished to commit the national ship to a gallant commander. I thought that was not his element, and I preferred another, who possessed, I believed, more skill and experience, and under whose command I thought the ship, and the crew, and the cargo, would be safer and happier.

You were actuated by one of the noblest of virtues. I too acknowledge its sway. But whilst military merit is no disqualification, but, when accompanied by other requisite attainments, may be a reason for civil promotion, standing, as it appeared to me, alone, I did not think we could prudently entrust the Chief Magistracy of this great country to the distinguished object of your choice. I felt with you the obligations of national gratitude. But I thought they should be fulfilled in other forms. Let the public gratitude manifest itself in just and adequate rewards, drawn from the public treasure. Let inspired poets sing the praises of our military and naval commanders. Let the chisel and the pencil preserve their faithful images for the gratification of the present and future generations. Let the impartial historian faithfully record their deeds of glory and renown, for the admiration and the imitation of posterity. I say, too, in the language of a departed sage, "honor to those who fill the measure of their country's honor."[11] But it should be appropriate, considerate honor—such as becomes its object, and such as freemen, jealous, cautious, and enlightened freemen, ought to bestow. If my suffrage is asked for the highest civil office of my country, the candidate, however illustrious and successful he may be, must present some other title than laurels, however gloriously gathered on the blood-stained field.

These are my principles, which governed me on the memorable occasion to which I have referred. I quarrel with no man for holding opposite principles. I ask only the humble privilege of acting upon my own. And that privilege I *will* exercise during life, in spite of all the detraction, calumny, and intimidation by which I have been, or may be assailed. Throughout a life, which is not now short, I have had the greatest confidence in the candor, the intelligence and the justice of the public. I do not speak of confidence in the abused sense of the affected demagogue, but of that confidence which lies at the bottom of all our institutions, which supposes a competency in the people to self government, without which, liberty is a mockery, and our system a splendid illusion.

I have yet another cherished resource, of which HE only can deprive me who gave it: It is the consciousness of the rectitude with which I *know* I have faithfully served my country.

I will not longer detain you. I ask permission to offer a sentiment:

The City of Pittsburg [*sic*]—The abundance, variety, and excellence of its fabrics attest the wisdom of the policy which fosters them.

Washington *Daily National Journal*, June 28, 1827, reprinted from *Pittsburgh Gazette* of June 22. The dinner, held at "Mr. Holdship's Anchor paper mill" (cf. above, Clay to Shaler and Mountain, June 19, 1827), was attended by over 600 persons, said to be a number larger than "ever assembled on a similar occasion in this city." William Marks presided. Clay rose in response to the eleventh toast.
   1 Genesis xl, 23. The quotation is garbled.   2 Cf. above, II, 178–86 *passim*, 826–47.
   3 The presidential election of 1824–1825; Andrew Jackson.   4 On the protest of the Virginia Legislature, cf. above, Brooke to Clay, January 31, 1827, note.   5 Article I, Section 8, paragraph 3.   6 Cf. above, I, 388, 389n, 643.   7 Article I, Section 8, paragraph 1.   8 Cf. above, II, 776n–77n.   9 Reference not found. Pennsylvania had vigorously opposed both the first (1820) and the second (1821) Missouri compromises. U. S. H. of Reps., *Journal*, 16 Cong., 1 Sess., pp. 276–77; 16 Cong., 2 Sess., pp. 277–78.
   10 See above, III, 645, a reference to Pennsylvania's role in the election of 1824–1825.
   11 The quotation has not been found. In the version of this speech published in *Niles' Weekly Register*, XXXII (June 30, 1827), 298–300, the last word of the quotation is printed as "glory."

From William C. C. Claiborne

Dear Sir,   Washington June 20th. 1827
   I reached this place on last Sunday evening[1] and was very sorry not to find you at home. The family were much surprised to see us; we were not expected so soon,[2] and though I met with the kindest reception, I brought one with me, who I suppose was still more welcome. This is your little grandson Duralde,[3] whom I have taken all the way round by sea, and delivered safe and sound into the hands of his grand Maman, who appears extremely happy to have him with her. He is the pet of all the family; John[4] is very kind to him, and seems delighted with Martin who is almost as large as his Uncle; they speak different languages, and it is very amusing to see them endeavouring to understand each other. I had the pleasure of finding Henry at home, he delayed his departure for a short time in consequence of our

arrival, and set off rather reluctantly yesterday morning to return to West Point.[5]

I am so far highly delighted with my visit to the North, but I travelled from New York to Washington in such haste, that I had not time to see much of the Cities through which I passed; I intend therefore after remaining here about a month, to return to New York, and proceed from thence, on a tour to the springs,[6] the falls of Niagara &c.

I hope that you will have no occasion to prolong your absence, unless it be from the great zeal of your friends; We look forward very anxiously to the day of your return. I left all my relatives at home, in good health, so is the family here, and we hope that yourself and friends in Kentucky enjoy the same blessing. I remain Most affectionately and respectfully your's   WILLIAM C. C. CLAIBORNE.

ALS. DLC-HC (DNA, M212, R2). Addressed to Clay at Lexington, Kentucky.
[1] June 18.   [2] Cf. above, Erwin to Clay, May 21, 1827.   [3] Martin Duralde (III).
[4] John Morrison Clay.   [5] Cf. above, Henry Clay, Jr., to Clay, June 16, 1827.
[6] Probably at Saratoga.

INSTRUCTIONS AND DISPATCHES   June 20, 1827

From ALBERT GALLATIN, London, no. 87. Reports that his conference with the British plenipotentiaries (William Huskisson and Henry U. Addington) "did not take place till yesterday [cf. above, Gallatin to Clay, June 13, 1827]," at which time they "expressed their assent to a renewal for ten years of the third Article of the Convention of 1818 [cf. above, Clay to Gallatin, February 24, 1827 (no. 18)], but with a declaration, on the part of Great Britain, to be entered in the Protocol, that, according to her understanding of the article, neither party could exercise exclusive jurisdiction in the territory in question." Adds that they also expressed willingness "to renew the Commercial Convention of 1815 for an indefinite time, but with a proviso that it might be annulled at any time on either party giving one year's notice, and with an additional article intended to prevent the laying a higher duty on rolled than on forged iron" (cf. above, Gallatin to Clay, May 29, 1827). Encloses copies of "the draughts of two Conventions and of the intended declaration," which they placed in his hands. Notes the objections stated by himself, both to the declaration and "to the proposed mode of" renewing the commercial convention, before saying that he "would take the papers into serious consideration" and not give his "final answer till at the next conference." Explains that his answer cannot change but that he wanted "one opportunity more of discussing amicably both subjects," so that, "if, as according to present appearances, the negotiation should fail in both respects, no blame should attach to us for precipitancy or want of every endeavour to obtain a more favorable result." States that, "With the same object in view, . . . [he] thought this to be the proper time to say that . . . [he] was authorized to take into consideration the substance of the nine articles, which had been offered by the British Plenipotentiaries at the 22d Conference of the negotiations of the year 1824" (cf. above, Clay to Gallatin, June 19, 1826). Encloses a copy of the papers (presenting the American view on these nine articles), which he placed in the hands of Huskisson and Addington.

William B. Lawrence adds, in a postscript, that "The protocol of the 8th Conference is enclosed." ALS (except for the postscript, AES). DNA, RG59, Dip. Disp.,

Great Britain, vol. 34 (M30, R30). Published, with enclosures, in *American State Papers, Foreign Relations*, VI, 675–77. Received August 14.

From SAMUEL HODGES, JR., "Consulate U. States, Cape de Verde Islands   Villa da Praya, St. Iago." Acknowledges receipt, "yesterday," of Clay's letter of June 20, 1826. Promises "to execute the Commission" when "Capt. Ephraim Merchant," now absent, returns. States that "one of the seamen impressed from the Brig Pharos" (cf. above, Hodges to Clay, March 16, 1826) had documentary proof that he was a native of Portland, Maine, but "It was not until after eleven days detention, and an order from Commodore [Charles] Bullen who arrived in the mean time, that Captain [D. C.] Clavering restored him." Adds that the other seaman, "Shipped by Capt. Merchant at Bonavista . . . had no protection, and was possibly an Englishman." ALS. DNA, RG59, Cons. Disp., Santiago, vol. 1 (M-T434, R1).

From JOEL R. POINSETT, Mexico, no. 93. Reports his understanding that the messenger, of whom he wrote in his last dispatch (above, June 16, 1827), "brought only the project or basis of an agreement between France and this country [Mexico], and information that the French had granted an *exequatur* to the Mexican Consul in Paris [Tomás Murphy] and appointed Mr. [Alexandre] Martin, who is now here, Consul for Jalapa and provisionally Consul General for Mexico." Admits having no precise knowledge of "the propositions sent by Mr. Camacho"; expresses pleasure in finding "that this government is not disposed to enter into any informal arrangement, which might have the effect of postponing the recognition of their independence"; and states that "France has offered to Mexico her friendly offices with the court of Rome." Adds that the troops in Veracruz are obeying orders to return to the capital (cf. above, Taylor to Clay, January 31, 1827). LS. DNA, RG59, Dip. Disp., Mexico, vol. 3 (M97, R4). Extract published in Manning (arr.), *Diplomatic Correspondence . . . Latin-American Nations*, III, 1662. Received August 2.

Mexico, like Colombia (see above, Everett to Clay, March 31, 1827), was seeking to re-establish relations with the Vatican. A conference on the matter had been held on April 18 between Monsignor Vincenzo Macchi, Archbishop of Nisibi, the Papal Nuncio in France, and Camacho, in the presence of the Baron de Damas. The Nuncio explained that the Pope, Leo XII, as head of State would not receive a Mexican emissary but that as the Pontiff of the Church he would accept a representative. Ernesto de la Torre Villar (ed.), *Correspondencia Diplomatica Franco-Mexicana (1808–1839)* (vols. 1–; Mexico, 1957), I, 53. The diplomatic ties were not improved, however, until 1830, when "a provisional modus vivendi" re-established relations; even then the opposition of the Mexican clergy delayed resolution of the problem. Rives, *The United States and Mexico*, I, 67.

Macchi, born in the diocese of Montefiascone in 1770, had been elevated to the archbishopric in 1818 and served as Nuncio to Paris from 1820 to 1828. In 1826 he had been made a cardinal. After a series of diplomatic and administrative posts in the Church, he was named to the episcopacy of Ostia as a deacon of the College of Cardinals in 1847.

Toasts and Address at Washington, Pennsylvania, Banquet

[June 21, 1827]

Our Guest, HENRY CLAY: the eminent statesman—the uniform patriot and the eloquent advocate of the true "American system,"—

amidst the fury of party conflict, and the calumnies of malevolent opposition, he enjoys the proud solace of an honorable mind.

... Mr. CLAY rose, and made a short address, (we regret that we are not able, and that he had not time to furnish a full statement of it.) He expressed, in feeling terms, his thanks for the kindness, which during a period of more than 20 years he had always experienced from the citizens of this county: He showed how the opponents of the American system, at different periods, had, in Congress, varied their modes of attack; sometimes charging its friends with embracing too many articles in their scheme of protection, and at others too few: He stated that, owing to amendments made in the Senate to the bill of 1824,[1] injustice was done to the article of wool, in its raw and fabricated form, and that the friends of the system then believed that future legislation would be necessary to place it on a footing of equality with other essential articles: he vindicated the power of the General Government to adopt the American system, in both of its branches of internal improvement and domestic industry: As to the first, repeated decisions of Congress, sanctioned by public opinion, had affirmed the authority. As to the other, it was delegated by at least two clauses in the Constitution, that which empowers Congress to regulate foreign commerce, and that which confers upon that body the right to lay imposts.[2] Both powers, under various Administrations, had been exercised to an extent far exceeding any thing now proposed. He expressed his firm conviction that, by a faithful adherence to the principles of the system, every hope, and every anticipation of its friends, would be completely realized. He expatiated on the utility of standing by our principles, of upholding the great interests of the country, and of avoiding the sacrifice of them to promote the cause of any man. The battle was again to be fought. Renowed [sic] hopes, fresh troops, other forms of assault was [sic] to be employed, but the issue of the contest was not doubtful, with firmness and fidelity. Finally, he thanked the company for the generous sympathy which they had expressed on account of the calumnies which had been directed against him. He had experienced, he thought, rather more than his share of bitterness and malignity. He bore them, he would not say always cheerfully or calmly—but he bore them under a firm persuasion that truth and justice would ultimately prevail, and, if they did not, he had a remaining consolation of which no human power could bereave him.

He concluded by proposing a sentiment which, although already substantially given, would bear repetition—

Pennsylvania and governor Shulze[3]—MEASURES, NOT MEN.

Washington, D. C., *Daily National Intelligencer*, July 2, 1827. Dated by reference in a letter signed "Recorder," dated June 19, in Washington *Daily National Journal*, June 21, 1827.

[1] See above, III, 756n.   [2] Both in Art. I, sec. 8.   [3] John Andrew Shulze.

To James Barbour

Dear Sir   Washn.[1] 21 June 1827.
A son of Mr. Parker Campbell of this place has been recd. at West point, but it is said that he wants a fraction of an inch of the requisite height. I knew his father well.[2] He was one of the most eminent and respectable members of the Bar, and the greatest interest is felt here in behalf of his bereaved family. If it be not absolutely inadmissible, I think it would be expedient to receive him, notwithstanding his want of that part of an inch, which he will quickly acquire   I should be very glad if you could receive him.[3]
I have been every where received in a manner far transcending my most sanguine expectations. Yr's truly   H Clay

ALS. DNA, RG77, Letters Recd., 1826–37, serial no. M-277. Addressed to Barbour on attached sheet.
[1] Pennsylvania.   [2] Parker Campbell had died August 7, 1824.   [3] The son, John Calhoun Campbell, was admitted to the United States Military Academy in 1828 but never graduated. He has not been further identified.

From John Quincy Adams

Henry Clay Esqr. Secretary of State
Dear Sir   Washington 21 June 1827
I enclose herewith two letters[1] for you which I have recently received; and which were left open for my perusal— Your lady and family are well   Yours faithfully—

Copy. MHi-Adams Papers, Letterbook, Private, no. 9, February, 1825–March 13, 1829, p. 158 (MR148).
[1] Not identified.

From Nicholas Biddle

Dear Sir,   Bank of the United States June 21. 1827
A letter received this morning from Messrs Baring Brothers & Co of London, contains the following passage.
"Mr T. Wiggin has deposited with us £ 1745.2. to be placed to the credit of the Institution subject to the order of the Right Reverend Philander Chase, the Honble Henry Clay, & Mr Bezoliel [sic] Wells, as a Committee of the Trustees of the Ohio Theological Seminary."[1]
This deposit was probably made in consequence of a letter from me to Mr Chase on the 15th of Jany last recommending this course & stating that if a deposit were thus made, "On receiving information from the Messrs Barings the Bank will settle at once with you at the rate of exchange of first rate private bills of exchange on that day."
In order to ascertain that rate I have procured & now inclose a certi-

ficate from the Exchange brokers by which it appears that the rate is 10 1/2 pr Ct. On that basis the £ 1745.2. will yield the sum of Eight thousand five hundred & seventy dollars & thirty eight cents which has accordingly been carried to the credit of the Committee, and awaits their order. I would not have ventured to disturb your retirement among your old constituents by any business letter of Church or State but it was proper to give to the Committee the earliest information of the State of their funds, & I do not know the residence of your colleagues. I will only add that I am Very respy yrs   N Biddle Prest. Honble Henry Clay. Secy of State Lexington Ky.

ALS. DLC-HC (DNA, M212, R2).
1 Cf. above, Clay to Chase, September 26, 1826, note; Wiggins to Clay, March 26, 1827.

INSTRUCTIONS AND DISPATCHES   June 21, 1827

From Albert Gallatin, London, no. 86. States that he wrote (Richard) Rush "two days ago. . . , respecting a vessel which had sailed from Belfast for Philadelphia with a greater number of passengers than is permitted by the laws of the United States (see above, Speech, January 20, 1827, note 14) and that (William) Huskisson, without knowledge of this case, spoke of "much alarm at Liverpool whence several vessels had lately sailed under similar circumstances: and he confirmed the fact that, there at least, there was no knowledge of the law of the United States, before the notice given by Mr [James] Buchanan, the British Consul at New York." Encloses a copy of a list, supplied by Huskisson, "of the Liverpool vessels in question. . . ." Observes that he has "every reason to believe that the parties have acted in ignorance of our law; and it would be a matter of regret, if there was no way to remit penalties in this case." Notes "Mr Huskisson's enquiry" regarding "the first provision of the law." LS. DNA, RG59, Dip. Disp., Great Britain, vol. 34 (M30, R30). Copy, in NHi-Gallatin Papers (MR20). Received August 15. Endorsed by Clay: "Send a Copy of these despatches to Mr Rush, and inquire what has been done with the vessels mentioned. H C."
    Later on August 15, "The Secretary of State" transmitted "to the Secretary of the Treasury" copies of Gallatin's letter and its enclosures and requested "information . . . concerning the Passenger-vessels referred to by Mr. Gallatin." Copy, in DNA, RG59, Dom. Letters, vol. 22, p. 29 (M40, R20). Copy also in MHi-Adams Papers, Letters Recd. (MR482).
    James Buchanan served as British consul at New York from 1816 to 1843.

From Daniel Webster

My Dear Sir,   *Private*   Boston June 22 [1827].
    We have heard of your departure from Washington, & are expecting daily, to see the account of your reception at Pittsburg.[1] This will find you, probably, at Lexington.
    Since I wrote you[2] nothing unexpected has occurred here. Mr Mills' letters, or those of his friends, caused some little difficulty, & gave *me* great pain, personally. He has been informed, however, of the con-

siderations which led to the actual result, and is entirely satisfied, & indeed professes to be highly gratified.[3]

The N. Hampshire Legislature is in session. That State is so absolutely *safe*, that one may as well laugh, as cry, at the strange management of our friends there, since no degree of imprudence can lose us its votes.

The degree of imprudence, however, which has been manifested, is surpassing. I took the liberty of suggesting to them, one & all, the expediency of bringing Resolutions in the Legislature at once, in which *all friends* could unite. Instead of taking this course, a meeting was called of the "Republican" friends of the Administration, at which Mr Bell[4] presided, & where he & Mr Bartlett & Mr Whipple made speeches.[5]

I send you, herewith, a copy of a letter which I recd. from my brother,[6] two or three days ago, who is a member of the Legislature. Mr Bell's good sense appears to me to have strangely forsaken him. He cannot, I am sure, go one step, without the votes of the Federelists [*sic*]. If he were now a candidate for re-election, it would depend on *them* to say whether he should be chosen. Yet he still adheres to *exclusive caucusses* [*sic*], & *party discipline*. This *party* confidence, & *party* blindness, which are so unworthy of so wise a man, will assuredly defeat all his objects. The *Resolutions* cannot be carried, in the way & by the means Mr Bell & his friends propose. I have before told you of the condition of the Legislature, & of the State, in regard to ancient party divisions; & it will all prove true. This administration meeting *was not* attended by the men of weight & influence, either in the Legislature, or out of it. The *People* are wholly averse to the perpetuation of their old differences; but a *union* meeting would have brought out everybody, of all sides, & carried every thing before it.—Enough of this.— In the end, all will be right, in that essentially *sound* State, tho' there will & must be some previous fermentations.

The New York Nat. Advocate has passed into other hands, & much good is hoped from its future operations.[7]

The Baron Mareuil & family passed yesterday with us. They embark at New York on the first of July. Our latest English dates are still only to the 8th. of May. No vote, indicative of the strength of the new Ministry, had been taken, in either House of Parliament. I am not so positive, as most people seem to be, that the new Premier[8] will achieve an easy triumph over his adversaries; and I cannot say that I feel quite so much interest in his success as I should do, if his feelings were more kind, or I may say, more just towards us— Yours very sincerely & truly

Hon: H. Clay Lexington   DANL. WEBSTER

ALS. DLC-HC (DNA, M212, R2).   1 See above, Toasts and Response, June 20, 1827. 2 See above, June 2, 1827.   3 Elijah Hunt Mills had reportedly addressed letters to his friends, announcing that he wished at the June meeting of the General Court to be

considered a candidate for re-election. *Albany Argus,* June 9, 1827, and cf. above, Clay to Everett, April 5, 1827, note. Upon learning that Webster had been elected in his stead, Mills had written to Webster on June 9, expressing gratification at the latter's election but adding that he had not known Webster's intent to be a candidate. Mills stated that he had been willing to run for the seat to prevent the election of John Mills and lamented that he now appeared "before the public as an unsuccessful candidate for an office which . . . [he] sincerely wished not to hold, and as having incurred an implied vote of censure for . . . past services." Charles M. Wiltse (ed.) and Harold D. Moser (assoc. ed.), *The Papers of Daniel Webster, Correspondence* (Hanover, New Hampshire: University Press of New England, 1974–), II (1976), 216–17.   4 Samuel Bell. Cf. above, Webster to Clay, April 14, 1827, note.   5 Ichabod Bartlett and Thomas Whipple, Jr., who had spoken in Concord, New Hampshire, on June 18.   6 Ezekiel Webster to Daniel Webster, June 17, 1827, published in Wiltse and Moser (eds.), *Papers of Daniel Webster, Correspondence,* II, 218–19. Ezekiel Webster, born in Salisbury, New Hampshire, and graduated in 1804 from Dartmouth College, was an eminent lawyer and for several terms a member of the New Hampshire Legislature. He died suddenly, of a heart attack, at Concord, April 10, 1829.   7 Cf. above, Porter to Clay, May 1, 1827, note.
     8 George Canning. Cf. above, Gallatin to Clay, February 22, 1827, note.

INSTRUCTIONS AND DISPATCHES   June 22, 1827

From JOHN JAMES APPLETON, Stockholm, no. 18. Acknowledges receipt, on May 27, of Clay's letter of April 11, with enclosures, and states that the Count de Wetterstedt informed him "that the act of Congress had been received thro' " Baron Stackelberg. Notes that he has had, since May 15, the date of his last dispatch, eight conferences with Wetterstedt "on the subject of the Treaty" (cf. above, Clay to Appleton, January 12, 1827) but that "In the absence of a trusty conveyance for" his letters, he has "abstained from" informing Clay of what occurred at these meetings. Reports that he and the Count have reached agreement on extension of the old treaty, "with an exception, however, in relation to the article of Salt. . . ." Adds that, if he can carry "this last point the signature of the Treaty will suffer no further delay." ALS. DNA, RG59, Dip. Disp., Sweden and Norway, vol. 5 (M45, R-T6). Published in *American State Papers, Foreign Relations,* VI, 725. Received August 26.

From ALEXANDER H. EVERETT, Madrid, no. 79. Acknowledges receipt of Clay's instructions of March 20 and April 5 and promises to "lose no time in renewing . . . representations" concerning the *Zulmé* and "recognition of our Consul for the Havanna [*sic*]." Reports an interview with "The Minister" (Manuel Gonzáles Salmón), who stated that his proposal, "to admit and recognise at the Havanna the Consuls of all friendly powers" (cf. above, Everett to Clay, June 4, 1827), "had not yet been presented to the Council" and who requested Everett to pen an official note, which would be added to the papers to be submitted. Adds that Salmón, in answer to an inquiry about the effect of Everett's letter to the King (cf. above, Everett to Clay, April 7, 1827), stated that he would soon reply officially to the "note containing that communication," which "had produced a good effect, and that steps would be taken to obtain the decision of the Council upon the Indemnity question within a very short time." Observes that "the Confirmation by the Pope [Leo XII] of the Bishops presented to the principal Sees in Columbia [*sic*] and Peru" (cf. above, Everett to Clay, March 31, 1827) has created "a great sensation" in Madrid and appeared to take "the Government in some measure by surprise." Discusses the timing and manner of the announcement; notes that Salmón requested the new Papal Nuncio (Francesco Tiberi) not to enter Spain "for the present" or to withdraw, if already there, and that "The latter has in consequence returned to France"; and predicts "that the difficulty will be easily adjusted through the mediation of France and terminate without producing any serious results." Summarizes "news . . . of a Ministerial Revolution in Portugal by the effect of which the Marquis of Palmella now Ambassador at London has been appointed Minister of Foreign Affairs (cf. below, Lawrence to Clay, October 13, 1827). Credits "the Minister of War Saldanha" with re-forming the administration, which is "understood to be more decidedly partial to the Constitution. . . ." LS. DNA, RG59, Dip. Disp., Spain, vol. 27 (M31, R28). Received August 22.

Monsignor Tiberi, archbishop of Athens, who was accepted as nuncio at Madrid in 1828, has not been further identified.

Pedro de Sousa Holstein, Duke of Palmella, born in Turin and reared in diplomatic circles, had accompanied the Portuguese Court to Brazil in 1820 and upon its return to Lisbon in 1823. Named Minister of State in the latter year, he was identified with the proponents of the Constitution of John VI and Pedro IV. During the Miguellite upheaval of 1828, Palmella returned to England and organized expeditions in support of Maria da Gloria. He subsequently was named to the presidency of the Council of Ministers from 1834 to 1836, again in 1842, and yet again in 1846. Forced to flee the country in October, 1846, he retired from politics and devoted his remaining years to writing.

João Carlos Gregório Domingues Vicente Francisco de Saldanha Oliveira e Daun had become a general while serving with the Portuguese forces in Brazil and had been governor of the Province of Rio Grande del Sur in 1821. Returning to Portugal in 1822, he had been military governor of Oporto from 1825 to 1826 and in the latter year had assumed the portfolio of Minister of War under the regency of Isabel Maria. An ardent defender of the constitution, he had been forced by ill health to relinquish his office from January to June, 1827. His return to power, marked as a triumph of liberalism, was brief. He was dismissed in July. He was active in leading the forces of Maria against Miguel but spent much of the period of Miguellite dominance in exile. For his services to Maria in this struggle he was accorded the titles of Marquis and Marshal after the fall of Miguel, in 1834. For a few months in 1835 he again held the Ministry of War and became president of the Council of State. In 1846 Maria conferred on him the title of Duke and called on him to establish a ministry in which he held the portfolio of Foreign Affairs. He was dismissed the following year, served for a time as Ambassador to Madrid, but returned before the end of the year again to the presidency of the Council, an office he held until 1849, subsequently from 1851 to 1856, and again in 1870. He served as Portuguese Ambassador to Paris from 1860 to 1869 and to London from 1870 until his death in 1876.

From WILLIAM TAYLOR, Veracruz, "Private." Reports that (John) Sergeant is near Veracruz awaiting the arrival of the brig *Eliza* (cf. above, Sergeant and Poinsett to Clay, June 14, 1827). Notes receipt of a letter from (Joel R.) Poinsett, who states that he has requested permission to return home in the fall. Observes that Poinsett has "been unpleasantly situated for some time past." Relates the circumstances attending an assault by the Lieutenant Governor of the Castle of Ulloa (not identified) upon the persons of Thomas Boldock, the captain of the British brig *Swallow*, and of the British vice consul (J. Welsh). Observes that he has remonstrated against "such abominable proceedings—not as the advocate of this or that person, but as threatening the peace and tranquility [*sic*] of all foreigners" and that the civil authorities were sympathetic but, as in former times, too fearful of the military to give satisfaction for the attack. Predicts that the Mexican Government will issue something like an apology, "but nothing more." ALS. DNA, RG59, Cons. Disp., Veracruz, vol. 1 (M183, R1).

Boldock and Welsh have not been further identified.

Greeting, Response, and Toast

[Steubenville, Ohio, June 23, 1827]

SIR:—On behalf of the workmen of this manufactory, I bid you welcome. We have long wished for an opportunity of tendering our respects personally to the untired advocate of domestic industry, which in you sir, we recognise.— We thank you for the zeal you have always manifested in behalf of a system, in which not only we, but the great mass of the citizens of Ohio, and of the west, feel deeply interested. When the policy of foreign nations has deprived our farmers of a market abroad for their products, they naturally look to the "American system" to supply its place; *they will feed us, we will clothe them,* and thus a home market will be created and an interchange of labour take place over which foreign nations will have no control. Although the woollen manufacture is at this time in a state of great depression; yet we look forward to no very distant day, when the government will (as in the case with cotton,)[1] render it effectual protection; and thus secure profitable employment to our manufacturers, and an invaluable market to the farmers and wool growers of the west.

[Clay's reply was locally reported as follows:]

After tendering his thanks for the kind reception he had met with, Mr Clay observed, that we had far overrated his exertions in behalf of the American system. He said that he had only been a humble co-operator with others, in that great cause; and adverted, particularly, to the exertions of the Ohio delegation and of our immediate representative in congress (Mr. Wright)[2]—but that we did him no more than justice in ascribing to him consistency, zeal and perseverance in its support. He further observed, that the station he now occupied, precluded him from any interference with legislative proceedings—but gave assurance that, in whatever situation he might be placed, we might always expect his cordial support of the American system. He lamented the present depressed state of the woollen manufacture and of the raw material, and expressed it as his opinion and conviction that this depression was owing to inadequat [sic] protection by Congress, and that he had no doubt but that the errors of legislation in that particular, would at no distant period, be corrected by a future legislature.

.   .   .   .

Mr. Clay, with other gentlemen present, were then invited by Mr Semple, in behalf of the workmen, to the table, provided with a variety of refreshments, where the company drank to the following toast of Mr Semple,

"The American system and its friends."[3]

Lexington *Kentucky Reporter,* July 11, 1827. The greeting was presented by Samuel Semple, a weaver, at the Wells and Dickinson Woolen Manufacturing Company, otherwise known as the Steubenville Woolen Mills, operated by Bezaleel Wells and William R. Dickinson.

1 That is, cotton goods. Cf. above, III, 756n.   2 John C. Wright.   3 Following this meeting, Clay visited several other manufacturing establishments in and near Steubenville before attending the public dinner reported below, this date.

Toasts at Steubenville Public Dinner

[June 23, 1827]

HENRY CLAY—We have met, not to flatter him, but to testify our admiration of his splendid talents, our gratitude for his indefatigable and successful efforts in the cause of Internal Improvements and Domestic Manufactures, and our entire confidence in the purity and correctness of his political course!

[Clay responded with a speech, "of about half an hour in length in his own superior style,"[1] and concluded by offering the following toast:]

The green clad hills of this beautiful region of country, their flocks and their fleeces.

Lexington *Kentucky Reporter*, July 11, 1827. "About 3 P.M. an assemblage of not less than 130 citizens of the place and the immediate vicinity, together with a number of distinguished gentlemen from Pittsburgh, Wheeling and the neighboring towns, sat down with Mr. Clay to a public dinner . . . at the Washington Hall, at which Bezaleel Wells, Esq. presided, assisted by N. Dike, Esq. A Sutherland, Esq. and Col. David Sloane Vice Presidents. A number of guests were invited, among whom were the Messrs. J[ames]. Ross, sr. and jr. [Henry] Holdship, and Craig, of Pittsburgh, and Mr. Bayard, of Wheeling." James Ross, Jr., at this time a very young man, was admitted to the bar but never practiced. Neville B. Craig, born near Pittsburgh and educated at Princeton College, had been admitted to the bar in 1810, was city solicitor from 1821 to 1829, and subsequently served in the Pennsylvania Legislature. He was most noted as the editor from 1829 to 1841 of the *Pittsburgh Gazette*, founded in 1786 and renowned as a Federalist organ. Bayard has not been further identified.

1 Not further reported.

To John Quincy Adams

Dear Sir   Steubenville 23d. June, 1827.

I have been received on this side of the Mountains with much more cordiality than I anticipated. I dine for the fourth time and at the fourth place to day, at a public dinner.[1] Crowds & eschorts [sic] have every where attended me, so as to leave me no command of myself or of my time. The dinner at Pittsburg [sic] exceeded any thing I ever witnessed of that sort. More than 500 dined at the public tables, and many could not find places. Upwards of 700 listened to a Speech which I addressed them, and which they repeatedly interrupted by long and enthusiastic bursts of applause

Our friends are divided in opinion as to the fact whether the Administration has *at this time* a majority in Western Pennsa. They are all agreed that, if there be no adverse tide, it will have the majority before the election. I find that it is among the new converts (of whom there are many) that doubt as to the present state of the fact most prevails. My opinion is that the Administration is stronger than is believed. Our friends are taking courage and coming out openly, and courage is what they wanted. They think that my visit will inspire confidence. Marks, Lawrence and Stewart[2] (each of whom was at the dinner of the place of his residence) have now openly committed themselves. The effect of the favorable opinion at Harrisburg[3] is manifest. Almost every officer holding his appointment from Govr. Shulze[4] (the Prothonotary [sic] &c &c &c) and they are generally the most efficient persons of their respective villages, are decided & open in support of the Administration.

The Mess Rapps[5] attended the dinner at Pittsburg, and were among the most delighted persons in the assemblage.

I hope to be able to descend the river in a Steam boat from Wheeling tomorrow.[6] I am with great respect Your ob. Servant   H CLAY
Mr. Adams.

ALS. MHi-Adams Papers, Letters Recd. (MR481).
[1] Cf. above, Toast, June 15, 1827; Toasts and Speech, June 20, 21, 1827; Greeting, this date; Toasts, this date.   [2] William Marks; Joseph Lawrence; Andrew Stewart.
[3] Cf. above, Crowninshield to Clay, March 14, 1827; Lacock to Clay, March 27, 1827; Markley to Clay, May 19, 1827; Clay to Everett, May 22, 1827.   [4] John A. Shulze.
[5] George Rapp and his adopted son, Frederick (né Reichert). The latter handled the business affairs of the Harmony Society. He had been a representative to the Indiana constitutional convention, in 1816, and an officer in the organization of several Indiana banks.   [6] Clay left Wheeling, June 24, on board the *Reindeer*, a vessel of 60 tons, built at Brownsvania, in 1826.

From Richard Rush

My dear Sir,   Washington June 23. 1827.

I have just read Lord Grey's speech[1] and cannot resist the desire I feel to send it to you. You will recognise in it sentiments I have expressed as regards Mr Canning and the new states. If Earl Grey had been better informed, he would have said that it was *you* who did most to call them into being. I say this in no idle spirit of praise, having always abroad and at home expressed the opinion that, next to their own exertions, the South Americans owe to you more than to any other man in either hemisphere their independence, you having led the way to our acknowledgment of it.[2] This is truth; this is history. Without our acknowledgment, England would not have taken the step to this day.[3] This is my belief. I give Mr Canning no credit for the part he acted. It was forced upon him by our lead, which he never had the magnanimity to avow, but strove to claim all the merit for England, or rather for himself. He esteems civil and political liberty no more than Lord Londonderry[4] did, though circumstances have made him appear to be somewhat more their champion. That *our* publick should be inclined to rejoice at Mr Cannings present triumph, is, I think the effect of his character not being understood among us.

Certainly, as regards the United states, he has been of all British statesmen the least disposed to do us justice; yes truly, the least of any that
ever we have had to deal with, without a single exception. Forgetting
if we can all that he has *said* of us, let us take his acts; for was it not *he*
who disavowed Erskine's arrangement, which, had it been sanctioned
in England, might have prevented a war?[5] was it not *he* who in 1823
infused the unfriendly tone into that long negotiation at London, almost refusing to listen to nine out of ten of our claims, obviously just
as the most of them were?[6] and was it not *he* who in 1826 most abruptly
closed the West India trade against us, upon pretexts the most unexpected and flimsy?[7] I could make the list longer, but that I should
make too long a letter of it, having intended to do nothing more than
send you Lord Grey's speech. I know how high you rate his speeches.
Mr Canning never liked the U. States or their institutions, and never
will; his Liverpool speech,[8] and the conclusion of his late despatch,[9]
notwithstanding. He will watch all our steps with a sharper and more
active jealousy, than perhaps any other English statesman living. Of
all their publick men *we* have the least to expect from him—Adieu—
Most Sincerely yours my dear Sir, RICHARD RUSH.
Mr Clay.

ALS. DLC-HC (DNA, M212, R2).
1 Charles Grey, second Earl Grey, Viscount Howick, and Baron Grey, born in Northumberland and educated at Cambridge University, had represented his birthplace in Parliament from 1786 to 1807 as an outstanding Whig leader and proponent of constitutional
reform. He had been First Lord of the Admiralty in 1806 and Secretary for Foreign
Affairs in 1806–1807; but when the Whig ministry fell on the issue of admitting Catholics into the Army and Navy, he had left office and remained out of power for the next
24 years. His accession to the peerage had brought him into the House of Lords in 1808,
and there he continued his leadership of the demands for governmental reform and
Catholic rights. He opposed Canning for both his conduct of foreign affairs and his views
on the Catholic question. Grey finally assumed formation of a ministry in 1830 and
held office until 1834. Grey's speech in the House of Lords on May 10, 1827, had assailed
Canning's motives in relation to Latin America as "looking only to some beneficial commercial intercourse" without regard for feelings of "natural right and national independence." He termed as an "idle" and "empty boast" Canning's claim that he had
"called the New World into existence to redress the balance of the Old" (cf. above,
Lafayette to Clay, December 29, 1826). The Latin-American states, Grey asserted, "were
called into existence by their own exertions—they were called into existence by the example of the United States of America—they were called and nurtured into existence
by the united wishes and encouragement of the people of this country [Great Britain]."
Meanwhile, Grey noted, Canning had been assuring Spain that her separation from her
colonies was a consequence of events "in which Great Britain took no part . . ." (cf. above,
McRae to Clay, December 13, 1825). Hansard (comp.), *Parliamentary Debates*, New
Series, XVII, 727–29. 2 Cf. above, II, 512–41; Forbes to Clay, July 1, 1825. 3 For
England's recognition of South American Governments, see above, Nelson to Secretary
of State, March 8, 1825, note. 4 Castlereagh. 5 Canning, as British Secretary
of State for Foreign Affairs in 1809, had repudiated the agreement made by David M.
Erskine. Cf. above, I, 746, note 6. 6 Probably a reference to the protracted negotiations on which Rush had been engaged in London over a wide gamut of topics—prohibition of the slave trade, commercial intercourse with the West Indies, boundary
disputes, fisheries, and maritime rights. The conferences, under instructions dated in
June, 1823, had not begun until January 23, 1824, and had been broken off as generally
unsuccessful on July 28, 1824. 7 Cf. above, Gallatin to Clay, August 19, 1826.
8 At a public dinner in the townhall of Liverpool, August 25, 1823, Canning had toasted
the health of Christopher Hughes with congratulations on the "full and uninterrupted
intercourse" between the United States and Britain. R[oger] Therry (comp.), *The*

Speeches of George Canning with a Memoir of His Life (6 vols.; London, 1828), VI, 413–14. On Hughes' visit to Britain, cf. above, Hughes to Clay, January 30, 1827, note 14.

⁹ Canning's letter to Gallatin, January 27, 1827, summarized in Gallatin to Clay, January 28, 1827, note.

INSTRUCTIONS AND DISPATCHES   June 23, 1827

From ALBERT GALLATIN, London, no. 88. Encloses a copy of "the draft of Protocol," handed to him by (Henry U.) Addington on June 21, of their "next preceding Conference" (cf. above, Gallatin to Clay, June 20, 1827). States that it includes "mention . . . of the intended British declaration, to be annexed to the renewal of the 3d Article of the Convention of 1818"; that at the "Conference of yesterday" he "said . . . that, if the British plenipotentiaries insisted on having the Protocol expressed in that manner, . . . [he] would decline altogether agreeing to the renewal"; and that "They agreed that the drawing of the Protocol should be suspended until" that subject had been disposed of. Encloses also copies of "two papers" which he gave the plenipotentiaries and which contain "the substance" of his "objections both to the declaration and to the proposed additional article of the Commercial Convention." Notes that the British negotiators intend giving "a definitive answer on both subjects . . . on Tuesday next 26th instant." Observes that they next turned to "the subject of the North East boundary and made some progress." Acknowledges, in a postscript, receipt of Clay's "despatches of 12th & 15th May Nos 28 & 29." Adds: "The No. 24 [above, March 29, 1827] is still missing." ALS. DNA, RG59, Dip. Disp., Great Britain, vol. 34 (M30, R30). Published in *American State Papers, Foreign Relations*, VI, 677–78. Received August 26, 1827.

From H[ENRY] MIDDLETON, St. Petersburg, no. 70. Reports that a fleet, including "nine sail of the line" and other vessels, sailed from Kronstadt two days earlier, bound for some English port, whence a part of it will proceeed "when joined by a British Squadron, to the Mediterranean Sea. . . ." Observes that this tends "to confirm the rumor that England Russia & France have engaged by Treaty [cf. below, Brown to Clay, July 12, 1827] to co-operate with a view to the pacification of the East" but that the conditions of the treaty "& what limits may have been marked out to the ambition of the contracting parties" are not yet clear. Notes that the treaty powers plan to cut Turkey off from her island possessions and Africa and to starve Constantinople into submission, but questions whether Austria, England, or France will allow Constantinople to fall into Russian hands.

States that "the Persian war [cf. above, Middleton to Clay, September 17, 1826, and note] appears to be faintly carried on" and that the Russian provinces "beyond Caucasus are suffering severely from famine." Includes, in a postscript, an extract of the protocol which the Duke of Wellington signed on his visit to St. Petersburg, mentioned in dispatch no. 60 (above, June 13, 1826). ALS. DNA, RG59, Dip. Disp., Russia, vol. 11 (M35, R11). Copy, in MHi-Adams Papers, Letters Recd. (MR481). Dated June 11/23, 1827; received September 8.

From WILLIAM H. D. C. WRIGHT, Rio de Janeiro. Cites a "general opinion . . . that a Peace will be concluded" between Brazil "And Buenos Ayres in a short time." Notes that (Manuel José) García has sailed for Buenos Aires on a British warship, "bearing with him the Emperor's [Peter I's] proposals for peace and such is the disaffected state of the interior provinces of Buenos Ayres, that it is thought she will be compelled to accept his terms. . . ." Adds that he has heard nothing further on the French Minister's (the Marquis de Gabriac's) demands (cf. above, Wright to Clay, May 25, 1827). ALS. DNA, RG59, Cons. Disp., Rio de Janeiro, (M-T172, R3). Received August 7.

From JAMES MAURY, Liverpool. States that, "Last winter," he guaranteed a bill for $500 drawn on Clay by (Edward) Weyer, after Maury, Latham and Company first had refused to accept it, and that he has "just heard this bill has been protested for non-payment." Acknowledges that he was not authorized to make the advance on "public account" but remarks that he acted only because Weyer was "a public messenger from our Government to this"; submits the case "to the liberality of our Government. . . : and, to . . . [Clay] the propriety of laying it before the President." ALS. DNA, RG59, Cons. Disp., Liverpool, vol. 4 (M141, R4).

From TIMOTHY PITKIN, Farmington (Connecticut). States that he is "Contemplating to present to the public, Sketches of the *political & civil* History of the United States" and requests "permission to examine some papers in . . . [Clay's] office, particularly those, heretofore ordered by Congress, to be published" (cf. above, Sparks to Clay, January 31, 1827, note). ALS. DNA, RG59, Misc. Letters (M179, R65).

Daniel Brent acknowledged, on June 29, receipt of this letter and informed Pitkin "that the Records of letters from our Ministers in Europe, during the period of the Revolutionary War, were lately put into the hands of the Revd. Mr. Jared Sparks, to make the selection for publication, contemplated by the Resolution of Congress. . . , and that Mr. Sparks . . . has carried these Records to Boston." He added that "The original letters . . . remain upon file" and that he presumes "the Secretary would be glad to extend to . . . [Pitkin] every accommodation, compatible with their not being withdrawn from the office, . . . tho' a reference to or an examination of them, in this way, must *necessarily* be found less agreeable and easy than in the Records." Copy, in DNA, RG59, Dom. Letters, vol. 21, p. 567 (M40, R19).

Pitkin published *A Political and Civil History of the United States of America from the Year 1763 to the Close of the Administration of President Washington. . .*, in two volumes, at New Haven in 1828.

Post Note to George Graham

24 June 1827.

Pay to Geo. Graham or order on the 3d. July next the sum of Two hundred and fifty dollars.   H. CLAY
Cashr. of the Off. B. U. S. Washington.[1]

ADS. DLC-TJC (DNA, M212, R16). Endorsed (AES) on verso: "Rcd. $236 63/100 Geo. Graham." Cf. above, Graham to Clay, May 12, 1827.
[1] Richard Smith.

Check to Richard Simms

Wheeling 24th June 1827

Pay to Richard Simms or order Twenty five dollars.
Cashr. of the Off. B. U. States Washington.[1]   H. CLAY

ADS. DLC-TJC (DNA, M212, R16). Endorsed on verso by Simms, who may have been a hotel proprietor.
[1] Richard Smith.

From Henry Clay, Jr.

Dr. father   W. Point—24h. June—27

I arrived here last Thursday the 21st. and have already been examined and I am glad to add have been admitted— Yesterday we came into camp; and I am now in my tent sitting on my knapsack and writing on my chair— I am better pleased than ever with the Academy— I was well recd. by the officers on my return and now start with the prospect of success hereafter— Am delighted with the hardships accompanying a military life but still give the civil the preference— My duties will prevent my writing more, although I had intended to have written a long letter concerning the discipline and course of study in use here   Give my respects to all my relations and friends— Tell Cousin Nannette[1] that I am daily expecting an answer to my letter which was written before I left Washington   believe me your grateful son   HENRY CLAY JR
H. C.

ALS. Henry Clay Memorial Foundation, Lexington, Kentucky.
[1] Nannette Price (Mrs. Thomas) Smith.

INSTRUCTIONS AND DISPATCHES   June 24, 1827

From JAMES OMBROSI, Florence. Cites, as "A fresh instance" of difficulties occasioned by refusal of the Tuscan Government to grant him "the Royal Exequatur" and "to acknowledge the due authority of American Consular Certificates in papers of this description," the case arising from an application made by "Mr. Geraume Patterson [*i.e.*, Jerome Napoleon Bonaparte] of Baltimore" to him "as Consul to give a voucher to certify to a power of attorney in favor of Mrs. Patterson [Elizabeth Patterson Bonaparte], his mother. . . ." Adds that when the "public Notary," who had witnessed Patterson's document, attempted "to have it deposited in the General Archives of Contracts of the City of Florence" and to have copies made for Mrs. Patterson's use, the Recorder refused to enter it, to allow copies to be made, and to return it. States that he has offered to have his "Certificate annulled," but the matter has not been settled. Notes that he has given "Mrs. Patterson a Certificate that the aforesaid instrument has actually been filed in the Office of General Archives" and that this step has been approved by Judge [Joseph] Hemphill of Pennsylvania, now in Florence, who "has kindly taken charge of this letter" and who may be consulted for additional information. Suggests "that some method should be devised whereby the Royal Exequatur should be obtained, and the power of the American Consulate here be duly recognized." ALS. DNA, RG59, Cons. Disp., Florence, vol. 1 (M-T204, R1). Received September 29.

To Charles Hammond

My dear Sir   (Confidential)   Ohio river Reindeer. 25 June 1827.

On passing Wheeling yesterday (where I slept only abt. an hour) I learnt that Carter Beverly had recd. the preceding evening a letter from Genl. J. which was then in Mr. Zane's[1] possession. I went to his house and perused the original letter in the hand writing of Genl. J. Mr. Zane furnished me with a Copy of it, and also a Copy of a letter which he had recd. from C. Berley² [*sic*], and I send you herewith Copies of both those Copies.

On my arriving in K. it is my intention to address a note to the public denying the charges and demanding the proof &c; and at the same time to publish the above Copies.³ I do not therefore wish them to be published by you, until they reach you through some other channel.⁴ I send you copies now that you may have the earliest intelligence.

I could not have wished the affair to take a more favorable turn. If it do not end in degrading Genl. Jackson, I am greatly deceived as to the character of the American public.

My reception in W. Pennsa was marked by the greatest cordiality. At Pittsburgh it was enthusiastic.⁵ I send you a paper⁶ from that City containing the a/c. which will probably be the first that reaches you.

I do not expect to remain long (not more than about a fortnight or three weeks) in K.

It is so difficult to write on board a Steam boat in motion that I will only add that I am   Truly Your friend   H. CLAY
C. Hammond Esq

ALS. InU.
¹ Andrew Jackson; Noah Zane. Jackson's letter to Beverley, variously dated as June 5 or 6, 1827, repeated and elaborated the charge made earlier by Beverley (cf. above, Report of Interview, *ca.* April 15, 1827, note). The date of June 5 appears on the letter as published in Bassett (ed.), *Correspondence of Andrew Jackson*, III, 355–57, based upon an unidentified transcript; that of June 6 appears on the version published in the Lexington *Kentucky Reporter*, July 4, 1827, based on Zane's transcript.   ² Carter Beverley to Zane, June 24, 1827. Announcing receipt of Jackson's letter, Beverley declared: "He [Jackson] most unequivocally confirms all I have said regarding the overture made to him pending the last Presidential election before Congress; and, he asserts a great deal more than he told me; going most circumstantially and minutely into the business. It was always his intention, he says, that if Mr Clay ever denied the facts, to give him up his authority. It is of the first character, and order, in our government and country. It only awaits Mr. Clay's denial now; the whole subject will then be brought to issue before the public." Lexington *Kentucky Reporter*, July 4, 1827.   ³ See below, Address to the Public, June 29, 1827. The above-mentioned copies were published with the Address in the Lexington *Kentucky Reporter*, July 4, 1827.   ⁴ The Address and copies of the letters were published in the *Liberty Hall and Cincinnati Gazette* on July 6, 1827, reprinted from the Lexington *Kentucky Reporter*.   ⁵ Cf. above, Toast and Speech, June 20, 1827; Clay to Adams, June 23, 1827.   ⁶ Probably the *Pittsburgh Gazette*.

To John Armstrong and Others

Maysville, June 26.

GENTLEMEN.—To be met at the very moment of touching the soil of Kentucky, by congratulations so friendly and respectful, and by an invitation so cordial and honorable, as those which are contained in your note¹ which I have this moment had the honor to receive, fills me with emotions which are absolutely inexpressible. I thank my fellow citizens of Maysville, again and again, for these hearty demonstrations of their confidence and attachment. They add to the many heavy obligations under which they have heretofore placed me. Their kindness and approbation are among the best consolations for the bitterness and malignity by which I have been and yet continue to be assailed.

My visit to Kentucky was for the natural purpose of paying necessary attention to my private affairs. If it afford me the opportunity of seeing and renewing professions of mutual attachment with my fellow citizens, I shall not be deterred from indulging in that gratification, by the fear or the denunciation of my enemies. I regret, however, that jaded as I now am by my journey and some of its agreeable incidents, and being moreover anxious to reach home, I cannot at this time, accept of the invitation to dinner which has been so handsomely and kindly tendered me. I will endeavor, on my return to my official duties, to have the honor of dining with my fellow citizens of Maysville, if at that time it should suit their convenience. In the mean time, I pray you to assure them of my very great sensibility to the kind and distinguished manner with which they have greeted my arrival. Tell them, that although my enemies are resolved to spare no exertion to destroy my public character, I will triumph over all their machinations, because truth is omnipotent, and public justice certain.

With assurances of my high regard and esteem for you, gentlemen, collectively as well as individually, I pray you to accept those also of my being, most truly, Your faithful and obedient servant,

H. CLAY.

MESSRS. *John Armstrong, Francis Taylor, James Morrison, Tho: G. Richardson, Peter Grant,[2] Sam. January, John Wood, Thomas Newman,[3] John Brown, Wilson Coburn, John T. Langhorne, Rich'd. Henry Lee.[4]*

Lexington *Kentucky Reporter*, July 4, 1827.   [1] Below, this date.
[2] Thomas G. Richardson was a physician, one of the founders of the Kentucky State Medical Society in 1851. Peter Grant, born in Connecticut, had settled at Maysville around 1807, was a partner of Armstrong as a salt merchant, also owned a tannery, and was reportedly "one of the wealthiest men of the West." U[lysess] S. Grant, *Personal Memoirs* . . . (2 vols.; New York, 1885–1886), I, 18–19. He drowned on the Kanawha River in 1829.   [3] Wood and Newman have not been identified as residents of this locale.
[4] Lee, a notary in Mason County in 1819, became editor of the Maysville *Eagle* from 1828 to 1830 and of the Cincinnati *Daily Commercial* from 1852 until his death in 1853. In the interim he was a member of the Kentucky Legislature in 1832, mayor of Maysville for a number of years, and an employee of the United States Treasury Department in 1851.

From John Armstrong and Others

HON. HENRY CLAY: *Maysville, June 26* [1827].

SIR—The undersigned, a committee in behalf of the citizens of Maysville, respectfully greet your arrival upon the borders of the state of your adoption, and invite you to partake of a public dinner at Capt.

Langhorne's Hotel,[1] on such a day as your engagements will enable you to gratify them with your presence.

The committee are not unmindful of the fact, that at the present period of political excitement and vituperation, your visit to Kentucky has been ascribed to a *political movement*, with a view of sustaining what is termed by the public journals of the opposition, *"a hopeless cause."*[2] This denunciation, however, given as it is in advance, shall not deter your fellow citizens from the free and unreserved expression of that attachment and undiminished regard they feel for your character as a legislator, a diplomatist and a citizen.

In a government like ours, where disappointment must necessarily follow competition for office, it is expected that the disappointed aspirants for power will give free scope to their splenetic animadversions. The good, the virtuous and the great, will be subjected alike to their indiscriminate censure and unqualified abuse. Under such circumstances as these, it was not unexpected by the committee that the course which duty prompted you to pursue in the choice of a President by the house of representatives,[3] would have subjected you to the lash of 'the scorpion hearted race' who live & batten on detraction. But they confess they were unprepared to meet the foul and calumniating charges of '*intrigue*' and '*corruption*,' which have been cast upon you by those who have either *imagined* or *felt* themselves injured by your vote. In common with the great mass of their fellow citizens of the United States, they have called for *the proof*—and the call has been answered by the reception of vague surmises and idle rumors—reiterated with a recklessness of spirit without a parallel in this republic.

But it is your fortune and your glory, sir, that you live in such times, and possess such exalted worth, that the envy of those whose duty it is to applaud you, can receive no other consolation than by withholding those praises in public, which all honest men, in private, acknowledge you have deserved.

We tender to you, individually, and in behalf of the citizens of Maysville, the renewed assurances of our highest regard and esteem.

JOHN ARMSTRONG,	JOHN WOOD,
FRANCIS TAYLOR,	THOMAS NEWMAN,
JAMES MORRISON	JOHN BROWN,
THO: G. RICHARDSON,	WILSON COBURN,
PETER GRANT,	JOHN T. LANGHORNE,
SAMUEL JANUARY,	RICHARD HENRY LEE.

Lexington *Kentucky Reporter*, July 4, 1827.

[1] Maurice Langhorne in 1823 had opened a tavern in Maysville, where Lafayette had been entertained two years later.   [2] The quoted reference has not been found. Opposition journals generally interpreted Clay's return to Kentucky as an electioneering maneuver, designed to influence events in areas traversed. See Washington *United States Telegraph*, April 4, 1827; *Albany Argus*, July 2, 6, 31, 1827.   [3] Cf. above, Clay to Brooke, January 28, 1825.

INSTRUCTIONS AND DISPATCHES   June 26, 1827

From ALBERT GALLATIN, London, no. 89. Informs Clay that "The heir presumptive, the Duke of Clarence, being now Lord High Admiral, . . . [he] thought that
the object of . . . [Clay's] despatch No. 28 [above, May 12, 1827] would be better
promoted by communicating it to him, rather than to the Foreign Office, where it
would remain on the shelf without producing any effect." Encloses a copy of his
letter to (John Wilson) Croker, "requesting him . . . to lay" a copy of Clay's
dispatch before the Duke. Adds: "An inquiry is set on foot to obtain the document
mentioned in your dispatch No. 29 [above, May 15, 1827]." ALS. DNA, RG59, Dip.
Disp., Great Britain, vol. 34 (M30, R30). Duplicate, in MHi-Adams Papers, Letters
Recd. (MR481). Received August 26.

From JOHN MULLOWNY, Tangier, no. 50. Describes an incident in which an officer
from a Colombian national vessel anchored in the bay, "on attempting to land,
was violently opposed by the Spanish Consul" (not identified), whose opposition
was successful until the Colombian revealed that a letter he wished to deliver to
"the American Consul" contained "one for the Bashaw [probably Mohamet
Omemon]," who was absent at the time. Adds that the acting Governor (probably
Sidi Hamet Temsumany, not further identified), upon receiving the letter, was
threatened by the Spaniard; that both of these men sent couriers to the Emperor
(Abd-er-Rahman II), who reportedly replied in a peremptory manner to the consul. Quotes a letter, dated June 20 and signed by Mohamet Omemon, written in
response to one directed to the Bashaw by Captain John Maitland, of a "Colombian Brig of War," stating, by direction of the Emperor: "you shall be permitted
to enter our dominions most willingly with all respects and protection, with your
vessels, and to send us your Consul. . . , also we will form treaties. . . ." ALS. DNA,
RG59, Cons. Dip., Tangier, vol. 4 (M-T61, R4). Received August 28.
    In an addition to the duplicate of this dispatch, Mullowny states that his ab-
sence, "some few miles in the country," when the above described incident occurred, prevented his challenging the behavior of the Spanish consul.

DIPLOMATIC NOTES   June 27, 1827

From the BARON DE MAREUIL, New York. Acknowledges receipt of Clay's letter of
May 26 (*i.e.*, 25); notes that the President's reception of the observations contained in his note to Clay, of May 16, leads him to hope they may bear fruit in
more reciprocally advantageous stipulations tbetween the two governments; refers
again to disadvantages suffered by French wines and silks exported to the United
States; and, believing that the President found in the letter of May 16 overtures
that seemed desirable, states his expectation that the United States Minister in
France (James Brown) has received instructions to prepare the way for "une
négotiation décisive." ALS, in French. DNA, RG59, Notes from French Legation,
vol. 10 (M53, R-T9).

INSTRUCTIONS AND DISPATCHES   June 27, 1827

From ALBERT GALLATIN, London, no. 90. Notes that "yesterday's Conference" (with
William Huskisson and Henry U. Addington) returned to "the same subjects"
discussed on June 22 (cf. above, Gallatin to Clay, June 23, 1827). Reports that he
replied to a suggestion by Huskisson, "that an article might be framed, respecting
the meaning of the words 'like articles' in the commercial Convention," by ques-

tioning whether one "could be so expressed as to permit" agreement and by observing "that if it was really believed that our discriminating duty between rolled and hammered iron was an infraction of the Convention [cf. above, Gallatin to Clay, February 24, June 20, 1827], it was extraordinary that the importers had never brought the case before the Courts. . . ."

Summarizes "A new suggestion . . . respecting the renewal of the agreement for the joint occupancy of the territory west of the Stony Mountains," pointing out that "The British Plenipotentiaries had it in contemplation to insert in the Protocol, a declaration purporting either that, according to their understanding of the agreement neither party had a right to take military possession of the Country, or that if the United States did establish any military posts in the Country, Great Britain would do the same." States that he replied that he "could not agreee to the renewal of the agreement, if accompanied with the insertion in the Protocol of any declaration purporting to attach any construction or interpretation whatever to the agreement" and that, if the British Government wished "to signify their determination of establishing military posts in that Country, in case it, [sic] was done by the United States," that determination should not be communicated by means of the protocol but through regular diplomatic channels. Notes that, following further discussion, in the course of which he stated his preference for "a simple renewal of the agreement, and nothing more," the "British Plenipotentiaries said that there was such an avowed intention on the part of the United States to establish a military post, that they thought, that they could not agree to a renewal of the former agreement, without making at the same time some declaration on that point, but that they would again consider the subject before they came to a definitive determination." Concludes: "We had afterwards a long conversation on the subject of the general map of the surveys of the North Eastern boundary. But we have not yet begun to discuss any of the other topics embraced by the informal Projet of Convention. I only understand that they have prepared a Counter Projet." ALS. DNA, RG59, Dip. Disp., Great Britain, vol. 34 (M30, R30). Published in *American State Papers, Foreign Relations*, VI, 680. Received August 26.

A bill authorizing United States "occupation of the Columbia or Oregon river" had passed the House of Representatives on December 23, 1824, but had been tabled in the Senate. President Adams having recommended such action in his first Annual Message, a bill "to authorize establishment of a military post . . . on the Pacific Ocean" had again been reported in the House on January 16, 1826. The measure had not come to a vote. Another bill to authorize occupation of the "Oregon river" was reported in the House on December 18, 1827, and finally rejected on January 9, 1829. U. S. H. of Reps., *Journal*, 18 Cong. 2 Sess., p. 78; 19 Cong., 1 Sess., p. 156; 20 Cong., 1 Sess., p. 65; 20 Cong., 2 Sess., pp. 140–41; Richardson (comp.), *Messages and Papers of the Presidents. . .* , II, 313.

From WILLIAM B. HODGSON, Algiers, no. 89. States that, since transmitting his dispatch of May 8, he is "without intelligence" concerning "the Consul General" (William Shaler). Encloses "a transcript of the Journal of the Consulate from the 1st of May, to the present date," which "records a State of Hostilities . . . between this Regency and France . . ." (cf. above, Brown to Clay, May 29, 1827, note). Summarizes the course of events that has led to the blockade of the port by a French squadron and to various acts of defiance by the Bashaw (Hosséin). ALS. DNA,, RG59, Cons. Disp., Algiers, vol. 11 (M23, R-T13). Received September 8.

From BEAUFORT T. WATTS, Bogotá, no. 31. Transmits copies of his recent diplomatic correspondence with Colombian officials, including that relating to his "letter to the President [Simón Bolívar]" (cf. above, Watts to Clay, June 14, 1827) and to the case of the *Josephine* (cf. above, Clay to Watts, March 8, 1827). States that, "In consequence of the unsettled State of the country," he will not avail himself of permission to take leave "until the arrival of the President who is expected in August. . . ." Expresses confidence that Bolívar "will tranquilize the various parties that now divide and distract the Country" and predicts, if he fails, "A seperation [*sic*] of the three great Provinces, Quito, Cundinamarca and Venezuela, into independent States. . . ." Notes that "The present system of government . . . has proved inadequate"; that "the politicians . . . think the federal System too complex for a people almost unacquainted with civil liberty, yet they are inclined to favour it"; and that "Bolivar has promised to call a convention for the purpose of adopting that System; whilst General˙[Francisco de Paula] Santander the Vice President, and his adherents, plume themselves upon their adhesion to the constitution and present form of government. . . ." Charges that the wish of this group is "to foil the views of the President," to bring about "seperation of the three Divisions," and to make Santander "the Chief of Cundinamarca." ALS. DNA, RG59, Dip, Disp., Colombia, vol. 4 (M-T33, R4). Copy, in MHi-Adams Papers, Letters Recd. (MR481); extract published in Manning (arr.), *Diplomatic Correspondence . . . Latin-American Nations*, II, 1319. Received September 3.

From James Brown

My dear Sir   Paris June 28. 1827

I hope you will find it convenient to return to Washington before the elections commence in Kentucky which I have every reason to fear will be very warm and turbulent this year.[1] You are neither in a condition of life nor a state of health to take the open decided and active share you formerly did in these unpleasant conflicts of popular opinion. The Southern portion of your State bordering on Tenessee [*sic*] will probably be favorable to General Jackson   the Counties on the North side of the river unless Johnstons influence shall preponderate in his District will no doubt vote in favor of the present Administration.[2] The latest accounts I have had from Louisiana induce me to think that it will support Mr Adams if the presince [*sic*] of the General on the 8 of January[3] does not produce a change. From this time until the result is known, the effect of these divisions will be felt at home, and abroad, in your domestic policy, and in your foreign relations. This state of things ought to be remedied but I know not how it can be done. If it continues it will ultimately corrupt our people and destroy our reputation as a nation.

I hope you will be able to preserve your health and with it your temper in all the trying situations in which you will be placed. Your life is of great importance to your family, to say nothing about your country, and therefore you ought to feel it to be your duty to preserve your cheerfulness and equanimity whatever may be the course of affairs. You will have many severe trials and all your good humour and

patience will be wanting to enable you to bear them. The real statesman must acquire the habit of letting fools and crooked politicians
pass without stepping out of his way to correct or expose them. Their
self love if wounded makes them bitter and implacable enemies
Whereas by letting them pass unnoticed the next popular breath may
throw them into your scale. I have had a very great friendship for
Benton[4] and thought until lately that he was one of your firmest
friends. Floyd[5] too appeared much attached to you and I had considered him as a man exceedingly steady in his friendships. The distance which separates me from my country conceals from my view all
the small machinery by which affairs are carrying on at home and only
presents to my mind the grand results.

The affairs of the Greeks have been almost desperate for some time.
It is now pretty certain that the grand powers will interpose in an efficient manner and terminate the disgracefull [sic] war[6]— A fleet of
Russian French English and as some suppose Swedish and Dutch Vessels will shortly appear in the Mediterranean and separate the Contestants.[7] God grant that this intervention may arrive in time to save
Athens and the remnant of the Greeks from destruction.

Failing to obtain a law to restrain the liberty of the Press Ministers
have reestablished the censorship.[8] The National guard has been disbanded some time ago[9] and the Press is now gagged until the ensuing
Session of the Chambers. General Lafayette has been elected for the
Department of Meaux as a deputy by a majority of only two votes.[10]
I am sorry he has again entered on a theatre where he can do no possible good and will be exposed to great obloquy and vexation. He
openly calls himself a Republican, and I cannot perceive what business a Republican can have in a Chamber of decided Royalists. On his
return I was disposed to believe that he would be contented with the
honors he had received in the United States and consider it as the *fifth*
and *last act* in his political life. Contrary to all the rules of the Drama
he has determined to exhibit in a *sixth* act[11] and after passing over to
the wrong side of seventy years.[12] The hatred felt in relation to him
in certain quarters may possibly react a little on his *distant* friends but
this is a delicate subject and must be passed over lightly. He is about
to marry two of his grandaughters [sic] and seems hightly [sic] pleased
with their choice.[13] He has every thing to make private life charming
and loving him as I do from my heart, I regret his meddling in public
affairs. As soon as the celebration of the 4 of July is over we expect to
be requested to attend the marriage at La Grange, where we shall only
remain one or two days.

I have lately collected a list of the Ships which have been subjected
to the payment of the discriminating duties in consequnece of the indirect voyage[14] and shall in two or three days address a letter to the

Minister of Foreign affairs[15] demanding the repayment of the money
and a promise to prevent similar abuses in future. The principle is
clearly with us and I should have pressed it last summer but I found
the Vessels had sailed from the United States without the necessary
proofs of the origin of their Cargoes. They have since that time obtained them and although I have some reason to fear that this circumstance will be laid hold of to keep the money yet I shall endeavor to
make an argument on the case which with a just government ought
in my opinion to be successful. It is strange that our Merchants who
ought long ago to have known how readily the absence of forms is laid
hold of to put a vessel in the wrong should be so very neglectful of the
usual formalities. I find the discriminating duties have been demanded
on the Cargoes of six American Vessels four from New Orleans and
one from Charleston laden with Cotton and one from Richmond with
Tobacco. In this last Case the Tobacco was bought by the Government
which buys exclusively *Virginia Tobacco*.[16] And yet they pretend to
doubt the *Origin* of the Cargo! The fact is that France would renounce
the Convention[17] tomorrow if she knew how to get along without it.
She finds we carry four fifths of the produce of both Countries. The
more she embarrasses our trade, the more she can restrict our rights
under the Convention, the more she imagines she will promote the
interests of her own Navigation. This indifference for the Convention
arising from her small share in the carrying trade renders the subject
delicate in its management as the people of our Country attach its full
value to it.

I informed you officially that a Squadron had sailed from Toulon
to demand satisfaction from the Dey of Algiers for some alledged insult to the French Consul upon the refusal of which the place was to
be declared in a state of Blockade and prizes made of Algerine Vessels.[18] The news received to day is, that the reparation asked was that
the French flag should be hoisted in Algiers and saluted by a discharge
of one hundred Cannon. This the Dey has refused and the Squadron
placed itself in a position to blockade the place. As a larger force has
been ordered round from the Brest Station it is probable that more
vigorous measures will be resorted to in the event of the Deys continuing refractory.[19]

Mrs. Brown will send Mrs. Clay a great many very fashionable things
by the Vessel which will sail on the 15 July. Some small articles which
are of value will be sent by Mrs. Rumpff formerly Miss Astor who goes
with her husband the Minister of the Hanse Towns to make a Commercial treaty at Washington.[20] I shall write by Mr Rumpff who is my
friend a most amiable and honorable man and who will sail about the
middle of August. I hope the necessary orders respecting his &c &c will
be at New York on his arrival. You know Mr Astor[21] and Mrs. Clay

will be pleased with his daughter who has considerable acquired and natural talent—

My health continues to be as good as it has ever been with the exception of some torpor in the left foot which interferes with the activity of my gait. I shall remain in Paris during the Summer and as our Hotel is large and airy our Court and garden extensive and the City abounds in agreeable public walks I shall pass the time very agreeably. I am often *home* sick but Mrs. Brown is I fear becoming too fond of France— She says she wishes to return in more tranquil times and that she wishes to stay two years longer in Europe. You know I delight in giving her her own way and therefore unless a better Envoy can be found, and indeed that is not a very difficult thing, I may remain here two years more. I hope our Countrymen who visit Paris go home satisfied with the reception we give them, for I feel conscious that neither my time nor my pecuniary means will permit me to do more for them.

I beg you to present our affectionate regards to Mrs Clay whilst I remain very truly Your Affte. friend   JAMES BROWN
Honb. H Clay.

We have this moment learned that Athens has fallen   The particulars not known.[22]

ALS. DLC-HC (DNA, M212, R2).
[1] The Kentucky elections were held on August 6–8, 1827; on Clay's return to Washington, cf. below, Clay to Erwin, August 4, 1827.   [2] Cf. above, Clay to Taylor, April 4, 1827, note. All but Chittenden Lyon and Joel Yancy of the Jacksonite Congressmen resided north of the Green River. The influence of James and Richard Johnson had already been indicated in the election of Robert McHatton.   [3] Anniversary of the Battle of New Orleans.   [4] Thomas Hart Benton.   [5] John Floyd.   [6] Cf. below, Brown to Clay, July 12, 1827.   [7] Cf. above, Brown to Clay, June 12, 1827, note; Middleton to Clay, June 23, 1827. The Swedish and Dutch fleets did not participate in the action.   [8] Cf. above, Brown to Clay, December 13, 1826, and note; April 27, June 12, 1827.   [9] Cf. above, Brown to Clay, May 12, 1827.   [10] Cf. above, Brown to Clay, April 12, 1827, and note.   [11] "Alexandrian precept, handed on by Horace, gave to the five act division a purely arbitrary sanction, which induced playwrights to mask the natural rhythm of their themes beneath this artificial one." William Archer, *Play-Making; a Manual of Craftsmanship* (Boston, 1913), 138. Lafayette, himself, had written to the Count de Maurepas, after the surrender of Yorktown: "The play is over, Monsieur le Comte; the fifth act has just ended. . . ." Brand Whitlock, *LaFayette* (2 vols; New York, 1929), I, 260.   [12] Lafayette was 70 years of age on September 6, 1827.
[13] For the wedding of Louise de la Tour-Maubourg, cf. above, Brown to Clay, June 12, 1827. The second wedding was that of Natalie Lafayette, a daughter of George Washington Lafayette, to Adolphe Périer in December, 1827. Young Périer came from a family of industrialists and politicians identified with moderate opposition to the government.
[14] Cf. above, Beasley to Clay, August 16, 1826; Brown to Clay, August 23 (1), September 11, 1826; Clay to Brown, March 21, 1827.   [15] The Baron de Damas.   [16] The French Government had maintained a tobacco monopoly since 1674, interrupted only for the period 1791 to 1811. A. W. Madsen, *The State as Manufacturer and Trader; an Examination Based on the Commercial, Industrial and Fiscal Results Obtained from Government Tobacco Monopolies* (London, 1916), 53–54.   [17] Of 1822. Cf. above, III, 53n.   [18] Above, June 9, 1827.   [19] Cf. above, Hodson to Clay, June 27, 1827; Brown to Clay, June 12, 1827, "Private."   [20] Mr. and Mrs. Vincent Rumpff. Cf. above, Hughes to Clay, March 9, 1827.   [21] John Jacob Astor.   [22] The Acropolis had been surrendered to Turkish forces on June 5.

INSTRUCTIONS AND DISPATCHES   June 28, 1827

From WILLIAM WHEELWRIGHT, Guayaquil. Reports that "Discord & civil war has [*sic*] raged throughout this section of the country since the revolution of April 16th [cf. above, Wheelwright to Clay, April 19, 1827] and there is but little hope of a speedy return to peace and tranquilty [*sic*]"; blames (Símon) Bolívar for these evils; and notes that the city is deserted. ALS. DNA, RG59, Cons. Disp., Guayaquil, vol. 1 (M-T209, R1). Extract published in Manning (arr.), *Diplomatic Correspondence . . . Latin-American Nations*, II, 1320. Received October 15.

On the emergence of opposition to the Peruvian role in the revolution in Guayaquil, cf. above, Marks to Clay, June 18, 1827; below, Cooley to Clay, July 3, 1827; Nones to Clay, September 17, 1827, note.

MISCELLANEOUS LETTERS   June 28, 1827

From EDWARD EVERETT, Boston. Encloses, at the writer's request, an extract from a letter received from Franklin Litchfield. Comments that Litchfield's view is "not without its grounds. . . ." ALS. DNA, RG59, Misc. Letters (M179, R65).

Litchfield urges in the enclosure, extracted from a letter of May 8, 1827, the appointment of an American "Agent" in Carácas and the payment of salaries to American consuls. Notes that the late R(ichard) C. Anderson, Jr., shared his opinion on both points.

Address to the Public

Lexington, 29th June, 1827.
TO THE PUBLIC.

On my arrival at Wheeling, on the 23d instant,[1] I was informed that Mr Carter Beverley, then at that place, had received the preceding night by mail, a letter from General Jackson, which he had exhibited to several persons, and left with my friend Col. Noah Zane, for my perusal,[2] and which I was told formed a subject of general conversation, and had produced much excitement in the town. The Captain[3] of the Reindeer having kindly detained his steamboat for my accommodation, and as I was unwilling longer to delay his departure, I had only time to obtain a hasty but I believe a correct copy of the letter, and I now seize the first moment, after my arrival at home, to present it to the public, together with a copy of another letter addressed by Mr Beverley to Col. Zane.[4]

I purposely forbear, at this time, to make several comments which these documents authorize, and confine myself to a notice of the charges which General Jackson has brought forward in his letter.

These charges are, 1st. That my friends in Congress, early in January, 1825, proposed to him that, if he would say, or permit any of his confidential friends to say, that, in case he was elected President, Mr Adams should not be continued Secretary of State, by a complete union of myself and my friends, we would put an end to the Presidential contest in one hour; and

2dly. That the above proposal was made to General Jackson, through a distinguished member of Congress, of high standing,[5] *with my privity and consent.*

To the latter charge, I oppose a direct, unqualified and indignant denial. I neither made, nor authorized, nor knew of any proposition whatever to either of the three Candidates who were returned to the House of Representatives at the last Presidential election,[6] or to the friends of either of them, for the purpose of influencing the result of the election, or for any other purpose. And all allegations, intimations and inuendoes that my vote, on that occasion, was offered to be given, or was in fact given, in consideration of any stipulation or understanding, express or implied, direct or indirect, written or verbal, that I was, or that any other person was not, to be appointed Secretary of State, or that I was, in any other manner, to be personally benefitted, are devoid of all truth, and destitute of any foundation whatever. And I firmly and solemnly believe, that the first of the two above mentioned charges is alike untrue and groundless. But if (contrary to my full belief) my friends or any of them made any such proposition or offer, as is asserted in that first charge, it was without my knowledge and without my authority.

The letter of Gen. Jackson insinuates, rather than directly makes, the further charge, that an arrangement was proposed and made between Mr Adams's friends and mine, by which, in the event of his election, I was to be appointed Secretary of State. I pronounce that charge also, as far as I know or believe, to be untrue and without the least foundation.

Gen. Jackson having at last voluntarily placed himself in the attitude of my public accuser, we are now fairly at issue. I rejoice that a specific accusation by a responsible accuser, has at length appeared, though at the distance of near two and a half years since the charge was first put forth, through Mr George Kremer.[7] It will be universally admitted, that the accusation is of the most serious nature. Hardly any more atrocious could be preferred against a representative of the people in his official character. The charge in substance is; that deliberate "propositions of bargain" were made by my Congressional friends collectively, through an authorized and distinguished member of Congress, to Gen. Jackson; that their object was, by these "means of bargain and corruption," to exclude Mr Adams from the Department of State, or to secure my promotion to office; and that I was privy and assented to those propositions and to the employment of those means.

Such being the accusation and the prosecutor, and the issue between us, I have now a right to expect that he will substantiate his charges by the exhibition of satisfactory evidence. In that event, there is no punishment which would exceed the measure of my offence. In the opposite event, what ought to be the judgment of the American public is cheerfully submitted to their wisdom and justice.   H. CLAY.

Lexington *Kentucky Reporter*, July 4, 1827.
[1] See below, Clay to Smith, July 10, 1827.   [2] Cf. above, Clay to Hammond, June 25, 1827.   [3] Bennett, not further identified.   [4] Dated June 24, 1827. See above, Clay to Hammond, June 25, 1827, note.   [5] James Buchanan. See below, Smith to Clay, August 1, 1827, note.   [6] See above, Clay to Brooke, February 10, 1825, note.
[7] See above, Clay to Gales and Seaton, January 30, 1825; Kremer to Clay, *ca.* February 3, 1825.

From Hector P. Lewis and Others

LEXINGTON, 29th June, 1827.

DEAR SIR:—Upon returning to your home, and mingling in the circle of your old friends, to whom you are endeared by an acquaintance of thirty odd years duration, you must readily perceive, that their attachment has been heightened, and their confidence in your virtue, independence, patriotism and philanthropy, strengthened more and more by each revolving year.

They are aware that in these days of indiscriminate revilings, there are none so pure as to be entirely exempt from the unhallowed approach of calumny; but its poisonous shafts, when hurled from the head of disappointed ambition, must fall harmless at the feet of him who has spent a long life devoted to the best interests of the great family of man.

That wise and liberal policy of which you have ever been the able and distinguished advocate, still displays itself in that administration in which you have been justly called upon to act an important and highly responsible part.

The shepherd upon our mountains who tends his little flock—the mechanic and manufacturer, who by their constant toil and labor, sustain and cherish a family, full of hope, though without comfort—the agriculturalist as he joyfully transports the fruits of his yearly industry to the markets—the friends of learning and of science, when they recollect that a people to be free must be virtuous, and to be virtuous must be enlightened—the philanthropist whose will to do good extends to the uttermost bounds of the earth, who is devoted to the freedom, independence, comfort and happiness of all mankind—all will with one voice proclaim, that you have been their able and efficient friend.

As a means of manifesting to you the entire and increased confidence of your former constituents in the county of Fayette, we have been appointed at a meeting at Capt. Postlethwaite's[1] Inn, their committee to solicit your acceptance of a dinner, to be prepared at Noble's Inn, on the 12th day of July next.

From us individually, accept assurances of that high respect and distinguished consideration, which has always been felt by your friends,

H. P. Lewis,	E. Milton,[3]	Robt. S. Russell,
Peter Gatewood,[2]	A. Young,	C. Carr,[6]
Roger Quarles,	M. Fishel,[4]	Jos. Robb,
David Sutton,	Rich'd H. Chinn,	E. Yeiser,[7]
Wm. C. Connett,	Jas. Shelby,	Walter C. Carr,
John Graves,	Thos. Bodley,	Henry C. Innis,
Jas. Rogers,	D. Barton,	Wm. Stubblefield,[8]
Robt. C. Boggs,	H. Bledsoe,[5]	W. H. Richardson.

To the Hon. H. CLAY.

Lexington *Kentucky Reporter*, July 14, 1827. Lewis, born in Virginia and educated at Transylvania University, operated a thousand-acre farm six miles north of Lexington. He had served with the rank of colonel in the Kentucky militia during the War of 1812.
 [1] John Postlethwait.   [2] Owner of a farm in Fayette County, seven miles south of Lexington.   [3] Graves, born in Louisa County, Virginia, had come to Kentucky as a youth, in 1787; had fought in the War of 1812, like Lewis as a colonel of militia; and at this time operated a farm on the Iron Works Road, seven miles north of Lexington.
 Rogers had a large farm near Bryan Station, five and a half miles northeast of Lexington. Boggs owned a 380-acre tract on the Richmond Road nine miles east of Lexington. Elijah Milton farmed in the South Elkhorn district of Fayette County.
 [4] Ambrose Young; Michael Fishel.   [5] David Barton was an elderly and well-to-do farmer residing on Iron Works Road, Fayette County. Bledsoe, a captain of militia, owned a share in a 181-acre farm near Athens, Fayette County.   [6] Charles Carr.
 [7] Englehart Yeiser.   [8] Walter Chiles Carr had a farm on the Tates Creek Road, at Hickman Creek, in Fayette County. Innis was probably Henry E. Innes, a native of Virginia who had come to Kentucky around the turn of the century, served as a surgeon in the War of 1812, and practiced medicine and farmed along the Russell Cave Pike at North Elkhorn Creek. He owned over a thousand acres. Stubblefield, also a native Virginian, had come to Kentucky in 1786, served in the War of 1812, and as a young man had lived near Bryan Station. He later served as sheriff of Mason County, Kentucky. His residence in 1827 has not been identified.

INSTRUCTIONS AND DISPATCHES   June 29, 1827

From JAMES BROWN, Paris, no. 70. Reports having "just heard that the Acropolis, and consequently Athens, have been taken by the Turkish forces." Refers to the expectation "that in a very short time a fleet of British, Russian and French vessels will assemble in the Mediterranean, and terminate this cruel and disgraceful war" and to a belief that a treaty to that end has "been signed at London . . ." (see below, Brown to Clay, July 12, 1827). Notes the blockade, by a French squadron, of the harbor of Algiers and adds: "As all the Algerine ships of war were within the port, no danger is to be apprehended from their cruisers." LS. DNA, RG59, Dip. Disp., France, vol. 23 (M34, R26). Copy, in MHi-Adams Papers, Letters Recd. (MR 481). Received August 22. Cf. above, Brown to Clay, June 28, 1827.

From JAMES COOLEY, Lima, no. 3. Reports that (Cristóbal) Armero, the Colombian Chargé d'Affaires, was expelled by the (Peruvian) Government on June 25 for reasons not yet clear, though rumors attribute the expulsion to Armero's friend-

ship with Simón Bolívar. ALS. DNA, RG59, Dip. Disp., Peru, vol. 1 (M-T52, R1).
Received October 28.

Armero was a merchant by trade.

From JOHN M. FORBES, Buenos Aires, no. 50. Reports that (Manuel José) García
has returned (cf. above, Forbes to Clay, April 12, May 24, 1827; Wright to Clay,
May 25, 1827), on a British vessel, with "the preliminaries" of the treaty of peace
he has signed with the Emperor of Brazil (Peter I); that public reaction to news
of peace was initially favorable; and, as information about the terms of the agreement leaked through the "veil of secresy [sic])" imposed by "the Executive Government," that "the most lively indignation" was aroused toward García and was, "in
no small degree, . . . extended to Lord [John Brabazon] Ponsonby and the English." Encloses a copy of the *Mensagero Argentino* of June 27, which contains accounts of "official proceedings" rejecting the treaty. Notes that the effect on Congress "of this ignominious peace has been to excite an enthusiastic spirit of patriotism and an apparently Cordial union of the hitherto discordant feelings of that
body"; that (Bernardino) Rivadavia's resignation (from the Presidency) "has been
referred to a Committee"; and that "it is said" the government of the Province
(of Buenos Aires) will be reestablished, and the Congress dissolved. Lists the names
of officers in "The proposed organization of the provisional government" and
predicts that "This happy change in national feeling will double the physical as
well as the moral energies and force of the army" to the extent that the Brazilian
Emperor will be compelled to propose new peace terms.

States that he received on June 20 "an official letter from Governor [Juan
Bautista] Bustos, of Cordova, protesting . . . against the assumed authority of
Mr. Rivadavia, and against any treaty or convention which . . . [Forbes] might
enter into with him in his pretended character of President" (cf. above, Forbes
to Clay, April 12, 1827, note). Transmits a copy of his reply to this communication and promises soon to forward a translation of the letter. LS. DNA, RG59,
Dip. Disp., Argentina, vol. 3 (M69, R4). Published in Espil (comp.), *Once Años
en Buenos Aires*, 468–70. Received October 3. The enclosures include, despite
Forbes' statement, a translation of Bustos' letter, dated May 31, 1827 (endorsed
on last page: "with Jn. M. forbes' No. 50.").

To Hector P. Lewis and Others

LEXINGTON, 30th June, 1827.

GENTLEMEN:—I have received your affectionate note of the 20th
instant, and regret the incompetency of any language that I can command, to express with sufficient sensibility, the feelings which have
been excited in my breast by the cordial, the friendly, the enthusiastic, reception which my old friends and neighbors have given
me, on my return home among them. I have perceived, gentlemen,
with much delight, that their attachment increases with the passing
years, and strengthens in a ratio equal to the force of the accumulated
malignity and calumny with which I am assailed. These demonstrations of friendship and confidence, alike honorable to the hearts of
those who make them and to their grateful object, afford a cheering
support. And seconded, as they are, by a consciousness of my having
endeavored, with zeal and fidelity, to serve my country, I stand fear-

lessly prepared for the issue of the assaults, which are so perseveringly directed against me.

The Administration ought to be judged by its measures. Any other rule would assume that the agent was more important than the agency. If the members of the administration shall be found arrayed in opposition to a national policy, which they had formerly sustained, they would deserve the public censure. But if the measures, foreign and domestic, which they now support are those that they have always espoused, they have at least the merit of consistency.

I thank you, gentlemen, for the too flattering estimate which you have been pleased to make of the effects of my public service. Sincerely believing that certain great measures would tend to the promotion of the general prosperity, I have anxiously labored for their adoption. Their success has, I think, abundantly confirmed the wisdom of the principles on which they depend.

I accept, with much pleasure, the invitation to a public dinner at Mr Noble's Inn on the 12th of next month, which you have been pleased to convey. And requesting you to accept assurances of my high respect and esteem, I am faithfully and cordially, your friend and fellow citizen,   H. CLAY.

MESSRS *H. P. Lewis, Peter Gatewood, Roger Quarles, &c. &c.*

Lexington *Kentucky Reporter*, July 14, 1827. Cf. above, Lewis and others to Clay, June 29, 1827.

Bill from St. John's Church

DR. Hon. Henry Clay.   [*ca.* June 30, 1827]
                    To St. John's Church,
For 1 .... quarter Pew rent, ending 30 June 27 $13. ....
        25 P C. on rent 1 qr. ....   3.12 ......
                                        $16.12

D, partially printed. DLC-HC (DNA, M212, R3).

From the Baron de Mareuil (1)

Sir,   New York 30h. June 1827.
    At the moment when I am about to depart, permit me to add to my official communications of this day,[1] some more particular expression of the sentiments which I bear away with me, and the better part of which is assured to you. I have often regretted that conversation was not more easy between us, being persuaded of the interest and pleasure which you would have been able to throw over it, and eager as I would have been to make myself understood in those things of which the pen cannot treat, but in which the heart and spirit may find satisfaction.

I hope, however, that I may not have been misunderstood by you, and that I have made an impression upon you, akin to that which you have left on me.

The extensive and beautiful tour which I have just finished, has much increased my admiration of North America.[2] I have regretted that I was not at Black Rock, and that I was unable to deliver in person to General and Mrs. Porter, the recommendations with which you honored me.[3]— Madame Mareuil begs that Mrs. Clay will be pleased to accept her adieus and compliments. I venture to add my homages, and to beg, sir, that you will accept, at the same time with my thanks for the welcome treatment which I received from you during my residence in Washington, the assurance of the invariable sentiments of high consideration which I have professed for you.

M. Clay. Secretaire d'Etat   THE BARON DE MAREUIL.

ALS, in French with trans. DLC-HC (DNA, M212, R2).   [1] Below, this date.
[2] Cf. above, Clay to Porter, April 20, 1827; and below, Porter to Clay, July 11, 1827.
   [3] See above, Clay to Porter, April 18, 1827.

Toast by Actor at Theater

[June 30, 1827]

Long life and happiness to those in affluence, who do not forget the distresses of the Poor, and who endeavor to alleviate those distresses by encouraging *Domestic Industry*.

Lexington *Kentucky Reporter*, July 4, 1827. Quoted in a "COMMUNICATION" by "A MECHANIC," who stated: "During the performance of the Blind Boy, at the Theatre on Saturday evening, which Mr. CLAY attended at the invitation of the Managers, the . . . toast in compliment to him was introduced by one of the actors [unidentified]. . . ." Following quotation of the toast, the statement continues: "The sentiment was warmly and very generally applauded by the respectable audience assembled on the occasion. Mr Clay on entering the box appropriated to his use, was welcomed by continued greetings— These manifestations of personal and political regard could scarcely have been more gratifying to the worthy object of them than to the author of this communication, and other old friends, who for the last twenty years have witnessed with delight the untiring exertions of this talented individual, to advance the true interests of his country, by supporting Internal Improvements and Domestic Manufactures." *The Blind Boy* was a melodrama written by James Kenney, an Irish dramatist, for production at Covent Garden, London, in 1807. Kenney's plays were at their peak popularity during the 1820's. Solomon F. and Lemuel Smith and Henry R. Crampton were the managers of the Lexington theater during a short season which had opened on June 25. "Sol." Smith noted that during the three-week series they had "but one good house and that was when *Henry Clay* attended the theatre." Solomon Franklin Smith, *Theatrical Management in the West and South for Thirty Years* . . . (New York, 1868), 48. S. F. Smith, born and reared in central New York, had been attracted to the theater at the age of 13 and, although he had studied and later occasionally practiced law, devoted most of his life to acting in and managing theatrical productions. He toured predominantly in the southeastern States, "built the first real theatre west of the Mississippi," at St. Louis, and dominated the theatrical business at that city, Mobile, and New Orleans for long periods during the years 1835 to 1853. In the latter year he settled in St. Louis and concentrated on the practice of law. William Glasgow Bruce Carson, in *Dictionary of American Biography*, IX, 346–47. His youngest brother, Lemuel, toured with him during much of the period from 1823 until 1832, when at age 27, Lemuel was murdered at Milledgeville, Georgia. Crampton had appeared in Lexington on several occasions during the mid-1820's and appears to have organized the venture in 1827. He and the Smiths had developed theatrical ties the previous year at Cincinnati.

DIPLOMATIC NOTES   June 30, 1827

From the BARON DE MAREUIL, New York (2). States that he will board a vessel on the next day; names, as Chargé d'Affaires during his absence, "M. le Comte de Menou, premier Secrétaire de la Légation du Roi [Charles X] aux Etats Unis"; and notes that this is not the first time such functions have devolved upon Menou (cf. above, III, 398n). ALS, in French with trans. in State Dept. file. DNA, RG59, Notes from French Legation, vol. 10 (M53, R-T9).

INSTRUCTIONS AND DISPATCHES   June 30, 1827

From ALEXANDER BURTON, Cádiz. States that the greater part of Spanish trade with Cuba and Spain's former American possessions has been carried by United States vessels despite the discriminatory tonnage duty (cf. above, Clay to Everett, April 27, 1825, note; Burton to Clay, January 10, 1826; Everett to Clay, February 27, 1827); notes that although most of the property shipped in these vessels "is for Spanish Account," he knows of no interference "by Colombian or other Privateers" cruising off the Spanish coast. Points out that the quarantine imposed by the French at Cádiz and Barcelona on American vessels during the summer (cf. above, Burton to Secretary of State, March 16, 1825; Burton to Clay, June 30, August 7, November 15, 1825; March 12, 1826; Everett to Clay, March 19, April 7, June 4, 1827) forces much of the trade "to pass by way of Gibraltar, at which place the Spaniards disguise the origin of their produce and manufactures, with a view to introduce them into Mexico and other points where the importation is prohibited." Reports that the importation "of grain and Breadstuffs" into Spain is forbidden; that hopes are entertained that the French garrison at Cádiz will be removed during the year; and that "An expedition is now fitting out, to add to the Spanish force at Havana. . . ." Credits (Alexander H.) Everett with making "every exertion to place our Shipping on a better footing as regards Tonnage Duty, and quarantine, but as yet without effecting any material alteration." ALS. DNA, RG59, Cons. Disp., Cádiz, vol. 4 (M-T186, R4). Received September 4.

From PAUL FROBERVILLE, "Port Louis, Isle of France." States that Prosper Froberville, who has gone to Europe, has appointed him acting consular agent for the United States. LS. *Ibid.*, Port Louis, vol. 1 (M-T118, R-T1). Cf. above, Prosper Froberville to Clay, March 7, 1827.

INSTRUCTIONS AND DISPATCHES   July 1, 1827

From DAVID DICKSON, "San Fernando de Bijar" (*i.e.*, San Antonio), Texas. Observes that inasmuch as (Joel R.) Poinsett advises him "of the Establishment of a Consular office at the Bay of Matagorda; *That* being the very key to the Commerce of this place . . . the office here is in effect abolished—" Laments his personal loss in the abandonment of "a lucrative practice in the United States" and tenders his resignation, "to take effect on the first of October; If the fact exists as stated by Mr. Poinsett." Postscript reports the massing of a "considerable Army" by Major General (Anastasio) Bustamente, "to operate against the Hostile Indians," who, however, have sued for peace. Encloses "a rough Table Exhibiting the different Tribes of Indians living in Texas—" ALS. DNA, RG59, Cons. Disp., Texas, vol. 1 (M-T153, R1). Received December 20. The enclosed table lists locations and number of warriors of 31 tribes.

From S[AMUEL] D. HEAP, Tunis. Refers to his letter (not found) of May 15, "via Marseilles." Observes: "our relations with this Regency continue on the most favorable footing— Our cruisers find it convenient to call here on their return from the Levant, as by procuring Pratic [*sic*] here, which they do immediately on their arrival, they reduce their quarantine ten or twelve days at Mahon and other European ports." Notes that (Charles D.) Coxe "may be daily expected" from Marseilles.

Reports having exceeded, "by a small amount," the limit imposed by his instructions for the purchase of a consular present (cf. above, Clay to Heap, April 20, 1826); explains the reasons for his action; and adds that "There are still two influential officers to be satisfied." Lists gifts of diamonds, cannon, "Spars &c" made to the Bey [Hassein] by the King of Sweden (Charles XIV) and states that "A cargo of equal value is daily expected from Denmark." Points out that "thus these governments continue to furnish the Barbary Regencies with the means of annoying the commerce of the Mediterranean, in preference to keeping a small naval force in this sea, the cost of which would exceed very little the tribute they are obliged to pay." Comments that, since "The naval force of this Regency . . . has for a long time . . . been employed in the service of the Sultan [Mahmud II], the Bey is not provided with the means of protecting his ports from the Greek Cruisers several of which have been committing depredations for some weeks past on this Coast–" ALS. *Ibid.*, Tunis, vol. 5 (M-T303, R5). Received December 20.

From JOHN C. JONES, JR., "Oahu   Sandwich Islands." Submits consular reports and calls attention to the "large . . . amount of American Property [that] anually [*sic*] comes to these Islands and is thought demands of the Government their constant protection in this remote quarter of the globe–" Cites "the whale Fishery on the coast of Japan," which has made "the Sandwich Islands . . . of indispensible [*sic*] importance to the American Commerce employed for that purpose. . . ." Elaborates: "At present the whale ships visit the Sandwich Islands in the months of March and April and then proceed to the Coast of Japan, they return again in October and November remain here about six weeks, and then proceed in different directions, some to the Coast of California, others cruise about the Equator when they return thither again in March and April and proceed a second time to the Coast of Japan; it usually occupies two seasons on that coast to fill a ship that will carry Three Hundred Tons.

"The number of hands generally comprising the Company of a whale ship will average Twenty Five; and, owing to the want of discipline, the length and the ardourous [*sic*] duties of the voyage, these people generally become dissatisfied and are willing at any moment to join a rebellion or desert the first opportu[nity] that may offer;—this has been fully exemplified in the whale ships that have visited these Islands, constant desertions have taken place and many serious mutinies both contributing to protract and frequently to ruin the voyage.— I would beg leave to suggest to the Government the propriety, as well as necessity, of a vessel of war, semianually [*sic*] visiting these Islands at the periods when the whale ships generally asse[m]ble— There are usually in the months of March April & May and again in October November & Decem[ber] collected at this harbour at one time from Twenty five to Thirty American ships and these ships are manned by not less than six Hundred Seamen.—such a body of men collected at one place in a land too where the only law is that might makes right, restrained but little by the authority of their respective commanders, dissatisfied and harrassed [*sic*] with hardship and oppressions, are ready to engage in any outrage that they imagine might improve their condition or free them from their bonds. Add to this there are generally on this Island from fifty to one Hundred lawless seaman [*sic*] of every nation, desserters [*sic*] from different ships, and a number of convicts from New Holland [Australia], and these are always on the alert to promote rebellion and encourage desertion."

Notes that recent "visits of the United States Schooner Dolphin & sloop of war, Peacock" brought "Good order" among the seamen of the whaling fleet, "a Treaty of Commerce" signed by "the Commander of the Peacock and the authoritys [*sic*] of this land," and an agreement under which "the King & Chieffs [*sic*]" have undertaken to pay debts due "certain citizens, of the United States. . . ." Adds that "The Island of Oahu is the principal one of the group visited by the shipping as it affords the most abundant supplies is the place of the Royal Residence, and possesses one of the safest Harbors in the known world" (Pearl Harbor) and declares: "This should be the station a [*sic*] vessel of war." Admits that "repeated solicitations of the Masters of America[n] shipping at these Islands" have led him "to make this communication," which, he hopes, "may have some influence to induce the Government of the United States to stretch fourth [*sic*] an arm of Protection to their commerce in this distant quarter of the globe." LS. *Ibid.*, Honolulu, vol. 1 (M144, R1). Received April 2, 1828 (duplicate [DNA, RG59, Misc. Dup. Disp., box 4, folder 30] received March 29, 1828).

Whaling off the eastern coasts of Japan had been opened by the Americans and the British in voyages extending from 1819 to 1822. Over the next decade this area became the most important grounds for such operations, with the Americans having 60 to 70 vessels a year in the north Pacific by 1835. George Brown Goode, *The Fisheries and Fishery Industries of the United States . . .* (7 vols.; Washington, 1884–1887), II, 69.

Thomas ap Catesby Jones, Master Commandant of the *Peacock*, had negotiated on December 23, 1826, "Articles of Arrangement" with King Kauikeaouli, through his guardians, Queen Kaakumanu and her ministers, at Oahu, declaring perpetual friendship and providing for trading privileges, protection of American citizens, and most-favored-nation status, among other measures. For the terms, see *House Reports*, 28 Cong., 2 Sess., no. 92, pp. 19–20.

A Virginian, Jones had entered the Navy as a midshipman in 1805, attained the rank of lieutenant in 1812, and won distinction in the War of 1812. He had subsequently served three years in the Mediterranean Squadron and five years as inspector of ordnance at the Washington Navy Yard. He had been sent to the Sandwich Islands (Hawaii) while on assignment with the Pacific Squadron in 1825. Promoted to captain in 1829, he commanded a South Seas surveying and exploring expedition in 1836. He also commanded the Pacific Squadron intermittently in 1842 and from 1844 to 1850; but much of his later career was embroiled in controversy with the Navy Department, stemming from his impetuosity and cavalier use of funds without official authorization, a characteristic evidenced in his negotiations in 1826. Suspended from service in 1850, he was restored to active duty in 1853 but retired in 1855.

Kaukeaouli, who nominally ruled from 1825 to 1854, ascended the throne in 1832 as Kamehameha III.

To John Quincy Adams

Dear Sir   Lexington 2d. July 1827

I reached this place on the 28h. Ulto. I find the state of public opinion pretty much as I believed it to be in this State before I left the City. In some instances less, in others more, favorable and they about counterbalance each other. The contest will be warm and animated, but I think that the Administration will not have a less number of friends in the next than it had in the last Congress, and there is not a bad prospect of having one or two more.[1]

A topic which I am told is employed now with more effect than any other in this State is that of your accounts.[2] It is to be regretted that some clear and satisfactory explanation of them, in the shape of a news paper article, has not been given. I understand that Mr. Dwight's defence of them, in the H. of R. last winter, which I remember to have heard at the time was thought quite sufficient, was either never published at all or imperfectly published.[3] The points which are pressed I am told are 1st. the magnitude of the amount and 2dly. that you settled them yourself. Whilst Ingham's Speech[4] and other similar matter is circulated with great industry, there is no opposing statement put forward. I think it is very desirable that such a statement should appear in the press at Washn. City.[5]

You must have seen that most strange letter of Mr. Watts inviting Bolivar to return to Bogota.[6] I think it is worthy of consideration whether he ought not to be immediately recalled. If Bolivar has the designs, which we have too much reason to apprehend he entertains, nothing could have been more indiscreet than that Mr. Watts, without instructions, should write a letter, which if the Govt. remain silent, will have the effect of throwing this Country into Bolivar's scale. Of Mr. Watts's incompetency I had before no doubt; and this new proof furnishes a just occasion to replace him by one more capable.

I am preparing to return to the City by the time I intended before I left it, and I hope to accomplish the object. My reception in K. is more warm and enthusiastic than ever. Indeed I find it extremely difficult to avoid their invitations to public dinners &c.

Carter Beverly [sic] recd. at Wheeling a letter from Genl. Jackson confirming and adding to his statements in his Fayetteville letter. I shall cause a Copy of it to be published in the Reporter tomorrow, with a note from me, making up an issue with the Genl.[7] I think it probable that it has been already published to the Eastward, and that you may therefore have seen it.[8] I am deceived if the American public does not condemn the Genl. for having written such a letter. I am with great respect and regard, truly Your friend & ob. Servt.

Mr. Adams.   H. CLAY

ALS. MHi-Adams Papers, Letters Recd. (MR481).
[1] Cf. above, Clay to Taylor, April 4, 1827, note.   [2] Cf. above, Johnson to Clay, April 8, 1827, and note.   [3] Explanation by both Henry W. Dwight and Daniel Webster on President Adams' accounts for the years 1813–1815 had been delivered in the House of Representatives on February 27, 1827, and published in the Washington Daily National Intelligencer, February 28, 1827, and the Register of Debates, 19 Cong., 2 Sess., 1446–51.   [4] The attack upon Adams' accounts had been initiated by Samuel D. Ingham, in a debate on the General Appropriation Bill, on February 14, 1827. Register of Debates, 19 Cong., 2 Sess., 1171–73.   [5] No such statement appeared in the administration organ, the Washington Daily National Journal, during the next six weeks.   [6] Cf. above, Watts to Clay, June 14, 1827.   [7] Cf. above, Clay to Hammond, June 25, 1827; Clay "To the Public," June 29, 1827.   [8] Jackson's letter to Beverley, dated as June 5, 1827, was published in the Washington United States Telegraph, July 2, 1827.

From THOMAS BROOKS, Santiago de Cuba. Reports having transferred the seal of office and books to Thomas Backus (cf. above, Wright to Clay, August 10, 1826; Clay to Backus, March 7, 1827); files returns of American vessels and cargoes to June 30; and attributes the increase in American trade during the last half year to the opening of the port as an entrepôt for breadstuff, lumber, and livestock destined for the adjacent British Colony (Jamaica—cf. above, Harrison to Clay, May 27, 1827). ALS. DNA, RG59, Cons. Disp., Santiago de Cuba, vol. 1 (M-T55, R1).

From ALBERT GALLATIN, London, no. 91. Notes that the King granted no audience "to any foreign Minister" from April 30 until June 30, "when he received Count d'Ofalia," and that "although Mr. [José Fernández] Madrid, the new Minister from Colombia has been waiting here for some time to deliver his letters of credence, his audience for that purpose was postponed." LS. DNA, RG59, Dip. Disp., Great Britain, vol. 34 (M30, R30). Copy, in MHi-Adams Papers, Letters Recd. (MR481). Received August 25.

From William McClanahan and Others

RICHMOND, July 3, 1827.

SIR:—At a very large and numerously attended meeting of your Fellow-citizens of Madison county, in the Court-house at this place on yesterday, it was resolved unanimously, as an humble tribute of respect for your long, distinguished and meritorious public services, and as an evidence of their undiminished confidence in your integrity and enlightened American policy, to invite you to partake with them, of a Democratic Republican Dinner at Wm. Rodes's spring[1] in this vicinity, at such time as might suit your convenience.

The resolutions[2] are herewith transmitted to you—to advise you of which and to solicit your attendance, the undersigned were appointed a committee.

No duty could have been assigned us by our fellow citizens, more agreeable to our feelings, than to be the medium through which to convey to you the friendly sentiments entertained by them, and by us individually, for your private worth and public usefulness,—we shall ever recur to it as amongst the happiest periods of our lives.

The present purturbed [sic] state of the political atmosphere in the United States is a loud call, it seems to us, upon the friends of Domestic Manufactures and Internal Improvements, of social order and the principles of universal liberty, of which you have been the long, the indefatigable and the powerful advocate, to unite, and in Spartan concert to resist, the novel, dangerous and extraordinary doctrines of the enemies of these measures.

You, sir, are considered one of the Doric columns of the "American System," and hither may be traced that unhallowed stream of vituperation and bitterness which has of late been poured out upon your character.

With you, the "Combination"[3] hope to see the American System sink, could they by calumniation and falsehood effect your downfall.

The prostration of the present distinguished chief magistrate of the nation, who, is, with you, upon the great principles of the 'American System' identified, and the elevation of another individual, whose views are supposed to be more in unison with theirs, is the real object, in our estimation of the enemies of domestic manufactures and internal improvements.

By adherence to those cardinal principles, (uncompromising integrity, boldness and independence,) which has always characterized your public life, both you and the great cause in which you are engaged, must and will triumph.

If unfortunately however, the phrenzied state of public sentiment should be such, as to surrender the principles for which you have been so ably and so zealously contending for the last twenty years, it will only be temporary. And should you go down amidst the extraordinary excitement of the times, you will only go down like the Sun of the South American and the Greek, whom you have sought to liberate,[4] to rise again with more effulgent splendour, hailed with acclamations of joy and gratitude by every friend to the "American System."

Permit us sir, to avail ourselves of this occasion to make a tender of the homage of our distinguished consideration.

WM. McCLANAHAN,	JOHN WHITE,
SQUIRE TURNER,	RICH'D. APPERSON[6]
WM. GOODLOE, Sen.	DAVID IRVINE,
JO. KENNEDY,[5]	W. H. CAPERTON.

HON: H. CLAY.

Lexington *Kentucky Reporter*, July 18, 1827. McClanahan, reared near Paris, Kentucky, was now a merchant in Richmond, Kentucky. He had served in the State House of Representatives in 1822.
[1] Probably at the home, "Woodlawn," built by William Rodes on the Big Hill Pike, near Richmond, in 1822. Rodes had been a member of the Kentucky House of Representatives for the Session of 1819–1820.   [2] The first stated: "*Resolved*, That the able and unremitted exertions of the Hon. H. Clay, in the great cause of Domestic Manufactures, Internal Improvements, and the cause of struggling Liberty in every quarter of the world, merit and fully meet our hearty approbation; and that our confidence in his talents integrity and enlightened policy is increased instead of being diminished." Three additional resolutions, in tribute to Clay's "talents, his exertions in promoting the best interests of his country, and his political firmness of all trying occasions," invited him to a "*Domestic* [sic] *Republican* Dinner, at Mr Wm. Rodes's spring," at a date to suit his convenience and provided for committees to conduct the affair. Besides the resolutions relating to entertainment of Clay, the assembly had expressed approval of the call to a general convention by "the friends of the American System in Pennsylvania," to meet at Harrisburg on July 30 (see above, Clay to Crowninshield, March 18, 1827, note), agreed "that Kentucky ought to be represented" in it, and provided for a committee to represent the county in selecting delegates if Kentucky should decide to participate. Lexington *Kentucky Reporter*, July 11, 1827, reprinted from Richmond *Farmer's Chronicle*. Delegates from several Kentucky counties, including Madison, did meet at Frankfort on July 14 and named representatives to the Harrisburg meeting. Lexington *Kentucky Reporter*, July 18, 1827.   [3] The phrase used by John Floyd (cf. above, Brooke to Clay, February 11, 1827) had now been adopted as a term referring to

the alliance of Jackson supporters, particularly its inclusion of those opposing a protective tariff.   4 See, *e.g.*, above, II, 512–62; III, 603–12.   5 Goodloe, born in North Carolina, had come to Kentucky at age 18, in 1787, and settled three miles east of Richmond.   Born in 1760, Joseph Kennedy had come to Kentucky in 1776, served through the Indian fighting of the Revolutionary War, in which duty he had attained the rank of captain, and held appointment as a judge of Madison County court under the jurisdiction of Virginia and later of Kentucky.   6 Apperson, born in Virginia in 1799, had moved to Madison County, Kentucky, in 1815, where he taught school, clerked in a store, and finally completed education for the law. In 1829 he removed to Mt. Sterling, Kentucky. There he continued an active career at the bar, served as a representative in the Kentucky General Assembly (1838–1839 and 1843–1844) and as a delegate to the Constitutional Convention of 1849, and became active in railway development.

INSTRUCTIONS AND DISPATCHES   July 3, 1827

From JAMES BROWN, Paris, no. 71. Transmits "the official notification from this [the French] Government, of the blockade of Algiers" (cf. above, Brown to Clay, June 9, 28, 29, 1827). LS. DNA, RG59, Dip. Disp., France, vol. 23 (M34, R26). Received August 28.

From JAMES COOLEY, Lima, no. 4. Theorizes that the Colombian Chargé d'Affaires (Cristóbal Armero) was probably expelled because of his correspondence with the leaders of "the late movements at Guayaquil" (cf. above, Wheelwright to Clay, June 28, 1827, and note; Cooley to Clay, June 29, 1827). Reports that the Peruvian Congress is debating a "decree of Amnesty." Adds, in a postscript that there is "a great degree of coolness" toward the Congress meeting in (Tacubaya) Mexico; that he doubts whether Peru would ratify any treaty made by the body; and that it will probably be "the end of the year before [Peruvian] Ministers can be commissioned & reach . . . the Congress" (cf. above, Tudor to Clay, June 15, 1827). ALS. DNA, RG59, Dip. Disp., Peru, vol. 1 (M-T52, R1). Received January 3, 1828.

To William McClanahan and Others

Gentlemen: LEXINGTON, 4th July, 1827.

I have received, by the hands of two of your body, your note of yesterday, inviting me, in behalf of your fellow citizens of Madison county, to a Domestic [*sic*] Republican Dinner, at Mr Rodes's[1] spring, and accompanied by certain resolutions which had been adopted by the meeting. For the too flattering sentiments which are borne by those papers, I pray my fellow-citizens, who composed the meeting, and you gentlemen, to accept my respectful and cordial thanks. An unaffected desire, which I have to visit Madison county, renders very painful the necessity which I am under of declining this invitation. I am obliged, if possible, to reach Washington City by the first of August,[2] which leaves me now only a few days to bestow necessary attention on my private affairs.

Although I cannot but feel that you have made too high an estimate of my public services, I concur entirely with you in your views of the dangers which threaten the subversion of those measures of national policy, to which I have zealously dedicated my best exertions. All who are opposed to the American System—all who are opposed to Internal Improvements, are now united with others in the endeavor to defeat the re-election of the present Chief Magistrate and to elevate another individual. Should they succeed, (of which I am happy, however, to believe there is no occasion for apprehension,) there cannot be a doubt that the most powerful element in this association would afterwards prevail in the conduct of public affairs, or that it would become the nucleus of a new opposition to the very person whom it had contributed to elect. Against such inauspicious results, the best security is the intelligence, candour and virtue of the People. A reliance upon this security has been the great maxim of my public life. I have never heretofore been deceived in it. And I am extremely glad to be authorised to assure you, that daily developments of public sentiment justify the confident anticipation, that the truth of the maxim will be again confirmed.

I hope, gentlemen, you will make acceptable to my fellow-citizens of Madison, the reason which I am compelled to offer for declining their friendly invitation. And I beg leave to present to the gentlemen of the committee my respectful acknowledgments for the sentiments of confidence, approbation and esteem, with which they have honored me.

I am, with great respect, Your friend and ob't serv't,

H. CLAY.

Messrs. W. McClanahan, Squire Turner, Wm. Goodloe, sen. Joseph Kennedy, John White, R. Apperson, David Irvine, Wm. H. Caperton.

Lexington *Kentucky Reporter*, July 11, 1827.   [1] William Rodes.
[2] Cf. below, Clay to Erwin, August 4, 1827.

To Samuel H. Woodson

My dear Sir   (Confidential)   Lexn. 4 July 1827.
I have this moment recd. your obliging favor of yesterday.[1] Govr. Kent[2] *expects* that extracts from his letter will be published. I wish that however done, without unnecessarily involving him. I would advise the omission of the part which relates to Mr. Randolph,[3] and *perhaps* that which relates to Genl. Sanders.[4] The residue would do good to be published at this moment, especially since the appearance of Genl. Jackson's letter.[5]

I fear I shall not have it in my power to visit Frankfort, which I regret very much as it may deprive me of the pleasure of seeing you and other friends. I am always Cordially Your friend   H. CLAY
Saml. H. Woodson Esq

ALS. DLC. Addressed, on separate sheet, to Woodson at Frankfort, Kentucky, where he had settled earlier this year, "with an intention to devote himself *exclusively* to his profession," law. Frankfort *Argus of Western America*, April 25, 1827.
[1] Not found.   [2] Joseph Kent. Cf. above, Kent to Clay, April 28, 1827.

3 Probably John Randolph.   4 Romulus M. Saunders. The letter from Kent to Woodson, dated May 15, 1827, was published, with reference to Kent as the author, in the Frankfort *Commentator*, reprinted in the Lexington *Kentucky Reporter*, July 11, 1827, in part as follows:

Our friend, Mr Clay, appears to be the chief object of persecution with the opposition. They are, with great industry, conducting a systematical attack upon him, which commenced with the Kremer story [see above, Clay to Gales and Seaton, January 30, 1825; Kremer to Clay, *ca.* February 3, 1825], which was an entire fabrication.

At the time the plot opened, I was a member of the House of Representatives, and heard Kremer declare he never designed to charge Mr Clay with any thing dishonorable in his life.

[Yet] the old man, naturally honest, was imposed on at the time, by a powerful influence, and constrained to act his part in an affair, which, from beginning to end, was as much a fiction as the merry wives of Windsor, or the School for Scandal.

The attack on Mr Clay, during the late session of Congress, by Gen. Saunders, as far as I could judge from the debate as published, proved an entire abortion, and I hardly know which surprised me most, the folly of the attack or the inconsistency of the General.

You have seen, no doubt, that Mr F. Johnson stated in his reply to Gen. Saunders, that at the time of the presidential election, in the House of Representatives, that he, Gen. S, was decidedly in favor of Mr Adams, in preference to General Jackson.

In confirmation of what Mr Johnson has stated, I well remember, that not ten minutes before the election, Gen. Saunders came to me, with an anxious countenance, discovering deep concern indeed, and used these emphatic words: "I hope to God you may be able to terminate the election on the first ballot, for fear we from North Carolina may be forced to vote for Gen. Jackson." North Carolina, you know, voted in the House of Representatives for Mr Crawford, whose prospect of success was hopeless, although the electors of that state gave their votes in favor of Gen. Jackson.

. . . .

Mr Clay I have known intimately for sixteen years; his public career is completely identified with every important event of the country, from that period to the present time, whether in peace or in war.

During the late war, I have seen the House of Representatives, after having gone out of committee of the whole, return to it again, for the sole purpose of affording Mr Clay an opportunity (then Speaker) of putting down the desperate, and infuriated advocate of British tyranny, insult and injury.

But his enemies say Mr Adams bargained with him—This is assertion without proof, and as destitute of truth, as it is of manly frankness.

His superior qualifications placed him in the department of State, and history furnishes no instance, when a superior mind ever had to bargain for a high station, for which, his peculiar fitness was evident to every one.

In Maryland, the administration is daily gaining ground, and by the time the election occurs, I hope we shall be able to present an undivided front in their support.

For Saunders' attack on Clay during the recent Session of Congress, see above, McGriffin to Clay, February 19, 1827, note. In the course of his reply (cf. above, Johnson to Clay, March 12, 1827, note), Francis Johnson had noted the opposition to the administration based "upon charges made against the President and Secretary of State, of coalition, &c." "The Secretary of State did vote for Mr. Adams," he had commented, "and I might ask many, who are now arrayed against the Administration, if they would not have done so? I might ask some—yes; the gentleman from North Carolina {Mr. S.}—if he does not know some who made earnest and solemn appeals to members who were uncommitted, saying, Save the nation, save the nation, by the election of Mr. Adams; and who are now to be found arrayed among the foremost of the Opposition?" *Register of Debates*, 19 Cong., 2 Sess., 1353.   5 Cf. above, Clay to Hammond, June 25, 1827.

INSTRUCTIONS AND DISPATCHES   July 4, 1827

From ALEXANDER H. EVERETT, Madrid, no. 80. Reports receiving, before he "had made any new communication to the Minister [Manuel Gonzáles Salmón] respecting the Columbian [*sic*] Privateer Zulmé [cf. above, Everett to Clay, June 22, 1827]," an answer of which a translation is here enclosed, to his former note (see above, Everett to Clay, April 7, 1827). Characterizes this answer as "anything but satisfactory." Charges that the Spanish Government refuses to come to a "decision upon the merits of the case under pretext of the necessity of sending to America for further information," although official reports in the Marine Department "can hardly fail to contain a statement of all the necessary particulars," and that "The concluding remarks" in Salmón's note "exhibit a want of information upon the common principles of National [*sic*] law, or rather an inattention to the subject which may be viewed as singular even in the proceedings of this Government, and which it would be hardly decent to qualify in a public despatch by the proper name."

Asserts that he has found the enclosure in Clay's "last instructions on this subject" (above, March 20, 1827) "so irregular in form and so unsatisfactory in substance that . . . [he has] concluded for the present not to make any use of it." Explains at length his objections to the document. Observes that "As the Government of the United States make this demand in their own character as an Independent power it seems to be proper that the evidence they offer in support of it should also be such as they can guarantee upon their own responsibility" and suggests the manner in which certain evidence should be gathered, authenticated, certified, and sent to him. Promises, meanwhile, to continue trying "to obtain a decision of the case. . . ." Transmits "copies of two notes" addressed by him "to the Minister [Salmón], one on the subject of the Consulate at the Havana and the other on the Quarantine laws." Notes that, since "the former question" is being submitted by Salmón to the Council of State, he "thought it unnecessary to make the application very urgent and contented . . . [himself] with transmitting a copy of the memorial enclosed in . . . [Clay's] last instructions" (above, April 5, 1827). LS. DNA, RG59, Dip. Disp., Spain, vol. 27 (M31, R28). Received September 8.

From JAMES LENOX KENNEDY, Mazatlan (Mexico). Reports that he arrived "yesterday" and awaits recognition by the Mexican Government. ALS. DNA, RG59, Cons. Disp., Mazatlan, vol. 1 (M159, R1).

MISCELLANEOUS LETTERS   July 4, 1827

From WILLIAM PHILLIPS, Philadelphia. States that his communication of May 12 (1827) was "mailed in Providence R. I. about the 21st. ulto." Complains "in the bitterest terms" of his treatment "by the Command. of Omoa" (not identified). Notes that he "left there on the 14th. of May in a dull sailing vessel, Suffered many privations in the passage of 40 days to the U States." Adds: "I have the Seal & cypher of Legation in my possession; my residence is at No. 19 Pine Street, any orders from the department will be attended to." ALS. DNA, RG59, Cons. Disp., Central America, vol. 1 (M219, R2).

From John Mills, James Brasfield, and Others

Hon. Henry Clay:—   WINCHESTER, July 5th, 1827.
    SIR: The undersigned, a committee in behalf of the citizens of Clark county; respectfully invite you to partake of a Public Dinner, at this place, on the 13th inst. The people resident in this part of your con-

gressional district wish to have the pleasure of seeing and greeting you; they desire another opportunity of giving you another proof of their continued attachment and unshaken confidence—an attachment and confidence based upon an acquaintance of thirty years, above twenty of which you have been in the public service. We offer you our cordial congratulations upon the success which has attended your public life. During the long time you presided in the House of Representatives in Congress,[1] all parties concurred in the ability and impartiality of your administration. When our country was involved in war, you crossed the ocean and assisted in negotiating an honorable peace.[2]— When our Union was threatened with severance in the unfortunate Missouri Question, you effected a satisfactory adjustment.[3] When South America was fighting for the rights of man, you were the first to propose the acknowledgment of her independence, and persevered in that glorious effort until it was crowned with success.[4] When our infant manufactures were about to be crushed under British competition, you flung over them a shield of protection,[5] and they are now seen floating on the "tide of successful experiment." When the powers of our government were about to be paralized [sic] with the doctrine that we could have neither roads nor canals, nor obstructions removed from our navigable rivers, you conspicuously aided in securing the triumph of the principle, which enables this people to improve the internal condition of this continent[6]—this grand theatre of human greatness—so as to promote the convenience, wealth and safety of the Republic. At an important crisis in our history, when our beloved country was divided and distracted by the rival contests for the high office of Presidency, you, with a promptness and decision which has ever characterised your course, aided in giving to this Nation a Chief Magistrate, who had demonstrated by his course of public service, during a period of above thirty years, that he was among the first statesmen in the world.[7] In this act of your life, like all that preceded it, you followed the illustrious lights that had gone before you. You reposed your confidence in the man that had previously received the confidence of Washington, Jefferson, Madison and Monroe.[8] The result has triumphantly justified you. Under his Administration, we occupy a proud station among the nations of the earth. We have liberty and unrivalled prosperity at home, and peace and respectability abroad. Throughout our vast country, the finger of oppression bears not on one single citizen. It is the glory of the present Administration, to have shaped its course in such caution and wisdom, that even its most violent opposers have not agreed among themselves which of all its numerous acts to condemn. That any portion of the citizens of these States should be politically discontented, at a time when we are so highly favored with all the blessings that freemen can desire—that there should exist a party organised for the purpose of changing the

Administration of the present government, would excite our astonishment, if we had not been apprised of the fact, that the Administrations of Washington, Jefferson and Madison, had been also assailed by faction. We are not astonished, because our whole history proves to us, that so long as ambitious men want office, and avaricious men want money, the purest patriots will be hunted for their places. When we look at the catalogue of vague assertions, insinuations and surmises against the members of the Cabinet, which darken and disgrace the press, we repose ourselves on known facts. We look at long lives spent in faithful and able services, and ask who it is that would rob grey-headed, patriot statesmen of their well-earned fame? We ask, who has filled the world with so much clamor? Where do they live? How long have they been known? Have they any reputation to lose if they should be convicted of slander? It is as much the duty and interest of freemen, to stand by and support, with just confidence and applause, integrity and talents in our public servants, as it is their duty to punish the faithless. For how is it possible to form or maintain a free government, by any other means than through the agency of able and honest representatives? And how are true statesmen to be sustained against the calumnies of office-hunters, unless the people will treat with indignation all charges unsupported with fair and satisfactory evidence? We believe in the justice of our country, and in the final triumph of a wise and prudent Administration, over the machinations of those who hunger and thirst for power and emolument.

We tender to you individually, and in behalf of the citizens of this county, the renewed assurances of our highest regard and esteem.

John Mills,	*C. Morrow,*[9]	*Richard Hawes, jr.*
Colby H. Taylor,	*Jams [sic] Simpson,*	*J B. Duncan,*[12]
Thomas R. Moore,	*Silas Evans,*[10]	*Chilton Allan,*
Sam M. Taylor,	*James Brasfield,*	*Matth. Anderson, jr.*[13]
James Bruton,	*Mathew Thompson [sic],*	*Benj. H. Buckner.*
John G. Stewart,	*Benjamin Harrison,*[11]	

Lexington *Kentucky Reporter,* July 14, 1827.

[1] November 4, 1811–January 19, 1814; December 4, 1815–October 28, 1820; December 1, 1823–March 3, 1825. [2] See above, I, 852–1006 *passim.* [3] See above, II, 669–788 *passim;* 911; III, 15–50 *passim.* [4] See above, II, 135, 155–56, 289–92, 343–44, 402–405, 492–507, 508–62, 817–18, 853–60; III, 22–24, 29–31, 44, 184, 186n. [5] See above, II, 134, 138–39, 178–79, 180, 182–84, 185–86, 824–25, 826–47; III, 635–38, 642–44, 647–51, 657–61, 664–65, 670–71, 675–81, 682–730, 733–34, 756. [6] Cf. above, II, 308–11, 322, 446–65, 467–91; see above, III, 568–69, 572–93, 619–27, 632–33. [7] See above, Clay to Blair, January 8, 1825; Clay to Adams, January 9, 1825, note; Clay to Brooke, January 28, February 10, 1825; Clay, Address to the People of the Congressional District, March 26, 1825. [8] George Washington had appointed John Quincy Adams as Minister to the Netherlands in 1794 and to Portugal in 1796. Jefferson's action in not including him as a commissioner of bankruptcy, when Congress shifted that authority in 1801 from the judges to the President, had had the effect of removing Adams from the appointment which he then held; but Jefferson had written to Abigail Adams that he did not know of her son's involvement in the action. Jefferson to Abigail Adams, September 11, 1804, in Jefferson, *Writings* . . . (Monticello edn.), XI, 49–53. Writing to an unidentified correspondent in 1826, Jefferson had stated: "I have never entertained

for Mr. Adams any but sentiments of esteem and respect; and if we have not thought alike on political subjects, I yet never doubted the honesty of his opinions. . . ." *Ibid.*, XVI, 154.   9 Bruton in 1840–1841 was a representative from Montgomery County in the State legislature. Stewart served in that body from Clark County in 1830–1831. Morrow has not been further identified.   10 Member of the Kentucky House of Representatives, from Clark County, 1824–1827, 1828–1829.   11 Matthew Thomson had come to Clark County as a youth, at least as early as 1792. Harrison was probably the nephew of the pioneer Benjamin Harrison, of Bourbon County, who had come to Kentucky as early as 1776 and had been active in the establishment of the State government; the younger Benjamin Harrison served in the Kentucky Legislature during the Sessions of 1829–1830 and 1831.   12 Probably James B. Duncan, who died in Clark County in 1841.   13 Not further identified.

From George Robertson

SIR:—   LANCASTER, 5th July, 1827.

I am instructed by the committee appointed in the 2d of the enclosed resolutions,[1] to invite you to a Public Dinner, proposed to be given you by the county of Garrard, at whatever time shall be most convenient to yourself during your sojourn in Kentucky: and I am also instructed by the committee to assure you of their individual respect and undiminished confidence, notwithstanding the calumnies of factious and disappointed men.

Allow me to add, that in making this communication, it is peculiarly gratifying to me, at this eventful conjuncture of our affairs, local as well as national, to be the organ of the good wishes for your welfare, and for the success of your cause, which are felt and have been most signally manifested, by my county—a county which, if distinguished for nothing else, has some acknowledged claims to a good name, for the constancy and disinterestedness, and (*I will say*) *consequently*, the general rectititude of its political opinions: and my gratification is in no small degree increased, by the fitness of the opportunity which this occasion offers me, to bear my humble testimony in your behalf, against the calumnious charges of Gen. Jackson and some of his disappointed friends.

Associated with you for years in a public service then full of peril and difficulty, I have ever found in your political conduct, unquestioned purity of motive, elevation of sentiment, undisguised frankness, and invincible intrepidity.[2] But these claims (strong and undeniable as they are) to the approbation and gratitude of your country, are multiplied and enhanced by the incidents connected with the last three years of your life.

The late Presidential election placed you in a situation singularly delicate and responsible. Unawed by threats, and unseduced by promises or hopes, you obeyed the dictates of a sound mind and a pure conscience, and fearlessly contributed by your vote, to the election of an individual eminently qualified in every way for the high trust—one who had served his country at home and abroad, for forty years, faithfully and successfully—one who enjoyed the confidence and friendship of Washington, Jefferson, Madison and Monroe[3]—one who concurs with you in the policy best adapted to promote the prosperity and ensure the union and harmony of these States—who cherishes and advocates, and will encourage to the limit of constitutional power, the American System of Roads and Canals, of Domestic Industry, and of a diffusive education—one who has administered the government, thus far, in a manner which could not be disparaged by a comparison with any preceding Administration—who is national and liberal in his principles, impartial in his favours, honest and patriotic in all his purposes—who was the choice of a large majority of the people of the United States, as a fair induction of acknowledged facts will demonstrate[4]—the choice of General Jackson himself (*next to himself*)[5]—the choice of your own District[6]—and, as I have never doubted, and as I believe events will shew, the choice (in preference to the "Hero") of the people of Kentucky.[7] Your knowledge of the disparity of the rival candidates, in fitness for so high a station—your devotion to the cause of Internal Improvement and Domestic Manufactures—your regard for the welfare and the Constitution of your country, left you no safe, or consistent, or honorable alternative. Even your enemies cannot deny, that they had no right to expect, from a knowledge of your principles and your opinions, that you would vote for Gen. Jackson, and many of them candidly admit, that you could not have done so consistently. And if you had suffered yourself to be tempted or provoked to such a suicidal and parricidal act, it would be quite easy to shew that you could not have made him President. I have personal reasons too, for knowing, if any man living can *know*, that in voting for Mr Adams, and accepting the station you now hold in his Cabinet, your motives were pure and patriotic, uninfluenced by any selfish aim or expectation.[8]

I never doubted that you would act as you did. I never doubted that the vote of Kentucky would not be given to Gen. Jackson, *under any circumstances*; or that the votes of Illinois and Missouri would not be given to him, *what ever your course might have been*.[9] And for the people of Kentucky, I will say, that I do not believe they ever were, are now, or ever will be, in favor of electing Gen. Jackson President of the United States—although in his famous Harrodsburg letter, he intimates that you and Mr Adams are corrupt and are engaged in a crusade against the people, and that HE is their great Atlas.[10]

Go on as you have done; "be just and fear not"—and that Government which is the best, and that Administration which is the cheapest in the world, will continue to prosper more and more, until their complete triumph. In ordinary times, it would not be proper, or consistent with my self-respect, to address you in a style so unusual, and which by some might be deemed adulatory. But I felt it due to this occasion, and to a just magnanimity, recollecting as I do, that our public intercourse and personal acquaintance commenced under circumstances not the most propitious to the interchange of kind feelings or favorable opinions.[11] Believing that the same intimate knowledge which I have acquired of your character, by long and scrutinizing observation, will produce the same effects on others that I am happy to avow it has had on me, I cherish the expectation that, ere long, many of those who, from prejudice or delusion, are counted your enemies, will be numbered among your friends, and feel regret and surprise that they ever doubted the *integrity* of your conduct.

Accept, Sir, for my colleagues of the committee, and for myself, our most respectful salutations   G. ROBERTSON.

Hon. H CLAY.

Lexington *Kentucky Reporter*, July 14, 1827.
[1] On July 4 citizens of Garrard County, Kentucky, at a barbecue near Lancaster, had resolved, first, to invite Clay to a public dinner at that town, "at such a time as . . . most convenient to him," and, second, that the committee to extend the invitation be composed of Robertson, John Yantis, Elijah Hyatt (Hiatt), Robert McConnell, William B. Parrow, Thomas Kennedy, Thomas Millan, Simeon H. Anderson, John Rout, Daniel Obannon, John Faulkner, and John B. Jennings. Lexington *Kentucky Reporter*, July 14, 1827. Hiatt, a well-to-do farmer, left an estate of 1,065 acres in Garrard County at his death in 1851. McConnell was a doctor and, during the Session of 1827–1828, a member of the Kentucky General Assembly. Kennedy (cf. above, I, 18) had come to Kentucky from North Carolina as a pioneer, had fought in the Battle of King's Mountain during the American Revolution and in Indian campaigns, had been named to the Virginia Legislature in 1778 and 1791, had been active in drafting the Kentucky Constitution of 1792, and then had served in the Kentucky General Assembly from 1799 to 1824. He died in 1836, owner of some 7,000 acres of land and a large retinue of slaves. Anderson had been admitted to the bar and practiced at Lancaster. He represented that district in the Kentucky Legislature, 1828–1830, 1832, 1836–1838, and was elected to Congress for a term beginning March 4, 1839. He died in August, 1840, at the age of 38. Obannon owned a small tract of land and a paper mill at his death in 1845. John B. Jennings was probably a grandson of William Jennings; the younger man has not been further identified. Millan and Parrow, not further identified.   [2] See above, II, 676n; III, 24.
[3] Cf. above, Mills, Brasfield, and others to Clay, this date.   [4] Since electors were still chosen by legislature in six States in 1824, the popular vote cannot be accurately measured. Cf. Schlesinger and Israel (eds.), *History of American Presidential Elections*, I, [409].   [5] Cf. Jackson to James Gadsden, December 6, 1821, in Bassett (ed.), *Correspondence of Andrew Jackson*, III, 140.   [6] Cf. above, Address to the People, March 26, 1825 (IV, 155–56), and notes.   [7] Cf. above, Clay to Brown, March 27, 1827 note.
[8] In a letter to James Davidson, December 17, 1827, Robertson stated that he had had "a frank conversation" with Clay as early as September, 1824, on the subject of the coming election and had "understood distinctly, that nothing could ever induce him to aid in or approve the General's [Jackson's] election." "Indeed," Robertson continued, "before the election by the House of Representatives, I had heard no one express the opinion that Mr. Clay would or could co-operate with General Jackson's friends." Published in Clay's *Supplement to the Address . . . to the Public, Which Was Published in December, 1827 Exhibiting Further Evidence in Refutation of the Charges against Him, Touching the Last Presidential Election, Made by Gen. Andrew Jackson* (Washington, 1828), 9 (cf. below, June 10, 1828). For Clay's *Address . . . to the Public*, see below, December 29, 1827. Cf. also below, Davidson to Clay, October 20, 1827.   [9] Cf. above, III, 889n; Clay to Brown, March 27, 1827, note.   [10] Cf. above, Hammond to Clay, October 26, 1826, and note.   [11] Reference not found, but cf. above, III, 24.

INSTRUCTIONS AND DISPATCHES   July 5, 1827

From ALBERT GALLATIN, London, no. 92. States that (William) Huskisson, "about a fortnight ago, intimated" that he intended going abroad for benefit of his health, "after the prorogation of Parliament," and that "It was understood that what related to the Commercial Convention, to the renewal of the 3d article of the Convention of 1818, and to the 'nine articles' [cf. above, Gallatin to Clay, June 20, 1827] might be concluded before that time, and that another person would be appointed in his place to terminate the negotiations on . . . the only remaining point, that which relates to the North Eastern boundary [cf. above, Gallatin to Clay, June 27, 1827]." Reports successive postponements of conferences and the receipt of word that "the state of" Huskisson's "health was so precarious" that a replacement for him might be necessary "before another Conference could take place." Observes that his own "stay here must be protracted longer than . . . expected, probably till the 1st of October." Adds that (Henry U.) Addington has informed him of the British Government's decision on one point: "It was utterly impossible for them to agree to a stipulation for the surrender of fugitive slaves." LS. DNA, RG59, Dip. Disp., Great Britain, vol. 34 (M30, R30). Published in Adams (ed.), *Writings of Albert Gallatin*, II, 377–78; extract, in *House Docs.*, 20 Cong., 1 Sess., no. 19, p. 4. Received August 25.

MISCELLANEOUS LETTERS   July 5, 1827

From SAMUEL L. SOUTHARD, Navy Department. Transmits "a communication (No. 15) received recently from Commodore James Biddle" and requests that Clay read it, copy "such parts as may be desirable," and return it. LS. DNA, RG59, Misc. Letters (M179, R65).

In the accompanying letter (as copied at the State Department), written May 15, 1827, on board the *Macedonian* at Rio de Janeiro, Biddle states that Brazil maintains enough vessels for a lawful blockade of the River Plate but that "It may . . . be doubted, whether the officers employed in this service are vigilant in the performance of their duty"; reports that he procured, while at Montevideo, "the release of twenty-five American Seamen from the different Brazil Men of War at that anchorage"; notes the departure from Rio of (Condy) Raguet, "a faithful, zealous, capable representative of his government"; encloses a letter from (John M.) Forbes, whose request that Captain (Beekman Verplanck) Hoffman visit Buenos Aires will not be granted; and adds that "Mr. [Manuel José] Garcia, appointed by the government of Buenos Ayres its Minister to the Court of London, arrived here on the 9th instant" and, instead of continuing his journey, "is at present engaged in negotiating with this [the Brazilian] government for peace" (cf. above, Forbes to Clay, June 29, 1827).

Executor's Note Account with Morrison Estate

[July 6, 1827]
As only acting executor of the estate of James Morrison, Clay files an account of the settlement in notes of the Bank of the Commonwealth from July 10, 1826, through July 6, 1827. A commission of five per cent on receipts of $1,267.73, amounting to $63.13, is allowed the executor. Examined and certified, July 6, 1827, by John Brand, John Bruce, and Benjamin Gratz. Fayette County, Will Book H, 132–34.

Executor's Specie Account with Morrison Estate

[July 6, 1827]
As the only acting executor of the estate of James Morrison, Clay files an account of the settlement in specie funds from July 10, 1826, through July 6, 1827. A commission of five per cent on receipts of $7,743.44, "exclusive of the items in the preceding Statement

of 450$ and 450$ (being the interest paid by the Executor on account of the proportion of the Legacy of the University in his hands). . . ," amounting to $387.17, is allowed the executor. Examined and certified, July 6, 1827, by John Brand, John Bruce, and Benjamin Gratz. Fayette County, Will Book H, 127–31.

MISCELLANEOUS LETTERS   July 6, 1827

From José IGNACIO DE MOLINA, Lima. Transmits copies of "La obra de Constitution de cumplimiento de la ley," published under the auspices of "los Estados libres de America" and dedicated to "los Unidos del Norte [sic]," the founders of liberty in this part of the world; requests that they be given to the President. ALS, in Spanish. DNA, RG59, Misc. Letters (M179, R65).

Molina, not further identified, had just published *Peru el Cumplimiento de la Ley por el Órgano Republicano; Proyecto* (Lima, 1827), a 76-page document.

To George Robertson

LEXINGTON, 7th July, 1827.

DEAR SIR:—Gen. Faulkner and Mr Anderson[1] delivered to me the resolutions adopted at a meeting of my fellow citizens of Garrard, and your obliging letter of the 5th instant, conveying an invitation to a public dinner, which they are pleased to tender me as a testimony of their confidence. I thank them for this honorable manifestation of their attachment, and it would afford me very high gratification, if I could accept their hospitality; but my engagements, public and private, preclude me from enjoying it. I beg you and your worthy colleagues, to render my excuse acceptable to those for whom you act.

I cannot avoid accompanying my regrets, on account of the necessity I am under to decline the invitation, with my respectful acknowledgments to the committee, for the friendly sentiments and feelings, which they have had the goodness to express.— Conscious of the purity of the motives with which I acted on the occasions to which you refer, I anticipate with confidence, from the candor and intelligence of the people, a decision founded in justice. I must add my particular obligations to you, as an old colleague with whom I had the honor to serve, at a period of great interest in the National Councils, for the spontaneous and generous testimony which you have rendered in my behalf.

With assurances of my personal esteem and friendship, I am truly your obedient servant.   H. CLAY.
G. ROBERTSON, Esq. &c. &c.

Lexington *Kentucky Reporter*, July 14, 1827.
[1] John Faulkner; Simeon H. Anderson.

INSTRUCTIONS AND DISPATCHES   July 8, 1827

From ALBERT GALLATIN, London, no. 93. States that he encloses copies of his "letter of 1st June to Lord Dudley, enquiring whether the British Government would be disposed to facilitate the passage through the African British Possessions of certain Natives of Africa [William Beach Lawrence adds, in a postscript, that the "letter referred to . . . was enclosed in No. 81" (above, June 4, 1827)], and of His Lordship's answer dated yesterday." Admits that, "Having but a very imperfect knowledge of the settlement of Liberia, and none of the connection of the Government of the United States with that establishment, or of the measures contemplated to carry their views into effect" (cf. above, Speech, January 20, 1827), he "could not give any explanation on the subject." Conjectures "that the British Government wishes to know with more precision what are the facilities expected from them, and will not pledge themselves for the support or expence [*sic*] attending the return to their native countries of the Africans in question." ALS. DNA, RG59, Dip. Disp., Great Britain, vol. 34 (M30, R30). Copy, in MHi-Adams Papers, Letters Recd. (MR481). Received August 26.

In the enclosure, Lord Dudley gave assurance "that His Majesty's Government have a very strong disposition to afford every practicable assistance to the Government of the United States, for accomplishing the humane object which they have in view"; but at the same time expressed "apprehension of the practicability of any general measure for restoring captured Africans to their homes"; and stated that "His Majesty's Government must hesitate in pledging themselves, decidedly, to an undertaking, which in the end they may find themselves unable to carry into execution; and the failure of which would only aggravate the misfortunes of the unhappy persons whom it was designed to relieve."

From J[OEL] R. POINSETT, Mexico, no. 94. Transmits "a copy . . . and translation of a manifesto issued by the Legislature of the State of Vera Cruz," which was "published, ostensibly, to vindicate the State from the charges of having acted rebelliously by expelling . . . a federal officer" (cf. above, Poinsett to Clay, June 16, 1827), but in reality "to expose what the Legislature of Vera Cruz suspects to be the policy of the United States towards Mexico, and . . . [Poinsett's] efforts to carry that policy into effect"; notes that he has "abstained from demanding satisfaction for this unprovoked and unjustifiable insult." Encloses a copy and a translation of his reply to the assertions of the manifesto, "proving them to be as false and unfounded as they are absurd and infamous." States that he refrained from demanding satisfaction from the federal government because, if it had not been "promptly and fully rendered," his request for his passports "would have placed the two governments in collision," thereby producing the effect desired by the promulgators of the manifesto.

Describes the development of political parties in Mexico between his arrival and the present: before he arrived, the Escoseses or Scotch Masons, comprised of a majority of the higher orders of the clergy, aristocracy, and monarchists, and including the Centralists, largely European Spaniards and wealthy merchants, were the only organized political party; they controlled all the power in the government and opposed a federal government, many of them preferring a monarchy based upon the House of Bourbon and viewing the United States as a natural enemy. Asserts that "a large majority of the nation was then and still is in favor of the federal and republican form of government; but that majority was not organized and its opposition to the views of the dominant party was unconnected and feeble."

Notes that, because of their hostility toward the United States, the Scotch party "has not hesitated to make use of the most unfair and even the basest means to prejudice the public mind" against both himself and his government, that calumnies have been "lavished" upon him "by the Gazette called the '*Sol*,' the organ of that party," and that there had even been attempts to induce the Friar Arenas to implicate him in that conspiracy (cf. above, Sergeant to Clay, January 26,

1827), a project which had been thwarted by the testimony of Arenas, "shortly before he was led out to execution, and which he repeated while on the way to the
place where he was shot." Argues that, because of the attitude of the Scotch party,
he, Poinsett, "was impelled" either to associate with the opposition or to withdraw
from society. Defends Free Masonry, describes his role as a Mason in assisting the
five Ancient York Masonic Lodges in Mexico to obtain a charter from the Grand
Lodge of New York, but adds: "from the moment the public voice accused them
of perverting this philanthropic institution to political purposes, I withdrew myself from their meetings."

States that "the two great parties which divide the country, are arrayed each
under the banner of its respective masonic rite. . ."; reports that since the Yorkist
Masons have gained control of the government, "the progress of liberal principles
has been most rapid—so much so as to lead the people to regard that progress as
the effect of some secret cause" and to attribute the success of the republican
party, the consolidation of the federal system, and the establishment of liberal
principles exclusively to . . . [his] influence"; adds that the Escoseses' control of
the Veracruz Legislature explains the issuance of the manifesto; and urges indulgence toward "the errors committed by these people . . . [since] the science of
government is new to them. . . ." Details his efforts "to convince the government
and people of this country of the friendly disposition cherished by the United
States towards them"; denies that he has ever attempted "to induce discord among
the inhabitants of the country"; and emphasizes that the general government "has
lamented the imprudent conduct of the Legislature of Vera Cruz." LS. DNA,
RG59, Dip. Disp., Mexico, vol. 3 (M97, R4). Extract published, as is Poinsett's
reply (dated July 4, 1827) to the manifesto, in Manning (arr.), *Diplomatic Correspondence . . . Latin-American Nations*, III, 1662, 1663–68. Received August 31.

To William Garrard and Others

Gentlemen   Lexington 9h. July 1827.

Agreeably to the promise which I made to Mess. Matson,[1] Duncan[2]
and Davis[3] when they delivered me your note of the 2d. inst.[4] inviting
me to a County dinner in Bourbon, I have now the satisfaction to
communicate my acceptance of the invitation, and to state that I will
dine with my fellow Citizens whose hospitality is thus kindly tendered,
on monday next, the 16h. instant.

I have to request, gentlemen, that you will make acceptable my acknowledgments as well for the distinguished honor which has been so
handsomely proposed to me as for the friendly motives which dictated
it. I offer you, gentlemen, individually as well as collectively, assurances of the high regard & esteem of Your faithful and obt. Servt.

H. CLAY

Will. Garrard   Thos. Matson   [John L.] Hickman[5] [. . . .]

ALS. Henry Clay Memorial Foundation, Lexington, Kentucky. MS. torn; apparently
four additional addressees were listed.

1 Thomas Matson had come to Bourbon County from Virginia, prior to 1810.

2 Not identified—the Duncan family, pioneer settlers of Bourbon County, was numerous.   3 Probably Garret Davis.   4 Not found.   5 On John L. Hickman's
role at the Bourbon County dinner for Clay, see below, Toast, July 16, 1827. Hickman
had served in the Kentucky House of Representatives during the Sessions of 1808–1809,
1816–1818, and 1820 and at this time sat in the Kentucky Senate (1821–1829).

To John Mills and Others

LEXINGTON, 9th July, 1827.

GENTLEMEN:—I have received the note which, as a Committee of my fellow-citizens of Clarke County, you addressed to me on the 5th instant, inviting me to a public dinner at Winchester on the 13th inst. I regret very much, that the necessity which I am under, of an early return to Washington City, will not allow me to accept the invitation. It would have been particularly agreeable to me, at the present time, in consequence of a new form which an old attack has received from a high source,[1] to have been able to visit all parts of my old Congressional district, and communicate freely with my former constituents. As I am prevented from having that satisfaction, I request, gentlemen, that you will do me the favor to convey to that portion of them, situated in Clarke county, my respectful acknowledgments and hearty thanks for their kind invitation, for the friendly sentiments with which its transmission is accompanied, and especially, for the repetition of the expression of their approbation of my vote on the late Presidential election. Subsequent events and developments of the character of the competitor of the candidate who was elected, have certainly not tended to weaken the strong conviction I felt, at the period of the election, of the unfitness of that competitor for that office.

The Administration, gentlemen, of which you have been pleased to express your approbation, has anxiously endeavored, by the exertion of all its energies, to promote the public good. That the public will judge and decide correctly of its acts I have no doubt. To their decision all are bound to submit. And I have entire confidence, that it will be in conformity with justice and the interests of our country.

I request, gentlemen, your acceptance of the assurance of the high respect for you collectively and individually, of your faithful friend and fellow-citizen,   H. CLAY.

Messrs. John Mills, Colby H. Taylor, Thomas R. Moore, &c. &c.

Lexington *Kentucky Reporter*, July 14, 1827.
[1] Cf. above, Clay to Hammond, June 25, 1827.

From Samuel L. Southard

Dear Sir: 9 July—[1827]

Several days ago I injured my finger so that I still write with great inconvenience & pain. This, by way of apology— We have little that is new & important— To the North every thing seems to promise fairly— I see nothing to create doubt of the final result. In N. York, the prospect brightens— New facts are daily added to those of which you were apprised before you left— The editorial article in the leading Clintonian paper in Albany is decisive & strong—& I am informed was *written* by Mr. C. himself.[1] If so, he does not doubt what the State will do.

The principal topic of the day is, the Genl's letter to Beverly[2]— The effect precisely what might well have been anticipated— The comee of Guardians[3] ought to keep nearer to the Genl.

I write in so much pain that I must stop— your family is well— mine as usual— respectfully &c &c   SAML L. SOUTHARD
Mr. Clay.

ALS. DLC–HC (DNA, M212, R6).
[1] The *Albany Daily Advertiser* on June 22, 1827, endorsed the candidacy of John Quincy Adams and the course of his administration. *Albany Argus*, June 23, 1827; Washington *Daily National Journal*, June 26, 1827.   [2] Cf. above, Clay to Hammond, June 25, 1827.   [3] Cf. above, Johnson to Clay, April 29, 1827, note.

INSTRUCTIONS AND DISPATCHES   July 9, 1827

From ALBERT GALLATIN, London, no. 94. Notes that he "alluded," in his dispatch of the preceding day, "to the settlement of Liberia, because it is possible that some jealousy of that establishment is one of the causes of the vague answer given by the British Government." Speculates, also, that the recent unpopularity in England of "British settlements on the Coast of Africa. . . , on account of the expence [*sic*], of the Ashantee War and above all of the immense waste of life amongst both whites and blacks not born in the Country," which have led to "Some enquiry . . . on the subject in Parliament" (a report of which is enclosed), "may have contributed to make this Government averse to enter into any engagement connected with these settlements." Reports that the British have advised the Dutch Government "that, owing to the notorious unhealthiness of Sierra Leone, the mixed tribunal for the trial of offences against the laws forbidding the Slave trade would be removed to the island of Fernando Po on the Benin Coast," to which "it seems they intend to transfer their principal garrison and civil establishments." Observes that the British "have taken possession of Fernando Po in a very summary way"— the island having been ceded by Portugal to Spain "about the year 1778" and "never . . . retroceded"; charges that "The present occupation by the British is a practical exposition of the doctrine asserted in respect of the territory west of the Stony Mountains." ALS. DNA, RG59, Dip. Disp., Great Britain, vol. 34 (M30, R30). Copy, in MHi-Adams Papers, Letters Rec'd. (MR481). Received August 26.

In 1824 British from Sierra Leone had invaded the Ashanti territory on the Gold Coast. Defeated in that campaign, the British had overcome the Ashanti in 1826, but peace was not effected until 1831. The warfare was resumed in 1863 and continued intermittently until Ashanti became a Crown Colony in 1902. Henry Wellington (not further identified) and James Rowan (a major of infantry) had been sent by Parliament as commissioners of inquiry in 1825. The first part of their report "into the State of the Colony of Sierra Leone" had been ordered for printing by the House of Commons on May 7, 1827, and is filed with Gallatin's dispatch. G. B. House of Commons, *Sess. Papers, 1826–1827*, VII, 267–377 (rept. no. 312).

Although the Spanish had held title to the island of Fernando Po since 1494, they had been so decimated by yellow fever there that they had withdrawn in 1781. Because of the island's strategic location for control of the slave trade, the British leased bases from the Spanish in 1827 and, in the absence of Spanish governmental authority, took over administration of the island. Efforts of the British to acquire the island were subsequently rejected by Spain, so in 1843 the British antislavery patrol base was shifted to Freetown in Sierra Leone.

From WILLIAM R. HIGINBOTHAM (Bermuda—1). Notes that his drafts of December 23, 1826, for $414.50 and of January 18, 1827, for $100 have been refused and returned protested, for "the reason alleged . . . that I was not to draw until authorized." Encloses a copy of a letter from the 5th auditor's office, Treasury Department, dated November 5, 1826, which shows him a credit of $521 standing on the books of the Treasury until claimed. Comments: "I have learned from a private source, that explanations are required by you—I beg leave to be informed of them by return of the Annapolis Packet." LS. DNA, RG59, Cons. Disp., Bermuda, vol. 1 (M-T232, R1).

On March 22, 1827, William Browne had written as follows to "Messrs. J. & J. Harper, Alexandria [District of Columbia]": "William R. Higginbotham [sic] . . . having been instructed under date of 23 June last to make no further drafts upon this Department, until he should receive authority to that effect, the Secretary declines making any payment on account of the draft of that gentleman, $414.50 which was presented by one of your House a few days since; I therefore return it herewith." Copy, in DNA, RG59, Dom. Letters, vol. 21, p. 502 (M40, R19). The Harpers have not been identified. Cf. above, Clay to Higinbotham, April 3, 1826; June 23, 1826.

On September 15, 1827, William Browne, by authorization of "the Secretary," informed John (G.) Vowell, of Alexandria, "that the sum of $243.38 is now ready to be paid on account of the Bill of $414.50 drawn upon this Department by Mr. Higinbotham" and held by Vowell (a prominent and wealthy merchant). Copy, in DNA, RG59, Dom. Letters, vol. 22, p. 50 (M40, R20).

From W. R. HIGINBOTHAM (Bermuda—2). Refers to his preceding letter of this date and notes that the holder of his draft of December 23, 1826, for $414.50 has called for immediate payment and has been instructed to return the original draft to the Department. States that, in addition to the Treasury balance of $521.90, reported as due to Higinbotham on November 5, 1826, a voucher for $110.61 subsequently should have been passed to his credit. LS. DNA, RG59, Cons. Disp., Bermuda, vol. 1 (M-T232, R1). Endorsed: "Amt due him per Statement 30. June 1827, $343.38."

MISCELLANEOUS LETTERS   July 9, 1827

From RICHARD DAVIS, Georgetown (District of Columbia). Submits an overdue account, amounting to $33.25, for purchases of clothing by "Mr. John Maul an old gentlemen whose Son . . . is messenger in . . . [Clay's] Office." Adds: "I was advised to let you know that the same remains unpaid, & that you have it in your power to cause the same to be paid through his Son"; and requests Clay's aid "in getting the money." ALS. DNA, RG59, Accounting Records, Misc. Letters.

In reply to this letter William Browne informed Davis, July 23, 1827, "relative to a debt due . . . from Mr. John P. Maul," that he was "directed to state that it has never been the practice of any Secretary of the Department to interfere in the private concerns, or pecuniary engagements, of persons attached thereto, and that he cannot, in the present case, make an exception to that rule.—" Copy, ibid., Dom. Letters, vol. 22, pp. 9 (M40, R20).

Davis was proprietor of a dry-goods store in Georgetown. John Maul, a native of Pennsylvania, had served in the Army as a resident of the District of Columbia from 1813 until 1815 and from 1816 until 1821, when he had been discharged with the rank of captain. Two Maul brothers, presumably William and John P., had been employed by the State Department (cf. above, Woodside to Clay, October 5, 1826).

From JAMES H. McCULLOCH, Baltimore. Transmits a letter received from Robert Monroe Harrison, whom he does not know personally, but with whom he has corresponded for several years; cites Harrison's "just & energetic efforts to obtain justice for our seamen," his difficulties "with the petty authorities" on the islands where he has been stationed, and the ill fortune that has followed him; and states that, with one exception, reports of him from American citizens who have had dealings with him have been good. ALS. DNA, RG59, Misc. Letters (M179, R65).

In the enclosure, dated May 18, Harrison expresses thanks for any "agency" McCulloch may have had in procuring for him the appointment as consul to St. Bartholomew (cf. above, McCulloch to Clay, February 9, 1827), states that he has heard that he will not be received there, and begs that McCulloch write his friends "to use their interest" with Clay to get him recognition.

To Thomas Smith

Lexington 10th July, 1827.

Mr Smith:—I will thank you to correct an unimportant mistake of date, in my letter of the 29th ult. addressed to the public, and inserted in the Reporter. It was on Sunday the 24th, and not on the 23d ult., that I arrived at Wheeling. Yours,   H. CLAY.

Lexington *Kentucky Reporter*, July 11, 1827.

From René Auguste Chouteau and Others

Honorable Henry Clay
Sir   St Louis July 10th. 1827

The profound respect which the undersigned Citizens of St Louis entertain for your talents, and the estimate which they place upon your eminent public services, would not permit them to behold otherwise than with deep concern the success of any attempt to paralize [*sic*] your usefulness. They deem the present therefore a conjunction which calls upon them to render to you that support which the audible expression of their approbation may be calculated to afford—a conjunction which imposes upon the good, upon the friends of correct principles throughout these States, an obligation to lift up their voices in support of our Administration, eminently entitled to their confidence.—

Hoping that considerations referable to your public duties may not be deemed to interpose obstacles to the gratification of their wishes, the undersigned beg leave to express the satisfaction which a visit from you to their infant City would afford them, if not inconsistent with your private arrangements, and to [r]equest that they may be favored with an opportunity to offer personally to you, the defender of the rights of Missouri the advocate of free governments, the friend of the liberties of the human race in every portion of the World, to you, the

Statesman of elevated views, of enlightened policy and liberal principles, those public manifestations of regard which would be most grateful to their feelings   AUG. CHOUTEAU

[. . . .]

LS by Chouteau and 216 other citizens of St. Louis. DLC-HC (DNA, M212, R2).

From James McBride and Others

To the Honorable Henry Clay.   HAMILTON, July 10, 1827.

SIR:—The citizens of Hamilton and Rossville, desirous to evince the
high sense they entertain of your public services, and having understood that, in returning to Washington City, you will pass through the
state of Ohio, have instructed the undersigned to express to you their
wish that you partake with them a public dinner, at such time as may
best comport with your arrangements.

In expressing to you this invitation, we take leave to assure you of
the high consideration we individually entertain of your character as
a citizen, and of your services as a public functionary.

JAMES M'BRIDE,   GEORGE BURNAP, }
SAM'L MILLIKIN,   DAVID HIGGINS.[1] } *Committee.*
J. C. DUNLAVY,

Lexington *Kentucky Reporter,* July 21, 1827. McBride, born near Greencastle, Franklin
County, Pennsylvania, had settled at Hamilton, Ohio, in 1806, at age 18, and had been
a member of the Ohio General Assembly, representing Butler County, in 1822. He acquired prominence for his archaeological investigations of the Indian mounds in the
region and supplied the data for the publication, *Ancient Monuments of the Mississippi
Valley,* issued by the Smithsonian Institution in 1848. He was also active in the founding
of Miami University at Oxford (established by legislative authority of 1809 but not
opened as a college until 1824) and served on its board of trustees.
   [1] Millikin, born in Pennsylvania, was a veteran of the War of 1812, a physician, and
a merchant. He had served four years (1821–1825) as sheriff of Butler County, Ohio.
   John C. Dunlavy (Dunlevy) was also a physician at Hamilton. He had moved there
and opened practice in 1823 after a residence in Lebanon, Ohio, to which town he returned in 1834. Burnap has not been identified. Higgins had been a member of the
Ohio House of Representatives from 1823 to 1826 and served as judge of the court of
common pleas at Sandusky from 1831 to 1837.

INSTRUCTIONS AND DISPATCHES   July 10, 1827

From ALBERT GALLATIN, London, no. 95. Encloses copies of "the five Acts [relating
to consolidation of the criminal law] of the last session of Parliament brought in
by" (Robert) Peel, along with a bill, "not yet enacted," introduced by him. Notes
that Peel has provided the United States Government "a complete set of all the
papers, connected with the consolidation and reform of British jurisprudence,
which have been *printed* under his sanction [Anthony Hammond, *A Treatise on
the Consolidation of the Criminal Law* (8 vols., London, 1825–29)]." Explains that
Peel "did not commit himself to the approval of them or of any thing on the
subject of criminal law, beyond what he had submitted to the consideration of
Parliament," but rather that he gave the author, "a general authority to proceed
in his work and to print the result of his labours. . . ." Promises to send these

"three folio volumes," plus "an important work which has just appeared [Henry Hallam, *The Constitutional History of England, from the Accession of Henry VII to the Death of George II* (2 vols., London, 1827)]," and the "Second edition of Humphrey [*sic*] on real property [James Humphreys, *Observations on the Actual State of the English Laws of Real Property; with Outlines for a Systematic Reform* (2d. edn., London, 1827)]," with "the other books for the Department." Predicts that Humphreys' work will "produce useful and important alterations" in British property law. ALS. DNA, RG59, Dip. Disp., Great Britain, vol. 34 (M30, R30). Copy, in MHi-Adams Papers, Letters Recd. (MR481). Received August 26.

The five acts to which Gallatin referred were 7 & 8 *Geo.* IV, c. 27–31, pp. 79–108, dated June 21, 1827. On June 20, Peel had also been directed, with others, to prepare a bill dealing with small debt recovery. G. B. House of Commons, *Journal*, vol. 82 (1826–1827), p. 586.

From HENRY MIDDLETON, St. Petersburg, no. 71. Transmits "the report of a Commission of inquiry instituted at Warsaw to examine into the proceedings of certain secret societies in Poland," which indicates that some Poles remember "their former independent political existence & the rights" lost "by conquest." Notes that, in consequence of this report, "the Emperor & King [Nicholas I] has convoked the high national Court of the Kingdom of Poland to bring to trial the accused" and those implicated in the "Polish provinces of Russia will be tried at St. Petersburgh [*sic*] by the criminal department of the Senate of the Empire." Comments that the report reflects the "vigilance and jealousy of the Governors," rather than "insurrectionary intention of the governed," who appear to have no hope of the re-establishment of Poland; expresses doubt that Russia need expect "any commotions" from the Poles. ALS. DNA, RG59, Dip. Disp., Russia, vol. 11 (M35, R11). Dated 28 June/10 July 1827." Received October 8.

An agreement, "couched in rather general terms," formulated at Kiev in 1825 by members of Russian and Polish secret organizations had come to light during the investigations resulting from the Decembrist uprising (see above, Middleton to Clay, January 2, 7, February 11, 1826). The Polish tribunal in 1828 "cleared all the accused from the charge of high treason" and sentenced them leniently "for their participation in clandestine organizations." Alexander Gieysztor and others, *History of Poland* (trans. from the Polish by Krystyna Cekalska and others; Warsaw, 1968), 445.

From George I. Brown and Others

JESSAMINE COUNTY, July 11th, 1827.

DEAR SIR:—We the undersigned, a committee appointed on behalf of a large number of the citizens of this county, are authorised to say, that they are still very desirous of manifesting the very high respect and regard which they now and ever have entertained for you, in your prompt and unwearied efforts in the great cause of Internal Improvements and National Industry; in your wise and philanthropic views in regard to Universal Liberty, and and [*sic*] in every other possible measure that could extend wealth, honor, or respectability to our common country. It is therefore the ardent and very anxious wish of this Committee, and their fellow citizens of this county whom they represent in sentiment on this occasion, once more to display that unbounded and unshaken confidence which they have ever reposed in you, without cause of regret; and we are instructed to invite you to an entertainment to be given in Nicholasville, whenever you shall signify your convenience to attend.

With sentiments of the highest regard and respect, your friends and fellow citizens.

George I. Brown,   Hugh Chrisman,
William A. Fry,[1]   Jacob Todhunter,[2]
B. Netherland,   A. Logan,
John Barkley,   Mason Singleton,[3]
John Downing.

The Hon. H. CLAY

Lexington *Kentucky Reporter*, July 18, 1827.
[1] Born in Albemarle County, Virginia, in 1761. A veteran of the Revolution, he was pensioned for this service in 1834 and died the following year, leaving farm land in Jessamine, Garrard, and Cumberland Counties of Kentucky and in Virginia.   [2] A farmer who died in 1832, at age 73.   [3] Born in the early years of Kentucky settlement, in the Keene area of what became Jessamine County, he was a veteran of the War of 1812. He had become a major of Kentucky militia in 1816.

From Peter B. Porter

Dear Sir,   Black Rock July 11th. 1827
    Thinking it possible that some of your friends in Kentucky may feel disposed to make a voyage through the western Lakes, I send you a number of the Black Rock Gazette,[1] containing a notice of the sailing of the Steam Boat, H. Clay,[2] for Green Bay, on the 7th. of next month. She will touch at Sandusky, on her outward passage, on the evening of the eighth. The Boat is stanch & safe, an admirable sailer, & has very comfortable accomodations [sic].

    I congratulate you on your late triumphant march through Pennsylvania,[3] exhibiting a very different state of feeling from that which prevailed there two years ago.[4] I cannot but hope that the change, obviously great, will be sufficiently so to produce the desired result. The political aspect of New York is at this time extremely favourable, & daily becoming more so. There can be no doubt but that a large majority of the people will go with the administration, but if our present system, of chosing [sic] electors by districts, is retained, as I think it will be,[5] Genl. Jackson will probably get some half a dozen votes.[6] The "American System" is extremely popular in every part of the State, with the exception perhaps of the city of New York, and we shall send a very numerous delegation to the Harrisburg Convention,[7] as well on account of the intrinsic importance of its objects, as because it will afford a favourable opportunity to the friends of the Admn for concerting the means of counteracting the systematic attacks of the opposition. The followers of Clinton & Van Buren are deserting them on the presidential question,[8] and we begin to be afraid that Clinton himself will desert his own standard & come over to the Administration.[9] I think however that he still entertains hopes that the supporters of Jackson will eventually give him up, & make him (Clinton) the opposing candidate to Mr Adams[10]—

We did not have the pleasure of seeing the French Minister & his family.[11] They were for two days at the Falls,[12] from whence he wrote me a very polite note (by Mr. Chavelier [sic] of Richmond[13] who passed a day with us) enclosing your letters & expressing his regret that the early sailing of the Steam Boat from Queenstown[14] in which he had taken passage prevented him from visiting Black Rock & Buffalo. It would have given pleasure to have seen them, but our disappointment was less on account of the peculiar condition of Mrs Porter's health which would have prevented her from bestowing on them all the attentions she could have wished.[15]

Mrs Porter, who still remains in statu quo, joins me in assurances to Mrs Clay & yourself of our great respect & regard.   P. B. PORTER
Hon. Henry Clay.

ALS. DLC-HC (DNA, M212, R2).
[1] Established as a weekly December 20, 1824.   [2] Cf. above, Clay to Porter, April 23, 1825, note.   [3] Cf. above, Clay to Adams, June 23, 1827; Clay to Hammond, June 25, 1827.   [4] Cf. above, Address, March 26, 1825, note 8; Cameron and Krause to Clay, February 6, 1826; Binns to Clay, May 10, 1826, note; Sergeant to Clay, September 28, 1826; Markley to Clay, May 30, 1826; Cameron to Clay, ca. October 15, 1826.   [5] Cf. above, Clay to Brooke, December 11, 1826, note.   [6] Cf. above, Degrand to Clay, February 8, 1827. In the election of 1828, New York gave Jackson 20 electoral votes and Adams, 16.   [7] Cf. above, Clay to Crowninshield, March 18, 1827, note. New York sent the largest delegation, 21, to the convention. Philadelphia United States Gazette, August 2, 1827.   [8] Cf. above, Rose to Clay, June 16, 1827.   [9] Cf. above, Porter to Clay, April 18, 1827; Southard to Clay, July 9, 1827.   [10] Cf. above, Porter to Clay, October 8, 1826; Webster to Clay, April 14, 1827; Clay to Webster, April 20, 1827.
[11] See above, Mareuil to Clay, June 30, 1827.   [12] Niagara Falls.   [13] Probably John A. Chevaille, of French birth, who had come to the United States as agent for Pierre Augustin Caron de Beaumarchais and resided in a mansion at the corner of Third and Cary Streets, Richmond, Virginia.   [14] Ontario.   [15] See above, Porter to Clay, May 1, 1827, note.

INSTRUCTIONS AND DISPATCHES   July 11, 1827

From J[OHN] J. APPLETON, Stockholm, no. 20. Announces, "with great pleasure," the signing "of a new Treaty of Navigation and Commerce between the United States and His Majesty the King of Sweden and Norway [Charles XIV]," a copy of which he encloses. Calls attention to the fact that the document "secures all the interests for which he had received instructions (see above, Clay to Appleton, January 12, 1827). States, more specifically: "By it, the Vessels of the United States are placed in the ports of Sweden, Norway & the Island of St. Barthelemey on a footing of perfect equality with the Vessels of those Countries, with reference to the general faculty of importing and exporting and to the duties and charges of all kinds payable in such cases on the Vessels and their Cargoes; the trade between Sweden and Norway and their West India Colony is open'd to the Citizens of the United States on the same footing as to natives of those Countries; and the produce of the United States are [sic] admitted in Sweden, Norway, and St. Bartholemy [sic] on the same terms as similar produce from any other foreign Country and moreover in Sweden and Norway on the same terms as similar produce from their West India Colony and in the colony as similar produce from the mother Country." Lists "The only exceptions to these principles":

"1. As regards vessels, the reserve made by each State of its own coasting Trade.

"2. As regards both vessels and produce, the reserve made by Sweden & Norway of their trade with Finland.

"3. As regards produce alone, the reserve made by Sweden & Norway of particular advantages to the Tallow, and Tallow Candles of Russia."

Explains the reasons for his agreement to the last two exceptions and for the insertion of various articles into the treaty; transmits documents relative to the negotiations; notes the circumstances through which the treaty was signed on July 4; praises (James) Cucheval, his secretary, who takes the treaty to Washington; and concludes with the hope "that in the negociation" he has "not misunderstood . . . [Clay's] instructions, and that its result will be advantageous to our dear Country. . . ." ALS. DNA, RG59, Dip. Disp., Sweden and Norway, vol. 5 (M45, R6). Published, with enclosures (except the treaty), in *American State Papers, Foreign Relations*, VI, 725–41; the treaty is found in *ibid.*, 707–13, and, again, 830–35. Received September 8.

Ratifications of the treaty were exchanged at Washington, January 18, 1828.

From J[OHN] J. APPLETON, Stockholm, no. 21. States that, since closing his earlier dispatch of this day, he has "received from the Count of Wetterstedt a letter and a box directed to the Baron of Stakelberg [sic]," which "will be forwarded by Mr. [James] Cucheval." Notes that "the box contains the instrument of the King's [Charles XIV's] ratification of the Treaty." Comments on the "distinguished attention and Kindness" with which he has been treated by the King and Cabinet" and adds: "To the Count of Wetterstedt, I should not do justice if I did not mention that during the negociation he has evinced all the frankness and liberality of an honest and enlightened mind. He holds our Country and its institutions in just estimation."

Reports in a postscript, for which he opened this communication, "the purport of a verbal communication . . . just received from the Minister of Foreign Affairs [Wetterstedt] at an interview which he had requested for the purpose": "The Minister stated that a serious misintelligence having existed between Mr. [Robert Monroe] Harrison our Commercial Agent at St. Barthelemy and the former Governor of that Colony [Johan Norderling—cf. above, Harrison to Clay, May 21, June 9, 1827], he had by order of the King instructed the Baron of Stakelberg to intimate that it would be agreable [sic] to H. Majesty that Mr. Harrison should not be appointed to that consulate. Owing no doubt to some failure on the part of the Baron, Mr. Harrison had contrary to the King's wishes received that appointment. The King had too much respect for the Government of the U: S: to refuse now an Exequatur to its Consul: He hoped however that sharing his anxiety for the maintenance of harmony and good intelligence between the Authorities of the two Countries in that distant Colony, it would see the propriety of recommending on any suitable occasion, to Mr. Harrison, more moderation in his conduct, that the disagreeable scenes which had occur'd might not be repeated. The Count added that he was far from believing that the former Governor, had himself been an example of prudence in the controversies to which he alluded but, that Mr. Harrison could claim his share of the blame that attach'd to them." ALS. DNA, RG59, Dip. Disp., Sweden and Norway, vol. 5 (M45, R6). Received September 8.

Toasts and Speech at Lexington Public Dinner

[July 12, 1827]

4. *Our distinguished Guest Henry Clay*—The furnace of persecution may be heated seven times hotter and seventy times more, he will come out unscathed by the fire of malignity, brighter to all and dearer to his friends; while his enemies shall sink with the dross of their own vile materials.

[Clay responded to the above toast as follows:]

MR PRESIDENT, FRIENDS AND FELLOW CITIZENS;

I beg permission to offer my hearty thanks, and to make my respectful acknowledgments, for the affectionate reception which has been given me during my present visit to my old Congressional district, and for this hospitable and honourable testimony of your esteem and confidence. And I thank you especially for the friendly sentiments and feelings expressed in the toast which you have just done me the honor to drink. I always had the happiness of knowing that I enjoyed, in a high degree, the attachment of that portion of my fellow citizens whom I formerly represented; but I should never have been sensible of the strength and ardor of their affection, except for the extraordinary character of the times. For near two years and a half I have been assailed with a rancor and bitterness which have few examples. I have found myself the particular object of concerted and concentrated abuse; and others, thrusting themselves between you and me, have dared to arraign me for treachery to your interests. But my former constituents, unaffected by the calumnies which have been so perseveringly circulated to my prejudice have stood by me with a generous constancy and a noble magnanimity. The measure of their regard and confidence has risen with, and even surpassed, that of the malevolence, great as it is, of my personal and political foes. I thank you, gentlemen, who are a large portion of my late constituents. I thank you, and every one of them, with all my heart, for the manly support which I have uniformly received. It has cheered and consoled me, amidst all my severe trials; and may I not add that it is honourable to the generous hearts and enlightened heads who have resolved to protect the character of an old friend and a faithful servant?

The numerous manifestations of your confidence and attachment will be among the latest and most treasured recollections of my life. They impose on me obligations which can never be weakened or cancelled. One of these obligations is, that I should embrace every fair opportunity to vindicate that character which you have so generously sustained, and to evince to you and to the world, that you have not yielded to the impulses of a blind and enthusiastic sentiment. I feel that I am, on all fit occasions, especially bound to vindicate myself to my former constituents. It was as *their* representative; it was in the fulfilment of a high trust which *they* confided to me, that I have been accused of violating the most sacred of duties, of treating their wishes with contempt, and their interests with treachery. Nor is this obligation, in my conception of its import, at all weakened by the dissolution of the relations which heretofore existed between us. I would instantly resign the place I hold in the councils of the nation, and directly appeal to the suffrages of my late constituents, as a candidate for re-election, if I did not know that my foes are of that class whom one rising from the dead cannot convince, whom nothing can silence, and who wage a war of extermination. On the issue of such an appeal, they would redouble their abuse of me and of you; for their hatred is common to us both.

They have compelled me so often to be the theme of my addresses to the people, that I should have willingly abstained on this festive occasion, from any allusion to this subject, but for a new and imposing form which the calumny against me has recently assumed. I am again put on my defence, not of any new charge nor by any new adversary, but of the old charges, clad in a new dress, and exhibited by an open and undisguised enemy. The fictitious names have been stricken from the foot of the indictment, and that of a known and substantial prosecutor has been voluntarily offered. Undaunted by the formidable name of that prosecutor, I will avail myself, with your indulgence, of this fit opportunity of free and unreserved intercourse with you, as a large number of my late constituents, to make some observations on the past and present state of the question. When evidence shall be produced, as I have now a clear right to demand, in support of the accusation, it will be the proper time for me to take such notice of it as its nature may require.

In February, 1825, it was my duty, as the Representative of this District, to vote for some one of the three candidates for the Presidency, who were returned to the House of Representatives. It has been established, and can be further proved that, before I left this State the preceding fall, I communicated to several gentlemen of the highest respectability, my fixed determination not to vote for General Jackson.[1] The friends of Mr Crawford asserted to the last, that the condition of his health was such as to enable him to administer the duties of the office. I thought otherwise, after I reached Washington City, and visited him to satisfy myself, and that that physical impediment, if there were no other objections, ought to prevent his election.[2] Although the Delegations from four States voted for him, and his pretensions were zealously pressed to the very last moment, it has been of late asserted, and I believe by some of the very persons who then warmly espoused his cause, that his incompetency was so palpable as clearly to limit the choice to two of the three returned candidates.[3] In my view of my duty, there was no alternative but that which I embraced. That I had some objections to Mr Adams, I am ready freely to admit;[4] but these did not weigh a feather in comparison with the greater and insurmountable objections, long and deliberately entertained against his competitor. I take this occasion, with great satisfaction, to state, that my objections to Mr Adams arose chiefly from apprehensions which have not been realized. I have found him at the head of the Government able, enlightened, patient of investigation, and ever ready to receive with respect, and when approved by his judgment, to act upon the counsels of his official advisers. I add, with unmixt pleasure, that, from the commencement of the Government, with the exception of Mr Jefferson's Administration, no Chief Magistrate has found the members of his Cabinet so united on all public measures, and so cordial and friendly in all their intercourse, private and official, as those are of the present President.

Had I voted for Gen. Jackson, in opposition to the well-known opinions which I entertained of him, one tenth part of the ingenuity and zeal which have been employed to excite prejudices against me would have held me up to universal contempt: and what would have been worse, *I* should have *felt* that I really deserved it.

Before the election, an attempt was made by an abusive letter, published in the Columbian Observer, at Philadelphia,[5] a paper which, as has since transpired, was sustained by Mr Senator Eaton,[6] the colleague, the friend and the biographer of General Jackson,[7] to assail my motives and to deter me in the exercise of my duty. This letter being avowed by Mr George Kremer,[8] I instantly demanded from the House of Representatives an investigation.[9] A committee was accordingly, on the 5th day of February, 1825, appointed in the rare mode of balloting by the House, instead of by the selection of the Speaker. It was composed of some of the leading members of the body, not one of whom was my political friend in the preceding Presidential canvass. Although Mr Kremer, in addressing the House, had declared his willingness to bring forward his proofs, and his readiness to abide the issue of the enquiry, his fears or other counsels than his own prevailed upon him to take refuge in a miserable subterfuge.[10] Of all possible periods that was the most fitting to substantiate the charge, if it was true. Every circumstance was then fresh; the witnesses all living and present; the election not yet complete; and therefore the imputed corrupt bargain not fulfilled. All these powerful considerations had no weight with the conspirators and their accessaries, and they meanly shrunk from even an attempt to prove their charge, for the best of all possible reasons—because, being false and fabricated, they could adduce no proof which was not false and fabricated.

During two years and a half, which have now intervened, a portion of the press, devoted to the cause of Gen. Jackson, has been teeming with the vilest calumnies against me, and the charge, *under every cameleon form*, has been a thousand times repeated. Up to this time, I have in vain invited investigation, and demanded evidence. None, not a particle has been adduced.

The extraordinary ground has been taken, that the accusers were not bound to establish by proof the guilt of their designated victim. In a civilized, christian and free community, the monstrous principle has been assumed, that accusation and conviction are synonymous; and that the persons who deliberately bring forward an atrocious charge are exempted from all obligation to substantiate it! And the pretext is, that the crime, being of a political nature, is shrouded in darkness and incapable of being substantiated. But is there any real difference, in this respect, between political and other offences? Do not all perpetrators of crime endeavor to conceal their guilt and to elude detection? If the accuser of a political offence is absolved from the duty of supporting his accusation, every other accuser of offence stands equally absolved. Such a principle, practically carried into society, would subvert all harmony, peace and tranquillity. None—no age, nor sex, nor profession, nor calling would be safe against its baleful and overwhelming influence. It would amount to an universal license to universal calumny!

No one has ever contended, that the proof should be exclusively that of eye-witnesses, testifying from their senses positively and directly to the fact. Political, like all other offences, may be established by circumstantial as well as positive evidence. But I do contend that *some* evidence, be it what it may, ought to be exhibited. If there be none, how do the accusers *know* that an offence has been perpetrated? If they do know it, let us have the *facts* on which their conviction is based. I will not even assert that, in public affairs, a citizen has not a right, freely to express his *opinions* of public men, and to speculate upon the motives of their conduct. But if he chooses to promulgate opinions, let them be given as *opinions*. The public will correctly judge of their value and their grounds. No one has a right to put forth the positive assertion, that a political offence has been committed, unless he stands prepared to sustain, by satisfactory proof of some kind, its actual existence.

If he who exhibits a charge of a political crime is, from its very nature, disabled to establish it, how much more difficult is the condition of the accused? How can he exhibit negative proof of his innocence, if no affirmative proof of his guilt is or can be adduced?

It must have been a conviction that the justice of the public required a definite charge, by a responsible accuser, that has at last extorted from Gen. Jackson his letter of the 6th of June, lately published.[11] I approach that letter with great reluctance, not on my own account, for on that I do most heartily and sincerely rejoice that it has made its appearance. But it is a reluctance excited by the feelings of respect which I would anxiously have cultivated towards its author. He has, however, by that letter, created such relations between us that, in any language which I may employ, in examining its contents, I feel myself bound by no other obligations than those which belong to truth, to public decorum, and to myself.

The first consideration which must, on the perusal of the letter, force itself upon every reflecting mind is that which arises out of the delicate posture in which Gen. Jackson stands before the American public. He is a candidate for the Presidency, avowed and proclaimed. He has no competitor at present, and there is no probability of his having any, but one.[12] The charges which he has allowed himself to be the organ of communicating to the very public, who is to decide the question of the Presidency, though directly aimed at me, necessarily implicate his only competitor. Mr Adams and myself are both guilty or we are both innocent of the imputed arrangement between us. *His* innocence is absolutely irreconcilable with *my* guilt. If Gen. Jackson, therefore, can establish my guilt, and, by inference or by insinuation, that of his sole rival, he will have removed a great obstacle to the consummation of the object of his ambition. And if he can, at the same time, make out his own purity of conduct, and impress the American people with the belief that his purity and integrity alone prevented his success before the H. of R. his claims will become absolutely irresistible. Were there ever more powerful motives to propagate,—was there ever greater interest, at all hazards, to prove the truth of charges?

I state the case I hope fairly; I mean to state it fairly and fearlessly. If the position be one which exposes Gen. Jackson to unfavorable suspicions, it must be borne in mind that he has voluntarily taken it, and he must abide the consequences. I am acting on the defensive, and it is he who assails me, and who has called forth, by the eternal laws of self-protection, the right to use all legitimate means of self-defence.

Gen. Jackson has shewn, in his letter, that he is not exempt from the influence of that bias towards one's own interests, which is unfortunately the too common lot of human nature. It is *his* interest to make out that he is a person of spotless innocence and of *un*-sullied integrity; and to establish, by direct charge, or by necessary inference, the want of those qualities in his rival. Accordingly we find, throughout the letter a labored attempt to set forth his own immaculate purity in striking contrast with the corruption which is attributed to others. We would imagine from his letter that he very seldom touches a newspaper. The Telegraph[13] is mailed regularly for him at Washington, but it arrives at the Hermitage very irregularly. He would have the public to infer that the post-master at Nashville, whose appointment happened not to be upon his recommendation,[14] obstructed his reception of it. In consequence of his not receiving the Telegraph, he had not on the 6th June 1827 seen Carter Beverley's famous Fayetteville letter, dated the 8th of the preceding March, published in numerous gazettes, and published, I have very little doubt, although I have not the means of ascertaining the fact, in the gazettes of Nashville.[15] I will not say, contrary to Gen. Jackson's assertion, that he had never read that letter, when he wrote that of the 6th of June, but I must think that it is very strange that he should not have seen it; and that I doubt whether there is another man of any political eminence in the United States who has not read it. There is a remarkable coincidence between Gen. Jackson and certain editors who espouse his interest, in relation to Mr Beverley's letter. They very early took the ground. in respect to it, that I ought, under my *own signature* to come out and deny the statements.[16] And Gen. Jackson now says, in his letter of the 6th of June, that he "always intended, should Mr Clay come out, over his own name, and deny having any knowledge of the communication made by his friends to my friends and to me, that I would give him the name of the gentleman through whom that communication came."

The distinguished member of Congress,[17] who bore the alleged overture, according to Gen. Jackson, presented himself with diplomatic circumspection lest he should wound the very great sensibility of the General. He avers that the communication was intended with the most friendly motives, "that he came as a friend," and that he hoped, however it might be received, there would be no alteration in the friendly feelings between them. The General graciously condescends to receive the communication, and in consideration of the high standing of the distinguished member, and of his having always been a professed friend, he is promised impunity, and assured that there shall be no change of amicable ties. After all these necessary preliminaries are arranged between the high negociating powers, the envoy proceeds: "He had been informed by the friends of Mr Clay, that the friends of Mr Adams had made overtures to them, saying if Mr Clay and his friends would unite in aid of the election of Mr Adams, Mr Clay should be Secretary of State; that the friends of Adams were urging as a reason to induce the friends of Mr Clay to accede to their proposition that, if I was elected President, Mr Adams would be continued Secretary of State (inuendo there would be no room for Kentucky.") {Is this Gen. Jackson's inuendo or that of the distinguished member of Congress.} "That the friends of Mr Clay stated the West does not want to separate from the West, and if I would say or permit any of my confidential friends to say that, in case I was elected President, Mr Adams should not be continued Secretary of State, by a complete union of Mr Clay and his friends, they would put an end to the Presidential contest in one hour; and he was of opinion it was right to fight such intriguers with their own weapons." To which the General states himself to have replied in substance, "that in politics as in every thing else my guide was principle, and contrary to the expressed and unbiassed will of the people or their constituted agents, I never would step into the Presidential chair; and requested him to say to Mr Clay and his friends (for I did *suppose* he had come from Mr Clay, *although he used the terms Mr Clay's friends*) that before I would reach the Presidential chair by such means of bargain and corruption, I would see the earth open and swallow both Mr Clay, and his friends and myself with them." Now all these professions are very fine and display admirable purity. But its sublimity would be somewhat more impressive, if some person other than Gen. Jackson had proclaimed it. He would go into the Presidential chair, but never, no! never contrary to 'the expressed & unbiassed will of the people, or their constituted agents:' two modes of arriving at it the more reasonable, as there happens to be no other constitutional way. He would see "the earth open and swallow both Mr Clay and his friends and myself," before he would reach the Presidential chair by "such means of bargain and corruption." I hope Gen. Jackson did not intend that the whole human race should be also swallowed up, on the contingency he has stated, nor that they were to guaranty that he has an absolute repugnance to the employment of any exceptionable means to secure his elevation to the Presidency. If he had rendered the distinguished member of Congress a little more distinguished, by instantly ordering him from his presence, and by forthwith denouncing him and the infamous proposition which he bore, to the American public, we should be a little better prepared to admit the claims to untarnished integrity, which the General so modestly puts forward. But, according to his own account, a corrupt and scandalous proposal is made to him; the person who conveyed it advises him to accept it, and yet that person still retains the friendship of Gen. Jackson, who is so tender of his character that his name is carefully concealed and reserved to be hereafter brought forward as a witness! A man who, if he be a member of the House of Representatives, is doubly infamous—infamous for the advice which he gave, and infamous for his willingness to connive at the corruption of the body of which he was a sworn member—is the credible witness by whom Gen. Jackson stands ready to establish the corruption of men whose characters were never questioned!

Of all the properties which belong to honorable men, not one is so highly prized as that of character. Gen. Jackson cannot be insensible to its value, for he appears to be most anxious to set forth the loftiness and purity of his own. How has he treated mine? During the dispensation of the hospitalities of the Hermitage, in the midst of a mixed company, composed of individuals from various States, he permits himself to make certain statements respecting my friends and me, which, if true, would forever dishonor and degrade us. The words are hardly passed from his mouth, before they are committed to paper, by one of his guests, and transmitted in the form of a letter to another State, where they are published in a newspaper, and thence circulated throughout the Union. And now he pretends that these statements were made, "without any calculation that they were to be thrown into the public journals."[18] Does he reprove the indiscretion of the guest who had violated the sanctity of a conversation at the hospitable board? Far from it. The public is incredulous. It cannot believe that Gen. Jackson would be so wanting in delicacy and decorum. The guest appeals to him for the confirmation of the published statements; and the General promptly addresses a letter to him, in which "he most unequivocally confirms (says Mr C. Beverley) all I have said regarding the overture made to him pending the last Presidential election before Congress; and he *asserts a great deal more than he ever told me.*"[19] I should be glad to know if all the versions of the tale have now made their appearance, and whether Gen. Jackson will allege that he did not "calculate" upon the publication of his letter of the 6th of June.

The General states that the unknown envoy used the terms "Mr Clay's friends," to the exclusion therefore of myself, but he nevertheless inferred that he had come from me. Now why did he draw this inference contrary to the import of the statement which he received? Does not this disposition to deduce conclusions unfavorable to me manifest the spirit which actuates him? And does not General Jackson exhibit throughout his letter a desire to give a coloring to the statements of his friend, the distinguished member of Congress, higher than they would justify? No one should ever resort to implication but from necessity. Why did he not ascertain from the envoy if he had come from me? Was any thing more natural than that General Jackson, should ascertain the persons who had deputed the envoy? If his shocked sensibility and indignant virtue and patriotism would not allow him to enquire into particulars, ought he to have hazarded the assertion, that I was privy to the proposal, without assuring himself of the fact? Could he not after rejecting the proposal, continuing as he did on friendly terms with the organ of it, have satisfied himself if I were conusant [sic] of it? If he had not time then, might he not have ascertained the fact from his friend or from me during the intervening two and a half years? The compunctions of his own conscience, for a moment, appear to have visited him towards the conclusion of his letter, for he there does say, "that in the supposition stated, I *may* have done injustice to Mr Clay; if so the gentleman informing me can explain." No good or honorable man will do another voluntarily any injustice. It was not necessary that Gen. Jackson should have done me any. And he cannot acquit himself of the rashness and iniquity of his conduct towards me by referring, at this late day, to a person whose name is withheld from the public. This compendious mode of ad-ministering justice, by first hanging and then trying a man, however justifiable it may be, according to the precepts of the Jackson code, is sanctioned by no respectable system of jurisprudence.

It is stated in the letter of the 6th of June, that the overture was made *early* in January; and that the second day after the communi-cation it "was announced in the newspapers that Mr Clay had come out openly and avowedly in favor of Mr Adams." The object of this statement is obvious. It is to insinuate that the proposal which was re-jected with disdain by Gen. Jackson was accepted with promptitude by Mr Adams. This renders the fact as to the *time* of the alleged an-nunciation very important. It is to be regretted that Gen. Jackson had not been a little more precise. It was *early* in January that the overture was made, and the *second day* after the annunciation of my intention took place. Now I will not assert that there may not have been some speculations in the newspapers about that time (although I do not believe that there were even any *speculations* so early) as to the probable vote which I should give; but I should be glad to see any newspaper which, the second day after early in January, asserted in its columns, that I had come out "openly and avowedly in favor of Mr Adams." I challenge the production of such a paper. I do not believe that my intention so to vote for Mr Adams was announced in the newspapers openly and avowedly during the whole month of January, or at any rate until late in the month. The only *avowal* of my intention to vote for him which was publicly made in the newspapers prior to the election, is contained in my letter to Judge Brooke, which is dated the 28th January. It was first published in the Enquirer at Richmond some time in the ensuing month.[20] I go further; I do not believe that any newspaper at Washington can be produced announcing, before the latter part of January, the fact, whether upon my avowal or not, of my intention to vote for Mr Adams.[21] Gen. Jackson's memory must deceive him. He must have confounded events and circumstances. His friend, Mr George Kremer, in his letter to the Columbian Observer, bearing date the *25th January*, has, according to my recollection of the public prints, a claim to the merit of being the first or among the first to announce to the public my intended vote. That letter was first published at Philadelphia, and returned in the Columbian Observer to Washington City on the 31st January. How long before its date that letter was written for[22] Mr Kremer does not appear. Whether there be any connexion between the communication made by the distinguished member of Congress and that letter, perhaps Gen. Jackson can explain.

At the end of more than two years after a corrupt overture is made to Gen. Jackson he now, for the first time, openly proclaims it. It is true, as I have ascertained since the publication of Mr Beverleys Fay-etteville letter, the General has been for a long time secretly circulating the charge. Immediately on the appearance at Washington of that letter in the public prints, the Editor of the Telegraph asserted, in his paper, that Gen. Jackson had communicated the overture to him about the period of the election, not as he now states but according to Mr Beverley's version of the tale.[23] Since I left Washington on the 10th of last month, I have understood that Gen. Jackson has made a similar communication to several other persons, at different and distant points.[24] Why has the overture been thus clandestinely circulated? Was it that through the medium of the Telegraph, the leading paper supporting the interest of Gen. Jackson, and through his other depositories, the belief of the charge should be daily and gradually infused into the public mind, and thus contribute to the support of his cause? The zeal and industry with which it has been propagated, the daily columns of certain newspapers can testify. Finding the public still unconvinced, has the General found it to be necessary to come out in proper person, through the thin veil of Mr Carter Beverley's agency?

When the alleged overture was made, the election remained undecided. Why did not Gen. Jackson then hold up to universal scorn and indignation the infamous bearer of the proposal, and those who dared to insult his honor and tamper with his integrity? If he had, at that time, denounced all the infamous parties concerned, demanded an enquiry in the H. of R. and established by satisfactory proof the truth of his accusation, there might and probably would have been a different result to the election. Why, when at my instance, a Committee was on the 5th day of February 1825, (only four days before the election,) appointed to investigate the charges of Mr Kremer, did not Gen. Jackson present himself and establish their truth? Why on the 7th of that month, two days before the election, when the Committee reported that Mr Kremer declined to come forward, and that "if *they knew* of any reason for such investigation they would have asked to be clothed with the proper power, but not having themselves any such knowledge, they have felt it to be their duty only to lay before the House the communication which they have received;"—why did not Gen. Jackson authorize a motion to recommit the report and manfully come forward with all his information? The Congress of the Nation is in session. An important election has devolved on it. All eyes are turned towards Washington. The result is awaited with intense anxiety and breathless expectation. A corrupt proposition, affecting the election, is made to one of the Candidates. He receives it, is advised to accept it, deliberates, decides upon it. A Committee is in session to investigate the very charge. The candidate notwithstanding remains profoundly silent, and, after the lapse of more than two years, when the period of another election is rapidly approaching, in which he is the only competitor for the office, for the first time, announces it to the American public! They must have more than an ordinary share of credulity who do not believe that Gen. Jackson labors under some extraordinary delusion.

It is possible that he may urge, by way of excuse for what must be deemed his culpable concealment of meditated corruption, that he did not like to volunteer as a witness before the committee, or to transmit to it the name of his friend, the distinguished member of the H. of R., although it is not very easy to discern any just reason for this volunteering now which would not have applied with more force at that time. But what apology can be made for his failure to discharge his sacred duty as an American Senator? More than two months, after the alleged overture, my nomination to the office which I now hold, was made to the Senate of the United States, of which Gen. Jackson was then a sworn member.[25] On that nomination he had to deliberate and act, in the most solemn manner. If I were privy to a corrupt proposal to Gen. Jackson, touching the recent election; if I had entered into a corrupt bargain with Mr. Adams to secure his elevation, I was unworthy the office to which I was nominated; and it was the duty of Gen. Jackson, if he really possessed the information which he now puts forward, to have moved the Senate to appoint a committee of enquiry, and by establishing my guilt, to have preserved the National Councils from an abominable contamination. As the conspiracy of Geo. Kremer & Co. had a short time before meanly shrunk from appearing before the committee of the H. of R. to make good their charges, I requested a Senator of the U. S. when my nomination should be taken up, to ask of the Senate the appointment of a committee of enquiry, unless it should appear to him to be altogether unnecessary.[26] One of our own Senators[27] was compelled, by the urgency of his private business, to leave Washington before my nomination was disposed of; and as I had but little confidence in the fidelity of the professed friendship of the other,[28] I was constrained to present my application to a Senator from another State. I was afterwards informed that, when it was acted upon, Gen. Jackson and every other Senator present was silent as to the imputations now made, no one presuming to question my honor or integrity. How can Gen. Jackson justify to his conscience or to his country this palpable breach of his public duty? It is in vain to say that he gave a silent negative vote. *He* was in possession of information which, if true, must have occasioned the rejection of my nomination. It does not appear that any other Senator possessed the same information. Investigation was alike due to the purity of the National Councils, to me, and as an act of strict justice, to all the other parties implicated. It is impossible for him to escape from the dilemma that he has been faithless, as a Senator of the United States, or has lent himself to the circulation of an attrocious [*sic*] calumny.

After the election, Gen. Jackson was among the first who eagerly pressed his congratulations upon his successful rival.[29] If Mr Adams had been guilty of the employment of impure means to effect his election, Gen. Jackson ought to have disdained to sully his own hands by touching those of his corrupt competitor.

On the 10th of February 1825, the very next day after the election, Gen. Jackson was invited to a public dinner at Washington, by some of his friends. He expressed to them his wish that he might be excused from accepting the invitation, because, alluding to the recent election, he said "any evidence of kindness and regard, such as you propose, might, by many, be viewed as conveying with it EXCEPTION, murmuring and feelings of complaint, which I sincerely hope belong to none of my friends."[30] More than one month after the corrupt proposal is pretended to have been received, and after, according to the insinuation of Gen. Jackson, a corrupt arrangement had been made between Mr Adams and me—after the actual termination of an election, the issue of which was brought about, according to Gen. Jackson, by the basest of means, he was unwilling to accept the honors of a public dinner, lest it should imply even an *exception* against the result of the election.

Gen. Jackson professes in his letter of the 6th of June—I quote again his words, "to have always intended, should Mr Clay come out over his own signature and deny having any knowledge of the communication made by his friends to my friends and to me, that I would give him the name of the gentleman through whom that communication came." He pretends never to have seen the Fayetteville letter; and yet the pretext of a denial under *my signature* is precisely that which had been urged by the principal editors who sustain his cause. If this be an unconcerted, it is nevertheless a most wonderful coincidence. The General never communicated to me his professed intention, but left me in entire ignorance of his generous purpose; like the overture itself it was profoundly concealed from me. There was an authorized denial from me, which went the circle of the public prints, immediately after the arrival at Washington of the Fayetteville letter.[31] In that denial my words are given. They were contained in a letter dated at Washington City on the 18th day of April last, and are correctly stated to have been "that the statement that his (my) friends had made such a proposition as the letter describes to the friends of Gen. Jackson was, as far as he knew or believed, utterly destitute of foundation; that he was unwilling to believe that Gen. Jackson had made any such statement; but that no matter with whom it had originated, he was fully persuaded it was a gross fabrication, of the same calumnious character with the Kremer story, put forth for the double purpose of injuring his public character, & propping the cause of Gen.

Jackson; and that for himself and for his friends he *defied* the substantiation of the charge before any fair tribunal whatever." Such were my own words transmitted in the form of a letter from a friend to a *known* person. Whereas the charge which they repelled was contained in a letter written by a person then unknown to some person also unknown. Did I not deny the charge under my own signature in my Card, of the 31st January 1825, published in the National Intelligencer?[32] Was not there a substantial denial of it in my letter to Judge Brooke, dated the 28th of the same month? In my Circular to my Constituents?[33] In my Lewisburg Speech?[34] And may I not add, in the whole tenor of my public life and conduct? If Gen. Jackson had offered to furnish me the name of a member of Congress, who was capable of advising his acceptance of a base and corrupt proposition, ought I to have resorted to his infamous and discredited witness?

It has been a thousand times asserted and repeated, that I violated instructions which I ought to have obeyed. I deny the charge; and I am happy to have this opportunity of denying it in the presence of my assembled Constituents. The General Assembly requested the Kentucky delegation to vote in a particular way.[35] A majority of that delegation, including myself, voted in opposition to that request.[36] The legislature did not intend to give an *imperative* instruction. The distinction between a request and an instruction was familiar to the legislature; and their rolls attest that the former is always addressed to the members of the House of Representatives, and the latter only to the Senators of the United States   But I do not rely exclusively on this recognized distinction. I dispute at once the right of the legislature to issue a mandatory instruction to the Representatives of the people. Such a right has no foundation, in the Constitution, in the reason or nature of things, nor in the usage of the Kentucky Legislature. Its exercise would be a manifest usurpation. The General Assembly has the incontrovertible right to express its opinion and to proclaim its wishes on any political subject whatever; and to such an expression great deference and respect are due; but it is not obligatory. The people, when, in August 1824, they elected members of the General Assembly did not invest them with any power to regulate or control the exercise of the discretion of the Kentucky delegation in the Congress of the United States. I put it to the candor of every elector present, if he intended to part with his own right, or anticipated the exertion of any such power by the legislature, when he gave his vote in August 1824?

The only instruction which I received from a legitimate source, emanated from a respectable portion of my immediate constituents; and that directed me to exercise my own discretion, regardless of the will of the legislature.[37] You subsequently ratified my vote by unequivocal demonstrations repeatedly given of your affectionate attachment and your unshaken confidence. You ratified it two years ago by the election of my personal and political friend (*Judge Clarke*) to succeed me in the H. of R. who had himself subscribed the only legitimate instruction which I received.[38] You ratify it by the presence and the approbation of this vast and respectable assemblage.

I rejoice again and again, that the contest has at last assumed its present practical form. Heretofore, malignant whispers and dark surmises have been clandestinely circulated, or openly and unblushingly uttered by irresponsible agents. They were borne upon the winds, and like them were invisible and intangible. No responsible man stood forward to sustain them, with his acknowledged authority. They have at last a local habitation and a name. General Jackson has now thrown off the mask and comes confessedly forth, from behind his concealed batteries, publicly to accuse and convict me. We stand confronted before the American people. Pronouncing the charges, as I again do, destitute of all foundation, and gross aspersions, whether clandestinely or openly issued from the halls of the Capitol, the saloons [*sic*] of the Hermitage, or by press, by pen, or by tongue; and safely resting upon my conscious integrity, I demand the witness, and await the event with fearless confidence.

The issue is fairly joined. The imputed offence does not comprehend a single friend, but the collective body of my friends in Congress; and it accuses them of offering, and me with sanctioning corrupt *propositions*, derogating from honor, and in violation of the most sacred of duties. The charge has been made after two years deliberation. Gen. Jackson has voluntarily taken his position, and without provocation. In voting against him as President of the United States, I gave him no just cause of offence. I exercised no more than my indisputable privilege, as, on a subsequent occasion, of which I have never complained, he exercised his in voting against me as Secretary of State. Had I voted for him, I must have gone counter to every fixed principle of my public life. I believed him incompetent, and his election fraught with danger. At this early period of the Republic, keeping steadily in view the dangers which had overturned every other Free State, I believed it to be essential to the lasting preservation of our liberties, that a man, devoid of civil talents, and offering no recommendation but one founded on military service, should not be selected to administer the Government. I believe so yet; and I shall consider the days of the Commonwealth numbered, when an opposite principle is established. I believed, and still believe, that now, when our institutions are in comparative infancy, is the time to establish the great principle, that military qualification alone is not a sufficient title to the Presidency. If we start right, we may run a long race of liberty, happiness and glory. If we stumble, in setting out, we shall fall as others have fallen before us, and fall without even a claim to the regrets or sympathies of mankind.

I have never done Gen. Jackson, knowingly, any injustice. I have taken pleasure, on every proper occasion, to bestow on him merited praise for the glorious issue of the battle of New Orleans. No American citizen enjoyed higher satisfaction than I did with the event. I heard it for the first time on the Boulevards of Paris;[39] and I eagerly perused the details of the action, with the anxious hope that I should find that the gallant militia of my own State had avenged on the banks of the Mississippi, the blood which they had so freely spilt on the disastrous field of Raisin.[40] That hope was not then gratified; and although I had the mortification to read the official statement that they had ingloriously fled,[41] I was nevertheless thankful for the success of the arms of my country, and felt grateful to him who had most contributed to the ever memorable victory. This concession is not now made for the purpose of conciliating the favor or mitigating the wrath of Gen. Jackson. He has erected an impassable barrier between us, and I would scorn to accept any favor at his hands. I thank my God that He has endowed me with a soul incapable of apprehensions from the anger of any being but himself.

I have, as your representative, freely examined, and in my deliberate judgment justly condemned, the conduct of Gen. Jackson in some of our Indian wars.[40] I believed, and yet believe him to have trampled upon the Constitution of his country, and to have violated the principles of humanity.—Entertaining these opinions, I did not and could not vote for him.

I owe you, my friends and fellow-citizens, many apologies, for this long interruption of the festivities of the day. I hope that my desire to vindicate their honored object, and to satisfy you that he is not altogether unworthy of them, will be deemed sufficient

. . . .

VOLUNTEERS

. . . .

By Charles H. Wickliffe.[43] HENRY CLAY—The Statesman and Orator, may his commanding talents and great exertions in the cause of Internal Improvements and Domestic Manufacturers, elevate him to the highest office in the gift of a free people.

. . . .

By Mr. A. F. Hawkins.[44] Henry Clay—It is not the ravings of his personal enemies nor the writhings of disappointed political aspirants that can destroy our confidence in the integrity of our faithful public servant.

. . . .

By Mr. John B. Coleman. The Roads and those who travel them—May the first be *MacAdamised,* and the last Adamised on a good Clay foundation.

. . . .

By G. W. Anderson. The SUN of Jack is rising, but Jack-SON is setting.

. . . .

Lexington *Kentucky Reporter,* July 14 (toasts), 18 (speech), 1827. Cf. above, Lewis and others to Clay, June 29, 1827; Clay to Lewis and others, June 30, 1827. Abraham Bowman presided over the affair, held at Noble's Inn, Lexington, Kentucky, for a throng variously estimated at "more than 700" (Lexington *Kentucky Gazette,* July 13, 1827) to "1500 or 2000 persons" (Lexington *Kentucky Reporter,* July 21, 1827). The vice presidents were John Fowler, John Postlethwait, Richard Pindell, A. F. Price, and Richard Higgins; the Reverend C(aleb) W. Cloud asked the blessing; and (Joseph) Robb was "Marshall [*sic*] of the day." William B. Rochester, who was toasted and who offered a toast to "Kentucky," was a guest (cf. above, Rochester to Clay, June 3, 1827). Bowman, born in 1749, had been one of the first justices of the peace, 1772 and 1773, in Shenandoah County, Virginia; had been to Kentucky in 1775; and had fought in the Revolutionary War, rising to the rank of colonel before he resigned in 1779. He had led a party of 30 families as settlers to Kentucky in the fall of 1779, and he himself had settled in Fayette County, in 1781. He had been one of the first justices of the latter county and a representative in the first Session of the Kentucky Legislature. He owned about 8,000 acres six miles southwest of Lexington, on South Elkhorn Creek, and had erected there one of the first brick houses in the State. At his death in 1837, his estate amounted to nearly 12,000 acres. Dr. Caleb Wesley Cloud (cf. above, II, 402n) was a Methodist minister, as well as a physician, and the founder of St. John's Chapel.

1 Cf. above, III, 906; "Address to the People," March 26, 1825 (IV, 144); Clay to Hammond, May 2, 1825. 2 Cf. above, Clay to Blair, January 8, 1825; Clay to Featherstonhaugh, January 21, 1825; Clay to Brown, January 23, 1825; Clay to Brooke, January 28, 1825. 3 Reference to this change in viewpoint has not been found. 4 Cf. above, III, 895, 901; Clay to Brown, January 23, 1825; Clay to Porter, January 23, 1825; Clay to Blair, January 29, 1825; Clay to Wharton, February 5, 1825. 5 See above, Clay to Gales and Seaton, January 30, 1825, and note. 6 John H. Eaton. Cf. above, Moore to Clay, February 10, 1827. 7 Cf. above, "Address. . . ," March 26, 1825, note 11. 8 Above, Kremer to Clay, *ca.* February 3, 1825. 9 Above, February 3, 1825. 10 *Ibid.,* note. 11 Cf. above, Clay to Hammond, June 25, 1827. 12 John Quincy Adams. On Jackson's candidacy, see above, Clay to Hammond, November 1, 1825. 13 Washington *United States Telegraph.* 14 On the opposition to the appointment of John P. Erwin as postmaster, cf. above, Williams to Clay, September 20, 1826; Hunt to Clay, January 8, 1827. 15 In his letter to Carter Beverley, June 6, 1827, Jackson had written "I have not seen your letter alluded to as having been published in the [Washington *United States*] Telegraph, altho' that paper, as I am informed, is regularly mailed for me at Washington; still I receive it irregularly, and that containing your letter has not come to hand, of course I cannot say whether your statement is substantially correct or not." Bassett (ed.), *Correspondence of Andrew Jackson,* III, 356 (where the letter pp. 355–57, is dated June 5, 1827). Beverley's letter had been published without signature, first in the Fayetteville, North Carolina, *Observer* (cf. above, Clay Interview, *ca.* April 15, 1827) ; and subsequently, still without identification of the author, in Washington *United States Telegraph,* April 13, 1827. It has not been found in the Nashville press. 16 See, *e.g.,* *Richmond Enquirer,* June 15, 27, 1827; Cincinnati *National Republican,* June 29, 1827; Cincinnati *Advertiser,* June 30, 1827. 17 James Buchanan. Cf. below, Smith to Clay, August 1, 1827, note. 18 Bassett (ed.), *Correspondence of Andrew Jackson,* III, 356. 19 Beverley to Zane, June 24, 1827. Cf. above, Clay to Hammond, June 25, 1827. 20 See above, Clay to Brooke, January 28, 1825, note. 21 The *Washington Gazette* had noted in an editorial of January 21, 1825, a rumor that Clay had decided to support Adams, "a determination which we," the editor commented, "are certain must be premature if not altogether without colorable foundation." On January 27, the same journalist announced that Clay had "deserted the cause of democracy; gone over to Mr. Adams"; and was "endeavoring to cast the die in his favor. . . ." The Washington *Daily National Journal* had first carried on January 31, 1825, comment on Clay's decision to support Adams. 22 Cf.

above, "Address to the People of the Congressional District," March 26, 1825 [IV, 146]; Eaton to Clay, March 28, 31, 1825; Clay to Eaton, March 30, April 1, 1825.   23 Duff Green had reported in the Washington *United States Telegraph* on April 26, 1827, that Jackson's statement "relative to the overtures made to him as to the formation of his cabinet, previous to the late election of President," had been "the subject of conversation at this city, in February and March, 1825. . . ."   24 Cf. above, Clay "To the Public," June 29, 1827, which indicates that the Beverley letter was being widely circulated; but references to other recent communications by Jackson on the bargain charge have not been found.   25 Cf. above, Commission as Secretary of State, March 7, 1825, note.   26 The request has not been found; the Senator was William Henry Harrison (cf. below, Clay to Harrison, September 6, 1827).   27 Richard M. Johnson had not been present when the vote was taken.   28 John Rowan, who had just become a Senator, had, however, voted for confirmation.   29 Adams, *Memoirs*, VI, 502; Margaret Bayard Smith, *The First Forty Years of Washington Society. . .* , ed. by Gaillard Hunt (New York, 1906; reprint edn., 1965), 183; S[amuel] G. Goodrich, *Recollections of a Lifetime, or Men and Things I Have Seen: in a Series of Familiar Letters to a Friend . . .* (2 vols.; New York, 1857), II, 403.   30 See above, Address, March 26, 1825, note 36.   31 Above, April 15, 1827. The item was reprinted in numerous journals, including the Washington *Daily National Journal*, April 26, 1827; the *Charleston Courier*, May 3, 1827; and, as an extract, the *Liberty Hall and Cincinnati Gazette*, May 11, 1827.   32 See above, Clay to Gales and Seaton, January 30, 1827.   33 See above, "Address to the People of the Congressional District," March 26, 1827.   34 Above, August 30, 1826. 35 See above, III, 901–902n.   36 See above, Kendall to Clay, February 19, 1825, note. 37 Cf. above, "Address to the People. . . ," March 26, 1825 (IV, 155–56).   38 Following Clay's resignation, March 6, 1825, from his seat in the United States House of Representatives, James Clark had been elected in August to fill the vacancy. *Niles' Weekly Register*, reporting this election, XXVIII (August 27, 1825), 405, identified Clark as "a most decided personal and political friend of" Clay. No correspondence from him to Clay during the interval of the election contest has been found, but cf. above, Micah Taul and others to Clay, June 3, 1825.   39 Cf. above, II, 11.   40 Cf. above, I, 814n.   41 See above, II, 11 and note.   42 See above, II, 636–62, 666–67.   43 At this time a young man, he became mayor of Lexington for two terms, in 1839 and 1840, and for many years, including the Civil War period, served as deputy city marshal.

44 Augustus F. Hawkins, born in Scott County, Kentucky, in 1796, had come to Lexington as a young man, had operated a dry-goods store from 1819 to 1822, and since then had been chief clerk of the Lexington Branch of the Bank of the United States. After the closing of that institution, he joined the Northern Bank of Kentucky, chartered in 1835 to operate at Lexington and at four branches. He became cashier of the latter bank in 1852.

From Alexander Miller

Dear Sir   Lexn. July 12th 1827

I arrive [sic] in town Last Evening & would have bean truly glad to have had the Honer of your Company a few Minuates [sic] but owing to the peculiar Circumstances the day will place you under[1] I decline wishing to trouble you personally & begs [sic] leave respectfully to in this way inform you that I have a great Anxiety to put my Son Cyrus C. Miller in the Military Accadamy at west Point[2]   I have left a letter from Mr. T. C. Howard of Richd. to you[3] & have left on [sic] for the Secretary at war[4]—   this is the first favour we have Ever asked at the hands of the general government & we claim nothing further then [sic] their Circumstances & opertunities may Enable them to grant,   to be sure Col. Barnett & my father has Served their Country in the most perilous times of the Revolution[5] but this was only their duty,   if dear Sir you Can forward My wishes in this Matter, it will be to me a

great gratification. I am dear Sir as before your Honers most devoted
& Obt. St.　　　　　　　　　　　　　　　Alexander Miller
Mr Clay

ALS. DNA, RG94, United States Military Academy, Cadet Applications, 1829/95.
Addressed to Clay at Lexington, "Care of Mr. [William H.] Caperton." Miller, a physician, had settled in Richmond in 1806.
　¹ Cf. above, Toasts and Speech, this date.　　　² The young man, not further identified, was rejected as an applicant. *House Docs.*, 21 Cong., 1 Sess., no. 79, p. 115.
　³ Not found.　　　⁴ James Barbour.　　　⁵ James Barnett, Miller's father-in-law, had
been a captain in the Virginia forces on the Continental Line during the Revolutionary
War and a colonel in the campaign of George Rogers Clark against the Indians in 1784–
1785. He had also been a justice of the peace when Madison County was organized in
1786. He resided on Silver Creek, in that county, where he died in 1835. Miller's father
has not been identified.

INSTRUCTIONS AND DISPATCHES　　　　　　　　July 12, 1827

From J[ohn] J. Appleton, Stockholm, "[Priv]ate." Encloses "a letter from the
Count of Wetterstedt which accompanied two engraved portraits of the King
[Charles XIV] presented" to Appleton "by order of H. M." Notes that he accepted
the gift, not deeming it in violation of the regulation against accepting "any thing
of intrinsic value" (cf. above, Clay to Poinsett, March 27, 1825; below, Clay to
Appleton, September 11, 1827 [2]). Calls attention to the request in Wetterstedt's
letter that he send to Clay and the President "a couple of medals from *his* foundery
[*sic*] in manifestation of his respect." Observes that the medals, which will be delivered by (James) Cucheval, "are fine specimens of what may be made with iron,
but they are not the only things here that bear a Spartan character." Refers to
his wish, expressed in his letter of April 7, for a leave of absence, now made impossible "by an earlier conclusion of the negociation, than . . . expected," and
requests further consideration "Should . . . any other proper occasion offer. . . ."
Asks that the laws and other printed documents stemming from the last two Sessions of Congress be sent him by Cucheval, whom he recommends highly to Clay's
"kindness." Concludes: "Please to accept my sincere wishes for your prosperity in
private & in public life, and those which I form for the U: S: in desiring them a
long continuance of your servic[es]." ALS. DNA, RG59, Dip. Disp., Sweden and
Norway, vol. 5 (M45, R6).
　In another private communication, dated July 13, 1827, Appleton enclosed the
letter from Wetterstedt, referred to above, "which, by inadvertance, was not
joined to that letter." ALS, *ibid.*

From James Brown, Paris, "Private." Notes that the five-power treaty designed to
end the war in Greece "has been signed at London"; that "The answer of the
Sultan [Mahmud II] to the pressing notes received from the Ambassadors at Constantinople [cf. above, Brown to Clay, April 13, 1826, March 23 (2), April 27,
1827] breathes a spirit of resistance to all propositions of accommodation"; and
that a Russian fleet "has sailed from Cronstadt, destined as it is believed, for the
Mediterranean" (cf. above, Middleton to Clay, June 23, 1827). Reports that it is
not known whether the allied vessels already in that sea (cf. above, Brown to Clay,
June 28, 29, 1827) will wait for this squadron but that, by the "latest accounts, a
fleet with troops and provisions on board, was nearly ready at Alexandria to sail
with the view of reinforcing the Turkish army in Greece." Comments that "The
Count Capo d'Istria, who has been elected President [of Greece], is said to have
left St. Petersburg on his way to take possession of his office"; that the British
Government reportedly is apprehensive that "he might be too much in the in-

terest of Russia"; and that "The Greek cause still excites much interest . . . in France" and "almost every other part of the continent. . . ."

Observes that "The renewal of the censorship (cf. above, Brown to Clay, June 12, 28, 1827) has not produced as much discontent as was expected by the leaders of the opposition"; that the people care little about politics; and that the Ministers "hold their places by a very firm tenure." Predicts that these officers "will obtain an overwhelming majority at the next election."

States that "The French Government seems inclined to do no more than blockade . . . [Algiers—cf. above, Brown to Clay, June 9, 28, 29, July 3, 1827] and to wear out the patience of the Dey [Hussein]. . . ." Expresses a belief that "more efficient measures" will be taken if the Dey continues "to refuse the reparation demanded."

Speculates "that the Spaniards and Portuguese malcontents promise themselves much from Don Miguel in October next, when he shall have attained the age of majority [cf. above, Everett to Clay, June 9, 1827], and that they will remain quiet and await his arrival." Adds that the Papal Nuncio (Francesco Tiberi) "has at last obtained permission to pass to Madrid" (cf. above, Everett to Clay, June 22, 1827). ALS. DNA, RG59, Dip. Disp., France, vol. 23 (M34, R26). Copy, in MHi-Adams Papers, Letters Recd. (MR481).

The culmination of protracted negotiations among representatives of the European powers, concerning the Greek war, occurred with the signing of the Treaty of London, July 6, 1827. By the terms of this document, France, Great Britain, and Russia agreed to offer mediation to Turkey and to demand an armistice in the war between Turkey and Greece; proposed self-rule by the Greeks under Turkish authority, an annual tribute to be paid by Greece to Turkey, and the transfer, with compensation, of Turkish property within Greece to the Greeks; provided a guarantee, by the signatory powers that wished to accept the obligation, of the settlement reached by "the Contending Parties"; and, in an "Additional Article," declared that, "In case the Ottoman Porte should not, within the space of one month, accept the mediation which is to be proposed to it, the High Contracting Parties" would form "a connection with the Greeks" and, if either of the contending parties refused an armistice, "the said High Powers" would enforce one and "continue to pursue the work of pacification, on the bases upon which they have agreed. . . ." Parry (ed.), *Consolidated Treaty Series*, vol. 77, pp. 307–15.

As contemplated in the Protocol of St. Petersburg, negotiated by the Duke of Wellington in 1826 (see above, Middleton to Clay, June 13, 1826), Austria and Prussia were to have entered into the proposed arrangements concerning Greece. Metternich had at first rejected any concessions to the Greeks. Although he had urged that the Porte yield to Russia's demands in April, 1826 (see above, Brown to Clay, April 27, 1826, note), he had failed to induce the Sultan (Mahmud II) to pacify the Greeks. Metternich had then rejected the invitation to attend London negotiations; and Prussia, following his leadership, had also refused to enter into the arrangements. Arthur Herman, *Metternich* (New York, 1932), 168, 171, 173–74, and above, Middleton to Clay, April 21, 1825, note.

Count Giovanni Antonio Capo d'Istria, born in Corfu and educated at Padua, had been Secretary of State for the Ionian Islands from 1803 to 1807, while they briefly constituted a republic under Russian protection. Upon the return of the islands to France, he had turned in 1809 to a career in the Russian diplomatic service, where he had attained distinction and, until 1821, considerable influence with Czar Alexander I. He had opposed, however, Russian participation in the Holy Alliance and had consequently incurred Metternich's hostility. The Greek revolt and the response of the Holy Alliance to revolutionary upheaval across south Europe (see above, III, 82n, 313n) had placed Capo d'Istria in an untenable situation. He had consequently retired from the Russian service in 1822 and for the next five years had resided in Switzerland, where he devoted himself to Greek relief efforts. In April, 1827, he had been elected to a seven-year term as President of Greece. He toured Europe, going to Russia in May, to Britain in August, and finally to France, in search of economic and diplomatic aid for his people, before he took office at Nauplia the following January. After four years of struggling to overcome the rivalries of local leaders and the criticism of the French and British, who viewed him as a tool of Russia, he was assassinated in 1831.

From CHRISTIAN GOEHRING, Leipzig. In forwarding the list of invoices certified from January 1 to July 1, 1827, notes that "much more" merchandise was exported from Saxony to the United States than he certified, because local manufacturers "fear the special insight and the judgment in their trade with America by a Consul in their vicinity, might prejudice the interest of their business and therefore prefer the Invoices for the most part to be certified either at Hamburg or at Bremen." ALS. DNA, RG59, Cons. Disp., Leipzig, vol. 1 (M-T215, R1). Received September 12.

To George Thompson

My Dear Sir   Lexington 13h. July 1827.
    I regret to hear of your indisposition,[1] and sincerely hope that you may soon have your health restored and be yet preserved to us many years.
    I should have taken great pleasure in visiting you, and my friends in Mercer, if I could, but the necessity of my returning to Washn. by an early fixed day will not allow me that satisfaction.
    I return Mr. Gooch's letter[2] handed me by your son.[3] It has several errors respecting me. He labors under a most egregious one in supposing that I refused to serve in Mr. Monroe's Cabinet,[4] because Mr. Adams was a member of it. There is no foundation for that statement. I am, truly Your friend.   H CLAY
Col. G. Thompson.

    ALS. ViU. Addressed: "Col. Geo. Thompson. Pleasantfields   Mercer [County, Kentucky]."
    [1] Cf. below, Toast at Public Dinner, July 14, 1827.   [2] Not found. Probably written by Claiborne W. Gooch in response to Thompson's letter to Ritchie and Gooch, February 7, 1827 (see above, Thompson to Clay, February 23, 1827, note).   [3] George C. Thompson.   [4] Cf. above, II, 391n.

MISCELLANEOUS LETTERS   July 13, 1827

    From ELISHA WHITTLESEY, "Canfield, Trumbull County, Ohio." Asks that the President's attention be called to Robert Eaton's prayer for relief "against a judgment—on a bond he executed—conditioned for the production of a certificate, of the Lawful Shipping of 200 bbs of salt from Oswego . . . New York to a port in Ohio; the Salt having been transported a part of the way through Canada." Relates the history of the case, which began during (James) Monroe's administration. ALS. DNA, RG59, Misc. Letters (M179, R65).
    Endorsed by Clay on cover: "Are there any papers in the office relative to this business? H. C.
    "Perhaps it wd. be best to forward the enclosed to the President."

Eaton, a resident of Ohio, had shipped in 1817 salt manufactured in New York State by way of Oswego to Queenstown and Fort Erie, Canada, en route to Sundusky, Ohio. Lacking a certificate from the port officers at Oswego, he had been required to post bond at Sandusky concerning the domestic manufacture of the salt. His failure to provide the proper documentation within six months had led to forfeiture of the bond and damage charges, amounting to $212, plus court costs of $76.73. By act of March 2, 1833 (6 *U.S. Stat.*, 541), Congress refunded to Eaton the $212 but not the costs of litigation, which the investigating committee concluded had "accrued in consequence of his own neglect, by which the Treasury was not benefited. . . ." *House Repts.*, 21 Cong., 1 Sess., no. 309.

Toast at Public Dinner[1]

[July 14, 1827]

6.   Our distinguished fellow citizen and guest, HENRY CLAY. His unabated zeal and untiring fidelity in the discharge of all his public duties; his devotion to the cause of freedom in both hemispheres; his herculean efforts to render his country emphatically independent, by the aid of a well regulated tariff and a judicious system of Internal Improvements, will embalm his memory in the hearts of millions of freemen yet unborn, and cause his name to be chanted with gratitude, when the names of his calumniators shall long have been forgotten.

Lexington *Kentucky Reporter*, July 21, 1827.
[1] This was one of 13 toasts offered at a dinner honoring Clay, at Versailles, Woodford County, Kentucky, with General Marquis Calmes presiding. Over 1000 persons attended by acceptance. Clay, "though laboring under a cold and hoarsness [sic]," spoke for about 45 minutes. Lexington *Kentucky Reporter*, July 18, 21, 1827. The invitation to the dinner, its acceptance, and a report of Clay's speech have not been found.   Virginia-born Calmes, a captain in the Revolution and a brigadier general of Kentucky Volunteers during the War of 1812, had arrived in Kentucky in 1785, had been one of the founders of Versailles, and had given the town its name.

To George I. Brown and Others

LEXINGTON 14th July, 1827.

Gentlemen:—I have great pleasure in acknowledging the receipt of your note of the 11th inst. transmitting resolutions adopted at a meeting of the citizens of Jessamine county, and an invitation to a public dinner which they have done me the honor to tender to me. I regret extremely that the nature of my public engagements is such as not to admit of my acceptance of it. Connected formerly with the people of Jessamine by a political relation, which will always be remembered by me with great satisfaction, I receive with uncommon gratification, the renewed expression of their confidence and attachment. I should have been very happy, by personal intercourse, to have assured them that I am the same unaltered person whom they once so highly honored. As I am not allowed that happiness, for the reason which I have stated, I hope gentlemen you will present to them my cordial thanks for the new as well as the old evidences of their affection and confidence, and assure them that I shall never cease to recollect with respect and gratitude, the people of Jessamine county. I offer you, also, the tender of the high respect and esteem of Your faithful and obedient servant   H. CLAY

Mess. *G. I. Brown, Hugh Chrisman, Wm. A. Fry, Jacob Todhunter, B. Netherland, A. Logan, John Barkley, Mason Singleton, and John Downing.*

Lexington *Kentucky Reporter*, July 18, 1827.

INSTRUCTIONS AND DISPATCHES   July 14, 1827

From ALBERT GALLATIN, London, no. 96. Reports that (William) Huskisson, "who has had a relapse and whose condition is considered critical," has left London to spend "some months on the Continent." Adds that he has learned unofficially that (Charles) Grant, vice president of the Board of Trade, will succeed Huskisson on the commission to negotiate with the United States and that, meanwhile, conferences "remain suspended." Notes, "positive declarations to the contrary notwithstanding," that Lord Dudley remains in the Foreign Office. Attributes Dudley's continuation to (George) Canning's inability to gain support for himself as both First Lord of the Treasury and Foreign Minister. Observes that Canning is surrounding himself with sycophants and men "without any weight" and that "the only efficient members of the Ministry are Messrs. Canning & Huskisson, Lords Lansdown [sic] & Goodrich [sic]." Expresses doubt that changes in policy toward the United States will come immediately, although they may be expected later, if Huskisson is "withdrawn altogether from public life."

States that the "treaty concerning Greece [cf. above, Brown to Clay, July 12, 1827] has been prematurely published, owing probably to some indiscretion or impropriety in a subordinate in the foreign office" and that the public articles "are almost the transcript of the Protocol signed at St. Petersburg in April 1826, between Count Nesselrode and the Duke of Wellington" (cf. above, Middleton to Clay, June 13, 1826), while the substance of the private articles was agreed on at Paris in October (1826) as he informed Clay "at the time" (cf. above, Gallatin to Clay, October 16, 1826). Asserts that the "constant and it may be said the exclusive object" of the British "has been to prevent a war between Russia and Turkey"; that Britain united with Russia to keep her from interfering with the affairs of Greece; but that the treaty should have been signed earlier to prevent the loss of Athens (cf. above, Brown to Clay, June 28, 29, 1827) and the near annihiliation of Greece. Notes that the Russian fleet on its way to the Mediterranean (cf. above, Brown to Clay, July 12, 1827) is expected daily. Remarks that Austria and Prussia were invited to join in the treaty but objected, "it is said," to the secret articles; expresses his own belief that Austria is averse to the whole of it. ALS. DNA, RG59, Dip. Disp., Great Britain, vol. 34 (M30, R30). Copies, in MHi-Adams Papers, Letters Rec'd. (MR481) and NHi-Gallatin Papers (MR20). Received August 26.

Charles Grant, titled as Baron Glenelg in 1835, had been born in Bengal and educated at Magdalene College, Cambridge. He had entered Parliament in 1811, where he remained a member of the House of Commons until 1835, then moved to the House of Lords. He had been named a lord of the Treasury in 1813 and in 1819 chief secretary for Ireland and a member of the Privy Council. He had been vice president of the Board of Trade since 1823 and in September, 1827, became president of that Board and treasurer of the Navy. He resigned with the fall of Canning's supporters in 1828 but was again president of the Board of Trade from 1830 to 1834 and was colonial secretary from 1835 to 1839.

Henry Petty-Fitzmaurice, third Marquis of Lansdowne, educated at Edinburgh and at Trinity College, Cambridge, had entered the House of Commons in 1802 and had become Chancellor of the Exchequer in 1806. He had succeeded to the inherited title in 1809 and continued his political career as a Whig leader in the House of Lords. He had been heavily instrumental in bringing about the support of a segment of the Whigs for Canning in the formation of the latter's Ministry in April, 1827 (see above, Gallatin to Clay, February 22, 1827, note), had entered the Cabinet without portfolio, and on July 16, 1827, assumed the Ministry of the Home Department. He was also active in the organization of the Goderich Ministry upon Canning's death in August (cf. above, Gallatin to Clay, February 22, 1827 note). Lansdowne left office with the fall of the Whigs in January, 1828, returned as president of the council from 1830 to 1841 and again from 1846 to 1852, and entered the cabinet without portfolio from 1852 until his death in 1863.

The treaty relating to Greece had been published in the London *Times*, July 12, 1827, on the basis of "Private Correspondence" from Paris, dated July 9.

From ROBERT MONROE HARRISON, Antigua. Acknowledges receipt of Clay's letter of May 14, 1827, and accepts the appointment. States that he will begin his tour immediately, as transportation among the islands is generally limited during the hurricane season, and will stop first at the Island of St. Bartholomew to appoint an agent to represent the United States. Encloses an exchange of letters with R. B. Eldridge, whom he asked for information on "the state of the West Indies colonies generally. . . ." Inquires, in a postscript, whether his tour should include Jamaica, and notes that he will visit the Windward Islands while awaiting a decision. ALS. DNA, RG59, Cons. Disp., Antigua, vol. 1 (M-T327, R1). Received August 10. Cf. below, Harrison to Clay, July 18, 1827, note.

Endorsement on Bill and Receipt

[*ca.* July 15, 1827]

Mathews rect. for instruction to H. C. Hart

AE. DLC-TJC (DNA, M212, R16). Clay's endorsement appears on verso of the following undated document: "Mr. H. Hart To Thomas J Matthews Dr. for 3 mos. Instruction from 27th April to 27: July $10.00   Recd. payment in full   Thomas J Matthews."

Statement of Farm Receipts and Expenditures

[*ca.* July 15, 1827]

A Memmorandum [*sic*] of articles sold of [*sic*] the farm[1]
since the 1st. of August. 1826

	Specie
One falin[2] [*sic*] Hide	$ 2 68 3/4
one ..Do.. ..Do	2 75
31 1/2 bushels wheat at 37 1/2 cents per bushel	11 81 1/4
20.. ..Do... ..Do..at.Do... per bushel	7 50
57 1/2 ..Do... ..Do..at Do...	21 56 1/4
for Meal from Mrs Hart[3]	1 62 1/2

for House rent from J. Diamond⁴ cash	6 00
from ..Do....in cash	3 00
one calfskin	1 31 1/4
one Veal calf	2 25
one Ton Hay	10 00
	$ 70 50

Expences [*sic*] of the farm from the 1st. Augut. 1826

	Specie
for Bristo & bills⁵ over work at mowing	$ 1 00
for Alum & salts for the Negros [*sic*]	„ 31 1/4
for Turning 34 rounds for the Horse [mill]	2 75
for 137 lbs. Bacon last fall at 4 cents per lb	5 48
for cutting 2 colts last fall	1 00
for 44 yards jains⁶ at 50 cents per yard	22 00
for Thread and Tape for T. W. Clay	„ 25
for 4 Horse collars	6 00
for 4 Blind bridles	6 43 3/4
for 14 yards Toa⁷ [*sic*] linen	2 6 1/4
for 2 1/2 lbs. saltpetter [*sic*]	„ 50
for 2 lb salts	„ 37 1/2
for 2 gallons whisky at Hogg Killing	„ 75
for 4 dozn. buttons	„ 25
for weaving 18 yards linsey	1 12 1/2
for midwifes fee for Darkey	3 00
for sole leather to mend the Negros shoes	1 18 3/4
for constables fee for executing a warant [*sic*] on a Negro for stealing Hoggs	1 25
for nails and paint for the Gate posts	„ 75
for weaving 33 yards Toa [*sic*] linen	2 75
for weaving and spooling 36 yards fine wide linen for Mrs. Clay	6 50
for cotton Cloth for the negro children	1 75
for two back bands	2 00
	$.69 48
for Dying wool for Mrs. Clay	50

AD, probably by John H. Kerr. DLC-TJC (DNA, M212, R16). Endorsed by Clay: "Mr. Kerr A/cs. rendered July, 1827." The endorsement and each account are on separate sheets.
¹ "Ashland."   ² Fallen, *i.e.*, dead carcass.   ³ Mrs. Thomas Hart, Sr.   ⁴ Not identified.   ⁵ The slaves, Bristow and Bill.   ⁶ Jeans.   ⁷ Tow.

INSTRUCTIONS AND DISPATCHES   July 15, 1827

From ALEXANDER H. EVERETT, Madrid, no. 82. Notes that "The affairs with Portugal remain substantially" unchanged; that "In the relations with Rome there has also been no material change, the Council of State not having yet given its opinion upon the line of conduct to be pursued" (cf. above, Brown to Clay, July 12, 1827); that "Mr. Labrador, an experienced diplomatist, . . . has been appointed Minister to the Pope [Leo XII]; but will probably not be despatched until the final determination is taken here"; and that "the Nuncio [Francesco Tiberi] remains at Bayonne [cf. above, Everett to Clay, June 22, 1827]," probably awaiting instructions "from his Government, should he even receive from this place in the mean time an invitation (which has not yet been forwarded) to proceed."

States that "no Bishop has been admitted by the Pope for Mexico" (see above, Poinsett to Clay, June 20, 1827) and explains the difficulty: "the existing Archbishop [Pedro José Fonte]" left Mexico at the outbreak of revolution and is now a "Councillor of State" in Spain; he cannot by "Canon Law . . . be superseded without a trial," which the Pope does not contemplate; and the (Mexican) President (Guadalupe Victoria) has refused to accede to a compromise, offered by the Pope, who proposed "appointing for the life of the incumbent an Administrator of the Diocese to be named by the Republic." Observes: "If it be the object of the Mexicans to maintain their connexion with the See of Rome on the acknowledged principles of the Catholic faith, the prudence of their conduct is very questionable. It is not unlikely, however, that they may be intending to separate from the Parent Church and to organize one of their own."

Encloses "a translation . . . of a note addressed by the late Nuncio to this Government," dated October 8, 1825, and signed "l'Archevêque de Tyr" (cf. below, Hughes to Clay, October 5, 1827, note), "which did not at the time fall into" Everett's hands and which, in the absence of further correspondence on the subject, caused "the Spanish Cabinet," to take "for granted that no step of importance was in immediate contemplation. . . ." Predicts that "the influence of the foreign powers will probably arrange the quarrel without much difficulty." Encloses also "translations of a circular letter addressed by the Government to the merchants who have emigrated from the Colonies and settled in other parts of Europe" (inviting them to return "to the Spanish territory. . . .") and of "a Memoir on the state of the Nation which was transmitted to the King [Ferdinand VII] more than a year ago [cf. above, Burton to Clay, June 30, 1826] by one of his subjects [Xavier de Burgos, identified in the enclosure as "H. M's. financial commissioner"] residing in an official capacity at Paris" and which, when "laid before the Council of State . . . was . . . received with . . . indignation and contempt. . . ." Refers again to the invitation issued to the merchants and states that "A request conceived in a different style has lately been transmitted to all the Grandees who are absent from the country, informing them that if they do not return before a certain day their estates will be confiscated."

Adds in a postscript, on July 26, that the Council of State, after "a good deal of angry discussion" concerning "the relations with Rome," decided that the King should write a letter of protest to the Pope, that "Mr. (Manuel Gonzáles) Salmon is to address a similar letter to the Cardinal Secretary of State to His Holiness" (Giulio Maria della Somaglia), and that "The question of the late proceedings in regard to the Nuncio is not to be" mentioned until "brought forward here by order of the Court of Rome," after which "Mr. Labrador will be despatched . . . as Ambassador to the Pope for the purpose of arranging the difficulty." Remarks that, according to intelligence from Rome, "the refusal here to admit the Nuncio" was thought to have affected "the Pope's health, as he suffered pretty severely about the same time from an attack of the Piles to which he is subject." Cites a rumor, which he questions, "that Cardinal Giustiani, the late Nuncio here, has been appointed Legate to America, for the purpose of completing the arrangement of the affairs of the Church in that quarter." LS, except for the postscript in Everett's hand. DNA, RG59, Dip. Disp., Spain, vol. 27 (M31, R28). Received September 16, 1827.

Pedro Gómez Havelo, the Marquis of Labrador, had been born in Paris in 1775 and, as one of the counsellors of Ferdinand VII accompanying the Spanish monarch to Bayonne in 1808, had been imprisoned by Napoleon. Following the latter's surrender, Labrador had participated in the Congress of Vienna and subsequently served as Spanish Ambassador in Naples and Rome. Upon the death of Ferdinand VII in 1833, he carried on diplomatic missions for the supporters of Don Carlos until his retirement.

Fonte, born in Aragon, Spain, had been vicar-general of Mexico from 1802 to 1811 and archbishop since 1816. He had returned to Spain in 1822 but did not relinquish his see until ordered by Pope Gregory XVI to return to Mexico in 1837.

Note Account, Private, with Morrison Estate

Henry Clay (in private Acct.)   Lexington Ky. 16th. July 1827
In A/C with J. Morrison's Estate

			Dr.	Cr.
1826		For Comms. Notes received and paid.		
Augt.	12	To Balance per A/C rendered[1]	2.901 79	" "
1827				
July	6	By 5 Pr. Ct. Commission on 1262$73 being amount of receipts on Acct. of the Estate since 10 July 1826, the period of the last settlement of his accounts	" "	63 13
		Balance	" "	2,838 66.
			$2.901 79	2,901 79
		To Balance	2.838 66	" "

E & O. E.

Robt. Scott

ADS. KyLxT.
[1] See above, Note Account, Private, with Morrison Estate, August 12, 1826.

Specie Account, Private, with Morrison Estate

Henry Clay (in private Acct.)   Lexington Ky. 16th. July 1827
In A/C with James Morrison's Estate

			Dr.	Cr.
1826		For Specie funds received and paid.		
Augt.	12	To Balance as per A/C rendered[1]	16.280 "	" "
Octr.	3	" J. Morrison's Estate for 6 Ms. interest on 15,000$. of the T. University Legacy in his hands[2]	450 "	" "

	9	By Cash pr. Check[3] on Office of Disct. & Depte. B. U S. Lexn.	" "		200 "
		To J. Morrison's Estate for 67$50. recd. of A Kendall on 26 Augt. 1826 for interest on his Note[4]	67 50		" "
	14	By Cash recd. of Jno. Tilford on Acct. of his Note[5]	" "		252 15
Novr.	8	" Cash recd. of Jno. Tilford the balance of ditto after deducting 150$. transmitted to W. City by Tilford[6]	" "		50 "
Decr.	18	" Cash in U S. B Check[7] 500$. Premm. on do 250c.	" "		502 50
1827					
Jany	16	To J. Morrison's Estate, for Amt of R. J. Breckenridges draft on Francis Preston, recd.[8]	676 12		" "
		" Ditto do recd. for U S. Stock & dividends[9]	289 69		" "
Mar.	20	" Ditto do recd. of Mr. Brieze[10] on Acct. W. Morrison[11]	1,000 "		" "
Apl.	2	" Ditto do for 6 Ms. interest on 15.000$. of the Ta. University Legacy in his hands	450 "		" "
May	25	" Ditto for Dividends recd. on U S. Stock	89 73		" "
July	6	" By 5 Pr. Ct. Commn. on 7743$44; being the amount of receipts on Acct. of the Estate since the 10h. July 1826 the period of the last settlement of his accounts	" "		387 17.
		Balance	" "		17.911 22
			$19.303 04		19.303 04

To Balance	17.911 22		" "

E & O. E

ROBT. SCOTT

ADS. KyLxT. Copy recorded in Fayette County Court, Will Book H, 127–31.
[1] See above, Specie Account, Private, with Morrison Estate, August 12, 1826.   [2] Cf. above, III, 496n.   [3] Not found.   [4] Cf. above, Kendall to Clay, July 8, 1826, and note.   [5] Cf. above, III, 785–86.   [6] Cf. above, Scott to Clay, November 21, 1826. No other record of the transaction has been found.   [7] Not found.   [8] Cf. above, Receipt to Robert J. Breckinridge, July 31, 1826; Clay to Francis Preston, same date.
[9] No record of the investment in United States stock has been found. Cf. above, Worsley to Clay, April 17, 1827, note.   [10] Sidney Breese.   [11] William Morrison

had been born at Doylestown, Pennsylvania, had trained under his uncle, Guy Bryan, a Philadelphia merchant, and around 1790 had moved to Kaskaskia as the representative of the firm of Bryan and Morrison. A decade later he had opened a store at Cahokia and in 1809 had been one of the backers of the Missouri Fur Company, of St. Louis. He had been active during the early political controversy in Indiana Territory and had engaged extensively in land speculation. His relationship to James Morrison has not been found.

Note Account with Robert Scott

The Honble Henry Clay   Lexington Ky 16 July 1827
In A/C with Robert Scott.

1826	For Coms. Notes[1] received and paid. Dr.		Cr.
Augt. 12	To Balance per settlement and A/C rendered[2]	576 43	" "
Septr. 9	Recd. of Mr. Ratel[3] for 1 qrs. House rent ending 12 Ulto.	" "	32 50
13	" John Deverin on Acct. of House rent due 1st. inst.	" "	77 "
23	Paid Mrs. Hart on Acct.[4]	125 "	" "
Octr. 5	Recd. of Jno. McCracken for Stable rent	" "	37 50.
	Paid Ditto for keeping Carriage & other Horses	40 "	" "
24	Recd. of John Deverin for bal. of 1 qrs. H. Rent due 1 Septr. 1826	" "	48 "
Novr. 3	" Wilkins & Co.[5] on Acct. of rent due in Augt. last	" "	66 "
20	" Docts. Caldwell &c.[6] for rent of Lecture Rooms &c.	" "	450 "
Decr. 22	Paid Mrs. Susan Hart on Acct.	125 "	" "
23	Recd. of Mr. Ratel for 1 qrs. H. rent due 12 Novr. Ulto.	" "	32 50.
	" John Deverin for 1 qrs. House rent due 1st. inst.	" "	125 "
28	" Jno. Mc.Cracken for 1 qrs. Stable rent	" "	37 50.
1827			
Feb 26	Recd. of P. Ratel for 1 qrs. House rent due 12 inst.	" "	32 50.
Mar 20	" John Deverin for 1 Qrs. House rent due 1st. inst.	" "	125 "
26	Paid Mrs. Susan Hart on Acct.	125 "	" "
April 3	Recd. of E. B. Pearson on Acct. of his Note[7]	" "	25 "
17	" P. Ratel for 1 qrs. House rent due 12 inst.	" "	32 50

June 5	„ Jno. Deverin, in full of House rent	„ „	125 „
July 16	„ Himself at Mr. Smiths[8]	„ „	20 „
	Balance	274 57	„ „
		$1266 „	1266 „
	By Balance		274 57.

E & O. E.

ROBT. SCOTT

ADS. KyLxT. [1] Notes of the Bank of the Commonwealth.
[2] See above, Note Account with Scott, August 8, 1826. [3] Philbert Ratel.
[4] Susannah Hart (Mrs. Thomas, Sr.). [5] Wilkins, McIlvaine and Company (cf. above, II, 786–87). [6] Charles Caldwell on behalf of the Transylvania University Medical Faculty (cf. above, III, 136–37). The other members of the faculty during the winter of 1826–1827 were Benjamin W. Dudley, Daniel Drake, William H. Richardson, Charles Wilkins Short, and James Blythe. [7] Cf. above, Memorandum, July 6, 1825.
[8] Probably Thomas Smith.

Specie Account with Robert Scott

The Honble Henry Clay. Lexington Ky 16 July 1827.
In A/C with Robert Scott.
For Specie funds received and paid.—

1826		Dr.	Cr.
Augt. 16	Paid L. G. Sturdevant[1] for 10 New Keys and repairing Locks	7 75	„ „
19	„ F. W. Breckenridge[2] for 5000 Shingles	12 50	„ „
24	„ William Wall[3] „ 4700 ditto	11 75	„ „
	„ Wright & Vance[4] „ 9675 ditto	23 04	„ „
	„ Negro's for carrying ditto up Stairs	1 25	„ „
26	„ M Kennedy for carpenters work &c. at Mrs. Cooks[5]	25 66	„ „
Septr. 1	„ V. Day[6] for repairing pavement at Mr. Ratels[7]	2 75	„ „
2	„ P. Weakley[8] for 5000 Shingles	10 „	„ „
	Recd. of Gratz & Bruce for 4„0„21 lb Hemp @ 6$.	„ „	25 12
	„ William Bell to pay expenses of patenting Bed Stead[9]	„ „	30 „
4	Paid John Price[10] for 5 Bbls Corn for Farm[11]	7 50	„ „

	6	„ M. Kennedy for 3750 Shingles	7 50	„ „	
	7	„ Gratz & Bruce for 200 lb milled Hemp got about 2 Ys. since	12 „	„ „	
	8	„ R Grinstead for Stone work at Hotel Stable[12]	41 „	„ „	
	11	„ Jno. Wirt, conste.[13] costs in case vs Mrs. Rollins[14]	1 25	„ „	
	18	„ D. Megowan for a Bbl Salt for Farm	3 38	„ „	
	23	„ T. K. Layton & Co. for Brick & work at Hotel Stable	100 87	„ „	
		„ Ditto ditto „ Wilkins's[15]	4 13	„ „	
	25	„ Henry Harvey for Glass & Glazing at Mrs. Cooks	5 18	„ „	
Octr.	9	„ A. K Smedes for the 1/3d. of a lot of Hemp delivered Mr. Jno. H. Kerr to rot and clean out on the shares	12 93	„ „	
	23	„ D Grisham for Hinges &c. for the Hotel Stable	5 „	„ „	
Novr.	1	„ Henry Harvey for Painting, Glass, Glazing &c. in the House rented to Postlethwait, Brand & Co.[16]	7 81	„ „	
	„	„ T. Studman for a Lock & repairing, others for ditto	2 50	„ „	
	7	„ T. W. Clay to pay for depositions	1 25	„ „	
		„ Thos. Mc.Cracken per request of M. Kennedy in part of repairs on Hotel Stable	132 25	„ „	
	10	Recd. of Mrs. Cook for 1 qrs. House rent due this day	„ „		41 25
		Paid Mrs. Cook for boarding &c. due by T. W. Clay	29 „	„ „	
	11	„ Lewis & George[17] for plastering Stair way of Lecture Rooms	6 „	„ „	
	13	„ J. H Kerr on Acct.	5 „	„ „	
	14	Recd. of Gratz & Bruce, balance of Meal Acct. to 11 inst.	„ „		78 „
		Paid B. Blunt[18] for 4 Bbls Salt for use of Farm	14 06	„ „	
	26	„ Pritchart & Robinson[19] for Linsey for Farm Negroes	6 „	„ „	
	28	„ John Hull for Leather „ ditto	8 75	„ „	

			Dr.	Cr.
	29	„ R. Mc.Nitt[20] for Glass & Glazing windows in Lecture Rooms which had been broken by the Carpenters when putg. on Roof	2 „	„ „
	30	„ T. K. Layton & Co. for Brick furnished and work at the House leased to Postlethwait, Brand & Co.	9 „	„ „
		Forwarded	519 06	174 37

1826			Dr.	Cr.
Novr.	30	Amounts forward	519 06	174 37
Decr.	23	Paid B. Kieser [sic] for binding Gregory's Dictionary,[21] pr. order of T. W. Clay	6 „	„ „
		Recd. of B. Keiser for 1 qrs. House rent due 23rd. Ulto.[22]	„ „	13 75
	28	Paid M. Kennedy, balance of his Bill for repairing Hotel Stable	120 84	„ „
	30	Recd. of Mrs. Morrison[23] for 6 Hogs 863 lb @ 1 3/4c.	„ „	15 10
		Paid R Henry for Black Smith work for Farm	16 88	„ „
1827				
Jany.	2	„ January & Huston for carriage of House hold goods	5 69	„ „
	4	Recd. of J. H. Kerr for 100 lb Pork sold old Mrs. Hart[24]	„ „	1 75
		„ Mrs. Morrison for Rye Straw	„ „	1 „
	6	Paid M. Fishel for Elbow to Tin Spout	„ 75	„ „
	11	Recd. of Jno. H Kerr for 606 lb Lard sold R. S. Todd @ 3 1/2c.[25]	„ „	21 21.
		Paid Jno. H. Kerr on acct. of his wages	50 „	„ „
	12	„ Jno. Sinclair[26] for plank got for Stable in Augt. last omitted	4 37	„ „
	25	Recd. of Jno. H. Kerr for 16„1„23 lb Hemp sold	„ „	125 25
Feby.	3	Paid Jno. H. Kerr on Acct. of wages	25 „	„ „
	5	Recd. of Jno. D. Dillon for 2 qrs. House rent[27] due 21 Decr. 1826	„ „	30 „

	Paid Jno. D. Dillon for Brick & paving	12 50	" "	
10	Recd. of M. H. Jouitt [sic] for 1 qrs. House rent[28] due 27 Nov. 1826	" "	15 "	
	" Mrs. Cook for 1 qrs. House rent due this day	" "	41 25	
26	Paid J. Winn[29] for 6 Bus. Hemp seed	21 "	" "	
	Recd. of Postlethwait, Brand & Co. for 1 qrs. House rent due 30 Ulto.	" "	30 "	
Mar 10	" B. Keiser in full of House rent due to 7 inst.	" "	15 25	
24	Paid Jno. H. Kerr to give hands for extra breaking Hemp	2 56	" "	
April 4	" Jno. H. Kerr to buy 45 1/2 Yds Linen for Negro Cloathing 910c. & 2 Boxes for packing Bacon for Washington City 150	10 60	" "	
5	Recd. of Jno. Mc.Cracken for 1 qrs. Stable rent due 31 Ulto.[30]	" "	37 50	
6	" Jno. H. Kerr for 18„2„20 lb Hemp Sold	" "	142 "	
16	Paid Wm. West J. P. for Warrant of Distress vs Mason[31]	" 50	" "	
24	" Jno. H. Kerr on Acct. of Wages	15 "	" "	
	Recd. of S. Buckner & Co.[32] for last years hire of Shadrack	" "	66 25	
28	" Jno. T. Mason for 1 Years rent of Ashland[33]	" "	150 "	
	Paid ditto for repairs at ditto as per Bills	30 82	" "	
May 10	" A. Mc.Clure & Co. for 48 Yds domestic Cotton got by Mr. Kerr to cloathe Negro women	8 "	" "	
15	Recd. of Mrs. Cook for 1 qrs. House rent due 9 inst	" "	41 25	
17	" Postlethwait, Brand & Co. for 1 qrs. House rent due 30 Ulto.	" "	30 "	
18	Paid D. Megowan for a Bbl Salt for Farm use	3 31	" "	
June 7	" A. Mc.Clure & Co. for a Scythe & 12 Yds Linen for Farm use	3 90	" "	

			Dr.	Cr.
	13	„ Jno. H. Kerr to pay midwife to Negro Sidney[34]	3 „	„ „
		„ Jno. O. Sprake[35] for Carding Wool in July 1826	2 80	„ „
	21	„ January & Huston for carriage of Bacon to Maysville &c.	8.75	„ „
	28	„ Jno. H. Kerr to pay hire of harvest hands	4 50	„ „
July	2	„ Jno. Taylor[36] for Hack hire &c to Paris	3 50	„ „
„		Recd. of J. Mc.Cracken for 1 qrs. Stable rent due 1st. inst.	„ „	37 50
	6	Paid S. Vanpelt[37] for repairing Pump at Farm	3 „	„ „
		Forwarded	$882 33	988 43

1827			Dr.	Cr.
July	6	Amounts forwards	882 33	988 43
	10	Recd. of M. H. Jouitt for 2 qrs. House rent due 27 May	„ „	30 „
	11	„ David Sutton for 1 Ton Hemp	„ „	152 „
	13	„ Jno. Tilford for balance of his Note of 25 June 1824 for 397$22[38] with interest to 25 June 1827 Two hundred having been paid on H. Clays order heretofore[39]	„ „	268 71.
		Paid himself in the Office	550 71	„ „
	15	„ Ditto, the balance in full	6 10	„ „
			$1439 14	1439 14

E. & O. E.

ROBT. SCOTT

ADS. KyLxT.   [1] Not identified.
[2] Not identified   [3] Possibly William K. Wall.   [4] There were numerous Wrights and Vances in Fayette County; no firm has been identified.   [5] Catherine B. Cooke (cf. above, Rental Agreement, August 8, 1826).   [6] Not identified.   [7] Philbert Ratel. Cf. above, III, 752–53.   [8] Not identified.   [9] Bell, of Lexington, a manufacturer of planes, had been granted a patent, November 7, 1826, for an improvement in bedsteads. *House Docs.*, 19 Cong., 2 Sess., no. 27, p. 18 (January 8, 1827).   [10] Probably John R. Price.   [11] "Ashland."   [12] Cf. above, I, 343–44, 356, 378.
[13] Constable.   [14] Possibly Mrs. Frances Rawlins. Record of the case has not been found.   [15] Cf. above, II, 786–87.   [16] Cf. above, Rental Agreement, October 31, 1826.   [17] Probably Lewis Barbee, plasterer, and George Kauck, a housejoiner—both of Upper Street in Lexington.   [18] Bartholomew Blunt, for some 30 years, until his death in 1843, a grocer on Upper Street, near Short, in Lexington.   [19] William Pritchartt; Robinson, not further identified. The partnership had been operating as Lexington merchants for several years.   [20] Robert McNitt was a Lexington butcher.

21 George Gregory, *A New and Complete Dictionary of Arts and Sciences, Including the Latest Improvement and Discovery and the Present State of Every Branch of Human Knowledge* (3 vols.; New York, 1819).   22 Cf. above, I, 826–27.   23 Esther Montgomery Morrison (Mrs. James).   24 Susannah Hart (Mrs. Thomas, Sr.).   25 Kerr's receipt of this date to Todd is located in DLC-TJC (DNA, M212, R16).   26 Not identified.   27 Cf. above, Rental Agreement, June 21, 1825.   28 Cf. above, Rental Agreement with Catherine B. Cooke, August 8, 1826, and note; Rental Agreement with Postlethwait, Brand, and Company, October 31, 1826.   29 Probably Jacob Winn.   30 Cf. above, Scott to Clay, January 13, 1827.   31 John T. Mason. Cf. above, I, 383–84; Bill of Complaint against Wickliffe, July 5, 1825; Clay to Wickliffe, Barry, and Mason, July 13, 1826. Mason's answer "to a Bill in Chancery exhibited against him & others in the Fayette Circuit Court by Henry Clay Complainant" was certified, February 19, 1827, and filed April 10, 1827. Fayette Circuit Court, File 823.   32 Probably Samuel Buckner, of Bourbon County, Kentucky, not further identified.   33 Cf. above, Clay to Mason, March 9, 1826.   34 Not previously identified.   35 Lexington wool manufacturer.   36 Probably the freedman in Deed of Emancipation, above, July 2, 1825. MacCabe, *Directory of the City of Lexington . . . for 1838 & '39*, 67, lists John Taylor, identified among "colored persons," as "hack driver," residing at "9, E Short st."   37 Samuel Van Pelt (Jr.), Lexington pump maker.   38 Cf. above, III, 785–86.   39 Record of this transaction has not been found.

Toast to Clay at Paris, Kentucky, Public Dinner

[July 16, 1827]

Our Distinguished Guest, HENRY CLAY—Father of the "AMERI-CAN SYSTEM," Mediator of Missouri; the friend of his Country, and of Man;—where is the Kentuckian who will not proudly say, *He is my Countryman?*[1]

Lexington *Kentucky Reporter*, July 25, 1827. This newspaper reported, on July 18, that attendance at the dinner was from four to five thousand people; in the issue of July 25 the figures were five to eight thousand. President of the affair, held "on the green below Paris" (Kentucky), was Captain William Garrard; John L. Hickman was vice president.

[1] The editor commented further: "After MR. CLAY'S health was drank [*sic*]; which was followed by long continued cheers, he addressed the company at some length; we regret that it is out of our power to lay before our readers this most splendid effort of genius—we will never forget the emotions we felt, nor the electric effect with which it transported the crowd—he was frequently interrupted by the enthusiastic applause of the people—his effort throughout was worthy of himself and the great cause he defended."

From Josiah Stoddard Johnston

Dr. Sir   Cincinnati July 16th. 1827

I arrivd [*sic*] here yesterday. The lateness of the Season & the low Water determind [*sic*] me at Louisville to proceed without delay to Washington   I regret I could not have had the pleasure to meet you at Lexington— I shall be at Maysville to night & expect the Albion[1] to follow us in two days in which I shall proceed to Wheeling— The River is falling but hopes are entertaind [*sic*] that we shall have Water enough to Carry us up

I can give you the most positive assurances that the vote of Louisiana is Safe[2]— If there was any doubt of public opinion, which there is not. The Electoral Ticket would Carry it— We have Villier [*sic*], The-

bideau [*sic*]—DuPre—Thomas—& Hughes³   These names alone will
elect the Ticket— The Cause is every Where falling off— The Struggle
has been made & failed— The people are becoming Convinced of this.
If Genl. Jackson had any chance of Success, his friends would ruin
him— at this place they openly joind [*sic*] the opposition to the woolens
Bill & to the Harrisburg Convention⁴ & it will perhaps become general— I wish it may— Their folly will be the precursor of their fall—

The Crawford party have driven the friends of Genl. Jackson into
all their views—& the people now begin to see that the Country will
be thrown into their hands if he Succeeds— The Genl. Carries too
much dead Weight—& they will sink him—

I am very glad to see the Letter to Beverly [*sic*]⁵   The precise
charge is now known— They have gaind [*sic*] much by the vagueness
of the Suspicions they have set afloat—& they would have gaind more
by leaving it as it was— The charge Now dwindles to nothing & does
not reach you. at most it was a proposition of one of his friends to
Corrupt you— Now let him disclose the name of this honest & *highly
respectable* member & see what he will make of it⁶— It will appear that
he had just as much foundation for his Suspicions as the Genl. had
for his— Such a proposition Cannot be traced to any man— Here they
will fail & the Calumny will recoil—

But how different is this charge from the accusation heretofore put
forth in the papers & Uncontradicted & not disavowd— It was once
asserted that you had told the Genl. that he would be elected—& that
the proposition was made by your friends direct to him⁷—

I am anxious to see the name of his friend—& his disclosures— With
great regard yr Obt Set   J. S. JOHNSTON

ALS. InU.
¹ The steamboat *Albion*, a vessel of 50 tons, had been built at Cincinnati in 1826 and
in the spring of 1827 had been run successfully some distance up the Allegheny River
in a test of the practicability of steam navigation on that extension of the Ohio-
Mississippi River system. Washington *Daily National Intelligencer*, April 30, 1827.
² Cf. above, Clay to Brown, March 27, 1827, note.   ³ Probably Jacques (James)
Philippe Villeré; Henry S. Thibodaux; Jacques DuPré; and Philemon Thomas. Hughes
has not been identified.   DuPré, of St. Landry Parish, Louisiana, amassed a fortune as
a stockraiser. He at this time represented his parish in the Louisiana Legislature, served
from 1828 to 1846 in the State Senate, and briefly in 1830–31 held office as acting Governor.
Early in July meetings were being held for the selection of delegates from each parish
to attend a State convention on the first Monday in November to name Adams electors.
Cf. Baton-Rouge *Gazette*, July 14, 1827. Only Villeré of those here listed was included
among the five Adams electors finally designated in November. Cf. *ibid*., November 10,
1827.   ⁴ On the woolens bill, see above, Pleasants to Clay, February 14, 1827; on the
Harrisburg Convention, see above, Clay to Crowninshield, March 18, 1827, note. At a
meeting held in Cincinnati on July 13 to name delegates to the Harrisburg Convention,
the supporters of Jackson had strongly opposed the action and had sought to adjourn
the meeting until too late for a delegate to reach Harrisburg. The meeting had been
so disorderly that it had been necessary to adjourn it temporarily. On July 16 the
Cincinnati delegates had been named. *Liberty Hall and Cincinnati Gazette*, July 16, 1827.
⁵ Cf. above, Clay to Hammond, June 25, 1827.   ⁶ James Buchanan. See below,
Smith to Clay, August 1, 1827.   ⁷ The Beverley letter of March 8, 1827, published in
the Fayetteville, North Carolina *Observer*, and repetition of its charges from Jacksonian
organs, reprinted in the *Richmond Enquirer*, April 10, July 3, 1827, had emphasized that
the reported bargain was a direct approach to Jackson's friends by Clay's friends. The

Jackson letter to Beverley on June 6, 1827, had now brought into the approach an intermediary who was not intimately identifiable with either group. Cf. below, Smith to Clay, August 1, 1827; Clay to Southard, August 12, 1827.

INSTRUCTIONS AND DISPATCHES   July 16, 1827

From ALFRED FOX, Falmouth. Transmits, in the absence of his brother (Robert Were Fox), the latter's consular report; notes that the depression is lifting and that an abundant harvest is promised. LS. DNA, RG59, Cons. Disp., Falmouth, vol. 2 (M-T202, R-T2). Alfred Fox, not further identified.

From WILLIAM TAYLOR, Veracruz, "private and inofficial." Transmits "two very Singular documents": "the Manifest [sic] of the Congress of Vera Cruz in justification of their Conduct for having expelled . . . Ignacio Esteva [cf. above, Poinsett to Clay, June 16, July 8, 1827]," which also questions "the friendly views of the U. S. towards Mexico" and attacks "the Conduct of Mr. [Joel R.] Poinsett;" and Poinsett's reply. Encloses also "a short paragraph from the Sol, a leading paper in opposition to Mr P——." ALS. DNA, RG59, Cons. Disp., Veracruz, vol. 1 (M183, R1). Copy in MHi-Adams Papers, Letters Recd. (MR481). Received August 20.

From James Erwin

Dear Sir   Shelbyville[1] July 17th. 1827.
    Inclosed you will receive a Bill drawn by W. Brashear[2] and accepted by Messrs. Howard & Merry of Boston[3] for $400 rec'd. by me in part payment for your Steam engine,[4]   the payers are men of Capital, & the Bill will Certainly be met at Maturity. We have just recd. an account of your visit to Pittsburg [sic],[5] your letter in reply to Jacksons to C Beverly [sic].[6] & an account of your reaching Lexington all by the same mail   all of which is calculated to give us great pleasure,   we are now looking with great anxiety for the Genls. Statement.[7]   his confidential Editors the Republican of Nashville[8] in a tell tale Editorial Squib[9] after the rect of your letter Remarks that the Genl. did not mean as much as you would intimate &C &C that he only Supposed you were privy &C. &C.   I have no doubt the Genl. feels the awkwardness of his Situation,   their violence in this State even is doing good.   on the 4th July at Nashville a Committee was organized to Make Suitable preparations to Celebrate the day. on which the Jacksonites perceivd. too many administration men— They called a meeting & voted them all off. because they were administration men— The consequence was that an Administration dinner was immediately set on foot and about 70 very Respectable men such as Fletcher Washington Tannehill & & [sic] others then openly manifested their disapprobation to the Genl. and the Course his friends are pursuing[10]—
    A vacancy is likely to happen there by the Resignation of Judge McNairy[11] of the Dist Court of the U S. and I learn there will be perhaps three or four very Respectable applicants   Genl. Gibbs called on me for a letter to you which I gave him[12] as I would have done

either of the others,   I learn that Gibbs. Judge Crabbe. & perhaps. Col. Williams.[13] will be the prominent applicants. they are all our personal & particular friend [sic]   Williams and Gibbs independant [sic] political ones. Crabbe only half way so.   holding on to both sides, with an eye to a Seat on the Supreme Bench of the U S. Court Should the Judiciary Bill pass[14] Gibbs & Crabbe both Stand high at the Bar, very little difference as to their qualifications.   and as to Character equal   Gibbs possesses the most independance & firmness Williams will be in a difficult place,   he is now a candidate for the Senate of [sic] Knox County & Judge White[15] has been using[16] every exertion against him— Some making Stump Speeches. abusing the Adm, and connecting him therewith,   it would destroy Williams election were it known that he had applyed [sic] for this office or any office from the Govt. & should they beat him it would be desirable to him to receive this appointmt.   the Chance is now in favr. of Williams success in which event I am not Sure he would Care to get this appointment, for if we Succeed pretty well throughout the State, the chance will be very soon for him to beat White for the Senate of the U S.[17] I mention these matters that you may understand the situation of the parties so [that you][18] may do the best for all concerned— [. . .]be a hard Contest between Bell & Grundy[19] the chances were altogether in fav. of Bell, but Grundy has got out the Story that Bell is secretly adm, which is not the fact but is having Some effect. I yet think Bell will beat him, & we think we will be able to beat Polk.[20] here, But with a poor Substitute, one however that will not like Polk make it a business to ride thro [sic] his Dist retailing falsehood unsparingly.

Anne and the children[21] are in good health. the youngest grows finely. Julias neck yet remains Sound. but I still have nagg[22] fears about it. Anne sends her love to you & her Mother to whom you will also remember me most affectionately. Very Truly   J ERWIN

ALS. DLC-HC (DNA, M212, R2). Endorsed by Clay: ". . . Answered"; see below, Clay to Erwin, August 4, 1827.
1 Tennessee.   2 Possibly Dr. Walter Brashear, who had moved from Lexington to St. Mary's Parish, Louisiana, in 1822. The bill has not been found.   3 Abraham Howard and Robert D. C. Merry were Boston shipping merchants.   4 Cf. above, II, 887, 889; III, 72; Clay to Erwin, April 28, 1826.   5 Cf. above, Toasts and Response, June 20, 1827.   6 See above, Clay "To the Public," June 29, 1827.   7 See below, Smith to Clay, August 1, 1827, note.   8 Allen A. Hall and John Fitzgerald, who had bought the *Nashville Republican and Tennessee Gazette* in 1826 and the *Nashville Gazette* in 1827, issued the combined journals in 1827 as the *Nashville Republican and State Gazette*, a Jackson organ. After the election of 1828, Fitzgerald sold his interest to Hall, who remained the editor until 1834.   Born in North Carolina, Hall had settled in Nashville to practice law and had been admitted to the bar in that city in 1824. His career was, however, primarily identified with journalism. From 1837 to 1841 he was one of the editors of the *Nashville Republican Banner*, formed in 1837 as a merger of the *Nashville Banner and Whig* with the *Nashville Republican*; in 1845 he acquired an interest in the *Nashville Whig*, founded in 1838; from 1849 to 1853 he edited the Washington, D. C., *Republic*, founded in 1847 as the administration organ for President Zachary Taylor; from 1853 to 1857 he again edited the Nashville *Republican Banner*; from 1857 to 1859 he founded and edited the *Nashville Daily News*; and in 1859 he became one of the founders and principal editor of the Nashville *Opposition*. Inter-

mittently he held political patronage appointments, as Chargé d'Affaires to Venezuela
from 1841 to 1845, Assistant Secretary of the Treasury from 1849 to 1850, and Minister
to Bolivia from 1863 until his death there in 1867.   9 Cf. Lexington *Kentucky Reporter*, July 25, 1827, reprinting editorial from *Nashville Republican* of July 14.

10 Reporting the July 4 festivities on July 7, 1827, the *National Banner and Nashville
Whig* expressed "regret that political dissentions were so far permitted to intrude, as
to create two public dinners, instead of that harmonious and united cooperation around
one festive board, which has been usual . . . on similar occasions heretofore." Jackson
and his family attended one gathering by invitation and heard an oration which vehemently attacked the Adams-Clay "bargain." The administration supporters, 65 in
number as reported by the *National Banner*, met separately for a dinner at which
Wilkins Tannehill presided and Thomas Washington and Dr. Boyd McNairy were vice
presidents. James Erwin was among those who presented toasts, several of which lauded
Clay. Thomas H. Fletcher was not mentioned as prominent in the celebration.   Wilkins
Tannehill, born in Pittsburgh, had resided briefly at Lexington, Kentucky, in 1810,
before settling later that year in Nashville, where he had opened a warehouse and sold
salt. He had branched into the grocery business and in 1818 had been cashier of the
Nashville Bank. Tannehill had become active in political journalism in 1818 and was
mayor of Nashville from 1825 to 1827. In 1830 he founded the *Nashville Herald* as a
Clay organ.   11 John McNairy. Cf. above, Clay to Callaway, May 24, 1826, note.

12 No letter has been found from Erwin to Clay, recommending George W. Gibbs.
13 Henry Crabb; John Williams.   14 Cf. above, III, 551n.   15 Hugh Lawson
White.   16 Word unclear.   17 Williams won election to the State Senate, 1827-
1829, but was not again returned to the United States Senate. He subsequently declined
appointment to the State Supreme Court.   18 MS. torn; two or three words missing
here and at the beginning of the next sentence.   19 John Bell and Felix Grundy
were candidates for a seat in Congress. On the outcome, cf. above, Carroll to Clay,
November 25, 1825, note.   20 James K. Polk's unsuccessful opponent in this election
was Lunsford M. Bramlett, a North Carolinian by birth, who had been reared in
Georgia and had settled in Tennessee as a young man in 1813. He had been admitted to
the bar at Pulaski the following year. He served as State Chancellor from 1836 to 1844.
21 Clay's daughter, Anne Brown Clay Erwin, and grandchildren, Julia D. and Henry
Clay Erwin.   22 Nagging.

INSTRUCTIONS AND DISPATCHES   July 18, 1827

From HEMAN ALLEN, Santiago de Chile, no. 55. Transmits copies of his correspondence with the United States consul, (Michael) Hogan, regarding the latter's proposal to return to the United States, "without permission," and "the appointment
of a person to perform the temporary duties of the Consulate." Indicates that unless the *Peacock* (cf. above, Jones to Clay, July 1, 1827) arrives before the end of
the month, he (Allen) intends to leave with his family on "some other conveyance."
Reports that the Congress of Chile did not recess (cf. above, Allen to Clay, June
14, 1827) "but adjourned *sine die*," after providing "for the assembling of a new
Congress" next February "to receive the instructions of the Provincial Assemblies
and Municipalities" regarding a new constitution. States that "The administration
of President [Francisco Antonio] Pinto [Diaz] has thus far been very tranquil. . . ."
Adds: "I hear that he contemplates many improvements in the government, and
that a full mission is soon to be sent to the United States; yet, my credulity has so
often been taxed on such subjects, that I fear, the day is still distant, for their
final accomplishment." ALS. DNA, RG59, Dip. Disp., Chile, vol. 2 (M-T2, R2).
Received December 13.

Among the reasons given by Hogan, in the enclosed correspondence, for his
desire to return to the United States is the following: "to justify myself against
the attacks that I too well know have been unjustly made against me." Cf. above,
Allen to Clay, December 22, 1826, June 14, 1827.

From J[OHN] M. FORBES, Buenos Aires, no. 51. Reports that the provincial government of Buenos Aires has been re-established, "[Bernardino] Rivadavia's resigna-

tion was accepted" (cf. above, Forbes to Clay, June 29, 1827), and Vicente López was elected provisional President; that López has named "General Marcos [sic] Balcarce, Minister of Foreign Relations and of War and Marine"; and that an election has been called to form "the Provincial Junto of this town and Province. . . ." States that General (Carlos Antonio José de) Alvear has been removed from command of the national army, to be succeeded by General (Juan A.) Lavalleja; describes this as a popular move which should "electrify" the Banda Oriental "and reunite many corps who have left the National army. . ."; adds that all the above events have transpired "in the utmost tranquility [sic] and good order. . . ."

Notes the arrival of a British brig of war bearing dispatches for Lord (John B.) Ponsonby and observes that the "extreme mystery" fostered by the crew's failure to communicate any news has given rise to several rumors, which include talk of an English occupation of Cuba and subsequent war between the United States and England, and of the Emperor of Brazil's (Peter I's) request for "the hand of another Archduchess of Austria."

Reports, on July 20, accounts of a conflict in the interior between forces led by Colonel (Gregorio Argoz de) La Madrid, "on the part of the Former Government," and Colonel (Juan Facando) Quiroga, "on that of the opposition," resulting in La Madrid's defeat; assesses the implications of this conflict as detrimental to unification of the provinces; and states that "the paper currency of this Country is threatened with almost total extinction." L, written and signed at dictation by J. Dickinson Mendenhall. DNA, RG59, Dip. Disp., Argentina, vol. 3 (M69, R4). Published in Espril (comp.), Once Años en Buenos Aires, 470–72; extract published in Manning (arr.), Diplomatic Correspondence . . . Latin American Nations, I, 661–62. Received October 26.

Vicente López y Planes, born in Buenos Aires in 1785 and educated at the Royal College of San Carlos, had received a doctorate in laws at Chuquisaca and in 1808 had published a lengthy poem, El Triunfo Argentino. He was also the author of the Himno Nacional Argentino, adopted by the Asamblea General Constituyente in 1813. Identified with the movement for Argentine independence from his youth, he had been elected a deputy for Buenos Aires to that Assembly and had held a number of civil posts over the years. He now served as provisional President for only a month, from July 7 to August 12, 1827. He became a member of the Senado Consultivo in 1832, was briefly Minister of Foreign Relations in January of that year, and for many years presided over the Superior Court of Buenos Aires. He was again Provisional Governor of the Province of Buenos Aires from February to July, 1852.

Juan Ramón Gonzalez Balcarce, born in 1773, had enrolled in the army as a youth, had been named commander of the armies of Tucumán in 1805, and had participated in the famous battle of that name in 1812. He had been named Governor-Intendant of Buenos Aires in 1816, a post from which he resigned within a few months. He had been elected in 1824 to the Congreso General Constituyente, was named to the post of Minister of War and Marine in 1827, and subsequently became Minister Plenipotentiary to effect peace with Brazil. He was again named Governor and captain-general of the Province of Buenos Aires in 1832 and charged with the handling of foreign relations; but, in the face of partisan upheaval, he soon retired to private life, in Buenos Aires.

Lavalleja had been born in Minas, now called Lavalleja, Uruguay, in 1788. He had joined the revolutionary forces of José Artigas in 1811 and, after the defeat of the Spanish, had fought against Brazil for independence of the Banda Oriental. The appointment of Lavalleja which Forbes here reports precipitated a revolt by one corps of the Argentine forces on December 1, 1828, which in its effects greatly aggravated the chaos in the administration of the country.

Quiroga, born in Rioja Province in 1788, was a military leader, known as the "Tiger of the Llanos." After a turbulent youth, he had become from March to July, 1823, head of the Province of Rioja and in 1824 had been a member of the Congreso General Constituyente. The province of Rioja, however, and Quiroga, had rejected the proposed constitution (cf. above, Forbes to Clay, April 12, 1827, note) and Rivadavia's Presidency. Quiroga's defeat of La Madrid at Tucumán ranked him among the leaders of the federal forces in the ensuing struggle over the issue of a strong central government for Argentina, but as the country was torn apart by rival caudillos in the succeeding years, Quiroga seems to have regretted this position. He was assassinated in February, 1835, while undertaking a mission for concilation to avert civil war between the northern provinces and Buenos Aires. On the troubled events of this period, see Levene, *A History of Argentina*, 387–90, 393–95, 401–402, 408–409.

From ROBERT MONROE HARRISON, Antigua. Encloses "a letter [not found] written by the Mercantile house of [William] Dawson of Baltimore which has been inserted in several of the Colonial papers and commented upon by all of them in pretty much the same Style." Asserts that, "Whatever may have been the intention of Government by sanctioning this *indirect trade* [*sic*]" (cf. above, Harrison to Clay, May 3, 1827; Editorial Article, May 9, 1827), he can see no "great advantage" to "the people of the U States or those of the Colonies. . . , the latter having no shipping and the former being now the Carriers for them." Predicts that "It may however be of some to the European Shipping which come to the West Indies in the early part of the Season before the crops come in, as they will be inabled [*sic*] to make a voyage to the U S while their Cargoes are preparing." Adds: "In order to Enforce upon the Owners or Commanders of vessels the necessity of touching at Neutral Ports, on the outward and return voyages, Consular clearances should be exacted as there is no dependence on any thing given by the Public Authorities of St Thomas, St Eustatia [*sic*] or St Bartholomews [*sic*]."

Requests Clay to inform him "as soon as possible" whether he should "extend" his "observations to Jamaica. . . " ALS. DNA, RG59, Cons. Disp., Antigua, vol. 1 (M-T327, R1). Received August 9. Endorsed by Clay on verso of last page: "Let a letter be prepared to Mr. Harrison informing him that it is the President's Wish that he shd extend his observations to Jamaica. H C"

Writing on August 9, 1827, Daniel Brent, by direction of "the Secretary," acknowledged receipt of Harrison's "Letters . . . of the 14. 18 and 19th. of July" and stated that the President wished him to include Jamaica among the "British Islands" that he was to visit. Copy, in DNA, RG59, Cons. Instr., vol. 2, pp. 437–38 (M78, R2).

On May 26, 1827, orders had been issued at Kingston, Jamaica, laying double duties on American produce imported through neutral islands after the first of June. *Niles' Weekly Register*, XXXII, (June 30, 1827), 291, citing private correspondence. Halifax newspapers during this summer were also reporting that American produce was "received in abundance" in the British islands, although at enhanced prices. *Ibid.* (July 21, August 25, 1827), 347, 416.

From FREDERICK JACOB WICKELHAUSEN, Bremen. Files his semiannual list of American arrivals and departures, reporting 31 vessels, which indicates an increase in commerce with Bremen. Reports that Hanover has sold to Bremen "a small tract of land, situated at the entrance of the Weser, about 40 Miles" from Bremen and that construction has begun there on "a Seaport for vessels of at least 240 tons Burthen." Encloses a copy of his letter to the collector at Boston (Henry A. S. Dearborn) concerning an "extraordinary case" and solicits Clay's reaction to his handling of the matter. Notes that he has received many applications "from the interior of Germany" from persons who wish to emigrate to the United States, which he approves if the applicants have enough property "to enable them to meet the first cost of a new establishment." Describes conditions imposed upon the emigrants by the German governments. Discusses the activities of Schaeffer (not further identified), Chargé d'Affaires of Brazil, in recruiting settlers to that nation; expresses belief that the Germans would adapt more readily to the United States; and advises that the United States could get no better immigrants than those from the German interior.

Recalls, in a postscript, that he requested from the State Department, on February 20, 1823, "a Certificate . . . in which is declared that no deduction or tax is exacted from persons or property, that are or is removing from the United States to a foreign country. . . ." Explains that "such a certificate will be serviceable to exchange against a similar one from the Government of the Dukedom of Oldenburg, in which country a deduction of 10 per Cent is existing still. . . ." ALS. DNA, RG59, Cons. Disp., Bremen, vol. 2 (M-T184, R2). Received September 12.

In the enclosure Wickelhausen informs Dearborn of the plight of the *Isis*, which arrived from Havana, June 3, without documents to prove its nationality—they having apparently been lost by the vessel's master, Elias Hulin, prior to his death on the voyage. Upon presentation by the mate and acting master, Thomas Russel, of evidence that the owners were Nehemiah Parsons and Israel Thorndike of Boston, Wickelhausen extended his protection to the *Isis*, upon condition that it "return direct to Boston . . ." and upon receipt of bond from the consignee that the vessel would so return to port.

On November 1, 1827, Daniel Brent, "By direction of the Secretary, acknowledged receipt of Wickelhausen's dispatch and transmitted the certificate he had requested. Copy, in DNA, RG59, Cons. Instr., vol. 2, p. 446 (M78, R2).

By a convention signed at Hanover January 11, 1827, Bremen had acquired the basic territorial cession whereby the port of Bremerhaven was constructed at the confluence of the Geeste River with the Weser. The harbor was opened in 1830, and the docks were greatly expanded in later years.

Hulin and Russel have not been further identified. The *Isis* had been built for the Boston merchant Nehemiah Parsons, at Medford, Massachusetts, in 1812. The vessel had been in Cádiz, Spain, at the outbreak of the War of 1812, and Richard W. Meade, as consignee, had arranged for a fictitious transfer of its registry to Spanish ownership through the connivance of the captain but apparently without the authority of the owner. The Spanish registration had been continued over the years. In 1828 the Committee on Commerce of the House of Representatives recommended that the nationality of the vessel be restored, though the Committee rejected Parsons' plea that the extra expenses of its foreign registration be refunded. A bill to this effect was introduced but failed to reach a vote. *House Repts.*, 20 Cong., 1 Sess., no. 132; U. S. H. of R., *Journal*, 20 Cong., 1 Sess., p. 270.

From Wyndham Robertson

Dear Sir   Washington City July 19, 1827

You will not I hope consider me to presume too far when I venture to ask of you the favor of some few letters of introduction to your friends in Europe   I am emboldened to do so, by the known courtesy that has always marked your course towards young Americans, and yet more by the friendly relations that have so long subsisted between yourself & more than one member of my immediate family.[1] I propose spending some months in Europe mostly in France, for the purpose of re-establishing my health and am desirous at the same time, to improve the opportunity it will afford of acquiring useful information and indulging a rational curiosity. Nothing would conduce more I feel assured, to procure me these advantages than to be introduced abroad under your auspices— and, I will add, no one's introduction would be more agreeable to me than yours. Knowing my views, you will yourself be better enabled to refer me to gentlemen whose station or character will tend to promote them, than I am to suggest them. If at the same time there be any objects within my reach while there, to which you may deem it worth whi[le] particularly to direct my attention, your kindness will be properly appreciated & acknowledged. It occurs to me at this moment that my stay in England will be so short as to preclude the possibility of receiving a letter from you while there. Should it be agreeable to you to write, you will be pleased, therefore, to address me at Paris—to which place, as my visit must be limited to a very few months, it is my present purpose to confine my self almost exclusively. In extending to me the favor I ask, you will confer on me an obligation I shall be always happy to acknowledge. I am Sir With the highest respect Your friend & fellow citiz[en]

                                                        WYNDHAM ROBERTSON

ALS. DLC-HC (DNA, M212, R2). Addressed to Clay and endorsed by him on verso: ". . . Sent the letters requested." The letters have not been found.
[1] Robertson was a brother of John and Thomas Bolling Robertson. Born near Richmond and educated at the College of William and Mary, Wyndham Robertson had been admitted to the bar in 1824. He became a member of the Executive Council of Virginia from 1830 to 1836 and, as senior member of the Council, succeeded to the Governorship of Virginia in 1837. From 1838 to 1841 he served in the Virginia House of Delegates. He retired at that time and returned to public affairs only during the Civil War crisis years, again as a member of the House of Delegates, from 1859 to 1865.

DIPLOMATIC NOTES   July 19, 1827

From PABLO OBREGÓN, Washington. Refers to Clay's note of February 19, 1827, and announces the dispersion from Nacogdoches of the insurgents, some of whom have taken refuge in the United States. Describes the actions of the insurgents and names American citizens involved (cf. above, Dickson to Clay, January 3, 1827, note; Obregón to Clay, April 25, 1827, note). Encloses a copy of a convention between the insurgents and certain Indians, identifies B(enjamin) W. Edwards as one of the principal trouble-makers, requests that Edwards and his companions be punished, and states that the difficulties in Texas have been ended. ALS, in Spanish with trans. in State Dept. file. DNA, RG59, Notes from Mexican Legation, vol. 1 (M54, R1).

INSTRUCTIONS AND DISPATCHES   July 19, 1827

From ROBERT MONROE HARRISON, Antigua. States that, "pressed . . . for time" when he acknowledged on July 14 Clay's "Despatch of the 14th May," he "very

uncourteously omitted to offer" his "personal thanks, for the handsome and flattering terms in which" Clay's "official communication was couched"; gives assurance of his "vast sense of obligation"; and notes that he will depart "on or
about the 22d inst." to begin his mission by visiting Barbados. ALS. DNA, RG59,
Cons. Disp., Antigua, vol. 1 (M-T327, R1). Received August 9.

MISCELLANEOUS LETTERS   July 19, 1827

From JONATHAN H. LAWRENCE, New York. Inquires whether the "arrangement,"
which he understands has been made between the United States and Brazil (cf.
above, Rebello to Clay, June 1, 1827; Clay to Rebello, June 2, 1827; Clay to Force,
June 3, 1827), "will embrace the case of the ship Spermo. . . ." ALS. DNA, RG59,
Misc. Letters (M179, R65). Cf. above, Raguet to Secretary of State, March 11,
1825, note; Lawrence to Clay, February 2, 1827.

   Daniel Brent replied to Lawrence, July 24, 1827, "In the absence of the Secretary," informing him that "no arrangement has hitherto been made between the
two Governments, concerning the claims" mentioned and expressing a "hope that
when the United States can be conveniently represented at Rio de Janeiro, just
satisfaction will be given by the Government of Brazil for injuries committed. . . ."
Copy, in DNA, RG59, Dom. Letters, vol. 22, p. 9 (M40, R20).

INTRUCTIONS AND DISPATCHES   July 20, 1827

From CHARLES BARNET, Antwerp. Reports the arrival of numerous American vessels without Mediterranean passports (cf. above, Clay to Nourse, November 11,
1825, note) and the claim of the ships' masters that the law requiring these documents has been repealed. Notes that, "Having found," upon entering his office,
"but a few numbers of the Acts of Congress and not having received the Sequel
since," he has "not been unabled [sic] to ascertain positively whether this law, was
obsolete or not. . . ."

   Requests instructions relative to the status of seamen absent over 48 hours
from their vessels which do not wait for them. ALS. DNA, RG59, Cons. Disp.,
Antwerp, vol. 1 (M-T181, R-T1).

   The House of Representatives had approved on December 29, 1826, a resolution calling upon the Committee on Commerce to investigate the expediency of
repealing legislation which required Mediterranean passports. No report was
filed and no action resulted from the investigation within the next few years.
U. S. H. of Reps., Journal, 19 Cong, 2 Sess., p. 107.

   The law concerning the responsibilities of seamen dated from July 20, 1790 (1
U. S. Stat., 133), and provided: ". . . if any seaman or mariner shall absent himself for more than forty-eight hours at one time, he shall forfeit all the wages due
to him, and all his goods and chattels which were on board the said ship or vessel,
or in any store where they may have been lodged at the time of his desertion, to
the use of the owners of the ship or vessel, and moreover shall be liable to pay
to him or them all damages which he or they may sustain by being obliged to hire
other seamen or mariners in his or their place, and such damages shall be recovered with costs. . . ."

From JOHN CUTHBERT, Hamburg. States that "Among the arrivals this year have
been several [American] vessels from the West Indies, not one of which has been
furnished with a Mediterranean Pass [cf. above, Barnet to Clay, this date], and
the excuse of the masters is, that when they left the United States, they had not

any intention of visiting Europe." Cites the case of one vessel which arrived here from Pernambuco without a Pass, and contrary to . . . [his] advice" has been chartered for a voyage to Smyrna.

Encloses copies of letters he has written concerning "the improper discharge of Seamen" and suggests that "The discharge of Seamen that are not on the Roll as Americans, or that have been Shipp'd out of the United States, is an evil that will probably require the interference of Congress—" Notes that "every master is informed on his arrival, that the Laws of Hamburg does [sic] not allow the discharge of Seamen without the consent of the Consul of the Nation to which the vessel belongs" and that "several of the vessels that have arrived here have been shamefully short manned. . . ." ALS. DNA, RG59, Cons. Disp., Hamburg, vol. 3 (M-T211, R3). Received September 25.

On the existing legislation for protection of "distressed seamen," see above, Clay to Quarrier, May 12, 1825; Williamson to Clay, April 3, 1827, note. No additional legislation on the subject was adopted during this period.

From ALBERT GALLATIN, London, no. 97. States that the draft of the protocol enclosed in his "despatch No. 88" (above, June 23, 1827) "was withdrawn" at his suggestion, his "wish being that no premature commitment on their [the British] part should prevent them from abandoning the ground they intended to take," and that, in consequence, protocols of conferences 9 through 11 "have not yet been adjusted and signed." Explains that, since the anticipated 12th conference has not been held and (William) Huskisson has left England (cf. above, Gallatin to Clay, July 14, 1827), "copies of the drafts . . . proposed and discussed" are now enclosed "in order that the situation in which he [Huskisson] left the negotiation may be fully understood." Transmits copies of the drafts (of protocols) submitted privately for his consideration by (Henry U.) Addington and of "the papers" returned in response. Reports that "The verbal alteration . . . [he] had proposed in the Protocol of the 9th Conference was agreed to," but that Addington informed him that "in consequence of the detailed observations respecting iron and other matters . . . inserted in" Gallatin's "draft, . . . they should of course find it expedient to throw in their counter observations. . . ." Notes further communications from Addington, who, in a letter of July 6, promised to try to "get the Protocols signed by Mr. Huskisson before he left London" and stated that Charles Grant had been appointed to replace Huskisson. Observes that he has not heard from Addington since "on the subject." Reports that on July 14 he "wrote . . . a private Note to Mr. [George] Canning asking him for a short interview" and explains his stated reason and "still stronger motive' for the request; that Canning, citing "a severe attack of lumbago," agreed to a conference "so soon as he was sufficiently well again"; that he has heard nothing further from Canning, who has "gone to Chiswick, a few miles from London"; and that Grant has informed Gallatin of his appointment and "agreed to meet in conference to morrow. . . ." Suggests that if Canning is "declining an interview, when it is notorious that the gentlemen with whom" Gallatin is "to treat will not take the least step without his approbation," his action "would seem to indicate a disposition not to renew the commercial Convention and generally unfavorable in every respect" (cf. below, Gallatin to Clay, August 9, 1827). Adds that, on the subjects of that convention and "the territory west of the Rocky Mountains," he could "have brought matters to a close during the three last conferences; and, in ordinary times, . . . would have done it. But . . . if a failure as probable took place, it should not on either point be liable to the imputation of its being owing to precipitancy on our part. . . ." ALS. DNA, RG59, Dip. Disp., Great Britain, vol. 34 (M30, R30). Extract and enclosures published in *American State Papers, Foreign Relations*, VI, 681–83; copy, in MHi-Adams Papers, Letters Recd. (MR481).

From JOHN RAINALS, Copenhagen. Reports the appearance "this morning" of a Russian fleet, which will remain several days to take on supplies before proceeding to a British port, "& from thence to the Mediterranean" (cf. above, Rainals to Clay, May 20, 1827; Middleton to Clay, June 23, 1827; Brown to Clay, June 28, July 12, 1827; Gallatin to Clay, July 14, 1827). Notes receipt of "a letter from Count Schimmelman [sic], stating the King's [Frederick VI's] being willing to permit and acknowledge" (John) Cuthbert as vice consul for Holstein, provided he will "reside, or have an office in Alton[a]" (cf. above, Rainals to Clay, May 20, 1827), and Cuthbert's reaction—"a wish to let the question rest for a time" rather than accept that condition. Adds that "The trade to the Baltic" has increased "and with appearance of more steadiness." ALS. DNA, RG59, Cons. Disp., Copenhagen, vol. 3 (M-T195, R3). Received September 10.

From Sidney Breese

Honble. Henry Clay
Dear Sir,   Kaskaskia July 21. 1827.
    I return you thanks for the acknowledgment of the receipt of my letter to you of the 7th ulti.[1] I should have written you long ere this had I not been absent attending the Courts in Missouri when your letter arrived here. Permit me to Congratulate you Sir, upon your return to the State, whose character you have so largely Contributed to establish, and whose confidence this [coil] and this good report you have Continued to retain.
    It is a Source of real pleasure to your friends to witness those marks of public approbation, by which you have on your journey been honored— we are gratified to see them, and feel rejoiced, that the most unjustifiable clamors which have been raised by evil and designing men, are fast changing to notes of applause, and we cannot but believe but that in proportion to your most unmerited persecutions will be the measure of your reward— Your reception at Pittsburgh[2] was truly gratifying, and gives evidence of a great change in public sentiment there Your speech is Much admired, and all admit it is well adapted to the Meridian of the place, the time, and the occasion. We confidently hope that the Storm which has so long raged against you, has spent its fury, and that hereafter in your onward Career, you will be favored with prospering gales, and with skies without a cloud.
    Since my return home, I have attended the Courts in the northern Circuit (the most populous part of our state) and have taken great pains to ascertain the state of feeling and opinion there, and the result is, as I believe that at the next election the present administration will be sustained by a large majority.[3] The grant of land for our Canal[4] has produced great unanimity of sentiment there, in favor of those under whose auspices, and by whose assistance the grant was effected— but apart from this, there is a decided majority there, in favor of the "American System," and will support no man or set of men, whose opinions on that subject are doubtful and not openly and fearlessly

expressed— There is too, a great mass of intelligence there, and men
Capable of discerning the true grounds of the opposition, and the real
reasons for the election of Gen. Jackson.

The Southern part of this State, from this County[5] down to the
mouth of the Ohio River, will give a majority for Genl. Jackson— so
will some of the Counties in the interior—they are however for the
most part thinly populated. The Ohio and Wabash Counties will be
much divided— If your friends there will support Mr. Adams, his
scale will preponderate—they do not generally in the state support him
unless it be there, of which I have no certain information. Some of
your friends, who seemed at one time to be most devoted to you, have
gone over to the enemy—deserted you in your utmost need, and all
forsooth, because they think Mr. Adams' re-election doubtful or impossible and wish to be on the strong side— such friends can be dispensed with—they Cannot be trusted. In this County, if the friends of
the Administration succeed in Obtaining the vote, it will be Contrary
to my expectations, as the Land Officers here, Gov. Bond[6] & Edward
Humphreys, are industriously though secretly exerting all the influence their offices give them against us. This influence the result of
their official stations, we have found to be at several elections irresistible— You may know how one must feel, when I state you the fact that
he Mr. H. declared, being a hot Crawford man,[7] that he would not
hold an office under Mr. Adams should he be elected. This I can
prove—— he is a secret insidious foe. As to Gov. Bond, he is pretending
to be in *favor* of the Administration, and there is no man more decidedly hostile to it— his appointment as well as that of Mr. Humphreys is soon to be made, and they are both very anxious to keep their
places and will do any thing to accomplish that object. I state it to
you, and pledge my word for the truth, that they are both hostile,
decidedly so, to the present Administration— they associate with none,
and have the Confidence of none, of its real friends. Mr. Kane[8] is their
friend, and it is well known that he has taken a stand against you and
identified himself with the opposition— all his friends here are of that
description— As for Mr. Kane, he is at open war, with the whole of us—
he has a *set* here, very clamorous against you more especially and who
believe every thing true, that is printed in the "Telegraph"[9]— that
paper is taken by Mr. Humphreys the receiver, & from which he and
his friends collect their texts for their "harangues" against the administration, and topics for abuse of you. Your friends here sincerely
hope and trust that you will be placed in a situation, by which their
removal from office can be effected— they are doing you all the injury
they can, and the first law of nature points to the Course I have dared
to suggest. Your friend Mr. Connar[10] the Marshal informs me that
Guy W. Smith, brother of John Speed Smith, Receiver of Public
Moneys at Palestine[11] is very violent for the opposition— the Register

there Mr. Kitchell[12] is a devoted friend of Mr. Kane and if he is not violent and open against you, it is for the same reason that activates Gov. Bond here, a desire *only* to secure his re-appointment.

The Contest in this state will be an animated one, and the result in my opinion doubtful. The opposition are an organized Corps, active and well disciplined, and will exert themselves to the utmost. The friends of the Administration will not be idle— we vote *now* by general ticket, and it is our design to bring out for Electors, this fall or winter, three of our most popular men,[13] and by industry and Concert we hope to succeed. We have erected the standard on which is inscribed "American System," and are determined to defend it. The opposition come out openly for the Virginia doctrines,[14] with some little modifications, they are disciples of Van Beuren [*sic*], and will if they can *Vanbeurenize* the state. Mr. Kane and the other master spirits of the party Lt. Gov. Kinney and Judge Smith[15] have Contributed a sum of money for the purchase and support of a Jackson Press to be located at Edwardsville,[16] with which they expect to do wonders— I send you some papers[17] by which you will see that Mr. Kane with his friend Gov. Bond at his back, has attempted upon our printer here, to introduce Van Beuren's system for the better regulating the paper of the County, or rather his own improvement upon it[18]— It is the general opinion that Mr. K. was intoxicated— They are very hostile to me, and wish to see me "put down"— this pleases me, as it gives me a license to do them all the injury I can— I have personally no Cause of quarrel with them, but political foes Cannot well be other than *personal* ones—at *least* in this County, and in *these* times.

Our representative to the next Congress—Genl. Duncan[19]—has been and is now I understand on a visit to Nashville— It is said he is Jacksonian— of this I much doubt. He has great respect for you, and I think unbounded Confidence in you. I do not believe he will oppose the Administration— Judge Thomas[20] has left our state much to our joy— he has gone to Ohio to reside, and declared he should not be a candidate for re-election. He told me last winter, he was determined, when he returned to this state to take *strong* ground in favor of the Administration— instead of which he has been the most of his time at St Louis, and not visited *our* people at all, and on his visit to this place he made his home and associates of our most inverterate [*sic*] and determined enemies. None of your friends or of Mr. Adams place any Confidence in him nor *can* they—*he is a man not to be confided in,* but can be *used* as occasion may offer.

We have great hopes of Pennsylvania— present appearances seem to justify the belief that her undivided support will be given to the Administration.[21] Will we be disappointed? *Missouri* may be Calculated on with safety— Judge Cook[22] who Resides in the southern circuit assures me that the southern Counties will generally go for Mr.

Adams— they will on the Upper Mississippi and if your friends on the Missouri, are true to you, and to principle, the vote of the state is certain. I saw Mr. Geyer[23] my friend a few days since, he is determined to visit those Counties—he is devoted to you— They are preparing to invite you, so, I understand, to St Louis— A paper for that purpose has been circulating there to which there were more than 150 names[24]— St Louis city is almost unanimously for the Administration—at least 9 tenths—

I hope Sir you will pardon the free manner with which I have addressed you, and also the length of this letter— I hope it may prove not uninteresting to you—it is well intended and I hope you will receive it in the same spirit you did some observations I made to you last winter.[25] Wishing you health and continued prosperity, and that you may succeed in crushing the force arrayed against you and finally triumph over all your foes. I remain dear Sir your friend & obt &c.

SIDNEY BREESE

ALS. DLC-HC (DNA, M212, R2).   [1] Neither communication has been found.
[2] Cf. above, Shaler and Mountain to Clay, June 19, 1827; Toasts and Response, June 20, 1827.   [3] Cf. above, Clay to Brown, March 27, 1827, note.   [4] The Illinois and Michigan Canal. Cf. above, Edwards to Clay, July 18, 1825, and note.   [5] Randolph.
[6] Shadrack Bond, a native of Maryland, had moved to Kaskaskia around 1791, had been a member of the Legislative Council of Indiana Territory, 1807–1808; the first Delegate of Illinois Territory to Congress, 1812–1814; receiver of public moneys in the general land office at Kaskaskia, 1814–1818; and first Governor of the State of Illinois, 1818–1822. He was register of the land office for the District of Kaskaskia from 1825 until his death, in 1832.   [7] During the presidential campaign of 1824–1825.   [8] Elias Kent Kane.   [9] Washington *United States Telegraph*.   [10] Henry Conner.
[11] Born in Kentucky in 1794, Smith had moved as a youth to Illinois, where he had held rank as a general of militia at his retirement in 1818 and represented Edwards County in the State Senate, 1818–1820. He held appointment as receiver of public moneys at the Palestine land office from 1820 to 1837. From 1842 to 1844 he sat in the Illinois House of Representatives.   [12] Joseph Kitchell, born in New Jersey, had settled in Crawford County, Illinois, shortly after the War of 1812, had been named justice for that county in 1818, and had represented it in the State Senate from 1818 to 1822. He had been named register of the Palestine land office in 1821 and held the appointment until 1841.   [13] Illinois electors had been chosen by district in the presidential election of 1824. Provision for their election by general ticket had been enacted January 11, 1827. Ill., *Revised Code of Laws . . . Enacted by the Fifth General Assembly . . . Commencing on the Fourth Day of December, 1826. . .* , 188–89. The Adams supporters named for the general ticket in 1828 were George Webb, Elijah Iles, and Samuel H. Thompson. Webb, born in Virginia, may have been the Winchester, Kentucky, tavern-keeper of 1807. He was postmaster at Bon Pas, White County, Illinois, from at least as early as 1825 until 1833. Iles, born in Fayette County, Kentucky, in 1796, had moved in 1818 to St. Louis, Missouri, and in 1821 to the area that became Springfield, Illinois. In the latter community he had opened a store, had invested in land, and had become postmaster. He served in the State Senate from 1826 to 1834 and became a Clay elector in 1832. Thompson was a Methodist minister, of Madison County, the defeated candidate for lieutenant governor in 1826.   [14] Cf. above, Brooke to Clay, January 31, 1827, note.   [15] William Kinney; Theophilus W. Smith. Born and admitted to the bar in New York City, Smith had moved to Edwardsville, Illinois, in 1816. He had been elected to the State Senate in 1823 and to the Illinois Supreme Court in 1825. He moved to Chicago in 1836 but remained on the Court until 1842.   [16] The journal, known as the *Illinois Corrector*, ran from October 14, 1827, until November 20, 1828. The printer was Robert K. Fleming, who had published for Kane the pro-Crawford *Republican Advocate*, at Kaskaskia, in 1823–1824. Born in Erie, Pennsylvania, Fleming had learned his trade at Pittsburgh and worked for a time in St. Louis before moving to Kaskaskia. He had resumed newspaper printing at Kaskaskia and Vandalia

in the interval prior to his move to Edwardsville, and following the cessation of the *Corrector* he returned to Kaskaskia as printer of the *Western Democrat*, apparently under the editorship of Breese, for some years after 1829. In 1833 he removed to Belleville, where he published a succession of journals over the next twenty years.   [17] Not found.   [18] Through May 30, 1827, the Kaskaskia *Illinois Reporter* had been published for Breese as editor and proprietor. L. O. Shräder, the printer and publisher, noted on June 6 that Breese had withdrawn from this connection. In the issue of July 11 Shräder reported that Kane had visited the newspaper office twice with the county sheriff (Thomas J. V. Owen) and on July 9 with Governor Bond, to demand, in great anger, the name of the writer of an editorial. Kane reportedly threatened to "blow up" the printing establishment. In commenting on the incidents, Shräder observed: "Our wonder is excited to know, if blowing up printing establishments be a part of Van Beuren's [*sic*] system for regulating the Press!" Cf. above, Sergeant to Clay, April 17, 1827, note. Shrader continued as publisher of the *Illinois Reporter* until 1829, when the journal was re-named the *Western Democrat* with Fleming as publisher. Owen, born in Kentucky in 1801, had been elected sheriff of Randolph County, Illinois, in 1823 and re-elected in 1826. He was elected to the Illinois General Assembly in 1830 and from 1831 to 1833 held appointment as Indian agent at Chicago. He became a member of the first board of trustees for the town of Chicago but died in October, 1835.   [19] Joseph Duncan.   [20] Jesse Burgess Thomas, born in Hagerstown, Maryland, had studied law at Washington, Mason County, Kentucky, from 1799 to 1803 and had opened practice at Lawrenceburg, Indiana Territory. He had served in the Territorial legislature from 1805 to 1808 and in 1809 had been named Federal judge for Illinois Territory. He had held that office until 1818, when he had become Senator for Illinois. He retained his Senate seat until March, 1829, but upon the expiration of his term moved to Mount Vernon, Ohio. From 1843 to 1848 he was a judge of the Ohio Supreme Court.   [21] Cf. above, Clay to Brown, March 27, 1827, note.   [22] John D. Cook, born in Orange County, Virginia, in 1790, had been taken shortly thereafter to Scott County, Kentucky. He had studied law in Frankfort and about 1815 had entered practice at Ste. Genevieve. He had been a delegate to the Missouri Constitutional Convention and one of the principal authors of the resulting document. In 1821 he had been appointed a judge of the State Supreme Court but two years later had resigned. From 1825 to 1849 he served as a circuit judge in the district covering southeastern Missouri, from then and until his death in 1852 he was Federal attorney for Missouri. He was a younger brother of Daniel Pope Cook.   [23] Henry S. Geyer.   [24] See above, Chouteau and others to Clay, July 10, 1827.   [25] Not found.

From Theodore Hunt

The Honble Henry Clay
Dear Sir   (Confidential)   Saint Louis July 21. 1827
Some few days since a letter[1] expressive of the feelings of your friends and the friends of the Administration was forwarded to you— The object of this communication is, to inform you that care was taken, that none other should be on the paper— I do believe Our State will be on the American System side of the question, *if it is not so at present*— Some of the people have been deluded, but are Comeing [*sic*] to their Senses— The Change is taken [*sic*] place, Slow but sure— If the handbill signed and published by Genl Jackson against Col Benton at the time of their dificulty [*sic*][2] could be procured, it would not only aid in the change here, *but elsewhere*. The latter person is at present in this Town, bold in his assertions, and active in his exertions. The Treasury arrangements with respect to depositing funds from the Land Offices, *and the collecting of drafts by disbursing officers*, are such, as to be detrimental to the Public Interests;[3] This fact may not press itself upon the Vigilent [*sic*] officer at the head of the depart-

ment,[4] but were an arrangement made by the Treasury, to have an Individual appointed here to receive deposits, and pay over the amount of drafts, it would afford a decent salary, say about one Thousand dollars per Annum, and save to the Government at least Ten Thousand dollars— He should be a Man of unimpeachable Character, and be heavily bonded— You will My Dear Sir please pardon the liberty I have taken in detailing my views to you— My desire to be of service to our Common Country and to yourself, must be my apoligy [sic]— I Remain with Great Respect Yr friend & Servant

THEODORE HUNT

ALS. DLC-HC (DNA, M212, R2). Hunt, born near Trenton, New Jersey, a brother of Wilson and John W. Hunt, had been commissioned a midshipman in the United States Navy in 1798 and raised to the rank of lieutenant in 1802. He had served in the Mediterranean from 1803 to 1806 and at the Norfolk Naval Station in 1806 to 1807, after which period he had entered merchant service. He had resigned from the Navy in 1811 and subsequently settled in St. Louis, where from 1814 to 1817 he had been a partner in the Missouri Fur Company. He had also operated a tanyard in St. Louis, at least as late as 1819. In 1825 he had been named recorder of land titles for the District of Missouri, a position from which he was removed by President Andrew Jackson in 1830. Hunt died in 1832.
    [1] See above, Chouteau and others to Clay, July 10, 1827.   [2] On the "difficulty," see above, I, 820n. Benton had published on September 10, 1813, a circular presenting an "Account of a Duel with General Jackson." THi.   [3] Under the law (3 U. S. Stat., 466), enacted April 20, 1818, receivers of public money at the land offices were to be paid $500 a year and a commission of one percent on the funds received, to a maximum compensation of $3,000 a year. Bernard Pratte, the receiver at the St. Louis Office, had been appointed in December, 1824, and was reappointed to another four-year term in 1829, but he was not reappointed in 1833. His compensation for the year as reported in 1827 was $947.96. Biennial Register, 1827, p. 65. The inspection system established for land office accounts had been overhauled in 1816 and has been viewed an exemplary. See White, The Jeffersonians, 524–26. Legislative revision of the compensation was not again enacted until 1862.   Pratte, born at Ste. Genevieve in 1771, was a St. Louis merchant and fur trader. He had been a territorial judge in 1807 and from 1812 to 1814 a judge of St. Louis County, a trustee of St. Louis from 1808 to 1820, and a member of the Missouri constitutional convention. He had also been a militia officer, commissioned brigadier general for the Territory in 1815. He retired from business in 1830.
    [4] Richard Rush.

From Robert Scott

Dr. Sir   Lexington 21st. July 1827
    Herewith enclosed, I transmit copies of the final settlement between the late Cols. Morrison and OHara[1] and the receipt of the latter for sundry [title] papers to lands &c. conveyed to him &c.
    That part of the land on the Kiskeminetas [sic] remaining to Colo. Morrison at his death was conveyed to my brothers and sister;[2] and I understand from them that the patent for a part has not yet been obtained— By the agreement and settlement between Cols. Morrison and OHara, it appears to me that the latter was bound to pay all expense necessary to the obtainment of the patent; but my brother informs me that Majr. Harmer Denny[3] of Pittsburgh, who is Colo. O.Hara's executor, is of opinion that it is doubtful [sic] whether

OHara's estate is bound for more than the office fees of taking out the patent— On examining the papers I apprehend you will be of a different opinion from Majr. Denny—

If you should, I will thank you in that case and when at leisure to write to Majr. Denny on the subject— You will observe by the agreement that Colo. OHara was bound to procure the patents and convey one equal moiety to Colo. Morrison and I beleive [sic] no deed has been made to O.Hara or his Reps. for half of the 1000 Acres on Green River[4]— Can the conveyances be made before your return to Kentucky? If they could, I would send on a deed for the Green River land for you to execute in Washn. to be delivered when OHara's executor shall make a conveyance for the land on Kiskeminetas—

Enclosed also I send you a copy[5] of an authority given by Colo. O.Hara to Colo. Morrison, to sell the land located by Gl. Lyttle [sic], being 500 Acres[6]— It bears even date with their settlement and is the only paper I can find on the subject— I fear we will have some difficulty in obtaining the title for this land—very respectfully Yr. obt. Servt

The Honble Henry Clay   ROBT. SCOTT

ALS. DLC-TJC (DNA, M212, R13).
[1] James Morrison; James O'Hara. The documents mentioned here have not been found.   [2] James Morrison had bequeathed $5,000 worth of land, each, to James Scott, William Scott, and Mary (Scott) Boyd, and had provided that they should be legatees for any residue of the estate if it amounted to $9,000. Fayette County Court, Will Book E, 64, 67. Samuel Scott was not mentioned in the will. Mrs. Boyd resided in Allegheny County, Pennsylvania, in 1838. William Scott may have been the Lexington merchant identified with the firm of Scott and Tilford.   [3] Born in Pittsburgh and graduated in 1813 from Dickinson College, Denny had been admitted to the bar in 1816 and was, from 1824 to 1829, a member of the Pennsylvania House of Representatives. He served in Congress from 1829 to 1837 and was a Presidential elector in 1840. He resumed the practice of law in 1837 and was an incorporator of the Pennsylvania Railroad and of other smaller lines in the vicinity of Pittsburgh.   [4] Cf. "Schedule of the Real Estate of James Morrison. . . ," Fayette County Court, Will Book F, 71–74.   [5] Not found.   [6] Presumably, half of the 1,000 acres mentioned by William Lytle, above, III, 878. Cf. also, above, Lytle to Clay, May 25 (and note), August 3, 1825, July 31, 1826; Jones to Clay, September 29, 1826.

MISCELLANEOUS LETTERS   July 21, 1827

From "DUFF GREEN By JNO C RIVES," "Office of U. S. Telegraph." Encloses "a letter just received from Mr. F. Stoever of Philadelphia"; requests that Clay state "whether the desired information will be given to Mr Stoever"; and adds that, "if it will be given," he will pay "for making out the papers." ALS by Rives. DNA, RG59, Misc. Letters, M179, R65. Addressed to the Secretary of State.

On the same date, Daniel Brent replied, returning Stoever's letter to Green and promising that "an authenticated copy of the circular letter, which was addressed to the several persons employed by the Secretary to publish the Laws of the last Session of Congress, including the Editor of the Democratic press of Philadelphia [John Binns] and containing the information requested by Mr. Stoever, will be transmitted to him on Monday, next, by this Department—" Copy, in DNA, RG59, Dom. Letters, vol. 22, p. 7 (M40, R20).

Two days later Brent, "in absence of the Secretary," wrote to Stoever, transmitting a copy of the circular letter in question and stating his belief "that it contains all the particulars required by" Stoever's letter to Green, "except as to the amount of compensation actually paid to Mr. Binns; and that is stated in the memorandum, enclosed, of Mr. William Browne, the Agent of this Department for disbursements." Notes that, "Besides this payment, however, other small ones may have been made to him for publishing notices and advertisements of this Department, having no connection with the service of the publication of the Laws." Concludes: "I presume that Mr. Binns will readily admit these two papers as evidence in the case to which you refer, without the formality of an official certificate; and I have deemed it unnecessary, therefore, upon reflection, to furnish one, especially as it seems to me that such a certificate would add nothing to their legal authenticity, unless given in pursuance of an Order of the Court, in which they are to be used." Copy, in *ibid.*, 8. The "memorandum" by Browne, also dated July 23, states that, "On the 11th. ulto.," he "remitted to John Binns . . . the sum of $95.50 . . . for publishing . . . the Laws. . . ." Copy, in *ibid.*

Brent transmitted to Binns, in a letter dated July 25, 1827, a copy of the communication sent to Stoever and informed him that the information was "to be used in a Court at Philadelphia, wherein the question was to be tried, whether the office of Alderman," held by him "under the Laws of Pennsylvania, was, or was not compatible, with this Agency of publisher of the Laws of the United States." Copy, in *ibid.*, 12–13.

Rives was now in the employ of the Washington *United States Telegraph*. Frederick Stoever has not been further identified.

In the case of *Commonwealth, ex relatione Bache vs. Binns*, the Pennsylvania Supreme Court on March 28, 1828, ruled that Binns' appointment as editor of a newspaper to publish the laws of the United States did not constitute an "appointment or employment under the *United States*, incompatible, by virtue of the act of assembly of the 12th of February 1802, with the office of alderman of the city of *Philadelphia*." Thomas Sergeant and William Rawle, Jr., *Reports of Cases Adjudged in the Supreme Court of Pennsylvania* (3rd edn., revd.; Philadelphia, 1875), XVII, 219–47. Binns had been alderman since 1822 and had been appointed to publish the laws since December, 1825.

From William H. Caperton

D. Sir   Richmond[1] July 23rd. 1827.

Mr Archd. Curle of this County[2] one of your early acquaintances and steady frinds [sic] has address [sic] the Secretary of war[3] soliciting the appointment of his Son Edwin Curle[4] a cadet in the Military School at West Point. He is a young man of fine appearance, good acquirements and most excellent character. The respectability of Mr Curle and his family and the anxiety of his Son to enter the Military School, enlists me very strongly in his favour, and I hope you will as Mr Curle has no other acquaintances at Washington, interpose your frindly aid in his behalf with the Secretary of War, which will place Mr Curle and myself under lasting obligations to you. With undiminished confidence I am Your frind   W. H. CAPERTON
Hon. H. Clay Secretary of State

ALS. DNA, RG59, United States Military Academy, Cadet Applications, 1827/11. Endorsed on cover by Clay: "Submitted to the Secy of War, with the earnest recommendation of H. Clay   10 Aug. 1827."

1 Kentucky.   2 Curle had been a justice of the peace of Madison County as early as 1798. He died in 1832, "at an advanced age." Lexington *Observer and Reporter*, January 20, 1832.   3 James Barbour.   4 Probably Edwin I. Curle, who subsequently moved from Madison County, Kentucky, to St. Charles County, Missouri, where he died in July, 1839. Lexington *Kentucky Gazette*, August 1, 1839. Curle was not officially listed as an applicant or appointee at the United States Military Academy. *House Docs.*, 21 Cong., 1 Sess., no. 79. He appears to have been still a resident of Madison County as late as 1831. Madison County Court, Will Book E, 235–38.

DIPLOMATIC NOTES   July 23, 1827

From CHARLES R. VAUGHAN, Long Branch (New Jersey). Informs Clay "that it is his intention to return to Washington immediately in order to make the final payment due on the 1st. August next to the Government of the United States, under the Convention concluded at London on the 13th. Novr. 1826" (cf. above, Gallatin to Clay, November 13, 1826; Vaughan to Clay, January 9, 1827); asks who is authorized to receive the payment. NS. DNA, RG59, Notes from British Legation, vol. 14 (M50, R15).

Clay replied, August 3, 1827, that he, "being authorized, to receive the final payment due this day, under the Convention. . . , will be ready at the Department of State, at one o'clock P.M. today, or at such other hour as may be more agreeable to Mr. Vaughan, to receive the same accordingly." N, in DNA, RG59, Notes to Foreign Legations, vol. 3, p. 374 (M38, R3).

A copy of the receipt, dated "Augt. 1st. [*sic*] 1827," signed by Richard Smith, cashier of the Washington branch of the Bank of the United States, acknowledging deposit by Clay "to Credit of the Treasurer of the United States" (Thomas Tudor Tucker) of the sum of Six hundred and two thousand, four hundred and eighty dollars," is found in *ibid.*, 380.

Tucker, born in Bermuda in 1745 and educated in medicine at the University of Edinburgh, had settled in Charleston, South Carolina, where he had been practicing at the outbreak of the American Revolution. He had served as a surgeon in the Continental Army, as a member of the Continental Congress (1787 and 1788), and as a member of the United States House of Representatives (1789–1793). He had been appointed Treasurer of the United States in 1801 and held the office until his death in 1828. He was an uncle of Henry St. George Tucker.

INSTRUCTIONS AND DISPATCHES   July 23, 1827

From W[ILLIAM] TUDOR, Lima, no. 72. Encloses report (not found) on "American commerce in the port of Callao" (cf. above, Tudor to Clay, January 15, 1827); calls attention to a decline in "The number of arrivals" but an improvement in "the general result of the voyages"; and notes "a very handsome profit" in the sale of flour and, largely because of the tariff, a smaller yield from other American manufactures, except "coarse cottons," which "are the chief article of our produce brought to this market." Reports that (the Peruvian) Congress has not begun consideration of the tariff (cf. above, Tudor to Clay, March 23, 1827); that the sale of English goods has declined; that French trade has increased—temporarily, in his opinion (cf. above, Tudor to Clay, April 26, 1827); that the Dutch have not found the market profitable; that "On the whole our trade has perhaps yielded a m[ore] favorable account than any other"; and that "whaling & sealing vessels" entering Callao for supplies have been exempted "from the operation of the tonnage duties." Alludes to the "revolution in the trade of these countries" that would result from the establishment of packet service "from our ports for the transportation of letters, passengers & merchandize to the Isthmus; & corresponding lines on this [western] side along the coast of Guatemala & Mexico on the one hand, & that of Colombia, Peru, & Chile on the other." Declares that the United States would "benefit much more than any other nation in the result" and urges "that this object may be fully considered at Washington, & that the government will stimulate private enterprize to ente[r] on the undertaking without delay, by every kind of encouragement that may be expedient" (cf. above, Tudor to Clay, April 9, May 28, June 11, August 1, 1826; Nixon, McCall and Company and others to Clay, May 28, 1826; Ralston to Clay, March 26, 1827). ALS. DNA, RG59, Cons. Disp., Lima, vol. 2 (M154, R2). Received December 19.

In a letter to the House Naval Committee in January, 1826, Samuel L. Southard had recommended that Congress establish communication with the Pacific by way of Panama; and that committee on January 24, 1827, had reported a bill authorizing construction of two schooners to be employed in such service. *House Repts.*, 19 Cong., 2 Sess., no. 56; U. S. H. of Reps., *Journal*, 19 Cong., 2 Sess., p. 408. No action had been taken on the proposal.

From Harrison Munday

TO HENRY CLAY, ESQ   ST. LOUIS, 24th July 1827.

SIR: My former friendship and high esteem for you as a man and a politician, connected with your vote in the late Presidential election, is the only apology I shall offer for addressing you through the public journals. I was once your friend and neighbor, and have felt a just pride in hearing you spoken of as among the most distinguished men in the nation. At present I am located in the youngest and most western State in the Union, and still hear you and *your friends* (not your old democratic friends of the school of Jefferson) but your new ones of Hartford Convention[1] memory, such as Webster, Osgood, Otis, Strong,[2] and to cap the climax *John Q Adams*[3] spoken of freely in every assemblage; but how changed the public sentiment! Then you was [*sic*] the compatriot of Jefferson and Madison, and now you are identified with the Hartford Convention and John Q Adams, whom you have denounced in the most unqualified terms. I remember well your opinions of the man, and will call your attention to a conversation held in your own office in Lexington, Ky. shortly after your return from Ghent, relative to Mr. Adams, in which you said, that *there was no doubt upon your mind, but that he was the greatest political hypocrite on earth; that he was as much a federalist at that time as he was in the days of his father's administration; that he was an opposer of the western interest, and that it was as much as the Commissioners associated with him at Ghent could do, to prevent him from giving away the free navigation of the Mississippi River to the British.*[4] You continued your remarks and said, that if ever Adams should become President, the people would see worse times than they had under the administration of his father. You called him an Eastern puritan, and indeed heaped so many opprobrious epithets upon him during your observations, that all who had the least regard for your veracity, must have looked upon Mr. Adams as the basest of men. With a knowledge of these things fresh upon my mind, I shall not undertake to describe the astonishment, pain and deep mortification I felt on learning that you, sir, was [sic] the very man who elevated John Q Adams In [sic] the first office in the gift of a free and independent people. The veriest hypocrite on earth could not have done more than this, and there was a time when I confided so strongly in you that no man would dare, with impunity, to tell me Henry Clay will [sic] commit this deed and betray his friends. But it is done; and I sincerely believe your fate is justly and irrevocably sealed by a much injured and insulted people, whose will you set at defiance; and which I could not have believed you ever would do, after hearing the speech you delivered at Higbee's mills against J. Pope, in which you said you "never had disobeyed the people nor you never would, know their will how you might."[5] And now, sir, I would ask in what way you are to atone for an open violation of this great ruling principle of our government? Are you prepared to say the people of Kentucky were in favor of Adams? Or rather on the contrary, can you deny but you had always been his deadly enemy and used your whole influence and successfully too, to poison and rivet the public mind against him up to the very hour of your apostacy? Far as you may have wandered from the line of your duty in voting for Mr. Adams, I am persuaded you cannot raise your voice against truths so notorious as these, and I willingly submit them, to that same *conscience* which admonished you there was danger in the elevation of a "Military Chieftain."[6] I might enlarge much on this subject and call your attention to many of your political opinions relative to men and measures, which, when compared with your present situation, would go far to establish your inconsistency and duplicity; but I am not disposed to dwell upon matters of this nature to any greater extent than the present times appear to require of every citizen who feels an interest in the purity and permanency of our government; and will conclude by remarking, that the contempt with which distinguished public servants treat the will of the people, and the repeated abuses of public confidence, assume the most alarming aspect, and strongly admonish the people of the necessity of an immediate reform. Impressed as I am with this belief, I hope you will not attribute my remarks to any thing but a wish to contribute, by all honorable means in my power, to the stability of a government to which I am devoted.

HARRISON MUNDAY.

Frankfort *Argus of Western America*, August 8, 1827. The document is introduced by the statement: "The following is a letter from a genuine 'Hunter of Kentucky,' as warm hearted and devoted a friend as Mr. Clay had in the world. He speaks the language of thousands who have been equally wounded by late political events. It is well known that Mr. Clay's language towards Mr. Adams after their return from Europe, was generally like that detailed by his old friend." Munday had been resident in Mercer County, Kentucky, in 1800 and in 1811 had been a surveyor on the Madison County end of the Tates Creek Road and a flatboat freighter on the Kentucky and Ohio Rivers. He had served briefly with the Kentucky forces in the War of 1812 and from 1819 to 1820 had been one of the proprietors of the Greenville Springs (cf. above, II, 701n). Written by Samuel Woodworth, who was also the author of "The Old Oaken Bucket," "The Hunters of Kentucky, or the Battle of New Orleans," was a popular song among the Jacksonians during the presidential campaign of 1828. For the full text, see *Magazine of American History*, 1884, pp. 548–49. On its significance in the campaign, see John William Ward, *Andrew Jackson, Symbol for an Age* (London: Oxford University Press, c. 1953; repr., 1968), 13–29.

1 Cf. above, II, 222n.   2 Daniel Webster; David Osgood; Harrison Gray Otis; Caleb Strong. As a Federalist member of Congress during the War of 1812, Webster had vehemently denounced the legislation which provided for raising military forces and, in particular, a proposal in 1814 which conscripted militia into the regular Army. He had then seen as one of the "highest obligations" of the States their duty "to interpose between their citizens and arbitrary power." But Webster had not himself been involved in the Hartford Convention, and he had opposed the sending of delegates to it. Richard N. Current, *Daniel Webster and the Rise of National Conservatism* (ed. by Oscar Handlin; Boston, [c. 1955]), 16–17 (quoted); Fuess, *Daniel Webster*, I, 170–72.

Osgood had likewise not been a delegate to the Convention, although he had been an ardent Federalist and had strongly opposed the war. Born in Andover, Massachusetts, and graduated in 1771 from Harvard College, he had been ordained for the ministry in 1774 and had been a clergyman until his death in 1822. In 1812 he had published a sermon highly critical of the war.   On Otis, see above, II, 433n.   Strong, Governor of Massachusetts from 1800 to 1807 and again from 1812 to 1816, had approved the calling of the Convention and its report, though he had not been a delegate. Born in Northampton and graduated in 1764 from Harvard College, he had been admitted to the bar in 1772, had served as county attorney from 1776 to 1800, and had sat in the General Court from 1776 to 1778 and in the State Senate from 1780 to 1788. He had been a member of the Federal Constitutional Convention of 1787 and had been active in the Massachusetts ratifying convention. From 1789 to 1796 he had served in the United States Senate.   3 Adams, who later described the New England protest of the embargo act of 1807 (above, I, 389n) as "the embryo conception of the Hartford Convention," had supported the Jefferson administration on this legislation and thereby so incurred the hostility of Massachusetts leaders that he had been forced to resign from the United States Senate in June, 1808. He was henceforth viewed by the Federalists as an apostate. Bemis, *John Quincy Adams and the Foundations of American Foreign Policy*, 143–49.   4 Cf. above, I, 999–1000n, 1003–1005n; II, 144–45, 372, 373n; III, 253–55.   5 Cf. above, II, 216–21n. The speech at Sandersville on July 25, 1816, there reported, appears to have embraced similar ideas.   6 Cf. above, Clay to Brooke, January 28, 1825.

From Robert Scott

Dear Sir,   Lexington 24th. July 1827

On last evening I returned from Frankfort where I had been according to appointment with Mr. Talbott[1] in order that we might visit the occupants of the land on Lacompts [*sic*] Run[2] to see if we could not effect a compromise with them; but he had an appointment in Woodford[3] and would not attend with me—

Whlst [*sic*] at Frankfort I had an interview with Mr. Crittenden and saw Mr. Waring[4]— By advice of the former I employed the latter to attend to the business with Higgins and Cockerell relative to the land in Union Cy[5]   Mr. Waring fears it is now too late for Waggoners heirs to tender a deed or deeds to Higgins and Cockerell, but has promised to exert himself and see what he can do with them and let me know— And Mr. Crittenden advised me to procure of you a Power of Attorney[6] duly authenticated and authorizing me to convey the land, in order that if any compromise or arrangement can be made I may be enabled to carry it into effect— I have given my bond for costs and intend Carry the suits the [sic] U S Court,[7] but unfortunately it is too late to operate as a supersedeas to the proceedings of the State Courts as to effect that it should have been done within ten days after the decision or adjournment of the Court—yet by taking the Appeal we may perhaps be better enabled to gain a compromise and the cost for the present will not be much—

The suits of Higgins and Cockerell against Waggoners heirs for the purchase money of the lands recovered by the Estate,[8] and from which they have not yet been evicted, is now in the Court of Appeals where they will probably remain a considerable time as they are far back on the docket— As they, Cockerell &c. have not been evicted, could they yet be compelled to receive deeds from Waggoners heirs do you suppose?

This business I confess seems to stand in an unfavorabbe [sic] attitude as regards the estate, but must do the best we can with it and possibly may get better out of it than present circumstances would seem to indicate—

Herewith is a memorandum describing the land should you deem it advisable to send me a Power of Attorney to convey it— Very respectfully Yr. obt. Servt.   Robt. Scott
The Honble Henry Clay

ALS. DLC-TJC (DNA, M212, R13). Endorsed by Clay: "Answd." Answer not found. [1] Isham Talbot.   [2] Cf. above, Agreement, March 11, 1806, note.   [3] County, Kentucky.   [4] John J. Crittenden; John Upshaw Waring.   [5] Cf. above, Scott to Clay, September 22, 1826, and note.   [6] Not found.   [7] Case not found.   [8] Of James Morrison. The suits have not been found.

From Daniel Webster

My Dear Sir,   Boston July 24. 1827
Your reply to Genl. Jackson's letter[1] is admirable, & has been most favorably recd. every where, at least on this side the Alleghany [sic]. It places the Genl. in a position where he cannot remain. He must move, in some direction; &, whatever movement he makes will either embarrass his friends, or still more embarrass himself. I have a suspicion, that the respectable member of Congress is Mr Buchanan.[2] If this should turn out so, it will place *him* in an awkward situation, since, it seems, he *did recommend* a bargain with your friends, on the

suspicition [*sic*] that such a bargain had been proposed to them, on the part of friends of Mr. Adams. I am curious to see how this matter will develope itself, &, in the meantime, am confident that Genl. Jackson is falling, in general estimation, daily & hourly. The present tide of things, if it should meet no counter currents of reaction, will & must overwhelm the opposition in another year. New York is growing stronger & stronger, daily, & at this moment I seriously doubt, whether, if the Elections were now to come on, Genl. Jackson could get *three* votes in the State. North of New York, from present appearances, there will be no such a thing as a Jackson Ticket found, except in New Hampshire. In that State our friends have, at last, opened their eyes, & seeing their danger, there is danger no longer.³ Govr. Peirce⁴ turns out to be a *thorough Jackson man*, & completely under Hills⁵ influence. This was predicted, to some of our friends, a year ago, but they would not credit the prophecy. However, since the Govr. so *turns out*, he himself will be *turned out*, at the next election, in March. Friends have agreed on this, & there is not the least doubt it will be done.⁶

Mr Gorham was elected yesterday, as my successor.⁷ The occasion created no great excitement & tho' some of us did not like the premature movement of the Gentlemen who nominated him, there is no objection to him. He is very acceptable to every body, except the Jacksonians, who set up a candidate, & rallied three hundred votes.

It is probable Mr Holmes will succeed Mr. Burleigh in the York District, in Maine.⁸ Yours always truly   DANL. WEBSTER
Hon H. Clay

ALS. DLC-HC (DNA, M212, R2). Addressed as *"Private."*
1 See above, Clay "To the Public," June 29, 1827.   2 James Buchanan. See below, Smith to Clay, August 1, 1827, note.   3 See above, Clay to Webster, May 28, 1827, note.   4 Benjamin Pierce.   5 Isaac Hill.   6 Pierce was defeated by John Bell, a merchant and sheriff of Rockingham County, 1823–1828. Born in Londonderry, New Hampshire, Bell had served in the New Hampshire House of Representatives, 1799–1800, the State Senate, 1803, and the State Council, 1817–1822. He was Governor only one term.   7 Benjamin Gorham with 1659 votes defeated three other candidates, including the Jacksonian David Henshaw, who received 459 votes. *Boston Daily Advertiser*, July 24, 1827. Gorham had been nominated on July 12 by a meeting of Federalists, who anticipated action by a previously called meeting of the Republican Administration Committee, set for July 15, thus marking a split in the coalition like that noted above, Webster to Clay, May 18, 1827, note. *Boston Daily Advertiser*, July 13, 16, 23, 1827.

Henshaw, born in Leicester, Massachusetts, and trained as a druggist's apprentice, had become wealthy in banking and insurance business and by 1828 was active in promoting railway development between Boston and Albany. In 1821 he had been one of the founders of the *Boston Statesman*, as a Republican organ, which supported Crawford's candidacy in 1824 and the Adams administration in 1826. But Henshaw advocated the "free bridge" proposal in 1827 (cf. above, Webster to Clay, May 7, 1827, note) and then swung his allegiance to Jackson. With the latter's support, Henshaw was named collector of the port of Boston in 1829 and through this office held control of Democratic patronage in the State until 1837. The failure of his bank at that time forced him into a brief political retirement, but in 1839 he was elected to the State legislature. Allied with the Tyler faction of the Democratic Party, he was named Secretary of the Navy, 1843–1844, and regained great influence in the party until his death in 1852.

8 William Burleigh had died July 2. John Holmes was defeated in the ensuing election by Rufus McIntire, who was also at that time identified as "a qualified friend of the

administration." *Boston Daily Advertiser*, September 3, 1827. Born in York County and graduated in 1809 from Dartmouth College, McIntyre had begun the practice of law at Parsonfield, Maine, in 1812, served in the War of 1812, and entered upon a political career as a member of the State House of Representatives in 1820. He was county prosecutor from 1820 to 1843 and a member of the United States House of Representatives, there identified as a Jacksonian, from 1827 to 1835. He was named State Land agent in 1839 and 1840, Federal marshal, 1845, and surveyor of customs at Portland, 1853 to 1857.

INSTRUCTIONS AND DISPATCHES   July 24, 1827

From VINCENT GRAY, Havana. Observes that "The affear [*sic*] of the Schooner Mary Elenore [*i.e.*, *Mary and Eleanor*—cf. below, Gray to Clay, August 3, 1827], has not yet been brought to a close; but" he anticipates "a favorable result." Notes the appearance in succession, off the port, of three United States naval vessels: the *North Carolina*, the *Hornet*, and (in a postscript) the *Grampus*. States that he has learned that "Commodore [David] Porter has not yet Issued any commissions, as it is not his Interest to do so"; that Porter's "Ship is now at Key West"; and that Porter has been at Pensacola, which he left on July 14. Reports that "Thomas Preble of Baltimore [cf. above, Gray to Clay, June 13, 1827]. . . , who had been condemned . . . for a crime not committed by him but by his mate . . . in 1825," has been released to him (Gray) and placed on board a vessel to work his passage home. Adds that more Americans have died (in Havana) of "the fever in one week . . . than . . . during the whole of the last season." ALS. DNA, RG59, Cons. Disp., Havana, vol. 5 (M-T20, R5). Received August 7.

INSTRUCTIONS AND DISPATCHES   July 25, 1827

From THOMAS L. L. BRENT, Lisbon, no. 42. Transmits "a copy of a note [not found] from the [acting] Minister of Foreign Affairs [the Marquis of Saldanha] respecting the complaint against the military Commandant at the Isle of Mayo" (cf. above, Hodges to Clay, May 19, 1826; Clay to Brent, June 12, 1826; Brent to Clay, March 16, April 24, 1827), in which the Minister upholds the commandant's "privilege" to ship four moios of salt "in every vessel that went there to load" but states that in order to avoid further " 'disagreeable incidents' " the privilege has been terminated; also forwards additional documents concerning this incident as well as other matters. LS. DNA, RG59, Dip. Disp., Portugal, vol. 7 (M43, R6). Received October 3.

From JOHN RAINALS, Copenhagen. Reports that "the Russian fleet" (cf. above, Rainals to Clay, July 20, 1827), joined by additional vessels, "Sail'd yesterday morning" and that "It is understood, they will be further join'd by one or two frigates on their arrival at Portsmouth." ALS. DNA, RG59, Cons. Disp., Copenhagen, vol. 3 (M-T195, R3). Received September 10.

From Simon Cameron

Sir   [*ca.* July 26, 1827]
    We annex our bill[1] for advertising, &c. during the last year, and for publishing the laws of the last session of congress, for which you will please send us a draft by an early mail
    You will see we have taken the field with vigor, and we have little

doubt that a very large portion of the citizens of this state will think with us, that the wise measures of Mr Adams and his able cabinet deserve the support of every disinterested Pennsylvanian. The military fever has much abated, and the toasts of the fourth of July as well as other "signs of the times" indicate astonishing changes.[2] The oldest and the best democrats among us are daily avowing their determination to support the American policy in opposition to the turbulent partizans of the military chieftain. Our people are beginning to reflect that their gratitude for the services of a successful and a gallant commander does not require them to give their suffrages for that, placing that commander in the highest civil station in the government. At the last election the vote of our state was carried entirely by feeling;[3] and the reflection which now is taking place will produce a contrary effect. I am not sufficiently sanguine to say that the vote of Pas.[4] will go for the admstr. but many of our people believe so, and I know sufficient changes among those who were the violent, rampant supporters of the "Hero" to almost make me believe the same thing.[5] The contest, however, I am certain will be so doubtful as to prevent any effect abroad favorable to the Govt.

Your letter[6] has completely silenced your opponents in this quarter. The sensible part of them admit that it is such an answer as does honor to you, and that it cannot be refuted   They endeavor to shift the accusation from Genl Jackson to his friends.

Please excuse my troubling you on this subject, and believe me Very respectfully yrs &c   SIMON [CAMERON]
Hon. H. Clay.

ALS. DNA, RG59, P. and D. of L. Undated; postmarked at Harrisburg, Pennsylvania, July 27, [1827].
    1 Omitted by the editors. The bill was for $28.00.   2 The Fourth of July toasts of the Democratic-Republicans of Harrisburg and vicinity had evidenced the importance of protective tariff legislation in the area. Several toasts, each, to Jackson, Adams, and Clay indicated a mixture of personal support. Harrisburg *Pennsylvania Intelligencer*, July 10, 1827.   3 Cf. above, III, 645–46n. Pennsylvania had given Jackson all her electoral votes and over three times the popular vote of his combined opponents in the 1824 election, Schlesinger and Israel (eds.), *History of American Presidential Elections*, I, [409].   4 Pennsylvania.   5 Cf. above, Clay to Brown, March 27, 1827, and note.   6 Above, "To the Public," June 29, 1827.

INSTRUCTIONS AND DISPATCHES   July 27, 1827

From JOEL R. POINSETT, Mexico, no. 95. Reports that, in compliance with Clay's instructions (above, May 31, 1827), he addressed a note to the Mexican Government relative to the presence of the Mexican squadron, under (David) Porter, at Key West but has received no reply. Notes that civil war continues in Guatemala (cf. above, Gonzalez to Clay, January 7, 1827) and that "troops under the command of President [Manuel José] Arce, were defeated in an attack upon the town of San Salvador," and charges that "The malcontents are led on by foreign officers." Refers briefly to uncertainties concerning the assembling of delegates to the Congress of Tacubaya. States that he has "received no notice . . . from this government on the subject of renewing the negotiations." Observes that "no essential change" has occurred "in the political state of things in this country" and that "The general government continues to take measures of precaution in the State of Vera Cruz." The legislature of that State, "to give a convincing proof of their attachment to the Federal Constitution, [have] invited the general government to send Genl. [Vicente] Guerrero to take the command. . . ." LS. DNA, RG59, Dip. Disp., Mexico, vol. 3 (M97, R4). Received September 30.

From James Brown

My dear Sir   July 28. 1827

Mrs. Brown has sent a large case containing the most bulky of the articles which you requested her to purchase[1] by the vessel which sailed from Havre on the 15 and addressed to the care of Mr Isaac Bell. I supposed you would have left Washington for Kentucky before they could arrive, and I therefore enclosed Mrs. Brown's letter[2] giving an account of the articles and of their prices under cover to Mr Lee[3] with a request that he would deliver it. His Excellency Mr Rumpff[4] whose intended visit I had some time ago announced to you officially,[5] will sail on the 1st. and he has been so kind as to take charge of a small box containing the residue of what you ordered which he has promised to hand to Mrs. Clay at Washington. You know that Mr Rumpff goes out under the impression that it will be practicable to form with the United States a Commercial Treaty resembling in its features those conclude [sic] with Guatemala and Denmark.[6] I have told him that I could not say what might be the disposition of our Government on that subject, but that it must have occurred to him that the Hanseatic Towns were not in the same condition with the Countries above mentioned having no productions of their own and being the carriers of those of other powers. Ministers have gone from those towns to Mexico, to the Central Republick and to the States of South America with a similar object in view.[7] These small States hope that the policy avowed by Mr Huskinson [sic][8] that of throwing the commercial or navigating advantages into the hands of the weak powers rather than giving them to those whose growth might produce rivalship, will be adopted in the New World. Of all this he will be better able to judge after he has seen you and whether he succeeds or not he will have an opportunity of seeing our country and the family of his lady at New York.[9] I have given him a letter to you[10] and can safely recommend him as a most intelligent polite and amiable man deserving the kind attentions of all who know him.

The Greeks hold out as well as can be expected considering the force against which they have to contend, and their want of money credit and indeed resources of every kind. The French fleet in the Mediterranian [sic] is already very powerful and is daily increasing by the arrival of Vessels of War from the Brest station. The English and

Russian Squadrons will soon appear there and the combined fleet[11] will be very formidable. In the mean time the Porte seems to discover no disposition to yield to this formidable interposition, but, strong in the *justice* of his cause, and sustained by the principles on which the Holy Alliance was founded, he is preparing to make a most vigorous resistance.[12] It is not easy to foresee the result. This coallition [*sic*] so difficult in its formation, and so indefinite in its ultimate objects may be dissolved by discordant opinions on questions of detail which have not yet been settled. From such Mediators Greece can promise herself neither real Independance [*sic*] nor rational civil liberty. The struggle has awakened some dormant talent, has increased the glory of those hallowed countries, but will for some time procure for their wretched inhabitants no solid advantages.

The winds of the British Eolus [*sic*][13] seem to subside rapidly, and instead of wafting all Europe safely into the haven of liberty he will suffer Portugal to sink into the calm of despotism.[14] Don Miguel after receiving an Austrian education at the Court of Vienna, will soon appear at Lisbon, and aided by the intrigues of his mother,[15] and the influence of the Priests, will overturn the Constitution of Don Pedro, and drive out the most prominent of its supporters.[16] Spain will be satisfied with nothing short of this, and if contented with this, will be sustained by the Continental powers. England will be too happy to withdraw from the contest, ardently as she seemed to embark in it. The only remaining hope of the Constitutionalists seems to rest on the expected arrival of Don Pedro, who it is thought, may when apprized of the designs of his brother, leave Rio Janeiro, and sail for Lisbon. Even in that event it is not certain that things may not have been carried too far in favor of Don Miguel to leave room for the establishment of the constitution. In truth the people are not prepared for the Representative system, and are so lost to all confidence in themselves, that they prefer the Government of a Despot, to the enjoyment of liberty. You may think this a gloomy picture but I sincerely believe that it is not overcharged. I would not be understood as saying that on the arrival of Don Miguel the Constitution will be abruptly overturned, on the contrary it will be nominally preserved but will soon undergo such modifications as will destroy its value.

I wish much to hear from the Western Country, in order to know how it will act in the approaching Presidential contest. If the accounts which reach me from New York be correct, that State will vote for General Jackson.[17] The coallition of Van Buren and Clinton[18] has been unexpected although I think I can account for it. Who will be Vice President? If I was at home, ambitious, and popular I would prefer this office to any other under our Government   I thought so before the last election, and I felt pretty confident that Mr Calhoun[19] would prove that my opinion was well founded. The event has not

sustained my opinion but has not changed it. His conduct as President
of the Senate has either been weak or worse. He has permitted debate
to take a range before unknown in that body and the publick has accused him of doing so in order, by unfair means to assail the character
of the Administration.[20] If he had acted impartially and independently, and called into activity those prepossessing manners of which
he has the command he might have preserved his friends and increased
their number. He has been too eager for premature elevation and has
I presume lost much of his popularity. Clinton & Van Buren will both
in case of the success of Mr Jackson take the lead of him. I am Dear Sir
very truly Your friend & Obedt. [Se]rv   J   B.
Honble Henry Clay.

ALS. DLC-HC (DNA, M212, R2). Endorsed by Clay on side of last page: ". . . James
Brown."
[1] Cf. above, Clay to Brown, May 30, 1827; Brown to Clay, June 28, 1827.   [2] Not
found.   [3] Probably either Theodorick or William Lee.   [4] Vincent Rumpff.
[5] Above, May 12, 1827.   [6] Above, Convention with Central American Federation,
December 5, 1825; Convention with Denmark, April 26, 1826.   [7] On the negotiation
of a treaty with Brazil, see above, Wickelhausen to Clay, January 19, 1827, note. A
treaty with Mexico was signed in 1828. Parry (comp.), *Consolidated Treaty Series*, vol. 78,
pp. 27–32. Probably because of the disorganization developing at this time in the Federation of Central America (cf. above, Gonzalez to Clay, January 7, 1827; Phillips to Clay,
March 2, 22, May 12, 1827; Sergeant and Poinsett to Clay, May 9, 1827), no treaty was
negotiated at this time.   [8] William Huskisson. Cf. above, Rush to Secretary of
State, March 26, 1825, note.   [9] The Astor family. Cf. above, Hughes to Clay, March
9, 1827.   [10] Not found.   [11] Cf. above, Brown to Clay, July 12, 1827; Middleton
to Clay, June 23, 1827; Pulis to Clay, July 6, 1827; Gallatin to Clay, July 14, 1827; Rainals
to Clay, July 20, 25, 1827.   [12] Cf. above, Middleton to Clay, April 21, 1825, note;
Ombrosi to Clay, May 16, 1827.   [13] Apparently a reference to George Canning.
[14] Cf. above, Brown to Clay, June 12, 1827 ("Private").   [15] Carlota Joaquina.
[16] Cf. above, Brown to Clay, April 12, 1827; Everett to Clay, June 9, 1827.   [17] Cf.
above, Clay to Brown, March 27, 1827, note.   [18] Martin Van Buren; DeWitt Clinton.
Cf. above, Hammond to Clay, January 28, 1827; Mallory to Clay, April 4, 1827; Porter
to Clay, April 6, 18, May 1, 1827.   [19] John C. Calhoun.   [20] Cf. above, Fendall
to Clay, March 22, 1826; King to Clay, April 12, 1826; Warfield to Clay, May 5, 1826, and
note. See also, editorial in *Baltimore Patriot*, April 11, 1826, and Adams, *Memoirs*, VII,
433.

INSTRUCTIONS AND DISPATCHES   July 28, 1827

From JAMES BROWN, Paris, no. 72. Acknowledges receipt of Clay's "dispatches Nos.
13 [May 28, 1827] and 14 [June 6, 1827]," as well as "a letter from Mr. [Daniel]
Brent with the printed schedules of claims upon this Government." Promises that
"The important subjects of these dispatches shall receive due attention." LS.
DNA, RG59, Dip. Disp., France, vol. 23 (M34, R26). Received September 11.
   Brent's letter to Brown was written June 18, 1827. Copy, in DNA, RG59, Dip.
Instr., vol. 11, p. 366 (M77, R6).

From ALEXANDER H. EVERETT, Madrid, no. 83. Transmits "the answer . . . received,
with less delay than usually occurs here," to his "late note on the affair of the
Colombian Privateer [*Zulmé*]" (cf. above, Everett to Clay, July 4, 1827). Comments that "Mr. [Manuel Gonzáles] Salmon disclaims the intimation conveyed in
his preceding letter that the United States were to be regarded as representing
the interest of the owners of the privateer, and assents to the construction of the
law of nations, applicable to this subject," as stated in Everett's note. Adds that

"notwithstanding the objections that may be urged with more or less justice against the form of the document" enclosed in Clay's "last instructions upon this affair" (cf. above, Clay to Everett, March 20, 1827; Everett to Clay, July 4, 1827), he has "transmitted it to the Minister with an accompanying note, of which a copy is annexed." Predicts that, although "The claim is . . . in substance fully established," the Spanish Government will "avoid restoring the Privateer as long as possible. . . ." Suggests that additional evidence be obtained and held in readiness for future use. Encloses also "an answer . . . lately received to the proposition contained in" his note of February 19 "for a reciprocal repeal by the Governments of the two countries of the extraordinary tonnage duties now imposed in each upon the Commerce of the other" (cf. above, Everett to Clay, February 27, 1827). Expresses surprise "at the tenor of the answer," which indicated that no change would be made until completion of a study of the matter by "the Board of Duties." Attaches a copy of his reply to Salmón, in which he points out "that the contemplated arrangement can only be effected by a mutual understanding between the two Governments and therefore belongs properly to the diplomatic department of the Administration." LS. DNA, RG59, Dip. Disp., Spain, vol. 27 (M31, R28). Received October 11.

From ALBERT GALLATIN, London, no. 99. Refers to documents transmitted with his "despatch No. 97" (above, July 20, 1827). Reports that, having agreed in subsequent conferences "to renew the 3d & 4th articles of the Convention of 1818 indefinitely, but liable to be abrogated at the will of either party on twelve months notice" (cf. above, Clay to Gallatin, June 19, 1826 [V, 475], February 24, 1827 [no. 18]; Gallatin to Clay, June 20, 23, July 20, 1827), the negotiators "agreed to curtail as far as practicable the Protocols, with the exception of that of the Ninth Conference, which had been signed by Mr. [William] Huskisson before he left town." Notes a meeting, the fourth since (Charles) Grant replaced Huskisson, scheduled for "to day in order to sign the Protocols and, if they are ready, the two Conventions [cf. below, Gallatin to Clay, August 6, 1827]." Expresses hope that he will be able to "send them by the packet of 1st of August, for which Mr [James] Cucheval, the bearer of the treaty with Sweden [cf. above, Appleton to Clay, July 11, 1827], affords a good opportunity." Summarizes a conversation with (George) Canning "on the various subjects pending between" the United States and Great Britain: little was said "on the Commercial Convention," on which agreement has been reached; the discussion "on the subject of the territory west of the Rocky Mountains, being in reference to the practicability of further arrangements calculated to preserve peace, whilst the question of a definite boundary remains unsettled, will be the subject of a distinct despatch" (none found). Canning also "opened the subject of impressment, and asked the usual question whether we had any new guarantees to propose," in response to which he was told that "he must expect none but the good faith of the United States and the interest they had in fulfilling the engagements they might contract in relation to that subject" (cf. above, Clay to Gallatin, June 19, 1826 [V, 444–46]). Expresses a belief that on this issue Canning is "as Lord Castlereagh was [see Rush to John Quincy Adams, August 15, 1818, in *American State Papers, Foreign Relations*, IV, 379], ahead of public opinion and national pride" and "that, notwithstanding his conviction that an agreement, such as we might accept, is extremely desirable, he is not prepared at this time to make the proposals." In regard to colonial trade, Canning replied negatively to a question whether Gallatin "might expect an answer to . . . [his] last official note on" the subject (cf. above, Gallatin to Clay, June 4, 1827) and expressed surprise that "there could be any doubt" as to "the ultimate views of" the British Government on the matter, after which Gallatin "only observed that the course adopted by the British Government was so contrary to the nature of things and to their avowed general principles, that we had naturally considered it as a temporary measure and founded in part on misapprehensions which . . . [he] had hoped we had succeeded in removing." Concludes: "I am confident that you may rely that no change will take place for the present, nor until the experiment of supplying their West India Colonies, through their own means, shall have failed and produced a reaction." ALS. DNA, RG59, Dip. Disp., Great Britain, vol. 34 (M30, R30). Copy, in MHi-Adams Papers, Letters Recd. (MR481); published in Adams (ed.), *Writings of Albert Gallatin*, II, 378–80. Received September 8.

MISCELLANEOUS LETTERS   July 28, 1827

From JOHN RODGERS, "U. S. Ship N Carolina Hampton Road [*sic*]." Encloses copies of a letter "received from the Capudan Pasha of the Ottoman Empire, in answer to" his communications of "July last" (cf. above, Rodgers to Clay, July 19, 1826; February 14, 1827), and of the response "which (considering the extent & importance of our Commerce at this time in the Archipelago, dependent for protection entirely on his good will)," Rodgers thought "prudent to make, notwithstanding his [the Pasha's] answer to the proposition . . . made him, on behalf of the Government of the United States, is neither as favourable or as explicit as his promises had led . . . [Rodgers] to expect." Attributes his failure to achieve the success anticipated "to the unexpected occurrence of a variety of unforeseen & unauspicious events, which soon after took place" and which he promises to explain later. States that he intends, as soon as he can leave his "present command," to see Clay in person and, meanwhile, refers him "to the bearer, Mr. Geo. B English," who was "present at both . . . conferences with the Pasha. . . ." ALS. DNA, RG59, Misc. Letters (M179, R65).

In the first enclosure (translation in State Department files), dated "Constantinople 7 Febrier [*sic*] 1827," Khosref Mehemmet Pacha acknowledges receipt of Rodgers' letter of December 19, 1826, and informs him that the Sultan (Mahmud II), although appearing to listen kindly to the proposals, is so "occupied with the New Military System" (cf. above, Moore to Clay, June 20, 1826, note) that he has little time to think of other things." Rodgers' reply is dated May 18, 1827.

George Bethune English, born in Cambridge, Massachusetts, graduated in 1807 from Harvard University, and awarded an M.A. degree at the Harvard Divinity School, had had a varied career—as newspaper editor, member of the New Harmony colony, lieutenant of United States Marines (appointed in 1818), officer in the Egyptian Army, and secret agent for the United States in negotiations for opening trade with Turkey. It was he who during the winter of 1823–1824 had entered into the arrangements for Rodgers' mission (see above, Clay to Rodgers, September 6, 1825, note), and he had served Rodgers as an interpreter. Returning to the United States in 1827, he died the following year.

INSTRUCTIONS AND DISPATCHES   July 29, 1827

From ALBERT GALLATIN, London, no. 100. Encloses "the Protocols of the 9th, 10th, 11th, 12th, 13th, & 14th Conferences as finally adjusted, together with the papers thereto annexed, vizt. the answer to the nine Articles proposed, in 1824, by the British Plenipotentiaries annexed to the 11th Protocol, and the Projets of Convention for the renewal of the 4th & 3d Articles of the Convention of 1818, respectively annexed to the 12th & 13th Protocols." Notes that the conventions were to have been signed yesterday (cf. above, Gallatin to Clay, July 28, 1827), "but the British Plenipotentiaries found that it was an invariable rule, at the Foreign

Office, to submit every Convention or Treaty to the King's Advocate before it was signed." Adds: "That officer [Sir William Rae] being out of town, a delay of two or three days will ensue, and the Conventions cannot be sent by the Packet of 1st of August." Predicts that "The nine articles, so called [cf. above, Gallatin to Clay, June 20, July 5, 1827], will soon be disposed of one way or another: and we will now enter seriously in [sic] the discussion of a Convention, having for object to prepare for trial that reference to a foreign State of the contested North Eastern boundary" (cf. above, Gallatin to Clay, July 5, 1827). Remarks that "The subject is somewhat complex"; that he has found (Henry U.) Addington "extremely difficult on all topics generally and far more on this than on any other"; that (Charles) Grant is "very intelligent and appears candid"; and that the latter's "substitution for Mr. [William] Huskisson [cf. above, Gallatin to Clay, July 14, 20, 1827] is not to be regretted." States that he failed in his "very hasty letter of yesterday to say that" he had discussed with (George) Canning "the subject of the North Eastern boundary." Observes that Canning "appears sincerely desirous that the proceedings may be simplified, so as to have a chance to find a Sovereign who will consent to decide the question." Reports his agreement with Canning's suggestions that further surveys should be dispensed with and that the arbiter should "decide on questions purely of law and what was the true construction of certain expressions in a treaty," rather than "give an opinion on the contested topography of the Country"; that "both sides" should abstain, "pending the suit, of [sic] any act of Sovereignty over the contested territory"; and that "the choice of an Arbiter ought to be postponed till after the ratification of the proposed preliminary Convention and when both parties are ready for trial." Expresses his relief at the last suggestion: "If obliged to come to a choice at this time, I would have felt much embarrassed between my instructions [see above, Clay to Gallatin, June 19, 1826 (V, 447)] and the present dubious state of the Republic of Colombia" (cf. above, Watts to Clay, June 27, 1827). ALS. DNA, RG59, Dip. Disp., Great Britain, vol. 34 (M30, R30). Copy, in MHi-Adams Papers Letters Recd. (MR481); published in *American State Papers, Foreign Relations*, VI, 683–684. Received September 8.

Gallatin's answer to the Nine Articles, appended to the Protocol of the Eleventh Conference, follows in content his instructions, above, of June 19, 1826. For the articles and the answer, see *American State Papers, Foreign Relations*, VI, 685–86.

Rae, born in Edinburgh, had been admitted to the Scottish bar in 1791, had succeeded to the baronetcy in 1815, had served in Parliament from 1819 to 1826, and had been lord advocate since 1819. He retained that office until 1830 and was reappointed to it from December, 1834, to April, 1835, and from September, 1841, until his death in October, 1842. He served again in Parliament from 1830 to 1842.

From NATHAN LEVY, St. Thomas. Transmits documents relating to the claims of a Captain Hammond against a privateer. Complains of the enmity of the Danish Governor General, (J.) Sobotker, who has been recently elevated to this post from his position as Governor of St. Thomas, carrying with him antipathies toward this consulate. LS. DNA, RG59, Cons. Disp., St. Thomas, vol. 2 (M-T350, R2). Received August 31.

The enclosed documents include a deposition by John Hammond and Caleb Jackson, master and mate of the American brig *Mohawk*, of Baltimore, dated July 18, 1827, relating to the seizure of the vessel and its cargo by a Captain Costa, sailing under Brazilian colors, later changed to those of Buenos Aires, who has been recognized here (in St. Thomas), and the answer of Sobotker to Levy, reminding him that consular duties do not encompass such a protest and that the offended party has access to redress in the courts.

Hammond was a resident of Baltimore in 1829; Jackson and Costa have not been further identified.

From Franklin Litchfield

To the Hon. Henry Clay Secy of State of the
United States   Washington City
Sir,   Private.   Puerto Cabello Colombia July 30th. 1827

I do myself the pleasure to transmit you a Case containing the Bust of President Bolivar, which is a most perfect likeness of this great South American Statesman.

This is the first Copy ever taken of him in this style, and was lately executed by an Italian[1] at the City of Caracas, and beg of you to accept the same in my name as a token of respect for your disinterested and patriotic Eloquence displayed on the floor of Congress in defense of the rights and independence of the native Country of this distinguished Liberator.[2]

Mr Royal Phelps Junior[3] is encharged with the delivery of said Bust in person, and if you have no objections, I have requested him to have a Portrait painting taken from it in *oleo* by one of our first Artists.[4]

I have also requested Mr Phelps to make several enquiries of you relating to my Consular Duties, and beg of you the favor to communicate to him your views frankly. I have the honor to be very respectfully Your most Obedient Servant & friend   FRANKLIN LITCHFIELD

ALS. DLC-HC (DNA, M212, R2).   [1] Not identified.   [2] See above, II, 155–56, 289–92, 402–405, 492–562 *passim*, 817–18, 853–60; III, 22–24, 29–31, 186n, 597, 764–65.
[3] Born in Sempronius, Cayuga County, New York, in 1809, young Phelps had been apprenticed as a boy to a tanner, had run away to sea, and had worked for a time for a coffee merchant on St. Croix. He opened his own mercantile business in Venezuela in 1840 and in 1847 transferred his headquarters to New York. He was a member of the New York Legislature from 1862 to 1863.   [4] Not found.

From Timothy Wiggin

London, July 30, 1827.
To the Honorable Henry Clay, State Department, Washington.

SIR:—Messrs. Hoares,[1] bankers and treasurers of the Ohio fund,[2] have just discovered a mistake that was made by the bankers at Oxford,[3] who remitted to them the subscriptions raised there for Ohio, and for the General Seminary,[4] and Hartford College.[5] They ought to have remitted to Messrs. Hoares only so much as was raised for Ohio, but they did remit what was raised for all these, and the consequence has been that I received and paid £160, 14s. 6d. too much. The only way to correct the mistake now, is for the trustees of Ohio to pay to the trustees of the General Theological Seminary at New York, and of the College at Hartford, what I paid to them in error, say £160, 14s. 6d. sterling, or what was realized from that sum. The enclosed lines to Bishop Chase[6] will inform him of the matter. Pray excuse the trouble, and believe me, most truly, your obedient servant,

TIMOTHY WIGGIN.

Chase, *Reminiscences*, II, 568.
¹ Hoare's Bank, founded as early as 1673, was a London firm, at this time headed by Henry Hoare of "Mitcham," who died in 1828.   ² Cf. above, Wiggin to Clay, March 26, 1827; Biddle to Clay, June 21, 1827.   ³ Not identified.   ⁴ The General Theological Seminary of the Episcopal Church in the United States of America had been established in New York in 1817, moved to New Haven, Connecticut, in 1820, and returned to New York in 1822.   ⁵ Washington College, renamed Trinity College in 1845, had been opened in the basement of a Hartford church in 1824. A year later it had been moved to its own campus, also at Hartford.   ⁶ Philander Chase. The enclosure has not been found.

DIPLOMATIC NOTES   [ca. July 30, 1827]

From CHARLES R. VAUGHAN, Washington. States that a copy of Clay's note (to Vaughan, March 26, 1827), acknowledging receipt of Captain (D. C.) Clavering's "explanation . . . of the alleged impressment of two American Seamen by that officer," which explanation "completely vindicated Captain Clavering from the imputation which was laid to his charge," was forwarded to the British Government, which directed Vaughan "to make some observations upon that subject." Continues: "The British law of impressment, has been so often under discussion between the two Governments, that His Majesty's Government had persuaded itself, that the Government of the United States, did not now need to be informed, that neither the Admiralty nor any Officers acting under their Authority are empowered, or at liberty, during Peace, to impress any British Subject, or, *à fortiori*, any alien, either within His Majesty's Dominions, or in any other part of the world:—and that any British Officer so misconducting himself, besides such punishment as might be inflicted upon him by the Admiralty, would infallibly subject himself, to have heavy damages awarded against him, in a Court of Law, at the suit of the individual aggrieved.

"His Majesty's Government having entertained a belief, that so much of the British Law of impressment was at least notorious to the Government of the United States, they have observed with much regret from Mr. Clay's note of the 15th. June [1826], that instead of inferring from the extreme improbability of the original charge, and from the report of the British Consul at Boston [George Manners—cf. above, Vaughan to Clay, May 22, 1826], that, if there was any foundation at all for the complaint, it was likely to be much exaggerated, Mr Clay appears to have strained the evidence before him, and to have drawn inferences from it, to the prejudice of the British Officer, which the facts do not seem fairly to warrant.

"The Government of the United States may be assured, that His Majesty's Government has studiously, and they believe successfully, endeavoured to instil [*sic*] into the minds of the Officers of His Majestys' Naval Service, the necessity of showing the utmost respect to the Officers of every Power in amity with His Majesty. But to insure the continuance of such respect, and the consequent interchange of good offices, it is necessary, that a corresponding good feeling should influence the conduct of the Foreign Powers.

"Anticipating the entire confirmation of the statement of Captain Clavering by the Master of the 'Pharos' [Ephraim Merchant], whenever the Government of the United States shall have an opportunity of communicating with him [cf. above, Clay to Hodges, June 20, 1826; Hodges to Clay, June 20, 1827], the Undersigned, is instructed, to represent to Mr Clay, that His Majesty's Government feel, that they have reason to complain of the conduct of Mr. [Samuel] Hodges [Jr.], the Consul of the United States at the Cape de Verd Islands, whose letter to Mr. Clay of the 16th. March 1826 containing the unfounded assertion as to the impressment of the two men, appears to have been the original cause of this unpleasant corre-spondence." NS. DNA, RG59, Notes from British Legation, vol. 14 (M50, R15). Dated "July 1827"; received August 2. In a communication to James Barbour, below, January 26, 1829, Clay refers to this note as "of July 20th. 1827." Copy, in MHi-Adams Papers, Letters Recd. (MR481).

INSTRUCTIONS AND DISPATCHES   July 30, 1827

From WILLIAM SHALER, Mahón (1). Reports his return "from the baths of Cata-lonia a short time since, Somewhat improved in . . . health"; states that he still can obtain relief from pain only "thro' the agency of opium." Transmits a copy (not found) of the report of the Dutch consul at Algiers (Fraissinet, not further identified), which demonstrates "the necessity of every government that aims at independence in their relations with Algiers, being represented by an honest and prudent man." Charges that "The deplorable dilemma, in which France is placed with those Barbarians [cf. above, Brown to Clay, May 29 (no. 1), June 9, 28, 1827], has been brought about by the interested intrigues of an unfaithful agent. . . ." Predicts that France can be saved from humiliation only by "the conquest of Algiers or the death of the Bashaw [Hosséin], whose successor by disavowing the past. . . , may . . . restore the status quo in . . . relations with France." ALS. DNA, RG59, Cons. Disp., Algiers, vol. 11 (M23, R-T13). Received October 21.

From WILLIAM SHALER, Mahón (2). Reports having recently spent time in Cata-lonia, observed that "Principality," and acquired "considerable information rela-tive to . . . the other provinces of that fine Kingdom, that borders on the Mediter-ranean." Recommends the negotiation of a commercial treaty with Spain "upon the principles of a fair reciprocity. . . ." States: "Those countries are teeming with immense masses of raw agricultural products, the transportation of which to the Markets of . . . America, in vessels of the United States, would be of im-mense benefit to our navigation; and if through negotiation we could obtain the importation into Spain on reasonable terms, of our grain, flour, Rice, and pulse, our exports would be greatly, and most beneficially, increased." Adds that "several articles of much importance that we export, and that are admissable there, are hardly known in their markets"; cites particularly "our Cottons." Expresses the opinion that although a Spanish-American treaty would be opposed by France and England, that obstacle could be overcome and comments: "we seem now to be favorites in Spain. . . ."
   Suggests that concessions on the part of the United States would be necessary to obtain such a treaty, by giving "all possible encouragement to the manufactures of Spain, that is compatible with our home policy, which . . . [he] trust[s] will never be abandoned. . . ." Recommends particularly that the United States re-ceive Spanish wool and silk fabrics. States: "I am not sufficiently well acquainted with the state of the wool growing business in the U. S. to form an opinion on the policy of prohibiting the importation of wool, and particularly of Spanish wool, but it is obvious that we should be very sure of an abundant and cheap home supply before resorting to such a measure; it would certainly appear rather invidious in a negotiation of a Treaty of Commerce with Spain should we refuse to receive her wools. we should in this case seek to obtain a repeal of the existing laws in their late Colonies against the importation of the agricultural products and fabricks of Spain. . . ." Argues that Spain "can never transport her produce to market in her own vessels, as cheap as we can do it for her" and, further, that Spain "is generally involved in some petty dispute with some one of the Barbary States, that paralyses the safety of her flag. . . ."

Asserts that Catalonia "furnishes a remarkable example of the advantages, and even of the necessity of protecting infant manufacturing establishments against the hostile rivalry of old and wealthy institutions of the same character and intent"; explains that Charles III fostered her industry, and, consequently, that she is "one of the best Cultivated and most wealthy Countries of Europe. . . ." ALS. DNA, RG59, Cons. Disp., Algiers (M23, R-T13). Received October 21.

Charles III, who had ruled Spain from 1759 to 1788, had sought to make the country a great colonial power and had implemented necessary administrative reforms to this end in both Spain and its colonies. Because of his economic policies, Spain's prosperity had increased greatly during his reign.

From WILLIAM TAYLOR, Veracruz, "Private." Surveys the struggle between York and Scotch Masons in the State of Veracruz (cf. above, Poinsett to Clay, July 8, 1827); observes that "The first overt act was on the part of the 'Escoseses' in the passage of the law, of the 20th April last against masons, passed in anticipation of the arrival . . . of [José Ignacio] Esteva," Yorkist leader, who had been appointed "Commissary General . . . for this State"; notes the expulsion of Esteva (cf. above, Poinsett to Clay, June 16, 1827); and cites the control exercised by the Escoseses over "the State Legislature & every Officer under the State," as well as over "the press." Discusses an attack by the *Veracruzano Libre* on "Colo. [José Antonio] Rincon an Officer . . . in the Confidence of the General Government" and the subsequent destruction of the press of that journal by ten or twelve masked men. States that "General [Miguel] Barragan Governor of this State & Military Commander under the General Government of this District," has refused demands that Rincon and his regiment be ordered from the city. Opines that the Escoseses party, "since the arbitrary expulsion of Esteva & usurpation of the press, . . . is losing ground daily." Characterizes "The expulsion of Esteva" as an unfortunate "precedent for the Country at large" but charges that "his object in Coming here was not so much the exercise of his Duties as Commissary General, as to organise [*sic*] & promote the interests of the Yorquinos." Adds that, until "things" are "more settled," he will "not Consider it prudent to absent . . . [himself] from this place."

Reports also an exchange of prisoners with a small Spanish naval squadron lying off the coast. ALS. DNA, RG59, Cons. Disp., Veracruz, vol. 1 (M183, R1). Copy, in MHi-Adams Papers, Letters Recd. (MR481). Received August 21.

The "law of the 20th April" was a decree issued by Miguel Barragán, prohibiting all Masonic associations and ordering banishment for five years of all persons concerned in such bodies and punishment by imprisonment for four years of all who furnished them a meeting place. *Niles' Weekly Register*, XXXII, (May 26, 1827), 214, citing Veracruz *Mercury*, April 22, 1827.

Born in Jalapa in 1776, Rincon was a political leader in the Province of Tabasco and had been Commandant General there from 1822 until May, 1824. He attained the rank of brigadier general in the Mexican Army in 1832.

MISCELLANEOUS LETTERS   July 30, 1827

From JOHN W. HOLDING, La Guaira. States that he has been informed of Clay's request that (Beaufort T.) Watts aid (Joseph) Karrick "in support of a claim . . . for reprisals made upon Spanish, and portiguese [*sic*] property, Seized by Colombian [*sic*] Government" (cf. above, Clay to Watts, January 7, 1827); that he considers himself "the legal representative of this claim, and property," which he has "been prosecuting . . . before the judiciary of this country for the last five years, not thinking for one moment that the United States was the least interested in the liquidation of the Foreign claims"; and that his agent fears "serious injury" to Holding from the use of Clay's name and "the influence of the representative. . . ." Asks that he be "placed upon the same ground with Mr Karrick" and that their difference be settled between themselves, "with or without . . . [Clay's] influence, on either side." Requests a reply. ALS. DNA, RG76, Misc. Claims, Colombia (MR1, frames 593–95).

On September 14, "by direction of the Secretary," Daniel Brent acknowledged receipt of this document and sent to Holding, with a request that he forward it, a letter under flying seal to Beaufort T. Watts (below, Clay to Watts, same date). Copy, in DNA, RG59, Dom. Letters, vol. 22, p. 49 (M40, R20).

Holding was a native of Maryland and a veteran of the War of 1812. From 1845 to 1850 he was consul for the United States at Santiago, Cuba.

From P[ETER] A. KARTHAUS, JR., Baltimore. Transmits documents (not found) sent by direction of his father, P(eter) A. Karthaus (Sr.), who "is constrained to ask the assistance of . . . Mr. B T Watts and as far as is consistent the aid of our government in obtaining redress with a citizen of Columbia [sic]. . . ." Asks to be informed whether Clay "will forward these documents and subjoin any instructions to Mr. Watts in relation thereto." LS. DNA, RG59, Misc. Letters (M179, R65).

Peter A. Karthaus and Son were Baltimore merchants. On the requested instructions, cf. below, Karthaus to Clay, August 17, 1827, note.

Receipt from Josiah Stoddard Johnston

[ca. July 31, 1827]

Recd. of H. Clay in July 1827 the sum of Forty dollars to defray the expences [sic] of Henry Clay Hart from Limestone[1] to Washington.[2]

J. S. JOHNSTON

DS in Clay's hand, signed by Johnston. DLC-TJC (DNA, M212, R16).
[1] That is, Maysville, Kentucky, where Johnston had apparently been from July 16 to 18. Cf. above, Johnston to Clay, July 16, 1827.   [2] On Hart's trip, cf. below, Clay to Rodgers, September 29, 1827, and note.

DIPLOMATIC NOTES   July 31, 1827

From CHARLES R. VAUGHAN, Washington. States, in reply to Clay's "request, that enquiries might be made respecting James Ringold [sic] Slemaker" (above, Clay to Vaughan, April 28, 1827), "that it appears that Slemaker was received on board the 'Sybille,' not as entering into the British Service, but out of charity, at Carthagena on the 25th. August 1822, & that he was landed at Jamaica on the 10th. November of the same year." Encloses "a copy of the letter from the Secretary of the Admiralty [John Barrow] upon this subject." NS. DNA, RG59, Notes from British Legation, vol. 14 (M50, R15). Copy, in MHi-Adams Papers, Letters Recd. (MR481).

Barrow, born in 1764, had risen from humble origins to appointment in 1804 as second secretary in the Admiralty Office, a post he held, with but brief intermission in 1806–1807, until 1845. He had been given an honorary degree by the University of Edinburgh in 1821 and was granted a baronetcy in 1835. He was renowned particularly for publications describing his travels to China, South Africa, and the Arctic. Point Barrow, Cape Barrow, and the Barrow Straits were named in his honor, in testimony to his support for exploration in these regions.

INSTRUCTIONS AND DISPATCHES   July 31, 1827

From HEMAN ALLEN, Santiago de Chile, no. 56. Reports taking his "final leave of the Court of Chile," presenting (Samuel) Larned as Chargé des Affaires, and delivering to him the records of the Legation. Encloses "a sketch of" his "address and of the reply of the [Chilean] President [Francisco Antonio Pinto Diaz] on that occasion." ALS. DNA, RG59, Dip. Disp., Chile, vol. 2 (M-T2, R2). Published in Manning (arr.), *Diplomatic Correspondence . . . Latin-American Nations*, II, 1118–20. Received December 13.

On the same date Larned informed Clay that his salary as Secretary of Legation terminated as of "this day" and that the following day he would enter upon his duties as Chargé. ALS, in DNA, RG59, Dip. Disp., Chile, vol. 2 (M-T2, R2), received January 18, 1828.

From JOHN J. APPLETON, Stockholm, no. 22. Acknowledges receipt of a letter, dated May 11 (1827), from the State Department instructing him "to take all the necessary steps to obtain an *Exequatur* for Mr. [Robert Monroe] Harrison, appointed Consul of the United States at St. Barthelemy." Refers to the postscript to his dispatch "No. 21" (above, July 11, 1827); states that he has received Harrison's exequatur and has accepted an offer of "the Count of Wetterstedt . . . to have it forwarded with his despatches to St. Barthelemy"; notes that Wetterstedt has since gone to "the country" but that "the Chancellor [David von] Schulzenheim," who has "assumed the direction of the Department of Foreign Affairs during the Count's absence," has given assurance that the packet for Harrison would be forwarded immediately; and encloses copies of correspondence concerning these matters. Comments on the continued refractory spirit of the Norwegian Storthing (cf. above, Appleton to Clay, March 25, 1827), which ends its session "this day," on the departure of the "Russian Ambassador General [Jan Pieter] de Suchtelen . . . to pay a visit to the new Emperor" (Nicholas I), and on the arrival of "The Count of Montalembert . . . as French Envoy." ALS. DNA, RG59, Dip. Disp., Sweden and Norway, vol. 5 (M45, R6). Received September 25.

The letter of May 11 had been written by Daniel Brent. Copy, in DNA, RG59, Dip. Instr., vol. 11, p. 312 (M77, R6).

David von Schulzenheim, born in 1788 and educated at Uppsala, had been named secretary of the Embassy at Paris in 1814, a cabinet secretary in 1817, Secretary of State in 1824, and Chancellor in 1825. In the last post he on numerous occasions substituted for the Minister of Foreign Affairs, and in 1838 he was named to that office in the Cabinet. He was given the title of baron in 1830.

Marc-René-Anne-Marie, Count of Montalembert, born at Paris in 1777, had fought against the forces of Toussaint L'Ouverture in Santo Domingo and had subsequently, as a leader of the emigrés, joined the British Army, with whom he had fought in the Peninsular campaigns. Under the Restoration regime of Louis XVIII in France, Montalembert had been named Secretary of Legation at London in 1814 and Minister to Stuttgart in 1816, to Copenhagen, from 1819 to 1820, and to Stockholm, from 1827 to 1829. He had been created a peer of France in 1819; and, during the months before his death in 1831, he participated actively as a member of the Chamber of Peers.

From FRANKLIN LITCHFIELD, Puerto Cabello. Acknowledges receipt of Daniel Brent's letter of June 8 (see above, Hawley to Clay, June 1, 1827, note); remarks that he received no communication from (Betsy) Hawley until July 23; and states that since the commission issued by the Colombian Government to her brother (Isaac P. Hawley) was not presented to him before his death, he was not entitled to any compensation other than for "Transport." Adds that he does not know whether the brother, who was engaged in privateering, was due any sums from that source. Notes that he has written to the sister. LS. DNA, RG59, Cons. Disp., Puerto Cabello, vol. 1 (M-T229, R1).

From JAMES OMBROSI, Florence. Reports a visit to Florence by "Capt. John B. Nicolson of the U. S. Sloop of war Ontario," who was granted an audience by the Grand Duke (Leopold II). States that, if he were "like the Consul of Prussia [the Count Lucchesini] . . . acting Chargé d'Affaires" (cf. above, Ombrosi to Clay, June 15, 1827), he "might have accompanied Capt Nicolson. . . ." ALS. DNA, RG59, Cons. Disp., Florence, vol. 1 (M-T204, R1). Received October 18.

MISCELLANEOUS LETTERS   July 31, 1827

From JOHN COWPER, Norfolk. Refers to the claims against France, for the period prior to 1800, that "will come before the next Congress." Asserts that "The amount of those claims, can have no effect on their justice, but . . . it will do them no service, to exhibit them for an amount greater than they are in fact"; states that he knows from his service as "an Agent for many claims under the Florida Treaty [cf. above, II, 678n], . . . that a very large amount was allowed by the Commissioners under that Treaty, for French Captures prior to the Convention of 1800" (cf. above, Clay to Adams, May 20, 1826); explains that "These claims were allowed, because the vessels were carried into Spanish Ports, and disposed of contrary to the Laws of Nations," and estimates that "Sixty per cent" of the money he recovered "was for claims of this character." Contends that, with the information accompanying each case now in Clay's office, "there can be no difficulty and very little trouble in ascertaining every claim, that ought not be presented to Congress as forming any part of the claims now set up." Professes to "have no doubt" that "Many . . . were paid under the Louisiana Treaty" (cf. above, Lawrence to Clay, December 15, 1827, note), although "in that" he admits to be "not so conversant," and adds that he is sending Clay "a Book, which will be found useful, in aid of any examination, that may be instituted." ALS. DNA, RG76, Misc. Claims, France (MR2).

Cowper had been a member of the Virginia House of Delegates from Nansemond County in 1791 and an alderman of Norfolk in 1800. He apparently acted on various occasions as an agent for claims collection. Cf. 6 *U. S. Stat.*, 660 (July 1, 1836), which allowed him commission for his work in prosecuting claims for indemnity under the Adams-Onís Treaty.

Following receipt of Clay's letter to John Holmes, above, January 22, 1827, the Senate Committee on Foreign Relations, on February 8, had introduced a resolution calling upon the President "to procure the evidence and documents relating to the claims . . . and to cause an abstract of the claims, and of the evidence and documents, to be laid before the Senate at the commencement of the first session of the next Congress." The resolution had not, however, been passed. U. S. Sen., *Journal*, 19 Cong., 2 Sess., pp. 163, 219–20. Cowper may have been indicating his knowledge that memorials by a number of claimants were to be presented to the 20th Congress, calling for the United States Government to provide the compensation considered due. Cf. *ibid.*, 20 Cong., 1 Sess., pp. 46, 474.

The book to which Cowper refers may have been *A Sketch of the Claims of Sundry American Citizens on the Government of the United States, for Indemnity, for Depredations Committed on their Property by the French, (Prior to the 30th of September, 1800), Which Were Acknowledged by France and Voluntarily Surrendered to Her by the United States, for a Valuable National Consideration, in the Convention of that Date*, by a Citizen of Baltimore (Baltimore, 1826). Sabin,

Bibliotheca Americana, XX, 44–45, suggests that the author may have been Robert Purviance, who had, however, died in 1806.

To Joseph Gales, Jr., and William W. Seaton

1 Aug. 1827.

Will you be pleased to insert in the Intellr. of tomorrow a note to the purport of the article annexed hereto? Yr's respectfly   H CLAY

For the Intellr. of the 2d.[1]

"We are informed that Mr. Vaughan,[2] the British Minister, paid to Mr. Clay, at the Dept. of State, yesterday, the second and last instalment, amounting to upwards of $600.000, under the Convention of Novr. last."[3]

ALS. Owned by Thomas D. Clark, Lexington, Kentucky. Addressed on attached sheet: "The Editors of the Intellr.   Present."
[1] As requested, the statement appeared in the Washington *Daily National Intelligencer* of August 2, 1827.   [2] Charles R. Vaughan.   [3] Cf. above, Gallatin to Clay, November 13, 1826; Clay to Adams, January 15, 1827.

From William B. Rochester

My Dear Sir   Rochester Aug: 1 1827

I arrived at home on the sixth day (27h)[1] after taking leave of you at Columbus[2]—   altho' your failure to return to Washington by this route was the cause of great disappointment and of general regret yet I think that in your exhausted state and considering the necessity on your part for an early arrival at Washington, you made a good escape— immense preparations were making at Buffalo & Black Rock for your entré into our State— At this place the corporation had made their dispositions, & were only waiting the annunciation of your arrival upon the frontier, in order to give them effect— I found for me various letters from divers points Eastward all indicating the note of preparation as you should advance, & the wishes & Expectations at different & contrary points.

It is all a mistake that this part of N. Y. feels any inclination for the "Hero"[3]—   there is here and there a solitary croak—   the most unpleasant incident to me which has transpired, is the fact that my friend Whittlesey late Editor & proprietor of the Monroe Repub: was reduced by his pecuniary necessities to sell out only two days before my return home, to two young adventurous Jacksonians, and could only extort a promise of neutrality—which in my opinion amounts to nothing[4]—   but we still have an efficient & powerful paper the daily Telegraph as well as the third paper printed here—the Album.

You may judge of the anxiety of many to see you When I mention the fact that from several of the interior towns in this & the adjoining counties vedettes were sent & stationed here to carry the intelligence of your arrival whenever ascertained— The only & best excuse I could make for you was the urgency of your public duties—the insurmountable detentions interposed to your progress by your Ken: friends & the prospect of your visiting the Niagara Falls next fall   Mr. Evans[5] will resign his seat in Cong:— I am told he is for the admin: in spite of V. Buren— I have always found him an unwavering self-poised politician[6]— he was not at home when I passed thro' Batavia.—

Our M. H. R. Col: Barnard[7] has just retd. from the City of N. Y. I was apprehensive that He would return thro' Albany somewhat poisoned by the Regency of that city— have as yet had no oppy. of a private interview with him— he called to see me immediately on his return but I was surrounded by visitors which precluded any direct declarations on his part— however when I was commenting upon the late demonstration of the Hero pretty freely, he himself voluntarily alluded in terms of disapprobation to one feature in the matter at issue between you, viz: that Genl. J. should make as the basis of his accusation of you[8] the communication of a man, whom Duff Green, says (as it were ex cathedra) is not worthy of credit[9]— I will write you more in extenso in a week or two— it seems that Clinton[10] is still mystified— a red mouthed admirer of Jackson & intimate friend of Clinton, passed thro' Rochester yesterday just from Albany & N York— he declares that Clinton is for the "hero" horse, foot, & dragoons— but quien sabé & it is of little importance now   I am told he is very sour & unamiable [sic] disposed to quarrel with his best friends & on good terms only with his decanter.

I have an hundred things to say but must conclude by assuring you that the Genl. administration never stood better in this part of the State than it does now— even John c [sic] Spencer, is about retracing his steps.[11] My best respects to Mrs. Clay   Yr friend
Hon H. Clay.   W B ROCHESTER

P.S.   You know my opinion of the professional merits of John Duer Esq.— his Brother the Circuit Judge[12] has desired me by letter to write you on his subject namely—that he is (as well as Ogden & Maxwell)[13] a candidate for the office of U. S. D. Atty, if Tillotson[14] declines— for the Judgeship, I thot. him, better qualified than Wheaton[15]— I am told that Ogden is *your* favourite— perhaps he is best qualified of the three— but all are abundantly competent.— I can only express my feelings (as I am indeed)—it is this that both personally & politically, I think either D. or M. preferable to O.

Capt. Elisha Ely of this place is entirely satisfied with his disappointment in the Consulship to S. M.[16]— he desires me to say so to you— he acquiesces freely—

ALS. DLC-HC (DNA, M212, R2) .   1 Of July.
2 Rochester had been in Lexington (cf. above, Toasts and Speech, July 12, 1827, note) and apparently had traveled with Clay until their paths diverged in Ohio.   3 Andrew Jackson.   4 Frederick Whittlesey, a cousin of Elisha Whittlesey, had joined Edwin Scrantom in editing the Rochester *Monroe Republican* early in 1827. Born in Connecticut and graduated in 1818 from Yale College, Frederick Whittlesey had been admitted to the bar in Utica in 1821, had begun the practice of law at Rochester in 1822, and in 1825 had become clerk of the circuit court. He became Monroe County treasurer (1829–1830), a member of Congress (1831–1835), Rochester city attorney (1838), vice chancellor of the eighth judicial district of New York (1839–1847), a justice of the State Supreme Court (1847–1848), and a professor of law at Genesee College (1850, 1851).   Whittlesey sold the *Monroe Republican* to Henry C. Sleight and Luther Tucker, who had taken over the *Rochester Daily Advertiser* the previous October. Sleight, born in New York City, had fought in the War of 1812, and had printed the Lexington, Kentucky, *Western Monitor* in 1814 to 1815, the Russellville, Kentucky, *Messenger*, from 1815 to 1817, and the Jamaica *Long Island Farmer* from 1821 to 1826. He refused to support Van Buren in the fall of 1828 but sold his interest to Tucker, who received the necessary backing from Van Buren's friends. Sleight subsequently engaged in a general publishing business, removed to Illinois, and in 1868 retired to Sag Harbor, Long Island.   Tucker, born in Vermont in 1802, had worked for Sleight on the Jamaica newspaper from 1824 to 1826, continued the *Rochester Republican* from 1827 to 1839, and also published the Rochester *Genesee Farmer* from 1831 to 1839. In the latter year he merged the *Genesee Farmer* with the Albany *Cultivator* and in 1840 removed to Albany. There he founded and edited from 1846 to 1852 the *Horticulturalist* and in 1853 began a weekly edition of the *Cultivator* under the title *Country Gentleman*, for which he served as editor until his death in 1873.   5 David E. Evans' resignation had been dated May 2, 1827, but it was not publicly announced until mid-September. *Albany Argus*, September 11, 1827.
   6 Cf. above, Rochester to Clay, May 9, 1826.   7 Daniel Dewey Barnard.   8 Cf. above, Report of Clay Interview, *ca*. April 15, 1827; Clay to Hammond, June 25, 1827; Address to the Public, June 29, 1827.   9 Cf. below, Smith to Clay, this date, note.
   10 DeWitt Clinton.   11 Reference to a change in Spencer's views has not been found.   12 William Alexander Duer. See above, Washington to Clay, February 15, 1826, note.   13 David B. Ogden; Hugh Maxwell.   14 Robert Tillotson.
   15 Henry Wheaton. On the judgeship, cf. above, Porter to Clay, October 8, 1826, and note; November 7, 1826.   16 Santa Marta, Colombia. Cf. above, Marvin to Clay, *ca*. January 5, 1827.

From John Sergeant

Dear Sir,   Philada. Augt. 1. 1827.
   Your absence from Washington, and the expectation of seeing you here on your return, have prevented me from writing to you during the few days I have been at home.[1] I now perceive from the newspapers that you will probably not pass this way,[2] which I the more regret as I think there was every disposition to give you a much more hearty greeting than you have ever before received in Philadelphia.
   I have brought with me a dispatch, of no great moment, from Mr. Poinsett and myself,[3] and a letter from Mr. P. to the President informing that the Mexican Govt. has signified to him that his presence there is not acceptable.[4] I shall also have one more dispatch to forward from myself, accompanied with copies of my notes to the several ministers and their answers.[5] Upon all these matters, I have a great deal to say to you, and, if you are not coming here, will take an early opportunity of seeing you at Washington, allowing you, however, some time after your return to dispose of the business accumulated during your absence. If you should wish to see me sooner, please to let me know.

I find myself very much in arrear as to home news. The latest papers I have seen, until within a few days past, were only of the middle of April. Appearances are, however, encouraging. Our friends here exhibit a much better countenance than they did some time ago.

In the Beverly [*sic*] business, you have a complete triumph, upon which I sincerely congratulate you. I am afraid Genl. Jackson will be in a dreadful rage when he reads your speech at Lexington,[6] for it will open his eyes to his own folly, and nothing is so provoking as such a discovery. Very respectfully & truly Dr. Sir, Yrs   JOHN SERGEANT
The Honble Henry Clay

ALS. DLC-HC (DNA, M212, R2).
[1] Sergeant had arrived in quarantine on July 27. Philadelphia *United States Gazette*, July 28, 1827.   [2] Newspaper reference not found. On Clay's return route, cf. above, Rochester to Clay, this date; on his arrival in Washington, see below, Clay to Erwin, August 4, 1827.   [3] Above, June 4, 1827.   [4] In this lengthy communication, dated June 8, 1827, Poinsett stated that petitions asking the Mexican President (Guadalupe Victoria) to send him "out of the Country" had been received from the States of Puebla and Veracruz; that Victoria "did not regard the conduct of the States in this particular as at all improper"; and that Poinsett informed him of his intention to request Adams to withdraw him "from a Country where the person of a foreign minister was exposed to such insults without the chance of receiving any protection from the general government." Observing, "I have thus submitted to you a faithful statement of . . . the reasons, which induce me to wish to withdraw from this Court," he, nevertheless, expressed willingness to remain if Adams thought he should. He added: "I am very far from wishing to resign the appointment so lately conferred upon me of Envoy Extraordinary and Minister Plenipotentiary to the Congress of Tacubaya— If you think proper to withdraw me from this Court, I will retire to that village, and remain there until after the meeting of the Congress, or rather until after its adjournment." MHi-Adams Papers, Letters Recd. (MR481).   [5] The dispatch has not been found, unless it was the "Private" letter, above, May 30, 1827. The cited enclosures, copy of Sergeant to José Mariano Michelena, José Dominguez, Antonio Larrazábal, and Pedro Gual, June 2, 1827, and translations of Dominguez to Sergeant, June 3, 1827; Larrazábal to Sergeant, June 4, 1827; Michelena to Sergeant, n.d.; Gual to Sergeant, June 5, 1827, are found in DNA, RG43, First Panama Congress, 1825–1827 (M662, R1).   [6] Above, July 12, 1827.

From Thomas Smith

Dr. Sir.   Lexington, August 1. 1827.
I enclose a letter[1] addressed to me by Mr. Simon Bradford of Nashville on the subject of an office expected shortly to be vacant. I do not know the individual recommended, but Mr. Bradford is a very respectable merchant, and an old acquaintance of mine. He is but remotely connected to our Bradfords.[2] The approaching election has become rather a flat topic. There is less of animation on our side than I could wish. This does not augur well, while on the other side there is great activity. But I know of no changes, or other unfavourable indication.[3] It is impossible for the Jackson party to succeed here, except by the aid of spurious votes from Scott and other counties. It will require great vigilance to prevent such imposition, as Morton[4] I have no doubt is prepared to do every thing, and no body denies that he is capable of doing any thing. The General's Reply[5] excites a feeling of

contempt. Although I cannot but think it has disappointed his friends, yet they pretend to regard it as very proper & very candid. He has in fact adopted a very ingenious course to keep alive the subject and to get clear of the imputation of slander—that is to say, with his heedless partizans, and the unthinking. Markley it is inferred is the member upon whom Buchanan will attempt to saddle the intrigue, and Markley we judge from the Telegraph, it is anticipated will disavow it.[6] If any thing occurs to throw light as to the course likely to be pursued by the antagonist party, I should be pleased to be apprised of it. Your course it is thought by your friends will be, to let them alone, for the present. I am advised that Moore, Wickliffe &c. will testify that you advised them not to commit themselves.[7]—   The Jackson dinner was no great things [sic]. The party from all quarters rallied, and the number, about 2500, was made up of strangers chiefly, and boys and negroes. The speeches of Pope and Barry, were more violent than can well be represented. They unpacked their morbid souls, and said every thing.[8]— The contest between Lee White & Wickliffe, & between McHatton and Sanford, will be very close. Henry will be defeated.[9]— Respects to Mrs. Clay. Yours truly,   THO. SMITH

[Endorsed on cover][10]

I have deposited $12 to your credit in Bank, which sum pay to the Colonization Society,[11] as the amt. collected in the Rev Mr. Marshall's Church.[12]   T. S.

ALS. DLC-HC (DNA, M212, R2). Addressed to Clay, "Private."   [1] Not found. [2] Simon was a son of Fielding Bradford. Born and reared in Lexington, he had served in the War of 1812 and for a time commanded a steamboat plying between Nashville and New Orleans. He settled in Nashville about 1818 and became a very successful cotton factor. About 1845 he removed to Memphis.   [3] On the Kentucky Congressional election, cf. above, Clay to Taylor, April 4, 1827, note; Brown to Clay, June 28, 1827, note. [4] Probably William R. Morton, deputy sheriff, and from September, 1827, to 1830, sheriff of Fayette County.   [5] Jackson's answer to Clay's Speech at the Lexington Public Dinner, above, July, 12, 1827, had been addressed "To the Public," July 18, 1827, and published in the *Nashville Republican*, July 20, 1827. Reprinted in the Lexington *Kentucky Gazette*, July 27, 1827, the letter named James Buchanan as the "member of Congress, of high respectability," who had reported to Jackson that he had been visited by Clay's friends. They had stated, as the General reported it: "the West did not wish to separate from the West, and if I would say, or permit any of my confidential friends to say, that in case I was elected President, Mr. Adams should not be continued as Secretary of State, by a complete union of Mr. Clay and his friends, they would put an end to the Presidential contest in one hour. . . ." Jackson challenged Clay's expression of satisfaction "that a specific accusation by a responsible accuser, has at length appeared." Jackson reminded his readers that George McDuffie had proposed the following resolution as an instruction to the special committee of the House of Representatives which had investigated the charges of George Kremer (above, February 3, 1825, note): "That the said committee be instructed to inquire whether the friends of Mr. Clay have hinted that they would fight for those who would pay best, or any thing to that effect; and whether overtures were said to have been made by the friends of Adams to the friends of Mr. Clay, offering him the appointment of Secretary of State for his aid to elect Mr. Adams; and whether the friends of Clay gave this information to the friends of Jackson, and hinted that if his friends would offer the same price they would close with them; and whether Henry Clay has transferred, or resolved to transfer his interest to John Q. Adams; and whether it was said and believed, that, as a consideration for this abandonment of duty to his constituents, Clay was to be appointed Secretary of State; and that the said committee be authorized to send for persons and papers, and to compel the persons so sent for, to answer upon oath." Jackson maintained that Clay's influence was such that according to those terms the inquiry would have been initiated at that time if he had supported it. McDuffie's resolution, according to Jackson, had been presented to the House of Representatives on February 4, 1825, and "negatived by a large majority," without recorded vote. Cf. *Register of Debates*, 18 Cong., 2 Sess., 482, 486.   6 The Washington *United States Telegraph* on July 21, 1827, noted that as early as July 17 the Philadelphia *Democratic Press* had named Buchanan as Jackson's Congressional informant. The *Telegraph* asserted that Philip Swenk Markley had given the identification to the editor (John Binns) of the *Democratic Press* and noted that Markley, "who was the agent of Mr. Clay," had been appointed Naval Officer at Philadelphia. As early as July 2, 1827, an editorial in the Washington *United States Telegraph*, without naming either Buchanan or Markley, had spoken of Clay's "confidential friend" in the episode as "a man of no pretensions to moral principle, has lived expensively for several years at the cost of others, borrowing money of whoever would trust him, without intending to pay, giving checks upon banks where he never had an account, defrauding militia officers of the late war of their compensation, keeping clients' money in his hands for years, and deceiving them by false information of their business." "This man," editor Duff Green had concluded, "may be induced to exculpate Mr. Clay, but he cannot be a competent witness in a court of conscience."   7 On Thomas P. Moore's purported statement, cf. below, Clay to Blackford, August 24, 1827; on Charles A. Wickliffe's testimony, cf. below, Johnson to Clay, September 9, 1827, note.   8 Reports of the Jacksonian dinner, at Fowler's Garden in Lexington, July 21, 1827, varied according to the politics of the journalists. Attendance estimates for this *"free dinner,"* as the Lexington *Kentucky Reporter* observed, July 25, 1827, ranged between two and three thousand, "including many from Scott, Woodford, Franklin, Jessamine, Mercer, Anderson, Madison, Clark, Montgomery, Bourbon, Harrison, &c. [counties]." The Lexington *Kentucky Gazette*, July 27, 1827, placed the attendance at 4,000. William T. Barry was the scheduled speaker, but before he arrived John Pope was invited to address the body. Pope's speech, which filled six columns in the *Kentucky Gazette*, August 3, lauded Jackson as a civilian first, although at times a glorious military leader; assigned to the hottest corner of Hell the authors of the "foul calumny" against Rachel Robards Jackson (cf. above, Clay to Hammond, December 23, 1826); and pointed to "the great and leading question before the nation" as centering on "whether the public will was improperly defeated in the last Presidential election." Barry's speech, nearly as long, defended Jackson's military career, castigated the Kentucky representatives who had supported Adams' election, criticized the judicial appointment of Robert Trimble, and emphasized the role of the people in choosing the President as distinct from the old policy of succession of Cabinet members to the office. Lexington *Kentucky Gazette*, August 31, 1827.   9 See above, Johnson to Clay, April 29, 1827. In the Fifth Congressional District Robert L. McHatton defeated Alfred Sanford by 319 votes. Frankfort *Argus of Western America*, September 26, 1827. Sanford, of Covington, Kentucky, had served in the State House of Representatives from 1813 to 1820, excluding only the Session of 1816–1817.   10 AEI.   11 American Colonization Society.   12 Born in Ireland in 1760, Robert Marshall had accompanied his family to western Pennsylvania in 1772 and fought in the American Revolution. At the age of 23 he had begun theological training as a Presbyterian in Virginia. He had come to Kentucky in 1791 as a missionary and in 1793 had been ordained pastor of Bethel Church in Fayette County and Blue Spring Church in Scott County. From 1803 to 1811 he had joined in the break from the Kentucky Synod; but, returning to the established order, he soon recovered his charge at Bethel Church, where he remained until his death in 1832. Lexington *Observer and Reporter*, June 21, 1832.

INSTRUCTIONS AND DISPATCHES   August 1, 1827

From JOSHUA BOND, Montevideo (1). Reports "that the regulation, which was some time ago adopted by the Brazilian Government, exacting bonds from all vessels sailing from this port with cargoes the productions of other countries which might be supposed to be wanting by their enemy, has been finally rescinded, at the instance, it is believed, of the British government." Encloses a copy of "an order of the Brazilian government directed to the authorities at this place, prohibiting the departure of any vessels which may have on board arms or munitions of war, and which, it is understood, will be extended to all merchant vessels that may enter this port with these articles in search of a market." Cites a case in which the order was enforced, involving removal of "a brass gun" from the schooner *Washington,* "which touched in here, bound from Valdivia to Boston," as "very trivial" but expresses apprehension as to future injurious effects of the order. ALS. DNA, RG59, Cons. Disp., Montevideo, vol. 1 (M71, R1). Received November 9.

On the imposition of the Brazilian blockade, cf. above, Raguet to Clay, December 23, 1825; April 12, June 27, July 17, 1826; Forbes to Clay, February 14, 1826. On January 21, 1826, the Viscount of Laguna had announced measures requiring that captains and consignees of vessels sailing from the port of Montevideo post bonds, "to the value of the goods which they might export," to prevent their entering "any ports of the Republic of Buenos Ayres, and affording succor to the enemy. . . ." Viscount of Baependy to Francisco de Paula Maggessi Navares de Carvalho, March 2, 1826, in *House Docs.,* 20 Cong., 1 Sess., no. 281, p. 145. James Biddle had notified Samuel L. Southard on February 21, 1827, that bonds were not exacted from foreign vessels that did "not break bulk" and that "vessels selling a part of their cargoes . . . [were] allowed freely to depart with the remainder." He expressed concern then, however, that the requirement of bonds might be extended to "all vessels whatever quitting the port." *Ibid.,* 140. The order which Bond now reports has not been found, but a decree of November 6, 1827, required that measures be taken to prevent any foreign vessel from sailing "from this Province during the present war, without previously giving sufficient security not to enter the ports of that Republic [Buenos Aires]." *Ibid.,* 113.

Carlos Frederico Lecor, Viscount Laguna, born in Portugal, had fought in the Peninsular War and had come to Brazil in 1816. As a follower of Dom Pedro he had been elevated to nobility in 1822. He held rank as lieutenant general commanding the Brazilian forces at Montevideo.

From JOSHUA BOND, Montevideo (2). Transmits "an extract from the Protest of the master [Albert P. Devalangin] of the Brig President Adams of Baltimore, whose vessel was seized by a Brazilian schooner of war" near Montevideo; notes that "The baggage of the passengers after much trouble has been given up, whilst that of the master and crew, who have suffered from ill treatment, has been detained. . . , notwithstanding repeated remonstrances . . . to the authorities against the proceeding"; and expresses a belief "that no change will be made by them in the practice, unless it be through the interference of the Government of the United States. . . ." ALS. DNA, RG59, Cons. Disp., Montevideo, vol. 1 (M71, R1). Received November 9.

Devalangin has not been further identified. The brig *President Adams* was a vessel of 199 tons, sailing at the time of seizure partly in ballast, the bulk of its cargo having been sold in Montevideo.

From Francis Scott Key, Jr.

Dear Sir:—   G. T.[1] August 2nd, 1827.

I have received a letter to-day from John Hart[2] in which he requests me to apply to you in his behalf on your arrival—

He only asks that his board should be paid for him in the prison, that he may not be turned into a room, appropriated to the common prisoners, which he states is filled with the most worthless & wretched creatures.— He says if the board he now owes is not soon paid, the keeper will make this disposition of him.

I have also a letter from one of his fellow prisoners, Edward Thompson, the famous tea-merchant. He unites recommending [sic] that his friends should grant him this indulgence—that it might have a dreadful effect upon him to confine him with the wretches who are subject to the ordinary treatment and discipline of the prison—that his conduct since his confinement has been quite unexceptionable—that at present he lives in Mr. Ruff's[3] family with the other debtors who are boarders, and is quite in *good society*; but that Mr. Ruff cannot keep him in this way without assurances of payment. He now owes $20.00 for four week's [sic] board. Mr. T. also says he will want a small sum for some articles of clothing, and that a remittance for these purposes may be properly made to Mr. Ruff the keeper, of whom he speaks as a reputable man. He says "he earnestly recommends a sufficient remittance to cover his board, otherwise he will be turned into the room occupied by the most miserable creatures on Earth, where his morals will no doubt be seriously injured."

I have thought it right to give you this information— at the same time it seems strange and wrong that he should require this assistance, for I presume he still draws his pay from the Navy,[4] and if so, it amounts to more than $20.00 per month, and ought therefore to support him.

I think of answering his letter by stating this to him, unless you consider it best to write to him yourself,[5] or to adopt some other course. Respectfully yours,   F. KEY.
Hon. Henry Clay, Sec'y of State, Washington.

Copy. InHi. The correspondent was probably the son of Francis Scott Key, the author of "The Star Spangled Banner." The elder Key, born in 1779, was practicing law in Georgetown and in the Federal courts; however, he seems rarely to have used a single initial in his signature. The younger "Frank," born in 1806, had been commissioned a midshipman in the Navy in May, 1823, and had served with the West Indies Squadron in 1825 and the Mediterranean Squadron in 1826. He had left the Navy in February, 1827.
[1] Georgetown, District of Columbia.   [2] John S. Hart. Cf. above, Watson to Clay, March 30, 1827; below, Clay to Meade, August 4, 1827.   [3] Not further identified.
[4] Young Hart was assigned to duty on the schooner *Shark*, in the West Indies, by December 31, 1827, but dismissed from service a year later.   [5] Cf. below, Clay to Meade, August 4, 1827.

From John Scott

Honble Henry Clay
Dr Sir   St [sic] Genevieve Missouri August 2d. 1827.
I here send you a Copy[1] of a Letter received Last night from Mr Robt. Scott.   When we Last talked on this Subject.[2] I Stated very frankly my embarrassed Situation, the Ampleness of the Security you

held, and my Sincere desire to meet this claim— I understood you then
to say that I should not be proceeded against for some two or three
years till I could turn round in my practice[3]— I presume from the tenor
of Mr Scotts Letter that you have felt compelled to alter your couse
[sic] and endeavour to enforce the Collection at an earlier day— This
determination on your part compels me to make in honour a fair and
open disclosure to you of my present Situation. Leaving you then to
act as duty shall dictate. because I do not doubt. that if Left to the
influence of feelings alone. I would have the most ample time—

Beside this debt I owed some seven or eight thousand dollars. suits
were commenced Last year on them all. and Judgments obtaind, and
after my departure for the City of Washington Last fall. evey [sic]
atom of my property down to the Most Minute of household furniture
was sold under the hammer even the reversionary Interest in the property Mortgaged to Col Morrison.— It gives me pain to say that the
Costs of a suit alone Could not be made from any thing I have in this
world. and that unless it is Intended to deprive me of my *personal
Liberty* and drive me to the Last resort of all unfortunate debtors. all
process at this time would be unavailing— I do not wish you to rest
on my statement alone for this fact, you can have unfortunately the
same assurances from any one to whom you will write on the Subject—
A Couse so rigid and persevering as this would be will only place it
further out of my power to meet the claim by entirely destroying my
credit. and capacity to act, or do busiess [sic] for even the collecting
busiess will not be given to a Lawyer. who has been released from
prison by operation of Law— Why not foreclose the Mortgage and buy
in the property Mortgaged for the estate.   it is very honestly worth
more than the debt.   the estate of Col Morrison cannot be pressed for
funds and this property will be fully good for the debt if you will have
the mortgage foreclosed and order the property to be purchased in for
the debt. it is worth it at Congress price.[4] independent of the salt water
and town site and wood yard on it— This place has the only place for a
deposit for all the Counties of Pery [sic]. Madison and the back parts
of Cape Girardeau. Ste Genevieve. and the whole of Wayne. You
would in my opinon [sic] do Justice to the Estate. and save me. if you
would forclose the Mortgage and buy in the property for the whole
debt,   Menard and Vallee[5] want to make an establishment there now,
and have been buying out the Interest of Hempsteads[6] heirs. and are
now petitioning for a division of the property with a view to make a
Commercial Stand at St Loro[7] on the tract—   do persue [sic] this
Couse and order your agent to buy it in for the debt. or as near the
debt as possible and I will try as early as possible to arrange any Ballance [sic] that may be due,   I know you are very busy. but try to Let
me hear from you. and do not if in your power to prevent it have me

eternally crushed. ruined. and destroyed in this matter,   I am sure the property is worth more than the debt. and before Long must and will command that much— I cannot give other or further Security. and if pressed personally must in the end resort to a Couse that finally and forever seals me up—   write me soon   Yr friend   JOHN SCOTT

ALS. DLC-TJC (DNA, M212, R13).   1 Not found.
2 John Scott's indebtedness to the estate of James Morrison, listed in the schedule of bonds and notes due the estate as $3,838.66, due June 24, 1821. Fayette County Will Book F, 235. On the Debt Account, above, ca. August 12, 1826, Clay listed the debt as "Bad."   3 His service in Congress had ended March 3, 1827. Cf. above, Clay to Adams, July 25, 1826, and note.   4 That is, $1.25 an acre, as a minimum.   5 The firm of Pierre Menard and Jean-Baptiste Vallé, founded at Kaskaskia in 1820, as an outgrowth of the business of Menard dating from 1791 at that town, had opened a store at Ste. Genevieve in the early 1820's under the management of Vallé's youngest son, Felix.   Menard, born near Montreal in 1766, had come to the Illinois country as a youth, prior to 1781, and engaged in fur trade. He had later become one of the partners in the founding of the Missouri Fur Company. He was a militia officer and had held a variety of civil appointments in the Territorial governments of Indiana and Illinois. He had presided over the Illinois Territorial Council from 1812 to 1818 and had served as Lieutenant Governor of Illinois from 1818 to 1822. He remained active in business until about 1839.   Jean-Baptiste Vallé, born at Kaskaskia in 1760, had served as commandant at New Madrid, 1803 to 1804, and briefly in the same capacity at Ste. Genevieve in 1804. In the latter year he had been named a judge of the Court of Quarter Sessions. His son Felix had been born at Ste. Genevieve in 1800.   6 Probably Edward Hempstead, born at New London, Connecticut, in 1780 and educated at law. He had opened practice in Rhode Island in 1801 but removed to St. Louis in 1804. He had been attorney general of the Territory of Upper Louisiana from 1809 to 1811, a member of the Territorial Assembly in 1812, and Delegate to Congress from 1812 to 1814. Enjoying a large legal practice, he had speculated heavily in land. He had been killed in 1817 by a fall from a horse.   7 Word uncertain.

INSTRUCTIONS AND DISPATCHES   August 2, 1827

From S[AMUEL] D. HEAP, Tunis. Encloses "the Copy of a correspondence [dated July 31] . . . between. Com. [William Montgomery] Crane, the French Consul [Constantine Guys] and Commander of the French Ship Maria Teresa [variously named as Forqué or Fourqué, not further identified] respecting a man [identified as Lewis Laporte] who deserted from the U. S. Ship Java and sought protection in the French Consulate." Notes that "Our Minister at Paris [James Brown] has been made acquainted with the case. . . ." ALS. DNA, RG59, Cons. Disp., Tunis, vol. 5 (M-T303, R5). Received December 20. The enclosures also include letters from Delacouray, "the second Captain of His Majesty's Frigate Maria Teresa," to Crane, July 30, 1827; Crane to Heap, July 31, 1827; and Crane to Brown, August 1, 1827; as well as a deposition, dated July 30, 1827, in which "Simon [*sic*] Laporte 32 years old, . . . says he is a native of Havre. . . ."

Crane, born at Elizabeth, New Jersey, in 1784, had entered the Navy as a midshipman in 1799, commanded vessels in the war against Tripoli and during the War of 1812, served as captain of the frigate *United States* from 1821 through 1823 and as commander of the navy yard at Portsmouth, New Hampshire, in 1824 and 1825. From June, 1827, to October, 1829, as captain of the frigate *Java*, he commanded the Mediterranean Squadron. He returned as commander of the Portsmouth Navy Yard, 1832 to 1840, became a Navy Commissioner, 1841 to 1842, and was Chief of the Bureau of Ordnance and Hydrography, 1842 to 1846.

The *Java*, built at Baltimore in 1813–1814, a frigate of 1508 tons, with 44 guns, had sailed for the Mediterranean from Boston on June 9.

From Thomas I. Wharton

My dear Sir   Philada. 3d August 1827
    I enclose you a letter from the Consul of the U. S. at Lisbon[1] re-
questing leave of absence which his brother Mr. Randal [sic] Hutchinson[2] of this City placed in my hands some time since to be forwarded
to you. They are both respectable men And if consistently with official
duties you can grant the request it will be very acceptable to them.
    I beg to offer my sincere congratulations upon the issue of the late
extraordinary proceedings & the triumphant position in which you
now stand before the people   The friends of the General here are
amazingly discomfited by your Speech.[3] Nothing could have happened
more fortunately than the publication of his letter. "O that mine
enemy had written a letter" Would have been the exclamation of Job
under such circumstances. A few more such evidences of malignity of
disposition and feebleness of mind will render the cause of the General entirely hopeless. I beg to offer my congratulations also upon the
prodigious improvement that has taken place in public opinion in this
state. The prospects are still brightening & if nothing occurs to *un
popularise* the administration I think we may safely calculate on giving you our 28 votes.[4] What has been done has been effected by a small
body of active men against great difficulties & unnatural discourage-
ments. We have had to contend not only with open enemies but with
professed friends, with post offices & custom houses & nearly all the
array of government patronage.[5] Such a state of things I venture to say
was never before witnessed. The 4th of July was thought to be a convenient opportunity to make the first show of our strength. Every
exertion of course was used to swell our ranks & give an imposing
appearance. I made great sacrifices individually of business & feelings
&c. and consented to deliver the Oration. But *one* officer under the
government subscribed to the dinner.[6] *Not one* attended the oration.
Mr. Walsh employed all his energies to decry our proceedings & prevent their being generally attended & afterwards did his best to turn
them into ridicule.[7] When I say that I made a sacrifice of feelings in
consenting to deliver the oration I mean plainly that I had made up
my mind to take no further public part in support of the administration seeing from abundant evidences that the road to its civilities was
in an opposite direction. No professional man in this community Can
take an active part against Gen. J. without the risk of incurring enmities which may be almost ruinous to his business. I perceived that
professional men were engaged at enormous fees to assist in U. S.
causes here with no other pretensions than such as public disclaimers
of attachment to the administration and contemptuous indifference
about the attempts to support them, while I with very slender means

and an increasing family was incurring the risk I have mentioned of wasting valuable time & professional hopes in the thankless office of their friend & advocate. I had determined therefore to leave the Admn to such support as it could derive from its District Attorney[8] & his Coadjutor Mr Randall,[9] from the Post Master[10] the Collector[11] the Naval officer[12] &c &c.— but the peculiar situation of things on the 4th of July & the urgent application of the Committee of Arrangement[13] made me deviate in that instance from the resolution I had adopted— The result of the celebration was very satisfactory— It produced an impression which will have a decided effect hereafter. I send a copy of my oration.[14] You will find it rather an argumentation than a declamatory performance— I have a thorough contempt for the flourish & bombast generally prevailing in 4th of July orations & I think I have probably gone into the opposite extreme.

Notwithstanding the cold blooded hostility of Walsh the P. was with him & his friends the greater part of the time he was here[15]— Yours very faithfully & sincerely.   T. I. WHARTON

ALS. DLC-HC (DNA, M212, R2).
[1] See above, Israel P. Hutchinson to Clay, April 24, 1827.   [2] Randall Hutchinson was at this time prothonotary of the district court of the city and county of Philadelphia.
[3] See above, Toasts and Speech at Lexington Public Dinner, July 12, 1827.   [4] Cf. above, Clay to Brown, March 27, 1827, note.   [5] See above, Clay to Jones, January 23, 1827; Degrand to Clay, February 8, 1827; McGiffin to Clay, February 19, 1827; Crowninshield to Clay, March 14, 1827; Clay to Crowninshield, March 18, 1827; Webster to Clay, March 25, 1827; Binns to Clay, April 28, 1827.   [6] John Binns, a publisher of the laws, had attended the dinner; no "officer under the government" has been identified among those prominent in the proceedings.   [7] Robert Walsh, Jr., had published several editorials, both before and after the occasion, lamenting "the plan of meeting under party-titles and banners on the anniversary of . . . National Independence." Philadelphia *National Gazette*, July 3, 7 (quoted), 1827.   [8] Charles Ingersoll.
[9] Josiah Randall.   [10] Richard Bache.   [11] William Jones.   [12] Philip S. Markley.   [13] Not identified.   [14] *An Oration, Delivered on the Fourth of July, 1827, in the State House in the City of Philadelphia* ([Philadelphia, 1827]).
[15] President Adams had left Washington on July 31 to spend the next two months at Quincy. He had arrived at Philadelphia late on August 1. His old Federalist friend, Robert Walsh, Jr., had invited him to lodge at his home; but Adams, declining, had agreed instead "to spend with him a part of the evening." After a visit with John Sergeant and his family, Adams had "passed the remainder of the evening at Mr. Walsh's, where . . . [he] met Jos. Hopkinson, N. Biddle, J. Vaughan, and several other persons with whom . . . [he] was not acquainted." Sergeant had accompanied him throughout the evening. In the morning Vaughan had ushered him to the boat. Adams, *Memoirs*, VII, 313.   In March, 1828, Walsh explained to Adams that he retained "a constant preference" for him in the Presidential election but that half his readers were Jacksonian; that he had nothing in common with "those in Philadelphia who plumed themselves upon being the special supporters of the Administration, and particularly with Binns," and accordingly that he discountenanced attacks on Jackson. Adams noted that Walsh's journal exhibited "constantly a hostile spirit to Mr. Clay. . . ." Adams concluded that Walsh was "personally friendly to" himself "from a congeniality of literary tastes and pursuits," but that "his vanity and his ambition . . . and perhaps his interest" drew him to the opposition. *Ibid.*, 492–93.   John Vaughan, English by birth, had come to Philadelphia in 1783 as a wine merchant. The following year he had been elected a member of the American Philosophical Society, founded by Benjamin Franklin in 1743. He was noted primarily for his affiliation with that body, as its vice president, 1785–1787, secretary, 1789–1791, treasurer, 1791–1841, and librarian, 1803–1841.

INSTRUCTIONS AND DISPATCHES   August 3, 1827

To HENRY WHEATON, Copenhagen, no. 3. Transmits "copies of two papers. . . .
One is Mr. Stephen Girard's statement of a claim . . . on the Danish Government
[concerning the case of the ship *Good Friends*]; and the other is a letter from
him in relation to that claim." Notes that the claim "had not before been transmitted to" the State Department and adds: "Additional information concerning
it will probably be personally given to you by Mr. Girard's friend and agent Mr.
[John] Connell." LS. DNA, RG84, Denmark, Official Correspondence, 1827–1835
(MR14, frame 333). Copies, in DNA, RG59, Dip. Instr., vol. 11, p. 370 (M77, R6);
DLC-HC (DNA, M212, R8).

Girard's letter to Clay (not found), dated July 30, 1827, had been acknowledged
by Daniel Brent on August 1, 1827. Copy, in DNA, RG59, Dom. Letters, vol. 22,
p. 18 (M40, R20).

Stephen Girard, born at Bordeaux, France, in 1750, had been a shipmaster in
the French merchant service, 1773–1776, had settled in Philadelphia about 1779,
and engaged in foreign trade. Becoming wealthy through operations in commerce, banking, insurance, and real estate, he strongly supported both the first
and the second United States Banks and had himself continued the former as a
private venture under the name, Bank of Stephen Girard. He died at Philadelphia
in 1831, leaving over $6,000,000 in trust for the foundation of Girard College.

The *Good Friends*, a vessel built at Bordeaux in 1786, "of the capacity of about
500 hogsheads of tobacco," had been seized under Napoleonic decrees in 1809 and
carried into Norway. The estimated losses, with interest, by 1826 totalled $68,-
529.93. Under the treaty of indemnity signed by Wheaton with Denmark in 1830,
Girard's executors were awarded $10,500, less than a quarter of the actual expenses,
without interest, incurred in obtaining the release of this vessel and another
seized at about the same time. John Bach McMaster, *The Life and Times of
Stephen Girard, Mariner and Merchant* (2 vols.; Philadelphia, 1918), I, 164; II,
86–98, 401–402.

From VINCENT GRAY, Havana. Reports that the schooner *"Mary and Eleanor,"* detained at Havana from July 15 to July 28, has been released free of costs and
charges, "with the right of prosecuting the Passenger who has been the cause of
her arrest, for detention and Damages." This, Gray has "advised against: as the
whole dispute on board, originated from their [o]wn silly and childish conduct
toward the passenger, a crazy man." States that the Captain General (Francisco
Dionisio Vives) acted in proper and friendly manner towards the Americans,
"who were not worthy of the [a]ttention bestowed upon them," and that he "never
saw such a set, in any vessel before." Notes that the schooner sailed that morning
for Charleston, without the captain and crew. ALS. DNA, RG59, Cons. Disp.,
Havana (M-T20, R5). Received August 14.

The vessel, identified in news accounts as the *Mary Eleanor*, under a Captain
Smith of Alexandria, not further identified, had been held at Havana after a
voyage from St. Iago de Cuba, during which a scuffle had ensued when a Spanish
passenger, unable to pay for his passage, had requested to be carried closer to
shore off the Isle of Pines, a notorious pirate haunt. Upon the captain's refusal,
the passenger had begun signaling to a vessel near the shore. The captain had
apparently threatened to fire on the passenger, and the latter had thereupon attacked with a harpoon. Overpowered, the Spaniard had been carried in chains to
Havana, where the captain had been arrested for cruelty. He and the crew, after
detention a few days, had been freed, but the captain did not rejoin the vessel.
Charleston Courier, August 4, 16, 1827.

From HENRY CHIPMAN, Detroit. Acknowledges "receipt of a Commission as one of the Judges of the Michigan Territory." LS. DNA, RG59, Acceptances and Orders for Commns. (M-T645, R2). Published in Carter (ed.), *Territorial Papers*, XI, 1110.

The commission had been sent by Daniel Brent, "in the absence of the Secretary," July 19, 1827. Copy, in DNA, RG59, Dom. Letters, vol. 22, p. 3 (M40, R20).

From WILLIAM MAUL, Washington (1). Encloses a letter received from a friend of his sister. Recalls that he told Clay "the cause of" his "being detained so long in the Western Country, and that" he had been ill "and not abble [*sic*] to travel." ALS. DNA, RG59, Misc. Letters (M179, R65).

The enclosure (ALS), written at Evansville (Indiana), December 28, 1826, by J(oshua) V. Robinson at the request of "Mrs Vernon" (presumably Maul's sister), contains information on the death of William W. Vernon, a description of the destitute condition of his family, and a plea that Maul come to assist the widow and children move "back" or, if that were impossible, "to furnish her with money sufficient to pay her expences [*sic*] on the way." Robinson and Vernon had both been listed as residents of Vanderburgh County, Indiana, in the Census of 1820 and were trustees of the town of Evansville during the early 1820's.

From WILLIAM MAUL, Washington (2). States that (Daniel) Brent has informed him that Clay had said he "had made or, would *make sum other appointment*" in his place. Continues: "As for you Sir I have had Very little to do with and during my absence my pay was stoped wich is a thing I never herd of before, but I have told you in one or too of my letters [see above, this date] the cause of my being detained in the Western Country so long—" Asserts that he has "been in a manner raised in the Office," with little opportunity for schooling, "and also deprived of a trade," and refers to Brent for substantiation of "every thing" he has said. Concludes: "If I am dismissed from your office Sir god only knows what the family will do, but if I had the money I would leave this part of the World and see if it was possible for me to get sum situation wich would get me a *livelyhood*." ALS. DNA, RG59, Misc. Letters (M179, R65).

Maul was replaced as assistant messenger and watchman by William H. Prentiss, a native of the District of Columbia who had been employed in 1822 at B. O. Tyler's Lottery Office. Prentiss was retained in the State Department at a salary of $350 annually from 1827 to 1833.

To James Erwin

Dear Sir   Washn. 4 Aug. 1827.

I recd. today your favor of the 17h. Ulto. I have forwarded[1] the bill which it inclosed for $400 on account of my Engine, and I hope it will be paid.

I found, on my arrival here last tuesday (the 31st Ulto) Mrs. Clay; Theodore, John, Martin Duralde and H. Clay Hart[2] (who had preceded me a few days) all well. James[3] accompanied me. So that we have now quite a smart family. Theodore will however diminish it in a few days.[4] We should be delighted to have yourself, Anne and children[5] with us (and our house affords abundance of accommodation) but we know not when we dare indulge the hope of that gratification.

I have not yet certainly heard the name of the member of Congress who, Genl. Jackson says, gave him the information contained in his letter to Beverley.[6] If I am to credit what I see and hear, my Speech[7] near Lexington has surpassed, in its effects, all my anticipations. The General is believed to be irrecoverably prostrate. That such ought to be the effect of *his* letter I know, and I hope such will ultimately be its effect. Some suppose that Genl. Jackson will be impelled by his passions into an instaneous [*sic*] challenge of me. There is no reasoning on *passion*, but I shall be prepared for any and every honorable event.

Mrs. Clay unites with me in love to yourself, Anne and our grand children. Yr's affectionately   H CLAY
James Erwin Esq

ALS. CtY-A. Conger Goodyear Collection.
  [1] Below, Clay to Frothingham, this date.   [2] Theodore Wythe Clay; John Morrison Clay; Martin Duralde III; Henry Clay Hart.   [3] James Brown Clay.   [4] Cf. below, Clay to Erwin, September 3, 1827.   [5] Julia D. and Henry Clay Erwin.   [6] See above, Smith to Clay, August 1, 1827.   [7] See above, July 12, 1827.

To Samuel Frothingham

Sir: Washington, August 4th, 1827.
    Enclosed I transmit to you an accepted bill for four hundred dollars, drawn by Walter Brashear on Howard & Merry, of Boston.[1] When payment is made be pleased to advise me thereof. If it should be protested, which is not anticipated, be pleased, without delay, to transmit a notice of the protest by the first mail, to Mr. Brashear, at New Orleans, and another to me, at this place. I am your obedient servant,
                                        H. CLAY

Cashier of the Office of the Bank of the U. States, at Boston.

LS. DLC-HC, Misc. Papers, United States: Finance (DNA, M212, R9).
  [1] Cf. above, Erwin to Clay, July 17, 1827.

To Richard W. Meade

Dear Sir   (Private & Confidential)   Washn. 4 Aug. 1827
    There is a young man, a nephew of Mrs. Clay, a Midshipman who, by a series of indiscretions, has at last got himself into Jail for debt in Philadelphia. His name is Jno. S. Hart.[1] I think myself that he had better remain there a while to bring him back to his senses, provided he is in no danger of losing his health or being thrown into the Felons' apartments. He writes[2] that he is under that danger;—that he now lives in the family of a Mr. Ruff, (who I understand to be the keeper of the Jail) but that if he cannot pay his board, amounting to about

$20 per month, he will be put out of the debtors Apartments &c. Now his pay as a Midshipman would pay that sum, and I therefore can not comprehend how he should be exposed to that danger.

The object of this letter is to ask the favor of you to ascertain the truth of his case; and if it be *necessary*, in your opinion, to advance any sum, not exceeding twenty five dollars, to pay his board, and prevent his removal from the debtors apartments. I have no means of his in my hands, nor any instructions from the nearer connexions of this young man. It is useless to trouble you with a long detail of his irregularities; but I am satisfied that a sense of suffering can alone recall him to his duty. I do not wish therefore any thing to be done for him, at my instance, but to preserve his health, or to guard him against the contamination of vicious persons. Your friend & ob. Servt
R. W. Meade Esq   H CLAY

ALS. PHC-Charles Roberts Autograph Collection. Addressed to Meade at "Walnut Street   Philadelphia."
[1] Cf. above, Key to Clay, August 2, 1827.   [2] No letter has been found.

From Timothy Wiggin

London, August 4, 1827.
To the Honorable Henry Clay, State Department, Washington.

Sir:—I wrote to you on the 30th ult., and requested you and your co-trustees to pay to the General Theological Seminary in New York, and the College at Hartford, £160,14*s*.6*d*., out of the Ohio Fund, that sum having been paid to it in error. I have now to confirm the error, but have also the pleasure to request you not to pay the money over without further advice from me, as a noble peer has given £100 to the Ohio Institution,[1] and I have hopes of raising the remaining £60. At present the donation is anonymous, but I believe it was made by Lord Goderich.[2] I am sorry to trouble you so frequently in this matter; but rely on a continuance of that kindness which you manifested from the first towards the good cause. I remain, truly, your obedient servant,
TIMOTHY WIGGIN.

Chase, *Reminiscences*, II, 568.   [1] Kenyon College.
[2] Frederick John Robinson, Viscount Goderich, first Earl of Ripon.

INSTRUCTIONS AND DISPATCHES   August 4, 1827

From ALEXANDER H. EVERETT, Madrid, no. 84. Notes the quiescent state of "public affairs ... at this Legation": "All disposition to take into serious consideration the great question of the Colonies seems to have ceased with the danger of an immediate invasion of . . . Cuba [cf. above, Everett to Clay, January 1, April 5, June 2, 9, 1826; Poinsett to Clay, September 23, 1826; Poinsett to Clay, May 12, 1827]. The two subjects of Commerce and Indemnities . . . have been urged . . . for about two years; and it would be . . . useless, not to say undignified, to pursue the same course any longer. The affairs of the Quarantine laws and the Colombian Privateer [cf. above, Everett to Clay, March 19, April 7, June 4, July 4, 1827] will probably be satisfactorily settled within a short time and there will then be no subject of much interest requiring immediate attention." Requests of the President, through Clay, a six-month leave of absence, beginning in the spring. LS. DNA, RG59, Dip. Disp., Spain, vol. 27 (M31, R28). Received October 11.

MISCELLANEOUS LETTERS   August 4, 1827

From BARING BROTHERS AND COMPANY, London. State that, on the advice of Albert Gallatin, they have honored a draft of Beaufort T. Watts for £200, dated June 1, but that they will "discontinue similar payments in future unless the needful credit be opened by . . . [Clay's] Department." LS. DNA, RG59, Misc. Letters (M179, R65).

On September 19, 1827, Daniel Brent acknowledged, "by direction of the Secretary," receipt of this letter and informed Baring Brothers of the "letter . . . just . . . written to Mr. Watts . . ." (see below, Clay to Watts, September 18, 1827). Copy, in DNA, RG59, Cons. Instr., vol. 2, pp. 443–44 (M78, R2).

Check to John Dickinson

6 Aug. 1827

Pay to John Dickingson Esqr. or order Twelve hundred dollars out of the deposit made to my credit by Genl. William Marks.
Cashr. of the Off. of B. U. States Washington City[1]   H. CLAY
$1.200—

ALS. DLC-TJC (DNA, M212, R16). Endorsed: "Jno. Dickinson" (not identified).
[1] Richard Smith.

To Joseph Gales, Jr., and William W. Seaton

6h. Aug. [1827]

Mr. Clay's Compliments to Mess. Gales and Seaton, with the letter from Wheeling inclosed.[1] He is obliged to them for the friendly motive which induced them to consult him in regard to its publication.

There are no more respectable persons than the three gentlemen who sign it; and the transaction which they relate is correctly related, at least substantially so.

I have no particular wish that it shd. be published. But I am inclined to think that it had better be published as that will be in conformity with the wishes of the gentlemen. Although the misrepresentations, which it corrects, have not found any place in the N. Intellr. they have nevertheless reached the public, and the correction may obtain the same destinction [sic] through the Intellr.

AN. KyU. Addressed on attached sheet: "Mess Gales & Seaton   Present."
[1] The letter, published in the Washington Daily National Intelligencer, August 8,

1827, had been written from Wheeling, July 28, addressed to Gales and Seaton by A(lexander) Caldwell, Moses W. Chapline, and Richard McClure. It responded to criticism in the Jackson press that Clay, knowing that Beverley had sent Noah Zane his letter from Jackson (see above, Clay to Hammond, June 25, 1827, note) as *"a private document, lent upon a positive assurance of the sacredness, and as a matter of favor,"* had imposed upon Zane in taking a copy and publishing it. Washington *United States Telegraph*, August 1, 1827, reprinting letter from Beverley to Moses Dawson, editor of the Cincinnati *Advertiser*, July 12, 1827. The Wheeling correspondents asserted that Zane had sent word asking that Clay call upon him when he arrived at Wheeling and had shown Clay the Jackson letter in their presence, that Zane had offered to furnish Clay with a copy, that McClure had suggested that the copy could be prepared before Clay left Wheeling and had added that he thought the covering letter from Beverley to Zane should also be copied, and that Clay had requested that both copies be attested.

Chapline, born in Virginia and a veteran of the War of 1812, was a prominent Wheeling lawyer.

From Thomas Finley

Dear Sir,   Baltimore 6th. Augt. 1827

Having occasion to address you an official letter[1] to day, I avail myself of this occasion to offer you my congratulations on your happy and well timed speech at Lexington[2]— This is in my estimation, one of the best efforts you have ever made, and I feel persuaded that it will produce a powerful effect— You have said every thing that is necessary to be said. you have now the "vantage ground" and it would be useless to say another word until there is another movement at the "Hermitage"—

So far as I have heard opinions expressed, your friends are delighted with this speech—and I am confident the opposition have not met with any thing to annoy them so much—

The prospect for the administration in this state is every thing that could be wished— and I know that in many districts in Pennsylvania it gains strength daily— and there are strong reasons to believe that before the election for President comes on, this great state will be found on the side of the administration— Or should the opposition obtain a victory, they will obtain it after a hard fought battle.[3]— I would like to see a new Republican paper, friendly to the administration established in Philadelphia[4]— my reasons for this I will take another opportunity to detail—

I beg you to be assured of my respect and good wishes—
Honl Henry Clay   THO FINLEY

ALS. DLC-HC (DNA, M212, R2). Endorsed on cover: "Private and confidential."
[1] Not found. The letter presented an inquiry concerning whether the Government would pay the costs due in its case against Francis LeBaron. Daniel Brent, replying on August 9, informed Finley that the order discharging LeBaron had not mentioned the costs of the suit and that in such case it was understood that the petitioner bore them. Copy, in DNA, RG59, Dom. Letters, vol. 22, p. 21 (M40, R20). LeBaron, a native of Massachusetts, who had been commissioned a surgeon's mate in the United States Navy in 1800, from which service he had resigned in 1802, had been named apothecary general of the Army in 1813 and honorably discharged from the latter service in 1821. During the subsequent years he had been endeavoring to settle his accounts, on which he was charged with a balance due of $11,555.92 in 1821. *Sen. Docs.*, 17 Cong., 1 Sess., no.

36, p. 8. Record of his discharge proceedings has not been found. ² See above, July 12, 1827. ³ Cf. above, Clay to Brown, March 27, 1827, note. ⁴ Cf. below, Johnston to Clay, September 14, 1827, note.

From Jules de Wallenstein

Dear Sir;   Philadelphia Aug. 6th. 1827.

In taking the liberty to enclose a letter for Baron de Maltitz and begging your pardon for the trouble I give you, I shd. be sorry not to improve this opportunity by tendering to you my sincere congratulations on the exalted testimonials of attachment, esteem, gratitude and admiration, which have been dispensed to you so abundantly, during your late excursion,¹ and which have found countless responsive voices in every part where I was. Every where, indeed, I had the pleasure of observing how highly your services to your country are appreciated. Had I had the honour to accompany you in your journey, I might perhaps have shewn you, better than I can express, how sincerely I rejoice in your merited success; but I could not have felt more than I did, while I accompanied you only with my best wishes.

Should you have news respecting Baron de Krudener's departure for America,² I wd. esteem it as a new proof of your extreme kindness, if you wd. relieve me from the complete ignorance in wh. I am in this respect. I intend to remain here some weeks, and wd. feel happy to receive your commands, & not less to see you, before my return to Washington.

Be pleased to accept the repeated assurances of the utmost respect with which I have the honour to be, Dear Sir, Your obliged and faithful obedient Servt.   WALLENSTEIN
To the Honble. Henry Clay Secretary of State.

ALS. DLC-HC (DNA, M212, R2).   ¹ Cf. above, Clay to Adams, June 23, 1827.
² Cf. above, Middleton to Clay, July 30, 1826.

INSTRUCTIONS AND DISPATCHES   August 6, 1827

From ALBERT GALLATIN, London, no. 101. Reports that at the conference, on August 2, "at which the two Conventions finally agreed on the 27th. ulto. [cf. above, Gallatin to Clay, July 28, 1827] were to be signed," he was told that "those instruments had not yet been returned by the King's Advocate [William Rae—cf. above, Gallatin to Clay, July 29, 1827]," and, instead, the conferees "discussed for three hours" Gallatin's "informal Projet of Convention, for carrying the 5th Article of the treaty of Ghent [cf. above, Gallatin to Clay, June 5, 1827, no. 82]. . . ." States that "On the 4th." he "was invited to meet to day" but, later, received a note requesting postponement to August 7—a delay that he suggests may be "the consequence of the critical situation of Mr. Canning, who has had a relapse [cf. below, Gallatin to Clay, August 9, 1827]. . . ." Refers to the impossibility of calculating "the consequences of his death both here and as to the policy of this Country towards other foreign Nations," and expresses an opinion that "As regards the United States there may be delay in concluding the minor arrangements now under consideration; but no immediate change on important points can be expected, whoever may be Mr Canning's successor." Adds, in a postscript: "5. o'clock—I have just returned from the foreign office. The two Conventions are signed, but cannot be forwarded by this packet. No hope of Mr Canning. Our negotiations are suspended. A. G." ALS. DNA, RG59, Dip. Disp., Great Britain, vol. 34 (M30, R30). Copy, in MHi-Adams Papers, Letters Recd. (MR482); published in Manning (arr.), *Diplomatic Correspondence . . . Canadian Relations*, II, 605–606. Received September 10.

From ALBERT GALLATIN, London, no. 102. Transmits "a Convention, extending indefinitely, but liable to be rescinded at the will of either party, the Commercial Convention of 1815 between the United States and Great Britain" (above, II, 57–59). Notes that the new Convention "was signed this day" (cf. above, Gallatin to Clay, no. 101). Refers to protocols of certain "Conferences for the progress of the Negotiation" and elaborates on discussions of some of the points at issue. ALS. DNA, RG59, Dip. Disp., Great Britain, vol. 34 (M30, R30). Copy, in MHi-Adams Papers Letters Recd. (MR482); published in *American State Papers, Foreign Relations*, VI, 689–91, with the enclosure on p. 639. Received September 16.

From JOSEPH PULIS, JR., Malta. Notes the arrival "of two English line battle Ships, . . . sent as a reinforcement of the Squadron in the Mediterranean in consequence of the alliance signed in London the 6th. of July ultimo . . ." (cf. above, Brown to Clay, July 12, 1827). States that "Yesterday the Java passed through this channel" and "proceeded on to Smyrna." Reports that he has been named Danish "Consul in these possessions." LS. DNA, RG59, Cons. Disp., Malta, vol. 1 (M-T218, R-T1). Received October 9.

The document is dated: "Malta the 6th of July 1827." The dating is here altered on the basis of the internal reference to the treaty and the evidence (above, Heap to Clay, August 2, 1827) that the *Java* was at Tunis, on its outward voyage, on July 30 through August 1.

MISCELLANEOUS LETTERS   August 6, 1827

From BARTOW AND BRANNAN, Washington. Request "written permission" for "free access to the Models, drawings specifications &c. deposited in the Patent Office" to prepare material for a proposed publication, *The North American Museum of Arts and Sciences*. LS. DNA, RG59, Misc. Letters (M179, R65).

Endorsed on verso: "Permission granted. H. C." Clay provided the requested written permission in a reply dated August 14. Copy, in DNA, RG59, Dom. Letters (M40, R20).

Bartow and Brannan were booksellers and stationers on Pennyslvania Avenue, Washington. John Brannan, the Washington partner, was also at this time a messenger in the Pension Office of the War Department. The other partner was probably William A. Bartow, a bookseller of New York City.

In November Brannan and Uriah Brown issued a prospectus for a new periodical under the title *Polyanthist, or American Museum of Arts and Sciences*. Washington *Daily National Journal*, November 23, 1827; *Daily National Intelligencer*, December 5, 1827; and cf. below, Testimonial, ca. November 22, 1827. Ichabod Lord Skinner, principal of a girls school and publisher of the *Columbian Register* in Washington, finally took over the venture and issued the publication as *The*

American Journal of Improvements in the Useful Arts, and Mirror of the Patent Office of the United States, dating from the beginning of 1828.

From CHARLES HAY, Navy Department. Transmits "copies of a correspondence between Commo. Charles G. Ridgely, Commanding the U: S: Naval forces in the West Indies, and David Porter Esqr. Commanding the Naval forces of the Republic of Mexico, the originals of which were received this morning." States that he sends them for Clay's "examination, in consequence of the reference, contained in the reply of the Mexican Commander, to a correspondence, touching the subject, now in the possession of the Minister of the Mexican Government [Pablo Obregón]." Asks whether Clay thinks the originals should be forwarded to the Secretary of the Navy (Samuel L. Southard), now at "White Sulphur Springs, Greenbriar County, Va." ALS. DNA, RG59, Misc. Letters (M179, R65).

Clay replied, on the same day, acknowledging receipt of the enclosures and advising that "a Copy of the correspondence" be sent to Southard. LS, in DNA, RG45, Misc. Letters Recd., 1827, vol. 5, p. 66.

The enclosures, both written at Pensacola, July 13, 1827, include a letter from Ridgely informing Porter of the Spanish charge "that the neutrality of the U States has been violated at Thompson's Island by the Mexican Naval Forces. . . , to the injury of . . . the Commerce of Spain" (cf. above, Rivas y Salmon to Clay, May 31, June 12, 1827) and the latter's denial of such violation. Porter continued: "I have been long aware that complaints have been made by the Spanish Authorities of the Island of Cuba against me, they were communicated to me by the Collector of the Port of Key West [William Pinkney], to which I have replied, and the Mexican Minister at Washington is furnished with a copy of the correspondence thereof." Porter stated that he would leave Key West if he were officially informed by the United States that the Mexican naval force was not welcome there and if he were "also officially informed that the blockade . . . [was] raised, and the Squadron now in pursuit of . . . [him had] retired to a Spanish port, and the sea left free. . . ."

To René Auguste Chouteau and Others

Washington, D. C., 7th Aug., 1827.

GENTLEMEN: Your obliging letter, under date at St. Louis, the 10th ultimo, and addressed to me at Lexington, having arrived there, after my departure for this city, has been received by me at this place. I pray your acceptance of my warmest acknowledgments for the invitation which it conveys, and for the friendly sentiments which have prompted it. The value of this testimonial is greatly enhanced by the high respectability of the gentlemen who have done me the honor to tender it, several of whom have been personally known to me for many years, and others by reputation a long time.

It would have afforded me very great satisfaction to have visited the State of Missouri, endeared to me by many circumstances, but especially by that to which you have been pleased to advert. I have long wished to see its commercial metropolis, and my regret at not having been able, during my late excursion to the West,[1] to gratify that wish, is much increased since the receipt of your very kind letter. The approbation, gentlemen, which you have been good enough to express, in too flattering terms, of my public conduct, is among the best rewards of past, and one of the highest incentives to future exertion. The General Administration will also derive much encouragement from the fact, of having such citizens as you among those who do justice to the motives which animate it.

With my best wishes for your happiness and prosperity, I am, with great respect, your obedient servant.   H. CLAY.

Col. AUGUSTE CHOUTEAU, for himself, And the other gentlemen who subscribed the letter, to which the above is an answer.

Washington *Daily National Intelligencer,* September 20, 1827. ALI draft, dated August 6, 1827, in DLC-HC (DNA, M212, R2).
[1] Cf. above, Clay to Erwin, June 3, 1827.

Order on Washington Office, Bank of the United States

Office of Discount and Deposit,   WASHINGTON, Aug 7. 1827
PAY to Jos Vance *or bearer, the nett proceeds of* his *note of* Two thousand dollars *discounted this day to my credit.*   H CLAY
$1.978 67/100

DS, partially printed. DLC-TJC (DNA, M212, R16). Cf. above, Order, June 5, 1827.

From John H. Farnham

Hon Henry Clay
My dear Sir,   Salem Indiana Aug. 7. 1827.
I beg the liberty of communicating to you and through you to the President a suggestion which I trust will find an apology in the sincerity of the feelings which prompt it. You are well aware that no inconsiderable quantity of land in this and the adjoining states, on which one or more payments have been made, has become forfeited to the Government.[1] The Legislature of this State at their last Session unanimously adopted Resolutions soliciting (among other things) Congress to allow to the holders of Certificates, which had been forfeited, the value of the payments thus lost; either in the lands forfeited, or other public lands.[2] The liberal policy heretofore pursued by government has authorised and encouraged the expectation that Congress would ultimately allow to all persons, who had thus lost their money, or to their assees. the value of the same. Hundreds, I may say thousands, have cherished the belief that a parental and indulgent government would never accept or retain the money of its citizens without allowing therefor a full equivalent. I beg leave to state that many of the friends of the Administration in this state have publicly expressed a confident belief that the Executive would recommend to

Congress a favorable consideration of this unfortunate class of the purchasers of public Lands. It would be to them a most gratifying & cheering circumstance to realize their fond predictions—to see this act of *liberality & justice combined* sanctioned & enforced by the President's recommendation.[3] They would revolt at proposing themselves and regret seeing recommended by the Chief Executive of the Nation any measure of the kind not founded on the broad basis of enlightened Equity. Believing the proposition above hinted at to be thus founded and convinced it would furnish copious and grateful relief to large numbers of our citizens and be duly appreciated by them, I avail myself of the honor of your acquaintance to convey to you the suggestion. Enclosed I send a copy of the Resolution of the General Assembly unanimously adopted at their last session and have the honor to remain With the highest consideration Your most obedient servant

JOHN H FARNHAM

P.S.   Permit me to say that the intelligence of Indiana is on the right side of all important questions— All that we want is a palpable appeal to the sober senses of those, who are governed more by *sensation* than *reflection*.

ALS. MHi-Adams Papers, Letters Recd. (MR482). Farnham, born in Massachusetts in 1791, had been graduated from Harvard University with an A.B. degree in 1811 and an M.A. in 1821. He was renowned as a lawyer and speaker, as a strong proponent of public education by free schools, and as one of the incorporators and first corresponding secretary of the Indiana Historical Society, founded in 1831. He died of cholera during the epidemic of 1833.

1 For evidence of Clay's earlier interest in this subject, see above, III, 47, 50, 52.

2 The resolutions, referred to the Committee on Public Lands of the House of Representatives on February 26, 1827, and on the following day ordered to be printed (*House Docs.*, 19 Cong., 2 Sess., no. 117), had incorporated two proposals. The first had called for a further extension "in the time of payment on all lands now forfeited, or liable to forfeiture," as a continuation of the relief to public land entrants first authorized by the act of March 2, 1821 (3 *U. S. Stat.*, 612–14), and extended by acts of May 18, 1824, and May 4, 1826 (4 *U. S. Stat.*, 24–25, 158–59–cf. above, Ewing to Clay, August 6, 1825, note), which were now scheduled to expire on July 4, 1827. The second resolution encompassed the idea presented by Farnham, providing that those public lands entrants who had made one or more payments, then forfeited their lands, or were about to forfeit them, might have "a privilege in the nature of a *right* of pre-emption . . . to repurchase the same, or other lands of equal value, at a sum which, added to . . . former payments, . . . [should] make the amount per acre not to exceed the *minimium* price of Congress lands. . . ." Both proposals were enacted by the Twentieth Congress. The first, continuing the force of the former legislation until July 4, 1829, was approved March 21, 1828 (4 *U.S. Stat.*, 259–60). The second measure required issuance of certificates for amounts paid "in all cases where one twentieth of the purchase money . . . [had been] deposited and forfeited to the United States" and acceptance of these certificates "as cash in payment of any public land" sold by the United States Government in the State or Territory in which the original purchase had been made.   3 Adams, whose comments in his *Memoirs*, VII, 187–88, on November 27, 1826, indicate that he recognized the political nature of the issue of relief to public land entrants and that he was not sympathetic to the proposals, nevertheless, in his annual message of December 4, 1827, called upon Congress to extend the term for payments under the act of March 2, 1821, and also submitted "to their consideration, in the same spirit of equity, the remission under proper discriminations, of the forfeitures of partial payments on account of purchases of the public lands, so far as to allow of their application to other payments." Richardson (comp.), *A Compilation of the Messages and Papers of the Presidents*, II, 391.

From Jared Sparks

Dear Sir,   Boston, Aug. 7th. 1827

Mr Pitkin[1] has written me, desiring permission to consult the Diplomatic Correspondence in my possession, with a view to make selections for historical purposes. He informs me, also, that he had written to you on the same subject.[2] I take the liberty to send you enclosed a copy of my reply,[3] which I trust you will approve. Since the papers are now in the way of publication, there would seem no good reason for bringing any part of them before the public, in any manner different from that pointed out by the resolution of Congress, even if the tenor of our contract did not preclude such a measure.

I shall spare no pains to do justice to the undertaking. In the spring I contemplate a short tour to Europe where I shall make an effort to procure such materials, as will throw light on that part of our revolutionary history, embraced in the Diplomatic Correspondence. I shall endeavor particularly to obtain access, as far as practicable, to such diplomatic papers in England, Holland, France, & Spain, as relate to our differences with Great Britain, and the acknowledgement [sic] of our independence by the European powers. This object may perhaps be wholly unattainable, but I will remit no exertion to accomplish it.

Permit me, Sir, to congratulate you on your return to Washington, and on the improved condition of your health, as stated in the newspapers.[4]

With perfect respect & sincere regard, I am, Sir, your friend, & most obt. sert.   JARED SPARKS
Hon. Henry Clay.

P.S.   An article on your "Speeches" is in hand by a gentleman well qualified for the task, which I intend shall appear if possible in the October number of the North American Review, though it may be deferred till January.[5]   J. S.

ALS. DLC-HC (DNA, M212, R2).   [1] Timothy Pitkin.
[2] See above, Pitkin to Clay, June 23, 1827.   [3] Not found.   [4] See, *e.g.*, Washington *Daily National Journal*, August 2, 1827.   [5] See above, Sparks to Clay, April 9, 1827, note. The unsigned review article appeared in the October, 1827, issue of the *North American Review*, XXV (New Series, XVI), 425–51. On the authorship by Edward Everett, cf. below, Sparks to Clay, August 25, 1827.

INSTRUCTIONS AND DISPATCHES   August 7, 1827

From ALBERT GALLATIN, London, no. 103. Transmits "a Convention, concluded yesterday [cf. above, Gallatin to Clay, August 6, 1827, no. 101]. . . , renewing indefinitely but liable to be annulled at the will of either party, the third Article of the Convention of 1818" (cf. above, II, 611n). Summarizes the successive stages of the negotiation. Concludes: "I beg leave here to observe that some of the most cogent motives, for having made the agreement in 1818, have now ceased to operate. The Country is still now, as it was then, almost exclusively occupied by the British traders. But the claim of the United States had not at that time been strengthened by the acquisition of that of Spain [cf. above, II, 678n, 816n]. The British Plenipotentiaries, unable for that very reason to sustain the British claim against the United States by the Nootka Convention [cf. above, Clay to Gallatin, June 19, 1826, note 29], did then assert a right of absolute Sovereignty, founded, as they said, on prior discoveries and Indian purchases, but which is no longer affirmed. They had also declared, that the order given by the British Government but not yet carried into effect for the restitution of Astoria [cf. above, Clay to King, May 10, 1825, note 19], had issued under an erroneous impression that that establishment had been captured, instead of having been, as they asserted, voluntarily transferred. For all those reasons it appeared necessary that, in a Convention, which established the 49th parallel of latitude as the boundary between the two Countries as far as the Stony Mountains, some provision should be inserted, recognizing the existence of the claims of the United States to the territory West of those Mountains. As there was no apparent reason, why that boundary should not, as the northern limit of Louisiana, have been extended to the Pacific Ocean [cf. above, Gallatin to Clay, November 16, 1826], absolute silence with respect to that territory might, under all the circumstances of the case, have had a tendency to weaken the claim of the United States.

"A renewal of the Agreement is no longer necessary for that object. But, in addition to the reasons, that were assigned in the course of the negotiation, in favour of continuing it in force, there is still one peculiar to the United States. They claim exclusive Sovereignty over a territory, a considerable portion of which is occupied by British traders, whom They could not dispossess without engaging in a war, whom, from their distance and other causes, They are not at this time prepared to remove. It is certainly more eligible that those persons should remain on the territory of the United, [sic] by virtue of a compact and with their consent, than in defiance of their authority.

"Although the prospect of paving the way for a more complete and satisfactory agreement has been one of the motives for concluding this Convention, no commitment has taken place in that respect. And the further observations which I have to submit on that topic . . . will be the subject of a separate despatch." ALS. DNA, RG59, Dip. Disp., Great Britain, vol. 34 (M30, R30). Copy, in MHi-Adams Family Papers, Letters Recd. (MR482); published in *American State Papers, Foreign Relations*, VI, 691–93, with the enclosure on pp. 641–42. Received September 16.

From VINCENT GRAY, Havana. Reports that he has obtained a promise of the release from prison of "James Johnson a native of Baltimore and his associates," captured while serving on board a Colombian privateer (further reference to the incident has not been found); describes their condition; and states that he has made arrangements to clothe them and return them to the United States. ALS. DNA, RG59, Cons. Disp., Havana, vol. 5 (M-T20, R5). Received August 24.

From SAMUEL HODGES, JR., "Consulate United States, Cape de Verd Islands   Villa da Praya, St. Iago." States that, after receiving the letter of May 24 from Clay's Department (see above, Hodges to Clay, March 31, 1827, note), he has appointed "Mr. David S. Ilsley, of Portland, now residing here [not further identified]" to assume the consular duties during Hodges' visit to the United States. ALS. DNA, RG59, Cons. Disp., Santiago, vol. 1 (M-T434, R1). Received October 4.

From BEAUFORT T. WATTS, Bogotá, no. 32. States that "this day the act for calling a Convention, to amend the constitution, with the view to adopt the federal System [cf. above, Watts to Clay, June 27, 1827], has rec'd the sanction of the Executive"; that "Another important act which ... only wants the Executive approbation" will reduce the size of the army; and that the President (Simón Bolívar) is on his way from Cartagena to Bogotá. Encloses newspapers. ALS. DNA, RG59, Dip. Disp., Colombia, vol. 4 (M-T33, R4). Received October 26.

MISCELLANEOUS LETTERS   August 7, 1827

From DANIEL W. COXE, Philadelphia. Explains the basis of a claim against Denmark for overcharge of duties on a cargo of sugar carried by his vessel, the *Thomas Wilson*, and sold in that country in 1810. States that he has authorized John Connell to act in his behalf and asks that (Henry) Wheaton be requested to aid Connell. ALS. DNA, RG59, Misc. Letters (M179, R65).

On August 13, Clay replied to Coxe, acknowledging receipt of this letter and enclosing "under a flying seal" the letter to (Henry) Wheaton, below, August 13, 1827. Copy, in DNA, RG59, Dom. Letters, vol. 22, p. 26 (M40, R20).

Coxe, an agent of Reed and Forde of Philadelphia, had formed a partnership in 1793 to engage in New Orleans trade, by which he amassed a fortune. He had numerous claims pending settlement of the issue of Napoleonic spoliations.

From CHARLES HAY, Navy Department, Washington. Transmits an extract of a communication from Commodore James Biddle, dated June 7, 1827 at Rio de Janeiro, reporting that the Argentine Foreign Minister (Manuel José) García has concluded a treaty and has taken it to Buenos Aires for ratification (cf. above, Forbes to Clay, June 29, 1827). ALS. DNA, RG59, Misc. Letters (M179, R65).

From EDWARD LIVINGSTON, Red Hook, New York. Notes that he has seen Gallatin's latest dispatches (above, Gallatin to Clay, January 4, 1827; February 13, 1827) regarding lighthouses on the Bahama Banks and off the Florida coast. Explains the importance of three resolutions he introduced concerning navigation in the Gulf of Mexico and off the Florida coast, including one which initiated the negotiations with Great Britian on the matter (cf. above, Rush to Clay, May 12, 1825, note). ALS. DNA, RG59, Misc. Letters (M179, R65).

Order on Washington Office, Bank of the United States

Washington August 8th, 1827.
Pay to check on Philadelphia or bearer sixty one dollars and eleven cents   H CLAY
Cashr. of the Off. B. U. States[1]

ADS. DLC-TJC (DNA, M212, R16).   [1] Richard Smith.

From Francis T. Brooke

My Dear Sir   Wanesborough [*sic*] August 8 [1827]
If I had known of your Safe arrival[1] before I left home I Should have congratulated you most cordially on an event so much desired by your friends   I am here on my way to the Springs with my friend Southard,[2]   I have the pleasure to inform you that the Lexington

Speech[3] has worked an unexpected change in public opinion in this quarter of Virginia,   I arrived at Charlottesville on their court day met Barber [sic] Rives & Gordon[4] there with woebegone faces,   Several of the most influential men in the county have now taken a decided an [sic] active part in your behalf,—as they were disappointed in your not coming that way—   my Son Robert[5] had Suggested to them to write you a letter expressing their regret—and at the same time their approbation of your course,   I think it is probable that you will receive one in Some Short time,[6] which will afford you a better opportunity of again repelling the charges against you than by a Dinner Speech as I think it is impossible to improve upon the one at Lexington,   Since I came here this evening Major Gibbon[7] who is here, informed me that he had Seen Genl Porterfield[8] who assured him that the change of public Sentiment Since the arrival of the Speech was miraculous— Rives & Gordon at Charlottesville compelled me to vindicate your conduct, for which I think they felt Some regret, you will excuse me for this hasty and Scribbled Letter by candle light—   if you find occasion to write me direct to the Sulpher [sic] Springs— Yours very Sincerely   F BROOKE

ALS. DLC-HC (DNA, M212, R6). Addressed to Clay at Washington; postmarked: "Waynesboro [Virginia] 9th August."
    [1] Cf. above, Clay to Erwin, August 4, 1827.   [2] Samuel L. Southard. Cf. above, Hay to Clay, August 6, 1827.   [3] Above, July 12, 1827.   [4] Either John Strode Barbour or Philip Pendleton Barbour; William Cabell Rives; William Fitzhugh Gordon. Gordon, a Charlottesville lawyer, had been a Commonwealth attorney in 1812, served in the War of 1812, and was a member of the Virginia House of Delegates, 1818–1829. He was a member of the State Constitutional Convention, 1829–1830, and of Congress from 1830 to 1835.   [5] Robert Spotswood Brooke.   [6] No letter has been found.   [7] James Gibbon.   [8] Robert Porterfield, born in Frederick County, Virginia, in 1752, had served in the American Revolution, had settled in Augusta County, Virginia, at the close of the war, and had been county magistrate there for over 50 years, twice sheriff.

From Joseph F. Caldwell

Palladium Office; Lewisburg Va. 8th Month 8th. 1827
Respected Friend
    Thy speech which was delivered at the Lexington Dinner[1] has been among us near a week; and has had the most astonishing effect. The many admirers of Gen. Jackson in this section of country are very much disatisfied [sic] with his letter to C. Beverly[2] [sic], and more so with the General's address to the public;[3] that they now openly say; they "cannot like J. Q. Adams and they only disliked Henry Clay because he had united his fortunes with those of the Codfish protector; but they [sic] I yesterday heard a man say, who is a great advocate for the claims of General Jackson and who has himself frequently aspired to the confidence of the people of this county *"that rather than submit to a northern policy he would assist in dissolving twine[4] this Union,"* and such are *many* of the friends of Gen. Jackson.

Military men from various sections of the United States who are now at the different Springs in this country say the difference between the General and thyself must result in a duel; I myself belieive [*sic*] it is the only way in which General Jackson would like to settle the affair, but my dear friend, I will *reason* with thee, would it be wise or politic to contend in a duel with a *desperate* man? A man who, when he finds he cannot be made president, and I trust he will find that he cannot be; his whole character declares him to be a man who is more regulated by his passions than his reason, and when he finds from the influence of his letters and thy speeches that he is loosing [*sic*] ground, (and to judge by the people here of those elsewhere,) this he will find to be the case, he will be disposed to appeal to arms to punish and destroy the man who has dared to expose his foibles to the public notice   now, I appeal to thy judgement if *honor* would require it of any man, particularly of Henry Clay to accept a challenge from such a desperado? If thou shouldst fall, those who now support and pretend to admire the General will see nothing in it to blame him with, but if he should fall, thou wilt in consequence, loose the respect of numerous friends; and if I judge correctly of thy conscience, that never erring Monitor will make thy after days miserable indeed

I see it is the intention of some gentleman to publish thy Speeches, I hope the one delivered at Lexington will be included,[5] I intend to have one copy procured to present to my son thy namesake,[6]

I was in hopes thou wouldst have returned home by this place, if thou hadst done so, it was the intention of the citizens of Union & Monroe to have given thee a dinner

I can not bring myself to beleive [*sic*] that Virginia will vote for Jackson in preference to J. Q. Adams   if she does, it will be by a division more equal than has yet ever existed in this State,[7]   Yet I have hopes that she will go for the administration,   she would certainly I think prefer Henry Clay to any others, although a majority of her citizens apparently do not like his principles,   I say apparently for, I am induced to beleive, if we had a convention[8] that would give us an equal representation [*sic*]   such resolutions as friend Giles proposed[9] never would have passed her Legislature

I am disposed to aid with my might & "mite" the principles thou hast so warmly advocated and always thy [*sic*] mayest depend on the friendship and good wishes of Thy Friend   J. F. CALDWELL

ALS. DLC-HC (DNA, M212, R2). Addressed to Clay, "*Private.*"
[1] See above, July 12, 1827.   [2] Cf. above, Clay to Hammond, June 25, 1827.
[3] See above, Smith to Clay, August 1, 1827, note.   [4] Word not clearly legible.
[5] Cf. above, Sparks to Clay, August 7, 1827, note. The speech of July 12 was not included.   [6] Henry Clay Caldwell, of Lewisburg, was nominated an assistant surgeon in the United States Navy in October, 1853, and the appointment approved in January, 1854. He passed the examination for surgeon in May, 1858, but died in December, 1859, before promotion.   [7] Cf. above, Clay to Brown, March 27, 1827. The popular vote in Virginia in 1828 was 26,752 for Jackson; 12,101 for Adams. Schlesinger and Israel (eds.),

History of American Presidential Elections, I [492].   8 Cf. above, Johnson to Clay, March 12, 1827, note.   9 See above, Brooke to Clay, January 31, 1827.

From John Sergeant

Dear Sir,   (Private)   Philada. Augt. 8. 1827.

Your favor of the 4th. inst. was duly received[1]   By this mail, I will forward the last dispatch from Mr. Poinsett and myself.[2] I shall have one more to send you, from myself, with a copy of my note to the several ministers at taking leave and their answers.[3] I beg to trouble you also with a letter for Madrid, which may be forwarded when you write to Mr. Everett.[4]

The final dispatch above mentioned, will not be sent at present, nor probably 'till after I shall have had the pleasure of seeing you.

I have received a printed copy, in a newspaper, of Mr. Poinsett's reply to the State of Vera Cruz. He will no doubt have sent you one.[5]

Every thing in this quarter looks well. Our friends are more numerous than they were, and show a much better countenance. There was an intention, if you had come this way, to give you a very cordial reception,[6] and it would have had a good effect. If you should make us a visit, I think you will find a very satisfactory change. But you will also find some disposition among individuals to complain, not altogether without reason, but still in an immoderate degree. The complaints are of each other, and are owing to the peculiar state of things here. You have probably been already importuned by them.[7] They are no [*sic*] otherwise formidable than as they may plague you, for notwithstanding these little personal feelings, our friends are more hearty than ever, and (which is of no little moment) are cheered by the confident expectation of triumph. Very respectfully and truly yrs.

The Honble Henry Clay.   JOHN SERGEANT.

ALS. DLC-HC (DNA, M212, R2).   1 Not found.
2 Above, June 4, 1827.   3 Cf. above, Sergeant to Clay, August 1, 1827, note.
    4 No subsequent letter to Alexander H. Everett was written from the State Department until that below, November 19, 1827; and no reference to Sergeant's enclosure has been found.   5 Cf. above, Poinsett to Clay, July 8, 1827.   6 Cf. above, Sergeant to Clay, August 1, 1827.   7 Cf. above, Wharton to Clay, August 3, 1827.

From Samuel L. Southard

My dear Sir: Waynesborough,[1] 8 Aug. 1827

You have set the whole world in commotion— Never did one speech[2] produce such an effect— It meets almost universal approbation. & with the wise & good there is no exception. I think they praise it too much—good as it is— a little envy you know is sometimes pardonable. I am informed that Genl. J. has given an answer[3] to your letter[4]— shall see it in the morning at Staunton— It is said to be mild, & to give up B.[5] as the Man.

I am satisfied that a rapid change is taking place in this State— and my hopes that even Virginia will be with [*us*] have been confirmed— they grow stronger every day.[6] I find many men with us whom I looked upon as aliens. You may depend that I shall endeavor to encourage the process which is going on. Cannot you give me some good news at the White Sulphur?[7] Respectfully &c &c   SAML L. SOUTHARD
Mr. Clay.

ALS. DLC (DNA, M212, R2).   [1] Virginia.
[2] See above, July 12, 1827.   [3] See above, Smith to Clay, August 1, 1827, note.
   [4] See above, Clay "To the Public," June 29, 1827.   [5] James Buchanan.   [6] Cf. above, Clay to Brown, March 27, 1827, note; Caldwell to Clay, August 8, 1827.   [7] Cf. above, Brooke to Clay, August 8, 1827.

INSTRUCTIONS AND DISPATCHES   August 8, 1827

From JOEL R. POINSETT, Mexico, no. 96. Observes that "The violent state of things . . . in the State of Vera Cruz [cf. above, Poinsett to Clay, June 16, July 8, 27, 1827; Taylor to Clay, July 16, 30, 1827], appears to be rapidly approaching a crisis"; summarizes recent events there; and expresses a belief that under General [Vicente] Guerrero, who has been sent to the area, "the affairs of Vera Cruz will be terminated favorably for the general government. . . ." LS. DNA, RG59, Dip. Disp., Mexico, vol. 3 (M97, R4). Copy, in MHi-Adams Papers, Letters Recd. (MR482). Received November 14.

MISCELLANEOUS LETTERS   August 8, 1827

From WILLIAM PHILLIPS, Washington. States that, "At the recommendation & with the approval of Coll. [John] Williams," he accepted in 1826 "the agency for" A. H. Palmer and Company, which had "obtained the contract for cutting the canals [*sic*] to open a communication between the Atlantic & Pacific oceans" (cf. above, Phillips to Clay, February 3, 1827) and that he suffered severe financial losses when his bills were protested and the "said Palmer . . . absconded now in London—" Notes that "the Seal & papers of the Legation of the United States near the Government [of the Federation of Central America]" were entrusted to him prior to the departure of Williams. Requests "some compensation for services rendered to the U States after the departure of Col. Williams. . . ; in order to alleviate in Some measure the loss of the funds . . . advanced on account of the canal (*too* important to the Government of the U States to fall into the hands of any other power as Mr Williams emphatically stated). . . ." ALS. DNA, RG59, Dip. Disp., Central America, vol. 1 (M219, R2).

Order on Washington Office, Bank of the United States

9 Aug. 1827

Pay to Mr Vance's[1] note or bearer thirteen dollars and 99 Cents.
Cashr. of the Off. of B U S. Washn.[2]   H. CLAY

ADS. DLC-TJC (DNA, M212, R16).   1 Joseph Vance. Cf. above, Order, June 5,
August 7, 1827.   2 Richard Smith.

From Robert H. Goldsborough

Myrtle Grove, near Easton E Shore of Mayld.
My dear Sir.   Augt. 9th. 1827.

I learn by the public prints that you are safely returned to your station of toil and high responsibility, after a journey, chequered with fatigues and gratifications, that has greatly improved your health.[1] I congratulate you Sir upon these events under the perfect assurances, that the good vastly preponderates over the inconvenience, and that the generous greetings of your friends have enabled you to defeat much of the sinister designs personal to yourself, and in part directed agt. the administration to which you are attached.

You will find, after you have leisure to look around, that Maryland has not been altogether lifeless during your absence from the adjacent territory, but that a most respectable and imposing Meeting has been held, that has taken an interest in the present and future state of our Country, so far as concerns the destinies under which it may be placed at the next Presidential election. Our Convention in Balte.[2] was a large body of highly respectable citizens, representing every part of the State but the distant County of Alleghany [sic], and it was conducted with so much dignified and harmonious good feeling, that our opponents entertain great fears, as they have reason to do, for the result. I am inclined to hope and believe, that it was one of the most successful delegations of the people that has taken place for a long time past.

I have the pleasure to inclose you one of the pamphlets containing these proceedings and address,[3] and hope you will find in it a temperate but firm expression of fair views and c[or]rect sentiment throughout. It is to be lamented that the address was necessarily so long—but where was it to stop shorter? To enter into a subject that embraced so much and to have left it, re infecta, wd. have thrown an air of ridiculous abandonment over the whole, like the review of the Jackson address of the measures of administration.[4] To have looked into the subject at all, required that a view of most of the strong points should be taken, and justice to them necessarily led to an extended exposition.

However, the whole proceeding seems to be well received and I have no doubt will be productive of salutary results.

With great respect and esteem I have the honor to be Dear Sir yrs very faithfully   ROBT H GOLDSBOROUGH
The Honble Henry Clay.

ALS. DLC-HC (DNA, M212, R2).
1 Cf. above, Clay to Erwin, August 4, 1827; Sparks to Clay, August 7, 1827.   2 Cf.

above, Clay to Everett, May 2, 1827, note.   3 Published in Washington *Daily National Journal*, July 30, 1827.   4 An address, drafted and adopted as part of the proceedings of a Baltimore convention of Jackson supporters on May 21–22, had denied that administration support for internal improvement and domestic manufactures constituted "the lines of separation between the supporters of Mr. Adams and General Jackson." The issue, according to Jackson's Maryland proponents, rested essentially upon the preservation of political liberty through the operation of the electoral process, when it devolved upon the Congressional representatives, "*to carry into effect,* so far as practicable, *the will of their constituents.*" Washington *United States Telegraph*, May 24, 30 (quoted), 1827.

INSTRUCTIONS AND DISPATCHES   August 9, 1827

From ALBERT GALLATIN, London, no. 104. Encloses "the Protocols of the 15th & 16th Conferences, which, in addition to some other matter, complete all that passed on the subject of the Commercial Convention and of the territory west of the Rocky Mountains." States that, he was "unexpectedly invited by the British Plenipotentiaries [Charles Grant and Henry U. Addington]" to a meeting on August 6 "for the purpose of signing the two Conventions [cf. above, Gallatin to Clay, August 6, 7, 1827] prior to Mr [George] Canning's death then every moment expected, although he survived till yesterday morning." Notes that Canning "had seen and approved those two instruments." Reports that "The British Plenipotentiaries . . . have declined to meet again in Conference until after the new administration shall have been formed." Observes that, "although the merits of Mr Canning may have been lately exaggerated, there is no one to fill his place immediately with equal effect as Premier, and still less as leader of the House of Commons." Cites expectations that "Lord Goodrich" (Goderich) will "be placed at the head of the new Administration" (cf. above, Gallatin to Clay, February 22, 1827, note) and that "the Duke of Wellington will return to his office, of Commander in Chief." Concludes: "Whatever changes may take place in the *personnel* I expect none in the general policy of Government." ALS. DNA, RG59, Dip. Disp., Great Britain, vol. 34 (M30, R30). Copy, in MHi-Adams Papers, Letters Recd. (MR482); extract published in *American State Papers, Foreign Relations*, VI, 693–94. Received September 16.

From ROBERT MONROE HARRISON, Barbadoes. Reports that he arrived on August 5 (cf. above, Harrison to Clay, July 19, 1827); that he visited Dominica and St. Lucia en route; and that he learned from planters that supplies at the latter place cost "at least 30 P C more now than when the Ports were open to our vessels; yet the merchants who alone are benefited by the trade being interdicted, avow, that they get those articles which were formerly supplied by the U States direct, through the Neutral Islands equally cheap at this moment!" Comments that, "Whilst the Ports were open the people of British North America as well as others interested in excluding our vessels from the trade, boldly asserted that they could supply the West India Colonies with all they required . . . yet strange to say fewer of their vessels have arrived in the different Islands since the interdict than before." Explains that United States supplies are coming through the neutral ports and asserts: "so long as the British Government permits it, I can hardly bring myself to believe that the interdict will be of any material injury to the U States." Notes, however, that there are not many neutral ports available and they are overstocked.

Cites duties on American vessels in the Danish, Swedish, and Dutch islands at an average of $70 to $120; in the British, "$400 to $1200, and sometimes $1500, and that too on a cargo which cost originally in the U States $800!" Claims that American merchants are getting "as much in the Neutral Ports as if they came here direct, & consequently save all the difference of cargoes; independent of which their cargoes are not traded out and left behind them, and in many instances *lose* the *whole*, in consequence of Banktruptcy [*sic*] or death which too often happens in these sickly Islands."

Promises to send a full report on observations in Dominica, St. Lucia, and Barbadoes in eight or ten days and notes his intention to prepare a "more minute and formal" review at the close of his "*Tour*."

States that this dispatch will be delivered by James Niel, for whom he has written a few lines of introduction (not found) to Clay, that Niel is attached "to the great and respectable House of Cavan & Co. well known in the U States and throughout Europe," and that James Cavan, senior member of the firm, resides in London "and for many years has possessed the *ear of ministers!*" Surmises that Niel's tour through the United States to Canada "is in some way connected with the views of the British Government, or some great and important speculation depending on the existing state of affairs. . . ," and promises that he will attempt to discover its purpose.

Notes, in a postscript, the expected arrival of 2600 barrels of flour from Danzig; remarks that he knows of "no cargoe such as the U States have heretofore furnished being introduced in other than British vessels"; and adds that two "cargoes of yellow cornmeal in Puncheon have arrived from Triest in British Vessels."

Reports, in a second postscript, dated the 14th, that the above-mentioned flour arrived "yesterday"; that bread made from it is "sweet but darker" than ours; that it is said to be "best when mixed with ours"; and that the cargo is offered at $8 1/4, the same price as flour brought here from neutral islands. ALS. DNA, RG59, Cons. Disp., Barbadoes, vol. 1 (M-T333, R1). Received September 26.

Neil and Cavan have not been further identified. William Cavan, a New York dry goods merchant, may have been the American partner.

From W[ILLIAM] TUDOR, Lima, no. 73, "*Confidential*." Begins: "Though I believe Mr [James] Cooley will write by this opportunity [below, Cooley to Clay, August 11, 1827, no. 5 and no. 6], I still venture to give you a sketch of the principal occurrences here since my last confidential letter of June 15h., as some of them may escape his notice, & as there is a considerable degree of interest attending the first steps of the only government Peru has yet known exempt from foreign influence." Devotes ten manuscript pages to a discussion of political events and personalities in Peru, Bolivia, and Colombia, in which he is highly critical of (Simón) Bolívar and his followers and is sympathetic toward the new regime in Peru and the advocates of popular self government in other areas. Mentions having been told "that the English & American Chargé [*sic*] d'Affaires [Alexander Cockburn; Beaufort T. Watts] interfered in" the question of acceptance by the Colombian Congress of Bolívar's resignation (on Watts' role in this matter, cf. above, Watts to Clay, June 14, 1827, and note; on Cockburn's relationship with Bolívar, cf. below, Nones to Clay, December 24, 1827) and declares that, if "the American agent . . . took the side of Bolivar against the patriotic party in Colombia, it was a most unhappy errour [*sic*]." Adds, in a postscript dated August 10, that he "saw yesterday with utter astonishment the letter of Mr Watts to Gen. Bolivar," which "has caused much surprise & disapprobation"; that he is "convinced from its intrinsic evidence, that Mr W. did not write it; neither the style nor the sentiments are those of an American"; that Watts "is probably intimate with some of the adherents of Bolivar," who "insidiously persuaded Mr Watts to this interference"; and that Watts, "perhaps distrusting his own knowledge of Spanish . . . incautiously signed" a letter drawn up for him. States that Cooley "has written a note to the Minister of Foreign Affairs" (Francisco Xavier Mariategui) disclaiming on the part of the United States the feelings expressed by Watts (cf. below, Cooley to Clay, August 11, 1827, no. 6) and that he, himself, intends publishing "a short notice . . . under the signature of an 'American citizen.' " Continues, with an account of a conversation with Serrano, Minister from Bolivia (possibly Francisco Javier Serrano Gomez), relative to whether (Antonio José de) Sucre (y de Alcalá) might leave that country and to future relations between it and Peru. ALS. DNA, RG59, Cons. Disp., Lima, vol. 2 (M154, R2). Received December 19.

Mariategui, born in Lima in 1793, had studied law and had been actively engaged in the movement for Peruvian independence. He had been a deputy at the first Constituent Congress and served as secretary in the drafting of the Constitution. In 1824 he had been named a judge of the Superior Court of Trujillo and the following year had become prosecutor of the Superior Court at Lima. He held the post of Minister of Foreign Affairs in 1827 and 1828 and subsequently served as Minister to Ecuador, beginning in 1832, and Minister to Bolivia, appointed in 1842. He was a member of the Peruvian Supreme Court from 1851 to 1870 and presiding judge during much of that period.

Serrano Gomez, popularly known as Dr. Parela, was a Catholic priest. Born in Bogotá, he had been active in the movement for Latin American independence since 1810.

MISCELLANEOUS LETTERS   August 9, 1827

From EDWARD LIVINGSTON, Red Hook, New York. Cites a House Resolution of January 13, 1825 (U. S. H. of Reps., *Journal*, 18 Cong., 2 Sess., pp. 128–29), requesting from the President "Statements 1st. Of the number of Convictions for offences against the law[s] of the United States   2d. The number of Executions. 3d. the number of [pa]rdons   4. an account of the Convictions for other offences." States that he "can not discover [tha]t any answer has been made to this resolution" and notes that the information requested "will probably become necessary in the discussion [of the] system of penal law now printing by order of the house for its consideration." Encloses forms which, he suggests, might be printed for use by "the Clerks and Marshals" in making "their returns" now and annually in the future. Concludes: "You may perhaps have heard of the task I very [unwisely] imposed upon myself in relation to the penal laws of the U. S. and will therefore I h[ope] excuse the indiscretion which perhaps I am guilty of, in this endeavour to procure the information necessary to aid me in the duty I have undertaken." ALS. DNA, RG59, Misc. Letters (M179, R65).

Livingston's work was published as *A System of Penal Law for the U. S. of America: Consisting of a Code of Crimes and Punishments, a Code of Procedure in Criminal Cases; a Code of Prison Discipline; and a Book of Definitions, Prepared and Presented to the H. of R. of U. S. . . .* (Washington, 1828).

On August 17 Clay addressed a circular to the Federal attorneys, enclosing tables to enable them to supply the desired information. Copy, in DNA, RG59, Dom. Letters, vol. 22, pp. 30–31 (M40, R20). His report to Adams (no letter of transmittal found), supplying the requested information, was presented to Congress on January 26, 1829, and published as *House Docs.*, 20 Cong., 2 Sess., no. 146.

From JOHN McDONALD, Portsmouth (Ohio). Recalls himself to Clay: "I am the same John McDonald whom you defended in the U S district court in a suit where the U S were plaintiffs" (cf. above, Creighton to Clay, November 9, 1825, and note 5). Requests Clay's aid in obtaining a release from prison for his youngest brother, William McDonald, who, as detailed in this account, served with distinction in the War of 1812, "was continued on the peace Establishment as an Assistant inspector Genl.," and "in an evil hour permited [sic] himself . . . to draw from two different officers pay for the same time,* for which offence he was degraded and his name stricken from the Army list, . . . and suit imeadiately [sic] brought against him for the money . . . improperly received from government—a Judgement was rendered against him and he now finds himself immured within the walls of a prison without any prospects of relief—except through the clemency of the president." States his reason for writing Clay: "Why Sir, you are the representative of the western people in the Cabinet, and when we have any Greveances [sic] to complain of, or request to ask of the Chief executive, we naturaly [sic] solicet [sic] your mediation, we can approach you with less awe, and more confidence, than we could other leaders, of whose private charector [sic] we know nothing." Explains, in a note appended under the asterisk, "the manner" in which his brother "commited [sic] the offence" and characterizes his conduct as "extreemly [sic] imprudent, but not monstrously wicked." ALS. DNA, RG59, Misc. Letters (M179, R65). Postmarked at Portsmouth, Ohio.

"By direction of the Secretary of State," Philip R. Fendall acknowledged, on August 21, receipt of this letter, explained that cases for such relief were "generally brought before the President in the shape of a petition from the party himself," and enclosed "a form from which . . . [the] brother can probably, prepare a petition to suit the present occasion." Copy, in DNA, RG59, Dom. Letters, vol. 22, p. 32 (M40, R20).

John McDonald, born in 1775, had been brought as a child of five from Northumberland, Pennsylvania, to the Mingo district of Ohio, had removed to Kentucky about 1790, and had been a ranger with General Anthony Wayne in 1794 and a captain in the United States Army during the War of 1812. He had several times held office as justice of the peace and had served for two terms from 1816 to 1818 as a member of the Ohio Senate. He had been sued by the Government for a deficiency in his accounts as paymaster of the Ohio militia. The verdict of the District Court had favored McDonald, but the case had been carried to the Circuit Court on appeal. U. S. H. of Reps., *House Docs.*, 17 Cong., 2 Sess., no. 32, p. 74. Subsequent court action has not been traced.

William McDonald had entered the War of 1812 as a lieutenant and had risen to the rank of major. He was listed as owing $742.76 on settlement of his accounts in January, 1819. His case had been reported for suit in December, 1820. U. S. H. of Reps., *House Docs.,* 17 Cong., 2 Sess., no. 32, p. 70.

To James Brown

My dear Sir   Washn. 10h. Aug. 1827.

I returned ten days ago from K. My reception in the West was distinguished by more enthusiasm than ever. It was difficult to resist the numerous invitations to public entertainment that poured in on me. Those which I could accept were attended by greater crowds than ever assembled before on any similar occasion.

If the zeal of my friends is great, so is the perseverance of my enemies. You will see from the News papers that Genl. Jackson himself has taken the field.[1] I send you a Copy of my Speech delivered at Lexington on the subject of his letter.[2] It has produced every where very great effect. And I anticipate, with entire confidence, as signal a victory over the General as he gained over the British at N. Orleans. As a part of a mass of evidence which I am accumulating, I am desirous to obtain from Genl. LaFayette a statement of a conversation I had with him about the Presidential election in Decr. 1824. I have no doubt that he recollects it, and I have this day written to him[3] to request (if he sees no impropriety in furnishing it, and I can see none) that he will furnish it. I would thank you to see him on the subject, and ask him to let you peruse my letter to him. I should be glad to get this statement as soon as the General can prepare and forward it.

Your letter of the 12h. May came to me whilst I was in Lexington. The part of it which relates to my payment of $450 for you to Mrs. Hart and Mrs. Price[4] brought tears of gratitude from the family. They say that it will make them perfectly easy. Indeed they were unwilling to receive it; but I insisted that it was according to your directions, and I should pay it to them, which I offered to do at that time, but as they said it would be soon enough to get it this fall, I will remit it to them before they want it. You enquire of me if more than the annual allowance of $300 to them hereafter is necessary to their comfort? They assure me positively that it is not; and that they would be unwilling to receive more of you. I pay Mrs. Hart regularly the annuity of $500, although I have no active funds of the Estate[5] in my hands.

We have around us in this City more of a family than usual. Theodore, James, Henry Clay Hart, Martin Duralde (our grandson) and John M. Clay are with us.[6] We have therefore quite a house full. We are all well; but Mrs. Clay's health is not as good as it used to be.

Poinsett has got himself into scrapes in Mexico,[7] as I anticipated he would. The Govt .of Mexico has even intimated its desire to him that he should be replaced by another.[9]

I think Mr. Adams will certainly be re-elected. He is gaining ground every where, and his competitor losing. The elections to Congress took place in K. this wek. I shall be disappointed if they do not eventuate in increased strength to the Administration.[10]

Mrs. Clay unites her respects with mine to Mrs. Brown. I am Yr's Respectfy   H. CLAY
James Brown Esq

ALS. KyLxT-Haupt Collection.   [1] Cf. above, Smith to Clay, August 1, 1827, note. [2] Above, July 12, 1827.   [3] See below, this date.   [4] Susannah Hart; Susannah Price.   [5] Of Colonel Thomas Hart.   [6] Cf. above, Clay to Erwin, August 4, 1827. [7] Cf. above, Taylor to Clay, June 22, July 16, 1827; Poinsett to Clay, July 8, 1827. [8] Cf. above, Clay to Brown, March 27, 1827.   [9] Cf. above, Sergeant to Clay, August 1, 1827.   [10] Cf. above, Clay to Taylor, April 4, 1827, and note.

Check to John Dickinson

OFFICE OF DISCOUNT & DEPOSIT, Washington,
No.   10h. August 1827
PAY to John Dickingson [*sic*] or order One hundred and twenty *Dollars,* /100
$120 DOLLARS, /100   H CLAY

ADS, partially printed. DLC, TJC (DNA, M212, R16). Endorsed on verso: "Jno. Dickinson   Credit my accot. Wm. J. Roberts Cashr [not further identified]."

To Lafayette

My dear General   Washington 10h. August 1827.

It has been a long time since I had the pleasure of receiving a letter from you. I have to reproach myself for not enjoying that satisfaction, being sensible that I did not acknowledge, with the regularity which I should have done, your several favors. I beg you to believe that my apparent neglect proceeded from any other cause than that of insensibility to their value, or of diminished respect and veneration. You are so completely identified with our Country and with Liberty, that want of affection for you would be a sort of treason against them. And I have too lively a recollection of the many proofs, which you have had the goodness to give me of your confidence and attachment to admit of the smallest abatement of my estem and friendship for you.

Poor Greece continues to bleed. A few weeks ago we had the highest hopes of the triumph of her arms; but the late accounts have afflicted us with the sad news of a dreadful defeat before Athens.[1] These accounts come from so many concurrent sources that one scarcely dares cherish the hope that they are fallacious. I had hoped that, long before this, there would have been some effective interference, in behalf of Greece, by the European powers. That such an interposition was designed, and is yet contemplated, we are assured by intelligence received from several quarters.[2] I fear it will be too late, if it should ever be rendered.

The Congress of the American powers, transfered [sic] from Panama to Tacubaya, has not yet been organized, nor have ministers, from more than two or three of them, yet assembled at the latter place.[3] This delay is attributed to the fact of the procrastination in the ratification of the treaties which were concluded at Panama; but I believe its real cause is the suspicions and distrusts which prevail among the new States in regard to the views and designs of Bolivar. You will recollect that, at the dinner which you did the members of the H. of R. the honor to accept and attend, on the 1st. of January 1825, I proposed as a toast Bolivar, the Washington of South America.[4] I must revoke or at least suspend that sentiment. And what has since transpired satisfies me that there is some hazard in pronouncing upon the character of any man, whilst he yet lives, or at least whilst he is in action. For I am sorry to be obliged to tell you that evidence has reached me from so many quarters, and of a kind so entirely satisfactory, that I can no longer resist the conviction, which I very reluctantly adopted, that he has conceived and actually commenced the execution of a vast project of ambition, which involved the overthrow of the liberties of South

America. That project was no less than the ultimate establishment of an Empire which should stretch from the Isthmus of Darien to Cape Horn.[5] The first movement was the Bolivian Constitution, with its President for life &c;[6] the next its adoption in Lima;[7] the third which he proposed was its introduction into Colombia;[8] and then he designed the union of Bolivia, Peru and Colombia,[9] which were to form a nucleus only for ulterior purposes. The subversion of the Bolivian Constitution in Peru[10] is the first check which the execution of this gigantic plan has encountered. And Bolivar finds in Colombia itself a degree of resistance[11] which he did not anticipate. He may now *possibly* abandon his project, or growing desparate [*sic*] and infuriate by unforeseen obstacles, he may plunge South America in civil War. He has grown, I understand, passionate, impatient and overbearing, and takes Bonaparte as his model.[12] Was ever man guilty of greater folly? What glory awaited him, if he had been true to Liberty and to his Country! Greater than ever man has acquired or can achieve. For where is there another quarter of the Globe to emancipate from so degrading a thraldom?

The effect of these designs of Bolivar has been to create jealously [*sic*] with the New Republics, and I fear it will lead to the disappointment or postponement, for a long time, of the fulfilment [*sic*] of the hopes and expectations which were entertained about the Congress.

Our own Country continues to prosper in all its great interests; and up to this time all parts of it have enjoyed this summer, unexampled health. Still there are great political heats and much rancor prevailing between political parties throughout the Country. These divisions grow out of that point, so difficult to adjust, and which may be considered as the desideratum in free Governments, the election of Chief Magistrate. You witnessed their origin, when you were among us. I do not think the result of the approaching election even doubtful; Mr. Adams will be re-elected and I believe by more than two thirds of the Union. We shall nevertheless have enough of trouble and turmoil until the event is decided; and I think it likely that the next Session of Congress will be characterized by more intemperance than any which preceded it. The causes which produce this unhappy state of things are the same as those which have unfortunately produced a like condition, in most free governments—the loss and love of power, military renown &c &c.

Ever since you have left us, I have been the object of constant and malignant attack and abuse. All present and future aspirants have united in attacking me, however they may be divided in other respects; and their desire to prostrate me appears more ardent than even that of defeating Mr. Adams. Many of them I have no doubt would be perfectly satisfied that Mr. Adams should succeed, if my downfall could be accomplished. I have nevertheless the satisfaction to tell you that I have been sustained by the people, and especially by those of the Western states, with great generosity and unanimity. During an excursion to the West, from which I have just returned, I have been received and treated with a degree of enthusiastic attachment, which has no example in the Country but that which was furnished in your own case.

The calumnies which have been propagated against me render it necessary to resort to you to establish a fact which I have no doubt remains in your recollection. During your visit to this City in December 1824,[13] and I think before you went to Annapolis, or immediately after your return from that City,[14] (I am confident it was in the month of December) I had a conversation, at your instance, on the subject of the approaching Presidential election. It commenced by your observing that you were here, as the guest of the Nation, enjoying the hospitalities of all parties; that you did not deem it proper therefore that you should take any part in our local politics or divisions; that you conversed with no body on that subject but me; that, taking a deep interest in all that concerned us, you could not but regard with solicitude the existing contest. And you asked me how the election would go and how I meant to vote. I observed that I would frankly tell you how I should vote; that I considered Mr Crawford's state of health, if there were no other objections, rendered it improper that he should be elected; that in my view, therefore, the contest was limited to a choice between Mr. Adams and Genl. Jackson. And I added that I could not think it proper to vote for Genl. Jackson, who I believed to be incompetent, and whose election, as he had no claim other than one founded upon exclusive military pretension, I believed would be injurious to the Republic, especially in this early stage of its existence. I should therefore vote for Mr. Adams.[15] I told you that I could not, with certainty, say how the election would terminate, but I believed Mr. Adams would be elected.

I shall be greatly obliged if you will, with as much particularity, as your memory may enable you, state the above conversation in a letter addressed to me[16] or to some other friend (in the latter case, advising me who) and mentioning with as much precision as you can *the time* when

AL. NNPM. The last part of the document is missing.
[1] Cf. above, Brown to Clay, June 28, 1827.   [2] Cf. above, Brown to Clay, June 12 (1, 2), July 12, 28, 1827; Gallatin to Clay, July 14, 1827.   [3] Cf. above, Sergeant to Clay, May 30, 1827; Tudor to Clay, June 15, 1827; Cooley to Clay, July 3, 1827.
[4] See above, Remarks and Toast, January 1, 1825, and note.   [5] See above, Clay to Sergeant and Poinsett, March 16, 1827, note.   [6] Cf. above, Crosby to Clay, September 17, 1825, note; Allen to Clay, August 7, 1826.   [7] Cf. above, Tudor to Clay, August 24, 1826.   [8] Cf. above, MacPherson to Clay, October 2, 1826.   [9] Cf. above, Tudor to Clay, July 5, 1826; Allen to Clay, August 7, 1826; Poinsett to Clay, November 15, 1826.   [10] Cf. above, Tudor to Clay, February 3, March 23, 1827.   [11] Cf. above, Poinsett to Clay, March 28, 1827; Williamson to Clay, May 9, 1827; Watts to Clay, June 14, 27, 1827.   [12] Cf. above, Tudor to Clay, July 5, August 24, 1826.   [13] Cf.

above, III, 868, 894n.   [14] Lafayette had left Washington for Annapolis on December 16 and had returned to Washington by way of Baltimore and Frederick. He had reached Washington December 31, 1824. Brandon (ed. and comp.), *Lafayette, Guest of the Nation*, III, 200, 216.   [15] Cf. above, III, 906; Clay to Adams, January 9, 1825, note.   [16] See below, Lafayette to Clay, October 10, 1827.

From John Clay

my dear Brother   Versailles[1] 10th august 1827
    I returned a few days ago from the Olymn. Springs[2] where I had remained for two weeks. my health has been much benefitted I have hopes of soon being reinstated.
    on my arrival here I found your letter from Maysville the 18th ulto[3] I regret sincerely I was deprived the pleasure of meeting you   I wished much to have conversed with you, even if it had been only for an hour. I received a letter from you last febry.[4] in which you make mention of a favorable termination of my suit with Smith[5]   nearly of the same date I received one from Mr Livingston[6] confirming what you had communicated   Mr L, further states he would be in New Orleans in april & bring on with him the decision of the Sup. Court & the mandate & I left N Orleans the 1st. of July, Mr L had not then arrived there, & I am not informed whether he will go thither the present year. I am therefore still in the dark as to the nature of the decision. If I had had it in time I could have procured some contributions from those similarly situated with myself, to aid me in paying Counsel & other expenses attendant upon this Suit. I may still get something contributed if I can be put into possession of the decision, mandate & [. . .].[7] Could you not send them to me? I know there will be some expence attending in getting them from the Clerks office but upon being informed of the amount, I will remit you the same.
    For the Spring of 1824 I felt confident of surviving my difficulties & have something remaining   the Subscrip—for the new Bank had opened[8] & I subscribed ten shares in the name of my namesake John Morrison Clay intending to pay up the installments & the whole for his benefit—   shortly afterwards my affairs took an unhappy turn numerous suits against me— I was forced into a Sale of all my property of whatever nature for the payment of my debts—   the great sacrifices which took place in the Sale of my property left me pennyless. in the winter of 1825–26 two further instalments on the stock was called. I was unable to meet them   I applied to Mr Duralde & Mr. Erwin[9] to aid me.   both refused—,   I wrote to you about the same time[10]   You never replyed. I thought at that time that this Stock would have been forfeited to the Institution. I find since that the dividends are only suspended. I feel much humiliated that I am not enabled to do what I would want to do for my little namesake, but poverty has intervened & prevents it. I have paid two hundred dollars

upon this Stock; it in its present predicament lays dormant & benefits no person— I may in my present difficulties be benefitted by receiving back that Sum. It may be done in this way   to wit   you must give me a power of Atty.[11] to make Sale of the Same   the Laws of Louisiana requires [sic] a further ceremony—a family meeting—to say Mrrs. [sic] Clays signature with one or two friends recommending the Sale. when these are furnished to me I then apply to the Probate Court. for an order to Sell the Stock which is necessary to Govern the Directors in making the transfer, in cases of Orphan Children[12]— This would be of great relief to me in my present situation— You will have sufficient time to forward me those papers. as well as those from the Sup. Court prior to my going to N. Orleans— I shall not leave here before the 1st. or 5th of October.

The Election is over since the 8th Inst.   having taken no part I know but little as to the result. only that the aggregate result will be in favr. of the Government[13]   riots & scenes too abominable have been witnessed[14]   I dont feel disposed to touch upon them   I feel too much humiliated   I presume you will have early & ample communications from your numerous friends in Kentucky

Our poor old mother[15] continues in a languishing state   I fear you will not see her again. She is now a burthen to her friends & herself I am devoting most of my time with her. Yr Affte. Brother

JOHN CLAY

ALS. DLC-TJC (DNA, M212, R10). Addressed to Clay at Washington.
[1] Kentucky.   [2] See above, I, 150n.   [3] Not found.   [4] Not found.
[5] Abraham Smith. On the case, see above, III, 338–39, and note.   [6] Edward Livingston.   [7] Word illegible.   [8] The Bank of Louisiana had been chartered April 7, 1824, with a capital of $4,000,000, half of it supplied by the State and the remainder offered to public subscription. John J. Knox, *A History of Banking in the United States* . . . (New York: B. Rhodes and Co., 1900, repr. A. M. Kelley, 1969), 611.   [9] Martin Duralde, Jr.; James Erwin.   [10] Letter not found.   [11] Not found.   [12] Under Louisiana law of 1825 a *tuteur subroge* was required to act when the interests of an infant and his principal guardian conflicted. Such tutorship could be filled by *conseil de famille*. The "family meeting" was to consist of five relatives of the minor or, in lieu of relatives, friends, all of whom must live in the parish in which the meeting was held. *Louisiana Law Institute*, compiled edn. of the *Civil Codes of Louisiana* (3 vols.; Baton Rouge, 1937–1940), arts. 247, 281; pp. 141, 159, 160.   [13] Cf. above, Clay to Taylor, April 4, 1827, note.   [14] The election was described as "one more violent and disorderly than was ever witnessed by the inhabitants of Lexington. . . ." Lexington *Kentucky Reporter*, August 8, 1827. The same editor on August 11, noted: "Much of the violence . . . is attributed to the active exertions of a few of Mr. Clay's personal enemies."
[15] Elizabeth Clay Watkins.

From Charles Hammond

[Cincinnati, August 10, 1827]

The old General's movements have been more extravagant than I expected.[1] From the best observation I can make, his conduct makes his leading supporters more and more violent. The more they feel that their confidence ought to be shaken, the more they are resolved it shall not be. Such is the course of the leaders here. They have had meetings and resolutions in abundance. Have resolved to support a tariff, such an one as no sensible man can support, and hope to throw the blame of rejecting it on the North.[2] Every day's experience confirms me in the opinion that the opposition leaders have lashed themselves into a state of desperate feeling: They would sacrifice any thing & any body to insure success, and they can give no better reason, than that of your Senator.[3] "By the Eternal, they will put down the Administration." My apprehension is, that the result in Kentucky is not so favorable as you anticipated.[4] Nothing under existing circumstances more fully displays the lengths to which men are prepared to go. That the Kentuckians should desert you, would be one thing. To deify Gen. Jackson is the most extraordinary. And I perceive among those who write in support of the General many who were once your friends and were never his.[5]

Copy. InHi. The text is incomplete (cf. below, Clay to Hammond, August 22, 1827).
[1] On Jackson's recently published letters, see Clay to Hammond, June 25, 1827; Smith to Clay, August 1, 1827, note.   [2] For an account of the political stratagem which underlay the introduction and passage of the tariff act of May 19, 1828 (4 *U. S. Stat.*, 270–75), the so-called Tariff of Abominations, see Calhoun's speech in the United States Senate, February 23, 1837, in Richard K. Crallé (ed.), *The Works of John C. Calhoun . . .* (6 vols.; New York, 1853–1855), III, 47–51. Cf. also, below, Clay to Crittenden, February 16, 1828.   A meeting of Jackson's supporters in Cincinnati, reported variantly as August 7 or 8, had determined to send a long memorial to Congress in support of a tariff. *Cincinnati Advertiser*, August 4, 1827; *Liberty Hall and Cincinnati Gazette*, August 16, 1827.   [3] Richard M. Johnson or John Rowan.   [4] Cf. above, Clay to Hammond, June 5, 25, 1827; Clay to Taylor, April 4, 1827, and note.   [5] For example, Francis Preston Blair and Amos Kendall.

DIPLOMATIC NOTES   August 10, 1827

To CHARLES R. VAUGHAN. Acknowledges receipt of Vaughan's note of July 31 and adds: "If the relations of that young man [James Ringgold Slemaker] have not the satisfaction of learning that he still lives, they cannot fail to feel grateful for the charitable consideration which prompted his reception on board His Britannic Majesty's Ship Sybille at Carthagena." Copy. DNA, RG59, Notes to Foreign Legations, vol. 3, pp. 378–79 (M38, R3). ALI draft, in CSmH.

INSTRUCTIONS AND DISPATCHES   August 10, 1827

From ALEXANDER H. EVERETT, Madrid, no. 85. Transmits "a copy of a pretty long note" he "addressed to the Minister [Manuel Gonzáles Salmón] on the 16th ult. on the health laws." Reports that Salmón informed him a few days later "that in consequence of" Everett's "last preceding notes on the same subject of the 4th and 29th ulto. [*i.e.*, June 4 and 29–cf. above, Everett to Clay, June 4, July 4, 1827] which had been referred to the Supreme Board, that body had determined to address a new circular Instruction to the Provincial Boards confirming with some slight modifications (and these of a favorable kind) the construction of the law" contained in Salmón's letter of May 30 (*i.e.*, May 25, copy enclosed with Everett's letter of June 4) to Everett. Notes that the circular "exempts altogether from Quarantine at all seasons all our vessels, when provided with the usual bills of health, excepting such as proceed from the ports of Georgia and the two Carolinas between the 1st. of June and the last of September, and these are only regarded as suspicious." Adds: "It has . . . been a matter of considerable satisfaction to me to have succeeded so well and so early in this preliminary question." Warns of possible difficulties with "French Military authorities," whose consent will be needed "to give effect to the new system at Barcelona and Cadiz. . . ." Encloses copies of a recent "note from the Minister respecting the privileges of public Couriers" and of his own reply, which "seem to have some connexion with the affair of Mr [Obadiah] Rich's detention last year [cf. above, Everett to Clay, February 13, April 19, 1827]. . . ." LS. DNA, RG59, Dip. Disp., Spain, vol. 27 (M31, R28). Received October 15.

In one of the enclosures, Salmón informs Everett "that in future no Courier, whether on horseback or in a carriage, shall be suffered to enter . . . the City whenever the extraordinary number or size of his portmanteaus shall afford reason to suspect they contain besides the official correspondence prohibited goods or others which it may be intended to pass free of duties. . . ."

From ALBERT GALLATIN, London, no. 105. Submits "the observations, on a more specific agreement with Great Britain respecting the Territory west of the Rocky Mountains," alluded to in his "despatch No 103 [August 7, 1827]":

The British have no wish to colonize that area, which "they view rather with indifference; . . . they do not believe that it will, when once settled, long remain either a British Colony or a part of the United States"; and, consequently, they attach little importance to the nationality of immigrants and "are willing to let the settlement of the Country take its natural course." Still, "they are not . . . prepared to agree to such a division of it between the two Powers, as the United States do ask and have a right to claim," and "the settlement of a permanent boundary" cannot be reached "until the citizens of the United States shall have acquired a respectable footing in the Country." Meanwhile, the British Government feels itself "bound to protect the existing establishments which have been created by British capital and enterprize. . . ." Barriers to a definitive settlement include "the Fur Company" (the Hudson's Bay Company), recollections of the Nootka affair (cf. above, Gallatin to Clay, June 19 [note 29], November 16, 25, 1826), and national pride; "but Great Britain does not seem indisposed to let the Country gradually and silently slide into the hands of the United States; and she is anxious that it shall not, in any case, become the cause of a rupture between the two Powers.

"It has been under the influence of those motives, that . . . the British Plenipotentiaries [William Huskisson, Henry U. Addington, Charles Grant] . . . have considered the Country as unoccupied and equally open to all, but have sedulously avoided to set up a claim of absolute and exclusive sovereignty to any part of it. And . . . this exposition of the *nature* of the claim of Great Britain is . . . far more important than the arguments adduced in support of it. To the same disposition must be ascribed the proposal, in the Projet of Convention offered at the sixth Conference [cf. above, Gallatin to Clay, December 20, 1826], that no settlement then existing, or to be formed during the fifteen ensuing years, should be adduced in support of any claims by either party to the exclusive Sovereignty of the Country: a proposal which, considering that the United States never had had but one settlement within its limits was on the whole favorable to them; but the principal object of which was, that Great Britain should not hereafter be prevented from adjusting the permanent boundary by settlements acknowledged by her to have been made with her sanction & under an expectation of support & protection on her part."

The objection of the British Plenipotentiaries to the proposed establishment by the United States of a territorial government (cf. above, Gallatin to Clay, November 27, 1826; Hoard to Clay, April 2, 1827, note) has been largely removed by "the explanation given and the comparison made, between that form of extending jurisdiction and that adopted by the Act of Parliament of July 1821" (cf. above, Gallatin to Clay, April 21, 1827, note), and "an understanding might take place in that respect without agreeing to any specific condition." Consequently, a territory might be created, with "its eastern boundary a line within the acknowledged boundaries of the United States, and describing the Country over which the jurisdiction was to extend, generally, or in terms similar to those used in the Act of Parliament," for which territory three restrictions have been suggested: "1. That no custom house should be erected" and no duties charged west of the Rockies; "2. That" Americans and Britons in the territory "should be amenable to the jurisdiction of their own Country. . ."; and "3. That no military post should be established by either party in the territory."

Observes that "The British Plenipotentiaries had expressed a decided preference for a compact of 20 or 25 years duration, if the two last mentioned conditions made part of it." Concludes by stating that he has, "in the course of the conversations on the subject matter of this despatch, suggested . . . that any negotiation for that object should be carried on at Washington; and that it should not be pressed immediately, as the subject being under several aspects of new impression, some time was necessary to take it under serious consideration and to mature the views of the Government of the United States respecting it." ALS. DNA, RG59, Dip. Disp., Great Britain, vol. 34 (M30, R30). Copy, in MHi-Adams Papers, Letters Recd. (MR482); published in *American State Papers, Foreign Relations*, VI, 694–96. Received September 16.

When the North West Company and the Hudson's Bay Company had quarreled (cf. above, III, 459n) over the monopoly accorded the latter, by its charter of 1670, granting it control of trade in British America north of the St. Lawrence River, the Crown had intervened and combined the companies under the charter and name of the older organization. In December, 1821, the merged Hudson's Bay Company had been licensed to "hold a monopoly of all rights of British trade with the Indians of the several 'parts' " of North America, one of which parts was the area west of the Stony (Rocky) Mountains. Frederick Merk (ed.), *Fur Trade and Empire, George Simpson's Journal* . . . (revd. edn., with a new introduction; Cambridge, Massachusetts: Harvard University Press, 1968), xi, xii.

From SAMUEL LARNED, Santiago de Chile, no. 57. Reports that he has entered upon his official duties and that (Heman) Allen has departed for the United States. States that he has been informed "of the appointment . . . of Don Joaquin Campino as Envoy Extraordinary and Minister Plenipotentiary to the United States, and of Don José Joaquin Perez as Secretary of Legation"; notes that Campino will "remain in the United States for a year or so, and then proceed to Europe; leaving Mr. Perez as Chargé d'Affaires"; surmises that Campino will depart soon "for his destination." Labels the political structure in Chile as "tranquil," notes that as yet there is no agreement on "the form of government to be adopted," but expresses certainty that "the decision will be in favour of popular institutions, and an elective Chief Magistrate." Summarizes news from Peru and Buenos Aires. ALS. DNA, RG59, Dip. Disp., Chile, vol. 2 (M-T2, R2). Published in Manning (arr.) *Diplomatic Correspondence . . . Latin-American Nations*, II, 1120–21. Received December 12.

Perez, born and educated in Santiago, was now, at age 26, beginning a distinguished diplomatic and political career. He served as Secretary of Legation at Washington until 1829, then moved to Paris as Minister Plenipotentiary until 1831, was soon afterward sent in the latter capacity to London, and in 1836 became Minister to Buenos Aires. In 1845 he entered the Chilean Cabinet as Secretary of the Treasury and in 1849 assumed the portfolio of Minister of Foreign Relations. After nearly a decade of service in the Chamber of Deputies and the Senate, he was elected President in 1861. He remained in that office for two five-year terms and from 1871 to 1876 served again in the Senate.

From JOEL R. POINSETT, Mexico, no. 97. Reports an interview on the preceding day with the Mexican President (Guadalupe Victoria), who "expressed his earnest desire" to resume negotiations with the United States as soon as possible, "hinted that this government was disposed to yield the points which, in the late negotiations, had been insisted upon as a *sine qua non*, and the insertion of which had occasioned the rejection of the Treaty by the Senate of the United States" (cf. above, Poinsett to Clay, July 12, 1826 [no. 50]; Clay to Poinsett, March 12, 1827), and stated his willingness "at once to enter into negotiations" on the subject of the boundary.

Adds: "In the course of conversation, he requested me to state to the President, that he had seen with regret the Manifesto of the Legislature of Vera Cruz [cf. above, Poinsett to Clay, July 8, 1827] and other indications of a hostile spirit towards the United States and towards me personally, and to assure him, that such were not the sentiments entertained in relation to us either by the government or by the people of Mexico. He assured me, *confidentially*, that he was now perfectly aware of the plans and intentions of the monarchical party and was determined to counteract them and to promote the success of the republicans by any means in his power." Poinsett expresses his belief in the sincerity of this declaration and asserts that "The late occurrences in Vera Cruz and the conduct of the *Scotch* party here [cf. above, Poinsett to Clay, August 26. 1826 (no. 55)] too clearly indicate the tendency of their plans to overthrow the existing institutions of the country for the most unwary to be any longer deceived by their professions of attachment to the federal government." LS. DNA, RG59, Dip. Disp., Mexico, vol. 3 (M97, R4). Copy, in MHi-Adams Papers, Letters Recd. (MR482). Received Noxember 14.

From J[OEL] R. POINSETT, Mexico, no. 98. Transmits a translation of the "*declarations*" signed at Paris by Baron de Damas and (Sebastián) Camacho (cf. above, Poinsett to Clay, June 16, 1827); notes that "The President [Guadalupe Victoria] yesterday . . . stated that France had held out the expectation that within . . . eighteen months she would be ready to conclude with Mexico a formal Treaty on the same conditions." Reports that "Similar Conventions have been . . . signed by Mr Camacho with Hanover and the Hans [*sic*] towns" (cf. above, Brown to Clay, July 28, 1827). LS. DNA, RG59, Dip. Disp., Mexico, vol. 3 (M97, R4). Copy, in MHi-Adams Papers, Letters Recd. (MR482).

The commercial treaty between Mexico and Hanover had been signed at London on June 20, 1827. Parry (ed.), *Consolidated Treaty Series*, LXXVII, 277–80.

From W[ILLIAM] H. D. C. WRIGHT, Rio de Janeiro. Reports that "The Government of Buenos Ayres rejected the Treaty [cf. above, Forbes to Clay, June 29, 1827] with great indignation" and that (Manuel José) García was forced into hiding. Notes that "Lord Ponsonby to whom the Buenos Ayreans attribute great agency in constructing the Treaty, was . . . apprehensive" for his own safety. Encloses a copy of the document. Attributes the false optimism in Rio about the treaty's prospects to an expectation that the discord in the interior of Buenos Aires (cf. above, Forbes to Clay, April 12, 1827, note) would force that nation to accept Brazil's terms. Adds that all negotiations have been terminated, that (Bernadino) Rivadavia has resigned, and that "Don Vincente Lopez has been appointed President of Buenos Ayres." Observes that "Brazil is evidently suffering more by the war than B'Ayres,   the Privateers of the latter, are completely destroying the commerce of the former, while the whole warlike operations of the former, are confined to an ineffecient [sic] blockage of the river La Plata."

Cites his letter of "the 23d Ulto" (not found), in which he reported "that the American Schooner Hero having entered the Island of St Catherines in distress, was there detained, and her Captain and Mate thrown into prison"; states that these men have been sent to Rio under a charge of piracy; and promises to give more information on their case "in a few days." Informs Clay that Captain (James) Biddle has sailed, hoping "to fall in with a Buenos Ayrean Privateer, by whom the Brig Hannah of New York has been taken, her Captain taken out," and the vessel sent to an unknown place of detention. ALS. DNA, RG59, Cons. Disp., Rio de Janiero, vol. 2 (M-T172, R3). Received October 3.

On the case of the *Hero*, cf. below, Wright to Clay, September 1, 1827; Clay to Tudor, March 19, 1828, Tudor to Clay, January 22, 1829. The Brazilian Government in 1829 issued warrants for reparations on claims involving several vessels, including the *Hero. House Docs.*, 25 Cong., 1 Sess., no. 32, pp. 145–46, 257.

The case of the *Hannah* has not been found as a claim against Buenos Aires. The vessel was one of several seized by Brazil and condemned at Montevideo, for which indemnity was granted by the latter Government in 1830 and 1831. *Ibid.*, pp. 79, 119, 121, 179, 190–91, 225.

The captain of the *Hero* was George Simmonds (or Simmons), Jr.; the mate, Mathias Mahorner. Neither has been further identified.

MISCELLANEOUS LETTERS   August 10, 1827

To WILLIAM RADCLIFF, "Consul of the United States at Lima, and for the Ports of Peru." Transmits his "Commission, accompanied with printed Consular Instructions and a blank Consular Bond. . . ." Copy. DNA, RG59, Cons. Instr., vol. 2, p. 438 (M78, R2).

On August 16 Radcliff acknowledged receipt of the commission and accepted the appointment. ALS, in DNA, RG59, Cons. Disp., Lima, vol. 2 (M154, R2). On December 20, he informed Clay of his intention to leave New York for Lima, "by way of Carthagena and Panama, on the thirtieth day of this month. . . ." ALS, in DNA, RG59, Misc. Letters (M179, R65).

Check to Thomas H. Gilliss

No.   OFFICE OF DISCOUNT & DEPOSIT,
                          Washington,

                                                        11 August 1827

PAY TO Tho. H. Gillis [sic] or order for pew rent &c sixteen *Dollars*, 12/100

$16 DOLLARS, 12/100   H. CLAY

ADS, partially printed. DLC-TJC (DNA, M212, R16). Cf. above, Bill from St. John's Church, *ca.* September 30, 1826.

Order on Washington Office, Bank of the United States

No.   OFFICE OF DISCOUNT & DEPOSIT,
                          Washington,

                                                      11 Aug. 1827

         PAY to Check on N. York, —, — *or bearer,*
Fifty —— *Dollars,*   /100

                                                      H CLAY

$50 DOLLARS,   /100

ADS, partially printed. DLC-TJC (DNA, M212, R16). Cf. below, Kip to Clay, September 3, 1827.

From William T. Barry and Robert Wickliffe

Mr Robert Scott agent for Henry Clay.   [August 11, 1827]

Take notice that on Saturday next, the 18th Inst we will attend at the office of the Clerk of the Fayette Circuit Court[1] between the hours of ten in the morning and six in the evening, to take the Depositions of James B. January and John Keizer [*sic*] and others, to be read in evidence in a suit in Chancery depending in the Fayette Circuit Court wherein Said Clay is Complainant and we and others are Defendants[2]

                                                      WILL. T. BARRY
                                                      RO. WICKLIFFE.

Copy. Fayette County Circuit Court, Box 823. Endorsed on verso: "Fayette County Sct Augt 13. 1827   This day H I Bodley made oath before me that he did on the 11th Inst deliver to R. Scott a true copy of the within notice. Given under my hand the day above Waller Bullock J P F C."

Bullock, born in Virginia about 1774, had settled in Fayette County, Kentucky, before 1803. He was a magistrate much of the period from 1815 to about 1849 and sheriff during the early 1830's.

[1] Thomas Bodley.   [2] Cf. above, Complaint, *ca.* July 5, 1825; Clay to Wickliffe, Barry, and Mason, July 13, 1826.

From John Bradford

Dr Sir   Lexington Augt. 11th. 1827

[Encloses his accounts against the State and Navy Departments for publishing documents. Inquires whether drafts forwarded by Clay include payments from the Navy and Commissary General Departments.]

The subscribers to a fund to procure a President to T. University are becoming clamorous; many declare tha[t] if one is not shortly appointed they shall not consider themselves bound for their subscriptions:[1] An opinion is entertained by many that Mr. McCaul[ey] of New York,[2] who it is said is eminently qualified, could be obtained if suitable propositions were made to him; but a majority of those who I have heard speak on the subject seem to prefer "Woods."[3]

The Idea of a military professorship in the University is still popular;[4] and since the publication of the favorable report of the visitors of
the Gymnasium at Washington,[5] seems to become more popular,—
Could you with convenience furnish us with the constitution or
principles of that establishment? If you can it will be very acceptable.
Yours very respectfully, I am Yr Obt Serv—   JOHN BRADFORD

The Kentucky Gazette has been transfered [*sic*] to A. G. Meriwether,[6] and all the emolument of that paper from and after the 1st.
day July 1827 said Meriwether is entitled to

JOHN BRADFORD

A. G. MERIWETHER

ALS. DNA, RG59, Misc. Letters (M179, R65). Addressed to Clay.
1 The Lexington *Kentucky Reporter*, April 11, 1827, had proposed that, because the
Transylvania University was "deficient at this time in its finances [cf. above, Clay to
Bradford, February 10, 1827] a suitable fund should be raised by the citizens to ensure
a competent salary to the president, until the institution can be restored at the ensuing
session, and the state authority be brought to bear upon it." The editor reminded his
readers that under an act of 1817 (Ky. Gen Assy., *Acts . . . 1817*, ch. CCXCIV, pp. 554–56,
approved February 3, 1818) Transylvania had been identified as a "state institution."
On the opposition of Governor Joseph Desha and the Relief Party toward the University, see above, IV, 818n; John D. Wright, Jr., *Transylvania: Tutor to the West* (Lexington: Transylvania University, 1975), 108–12. In January, 1828, under authorization by
the Lexington Town Trustees, a referendum was held on the issue whether the city
should subscribe $500 to "the subscription paper" circulated for the purpose of insuring
adequate salaries for the president and faculty. The proposal was then rejected; but,
upon authorization by a town meeting March 15, 1828, the town trustees agreed to subscribe $500 a year for four years. Lexington Town Trustees, Minutes, Book 3, p. 340;
Lexington *Kentucky Reporter*, December 19, 1827; March 19, 1828. Over the period
1827 to 1829 the city and a number of its citizens contributed $3500 a year as a salary
fund for the University. Peter, *Tranyslvania University*, 156n.   2 Thomas McAuley,
born in Ireland in 1778, had come to the United States as a young man and had been
graduated in 1804 from Union College, Schenectady, New York. He had remained at
that institution as tutor, lecturer, and professor until 1822. Having been ordained by
the Presbytery of Albany in 1819, he had become pastor of the Rutgers Street Church
of New York City, where he was currently serving. Although invited to the presidency
of Transylvania University, he accepted instead a call to the Tenth Presbyterian Church
in Philadelphia, held the pastorate there until 1833, and then returned to New York
to lead the Murray Street Church. McAuley had been moderator of the General Assembly of the Presbyterian Church in 1826 and held that position again in 1837. He
was active in the movement to found Union Theological Seminary (New York Theological Seminary) and became its first president, from 1837 to 1840. In 1845 he resigned
his pastorate and passed the remainder of his life in retirement.   3 Alva Woods.
4 The Lexington *Kentucky Reporter* of April 11, 1827, had reported, and endorsed,
a proposal that Captain (Alden) Partridge, "now teaching" at the American Literary,
Scientific, and Military Academy at Middletown, Connecticut, operate such an institution "as a valuable auxiliary to the preparatory department of the University." On
June 1, 1827, the Lexington *Kentucky Gazette*, which on April 13 had reprinted the
Reporter item, carried an editorial referring to "The solicitude which has been ex-
pressed by many of the warm friends of Transylvania University, that a Military Pro-
fessorship should be added to that institution," and published a Prospectus on the
Connecticut institution. Partridge, it was then reported, had "offered to furnish a competent military teacher, if such a professorship should be established by the trustees."
Partridge, born in Norwich, Vermont, had attended Dartmouth College and the United
States Military Academy. Commissioned in 1806 as a first lieutenant of engineers, he had
remained at the Academy until his resignation from the Army in 1818, meanwhile holding professorships in mathematics and engineering and for two years serving as acting
superintendent. His administration had been terminated after a bitter struggle and court
martial growing out of his replacement by Sylvanus Thayer. The following year Partridge
had founded the American Literary, Scientific and Military Academy at Norwich and

in 1825 had moved it to Middletown, where it had three or four hundred students in 1827. The institution was moved back to Norwich in 1829 and chartered in 1834 as Norwich University. Partridge devoted much attention to promoting the establishment of military academies throughout the nation and has been acclaimed as the founder of that concept of preparatory school education. He was surveyor-general of Vermont in 1822–1823 and a member of the Vermont Legislature in 1833, 1834, 1837, and 1839.

5 The Washington Literary, Scientific and Military Gymnasium, under the superintendence of James D. Cobb, had been reviewed favorably by the board of visitors in a report dated May 26, 1827, published in the Washington *Daily National Intelligencer*, July 3, 1827, and in the Washington *Daily National Journal*, July 7, 1827. The board had included among others, such prominent figures as James Barbour, John McLean, Alexander Macomb, and Isaac Roberdeau. Cobb, a native of Vermont, and a graduate of the United States Military Academy,, had been brought before court martial and dismissed from the Army in March, 1814. Under a special act of Congress, February 11, 1830 (6 *U. S. Stat.*, 405), this action was declared illegal and Cobb was awarded the "pay, subsistence, and other emoluments of a first lieutenant" for the period from his dismissal until 1821. An educator and lawyer of some prominence, he petitioned for further redress as late as 1859 but without success. *House Reports*, 35 Cong., 2 Sess., no. 204.

6 Albert G. Meriwether, born in Virginia and brought to Kentucky in 1806, had become one of the publishers from 1821 to 1822 of the Louisville *Western Courier*, established in 1811, and until March, 1827, of the Frankfort *Argus of Western America*. Two months later he had issued proposals for a weekly newspaper at Lexington, to be known as *The Liberal* and to support Jackson's candidacy. The first number of the new publication was to have appeared around June 15, but on June 29 Meriwether announced that he had taken over the Lexington *Kentucky Gazette* and that subscribers to *The Liberal* would "be furnished with" the *Gazette* instead, the name being "The only difference. . . ." Lexington *Kentucky Gazette*, May 25, June 29, 1827. Unable to repay his backers he lost control of the Lexington paper at the beginning of October, 1828, and resumed his work with Amos Kendall in Frankfort. Under the Jackson administration Meriwether held appointment as a clerk in the examiner's office of the Post Office Department in Washington from 1833 to 1836. He remained in Washington thereafter until his death in 1848. Dwight Lawrence Mikkelson, *Kentucky Gazette*, 1787–1848: "The Herald of a Noisy World" (Ph.D. dissertation, University of Kentucky, 1963), 208–11.

From Edward Ingersoll

Dear Sir   Philadelphia August 11. 1827.

It is so long since my last intrusion upon your attention—at least to me it seems so long—that I fancy myself privileged to address a few words to you of very cordial congratulation on the present cheering aspect of political affairs—and particularly on the triumphant position in which you are placed by the recent exposure and discomfiture of the base attempt made by General Jackson, and his abettors, to undermine and destroy your character.[1]

You have so good a memory, even for *minutiae* that it is quite possible you recollect that I have not been always very confident in my hopes of a happy result to the warfare carried on by the powers of darkness against the best and wisest of administrations that this nation yet has known.[2] You will nevertheless allow me credit for sincerity when I say that I have *now* come—(though slowly)—to the full belief that all is going right; and that we,—the friends of justice truth and the administration,—are going to gain a victory of immeasureable [*sic*] benefit to the nation and of unbounded honor to you, on whose fame it mainly depends whether the good cause shall be successful or defeated.

I think a reasonable foundation for this gratifying anticipation may be seen in the gradual development of the true character of Jackson, as well as of his most anxious supporters, the accumulating proofs of his imbecility and their profligacy, and also in the progressive awakening of the public mind, in the middle states, to the only wise system of of [sic] policy which you long since recommended[3] and which is now as inseparably connected with your name and character as a statesman, as the New York Canal[4] is with the fame of Dewitt Clinton, or the battle of New Orleans with that of General Jackson.

I have the greater reliance on my present opinion because I have not come to it hastily, nor merely by following my wishes. When, just before the Presidential election, the unexpected vote of the Louisiana legislature excluded your name from the consideration of the House of Representatives as a candidate,[5] I speculated, as others took the liberty to do, on the course you would probably adopt; and I well remember expressing an expectation and hope—(though at variance, in so doing, with some of my most active co-labourers in the then recent election effort here) that you would vote for Mr Adams—. And when after the election it was said the Department of State was urged upon your acceptance I uttered my opinion, as positively, (against a much more earnest contrariety of judgment than before) that you would, and ought to, sustain the administration of the candidate whom you had joined in electing—, and for this purpose ought to take the chief place in the new cabinet.

Pardon this little egotistical retrospect— I wish to explain that I was not then blind to the dangers and difficulties that were to be expected; that the bitter hostility of a powerful opposition would beset your path was plainly to be anticipated—but—I confess, I did not believe that so much malignity dishonesty and activity would be brought to bear their parts in the desperate war against your reputation and your prospects. I have had my fears that the perseverance audacity and cunning of your enemies would produce an effect upon the minds of the people and would mislead them. But an anxious observation of all safe indications within the scope of my vision leads me *now* to a more comforting belief; and I do trust that the machinations of the unprincipled will be foiled. The precipitate malice of Jackson has put the whole of the much trumpetted [sic] calumny about *bargain* &c on such an issue that it can be made intelligible to every understanding; and must lead to the exposure and disgrace of the whole cabal. It is now *our* time to cry aloud and spare not— we must now carry the war into the enemy's country and dispensing with defensive measures, now no longer necessary, apply ourselves to the much more agreeable operations of offensive warfare. I think it is now an easy matter to make any Jacksonite, who will listen, ashamed of his candidate and his party. I omit no opportunity of doing so. But we want opportunity sadly, in this place—; there is an odium about the character of Mr Binns[6] that blurs everything which he publishes, and dulls it's [sic] point—; the Society which was formed here, while I was ill, of the friends of the gen. and state administrations[7] is perfectly useless. I have in vain endeavoured to persuade them to turn into a *tract* society; convinced, myself, that much light may be shed by publications *not* in newspapers,—and recollecting the sensation which I excited by the little performance of the tract kind, which I published of my own mere motion, last autumn;[8] which I do believe had upon Gov. Shulze[9] and some other of our public men almost a decisive influence. The Governor even lately spoke of that little affair again, and expressed a wish to see it republished, *in German*; but circumstances have changed—, it was the policy I thought *last year*, to speak of General Jackson with cautious reserve, in Pennsylvania, and to spare predilections in his favour, but *now* the whole iniquity of his conduct and paltriness of his character ought to be fully exposed.

I think I must go to the legislature this coming session—which I have heretofore avoided—for the mere sake of lo[ok]ing at the opposition.

The grand mainoevre [sic] in the recent movement of the 'hero of New Orleans,' is the invoking Mr McDuffie's name and thrusting him forward to the front, as the first and chief accuser[10]— [I] have been shewing up, for the use of some of the editors, the impudent falsehood involved in this attempt; and by an abstract of the debate of the 4th. of February pointed out, as it is very easy to do, how very far that gentleman was from desiring to occupy the bad eminence to which general Jackson would thrust him, and how unwilling he was indeed to be a[n] accuser at all, or to admit that any accusation had been m[ade][11]   People are looking with curiosity for Mr Buchanan's statement,[12] chief[ly] I think to see how he will take the *kindness* done to him by his frien[d] and idol the general. His situation is mortifying enough, but, a[s] I esteem him, not undeserved. I have no confidence in his ca[n]dour, but he cannot falsify now without imminent danger of dete[ct]ion. My suspicion is that he left the general at the close of their only conversation not quite impressed with the idea that his advice had met with so indignant a rejection as the general now de-[s]cribes, but on the contrary supposing himself encouraged to make such discreet overtures as the general and his particular friends who estimated the political integrity of others by the standards of their own thought, would meet with such a reception as to lead to others more distinctly tending to an arrangement. Some expressions used by Buchanan which I heard of at the time, or very shortly after, taken in connection with the fact, not then disclosed, of his having held a private conference with the general, seem to justify such a suspicion. But he will not tell whether I am right.

I have lately seen a letter which relates, on the authority of Walter Forward, lately a member from Pittsburg,—this anecdote of Mr Buchanan. When the debate on the 'Speaker's Appeal' (Feb. 3. or 4) was going on, Forward accosted Kremer "Why Mr Kremer you surely do not mean to charge any corruption or dishonorable conduct to Mr Clay, do you?" To which Kremer answered "No indeed, I had no such idea, and I am willing to say so to the House." Just then Buchanan came up and Mr Forward said to him "Well Mr Buchanan we are likely to get rid of this disagreeable business very easily, here is Mr Kremer ready to say that he meant to charge nothing dishonorable to Mr Clay"— Mr Buchanan replied "Mr Forward you had better let Mr Kremer alone, he is in the hands of his friends and *they* will take care of him"—and walked off in private talk with Kremer.

Perhaps you heard of this.[13] It was new to me and seem'd an additional proof of the existence of a vile cowardly conspiracy to get up and keep up, by means of an irresponsible name, a foul slander against you which none of the conspirators dared openly to avow that they believed; to poison the public mind suppress the truth and prevent investigation. I did not know, before, that Buchanan joined in all this iniquity; and when I compare this conduct with his professions when he called to take leave of you at the close of the long Session—May 1826[14]—, I cannot hold him in much respect.

I lately made a visit to Miner[15] and found him very happy and very busy, keeping up his paper[16] with spirit and ability, writing enquiring letters and receiving satisfactory answers touching the public sentiment in this State, of which he has great hopes, but apprehends as I do that the deceptive magic of party organization will be against us.

I have laid an unwarrantable tax on your patience under pretence of a few words—, Yet I cannot refrain from turning from subjects of public interest to say that I have lately lost by death a most excellent friend in my father in law John H. Brinton,[17] a man of as clear an understanding and honourable a spirit as I have ever known, with whom I was in habits of intimate and confidential intercourse, and whose unexpected decease at the early age of fifty four {early to close a life of usefulness and virtue} has not only been an affliction to me in my domestic circle and by the loss of a true friend, but has devolved on me, as an executor of his will, the burthensome care (in part) of his large but dispersed and much encumbered property.

Excuse me for forcing on you this last appeal to your friendly sympathies, as well as for the unreasonable length of this epistle, and believe me very faithfully and respectfully Yours

To the Hon: H. Clay.   EDWARD INGERSOLL

PS   Since writing my letter I have seen Mr Buchanan's statement in the evening's paper. It is all sufficient and satisfactory. Surely as a gentleman general Jackson is disgraced—, as a candidate perhaps he may live through it. My suspicion is not removed that he intended to give Buchanan authority to make overtures. From the statements of the two it appears that Jackson was told 'Mr Clay wants to be Sec. of State, Mr Clay's friends are attached to him— they will vote to-gether— they will decide the election— they will not vote for you if they think *you* certainly will not appoint him— they desire a declara-tion from you which will influence their vote in your favour— All this he understood and believed came as a message from Mr Clay and his friends'— and therefore the dignity & propriety of the answer is to be estimated as if it had been actually so. Well, the general gives '*all the answer*' that the supposed emissary says is necessary to influence the vote of those from whom the general supposes him to have come—and the general is quite sure that he desired the answer, whatever it was, should be communicated by the emissary to the persons whose votes he was thus assured would be influenced by the *all* sufficient declaration.

This is my prima facie [*sic*] view of it. I do not know how evidence much stronger than this could exist of a design to tamper with votes— Any jury in Christendom would convict the general on such testimony. Again I say pardon my *long* talk.

ALS. DLC-HC (DNA, M212, R2).
1 Cf. above, Report of Interview, *ca.* April 15, 1827, and note; Clay to Hammond, June 25, 1827; Smith to Clay, August 1, 1827, note.   2 Cf. above, Ingersoll to Clay, Sep-tember 22, 1826.   3 The "American System"—cf. above, III, 688, 701.   4 The Erie Canal.   5 See above, III, 900.   6 John Binns.   7 Cf. above, Clay to Crownin-shield, March 18, 1827, and note.   8 Cf. above, Ingersoll to Clay, September 22, 1826.   9 John A. Shulze.   10 See above, Smith to Clay, August 1, 1827, note.
11 McDuffie had opposed the proposal to conduct the investigation as requested by Clay, above, "Appeal to the House," February 3, 1825. He had questioned whether Con-gress had authority to take any action as a result of its investigation. He did not be-lieve the (Kremer) letter presented any specific charge but rather rested upon rumor. He maintained that the inquiry threatened the liberty of the press. His amendment, therefore, had been intended to provide specificity to counteract the vagueness of the directive for the investigation: ". . . if the House determined to have an investigation, he hoped some points would be prescribed to which the attention of the committee should be exclusively directed." *Register of Debates*, 18 Cong., 1 Sess., 469–83 (quotation on 483) *passim*. Ingersoll's editorial comments on McDuffie's action have not been found.   12 Buchanan's statement, dated August 8, was published in the Lancaster, Pennsylvania, *Journal* and reprinted in the Philadelphia *United States Gazette*, August 13, 1827. In it Buchanan recounted the circumstances which had caused him to inquire of Andrew Jackson on December 30, 1824, whether, if elected President, he intended to appoint John Quincy Adams as Secretary of State. Buchanan explained that he had been alarmed that this appointment would alienate the supporters of Clay and other candidates and that he had discussed his fears with (Philip Swenk) Markley, who had "urged" that the question be presented to Jackson. After hearing the inquiry, Jackson had stated that he would keep such secrets to himself, that he would "go into office perfectly free and untrammeled. . . ." Buchanan maintained that he had called upon Jackson "solely as his friend," upon his own responsibility, "and not as the agent of Mr. Clay, or any other person." He reminded his readers that he had not been "the political friend of Mr. Clay, since he became a candidate for the office of President." He added, moreover, that, in answer to an inquiry, he had informed the editor of the Washington *United States Telegraph* (Duff Green) last October 16 that he (Buchanan) "had no authority from Mr. Clay, or his friends, to propose any terms to General Jack-son in relation to their votes" and that he had never made such a proposition.   13 Cf.

above, Clay to Adams, February 11, 1825, note.   14 No reference has been found.
15 Charles Miner.   16 The West Chester *Village Record.*   17 Ingersoll had
married in 1816 Catharine Anne Brinton, the daughter of John Hill Brinton, who among
his property holdings owned the southeast corner of Broad and Chestnut Streets, Philadelphia.

INSTRUCTIONS AND DISPATCHES   August 11, 1827

From JAMES COOLEY, Lima, no. 5. Encloses copies of correspondence between
(Cristóbal) Armero, the Colombian Chargé d'Affaires, and the Peruvian Government, concerning Armero's expulsion (cf. above, Cooley to Clay, June 29, July 3,
1827), and of his own correspondence with Armero. Reports that intelligence has
been received of General (José de) Lamar's acceptance of the Presidency (cf.
above, Tudor to Clay, March 23, 1827; Cooley to Clay, June 14, 1827) and of his
recovery from the "sickness which had alone detained him at Guayaquil." Notes
that the presence of Lamar, whose arrival is "hourly expected," is necessary for
the formation of a Cabinet and to cope with the problems of "an exhausted
Country & a Treasury greatly embarrassed. . . ." Adds that in Cuzco and one or
two adjacent provinces, areas loyal to General (Andrés) Santa Cruz, disturbances
occurred upon Lamar's election but resulted in "nothing serious." Forwards a
copy of the "decree of 'amnesty' as it was called" (cf. above, Cooley to Clay, July 3,
1827), but notes that the Congress abandoned it and vested in the Executive the
power temporarily to exile "suspected persons." States that "On the subject of
a Constitution it seems to be settled not to adopt the Federal system." ALS. DNA,
RG59, Dip. Disp., Peru, vol. 1 (M-T52, R1).

From J[AMES] COOLEY, Lima, no. 6. *"Private & confidential."* Notes that on August
9 he read in an issue of the *Mercurio Peruano* (enclosed) a letter (cf. above, Watts
to Clay, June 14, 1827; Clay to Adams, July 2, 1827) "purporting to be written" by
(Beaufort) Watts, at Bogotá, to General (Simón) Bolívar; alludes to Watts' letter
as "singularly indiscreet" in light of local "apprehension, however groundless
that Bolivar may attempt to regain his lost power"; and reports that, since he
"could not doubt for a moment that such a note was unauthorized," he so informed the Peruvian Government. Transmits copies of his disclaimer and the
response. ALS. DNA, RG59, Dip. Disp., Peru, vol. 1 (M-T52, R1). Received
December 18.

From ALBERT GALLATIN, London, no. 106. Encloses "Lord Dudley's answer to"
Gallatin's "notes on the subject of light houses & buoys on the Bahama Banks" (cf.
above, Gallatin to Clay, June 8, 1827). Notes that "the British Government concurs with that of the United States, in the expediency of erecting light houses,
floating lights and buoys on the British side of the channel between the Bahama
Banks and Florida, and that directions have been given for taking the preliminary
steps towards carrying that measure into effect." ALS. DNA, RG59, Dip. Disp.,
Great Britain, vol. 34 (M30, R30). Copy, in MHi-Adams Papers, Letters Recd.
(MR482); published in *American State Papers, Foreign Relations,* VI, 756. Received September 16.

From WILLIAM TAYLOR, Veracruz (1). Reports that the Mexican regulation requiring consular certification at certain ports in the United States for goods
shipped to Veracruz (cf. above, Taylor to Clay, June 15, 1827) has been "virtually
rescinded" and is no longer enforced. Attributes the change to the influence of
the French consul (Alexandre Martin), whose flag was the first from Europe to
come under the regulation which was adopted in July. Notes that, because of a
quarrel between Colonel (José) Rincon and four lieutenant colonels, which re-

sulted in Rincon's allegedly ordering the print shop of their newspaper, the
Veracruzano Libre, destroyed (cf. above, Taylor to Clay, July 30, 1827), General
(Miguel) Barragán ordered Rincon's arrest; that Rincon fled to join his regiment
at their barracks; and that the General Government subsequently ordered the
junior officers to Jalapa, Rincon to Boro del Rio, and Barragán to Mexico, with
General (Vicente) Guerrero being named to succeed him as the military commander of the district. Reports that in the course of these disturbances he requested and obtained assurances from each side that the persons and property of
the foreign community would be protected in the event of violence. ALS. DNA,
RG59, Cons. Disp., Veracruz, vol. 1 (M183, R1).

From WILLIAM TAYLOR, Veracruz (2), "private & confidential." Reports that the
conflict among the military authorities of Veracruz increased in violence until
the General Government on August 8 issued orders by which the disputants were
sent away to different assignments (cf. above, Taylor to Clay, this date). Explains
that the personal feud became generalized under the banners of the two contending factions, the Escoseses and the Yorkinos. Excuses Colonel (José) Rincon's
retaliation (destroying the *Veracruzano Libre* press and type) on grounds that
he acted only after Governor Barragán refused to do him justice (in quieting the
journal's attacks). Notes that his letter to Colonel Rincon inquiring about the
safety of foreigners and their property was "personal & private." Notes that
Rincon "communicated unhesitatingly his intentions to obey" (the orders to take
his regiment out of the city).
    Expresses mortification that the French agent (Alexandre Martin) was able to
use his influence with the government to rescind an order respecting consular
certificates (cf. above, Taylor to Clay, this date), a matter about which the American Minister (Joel Poinsett) had "done nothing—. . . [had] not been able to do
anything & less now than ever." Recalls that upon Martin's arrival, he (Taylor)
opposed permitting him to reside in Mexico (City), that Poinsett welcomed him,
and that the Frenchman became one of Poinsett's "greatest enemies."
    Encloses copies of "all the proclamations manifests [*sic*] &c &c issued during the
late disturbance." In a postscript, advises that should Poinsett return home he
not be replaced as Chargé des Affaires by (John) Mason (Jr.), whose "friends &
ennemies [*sic*]—likes & dislikes would be the same." ALS. DNA, RG59, Cons. Disp.,
Veracruz, vol. 1 (M183, R1). Received September 22.

MISCELLANEOUS LETTERS   August 11, 1827

From T[HOMAS] D. PORTER, New York. States that he is "about to undertake the
publication of a Price-Current, & Commercial Journal on a novel plan," for which
he has "taken a copyright . . . according to the forms of the law." Cites the requirement (under act of May 31, 1790, 1 *U. S. Stat.*, 125) that "a copy of the
work" be forwarded "to the Secretary of State" and solicits Clay's interpretation
of that requirement. Requests, also, an opinion concerning "the *legal* security . . .
obtained by taking the Copy-right," a subject on which he has "strong doubts."
ALS. DNA, RG59, Misc. Letters (M179, R65). Endorsed by Clay on verso of last
page: "☞. Write that it is the safest course to forward a copy of each *number*
of the work; and that alone would be a strict compliance with the Law.
    "On the other point, the sufficiency of the seccurity which the patent gives, for
the enjoyment of the right, I cannot offer any opinion. It depends upon the decision of the Courts, should they be resorted to, and what that would be it is no
part of my official duty to anticipate. H C."
    Daniel Brent acknowledged, on August 27, receipt of Porter's letter and in-

formed him of Clay's opinion. Copy, in DNA, RG59, Dom. Letters, vol. 22, p. 37 (M40, R20).

Porter and Eustis Prescott of New York City (not further identified) issued the first number of their *Comparative Price Current and American Commercial Reporter* on August 16. It provided "a statement of the wholesale prices of the principal articles of trade, in about fifty different markets, in Europe and America, . . . the rates of exchange between the several countries . . . prices of freight . . . premiums of insurance . . . seamen's wages—port charges—tariff duties. . . ." New York *Daily Advertiser* August 18, 1827.

To Samuel L. Southard

My dear Sir   Washn. 12h. Aug. 1827.

I received your obliging favor of the 8h. inst. under date at Waynesborough. I am glad to learn that my Speech at Lexington[1] has produced good effect, although I cannot but think that there is some exaggeration of it, from the partiality of my friends. You will have seen the Genls. epistle of the 18h. Ulto. addressed to the public.[2] It will be necessary that you should bear in mind that when he wrote it, he had not seen my Lexington Speech. My opinion is that his case is not improved, but rendered worse by that epistle. It is written with more cunning than his letter to Carter Beverley,[3] but it is the miserable cunning of a County Court lawyer. What an unenviable situation has he placed *his* friend Buchanan[4] in! Among the disingenuous characteristics of the Genls. last letter is that of his representing Mr. B. as my familiar friend &c. He never was my friend, personal or political; nor did there ever exist any intimacy between us. We are in hourly expectation of hearing from B. Rumor says he will not confirm the statements of the General.[5]

You will have seen, travelling the Jackson circuit, a Speech attributed to Mr. Trimble, affirming that my friends distinctly ascertained that Mr. Adams would appoint me Secy of State &c. I have no doubt that it is a vile fabrication. As far as I have been able to trace it, it originated in a paper published in Winchester (Virginia) where it is given as the hearsay of a hearsay.[6] In the subsequent mutations through which it passed, it is divested by the Jackson Editors of the drapery which exhibits it in its questionable shape, and they present it to their credulous partizans as a downright and veritable speech of Mr. Trimble.[7]

We are anxiously waiting to hear the result of the K. elections. It ought to reach you before it gets here.

We have no news. I believe all public matters here go well. You will have heard that your son Henry and the infant[8] have been ill. I believe neither of them was ever in any danger; and I have this moment upon enquiry been informed that they continue to get better.

Be pleased to make my respects to Judge Brooke and say to him

that I recd. his obliging letter from Waynesborough,[9] and I will write to him tomorrow or next day.[10] I will thank you also to give my best respects to Mr. Caldwell.[11] I am faithfy & Cordially Yr's   H CLAY
Mr. Southard.

ALS. NjP-Samuel L. Southard Papers. Endorsed: "Ansd 23 Augt." Answer, not found.
   [1] Above, July 12, 1827.   [2] Cf. above, Smith to Clay, August 1, 1827.   [3] Cf. above, Clay to Hammond, June 25, 1827.   [4] James Buchanan.   [5] Cf. above, Ingersoll to Clay, August 11, 1827.   [6] The Winchester journal has not been found. On August 9, 1827, the Washington United States Telegraph attributed to the American Sentinel a news item reporting that Representative (David) Trimble of Kentucky "in a recent speech, openly avowed. . . : " 'When we got to Washington, we found that Crawford was out of the question. We ASCERTAINED, that if GENERAL JACKSON was elected, he would not appoint our friend Clay Secretary of State. We THEN ascertained DISTINCTLY, that if Mr. Adams should be elected, he would appoint Mr. Clay his Secreary of State. Under these circumstances, we determined to vote for him.' "   [7] For Trimble's denial that he made the statement, cf. below, Clay to Gales and Seaton, September 26, 1827.   [8] Probably Henry H. Southard, who was admitted to the United States Military Academy from New Jersey in 1828 but was not graduated, and a daughter Ann, born in January, 1826, died in February, 1829.   [9] Above, August 8, 1827.
   [10] See below, August 14, 1827.   [11] James Calwell.

From John P. Erwin

Dear Sir   Nashville 12 Augt. 1827.
   I had the pleasure of receiving your letter[1] (on yesterday) dated near Wheeling—and will as soon as practicable make the investigation,[2] and communicate the result, as desired— I believe that many of the Genls. supporters would greatly prefer that he had remained silent and not committed his fortunes to paper.[3] They seem to apprehend no good consequences to their cause, from this Beverly [sic] affair— The address at Lexington was republished in the Whig & Banner[4] which has more than 2000 subscribers, and has been read all over the country— It has had its effect too, even here— The elections have terminated in this State pretty much as I could have anticipated, altho not in every instance as I would have wished— The defeat of Grundy[5] is seriously felt here, because not only the near relatives, & devoted friends of Genl J—— but even himself took an active part in the contest— He did not go about electioneering but whenever an opportunity was offered, he expressed his anxiety in favor of Grundy, and on the day of the election, when the greatest crowd was in the Court House, he moved up to the polls with considerable ceremony, attended by your Marshal (Genl Purdy)[6] and several intruders—or runners,—and when there after holding an open ticket for Grundy, for some time in his hand, under the pretence of allowing others to vote before him, he & Purdy voted open tickets for Grundy— Crockett[7] the bear hunter who voted for Colo. Williams[8] for Senator, in opposition to Genl J—— is elected 2 to 1   Marable is said to be reelected by 1 or 200 over

Reynolds[9]— And in the Knoxville District, Arnold, who has said so many clever things of Genl J—— & his lady, came within 300 votes of being elected,[10] in opposition to all the interest of Hu L. White & Co— Colo. Williams has obtained a decided victory   His majority being much larger than is usual in that county[11]— Several others of independent principles have been successful in different counties—viz—Bradford, Senator in Bedford—Genl. Smith, Senator—Huntsman Senator, who in a former Legislature moved to throw Genl Jacksons intemperate remonstrance against a Bank, under the table[12]—

You will have three Judicial appointments to make in this State, during the present year—viz—a marshal for West Ten—a District atto for East Ten—and in all probability, a *District* Judge—it being generally understood that Judge McNairy would resign ere long[13]—

By the latest information, James & family[14] were quite well—

I will certainly attend to your last letter, with the least possible delay—very respectfully   JNO. P. ERWIN

ALS. DLC-HC (DNA, M212, R2). Addressed to Clay and endorsed on cover: "*private* letter."

[1] Not found.   [2] Probably an inquiry concerning Jackson's access to publication of the letter of Carter Beverley. Cf. above, Toasts and Speech, July 12, 1827.   [3] Cf. above, Smith to Clay, August 1, 1827.   [4] Nashville *Banner and Whig*, July 28, 1827.   [5] Felix Grundy. Cf. above, Carroll to Clay, November 25, 1825.   [6] Robert Purdy.   [7] David Crockett, born near Rogersville, Tennessee, in 1786, had run away from home at age 13, married young, farmed for a time unsuccessfully, served under Jackson in the Creek campaign of 1813–1814, and in 1815 settled in western Tennessee, where he held office as a magistrate. Distinguished primarily by his claim to have killed 105 bears in only eight or nine months, he had been elected to the State legislature in 1821 and again in 1823 and was now entering Congress, where he served from 1827 to 1831 and again from 1833 to 1835. He consistently opposed Jackson and was defeated for re-election by Jackson's forces. He thereupon joined the movement for Texas independence and was killed in 1836 in the assault on the Alamo.   [8] John Williams. Cf. above, Carroll to Clay, October 1, 1823.   [9] John H. Marable; James B. Reynolds.   [10] Cf. above, Penn to Clay, *ca.* June 19, 1827. Pryor Lea defeated Arnold by 352 votes. Washington *Daily National Intelligencer*, August 21, 1827.   [11] Williams, with a total of 1585 votes, won election by a margin of 369, in the district which covered Knox and Anderson Counties. Leota Driver Maiden, "Colonel John Williams," East Tennessee Historical Society *Publications*, XXX (1958), 40.   [12] Theodorick F. Bradford; Samuel G. Smith; Adam Huntsman. Smith, born in 1794, had been clerk of Jackson County around 1825 and was the first mayor of the town of Gainesboro. He represented Jackson, Fentress, Overton, and White Counties in the State legislature from 1827 to 1831 and was secretary of state for Tennessee from 1832 until his death in 1835. Huntsman, born in Virginia in 1786, had moved first to Knox County, Tennessee, and around 1809 to Overton County, where he had begun the practice of law. He had been elected as a State Senator for White, Overton, and Jackson Counties in 1815, 1817, and 1819, and then moved to Madison County, whence he was again returned to the State Senate in 1827. He was elected to Congress as a Jacksonian, serving there from 1828 to 1830. He was also actively engaged in land speculation and attained wide reputation as a criminal lawyer. Huntsman's early opposition to Jackson had been occasioned by the General's attempt to influence the legislature against a loan office bill, designed as relief legislation in 1820. The Senate had tabled a resolution expressing Jackson's views, and Huntsman had denounced it as "dictatorial, indecorous and intemperate." Joseph Howard Parks, *Felix Grundy, Champion of Democracy* (University: Louisiana State University Press, 1940), 142–43.   [13] On these contemplated appointments, cf. above, Power of Attorney, June 6, 1825, note; Clay to Callaway, May 24, 1826, note; below, Williams to Clay, August 23, 1827, note.   [14] James and Anne Brown Clay Erwin and their children, Julia D. and Henry Clay Erwin.

From Lafayette

Paris August 12th 1827

These few lines, by dear friend, are entrusted to Mrs Shaw, a daughter of General Greene,[1] and Mrs Greene Her Niece and Cousin[2] Who Have past [sic] With us Most of the time of their Sojourn in Europe, and Who Have inspired My family and Myself With the Sentiments of Highest Respect, Warm Affection, and Every Wish for their Welfare. Mrs Shaw Will go to Washington in pursuit of a claim on British Compensations[3] and I Beg You to favour Her With Your kind advices,   Both ladies, as our intimate friends, Will tell you More about La Grange and its inhabitants than I could do in a long letter. I Have writen [sic] to the president about my family and Election Concerns;[4] Mr Brown[5] gives you an Account of public affairs. I Shall therefore Content Myself With Requesting My Respects to Mrs Clay, a Remembrance of me to Your family, Colleagues, and other friends, Being Most truly and affectionally [sic]   Yours   LAFAYETTE

ALS. DLC-HC (DNA, M212, R2). Addressed to Clay.
[1] Louisa Greene (Mrs. James) Shaw; Nathanael Greene.   [2] Cf. above, Brown to Clay, June 25, 1826.   [3] Mrs. Shaw had claims for loss of slaves, cotton, buildings, and provisions, for which she sought reimbursement, under the Treaty of Ghent, from the commissioners acting under the Convention of November 13, 1826 (cf. above, Clay to Gallatin, December 28, 1826). *House Docs.*, 19 Cong., 1 Sess., no. 122, pp. 150, 157.
[4] In a letter dated August 12, 1827, Lafayette had told of the marriage of Louise de la Tour-Maubourg, the engagement of Natalie Lafayette (cf. above, Brown to Clay, June 12, 28, 1827, note), and a visit by George Washington Lafayette to Auvergne. Lafayette noted his personal reluctance to enter the Chamber of Deputies but described his election. MHi-Adams Papers, Letters Recd. (MR 482).   [5] James Brown.

INSTRUCTIONS AND DISPATCHES   August 12, 1827

From HEMAN ALLEN, Valparaiso. Explains his difficulties in finding passage to the United States; proposes now to sail on the *Vincennes* for Acapulco; and expresses a hope that his accounts will be approved to the time of his embarkation. Encloses "a letter [not found], from President [Francisco Antonio] Pinto [Diáz] to the President of the United States and notes that (Joaquín) "Campino has been appointed Minister to the United States." Renews his appeal for another appointment. ALS. DNA, RG59, Dip. Disp., Chile, vol. 2 (M-T2, R2). Received December 13.

From James Brown

Dear Sir,   Paris August 13. 1827

I have had a conversation with the Baron de Damas respecting the discriminating duties demanded last year on Vessels which had touched for orders at the port of a third power on their voyage to France.[1] I have some hope that the principle may be abandoned and that the construction placed on the Treaty at Washington may be adopted here. I sent him a letter insisting that this should take place and urged the return of the duties illegally exacted. I find that the owners of these cargoes have been negligent in complying with the usual formalities having omitted to procure any certificate of origin either from the French Consul or the Collector of the Port. Should the objection therefore of the indirect voyage be overcome, I apprehend we shall have to encounter another arising from the want of proper proofs of the origin of the cargo. It is astonishing that our Merchants who ought to understand the rigor of this Government in taking advantage of the slightest informality on the part of the owners of ships and cargoes should omit documents which are considered essential by every Government.

I shall endeavor to have an interview before the sailing of the next Packet with the Minister of Foreign Affairs and also with the President of the Council.[2] This last gentleman has had his attention more frequently centered to our claims and perhaps understands them better than the Baron de Damas. The proposal to submit the question under the Louisiana Treaty to arbitrators (not sovereigns)[3] may startle this Government as being a step beneath its dignity. It will be my plan at our interviews to talk the affair over carefully and feel my way before I write. The treaties made with Denmark and Sweden and Guatemala[4] are known here and perhaps this Government may insist on being placed on the same footing with those and urge that in case of an arbitration this view of the subject may be submitted.

The death of Mr Canning[5] excited a considerable degree of feeling for the first two or three days and had some effect on the stocks. This feeling now rapidly subsides and it was believed that the event will have no material influence on the affairs of Europe or even on those of England. It appears pretty certain that France has entered into the policy of Austria in relation to the affairs of Portugal.[6] Don Miguel will arrive and be declared Regent in October[7] unless England shall oppose it by force and thus incur the risk of a war with France and Spain and Austria. It is generally believed that England will consent to the Regency of Don Miguel and withdraw her troops from Portugal, France consenting to evacuate simultaneously the Garrisons she occupies in Spain.[8] The constitution is a subject of minor consideration, but perhaps some stipulation may be made for its preservation until it shall be found convenient to annul it.

The Russian fleet is slowly advancing towards the Mediterranean[9] having arrived in the Downs. The French have already a really considerable Squadron in that sea sufficient to separate the Combatants and spare the further effusion of blood. But the parties to this humane alliance proceed with such deliberation that if the troops of the Porte are active they may, before the intervention is felt, exterminate the residue of the wretched Greeks

I hope when this letter arrives you will have returned from your western tour with reestablished health and spirits.[10] The fatigues of your place are too great for you and you ought to insist on the establishment of a home department.[11] The increased duties of the Secretary of state in consequence of the acknowledgment of the Independence of the former Spanish Colonies make it sufficiently laborious for one man to attend to our foreign Affairs.

I inclose you a letter for Mrs Clay from her sister on the subject of her orders for this Country   I am Dear sir with sincere regard your faithfull [sic] & Obedt Servant   JAMES BROWN
Honorable Henry Clay Secretary of State

ALS. DLC-HC (DNA, M212, R2).
[1] Cf. above, Beasley to Clay, August 16, 1826; Brown to Clay, August 23 (1), September 11, 1826; Clay to Brown, March 21, 1827; Brown to Clay, June 28, 1827.   [2] Damas; the Count de Villèle.   [3] See above, Clay to Brown, May 28, 1827.   [4] See above, Convention, December 5, 1825; Convention, April 26, 1826; Appleton to Clay, July 11, 1827.   [5] George Canning. Cf. above, Gallatin to Clay, August 9, 1827.   [6] Cf. above, Brent to Clay, June 30, July 10, 16, November 2, December 25, 1826; Brown to Clay, July 28, 1827.   [7] Cf. above, Everett to Clay, June 9, 1827; Brown to Clay, July 12, 1827.   [8] Cf. above, Everett to Clay, March 19, 1827; Gallatin to Clay, April 14, 1827 (no. 68).   [9] Cf. above, Rainals to Clay, May 30, July 20, 25, 1827; Middleton to Clay, June 23, 1827; Brown to Clay, June 28, July 12, 28, 1827; Gallatin to Clay, July 14, 1827.   [10] See above, Clay to Erwin, August 4, 1827.   [11] Cf. above, Brown to Clay, January 30, 1826; Clay to Webster, February 16, 1826, note.

From Asher Robbins

Dear Sir   Newport, (R.I.) Aug. 13, 1827
Your letter of the 6th inst:[1] arrived here in my absence; and it has but this moment been put into my hands. Personally, I am but slightly acquainted with Proffessor [sic] Woods;[2] but from that acquaintance should doubt, whether he possesses all those qualifications which would be desireable [sic] in a President of a University. He is Professor of natural philosophy & the mathematics;[3] and I should presume, from his reputation that he is well acquainted with those branches of learning; I have conversed with him a little on the subjects of both, but not enough to be myself a Judge of the extent of his proficiency in them. As to general science; and as to literature ancient & modern; or what are called *belles lettres*; I take it his attainments are not great; and I doubt if either his genius or taste lead him to their cultivation. He appears to me to possess a plain good understanding; but not one of uncommon force, nor of any brilliancy. His standing for scholarship and capacity is respectable; but not very distinguished. I understand him to be studious, attentive & strict in his discipline; and to give satisfaction in his department. There is nothing exceptionable in his manners and deportment; these are decent & proper; neither is there any thing, I beleive [sic] exceptionable in his temper.

Such are my impressions as to Mr Woods; perhaps they are not so favorable to him as they ought to be; and I beg you would not act upon them till you hear from me again on the subject. I will ascertain & very shortly, & from those whose opportunities have made them more competent Judges than I am of his qualifications, for the place in contemplation; and write you again;[4] in the mean time please to consider this letter as confidential; & believe me yr. devoted friend
Hon. Mr Clay   ASHER ROBBINS

ALS. KyLxT.   [1] Not found.
[2] Alva Woods.   [3] At Brown University.   [4] See below, August 22, 1827.

From John Sergeant

Dear Sir,   (Private)   Philada. Augt. 13. 1827.
   I have received your favor of the 10th.,[1] and enclose to you the manifesto and reply,[2] which reaching you unofficially, you can read or not according to your convenience. The former came to me in a letter from Vera Cruz dated the day after I left there, and the latter came only two days ago. They would have been sent to you before now, but I took it for granted you had received copies by the same opportunities.
   The President's *visit* in the quarter you mention,[3] was probably one of those things which could not be avoided. I presume he was seized upon at the moment of arrival and had no choice. This is only my own notion. The thing, however, is of no great moment.
   We are in doubt here what will be the Governor's[4] decision as to the election, whether he will order one in October, or wait 'till after the meeting of Congress and some order of the House upon the former election.[5] In either case, I expect to be a candidate, and of course hope to succeed. The friends of the Administration are certainly increasing.
   The Palladium of this morning (as I have heard) speaks of a letter from Mr. Jefferson to Mr. Giles upon the subject of the arrangement of the Administration at Mr. Adams's coming into office.[6] If Mr. Jefferson stated what I am told the paper says is contained in his letter, he must have been grossly imposed upon, for there is not a word of truth in the statement. The chief object I suppose is to array his name against you. It can have no effect. The great battery having been silenced, irreparably destroyed, a petty reserve like this will not avail. I am a little curious to see how Genl. Jackson's friends will treat Mr. Buchanan.[7]
   From all I have heard and seen, I think you would find a visit to Philadelphia neither unpleasant nor unprofitable. Very respectfully and truly yrs.   JOHN SERGEANT.
The Honble Henry Clay.

ALS. DLC-HC (DNA, M212, R2).   1 Not found.
2 Cf. above, Poinsett to Clay, July 8, 1827.   3 Cf. above, Wharton to Clay, August 3,
1827.   4 John A. Shulze.   5 Cf. above, Sergeant to Clay, September 28, 1826,
note.   6 No copy of the Philadelphia *National Palladium* for this date has been
found. The Washington *United States Telegraph* on August 15 reprin'ed the following
excerpt from the *National Palladium*: "We understand that a letter from Mr. Jefferson,
shortly before his death, to a distinguished person in Virginia, will be published soon,
expressing Mr. Jefferson's high disapprobation of Mr. Adams' conduct, with an account
of the manner by which Mr. Adams was apparently brought round to the democratic
ranks." William B. Giles was not named in the account. A letter from Jefferson to Giles,
dated December 26, 1825, was released on September 7, 1827 (cf. below, Johnston to
Clay, September 14, 1827, note); but it does not concern "the arrangement of the Administration at Mr. Adams's coming into office." For correspondence centering on the
controversy which developed over Jefferson's views on the administration, see also, below, Hammond to Clay, August 29, 1827. The *National Palladium and Freeman's
Journal* had been established in January, 1827, as a continuation of the *Freeman's
Journal and Philadelphia Mercantile Advertiser* (founded in 1775) and represented
Jacksonian interests.   7 Cf. above, Ingersoll to Clay, August 11, 1827, note.

INSTRUCTIONS AND DISPATCHES   August 13, 1827

To WILLIAM SHALER, Algiers. Acknowledges receipt of his letter of May 14 and
states that the President grants permission for him to return to the United States,
on leave with pay, "leaving Mr. [William B.] Hodgson in charge of the Consulate. . . ." Clay. DNA, RG59, Cons. Instr., vol. 2, pp. 439–40 (M78, R2).

To HENRY WHEATON, "Charge d'Affaires of the U. S. to Denmark," no. 3 (*i.e.*, no.
4). Recommends to his "favorable attention" the claim of Daniel W. Coxe "upon
the Danish Government, the prosecution of which will be managed by Mr. John
Connell," and states that Coxe has been informed that Wheaton will aid his
cause. LS. DNA, RG84, Denmark, Official Correspondence, 1827–1835 (MR14,
frame 334). Received October 2, 1827. Cf. above, Coxe to Clay, August 7, 1827,
and note.

From SAMUEL HODGES, JR., Santiago (Cape Verde Islands). Encloses copies of correspondence with the Governor (Caetano Procopio Godinho de Vasco, not further
identified) relating to the quarantine practices of the local government. Complains that it is "ridiculous that a health visit should be established here where
originates most tropical diseases, and particularly when it is made a part of
Speculation." Has requested assistance from (Thomas L. L.) Brent in approaching
the Portuguese Government on this matter. ALS. DNA, RG59, Cons. Disp., Santiago, vol. 1 (M-T434, R1). Received October 14.

MISCELLANEOUS LETTERS   August 13, 1827

From ANDREW BROWN AND OTHERS, Hamburg. Complain of the treatment they, as
distressed seamen, receive at the hands of John Cuthbert, "whose cold heart, dares
to insult, dares, (instead of [assisting] us), to threaten us with a *treading mill*!"
Charge that he "allows American Captains, to ship Germans, Danes, &c., and
leaves . . . [American seamen] unprotected on a foreign shore." Ask that their
complaint be laid "before the President, so that the necessary orders m[ay] be
handed to Mr. Cuthbert, to behave in future as becomes [the] dignified situation
he fills—to give assistance to distres[sed] seamen, to receive them kindly, and not
with his usua[l] imprecations of "G—d d——n you, Sir, you are a blackguard and
I will send you to prison, to a *treading mill*!" LS, signed by Brown and 26 others.

DNA, RG59, Cons. Disp., Hamburg, vol. 3 (M-T211, R3). Received October 31. Tape and binding obscure margins.

"By direction of the Secretary," Daniel Brent sent to Cuthbert, on November 23, 1827, a copy of this document in order to allow him to submit "such explanations or statements in regard to the allegations" as he could give. An early reply was requested. Copy, in DNA, RG59, Cons. Instr., vol. 2, pp. 450–51 (M78, R2).

Brown gives his home address as New York and his age as 30 years.

To Francis T. Brooke

My Dear Sir: Washington Aug. 14. 1827.—
I received your obliging favor from Waynesborough.[1] I should be very glad if I could participate with you & Mr. Southard in the pleasure & benefit of the Springs. My health is, however, not bad.—

I hope you are not mistaken in the good effect of my Lexington Speech.[2] Mr. Buchanan has presented his communication to the public;[3] & although he evidently labors throughout the whole of it to spare & cover Gen. Jackson, he fails in every essential particular to sustain the General.— Indeed, I could not desire a stronger statement from Mr. Buchanan. The tables are completely turned upon the General. Instead of any intrigues on my part & that of my friends, they were altogether on the side of Gen. Jackson & his friends.— But I will leave the Statement to your own reflections. I directed a copy to be inclosed yesterday to Mr. Southard.— It must confirm any good impressions produced by my speech.

Tell Mr. Southard that his children are much better, & that he need not entertain any fear about them[4] —

With my best wishes that you may both realize much benefit from the mineral waters, I am alway [sic] your friend.   H. CLAY
The Honble F. Brooke.

Copy. DLC-TJC (DNA, M212, R13) . Published in Colton (ed.), *Private Correspondence of Henry Clay*, 169.
[1] Above, August 8, 1827.   [2] Above, July 12, 1827.   [3] See above, Ingersoll to Clay, August 11, 1827.   [4] Cf. above, Clay to Southard, August 12, 1827.

To Jared Sparks

Dear Sir   (Inofficial)   Washington 14h. August 1827.
I received your favor of the 7h. instant transmitting a copy of your answer to Mr. Pitkins application for access to the Diplomatic Correspondence. During my absence, on my late excursion to the West, he had addressed a letter on that subject to the Department, to which an answer from Mr. Brent was returned by the direction of the President.[1] This answer gave him some qualified permission to examine

the correspondence at the Dept. of State, of which he has not availed himself yet. I certainly shall do nothing intentionally which shall interfere with the engagement which, in behalf of the public, I have made with you.[2] Should you execute your intention of going to Europe in the Spring,[3] I will take pleasure in furnishing you with some letters, which may possibly be of some service to you.

My health, to which you kindly allude, is better than it has been at this season of the year, for several past years. I had however too little repose on my late journey to derive all the benefit which I usually experience from travelling. I am with high regard Your ob. Servt.

Mr. Sparks.   H. CLAY

ALS. MH.   [1] See above, Pitkin to Clay, June 23, 1827, and note.
[2] Cf. above, Sparks to Clay, January 31, March 13, May 7, 1827.   [3] Sparks was a year in Europe, arriving at Liverpool on April 14, 1828, and returning to New York on May 11, 1829. While there, he examined documents in British and French archives concerning the American Revolution.

From James Barbour

Washington August 14th. 1827.

I certify that in the early part of the Session of Congress 24–5. I dined at the Columbian College with Genl. La Fayette Mr Clay and others[1]— on returning from that dinner to Town Mr Clay and myself (there being no other person with us) came in the same hack— During the ride our conversation turned on the then depending presidential election— I expressed myself in the event of the contest being narrowed down to Mr Adams and General Jackson in favor of Mr Adams— And Mr. Clay expressed a coincidence of opinion—

JAMES BARBOUR

ADS. DLC-HC (DNA, M212, R2). Not addressed; endorsed by Clay on verso: "J. Barbour." Published in Appendix, p. 55, of Clay, *Address . . . to the Public*, below, December 29, 1827.
[1] The first commencement of Columbian College had been held on December 15, 1824. The ceremony had occasioned a dinner attended by General Lafayette, President Adams, members of the Cabinet, and several Senators and Representatives. Washington *Daily National Intelligencer*, December 16, 18, 1824.

From Tristam Burges

Sir   Providence August 14th 1827

I can not answer every part of your letter of the 5th Inst.[1] With the scientific & literary attainments of Professor Woods I am not acquainted. As a Preacher he is certainly respectable; & in his Professorship has given Satisfaction. His character is good his temper amiable his general deportment that of a gentleman & a Christian. He presided pro tempore in Brown University & I never heard his conduct called in question. Professor William G. Goddard of this town[2] can tell you what are his attainments.

I have the honour to be with much respect your obt sert

TRISTAM BURGES

ALS. KyLxT. Addressed, on attached sheet, to Clay.
[1] Not found. Cf. above, Robbins to Clay, August 13, 1827.   [2] Born in Rhode Island in 1794 and graduated from Brown University in 1812, Goddard was professor of moral philosophy and physics at that institution from 1825 to 1834 and of rhetoric and belles-lettres from 1834 to 1842. He had been editor and publisher of the Providence *Rhode Island American* from 1814 to 1825.

From George W. Jones

Agency Office Bank U States.
Hon. H. Clay   Cincinnati August 14. 1827
Sir   I had the pleasure to address you on the 29th. June at Lexington, but presume the letter[1] did not get to your hands. and am therefore again under the necessity of soliciting your attention to the Surveys No 4251 patented to James Morrison, and No. 4451 patented 3/5 to James O'Hara,[2] and 2/5 to Nicholas Bowsman[3] Each Survey being for 500 Acres of Land.

The Bank of the United States is the unconditional Assignee of all William Lytle's one third, or Locators Share, in said Survey without limitation or Condition,   No other person, or body has any right or title to said Share or the proceeds thereof,   The letters of Col. Morrison which I hold fully recognize the Claim, and my duty as Agent leads me to request you will admit or reject the right of the Bank to One third of those Surveys— Or if you prefer, an Engagement to pay a Sum to be agreed upon for a release of the Bank right—Should it be a matter of Choice not to relinquish the Land—   in that Event I would on the part of the Bank agree to fix the Sum to be received from the Estate of Col. Morrison at Five hundred dollars with interest until paid—   the sooner this matter can be finally closed, the less trouble will be given to all parties interested   You will therefore particularly oblige by giving it your attention   I am with great respect Yr. Obt. Svt.   GEO: W. JONES AGT.

ALS. DLC-TJC (DNA, M212, R13). Cf. above, Jones to Clay, September 29, 1826.
[1] Not found.   [2] Cf. above, Scott to Clay, July 21, 1827.   [3] That is, Bausman.

From Richard B. Maury

My Dear Sir.   *Private*   Orange Springs Va. 14h August 1827.
I have recently, at the request of Mr. Forbes,[1] assumed the management of his accounts with your Department, and having occasion to

communicate with him upon the subject of them, I have taken the liberty of sending the inclosed letter[2] to your care.

I beg that I may, at the same time, be permitted to tender you my humble, tho' sincere felicitations upon the triumph which I believe is soon to be consummated over your vile and slanderous Calumni-ators. I use not the language of flattery, when I assure you, that your Lexington speech is considered by all unprejudiced men, with whom I have conversed, as one of your happiest, mightiest efforts, and I am confident it has not passed away without its effect. The physic is evi-dently at work even in this *infected region*, for I have found on count-ing noses in a company of 30 or 40, now visitors here, that the balance is in favor of the "Coalition."[3]

The People are put to it to reconcile the conflicting statements of the General and hi[s] meddling guest,[4] and want further explanation. Unfortunately for the General's cause, his friend Mr. B, (as I dare say you know) is looked upon by many as little better tha[n] a Swindler.

With assurances of my most exalte[d] respect I am Dear Sir Yr Mo obt Serv[t]   R. B. MAUR[Y]
Hon. Henry Clay Washington

ALS. DNA, RG59, Misc. Letters (M179, R65). Maury, a Virginian and a veteran of the War of 1812, had been private secretary to President James Monroe and since 1825 had been a clerk in the Navy Department. He was a nephew of James Maury and now re-sided in Georgetown.
    [1] John M. Forbes.   [2] Not found.   [3] Cf. above, Hammond to Clay, March 28, 1827.   [4] Andrew Jackson; James Buchanan. Cf. above, Smith to Clay, August 1, 1827; Ingersoll to Clay, August 11, 1827.

INSTRUCTIONS AND DISPATCHES   August 14, 1827

From ALBERT GALLATIN, London, no. 107. Comments: "It is now understood that the new Administration of this Country is to be but a continuation of that of Mr. [George] Canning [cf. above, Gallatin to Clay, August 9, 1827], to act on the same principles, and no new appointments to be made but those that are strictly necessary." Notes that "Lord Goodrich [*sic*] is first Lord of the Treasury"; that "Lord Harrowby President of the Council, retires from office"; and that ". . . the other Ministers, with the exception perhaps of Mr [William] Huskisson, remain in their respective offices." Speculates that Huskisson will have the option of two offices—Chancellor of the Exchequer, "for which he is best qualified and to which he is called by public opinion," or the Colonial Department, which "his precarious health will probably induce him to take. . . ." Discusses the possibilities for a suc-cessor to Canning in the House of Commons and concludes that Huskisson "is . . . looked on and intended as the Ministerial leader in the House." Conjectures that "Power will be more divided than under Mr Canning"; that "the great political questions will be decided by the Cabinet"; and, in view of Huskisson's "weight in those [questions] affecting the finances of the Country," that "There will . . . be no change in the policy of Great Britain toward us." Comments further on Huskis-son's health; states expectation that "The present administration will . . . last till after the next meeting of Parliament in January," and beyond; and adds that "The critical situation of affairs in Portugal is at this moment the principal cause of embarrassment" (cf. above, Brown to Clay, July 28, August 13, 1827). ALS. DNA, RG59, Dip. Disp., Great Britain, vol. 34 (M30, R30). Copy, in MHi-Adams Papers, Letters Recd. (MR482); published in Adams (ed.), *Writings of Albert Gallatin*, II, 380–83. Received September 16.

Dudley Ryder, first Earl of Harrowby and Viscount Sandon, had been elected to the House of Commons in 1784, had been named to the Privy Council in 1790, and had entered the House of Lords in 1804. He had been for many years vice president of the Board of Trade, for a few months in 1804, Foreign Secretary, and from 1812 to 1827 minister-president of the Council. Retiring from office at this time, he refused to become Prime Minister when Goderich resigned (cf. above, Gallatin to Clay, February 22, 1827, note) but continued active in Parliament.

From VINCENT GRAY, Havana. Notes that Commodore (Angel) LaBorde has returned from the coast of Mexico and Veracruz, where he conducted an exchange of prisoners. Reports that the "autos" of (John) Hollins have been returned from Spain, that Hollins' attorney, (Richard R.) Keene, has arrived to attend his case in Havana, and that "Appearances are favorable for Hollins. . . ." ALS. DNA, RG59, Cons. Disp., Havana (M-T20, R5). Received August 28. Cf. above, Hollins to Clay, January 27, 1827.

MISCELLANEOUS LETTERS   August 14, 1827

From WILLIAM B. ROCHESTER, Rochester (New York). States that he is preparing to leave for Guatemala "very early in September"; suggests that, in view of "the lapse of time, since receiving . . . [his] instructions" (cf. above, Clay to Rochester, March 11, 1827), they may need to be extended; and asks how to draw for his outfit (cf. above, Rochester to Clay, June 3, 1827). ALS. DNA, RG59, Dip. Disp., Central America, vol. 1 (M219, R2).

From CHAUNCEY WHITTELSEY, Middletown (Connecticut). Reminds Clay of their discussion of the case of the schooner *Esther* (cf. above, Dorr to Clay, October 7, 1825, and note) in September, 1826, and that Clay asked him for a statement of facts from which to draft instructions to the Chargé on the matter. Notes that he requested (Jonathan) Barnes to supply the information and was assured that he had (cf. above, Barnes to Clay, November 10, 1826). Reports that his brother-in-law, the principal owner of the *Esther*'s cargo, Henry D. Tracy, now living in Lima, has learned that the Chargé has arrived and that his instructions (above, Clay to Cooley, November 6, 1826) contain no mention of the claim. Requests that Clay inform him "whether the Petition was received & if received, whether any instructions have been given to the charge des affaires—& if not whether any further procedings [*sic*] are necessary on the part of the Claimant—." ALS. DNA, RG76, Misc. Claims, Peru (MR83, frame 538). Received August 18.

The State Department had received the above-mentioned statement from Barnes eight days after the date of Clay's instructions to Cooley.

To Charles R. Vaughan

Rt. Honorable Charles R. Vaughan.
Envoy Extraordinary &   Department of State, Washington,
Minister Plenipoty. from Great Britain.   August 15th. 1827.

The undersigned, Secretary of State of the United States, has the honor to acknowledge the receipt on the second instant, of the Note of Mr. Vaughan,[1] His Britannic Majesty's Envoy Extraordinary and Minister Plenipotentiary under date in the last month, communicating some observations which he is directed by his Government to make, in relation to the impressment of two seamen from on board the American Brig Pharos by Captain Clavering of His Britannic Majesty's Ship Redwing.

The Undersigned regrets extremely the unavoidable circumstances which have hitherto prevented the procurement of the deposition of Captain Merchant,[2] who commanded the Pharos at the time the two seamen were taken from her; and he now transmits herewith, for the perusal of Mr. Vaughan and the use of his Government a copy of a Letter just received from Mr. Samuel Hodges Junr., the American Consul at the Cape de Verd Islands, under date the 20th. of June last, from which it appears that there was great and unaccountable delay in Mr. Hodges' receipt of the Letter from this Department, of the 20th. of June of the last year, directing him to take Captain Merchants deposition. But the Letter also shews a determination of the American Consul to execute the direction which he has received as soon as Captain Merchant, then on the Coast of Africa, shall have returned to the station of Mr. Hodges. The Letter also states the additional fact that one of the two Seamen, in question, appeared on the Roll of Equipage of the Pharos to be a Citizen of the United States, and his protection represented him as a native of Portland, in the State of Maine.

In this incomplete state of the evidence of the transaction, the undersigned would have gladly abstained, at this time, from any further observations upon the case but for what he must consider the extraordinary character of some of those which have been communicated through Mr. Vaughan, by the command of his Government.

Whilst the American Government does not hold itself bound to possess a perfect knowledge of the Municipal Laws of Great Britain, it was not entirely without information that the British practice of Impressment is not usually enforced in a season of Peace, and in the first note which the Undersigned, on the 8th. day of May, 1826, had the honor of addressing to Mr. Vaughan, on the subject of this correspondence, the following expressions are used: "If, as we are bound at present to believe, they {the facts attending the impressment of the two seamen} are well founded, Captain Clavering must not only have acted without, but contrary to, the orders of his Government: for it is otherwise impossible to believe, that the outrage which they disclose should have been attended with the aggravating circumstance of being perpetrated in a season of profound peace between Great Britain and the rest of Christendom." Notwithstanding the existence of that general interdict, the Undersigned did suppose it possible that an Officer of the British Navy, without the authority of his Government, might have undertaken, in a particular case, to impress two American seamen. And the demand which was made on that supposition, of animadversion upon the conduct of Captain Clavering, was founded, not merely on the alleged outrage itself, but, also, upon the belief that it had been committed without authority.

If Mr. Vaughan had been instructed to make a specific statement in support of his general allegation, that the Undersigned had in his note of the 15th [sic] of June, of the last year, strained the evidence before him, he would have been enabled to judge of the correctness of that general assertion. Without the benefit of any such specification, he can only say that he has received the evidence referred to, and cannot admit that any conclusion that he has drawn from it, is unwarranted.

The Government of the United States would be very unwilling to believe, and, during this correspondence, has certainly been far from charging, that that of His Britannic Majesty had failed to inculcate on the Officers in His Britannic Majesty's Naval service, the observance of due respect towards the officers of every power, in amity with his Majesty. It was, therefore, altogether unnecessary that the condition should have been intimated in Mr. Vaughan's Note, that "to ensure the continuance of such respect, and a consequent interchange of good offices, it is necessary that a corresponding good feeling should influence the conduct of the Foreign Powers." If this intimation were thrown out with the intention of repressing well founded complaints which the American Government may, from time to time, suppose itself to be justified in making to that of Great Britain against the conduct of any of its officers, it cannot be allowed to have that effect, even if the exhibition of any such complaint should be unhappily followed by any diminution of that courtesy and respect customary in the intercourse between the officers of friendly Maritime powers, and which none are more uniformly in the habit of practising than those of the American Navy. If in the process of investigating any complaint which shall have been so preferred, it shall be made to appear that any officer of the United States has acted with impropriety, the American Government will ever be as ready to reprehend his conduct, as it would be prompt in demanding the punishment of a foreign officer, who shall have violated the rights of the United States, or of any of its Citizens.

After all that has heretofore passed between the two Governments in relation to the British claims and practice of impressment, as applied to the Navigation of the United States, it ought not to excite surprize that their Government should instantly remonstrate against the very first renewed example of the practice, or any semblance of it: And the Undersigned hopes that the sensibility which has been manifested to the vindication of Captain Clavering, authorizes a conclusion favorable to the preservation of a good understanding between the two Countries on that most interesting and delicate subject.

The Undersigned tenders to Mr. Vaughan, on this occasion, assurances of his most distinguished consideration.　　　　　H. CLAY.

Copy. DNA, RG59, Notes to Foreign Legations, vol. 3, pp. 379–83 (M38, R3). Draft (the first two paragraphs in Clay's hand), in CSmH; copy, in MHi-Adams Papers, Letters Recd. (MR482). For Adams' approval of Clay's stand, cf. below, Adams to Clay, August 23, 1827.
1 Above, *ca.* July 30, 1827.　　2 Ephraim Merchant.

From John Quincy Adams (1)

Henry Clay—Secretary of State
Dear Sir.　　　　　　　(Private.)　　　　　　Quincy 15. August 1827.
On my passage through Philadelphia,1 Mr Sergeant put into my hands the enclosed private Letter from Mr Poinsett to me,2 which was transmitted to him, after he left the City of Mexico, but before he sailed. I communicate it to you for your information, and wish it may also be perused by the other members of the Administration　It seems to me that there is no occasion for any thing to be done on our part, until the affair shall assume a more public and official shape. In the meantime it may be advisable to reflect upon the course to be pursued in that event— Have the goodness to keep Mr Poinsett's Letter to be returned to me on my arrival at Washington. Faithfully yours
　　　　　　　　　　　　　　　　　　　J. Q. ADAMS

ALS. MHi-Adams Papers, Letters Recd. (MR482). Clay acknowledged receipt of this letter and of one below, this date, in a routine note of acceptance, August 20, 1827. ALS, in *ibid.*; copy, in DNA, RG59, Unofficial Letter-Book of H. Clay, p. 13.
1 Cf. above, Wharton to Clay, August 3, 1827, and note.　　2 Cf. above, Sergeant to Clay, August 1, 1827, and note.

MISCELLANEOUS LETTERS　　　　　　　　　　　　August 15, 1827

To "George Blake Esqr., Atty. of the U. S. for the D. of Massachts. or [Henry] A. S. Dearborn, Collr. of the Customs Boston." Recalls: "A letter was written to you [Blake] from this Department on the 30th. of May 1826. . . ; and a letter was soon afterwards received from you, or the Collector at Boston in reply [see above, Blake to Clay, June 7, 1826]," relative to obtaining a statement from Captain (Ephraim) Merchant. Adds: "Circumstances make it very desirable that this should be done without delay, if Captain Merchant be now in Boston, and in that case I have to request you to procure his deposition immediately and forwarded [*sic*] to this Department." Copy. DNA, RG59, Dom. Letters, vol. 22, pp. 27–28 (M40, R20). Cf. above, Clay to Vaughan, this date.

From [JOHN QUINCY ADAMS], Quincy (2). Encloses a "Petition of James Hall, of the Eastern District of Florida, complaining of certain proceedings of Waters Smith, the Marshal of the United States for that District," and enclosing a deposition of Hall and "copies of two other depositions relating to the subject." Suggests that copies of the papers be sent to Smith, with a request for explanations. ALS. DNA, RG59, Misc. Letters (M179, R65).

Daniel Brent, on August 24, transmitted to Smith, "by direction of the Secretary," copies of these documents "exhibiting a complaint . . . for an alleged interference . . . [by Smith] with regard to a quantity of timber sold by . . . [Hall] from a tract of land in East Florida, claimed by him as his property, and by . . . [Smith] in behalf of the United States as public property. . . ," in order to give Smith "the opportunity of making explanations to this Department, with reference to the facts alleged." Copy, in DNA, RG59, Dom. Letters, vol. 22, p. 34 (M40, R20).

Hall, born at Keene, New Hampshire, in 1760, was a veteran of the Revolutionary War and had settled at Plummer's Cove, Florida, in 1798. He is supposed to have been the first American physician to practice medicine in that territory. He was named justice of the peace for St. John's County in 1822, of Duval County in 1832, and of Gadsden County in 1835 and continued in medical practice until his death in 1837.

From SAMUEL MOORE, Philadelphia. Acknowledges receipt of a letter "accompanied by a copy in Brass, of the 'Mark of Castile'—the standard weight by which the coinage of the Spanish Mint is regulated," which the United States Minister in Spain, (Alexander H.) Everett, has sent through Clay. Explains that the weight arrived too late for the purpose for which he had requested it, the preparation of a report required by a resolution of the Senate "relative to the foreign coins circulating in the United States [*Sen. Docs.*, 19 Cong., 2 Sess., no. 23]," but that "it is, otherwise, acceptable and will be useful." Asks that the enclosed letter, expressing appreciation, be forwarded to Everett. ALS. DNA, RG59, Misc. Letters (M179, R65).

Moore, who had served in the United States House of Representatives from 1818 to 1822, was director of the United States Mint from 1824 to 1835.

To John Quincy Adams

Dear Sir   (Confidential)   Washington 16h. August 1827

I sent you a few days ago[1] the last dispatches from Mr. Gallatin, according to which it would appear probable that his negotiation will fail on both the points of the N. Western boundary and the renewal of the Commercial Convention. The British require, in effect that neither party should exercise any exclusive Sovereignty over the disputed territory; and that a new clause should be added to the Commercial Convention sustaining the British interpretation of the treaty of 1815 as to Rolled iron. Mr Gallatin gave an answer declining to accept the British proposals, but took time for further consideration before he should render his answer definitive.[2] He has probably before this time communicated his final answer, and the negotiation is concluded, one way or the other, on those two points.[3] It does not strike me therefore as necessary to give him any instructions in regard to them, other than to approve what he has done. I think he was right in both particulars. There was still a chance of the British receding;

and if that shall not have happened, there will be yet an opportunity of the two parties coming to an agreement before the month of October 1828, when the existing Convention[4] will expire.

I confess I begin to think that the B. Government is disposed to quarrel with us, and with this view it is increasing the number of the subjects of difference and misunderstanding.

I received a note some days ago from Mr. Vaughan,[5] in respect to the two Seamen impressed from on board the Pharos on the coast of Africa, written in rather an offensive tone. I suspect that character has been communicated to it by the Lord High Admiral, the Duke of Clarence. I transmit a copy of the note, together with a copy of the answer[6] which I returned, and which I hope will meet your approbation.

I think Mr. Gallatin ought to have more strictly executed the last instruction, respecting the Colonial question.[7] He has, in his note to the British Secretary,[8] left out parts, particularly the reproof of Mr. Canning for the sentiment that he *would not* be drawn into any further discussion of the Subject, which I think ought not to have been omitted. I am, Sir, with great respect Faithfully Your obt. Servant Mr. Adams.   H. CLAY

ALS. MHi-Adams Papers, Letters Recd. (MR482). Copy, in DNA, RG59, Unofficial Letter-Book of Henry Clay, 12–13.
[1] The letter of transmittal has not been found.   [2] See above, Gallatin to Clay, June 20, 1827.   [3] Cf. above, Gallatin to Clay, August 6, 7, 1827.   [4] Cf. above, II, 611n.   [5] Above, Vaughan to Clay, July 30, 1827.   [6] Above, Clay to Vaughan, August 15, 1827.   [7] Above, Clay to Gallatin, April 11, 1827.   [8] Cf. above, Gallatin to Clay, June 4, 1827, and note.

From Francis Wayland, Jr.

Sir   Brown Univ'y. Providence Aug. 16. 1827.
I have the honor to acknowledge the receipt of your favor of Aug. 7,[1] and will as you have requested assure you frankly and explicitly upon the question, which it suggests.—

With regard to myself I am able to speak decidedly. My connexions with this Institution are of such a nature and I have been so identified with the changes which have taken place in its discipline and which are yet in prospect that I could not remove to any other situation without material sacrifice of Character. Feeling satisfied that such is the fact further discussion of this topic would be useless.—

With Prof. Woods[2] I have been acquainted as an officer only during my residence here, about 6 months. His advantages have been greater than those of Americans of his age generally. He has received a regular Academical & Theological Education in the best seminaries in this country & in every part of his course as I have been informed has stood among the first. He has also spent a year or more in Europe— He is a man of entire kindness of heart, of amiable manners of unusual prudence, and of true but conciliatory piety. In a N England College I think he would make a safe and judicious President, and should not be surprized if he should be elected at any time to the charge of any one of our younger Colleges. As a belles lettres scholar I should not think him specially distinguished. He is always accurate but not often splendid. Nor has he particular power in Conversation. In these respects as in most othe[r]s he is very much the reverse of the late Dr Holley whose death[3] I regret very much to have heard.—

What the difference may be between a Western and N England College I do not know and therefore am unable to decide respecting Prof W's capacity for the former situation. If he be a prominent Candidate I am of opinion that it would be well for some gentleman who knows the situation of Transylvania Univ'y to see him before an election.—

I observe it is mentioned in the papers of today that you are expected somewhere at the North in a few days.[4] Could you not make it in your way to attend our Commencement on the 1st. Wednesday the 5th of Septr. You would probably meet on that occasion many of your N. England freinds [sic].—

I trust I need not add that it will always give me pleasure in any manner in my power to subserve the interests of Transylvania University. I am Sir Yours respectfully   FR WAYLAND JR.
The Hon Henry Clay.—

ALS. KyLxT. Cf. above, Robbins to Clay, August 13, 1827; Burges to Clay, August 14, 1827. Wayland, born in New York in 1796 and graduated from Union College in 1813, had studied medicine briefly and in 1816 attended Andover Theological Seminary. He had tutored at Union College from 1817 to 1821, served as pastor of the First Baptist Church of Boston from 1821 to 1826, returned as professor of mathematics and natural philosophy at Union for a few months, and in February, 1827, had become president of Brown University. He retired from a distinguished career in that office in 1855 and for a time held the pastorate of the First Baptist Church of Providence.
1 Not found.   2 Alva Woods.   3 Following his resignation from the presidency of Transylvania University (see above, Clay to Bradford, February 10, 1827, note), Holley had left Lexington on March 27, had moved to New Orleans, and at mid-July had embarked for New York by sea, seeking relief from an illness and the summer heat. On July 31, ten days out of port, he had died of yellow fever off the coast of Florida. The *Washington Daily National Intelligencer*, on August 13, 1827, had reprinted a dispatch from the *New York American* of August 11, announcing the event.   4 The Philadelphia *United States Gazette*, on August 13, 1827, had commented: "We understand that the Hon. Henry Clay . . . is expected to be in this city in a few days." Cf. below, Sergeant to Clay, August 17, 1827.

DIPLOMATIC NOTES   August 16, 1827

From CHARLES R. VAUGHAN, Washington. Acknowledges receipt of Clay's note of August 15 and remarks that "there are some points in it, which he cannot allow to pass without observation." Contends that, although the statement of the British consul at Boston (George Manners—cf. above, Vaughan to Clay, May 22, 1826) "was an ex parte one, and the evidence which he adduced, was not certified on oath, . . . surely there was enough in it, to induce a suspicion, that the facts which had been laid before the Government, of the United States [cf. above, Hodges to

Clay, March 16, 1826], might have been misrepresented, and to induce a suspension of judgment on the merits of the case." Asserts that he "could never consent to believe, that it was possible, that a British officer could have ventured under any circumstances, to impress Seamen of any Nation, during a time of Peace, in defiance of the Laws of his own Country." Contends "that the general tone of his [Clay's] Note of the 15th. June fully justified the observations which he [Vaughan] was instructed to submit to him." Expresses regret "that Mr. Clay is pleased to imagine" that Vaughan sought to repress "in future well founded complaints," when in his note of August 2 he intimated that, "to ensure the continuance of . . . respect [by British naval officers toward officers of every friendly power], a corresponding feeling should influence the conduct of the latter. . . ." Adds: "Surely it cannot be necessary seriously to disclaim any such motive imputed to His Majesty's Government."

Admits that "it is very natural that the Government of the United States should be disposed to remonstrate against any semblance of" impressment and states that "it must be expected, that the British Government will vindicate the conduct of it's [sic] officers, particularly when, as in the present case, there shall be good reason to apprehend that their conduct has been misrepresented." Absolves Captain Clavering of all blame in the incident and reiterates the British complaint against (Samuel) Hodges (Jr.), who, he trusts, "will be made to account for his assertion, of the impressment of two American Seamen, which has caused the unpleasant correspondence, which the Undersigned has been called upon to carry on, with the Government of the United States." LS. DNA, RG59, Notes from British Legation, vol. 14 (M50, R15). Copy, in MHi-Adams Family Papers, Letters Recd. (MR482).

INSTRUCTIONS AND DISPATCHES   August 16, 1827

To SAMUEL HODGES, JR., "Consul U. States for the Cape de Verd Islands, Villa de Praya." Encloses "transcripts of a communication from the British Minister [Charles R. Vaughan], upon the subject of the Impressment of some seamen from the American Brig Pharos into the British Ship of war Redwing" (above, Vaughan to Clay, ca. July 30, 1827), referred to in Hodges' letter (above) of March 16, 1826. Requests a deposition from Captain Ephraim Merchant upon his return to Hodges' district from Africa (cf. above, Hodges to Clay, June 20, 1827). Copy. DNA, RG59, Cons. Instr., vol. 2, pp. 438–39 (M78, R2).

On August 22, Daniel Brent wrote to Hodges, at Clay's direction, transmitting a copy of another letter from Vaughan (to Clay, below, August 21, 1827) and requesting that depositions be obtained from "the Mate or any of the Hands of the Pharos, who may be" available. Brent added: "The sooner this is done the better." Copy, in *ibid.*, 440–41.

From ALEXANDER H. EVERETT, Madrid, no. 86. Reports that, since he last wrote (above, August 10, 1827), "The relations with the Court of Rome [cf. above, Everett to Clay, June 22, July 15, 1827] have taken (as was anticipated) a pacific turn. . . ." Notes an exchange of autograph letters between the Pope (Leo XII) and the King (Ferdinand VII), which, he expects, will be followed by admission of the Nuncio (Francesco Tiberi) into Spain, the reception of "Mr Labrador" as Ambassador to Rome, and "settlement of the affair . . . with no farther [sic] trouble." Praises the astuteness and skill of (Ignazio Giovanni) "Cadolino [sic]", late Secretary to the Roman Embassy, whose influence over the Duke del Infantado contributed to the beginning and the success of the negotiations.

States that "the attention of this Government, and indeed of the whole political world of Europe, is now directed with anxious expectation to the consequences that may ensue upon the arrival of the Infante Don Miguel at his legal majority on the 25th of October." Discusses at length differing views concerning possible events to transpire in Portugal: Miguel has the right, under the Constitution, to claim the character of Regent, "supposing the abdication of the Emperor of Brazil [Peter I] to have taken effect, and the throne to be now occupied by his daughter [Maria da Gloria—cf. above, Raguet to Clay, May 6, 1826]"; the Emperor, however, "construes the decree of abdication, which is somewhat obscurely worded, to mean that," until the marriage of "Miguel and the future Queen . . . shall be solemnized by both the parties in person," "the Emperor is still King of Portugal," as "is in fact acknowledged . . . in all the public proceedings of the present Regency [cf. above, Brent to Clay, March 6, 1826]"; Miguel, invited to visit Brazil, but "averse to the voyage," has expressed "his wish to return to Portugal upon reaching his majority," and the Austrian Government has informed "the other courts" that it will not prevent that action—a decision with which the other continental powers agree (cf. above, Brown to Clay, July 28, August 13, 1827); an anonymous "elaborate pamphlet published at Paris under the title of '*An Examination of the Constitution of Dn Pedro and the rights of Dn Miguel*,'" which (Everett intimates) originated in "the Chancery of Prince Matternich," contends that "Dn Pedro as a foreign Prince has no pretentions [sic] to the Crown of Portugal, which . . . devolved at the death of the late King [John VI] upon Dn. Miguel," who is "at this moment *de jure* King" and that "the Treaty of separation between Portugal and Brazil was void [cf. above, Raguet to Clay, March 11, 1825, note]"; and, in any event, "the period when the crisis must occur is now only months distant, and . . . it is one of such importance that its consequences may involve a general war."

Observes that "The troubles in Catalonia [cf. above, Everett to Clay, April 19, 1827] . . . still continue, and appear to be growing more rather than less alarming." Encloses a translation of a note from (Manuel Gonzáles) Salmón, and a copy of his reply, relative to "the capture of a Spanish vessel by a Colombian Privateer," which "case will be more fully represented . . . by the Spanish Chargé d'Affaires at Washington. . . ." Adds in two postscripts (the second written August 17) information concerning the removal from office of (Juan Josef) Recacho, Superintendent of Police, which, "under present circumstances, and viewed in connexion with the troubles in Catalonia, must be considered as indicating the complete triumph of the Apostolical interest. . . ." LS, except for the second postscript, which is in Everett's hand. DNA, RG59, Dip. Disp., Spain, vol. 27 (M31, R28). Received October 11.

In the first enclosure Salmón informed Everett of the capture "of the Spanish Merchant Schooner Dolores . . . by a Privateer belonging to the self styled Republic of Colombia," which privateer was manned by "a crew of from twenty to four and twenty men, all, except one, citizens of the United States," and added that "the Spanish Chargé d'Affaires at Philadelphia" had been directed to make to the American Government "a representation of the circumstances of the case wherein the laws of neutrality which the U. S. have so repeatedly and solemnly declared it to be their intention to observe, during the war between the Mother Country and her rebel Colonies, have been so openly violated."

Francisco Tacón had filed his credentials as "Minister Residento" from Spain to the United States on July 23, 1827 (LS, in Spanish with trans. in State Dept. file, in DNA, RG59, Notes from Spanish Legation, vol. 9 (M59, R-T12), replacing Hilario de Rivas y Salmon, the Chargé. The Spanish Legation was at this time located in Philadelphia.

From ROBERT MONROE HARRISON, Barbados. In accordance with instructions contained in Clay's letter of May 14, last, reports on the trade conditions on the islands of Antigua, Dominica, St. Lucia, and Barbados. Notes the number of various classes of the population; the amount and kinds of production and of supplies necessary to be imported, from what countries these are obtained, the prices paid for them, the competitive position of the United States in these markets with and without the British trade restrictions (cf. above, Clay to Vaughan, March 17, 1827), and the possibility and probable effect of popular remonstrance concerning these barriers. Comments: "If the direct intercourse remains interdicted, the Islands will continue (if permitted) to draw their supplies almost entirely from the Foreign Islands in the Neighbourhood . . . consisting of the products of the U States; with the exception of White pine and Spruce lumber, Cedar and laying shingles (commonly called Boston chips) which will cheaply be supplied from British America; a few Red oak staves might also be derived from the same source: The disadvantages of the indirect Trade are considerable, in the first place the domestic markets are supplied irregularly, thus creating considerable fluctuations of price—rarely in favor of the consumer— Secondly every article so imported is sadled [sic] with the double charges of freight, agency, and probably Storage, and all this falls on the unfortunate Colonist without any equivalent to the Nation," except for the drogher trade from the foreign to British islands. With respect to Antigua, it is thought "that remonstrance would be unavailing, invasions of the rights of the West India property, by the Mother Country, have of late become so frequent, and memorials praying for relief . . . have been so entirely and shamefully disregarded. . . ." The Salt Islands, "who depend so entirely on the intercourse with the U States," might afford an exception. "Merchants (who are interested in the continuance of the interdict) seem to think no relaxation is to be expected; they however suppose that the circuitous trade between the U States and British West India Colonies [through neutral colonies] will be *tolerated.* . . ."

Particularly emphasizes the severity of hurricanes and floods on Dominica and the numerous, extremely poisonous snakes on St. Lucia. Observes that the inhabitants of these islands, of French background, are more high-spirited than those of Antigua and more likely to protest the restrictions.

Barbados, the oldest of the colonies, headquarters of all the British forces in the Windward Islands, is most lavishly and elegantly developed. Here a cargo of Danzig flour has been received. Used as a mixture with American flour, it costs 50 cents a barrel more than American flour coming circuitously through the neutral islands; but some 1600 barrels of the 2600 imported could not be sold and were sent to Jamaica. Generally the people of this island have not been hurt by the interdict because the island was better stocked than the others discussed and it is more productive. Comments: "they in general applaud the measure of their Government in the present instance as regards the U States, but concur in the fullest manner with the people of Antigua on the subject of *oppression* Invasion of rights &c. by the Mother Country; and go far beyond them in expressions of manly sentiments of feeling and disapprobation, of the recent measures of Parliament as regards the Slave population."

Concludes: "Known as I am throughout the Islands, It is natural to suppose that the curiosity of some persons will be exited [sic] by seeing me travelling at this season of the year; but whatever may be their Ideas, no impertinent remarks, or enquires [sic] have been made! I therefore flatter myself to be able to accomplete [sic] my observations through the Islands in the same way they have commenced, not perhaps with the talent that others would have performed them, but with *privacy* and *zeal* to be useful to my Country, (well knowing that in your Eyes, as well as those of that great and good Personage who is now at the head of our Government), that these *two qualities* were the best recommendations to its favor." Explains that he will proceed to Demerara and Berbice (British Guiana) and then back to Barbados to get a passage to Trinidad, "as there is no conveyance from Demerara to the latter place."

Postscript dated September 13, 1827, acknowledges receipt of a letter written by (Daniel) Brent, at the direction of the President, dated June 16 and received on August 29.

A second postscript, undated, notes that the governments of Guadeloupe and Martinique, "having percd. that the English Islands were receiving their Supplies from St. Bartholomew St. Eustatia and St. Thomas (although far to leeward) in preference to taking them at either of the two *first* named *places,* although immediately at their doors, have thought proper to allow cargoes to be sold from *board* to *board* by paying *one half duties.*" Comments that this will prove advantageous both to the English purchasers and to the American trader, "as the expenses of landing Storing &c, at both those places are great, independent of the risk in *Hurricane Months* as the Sea in the open Roadsteds [*sic*] of those two Islands is at times so heavy that vessels are prevented from landing for days." But notes: "The above arrangement with several similar facilities, which have been afforded to the commerce of the U States, and that of England by the *Neutral Islands*; serves in a great measure to *perpetuate* the *Interdict,* as the Colonies will hardly remonstrate to the Mother Country unless such a measure is Justified by necessity." Reports that merchants are profiting by the interdict, since their vessels are kept employed, that planters are the ones hurt by the arrangement; that the latter have the majority in the legislatures of the colonies but are held in check by their involvement with the mercantile houses in England and the extent to which their mortgages are held by local representatives of those establishments. ALS. DNA, RG59, Cons. Disp., Barbados, vol. 1 (M-T333, R1).

The British House of Commons by resolutions of May 15, 1823, had declared it "expedient to adopt effectual and decisive measures for ameliorating the condition of the slave population in his majesty's colonies," that "through a determined and persevering, but at the same time judicious and temperate enforcement of such measures the House anticipated an improvement in the character of the slave-population" which would prepare it "for a participation in those civil rights and privileges which are enjoyed by other classes of his majesty's subjects," and that the House was "anxious for the accomplishment of this purpose, at the earliest period . . . compatible with the well-being of the slaves themselves, with the safety of the colonies, and with a fair and equitable consideration of the interests of private property."

In 1824 an order in council specifically directed at Trinidad, had called to the attention of the colonial legislatures the "expediency of adopting such measures" as might establish "the principles of improvement in the condition of the slave-population generally." Nine propositions relative to the treatment of slaves had been recommended for adoption by the colonists; and on Barbados an act of September 18, 1825, had provided "many important provisions on all these several heads." Antislavery proponents during Parliamentary debate in 1826 were highly critical of the effect of such measures. Henry Peter Brougham, on May 19, referring specifically to the Barbados legislation, had commented: ". . . when these provisions were compared with previous acts, it would be found, that some of them would not prove of the slightest advantage to the slaves; that many of them were verbally copied from previous enactments—that many of them made worse what was already bad, and, where they differed from the earlier legislation, it was, in most cases, to the disadvantage of the negro." Efforts to press for more vigorous reform legislation were, however, defeated at this time. *Annual Register, 1826* (vol. 68), pp. 148–63.

MISCELLANEOUS LETTERS   August 16, 1827

To EDWARD LIVINGSTON, New York. Acknowledges receipt of his "letter [above, August 9, 1827] calling . . . attention to the resolution of the House of Representatives in regard to the collection of information relative to the penal laws of the U. States" and promises "immediately [to] give the subject proper attention." Adds: "I was not aware of the existence of such a resolution, which I think was not communicated to this Department, in the customary manner." Acknowledges receipt, also of his "letter with the accompanying map, respecting the lights wanted by the trade of the Gulf of Mexico" (cf. above, August 7, 1827), copies of which will be sent to (Albert) Gallatin for use in his negotiations "on that subject." Copy. DNA, RG59, Dom. Letters, vol. 22, p. 28 (M40, R20).

From SAMUEL S. CONANT, New York. States that he has been informed that "there is in the possession of the Government, surplus copies of the Public documents" and that "Conductors of news papers have sometimes been furnished with them." Notes that he feels "extremely the want of authentic sources of information, as for instance in the proceedings of Congress in relation to Genl. Jackson & the Seminole war" (cf. above, II, 612–13n; Toasts and Speech, July 12, 1827) and inquires whether . . . [he] can be supplied with the public documents & Journals of Congress for the use of the [New York] *National Advocate*." ALS. DNA, RG59, Misc. Letters (M179, R65).

   Endorsed by Clay on verso (several words obscured): "[*Public documents*] which are sent to this Dept. are to be distributed among persons designated by the orders of Congress; and he not being one of them, we regret that we cannot supply him— We have no surplus Copies. H C" Cf. above, Porter to Clay, May 1, 1827; Webster to Clay, June 22, 1827.

   Daniel Brent, as "directed by the Secretary," acknowledged receipt of Conant's letter, stated that he was sending him "a volume containing the Debate in the House of Representatives . . . on the Seminole War," and added: "It is a difficult matter to collect together a set of the official Documents that was printed by order of either House upon that Subject, otherwise it would likewise be transmitted, conformably to your request." Copy, in DNA, RG59, Dom. Letters, vol. 22, p. 33 (M40, R20).

To John Quincy Adams

My Dear Sir   Washington 17h. Aug. 1827.
   The inclosed P. S. was intended for my last letter.[1]
   Mr. Sergeant having informed me that he was charged with a letter to you from Mr. Poinsett, communicating the wish of the Mexican Government that he should be replaced by another,[2] I mentioned the fact a day or two ago to Mr. Rush; and I have had to day a long conversation with this gentleman, in which he expressed again his desire to leave the Treasury, and signified that he should be glad to be ap-

pointed to the Mexican mission. Mr. Rush put his inclination for the change of situation on the old grounds,[3] and upon the additional one, that he is becoming seriously apprehensive about the continuance of his health, from his incessant labors. I think myself that there is reason for that apprehension.

On the point of descending from his present more elevated position, he thinks that the junction of the mission to Mexico with that to Tacubaya will make the foreign equal to the domestic station. He moreover considers Mexico, the most important of all the Foreign American powers, and that we have highly interesting matters pending with it.

I do not think that the public would be better served at Mexico than by Mr. Rush. Indeed I think him peculiarly qualified to efface the bad impressions which Mr. Poinsett will have left there. And I give my hearty concurrence in his appointment, if you should think it expedient.

I have thought proper to communicate this conversation with Mr. Rush that you might deliberate as well upon the propriety of sending him to Mexico as upon the selection of his successor in the Treasury. Altho' Mr. Rush is not entirely unapprized that I might mention this subject to you, the communication is not made at his instance. I am faithfully Your friend & ob. Servt.   H CLAY
Mr. Adams.

P.S. I have a letter from Philada., written by one of the best and most efficient friends of the Administration, complaining that whilst there you were surrounded and engrossed exclusively by Mr. Walsh and his friends, of whom the letter speaks in unfavorable terms not necessary to be repeated.[4] I have thought it right to let you know what is said. You will be best able to decide if the statement be true, and to appreciate it properly.   H. C.

ALS. MHi-Adams Papers, Letters Recd. (MR482).   [1] Above, August 16, 1827.
[2] See above, Sergeant to Clay, August 1, 1827. Cf. above, Adams to Clay, August 15, 1827 (1).   [3] In accepting appointment to the Treasury Department Richard Rush had expressed fear of his inadequacy to fill the office because of inexperience in finance and long absence from the country. Two weeks later and again upon his return from London in July he had reiterated his concern and at the latter date suggested that he exchange appointments with Samuel L. Southard as Navy Secretary. Rush to Adams, April 14, 28, 1825, MHi-Adams Papers, Letters Recd. (MR479); Adams, *Memoirs*, VII, 38.
[4] See above, Wharton to Clay, August 3, 1817.

From Benjamin Winslow Dudley

Dear Sir,   Lex   Aug 17. 1827
For a Considerible [*sic*] time past I have contemplated addressing you a letter on the propriety of removeing [*sic*] from office the Post Master of this place[1]— All those with whom I have had conversation

in relation to the office unite in a desire to see it placed in other hands—
I have sufficient evidence of *his want of moral responsibility* to convince my mind that his integrity in the discharge of his duty is unworthy of trust— He was without our knowledge forced upon us by a
species of bargain & management, as you will see by the enclosed letter
from Colo Combs,[2] at a time when a highly competent & responsible
citizen of this place had been recommended for the appointment—
The manner & circumstances by which he came into office cannot but
be deprecated by the honest & virtuous[3]— Our citizen for whom the
appointment was solicited could not be bought—but Mr. Ficklin, a
stranger, who was bankrupt in purse & credit was found to answer the
purpose— The facilities afforded by the office of diffuseing [*sic*] information enables Mr. Ficklin to render important services to the
Jackson party; while he cautiously watches & peremptorily forbids the
Post riders from takeing [*sic*] any bundles or papers or handbill [*sic*]
suspected to be in favor of the administration

   A Government like ours must be sustained by its inferior officers—
It is due to every administration to secure for itself a fair trial of its
policy; nor is the experiment made, when the inferior officers are suffered to array themselves in all the strength of office against the measures of government— The correct policy of vacateing [*sic*] all offices
held by individuals hostile to the administration, & who take advantage
of their situation to prejudice the public mind against its measures
cannot be questioned—

   Should the Post Master General[4] dismiss Mr. Ficklin there is no individual who could be named as his successor; that would unite the
feelings & confidence of our town so generally, as Harry I Bodley esqr.

   Mr. B. is irreproachibly [*sic*] correct & upright in his conduct active
& of industrious habits, well educated, a fine capacity for business, &
universally beloved by all who know him—

   Except with the Jacksonians, who would put down an angel in favor
with the administration, the appointment of Mr. Bodley would be
peculiarly gratifying— I transmit you inclosed a letter from Colo.
Combs containing an extract of a Communication from S. H Woodson, our representative, at the time Mr. Ficklin was put into office—
I have the honor to be sincerely Yours   B. W. DUDLEY
H. Clay &c &c

ALS. DLC-HC (DNA, M212, R2).   1 Joseph Ficklin.
2 Probably Leslie Combs. The letter has not been found.   3 Cf. above, III, 33, 34n.
At the time of his removal John Fowler was in default on his accounts by about $10,000.
William T. Barry, one of Fowler's securities, had been supplied a blank commission of
appointment, through the intercession of Senator Richard M. Johnson, with Return J.
Meigs, the Postmaster General, and had named Ficklin to the Lexington office. Rumor
asserted that Ficklin had been granted the appointment under an understanding to
protect Barry from liability for Fowler's debt. Ficklin in 1824 had initiated a libel suit
in Bourbon Circuit Court for $20,000 against the Reverend John McFarland, pastor of
the Paris Presbyterian Church from 1820 until his death in 1828, concerning these circumstances, but the suit had been dropped. The issue became a matter of political

controversy in the autumn of 1829 and again at the time of Ficklin's removal from the Lexington postmastership in 1841 and reinstatement in 1843. Clay was known to have supported retention of Fowler in 1821; Johnson, Barry, and Ficklin were all Jackson supporters. See Ficklin to the Editor of the Frankfort *Commentator* [James G. Dana], September 8, 1829, in Lexington *Kentucky Gazette*, September 11, 1829; Lexington *Kentucky Reporter*, September 16, 1829; Frankfort *Argus of Western America*, September 9, 1829; Mikkelson, "Kentucky Gazette," 129.   4 John McLean.

From "Marcus"

TO THE HON. HENRY CLAY.   [*ca*. August 17, 1827]
SIR: The die is cast; your enemies have fallen; and the dark and insidious attack upon your public character frustrated, leaves them to the indignation and contempt of an enlightened community. In vain now will *ingenious* slander and *industrious* falsehood shift the scene. A liberal, and I trust unprejudiced, public can no longer be alarmed by the cry of "wolf, wolf," when there is no wolf. The American People are too high-minded not to appreciate *truth* and dispense *justice*: And be assured that while the liberty and glory of our Republic continue the objects of your ardent devotion, and while with fearless honesty you labor to advance the great interests of your fellow-citizens, they cannot, they will not desert you.

Pensioned presses may again assail you with abuse; a clamorous and disappointed faction may still load you with "corruption;" the Hero of Orleans once more may charge you, through his *illustrious* friends with high crimes and misdemeanors; all this you may soon expect. But, sir, the honor of the country, your own character, and the sacred cause of truth and justice, require from you no further vindication. Your part has been performed; and out of their own mouths are they condemned. A distinguished member of Congress[1] unequivocally has declared that he "called upon Gen. Jackson *solely* as his *friend*, upon his individual responsibility, and not as the agent of Mr. Clay, or any other person." For the last two years you have triumphantly challenged your accusers. But in vain. They, with more than *Parthian* cunning, *willing* but *unable* to adduce evidence against you, have meanly retreated from every investigation, flinging behind them the poisoned arrows of defamation.

From the time that the artful libel *formed* in conclave—"*spargere voces, in vulgum ambiguas*"—was ushered into the world under the *formidable* name of Kremer,[2] to the present auspicious period, when, after slumbering for a season, it is revived under the sanction and name of Andrew Jackson[3]—in this long interval you have been the victim of the most atrocious calumnies; unable to find a "local habitation and a name" for your accusers, you have patiently suffered, confidently relying on the magnanimity and justice of a free People. Before the unerring tribunal of Public Opinion, you have at length brought your illustrious *accuser*.[4] To support his "*conversation*," or charges, he refers to an *ardent* friend. This *friend* gives his testimony. It is now before the American public; and I call upon every American citizen to decide between the accuser and the accused. The evidence before them is clear and precise. I already anticipate their verdict. The unprejudiced portion of your countrymen pronounce you guiltless; and each day will add new proofs in your favor. But there is error somewhere; and would, for the honor of my country, that the name of Jackson was unconnected with this matter. If indeed he had emulated the virtues of Washington, and made the character of this immortal man the model of his own, we should not now have cause to suspect or censure him. The Father of his Country sought not office, but, with a modesty inseparable from a great mind and a good heart, shrunk from its responsibilities. No mad and interested party labored to elevate him; his rise was not on the ruins of other men's reputations; no, his was the majestic and almighty sway of virtue over the affections of an admiring nation; and the *Telegraph*[5] of his fame is the liberty and glory of the country he emancipated. This is a digression. I will not compare Jackson with Washington, for the fear of doing injury to one, and injustice to the memory of the other.

Unfortunately for Gen. Jackson, his friends do not benefit him much. They have already clouded the brightness of that military halo which encircles his brow, and will leave him at last the object of pity, not of admiration. Grateful for his services, I honored him; mindful of his valor, I respected him; and on the return of that anniversary, distinguished by the triumph of our arms, joined in the festivities and praise bestowed on the gallant defender of Orleans. His biography has been written, truly worthy the hero and the author.[6] Another is soon to be presented to the public, in more glowing colors, by a master hand.[7] It is well—but far better could the General have enjoyed in retirement the gratitude and admiration of his country. Then, with unfaded laurels, he might have passed down to posterity, not in a labored biography, but on the fairer page of his country's history.

In conclusion, Sir, I must claim your indulgence for thus publicly expressing myself. A long and increasing conviction of your integrity, at this time established beyond doubt, besides the great respect and admiration your firmness and eloquence in the cause of liberty and man, must excite in every bosom uninfluenced by prejudice and passion, constitute my only excuse. The path to fame, and your country's lasting remembrance, is before you—advance boldly, as you have done —a bright reward awaits you. With great consideration, your very obedient servant,   MARCUS.

Washington *Daily National Journal*, August 17, 1827. Headed: "For the National Journal." "Marcus" may have been Joseph Blunt, who had written under that pseudonym in 1819 and was now becoming actively concerned in the election campaign. Cf. below, Clay to Blunt, September 11, 1827.

1 James Buchanan. See above, Ingersoll to Clay, August 11, 1827, and note.

[2] George Kremer. See above, Clay to Gales and Seaton, January 30, 1825; Kremer to Clay, February 3, 1825; Appeal to the House, February 3, 1825, and note.   [3] See above, Report of Interview, *ca.* April 15, 1827; Clay to Hammond, June 25, 1827.
[4] Cf. above, Address to the Public, June 29, 1827; Toasts and Speech, July 12, 1827.
[5] Allusion to the Washington *United States Telegraph.*   [6] See above, Address to the People of the Congressional District, March 26, 1825, note 11.   [7] Henry Lee had announced in March, 1827, proposals for publishing by subscription a biography of Jackson. Washington *United States Telegraph*, March 7, 1827. The advertisement was continued through the issue of December 17, 1827, but the biography was never published. Bassett (ed.), *Correspondence of Andrew Jackson,* III, 362n.

From John Sergeant

Dear Sir,   (Private)   Philada. Augt. 17th. 1827

My object in writing is only to inform you of what has been doing here, so that you may be prepared for an application which will be made to you.

Some one very well disposed, having heard that you were shortly to be in Philadelphia,[1] called a meeting two or three days ago to make preparations for giving you a suitable reception. A large committee was appointed and met last evening. A question immediately arose whether any one knew of your intention to come, and this appearing to be doubtful, a further question presented itself as to the course to be pursued. Finally, a complimentary resolution was passed, and a small committee appointed to forward it to you and make inquiry as to your intentions.[2] So the matter now stands. You will therefore be called upon.

A few of those who were present, seemed inclined to send you an invitation. Others, more numerous, and I rather think, more judicious, were of a different opinion. They say, that if you had been passing this way, it would have been proper not to let you pass without a demonstration of respect and regard. They might add, that if there were any occasion for a public dinner here, at this time, it would be very fit to give you an invitation to it. But they doubt the propriety of inviting you merely to give you a dinner, and they doubt the propriety of enquiry and preparation which might be considered as only another mode of doing the same thing. They say that your position now is as fine as possible, and that such a step cannot improve it, while at the same time it is liable to the objection that it may embarrass you, and that it may seem like seeking an occasion which you neither wish nor stand in need of.

These views appear to have some force, and I have thought it best to state them to you, as they are entertained by many of your most zealous friends. If you should think differently, they will all cordially cooperate in every expression of respect and regard. The only objection has been to the manner of the thing, and of the weight of that objection you are well able to judge. I was not apprised of the first meeting 'till after it was held, and to the second (of the Committee) I was not invited.

Interruptions have kept me from closing this letter in time for the mail of today. It will probably be too late for its purpose.

The public mind is occupied with Genl. Jackson and Mr. Buchanan.[3] You are now out of the case, for it seems to be agreed that all ground of imputation is entirely removed, so far as you are concerned, and you are upon much higher ground than if you had never been assailed. The question is between Genl. J. and Mr. B., and I confess I feel some curiosity to see how it will here after be treated. There is a great effort at present to be amicable, but I do not think this disposition can continue, Very respectfully & truly yrs.

The Honble Henry Clay.   JOHN SERGEANT.

ALS. DLC-HC (DNA, M212, R2).   [1] Cf. above, Wayland to Clay, August 16, 1827.
[2] A meeting, held at the old Masonic Hall, Philadelphia, on August 13, had elected officers and adopted a resolution calling for appointment of a committee of 100 "to carry into effect some appropriate plan of receiving and demonstrating . . . [the body's] respect to Mr. Clay. . . ." On August 16, the designated committee had met, again at the old Masonic Hall, and adopted resolutions stating that, in view of their hope that Clay would "visit Philadelphia within a few days, . . . the friends of the American System, would gladly avail themselves of such an opportunity to give him a public demonstration of their respect." A subcommittee of 14 had then been appointed to act in "such a contingency." Philadelphia *United States Gazette*, September 4, 1827.
[3] Cf. above, Ingersoll to Clay, August 11, 1827, and note.

INSTRUCTIONS AND DISPATCHES   August 17, 1827

From ALEXANDER H. EVERETT, Madrid, "Confidential." Transmits, "for the President's information" a "copy of a confidential despatch addressed to the Minister of State [Manuel Gonzáles Salmón] by the Conde de Alcudia, Spanish Minister at London," and requests "that it . . . not be placed on the public files of the Department of State." Explains: "In this letter the Spanish Minister informs his Govt of a plan conceived by that of England, and already in a state of partial execution, for effecting a revolution in the Canary Islands & in Cuba [cf. above, Everett to Clay, June 9, 1827, and below, December 12, 1827]. The sources from which the Count de Alcudia derived his knowledge upon the subject are, as you will perceive, of the most respectable character, and such as to leave no doubt of the reality of the facts. The object seems to be to establish the British influence in those islands—in the end probably to obtain territorial possession of them; & the cover of a spontaneous declaration of independence by the inhabitants is to be employed in order—as is expressly stated—to avoid awakening the jealousy of the Govt. of the U. S." Notes two singularities: "that the Duke of Wellington should have made known to the Spanish Minister a plan formed & acted on while he was himself a member of the cabinet" and "that Mr. Salmon himself should have made no communication to . . . [Everett] upon a project, which is certainly not indifferent to the U. S. and in regard to which he might naturally expect that their cooperation would be useful to Spain." LS. DNA, RG59, Dip. Disp., Spain, vol. 27 (M31, R28). Published, with enclosure, in Manning (arr.), *Diplomatic Correspondence . . . Latin-American Nations*, III, 2146–48. Received October 11.

The enclosure, dated June 1, 1827, and naming the Duke of Wellington as the source of information, asserts that the British Government had sent agents to report on "the state of defence of the islands & the sentiments of the inhabitants," that having learned the strength of the garrison, the British had "concluded to prepare the public opinion in favour of England by means of emissaries, to the end that the inhabitants . . . [might] declare themselves independent and call in the British to their assistance," and that the plan was "connected between the revolutionists residing here (at London) and in the islands," including "a Spanish General now at this place . . . fixed upon for taking the command at the Havana."

MISCELLANEOUS LETTERS   August 17, 1827

From PETER A. KARTHAUS, JR., Baltimore. Having perceived from the "public prints" that B(eaufort) T. Watts is leaving his post at Bogotá, inquires whether the report is true and, if so, who will succeed him. States that he (Karthaus) has prepared documents relative to his father's claim against Colombia (cf. above, Karthaus to Clay, July 30, 1827) in which the "Power has been made in his [Watts'] name &c to appoint other attornies [sic] under him." ALS. DNA, RG59, Misc. Letters (M179, R65). Endorsed on verso: "Let an ansr. be written that Mr. Watts has not [a] leave of absence and that if he shd. come home, it is not known if he will return. H C."

Daniel Brent wrote Karthaus, on August 20, as follows: "We have no information other than that which the public prints furnish, that Mr. Watts is coming home soon, tho' a conditional leave of absence, for a short period, was given to him by the President some time ago [see above, Clay to Watts, March 8, 1827]. I presume your father's power to him will be available for his successor, when one is appointed, but it is not known that this will be the case soon, or that Mr. Watts will not return to his post, if he should come hither, under the leave which he has to do so." Copy, in DNA, RG59, Dom. Letters, vol. 22, p. 31 (M40, R20).

In reply to another letter from Karthaus, dated August 27, 1827 (not found), which was accompanied by one to Watts, with enclosures, Brent wrote that the communication intended for Watts would be forwarded, but without official instructions, since the claims appeared to be of a "private nature . . . against an inhabitant of Colombia," and added that he would receive and transmit to Watts a letter under flying seal, with enclosures. Copy, in *ibid.*, p. 40.

On August 31 Brent sent Watts, "by direction of the Secretary, a letter from Karthaus, "accompanied by a power of attorney . . . to recover from John B. Elbers of Bogota the amount due to him, as the holder of certain protested Bills of Exchange drawn upon Baring Brothers and Company . . . by the said Elbers," and added: "We have informed Mr. Karthaus that we would transmit these papers to you *as his private agent. . . .*" LS, in DNA, RG84, Colombia (MR14, frame 269).

The Baltimore *American and Daily Advertiser*, August 10, 1827, had reprinted an item from the *New York American*, quoting a letter from José A. Torrens, in Bogotá expressing regret at Watts' "departure" and stating that Torrens had honored him with a dinner attended by the dignitaries of Colombia.

From RICHARD RUSH, Treasury Department. Acknowledges receipt of Clay's note of August 15 (cf. above, Gallatin to Clay, June 21, 1827, note). Reports that three ships violated the Passenger Ship Act (see above, Speech, January 20, 1827, note 14), but that their penalties, collected at New York, were remitted when it was shown to "the satisfaction of the President" that the infractions had occurred "through ignorance of the law. . . ." Predicts that the other ships on

Huskisson's list will be dealt with individually by the President. Adds that the Passenger Ship Act is not confined to Great Britain, "as seems to be supposed," but applies to all nations with which the United States trades. LS. DNA, RG59, Misc. Letters (M179, R65). Copy, in MHi-Adams Papers, Letters Recd. (MR482).

To John F. Henry

Dear Sir   Washn. 18h. August 1827.
   Your favor of the 29h. Ulto.[1] is just received. I regret extremely the failure of the arrangement between Col New and yourself, because I apprehend it may occasion the defeat of you both.[2] If however there should be a different result, and you should be elected (which will have been ascertained before the receipt of this letter) I pray you to accept my hearty congratulations.
   Buchanans statement[3] is before the public. He was the designated witness, deliberately summoned by Genl. Jackson, to establish his charges against me; and you will have seen that he has failed, in every material particular, to confirm the General's statements. With respect to the new tale[4] which you inform me has just taken wings at the Hermitage, it has not the merit of a misrepresentation—it is a gross fabrication.
   I feel great anxiety to hear the result of our elections in K.[5] The first day's termination from Fayette has only reached me this morning. From that I conclude there was a close contest. I am respectfy Yrs
Dr. J. F. Henry   H. CLAY

   ALS. DLC-Short Family Papers.   [1] Not found.
[2] Cf. above, Johnson to Clay, April 29, 1827, note.   [3] Cf. above, Ingersoll to Clay, August 11, 1827, note.   [4] Probably an allusion to Jackson's answer to Clay's Speech at the Lexington Public Dinner. Cf. above, Smith to Clay, August 1, 1827, note.
   [5] Cf. above, Clay to Taylor, April 4, 1827, note; below, Clay to Adams, August 19, 1827, note.

Check to "Joseph"

                                                        18 Aug. 1827
No.   OFFICE OF DISCOUNT & DEPOSIT, Washington,
   PAY to Joseph *or bearer*, Fifty *Dollars*,   /100
$50 DOLLARS,   /100   H CLAY

   DS, partially printed. DLC-TJC (DNA, M212, R16). Joseph, not identified, was probably a servant. Cf. Clay to "Charles," above, April 8, 1826; below, October 6, 1828. On the latter, Clay struck out the name "Joseph" and substituted "Charles," probably Charles Dupuy. Clay subsequently wrote, without reference to purpose, additional checks to "Joseph" as follows: during 1827, September 29, $120; October 13, $100; October 16, $100; December 28, $50; and during 1828, January 2, $25; January 7, $75; March 13, $100; March 28, $100; April 5, $100; April 17, $50; April 22, $50; May 2, $150; May 3, $150, May 16, $25; June 3, $25; June 18, $50. All DS, partially printed, in *ibid.*

To Bezaleel Wells

Dear Sir   Washn. 18 Aug. 1827.

I have received the inclosed Check from Bishop Chase, which I am willing to subscribe, whenever the deed is made by Mr. Hoge for the Land.[1] I think the payment of the purchase money and the execution of the deed ought to be simultaneous. Have you made any arrangement about the execution of the deed? Mr. Hammond[2] promised me at Columbus last month to prepare and send me a deed, but I have not received it. As I passed through Brownsville, I obtained from Mr. Hoge's nephew the deed for the land from Col. Howard,[3] which I now have, and from which I could myself prepare a deed *if I had the Corporate name* given to the Episcopal Church by the act of the Ohio Legislature,[4] which I have not. Could not Mr. Wright[5] be gotten to prepare a deed, with the proper Certificates of the magistrates both as to its execution, and the relinquishment of dower? If such a deed is sent to me, I can fill it up with the abutments & description of the Land.

Whenever the inclosed Check is executed, it ought to have your Signature, as well as that of the Bishop's and mine. I am respectfully Your obedient Servant   H. CLAY
B. Wells Esq

ALS. Kalamazoo Public Museum, Kalamazoo, Michigan.
[1] Bishop Philander Chase had entered a conditional contract with William Hogg (or Hoge) on March 8, 1826, for purchase of "section 1, in township 6, and section 4, in township 7, and [*sic*] the 12th range of United States military land, containing each four thousand acres. . . ." Chase, *Reminiscences*, II, 511; Washington *Daily National Intelligencer*, July 3, 1826; and cf. above, Chase to Clay, January 27, 1825, note. Hogg, born in England, was an uncle of George Hogg, had induced the family of the latter to emigrate to the United States, and was engaged with his nephew in a variety of commercial enterprises in the vicinity of Brownsville, Pennsylvania. On the location and distribution of the United States military bounty lands by act of June 1, 1796 (1 *U. S. Stat.*, 490–91), see Paul W. Gates, *History of Public Land Development* . . . (Washington, 1968), 259–60.   [2] Charles Hammond.   [3] Possibly John Eager Howard, a lieutenant colonel in the American Revolution, who had been awarded a medal and the "Thanks of Congress" for his services in the battle of Cowpens (1781). Born at Baltimore in 1752, Howard had been later a delegate to the Continental Congress, Governor of Maryland (1788–1791), and a United States Senator (1796–1803). He died in October, 1827.
[4] Bishop Chase, as "Bishop of the Protestant Episcopal Church in the diocese of Ohio," and the current trustees of the seminary were "constituted a body corporate and politic . . . by the name of the Theological Seminary of the Protestant Episcopal Church in the Diocese of Ohio. . . ." Ohio, *Laws, 1824–1825 (Local Laws)*, XXIII, 12 (approved December 29, 1824).   [5] Probably John C. Wright.

From Hugh Mercer

My dear Sir,   (*Confidential*)   Fredericksbg, Augt 18th. 1827—

I cannot longer refuse obedience to my feelings & wishes— I tender you in great & sincere heartfelt Sincerity, my cordial congratulations upon the signal Triumph afforded you over the "machinations of your enemies," by the publication of Mr Buchanan[1]— "Truth is indeed omnipotent & public Justice certain"[2]—   already are the wavering here, decided—men of Character & intelligence, have left the cause of Genl J——n since this developement [sic]— Your address to the people of Lexington[3] has had, & must have thro' the United States, a powerful effect— Mr Jefferson's views & *alarm* upon the elevation of Genl J——n to the Presidency, must also have great influence

This authority, known to me to be most direct & authentic, I have put in circulation thro' Gales & Seaton, *confidentially*[4]— I am preparing a piece, exposing the causes of the Correspondence between Genl J—— & Mr Southard,[5] which originated here, which will do great good to the cause of the admin—& expose Genl J—— & a *particular* & very weak *Partizan* of his here, not a little—

My friend Colo Barbour,[6] the Secy, was here this morning, & was at my house— I shewed him the rough Draft of the piece— he approves it highly, & urges its early publication—in two or three weeks perhaps —either in the "nat-Intel"—or "nat-Journal"—   I wish not of course to be known as the author—   it will produce, if I mistake not, much additional excitement against Genl J——n in the U. States— He & his Partizans deserve the exposure given by this piece— I was at Washington late in July, to comply with a particular request from Colo Trumbull,[7] in obedience to my Duty, as I thought, to my Country, & I saw Mr Southard upon this Subject— He has no objection whatever to the publication of the correspondence—on the contrary, would desire it, if the J——n party here can be *forced* to publish it[8]— I left Washington the Day you were expected & on which you arrived[9]— my engagements here hurried me home— I greatly wished to have remained until I could have taken you once more by the hand.

The persecutions you have encountered will now have a reaction— & the consequence be inevitable.

You will henceforward have more enviable & higher standing in the confidence & affection of the Country, much higher than you have ever had.

Colo B— informed me of the invitation to you from the thousands in Philada., to give them an opportunity of testifying to you, their increased confidence & attachment—& said you were deliberating whether to accept— It is a distinguished proof of high & merited confidence, from an enlightened, refined & populous City— You will be best able to decide— I can only wish that it may comport with your own views, to accept the invitation[10]— I am, my dear Sir, very truly & faithfully, your friend— (In haste) (please destroy this—)

                                                              HUGH MERCER

—19th.

The proposed & contemplated convention at Richmond,[11] the first of Jany, of the friends of the admin. & the *opponents of Genl J——n to the Presidency*, named to me by Colo. B. will be I think a most useful Measure— I have for some time past, been thinking of proposing such a meeting— The majority in Va. (if there is a majority at all against the admin.) is not so large & decided, as Mr Ritchie & the aspirants after office & power, would have the country to believe[12]—   H. M.

I shall be incouraged [*sic*] in future, to have more confidence in my political anticipations— I predicted six years ago, that you would be the President of this Country, if you lived— others, who were then & are still among your friends, did not think with me— my personal attachment may have had some influence in forming this opinion— passing events now look strongly & forcibly to this issue— In truth, the violent opposition to the admin. with the principal leaders in the U States, has been with a steady eye to defeat, if possible, this issue— your elevation to the chief magistracy of the country—to keep room for themselves—

ALS. DLC-HC (DNA, M212, R2).   [1] Cf. above, Ingersoll to Clay, August 11, 1827. [2] Source of quotation has not been found.   [3] Above, Toasts and Speech at Public Dinner, July 12, 1827.   [4] The Washington *Daily National Intelligencer*, on August 4, had published a strong editorial expressing fear of the effort "to place a merely military man at the head of our Republic." In conjunction with this statement, the editors quoted an observation purportedly made by Thomas Jefferson, "not many weeks before his death," to a friend: "that his faith in the self-government of the People had never been so completely shaken as it had been by the efforts made, at the last election, to place over their heads one who, in every station he ever filled, either military or civil, made it a point to violate every order and instruction given him, and take his own arbitrary will as the guide of his conduct." For a summary of other statements at this time reporting Jefferson's disapproval of Jackson, see William H. Gaines, Jr., *Thomas Mann Randolph, Jefferson's Son-in-Law* ([Baton Rouge], [c. 1966]), 179–80.   [5] Three letters—Jackson to Samuel L. Southard, January 5, 1827; Southard to Jackson, February 9, 1827; and Jackson to Southard, March 6, 1827—had resulted from a conversation "at the table of Mr. John S. Wellford of Fredericksburgh Virginia [not further identified]," on which occasion Southard had maintained that James Monroe, rather than Jackson, should be credited with the American victory in the Battle of New Orleans—"*that just before our troops were ordered to New Orleans Genl Jackson left the army and was returning home when Mr. Monroe sent him a peremptory order to return to the defence of that place, and that this, with other energetic measures of Mr Monroe was the salvation of New Orleans.*" Jackson, pronouncing the allegation "false and unfounded," demanded to know the basis on which Southard had made the statement. Southard denied that he had ever charged Jackson "with neglect or desertion of . . . military duties" but asserted that he had defended Monroe against the "extremely unjust" implication that the War Department under his administration had neglected to supply Jackson with the means and money to fight the battle. Jackson's reply was tart, sarcastic, and very critical of the War Department's operations in providing for the defense of New Orleans. Bassett (ed.), *Correspondence of Andrew Jackson*, III, 329–30, 342–44, 345–48. The Washington *Daily National Journal*, on September 8, 1827, published an item, signed "Jefferson" and dated merely as August, 1827, which claimed that Jackson had supplied a copy of the correspondence "in April last, to a very zealous partizan of his in Fredericksburg, one of the medical faculty, who is more remarkable for his zeal in this cause, than for the strength of his intellect, or his influence." This appears to be the "piece" which Mercer was "preparing," and the Jackson supporter to whom he alluded was John Hooe Wallace, a Fredericksburg physician, whose advocacy of Jackson at the Wellford gathering had precipitated Southard's remarks.   [6] James Barbour. [7] John Trumbull, born in Connecticut in 1756 and graduated from Harvard University, had held rank as a colonel in the American Revolution. In 1780 he had sailed for France and thence to Britain, where despite his arrest on suspicion of treason, he had begun to study painting under Benjamin West. Under the latter's guidance Trumbull had completed in 1786 "The Battle of Bunker Hill" and "The Death of General Montgomery in the Attack of Quebec." During the next three years he had begun paintings on "Declaration of Independence," "Surrender of Lord Cornwallis at Yorktown," and "Death of General Mercer at the Battle of Princeton." Much of Trumbull's later activity centered upon efforts to arrange for engraving of these works and, from 1816 to 1824, the painting of four scenes of life-size dimensions in the Rotunda of the National Capitol. In financial distress, Trumbull had unsuccessfully sought in the fall of 1826 a commission to paint four additional scenes, including the one on the "Death of General Mercer at the Battle of Princeton," which related to Hugh Mercer's father, General Hugh Mercer. Adams, *Memoirs*, VII, 188.   8 Early in July administration and Jacksonite journals had published allusions to the correspondence, with the Washington *United States Telegraph* denouncing the implication imputed to the Washington *Daily National Intelligencer* that Jackson had challenged Southard to a duel. Washington *Daily National Intelligencer*, June 29, 1827; Washington *Daily National Journal*, July 9, 12, 1827; Washington *United States Telegraph*, July 7, 1827. Although the editor (Duff Green) of the *United States Telegraph* admitted that he held copies of the correspondence, he did not publish it. In deference to the wishes of James Monroe, who subsequently explained that he had desired to "take no part in the pending election. . . ," Southard also withheld the correspondence. When Southard in 1829 sought Monroe's support for its publication, the ex-President somewhat stiffly reiterated his concern that such action might jeopardize his relationship with one or the other of the parties, with both of whom he remained "friendly." Monroe to Southard, April 17, 1829, in James Monroe, *The Writings. . .*, ed. by Stanislaus Murray Hamilton (7 vols.; New York, 1898–1903), V, 195–98.   9 Cf. above, Clay to Erwin, August 4, 1827.   10 No formal invitation has been found. Cf. above, Sergeant to Clay, August 17, 1827, note; below, Sergeant to Clay, August 23, 1827.   11 Thomas Ritchie, editor of the *Richmond Enquirer*, cited as "the first step" in this movement for a Richmond convention, a notification which appeared in the Fredericksburg newspapers September 11, inviting the people of that town, and of Spotsylvania County to meet on September 29 for the election of delegates. *Richmond Enquirer*, September 18, 1827. By December, 90 of the 102 counties in Virginia had named delegates, and the remainder were expected to do so. *Niles' Weekly Register*, XXXIII (December 1, 1827), 212. The convention date was ultimately changed to January 8, 1828, when the body met under the presidency of Francis T. Brooke, endorsed the candidacy of Adams and Richard Rush, named Presidential electors pledged to their support, and drafted an "Address" explaining their views. *Richmond Enquirer*, January 15, 17, 1828. This nomination in effect served as an administration endorsement of Rush for the Vice-Presidency. Cf. Remini, *Election of Andrew Jackson*, 133.   12 On August 21, 1827, Ritchie wrote in the *Richmond Enquirer*: ". . . the great majority of the people are for General J. Several counties and towns may have a majority of votes for Mr. A., and among them we might include the city of Richmond. . . . But taking the voters of the State together, we hazard nothing in saying that two-thirds, if not three-fourths of them are opposed to Mr. Adams." On the outcome of the Virginia election, cf. above, Clay to Brown, March 27, 1827, note.

INSTRUCTIONS AND DISPATCHES   August 18, 1827

To ALBERT GALLATIN, "Envoy Extraordinary and Minister Plenipotentiary of the U. S. to Great Britain," no. 33. Transmits a "copy of a letter from the Secretary of the Treasury" (above, Rush to Clay, August 17, 1827); notes that it "is calcuicated to remove entirely the apprehension expressed by Mr. [William] Huskisson in the conference referred to in [Gallatin's] . . . Despatch No. 86" (above, June 3, 1827); and instructs him to "take an early opportunity to communicate it to Mr. Huskisson." LS. NHi-Gallatin Papers (MR15). Copy, in DNA, RG59, Dip. Instr., vol. 11, pp. 371–72 (M77, R6).

To John Quincy Adams

My dear Sir   Washn. 19h. Aug. 1827.
      Partial accounts of the Kentucky elections reached me last night. They authorize the belief that Metcalfe, Trimble and Clarke are re-

elected.[1] They do not extend sufficiently into other districts to justify any certain conclusion. Travellers say that Le Compte has been beaten by Crittenden; and that McHatton, if not left out, has been run hard.[2] Judging from what I have seen, I think the next legislature will be friendly.[3] I remain truly Your friend   H. CLAY
Mr. Adams.

ALS. MHi-Adams Papers, Letters Recd. (MR482).
[1] Thomas Metcalfe; David Trimble; and James Clark. On Trimble's defeat, cf. above, Clay to Adams, July 25, 1827, note. Clay probably had seen the Lexington *Kentucky Reporter* of August 8, 1827, but not the issue of August 11.   [2] Joseph Lecompte; Henry Crittenden; Robert L. McHatton. Cf. above, Clay to Taylor, April 4, 1827, note; Smith to Clay, August 1, 1827, note.   [3] The Lexington *Kentucky Reporter*, September 1, 1827, identified members of the Kentucky Legislature as favoring the Adams administration over Jackson by 21 to 17 in the Senate and 54 to 45 in the House of Representatives.

To Edward Everett

My dear Sir   Washington 19h. Aug. 1827.
I was glad to find by your letter of the 13h. that your sight had returned to you.[1] I hope it will soon be perfectly restored.

We have just recd. partial accounts from the Congressional districts in K. nearest to us, Trimbles, Metcalfes and Clarkes. There is reason to believe that they are all re-elected; and the intelligence otherwise looks well. It is rumored, 'though I do not yet credit it, that Lecompte is beaten, and McHatton run hard, if not also beaten, by two friends.[2]

I thank you for the Engraving.[3] An extensive circulation of them to the West and Pennsa. would have good effect. Could not the author of it, make something out of the six Militia?[4]

Blunt's notion is idle.[5] They dare not displace Jackson. What would Pennsa do? What the South? Any attempt to supplant him would, strange as it may appear, bring his friends in masses to Mr. Adams.

The affair of the V. Presidency ought not to be much longer postponed.[6] There ought to be, at all events, an early decision after the commencement of the approaching Session. Your's Cordially & faithfully   H. CLAY
The Honble Mr. Everett.

ALS. MHi. Cf. above, Clay to Adams, this date.
[1] The letter has not been found. Everett's diary reports illness which affected his eyes from about July 12 to August 5. MHi-Edward Everett Papers, vol. 139, pp. 163–64 (MR36).
[2] Cf. above, Clay to Adams, this date.   [3] Not found.   [4] Cf. above, Watkins to Clay, September 30, 1826, note. John Binns was supposed to have been the author of a pamphlet which, according to the *Huntingdon Gazette*, contained "all the slanders and falsehoods put in circulation for some years, by the enemies of General Jackson, against his reputation. . . ." The pamphlet had "been in circulation, for some time," when the *Gazette*'s comment was reported in Washington *United States Telegraph*, November 27, 1827. Binns subsequently published the famous "Coffin Hand Bill," bordered in black and illustrated with several groupings of coffins—six at the top, then seven just below mid-page, followed by one and then four more at the bottom of the page—bearing the title *Some Account of Some of the Bloody Deeds of General Jackson*. The latter document is not dated but the *New Hampshire Patriot* of February 25, 1828, mentioned that

it had been recently published. It is possible that an earlier version had appeared in the spring of 1827 (cf. above, Binns to Clay, April 28, 1827). In the Philadelphia *Democratic Press*, March 26, 1828, Binns described a version different from that noted above— "When we published, with a small coffin at the head of it, an account by 'An Eye Witness,' of the execution of the six militia men. . . ." The "Eye Witness" statement presented in *Some Account of Some of the Bloody Deeds* . . . lies below the grouping of six coffins.   5 Probably Joseph Blunt. Late in the summer "Some movements were made in Virginia, Ohio and at Buffalo, and at two or three other places in the state of New York, to bring forward Mr. Clinton as a candidate for the presidency. . . ." Hammond, *History of the Political Parties of New York.* . . , II, 256. Cf., also, Southard to Adams, August 25, 1827, in MHi-Adams Papers, Letters Recd. (MR482).   6 Cf. above, Mercer to Clay, August 18, 1827, note.

To Josiah Stoddard Johnston

My Dear Sir   Washington 19h. August 1827.

We have only imperfect accounts from some of the Congressional districts in Kentucky. These authorize a belief that Metcalfe, Trimble and Clarke are re-elected. And as far as I learn the Administration tickets have generally prevailed in their districts. Capt. Byers' appears to have declined; and Beatty and Morris were elected without any great struggle.[1] The inclosed letter from Mr. Robertson, late Speaker of the H. of R. of K., on his return home from Harrisburg,[2] would justify the hope that Mr. Crittenden is elected, and McHatton defeated by the Admon Candidate in his district; but I do not think we ought yet to count upon those auspicious results.

The City has been extremely hot since you left us; but, for the last two days, the heat has been tempered by misty weather. I think you have made a lucky escape. I should find it very loansome, if the occupations of business did not constantly engage me.

My best respects to Mrs. Johnston; and I pray you also to communicate them to Mr. and Mrs. Madison and to Mrs. Cutts.[3] I am Cordially Your friend   H. CLAY
The Honble J. S. Johnston

ALS. PHi. Cf. above, Clay to Adams, this date.
1 James Byers, who appears not to have entered the Kentucky Legislature until 1833; Adam Beatty; David Morris. The latter two were identified as administration supporters. Lexington *Kentucky Gazette*, August 10, 1827. Morris, who in 1788 had moved to May's Lick, Kentucky, as a boy with his family from Plainfield, New Jersey, served in the Kentucky Legislature during the Sessions beginning in 1827, 1832, and 1833.
2 George Robertson's letter has not been found. He had been Speaker of the Kentucky House of Representatives from 1823 to 1824 and from 1825 to 1827. He had also been a delegate to the Harrisburg Convention (cf. above, Clay to Crowninshield, March 18, 1827, note).   3 Mr. and Mrs. James Madison; Anna Payne (Mrs. Richard) Cutts, sister of Mrs. Madison.

To Samuel L. Southard

My dear Sir   Washington 19h. Aug. 1827.

You ought to hear, at the White Sulphur Springs,[1] from K. before we do at this place. Partial accounts of the Congressional elections only have reached us. They authorize the belief that Clarke, Trimble and Metcalfe (the only districts from which we have many returns) are re-elected. Travellers say that Lecompte is beaten, and McHatton, if not beaten, very hard run. Upon the whole I think it will appear that we have not lost, perhaps have gained, ground.

Your family is better. I understand that the children are all well, but Henry and he not bad.[2]

The inclosed is sent to amuse you. I received it from Boston.[3] After you have laughed at it, give it to Mr. Caldwell, keeper of the Springs, but not as coming from me.[4] Your's faithfully   H. CLAY
The Honble Mr. Southard

ALS. NjP-Samuel L. Southard Papers. Cf. above, Clay to Adams, this date.
[1] Cf. above, Hay to Clay, August 6, 1827; Southard to Clay, August 8, 1827.   [2] Cf. above, Clay to Southard, September 24, 1826, note; August 12, 1827, and note.   [3] The enclosure, not found, may have been "the Engraving" sent to Clay by Edward Everett. See above, Clay to Everett, this date.   [4] James Calwell.

To Daniel Webster

My dear Sir   Washn. 19h. Aug. 1827.

We have partial accounts from K. Congressional districts nearest to us. Clarke and Metcalfe are certainly and Trimble probably re-elected. The accounts do not furnish us with much information from the other districts, but our intelligence, such as it is, is not unfavorable. Judging from what I have seen, I think we shall be stronger than ever in the next Legislature of K. and that, if we do not gain (of which there is some hope) we shall not loose [sic] ground in Congress.

(Confidential)

C. Hammonds paper in Cincinnati[1] (published by Morgan Lodge and Fisher)[2] is I think, upon the whole, the most efficient and discreet gazette that espouses our cause. He is poor, disinterested, and proud. His paper is now published daily.[3] I think he is every way worthy of encouragement and patronage. The only assistance he would receive would be in the extension of his subscription list. Perhaps he might receive a present of a new set of types. I write without his knowledge, and from a strong sense of his worth and merits. Can not there be something done for him in your quarter? I am truly Your friend
Mr. Webster   H. CLAY

ALS. DLC—Daniel Webster Papers (DNA, M212, R22). Cf. above, Clay to Adams this date.
[1] *Liberty Hall and Cincinnati Gazette.*   [2] Ephraim Morgan; James Lodge; Brownlow Fisher. Morgan, a Quaker, had come west from Hampden County, Massachusetts, about 1804. After several successful printing ventures, he had become in 1816 at the age of 26, one of the publishers of the *Liberty Hall.* Lodge, born in Westmoreland County, Pennyslvania, had resided briefly in Dayton, Ohio, and Corydon, Indiana, before settling in Cincinnati about 1814, at age 22. He had joined Morgan as a publisher of *Liberty Hall* in 1817. Fisher, born in England, had joined the partnership in 1825. Lodge left the journal from April, 1827, until June, 1828, and was replaced by Stephen S. L'Hommedieu,

born in Sag Harbor, New York, in 1806 but resident in Cincinnati since 1810. In June, 1828, Morgan and Fisher left the firm; Lodge then returned, continuing the business with L'Hommedieu.   3 Beginning with the issue of June 25, 1827, under the title *Cincinnati Daily Gazette.*

From Peter B. Porter

Dear Sir,   Black Rock Augt. 19th. 1827

The mail of last evening brought us Mr. Buchanan's explanation;[1] and although I was prepared to believe that this anxiously expected document would give no countenance to the charges against you, I confess I had little hope of finding it, what it has happily turned out to be, a full & *affirmative* exculpation of yourself & friends from all participation in the alledged [sic] overtures, or, as the the [sic] General calls them "propositions of bargain."[2]

I have long been of opinion that the Combination[3] would eventually abandon Jackson, & take up some new Candidate; and his disgracefull [sic] failure in this assault upon the reputations of yourself & Mr Adams, strengthens that opinion. I believe that I have heretofore, & probably more than once, intimated to you my conviction that Mr Clinton's support of Jackson,[4] & the demonstrations made in his recent public speeches, favourable to Southern Men & Southern policy,[5] were founded on the calculation that Jackson would ultimately be withdrawn, and that *he* might be substituted as the opposing candidate to Mr Adams. Such, unquestionably, are still his calculations, and as I think with a greatly increased probability of their being realised. I hope therefore that you & your friends will be prepared for such an event.

My own impressions are that the politicians of the Southern atlantic States, who are very important men in the affairs of the "combination," would prefer Clinton to Jackson[6]—but I cannot believe that they would be able, by such an arrangement, to bring either the New England states or Ohio, on which they would make great calculations, into their views. In the State of New York the substitution of Clinton for Jackson, would change, in some degree, the component materials of the two parties, but I doubt whether it would essentially vary the aggregate strength of either. Many of the Federalists & Clintonians who are disposed to support Adams against Jackson would give their votes for Clinton—but, on the other hand, an equal number of those Bucktails who have been ordered by Van Buren & his friends into the support of Jackson, would probably, if Clinton were a candidate, go for his opponent. There is still, I am satisfied, a secret understanding and co-operation between Clinton & Van Buren. Whether this alliance will continue or be broken, will depend upon the estimates which they may severally make of the effects of one or the other course on their respective political fortunes. If Clinton is the candidate, Van

Buren I think will support him— But if Van Buren should be the candidate—and I am persuaded that he has some expectations of such a result—it is more doubtfull whether Clinton can be induced to go with him.

I am in daily expectation of receiving a letter from Mr Barclay, who is now in New York, advising me that he is ready to meet me at that place, and close our commission.[7] He has informed me through Maj. Delafield, that the instructions which he received from his Government in the spring were unsatisfactory, and that he is daily expecting others, untill the receipt of which he could not be prepared for our last meeting.

I know, my dear sir, that you will pardon the liberty I take in intreating you to avoid being led into *personal contests* with your political enemies. They are resolved to get rid of you if possible—and as they have failed in [. . .],[8] they will probably now attempt to shoot, you down. From McDuffie's deportment toward you for two years past in the House of Reps.[9]—from his insolent attack upon you at a late 4th. of July dinner[10]—and from the extraordinary manner in which his name is introduced into Genl. Jacksons late *bulletin*,[11] it is evident that he is [the] champion selected to fight you first. But I [trus]t that you will treat his *bullying* with the contempt it deserves.

Mrs Porter, who has a fine healthy Boy about five weeks old,[12] joins in assurance of respect & regard   P. B. PORTER
Hon. H. Clay

ALS. DLC-HC (DNA, M212, R2). Addressed: *"Private."*
[1] Cf. above, Ingersoll to Clay, August 11, 1827, note.   [2] Cf. above, Clay to Hammond, June 25, 1827, note.   [3] Cf. above, McClanahan and others to Clay, July 3, 1827, note.   [4] Cf. above, Porter to Clay, October 8, 1826; July 11, 1827.   [5] Not found.   [6] Cf. above, Clay to Everett, this date, note: William Hoffman, "Andrew Jackson and North Carolina Politics," *The James Sprunt Studies in History and Political Science*, XL (1958), 12.   [7] Anthony Barclay—see above, Porter to Clay, April 20, 1827.   [8] Word illegible.   [9] Cf. above, Binns to Clay, February 27, 1825; Toast and Speech, August 30, 1826, note 17.   [10] McDuffie had delivered two addresses at Hamburg, South Carolina—the first, at a Mechanics Festival on July 2; and the second, a Fourth of July oration. The former was considerably more virulent and personally abusive of Clay. Mistakenly, the Washington *Daily National Journal*, August 1, 1827, attributed to the second address the following excerpt, from the first oration, which was probably the version Porter had seen: "I . . . assert, and am willing to stake my humble stock of political reputation upon the truth of the assertion, that the circumstances of the extraordinary coalition between Mr. Adams and Mr. Clay, furnish us strong evidence of an abandonment of political principle on the part of Mr. Clay and corrupt political bargain between him and Mr. Adams, as is ordinarily required, in courts of justice, to establish the guilt of those who are charged with the highest crimes known to the law." Washington *United States Telegraph*, July 20, 1827. The speech of July 4 was more critical of the administration program and of Adams' commitment to the protective tariff and internal improvements, measures, McDuffie asserted, which Adams had not supported in 1824 but had now adopted as a political ploy. McDuffie maintained that his opposition rested less on the program than on its purpose: "They are the first American statesmen who have entered the arena of the Presidential canvass offering millions of extorted bounties to the manufacturing sections of the country, and millions of appropriation for Internal Improvements, to other sections of country, as a reward for their suffrages. I know it is the confidential calculation of Mr. Clay that nothing can resist this comprehensive scheme of corruption, which proposes under the form of law and under the assumed guise of patriotic motives to purchase up one half of society

with the wealth plundered from another." *Ibid.*, July 21, 1827.   11 Cf. above, Ingersoll to Clay, August 11, 1827.   12 Peter Augustus Porter, the Porters' only son, had
been born July 14, 1827. He was educated at Harvard University and in Germany, became a member of the New York Legislature in 1861–1862, was commissioned a member
of the United States Army in August, 1862, and was killed in battle in June, 1864.

To Charles R. Vaughan

Department of State, Washington 20. August 1827.

The Undersigned Secretary of State of the United States, in acknowledging the recept [*sic*] of the note of Mr. Vaughan, of the 16th. of the
current month, will restrict himself to one or two remarks only, in
closing on his part for the present, a discussion into which he has been
prematurely drawn by the note of Mr. Vaughan, of the last month,
transmitted at the instance of his Government.[1]

If Mr. Vaughan, in bringing forward the British Consul's statement,
on the 22d. day of May, in the last year,[2] had contented himself with
a simple exhibition of it, as he now admits it to be, as an ex parte statement, not certified on oath, and, consequently not to be considered
as deciding any point whatever in the case especially when opposed,
as it was by a contrary Statement from the American Consul,[3] the
Undersigned would have forborne to make any observations upon
that ex parte statement, until the evidence was completed. But Mr.
Vaughan must recollect that he communicated it "as a satisfactory
explanation of the transaction complained of," which seemed to require that it should be placed in its true light.

The Undersigned was unable clearly to comprehend the object for
which the intimation was given by Mr. Vaughan of a contingent withdrawal of the respect which the British Naval Officers are in the habit
of paying to the Officers of other friendly powers. He is happy to find
from Mr. Vaughan's last note, that it was not with any intention of
repressing complaints, which any Foreign power might feel itself justified in urging as well founded, to the British Government. But the
Undersigned still unable to perceive the purpose, or bearing of that
intimation, must think that the interpretation which he ventured to
suppose might have been intended, was not very unnatural.

When the Undersigned shall receive the further testimony which he
expects,[4] and which he will certainly continue to endeavour to obtain,
he will transmit it to Mr. Vaughan in full confidence that the Government of His Britannic Majesty will promptly cause such reparation to
be made as may appear, from the whole case, to belong to the United
States. Nor is this confidence weakened by the satisfaction which Mr.
Vaughan derives from the explanation of Captain Clavering—an explanation which, contrasted with the statement furnished by the
British Consul, renders, to say the least of it, a very imperfect account
of the transaction to which it relates.

If upon a full investigation it shall turn out that Mr. Hodges, the American Consul has conducted himself in an improper manner towards the British Government or towards Captain Clavering, Mr. Vaughan may be assured that he will receive just animadversion from the Government of the United States.

The Undersigned requests Mr. Vaughan will accept assurances of his distinguished consideration.   H. CLAY.

Copy. DNA, RG59, Notes to Foreign Legations, vol. 3, pp. 383–85 (M38, R3). Copy, initialed, in CSmH; copy, in MHi-Adams Papers (MR482).
1 Above, *ca*. July 30, 1827.   2 That is, the statement of George Manners, enclosed in Vaughan to Clay, May 22, 1826.   3 Samuel Hodges, Jr.   4 Cf. above, Clay to Hodges, June 20, 1826; August 16, 1827; Clay to Blake or Dearborn, August 15, 1827.

From Andrew Marschalk

Sir   Natchez (M) 20h Aug. 1827

I have the honor to Acknowlege [*sic*] the receipt of a letter from Mr Brent of the Department of State of the 12h. ult.[1] in relation to the case of an Aged moor,[2] a Slave belonging to Mr Thomas Foster, of this State, and claiming to belong to the Royal family of his country.

In pursuance of the directions of the President, I immediately waited on Mr. Foster, and made the enquiries suggested: He promptly replied, that he had signified to Prince (the Slave) four years ago, his willingness to permit him to return to his native country, if it could be effected without any expence to him (Mr. F.) and that he *was at present* equally willing to *give him his liberty*, conditioned however, that he should only enjoy that liberty in his Native country, conceiving that the possession of it here might operate to his, (Mr. F.'s) inconvenience by an improper influence over his children,[3] remaining with him, as Slaves. In the interview with me, Mr. Foster declined complying with my request to signify his wishes and intentions in writing. He is a planter of very retired habits, but of proverbial strictness and integrity. I however repeated my request to him thro' the medium of Henry Daingerfield, Esq. a young gentleman of the Bar, of the highest respectability.[4] Mr. F. again declined writing on the Subject, but reiterated his declarations respecting Prince— By my request, Mr. Daingerfield gave me, in writing the Substance of his conversation with Mr. Foster which I do myself the honor to enclose to you for the information of the President.[5]

I have communicated to the Old Man the benevolent intentions of the President toward him. He expresses the most grateful acknowledgements to him—and also feelings of the most profound friendship and respect to *all* the white men of America: but most particularly those of the state of Mississippi—and of Natchez, where as he expresses himself, all have been his friends and that he has by their general Kindness to him, known Slavery only by name.

By the aid of a literary Gentlemàn, (now absent for a few days from this city on professional business) who has taken a peculiar interest in the welfare of the Old Man—I expect to be enabled to lay before the President, the very interesting narative [sic] of Prince, anterior to his captivity, in battle, with the enemies of his country, in which he declares that he acted as a colonel of regiment of Cavalry.[6] Altho at the Advanced age of 65, his faculties are in full vigor—and his Geographical and other details accurately correct with the known histories of his country.

Altho by birth and education a strict Mahometan [sic], he expresses the most reverential respect for the Christian Religion—the moral precepts of which he appears to be well informed, and speaks of having read some of the Christian Scriptures of the Old Testament in his own Country, in the Arabic language. He has very often enquired of me the possibility of procuring a New Testament—(or in his own language) the history of Jesus Christ—for which, he says he would be willing to pay any price. In a recent conversation with him, on this Subject, I expressed a wish that he would yet become a Christian: he promptly replied, that "He thought he would,"—and repeated, as he always did, when conversing on that Subject, his wish for a testament. Should it be practicable to obtain one for him, and the President think proper to cause it to be sent here for him. I would feel particularly gratified in presenting it to him— The Advantages to be derived, from a comparison of the English Version, by the examination and reading of a person, in whom he has implicit confidence, would establish the correctness of the Arabic copy to his mind.

Permit me, Sir, to tender through you, to the President, my most respectful acknowledgement [sic] for the benevolent interest he has been pleased to take in the cause of this very interesting Old Man— who has been thirty-nine long years deprived of that inestimable blessing which the citizens of our happy country so abundantly enjoy—and who after so long a period of slavery & privation in a distant country, waits with the most pleasing Anticipations a return to the land of his fathers—and invokes blessings in his daily prayers, on that Country whose bounty is about to confer on the remnant of his days the Boon of Liberty   I have the honor to be Sir Very respectfully Your mo. Ob. Hl Servt.   Andrew Marschalk
Hon. Henry Clay

ALS. DNA, RG59, Misc. Letters (M179, R65). Copy, in MHi-Adams Papers, Letters Recd. (MR482). On December 18, Marschalk, fearing that the original had been lost, sent Clay a duplicate of this letter. ALS, in DNA, RG59, Misc. Letters (M179, R65).
1 See above, Mullowny to Clay, March 24, 1827, note.   2 Prince (Abduhl Rahahman). Cf. above, Reed to Clay, February 2, 1827.   3 There were five children and eight grandchildren left at Natchez when Prince and his wife departed. Subsequently

eight of them were purchased by the American Colonization Society and sent to Liberia in 1830. "The others presumably remained in slavery." Sydnor, "Biography of a Slave," *South Atlantic Quarterly*, XXXVI (1937), 72.   4 Henry A. Daingerfield, not further identified.   5 The enclosure is in the form of a letter from "H. A. Daingerfield" to Marschalk, dated at Natchez, August 20, 1827.   6 No statement has been found.

From Robert Scott

Dear Sir,   Lexington 20th. Augt. 1827

Your favor of the 4th. inst[1] came to hand in due course—

In the cases of Cockerell and of Higgins,[2] I have obtained Writs of Error from Judge Trimble[3] and will have the Citations served as soon as I can prevail on the Marshal[4] to do it   Fearing he may not do it as soon as desirable I have requested Mr Hanna[5] to send me official copies which I will forward to Mr. Waring[6] under the hope that they may facilitate a compromise and perhaps induce Cockerell and Higgins to suspend proceedings under the Judgments which I presume they will have entered in the Union Ct. Ct. about the middle of Septr.[7] It is unfortunate that application was not made for the Writs in time for them to operate as Superces. but as I have been advised by Mr. Crittenden[8] and others the time was suffered to pass— We must therefore do the best we can in the matter— When I hear from Waring I will see Mr. Crittenden and obtain his advice how to proceed—

Respecting the negro woman,[9] you observe you do not feel entirely satisfied with my conduct and you might as well say so— Feeling as you did it was right to make it known— With respect to this transaction I remain perfectly tranquil—feeling a perfect consciousness of of [sic] correctness in it from first to last— No one had a preference of purchase in the woman except Mrs Morrison[10] and she declined it altho' repeatedly applied to   I had therefore an undoubted privilege of making it and did so and with my own means— It is true, as heretofore stated, that my intention was to accommodate her and let her have the woman at the price I gave for her, but it does not at all follow that because I chose to accommodate Mrs Morrison I am bound to accommodate all and any other— Suppose the woman had died whose loss would it have been—the answer is obvious and as obviously determines the question   all good rules work both ways   However the difference is not much and suppose [sic] you must have her at the price you state, but I might as well give 25$. away as I could get 350$ for the woman in an hour—

Mr. Postlethwaite [sic] has replevied the debt assigned me by Garrett[11] for the benefit of his securities for 12 Months— It was enjoined by Trimble and the Montgomery Ct. Ct. has appointed Mr. Hawes receiver[12] as he informs me—

I have setled [sic] with Wier [sic] on 25th ulto.   Amt $6888,,92 of which he paid me 278$92 to pay costs &c. and 6610$ in his Notes payable in 1. 2. 3 & 4 years with interest included, 1900$ each secured by Mortgage on real estate[13]— As some notices were served on me relative to these debts, I was advised that my safest course was to take the notes in my own favor as Trustee &c. which I have done—and by the time the first becomes due the business will I suppose be finally setled as to those claiming from Garrett, when I can and will transfer the notes—

On examination in Mr. Hanna's Office, I find judgmt. has not been obtained against either of Garretts securities, though Judgment has been rendered against him[14]— In this state of the case, may not a question arise whether or not his securities have a right to obtain and appropriate his funds—having *as yet* sustained no damage? To enable you to determine this question, I send herewith a copy of the assignment[15]—

[. . .][16] survey of the land laid off for Holmes & Beckett[17]—which I trust you will approve assent to and return—as it is for reasons heretofore made known to you, of great importance to them and no loss to the estate I apprehend as they complained much of the quality of the land— they are men in moderate circumstances, with large families, but quite industrious and of good moral habits—

Your domestic affairs are I beleive [*sic*] doing as well as can be expected— I have not been able to rent the Hotel[18] yet, nor have I had an offer for it— Beach[19] has not paid me, but says he has some work made and bespoken, which he expects will be taken and paid for very Soon when he will pay from six to 700$. You will recollect leaving with me the written promise of Jno. T. Hawkins[20] to give an order on Jas. Barbour of Va. for 100$. A day or two since—I applied to Hawkins admr.[21] for the order and he informed me he some how understood— that the decd. Hawkins had put into your hands for collection some accounts or claimes [*sic*] against said Barbour— Is he correct? Very respectfully Your obt. Servt.   ROBT. SCOTT
The Honble Henry Clay

ALS. KyLxT.   1 Not found.,
2 William Cockerell; ———— Higgins. Cf. above, Scott to Clay, September 22, 1826; July 24, 1827.   3 Robert Trimble.   4 Chapman Coleman.   5 John H. Hanna.
6 John U. Waring.   7 No report of the judgments or of proceedings under them has been found in Union Circuit Court records.   8 John J. Crittenden.   9 The Morrison estate specie account for the quarter ending October 1, 1827, includes on September 15 a debit entry of $325 paid to Scott "for negro woman, Winney, purchased of him." The entry was omitted in the assembling of the account on an annual basis, summarized below, Morrison Estate, Specie Account, August 8, 1828.   10 Esther Montgomery (Mrs. James) Morrison.   11 John Postlethwait; Ashton Garrett. Cf. above, Debt Account, *ca.* August 12, 1826. The securities were Joseph H. Hawkins, George R. Tompkins, and Morrison.   12 Robert Trimble; Richard Hawes, Jr.
13 This seems to be a debt owed by James Weir to the Morrison estate, rather than the one owed by Weir to Clay personally (cf. above, III, 550n). No previous report of the debt has been found in the Morrison estate records.   14 Judgment against Garrett had been awarded on May 14, 1822. U. S. District Court of Kentucky, Order Book H, 193. Suit against Tompkins had been abated October 13, 1823, because of his death

(September 16, 1823). *Ibid.*, 295. Record of actions against Hawkins and Morrison has not been found.   15 Not found.   16 MS faded; three or four words missing.

17 Samuel Holmes and Samuel Beckett, both of Pendleton County, Kentucky, where they resided on a tract of 250 acres devised to them by James Morrison. Fayette County Court, Will Book F, 65. Holmes, brother of James and father of James Morrison Holmes, was a nephew of Morrison; Beckett, a brother-in-law of Holmes, had married Morrison's niece, Mary Holmes.   18 The Kentucky Hotel. Cf. below, Scott to Clay, September 10, 1827.   19 Jabez Beach. See above, Property Deed, August 2, 1826; Mortgage Deed, same date.   20 Cf. above, III, 484.   21 On December 11, 1826, Alexander Rigg had been named administrator for the estate of John T. Hawkins. Fayette County, Order Book 6, p. 319. A son of Jonathan Rigg, Alexander was a brother-in-law of Hawkins, who in 1818 had married Mary Rigg.

INSTRUCTIONS AND DISPATCHES   August 20, 1827

From THOMAS L. L. BRENT, Cintra (Portugal), no. 43. Gives illness as the reason he has not "written lately more often. . . ." Notes the concern, caused by the serious illness of "the Infanta Regent" (Isabel Maria) in May (cf. above, Brent to Clay, May 5, 1827), that in case of her death Dom Miguel would "have been entitled to the Regency" upon reaching the age of 25 in October (cf. above, Everett to Clay, June 9, August 16, 1827; Brown to Clay, July 12, 28, August 13, 1827), and the "very general opinion that" his "mere arrival . . . would give a severe blow to the constitutional cause. . . ." Explains "the declining confidence in the Ministry" among the "Liberals"; blames "the intrigues of the ultra-royalist party" and the "discontent of the garrison on account of their pay being much in arrear" for "a very serious disturbance . . . at Elvas," which was "quelled immediately." Traces events leading to the resignation of (João Carlos) de Saldanha (Oliveira e Daun) from the War Department (cf. above, Everett to Clay, June 22, 1827, note), which caused "a very great excitement" among the people of "the City," who proclaimed their support for him and the Constitution but were dispersed and, later, criticized by "the acting Minister of foreign Affairs Count da Ponte in the circular addressed to the diplomatic corps. . . ." Encloses a copy of the circular. Lists the members of the Ministry. States that Miguel, who refused to comply with the order to go to Brazil (cf. above, Raguet to Clay, July 17, November 27, 1826; Brown to Clay, April 12, 1827; Everett to Clay, June 9, August 16, 1827), is under the influence of Austria" and that "This power upholds his pretensions to enter upon the Regency immediately on his attaining his twenty fifth year. . . , which it is understood will be opposed by the Princess Regent, unless she is directed by the Emperor [Peter I] to give it up." Adds: "It is the universal opinion that unless the Emperor come soon to Portugal the power that he has over the crown of this Kingdom will be taken from him. . . ."

Reports that relations with Spain "have assumed a less hostile character"; that "There is at this moment no insurrection or disturbance in . . . Portugal: but the country is kept in a state of injurious suspense, uncertain whether the Infante don Miguel or the Emperor don Pedro will finally govern this Country, and whether the political institutions will continue to be upset"; and that nothing more is heard "of the negotiations . . . respecting the evacuation of the Peninsula by the french and english troops" (cf. above, Gallatin to Clay, April 14, 1827; Brown to Clay, April 27, 1827). ALS. DNA, RG59, Dip. Disp., Portugal, vol. 7 (M43, R6). Received October 18.

Manuel de Saldanha da Gama Melo Tovas Guedes de Brito, the seventh Count of Ponte, succeeded his uncle, Saldanha d'Oliveira e Daun, as Minister of War and from July 27 to November 7, 1827, was also Minister of Foreign Affairs.

From JOHN M. FORBES, Buenos Aires, no. 52. Transmits a translation of the note addressed to him by (Bernardino) Rivadavia, upon his retirement from office (cf. above, Forbes to Clay, June 29, 1827), expressing friendship for the United States but, also, "disappointment . . . at not having received . . . replies to the political questions" contained "in the note of the Minister of Foreign Affairs [Francisco de la Cruz] . . . of 24th August of last year." States that (Juan Baptista) Bustos, while "applauding the character of Mr. [Vicente] Lopez, the new Provisional President, declined adhering to the arrangements made here [cf. above, Forbes to Clay, July 15, 1827], without the previous Consent of the provinces with whom he stands Confederated," and that, "subsequent to the reorganization of the Provisional Government and the election of Col: Manuel Dorrego as Governor of this Province," Lopez resigned. Adds that "One of the first acts of the Provisional Junto was" to withdraw "the deputies of this Province from the General Constituent Congress," which dissolved on August 18. Forwards translation of a note, received from the Department of Foreign Affairs, informing him of the latter event.

Reports that Governor Dorrego, previously "distinguished for the virulence of his hostility towards the English," has reversed his position; attributes the reversal to the influence of Manuel José García; notes that the first indication of the change in political opinions "was . . . the nomination of Manuel Moreno as Minister of Government"; recounts Moreno's career and his devotion to British interests; points to the nomination of García's brother-in-law, Manuel H. Aguirre, to be Minister of the Treasury, as confirmation of García's influence over Dorrego; and describes "the confident prediction circulated in public, of the almost certain prospects of an early peace," which however, is to be effected "through the renewed mediation of Lord [John Brabazon] Ponsonby . . . to obtain a renewal on the part of the Emperor [Peter I] of those institutions which this Government so recently rejected with indignation" (cf. above, Forbes to Clay, August 10, 1827).

Continues later the same date, noting Aguirre's resignation, because of an empty treasury, and the appropriation of $20,000 by the Provisional Junto for the purpose of sending "deputies . . . into the provinces, to accomplish the so much desired concilation, and to concert the best means of carrying on the war against Brazil." Cites the difficulties in the way of bringing conciliation among the provinces and expresses apprehension concerning "the Congress which has been summoned by Bustos for the 1st. of September." Refers to a rumor that Lord Ponsonby intends "resuming his mediation through Sir William [i.e., Robert] Gordon, in endeavouring to procure some modification of the Emperor's terms. . . ." Observes that reports from Brazil of declining public credit and depreciating "funds and currency" have "effected a total change in the views of this Government [of Buenos Aires], who had previously determined to make another effort to obtain peace; but have now resolved to turn all their energies to vigorous prosecution of the war." L, written and signed at dictation by J. Dickinson Menderhall. DNA, RG59, Dip. Disp., Argentina, vol. 3 (M69, R4). Published in Espil (comp.), Once Años en Buenos Aires, 472–75, where the addendum is dated Auguust 26.

The "note . . . of 24th August of last year," to which Rivadavia referred, was enclosed in Forbes' dispatch, above, of September 5, 1826. In it, Forbes was asked to submit to his Government two questions: "1st. Whether the declaration of the President of the United States in the message to the Houses of Congress on 2d December 1823 . . . is, or is not applicable in the case where any European Power may assist . . . the Emperor of Brazil to sustain the war which he has declared against the United Provinces of the River Plate?—

"2d. If such declaration is equally applicable in the case where the Emperor of Brazil, as King of Portugal, may attempt to draw from that Kingdom, or from any of the dominions belonging to the Crown of Portugal and Algarves, any kind of aid for sustaining the said war?—"

Dorrego, born in Buenos Aires in 1787 and educated in law at the University of San Carlos, had become involved in the Chilian movement for independence while completing his studies at Santiago. He had subsequently fought against the Spanish in Upper Peru and northern Argentina but had been banished in 1816 by Juan Martin de Pueyrredon for military insubordination. He had spent the next four years in the United States, had returned to Argentina in 1820, and had been elected to a succession of political offices—governor of Buenos Aires (1820), member of the Junta de Representantes (1823), member of the constitutent congress (1826), and again governor of Buenos Aires (1827). In December, 1828, his government was overthrown, and Dorrego was shot.

Governor Bustos, of Cordoba, had on July 21, 1827, called for a meeting of the disaffected provincial leaders (cf. above, Forbes to Clay, April 12, 1827, note) to assemble in September for organization of a new general congress. The proposed meeting did not take place until September, 1828, when at Santa Fé controversy continued to disrupt the attempt at unity. Zinny, *Historia de los Gobernadores de las Provincias Argentinas*, III, 58, 453n.

From A[BRAHAM] P. GIBSON, St. Petersburg. Transmits "C. R. Lenartzen's certificate of protest against Capt. George Winsor Jr. of the Ship United States, of Boston, for his having left at Cronstadt one of his seamen, John Greggs, without discharging him agreeably to the Laws of the United States" (cf. above, Williamson to Clay, April 3, 1827, note). LS. DNA, RG59, Cons. Disp., St. Petersburg, vol. 2 (M81, R-T2). Received November 16.

Endorsed in Daniel Brent's hand, on separate sheet: "Papers enclosed sent same day to Geo Blake, Dist Atto at Boston." For a copy of Brent's letter, "by direction of the Secretary," see DNA, RG59, Dom. Letters, vol. 22, p. 84 (M40, R20).

Winsor and Greggs have not been further identified.

From J[OSEPH NICHOLAS] MORILLO, Tripoli. Reports that, under instructions from (Thomas D.) Anderson, who was unable to be present when his successor, (Charles D.) Coxe, arrived (cf. above, Shaler to Clay, October 6, 1825, note), he closed Anderson's affairs, both consular and private, and turned the office over to the new appointee. Charges that "Mr. Coxe was no sooner in possession of the establishment than he seized and detain'd the furniture of Mr. Anderson under the pretext that it belonged to the United States," although "every person in Tripoli knows" that Anderson bought the furniture from his predecessor, (Richard B.) Jones. Accuses Coxe of other acts of high-handedness which "created a great excitement, and amongst the Consuls the highest disgust. . . ." Explains that he makes this report "in order that Mr. Anderson may have an opportunity to recover the property . . . of which he has been robbed by the abuse of Official Authority." Notes that Coxe's conduct, of which his own wife (not further identified) has been critical, can only be accounted for "on the ground of insanity or habitual intoxication. . . ." Adds that "Many of the Consuls" of other governments at Tripoli have informed him "that they would have no further intercourse with Mr. Coxe than Official etiquette absolutely required, and others expressed their great regret that a Government such as that of the U. S. should be represented by so improper a person." ALS. DNA, RG59, Cons. Disp., Tripoli, vol. 4 (M-T40, R-T5). Received March 25, 1828. Endorsed by Clay on separate sheet: "To be laid before the President— Should not Mr Coxe be removed? H C"

Jones, of Philadelphia, had been appointed United States consul at Tripoli in 1812 and had been succeeded by Anderson in 1816. Jones subsequently held a post from 1852 to 1854 as consul general at Alexandria, Egypt.

MISCELLANEOUS LETTERS   August 20, 1827

To WILLIAM B. ROCHESTER, "Appointed Charge d'Affaires to Guatemala." Acknowledges receipt of his letter of August 14; states that "if any additional instructions be necessary. . . , they will be forwarded to . . . [him] at New York"; tells him how to obtain his "outfit and six months salary"; and requests that he inform the State Department of his "movements, particularly . . . that of . . . [his] departure from home." LS. NRHi. Copies, in DNA, RG59, Dip. Instr., vol. 11, p. 372 (M77, R6); DLC-HC (DNA, M212, R8).

To John Jacob Astor

Jno. Jacob Astor Esqr. N. Y.
Dear Sir,   Dept. of State, Washington 21 Augt. 1827.—
    A letter which I received this day from Mr. Brown[1] informs me that Mr. Rumph,[2] your son in law, was to be sent about the 15th. of this month for the Port of New York, on a mission to the United States. Upon his arrival, the Collector would, probably, without special orders, extend to his baggage the usual privileges belonging to his diplomatic character, but to ensure his enjoyment of them, I have the pleasure to transmit to you enclosed a letter which may be used if necessary.[3]— I am truly & faithfully, Your obedt. Servant,   H. CLAY.—

    Copy. DNA, RG59, Dom. Letters, vol. 22, p. 32 (M40, R20).
    [1] See above, Brown to Clay, June 28, 1827.   [2] Vincent Rumpff.   [3] A routine letter from Clay to Jonathan Thompson, on this date, informed the Collector of Rumpff's diplomatic character. Copy, in DNA, RG59, Dom. Letters, vol. 22, p. 33 (M40, R20).

Promissory Note to Daniel Brent

$ 6.000—   August 21. 1827
    Sixty days after date, I promise to pay to Daniel Brent or order Six thousand dollars for Value received—payable at the office of Discount & Deposit   Washington   H. CLAY

    DS. DLC-TJC (DNA, M212, R16). Cf. above, Promissory Note, June 19, 1827.

From Thomas Corwin

Dear Sir,   Lebanon 21st. August 1827
    You are no doubt surprised that I should have delayed till now an answer to your very welcome letter of the 21st. Ult.[1] The information necessary for a correct answer to some of your enquiries was not in my power at the receipt of your letter & I have been since endeavoring to ascertain with certainty whether the P M g[2] had removed any of his

deputies in this neighborhood and for what reasons.[3] I have not been able to learn that any such removals have been made, indeed I am certain that no instance of the kind has occurred,   I have not corresponded with Judge McLean since early in 1823   he then dropt all intercourse with me in consequence of my participation in the caucus in the Ohio Legislature[4]   at least I never could assign any other reasons for the very sudden change in his conduct towards me   My intercourse with Judge McLean during his visit to this place[5] a few months since was limited to a very ceremonious kind of visit by me & I had no conversation with him on the common political topics except in a promiscuous company one evening at the post office   I found him opposed to any further encouragement to our Manufactures upon the ground that the present Tariff is a "Judicious" one,   I have heard but do not know the fact, that he has condemed [sic] the Panama Mission & that the colonial trade bill of last Session did by no means meet his approbation,[6]   These Circumstances all seem [to] designate him as one opposed to the general Measures of the present administration— I expect you have heard that he is *secretly* doing much to aid the election of Genl. Jackson at the coming contest,   I can hardly beleive [sic] this is the case at least to the extent of the rumors I have heard   He must be too proud of himself to submit to the feelings & self reproach that such a course must bring upon him,— I have no doubt however but Judge McLean most ardently wishes to see Genl. Jackson elected, not because he dislikes Mr. Adams or his principles so much, but you sir are the "Lion in his path"[7]   of this I think you must be sensible, you know him & he is aware of it,   I have heard a rumor which supposes he may be removed sometime soon— I cannot but feel a deep interest in every thing however trivial that may have any influence upon the Approaching contest & this must be my excuse for obtruding upon your notice a single observation on this subject. It seems to be admitted every where that Judge McLean has filled his present station with much credit to himself & benefit to the country,   I am satisfied he has gained much more applause than he intrinsically Merits— His removal would have the effect to rouse all his "Minions & the howl of persecution would resound throughout the Union"[8]   what it might do in Ohio I know not, but I should fear its consequences— At present we are as safe as Massachusetts—   if the public service did not most imperiously require it as this Measure might produce in the way I mention a serious public calamity (for such I do think would be the true Character of the act that would place Genl Jackson at the head of our officers) might it not at least be defered [sic]— I hope you will allow the interest I feel in the affairs of our common country to sheild [sic] me from the Charge of impertinent & uncalled for council in a Matter where I have no *right* to be heard—

We have this Morning received Buchanan's letter upon the "bar-

gain"[9]   What must be the verdict on this evidence— Is the great
American jury so stupid as not now to see that this All conquering
Hero this paragon of truth & integrity has sunk to the level of a contemptible & I must add perjured informer   Can the hot house laurels
of a single battle sustain themselves against the blight this Mildew
threatens to bring upon them,   I think not,   such I beleive is not
now the expectation of his friends— We did hope to see you in the
Miami country somewhere during your stay in the west   you would
have been received with unbounded enthusiasm   your persecutors
have made you better known to the people of Ohio than they expected or hoped,   your conduct motives & principles are every day
more & more admired— I speak freely because I have watched the
progress of public opinion with much anxiety & am not deceived— I
do not trouble you often. but you will see that when I do write it is
not out of mere compliment but a downright matter of business— I
remain your very obliged & humble Servt.   THOMAS CORWIN
Hon H Clay Washington City

ALS. DLC-HC (DNA, M212, R2).   [1] Not found.
[2] John McLean.   [3] Cf. above, Hammond to Clay, March 28, 1827, note.   [4] Cf.
above, III, 341, note; 351, note.   [5] McLean had visited his home at Ridgeville, in
Warren County, Ohio, between June 1 and July 26, 1827, his first return visit in four
years. He had been entertained at a public dinner in Lebanon June 19.   [6] Cf. above,
Clay to Porter, November 28, 1825; Clay to Anderson, March 15, 1826; Clay to Force,
February 25, March 25 (enclosure), 1827.   [7] Proverbs 26:13; and cf. above, Hammond
to Clay, March 28, 1827, note.   [8] Source of quotation has not been found.   [9] Cf.
above, Ingersoll to Clay, August 11, 1827, note.

From Nehemiah Rice Knight

Hon. H. Clay
Dear Sir,   Providence August 21. 1827—
    Your letter of the 6th instant[1] requesting information of Mr Woods[2]
of Brown University has been recd. and in reply thereto can [sic] only
say, that I have not the pleasure of a personal acquaintance with that
gentleman, but am informed he is considered a good scholar, of irre-
proachable character, amiable and unassuming in his general deportment—   But of his aptitude or peculiar fitness to preside over such
an institution as that of Transylvania University, I am not sufficiently
informed to give the particular information desired—With the most
respectful consideration, I have the honour to be, Sir, your Obt Servt.
                                             N, R, KNIGHT

ALS. KyLxT.   [1] Not found.
[2] Alva Woods.

DIPLOMATIC NOTES   August 21, 1827

From CHARLES R. VAUGHAN. Acknowledges receipt of Clay's note of August 20.
States that he regrets "any Misunderstanding" that may "have arisen in the Course
of his Correspondence respecting the alleged Impressment of American Sailors"

and that he "cannot but repeat his Conviction, that from all that has already come to his Knowledge, the Transaction in Question cannot by any means be regarded as an Act of Impressment." Adds that "He is prepared however to receive whatever Proof Mr. Clay may hereafter offer to invalidate that Conviction." LS. DNA, RG59, Notes from British Legation, vol. 14 (M50, R15). Copy, in MHi-Adams Papers, Letters Recd. (MR482).

INSTRUCTIONS AND DISPATCHES   August 21, 1827

From ALBERT GALLATIN, London, no. 108. Encloses "the copy of a Note to Lord Dudley, on the subject of the Colonial Intercourse, which, though dated the 17th, was only transmitted to day." States that "As soon as it was fully ascertained that this Administration was to be, to all intents and purposes, a continuation of that of Mr [George] Canning [cf. above, Gallatin to Clay, August 14, 1827] . . . there was no motive for delaying the enquiry." Speculates whether the Ministry will consult (William) Huskisson (cf. above, Gallatin to Clay, July 14, 20, 1827) or immediately "answer in the negative." Adds that he has "asked an interview from Lord Dudley" and "will also try to see Lord Goodrich [Goderich] and Marquis Lansdown [sic]. . . ." Reports that "Unfortunately no inconvenience has yet been felt from the measures that have been adopted [cf. above, Gallatin to Clay, August 19, 1826, and note; Clay to Vaughan, March 17, 1827]"; that "no remonstrance has yet been made from" the British West Indies; and that "The shipping interest . . . believes that it will be benefitted by an adherence to the system," which "is therefore supported . . . by . . . public opinion" (cf. above, Harrison to Clay, August 9, 16, 1827). Discusses Canning, with whom he "had much rather have had to deal . . . at this moment than with the present Cabinet. . . ." Encloses "a London Gazette [not found], containing an order of Council of 16th of July last, issued in conformity with the Act of Parliament of last Session" (see above, Gallatin to Clay, June 13, 1827, and note). Calls attention to the circumstance that to the nations "that had not complied [with the Act of July 5, 1825—cf. above, Rush to Secretary of State, March 26, 1825, note], (France & Russia) the privileges of trade and intercourse with the British Colonies have nevertheless been extended." Adds: "This invidious distinction as contrasted with our exclusion is one of the topics on which I intend to dwell." Appends a list of members of the "*Present Cabinet*." ALS. DNA, RG59, Dip. Disp., Great Britain, vol. 34 (M30, R30). Published in *Sen. Docs.*, 22 Cong., 1 Sess., no. 132, p. 27. Received September 25.

In the note to Dudley, Gallatin stated that he had "been instructed [see above, Clay to Gallatin, April 11, 1827] to enquire, whether if Congress should, during its next session, pass a law" opening American ports to British vessels, from British colonies, carrying British or colonial produce, and repealing the act of March, 1823 (cf. above, III, 729n), the British would revoke "the Order in Council of the 27th of July 1826," abolish "the discriminating duties on American vessels in the British Colonies," and allow "these vessels . . . to enjoy the privileges of trade and intercourse with those Colonies, according to the Act of Parliament of the 5th. of July 1825."

The British order in Council of July 16, 1827 "confirmed and continued in force" orders in Council relating to the privileges accorded foreign countries trading with British possessions abroad. Prussia, Hanover, Sweden and Norway, Oldenburgh, Lübeck, Bremen, Hamburg, Colombia, the United Provinces of Rio de la Plata, the United States of Mexico, and Russia were authorized to enter their domestic produce into British possessions and to export from the latter territories "into any Foreign Country whatever." France was accorded the privilege of importing French productions of certain enumerated items into the British West

Indies and America but specifically barred from importing French wine into those territories. The closing of the trade of the United States with the British possessions in the West Indies, the Bahamas, Bermuda, Newfoundland, and on the continent of South America, effective on December 1, 1826, by order in Council of July 26, 1826—and the similar prohibition to operate at somewhat later dates in respect to American trade with British possessions elsewhere—was reaffirmed. *British and Foreign State Papers 1826–1827*, pp. 666–71.

To John Bradford

Dear Sir   Washn. 22d. Aug. 1827.

Inclosed I send you a letter from Professor Wayland, President of Brown University,[1] whom I took the liberty to sound as to the practicability of engaging him to go to Transylvania. I regret that his answer is unfavorable.

I think I shall write to Mr. McCalla[2]— Of course I shall not commit the Board, having no power to do so. I am Yr. ob. Servt.   H. Clay
Jno. Bradford Esq

ALS. KyLxT.   [1] Above, August 16, 1827.
[2] Thomas McAuley. Cf. above, Bradford to Clay, August 11, 1827.

To Charles Hammond

My dear Sir   Washington 22d. August 1827.

I recd. your favor of the 10h. inst. with directions for preparing the Seminary deed,[1] which has been done accordingly; and I shall forward it today to be executed.

The accounts which have yet reached me of the K. elections are very imperfect. You apprehend that their result will be less favorable than I anticipated. Perhaps so; but, judging from what I have seen, I am inclined to believe that the general issue of the elections will be favorable.[2] I shall be deceived greatly if there be not a majority in both branches of the General Assembly friendly to the Administration;[3] and that is a most important point. The elections in No. Carolina have not turned out badly;[4] and those at Knoxville and Nashville in Tennessee are far from being agreeable, in their issue, to Genl. Jackson.[5]

On this side of the Mountains there has been a great and manifest decline of the General's cause, since the letter to C. Beverley was published;[6] and this decline is not confined to the North but extends to the South. Letters of congratulation have poured in upon me from all quarters. And some of my friends, who heretofore despaired of the vote of Virginia, now express sanguine expectations that it will be given to Mr. Adams. Mr. Southard, who is now at the White Sulphur Springs, writes me to that effect.[7] Your's, with great regard
C. Hammond Esq   H. Clay.

ALS. InU.
1 The complete text of the letter, published above, has not been found. For an additional reference to the deed, see above, Clay to Wells, August 18, 1827.   2 Cf. above,
Clay to Taylor, April 4, 1827, and note.   3 Cf. above, Clay to Adams, August 19,
1827, note.   4 Seven Jacksonians and six supporters of the administration had been
elected to Congress in North Carolina. The issue of Presidential support had not, however, been decisive in the election, which hinged primarily on the personal popularity
of the contestants. Hoffman, "Andrew Jackson and North Carolina Politics," *James Sprunt
Studies in History. . . ,* XL, 13–14.   5 See above, Erwin to Clay, August 22, 1827.
6 Cf. above, Clay to Hammond, June 25, 1827.   7 Above, August 8, 1827. See also
Brooke to Clay, August 8, 1827; Caldwell to Clay, August 8, 1827; Mercer to Clay, August
18, 1827.

From Asher Robbins

Hon. Mr. Clay—   Newport. R. I. Aug. 22d. 1827
    Dr. Sir.   Since my last¹ I have made the enquiries which I therein
promised to make concerning Mr Woods.

    I have learnt nothing to vary the sentiments then communicated.
Those whom I have consulted agree in thinking, that he is not well
fitted for such a place; tho very well fitted for a subordinate place;
such, for instance, as he now occupies.

    If your University is not restricted to any particular School of
Theology;² as too many of our learned Institutions are; I could mention several whose qualifications for the Office, I think, would entitle
them to a decided preferrence [*sic*] over Mr Woods; whose qualifica-
cations indeed, eminently fit them for that Office;   But whether or not
they could be obtained I know not. I remain Dr Sir yrs. truly
                                                      ASHER ROBBINS

    ALS. KyLxT.   1 Cf. above, Robbins to Clay, August 13, 1827.
2 The criticism of Horace Holley had centered upon his theological background. Cf.
above, II, 583n; Sonne, *Liberal Kentucky,* 191–241. To counteract the criticism, the
faculty and trustees had concluded in 1824 that, while a State university should be non-
sectarian, "the great doctrines of our *common religion,* those in which the good and
pious of all denominations agree, should be taught. . . ." The Roman Catholics, Baptists,
Episcopalians, and Methodists had agreed to rotate preaching in chapel; the Presbyterians had refused to co-operate. Sonne, *Liberal Kentucky,* 232–3.

From Robert Scott

Dear Sir,   Lexington 22 August 1827
    Your favor of the 10th. inst¹ came to hand today.

    I observe what you say in relation to the business between the estates
of Colo. OHara and Colo. Morrison² and will consider kind in you
when leisure will permit, if you will look into the papers which I
sent you³ and write to Majr Denny on the subject should your opinion
concur with mine— It will I have no doubt, have a good effect in
hastening the completion of the title to the land—

    The record in the cases of Cockerell &c. shall be sent on to you in
due time, provided a compromise cannot be effected with them⁴—

946 SECRETARY OF STATE

Knowing as I do, that you have so much important business before you, I regret troubling you so often upon affairs which comparatively are of but little importance; but it seems I cannot otherwise get on without neglecting the interests of the estate— It is necessary that you should answer Cooper and Boswells Bill in Chancery—a copy of which is herewith and all the information which I can give you[5]— Our Chancery docket I understand is to be gone thro' at or during our Septr. term—which begins on the 3rd Monday. If you can send it on in time I will thank you and please return the papers herewith enclosed— I know nothing of the transactions which they alledge [sic] in their bill, to have taken place between them and Colo. Morrison— never having heard any thing of them until since suit was brought— I know of no other than what took place with my self— nor do I now recollect the tender which they state having been made to me—tho' it may have been made— The reason I did not submit the controversy to arbitration, nor an agreed case to the Court, was because we could not agree on the facts—

Enclosed herewith is a letter[6] I recd. from Jno. Scott of Missouri, from which you will perceive the chance of payment from him is but slender[7]— I have written him in answer that the lien of the mortgage would readily be relinquished to any one who would give good security for the debt payable at a future day, with interest, and referred him to Colo Sullivan.[8] By his letter you will observe he appreciates the land and Saline much above the amount for which it is mortgaged   I have understood far otherwise lately, from a Mr. Timy. Davis[9] who lives at St. Genevieve, and who with others wishes to buy a part of the tract— I have referred him also to Colo. Sullivan who I presume will be on the spot and can better judge of what is expedient in the matter than those at such a distance as you are— Mr. Davis informs me the title to the land has never been confirmed— consequently the claim is less valuable than if confirmed, as there is almost always some doubt as to the confirmation of such claims—

The Hotel is stil [sic] unoccupied[10]—   Your other domestic affairs are all doing well I beleive [sic]— The News Papers will inform you our elections in several cases have eventuated contrary to our expectations and wishes[11]— It is really strange that the Jackson mania should prevail to such an extent in Kenty.— before the result of the elections I could not have beleived [sic] it. very respectfully Yr. obt. Servt

The Honble Henry Clay   ROBT. SCOTT

ALS. DLC-TJC (DNA, M212, R13).   [1] Not found.
[2] James O'Hara; James Morrison.   [3] Cf. above, Scott to Clay, July 21, 1827.
[4] Cf. above, Scott to Clay, September 22, 1826; July 24, 1827; August 20, 1827.   [5] Not found. The answer of Clay as executor of James Morrison, deceased, in response to Spencer Cooper and Company, complainants, was filed on September 17, 1827. The case was finally submitted to an arbitrator in 1830, and on February 20, 1832, the arbitrator's award was made the decree of the court. The injunction awarded the complainants was dissolved. their bill was dismissed, and they were required to pay the defendant $22.40,

"being ten per centum on the amount enjoined," and his costs. Fayette Circuit Court, Civil Orders, Book 6, p. 248; Book 10, p. 26; Book 13, pp. 92–93.   6 Not found.
    7 Cf. above, John Scott to Clay, August 2, 1827.   8 John C. Sullivan.   9 Born in Newark, New Jersey, Davis had come to Kentucky in 1816, studied and practiced law there for several years, then removed to Missouri and in 1837 to Dubuque, Iowa, while continuing legal practice. Identified politically as a Whig, he was a member of Congress from 1857 to 1859.   10 Kentucky Hotel. Cf. above, Scott to Clay, August 20, 1827.
    11 Cf. above, Clay to Taylor, April 4, 1827, and note; Clay to Adams, August 19, 1827, note.

From Henry Shaw

My Dear Sir   Lanesborough[1] Aug. 22. 1827
    I hope you have not believed, that because I have for borne for a long time to vex you with Troublesome letters, that I have been un-mindfull [sic] of your course, or indifferent to any thing that could bear upon your present fame or future prospects— I have felt that a bad policy has been pursued in relation to our own State, most certainly one that has effectually displaced the old Republicans and given the power into hands that may not abuse it, but not as reliable as I could wish[2]— I urged upon Mr. Websters friends the impolicy of placing him in the Senate— I had various reasons for it, but the one most operative with me was, that he was too strong a Man to be made too Independant [sic]— I thought it would have been better to have had him for the present checked by the people of Boston— but his great anxiety prevailed against any other consideration— it was more-over too soon to commit so great a violence upon the old Republican feelings of the State— I hope however that he may be faithfull [sic]— I hope to acquire more confidence in him he[re]after— I say this much in relation to gone bye things, that you may understand that altho there has not been yielded to every call or intimation from Wer. The support that might have been expected, it has not been witheld [sic] from any wish to embarriss [sic] but from an anxious desire to have every thing done with an Eye to the future, while the reasonible [sic] wishes of the present was [sic] not entirely disregarded— the great body of your friends in this State are rapidly gaining strength—and depend upon it there will be left untouched, no chord to [. . .][3] to them, a still more powerfull [sic], and in the end a Triumphant body— I have alwas [sic] sought preserve [sic] among your friends an understanding of common feelling [sic] and interest, for reasons which have [sic] heretofore suggested— In some things I may have been led too far by my anxious desires to promote what appeared to me to be the interest of the Nation, by promoting your own— this however will be to you unpardonable offence—
    I saw Mallery [sic],[4] & was through the great part of Vt. recently and from what I have seen, I can say with Truth, that in regard to yourself a class of feelings that have existed personal to yourself, are fast sub-

siding, and a degree of enthusiasm prevailing— An Enthusiasm that I hope will forever distiguish [sic] your friends, from the cold and calculating ones of common statesmen— Mallery gives a good account of Harrisburg⁵— this you have had from others long before this. Van B.⁶ I saw last week— he feells [sic] divided— hopes for some reasons, that old Hic, will loose [sic] ground, & fears at the same time the consequence of it— he said, a few more letters from the old Man,⁷ would do the business for him— he will support the Tariff in some form, and is working hard to lessen the opposition of the South— he fears the state of that question— I rejoice to see the Jackson Dinner at Lexington,⁸ a few more such Dinners and the game would be finished— but they will take a different course— your Triumphant appeal to the Nation made at the Festive Board at Lexn.⁹ has done wonders, and will crown all the hopes of the most devoted friends—if—and pardon me for saying it, the triumph is not pushed *too far*— but it will not be— from all this region the prospect has never looked better—and as far as we can learn throught [sic] the Country—

I want you to bear in mind one thing, which will perhaps explain to you some others as they pass—, that the old lines of party are not wholly extinct among us, and it is proper that the Republicans should at times protect themselves by acting in concert— old feelings are to be respected, and we are to be brought not in a lump but by degrees, to amalgamate— If there is nothing said about Amalgamation, we shall unite of course— I must go with old associates, but they will in the end all go right, if treated kindly—

I should be happy to hear from you occasionally, & when I do fail in courtesy, depend upon it I shall not fail in devotion—

H: SHAW

ALS. DLC-HC (DNA, M212, R2).   1 Massachusetts.
2 On the general problem of Daniel Webster's move to the United States Senate, cf. above, Webster to Clay, June 8, 1826, note; May 7, 18, June 2, 1827; Clay to Everett, May 2, 1827; Clay to Webster, May 14, 28, 1827; Silsbee to Clay, May 23, 1827. The resentment of old Republicans against the movement for amalgamation with former Federalists is evidenced, above, in Mundy to Clay, July 24, 1827.   3 Word illegible.
4 Rollin C. Mallary.   5 The Harrisburg Convention (cf. above, Clay to Crowninshield, March 18, 1827, note).   6 Martin Van Buren.   7 Cf. above, Smith to Clay, August 1, 1827, note.   8 *Ibid.*   9 Above, July 12, 1827.

From Daniel Webster

My Dear Sir   Boston Aug 22. 1827

My letter to Col Johnson¹ was not important & the delay, in its transmission is of no moment.

You speak very modestly of recent events, in which you have borne so distinguished, & so *successful*, a part. I cannot think Genl. Jackson will ever recover from the blow which he has recd. Your speech at Lexington,² in point of merit, as a clear & well stated argument, is certainly at the head of all your efforts; & its effects on public opinion have not been exceeded by those of any political paper, I may almost say, within my recollection. Buchanan[3] is treat'd too gently. Many persons think his letter[4] *candid*. I deem otherwise. It seems to me he has labored very hard to protect the Genl, as far as he could without injury to himself. Although the Genl's friends this way, however, *affect* to consider Buchanan's letter as supporting the charge, it is *possible* the Genl. himself & the Nashville Comee. may think otherwise, & Complain of Buchanan.[5] I should expect this, with some confidence, if they recd. the letter a little earlier than they may have seen the turn which the Atlantic Editors have attempted to give it. As these last have pretty generally agreed to say that the letter does support the Genl.,[6] the Nashville Commentators, if they see the example in season, may be disposed to follow it. I do not yet learn what answer comes from that quarter to your *Speech*.

We must soon hear from Kentucky, & make up our minds to whatever comes. It would be bad, on many accounts, if we should lose any votes, in that State.[7] In the first place, we have none to spare, & in the second place the general impression, produced by such a result, would be more or less injurious. Nevertheless, no extent of misfortune there, in these elections, would shake my faith in the final success of the Administration. With activity, zeal, & prudence, we shall succeed.

The President & Govr. Kent[8] dined with me yesterday, both in good health, & excellent spirits. The President is fast recruiting.

I go to Barnstable County tomorrow, to pass a week or ten days, on the Sea Shore. Ever truly yours   DANL. WEBSTER
Hon Mr Clay

ALS. DLC-HC (DNA, M212, R2). Endorsed on cover: "*Private*."
1 Francis Johnson, from whom Webster had received a letter cited in Webster to John W. Taylor, July 15, 1827. Wiltse and Moser (eds.), *Papers of Daniel Webster*, II, 230, 239, 240n. Webster's letter to Johnson, the letter transmitting it to Clay, and Clay's reply to Webster have not been found.   2 Above, July 12, 1827.   3 James Buchanan.
4 Cf. above, Ingersoll to Clay, August 11, 1827, note.   5 For Jackson's initial reaction to "The outrageous statement of Mr. Buchanan," see Remini, *Election of Andrew Jackson*, 66–67. By September 4 he had cooled to the degree that he wrote Amos Kendall: "I have seen Mr Buchanan [*sic*] address, it is such a production as surely I had not a right to expect from him; but we live in days of wonder." Bassett (ed.), *Correspondence of Andrew Jackson*, III, 381. John H. Eaton, for the Nashville Committee, subsequently undertook to counteract the effect of the discrepancies which Buchanan's statement had made evident. Cf. below, Ingersoll to Clay, October 6, 1827, note.   6 The *Boston Statesman* reprinted from the New Hampshire *Concord Statesman*: "Mr. Buchanan's letter . . . is an ample and triumphant vindication of Gen. Jackson's assertions and character." Quoted in Washington *Daily National Journal*, August 30, 1827. The Philadelphia *National Palladium* maintained: "Every line and every word of this letter go to establish the fact, that General Jackson believed that Mr. Buchanan's remarks and questions were made in consequence of suggestions to him by Mr. Clay's friends. . . ." Reprinted in Washington *United States Telegraph*, August 15, 1827. The *New York Enquirer* found that Buchanan's letter "confirms every declaration made by Gen. Jackson, denying at the same time that he [Buchanan] was authorized by Mr. Clay, and differing with Gen. Jackson as to some circumstances. . . ." Reprinted in *ibid.*, August 17, 1827. Cf. also, below, Crittenden to Clay, September 6, 1827, note.   7 Cf. above, Clay to Taylor, April 4, 1827, and note; Clay to Adams, August 25, 1827, note; Scott to Clay, this date.   8 Joseph Kent.

INSTRUCTIONS AND DISPATCHES   August 22, 1827

From W[ILLIAM] H. D. C. WRIGHT, Rio de Janeiro. Reports that he has "learned nothing further relative to the case of Capt. [George] Simmonds [Jr.] and his mate, of the American Schooner Hero, who are now in confinement at this place, charged with Piracy." States his belief that peace negotiations (with Buenos Aires) have begun again, with (Sir Robert) Gordon playing an active role (cf. above, Forbes to Clay, March 8, August 20, 1827); notes a rumor "that the terms have been agreed upon" but hesitates to predict the results. Observes that locally there is little preparation for war. ALS. DNA, RG59, Cons. Disp., Rio de Janeiro, vol. 2 (M-T172, R3). Received October 27.

MISCELLANEOUS LETTERS   August 22, 1827

From GEORGE BLAKE, Boston. Acknowledges receipt of Clay's letter of August 15 and reports that Captain (Ephraim) Merchant is not expected to return from a voyage to Africa "in less than a year from [*sic*] the present time." ALS. DNA, RG59, Misc. Letters (M179, R65).

To John Quincy Adams

Dear Sir   Washington 23d. August 1827.
     Mr. Rush, Mr. Wirt[1] and I had a meeting yesterday on the subject of Mr. Poinsetts letter.[2] You are aware that Mr. Barbour and Mr. Southard[3] are absent from the City. My object now is to communicate the opinions which we formed in that conference. Mr. Rush did not take much part in the conversation from reasons which may be inferred from a former letter.[4]
     Mr. Wirt and I both thought that it was expedient to have Mr. Poinsett replaced by some other Minister from the U. S. whose relations with the Mexican Government were not of the same unfriendly character as those which unhappily exist between Mr. P. and it. Mr. Rush coincided in that opinion. There are important interests of this Country now confided to Mr. P.; the modification of the Commercial treaty; the negotiation about our limits, Texas, &c &c.[5] With the state of feeling which exists between him and that Government (and it is not material to determine which party is in fault) it is almost certain that Mr. P. can do nothing. But are we sure that Mr. P. has not given some cause for dissatisfaction? Is there not reason to believe that he has throughout conducted his mission on the erroneous principle of forming a party, within the Country, for the purpose of influencing the Government?[6]
     Mr. Wirt apprehended that if Mr. P. were recalled it might have the effect of souring him and throwing him into the ranks of our opponents. But, as he stated to the Mexican President,[7] that he should de-

sire his recall, it may be placed upon that ground. It is not necessary to express any dissatisfaction with him. His return may be ascribed to the fact of unfriendly relations, no matter how created, between him and that Government, and to his own desire expressed in his letter to you. It is true that is coupled with the wish of his retaining the Tacubaya appointment. But he may be told that this latter is an incident to the Mexican Mission; and that considerations of public economy, considering the uncertain issue of the Congress of Tacubaya, forbid two distinct missions.

After his intimation to the President of Mexico that he should ask of you his recall, and the President's acquiescence in that course, can he be continued there longer with propriety?

Will not the President of Mexico expect, and has he not a right to expect, his recall?

Reverse situations, suppose a Foreign Minister unacceptable to this Government, were to inform you that he should desire his recall, would it not be regarded as a thing that would certainly take place, without any official movement on our part?

I confess, Sir, that I think it fortunate that an opportunity has fairly occurred of our being represented at Mexico by some more suitable person than Mr. Poinsett. And as he cannot justly blame this Government for any part of that state of things which he finds himself in at Mexico, I think it is advisable not to let this opportunity pass, without embracing it. It appears to me indeed that we shall assume the consequences of any mischief happening in our relations with Mexico by Mr. Poinsetts continuance there, if he is not now taken at his word, and suffered to return.

And I respectfully suggest, Sir, whether his letter to you is not a sufficient official basis to act upon? By turning that letter over to the Dept. of State, and directing that Mr. Poinsett be informed that, according to the intimation which he gave to the President of Mexico, he is permitted to return, it seems to me that there would be no necessity for waiting any other official communication. The Mexican Government, I should suppose, will not make any further movement, because it will anticipate Mr. Poinsett's recall, from what he himself told the President of Mexico. At least it will not make a formal application for his recall until it has a certained [sic], after the lapse of a considerable time, that our Government means to continue Mr. P. at Mexico. Mr. Poinsett will not ask his recall, by an official despatch to the Department of State, because, if you remain silent, he will infer your acquiescence to his remaining.

Our accounts from K. as to the late elections are still imperfect. I believe the result will be such as to leave the two parties in our delegation, in the next Congress in the same relative strength that they were in the last.[8] Judging from the returns which I have seen, there will be a decided majority of friends to the Administration in both branches of the General Assembly.[9] The election in my old district, both to Congress and to the State Legislature, turned out as my friends wished.[10] I am, with great respect, faithfully Your ob. Servt.

Mr. Adams.   H. CLAY

ALS. MHi-Adams Papers, Letters Recd. (MR482).   [1] Richard Rush; William Wirt. [2] See above, Sergeant to Clay, August 1, 1827; Adams to Clay, August 15, 1827. See, also, Adams, *Memoirs*, VII, 312–13.   [3] James Barbour; Samuel L. Southard.   [4] Above, Clay to Adams, August 17, 1827.   [5] Cf. above, Clay to Poinsett, March 12, 15, 1827.   [6] Cf. above, Poinsett to Clay, July 8, 1827.   [7] Guadalupe Victoria.   [8] Cf. above, Clay to Taylor, April 4, 1827, and note.   [9] Cf. above, Clay to Adams, August 19, 1827, note.   [10] Cf. above, Crittenden to Clay, March 3, 1827, note. Robert J. Breckinridge, James True, and Leslie Combs, all identified as administration supporters, had been elected from Fayette County to the Kentucky House of Representatives. True, a Fayette County farmer, had been a member of the legislature in the Sessions of 1815 through 1817 and since November, 1823. He remained in that body until 1831. He was also sheriff of Fayette County at the time of his death in July, 1831.

Order on Washington Office, Bank of the United States

No.   OFFICE OF DISCOUNT & DEPOSIT, Washington,

                                                          23 Aug. 1827

PAY to Draft on Balto— *or bearer,*

Nine Dollars,   /100   H CLAY

$9—DOLLARS,   /100

ADS, partially printed. DLC-TJC (DNA, M212, R16) .

From John Quincy Adams

Henry Clay, Secretary of State Washington—

Dear Sir—   (Private and Confidential)   Quincy 23. August 1827.

Your Letters of the 16th. and 17th. instt. were received this Morning— Mr Poinsett's Letter[1] was enclosed to you with mine of the 15th. As he does not ask to be recalled, it seems expedient to wait for an official movement from the Mexican Government, before taking any decisive step.[2] I shall not be unmindful of Mr Rush's wishes, in the event of a vacancy in the Mission to Mexico.

I perceive with much concern, the *temper* which the present Administration of the British Government is infusing into their Negotiations with us— Your Note in reply to Mr Vaughan[3] upon the impressment of the Seamen appears to me altogether proper. With regard to the Instructions to be given to Mr Gallatin although his course of referring the two points claimed by the British Plenipotentiaries on the renewal of the Convention of 1818 was proper,[4] I wish it to be considered whether it may not be advisable to authorize him to accede to them both. There is so much weight in the British argument against the discrimination between rolled and hammered iron, that I think the point may be conceded without derogation, and the stipulation to forbear exclusive Legislation for ten years, on condition that the British Act of exclusive Legislation shall itself be repealed, may be safely acceded to—especially with the additional Article that either party with twelve Months Notice may put an end to the Convention— Its renewal seems to me highly important, not only because its operation is advantageous to us; but because it will at least put off the quarrel, which they may be seeking—

I arrived at Philadelphia, at 6 O'Clock in the Evening; and left it at 6 the next Morning— I spent half the Evening with Mr Sergeant, at his house, and the other, also with him and some other friends at Mr Walsh's.[5] This latter Gentleman is friendly to the Administration *in his way*, though not always happy in his manner of shewing it, and sometimes perhaps over charitable to its enemies— In Philadelphia, as elsewhere, it is a great desideratum that the friends of the Administration should understand, and not counteract each other   I believe Mr Walsh might be made sensible of this, if hostilities should be suspended *against him*.[6] Yours ever faithfully   J. Q. ADAMS.

ALS. InU.   [1] Cf. above, Sergeant to Clay, August 1, 1827, and note.
[2] Cf. above, Clay to Adams, this date.   [3] Above, August 15, 1827.   [4] Cf. above, Gallatin to Clay, June 20, July 28, 1827.   [5] Cf. above, Wharton to Clay, August 3, 1827, and note.   [6] Cf. above, Clay to Webster, April 14, 1827.

From John D. Godman

Dear Sir,   New York 23d Augt. 1827.

The extract has been in the hands of Mr. King[1] for some days. He intends to make a better use of it than merely to publish it singly, being at present engaged in preparing an article containing a fair review of the public services and consistency of the party in question; in which along with other testimonials, the extract will be introduced.[2] This will without doubt be an able and useful paper.

It is greatly to be feared that Kentucky will lose the advantage of her medical School, as Drake has resigned and Dudley is appointed at Baltimore.[3] These circumstances, together with its location, which is rather unfortunate in relation to anatomical and surgical facilities, may operate very prejudicially. Had it been possible to have established the institution somewhere on the Ohio, its destiny, with the talent it has thus far employed, must have been very different. In medical politics, I believe, we are on the eve of having another Explosion in New York.[4]

Hoping to have the pleasure of seeing you here, I remain very faithfully yours   J. D. GODMAN.
H. Clay Esqr.

ALS. DLC-HC (DNA, M212, R2).   1 Charles King.
2 Reference has not been found.   3 Daniel Drake had resigned from the Medical Department of Transylvania University on March 19, five days after the resignation of Horace Holley as president of the University. Drake's biographer found "no explanation for the concurrence of these resignations" but surmised that Drake "probably anticipated the deterioration of Transylvania as a result of Holley's departure. . . ." Emmet Field Horine, *Daniel Drake, 1785–1852, Pioneer Physician of the Midwest* (Philadelphia, [c. 1961]), 214, 216.   Benjamin W. Dudley was appointed Professor of Surgery at the University of Maryland by action of the trustees on August 15, 1827, but declined the chair and remained at Transylvania. *Baltimore American and Commercial Daily Advertiser*, August 16, 1827; Lexington *Kentucky Gazette*, August 31, 1827.   4 The College of Physicians and Surgeons, established in 1807 as a department of the University of New York and combined with the Columbia Medical School in 1811, had been disrupted for nearly a decade by controversy over the role of the faculty in administration. In 1826 provision had been made for a board of trustees to be composed of 13 laity and 12 medical practitioners. The faculty, in protest, had resigned as a body on April 11. The following September five of the faculty had proposed to the trustees of Rutgers College that a medical school be organized under their administration in New York. Rutgers Medical College was accordingly established. The New York Legislature in 1827, however, passed an act denying authorization to practice medicine or surgery within the State under a diploma "granted by any authority out of this state to an individual who . . . [had] pursued his studies in any medical school within this state, not incorporated and organized under its laws. . . ." The Rutgers Medical College held only one significant graduation ceremony and passed into oblivion; the New York institution replaced the disaffected faculty. Godman, who had been one of the seceders and was a member of the Rutgers institution, opened a private medical school during the summer of 1827. James J. Walsh, *History of Medicine in New York* (5 vols.; New York, 1919), II, 415–23; William H. S. Demarest, *A History of Rutgers College, 1766–1924* (New Brunswick, 1924), 294–97 (297 quoted); *New York American*, May 8, 1827.

From John Sergeant

Dear Sir,   Philada. Augt. 23. 1827.

Your favor of the 19th.[1] was duly received. I fully agree with you in opinion as to the propriety of your coming, or rather, of your not coming here[2] at present, for the reasons you state. You will perceive, however, that this matter has now assumed a new aspect, in consequence of the ferocious course pursued by the Jacksonites. Their conduct has produced a strong feeling in the City, as it ought to do, for it is really a gross and indecent outrage. In what manner it is to be treated, remains yet undecided.[3]

Mr. Markley, whom I accidentally met with at Norristown about ten days ago, seemed to have made up his mind with the advice of his friends that it was not necessary for him then to come out.[4] I told him I was of the same opinion, but that the time would come, and was not very far off, when his statement would be required. Yesterday, I saw him again, and told him the thing had now taken its shape, and it was evident that Genl. J's case was to be supported by presumptions against him.[5] He is manifestly desirous to remain quiet, tho' he says distinctly he should clearly acquit you and your friends, and says too that the conversation between him and Buchanan was introduced by that gentleman, who called upon him at his lodgings. He has promised to call upon me. There are difficulties as to bringing him out, which I cannot at present understand or explain.

We are in the same disjointed state here as formerly.[6] A great many well wishers[, some][7] zealous friends, and, no doubt, a large majority in the City, but no organization. This is owing in part to the state of parties. The old names are kept up, the old machinery is employed, and elections turn entirely upon this distinction, so that there is no effective mode of operating in mass, or even of encouraging and animating each other. I was in hopes that before this time some thing would have been done at Harrisburg, but there is no sign of movement. We must therefore try to do something for ourselves, Very respectfully & truly Yrs.   JOHN SERGEANT.
The Honble Henry Clay.

ALS. DLC-HC (DNA, M212, R2).   1 Not found.
2 Cf. above, Sergeant to Clay, August 17, 1827; Mercer to Clay, August 18, 1827.
3 Reacting to the news of arrangements undertaken for welcoming Clay should he come to Philadelphia, Jackson's supporters had met on August 17 and adopted a resolution for appointing a committee of 113 "to ascertain whether any attempt to misrepresent the feelings and opinions of the citizens of the district by a public entertainment to Henry Clay be contemplated:—with full power at their discretion to take such measures as may afford the people an opportunity in a signal manner to *counteract* the designed effect of any such movement. . . ." A meeting of that committee on August 20 had called an assembly to express such feelings "*immediately*" upon receiving information of the arrival of HENRY CLAY IN, OR NEAR, THIS CITY. . . ." Clay's friends, meeting August 28, regarded these pronouncements as inhospitably designed "to prevent the contemplated visit" and conducive to violence. Accordingly they adopted a series of resolutions, asserting their rights "to express . . . approbation of the principles and conduct of public men" and "to exercise decorous hospitality towards eminent citizens of other states" who might visit the city; voiced their "indignation [at] the recent proceedings" of the Jacksonites; announced their "intention to offer Mr. Clay a tribute of well earned respect in the event of his passing through this city"; and increased the number of their committee to 200 or more. Philadelphia *United States Gazette*, September 4, 1827.   4 Philip Swenk Markley—cf. above, Smith to Clay, August 1, 1827, and note.
5 Cf. above, Webster to Clay, August 22, 1827, note. An editorial in the Washington *United States Telegraph* on August 17, 1827, had emphasized the linkage between Markley and Buchanan in the inquiry about Jackson's nominee for appointment to the State Department; had asserted that "Mr. Markley was, before the election devolved upon the House, a passive instrument in the hands of Mr. Clay . . ."; and had called attention to Markley's appointment to the "office worth $3000 per annum," as Naval officer in the Philadelphia customs house.   6 Cf. above, Sergeant to Clay, August 8, 1827.
7 Punctuation and word obscured on MS.

From John Williams

Dear Sir,   Leas Springs[1] Augt. 23d. 1827.
You will herewith receive my letter recommending Mr John A. McKinny[2] for the office of U States Atto. in the district of East Tennessee— I understand that Mr. Lea[3] will not resign the office until after the October term & then expects to take his seat in Congress in December— Judge White Mr. Lea & others will unite in pressing on your Department the appointment of some one of their violente [sic]

partizans[4]— The principal recommendation that their candidate will have is that he is engaged in, retailing the Slanders of Duff Greene [sic] & co.   It can with truth be said that Mr. Adams is & has always been the favorite candidate with Mr. McKinney— Its [sic] probable that some persons in this State may recommend Wm. B Reese[5] Son in law of Genl. Cocke[6] or my brother Tho: L Williams who is now absent on a visit to North Carolina— In the present condition of things in Tennessee neither of those gentlemen ought to be appointed— Great exertions will be used by Judge White & Co. to force on the administration some one of their underlings— If the President should have any difficulty on this subject permit me to suggest that he offer the appointment to Genl. Cocke—   After the Octo. term there will be nothing for the United States Atto. to do for ten months. Your friend Mr. Clay   JOHN WILLIAMS

ALS. DNA, RG59, A. and R. (M531, R5). Addressed: "Private."   [1] Tennessee.
[2] ALS, in DNA, RG59, A. and R. (M531, R5). A Rogersville lawyer, McKinney had entered practice about 1807. He was nominated by President Adams for the recommended office on December 27, 1827, and the appointment was approved on January 9. Andrew Jackson reappointed him in 1831 and 1835. From 1839 to 1844 McKinney was a partner in a firm of iron manufacturers in Washington County, Tennessee.   [3] On Pryor Lea's election to Congress, see above, Erwin to Clay, August 12, 1827, note; on his resignation as United States attorney, see below, Lea to Clay, October 13, 1827.
[4] White to Clay and Lea to Clay, both dated September 5, 1827, ALS, in DNA, RG59, A. and R. (M531, R2).   [5] William B. Reese, born in Jefferson County, Tennessee, in 1793, educated at Blount and Greeneville Colleges, and in 1817 admitted to the bar, was a prominent Knoxville lawyer and farmer. He was elected judge of chancery court of the Eastern District in 1832 and a judge of the State Supreme Court in 1835. He retired from the bench in 1847, and in 1850 assumed the presidency of East Tennessee University, where he remained until failing health forced him to resign in 1853.   [6] John Cocke.

INSTRUCTIONS AND DISPATCHES   August 23, 1827

From JAMES COOLEY, Lima, no. 7. Reports that "General [José de] LaMar arrived here privately on the morning of the 19th." and that, "Yesterday, the General took the oath as President of the Republic." ALS. DNA, RG59, Dip. Disp., Peru, vol. 1 (M-T52, R-T1). Received December 29.

From W[ILLIAM] TUDOR, Lima, no. 76, "Confidential." Reports the arrival of General (José de) Lamar, who has taken the oath of office as President, "& thus for the first time since the revolution, Peru has a regularly constitutional, organized government, emanating from the will of the people, uninfluenced by any foreign interference." Notes that a number of toasts at "a large public dinner" for Lamar contained complimentary references to the United States, whereas "In the days of [Simón] Bolivar, especially after his system of usurpation was matured, every allusion of this kind was carefully avoided." Comments on the good effect produced by (James) Cooley's communication with reference to (Beaufort T.) Watts' letter (cf. above, Cooley to Clay, August 11, 1827, no. 6). Compares the annual disbursements by the English vice consul (not identified) for seamen (about $9,000) with his own for the same purpose (some $400); discusses charges for hospitalization of ill seamen and interment of the dead; and refers to English efforts "to obtain leave to have a protestant chapel, or at least a protestant bury-ing ground. . . ." ALS. DNA, RG59, Cons. Disp., Lima, vol. 2 (M154, R2). Received December 27.

To William Matthews Blackford

Sir   Washington 24h. August 1827.

Without resorting to either of the Gentlemen to whom, in your letter of yesterday,[1] you have refered [sic] for information of your character, I cannot doubt its respectability, nor the sense of justice which induced you to address that letter to me. I thank you most heartily for it. I know not whether Mr. J. S. Barbour has or has not such a letter as he describes from Majr. Moore;[2] but the assertion, by whomsoever made, is altogether untrue, "that at a meeting of Mr. Clay's Congressional friends in Washington he (Majr. Moore) had heard Mr. Clay tell them that if they thought his (Mr. Clay's) services in the Cabinet important, those services could be secured by the election of Mr. Adams to the Presidency." I never made such a communication, nor one of any similar import to my friends. When the office of Secy. of State was tendered to me, some time after the election was over, I consulted my friends as to the propriety of my accepting it, as stated in the Circular addressed to my Constituents;[3] and it is possible that it is to that fact that Mr. Barbour or Majr. Moore may have intended to allude.

I do not think that, in the present state of this new calumny it is encumbent on me to take any public notice of it. As one falsehood is detected, others, in relation to me, will follow in endless succession, until the election shall terminate which they are intended to affect. There is some difficulty in discriminating between those slanders which a public man should, and those which he should not, take personal notice of. One thing however is very clear that it is impossible for me, if it were even proper, to answer and expose all the calumnies of which I have been, and may yet expect to be, the object. I have neither the physical nor moral ability to do it. It could only be done by a being possessed of supernatural powers. I must place some reliance on my own character, and a great deal on the intelligence of the public. If both these fail me, I must content myself with the consciousness of having deserved better treatment, and with the further consolation that I shall not be the first instance of a man, who has faithfully served his Country, being sacrificed by the vilest arts of detraction.

The present tale carries its own means of proof or refutation. It was "at a meeting" of my "Congressional friends." If true, it can be established by at least some half a dozen or more. If false, it can be dis-

proved by an equal number. I am perfectly willing to let it rest on that issue. I am respectfully Your obedient Servant   H. CLAY
Wm. M. Blackford Esqr.

ALS. NcD. Born in Frederick County, Maryland, in 1801, Blackford had been educated for law but subsequently turned to journalism. In 1830 he became editor and publisher of the Fredericksburg, Virginia, *Political Arena*, founded July 4, 1827, as an organ of the Adams administration. From 1842 to 1844 he was Chargé d'Affaires at Bogotá and from 1851 to 1853 postmaster of Lynchburg, Virginia. During the intervening period, 1844 to 1851, he was editor and, in the latter years, part owner of the Lynchburg *Virginian*. From 1851 until his death in 1864 he was cashier of a Lynchburg bank.
    1 Not found.   2 Thomas P. Moore.   3 The statement is not included in the Address to the People of the Congressional District, above, March 26, 1825. It is found, above, in Clay to Brooke, February 18, 1825, and in Toasts and Speech at Public Dinner, Lewisburg, Virginia, August 30, 1826.

DIPLOMATIC NOTES   August 24, 1827

From BARON MALTITZ, Washington. Forwards to Clay "the papers which he [Maltitz] mentioned to him yesterday." N. DNA, RG59, Notes from Russian Legation, vol. 2 (M39, R2).
    The enclosures, all copies, include a letter, dated "New York 14 July 1827," to the Russian Minister from Dwight, Townsend, and Walker, to which is annexed a bill for a subscription to the New York *Daily Advertiser* from October 20, 1821, to August 20, 1824, amounting to $27.30. With reference to the obligation, the firm declared: "We cannot divine the reason why it should not be paid, we have sent the papers, & the department has had the benefit of it—   Our Bills against the French, Spanish, & English Ministers have always been paid. . . ." An unsigned note dated July 19, 1827, written in reply, informed Dwight, Townsend, and Walker that their claim "is of a private nature and can therefore be satisfied only by those persons who, according to the statement of the above gentlemen, have been subscribers to the daily advertiser. . . ." On July 23 William B. Townsend gave notice that he would "arrest the Minister, on his arrival or departure, as opportunity may offer for the principal & interest, if the same be not discharged." Cf. below, Clay to Tillotson, August 25, 1827.
    The firm was comprised of Theodore Dwight, Sr.; William B. Townsend; and John W. Walker. The latter two partners have not been further identified.

INSTRUCTIONS AND DISPATCHES   August 24, 1827

From ISAAC COX BARNET, Paris. Notes the death, in London, on May 26, of James Reid, who had resided in Paris "for the last six years"; reports finding among the decedent's papers "a Certificate of Bankrupt [*sic*]—dated Philadelphia—Decr. 1800 —and . . . a Schedule of losses from May 1796, shewing a total of $.233,741.62.c" but "no certificate of discharge"; asks whether he is correct in thinking "that, unless such certificate be produced," or he receives instructions from Clay or the Secretary of the Treasury (Richard Rush), he "ought not to pay over the avails of the said Estate to the heirs—but remit it to the Treasury of the United States as provided by Law." Encloses copies of various documents. ALS. DNA, RG59, Cons. Disp., Paris, vol. 6 (M-T1, R6). Received October 11, 1827. Cf. below, Barnet to Clay, September 29, 1827.

From ALBERT GALLATIN, London, no. 109, "Confidential." Admits that in his earlier statement "that the present administration might be considered as permanent till at least the next meeting of Parliament" (above, Gallatin to Clay, August 14, 1827), he "had not paid much attention to some subsequent floating rumours to the contrary, having had direct information, corroborating the general opinion." Reports having discovered, during a conversation with Lord Dudley, "that the arrangements were not completed and that there was cause of uneasiness amongst themselves." Adds that Dudley "said emphatically that they had no head" and that (William) Huskisson "was anxiously expected and wanted." Expresses a belief that "The unsettled state of the administration can produce no other inconvenience to us than delay. . . ." Conjectures that "the Whigs are dissatisfied, and that the opposition to Mr. Tierney's pretensions to the Chancellorship of the Exchequer [cf. below, Gallatin to Clay, August 30, 1827] may have contributed to their displeasure." ALS, partly in code, deciphered in State Dept. file. DNA, RG59, Dip. Disp., Great Britain, vol. 34 (M30, R30). Published in Adams (ed.), *Writings of Albert Gallatin*, II, 385–86. Received October 2.

George Tierney, born at Gibraltar in 1761, had been educated at Cambridge University and had held a seat in the House of Commons for over thirty years. Long prominent for his opposition to William Pitt, even to the extent of personal encounter in a duel in 1798, he had nevertheless risen to the forefront of the Whigs and by 1817 was an acknowledged spokesman for the party. But the Whigs never entirely accepted his leadership, and many resented his support of George Canning's coalition government in 1827 (cf. above, Gallatin to Clay, February 22, 1827, note). He entered Canning's Ministry as master of the mint and retained that office until the fall of the Goderich Ministry in January, 1828.

From WILLIAM B. HODGSON, Algiers, no. 90. Transmits a copy of the consular journal; notes receipt of a letter "from the Consul General" (William Shaler), who expects "to return to Algiers, in October next" (cf. above, Hodgson to Clay, May 2, 1827); reports a visit by Commodore (William Montgomery) Crane, who left a letter "communicating his appointment to the Command of the U. States' Squadron in the Mediterranean, and after informing himself of the state of our Relations with this Regency, . . . sailed for Mahon." Comments on the amicable relations existing between the United States and Algiers and on the high regard with which the Bashaw (Husséin) views Shaler. States that the French blockade (cf. above, Brown to Clay, June 9, 1827) has ben "negligently enforced" and that, expectations "that France would signally chastise these presumptuous Banditti" to the contrary, "The temper thus far displayed by the Algerines, and their active preparations for defence, does [*sic*] not justify the supposition, that they will evade that chastisement, by a humiliating concession." ALS. DNA, RG59, Cons. Disp., Algiers, vol. 11 (M23, R-T13). Received October 31.

To John Quincy Adams

Dear Sir   Washington 25h. August 1827.

I cannot better comply with the request contained in the inclosed letter[1] than by transmitting it to you. It will not be necessary to return it.

I am sorry to say that the elections in Kentucky have not turned out as favorably, as the first accounts indicated.[2] Intelligence received last night informs us that Trimble[3] and F. Johnson have both been defeated, by not large majorities, and that Dr. Henry[4] has also lost his election, owing to two candidates being run on the side of the administration against one Jackson man.[5] We have not the final result in Mr. Letcher's district, but there the contest was between two both equally friendly.[6] I have still hopes ('though of that we have yet no certainty) that we have majorities in both branches of the General Assembly.

This result does not destroy 'though it weakens the confidence I had in the Electoral vote of the State.

It is to be remembered that Buchanan's communication did not get to Kentucky until after the election.[7] I am with great respect Your's faithfully   H. CLAY
Mr. Adams.

ALS. MHi-Adams Papers, Letters Recd. (MR482).
[1] Above, Farnham to Clay, August 7, 1827.   [2] Cf. above, Clay to Taylor, April 4, 1827, and note; Clay to Johnston, August 19, 1827; Clay to Adams, August 19, 23, 1827.   [3] David Trimble.   [4] John F. Henry.   [5] See above, Johnson to Clay, April 29, 1827.   [6] Robert P. Letcher defeated William Rodes in the Fourth Congressional District.   [7] James Buchanan's letter (see above, Ingersoll to Clay, August 11, 1827, note) was not published in the Lexington *Kentucky Reporter* until August 25 and not until August 31 in the Lexington *Kentucky Gazette*.

From Martin Duralde, Jr.

Dr. Sir,   New Orleans 25th. August 1827
I had the pleasure of receiving your letter of the 20th. Ultimo[1] and in compliance with your request I send you under this Cover a notarial Copy[2] of Mr. Mathers Notes[3] together with the Copies of two Acts the one transfering these notes to Mr Hawkins,[4] the Attorney of Js. Morrison, and the other fixing the final payment of Said notes to the year 1831.

I consider these notes as excellent and have not the least doubt but that they will both be paid on the their [sic] falling due in the year 1831 and perhaps Sooner. The interest mentioned in the body of these notes will be paid punctually every year by Mr. James Ramsay[5] [sic], the agent of Mr. Mather in New Orleans. These notes, as you will perseive [sic], are secured by a mortgage on Mather's Sugar Plantation and have priority over any other mortgage should there exist any.

You will remember that the interest which these notes will produce this year are [sic] to pay Mr. Hennen's Claims against the Estate of Col. Morrison, as an Attorney employed at the time by Mr. Hawkins in the case of Morrison *vs* Smith.[6] The Estate owes me also $100 which I have advanced for it. I will address you by the next Mail. Kiss my dear child[7] for me and present my respects to Mrs. Clay   I am respectfully your Most Hble. Servant   M. DURALDE
Henry Clay   Secretary of State   Washington

P.S.   Instead of one I send you two notarial Copies of the above mentioned notes. You will find a difference in the two Certificates of the notary at the bottom.

ALS. DLC-TJC (DNA, M212, R13).   1 Not found.
2 None of the copies mentioned in this letter has been found.   3 For earlier references to George Mather's notes, see above, Whittelsey to Clay, December 22, 1826; Clay
to Whittelsey, January 20, 1827; Clay to Erwin, April 21, June 3, 1827; Erwin to Clay,
May 21, 1827.   4 Joseph H. Hawkins.   5 New Orleans merchant.   6 For
Alfred Hennen's connection with the case of *Morrison vs. (John K.) Smith's Syndic*, see
above, Account with Nathaniel Cox, *ca.* May 27, 1826.   7 Martin Duralde III. Cf.
above, Erwin to Clay, May 21, 1827; Henry Clay, Jr., to Clay, June 16, 1827.

From Ralph Lockwood

Hon. Henry Clay
D Sir,   New York August 25. 1827—
   I trust that the subject of this letter and my motives will excuse my
freedom in addressing you. The latter I am certain you cannot fail
duly to appreciate.
   A rumor has been circulated here for this day or two, which I treated
till this moment as the idlest invention in the world, that Mr. *Elias
Kane*, late of albany, now of this City, was about to be appointed Post
master in this City, in place of Gen. Bailey, about to resign.[1] I am assured, this moment, that it is the open conversation in that Office and
that is [*sic*] confidently expected to take place. Though I cannot credit
it, I have thought it my duty to state to you that such an appointment
would alienate at least 9 tenths of the *democratic* supporters of the
administration in this City and give no particular satisfaction to any
other party. I am sure that this appointment, at this period, would put
it out of the power of the friends of the Administration with whom I
have the honor to act, to make even the *show* of opposition to the
Jackson party, which already claims a victory. Its influence upon the
State at large would be scarcely less disastrous.
   Mr. Kane is said to be a very respectable man. He is and has always
been the warm devoted partisan of Mr. Clinton[2] and a most *bitter* and
contemptuous federalist.
   I cannot believe that any such measure will be sanctioned by the
President— But the report has created, coming from the confidential
deputy[3] of the Post master, a great deal of uneasiness and alarm among
our friends, this morning.
   That a change might be in contemplation, we have all readily believed. At the same time, we have thought it possible that great exertions might be made by the present incumbent to appoint his successor,
and that, perhaps, Mr *Kane* might be his man. Under these circumstances, I have thought it would be pardonable in me to state the effects which would inevitably follow from it in this City, and as I think
in the State. With the greatest respect, I have the honor to be, Sir Your
obedient, faithful servant   RALPH LOCKWOOD

ALS. MHi-Adams Papers, Letters Recd. (MR482). Addressed: "Private."
   1 Cf. above, Kane to Clay, March 30, 1825, and note.   2 DeWitt Clinton.   3 Not
identified.

From Jared Sparks

Dear Sir,   (Private)   Boston, Aug. 25. 1827

I write only to acknowledge your very kind letter of the 14th. inst, and particularly to thank you for your obliging offer to furnish me with letters for Europe. The truth is, my main object in going abroad at present is to further my historical projects, by gathering materials not to be had in this country. The public in the end I hope will be benefited [sic]. I intend to inspect thoroughly the papers in the office of Trade and Plantations, and I should feel abundantly compensated if I could succeed in making such a representation, as to induce Congress to see the wisdom of procuring a full copy for their library, or some other public depository.[1] At all events I trust my objects will be worthy of your countenance and encouragement, and letters from you to this effect will be of the utmost importance to me. I shall be in Washington in January, & will explain to you more at large my purposes.

The review of your Speeches is in in [sic] the press. It is from the pen of Mr E. Everett, and contains some remarks on the different modes of debating in the English Parliament & our Congress, which are interesting.[2] I am, Sir, with very great respect and esteem, your most obt. sert.   JARED SPARKS

Honble. Henry Clay.

ALS. DLC-HC (DNA, M212, R2).
[1] No record of such a compilation at this time has been found. Cf. above, Rush to Secretary of State, March 16, 1825; Rush to Clay, April 19, 1825, and below, Gallatin to Clay, August 25, 1827.   [2] Cf. above, Sparks to Clay, August 7, 1827, and note.

INSTRUCTIONS AND DISPATCHES   August 25, 1827

From ALBERT GALLATIN, London, no. 110. Reports receipt of the "letter from the Governor of North Carolina [Hutchins Gordon Burton], . . . requesting . . . [him] to apply to the British Government for leave to procure copies of such documents, in the public offices here, as relate to the Colonial history of North Carolina" (cf. above, Burton to Clay, April 19, 1827). Praises the cooperation received from the British: "Not only the leave was granted; but the Board of Trade had an Index prepared of all the Records that had reference to the Province of North Carolina, in order that the State might point out those documents of which copies should be wanted." Transmits his "answer to the Governor, enclosing the Index and other papers relative to the subject" and requests "that the packet . . . be forwarded."

Notes that he has procured, at the request of the Director of the Mint (Samuel Moore), "a brass troy pound weight . . . an exact copy of the British standard as established by Act of Parliament," which he has transmitted. Encloses a "statement of the manner in which the weights were compared and of the certificate . . . annexed to it." ALS. DNA, RG59, Dip. Disp., Great Britain, vol. 34 (M30, R30). Received October 2.

A letter from Daniel Brent, dated October 2, transmitted Gallatin's letter and packet to Burton. Copy, in DNA, RG59, Dom. Letters, vol. 22 (M40, R20).

From SAMUEL HODGES, JR., Cape de Verd Islands, "Villa da Praya St. August [sic]."
Transmits in response to Clay's letter of June 20, 1826 (cf. above, Hodges to Clay,
June 20, 1827), the deposition of "Capt Benjamin Homer, . . . mate of the Brig
Pharos . . . at the time of the impressment of the two men from that Vessel by
His B. M. Ship Redwing at Sierra Leone. . . ." Adds that "Capt. [Ephraim] Mer-
chant has not yet returned from the Coast of Africa. . . ." ALS. DNA, RG59, Cons.
Disp., Santiago, vol. 1 (M-T434, R1). Received October 14.

In the enclosed deposition Homer, now "Master and Commander of the Brig
Union of Portland [Maine]," recounted the voyage of the *Pharos* in 1825, the
forcible removal from that vessel to the *Redwing* of Studson Roberts and another
seaman, whose name deponent was unable to recall, and the return of Roberts by
order of Commodore (Charles) Bullen.

MISCELLANEOUS LETTERS   August 25, 1827

To ROBERT TILLOTSON, "D. Attorney, N. Y." Encloses a copy of "the correspondence . . . between the Editors of the New York daily Advertiser and the Russian
Legation" (cf. above, Maltitz to Clay, August 24, 1827). Continues: "Whether the
demand is, or is not, well founded, the Russian Minister [Baron de Maltitz] is protected from any species of arrest, by his public character. As he is expected shortly
at New York, I have to request your official interposition, if it should be necessary,
to prevent, or relieve him from the arrest. Perhaps, if you could see the Editors
(Theodore Dwight, Sr., William B. Townsend, and John W. Walker), you might
dissuade them from a purpose which, if executed, may involve them in some
trouble. Without venturing to give any opinion upon the validity of the demand,
it may be remarked that, even if the Russian Minister were not entitled to the
protection, which the public law extends to his character, the demand must be considered as existing either against the Russian Government, or against the person,
in his private capacity, who ordered the paper, and in either case, the present Russian Minister, who is not that person, cannot be held liable for the demand—"
Copy. DNA, RG59, Dom. Letters, vol. 22, pp. 36–37 (M40, R40).

From WILLIAM WIRT, Washington. Transmits record of Joseph Roffignac's case (cf.
above, Roffignac to Clay, June 1, 1827) and his own opinion, noting that he has
shown the material to Senator (Charles Joseph Dominique) Bouligny, since Adams
instructed him to consult with the Senator for explanation, if needed; requests,
since Bouligny made no suggestions and the decision was adverse to Roffignac, that
the papers be placed "in the Department of State, either to be forwarded to the
Prest. or retained in the Department 'till his return. . . ." ALS. DNA, RG59, Misc.
Letters (M179, R65).

From Seth Hunt

Henry Clay Esqr
Dear Sir   *Confidential*   New York Sunday Morning August 26. 1827
There is a report current this day & yesterday, that General Baily
the Post Master of this City is to be removed and Mr. Eliaz [sic] Kane
OF ALBANY appointed in his place[1]—   Without offering any apology
for addressing you—I take the liberty most Earnestly to recommend,
that it be well ascertained *before* making this change, that it will be

satisfactory to the public and popular with the friends of the Administration— I have Sir, as all who know me know, no political views but such as are wholly disinterested and free from personal interests or feelings and that in all things I act purely from the desire to promote and Sustain the cause of the administration against the unprincipled combination that is arrayed against—wanting nothing for myself, or my friends, & considering myself a Citizen of Alabama, I feel persuaded that you will do me the justice to believe, that I would not presume to address you, was [sic] it not for the purpose of preventing if possible, the adoption of a Measure, that, I feel confident will dissatisfy the great body of the Citizens of all parties and most especially the old democracy, to which ever *personal* party they may belong— Mr. Kane & his whole family were *tories* during the revolutionary war. & I feel confident that Mr Elias Kane accompanied his father and brothers to England[2]—the father was one of the Loyal Americans who rec'd. compensation of the British Government for his losses[3]— Mr Elias Kane was an ultra federalist in 1798–1800. & is now a Clintonian—   I do not mention these facts with any unfriendly feelings towards Mr Kane—but because I desire to preserve the administration from the adoption of a Measure which cannot fail to render them unpopular— General Baily is a friend of Mr Adams, but if it should be thought adviseable [sic] to remove him thus on account of his advanced age policy requires that his successor should be selected from among the democratic republicans in this City—and if I know any thing of the public feeling he should be free from the imputations of ancient federalism—

In haste   Respectfully Yours   SETH HUNT

P.S.   Among the reasons assigned for the selection, of Mr Elias Kane, is the gratification of his *putative* son[4] in Illinois.

ALS. MHi-Adams Papers, Letters Recd. (MR482).
[1] Cf. above, Lockwood to Clay, August 25, 1827.   [2] John Kane, the father, had come to America from Ireland in 1752 and settled in Dutchess County, New York, where he had been prominent in land riots of 1764–1765. During the American Revolution he had joined the British forces, his property had been confiscated, and following the war he had returned to England, while his family had fled to Nova Scotia. But his five sons returned to the United States and subsequently became prominent as merchants—Charles at Schenectady, James at Albany, Oliver in New York, Elias in Philadelphia, and Archibald in the West Indies. Weed, *Autobiography*, I, 153.   [3] Reference to this compensation has not been found.   [4] Elias Kent Kane.

INSTRUCTIONS AND DISPATCHES   August 26, 1827

From THOMAS L. L. BRENT, Cintra (Portugal), no. 44. Reports that, at the request of I(srael) P. Hutchinson, United States consul at Lisbon, he has addressed to the Portuguese Government a note "on the subject of the excessive export duty, port charges and regulations in regard to the article of salt exported in american Vessels." Encloses copies of the note and of Hutchinson's letter to him. ALS. DNA, RG59, Dip. Disp., Portugal, vol. 7 (M43, R6). Received October 15.

From JOHN WILLIAMS, Knoxville, Tennessee. States that, since "writing . . . a few days ago" (above, two letters, August 23, 1827), he has learned that "Mr. [John A.] McKinney intends to visit Washington about the meeting of Congress" and that "The object of this note is to make . . . [Clay] personally acquainted with this worthy & highly respectable gentleman." ALS. DNA, RG59, A. and R. (M531, R5).

To John Quincy Adams

Dear Sir   Washington 27h. August 1827.

The inclosed letter,[1] this day received, gave me the first intelligence of the vacancy in the P. Office at N. York and of the reputed successor of Mr. Bailey. Afterwards I heard the same rumors from a friend,[2] who had lately left N. York, and who concurs entirely with the writer as to the inexpediency of Mr. Kane's appointment.

The selection, in that great city, of a P. Master is a matter of some consequence. If I were to offer an opinion, as to the person who should be appointed, it would be that he should, besides the indispensible [*sic*] qualities of integrity and competency, possess the further recommendations of having been and now being your friend and a Republican. I am truly & faithfy Yrs   H. CLAY
Mr. Adams.

ALS. MHi-Adams Papers, Letters Recd. (MR482). Endorsed by Clay on address sheet: "With Mr. Clay's respectful compliments."
[1] Lockwood to Clay, August 25, 1827.   [2] Not indentified.

To John Bradford

Dear Sir.   Washington, D. C. 27th Augt. 1827.

I transmit to you, enclosed, a letter from Mr. Senator, (late Governor,) Knight;[1] and, also, another letter from his colleague, Mr Senator Robbins,[2] both relating to Professor Woods. These letters, together with those which I lately sent you, now puts [*sic*] the board[3] in full possession of all the information to be derived from the whole delegation in Congress from the State of Rhode Island.[4] I am sorry that this information is not of a nature to remove the doubts which I entertained of the expediency of appointing Professor Woods to the Presidency of Transylvania.

I expect, in a few days, to receive an answer to a letter which I wrote to New York for the purpose of sounding the disposition of Mr. McCauley,[5] of which I will give you due information   I am, respectfully,
Your obedient servant,   H. CLAY
John Bradford, Esq. Chairman, &c. &c. &c.

LS. KyLxT.   1 Above, August 21, 1827.
2 Above, August 22, 1827.   3 Of trustees, Transylvania University.   4 Though
no letter of transmittal has been found, it appears that Clay had sent Bradford the letters from Asher Robbins, of August 13, and from Tristam Burges, of August 14. No
communication on this matter from Dutee J. Pearce, the remaining member of the congressional delegation from Rhode Island, has been found.   5 Thomas McAuley.
Clay's letter to him has not been found. Cf. above, Bradford to Clay, August 11, 1827;
Clay to Bradford, August 22, 1827.

To Edward Everett

My dear Sir   Washington 27 Aug. 1827.
    Your favor of the 21st. inst[1] inclosing a letter to Mr. Tudor[2] has
been recd., and the letter shall be expedited to its destination.
    Mr. Little[3] held no Clerkship, as has been erroneously supposed, in
the patent office, and his death therefore has created no vacancy to fill.
He had last year been occasionally employed in that office on extra
business, but had no regular appointment; and since the last adjournment of Congress he has not been employed at all.
    Our late news of the elections in K. has not been as good as the first
was. Trimble and Johnson have both lost their elections by small
majorities,[4] and Henry also by a division among the friends of the Administration who run [sic] on our side two Candidates whilst only
one[5] was set up by the Opposition. Metcalfe, Clarke, Letcher, Buckner
and Young[6] are re-elected; and I fear the others may be set down
against us.[7] Buchanan's communication[8] bears date the last day of our
elections, and of course it did not reach K. until after their termination. It is believed (though that it is not certainly ascertained) that the
friends of the Administration are the majority in both branches of the
General Assembly.[9] I yet believe the State will ultimately go right.[10]
Yr's faithfully   H CLAY
Edwd. Everett Esqr

P.S.   I accidentally wrote on a half sheet.   H. C.

ALS. MHi.   1 Not found.
2 Not found.   3 Robert Little   4 David Trimble lost by 355 votes; Francis Johnson, by 99. Washington Daily National Intelligencer, September 27, 1827, reprinted from
Frankfort Commentator.   5 John F. Henry—cf. above, Johnson to Clay, April 29,
1827.   6 Thomas Metcalfe; James Clark; Robert P. Letcher; Richard A. Buckner;
William S. Young.   7 Cf. above, Clay to Taylor, April 4, 1827, and note.   8 Cf.
above, Ingersoll to Clay, August 11, 1827, and note.   9 Cf. above, Clay to Adams,
August 19, 1827, note.   10 Cf. above, Clay to Brown, March 27, 1827, note.

From Robert P. Letcher

My Dear Sir   Lancaster[1] 27h. Augt. 1827
    Yours of the 9h. Inst came to hand last night[2]— The one by Mr. A.
I recd. a few days since by private hand from the county of Harlan.[3]
With your letter of the 9th. Mr. Buckhannans [sic] response to the

Hero[4] was receivd. This answer is well put together. As they say, in Connecticut, "there is a great deal of good reading" in Buck's reply— Its [*sic*] modest and genteel, yet strong and conclusive. I am truly delighted with the manner in which B. has acquited [*sic*] himself— I really feared and believed he was placed in such a dilemma, by the Genl. that he could not extricate himself with any sort of credit— But he has come forth victoriously— I am sincerely gratified with the result, and must believe it will have a happy effect upon the P. election. It is impossible it should turn out otherwise. Virginia after this, will not— cannot support the Gel.[5] I never had the least hope of Vira. until now. I presume Buck.s Reply supersedes the necessity of any reference to the conversation in my room.[6] I am glad of it.

Your forebodings in relation to the elections in this state, were realized[7]— We have not succeeded quite as well [as] I expected, but very nearly— You need not think of loosing [*sic*] Ky.[8] This defeat will have a good effect upon the Admn. men, and wake them up from the sleep of confidence in which they have been reposing for some time past. You know I have always entertained doubts of this state, but strange as you may think it, My hopes are stronger and my confidence greater *now* than heretofore, of success.

Be so good as to offer my best wishes to Mrs. Clay, not forgetting John.[9] Your friend   R. P. Letcher

ALS. DLC-HC (DNA, M212, R2).   1 Kentucky.
2 Not found.   3 No letter of recent date from John Quincy Adams to Letcher has been found, and no bearer has been identified.   4 Cf. above, Ingersoll to Clay, August 11, 1827, and note.   5 Cf. above, Clay to Brown, March 27, 1827, note.   6 See below, Johnson to Clay, September 9, 1827.   7 Cf. above, Clay to Taylor, April 4, 1827, note.   8 Cf. above, Clay to Brown, March 27, 1827, note.   9 John M. Clay.

From William B. Rochester

Hon H. Clay
My Dear Sir   *private*   Rochester 27. Aug: 1827.

Your favour of the 21st inst.[1] arrived this moment— I did not carry into execution the threat contained in my letter of the 1st. inst., i,e, to inflict upon you another in a few days— the fact is—I have been constantly making excursions in different directions with Mrs. R. & our children[2] for the last month & they will accompany me part of the way to New York, for which city I shall leave home tomorrow evening to proceed on my mission[3]— of this determination I will advise your Department by letter tomorrow morning in reply to yr. communication (official)[4] which arrived two days earlier than yours of the 21st. inst—

I hope arrangements will be made to let me have my outfit $4500. at the U. States' Branch Bank in the city of N. York by the 20. Sept. next   I have given notes for $3350 to be *on that day there paid*— my

sole reliance is upon the outfit— for my salary say 6. mos. in advance I
will draw directly on your Dept. from N-Y.— this request however will
be submitted in the letter which I shall address to the Dept. of State
tomorrow.

Your friends in this quarter (and they are not few) became reconciled to the disappointment, for the satisfactory causes which required
your presence at Washington[5]   I am gratified to learn that Mr. Tuder
is appointed [6]— By the Bye—if a certain ------ Wilkison[7] of Buffalo, shall
become an applicant for office let me caution you as a personal friend
and as a friend to the administration agt. him   there is not a more
unprincipled fellow in our State—and he now lacks popularity as much
as he always lacked principle— withal he is grossly illiterate a Jacksonian in disguise. Genl. Porter[8] knows him well & despises him. he
wants a birth [sic] in the diplomatic corps & has been boring me for a
letter to you! when I repeat beware of him! let my motive be my
apology for taki[ng] such liberty—

Wilkison, (like Lewis)[9] may possibly get respectable signatures—but
men will only recommend him in order to get rid of him—

It was well done not to appoint Lewis—he is however a gentleman
and compared to Wilkison a saint—

I fear that the habits of poor Elisha Ely, who was appointed consul
to Santa Martha,[10] unfit him for any responsible post— I have been
soundly rated for contributing to his appt. tho' I had no agency whatever in recommending him— he however is an honest man & a friend
&c—

As my family go with me part of the way, I shall necessarily travel
slowly to New-York— I am very desirous of spending a day or two at
Albany whilst the legislature is in Session— they meet in a few days[11]—

I should write more at length touching political prospects, movements &c but it is late & I am tired out— just returned from Steuben &
find things there as they should be— I must do Genl. McClure[12] the
justice to say that he is unequivocally agt. the hero— he & Magee &
Woods[13] &c all of whom supported Clinton last fall,[14] condescended to
apologize by giving as a reason that they thought my election hopeless— they offered me a public dinner which was declined— all seem
anxious to make amends for recent defection—& seemed to be determined that I must succeed Clinton whether or not— this however
does not "jump with my humour"[15]

Late as it is I should write you more in detail now, but expect to
write you from Albany & New York— indeed, if time be allowed me,
between the time of arriving at New York & the departure of the vessel
in which I shall take my passage, I shall hope to see you, as in such
case I will go to Washington to put my late accounts with government— if you should (as you contemplated) leave Washington for the
North,[16] I shall hear of your movements thro' the papers & perhaps

meet you somewhere on the road— Judge Beatty[17] has written particular accounts of Ken: elections— the result might have been better— but is very well— Buchanan has spread consternation in the camp[18]— my Father[19] desires to be remembered to you— truly & sincerely yr. Friend   W B ROCHESTER

ALS. DLC-HC (DNA, M212, R2).   [1] Not found.
[2] Rochester had been married in 1816 to Amanda Hopkins, of Oneida County, New York. Their children in 1827 included James Hervey, born in 1819; Harriet Louisa, born in 1821; and William Beatty, born in 1826. *Rochester Historical Society Publication Fund Series*, III, p. 343.   [3] Cf. above, Clay to Rochester, March 11, August 20, 1827; Rochester to Clay, May 12, August 14, 1827.   [4] Above, Clay to Rochester, August 20, 1827.   [5] Cf. above, Rochester to Clay, August 1, 1827.   [6] William Tudor—cf. above, Rogers and Van Winkle to Clay, June 14, 1827.   [7] Samuel Wilkeson, born in Carlisle, Pennsylvania, in 1781, and reared on a farm near Pittsburgh, had removed to Ohio in 1802 and to the vicinity of present-day Westfield, New York, in 1809. He had built keel boats, had engaged in lake and river trade, and had become an iron founder and manufacturer. In 1820 he had, without engineering training, successfully constructed a pier and harbor for the western terminus of the Erie Canal at Buffalo Creek. He had been appointed the first judge of common pleas for Erie County (New York) in 1821, had been elected a State senator in 1824, and became mayor of Buffalo in 1836. He was active in support of the American Colonization Society, for some time was president of its board of directors, and for two years edited the *African Repository*. He died at Kingston, Tennessee, in 1848.   [8] Peter B. Porter.   [9] Daniel W. Lewis.   [10] Santa Marta, Colombia—cf. above, Marvin to Clay, *ca.* January 5, 1827, note.   [11] The New York Legislature convened in special Session on September 11, to consider a revised code of laws. *Niles' Weekly Register*, XXXII (April 28, 1827), 151; XXXIII (September 22, 1827), 54.   [12] George McClure.   [13] John Magee; William Woods. Magee, born in Easton, Pennsylvania, in 1794, had served in the War of 1812 and at that time settled in Bath, New York. He had been constable of Steuben County from 1818 to 1820 and sheriff since 1821. He was elected to Congress in 1827 and held that seat until 1831, when he declined re-nomination. During the remainder of his life he was active in banking, mining, and railway development.   [14] Cf. above, Rochester to Clay, November 18, 1826, and note.   [15] Shakespeare (Furness [ed.], *A New Variorum Edition*), *Henry the Fourth, Part I*, Act 1, sc.ii, lines 65–66.   [16] Cf. above, Wayland to Clay, August 16, 1827.   [17] Adam Beatty.   [18] Cf. above, Ingersoll to Clay, August 11, 1827.   [19] Nathaniel Rochester.

MISCELLANEOUS LETTERS   August 27, 1827

To WILLIAM THORNTON, "Superintendent of the Patent Office." Daniel Brent writes: "The Secretary desires me to inform you, as I have the honor to do, that he thinks Mr. John M. Benham is entitled to a patent for the application of the water proof cement, in the manner and for the objects, stated in his specification, and that he wishes you to give him a patent, accordingly, upon his complying with the requisitions of the Law." Copy. DNA, RG59, Dom. Letters, vol. 22, p. 39 (M40, R20).

Benham, of Bridgewater, Oneida County, New York, was awarded a patent on August 29, 1827, for "Aqueducts, of water-proof lime." The patent, reissued on October 1, 1830, provided for a "conductor, formed of water-proof lime, as a cement for stone, wood or brick. . . ." Burke (comp.), *List of Patents. . .* , 191; *Franklin Journal*, V (January–June, 1828), 210.

From CHARLES HAY, Navy Department. Transmits "copies of a correspondence between Commo. C. G. Ridgely, Commander of the U.S. Naval forces in the West Indies, and William Pinkney, Esqr. U.S. Collector at the port of Allenton or Key West, received this morning, touching the alleged infractions of neutrality committed within the jurisdiction of the United States by the Naval forces of the Re-

public of Mexico under the Command of David Porter Esqr:." Requests "instructions on the propriety of transmitting copies to the President of the United States."
LS. DNA, RG59, Misc. Letters (M179, R65). Cf. above, Hay to Clay, August 6,
1827. The enclosures have not been found.

When the United States in 1822 took possession of the island now known as
Key West, it was named Thompson's Island, in honor of Smith Thompson, then
Secretary of the Navy, and the harbor was named Port Rodgers in honor of John
Rodgers, then president of the Board of Navy Commissioners. Commodore Porter,
however, dated his letters from Allenton, in reference to Key West. None of the
names was long current; the older Spanish name of *Cayo Hueso*, anglicized as
"Key West," persisted. Jefferson B. Browne, *Key West, The Old and the New*
(Gainesville, 1973), 9.

To John Sloane

Dear Sir   (Confidential)   Washington 28h. Aug. 1827.

I thank you for the friendly congratulations contained in your letter
of the 21st. inst.,[1] just received, on account of our recent victory over
Genl. Jackson— a victory it is and must be ever considered, altho' his
partizans are here endeavoring to make out that the statement of Mr.
B.[2] is to be received as a confirmation of the assertions of the General.[3]
I am curious to see what course will be taken at the Hermitage. If that
shall be decided & promulgated, before it is seen, there what turn on
this side of the Mountains has been taken by the presses devoted to
the Hero, it will be to impeach Buchanan. But if the councils of the
Hermitage wait to be enlightened by those of the Telegraph[4] &c. they
may conclude to acquiesce in Mr. B.s evidence & endeavor to argue
the American people into the belief that it sustains the General.

The news from K. as to the Congressional elections is not good.
The loss of the elections of Trimble[5] & F. Johnson has affected me
personally much more than politically. If, as I am induced to believe
from the returns which have reached this place, we have gained a
decided majority in the Legislature it will counterbalance our loss in
Congress.[6] Still that must be regarded as a loss, which *I* feel most in-
tensely. We must not however despair even of Kentucky much less of
the general cause.

On the subject of the V. Presidency every thing will abide, I presume, the meeting of Congress. The wish I have all along had is still
my wish, that the best selection should be made, which can be made,
to promote the more important object. As to the P. M. G.[7] I do not
think he is seriously thought of any where by *our* friends, and it would
be rather awkward for him to come into collision with his patron &
idol.[8] The idea of the Pennsylvanian[9] has been one that I have always
had an inclination to.

I presume that all our friends will be aware of the necessity of a

punctual attendance on the first day of the approaching Session. I am
Cordially Your friend   H CLAY
J. Sloane Esq

ALS. MH-Houghton Library.   1 Not found.
2 James Buchanan—cf. above, Ingersoll to Clay, August 11, 1827.   3 Cf. above, Webster to Clay, August 22, 1827, and note.   4 Washington *United States Telegraph.*
    5 David Trimble.   6 Cf. above, Clay to Taylor, April 4, 1827, note; Clay to Adams,
August 19, 1827, and note.   7 John McLean.   8 John C. Calhoun. Cf. above, III,
259 and note; McGiffin to Clay, February 19, 1827.   9 Probably Richard Rush—cf.
above, Mercer to Clay, August 18, 1827, note; but cf. also, above, Pleasants to Clay, May
4, 1827, where John A. Shulze was proposed.

To Samuel L. Southard

My dear Sir   Washn. 28h. Aug. 1827.
    Trimble and Col. F. Johnson have lost their elections by small ma-
jorities.[1] I fear Henry has also lost his in consequence of there being 2
candidates on the side of the Admon and only one for Jackson.[2] On
the other hand, returns of 75 out of the 100 members to the H. of R.
give us 48 to 27 if they are to be relied on. I think we shall have a decided majority in both branches of the Legislature.[8] I think therefore
that the electoral vote of the State may be considered as safe.[4] In the
Congressional district within which Col. R. M. Johnson resides, our
candidate was beaten by only about 100 votes;[5] and in that District
the Jackson interest was supposed to be overwhelming.
    Your family is well. I am faithy Yr's   H CLAY
Mr. Southard.

ALS. NjP-Samuel L. Southard Papers.
    1 David Trimble; Francis Johnson. See above, Clay to Everett, August 27, 1827, note.
    2 On John F. Henry's defeat, cf. above, Johnson to Clay, April 29, 1827, and note.
    3 Cf. above, Clay to Adams, August 19, 1827, note.   4 Cf. above, Clay to Brown,
March 27, 1827, note.   5 On Alfred Sanford's defeat, cf. above, Smith to Clay, August
1, 1827, and note.

From John Bailhache

Sir,   Chillicothi [sic], August 28, 1827
    Having, in January, 1826, at the urgent solicitation of Thomas
Scott, Esq. of this town, taken the liberty of recommending him to
your favorable notice,[1] as an applicant for a seat on the Bench of the
Supreme Court, in the event of the passage of the bill to provide for
the extension of the Judicial System of the United States, then pending before the House of Representatives,[2] a deep sense of the duty I
owe to you, as well as to myself, now compels me to withdraw that
recommendation.
    The circumstances under which my communication was penned,

being familiar to you, need not be recalled to your recollection. Suffice it to observe, that my confidence in the sincerity of Judge Scott's political professions has gradually declined for some time past; and that my visit to Columbus, during the late sitting of the Federal Court, has confirmed my worst suspicions in their fullest extent—that gentleman having, in a conversation I overheard accidentally, openly avowed his attachment to the opposition. This fact, together with the firm belief that he has been of late in the habit of attending the secret meetings of the Jackson party in this place, and that he is the author of a handbill, a copy of which is enclosed,[3] issued here a few days since, for the purpose of keeping alive the odious charge originally promulgated by Geo. Kremer[4] reduce [sic] me to the mortifying necessity of acknowledging, that this individual is no longer worthy of the countinance [sic] of an honest and virtuous administration, and of retracting whatever I may heretofore have urged in his behalf.

With much regret for having thus inadvertently, though I trust, innocently, committed myself; and a sincere desire that your personal happiness and political prosperity may continue long to increase, I have the honor to be: Sir, Your very obedt. hume. Servt

JNO. BAILHACHE

Hon. H. Clay, Esq. Secretary of State, Washington City.

ALS. DNA, RG59, A. and R. (M531, R7).　　1 The letter has not been found.
2 Cf. above, III, 551, note; Hammond to Clay, January 4, 1826, and note.　　3 Not found. "A Voter," writing from Chillicothe on August 25, 1827, had publicly questioned whether Scott was the author of the handbill and subsequently noted that Scott had replied without clarifying the authorship. Chillicothe *Scioto Gazette*, August 30, September 6, 1827.　　4 Cf. above, Clay to Gales and Seaton, January 3, 1827, and note.

INSTRUCTIONS AND DISPATCHES　　　　　　　　August 28, 1827

From J[OHN] M. FORBES, Buenos Aires, no. 53. Reports the substance of a conversation which took place during "a formal official visit from Mr. Bustos [not further identified], the nephew of the Governor of Cordova [Juan Bautista Bustos] and Commissioner of that Province near this Government," who observed "that the political course of the provinces was the more easy, inasmuch as they had a model before them which they had determined to adopt"—referring to "the wise Constitution of the United States and its happy Administration." Notes that to Bustos' expression of regret that the United States had furnished two frigates to "the Emperor" (Peter I of Brazil—cf. above, Wright to Clay, March 12, 1827) he explained that American shipyards are free of government interference and would have constructed vessels for "this Government" had they been commissioned, "with the same punctuality as in other cases—but entirely without any agency or interference on the part of our Government." Adds, on September 9, that "The government here has succeeded in raising a loan of six millions of dollars to carry on the war." L, written and signed by J. Dickinson Mendenhall "at request of J. M. Forbes Esqr." DNA, RG59, Dip. Disp., Argentina, vol. 3 (M69, R4). Published in Espil (comp.), *Once Años en Buenos Aires*, 475–76. Received January 8, 1828.

From VINCENT GRAY, Havana. Reports, "In *confidence.* . . , that the [British] Admiral on the Jamaica Station [probably Charles Elphinstone Fleeming], has announced to the Captain General [Francisco Dionisio Vives] . . . his intention to send an armed vessel to Key Sal, for the purpose of driving away. . . , all the American vessels who may be procuring salt at that Key, and to prevent in future the American vessels from procuring any more there; as the Said Key belongs to H. B. M. [George IV]," to which the Captain General replied "that Key Sal did actually belong to H. C. M [Ferdinand VII], and that if he did drive from thence any vessel, belonging to Citizens of the United States, or any other neutral frindly [*sic*] Nation," he and his nation would be held answerable for injuries committed. Adds: "Much salt is procured for the U States there, as well as for this Island." ALS. DNA, RG59, Cons. Disp., Havana, vol. 5 (M-T20, R5). Received September 14.

Fleeming, born in 1774, had become commander of a sloop at the age of 20 and had served with distinction throughout the war with France. He had been promoted to rear admiral in 1813 and to vice admiral in 1821. He held the command in the West Indies in 1828 but has not been so identified earlier.

MISCELLANEOUS LETTERS   August 28, 1827

From JOHN QUINCY ADAMS, Quincy (Massachusetts). Acknowledges receipt of Clay's "Letters of the 19th. and 20th. inst.," as well as "the sequel" of Clay's "Correspondence with Mr [Charles R.] Vaughan, upon the case of the two seamen stated to have been impressed by Captain [D. C.] Clavering" (above, Clay to Vaughan, August 15, 20, 1827; Vaughan to Clay, August 16, 21, 1827). ALS. DNA, RG59, Misc. Letters (M179, R65).

From WILLIAM B. ROCHESTER, "Rochester, Monroe Co. N. Y." Acknowledges receipt of Clay's reply (above, August 20) to his letter of August 14; discusses his financial arrangements; states that he will "set out this evening . . . to proceed on . . . [his] mission"; notes receipt of "a long & satisfactory letter from Capt. Philips [William Phillips] of Philadelphia, who lately returned from Guatemala" and with whom he hopes "to have a personal interview . . . before sailing." ALS. DNA, RG59, Dip. Disp., Central America, vol. 1 (M219, R2).

From Jabez D. Hammond

Sir,   Albany August 29. 1827

In passing through Massachusetts a few days ago I saw for a short time the President[1]— In the course of his conversation he stated that he had been informed you intended to visit Albany this season[2]— I need not say I was highly gratified to learn that you had projected such a journey— —Allow me to suggest that if this is your determination I hope you may be here during the Session of our Legislature which will commence on the 11th. September next and probably continue five or six weeks[3]— —Many of the members I know are extremely desirous to see and become acquainted with you— I have no doubt that much good might result from such a visit while I have every reason to believe that a Tour from New York to this place in the month of September will not only be a pleasant and agreeable one but advantageous to your health which I am rejoiced to be informed has improved within the last year—

The Singular combination of which the opposition is formed by their continued unfounded and unprecedented attacks upon you afford evidence that they believe if you were broken down the Administration would of course be prostrated— —A stronger demonstration of your personal wort[h] and influence could not be furnished— I am with great respect Your Obedt. Servt.   JABEZ D. HAMMOND
The Hon. H. Clay—

The letter of that poor unprincipaled [*sic*] & besotted old man Gov. Randolph can not injure you nor the Administration nor I hope the reputation of Mr. Jefferson[4]—

I have been credibly informed that this same Mr. Randolph declared in N. York in the Autumn of 1823 I believe, that Mr. Jefferson thought Mr. Clinton ought to be the then next President[5]— I suppose he was then endeavouring *to borrow money*[6]—

ALS. DLC-HC (DNA, M212, R2). Addressed: *"Private."*
[1] Hammond had seen Adams on August 16. Adams, Diary, November 11, 1825–June 24, 1828, p. 268 (MHi-Adams Papers [MR40]).   [2] No other reference to a projected visit to Albany has been found. Cf. above, Wayland to Clay, August 16, 1827; Sergeant to Clay, August 17, 23, 1827.   [3] Cf. above, Rochester to Clay, August 27, 1827, note.

[4] The efforts of the opposing parties to place their leaders under the mantle of Thomas Jefferson (cf. above, Sergeant to Clay, August 13, 1827; Mercer to Clay, August 18, 1827, and note) had led Thomas Mann Randolph to address Thomas Walker Gilmer, editor of the Charlottesville *Virginia Advocate*, a letter published in that journal on August 18, asserting that Jefferson had had great respect for President Adams prior to his election but that he had been very disturbed by the assumption of Federal powers under his administration. Jefferson, reportedly, had remarked in August or December, 1825, "that it was fortunate for the country that Gen. Jackson was likely to be fit for public life four years after, for it seemed to him to be the only hope left of avoiding the dangers manifestly about to arise out of the broad construction now again given to the Constitution of the United States. . . ." Randolph had added that Jefferson "often said that he [Jackson] was an honest, sincere, firm, clear-headed, and strong-minded man; of the soundest political principles. . . ." He had continued by noting that Jefferson "Towards Mr. Clay, as a politician, . . . constantly manifested a very strong repugnance, and often said that he was merely a splendid orator without any valuable knowledge from experience or study, or any determined public principles founded in sound political science, either practical or theoretical." He had concluded with a belligerent challenge: "If what I have said should excite resentment, I shall hold Mr. Clay, and him only, responsible to me, for any improper expression of that feeling." Reprinted in *Richmond Enquirer*, August 24, 1827. For subsequent developments on this matter, see below, Barbour to Clay, August 30, 1827; Randolph to Clay, September 1, 1827; Clay to Randolph, September 1, 1827; Randolph to Clay, September 12, 1827; Clay to T. J. Randolph, September 15, 1827. Gilmer, born in Albemarle County, Virginia, in 1802, and trained at law, had settled in Charlottesville and in July, 1827, had taken over the *Central Gazette*, established in 1820, and converted it to the *Virginia Advocate*, a Jackson organ. He served in the Virginia Legislature from 1829 to 1834 and from 1835 to 1839, was Governor of Virginia from 1840 to 1841, and sat in Congress from 1841 until 1844. Breaking with Jackson on the issue of State rights, he became identified with the Tyler wing of the Whig Party in 1841, as a member of Tyler's so-called "Corporal's Guard." He was appointed Secretary of the Navy in February, 1844, and was killed in the explosion aboard the *Princeton* later that month. Seager, *And Tyler Too*, 152, 205.

[5] DeWitt Clinton reported in his diary that autumn that Jefferson "said the President ought to be the greatest man in America," and, "asked who was, he said D. W. C." Randolph and Clinton had "sat up late together" discussing "people and things in

general." Bobbé, *De Witt Clinton*, 257.   6 Randolph had been in New York for a month attempting to borrow money on "Varina," one of his plantations. He had obtained only temporary relief; by the following spring his debts, then amounting to over $23,000, had been taken over with his property, held under deed of trust, by his son, Thomas Jefferson Randolph. Gaines, *Thomas Mann Randolph*, 142, 148.

INSTRUCTIONS AND DISPATCHES   August 29, 1827

From JOHN RAINALS, Copenhagen. Encloses semi-annual shipping report; notes that "the Trade to the Baltic Sea has this Season been more extensive than it was last year to the present period, under the flag of all Nations"; adds that the harvest turned out well; and states that Henry Wheaton has reached England, from which place he will depart for Copenhagen about September first. ALS. DNA, RG59, Cons. Disp., Copenhagen, vol. 3 (M-T195, R3). Received December 2.

To John Quincy Adams

Dear Sir   Washington 30h. August 1827.

I received yesterday your letter of the 23d. instant. After its date you must have received other despatches from the Department of State transmitted by Mr. Gallatin. From these you will perceive that he did not take the two points, proposed by the British Plenipotentiaries,[1] for reference to his Government, but for his own consideration (see his despatch No. 87;)[2] and that he afterwards decided to reject them, and gave to the B. Plenipo's: two written arguments, one relating to the point respecting the Commercial Convention and the other to that respecting the N. Western boundary (see his despatch No. 88.)[3] In this state of the case the matter stands. It does not appear that the B. P. had, in consequence of that determination of Mr. Gallatin, refused to renew the Convention of 1818; but that, on the contrary, they had again taken the subject of the N. W. boundary into consideration. So the affair I understand was left on the 14h. of July 1827 when Mr. Huskisson was compelled by indisposition to withdraw from the negotiations. It was expected that Mr. Grant[4] would be substituted to [*sic*] him, (see Mr. Gallatins despatch No. 96.)[5]

Under these circumstances shall I instruct Mr. Gallatin to accede to the British demands on the two points refered [*sic*] to? I shall await your further directions, founded on the despatches which must have been received by you subsequent to the date of your letter. Shall I confer with the other members of the administration who may be here?

I am inclined to think the British Government may waive both points.[6] I should be sorry that the negotiation should break off on those points, but then there will be still another year to go upon.[7] As to the discrimination between rolled & hammered iron, I am inclined to think the weight of the argument is with the British; but Congress has at least twice decided otherwise.[8] You will recollect Mr Baldwin's argument, which however I think was refuted by that of Mr S. Canning.[9]

On the other point, we should, by consenting to the restraint which the B Government wishes to impose against our military occupation of any part of the Territory on the N. W. Coast, come into direct collision with the H. of Representatives.[10] What shall we lose if that part of the Convention is not renewed? What danger shall we encounter? None, unless from our own acts. What shall we gain by the renewal with the British modification? What danger avoid? None. We shall only have tyed those hands by a treaty, which we may keep still without it. And it will be the Executive who will have co-operated in fastening the hands of Congress.

I do not think that we ought to be hastening any settlements beyond the Rocky mountains. We ought to do nothing more in my opinion there than may be necessary to preserve our rights for posterity. I am faithfully Your obedient Servant   H CLAY
Mr. Adams.

ALS. MHi-Adams Papers, Letters Recd. (MR482).
[1] William Huskisson; Henry U. Addington.   [2] Above, June 20, 1827.   [3] Above, June 23, 1827.   [4] Charles Grant.   [5] Above, July 14, 1827.   [6] Cf. above, Gallatin to Clay, July 28, 1827.   [7] Cf. above, II, 59n; III, 60n; Clay to Gallatin, February 24, 1827 (no. 18).   [8] Cf. above, Gallatin to Clay, December 21, 1826, and note.
[9] Clay's allusion to Baldwin's views is obscure. Stratford Canning in a letter to Secretary of State Adams, November 26, 1821, had contended that, "for all the ulterior purposes to which bar iron, as such, is applicable, the rolled is equally good with the hammered; that both the one and the other are sent to market in the same stage of manufacture, and that the only difference between them is one of a retrospective nature, not affecting the identity of their present state, but relating solely to the process by which they were brought to the same point." He argued that the British bar iron was "at least equal to that of Sweden and Russia" and that the efficiency of the British technique in manufacturing it by rolling, rather than hammering, was irrelevant as a consideration in taxing the *"like articles"* in accordance with the most-favored-nation principle of the Commercial Convention of 1815 (see above, II, 57). Since Britain alone exported rolled iron, Canning considered the provisions of the American tariff law discriminatory. *American State Papers, Foreign Relations*, IV, 871–72. Henry Baldwin, as chairman of the House Committee on Manufactures, had proposed raising the duty on rolled iron in 1820. As reported, his speech of April 21, 1820, had alluded to the difficulty of defining whether bar iron was a raw material or manufactured, but, according to the somewhat garbled, reported version of his speech, he had conceded that the rolled iron was manufactured: "I believe the safer rule is to consider that which is taken from the earth as the raw material, and every change in its form or value, by labor, as manufacture, equally entitled to encouragement." His argument had consequently rested upon the importance of protection for domestic manufactures. *Annals of Congress*, 16 Cong., 1 Sess., 1934–35.   [10] Cf. above, Gallatin to Clay, November 5, 1826, note; Hoard to Clay, April 2, 1827, note; Gallatin to Clay, June 27, 1827, note.

To James Barbour

Sir: Washington, D. C. 30th Augt. 1827.

In compliance with a request received from a very respectable source,[1] I take pleasure in recommending for the appointment of Cadet at the military academy, Cyrus C. Miller, son of Dr. Alexander

Miller, of Madison county, Ky. I am, with great respect, Your obedient
servant,   H. CLAY
Honble James Barbour, Secretary of War.

LS. DNA, RG94, United States Military Academy, Cadet Applications, 1827/126.
[1] See above, Miller to Clay, July 12, 1827.

From James Barbour

Dear Sir   Barboursville[1] Augt. 30h. 27
    The enclosed paper[2] was delivered me yesterday by a servant who
immediately disappeared on its delivery—so that I know not from
whom it comes[3]—   Yet the information it contains and the anxiety
manifested by the writer induce me to transmit it by the earliest opportunity afforded by the Mail—
    Mad as R—[4] is I can scarcely believe he will move in the subject—
But surely you can have no difficulty in deciding should he do so to
treat his call with contempt—
    If you have anything new let me hear from you. My best respects
The Hon. H. Clay—   JAMES BARBOUR

ALS. DLC-HC (DNA, M212, R2).   [1] Virginia.
[2] The enclosure reported that Thomas Mann Randolph had seen a piece, abusive of
himself, in the Washington *National Journal* (cf. below, Randolph to Clay, September
1, 1827), which he believed Clay had written, and warned that Randolph had boarded
a stagecoach for Washington "determined that he would make Mr. Clay fight him" and
that he was "exceedingly exasperated, and . . . capable of any violence." Colton (ed.),
Private Correspondence, 173–74.   [3] Colton asserts that Clay endorsed the envelope
(not found): " 'Supposed to be from T. J. R.' " (Thomas Jefferson Randolph). *Ibid.*, 172n.
[4] Thomas Mann Randolph.

From James Brown

Dear Sir   Paris August 30 1827
    I hope that before this letter can reach Washington you will have
returned from your western tour in possession of a sufficient stock of
health to enable you to support the fatigues of the next winter's campaign. It will certainly be long, and probably very warm, as the violence of parties may be expected to increase until the Presidential
election shall have been made. I greatly fear your journey to Kentucky
has been rendered disagreeable to you by the situation of affairs in
that agitated quarter.[1]
    It is now more than a month since I had an interview and very free
conversation with the Baron de Damas on the subject of the discriminating duties demanded at Havre on Vessels which had on their voyage
touched for orders at the Port of a third power.[2] I told him that when
Mr. Villele had sustained that decision of the Director General of the
customs,[3] I had assured him that my Government would not acquiesce

under it,[4] but that the French Government had been the first [to] make a formal remonstrance against the principle and I then stated what had passed at Washington between you and the Baron de Mareuil.[5] He said that it [was] very probable the French Government had made a mistake in the course taken at Havre. I remarked that the exemption from the discriminating duties was not made, by the Convention of 1822 to depend on the direct or circuitous voyage but on the character of the Vessel and its Cargo—that if both belonged to the nation the one owned the other produced in that nation, the right to the exemption was perfect.[6] I admitted the right of the two nations respectively to frame rules for the prevention of fraud, but I insisted that in doing so care must be taken not to annul, or even narrow, the privileges conferred by the Treaty. That the right of touching at some intermediate point on a voyage was one of great importance to both nations, and where no commercial exchange took place at such intermediate port, could not injure either party. It would prevent vessels from going to bad markets and consequently from making unprofitable voyages. I told him that France would lose more than the United States by putting an end to this practice of touching for information, and I called his attention to the instance of French vessels bound to some port in the Gulph of Mexico— At Havannah [sic] it would be easy to ascertain the State of all the markets of the Gulph and direct the Vessel to the one at which the Cargo on board would find the most ready and beneficial sale. He did not attempt to oppose any arguments to those I offered. I told him I should address to him a note on that subject which I did soon after. Although nearly a month has elapsed since the date of my note the answer has not yet arrived. I have demanded the return of the discriminating duties on four vessels amounting to nearly fifty thousand francs. It is not probable they will continue to insist on the principle, but it is to be apprehended that as our Merchants have in these instances sent their vessels without the proper certificates of origin, although that origin cannot be doubted, the French Government may, on that account, refuse to refund the duties. It is real[ly] surprizing [sic] that some of our most experienced Merchants are exceedingly remiss in complying with custom house formalities which if insisted on may be seriously injurious to the parties interested.

I have devoted much attention to the instructions you sent me respecting our claims on France.[7] I have prepared a note to the Minister of foreign Affairs[8] but intend in two or three days to have a conference with him before I send it   Either the arbitration will be rejected altogether, or the French Government will insist on submitting the 8 art generally, or it will insist on submitting all the points in dispute between the two Countries. If the first course is chosen perhaps the United States will improve their ground by having made the offer, but if the second or third mode of submission is preferred, and we decline accepting them, will not our situation be made worse by it? Will not the Claimants ask why refuse to submit our claims to the decision of arbitrators who if they are just, will award in our favor and will direct them to be paid whereas if we leave the decision of them to the French Government they will either be constantly postponed or rejected as not being payable by the actual dynasty. If this Government suspects we would refuse to submit the claims they will certainly insist on leaving them also to arbitration. I confess I cannot perceive how we shall gain any thing in public opinion by making only a partial submission of the 8 art and by refusing altogether to submit the claims— These however are but the opinions of a [sic] individual whose duty it is to act as he is instructed and to yield up his own opinions to those of more capable persons. I do not believe it was at any one given period since the restoration the intention of the French Government to pay these claims, and the intimations to that effect held out by some of the Ministers, had delay more in view than any other object. They did not wish us to press at the time when they were not sure that they would not be compelled forcibly to resist the claims of the Allied Sovereigns and they did not desire even our weight thrown into the same scale. With the exception of some loose observations from one of the most conscientious but certainly not one of the most influential of the Ministers,[9] we have had no encouragement for hope ever since the country has been evacuated by the army of occupation. Indeed I cannot see much use in doing more at present than keeping up *continual* claim and hoping that in some future contingency we might *demand* effectually our rights.

The sensations of joy and of sorrow awakened by the death of Mr. Canning[10] have subsided and it is now pretty certain that no very great event will grow out of the loss of this statesman. Indeed when the friends of liberty review his life and actual sentiments they will be at a loss to discover why he has been looked up to as the friend of civil and religious freedom. On all questions for the last thirty years (the Catholic question excepted)[11] he has steadfastly opposed every thing like liberty in every part of the world[12]— It is thot [sic] he boasted that he had obtained compensation for the Military occupation of Spain by France in the erection of the former Spanish Colonies into independant [sic] Republics.[13] But it is equally true that in 1825 he wrote to the Spanish Ambassador at London that the Independance of the Spanish Colonies was neither the act nor wish of the British Government.[14] I cannot believe we have lost a friend in the death of that Minister. Few of those who have as the Representatives of foreign nations had diplomatick relations with him at London speak of him with much regret.

You will perceive from Mr Everetts[15] dispatches that the State of Spain is far from being satisfactory. That of Portugal is still worse, and from both a superficial observer would infer that there was immediate danger of a continental war. I think very differently, and feel confident that the Sovereigns will make great exertions and even heavy sacrifices rather than permit war to break out at this time   England, ever so formidable, is now mild and conciliating in her views and conduct. She perceives that her whole paper system would burst on the firing of a single cannon.[16] In this country the status quo is very agreeable to the Royal family and employe's [sic] and that cannot be more secure in war than during the existence of peace. If therefore Don Pedro arrives legitimacy will bear down all before it and Don Miguel and the Austrian policy[17] must give way to preserve peace and a *principle*. If Don Pedro remains where he is Don Miguel will arrive supported by Austria at the head of the Continental sovereigns, and the friends of the Constitution, English troops, English influence and even the Charter itself, will, for the preservation of *order* and *peace* be driven from the Peninsula. Perhaps it would be more correct to say that England to avoid war will *voluntarily* withdraw her troops endeavoring to stipulate as well as she can for the safety of the friends she leaves at Lisbon—

The Russian fleet has sailed for the Mediterranean[18]— The first Squadron is already very strong in that sea.[19] The Blockade of Algiers requires several Vessels and is said to have been so loose that some algerian Cruisers have escaped and made one or two French vessels prizes the crews fortunately escaping in their boats.[20]

Colo. Delaunay[21] has been here for some days with six Osage Indians four men and two women. He told me he intended to exhibit them for money. I have feared that it would be a bad Speculation and that it would not afford sufficient funds to enable the party to return to their nation.[22] They have been presented to the King[23] have breakfasted and dined with the Minister of Foreign affairs visited some of the Convents &c and the news papers state that they have dined with me in Company with the Corps diplomatique.[24] I had it is true a Diplomatic dinner on the day mentioned in the Journals but the Osages were not invited. They called on me without ceremony a day or two past and I gave them breakfast with which they appeared well satisfied. Mr Gallatin had a great deal of vexation and trouble in sending home a party of Oneida, who came here with the same object.[25] Would it not be well if our Agents in the Nations were instructed to use their influence to prevent such unworthy speculations? If the interpreter[26] should die, there is no one on this side of the Atlantic who can explain their wants or convey a knowledge of their sufferings. Colo. Delaunay says he has been aid de camp of Genl Howard[27] has resided twenty three in [sic] the State of Missouri and is a citizen of the United States. Mr Derbigny[28] of New Orleans recommends him as a very respectable man— He proposes to return by New York and Washington—

Before this letter can reach you Mr. Rumpff and his Lady[29] will have arrived   They will soon be followed by Baron de Krudener[30] Russian Minister for the U States who proposes to sail in a few weeks. I have had the pleasure of making his acquaintance and find him intelligent and amiable. It is unfortunate that he hears badly and speaks the English language very imperfectly. He was much esteemed in Switzerland where he has been chargé d'Affaires for the last several years. He goes with strong prepossessions in favor of our country and I hope he will be pleased with it.

My health has been very good for the last twelve months. Mrs. Brown suffers very much from a pain in her face, the cause of which we have been unable to discover. I think it is rheumatic as we always find it increased by exposure. She is however so fond of society, and indeed is so great a favorite, that she is invited every where and seldom notwithstanding all she suffers declines an invitation.

I am much obliged to you for your attentions to my accounts which Mr Pleasonton[31] writes me have been settled to the end of the last year. I have no wish to fall into the hands of men who are always ready when an account is not settled to cry out *defaulter*.

Mrs. Brown requests me to say to Mrs. Clay that she has sent on all her sister directed and that from the pains she has taken in the selection she hopes qualities and pieces will be satisfactory. The account would have been sent by the packet which will sail on the first but the expenses of packing and sending to the ship could not be obtained in time— You will have them by the next Packet. I shall present the Copy of your speeches as you request as soon as it shall have been handsomely bound   I thank you for that sent to me[32]— I am Dear Sir very sincerely Your friend &c &c.   JAMES BROWN

Hon H Clay Washington

ALS. DLC-HC (DNA, M212, R2).
[1] Cf. above, Brown to Clay, June 28, 1827; Clay to Adams, June 23, 1827; Wallenstein to Clay, August 6, 1827.   [2] Cf. above, Brown to Clay, August 13, 1827.   [3] Cf. above, Brown to Clay, September 11, 1826.   [4] Cf. above, Brown to Clay, October 22, 1826 (1).   [5] Cf. above, Mareuil to Clay, March 13, 1827; Clay to Mareuil, March 20, 1827; Clay to Brown, March 21, 1827.   [6] Cf. above, III, 53n. See, in particular, Article 3. Parry (ed.), *Consolidated Treaty Series*, vol. 72, pp. 387–88.   [7] Above, May 28, 1827.   [8] Damas.   [9] Viscount Mathieu Jean F. Montmorency (cf. above, Brown to Clay, November 29, 1826, note).   [10] George Canning.   [11] Cf. above, Gallatin to Clay, February 22, 1827, note.   [12] For earlier, contrary views, cf. above, Clay to Smith, May 4, 1825; Brown to Clay, August 26, 1825.   [13] Cf. above, Lafayette to Clay, December 29, 1826, and note.   [14] For reference to Canning's note to the Chevalier de los Rios, see above, McRae to Clay, December 13, 1825.   [15] Alexander H. Everett.   [16] Cf. above, Hughes to Clay, June 14, August 18, 1826; Biddle to Clay, February 8, 1827.   [17] Cf. above, Brown to Clay, August 13, 1827; Everett to Clay, August 16, 1827; Brent to Clay, August 20, 1827.   [18] Cf. above, Middleton to Clay, June 23, 1827; Brown to Clay, July 12, August 13, 1827; Rainals to Clay, July 20, 25, 1827.   [19] Cf. above, Brown to Clay, July 28, 1827.   [20] Cf. above, Brown to Clay, May 29, June 9, 28, July 12, 1827; Hodgson to Clay, August 24, 1827.   [21] David Delaunay.   [22] See below, Brown to Clay, November 13, 1827, and notes.
[23] Charles X.   [24] The basic account of the Osage entertainment as reported in the United States appeared in the Philadelphia *National Gazette*, October 12, 1827, and

was reprinted in the New Orleans *Courrier de la Louisiane*, November 5. It noted that the Indians had been "introduced at Court, caressed at diplomatic dinners, admired at the grand opera, and, in short, distinguished as the lions of the day." It did not, however, mention any involvement of Brown in these festivities.   25 Six men and two girls of the Oneida Indians and an interpreter had sailed for Havre in April, 1819. *Niles' Weekly Register*, XVI (April 24, 1819), 160. Reference to their subsequent activities has not been found.   26 Paul Loise, a Frenchman, who had been appointed in 1808 as "resident Interpreter of the Osage Indians." Carter (ed.), *Territorial Papers*, XIV, 231.
     27 Delaunay had been adjutant general with the rank of major, in the militia of Louisiana Territory in 1806 and 1808. Benjamin Howard had been appointed Governor of the Territory in 1810 and thereby became commander of the militia. Carter (ed.), *Territorial Papers*, XIII, 549; XIV, 403–404. The cited relationship may well have existed between them in militia service.   28 Pierre Auguste Charles Derbigny.
     29 Mr. and Mrs. Vincent Rumpff—cf. below, Rumpff to Clay, September 20, 1827.
     30 Paul de Krudener.   31 Stephen Pleasonton. Cf. above, Brown to Clay, March 23 (2), 1827.   32 Cf. above, Clay to Brown, May 30, 1827.

From Porter Clay

Dr. Sir,   Frankfort[1] 30h August 1827
     To our great mortification your political enemies have triumphed in the congressional elections which you no doubt have heard ere this[2]   falsehood and detraction has for once succeeded to place matters in a confused state here,   But I apprehend it will have the effect to rouse every honest man in the community to double diligence and as I informed you last winter[3] I have no doubt if an organized effort is made all will be well in Kentucky yet but without it—Jackson will get the entire vote of this state[4]   It is too early for me to say what will be the effect of Buckhannons [sic] communication,[5]   the friends of the General here as well as to the eastward contends [sic] for its support of his allegations against you[6]   but this is as it should be   if the People of the UN States can be made to believe in such a pervertion [sic] of Truth they deserve to be governed by a military despot—
     I am desireous [sic] that you should fortify yourself with as strong evidence as you can in relation to the declarations you made in Kentucky just before the presidential elections who you had determined to support in the event of your being excluded from the number that would enter the house of Rep[7]   amongst the number you have publickly named[8] you have not mentioned Col James Davidson our Treasurer   you can address him a note upon that subject and I am almost certain if I am not very much mistaken that he heard you[9] Express your mind Just before you left his place   I have had no conversation with him of late upon the Subject but I feel confident he has named it repeatedly about the time that the dispute first arrose [sic] in relation to that subject   yours &c   PORTER CLAY
H Clay Esqr

     ALS. DLC-TJC (DNA, M212, R10).   1 Kentucky.
2 Cf. above, Clay to Taylor, April 4, 1827; Clay to Adams, August 19, 25, 1827.   3 See above, Porter to Clay, February 22, 1827.   4 Cf. above, Clay to Brown, March 27, 1827, note.   5 Cf. above, Ingersoll to Clay, August 11, 1827.   6 Cf. above, Webster

to Clay, August 22, 1827.   7 Cf. above, Clay to Sloane, May 20, 1827, and notes; below, *Address . . . to the Public*, December 29, 1827.   8 Public reference prior to this date concerning such a list has not been found. Cf. above, Speech at Lexington Public Dinner, July 12, 1827.   9 See below, Davidson to Clay, October 20, 1827.

INSTRUCTIONS AND DISPATCHES   August 30, 1827

From ALBERT GALLATIN, London, no. 111. Corrects statement, made in dispatch no. 109 (above, August 24, 1827), that "[George] Tierney had pretensions to the Chancellorship of the Exchequer." Notes that the "Cabinet was formed . . . on the principle of amalgamation between . . . [the Whigs] and the moderate Tories, with whom they do not differ on any practical important questions." Reports that since such a situation involved the exclusion of the High Tories from office, the King's (George IV's) designation of (John Charles) Herries as Chancellor, without consulting the Cabinet, caused Lansdowne and others to threaten resignation and led to much discussion concerning the limits of the King's appointing powers. Comments that until the ministerial crisis is resolved, the diplomatic negotiations remain "suspended."

Reports that the Emperor of Brazil (Peter I) has appointed Dom Miguel Regent of Portugal and that the fact will be made public in "this morning's 'Times' "; denies knowledge of any agreement among Austria, France, and England on the matter. Expresses opinion that "Great Britain has had no other object in view, with respect to Portugal, than to preserve her influence over that Country, without caring at all by what Constitution it was governed."

Acknowledges receipt of Clay's no. 24 (above, March 29, 1827). ALS. DNA, RG59, Dip. Disp., Great Britain (M30, R30). Published in Adams (ed.), *Writings of Gallatin*, II, 386–87. Received October 2.

Herries, born in London in 1778, had entered governmental service at the age of 20, as a junior clerk in the Treasury. After a quarter century of service in subordinate posts dealing with financial concerns, he had attained prominence in 1823 through appointment as financial secretary to the Treasury and election to the House of Commons. He had remained in the government under the Canning Ministry. A disagreement between himself and William Huskisson over the nomination of a chairman for the Finance Committee of the House of Commons contributed to the fall of the Goderich Ministry and the transfer of Herries to Master of the Mint in February, 1828. In 1830 he was named also president of the Board of Trade, but he resigned both the latter offices with the ministerial change in November of that year. For a few months in early 1835 he was Secretary of War. From 1841 to 1847 he was out of office and out of Parliament, but he was returned to the House of Commons in 1847 and continued there to pursue an active interest in financial affairs until his retirement in 1853.

The London *Times*, August 30, 1827, reported the arrival in London of a messenger (Carlos Mathias Pereira—see below, Brent to Clay, October 11, 1827) en route from Peter I to Miguel, supposedly as bearer of a dispatch appointing the latter Regent of Portugal. Question was raised whether this signified merely that he was appointed "Regent under the charter in the name of Donna Maria," during her illness, or whether he was to represent Peter as ruler of Portugal, a position which must also be temporary, since the two states had been separated by treaty (see above, Raguet to Secretary of State, March 11, 1825, note).

From SAMUEL LARNED, Santiago de Chile, no. 58. Reports the status "of the several claims that have, at different times, been committed to the management of" the Legation: no progress has been made in the cases involving the *Macedonian* (cf. above, Allen to Clay, June 24, 1825; May 4, June 10, July 26, 1826) and the *Warrior*

984 SECRETARY OF STATE

(cf. above, Allen to Clay, November 5, 1825; January 24, 26, 1826). In regard to cases of less importance: the claim of the representatives of John Campbell (cf. above, Allen to Clay, December 2, 1825; Van Buren to Clay, April 19, 1826) is "not of a nature to warrant . . . official interference in its recovery"; a "demand instituted by Mr. [Heman] Allen . . . at the solicitation of Mr. J[oel] R. Poinsett" for $2,000 to satisfy a note "given him by the Late Jose Miguel de Carrera has been arranged . . . with the Executor of the deceased, and the money remitted . . . to the claimant"; and the claim for $1,000 lodged by Captain George W. Lewis, of the brig *Garnet* of Boston, for an unjust exaction of duties, has not been settled. Observes that the financial condition of the Chilean Government will prevent immediate payment of these claims and suggests that he press for recognition of the obligations and for future payments. ALS. DNA, RG59, Dip. Disp., Chile, vol. 2 (M-T2, R2). Received January 18, 1828.

Captain Lewis was long prominent in the American merchant marine. In 1845 he commanded the first American steam vessel that sailed to British India and China. *New England Magazine*, XXVI (July, 1872), 274–75.

Settlement of the claim of the *Garnet* has not been found.

From John Quincy Adams

Henry Clay—Secretary of State
Dear Sir   Quincy 31 August 1827.
Your letter of the 23d instt has been received—with copies of the Letter of 29. June from Mr Brown,[1] and of the private Letter of 16 July from Mr W. Taylor—The translation of the manifesto of the Congress of Vera Cruz and the Exposition of Mr Poinsett—as also the translated Article from the Newspaper.[2]

I have considered with great attention your observations with regard to the expediency of immediately recalling Mr Poinsett, and have thought it best to postpone my final determination, till my return to Washington— The Manifesto of the Congress has rather increased my repugnance to acting so decisively against Mr Poinsett, at this stage of the controversy— The charges of the Congress are vague, indefinite and sustained ·by no better evidence than morbid suspicions— The only fact alledged [sic] specifically against him, he very distinctly denies, and although I regret that he should have established *any*, special relations between himself and a Society in which the mysteries of the masonic fraternity were connected with political movements, yet there appears nothing in his conduct, leading to doubt of the integrity of his intentions, and he declares that he withdrew from the Meetings of the Society immediately on finding that they were assuming a political complexion[3]— To recall him now would seem not only to sacrifice him to the unfounded jealousies of the Congress, but to sanction their unjust complaints and as they themselves indicate an excess of patriotic zeal, as the supposed cause of his proceedings, it would appear harsh treatment of him by his own Government, to take part against him by a recall which could not be altogether divested of the aspect of censure— These sentiments shall however be fully reconsidered when we meet.—

With high and undeviating regard and esteem, I remain faithfully your's—

Copy. MHi-Adams Papers, Letterbook, Private, no. 10, pp. 90–91 (MR149).
[1] James Brown.   [2] Cf. above, Taylor to Clay, July 16, 1827, and note.   [3] Cf. above, Poinsett to Clay, July 8, 1827.

MISCELLANEOUS LETTERS   August 31, 1827

From JOHN ADAMS SMITH, Madrid. Encloses a copy of a letter from S(tephen) Pleasonton, dated June 8, 1827, stating that a settlement of Smith's "account as late United States Secretary of Legation and Chargé d'Affaires at London" (cf. above, Clay to Rush, April 11, 1825, note; Clay to Smith, April 11, 1825) shows a balance of $552.74 due to the Treasury. Notes that "the item of outfit as charged in . . . [his] account as Chargé d'Affaires at London in 1825" was not allowed because of "the Secretary of State not having decided upon" it and that "the outfit charged as Secretary of Legation in 1815 of $500 One Quarters Salary has also been omitted. . . ." Points out that in 1825 he "acted as Chargé d'Affaires for five months . . . subject to all the incidental expences [*sic*] of that appointment" and that for the outfit in 1815 he had the authority of a letter from Secretary of State James Monroe, as well as a letter from Clay, April 11, 1825. Presents a calculation showing a balance in his favor of $4,447.26, which he wishes transmitted as "a credit" for himself "upon the Messrs Barings Brothers & Co. . . ." ALS. DNA, RG59, Dip. Disp., Spain, vol. 27 (M31, R28). Received November 13.

To William S. Dallam

Washington 1st. Septr. 1827.

I thank you, my dear Sir, for your kind and obliging letter of the 21st. Ulto.[1] The results of the Congressional elections in K.[2] have personally mortified me more than they would have done, from a mere estimate of their political influence. The loss which has occurred, in them, to the Administration, is perhaps compensated by the clear majorities of its friends which you say have been elected to the Legislature.[3] At all events, it must be borne with manly fortitude. In politics as well as in War reverses some times happen. The regret, which they occasion, will be always less when it is known they have not been deserved; and then they will stimulate to fresh exertion.

Unless I am greatly deceived, if Mr. Buchanan's statement[4] had arrived before the elections in K. it must have materially affected them. The chain of recent events, of which that was the last link, has produced great effect on this side of the mountains. Yr's faithfully
Majr. Dallam.   H CLAY

ALS. NcD.   [1] Not found.
[2] Cf. above, Clay to Taylor, April 4, 1827, note.   [3] Cf. above, Clay to Adams, August 25, 1827, note.   [4] Cf. above, Ingersoll to Clay, August 11, 1827.

To Thomas M. Randolph, Sr.

Sir   Washington 1st. September 1827
    Mr. Wheaton[1] having delivered to me this day a letter from you,[2] in which you have called upon me to declare whether your belief be well founded or not in each of the cases therein stated, I take much pleasure in saying 1st. that I have no recollection of having, before or since the month of Decr. 1824, made use of any expressions insulting in their purport and injurious in their consequences with regard to you. 2dly that I am fully persuaded you labor under an entire mistake in supposing that, by any expressions or representations of mine, the Department of War was induced to adopt a line of conduct in respect to you, which defeated the object of your mission to Florida last winter. I had no agency in your appointment, nor had I any thing to do with the relations which subsequently arose between the Dept. of War and yourself. I remember to have heard with satisfaction of the appointment about the time it was made, and I assure you that I could not possibly have entertained any other wish in regard to your mission, but that it should have been attended with full success. And, thirdly, so far from being the author of the piece to which I understand you to refer in the National Journal of the 25h. Ulto (the piece under the Editorial head) I had not even read it, until since I have received your note. That paper is generally left at my house before breakfast, and I do generally throw my eye over it; but the number containing the article in question was either not left as usual, or was not seen by me. I am Your obedient Servant   H C.
Tho. M. Randolph Senr. Esqr

    ALS (possibly a draft). DLC-TJC (DNA, M212, R10).
    1 Possibly Joseph Wheaton, of Rhode Island, a veteran of the American Revolution and of the War of 1812, who had for some time been a resident of Washington while attempting to settle his accounts as deputy quartermaster general in the United States Army. He died in November, 1828, at Baltimore.   2 Below, this date.

From Edwin Upshur Berryman

My dear Sir   New York Sepr. 1st. 1827
    In consequence of my not having had an interview with the Revd. Mr Maccauley [sic][1] until very lately. I have been prevented replying to your favor of the 23d August[2] until to day. I now enclose you letter[3] [sic] which I recd from him on the Subject referred to by you.
    From the conversation which I had with him previous to the reception of his note I have no hesitation in saying that he would accept the situation, provided he were satisfied upon the points suggested by him. Docr Hosack[4] is at present Absent from our city & will not return for a few days. I will consult the Gentleman mentioned by you so soon as he arives [sic].— as to Mr. Maccauleys competency for the

office, and advise you of the resuls [sic].[5] From his General reputation as a Man of Piety & Talents as also from his appearance Manner &C I have no doubt but that he would meet the expectations of our friends in Kenty over[6]

With My respects to Mrs Clay & family accept assurances of warmest Friendship. Very Respectfully Yrs E. U. BERRYMAN

Honl H Clay Washington City

ALS. KyLxT. [1] Thomas McAuley. Cf. above, Bradford to Clay, August 11, 1827. [2] Not found. [3] Not found. [4] David Hosack, born in New York in 1769 and graduated from Princeton in 1789, had taught botany and materia medica at Columbia University from 1795 to 1811 and the practice and theory of medicine at the College of Physicians and Surgeons from 1811 to 1826. [5] Cf. below, Berryman to Clay, September 29, 1827. [6] To verso.

From Philip Ricard Fendall

Dear Sir, Saturday 4 P. M. [September 1, 1827]

I found Mr. Randolph at Mr. Wheaton's,[1] where I handed to him your note.[2] On his invitation I took a seat while he read it, which he did with great gravity. He then thanked me for bringing it, and I took my leave. His manner was courteous, but his eye indicated insanity, in the most unequivocal manner. Very resply. and faithfully,

P R FENDALL.

ALS. DLC-HC (DNA, M212, R2). Addressed to Clay.
[1] Thomas M. Randolph; possibly Joseph Wheaton. [2] Above, this date. See also, Randolph to Clay, below, this date.

From Thomas M. Randolph, Sr.

Sir, Washington City Saturday September 1st. 1827.

Upon what I think sufficient ground I believe, that you have, several times since the month of December 1824, made use of expressions insulting in their purport, and injurious in their consequences, with regard to me.[1]

I believe that by such expressions and by unjust representations you occasioned that conduct towards me from the Department of War, which defeated the object of my mission to Florida last Winter.[2]

Lastly, I believe that you are the author of the piece in the National Journal of last Saturday August 25th., in which such abusive language is used towards me.[3]

With respectfull [sic] feelings I call upon you to declare whether my belief be well founded, or not, in each of the cases stated.

Henry Clay Esqr. Sec:ry St THO M RANDOLPH Senior

ALS. DLC-TJC (DNA, M212, R10). [1] Cf. above, Clay to Randolph, this date.
[2] On Randolph's appointment as commissioner to run the boundary between Georgia and Florida and on Secretary of War James Barbour's efforts to obtain relevant documents for his use, see above, Barbour to Clay, December 23, 1826, note. Randolph had

returned to Virginia by early June and charged, in the Charlottesville *Central Gazette*, that he had been unable to perform his duties because he lacked a copy of the report drawn up by Andrew Ellicott and Stephen R. Minor, as commissioners to run the Florida boundary under article 3 of Pinckney's Treaty of 1795. He blamed Clay, as Secretary of State, for the failure of the War Department to supply him the requested document. *Richmond Enquirer*, July 6, 1827. On Clay's explanation of the difficulty, see below, Clay to Adams, February 13, 1828. Minor, Virginian by birth, was a naturalized Spanish subject, secretary to the Governor, Manuel Gayoso de Lemos. Minor had been appointed in 1798 as the Spanish commissioner for running the boundary.   3 In the cited issue of the Washington *Daily National Journal*, editor Peter Force had alluded to Randolph's report of Jefferson's criticism of the Adams administration and, particularly, to Randolph's menacing references to Clay (see above, Hammond to Clay, August 29, 1827, note) as the product of "impotent malice and disgusting vanity," "an electioneering fetch." The editor had queried in turn about Jefferson's opinions of Randolph and commented: "It is fortunate, as Mr. Jefferson is dead, . . . that the world knows that Mr. Th. M. Randolph never enjoyed his confidence, and that he has defects of character which excite commiseration rather than resentment." On September 5 the editor, noting that Randolph believed the first editorial unjust, published at the latter's request a series of letters written by Jefferson to his son-in-law during 1825 and 1826. On July 9, 1825, Jefferson had urged Randolph to return home and asserted that he had "never heard a word from anyone, neighbor or stranger, but of esteem and respect for" him.

INSTRUCTIONS AND DISPATCHES   September 1, 1827

From JAMES OMBROSI (Florence—1). Reports that "the Granduke [*sic*] of Tuscany [Leopold II] has determined to promote in conjunction with the French Government the design of exploring Egypt and the neighbouring Nations," has allocated 53,000 francs for that purpose, and has "appointed a Botanist and an Antiquary who are to go there in company of Champollion, who presides [*sic*] the french expedition." ALS. DNA, RG59, Cons. Disp., Florence, vol. 1 (M-T204, R1). Received October 26.

Jean François Champollion, born in 1790, had been appointed in 1809 professor of history in the lyceum of Grenoble. There he had begun studies in the deciphering of hieroglyphics which later brought him recognition as one of the translators of the Rosetta Stone. In 1828 he conducted a French-Tuscan scientific expedition to Egypt. Included in the party was Ippolito Rossellini, an Italian antiquary (the botanist has not been identified). Champollion was named to the chair of Egyptian antiquities in the College de France in 1831 but died the following year while preparing his notes on Egypt for publication.

Rosellini, born at Pisa in 1800, was professor of oriental languages at the University of Pisa and an admirer of Champollion's work. Following the Frenchman's death, Rosellini took over the task of publishing the report of their expedition. This study, *I Monumenti dell' Egitto e della Nubia* . . . (11 vols.; Florence, 1832–1840), became the basis for the modern study of ancient Egypt. Jean Chrétien Ferdinand Hoefer, *Nouvelle Biographie Générale depuis les Temps les Plus Reculés jusqu'à Nos Jours* . . . (46 vols.; Paris, 1842–1866), vol. 42, cols. 642–43.

From JAMES OMBROSI, Florence (2). States that he has forwarded to Richard Rush certain documents placed in his hands by "Emanuel Fenzi & Co." (not further identified), concerning "an assortment of straw hats sequestered by the Customs house officers" at Boston. Refers to the difficulties explained in his dispatch of June 24, 1827, and reports that a decision has been reached to allow Mrs. Patterson (Elizabeth Patterson [Mrs. Jerome] Bonaparte) to take copies of the certificate he had given. Urges, notwithstanding this adjustment, that the United States Government "find the way to let . . . [him] have the Royal Exequatur," in order "that the power of an American Consul might be acknowledged in this City." ALS. DNA, RG59, Cons. Disp., Florence, vol. 1 (M-T204, R1). Received October 26.

From W[ILLIAM] H. D. C. WRIGHT, Rio de Janeiro. Observes that, since (Condy) Raguet's departure (cf. above, Raguet to Clay, March 12, 1827), he has considered it his "duty on several occasions to remonstrate against the Acts of this Government"; transmits "copies of the correspondence in each case"; and comments on the disregard, shown by Brazilian authorities, for personal liberty. Notes that the enclosures relate to the case of "Isaac Perry (a Native Black of the U. S.) who was forcibly taken from on board the American Brig Leopard, and kept in irons for several weeks" on a trivial, unsubstantiated charge and who, with an Englishman (John Finchem), also imprisoned, has been "delivered up . . . and . . . received on board the Macedonian by Come [James] Biddle"; the case "of the Schooner Hero" (cf. above, Wright to Clay, August 10, 22, 1827), in which "The Conselho Supremo de Gustiça has decided that the charges . . . are unfounded. . ."; "the sentences in the cases of the Brigs Pioneer and Sarah George" (cf. above, Raguet to Clay, October 2, 1826, note; Bond to Clay, October 28, 1826); "some information relative to the Prize Court, (the Conselho Supremo de Gustiça)"; "Copies of the instructions given to Admirals Lobo and Guedes"; and the semiannual report of shipping at the port (of Rio de Janeiro). Adds in a postscript: "This Government has offered to the English & French Ministers [Sir Robert Gordon; probably Count A. M. de Gestas] to give up the Prize Vessels of their respective Nations, upon the condition that they abandon all claim to damages— The terms have not been accepted." ALS. DNA, RG59, Cons. Disp., Rio de Janeiro, vol. 2 (M-T172, R3). Received October 25.

Enclosures (in Portuguese with translations in State Department files) indicate that "the Supreme Council of Justice had upheld, June 15, 1827, a decision of "The Auditor General of Marine of Monte Video" declaring "the Brig Sarah George and her cargo to be a good prize to the captors" and, on June 20, another decision of the same official that, there being no cause to consider the *Pioneer* guilty of violating the (Brazilian) blockade, this vessel and cargo were "adjudged to be released, and the costs to be paid by the captors." Another enclosure reveals that, on August 22, "the Supreme Military and Admiralty Council" had ruled that the costs in the latter case must be paid by the appellees.

In a letter to Samuel L. Southard, August 27, 1827, Commodore Biddle reported that Perry and Finchem had betrayed to a boarding party of a Buenos Aires privateer the presence of a Brazilian officer "secreted below in the schooner [the *Leopard*]; in consequence of which the Brazil officer was taken on board the privateer and detained." For this action the two seamen had been imprisoned when the *Leopard* arrived at Rio de Janeiro. They had been released to Biddle "upon an implied condition that they be remitted to our Government for punishment"; but since they owed no duty to the Brazilian authorities, Biddle held them blameless. *House Docs.*, 20 Cong., 1 Sess., no. 281, pp. 164–65.

MISCELLANEOUS LETTERS   September 1, 1827

From JAMES LINSEY, Westfield, New York. Cites his physical infirmities at the age of 60; laments his loss of property to "those who have usurped . . . [his] rights and lived in indolence on . . . [his] earnings"; notes that he has been "deprived of the benefit of a Patent Obtained February 4th, 1809," recorded "in the Patent Office"; concedes that his "bodily infirmities Secureth a lawfull support at public expence [*sic*] (. . . to the prais [*sic*] of what virtue and humanity exist in our established authorities)"; and asks that "all the Oficers [*sic*] of Government and Cabinet" use their influence in support of the petition which he plans to bring "before the national legislature. . . ." ALS (largely illegible). DNA, RG59, Misc. Letters (M212, R65).

Linsey, a veteran of the Revolution, had been a resident of Cazenovia, New York, in 1809, when he had been awarded a patent for inventing a circular saw for cutting timber. *House Docs.*, 21 Cong., 2 Sess., no. 50, p. 294.

His petition to Congress, filed December 8, 1828, claimed that he had "purchased sundry tracts of land sold under authority of the United States, of which he . . . [had] been unable to get possession . . ." (cf. below, Linsey to Clay, September 11, 1827). The House Committee on Judiciary reported unfavorably on December 15, and the petition was tabled. Revived the following year, it was sent first to the Committee on Claims and subsequently again to the Committee on Judiciary. On January 4, 1830, the latter body reported Linsey's claim "wholly without foundation: if allowed, it could only be upon the monstrous principle, that the United States, by selling the lands of an individual, for the payment of his direct tax, became the warrantor to the purchaser, and his heirs and assigns, for the validity of the title." U. S. H. of Reps., *Journal*, 20 Cong., 2 Sess., pp. 33, 62; 21 Cong., 1 Sess., pp. 83, 101, 125; *House Reports*, 21 Cong., 1 Sess., no. 48.

From JOHN WILMOT, Baltimore. States that "During the Spring of 1824, arrangements were entered into on the part of Mr. James Rice, and the subscriber; aided by the counsel and co-operation of Samuel Smith and James Loyd [*sic*] Esqrs, with the then Secretary of State [John Quincy Adams]; for the immediate appointment of Commodore [David] Porter, and Mr. Jabez Boothroyd, a resident of Cape Haytien; as joint commissioners, in behalf of the numerous Sufferers, by the seizure and confiscation of American property by the order of King Christophe; to make a further effort toward the adjustment and settlement of this distressing, and long suspended claim." Notes Porter's recall (cf. above, Nelson to Clay, April 6, 1825, note) and the expectation of the claimants that his successor [Lewis Warrington] would be instructed to demand "a restoration of" their "property." Observes that the claimants do not know what, if anything, has been done in their behalf; refers to the President for his knowledge of their case; and summarizes the failure of private efforts to adjust the matter, Expresses the wish of the claimants to know why the "project" entrusted to Porter was abandoned and "whether any reasons of State . . . forbid its revival in another Shape. . . ." ALS. DNA, RG59, Misc. Letters (M179, R65).

Wilmot, born at Annapolis in 1778 and educated at St. John's College, was a veteran of the War of 1812 and a merchant in Baltimore. Neither his interest nor that of Rice, who was active in the Maryland State Colonization Society (founded in 1831), has been further identified.

Boothroyd, who had resided in Baltimore in 1816, had been part owner of the schooner *Mariner*, which sailed from Philadelphia in 1810. The vessel was one of those seized under decree of embargo issued by Henri Christophe, on October 6 of that year, against all American vessels then at Cape Henry, in an effort to recoup funds which he believed had been unjustly withheld from him on remittance to a firm of Baltimore merchants. Controversy over the claims continued as late as 1842 (see *House Docs.*, 27 Cong., 3 Sess., no. 36), and no record has been found of their settlement.

INSTRUCTIONS AND DISPATCHES   September 2, 1827

From WILLIAM SHALER, Mahón. Reports having learned, "by the arrival of a Dutch Brig of war from the Bay of Algiers," that the Algerines have been so elated by their success in getting two prizes through the French blockade that they have "sent out all their light Cruizers from Corvettes downwards." Criticizes the lack of "energy, and professional intelligence in the prosecution of this defensive war" by the French, who are not likely to obtain "an honorable peace" without a stroke of good fortune or the landing of troops, hardly possible "before next Spring," and whose "Commerce in this Sea may be considered as suspended," owing to rising insurance rates. Expresses belief in "the safety of . . . [American] relations with Algiers" during the war; notes that "much will depend on the character of the peace which terminates it"; recommends "special instructions" to stimulate "the vigilance of . . . [American] Commanders on this Station"; and encloses copies of his "official correspondence . . . with Captain [William Montgomery] Crane on this subject." Mentions discouragement in regard to his personal health and his use of opium "to obtain a respite from pain even to write a letter. . . ." States his intention of returning "next month" to his post, where, he thinks, his life will be endangered if he remains later than May, and his hope of receiving, before leaving for Algiers, the President's approval of his "request for leave to return home. . . ." ALS. DNA, RG59, Cons. Disp., Algiers, vol. 11 (M23, R-T13). Received November 18. Endorsed by Clay on verso of last page: "Has permission been given to Mr S to return?"

Check to Edward Cutbush

3d. Septr. 1827.

No.   OFFICE OF DISCOUNT & DEPOSIT, Washington,
PAY to Dr. Edward Cutbush or order Sixty four *Dollars*, 50/100
$64 DOLLARS 50/100

ADS, partially printed. DLC-TJC (DNA, M212, R16). Cf. above, III, 416.

To James Erwin

Dear Sir   Washington 3d. Septr. 1827.
I have some thought of applying the debt of Mathers due to Col. Morrisons estate[1] to my own use, and crediting the Estate with the nominal amount of it. You have informed me that it could not be sold in the market for so much,[2] and consequently that arrangement would be better for the Estate than if I were to sell the debt to any other person. But, what I wish you to inform me is, whether I should be safe in making the proposed disposition of the debt? Whether you regard the debt as well secured?

My family is well. My own health is pretty much as usual. Theodore[3] is yet with us, but talks of returning to Kentucky this week. Little Duralde[4] has made great progress in English. He is a fine boy, blessed with a good constitution and a stout frame.

I have been much concerned with the results of some of the Kentucky elections.[5] Every where else public affairs look well, and even there I cannot but still hope. Buchanan's statement[6] has produced an effect on Genl. Jackson's cause, from which it is believed by many it can never recover.

When are we to see you and Anne?[7] Mrs. Clay joins me in affectionate remembrance to both of you. Yr's Sincerely   H CLAY
James Erwin Esq

ALS. THi.   [1] Cf. above, Whittelsey to Clay, December 22, 1826, and note.
[2] Cf. above, Erwin to Clay, May 21, 1827.   [3] Theodore Wythe Clay.   [4] Martin
Duralde, III.   [5] Cf. above, Clay to Taylor, April 4, 1827, note; Clay to Adams, August
25, 1827.   [6] Cf. above, Ingersoll to Clay, August 11, 1827.   [7] Anne Brown Clay
Erwin.

Order on Washington Office, Bank of the United States

Offe. B U States   Washn   Sep. 3d 1827
Pay to first payment on lot No. 9 in sqr. 221.[1] or bearer one hundred
& Seventy nine dollars—
$179   H CLAY

DS. DLC-TJC (DNA, M212, R16).
[1] Square 221 in the Washington plat was bounded by Madison Place and Pennsylvania
Avenue, diagonally across from the White House. Clay is known to have owned "Madison
Place 15½ west," a lot which he reportedly transferred to John Rodgers "for a remarkable
Andalusian jackass which Rogers [sic] had picked up in Spain. . . ." Federal Writers'
Project, Washington City and Capital (Works Progress Administration, American Guide
Series; Washington, 1937), 652–53.

From John J. Crittenden

My Dear Sir,   Frankfort Septr: 3rd 1827
I have received your letter of the 23rd of July last,[1] & can not hesitate to give you the statement you have requested.
Some time in the Fall of 1824, conversing upon the subject of then [sic] pending Presidential election, & speaking in reference to your exclusion from the contest, and to your being called upon to decide & vote between the other candidates who might be returned to the House of Representatives, you declared that you could not, or that it was impossible for you to vote for Genl Jackson in any event. Such, I think, was nearly the language used by you, and, I am satisfied, contains the substance of what you said.[2] My impression is that this conversation took place at Capt: Weisigers[3] tavern in this town, not very long before you went on to Congress in the Fall preceding the last Presidential election, and that the decleration [sic] made by you as above stated,[4] was elicited by some intimation that feel [sic] from me, of my preference for Genl. Jackson over all the other candidates except yourself—
It was one of the many casual conversations we had together upon the subject of that election, & various other subjects, & had entirely escaped from my mind, untill [sic] my attention was particularly recalled to it after the election.[5]

I will only add, Sir, that I have casually learned from my friend Coln: James Davidson, our State Treasurer, (what you may probably have forgotten)[6] that you conversed with him about the same time upon the same subject, & made to him, in substance, the same declaration that you did to me.[7]

Notwithstanding the reluctance I feel at having my humble name drawn before the public, I could not, in justice, refuse to give you the above statement of facts, with permission to use it as you may think proper for the purpose of your own vindication. I have the honor to be Yr's &c   J J CRITTENDEN

Hon: H— Clay Secty: of State

ALS. NcD. Published as supplementary material, Appendix, p. 50, with Clay's *Address . . . to the Public,* below, December 29, 1827. Copy of variant in hand of Mrs. Chapman Coleman, Crittenden's daughter, NcD; for explanation of variation, cf. below, Crittenden to Clay, October 30, 1827.
[1] Not found.   [2] In the variant version this sentence appears as: "This contains the substance of what you said."   [3] Daniel Weisiger.   [4] In the variant version the passage following "took place" reads: "not long before you went on to Congress & your declaration. . . ."   [5] This entire paragraph was omitted in variant version.
[6] Parenthetical clause omitted in variant version.   [7] Cf. above, Porter Clay to Clay, August 30, 1827, note.

From Leonard Kip

Sir   New York Sep. 3 1827.

In consequence of my absence from the City I did not receive yours of 11th Augt.[1] before this day. The draft of $50[2] has been placed to the Cr. of Bishop Chase[3] account of which I shall inform him   I am respectfully Your Obt. Sert.   LEONARD KIP

ALS. DLC-HC (DNA, M212, R2). Addressed to Clay; endorsed by him on cover: ". . . Rect. for my subscription of $50 to Episcopal Church of Ohio."
[1] Not found.   [2] Cf. above, Order on Washington Office, Bank of the United States, August 11, 1827.   [3] Philander Chase.

From Robert Scott

Dear Sir,   Lexington 3rd. Septr. 1827

On the first inst. Messrs. Gratz & Bruce paid their Note of the 26 June 1823.—9452$71[1] and the interest thereon since the 23rd. April last—201$66.

And Doctr. Boswell[2] has paid 2068$. on Account of his Note[3]—2000$ being principal and 68$ the interest thereon since the 6th. Feby. last— What shall I do with these sums—remit them to you?—

Mr. Kendall has sold two of the negroes morgaged [*sic*], and paid me the proceeds—say 987$50 in the Currency and on Account of his debt[4]—

Mr. Kerr[5] was in town on the 1st. inst.   says the hemp crop is good

and is in stack— I advanced him 20$ on Acct. of his wages— should he want any further Small Sum, shall I let him h[ave it?   I] have been unable to lease out the hotel⁶— very respectfully Your obt. Servt.
The Honble Henry Clay   ROBT. SCOTT

ALS. KyLxT. MS. torn.   ¹ See above, III , 443–44.
² Joseph Boswell.   ³ Cf. above, III, 668.   ⁴ Cf. above, Kendall to Clay, July 8, 1826, and notes.   ⁵ John H. Kerr.   ⁶ The Kentucky Hotel.

INSTRUCTIONS AND DISPATCHES   September 3, 1827

From VINCENT GRAY, Havana. Reports that Commodore (David) Porter's squadron has left Key West; that about 3,000 Spanish troops are expected to arrive soon on a ship of the line and a frigate; and that "[Francisco Tomás] Moralles [sic] is loaded with Titles and Honors and made Cap. General of the Canaries." Notes that "[Angel] Laborde has returned to port, with all his vessels & only in time to save him from a similar fate to that he suffered in 25 & 26." States that he has "heard nothing more on the Key Sal affair" (cf. above, Gray to Clay, August 28, 1827). ALS. DNA, RG59, Cons. Disp., Havana, vol. 5 (M-T20, R5). Received September 17.

On Laborde's difficulties in 1826, cf. above, Gray to Clay, October 20, 1826, note; reference to those in 1825 has not been found.

MISCELLANEOUS LETTERS   September 3, 1827

From ENOCH LINCOLN, Portland (Maine). States that, since his last letter concerning the northeastern boundary (above, May 29, 1827), he has received information that impels him "to solicit the attention of the President," since it proves that "the representation made to" Clay and communicated to Lincoln on March 27, 1827, "that the British Government has abstained from the performance of any new acts which might be construed into an exercise of the rights of sovereignty or soil over the disputed territory was entirely incorrect." Contrasts the "forbearance" of Maine "with the opposite course by Great Britain"; cites treatment by "the government of New-Brunswick" of settlers "Along the St. John's river, following it up westwardly from the junction of the Matawascah [sic]"; and calls "attention to the sacrifice to which Maine is submitting" in being forbidden to use "the vast resources" of "a tract of not less than six millions of acres" while "a foreign power . . . is in the mean time applying its jurisdiction in the same manner as if the representations of its Minister created no pledge and no obligations to sustain their correctness." Asserts that "It has been the doctrine of the government & of a great portion of the people of the United States, at times when Great Britain was heretofore prosecuting claims against this country more extensive but not less unjust than the present, that an injury to a single citizen inflicted a wound upon the body politic, and that an evil inflicted upon a part demanded the making a common cause for its remedy." Presents a view, "omitted purposely on former occasions," in the form of an "analogy of the opinions . . . uniformly entertained by our statesmen and jurists in the case of the Mississippi," and argues that "the value of the property at stake" is "beyond calculation" under "the doctrine applied to the navigation of the Mississippi that the ownership of the head waters of rivers gives the right of free navigation to their sources" (cf. above, I, 624; Clay to Gallatin, June 19, 1826 [V, 456–57]). Invites attention to the resources of forest and soil in the disputed area and declares "that there will be," if the British claim be defeated, "a facility of artificial water communication which regarding its extent is unparallelld [sic] in the geography of this country. It will embrace all the waters of the St. John, Penobscot, Kennebec & St. Lawrence." Concludes by asserting his "confirmed belief that Maine will never assent to an arbitration unfavorable to her interests in the great concern. . . ." LS. DNA, RG76, Northeastern Boundary, env. 4, item 17. Copy, in MHi-Adams Papers, Letters Recd. (MR482). Published in *American State Papers*, VI, 930–31.

Governor Lincoln apparently alluded to a proposal evidenced by a resolution of December 28, 1826, in the United States House of Representatives, calling upon the Secretary of War to report on engineering surveys of the Kennebec River and of contemplated canals to link the Kennebec, Androscoggin, and Connecticut Rivers with Merry-Meeting and Casco Bays. The only segment of the survey found related to the lower Kennebec, although a full report was promised by the end of January, 1827. *House Docs.*, 19 Cong., 2 Sess., no. 103.

From CHARLES J. NOURSE, "Department of War." Transmits an extract of a letter from Governor (George) Izard (of the Territory of Arkansas). ALS. DNA, RG59, Misc. Letters (M179, R65). In the enclosure, written to James Barbour on July 31, 1827, Izard reports having learned "that an expedition has been set on foot by two white men, named Burhman [Charles Burkham] & [Nathaniel] Robins for the ostensible purpose of attacking the Camanche [sic] Indians in the Mexican Republic, and that the party was to be composed of American Citizens." He adds that "The proceeding seems to be sanctioned by Jose Antonio Caucedo [i. e., Saucedo], Chief of the Department of the Province of Texas"; that, should the attack occur, settlers "on Red River apprehend reprisals" from the Indians, who have been friendly; and that, since "the members of the expedition are to rendezvous . . . within the Territory of Mexico," he does not know how "to interfere with it. . . ."

On the outcome of the disturbance here reported, see below, Izard to Clay, October 16, 1827, and note.

Burkham with his family had settled in Miller County, Arkansas Territory, in 1816 as emigrants from Indiana. They had crossed into Texas to reside at the mouth of Mill Creek, in present Bowie County, in the spring of 1820. They apparently did not remain long in Texas, for Burkham was identified as of Miller County, Arkansas, in 1827; he resigned as sheriff of that county in 1830 and served as magistrate there in 1835.

Robins (or Robbins) had moved from Arkansas to Pecan Point, on the Red River in Texas, around 1826. He later moved to the Trinity River and in 1834 applied for a land grant at the crossing of the Old San Antonio Road, a tract which included a ferry site. He helped to organize the provisional government in 1835 and fought in the revolution the following spring.

From Thomas Adams

Sir,   Philada. Sept. 4th, 1827

In taking this liberty of addressing you, altho' agreeable to your kind permission, I feel sensible of its encroachment upon your invaluable time—which nothing short of an axiety [sic] I feel for a Brother's interest would justify me in So doing; but the personal interview I had the honor of having with you at Washgton in May last,[1] taught me to approach you with a confidence that no reasonable and

I may perhaps call the present just claim of a Citizen would be viewed with indifference.

during the last five Years or more, Several unSuccessful applications have been made in behalf of my Brother Geo. B Adams to his Government for the Consulate of Alicante[2] & I feel the greatest confidence in declaring to you Sir, no claims to that situation have been superior,   for the truth of which I beg reference to the Archives of your Dept. & I beleive [sic] it has been readily acknowledged & admitted as the only ground on which the present incumbant[3] [sic] recd a preference over my Brother was the Letter of Mrs. Montgomery to Mr Monroe added to his personal freindship [sic] for the family.[4]— You had the kindness to allow me to remind you of the length of time Mr Montgomery should be absent from his Station and you were then pleased to say a few months of which would determine you in recommending another candidate—   Mr M has now been absent at Sta. Martha's (from which place it may be in Your recollection he made application for the consulate thereof) Since the 23d of Nov last[5]—   Mr Brent[6] who has long been I beleive a frd to Mr Montgomery (through his nephew. T L. L Brent Esq our charge de Affairs [sic] at Lisbon & to whom Mr M was once private Secretary)[7] & to Whom I have often been refered [sic] for advice with regard to Mr Montgomery's locating himself at St Martha, will I hope confirm this to you— I therefore beg most respectfully to renew the Application in behalf of my Brother who is enthusiasticly [sic] attached to the present ad-administration [sic], and in this instance asks but the honor of his country's confidence which is the height of his ambition to serve   and if any further weight in favor of his claim I feel justifiable under circumstances of adding that of my own personal & industrious exertions in behalf of the happy success of the present admistrn. using my utmost to avert the ruin that must inevitably follow the unnatural & fanatic promotion to power (which however I hope we have now but little to fear) of the candidate[8] to be offered in opposition to our good & able present cheif [sic] magistrate   and I feel a secret pride also in saying to you alone Sir, it happily falls within my power to act for one individual Citizen no inconsiderable part,   while others may write & talk whether to the purpose or not I can (and beg not to be considered as boasting of too much) *silently* count my numbers & what is more depend upon their votes—   With great-respect I am Sir Yr Mo Obt Sert

The Honble. Henry Clay Secretary of State   THOS. ADAMS

ALS. DNA, RG59, A. and R. (M531, R1). As directed by Clay, Daniel Brent acknowledged, on September 7, receipt of this letter and stated that George B. Adams would be recommended to the President for "the appointment. . . , if it shall appear that Mr. Montgomery has established a permanent abode elsewhere." Copy, in DNA, RG59, Dom. Letters, vol. 22, p. 46 (M40, R20). Cf. below, Clay to George B. Adams, November 9, 1827.

1 Cf. above, Degrand to Clay, April 14, 1827.   2 Cf. above, Cook to Clay, August 3, 1825; Carey to Clay, August 26, 1825; Godman to Clay, September 4, 1825; Everett to

Clay, December 25, 1826.   3 Robert Montgomery.   4 On September 6, 1823, Elizabeth Montgomery, the widow of Robert Montgomery, Sr., had requested of President
James Monroe that her eldest son, Robert, Jr., be appointed to replace his father as
consul at Alicante, Spain. DNA, RG59, A. & R. (M439, R12). Robert Montgomery, Sr.,
had been appointed consul at Alicante as a resident there in 1793.   5 Cf. above,
Montgomery to Clay, December 24, 1826.   6 Daniel Brent.   7 Thomas Ludwell
Lee Brent was a cousin, not a nephew, of Daniel Brent. *Virginia Magazine of History and
Biography*, XVII (1909), 195; XIX (1911), 95–96. Montgomery had been secretary in the
Legation at Madrid when Brent temporarily served as Chargé during the absence of
John Forsyth from his post, on a return to the United States, in the winter and spring of
1820–1821. Montgomery to Clay, December 24, 1826 (passage omitted in editorial sum-
mary). Alvin Duckett, *John Forsyth. . .* , 66–69.   8 Andrew Jackson.

From George W. Kouns

To any of the Executors of the last will
and testament of the late Col. James   Catlettsburgh [sic], Greenup
Morrison Dec. late of Lexington Ky.   County Ky¹ Sept 4th 1827

Gentlemen—On the 3d of July 1811, in pursuance of the provissions
[sic] of an act of Congress approved on the 3d of March 1803,—entitled,
"an act for the relief of insolvent debtors within the district of Columbia,"—(for acts of the 2d Session of the 9th Congress, page 294)²
The late Genl. James Wilkinson conveyed in trust for the benefit of
his creditors, to Eli [sic] Williams and Elias B. Caldwell, late of Washington City, all his lands in Ohio & Ky³—   On the 22d of May 1816
Williams & Caldwell, trustees as aforesaid, executed to the late Col.
James Morrison, a power of atty. to sell the Generals lands in Ky—
And by virtue of that power of atty. Col. Morrison conveyed in 1820
to Robt Pogue [sic] of Mason Cty. Ky. 5000 acres of the Generals lands
in this County for the sum of $1500,⁴—for which sum I am informed
that Pogue executed his note to Morrison, and afterwards discharged
the same by assigning to Morrisons executors a note on Messrs Shreve
& Co. of this County, for that amount, which had been executed to
A. Dougherty and by Dougherty transfered [sic] to Pogue, who transfered it to Morrisons executors, who afterwards sued in Jessamine
County Ky and recovered the same from Messrs Shreve & Co.⁵ Both
Williams and Caldwell departed this life, some time since,⁶ and on the
9th of Augst. last I was appointed the sole trustee to supply the vacancy
occasioned by their death.— The executors of Genl. Wilkinson are
entitled to the aforesaid sum of $1500, and my duty as trustee under
the act of Congress before recited, makes it incumbent on me to adopt
measures to obtain it

[Inquires "whether the aforesaid sum of $1500 with its legal in-
terest, will be paid . . . [to him] with or without suit"; notes that
Wilkinson's deed to Williams and Caldwell "and the power of Attorney from Williams and Caldwell to Col. Morrison" are recorded
in the office of the clerk of the Kentucky Court of Appeals, while
Morrison's deed to Poague "is on record in the clerks office of this

county"; and adds that "The evidence" of his own "appointment as trustee" is in his possession.] Your early attention to the subject of the foregoing communication, will oblige   Yours, Very Respectfully Col. Morrison's Executors   GEORGE W. KOUNS

ALS. DLC-TJC (DNA, M212, R13). Kouns has not been further identified.

1 Catlettsburg is now in Boyd County, created in 1860 from parts of Greenup, Carter, and Lawrence Counties.   2 2 *U. S. Stat.*, 239–41. Wilkinson had become heavily indebted in the course of defending his career before two Congressional investigating committees and, in July, 1811, a military court martial.   3 Wilkinson was grantor by deeds dated November 17, 1810, and July 3, 1811, conveying lots in Frankfort and 64,659 acres in Ohio and Kentucky and a tract on Dauphin Island, Mobile Bay, Alabama. Jillson (comp.), *Old Kentucky Entries and Deeds*, 542.   4 Greenup County Court, Deed Book C, 380–81. A copy of the power of attorney from Williams and Caldwell to Morrison, dated May 22, 1816, is recorded *ibid.*, 382.   5 See above, III, 594, and note.

6 Williams had died in 1823 (Scharf, *History of Western Maryland*, II, 1233); Caldwell, in 1825 (Washington *Daily National Intelligencer*, June 2, 1825).

DIPLOMATIC NOTES   September 4, 1827

From JOSÉ MARÍA SALAZAR, Baltimore. Announces receipt of his letters of recall, to be presented to the President, and of a letter from his government addressed to Clay, all of which he will hold until the President returns to Washington, if that event be not long delayed. Asks when the President is expected. LS, in Span. with trans. in State Dept. file. DNA, RG59, Notes from Colombian Legation, vol. 1, pt. 2 (M51, R2).

Clay replied on September 5, informing Salazar of the President's expected return "the first of next month" and adding: "Should you desire to take your departure prior to that time, you may if you think proper, deliver your Letters of recall to me." Copy, in DNA, RG59, Notes to Foreign Legations, vol. 3, p. 385 (M38, R3).

Adams returned to Washington on October 17. Adams, *Memoirs*, VII, 339. Salazar took leave of Clay on October 13 but remained at his residence in Philadelphia for another six months. Washington *Daily National Journal*, October 15, 1827.

INSTRUCTIONS AND DISPATCHES   September 4, 1827

From A[LEXANDER] H. EVERETT, Madrid, no. 87. Gives an account of the departure of (Juan Josef) Recacho from Madrid (cf. above, Everett to Clay, August 16, 1826) despite the efforts of a mob to apprehend him; reports a rumor that Recacho has since been imprisoned, as has "the Intendant of Madrid Balbao, who was removed at the same time"; and encloses "translations of the decrees by which these changes were effected. . . ." Attributes the removals to (Francisco Tadeo) Calomarde, whose objectives are subject to differing interpretations; notes that, although further changes in the Ministry have been rumored, none has occurred since the dismissal of Recacho. Lists the persons "likely to come into power, should the Council of State ultimately carry the day." Views the outcome "of the troubles in Catalonia" (cf. above, Everett to Clay, April 19, August 16, 1827) as determining whether further changes will be made. Encloses "translations of three documents of recent date which serve to shew the extent of" the Government's "apprehensions, and in part the measures that have been adopted in consequence." Cites the unreliability of regular troops and Royalist volunteers as one cause of concern. Encloses "an estimate of the revenue of the Kingdom for the last year" and notes that the Council of State is "exclusively engaged in digesting plans for the improvement of the Revenue. . . ." ALS. DNA, RG59, Dip. Disp., Spain, vol. 27 (M31, R28). Received November 23.

"Balbao" was probably Trinidad Balboa, chief of police during the absolutist second phase of Ferdinand VII's reign. Balboa was reputedly dismissed because he criticized the nocturnal escapades of the King. During the period of political instability following Ferdinand's death, Balboa attained the military rank of general and for a time headed the government, but he was again quickly driven from office and deported. *Diccionario de Historia de España desde sus Orígenes hasta el Fin del Reinado de Alfonso XIII* (2 vols.; Madrid, 1952), I, 356.

From HENRY MIDDLETON, St. Petersburg, no. 72. Acknowledges receipt of Clay's "Despatch No. 6 [above, February 12, 1827] . . . by Mr. J. Tilton Slade"; states that he "had not been unmindful of this affair" (the case of the *Hector*), but had, until recently, considered "its being urged inadvisable"; adds that he "took occasion sometime in February last to make an application to this Government" and "was promised" that it "should be attended to." Reports that Slade, upon being informed of the situation, "agreed to leave the matter in the hands of the Consul *A. P. Gibson*, who had already appeared in the Character of Agent for this claim." Cites an exchange of notes with Count (Karl Robert) Nesselrode, with whom he expects soon "to discuss . . . the above-mentioned claim—" ALS. DNA, RG59, Dip. Disp., Russia, vol. 11 (M35, R11, 2d. page only). Dated 23 August/4 September.

To James Barbour

Sir: Washington, D. C. 5th Sept. 1827.

I take pleasure, in compliance with a request[1] I have received from a highly esteemed friend in Kentucky, in recommending Frederick B. Trimble,[2] residing at Mount Stirling [*sic*], in Kentucky for the appointment of a cadet in the West Point Academy. He is a nephew of the Honorable Robert Trimble of the Bench of the Supreme Court, and, I understand, is a promising youth of seventeen years of age. I am, with great respect, Your obedient servant,   H CLAY
Hon. James Barbour, &c. &c. &c.

LS. DNA, RG94, United States Military Academy, Cadet Applications, 1827/34.
[1] Not found.   [2] Young Trimble, not further identified, was rejected as an applicant for the Military Academy. *House Docs.*, 21 Cong., 1 Sess., no. 79, p. 115.

Check to Philip Hines

5 September 1827.
Pay to P. Hines or order one hundred and fifty eight dollars.
Cashr. of the Off. Bank U. States Washington[1]   H. CLAY

ADS. DLC-TJC (DNA, M212, R16). Philip Hines was a baker in Washington, D. C.
[1] Richard Smith.

To Duncan McArthur

My Dear Sir   Washington 5h. Sept. 1827
I recd. your favor of the 24h. Ulto.[1] and had on the same day an op-

portunity of conversing with Mr Rush[2] about the writ of error in your Land suit.[3] He has every disposition to do what is right that you could wish him to possess. But he feels a difficulty in directing the whole proceedings, depositions &c. to be taken up to the Supreme Court as you desire. He doubts (and I must add so do I) whether the Supreme Court must not decide on the bill of exceptions, as it has been taken; and whether it could take any notice of what is not in, or refered [sic] to by, the bill of exceptions, if it were brought up. If, for the purpose of understanding the case, it be necessary to refer to papers not made a part of the bill of exceptions, ought not these papers to have been incorporated in the bill of exceptions, when it was drawn? Mr. Rush moreover thinks that he ought not to interfere with the Counsel of the U. S. in the management of a cause which has been confided to their direction.

If, as you think, the Supreme Court can not comprehend the case from the bill of exceptions, it will not follow that the Court will reverse the judgment, but I should suppose the reverse.

I urged Mr. Rush to interpose so as to get a trial at the approaching term, and I think he will as far as it may be delicate and proper for him to interfere

Believing, my dear Sir, that you have sustained much injustice, by delay in this business, and that you have had to encounter men, acting from bad motives, I should be extremely sorry if the cause has been so managed in the Court below as to occasion still further procrastination. I was pleased to hear that the Agent of the Treasury Department had been changed.[4] I hope the one that has been substituted is actuated by less inimical feelings towards you.

Your request to Dr. W.[5] shall be attended to.

I think with you that the statement of Mr. Buchanan[6] entirely exonerates both my friends and myself, and it *may* supersede the necessity of any further exposition of the calumny; but that may not be the case; and I wish to accumulate materials for future use, if contingencies should render them necessary.[7] I remain Cordially Your friend   H. CLAY

Genl. McArthur.

ALS. DLC-Duncan McArthur Papers (DNA, M212, R22).   [1] Not found.
[2] Richard Rush.   [3] Cf. above, McArthur to Clay, April 18, 1827, and note.   [4] The replacement for Cadwallader Wallace has not been identified.   [5] Tobias Watkins. Cf. above, McArthur to Clay, May 14, 1827.   [6] James Buchanan—cf. above, Ingersoll to Clay, August 11, 1827, and note.   [7] Cf. above, Clay to Sloane, May 20, 1827.

From Edward Church

Henry Clay Esqr. Secretary of State &ca &ca &ca, Washington.
Sir,   Prangins, Canton de Vaud,[1] September 5th. 1827.
It is now more than ten years since I obtained the appointment of

Consul for l'Orient, an honor which I owe in a great measure to your interposition in my behalf,[2] I shall ever have a grateful recollection of this, & other testimonies of your friendship which I had previously received—

You are aware that the motives which led me to ask for this Office, and to forsake the asylum which I had sought in Kentucky,[3] were such as would not admit of my remaining long in Europe without some profitable employment, & such, it was soon evident to me, I was not to expect in any port of my Consular division, no one of which is ever visited in time of peace by our flag, except through some casualty; a personal residence there would therefore have been fatal to the hopes which had led me to c[ross] the Atlantic once more with my Family, without i[n] the smallest degree benefiting my Countrymen,   such a useles[s] sacrifice of my prospects I was conscious it could neve[r] be the will of my Government to impose,   in cons[equence] after taking proper advice, I appointed such agents as would suitably fulfill the duties of the office in case of need, & notified Government therewith; since then I have heard nothing that could lead me to suppose that I had been disappro[ved.]

My next object was to look about me for some mean[s] of profitable exertion,   at this time (1817) the invention of our ingenious countryman Fulton,[4] had been turned to but little account on this continent, & indeed had made but little progress in Great Britain,   it seemed to me to offer a fair & honorable field for American enterprise.   appaling [sic] obstacles presented themselves on every side, & amongst these, the paucity of my own pecuniary means, was not the least formidable,   an effort was indispensable,   I took courage, put my shoulder to the wheel, and I have the satisfaction at this time to know that I have introduced Steam navigation into France, Switzerland, Germany & Italy, in which countries every attempt that had been previously made had proved completely abortive, and involved in ruin many of the interested, and consequently could only tend to discourage farther Enterprise;   I have myself built upwards of twenty Steam Boats, all of which have rendered, & continued to render important services in the countries where they are established,[5] of which I have received from their respective Governments the most ample testimony;   I shall certainly have paid much too dear for all these advantages, if by absenting myself from my Consulate in pursuit of them, I have incured [sic] the blame of the Executive;   I am proud of the commission I hold & would never neglect my public duty for any object of private interest, as it will be seen should it ever be my good fortune to be placed in a Station to serve my Country efficiently.—

For the last four years I have made Switzerland my home,   its Republican Institutions, and the blessings which flow from these to every class of the community distinguish this paternal Government from every other in Europe, & cause it so peculiarly to harmonize with the feelings of an Ameri[can] that he almost believes he has found once m[ore] his native land,   at least it renders an absence from this more tolerable. I have the honor to be Sir with the highest esteem & grati- tude Your most obedient & obliging Servant   EDWD CHURCH.

If you should honor me with a line to satisfy me that I am not dis- approved by Government pray address it to the care of Messr. Delessert & Co.⁶ Paris, my Bankers, who will take care to forward it immedi- ately.—

ALS. DNA, RG59, Misc. Letters (M179, R65). Received October 26. MS. torn. En- dorsed by Clay on verso of cover: "Is there a Consul at L Orient appointed in place of Mr. Church? H C."
    ¹ Switzerland.   ² Church had been named consul at L'Orient in January, 1817, and retained the appointment until 1831.   ³ Cf. above, I, 559.   ⁴ Robert Fulton.
    ⁵ Church had written to David Meade, Sr., of Jessamine County, Kentucky, on June 4, 1823, reporting the construction of his eighth steamboat, the *William Tell*, on Lake Geneva, Switzerland, and a proposal "to establish a boat on the Lake of Constance" later that summer. Lexington *Kentucky Gazette*, October 30, 1823. He obtained a patent "for a gandole [*sic*] to sail by steam" from France in the spring of 1827, and a letter from London in March of the latter year noted his talk about steamboats in London at that time. *Franklin Journal and American Mechanic's Magazine*, V (1828), 143; *Niles' Weekly Register*, XXXII (June 30, 1827), 292.   ⁶ Banking house established in Paris by Etienne Delessert in 1777. Etienne had died in 1816, but the business was continued by his sons Benjamin, born at Lyon in 1773, and François-Marie, born at Paris in 1780.

INSTRUCTIONS AND DISPATCHES   September 5, 1827

To JOHN MULLOWNY. States that his draft, of which notice was given in his "Letter of the 7th. [*i.e.*, 11th] June last" to Clay, has been paid, and the amount charged to him "on the Books of the Treasury." Warns: "This is not to be considered, however, as at all dispensing with or affecting the limitation in the expenditures of your Consulate, prescribed by my letter of the 22nd. October 1825, but as simply a payment upon account." Copy. DNA, RG59, Cons. Instr., vol. 2, p. 441 (M78, R2).

From THOMAS BACKUS, Santiago de Cuba. Requests instructions relative to the *Mohawk*, Captain (John) Hammond; questions its ownership, although sup- posedly it is an American vessel, and its activities in and out of the hands of Buenos Aires privateers; and notes that the problem of vessels sailing under two flags, Spanish in port and American at sea, requires clarification. LS. DNA, RG59, Cons. Disp., Santiago de Cuba, vol. 1 (M-T55, R1).
    On March 25, 1828, Daniel Brent wrote to Backus, "By direction of the Secre- tary," transmitting a copy of a letter (not found) addressed to the Secretary by C(harles) J. Ingersoll and instructing the consul, "if Captain Hammond shall substantiate the case stated in that Letter to afford him such official aid as may appear proper, and conducive to his obtaining redress." Copy, in DNA, RG59, Cons. Instr., vol. 2, p. 462 (M78, R2).

From J[OEL] R. POINSETT, Mexico, no. 99. Transmits translation of a speech de- livered by the President (Guadalupe Victoria) to the Special Session of Congress which convened September 1; reports that "Tranquillity is restored to the State of Vera Cruz"; notes that in some of the State legislatures "propositions have been discussed for the expulsion of the European Spaniards"; expresses his opinion that their expulsion is not at this time necessary for the nation's safety and that, since the Spaniards are the "only large capitalists" engaged in commerce, their expulsion would damage Mexico's trade; adds that in the neighborhood of Acapulco the Creoles have risen against the European Spaniards, but few lives have been lost (cf. above, Sergeant to Clay, January 26, 1827, note; below, Taylor to Clay, November 2, 1827, note); relates that accounts from Guatemala indicate the "constituted authorities are likely to prevail. . ." (cf. above, Poinsett to Clay, July 27, 1827). LS. DNA, RG59, Dip. Disp., Mexico, vol. 3 (M97, R4). Received November 14.

MISCELLANEOUS LETTERS September 5, 1827

To ALBERT GALLATIN. Introduces the bearer, "Mr. John Campbell of Virginia," a lawyer "with whom . . . [Clay] was well acquainted in early life," who "goes to England for the purpose of looking after an Estate to which he or his nephew, he has reason to believe, has become entitled by the English laws of inheritance." Invokes "any aid or attentions which . . . [Gallatin] may find it convenient to afford Mr. Campbell." ALS. ViHi.

Campbell was appointed Treasurer of the United States in 1830 and removed in 1839 because of ill health. Although he practiced and resided in Richmond, he noted that all his "near relatives and most intimate friends" lived in the southwestern area of the State. Campbell to Martin Van Buren, April 21, 1829 (DLC-Van Buren Papers; M660, series 2, R8).

To William Henry Harrison

Dear Sir: Washington City, 6th September, 1827.

A speech of Mr. Senator Branch of North Carolina, (of which I transmit you a copy herewith,) has been recently published as having been delivered by that gentleman on the occasion of the Senate's confirmation of my nomination to the office which I now hold.[1] It is brought forward to impugn a statement contained in a speech[2] which I delivered in July last at Noble's near Lexington. In the course of an argument which I urged against the improbability of any such overtures having been made, as General Jackson stated himself to have received from my friends, I contended that if they had been received Gen. Jackson was bound when, as a Senator of the United States, he was required to act upon the nomination to have disclosed them to the Senate and to have moved the appointment of a committee of Inquiry, and that it was especially incumbent on him to have adopted that course, as it did not then appear that any other Senator knew of the alleged overtures. I observed that I had requested a Senator of the United States, when my nomination should be taken up, to ask of the Senate the appointment of such a Committee, unless it should appear to him to be altogether unnecessary. And I added that I was afterwards informed, "that when it was acted upon, General Jackson, and every other Senator present, were silent as to the imputations now made; no one presuming to question my honor or integrity."

Although it cannot be regarded material to the validity of the argument, as urged against General Jackson, whether Mr. Branch did or did not make a speech in opposition to my appointment, I am desirous that in the statement of any matter of fact made by me, even on a collateral or unimportant point, there should be perfect accuracy; or that, if a mistake has been committed, it should be rectified. You will I think, recollect, that I desired you, as my friend, with much earnestness, to ask from the Senate the appointment of a Committee of Investigation into Mr. Kremer's charge,[3] if, from the course the nomination should take in the Senate it should appear to you to be at all necessary; that you afterwards informed me that nothing had occurred to render the appointment of such a Committee necessary; and that you had, therefore, forborne to ask it. The Senate acted as usual, with closed doors, and consequently no one was present but the members and the officers of the body. The injunction of secrecy was removed after the decision upon the nomination.

After the publication of my speech at Noble's, upon seeing a statement in some of the public prints, that Mr. Branch had addressed some observations to the Senate, in opposition to my nomination,[4] an indistinct recollection occurred to me that you did inform me that no Senator but Mr. Branch had said any thing on the subject of my appointment; That he made a few remarks, which were but little attended to, and which appeared to produce no impression. I think you did not state, particularly, what they were, for I am quite sure if you had mentioned that Mr. Branch had assigned the reasons which he now puts forward, a more distinct and durable impression would have been made on my mind. It would, however have been too late, at that time, for me to have applied to the Senate for the appointment of a committee if I had even thought it to be necessary as the Senate had finally acted upon the nomination.

My object in addressing this letter to you being to obtain from you a statement according to your recollection, of the above transactions, so far as you had an agency in them, I shall be very much obliged to you to furnish me with a reply[5] as soon as may be convenient.—I am, with great respect, Your friend and obedient servant

Copy. DLC-HC (DNA, M212, R2).

1 On September 3, 1827, the Washington *United States Telegraph* had reprinted from the *Raleigh Star*, of North Carolina, a letter addressed to the editors, (A. J.) Lawrence and (Thomas J.) Lemay, August 27, 1827, by John Branch, enclosing the text of what he described as "the only remarks that were made" on the occasion of Clay's confirmation as Secretary of State. In that speech Branch had expressed his unwillingness "to advise and consent to this appointment" because of the Constitutional restriction against a Senator or Representative being appointed to civil office under the Federal government " 'which he has assisted to create, or the emoluments of which have been increased by his vote.' " Branch queried whether, in view of such a policy, a member of Congress might "not with as much propriety be suspected of voting from sordid or interested considerations, when he makes an officer, who, in turn, gives him an office?" While not himself prepared "to assert positively that corruption . . . mingled with this transaction," he thought the circumstances were "sufficient to fix on the public mind the strongest

suspicions that they . . . [had] been cheated out of their rights by corruption and intrigue. . . ." Lawrence had become a proprietor of the *Raleigh Star and North Carolina
State Gazette* (founded in 1808) in 1823. Lemay had acquired the other half interest in
1826. In 1835 Lawrence sold his share also to Lemay, who continued the journal until
1852.   [2] Above, July 12, 1827.   [3] See above, Clay to Gales and Seaton, January
30, 1825; Kremer to Clay, *ca.* February 3, 1825.   [4] The *Raleigh Star* of August 23 had
called upon Branch to publish his speech. Editorial reprinted in *Richmond Enquirer*,
August 23, 1827, and Washington *United States Telegraph*, August 30, 1827.   [5] Before
replying, Harrison consulted Josiah Stoddard Johnston about the incident. Johnston asserted that Branch had merely insinuated his accusations and that therefore the obligation of proof rested with him, not Clay's friends. Harrison did, however, on November 4,
1827, issue a public statement conceding that he had not heard the Senate proceedings
distinctly but had not considered and still did not believe that Branch's remarks warranted inquiry. Goebel, *William Henry Harrison. . . ,* 251; Washington *Daily National
Intelligencer,* November 24, 1827.

To George Izard

To His Excellency George Izard
Governor of Arkansas, Saline.
Sir,   Dept. of State, Washington 6 Septr. 1827.
   Your letter of the 31st. Ulto. addressed to the Secretary of War, now
absent from the City, has been shewn to me,[1] stating that an expedition has been set on foot by two white men named Burkman and
Robins[2] for the ostensible purpose of attacking the Camunche [*sic*]
Indians in the Mexican Republic, and that the party was to be composed of American Citizens.— Such an enterprize is incompatible with
the obligations and duty of an American Citizen, and may, as you
justly observe, involve us in difficulties. If there be any Citizens of the
Territory of Arkansas about to engage in such an expedition, and
proof can be made of their purpose, I beg leave to suggest the expediency of instituting prosecutions against them under the act of
Congress, which forbids any person, within the territory, or jurisdiction of the United States, from enlisting or entering himself in the
service of any foreign State, as a Soldier[3]— I am with great respect,
Your Excellency's obedt. Servt.   H. CLAY.

Copy. DNA, RG59, Dom. Letters, vol. 22, pp. 44–45 (M40, R20). Cf. below, Izard to
Clay, October 16, 1827, note.
   [1] See above, Nourse to Clay, September 3, 1827.   [2] Charles Burkham and Nathaniel
Robins (or Robbins).   [3] Cf. above, II, 289–90.

From James Brown

My dear Sir,   (private)   Paris Sept 6, 1827
   Mr Perkins who has been in Paris for some time called on me and
informed me that he had obtained Patents from this Government for
his new Steam Engine and Steam Cannon.[1] He represents the former
as being of only one fourth of the bulk and weight and consuming
only one third of the fuel consumed by the Engines now in use and

performing the same work. It seems too that he has contrived to remove all danger from the explosion of his boilers by generating his
steam in a great number of tubes or pipes the explosion of one of
which would be innoxious [sic] whilst the explosion of more than one
at a time would be impossible. I have seen Gentlemen who have assured me that they have seen one of these Engines in operation in London, placed near one of the best of Watt & Bolton[2] [sic] and employing
[sic] in pumping water, and that Perkins Machine with one fourth of
the weight and bulk and one third of the fuel was equally powerful
with that of W & B. His steam musket has been tried in presence of
the Duke of Wellington and some french Engineers and has discharged one thousand balls in one minute with a force greater than
that given by the best gun powder. His cannon is contrived to discharge one hundred balls in one minute with almost incredible force.
The French Government has taken a great fancy to him and has I
understand engaged him to come over and work for them. He told
me *in confidence* that they had proposed to employ him to build a
Vessel armed with steam guns carrying cannon to discharge balls of
one hundred weight in rapid succession and that he should come over
to commence his labors for France in the course of a few weeks.[3] He
gave me permission to state this to you in confidence and to assure you
that his own Government should not be left unarmed against what he
thinks the most formidable arm yet known. He assures me that the
Duke of Wellington on witnessing the effect of his Gun declared that
henceforth the weakest nation might defend itself against the most
powerful. I know Mr Perkins like all other projectors is very sanguine
and enthusiastic but I have reason to believe that his gun may be
employed with great effect on our batteries and in defending our harbors. I have urged him to send over his models and specifications to
obtain a patent in the United States although I am not sure that he
can now obtain it after having patented it in England and France.[4] At
all events I hope we shall be made acquainted with the discovery so as
to avail ourselves of it should it answer his expectations. It is his intention to obtain Patents in Holland and Russia.[5]

I have not time to write to Mr Rush[6] by this opportunity. I have
mentioned the subject of the looms to Mr Barnet[7] who thinks it will
be very difficult to obtain either drawings or models of them as the
exportation is strictly prohibited. He will however do all he can to
obtain the one or the other.

Mr Warden our former consul here is really a modest excellent man
and has on all occasions endeavored to render himself useful to our
Country and to our countrymen. He is very poor and supports himself
by his pen. I wish he could be thought of should any opportunity offer
to notice him.[8]

Mrs. Brown suffers very much from a pain in her face with which she has been occasionally afflicted for several years. She sends a letter to her sister,[9] having already sent on all the objects you asked. You have now a delightful house[10] and will be able by cheerfulness and good company to mitigate the *horrors* of the next winter. The election so far has been conducted in a manner calculated to give pain to every honorable mind. Mr Sontag[11] tells me that you have become exceedingly sensitive and that you have less command of your countenance and feelings than ought to belong to your station. He adds that Mr. Adams on the contrary supports the attack with truly philosophical firmness. I presume your bad health may account for this circumstance.

I have not since the month of April received a single line from either of my brothers. Doctor Brown has always hitherto been exceedingly exact in his correspondence and his silence now gives me great anxiety. Do you know where he is?[12] Any news respecting my family will be very gratifying to me. My brother John is now so advanced in life and has had so much trouble and affliction in consequence of the melancholly [sic] event of the last year that I cannot expect him to write to me[13]—

Make my best respects to my friend Johnston[14] and tell him that he is indebted to me for several letters since I last heard from him. If you see Mr Skinner who conducts a useful agricultural Journal at Baltimore[15] tell him that the society[16] ought to send out some intelligent young man to remain two or three years in the South of France and apply himself closely to the study of the production of raw silk.[17] The Southern states are ruined if they do not diversify their industry by producing olives silk and Wine. The trees ought to be planted immediately or the seeds sown and the nurseries prepared which in four or five years will yield mulberry leaves in abundance. Negro women and children can manage the raising of silk as well as that of cotton and it will be more productive   But this cannot be learned from books. The practice might be acquired by visiting and working at establishments of that kind. So soon as the South shall produce the silk the Eastern people will discover the art of manufacturing it.

Mrs. Brown begs me before I close this letter to say to Mrs. Clay that she forgot to give her credit for twenty francs which she had retained out of the former account to send [sic] on the Caisse— You will please deduct it from the amount stated in the account now sent you.[18] Present our love to Mrs. Clay   I am Dear Sir your friend & faithful servt   JAMES BROWN
The Hon Henry Clay.

ALS. DLC-HC (DNA, M212, R2).
[1] Born at Newburyport, Massachusetts, in 1766, Jacob Perkins had been apprenticed to a goldsmith and by 1781 had taken over management of the business. His enterprise as an inventor had been shortly evidenced in a method of silver plating, a machine for cutting nails, and a plate for engraving. The last of these developments had led to his formation of a company in 1819 for the printing of bank notes and, beginning in 1840,

postage stamps by a process which continued in use until near the turn of the century.
    Perkins had begun experiments with steam under high pressure about 1822. By 1827
he had attained operating pressure of 800 pounds to the square inch in a single cylinder
engine and 1,400 pounds in a compound engine. About 1836 he patented a boiler and
engine for a steam vessel using steam at 2,000 pounds pressure. He also received patents
in 1829 for an improved paddle wheel and in 1831 for a method of circulating water in
boilers, the latter of which served as the precursor of the modern water-tube boiler. Carl
W. Mitman, in *Dictionary of American Biography*, VII, pt. 2, pp. 472–73.   [2] Cf.
above, II, 887n.   [3] An account of Perkins' experiments with steam artillery and
musketry, as tested at Greenwich, England, before French engineers appointed by the
Duke d'Angoulême, "together with one of his aids and Prince Poulignac," had been
published as a letter from Perkins to Thomas P. Jones, editor of the *Franklin Journal*,
March 8, 1827, reprinted in Washington *Daily National Intelligencer*, August 7, 1827.
Perkins there stated that he had been hired by the French to construct a "piece of
ordnance . . . to throw sixty balls, of four pounds each, in a minute, with the correctness of the rifled musket, and to a proportionate distance." A musket was to be "attached
to the same generator for throwing a stream of lead from the bastion of a fort, and . . .
made so far portable as to be capable of being moved from one bastion to another,"
the musket "to throw from one hundred to one thousand bullets per minute. . . , and that
for any given length of time." *Niles' Weekly Register*, which on July 28, 1827 (XXXII,
360), had carried a report of the Greenwich tests, noted on January 3, 1829 (XXXV, 301),
that later experiments were disappointing, that "the steam gun sold to the French
government . . . [did] not possess the power of throwing a ball more than half the
distance that a common cannon of the same calibre did. . . ." Jones, born in England
in 1774, had come to the United States as a young man. In February, 1825, he had been
one of the founders of the *American Mechanics' Magazine* and later that year had become sole owner as well as editor of that journal. Appointed in 1826 professor of
mechanics and natural philosophy at the Franklin Institute for the Promotion of the
Mechanic Arts and placed in charge of the *Franklin Journal*, he had then merged the
publications and continued as the editor until his death in 1848. He was also named
superintendent of the Patent Office in the State Department on April 12, 1828, served
there until 1829, and was from 1837 to 1838 an examiner in the reorganized Office.
    [4] On Perkins' British and French patents, cf. Robert Stuart [*i.e.*, Robert Meikleham],
A Descriptive History of the Steam Engine (3d. edn.; London, 1825), 218; *Franklin Journal
and American Mechanics' Magazine*, IV (September, 1827), 216; VII (February, 1829),
151, 152. No record has been found that Perkins received American patents for these
improvements.   [5] No record found.   [6] Richard Rush.   [7] Isaac Cox Barnet.
    [8] David Bailie Warden, born in Ireland, had emigrated to the United States in 1799,
taught for a time at an academy in New York State, acquired United States citizenship
in 1804, and in the latter year moved to Paris, France. He had been private secretary to
the American Minister, John Armstrong, until 1808, when he had been named consul
pro-tempore. From 1810 to 1814 he had held appointment as consul. During the remainder of his life, which he spent in France, he published numerous descriptive, statistical, and historical accounts on the United States as interpreted for the French. He did
not receive further American appointment.   [9] Mrs. Clay.   [10] The Washington
property rented from Mrs. Stephen Decatur.   [11] Fortuné de Sontag.   [12] Samuel
Brown had resigned from the faculty of Transylvania University in 1825 and retired to
his former home in Alabama. There he had suffered a paralytic stroke the following
year. Though in ill health, he lived until January, 1830.   [13] Another brother,
Preston W. Brown, had been murdered the previous year (see above, Clay to James
Brown, October 8, 1826). John Brown was now 70 years of age.   [14] Josiah Stoddard
Johnston.   [15] John Stuart Skinner; the *American Farmer*.   [16] Probably the
Maryland Agricultural Society, founded in 1786. The organization had adopted a resolution in 1821 endorsing Skinner's efforts through the *American Farmer* "to advance the
interests of agriculture," and in 1824 the editor had served as corresponding secretary
of the Society. Albert Lowther Demaree, *The American Agricultural Press, 1819–1860*
(New York, 1941), 29; Edith Rossiter Bevan, "Gardens and Gardening in Early Maryland," *Maryland Historical Magazine*, XLV (December, 1950), 267.   [17] No reference
to such a project has been found. Lafayette, however, sent a book *On the Rearing of
Silk Worms* and a quantity of silkworm eggs to Joseph Y. Tomkins, of Baltimore, in 1829.
Lucretia Ramsay Bishko, "Lafayette and the Maryland Agricultural Society, 1824–1832,"
Maryland Magazine of History, LXX (Spring, 1975), 65. A factory for manufacturing silk
ribbons was started at Baltimore in 1829 but existed only briefly. In 1827–1828 the
Mansfield Silk Company, cited as the first successful silk mill in the United States, was
founded at Mansfield, Connecticut. L[inus] P. Brockett, *The Silk Industry in America, a
History* . . . ([New York], 1876), 52–53.   [18] Not found.

From John J. Crittenden

Dear Sir,   Frankfort Septr: 6th 1827

The result of our Congressional elections[1] was so contrary to my expectations & wishes, that I have hardly yet regained spirits enought [*sic*] to write you— I am indebted however to Mr Buckhannon [*sic*] for some revival of my spirits[2]— And I do most cordially congratulate you on result [*sic*] of Genl Jackson's appeal[3] to that gentleman— It seems to me that if you had dictated his letter you could have made it but little more favourable to your own purposes— It is really matter of astonishment to me thus to see the gross attempt which is making in all the opposition papers that I have seen, to represent B—'s letter as corroborating the statements of Genl. Jackson[4]— It surely can not be possible for them to maintain that ground before the people, and by assuming it they have precluded themselves from any attack upon his veracity— I can hardly think that Genl Jackson will be satisfied with B—'s statement, and if he, or Genl Eaton should come out with a con- tradiction of it, would it not produce a most awkward dilemma for the party?

We are looking towards Nashville, & expecting to hear something from Genl. Eaton at least upon the occasion[5]—

Buckner[6] has been here several days— I parted with him this morn- ing— He is about publishing, in the form of an address to his con- stituents, a reply[7] to a letter addressed to his competitor Billy Owings by Genl Jackson a short time before the election, & circulated in hand bills throughout the District for the purpose of prejudicing Buckner[8]— In this letter Buckner is charged with falsehood— His reply is a severe animadversion, personal & political,— You will see it in the next Commentator.[9]

I doubt the propriety of delivering yr. letter to White[10]— I have not seen him since I received it, when I do I shall probably hand it to him— Perhaps it is the safer course— He did certainly express himself in terms of the most unqualified approbation & admiration of your conduct, at the time of & after the Presidential election— And de- nounced as false &c the charges of corruption & intrigue made against you & your friends— I think that I am well informed as to this matter, & that I can refer you if it becomes necessary to gentlemen who can establish the fact.

The inclosed letter[11] contains the statement you desired from me— I have read it to Davidson, particularly that part of which relates to him & he acquiesces in it— He will furnish you, no doubt, if applied to with a direct statement upon the subject— And I hope you will write to him for one[12]— You have few friends that more deserved to be valued & esteemed by you— He is a man of solid worth, & to be de- pended in every extremity [*sic*].

Our friend Denny, who is now the attorney General of Kenty:, wishes to be made a judge in Florida— He has written you on the subject[13]— He is a clever man, superior to most of your Territorial judges, and I wish that you may find it convenient & proper to give him the appointment.

We have just seen Mr. T. Randolph's expose of Mr. Jefferson's opinions about men & things[14]— It is considered a most strange & Madmanlike production— You must not, it seems, say a word about it— But I do hope it will bring forth those testimonials of Mr. Jefferson's real sentiments, which have been so frequently alluded to, & some of which I understand from a paragraph in the Nat: Intel:[15] to be in possession of the Editors of that paper— I am with great esteem &c Yr's &c.   J J CRITTENDEN

Hon: H Clay Secty: &c

ALS. NcD.   [1] Cf. above, Clay to Taylor, April 4, 1827, note.
[2] Cf. above, Ingersoll to Clay, August 11, 1827.   [3] Cf. above, Smith to Clay, August 1, 1827.   [4] See, for examples, the Washington *United States Telegraph*, August 28, 1827, reprinting an article from the Charlottesville *Virginia Advocate*, and above, Webster to Clay, August 22, 1827, note.   [5] Cf. above, Webster to Clay, August 22, 1827, note; below, Ingersoll to Clay, October 6, 1827.   [6] Richard A. Buckner.
[7] Published in Lexington *Kentucky Reporter*, September 12, 1827.   [8] See Jackson to William Owens, July 25, 1827, published in Lexington *Kentucky Gazette*, July 31, 1827, and Bassett (ed.), *Correspondence of Andrew Jackson*, III, 375–76. Owens, born in Fauquier County, Virginia, in 1773, had come to Kentucky with Simon Kenton at the age of ten, had fought in the Indian campaigns of the early 1790's, then had studied law and opened practice at Danville. In 1807 he had removed to Columbia, Kentucky, where he resided until his death, in 1847. He had been a State Senator from 1815 to 1824, a commonwealth's attorney for many years, and Buckner's opponent in the recent Congressional election (cf. above, Clay to Everett, August 27, 1827).   [9] Frankfort *Commentator*, September 8, 1827.   [10] David White, Jr. Cf. below, Crittenden to Clay, October 30, 1827, and note.   [11] Above, Crittenden to Clay, September 3, 1827.   [12] See below, Davidson to Clay, October 20, 1827; Clay's letter to Davidson, not found.   [13] No application from James W. Denny has been found.   [14] Cf. above, Hammond to Clay, August 29, 1827, and note.   [15] Cf. above, Mercer to Clay, August 18, 1827, and note.

INSTRUCTIONS AND DISPATCHES   September 6, 1827

From THOMAS D. ANDERSON, Leghorn, "Duplicate." Notes that he has remained in his present location "by permission from the State Department for the benefit of" his eyesight and that he is "in daily expectation of the arrival of . . . Mr. [Charles D.] Cox [*sic*] in Tripoli when the seals and records of the [consular] Office will be delivered to him by Mr. [Joseph Nicholas] Morillo. . . ." States that he has "experienced much embarrassment for want of funds," owing to suspension of his credit in London "on acct. of the delay in adjusting . . . [his] accts. with the Government." Explains that the vessel on which he sent his accounts has apparently been lost at sea and that for "upwards of five years" he has "not rec'd. any . . . salary or any funds for the contingencies of the Consulate." Expresses trust that his "bills on the State Dept. for the amount of four years salary" will be honored. ALS. DNA, RG59, Cons. Disp., Tripoli, vol. 4 (M-T40, R-T5). Received March 25, 1828.

From ALBERT GALLATIN, London, no. 112. States that Clay "will perceive by the news papers that the difficulties, in making a definitive arrangement of the new Administration [cf. above, Gallatin to Clay, August 30, 1827, and note], have been removed." Explains that "The Whigs have yielded," although "it is very clear that" the decision to appoint (John Charles) Herries was made without consulting them. Predicts that, despite some dissatisfaction, the Cabinet will remain intact "till after the meeting of Parliament." Encloses a copy of a note he sent to Lord Dudley. Reports that his conferences with the British plenipotentiaries will resume on September 12. ALS. DNA, RG59, Dip. Disp., Great Britain, vol. 34 (M30, R30). Copy, in NHi-Gallatin Papers (MR21). Received October 14.

To John W. Taylor

My dear Sir   (Confidential)   Washington 7h. Septr. 1827.

The unfortunate result of some of our elections in K. has no doubt reached you.[1] It is bad, but I still hope and believe the State will be ultimately safe. We are the majority, it is alleged, in both branches of the General Assembly.[2] This issue of those elections makes it more important, in reference to the choice of a Speaker of the H. of R. to ascertain the disposition of the new members from N. York. Have you any information tending to shew what it is? I should be glad to receive it, if you have. We have gained some additional strength in North Carolina;[3] and I hope we shall get Delaware, but for the divisions between our Federal & Republican friends I presume it would be certain.[4] Yr's with great regard   H CLAY
Jno. W. Taylor Esq

ALS. NHi. Endorsed by Taylor: ". . . Recd. & Ansd. 12. 1827 [answer not found] Copy table of N. Y. Rep. to 18. 19. & 20h Cong. enclosed & opinion that 18 or 20 Votes may be safely counted on for Ad. Speaker at next session—" In fact only 16 New York Congressmen voted for Taylor's election as Speaker; 17 and the absent Thomas Jackson Oakley were identified as supporters of Andrew Stevenson when the House voted on December 3, 1827. *Albany Argus*, December 10, 1827, reprinted from the New York *Commercial Advertiser*. Stevenson won the Speakership by a vote of 104 to 94 over Taylor. *Register of Debates*, 20 Cong., 1 Sess., 811.
[1] Cf. above, Clay to Taylor, April 4, 1827, note.   [2] Cf. above, Clay to Adams, August 19, 1827, note.   [3] Cf. above, Clay to Hammond, August 22, 1827, and note.
[4] On the vote of Delaware for the Presidency in 1828, cf. above, Clay to Hammond, June 1, 1827, note. On the Federalist support for Jackson in Delaware, cf. above, Markley to Clay, April 28, 1827. Louis McLane and Henry Ridgely, prominent Federalists, exerted leadership for Jackson (cf. above, Hammond to Clay, March 28, 1827); but John M. Clayton, who had emerged as a young Federalist partisan after the War of 1812, now organized a pro-Adams party, merging Federalist and Republican support, which successfully carried the election in October, 1827, for both houses of the General Assembly and the congressional seat vacated by Louis McLane. Richard Arden Wire, "John M. Clayton and the Rise of the Anti-Jackson Party in Delaware, 1824–1828," *Delaware History*, XV (April, 1972), 257, 259–64; Munroe, *Louis McLane*, 219–20; and cf. above, Clay to Webster, May 14, 1827, note; below, Sergeant to Clay, September 18, 23, 1827. Clayton, a cousin of Thomas Clayton, had been born in 1796, in Sussex County, Delaware, graduated in 1815 from Yale College, trained for law at the Litchfield Law School, and admitted to the bar in 1819. He had been a member of the State Legislature in 1824 and was secretary of state for Delaware from 1826 to 1828. He served in the United States Senate, first as a National Republican, later as a Whig, from 1829 to 1836, from 1845 to 1849, and from 1853 until his death in 1856. From 1837 to 1839 he was chief justice of Delaware, and from 1849 to 1850, Secretary of State for the United States.

From John Williams

Sir,   Knoxville, Sept. 7th 1827.

It is now reported that Mr. Spencer Jarnagin is to be supported for the office of United States Atto. in the district of East Tenn— Mr. Jarnagin possesses respectable talents, but he is unworthy of the office— He has been notorious for his disregard of the truth from his boyhood— He has been distinguished during the past Summer for circulating the slanders of Duff Green in relation to yourself & Mr. Adams— You are at liberty to shew this letter to Mr. Jarnagin or his friends— This will be handed you by Mr. Calvin Morgan one of the most wealthy & respectable merchants of Tenn[1]— He can give you the news of this part of the Country— Yours respectfully

Mr. Clay—   JOHN WILLIAMS

ALS. DNA, RG59, A. and R. (M531, R8).

[1] Born in Litchfield, Connecticut, an older brother of Gideon Morgan, Jr., Calvin had been reared in Virginia, had moved to Knoxville, Tennessee, in 1806, and the following year had obtained a merchant's license. He was also active in banking, became a tax assessor in 1816, and served as a trustee of numerous educational and civic bodies.

INSTRUCTIONS AND DISPATCHES   September 7, 1827

From BEAUFORT T. WATTS, Bogotá, no. 33. Transmits copies of correspondence between "the president of the Republic" (Simón Bolívar) and the president of the Senate (Jerónimo Torres); between himself and "the minister of War Genl. [Carlos] Soublette"; and between himself and "the Minister of Foreign Affairs" (José Manuel Restrepo). Notes that "From the correspondence between President Bolivar and the President of the Senate," Clay "will learn the unfortunate State of the Republic." Adds: "The President has not yet reached the city, but is expected in a few days—when I hope I shall be able to give you a more favourable account of political events." ALS. DNA, RG59, Dip. Disp., Colombia, vol. 4 (M-T33, R4). Received October 26.

A translation of Bolívar's letter (undated in the enclosure, but dated August 24, 1827, in the published version) may be found in Lecuna (comp.) and Bierck (ed.), *Selected Writings of Bolivar*, II, 658–61. In the enclosed copy of his letter to Soublette, Watts requests information concerning two Americans who had fought for the Patriot cause in Colombia. The Secretary of War replied that inquiries about one of them, John B. Haw, "proved fruitless" but traced the career of the other, Alexander Macauley of Virginia, from his arrival in 1811 to his execution by the Royalists in 1813. The enclosed correspondence with Restrepo relates to the effects of H. E. Fudger (cf. above, Watts to Clay, July 19, 29, 1826; Bürklé to Clay, October 19, 1826), to exequaturs for William Radcliff (cf. above, Clay to Radcliff, August 10, 1827) and William J. Seaver (*i.e.*, Sever—cf. above, Clay to Sever, March 21, 1827); and to a claim by David Y. Lanman, about which Watts had written earlier (cf. above, Watts to Clay, June 14, 1827).

Torres, born and educated in Popayán, had received a law degree at Quito and, after participating in the revolution against Spain from its early stages, had held a number of judicial and administrative posts under the republican government. He had been imprisoned by the Spanish for three years for this involvement. Following the triumph of Bolívar, Torres had entered the Colombian Senate in

1821 and retained his seat until 1828. He was identified as a strong supporter of the Liberator and at various times a member of the Colombian debt commission, an associate judge of the Supreme Court, counselor of state, director of the mint, a commissioner to France, and chief auditor of the Treasury.

Haw and Macauley (or McCauley) have not been further identified.

To John Quincy Adams

Dear Sir   Washington 8h September 1827.

I hasten to inform you that despatches from Mr. Gallatin[1] received this day communicate the intelligence that the B. Government has agreed to renew the provisions of the Convention of 1818, in relation to the N. West and to Commerce between the U. States and G. Britain for an indefinite period, with the priviledge [sic] to either party to terminate the agreement by giving one year's previous notice. This will supersede the necessity of fresh instructions on those two subjects. A copy of the despatches shall be sent you as soon as it can be prepared.

I have also received today a new treaty with Sweden[2] which, as far as I am able to judge, from a very hasty perusal, is in substantial conformity to the instructions given to Mr. Appleton,[3] and embraces some of our late liberal principles to a very satisfactory extent. Copies of the treaty and of Mr. Appleton's despatches shall also be sent to you, as soon as they can be prepared.

Mr. Southard[4] has returned. I am, with great regard faithfully Your obt. Servt.   H. CLAY
Mr. Adams.

ALS. MHi-Adams Papers, Letters Recd. (MR482).   [1] Above, July 26, 28, 29, 1827. [2] Cf. above, Appleton to Clay, July 11, 1827.   [3] Cf. above, Clay to Appleton, January 12, 1827.   [4] Samuel L. Southard. Cf. above, Hay to Clay, August 6, 1827.

INSTRUCTIONS AND DISPATCHES   September 8, 1827

From JAMES BROWN, Paris, no. 73. States that he requested an interview, held on September 7, with the Baron de Damas for the purpose of complying with Clay's instructions of May 28. Notes that he reviewed, during the conversation, the negotiations relative to American claims against France and informed Damas that the United States "would not admit the propriety of associating in the same negociation, the disputed demand under the 8th. article of the Louisiana treaty and incontestable claims of American citizens, a large portion of which . . . had been admitted by France to be just," but that he had been instructed to propose that "the question under that treaty . . . be referred to arbitration. . . ." Reports that Damas expressed doubt that the proposal would be accepted by France; inquired whether the United States would be willing also to submit the question of claims to arbitration, although he was not prepared to commit his own government to that step; and appeared "strongly inclined to think that . . . [the United States] had no just claim for indemnity on the present Government of France, on account of injuries done to . . . commerce under the authority of Napoleon." Damas also observed that, despite the spoliations, American commerce during the European war had been profitable, the United States had acquired Louisiana for a comparatively small price, and "since the restoration, . . . France had given to the United States no just cause of complaint." Summarizes his response to Damas' statement and reviews the further discussion of commerce and claims, at the conclusion of which Damas stated that he would consult the King [Charles X] on Brown's "proposition." Concludes: "I could not discover that conciliatory disposition on the part of France, which the United States had a right to expect from the manner in which they have conducted the negociation. I confess from the time at which I received the Baron de Damas' letter of the 11th. of November 1825 [cf. above, Brown to Clay, November 28, 1825], I have not been very sanguine in my hopes of a satisfactory arrangement with France. LS. DNA, RG59, Dip. Disp., France, vol. 23 (M34, R26). Received October 26.

From Francis Johnson

Dear Sir   (Private)   Bowling Green Ky 9h Sept. 1827

Inclosed I send you a Copy of a letter I recd. from Mr Ch A Wickliffe and my answer[1]— I felt some what surprized [sic], I must own, at his making such inquiries of me, and especially that he should call on me for statements in regard to conversations, which if they ever took place have in truth wholly escaped my recollection— It strikes me, more is meant by the month of '*January*' than to bolster up his statements— It may be found necessary to support the Hero—in his "Month of *Jany*,"[2] if not early in *January*—it is probably thought, "some time in *January*," is better than no time in *January*—

The circumstances to which I have alluded, as making it highly improbable, that you should have held such a conversation, in Jany are, these, first, I do not remember, that you ever stated, who you would vote for until the evening at Letchers[3] room, which must have been very late in January, perhaps the 29—that some few days before the Election, I urged you, for considerations that I named, to use your influence if you had any, to advance the side we had espoused, and that we deemed so essential to the best interest of the Country & the West, should succeed, that the peace safety & happiness of the country depended on Mr Adams Election, as I then clearly perceived & fully beleived [sic], and I thought it a duty every man owed the Country, to use all fair & Honorable means for success— That you replied, that you did not like, to do more, than to give your vote, that you thought it was as far as you ought to go—(substantially I mean) and I may have added and probably did; that since you had avowed your determination to support Mr Adams, I was well convinced your prostration was determined on—

another reason why I suppose you could not have *persuaded* Mr W. to vote for Mr A[4]— is, it was well known he had declared himself, early for Genl J, and added, that he had committed himself, by promising if you were not retd. to vote for the Genl.— Though I certainly can not say; that you did not converse with him on the subject & try to convince, him, but if you ever did do so—and that in my presence I have certainly forgotten it— I know my memory is not very retentive of circumstances, unless they make some impression at the time— Nor do I recollect the circumstance of Storrs,[5] telling you the N Y Jackson men had determined to Vote for Adams; tho, it strikes me Warfield[6] said certain members of N Y would vote for Mr Adams. Respectfully Yr friend   FR. JOHNSON

Hon. H. Clay

ALS. DLC-HC (DNA, M212, R2).
[1] Wickliffe, seeking corrobation for his claim, made to some of his constituents the previous summer, that Clay had twice tried to persuade him to vote for Adams, asked Johnson for a statement on the matter. Asserting that Johnson was present on both occasions, Wickliffe cited the "back room of Mr. [William H.] Prentiss' on the Pennsylvania Avenue" as the location for the first entreaty, while the second he remembered as having occurred "at Mr. Clays own room in the night some time in January." According to Wickliffe's version, Clay had left the latter meeting with "some person" who had knocked at the door and, upon returning, had told the company that "Mr [Henry R.] Storrs of N. Y. had just informed him that the Jackson members of N York had assured him that they would vote for Adams. . . ." Johnson denied having been present on either occasion and asserted that it was "highly improbable, that Mr Cl[ay] held conversations of that character with any one, at any time 'in the month of January,' preceding the Presidential Election—" Copies of Wickliffe to Johnson, September 4, 1827, and Johnson to Wickliffe, September 9, 1827, in DLC-HC (DNA, M212, R2).   [2] Jackson's dating of the purported overture on behalf of Clay as "Early in January, 1825," appeared in his letter to Beverley, June 6, 1827. In his letter "To the Public," of July 18, 1827 (see above, Smith to Clay, August 1, 1827, note), Jackson referred more loosely to the incident as "in January, 1825."   [3] Robert P. Letcher.   [4] Wickliffe; John Quincy Adams.   [5] Henry Randolph Storrs.   [6] Henry R. Warfield.

MISCELLANEOUS LETTERS   September 9, 1827

From ARTHUR LITHGOW, Boston. States that John Larkin Payson's commission as consul for Messina "has never reached him." Asks that another be forwarded; notes that "Hon Mr [Edward] Everet [sic] writes . . . on the Subject" (below, September 11, 1827); and adds: "Mr Payson is a near connextion [sic] of mine." ALS. DNA, RG59, Misc. Letters (M179, R65). Endorsed on cover by Daniel Brent: "Mr TH [Thomas L. Thruston] will please prepare & send a duplicate Commn. &c &c."

Lithgow, born in Maine, had been for several years sheriff of Kennebec County in that State before removing to the Charlestown area of Boston, where he was now inspector of customs. His daughter, Frances, had married Payson.

From John Bradford

Dr Sir   Lexington Sepr. 10h. 1827

Inclosed is an a/c for two publication's [sic], which I presume were not embraced in the draft you forwarded me.

There is also inclosed an a/c for two publications for the Navy dept—with copies cut out of the news papers in which they were published agreeably to the request of the Agt.[1]

I recd. a copy of the laws &c of the Washington Gymnasium,[2] for which accept my thanks;— I have also recd. from Wayland and others whose names I do not recollect the letters you forwarded respecting professor Woods.[3]— Mr Tilford has recd a letter from Mr. McCauly [sic] of New York to a Mr. McGoffin[4] a relation of his in Philadelphia in answer to a letter from Mr. Wilkins[5] to Mr. Tilford, which was put by Mr Tilford in the hands of McGoffin in order to ascertain whither [sic] McCauley could be obtained— From Mr. McCauleys letter to his friend a principle [sic] object with him seems to be salary, as well as to use his own discretion with regard to religious tenets, as he inquires whither any and what are the restrictions with regard to them.— From present prospects I despair of getting the University again into oporation [sic]. Accept the assurances of my sincere respects.

                                                      JOHN BRADFORD

P.S.   Since writing the above I recd. yours of the 27h ult covering the letters to you from Governor Knight & Senator Robins [sic].[7]

                                                              J. B.

ALS. DNA, RG59, Accounting Records. Addressed to Clay.
[1] On September 29, 1827, William Browne sent Bradford a draft for $14 for State Department advertizing and $23 to settle his account against the Navy Department. Copy, in DNA, RG59, Dom. Letters, vol. 32, p. 58 (M40, R20).   [2] Cf. above, Bradford to Clay, August 11, 1827.   [3] Francis Wayland, Jr.; Alva Woods—cf. above, Clay to Bradford, August 22, 1827.   [4] John Tilford; Thomas McAuley. McGoffin has not been identified.   [5] Charles Wilkins.   [6] Tranyslvania University.   [7] Nehemiah R. Knight; Asher Robbins.

From Robert Scott

Dear Sir,   Lexington 10 Septr. 1827.
    Your favor of the 27 Ulto.[1] has been received and also Mr. Jones's letter to you of the 14th.[2] on the subject of the land located by Genl. Lytle—
    In the schedule annexed to Colo. Morrison's Will, he states, "934 Acres located by Genl. Wm. Lytle on the Miami—in the location there is 1400 Acres, and Genl. Lytle is entitled to the balance for locating— @ 2$.—1868$""[3]—being one third. Those 934 Acres were conveyed to James Holmes in part of his legacy[4]— On examination of Genl. Lytle's accounts and Colo. Morrison's letters to him, I found that Colo. M.s 2/3 ds. of the 400 Acres had been sold by his authority and nearly accounted for by Genl. Lytle—perhaps quite accounted for—see his Accts. you have them— It appears then, that instead of 934 Acres, there remained to the estate but 2/3 ds. of 1000 or 666 2/3 Acres—leaving a deficit in the quantity conveyed to Holmes of 267 1/3 Acres— In May and June 1825 I recd. two letters from a Mr Henry Avery on the subject of this land[5]—they are enclosed herewith— I do not know what to advise as to the price of the land, I should suppose it high—but it

would be advisable I think to acquire it, even at a Small sacrifice and confirm the title to Holmes—

Enclosed herewith also, is a letter from a Mr Kouns, who states himself successor to Williams & Caldwell, Trustees of the late Genl. Wilkinson[6]—and a copy of an agreement between said Williams & Caldwell and Colo. Morrison[7]— What Mr. Kouns states of the sale of the land by Colo. Morrison to Genl. Poague for 1500$. and transfer of the Notes on Shreve &c. is correct— The amt recd including interest is 1809.$90 and charges paid 92$81 leaving—1717$09—net balance— The General, Wilkinson, is indebted to Colo. Morrison's estate on an Acct. 144$69[8]—that I suppose we cannot retain— I have not answered Mr. Kouns— please instruct me—and say what evidence of his authority you will require and whether the charges according to the agreement, are not first to be deducted from the gross rects. and the net balance divided[9]—

On enquiry Mr. Harper[10] informed me that on the 22nd. Ulto. he forwarded to you, a statement of your Bank Acct.[11] On the 5th inst. I deposited to your credit 50$—making your Acct there equal to your check in favor of Mrs. Morrison[12]— she did not stand in need of the money, but supposing you had enough in Bank to meet it I took it in and did not like to bring it back— Mr. Beach[13] has not yet paid me & have no money on hand— He claims 25$— for conveying you to Maysville[14]—is it right? As to your check for 248$ in favr. of Theodore,[15] it will make no odds at present— I will hold it up until money comes in— I will attend to the collection of the notes in Genl. Bodleys[16] office, taken on acct. of your Dallam business[17]—

I have leased that part of the hotel occupied by Deverin[18] for 12 Ms. for 225$. excluding the Billiard room and including the Ice house until it may be wanting for the other tenement—

Henry Daniel has dismissed the suit brot. against me in the Montgomery Ct. Ct. relative to the negroes recovered of Garrett[19]—so I hope we are clear of that perplexity—

Mrs. Morrison speaks of setting out for Balto. in the course of the week— I shall however beleive [sic] her going doubtful until I see her off— very respectfully Your obt. Servt   ROBT. SCOTT
The Honble Henry Clay

ALS. DLC-TJC (DNA, M212, R13).   1 Not found.
2 Above, George W. Jones to Clay, August 14, 1827.   3 Fayette County Court, Will Book F, p. 73.   4 Cf. above, Lytle to Clay, August 3, 1825, and note.   5 Cf. above, Lytle to Clay, May 25, 1825. The letters have not been found.   6 Cf. above, Kouns to Executors, September 4, 1827.   7 Not found.   8 The item was listed as a "Bad" debt in Clay's Debt Account of Morrison's Estate, noted above, ca. August 12, 1826.
9 Clay's answer has not been found.   10 James Harper.   11 The statement, from the Lexington Branch of the Bank of the United States, has not been found.
12 Esther Montgomery Morrison. The check has not been found.   13 Jabez Beach (cf. above, Property Deed to Beach, August 2, 1826; Mortgage from Jabez and Ann M. Beach, same date; Scott to Clay, August 20, 1827).   14 On Clay's journey back to Washington in July of this year, cf. above, John Clay to Clay, August 10, 1827.

15 Clay's son. The check has not been found.   16 Thomas Bodley, Fayette County Circuit Clerk.   17 Cf. above, III, 296–98, 492, 882, 883; Receipt from Richardson, July 31, 1826, and note; Account with Smith, *ca.* August 12, 1826, and note.   18 John Deverin. Cf. above, Scott to Clay, August 20, 1827. On September 23, Norwood and Coghlan, not further identified, announced that they were opening "a Coffee House in the building formerly occupied by Mr John Deverin, on the North East side of the Public Square, where they . . . [would] constantly keep on hand a supply of the best liquors . . . [and] very superior beer. . . ." Lexington *Kentucky Gazette,* September 23, 1827.   19 Ashton Garrett. Cf. above, Scott to Clay, August 20, 1827. Presumably Daniel acted as attorney for the plaintiff.

To John J. Appleton

No. 4   John J. Appleton Chargé d'Affaires to Sweden
Sir   Department of State Washington 11th. Septr. 1827.

Mr Cucheval[1] arrived in this city on Saturday last (the 9th.[2] Instant), and delivered the Treaty of Commerce and navigation[3] which you had recently concluded and signed at Stockholm, together with your despatches No 18. 19. 20 & 21 with their accompaniments[4]— Numbers 1 to 17 inclusively had been previously received.

The absence of the President[5] from this city prevents my transmitting to you his opinions of the treaty, without subjecting Mr. Cucheval, who appears very anxious to return, to a longer detention than would be agreeable, or is, perhaps necessary— The few observations which I shall make must therefore be regarded as my own.

The provisions of the Treaty appear to me to be characterized by great liberality, and to come up entirely to any expectations which I had formed. The exceptions to the operation of its general principles are unimportant, and such as will not, I apprehend, create any difficulty in the ratification of the treaty— Although the trade of the Island of St Barthelemy is not very important, the principle which has been adopted in respect to it of perfect equality between the navigation of the two countries, must be considered as particularly acceptable.

I regret that the Treaty has not been signed in the English, as well as in the French language, as was the case with the two former treaties which were made with Sweden.[6] We ought always to insist upon the use of our own language, in forming our national engagements. The clause which you have introduced for the mutual surrender of deserters,[7] I think will create no difficulty, as it is in conformity to a spirit of liberality which has always actuated this Government.

I also regret that you did not succeed in prevailing upon the Swedish Government to consent to a restriction of the principle that free ships shall make free goods, to the nations that recognize it. The want of such a limitation in a treaty which we lately concluded with Mexico, was one among several objections which operated on the Senate of the United States, and induced it to ratify the Treaty upon the condition of its alteration in that, and some other, respects[8]— As neither the treaty of 1783 negotiated by Franklin,[9] nor that of 1816, which continued its principal stipulations contained any such qualification of the principle, I hope the want of it, in the present treaty will not be deemed by the Senate an insuperable objection.

Mr. Cucheval appears to have executed the trust you confided to him as a bearer of despatches, with zeal and precision— The arrangement which you made with him in regard to his compensation is approved, the amount which you stipulated to pay him, not exceeding that to which he would have been entitled, according to the long established allowances which are usually made to Bearers of despatches— We have advanced to him here the sum of $450, which with the $394.70 paid by you to him, are to be credited against the $1320 which you agreed to pay him, and the residue you will pay him and charge to the Government, on his arrival at Stockholm and delivery to you of the despatches with which he is now entrusted. From your representation of the assistance which he rendered you as a copyist during the negotiation there has been allowed and paid him the further sum of $100.—

In relation to the person who has been selected as Consul for the Island of St. Barthelemy,[10] you will express to the Minister of Foreign Affairs of Sweden,[11] due acknowledgments for the friendly spirit which has been manifested by the Swedish Government, in waiving any obj-ection which it might have felt itself authorized to make to the person selected. You will assure Count Wetterstedt that nothing was further from the intention of the President than the nomination of a person unacceptable to the King of Sweden and Norway.[12] It was believed that the difficulty which formerly arose between Mr. Harrison and the Governor of St Barthelemy,[13] was of a personal nature; and that it was, therefore altogether obviated by the removal of the Governor from the Island— Mr Harrison was designated on account of the confidence reposed in his zeal, experience and ability; and it is hoped his deportment will hereafter be entirely satisfactory both to the local authorities of the island and to the parental Government: But, if it should prove otherwise, the President will not fail effectually to interpose his authority— I am with great respect Your Obedt. Servant   H. Clay

Copy. DNA, RG59, Dip. Instr., vol. 11, p. 374 (M77, R6). LI Draft, partly in Clay's hand with his interlineations, in DLC-HC (DNA, M212, R8).
    [1] James Cucheval.   [2] That is, 8th.   [3] Cf. above, Appleton to Clay, July 11, 1827 (no. 20), and note.   [4] Above, Appleton to Clay, June 22, 1827, which bears a received date of August 25, Appleton to Clay, July 11, 1827 (two of the same date). No. 19, dated July 1, has been omitted by the editors as routine.   [5] Cf. above, Wharton to Clay, August 3, 1827, note.   [6] A treaty of amity and commerce, signed at Paris, in 1783, had expired 15 years after its ratification. Many of its provisions had been renewed in a treaty of amity, commerce, and navigation, signed September 4, 1816. Miller (ed.), *Treaties. . .* , II, 123–50, 601–16. Clay's statement is erroneous. Both these treaties had been written in French and that version signed. *Ibid.*, III, 305.   [7] Article 14 provided that consuls, vice-consuls, and commercial agents be "authorized to require the assistance of the local authorities for the arrest, detention, and imprisonment" of

deserters from "ships of war and merchant vessels. . . ." Upon demand "in writing,"
with documentary proof, surrender of the deserter was not to be refused. If he were not
sent back to his ship within two months, he was to be freed. If he had been charged
with a crime his release might be delayed until the proper tribunal announced sentence
and that sentence had been carried into effect. *Ibid.*, 294.   8 Cf. above, Poinsett to
Clay, July 12, 1826.   9 Benjamin Franklin.   10 Robert Monroe Harrison.
    11 Count Gustave de Wetterstedt.   12 Charles XIV.   13 Cf. above, Harrison to
Clay, May 21, June 9, 1827; Appleton to Clay, July 11, 1827 (no. 21).

To John J. Appleton

J. J. Appleton
Dear Sir,   (Private)   Dept. of State, Washington Septr. 11th. 1827.
    Since the arrival of Mr. Cucheval with the despatches, which he
bore,[1] I have received your letter of the 13th. July,[2] transmitting, enclosed, that of the Count of Wetterstedt, referred to in your letter of
the 12th. but which did not accompany it, as was your intention. In
respect to the two engraved portraits of the King,[3] to which the Count's
letter refers, although their value be inconsiderable, it would have
been better if you had declined their acceptance. The rule of the
Constitution, which prohibits the acceptance of presents,[4] is simple,
inflexible, and without any qualification. If it once be departed from,
and another rule, that of the value of the donation, be substituted,
there will be great difficulty in its practical application; and in the
end there is danger, that Articles of value will come to be considered
as acceptable, which, in the beginning would have been promptly declined. The same observations apply to the iron medal, which Count
Wetterstedt designed for me.— Although my acceptance of it is not,
perhaps, strictly within the prohibition of the Constitution, I should
have been better satisfied, if it had not been received. As it is, I shall
deposit it in the Department of State, and I will thank you to make
my acknowledgments to the Count de Wetterstedt for his recollection
of me. The Medal is a beautiful Specimen both of the flourishing
State of the Arts in Sweden, and of one of its richest productions.—
    I communicated, in due time, to the President the wish which you
expressed to me of bringing home, yourself, the Treaty which has
been lately concluded.[5] With every disposition to accede to any reasonable request which you might make, as you had not the plea of
sickness to offer, nor that of visiting your own proper family, and as
you had but lately reached Stockholm, the President did not think it
expedient that you should leave your post. I did not inform you at
the time, because you intimated the alternative you would pursue, in
the event of your not obtaining permission to return home. After the
treaty shall be mutually ratified, and put into operation, you will
have been longer at Stockholm, and the obstacles to your return will
be diminished.—

Mr. Cucheval takes with him the Acts of the two last Sessions of Congress as desired by you, to which Mr. Brent[6] will add such of the public documents as belong to your mission, and which have not been, hitherto, transmitted— An advance has been made to Mr. Cucheval of such a sum, on account of the compensation which you have stipulated him to receive, as was satisfactory to him— I have also made him an allowance for the assistance which he had rendered you as a clerk, during the progress of your late Negotiation.—

Reciprocating the friendly sentiments and wishes which you have expressed toward me.— I am with great respect, Your obedt. Servant,

H. CLAY.

Copy. DNA, RG59, Unofficial Letter-Book of Henry Clay, 13–14.
[1] James Cucheval—cf. above, Clay to Appleton, this date.   [2] Cf. above, Appleton to Clay, July 12, 1827, note.   [3] Charles XIV.   [4] Art. I, sec. 9.   [5] Cf. above, Appleton to Clay, April 7, July 11, 1827.   [6] Daniel Brent.

To Joseph Blunt

Dear Sir   (Private)   Washington 11h. September 1827

I recd. your favor of the 8h. inst.[1] which I have deliberately perused. I regret exceedingly the existence of the differences between the friends of the Administration, to which you refer, and agree entirely with you in thinking that the time has arrived when it is highly desirable that they should be buried. I cannot admit that the Admin is justly chargeable with neglect towards its friends, but I have neither time nor is it necessary, I hope, to enter in its vindication.

I have no doubt of the good effect which would follow from the adoption of the measures you suggest by the Legislatures of the different States to which you refer. The difficulty is in our friends prevailing on the Magistrates to adopt them. The election has not yet taken place in Maryland of members to their Legislature. It occurs next month. There is much reason to hope for a decided majority.[2]

I think myself that the great struggle is now to be in your State. Without intending it, the course which has been pursued there of re-electing Mr. V. Buren[3] &c. &c. has done more than any thing else to invigorate the cause of the Opposition.

If the vote of N. York should be given to Mr. Adams,[4] he is safe, but if he should lose it, or a majority of the elections, there is great probability of the election of his competitor.

This being the case, I should think, that the great aim of Mr. Adams's friends in N. York would be to give such a character to the next legislature as will ensure the passage of a general but popular ticket. If that object were effected, there would be an end of all troubles. Otherwise we shall have more turbulence, more bitterness and more exasperation between parties than have ever been seen in this Country heretofore.

Our information from the City of N. York is that it is very uncertain which way the majority is. From the Country, and especially from the Western part of your State accounts are more favorable.[5] I am respectfy Your ob. Servant   H Clay

J Blunt Esq

ALS. DLC-HC (DNA, M212, R2).   [1] Not found.
[2] Held on October 1, the election brought victory to 49 administration supporters and 31 Jacksonians. The administration forces triumphed in both the eastern and western districts of the State. Washington *Daily National Intelligencer*, October 8, 1827.
[3] Cf. above, Clay to Porter, June 22, 1826, note.   [4] Cf. above, Clay to Brown, March 27, 1827, note.   [5] Cf. above, Porter to Clay, May 1, 1827, note; Rose to Clay, June 16, 1827; Rochester to Clay, August 1, 1827.

From John Quincy Adams

Henry Clay—Secretary of State—Washington.

Dear Sir   Quincy 11 September 1827.

I have received your Letters of the 25th. 27th. and 30th. ulto. with copies of despatches from Mr Gallatin and Mr Appleton;[1] and two Letters relating to the Post Office at New York.[2] On my passage through that City I saw General Bailey[3] who did not indicate any intention of resigning and I understood that he had no such intention.

Since the perusal of Mr Gallatin's despatches it appears to me to be most advisable to wait until we hear further from him before we give him new instructions with regard to the modifications proposed by the British Government to the Convention of 1815 upon its renewal. The discrimination between rolled and hammered iron[4] is an object not of magnitude to stake upon it the renewal of the whole Convention. From the experience we have had it seems scarcely possible that any project of Settlement on the North West Coast should within ten years receive the sanction of Congress— But if it should the stipulation, that either party may with twelve months notice annul the Convention,[5] would enable them to undertake it as freely as if we had no engagement of forbearance— I should nevertheless prefer the renewal of the Convention unaltered   Yours sincerely.

Copy. MHi-Adams Papers, Letterbook, Private, no. 10, pp. 94–95. Copy, dated September 4, 1827, in InHi-William H. Smith Collection.
[1] Albert Gallatin; John J. Appleton. Clay does not mention, in his letters to which Adams refers, the transmittal of any dispatch from Appleton. Presumably, Appleton's no. 18 (above, June 22, 1827), received August 26, was enclosed with Clay's letter of August 27 or that of August 30.   [2] Clay mentions (above, August 27) the enclosure of only one letter on this subject; he probably transmitted the communication from Seth Hunt (above, August 26, 1827), now in the Adams Family Papers, with his letter of August 30.   [3] Theodorus Bailey.   [4] See above, Gallatin to Clay, May 29, June 20, 1827; Clay to Adams, August 16, 30, 1827; Adams to Clay, August 23, 1827.   [5] Cf. above, Gallatin to Clay, June 20, 23, 27, 1827.

From John Sergeant

Dear Sir,   (Private)   Philada. Septr. 11. 1827.

Mr. Markley has never called upon me, notwithstanding his promise.[1] For some days, he has been out of town. If you think it of importance, I will endeavour to get hold of him. For reasons which I cannot well explain, it appears to me of little moment. Mr. Roberts,[2] however, who is now in the City, is of a different opinion.

Every thing here (in the City) is going on as well as possible. Every difficulty is yielding, and the election will afford an opportunity of bringing out our whole strength in the most favorable manner, so that the appearance will be fully equal to the reality, and I hope very imposing. The truth is, that in the City, the administration is strong, and there is much zeal among a class of people from whom I expected little more than a cold vote. The *mode* of combining, has occasioned the most trouble, and is not yet entirely settled; but it is every moment becoming easier, as men become more earnest about the object.[3] Some of our friends now calculate upon a majority of 1500 to 1800. That is too large. The whole vote will not be more than 4500.[4]

Some progress seems also to be making in the County of Philadelphia. Our friends have organized themselves, and are rallying in more strength than was anticipated. They talk now with confidence of carrying their ticket. I am afraid they are too sanguine. But they will have a good vote.[5]

In other parts of the State, there is not as much gain as I hoped for, and there are some *relapses*. You have perhaps heard of the fate of Ritner, of Washington County, Speaker of our Legislature. (H. R.) After leading every one to believe he was with us, he lately came out for Jackson, the election in his County being near at hand.[6] He has been left off the ticket, by common consent, a fate he well deserved, and nobody will now care which side he takes. I firmly believe, however, that we shall have the vote of this State.[7] It will require steady and patient exertion. Very respectfully & truly Yrs.   JOHN SERGEANT.

The Honble Henry Clay.

ALS. DLC-HC (DNA, M212, R2).   [1] Cf. above, Sergeant to Clay, August 23, 1827.
[2] Probably Jonathan Roberts.   [3] Cf. above, Markley to Clay, April 28, 1827, and note.   [4] Sergeant won the Congressional election (cf. above, Sergeant to Clay, September 28, 1826, note) in the city of Philadelphia by a scant margin, 2702 votes for Sergeant to 2557 for his opponent, Joseph Hemphill. Philadelphia *United States Gazette*, October 10, 1827. The whole Republican ticket was, however, elected over "the martial one" in Philadelphia city. Washington *Daily National Intelligencer*, October 14, 1827.

[5] Three new delegates were elected to the legislature from the county. All were identified as Democrats, as opposed to Federalists, but their attitude toward administration policies has not been found. The Washington *Daily National Intelligencer*, October 17, 1827, reported a marked increase in administration support in both the city and the county of Philadelphia and the adjacent counties of Montgomery and Berks. Cf. also, Klein, *Pennsylvania Politics*, 226.   [6] Joseph Ritner had published a letter "To the Public," dated August 22, 1827, announcing that he had voted for Jackson in 1824 and

that he intended to vote for him "at the ensuing election." *Harrisburg Chronicle*, reprinted in the *New York Evening Post*, September 7, 1827.   7 Cf. above, Clay to Brown, March 27, 1827, note.

INSTRUCTIONS AND DISPATCHES   September 11, 1827

To ALBERT GALLATIN, no. 34. Transmits "the copies of a letter and map" sent by Edward Livingston (see above, Livingston to Clay, August 7, 1827) "to aid . . . in the proposed arrangements respecting the establishment of Lights on the Bahama Banks for the security of navigation in that quarter." LS. NHi-Gallatin Papers (MR15). Copy, in DNA, RG59, Dip. Instr., vol. 11, pp. 376–77 (M77, R6); L draft, in Daniel Brent's hand, in DLC-HC (DNA, M212, R8).

To FRANKLIN LITCHFIELD. Quotes, in reply to (Litchfield's) letter of July 20, 1826, "The 4th. Section of the Act of Congress of Feby. 28th. 1803" and concludes: "As neither this section, nor any other provision of the Laws on the same subject deprives an American seaman, because he has acted in a foreign service, of his title to the protection of the Consuls and other Commercial functionaries of the United States, you will therefore continue to extend it to all seamen being Natives as well as Citizens of the United States, who may appear before you, or be found under destitute circumstances. In every such instance it is expected, however, that you will act with strict regard to economy." Copy. DNA, RG59, Cons. Instr., vol. 2, pp. 442–43 (M78, R2).

   Article 4 of 2 *U. S. Stat.*, 203–205, provided the basic instruction requiring consular assistance to distressed seamen (cf. above, Pleasonton to Clay, April 19, 1825, note).

From ALBERT GALLATIN, London, no. 114. Reports his inability to obtain a copy of the document requested in Clay's "despatch No. 29" (above, May 15, 1827); encloses a "copy of the Report, as it was first published." Encloses also "a letter from the Board [of Trade] to the ship owners [of London], dated 21st March 1827, with the report thereon of their Committee, which . . . will elucidate the views of both the ship owners and Government on the navigation laws of this Country." ALS. DNA, RG59, Dip. Disp., Great Britain, vol. 34 (M30, R30). Received November 3.

MISCELLANEOUS LETTERS   September 11, 1827

From EDWARD EVERETT, Boston. States that "Mr [John Larkin] Payson, lately appointed Consul of the U.S. at Messina, has not received his Commission" and requests that another be issued (cf. above, Lithgow to Clay, September 9, 1827). Encloses, in response to the letter (from Daniel Brent) to Nehemiah Foster, June 11, 1827 (see above, Foster to Clay, June 4, 1827, note), the latter's "Original papers" relative to his claim against Colombia. Notes that Foster's "claim is for about $200, which is to him a great sum," and invites "the attention of the Department to it. . . ." ALS. DNA, RG76, Misc. Claims, Colombia (MR1). In another letter to Clay, dated September 28, 1827, Everett asked that Payson's commission be sent to himself (Everett). ALS, in DNA, RG59, Misc. Letters (M179, R65).

From JAMES LINSEY, Westfield (New York). Alludes to his letter to the Secretary of State "dated the 1st of this instant," which enclosed a copy of the deed that "secured" to him a tract of 8,000 acres in Harrison County, (West) Virginia, by transfer of rights obtained under act of Congress of July 14, 1798 (1 *U. S. Stat.*,

597–604). States that he wants the matter brought to the attention of every active officer in the United States, that they "should be made aquinted [*sic*] with the Circumstances of the land business. . . ." Protests that he has lost 15 years improvement, the expense of survey, and court costs. ALS. DNA, RG59, Misc. Letters (M179, R65).

The cited statute provided for the levy of a direct tax and included authorization for property liens for unpaid taxes.

From Thomas J. Randolph

Dear Sir   Edgehill Sep 12 1827

About a month since and after my departure to the springs whither I had gone in pursuit of health, a piece[1] appeared in the Virginia Advocate printed in Charlottesville, signed Th. M. Randolph senr., purporting to be the opinion of my grand-father,[2] relative to certain men and measures. I had hoped to have seen our mutual friend Judge Brook [*sic*] at the springs,[3] thro whom I proposed to communicate to you the views and feelings of my grand-father's family upon the subject; but he had left there by a different rout [*sic*] before I reached there. We feel it due to ourselves, and to the memory of my grandfather, to enter an entire disclaimer as to the opinions expressed therein, and I feel assured that you will not require our solemn asseveration to believe, that as to yourself particularly, my grandfather never expressed or entertained the opinions therein ascribed to him. The unfortunate tone and temper of my father's mind had for 20 years precluded confidential communication between them. There were long intervals, one of two years at one time, in which breakfasting, dining and supping, at the same table there was no communication, and for the twelve months preceding his death with a short interval of a few weeks about August 1825 none whatever. During his illness he saw him but once, for a few moments, until the night immediately preceding his death when he was insensible. These facts shew that he was at least not likely, to be a correct reporter of his opinions. As the husband of his only child[4] who with her children[5] had lived with him from their cradles, and were to him as his own children, his letters of June, July 25 and Jany. 26 now published,[6] shew but but [*sic*] futile efforts to reclaim the husband of that daughter.

Unpleasant as the task is I have felt it due to you, and to the memory of my grandfather, to sever ourselves from my father in this matter and *confidentially* to state the above facts, which altho notorious in the vicinity, would not be proper to be publicly divulged by a member of my father's family and particularly by myself who have ever been peculiarly the object of his bitterest hatred.[7] With great respect, Yours, The Hon'bl. Henry Clay, Washington.   TH. J. RANDOLPH.

Copy. InHi.   [1] Cf. above, Hammond to Clay, August 29, 1827, note.
[2] Thomas Jefferson.   [3] Cf. above, Brooke to Clay, August 8, 1827.   [4] Martha

Jefferson Randolph, of Jefferson's six children, alone survived him.   ⁵ Twelve in number, identified in Gaines, *Thomas Mann Randolph*, 37, 44, 51, 71, 78, 94, 104, 106.
    ⁶ Cf. above, Randolph to Clay, September 1, 1827, note.   ⁷ For a discussion of the relationship between the father and son, see Gaines, *Thomas Mann Randolph*, 155–57, 159–60, 186.

INSTRUCTIONS AND DISPATCHES   September 12, 1827

To ALBERT GALLATIN, no. 35. Acknowledges receipt of his dispatches "to No. 101" (above, August 6, 1827); notes that "it appears from the last" that he "had concluded and signed conventions for the renewal of the Commercial Convention of 1818, and upon the subject of the North Western Boundary line"; promises to "again peruse all . . . [his] dispatches very soon, and . . . then transmit . . . any remarks which they may seem to call for"; and congratulates him "upon . . . having brought the negotiations upon the two subjects to a conclusion which . . . must prove satisfactory to the Government of the United States." LS. NHi-Gallatin Papers (MR15). Copy, in DNA, RG59, Dip. Instr., vol. 11, p. 377 (M77, R6); L draft, in Daniel Brent's hand, with interlineations by Clay, in DLC-HC (DNA, M212, R8). Published in Manning (arr.), *Diplomatic Correspondence . . . Canadian Relations*, II, 135.

MISCELLANEOUS LETTERS   September 12, 1827

From SAMUEL BLAIR, St. Augustine. Reports the arrival of a communication from the State Department to Waters Smith, enclosing the petition of James Hall (cf. above, Adams to Clay, August 15, 1827); requests, as Smith's representative "in all cases of this nature," that since Smith has "gone to Key West in the discharge of his official duty," further action be postponed until his return, so that he can forward pertinent documents; explains that Smith stopped the cutting of timber on the land which Hall claims, pending review before the Board of Commissioners for the Adjustment of Land Claims. ALS. DNA, RG59, A. and R. (M531, R7).

From E[DWIN] LEWIS, Mobile, Alabama. Protests the refusal of the United States Government to recognize his claim, under a Spanish grant, to a large amount of land. Notes that he had "before stated" to Clay his interest in this matter (no earlier communication of this nature has been found); cites (James) Madison's "proclamation in 1810" which promised protection to the inhabitants of the area annexed; charges that "intruders," rather than the early claimants, receive governmental protection; states that a bill before Congress "last year was very excellent except the limiting the power of the Commissioners to confirm only 10,000 acres"; and closes with his "warmest wishes" to Clay. ALS. DNA, RG59, Misc. Letters (M179, R65).
    No reference has been found concerning the Lewis claim. President Madison's proclamation, of October 27, 1810, extended the government of the United States over the Territory "south of the Mississippi Territory and eastward of the river Mississippi and extending to the river Perdido. . . ." Richardson (comp.), *A Compilation of the Messages and Papers of the Presidents*, I, 480–81.
    Lewis's reference to the proposed legislation probably alluded to House Bill no. 19, "An Act to confirm certain claims to land in the Territory of Florida, founded on habitation and cultivation," which had passed the House of Representatives but had been indefinitely postponed in the Senate. U. S. H. of Reps., *Journal*, 19 Cong., 1 Sess., p. 606.

From James Brown

My dear Sir,   (private and strictly confidential)   Paris Sept. 13. 1827

You will receive by this opportunity a dispatch from me[1] by which you will find that the proposed arbitration is in a fair way of experiencing the fate you anticipated[2]— I did myself apprehend that France presuming from the strenuous and persevering manner in which we had refused to connect the treaty question and claims in the same negociation might have offered to submit them to the same reference in hopes that we would reject that offer— It was my intention at first to have sent a note to the Minister of foreign affairs[3] in which I should have engrafted your Instructions[4] so far as they contain a narration of the facts and arguments and circumstances of the negociation. I thought however that you had prepared that paper with a view of submitting it in extenso to Congress whenever circumstances might require it[5] and I therefore to leave you the credit of an excellent State paper preferred in the first instance to relate its contents in a conference and refer to them generally as you find I have done in the Dispatch which I now send you. Tell me candidly whether in doing so I have complied with your expectations. It would seem as if France has no wish to leave the ground on which she now stands and I sometimes doubt whether that the ground now taken by Baron de Damas was not always kept in view as one to which she would retreat and obstinately occupy when driven from every other. How long Baron de Damas may delay a definitive answer* I am unable to say but I have feared ever since his letter of 11 Novr. 1825 that he had irrevocably made up his mind to adhere to the principle stated in that letter.[7]

It is with you to judge what will be done in that event. Your claimants will ask for vigorous measures, perhaps for war or for some thing that will end in an appeal to hostilities. The first effect of war will as I think be the entire loss of their claims that is if the present State of things in Europe undergoes no change. For it is obvious to every man of reflexion that we are not in a situation to force France to acknowledge our claims after putting her to the expence [sic] of a war on account of them. In a maritime War we have as much to lose and more than France as our commerce is more widely spread upon the face of the Ocean and as she may resort to means which have lately been in use in destroying commerce[8] and for which she would find ready instruments in the unprincipled population of other nations. You will reflect that the party spirit now prevailing in Congress may possibly give auxiliaries to the French manner of looking at the subject and that the commercial and agricultural interests may revolt at the idea of increasing the debt and of interrupting the commercial pursuits of our Merchants. It is worthy of consideration whether we ought not to wait for a more favorable state of opinion at home and of circumstances abroad before we advance so far on certain questions as not to be permitted to make an honorable retreat should we be found unwilling to go all lengths. These points are made with much diffidence I have the highest confidence in the prudence of the administration and in the calm good sense of the people.

As to my own standing here I have personally every reason to be satisfied with it— I have however felt a great deal of mortification at my inability to be useful to my country and would cheerfully return if the Government thought that a change in a Minister here could promote the public interests. Mr. Adams told me when I had last the pleasure of seeing him that the French Government would give me a great deal of trouble and I believed what he said because I supposed I should soon after my arrival be engaged in an active and perplexing correspondence. I have not been disappointed in the anxiety, and vexation but in the cause of that anxiety. I have been vexed and mortified that I have never had the field of discussion fairly opened to me, but have been kept aloof from it by the unwillingness of this Government to discuss any thing. I fear Mr Gallatin[9] will not succeed much better in England than I have in France   I am told Mrs. Gallatin wishes very much to come to France and Mr. Gallatin to return to the United States.[10]

I was pleased to find in the papers your denial of the charge contained in General Jacksons letter to Beverley.[11] It will be difficult to persuade any reflecting man that you have compromitted [sic] yourself by a proposal of that kind to your political enemy & it will puzzle the General to assign a good reason for witholding [sic] the accusation when he could have made such use of it if true on the Kremer controversy[12] and when your nomination was before the Senate.[13] Mr Astor[14] writes me that the opinion of New York is rapidly changing in favor of Mr Adams. I hope you will preserve your temper and health throughout the trial which will I believe terminate as you have always predicted.

Mr Mareuil[15] is here and I have heard is not very well pleased with his residence in America. Baron de Damas asked me if I had received instructions from you to make some alterations in the conventions [sic].[16] I told him that I had received a Communication of the Correspondence of Mr Mareuil and yourself respecting the duties, but that I presumed the Count de Menou had received instructions relative to that subject He said he had, and that the French Govt. could not continue the Convention unless they could obtain from us some commercial advantages. He complained of the high duties.[17] I told him that I could consume French wines at a lower price in New York than that at which they sold in Paris and that it would seem extraordinary, that when our duties were not half [. . .][18] as the duties for entering Paris, that any complaints of excess over duties should be heard— He

observed that the complaint was more particularly of the duty demanded on Brandy and Silk.[19] I told him that the agricultural portion of our population in consequence of the prohibition on their bread stuffs[20] were obliged to sell them in the form of spirits and that they wished to increase the consumption of their own spirits by imposing certain duties of [sic] those imported from other Countries. I observed that an influence of the same kind exerted in France by the producers of Laces was no doubt the cause of the high duties or rather of the Monopoly on that article. I told him that the United States had always felt, and still felt disposed, to do all that that was consistent with the interest of their own agriculture, commerce, and revenue, to increase the imports from France and that any propositions having that for their object would receive the deliberate consideration of my Government. I hope to hear from you as soon as possible on these points and also respecting the claims if an answer is not pressed upon me before your letter arrives. Yours, truly   J. B.
Hon. Henry Clay.

* The King has gone to St. Omer[6] and will not return before the last of this month.

ALS. DLC-HC (DNA, M212, R2).   [1] Above, September 8, 1827.
[2] Cf. above, Clay to Brown, May 30, 1827.   [3] Baron de Damas.   [4] Above, Clay to Brown, May 28, 1827.   [5] If submitted to Congress, the instructions were not published during the Adams administration. The document was included in the papers transmitted to Congress by Andrew Jackson on January 17, 1833, and published as *House Docs.*, 22 Cong., 2 Sess., no. 147, pp. 5–18.   [6] Charles X had gone to St. Omer to review the army, assembled in a resplendant display to counteract the agitation which had accompanied the disbanding of the Parisian National guard (cf. above, Brown to Clay, May 12, 1827). See J. Lucas-Dubréton, *Le Comte d'Artois, Charles X, Le Prince, L'Emigré, Le Roi* ([Paris, c. 1962]), 164–66.   [7] Cf. above, Brown to Clay, November 28, 1825.   [8] Privateering.   [9] Albert Gallatin.   [10] Cf. above, Gallatin to Clay, December 30, 1826; April 7, 1827; Clay to Gallatin, February 24, 1827; Clay to Webster, April 20, 1827.   [11] Above, "To the Public," June 29, 1827.   [12] Cf. above, Clay to Gales and Seaton, January 30, 1825; Kremer to Clay, *ca.* February 3, 1825; Appeal to the House, February 3, 1825, and note.   [13] Cf. above, Commission as Secretary of State, March 7, 1825, note.   [14] John Jacob Astor.   [15] Baron Durant de Mareuil.
[16] Of 1822. Cf. above, III, 53n; Brown to Clay, June 28. August 13, 30, 1827.
[17] Cf. above, Mareuil to Clay, April 28, 1826, note. For the specific American rates on wines, see *Niles' Weekly Register*, XXXIV (June 14, 1828), 251.   [18] Probably two words obliterated by tear in MS.   [19] The tariff on spirits made from materials other than grain, as enacted April 27, 1816, ranged up to 70 cents a gallon "of fifth proof." 3 *U. S. Stat.*, 312 (April 27, 1816). Under the legislation of 1824 the American duty on silks imported from nations other than those "beyond the Cape of Good Hope" was 20 per cent ad valorem. 4 *U. S. Stat.*, 26.   [20] In 1819 the French had introduced a scale of import duties on cereals that, like the British corn laws, fluctuated according to the domestic price level and prohibited imports when the price fell below a fixed limit. Frank Arnold Haight, *A History of French Commercial Policies* (New York, 1941), 18.

From Josiah S. Johnston

Washington [*i.e.*, Philadelphia] Thursday Morng.
Dear Sir   [September 13, 1827]
I have seen many of our friends here & I perceive a higher tone & finer spirit, than has been manifested here before.

I saw Mr. Sargeant [sic][1] last evening he says there is an increased Animation in the Cause throughout this State and attended with the best affect— Several Presses are establishing at important points— There will be one in this City, one in Lancaster (& one in Carlisle as soon as possible) & several others are expected[2]— They begin to form meetings & to Unite & ascertain their strength— He says all [th]ings are now working well— The excitement in this State [h]as been as it has every Where else on one side—& if the people are not Aroused, that side will Controul the Elections & govern the Country by this sort of violence[3]— In this City Causes are now Working to bring the parties to the sticking point— The Election for Congress is to be re-newed[4]—   The Federal party have had a meeting to Consider of the nomination of Mr. Sargeant[5]— They can hardly forgive the refusal before[6]—& they are very obstinate— I have no doubt they will either Nominate him or from pride refuse to nominate While [th]ey will determine to support him   The democratic party will nominate him[7]— There is no doubt entertained here of the result[8]—& it will have the happyest effect upon the State—   a Triumph here is very important in its influence & it is desirable Now More than ever, Since the Late occurrences here

The resolutions relative to your visit have roused a better spirit here— But I believe these Jackson Men are ready for any thing— They marshall in their ranks a class of Men, not easily Contrould—in popu-lar excitement— It appears to me that in this City & probably in the State Society is Cut horizontally, leaving only a few political Leaders.

I have seen Markley—he says that Buchanan, Came to him & held such a Conversation[9]— That B. by making him the principal speaker & the most Conspicuous figure—has misrepresented the thing— But Markley thought as the affair now stands between B & the Genl. it was wiser to say nothing, Until we see how it will turn between them[10]— & in this opinion Mr. Sargeant Concurred— It is extremely Uncertain what Course the General will persue [sic] on reading Buchanans Let-ter— If he denounces Buchanan—it will be well to Let them fight the intriguers with their own weapons— We will stand by— Markley will when the proper time Comes, make a statement.[11]

It is said here that one of the principal duties of the Committee at Nashville is to keep the Genl. Cool—by keeping from [him] all papers & Letters calculated to excite him—

The Louisville paper I am told menaces Buchanan[12]   They threaten if he denies the fact, to come out upon him—   from this hint, which must be from authority, I augur they mean to sustain the Charge against Buchanan—& as they have without apology exposed him, they will not hesitate to Sacrefize [sic] him— We shall in a few days hear from Nashville   With great regard yr Obt Sert   J. S. JOHNSTON

ALS. InU. Addressed to Clay; postmarked: "13 SEP."   ¹ John Sergeant.
² On October 1 the *Pennsylvania Gazette* was begun at Philadelphia, published by
G. Taylor and Company, as an administration organ. On October 3, Cyrus S. Jacobs
issued the first number of the Lancaster *Reporter*, in support of the administration.
A. B. and R. K. Grosh about the same time acquired the *Marietta Pioneer* founded a
year earlier, also in Lancaster County, and pledged to convert it from political neutrality
to administration backing.   No new journal has been found at Carlisle, but two administration organs shortly appeared at Doylestown, in Bucks County—the *Bucks County
Intelligencer*, renamed when Elisha B. Jackson and James Kelly acquired the *Bucks
County Patriot* in early October, and the Bucks County *Political Examiner*, established
by F. B. Shaw and J. W. Bartleson in November.   Of the above-mentioned editors, the
Groshes were identified with an old Lancaster County family; Kelly later (1838) served
as clerk of the Bucks County Court of Quarter Sessions; and Francis B. Shaw, admitted
to the bar in 1800, was county district attorney from 1812 to 1850. The others have not
been identified.   ³ Cf. above, Sergeant to Clay, August 23, 1827, note.   ⁴ Cf.
above, Sergeant to Clay, September 28, 1826, note; below, Sergeant to Clay, September 13,
18, 21, 26, 1827.   ⁵ "Federal Republicans," as the party was denominated in Philadelphia, had met in ward meetings on August 28 to elect conferees to sit as a General
Board of Conferees for the ensuing election. Philadelphia *United States Gazette*, August
30, 1827. On September 21 the Board concluded that it was inexpedient to recommend
any candidate for the Congressional election. Federal Republicans friendly to the election of Sergeant, meeting on the 26th, endorsed this decision, but at the same time called
for support in Sergeant's behalf. *Ibid.*, September 27, 1827; Washington *Daily National
Journal*, September 25, 1827.   ⁶ See above, Sergeant to Clay, October 2, 1826.

⁷ The Democratic Party, like the Federalists, split on the nomination in Philadelphia.
The "Democratic General Ward Committee opposed to the election of General Jackson
as president" met some time before September 19 and nominated Sergeant as their
Congressional candidate. On September 20 their followers formally endorsed the stand
and appointed election officers. Philadelphia *National Gazette*, September 19, 1827;
Philadelphia *United States Gazette*, September 22, 1827.   This faction had, however,
been formed in reaction to the strong pressure of Jackson's supporters in ward meetings.
The Democratic Party, "through its regular [*sic*] constituted organs, expressly declined
nominating candidates for the twentieth Congress. . . ." Accordingly, on September 27
the friends of Jackson, in counteraction to the nomination by "the friends of the existing
administration," nominated Joseph Hemphill. Philadelphia *United States Gazette*, September 29, 1827.   ⁸ See above, Sergeant to Clay, September 11, 1827, note.   ⁹ Cf.
above, Smith to Clay, August 1, 1827, note.   ¹⁰ Cf. above, Webster to Clay, August
22, 1827, and note.   ¹¹ See below, Sergeant to Clay, October 31, 1827, note.

¹² Shadrach Penn's *Louisville Public Advertiser*, on August 25, 1827, concluded that
Buchanan's statement was "not one of that pointed and unequivocal character, which
his high standing as a gentleman and politician, authorised us to expect. . . ." It warned
that "Buchanan and the coalition" might be placed in "unenviable situations" if his
statements "proved to be directly at war with the tenor of his conversations . . . in
January, 1825. . . ."

From John Sergeant

Dear Sir,   (Private)   Philada. Septr. 13. 1827.

Our little affairs here are subject to the like changes as greater ones.
When I wrote a few days ago,¹ appearances were as favorable as possible. They have now become a little obscure, and there is some reason to apprehend confusion may ensue. What is most extraordinary is,
that a part of the disturbance proceeds from a quarter where (if it
had not been for the occurrences of last fall)² we should very naturally
have looked for cooperation. I hope every thing will yet go well. Of
course, I feel some interest in the matter on my own account. But this
consideration is of little weight in comparison with the great object

of giving support to the administration in Pennsylvania. Every thing admonishes us of the necessity of exertion, and yet some who profess to be with us, are so wedded to their own views, that one is really led to doubt their sincerity. We will do all we can, and will do it with the zeal which a good cause deserves, and we will not yield 'till we are clearly beaten. The greatest difficulty we can meet with, will be from the Federalists taking up some one who avows himself to be a friend of the administration.[3] In that case (which possibly may happen) the question will be, what course we shall pursue. The nomination will be made with no friendly view, it will not be acceptable to our best friends, and, upon a large scale, it will do no good. Yet, to oppose it by a separate nomination, may have the effect of bringing in the Jackson candidate.[4]

From these hints you will be able to perceive in some degree how matters now stand, and to understand what may turn up. I hope all may go well, but am not so confident as I was two days ago, Very respectfully and truly yrs   JOHN SERGEANT.
The Honble Henry Clay.

[Postscript]   Sept. 14.
I have just received your letter of the 12th.[5] The Kentucky elections[6] have done us some harm, undoubtedly, but that is only an additional motive for exertion with all who are not *rats*. I have never known a man suffer in his character, his conscience, or his peace of mind, by maintaining a good cause, whatever might be the issue, but I have known many a man ruined by success in a bad one. We are sure, therefore, sure of our own approbation, and that is the main point.

ALS. DLC-HC (DNA, M212, R2).   1 Above, September 11, 1827.
2 Cf. above, Sergeant to Clay, October 2, 1826.   3 Cf. below, Sergeant to Clay, September 21, 1827.   4 Joseph Hemphill.   5 Not found.   6 Cf. above, Clay to Taylor, April 4, 1827, note; Clay to Adams, August 25, 1827.

From Elizabeth Clay Watkins

My Dr. Son   Woodford[1] Kentucky Sept, 13th, 1827
    your Kind favour of the 14h. of August[2] Last by mail Came safe to hand a few days ago, I feal glad that you have got again to the bosom of your familey and found them all well   rest ashourd my Son I have been a grate deal worse since you last saw me then [sic] I was when I had the pleashure of seeing you,[3]   I am still very low   I can make out to woulk acroce the House with the help of a caine or some one to help me   I feal to day some what better having a good nights rest my Caugh is not as bad as it has been,—   your aunt Moss is very porley [sic] and has bien for 2 or 3 weeks   also her son Phillip is very low,[4] at present very little hope of their recovery   Mr. Blackburn[5] has been very poreley [sic] but is geting better so that he is able to attend to his

business also your sister[6] is well as to your brother Jno,[7] I have not seen him for 2 weeks I Expect him in a few days he was quite well when he left me, Mr. Watkins[8] still injoues his usuall health but much worne out by attending on me both night & day Mr. Watkins joines me in Love to you and Lucretia and the rest of the familey pray my right [sic] me when conveaniant and may God bless you all is the sincear [. . .][9] of your Mother ELIZABETH WATKINS Mr. Henry Clay

ALS. DLC-TJC (DNA, M212, R10). [1] County. [2] Not found. [3] During his last visit to Kentucky (cf. above, Clay to Erwin, June 3, 1827). [4] Elizabeth Watkins, born in 1755, an elder sister of Clay's stepfather, Henry Watkins, had married Edmund Wooldridge in Cumberland County, Virginia, in 1774. She had joined her husband in Kentucky at about the same time that Henry Watkins and his wife had moved to Woodford County. After Wooldridge's death in 1791, the widow had married John Moss, who also had died, in 1809, leaving, besides older sons and daughters, Phillip and Nashville Moss, not yet of age. Woodford County Court, Will Book A, 34–35, 99–100; C, 195–200. Phillip Moss, with whom his mother resided, on a farm of 200 acres in Woodford County, died October 20, 1827. Kentucky State Historical Society, *Register*, L (1952) 150. [5] William B. Blackburn. [6] Martha Watkins (Mrs. William B.) Blackburn. [7] Cf. above, John Clay to Clay, August 10, 1827. [8] Henry Watkins. [9] Word obliterated.

INSTRUCTIONS AND DISPATCHES September 13, 1827

From JOHN MULLOWNY, Tangier, no. 51. States that "Yesterday an Agent from His Majesty the Emperor [Abd-er-Rahman II] . . . sailed for Gibraltar in pursuit of vessels to equip for war, said to be of a small class, . . . probably of about 60 to 100 tons. . . ." Notes that "The British and Spanish affairs are both under difficulties which are on the increase" and that his "prediction [above, to Clay, May 22, 1827] relative to the British Consul [J. Douglas] . . . is verified, he left here on leave of absence" and, by order of the Emperor, will not be readmitted "to any port in the Empire." The Spanish consul, as expected (cf. above, Mullowny to Clay, June 26, 1827), has been directed "not to trouble His Majesty in future relative to any concerns of the South American States, as he had ascertained to his own satisfaction, that the United States of N. America had acknowledged them Free & Independent, at present his ports should be for their use, till a Consul from either should appear, and . . . he was prepared to do the same as the United States of N. America has done." Refers to further trouble between the Spanish Consul and the Bashaw (Mohamet Omemon) and to difficulties the French consul (Sourdeau) has brought on himself. Notes the advantage accruing to American shipping as a result of increased costs of "Insurance on french commerce . . . in the Mediterranean" (cf. above, Shaler to Clay, September 2, 1827); the appearance of an Algerine vessel off the port (of Tangier) despite the French blockade of Algiers (cf. above, Brown to Clay, May 29, June 9, 28, August 30, 1827; Shaler to Clay, September 2, 1827); and his continuing belief in the friendship of "His Majesty Muley Abdrahaman" for the United States. Recommends "a more liberal allowance to this Consulate in order to secure national respect as well as . . . personal security and comfort"; calls attention to his dispatch of February 15, 1826; and adverts to the benevolence shown to American citizens by "these people unjustly called Barbarians. . . ." Suggests that he be allowed "$4000 salary included [sic] say $2000 instead of the one under the letter of Octr. [22] 1825. . . ." Reports that "on the 5th. Inst. 9 Ships of war . . . passed up the Straits under Russian colours" (cf. above, Rainals to Clay, May 20, July 20, 25, 1827; Middleton to Clay, June 23, 1827; Brown to

Clay, June 28, July 12, 28, August 13, 30, 1827; below, Hughes to Clay, September 16, 1827; Lafayette to Clay, October 10, 1827; Ombrosi to Clay, November 6, 1827). ALS. DNA, RG59, Cons. Disp., Tangier, vol. 4 (M-T61, R4). Received November 17.

Sourdeau, not further identified, had been consul general for France in Morocco since at least 1818 and died there in 1829.

To Josiah S. Johnston

Dear Sir   Washn. 14h. Sept. 1827.

I have recd. your favor of yesterday, and thank you for the agreeable intelligence which it communicates. If we can succeed in the coming Maryland elections,[1] in the Delaware election,[2] and in that in the City of Philada.[3] our cause will be again put in good heart. From K. my late information is more encouraging. The partial defeat in the Congressional elections[4] has aroused our friends, and they think it will have ultimately good effect. Letcher[5] says he is more than ever confident of our cause prevailing. I think the exultation on the one side and the depression on the other will be found to be without any sufficient ground and that it will be temporary.

I am glad that you conversed with Markley. It may be necessary for him to come out in the end with *his* statement; 'though I think that not necessary until we hear from the Hermitage.[6] At the last date I saw from Nashville, Buchanan's statement had just reached there.[7]

If it won't give you any trouble, I will thank you to get Watson[8] to make me a couple of pair of pantaloons of Casimere [sic] (some dark color or mixt) that will answer for the fall and to wear with shoes exclusively, as I never wear boots. Ever Cordially Your friend
Mr. Johnston.   H CLAY

ALS. PHi.   1 Cf. above, Clay to Blunt, September 11, 1827, note.
2 See above, Clay to Taylor, September 7, 1827, note.   3 Cf. above, Sergeant to Clay, September 11, 1827, note.   4 Cf. above, Clay to Taylor, April 4, 1827, note.   5 Cf. above, Letcher to Clay, August 27, 1827.   6 Cf. above, Johnston to Clay, September 13, 1827, note.   7 Published in the *National Banner and Nashville Whig*, September 1, 1827.   8 Probably Charles C. Watson.

From Josiah S. Johnston

Dear Sir   Phil. Friday [September 14, 1827].

Mr. Fearne[1] a very respectable Gentleman & a Warm friend of the admt. invited me to meet last evening several persons, Zealously engaged in the Cause. I met Judge Burns, Mr. Trevors, Mr. Conner the Marshall [sic], Mr. McIlvain[2]— I found them indeed ardently espousing the Cause, & of great knowledge of men & parties through the State. Mr. McIlvain is a young Gentleman of Talent, of ardent character, & of extensive personal acquaintance He is Connected with the Board of Canal Commissioners[3] & has made a long excursion through the several Counties & has had intercourse with the principal men. He has promised me a Statement in Writing, which I will bring with me.[4] This is yet a Jackson State—but the Admt. is stronger & its friends more alive & active than I expected   There are decided majorities in many Counties. & the reaction is going on steadily— He thinks that Lancaster County is now with us. & that the Germans, slow to move, are turning to the admt.— In which he believes the Governor[5] will Continue to use his influence— These Gentlemen have the highest hopes of this State.

Mr. McIlvain is of Opinion, that the course which Genl. Jackson may persue [sic] towards Buchanan,[6] will have a decisive effect. Buchanan is waiting & many of his friends with anxiety for the Generals reply to his Letter— They are not satisfied with the Conduct of the General—They think it was an Unnecessary exposure & a violation of the Confidence of friends— That it was intended to sacrifize [sic] him— It is thought the Genl. has written him since the Beverly [sic] Letter,[7] that he must Corroborate it & that they have other evidence against him—& an article from a Louisville paper threatens him[8]— It is expected therefore that the Genl. will denounce him, & Buchanan [sic] friends are determind [sic] to adhere to him—& in that event they will have exposures to make— In this state of things nothing ought to be said about Buchanan— The prudence of the Committee,[9] may restrain the Genl.—otherwise we should have an open breach—& I am not sure there are not men here, who wish & who will advise the Genl. to Come out upon him—   he will want no advice   he will see & feel that he is in all material points Contradicted—   the story of Beverly is flatly Contradicted. He will not suffer himself to be placed in that situation, if he is at Liberty—

If he comes out openly upon B. it will then be a Struggle, between the friends of both—& B.s friends will turn against him— We may expect Some thing in a few days[10]—

I have advised them of the expediency of dividing their Counties into small divisions & appointing at least 100 men in each County to Conduct & superintend the Election & bring the people to the polls[11]— They say it will be Communicated to their friends & they will recommend a perfect Organization—   this is indispensable—

The Federalists will Support Sergeant although it is not determind to nominate him yet & I have no doubt of his Election[12]

You will See in Washington Mr. LeBriton [sic]—The clerk of the Supreme Court N. orleans—& his wife the daughter of Judge Derbigny[13]— I commend them to you but I believe Duralde[14] has written—

I believe I shall have to go to N. York tomorrow—

Nothing could be more Unwise than the publication of Mr. Jeffersons Letter with Giles notes in this State[15]   What can intimat [sic] more clearly the views of the Southern politicians. & What can be more fatal to the interests of this State. I shall give them the Commentary in this Letter— With great regards   J. S. JOHNSTON

ALS. InU. Addressed to Clay; postmarked: "SEP," with the date not clearly legible.
¹ Not identified.   ² Probably Joseph Burns; John Bond Trevor; John Conard; Abraham Robinson McIlvaine. Trevor, a merchant and banker, was appointed a director of the Bank of the United States in December, 1827, and for several years served in the Pennsylvania Legislature. McIlvaine, born in Delaware County, Pennsylvania, in 1804, was a Chester County farmer, member of the Pennsylvania House of Representatives (1836 and 1837), and of Congress (1843–1849).   ³ Cf. above, Sutherland to Clay, February 13, 1826, note.   ⁴ Not found.   ⁵ John A. Shulze.   ⁶ Cf. above, Webster to Clay, August 22, 1827, note.   ⁷ Cf. above, Report of Interview, ca. April 15, 1827. Jackson had written to Buchanan on July 15, expressing his hope for a statement upon the events of the "bargain." Basset (ed.), Correspondence of Andrew Jackson, III, 373–74.   ⁸ Cf. above, Johnston to Clay, September 13, 1827, note.   ⁹ Nashville Central Committee.   ¹⁰ Buchanan was the leader of the Jackson Federalists in Pennsylvania. Livermore, Twilight of Federalism, 238. Cf. above, Johnston to Clay, September 13, 1827, note.   ¹¹ On the lack of party organization encompassing the administration supporters in Pennsylvania, see Klein, Pennsylvania Politics, 218.   ¹² Cf. above, Johnston to Clay, September 13, 1827, note,   ¹³ Pierre Auguste Charles Derbigny; LeBretons, not further identified.   ¹⁴ Martin Duralde, Jr. His letter has not been found.   ¹⁵ On December 26, 1825, Thomas Jefferson had expressed to William B. Giles his "affliction" at observing "the rapid strides with which the federal branch of our government, is advancing toward the usurpation of all the rights reserved to the states, and the consolidation in itself, of all powers foreign and domestic, & that too by constructions, which if legitimate, leave no limits to their power." He had then proceeded to criticize the Federal support of protective tariffs and internal improvements, as well as the younger Federalist recruits, who "now look to a single and splendid government of an Aristocracy, founded on banking institutions and moneyed incorporations, under the guise and cloak of their favored branches of manufactures, commerce and navigation, riding and ruling over the plundered ploughman & beggared yeomanry." The letter had been published in the Richmond Enquirer, September 7, 1827, with a lengthy introductory comment by Giles pointing to Clay's "desideratum in political economy" as sketched in his speech upon the tariff of 1824 (see above, III, 695). For the full text of the letter, see Ford (coll. and ed.), Works of Thomas Jefferson, XII, 424–28.

DIPLOMATIC NOTES   September 14, 1827

To CHARLES R. VAUGHAN. Transmits an extract from Enoch Lincoln's letter to Clay, of September 3; notes the allegation, in that extract, concerning the acts sanctioned by New Brunswick "within the territory respectively claimed by the United States and Great Britain, inconsistent with that mutual forbearance which it has been understood . . . would be inculcated and practised on both sides"; and states that "a confident reliance is placed in the Government of His Brittanic Majesty to cause an immediate correction of the irregular proceedings of which complaint is made." Copy. DNA, RG59, Notes to Foreign Legations, vol. 3, pp. 387–88 (M38, R3). ALI draft, in CSmHi. Published in Manning (arr.), Diplomatic Correspondence . . . Canadian Relations, II, 136–38.

In a communication to Clay, marked "Private", dated September 16, 1827, Vaughan wrote: "The inclosed Note which I had the honour to receive from you yesterday has not been signed, by some accident— Pray have the goodness to sign it & send it back to me—" ALS, in DNA, RG59, Notes from British Legation, vol. 14 (M50, R15).

INSTRUCTIONS AND DISPATCHES   September 14, 1827

To BEAUFORT T. WATTS, Bogotá, no. 4. States that he has received a letter from John W. Holding (above, July 30, 1827) and adds: "Your interposition, if employed at all, is to be understood as for the benefit of the rightful claimant, being a citizen of the United States, whoever he may be, without undertaking to decide any controversy which may unhappily exist as to the real proprietor of the claim." L, signature removed. DNA, RG84, Colombia (MR14, frames 270–71).

From ALBERT GALLATIN, London, no. 115. Reports resumption of conferences (cf. above, Gallatin to Clay, August 9, 1827) on September 12. Reports, also, "an interview [on September 13] with Lord Dudley and Mr [William] Huskisson on the subject of the Colonial Intercourse [cf. above, Gallatin to Clay, August 21, 1827]," during which "Mr Huskisson said, that it was the intention of the British Government to consider the Intercourse with the British Colonies as being exclusively under its controul, and any relaxation from the Colonial system as an indulgence to be granted on such terms as might suit the policy of Great·Britain at the time, when it might be granted; that he was not prepared to say whether, or on what terms, it might be found expedient to open again the intercourse to American vessels, in case it was open on the part of the United States and their laws laying restrictions or imposing extra duties on British vessels [cf. above, II, 564–66; III, 729, note 21] should be repealed; and that an answer to that effect would be given to . . . [Gallatin's] Note of 17th. of August last, if his colleagues agreed with him in opinion." States that, in reply, he "said that every question of right had on this occasion been waived on the part of the United States, the only object of the present enquiry being to ascertain whether, as a matter of mutual convenience, the intercourse might not be opened in a manner satisfactory to both Countries," and added an intimation that Great Britain, by "opening the trade to other Countries that had not complied with her terms [cf. above, Gallatin to Clay, August 21, 1827], and declining to open it to the United States even in the event of such compliance," intended "to inflict a wanton injury, or at least to evince an unfriendly disposition towards them." Cites Huskisson's denial of "unfriendly feeling towards the United States"; his explanation of the opening of the trade to Russia, "the only Power to whom" it had been opened; and his view that the manner in which the United States had met "the advances made by the Act of Parliament of the year 1822" appeared to indicate that "America had entertained the opinion that the British West Indies could not exist without her supplies, and that she might therefore compel Great Britain to open the intercourse on any terms she pleased." Adds that he "disclaimed any such belief or intention on the part of the United States"; that he "intimated . . . to Mr Huskisson, that he was acting under the influence of irritated feelings"; that Huskisson denied the charge but "remained immoveable [sic] in the position he had assumed"; that "Lord Dudley, without taking a share in the conversation . . . acquiesced in the opinion of his Colleague"; and that "Mr Huskisson explicitly declared that neither of the two bills, which were under the consideration of Congress during its last Session, would, if passed into laws, have induced this Government to remove the interdict on American vessels" (cf. above, Clay to Force, February 25, 1827, and note; Gallatin to Clay, April 21, 1827). ALS. DNA, RG59, Dip. Disp., Great Britain, vol. 34 (M30, R30). Published in *American State Papers, Foreign Relations*, VI, 978–79. Received November 3.

MISCELLANEOUS LETTERS   September 14, 1827

To ENOCH LINCOLN, Portland, Maine. Acknowledges receipt of Lincoln's letter of September 3 and states that he has transmitted a copy to the President and to the British Minister (cf. above, Clay to Vaughan, this date) with an "expression of a confident expectation that the necessary orders will be given, on the part of the

British Government, to enforce that mutual forbearance from any new Acts, tending to strengthen the claims of either party to the disputed territory. . . ." Copy. DNA, RG59, Dom. Letters, vol. 22, p. 50 (M40, R20). Published in *American State Papers, Foreign Relations*, VI, 931–32.

To Thomas J. Randolph

Dear Sir   Washington 15h. Sept. 1827.
    I duly received your favor of the 12h. inst.; and I feel greatly obliged by the friendly feelings which dictated it. At the same time, I must say, that it was not necessary to convince me that the opinions, attributed to Mr Jefferson, in a late publication of T. M. Randolph Senr. Esqr.,[1] were somewhat colored by the medium through which they were reflected, without perhaps any actual design to misrepresent. It is highly probable that some of the opinions which I hold on public affairs did not meet your grandfather's approbation; and it is not unlikely that he may not have entertained a very high opinion of my capacity as a Statesman. No one has a stronger Consciousness than I have that he ought not to have made a high estimate of me. But I cannot believe that, on any occasion, he ever allowed himself to speak unkindly of me, or with any feelings of strong repugnance. I read, therefore, the publication in question, without the slightest feelings of resentment towards its author, and without the least abatement in the veneration which I feel for the character of your illustrious Grandsire, or diminution of the interest which I take in the welfare of his only daughter[2] & her children.
    Your letter has been justly appreciated. Nor is its value lessened from those considerations of evident propriety which recommend that it should be regarded as confidential, at least until an event shall take place which I hope is far distant.
    With my best wishes that, if your health were not re-established during your late visit to the Springs, it may be speedily restored, I am with great respect Yr's faithfully   H. CLAY
T. J. Randolph Esqr

    ALS. NNPM.   [1] Cf. above, Hammond to Clay, August 29, 1827, note.
[2] Martha Jefferson Randolph.

From Susan Decatur

My dear Mr Clay   Manor, Sept 15th 1827
    I am sorry to hear that any thing has occurr'd to render your habitation[1] less convenient; and I wou'd gladly consent to the remedy you propose,[2] but that the property has already prov'd so ruinous to me[3] that I determin'd some time since never to disburse another dollar

upon it, and to sell it at almost any sacrifice the moment I can find a purchaser—

Before the House was built, my belov'd husband took the precaution to have the Lot graduated by the City Surveyor, and if the Corporation have chang'd their plan, or their Surveyor committed an error, I think they ought to pay for the alteration—the pavement alone cost us an hundred dollars

If I shou'd recover my claim[4] during the next Session of Congress it will put me more at my ease; but at present I require every dollar I can command to keep me from starving!

I beg you to believe me always, very sincerely and respectfully Yours
S. DECATUR

Have the goodness to offer my affectionate remembrance to Mrs. Clay if she does not disown any acquaintance with me!

ALS. DLC-HC (DNA, M212, R2).
[1] Cf. above, Clay to Henry Clay, Jr., April 2, 1827.   [2] Proposal has not been found.
[3] Cf. above, Decatur to Clay, March 30, 1826.   [4] Mrs. Decatur had filed a petition with Congress on December 19, 1825, asking compensation as the widow of Stephen Decatur in reward for his services in leading a party of volunteers on the night of February 16, 1804, to board and destroy the frigate *Philadelphia*, in the harbor of Tripoli, after its capture by the enemy. A Senate committee in January, 1828, recommended legislation which would have appropriated $100,000 for compensation to the officers and crew involved, an arrangement intended to provide Mrs. Decatur with $5,000 as a share; but the House Committee reported unfavorably on the bill and the House, after sending the report to Committee of the Whole, failed to revive it during the Session. The measure was brought up again during the Second Session but did not come to House vote before adjournment. Although Andrew Jackson recommended in his first annual message that the claim be paid, the proposal was finally rejected by a decisive vote on May 1, 1830. *Sen. Docs.*, 20 Cong., 1 Sess., no. 23; *House Repts.*, 20 Cong., 1 Sess., no. 201; U. S. H. of R., *Journal*, 20 Cong., 1 Sess., p. 423; 20 Cong, 2 Sess., p. 364; 21 Cong., 1 Sess., pp. 28, 590.

From Robert Scott

Dear Sir,   Lexington 15th. Septr. 1827

In December last I think it was, when under considerable depression of spirits,[1] I caused Mr. Deweese[2] to write you a letter in which he assumed the responsibility of causing to be accounted for all monies which I might from that time until your next subsequent return to Kentucky, receive either on your acct. or that of Colo. Morrison's[3] estate— And to indemnify him I put into his hands some securities, which I now wish to withdraw— Not in the least doubting that you were perfectly sattisfied [sic] with the accounts as exhibited when here,[4] I now solicit the favor of you to return under cover to me that letter—or if you cannot conveniently lay your hand on it, a few lines addressed to him signifying what I wish— I beg you will not neglect this request and very much oblige Sir, your obt. & Hble Servt
The Honble Henry Clay   ROBT. SCOTT

ALS. DLC-HC (DNA, M212, R2). Endorsed by Clay on verso: "Retd. the letter of Mr. Dewees as requested."
    1 Cf. above, Scott to Clay, December 25, 1826 (2).   2 Farmer Dewees. The letter has not been found.   3 James Morrison.   4 Cf. above, Clay to Erwin, June 3, 1827, and note; Note and Specie Accounts with Morrison Estate and Note and Specie Accounts with Scott, July 16, 1827.

INSTRUCTIONS AND DISPATCHES   September 15, 1827

From THOMAS L. L. BRENT, Cintra. Reports having been "informed that the Marquis of Palmella [cf. above, Everett to Clay, June 22, 1827] . . . has written here that a messenger [Carlos Mathias Pereira—see below, Brent to Clay, October 11, 1827, note] had arrived at London on his way to Vienna with letters from the Emperor [Peter I] to the Infanta don Miguel appointing him Regent of Portugal" (cf. above, Gallatin to Clay, August 30, 1827). Encloses an extract from his last letter to (Alexander H.) Everett. ALS. DNA, RG59, Dip. Disp., Portugal, vol. 7 (M43, R6). Received November 12.

MISCELLANEOUS LETTERS   September 15, 1827

From GEORGE W[ILLIAM] HUBBELL, Bridgeport, Connecticut. States that he is about to leave for Manila, where he has been United States consul for five years; that he has been detained at home, "by Ill Health & Business," longer than expected; and that he wishes to know whether the Government will allow him to retain his commission or require him to resign it. ALS. DNA, RG59, Misc. Letters (M179, R65).
    Hubbell, born in 1796, had been trained in a counting house and at the age of 20 had embarked upon the first of several voyages as a supercargo on vessels sailing to Portugal, Gibraltar, and South America. In 1821 he had gone to Manila to establish a mercantile firm, which continued at least as late as 1881. Hubbell had been named consul in 1822 and retained the post until his death, in 1831. Walter Hubbell, *History of the Hubbell Family* (New York, 1881), 126–35 *passim*.
    On April 6, 1825, Hubbell had addressed a letter to "John Quincy Adams Secretary of State," stating that "In consequence of Ill Health" he was leaving Manila "for Europe, and from thence to the U. States"; that he would return to his post as soon as his health was restored; that he was unable to appoint an acting consul, "there being no American Citizens in Manila"; and that he would, upon reaching the United States, "immediately communicate with the Department of State. . . ." ALS, in DNA, RG59, Cons. Disp., Manila, vol. 1 (M-T43, R1).
    Daniel Brent acknowledged for Clay, on September 22, 1827, receipt of Hubbell's letter of September 15, stated that his commission was still in force, and asked that he inform Clay whether he intended returning to his post. Copy, in DNA, RG59, Dom. Letters, vol. 22, p. 52 (M40, R20).

From THOMAS D. PORTER, New York. Requests that the Secretary take steps to insure that his letter of "—— August" (cf. above, Porter to Clay, August 11, 1827) is answered and the other requirements of the law are fulfilled. ALS. DNA, RG59, Misc. Letters (M179, R65).
    No reply has been found.

From Christopher Hughes

My dear Sir.   Private   Brussels; September 16th. 1827.
    It is a very long while since I have had the pleasure to hear from

you; but I have heard from others, that your health has become much better;[1] and I sincerely hope, that your late journey home,[2] and relaxation from the daily labours of the Department, will have given you a stock of strength and spirits sufficient to carry you through the severe business of the approaching winter.

I have no political news to send you; the newspapers tell all that passes in Europe; nothing can be more quiet and settled, than the calm that reigns in every quarter; no sort of uneasiness seems to be felt as regards Portugal, since the nomination of Miguel to the regency;[3] it is believed to have been the desire of England, that he should be withdrawn from Vienna & put at the head of the Portuguese Government;[4] England counting, with confidence, on making him tractable, at home; and counting also, on such a combination and cooperation with the other great powers, in the great work of preserving the peace of Europe, as completely to frown down, any thing like a hostile policy, on the part of Miguel towards Spain! Spain and Portugal will not be allowed to quarrel; England will be glad of an opportunity to withdraw her troops; and it is supposed, that France will enable her to do so, save the point of honour, by entering into engagements for the gradual evacuation of Spain.[5] In a word every thing will be done, to preserve the peace of the World.

There is some doubt, and uneasiness, as to the course that may be taken by the Grand Seigneur;[6] as yet, he has shown a spirit of determined repugnance to the interference of France, Russia & England, in his affairs with the Greeks; if he persist, strong & immediate measures will be taken to bring him to reason; but many politicians, and especially the French, think, that he will be awed, into compliance with the terms prescribed to him, by the formidable coalition with which he is menaced;[7] and not a little influenced by the divisions & distraction, that still exist within his own territories; the effects of his late reform in his military establishment.[8] This is the only point in the affairs and politics of the old world, about which any anxiety is felt at this moment.

Mr. Canning has left a very infirm Ministerial-posterity behind him;[9] much doubt is felt as to the stability of the Ministry as lately arranged.[10] with the exception of Mr. Peel,[11] their assailants are not formidable, as to talents and address; but Tories are always formidable; Tory is another word for aristocracy, wealth and influence; the first ten days of the next session of parliament will decide either the permanency, or the fall of the Ministry. Amongst the present race of British Statesmen, there are none who enjoy the consideration and weight that were accorded, by the nation & the world, to that class of public men, of which, Mr. Canning was the last. I have had opportunities, in the course of the summer, of talking with many Englishmen of the highest rank & connection; and there is scarcely one of

them who did not express the above opinion, & who did not manifest
a sort of mortification, in speaking of the very inferior & second-rate
set of men, now at the head of the affairs of their country; and they
went farther by stating, that even among the younger & growing class
of politicians, they would be at a loss to place their hands upon one
man of promise; or on whom, they could found, any sort of flattering
expectation.

Every thing is flourishing and prosperous in this Kingdom, so much
so, as to make it the envy & the admiration of the neighbouring countries. Numbers of skilful [sic] artists emigrate from England & from
France bringing their talents & their capital, and establish themselves
in this favoured part of Europe. The King[12] holds out every desirable
encouragement to them; and in many cases, has not merely given the
benefit of his royal countenance, but made large advances of money,
to enable ingenious strangers to erect buildings, and to lay the foundations of extensive manufactories; He has even taken shares, and
made himself *a partner*, in several extensive manufacturing concerns,
that have been lately established in his dominions. He finds his reward
in the signs of prosperity, and of cheerfulness and content, that meet
his eyes, no matter in what quarter he may cast them; & in the hearty
proofs, of confidence in his wisdom and love for his person and for his
family, which are lavished on him by his subjects. Ten, nay, even five
years ago, the very reverse of this was the Fact.

I never, by any *chance*, see an american paper, now more than 4
months since I received the last from Washington, via N. York & Amsterdam, and they were 4 months old; if I could only prevail on Mr.
Brent,[13] to order them to be differently put up; that is, under a broad-
cross-*band*, & *not* under an envelope, (for an Envelope gives them the
guise of a *despatch*:) & to request the Collector at New York[14] to send
them by the Havre packets; Mr. B[15] easily would forward them to me
here, by the Diligence; I should get them then, regularly, at a very
trifling expense, and 3 days after their arrival in Europe. Perhaps, my
dear Mr. Clay, you would have the kindness to mention this to Mr.
Brent; I am sure Mr. Thruston[16] will take all the trouble of changing
the manner of putting them up. The only glimpse of home news that
I ever catch, is in mutilated scraps in the English Newspapers. I had
to write to Mr. Brown[17] & beg him to send me your letter,[18] in reply to
Genl. J.s,[19] shown you on your journey to Lexington. I had seen a
notice of it in a London print, & was very anxious to see it. I shewed
it to Bagot,[20] who takes a great interest in our politics, and always enquires about you, in the most friendly terms. I hope I am not asking
too much, when I repeat my request, that you will have this newspaper matter arranged, as I have pointed out.

Young Huygens[21] is still travelling in the north; I believe he is at

Copenhagen; the Sec. of State[20] told me, a few days ago, that the time, of his return to America is not yet fixed.

The Court will move to the Hague in a few days, & take up their residence for the coming year. We have been officially notified of the translation.

I understand that Count George de Caraman, (formerly at Washington, with Mr. Serrurier [sic]:)[23] is very desirous of becoming the Successor of Mr. de Mareuil,[24] & very probably, will be named to Washington. He has been for several years, Minister at Stutgardt, & was lately named to Dresden; he did not think the step a promotion; and is now soliciting the place of Mr. Mareuil.[25] Mr. de Caraman is an old friend & correspondent of mine, and I have reason to think him very friendly & well disposed, towards our country. The person whom I should like to see at Washington is Mr. de Cabre,[26] who desires it of all things; but his health is wretched, and his family connections, especially his Brother in Law, Ct. Alexr. de la Borde,[27] are not at all in favour. Cabre is now at Cassel, & confined more than 1/2 the year to his Sofa, by the gout! Caraman is considered to be very clever; He married a woman of Fortune, a few years ago; has children, and, if named, he will take his family, with a view of passing several years in america. His Father,[28] an ancient diplomatic Servant, is still Minister at Vienna. The French Minister (Count d'agoult, formerly at Stockholm) here is named to Berlin; We are to have in his place, Mr. de la Moussaye,[29] now at Munich; & my old Colleague, & a friend of Mr. Adams Ct. Rumigny, goes from Dresden (the succession that Caraman declined;) to Munich. There is not a Government in Europe, unrepresented at present, in the Netherlands. I am in daily expectation of hearing of the arrival in Europe, of Mr. Wheaton,[30] & of receiving from you final orders about the House at the Hague.[31] I pray you to believe me, my dr. Sir, respectfully & faithfully, yr. obet sert

To Henry Clay Esqr. Washington   CHRISTOPHER HUGHES.

ALS. DLC-HC (DNA, M212, R2).
[1] Cf. above, Clay to Brooke, August 14, 1827; Clay to Sparks, same date; Clay to Erwin, September 3, 1827.   [2] Cf. above, Clay to Erwin, June 3, 1827.   [3] Cf. above, Gallatin to Clay, August 30, 1827; Brent to Clay, September 15, 1827.   [4] George Canning had refused to guarantee the succession to Portuguese Liberals, but he had viewed the succession of Dom Miguel through foreign force or intrigue as "a deadly disgrace as well as a lasting injury to England." Quoted in Robert William Seton-Watson, Britain in Europe, 1789–1914, a Survey of Foreign Policy (New York, 1938), 95. The negotiations for Miguel's return were conducted in Vienna, under Metternich's auspices, without British intervention. Ibid., 142.   [5] Both the French and the English accomplished these respective evacuations during 1828. The British were embarking troops for their withdrawal in early March when Sir Frederick Lamb, upon learning of Dom Miguel's activities to overthrow the constitutional regime, countermanded the order. Very shortly, however, fresh instructions arrived which required the removal of the British troops. Cádiz, the last position retained by the French in Spain, was relinquished in September. Annual Register, 1828, pp. 190–91, 208–209.   [6] Mahmud II, Sultan of Turkey.   [7] Cf. above, Brown to Clay, July 12, 1827, and note. The Ambassadors of Great Britain, France, and Russia—Stratford Canning, the Count de Guilleminot, and Alexander Ribeaupierre

—had presented to the Reis Effendi (Saida) on August 16 a request for an answer to their proposed intervention and had demanded an answer within 15 days. The Turkish Foreign Minister on August 30 had refused to alter his answer of June 9 (see below, Middleton to Clay, September 29, 1827). On August 31, the Ambassadors had delivered another note, detailing the measures which their governments proposed "to take to restore peace in the East," had then dispatched fresh instructions to their fleet commanders (see below, Lafayette to Clay, October 10, 1827, note), and had terminated the conferences. London *Times*, September 25, 1827, reprinting dispatch from Paris *Gazette de France*, September 23, 1827.
8 Cf. above, Moore to Clay, June 20, 1826, note.   9 Cf. above, Gallatin to Clay, August 9, 1827.   10 Cf. above, Gallatin to Clay, August 14, 24, 30, September 6, 1827.
11 Robert Peel.   12 William I.   13 Daniel Brent.   14 Jonathan Thompson.
15 Reuben G. Beasley.   16 Thomas L. Thruston.   17 James Brown.
18 Above, "To the Public," June 29, 1827.   19 Jackson's letter to Carter Beverley, June 6, 1827. Cf. above, Clay to Hammond, June 25, 1827, and note.   20 Sir Charles Bagot.   21 Roger Bangeman Huygens.   22 John Gijsbert Verstolk Van Soelen.
23 Louis Barbé Charles Serurier, born in 1775, had been French Minister to the United States from 1811 to 1815 and returned to that post from 1831 to 1835.   24 Baron Durant de Mareuil. Cf. above, Brown to Clay, November 29, 1826; March 23, 1827, note.
25 Cf. above, Hughes to Clay, January 21, 1827, note.   26 Jean Antoine de Cabre.
27 Born in Paris in 1773, Laborde had served in the Austrian Army during the French Revolution. For nearly a decade after 1797 he had travelled extensively in England, Holland, Italy, and Spain and had published two multi-volumed accounts of the last country. He had returned to public life in France in 1808 and in 1822 had been elected a Deputy, re-elected in 1827. He held the favor of Louis-Phillipe after the Revolution of 1830 but remained relatively free of politics during the remainder of his life.
28 Victor-Louis-Charles Riquet, first Duke of Caraman, had been born in Paris in 1762 and, after a nominal military career, had served during the French Revolution in the Prussian Army. Because of this service he had been seized and detained for some five years by Napoleon but in 1814 had been named Minister Plenipotentiary to Berlin to effect the repatriation of French prisoners. He had been elevated to the peerage in 1815 and the following year had been sent as Ambassador to Vienna. He retired in December, 1828, and was then given the hereditary title of Duke.   29 Born in 1778, Louis-Toussaint, later Marquis de la Moussaye, also had emigrated from France during the Revolution but had returned to fight under Napoleon and had held a succession of minor administrative and diplomatic appointments. He had become Minister to Stuttgart in 1817 and to Munich in 1821. Because of his opposition to the reunion of Belgium with France in 1830, he was recalled from the mission which he began in the Netherlands in 1828. Meanwhile he had served as a member of the French Chamber of Deputies, from 1820 to 1830. In 1835 he was created a peer.   30 Henry Wheaton. Cf. above, Rainals to Clay, August 29, 1827.   31 Cf. above, Willink and Van Staphorst to Clay, September 13, 1825; Clay to Forsyth, March 7, 1826; Clay to Hughes, December 12, 1826; Hughes to Clay, April 14, 15, 1827.

MISCELLANEOUS LETTERS   September 16, 1827

From JOSEPH C. MORGAN, Glen Morgan Mill, White Marsh Post Office, Montgomery County, Pennsylvania. Notes that he has heard nothing regarding the claim of S. H. Van Kempen (cf. above, Morgan to Clay, December 26, 1825), for "Upwards of an year," and inquires whether or not the American Chargé to the Netherlands (Christopher Hughes) has made a "peremptory demand" against that Government. ALS. DNA, RG76, Misc. Claims, Netherlands (MR3).

From Thomas Law

Dear Sir—   Sepr 17th 1827—
    The Stocks of two banks in Alexandria are 40 or 50 p Ct. below par— if you employ any one to investigate you will ascertain that there is a lamentable scarcity of money— Merchants are becoming

more in debt to Govt for duties— Banks are in general reducing their notes in circulation— Every 23 or 25 years our circulating medium ought to be doubled, for doubled population— Our circuland, in Estates, houses, mills, factories Slaves &ca. ought to be more than double— We want Canals & railways & roads to unite our Western brethren. Can we expect to accomplish these important permanents [sic] improvements with our present pecuniary resources—   has not our Cotton fallen in price 15,000,000 Ds. a large deduction from domestic exports of 50,000,000— Tobacco also has fallen— & wheat &ca. If you wish the Tariff to operate give men the means to set up factories— Gold & silver defy the regulations of a Govt   a national Currency always stays at home, it promotes marriages, schools & industry of all kinds—

I enclose three Tracts which I have given away[1]— the first was hurried the second I took great pains about,   many members of Congress attended who came to hear an Address[2] displaying flights of imagination,   they went away converts to solid reasoning— No 3 is a mere make weig[ht]   I took pains with No 2 & my son Edmund cooperated who had long been a Bullionist & who can shrewdly argue to baffle where he cannot convince,   as he has a strong judgement his change of opinion gave me great joy, more indeed than if a host of objectioners had yeilded [sic]—

If you wish your Tariff to operate well, let manufacturers have money at moderate interest to set up manufacturers [sic]—

Political economy you are master of, one important branch of it excepted— I allude to finance, which now elevates men in England to the highest Stations— Lord Goodrich[3] is a financier— If you will submit my pamphlets to judicious men & objections arise, if they are imparted to me, I will either invalidate them or acquiesce in their solidity— Collision will elicit light   I seek only for Truth— God has given immutable principles for every Science— Humanity says to Legislators, study to have all your Citizens well occupied—fifty. years of my life have been given to political economy, the accompg Copy of a Letter[4] encourages me cum multis aliis to persevere—

Do not apprehend that I shall trouble you with numerous intrusions I am aware of your multiplicity of business, for Heads of Departments in this Country, have the trouble of details—

I feel that the crisis justifies my endeavors to avert approaching calamities,   I sympathise with sufferers, & I am anxious to see this Country have all its energies called forth & enjoying unparalell'd [sic] prosperity, before I go hence & am no more seen— pray preserve my pamphlets,   if you arrive at my age, a reperusal of them will prove that they recommend what would give millions on millions to the industry, & destroy discontent blindly wishing for a change   I remain with respect esteem & unfeigned regard   THOS LAW

ALS. DNA, RG59, Misc. Letters (M179, R65).
  1 Cf. above, Law to Clay, March 18, 1827, and notes.   2 Probably at the Columbian
Institute. Papers published by Law in 1828 and 1830 concerning his views on money were
initiated as addresses to that organization.   3 John Frederick Robinson, Viscount
Goderich.   4 Not found.

From William B. Rochester

Hon: H. Clay
My dear Sir   (private)   Albany 17. Sept. 1827.

Upon my arrival at this place I found your last favour[1] in the post
office, but with the seal broken—most probably by accident—

I find it difficult to ascertain with precision the State of parties in
the assembly— in that body the doctrine of non-committal seems to
have obtained to some extent— not so in the Senate   in the latter body,
of the 30—they stand at present 16. for J. 14. for the administration—
of the 16—6. are clintonians—of the 14. 4. are Clintonians— Clinton
himself is undoubtedly decidedly for the hero & expects to be V. P.—
he will make no public demonstration until after our fall election[2]—
in the interim unwearied pains will be taken to get Jacksonian candidates returnd [sic] to the Succeeding Legislature— in the 4h. Senate
Distr: both the parties—Bucktail & Clintonian have already made their
Senatorial nominations   each convention had nominated a Jacksonian[3]—. this I get from Martindale[4]—   I fear that our Lieut. Govr.
(Pitcher)[5] goes for J.—yet he professes great regard for you!— as I wrote
you before, there can be no doubt of the attachment of our western
people to the policy & men of the existing administration with the
exception of some sections of Counties bordering on the Penn: line—
for the Southern part—especially the city of New York I should not
like to be responsible— Chs. King has (I think imprudently) thrown
down the Gauntlet[6]— Jackson's friends urge it with apparent eagerness
& seem to [sic] determined to draw the line where they think it will
(as in the city) answer their purpose—

I should with much reluctance abandon the hope & belief, long
cherished, that the Body of the People in our State are disposed to continue their support of the Measures, now pursued and with which I
conscientiously believe the great interests of the Nation and especially
those of N. Y. are identified— like yourself, I have always, relied much
upon the intelligence of the People—but I cannot shut our eyes against
the fact that upon the surface here, there appears at present a tendency
to be carried along with the current of Virginia politicks,[7] in defiance
of all former professions & practice.—

I have been confined to my room two days, in consequence of cold
contracted by sudden change of weather— Shall start for the Cty of
N. Y. to day—whence I shall write you more in extenso unless (as is
probable) I find I shall not be able to get a passage to Omoa in all

Sept.— in that case I will go to Washington to spend a day—to settle my account &c

this scroll must assure you, that neither my head, my nerves or my spirits are in tune for writing— do not trouble yourself to reply to the many hasty letters which I am in the habit Of inflicting upon you— Sincerely yr. friend   W B Rochester—

ALS. DLC-HC (DNA, M212, R2).   1 Not found.
2 The election was not held until November 11, but the *New York American*, September 17, 1827, commented that the *New York Evening Post*'s "annunciation, almost official" (on September 12), of Clinton's support for Jackson was causing excitement in the State. Another item in the same issue of the *American* reported information in a letter from Albany that Martin Van Buren had stated Clinton would run for Vice President and that the Governor had agreed to be a candidate. Cf. also, below, Hammond to Clay, October 29, 1827.   3 Reuben Sanford, of Essex County, a veteran of the War of 1812, a farmer, merchant, and manufacturer, had been nominated by the Republicans of the Fourth District on September 8. His opponent was George Throop, a Federalist and Clintonian (not further identified), who was defeated in the November election.
4 Name unclear—probably Henry C. Martindale.   5 Nathaniel Pitcher.   6 Cf. above, Thomas to Clay, May 13, 1827. The editor of the *New York American*, August 30, 1827, had advised that the choice of State legislators "be made with distinct reference to the Presidential question. . . ." An editorial in the Albany *Argus*, September 6, 1827, had observed: "The American assumes to itself the direction of the affairs of the friends of the administration in this state" and commented: "The magisterial command of the American (which savors more of arrogance than good sense) will be treated therefore, with the disregard, if not contempt, which it deserves."   7 Cf. above, Kent to Clay, January 26, 1827; Mallory to Clay, April 4, 1827; Clay to Porter, May 13, 1827, note.

DIPLOMATIC NOTES   September 17, 1827

From CHARLES R. VAUGHAN, Washington. Acknowledges receipt of Clay's note of September 14; recalls his past remonstrances "against the Conduct of Persons calling themselves Agents accredited by the States of Maine and Massachusetts, for offering to sale in the British Settlements upon the Madawaska River, grants of Lands, and for Surveying and laying out New Settlements" in the disputed territory (above, Vaughan to Clay, November 15, December 2, 1825; January 16, 1827); states that inasmuch as the disputed territory has been considered part of the Province of New Brunswick since 1784, and before that part of the Province of Nova Scotia, Great Britain cannot accept the "validity of any title to Lands" in the area "until a change in the Right of possession shall have been effected, in consequence of the fifth Article of the Treaty of Ghent" (cf. above, I, 1006); asserts that "no Act of Jurisdiction," including conscription, "can influence, in any shape, the decision of the question of Boundary under the Treaty of Ghent"; promises to transmit copies of Clay's note and Enoch Lincoln's letter to Sir Howard Douglas, Lieutenant Governor of New Brunswick, who, Vaughan claims, "has abstained from exercising any authority over the unoccupied parts of the disputed Territory, excepting for the purpose of preserving it in it's [*sic*] present State"; encloses copies of a letter of instructions to the "Magistrates residing in the Neighbourhood of the disputed Territory" from the government of New Brunswick and another in which Douglas informed Vaughan that "he had directed the Attorney General of New Brunswick to prosecute some British Subjects who had cut down Timber upon the St. John's [*sic*] River"; and expresses hope that the question of boundary will be speedily resolved. LS. DNA, RG59, Notes from British Legation, vol. 14 (M50, R15). Published in Manning (arr.), *Diplomatic Correspondence . . . Canadian Relations*, II, 628–31.

In the first enclosure, dated March 9, 1827, W(illiam) F. Odell, Provincial Secretary of New Brunswick, states that he has been "commanded by H. E. the Lt. Governor" to request vigilance and utmost diligence to discover any attempt which may be made by any of H. M.'s Subjects to intrude upon that Territory with a view to make settlements, or to procure Timber, & to make immediate representation thereof to H. M.'s Attorney General that legal steps may be taken to punish such intruders & trespassers." In the second letter, dated April 13, 1827, Douglas informs Vaughan of the circulation of the Odell instructions.

Odell, born in Burlington, New Jersey, had studied law and had been admitted to the New Brunswick bar in 1806. He had been named provincial secretary in 1812 and held the position until his death in 1844.

INSTRUCTIONS AND DISPATCHES   September 17, 1827

To ALBERT GALLATIN, no. 36. Acknowledges receipt of his "despatches, Nos. 102, 3, 4, 5, 6 and 7 [above, August 6, 7, 9, 10, 11, 14, 1827] . . . together with the two conventions, signed on the 6th ultimo. . . ." States that he cannot communicate the "opinion of those two instruments" held by the President, who "is expected to return [to Washington] about the 1st. of next month," but he does "not doubt they will meet his full approbation." Notes the necessity of "a proper understanding" in regard to "the place where, in the event of their ratification by both Governments, the ratifications are to be exchanged. . . ." LS. NHi-Gallatin Papers (MR15). Copy, in DNA, RG59, Dip. Instr., vol. 11, p. 379; L draft, in DLC-HC (DNA, M212, R8). Published in Manning (arr.), *Diplomatic Correspondence . . . Canadian Relations*, II, 138.

From A[BRAHAM] B. NONES, Maracaibo. Reports having learned that the troops accompanying (Simón) Bolívar, which were moving slowly toward Bogotá (cf. above, Watts to Clay, August 7, 1827), have been halted after receipt by that leader of "a strong remonstrance addressed by" the Secretary of War of Colombia (Carlos Soublette) "by order of the Executive power, declaring the impossibility of supporting an augmentation of Troops in the Interior in Consequence of the want of money in the national Treasury. . . ." Notes confirmation of "the report of the Seperation [*sic*] of the Departments of Guayaquil, Ecuador and Asuay from the Republic [cf. above, Allen to Clay, June 14, 1827] and that . . . [Juan José] Flores has been proclaimed chief or President of the three seperated departments. . . ." Predicts also the separation of Venezuela (cf. above, Litchfield to Clay, May 23, 1826, note) and observes: "the fact is the confusion increases every day and affairs are drawing to a Crisis." LS. DNA, RG59, Cons. Disp., Maracaibo, vol. 1 (M-T62, R1). Received October 14.

Flores (or Florez), born at Puerto Cabello in 1800, had been imprisoned at the early age of 14 for revolutionary activity against Spain and had subsequently had a distinguished military career in the Colombian forces. He had been given the rank of brigadier general in 1826 and in 1827 had led one of the divisions which seized Guayaquil (cf. above, Tudor to Clay, April 25, 1827). With the outbreak of war between the northern provinces and Peru in 1829, he contributed significantly to the victory of the former at Tarqui (see above, Tudor to Clay, February 23, 1826, note) and was then promoted to general. He became the first president of Ecuador and held that office from 1830 to 1834 and again from 1839 to 1843.

From John Newnan

Worthy Sir,   Nashville Sepr. 18th. 1827.
    I assure you my feelings have been not a little excited on reading

in our Banner and Whig, the mean and truly contemptible statement which Thos. M. Randolph has been induced to publish[1] for the gratification of a faction which is betraying great despair lately, if we are to Judge from the efforts now used, to suppress truth and in fabricating falsehoods and perversion in support of their bad cause. Altho I have addressed my statement to Mr Force,[2] and do not regard paying the postage, yet as I am unwilling that the contents shd. be published without being first submitted to yr inspection and examination, as a part therof [sic] respects yourself,   I have taken the liberty to enclose to you, that you may direct yr friend Force or some other Editor to make any alteration that may be necessary, previously to the publication,[3] and which I am desirous may be before the appearance of the long Bulletin of Eaton, Jackson and Magor [sic] Lee[4] now hatching at the Hermitage, in answer to Buchanan[5] and others on the subjects of the charges and wicked accusation agt Mr Adams, yourself and friends.

I would be glad Mr Joseph Pearson of Washington[6] who is an old acquaintance of mine and has been raised and educated in the part of No. Carolina that I came from, if you think it advisable and safe, could see the reply to Randolph & Co. Our friend Erwin[7] will write a short letter on the subject now before you. With much regard and este[em] I am, Sir, sincerely—yrs   J. NEWNAN

ALS. DNA, RG59, Misc. Letters (M179, R65). Addressed to Clay.

Newnan, of Scotch descent, had come to Nashville from Salisbury, North Carolina, about 1810. He was a distinguished physician in the Tennessee community until his death in 1833.

[1] Cf. above, Hammond to Clay, August 29, 1827, note. The Randolph letter had been published in the National Banner and Nashville Whig on September 8.   [2] Peter Force.   [3] The enclosure has not been found and has not been identified in the Washington Daily National Intelligencer.   [4] John Henry Eaton; Andrew Jackson; Henry Lee. Cf. above, Webster to Clay, August 22, 1827, note.   [5] James Buchanan. Cf. above, Ingersoll to Clay, August 11, 1827, note.   [6] The North Carolina Congressman (1809–1815) was a lawyer who had opened practice in Salisbury around the turn of the century and died there in 1834. His identification as a resident of Washington has not been found other than for the period of his congressional service.   [7] Probably John P. Erwin. The "letter" has not been found in the National Banner and Nashville Whig.

From John Sergeant

Dear Sir,   (Private)   Philada. Septr. 18. 1827.

I received to day your letter of the 16th. inst.[1] When my last[2] was written, appearances here were very unfavorable. They have become better again, and there is reason to believe all will go right. The federalists are now organized and are making their preparatory arrangements. Individually, they are for the most part well inclined, and even zealous; but as a body they are operated upon by motives which I need not take up your time in explaining, having their root chiefly in the occurrences of last fall. The probability now seems to be that they will endeavour to escape from their perplexity by making no nomination for Congress.[3] Next to a nomination such as we wish (the only one they will make if they do nominate) this is the most favorable course they can take. It will leave individuals of the party to follow their own inclination, uncommitted by any party engagement such as we felt the effects of at the last election,[4] and it will be nearly as decisive an indication of the wishes of the body of the party as a nomination would be. The latter, however, would have the advantage of stopping the mouths of the malcontents among themselves, of whom there are some— The federalists will nominate for all other elective offices, Legislature, City Councils &c. The friends of the administration among the democrats (now organized) will immediately proceed to nominate for Congress, and probably make no other nomination.[5] There will thus be no interference, and I hope all who have one object, will cordially cooperate. If they do, we shall certainly succeed, and I think by a handsome majority. You may rely upon it we will do our best.

The consequence you give to my being in Congress, tho' it is very flattering, is somewhat distressing. I do not feel myself equal to the task, and am sure I am not qualified for such times as are coming. I do not say this from affected modesty, but in sincerity and truth after some deliberation. But I am sufficiently impressed with the importance of the crisis to be willing to do all I can, and this is the utmost I can promise.

There has been a respectable meeting of the democratic friends of the administration in Chester County.[6] Appearances there are favorable. It is said, too, that we are doing well in Lancaster County,[7] heretofore supposed to be one of the strongest holds of Jacksonism in the State. Our friends say we may calculate upon a large majority in that County. There are other parts of the State (Cumberland for example) where an open and manly stand has been taken and will be maintained. In Philada. County, our adversaries have just now a violent quarrel among themselves.[8] If they do not settle it soon, we will beat them. In general, however, I do not think our strength can be fairly produced 'till after the coming election in October. Measures will then be adopted for a convention in March to form an electoral ticket,[9] which will bring the matter fairly to issue disentangled from all those circumstances which have given the timid and time serving an apology for shrinking from their duty.

I have great apprehensions about Delaware, tho' the accounts are contradictory. I presume you know the position of the parties there. The federalists in the usual way nominated Mr. Johns.[10] The Democrats regularly nominated Doctor Naudine,[11] and as the integrity of the parties has always been strongly insisted upon, it was supposed they would take the old ground of Federalist against Democrat. But these gentlemen are both friends of the Administration, and known to be such. The Jacksonites, therefore, of both parties, abandoning their ancient party feelings, have united in a nomination of a Jackson candidate.[12] He will take the field against the other two with manifest advantage. Some time ago, it was said one of the Administration candidates would retire, but it has not yet been done. Perhaps there are doubts of the expediency of the step.

This is already a very long letter. I will close it with saying that I do not know of any service you can render us here, except as you are every day assisting us by maintaining your claim to the attachment and respect of your friends and the confidence of our Country, Very respectfully and truly Yrs. JOHN SERGEANT.

P.S. I do not expect you to be at the trouble (occupied as you are) of answering my letters, unless there be something that requires an answer. My object, generally, is to let you know what is going on, and sometimes, you will think, to unburthen my mind.

ALS. DLC-HC (DNA, M212, R2). Endorsed by Clay for filing. [1] Not found. [2] Above, September 13, 1827. [3] Cf. above, Johnston to Clay, September 13, 1827, note. [4] Cf. above, Sergeant to Clay, September 28, 1826, note. [5] Cf. above, Johnston to Clay, September 13, 1827, note. [6] Held on September 15. Philadelphia *Democratic Press*, September 5, 1827; Washington *Daily National Journal*, September 24, 1827. [7] Cf. above, Johnston to Clay, September 14, 1827. [8] Cf. below, Sergeant to Clay, September 26, 1827. [9] The Pennsylvania convention to name electors in support of the administration met at Harrisburg on January 4. *Niles' Weekly Register*, XXXIII (January 12, 1828), 316. Meetings to select delegates to the convention had been vigorously pressed from early November. See Washington *Daily National Journal*, November 10, 15, 1827. [10] Kensey Johns, Jr. [11] Arnold Naudain, born near Dover, Delaware, in 1790 and graduated from Princeton College in 1806, had received his diploma in medicine from the University of Pennsylvania in 1810 and served as surgeon general of Delaware militia during the War of 1812. He had been a member of the State Legislature from 1823 to 1827 and held the speakership in 1826. He was elected to the United States Senate from 1830 to 1836, then to the State Senate from 1836 to 1839, and from 1841 to 1845 was collector of the port of Wilmington. He moved to Philadelphia and resumed the practice of medicine in 1845. [12] James A. Bayard, Jr. On the developments in the election, cf. above, Clay to Taylor, September 7, 1827, note; below, Sergeant to Clay, September 23, 1827. Bayard, the son of Clay's colleague at Ghent, had been born in Delaware in 1799, studied law, and opened practice in Wilmington. Identified as a Federalist, he was nominated by the Jacksonian Democrats as a fusion effort. See McCormick, *Second American Party System*, 152–53. Bayard became Federal attorney for Delaware from 1838 to 1843 and a United States Senator from 1851 to 1864 and from 1867 to 1869.

INSTRUCTIONS AND DISPATCHES September 18, 1827

To BEAUFORT T. WATTS, no. 5. Informs him of the receipt of the letter (above) of August 4, 1827, from Baring Brothers and Company. States that, inasmuch as Watts has no authority from the State Department "to draw upon these Bankers" and his salary and contingent expenses have been paid at the Department to holders of his drafts, "Baring, Brothers and Company have been advised no longer to honor" his bills. Explains the necessity, "for the safety of the Treasury" and "the more convenient adjustment of the accounts of diplomatic agents," of having only one source for the payment of these accounts. LS. DNA, RG84, Colombia, Dispatches, vol. 3 (MR14).

From ALBERT GALLATIN, London, no. 116. Reports the death, on September 11, of William Davy and states that he has "given a temporary appointment to" Davy's son Albert, who "is a candidate for the permanent appointment and in every respect qualified for it." ALS. DNA, RG59, Dip. Disp., Great Britain, vol. 34 (M30, R30). Received October 31. Cf. below, Clay to Davy, November 9, 1827.

William Davy, a Philadelphia textile merchant, had been appointed consul at Leeds, England, in January, 1817.

From SAMUEL LARNED, Santiago de Chile, no. 59. Reports that (Joaquín) Campino "only awaits an opportunity to proceed on his Mission" as Minister to the United States (cf. above, Allen to Clay, March 20, 1826; Larned to Clay, August 10, 1827) and that his instructions, which he allowed Larned to read, indicate that "almost the sole object of his Mission is to reciprocate . . . the courtesy of the United States in sending a Minister Plenipotentiary to this country. . . ." Notes that "Mr. Campino is authorized, in general terms, to enter into 'preliminary stipulations,' should the government of the United States propose" negotiation of a commercial treaty, but that such a proposal is not expected. Expresses an opinion that the Chileans would prefer that negotiations, when begun, be carried on in their own capital. Adds that, in regard to claims, Campino "is merely authorized to assure the President, that they shall meet the prompt and candid attention of this government whenever the discussion of them shall be again renewed by" Larned (cf. above, Larned to Clay, August 30, 1827). States that the treaty negotiated between Chile and "the United Provinces of the Rio de la Plata [cf. above, Allen to Clay, December 23, 1826] . . . was finally rejected by the National Commission of this country, a few days ago." Discusses a series of incidents, beginning with a dispute between a native of Chile and a British naval officer over a seat "in the Theatre of Valparaiso," which resulted in the death of one Chilean soldier, in "a violation of the territory of Chile by an armed British force," and in "much excitement here," which will engender "bad feeling . . . not only towards the British, but . . . towards all foreigners. . . ." ALS. DNA, RG59, Dip. Disp., Chile, vol. 2 (M-T2, R2). Received January 18, 1828.

MISCELLANEOUS LETTERS   September 18, 1827

From BARING BROTHERS AND COMPANY, London. State that Beaufort T. Watts has "further drawn upon" them, "for, £200. under date of 7 August," and that they have honored the draft. Call attention again "to the necessity of placing this Legation, on the proper footing. . . ." ALS. DNA, RG59, Misc. Letters (M179, R65). Cf. above, Clay to Watts, this date; Baring Brothers and Company to Clay, August 4, 1827.

From P[AUL] SIEMEN FORBES, New York. Inquires whether John M. Forbes, whose health is "in a very precarious state," has been granted permission to return to the United States, as the information "will decide a family question of some importance." ALS. DNA, RG59, Misc. Letters (M179, R65).

On September 22, Daniel Brent acknowledged for Clay, who was "indisposed and confined at home," receipt of this letter and replied that John M. Forbes had already been informed (above, Clay to Forbes, April 20, 1827) of the President's refusal of his request for a leave of absence. Copy, in DNA, RG59, Dom. Letters, vol. 22, p. 52 (M40, R20).

Paul Siemen Forbes, a cousin of John Murray Forbes, was a merchant and in 1844 became United States consul at Canton.

Order on Washington Branch, Bank of the United States

19 Septr 1827

No.   OFFICE OF DISCOUNT & DEPOSIT, Washington,
    PAY to Check on Philadelphia———or bearer, Seventy five———
Dollars, /100

H CLAY

$75 DOLLARS, /100

ADS, partially printed. DLC-TJC (DNA, M212, R16).

DIPLOMATIC NOTES   September 19, 1827

To CHARLES RICHARD VAUGHAN, Washington. Acknowledges receipt of Vaughan's note of September 17; promises to send a copy to the Governor of Maine (below, Clay to Lincoln, this date) and request from him further information regarding American settlements on the St. John River; comments that the enclosed letters of Sir Howard Douglas "manifest a just solicitude on the part of that officer" in fostering good relations between the United States and Great Britain; and expresses participation in Vaughan's desire that a settlement of the boundary may soon be achieved through negotiations. Copy. DNA, RG59, Notes to Foreign Legations, vol. 3, pp. 388–89 (M39, R3). ALS draft, in CSmH; published in Manning (arr.), *Diplomatic Correspondence . . . Canadian Relations*, II, 138–39.

INSTRUCTIONS AND DISPATCHES   September 19, 1827

From HEMAN ALLEN, Valparaiso. Reports that, since he has not been able to take passage on a United States naval vessel, he plans to depart on a French merchant ship which sails for Rio de Janeiro on September 22. ALS. DNA, RG59, Dip. Disp., Chile, vol. 2 (M-T2, R2). Received January 18, 1828.

From J[AMES] COOLEY, Lima, no. 8. States that the Peruvian Congress recently appointed a committee, which has not yet reported, on the Congress at Tacubaya. Reports "an informal interview with Gen. [José de] LaMar," at which (Francisco Javier Luna) Pizarro, "lately appointed to negotiate a Treaty with the Minister Plenipotentiary from Chile [not identified]," and "the present Secretary of State, Mr [Francisco Xavier] Mariatiguy [*sic*] were present" and (William) Tudor accompanied Cooley. Notes that when he brought up the subject of American spoliation claims (cf. above, Clay to Cooley, November 6, 1826), the Peruvians "seemed perfectly apprized of the nature of those claims & that they would be pressed, but expressed no opinion"; that he gathered from the conversation that Peru would not ratify "the Treaty that had been concluded at Panama" (cf. above, Salazar to Clay, November 20, 1826); and that "a Minister may be sent to Tacubaya to announce the determination of this Government," after which he "*might* be directed to proceed . . . to Washington, tho' the sad state of their finances was alluded to" as a barrier "to making Diplomatic Appointments at present." Reports that he believes "they are sincerely desirous of treating with us"; that he regrets that "it had not been determined [by the United States] to propose to treat at once here," when the men in power were "favorably inclined towards us" and "unshackled by Treaties with the neighboring Republics"; and that treaty negotiations "would afford the best opportunity of adjusting the claims of our Citizens upon this Gov-

ernment." Notes that, in response to an inquiry by Pizarro concerning "the sentiments" of the United States "upon the subject of the New Republics late Spanish
Colonies giving to each other a preference in their ports over the vessels of other
nations," he replied that, though without specific instructions, he had "no hesitation in giving . . . [his] opinion, that the Government of the United States would
not treat but upon the basis of the most favored nation." Surmises that "This
subject [of preferential treatment] has no doubt been proposed by the Minister
from Chile." Encloses "a paper containing the Proclamation of Gen [Simón] Bolivar at Caraccas [sic], the publication of which excited considerable indignation
here." ALS. DNA, RG59, Dip. Disp., Peru, vol. 1 (M-T52, R1). Extract published
in Manning (arr.), *Diplomatic Correspondence . . . Latin-American Nations*, III,
1835. Received January 3, 1828.
    The enclosure, *Mercurio Peruano*, September 18, 1827, contained a copy of a
proclamation by Bolívar, dated June 12, 1827, and directed to Colombians, charging their enemies with threatening destruction of the Republic, promising to
sacrifice himself in its defense, referring to "los nuevos pretorianos" who assume
power in violation of law, pointing specifically to rebellious activities of the Colombian troops who had been stationed in Peru (cf. above, Tudor to Clay, February 3, 1827), and calling for a national convention. Published as a proclamation
dated June 19 in *Niles Weekly Register*, XXXII (July 21, 1827), 351–52.

From W[ILLIAM] TUDOR, Lima, no. 77, "*Confidential.*" States that since (James)
Cooley is also writing at this time (above, this date), he (Tudor) has "only to
offer a few details on some poli[ti]cal occurrences, which may not be communicated by [h]im." Praises the reforms instituted by (José de) Lamar; comments on
the work of the Congress; reports a conversation with Lamar concerning the Congress of Tacubaya, after which the President caused the subject to be called up
in Congress, where no action has been taken on it; observes that "Dr [Francisco
Javier] Luna [Pizarro] showed . . . [him] in confidence the Treaties [cf. above,
Salazar to Clay, November 20, 1826] & journal of proceedings in Panama, & those
treaties seem to be null by the attempted autocracy of Bolivar, which violated one
of their conditions, & by the actual situation of Colombia & Central America" (cf.
above, Litchfield to Clay, May 22, 1826, note; Nones to Clay, September 17, 1827;
Sergeant and Poinsett to Clay, May 9, 1827); and adds that "the Dr has told [him]
. . . that Peru would not ratify those treaties, & that a Minister will be sent from
here, to declare her secession from the Congress & all further proceedings of that
Assembly at the present period."
    Disclaims any intention of assuming the duties of Cooley, who "is embarrassed
by his not speaking the language" and whom Tudor accompanied to an interview
with Lamar.
    Discusses events in Guayaquil and Bolívar's "proclamation of June 1 [sic]." As-
serts that "Peru is safe with La Mar at the head & she stands between Bolivar &
the enslaving of all South America." Refers to the increasing difficulties of (Antonio José de) Sucre. ALS. DNA, RG59, Cons. Disp., Lima, vol. 2 (M154, R2). Received January 3, 1828.
    Tudor's allusion to Bolívar's "attempted autocracy," as a violation of the trea-
ties, related to the demand by Colombia's delegates that article 29 of the proposed
Treaty of Union, League, and Confederation be amended to eliminate the requirement that none of the allies substantially change its form of government,
upon pain of expulsion, with "reinstatement only upon the unanimous consent
of the parties concerned." Although the final draft had been modified to remove
this restriction, Bolívar had subsequently criticized the treaty as containing "articles which might hamper the execution of certain projects that . . . [he had] in
mind. . . ." Bolívar to Pedro Briceño Méndez, September 14, 1826, in Lecuna

(comp.) and Bierck (ed.), *Selected Writings of Bolívar*, II, 637. See also Lockey, *Pan-Americanism. . .* , 341–48; Salvador de Madariaga, *Bolívar* (New York, 1952), 536.

From J[OHN] G. A. WILLIAMSON, LaGuaira. Transmits, in the belief "that a Garbled statement of a personal affair which took place on the evening of the 14th. inst may reach the U. States, between a Mr Robinson and" himself, "a copy of the correspondence which had occured [*sic*] previously—" Admits striking his antagonist. ALS. DNA, RG59, Cons. Disp., LaGuaira, vol. 1 (M84, R1). Received October 14. Endorsed on cover: "*Private.*"

Enclosures reveal that the controversy, with Edward W. Robinson (not identified), concerned a *vale*, which had been embargoed, "owing," according to Robinson, "to *neglect*, which the parties interested will be able to place to its proper source." Williamson had pronounced the charge "false."

MISCELLANEOUS LETTERS   September 19, 1827

To ENOCH LINCOLN, Portland, Maine. Transmits a copy of a letter from the British Minister (above, Vaughan to Clay, September 17, 1827) with its enclosures; notes that Vaughan "states that the American Settlers on the St. Johns [*sic*] have recently established themselves there, within an ancient British Settlement, and that their titles have been lately obtained from the agents of the States of Maine and Massachusetts"; asks "to be put in possession of any information" which demonstrates whether or not Vaughan's statement is correct. Copy. DNA, RG59, Dom. Letters, vol. 22, p. 51 (M40, R20).

From Samuel L. Southard

The Hon: Henry Clay Secretary of State
Sir   Navy Department 20th. Septemr. 1827

I have given to the letter of Henry F. [*sic*] Duncan Esqr. of Paris Ky. which you submitted to me and, which is herewith returned,[1] a careful perusal.—

Mr. Duncan expresses a wish to enter into a contract to furnish *Tarred Yarns* for the use of the Navy.— The Department contracts for *Cordage only*, having no rope walks or convenience for the Manufacture of the article.— The necessary supply of Cordage is procured annually by contract— Public Notice is given of the quantity and kinds required at the several depots; proposals will soon be issued for the supplies required during the ensuing year.— The specimen of Water rotted hemp sent by Mr. Duncan appears to be of good texture and quality.— Prepared in this manner, the hemp of American growth is not inferior to that produced in Russia. The Department will give it a decided preference; as by fostering its production for a few years, our Navy will be rendered completely independent of foreign Markets for a supply of the article.— I am Respy &c   S. L. S.

Copy. DNA, RG45, Executive Letterbook, 1821–1831, p. 268.
[1] The letter has not been found. It was probably from Henry Timberlake Duncan,

born in 1800 at Paris, Kentucky, a farmer, later noted for his interest in thoroughbred stock. He became a personal friend of Clay and was named in his will.

From Vincent Rumpff

Sir,   New York. September 20. 1827.

I hasten to offer You my best thanks for Your Kindness in sending an Order for the free admittance of my baggage to the Custom House of New York,[1] which my father in law[2] delivered to me at my arrival at this place.

As I propose making a tour to the falls of Niagara, and visiting the northern parts of this interesting country before I go to Washington, I have the honor to enclose a letter which Mr Brown has given me for You,[3] and though it is to serve me as an introduction, still it may contain other matters of interest to You. Mrs Brown has also confided to my care a small box for Mrs Clay,[4] which she wished to have soon delivered. I therefore send it by this day's stage.

I am very anxious to have the honor of making Your acquaintance and of renewing to You the assurances of the greatest regard and consideration with which I am, Sir, Your most obedient servant

V. RUMPFF

The Honorable Henry Clay Secretary of State of the United States Washington.

ALS. DLC-HC (DNA, M212, R2).   [1] Cf. above, Clay to Astor, August 21, 1827, note. [2] John Jacob Astor.   [3] Cf. above, Brown to Clay, July 28, 1827, and note.   [4] Cf. above, Brown to Clay, June 28, 1827.

INSTRUCTIONS AND DISPATCHES   September 20, 1827

From ALEXANDER H. EVERETT, Madrid, no. 88. Reports that the 18,000 troops mentioned in his last dispatch (above, Everett to Clay, September 4, 1827) as having been raised to crush the rebellion in Catalonia "have since been moving into that province"; that the rebellion is represented in recent intelligence "as constantly gaining ground"; that the "King [Ferdinand VII] has determined to take the field in person against the Insurgents" and left for Tarragona on the 22nd, accompanied by the Minister of Grace and Justice (Francisco Tadeo Calomarde), now his "only confidential Counsellor"; and that the King decided to go when he heard of "the excesses and horrors . . . perpetrated by the insurgents" and the circulation of some gold coins stamped with the head of Carlos 5" (cf. above, Brown to Clay, August 26, 1825, note). Notes that Madrid and "its neighbourhood are now almost wholly destitute of any armed protection except the Royalists volunteers" and that "these have hitherto joined the Rebels wherever the latter have shewn themselves"; that if the Insurgents lack the resources and enterprise to strike at the capital and "confine their operations to the same districts where they now are, it is not improbable that the Kings [sic] presence may, as he appears to anticipate, produce a good effect." ALS. DNA, RG59, Dip. Disp., Spain, vol. 27 (M31, R28). Received November 20.

From SAMUEL LARNED, Santiago de Chile, no. 60. Notes that (Heman) Allen, the bearer, "finally concluded to take passage on a French merchant ship, bound for

Rio de Janeiro, thence to reembark for the U. States." Reports that "The French Inspector General, resident here [Charles A. L. de La Forest]," is now designated as "Consul General" and given a higher salary. Suggests that "the government of France has some particular object in view and cites, as further evidence, "The profuse and studied hospitalities, and marked court of the consular family towards the natives, . . . the ostentatious display of . . . *trappings* of royal government, . . . [and] the politick and captivating offer . . . to grant a free passage" on French war-ships "to all the respectable youth of Chile whose parents may be desirous of sending them to France for education [cf. above, Tudor to Clay, February 28, 1826]. . . ." Adds: "A similar offer has been made in Peru, and, I have no doubt, in all the rest of these countries." Transmits "sundry" documents relative "to the affairs of Peru and Colombia. . . ." ALS. DNA, RG59, Dip. Disp., Chile, vol. 2 (M-T2, R2). Received January 29, 1828.

From J[OHN] G. A. WILLIAMSON, LaGuaira. Transmits "a pamphlet which has just been published—" Adds: "It requires no comment of mine." ALS. DNA, RG59, Cons. Disp., LaGuaira, vol. 1 (M84, R1). Received October 14. Endorsed by Clay on cover: "The pamphlet to be translated."

The pamphlet has not been found; the translation is a document of 29 pages, entitled "A brief Narrative of the acts of violence which grew out of the trans-actions at Panama on 13th. September and 14th. October 1826," consisting of an official report of "The Municipality (Corporation) of Panama" directed "To the Secretary of State of the Home Department" (José Manuel Restrepo), concern-ing a period in which military dominance over the local government was estab-lished in the name of the Liberator (Símon Bolívar).

Order on the Bank of the United States, Washington Branch

No.　OFFICE OF DISCOUNT & DEPOSIT, ⎱ 21st. Septr 1827
　　　　　　　　Washington,　　　　　　⎰

　PAY to Check on New York　　　　　or bearer, Forty four
Dollars, 31/100

　　　　　　　　　　　　　　　　　　　　　　H CLAY

$44 DOLLARS, 31/100

ADS, partially printed. DLC-TJC (DNA, M212, R16).

To Lewis Sanders

Dear Sir:　　　　　　　　　　　Washington, D. C. 21 Sept. 1827.
　I received your letter this morning of the 12th ultimo.[1] On the subject to which it refers, water-rotted hemp, Mr. Southard[2] will I presume, write you, as he mentioned to me the other day his having received a letter from you in regard to it. He is now out of the city.[3] If you will prepare your hemp by water rotting, and put it up neatly, you need have no fears of not being able to get the price of the best Russia hemp:[4] And as this latter is subject to a duty,[5] the American article will have a decided advantage in the competition.

I am sorry I cannot supply you with the ram which you want. Mine was killed last Winter,[6] and when I left home I had to depend upon getting one from Mr. Price of Clark.[7] I am, respectfully, your obedient servant,   H. CLAY
Lewis Sanders, Esq.

LS. Owned by Miss Anna V. Parker, Ghent, Kentucky.   [1] Not found.
[2] Samuel L. Southard.   [3] Apparently on a tour of inspection. He was in New York early in October, visited the Philadelphia Navy Yard on October 10, and returned to Washington on October 14. Washington *Daily National Intelligencer*, October 15, 16, 1827; Adams, *Memoirs*, VII, 329.   [4] Cf. above, Southard to Clay, September 20, 1827.
[5] Cf. above, III, 756, note.   [6] Cf. above, Scott to Clay, November 21, 1826.
[7] Probably John Price, a son of Pugh Price. Born in Prince Edward County, Virginia, in 1764, John had served in the Revolutionary War and moved to Kentucky around 1793. He had first located in Bourbon County on an 1800-acre tract for which Clay had represented him in litigation over the title. Unsuccessful in holding that land, Price had moved to Clark County, where he resided six miles west of Winchester. Benjamin Leather Price, *John Price, the Emigrant, Jamestown Colony 1620, with Some of his Descendants* (Alexandria, Louisiana, [c. 1910]), 23–25.

From John Jacob Astor

Dear Sir   New York Sept 21. 1827
    Mr Rumpff Left a Small Box with me Rec'vd from Mrs Brown[1] Directed to you for Mrs Clay   will you please to Direct me me [*sic*] what to do with it—Whether to Send it now or wait till Mr Rumpff gos [*sic*] on which will be Some weeks first— I am Dear Sir most Resptfully [*sic*] Your obedt Servant   JOHN JACOB ASTOR
The Honbe Henry Clay

ALS. DLC-HC (DNA, M212, R2).
[1] Vincent Rumpff; Mrs. James Brown. See above, Brown to Clay, June 28, July 28, 1827; Rumpff to Clay, September 20, 1827.

From Francis T. Brooke

My Dear Sir   St Julien Sepr 21 1827
    I have no doubt our friend Southard[1] gave you a full account of our Tour to the Springs[2] in which I am Sure he would do justice to my Zeal in the Cause of truth & patriotism— you will See by the papers that an attempt is to be made to form an electoral ticket by a convention at Richmond[3] in opposition to the Caucus Ticket there, I wish you would give me your idea of it— I endeavoured to impress it on your friend Genl Breckenridge[4] that Something of the Sort was necessary—that the people in Some Shape ought to be brought out to control the legislature or at least to influence it— I confess I am alarmed by the accounts from Kentuckey [*sic*]   indeed if Ritchie is correct in his expose in the last Enquirer the Battle is over[5]— whatever may be the event, if our institutions are to fail, I am yet anxious that the charge of corruption in the formation of the Cabinet Should be completely refuted,   he himself from the tone of his last paper

Seems to forbear at least to insist on it,   in looking over my letters
I found one of yours[6] (which if my Zeal has not blinded my judgment,
the publication of) [*sic*] would have a good effect   the dificulty [*sic*]
will be to get it before the public in a way to give it its due weight,   I
inclose it to you for your consideration— let me have a line from you—
Your friend   FRANCIS BROOKE—

ALS. InU. Addressed to Clay.   1 Samuel L. Southard.
2 Cf. above, Brooke to Clay, August 8, 1827.   3 Cf. above, Mercer to Clay, August 18,
1827, note.   4 Probably James Breckinridge.   5 In an editorial in the *Richmond
Enquirer* of September 18, 1827, Thomas Ritchie had alluded to a forfeiture of public
confidence in the administration and to corruption in the election of 1824, but had based
his own opposition upon the failures of the administration's program. The union of De-
Witt Clinton and his friends with "the distinguished members of the other party" in
New York was cited as assurance that Jackson would carry 20 to 25 electoral votes in that
State. The prediction was accurate; the General received 20 votes to Adams' 16.
6 Cf. above, Clay to Brooke, February 4, 1825.

From John Sergeant

Dear Sir,   (Private)   Philada. Septr. 21. 1827.
    The federal conferrees [*sic*] decided, this evening, to make no nomi-
nation for Congress. This is not quite as satisfactory as if they had
concurred in the nomination already made, but much better than if
they had made any other nomination. The mass of the federalists will
give us their support, and I suppose meetings will immediately be
called to display their strength and concentrate their action.
    The Jackson party have made no nomination yet. Besides Mr. Horn,
(the candidate of last year), they are understood to be thinking of
Mr. Wurts and Mr. Hemphill,[1] both of whom are in their offer. If
they take up the latter, it will be for the purpose of gaining federal
votes, but they will be likely at the same time to lose some of their
own party, which will also happen if they should take up Mr. Wurts.
Mr. Horn and his friends will be dissatisfied. There is a great deal of
distraction and division among them upon this point.
    Our friends are very confident of success, and I think the prospect
is good. If we come out strong, the effect will be felt throughout the
State. But, as respects myself, I am prepared for whatever may happen,
being entirely satisfied to stand or fall with the cause! Very respectfully and truly yrs.   JOHN SERGEANT.
The Honble Henry Clay.

ALS. DLC-HC (DNA, M212, R2). Cf. above, Johnston to Clay, September 13, 1827,
note.
1 Henry Horn; John Wurts; Joseph Hemphill.

INSTRUCTIONS AND DISPATCHES   September 21, 1827

From ALBERT GALLATIN, London, no. 117. Reports agreement "on the terms of the
intended Convention, for regulating the proceedings of the reference to a friendly

Sovereign or State of the North Eastern boundary, in conformity with the 5th Article of the Treaty of Ghent" (cf. above, Gallatin to Clay, July 29, 1827). Notes some minor points "in the general Map" still to be adjusted. Expresses an expectation that the convention and accompanying documents can be sent "by the packet of the first of October." Explains some features of the agreement and adds that "The British Plenipotentiaries will not entertain any proposition respecting the navigation of the St Lawrence founded on the right claimed by the United States to navigate that river to the Seas" (cf. above, Clay to Gallatin, June 19, August 8, 1826; Clay to Porter, November 13, 1826; Clay to Vaughan, November 15, 1826). States his opinion "that, for the present at least and whilst the intercourse with the British West Indies remains interdicted [cf. above, Gallatin to Clay, August 19, 1826], it is best to leave that by land or inland navigation, with the North American British Provinces, to be regulated by the laws of each Country respectively." Concludes: "I have not received the answer of this Government to the enquiry respecting the Colonial Intercourse [cf. above, Gallatin to Clay, August 21, 1827, and note], nor that of the British Plenipotentiaries on the *Nine Articles* [cf. above, Gallatin to Clay, July 29, 1827]. These are the only subjects remaining unfinished." ALS. DNA, RG59, Dip. Disp., Great Britain, vol. 34 (M30, R30). Extract published in *American State Papers, Foreign Relations*, VI, 768. Received October 31.

From W[ILLIAM] H. D. C. WRIGHT, Rio de Janeiro. Reports rejection by the British and French Ministers (Sir Robert Gordon; probably Count A. M. de Gestas) of the proposal, made by the Brazilian Foreign Minister (the Marquis of Queluz) immediately after (Izidoro da Costa) Oliveira's return from the United States (cf. above, Raguet to Clay, May 31, 1827, and note), on August 23, "that all the captured vessels of their respective Nations, would be restored, provided they would abandon all claims for damages" (cf. above, Wright to Clay, September 1, 1827), and the offer of a second scheme whereby "the cargoes of all the vessels shall be landed, and . . . the duties arising upon them, shall be . . . applied to the payment of the damages. . . ." Surmises that the latter proposal is not acceptable to the French Minister but probably is to his British counterpart. Explains that many British merchants, having settled "with the Insurance Company for 60 per Cent," are eager to compromise with the Brazilian Government but that such a transaction "should be viewed, rather as a Mercantile settlement between individuals . . . and this Government, than as a National Adjustment of the Prize Question." Notes "the general opinion here . . . that the object of this Government, is to obtain the best terms of England and France, before the demands of the United States are known." Summarizes news brought by "The British Packet from Buenos Ayres." Adds that the *Matilda* "has been condemned," while the *Hero* "has been acquitted, delivered up, and the Capt [George Simmonds, Jr.] & Mate put at liberty." Encloses "some . . . documents in relation to the Hero." ALS. DNA, RG59, Cons. Disp., Rio de Janeiro, vol. 2 (M-T172, R3). Received November 7.

On November 20 Wright transmitted to Clay "a copy of the decision on the case of the Schooner Hero, and two letters" received from Simmonds "while in prison." ALS. *Ibid.*

MISCELLANEOUS LETTERS   September 21, 1827

From STEPHEN H. DESFORGES, Lexington (Kentucky). Expresses gratitude for the help given him from the beginning of his correspondence with (Charles Peter Stephen) Wante (cf. above, Brown to Clay, February 13, 1827) and requests Clay to continue recommending his interests to "Monsieur l'Ambassadeur" (James Brown), who has named (Isaac) Cox Barnet as Desforges' "chargé de Procuration" (cf. above, Desforges to Clay, March 12, 1827). ALS, in French. DNA, RG59, Misc. Letters (M179, R65).

From AUGUSTUS JOCELYN, Brookville, Indiana. Appends, to a letter concerning his account for publishing the laws, the following: "P. S. political matters and things are working well in Indiana— Our Senator Gen. [James] Noble is not an idler, in the good cause— He is popular and eficient [sic]—" ALS. DNA, RG59, P. and D. of L.

From CONDY RAGUET, Philadelphia. Encloses a receipt from (William H. D. C.) Wright for books and other property of "the late American Légation" in Brazil. Adds that he has retained copies of his correspondence as Chargé d'Af[f]aires and "all the original notes of the Brazilian Ministers to" him prior to his departure and that he is "under t[he] impression, that" these documents belong to him. Requests to be informed whether "th[is] impression be erroneous. . . ." ALS. DNA, RG59, Dip. Disp., Brazil, vol. 5 (M121, R7). Cf. below, Clay to Raguet, September 24, 1827.

From WILLIAM B. ROCHESTER, New York. Reports having spent several days in New York City making preparations for his departure to Central America; states that he will "start for Phila: tomorrow" and try to obtain passage; and encloses "for the Treasurer [Thomas T. Tucker] an ackwt. of the rect. of his draft for $6750" (cf. above, Rochester to Clay, August 27, 1827). ALS. DNA, RG59, Dip. Disp., Central America, vol. 1 (M219, R2). Received September 24.

DIPLOMATIC NOTES   September 22, 1827

From JULES, CARDINAL OF SOMAGLIA, Rome. Acknowledges receipt of Clay's letter of May 24, 1827, and states that complete credit will be given to "déclarations" of the men mentioned in it. LS, in French with trans. in State Dept. file. DNA, RG59, Notes from Foreign Consuls, vol. II.
    Daniel Brent sent to Mathew Carey, on December 22, 1827, "by direction of Mr. Clay, with a request that" it be communicated to (John J.) Borie, a translation of the Cardinal's letter. On the same date Brent also transmitted a copy of the translation to Richard W. Meade. Copies, in DNA, RG59, Dom. Letters, vol. 22, pp. 109, 110 (M40, R20).

INSTRUCTIONS AND DISPATCHES   September 22, 1827

From MICHAEL HOGAN, Valparaiso. Encloses new commercial regulations in force at the Valparaiso customhouse. ALS. DNA, RG59, Cons. Disp., Valparaiso, vol. 1 (M146, R1).

MISCELLANEOUS LETTERS   September 22, 1827

From ROBERT BARRY, Baltimore. Requests that Clay review the decision of James H. McCulloch, Collector at Baltimore, which refused to allow the Spanish merchant vessel Volador, "owned by Merchants at Havana," to replace, while in port for repairs, guns lost in a storm. ALS. DNA, RG59, Misc. Letters (M179, R65). Received September 24.

Daniel Brent acknowledged the letter for Clay on September 24 and informed Barry that the Secretary of State regretted that the permission could not be granted. Copy, in DNA, RG59, Dom. Letters, vol. 22 (M40, R20) p. 53. Cf. below, McCulloch to Clay, September 22, 1827, and note.

Barry was a Baltimore auctioneer and commission merchant. The *Volador*, a brig, was later infamous as a slaver. *Sen. Docs.*, 28 Cong., 2 Sess., no. 150, p. 132.

From JOSEPH DELAFIELD, New York. Reports that (Anthony) Barclay has notified him that Barclay has written (Peter B.) Porter "of his readiness to hold a Board for the purpose of closing the [Northern Boundary] Commission in October next" and that he understands Barclay "has received such instructions from his Government upon the points submitted as will enable him to act definitely"; adds: "in the course of the ensuing month it will be in my power to lay before you the result of their final deliberations." ALS. DNA, RG76, Northern Boundary: Treaty of Ghent, Arts. VI and VII, env. 1, folder 2.

From JAMES H. McCULLOCH, JR., Baltimore. States that Baltimore customs officials believe that the "Law of 20th April 1818 [cf. above, II, 507n]—sections 5 & 8 especially seem to prohibit" augmentation of the *Volador*'s armaments in an American port. ALS. DNA, RG59, Misc. Letters (M179, R65).

Daniel Brent acknowledged on September 26, 1827, the Secretary's receipt of the letter from the collector's office and informed him that "the Secretary is of opinion that the Law forbids the augmentation of the number of guns of any foreign vessel in our ports. . . ." Copy, in DNA, RG59, Dom. Letters, vol. 22, p. 56 (M40, R20).

From John Sergeant

Dear Sir,   (Private)   Philada. Septr. 23. 1827.

The accounts from Delaware are very favorable. At the election of inspectors in Kent (where the Jacksonites thought themselves strong) our friends carried every district but one, with a total majority of 199. I have seen a statement of the results in a letter. In Newcastle, it is said we have been equally successful, carrying every hundred but one. Of this, however, I have seen no authentic evidence. In Sussex, the only remaining County, our strength was admitted.[1] You are aware that Doctr. Naudain has withdrawn, and Mr. Johns will unite the votes of all our friends.[2] The prospect there seems good.

Every thing here, in Philada., is going on well. Our friends are harmonious, united and active. On the other side, there is great distraction about a candidate, and I do not believe they can agree upon one who will unite all their own votes. Do as they may, the general impression is that we shall beat them handsomely.[3]

In New York, the intriguers, it would seem, are beginning to work. It is believed, but I know not on what authority, that Mr. Clinton is to be brought forward for Vice President,[4] and it is supposed that his name may have some influence in Ohio and New Jersey. I should think that it could have no influence any where, and am not without hopes that the intriguers will (as they often have done) outmanage themselves.

In Pennsylvania, we seem to be gaining, but I cannot speak on that point with any certainty. There is increased exertion, undoubtedly, as is evident from the fact that applications have been made from the interior for two German editors to conduct papers favorable to the Administration.[5] We shall be able to see more clearly after the election. Nothing, of a local kind, has done us so much good as the vulgar and offensive proceedings of the Jacksonites upon the occasion of your expected visit.[6] *They* are not ashamed of it; but they are very sensible of the mischief it has done them, and of the necessity of trying to be a little decent. Mr. Hemphill[7] will find himself in strange company if he should get among them, especially as he has nothing commanding in his nature, and will therefore be obliged to submit.

You will have to consider about a Vice President from the South or the West, Very respectfully and truly yrs. JOHN SERGEANT.
The Honble Henry Clay

ALS. DLC-HC (DNA, M212, R2).
[1] Cf. above, Clay to Taylor, September 7, 1827, note. [2] Arnold Naudain; Kensey Johns, Jr. [3] Cf. above, Johnston to Clay, September 13, 1827, note. [4] Cf. above, Rochester to Clay, September 17, 1827. [5] The Philadelphia *Democratic Press*, September 26, 1827, carried an advertisement for "A person who can give satisfactory evidence of his capacity and qualifications to conduct a German newspaper, and who would have no objections to settle in Pennsylvania, within a hundred miles of Philadelphia. . . ." The Reading *Berks County Adler* was established on December 1, 1827, by Charles F. Egelman and continued as an anti-Jackson organ through 1837, when the title was changed to the *Berks County Demokrat*. Daniel Miller, *Early German American Papers* (Lancaster, Pa., 1911), published as Pennsylvania German Society, *Proceedings*, XIX (1908), pt. 22, p. 59. At Aaronsburg, *Der Centre Berichter*, cited in 1828 as published by Adam Gentzel (not further identified), was begun in 1827 and continued until 1847.
Egelman, born at Osnabrück in Hanover, had emigrated to the United States in 1802, at age 20. He had worked as a coachmaker at Baltimore for some time and then removed to Berks County, where he was a teacher. He was known primarily as an astronomer and for many years supplied the data for the principal American almanacs. [6] Cf. above, Sergeant to Clay, August 23, 1827, note. [7] Joseph Hemphill—cf. above, Johnston to Clay, *ca.* September 13, 1827, note.

To John Quincy Adams

Dear Sir   Washington 24h. September 1827

I have been confined several days by a slight indisposition[1] from which I have so far recovered as to be able to attend at the office today. I yet feel considerable debility, and believe it will be necessary to absent myself a week or ten days from the City to regain my strength.

Copies of the treaty with Sweden and the Conventions with England, together with all the Foreign Correspondence, deemed necessary to be seen by you, have been regularly transmitted.[2] I regret that Mr. Appleton did not sign the treaty in an English as well as a French version;[3] but I presume that omission, which I am at a loss to account for, will not be considered an insurmountable objection to its ratification. I have thought it expedient to authorize short notices of these compacts to be inserted in the Gazettes.[4]

Mr. Poinsett asks instructions in regard to the Manifesto of the Congress of La Vera Cruz.[5] Of what nature shall they be? Can we regularly take any notice of it? Must we not regard the attack on our Minister, however reprehensible, as in the nature of those effusions of the Press and of public opinion which, when analogous occurrences happen among ourselves, are considered as irredressible?

Govr. Lincolnn [sic] still scolds and complains. I have made one of his late communications the basis of a note to Mr. Vaughan who promptly and I think satisfactorily replied.[6] I have transmitted to the Governor the Ministers Answer.[7]—

Mr. Barclay has at length obtained the expected instructions which will enable him to come to a definitive settlement, probably next month, with Genl. Porter, on the subject of the boundary,[8] the adjustment of which is confided to their joint agency. I am with great respect Faithfully Yr's   H CLAY
Mr. Adams.

ALS. MHi-Adams Papers, Letters Recd. (MR482).
1 Cf. above, Forbes to Clay, September 18, 1827, note.   2 Cf. above, Clay to Adams, September 8, 1827.   3 Cf. above, Clay to Appleton, September 11, 1827.
4 Washington *Daily National Journal*, September 10, 24, 1827; Washington *Daily National Intelligencer*, September 11, 24, 1827.   5 Cf. above, Poinsett to Clay, July 8, August 10, 1827; Taylor to Clay, July 16, 1827; Adams to Clay, August 23, 1827.   6 See above, Clay to Vaughan, September 14, 1827; Vaughan to Clay, September 17, 1827.
7 See above, Clay to Lincoln, September 19, 1827.   8 Anthony Barclay; Peter B. Porter. Cf. above, Delafield to Clay, September 22, 1827.

To Francis T. Brooke

My dear Sir   (Confidential)   Washington 24h. Septr. 1827.

I received your obliging favor of the 21st. inst. with its inclosure. Mr. Southard, on his return from the Springs, brought home with him high spirits and good health, and communicated to me all interesting occurrences on his journey. The result of the Kentucky elections,[1] 'though in some respects to be regretted, ought not to be regarded in the discouraging light in which it is. It should be recollected that they took place before Mr. Buchanan's statement[2] reached the State, and before the extensive circulation of the Speech[3] which you and Mr. S. too highly extolled.[4] Many local and other causes had also an inauspicious effect, which it is believed will not operate in future. Notwithstanding all circumstances, the Legislature, in both of its branches, is decidedly friendly to the Administration, and of those who actually voted for members of Congress, there is a considerable majority for Mr. Adams.[5] This happened by the Jackson members being elected in several instances by small majorities, and the Adams, either without competition, or by large majorities. My letters speak with great confidence of the final vote of the State. Mr. Letcher writes that his confidence is greater now than ever.[6]

As to Mr. Ritchies boastful statement that is all a russe [sic] de guerre. My belief is that Mr. Adams will be re-elected, and with ease. I speak of course with all the diffidence which one ought to feel in expressing himself on such a subject   It is a part of the system of the friends of Genl. Jackson to make demonstrations—speak bodly [sic]—claim every body & every State and carry the election by storm. The circumstance most to be deprecated is that this system has too much success in disspiriting our friends.

You ask my opinion as to the project of a Convention in Virga. to nominate in January next electors for Mr. Adams. It appears to me to be an excellent project, and one that cannot fail to have good effect, even if it should not succeed. It will strike by its novelty; and it will command respect by its fairness. There is a great portion (I believe a majority) of the population of Virginia opposed to the domination of the Richmond party. That majority is kept down by the principle of representation, according to territorial division instead of population. The election of electors is the only election in Virginia, in which that principle does not prevail, and in which the decision is according to numbers without regard to Counties. There is reason to believe that the greatest strength of the Administration in Virginia is where there are the greatest numbers; and consequently it will be manifested in the vote for electors. This is or will be known; and the desire of putting down the Richmond influence will stimulate many to the greatest exertion, and may operate in numerous instances to induce men to discard their preference for Genl. Jackson in order to defeat the party of the Metropolis.

In every view of the matter, I think it of the first importance to push the plan. You are to have the first meeting I understand at Fredericksburg.[7] There should be great exertion to make it respectable— So matters strike me.

I thank you for the opportunity of perusing my letter of 4 Feb. 1825. I think its publication would have good effect. Perhaps it had better be defered [sic] a little while. You could take it with you to Richmond, shew it to Pleasants,[8] and he could at a proper time publish it by your permission. When published it ought to be accompanied with this explanation of the first paragraph—that my letter to you of the 28 Jan. 1825 (the letter refered [sic] to in that paragraph) had found its way into the Enquirer, where it was not correctly represented, owing no doubt to the erroneous information of its contents recd. by the Editor;[9] that you wrote to me expressing regret that it had been the subject of newspaper animadversion; and hence my letter of the 4h. Feb.

I return the letter, having retained a Copy.

Are you coming here, as Southard, now absent, told me was probable? Or are you going shortly from home? If you come, pray come at once to my house, where there is always a bed for you.

I have been a little indisposed; and I have some thought of an excursion of a week or ten days to get out of the dust of the office and the smoak of the City— I know not whether I shall be able to get off; but if I do I have a thought of a little tour first to Harper's ferry and then round by Mr. Monroes[10] & possibly to your house. I beg you not to mention my wish in this respect, first because I do not know that I can execute it, and 2dly. if I should I desire to go as much incog: as possible. I am ever Cordially Your friend.   H CLAY
The Honble F. Brooke.

ALS. KyU.
[1] Cf. above, Clay to Taylor, April 4, 1827, note; Clay to Adams, August 25, 1827, note. [2] Cf. above, Ingersoll to Clay, August 11, 1827, note.   [3] Above, July 12, 1827.
[4] Cf. above, Brooke to Clay, August 8, 1827; Southard to Clay, August 8, 1827.
[5] The Frankfort *Commentator* of August 18, 1827, had published figures on the margin of victory in the various Congressional races in Kentucky, showing a majority of 8,687 votes for administration candidates over the Jackson supporters. Washington *Daily National Intelligencer*, September 1, 27, 1827; *Niles' Weekly Register*, XXXIII, (September 22, 1827), 50; Philadelphia *Democratic Press*, September 25, 1827. The Frankfort *Argus of Western America*, September 26, 1827, by omitting the votes in two districts where the opposing candidates were both administration supporters concluded that the Jackson forces had a majority of almost a thousand.   [6] Above, August 27, 1827.
[7] The meeting, to which citizens of Spotsylvania County and the town of Fredericksburg who opposed the election of Jackson had been called, was held on September 27, 1827, with Brooke presiding. With one dissenting vote they adopted resolutions calling for a convention to form an electoral ticket, requesting that the assembly select two delegates to represent them at that meeting, and urging that the citizens of other counties who shared their opinions take similar action. Brooke and Hugh Mercer were then unanimously chosen as the local delegates. Washington *Daily National Journal*, October 4, 1827, reprinting item from Fredericksburg *Argus*.   [8] John H. Pleasants. Clay's letters to Brooke of January 28 and February 4, 1825, were both published in the Richmond *Constitutional Whig*, and reprinted in the Washington *Daily National Intelligencer*, March 28, 1828, with the explanatory note that the editor had requested permission to publish the letters after allusion to the content during the controversy occasioned by Thomas Mann Randolph (cf. above, Hammond to Clay, August 29, 1827, note).
[9] Thomas Ritchie. Cf. above, Clay to Brooke, January 28, 1825, note. The differences in the *Enquirer*'s version were insignificant—substitution of the word "contest" for "election" in the first sentence and of the word "view" for "risk" in the next to last sentence of the first paragraph.   [10] James Monroe.

To James Davidson

Dear Col.   Washington 24h. Decr. [*i.e.*, September] 1827.
Mr. Crittenden and my brother have both reminded me of a conversation which I had with you, in the Fall 1824, prior to my departure from Kentucky to attend Congress in this City, on the subject of the pending Presidential election, in the course of which I avowed to you my decided preference for Mr. Adams over Genl Jackson, and expressed my determination, in the event of my being called upon to choose between them, to vote for Mr. Adams. The particulars of this conversation had escaped me, but from my friendship and intimacy

with you, there is no man with whom it is much more likely that I should have conversed on such a subject, and I have no doubt that I did. Will you do me the favor to transmit me a written statement of what passed between us on that subject, according to the best of your recollection? Your faithful friend   H CLAY
Col. Davidson.

ALS. MB. On the dating of this document, cf. above, Porter Clay to Clay, August 30, 1827; Crittenden to Clay, September 3, 6, 1827; and below, Davidson to Clay, October 20, 1827; Clay to Davidson, November 5, 1827.

To Samuel Southard

My dear Sir   Washn. 24h. Septr. 1827.
    I am better than when you left here, feeling no other effect from my indisposition but that of the loss of some strength.
    John Jacob Astor Esq. of N. York has a small box in his possession for Mrs. Clay sent her by her Sister[1] in Paris. We shall be much obliged to you, if you would take charge of it on your return from Troy and bring it with you to this City. Mrs. Clay attaches much value to it on a/c. of the source whence it comes. I hope it will subject you to no inconvenience. Wishing you a pleasant trip, I am Yr's truly
Mr. Southard.   H CLAY

ALS. NjP-Samuel L. Southard Papers. Endorsed by Southard: ". . . recd. and ansd. in Trenton 7 Oct. & wrote to Mr. Governeur [sic] to bring the box to me." Samuel Lawrence Gouverneur was a nephew of Eliza Kortright (Mrs. James) Monroe and private secretary to the former President. Gouverneur had married Maria Hester, the youngest daughter of the Monroes, in 1820. He had been appointed postmaster of New York in 1825 and held that post until removed by Jackson in 1836. Southard and Gouverneur were close friends.
[1] Ann Hart (Mrs. James) Brown—cf. above, Astor to Clay, September 21, 1827.

From John Quincy Adams

H. Clay. Secretary of State. Washington
Dear Sir   Quincy 24 September 1827
    Since my letter to you of the 11th instt. I have received yours of the 8th and from the Department copies of Mr Gallatins despatches to N 107[1] inclusive, with several others from Messrs Brown, Middleton, Appleton, Watts and Cooley.[2] Also of the letter to you from Governor Lincoln of Maine and of your answer[3]—
    Upon this last subject I presume that in addition to the extract from the Governors letter communicated to Mr Vaughan,[4] you have given instructions to Mr Gallatin, to press the complaint, upon the consideration of the British Government.[5] In one of Mr Gallatins latest despatches, I think he mentions that Mr Canning in the last conference which he held with him urged the point that no exclusive jurisdiction

should be exercised by either party over the controverted territory, until the question of boundary should be settled.[6]

I am relieved from much anxiety by the conclusion of the two conventions;[7] and if any thing could warrant *us*, in regretting the decease of Mr Canning, it is that it happened precisely at the moment when he was relaxing from his feelings of hostility to this Country, and *beginning* to listen to reason. Mr Huskissons[8] enmity is cooler, and more systematic. I should have great hopes of Lord Goodrich [*sic*] if I thought it probable he would long continue at the head of the Ministry.[9] Mr Brougham has told us distinctly enough that we are to expect nothing from the whigs[10]

My present purpose is to leave this place on my return to Washington the 4th of next month. It may perhaps be the 15th before I shall arrive there— Yours faithfully—

Copy. MHi-Adams Papers, Letterbook, Private, no. 10, p. 107 (MR149).
[1] Above, Gallatin to Clay, August 14, 1827.   [2] James Brown; Henry Middleton; John James Appleton; Beaufort T. Watts; James Cooley.   [3] Above, Lincoln to Clay, September 3, 1827; Clay to Lincoln, September 14, 1827.   [4] See above, Clay to Vaughan, September 14, 1827.   [5] The instructions had not been sent to Gallatin. On October 23 Adams noted that Clay had "again" discussed with him instructions to be sent "relating to the Northeastern frontier," but nothing further on that subject was directed to Gallatin before he left London. Adams, *Memoirs*, VII, 343.   [6] Cf. above, Gallatin to Clay, July 29, 1827.   [7] Cf. above, Gallatin to Clay, August 6 (101 and 102), 7, 1827.   [8] William Huskisson.   [9] On the Ministry of Frederick John Robinson, Viscount Goderich, cf. above, Gallatin to Clay, February 22, 1827, note.   [10] Henry Peter Brougham had incurred the anathema of Americans when he had spoken in the House of Commons, on April 9, 1816, of the value of incurring "a loss upon the first exportation [of British goods after the War of 1812], in order, by the glut, to stifle in the cradle those rising manufactures in the United States, which the war had forced into existence contrary to the natural course of things." T. C. Hansard (comp.), *Parliamentary Debates. . . ,* XXXIII, 1099; *Niles' Weekly Register,* XI (January 11, 1817), 298.

INSTRUCTIONS AND DISPATCHES   September 24, 1827

From ALBERT GALLATIN, London, no. 118. Transmits "The second edition of the Report of the Board of Trade of   1791, as published by the ship owners"; explains why he could not find it earlier. ALS. DNA, RG59, Dip. Disp., Great Britain, vol. 34 (M30, R30). Copy, in NHi-Gallatin Papers, vol. 15, p. 72 (MR21). Received November 3. Cf. above, Clay to Gallatin, May 15, 1827; Gallatin to Clay, September 11, 1827.

From J[OHN] G. A. WILLIAMSON, LaGuaira. Notes having "been several times applied to by Citizens of the United States, to Christen their Children, born since they have been residents of this Country"; inquires "how far such an act . . . would go, to make them Citizens of the U. States," and how far his authority extends in this connection. ALS. DNA, RG59, Cons. Disp., LaGuaira, vol. 1 (M84, R1).

MISCELLANEOUS LETTERS   September 24, 1827

To CONDY RAGUET. States, in answer to Raguet's letter of September 21, that it has been "customary for the Foreign Ministers of the United States to retain the entire correspondence of their Legations" and that the rule applies to Raguet as

Chargé to Rio de Janeiro; commends Raguet's action in leaving the "records and papers" of his "Consular office" with (William H. D. C.) Wright. Copy. DNA, RG59, Dip. Instr., vol. 11, p. 361 (M77, R6).

DIPLOMATIC NOTES   September 25, 1827

From JOSEPH R. REVENGA, Bogotá. States that the Liberator President (Simón Bolívar) has directed him to explain why (Beaufort T.) Watts' letter was published (cf. above, Watts to Clay, June 14, 1827, note); reports that Bolívar viewed the letter as evidence of the interest which the United States held for Colombian welfare and, "as it was calculated to produce some good . . . thought that to refrain from giving it publicity, merely because it is not customary to do so, would have argued a misconception of the zeal and philanthropic views of the [American] Government. . . ." LS, in Spanish with trans. in State Dept. file. DNA, RG59, Notes from Foreign Legations, Colombia, vol. 1, part 2 (M51, R2).

MISCELLANEOUS LETTERS   September 25, 1827

To GEORGE HANCOCK. Acknowledges receipt of his letter of September 19 (seeking appointment of his nephew, William Preston Griffin, as a midshipman). States that he (Clay) has made the requested recommendation, that (Secretary of the Navy Samuel L.) Southard "is at present out of the city," and that, upon his return, a decision will be made on the application. LS. CtY-John Mason Brown and Preston Brown Papers.

Hancock, a Virginia planter, operated "Fotheringay," in Montgomery County. Griffin was the son of Hancock's oldest sister, Mary (Mrs. John Caswell Griffin), who had died in 1826, at Fincastle, Virginia. Born in 1810, the youth was admitted to the Navy as a midshipman on October 1, 1827, passed midshipman's grade in 1833, and was commissioned a lieutenant in 1838.

To W[ILLIAM] HASELL HUNT, "Clerk of the U. S. Superior Court for W. Florida, Pensacola." Acknowledges receipt of Hunt's "letter of the 4th. instant" (not found) and informs him that a set "of the Laws of the United States," which he requested, is being forwarded. Concludes: "I am greatly obliged to you for the intelligence concerning Mrs. Woodrow, which your letter communicates— When you see her, will you have the goodness to inform her from me, that her son was well two weeks ago, in Stafford County Virginia when we last heard of him?" Copy. DNA, RG59, Dom. Letters, vol. 22, p. 55 (M40, R20).

Hunt, who had been born in Boston and had attended Harvard College, had joined his older brother, William Gibbes Hunt, in Lexington, Kentucky, in 1816. Six years later W. Hasell Hunt had removed to Pensacola, where he published, from 1824 to 1829, the *Pensacola Gazette*. He had been tax assessor of Escambia County in 1824, was clerk of the Superior Court of West Florida, and became a member of the Florida Legislative Council in 1829. He had been appointed postmaster at Pensacola in 1826 or 1827 and was removed from that office in 1829 under the Jackson administration. In 1830 he joined his brother at Nashville, Tennessee, as a publisher of the *National Banner*, and there he established in 1834 the *Kaleidoscope* magazine. Douglas C. McMurtrie, "The Beginnings of Printing in Florida," in *The Florida Historical Quarterly*, XXIII (October, 1944), 76–77.

Mrs. Woodrow, at this time a resident of New Orleans, was a sister-in-law of Robert and Daniel Brent. Born Mary Fitzhugh, she had first married their eldest brother, George of "Woodstock," a veteran of the Revolutionary War and member of the Virginia House of Delegates from 1787 to 1789. Following his death in 1804, she had married Henry Woodrow (not further identified).

Mrs. Woodrow's son was Robert Carroll Brent, who had been graduated from the United States Military Academy at West Point in 1815, had risen to the rank of first lieutenant in 1819, but had resigned from the Army in 1823. He resided on the family estate in Stafford County until his death in 1837.

From HENRY KING, near Northumberland Courthouse, Virginia. Requests Clay's aid in claiming bounty land, the warrant for which King entrusted to a man who was to have it "designated," and who, he supposes, got and sold the patent. A farmer, he states he wishes to move his family to the tract. ALS. DNA, RG59, Misc. Letters (M179, R65).

In Clay's absence, Daniel Brent acknowledged, on October 9, 1827, receipt of this letter, which, he wrote, he had forwarded to the General Land Office with a request for information to transmit to King. Brent enclosed the reply, which stated the procedure King should follow in order "to remedy any fraud, which may have been committed. . . ." Copy, in DNA, RG59, Dom. Letters, vol. 22, p. 61 (M40, R20).

King had been a member of the House of Burgesses in 1775 and had served in the Virginia forces throughout the Revolutionary War.

To Joseph Gales, Jr., and William W. Seaton

Wednesday morning [September 26, 1827].

Mr. Clay's respects to Mess. G. & S. with the letter[1] returned which they were good enough to send for his perusal.

He never doubted, from the moment he saw it, that the Speech attributed to Mr. T.[2] was a gross fabrication or a wilful [sic] misrepresentation. He advised Mr. T. (if that were the case) to contradict it; and Mr. C. yet expects to see from Mr. T. himself a formal and positive contradiction.[3] In the mean time Mr. C. has recd. the letter herewith sent,[4] before Mr. T. could have gotten his (Mr. Cs) letter.[5] In this letter (see the ☞) Mr. Trimble says: "I have lately seen &c.

If Mess. Gales & Seaton choose they may say in the Intellr (and insert the paragraph in consequence of a letter from a respectable correspondent) "We have before us a letter from D. Trimble Esq. under date the 21st. Ulto. in which he says: 'I have lately seen a statement which is making the tour of News papers, said to be a part of some observations made by me at Lewis Court House in a Speech which I made there in the Spring of 1825 after my return from Congress. The statement is utterly false. . . .' 'I never used such language to any man on any occasion.' ["][6]

It will hardly be necessary to extract the whole paragraph, or to use the name of *Tom* Marshall[7]—

P.S.   Be pleased return [sic] Mr. Trimbles letter.

AN. NN-Ford Collection.

1 Not found—possibly the letter of John McLean to the editor of the Shawneetown *Illinois Gazette,* cited below, Street to Clay, October 8, 1827. 2 David Trimble—cf. above, Clay to Southard, August 12, 1827. 3 Trimble's statement, addressed to Tobias Watkins, August 12, 1827, was published in the "Appendix," to the pamphlet edition of Clay's *Address . . . to the Public,* December 29, 1827, 38–42. In the main body of the *Address,* 11–12, Clay quoted Trimble's testimony as follows: "I do not know of my own knowledge, nor have I been informed by others, that offers, propositions, or overtures such as are spoken of by Gen. Jackson in his letter to Beverly [*sic*—cf. above, Clay to Hammond, June 25, 1827, note], or similar thereto, or of any kind whatever, were made by Mr. Adams or his friends, to Mr. Clay or his friends; or by Mr. Clay or his friends, to Gen. Jackson or his friends. I do not know, nor do I believe that Mr. Adams or his friends made overtures or offers, directly or indirectly, to Mr. Clay or his friends to make him Secretary of State, if he and his friends would unite in aid of the election of Mr. Adams. Nor do I know or believe that any pledge or promise of any kind was made by Mr. Adams or his friends to Mr. Clay or his friends, to procure his aid in the election. I never heard from Mr. Clay, or any of his friends, or any one else that he was willing to vote for Gen. Jackson, if the General would say, or any of his friends for him, that Mr. Adams should not be continued Secretary of State. Nor do I know or believe that Mr. Clay ever expressed a willingness, or any of his friends for him, to support or vote for Gen. Jackson, if he could obtain the office of Secretary of State under him.

"I do not know or believe that any overtures or offers of any kind were made by Mr. Clay or his friends to Mr. Adams or his friends to vote for him or support him if he would make Mr. Clay Secretary of State; or to Gen. Jackson or his friends to vote for him or support him, if he could obtain the office of Secretary of State under him; nor do I believe that Mr. Clay would have taken office under him if he had been elected." Elsewhere in the same text, 15–16, Clay alluded to Trimble's letter as follows: "David Trimble Esq. states that, about the first of October 1824, he held a conversation with me at Frankfort, in Kentucky, on the subject and prospects of the pending election, which he details minutely, and that in the course of it I said 'that I could not consistently with my principles vote for Gen. Jackson, *under any possible circumstances.*' I urged to him all the objections which weighed on my mind, and which have been so often stated, and especially that which is founded upon Gen. Jackson's possession of military pretension only. And, in reference to an objection which Mr. Trimble understood me as entertaining against Mr. Adams growing out of the negotiations at Ghent, Mr. Trimble states that I remarked that it had been 'greatly magnified by the friends of his competitors' 'for electioneering purposes;' 'that it ought to have no influence in the vote which he might be called upon to give; that, if he was weak enough to allow his personal feelings to influence his public conduct, there would be no change in his mind on that account, because he was then on much worse terms with Gen. Jackson about the Seminole war [above, II, 636–62], than he could ever be with Mr. Adams about the treaty of Ghent [above, II, 322–23, 409]; that in the selection of a chief Magistrate for the Union he would endeavor to disregard all private feelings, and look entirely to the interests of the Country and the safety of its institutions.' " 4 Not found. 5 Not found.

6 The paragraph, as quoted, appeared in the Washington *Daily National Intelligencer,* September 27, 1827. Internal quotation marks were written and published as double marks; they are here changed by the editors for clarification. 7 Possibly Thomas A. Marshall.

From Amos Kendall

TO HENRY CLAY, ESQ. LETTER I. [*ca.* September 26, 1827]

[Relates how he "came to the knowledge near three weeks before the election"[1] that, if Adams became President, Clay would be Secretary of State: a "confidential friend and correspondent"[2] of Clay had requested Kendall, about January 20, 1825, to write his Congressman[3] in favor of Adams, as the latter would make Clay Secretary of State; on the man's third visit Kendall had agreed, having been convinced that the alternative would be Jackson as President with Adams as Secretary of State. Since Adams offered the appointment to Clay, Kendall concludes that the arrangement had been made, probably by January 15.]   AMOS KENDALL.

Copy. Frankfort *Argus of Western America*, September 26, 1827.
1 By the House of Representatives—cf. above, Clay to Brooke, February 10, 1825, and note.   2 Francis P. Blair—cf. below, Blair to Clay, October 3, 1827.   3 David White, Jr.

From John Sergeant

Dear Sir,   (Private)   Philada. Septr. 26th. 1827.

I received to day your letter of the 23d.[1] The federal meeting in support of the nomination already made was held this afternoon, and in weight and numbers was all we could wish.[2] It will have a decisive effect upon the body of the party. Some of our friends are a little dissatisfied that the meeting avoided the Presidential question, adhering to strict federal ground. Not having seen their resolutions, I am not able to say how far this is well founded. I am well persuaded, however, that the course taken was deemed the most politic, and upon that point we cannot deny their right to judge for themselves— The Jackson meeting will be held to morrow.[3] It will be large, no doubt, for it will be drawn from all quarters, without regard to the limits of the district, and be composed of all sorts and sizes, voters or not voters. It is said they will take up Mr. Hemphill (who returned last evening) if he will consent, and if not, Mr. Kittera.[4] In either case, they will lose their strong position as the democracy of Pennsylvania, which has hitherto been of great avail to them. Whatever may be the result of the election here, this movement will relieve us from one of our greatest difficulties— As to the election itself, we are very confident, but not unmindful of the necessity of exertion. I think the prospect now encouraging— Measures have already been taken for printing in German and distributing ten thousand copies of the most material of the papers you mention.[5] We shall have an additional news paper here in a few days,[6] and two German papers are about to be set up, in the interior.[7] Our friends are becoming more zealous every day, and we shall be upon a par, in point of activity, with our opponents, Very respectfully and truly yrs.   JOHN SERGEANT.

The Honble Henry Clay.

ALS. DLC-HC (DNA, M212, R2).   1 Not found.
2 Cf. above, Johnston to Clay, September 13, 1827, note.   3 *Ibid.*   4 Joseph Hemphill; Thomas Kittera.   5 Publication not found.   6 The Philadelphia *Pennsylvania Gazette.*   7 Cf. above, Sergeant to Clay, September 23, 1827, and note.

INSTRUCTIONS AND DISPATCHES   September 26, 1827

From ALBERT GALLATIN, London, no. 119. Reports that, at a conference "yesterday" (the Protocol of that conference was dated September 24, 1827. Manning [arr.], *Diplomatic Correspondence . . . Canadian Relations*, II, 633, 634n), "the British Plenipotentiaries [Charles Grant; Henry U. Addington] took up the subject of the 'Nine Articles' " (cf. above, Clay to Gallatin, June 19, 1826 [V, 471–75]; Gallatin to Clay, June 20, 1827). States that "They reiterated the declaration, which they had already intimated [cf. above, Gallatin to Clay, December 21, 1826; July 5, 1827], that their Government could not accede to the proposal of a mutual surrender of fugitive slaves. . . ." Observes that he was told "informally that, such was the state of public opinion here on that subject, that no Administration could or would admit in a treaty a stipulation such as was asked for." Continues: "They further stated that, one of the most material articles having been rejected (the second) [cf. above, V, 473] and the two Governments not being agreed on several of the others, they did not consider the subjects embraced by the Articles to be of sufficient importance or urgency to be the subject of a separate Convention." Notes that he explained that the amendments offered by him were "only for consideration," that he had instructions to insist on only two, and that "there would be no difficulty if the apparent disagreement on some points was the only objection." Adds that "They then said they really did not think it worth while to make a Convention for such purposes only as the Articles embraced, that most of the provisions therein contemplated (Art. 3 to 8) were such as would, between Great Britain & the United States, be naturally acted on without a treaty; And that when the propositions had been made in 1824, it had been with the expectation that they would be appended to a Convention embracing more important objects." Concludes: "Although the reasons assigned did not in every respect appear conclusive, I could but acquiesce in the determination of the British Plenipotentiaries." ALS. DNA, RG59, Dip. Disp., Great Britain, vol. 34 (M30, R30). Published in Adams (ed.), *Writings of Albert Gallatin*, II, 389–90. Received November 1.

To John F. Henry

My dear Sir: (Confidential.)   Washington, D. C. 27 September, 1827.

I transmit you, herewith, a paper containing some hasty reflections on the subject of a more united and vigorous coöperation of our friends, to which I request your deliberate attention. I am so strongly penetrated with the necessity of more concert, that I hope our friends will adopt the plan now suggested, or some other, more efficacious. I have sent counterparts of this paper to J. J. Crittenden, F. Johnson, D. Trimble, T. Smith, G. Robinson,[1] and some other friends, and requested their execution of the plan if it meet their approbation.

Prior to the result of the late Congressional elections in Kentucky,[2] the Jackson cause, if not prostrate, was rapidly on the decline. That result has excited[3] new hopes amongst its partisans, and, for the moment, created some depression amongst our friends. The effect is gradually subsiding, and giving way to a conviction, among the well informed and reflecting, that the success of Mr. Adams' re-election is certain, with proper exertions. Even in quarters from which little was expected, an encouraging spirit begins to shew itself. But I have not time to dwell on the subject, and I will, therefore, conclude with again earnestly requesting your full consideration of the expediency of some system by which the exertion of our friends may be rendered more efficacious. I am, with great regard, faithfully, Your obedient servant, Dr. Henry.   H. CLAY

[Enclosure]
If the result of some of the Congressional elections in Kentucky is not in accordance with our wishes and expectations, that of the whole of the elections, Congressional and State, is far from being discouraging. We still have the majority.[4] Our opponents have come nearer obtaining it than could have been expected or desired: But, looking at the whole State, as a whole, they are still in the minority. How have they approached so near us? The solution of this question is very important, and upon it depends the direction which we should give to our future efforts. Let such a solution be here attempted. They owe their success, mainly, to an efficient organization of their party. If there be a system of concert and coöperation on one side, and a want of it on the other, the side having it will forever prevail in all political struggles in which there is any thing like an equal division of the community. Discipline and systematic exertion do not more certainly lead to victory in war, than union, concert, and organization must always command success in politics. We have been nearly beaten at the late elections for the want of this union; and we shall certainly be beaten, in the great struggle of the coming year, if we continue in this unequal condition. We must learn, as others have done before us, from our adversaries; and practise, in support of our cause, at least those honorable and legitimate tactics which they employ to further theirs.

Our opponents have, no doubt, in some instances, employed means of detraction and corruption, which we would scorn to use, and with which we would not sully our cause. They may, and probably have, by such means, effected one or two elections. Let them enjoy their triumph, with no other feelings, on our part, than those of regret that any portion of our fellow citizens should allow themselves to use, and should find willing subjects of, base and dishonorable instruments. But, let it be repeated, *organization* has been the efficient cause of the degree of success which our opponents have lately obtained. There is a double advantage in organization: it admits of a ready and easy distribution of intelligence through all the persons associated, and it ensures regular, united, and systematic exertion, on the important day of the election. With this strong conviction, that unless our friends organize themselves they are in imminent danger of being beaten hereafter, allow me to suggest an arrangement which strikes me as being worthy of consideration.

Let there be a public meeting called in every county of the State of the friends of the administration, of the American System, and of H. Clay, if it is thought expedient to use his name. Let them adopt resolutions of approbation and support; and, particularly, resolutions expressive of their detestation of the calumny by which their fellow-citizen has been assailed; of their confidence in him, and of their conviction of the entire failure to establish, through Mr. Buchanan,[5] any thing injurious to his character.

Let there be appointed at those meetings a Committee of active, intelligent residents of the county-town and its neighborhood, to be composed of some ten or a dozen persons, and to be denominated the committee of Correspondence. Let there be a large Committee of Vigilance established, embracing one hundred or more persons, and so distributed throughout the county that there shall be one or more of the Committee in every neighborhood.

The duty of the Committee of Correspondence, (which should be organized by appointing the most active and influential man of their number as President,) may be to correspond with other similar Committees, or with individuals, in the same State, or in other States: And it should be especially their duty to collect, and distribute, thro' the members of the Committee of Vigilance, political essays, tracts, and newspapers, calculated to advance the success of the cause. The Presidents of the Committees of Correspondence will form so many rallying points, to which could be transmitted, from friends in other States, useful documents and information: And every neighborhood would have, in the persons forming the Committees of Vigilance, so many repositories, to which the vicinage could resort, for the purpose of support, vindication, and refutation. It must never be forgotten that the principle on which all our institutions are based, is the capacity of the people to govern themselves. To their judgments, properly enlightened by information, the appeal must always be made for a correct decision of any matter connected with their government. And the great object of every patriot should be, to carry such information and knowledge home to the people as will enable them to comprehend, clearly, the truth, and to pursue their own best interests.

The object of a Committee of Vigilance, collectively and individually, should be to watch over the interests of the cause; to vindicate it from error and aspersion; to disseminate information and documents received from the Committee of Correspondence; to animate their neighbors, and to stimulate and encourage them to attend the elections. It would not be very important that the Committee should assemble in their collective capacity very often: And a provision might be made that the Chairman of the Committee, and a small portion of its members, would be sufficient to form a quorum for the transaction of business.

The Committee of Correspondence, or of Vigilance, ought to be invested with powers to call meetings of the people friendly to the cause, when deemed necessary.

Besides the advantages already suggested in such an organization as is here faintly sketched, there are others not unworthy of notice. Every member of the two Committees would feel himself flattered by the appointment, and impelled by the confidence reposed in him, to make the greatest exertions. Intelligence would be rapidly and certainly communicated throughout the whole community: and there would, at the period of the election, instead of an uncertain, disjointed, and ill-directed exertion, be union, harmony, and certainty in action. An estimate could, at all times, be correctly made of the number and strength of friends in every neighborhood. In such a system of concert and coöperation, success would be certain and inevitable.

The sooner the work is begun the better. It ought not, it is conceived, to be delayed beyond this Fall. No matter whether many or few attend the first initiatory meetings which are called: All that is required, is, that you should have enough to give form to the proceeding, and that you be sure of the persons appointed on the two Committees, and who may be designated whether present or absent.

Is it worth while to conceal this movement from the other party? Not at all. Concealment is itself impossible, and is altogether unnecessary. If it were attempted, it would fail, and the other party would claim credit and obtain advantage by the exposure of the design.

The importance of such a plan of coöperation as has been here suggested, will quickly develope itself in all parts of the State—but especially in those Congressional districts which are represented by unfriendly members. During the ensuing session of Congress those districts will be deluged by inimical documents and papers transmitted by those members, and the effect of this one-sided intelligence will be very great, unless it be counteracted by the distribution of information on the opposite side. The Committees which have been proposed will form regular and legitimate channels for carrying counteracting information to the body of the people in those districts.

It would be an improving addition to the preceding plan of coöperation if there were a Central Committee of Correspondence established at Frankfort, to communicate with the other committees throughout the State. Such a Central Committee would at all times be highly useful, but especially so during the period of the session of the Legislature.

LS. Owned by William P. Foster, Portland, Oregon.   1 George Robertson.
2 Cf. above, Clay to Taylor, April 4, 1827, note.   3 Clay substituted, by interlineation, this word for "created."   4 Cf. above, Clay to Adams, August 19, 1827; Clay to Brooke, September 24, 1827.   5 Cf. above, Ingersoll to Clay, August 11, 1827, note.

From Francis T. Brooke

My Dear Sir   St Julien Sepr 27 1827
  I received your letter of the 24 this morning   I fear it will be im-

possible for me to visit Washington before I go to the court which will meet on the 10h proximo,   nothing could afford me more pleasure than to See you here,   your views of the effect of a convention at Richmond to form an Electoral ticket in opposition to the caucus ticket accord with my own perfectly— the hostility in the populous parts of the State to the Richmd party is very Strong—and may be made to operate well— the convention question, also if well managed by the friends of the admn will do Some Service,   I fear the meeting in Fredg will turn out unfavorably, it ought to have been called to the county courthouse, and longer notice Should have been given,   it will have a good effect however in prompting other counties to adopt the plan from which I promise myself the best effects— I wish you could See Mr Madison[1] on your tour,   if his Sentiments could be known they would have a wonderful effect not only in Virginia but in the Union,   I have written a long letter to my friend Joseph C Cabell on that Subject who has more access to his opinions than any body else that I know[3]— let me know your movements and excuse this hasty letter— Yours very truly   FRANCIS, BROOKE

ALS. InU.   [1] James Madison.
[2] Cf. below, Mifflin to Clay, October 21, 1827, note.

Bill from Lemuel Franklin

Honbl. Henry Clay   Philadelphia Septr. 27th 1827
                    Bought of Lemuel Franklin
        Four pairs calf skin Shoes @ 2.75   11..00
              One pair Velvet Shoes   3.50
                                                  ─────────
                                             $ 14.50
                                                  ─────────

per Order of R. W. Meade Esqr.

ADS. DLC-TJC (DNA, M212, R16). Addressed on cover: "Honourable Henry Clay Secretary of State Politeness of R. W. Mead [*sic*] Esqr." Endorsed by Clay on cover: "Sent a check for the within 22d. Oct 1827." Franklin was a Philadelphia boot and shoe maker.

From Joseph Durham Learned

Dear Sir,   (Confidential)   Baltimore Sept. 27th. 1827
    Since I had the pleasure of seeing you, I have recd. the proposals of Mr. Force, to take an interest in the National Journal.[1] Those proposals require some little consideration from me, and before I come to a conclusion upon the subject, I have taken the liberty of addressing this communication confidentially to you. The interest I feel in the political contest that now agitates the country, is the only apology I have to offer, for intruding it upon your notice.
    Perhaps you may recollect an interview that I had with you, in the

City of Washington, previous to the late Presidential election, when you were a conspicuous candidate for the Presidency; and the disposition I then expressed, to lend you my feeble aid, by devoting the Columns of the Federal Republican, (in my hands a decided republican paper) to your interest. You had *then* my preference, although I entertained doubts of your success at that election. Mr. Adams was my next choice, and I early determined so to shape my course, as not to loose [sic] the influence of my paper to the cause of my favorite Candidate. Consequently, I commenced in a series of numbers addressed to the people of the United States, calling the attention of the public to the principles that should govern the People in making their choice, and to the requisite qualifications of the man who *ought* to be elected to this high station, without, at first, directing their application to any one. These communications had their effect, for they advocated, principles that could not be controverted. They led the way to their successfull [sic] application, and were mostly republished elsewhere, by all parties. In the course of the canvass, when I became convinced that you could not succeed *at that time*, in opposition to Mr. Adams or Genl. Jackson, I brought out my paper for Mr Adams, and made my previous numbers bear upon him, by the test I had laid down and until the election was over, I suffered no effort of mine to be wanting, to sustain his cause. I can appeal to the leading friends of the Administration throughout this State to bear testimony, to the energy and effect of my exertions, with confidence, that they will give me a liberal share of commendation.

Long before the contest was ended, and until the cabinet was formed, the people of the United States naturally looked to you as the successor of Mr. Adams as Secretary of State, in the event of his election; and your appointment, therefore, created no surprise, and was universally popular, except with the disappointed, whose approbation could not have been expected. From the circumstances connected with the election, you became at once identified with Mr. Adams, and it is not strange that you were marked out for the same fate. Every ungenerous feeling that disappointed ambition could engender, united with all the political considerations that combined to embitter the rancour of the moment, were indiscriminately levelled [sic] at you both. It is easy to see why so much of their animosity, is now directed, pointedly at you. Mr Adams has gained his elevation, and unless the opposition can reach *you* through *him*, and enable them to crush you, both at a blow, *you* stand in the way of their future success. They would gain but half their object, by defeating the reelection of Mr Adams, while you were left in the way to occupy his station. Success, therefore, answers a double purpose; it sinks you both together, while defeat blasts their prospects forever. To accomplish this, is the great effort of their policy, and upon its success, rests the foundation of their political hopes. Your friends, and the friends of Mr. Adams see this. They see too, that the Executive favors have not been bestowed upon the friends of the Administration, although possessing *equal* qualifications, and *superior* pretentions.[2] They have felt this neglect with sensibility, from one end of the continent to the other. They are not satisfied with either the Justice or propriety of this policy. And the result is, that while his appointments may have served to neutralize a *few* political opponents, they have alienated the affections, and cooled the ardour of a *host* of friends. I state the fact confidently, that were not your fate too closely linked with that of Mr. Adams to be separated hundreds of his former friends, in Maryland, would not turn on their heels to promote his reelection. And this is not because they are dissatisfied with the conduct of the Administration generally, or because they distrust his moral or political integrity. Their confidence here remains unshaken. Neither do they question the purity of his motives; but the correctness of this policy. It is not the way to sustain his cause. I like the Jeffersonian system, "take care of my friends, and let my enemies take care of themselves."[3]

Much may yet be done in Pennsylvania, but it must be by different measures from those hitherto pursued. The people of that state are a little peculiar in their *notions*. Their political prejudices are stubborn and inveterate. They are not to be overcome by appeals directly made to themselves, but through the influence of the leading republicans of the State, to whom they have been accustomed to look for favor and information, and in whom they have confidence. The old Federal prejudice is yet warm & inveterate there, and every effort is making by the friends of Genl. Jackson, to identify the Administration with the most odious relics of that party. The effort has been thus far, successfull [*sic*], and will continue to be so,[4] while the great republican interest of the State is overlooked or neglected, as it has been. If the heads of the departments of the Government were as numerous as hydra, and filled by men from the north of the Potomac, they would be attacked, in succession one after another, if not to destroy, at least to weaken the confidence of the people in the Administration. Talents, integrity, experience in Government, purity of motives, and unexceptionable conduct, are no shield against the daring calumnies, and insidious sneers of men, unawed by principle, and ambitious of power, with success in view. The course of policy pursued by the Administration is not calculated to combat with such men, upon equal terms, when aided alone by interested enemies, or lukewarm friends. I am not vain enough to suppose that these suggestions are new to you; that they have not come within the range of your keen observation. But men in power do not always find friends who will speak their opinions boldly, with a single eye to the facts and their results.

But to the point, what is to be done? The National Journal is not now aiding the cause of the Administration; and its expences [sic] under the present management exceed its receipts.⁵ It is not worth more therefore, than the value of the materials. I have never asked a favor of the Government either directly or indirectly, nor do I intend to ask one now. Yet I feel a deep interest in your success, and some confidence in my ability to serve the cause of the Administration. But I have a large family dependent alone upon me for education and support. Their interest and my own I am bound to observe. By coming into the concern of the Journal I could retrench its expences, and increase its power and patronage. But to do this entirely upon my own responsibility, would exhaust my weak rescourses [sic], and leave me & my family without support, before the concern would yield me an indemnity. If I could receive some aid not as a favor, but as a compensation for services I am competent to render, independent of the paper, until it would yield me support, I would not hesitate to risk the result. The favor would then be reciprocal, and I could give up my profession and sustain myself without incurring pecuniary embarrassments. If the public interest is to be promoted, by sustaining the Administration, as every considerate man in the nation believes, it must be paid for to some one. He who promotes it most is best employed. Whether I could do that is not for me but others to decide. Could I see this point clearly arranged, nothing would give me more pleasure than to remove to Washington. Any thing short of that would require a sacrifice from me, that I could not, in Justice to myself, encounter.

The Georgetown paper,⁶ is also offered to me. But that has now but a very limited circulation, and the only way to render it of essential service to the Administration, would be to print two or three thousand papers, regularly, and put them in circulation, without regard to the subscription— Most of those who might receive the paper, if it was ably conducted, would become subscribers, and in the end would render the establishment profitable. But this could not be done, by the proprietor alone. The expense would be too heavy. If the *friends* of the Administration, would do what their opponents are doing,⁷ combine to meet the expense of such a measure—There would be no difficulty. It might be made a Stock concern, and the establishment pledged in trust to refund the money advanced. Such a plan was, some time since, gotten up in this city, and most of the stock subscribed for, but some of the friends of the Administration are now so lukewarm, that it could not be carried into effect without aid from abroad. I could, indeed, render a paper in Georgetown, of as much use to the Administration, if conducted upon my plan, as if published in Washington. But while I should be laboring with all my energies for the general cause, and to establish a paper to give it influence, I should be totally destitute of support myself, unless I had some other reliance than the paper.

I have thus Sir explained my views and opinions, upon a subject, that is *here*, deemed of the highest importance. But in making this communication to you, I do not seek to draw you into a correspondence. I know the delicacy of your situation, and the severe, and often, invidious scrutiny to which your acts and declarations are subjected. I do not require you to answer this letter, therefore, unless you may think proper to do so, and it may comport with your pleasure and convenience; while, if you can render it of service to yourself, you are at liberty to use it as you may think proper. It is written in frankness and sincerity, and I am sure you will appreciate the motive, even if you should not agree with me in opinion   I have the honor to be Sir yours Sincerely   J. D. Learned
Hon. Henry Clay

ALS. DLC-HC (DNA, M212, R2). Learned, born in 1780, had been graduated from Middlebury College in 1805, had read law in Massachusetts, and had entered practice in Portland, Maine, in 1810. He had served as a colonel of militia through the War of 1812 and afterward resumed practice of law in Baltimore and edited the *Federal Republican and Baltimore Telegraph* (founded as the *Federal Republican and Commercial Gazette* in 1808, merged in 1816 with the *Baltimore Telegraph and Mercantile Advertiser*, and continued under joint title until 1834).

[1] Peter Force; Washington *National Journal*.   [2] Cf. above, Clay to Peters, October 16, 1826; Peters to Clay, October 24, 1826; Webster to Clay, March 25, 1827; Clay to Webster, April 14, 1827; Worsley to Clay, April 17, 1827; Binns to Clay, April 28, 1827; Wharton to Clay, August 3, 1827; Shaw to Clay, August 22, 1827; Hunt to Clay, August 26, 1827; Clay to Adams, August 27, 1827.   [3] Quotation not found. For comment on Jefferson's appointment policy, see White, *The Jeffersonians*, 351–58; Carl Russell Fish, *Civil Service and the Patronage* (Cambridge, Massachusetts, 1920), 29–51.   [4] For a contrary assessment of the administration's chances in Pennsylvania, see above, Cameron to Clay, *ca.* July 26; Wharton to Clay, August 3; Finley to Clay, August 6; Sergeant to Clay, September 11, 23, 26; Johnston to Clay, September 14, 1827.   [5] On April 29, 1828, Tobias Watkins suggested that he, himself, purchase and edit the *National Journal*. Adams, noting this proposal, commented: "Force has been unfortunate with it, and has neither funds nor credit to sustain it any longer." *Memoirs*, VII, 523–24. Force continued, however, as publisher of the *National Journal* until the newspaper was discontinued in January, 1832.   [6] The *Metropolitan and Georgetown Commercial Gazette*, founded in 1820, was merged in July, 1828, with the Georgetown *Columbian Gazette*, established in November, 1826, and published since March, 1827, as the *Georgetown Columbian and District Advertiser*. Learned had probably been approached to take over the older journal.   [7] Cf. above, Moore to Clay, February 10, 1827, note; Whittlesey to Clay, March 13, 1827; and see, also, Remini, *Election of Andrew Jackson*, 76–80.

From Robert Scott

Dear Sir,   Lexington 27 Septr. 1827
    Your two favors of the 7 & 14 inst.[1] have been received—
    I have for some time past, been in correspondence with Mr. Cox[2] in relation to the case of Sanders against Ogden—   And he has informed me that he has received the mandate of the U S. Supreme Court in that case;[3] that the Judgment affirmed is 4017$64 but that it is beleived [*sic*] to be a question of some doubt whether it carries interest, and that Ogdens security[4] has abundance of property of which to make the debt; but he beleives payment will be with held as long as possible—

The assignment of Sanders to Stainton and by him to Morrison,[5] was transmitted to Mr. Cox for collection, early in the year 1821—

Of the Ogden debt, Mr. Cox claims about 1600$ and 900$ of it has been assigned to me, with costs, damages and interest on a bill of Exchange to that amount, protested in 1819— whether Mr. Cox's claim bears interest or not, I do not know, but if it should, and I suppose it does, and the Judgment against Ogden should not, there will be but little left for Colo. Morrison's Claim.

Enclosed is a check[6] of the Office of Discount & Deposit of this place on the Bank of the U States, for Six thousand dollars, which is to the debit of your private acct. with Colo. Morrisons estate— It cost ½ pr. Ct premm.   say 30$—

Mr. S. Hickey, requested me to say to you, that a lock which you know something about, will be finished in 2 or 3 weeks— Very respectfully Your obt. Servt.   ROBT. SCOTT
The Honble Henry Clay

ALS. DLC-TJC (DNA, M212, R13).   [1] Neither letter has been found.
[2] Probably Nathaniel Cox.   [3] Cf. above, Boyle to Clay, January 10, 1825, and note; Scott to Clay, March 9, 1825; Wheaton to Clay, May 29, 1827, note. In outcome Sanders had won his case against Ogden, for in a ruling on several "reserved points" Chief Justice Marshall had been joined by two colleagues in holding that a State bankruptcy law could not relieve a debtor from claims owed in another State when prosecuted in the courts of that State or in a Federal court. 25 *U. S.* (12 Wheaton) 356–68.
[4] Probably Thomas L. Harman, who with Peter V. Ogden had jointly signed as securities to George M. Ogden's bond on appeal from the judgment of the District Court of the United States for Louisiana, December 13, 1819. DNA, RG267, Series 21, Appellate Case Files. Ogden, born in 1785 and graduated from Princeton College in 1804, was George M. Ogden's brother and had been his partner in a New Orleans mercantile firm. Peter V. Ogden had died, of yellow fever, in 1820. Harman, a New Orleans banker, has not been further identified.   [5] Andrew Stainton; James Morrison.   [6] Not found.

INSTRUCTIONS AND DISPATCHES   September 27, 1827

From JAMES BROWN, Paris, no. 74. States that in the course of his interview with the Baron de Damas on September 7 (cf. above, Brown to Clay, September 8, 1827), the Baron remarked "that France was very far from being satisfied with the operation of the Convention of June 24th. 1822; that it had been discovered . . . to have had an unfavorable effect on French navigation, and that it must shortly terminate unless the United States could consent to diminish the duties on certain articles of French production." Adds that to Damas' inquiry whether Brown had received from Clay "any recent instructions . . . on that subject," he replied that Clay had sent copies of the exchange of letters with the Baron de Mareuil (above, Mareuil to Clay, May 16, 1827; Clay to Mareuil, May 25, 1827; Clay to Brown, June 6, 1827), "from which, as well as from what . . . [the United States] Government had already done in regard to French silks and wines" (cf. above, III, 675n; Clay to Mareuil, April 28, 1826, note; Brown to Clay, September 13, 1827, note), Brown had "inferred its disposition to meet the French Government in any plan which would give the greatest degree of activity to the commercial intercourse between the two nations, and to consent to any measures which could be devised, consistently with their mutual interests, to increase the consumption of their respective commodities."

Reports that, apprehensive that the French intention might be to "terminate the Convention, and wishing in that event to discover what course it was their intention to pursue," he requested another interview, which took place on September 20. Outlines his presentation at that time of the American view concerning duties and restrictions affecting trade between the two countries, after which Damas "admitted that the subject . . . was not free from difficulties, but at the same time very delicately hinted . . . that we were disposed to entertain no very friendly feelings towards the French commercial marine." Summarizes his efforts, in reply, to give reassurance on that point. Notes that, after requesting a reply to his note of August 1, "respecting discriminating duties . . . on American vessels arriving at Havre, on account of their having on their voyage touched at the port of a third power" (cf. above, Brown to Clay, August 13, 30, 1827), he took his leave. Observes that, although he received from the interview "no positive assurances as to the intentions of France respecting the Convention," it left on his mind "a strong impression . . . that France will not, for some time at least, take any step to release herself from its obligations." LS. DNA, RG59, Dip. Disp., France, vol. 23 (M34, R26). Received November 18.

MISCELLANEOUS LETTERS   September 27, 1827

From JOSEPH M. WHITE, Harrodsburg, Kentucky. Having "just heard of the death of the Marshal of West Florida Wm. Sebree," requests "that if the vacancy has not been filled in time for the November Court . . . it may be delayed until" he reaches "Washington, . . . early in Nov." Warns: "There will be presented, some persons, who are not qualified in any respect for the office." ALS. DNA, RG59, A. and R. (M531, R8-James Webb file). For the appointment, cf. below, Clay to Wilson, November 27, 1827.

From Daniel Mallory

D Sir,   New york, Sept. 28. 1827.

I have been very desirous of seeing you here, more perhaps from a selfish wish to consult you on my own private affairs than for any other purpose; tho. among your friends the feeling is universal that your presence would harmonise and concentrate a great many who only wait for a motive to act openly & effectively.

Having accepted of a temporary interest in the "National Advocate,"[1] business connected with the paper call'd me lately to Paterson, where I spent a few days. I had there an opportunity of freely exchanging opinions with many influential gentlemen;—they were unanimous that a visit from you would render the Administration Stronger in New Jersey; and they were most anxious to have an opportunity to offer you publicly their unfeigned thanks for your distinguished and effectual support to the policy that has made their town rich and populous.

The opposition prints here would lead people at a distance to suppose our population were largely in favour of Gen. Jackson, when, if we are not greatly deceived we shall elect all our men friends to the Administration.[2] The truth is our friends are mostly quiet moral people—men of weath [*sic*] and influence; and this remark is general through the nation.

To recur again to the subject of your visit. Is there any probability of your visiting this part of the Country this fall?—

I had made up my mind that so long as there was any feasiable [*sic*] way of employing my time and faculties I would never make another application to the government for employment;[3] but, being sadly disappointed in realizeing [*sic*] some expectations,—well founded indeed—and having as you know others dependent on me for support, I ask you, Sir, if there is any place in the gift of the government, that could be given to me, that would suit my humble capacity?— I am very well aware of the impossibility of finding places for even a very small number of the numerous friends that apply; yet it sometimes happens that a vacancy occurs that will only suit certain persons.

I have very lately had the pleasure of seeing Judge Rochester,[4] who I suppose has been with you for, if I mistake not, he is expected back here about this time[5]—

Mrs M. and the children[6] are at Troy, where they have been since May. Respectfully and Sincerely, yours   D. MALLORY
Hon. H. Clay Washington

ALS. DLC-HC (DNA, M212, R2). Addressed: *"Private."*
[1] Mallory's connection with that journal has not been found.   [2] Cf. above, Clay to Blunt, September 11, 1827; Rochester to Clay, September 17, 1827.   [3] Cf. above, III, 452.   [4] William B. Rochester.   [5] Cf. above, Rochester to Clay, September 21, 1827.   [6] Not identified.

From Daniel Webster

My Dear Sir,   Confidential   Boston Sep. 28. 27

I hope you are recovered from such a *shock*, as the disappointment in Kentucky would naturally produce.[1] There is, doubtless, much cause for regret, but *none for despair*. We have a year yet, before us, & I trust time will aid our efforts.

For the last 3 or 4 weeks I have been with my wife & children[2] down on our Southern shore, to get a little quiet. Professional duties have now called me home, & I expect to be a good deal engaged, till my departure for Washington. Not so much, however, as not to be able to attend to any thing which the *general good* may require. I am willing to make an effort to do something for Hammond.[3] His paper[4] is certainly ably & vigorously conducted. It is not a little difficult to excite an interest for objects so distant. Yet there are a few Gentlemen here who would be willing to bear a part. A tolerable set of types, I learn, could be furnished at the foundery [*sic*] here for abt. 5 or 6 hundred Dollars. I will undertake to say that a fount to that expense shall be placed to his order, here, or transmitted elsewhere, if you think that such a mode would be the best way of serving him. I am not myself much acquainted with H. & do not know his feelings towards me.

If you can correspond with him freely, & can learn whether he can be better served, to the same extent, in another way, it will be equally easy & agreeable to me. At your convenience, let me have your opinions & wishes, in regard to this matter, & they shall be promptly attended to—

The few elections which have recently taken place, in this quarter, have resulted well enough. I have no fears of McIntyre,[5] & on the whole, am reconciled to his election. Butman,[6] elected in Kidder's District, is a very true man.— In the House there will be three, & only three, whose votes, in electing a Speaker I fear will be agt. Taylor; Anderson & Ripley from Maine & Harvey from N.H.[7]— If Johns shall be chosen in Delaware, & Sergeant in Philadelphia,[8] they, with what has happened in N. Carolina,[9] will make good the losses in Kentucky. Mr Taylor thinks a *majority* of the N York Members will be disposed to support him. If it should be but a *bare* majority, the Election will be very close.[10] All our friends, I fear, do not rightly estimate the importance of this election; I hope we shall be able to impress it on them in season.—

The President is yet with [us]. His health seems better, but he is not yet so well as I should wish to see him.[11] I am, Dr Sir, mo truly Yours   DANL. WEBSTER

Mr. Clay

ALS. DLC-HC (DNA, M212, R2).   [1] Cf. above, Clay to Taylor, April 4, 1827, note.
[2] Webster had married Grace Fletcher, of Hopkinton, Massachusetts, a schoolteacher, in 1808. She had become ill in June, 1827, and had been recuperating on Nantucket Island and at Sandwich through the summer. She again became very ill as they returned to Washington in November and died in New York January 21, 1828. Their children still living at this time were Daniel Fletcher, born in 1813, Julia, born in 1818, and Edward, born in 1820.   [3] Charles Hammond. Cf. above, Clay to Webster, August 19, 1827; below, Clay to Webster, October 17, 1827.   [4] *Liberty Hall and Cincinnati Gazette.*
[5] Rufus McIntire.   [6] Samuel Butman, successor to David Kidder, who did not offer for re-election, had been born in Worcester, Massachusetts, but had moved to Penobscot County, Maine, in 1804, had served in the Maine Legislature in 1822, 1826, and 1827, and now entered the United States House of Representatives. He remained in Congress until 1831 and subsequently (1853) became a member and president of the Maine Senate.   [7] John W. Taylor; John Anderson; James W. Ripley; Jonathan Harvey. The individual vote was not published. Cf. above, Clay to Taylor, September 7, 1827, note. Ripley, born in Hanover, New Hampshire, in 1786, had entered the practice of law in Fryeburg, Massachusetts (Maine). After service in the War of 1812, he had been a member of the Massachusetts House of Representatives (1814–1819) and entered Congress in 1826. He resigned from Congress in 1830, returned to legal practice, and held the post of collector of customs at Passamaquoddy from 1830 until his death in 1835.   [8] Kensey Johns, Jr.; John Sergeant. Cf. above, Sergeant to Clay, September 28, 1826, note; Clay to Webster, May 14, 1827, note.   [9] Cf. above, Clay to Hammond, August 22, 1827, note.   [10] Cf. above, Clay to Taylor, September 7, 1827, note.
[11] Upon his departure from Washington (cf. above, Wharton to Clay, August 3, 1827, note), Adams had complained that his health was "languishing without sickness." He described his symptoms over the past several months: "From four to five hours of sleep, not of good repose; a continued habit of costiveness, indigestion, failure of appetite, uncontrollable dejection of spirits, insensibility to the almost unparalleled blessings with which I have been favored; a sluggish carelessness of life, an imaginary wish that it were terminated, with a clinging to it as close as it ever was. . . ." *Memoirs,* VII, 311.

DIPLOMATIC NOTES   September 28, 1827

From CHARLES R. VAUGHAN, Washington. Encloses a copy of a letter he received from the British consul in Baltimore (John Crawford) and a copy of one to that official from the consignees (Richard H. Douglass and James Ferguson) of two British brigs; states that the harbor master (probably Alexander Macdonald) at Baltimore demanded a greater fee of British vessels than American. Reports that Douglass and Ferguson refused to pay the fee and are threatened with judicial proceedings; protests the harbor master's action as a violation of the 2nd Article of the Convention of 1815 (see above, II, 57–58). LS. DNA, RG59, Notes from British Legation, vol. 14 (M50, R15).

Macdonald was identified as "superintendent of navigation," a State appointee. *Matchett's Baltimore Directory for 1827*, 178. Cf. below, Clay to Kent, September 29, 1827.

INSTRUCTIONS AND DISPATCHES   September 28, 1827

From JAMES BROWN, Paris, no. 75. States that, "Agreeably to . . . [Clay's] letter of the 25th. of May last (No. 12), . . . [he has] caused the books therein mentioned" to be shipped "to the Collector of the Customs at New York" (Jonathan Thompson), who is being asked to hold them subject to Clay's orders. Appends a list. Adds that the shipment also includes "a small bundle of books addressed to the President, by Count Vidua, the traveller, who was about two years since at Washington, and who has recently departed to pursue his travels in Hindostan." LS. DNA, RG59, Dip. Disp., France, vol. 23 (M34, R26). Received November 18.

Count Charles Vidua, 1785–1832, of Piedmont (Italy), was a writer of philosophical discourses and travel accounts, notably in the early 1820's concerning his voyages to Greece and Asia Minor.

From ALBERT GALLATIN, no. 120. States his expectation that the Northwest Boundary Convention (cf. above, Gallatin to Clay, September 21, 1827) "will be ready tomorrow or early next week," when the negotiators (Gallatin, Henry U. Addington, and Charles Grant) will hold their "last Conference, all the subjects on which . . . [they] were respectively instructed being exhausted." Promises to "transmit the Protocols at the same time with the Convention. . . ." Observes that he has received no answer to his note of August 17 (cf. above, Gallatin to Clay, August 21, 1827); that he does "not know whether there is any intention to delay it, although" he is "certain" judging from a conversation with (William) Huskisson on the preceding day, "that there is none to change the determination already announced on that subject" (cf. above, Gallatin to Clay, September 14, 1827); and that, "This being the only thing which, after signing the Convention will detain . . . [him, he] will, when it shall have been received, avail . . . [himself] of the permission of the President to return home [cf. above, Clay to Gallatin, May 5, 1826; February 4, 1827 (no. 19)]. . . ."

Notes that, having "reason to believe that, had Mr [George] Canning lived, he would have opened a negotiation on the subject of Impressment" (cf. above, Gallatin to Clay, July 28, 1827), and, "Understanding from an authentic source, that there was some disposition to that effect amongst two or three Members of the Cabinet, . . . [he] sought an interview with Mr. Huskisson in order to ascertain the fact. . . ." Reports that Huskisson, although expressing "himself in the most decided terms in favour of an arrangement founded on the basis heretofore proposed by the United States (cf. above, I, 1000; Clay to Gallatin, June 19, 1826 [V, 444–46]), did not believe "this was . . . the time to take up that subject," which "must be postponed to a more favorable opportunity." Explains the reasons for Huskisson's view.

Points out that he has "not been able to arrange any subject but such as did not admit of being delayed" and that decisions in regard to "the Colonial Intercourse" (cf. above, Gallatin to Clay, August 19, 1826) and navigation of the St. Lawrence River (Clay to Gallatin, June 19, 1826 [V, 451–64]; Gallatin to Clay, November 14, 1826 [no. 24]) had been made before his arrival (in England), "and, on both points this Government was immovable" but that "In other respects and in their feelings generally towards the United States, . . . they are in a better disposition than . . . [he] found them."

Adds, in a postscript: "I send herewith Gifford's [sic] abstract of Acts of Parliament of last Session, and Hume's Laws of Customs, an official work, with the supplements of 1826 & 1827. This volume contains all the alterations subsequent to the last edition of the Commercial Digest of the United States and supersedes the necessity of any other report from this Legation on that subject." LS, except for postscript in Gallatin's hand. DNA, RG59, Dip. Disp., Great Britain, vol. 34 (M30, R30). Published in Adams (ed.), *Writings of Albert Gallatin*, II, 390–92. Received November 1.

Stanley Lees Giffard, born in Dublin in 1788, graduated with the M.A. degree from Trinity College in 1811, and admitted to the bar at the Middle Temple in the latter year, had founded the London *Standard* in 1827. He edited the journal for over 25 years.

James Deacon Hume had compiled *The Laws of the Customs. . .* , published at London in 1825. Supplements for 1826 and 1827 were appended to an edition also published at London, in 1827. Born in Surrey, England, in 1774, Hume had become a clerk in the Thames Street customs house in 1791. Rising to the rank of controller of customs, he had conceived in 1822 the idea of consolidating all the customs laws, and it was he who had assembled the codification enacted in July, 1825 (cf. above, Gallatin to Clay, August 19, 1826, note). He was appointed joint secretary to the Board of Trade in 1828 and remained in that office until 1840.

John Brice, a Baltimore commission merchant, had published at Baltimore in 1814 *A Selection of All the Laws of the United States, Now in Force, Relative to Commercial Subjects. . . .* He had added *A Supplement. . .* , published in 1816, continuing the survey through the First Session of the Fourteenth Congress. No subsequent edition has been found prior to 1830, when another digest was commissioned by the Secretary of the Treasury (Samuel D. Ingham).

From BEAUFORT T. WATTS, Bogotá, no. 34. Reports the arrival, on September 10, of "the President of the Republic" (Simón Bolívar), who has taken the oath of office. Praises the "promptness and energy" of Bolívar's administration but notes the exhaustion of a 36 million dollar loan borrowed from England while "he marched to assist Peru in her War of Independence." Encloses a translation of the letter from (Joseph R.) Revenga to Clay (September 25, 1827), the original of which, Revenga informs him, "will be forwarded through their Representative in the United States" (José María Salazar). ALS. DNA, RG59, Dip. Disp., Colombia, vol. 4 (M-T33, R4). Received December 3.

The above-mentioned Colombian loan had been negotiated in London in the spring of 1824. *Annual Register, 1824*, p. 224.

To John Quincy Adams

Dear Sir   Washington 29h. Sept. 1827.

According to information from the West, our Indian relations with the Winnebagoes[1] on the Ouisconsin wear an aspect more and more hostile. Their condition is such that I should not be surprized if we shortly heard of an action with Genl Atkinson. I have advised Mr. Barbour[2] to return forthwith to the City to be prepared for any emergency. The nature of Genl. Atkinson's force is less adapted to offensive operations than to defensive. Genl. Gaines[3] is however authorized to call for mounted men, the most effective in Indian warfare.

I regret the necessity I feel, at such a juncture, to leave the City for a few days; but the state of my health allows me no other alternative.[4] I hope not to be absent beyond ten or twelve days, and I shall at no time be farther than within a day and a half's journey from the City. I am respectfully & faithfy Yr's   H. CLAY
Mr. Adams.

ALS. MHi-Adams Papers, Letters Recd. (MR482).
[1] The Winnebagoes, restive for several months because of encroachments on their lands by lead miners, failed to win the support of other northwestern Indians for a general uprising. Red Bird, leader of a small Winnebago band, had, however, with two companions murdered several whites in June, 1827. On September 1, he and some of his warriors surrendered at the Fox-Wisconsin portage to Thomas L. McKenny and a combined force of regular Army troops, militia, and friendly Indians. He was, therefore, in custody prior to the arrival of General Henry Atkinson. Tried and convicted, but not yet sentenced, Red Bird died in prison on February 16, 1828; his companions were pardoned by President Adams in November, 1828. *Niles' Weekly Register*, XXXIII (November 10, 1827), 162; Herman J. Viola, *Thomas L. McKenney: Architect of America's Early Indian Policy, 1816–1830* (Chicago, 1974), 155–67; Frederick W. Hodge (ed.), *Handbook of American Indians North of Mexico* (Smithsonian Institution, Bureau of Ethnology, *Bulletin* no. 30; 2 pts., Washington, 1912), pt. 2, p. 358.   [2] James Barbour.
[3] Edmund P. Gaines.   [4] Cf. above, Clay to Adams, September 24, 1827; Clay to Brooke, September 24, 1827. Richard Rush wrote Adams on September 29: "Mr Clay expected to leave town this morning on a short absence in the hope of recruiting [*sic*] after his late indisposition." MHi-Adams Papers, Letters Recd. (MR482).

To Joseph Kent

His Excellency Joseph Kent,
Governor of Maryland, Annapolis.
Sir,   Dept. of State, Washington 29 Septr. 1827.
I have the honor of enclosing the Copy of a Note just received at this Office with its Enclosures from the British Minister[1] at this place, stating that the Harbour Master of Baltimore[2] has made a charge upon two British vessels, which had arrived at that Port, that is over and above what is paid by vessels of the United States, and that the payment of the charge being repugnant to the 2d. Article of the convention of 1815 between the United States and Great Britain, is resisted upon that ground.—

It being understood that the charge, in question, is repugnant to the Convention referred to, and it being within the exclusive jurisdiction of the Authorities of the State to ensure the observance by the Harbour Masters of that Port, of the engagements of the United States contracted in this respect by that Convention, I have the honor to submit the case to your Excellency's consideration, that such measures may be adopted, as you shall judge necessary and proper to carry into effect with good faith the obligations of the United States.—I have the honor to be, with Great respect, Your Excellencys Obedt. Servant,

H. CLAY.

Copy. DNA, RG59, Dom. Letters, vol. 22, pp. 57–58 (M40, R20).
[1] Above, Charles R. Vaughan to Clay, September 28, 1827.   [2] Alexander Macdonald.

To John Rodgers

Dear Commodore   29h. Sept. 1827.

Will you have the goodness to inform me whether your son[1] has gone to the U. S. Ship North Carolina,[2] and if not when it is your purpose to send him? Our nephew H. C. Hart about whom I spoke to you, is about to proceed to the same vessel,[3] and, if the youths can accompany each other, I have thought that it might perhaps be agreeable to both. We should be glad of such an arrangement, as young Hart is an entire Stranger at Gosport.[4] Yr's faithfully   H. CLAY

ALS. DNA, RG45, Office of Naval Records and Library Area File, no. 11, 1775–1910. Upon his return from sea duty aboard the flagship *North Carolina* at the end of July, 1827, Rodgers had been re-assigned to the Board of Navy Commissioners, as president.
[1] John Rodgers, the son, born in 1812, was not appointed a midshipman until April, 1828. He began active service on the *Constellation* in the Mediterranean. In 1833 he returned, on leave of absence to study for his midshipman's examinations, which he passed in 1834. He was promoted to lieutenant in 1840, captain in 1862, and rear admiral in 1872.   [2] Cf. above, Gray to Clay, July 24, 1827. The *North Carolina* had arrived at Hampton Roads July 28, 1827, and was held "in ordinary" that autumn.   [3] Henry Clay Hart, who entered service as a midshipman September 1, 1827, was listed at the Naval School at Norfolk on December 31. He was assigned to the *Delaware*, a ship of the line of 2633 tons, built at Norfolk, launched in 1820, but not commissioned until February, 1828. Hart served in the Mediterranean from 1828 to 1830 and in the Pacific from 1831 to 1834. After some months on leave of absence he resigned from the Navy on December 29, 1834.   [4] The Navy Yard at Norfolk.

To Samuel L. Southard

My Dear Sir   Washington 29h. Decr. [*i.e.*, September] 1827.

Our Indian affairs in the N. W. wear a more hostile aspect.[1] I think it desirable that the President and all of us should be on the ground, as soon as practicable, for any emergency. I go away today, from indisposition, but I think I shall return by the 10h.

A letter just recd. from Dr. Drake[2] requests me to remind you of the promise you made to appoint his son[3] a Mid Shipman, and to send him in the Delaware. I wish you would forward him to Cincinnati the appointment. The Dr. has the subject much at heart.

Barbour[4] will be here on tuesday.

I hope to return with more strength and to find you and our Colleagues all here. In the mean time I am faithfully Your friend & ob Servt.   H CLAY

Mr. Southard

ALS. NjP-Southard Papers. On the dating of this letter, cf. Adams, *Memoirs*, VII, 329. Endorsed: "Ansd."; the answer has not been found.
¹ Cf. above, Clay to Adams, this date.   ² Daniel Drake. The letter has not been found.   ³ Charles Daniel Drake, born in 1811, had been commissioned April 1, 1827, but he was "Waiting orders." *Biennial Register, 1827*, p. 124. Dismissed from the Navy in October, 1829, he was admitted to the bar in Cincinnati in 1833 and the following year opened practice at St. Louis. He became a member of the Missouri Legislature in 1859 and 1860 and a United States Senator from 1867 to 1870, when he resigned to become chief justice of the United States Court of Claims.   ⁴ James Barbour.

From Edwin U. Berryman

My dear Sir   New York Sepr 29th. 1827

I have had an interview with Doctrs. Hosack & Godman & Professor Renwick¹ upon the subject proposed in your favor of the 3d Inst.² They concur in the opinion, that I have heard expressed by all those whom I have conversed with, who know him.³ That he is entirely competent & efficient.to the duties that will be imposed on him, in the event of his acceptance of the situation. Indeed I have not as yet heard a disputing voice as to his Talents & capacity—

Your friends here are industrious & sanguine in carrying this State for the administration. The Clinton & Van beuren coalition⁴ notwithstanding. During the ensuing week they proposed taking a decisive Stand, the result of which you will see published in the next weeks papers.⁵ With My Particular respects to Mrs Clay & family Believe me Yr Friend & Obt St   E. U. BERRYMAN

P.S.   I inclose you a Note from Doct. Godman⁶ in which he expresses his opinions more fully on the Subject. Yrs Sincerely

To/The Honb. H. Clay Washington City   E. U. BERRYMAN

ALS. KyLxT.
¹ David Hosack; John D. Godman; James Renwick. Born in England in 1792 and brought to the United States as a child, Renwick had been graduated from Columbia College in 1807 and awarded the M.A. degree at that institution in 1810. He had taught there briefly in 1812 and returned in 1820 to resume a life-time career as professor of natural philosophy and experimental chemistry. He had served as a topographic engineer for the Government in 1814, and he subsequently attained distinction by a report on the feasibility of the Delaware and Hudson Canal (1826) and service as a commissioner to survey the northeastern boundary between Maine and New Brunswick (1840). He retired from Columbia in 1853.   ² Not found. Cf. above, Berryman to Clay, September 1, 1827.   ³ Thomas McAuley. Cf. below, Clay to Bradford, October 14, 1827.
⁴ DeWitt Clinton; Martin Van Buren. Cf. above, Hammond to Clay, January 28, 1827, note.   ⁵ A series of ward meetings friendly to the administration was held in New York during the next two or three weeks. Most notably, the "Republican Young Men" friendly to the administration within the Tammany organization met on October 13 and adopted resolutions of support. Washington *Daily National Journal*, October 18, 1827.   ⁶ Not found.

From James Brown

My dear Sir,   (Private)   Paris Septr 29. 1827

I have had the pleasure to receive your letter of the 7th of August[1] and feel happy that you have augmented your stock of health by your journey,[2] that you found all your family well and that you see your fireside surrounded by so many of your children. It is in the domestic circle at last, and not in the bustle of business, or in the perplexing pursuits of ambition, that real enjoyment is to be found. I hope during the dreadful winter which is fast approaching you will possess at home an effectual antidote against the disgust created by bitter enemies and hypocrital [sic] friends abroad. Of these last, you in common with many other politicians, have your full share.

General Jacksons conduct has certainly disappointed me. I knew he could never prove his accusation as stated the [sic] Beverley letter,[3] but I did really fear, that some of your ardent but indiscreet friends, might have equally compromitted you and themselves. From the manner in which he had mentioned the proposal made to him, I could never have imagined that he would cite one of his own especial friends[4] as his authority, and still less that he would have been so blind as not to perceive that he was deeply implicated in the turpitude of the proposal by receving [sic] it so well, by concealing it so carefully, and by speaking so very respectfully of the individual by whom it was made. The manner in which he has retreated from supporting the charge is not in keeping with the frank, manly, and fearless character which I had attributed to him. If party spirit could for a moment slumber, I think the enemies of Mr Adams would now abandon General Jackson, and select another Candidate.[5] Much of the sympathy which had been awakened by the ungenerous attacks made on the General and on his nearest connexion[6] will be allayed by finding him placed in the character of an accuser who has failed in supporting his accusation. As you have at home enough, and indeed too much, of this unpleasant subject, I shall leave it on the other side of the Atlantic, and merely tell you that I have read the letter you wrote to General Lafayette[7] and conversed with him on the subject of it. He stated that he recollected the conversation to which you allude and, with the exception of the precise date, about which he did seem certain, he could at that time perceive no impropriety in stating what had passed. He asked me if you attached any importance to receiving what he had to state by the Packet which carries this letter, and whether it would do as well by the one which will sail from Havre on the 15 of next month. I told him that I knew you wished to receive it as soon as he could conveniently prepare it, and that my Despatches would leave paris this morning at 12 oClock. If it comes in time I shall send it to you.[8]

We have, as you see by the papers, sent with this, News from Constantinople to the 1st. of Septr. The Porte, at that date, persisted in refusing the mediation, and protesting against the interference of the three allied powers in the affairs of Greece.[9] The Ambassadors[10] had when the courier left Constantinople embarked their wives on board of Vessels to carry them to their respective destinations. The fleet from Egypt had sailed some days but we have heard nothing of it since.[11] This news has had little or no effect upon the stocks, the opinion being general, that the Porte was not so rash as to risk hostilities with the combined forces in the Mediterranean, threatened as he is by a large Russian army in his vicinity.[12] I do not for my own part believe this affair will end in war. Russia is the only power which seriously wishes such a result. Austria England and France will use all their influence to prevent it,[13] for reasons too obvious to require mentioning. The Greeks will cease to be massacred or governed à la Turc, but will be disposed of according to the good pleasure of their new masters. Indeed they seem to be about as well prepared for free Government as the Spaniards, the Portugueze [sic], or our good neighbours on the American Continent.

The insurrections in Catalonia[14] had become so formidable as to require vigerous [sic] and extraordinary measures to suppress them. The King[15] has resolved to accomplish this in person and will probably accomplish it without striking a blow. He has set out from Madrid with Colomarde and a small escort[16]— He will present himself in the Camp of the Insurgents and say my faithful subjects what object have you in view in arming without my orders. Sire, we have assembled in military array to liberate your sacred person from Captivity. My subjects you see that I have travelled from Madrid to Catalonia without troops and without molestation and consequently that I am not now, nor have I ever been a Captive. What other object has assembled my liege subjects? Sire we wish to make you an Absolute King. If my subjects wish me to be Absolute their wishes correspond with my own, and if you can tell me how I can become more absolute than I have always been since the surrender of Cadiz[17] I shall cheerfully comply with your desires. Sire we wish you to exterminate the free masons and constitutionalists and to establish the Inquisition.[18] My subjects must reflect that these detested classes are numerous and very much dispersed over the face of Spain and that I have done, and am still doing, all I can to destroy them, and you may rest assured of my desire at a convenient season to re establish the Holy Inquisition. Should some rash apostolick mutter an intention of conferring the crown on Don Carlos[19] he will be ready to thank them for their kin[d] intentions and assure them that he prefers waiting for the death of his Brother *whom God preserve for many years*— The faithful Catalonians will then shout long live our absolute King! and the Holy Inquisition! and the Insurrection will terminate much to the satisfaction of all parties. The leaders will be taken into favor and the lower classes will continue to rob and murder and plunder to gain an honest livelihood.

By the latest accounts from Vienna we learn that Don Miguel would set out in few [sic] days for Lisbon in order to assume the regency.[20] His sister and mother[21] have prepared everything fo[r] his reception. The Constitutionalists who have been encouraged by the enthusiastic speech of Mr Canning[22] to look to England for support and who have braved the fury of the Queens party will be deserted on all hands and exposed to persecution, exile, and destruction in every form. So much for foreign interference the lamentable effects of which are seen in Spain and Portugal.

The Baron de Krudener Russian Minister to the United States will sail for New York by the same Vessel which carries this letter. He appears to be a plain frank, honorable man, is much esteemed by all who know him, and was greatly in favor in Switzerland where he resided many years as Charge d'Affaires. It is to be regretted that he is very deaf and I fear not very well acquainted with the English language. As far as I can judge he goes on with the wish to please and to be pleased with our Country, and as the friendship of Russia is of much importance to us, I hope you will think it worth cultivating through this very excellent minister.

The Minister of foreign Affairs here[23] either has more business on his hands than any of his Predecessors, or is more tardy in his operations,— I have written a letter to him early in August respecting the discriminating duties demanded at Havre on American Vessels which had touched at the Ports of a third power on their passage to which notwithstanding all my sollicitations [sic] I have not yet received his answer.[24] I have found so much delay in answering letters, that I transact all the small business of the Legation by conversations as being much more expeditious. If Mr Villele was at the head of the foreign affairs business would meet with more dispatch. The Baron de Damas has been educated a soldier and until after the Campaign in Spain had not as I have heard paid much attention to political affairs. Personally I have every thing to satisfy me, but I fear I shall return without being able to render any very important services to my country.

The Manufactures of France are making rapid proficiency as well in their quality as in the reduction of their price. The exposition of objects of domestic industry at the Louvre[25] has been unusually splendid and has attracted multitudes of strangers from every part of Europe. The Silks and Woolens surpass every thing of this kind which I have seen in solidity, finish, coloring and taste. Young Hulme[26] is now here. He is much pleased with his opportunities at the Sedan Manufactory where I was so fortunate as to place him,[27] and will return & remain there until he has acquired a perfect knowledge of the making and finishing the best of broadcloths. I wish some Virginian Carolinian or Kentuckian would acquaint himself with the French language and reside two or three years in the South of France in order to learn how to cultivate the Vine & the olive and to make Silk.[28] I have instructed Mr Barnet[29] to use every fair means to procure models of the best silk looms but I fear he will not find it an easy matter to send them out of the Country.

Mrs. Brown has suffered severely during the last two months from a recurrence of the pain in her face with which she has been occasionally afflicted during the last ten years.[30] She hopes Mrs. Clay will receive all her things[31] in time as they were sent to my obliging friend Mr Isaac Bell of New York, Greenwich Street No 72.

Mr Johnston[32] is still in Paris but not finding his health as good as he could wish, talks of passing the winter in Italy. I shall do every thing to enable him to pass his time agreeably in Paris which is generally considered as no very difficult matter. Since his arrival the Court has been at St Cloud[33] or rather the King has been absent on a journey to St Omers.[34] If Mr Johnston wishes it I shall present him at Court and I have no doubt of being able to introduce him at some very agreeable houses. His bad health has affected his spirits and I fear the Atmosphere of Paris during the winter is not calculated to raise them. I have never liked this climate as well as our own. I have however become more accustomed to it, and since the restoration of my health,[35] I never allow myself to complain.

You will receive by this opportunity a despatch relative to the Convention of 1822.[36] From the manner in which the Baron de Damas introduced the subject in a Conference relating to the Claims I was apprehensive this Government either had given or intended to give notice that it must terminate. In my interview of the 20th I used such language with him as I thought calculated to prevent that event and I hope it will have some effect. It appears probable that France will be contented if you can make some reduction on the duties on Brandy and perhaps it might be as well to consent to it. I do not believe it would greatly interfere with the producers of domestic Spirits as those who are in the habit of drinking Brandy will not be prevented from doing so by the present duties. We certainly have every advantage in the navigation and will under the convention continue to possess it. Our revenue can admit perhaps of a small sacrifice to prevent the recurrence of the state of things of 1820.21..[37]

The King has been much flattered and gratified by his tour to St Omers. I think he is more popular in the provinces than in the Capital. The press is under Censorship and the people seem to bear it better that [sic] I had expected. This will encourage the Chambers at their next Session to pass a pretty strong law restraining the liberty of the Press.[38] The people are generally active and prosperous, and the crops of all kinds abundant. The laws are well administered, and the Government upon the whole more mild and just than at any former period. So long as this state of things continues the Country will remain tranquil even should some occasional violations of the Charter take place.

As I receive my despatches regularly, if you have time during the sitting of Congress, I would be much obliged to you if you would enclose me the News papers which you receive from different parts of the Union for which you have no longer any use. Every thing from home amuses us here. Mrs Brown joins me in love to Mrs. Clay and your family. I am Dear Sir your friend   JAMES BROWN
Hon. Henry Clay.

ALS. DLC-HC (DNA, M212, R2).
[1] Not found. Cf. above, Clay to Brown, August 10, 1827.   [2] Cf. above, Sparks to Clay, August 7, 1827; Clay to Brooke, August 14, 1827; Clay to Sparks, August 14, 1827.   [3] Cf. above, Report of Interview, *ca.* April 15, 1827; Clay to Hammond, June 25, 1827.   [4] James Buchanan. Cf. above, Smith to Clay, August 1, 1827.   [5] Cf. above, Clay to Everett, August 19, 1827.   [6] Mrs. Rachel Donelson Robards Jackson. Cf. above, Clay to Hammond, December 23, 1826; Penn to Clay, *ca.* June 19, 1827.   [7] Above, August 10, 1827.   [8] For Lafayette's letter to Clay, see below, October 10, 1827.   [9] France, Great Britain, and Russia. Cf. above, Brown to Clay, July 12, 28, 1827; Hughes to Clay, September 16, 1827; below, Middleton to Clay, this date.   [10] The Count de Guilleminot; Stratford Canning; Alexander Ribeaupierre.   [11] Cf. above, Brown to Clay, July 12, 1827; below, Ombrosi to Clay, November 6, 1827.   [12] Cf. above, Middleton to Clay, September 17, 1826, and note.   [13] Cf. above, Middleton to Clay, June 23, 1827.   [14] Cf. above, Everett to Clay, April 19, August 16, September 4, 1827.
[15] Ferdinand VII.   [16] Cf. above, Everett to Clay, September 20, 1827.   [17] Cf. above, III, 313n, 498; Burton to Clay, March 16, April 12, 1825; Hughes to Clay, September 16, 1827, note.   [18] Cf. above, Sergeant to Clay, April 17, 1827, note. Despite agitation by the Apostolic party for reinstitution of the Inquisition under Government auspices, Ferdinand withheld State support—partly because he recognized the unpopularity of the "Holy Office" and, probably in greater degree, because the Crown had taken over its domains. See *Annual Register, 1827,* p. 231. The Inquisition was again formally, and finally, banned in 1834, by Isabella II.   [19] Carlos María Isidro de Borbón. Cf. above, Brown to Clay, August 26, 1825, and note.   [20] Cf. above, Gallatin to Clay, August 30, 1827; Brent to Clay, September 15, 1827.   [21] Isabel Maria; Carlota Joaquina.   [22] George Canning. Cf. above, Gallatin to Clay, December 13, 1826; Brown to Clay, December 23, 1826; April 12, 1827; Everett to Clay, January 7, 1827; Hughes to Clay, January 21, 1827.   [23] The Baron de Damas.   [24] Cf. above, Brown to Clay, August 30, September 27, 1827.   [25] Louis XVIII had decreed that industrial exhibitions should be held every four years. Three were held, in 1819, 1823, and 1827, all at the Louvre, in Paris. They were designed to bring together representative products from each Department of France. Kenneth W. Luckhurst, *The Story of Exhibitions* (London, 1951), 80.   [26] Cf. above, Hulme to Clay, August 24, 1826. The young man was probably Thomas Hulme, Jr., of Pennsylvania, who became United States consul at Sedan, France, from 1841 until his death in 1845.   [27] Cf. above, Brown to Clay, September 12, 1826. Sedan was a center of cloth manufacture in France, particularly notable for its woolens.   [28] Cf. above, Brown to Clay, September 6, 1827.   [29] Isaac Cox Barnet.   [30] Cf. above, Brown to Clay, August 30, 1827.
[31] Cf. above, Clay to Brown, March 27, May 30, 1827; Brown to Clay, May 27, June 28, July 28, August 30, September 6, 1827.   [32] Not identified.   [33] The family property of the dukes of Orleans was located at St. Cloud.   [34] Cf. above, Brown to Clay, September 13, 1827.   [35] Cf. above, Brown to Clay, June 25, July 15 (1), August 26, September 19, October 13, 1825.   [36] Above, Brown to Clay, September 27, 1827.
[37] Cf. above, II, 846n; III, 53n.   [38] Cf. above, Brown to Clay, June 12, 1827, note. Contrary to Brown's expectation, the Chambers in 1828 approved a bill authorizing any French citizen to establish a journal or periodical and renouncing "the discretionary power of establishing a censorship." *Annual Register, 1828,* p. 170.

DIPLOMATIC NOTES   September 29, 1827

To [CHARLES R.] VAUGHAN. Acknowledges receipt of Vaughan's note of September 28 and informs him of the "Official Letter" addressed "to the Governor of the State of Maryland [above, Clay to Kent, this date] under whose authority the Harbour-Masters of the Port of Baltimore are appointed. . . ." Copy. DNA, RG59, Notes to Foreign Legations, vol. 3, p. 390 (M38, R3). L draft, in CSmH.

INSTRUCTIONS AND DISPATCHES   September 29, 1827

From ISAAC COX BARNET, Paris. States that he has received, since his last dispatch (above, August 24, 1827), a copy of the "Certificate of discharge," found among the papers of James Reid; reports that (Thomas) Aspinwall, who sent the certificate, informs him that George Joy of London "sets up a claim against Mr. Reid's estate for upwards of £.1100 Stg.—which originated in 1797—that he . . . [Aspinwall] thinks it founded in equity and that Mr. Joy intends coming over to Paris to sue for payment.—" Reports that he has replied to Aspinwall that he will defend the estate, since the certificate was "granted under the late general Bankrupt Act" (cf. above, Shaw to Clay, August 27, 1826, note) from all "old claims of the kind," and that "the French tribunals take no cognizance of controversies originating abroad between foreigners. . . ." Encloses a duplicate (not found) of his letter to the district attorney at New Orleans (John W. Smith), which he hopes will be effective in checking "an *illegitimate* trafic [sic] in human flesh," and solicits Clay's advice on the matter. ALS. DNA, RG59, Cons. Disp., Paris (M-T1, R6). Received November 18.

From FELIX CICOGNANI, Rome. Transmits "a letter [the Cardinal of Somaglia to Clay, above, September 22, 1827]. . . , which the Cardinal Secretary of State has" requested that he forward to Clay, and "a copy of the letter" received from that official "in answer to the communication . . . made to him of the Proclamation . . . of the President of the United States exempting the vessels and merchandise of the Roman States from the foreign discriminating duties of tonnage and impost in the United States" (cf. above, Lucchesi to Clay, May 30, 1827, note). Reports that from July 1, 1826, no American vessels have entered "the ports of the Papal States" and expresses "hope that in consequence of the reciprocity now existing between the two Countries this state of things will change. . . ." ALS. DNA, RG59, Cons. Disp., Rome, vol. 1 (M-T231, R1). Received December 20. Addressed to "[The] Honourable John Henry Clay."

From ALBERT GALLATIN, London, no. 121. Acknowledges receipt of Clay's "letter No. 33 of 17th [*i.e.*, 18th] August last"; states that he "communicated the substance of it to Mr [William] Huskisson, transmitting at the same time to him the copy of Mr [Richard] Rush's letter to" Clay of that date; and encloses a copy of Huskisson's reply. LS. DNA, RG59, Dip. Disp., Great Britain, vol. 34 (M30, R30). In the enclosure Huskisson praised Rush's reply "as fulfilling every reasonable expectation that could be formed by the Parties, and as affording a satisfactory proof of the spirit of equity by which the Govt. at Washington is actuated in dealing with a transaction of this nature."

From HENRY MIDDLETON, St. Petersburg, no. 73. Transmits a copy of "The note of the Reis Effendi [Saida Efendi] delivered to the ambassadors of the Christian powers" on June 9 (cf. above, Brown to Clay, this date); states that, according to "The latest accounts from Constantinople," the Reis Effendi has rejected "a joint note grounded upon the Treaty lately signed at London between England Russia

& France" (cf. above, Brown to Clay, July 12, 1827) and "presented by the ambassadors of those Powers [Stratford Canning; Alexander Ribeaupierre; the Count de Guilleminot] to the Porte, urging the proposition of an Armistice with the Greeks and requiring an answer to be given in 15 days" (cf. above, Hughes to Clay, September 16, 1827). Conjectures that the Turks may fall "upon the Russians on the Caucasian frontier, where the Persians appear to have obtained some advantages, and heat and famine have combined to destroy a considerable part of the Russian force" (cf. above, Middleton to Clay, June 23, 1827; *Niles' Weekly Register*, XXXIII [September 8, 1827], 18). Observes that "The question of highest interest in the west of Europe of late" relates to "the military occupation of Portugal by the English.& of Spain by the French forces, or of the simultaneous evacuation of both those Countries." Notes that Spain has sought the advice of Russia, which recently responded in the form of "an instruction" (enclosed) to the Russian Ambassador in Paris (Charles André, Count Pozzo di Borgo). Surmises that "the appointment of Don Miguel to the regency [cf. above, Gallatin to Clay, August 30, 1827] will . . . probably bring these matters to a *dénouement* little agreeable to the feelings of the friends of human happiness." Predicts that "If England should consent to withdraw her troops, the reestablishment of *absolutism* may be expected throughout the regions of the West of continental Europe, unless it be averted by an armed opposition." ALS. DNA, RG59, Dip. Disp., Russia, vol. 11 (M35, R11). Dated September 17/29, 1827; received January 4, 1828.

In the first enclosure the Reis Effendi rejected mediation in the struggle between Greece and Turkey as interference in an internal issue; the second reveals that the Emperor (Nicholas I) advises against the dangers that would attend an immediate evacuation of foreign troops from Spain and Portugal.

From HENRY WHEATON, Copenhagen, no. 1. Reports his arrival on September 19 and accreditation and reception ceremonies of September 20 and 26. States that he learned, while in Lübec, that (Joseph H.) Clark, "who was appointed Consul for that port, does not reside there, and never has resided there"; promises since the United States is "about to establish more intimate commercial relations with the Hanseatic towns [cf. above, Hughes to Clay, March 9, 1827, and note] . . . to look about for some proper person to be recommended . . . for that station." ALS. DNA, RG59, Dip. Disp., Denmark, vol. 1B (M41, R3). Received November 30.

MISCELLANEOUS LETTERS   September 29, 1827

From HENRY PRATT, Philadelphia. States, as owner of the brig *Ruth* (cf. above, Raguet to Clay, September 1, 1826), that because of a belief "justified by the publications in the newspapers at Washington [cf. above, Clay to Force, June 3, 1827, attachment], that the Emperor of Brazil [Peter I] had made to our government, such assurances, as would lead to a full Satisfaction" for the damages done by Brazilian cruisers, he has forborne pressing his claim. Requests "any information . . . which it may not be improper to grant" and asks whether "it may not be necessary for the more complete vindication of our rights, to lay before Congress at thier [*sic*] ensuing Session, a detailed statement of the plunderings, detentions & insults, American vessels have endured, from the authorities, & armed force of the Brasilian Emperor." LS. DNA, RG76, Misc. Claims, Brazil (MR1, frames 82–83).

On October 25, Pratt, fearing that the letter had escaped Clay's notice, because of his absence from Washington (cf. above, Clay to Adams, September 29, 1827, note) wrote again and enclosed a second copy. *Ibid.* (frames 39–41). In reply, Daniel Brent informed him, "by direction of the Secretary," on October 29, 1827, that William Tudor had been appointed Chargé at Rio de Janeiro, that there was "reason to believe. . . , if indemnity . . . [should] be found to be rightfully due in it [the case of the *Ruth*], it . . . [would] be awarded. . . ," and that Pratt should instruct his agent in Rio to give Tudor documents and a statement relative to the case. Copy, in DNA, RG59, Dom. Letters, vol. 22, pp. 33–34 (M40, R20).

Pratt (1761–1838) was a Philadelphia merchant and banker.

In response to a resolution adopted April 30, 1828, introduced by Richard Coulter, of Pennsylvania two days earlier, the House of Representatives called for publication of the correspondence between the "late Charges des Affaires, at the Court of Brazil [Condy Raguet] and the Brazillian [sic] Government, in relation to the alleged blockade . . . of the Buenos Ayrean Republic" and the imprisonment of Americans by Brazil; correspondence between the Chargé and his own Government concerning those subjects and his demand for his passports; also, "any information that may have been recently received by the Government concerning a paper blockade of the whole coast of the Buenos Ayrean Republic, by the Government of Brazil"; and a statement of measures taken by the United States "to countervail the illegal system of blockade. . . ." U. S. H. of Reps., *Journal*, 20 Cong., 1 Sess., pp. 640–41. On May 23, 1828, the requested information was supplied; it was published as *House Docs.*, 20 Cong., 1 Sess., no. 281.

From James Erwin

Dear Sir   Shelbyville Sept 30th. 1827.

Inclosed you have a reply to your inquiry relative to the notes of Mather,[1]   While in Nashville last week I met with Col. Crockett[2] Member elect to Congress. from the Western District of Ten,   he was desirous of making your acquaintance, as he Said, & at the suggestion of a friend I gave him a letter to you.[3] which may require some explanation, lest you might think I was rather indiscriminate in Sending you acquaintances,   Col. Crockett is perhaps the most illiterate Man, that you have ever met in Congress Hall   he is not only illiterate but he is rough & uncouth, talks much & loudly, and is by far, more in his proper place, when hunting a Bear, in a Cane Brake, than he will be in the Capital,   yet he is a man worth attending to,   he is independant [sic] and fearless & has a popularity at home that is unaccountable,   he obtained at the last election 6000 Votes beating both his opponents with their joint votes— he voted against Genl. Jackson & for Col. Williams[4] for Senator While in the Legislature   And he now goes to Washington determined to pursue his own Course. he has promised to vote for Mr Taylor[5] for Speaker if he is a candidate or if he is not for such other person as you may advise him, as he is more willing to trust your experience than his own,   and strange as he may appear to you. he is the only man that I now know in Tennessee that Could openly oppose Genl. Jackson in his District & be elected to Congress— The day before I left Nashville the Legislature was occupied in debating the propriety of electing a Senator for 1829. Judge White was there & hea [sic] and Eaton[6] had the matter arranged, & he will be reelected,

I sent you a paper Containing Eatons publication,[8]   it has excited little or no attention in Tennessee. his friends even seem disappointed— They appear willing to let it pass in Silence.

I leave here in a few days by way of Alabama, for N Orleans. accompanied by my family & Mrs. Hitchcock,[9]   we will delay on the road until we have full confidence in the health of the City.[10] both the Children as well as Anne[11] enjoy excellent health, our Son is a remarkably fair child   Anne is quite impatient to exhibit him to you & her mother & I hope the time not far distant When she will have that pleasure— Present us most affectionately to Mrs. Clay & all the family
Yrs Truly   J ERWIN

ALS. DLC-HC (DNA, M212, R2). Addressed: "private."
[1] George Mather. The enclosure has not been found. Cf. above, Whittlesey to Clay, December 22, 1826; Clay to Erwin, September 3, 1827.   [2] David Crockett. Cf. above, Erwin to Clay, August 12, 1827.   [3] Not found.   [4] John Williams.   [5] John W. Taylor. Cf. above, Clay to Taylor, September 7, 1827, note.   [6] Hugh Lawson White; John Henry Eaton.   [7] Cf. above, Carroll to Clay, October 4, 1825, note.   [8] Cf. above, Webster to Clay, August 22, 1827, note.   [9] Anne Erwin Hitchcock.
[10] Yellow fever had occasioned about double the usual mortality in New Orleans at mid-August, 1827. *Niles' Weekly Register*, XXXIII (September 22, 1827), 50.   [11] Julia D., Henry Clay, and Anne Brown Clay Erwin.

From William B. Rochester

Hon H. Clay
My Dear Sir   *private*   Baltimore 30. Sept. 1827.
Having been attacked by a most unaccountable vertigo on the even'g when I last left your house,[1] I did not deem it prudent to travel quite so soon or so rapidly as I then intended— I consequently did not reach Baltimore until yesterday and (the day-boat being discontinued) shall depart hence for Phila: & N. York tomorrow at 5. P. M.— At the latter city I shall undoubtedly arrive by the 4th. inst. [*sic*] which will give me a day in Phila: for Capt. Phillips[2] & others

Any communications from your Dept. for me, will be, of course directed to N. York— Upon examining the latest N. Y. papers I find that the destination of the little vessel which I spoke of, is changed from Omoa to Havanna [*sic*]—

I do not think I shall *urge* Capt. Phillips to take me out, as he evidently seems to put *his* going out *at all* upon the footing of accommodation & compliment to me!—

It is supposed that the contest here tomorrow will be close— I hear good news from Phila: and from Delaware— accounts from Hagers Town[3] are not so favourable—

I am very sorry that you are again troubled with the enclosed account— Pleasonton[4] said you had only to indorce [*sic*] on it *"approved"*— i,e, as I intimated to him, making yourself, in lieu of him the Auditor— his excuse was, that it would save trouble with the Comptroller[5]— I am Sir Very truly Sincerely yrs.   WM B ROCHESTER

ALS. DLC-HC (DNA, M212, R2).
1 Cf. above, Rochester to Clay, September 17, 1827.   2 William Phillips.   3 Cf. above, Rochester to Clay, September 21, 1827. For sentiment in Philadelphia, cf. above, Johnston to Clay, *ca.* September 13, 1827, note; in Delaware, cf. above, Clay to Taylor, September 7, 1827, note; in Maryland, cf. above, Clay to Blunt, September 11, 1827, note. In the Maryland legislative contests to which Rochester referred, however, the Jacksonites were completely victorious, electing two of their supporters in Baltimore City, four in Baltimore County, and four in Washington County (including Hagerstown) while no Adamsites were elected in those districts. Washington *Daily National Intelligencer*, October 5, 1827.   4 Stephen Pleasonton.   5 Joseph Anderson.

Bill from St. John's Church

DR. Hon. Henry Clay   [*ca.* September 30, 1827]
                         To St. John's Church,
   For 1 . . . . . quarter, Pew rent, ending 30 Sepr. 27, $13.—
      25 PCt. on rent. 1 qr 3.12
                                                           —————
                                                           $16.12

D, partially printed. DLC-HC (DNA, M212, R3).

INSTRUCTIONS AND DISPATCHES   September 30, 1827

From ALBERT GALLATIN, London, no. 122. Transmits "a Convention with Great Britain for the regulation of the reference to Arbitration of the North East boundary Question, which after a long, protracted and arduous negotiation, was concluded yesterday." Discusses, in about 24 manuscript pages the course of the negotiations and the difficulties involved in them. Advises, in view of "the numerous difficulties" encountered, "that there is no other alternative but to adopt" the convention "or a reference of the Reports of the Commissioners and of all the papers thereto annexed, such as they are." Observes, with reference "to the most important question, that of the North West angle of Nova Scotia and of the line thence along the highlands," that "there is no proposition in Mathematics more conclusively demonstrated, than that the line contended for by Great Britain is altogether inconsistent with the Treaty [of Paris] of 1783." Adds: "The only danger is that the Arbiter may decide that the conditions of that treaty are contradictory and that it cannot be executed. It is morally impossible that he should give a decision in favour of Great Britain." Encloses copies "of the Protocols of . . . [the negotiators'] five last conferences and of the Map A." Notes that "The original of this Map and of that of Mitchell [cf. above, Delafield to Clay, September 23, 1825, note] procured here being both intended to be laid before the Arbiter will remain in the Archives of this Legation subject to . . . [Clay's] orders. . . ." LS. DNA, RG59, Dip. Disp., Great Britain, vol. 34 (M30, R30). Published, with enclosures (except for the convention), in *American State Papers, Foreign Relations*, VI, 696–705.

The convention, found in *ibid.*, 643–44, comprises eight articles: the first denotes agreement to refer "the points of difference . . . in the settlements of the boundary between the American and British domains, as described in the 5th article of the treaty of Ghent, . . . to some friendly Sovereign or State" and to try "to obtain a decision . . . within two years after the Arbiter shall have signified his consent to act as such"; the second provides for the substitution, for the "voluminous and complicated" documents assembled by "the Commissioners appointed to carry into execution the 5th article of the treaty of Ghent," of a new statement of the case, drawn up by each party and communicated to the other party within fifteen months, and for the exchange "of a second and definitive statement" if it should be found desirable; the third obliges each party to "communicate to the other . . . all the evidence intended to be brought in support of its claim. . ."; the fourth designates "Mitchell's map . . . and the map A, which has been agreed on by the contracting parties," as "the only maps that shall be considered as evidence mutually acknowledged by the contracting parties of the topography of the country"; the fifth requires all documentation to be delivered to the arbiter within two years after ratification of the convention, or, if he has not consented within that time to act, within six months after his consent shall have been obtained; the sixth designates procedures by which additional "elucidation or evidence" desired by the arbiter might be furnished to him; the seventh declares: "The decision of the arbiter, when given, shall be taken as final and conclusive, and it shall be carried, without reserve, into immediate effect. . ."; and the eighth sets a limit of nine months, from the date of the convention, for the exchange of ratifications.

From John Quincy Adams

Henry Clay. Secretary of State. Washington
Dear Sir   Quincy 1 October 1827
Your letter of the 24th ulto confirms the Report which I had heard with great concern of your indisposition and partly relieves me by the information of your convalescence. I hope it has been ere this complete—

By my letter of the same day you will have seen that all the documents which had been transmitted to me from the Department had been received. Since which copies of the correspondence with Mr Marschalk at Natches [sic] and of the recent despatches from Mr Poinsett have come to hand.[1]

I believe our first Treaty with Sweden was in the French Language only;[2] but the general and better practice has been to sign in both languages. If Mr Appleton has not sent with the Treaty a Translation it will be necessary that great care should be taken in making that which is to be communicated to the Senate; and particularly with regard to those articles which are additional to or vary from the former treaties

By the last despatches from Mr Poinsett there appears to be a probability that the differences between the Government of the Mexican Federation and that of the State of Vera Cruz will terminate in a conflict of arms. It may perhaps be proper to instruct Mr Poinsett to express rather informally than in a public Memorial the regret which we have experienced, on observing the unfounded suspicions of the Government of Vera Cruz both with regard to the policy of this Union, and to the conduct of our Minister. That while we take a deep and always friendly interest in the welfare of the Mexican Federation, we abstain as a consequence of that principle itself, from all interposition in their internal political concerns, earnestly wishing them to result in the Peace, Union, and Prosperity of the whole. That influenced by the same disposition we forbear to make any formal complaint of the injustice done to us by the manifesto of the Congress of Vera-Cruz: but that we owe it to our own honor, and to the sincerity of our friendship for the Mexican Union, to declare that their representation of our views and feelings contained in that document is altogether unfounded— That we think they have equally misunderstood the conduct of our Minister who has disclaimed all interference on his part in the internal concerns of Mexico, and who could only by such forbearance fulfil the purposes and conform to the wishes of his own Government[3]—

I have had several conversations with the Governor of this State[4] upon the subject of the recent communication to the Department of State from the Governor of Maine.[5] The former is now upon a visit to his brother at Portland; and on his return I expect on my passage through Worcester to see him again—

I am still intending to leave this place next Thursday and Boston on Saturday. My expectation is to reach Washington the 13th;[6] should you have occasion to write me your letter might meet me on the 10th at New York— Yours with great respect and regard—

Copy. MHi-Adams Papers, Letterbook, Private, no. 10, pp. 111–12 (MR149).
[1] Above, Marschalk to Clay, August 20, 1827; Poinsett to Clay, June 20, July 8, 1827.
[2] Cf. above, Clay to Appleton, September 11, 1827 (no. 4), note.   [3] Cf. below, Clay to Poinsett, November 19, 1827.   [4] Levi Lincoln.   [5] Cf. above, Enoch Lincoln to Clay, September 3, 1827.   [6] Cf. below, Clay to Webster, October 17, 1827.

From Jonathan Elliot

OCT. 1, 1827.

SIR, Being the *first* representative, in the national legislature, who advocated the recognition of the independent governments of South America, by this republic,[1] and having taken a prominent and conspicious [sic] part in opening a new and extensive field of political and commercial intercourse, with the most interesting and fertile portion of this vast continent, you are fairly entitled to the enviable distinction of an *American Statesman*, whose intrepid patriotism, public virtue, and political philanthrophy, is not confined to your own country, but extends to the whole universe; and, thus, by excellence, your claim to precedence is established among the most eminent public men of the age. When eloquently maintaining the cause of South America, in the Halls of Congress, you were not mistaken in trusting to the patriotic spirit of your countrymen, or to the liberal principles of our government, that, in the end, you would be supported, and successfully attain the object of your anxious solicitude: and, confiding in the moral influence and temperate wisdom of the distinguished body over which you then presided, you clearly foresaw, that the United States, (destined to be the leading nation in the new world) could not long let their national character be suspected of indifference to the political welfare of their brethren of the South: for, after some years persever-ance, your policy and councils prevailed; whilst, in the mean time, the South American patriots illumined their hemisphere by a succession of brilliant achievements, and proved themselves worthy of your un-wearied efforts in their cause.

In the exalted height of our political prosperity, and pursuing the peaceful paths of commerce, it is now, happily, in the line of your of-ficial duty, to aid in consummating the great work you had the honor to commence, in framing and negotiating, with the new nations of the South, Conventions of Amity and Commerce, on the most liberal basis;[2] and, in extending and cementing those ties of friendship and national interest, that, under your administration of foreign affairs, not only commands respect for our national character abroad, but adds to our happiness, and promotes our prosperity, at home.

Such, Sir, are the motives that prompt me to take the liberty of dedi-cating to you the following work. With due respect, &c. &c. &c.

JONATHAN ELLIOT.

Jonathan Elliot, *Diplomatic Code of the United States of America: Embracing a Col-lection of Treaties and Conventions between the United States and Foreign Powers, from the Year 1778 to 1827* . . . (Washington, 1827) , [iii] (dedication).
[1] Cf. above, II, 135–36, 155–56, 289–92, 343–44, 402–405, 492–507, 817–18, 853–60; III, 22–24, 29–31, 44, 80, 186n.   [2] See above, Clay to Poinsett, March 26, 1825; Clay to Anderson, September 16, 1825; Convention with Central American Federation, December 5, 1825; below, Clay to Tudor, October 23, 1827.

INSTRUCTIONS AND DISPATCHES   October 1, 1827

From ALBERT GALLATIN, London, no. 123. Notes that, having ascertained the im-practicability of attempting to negotiate an "arrangement, founded on a recog-nition of the right of the United States to the navigation of the river St. Lawrence to the sea," and the "sensibility" of the British "on that subject" (cf. above, Gallatin to Clay, November 14, 1826), he did not bring that question forward officially until "after it had been distinctly ascertained . . . that there was no chance left of the Intercourse with the British West Indies being opened [cf. above, Gallatin to Clay, September 14, 1827], and after the principles of the Conven-tion respecting the North East boundary had been substantially agreed to [cf. above, Gallatin to Clay, September 21, 1827]. . . ." States that he had no hope of success but "apprehended that to omit altogether this subject might be construed as an abandonment of the right of the United States." Reports that, upon his bringing up the matter, the British Plenipotentiaries (Charles Grant; Henry U. Addington) informed him of their instructions not to enter into any discussion of it so long as the United States claimed free navigation of the river as a right; that he did not think it wise to commit his Government to "any specific proposal with the certainty of its being rejected, or to make this Government commit itself still further by reiterating its positive refusal to treat on the ground of a right on the part of the United States"; and that he "therefore made the entry" contained "in the Protocol of the 20th. Conference. . . ." Refers to Clay's instructions to him of August 8, 1826, with regard to "the admission of American produce at Quebec or Montreal free of duty"; observes that neither of the alternatives was attainable "in the present temper of this Government"; and expresses a belief that "we may with confidence rely on the obvious interest of Great Britain to remove every restriction on the exportation of American produce through Canada, and need not resort to any treaty stipulation short of at least a *liberty* in perpetuity to navigate the river through its whole extent." Points out that circumstances have changed and that "In consequence of the extension of the warehousing system to the ports of Quebec, Montreal & St. John's, places of deposit are in fact allowed for every species of American produce free of duty in case of exportation [cf. above, Clay to Ogden, June 17, 1826, and note; Gallatin to Clay, June 13, 1827]; which is all that in that respect we could ask as a matter of right" but that the navigation between Montreal and Quebec to and from the sea "cannot now be obtained by a treaty stipulation without . . . a disclaimer of the right." Expresses a belief, however, that "in practice" the navigation will not "be much longer denied" and cites "a disposition, not evinced on former occasions to make the navigation of the river free, provided it was not asked as a matter of right, and generally to encourage the intercourse between the United States and the adjacent British provinces." Attributes "This change of disposition" to the desire of the British to obtain "supplies for the West India Colonies" and "to more correct views of what is so clearly the interest and ought to be the policy of Great Britain" with regard to "the American inland commerce." States that "It is therefore to that mode of attaining the object in view that" he has turned his attention; summarizes his arguments in an interview "to day" with Lord Dudley; terms "somewhat remarkable" the doubt, expressed by Dudley "and several of the other Ministers, . . . that the navigation of the river was interdicted to our boats between Montreal and Quebec"; and concludes with "great hopes that setting aside the abstract question of right, . . . our citizens will ere long and through the acts of Great Britain alone, enjoy all the benefits of the navigation. . . ." Suggests, "should this expectation be disappointed," retaliation "above St. Regis." ALS. DNA, RG59, Dip. Disp., Great Britain, vol. 34 (M30, R30). Published in *American State Papers, Foreign Relations*, VI, 768–69.

The "entry . . . in the Protocol of the 20th. Conference," to which Gallatin refers, makes note of his statement "that having satisfied himself that there was no probability of forming, at the present moment, any arrangement with respect to the free navigation of the river St. Lawrence on the principles heretofore, and still, urged by the United States, he would abstain from submitting, as he had intended, any proposal on that subject." True copy, by William B. Lawrence, in DNA, RG59, Dip. Disp., Great Britain, vol. 34 (M30, R30).

From Robert Scott

Dear Sir,   Lexington, 2nd. Octr. 1827

On the 27th. Ulto. I remitted you in a check of the Office here on the Bank of the U States Six thousand dollars of the funds of Colo. Morrison's estate.[1]

Herewith please receive statements of your Accounts with Colo. Morrisons estate, and also with me down to the 1st. inst.[2]

I have called upon Mrs. Hart[3] to make her a quarterly payment, but she says she has received some money from Orleans.[4] 150$ I beleive, which will serve to lay in her wood &c., and be sufficient for the present— When she has use for more she will inform me—

Aunt Morrison[5] and family are well— It is uncertain when or whether this season she will get off for Baltimore. &c. Very respectfully Your obt. Servt.   ROBT. SCOTT
The Honble Henry Clay

ALS. KyLxT.   [1] James Morrison; the check, not found.
[2] These quarterly statements (those on Clay's private account with Morrison's estate, not found; those with Scott, separate note and specie accounts, dated October 1, 1827, AD, in KyLxT) have been omitted by the editors. They are incorporated in the annual statements, below, Specie Account with Scott, August 6, 1828; Note Account with Scott, August 15, 1828; Private Account with Estate, August 15, 1828.   [3] Susannah Gray Hart.   [4] Cf. above, Brown to Clay, May 12, 1827 (1); Clay to Brown, August 10, 1827.   [5] Esther Montgomery Morrison.

From John Sergeant

Dear Sir,   (Private)   Philada. Octr. 2. 1827.
Your favor of the 28th. ulto[1] (confidential) was received yesterday. A death in the family[2] has kept me confined to the house, but I sent for the gentleman mentioned[3] and he called upon me. He stated various objections to coming out *at this time*, but after a good deal of conversation agreed to draw up a full statement, embracing all the points suggested, and to bring it to me to day. Upon most matters, he is sufficiently satisfactory, adhering, however, to this, that he had a great desire to promote your advancement, and that this was one of the motives which influenced him— I will forward you a copy as soon as the statement is obtained. In the mean time, consider a little the standing and official station of the witness, and whether in putting him forward, we may not offer a weak point to the enemy. I cannot say more at present, being engaged with the event first mentioned, but I feel extremely anxious about the step to be taken— Our local affair[4] looks tolerably well. There is no certain calculation, however, to be formed, as small things may have a great influence, Very respectfully and truly yrs.   JOHN SERGEANT
The Honble Henry Clay.

ALS. DLC-HC (DNA, M212, R2).   [1] Not found.
[2] Sergeant's mother-in-law, Anna Carmick (Mrs. James Horatio) Watmough, a widow since 1812, had died on September 30, at the age of 71.   [3] Philip S. Markley—cf. above, Johnston to Clay, September 13, 1827, note.   [4] Cf. above, Johnston to Clay, September 13, 1827, note.

INSTRUCTIONS AND DISPATCHES   October 2, 1827

From ALBERT GALLATIN, London, no. 124. Transmits "an Atlas containing several Maps intended to be laid before the Arbiter on the North East Boundary" (cf. above, Gallatin to Clay, September 30, 1827), additional engraved maps, "the annual Register for 1763 with a map, and Pownall's topographical account"; explains that duplicates of the maps remain in the Legation archives, "those sent . . . being intended to enable . . . [Clay] to make the necessary communications to the British Minister in conformity with the Convention"; and notes certain other maps that are not enclosed at this time. ALS. DNA, RG59, Dip. Disp., Great Britain, vol. 34 (M30, R30). Published in *American State Papers, Foreign Relations*, VI, 706.

The *Annual Register, 1763*, p. 208, carried a proclamation by George III, dated October 7 of that year, delineating the southern boundary of Quebec, recently acquired under the treaty of Paris, and a folded map, engraved by the geographer T. Kitchin, entitled "A New Map of British Dominions in North America, with the Limits of the Governments Annexed Thereto by the Late Treaty of Peace, and Settled by Proclamation, October 7th 1763."

Thomas Pownall had published at London in 1776 *A Topographical Description of Such Parts of North America as Are Contained in the (Annexed) Map of the Middle British Colonies, &c. in North America.*

From Francis P. Blair

Frankfort, October 3, 1827.

DEAR SIR: On returning home from Canewood[1] yesterday, (where I have been for some time for the purpose of restoring my health, which has recently suffered under a bilious attack,) I found an allusion to me in a letter from Mr. Kendall to you, contained in the last week's Argus,[2] which greatly surprised me. Nothing on my part ever authorized the course he has adopted. Before I left home, Mr. Kendall and Mr. ———[3] informed me that one of your political supporters (Thomas Y. Bryant) had, in order to charge me with inconsistency, informed them that I had been instrumental in getting some of the Kentucky delegation to vote for Mr. Adams, and that I had obtained a letter of instruction from him to Mr. White,[4] by the assurance that you would be made Secretary of State.[5] Mr. Kendall also stated that I had got his letter to White by making the same representation. I admitted that I might have given such an assurance, although I did not recollect it.

My estrangement from you in politics has given rise to many unworthy conclusions with regard to my motives. Your friends, and some of your relations, seem disposed to place the very worst construction on my conduct. They do me injustice. I have nothing to expect from General Jackson; and I know I never would have been disappointed in obtaining from your hands any personal benefit which I could have any right to expect from you. I think I gave some proof of disinterestedness in adhering to a defeated party against a triumphant one, when I might have ushered myself into the latter under the passport of your imposing name, and the recommendation of having always supported one, to support whom is now its only avowed object. Indeed, I adhered to you while your principles and declared opinions militated directly against the most important pecuniary interests[6] I ever had, or ever

shall have at stake. And I never deserted your banner until the questions on which you and I so frequently differed in private discussion—(State rights, the Bank, the power of the Judiciary, &c.)—became the criterions to distinguish the parties, and had actually renewed, in their practical effects, the great divisions which marked the era of 1798. Whatever others may say, then, I hope you will do me the justice to believe that I am operated on by a sincere political faith, although you may consider it a delusion; and if you will not allow that the principles of Democracy sway me, you may charge it to a sort of party instinct, in which reason has no part   My personal partialities have always led me towards you. My affections are still on your side, and if admiration of your genius had not been counteracted by the apprehensions that its powers are directed to destroy the political creed to which I had given my faith, I should have been proud always to have paid it my homage. Your most obedient servant,   F. P. BLAIR.
To H. CLAY, esq.

Copy. First paragraph published in Washington *Daily Globe*, October 12, 1844; the remainder in *ibid*., March 16, 1841.
[1] "Canewood," in Clark County, Kentucky, was the family home of Blair's wife, Eliza Violet Gist, whose sister, Maria C. Gist (Mrs. Benjamin) Gratz, had inherited the property and with her husband used it as a summer home.   [2] Above, September 26, 1827.
[3] The unnamed individual was not identified in the text of the inquiry conducted by the Kentucky Senate between January 31 and February 6, 1828, concerning the charges of bargain and corruption. Ky. Sen., *Journal* . . . *1827*, 298–339 *passim*. Cf. also, below, Blair to Clay, January 22, February 4, 1828, notes.   [4] David White (Jr.).   [5] Cf. above, Blair to Clay, January 24, 1825.   [6] See above, Blair to Clay, August 30, 1825, and note.

INSTRUCTIONS AND DISPATCHES   October 3, 1827

From JOSHUA BOND, Montevideo. States that, since he is "about to make a short visit to . . . the United States," he has appointed his brother, Dr. James Bond, acting consul. ALS. DNA, RG59, Cons. Disp., Montevideo (M71, R1). Received January 9.

From ALBERT GALLATIN, London, no. 125. Encloses Lord Dudley's answer, dated October 1, to Gallatin's notes of June 4 and August 17 (cf. above, Gallatin to Clay, June 4, August 21, 1827). Reports that he "had anticipated the negative answer to the enquiry contained in the last mentioned Note, having had two interviews with Mr [William] Huskisson" (cf. above, Gallatin to Clay, September 14, 28, 1827), who was "immoveable [*sic*]," who gave no "satisfactory explanation of the motives for persevering in the measures adopted in regard to the Colonial Intercourse," and who evinced "irritation not yet extinguished, on account of the United States not having met, especially in 1823 and 1824, the overtures of Great Britain [cf, above, III, 729, note 21]. . . ." Adds: ". . . it seems to me that there is also some obstinacy in the way." States that he "had not expected that Lord Dudley would have reverted to topicks already so much debated and again tried to raise doubts on points which had been satisfactorily explained." Asserts that "Mr [George] Canning had explicitly told . . . [him] that he thought it was time to close the controversy and that he would not make any answer to . . . [Gallatin's] Note of 4th of June." Encloses a copy of his reply to Lord Dudley. Observes that,

"Although they ought not to have again controverted our statements, the answer was intended to be very civil to the United States." ALS. DNA, RG59, Dip. Disp., Great Britain, vol. 34 (M30, R30). Published in Adams (ed.), *Writings of Gallatin*, II, 392–93.

DIPLOMATIC NOTES   October 4, 1827

From FRANCISCO TACÓN, Washington. Refers to the notes addressed to Clay by Hilario de Rivas y Salmon on May 31 and June 12 (1827); reports that Commodore David Porter is now in New Orleans, where, according to an extract (enclosed) of a letter from the Spanish consul at that port (Antonio Argote y Villalobos), he continues his illegal activities against Spanish commerce. Encloses also a copy of a newspaper which carries a letter from Porter in relation to his activities in recruiting men for his forces. Asserts that these activities violate the treaties between Spain and the United States and requests that his protest be brought to the attention of the President. LS, in Spanish with trans. in State Dept. file. DNA, RG59, Notes from Spanish Legation, vol. 9 (M59, R-T12).

Villalobos had formerly served as Spanish vice consul at Norfolk and, appointed in 1821, at Charleston.

The enclosed newspaper, the *Baltimore Gazette and Daily Advertiser* of September 12, 1827, in fact carried two documents relating to Commodore Porter's activities at New Orleans: one, a notice dated August 18, by J(ohn) W. Smith, the United States Attorney (for the Eastern District of Louisiana), setting forth precisely the terms of United States neutrality legislation (cf. above, II, 507n) and warning of its penalties; another, a letter dated August 20 by Porter, explaining why he had published a handbill relating to recruitment and including the handbill, which stipulated the pay for enlistment in the Mexican Navy and the manner by which the United States neutrality law might be circumvented.

INSTRUCTIONS AND DISPATCHES   October 4, 1827

From ALBERT GALLATIN, London, no. 126. States that, having concluded the negotiations entrusted to him (cf. above, Clay to Gallatin, June 19, 21, 1826; February 24 [no. 18], April 11, 1827; Gallatin to Clay, November 13, 1826; August 6, 7, September 26, 30, 1827) and having "received the definitive answer of this Government to the proposal which . . . [he] had been authorized to make on the Subject of the Colonial Intercourse" (cf. above, Gallatin to Clay, October 1, 3, 1827), he "will avail" himself "of the permission of the President to return to the United States" (cf. above, Clay to Gallatin, February 24, 1827 [no. 19]). Reports that he is leaving (William Beach) Lawrence as Chargé d'Affaires. Notes that "The current business of this Mission is much less than . . . anticipated and there will be none of a public nature till some time after the meeting of Parliament." ALS. DNA, RG59, Dip. Disp., Great Britain, vol. 34 (M30, R30). Published in Adams (ed.), *Writings of Albert Gallatin*, II, 393.

From JOEL R. POINSETT, Mexico, no. 100. Reports that, in an effort to ascertain "the probable period of the meeting of the Congress of American States at Tacubaya," he sent a note (dated August 7, 1827), a copy of which is enclosed, to the Mexican Plenipotentiaries (José Dominguez; José Mariano Michelena) to that body; explains that he "was further induced to send the note from having" learned of "a correspondence . . . between the Mexican Plenipotentiaries and Dr. [Pedro] Gual, the Representative of Colombia," on the question whether Gual was authorized to act alone or had to await the return of "the Minister [Pedro Briceño Mendez] who carried the Treaties of Panama [cf. above, Salazar to Clay, November 20, 1826] to Bogota"; notes that Gual, without answering this question, remonstrated "against the conduct of" Mexico for "not acting upon the treaties of Panamá, and declines taking any part in . . . the Congress . . . until the Convention [cf. above, Poinsett to Clay, May 10, 1827] . . . shall have been ratified." Expresses disappointment that his own note did not draw "from the Mexican Plenipotentiaries copies of the correspondence," to which they did not allude "in their reply, a translation of which" is enclosed. LS. DNA, RG59, Dip. Disp., Mexico, vol. 3 (M97, R4). Received November 9. In their reply, Dominguez and Michelena wrote that they could only repeat what they had told John Sergeant (see above, Sergeant to Clay, March 27, 1827, note).

From Christopher Hughes (1)

My dear Mr. Clay,   *Private*   Brussels; October 5th. 27.

I wrote to you a few days ago;[1] I have nothing new to communicate; the only public event of any importance, you will find stated in my despatch of this date;[2] i.e. the Concordat between H. R. Majesty & H. H. The Pope;[3] & this is an event of vital importance;   the King has been *bullied*, by his Catholic subjects, into a complete concession of all authority over the church, to the Pope; & all control over the education of his catholic subjects, to the priests. There has been carried on a sort of, schismatic war, between the king & the Priests, for the last six or eight years: the latter, as usual, claimed everything; and chiefly, the entire guidance of public instruction, of all persons, destined for the church, from the primary start of their education, up to the moment of their ordination & admission into the priesthood. H. M. resisted; He founded a College of Philosophy, at Louvain,[4] for the education of all classes of his subjects indiscriminately; & especially, for such as were meant for Divines; the influence of the Priests kept back the great mass of the Youth, under the threat of refusing them *orders*, from going to this Institution; but still some hundreds pursued & perfected their studies at the University; the Priests were firm in their grounds, & absolutely have persevered in refusing *to receive* into the Church, all Graduates of the College of Philosophy, who presented themselves for examination & ordination; the King would not yield & a complete episcopal interregnum has existed for several years; threatening, at any moment, to produce some serious explosion; as you may conceive, when you reflect on the very dense population of this part of H. M.s dominions; that 999, of 10,000 [*sic*] are rigid & even bigoted catholics; and that the apostolical & jesuit cause has been most manifestly gaining ground, & is gaining ground every hour.—throughout catholic Europe! The affair began to look very grave, and the disorder and numerous vacancies in the Church were felt to be inconveniences, not merely uncomfortable in themselves, but alarming as

to the effects they might produce on the mind of this large, unenlight-
ened & wilful [sic] portion of H. M.s subjects. The King was induced
by all these considerations, to send a very pompous Embassy last winter, to Rome;   He selected the Count de Celles,[5] one of Napoleon's
Prefects & a Peer; a man of rare wit & eloquence; perfectly versed in
public & knotty affairs; of a catholic family, but notoriously careless
as to religion himself, a diseur des bons-mots; a bon-vivant; crippled
by the gout; and one of the most notorious *Roués* in Europe; but, as I
have said, a man of commanding talents—a most delightful companion
& with a most plastic tongue & conscience;   Cte. de Celles is reported
to have said, on receiving the appointment, "is it not quite unaccountable, that his Majesty should select, for the settlement of a religious
quarrel, le plus *mauvais sujet* de tout le Royaume?" However, off he
went to Rome; kept a splendid House; pleased every Body, society,
Pope & Cardinals; observed, most vigorously, all the fasts & festivals;
& concluded the work, I now send you, in which, as it seems to me, He
has made his Master give *up & yield every thing*.

The Count de Celles will return to Rome, and reside there, as His
Majestys ambassador; & of course, he shall have a regular Nuncio at
this Court; where, in consequence of the above described episcopal
strife, there has been no papal legation for several years.[6]

I enclose you an extract[7] of a letter from *Odessa*, in which you will
perceive complimentary notice of our naval architecture, it is marvel-
lous [sic], in what terms of respect, admiration, & *anticipation*, all
points connected with our maritime character & capacities, are spoken
of in Europe; even by the *reluctant* English, including their Naval officers! Perhaps Mr. Southard[8] may like to read the enclosed; I *hope* he
has read "Lieut: de Roos's Book";[9] it has been read by all England;
chiefly because Mr. de Roos is of a very distinguished noble family, &
he, himself, one of the most notorious fashionables & Dandies, as they
say, "*about Town*." Count Pahlen[10] retains an admiration, for other
points belonging to our country, besides the Navy;   He was supposed
to have imbibed political principles, during his residence in the U. S.
too free & liberal to fit him for such duties, as the Emperor of Russia[11]
expects & exacts from his Diplomatic Ministers;   He was recalled,
some years ago, from his mission at Munich & "put upon the shelf."
His Brother Nicholas,[12]—was erased from the list of diplomatic em-
ployes [sic], & has not resided in Russia, since his return from America; either because he did not like, or did not feel it *safe* to do so.

Ct. Caraman has accepted the place at Dresden.[13] Baron Mareuil is
at Paris, & will find very great difficulty, as I learn, to get an acceptable
diplomatic place in Europe.[14]

Young Huygens[15] is here; but no time is fixed yet for his return to
america; though, I imagine, he will start via Havre, in 2 or 3 weeks.
He has managed to be made a chevalier, in some Household order of

the reigning Duke of Saxe Weimar[16] & wears a red ribbon at his button hole; with which, he appears to be amazingly tickled; & he has also managed to prevail on a Brother of his Mother,[17] a Danish Colonel, a Count de Lowendahl, (one of his ancestors was a French Marshal of that name:)[18] to adopt him & give him his title;   he is now *trying* to manage, what will be, I suspect, most difficult of all, i.e. to prevail on the King of the Netherlands to authorize the inscription of his name & title, as "Count de Lowendahl," at the Herald's office here;[19] & thus to glide in among the native nobility. Both the King of Denmark[20] & the King of the Netherlands make no objection to the act of adoption on the part of his uncle, the Colonel; who has a very numerous family himself; but unfortunately, they are all illegitimate!

I had a letter from Mr. Connell,[21] dated a few days ago, at Hamburg: Mr. Wheaton[22] had gone on; I regret, & am rather surprised, that he did not come through Brussels;   I *think* I could have given him some information, general and personal, that might prove useful to him in his mission at Copenhagen. If you had given him the rank of Envoy Extr. he might do something; as it is I doubt his success.

I met your old friend, Made. Greban, & had a long talk with her yesterday: she desired to be particularly remembered to you & to Mr. Adams! I had the happiness, on the 2d. of this month, to *assist* at the wedding of *one* of my young *old* Ghent favourites. Madse. Jeanette de Bay,[23] niece of the Meulemeesters;[24]   she were [*sic*] married three times; 1st. at the Hotel de Ville— 2d. at the Protestant & 3d. at the Catholic Church;   her husband is a very respectable Swiss Merchant.[25] N. B. I yesterday received *70* national Intelligencers & journals, *at once*, via Amsterdam! last date, 29 July! With the kindest messages from Mrs Hughes to Mrs. Clay, & my sincere respects to the President, I am, my dr. Mr Clay, as ever, Yr. frd. & servt.   CHRISTOPHER HUGHES—
Henry Clay Esqr. Washington.

ALS. DLC-HC (DNA, M212, R2).
[1] No letter since that, above, of September 16, 1827, has been found.   [2] Below.
[3] William I; Leo XII.   [4] Founded in 1425 but suppressed in 1797, the University of Louvain had been reopened by William I in 1816 as a state institution. It survived in this form only briefly and in 1835 became officially the Catholic University of Belgium.
[5] Born in Brussels in 1779, Antoine-Charles-Fiacre-Ghislain, Count de Wisher de Celles, had been a member of the Estates General and active in the negotiations which attached the Netherlands to France under Napoleon. Having impressed the Emperor, De Celles had been prefect of several departments, successively, including Zuiderzée, where he had incurred much local protest over his commitment to French designs. He had continued active in politics, as a member of the opposition, after the accession of William I and was named Minister to France in 1830. Shortly thereafter he was naturalized a Frenchman and in 1833 became a member of the French Council of State.   [6] Ignace Nasalli, born in Parma in 1750, a Jesuit from early youth, had been sent as an envoy to Spain in 1815 but, barred from entry to that country, had been named apostolic delegate to the Greeks in 1818 and preconized the following year as Archbishop of Tyr, *in partibus*. He had been named in 1823 as a plenipotentiary to conclude a concordat with the Netherlands but had failed in such efforts there as well as at Berlin during the succeeding years. He had been raised to a cardinalcy in June, 1827, and was the Papal delegate to the Hague in 1827 and 1828.   [7] Not found.   [8] Samuel L. Southard.
[9] John Frederick Fitzgerald De Roos, a lieutenant in the British Navy, had published

at London in 1827 a *Personal Narrative of Travels in the United States and Canada in 1826, . . . With Remarks on the Present State of the American Navy.* [10] Count Frederick Pahlen had been appointed Russian Minister to the United States in 1809 and still held the post in 1811. He was subsequently named Minister at Munich and then became Governor of Kherson in Russia. In 1829 he was one of the signers of the Treaty of Adrianople between Russia and Turkey. [11] Nicholas I. [12] The career of Count Nicholas Pahlen, located in Paris in 1815, has not been traced subsequently. [13] Cf. above, Hughes to Clay, September 16, 1827. [14] Mareuil next headed the French Mission in Portugal. In 1830 he returned to the Netherlands, where he had served as Minister in 1820. He was interim French Ambassador to London in 1832 and Minister to Naples in 1834. [15] Roger Bangeman Huygens. [16] Karl August. [17] Mrs. C. D. E. J. Bangeman Huygens, not further identified. [18] The marshal was Ulric-Frédéric-Woldemar, Count de Lowendahl (1700–1755), who had had a distinguished military career in the service of Poland, Russia, and France. He had had a son, born in 1742, who had commanded a corps of French émigrés during the French Revolution and may have been young Huygens' uncle. [19] The title is not listed in *Annuaire de la Noblesse et des Familles Patriciennes des Pays-Bas . . . le Année, 1871* (Rotterdam and La Haye, 1871). [20] Frederick VI. [21] John Connell. [22] Henry Wheaton. [23] Not further identified. [24] Mr. and Mrs. Jean de Meulemeester. [25] Not further identified.

From John Sergeant

Dear Sir,   (Private)   Philada. Octr. 5. 1827.

Since my last, Mr. Markley has called twice, but has not yet made out the statement.[1] We have arranged the *mode*, however, in which he is to come out, and I think it good. He will be written to, by one of the most important personages in the State, and in his answer will give a full narrative.[2] He shewed me yesterday a letter he had received from one of our friends at Harrisburg. I was delighted with the bold, manly and at the same time judicious counsel it gave him.

I congratulate you upon the triumph in Delaware.[3] It is of great consequence in every point of view, and, among other things, I hope will have its effect upon the Senators of that State.[4]

Every thing here looks well. Our friends are zealous, active and true, and I believe very numerous. It is an untried state of things, however, and no *certain* calculation can be made. But I hope, and believe, we shall give you a victory.[5] The Jackson presses here are a little abusive, but what of that? I am proud of being abused in such a cause, and never felt happier in communing with myself than I do at this very moment.

Some one told me within a few days that you seemed depressed by the Kentucky elections.[6] It is natural that you should have felt a little the disappointment. But there is one thing you may rely upon, that whatever may be the issue of this contest (and for the sake of the Country I do trust it will be as we wish) you will be a great gainer by it, tho' I have not time now to explain why and how, Very respectfully and truly yrs.   JOHN SERGEANT

The Honble Henry Clay

ALS. DLC-HC (DNA, M212, R2).
[1] Cf. above, Johnston to Clay, September 13, 1827, note. [2] Cf. below, Sergeant to Clay, October 31, 1827, note. [3] Cf. above, Clay to Taylor, September 7, 1827, note.

4 Henry M. Ridgely; Louis McLane.   5 Cf. above, Sergeant to Clay, September 28, 1826, note.   6 Cf. above, Clay to Taylor, April 4, 1827, note; Clay to Adams, August 25, 1827, note.

DIPLOMATIC NOTES   October 5, 1827

From FRANCISCO TACÓN, Washington. States that the efforts of the United States Government have been "ineffectual" in preventing the use of its harbors by belligerents for "the construction or purchase of ships, and in arming, equipping and fitting them out to carry on war against Spain. . . ." Reports that a corvette, "armed with thirty twenty-four pounders, named provisionally the Kensington, and lying at anchor in the port of Philadelphia" was built "by order of the government (so called) of Mexico" and "is detained solely because the amount of the funds hitherto obtained from Mexico has not been sufficient to complete the payment of her cost; that, in anticipation of payment of the balance, the enlistment of the numerous crew corresponding to the force of the Corvette has been commenced, and advantage has been taken of the discharge of seamen from the United States ship 'North Carolina'"; notes that "[Henry B.] Chew, of the former house of Luke and Chew in that city, was foremost in the building and equipment of the Corvette, until, having removed his residence to Baltimore, he left his brother [Samuel Chew], a lawyer, in charge of the business and its details"; that the corvette, "commanded by Captain Thomas Hayes, a citizen of Philadelphia, and manned with American sailors, is now about to sail, in order to join the Mexican navy, under the protection of the flag of the Federation, which she has hoisted"; concludes, since the United States declared its neutrality in the Act of April 20, 1818 (cf. above, II, 507, note), "that the Government of Mexico and the brothers Chews [sic] have infringed the laws of the United States"; requests that Clay bring the case of the *Kensington* before the President. LS, in Spanish with trans. in State Dept. file. DNA, RG59, Notes from Spanish Legation, vol. 9 (M59, R-T12).

The firm of William Luke and the Chews were merchants, located on Chestnut Street, Philadelphia.

INSTRUCTIONS AND DISPATCHES   October 5, 1827

From WILLIAM B. HODGSON, Algiers, no. 91. Describes an engagement on October 4, between attacking Algerine vessels and the French blockading force, which ended when the Algerines returned to port. Comments: "It remains to be seen, whether this combat will have the effect of elevating the French Marine, in the estimation of the Algerines, to the rank of the American and English, for which alone, they affect to have any fear or regard."

Notes that he received "a letter from the Consul-General [William Shaler] dated Sept. 17h at Mahon," stating that the latter would "return to Algiers, during this month." ALS. DNA, RG59, Cons. Disp., Algiers, vol. 11 (M23, R-T13).

From CHRISTOPHER HUGHES, Brussels (2). Transmits "the official Gazette of yesterday, containing a copy of the Concordat," arranged at Rome, June 18, 1827, between the King of the Netherlands (William I) and the Pope (Leo XII), "for the Government of the Catholic Church within H. M.'s dominions." Remarks on "some very unpalatable concessions" to which the King "has been obliged to consent. . . ." ALS. DNA, RG59, Dip. Disp., Netherlands, vol. 8 (M42, R12). Received November 30.

The concordat provided for the mode of appointing archbishops and bishops in the Catholic provinces. The king was to have an opportunity to review the names of candidates proposed by the cathedral chapter for such appointments and, if he found any not agreeable to him, their names were to be withdrawn. The chapter was then to elect the new prelate from the remaining nominees and communicate its choice to the pope, who would in turn conduct an inquiry into the candidate's qualifications and make the appointment. The king could not then veto the selection. All such officers in the Netherlands were required to take an oath of allegiance to the king. Three new sees were also to be created. *Annual Register, 1827*, pp. 285–86.

From HENRY MIDDLETON, St. Petersburg, "Private." Introduces Baron (Paul de) Krudener; notes that although he is deaf, Krudener has served in several Russian diplomatic missions; describes his background and character; and notes that "he is a man of observation and his opinions will carry weight here. . . ." ALS. DNA, RG59, Dip. Disp., Russia, vol. 11 (M35, R11). Dated September 23/October 5, 1827; received January 4, 1828.

From J[OEL] R. POINSETT, Mexico, no. 101. Transmits copies and translations of his correspondence with the Mexican Government "on the subject of the permanence of the Mexican squadron under the command of Commodore [David] Porter in the port of Key West." LS. DNA, RG59, Dip. Disp., Mexico, vol. 3 (M97, R4). Received November 9. Poinsett's note of July 10, addressed to the Secretary of State (Juan José Espinosa de los Monteros), complained of the violations of the law of neutrality committed by Porter in his "belligerent use of a port within the jurisdiction of the United States" to harass Spanish commerce. The Mexican reply claimed that Porter had "retired from the anchorage at Key West" and that any Mexican vessels still in that port were forced to remain there by the Spanish blockade.

To Josiah Stoddard Johnston

Dear Sir   Bath[1] 6h. October 1827

Prior to my departure from the City,[2] I promised to give you an account of my acquaintance and personal intercourse with Genl. Jackson. Detained here by an indisposition, which I hope will be slight, I avail myself of the leisure which is thus afforded me to fulfill my promise.

Before the year 1815 I did not personally know Genl. Jackson.[3] My acquaintance with him was made, in the fall of that year, at the City of Washington. We separated with favorable impressions towards each other, and he promised to pass a week of the ensuing summer at my house[4] in Kentucky. He was prevented from executing that intention, and wrote me a letter of regret[5] on the occasion. I again saw him in Washington during the Session of Congress at which the debate on the Seminole War took place.[6] He arrived, in the midst of the debate, and after I had pronounced, but before the publication of, the first Speech which I delivered on that subject. To evince that I was not actuated by any personal enmity towards him, in the opinions and sentiments which I had expressed to the House of Representatives, I waived the ceremony of the first call to which, as Speaker of that house, I was entitled, and visited him in the first instance. My visit was not returned and, unless it was at a distance, I have no recollection of again seeing Genl Jackson, during that Session, nor until the summer 1819. In that summer, President Monroe performed his Western tour, and he was attended in Kentucky by Genl. Jackson. When they were at Lexington, the place of my residence, I was absent, on my return from Louisiana.[7] They called, as I afterwards learnt, on Mrs. Clay at my house, and partook of some little refreshments. I was compelled, from the low state of the river, to leave the steamboat at the mouth of Cumberland, and to proceed thence by land to Lexington.[8] On my way thither, sitting one July morning at the door of a tavern in the little village of Lebanon near Green river in Kentucky, where I had breakfasted, the approach of Genl. Jackson and his suite was announced. As he ascended the steps, on which I was seated reading, I rose from my seat and saluted him in the most respectful manner. He hurried by me, slightly inclining his head, and rapidly uttering How do ye do Sir entered the tavern. Some of his suite paused and conversed with me some time, giving me the first intelligence I had received for several weeks of my family. After remaining a short time at the door, I entered the front room to get my hat and take something to drink. There I perceived Genl. Jackson sitting reading a newspaper, from which he did not appear to take his eye. After remaining in the room a few minutes, I left it, without speaking or being spoken to by the Genl., and resumed my journey home.

I saw no more of Genl. Jackson until the Session of Congress 1823–4, the first of the two Sessions in which he served in the Senate. Early in the Session, I was visited by the greater part of the Tennessee delegation (all I think but Genl. Cock [sic] and Mr. Eaton),[9] in a body, for the express purpose as they stated of producing a reconciliation between Genl. Jackson and myself. I gave them, in substance, the preceding account of my relations and intercourse with him. They stated that, when we met at Lebanon, they had been informed, that the Genl. was laboring under a complaint which rendered necessary a quick retirement to the back yard. I remarked that the opinions which I had expressed, in the Seminole debate, were sincerely entertained, both at that period and at the present time, but that they were opinions relating altogether to public affairs, and as they did not then, neither did they now, appear to me to render it necessary that there should be any personal hostility between us. On my part there had been no such feelings, and consequently there was no obstacle, with me, to prevent a respectful and courteous intercourse. They stated that such was exactly Genl. Jackson's feeling, and it was proposed that we should meet and, without adverting to the past, exchange friendly salutations, and be on terms of amicable intercourse for the future. For the purpose of producing a meeting between us, the Tennessee delegation (all of whom except Mr. Eaton and Genl. Jackson, I believe) boarded at Mrs. Claxtons on Capitol Hill,[10] gave a dinner, at which we both attended, shook hands and sat at dinner together.[11] I think Mr. Senator White (then a Commissioner under the Florida treaty)[12] was also of the party. I retired early and was followed to the door by Genl. Jackson and Mr. Eaton, and as their carriage and mine were both in waiting, they insisted that I should take a seat with them, which I did, and they sat me down at my door. After this we mutually dined with each other, at our respective lodgings. Among others I recollect that the present President of the U. States and the Vice President were of the party at Genl. Jacksons.[13]

Early in the Session of 1824–5, Genl Jackson called at my lodgings and left a visiting card. Shortly after I returned the visit, and I was under an impression that I did not find him at home, but as I have been since told that I saw him at his lodgings, it is quite probable my impression was erroneous. I saw but little of Genl. Jackson, during that Session. I have no recollection of meeting him any where but at public places or on public occasions, with the exception of the Birthday dinner given by the Russian minister (the 24h. Decr. 1824) in honor of the Emperor Alexander.[14] It was on that occasion that the only allusion occurred that ever was made, within my recollection, by me to the approaching Presidential election, in presence of Genl. Jackson, and that happened in this way: A groupe [sic] of some six or seven gentlemen, of whom Genl. Jackson and myself were two, were standing together conversing on the subject of Internal Improvements, just before dinner was announced. I observed, in the hearing of the Company, but directing myself principally to the General, "if you should be elected President, I hope the cause will flourish under your administration." To which he answered that it was a question merely of how much revenue could be appropriated to the object.

It has been said, in a quarter not entitled to much respect that, prior to my departure from Kentucky in November 1824, for Washington City, I addressed a letter to Genl. Jackson inviting him to join me in the contemplated journey to the Metropolis. I do not believe I wrote any such letter, but it is as possible as it is unimportant. I heard a few days, before I left Lexington that Genl. Jackson was to pass that way. We had been reconciled the preceding fall. It was, therefore, a matter of regret with me that my duty as Speaker, requiring punctual attendance, prevented my remaining at home to extend to Genl. Jackson that hospitality which I should have taken pleasure in dispensing.[15] And most certainly there was nothing, at that time, in the state of our relations to prevent us from travelling in Company. At that period I did not certainly know the result of the Presidential election in any one of the twenty four States. Although I did not doubt what it was in my own State, the returns had not come in.

Equally unfounded is the assertion, emanating from the same quarter, that I crossed the Pennsylvania Avenue to express to Genl. Jackson my congratulations on the vote he had obtained.

Such, my dear Sir, is a true and faithful, if tedious, narrative of the material incidents of my acquaintance and intercourse with Genl. Jackson. Your own desire to possess it will I hope excuse the latter quality. I am ever   Cordially Your friend   H. CLAY
The Honble J. S. Johnston.

ALS. PHi.
1 (West) Virginia, site of the Berkeley Springs, long acclaimed for their therapeutic waters. The land had been granted in 1756 by Lord Fairfax to the Colony of Virginia for a public resort.   2 Cf. above, Clay to Adams, September 29, 1827, note.   3 Cf. above, I, 250.   4 "Ashland."   5 Not found.   6 Cf. above, II, 490n, 612–13, 636–67 passim.   7 Cf. above, II, 700, 701n.   8 Cf. above, II, 697, 698.   9 John Cocke; John Henry Eaton.   10 Not further identified.   11 Cf. above, III, 535.   12 Hugh Lawson White—cf. above, III, 326n.   13 Cf. Adams, Memoirs, VI, 258.   14 Baron de Tuyll van Serooskerken; Alexander I. Cf. Adams, Memoirs, VI, 453–54.   15 The Washington United States Telegraph, August 7, 1827, had stated that Clay had written a letter inviting Jackson to travel through Lexington and to accompany him to Washington. The Lexington Kentucky Gazette had published a similar statement on August 17, 1827. The episode was brought into the inquiry conducted by the Kentucky Legislature, on January 31, 1828, when Oliver Keen(e) and Francis McAlear (or McLear) both testified that Clay had informed them in the fall of 1824 that he had written to Jackson, extending such an invitation. Frankfort Argus of Western America, February 13, 1828. No letter of such import has been found. Clay reiterated his view of the incident in his Address . . . to the Public, below, December 29, 1827. He had left Lexington before General and Mrs. Jackson arrived there, on November 16, and were entertained at "A splendid Ball . . . as a tribute of respect." Lexington Kentucky Gazette, November 18, 1824. Just when Clay had left town is not clear—cf. above, III, 886–88; Washington Daily National Intelligencer, November 30, 1824, reprinting item from the Lexington Monitor, November 17, 1824. According to the latter account, Clay had left Lexington on November 11.   McAlear, who in 1824 had been a New Court partisan, was probably the Fayette County justice of the peace identified in 1838 as McLear, owning 200 acres on the Old Frankfort Pike, 4¼ miles outside Lexington. MacCabe, Directory of the City of Lexington, 129.

To Richard Smith

Dear Sir   October 6h. 1827.
I omitted, prior to my departure from the City, to speak to you about a notice I recd. from the office[1] respecting the note of Genl. Vance.[2] You will recollect that I left one with you to renew it, which I hope will be done; and if he has not made provision to pay the discount, I must advance it for him; and in that event you will be pleased to charge it to my account. I am respectfully Your ob. Servant
Mr. Smith   H. CLAY

ALS. DLC-TJC (DNA, M212, R13). Addressed on cover: "R. Smith Esqr. Cashr. &c. &c. &c. Washington City." Postmarked at Hancock, Maryland. Endorsed, in an unidentified hand: "Charge Mr Henry Clay $21 33/100 being for the discount on Jos Vance note for 2000$ as per request October 13th 1827." Cf. below, Order on Washington Office, Bank of United States, October 9, 1827.

1 Not found.   2 Cf. above, Order on Washington Office, Bank of the United States, June 5, August 7, 9, 1827.

From Edward Ingersoll

Dear Sir   Philadelphia Oct. 6. 1827.

I send you a copy of an Address which as chairman of a committee I prepared for the Democratic citizens opposed to Gen. Jackson's elevation.[1] If you will take the trouble to look over it you will see that my aim was to carry the war into the enemy's country and hold up the hermit and his followers to the light. The appointment of the committee was only on Monday night— I did not know until Wednesday that my colleagues intended to throw the whole preparation of it on me—and with constant interruptions I had no time for making it what it ought to have been. But as the attention of the State is just now very much turned towards Philadelphia on account of our impending election of a member of Congress, and the new circumstances under which the contest is to take place,[2]—I thought it best to attempt an exhibit, crude though it must be, of the prominent performances and professions of the great idol of the opposition.

Plenty of matter is left for future use—and I do not mean to dismiss the subject yet. At the meeting, yesterday, which was really numerous and respectable, the Address was received with applause, and manifestly had good effect. I hear also today of its' [sic] having made some noise among the sovreign [sic] people at various convocations last evening

We hope to elect Mr Sergeant, and all the movements relative to the getting up of the ticket of the Democratic friends of the Administration,—or opponents of Jackson, have proceeded with that view.[3] Some disinterested patriots being willing to become candidates with the certain prospect of being not only beat, but distanced, for the sake of bringing out, as we trust we shall be able to do, a larger vote thereby for Mr Sergeant.

I have just seen Gen. Eaton's abortion.[4] Some parts are droll and amusing—. The solemn narration of your passing him and the other general on the steps and your momentous interrogatory "how are you to day General"? is so characteristic of the biographer and so fine a specimen of the mock heroic![5] Of all your *speeches*, I presume, this was one that you least thought to be destined to immortality. The floundering attempt to explain the loan to Simpson[6] is also very diverting. With sincerest wishes for your health & happiness, Most faithfully Yours
Hon. Henry Clay.   EDWARD INGERSOLL

ALS. DLC-HC (DNA, M212, R2).
¹ The address, not found, appears to have been published as a supplement to the Philadelphia *United States Gazette*, October 8, 1827. Cf. *ibid.*, October 6, 1827; Philadelphia *National Gazette*, October 8, 1827. ² Cf. above, Sergeant to Clay, September 28, 1826, note. ³ Cf. above, Johnston to Clay, September 13, 1827, note.
⁴ Published in *Niles' Weekly Register*, XXXIII (October 6, 1827), 94–96. John H. Eaton argued that the differences between Buchanan's statement (see above, Ingersoll to Clay, August 11, 1827, note) and that of Jackson were "principally verbal, and not material." The dating of Buchanan's conversation with Jackson is here given on Eaton's recollection, as early in the week ending January 22, on which latter date Clay and his friends purportedly determined to support Adams. Eaton cited Clay's letter to Brooke, above, January 28, 1825, "and, not earlier," as Clay's "declaration . . . of the course he had concluded to take." "Why," Eaton queried, "the necessity of a silence so long, and so rigidly preserved?" Cf. above, Clay to McClure, December 28, 1824; Clay to Blair, January 8, 1825; Clay to Adams, January 9, 1825, note; Clay to Featherstonhaugh, January 21, 1825; below, Clay to Benton, December 6, 1827, note; *Address . . . to the Public*, December 29, 1827, *passim*. ⁵ Eaton concluded that the meeting with Jackson on the Capitol steps on Monday, January 24, was a matter of embarrassment to Clay following the action taken two days previously. ⁶ Stephen Simpson—cf. above, Moore to Clay, February 10, 1827, note. Eaton maintained that he had "assisted," not "sustained," the journal, that there had never been any "agreement, or understanding, expressed or otherwise, as to any political course which they [the editors] should pursue."

DIPLOMATIC NOTES　　　　　　　　　　　　　　　　October 6, 1827

From PABLO OBREGÓN, Washington. Inquires whether foreign diplomatic agents in the United States are permitted to hoist their national flag. LS, in Spanish with trans. in State Dept. file. DNA, RG59, Notes from Mexican Legation, vol. 1 (M54, R1).

INSTRUCTIONS AND DISPATCHES　　　　　　　　　October 6, 1827

From ALEXANDER H. EVERETT, Madrid, no. 89. Encloses a copy of a letter he addressed to the Count de Beaurepaire, protesting the action of the Viscount de Gudin, commander of occupation at Cádiz, written after he learned from the consul at that port (Alexander Burton), that the Viscount had declined to enforce the "new circular from the Supreme Board of Health" (cf. above, Everett to Clay, August 10, 1827); states that Beaurepaire, the French Chargé, "has since acknowledged the receipt of it and states in his answer that not having any authority himself to interfere in the matter he would immediately refer the complaint to his Government"; reports having sent a copy of his letter to (James) Brown and "desired him (should he consider it expedient) to support the application" and that (Manuel Gonzáles) Salmón has assured him "that he would instruct the Spanish Chargé d'Affaires at Paris to do the same" (cf. below, Everett to Clay, November 26, 1827, where it is apparent that the instructions were issued to the Duke of San Carlos, the Spanish Minister, not Chargé, in Paris.

Expresses the opinion that "the late turn of affairs in Portugal" (cf. above, Hughes to Clay, September 16, 1827) increases "the probability of an early evacuation of the Peninsula by the French troops" but cautions that "the time when this event may take place is nevertheless still quite uncertain."

Adds, in a postscript dated October 10, that he encloses "translations from the Gazette of the official accounts of the King's [Ferdinand VII's] movements since he left this place" (cf. above, Everett to Clay, September 20, 1827) and reports that "It is understood that there has been a good deal of skirmishing in the immediate neighbourhood of Tarragona; but it is generally believed here that the rebels are likely on the whole to give way." LS, postscript in Everett's hand. DNA, RG59, Dip. Disp., Spain, vol. 28 (M31, R29). Received December 16.

The Count de Beaurepaire has not been further identified. Baron Pierre-Cesar Gudin, born in 1774, had won the rank of brigadier general in 1812 as an officer of Spanish forces fighting the English. He had returned to France in 1814 and had been accorded the title of chevalier. Under the Restoration government he had been raised to the rank of lieutenant general in 1821 and the following year had been placed in command of the military division based at Grenoble.

From J[OEL] R. POINSETT, Mexico, no. 102. Reports the end of disturbances in Veracruz (cf. above, Poinsett to Clay, June 16, July 8, 27, August 8, 10 [no. 97], 1827) and Durango (cf. above, Poinsett to Clay, March 24, 1827); notes agitation among "The people" for expulsion of European Spaniards; and discusses legislation, adopted in one State and under consideration in others, that "is likely to bring into collision the state and federal governments." Predicts that, if the policy continues, the European Spaniards will concentrate in Valladolid and Veracruz, where they are welcome, and thus become "much more formidable enemies of the liberties of the Republic." Adds that the anti-European feeling "has been . . . augmented . . . by the information the government pretends to have received of the arrival at Havana of General [Francisco Tomás] Morales with a reinforcement of ships and men and money" (cf. above, Gray to Clay, September 3, 1827). Suggests: "if we have an Agent in Havana, . . . he should be instructed to correspond with this Legation."

States that the Mexican Congress has appropriated $15,000 to defray the expenses of General (Manuel de Mier y) Terán, appointed "to examine and report upon the country which lies near and upon the boundary" (cf. above, Poinsett to Clay, July 12, 1826 [no. 50], and note); that José Ignacio Esteva and Juan José Espinosa (de los Monteros) have been appointed to treat (with Poinsett–cf. above, Poinsett to Clay, April 30, 1826); but that negotiations will not recommence until (Sebastián) Camacho returns from London (cf. above, Poinsett to Clay, April 8, August 26, 1826; June 16, 1827: Gallatin to Clay, December 16, 1826; Brown to Clay, April 27, 1827). Analyzes the "pecuniary distress of the government"; notes that the new tariff bill is still before the Congress; and expresses apprehension that prohibitive duties will be placed on low-priced cotton goods, a measure, however, which he believes "will affect the British manufacturers and traders even more than those of the United States."

Assesses the state of affairs in each of the South American nations and concludes that, in spite of her problems, "Mexico is better off than her Sister Republics." Mentions, as an afterthought, disorders "in the neighborhood of Acapulco," committed by both opponents and partisans of "the European Spaniards" (cf. above, Poinsett to Clay, September 5, 1827). LS. DNA, RG59, Dip. Disp., Mexico, vol. 3 (M97, R6). Received November 9.

From Thomas Smith

Dr. Sir. Lexington, Oct. 7. 1827.

I submitted your paper on the subject of county meetings,[1] immediately after it came to hand, to a small party of friends at my house—(Bodley, Harper, Chinn, Palmer, Gratz & Dudley)[2] who approved of the suggestions & promised their cordial cooperation in carrying them into execution. Last evening we had another meeting, with the addition of Combs, Matthews, Cowan and Wickliffe,[3] to arrange our proceedings. It was agreed to have our County meeting tomorrow week. Wickfe & Matthews will prepare an address—Chinn & myself resolutions.[4] The Jackson meeting will be held to:morrow.[5] Those friends first named & Wickliffe of the last, *only* were apprized of the existence of the paper from you. It was thought best to confine that fact to a limited number. There is no difference of opinion, except as to the policy of the large Come. of Vigilance. It was apprehended by some that the appmt. of such a come. would excite the animadversions of our adversaries. But the plan in effect will be carried out. You will have perceived that it has been in some measure anticipated at Louisville.[6] We shall cooperate with our friends there, as to the Convention at Frankfort for the nomination of an Electoral Ticket. It is possible the nomination of a candidate for Govr. will be included.[7] Gabriel Slaughter is talked of. Trimble[8] is somewhat averse to engage in the campaign. C. Allan is not objected to except on account of his votes on the occupant laws.[9] The objection to Robinson[10] is his former avowal of federalism. Col R. Taylor[11] has been thought of. It is believed however than [sic] Slaughter could be elected with least difficulty. McAfee[12] will be the opposing candidate. Pope[13] if he yields his pretensions will do it very reluctantly.

Wickliffe cooperates very cordially. He has promised to write to Speed, Eph: Ewing[14] &c. on the subject of county organization & meetings. I have written to C. Allan, and Major Thompson,[15]—and made some arrangements personally towards meetings in Bourbon & Scott.[16] You may rely upon it, we shall beat, if our friends can be kept in action.

I hope each of your Correspondents may be on their guard, and not expose improperly your com'n. The adverse party seize with avidity, every thing & expression that can be distorted to your prejudice, and they are not at all scrupulous as to the means employed. Penn lately got possession of a private letter of yours addressed to Crittenden.[17] Kendall I have very little doubt is in possession of letters to Blair. I say in my paper, that B. does not countenance K's reference to his letters.[18] I could not say otherwise on account of my respect for Gratz, who appears still to like B. But my private opinion is the reverse. I believe B. & K understand one another perfectly in this matter. I do not suppose you have ever written any thing to Blair that might not be published, if done fairly—but to guard against perversions and garbleing [sic], would it not be well to instruct some frd. at Frankfort to demand the originals? Copies will suit their purposes, & you would then know that no forgery could be passed off as a genuine letter.

I doubt whether we can do more than to ask the removal of the P.M. on the ground of his appt. in the first instance improperly[19]—and 2dly his want of responsibility, being notoriously insolvent: To which might be added a general expression of a want of confidence in him, on the part of many respectable Citizens. Charges against his admn. of his office, might be explained, perhaps refuted. But really he is so ardent a partizan, in such close & exclusive alliance with the most outrageous enemies of the President & yourself, who carry their hostility to such lengths, that he ought unquestionably to be removed. I do not know that he opens and reads letters, but I commit mine to his hands with constant apprehension that he will do it. He is the gran[d] pivot of the party for the whole state. He disseminates intelligence to the leaders of the party in every section. Such an enemy Mr. Jefferson would not have permitted to remain in office a single day. The President, I think, if he knew the character of the man, would not hesitate one moment to act on the general principle. But if he does not dismiss him voluntarily, a representation such as I have alluded to, must be made. Then you know how easy a counter remonstrance with the names of every Jackson man, can be got up. Respects to Mrs. Clay. Yours truly.   THO. SMITH

[Postscripts]
Excuse the broken sheet and hasty writing

A bloody affray lately took place near Natchez, which will give your friend Judge Johnson[20] pain. A duel, long talked of, between two of his constituents from Alexandria, terminated without bloodshed in the neighbourhood of that place: But the friends and attendants of the parties became engaged on the ground. Majr. N. Wright & Genl. Cuney were killed; Mr. Bowie and A. Blanchard dangerously wounded.[21]— These are all the particulars received in the Natchez paper by last mail.

                                                                              T. S.

ALS. DLC-HC (DNA, M212, R2). Addressed: *"Private."*
[1] Above, September 27, 1827.   [2] Either Thomas or Harry I. Bodley; James Harper; Richard H. Chinn; James W. Palmer; Benjamin Gratz; Benjamin W. Dudley.
[3] Leslie Combs; probably Matthews Flournoy; James Cowan; and Robert Wickliffe.
[4] At the meeting, held on October 15 at the Fayette County courthouse, Harry I. Bodley and Cowan were secretaries; Thomas Bodley was one of the delegates elected to attend the State convention; Wickliffe, Chinn, Cowan, and Gratz were appointed, with others, to a committee of correspondence; and Flournoy was included on a committee "to report resolutions and an address to the people of Kentucky on the subject of the next Presidential election." The resolutions, as adopted, lauded Clay's "honesty, purity and high-mindedness, condemn[ed] unfounded attacks upon him; support[ed] Adams & especially his" policy of protecting a home market for the productions of American labor, and approved the plans for county meetings to send delegates to a State convention, to be held at Frankfort, December 17. Lexington *Kentucky Reporter*, October 17, 1827.
[5] A committee of correspondence was also appointed at the Jackson meeting in Lexington on October 8. Frankfort *Argus of Western America*, October 17, 1827.   [6] The Lexington *Kentucky Reporter* of September 22, 1827, had reprinted a letter from "Many Citizens," addressed to the Louisville *Focus* and dated September 12, urging organization of the friends of the administration "to refute misrepresentations & providing [*sic*] correct information." The writers proposed that meetings in each county appoint delegates to a State convention and elect a county committee to "diffuse the information collected completely among the people."   [7] At the State meeting in Frankfort on December 17 Adams was nominated for the Presidency; the convention declined acting on a nomination for the office of Vice President; and Thomas Metcalfe and Joseph R. Underwood were endorsed for the Governorship and Lieutenant Governorship, respectively. Frankfort *Argus of Western America*, December, 19, 26, 1827.   [8] David Trimble.

9 On the occupying claimant law of 1824, cf. above, III, 803n. That measure had been amended by legislation of January 12, 1825, to expand the provisions for evaluation of and compensation for improvements made by the "bona fide Occupants of Land within this Commonwealth." Ky. Gen. Assy., Acts . . . 1824–1825, ch. 217, pp. 206–211. On the significance of this legislation, see Paul W. Gates, "Tenants of the Log Cabin," Mississippi Valley Historical Review, XLIX (June, 1962), 9–27. Chilton Allan had opposed passage of the law of 1824 and had voted to table the measure of 1825. Ky. Sen., Journal . . . 1823–1824, pp. 298–99; Journal . . . 1824–1825, p. 446. The individual vote on final passage of the latter measure was not recorded.   10 George Robertson.
        11 Richard Taylor.   12 Robert B. McAfee.   13 John Pope.   14 Probably Thomas Speed; Ephraim McL. Ewing.   15 George C. Thompson.   16 Meetings were scheduled in Bourbon County on November 5 and in Scott County on November 3. Lexington Kentucky Reporter, October 31, November 14, 1827.   17 Shadrach Penn, Jr.; John J. Crittenden. Clay's letter has not been found. Cf. below, Crittenden to Clay, November 15, 1827.   18 See Lexington Kentucky Reporter, October 6, 1827.
        19 On the controversy about Joseph Ficklin's appointment, cf. above, Dudley to Clay, August 17, 1827, note.   20 Josiah S. Johnston.   21 This, the famous "Sand Bar Fight," held on the first sand beach above Natchez, on September 19, 1827, was widely reported contemporaneously. See, e.g., Niles' Weekly Register, XXXIII (November 17, 1827), 182. For lengthy accounts, see Robert D. Calhoon, "A History of Concordia Parish," Louisiana Historical Quarterly, XV (1932), 638–42; G. P. Whittington, "Rapides Parish, Louisiana—a History," ibid., XVI (1933), 628–34; Harnett C. Kane, Gentlemen, Swords and Pistols (New York, 1951), 83–95. The principals were Dr. Thomas H. Maddox and Samuel Levi Wells, who, after exchanging two shots, were reconciled. The other participants here cited were Norris Wright, Samuel Cuny, James Bowie, and Alfred Blanchard.   Maddox, born in Maryland and graduated in medicine in 1816 from the University of Edinburgh, had practiced briefly in his native State before resuming his profession in Rapides Parish, Louisiana. Wells, born in St. Landry Parish, Louisiana, represented a faction of long term residents in the area who were now being challenged economically and politically by newcomers. He died of fever shortly after this encounter. Cuny, like Wells, reared in St. Landry, had also moved from there as an early settler in the Red River district.   Wright, one of the new faction in the Red River district, had come there from Baltimore, Maryland, and clerked in and subsequently operated a shoe store in Alexandria. That business had been dissolved in March, 1825, and Wright had been serving since 1823 as sheriff. He was also a director of the local bank and an owner of town property and a plantation.   Bowie, born in Kentucky in 1796, had been brought to Catahoula Parish, Louisiana, in 1802. While yet a youth he had left home and about 1814 settled in Rapides Parish. Rumored to have been involved in slave smuggling, he was at this time in financial difficulties and attributed to Wright his inability to negotiate a bank loan. During the encounter, after Wright and Bowie had exchanged shots, Wright stabbed Bowie with a sword cane, and the latter killed his assailant with a heavy blade distinguished by a curved point, subsequently identified as a "bowie knife." Bowie, severely wounded, recovered slowly and removed to Texas. There he was involved in skirmishes with the Mexicans as early as 1831 and, in the rank of colonel in the Texas forces, was killed at the Alamo in 1836.   Blanchard, a Virginian by birth, had recently settled on Bayou Jean de Jean. He suffered only a shot in an arm; his wound was not serious.

INSTRUCTIONS AND DISPATCHES   October 7, 1827

From BEAUFORT T. WATTS, Bogotá, no. 35. Notes his attendance, by invitation issued to himself and "the other foreign representatives," at the Foreign Office on September 13, "to be presented to the President of the Republic [Simón Bolívar]. . . , who had reached the Capital on the 10th. and had been installed into office." Reports his remarks, in which he congratulated Bolívar on his "return to the Capital," noted with pleasure the presence of the Vice President (Francisco de Paula Santander), stated that "The unfortunate divisions which had thus long prevailed" were regretted by the United States, and expressed hope that "These dissentions [sic] . . . will be removed. . . ." Explains that his object "was to conciliate the Vice President," who was pleased with his remarks. Credits the presence of Bolívar in the capital and "at the head of the administration" for the tranquillity that prevails in Guayaquil and Caracas. Encloses translations of congressional decrees, "A statistical account of" various aspects of the Republic, a note from (José Manuel) Restrepo informing him of (Joseph R.) Revenga's resumption of the duties of Foreign Minister, and other documents. ALS. DNA, RG59, Dip. Disp., Colombia, vol. 4 (M-T33, R4). Received January 9, 1828.

From Joseph M. Street

My dear friend,   St Louis 8 Octo. 1827.—
    Do not be startled at the familiarity of my commencement. You have *lastingly obliged me,* and *I never can forget it.* Whether I may be permitted to call you "my dear friend" or not—I shall ever *feel* that you have been a *friend* in the critical hour of *need.* I know well that it is mainly to you I owe my appointment, and whatever may be my deservings your heart will swell with the belief that you have been instrumental in rescuing from poverty an amiable woman, and a fine promising family of 6 Sons & 2 daughters.[1] It would be useless to assure you how grateful we both feel to you, when I inform you that all we have we owe to your goodness upon this occasion. With Hamlet I will say—"a little too much of this."[2] I am now with Genl. Clark[3] making out estimates for the current year ending 1 Sep. 1828. I shall be off to the Prairie du Chien in 2 or 3 days.— I will not trouble you at this busy period; but at some future day I hope to be able to shew you, (and the department under which I am placed) that the Indian Agency at Prairie du Chien is the most important in the West, except those on the Missouri, and that it is the only place where suiteable [*sic*] impressions can be made on as many Indian Tribes. It is the *Key* to the *only* convenient pass between the Lakes & the Mississippi. From the Mississippi to Buffaloe [*sic*], there is only one portage of *One mile and a half.* There are some small rapids in the Fox River making the whole portage about 8 miles.
    I have been but a few days here and am illy able to judge of this States vote. In this town there is much diversity of opinion in relation to the State's vote. Your friends confidently calculate that they have the majority. The friends of Jackson as positively say not. Both sides admit you have the Majority of the Town of St Louis.[4] I mean the Administration. I have met with but few who do not believe you have come off with flying colours in the contest with Jackson   However Editors of hired presses may amuse themselves with metephisical [*sic*] speculations, going to shew that when Buckhanin [*sic*] *positively* negatives a *positive* assertion of Jackson,[5] they both *mean* the same thing, the people cannot be so easily drilled into so mostrous [*sic*] an absurdity. Genl. Jackson's assumed (and believed) candour upon all occasions was the strongest prop that braced up his fortuitous elevation in the public mind. He grew upon the sensitive feelings of a grateful

people— In the late war, he was a brave & determined Soldier, whose fortune it was to lead an army of *higminded* [*sic*] *freemen* to victory and elevated triumph over a well appointed, and veteran army. Unfortunately, he soiled the glorious character of a victorious General acting under the mild and equal government of the people's choice, by acts of Sanguinary cruelty, and unessary [*sic*] rigour.[6] Yet, what was felt to be wrong, was gently passed over in the moment of victory & rejoycing [*sic*], and a grateful people awarded the laurel crown to the victorious chief.

Here many believed the warrior chief would repose, satisfied with the high honors conferred upon him. And when he asserted higher claims there was a feeling in many hearts in favour of the plain *matter of fact* Warrior. Some were ready to overlook the want of civil talent for the sake of military fame, and the best feelings of the human heart that hailed him conqueror, were almost ready to raise him to the presidential chair. But now—the contest has assumed a new character— The Chieftain has drank [*sic*] the praises of the people, and is drunken with mad ambition, and enfuriate [*sic*] love of power, & dominion. Not content to be raised to eminen [*sic*] by the people, his over bearing mind would tempt him to strike his opponents down, in his mad carrier [*sic*], and *violently seize the prize*, that heretofore has been *given* by the nation to whom they please.— A man entering the lists, and openly canvassing for the presidential chair, is new, and disgusting in our County. How odious then must he appear who is spreading the torch of defamation *clandestinely* against his *only* opponents, and striving to rise upon the ruined character of his competitor. This course is *seen & felt*, and amongst such a people as we are it cannot fail to have its effect.

I have insensibly slid into a long letter.— Appropos—McLean is the Writer of the letter to Eaton extracted in his prompous windy nothing.[7] What a prodigious man E. is in his own *humble* opinion. Unfortunately for McLean as you may see from the Shawanee [*sic*] town paper his *own letter* written from Washington on the first Feby 1825, gives the direct lie to his letter to Eaton.[8] He has done for his political character completely. He is looking to the Senate of the U. S. But he will see when the Senator is to be chosen in 1828–9   He will be in the back ground a long way. His conduct in this case will completely place him as he Says in his letter Crawfords [*sic*] friends were.[9]— Sincerely, respectfully & with a full Senese [*sic*] of gratitude   Yours in haste.

                                                    JOS. M. STREET

[Postscript] 11th.

It is some what drole that in all the recommendations to office from this place that decided friends of Jackson are recommended and in fact, are in office here. Supported by the public monies, drinking in the favour of the Administration & warmly engaged in electioneering against them & for Jackson. I could give you a list of names to that effect.— But Judge Lucas[10] who you know will be through Pensylvania [*sic*] to the City of W. about the first of Feby.—I am entirely unknown to him personally yet I can tell you confidently that what he says to you may be relied upon. And with regard to any information I may give of persons or things apply to him and he will explain it all. He wants no office nor will he accept one I am informed— He is devoted from principle to the cause he has expoused [*sic*] and will stand clear of all enthrallments. I will in a subsequent letter[11] give you some details— I ask no answers, nor do I wish to become the repository of any thing from you, who have much business upo[n] your hands— I wish to look into things here cautiously, and from time to tim[e] lay before you whatever information I can, that you may select from the facts communicated such as may be useful to you to know. I believe I can say confidently I am in the confidence of some of your warm friends here who have promised to aid my efforts.

A great part of the officers and commissioners here are for Jackson. Kenerly[12] who was sub Agent up the Missouri, and is now Sutler for the Troops at the Jefferson Baracks [*sic*] is a strong Jackson man   He also was an applicant for the Agency at Prairie du Chien.— He lives upon the Administration—tries to dip deeper into the public purse, and is actively engaged in vilifying the Admrs. The *Strong* [&] decided friends of the Admrs here (and your warm personal friends) ar[e] W. P. Hunt, T. Hunt, Peck, Biddle Brant, Simonds.[13]

I will at more leisure give you a curious peice [*sic*] of secret history about Paymasters & the manner in which the business is so managed as to fleece the government of 8 or 9000$ in *Milage* [*sic*]. Also in respect to Genl. Greens[14] Contract for the mail rout [*sic*] from this to[15]

ALS. DLC-HC (DNA, M212, R2).
[1] Cf. above, Street to Clay, January 11, 1827.   [2] Cf. Shakespeare (Furniss [ed.], *A New Variorum Edition. . . ,* III) *Hamlet,* Act III, sc. 2, line 79: "Something too much of this."   [3] William Clark.   [4] On the Missouri vote in the Presidential election of 1828, cf. above, Clay to Brown, March 27, 1827, note. Jackson also carried the electoral vote of St. Louis County with 609 votes to 443 for Adams. Washington *United States Telegraph,* December 11, 1828.   [5] See above, Webster to Clay, August 22, 1827, and note.
[6] See above, Watkins to Clay, September 30, 1826, and note.   [7] In his long statement concerning James Buchanan's version of his conversation with Jackson (see above, Ingersoll to Clay, August 11, October 6, 1827, notes), John H. Eaton had quoted a paragraph from a letter by "a gentleman, formerly of Congress, (not from this state [Tennessee]) and heretofore the friend of Mr. Clay," received in reply to one "lately written to him" by Eaton. The correspondent, whom Ingersoll identifies as John McLean, of Shawneetown, Illinois, mentioned the rumors of a "bargain of 1825," between Messrs. Adams and Clay . . . freely spoken of by many members of Congress," noted that he had had "no personal knowledge of any fact, which would warrant the belief, that the contract existed," but cited "some circumstances of unfavorable appearance." Those circumstances "were the continued silence and lengthy reserve of Mr. Clay's friends, in publishing or letting it be known, how they would vote; and the fact that the Kentucky delegation had a meeting to determine upon their course. . . ." There Clay had reportedly informed them "in substance, 'that in case General Jackson should be elected he believed the administration with its weight would be opposed to him, to prostrate him; that should Mr. A. be elected he felt satisfied it would not be so; but that he hoped no per-

sonal considerations for him would induce them to act contrary to their desire.' "

⁸ A letter dated February 3, 1825, from McLean to the editor of the Shawneetown *Illinois Gazette* (Henry Eddy), published in that journal on September 3, 1827, was reprinted in the Washington *Daily National Intelligencer*, September 27, 1827. It reviewed the Kremer charges (see above, Clay to Gales and Seaton, January 30, 1825, note; Kremer to Clay, *ca.* February 3, 1825) and concluded: *"No man, I think, believes that there is the least foundation for the accusation against Mr. Clay, and no man affects to credit it but Mr Kremer, at any rate I know of none who does."* Eddy, who had edited a journal in Pennsylvania, in 1817, had come to Shawneetown the following year and had begun editing the *Illinois Gazette* in 1819. He also practiced law with distinction for nearly thirty years and in 1835 was elected to a judgeship, from which he resigned after brief service.

⁹ McLean had commented: (William H.) "Crawford and his friends being looked upon as *hors de combat*, have little or nothing to do with the war." He had added, however, that, in view of the uncertainty of the situation, Crawford's election "would not be astonishing."   ¹⁰Jean Baptiste Charles Lucas, born and educated at law in France, had come to the United States in 1784, had settled first near Pittsburgh, and had been elected to the Pennsylvania Legislature from 1792 to 1798 and to the United States Congress from 1803 until 1805. He had resigned the latter seat to accept appointment as Federal judge for the northern district of Louisiana and had then removed to St. Louis. After continuing on the bench until 1820, he was now in retirement as a farmer near St. Louis.   ¹¹ See below, Street to Clay, October 16, 1827.   ¹² George Hancock Kennerly, born in Botetourt County, Virginia, in 1790, had been commissioned from Indiana as a first lieutenant in the United States Army during the War of 1812. He had resigned from the Army with the same rank in 1819 but carried the title of captain, probably a militia rank, in Missouri during the 1820's. Around 1817 he had opened a store in St. Louis and in 1827 removed to Jefferson Barracks, established the previous year on the west bank of the Mississippi River ten miles below that city. He was appointed postmaster at the military post in January, 1828, and retained that office through the Jackson administrations. For some 40 years, until his death in 1867, he operated a stagecoach service from Jefferson Barracks and during the Mexican War held a commission in the regular Army as captain and assistant quartermaster general, 1846–1848.

¹³ Wilson Price and Theodore Hunt; Thomas Biddle; James H. Peck; Joshua B. Brant; John Simonds, Jr. Wilson Price Hunt, a cousin of Theodore and John Wesley Hunt, had been born in Hopewell, New Jersey, in 1783 and had moved to St. Louis in 1804. For five years he had conducted a general store in the Missouri City, but in 1810 he had entered into partnership with John Jacob Astor in organizing the Astoria venture (see above, King to Clay, May 10, 1825, note) of the Pacific Fur Company. Hunt had commanded the overland expedition of 1811–1812 which blazed the Oregon Trail. Following the sale of Astoria to the British, Hunt had returned to St. Louis, where he operated a farm and grist mill. In 1822 he had been appointed postmaster of that city, a position which he retained until 1840. Brant, born at Hampshire, Massachusetts, in 1790, had moved in 1808 to New York State, where he had operated a drug store and a distilling business prior to 1813. Entering the Army at that time, he remained on active service until he resigned at the rank of lieutenant colonel, in 1839, after conviction by court martial of fraud and neglect of duty. He had come to St. Louis in 1823 and was attached to the quartermaster department.   ¹⁴ Duff Green.   ¹⁵ The remainder of the letter is missing.

INSTRUCTIONS AND DISPATCHES   October 8, 1827

From J[OEL] R. POINSETT, Mexico, no. 103. Transmits copies of his correspondence with the Mexican Government "on the subject of the right of the Consuls in the respective countries to hoist the flag of their nation in the places where they may reside." LS. DNA, RG59, Dip. Disp., Mexico, vol. 3 (M97, R4). Received November 9.

On February 3, 1827, Juan José Espinosa (de los Monteros) had informed Poinsett that Mexico could allow foreign agents in the Republic to hoist their native flag whenever the same privilege was extended Mexican agents in their country. Poinsett replied on October 7, 1827, that the United States had "no law or regulation to permit or prevent a foreign Consul from hoisting the flag of his nation on the house he may occupy." Cf. above, Obregón to Clay, October 6, 1827.

From J[OEL] R. POINSETT, Mexico, "*private & confidential*." Reports settlement of "the accounts of Mr. [Seth] Hayden's estate with Mr. [James Smith] Wilcocks" (cf. above, Storrs to Clay, June 20, 1826; Brent to Poinsett, April 24, 1827). Notes that "Wilcocks may resign the situation he holds" (cf. above, Clay to Poinsett, March 27, 1825, and note) and suggests that the vacancy not be filled. Asserts that the appointment "is certainly unnecessary [,] . . . there is no American citizen here at all fit for the office," to which the Mexican Government attaches unmerited importance, "and as the Consul of Great Britain receives a salary of twelve thousand dollars a year and lives in a style corresponding, the contrast would not only be painful and mortifying to us here, but would seriously affect our influence." Adds that, since learning the condition of Wilcocks' "private affairs," he has himself performed "all the duties of the consulate" and found them "triffling [*sic*]." ALS. DNA, RG59, Dip. Disp., Mexico, vol. 3 (M97, R4).

MISCELLANEOUS LETTERS   October 8, 1827

From ASA FITCH, Salem, New York. Introduces "the bearer . . . James D Doty a Territorial Judge in Michigan," who "attends the approaching Session of Congress to transact Business of Importance to many of the Inhabitants of Michigan Territory"; terms him "a friend & Connection"; and solicits for him "any assistance" Clay can render. ALS. DNA, RG59, A. and R. (M531, R2).

Fitch, a native of Connecticut and a veteran of the Revolutionary War, was a physician in Salem. He had filled local political offices and had been a member of Congress, 1811–1813.

Order on Washington Office Bank of the United States

Office B U States   Washn Oct 9 1827
    Pay to Jos. Vance or bearer proceeds of this note for $2000—
$1978 67/100   H CLAY

DS. DLC-TJC (DNA, M212, R16). Cf. above, Clay to Smith, October 6, 1827.

From William B. Rochester

My Dear Sir   New York 9. Oct. 1827.
    After diligent inquiry made since my return to this City[1] I have not been able to learn that it will be in my power to obtain an early conveyance to the bay of Honduras unless Capt Phillips[2] shall take a cargo from Philadelphia for Guatemala this fall—this I am pretty certain he means to do—so I was told by a young gentleman who is to be concerned with him— yet all that Phillips would say to me on this point, was, that *if* he went, he would be glad to take me &c   the man has some peculiarities   I think however, meaning well all the time—
    In the meantime I shall keep my station here, where my orders have been so far complied with, that I can take my departure on very short notice— I have no other intention, but to go and to that end have writ-

ten my Cousin Wm R Beatty[3] to come on, with my Mexi. Servant, to this City, immediately—

On one occasion during my late visit to Washingtn [sic] you observed that you had proposed for me (without knowing the President's views on the subject) a different destination—Bogota—

I would not now trouble you on this subject, but for the purpose of preventing, what shd., if possible, never exist among Friends, any misconception— I have always understood that the appt. of Colo. Watts,[4] was only temporary, and that it was in the contemplation of the President, so soon as the condition of Columbia [sic] shd. invite to it, to send there, as formerly, a Minister of higher grade than a Chargé— For such a station, I can only say, as in a previous private communication to you, that I advance no pretensions,[5] yet must say that after having been abroad & seen of what materials resident Plenipotentiaries are composed, my misgivings would not be so terrible— Whatever desire I may have indulged in on the subject, arises more out of regard to my friends & consideration for their opinions & wishes than out of individual ambition— I was blamed by many, after having recd a respectable support for the Chief Magistracy of our State, for consenting to retain my situation as Secty. of Legation and at this time there are those who deem the mission to the *terra incognita* for which I am destined, little superior, on the score of consequence— I pray you not to mistake me. I do not myself adopt this language— so far as I am concerned I feel & know that the Government have extended to me quite as much—more than I deserved—

You are aware however of the common topic of complaint in this State ags. the Genl. Administration— its friends say that their opponents are generally preferred for office— both sides complain that N. York has no officer of distinguished rank at home or abroad under appt. from Mr. Adams—

Certain it is however that the men who are most clamorous on these grounds are such as would be in opposition under any circumstances— would go as far as Col. R. M. Johnson—yet there are some well disposed to lend their support upon whom an impression has been made— For my part I always justified the offer made to Mr. Clinton,[6] tho', when he declined, I prophecied [sic] that he possessed neither magnanimity nor stability enough to appreciate the laudable motives of the President, or to remember his own professions   And as for the appt. of Mr. Conkling,[7] now harped upon by a certain class more than any other (for it is their policy at this juncture to treat Mr. Clinton gently) *time* will, I am confident, devellope [sic] that it was a judicious one—

I will extend this letter for the purpose of volunteering a suggestion —viz: in the possible event of my destination being changed would it not be well to send Mr. Mason[8] to Guatemala? his supposed knowledge of the Spanish American character & language and his services, probably give him some claim   this however is not the ground upon which I venture to make this suggestion, for he is almost an entire stranger to me.

But, whenever Mr. Poinsett[9] shall return from Mexico (which he doubtless will, as early as next spring, if not before) it has occurred to me that Mr. Mason would succeed him there for some time, in the capacity of Chargé des Affaires

Now I am decidedly of opinion, from observation made whi[le] in Mexico, that, unless a favourable change has ta[ken] place there recently, neither Mr. P. nor Mr. M. is calculated to advance our best interests in & with that Republick— The dislike of Mr. Poinsett is extended to those immediately around him & connected with the Mission— they are identified.   again—(I mention this in great confidence tho' notorious at the city of Mexico) Mr. Mason unfortunately had, just before he left the Country a violent quarrel with Ramos Arispe[10]— a member of the Cabinet—a man of strong passions—one of the most intriguing & dangerous of their Statesmen— Mr. M. accused him in his office of deliberate falsehood

I have much less doubt of the truth of the accusation, than I had of the propriety of making it— Spanish Priests seldom forget & never forgive unless the pardon is *purchased*   I am Dr Sir very respectfully & truly yours   WM B ROCHESTER
Hon: H. Clay

P.S.   I have not yet succeeded in seeing Mr. Gonsalez [*sic*],[11] but shall make it a point to see him in a day or two— intend to spend the evening with Judge Thompson,[12] if I can find him at home— —.

[Note on bottom of last page—margin obscured]
Since writing this letter I have been favoured with a visit by the venerable [M]ajr. Fairlie[13] of this City— he assures me that measures are in active preparation [to] counteract the Jacksonian current which appears upon the surface of our political [w]aters, and to keep from destruction the actual strength of the Administration—that a meeting is to take place to night[14] at which efficient steps will [be] taken, calculated to give a tone to the state—the evident *policy* of the Hero's [f]riends is to keep up a hue & cry, as evidence of strength—& whenever they can, [by] stratagem, they get in a Jacksonian constable even! & then boast of their Strength!

ALS. DLC-HC (DNA, M212, R2). Addressed: *"private."*
1 Cf. above, Rochester to Clay, September 30, 1827.   2 William Phillips.
3 William Rochester Beatty (1805–1848), of Washington, Kentucky, the eldest son of Adam Beatty. Also a lawyer, the young man succeeded to his father's practice in 1835.
4 Beaufort T. Watts.   5 Cf. above, Rochester to Clay, November 18, 1826.
6 Cf. above, Stuart to Clay, March 15, 1825, note.   7 Cf. above, Clay to Conkling, December 20, 1825.   8 John Mason, Jr.   9 Joel R. Poinsett.   10 José Miguel Ramos Arizpe.   11 Pedro Gonzales.   12 Smith Thompson.   13 James Fairlie, born in New York in 1757, had been an officer in the American Revolution, serving as

aide-de-camp to General Friedrich von Steuben from 1778 until the end of the war. Fairlie died in New York in 1830. ¹⁴ A meeting of Republican young men friendly to the administration was held at Tammany Hall in New York on October 13 and adopted resolutions "to resist the system of denunciation introduced by the advocates of General Jackson. . . ." Washington *Daily National Journal,* October 18, 1827. No report of the earlier meeting has been found. Neither it nor the meeting of October 13 is noted in Muskat, *Tammany,* 106, which does discuss the struggle between the rival partisans for control of the Hall in this period.

From Amos Kendall, Letter II

[*ca.* October 10, 1827]

[Alleges that Clay expected in the fall of 1824 to be eliminated as a presidential candidate and before he left Kentucky was "already making arrangements to turn the event of . . . [his] exclusion to the best advantage"; that, while publicly professing neutrality, he had told confidential friends that, in a contest between Adams and Jackson, he would vote for Adams; that he "made *personal* efforts to prevent any movement in the General Assembly of Kentucky on the subject of the presidential election [cf. above, Kendall to Clay, December 22, 1824, note]"; that he had, some time during December, 1824, or during the first half of January, 1825, avowed to a friend of (William H.) Crawford that he had weighed the pretensions of both candidates, and was "puzzled" as to which he should select; that in his letter to (Francis T.) Brooke (above, January 28, 1825) and in his letter to his constituents (above, March 26, 1825) Clay had discussed consulting his conscience and "weighing the pretensions of the two candidates."

[Charges that, despite this evidence, Clay has attempted to prove that he had determined to vote for Adams before he left Kentucky; that after failing to reach an understanding with Jackson, Clay turned to Adams; that an arrangement between Clay and Adams "was complete about the first of January"; that the arrangement was explicit as "Adams was to throw off his reserve about the Tariff and Internal Improvements, and mount the 'American System,' behind . . . [Clay], as a hobby," in order to gain Pennsylvania and the Middle States; that "The same hobby, with the aid of . . . [Clay's] personal audience and the dispensation of public patronage . . . would secure all the western States above Tennessee, while Mr. Adams, with the aid of [Daniel] Webster and his other managers, was to bring New England into the same combination"; that some members of the House of Representatives changed their vote to Adams upon learning that the latter would appoint Clay Secretary of State; that "Nearly all the Kentucky delegation declared, after their return home, that they voted for Mr. Adams because it was ascertained that he would appoint . . . [Clay] Secretary of State"; that (George) Kremer (cf. above, Appeal to the House, February 3, 1825), after his exposure of the bargain, declined Clay's demand for an investigation because the bargain was not yet executed;

and that Clay learned of the Beverley letter (cf. above, Report of Interview, *ca*. April 15, 1827) and became Jackson's "public accuser." Concludes by challenging Clay to appear at a Congressional investigation.]

Frankfort *Argus of Western America*, October 10, 1827.

From Lafayette

My dear Sir   La Grange October 10th 1827

Having Accidently missed the last Opportunity to Answer your most Valued favor August 10th, I avail myself of the next packet to offer my Affectionate thanks, and Request, as much as the pressure of Business allows it, the very High Gratification of Your Correspondence.

Your diplomatic Accounts from Europe leave little to Say, and altho' a Member of that House, By Courtesy, Called Representative, I am not the Wiser nor shall I Be the More useful for it. a dissolution of the House is much Spoken of.[1] the ministry are Recording the new electoral lists, in Consequence of a late Bill Mingling the Vote of election, With the duties of juror, to Which However Some additions Have Been Made.[2] as the public mind is progressing, and Several Wilful errors Have Been forcibly Rectified, A liberal opposition Cannot fail to Be more numerous; the question With Government is Whether they Will this year meet a large Minority, With a Seven Years New lease, or Herafter [sic] Risk to Have a Majority Against them, or at Least a Stronger opposition than that to Which, in Case of dissolution, they must Now submit.[3]

the Account of the funerals of Manuel Having Been Indicted Before an inferior tribunal, and our Speeches on His Tomb making a part of the impeachment of the publishers, it Became the duty of Mm. Laffitte, de Shonen, and myself to claim our share in the trial, Which We Could not obtain, But a judgment of the Court, Very properly and liberally Worded Has Acquitted the Selected objects of the Accusation. an Appeal from that decision, to the Superior Court, Has, it is Said, taken place.[4]

The intervention of three Great powers in the affairs of Greece Seem to promise a Respite, altho' it Has not prevented the Arrival of an Egyptian fleet and a Body of Soldiers. there is However Some good in the Notifications made By the french and English Admirals impeding further progress. the Mediation Has Been Accepted By the Greeks. the ottoman porte Hitherto Repells it.[5] So far they oblige the mediators to Commit themselves a little more, and if they are Sincere the porte must Yeld [sic] at last. it is obvious to Every looker on that those powers are jealous of liberty, of Complete Emancipation, and jealous of Each other. if Any Body Can play the difficult game, it must Be Capod'istria Who is now on His third Station, that of paris, Before He proceeds to the presidential Chair. He united in His person an Exclusive Coincidence of Happy Circumstances.   after He Has managed those discordant Elements, there Will Be other discordances to Be Managed at Home, for which He also Seems to Be the proper, and Exclusive Man. Upon the Whole, the Existence of Greece is Rather more Secured than it Has Been of late.

I Have Received a letter from our friend poinsett[6] [sic] and Cannot But observe With Him the general, and Especial attempts that Have Been lately directed Against the peace, Harmony, and institutions of the Republican states of South America and Mexico.· it is Very Natural to See the Republican Minister of North America a But [sic] to those Monarchical and Aristocratical factions.[7]   that the impulsion is given from Europe is Not, I think, to be questioned   But I Have Received With deep Regret the part of Your letter alluding to a Man[8] Whose glory, great talents, and Hitherto Experienced patriotism I Have delighted to cherish. Several painful informations Had Reached me, Which all together, and Many More Besides, Could Not Weigh So much With me as Your own Sense of the Matter. I Beg You to Continue to Write on the Subject, and on Every Matter Relative to public Concerns, to my friends, and particularly to you who know my old, grateful, and Sincere affection.

Blessed as I Have lately Been With the Welcome, and Conscious, as it is my Happy lot to Be, of the Affection and Confidence of all parties, and all men in Every party Within the U. S., feelings Which I most Cordially Reciprocate, I Ever Have thought myself Bound to Avoid taking Any part in local or personal divisions.   indeed, if I thought that, in these matters, my influence Could Be of Any avail, it should Be Solely Exerted to deprecate, not, By far, the free, Republican, and full discussion of principles and Candidates, But those invidious Slanders Which, altho' they are Happily Repelled By the Good Sense, the Candor, and in domestic instances By the delicacy of the American people, tend to Give Abroad incorrect and disparaging impressions. Yet that line of Conduct, from Which I must not deviate, Except in imminent Cases Now out of the question, does not imply a forgetfulness of facts, nor a Refusal to state them Occasionaly [sic]. My Remembrance Concurs With Your own on this point that in the later End of december, Either Before or after my visit to Annapolis, You Being out of the presidential Candidature, and after Having Expressed My above Mentionned [sic] motives of forebearance, I, By Way of a Confidential Exception, allowed myself to put a Simple Unqualified Question Respecting Your Electioneering Guess, and Your intended Vote. Your Answer Was that in Your opinion, the actual State of Health of Mr Crawford[9] Had limited the Contest to a choice Between Mr Adams and General Jackson, that a Claim founded on Military

Atchievements [*sic*] did not Meet Your preference, and that You Had Concluded to Vote for Mr Adams. Such Has Been, if Not the litteral [*sic*] Wording, at least the precise Sense of a Conversation Which it Would Have Been inconsistent for me to Carry farther and not to keep a Secret, While a Recollection of it, to assist Your Memory, I should not now deny, Not only to You, as my friend, But to Any Man in a Similar Situation.

present my affectionate Respects to Mrs Clay, Remember me to all your family and to our friends in Washington; I Will write By the Same packets the president, Believe Me forever Your Sincere obliged friend   LAFAYETTE

ALS. DLC-HC (DNA, M212, R2). Published in Clay, *Address . . . to the Public* (cf. below, December 29, 1827), "Appendix," 55–57.
1 On October 20, the Count de Villèle recommended to the King, Charles X, that the Chamber of Deputies be dissolved. The dissolution was ordered on November 6, with new elections to begin on November 17.   2 A bill initiated December 29, 1826, as the Ministry's proposal to reform jury selection, had been taken over and amended by opposition leaders so that the jury and electoral lists were consolidated, with provision that they be compiled annually. The measure had been approved by the King on May 2, 1827. Sherman Kent, *The Election of 1827 in France* (Cambridge, Mass., 1975), 18–30.
3 Under legislation of June 9, 1824, the term of Deputies had been lengthened from five to seven years. *Ibid.*, 33n. Authorities differ in reckoning the distribution of party vote after the November elections but agree that Villèle could no longer command a majority of the 428 Deputies in the Chamber. Kent finds 195 who might "in most foreseeable cases" have supported him, 199 "whose sympathies lay leftward of him . . . and who would have opposed him," and 31 "of the counter-opposition who were opposed to him from their position on the far right." Beach attributes 175 seats to the ministerial party, 170 to 180 to the liberals, and about 75 to the "royalist opposition." *Ibid.*, 161; Vincent Woodrow Beach, *Charles X of France, His Life and Times* (Boulder, Col., 1971), 249.
4 Jacques-Antoine Manuel, a lawyer and from 1814 to 1823 a member of the Chamber of Deputies, had protested the restoration of the Bourbons in 1815 and the French invasion of Spain in support of Ferdinand VII in 1823. Because of his violent oratory on the latter occasion, he had been expelled from the Chamber. His death, August 20, 1827, had provided the occasion for speeches by Lafayette, Jacques Laffitte, and Baron Auguste-Jean-Marie de Shonen pledging commitment to Manuel's public ideals. A description of the ceremony and report of the speeches had been published by Mignet, probably François-Auguste-Marie, French historian and editor of the Paris *Courrier Français*. He, the orators, the printer, and the bookseller (the latter two, not identified) were brought before the tribunal of Correctional Police, but all were acquitted and the seized publication released. *Annual Register, 1827*, pp. 222–23. Laffitte, born in Bayonne in 1767, had become head of a Paris banking house in 1804 and governor of the Bank of France in 1814. He had been elected to the Chamber of Deputies in 1816, had been conspicuous in defense of freedom of the press, and had been removed from the governorship of the Bank in 1819. He actively supported the revolution of 1830 and the accession of Louis Phillipe. For several months during the winter of 1830–1831, he was Minister of State. Continuing as a member of the left opposition in the Chamber of Deputies, he died in 1844. The Baron de Shonen, born in 1782, was a lawyer, named in 1819 councillor to the royal court. He had been elected a Deputy in 1827 and sat with the liberal opposition. In 1830, as a supporter of the revolution, he was named attorney general to the Court of Accounts and later raised to the peerage.   5 Cf. above, Brown to Clay, July 12, 1827; Middleton to Clay, September 29, 1827; Hughes to Clay, September 16, 1827, note; below, Ombrosi to Clay, November 6, 1827. The Greeks had proclaimed on August 21 their acceptance of the intervention. The Egyptian fleet with 5,000 troops and several French officers had arrived at the port of Navarino at the end of the month. On September 19 a part of the fleet, sailing out of the port, had been turned back by Sir Edward Codrington, commander of the British naval force. On September 22 the French Admiral, Henri Gauthier Rigny, had repeated the warning. Three days later the two officers had met with Ibrahim Pasha, informed him of the Greek decision, and warned him of their in-

tention to stop the fighting, by force if necessary. The pasha had agreed to a 20-day armistice while he consulted Turkish and Egyptian authorities. *Annual Register, 1827,* pp. 312–14; *Niles' Weekly Register,* XXXIII (December 8, 1827), 229. Codrington, born in 1770, had entered the Navy as a boy of 13 and commanded a vessel at 24. After distinguished service during the war with France, he had been knighted in 1815. He was raised to the rank of admiral in 1837 and retired from active duty in 1842. Rigny, born in 1782, had entered the Navy in 1798, had been assigned to land duty during most of the period of the Napoleonic wars, but in 1811 had become captain of a frigate. He had been placed in command of the French naval forces in the Levant in 1822 and raised to rear admiral in 1825. After the action at Navarino he was elevated to the rank of vice admiral and given the title of Count. He was named Minister of Marine and was elected a Deputy in 1831 and from April, 1834, to March, 1835, served as Minister of Foreign Affairs.   6 Joel R. Poinsett.   7 Cf. above, Poinsett to Clay, July 8, 1827.
        8 Simón Bolívar.   9 William H. Crawford.

DIPLOMATIC NOTES   October 10, 1827

From C. N. BUCK, Philadelphia. States that he is "instructed by the Senate of Hamburg" to inform Clay "that it is their intention to negociate a convention of commerce and navigation with the government of the United States of America, in conjunction with the Hanstowns [*sic*] of Lubeck and Bremen, for which purpose they have appointed a minister to Washington, in the person of the Hanseatic minister at Paris Mr. [Vincent] Rumpff." ALS. DNA, RG59, Notes from Foreign Consuls, vol. 2.

INSTRUCTIONS AND DISPATCHES   October 10, 1827

From ROBERT MONROE HARRISON, Demerara (British Guiana). Reports his arrival on October 6, acknowledges receipt of the Department's letter of August 9 (see above, Harrison to Clay, July 18, 1827, note), and promises to visit Jamaica and other British islands. Comments on the value, to Britain, of "this Colony [British Guiana]" and observes that, because it could supply many products for which the British West Indies have been dependent on the United States, his report on it will be detailed. ALS. DNA, RG59, Cons. Disp., Demerara, vol. 1 (M-T336, R-1).

MISCELLANEOUS LETTERS   October 10, 1827

From CHARLES F. MAYER, Baltimore. Reports receipt of "a letter from Mr. [Henry H.] Williams, now at Laguayra, stating that" Mayer had "committed an error, in" his letter to Clay (above, March 31, 1827), "in alleging that the Capture [of the *Morris*] took place before the ratification of the Treaty [with Colombia—cf. above, Clay to Salazar, March 21, 1825, and note];—the fact being, on the contrary, that it occurred after the ratification, tho' . . . before the *exchange* of the ratifications." Continues: "The property was captured on 12 May;—the Treaty was ratified by both Governments early in March. The vessel arrived at the port of her captors after the ratifications were exchanged." Refers to Clay's opinion, stated in the reply to Mayer's communication (see note appended to that document); expresses a hope that, "with the present corrected data," this view may change; and asks further instructions to "our Chargé des Affaires at Bogota [Beaufort T. Watts], in behalf of the claim. . . ." LS. DNA, RG76, Misc. Claims, Colombia, env. 5, case 37 (MR1).

        Replying on October 20, by direction of "the Secretary," Daniel Brent informed Mayer that Clay had already instructed Watts to "make every proper exertion with the Colombian Government" and that a copy of the letter of October 10 would be sent to him. Copy, in DNA, RG59, Dom. Letters, vol. 22 (M40, R20). On the same date Brent transmitted Mayer's letter to Watts, as promised. Copy, in DNA, RG59, Dip. Instr., vol. 11, p. 381 (M77, R6).

To Francis Preston Blair

[October 11, 1827]

I never wrote a letter in my life, on a political subject, to the publication of which, with the circumstances under which it was written, I could object; BUT I CERTAINLY WILL NOT CONSENT, *upon such a threat or demand as Mr. Kendall has thought proper to make,[1] to give my sanction to the violation of the confidence of private and friendly correspondence which would be produced by publishing the letters which have been interchanged between you and me, or between any friend and myself.*

Extract, dated and quoted in a letter addressed without date by Blair to Benjamin Watkins Leigh. Washington *Globe*, October 12, 1844.
[1] See above, Kendall to Clay, September 26, 1827.

INSTRUCTIONS AND DISPATCHES   October 11, 1827

From THOMAS L. L. BRENT, Lisbon, no. 45. States that "the tumult arising from the dismissal of General Saldanha" (cf. above, Brent to Clay, July 25, 1827) resulted in many arrests; that "The Intendant of Police Bastos, has pretended to discover a plan for erecting a Republick" but, though "the Princess Regent [Isabel Maria] . . . has been credulous enough to believe in his report," no substantiating evidence has been found; and that the actions of the Intendant, who "is believed to join in the views of the anti-constitutional party," were "a trick of his, having for object to discredit the constitutional party generally, and to acquire an ascendant over the Princess Regent. . . ." Refers to the discouragement of the constitutional party, the censorship of the press, and the suspension of newspapers until the only one "that now appears is the 'Gazeta de Portugal'" (established in 1822). Notes that the anticipation of Miguel's arrival creates "in the constitutional party considerable despondency" (cf. above, Brown to Clay, July 28 (1), 1827; Brent to Clay, August 20, 1827), although disappointment occasioned by the "notorious" private conduct of the Princess Regent and "the unsteadiness" of her public administration will lessen the regret. Lists recent changes in the Ministry, including the removal of "The Count da Ponte, Minister of war and ad interim Minister of foreign affairs," and the appointment of "Candido Xavier . . . ad interim to both offices." Reports having learned "that Carlos Mathias Pereira, the messenger bearing the letters" from Peter I to Miguel, reached Vienna (cf. above, Brent to Clay, September 15, 1827). Encloses "a translation of the decree of don Pedro dated at Rio Janeiro the 3rd of July of this year appointing his brother in these words 'his Lieutenant granting (othorgando) to him all the powers that as King of Portugal . . . [Peter was] entitled to and . . . specified in the constitutional charter in order that he may govern and administer those kingdoms [Portugal and Algarve] in conformity to the abovementioned charter.'" Adds that "Monsigneur Giustiniani, Archbishop of Petra newly appointed Nuncio at this Court has arrived. . . ." ALS. DNA, RG59, Dip. Disp., Portugal, vol. 7 (M43, R6). Received December 15.

On October 12 Brent sent to Clay an unnumbered letter of transmittal enclosing a translation of an extract from the Lisbon *Gazette* of October 10, 1827, providing yet another copy of the decree of July 3, 1827, and a report that the Portuguese Ambassador in London (the Duke of Palmella) had transmitted a dispatch, dated September 26, which informed him that Pereira had arrived in Vienna and delivered the documents to Miguel. ALS, in *ibid.*

José Joaquim Rodrigues de Bastos, born in 1777, had studied law and served as magistrate of Porto. A member of the constituent assembly of 1821, he had subsequently become identified with the supporters of Dom Miguel. He had been appointed Intendant of Police in 1827 and remained in office until the re-establishment of constitutional government in 1833. He thereupon retired to Porto and devoted himself to letters.

Candido José Xavier, born in Lisbon in 1769, was an army officer and had been forced into exile in Paris during the political upheaval from 1810 to 1820. Returning to Portugal as a supporter of constitutionalism, he had held posts as Minister of Marine and Minister of Foreign Affairs as well as, provisionally, Minister of War for brief periods in 1822 and in 1823, had been named sub-director of the Military College in December, 1822, and later, director of that institution, where he had remained until he assumed the portfolios as Minister of War and of Foreign Affairs, ad interim, in 1827. He continued in the Cabinet until February, 1828, when, following Dom Miguel's accession to power, Xavier retired to England. There he was active in support of the refugees from Portugal and in 1833 was named Minister of the Realm and provisional Secretary of Foreign Relations of the government in exile.

Pereira had earlier been Portuguese Chargé to the Holy See.

From W[ILLIAM] B[EACH] LAWRENCE, London, no. 1. Reports that (Albert) Gallatin informed Lord Dudley, on October 4, of "his intended return to America, on leave of absence," and requested that Lawrence "be recognized as the Chargé d'Affaires of the United States." Adds that "On the same day, Mr. Gallatin and family left . . . for Liverpool, from whence . . . [they] embarked . . . [on] the 8th. for New York." Enumerates the contents of the Legation archives, noting that the file of instructions is incomplete and "that the Laws of the United States for 1825–6 and 1826–7 have not been received. . . ." Requests the missing volumes of laws and regular transmittal of "the Congressional documents." Appends a list of "books, purchased in reference to the North West Boundary question," which "are retained . . . subject to" Clay's orders, and a list of maps, relative to "the North East Boundary," which are being forwarded. States that "certified Copies of Mr. Gallatin's" last six dispatches and "A despatch from Mr. [Henry] Wheaton [probably above, September 29, 1827], which was put under cover to" Lawrence, will be sent later. ALS. DNA, RG59, Dip. Disp., Great Britain, vol. 35 (M30, R31). Extract published in Manning (arr.), *Diplomatic Correspondence . . . Canadian Relations*, II, 650–51. Received November 30.

MISCELLANEOUS LETTERS   October 11, 1827

From BETSEY HAWLEY, "No. 77 Laurens Street," New York. Acknowledges receipt of "a polite note of the 8th. of June last, from the Department of State" (cf. above, Hawley to Clay, June 1, 1827, note); states that she forwarded the enclosures but has received no reply from (Franklin) Litchfield; charges that (Caleb) Brintnall refused, "on learning the heiress was a single female," to answer her letter to him; voices suspicion of connivance between Litchfield and Brintnall to deprive her of her late brother's property; and requests advice. ALS. DNA, RG59, Cons. Disp.,

Puerto Cabello, vol. 1 (M-T229, R1). Endorsed by Clay: "Mr. [Daniel] B[rent] will please ansr." No answer has been found.

From James Brown

Dear Sir   Paris Octr. 12. 1827

Our latest accounts from Constantinople were down to the 17 Ulto. The families of the Ambassadors[1] of the three allied powers remained on board of Vessels in the Harbor, waiting the result of the negociations.[2] The Porte Continued to refuse to admit any Mediation and declared that although he would avoid hostilities on his part, yet that in case of their commencing on the part of the Allies he would endeavor to repel them. His tone, if some private accounts may be credited had become moderate on hearing that the Egyptian fleet with four thousand troops had been blockaded in the port of Macri [sic] by the Allied Squadron. This intelligence however is incorrect for we have learned that the Egyptian fleet had landed at Navarino the army sent to to [sic] re-enforce Ibrahim Pasha. It is now feared that on being informed of this event he may again assume a high tone and repel pacifick proposals. We have heard but not from any very authentic source that Admiral Codrington had given notice to the commander of the Naval forces of Egypt at Navarino[3] that hostilities must cease and had actually blockaded the port. Knowing as the Porte must that two out of the three powers are not very hearty in the cause and that Austria feels a strong leaning in favor of Turkey, it is possible he may temporize and even make some resistance in order to try whether the jealousy felt by the European sovereigns of the gigantic power of Russia may not dissolve an Alliance composed of materials so discordant, and so little formed to act in concert.[4] It is well understood that the Treaty of the 6 July had its origin not so much in motives of humanity as of policy. Russia has long threatened Turkey, and had perhaps just cause of complaint and even of War on account of the disputes which through the influence of the other powers were settled by the Treaty of Ackerman.[5] Whilst those negociations were carrying on little was said or thought of the suffering Greeks. As soon as they had been brought to a conclusion and when England and France & Austria believed that all the complaints of Russia had been silenced, the Emperor[6] declared that he could not quietly permit his co-religionaires, the Greeks to be butchered without interfering to save them.[7] The idea then presented itself to England and France, to offer their co-operation in pacificatory measures, provided each of the powers would engage to refrain from aggrandizing itself in consequence of any hostilities to which the projected interference might give rise, and thus it was hoped that the ambitious views of Russia might be counteracted.

It was believed on all hands that by assuming a lofty tone with Turkey
and sending an imposing fleet into the Mediterranean the pacification
of Greece might be effected without striking a blow. It is now evident
that England is somewhat alarmed at the course of things and Mr Canning has been severely censured for the policy which has brought the
Country into the difficulty.[8] It is said that new negociations will be
opened at London, in the event of the parties proving obstinate, to decide on ulterior measures. It is not altogether certain that either England or Russia may not in the end be considered as the dupe in these
transactions.

At the last accounts from Spain the King[9] had arrived at Terragona
and issued a very spirited Proclamation commanding the Insurgents[10]
to lay down their arms on pain of being punished with death. The
rebels had in some quarters dispersed, yet still their numbers were
considerable. It is not improbable as the King has determined to consult the High Clergy and the superiors of the convents it may terminate
either in re establishment of the inquisition[11] or in making considerable concessions to the Clergy. Indeed some suspicions are afloat that
he will not be sorry with the apparent necessity of satisfying their
claims however unreasonable

The Count de Villa [sic] Real late Ambassador of Portugal at London has gone to Vienna for the purpose of conducting the Infanta Don
Miguel to Lisbon.[12] His mother[13] is now in high favor & has prepared
the publick mind for a change in the Government. The Consitution
[sic] will be abolished and its adherents persecuted.[14] The English
troops unless re enforced will in all probability be forced to quit the
Kingdom.

The King[15] has for the last month been absent on journies first to
St Omers [sic] and afterwards to Compiegne   He will not fix himself
at the Tuilleries [sic] until his birth day 4 of Novr. He has been received every where with great demonstrations of joy and appears to
be very popular. The Country is prospering from twelve years of peace
and ten of abundance not having had a scanty crop since 1817. The
Navy increases rapidly in the number and structure of their vessels;
and the number and the character of their seamen is creditable to
them. Their manufactures are flourishing and their Commerce is gradually but steadily extending itself. They are not in a situation to fear
any thing from popular commotion or from war with their neighbors.

I fear you will have a bad account to render of our foreign relations
in every quarter. Mr Gallatin has left London I believe without accomplishing the objects of his mission.[16] You know what my prospects
are and I find Poinset [sic][17] is tired and disgusted with Mexico— If
we are wise we will cultivate peace and increase our resources at home.
These will be a source of prosperity as is proved by the present con-

dition of France so enviable when compared with that of England. All my letters represent the state of our internal affairs, as being prosperous. The divided State of our Senate and house of Representatives renders the failures in our diplomacy more embarrassing. These divisions are well known in Europe and have their influence.

The Baron de Krudener leaves Paris this evening to embark on the 15th. I have given him a letter to you.[18] He appears to be a worthy man and goes out with a determination to be pleased with every thing— I am sorry to find that he is very deaf and but imperfectly acquainted with our language. If we can please him it will be worth while to do so as Russia has the most friendly dispositions in regard to us. Their Ambassador here[19] has frequently told me so and his conduct to me has given me confidence in his assurances.

The Baron de Damas has spoken to me again on the subject of the reduction of the duties on Silk and Brandy and observed that a slight concession on that point would satisfy France and give permanence to the Convention[20]—I have not been able to draw from him an answer to my letter respecting the discriminatory duties demanded on the Vessels which touched at Cork and Cowes, although I have asked it at three or four different times.

I have received a letter from Mr. Poinset who is I find disgusted with Mexico and anxious to return to the United States. I am not very sure that he would not be more satisfied with a residence at London or Paris. The certainty that we can accomplish little for our Country harrasses [sic] the mind and awakens feelings of discontent. I think it probable that I may in a few months ask the President to give me permission to return. Of this however you need say nothing at present. I am Dear Sir Your affte. friend & Obedt Servant   JAMES BROWN
Honble Henry Clay.

ALS. DLC-HC (DNA, M212, R2).
1 Stratford Canning; Alexandre Ribeaupierre; the Count de Guilleminot.   2 See above, Brown to Clay, July 12, September 29, 1827; Hughes to Clay, September 16, 1827, note; Lafayette to Clay, October 10, 1827.   3 Moharrem Bey, a brother-in-law of Ibrahim Pasha.   4 See above, Middleton to Clay, April 21, 1825; May 30, June 13, 1826.   5 See above, Moore to Clay, November 18, 1826.   6 Nicholas I.   7 Cf. above, Brown to Clay, March 23, 1827 (2).   8 On criticism of George Canning, cf. below, Lawrence to Clay, October 13, 1827. The London *Times* on September 5, 1827, had editorially responded to the implication that Stratford Canning, also, was censurable because the Ambassadors had allowed the Turkish Government only 15 days to reply to their note before terminating the negotiations (see above, Hughes to Clay, September 16, 1827, note). Under the treaty of June 6 the three powers had agreed to allow 30 days for the Turkish Government to respond. The editorial noted that, since Turkey was not a party to the treaty arrangement and could not officially know of the secret article covering the arrangements, she had no grounds to take offense.   9 Ferdinand VII.   10 Cf. above, Everett to Clay, October 6, 1827.   11 Cf. above, Brown to Clay, September 29, 1827, note.   12 Cf. above, Brent to Clay, October 11, 1827.   13 Carlota Joaquina.   14 Cf. above, Raguet to Clay, May 6, 1826, note.   15 Charles X.   16 Cf. above, Gallatin to Clay, October 4, 1827.   17 Joel R. Poinsett.   18 Not found. Baron Paul de Krudener arrived in Washington on December 18 to enter upon his duties as Russian Minister to the United States.   19 Charles André, Count Pozzo di Borgo.
20 Cf. above, Brown to Clay, September 13, 27, 29, 1827.

From William B. Rochester

Hon H Clay,
My Dr. Sir   *private*   New York 12h. Oct: 1827.

Judge Thompson[1] has just left my room, and by his permission and indeed request, I hasten to give you his suggestions on the subject of the Vice-Presidency a subject which I had intended myself to have introduced to you when at Washington, but omitted as nothing transpired which led to it—

Mr. Thompson has evidently taken much pains to inform himself touching the political matters of the day, all with a view to aid, & sustain the administration which possesses his unqualified confidence and receives his most zealous support—

he is clearly of opinion that you ought to be a candidate and was apparently much gratified when I ventured to express an opinion, founded upon what passed between us in travelling thro' Ohio last summer that you would submit to the wishes of your friends on that subject[2]—   it seems that he has lately had a free conversation with Genl. Scott[3]—   the latter has satisfied him that your name would secure Missouri, Illinois & Indiana & fix with those certainly Ken: Ohio & Louisiana besides doing more good in Penn & N. York that [sic] any other name possibly could—I hinted to Judge T. at the possibility of some of your friends in Penn, Louisiana & Missouri, and even in N. Y. separating you from Mr. Adams—   this he treats as an idle fear—

He has no doubt but that Calhoun will be the Jacksonian candidate for the V. Presidency unless the latter can satisfy himself beyond a reasonable doubt that Genl. J. will be elected, in which case he says Calhoun would prefer the Treasury. Department under Genl. J. with some individual at the head of the State Department, who would not be likely to interfere with his ulterior pretensions—   he thinks too that on this point Calhoun calculates with some judgment, as the order of the day seems to be against making the State Department any longer the passport to higher preferment, and maintains that this is a consideration which ought to be weighed by your friends—

The Judge is evidently somewhat uneasy about our State—   he is alarmed at appearances in the two cities of N York & Albany—   he says the administr. is not nigh so strong in either of them as it was six weeks ago, but confidently predicts a re-action before the lapse of many months, i,e, "when the fever of the moment is over and the people come to their senses"—

Notwithstanding he deprecates in the most unequivocal terms the possibility of the Hero's elevation, yet he consoles himself with the reflection (one which I confess is equally consoling to me & one which I have cherished for some weeks) that his administration & the policy which will be dictated to him by the Virginia School,[4] must undeceive the Western, the middle & northern States in a very short time, unite those states in a firm phalanx for ulterior operations, and put down in their respective States forever V Buren, Clinton, Woodbury, Benton, Johnson[5] & id omne genus—

Entre nous—Mr. Thompson forbodes ill of Sanford,[6] but I think such are the views of Mr. Sanford, such the current of things in N York, and such Mr. Sanfords characteristic indecision, that he will not break ground strongly in any direction—

He seems to dislike the idea of making Taylor,[7] Speaker—& finding that Mr. Sergent [*sic*] & I are in the habit of corresponding, has submitted a request that I would break the subject to Mr. Sergeant on this subject, (a delicate one) he seems to be sensible that great circumspection ought to be used, in regard to Mr. Taylor—I shall not comply with his request for the present at least,[9] tho' as between the two men S. & T. I should not hesitate to prefer the former, if in Congress, & I supposed his chance of success as good— Judge T. says that *he* could not vote for Taylor under any circumstances— on this subject he is quite fastidious— I have no room left for my own reflections in relation to the above matters—and give those of Mr. T. very rapidly tho' correctly—

Be pleased to present my respects to Mrs Clay   Yours very respectfully & truly   W B ROCHESTER

ALS. DLC-HC (DNA, M212, R2).   [1] Smith Thompson.
[2] Cf. above, Clay to Hammond, April 21, 1827; below, Rochester to Clay, November 4, 1827.   [3] Winfield Scott.   [4] See above, III, 341n.   [5] Martin Van Buren; DeWitt Clinton; Levi Woodbury; Thomas Hart Benton; Richard M. Johnson.
[6] Nathan Sanford.   [7] John W. Taylor.   [8] John Sergeant.   [9] Cf. below, Rochester to Clay, November 4, 1827.

INSTRUCTIONS AND DISPATCHES   October 12, 1827

From JAMES BROWN, Paris, no. 76. States that "Mr. Decourdemanche, avocat à la Cour Royale de Paris," has sent him "a model of a newly discovered method of book-binding, and also a letter respecting it," which letter is being forwarded to Clay. Transmits also "a printed notice" concerning it. ALS. DNA, RG59, Dip. Disp., France, vol. 23 (M34, R26). Received December 7. Neither of the enclosures has been found.

The donor was probably Alphonse Decourdemanche, who, beginning in 1828 and continuing as late as 1870, published numerous works on business law and governmental economic policy.

MISCELLANEOUS LETTERS   October 12, 1827

From JOSEPH KERSHAW, Camden (S. C.). States that the Revolutionary War prevented remittances being paid on a debt owed by the firm of "Kershaws, Chesnut

& Co," consisting of Joseph and Eli Kershaw, John Chesnut, William Ancrum, and Aaron Loocock, trading at Charleston, Camden, Cheraw, Granby, and Rocky Mount, to the firm of (William) Greenwood and (William) Higginson, "Merchants of London"; that the latter firm obtained in 1794 a judgment against Chesnut and Ancrum, the surviving partners, for $76,180.60; that his grandfather, Joseph Kershaw, had lost a fortune of more than 50,000 pounds sterling, because of British destruction of his property during the war, and, pleading insolvency, had advised Greenwood and Higginson "to present their claim to the Commission appointed under Jays [sic] Treaty" (cf. above, Clay to Gallatin, June 21, 1826, note). Notes that the "Representatives" of Chesnut have now filed a suit in "Court of Equity" against the Kershaw family "for the amount paid by him towar[d] the satisfaction of the judgement of Mes[srs.] Greenwood & Higginson—" Requests that Clay determine through the American Minister in Great Britain (Albert Gallatin) whether or not Greenwood and Higginson submitted the Kershaw claim to the Commissioners under Jay's Treaty and, if so, how much, if anything, was paid. ALS. DNA, RG59, Misc. Letters (M179, R65).

Daniel Brent acknowledged receipt of the letter on October 20, and, at the direction of the Secretary, stated that the requested inquiry would be made. Copy, in DNA, RG59, Dom. Letters, vol. 22, pp. 69–70 (M40, R20). On October 30, 1827, ". . . with the permission, and by direction of the Secretary," Brent requested Albert Gallatin "to cause the information required to be procured from the proper office in London. . . ." Copy, in DNA, RG59, Dip. Instr., vol. 12, pp. 22–23 (M77, R7).

The younger Kershaw has not been identified. The grandfather, Joseph, with his brother Eli, had come from Yorkshire, England, to Charleston about the middle of the eighteenth century and in 1758 had founded the village which became Camden. Joseph had opened a store there as a branch of a Charleston firm which included William Ancrum and Aaron Loocock. Eli in 1766 had located on land which developed as Cheraw, had opened a branch of the firm there, but in 1744 had closed out the operation and joined his brother at Camden. They had been active in the American Revolution, had been taken prisoner and deported, and Eli had died en route to Bermuda in 1780. Joseph had become prominent in the development of Camden and owned saw, grist, and flour mills, an indigo works, a tobacco warehouse, as well as the mercantile establishment. He had been mayor at the time of his death in 1791. One of several sons, John (1765–1829) had been prominent in South Carolina politics and a member of Congress (1813–1815). He was agent for the settlement of his father's estate and, alone, of Joseph Kershaw's sons left descendants. None, however, has been found of an age appropriate to have been this correspondent. Thomas J. Kirkland and Robert M. Kennedy, *Historic Camden* (2 vols.; Columbia, South Carolina, 1905, 1926), I, 11, 88, 109–11, 116, 203, 376–83.

Ancrum, a native of Northumberland, England, had been a wealthy Charleston merchant prior to the Revolution and had died in 1808. Loocock, his partner in the Charleston operations, had been one of the original proprietors of the land in the area of Camden. While both men had been active in the early stages of the Patriot cause, their property had been confiscated at the end of the war because of their collaboration with the British occupying forces.

Chesnut, born in the Shenandoah Valley of Virginia in 1743, had entered Kershaw's Camden store as an apprentice and had been taken into the firm by 1776. He also had been active in the Revolution and afterward had been a member of the State convention for ratification of the Federal Constitution and twice a member of the State Senate.

From James Brown

My dear Sir,   (Confidential)   Paris Octr. 13. 1827

The State of Mrs. Browns health has for some time been very bad and yet gives me much uneasiness. She has suffered much from an obstinate pain in her face with which she has [been] occasionally afflicted ever since our former journey to Europe.[1] This however painful is by no means alarming and after a confinement of three or four weeks is giving way to remedies. What gives me serious concern is a tumor in her right breast which although giving no pain must if not dispersed lead to dangerous consequences. I have employed two of the most distinguished Physicians who are applying poultices to dismiss the tumor but as yet with no very apparent benefit. It will be useless to speak of this to her family as it can do no good and as we hope to give you better news by the next opportunity of writing to you. She has been ordered to confine herself to the House, and only to receive a few friends witht[2] attending to her toillette [sic]. You Know her sociable and hospitable disposition and can easily suppose she is not very patient under this prescription. The idea that her complaint may not yield to the remedies tortures my mind and really almost disqualifies me from thinking on any other subject. Mr. Johnston[3] is here and has become very intimate with Mr Harris[4] formerly of St Petersburg. I took Mr Johnston with me and introduced him to Lord Granville and to the family of the Duke of Orleans and have asked leave to present him to the Royal family. He is an honest fellow but being a *malade imaginaire* and withall a little fastidious is not very easily satisfied with attentions. We find our countrymen generally grateful for attentions and easily satisfied, whilst a few consider their Minister as under obligations to become their Guardian and guide and are discontented after all that you can do for them. Mr Johnston will leave this for Italy in a few days. Mr H has many acquaintances and will pass the winter in Paris. He is a restless little fellow and somewhat of an intriguer.

I hope your things arrived safely. I sent them to the care of our obliging friend Mr Isaac Bell.

Are you all prepared for the state in which your foreign relations are about to be placed? You know in which mine will probably end by my last dispatch.[5] Would it not be better to delay an explosion until matters were more smooth and harmonious at home? And will they probably be better for some time? I wish you would direct me whether I ought to press and insist on a written answer or let the thing rest knowing what that answer will be if obtained from the present Ministry. If it be what we have a right to expect what next?— I am dear Sir very sincerely your friend &c.   J. B.

ALS. DLC-HC (DNA, M212, R2).   [1] See above, II, 331, 379, 431.
[2] Without.   [3] Cf. above, Brown to Clay, September 29, 1827.   [4] Levett Harris.
[5] Above, September 27, 1827.

DIPLOMATIC NOTES   October 13, 1827

From José SILVESTRE REBELLO, Wahington. Requests an interview with the President to present an autographed letter from the Emperor of Brazil (Peter I), communicating news of the death of the Empress, Maria Leopoldina Josepha Carolina, on December 11, 1826. ALS, in Portuguese with trans. in State Dept. file. DNA, RG59, Notes from Foreign Legations, Brazil, vol. 1 (M49, R1).

On October 20 Clay replied to Rebello that President Adams had directed that the letter be transmitted through the State Department. Copy, in DNA, RG59, Notes to Foreign Legations, vol. 3, p. 391 (M38, R3); ALI draft, in CSmH. Acknowledging Clay's note, on October 22, Rebello stated that he had sought "the personal admission to deliver the said Letter under the conviction that the public act would prove more clearly the permanent, and good harmony between the Government of H. M. the Emperor, and the Government of the United States." ALS, in Portuguese with trans. (AL) in State Dept. file. Clay responded, on the same day, with assurances that he "would take an early opportunity to lay before the President" the Emperor's letter. Copy, in DNA, RG59, Notes to Foreign Legations, vol. 3, p. 392 (M38, R3); L draft, in CSmH. For the significance of Rebello's effort to emphasize the "good harmony" existing between the two governments, cf. above, Pratt to Clay, September 29, 1827, note.

INSTRUCTIONS AND DISPATCHES   October 13, 1827

From W[ILLIAM] B[EACH] LAWRENCE, London, no. 2. Reports that "Greece and the [Iberian] Peninsula are now objects of great, almost indeed of engrossing attention." Cites reports of "the renewal of negotiations," the adherence of "the Porte ... to the resolution of resistance," and the existence among the allies of "the most contradictory interests" (cf. above, Hughes to Clay, September 16, 1827, note; Brown to Clay, October 12, 1827 [1]). Notes doubts concerning the wisdom of "the policy of this country's interfering at all in the affairs of Greece" and observes that "Many ascribe the Adhesion of England to the late Treaty [cf. above, Brown to Clay, July 12, 1827, and note] to the ardent character of Mr [George] Canning and to that love of effect, to which they also attribute the Portuguese expedition" (cf. above, Gallatin to Clay, December 13, 15, 1826). Asserts that "The truth is that the unfortunate result of the loans and the conduct of those who, in this country, first advocated the cause of the Greeks has created an apathy for the fate of that people, while apprehension of the effect, which the liberation of the Morea from the Turkish yoke, may have on the future maritime power of Russia is quite a predominant feeling." Refers to "The singular Character of the relations between England and France," which two countries are "allies in the Levant, while, in another section of Europe [the Iberian Peninsula], they are almost contending belligerents." Speculates that "the almost daily conferences ... between the French Chargé d'Affaires [Roth] and Lord Dudley would appear to imply the transaction at this moment of delicate and complicated business."

Praises "Villa [*sic*] Real, who is gone to accompany Don Miguel on his return to Portugal," as "a man of character, attached to liberal institutions and well regulated government," and gives the reason for his presence in London: "He is the brother in law of the Marquis Palmella, the Ambassador in London and probably the most enlightened of his countrymen. Villa Real was appointed several months since to replace the Marquis, on the nomination of the latter to the Department of Foreign Affairs at Lisbon [cf. above, Everett to Clay, June 22, 1827] and he actually came to England for the purpose. After he arrived, however, Marquis Palmella obtained permission to retain his present office and Villa Real was accredited here as a Special Minister."

States his understanding that Miguel "will pass some time in England," where "the influence of Palmella and others, by whom he would in this country be surrounded, might be productive of much good" and might "have the effect of softening asperities towards those who have heretofore thwarted the Prince's views. . . ." Points out, however, that, "though not a year has yet elapsed since . . . the two houses of Parliament manifested their confidence in the stability of Portuguese liberty, there is at this day scarcely an individual in England, who believes that the Constitution can be upheld." ALS. DNA, RG59, Dip. Disp., Great Britain, vol. 35 (M30, R31). Received November 30.

The London *Times* almost daily during the month of October reported that Roth, the French Chargé (not further identified), was transacting business at the British Foreign Office.

MISCELLANEOUS LETTERS   October 13, 1827

From PRYOR LEA, Knoxville. Resigns his post as United States attorney for East Tennessee because of "recent occurences (cf. above, Erwin to Clay, August 12, 1827)." ALS. DNA, RG59, Letters of Resign. and Declin.

Lea wrote again, on December 3, 1827, to inquire whether his resignation had "been received and accepted." ALS, in DNA, RG59, Misc. Letters (M179, R65). On December 4 Clay acknowledged receipt, on "the 29th. ulto.," of Lea's letter of October 13 and stated that it had been "immediately communicated to the President," who had accepted the resignation. Copy, in DNA, RG59, Dom. Letters, vol. 22, p. 103 (M40, R20).

To John Bradford

Dear Sir: Washington, D.C. Oct. 14, 1827.

I had requested Mr. Berryman to obtain the opinions of Professors Hosack and Renwick, and Dr Godman, as to the competency of the Revd. Mr. McCauley [*sic*] to discharge the duties of President of Transylvania.[1] Although the trustees have made the appointment[2] it may be satisfactory to them to peruse the enclosed letters, containing the information I desired Mr Berryman to procure and for that purpose, I now transmit them. I am, with great respect, Your obedient servant,
John Bradford, Esq.   H. CLAY

LS. KyLxT.   [1] Cf. above, Berryman to Clay, September 1, 29, 1827.
[2] The trustees of Transylvania University on September 15 had elected Thomas McAuley as president. Lexington *Kentucky Reporter*, September 19, 1827.

To John Sloane

Dear Sir: Washington, D.C. 14 Oct. 1827.

Your favor of the 23d ultimo[1] reached this place during my absence, for a short period, from the city.[2] You will have seen, subsequent to its date, that Mr. Eaton has presented himself to the public.[3] His abortive piece appears to have the double, though conflicting, object, of sustaining the statements of General Jackson, without impeaching those of Mr. Buchanan.[4] There is one circumstance attending the publication of Mr. Eaton, which deserves to be known. You will observe that he suppresses the name of the member of Congress from whose letter he gives an extract. Now I have in my possession satisfactory proof that that member is the same J. Mc.Lean, Senator from Illinois whose letter[5] was published a few weeks ago, in which he declares, from Washington, that nobody here, at that time, believed any thing of the Kremer story.

I have thought it worthy of consideration whether some act emanating from my friends, or from a certain portion of them, those from Ohio, for example, might not be expedient to vindicate themselves from the charges which have been directed alike against them and me. The next Session of Congress will afford a fit opportunity for determining on the propriety of such a proceeding.

I felt greatly concerned at the issue of some of the Kentucky elections.[7] More on a personal than a political account. The recent elections in Maryland[8] have terminated with so much success that it will efface all bad impressions produced by our loss in Kentucky.

The closeness of the contest for the Speaker's Chair,[9] will, I presume, occasion a very full attendance of the members at the commencement of the Session. In reference to that and other objects the election to supply the place of Mr. Wilson in Columbus district,[10] is of some importance. But there, I fear, as in some other instances, we are likely to be defeated by the multitude of our friends, who are eager to serve the public.[11] I am, my dear Sir, with great regard, faithfully, your friend, and obedient servant, H. CLAY
Hon. J. Sloane.

P.S. I am obliged, by the effects of my sedentary habits, to employ the friendly pen of an amanuensis,[12] but it is one entirely to be confided in. H. C.

LS, with postscript in Clay's hand. MH-Houghton Library. [1] Not found.
[2] Cf. above, Clay to Adams, September 29, 1827. [3] Cf. above, Ingersoll to Clay, October 6, 1827, and note. [4] Cf. above, Smith to Clay, August 1, 1827, and note; Ingersoll to Clay, August 11, 1827, and note. [5] Cf. above, Street to Clay, October 8, 1827, note. [6] Cf. below, Clay, *Address . . . to the Public*, December 29, 1827.
[7] Cf. above, Clay to Taylor, April 4, 1827, note. [8] Cf. above, Clay to Blunt, September 11, 1827, note. [9] Cf. above, Webster to Clay, June 2, 1827, note; September 28, 1827; Clay to Taylor, September 7, 1827, note. [10] William Wilson, born in Hillsboro County, New Hampshire, in 1773 and graduated from Dartmouth College in 1797, had studied law in Johnstown, New York, and about 1805 opened legal practice at Chillicothe, Ohio. From 1808 to 1823 he had held appointment as chief judge of the court of common pleas at Newark, Ohio. He had been a member of Congress from 1823 until his death June 6, 1827. [11] Two administration candidates, Daniel S. Norton, of Knox County, and Lyne Starling opposed one Jacksonian, William Stanbery (or Stanberry), who won by a plurality. *Liberty Hall and Cincinnati Gazette*, October 11, 25, 1827. Norton has not been further identified. Stanbery, born in Essex County, New Jersey, in 1788, had been admitted to the bar first in New York City and in 1809 at Newark, Ohio, where

he practiced until shortly before his death in 1873. He was a member of Congress from 1827 until 1833. Starling, born in Virginia, had settled at Franklinton, Ohio, in 1805 and engaged in general mercantile business. In 1809 he had bought a large tract of land on the east bank of the Scioto River and with other proprietors in the area had initiated a campaign, effected in 1812, to have the site designated for the State capital. When Starling's claim had been contested in 1820, he had reportedly employed Clay as counsel for the defense, an arrangement terminated, however, when Clay assumed office in the State Department. Starling's title was subsequently upheld. Andrew Denny Rodgers, III, "Lucas Sullivant and the Founding of Columbus," *Ohio Archaeological and Historical Society Publications*, XXXVII (1928), 172.   [12] Probably Richard Forrest.

From John Sergeant

Dear Sir,   (Private)   Philada. Octr. 14. 1827.

I have not written to you since our election, because I knew you would see the result in a newspaper as soon as a letter could reach you. It has been highly gratifying, and will have a good effect. Our friends in the interior looked to it with great interest, mixed with not a little apprehension. I confess, too, I had my misgivings. The combination against us was formidable, and there were circumstances operating against us which ought to have been of little weight, but nevertheless had some effect. Tho' the majority is small, the victory is decisive.[1] Our friends are elated and confident, and the enemy depressed, exhausted and I think very much broken. The intelligence from other parts of the State is also encouraging. Wherever a stand has been made, we have displayed a strength even beyond our own expectation. This is particularly the case in Montgomery, Lebanon, Lancaster and Franklin, and I believe in Bucks.[2]

We are now upon the alert to improve these advantages for the purpose of the general contest. But here a very perplexing difficulty occurs as to the *mode*, upon which there is some difference of opinion. You know already what it is. It will receive the most deliberate consideration, with all the light we we [sic] can obtain, and I hope we shall hit upon the right course.[3] I am persuaded we have a majority in the State, if we can only bring it out, and the success we have had here, in Maryland and in Delaware,[4] will help to smooth our way.

The President left us yesterday at noon. He was greeted at his arrival with unaffected kindness and respect, and at his departure had sufficient evidence of the number and enthusiasm of his friends.[5] Judge Southard[6] will be able to tell you all about that. You need be under no apprehension of being "counteracted" hereafter. Our opponents have been made sensible of the error of their conduct, and tho' I hope they will yet make many mistakes, they will not repeat exactly the same of which they were lately guilty.[7] If shame do not restrain them, fear will. They begin to know that their strength is not so overbearing as they supposed it to be, and that every move is material. If I am not much deceived, the good sense of the community is every where coming fairly into action, excited not a little by the violence of our adversaries, and

if this be so, how can there be a doubt of the issue? We have the whole of the argument, and they have nothing but a Hurra,   Very respectfully and truly yrs.   JOHN SERGEANT.
The Honble Henry Clay.

ALS. DLC-HC (DNA, M212, R2).
[1] Cf. above, Sergeant to Clay, September 11, 1827, note.   [2] While virtually the same statement as Sergeant made had appeared in the Philadelphia *National Gazette and Literary Register* on October 13, three days later the reports were described in that journal as "contradictory." The administration candidate for State Senator in Montgomery County had won a narrow victory, but Jacksonians had triumphed in all three contests for assemblymen from that county. *Ibid.*, October 15, 1827. Administration candidates had been generally successful in Bucks and Franklin. In Lancaster the retention of old party labels, as Democrat or Federalist, still obscured affiliations in the presidential contest. *Ibid.*, October 18, 1827; Philadelphia *United States Gazette*, October 12, 13, 16, 1827.   [3] Cf. above, Sergeant to Clay, September 26, October 31, 1827; Johnston to Clay, September 14, 1827, and note.   [4] Cf. above, Clay to Brown, March 27, 1827, note; Clay to Blunt, September 11, 1827, note; Clay to Taylor, September 7, 1827, note.   [5] The President was en route from Quincy, Massachusetts, to Washington. For his account of the Philadelphia visit on October 12–13, see Adams, *Memoirs*, VII, 329–31.   [6] Samuel L. Southard. Cf. above, Clay to Sanders, September 21, 1827, note.   [7] Cf. above, Sergeant to Clay, August 23, 1827, note.

From Porter Clay

Dr Brother   Frankfort 15h October 1827
I went up to Versailles the day before yesterday to see our old mother[1] who is considerably improved in health and is now able to walk about and attend to her domestick concerns   while there the sheriff[2] paid me $400 in part of Smiths debt vs Haggan[3] the balance will be paid before I can get an answer to this   you will therefore signify what disposition I shall make of the money   I did not ascertain what was the balance precisely but suppose it to be about $30 or $40
I have seen an advertisement in the Richmond papers offering our land for sail at auction which must have taken place some time in the latter part of August[4]—   I presume if a sail was effected that the agent must have informed you of the amout [sic] before this— I should be glad to here from you on that subject—   I am apprized it was sold on a credit of 12 months and if the amout is any thing of importance I should be enabled possibly to profit by the information
The political movements which are now takin [sic] place in this country indicate that there will be a vigorous effort on the part of the friends of the administration at our next election and I think the result need not be dreaded— If corruption is not used to draw off some of the friend [sic] of the Admn in the Legislature measures will be used to sustain the General government upon the subject of the Tariff and internal improvements[5] which cannot fail to have its influence upon the sober virtues and thinking part of the state— but as I do believe the leading Friends of the Heroe [sic] in this state are as unprin-

cipaled and corrupt as any set of men that ever disgraced any country I am confident that nothing will be left undone on there part to draw off and detach from the majorriety [*sic*] as many as they can to effect there purposes, and God only knows what they may effect in that way—I do most sincearly believe that the peculiar situation of the two contend [*sic*] parties in this state (to wit) releaf and anta [*sic*] Releaf[6] was the sole cause of the partial success of the friends of Jackson   your affectionate Brother   PORTER CLAY

ALS. DLC-TJC (DNA, M212, R10).   [1] Elizabeth Watkins.
[2] Thomas Stevenson, born in Woodford County, Kentucky, in 1783, had been a member of the Kentucky House of Representatives during the Sessions beginning in 1816, 1819, and 1820.   [3] Smith, not identified; probably James Haggin. No suit has been found.
    [4] On July 27, 1827, and ensuing dates, the *Richmond Enquirer* had carried an advertisement by L(awson) Burfoot, "By authority from Henry Clay," giving notice of the sale at auction on August 27, "next," of "the tract of land lying in the county of Henrico, on the Richmond Turnpike Road, about eight miles from the city of Richmond, belonging to Henry Clay, Porter Clay, and John Clay, being the land lately recovered by them, by a judgment of the Circuit Court of the United States, from the heirs of Richard Cocke, sen., dec., supposed to contain about 300 acres [*i.e.*, "Euphraim'—cf. above, Clay to Leigh, December 7, 1819; July 31, 1824]. . . ." Twelve months' credit, bonded "with approved security," had been authorized, and title was to be withheld until the purchase price was paid.   [5] On December 12, 1827, Adam Beatty, representative from Mason County, proposed that the Kentucky House of Representatives adopt a lengthy series of resolutions instructing the State's Senators and Representatives in Congress to support a "comprehensive system of internal improvements, commenced by the general government," and "more effectual protection" for domestic products "by increasing the duty on foreign hemp, flax, wool and spiritous liquors." The resolutions cited the need for protection, specifically, in aid of the manufacturing of iron, wool, "the finer kinds of cotton fabrics, including calicoes," hemp, and flax. As an "act of justice to the South Western States," the government was urged, to extend a branch of the national road from Zanesville, in Ohio, to Maysville, in Kentucky, and thence through the States of Kentucky, Tennessee, Alabama, and Mississippi, to New Orleans" and to commence "as early as practicable," the section between Maysville and Lexington (cf. above, Kercheval to Clay, November 8, 1826).   An attempt to amend the first resolution so as to require the consent of States through which proposed internal improvements should pass was narrowly defeated, by a vote of 49 to 46, on February 5; and on February 12 Beatty's package of resolutions was tabled. On the latter date the specific recommendation proposing to extend the National Road through the Southwest and to begin the construction between Maysville and Lexington was adopted. The Senate on the same day accepted the limited resolution, and it was approved on February 13. Ky. H. of Reps., *Journal . . . 1827–1828*, pp. 88–92, 352–53, 415; Ky. Sen., *Journal . . . 1827–1828*, p. 433; Ky. Gen. Assy., *Acts . . . 1827–1828*, p. 239–40. See also, below, Blair to Clay, February 4, 1828, note.   [6] See above, III, 902n.

From John H. Kerr

Sir   Ashland Oct. 15th. 1827

I wish to let you know How I am geting [*sic*] along at Ashland,   I Have a very good crop and cummenced [*sic*] this morning to gather it in,

I put a parcel of Hemp down[1] in Septr. it is now almost fit to take u[p] and another parcel last week

The Negros [*sic*] are all in good Health, and one more of an incrs [*sic*] since you left Here

The Stock are all in fine order

I got a very fine young ram from Mr. Price,[2] which I put with the Ewes 4 days ago— I would Here remark that there is a very fine young jack to be sold in the naborhood [sic], the price is $250　The man (I believe) would take the Gray Horse at $100 in part of the price,　I just mentioned this becaus [sic] I think it would be good policy to Have one on the farm

T. W. Clay lives at the farm when He is at Home. He is at this time gone some where and has got the Gray Horse

I Desire staying with you next year if you say so, if not let me know in time

Mr. R, Scott is unwilling to pay me my wages without your say so,[3] if you want any bacon for next year you will let me know when you next write　{your [sic] truly　　　　　　　　　　JNO. H, KERR

ALS. DLC–TJC (DNA, M212, R13). Addressed to Clay.
[1] Spread on the ground, to undergo the process of dew-rotting.　　[2] Probably John Price. Cf. above, Clay to Sanders, September 21, 1827.　　[3] Cf. above, Scott to Clay, September 3, 1827.

INSTRUCTIONS AND DISPATCHES　　　　　　　　　October 15, 1827

From VINCENT GRAY, Havana. States that Don Ignatio Duran (not further identi-fied), sent from Madrid to procure a million dollars for the public service, will raise seven or eight hundred thousand, which is "a much greater sum than they could have anticipated." Adds that, since the smugglers have been suppressed, the island's revenue should double. Reports that Lt. (Alexander) Thompson and Midshipman (Charles F. M.) Spotswood have been exchanged and are in Havana and that "Commodore [David] Porter had sailed from Pensacola the day before they left it" (cf. above, Gray to Clay, June 13, July 24, 1827). ALS. DNA, RG59, Cons. Disp., Havana, vol. 5 (M-T20, R5). Received October 31.

MISCELLANEOUS LETTERS　　　　　　　　　　　　October 15, 1827

From JAMES AND THOMAS H. PERKINS, Boston. State that, since their letter to Clay of October 10 (not found), the brig Nile has been released from its 23-day deten-tion at Montevideo by the Brazilian authorities and has arrived safely at Boston. LS. DNA, RG59, Misc. Letters (M179, R65).

On October 16, Daniel Brent "by direction of the Secretary," acknowledged receipt of the letter of October 10 and stated that the case would "receive due at-tention at his [Clay's] hands, and at this Department." Copy, in DNA, RG59, Dom. Letters, vol. 22, p. 63 (M40, R20).

The Boston brig Nile, bound from Canton to Buenos Aires, had been seized "in the river Plate" for violating the Brazilian blockade. The owners' claim for demurrage and interest on the value of the cargo was subsequently settled in full by the Brazilian Government. House Docs., 25 Cong., 1 Sess., no. 32, p. 160.

From S[AMUEL] L. S[OUTHARD], "Navy Department." Encloses "a correspondence between the Commander of our Squadron in the Mediterranean [William Mont-gomery Crane] and the French Consul at Tunis [Constantine Guys] respecting a deserter [Simon Laporte]" and requests Clay to "communicate" his "wishes" should he "think any instructions on the subject necessary." Copy. DNA, RG59, Exec. Letterbook, 1821–1831, p. 270. Cf. above, Heap to Clay, August 2, 1827.

From John Sergeant

Dear Sir,   (Private)   Philada. Octr. 16. 1827.

Your favor of the 14th.[1] was received, this morning. Under the same date, I wrote you a letter which I suppose you have by this time received. I have nothing now to add to it, except that we continue in good spirits and think we have ground for encouragement and hope in Pennsa. The election here will confirm and strengthen our friends, and will, I hope, be a lesson to them upon the value of exertion.

Mr. Markley[2] is slow, but he is at work, and says he will be ready in a day or two with his manuscript,[3] which he is to bring to me. I will endeavour to send you a copy. We hear of great preparations in Baltimore for doing honor to the President.[4] Very respectfully and truly yrs.
The Honble Henry Clay.   JOHN SERGEANT.

ALS. DLC-HC (DNA, M212, R2).   [1] Not found.
[2] Philip Swenk Markley.   [3] Cf. Sergeant to Clay, above, October 2, 5, 1827; below, October 31, 1827, note.   [4] En route to Washington from his home at Quincy, Massachusetts, Adams arrived in Baltimore on Sunday, October 14. A welcoming committee who had expected to entertain him on Monday expressed some embarrassment that the scheduled funeral of John Eager Howard "would necessarily occupy a great part of the day" and urged that Adams remain longer. He agreed, attended both Presbyterian and Catholic church services on Sunday, went to Howard's funeral on Monday, dined with the committee and some 30 of their friends on both Monday and Tuesday, and received visitors during most of the intervening time of the three days. He left Baltimore for Washington on October 17. Adams, *Memoirs*, VII, 333-39; Baltimore *American*, October 15, 16, 1827.

From Joseph M. Street

                          On Board the Steam Boat Josephine[1] On my way to
Dear Sir,   Prairie du Chein [sic] Octo. 16. 1827.

I closed my last[2] refering [sic] you to a subsequent letter for some further details. Whether interesting or not you can Judge. One thing I hope to effect—to give you some idea of men and things in this section of Country   I feel that you are deserving the highest honor that a grateful people can confer on you,—that personally I am indebted to you for favours that I ought not to have expected from you, and I am resolved to lay before you from time to time the judicious collections I can safely and unperceived make. As I before remarked I do not look for your responces [sic].— All I hope or desire is—that when assured of the correctness of my information, and the faithfulness of your *true friends*, you will act accordingly so as to sustain them. In weighing all my information I again refer you to a man I never saw or conversed with—yet he is your *true friend*, stands high, and has a phalanx that cannot be moved. He and this phalanx are your warm friends. I mean *Judge Lucas*.[3] He will on his way to Washington I am assured by a common friend to you & to him, visit all his old influential Pensylvania [sic] friends (he is a Pensylvanian) and greatly exert himself for the administration. His friends say,—that he is entirely disinterested & would not accept office least [*sic*] it might do his efforts an injury. Rest assured he is no inconsidera[ble] man in Missouri.— Converse freely & confidentially with him.

It would amuse you to have a peep behind the opposition curtain here, if you could be amused under the view of the deepest schemes of viliany [*sic*]. To me it is painful to see men who ought to have their countries interest at heart, striving as for life to unhinge the very sinews of the Country, and smile whilst endeavouring to bring ruin and desolation down upon their own Country. In 1824 the mail contracts for the line from St Louis to Franklin were taken. There were several bids. Genl. Green's was the lowest, and took the contract. He notified the P. M. Genl. that he had taken it too low & could not comply,—the P. M. G. then let him have it at a *higher price* than two other very reputable & perfectly responsible men—more so than Genl. Green—that were desirious [*sic*] to get at their bids. And this too without letting them know any thing of the matter.— I have seen the correspondence between Genl. Green & the P. M. Genl.—the *original letters of the P. M. G. were shewn to me.*[4] There is no mistake in this. I know this is out of your department—but how comes it that *your friends*—the friends of the Admns, cannot get a contract at a fair price—And Genl. G. can get the same contract at a *higher price than they were either of them willing to give & actually bid?* This does not look well. This is not the only case of apparent *leaning* in the P. M. G. towards the *friends of Genl. Jackson.* How is this?— Can the P. M. G. be opposed to the admns of which he is a member?[5]— I want no answers to these questions— I wish you to ask them for your own interest. In the military department too— T.[6] the paymaster Genl. appears *some how*, to have *chanced* upon the enemies of the admns in all his paymasters. And a complete system of *money making* I had almost said Sw——g[7] appears to prevail in paying out the money of the Government.— A paymaster for instance at Cincinatti [*sic*] pays the troops at this place— a paymaster here (St Louis) pays the troops at Counil [*sic*] Bluffs &c. &c. Money is obtained not at the Land offices here, or in Ill. or Arkansaw [*sic*]. But at New Orleans, and milage [*sic*] paid from the Council Bluffs to New Orleans & back again for a man going after money. *This is monstrous* yet if you will just get a peep at the paymasters returns from this quarter, I assure you—my dear sir, it is so. These men—from T. Pay M. G. to Whitmore [*sic*], & Colo., McRee[8] are enemies to the Admns.

See too the Depart of Indian affairs—I mean the Agents & sub-Agents —some of them are your friends—but more are your inimies [*sic*]— And for this very Agency (which I owe to your goodness) & frindly [*sic*] partiality) the very decided inimies of the Admns were warmly recommended for the place. I believe only one frind [*sic*] of the admns was recommended—and that was a very clever fellow, the sub-Agent John Marsh, who Gov. Cass[9] recommended. It is mortifying to your friends to see the friends of Genl. Jackson fattening on the loaves & fishes here, and using the very money which they receive at the hands of the admnson [sic] to hire men to abuse them. The suttler of the Troops at the Jefferson Baracks [sic], I am told is very active against the admns— lately a sub-Agent up the Missouri.—Capt. Kenerly.[10]—

These things are for your private use. I give them not entirely of myself but at the instance of *common warm joint friends* at St. Louis. For myself I candidly confess that originally I was not Mr. Adams' friend—I was perhaps prejudiced against him.— But when I saw *you* in the admnson—I did not hesitate to give it my warm support, so soon as Crawford was lost. And every day has more convinced me of the proprierty [sic] of my decision.

I wish, if possible, to be sustained in this country, not so much now on my own account as on account of the cause of the Country. I have seriously set my hand to the plough & I mean not to look back or flinch. I feel that I can & will be useful to the Government in this department —& I hope shew my gratitude to my friend who raised me to it. This is a very important Point (Prairie du Chein) and the Agency can be made more benificial [sic] to the U. S. than any other except those on the Missouri.

From the arrangements made by Genl. Atkinson with the Indians (Winebagoes [sic])[11] there will probably be a Treaty held during the ensuing year with them, for the purchase of the lands including the Mining district at Fever River, or below Prairie du Chein to our present boundary in Illinois. If so I should very much like to be one of the Commissioners,[12] and my appointment would particularly be agreeable to a great part of Illinois. Particularly the Northwestern part of the State on Ill. River. This is getting to be the strength of the State and is decidedly for the Admns. I purchased a plantation in Sangamo this last Spring and am improving it, and have a warm interest there. The people had applied to me to move amongst them & I intended to have done so this winter. And now shall move my family there & reside a part of my year. This Country is as rich soil as Fayette Co. Ky and is settling beyond any thing you can conceive. With good valuable setters [sic]. The military tract[13] is also settling with friends to the admnson. And the lead mines at Fever River is [sic] settling beyond any thing you can possibly conceive and bringing quantities of money into the country.

My appointment to the commission (for a treaty) that I speak of would *increase my means of being useful to the admnson.*

I remain with unbounded friendship to you, & entire devotion to the cause of the Admnson which I believe to be the Cause of my Country Your obliged friend & Hble Servt.   Jos. M. Street

P.S. You will perceive my appointment approved, and my nomination sustained by Rowan, Kane,[14] &c. on the oppositio[n] side. They are my *personal friends*—and wd. sustain me on that score, where it does not (as in this case) infringe upon their opposition. Their political course I condem [*sic*], and have freely said so, in my letters to them, this fall.   J. M. STREET

ALS. DLC-HC (DNA, M212, R2).
[1] Built at Cincinnati in 1827, its home port was New Orleans. The vessel was abandoned in 1829.   [2] Above, October 8, 1827.   [3] Jean Baptiste Charles Lucas.   [4] A similar account was reported in Beverly Tucker to Martin Van Buren, April 2, 1831, DLC-Martin Van Buren Papers (Presidential Papers—Martin Van Buren, MR10). Tucker maintained that Duff Green had received the contract from Postmaster General John McLean through the intervention of John C. Calhoun and that Green's remuneration had been "far beyond the price formerly paid" on the St. Louis to Franklin mail route. [5] Cf. above, Hammond to Clay, March 28, 1827.   [6] Nathan Towson.
[7] Swindling.   [8] Alphonso Wetmore; William McRee. Wetmore, born in Connecticut and commissioned from New York as an officer of the Army in 1812, held the rank of major and paymaster from 1815 until 1833, when he resigned under pressure to reimburse the Government some $14,701. *House Repts.*, 23 Cong., 1 Sess., no. 223.   [9] John Marsh; Lewis Cass. Marsh, born in South Danvers, Massachusetts, in 1799, and graduated from Harvard University in 1823, had found employment as a tutor at Fort St. Anthony (now St. Paul, Minnesota) and in 1824 and 1825 as sub-agent to the Sioux. In 1826 he had become sub-agent and justice of the peace at Prairie du Chien. Involved as a Sioux leader in the Black Hawk War (1832), he resigned his offices and engaged in general merchandizing for a time at St. Louis. In 1835 he moved to Santa Fé and the following year pushed on to California, where he acquired a ranch in the San Joaquin Valley. He hunted gold, practiced medicine, and was renowned as a publicist encouraging American settlement in that region during the mid-1840's.   [10] George H. Kennerly.
[11] Henry Atkinson—see above, Clay to Adams, September 29, 1827.   [12] Articles of agreement setting provisional boundaries between the Indians and the Americans in the area were arranged at Green Bay, August 25, 1828, and a formal treaty of cession was signed at Prairie du Chien, August 1, 1829. Street was not a commissioner in either negotiation, although he signed the treaty as Indian agent, a witness. Parry (ed.), *Consolidated Treaty Series*, vol. 78, pp. 496–98; vol. 80, pp. 34–37.   [13] The tract lay between the Illinois and Mississippi Rivers, from their confluence to the northern boundary of Mercer County, Illinois, continued east to the Illinois River. Of the total area, comprising 5,360,000 acres, 3,500,000 acres were appropriated in quarter sections as bounties to non-commissioned officers and men who had volunteered service in the War of 1812. *Illinois State Historical Society Journal*, VII (October, 1914), 297–98.   [14] John Rowan; Elias Kent Kane.

MISCELLANEOUS LETTERS   October 16, 1827

From GEORGE IZARD, Little Rock, Arkansas Territory. Acknowledges receipt of Clay's letter of September 6. Reports that "the alarm which prevailed in the Vicinity of Red River has ceased" and that "The Party under Burkman [Charles Burkham] & [Nathaniel] Robins dispersed of their own Accord before they had marched far into the Interior of Texas." Notes having heard that "the great Majority of" participants in the expedition "suspected the Object of their Leaders to be the Plunder of the Caravan which conveys Silver from Santa Fe to the City of Mexico. . . ." Recommends, in view of the assembling of Indian tribes across the border in Mexican territory, the adjustment of differences between the Comanches and "some of these People," and the impracticability of organizing an effective militia, that reinforcements be sent immediately, if possible, to military posts within the area. LS. DNA, RG59, Misc. Letters (M179, R65). Published in Carter (ed), *Territorial Papers*, XX, 543. Endorsed by Clay: "To be submitted to the President. H. C."

An investigation by the Arkansas Territorial Legislative Council, reported on October 19, revealed that Robins and Dr. Lewis R. Dayton, claiming to represent residents of Pecan Point, had written to José Antonio Saucedo the previous February, pointing to the uncertainty of the boundary between the United States and Mexico (cf. above, Clay to Adams, August 23, 1827), expressing the belief that they were on Mexican soil, and requesting protection from the Indians. Saucedo had appointed Robins and Dayton as commissioners and on April 19 had granted the settlers permission to organize a provisional government. On June 12 Charles Burkham, professing to act as a captain in the Mexican Army, had issued a proclamation to the inhabitants of Lost Prairie, in Miller County, Arkansas, calling for enlistment to fight hostile Indians and promising both compensation and a share in the plunder. Failure of the local settlers to respond to either the governmental or the military proposals had ended the incident. White, "Disturbances on the Arkansas-Texas Border," *Arkansas Historical Quarterly*, XIX (1960), 95–100.

Dayton, not further identified, may have been the troublemaker identified as Dr. Lewis B. Dayton, driven from the Austin Colony later in the summer of 1827. Malcolm D. McLean (comp. and ed.), *Papers Concerning Robertson's Colony in Texas* (3 vols., to date; Fort Worth: Texas Christian University Press, 1974–), III, 269n; Eugene C. Barker (ed.), *The Austin Papers* (2 pts.; American Historical Association, *Annual Report for the Year 1919*, II; Washington, 1924), pt. 2, pp. 1633, 1677, 1680.

From JOSIAH RANDALL, Philadelphia. Recommends Samuel Israel, a Pennsylvania native, for appointment as United States consul at Cap Haitien.

Adds: "We are in truth looking up in Penna. & for the first time I begin to think we shall shake Jackson to the centre. If the Current increases we are safe." ALS. DNA, RG59, A. and R. (M531, R4). Cf. below, Clay to Israel, November 9, 1827.

To Daniel Webster

My Dear Sir   Washn. 17h. Oct. 1827

Your favor of the 28th. Ulto. reached here whilst I was absent on a short excursion, undertaken to recover some strength which I had wasted during my devotion to business in the months of August and Septr.

I congratulate you on the present prosperous aspect of public affairs. The auspicious results of the elections in Maryland, Delaware, Philada. and of some other parts of Pennsa. have more than counterbalanced that of the K. elections[1] which affected me personally more than its political importance merited. I hope the election of Speaker is safe; but this, in some measure, still depends on the course which a majority of the N. York delegation may take. Should that be adverse to Mr. Taylor, it is to be feared that an Opposition Speaker may be elected. A strong effort should be made on the three members from Maine and N. Hampshire to prevail on them to vote, on that election, in conformity with the sentiments of their section and Constituents.[2] I have impressed some of our Western friends with the necessity of punctual attendance at the first of the Session.[3]

As to the affair of Mr. Hammond and the types,[4] be pleased to let it rest until you come here. Another & perhaps a better mode of accomplishing the object in view has presented itself. And that matter, therefore, had best remain over with others on which we will converse when you come here.

The President is expected to day. The incidents of the administration of the Government, during the current year, will enable him to exhibit a very satisfactory exposé to Congress.

In Virginia the indications are good,[5] and such as to authorize at least strong hopes. I remain Cordially & faithfy Yrs   H CLAY
D. Webster Esq

ALS. DLC-Webster Papers (DNA, M212, R22).
[1] For the Maryland election, cf. above, Clay to Blunt, September 11, 1827; for Delaware, Clay to Taylor, September 17, 1827; for Philadelphia, Sergeant to Clay, September 28, 1826, note; for other parts of Pennsylvania, Sergeant to Clay, October 14, 1827, and note; for Kentucky, Clay to Taylor, April 4, 1827, note.   [2] Representatives John Anderson, James W. Ripley, Jonathan Harvey—cf. above, Webster to Clay, September 28, 1827; Clay to Taylor, September 7, 1827, note.   [3] Cf. above, Clay to Sloane, October 14, 1827.
[4] Cf. above, Clay to Webster, August 19, 1827.   [5] Cf. above, Caldwell to Clay, August 8, 1827.

From Francis T. Brooke

My Dear Sir   Richmd Octor 17 1827

My Son in law Doctor Berkely [sic][1] wishes to remove to some new State to better his condition in the practice of Medicine   he has had flattering accounts of the opening for the faculty at Cincinnati,[2]   will you do me the favour to give me any information you may have on that Subject, and if you have none to be relied on, to write to Some friend there who may be depended on for accurate information,   if you know of any other place affording a prospect of Success in his profession be so good as inform [sic] me,   you will see by the papers how the convention[3] gets on,   in Albemarle there will be strong [sic] meeting my informer Says at least 300 voters and Judge Carr of the court of appeals will be one of its representatives,[4]   Chapmn Johnston will be elected for Augusta, but he will I hope be first elected here,   the meeting will take place the next week, as Soon as he arrives[5]— if we act with moderation there is every prospect of ultimate Success—   The Lynchburg resolutions[6] have done us mischief,   the personalities in them have excited some feeling against us,   I inclose you a letter from my friend Cabel[7] which you can return to me,   I hope Mr Madison[8] will not be found so inaccessible as is believed   Yours very truly
FRANCIS BROOKE

ALS. InU.
[1] Edmund Berkeley, of Staunton, Virginia, who had married Mary Randolph Spotswood Brooke.   [2] Either the Medical College of Ohio (above, III, 448n) or the Cincinnati Eye Infirmary, founded by Dr. Daniel Drake and Dr. Jedediah Cobb in 1827. For the latter, see Otto Juettner, *Daniel Drake and His Followers* . . . (Cincinnati, 1909), 58.
[3] Cf. above, Mercer to Clay, August 18, 1827, and note.   [4] The meeting of adminis-

tration supporters of Albemarle County was held at Charlottesville, Virginia, on November 15 with about 60 people in attendance. Jonathan Boucher Carr, not Dabney Carr, was elected the representative to the coming State convention. Jonathan Boucher Carr, educated as a lawyer, was not actively in practice. He subsequently moved to Lincoln County, Missouri. Dabney Carr, a nephew of Thomas Jefferson, had been named in 1812 head of the district chancery court at Winchester in Frederick County, where he had then taken up residence. In 1824 he had been appointed to the State Supreme Court of Appeals, and he remained on that bench until his death in 1837.   5 Chapman Johnson was elected by Adams supporters of the city of Richmond, who met on October 24, to select local delegates to the State convention. The Augusta County meeting of Adams partisans had, on October 22, named Johnson with five others, any two of whom might serve as delegates to the State meeting. Washington *Daily National Journal*, November 2, 1827, reprinting report from the *Staunton Spectator* (Virginia). Cf. below, Brooke to Clay, November 4, 1827, note.   6 According to the *Richmond Enquirer*, October 16, 1827, the meeting of Jackson's opponents in Lynchburg, Virginia, on October 9, produced resolutions so vitriolic in tone and questionable in accuracy, that Virginians could be expected to react only in support of the Tennesseean.   7 Joseph Carrington Cabell.
          8 James Madison—cf. below, Brooke to Clay, December 27, 1827, and note.

INSTRUCTIONS AND DISPATCHES   October 17, 1827

From VINCENT GRAY, Havana. Reports that Commissioner [Ignatio] Duran has sailed for Cádiz aboard the Spanish frigate "Pearla" (probably *Perla*) with $700,000 in specie and products of equal value. ALS. DNA, RG59, Cons. Disp., Havana, vol. 5 (M-T20, R5). Received November 5.

MISCELLANEOUS LETTERS   October 17, 1827

To CHARLES J. INGERSOLL, Philadelphia. Transmits "a translation of an Official Note received from the Spanish Minister" (above, Tacón to Clay, October 5, 1827) and requests that Ingersoll "enquire into the alleged circumstances of the case of this vessel, . . . institute such prosecution, or proceedings . . . as are warranted by law," and "report to this Department, as soon as may be convenient, the result of any Enquiry. . . , and an account of any steps . . . to preserve the neutrality, and enforce the laws of the United States.—" Copy. DNA, RG59, Dom. Letters, vol. 22, p. 64 (M40, R20).

To SAMUEL L. SOUTHARD. Returns the papers transmitted in Southard's "letter of the 11th. [*i.e.*, 15th] instant" and states that no instructions are necessary. Explains: "It is a case of desertion which is not provided for by our late Convention with France" (cf. above, III, 53n). Copy. DNA, RG59, Dom. Letters, vol. 22, p. 65 (M40, R20).

From WILLIAM B. GILES, Richmond (Virginia). Notes that he has been required by the Virginia General Assembly "to cause certain Journals of that body to be printed" but that "the Journals of the May Session of 1778, 1779 and 1784" are missing from "the proper rolls Office." Inquires whether "Copies of the missing Journals Can be obtained from the Library of the United States. . . ." Adds that the printer will need them "in five or six days. . . ." LS. DNA, RG59, Misc. Letters (M179, R65).
          Endorsement on cover, in Brent's hand, states that a copy of the resolution (enclosed with Giles' letter) in which the Governor's Council directed him to present this inquiry had been "Sent to the Librarian of Congress, with an order from the President for the Journals." A note, in Brent's hand, written on the copy of the resolution identifies the missing Journals as those for "The May Sessions of 1778,

1779 and 1782 [*sic*]." A further endorsement, in Brent's hand, on the copy of the resolution, states: "20 October 1827—Received from Mr. [George] Waterston [*sic*], Librarian of Congress, upon the Order of the President, The Journals of 1778, 1779, 1780, 1781 and 1784, and sent to Govr Giles on the same day."

The *Journals* of the May sessions of the Virginia House of Delegates for 1778, 1779, and 1784 were published by Thomas W. White in Richmond in 1827, 1827, and 1828, respectively, listed as items no. 7090, 7120, and 7392 in Earl G. Swem, *A Bibliography of Virginia*, Part II, *Containing the Titles of the Printed Official Documents of the Commonwealth, 1776–1916*, in Virginia State Library, *Bulletin*, X (1917), 9–10, 12, 35.

From B[ARTHOLOMEW] SHAUMBURGH, New Orleans. Solicits Clay's aid in favor of Dr. James S. McFarland, "who will apply to fill the vacancy made by the death of the Port Physician Doctor [William] Barnewell, . . . about four da[ys] ago—" States: "Doctor McFarland stands in the first rank with our Medical Men, & is very fortunate in his practice,　He is a man of Family, a Gentlem[an] & what is Still better *A friend of Ours*—."

Reports that an administration meeting, held October 13 to select "delegates to meet in Convention at Baton Rouge on the first Monday in November next" was "very respectable, & as numerous as Could be expected at this season." Concludes: "I flatter myself that all things will succeed as we wish it, & as it ought to be—" ALS. DNA, RG59, A. and R. (M531, R5).

Barnewell, originally a Philadelphian, had served as director and surgeon of the New Orleans Marine Hospital from 1804 to 1807. Later appointed port physician, he was followed in that post in 1827 by McFarland, who remained there until 1841. The latter practitioner, at least in later life, was highly controversial in his medical views. He opposed both the board of health and the quarantine regulations by challenging the idea that yellow fever was in some way connected with sanitary conditions. In 1854 he publicly condemned the draining of the swamp back of New Orleans as contributing to the yellow fever outbreaks. John Duffy (ed.), *The Rudolph Matas History of Medicine in Louisiana* (2 vols.; Baton Rouge, 1958), II, 17, 184.

Check to Josiah Stoddard Johnston

No.　OFFICE OF DISCOUNT & DEPOSIT, ⎱
　　　　　　　　　　　　Washington, ⎰ 18th. Octr 1827
　PAY to J. S. Johnston *or bearer*, Fifty *Dollars*, —/100
$50 DOLLARS, /100　　　　　　　　　　　　　　　H. CLAY

ADS, partially printed. DLC-TJC (DNA, M212, R16).

To Samuel L. Southard

My dear Sir　　　　　　　　　　　　　　　　18h. Oct. 1827
　Will you dine en famille to day at my house with Col. Mercer[1] &c.? I hope you will be able to come at 4 OClock. Yr's faithfy　　H CLAY
Mr. Southard.

ALS. NjP—Southard Papers. Endorsed: ". . . Accepted—"　　1 Hugh Mercer.

From Charles Hammond

My Dear Sir.   Cincinnati. Oct. 18, 1827

I learned yesterday evening, for the first time, that the Senator referred to, in your Lexington Speech,[1] as reporting to you that no attack was made upon your character at the time of your nomination was Gen Harrison, and that a correspondence had taken place between you in respect to it. I learned, too, that at a public meeting two weeks ago this day Gen. Harrison had Spoken of the fact, and Stated his Explanation.[2] It is possible that the facts I am about to state may be of importance to you in your future movements,: [sic] it is more than probable that they can be of no account. I nevertheless think it best to make them known.

In the Liberty Hall of March 22d. 1825 there is the following editorial paragraph, in reference to your nomination and the Vote upon it: "A violent Speech was made by Mr Branch[3] of North Carolina against Mr Clay. Mr. Macon,[4] from the Same State, it is understood voted in the negative expressly on the ground of Mr Clays views of the constitution" This paragraph was predicated upon a letter from Gen. Harrisson [sic] to myself, of which the following is an extract. "A most violent Speech was made by Mr Branch of North Carolina against the nomination. Those who voted against it were all the friends of Jackson and some of Crawfords. Yesterday the injunction of secrecy was removed So that the proceedings will be published to day. Mr Macon told Rowan[5] and myself yesterday that his vote against Clay was not on account of his conduct on the election of President, but for his construction of the constitution, I suppose in relation to internal improvements" The letter from which this extract is made is dated Washington March 9.

Many of your friends here think you would do well to make another appeal to Congress, more especially as the Heroites Seem to demand Such a course, as heretofore they called for a denial "over your own signature" They think the Speech of McDuffie, the publication of Branchs Speech, of Izaacs's [sic] and Eaton's statements, the Generals own "innuendo" &C.[6] give you just ground to ask an investigation. I do not See myself that Congress can properly take any jurisdiction of the matter, though possibly a corrupt agreement to obtain office may be proper ground of impeachment. I believe Such an appeal would confound and perplex them much. It cannot greatly interfere with public business, for nothing is to be done next winter in Congress but canvass for the Presidency. But I do not mean to assume the character of an Adviser— Were I President Adams I think I would decline the canvass, and let the opposition divide as they would do, to their own destruction

Our Elections in Ohio give no indication that the State is in danger. It must not be concealed that there is some Evidence of a gain for Jackson. This proceeds more from petty Strifes at home than from attachment to the cheif [*sic*] or his adherents.[7] We Shall not be able to obtain Victory without a tough Struggle which we shall very soon commence.

I can tell you one thing. The Heroites derive a vast advantage from their controul of the Post office in this City. Nothing would embarrass their movements in this State & Indianna [*sic*] so much as an administration Post Master in Cincinnati. Not long Since the present incumbent[8] was reported a defaulter, upon apologies not founded in fact. He is a man with no family but a wife: a professed Minister of the Gospel, disowned by the Methodist Church, and who has Set up a church of his own. And is supposed to have invested the public funds in the Edifice. *Inter nous* his removal would displease none, but those who would feel it in the movements of the election. My impression is that he is now a defaulter, and I should not be Surprised were McLean to remove him and Substitute another Jacksonian the present chief clerk.[9] I think the proceeds of the office Exceed 2000 Doll, consequently comes under the Surveillance of the President. Any Stir or commotion about a removal would be bad. We should have forty candidates. The quiet Substitution of William Ruffin,[10] or Benjn. F. Powers, would do us much service. I am poor enough to want Such an office for myself. But I do not. And I speak only what I know is for the common good.

Although the results of the election in Maryland and Delaware are highly gratifying,[11] it is not to be disguised that they give evidence of a very formidable opposition. According to present arrangments [*sic*] it would Seem that Jackson has a pretty fair Chance for five Electors in Maryland.[12] I am afraid too that you and your friends are over sanguine about Kentucky.[13]

Induldge [*sic*] me in making one Enquiry. What is the fact in respect to the allegation that you wrote to Jackson in oct 1824, to travel with you to Washington?[14]

Not long since the Postmaster General wrote a long letter to Mr Woods[15] of Butler. From you he says he has nothing to hope or fear. But he professes great regard for Mr Adams and insists that he is a general Supporter of the administration;[16] Finally requests Some of his old friends to write to the President in his behalf— Has there been any discovery that the Telegraph[17] is franked, or what has excited apprehension? Sincerely Yours   C. HAMMOND

ALS. OHi. Addressed to Clay.   [1] Cf. above, July 12, 1827.
[2] William H. Harrison—cf. above, Clay to Harrison, September 6, 1827, note.   [3] John Branch.   [4] Nathaniel Macon.   [5] John Rowan.   [6] For George McDuffie's speech, see above, Porter to Clay, August 19, 1827; for John Branch's speech, above, Clay to Harrison, September 6, 1827, and note; for Eaton's statement, above, Ingersoll to Clay, October 6, 1827; for Jackson's statement, above, Clay to Hammond, June 25, 1827, note.
Jacob C. Isacks on September 5, 1827, had written a letter for publication in the *Sparta Review* (Tennessee), reporting conversations he had had with Philip S. Markley and James Buchanan, "In the winter of 1824–5 after it was known that Mr. Clay had not re-

ceived a sufficient number of electoral votes to bring him before the house of representatives as a candidate for president; and before . . . [Isacks] had heard of any indications being given by him, and his friends, of the course which they ultimately took in the election. . . ." Isacks thought the conversations "might have" taken place "a week or two later" than the December 30, 1824, date, which Buchanan had recently indicated (cf. above, Ingersoll to Clay, August 11, 1827, note). According to Isacks, Markley had, "with more than ordinary interest and earnestness, . . . insisted that general Jackson, if elected, *ought to appoint Mr. Clay secretary of state, and urged . . . the necessity of having the thing so understood*; and said that he wished to see Mr. Eaton about it." On the same day Buchanan, according to Isacks, had also raised the issue but with the concern shifted so as to seek "assurance to be relied on, *that Mr. Adams not be continued in the state department*." As Isacks understood the situation, Buchanan feared that, "If nothing was communicated on which Mr. Clay and his friends could rely: That Mr. Adams would have a manifest advantage over general Jackson in the contest; because it had already been rumored, that if elected, general Jackson would continue Mr. Adams in his (then) present office. . . ; on the other hand the election of Mr. Adams would necessarily leave the department of state vacant." Isacks had protested that he was "so well apprised of the general's determination to remain silent upon all subjects calculated to give direction to the progress of the election till it was over" that he could not discuss the matter with him. He had therefore advised Buchanan himself to go to Jackson, "if he, (Mr. B.) thought it indispensable. . . ." *Niles' Weekly Register*, XXXIII (September 29, 1827) , 78–79.

   7 Cf. above, Clay to Sloane, October 14, 1827, note; below, Hammond to Clay, October 29, 1827.   8 William Burke, who held the office from 1815 until 1841, when he was removed as the Whigs came into political power.   9 Elam P. Langdon, born in Vermont in 1794 but resident in Ohio since the age of 10, had been assistant in the Cincinnati Post Office since 1816. He was best known as the founder and operator of the Cincinnati Reading Room, a repository of foreign and domestic newspapers, maintained in the rear of the post office.   10 William Ruffin, one of the organizers and first president of the Miami Exporting Company, had been postmaster of Cincinnati during the opening decade of the century and more recently had held local office as clerk of city court (1819) and sheriff (1825).   11 Cf. above, Clay to Blunt, September 11, 1827, note; Clay to Taylor, September 7, 1827, note.   12 Cf. above, Clay to Hammond, June 1, 1827, note.   13 Cf. above, Clay to Brooke, September 24, 1827, note.   14 Cf. above, Clay to Johnston, October 6, 1827, note.   15 John Woods, born in Johnstown, Pennsylvania, in 1794, had been admitted to the bar of Hamilton, Ohio, in 1819. He had been prosecuting attorney of Butler County from 1820 to 1825 and was a member of Congress from 1825 to 1829. Defeated for re-election as an administration supporter, he became editor and publisher of the *Hamilton Intelligencer*, established in 1828. He returned to politics as State auditor from 1845 to 1851.   16 On Adams' analysis of John McLean's relationship to Clay and the administration, cf. above, Hammond to Clay, March 28, 1827, note.   17 Washington *United States Telegraph*, the Jackson organ.

From Andrew Scott

Honbl. Henry Clay
Sir,   Little Rock Arks. Territory October 18th. 1827
   Although I was apprized that you were friendly to my reappointment as one of the Judges for this Territory;[1] yet, I did not know till recently to what extent you had used exertions in my behalf[2]— From my Brother John Scott who is now here examining the Land Office,[3] I have learned that you did particularly interest yourself for me, and that both you and the President, after my nomination to the Senate had been defeated, were so kind as to say that, if there was any other in this country vacant, my peculiar Situation would render me the most prominent candidate, and entitle me to the first consideration.— I ask you to accept my sincere thanks for this manifestation of your regard for my unprecedented Situation.— In moderate circumstances

with a large family, and unexpectedly thrown out of office upon a mere technical exception without trial or notice; permit me to solicit, that you will embrace the first opportunity to restore me to office within this Territory or, any where else that you can with propriety & according to those rules governing appointments place me—

Will you be good enough to name my situation to the President, or, lay this letter before him   Very Sincerely Your obdt. Servt.

Honbl. H. Clay Secty of State of the U. S.   ANDREW SCOTT

ALS. DNA, RG59, A. and R. (M531, R7).
[1] Cf. above, Van Buren to Clay, January 12, 1827, note.   [2] Scott had apparently been named one of the examiners under the law (2 *U. S. Stat.*, 282) which required annual examination of the books of the public land offices.   [3] Scott held a War Department appointment in 1830, "leasing out or rather assessing rents on the improved lands acquired from the Cherokee Indians." When he received this position has not been learned, but the office was abolished in November of that year. Carter (ed.), *Territorial Papers*, XXI, 248, 288.

INSTRUCTIONS AND DISPATCHES   October 18, 1827

From VINCENT GRAY, Havana. Reports that he has arrested "Several" vessels for "fraudulent use" of United States registry (cf. above, Gray to Clay, August 8, 1826) and has thereby "received more funds than sufficient to pay the Disbursements of this Department for distressed seamen, during the present half year." Recommends the appointment of "an agent" in Principe, "the seat of Government of this Island," for the purpose of detecting and preventing . . . Piracy . . . at, and near the Port of Nuevitas: as well as the fraudulent trade carried on in that place with vessels, with American and Spanish papers." Recommends also, if the agency be established, the appointment, to the position, of John Owen, "a native of New London" and long a merchant at Principe. Encloses several letters from Owen (written from "Puerto del Principe") in order to show "his fitness to fill the office." Encloses also an extract from a letter received from Mexico. ALS. DNA, RG59, Cons. Disp., Havana, vol. 5 (M-T20, R5). Received November 14.

Owen was appointed consular commercial agent at Puerto del Principe on June 27, 1828. He served in that capacity until 1832, at which time he was named United States consul there, a position he held until 1835.

To Francis Preston Blair

DEAR SIR   WASHINGTON, 19th October, 1827.

. . . .

It was a circumstance of the deepest regret with me, that you found yourself obliged to adopt the course you have, in relation to general politics. I had scarcely a friend breathing with whom I could have differed with more pain. I have never myself imputed to you bad motives, or spoken harshly of you, on account of that course. If any of my friends or relations have, they have done so, not only without my concurrence, but against my wishes. I know enough of the bitterness of political strife, to be sensible that private friendship should never be sacrificed on account of any difference of opinion on public affairs, if it be possible to prevent the sacrifice. I have neither felt or seen any necessity for such personal alienation in our case. As to the points of difference of opinion between us, it would be altogether useless here to enter into a discussion of them. Whilst I am ready to admit that you have pursued the path which your duty appeared to you to mark out, I claim for myself a conformity of my conduct with the most solemn dictates of a pure and disinterested patriotism.

.   .   .   .

With great regard, I remain, faithfully yours,   H. CLAY.
F. P. BLAIR, esq.

Extract in Washington *Daily Globe*, March 16, 1841. Cf. above, Blair to Clay, October 3, 1827.

Promissory Note from Clement R. Dunkin

19 Octr. 1827

One month after date I promise to pay Henry Clay or order, three dollars; being for the hire of his Negro woman Phillis for one month commencing this day—   C. R. DUNKIN

DS, in Robert Scott's hand. DLC-TJC (DNA, M212, R16). Endorsed by Scott on verso: "Phillis remained until the end of the year, being 2 Ms. 12ds.—$7— Dead and insolvent."
Dunkin, of a pioneer Lexington family, had been married in February, 1825. His death was not recorded in Fayette County documents.

From Daniel W. Lewis

Geneva[1] October 19 1827—

Mr. Clay. It is now about four years since, for reasons it would be useless to state to you, I formed the design of living in the Michigan territory. Nothing has prevented me, at any time since, but that I was too poor to live there, without immediate employment, & could not have been contented with out such employment, as, in my own belief, would have rendered me useful. Soon after you became Secretary of State, I applied to a friend—Mr. Robert S. Rose, with a request that, while at Washington, he would make to you,[2] such representations relative to my fitness for a judicial office, as he might think proper, in order that I might be considered by the administration, a candidate for the next place that should become vacant upon the bench of the Supreme Court of Michigan territory. I did not request, nor did I wish that any person, at the stated time for renewing the appointment of judges—once in four years, should be left out to make place for me. Mr. Rose, on his return home, informed me that he had made the application I requested, & told me it only be [*sic*] necessary to remind you of it, when a vacancy should occur. Mr. Rose told me that, when he made the application, you said to him "I may forget this, remind me of it by letter." I wrote also to a friend in Detroit, whom I had met with at that place, & with whom I had formerly been acquainted—a man in whom the government have [sic] placed confidence—who is well informed, & has the welfare of that country at heart, informing him of my earnest desire to live there, & requesting of him such information & advice as he might think fit to give me upon the subjects stated in my letter to him. He wrote me a plain account of the State of their judiciary, kindly offering to do any thing in his power to promote my views; conceiving them to be consonant with the advantages every portion of our common country has a right to derive from her judiciary establishments— Extracts from his letter were made, and, as Mr. Rose informed me, sent, in a letter written by him to you at Washington.— As soon as I heard of the decease of Judge Hunt,[3] I requested my friend Gen. Peter B. Porter of Buffalo to write you in my behalf, as he might think proper. He did so:[4] & to these communications I beg leave to solicit your particular attention.— I did expect the appointment, & was supported in that expectation by the opinions of those on whose judgment I have found it safe to place much reliance. A disappointment of this sort, to a man in my circumstances, & at my time of life, is no ordinary calamity: And, I hope I may say without arrogance, that I had no reason to apprehend that I should be disappointed, by the administration' [sic] filling a vacant seat, with a person[5] who, his time of life considered, could not reasonably be expected, in the usual progress of legal acquirements, to be overfurnished for the office & duties of a judge, when a time would arrive, at which, were I there, it would be right & desirable for me to retire.

Soon after the decease of Judge Hunt, a petition[6] signed by some of the most respectable inhabitants in the territory, was, without my request or knowledge, (for I had not thought of such a measure) forwarded to Washington, directed to you—Just before the appointment of Mr. Chipman was known here, I was told by a gentleman from Detroit, that my appointment was expected, & would be thought certain, but for a rule, as he expressed it, which he understood the administration had adopted, not to appoint, a person living out of the territory, to an office, provided one qualified for the office could be found in it.[7] This was the first intimation I ever had of such a rule. I think it could not have existed when Mr. Rose spoke to you on the subject, or you would have mentioned it to him, & he would have informed me of it. Now sir, if such a rule exist, it is obvious that the condition will never be wanting, for it is not supposable but that some person living in the territory can get himself respectably recommended to the administration— There are many men—respectable & worthy men, who do not see the necessity of a man's being educated a lawyer even, to qualify him for being a Judge; And (the truth of the remark is too well known to require an apology for making it) practitioners at the same bar, too often find motives, to prefer the advancement in court, of one of their own body— But I could not suppose, nor can I believe, that the administration will practise upon any rule that shall not be calculated to give the people every benefit they can possibly derive from any institution of which the management is committed to the administration. That such a rule should be adopted to avoid the trouble of choosing from an extensive field—of selecting from a large number, is not to be admitted, because it is obvious that, by thus confining their selection, they must neglect a great portion of the means in their hands, to benefit those for whose use the appointing power is entrusted to them. Nor is it to be apprehended that the principal officers of the government lack sagacity or judgment to select from an extensive field, any more than that they are too indolent to explore it.—

I am utterly at a loss for the reason of such a rule, if it exist. With regard to the present case, I believed enough had been done to shew that the welfare of the territory required the appointment of such a man as, I suppose my friends described me to be, in preference to any one residing within the territory; & I still think that, if you will recur to the extracts contained in Mr. Rose's letter, above alluded to, you will be satisfied that, the circumstance of residence, instead of affording a reason for appointing to the office of judge there, a person residing in the territory, furnishes a pretty strong objection against it.

Mr. Wing[8] the delegate from the territory, as I am informed by Mr. Rose, in a conversation between them on the subject at Washington, long before the vacancy happened, expressed himself fully in favour of appointing me a judge of their Supreme Court. Mr. Chipman, I am well informed edited & directed the paper[9] employed in support of Mr. Wing's last election. The parties are, I believe nearly balanced;

In the appointment of a judge, party, surely, should be laid out of the question; but, if the preponderance of one party be at all considered, it should not either in justice or policy, be thrown into the heavier scale. A man who had written, published, made every effort—all on one side, in a warmly contested election, would seem to a plain, honest man, to be the most unfit person for a judge among that very people, against nearly half of whom he must have acquired, if not prejudicies, certainly pretty strong feelings. The more strenuous party efforts electioneering struggles, are, with the less decency can they be rewarded by any office, especially a judicial office. I understand the administration are in the habit of allowing great weight to the opinions & representations of representatives & delegates. I am not disposed to question the propriety of this practice; When the nomination of Mr. Chipman was made, I presume the facts above stated, were not contemplated, nor known. The grounds of such a practice must surely be the fact of these men being well informed, together with the still more important fact of their being disinterested—free from every obligation except what is induced by a candid & patriotic view of their duty as representatives of the people. If the administration were known to rely upon the opinions of representatives, without regarding the circumstances under which those opinions were given, they might I think, be fairly understood to declare to every candidate for the place of representative or delegate "If you succeed in your election, you may rest assured, we will afford you the means of rewarding those to whom you may find yourself under obligation for their successful endeavours to promote it: We confine ourselves to your district in our selection of the candidate to fill any office that may become vacant in it. & we will be governed in our choice, chiefly by your recommendation; to which your place, we know will always procure you a decent, & commonly a respectable support." Permit me to look again, for a moment at the supposed rule. Here is a tract within the immediate jurisdiction of Congress not yet, nor perhaps for many years likely to become, a state, a frontier—not half peopled: needing, in its present state, the best aid in every branch of its concerns, & yet can have no choice of any of its public servants, but from among those who happen already to have become settled in their territory. When this territory was first organized appointments could not be confined to it: And while it remains such, I apprehend it will be impossible to designate the time when it may be fit so to confine them. When these people form a state, they may be supposed able to furnish the needful officers; at least, they will be at liberty to seek either at home or abroad, as they may judge most conducive to their welfare.

From some of my observations you might perhaps, infer that those in the territory who wish my appointment are, all, of the party opposed to Mr. Wing: I think it right therefore to state, that, as I am well informed, a number, perhaps one half (& they as respectable supporters as Mr. Wing had) who petitioned for my appointment, at the election of their delegate, voted for Mr. Wing—(certainly without intending thereby to make Mr. Chipman judge.)

I am unacquainted with proceedings to obtain places. It was my desire to proceed in conformity with the forms of office so far as I knew them, & I have done so. I was told by those who ought to know, that it would be improper to address the president directly—that the Secretary of State was the only proper person to be addressed: Yet, upon considering the time & circumstances of Mr. Chipman's appointment, I am led to believe it must have been made in consequence of application received by the President in your absence.[10]—

. . . .

To you sir, if I justly appreciate you, no apology can be necessary for the free & plain manner in which I address you. I owed it to myself, to my friends, &, may I be permitted to say? to the administration. You will readily believe, I do not mean to offend you, either by the matter

or in the manner of my letter. I know of no person, except yourself, to whom I am a stranger, that I could have written to, with so much freedom & confidence inspired by what I have learned of you, from some of my friends; not of your talents, but of your heart. I am sir, with very great respect, your obd't. Servt.   DANIEL W LEWIS.
Geneva Ontario County State of New York.

Some fifteen years since, I had an acquaintance of the name Daniel LeRoy, of whom, within that time I had not heard, until since the decease of Judge Hunt—When a friend from Detroit informed me that Mr LeRoy lived in the Michigan teritory, & that he voluntarily & very promptly engaged to him that he would write to Washington, recommending my appointment to the vacant seat.[11] Now sir, I desire to know whether any communication has been received at your office, directly from Mr LeRoy, or through any other person, & if so the purport of that communication. Permit me sir to request this information, & any thing more you may be kind enough to say to me, from under your own hand.   D W LEWIS—

ALS. DNA, RG59, A. and R. (M531, R5).   [1] New York.
[2] See above, Rose to Clay, June 16, 1827.   [3] John Hunt.   [4] Porter to Clay, July 3, 1827—ALS, in DLC-HC (DNA, M212, R2).   [5] Henry C. Chipman.   [6] Cooper and others to Clay, June 29, 1827—DS, in DNA, RG59, A. and R. (M531, R5).   [7] Cf. above, Clay to Brooke, November 30, 1825.   [8] Austin E. Wing.   [9] The Detroit *Michigan Herald*, of which Henry C. Chipman was one of the founders, ran from May, 1825, until April, 1829, and held a contract to publish the laws from the Second Session of the Nineteenth Congress through the remainder of the Adams administration.
[10] Cf. above, Chipman to Clay, August 3, 1827, and note. The remainder of this paragraph and the next, urging rectification of the "mistake," has been omitted by the editors.
[11] LeRoy to Clay, July 12, 1827—ALS, in DNA, RG59, A. and R. (M531, R5).

INSTRUCTIONS AND DISPATCHES   October 19, 1827

To LOUIS PAIMBOEUF, "Consul of the U States at the Island of Curacoa [*sic*]." Transmits his "Commission, together with printed Circular Instructions, and a blank Consular bond. . . ." Copy. DNA, RG59, Cons. Instr., vol. 2, p. 445 (M78, R2). Cf. above, Robinson to Clay, June 12, 1827.
    Paimboeuf, at this time a resident of New York, was a naturalized citizen of French birth. He had lived in New Orleans and had served in Louisiana volunteer units during the War of 1812. He held the consulship at Curaçao until 1833.

From A[LEXANDER] H. EVERETT, Madrid, no. 90. Transmits "the accounts furnished by the Gazette of the proceedings in Catalonia" (cf. above, Everett to Clay, September 20, 1827), where "the troubles" appear to be "subsiding." Cites a rumor that the King (Ferdinand VII) would "pass the winter" in the "neighbourhood" of Barcelona. Names, among persons arrested "on suspicion of being concerned in the insurrection," J(uan) J(osé) Marco del Pont, whose papers are said "to give a pretty complete disclosure of the origin of the troubles" and to implicate "various persons of the highest consideration, including Bishops and other Clergymen, Counsellors of State, Ministers &c. . . ." Notes, however, that no additional arrests have been made since that of Marco. States that "It is understood that the Minister [Francisco Tadeo] Calomarde and the Infante Don Carlos are committed by these discoveries; and the rumour continues to circulate that the latter will be removed from Court." Expresses doubt that "the persons implicated by the late discoveries will be very severely dealt with" and compares the disclosures with those "made at the time of the Conspiracy and revolt of [Jorge] Bessières in . . . 1825" (cf. above, Brown to Clay, August 26, September 19, 1825), which had been followed by "a change of Ministry" in favor of "the party which organized that movement" (cf. above, Everett to Clay, October 26, 1825, and note; Brown to Clay, October 30, 1825). Encloses copies of letters exchanged by the French Chargé d'Affaires (Count de Beaurepaire) and himself relative to quarantine laws. ALS. DNA, RG59, Dip. Disp., Spain, vol. 28 (M31, R29). Received December 17.

Beaurepaire informed Everett, by letter on October 11 (copy, not dated; the date is cited in Everett's reply), that, in addition to transmitting to his government Everett's note (cf. above, Everett to Clay, October 6, 1827), he "also applied to the Viscount Gudin for an explanation on the subject." Summarizes Gudin's reply, from which "it appears that the facts reported . . . by the Consul of the United States at Cadiz [Alexander Burton] are far from being correct." When acknowledging, on October 14, receipt of this communication, Everett asserted that the explanations were "in several particulars at variance with the official documents in . . . [his] possession," added that he was sending a copy of Beaurepaire's letter to the consul at Cádiz, and promised to write again upon receipt of the latter's reply.

On Marco del Pont, cf. below, Everett to Clay, this date. He has not been further identified.

From A[LEXANDER] H. EVERETT, Madrid, "Confidential No. 2." Reviews at length his conversations, which took place intermittently from "about the last of March," with a Colonel Cluet, who represented himself as a former inhabitant of Louisiana, "the proprietor" of extensive land holdings "on the south coast of" Cuba and a frequent visitor to Spain, and with (J. J.) Marco del Pont, whom Cluet introduced as "a wealthy merchant of the highest respectability and one who enjoyed in a very particular manner the confidence of the King [Ferdinand VII]. . . ." Reports that Marco "dwelt," in his first interview with Everett, "at great length upon the danger that threatened the island of Cuba in consequence of the probability of the war with G. Britain, which then appeared to be impending [cf. above, Clay to Biddle, March 13, 1827; Clay to Vives, March 14, 1827], and intimated that it would be highly agreeable to H. M. if the U. S. would guarantee the island to Spain, and that in that case a secret arrangement might be made which would secure to us commercial advantages of high importance." Adds that Marco "also enlarged repeatedly and earnestly upon the incapacity and corruption of the present Ministry. . . ." Notes that Cluet and Marco were never able to obtain authorization from the King to negotiate; admits doubt as to the real intentions of the two; and concludes that "the interviews . . . with them is [sic] not likely to produce any results of consequence. . . ." Explains that he would not have troubled Clay with this account "were it not for the confirmation it gives to the prevalent opinion respecting the origin of the insurrection." Asks that this letter be considered "as strictly confidential" and that it not be placed "upon the public files of the Department of State." LS. DNA, RG59, Dip. Disp., Spain, vol. 28 (M31, R29).

Louis Bronier Cluet [Declout], born into a wealthy Creole family in Spanish Louisiana about 1764, had been a career Spanish Army officer, rising to the rank of brigadier general. Following the American purchase of Louisiana, he had attempted to establish new Spanish colonies in remote areas of Texas and Cuba and in 1814 had proposed to Ferdinand VII the Spanish reconquest of Louisiana. Although his schemes had been discountenanced, his loyalty to the Crown had been rewarded by his appointment as Governor of the Province of Hagua, in Cuba, with the title Count de la Fernandina de Hagua. Shortly before his death in 1848, Queen Isabella named him to the Spanish Senate.

From WILLIAM SHALER, Mahón. Reports that he is "on the point of returning to Algiers" (cf. above, Shaler to Clay, December 1, 1826); that, though his "health is somewhat improved since the return of cool weather," he is "ill, unfit for business and compelled to the daily use of opium." States that he has not received a reply to his request for a leave of absence (above, May 14, 1827) "and as the war continues between France and Algiers [cf. above, Brown to Clay, May 29, June 9, 1827; Hodgson to Clay, June 27, 1827], the consequent blockade of the latter, will prevent all expectation of receiving it in time to be governed by it." Believing that the "President will not hesitate to grant so reasonable a prayer" and that remaining in Algiers another year would cause his life to "fall a sacrifice without an object," he expresses the intention to return to the United States the following April. ALS. DNA, RG59, Cons. Disp., Algiers, vol. 1 (M23, R-T13). Received December 20.

MISCELLANEOUS LETTERS   October 19, 1827

To WILLIAM PLUMER, JR., Epping, New Hampshire. Informs Plumer that the President has appointed him United States attorney for the District of New Hampshire and forwards his commission. Copy. DNA, RG59, Dom. Letters, vol. 22, p. 65 (M40, R20).
   Plumer declined the appointment. Cf. below, Clay to Christie, April 28, 1828.

Check to "A. B."

20h Oct 1827

No.   OFFICE OF DISCOUNT & DEPOSIT, Washington,
   PAY to A. B. *or bearer,* Twenty five *Dollars,* /100
$25 DOLLARS, /100   H. CLAY

   ADS, partially printed. DLC-TJC (DNA, M212, R16). A. B. has not been identified.

To John F. Henry

My dear Sir   Washn. 20h. Oct. 1827.
   I recd. your favor of the 15h. Ulto.[1] which reached this place during my temporary absence from it. I regretted your defeat very much. Indeed I have hardly yet recovered from the mortification which I felt on account of late events in K.[2] I lamented the disagreement between Col New[3] and yourself and feared its consequences. I hope it will have the effect of leading to more union and co-operation hereafter. It appears to me that, as the other side is so completely organized, unless we imitate in that respect their example our cause will be in danger in Kentucky. Concert on one side and disunion on the other is always likely to be attended with an effect similar to that of your late election.
   I observe what you say respecting Reynolds.[4] There is no better fel-

low nor any that I would take more pleasure in serving on a proper occasion. The vacancy has not yet occurred in the office to which he refers, and the competition for it, among some of the first members of the Bar in Tennessee is very great.[5]

You will have seen that our cause has triumphed in Maryland, Delaware, New Jersey, Philada. and some other parts of Pennsa.[6] I do believe, if it had not been for the issue of some of the K. elections, the Jackson cause would now have been at an end. It has recd a check, on this side of the mountains, from which I think it will not recover. I do not despair of Virginia.[7] And I hope that in August & Novr. of the next year[8] we shall recover the ground we lost in K. in the August of this year.

I have seen your brother[9] but once, owing to my absence from the City since his arrival here, but I hope to see him again before his departure. I am Yr's faithfy & Cordially   H CLAY
Dr Jno. F. Henry.

P.S.   Be pleased to make my respects to Capt. Hawkins[10] & Young Ewing Esqr   H C.

ALS. Owned by William P. Foster, Portland, Oregon.   1 Not found.
2 See above, Clay to Adams, August 25, 1827.   3 Richard B. New. Cf. above, Johnson to Clay, April 29, 1827, note.   4 Probably James B. Reynolds.   5 Cf. above, Williams to Clay, August 23, 1827; Lea to Clay, October 13, 1827.   6 For the results of the Maryland election, cf. above, Clay to Blunt, September 11, 1827, note; for Delaware, Clay to Taylor, September 7, 1827, note; for Philadelphia, Sergeant to Clay, September 11, 1827, note; Johnston to Clay, ca. September 13, 1827, note; for other parts of Pennsylvania, Sergeant to Clay, October 14, 1827, note. The elections in New Jersey resulted in administration victories for both houses of the legislature. The Trenton *True American* estimated that there would be a majority "of 17 at least in Joint meeting." Quoted in Washington *Daily National Intelligencer*, October 17, 1827.   7 Cf. above, Caldwell to Clay, August 8, 1827, and note.   8 In August, 1828, pro-administration candidate Thomas Metcalfe defeated William T. Barry for Governor by a vote of 38,940 to 38,231; for the November election, cf. above, Clay to Brown, March 27, 1827, note.
9 Gustavus A. Henry.   10 Probably John Hawkins, who was active at various times in the affairs of Transylvania University, the Lexington Light Infantry, and Kentucky Freemasonry.

From James Davidson (1)

Frankfort [ca.] October [20] 1827
Sir   I have taken the liberty of enclosing[1] to you the substance of a conversation which I had with you in the fall of 1824 on the subject of the then presidential election. You will no doubt find many imperfections both in the style as well as in the orthography, but in the correctness of the expression used by each of us I am confident there is no material variance; indeed I think I have employd [sic] the precise words. I have been induced to enclose it to you from various considerations, but more especialy [sic] on account of a misconception of a portion of a newly organised set of politicians who either do, or effect to believe you had not made up your oppinion [sic] in relation to

Genl Jackson prior to your leaving Ky.[2] It is certainly true that a large majourity [*sic*] of the legislature of 1824 did not expect you to suport [*sic*] the Genl. but some (as I thot.) from envy and others from an expectation to promote their own popularity and some wishd [*sic*] an occasion to abuse you, and as some said set a trap for you, these and other means were used to get a majourity to pass the resolutions[3] and I may add some were honestly in favour of the "hero". I have no recolection [*sic*] of your having said you would suport Mr. Adams: but I did infer you would   the conversation led to that inference   I commenced the conversation in Jocular way, that you might answer it in that way or not   you however answered me ernestly [*sic*] and with a freedom which has always been characteristic of your political course. although nothing was said as to its being confidential. yet I so considered it as I do all such comunications [*sic*] and I believe to Mr George Robertson the communication was first made but I thought it necessary at that time to assure my friends that you could not nor would not suport Genl Jackson and that the only effect of [*sic*] the resolutions would have [*sic*] would be, to give your enemies a pretext to assail you an advantage I did not wish them to get. I will close this desultory letter by saying we are all active and I think our efforts will be successful. your [*sic*] with essteem [*sic*]   JAMES DAVIDSON
H Clay Esqre.

ALS. DLC-HC (DNA, M212, R3). Cf. above, Clay to Davidson, September 24, 1827.
1 Below, Davidson to Clay, this date.   2 Cf. above, Clay to Sloane, May 20, 1827.
3 Cf. above, III, 902.

From James Davidson (2)

Sir,   Frankfort, 20th October, 1827.
During a visit you made to this place, in the fall of 1824, and I think, only a few days prior to your leaving Kentucky to attend the Congress of the United States, you and myself were in conversation about the then pending presidential election; in the course of which I remarked "Mr Clay, you will have to encounter some difficulty in making a selection amongst the candidates, should you be excluded from the house". You replied "I supose [*sic*] not much; in that event, I will endeavour to do my duty faithfully." I then observed, "I know you have objections to Genl. Jackson, and rumor says you have some to Mr Adams also, and the health of Mr Crawford is said to be very precarious. these are the reasons which induced me to supose there would be some difficulty." You in reply remarked, "I cannot conceive of any event that can possibly happen which could induce me to suport [*sic*] the election of Genl Jackson to the presidency. For if I had no other objection, his want of the necessary qualifications would be sufficient." Your remarks made a strong and lasting impression on my mind; and when the resolutions instructing our senators and requesting our rep-

resentatives in Congress to vote for Genl Jackson were under discussion in the House of Representatives, I informd several of my friends, that I had had a conversation with you on the subject to which the resolutions refer'd, and that I was convinced you would not suport the Genl; and to George Robertson Esqr (late speaker of the H R of this state) I gave the substance of your remarks to me, and he concured [sic] with me in the oppinion [sic] that you could not consistently, under any circumstances, vote for the Genl. and when the resolutions above mentioned were before the Senate (in which I then had the honor of a seat) I opposed them, and amongst other views I then took, I stated to that body "that all the resolutions we could pass during the whole session would not induce you to abandon wha[t] you conceived to be your duty, and that I knew you could not con[cur] with the majourity [sic] of the Legislature on that subject. Yours Respectfully
H Clay Esqr   JAMES DAVIDSON

ALS. DLC-HC (DNA, M212, R2). Published in "Appendix" of Clay's *Address . . . to the Public* (see below, December 29, 1827), p. 50. Cf. above, Davidson to Clay, this date.

INSTRUCTIONS AND DISPATCHES   October 20, 1827

From FRANKLIN LITCHFIELD. See undated letter, below, November 1, 1827.

MISCELLANEOUS LETTERS   October 20, 1827

"To His Excellency W. B. Giles, Richmond. Va." Acknowledges receipt of his letter of October 17. States that a search "in the Library attached to . . . [the State] Department" was unsuccessful, and adds: "Thinking it probable; that they might be among the books transferred by Mr. [Thomas] Jefferson to Congress, I directed a search to be accordingly made in the public Library at the Capitol, and I am happy to inform you that it was attended with success. The President directed the Librarian of Congress [George Watterston] to place them under my direction, and I now have the pleasure to transmit them herewith, bound up with some other Journals, from which they cannot be conveniently separated." Asks that they be returned, and appends a list. Copy. DNA, RG59, Dom. Letters, vol. 22, p. 66 (M40, R20).   For Jefferson's role in establishing the Library of Congress, see Bernard Mayo (ed.), *Jefferson Himself, the Personal Narrative of a Many-Sided American* (Boston, 1942), 310–11.

From W[ESTON] F. BIRCH, Mount Sterling (Kentucky). States that he is "a candidate for publisher of the Laws in Kentucky"; that he is induced by friends, including (David) Trimble and Chilton Allan, "a relation," to make this application; that he is "situated about the centre of the District"; and that his "subscription is large; and rapidly increasing. . . ." Continues: "It is presumable that the [Lexington *Kentucky*] Gazette, will be no longer continued, as its subscription is on the wane, and influence entirely gone; being conducted by a young man [Albert G. Meriwether] devoid of character and literary attainments [cf. above, Bradford to Clay, August 11, 1827, and note]. Before I could be induced to make this application, I was informed that to appoint Mr. [Thomas] Smith would be impolitic, as he was your relative [cf. above, I, 850–51; Scott to Clay, November 21, 1826, note], and would make a serious impression upon the Kentucky election, as it hangs upon a hair.

"The Georgetown Sentinel, Maysville Eagle, and [Paris] Western Citizen are respectable papers, but are thought to circulate too much in conjunction with the [Frankfort] Commentator, in the rich counties along the state road [the Maysville Road]; this fact I am personally acquainted with, and has stimulated me to lay before you my claim."

Notes that he will "continue to forward" his paper to Clay, who "can gather its political character." ALS. DNA, RG59, P. and D. of L.

Birch had edited in 1826 the *Cynthiana Advertiser* (Kentucky), a journal which was continued at least until February, 1827. He had married Harriet Ann Campbell, of Mount Sterling, in September, 1826, and for a time published a journal at that town called *The Western Beacon* (no copy found). Richard Reid, *Historical Sketches of Montgomery County* (Lexington, Ky., 1926), 23. Neither journal received the contract, which during both Sessions of the Twentieth Congress, was shifted from the Lexington *Kentucky Gazette* to the Louisville *Focus*, edited by William W. Worsley.

The Georgetown *Kentucky Sentinel* has been found in 1832; no other copy has been located. The Paris *Western Citizen*, continued under that title until 1886 and as the *Kentuckian-Citizen* until 1966, had been established in 1808.

The powers of the Maysville and Lexington Turnpike Company as originally chartered (see above, II, 569n) having lapsed because of non-compliance with the terms of its organization, a second company of that name had been incorporated by act of January 22, 1827. Ky. Gen. Assy., *Acts, 1826–1827*, ch. 74, pp. 81–95. Under both incorporations the State had been authorized to subscribe for stock, in the latter case, 1,000 shares.

From Samuel Mifflin

Dr S,   Phila October 21. 1827

The returns of the Elections in this State will exhibit a result very unexpected by our opponents & gratifying to the friends of the Administration, as certainly 12 months ago, the friends of the General claimed with some foundation the entire vote of the State in their favor—

It is true they now venture to make the same claim, but it is made in the voice of almost dispair [*sic*], as they cannot deny that unexpected & great changes have taken place against them— Witness Franklin Lebanon—Montgomery & Lancaster Counties[1]— In the latter, I could not in May or June last discover an individual who would venture an opinion in support of the Ad. & certainly we may now claim two if not three of the Representatives from that County. I have been informed by a Gentleman from Northumberland, that, that County, Columbia, Lycoming, Lucerne Susquehanna, Bradford & Tioga *together* would give us an [*sic*] majority.[2]

I have always considered however that the great effort should be made to place the matter fairly before the Germans for upon their vote must the decision of the contest depend— The changes which have already taken place among those people give us the strongest hopes of success & the steps now taking in Berks County present the most flattering prospects—

At the suggestion of Mr. Getz, of the Berks & Schuylkill Journal,[3] we have supplied him, with German type & he intends, to publish in his paper & in a Pamphlet (probably) from the Virginia letters[4] & such other leading matter as will bear favorably on our Cause— He writes me under date the 12h.

"We have concluded to hold an Ad. meeting on Tuesday 6 Novr (2d Court day) & from the Zeal already manifested it will be perhaps one of the largest meetings ever held on a similar occasion— Two of the Jackson Delegates have declined serving[5]— Our idea is to support thorough going Demos. I am daily importuned about the Virginia letters & the type arriving, I will make a demonstration by the by["]

Mr. Getz is a Gentleman of great respectability & possibly a warm supporter of the Gen. whose cause his judgment now forbids him to promote— Rely upon it we have the best hopes of securing the votes of this State & as I consider, the cause a most holy one, in which the honor & I believe the safety of my Country is involved—no effort shall be spared on my part to secure our success— With great respect, I remain Your friend & obt. Sert   SAML. MIFFLIN
Henry Clay Esq Washington

Can you favor me with a copy of the report of our foreign claims. made during the last Session[6]

ALS. DLC-HC (DNA, M212, R2). Addressed: "Private."
[1] Cf. above, Sergeant to Clay, October 14, 1827, and note.   [2] Susquehanna and Luzerne Counties had elected three administration candidates to the State Assembly. Philadelphia *United States Gazette*, October 19, 20, 1827. Political affiliations have not been identified for those elected in the other cited counties. On November 1, 1827, the Washington *Daily National Journal* claimed an increase of 20 to 30,000 votes for Adams supporters over the returns at the previous election.   [3] George Getz, born in Lancaster, Pennsylvania, in 1789, a naval veteran of the War of 1812, had founded the Reading *Berks and Schuylkill Journal* in 1816 and continued as its editor and publisher until 1832. The financially troubled weekly strongly supported Adams in 1828 and opposed Jackson so long as Getz was the proprietor. Following his sale of the paper in December, 1832, Getz became a bookseller in Reading and later, 1849–1853, mayor of that town. Marshall Selikoff, "The Editorial Policies of George Getz," *Berks County Historical Review*, V (1939), 7–13.   [4] A letter from James Madison to Joseph C. Cabell, March 22, 1827, in supportive response to Cabell to Madison, March 12, 1827, had declared the tariff resolutions, recently adopted by the Virginia General Assembly (see above, Brooke to Clay, January 31, 1827, and note) "extreme" and "deeply to be regretted," "a ground which cannot be maintained, on which the State will probably stand alone, and which by lessening the confidence of other States in the wisdom of its Councils, must impede the progress of its sounder doctrines." Madison had then pointed to the precedents in the United States, as well as "every existing Commercial Nation," for the use of governmental power" in the form of a tariff to the encouraging of particular domestic occupations" and noted that "The inefficacy of the power in relation to manufactures as well as to other objects, when exercised by the State separately, was among the arguments and inducements for revising the Old Confederation. . . ." Continuing, he argued that "A Construction of the Constitution practised upon or acknowledged for a period, of nearly forty years, has received a national sanction not to be reversed, but by an evidence at least equivalent to the National will." He conceded that a "Tariff for the encouragement of Manufactures may be abused by its excess, by its partiality, or by a noxious selection of its objects" and suggested that this "distinction" might "be a key to the language of Mr J[efferso]n, in the letter . . . alluded to" (probably the recently published correspondence with Giles, noted above, Johnston to Clay, September 14, 1827). In Madison's view such abuse "cannot be regarded as a breach of the fundamental compact, till it reaches a degree of oppression, so iniquitous and intolerable as to justify civil war, or

disunion. . . ." Gaillard Hunt (ed.), *The Writings of James Madison* (9 vols.; New York, 1900–1910), IX, 284–87. In a subsequent letter on the subject, addressed to the editors of the Lynchburg *Virginian* (Elijah Fletcher and Richard Henry Toler), October 10, 1827, Madison had reiterated these views while protesting against the journalists' inaccuracy in summarizing his remarks and, particularly, against their implication that he had alluded "by name to the governor of the state. . . ." Reprinted from the Lynchburg *Virginian* in *Niles' Weekly Register*, XXXIII (October 27, 1827), 135.   5 The meeting, held in Reading courthouse on Tuesday, November 6, drew some 250 Adams partisans. A Jackson meeting, held the following day in the same building, resulted in a dispute which threatened to disrupt the assembly. Philadelphia *United States Gazette*, November 12, 1827.   6 Cf. above, Clay to Holmes, January 22, 1827.

INSTRUCTIONS AND DISPATCHES   October 21, 1827

From Christopher Hughes, The Hague. Reports that he asked the Minister of Foreign Affairs (Baron Verstolk Van Soelen), "yesterday," whether "the instructions that young Mr. [Roger Bangeman] Huygens, (who is about to return to America) would take to His Majesty's Minister, at Washington [C. D. E. J. Bangeman Huygens], would be of a nature, to meet the just expectations of the President by restoring and establishing that perfect equality, in the treatment of American and Dutch vessels, and their cargoes, in the Ports of the Netherlands, which . . . [the United States] Government had considered to be the well-understood basis of our commercial intercourse; which had been invariably observed on our side; and which had been infringed here, by the return of 10. per. Ct., on the duties, to Dutch owners." Gives the substance of Verstolk's reply, in which he stated that "the grounds taken by His Majesty's Minister, in his correspondence with" Clay (above, Clay to Huygens, December 10, 1825; October 25, 1826; Huygens to Clay, September 15, November 11, 1826), "were perfectly satisfactory to this Government"; explained the Dutch view of the points at issue; and "made several observations . . . upon the grave inequality in the Tariffs of the two Nations; an inequality that has, according to his view, driven the Dutch Shipping out of our Ports. . . ." Points out that "This present despatch will confirm . . . [his] previous reports on the above subject [above, July 11 ("Private"), August 12, 1826; January 21 ("Private"), April 15, June, 12, 1827]. . . ." ALS. DNA, RG59, Dip. Disp., Netherlands, vol. 8 (M42, R12). Received December 11.

Order on Washington Branch, Bank of the United States

No.   OFFICE OF DISCOUNT & DEPOSIT,⎫
                        Washington,   ⎬
                                                            22d. Oct 1827
    PAY to Check on Philada *or bearer*, fourteen *Dollars*, 50/100
14 dollars, 50/100   H Clay

ADS, partially printed. DLC-TJC (DNA, M212, R16). Cf. above, Bill from Lemuel Franklin, September 27, 1827.

To Thomas H. Gilliss

Washington, D.C. 22 October 1827.
    Mr Clay presents his respects to Mr Gilliss, and encloses him a check[1] for $16 12/100, the amount of Mr. Clay's pew rent, &c. in Saint John's Church for the quarter ending on the 30th September last.—

N. DLC-HC (DNA, M212, R3). Endorsed by "T. H. Gilliss" on October 22: "Received the above mentioned Check...."
  1 Drawn on the Office of Discount & Deposit, Washington, D. C., October 22, 1827. ADS, partially printed, in DLC-TJC (DNA, M212, R16).

From George McClure

Confidential   [October 22, 1827]
  I find that since the publication of your corraspondance [*sic*] with your Western friend[1] whose name I do not recollect at present that there are many who had doubts of the purity of your motives in giving Adams the preference, are now sattisfied [*sic*] that your mind had been made up on that subject, long before the final question was agitated,— I have stated the same fact, that as early as november 1824, that you had unequivocally stated that if the contest should be reduced to Adams and Jackson, you had no hesitation in giving Adams the preference,
  What I would now beg leave to sugest [*sic*] for your consideration is, the propriety of addressing me a letter on that subject, of the date of November 1824 about the time we met to choose Electors, and after your return to Washington, it might be so worded as to be in answer to my inquiries on that head, which with your liberty I would pubish [*sic*]. It would be a knock down argument against your bitter Enemies. It is at you the fatal blow is aimed, and not Mr. Adams,   if they succeed against you, they well know that Adams will inevitably fall with you. He would become an easy prey, and could not stand a moment.—
  I trust that you will not be offended at my sugestions, whether you approve or disapprove of them, when I assure you, that I am actuated through motives of friendship, a friendship Sir, that cannot easily be shaken,— Should you think proper to make the communication it shall be sacred,— It would be well to suspend any communication to me until you hear of my return to this place, of which I will duly apprise you,
Yours—   G. Mc. C.—

ALI. DLC-HC (DNA, M212, R3). Addressed to Clay; dated by postmark. Endorsed by Clay on cover: "I was shocked by the proposal in the letter—   I need not say that it was impossible to comply with it."
  1 Probably Daniel Drake. Cf. above, Address, March 26, 1825 (IV, 144). On October 6, 1827, the Washington *Daily National Intelligencer* had republished a letter, which it had first printed April 4, 1825, in which Drake on March 21, 1825, had reported to the editors, Joseph Gales, Jr., and William W. Seaton, that Clay in mid-November, 1824, on the day before he had left Lexington to return to Congress, had asserted "that nothing should deter him from the duty of giving his vote, and that no state of things could arise that would justify him in preferring General Jackson to Mr. Adams, or induce him to support the former."

INSTRUCTIONS AND DISPATCHES   October 22, 1827

From W[ILLIAM] B[EACH] LAWRENCE, London, no. 3. Comments on the uncertainty of settlement of "the affairs of Greece" and "The affairs of Spain. . . ." Reports, in regard to the latter: ". . . it has been intimated to me from a highly respectable source, that the repeated conferences of Mr. Roth with the Foreign Secretary [Lord Dudley], to which I alluded last week [above, October 13] and which still continue, have reference to an arrangement for the mutual withdrawal by France and England of their troops from Spain and Portugal." Notes the credence given to "The intelligence of renewed negotiations between Brazil and Buenos Ayres" and represents "The Chargé d'Affaires of the latter power" (Juan Francisco Gil) as having informed him "that there would be no difficulty on the part of his country in effecting an arrangement founded on the independence of the disputed territory [Banda Oriental], though he conceived the treaty entered into by [Manuel José] Garcia in the highest degree disgraceful & that even a cession of the Banda Oriental to Spain itself would accord better with the feelings of his fellow citizens than its incorporation with the Brazilian Empire" (cf. above, Forbes to Clay, June 29, 1827; Wright to Clay, August 10, 1827; and below, Tudor to Clay, August 27, 1828, and note). Adds that "He [Gil] regarded the report of the contemplated guaranty of the independence of the new State by Great Britain not entitled to belief." Summarizes a conversation with Lord Dudley, who "took occasion to express himself in high terms of Mr. [Albert] Gallatin and particularly of his last note on the West India question [cf. above, Gallatin to Clay, June 4, 1827], which, he said, contained a most able argument." Notes that, a few days later, "Mr. [John] Backhouse, Under Secretary of State," brought up "the same subject, which, he said, seemed to excite much discussion in America," and cited a lengthy article "in a late number of the American Quarterly Review . . ." (cf. above, Clay to Carey and Lea, December 29, 1826, note). Observes that "It is perfectly clear that the decision of this Government was definitely made before the last note was addressed to Mr. Gallatin [cf. above, Gallatin to Clay, October 3, 1827], and that it will not, probably, be changed for some time to come." Explains that he "only alluded to this topick, in consequence of the remarks of Mr. Backhouse, which go to prove that the Administration here is alive to the public opinion in America in relation to the West India question. . . ." ALS. DNA, RG59, Dip. Disp., Great Britain, vol. 35 (M30, R31). Received December 3.

Gil, Argentine journalist and politician, had been made Secretary of Legation in London in 1826 and, upon the return home of Manuel de Sarratea later in that year, had become Chargé.

MISCELLANEOUS LETTERS   October 22, 1827

From JESSE D. ELLIOTT, Carlisle (Pennsylvania). Reports having observed in the Washington *National Journal* of October 17 a republication of an article from the *Boston Daily Advertiser* (October 12, 1827) which discussed the capture of the American brig *Nile* (cf. above, J. and T. H. Perkins to Clay, October 15, 1827). States: "There never had been a distinct and decided understanding between our resident Diplomatic Agent [Condy Raguet] and the court of Brazile [sic], other than that implyed [sic] in the acquiescence of His Exelency [sic] Vice Admiral [Rodrigo José Ferreira] Lobo . . . of the exact rule which should apply in the seizure of our commercial Vessels—"

Reports that while the Empress (Maria Leopoldina) lay dying (cf. above, Raguet to Clay, December 4, 1826), (James) Biddle had expected a revolution and consequently remained at Rio de Janeiro and ordered Elliott to Montevideo; that while there he (Elliott) "had opened a pretty fair understanding with the Marquis of Paranagua, Minister of Marine, as also with the Marquis of Queluz. . ."; that the former had asked him directly what would be the decision "of our Government in the event of their judging our Merchant Vessels under the European principles of Blockade"; and that he had replied that he could give no precise answer but that "the grounds taken and already maintained in the correspondance [*sic*] previously conducted with Vice Admiral Lobo had been in unison with the feelings of our government ever since its establishment and that such were the views of the President of the U. States. . . ." Paranaguá then had declared "that these views should prevail, and that orders to that effect should be dispatched to Vice Admiral [Rodrigo] Pinto [Guedes] then in command of forces at the La Plata. . . ." Notes that upon his arrival (at Montevideo) he had "found two Vessels under seizure," both of which had been released after he "opened a correspondence with Admiral Pinto. . . ." Expresses confidence that he can conclude an "advantageous treaty" with Brazil if Biddle is relieved in the spring, at the end of the term of enlistment for his men, and states: ". . . indeed I was requested to say to our government that Brazil was both anxius [*sic*] and ready to conclude a Treaty with us. . . ." ALS. DLC-HC (DNA, M212, R3).

The newspaper article to which Elliott alludes describes the capture of the *Nile* as a "case of aggression" and contrary to "an understanding . . . established between the Brazilian Government and Capt. Biddle, our representative in the La Plata, that American vessels bound to Buenos Ayres, should not be considered as liable to arrest, unless being warned off and their papers endorsed they should attempt a second time to enter the blockaded port."

Biddle was placed in command of the Mediterranean Squadron in 1830, after a year's leave from duty. Elliott, however, was assigned to shore service in 1829 and then to command of the West India, not the Brazilian, Squadron from 1830 to 1832. On the opening of negotiations for a treaty with Brazil, cf. below, Clay to Tudor, March 29, 1828.

From CHARLES J. INGERSOLL, Philadelphia. Acknowledges receipt of Clay's letter of October 17 and states: ". . . I have no official means of ascertaining the facts on which my [o]pinions and proceedings must be founded." Requests "to be more particularly . . . acquainted with the precise state of the case as respects the ownership, armaments, flag, crew[,] and belligerent force of the Vessel [*Kensington*], together with your judgments on the application of the law to such circumstances—" ALS. DNA, RG59, Misc. Letters (M179, R65).

To William Tudor

No. 1   William Tudor Esq.   Appointed Chargé des Affaires
of U.S. to the Emperor of the Brazils.
Sir: Department of State, Washington, D.C. 23 Oct. 1827.

On the 29th of June last, a letter was addressed to you, at Lima, from this Department, acquainting you with your appointment by the President, of Chargé des Affaires at Rio de Janeiro, transmitting a commission for you in that character, and requesting you to repair to Rio de Janeiro as soon as convenient.[1] You were also informed, by the same letter, that instructions would be forwarded to you upon my return to this city. Presuming that you have received that letter, and hoping that you have consented to accept the appointment thus conferred, and accordingly proceeded to the place of your destination, I shall now, by direction of the President, communicate to you the instructions which were promised in the above letter.

Our commercial relations and intercourse with the Brazils are very important. They have been constantly increasing, and are susceptible of much greater extension. It is desirable, for the interest of both parties, that a good understanding between them should be cultivated and maintained. During almost the whole period of the mission of your predecessor, causes of complaint and irritation were constantly arising, until he finally thought himself justified to demand his passports and return to the United States.[2] The immediate occasion of that step was the wrongful seizure of the Brig Sparks [*sic*], under circumstances of a highly aggravating character. After Mr Raguet had decided to return to the United States, and obtained his passports, instructions were transmitted by the Government of the Brazils to Mr Rebello, its Chargé des Affaires near this Government, and in consequence of them, a correspondence was opened between him and this Department, of which a copy has been already transmitted to you.[3] [Quotes from Rebello's notes of May 30 and June 1, 1827, and from Clay's replies, of May 31 and June 2.][4]

From the preceding review of the correspondence between Mr Rebello and myself, you will perceive that the appointment of a successor to Mr Raguet is asked for the purpose of enabling the Government of the Brazils to make, at Rio de Janeiro, arrangements for indemnity due to the citizens of the United States for the wrongs they have suffered, and the President consents to the appointment of a successor of Mr Raguet upon the express condition that, upon his arrival at Rio de Janeiro "a full and adequate indemnity will be promptly made for *any* injuries which have been committed upon the persons or property of citizens of the United States, in violation of the public law, under color of authority derived from his Imperial Majesty, the Emperor of Brazil." The engagement on the part of the Brazilian Government which that correspondence imports, to afford indemnity, is full, clear, and explicit. It could not rest upon a more solid basis of honor and good faith if it had been thrown into the shape of a solemn convention. The President, therefore, cannot, and does not, doubt, that you will be able to procure a prompt compliance with it. The only questions which it leaves open for settlement, are, First, the instances in which the public law has been violated to the prejudice of the persons or property of our citizens; and, Secondly, the just amount of indemnity which is due in consequence of such violation.

I transmit you, herewith, a full copy of all the correspondence which has passed between Mr Raguet and the Government of Brazil, which will put you in possession of the principal part, if not all of the claims of our citizens. These claims originate chiefly from groundless allegations of breach of blockade, instituted by the Government of Brazil and from injuries committed by the public vessels and cruisers of that Government. The principles of the law of blockade, invariably contended for by the United States, are discussed in the course of that correspondence, and appear to be substantially admitted by the Government of Brazil. According to those principles no place can be considered as lawfully besieged or blockaded, which is not invested by a competent belligerent force, capable of preventing the entry of a neutral; and such neutral cannot be lawfully captured without having been notified of the existence of the blockade; and, if he attempt to enter the blockaded port, being warned off. The first case which occurred was that of the Spermo. [Recounts details of this seizure.][5] The seizure of that vessel was in manifest violation of the law of nations; and the owners[6] are entitled not only to have their bond cancelled, but to full damages for the injury which they have sustained. You will require payment of damages, as well in the case of that vessel as in all other instances of the infraction of the law of nations to the prejudice of our citizens, which the correspondence of Mr Raguet discloses, or of which you shall receive other satisfactory information, either from this Department, or from the parties aggrieved. And you will, also, in all such cases, where bonds have been taken to await the final decision, require their surrender, to be cancelled.

Among the instances of aggression detailed in the correspondence of Mr Raguet, the case of the Brig Ruth, of Philadelphia, and her crew, is marked with peculiar circumstances of aggravation. . . .[7] The case of this vessel should also command your especial attention, as amongst those which are entitled to full indemnity.

The case of the Brig Sparks[8] will receive your particular attention, as having been that which occasioned the return of Mr Raguet, and was the immediate cause of the engagement, which was made by Mr Rebello, with me at this place. That Brig arrived at Rio Janeiro [sic] in March last, having cleared out from the port of New York. She had formerly been in the public service of the United States, but was sold, and purchased by J. H. Clark,[9] an American Citizen; and she sailed to South America with a short crew and several guns on board, but not mounted for action. She was probably intended to be sold, and in pursuit of a market. On her arrival at Rio, she was regularly entered, and conformed to all the local laws. There does not appear to have been any concealment in the conduct of her owner or commander, as to their designs, or her destination. A sale of her was actually offered to the Brazilian Government, and a negotiation took place about the terms of purchase. The parties not being able to agree upon them, an offer was made by the Brazilian Government to purchase her guns, the acceptance of which was declined. The commander of the vessel then determined to proceed to Monte Video, and the crew of the vessel having been found, on the voyage from New York, to be incompetent to man her, an addition of American sailors was made to it, in the port of Rio. The vessel then regularly cleared out at the Customhouse, without any objection being made as to the conduct of her owner or commander, or any suspicions being expressed as to the object of her destination. After she had actually got out of the harbour, she was forcibly seized by a public vessel of the Government of Brazil, taken possession of, brought back into the port, and her crew and cargo treated with great outrage and wanton violence. This aggression appears to have taken place upon the assumed ground that the vessel was piratical, and that she was designed to cruize against the subjects of the Emperor of Brazil. There does not appear to have been the slightest color for these imputations. It was, also, alleged against her, that she had on board more guns than appeared in her manifest, and that she had increased her crew at Rio. As to the first allegation, it appears that the number of guns beyond what was mentioned in the manifest, were immediately landed when the objection was first made, and before the vessel cleared out. The fact, at any rate, could only be regarded as a violation of the laws of the United States, and conferred no right upon the Government of Brazil to seize or condemn the vessel. As to the augmentation of the crew, that was a matter which belonged exclusively to the owner or commander of the vessel, with which no foreign Government had a right to interfere. That there was no design to employ the vessel in hostilities against the commerce of Brazil was manifest from the offer to sell her to that Government, and from the open and undisguised conduct of her commander[10] throughout. If there had been any ground for the seizure of the vessel, she ought to have been detained whilst she was yet in port, and not suffered to leave it with a regular clearance. The seizure of her, with a number of passengers on board, (a circumstance which indicated that there could have been no design to employ her in warfare,) was made in the most aggravating manner, and justifies the conclusion, that it was intended to acquire by force what could not be obtained by purchase. After the vessel was brought back into port, some of her crew were confined and treated with great cruelty, and she was abandoned by her commander to the Government of Brazil. Sensible of the injustice which had been done, an offer was made to pay for the vessel; but as the parties could not agree as to the terms or mode of payment, the commander of the vessel left her at Rio de Janeiro, and returned to the United States without obtaining any satisfaction. I transmit you, herewith, all the papers[11] received from the owner of the vessel, relating to this transaction. You will be able to ascertain, on the spot, the truth of a statement which has been made here, that the vessel has been taken into the service of the Emperor.[12] Whether that be true or not, the owner has a perfect right to full indemnity. The amount which he claims for the vessel and cargo is $30,000, and $5,000 for damages. From the means of judging of this demand which we possess, the amount does not appear unreasonable. But if it should be found practicable to obtain satisfaction without the formality of a convention, it will deserve consideration whether a somewhat less amount of indemnity ought to be refused. On that subject you will confer, if necessary, with the owner or his agent, who will be best able to decide whether a present and certain satisfaction is not better than one which is remote, uncertain, and contingent.

There are several modes according to which the citizens of the United States, who have suffered wrongs under color of authority from the Brazilian Government, in violation of the public law, may receive the indemnity to which they are entitled, in conformity with the assurances contained in Mr Rebello's letters. The most direct and least expensive mode would be that of the Brazilian Government voluntarily rendering justice itself in each individual case. You are authorized to suggest that course; and, if it should be adopted, you will afford to the respective claimants any official assistance in your power. In cases where the parties may differ about the quantum of indemnity, it will be easy to fix the amount by amicable arrangements, and by appeals to the judgment of impartial men.

Another, and the simplest mode, would be by a Convention in which the Government of Brazil should stipulate to pay a gross sum, in full satisfaction of all claims of American citizens; which sum should be subsequently distributed amongst them under the direction of the American Government. The only difficulty which is perceived in adopting this mode, is that of arriving at an amount which would do justice to all parties. The data in the possession of this Department do not admit of the ascertainment of that amount. Perhaps you will be able, from the documents now transmitted to you, and from such other information as you may have it in your power to acquire from the parties themselves, or their agents, to fix on a proper sum. In that case you are authorized to conclude a convention stipulating its payment on the part of the Brazilian Government. But it may happen that you will neither be able to satisfy yourself on that subject, nor to agree with the Brazilian Government on the principles which should regulate the claims for indemnity. In that contingency the only remaining mode of settlement which presents itself, is that of concluding a Convention by which a commission shall be instituted for the purpose of deciding the claims to indemnity. You are authorized to conclude such a convention, if, under all the circumstances of the negotiation with which you are charged, it shall appear the most expedient. A model for the appointment and organization of such a commission, which you may safely follow, is to be found in the Sixth and Seventh articles of the treaty with Great Britain, in 1794;[13] except that, instead of the commission being composed of five persons, as is provided for in those articles, it would be best that it should consist of only three. And you may follow, in describing the instances in which indemnity is to be made, the language of the before mentioned correspondence with Mr Rebello. The place of the meeting of the commission may be fixed at Rio; and a reasonable time may be limited, within which the claimants must present their demands for indemnity before the Board. A full power authorizing you to conclude a convention in either of the two modes which have been suggested, is herewith transmitted.[14] Should you conclude a convention, it will be executed in duplicate, and you will recollect, that in the counterpart which is transmitted to this Government, the United States must be first named, and your signature first placed to the convention, according to established usage. In that which shall be retained by the Brazilian Government the opposite course will be pursued, agreeably to the same usage.

The President and Directors of the New York South American Steamboat Association, have addressed to this Department a remonstrance, herewith transmitted, stating that they have sustained a loss amounting to at least $150,000, by a breach of good faith upon the part of the Brazilian Government, by not complying with its engagements, made with that association.[15] As this a [sic] claim arising out of contract, the Government of the United States can only interpose by its good offices. These you will render as far as it may appear to you to be proper to sustain the representations of the company, and to procure them the justice to which they may appear to be entitled.

It is understood that our commerce and manufactures do not enjoy, in the ports of the Brazils the same advantages as the commerce and manufactures of some other Foreign Nations, and particularly those of Great Britain and France. You will represent this unequality, if it shall continue to exist, and urge its removal. After the settlement of the question of indemnities, the President intends to cause a negotiation to be opened at this place, or at Rio, for the arrangement of the commerce and navigation of the two countries by treaty, if it be likely that an overture for such a negotiation will be favorably received. On this subject, you will, at some suitable time, sound the disposition of the Brazilian Government. I am, with great respect Your obedient servant,

H. CLAY

LS. DNA, RG84, Brazil, Instructions, vol. 1 (MR14). Copy, in DNA, RG59, Dip. Instr., vol. 12, pp. 1–13 (M77, R7); L draft, with occasional interlineations and the last paragraph in Clay's hand, in DLC-HC (DNA, M212, R8).
    1 The letter, written by Daniel Brent, "by direction of the President, and in the absence of the Secretary," is dated June 28, 1827. LS, in DNA, RG84, Brazil, Instructions, vol. 1 (MR14); copy, in DNA, RG59, Dip. Instr., vol. 11, pp. 366–68 (M77, R6).   2 Cf. above, Raguet to Clay, March 12, 17, 1827.   3 With the letter from Brent to Tudor, June 28, 1827.   4 Two and a half pages omitted by editors.   5 Half a page omitted by the editors. On the incident, cf. above, Raguet to Secretary of State, March 11, 1825, note.   6 Thomas Buckley and Son.   7 Cf. above, Raguet to Clay, September 1, 1826. Approximately half a page, recounting the history of the case, omitted by the editors.   8 Cf. above, Raguet to Clay, March 12, 1827.   9 Possibly Joseph Hill Clark.   10 Captain Clark.   11 J. H. Clark to Secretary of State (Clay), from New York, August 27, 1827, and Clark to Secretary of Navy (Samuel L. Southard), August 28, 1827, with a schedule of papers and papers endorsed no. 1 to no. 20, listed as sent to

Tudor but not found.   [12] Peter I.   [13] The Jay Treaty.   [14] Dated November 1, 1827. Copy, in DNA, RG59, Ceremonial Communications, II, 70.   [15] See above, Rogers and Van Winkle to Clay, June 14, 1827.

Order on Washington Branch, Bank of the United States

24h. Oct. 1827.

Pay to Check on Norfolk Twenty dollars.
Cashr. of the Off. of Dt. & Dt.   Washn.[1]   H CLAY

ADS, partially printed. DLC-TJC (DNA, M212, R16). Cf. above, Clay to Rodgers, September 29, 1827, note.
[1] Richard Smith.

From John Sergeant

Dear Sir: (Private)   Philada. Octr. 24. 1827.

Your favor of the 21st.[1] was received this morning, and the letter enclosed in it, having been first attentively read, is now returned. The course so forcibly urged by the writer has already been agreed upon, and will be followed here and in the neighboring counties without delay, under the recommendation of a very respectable (private) meeting[2] held in this City about a week ago in which this point was considered and decided upon the grounds stated by the writer. There were present at that meeting, gentlemen from Lancaster, Chester, Bucks and Montgomery, as well as from the City and County of Philadelphia, all earnest in the cause.

We have had an alarm about New York. The managers are said to have arranged so as to secure Jackson nominations to the Legislature, and thus a majority in that body.[3] If they succeed in this, we shall have every thing to fear. "Shadows, clouds and darkness"[4] you know rest upon all political prospects in that State, at all times,   Very respectfully and truly Yrs   JOHN SERGEANT.
The Honble Henry Clay.

ALS. DLC-HC (DNA, M212, R3).   [1] Not found.
[2] Not identified.   [3] Administration supporters were particularly concerned that a victory for the Jackson forces in the election, November 5–7, for the New York Legislature would permit the latter to change the State electoral law. See Washington *Daily National Journal*, November 5, 1827, and cf. above, Clay to Brooke, December 11, 1826, note. The bitterness of the struggle underway during the month of October for the control of Tammany (see above, Porter to Clay, May 1, 1827, note) and the triumph of the Jacksonites in New York City had far-reaching effects upstate. While the issue of the coming Presidential election was not then enunciated, the coalition of Clinton and Van Buren forces decisively defeated those who supported the administration. As early as November 17, *Niles' Weekly Register* reported: "The friends of General Jackson calculated upon at least two thirds of the members of the legislature, and from what is known, will certainly have a large majority. . . ." The same observer noted, however, that in many instances local matters had so clouded "the leading question, that no other than some act in the legislature itself . . . [would] decide the character of a number of the members." Cf. below, Webster to Clay, November 5, 1827; Clay to Brooke, November 6, 1827. See also Mushkat, *Tammany. . .* , 106–108.   [4] Source of quotation has not been found. Cf. Psalms 97:2.

DIPLOMATIC NOTES   October 24, 1827

To PABLO OBREGÓN, Washington. Acknowledges his letter of October 6 and states:
". . . it has not been customary here for Diplomatic Agents to avail themselves of
that privilege, nor is the utility of its exercise perceived, except in the event of
civil commotion, or of War raging in the bosom of the Country; but if any Diplomatic Agent thinks proper to hoist the flag of his Country, no Law is believed to
exist which would prohibit him from so doing." Copy. DNA, RG59, Notes to
Foreign Legations, vol. 3, p. 393 (M38, R3). ALI draft, in CSmH.

INSTRUCTIONS AND DISPATCHES   October 24, 1827

From J[OEL] R. POINSETT, Mexico, no. 104. Transmits translation of a note from
the Mexican Government requesting a passport for Brigadier General (Manuel
de) Mier y Terán and his party and a copy of his answer accompanying the passport. LS. DNA, RG59, Dip. Disp., Mexico, vol. 3 (M97, R4). Received December
10. Cf. above, Poinsett to Clay, July 12, 1826, and note.

From JOEL R. POINSETT, Mexico, no. 105. States that (Sebastián) Camacho's return
from London has coincided with a "marked . . . change in the conduct of the
President [Guadalupe Victoria]. Notes that "[Tomás] Salgado has been appointed
one of the Judges of the Supreme Court. . . , and has . . . resigned the office of the
Treasury"; that (Francisco) García (Salinas) has been appointed to Salgado's
former post; and that Secretary of War (Manuel) Gómez Pedraza, who "is about
to resign" because he was not consulted on changes in military personnel, may be
replaced by (Miguel) Barragán, "now Governor of Vera Cruz." Discusses the
changes in military commands; expresses concern that the President "seems disposed to reconcile both parties and to divide the command between them"; and
predicts that "the insurrectionary movements on the Southern Coast . . . will now
become formidable" (cf. above, Poinsett to Clay, October 6, 1827).
   Reports having learned, since beginning his dispatch, that "Gomez Pedraza
remains in the Ministry, but Ramos Arizpe, the Minister of Grace and Justice,
goes out, after doing all the mischief he could," and that "Camacho will resume
the department of foreign relations. . . ." LS. DNA, RG59, Dip. Disp., Mexico, vol.
3 (M79, R4). Received December 10.

MISCELLANEOUS LETTERS   October 24, 1827

To CHARLES J. INGERSOLL, Philadelphia. Acknowledges receipt of Ingersoll's letter
of October 22. States that the Department has no further information regarding
the *Kensington* case; that Clay "supposed . . . [Ingersoll] could obtain through the
Collector [William Jones], and the Officers of the Customs, or through the Marshal
[John Conard]" the necessary information; that he wrote his letter "with the intention" that the inquiry should be initiated, "and if, upon such enquiry, it should
appear that any thing was doing, which is forbidden by law, and contrary to our
neutral obligations," the requisite prosecution should be commenced. Continues:
"To bring the case within the act of Congress, I presume there must be a fitting
out and arming of the vessel, or an attempt to do it, with intent that she shall
cruize or commit hostilities upon the subjects of Spain or their property." States,
however, that Ingersoll's opinion and "that of the court" are more important than
his own; that "The duty of the Government is to prevent any deviation from a

line of strict neutrality, and, with that view, to examine carefully into the condition of any vessel which it is informed, or has reason to believe, may probably be designed to assist contrary to law, one of the belligerents in a War to which we are neutral"; and that "a full examination, even if such examination should result in a conviction that the law has not been broken," will be satisfactory. ALS. DNA, RG59, Dom. Letters, vol. 22, pp. 67–68 (M40, R20).

To Daniel Webster

My dear Sir   (Private and Confidential)   Washington 25h. Oct. 1827.

The course adopted by the Opposition, in the dissemination of Newspapers and publications against the Administration,[1] and supporting presses leaves to its friends no other alternative than that of following their example, so far at least as to circulate information among the people. At this moment, when at no former period was the prospect brighter in Virginia, there is danger, I understand, of losing the most efficient cause of the existing auspicious state of things, Mr. Pleasants and the Whig,[2] from the want of pecuniary means. What ought to be done? It seems to me that our friends who have the ability should contribute a fund for the purpose of aiding [th]e cause; and if that be deemed advisable, the appeal should be made in the large Cities where alone the capital is to be found. You stated, I think, last winter that such a fund would be raised,[3] and that I was authorized to address you on the subject. I have not felt that I ought to avail myself of the authority, fearing that your own means might be encroached on too much. As for myself, if it were otherwise proper, I am too poor. I have not the pecuniary ability.

The best form of affording aid to struggling presses is to supply it, and to require that a number of additional papers shall be circulated gratis, bearing some proportion to the contribution made. In this way the cause will be doubly served. I do not believe there is any part of the Union in which as much can be done, by the increase of the circulation of any paper, as can be effected, at this time, by extending that of the Whig in Virginia. Other papers (Mr Hammond's[4] for example, and some others to the West) might be assisted with advantage in the same way.

If you coincide in these views, would it not be well for you to give an impulse to the creation of a fund for the above objects by conversation or other communication with some of our friends?

I think our cause stands well at present; but, we shall greatly deceive ourselves, if we think the time has yet arrived, or will for some months arrive, when exertions may be safely relaxed. Always and truly Yrs.   H CLAY
D. Webster Esqr

ALS. DLC-Webster Papers (DNA, M212, R22).
1 Cf. above, Moore to Clay, February 10, 1827, and note; Phelps to Clay, April 21, 1827.   2 John H. Pleasants; Richmond *Constitutional Whig*.   3 Cf. above, Clay to Webster, August 19, 1827; Webster to Clay, September 28, 1827; below, Webster to Clay, October 29, November 5, 1827; Clay to Webster, November 8, 1827.   4 Charles Hammond; *Liberty Hall and Cincinnati Gazette*.

INSTRUCTIONS AND DISPATCHES   October 25, 1827

From SAMUEL LARNED, Santiago de Chile, no. 61. Describes his success in having the Chilean Government extend the terms of deposit for 100 barrels of related provisions belonging to the United States Navy, and notes his intention to negotiate with the Chilean Vice President (Francisco Antonio Pinto Diaz) "for a more convenient and advantageous regulation of this business." Notes that (Joaquín) Campino, in Valparaiso awaiting passage to the United States, "hopes to arrive before the rising of Congress." Indicates that "the Provincial Assembly of Aconcagua has manifested a disposition to establish a species of independence of the general government as a preparatory step to federation:—but it is hoped . . . that the Province will eventually subscribe to a *Municipal Federation*, towards which system most of the Provincial Assemblies seem inclined." Asserts that their system, "which may be made to combine the advantages of both the central and federal plans, is the one best calculated for the present condition of these countries" and explains the reasoning that has led him to this conclusion. States that Luna Pizarro informs him "that the Constituent Congress" of Peru "have it in contemplation to adopt their plan. . . ." Adds that "there is reason to believe that the United Provinces of the Rio-de-la-Plata, and a part at least of Colombia, will finally settle down upon a similar organization." Forwards back file (not found) of the Bogotá *Conductor*, a "paper . . . understood to be edited principally by Vice-President [Francisco de Paula] Santander. . . ." ALS. DNA, RG59, Dip. Disp., Chile, vol. 2 (M-T2, R2). Received January 30, 1828.

MISCELLANEOUS LETTERS   October 25, 1827

From CHARLES J. INGERSOLL, Philadelphia. Transmits a letter to himself from William Jones, Collector at Philadelphia, enclosing a report from Deputy Collector John Kerne on his investigation of the *Kensington* case (cf. above, Tacón to Clay, October 5, 1827; Clay to Ingersoll, October 17, 1827). ALS. DNA, RG59, Misc. Letters (M179, R65).

In the enclosure Kerne states that the *Kensington*, a corvette of 1418 18/95 tons, "has thirty iron guns," called "24 pounders but supposed to carry balls of 28 lbs. the Caliber about 6 Inches"; that he "saw no small arms, balls or ammunition of any kind on board, but understood that a small quantity of boarding pikes and tomahawks were in the lower hold." Reports that inquiries made of "the only person on board, who appeared to have any charge of the Ship" indicated that Samuel Chew owned it; that "no men had been shipped or enlisted"; that the ship "will leave the United States under a Certificate of Registry, as the property of a Citizen thereof—to proceed to Mexico and on her arrival there, would, on being paid for, be delivered to the purchaser"; that "on leaving the United States, she would not be in a situation to commit any Acts of hostilities—her armament would not be complete—and that no gunpowder was to be taken on board"; that 100 men would be needed to take the vessel to Mexico while 400 would be necessary "for warlike purposes."

From Peter B. Porter

Dear Sir,   New York October 26th. 1827

After consuming nearly a year in a correspondence with his Government on the subject of our differences, Mr Barclay[1] has concluded (by the instructions no doubt of that Government) to insist on his claims to St. George's Island by the establishment of the Boundary through the American channel.[2] As I could not yield to this most extraordinary and unreasonable claim, without abandoning some of the most important as well as most obvious rights of the U. States, we have closed the commission by an ultimate disagreement as to this & some other portions of the line, & an agreement as to the residue.

On a final adjustment of the accounts of the commission, it was found that the expenditures of the British party had exceeded those of the American by $8530 12/100. To equalise [sic] the expenses therefore, according to the provisions of the treaty,[3] I have given Mr Barclay a draft on you in favour of the Cashier of the the [sic] Phoenix Bank, M. Delafield[4] for $4265 6/100 equal to one half of their excess of expenses.

I hope you may find it convenient to pay this draft on its presentation, as Mr Barclay has been waiting some time for this money, and is I believe in immediate want of it to pay off his assistants. I should think the draft ought be paid out of the balances of the appropriations of former years, during which most of the expenses which it is to cover, were incurred, & became chargeable to our Government. The draft itself expresses the purpose for which it was given.

I shall write you officially & at length on the subject of the Commission in the course of three or four days. And as soon as my seperate [sic] report on the points of disagreement is made up, I propose to go to Washington with Major Delafield[5] to settle our accounts.

The electioneering campaign is going on in this city with great animation[6]—each party confidently claiming the ascendancy. There is I think every reason to beleive [sic] that the Administration ticket will succeed. What will be the result in the *Country* it is impossible to foretell—for, although the *material* of the elective body in the country is much more favourable to the Administration, than in this city, it is not impossible that the Jacksonians may outnumber us in the next legislature. If so, it will be owing to their extraordinary exertions, & to the inactivity of their opponents—and, I may add, to the circumstance that most of the partisan presses are at present under the controul of Van Buren or Clinton. It has been the policy of Mr Van Buren to keep the presidential question, as much as possible, out of sight, and he has succeeded in several instances, in getting Jackson men nominated for the Legislature, when a majority of the nominating convention were administration men; but who did not think it worth while to enquire, and perhaps did not care what the opinions of the candidate were in regard to this particular question. Whatever may be the result of the present election I cannot for a moment doubt but that a decided majority of the electoral votes of this state will, next year, be for Mr Adams.[7] The *Eighth* district in which I reside (comprising 7 or 8 of the most western counties of the state) is I believe entirely sound. There is in this Presidential contest, one strong source of consolation derived from the fact that the *Jackson fever* has invariably proved most violent in its commencement—and this state has but just taken it. With the highest respect & regard, your Obt Servt.

Hon. Henry Clay.   P. B. PORTER

ALS. DLC-HC (DNA, M212, R3).
[1] Anthony Barclay. Cf. above, Porter to Clay, October 18, 1826; April 20, 1827; Delafield to Clay, March 22, April 6, 13, September 22, 1827.   [2] Cf. above, Porter to Clay, October 31, 1826; Clay to Vaughan, November 15, 1826.   [3] Cf. above, Porter to Clay, November 8, 1826. Article VIII of the Treaty of Ghent stipulated the arrangements for payment of expenses.   [4] John Delafield, elder brother of Joseph, had been born in New York City in 1786, graduated from Columbia College in 1802, and trained in the family mercantile business. After twelve years as a successful merchant and banker in London, England, he had suffered financial reverses and returned to the United States in 1820. He had then become cashier of the Phoenix Bank in New York and later was named president of that institution. Again stricken by financial disaster around 1838, he removed to Seneca County, New York, and engaged in farming. Before his death in 1853, he won recognition as an exponent of improved agricultural technology.   [5] Joseph Delafield.   [6] Cf above, Sergeant to Clay, October 24, 1827, and note.   [7] Cf. above, Clay to Brown, March 27, 1827, note.

DIPLOMATIC NOTES   October 26, 1827

From CHARLES R. VAUGHAN, Washington. Refers to his note to Clay, "dated the 16th. [*i.e.*, 17th.] Septr.," and transmits "a copy of a letter" he has just "received from Sir Howard Douglas, the Lieutenant Governor of New Brunswick. . . ." NS. DNA, RG59, Notes from British Legation, vol. 14 (M50, R15). Published in Manning (arr.), *Diplomatic Correspondence . . . Canadian Relations*, II, 651–52 (the enclosure, 652n–53n).

In the enclosure, dated October 4, 1827, Douglas commends Vaughan for his "Note of the 16th. [*sic*] Septr." to Clay and gives "assurances that all the Acts of . . . [his] Govt. are in strict conformity with the positions and statements contained in" that note. He further asserts that he has done "nothing that can change the state of the question as it existed when the Treaty of Ghent was executed," that he has permitted no British encroachments into the disputed area, that, at the same time, he can not abandon "Territory, located and held as British settlements, before the Treaty of Ghent was executed"; further, that he has protested against American encroachment in 1825 "in one of these" (cf. above, Vaughan to Clay, November 15, 1825), on which "Mr. [Enoch] Lincolns representations are grounded," that "This Settlement" he is "bound to consider as a Part of New Brunswick," that no solution of the problem is possible "until a final decision be made of the question of right under the Treaty of Ghent," and that further American encroachment would constitute "a direct departure, on the part of the United States, from that course of mutual forbearance which has been here *strictly* observed."

Receipted Bill from John Schlecht

Henry Clay Esqr.   [October 27, 1827]
    1827.   Dr. To John Schlecht
Octr. 27th.   To Cask Wine 33 1/2 Gal. @ 2$ pr. Gal. $67.00
Recd. payt.   JOHN SCHLECHT

ADS. DLC-TJC (DNA, M212, R16). On the same date Clay drew an order for $67 on the Office of Discount and Deposit in Washington, payable to Schlecht. ADS, *ibid*. The handwriting on the signature of the receipted bill differs from that of the endorsement on verso of the draft.

INSTRUCTIONS AND DISPATCHES   October 27, 1827

From A[BRAHAM] P. GIBSON, St. Petersburg. Transmits "a french translation of an Ukase . . . relative to the quarantine of Vessels bound to this country and coming from any infected or suspected ports. . . ." Suggests that "these new regulations" be published and that "vessels coming direct from the United States . . . be furnished with Bills of health. . . ." LS. DNA, RG59, Cons. Disp., St. Petersburg, vol. 2 (M81, R-T2). Received February 21, 1828.

From ROBERT MONROE HARRISON, Demerara (British Guiana). Submits report on British Guiana, "out of which the Colonies of Demerara, Essequebo, and Berbice have been formed." Discusses the geography, history, agriculture, trade, plantation economics, and natural resources of British Guiana. Stresses the importance, to the planters, of barter trade with the United States, a trade made desirable because of convenience, regularity, and lower prices. Quotes one of the most respectable men of the colony concerning the undesirable economic consequences of placing their goods in the hands of the English merchants, who often hold mortgages on the plantations and thus can collect their debts directly and on their own terms. Expresses belief that the United States may have to make "very considerable concessions" to get the British to lift their interdiction of United States trade to the British West Indies but that the circuitous trade (through the neutral colonies) "will be tolerated for the present on account of the Salt Islands" (cf. below, Harrison to Clay, December 14, 1827). ALS. DNA, RG59, Cons. Disp., Demerara, vol. 1 (M-T336, R1). Received February 4, 1828.

From W[ILLIAM] H. D. C. WRIGHT, Rio de Janeiro. Reports the capture of "The Brig Ruth of Philadelphia . . . off Santos . . . by a Buenos Ayrean Privateer" (for the earlier capture of this vessel by Brazil, see above, Raguet to Clay, September 1, December 5, 1826; Clay to Tudor, October 23, 1827) and encloses a "copy of a protest made by her late Mate" (Charles Bayard, not further identified). Notes, also, the arrival, from Bahia, of "The Brig Patrick Henry of Boston," which has "Been plundered on her passage of eight hundred and twenty four kegs of gun powder by a Buenos Ayrean Government Corvette." Adds that "Nothing more has been done in the prize cases, but" he has been informed that "the arrangement" mentioned in his dispatch of September 21 "as likely to take place in relation to British Vessels, has been positively entered into." Observes that he views the recent appointment by "This Government" of "a Consulting Junto, to revise the Prize decisions" as "a step preparatory to the restoration of the Captured Vessels." ALS. DNA, RG59, Cons. Disp., Rio de Janeiro, vol. 2 (M-T172, R3). Received December 18.

    The *Ruth* had been seized by Argentine privateers in September, 1827 (cf. below, Forbes to Clay, October 30, 1827). John M. Forbes, as Chargé des Affaires, in the fall of 1828 submitted an estimate of damages and expenses amounting to some $57,000 in Argentine currency. The Argentine Government in 1829 and 1830 appointed two separate commissions to review claims for damages by its privateers, and those for the *Ruth* were admitted by the commissioners; but no record of a settlement has been found. *Sen. Docs.*, 35 Cong., 2 Sess., no. 189, p. 255; Harold F. Peterson, *Argentina and the United States, 1810–1960* ([New York]: State University of New York, 1964), 93–94.

A claim for the brig *Patrick Henry*, built at Newcastle, Maine, in 1820 and registered by William Gray, has not been found.

To Adam Beatty

My dear Sir   (Confidential)   Washn. 28h. Oct. 1827.

I have received and perused with much interest and attention your obliging letter of the 15h. inst.[1] On the point of an appeal from *me* to the H. of R.[2] I concur entirely in the view which you have taken. I have no idea of making any such appeal, unless it should be advised by my friends generally. My friends and myself have collected a mass of proof to establish that I uniformly, on various occasions, expressed a preference for Mr. Adams to Genl. Jackson, and on other points. I expect still more; and I *may* (for I have not positively decided to do so) publish the whole, together with some strictures, in a temperate address to the publick.[3] The only doubt I have is whether enough has not been already said and written, and whether I might not appear to be too sensitive. It is extremely difficult for a public man always clearly to distinguish the occasions in which he should speak out in his defence from those in which he ought to remain silent. I shall be guided, in my ultimate determination, by the opinion of my friends and among them that which you have kindly expressed will have much weight.

I am glad to see that our friends are bestiring [*sic*] themselves in K. with a view to more co-operation & concert. On that point I think mainly depends our success next year.

The result of late elections in Maryland, Delaware, New Jersey and Philada. has been very auspicious. Wherever the question was made in other parts of Pennsa. the Admon exhibited a strength which surprized both friends & foes.[4] But for the events in K.[5] during the past summer, the Jackson cause would now be at an end. Yr's faithfy & Cordially
A. Beatty Esq.   H CLAY

ALS. Owned by Earl M. Ratzer, Highland Park, Illinois. Endorsed on cover: "Answered 29th. Novr. 1827." The answer has not been found.
[1] Not found.   [2] Cf. above, Hammond to Clay, October 18, 1827.   [3] See below, *Address . . . to the Public*, December 29, 1827.   [4] For the Maryland election, cf. above, Clay to Blunt, September 11, 1827, note; for Delaware, Clay to Taylor, September 7, 1827, note; for New Jersey, Clay to Henry, October 20, 1827, and note; for Philadelphia, Sergeant to Clay, September 11, 1827, note; for other parts of Pennsylvania, Sergeant to Clay, October 14, 1827, note.   [5] Cf. above, Clay to Taylor, April 4, 1827, note.

To James Brown

My Dear Sir   (Private & Inofficial.)   Washington 28h. Oct. 1827

I recd. your two favors of the 13h. and the 6h. Ulto. Your official despatch giving an account of your interview with the Baron de Damas[1] is also received. It appears to me that it was very well to have that interview, but I think it is desirable that you should obtain a *written* answer to the offer to refer the Louisiana question. With that view, after waiting a reasonable time (as usual I suppose there will be much delay in the decision of the French Government on the proposal, and in the communication of it to you) for the answer, it seems to me that you would do well to address a note refering [*sic*] to the interview, and repeating the offer. In that note you might insert the historical review of the various negotiations &c &c which is contained in my despatch.[2] It is due, I think, to this government, and to the claimants to have a written answer from France. The French Minister will be less disposed to commit his Government to a rejection of the offer in writing than by parol [*sic*]. You very properly evaded a direct answer to the enquiry whether we would refer the claims as well as the other question. The French Minister, in that stage of the business, had no right to ask such a question. If they should, contrary to what now appears probable, decide to accept the proposal to refer, on the condition that we will consent also to refer the question of the indemnities, you ought to oppose, as long as possible, the connection of the two subjects, and if they persevere, you had better take their offer ad referendum. If they persist in rejecting the reference, I am desirous that the whole correspondence should be laid before Congress during the approaching Session;[3] and it is for that reason also that I think we ought to have a written answer.

As to what Congress will do, I cannot say. I believe they will do nothing at the present period. You may dismiss all apprehensions of War, at least for some time. If Congress (which I doubt) could ever be induced to go to War on a/c of the claims, the present is not the season for it.

The President has not, I believe, the slightest wish to replace you by any other person. He never, on any occasion, expressed any such desire to me. I believe he is perfectly satisfied with your Ministry. Your retirement at this time would rather embarrass than gratify us. I am quite sure that you may consult exclusively your own inclination and wishes as to the duration of your Mission.

We have no thought of giving you any instructions about a modification of the Convention.[4] We will hear, with a friendly ear, any proposals on that subject which France has to make, either at Paris or Washington. We have none ourselves. We should regret that France should put an end to the Convention; but if she does the responsibility must rest with her. I think myself that the duties on French wines and silks might be somewhat lowered, but that is an affair for the consideration of Congress. The reduction of the duty on brandy is impossible.

Lucretia has recd. and is highly pleased with the articles which her sister purchased for her.[5] They all came safely. The Lustres[6] &c have arrived at New York & we shall get them in good time. I have directed $450 to be paid to Mrs. Price and Mrs. Hart,[7] according to your request, or rather authority, and I will remit your bill as soon as I can procure one for the residue of the advances you have kindly made for me.

I can give you no account of Dr. Brown;[8] but I think some letters for you from Mr. John Brown, and probably from the Dr. passed some weeks ago through the office. Mason Brown has I have understood lost his wife.[9]

I sent you in Aug. a letter to Genl. La Fayette[10] the object of which was to recall his recollection to a conversation I had with him in Decr. 1824 in which I avowed my determination to vote for Mr. Adams. I am very anxious to get his ansr.[11] and will thank you to make my respects to him, and urge him to ansr. if he shall not have done it.

Elections this month in Maryland, Delaware, New Jersey and Philada. have turned out favorably to the Admon. In Pennsa. we exhibited a strength which surprized friends and foes. If the current there is not checked, Mr. Adams will get the vote of that state.[12] In Virginia our friends are every where in motion. A great meeting of them took place at Richmond this week, which was attended by four of the five Judges of the Court of Appeals.[13] They will hold a Convention in Jany to nominate electors for Mr. Adams,[14] and I am not without strong hopes of that State. But it is not to be disguised that the Opposition is powerful and the influence of the Military renown of Genl. Jackson great. We shall have another year of turmoil, & party strife, embittered beyond all example. My confidence in ultimate success is unshaken.

My health is not good, but not so bad as to prevent my attention to my customary duties. It is more owing to that cause than to politics that I some times display the impatience of which Mr. Sontag[15] spoke to you. Neither is Lucretia's health as good as she enjoyed in K. We are both getting old, and both feel it. Be pleased to make our best regards to Mrs. Brown and believe me Faithfy Your friend
James Brown Esq.   H. CLAY.

ALS. KyLxT.   [1] No. 73, above, September 8, 1827.
[2] Above, May 28, 1827.   [3] The subject was not submitted to the Twentieth Congress. Cf. above, Brown to Clay, September 13, 1827, note.   [4] Cf. above, III, 53n.
[5] Ann Hart Brown.   [6] Cf. above, Clay to Brown, March 27, May 30, 1827; Brown to Clay, May 12, June 28, July 28, 1827; Astor to Clay, September 21, 1827.
[7] Susannah Price; Susannah Gray Hart.   [8] Samuel Brown.   [9] Judith Ann

Bledsoe Brown had died September 28, 1827.   10 Above, August 10, 1827.
    11 Above, October 10, 1827.   12 Cf. above, Clay to Brown, March 27, 1827, note.
    13 Cf. above, Brooke to Clay, October 17, 1827, note. The judges in attendance were
Brooke, William H. Cabell, Dabney Carr, and, probably, John W. Greene. Cabell, born
in Cumberland County, Virginia, in 1777, and graduated in law at William and Mary
College in 1793, practiced and now resided in Richmond. He had been elected to the
Virginia Legislature in 1796, had been re-elected four times, and had been Governor of
the State from 1805 to 1808. His tenure on the Court of Appeals had begun in 1811. He
was the presiding jurist from 1842 to 1851.   14 Cf. above, Mercer to Clay, August 18,
1827, note.   15 Fortuné de Sontag.

INSTRUCTIONS AND DISPATCHES   October 28, 1827

From JAMES BROWN, Paris, "Private." Reports an expectation that the Chamber of
Deputies will soon be dissolved (cf. above, Lafayette to Clay, October 10, 1827)
and that "a considerable number of new peers" will be created in order to increase
in their chamber "a ministerial majority" and to fulfill "certain promises said to
have been made to some of the members of the existing chamber of deputies." Explains why "ministers should advise the dissolution of a chamber which has supported all the measures proposed by Government": despite "the septennial law"
(cf. above, Lafayette to Clay, October 10, 1827, note), more than a hundred deputies believe their terms expire at the end of the five-year period for which they were
elected; the Ministry thinks that an election held while "the public mind" is
"favorably disposed towards them" will "thereby secure their majority for the
next seven years"; and the Government expects to gain popularity by "referring"
to the people "the choice of a new chamber. . . ." Expresses his opinion that "In
a nation where, out of a population of thirty millions, not more than eighty thousand enjoy the right of suffrage, and where a very large proportion of these are
either employed by, or dependent upon the Government, it is by no means probable that a choice unfavorable to the Ministry will take place." States that he "has
heard it suggested . . . that the President of the council [the Count de Villèle]
wishes to obtain a more constitutional chamber, or at all events one less devoted
to the interests of the congregation, . . . to enable him to resist the claims of the
ecclesiastics" for higher salaries "and perhaps an indemnity for the loss of the
church property sold during the revolution." Encloses "a specimen" of letters
distributed by opponents of the Ministry.
    Notes "confused and contradictory accounts" from Catalonia (cf. above, Everett
to Clay, April 19, August 16, September 20, October 19, 1827; Brown to Clay,
September 29, 1827), "the wretchedness of all classes" there, and the diminishing
"means of repression" owing to "the want of money to pay the regular army."
    Adds that the Egyptian fleet attempted "to escape from Navarino" but has been
"compelled to return and anchor in the port"; that "the Porte" (i.e., Mahmud II)
is said to be "less averse to the mediation than he has heretofore been" (cf. above,
Brown to Clay, July 12, 1827; Hughes to Clay, September 16, 1827, note); and that
"it is believed that the allied sovereigns will take vigorous measures to terminate
the war. . . ." Cites "discordant interests and . . . jealousies" among the allies who
must decide, at the end of hostilities, "the disposition to be made of Greece. . . ."
Points out that the policy of Russia, which "seems to have bestowed her confidence
on the Count Capo d'Istria," is to make "Greece independent," while France appears to be "utterly opposed to the independence of Greece, more especially should
her Government assume the republican form." LS. DNA, RG59, Dip. Disp., France,
vol. 23 (M34, R26). Received December 13.
    A brief sortie by units of the Turkish fleet out of Navarino harbor on September
30 had been intercepted and turned back by British Admiral Codrington without
bloodshed. *Annual Register, 1827*, p. 315.

From BEAUFORT T. WATTS, Bogotá, no. 36. Transmits "a hasty translation of the Exposé of the Secretary of Foreign Affairs [Joseph R. Revenga], of the President's [Simón Bolívar's] Administration, in the four Departments which had separated from the General Government; and which has been approved of by Congress." ALS. DNA, RG59, Dip. Disp., Colombia, vol. 4 (M-T33, R4). Received January 9, 1828.

The enclosure includes Revenga's very lengthy report, dated September 10, 1827, on "the state in which the Departments of Maturín, Venezuela, Orinoco and Lulia, were at the time when His Excellency took them in December last under his immediate orders, and the measures which were thought indispensible [sic] to remedy the retrogradation and disorder, in the administration," and the document by which the Congress approved "The measures adopted by the Liberator President" with regard to these Departments.

MISCELLANEOUS LETTERS   October 28, 1827

To R[ICHARD] RUSH, Treasury Department. States that the corvette *Kensington* "is fitting out in the Port of Philadelphia, evidently for the purpose of being employed in War." Transmits a "report of an officer of the Customs describing her condition" (cf. above, Ingersoll to Clay, October 25, 1827, note); reports that the "case of the vessel has been made the subject of a formal complaint on the part of the Spanish Minister" (cf. above, Tacón to Clay, October 5, 1827); solicits Rush's opinion as to the "propriety of directing the Collector of Philadelphia [William Jones] to demand a bond, with adequate sureties, from the owners of the vessel, according to the provisions of the Act of Congress applicable to the case" (cf. above, II, 507, note); and expresses his own opinion that "such a measure" is "expedient." Copy. DNA, RG59, Dom. Letters, vol. 22, pp. 70–71 (M40, R20).

Rush addressed Clay on October 29, stating that he had "received, on Saturday," his "letter of the 27th [sic] instant relative to the case of the corvette Kensington" and enclosing "the copy of an instruction . . . addressed to the Collector of the port of Philadelphia upon the subject of it." LS, in DNA, RG59, Misc. Letters (M179, R65). The enclosure is a copy of an order by Rush to William Jones to "require the owners or consignees of the said Corvette to enter into bonds . . . that she shall not be employed . . . to cruise or commit hostilities against the subjects, citizens or property of any foreign prince or state, or of any colony, district or people, with whom the U. States are at peace."

On the same date Rush also wrote an unofficial letter to Clay: "Your letter to me about the Corvette Kensington, was inadvertently dated the 28th, which having been Sunday, I have ventured to alter the date, to the 27th, as you will see." ALI, *ibid.*, "private."

From CHARLES SAVAGE, Boston. Reports his intention to depart "for Omoa and *Guatemala* on or about November 15," to resume his consular duties. ALS. DNA, RG59, Cons. Disp., Guatemala, vol. 1 (M-T337, R1).

To Samuel S. Conant

Dear Sir　　(Private and Confidential)　　Washington 29h. Oct. 1827.

Your favor of the 26h. inst.[1] is received. A common friend[2] had suggested the utility of a correspondence with you, to which I urged no other objection than that of the very great extent of the Correspondence by which I am already oppressed. I shall nevertheless always receive any communication from you with pleasure, and I shall be happy to transmit from this place any information which I can, with propriety, communicate.

I hope your anticipations of success in the City of N. York will be realized. It is the most important election, now pending, which is near at hand.[3] The result of it will have much influence. From the interior of N. York our information is not good. And now, that the aspect of public affairs, every where else almost is, auspicious, it is mortifying to hear bad, where we had expected good, news. In Virginia there is a movement of the most encouraging kind, and which, unless checked, by discouraging events elsewhere, will I think carry the vote of that State to Mr. Adams.[4]

The attempt to enlist the *Republican* party in your State in favor of Genl. Jackson is the most extraordinary of all the political incidents of the day. The Republican party! which has always been animated by a love of liberty to lend itself to the establishment of a principle which has subverted all Republics.[5] I am with great respect Yr's truly
Saml. S. Conant Esq   H. CLAY

ALS. KyU.   1 Not found.
2 Not identified.   3 See above, Sergeant to Clay, October 24, 1827, note.   4 Cf. above, Brooke to Clay, August 8, 1827; Caldwell to Clay, August 8, 1827, note; Southard to Clay, August 8, 1827; Mercer to Clay, August 18, 1827.   5 The "Republican party" in New York, according to the *New York American* of September 27 and 29, 1827, represented a coalition of Martin Van Buren's "Republicans" and De Witt Clinton's "Clintonians" that had been formed to support Jackson's cause in the State. Thus the "Republicans," a group long "enlisted in support of a cause and principles," had allied themselves with "those who were the supporters of a particular man [Clinton]" and had become "not the advocates [of a] principle or of a public cause, but of another man!"

To Daniel W. Lewis

Daniel W. Lewis Esq. Geneva N.Y.   Department of State.
Sir,   Washington 29th. October 1827.
Your letter of the 19th. inst. in relation to the appointment of a Judge in the Michigan territory, has been received and attentively perused by myself, and afterwards submitted to the president. In designating Mr. Chipman for that office, the President was influenced by a very powerful recommendation in behalf of that gentleman, which it would have been extremely difficult to resist. The recommendations in your favour were also numerous and respectable. Among them was a letter from Mr. Le Roy recommending Mr. Woodbridge[1] or yourself to be appointed.

Your own good sense and reflection must satisfy you how painful it often is to decide on the conflicting applications of respectable gentlemen for the same public employment; and your candour, I am sure, will induce you justly to appreciate the public considerations which may point to the selection of one gentleman in preference to another I am respectfully Your obt. servt.   H. Clay.

Copy. DNA, RG59, Dom. Letters, vol. 22, p. 71 (M40, R20).   1 William Woodbridge.

To Francisco Tacón

The Chevalier Don Franciso Tacon,
Minister Resident, from Spain: Department of State,
Sir,   Washington D, C. October 29th. 1827.

I have the honor to acknowledge the receipt of your Note of the 4th. instant, and to inform you, that I have, according to the request which it contains, submitted to [sic] the President of the United States.

The entry of Commodore Porter, and the Mexican Squadron under his command, first into the port of Key West, and afterwards, into that of Pensacola,[1] was in the pursuit of that hospitality which the United States are ever ready to extend to thier [sic] friends, and to none more promptly than to Spain. That the Commodore remained so long a time in the former port is believed to have been owing chiefly to the fact that his egress would have been attended with the most imminent danger, if not certain capture from the presence of the Spanish Squadron, commanded by Commodore Laborde.[2] Upon the very first suggestion that some of the proceedings of Commodore Porter, while he was in Key West were contrary to the neutral obligations of the United States, immediate inquiry into them was ordered by the President, and the necessary measures adopted to prevent them, should they be attempted.[3] It is not known to this Government, whatever might have been the intentions of Commodore Porter, that he performed any act, whilst he was within the jurisdiction of the United States, forbidden by the Laws of neutrality. Both the Letter from the Spanish Consul at New Orleans, and the Gazette,[4] containing the publication of Com. Porter, which you have communicated display the zeal and vigilance of the officers of the United States, in preventing and punishing any acts on the part of Commodore Porter, contrary to Law. In that very publication the Commodore himself professes every disposition to pay the strictest attention to all the rights of neutrality, and the Laws of the United States. As to the fact of that publication, if considerations of delicacy ought to have restrained Commodore Porter from making it, I have to observe that according to the perfect freedom of the press which prevails in this Country, there is nothing in the Law which forbade it. But even in that publication the Commodore holds out no invitation to any direct violation of our Laws. If he suggested means by which their provisions might be eluded, the United States Attorney for the District of Louisiana,[5] appears, in a contemporaneous publication to have promptly called the public attention to the enactment of the Law applicable to the case, and thus to have guarded the community against any misconception of its duty which Commodore Porters publication might have tended to produce. In short, Sir, whilst it is freely admitted that Commodore Porter's conduct was not, in all respects, whilst he was lately in the Ports·of the United States, in conformity with the duties of that hospitality which was freely extended to him, the President is not aware that any part of it affords to Spain just ground of complaint.

I avail myself of this occasion to offer to you assurances of my distinguished Consideration.   H. CLAY.

Copy. DNA, RG59, Notes to Foreign Legations, vol. 3, pp. 394–95 (M38, R3) .
[1] See above, Gray to Clay, July 24, October 15, 1827.   [2] Angel Laborde.   [3] Cf. above, Clay to Obregón, May 21, 1827; Clay to Poinsett, May 31, 1827; Clay to Rivas y Salmon, June 9, 1827, note; Poinsett to Clay, October 5, 1827; Hay to Clay, August 6, 27, 1827.   [4] Antonio Argote y Villalobos; Baltimore *Gazette and Daily Advertiser*.
[5] John W. Smith.

From Charles Hammond

My Dear Sir.   Cincinnati Oct. 29. 1827.
From the best information I can obtain the final results of the Ohio election[1] Shows [sic] that Jackson is making Some advances. These are not sufficient to indicate any Serious danger, but are of a character to impress upon us the necessity of activity. We have accordingly taken measures to dicipline [sic] and organize our friends for action. Before the suggestion of a convention, made in the Columbus papers had reached us here, we had issued a private circular of which I send you a copy. We have no doubt but that the day named in it will be finally and generally adopted. A proper address will be prepared to be made by the convention to the people of the State, and Such other measures I trust will be commenced, as may enable us to meet our opponents on equal ground.[2] The Next Ohio Legislature will be about one third Jacksonians.[3] The Senate consists of thirty Six. Twelve are decidely for the Hero. Twenty two for the administration, and two— Gardener of Xenia, and Slaughter of Fairfield[4] on the fence. The House consists of 72 members. I am enabled to number but 23 for the Hero. In the Senate Some of the most persevering and artful men, Dr. Hamm[5] for Example, are against us. The Strong men of the House are with us.

It Seems there is no more chance to put down and Silence the lies of the Opposition, on the Subject of bargain and corruption, than there was of old to destroy the heads of the fabled dragon. Indeed for One lie contradicted two new ones are immediately got up. Before the labours of Jackson Branch Mc Duffie and Eaton[6] have compleated the rounds of circulation, the new story of a Baily & Webster intrigue is Set on foot.[7] And whilst contradiction is on the heels of that, we have another one started here which I suppose the Richmond Enquirer and the Evening Post will think it worth while to retail. I send you, with this, an Editorial article cut out of Dawsons paper of Saturday, in which you are accused of buying the Support of Wright and myself, by bartering to us the rights and interests of your client, the Bank of the United States, in her controversy with the State.[8] For this libel I have commenced a Suit against the author & publisher, being determined to bring to the test of legal investigation one charge of corruption and coalition.[9] I do this, not because I apprehend the tale will gain credence but for the purpose of ascertaining which is the true state of public Sentiment, as it may be found through the courts of justice, upon this Subject of libelous falsehood. This is a case of private conduct, in some degree separated from the matters that now agitate the public mind. A proper example of punishment may have a Salutory [sic] effect.

There is no question that Governor Clinton has determined to take the field for Jackson. He has so written to Atwater, and copies of his letter are circulated to produce effect. We have one in this City—dated Sep. 17. He says he has never *disguised* his preference for Jackson. He adds that New York will assuredly give him her vote.[10] We know, however, that the Governor must of necessity think So. I cannot but smile whenever I think how compleatly Van Buren has overreached the Governor.

The election of Mr Sergeant is a matter of much Gratulation for the Country. I have heard him named for Speaker.[11] This must not be. He cannot be spared from the floor. Do you not anticipate a majority against you?[12] I apprehend nothing from Such a State of things but its bad effect upon the timid and the wavering through the land.

Allow me to Say that the events of every day confirm me more and more in the opinion expressed in my letter,[13] that you should demand an investigation. It is the common opinion of those who converse here. Sincerely yours   C. HAMMOND.

ALS. OHi. Addressed to Clay.   [1] Cf. above, Clay to Sloane, October 14, 1827, note. [2] Urged by the *Ohio State Journal and Columbus Gazette* on October 18, a preliminary meeting of the "friends of the Administration" was held in Columbus on November 10. From this rally came a call for the selection of delegates to a statewide convention to draw up an electoral ticket supporting Adams for the Presidency in 1828. Some 220 delegates, including Hammond and representing 66 of Ohio's 73 counties, attended this convention in Columbus on December 28, 1827. *Ibid.*, October 25, December 29, 1827; January 2, 1828.   [3] The incoming Ohio Legislature showed 22 Administration supporters and 13 Jacksonites in the Senate and 44 Administration supporters and 28 Jacksonites in the House of Representatives. One member in each house was reported to be "on the fence." *Niles' Weekly Register*, XXXIII (February 2, 1828), 374.   [4] James B. Gardiner; Robert F. Slaughter. The latter had served in the Ohio House of Representatives in 1817, in 1819, and from 1821 to 1824 and in the Ohio Senate from 1803 to 1804, from 1810 to 1811, and since 1826. He remained in the latter body until 1832.   [5] John Hamm.   [6] For "the labours of Jackson," cf. above, Clay to Hammond, June 25, 1827, note, and Smith to Clay, August 1, 1827, note; of Branch, Clay to Harrison, September 6, 1827, note; of McDuffie, Porter to Clay, August 19, 1827, note; of Eaton, Ingersoll to Clay, October 6, 1827, note.   [7] On October 6, 1827, the Philadelphia *National*

Palladium had reported that Daniel Webster's influence in winning Federalist support for Adams' election "during the winter of 1824–25" had been obtained through the intercession of Representative John Bailey of Massachusetts, who professed that he had been authorized to promise "that if Mr. Adams was made President the claims of that party to office should have all and every proper consideration." Reprinted in New York *Evening Post*, October 9, 1827. Bailey on October 11, had denounced the account as a "gross fabrication." Reprinted in *Liberty Hall and Cincinnati Gazette*, October 31, 1827. Cf. Livermore, *Twilight of Federalism*, 214.   8 For the case of Ohio, that is, *Osborn vs. The Bank of the United States*, and Clay's role therein, see above, II, 721, and note; III, 646–47, and notes. The offending editorial had appeared in Moses Dawson's Cincinnati *Advertiser*, October 27, 1827.   9 No record of the suit has been found. Cf. below, Clay to Hammond, November 16, 1827.   10 See below, Hammond to Clay, November 5, 1827, and cf. above, Rochester to Clay, September 17, 1827.   11 John Sergeant—cf. above, Sergeant to Clay, September 28, 1826, note; Rochester to Clay, October 12, 1827; below, Rochester to Clay, November 4, 1827.   12 Cf. above, Clay to Taylor, September 7, 1827, note.   13 Above, October 18, 1827.

From Daniel Webster

My Dear Sir,   Private & Confidential   Boston Otr. 29. 1827

I recd the enclosed[1] this morning, & prefer directing a short answer, (which is all I have time for, as I am bound into Court) directly to yourself. I do this for reasons of prudence, not knowing the writer.[2]

Towards relieving the Gentleman[3] mentioned, I have already done what I thought I could afford. The Case, however, seems a pressing one, and I suppose friends here might be induced to lend a helping hand, if there were time & opportunity for consulting them. Indeed no difficulty would be felt about it, if there were not so many other similar cases— As it is, I will say to you, that $250 shall be forthcoming from this quarter, if eno more should be obtained to ensure the accomplishment of the object. That you or others must judge of, & I shall be content with the result. A line from you,[4] saying that you think there may be a fair chance of effecting good, by such a measure, on our part, shall be answered by an immediate transmission to you of the amt. above mentioned—Yrs   D WEBSTER

ALS. DLC-HC (DNA, M212, R3).
1 Not found. Cf. below, Webster to Clay, November 5, 1827.   2 Marcellus Smith, who was at this time one of the editors and publishers of the Richmond *Whig*.
3 John H. Pleasants.   4 Below, November 8, 1827.

INSTRUCTIONS AND DISPATCHES   October 29, 1827

From W[ILLIAM] B[EACH] LAWRENCE, London, no. 4. Acknowledges receipt of Clay's "despatches Nos. 34, 35, and 36 [September 11, 12, 17, 1827] addressed to Mr. [Albert] Gallatin"; adds that, "agreeably to that gentleman's instructions, copies have been taken and the originals forwarded to him." States that "the Map and letter furnished by Mr. [Edward] Livingston will afford valuable aid, should further communication with the British Government" on the subject of lights between the Bahama Banks and Florida "become necessary." States that "The same omission as to the place for exchanging the ratification," noticed by Clay "in the Conventions signed on August last, will be found on the one recently concluded respecting the North East Boundary" (cf. above, Gallatin to Clay, September 30, 1827). Expresses an assumption that Gallatin will inform Clay of "the understanding of the Plenipotentiaries" (cf. below, Gallatin to Clay, November 11, 1827) and notes that he, himself, does "not feel authorized . . . to make inquiries on this point from the British Government. . . ." Reports having been told, however, by [Sebastián] Camacho, "last spring," of "a circular from the [British] Foreign Office, by which he was informed that this Government had determined, on making Treaties with States, where the assent of the Legislature or one of its branches was necessary, that the ratification of such State should precede that of the King of Great Britain." Recalls that "This . . . agrees with the suspicions intimated by Mr. Gallatin, when transmitting the Slave Indemnity Convention" (cf. above, Gallatin to Clay, November 11, 13, 1826). ALS. DNA, RG59, Dip. Disp., Great Britain, vol. 35 (M30, R13). Received December 11.

MISCELLANEOUS LETTERS   October 29, 1827

To CHARLES J. INGERSOLL, "U. S. Attorney for the E. District of Pennsylvania." Acknowledges receipt of his letter of the 25th. instant" and notes that Clay had "previously on the 24th. instant" replied to Ingersoll's letter of the 22d." States that Clay has "requested the Secretary of the Treasury [Richard Rush—above, October 28, 1827] to instruct the Collector [William Jones] to require of the owners of that vessel [the corvette *Kensington*] bond, with sureties, agreeably to the Act of Congress applicable to such cases." Submits to Ingersoll's judgment whether the facts reported "warrant a prosecution" and advises at least a warning to the collector to exert vigilance. Copy. DNA, RG59, Dom. Letters, vol. 22, p. 72 (M40, R20).

From W[ILLIAM] B. GILES, Richard (Virginia). Acknowledges, with an expression of thanks to Clay and the President, the receipt of Clay's letter of October 20, "accompanied with certain Journals of the House of Delegates of this State"; notes "a mistake . . . in the transmission of one of the volumes— The Volume containing the Journals of 1804–1805, was transmitted, instead of that containing the Journal of 1782; which is the one wanted"; and asks that the latter volume be sent to him. LS. DNA, RG59, Misc. Letters (M179, R65).

From CHARLES S. HEMPSTEAD, St. Louis. Forwards a "Statement of facts" from himself and his father (Stephen Hempstead, Sr.), together with a letter from "several of . . . [the] most respectable [citizens of Missouri—documents not found]," concerning the imprisonment of his brother, Thomas [W.] Hempstead, at Cádiz, Spain (cf. below, Hempstead to Clay, November 20, 1827, note). Adds that the latter may be moved to Havana. Requests that the Government's representatives in Spain or Cuba "advance to him such sum as he may need, and it shall be reimbursed—" Asks that letters, enclosed, for his brother be forwarded "to Spain and Cuba." ALS. DNA, RG59, Misc. Letters (M179, R65).

Stephen Hempstead, Sr., a veteran of the Revolutionary War, had emigrated in 1811 from his native Connecticut to Missouri Territory, where he played a prominent role in the establishment of the Presbyterian Church.

To Charles Hammond

My dear Sir   (Confidential)   Washn. 30h. Oct. 1827.
I have to thank you for your obliging letter of the 18h. inst. There has been a correspondence between Genl. Harrison and myself in re-

spect to Mr. Branch's Speech. When I spoke at Noble's,[1] on the subject of my nomination to the Senate, the point, that I was laying stress upon, was the *silence* of Genl. Jackson, in regard to that nomination, at the time he acted upon it, and it did not then occur to me that Genl. Harrison had informed me that Govr. Branch had opposed it. The fact of an opposition to it by any other Senator than Genl. J. was not material to the argument I was pressing. Afterwards, when I saw it asserted that Branch had opposed it, I was satisfied that Genl. Harrison had stated to me, in general terms, that Mr. B. had opposed it, but I am convinced that he did not give me any detail of Mr. B.s speech, and that he spoke of it as one characterized by great malignity, which had made no impression, and of which my friends did not deem it necessary to take any notice— It must be evident that I could not have intended to assert that which could be contradicted by every Senator present on the occasion. Mr. Johnston of Louisiana recollects[2] having told me, the evening after the nomination was approved, that nothing had occurred in the Senate, on the subject of it, which was necessary to be noticed by my friends or me.

In respect to another Appeal to Congress, my present purpose is to present to the public, at a suitable time, during the approaching Session, a mass of testimony which has been collected, in exculpation of my friends and myself, and exposing the conduct of Genl. J.[3] but to make no further appeal to Congress myself. I shall, at the same time, be ready to express my hearty concurrence in any inquiry which may be proposed to the H. of R. by the other party. If I were to ask the enquiry, it would give *color* to the recent movements, and thereby at least tacitly admit that they had proved something. It would moreover take the affair out of the hands of Genl. Jackson and relieve him, and make me responsible for throwing a firebrand into Congress. Such are my own impressions, but I am ready to yield to a contrary course, if my friends shall think it expedient.

You ask what is the fact about the allegation of my having written to Jackson in the fall 1824 to travel with me to Washington?[4] In the fall 1823 we had become reconciled, so far as least as to be upon terms of civil intercourse, at the instance and upon the advance of *his* friends. *They* (the Tennessee delegation) made a dinner for that express purpose at Mrs. Claxton's Boarding house, to which we both were invited and at which H. L. White, then acting as Commr. under the Florida treaty, attended. These facts you are at liberty to use. In the succeeding fall, just before I sat [*sic*] out on my journey from Lexn. for this City, I heard that Jackson was coming that way. It was my wish that he should arrive there before I took my departure; and it was my intention if he did to shew him marked attention. To this I was impelled by the fact of the reconciliation, in the previous fall, by that of his being in the State in which I resided, at my home, and by that of our being competitors for the same office. I regretted, therefore, that I was compelled, from the necessity of my punctual attendance as Speaker, to leave home before the Genl. reached Lexn. I have no recollection, nor do I believe, that I wrote him any note whatever. If I did, let it be produced. I was certainly in a state of relation towards him at that time which would have permitted my addressing such a note to him, without any sinister motive whatever. Recollect that at that time I did not know the electoral vote of one State in the Union, not even my own, except by conjecture. I did not hear the result in Ohio until I reached the Kanawha. Equally false is the assertion that I crossed the Pennsa. Avenue to congratulate the General on his Electoral vote. The truth is, that from the fall 1823 up to a short period before the election, when my decision was known, *there were a succession of wooing advances from Jackson and his friends to me and mine.*

The P. Office at Cincinnati is in a condition to be regretted. That at Lexington is in the same state.[5] I do not believe it practicable to prevail on the President to move in the affair. He has great, if not inconquerable repugnance to turning any man out of office, merely for opinion. He believes it impolitic. The P. M. General[6] will not act because the state of things is agreeable to him. I do not know, whence his fears proceeded, which induced him to write to Mr. Woods, unless from his own consciousness. There has been no Cabinet consideration of the question whether he ought to be displaced or not; and he professes to and deceives the President.[7] I have defended the P.M. in private conversation as long as I could, and when I could no longer I have not accused him.

Our prospects are every where auspicious on this side of the mountains, except in N. York,[8] and there there are so many clouds that one cannot distinctly see what they are. We shall know after next week. In the City of N. York our friends are sanguine of success. Even in the antient dominion a powerful movement is making.[9]

Among the facts which I am endeavoring to establish is that of Jackson having freely, on board a Steam boat, at taverns and other public places, in the Spring 1825, on his return from this City to Nashville, asserted that Mr. Adams had succeeded in the election by a corrupt agreement with me. I shall be able to prove his assertion to that effect at Washn. in Pennsa., on board a steam boat, and at the Bowling Green in K. I have understood that he made the same statement at Cincinnati. Can you procure me from some respectable person a certificate of his having heard him make it at Cincinnati?[10] If you can I will be greatly obliged to you—

Will you be here this winter? Truly Your friend   H CLAY
C. Hammond Esq

ALS. InU.   1 See above, Toasts and Speech, July 12, 1827.
2 Cf. below, Johnston to Clay, November 17, 1827.   3 Below, *Address . . . to the*

Public, December 29, 1827.   4 Cf. above, Clay to Johnston, October 6, 1827.
     5 Cf. above, Dudley to Clay, August 17, 1827; Smith to Clay, October 7, 1827.   6 John
McLean.   7 Cf. above, Hammond to Clay, March 28, 1827, note.   8 Cf. above,
Sergeant to Clay, October 24, 1827, note.   9 Cf. above, Brooke to Clay, August 8,
1827; Caldwell to Clay, August 8, 1827; Southard to Clay, August 8, 1827; Mercer to Clay,
August 18, 1827.   10 In his *Address . . . to the Public,* below, December 29, 1827
(pamphlet edition, 20–22) Clay used this documentation to refute Jackson's claim, in
his public statement of July 18, 1827 (see above, Smith to Clay, August 1, 1827, note),
that his charge of a corrupt bargain in connection with the Presidential election of
February, 1825, had originated at his "own house and fireside" in March, 1827, in the
conversation reported by Carter Beverley (see above, Clay to Hammond, June 25, 1827,
note). The "indiscretion" was therefore not the result of "an unguarded moment of
hilarity, amidst his convivial friends, in his own domicil [*sic*]. . . ," Clay concluded. For
Jackson's remarks at Washington, Pennsylvania, see Andrew Wylie to Thomas McGiffin,
February 15, 1828; for those at Bowling Green, Kentucky, see John Keel to Francis Johnson, February 23, 1828—both published in the pamphlet edition of Clay's *Supplement to
the Address . . .* (cf. below, June 10, 1828), 6–7. For the incident aboard the steamboat,
see Daniel Large to Samuel Wetherill, October 2, 1827, with endorsement by William
Crowsdiil, October 5, 1827, published in Clay's *Address . . . to the Public,* "Appendix,"
58. No testimony has been found concerning such a statement at Cincinnati. Wylie, born
in Washington County, Pennsylvania, and graduated in 1812 from Jefferson College at
Cannonsburg, in that State, was a Presbyterian minister. He had been president of Jefferson College from 1813 to 1817 and of Washington College since the latter date. From
1828 to 1851 he was president of Indiana University, at Bloomington, Indiana. Keel
(or Kiel) has not been identified. Crowsdill (also cited as Crosdell and Croasdill) was a
resident of Philadelphia.

To Enoch Lincoln

His Excellency, Enoch Lincoln, Govr.
of the State of Maine, Portland.
Sir,   Dept. of State, Washington 30 Octr. 1827
    I have committed to the charge of Mr. William Prentis [*sic*],¹ who
will have the honor to deliver them and this letter to your Excellency,
and who is employed for that purpose, twenty four Manuscript Volumes of Books, according to the accompanying list,² on the subject of
the North, and North Easterly Boundary Lines of the United States,
prepared at this Office for the State of Maine, conformably with the
suggestions and desire expressed by your Excellency.³ From the extent
of these Manuscripts, it is more than probable, that they embrace
copies of a great deal more, in documents, discussion and Argument
than was in the contemplation of your Excellency, or than was desired
for the use of your State; but to secure a full compliance with your
Excellency's views, and to guard against any deficiency, I gave directions to have a Transcript made of everything which might by possibility, be useful or interesting upon the occasion, having the remotest bearing upon the subject, with the limitation stated in my
previous correspondence;⁴ and as the selection was necessarily committed to others, who may not have had a very accurate view of the
extent of the commission entrusted to them, it is not improbable that
it may comprise much which may be found superfluous. I send also
forty two copies of Maps likewise prepared with the same views, and
under the same circumstances, which Mr. Prentis will, also, have the

honor to deliver to your Excellency. I am, with great respect, your Excellys. obedient, humble Servant,   H. CLAY.

Copy. DNA, RG59, Dom. Letters, vol. 22, pp. 323–24 (M40, R20).
1 William H. Prentiss.   2 Not found.   3 See above, Lincoln to Clay, March 20, April 18, May 29, 1827.   4 See above, Clay to Lincoln, March 27, May 7, June 8, 1827.

From John J. Crittenden

Dear Sir,   Frankfort Octr: 30th 1827

It would take more time than it is worth, to make a sufficient apology for my long negligence in writing to you. I dare say you have almost considered it as some evidence, that the treachery of the times, which has swept from you so many of your old friends, has overtaken me also— It is not yet quite so bad as that.

Early in Septr:, at the Woodford Circuit Court I delivered your letter to Mr White[1] after a conversation with him on the subject to which it related— After he had read it, he told me that he would write to you, & from what he said I did not doubt but that his answer would be entirely satisfactory to you— I met with him again lately at this place, & was surprised to learn that he had not yet written— After another long conversation about the matter he concluded by saying that he would write to you as soon as he went home— I hope he has done so before this time— In conversation with me he says every thing you could desire, but seems to have some obscure fear of committing it to writing— He requested me to say to you "that you had nothing to fear from him." I told him that he had better write to you himself, & he concluded that he would. So the matter stands with him. If he does not give you the statement you wish,—he will not come out against you— He can not, nor, do I believe, he is disposed to do it, tho' the contrary has been thought.[2]

You seen [sic] the letters with which Mr Kendall has honored you in the Argus[3]— Blair & myself are of course the two confidential friends & correspondents of yours to whom he alludes— And Blair, the one spoken of as having prevailed on him to write— I have had but little to say with Mr. B— upon the subject— Indeed I hardly knew how to talk with him, or upon what terms to meet him— We had some conversation to day, & I learn from him that he has written to you fully[4]— That Kendalls publication was made without his knowledge—that nothing should induce him to act treacherously, or extort his private letters &c   He has no doubt explained more at large to you. For myself I beleive [sic] I received no letter from you during the month of Jany: 1825, nor any before the Presidential election, touching your appointment to the office of Secty: of State— For the purpose of replying to this reference of Mr. Kendall, & of vindicating myself from charges & animadversions that have been made on me for certain letters which I wrote to Genl Call & Mr White, I have prepared a piece for publication, & intended it to appear in the papers of this week— But have determined to with-hold it one week longer for further consideration[5]— I feel as if it were steping [*sic*] into the fire,—tho my determination is at present strong to take that step. I feel now as if it was required of me by duty, & that I ought therefore to be regardless of consequences.

County meetings are taking place throughout the State, on the part of the friends of the administration, & th[ey] appear determined to be well organized & prepared for the approaching contest[.]

Affairs remain with us as they were—there is no visible change that I can perceive— The news of the elections in Maryland, Delaware &c[6] have much encouraged your friends here, & have for the time given them more spirit.—

I wish you to return me the letter I some time ago wrote you containing my statement of your decleration [*sic*] to me that you could not vote for Jackson &c   I wish to make an alteration or addition in it, not affecting the substance of it, but which is nevertheless conformable to the truth, & material to me[7]— It shall be forthwith sent back to you. Yr's &c   J J CRITTENDEN
Hon: H Clay, Secty &c

ALS. NcD.   [1] David White, Jr. The letter has not been found.
[2] White did not provide Clay with the desired letter; but he did issue a statement to the public, dated February 17, 1828, which Clay included in his *Supplement to the Address . . . in December, 1827* . . . (Washington, 1828), 19–20 (below, June 10, 1828). There White denied any connection "in the alleged *management, bargain, sale, &c.* in the election of the President, and in the formation of his cabinet," and asserted that he believed his vote for Adams conformed to the will of his constituents. He stated: "I shall, in the exercise of my constitutional right of suffrage, vote for the Jackson ticket, and I will support it with zeal. Any opposition I may offer to the re-election of Mr. Adams, grows out of circumstances foreign from, and entirely unconnected with, his late election by the House of Representatives."   [3] Above, September 26, October 10, 1827.   [4] Above, Blair to Clay, October 3, 1827.   [5] Crittenden's statement, published in the Frankfort *Spirit of Seventy Six* and reprinted in the Lexington *Kentucky Reporter*, November 14, 1827, noted that "In the last presidential election" he had had "some partialities for" Jackson and "some prejudices against" Adams but that he had "greatly preferred Mr. Clay to both of them, and," he had continued, "it was my opinion that either of them, with Mr. Clay associated in the executive department, would form a safer and better administration for the country, than the other without him." Crittenden denied that his letters to Richard K. Call or to White were inconsistent with these views "or at variance with each other."   Alluding to current suggestions that he had received from Clay "in the month of January 1825" letters which conveyed information that Adams "had promised, if elected President, to make him secretary of state," Crittenden protested against the agitation to induce him to reveal private correspondence but asserted as the best of his recollection that he had received no letter from Clay during the month of January, 1825. "And," he stated, "neither then nor at any other time did I ever receive from him or any other correspondent of mine any letter containing information of such a promise, or of any such bargain or compact upon the subject."   [6] Cf. above, Clay to Henry, October 20, 1827, note.   [7] See above, Crittenden to Clay, September 3, 1827, and notes.

From Peter B. Porter

Sir,   New York October 30th. 1827.

Having closed the Commissions under the 6th. and 7th. Articles of the Treaty of Ghent,[1] it may be proper that I should give you a condensed history of our recent proceedings, many of the particulars of which have already been, from time to time, seperately [sic] communicated to you.

I had confidently calculated to close the Commission at the meeting of the Board which took place about a year ago;[2] but various circumstances concurred in recommending, at that time, to both parties, its further continuance.

[Explains three reasons for the delay: disgreement on "some portions" of the boundary line, principally that "to be run along St. George's island"; the necessity of waiting for a reply from the British Government to a proposal that the surveyors, delegated "to trace a meridian line" from the Lake of the Woods to the forty ninth parallel, should also trace that parallel "as far west as the Red River"; and the time required for the British surveyor to make enough copies of his maps for exchange.

[Notes the decision "to adjourn the Board" until March, 1827 (cf. above, Delafield to Clay, November 15, 1826), and refers to his journey to New York, in April, and the letter from (Anthony) Barclay to (Joseph) Delafield (cf. above, Porter to Clay, April 20, 1827). Continues:] I thereupon immediately wrote to him[3] requesting a meeting for closing the Commission, as early as he could be prepared, of which I requested him to advise me. In his reply dated on the 30th. of April, he agreed to give the information, and accounted for the delay of certain other dispatches which he was expecting from his government, by the then unsettled state of its Cabinet.[4] On the 18th. of September I received a letter from him dated on the 13th. of that month, proposing a meeting at New York in October, which accordingly took place on the 22d. instant, and the proceedings of which will appear from the copy of our Journal which will be forwarded to you by Major Delafield—

You will perceive from this Journal that I have been disappointed in the expectation I had encouraged, that the British Government would instruct its commissioner to relinquish his claim to St. George's Island— Indeed, I am now entirely convinced (and I trust there is no impropriety in expressing this conviction to you) that their claim to this island was originally made, and is still persisted in, in compliance with private instructions from the British Government; and these instructions not founded on any intrinsic merits which the claim itself is supposed to possess, but merely intended to lay the foundation of a negociation, by which they hope to alter a part of the line already established under the sixth Article[5]—with which the people and Government of Canada are much dissatisfied, and against which they have made strong remonstrances to their Government at home.[6]—

I flatter myself that the President, after reading my seperate report and the documents which will accompany it, will not be dissatisfied that I have resisted the extraordinary pretensions of my colleague in regard to St. Georges island, although it has resulted in an ultimate disagreement. This disagreement however will be attended with but little practical inconvenience to us, as we shall continue to enjoy the same common right to the navigation of the eastern channel, as we should, had the line been established through it, in conformity with my opinion: And as to the island itself—being situated in the immediate vicinity of our Fort at the Saulte de St. Marie[7]—it is, I believe, already in the possession of the garrison, and no attempt will probably be made by the British to dispossess them. That portion of the line, west of Lake Superior, in regard to which we have disagreed, is through a section of Country, uninhabited, and I might perhaps add, uninhabitable; and therefore not likely to be a cause of future collision.

[Asserts that "It is difficult to ascertain . . . the precise grounds" on which Barclay will "sustain his claim to St. George's island" but conjectures that "The substance . . . of his argument may . . . be gathered from" (Charles R.) Vaughan's letter to Clay, "in October last" (above, October 23, 1826), to "some parts of" which, with Clay's permission, he "may have occasion . . . to refer . . . as bases for observations . . . on the principles and facts it advances."]

Having minutely described on our Journal, all that portion of the boundary under the seventh article upon which we were agreed, and specified the points in difference (in regard to which all hopes of compromise had ceased) and having also adjusted our accounts, we proceeded, on Saturday last, to close the Commission, by an adjournment *sine die.*

[Reports agreement with Barclay to exchange, "on the 24th. December next," duplicates of their reports, at which time both reports will be forwarded to the State Department. Calls attention to entries in "the Journal" showing that (John) Hale ceased to act as "British Agent to the Commission," and attributes "His discharge" to "some personal dissatisfaction" (cf., however, above, Vaughan to Clay, May 12, 1826; Delafield to Clay, May 25, June 23, 1826). Cites the need for "an intelligent Agent" at the time of closing of the Commission.]

I have the honor, to be, with great respect, Your Obedient Servant
Honorable Henry Clay Secretary of State   PETER B. PORTER

P.S.   [Proposes that Major Delafield and he postpone settlement of their accounts in Washington "for two or three months. . . ."] As regards myself, if my personal convenience is entitled to any consideration, I would remark, that I propose making a journey to the south, with my family, as soon as the navigation opens in the spring, when I could very conveniently attend to these accounts; and you may therefore suppose that I would gladly dispense with a previous journey of 1500 miles, (going and returning) to be performed in the depth of winter and all the way over land.   PETER B. PORTER

Hon. Mr Clay, Secretary of State.

LS. DNA, RG76, Northern Boundary: Treaty of Ghent, 1814, Articles VI and VII, env. 1, folder 1.
    1 Cf. above, Clay to Vaughan, November 15, 1826; Porter to Clay, October 26, 1827.
    2 Cf. above, Delafield to Clay, September 23, 1826; Porter to Clay, October 8, 1826.
    3 That is, Barclay.   4 Cf. above, Gallatin to Clay, February 22, 1827, and note.
    5 Cf. above, Porter to Clay, November 4, 1826; Clay to Vaughan, November 15, 1826. A settlement signed by Barclay and Porter on June 18, 1822, had provided for a boundary under Article VI of the Treaty of Ghent to run from the point at which the 45th parallel of north latitude intersects the St. Lawrence River to the foot of the Neebish Rapids. Parry (ed.), *Consolidated Treaty Series*, vol. 72, pp. 368–72. The boundary under Article VII was to run thence to the northwestern point of the Lake of the Woods. On the remaining area of disagreement, cf. below, Delafield to Clay, November 6, 1827.   6 The "strong remonstrances" came from Lower Canada, where the people were reportedly "crying out at what they term the encroaching spirit of the government of the United States. . . ." *Niles Weekly Register*, XXXIII (February 23, 1828), 438. See also above, Porter to Clay, November 2, 1826.   7 Fort Brady. Cf. above, Porter to Clay, November 7, 1826.

From Isaac Russell

Mr Henry Clay
Dr Sir   Cincinnati October 30th 1827

[Reminds Clay that his "last lines" to him reported "no prospect of employment" for him in the State Department (letter not found) but urges that Clay not forget him. Cites the necessity of "getting to the Atlantic board" and his desire "to live again in Washington" because of a chronic pulmonary "affection," which he believes would be aided by a diet of "principally Oysters." Notes his skills at architectural drawing and composing letters.]

There was a great stir or fuss here, a few days ago; carriages gratis, filled with the halt, the lame & & [sic] the blind; nearly all drunk, to vote for Jackson, or to try his strength in the State Appointments of Ohio; such as these preponderated;[1] yet I do believe, as I did before at Hagerstown, that his Excellency the President will succeed at his 2nd Election— the friends of the Administration make no display, they are above imitating the vociferations of the rabble—

I was sorry Sir I was not at Pittsburgh when you dined there at Holdship's;[2] as I intended to have the pleasure of waiting on you; but this is my apology.— I had to go down to Jeffersonville land Office previous to 4th last July to save my Indiana tract, below Louisville, on which I ow'd Congress 50 Dolls.; which you might have observ'd I serv'd diligently for at the Lexington factory;[3] I went down in the Maryland

Stm. Bt. belonging to Stuart of Pittsbg.⁴— We ran aground, which prevented me to get to Mr Gwathmey⁵ till after 4th July, when he could not receive my balance,—*it reverted*! ! it was 80 Acres, as I relinquish'd 80 Acres, I set a great value on it; I intended to have thereon, a little Mill, a little Store & a little School; it is opposite Salt River in Inda.—

Mr Gwathmey gives me to hope that Congress next Session will extend the payments for another year or session— Ah Sir! how desirable this would be; our income now coming out, would this fall liquidate it, and it would be my own again, and I would receive my patent from President Adams— I wish and I want Sir your advice how I may act in this Case; whether you think that Congress may relieve me by a continuation of last Act "for relief of purchasers of public land"⁶   there are many poor distressed men in Indiana who have not been able to come in this Summer. I have been in Inda some days and did not see a dollar circulate there— Or shall I present a private petition *through you Sir* or our Indiana representatives, *Mr Noble, Mr Jennings, Mr Test.*⁷

I pray you Sir communicate your Suggestions to his Excellency Mr Adams, that perchance he may, with his council, see fit to recommend the poor Debtors of Pc. Ld. to Congress for amelioration & relief   I know he's a good man, let others say as they may;—   by so doing, he will have the blessing of future generations   With great respect, Mr Clay, I have the pleasure to conclude, your ever assured friend

ISAAC RUSSELL

☞ I have been here since June waiting for a rise of water.— The river is rising now rapidly

But please dictate to one of your clerks a letter in answer to this to this City— I dont feel strong enough yet to go up. I have a very fine double barrelld gun, & elegant fishing pole; but I dont go out— my fort [*sic*] is, to stay within to write, &c.

I R

PS—   I would be willing to receive as a salary from 4 to 800 Ds; I had at Lexington 700, at Louisville 900$,— if *you* wd be so friendly as to send me on 50 Ds to travel to Washn. it would be expediting me quikr [*sic*] I got 70 Ds. from James Prentiss at Phila. to come out to Lexn., not charg'd to me— officers travelling expences, 10 P Centum Per [. . .]⁸

ALS. DLC-HC (DNA, M212, R3). ¹ A meeting of Jackson's Hamilton County supporters had been held in Cincinnati on October 27 to select delegates to a State convention to meet at Columbus on January 8 "for the purpose of forming an Electoral Ticket, for the State." Ten delegates were named, with the proviso that if they could not attend the convention the members of the General Assembly from the county should serve as delegates. Cincinnati *Advertiser*, November 3, 1827.   ² Above, Toasts and Speech, June 19, 1827.   ³ The Lexington Manufacturing Company, founded by James Prentiss and operated from 1815 to 1818 for the manufacture of paper and woolen and cotton goods.   ⁴ The *Maryland*, a sidewheeler of 160 tons, had been put in service this year, 1827. It was still in operation a decade later. James Hall, *Statistics of the West, at the Close of the Year 1836* (Cincinnati,

1836), 258. It had probably been built by the Pittsburgh iron merchant, Robert T. Stewart, whose firm manufactured steam engines and boilers.   5 Probably Samuel Gwathmey, former (1805–1808) member of the Legislative Council of Indiana Territory and at this time Register of the United States Land Office at Jeffersonville, Indiana, a town he had helped found in 1802. In 1829 he lost his patronage job in the land office and moved to Louisville, Kentucky, where he was active in merchandizing and banking.   6 Cf. above, Farnham to Clay, August 7, 1827, note.   7 James Noble; Jonathan Jennings; and John Test.   8 Word illegible.

From John Scott

Honble Henry Clay
Dr Sir   St Louis. October 30th 1827

Our mutual friends John Perry and company[1] have become the proprietors of the only furnace in operation in Missouri—   This furnace is well Situated about thirty five miles from the Mississippi River; is in the Midst of the best Iron bank known—   This Establishment is young but very useful, and bids fair if properly encouraged to promote that System for which you have so long and ably contended— Those gentlemen are very desirous to make a Contract with the government to furnish any quantity of Cannon shot and shells that may be wanted in the west, or any where else; they can deliver them at any point, at any time, and cheap—   This Contract would encourage new beginners, and the State, bring other Lands into market, and be very useful to the govt.—   As this is a national matter to be prepared with the means of defense they request. as I do for them. that you will State to the Secretary of war.[2] or others your views of the advantages, propriety and Utility of Such, a Contract   I have the honor to be Truly yours   JOHN SCOTT

ALS. DNA, RG45, Misc. Letters Recd., 1827, vol. 7. Cf. below, Clay to Southard, January 5, 1828.
1 Perry had arrived in Missouri as a child in 1806, when his father, James, settled on a large grant of land near Potosi. Perry inherited the bulk of his father's estate, opened mines on the lead-rich land, and by the time of his death in 1850 had become "a man of large affairs." Howard L. Conard (ed.), *Encyclopedia of the History of Missouri* (6 vols.; New York, 1901) , V, 89–90.   2 James Barbour.

From John Sergeant

Dear Sir,   (Private)   Philada. Octr. 30. 1827.

Notwithstanding all reasonable efforts on my part, and repeated promises on the part of Mr. M.,[1] he is on the point of publication without shewing me the Mss. I have known for some time that he was in the hands of a person[2] who is quite competent to give him the right direction, and to that person I have from time to time communicated what appeared necessary. Still, I was surprised at Mr. M. calling upon me this morning, just as I was going to Court (where I am now writing) to say he should be out to morrow, but would endeavour to shew me the Mss. in the course of the day. I doubt whether he will do it, but feel no great anxiety, because I am confident the thing is right.

Appearances just now are in some quarters rather squally. New York seems to be in the hands of demagogues, bound with the chains of party.[3] She is, as usual, altogether mysterious. At Harrisburg, you will have perceived the somerset the Pennsa. Intelligencer is making, frightened by the threat of losing the Legislative printing.[4] We had not the least intimation— In Ohio, selfishness has given our adversaries an advantage in the election of a member of Congress[5]— On the other hand, Virginia is taking a noble stand,[6] and in Pennsylvania, we do not despair.[7] The convention will meet in force, I have no doubt, and we will offer an electoral ticket of the highest character for private worth and political standing.[8] We have the right of the matter; and as before intimated, will never yield 'till we are beaten,   Very respectfully and truly Yrs.   JOHN SERGEANT
The Honble Henry Clay.

ALS. DLC-HC (DNA, M212, R3).
[1] Philip Swenk Markley. Cf. above, Sergeant to Clay, August 23, October 2, 5, 16, 1827. [2] Not identified.   [3] Cf. above, Sergeant to Clay, September 23, October 24, 1827; Porter to Clay, October 26, 1827; Hammond to Clay, October 29, 1827.   [4] The "somerset" (that is, somersault) of the Harrisburg newspaper had begun at least as early as October 2, when owner-editor David Krauss (Kraus, Krause) announced editorially that the *Pennsylvania Intelligencer* would support the Adams administration at the national level and the Democratic ticket at the local, Dauphin County, level. Good Democrats, he argued, need not support Jackson in the coming October 9 elections for State and local offices. On October 16, following the Democratic victory in Pennsylvania in those elections, Krauss withdrew from the ownership and daily editorial management of the paper, turning those duties and the paper itself over to his partner, senior editor Simon Cameron. A month later, on November 17, Cameron merged the *Intellingencer* into the Harrisburg *Pennsylvania Reporter and Democratic Herald*.   [5] William Stanbery. Cf. above, Clay to Sloane, October 14, 1827, note.   [6] Cf. above, Brooke to Clay, August 8, October 17, 1827; Caldwell to Clay, August 8, 1827; Southard to Clay, August 8, 1827; Mercer to Clay, August 18, 1827.   [7] Cf. above, Sergeant to Clay, September 23, October 14, 16, 1827; Mifflin to Clay, October 21, 1827.   [8] Cf. above, Sergeant to Clay, September 18, 1827, note.

INSTRUCTIONS AND DISPATCHES   October 30, 1827

From J[OHN] M. FORBES, Buenos Aires, no. 54. Mentions secret negotiations of the Government of Buenos Aires "with the several interior provinces. . . ." Discusses the controversy surrounding the order issued by General (Juan Antonio) Lavalleja, the commander-in-chief of the Army, to arrest Drs. (Juan Andrés) Ferrera and (Gabriel) Ocampo, two "distinguished magistrates" of the Banda Oriental; the resignation of (Joaquín) Suárez, Governor of that Province; and the release of the doctors, whose imprisonment was resisted on the grounds that, since no "National Government" existed, "among equal sister provinces, no one could arrogate the power of judging on facts and occurrences arrising [*sic*] in another." Notes, however, that the Provincial Junta of the Banda Oriental has been suppressed on General Lavalleja's order. Reports that, contemporaneous with these events, "several of the interior Provinces . . . have organized their contingents of troops for the National army."

Mentions the public attack by the Government "induced, as is supposed, by the influence of [Manuel José] Garcia," upon (Bernardino) Rivadavia's Ministry to London (cf. above, Smith to Clay, July 2, 1825, and note) and (Carlos) Alvear's command of the Army, and encloses "a copy of the message and of Mr. Rivadavia's answer" (documents not found). Comments that "the British Mission here, in close league with Manuel J. Garcia, are still hovering about the Government, endeavoring to press them into the conclusion of a patched-up peace [with Brazil], dictated principally by British cupidity and unchristianlike coveting of the Banda Oriental," but expresses his opinion that (Manuel) Dorrego (cf. above, Forbes to Clay, August 20, 1827) is instead "determined to try the fortunes of the field."

Reports "the first case of the capture of one of our vessels [the brig *Ruth*] by a privateer under this flag" (cf. above, Wright to Clay, October 27, 1827). States that he "made prompt and urgent representations of the case," but that the agents of the privateer immediately put the case into prize court, and that the answer he received from the Government contained only their promise of a "prompt and just decision. . . ." Encloses copies of his letter and the response. Explains that the *Ruth* was seized upon the grounds, established by Article 6 of "certain secret instructions *(instrucciones reservadas)* said to have been given to all" Buenos Aires privateers, that "the whole Coast of Brazil was to be considered in a state of blockade"; asserts that he attacked this "perfidious measure . . . in an anonymous article" in the press and addressed a note to the Minister of Foreign Affairs (Manuel Moreno) questioning the authenticity of the secret instructions and the Government's intention to carry them out; and transmits a copy of his note and a translation of the reply, attesting to the validity of the instructions but announcing a decree ordering the repeal of Article 6. Forwards, also, the translation of a Government note announcing that, by "resolution of the provinces," the Buenos Aires Government is charged with conducting "every thing relating to the war and the Foreign Relations. . . ."

Continues on December 3: notes the progress in the provinces of electing members to the General Convention; adds that "The affair of the *Ruth* remains still under trial," although "By an interlocutory sentence" she has been restored to her owners; and transmits minutes of a conference held on November 20 with Moreno. Forwards intelligence that Moreno has "separated himself from the Government," and indicates that "Doctors, Don Manuel Castro, now President of the High Court of Justice, and D. Gregorio Tagle, . . . formerly Secretary of State," are being considered as his successor. Mentions his intention of travelling to Montevideo for a three-week vacation, leaving John Dickinson Mendenhall in charge of the Legation. LS. DNA, RG59, Dip. Disp., Argentina, vol. 3 (M69, R4). Published in Espil (comp.), *Once Años en Buenos Aires*, 477–82. Received February 26, 1828.

Subjects discussed at the conference with Moreno, as reported in the enclosed minutes, included the cases of the *Hope*, the *Pizarro*, and the *Ruth*.

Ferrera, born at Buenos Aires in 1789, had been trained in law at Córdoba and in 1819, upon his return to Buenos Aires, had become an official in the Police Administration. Known as a supporter of national unification, he was forced to flee to Montevideo by the opposition to that movement. There he was active in the efforts to overthrow Juan Manuel de Rosas as head of the provincial forces who came to power in December, 1829, and dominated Argentine affairs for the next 20 years. Ferrera returned to Buenos Aires in 1853, was named prosecuting attorney, and the following year was elected a representative to the first Constitutional Assembly of the new government.

Ocampo, born in Santiago, Chile, in 1798, had also studied at the University of Córdoba and received his doctorate in 1819. In 1822 he had been elected a deputy for the province of Colchagua, Chile, but in 1826 had moved to Montevideo. He subsequently removed to Buenos Aires, where he also became an active opponent of Rosas. Forced to flee Argentina in 1838, he returned to Chile, where he became dean of the Faculty of Laws and Political Sciences of Santiago and was distinguished as one of the editors of both the civil and commercial codes.

Suárez de Rondelo, born in the Banda Oriental in 1781, had been active in the movement for national independence first from Portugal, then from Brazil, since 1810. He had been one of the principal members of the Assembly of Uruguay in 1825 and was later named interim governor under the Constituent Assembly. He became Minister of War in 1831 and, as Deputy or Senator, served in the legislature from 1834 until 1841, when he became provisional President. In the latter office he organized the defense of Montevideo against Argentine attack, initiated by Rosas, from 1843 until 1851. Suárez retired only after the abandonment of the long-standing siege and the fall of Rosas.

Castro, born in Salta in 1772, had come to Buenos Aires in 1809 and had been one of the early proponents of independence. He had been Intendant-Governor of Córdoba from 1817 to 1820, editor for one year of the Buenos Aires *Gaceta*, and in 1824 a deputy to the National Congress, over which body he had presided. He had founded and was permanent director of the Academy of Jurisprudence, and he remained president of the Chamber of Justice until his death in 1832.

Tagle, a native of Buenos Aires, had begun the practice of law in 1800, had been active in public administration during the last years of the viceroyalty, and had served as Secretary of State under Juan Martin de Pueyrredón, from 1817 to 1819. After several periods of exile, he had been invited to return to Buenos Aires in 1823, had been named to the Court of Appeals, and succeeded Castro as president of that tribunal in 1832. He was removed from that position by Rosas in 1835 and retired from public affairs.

MISCELLANEOUS LETTERS   October 30, 1827

From GEORGE H. HUBBELL, New York. Acknowledges receipt of the letter of September 22 (see above, Hubbell to Clay, September 15, 1827, note) and states that he will "repair immediately" to Manila. ALS. DNA, RG59, Cons. Disp. Manila, vol. 1 (M-T43, R1).

To Francisco Tacón

Chevalier Francisco Tacon, &c. &c. &c.   Department of State,
Sir,   Washington, D. C. 31st. Oct 1827.

I have submitted to the President of the United States the Letter which you did me the honor to address to me on the 5th. instant. Having conveyed the first information which was received at this Department of the equipping of the Corvette Kensington, in the port of Philadelphia, shortly after the receipt of it, an inquiry was directed into the condition and circumstances of that Vessel, and the proper Law Officer of the Government was instructed, if they were found to be such as were prohibited by Law, to institute the requisite prosecutions.[1] An order has been issued from the proper Department to the Collector of the port of Philadelphia, to require of her owner or Consignees, if necessary, bond, with sufficient sureties, in conformity with the provisions of the act of Congress of the 20th. April, 1818, that the vessel shall not be employed by the Owners to cruize or commit hostilities against any Nation with which the United States are in peace.[2]

Perhaps I ought to content myself with the above statement, as presenting a sufficient answer to your Note. But the Government of the United States, participating most sincerely in the desire expressed by you, that all causes of complaint which might impair the friendly relations happily subsisting between the two Countries, should be removed, or satisfactorily explained, I will add a few general observations.

It is certain that the United States from their proximity to the theatre of the existing war between Spain and the Southern Republics, offer in their commerce, their manufactures, and their navigation, greater facilities to its prosecution than any other nation. This Government has nevertheless, been most anxious that neither party should draw from the United States any resources contrary to the public Law, and to the duties of an impartial neutrality. Nor can it be admitted that the efforts of the Federal Government, to prevent the violations of neutral obligations, have been ineffectual. Of the aids which the fair commerce of the United States supplies, both belligerants have occasionally taken free advantage. If the Citizens of the United States had sold objects of their legitimate commerce and industry to one party, and refused a sale of similar objects to the other party, there would have existed just ground of complaint. But no such partiality has been practised.

With respect to the particular articles or Ships, as stated in the Letter which I had the honor of addressing to your predecessor, under date the 3d. [sic] day of June last,[3] both Spain and some of the Southern Republics are believed to have freely availed themselves of the industry and commerce of the people of the United States in the procurement of them. Nor is it believed that the public Law or usage among Nations is opposed to the sale of Ships, as an object of commerce to either belligerent.

Ship Building is a great branch of American Manufactures, in which the Citizens of the United States may lawfully employ their capital and industry. When built, they may seek a market for the article in foreign ports as well as their own. The Government adopts the necessary precaution to prevent any private American vessel from leaving our ports equipped and prepared for hostile action; or, if it allow, in any instance, a partial or imperfect armament, it subjects the owner of the vessel to the performance of the duty of giving bond, with adequate security, that she shall not be employed to cruise or commit hostilities against a friend of the United States.

It may possibly be deemed a violation of strict neutrality to sell to a belligerent, vessels of war completely equipped and armed for battle: and yet the late Emperor of Russia could not have entertained that opinion, or he would not have sold to Spain during the present war, to which he was a neutral, a whole fleet of Ships of War; including some of the line.[4]

But if it be forbidden by the Law of neutrality to sell to a belligerant an armed vessel completely equipped and ready for action, it is believed not to be contrary to that Law to sell to a belligerant [*sic*—spelling varies throughout MS.] a vessel in any other state, although it may be convertible into a ship of war. To require the Citizens of a neutral power to abstain from the exercise of their incontestable right to dispose of the property which they may have in an unarmed ship to a belligerent, would, in effect be, to demand that they should cease to have any commerce, or to employ any navigation, in their intercourse with the belligerent. It would require more—it would be necessary to lay a general embargo, and to put an entire stop to the total commerce of the neutral with all nations. For if a ship, or any other article of manufacture, or commerce, applicable to the purpose of war, went to sea at all, it might, directly or indirectly, find its way into the ports, and subsequently become the property, of a belligerent.

The neutral is always seriously affected in the pursuit of his Lawful commerce by a state of war between other powers. It can hardly be expected that he shall submit to a universal cessation of his trade, because, by possibility some of the subjects of it may be acquired in a regular course of business by a belligerent, and may aid him in his efforts against an enemy. If the neutral show no partiality; if he is as ready to sell to one belligerant as the other; and if he take, himself, no part in the war, he cannot be justly accused of any violation of his neutral obligations.

So far as an investigation has been yet made, it has not resulted in the ascertainment of the fact stated by you, that the Kensington belongs to the Mexican Government. On the contrary, it appears that she is the property of American Citizens, built with their capital, and by their industry. They affirm that they neither have engaged, nor intend engaging, a single sailor to man her for any other purpose than that of peaceful commerce.[5]

The alleged inefficiency of the bonds which have been exacted of the Owners or Consignees of vessels, according to the enactment of the act of Congress of the 20th. April, 1818, to accomplish the purpose for which they were executed, cannot be admitted. If in any instance, those bonds have been violated, it is unknown to the Government of the United States. And if you will communicate any evidence, or information by which evidence may be acquired to establish the fact that the obligors have deviated from their obligation, in any case, a prompt enforcement of it will be ordered.

Such, Sir, is a candid exposition of the views and principles which have guided the Government of the United States. I cannot doubt that it will be received by His Catholic Majesty as a further evidence of the fairness and justice which the United States have uniformly observed throughout the whole progress of the present unhappy war.

I avail myself of this occasion to renew to you assurances of my distinguished consideration.   H. CLAY.

Copy. DNA, RG59, Notes to Foreign Legations, vol. 3, pp. 396–99 (M38, R3). L draft, in CSmH.
    [1] See above, Clay to Ingersoll, October 17, 1827.   [2] Cf. above, II, 493–507n; Clay to Rush, October 28, 1827, and note.   [3] Cf. above, Clay to Rivas y Salmon, June 9, 1827.
    [4] For the sale of Russian warships (five of the line and three frigates) to Spain in 1817–1818, ships to be used by Spain in her wars in Latin America, see Andrei Lobanov-Rostovsky, *Russia and Europe, 1789–1825* (Durham, N. C., 1947), 390.   [5] Cf. above, Ingersoll to Clay, October 25, 1827, and note.

From John Sergeant

Dear Sir,   (Private)   Philada. October 31. 1827.
    Mr. Markley is out to day,[1] as you will see. I have never seen the Mss. tho repeatedly promised that it should be shewn to me.[2] I hope you will find it satisfactory.

My chief object in writing, however, is to say that I have not availed myself of your permission, in two of your letters,[3] to use your name in conversation with him. It seemed the less necessary, because he told me a few days ago that he had not written to you, assigning as a reason the same which you had mentioned, that is, the peculiar relation in which you were placed by the recent publications. If he felt its force as applied to himself, he could not fail to feel it in application to you. There was no necessity, therefore, to say any thing, and I thought it well that you should be able to say you had had no communication with him, directly or indirectly— He has not come out in the form some time ago talked of. I suspect the personage he wished to correspond with, was shy.[4]

We have not yet got rid entirely of our stumbling block here, but are gradually putting it out of the way. Our friends are active and increasing. We are in hopes of having a very full convention, so arranged as to ensure its effect, which you will understand to be a matter not without its difficulties, owing to the state of parties in Pennsylvania. But I trust we shall overcome all difficulties, and find the State at last on the right side.[5] I shall be mortified extremely if she stultify herself.

Mr. Markley (to return to him) has very truly and clearly stated how

you stood, as to your pretensions to the office you hold, at the time of the election. That part of his address is well conceived, and, I think, well executed, and well calculated to remove public prejudice upon a point which does not seem heretofore to have been sufficiently put forward, Very respectfully and truly Yrs.   JOHN SERGEANT.
The Honble Henry Clay.

ALS. DLC-HC (DNA, M212, R3).
1 Cf. above, Smith to Clay, August 1, 1827; Johnston to Clay, September 13, 1827; Hammond to Clay, October 18, 1827, note. Markley's letter, addressed "To the Public" under date of October 30, fixed his conversation with Buchanan relative to Clay's role in the election only as "The latter end of December, 1824." He stated that Buchanan had expressed "great anxiety that he [Clay] should vote with Pennsylvania," that is, in support of Jackson, and that he [Markeley] and Buchanan had discussed the report currently circulating that Adams' friends were "holding out the idea that in case he should be elected, Mr. Clay would probably be offered the situation of secretary of state, and that in case general Jackson was elected, he would appoint or continue Mr. Adams" in the office. Markley admitted that he had agreed to ascertain from Clay whether his "views were favorable to general Jackson's election" as a preliminary to Buchanan's approach to Jackson or to Eaton "on the subject." But Markley maintained that he had not found Clay at his lodgings that evening and that, when he later called, he had been unable to discuss the matter because Clay was engrossed with friends. He asserted that he had not had opportunity for "any conversation with him [Clay] until the evening of the 10th or 11th of January. . . ." The discussion at that time, according to Markley, "was of a very general character; no mention was made of cabinet appointments, and I did not ascertain which of the candidates Mr. Clay would support." Markley charged that Jacob C. Isacks' statement of their conversation was "incorrectly reported." He stated that Isacks had expressed a belief, in which he himself concurred, "that a large portion of the western delegation . . . wished Mr. Clay to be secretary of state, in which desire they were joined by a large portion of the delegation [sic] from other states friendly to gen. Jackson's election." He contended that there had been "amongst the friends of all the candidates . . . much speculation on the subject . . . of cabinet appointments" and that "the general voice was raised in favor of, and the general eye always fixed upon, that distinguished statesman, and inflexible republican, Henry Clay, as the first officer of the government. . . ." He expressed belief "that which ever of the candidates had been elected, he [Clay] would have had the offer of the most prominent situation in the cabinet. . . ." Markley denied that he had been informed when Buchanan "called on" Jackson. He could not recall that he had had any subsequent discussion with Buchanan between December 30th and January 30th, during most of which period he had been out of Washington. He argued that such an absence could not be viewed as appropriate to the role of a "negotiator" during that critical period: "If I had been acting as the author and friend, or agent, of Mr. Clay, it would have been indispensable that I should have remained on the spot, where my services might have been useful. Frequent intercourse would have been absolutely necessary, to communicate what was said and done, and contemplated to be done." Philadelphia *Democratic Press*, reprinted in *Niles' Weekly Register*, XXXIII (November 10, 1827), 167-70.   2 Cf. above, Sergeant to Clay, October 30, 1827.   3 Not found.   4 Cf. above, Sergeant to Clay, October 5, 1827.
5 Cf. above, Sergeant to Clay, September 18, 1827, and note; Clay to Brown, March 27, 1827, note.

INSTRUCTIONS AND DISPATCHES   October 31, 1827

From W[ILLIAM] B. LAWRENCE, London, no. 5, Transmits "an order in Council, dated the 18th. instant, and which first appeared in the London Gazette of last night." Notes that "It authorises American Ships to go in ballast to the Bahama islands and export from thence fruit and salt" and that, "Though this modification of the British restrictions . . . is too unimportant to demand serious consideration," it is "the first relaxation since the order of July last [cf. above, Gallatin to Clay, August 21, 1827]. . . ." Reports that, seeking a better understanding of the matter, he "called this morning at the Foreign Office," where (John) Backhouse informed him "that the whole measure emanated from the Colonial Department, and that none of the offices had the subject before them except the Board of Trade." Backhouse, "inofficially, added that he presumed the order to be intended merely for the relief of the people of the Bahamas . . . and that it was in no way connected with our recent discussions" (cf. above, Gallatin to Clay, October 3, 1827). States further that Backhouse observed that, if information for communication to the United States Government were desired, "it would be requisite for the Foreign Department to procure it before replying to . . . inquiries, but that . . . [Lawrence] would be able to obtain all the desired explanations from Mr. [Charles] Grant." Summarizes his conversation with the latter, who confirmed "the Colonial nature of the order" and "expressed generally his regret that this matter had not been as successfully settled as the other points discussed with Mr. [Albert] Gallatin." In response to an inquiry "whether there was now any legal impediment to prevent our produce, which may be brought to a Danish island, from being taken thence in British vessels to Jamaica and the other islands," Grant said that "this was the manner in which he had supposed the trade to be conducted." Cites "other sources" for information that a report "in the '*Times*' of yesterday" of "a quarrel between the Russian and British Ambassadors [Alexandre Ribeaupierre; Stratford Canning] at Constantinople" is erroneous. ALS. DNA, RG59, Dip. Disp., Great Britain, vol. 35 (M30, R31). Received December 11.

To Jonathan Elliot

To Jonathan Elliott, Esq.   Washington, 1st November, 1827.

Sir: I have, according to the request contained in your letter of the 16[t]h ultimo,[1] examined the volume which accompanied it, containing a Collection of Treaties and Conventions between the United States and Foreign Powers, and other interesting matter.[2] The work, as far as I have been able to look into it, appears to me to have been accurately executed, and well arranged. It is, I believe, the first complete collection, in one volume, of our Treaties with Foreign Powers, which has been made; and I have no doubt that it will be found one of much utility to our public agents abroad, and public functionaries generally, as well as to the mercantile community. I am, respectfully, your obedient servant,   H. Clay.

Washington *Daily National Intelligencer*, December 19, 1827.   [1] Not found.
[2] Cf. above, Elliot to Clay, October 1, 1827, and note.

DIPLOMATIC NOTES   November 1, 1827

From Charles R. Vaughan, Washington. States that local authorities at Pensacola have impounded the "official papers and correspondence" of former British Consul (John Home) Purves upon his death on September 9; that Vice Consul John Innerarity's application for these materials was refused; and that the judge of the county court (Timothy Twitchell) set a bond of $2,000 on the documents. Declares that "Mr. Innerarity was justified in refusing to enter into a Bond, or to pay Costs, for the restitution of papers and effects, unjustly withheld from his custody"; requests "that such redress may be afforded to Mr. Innerarity as may be in conformity with the custom observed by the respective governments, and that the authorities of Pensacola may be directed to restore without costs the effects and papers of Mr. Purves, to Mr. Innerarity, who has been directed by the Consul General [Anthony St. John Baker] to take charge of the Consulate at Pensacola." Encloses correspondence relating to the case. LS. DNA, RG59, Notes from British Legation, vol. 14 (M50, R15).

Purves had died at age 42, following four years of consular service in Pensacola. Innerarity, his successor, was a native of Scotland, who had come to West Florida in 1802. He had long been identified with the British trading firm of Panton, Leslie, and Company, later John Forbes Company, as a clerk from 1802 to 1811 and subsequently as a partner.

Timothy Twitchell, judge of the Escambia County court, was active in legal and political affairs in the Pensacola area during the 1820s. In 1825 he had served as a timber agent for the United States Navy on the Gulf Coast. Appointed judge in 1827, he was elected to that post in 1830.

INSTRUCTIONS AND DISPATCHES November 1, 1827

From SAMUEL LARNED, Santiago de Chile, no. 62. Reports that the Chilean Government has received a copy of the treaty between Great Britain and Mexico, which contains an article reserving to Mexico "the privilige [sic] of granting special advantages to the new American States (cf. above, Poinsett to Clay, September 13, 28, 1825; Clay to Poinsett, December 9, 1825); that (Joaquín) Campino, then Minister of Foreign Relations, "desirous of expressing to the Mexican government the thanks of that of Chile for this friendly disposition, and also its views touching the matter," consulted him (Larned), who recommended Campino "to thank the government of Mexico, in general terms, for this manifestation of national regard; but not to compromise that of Chile, either to an admission of such special advantages, or to, what would be consequent thereupon, a reciprocation of them"; and that he "stated to Mr. C. that the acceptance of the proffered boon, and the granting of like privileges in return, would tend to embarrass Chile in her treaty stipulations with other countries, without affording her any real advantages,—that the policy was an invidious and unsound one," and that commercial treaties should be based on "perfect equality and the most exact reciprocity. . . ."

States that Campino did not follow his advice entirely but assured him that "his note [to the Mexican Government] should contain a virtual exception, from the rule in question, in favour of the United States"; copies an excerpt from the note, which states that Chile will follow the principle in commercial negotiations " 'with Great Britain or any other of the *European* nations' "; notes that Chile has not yet acted upon the principle; and recommends that the United States negotiate a commercial treaty with Chile as soon as possible, because, then, "the stipulation that they were to be placed on the footing of the most favoured nation, would foreclose the concession of any special privileges, either to Mexico or any other of the new States,—without clashing with the tenour of Mr. C's note."

Warns that negotiation between Chile and Peru "in accordance with the new principle," if successful, "would not only offer fresh embarrassments in the way of our future conventional arrangements . . . but . . . be detrimental to our trade in some of the staple products of our country . . ." (cf. above, Cooley to Clay, September 19, 1827, note). ALS. DNA, RG59, Dip. Disp., Chile, vol. 2 (M-T2, R2). Extract published in Manning (arr.), *Diplomatic Correspondence . . . Latin-American Nations*, II, 1122–23. Received February 19.

From FRANKLIN LITCHFIELD, Puerto Cabello, Colombia. Reports that (Simón) Bolívar returned to Bogotá on September 10, has taken "the oath prescribed by the 185th. and 186d. [*sic*] Articles of the Constitution of Colombia as President, and as such has taken charge of the Executive Authority. . . ." Congratulates Clay upon "this pleasing and auspicious occurrence" and adds: "as you have ever been the distinguished champion of South American Emancipation, and in particular to espouse [*sic*] the cause of the Independence of Colombia with the most ardent vows for her liberty and prosperity, I hasten to communicate this grateful intelligence. . . ." ALS. DNA, RG59, Cons. Disp., Puerto Cabello, vol. 1 (M-T229, R1). Undated. For dating, cf. below, Litchfield to Clay, November 23, 1827. Received December 3, 1827.

From JOHN MULLOWNY, Tangier, no. 52. Reports that "passes" have been "granted to two Brigs of war, . . . under the orders of His Majesty Muley Abdrahaman Emperor of Morocco to cruise"; surmises that "they are intended against the flags of the Hanseatic Towns, Prussia, Tuscany, and some others that have no Agents, to represent them here"; and notes that "it is whispered, that the South American States are included. . . ." Quotes from his request to the Bashaw (Mohamet Omemon) that "Commanders of armed vessels under the flag of . . . the Emperor . . . be instructed not to interrupt the peaceful passage of any American vessel, nor to board them unnecessarily as that will increase the quarantine in any European ports they may be bound to," and from the reply, "That it would strictly [*sic*] attended to." Notes that he furnishes Commodore (William M.) Crane and William Shaler "with information of all those movements. . . ." Appends a note stating that he has "obtained accurate information that the South Americans are not included as prize.—" ALS. DNA, RG59, Cons. Disp., Tangier, vol. 4 (M-T61, R4). No received date; "*Duplicate*," received December 27.

MISCELLANEOUS LETTERS   November 1, 1827

To WILLIAM B. GILES, "Governor of Virginia." Acknowledges receipt of Giles' letter of October 29; points to a discrepancy between his preceding letter, of October 17, in which he requested the volumes for "the May Sessions of 1778, 1779 and 1784, and "the memorandum at the foot of the resolution" enclosed with it, describing them as "those of 1778, 1779 and 1782"; reports that "the Journals of 1782" cannot be found; asks whether his (more recent) letter acknowledging receipt of "the Journals of 1804–1805," was correctly transcribed; and explains: "It was our intention to send, and the memorandum which we keep states that we did transmit the volume containing the Journals of 1784."
    Concludes: "The President is gratified (and I beg leave to add my participation in the feeling) that the attention which has been paid here to the request of your Excellency has been seen in the friendly spirit in which it was rendered. It would have been very satisfactory to him if we could have been able to supply the Journals of 1782." Copy. DNA, RG59, Dom. Letters, vol. 22, pp. 75–76 (M40, R20).

From THOMAS D. ANDERSON, Leghorn. Alludes again (cf. above, Anderson to Clay, September 6, 1827) to his accounts and states that his "salary alone," during the eight and one half years he served as consul at Tripoli, exceeds the money received from the United States "by nearly $2000—"; that he has received no funds from the United States Government for "Upwards of five years"; and that he has been unable to make the usual consular present to the Bashaw (Yusuf Karamanli). Explains that, by using "the small means" at his disposal to give "presents to the influential persons around the Bashaw who readily reconciled him to the policy of not taking any present, rather than receive one which did not amount to the sum establish'd by usage," he "saved to the U. S. upwards of $1000," "preserved the most harmonious relations," and "establish'd a precedent, which if the Government thought proper to follow up, would exonerate us from the expense of presents whenever a new Consul was appointed." Cites ill health as his reason for not being at Tripoli to receive his successor (Charles D. Coxe), to whom (Joseph N.) Morillo was instructed to deliver the consulate. Notes having received from Morillo and others "a statement of the proceedings of Mr Cox [sic] on his arrival" (cf. above, Morillo to Clay, August 20, 1827) and adds: "I hope the Government will take such steps as will restore my property to me, & prevent the character of a worthy man like Mr. [Richard B.] Jones remaining under the dishonorable imputation of having sold the public property & appropriated it to himself." ALS. DNA, RG59, Cons. Disp., Tripoli, vol. 4 (M-T40, R-T5). Received March 25, 1828.

From NINIAN EDWARDS, Belleville, Illinois. Informs Clay of the death, on October 15, of (Daniel Pope) Cook, who was on his way from Belleville to Washington but was prevented by illness from "getting any farther than Lexington [Kentucky]." Continues: "His family have just returned to this place, bringing with them, papers which he had intended personally to deliver to you, and among them a letter from Governor [Francisco Dionisio] Vives [above, May 4, 1827], which he was compelled to pledge his honor to deliver to you *with his own hands*. . . . I learnt from him before he left this place, that Govr Vives considered his situation as so delicate & critical, that nothing but such a promise could have induced him to send the letter at all. I shall therefore keep it . . . until I can have the honor of knowing your pleasure on the subject." Transmits "a part of a letter which, with the aid of his wife [Julia Edwards Cook] as his amanuensis, Mr Cook had commenced writing to . . . [Clay] & a copy of his letter to Govr Vives. . . ." ALS. DNA, RG59, Dip. Disp., Special Agents, vol. 9 (M37, R9). Endorsed by Clay: "To be submitted to the President. H. C."

In the enclosed, undated and uncompleted, letter intended for Clay, Cook states that he "sat [sic] out from home for Washington, for the purpose of delivering the communication . . . from Genl. Vives" and of reporting on his mission to Cuba; that he was "seized with the Dysentary, a new disease, which superadded to the remains of the old," has "prostrated" him; and that, unable "to proceed with any degree of comfort or convenience to Washington," he thinks that even Vives would not complain of him for adopting a different course for delivering the letter with which he was entrusted. Sketches his activities during his brief stay in Cuba; cites deteriorating health and medical advice as reasons for his returning home; explains why he has not filed a full report, which he intends doing "at a further day"; and states that he intends leaving home in October, since he wishes to continue his mission; asks that funds be sent to him at New Orleans for the purpose of returning to Cuba.

Cook died in Scott County, Kentucky, on October 16, 1827.

INSTRUCTIONS AND DISPATCHES   November 2, 1827

From HENRICH JANSON, Bergen (Norway). Refers to his communication of April 3 and lists "the . . . alterations which have since taken place. . . ." Adds that "The Tonnage of vessels is reduced 12 1/2 pCt., and the prohibition against importing Coffee berries in less packages than 200 lb weight, is annulled." LS. DNA, RG59, Cons. Disp., Bergen, vol. 1 (M-T369, R1). Received January 11, 1828.

From WILLIAM TAYLOR, Veracruz. Notes that there has been "no further disturbance in Vera Cruz" since his letter of August 11; that "Colonel José Rincon, undergoes a trial for form [sic] sake and proceeds to the Metropolis to be promoted";
and that "One of his late opponents, one of the Military Editors, is charged with
Conspiracy, and it is generally believed he will be . . . shot." Reports increasing
"out cry against the Spaniards," whose expulsion, "it is believed by many," will be
insured by "the election of Genl. [Vicente] Guerrero to the Presidency. . . ." States
that "Come. [David] Porter arrived here 26th Ultimo," driven in by "the want of
money," and that he will probably remain "Some 2 or 3 months." ALS. DNA,
RG59, Cons. Disp., Veracruz, vol. 1 (M183, R1).

Although Guerrero did not become President until 1829, Spanish nationals were
expelled from Mexico by legislative decree, dated December 20, 1827. Excepted
from the expulsion order were those married to Mexican wives, those having
children who were not Spanish nationals, the aged and infirm, those who had
loyally served the independence movement, and certain professionals in the sciences, arts, and industry. Bancroft, *Works*, XIII, 60–61n.

MISCELLANEOUS LETTERS   November 2, 1827

From ENOCH LINCOLN, Portland (Maine). Transmits copies of two affidavits, "to
the truth of the statements in which" he attaches "full credit," and "of a Proclamation relating to the same subject." LS. DNA, RG76, Northeast Boundary: Misc.
Papers, entry 84, env. 4, item 18. Published, with enclosures, in *American State
Papers, Foreign Relations*, VI, 631–32.

The enclosed affidavits attest to oppressions committed by provincial and British
officials on settlers in the disputed territory (cf. above, Lincoln to Clay, September
3, 1827). The proclamation, by Lincoln, emphasizes "trespasses . . . on the sovereignty of Maine"; states that, "relying on the government and people of the
Union, the proper exertion will be applied to obtain reparation and security";
and calls for "forbearance and peace, so that the preparations for preventing the
removal of our land-marks, and guarding the sacred and inestimable rights of
American citizens may not be embarrassed by any unauthorized acts."

MISCELLANEOUS LETTERS   November 3, 1827

From WILLIAM B. QUARRIER, Norfolk (Virginia). Acknowledges receipt of Clay's
"Letter on the Subject of the draft of W. R. Higinbotham for $100 . . . as also
the former one of the 15th Ulto [sic]." States that "The person to whom the draft
belongs" has directed him "to forward the same to a friend in Bermuda for adjustment. . . ." ALS. DNA, RG59, Accounting Records, Misc. Letters. Cf. above,
Babson to Clay, March 29, 1826; Clay to Higinbotham, April 3, June 23, 1826;
Quarrier to Clay, November 6, 1826; Caldwell to Clay, December 15, 1826; Higinbotham to Clay, July 9, 1827.

On September 15 William Browne, under Clay's authorization, had assured
Quarrier that Higinbotham's bill for $100 would be paid on presentation. Copy,
in DNA, RG59, Dom. Letters, vol. 22, p. 51 (M40, R20). On October 29 Browne
had reiterated that Higinbotham's bill for $100, "which had been held by . . .
[Quarrier], and payment of which had been refused, would be paid on presentation at the Department. . . ." Browne requested to be informed "by return of the
mail" whether Quarrier still held the bill or had returned it to Bermuda. Copy,
ibid., 72–73.

From Francis T. Brooke

My Dear Sir   Richmd No 4 1827

You see by the papers what we are doing in Virginia,   as an example of our Zeal I inclose you a letter from Judge Stewart[1] which you can return at some convenient time,   unless something sinister should occur to produce a counter current in the public mind, there can be little doubt I think that Virginia will not give her vote to Gen Jackson[2]— I have just seen Markleys[3] letter it will be much perverted as everything true is, but it will do great good— My friend Mr Johnsons protest[4] will do him more harm, than the cause,   the administration is more popular than he Seems to think—   the convention[5] here will approve I think of every sentiment in the preamble to the resolutions here,   time will shew, [sic]   I do not think that anything can be done with judge Stewarts Suggestion as to the Chief Justice,   we should rejoice much to have his Support but fear we shall not get it,[6] Your friend very truly   F, BROOKE

ALS. InU. Addressed to Clay.
[1] Archibald Stuart, born near Staunton, Virginia, in 1757, had fought in the Revolutionary War and subsequently read law under Thomas Jefferson. He had served terms in both houses of the Virginia General Assembly and had been active in passage of the Virginia Resolutions of 1798 (cf. above, II, 170n). Appointed to the General Court of Virginia in 1800, he remained on the bench until shortly before his death in 1832. He was a delegate from Augusta County to the Richmond Convention of administration supporters in January, 1828. His letter, enclosed by Brooke, has not been found.
[2] Cf. above, Caldwell to Clay, August 8, 1827, note.   [3] Cf. above, Sergeant to Clay, October 31, 1827, note.   [4] In a letter addressed to William H. Cabell on October 27, 1827, published in the *Richmond Enquirer* on November 2, Chapman Johnson had expressed "concern" and "gloomy forebodings" at "the prospect of General Jackson's elevation to the final office in the government. . . ." While he would be gratified "to be instrumental in preventing it," he continued, he had little confidence in Adams and therefore declined participation as a delegate in the Richmond Convention of January, 1828. He concluded: "I wish it distinctly understood, that my preference is not founded on an opinion of the fitness of Mr. Adams, or my confidence in his Cabinet,—but in a solemn conviction that General Jackson is altogether unfit, and eminently dangerous."
[5] Cf. above, Mercer to Clay, August 18, 1827, note; Brooke to Clay, October 17, 1827, note.   [6] Although John Marshall had not voted for twenty years, he was induced to come forward in 1828 and protest the attacks being made by the Jacksonians on the Adams administration.

From Benjamin S. Forrest

Dear Sir   Rockville 4h. Nov. 1827.

Too late for the mail of last evening I recieved [sic] the statement promised me by Mr. Braddock,[1] who is a rich respectable & intelligent merchant of this County.—

If it will be useful to you I lament deeply that you have not been heretofore furnished with it. To my mind it is a most important disclosure of the hopes and opinions of Genl. Jackson, through his most confidential friend, and always since you have known that the proof could be obtained, I have been astonished that you did not provide yourself with it.

After I recieved Mr. Braddock's letter of yesterday, I had a conversation with him, in which he told me that Mr. John T. Johnson was in company with Genl. Call² and that he (Mr. Johnson) declared that Genl. Jackson had not been & would not be considered the Candidate of the West; I believe Mr. Johnson voted for Genl. Jackson.³— I proposed that he should embody this opinion of Mr. Johnson's in his statement, but upon reflection I thought it probable that you might not wish the declarations of those two gentlemen connected, and I do not know what relations subsist between Mr. Johnson & yourself.— If it will be of service Mr. Braddock will so amend his statement as to embrace this notion Mr. Johnson's [sic]; there is no man upon whose memory I would more implicitly rely.—

I enclose also my own statement of Colo. Benton's expressions upon the subject of your vote for President, those underscored are literally his; they made stronger impression upon me in consequence of your having been the Candidate of my choice for President; and they presented themselves green and fresh to my mind when I read Colo. Benton's extraordinary letter to Mr. Scott of Missouri;⁴ I at that time and often afterwards mentioned them to my acquaintances.—

It is possible that we have not given to the statements, the form & shape most agreeable to you;—if so, my anxiety to serve you has so increased by the vil[e] and malignant assaults made up[on your re]putation and the falsehoods vomited for[th] by the "Trays, Blanches & Sweethearts"⁵ of Genl. Jackson, that I will wait upon you in your office any day this week, and bring Mr. Braddock with me, when you can prescribe the form you prefer, we regarding only the substance.— I say this week because our Court will sit on Monday the 12th. inst.— I am Dear Sir, with great respect Yr Mo. obdt. Servant

The Honble H. Clay   B. S. FORREST

[Enclosure]

Late in the Autumn of 1824 I met with Colo. Benton & Genl. Beecher,⁶ members of Congress at Dawson's Tavern in RockVille Maryland on their way to Washington.— I had not the pleasure of a personal acquaintance with either of those Gentlemen, but heard who they were from others, and afterwards seeing them in Washington ascertained that I was correctly informed.—

It was believed by most of the persons present that the election of a President would devolve upon the House of Representatives and that Mr Clay was not one of the number, from which, the House would be authorized to make its selection.— At that moment, the Presidential election was a most interesting subject of conversation, in which all present participated; there was much speculation upon the course which would probably be adopted by Mr. Clay & his friends; it was suggested by some Gentleman that Mr. Clay would vote for Genl. Jackson, I thought differently myself and entered into some of the considerations which I believed would forbid such a vote.— I was very glad to find that Colo. Benton agreed with me, he declared *it was impossible that Mr. Clay could vote for Genl. Jackson* and expressed much surprize at the suggestion.—

I had been under the impression that Colo. Benton was the friend of Mr. Clay and the conversation of the evening tended to fasten that impression on my mind.—   B. S. FORREST
RockVille Nov. 4h. 1827.

ALS. DLC-HC (DNA, M212, R3). Postmarked: "RockVille md   Free."
   1 John Braddock to Forrest, November 3, 1827, in DLC-HC (DNA, M212, R3). The letter was included as a supportive statement to Clay's *Address . . . to the Public* (below, December 29, 1827), "Appendix," 57. Braddock, of Montgomery County, Maryland, has not been further identified.   2 Richard K. Call.   3 Cf. above, Kendall to Clay, February 19, 1825, note.   4 On February 5, 1825, John Scott had written to Thomas Hart Benton, informing him that he intended to vote for John Quincy Adams. Benton had replied on February 8, reminding him that his vote belonged "to the people of the state of Missouri. . . ." "They are against Mr. Adams," he had protested. Noting that they had for nine years "been closely connected" in politics, Benton had then announced that the connection was "dissolved." "To-morrow," he had concluded, "is the day for your self-immolation." The correspondence, widely published, appeared in *Niles' Weekly Register,* XXVIII (March 26, 1825), 51.   5 Cf. Shakespeare (Furness [ed.], *A New Variorum Edition*), *King Lear* (3d. edn.), Act III, sc. vi, line 61.   6 Philemon Beecher.

From William B. Rochester

Hon. H. Clay
My Dr. Sir   (confidential)   New York 4 Nov: 27   Sunday Evg.
   I beg leave to refer you to the enclosed for Mr. Southard,[1] after perusing which please be good eno [*sic*] to cause it to be sealed & sent to him, unless indeed I have said something in it, which should not have been said—in which case I will thank you to consider it as addressed to Yourself exclusively—

It will be doubtless sufficient for my purpose of endeavouring to go out in one of the Public Vessels,[2] that your Dept. should be apprized of my views and wishes— my chief object is to know pretty soon which it will be? how soon &c?

Your favour of the 16h. ulto.[3] came duly to hand upon a reperusal now I think its safe arrival ought to have been promptly acknowlgd. yet, as it did not seem to call for an immediate answer, I had intended to defer my reply until aftre [*sic*] our election when I could combine therein the result &c &c—

My a/ct as Secy. of Legation has all been satisfactorily adjusted. I regret than [*sic*] you did not derive all the benefit you had anticipated from your late journey to Bath Va[4]— We have had a most unpropitious Season (as I can testify) for Valetudinarians among whom, by the bye

I do not mean to class you—on the contrary I trust & pray that your health may be completely re-established—that you may out-live the Slanders which have been propagated against you and put the authors to shame—and that you may go on, as heretofore, prosperously, conferring honour and benefactions upon our common Country—

I made known to Judge Thompson[5] that part of your letter wherein you allude to the question of the Vice-Presidency, in reply to his suggestions as communicated through me— he appears more & more confirmed in his opinions & wish on that subject,[6] for the obvious reasons which gain strength every day & is evidently much gratified with the frank manner in which you leave it to the decision of the friends of the administration, having a view to the "good of the cause." Genl. Porter,[7] with whom I have spent many hours during the last fortnight, left here this morng. for home via Albany.

The General's impressions on the subject of the V. Presidency correspond with those of Judge Thompson— in case the policy of such a step shd. be approved, after mature consideration, the difficulty will remain when the first public movement shd. be made— certainly it ought not to start in the West tho' the West must be satisfied— I am clearly of opinion that it could not originate any where so auspiciously as in the State of N. YK. or Penn—and as between those two States, the former would rather lead than follow the latter—

I do most conscientiously beleive [sic] that it is of last [sic] importance to the success of the cause in this State— Some 8 or 10 electoral votes in it alone will probably depend upon your name being on the ticket— Our people will not come out with such hearty goodwill and Spirit for A. & Shultz [sic] or for A. & Barbour[8]— Even now our friends have to call their meetings by inviting such as are "opposed to Jackson"— The Venerable Majr. Fairlie[9] an officer of the Revolutry. army, who heads the Repub: assembly ticket in this City and who is warm and active, has declared to me over & over again that he does not like Mr. A. but can never support Jackson—moreover that if you were not identified & connected with the administ., he would not stir an inch one way or the other— Believe me, he speaks the feelings of a vast many of that portion of the more influential democratic Republicans who now support the Genl. administration   No remark is more frequent here nowadays (its truth frequently conceded by Jacksonians) than that if you were the Candidate for the Chief office ags. the hero instead of Mr. Adams, there would be little or no contest in this State—

Yet no friend of yours has ever dreamed that you ought to be such candidate now or has done you so much injustice as to suppose, for a moment, that you wished to be—

Chas. King has so completely, I may add so inseparably identified himself with Mr. Davis,[10] by vain givings out (probably true) about the extraordinary confidence & personal regard of the President centering in himself to the exclusion of almost every other individual in the State, that our friends (his friends too) will not consent that he make his appearance at the public meetings—yet no one doubts Charles' sincerity & zeal—

Genl. Porter will probably be a member of our assembly next winter[11]— if he succeeds, as he thinks he will, in bringing over Root[12] to act in harmony with himself they will head the Rep: party with effect on the Legislature— permit me to intreat you to advise with the General (Porter) if your feelings undergo any change in reference to the Vice Presidency—

Judge Edwards[13] spent three hours with me alone in my room the other day— tho' a yankee to the hub he holds precisel[y] the same language with Maj. Fair[lie.] Without intimating to him that any thing had transpired between you & me on the question of the V. Presidency, I told him (knowing his & Judge Thompsons respect for each other) What were Judge T's views on that question as expressed by him to me— he seemed delighted that such were T's views— at last I gave him T's reasons— E. declared they were the very reasons which he himself had urged upon T. some weeks ago the force of which Judge T. (according to Judge E.) did not then seem to perceive so clearly as he (T.) now does— E. takes credit to himself for having made the impression upon T. tho' the latter to me quoted only Genl. Scott[14]— Edwards is as as [sic] honest a man as Thompson—and that is high praise—with less talent—with equal decision of character and more political efficiency—

G. A. Worth tells me he means to take up *his* pen— I have not even whispered to *him* about the V. Presidency— he has, you know, been a Clintonion— he now adopts the denunciation of Martindale[15] and denominates the Magnus Apollo,[16] a "chilled adder"— Clinton has been in this city for the last three days— a personal friend tho' political opponent of mine, told me last night, that Clinton took occasion yesterday to say to several visitors that altho' Govr. he possessed & claimed certain rights as a citizen—and as such should strain every nerve to advance the election of Genl. Jackson— his own nomination was not to take— he discovered this— I have not done so gratuitous & foolish a thing as to write to Mr. Sergeant about the Speaker-ship[17]— I am satisfied if Taylor[18] cannot succeed no other friend of the admin: can—Tho' *he* may lose some one or two present friends of the admin: from this State, yet I am induced to think he will get some two or three which Sergeant could not—of our delegates.—

Not knowing the Presidents reasons for his opinion in reference to the expediency of sending a Min: Plenipo: to Bogota[19] I cannot undertake to pass upon the wisdom of his determination and even if I did know them, shd. not presume to condemn his decision but of one thing I feel well assured, i,e if it were necessary to send one and the selection to fall upon this State there are hundreds in it with whose pretensions my humble ones bear no sort of comparison— so deep an impression has this conviction made upon my mind that (after the most deliberate, not to say, oppressive reflection and consultation with one single fast friend) I had come to the conclusion, if the President had been so inconsiderate (I crave *your* pardon) as to have tendered it to me, I must & should have declined it—I should only have asked that some suitable employment (ex: gr: private Secy) abroad might have been assigned for my amiable young friend & relative Wm R. Beatty— Believe me I feel greatly releived [*sic*] by the contents of your last letter— We hardly know how to trust ourselves in this world, (tho' few are willing to give it up for another)— the Author of the prayer which says "lead us not into temptation" well understood poor human nature— Yet such was my fixed determination and if I know myself, it would not have been departed from.

Perhaps *you* are obnoxious [*sic*] to a little chiding that such a thing was ever conceived—yet after making the foregoing declaration it is due to your indulgent partiality & personal friendship to explain— then—in the first place and chiefly I felt my incompetency for such a Station, & 2dly. many friends in all parts of the State, especially in Western Sections, have wished me to remain at home during the next Year, that is, they have importuned me to make a sacrifice for the sake of an experiment holding out but a barely possible prospect of success—

I need hardly say that allusion is made to our next Gubernatorial elections, nor will I deny nor have I denied a readiness to make such sacrifice, was there a reasonable probabity [*sic*] that the object was attainable—but that I consider out of the question— there will be Richmonds enough in the field[20]—a man does not feel desirous of being twice beaten— besides the situation of Governor is one to which I never aspired of my own free will and accord—nor do I see any charms in it yet notwithstanding had such a mark of Executive confidence been exhibited towards me (undeserving as I am) as had been towards my distinguished & successful competitor on a former occasion,[21] I admit that I was prepared to agree that my friends might venture upon the experiment— as it is—I plainly perceive that my presence at home in a political point of view can neither tend to serve my friends nor to advance me individually and as my necessities (not so imperious however but that they might have been foregone under different and better auspices) seem to require it, I go to Guatemala, there to take care of my crazy constitution and to represent my Govt. as Chargé &c to the best of my poor abilities until the 4h. March 1829— unless sooner recalled—

I ought to have made an effort to reach Guatemala from Mexico last Summer—but my instructions left me at liberty & I thought I could discern in your letter, but more especially in Theodore's[22] statement to me, an expectation on your part that I would return to the U. S. previously—

I do not mean any thing like reproach—far from it—I gratified myself in returning—but I will trouble you with this egotistical strain no longer than to say that I am Dr Sir, very respectfully & gratefully Your Friend   WM B ROCHESTER

ALS. DLC-HC (DNA, M212, R3).   1 Samuel L. Southard; the letter, not found.
2 For Rochester's efforts to obtain passage to Central America, cf. above, his letters to Clay, June 3, August 27, 28, September 17, 21, 30, October 9, 1827.   3 Not found.
4 Cf. above, Clay to Adams, September 29, 1827, and note.   5 Smith Thompson.
6 Cf. above, Rochester to Clay, October 12, 1827.   7 Peter B. Porter   8 Adams; John A. Shulze; James Barbour.   9 James Fairlie.   10 For the Charles King-Matthew L. Davis connection and its relationship to the political fortunes of the Adams party in New York, see Mushkat, *Tammany*, 107; cf. also, above, Porter to Clay, May 1, 1827, note.   11 Cf. below, Porter to Clay, November 6, 22, 1827.   12 Erastus Root.   13 Ogden Edwards.   14 Probably Winfield Scott.   15 Henry C. Martindale.   16 DeWitt Clinton.   17 John Sergeant. Cf. above, Rochester to Clay, October 12, 1827.   18 John W. Taylor.   19 Cf. above, Rochester to Clay, October 9, 1827.   20 Cf. Shakespeare (Furness [ed.], *A New Variorum Edition . . .*), *Richard III*, Act V, sc. iv, line 15.   21 Cf. above, Stuart to Clay, March 15, 1825; Rochester to Clay, November 18, 1826, and note.   22 Theodore W. Clay.

To James Davidson

Dear Sir   (Confidential)   Washington 5h. November 1827.

I recd. your favor of the 20h. Ulo. transmitting your statement of the conversation which passed between us in the fall of 1824 on the subject of the P. election. I am greatly obliged to you for it. It is very satisfactory, and required no apology, either for the stile [*sic*] or the orthography. I have collected, and am yet collecting a mass of evidence upon that, and some other points which I shall probably publish,[1] and which will be as gratifying to my friends as mortifying to my enemies.

The aspect of public affairs on this side of the Mountains is good. A powerful reaction is taking place against the Jackson cause, and I confidently anticipate its defeat. But I feel an anxiety about the course of my own State, which I cannot express.[2] Your's cordially
Col. Davidson   H CLAY

ALS. KyHi.   1 Below, *Address . . . to the Public*, December 29, 1827.
2 Cf. above, Clay to Brown, March 27, 1827, and note.

To Hezekiah Niles

Dear Sir   Washington 5h. Nov. 1827.

I received your favor of the 3d. inst.[1] with the Copies of the Address in behalf of the Harrisburg Convention,[2] which you had the goodness to send me. I shall seize the first leisure moments to peruse it, and I have no doubt that I shall find in it an able exposition of facts and views in support of the American System.

Mr. Markley's publication[3] ought to remove any prejudices or

doubts which that of Mr. Buchanan[4] did not eradicate. With Mr. M. I have had no communication, direct or indirect, since his name was brought out in the course of the past summer.[5] I shall, with you, be greatly disappointed if the American public, however much it has been excited, does not ultimately decide according to truth and justice. With great regard I am truly Yr's　　　　　　　　　　　H. Clay
H. Niles Esq

ALS. ViU.　　　1 Not found.
2 Cf. above, Clay to Crowninshield, March 18, 1827, note. Niles' contribution was titled "Address of the Committee . . . Assembled at Harrisburg, 30th July, 1827 . . ." and was signed by Niles as chairman, October 10, 1827.　　　3 Cf. above, Sergeant to Clay, October 31, 1827, note.　　　4 Cf. above, Ingersoll to Clay, August 11, 1827, note.
5 Cf. above, Smith to Clay, August 1, 1827.

From Charles Hammond

Dear Sir.　　　　　　　　　　　　　　　　　　Cincinnati Nov. 5. 1827.
My principal object in writing this letter is to Send you an extract from a letter written by Dewit [sic] Clinton to Caleb Atwater.[1] It places Mr Clintons present Views beyond all dispute. I have so considered them for two years. The extract is as follows.

"As it regards the Presidential question I have never concealed my preference for Gen. Jackson: but I have observed that circumspect demeanor which becomes my official station, and that dignified moderation which belongs to a great and good cause.— The people of this State[2] are decidely [sic] in favour of the Hero of New Orleans, a determination equally honorable to their patriotic Spirit and republican Virtue."

What think of you [sic] of the proceedings of the Tennessee Legislature?[3] My opinion is that all the States, where a majority are certain, will be required to do likewise. You may look for the denunciations of Virginia and of the States South of her. If there is no reaction, if public Sentiment continues to Sustain a course like this, depend upon it our days are numbered as one Government. The Success of the opposition Seals the fate of the country. Men who make up their minds to obtain power by Such means, cannot fail to take Such measures as Shall prevent themselves becoming the Victims of Similar assaults. Here, we are bracing ourselves to Sustain the Shock. I send you the prospectus of a new work,[4] intended to be conducted with Spirit and calculated to travel into all the bye ways of politics. It will be adapted to the meridian of Ohio Indian [sic] and Illinois, and not unsuited to Pennsylvania. If the press can effect any thing we are determined to do what we can in that way—

I wish Mr Adams's *ebony and topaz*[5] were Submersed in the deepest profound of the bathos. You great men have no priviledge [sic] to commit blunders. You belong to others, whom you cannot allways [sic] consult, and whom it is not allways safe to confide in. I had Said to myself. Mr Adams wrote for Walsh[6] the article on the colonial trade,[7] and I am resolved to have him in high estimation, and here comes this—I have no name for it,—to mar all my resolutions.— Is there no sop for Walsh? I wish he were pleased or would go over to the Enemy. Sincerely yours   C. HAMMOND

ALS. OHi. Addressed to Clay: "Private."
[1] The extract from a letter "dated about the 17th of September" had been published in *Liberty Hall and Cincinnati Gazette*, October 31, 1827. The *Knoxville Register* of January 9, 1828, citing the New York *National Advocate*, dated the letter as September 21, 1827.   [2] New York.   [3] On October 19, 1827, the Tennessee Senate, joined on October 22, by the State House of Representatives, had again passed the so-called "Tennessee Resolutions," which called for amendment of the United States Constitution to provide for popular election of the President and Vice President (cf. above, Hammond to Clay, November 1, 1825, and note). On October 24 the latter body had also entertained a motion to impeach President Adams, a measure that failed (34 to 2) largely on grounds that it was "inexpedient" and "might injure the cause of general Jackson" by giving credence to charges of "intolerance and violence" against him. *Niles' Weekly Register*, XXXIII (November 17, 1827), 183–86.   [4] The enclosure (not found) related to the Cincinnati *Truth's Advocate and Monthly Anti-Jackson Expositor*, published, January-October, 1828, by (James) Lodge, (Stephen S.) L'Hommedieu, and Hammond.
[5] At a dinner in Baltimore on October 16 (cf. above, Sergeant to Clay, October 16, 1827), where he dined with the officers and men who had been wounded at the Battle of North Point in September, 1814, the President had given a toast, "Ebony and Topaz— General Ross's posthumous coat of arms, and the republican militiamen who gave it," followed by an awkward effort to explain it. Adams, *Memoirs*, VII, 338. Born in 1766, Robert Ross had entered the British Army as ensign in 1789. Promoted to the rank of major general in 1813, he had led the brigade that sacked Washington in August, 1814. From that victory he had proceeded to Baltimore via Chesapeake Bay, landed his troops at North Point on September 12, and on that day had been killed in action. In gratitude for his service and sacrifice, the King had ordered a posthumous addition to his coat of arms and conferred the title "Ross of Bladensburg."   The "Ebony and Topaz" toast was an obscure allusion to Voltaire's *Le Blanc et le Noir*. The President explained to his bewildered audience that "Ebony" represented the spirit of evil (Ross) and "Topaz" the spirit of good (the American militiamen at North Point). The Democrats immediately poked fun at "old Ebony" Adams for his pompous literary erudition, the *Richmond Enquirer* on October 30, 1827, noting that "The Adams ticket in N. York is styled, 'The Ebony and Topaz Ticket'. . . ." See also Remini, *Election of Andrew Jackson*, 122–3.
[6] Robert Walsh, Jr.   [7] Cf. above, Clay to Carey and Lea, December 29, 1826, note.

From Daniel Webster

New York Nov. 5 [1827]
My dear Sir   Private & Confidential   Monday Morning
Professional business brought me to this City three days ago. Your first letter, on the subject of the Whig,[1] came to hand the day before my Departure; & your second, enclosing the letter to Mr Smith,[2] has been forwarded to me here. You will have recd one from me, on the same subject, covering Mr Smith's letter to myself.[3]

I look upon it as of great importance to support the *Whig*, & am disposed to do all in my power to that end. To what I said in my last, I will now add, that, under the pressing circumstances of this case, I will undertake for a remittance (to you) on my return, to twice the sum stated in that letter. I left some friends at work on the business,

& have no doubt that as soon as I reach home they will be ready with, at least, the sum now mentioned. Indeed this matter is so material, & so urgent, that we must do what the case requires; & if it be absolutely necessary that even a thousand Dollars be forthcoming from our quarter, it will come forth. Nevertheless, there are so many other calls, & so few persons who feel the importance of aiding objects so distant, that we have hardly courage to be *generous* & *bountiful*, lest the burden should fall too heavily on the willing few. We should be glad therefore if some part of the thousand could be successfully looked for elsewhere— But at any rate, this establishment must not go down, nor its conductor[4] be left in distress, for such a sum.

As to other more general arrangements, we are attempting to do what we can. I hope we may meet at W. with some settld [*sic*] System, and some ascertained means. Is there no danger in *writing* on these subjects? I hope your office is all confidential & trustworthy— All is safe at my end, because no one opens my letters.

Today is the beginning of the Election here. I should be glad to tell you what the prospect is, if I knew, but I can form little opinion. There has either been a strong access [*sic*] of the Jackson fever in this State, since the Spring, or else the clamour is so loud as to frighten our friends needlessly. Mr. Clinton, most unquestionably, is acting for Genl. Jackson, as far as he can. Mr. Van Buren, & his friends have the utmost confidence, in the result. They say, that all, or all but one, of the Senatorial Elections will terminate favorably to them; & that two thirds the H. of Assembly will be Jacksonians. The City, say they, will give a majority on that side, of 2 to 3 thousand votes.[5]

On the other hand, the friends of the Administration hope to divide the City, nearly Equally; to elect Sundry Senators, favorable to them; to elect such a House as shall not interfere with the Electoral Law.—

My own impressions is [*sic*];

that the Jackson party will carry the City, but not by any great majority

that in the Counties, where the question is fairly put to the people, on the Administration question, such as Albany, Columbia, Rensselaer &c, the Administration Ticket will, in a majority of instances, prevail;[6] that in many Counties, non committal men will be chosen; all of whom Mr V. B. will of course claim, & most of whom he will untimately control; & that in parts of the west, the Masonic & Anti Masonic dispute,[7] will supersede all other questions; that the Anti Masonic side will be found generally the strongest; & that the collateral bearing of the results of this singular contest will not be unfavorable to the Administration.

On the whole, I anticipate from this election some increase of hope, & much of exertion, among Genl. Jackson's friends; but nothing which need shake our expectation of carrying a majority of the Districts next Fall.[8]— You have doubtless, however, much fuller information than I have, although, for the moment, I am on the spot. Genl. Porter has been here. Unfortunately I did not know of it, in season to see him. He left yesterday morning. He will be himself in the legislature, as is expected;[9] which will be of some importance—

I hope to be able to get home at the end of this week, when I shall probably here [sic] from you.— By the 19th, it is my intention to set off, with my family, for Washington. Yours always truly

Mr Clay   DANL. WEBSTER

P.S. There is no part of the Country, in my judgt., in which our cause has been so badly managed as here. If it survives, it will be because it has power to hold out against both the disease & the doctor.— The prevailing error has been *timidity.*

ALS. DLC-HC (DNA, M212, R3). Addressed to Clay.
[1] Richmond *Constitutional Whig*—see above, Clay to Webster, October 25, 1827.
[2] Marcellus Smith. Neither letter has been found.   [3] Above, October 29, 1827.
[4] John H. Pleasants.   [5] Cf. above, Sergeant to Clay, October 24, 1827; Porter to Clay, October 26, 1827; Hammond to Clay, October 29, 1827; Clay to Conant, October 29, 1827, note; Rochester to Clay, November 4, 1827.   [6] On Columbia County, see below, Strong to Clay, November 12, 1827, and note. It was the only county which "failed to respond to the managing skill of the Regency [Van Buren's forces]." Remini, *Martin Van Buren...*, 158.   [7] A body which a coroner's jury declared to be that of William Morgan had recently been found on the shores of Lake Ontario. Morgan, a Batavia, New York, brick-and-stone mason, who had written a book, *Illustrations of Masonry*, purportedly to reveal the secrets of the Order, had been kidnapped in September, 1826, from a Canandaigua jail, where he had been incarcerated for petty theft. Great excitement had ensued during the search for his body and during the trials of those involved in the kidnapping. By the fall of 1827 the affair had assumed a political character. For a full discussion of the beginnings and scope of the Antimasonic movement, see Lee Benson, *The Concept of Jacksonian Democracy: New York as a Test Case* (New York, 1965), 15–46; Charles McCarthy, *The Antimasonic Party: a Study of Political Anti-Masonry in the United States, 1827–1840* (American Historical Association, *Annual Report, 1902*, I; Washington, 1903), 367–574.   [8] Cf. above, Clay to Brown, March 27, 1827, note.
[9] Cf. below, Porter to Clay, November 6, 1827, and note.

INSTRUCTIONS AND DISPATCHES   November 5, 1827

From J[OHN] J. APPLETON, Stockholm, no. 24. Reports a misconception, on the part of the Count of Wetterstedt, "respecting the object of one of the Articles of the Treaty recently signed" (cf. above, Appleton to Clay, July 11, 1827): "The Count [during a discussion on October 22] . . . only mentioned the Treaty to observe that as it was signed and probably now in the hands of my Government, it was too late to talk of changes or to regret any thing which it contained, still he could not conceal from me that the Norwegians had found great fault with the 8th. Article [quotes the Article in a footnote], which they chose to understand in a manner which would oblige them to abandon their present system of Duties on Navigation. They contended he said that in consequence of this Article Vessels coming from America might claim to be admitted in the Ports of Norway on paying no higher tonnage duty than if they had come from any other foreign County, even the nearest to Norway. As he (the Count) did not so understand the Article but considered it as placing merely the Vessels of the two Contracting Powers when engaged in the trade between either of them and any third Power upon the same footing in regard to Navigation duties as National Vessels, he had not hesitated to tell them that their apprehensions were groundless, and he did not doubt that my interpretation of the article, would confirm that which he had thus given it." States that he replied to the effect that his interpretation of the article agreed with that of the Norwegians and added that he had presented the Article for the purpose of obtaining "for the Vessels employed in the trade between the treating Countries as favourable terms of admission as were, or might be, enjoyed by those engaged in the trade between either of them and any other Foreign Country. . . ." Summarizes the explanations and illustrations used by him in bringing the Count to a change of opinion. Reports another interview, on October 29, at which Wetterstedt handed him a schedule of existing tonnage duties paid in Norway, which gave a distinct advantage to vessels from nearby ports; said that he had told the Norwegians "they would gain more than they lost by the 8th. Article, understood as they had interpreted it"; and added: "They were, however, much embarass'd [sic] how to proceed to effect the equalisation [sic] which it contemplated; they could direct that Vessels coming from Denmark should pay henceforth as much as those arriving from America, but that it was evident that so short a navigation could not bear such a burthen—" Observes that he "suggested the other alternative that Vessels coming from America should pay the minimum of the Foreign Tonnage Duty." Concludes: "Things remaining thus, we shall on the going of the Treaty into effect, have the right to claim that our Vessels be placed on the same footing as those coming from the nearest European Ports: a reduction of nearly 2/3 on the amount now paid, which will be particularly acceptable to such of our Vessels, as on their passage out may be driven, as it not infrequently occurs, in the Ports of Norway by Stress of weather, or by losses at Sea."

Encloses "a printed copy of a convention [concluded May 28, 1827; ratified, August 25] by which the Swedes and Norwegians have had the right to enter in the black [sic] Sea, and to tranship [sic] at Constantinople secured to them on the payment of stated duties." ALS. DNA, RG59, Dip. Disp., Sweden and Norway, vol. 5 (M45, R6). Received February 23, 1828.

Article VIII of the United States Treaty of Commerce and Navigation with Sweden and Norway stated that neither of the signatories would "impose upon the navigation between their respective territories, in the vessels of either, any tonnage or other duties, of any kind or denomination, which . . . [should] be higher or other than those . . . imposed on every other navigation except that which they . . . reserved to themselves, respectively, by the sixth article of the present treaty." Article VI excepted from the treaty the coastwise navigation of the contracting parties and that "from one port of the Kingdoms of Sweden or of Norway to another" and "between the two latter countries. . . ." A "Separate Article," appended to the main body of the treaty, also excepted from Article VIII the "special stipulations" of an earlier treaty between Sweden-Norway and Russia which regulated trade with the Grand Duchy of Finland on a basis recognizing "Certain relations of proximity and ancient connections." Parry (ed.), *Consolidated Treaty Series*, vol. 77, pp. 293–94, 304–306.

From JOHN CUTHBERT, Hamburg. Reports having sent to Clay's address "the Atlas Universel, published at Brussels, on 400 sheets Imperial, and according to the plan of the Publisher, when framed is to form a circle. . ."; expresses willingness "to present it to the National Library. . . ." ALS. DNA, RG59, Cons. Disp., Hamburg, vol. 3 (M-T211, R3). Received December 28.

Philippe Marie Guillaume Van der Maelen, a Belgian geographer, had published the *Atlas Universel de Géographie Physique, Politique, Statistique et Minéralogique. . .*, consisting of six parts, in three volumes, in 1827.

On the National Library, see above, Everett to Clay, March 25, 1826, note.

From W[ILLIAM] B. ROCHESTER, New York. Mentions that he wrote "at length" a letter "sent to the post-office about an hour ago" (cf. above, Rochester to Clay, November 4, 1827) but that he "entirely forgot to mention" that he was "looking impatiently for the copy of the correspondence of Col. [John] Williams &c." which Clay has promised. ALS. DNA, R59, Dip. Disp., Central America, vol. 1 (M219, R2).

To Francis T. Brooke

My dear Sir   Washington 6h. Nov. 1827.

I return, after having perused with no ordinary satisfaction, the excellent letter of Judge Stuart. The information which it communicates is very encouraging, and the zeal which it manifests is truly patriotic. My hopes of our parent State are greatly revived, by what I see and hear passing there. It may fall to her lot to preserve the Republic from the fatal rock on which so many free states have perished.

Mr. Johnson's letter excited with me no other feeling than that of surprize—not at the estimate which he has made of the President and the Administration—but that he should have thought that a politic occasion to announce his judgment.

Markley's publication,[1] as you suppose, I have no doubt will be much perverted; but I think the internal evidence, which it carries, of candor and truth cannot fail to make a deep impression.

From what I learn from N. York[2] I should not be surprized if a majority of Jackson members is returned at the elections this week, to the Legislature, notwithstanding my conviction, from all the testimony that reaches me, that an overwhelming majority of the people of the State are in favor of Mr Adams. If such should be the result, it will be owing to the fact that, at the Conventions which nominate the candidates for the Legislature, it has been so artfully contrived as to get Jackson candidates designated— Sometimes by the friends of both parties, and, in some instances, by Conventions composed of majorities favorable to Mr. Adams   Should the Legislature be so constituted, I do not yet doubt that a large majority of the Electors will be given to Mr. Adams at the next fall.[3] I remain truly Your friend
The Honble F. T. Brooke.   H CLAY

ALS. NcD. Cf. above, Brooke to Clay, November 4, 1827.
[1] Cf. above, Sergeant to Clay, October 31, 1827, note.   [2] Cf. above, Sergeant to Clay, October 24, 1827, and note; Porter to Clay, October 26, 1827.   [3] Cf. above, Clay to Brown, March 27, 1827, note.

To Jabez D. Hammond

Dear Sir   Washn. 6h. Nov. 1827.
I thank you for your letter of the 1st. with its inclosure,[1] containing

the proceedings of the interesting meeting at Albany.[2] Should the friends of the Administration follow up that example—should they act, in your State, with vigor concert and union, I can not doubt the course of the vote of the State;[3] but if they allow a system of complete organization and management to be executed on the other side, without co-operation on theirs, there is every thing to apprehend. Discipline on one side, with disorganization on the other, will ever prevail where there is any thing like an equal division.

The event which you announce as probable, that of a Legislature of a Jackson complexion,[4] will be much to be deprecated. It was not expected out of N. York; and is it not to be feared that the same means which have produced it may lead on to other similar successes? You say that it will not dare repeal the electoral law.[5] My dear Sir that party dare do any thing. If they believed that by assuming the power in the Legislature to appoint the electors they could ensure the election of their favorite, do you think, whatever professions are now made they would hesitate a moment? Would they not argue that success sanctions the deed? And have they not already a precedent derived from an adjoining State of a similar preceding [sic].[6] The state of things in N. York is more to be regretted because almost every where else bright prospects were chasing away those of an opposite character—

But I still hope for the best. We must not despair but continue, like men, to do our duty to the last. Ever Your's truly & faithfy
Jabez D. Hammond Esq   H CLAY

ALS. PHi.   [1] Neither has been found.
[2] A meeting of Adams supporters had convened in Albany on October 19 to select a candidate for the State Senate from that district. After a close contest John Gebhard, of Schoharie, had been named over Herman Knickerbocker, of Rensselaer. *Albany Argus*, October 20, 1827. Born in Columbia County, New York, Gebhard was a lawyer and had been surrogate of Schoharie County from 1811 to 1813 and from 1815 to 1822. From 1821 to 1823 he had been a member of the United States House of Representatives. Knickerbocker, also a lawyer, was prominent as a descendent of one of the early Dutch settlers and a man of great wealth. He had been town supervisor of Troy intermittently since 1802, a position which he held at this time. He had served in the United States Congress from 1809 to 1811 and in the State Assembly in 1816. In 1828 he became judge of common pleas for Rensselaer County.   [3] Cf. above, Clay to Brown, March 27, 1827, note.
[4] Cf. above, Sergeant to Clay, October 24, 1827, note.   [5] Cf. above, Clay to Brooke, December 11, 1826, note.   [6] By act of October 25, 1824 (Vermont, *Acts . . . 1824*, ch. 2, pp. 4–5) the Vermont Legislature had provided that electors for the President and Vice President of the United States, beginning with the canvass of 1828, should be selected by vote of "freemen's" meetings in the various towns. Members of the legislature had, however, met in caucus on November 9, 1827, and drafted a slate of candidates "almost unanimously recommended to the freemen of this State." Washington *Daily National Journal*, November 21, 1827, citing Woodstock (Vermont) *Herald*.

From Joseph Delafield

Hon. Henry Clay Secretary of State.
Sir.   New York. Novr 6. 1827.
The Boundary Line commission held its final meeting in this city

on the 22d ultimo. and adjourned on the 27th sine die, having brought all its joint proceedings to a close.[1] I have the honor to transmit herewith a copy of those proceedings.

The British commissioner[2] stated that his correspondence with his Government since the meeting in October 1826 had ended in an instruction "to proceed to close the commission in the manner described in the Treaty."[3] He gave no other information concerning his instructions, nor acknowledged any specific reply to the propositions submitted by him.[4] On the contrary it is made to appear that the foregoing is his only instruction, and consequently the business of the commission is brought back to the same position in which it was at the meeting in October 1826, and the whole subject has been concluded in conformity with the Views of the respective commissioners as recorded at the meeting and heretofore transmitted.[5] The Boundary line under the seventh article of the Treaty therefore is agreed to and determined through the St Marys River from the head of St George, or Sugar Island to Lake Superior, through Lake Superior to the northward of Isle Royale, and in the interior through Rainy Lake, Rainy River, and the Lake of the Woods including its most north-western point.

The disagreements are to St Georges or Sugar Island in the St Marys River, and the water communication from Lake Superior to the Rainy Lake. The merits of these two questions remain as at the previous meeting, no new evidence or arguments having been advanced on the part of the British, and none were deemed necessary on ours. The respective commissioners have agreed to exchange their separate and final reports on the 24th day of December next, when I have no manner of doubt it will appear, that the claims I have had the honor to prefer and advocate will be amply sustained and justified, and those of the British Agent shown to be [ex]travagant and unsupported.

At the same time, "duplicates of their respective reports declarations statements and decisions and of their accounts and of the Journal of all their proceedings" will be delivered to me, as directed in the Treaty, which together with a Very extensive series of maps of actual surveys, including those which have the Boundary Line (so far as it is determined) marked upon them, I shall as soon thereafter as practicable present to you at the Department of State.

The balance due from the United States to the British Government by reason of the excess of the expenses of the British Commission over ours, amounting to Four Thousand two hundred and sixty five dollars and six cents, being a moiety of such excess has been received and paid. With the greatest respect. [I] have the honor to be. Your mo: obed: servant   JOS: DELAFIELD
Hon. Henry Clay. Secretary of State.

ALS. DNA, RG76, Northern Boundary: Treaty of Ghent, 1814, Articles VI and VII, entry 142, env. 1, folder 2.

1 Cf. above, Porter to Clay, October 26, 30, 1827.   2 Anthony Barclay.   3 Of
Ghent.   4 Cf. above, Porter to Clay, October 18, 1826; Clay to Porter, October 22,
1826.   5 Cf. above, Delafield to Clay, November 15, 1826.

From Peter B. Porter

Dear Sir,   Utica Nov. 6. 1827

I left New York on Sunday, & am thus far on my way home. Having stopped for an hour I thought I would drop you a line on the subject of our pending election, in regard to which you cannot but feel some interest—altho' it is wholly out of my power to give you any information that can be depended on.

My own *conjecture* then is, as it has been for several weeks past, that the character of our next Legislature, if not absolutely Jacksonian, will at least, be confidently claimed as such by Mr Van Buren & Clinton,[1] who have been extremely active, and command most of the party presses in the State; while the Admn party have been without the means, even if they had avowed a disposition, to act with effect. as regards this state alone, Jackson success *at this present election* might perhaps be desirable, as it would rouse our friends to some energy. I cannot for a moment doubt but that this state will, long before the presidential election shew itself to be decidedly for the admn.

The policy of Van Buren has been to get Jackson candidates nominated when he could—&, when he could not, to take such as he deemed most promising subjects of *conversion*. In this way, probably one third of our members will come to albany "uncommitted"   prepared to go either way, as prospects between that time & the close of this session may invite.

I learnt last week, in N. York that I had been put in nomination for the Assembly[2] by some of my political friends, & the nomination persisted in, against the advice & remonstrances of my personal friends. It is too in opposition to the regular caucus nomination,[3] the machinery of which is controlled not by me, but by my enemies in Buffalo. Had I been at home I should have refused the nomination— But as it is, I am not without hopes of an election,[3] as I might by being in the legislature, be of some use in producing concert among our friends, and rousing them to energy. I beg you to excuse this scrawl which, I have written in great haste, & have not time to copy— Please burn it. respectfully   P. B. PORTER

ALS. DLC-HC (DNA, M212, R3). Addressed: "private."
1 Cf. above, Sergeant to Clay, October 24, 1827, note.   2 Cf. above, Clay to Brown,
March 27, 1827, note.   3 Porter had been nominated at a "public meeting" in contradistinction to candidates nominated "by a convention of delegates held on the 25th
ult." Although the *Black Rock Gazette* maintained that the latter nominees as well as
Porter, were "all friendly to the administration. . . ," the caucus candidates were defeated; while Porter was elected.   *Albany Argus*, November 2, 1827; *New York American*, November 20, 1827.

From JAMES OMBROSI, Florence. Transmits "the annexed very important news received before yesterday [sic] by a dispatch of Admiral [Edward] Codrington to this [sic] British Ambassador, written off Navarino's harbour, in [sic] date of the 20th. and 21st. October last . . . by which we have been informed that the Turkish and Egyptian fleet is entirely destroyed. . . ." Adds that "The battle was entirely provoked by the conduct of the Turks and the cruelty of Ibrahim Pasha, who during the Short truce never ceased to make a war of extermination in the interior of the Morea, and was rendered necessary to Obtain the results contemplated in the Treaty of mediation" (see above, Brown to Clay, July 12, 1827, note). ALS. DNA, RG59, Cons. Disp., Florence, vol. 1 (M-T204, R1). Received February 7, 1828. Enclosed is a copy of the *Gazzetta di Firenze*, of November 6, 1827.

The British Ambassador in Florence was John Fane (1784–1859), Lord Burghersh [Burgherst], later (1841) eleventh Earl of Westmorland. A distinguished soldier in the wars against Napoleon, he had attained the rank of major general in 1825 and became a lieutenant general in 1838. He was also an accomplished historian and musician, the author of several military histories of the Napoleonic Wars and seven operas. His various high-level diplomatic assignments culminated in service as resident Minister in Berlin, 1841 to 1851.

The Battle of Navarino had pitted the combined British, French, and Russian fleets against a Turco-Egyptian force which outnumbered them by four to one. Ibrahim, unable to put to sea (cf. above, Brown to Clay, October 28, 1827, note), had opened a bloody land campaign on October 19. To enforce their mandate to stop the war the allies had determined to confront the Turkish and Egyptian fleets in Navarino harbor. The engagement, fought at anchor, had begun when the Turco-Egyptians opened fire on Vice Admiral Sir Edward Codrington's force soon after it came to anchor. In the ensuing action, 53 of some 82 Turco-Egyptian vessels had been sunk or disabled. Allied losses had been light. The victory of the allies eventually led to the withdrawal from Greece of the Sultan's strategically isolated land forces and to the ultimate independence of Greece from Turkish rule. William Miller, *The Ottoman Empire and Its Successors, 1801–1927* . . . (revd. and enld. edn., London, 1966), 97–98; Edwin M. Hall, "The Battle of Navarino," in E. B. Potter and J. R. Fredland (eds.), *The United States and World Sea Power* (Englewood Cliffs, N. J., 1955), 274–76.

To Edward Everett

My dear Sir   Washn. 7h. Nov. 1827.
     I recd. your friendly letter of the 30h. Ulto.[1] and was glad to learn that your health was better. I regret very much, and so do other friends, that you mean to leave your better part[2] behind. The presence of as many of the softer sex as possible this winter is peculiarly desirable, to calm and soothe the turbulent passions which may be expected.
     As to politics, every thing appeared to be doing well of late, until recent developements [sic] in N. York.[3] How far they are to be regarded unfavorable we cannot tell here until the lapse of some days. In the mean time the most encouraging movements are making in Virginia.[4] The contest there will be, as in some measure it is every where in the

Union, one between the united intellect of the Country, and prejudice, ignorance and a blind attachment to an individual. If no counter current arises, my hopes of ultimate success in that State are very strong. Pennsa. is doing better than the late elections would indicate.[5] In Ohio we have about two thirds of each branch of the Legislature.[6] Louisiana, at this time is one of the safest and best organized States in the Union.[7] In Kentucky we have the Legislature and, altho' I am not without my fears as to a part of the vote of that State, our friends there continue sanguine.[8]

I must reserve other matters for the occasion of seeing you here. Until then and always believe me Sincerely & faithfly Yr's
The Honble E. Everett.   H CLAY

ALS. MHi.   [1] Not found.
[2] Charlotte Gray Brooks Everett.   [3] Cf. above, Sergeant to Clay, October 24, 1827;
Porter to Clay, October 26, 1827.   [4] Cf. above, Mercer to Clay, August 18, 1827, note;
Brooke to Clay, September 27, October 17, November 4, 1827.   [5] Cf. above, Sergeant
to Clay, October 14, 16, 30, 31, 1827; Mifflin to Clay, October 21, 1827.   [6] Cf. above,
Hammond to Clay, October 18, 29, 1827.   [7] Cf. above, Johnston to Clay, July 16, 1827;
Shaumburgh to Clay, October 17, 1827.   [8] Cf. above, Clay to Adams, August 19,
1827, and note; Letcher to Clay, August 27, 1827; Smith to Clay, October 7, 1827; Clay
to Beatty, October 28, 1827; Crittenden to Clay, October 30, 1827.

INSTRUCTIONS AND DISPATCHES   November 7, 1828

From J[AMES] COOLEY, Lima, no. 9. Pictures the internal condition of the country as "very deplorable," with bands of armed and mounted "robbers" active in around Lima. Reports the seizure of a vessel carrying a Colombian officer with dispatches from General (Simón) Bolívar to General (Antonio José de) Sucre in Bolivia; assesses Peruvian fears of invasion by foreign troops; mentions Peru's efforts to ready its "small Navy," organize a "National Militia," and by impressment increase the size of the army in order to resist any attempted invasion by Bolivar's forces. Notes that the Peruvian Congress has not appointed a member to the Congress at Tacubaya; adds that General (José de) Lamar, in a recent conversation, observed that Peru was too poor to dispatch ministers abroad; and concludes that "the prospect of Peru being represented either at Tacubaya or Washington at present is exceedingly problemmatical [sic]." ALS. DNA, RG59, Dip. Disp., Peru, vol. 1 (M-T52, R1). Extract published in Manning (arr.), *Diplomatic Correspondence . . . Latin-American Nations*, III, 1835–36. Received February 23, 1828.

From W[ILLIAM] TUDOR, Lima, no. 78, "*Confidential.*" Remarks that "Absence from this city for a few weeks" on account of impaired health has kept him from writing "since the 12h [*i.e.*, 19th] of Septr., which however is of little moment" since his "letters are merely supplementary to those of Mr. [James] Cooley. . . ." Devotes ten manuscript pages to a discussion, severely critical of (Simón) Bolívar and his adherents, of political developments and leaders in Peru, Bolivia, and Colombia, with some mention of other parts of Spanish America. Speculates on the disastrous results, including war against Peru (cf. above, Cooley to Clay, this date), to be apprehended from Bolívar's course of action and expresses an opinion that it "is not impossible that some steps might be taken by the U.S. & England, that would check his career, and avert long and dreadful suffering to these countries." Reports "a confidential conversation on this subject the other evening with

Gen. [José de] Lamar & Dr. [Francisco Javier] Luna Pizarro—in which . . . [he] suggested the policy of making some confidential communications to the government of the United States and that of England" and an agreement "that Dr. Luna Pizarro should draw up the documents mentioned." Notes that the Peruvian Congress, "still in session," does "almost as little as ours did last session at Washington"; that "the Committee in Congress differ in opinion as to the expediency of ratifying the [Panama] treaties" (cf. above, Tudor to Clay, September 19, 1827); and that the President (Lamar) told him there were no funds with which to send a Minister to Tacubaya. ALS. DNA, RG59, Cons. Disp., Lima, vol. 2 (M154, R2). Received February 21, 1828.

From BEAUFORT T. WATTS, Bogotá, no. 37. Transmits a copy and a translation of a letter from the Colombian Foreign Minister (Joseph R. Revenga) to Clay (above, September 25, 1827), an extract of a congressional decree of July 26 declaring Buenaventura a free port, and a copy of the decree of August 29 "Regulating the Interior and public debt."

Acknowledges receipt of (Daniel) Brent's note on President Adams' views concerning Watts' letter to (Simón) Bolívar (cf. above, Watts to Clay, June 14, 1827, and note); argues that the explanation contained in his dispatch no. 30 (*ibid.*) and supported by Revenga's of September 25, should be satisfactory; and encloses, in support of his conduct, a letter from the Vice President of Colombia (Francisco de Paula Santander) to the Liberator. Announces: "I shall take the earliest opportunity to explain again to my government the reasons that urged me to write to the Liberator, and can but hope that they will be satis satisfactory [*sic*]." ALS. DNA, RG59, Dip. Disp., Colombia, vol. 4 (M-T33, R4). Received January 9, 1828.

To Daniel Webster

My dear Sir   Washington 8h. Nov. 1827.
I recd. both your favors of 29h. Ulto. from Boston, and monday morning last from N. York.[1]

There is perfect security to your letters after they arrive at the office. They are opened by no one but by myself, especially when marked "private." Mr. Brent,[2] who is worthy of all confidence, is some times charged by me with opening the Mail, but he never opens letters so marked.

I am glad that you are enabled to procure a contribution for the Whig[3] to the amount mentioned in your last letter. It will afford at least present relief, and until some other arrangement can be made. I would prefer (if you have no objection) that the sum should be remitted to the Honble J. S. Johnston, who is here, animated by the greatest zeal in the cause, doing more than any other person that I know, and who is in habits of correspondence with the Editors of the Whig. He knows the situation of the Editors,[4] and has contributed himself handsomely to their relief. He will immediately pass the sum to its destination.

I regret very much the state of things in N. York.[5] It was not expected until within a few weeks. It comes at a moment when almost every where else prospects were bright or brightening. In Virginia especially there is much reason to hope that the reaction, of which we have evidence in all quarters, will carry the vote to Mr. Adams.[6]

The elections in Ohio place about two thirds of our friends in each branch of the Legislature. The same want of organization which exists in N. York is wanted in Ohio, but the evil is about to be remedied.[7]

I have a letter from Warfield which I was glad to receive on your account. I have advised him to publish nothing for the present[8] and until McLean,[9] who I take to be at the bottom of the business chooses, to come out. Expecting the pleasure of soon seeing you, I postpone for that occasion many things which I would otherwise now say, and remain   Cordially Your friend   H CLAY
D. Webster Esq

ALS. DLC-Webster Papers (DNA, M212, R22).
1 Only the New York letter of November 5, 1827, has been found.   2 Daniel Brent.
3 Richmond *Constitutional Whig.*   4 John H. Pleasants; Marcellus Smith.
5 Cf. above, Sergeant to Clay, October 24, 1827, note.   6 Cf. above, Mercer to Clay, August 8, 1827, and note; Brooke to Clay, September 27, October 17, November 4, 1827.
7 Cf. above, Hammond to Clay, October 18, 29, 1827.   8 Henry R. Warfield. Neither the letter nor Clay's reply has been found. Cf. above, Warfield to Clay, July 5, 1826, and note.   9 Louis McLane. See W[illiam] Coleman to Timothy Pickering, not dated; postmarked March 18 and endorsed as March 18, 1825 (ALS, in MHi-Pickering MSS.). Coleman reported that shortly "before going into ballot" (in the vote of the House of Representatives for the Presidency, in February, 1825), Webster had taken "Mr. L. Mc-Lean [*sic*] of Delaware a one-side" and offered to show him a letter "written to a member of the House [Warfield] in which Mr Adams . . . expressly committed himself & designedly as to the course he . . . [would] pursue towards the federalists if he . . . [were] elected." McLane, Coleman continued, had declined to see the letter because "his mind was conclusively made up." See, also, Livermore, *Twilight of Federalism,* 179, 214.

From Mary Austin Holley

Dear Sir,   Baltimore November 8th., 1827.
In addressing you on the present occasion, so interesting to me, I make no appeal to your benevolence or your friendship, since the one is spontaneous, and the other will not be withdrawn in the moment of trial. In rising from my late affliction[1] I find I have still one remaining care. The education of my son[2] claims my whole attention and I am desirous of securing to him every advantage. In sketching a plan for this purpose I have included the course at West Point, and understanding that *favour at Court* is all-important in such cases as well as in those of greater concern, I ask of you, my dear Sir, some assistance in obtaining a place for him there. By such an early application, the boy is not yet ten, and such good friends as yourself and Mr. Johnston,[3] I may hope to succeed either through Kentucky or Louisiana, unless, indeed, *the military dynasty should supersede* the civil, and then, my bright prospects failing, I should have to make interest, if not with *ebony,*[4] at least with as hard a substance—Old Hickory.

I will thank you to drop me a line on the subject and inform me what I may expect, and whether there is any formality to be attended to, directed to the care of James Dall Esq Baltimore, where I am staying, with my sister, Mrs. Dall,[5] till a suitable opportunity offers for returning to our unfortunate Lexington.[6] I hope you will not think me troublesome in calling your attention to my individual concerns when your mind is so much engrossed by the weightier matters of the State. I do it with diffidence, and shall acknowledge the favour with gratitude. I have had the resolution to leave my son at Cambridge, in the best possible situation,[7] and shall spare no pains to supply to him, as far as may be, his irreparable loss, and to ensure his success in life. It shall not be said, *his mother spoiled him.*

Present me most affectionately to Mrs Clay. I heard of Mr Claiborne[8] in Boston, and regretted that I did not arrive there soon enough to see him. Has anything been heard lately from Mr Duralde?[9] I wrote to him a long time since, on business, and have received no answer.

Wishing you all good, physically, morally and politically, I am, dear sir, with great respect yours, M A HOLLEY
To, Henry Clay Esquire

ALS. DLC-HC (DNA, M212, R3).
[1] The death of Horace Holley, her husband. Cf. above, Wayland to Clay, August 16, 1827, note. [2] Horace Austin Holley. [3] Josiah Stoddard Johnston. [4] Cf. above, Hammond to Clay, November 5, 1827, and note. [5] Henrietta Austin (1788–1866) had married in 1812 James Dall, son of a well-to-do Boston merchant, and soon afterward moved with him to Baltimore. [6] Probably a reference to the circumstances attending Holley's separation from the presidency of Transylvania University (cf. above, Clay to Holley, February 21, 1826, and note; Clay to Bradford, February 10, 1827, and note; Chase to Clay, April 19, 1827, note). Mrs. Holley did not return to Lexington until the spring of 1828, when she remained there only briefly. [7] Horace Austin Holley, then nine years old, was placed with a private tutor in Cambridge, Massachusetts, for a few months. In 1828, his mother moved him to the Garrison Forest Church school in Baltimore, run by her brother, Charles Austin, an Episcopal clergyman. Later, young Holley attended various schools in Lexington and New Orleans with indifferent success. By 1838 he had given up medical studies in New Orleans and had returned to Lexington, where he was "idle and immature and unhappy" and was considered "no count." Lee, *Mary Austin Holley,* 187, 195, 288, 296. He never attended the United States Military Academy. [8] Probably William C. C. Claiborne. Cf. above, Claiborne to Clay, June 20, 1827. [9] Martin Duralde, Jr.

INSTRUCTIONS AND DISPATCHES November 8, 1827

From A[LEXANDER] H. EVERETT, Madrid, no. 91. Notes the arrival at Valencia of the new French Ambassador, the Count de Saint Priest, "not . . . in his official character, but as a sort of private Commissioner from the King of France [Charles X] bearing an autograph letter from that Sovereign to His Catholic Majesty [Ferdinand VII]," which states that, if the latter wishes to visit Barcelona (cf. above, Everett to Clay, October 19, 1827) and feels "any repugnance at the presence of the French Garrison of that City [cf. above, Everett to Clay, June 4, 1827], it will be withdrawn during the time of his stay."

Reports that published accounts and private letters "from the theatre of the insurrection" (in Catalonia—cf. above, Everett to Clay, April 19, August 16, September 20, October 19, 1827) agree that "the Royal Troops have uniformly had the advantage" and that the insurgents "are reduced to a few small companies who are straggling about the mountains." Credits "the energetic" action of the

Government and "the Kings determination to take the field in person" with crushing the rebellion. Encloses a translation of a proclamation by one of the rebel leaders, who "complains bitterly of the deception practiced upon him by the Clergy. . . ." Discusses the roles of certain prelates in the "conspiracy," including that of "a certain Father Alvarez resident at Rome," who "was employed . . . as the agent of the apostolic party with the Pope [Leo XII], and was now engaged in enterprises of the most dangerous and treasonable character." Adds that the Pope acceded to a demand from the King for the arrest and delivery of Alvarez, who is now imprisoned in Spain. Laments the fact that, despite revelations of involvement of "the Clergy and the violent Royalist party . . . in the late troubles," there has been "no appearance of . . . a reaction in favor of Constitutional ideas, or even of a more liberal spirit in the conduct of the Administration." Cites, as evidence "of an augmentation of intolerance in regard to individuals suspected of holding liberal opinions," the practice "of the purification, as it is called. . . , of persons who had served the country during the period of the Constitution," and the operation under a decree, not yet published, of "two or three purifying Juntas."

Notes that "The late difficulty with the Pope in regard to the affairs of South America [cf. above, Everett to Clay, March 31, June 9, 22, July 15, August 16, 1827] seems to be amicably settled" and that "The new Nuncio [Francesco Tiberi], who takes the title of Archbishop of Athens, arrived here a week or two since. . . ." Casts doubt on a rumor "that the Court of Rome has consented to defer for a year the formal installation of the Bishops, lately named for Columbia [sic]" and denies the accuracy of reports of "negotiations for peace between Spain and her Colonies. . . ."

Encloses a copy of his further correspondence (cf. above, Everett to Clay, June 4, August 10, 1827) with "the Charge d'Affairs of France [Count de Beaurepaire] . . . on the subject of the quarantine laws enforced at Barcelona and Cadiz." Admits to "but little chance of success in this application" but expresses belief that it is his "duty to pursue it, and to show the French authorities that if we cannot in every instance secure our rights we at least know what they are." Appends a postscript to say that "The copy of the letter to Count de Beaurepaire . . . could not be prepared in season for this despatch." LS, except for postscript in Everett's hand. DNA, RG59, Dip. Disp., Spain, vol. 28 (M31, R29). Received January 19, 1828.

Emmanuel-Louis-Marie Guignard, Viscount de Saint-Priest, born in Paris in 1789, had fought with the Russian Army against Napoleon and, after the restoration of Louis XVIII to the French throne, had been honored for his services to the Royalist cause. He had commanded a brigade under the Duke d'Angoulême during the French occupation of Spain in 1823 (see above, III, 313n) and had then been raised to the military rank of lieutenant general. After the fall of Cádiz he had returned to France and from 1825 to 1827 had held appointment as Ambassador to Berlin. He remained in the post at Madrid until 1830.

Father Alvarez, a monk who had formerly acted as confessor to Queen Maria Louisa of Parma, was reportedly imprisoned "for life" in Rome by the Pope early in 1828. *Niles' Weekly Register*, XXXIV (March 15, 1828), 36.

MISCELLANEOUS LETTERS   November 8, 1827

From JABEZ D. HAMMOND, New York. Introduces James Duane Doty, "U. S. Judge of the Northern District of Michigan," who "will remain at Washington some time on business in which the people of Michigan Territory are interested." States:

"He is perfectly well acquainted with the public men in this (his native) State and is competent to give you any information you may desire respecting the State of parties here—" ALS. DNA, RG59, A. and R. (M531, R2).

From BETSEY HAWLEY, "No. 77 Norfolk Street, New York." Requests information on the procedure for taking out papers of administration on the property of her late brother (Isaac P. Hawley).

Refers briefly, in a postscript, to her complaints (against Franklin Litchfield and Caleb Brintnall—see above, Hawley to Clay, October 11, 1827) of mistreatment and concludes: "And as you have not answered my last communic[ation] on this Subject, I would ask, what in Such circumstances you expect me to do[?] Must I appeal to the public?" ALS. DNA, RG59, Cons. Disp., Puerto Cabello, vol. 1 (M-T229, R1).

Endorsed by Clay: "Mr. [Daniel] B[rent]. will report to me the particulars of this case   H C."

Daniel Brent acknowledged, on November 15, receipt of Miss Hawley's letter; stated that "The Secretary is sorry that he is unacquainted with the regulations of Colombia upon this subject, and . . . is unable, therefore, to give you the advice and directions which you solicit"; encloses an extract of Litchfield's reply (above, July 31, 1827) to the instructions given him (cf. above, Hawley to Clay, June 1, 1827, note); and indicates the possibility that "Mr. Litchfield may be enabled hereafter to communicate a more satisfactory result." Copy, in DNA, RG59, Dom. Letters, vol. 22, pp. 83–84 (M40, R20).

From James Wilson

My dear Sir,   Steubenville, Novr. 9. 1827.

I do not know whether it is the fashion for the "By Authority" printers to apply for re-appointment—but, lest it should be, I take the liberty of soliciting a renewal of mine.[1]

We have just recd. Markley's letter[2] here. It has given much satisfaction, & has taken from the opposition their last foot-hold.— I hope our friends at a distance have no fears as to Ohio. We have none here. All we want is organization, and *that* we are preparing for.[3] Your friend,   JAS. WILSON.

☞ Your little namesake,[4] of whom you were so kind as to enquire, in your last letter,[5] is well, as are all the family.
Hon. H. Clay.

ALS. DNA, RG59, P. and D. of L. Addressed: "Private."
[1] Cf. above, Wilson to Clay, November 3, 1825, note.   [2] Cf. above, Sergeant to Clay, October 31, 1827, note.   [3] Cf. above, Hammond to Clay, October 29, 1827, and note.   [4] Henry Clay Wilson (1827–1875) grew up to serve as a customs official in the Territory of Washington and as an officer in the commissary of subsistence in Ohio during the Civil War. He was a great uncle of President Woodrow Wilson.   [5] Not found.

INSTRUCTIONS AND DISPATCHES   November 9, 1827

To GEORGE B. ADAMS, "Consul of the U. States for the Port of Alicant [*sic*], in Spain." Transmits his "Commission, together with printed Circular Instructions, and a blank Consular Bond. . . ." Copy. DNA, RG59, Cons. Instr., vol. 2, p. 447 (M78, R2). Cf. above, Cook to Clay, August 3, 1825, note.

To ALBERT DAVY, "Consul of the U. States for the Port of Kingston upon Hull, in Great-Britain." Transmits his "Commission, together with printed Circular Instructions, and a blank Consular Bond. . . ." Copy. DNA, RG59, Cons. Instr., vol. 2, p. 447 (M78, R2). Cf. above, Gallatin to Clay, September 18, 1827.

On December 17, 1827, Davy acknowledged receipt of his commission and returned his bond. ALS, in *ibid.*, Cons. Disp., Leeds-upon-Hull, vol. 1 (M-T474, R1).

To WILLIAM GORDON, "Consular Commercial Agent at Aux Cayes." Transmits "the evidence of" his "appointment, together with a Copy of the printed Circular Instructions to Consuls." Copy. DNA, RG59, Cons. Instr., vol. 2, p. 448 (M78, R2).

Eighteen Philadelphia merchants had signed a memorial, dated November 5, 1827, and addressed to the President, recommending Gordon, "of the House of Graham, Gordon & Co American Merchants at Aux Cayes . . . to fill the vacancy occasioned by the death of James A. Holden. . . ." DS. DNA, RG59, A. and R. (M531, R3).

Neither Gordon nor his firm has been further identified.

To SAMUEL ISRAEL, "Consular Commercial Agent at Cape Haytien." Transmits "the evidence of" his "appointment together with a Copy of the printed Circular Instructions to Consuls." Copy. DNA, RG59, Cons. Instr., vol. 2, p. 448 (M78, R2).

Israel, member of a family of Philadelphia merchants, was himself a merchant at Cape Haitien.

From J[OEL] R. POINSETT, Mexico (City), no. 106. Transmits copies of his "correspondence with this government on the subject of the capture of the two American vessels Liberty and Superior." Points out that "the Mexican Secretary of foreign affairs [Juan José Espinosa de los Monteros] . . . takes the ground, that the officers who make captures are liable to be sued in the Mexican courts"; notes that "This principle is established by the laws of Spain, which still prevail . . . whenever they are not contrary to the Constitution of the United Mexican States"; declares that he would not advise owners of vessels "To sue officers who are worth nothing, in the courts of Mexico, where litigation is so very expensive and subject to no fixed rules"; and confesses that, "until this form is complied with," he does not "understand on what ground" he "can prosecute these claims. . . ." Requests instructions, "as similar cases may again occur." LS. DNA, RG59, Dip. Disp., Mexico, vol. 3 (M97, R4).

On the case of the *Liberty*, cf. above, Gracie to Clay, February 7, 1826; Clay to Poinsett, May 11, 1826.

The schooner *Superior*, according to the enclosed copy of Poinsett's letter, of September 13, 1827, to the Mexican "Secretary of State and of Interior and Exterior Relations," had been captured by a Mexican gunboat "in the port of Laguna on the 23rd of February, 1826," under the pretext "that the said schooner was the Superior of Philadelphia, and had been engaged in smuggling." Poinsett contended that the vessel was, in fact, of New York, that there was "no evidence of her having been engaged in smuggling," and that she had "not been condemned." He explained the delay in presenting the claim on the part of the owners as arising "from the seizure of the schooner and the abandonment made of her by the captain in consequence of her being wormeaten from remaining so long in the port of Laguna." The claim for damages, estimated at $8,092.72 in 1826, was continued until commissioners under the settlement with Mexico in 1848 finally awarded the sum of $5,447.92. *Sen. Docs.*, 35 Cong., 2 Sess., no. 981, p. 61.

To Mary Austin Holley

My dear Madam   Washington 10h. November 1827
If I had known, prior to the receipt of your letter of the 8h. inst. where to address you, I should have communicated to you my sincere condolence on your late afflicting bereavement. I shared largely with your numerous friends in the regrets which that dispensation of Providence excited, and particularly in sympathies for you. It is passed; and philosophy, religion and reason all inculcate resignation and submission to the irreversible decree.

In respect to your little son,[1] and your wish to place him at West point, all that I can now say is that I should be most happy to be able to promote your wishes. I presume, of course, that you do not think of putting him there for some years, as he is now entirely too young. When the proper time arrives, you may rely upon my doing whatever I can to testify in his behalf the respect I feel for you and for the memory of his deceased father.[2] I must correct you in one particular. The selection of Cadets is regulated by established principles of distribution among the States, as far as is practicable, and not by any feeling of favoritism.

I seldom hear from Duralde.[3] My last letter is of date the 12h. of September.[4] He is at the same time one of the best and most indolent of men, at least in regard to his correspondence.

Wm. Claiborne[5] is here with us, and both he and Mrs. Clay unite their cordial respects and good wishes to those of Your faithful & obt. Servant   H Clay
Mrs. Holley.

ALS. KyLxT.   1 Horace Austin Holley.
2 Horace Holley.   3 Martin Duralde, Jr.   4 Not found.   5 William C. C.
Claiborne.

INSTRUCTIONS AND DISPATCHES   November 10, 1827

From W[illiam] B[each] Lawrence, London, no. 6. Refers to the apparent lack of any "provision for the reimbursement of expenses incurred by the owners of foreign vessels in furnishing subsistence to American mariners taken from wrecks at sea and brought into port"; observes that the "motives of policy" and "dictates of humanity" that led "to the enactment of the laws for the relief of seamen in distress [cf. above, Pleasonton to Clay, April 19, 1825; Clay to Quarrier, May 12, 1825; Williamson to Clay, April 3, 1827, note] would appear . . . to govern in such cases"; and suggests that United States consuls, who are not "restricted to the relief of such seamen, as may be found destitute within *their respective districts*," be authorized to settle "claims of the Masters or owners of foreign ships for subsistence furnished to American seamen, saved from wrecks and brought into their Consulates. . . ." Explains that his concern in the matter results from an application made to him by (Thomas) Aspinwall, to whom, as consul at London, a claim of this nature was submitted, and reports that, relying for a precedent on a decision made by (Albert) Gallatin in a similar case, he directed Aspinwall to settle the account. Encloses the relevant correspondence. ALS. DNA, RG59, Dip. Disp., Great Britain, vol. 35 (M30, R31). Received December 20.

From J[OEL] R. POINSETT, Mexico, no. 107. Reports that the Cabinet changes which he announced in dispatch no. 105 (above, October 24, 1827) "have all taken place, except that of the Minister of Grace and Justice.— [José Miguel] Ramos Arispe [sic] is still in office, although his separation is talked of as certain." Adds that General (Manuel) Rincon, the new temporary chief of staff, will likely be succeeded by General (Vicente) Guerrero; that José Ignacio Esteva will probably replace (Juan Manuel de) Elizalde as "Governor of the District"; and that the next elections will establish the ascendancy of "the popular or republican party . . . for some time."

Indicates that the insurrection of anti-European Spaniards on the Pacific coast (cf. above, Poinsett to Clay, October 6, 24, 1827) has been "calmed, but is not put down," and another has arisen in the State of Michoacán; predicts that the (Mexican) Congress, in order "to comply with the wishes of the people," will "pass a law expelling the Spaniards from Mexico" (cf. above, Taylor to Clay, November 2, 1827, note); notes that "The measure in contemplation is to expel . . . all the unmarried European Spaniards, giving to those who are married to Creoles the strongest guarantees for their future protection"; and comments that the latter group, "by their industry and capital, must be regarded as the most useful members of the community." Cites statements by the Secretary of War (Manuel Gómez Pedraza) and by (Francisco) García (Salinas), critical "of the intentions of the Scotch party [Escoceses]."

States that he wrote privately to General Guerrero, at the request of the latter's friends, urging him not to sustain by force the efforts of those seeking to expel the European Spaniards, but rather "to await patiently the effects of the efforts of his friends in his favor to elect him the successor of [Guadalupe] Victoria." Encloses a translation of Guerrero's reply (dated November 1, assuring Poinsett that he would not engage in rebellion against the Government). Emphasizes that he has "never taken any step, that could be interpreted as an interference in the domestic concerns of the country, without the knowledge and consent and, generally, at the solicitation of the government; and that all . . . [his] efforts have been directed to preserve the existing institutions of the country and to prevent civil war."

Summarizes the instructions of the Envoy to Rome (Francisco Pablo Vazquez). Explains that (Sebastián) Camacho's illness has delayed resumption of negotiations (between the United States and Mexico) but that "The President repeated . . . the other day his disposition to conclude them as soon as possible, and his willingness to cede the points in dispute between the two governments." Professes to "see no cause to apprehend a civil war in Mexico"; discusses the Mexican Government's need for money and its efforts to raise a loan; and observes: "there exists such a disposition to prodigal waste, such excessive corruption on the part of those who collect and administer the finances of the State, and such an insatiable desire for places and pensions, that no income, however great, can suffice." Notes the arrival at Veracruz of "Commodore [David] Porter . . . with his squadron," (cf. above, Taylor to Clay, November 2, 1827). Requests Clay to send "Melish's Map published in 1818, which is cited in the Treaty of Limits [cf. above, Clay to Poinsett, March 26, 1825; IV, 172]," and which the President (Victoria) has asked Poinsett to obtain. LS. DNA, RG59, Dip. Disp., Mexico, vol. 3 (M97, R4). Received December 5.

Elizalde had earlier, 1821, been appointed the first Mexican Minister Plenipotentiary to the United States but had been replaced when illness delayed his departure.

Vazquez, born in Puebla in 1769, had moved to Mexico City in 1790. There he had received his doctorate and had been ordained in 1795. He had been named Minister Plenipotentiary to the Holy See in 1821 but had not received his credentials until 1825. His mission centered upon the problem of winning recognition of Mexican independence and the appointment of bishops (cf. above, Poinsett to Clay, June 20, 1827; Everett to Clay, July 15, 1827, note). He was himself named at the consistory of 1831 as one of the first six bishops of the Mexican Republic. Vazquez then returned to Mexico, reorganized the Mexican hierarchy, and consecrated the other bishops.

MISCELLANEOUS LETTERS November 10, 1827

To ENOCH LINCOLN, "Governor of the State of Maine." Acknowledges receipt of Lincoln's letter of November 2 and its enclosures. Requests information "as to the periods when the settlements were first respectively formed on the Madawasca, and the Aroostic [sic], over which the British Government is now attempting to exercise jurisdiction, and also whether they were established under British or American authority, whether they were made by American citizens or British subjects, and when the British Government first began to exercise any jurisdiction within them." Reports that "it is probable that a convention has been concluded at London making provisions in regard to the reference of the dispute between the two countries to arbitration, agreeably to the stipulations of the treaty of Ghent" (cf. above, Gallatin to Clay, September 30, 1827, and note). Copy. DNA, RG59, Dom. Letters, vol. 22, pp. 80–81 (M40, R20).

To PELEG SPRAGUE. Discusses the "difficulties which have arisen out of a conflict of jurisdiction between the British and American authorities, within the disputed territory belonging to the State of Maine but claimed by Great Britain" (cf. above, Lincoln to Clay, September 3, 1827); transmits affidavits on the matter received from Governor (Enoch) Lincoln (cf. above, Lincoln to Clay, November 2, 1827); and asks for information (of the same tenor as also requested of Lincoln, above this date). Copy. DNA, RG59, Dom. Letters, vol. 22, pp. 79–80 (M40, R20).

From JOSEPH KENT, Annapolis. Acknowledges receipt of Clay's letter of September 29 and its enclosures. Transmits a copy of a letter from the clerk of the (State Executive) Council (Thomas Culbreth) to Jacob Small, mayor of Baltimore, "who has the appointment and immediate controul" of the Harbor Masters, which he predicts "will put a stop to similar demands in future." States: "Should it be found necessary the attention of the Legislature will be called to the subject at their annual meeting next month—" ALS. DNA, RG59, Misc. Letters (M179, R65).

In the enclosure, dated October 18, Culbreth explains to Small that the Governor "considers the claims of the Harbour Master [Alexander Macdonald] forbidden by the Convention with Great Britain," cited in Clay's letter to Kent, "and consequently illegal," since the Convention operates "as a repeal of all Laws inconsistent with its provisions." He continues: "His Excellency therefore, respectfully requests, that as the demands have been made by An Officer under your Jurisdiction and authority, that you will interfere . . . to prevent any such demand in future."

From CHARLES F. MAYER, Baltimore. Recommends Charles L. Siegfried, who resides near Königsberg, as American consul in that place. States that Siegfried, a retired merchant, "resided for some time" in the United States and became a citizen while living in Georgia.

Asks "what steps have been taken by our Government" in the case of the schooner

Antelope, Peter Care (Jr.), master (cf. above, Care to Clay, May 28, 1827). ALS. DNA, RG59, Misc. Letters (M179, R65).

Siegfried has not been further identified. No consular appointment was made to Königsberg at this time.

From James Strong

Dear Sir,   Hudson[1] Nov. 12th. 1827

Your letter of the 14th of Sept.[2] reached me many days ago by the way of Albany, where it received a passing notice from the Editor of the Argus,[3] as you may have perceived. I should have answered it sooner, but that the approaching election occupied most of my time and attention. By hard work, we have beaten the Jacksonites in this County, and elected three (our whole number) able and decided administration men to the Legislature.[4] Untill [*sic*] about 6 weeks ago, most of the leading Bucktails in this county were for the administration— Mr. Van Buren made them a visit—they vered [*sic*] about— raised the Jackson flag—and by abusing you and Mr. Adams, succeeded in deceiving many.

I suppose two thirds of our Legislature will be Jacksonites[5]— Still I do not give up the cause. Our people have not reflected for a moment upon the consequences of giving up the administration of the government again to their southern Brethren, who are opposed to the protection & defense of northern interests. Van Buren sought this result of the election—and hopes that it will influence my colleagues in Congress—arrest the changes going on in Pennsylvania and Virginia[6]— and, if the Legislature can be pushed up to repeal the Electoral Law,[7] enable him to controul the Electoral vote of the State. But, thank God, we are twelve months sail from land—and in a deep sea—and tho' the storm may rage awhile, prudent & fearless conduct will yet save the Ship.

This concerted action between Gov. Clinton & Mr. Van Buren[8] has produced its first effect— But I think in the end it will ruin them both— Both cannot live and triumph— The ultimate success of the one will be the final overthrow of the other.

Mr. Oakley, I take it, will be a Jacksonite[9]— What the majority of the delegation from this state will think or do no mortal can tell. Most of them were elected as being friendly to the administration— And a majority of them, I am told by good authority, have said, within the last three months that they were still friendly to it, and meant to support it. If Taylors election, as Speaker, can be defeated—Van Buren and Clinton will defeat it.[10]

I was in Albany in September— There the majority of the Legislature were with us[11]—but they were afraid to act. It was apparent to me that Van Buren must be combated [*sic*] with his own men—that is,

Bucktails. By request, I went to see senator Sanford[12]—had a long—but general, conversation with him—and soon found out, what I supposed I should, that he had neither the courage nor stability to oppose the man he distrusted and hated. They were in want of a paper & a leader. I urged them to establish the one—and agree upon the other. Had they done so, I believe Van Buren might have been kept at bay— It is more difficult now— Still I think if they would do so even now, the state might be saved.[13]

While I hope the President will not overlook the protection of our domestic industry—the "American System"—I likewise hope he will not broach any new subject, which will necessarily come up in array as an executive measure— My hints may be useless, as probably all these things will be thought of—and thought of aright. Still the opinions of friends do not always come amiss.

I shall leave here for New York in the course of a week—and intend to be in Washington 5, or 6 days before the session begins.

We have had a severe snow storm—but the snow has nearly all gone off. Give my best respects to Mrs. Clay—　　Your friend
The Honble H. Clay Washington　　　　　　　　　　JAMES STRONG

ALS. DLC-HC (DNA, M212, R3).　　　　1 New York.
2 Not found.　　　　3 Edwin Croswell; *Albany Argus*. The reference has not been found.
4 The winning margins of the pro-administration (Federal ticket) legislative candidates in Columbia County were, however, razor-thin. See *Albany Argus*, November 17, 1827.
5 Cf. above, Sergeant to Clay, October 24, 1827, note.　　　6 For Pennsylvania, cf. above, Sergeant to Clay, September 23, October 14, 16, 1827; Mifflin to Clay, October 21, 1827. For Virginia, cf. above, Mercer to Clay, August 18, 1827; Brooke to Clay, October 17, November 4, 1827.　　　7 Cf. above, Clay to Brooke, December 11, 1826, note.　　　8 Cf. above, Porter to Clay, March 4, 1826; April 6, 1827.　　　9 Cf. above, Webster to Clay, June 2, 1827, and note.　　　10 Cf. above, Clay to Taylor, September 7, 1827, note.
11 Cf. above, Rochester to Clay, September 17, 1827.　　　12 Nathan Sanford.
13 Cf. above, Clay to Brown, March 27, 1827, note.

From John Williams

Sir　　　　　　　　　　　　　　　　　　Nashville Nov: 12th 1827.
From an intimation in the Journal recd. a few days ago, it is supposed that the administration intend for the future to confer appointments on their friends to the exclusion of their enemies[1]— If I am correct in this permit me to name my friend Theoderic [sic] F. Bradford of Bedford County as a suitable person for the office of Marshall [sic] in the district of West Tennessee— The present incumbants [sic] term of service will expire during the next winter[2]— The duties of this office are now performed by a deputy named Smith[3] who I understand is Duff Greens agent in this part of Tennessee— Mr. Bradford is a highly respectable Senator in our State Legislature— And his appointment would be highly gratifeing [sic] to many of your friends in this State　Respectfuly [sic] your Obt. Servant　　　　JOHN WILLIAMS
Honb H. Clay.

ALS. DNA, RG59, A. and R. (M531, R1). This letter and those, below, to Clay from Thomas H. Fletcher, November 18, 1827, and from John P. Erwin, November 20, 1827, with several other statements at this time recommending Theodorick F. Bradford to the favorable consideration of the Adams administration, figured in the correspondence of James K. Polk to Andrew Jackson Donelson, April 28, 1835, and Andrew Jackson to Polk, May 12, 1835, as identification of Bradford's Whig affiliations. Cf. Bassett (ed.), *Correspondence of Andrew Jackson*, V, 345; Herbert Weaver (ed.) and Kermit L. Hall (assoc. ed.), *Correspondence of James K. Polk* (4 vols.—; Nashville: Vanderbilt University Press, 1969–), III, 170–71.

1 An editorial in the *Washington Daily National Journal* of October 19, 1827, had replied to criticism of the *New York National Advocate* that they had "to contend with the opposition of nearly all the office holders in this city, especially those attached to the Custom-house." Deploring "the whole doctrine and course of the Jackson party, which aims at the suppression of all independence of opinion," and pointing to a resolution of New York Jacksonians that an individual should not "be put in nomination for ANY OFFICE, who is not opposed to the present Administration," the *Journal* editors asked whether "those who have set the example" could complain "If the friends of the Administration were to meet this by a resolution that none shall HOLD OFFICE who are opposed to the Administration. . . ?" On October 30, the *Journal* editors noted that their comment had been under attack by the New York *Evening Post*. Defending their stand, they argued that the President had responsibilities which required that he not "be fettered and harassed in his administration by the disaffection of his subordinate[*sic*] in office. . . ." "It is not only his right, but his duty," they continued, "to take the most efficient individuals; and they are not the most efficient who, instead of attending to the public interests, are using the facilities of office to subserve the views of a faction which is seeking every opportunity to impede the measures of the Administration."

2 Robert Purdy, the incumbent marshal, was reappointed. Cf. above, Power of Attorney, June 6, 1825, note.   3 Joel M. Smith, a city alderman, 1827–1828 and 1837–1838. In 1831 he was appointed by the Jackson administration as surveyor and inspector of revenue for the port of Nashville, a post he held until 1840. He became a proprietor of the *Nashville Union*, established in 1835, but sold his interest in 1839. He, nevertheless, continued active in local political affairs and during the 1840's held appointment as Federal pension agent in Nashville.

DIPLOMATIC NOTES   November 12, 1827

To CHARLES R. VAUGHAN, Washington. Acknowledges receipt of Vaughan's note of November 1, with its enclosures. Disagrees with Vaughan's position that the vice consul (John Innerarity) was entitled to the papers and effects of the deceased consul (John H. Purves), "according to general usage." Asserts belief that there is "no difference between the death of a Consul and that of any other private foreigner in respect to his effects"; that when a foreigner dies without family or relations "to take charge of his Estate at the place of his death, a practice prevails to allow the Consul of the Country of the deceased to put his official seal upon the effects of the deceased, until the local law operates upon them by a grant of administration, or if no such administration be granted, for the purpose of transmission to the kindred of the deceased"; and that "the Sheriff [Charles Mifflin] took possession of the papers and effects of the deceased, probably for safe keeping only, and under the Laws of the territory." Notes that Innerarity had not received an exequatur at the time of Purves's death and that Innerarity's "claim to be exempted from a compliance with an ordinary condition [the bond set by the Judge of the County Court (Timothy Twitchell)] is not believed to be warranted by public law or usage." Concludes: ". . . the case . . . does not seem to be one on which the President can, with propriety, interfere with the regular administration of the law, so far as regards the private papers and effects of the deceased. In respect to his official papers, they ought not to be withheld from his successor or other person acting as British Consul at the port of Pensacola; and measures will be taken for their being delivered up free from charges, if desired by Mr. Vaughan." Copy. DNA, RG59, Notes to Foreign Legations, vol. 3 pp. 400–402 (M38, R3).

From Francisco Tacón, Philadelphia. Acknowledges receipt, on November 8, of Clay's note of October 29; comments on the difference of opinion of the two governments relative to the legality of (David) Porter's acts; and cites the note of Hilario de Rivas y Salmon to Clay, June 12, 1827, for an explanation of the Spanish view of the matter. LS, in Spanish with trans. in State Dept. file. DNA, RG59, Notes from Spanish Legation, vol. 9 (M59, R-T12).

INSTRUCTIONS AND DISPATCHES   November 12, 1827

From James Brown, Paris, "Private." Transmits "public journals" in which "two ordinances" are published: "the first dissolving the Chamber of Deputies, the second, creating seventy six peers." Predicts that the opposition will gain "a few votes in the next chamber" without attaining a majority, while "The newly created peers will secure to the ministers a majority in the aristocratic branch of the Legislature." Notes that "The press is now free" and "The editors . . . seem disposed to press" their freedom "to the verge of licentiousness." States, as his opinion, that no important changes will occur in the ministry, that "The influence of the court is increasing," and that "The administration will carry all its measures in both chambers by overwhelming majorities" (cf. above, Lafayette to Clay, October 10, 1827, note).

Observes that "Miguel is daily expected in this city, whence he will proceed by the way of London to Portugal to assume the regency" (cf. above, Lawrence to Clay, October 13, 1827), a step that "has received the approbation of all the great powers including England." Refers to Miguel's promise to support the (Portuguese) Constitution (cf. above, Brent to Clay, November 2, 1826) and to a report that, upon his arrival, British and French troops will be withdrawn from Portugal and Spain, except for Cádiz, which France "will continue to occupy until the debt due to her from Spain shall have been discharged."

Interprets the assistance to "Russia in her negociations with Turkey" as designed to prevent the former from "making war in the east and aggrandizing herself by conquests in that quarter." Discusses, in this connection, the recalcitrance of "the Porte" and events culminating in the naval battle at Navarino (cf. above, Hughes to Clay, September 16, 1827, note; Brown to Clay, October 12, 1827, note; Ombrosi to Clay, November 6, 1827, note). Characterizes the outcome of this battle as "agreeable to the people" but "embarrassing to the cabinets of Europe," whose object "has been to preserve peace and to sustain Turkey as a power to serve as a counterpoise to the weight of the Russian empire." Declares that "After what has taken place the Ottoman power must either resist or submit and descend to the last state of degradation." LS. DNA, RG59, Dip. Disp., France, vol. 23 (M34, R26). Received December 20.

From W[illiam] B[each] Lawrence, London, no. 7. Summarizes in 14 manuscript pages British commercial regulations as found in Orders in Council, published in "the London Gazette from July 1823 to the present day," and in "the Acts of Parliament to which they [the Orders] refer, and from which they derive their force." Explains in conclusion: "Having . . . examined the commercial system of this Country, in order to enable me to discharge the public duties which may be confided to me, I have thought that the results of my inquiries might perhaps form not altogether a useless Appendix to the British Digest [see above, Gallatin to Clay, September 28, 1827], heretofore transmitted from this Legation. . . ." ALS. DNA, RG59, Dip. Disp., Great Britain, vol. 35 (M30, R31). Received December 20.

Memorandum to John Quincy Adams

[*ca*. November 13, 1827]

Subjects for communication to one or both branches of Congress by the President, if he think proper.

England.—The slave Convention made in Nov. 1826.[1]

Payment of the two instalments according to its stipulation.[2]

Proclamation of the President issued in March last for enforcing the acts of Congress to interdict the entry of British vessels from Colonial ports.[3]

Colonial question.

Convention respecting the N. W. Boundary.[4]

do.   in relation to Commerce.[5]

do.   in respect to the N. Eastern boundary, if received.[6]

France—Renewal of the negotiation for indemnities at Paris, the issue of which is not known.[7]

Sweden—Convention to Regulate the Commerce & Navigation between the two Countries.[8]

Brazils—The return of the Chargé des Affaires to the U. S. in consequence of aggressions,[9] and the appointment of a Successor[10] on assurances of the Brazilian Chargé d'Affaires that he should be recd. and treated with the respect due to his character, and that indemnity should be promptly made for all injuries inflicted on Citizens of the U. S. or their property contrary to the public law.[11]

Denmark—Chargé d'Affaires has been sent to Denmark with instructions to renew the demand upon that Government for indemnity on account of injuries so long suffered by Citizens of the U. S.[12]

AD. MHi-Adams Papers, Letters Recd. (MR483). Adams noted, on November 13 (*Memoirs*, VII, 353): "Mr. Clay brought the minutes I had requested him to make of the subjects under direction of the Department of State which it may be proper to notice in the message. Two or three of them had escaped my attention."
[1] See above, Gallatin to Clay, November 13, 1826.   [2] See above, Vaughan to Clay, January 9, July 23, 1827; Clay to Gales and Seaton, August 1, 1827.   [3] See above, Clay to Vaughan, March 17, 1827.   [4] See above, Gallatin to Clay, August 7, 9, 1827.
[5] See above, Gallatin to Clay, August 6, 1827.   [6] See above, Gallatin to Clay, September 30, 1827.   [7] Cf. above, Clay to Brown, May 28, 30, October 28, 1827; Brown to Clay, September 8, 13, 1827.   [8] See above, Appleton to Clay, July 11, 1827, nos. 20, 21.   [9] See above, Raguet to Clay, March 12, 17, May 31, 1827.   [10] William Tudor. See above, Rogers and Van Winkle to Clay, June 14, 1827, note; Clay to Tudor, October 23, 1827.   [11] See above, Rebello to Clay, May 30, June 1, 1827; Clay to Rebello, May 31, June 2, 1827.   [12] Above, Clay to Wheaton, May 31, 1827.

From James Brown

My dear Sir   (Private)   Nov. 13. 1827

I have in my dispatch of this day[1] given all the news of the last two weeks and I believe you will find it sufficient to gratify your taste for the novel and the extraordinary and also to give full scope to your ingenuity in prognosticating its influence on the future. The event at Navarino was unexpected here and I believe even there until the commencement of the conflict. It was difficult to admit the beliefe [*sic*] that the Turks would stake their fleet on the issue of a battle where the odds were so fearful in strength of vessels and discipline of crews in favor of the assailants. It is doubtful whether the Greeks will be placed in a better situation by this victory. The question will hereafter, in case the Porte remains obstinate, become a very perplexing one for Europe. The first object will be to satisfy Russia without an entire overthrow of the Ottoman Empire— the next will be to secure the existence of peace— If war becomes unavoidable will Greece and the Ottoman Empire become the price of an adjustment and in what proportions will they be parceled out among the parties? I cannot persuade myself that war will grow out of this. I mean a war among the European powers. Fortunately for us we are at a distance from the scene and will long I trust be permitted to increase[2] our resources and see our Country advancing to wealth and grandeur. As it is now well understood that our settled policy is that of not interfering in the affairs of Europe or giving just cause of offense to any nation I hope we shall be favored with the blessings of peace.

I have not had a line from you since the 7th of August[3] at which time you mentioned that Mrs. Clays health had not been so good as formerly. When you write again be so good as to relieve our anxiety on this subject. Mrs. Browns complaint[4] is undergoing a favorable change and I have reason to hope will in the course of a few weeks be removed. It has given me inexpressible uneasiness— I am afraid that with the labors of your office and the feelings produced by the illiberal attacks of your enemies, your own health will be impaired. It has excited my surprize to hear that you had become exceedingly sensitive to these attacks[5]— I hope you will heed them with contempt— I rather think from what I hear that New York and Pennsylvania will vote in favor of General Jackson in which event the election will be very doubtful. At this distance however we know but very little of what is passing with you—except from the Newspapers Editors or from travellers both of whom give us rather an expression of their own wishes than of the public opinion. Mr. Gallatin[6] wrote me from Liverpool and is now probably arrived. He was by no means pleased with his residence in England, and must be happy in returning to America. I am afraid that the state of foreign relations is not such as will give the President any advantages at the ensuing election.[7] Our South American neighbours are not likely to do us much credit. Mr. Poinset [*sic*][8] writes me that he is disgusted with the state of affairs in Mexico. The movements of Bolivars [*sic*] are by no means satisfactory. These Republicks are now filled with Agents who are not not [*sic*] friendly to the forms of Government which they have adopted. This nation will in all probability obtain a considerable influence now that they have agents in these Republicks.[9] General Lafayette and his son are both Candidates for the Chamber of Deputies. The former is very confident that he will be elected.[10] It is supposed that the opposition will compose about a fourth of the next Chamber. This opposition will be made up of about two thirds of ultra Royalists and one third liberals. If the General studied his own happiness he would retire from the unavailing contest.

I hope you have received the articles sent by Mr Rumpff and also the Lustres which went out in another Vessel.[11] If you want any thing which can be had at Paris we shall feel to [sic] happy in purchasing it for you.

You have no doubt received a Letter from General Lafayette containing a statement of his conversation with you shortly before the election.[12] He read me a copy of it and I hope you will find it satisfactory. Enough has already been proved to establish your innocence if the people would appeal to their reason instead of their passions. As it is you can make little impression on a large portion of them.

I have heard that an arrangement has been made between the Governments of France and the United States directing that the mail for Havre shall be sealed at New York and opened by the post Master at Havre.[13] If you send your dispatches in that way I should feel some apprehensions that they might run some risque— At all events the postage here will be enormous as so many letters are put up with the papers I receive. The postage on packages is very high— I have hitherto had no reason to complain of the manner in which I have received my dispatches and News papers. Will you be so obliging as to state to me what is the present arrangement?

I informed you sometime ago that a Mr Delaunay who says that he had been naturalized in Missouri as an American Citizen had brought out six Savages of the Osage tribe to be exhibited for money in Paris.[14] As Mr Delaunay has presented no American passport at this Legation, and as I disapproved the speculation I received him very cooly telling him at once that I was sorry that he had engaged in it. You may have seen in the papers that these Indians were received by the King and had breakfasted and dined with the Minister of foreign Affairs.[15] This account I have been told is correct. But you have seen also what is absolutely false that they had dined with me in company with the Diplomatic Corps   It is true that the Ambassadors and Ministers dined with me on the day mentioned in the newspapers but the Osages were neither invited nor present. They came with Mr Delaunay once in the morning and I gave them a breakfast without inviting any company to meet them. Mr Delaunay is now confined in Se Pelagie for an old debt and I apprehend these miserable savages will be exposed to want as they cannot speak a word of any language except their own.[16] In case of their being left in this situation what ought I to do? It will cost

nearly one thousand dollars to reconvey them to America and I have no authority to advance it for them— Our Agents ought to use their influence to prevent these situations. I am Dear Sir very truly Your friend & obedt. Servant   JAMES BROWN
Hon. H. Clay.

ALS. DLC-HC (DNA, M212, R3).   1 That is, November 12.
2 Word not clearly legible.   3 The letter to which he refers is that, above, of August 10, 1827.   4 Cf. above, Brown to Clay, October 13, 1827.   5 Cf. above, Brown to Clay, September 6, 1827; Clay to Brown, October 28, 1827.   6 Albert Gallatin.
7 Cf. above, Brown to Clay, October 12, 1827 (1).   8 Joel R. Poinsett.   9 Cf. above, Brown to Clay, January 11, 1826, note.   10 On the General's election, cf. above, Brown to Clay, April 12, 1827, note. George Washington Lafayette was also elected in 1827, as Deputy for the town of Coulommiers, which he represented for the next 20 years.
11 Vincent Rumpff. Cf. above, Rumpff to Clay, September 20, 1827; Astor to Clay, September 21, 1827; Clay to Brown, October 28, 1827.   12 Cf. above, Lafayette to Clay, October 10, 1827.   13 Cf. below, McLean to Clay, December 3, 1827.   14 See above, Brown to Clay, August 30, 1827.   15 Charles X; Baron de Damas.
16 Sainte Pélagie, built in 1665 as a shelter for young girls, had been converted to a prison in 1792 and from 1797 to 1834 served primarily to confine debtors. Delaunay had been sued for a debt of 9,385 francs, claimed due on commercial operations in France dating from 1799. The Indians, thus cut off from their sponsor, wandered over Europe, the objects of charity. One group, of which two died of smallpox en route, returned to Washington via Norfolk in the winter of 1829–1830; the other members of the party reached New York in April, 1830, and rejoined those in Washington. In May the survivors were returned to their tribe. For accounts of this venture, see "Mohongo's Story," in *Missouri Historical Review*, XXXVI (January, 1942), 210–14; and John Joseph Mathews, *The Osages, Children of the Middle Waters* (Norman [Oklahoma], [c. 1961]), 539–47.

DIPLOMATIC NOTES   November 13, 1827

From CHARLES R. VAUGHAN, Washington. Replies to Clay's note of November 12. Concedes that (John) Innerarity "was not entitled, certainly, to officiate as Vice Consul, an Exequatur not having been granted to him," but expresses his view that Innerarity should have been allowed "to keep in his custody the papers and effects of the deceased Consul [John H. Purves], on account of his long continued intercourse with him—of having formerly officiated as Vice Consul, & as he had been authorized by the Consul General [Anthony St. John Baker] to take charge of the Consulate, as soon as the death of Mr. Purves was known at Washington." States belief that "Mr Innerarity was ostensibly the proper person, to take care of the effects of the deceased, until the Heirs should claim the administration, & that he could not enter into bonds, or become answerable for expenses as he could not be considered an administrator." Disclaims "any intention of supposing, that forms were to be observed upon the death of a Consul, which do not equally apply upon the death of a British Subject, in a Foreign State, according to the usages which prevail in Foreign Countries." Argues, however, that "the local law should not operate until administration is required by the Heirs to the Property, or others interested in the succession, and until that event, the effects of the deceased ought to remain under the seal of the Consul." Requests that Clay fulfill his offer to direct that the official papers of Purves "be placed in the hands of Mr Innerarity" (cf. below, Clay to Wright, November 14, 1827). LS. DNA, RG59, Notes from British Legation, vol. 14 (M50, R15).

INSTRUCTIONS AND DISPATCHES   November 13, 1827

From W[ILLIAM] H. D. C. WRIGHT, Rio de Janeiro. Reports having denied certification of the ship papers of the *Canton*, of New Orleans. Explains that he found the papers irregular and encloses them (not found) for review. Notes that, when denied the certification, the ship's supercargo (a Chilean, not further identified) disclosed that he was owner of both the vessel and the cargo and thereupon sold the ship at Rio. Observes that he has learned from a newspaper source that the *Canton* was condemned by the United States Court at New Orleans in June last (record not found). ALS. DNA, RG59, Cons. Disp., Rio de Janeiro (M-T172, R4). Received January 19, 1828.

From Francis P. Blair

Dear Sir: Frankfort Novr 14. 1827

I have copied for Mr. Crittenden the letter in which you desired me to write to Mr White in regard to his vote in the presidential election[1]— I should have complied with your request[2] much more promptly, had I not been prevented by the circumstance of seeing your letter while on a hunting tour, from which I did not return until yesterday.

In explaining to you the grounds on which I had ventured to make the declaration with regard to your being appointed Secretary[3] which has been laid hold of by Mr. Kendall,[4] I did not mean to say that I understood there was "an arrangement" entered into on that subject, far less did I intend to intimate to you that your letter contained any such information— From it however I felt assured that Mr Adams had relinquished his hostility to you & that his friends had given indications that he & they were willing to promote your interests by advancing you to any Station, that might be thought best calculated to effect that object— I might not have felt myself authorized from the style of badinage in which your letter was couched to conclude that Mr Adams had given any decisive manifestation of the change in his disposition towards you, had I not previously known that one of the Kentucky delegation, most devoted to you[5] intimated the same thing in his letters, & evinced a zeal for the election of Mr Adams, which I knew could only proceed from a disposition to serve you. But you see that I was not singular in having acted on this belief—Mr Crittenden has avowed in his recent publication[6] that his preferences were for General Jackson—his prejudices against Mr Adams, and that he relinquished both to *associate you in the* executive department. How far such a declaration is proper at this juncture, does not become me to decide— I advised Mr Crittenden (being spoken to by him) from offering any explanation of the apparently contradictory recommendations contained in his letters to Call[7] & White— the advice I gave I am sensible would seem to come from a sinister quarter & probably he did right to reject it. But if there is no impropriety in your friends *now* making public such a motive for their conduct, I trust I shall be excused for the similar declarations which I made at a time I thought them essential to your service—

It gives me pain to perceive that any part of my conduct while I acted as your friend can be made to operate to your disadvantage— I am as ready now as I could have been then to prevent such a result. My opinion at first was that any attempt to pry into private intercourse & confidential correspondence ought to be met with nothing but resistance— Answering to one set of interrogations is but to invite a fresh swarm, like Esop's flies & in the end it would be found that no fox could escape from the ingenuity of such multiplied pursuers without making a surrender of his last drop— My opinion, sincerely given, was to repel by silence every attempt to approach that information to which the public is not entitled. Mr Crittenden by responding to Mr Kendall's call, declaring that he had no letters from you in Jany 1825 will notwithstanding his protestation, be considered as making a virtual admission of the necessity of answering such questions, & as I am the other person pointed at, will render the propriety of my reserve more questionable, & it will make my silence the more remarkable; But I am still of the opinion that I should say nothing of your letters to me for although they contain much to indicate the motive of your vote in the presidential election, yet as I said in my former letter I do not think your correspondence should be submitted to the mal-construction of those who might wish to use it against you—

You say it gives you pain to part with me in politics—   What must my regret be, to lose both you & Crittenden in whom my pride, my partiality & every political wish centered— My affectionate regards will always attend you both— but Alas! Alas! you have made sad work for the poor Republicans. Here we have been vanquished by division & the main body of us subjected, without a limitation on their power to the same masters who had driven us into a sort of rebellion— we cried out for quarter, but it would not be allowed— unsparing proscription was the order of the day. Upon the great scene where your voice once rallied the power of the democratic party to defeat the domestic enemy arrayed against you by foreign influence during the second war you made for Independence, we now find you have made Webster & Sergeant[8] "the lords of the ascendant—" That you have left your mantle to those men, is withering to the hopes of many who once followed you as the great Champion of their Cause— For myself however I must say that I do not question that you are actuated by the purest patriotism—   if you discard the means once employed by you to effect the public good, I readily believe that those you have at present adopted are thought to be the best— I am Dr Sir yr mst ob. st

The Honble H. Clay Secretary of State   F. P. BLAIR

ALS. DLC-HC (DNA, M212, R3).
1 John J. Crittenden; David White—see above, Clay to Blair, January 8, 1825.
2 Probably contained in the letter of which only the extract, above, Clay to Blair, October 19, 1827, has been found.   3 See above, Blair to Clay, October 3, 1827.

4 See above, Kendall to Clay, September 26, October 10, 1827.   5 Probably Robert
P. Letcher.   6 Cf. above, Crittenden to Clay, October 30, 1827, and note.
7 Richard K. Call.   8 Daniel Webster; John Sergeant.

Receipt from Susan Decatur

George Town, Nov. 14th 1827

Receiv'd from The Honble. Henry Clay two hundred dollars for one quarters House rent ending on the 15th of October 1827 [1]

SUSAN DECATUR

ADS. DLC-TJC (DNA, M212, R16).
[1] Cf. above, Clay to Henry Clay, Jr., April 2, 1827.

DIPLOMATIC NOTES   November 14, 1827

To CHARLES R. VAUGHAN, Washington. States that, "in conformity with the request contained" in Vaughan's note of November 13, "a direction has been this day transmitted to Mr. [Benjamin D.] Wright, United States Attorney in West Florida, to cause the official papers of the late Mr. [John H.] Purves . . . to be delivered over to Mr. [John] Innerarity free from all charges" (cf. below, Clay to Wright, this date). Copy. DNA, RG59, Notes to Foreign Legations, vol. 3, pp. 402–403 (M38, R3). L draft, in CSmH.

From JOSÉ SILVESTRE REBELLO, Washington. Charges that, from the outbreak of the current war between Brazil and Buenos Aires "the people of the United States began to manifest a scandalous wish that it might terminate in a manner unfavorable to" Brazil and "glorious" for Buenos Aires, "without any cause to justify such an unfair wish other than the deplorable political intolerance fomented by many of the Citizens of these States—" Comments that, since the trade between Brazil and the United States has increased during the conflict, "it is evident that this solicitude for the success of the enemies of His Majesty the Emperor [Peter I] does not proceed from any injury to their interests and can, therefore, only be attributed to the Republican intolerance." Cites the interpretation of the war by newspaper editors, "not one of them having shown that impartiality professed by the Government of the United States," and complains that "some citizens and inhabitants of these States have fitted out privateers, and, with letters of marque purchased in the United States themselves, have cruized against, and plundered Brazilian vessels and property. . . ." States that "These manifestations of gratu-gratuituous [sic] hostility . . . have, in addition to the individual character which they previously possessed, become in some measure national, by the act of an American Naval Commander, who, with an air of menace, demanded the surrender of property belonging to citizens of Buenos Ayres, which had been lawfully captured by the cruizers of H. M. the Emperor of Brazil, on the mere allegation of its being covered by the American flag, which act became for the american newspapers, a great subject of boast; and by that of another commander [James Biddle] who carried his interference in the transactions between the belligerents so far as taking away, as it were forcibly, from on board a vessel, which, having been captured, had, in some manner, acquired the character of a national vessel, several seamen calling themselves Americans; this act of violence being committed within one of the ports of the Empire of Brazil" (cf. above, Rebello to Clay, February 21, 1827). Presents, as additional evidence of "the unfriendly feelings nourished by the People of the United States," the case of an American citizen (H. T. Whittredge), "who, in a privateer [*Lavallega*] fitted out and commanded by himself, and provided with a letter of marque purchased in the United States, plundered" Brazilian subjects "to the amount of fifty thousand dollars, or more," even though the Brazilians had placed both the property and their persons "under the safe guard of the American flag. . . ." Alludes to the principle, agreed to by the United States in a treaty with another nation, "to restore such individual property as might, at the time of the ratification, happen to be in possession of the adverse parties" (Article I of the Treaty of Ghent, above, I, 1006) and argues that such a "mode of proceeding . . . leads to the clear inference that they [the United States] had recognized, as a principle of public law, the illegality of the capture of individual property—" Asks whether Brazil may not, under the principle, "claim the restitution of the private property of Brazilian Subjects so scandalously plundered from on board of American vessels, and under the American flag?"

Concludes by requesting that the Government of the United States "cause the property which was plundered from on board the Brig Ontario, to be restored to its owners" and "take proper measures to redress all injuries committed by Citizens and inhabitants of the United States, upon the Citizens of Brazil, as soon as the Government of H. M. the Emperor" shall transmit "the documents necessary to prove these acts of violence. . . ." Translation. DNA, RG59, Notes from Brazilian Legation, vol. 1 (M49, R1). Published in Manning (arr.), *Diplomatic Correspondence . . . Latin-American Nations,* II, 862–64. Endorsed by Clay on wrapper (AEI): "Translation of a note transmitted by Mr. Rebello, the Brazilian Chargé des affaires, which was returned to him the 16h. Nov. 1827 as being altogether inadmissible and offensive in its language. He was informed that it would not be received & he took it back—   H.C."

The unidentified American Naval Commander may have been Jesse D. Elliott; incident, not found.

INSTRUCTIONS AND DISPATCHES   November 14, 1827

From VINCENT GRAY, Havana. Transmits a copy of "a very Important Decree deeply effecting [sic]" American shipowners in the Spanish trade, an order not yet officially received. Reports that Commodore (Angel) Laborde will soon mount an expedition to Colombia and that a crew of 500 men for the recently repaired "ship of the line Gerara [sic]" will arrive soon from Cádiz. Suggests that Commodore (David) Porter, not heard of lately, may be in pursuit of a specie-laden frigate (*Perla*) that recently sailed for Spain. Calls for an amendment in the Distressed Seamen's Act to guard against shipmasters' discharging American seamen privately and then representing to the consul that the men in question have deserted (cf. above, Williamson to Clay, April 3, 1827, and notes). Argues that masters should be required to submit cargo manifests to the (commercial) agent, who should "be prohibited by Law, to grant a Certificate for Drawbacks" for articles not listed on the manifests, "as the frauds now committed upon the Revenue of the U States is [sic] truly great, and calls [sic] for a remedy"; cites an example in which he saved the government $3000 on one cargo by denying his signature to the shipmaster; and expresses belief that his letter concerning this case to the Secretary of the Treasury (Richard Rush) was not received, since that official failed to recommend to Congress changes in the "Drawback Law." Notes that Spanish authorities are enforcing their revenue laws more closely.

Mentions two cases on which he has recently taken action—one, return of a seaman to Rhode Island for trial on a charge of mutiny; the other, recovery of a Negro stolen at Charleston. Expresses fear that these incidents may be falsely reported and refers the Department to authorities who have been supplied with the pertinent documents. ALS. DNA, RG59, Cons. Disp., Havana, vol. 5 (M-T20, R5). Received December 22.

The enclosed decree, dated August 30, 1827, noted that a request had been received that vessels built in Catalonia but flying Tuscan and Sardinian flags be treated as Spanish when trading with Spain or her colonies, denied the petition, and directed that no more concessions be made in colonial commerce.

The *"Gerara"* (or *Guerrero*), as a Spanish "ship of the line" has not been identified. A Spanish brig involved in the African slave trade and a Mexican warship, also a brig, bore that name contemporaneously.

From W[ILLIAM] B[EACH] LAWRENCE, London, no. 8. Encloses "a Gazette Extraordinary," containing "the only official account of the battle of Navarino [cf. above, Ombrosi to Clay, November 6, 1827], which has yet been received by the British Government. . . ." Notes that "the weekly files of newspapers transmitted from the Legation will" give additional information. Reports that in England "All parties seem . . . apprehensive of the effect which the defeat of the Turks may have in advancing the power of Russia"; that Prince [Paul Anthony] Esterhazy has told him that Austria and Prussia were "acting in concert" in support of "the proferred [*sic*] mediation" by the allies (cf. above, Brown to Clay, July 12, 1827); that "Indeed the commencement, at this time, of open hostilities was wholly unexpected by everyone"; and that the British Government "is not yet without hope that arrangements will be effected without further hostile proceedings." States that (John) Backhouse told him "this morning that the last despatches from Lord [John Brabazon] Ponsonby" indicate the possibility of a truce between Buenos Aires and Brazil and that "he supposed . . . that the negotations which would be entered into would result in the independence of the Banda Oriental" (cf. above, Lawrence to Clay, October 22, 1827). Adds: "Don Miguel is expected here in a few days" (cf. above, Lawrence to Clay, October 13, 1827). ALS. DNA, RG59, Dip. Disp., Great Britain, vol. 35 (M30, R31). Received December 20.

MISCELLANEOUS LETTERS   November 14, 1827

To BENJAMIN D. WRIGHT, "Atty. of the U. S. for the Dist. of W. Florida." Transmits correspondence concerning the papers and effects of the late [John H.] Purves (see above, Vaughan to Clay, November 1, 13, 1827; Clay to Vaughan, November 12, 14, 1827) and requests, by the President's direction, that Wright "communicate this opinion to the officer having the direction or possession of those papers, and desire that he will deliver them to Mr. [John] Innerarity, without charge." Requests to be informed "of the result of this direction without delay" and whether his supposition "that the custody which the Sheriff [Charles Mifflin] acquired of the papers and effects of Mr. Purves was in conformity with the law, or some prevailing usage of the Territory; and, if not, by what authority he obtained them." Copy. DNA, RG59, Dom. Letters, vol. 22, p. 82 (M40, R20). Cf. below, Wright to Clay, December 7, 1827.

From John J. Crittenden

Dr. Sir   Frankfort Novr: 15th 1827

I have on this evening received from Mr Blair a letter for you which I shall place in the post-office with this, & also the inclosed copy of a former letter from you to him[1]— I have examined this copy with critical interest & attention; The temper of the times, & the malevolence of party spirit, could alone interpret it to your disadvantage—

The general sentiments it expresses, are such as you have avowed, & such as can not be considered otherwise than pure & honorable— The lightness & freedom in which you have indulged in some parts of the letter, is precisely that which belongs to private & friendly correspondence, & which at the same time renders us averse to their publication. I think the evidence which your enemies have extorted in the hopes of establishing your misconduct, have given the mortal blow to all their accusations & calumnies— By the very evidence which they have appealed to, your innocence is established— They grow weary of the subject, & find that the stone which they have so ignominiously laboured to roll up the hill, is likely to return upon their own heads— As far as proof can go—proof called out by your accusers—given by your opponents—you stand triumphant— All that is wanting is a little silence & a little time, that this evidence may be heard & considered by the people. Some of your most judicious friends here, think that you should make no further publication upon the subject— That your personal participation in the contest is neither necessary nor politic— That enough has appeared for your vindication, & that the justice & sympathy of the public will operate more speedily & more powerfully in your behalf, if left to itself, than if attempted to be enforced by any appeal you could make. I am of this opinion— Give it just so much weight as it deserves.

The friends of the administration in this State are acting; with spirit, & more confidence, I think than at any former period— The disappointments they have suffered in the last elections,[2] are attributed to their want of energy & concert, & have determined them to more systematic & resolute exertions. County meetings are every where taking place with great spirit, & the convention to be held here on the 17th of Decr:[3] will be one of the ablest & most respectable ever held in any State. These proceedings are every where inspiring strength & confidence. We shall have at our next elections a full expression of the Will of the people, & I hope for the best results.

Nothing has lately occurred more encouraging to the friends of the administration than the recent meeting of its supporters in Richmond, Va:[4]— It gives me strong hopes that the State will go for the administration.[5] If some popular man should start up there for the Vice-Presidency, I should think it very probable that it would be decisive of the course of that State.

Clinton, I take it, is against the administration— And his union with Van Buren, excites doubts & fears about the vote of New-York. What is to be the result of it?[6]

You inquire[7] about your letter to me which our friend Penn, of Louisville, lately got hold of[8]— It contained nothing very harmful of course, or our said friend would have admonished us of it, by publishing it in his News-paper.[9] It was dated in Feby: last, & contained only the speculation or statement, then current at Washington, of the probable vote of the several States at the ensuing Presidential election.

I have ascertained how Mr Penn got it. The children of a creature that lives near me, & who were some times playing about my house, some how or other got hold of it & bore it off—their father discovered it in their hands, & as silly as mean sends it to Mr Penn— Upon its receipt by him, there was at once a formadable [sic] buss [sic] through all Louisville, & great discoveries were expected— I was instantly informed of it by letters from several friends— And immediately wrote to Mr Penn, a letter which I intended for publication, but which was not published owing to some little want of management on the part of my friends— I stated to Mr Penn that the letter which had been sent to him, if genuine, contained nothing which I or you cared that the World should see—that defiled & dishonored as it was by the vile hands through which it had passed, I hardly wished to receive it back &c &c and to prevent injurious surmises I desired that he would immediately publish it &c. Mr Penn however being able to make nothing out of your letter, returned it to me by the same mail that carried mine to him. The creature who sent it to him, is too insignificant & mean, even for contempt. He has begged my forgiveness for it.

You will have seen by the time this reaches you the publication I have made— I had at first determed [sic] to publish my letter to White &c but finally concluded to take the course I have done.[10]

I have not seen Blair since he recd your last letter[11]— But in a conversation I had with him a short time previous, he stated to me that in the Fall 1824 you had told him that you should vote for Mr Adams, & expressed his willingness to give you a statement to that effect. Perhaps you had better obtain it. I wish you to return me the letter in which I gave you a statement on that subject,[12] in order that I may make a slight correction, or rather addition to it, which it is necessary & proper I should make— It shall be sent back to you without delay—

I hope you have before this, heard from White.[13] I have not seen him since I last wrote to you. In the worst event, you have nothing to fear from him.

Calhoun (an administration man) is elected in place of Doctr Young deceased.[14]

This is too long a letter, I know, to be written to a minister of State, but it can not now be amended. I am yr. Friend   J J CRITTENDEN
Hon: H Clay Secty: &c

ALS. NcD
[1] See above, Blair to Clay, November 14, 1827; Clay to Blair, January 8, 1825.   [2] Cf. above, Clay to Taylor, April 4, 1827, and note.   [3] Cf. above, Smith to Clay, October 7, 1827, note.   [4] Cf. above, Brooke to Clay, October 17, 1827, note; Clay to Brown, October 28, 1827.   [5] Cf. above, Caldwell to Clay, August 8, 1827, note.   [6] Cf. above, Clay to Brown, March 27, 1827, note.   [7] The inquiry has not been found.   [8] Shadrach Penn—cf. above, Smith to Clay, October 7, 1827.   [9] Louisville *Public Advertiser*.   [10] David White, Jr.—cf. above, Crittenden to Clay, October 30, 1827,

and note.   11 Above, Clay to Blair, October 19, 1827.   12 Above, September 3, 1827.   13 Cf. above, Crittenden to Clay, October 30, 1827, and note.   14 John Calhoon; William S. Young. Cf. above, Johnson to Clay, April 29, 1827, note.

From Mary Austin Holley

Dear Sir,   Baltimore Nov 15th. 1827

It would be unnecessary again to call your attention to my concerns, even to thank you for your letter[1] and the interest it expressed were it not that you misunderstood me and also need correcting. You took my joke[2] seriously and no wonder. You had a right to expect from me nothing that was not serious. I can not however but smile at the idea of being placed in the ranks of the idle, noisy, declaimers against the administration, whose unholy alliance I would not join even in jest.

Heaven knows that I am "all unused to the mirthful mood,"[2] but it so happened that I wrote to you under an elasticity of feeling which I imagined had passed from me forever. I had just arrived among friends who were glad to see me, and from whom I had been long separated, and on my way hither I had a letter informing me that my dear daughter,[4] whom I was hastening to attend, had been made happy by the birth of a second infant;[5] and as I advanced, another which said that my son,[6] the parting from whom had nearly dispossessed me, was not only reconciled, but quite contented and happy in his new situation. Hope seemed to be dawning upon me, and my prospects brightening, as much as, under existing circumstances, I had a right to expect. I was grateful. With these lively impressions my letter was written, and I was myself surprised, when I had done to find that I could trifle, but, pleased that any thing could for an instant divert me from myself, let it pass as if it would also amuse you.

My son is in the best situation I could find for him the school of Mr Wells (of the house of Wells & Lilly)[7] in Cambridge recently established. Some of my little Louisianians are also there. There he will remain till he is old enough, and he is altogether qualified, for the Academy at West Point, which I selected as safe in a moral view, and from economy. Does your son[8] suffer there in his health from a too rigid discipline? Having arranged every thing to my satisfaction so far, and pleased with the consciousness of having done my duty with respect to him, I thought, for greater security, and not knowing exactly what steps were necessary, I thought I had better make an early application, and from here as a more convenient point of communication.

If the regrets of the publick, and the dearer sympathy of friends, had entire power over grief I long since had ceased to mourn. That which I experienced in Boston as well as elsewhere was deep and affecting. I have been placed in situations peculiar and trying, calling forth all the energies of my soul. Entirely prostrate, one cannot but struggle gradually to rise. I had no time to brood over my sorrows. I had no rest, all was action, as if impelled by some unseen, irresistible agency. There is that in the human mind, when worthy of its high origin, which enables it to go on under all circumstances, adverse as well as prosperous. If I have no religion, as some contend, and with such my name is a reproach, I am not without the influence and support of that philosophy which he, whose memory I shall ever delight to honour, was proud to teach, and of which I should choose to give a practical illustration.

It would gratify me, my dear Sir, to hear from you, but unless you have an idle moment, which is hardly supposable, do not trouble yourself further with this correspondence. For yourself and Mrs Clay I shall ever cherish an affectionate and grateful regard. In my various wanderings and sojournings, and they have not been few nor far [betwee]n, I am frequently questioned respecting [you a]nd have opportunities of correcting mistakes. It is my happiness that I know you both so well, and however situated, in this changing scene, I shall ever pay you the tribute of a Sincere and entire respect.   M. A. HOLLEY

ALS. DLC-HC (DNA, M212, R3). Addressed to Clay.   [1] Above, November 10, 1827.
[2] Contained in her letter to Clay, above, November 8, 1827.   [3] "Albeit unused to the melting moode"—Shakespeare (Furness [ed.], *A New Variorum Edition*), *Othello* (11th edn.), Act V, sc. 2, line 423.   [4] Harriette Williman Holley Brand.   [5] Elizabeth Hay Brand, who in 1846 married Elisha Nichols Warfield, a son of Benjamin Warfield.
[6] Horace Austin Holley.   [7] William Wells, born in England and graduated in 1796 from Harvard College, had been a bookseller in Boston since the early 1800's. In 1815 he had entered into partnership with Robert Lilly, who continued the business after Wells retired in 1827 to Cambridge, where he established a school.   [8] Henry Clay, Jr.

INSTRUCTIONS AND DISPATCHES   November 15, 1827

From HENRY PERRINE, Campeche. Announces his arrival at "San Juan de Bautista," capital of Tabasco, on June 18; explains that the delay in reaching his post until November 7 was occasioned by a period of service as an arbitrator between United States and Mexican disputants, by personal illness, and by activities as a physician to various "distinguished individuals of the General & State Government who needed . . . aid." ALS. DNA, RG59, Cons. Disp., Campeche, Mexico, vol. 1 (M286, R1).

From BEAUFORT T. WATTS, Bogotá, no. 38. Recalls that when he received his commission as Chargé, he informed (José Manuel) Restrepo, the acting Minister of Foreign Affairs, "that it was 'not the intention of the President to make any permanent change in the rank of our diplomatic representative, but that he intended at some future and not distant day to nominate an Envoy Extraordinary and Minister Plenipotentiary.' " Reports that he has now learned that (Simón) Bolívar, for reasons of economy, feels "compelled at *present*, to recall the greater number of their [Colombia's] diplomatic agents, and that he could not continue at Washington a representative of higher rank than a Chargé d'Affaires." States: "The Minister in England will be continued, doubtless, for positive reasons; besides the probable influence that a Minister resident in London might have upon the other powers of Europe in recognizing their Sovereignty—The thirty three millions of debt due English merchants would be alone sufficient." Notes that "The object of the [Colombian] mission to Brazil which related principally to the subject of the boundary between the two Countries has failed" because Brazilian Emperor (Peter I) was not "prepared for the negociation." ALS. DNA, RG59, Dip. Disp., Colombia, vol. 4 (M-T33, R4). Received February 11, 1828.

From BEAUFORT T. WATTS, Bogotá, no. 39. Acknowledges receipt of (Daniel) Brent's "communication" regarding Watts' letter to (Simón) Bolívar (cf. above, Watts to Clay, June 14, 1827, and note). Refers to his dispatch no. 30 (above, June 14, 1827) and expresses hope that "in that explanation the reasons given were satisfactory to the President.—" Denies any breach of "international usage" and states: "I had no idea that the letter could possibly have resulted in a dangerous imprudence, particularly as I intended it as a private appeal to the President at a moment of political peril." Reports that Colombia has for.two years "been on the verge of dissolution" and that it looked to Bolívar and "to him only, as its deliverer." Offers evidence that the Colombians are pleased with his conduct and that Bolívar's return aided the nation. Concludes: ". . . it will be seen that all I desired or could have expected has been happily realised [sic] by the President's having taken charge of the government, and that the Vice President [Francisco de Paula Santander] as I informed you in my No. 35. [above, October 7, 1827] was perfectly satisfied with my conduct. I can but hope therefore, that this explanation will be still more satisfactory than the one already given.—" ALS. DNA, RG59, Dip. Disp., Colombia, vol. 4 (M-T33, R4). Received February 11, 1828.

MISCELLANEOUS LETTERS   November 15, 1827

From LEWIS WILLIAMS, Panther Creek, North Carolina. Introduces James R. Dodge, who "is taken to Washington on business and will thankfully receive any civilities. . . ." States: "Col [David] Crockett of Tennessee is now with me,—We expect to be in Washington before the meeting of Congress—" ALS. DNA, RG59, Misc. Letters (M179, R65).

Dodge, formerly engaged in business at Stokes, North Carolina, and later located at Raleigh, has not been further identified.

To Charles Hammond

My dear Sir   Washn. 16h. Novr. 1827

I have duly recd. both your favors of the 29h. Oct and the 5h. current, with their respective accompanyments [sic]. I am glad to see that our friends in Ohio have resolved upon organization and systematic exertion, in future. The other side is completely disciplined. And where there is system on the one side, and no concert with the opposing party, defeat is inevitable, at least when the community is nearly equally divided.

The libel against you and Wright[1] about the Bank suit is most false and base. But are you sure that you can maintain the suit upon what Dawson has published?

I think a mass of evidence which I shall cause to be published during the winter,[2] and a great part of which is already collected, will supersede the necessity of another appeal to Congress.[3] But on that point I shall be exclusively governed by the opinion and advice of my friends.

Govr. Clinton has come out in N. York[4] as well as to his respectable correspondent (Caleb Atwater) explicitly in favor of Genl. Jackson. The elections have just terminated in that State, and as far as they have been heard from the news is not good.[5] They develope [sic] the fruits of the secret coalition, long since suspected and announced, between Mr. Clinton and Mr V. Buren, and the arrangements consequent upon it. In that State, you know, they have but two electioneering systems in practical operation—the one Bucktail & the other Clintonian. It was so contribed [sic] that each of those two parties brought out Jackson Candidates even where they were in opposition for the same office. The settled habit of voting for the persons nominated by their Conventions lead [sic] the people to vote for the one ticket or the other accordingly as they belonged to the House of York or Lancaster, and which ever prevailed Jackson Candidates were elected.[6] Mean time the Administration party was without system, without organization. The result is, I have no doubt, the election of a Legislature decidedly Jacksonian. Our friends in N. York have at last begun to do, what they should have done six months or a year ago, that is to adopt a plan of co-operation. Whether it is too late or not time must disclose.

The Tennessee proceedings about impeaching the President will do good. By the bye, I am told that Mr. Weems of Maryland has pledged himself to move an empeachment [sic] against me, if no one else does.[7]

The Ebony toast and Speech were not felicitous; but it is a small affair—only a flash.

I agree with you that the success of the Opposition is pregnant with the fate of the Republic. I shall tremble, in that event, for its durability. These are the darkest pages of our history. Every man should awaken to the impending danger. None should under rate it; for it is perilous and alarming.

I have read with great pleasure the prospectus forwarded. If the work is executed with the ability which that displays and promises it will effect a great deal. Is there no fair way to disseminate it in Kentucky and especially in the adjoining Congressional district to Cincinnati? I think a great deal may yet be done in that State and district.

Virginia, depend upon it, is not idle. A spirit is getting up there worthy of the best days of Rome. There is much reason to hope and believe that it will conduct [sic] to final success. I am truly Your friend
C. Hammond Esqr   H. CLAY

ALS. InU.   1 John C. Wright.
2 See below, *Address . . . to the Public*, December 29, 1827.   3 For Clay's earlier "appeal to Congress," see above, February 3, 1825.   4 DeWitt Clinton. Cf. above, Rochester to Clay, November 4, 1827; Webster to Clay, November 5, 1827.   5 Cf. above, Sergeant to Clay, October 24, 1827, note.   6 Cf. above, Rochester to Clay, September

17, 1827.   7 Such action, by John C. Weems or by any of his colleagues in the Twentieth Congress, has not been found.

To Josiah Stoddard Johnston

Dear Sir   Washington 26h. [*i.e.*, 16th.]¹ November 1827.
Shortly after my arrival in this City in the Fall 1824 to attend Congress, and before the commencement of the Session, I conversed with you freely, on the subject of the Presidential election, more than once. I think one of these conversation [*sic*] was after I had seen Mr. Crawford,² on whom I called the next day after that on which I reached the City. In the course of these conversations I fully expressed to you my views and opinions as to Mr. Adams, Mr. Crawford and Genl. Jackson, and stated for which of them I should vote if I were called upon to decide between them. I shall be greatly obliged, if you would state, in writing, the purport of the above conversations, or of any other which I had with you, in November or December 1825 [*sic*], in reference to the Presidential election. It is proper to apprize you that I may make a public use of the statement. With great regard I am Your's truly
The Honble J. S. Johnston.   H CLAY

ALS. PHi.   ¹ Cf. below, Johnston to Clay, November 17, 1827. Clay's letter to Johnston is also dated November 26 as published in Colton (ed.), *Private Correspondence of Henry Clay*, 184.   ² William H. Crawford.

DIPLOMATIC NOTES   November 16, 1827

From F[RANCISCO] I. MARIATEGUI, Lima (Peru). States: "The Undersigned, Minister of Foreign Relations of the Peruvian Republic, has received orders from his Government to give to His Excellency, the Minister of the corresponding Department in the United States of North America, a slight idea of the events which prepared the recent political innovations by which Peru was placed in a situation to govern itself, and in the danger which threatens it, of a new war." Traces the actions of his country in the face of abuses of power by (Simón) Bolívar; cites the threat of hostilities by Colombia and, should that threat develop, the expectation of an attack by (Antonio José de) Sucre "in the South"; and asserts: "Resolved to leave nothing undone, on her part, which may remove all motives of war,—bathe the nation in American blood, and prolong her misfortunes, Peru will exhaust all reasonable and conciliatory expedients afforded by her situatio[n] and ability, to avoid this extreme; and hopes that the Government of the United States, impelled by a congeniality of principles, and by the love of humanity, will interpose its powerful mediation in defence of the peace and freedom of Peru." LS, in Spanish with trans. in State Dept. file. DNA, RG59, Communications from agents of Peru —Notes, vol. 1 (M-T802, R1). Translation published in Manning (arr.), *Diplomatic Correspondence . . . Latin-American Nations*, III, 1837–39. Received May 1 (1828); enclosed in Tudor to Clay, below, December 7, 1827.

INSTRUCTIONS AND DISPATCHES   November 16, 1827

To WILLIAM R. HIGINBOTHAM, "U States Commercial Agent, Bermuda." Informs him that his bill, for $414.50, drawn December 23, 1826, has been paid in part (cf.

above, Higinbotham to Clay, July 9, 1827, note) and that the balance will be paid, before any further drafts from him will be honored, as soon as he "may be entitled to a correspondent Credit on public account"; refers to the letter to him "of 26 [*i.e.*, 23] June 1826"; and cautions him against issuing drafts beyond "the clear and ascertained sum" credited to him. Copy. DNA, RG59, Cons. Instr. vol. 2, pp. 448–49 (M78, R2).

MISCELLANEOUS LETTERS   November 16, 1827

From GEORGE BETHUNE ENGLISH, Washington. Submits his financial statement, since the President has informed him "that it was not probable that the business which occasioned . . . [his] going to the Levant would be farther prosecuted at present." ALS. MHi-Adams Papers, Letters Recd. (MR483). Cf. above, Rodgers to Clay, July 28, 1827.

From ENOCH LINCOLN, Portland, Maine. Acknowledges receipt of documents (see above, Clay to Lincoln, October 30, 1827) and Clay's letter of November 10. States, in reference to the latter: "I am made sensible that the objections I have had the honor to urge against the submission to a foreign umpire of the territorial and jurisdictional rights of Maine, without consulting or advising her as to the conditions, have not been deemed available.— If any injury shall result to her, the appeal will be made to the people of this Country and to posterity. It has not seemed arrogant or presumptuous to have asked that if she is to be made a sacrifice she might not be devoted without some consideration on her part of the terms."
　Continues: "When you cautioned us against suggestions of compromise and acts of precaution, it was not believed that it was that you might the more easily throw us within the power of an umpire, but that you intended to intimate that the powerful arm of the federal government was holding its ample shield before us. At last we learn that our strength, security and wealth are to be subjected to the mercy of a foreign individual, who, it has been said by your minister, 'rarely decides upon strict principles of law,' and 'has always a bias to try, if possible, to split the difference' [cf. above, Gallatin to Clay, October 30, 1826, quotation omitted in this summary]. I cannot but yield to the impulse of saying most respectfully that Maine has not been treated as she has endeavored to deserve.—"
　Anticipates "that the violence committed has been but the commencement of a system" and calls attention to "the case of John Baker, who is stated to have been arrested on land conveyed to him in fee simple in the year 1825, by the Commonwealth of Massachusetts and the State of Maine. The conveyance was, virtually, a certificate of citizenship and a pledge for protection. It was also an act of State policy, a deliberate political measure, and the 'old Commonwealth' and this Republic may well call upon the President and Secretary of State to be their protectors." Encloses "communications to the Lieutenant Governor of New Brunswick [Sir Howard Douglas] and other documents. . . ." LS. DNA, RG76, Northeast Boundary, Misc. Papers, entry 84, env. 4, item 19 (frames 213–16). Published in *American State Papers, Foreign Relations*, VI, 933.
　John Baker, born in Moscow, Somerset County, Massachusetts (Maine), in 1796, had moved into the Madawaska region in 1820 as a lumberman. He had received title to his land from the States of Massachusetts and Maine under date of October 4, 1825, but British agents had seized his cut lumber as taken from Crown land. On July 4, 1827, Americans in the area had raised the United States flag and on July 5 organized a provisional government to operate for one year, pending establishment of constituted authority. Baker had subsequently stopped a British mail carrier from crossing his land and, although he had then permitted the carrier

to continue, had warned him against repeating the trespass. On September 25, 1827, New Brunswick authorities had arrested Baker and imprisoned him in Fredericton, where he remained until brought to trial May 8, 1828. He was found guilty and sentenced to imprisonment for two months in addition to payment of a fine of £25, for which he was to remain committed until payment was received. In all, he was imprisoned for over a year. Meanwhile his property, a cleared farm and mills, was seized and conveyed by the New Brunswick Government to other parties. George S. Rowell, "John Baker, the Hero of Madawaska," *The Magazine of History*, XXII (April–June, 1916), 122–25, 161, 217, 219; XXIII (July, 1916), 9.

Stipulation to William S. Dallam

17h. Nov. 1827.

Will S. Dallam having fully relinquishd to me his claim with an authority to sell the Land at my discretion after deducting my Debt therefrom[1]   I will arrange the balance of the proceeds to his order, whenever received.   H. CLAY

DS (the phrase, "whenever received," date, and signature in Clay's hand). NcD.
[1] Cf. above, III, 296–98, 861, 882, 892; Receipt from Richardson, July 31, 1826, note.

To Charles R. Vaughan

The Rt. Hon: C. R. Vaughan, &c. &c. &c.
Sir,   Department of State, Washington 17th. Novr. 1827.

In the note which I had the honor to address to you on the 19th. day of September, last, I informed you that I would transmit a copy of yours of the 17th., in answer to mine of the 14th of the same month, to His Excellency Enoch Lincoln, Governor of Maine, to obtain from him such information on the subject to which that correspondence related as he might communicate. I now transmit to you an extract from a Letter of Governor Lincoln, under date the 2d. instant, together with copies of two affidavits to which he refers. From one of those affidavits (that of William Dalton)[1] it would appear that he had resided during three years on the Aroostic River, thirty miles within the Line on the American side, that the constables and officers of the Province of New Brunswick have been in the habit, under the pretence of collecting debts, of coming to the settlement where he lived with precepts, and taking and carrying away every species of property they could find; that they generally carried it to the parish of Kent or Frederickton and there sold it at auction; that in a particular instance, of which the circumstances are declared in the affidavit, the acting British Officer declared that he did not care whether he was within or without his jurisdiction, for that a higher officer would bear him out in any thing he did; that he even employed a menace of resorting to physical force using at the same time approbious [*sic*] language; that the witness in consequence of the disturbances created in the Settlement by British Officers, sold his possessions at a great sacrifice in their value; and removed to another part of the State of Maine, and that the inhabitants of the Aroostic settlement have been unwilling and afraid to sleep in their own Houses, and have spent the night on the banks of the river and in the woods, and kept watch night and day as is customary in Indian warfare.

The affidavit of the other witness (Jonathan Wilson)[2] states that, at Woodstock in the province of New Brunswick, he learnt that Mr. Baker[3] had been arrested by the British authorities, with the agency of 45 men sent up in barges armed; that he was taken from his bed in the night; that the charge against him was for refusing and objecting to permit the British Mail to pass over his land; that he was confined in a jail, which is known to the witness to be extremely loathsome, filthy and dangerous to health; that he has been tried and sentenced to six months imprisonment and to the payment of £150; that he lived on Madawasca river, within the American line; and that the witness had learnt from his son,[4] who had recently been on the Aroostic, that the Settlers there complained bitterly of the oppression of the Officers and subjects of the British provinces; that their property was taken forcibly from them and carried off to the last Cow.

Such is the case made out by this testimony. I shall abstain at this time, from particular comments upon it. The proceedings which it discloses being incompatible with the rights of the United States, at variance with that forbearance and moderation which it has been understood between us were to be mutually observed, and exhibiting the exercise of rigorous acts of authority within the disputed territory, which could only be justified by considering it as constituting an incontestable part of the British dominions, I have to request such explanations as the occasion calls for. In the mean time I avail myself of the opportunity to tender to you assurances of my high Consideration.   H. CLAY.

Copy. DNA, RG59, Notes to Foreign Legations, vol. 3, pp. 403–405 (M38, R3). ALI draft, in CSmH.
1 Born in Somerset County, Maine, Dalton had re-located in Kennebec County after departing from the Aroostook.   2 A resident of Fairfield, Somerset County, Maine.
3 John Baker.   4 Leonard Wilson, not further identified.

From Josiah Stoddard Johnston

Dear Sir,   Washington Nov: 17th. 1827
In answer to your letter of the 16th.[1] I have no hesitation to state the purport of the several conversations that I had with you in relation to the Presidential election during the session of 1824·5.

I met you for the first time on your return to Washington in December 1824, on the Saturday or Sunday evening previous to the meeting of Congress, and at that time we had a long and free conversation on the approaching Election. I said to you it was still uncertain whether you, or Mr. Crawford[2] would be returned to the House of R., but from the information I had, I believed that you would receive the vote of Louisiana[3] and be returned as the third Candidate.

I expressed to you some solicitude about the Election, and the hope that we should pass quietly through it; I said that I apprehended a protracted struggle; that while three Candidates remained before the House it would be difficult for either to obtain a majority. That the excitement which the contest naturally produced would daily increase, that the parties would become obstinate, that the people might be dissatisfied, and that some agitation might be produced. That for the Character as well as the tranquillity of the Country, it was desirable that we should pass through it safely— You replied, that you would not permit the Country to be disturbed a day on your account, that you would not allow your name to interfere with the prompt decision of the question by the House. I said, if it becomes necessary the Country has a right to expect, and will expect that of you.

You informed me you had seen Mr. Crawford, that you had been shocked with his appearance, that notwithstanding all you had heard, you had no idea of his actual condition. And after expressing the sympathy which his misfortunes excited— You said he was incapable of performing the duties of the executive, and it was out of the question to think of making him President.

I remarked to you that in all probability the contest would be finally reduced to Mr. Adams & Genl. Jackson, and the conversation turned upon their comparative merit and qualifications, and a long discussion ensued; You drew a parallel between them, in a manner I thought, very just and respectful to both. You concluded by expressing a preference for Mr. Adams, which turned principally on his talents and experience in Civil affairs. I alluded to your critical position between the two parties, and the great personal responsibility under which you would act. You said it was true, but it could not be avoided, it was a duty imposed by your situation, and that you would meet it as any other Public duty.

I intimated to you, that in the present stage it would be improper to make known your sentiments, that there were strong motives for your not taking an active part in the contest. I suggested the relation in which you stood to the House, to the parties and to the Country, and said that great influence would be attributed to your opinion, that all parties would look to your course with interest, and that you would act under great responsibility. I thought there was no necessity for increasing the difficulty of your situation, by taking a part in the Election, and that it would be better to let it take its course. I left you under the impression that you concurred in these views.

I saw you again on the return of the votes from Louisiana, by which it was ascertained that you were excluded from the House. I then took the liberty of repeating to you all that I had before said in regard to the course you ought to pursue. I urged the consideration of your being the presiding officer of the House, where new questions might arise during the Election, and such other reflections as occurred to me. You said you were aware of the danger, as well as the delicacy of your position, and that you would leave your friends perfectly a [sic] liberty to exercise their own judgements [sic]. I will add that no instance came within my knowledge in which you deviated from this course. My opinion was and still is that you behaved with the greatest propriety, in the situation in which you were placed.

I conversed with you in a walk to the Capitol on the instructions of the Legislature of Kentucky.[4]— You still expressed your determination to vote for Mr. Adams. You said the Legislature had no right to direct you in the discharge of your duty; That you had received no instructions to vote for Genl. Jackson from your own district, that the instructions and letters you had received, directed you to pay no attention to the Legislative instructions, but to act upon your own judgement and do the best for the Country. You said you were not only free to choose, but you were under a great personal responsibility. That you would acquit yourself in the discharge of this duty, by making the best choice under all circumstances. That you believed Mr. Adams was the ablest and safest man, and you would act under that conviction.

I called on you on the morning of the publication of your card.[5] You said that I would now see that the delicacy you had observed had procured no respect or forbearance towards you; You spoke with some indignation at the means which had been employed, as well as the motives of those by whom you were assailed. You spoke of anonymous letters full of abuse and menace, letters written at Washington, to be published at different places, & of the letter which had been noticed in your Card &c.— I observed, you must expect all this,— You must have foreseen that at some time the storm would burst on your head— You must prepare to meet it firmly and bear it patiently. A public man must rely upon the weight of his Character, and the justice of his Country, & I added that I still believed the course you had pursued in the Election the most correct. You said you should continue as you had done to disregard Newspaper & anonymous abuse, but this paper was published on the authority of a member of the H. of R.[6] and therefore deserved to be met openly.

In referring to the terms of this letter, you observed that you did not know that you would be offered a place in any administration, nor did you know who would compose the cabinet of either Candidate. That you could not be the Member of any cabinet that would require you to advocate principles different from those you had always maintained before the Public, and for the support of which your public character was pledged.

On the tender of the office of Secretary of State, you consulted with me on the acceptance or refusal of the office. You stated all the reasons private and public, for and against the acceptance & asked my opinion.— I said it was an occasion in which you ought to consult freely your friends and act by their advice.— My own opinion is, you must accept; in the situation in which you have been placed by circumstances you have no choice;— And I suggested some reasons of a public nature why you ought to accept [to] be a member of the Cabinet.

After your nomination was confirmed, you informed me that you had requested Genl. Harrison to move for a Committee in the Senate if any thing occurred to make it necessary.[7] I replied that I did not think any thing had occurred to require a Committee on your part.

The foregoing is the purport, of several conversations; I cannot preserve the language, but it is a true and faithful statement of the substance of your opinions and views so far as they were known to me.

I avail myself of the occasion, although not called for by your letter, to state that I had occasional communication with you and several of your friends in which the conversation was free and unreserved.

That, no fact ever came to my knowledge, that could in the slightest degree justify the charge which has been exhibited. On the contrary I know that your opinion did not undergo any change from the time I first saw you on your return to Washington.— I have reason to believe that any silence and reserve which you observed during the contest, was dictated by a sentiment of delicacy to the Candidates, and by a sense of self respect, as well as of duty to the office you held in the House.

I will add that during the present Summer I met with two Gentlemen in the State of Mississippi, who voluntarily told me that they heard you express your decided preference of Mr. Adams at Lexington, before you left home for Washington. with great regards Yr. Obt Sert   J. S. Johnston

ALS. DLC-HC (DNA, M212, R3). Published as supportive material, in "Appendix", pp. 51–54, to Clay's *Address . . . to the Public*, below, December 29, 1827.
[1] As published by Clay in the "Appendix" to his *Address . . . to the Public*, this date is "26th."   [2] William H. Crawford.   [3] Cf. above, Clay to Brooke, December 22, 1824.   [4] Cf. above, Kendall to Clay, December 22, 1824, and note.   [5] Above, Clay to Gales and Seaton, January 30, 1825.   [6] George Kremer.   [7] Cf. above, Clay to Harrison, September 6, 1827, and note.

From Henry Shaw

My Dear Sir   Lanesboro[1] Nov 17th. 1827.

Yours of the 5.[2] was duly received, and I assure you that "laying upon the Table" for a few months was only regarded as a Parliamentary habit— It must be something more positive in its character than a post-*ponement* of the kind, that would disorder in the least degree the sentiments I entertain towards you— God forbid that I should tax you— I know something of your condition officially, I felt too sensibly the weight of your perplexities Politically, to wish, for my personal gratification, that your labors should be increased, or your cares multiplied— To add to either is not according to my notions of friendship— But I hope proffessions [*sic*] from me are unnecessary, as most certainly are any apologies from you— If I thought a line you write me, took one moment from your repose, or turned aside the current of reflections that might result in your benefit, I would burn it. When you can, with convenience spare one moment, it will add largely to my happiness— Your continuance in Publick life, upon terms gratefull [*sic*] to yourself, & in a Station worthy of your fame, is the single motive that governs me politically— There is nothing intimated, otherwise, that has, thus far, and as you will find, will hereafter appear in my conduct— I am pleased that what I wrote[3] "has served to explain some things" which you did not before fully understand— Is it not best always to try our friends by what we know of them, rather than by what others may say, or insinuate— I may find it necessary to pursue courses, which to you and to others may appear inexplicable—and if there should seem to be somewhat of inconsistency, there will be nothing of insincerity—

I still think the Election of Webster[4] impolitik—and perhaps before New Years you may think so— I have no faith in the friendship of the P[5]—nor any great confidence in the integrity of the Senator[6]— If the opposition succeed they the P & Co will charge their defeat to you— if oppon. fail you may or may not be sustained— now I will give you what will be deemed, I presume a strange opinion— It is this, that the Election of Jackson, *will secure to you the succession*! how is this— it would be a long story, and as the position will not be very gratefull to you, the reasons for it would be less so— In short, however this People are given to follow favorites—They have a strange mixture of cool sense, and wild enthusiasm. The one enables them to see their errors, the other prompts to a hearty correction of them— The P. is not, nor never was a favorite— he is Tolerated, but not supported— he has admirers, but not friends— he is a usefull [*sic*], and probably a virtuous publik man—but he would travel from Wn. to Quincy without awakening a sentiment of sorrow— The Fedsts. all hate him, & the Republicans never knew him— he could never again be brought forward— the "*Chieftain*"[7] would hardly get to the Palace, before the Enthusiasm that carried him there would begin to subside— there would be quarrels among the Managers— and disgust among the People— a revulsion would succeed— for promises that have been made could not be fulfilled— Intests [*sic*] that have been made to harmonize in an Opposition would recoil in power— the sober sense of the Nation would revolt at the vulgar display of wild Democracy at the Head, while Taste and decency and Principle would combine to ridicule its party colored vestments— Reaction begun would terminate as predicted— You are beloved by this Nation. And your present connexion is the only drawback upon your popularity— You'l [*sic*] say I am mad—stark mad— not quite so bad—what say you to the opinions that V. Buren had rather the Old Man should fail than win. now I fell [*sic*] quite sure such is the fact— but this if asserted would appear more wild than the other opinion—   what has Admn. done, or what has it failed to do, that can really be blamed— in what can Oppn. alter the general policy. These reflections will come over the Country, & he knows it. his power is factitious, & he dreads the effort to sustain another when the result may not be as personal as he could wish— There is no madness in either of the opinions— you speak of Parties as the power— I think I see the thing right—but there is a difference between that & making others see— It costs me no pain to act with Old Fedst. for legitimate ends— but the power is given where it should not go— I am hardly thought in this State to be An Adn. Man— because I opposed The P. in the first Battle, & have disliked him always. I tell them I was & am a Clayite— they may make what they will of it— the dirty Minions of the——[8] will have implicit faith in their Idol— this they do not get from me—and they are obliged to take things as they are— You have before you a laborious and difficult Task, and from present appearances, the chances are against success— but dont take my opinions, as is usual, for my hopes—altho' I do not fell [*sic*] exactly as many may, for I sincerely believe present defeat will prove ultimate Triumph—

No you have not pushed it too far—and every effort both of friends & foes has served to establish the purity of your conduct— defend your fame as heretofore and your friends will glory in that Tittle [*sic*]— I wish you to remember one thing, that the great mass of Adams men in this State were at the last Election your most bitter Enemies, and it was with these men that your friends had to contend— If we do not fell quite *lamb like* towards them them [*sic*] now it must be laid to the account of poor *human Nature*— They profess great zeal for you now but would make any other disposition of themselves if *so ordered*— If it was not too humbling a business, I should like it if you knew some of them— but let it pass— As near as I understand N. York at present, V. B. & Co. have formed An alliance with the South— by the Terms of the Treaty N. Y. is to controul nominally, and to have the next President,— the Young Men, and the Politicians, have been told, that this is the only scheme by which they can expect any advancement— That N, England are [*sic*] jealous of them, & the west would not be strong enough if they would [. . .][9]— bind[ing] the Alliance will accomplish the great aspirations of Patriotism—the preservation of the Union— it will abolish *Mason & Dixon's line*, & by mingling Slave & free States forbid a local division ruinous to our peace— it has been thus far well managed [as] you will have felt fast enogh [sic] from this Election— but the coutry [sic] may yet hold on to the Electoral Laws—

Our old friend Russell is out in some Letters in the States Man over "Sackville"— in which he strives to be very severe[10]— I say Russell, I suppose it is him— you will see them probably—

By the way—how gratified you must have been with the Baltimore display—it is every th[ing] the old woman said to have *"larnin"*[11]— it was a very unfortunate effort— 'tis strange, but such things must needs be—

Now if you survive this Epistle you may possibly weather the Opposition— but take it leasurely, & when you have fairly finished, just tell me of it— God speed you in all your wishes— Your FRIEND

H: SHAW

ALS. DLC-HC (DNA, M212, R3). Addressed to Clay. Margin of last page partially obscured.
[1] Massachusetts.   [2] Not found.   [3] Probably in his letter, above, August 22, 1827.   [4] Daniel Webster. Cf. above, Clay to Everett, April 5, 1827, note; Shaw to Clay, August 22, 1827.   [5] The President. Cf. above, Shaw to Clay, August 27, 1826.
[6] Webster.   [7] Jackson.   [8] Word omitted in text.   [9] Word illegible.
[10] Probably Jonathan Russell. The Boston *American Statesman and City Register*, on August 23, September 4, November 8, 1827, carried a series of letters, signed "Sackville" and dated from Roxbury, August 15, 27, November 3, 1827, respectively. All were severely critical of the administration. The first, in particular, attacked Clay and attributed Adams' election to corruption.   [11] Cf. above, Hammond to Clay, November 5, 1827, and note.

INSTRUCTIONS AND DISPATCHES   November 17, 1827

From THOMAS L. L. BRENT, Lisbon. Encloses translations of "an official article from the Portuguese Gazette shewing the preparations making in England for the reception of the Infante don Miguel" (cf. above, Lawrence to Clay, October 13, 1827); of "an amicable measure on the part of Spain as regards her relations with this Country" (Portugal); and of a letter from Miguel "to his sister the Princess Regent" (Isabel Maria). ALS. DNA, RG59, Dip. Disp., Portugal, vol. 7 (M43, R6). Received February 21, 1828.

The Spanish measure, here mentioned, provided for removal of military and other Portuguese refugees farther from the border between Spain and Portugal. Shortly afterward, according to this enclosure, the Spanish King (Ferdinand VII) decreed that "those portuguese refugees who after having returned to Portugal should again" ask asylum in Spain be refused entry.

From JOSHUA DODGE, Marseilles. Expresses opinion that "the Independence of Greece is unquestionably assured by" the Battle of Navarino (cf. above, Ombrosi to Clay, November 6, 1827); that a "general Struggle" may ensue, because Russia will probably seize the opportunity occasioned by the defeat of Turkey "to carry into execution the ancient projects of her Government against Turkey which will be opposed by the other European Powers"; and that Russia will increase "her fleet in the Black Sea." Reports that Ibrahim Pasha was not at Navarino and remains alive; that his survival "may be the means of saving the Europeans in Egypt from a general Massacre," because, "had he fallen, the Pacha of Egypt [Mehemet Ali], in despair might have permitted the sacrifice of the Europeans on first receiving the news"; that it is feared that "few or none" of the Europeans in Constantinople and Smyrna will escape; and that the Egyptians in Greece will struggle desperately, as "their means of escape from that Country are compl[etely] cut off." Advocates a "Strong American force in the Mediterranean" to counter the Barbary Powers, whose "fear . . . of our Gallant Navy has saved a number of ou[r] Merchantmen from being boarded by their Cruise[rs] which would have subjected them to a long quara[ntine] on their arrival in an European Port." ALS. DNA, RG59, Cons. Disp., Marseilles, vol. 2 (M-T220, R2). Margin obscured. Received February 7, 1828.

MISCELLANEOUS LETTERS   November 17, 1827

From ELIPHALET LOUD, Weymouth (Massachusetts). Reviews briefly "the case of the Ship Commerce" (cf. above, Hobart to Clay, December 15, 1825; Clay to Maltitz, June 19, 1826); notes that "Col. [Israel] Thorndike," having a similar claim against Russia (cf. above, Thorndike to Clay, March 13, December 19, 1825; February 7, 1827; Clay to Middleton, February 12, 1827; Middleton to Clay, April 30, 1827), employed as agent (Jacob Tilton) Slade, who has said in a letter to friends that (Pierre de) Polética had agreed to an interview with (Henry) Middleton on the subject; states: "I am now about sending a full power to Mr. Slade in Case the department of State recommend [sic] that way of procedure, & also whether [sic] Mr. Middleton had instructions to press Col Thorndikes Claim and not ours"; asks advice on several points. ALS. DNA, RG76, Misc. Claims, Russia (MR3).

INSTRUCTIONS AND DISPATCHES   November 18, 1827

From SAMUEL LARNED, Santiago de Chile, no. 63. Refers to his "dispatch No. 60" (above, September 20, 1827), in which he "touched incidentally on the subject of the offer of His Most Christian Majesty [Charles X] to grant a free passage on board of his ships of war, to such of the youth of this country as might be sent to France for their education; and promised to resume this matter in a subsequent communication." Inserts a translation of a note on this subject, addressed "To the Minister of Foreign Relations of the Republic of Chile" (office at this time vacant—cf. below, Larned to Clay, December 15, 1827) by (Claude-Charles-Marie Ducampe de) Rosamel, "The Rear Admiral, commanding the Naval forces of H. M. C. M. on the South American Station," December 10, 1825, and cites the "very flattering and polite reply, in which, amongst other things, the Minister says, that 'Chile persuades herself there will very shortly exist between the two countries other relations than those of pure friendship and benevolence.' " States that "many young men, of the wealthiest and most influential families, have been sent to France for the completion of their education"; voices alarm at "the effect of a practice of this nature" on "Chile, and the other late Spanish American colonies, possessing, already, in their social constitutions so many elements of servitude and anti-republican organization"; elaborates on his apprehensions in this regard; and recommends that his own Government follow the example of the French by offering "free passage . . . to such of the youth of these countries as might be destined to the United States for education" and admission of "a determinate number from each of them into the Military Academy at West Point. . . ." Observes that (Joaquín) Campino, who may "make some communications" on this subject, "will probably take passage in the vessel by which this despatch goes." ALS. DNA, RG59, Dip. Disp., Chile, vol. 2 (M-T2, R2). Published in Manning (arr.), *Diplomatic Correspondence . . . Latin-American Nations,* II, 1123–28. Received February 16, 1828.

Rosamel, born in 1774 near Calais, had served as a captain in the French Navy during the Napoleonic Wars and had been raised to the rank of rear admiral in 1823, when he had assumed command of the fleet off South America. In 1828 he was transferred to the Levant and placed in charge of the flotilla to uphold French honor at Tripoli. He was promoted to the rank of vice admiral in 1831 and from 1836 to 1839 held the post of Minister of Marine.

MISCELLANEOUS LETTERS   November 18, 1827

From J[OHN] J. CRITTENDEN, Frankfort (Kentucky). Recommends Felix Huston for appointment as United States attorney for the District of Mississippi. States: "His politics may however create some opposition to him at home. He is a decided Administration man—   And tho' that may be no great recommendation in Mississippi, it will not I hope be a prejudice to him in Washington. I know him well— He will make a good officer. He is a keen sagacious, bold, highspirited & efficient man." Requests that Clay "consider this as a private letter, & not a recommendation for the files of" his office. Adds in postscript: "Huston is the nephew of your old friend [Colonel] John Allen [of Frankfort]." ALS. DNA, RG59, A. and R. (M531, R4). Cf. below, Clay to Huston, February 21, 1828.

From THOMAS H. FLETCHER, Nashville. Notes that (Robert) Purdy's term as marshal for the District of West Tennessee will expire in January and that the "friends of the administration in this State are anxious that that office should be confered [*sic*] upon Theodorick F. Bradford." Asserts: "He is eminently qualified to discharge the duties incident to that office. Mr Bradford is now, and has been for six years a Senator in the General Assembly of this State. He is a devoted friend to the Administration, and is perhaps, with the exception of Colo [John] Williams, more obnoxious to the Jackson party than any other man in Tennessee. This distinction he has acquired chiefly from his unqualified support of your course about the late Presidential election—a support which he has unhesitatingly given in all places and upon all occasions. That his appointment will be strenuously opposed by every Member of Congress from this state is most certain—his political course in the Senate of this State has secured him that opposition." ALS. DNA, RG59, A. and R. (M531, R1). Cf. above, Power of Attorney, June 6, 1825, note.

To Samuel B. Barrell

To S. B. Barrell, Esq.

Sir,   Department of State Washington 19th. November 1827.

Some difficulties having arisen on our North Eastern border between the Government and people of New Brunswick and the State of Maine, in regard to certain settlements within the territory mutually claimed by the United States, and Great Britain,[1] the President is desirous of possessing information on particular points, which it is thought can be best acquired by sending some person to collect it on the disputed ground. He has accordingly authorized me to engage some person in this service; and as you have consented to accept it, I will now direct your attention to the particular points regarding which information is desired.

From the perusal of the affidavits,[2] copies of which you will receive herewith, you will perceive that collisions have arisen between the British authorities of New Brunswick, and some of the settlers on the Madawasca and the Aroostook, branches of the St. Johns; that these authorities claim to excercise a jurisdiction over those settlements although they are within the above disputed territory, and that they have, in fact, exercised it in various ways, and finally by the arrest of an American citizen, by the name of John Baker, who, after being carried from his home some distance to Frederickton, was there tried, convicted, and sentenced to an imprisonment of six months, and the payment of a fine of £150. The President wishes to know when, and by whom, these settlements on the Madawasca and Aroostook were first made? Whether they were under American or British authority or of French origin? By whom have they been governed? Have both the American and British governments exercised acts of jurisdiction over them; or only one government, and which, exclusively? Have the settlers generally acquiesced in the exercise of that authority, whether British or American, which has been extended over them? If these settlements were originally American, when did the British authorities first attempt to exercise jurisdiction over them? If they were originally British, when was an objection first made to the exercise of British jurisdiction over them? And when was the right first asserted, if it has been asserted at all, to exercise authority from the State of Massachusetts, or of Maine, over them? From what government do the settlers deduce their land titles? If both from an American and a British source, from which has the greater number been obtained? Which are the oldest?

You are also requested to inquire particularly into the causes of the arrest and condemnation of John Baker, and his present situation, and to procure official copies of the process and judicial proceedings against him. It being alleged that he is confined in a loathsome and unhealthy jail, you will examine, as far as you can, into his condition; and for that purpose, if you shall deem it necessary, you will proceed to the place of his confinement, and apply to the proper authority for permission to see him, and to ascertain the circumstances of his situation.

If it should turn out upon investigation, that the above-mentioned settlements were made and have been governed under the authority of Massachusetts and Maine, or either of them, you will please to take the affidavits of some three or four, or more persons, to establish that fact.

Measures being in a course of adoption, or operation, to settle between the United States and Great Britain the question of right in the disputed territory,[3] it is the wish of the Government of the United States, and it is professed to be that of the Government of Great Britain, that nothing should occur within the disputed territory to disturb the harmony between the two countries. We have inculcated forbearance and moderation on our side, and we are officially assured that it has been and will be practised on the other. Should you have intercourse with any of the inhabitants of the disputed territory, you may explain to them this mutual understanding between the two Governments. Whilst measures are in progress to adjust, in a regular way, by the two Governments themselves, the disputed boundary, abstinence from all acts of individual violence, and from all unnecessary collision, is the interest on both sides. Such acts and collisions might retard, but are not likely to advance, the work of amicable settlement between the two nations.

You will proceed, in the first place, and before you go upon the disputed ground to his excellency Enoch Lincoln, Governor of Maine, and explain to him, fully, the object of this commission. You will request of him such assistance and information in the execution of it, as he may be able and think proper to render. A letter of introduction to Governor Lincoln is herewith delivered to you;[4] and I expect also to procure for you a letter of introduction to Sir Howard Douglas, the Governor of New Brunswick, from the British Minister,[5] which will be delivered or forwarded to you.

The sum of $300 is now advanced to you on account of your expenses. On your return a reasonable allowance will be made for your services, and your reasonable expenses, will, also, be reimbursed you. I am, Sir, &c. &c. &c.   H. CLAY.

Copy. DNA, RG59, Dom. Letters, vol. 22, pp. 91–94 (M40, R20). Barrell, the name previously read erroneously as Samuel R. (cf. above, Barrell to Clay, December 11, 1826), was in 1827 a Washington attorney.
[1] Cf. above, Lincoln to Clay, September 3, 1827.   [2] Cf. above, Lincoln to Clay, November 2, 1827.   [3] Cf. above, Gallatin to Clay, September 30, 1827.   [4] Below, this date.   [5] Cf. below, Clay to Vaughan, this date.

To Joel R. Poinsett

No. 25.   Joel R. Poinsett, Esquire &c. &c. &c.
Sir.   Department of State Washington 19. Nov. 1827.

Your dispatch, No 94, under date the 8th. of July last, transmitting the manifesto of the Legislature of the State of Vera Cruz, with your answer to it, has been received and submitted to the President.[1] The propriety of a Foreign Minister abstaining from taking any part in the politics of the country where he is accredited, is perfectly obvious. The President learns from you, with satisfaction, that you have conformed to that rule of conduct; and that when the order of Masonry[2] which you assisted in organizing in Mexico, took a political direction, you withdrew from all participation in its proceedings. The President has seen with both surprize and regret the attack made upon you by the Legislature of la Vera Cruz. A Foreign Minister is responsible to his own Government, and only in a certain degree answerable to that which receives him. If this latter Government has just cause to complain of his conduct, established usage requires that it should communicate its complaint to his Government, and ask his recall. No such communication has been received from the Government of Mexico. Its silence, on the contrary, authorizes a belief that your conduct whilst residing near it, has afforded no just ground of complaint against you. Whilst the Government of the whole of the Mexican States is, therefore, to be presumed to be satisfied with the manner in which you have discharged the duties of your Mission, the irregularity of the Government of only one of those States, to which you are not accredited, and between which and the United States there is no direct diplomatic intercourse, undertaking publicly to arraign your conduct, is manifest. The example of such an interference might lead to the most pernicious consequences. The President, however, thinks it most expedient that you should not make the extraordinary course which the Legislature of Vera Cruz have thought proper to adopt, the subject of a formal complaint. Its impropriety is so evident and unwarrantable, that the hope may be fairly indulged that it will be neither repeated nor imitated. But it is due to the occasion that it should not pass altogether unnoticed. The President, therefore, directs that you will seek some early and suitable opportunity, informally to express to the President of the United Mexican States[3] the surprize and regret with which the manifesto in question has been seen here; to remonstrate against such a practice in future, and to say that the Government of the United States has seen nothing in your conduct, during your mission, to disapprove; but that it would, nevertheless, have been, at all times ready, if any complaints existed against you, on the part of the Mexican Government, to have received them through regular and established organs of communication, and given to them the fullest investigation, and the most friendly consideration.

The President does not desire that you should terminate your mission and return to the United States, but wishes, on that subject, that you should conform to your own inclination. He does not, on the other hand, if your residence there, from any cause, has become unpleasant, and uncomfortable, desire that you should remain against your own wishes. This subject would not have been adverted to, if intelligence had not indirectly, reached us, that you intended, and were making preparations, shortly to return home.[4] You will understand that the decision of that question is submitted exclusively, to your own feelings and discretion.

Your dispatches from No. 81 to No. 99,[5] inclusively, have been received. I am, with great respect, Your obedient Servant

H. CLAY.

LS. DNA, RG84, Mexico (MR17). Copy, in DNA, RG59, Dip. Instr., vol. 12, pp. 36–39 (M77, R7); L draft, in DLC-HC (DNA, M212, R8). Clay had submitted a draft of this dispatch to the President on November 13. Adams, *Memoirs*, VII, 353.
[1] For the correspondence on this matter between the President and the Secretary of State, see above, Adams to Clay, August 15 (1), 23, October 1, 1827; Clay to Adams, August 17, 23, September 24, 1827.   [2] The York Rite, or Yorkinos.   [3] Guadalupe Victoria.   [4] Cf. above, Taylor to Clay, June 22, 1827; Sergeant to Clay, August 1, 1827; Rochester to Clay, October 9, 1827; Brown to Clay, October 12, 1827.   [5] March 28 through September 5, 1827.

From John J. Crittenden

Dr Sir   Frankfort Novr: 19th 1827
I have just discovered that I omitted to return you Mr Blair's letter[1]– You will find it enclosed.

The friends of the Administration have just held their meeting in this place– It was very respectably attended, tho the weather was bad. The usual resolutions were adopted for future concert &c.[2]

The whole country resounds "with fearful note of preperation"[3] [*sic*] for the ensuing contest. It will be an arduous one, but with the spirit that now prevails, among the friends of the Administration, I shall be sanguine of success.

During the last winter & Spring John J Marshall & myself determined together to endeavour to get our sons[4] into the Military School at West-Point, & made applications accordingly– Through the kindness of my friend Barbour[5] I succeeded– But Marshall failed– And I almost regretted the success of my application, as it was a circumstance that probably added to his disappointment & mortification on the occasion.

His situation entitled him to expect the success of his application– And the denial of so small a favour, earnestly & with good reason solicited, was well calculated to chagrin him– I have very earnest & particular reasons for wishing that he may yet obtain an appointment for his son, and as he has, notwithstanding ancient feuds, displayed magnanimous & friendly feelings towards you, I could wish that he might obtain it through your agency– Do get the appointment for his son, & send it to him yourself. You were formerly written to[6] in relation to this business, by him or some of his friends– He does not know of this letter, & shall not, as perhaps his pride might be wounded at the renewal of any solicitations on the subject– Act in the matter as of your own motion– Barbour will not hesitate to grant your request, & small as the affair is I am very solicitious [*sic*] that you should attend to it, & without delay– And write directly to Marshall.[7]

Let me have a line on the subject. I am very sincerely Yr Friend
Hon: H. Clay Secty: of State   J. J CRITTENDEN

ALS. NcD.
¹ Cf. above, Blair to Clay, November 14, 1827, and note; Crittenden to Clay, November 15, 1827.   ² The Franklin County meeting of "The friends of the Administration" had been held in Frankfort on this date, with John Harvie as chairman and James W. Denny, secretary. They had adopted resolutions criticizing the intervention of "a military leader" in non-military affairs, approving the actions of the Adams administration, endorsing the "American system," and expressing faith in Adams and Clay "as pure, patriotic, uncorrupted and incorruptible republican [sic] and accomplished statesmen." They had also approved the calling of a State convention and appointed delegates and a committee of correspondence (cf. above, Smith to Clay, October 7, 1827, note; below, Davidson to Clay, December 25, 1827). Lexington *Kentucky Reporter*, November 24, 28, 1827.   ³ "Give dreadful note of preparation"—Shakespeare (Israel Gollancz [ed.], *The Works of Shakespeare* [12 vols., London, 1899–1900]), *King Henry V*, Act IV, Prologue, line 14.   ⁴ George Bibb Crittenden; Humphrey Marshall. Young Crittenden, born in 1812, was graduated from the United States Military Academy in 1832, resigned from the Army after a year of service, and then studied law under his father and at Transylvania University. He subsequently emigrated to Texas, was captured by the Mexicans as a member of the Texas Army in 1842, and was imprisoned for nine months. Returning then to Kentucky, he was commissioned a captain in the United States Army in 1846 and fought in the Mexican War. He held the rank of lieutenant colonel in 1861, when he resigned to join the Confederate forces as a brigadier general. Some six months later intemperance, which had repeatedly jeopardized his career, led to his censure by military court and forced his resignation. He served through the remainder of the war as a volunteer and afterward resided in Frankfort.   Marshall, also born in 1812 and graduated from the United States Military Academy in 1832, resigned his commission, studied law, and was admitted to the bar in 1833. He settled in Louisville the following year, practiced law, and was active in politics. He was commissioned a colonel of Kentucky volunteers in 1846 and served in the Mexican War. He was farming in Henry County, Kentucky, when he was elected to Congress in 1849. He served until 1852, resigned to become Minister to China from 1852 to 1854, and then returned to Congress from 1855 to 1859. He was a brigadier general in the Confederate Army from 1861 to 1863, represented Kentucky in the Confederate Congress from 1863 to 1865, practiced law in New Orleans from 1865 to 1867, and subsequently returned to legal practice in Louisville.   ⁵ James Barbour.   ⁶ Not found.   ⁷ Not found. Cf. below, Clay to Crittenden, December 16, 1827; Clay to Barbour, December 29, 1827.

DIPLOMATIC NOTES   November 19, 1827

To C[HARLES] R. VAUGHAN, Washington. Describes briefly the mission of S(amuel) B. Barrell (cf. above, Clay to Barrell, this date) and "requests of Mr. Vaughan a Letter of introduction for Mr. Barrell to Sir Howard Douglas, communicating the above object of this commission, and soliciting such assistance, in the execution of it, as Mr. Barrell may desire and Sir Howard may think proper to render." Copy. DNA, RG59, Notes to Foreign Legations, vol. 3, p. 405 (M38, R3). Published in Manning (arr.), *Diplomatic Correspondence . . . Canadian Relations*, II, 140–41, and *American State Papers, Foreign Relations*, VI, 838–39.

Vaughan acknowledged, on November 20, receipt of Clay's note and stated that he was "transmitting to him immediately" the letter requested. LS, in DNA, RG59, Notes from British Legation, vol. 14 (M50, R15). Published in Manning (arr.), *Diplomatic Correspondence . . . Canadian Relations*, II, 655.

INSTRUCTIONS AND DISPATCHES   November 19, 1827

To A[LEXANDER] H. EVERETT, no. 10. States that his "despatches from No. 36 [June 2, 1826] to No. 87 [September 4, 1827] . . . have been received, and submitted to the President," who "has given to the request contained in that of the 4th. August 1827 (No. 84) attentive and friendly consideration." Informs him that, "in believing it [a leave of absence] to be a matter of course, . . . [he is] under some misapprehensions." Explains the grounds on which short leaves have been granted to United States Ministers abroad and the necessity for each of these officials to "be always present at his post, or if allowed to be absent, that there should be a strong necessity for his temporary withdrawal." Reports that, "Entertaining these views, the President regrets that he cannot accede to . . . [Everett's] request" and adds that a similar application from (Henry) Middleton was also rejected (cf. above, Middleton to Clay, January 7, 1826; Clay to Middleton, April 21, 1826). Transmits "Copies of a correspondence with Mr. [Hilario de Rivas y] Salmon during the last summer, and also copies of one more recent with Mr. [Francisco] Tacon." Copy. DNA, RG59, Dip. Instr., vol. 12, pp. 39–40 (M77, R7). ALI draft, in DLC-HC (DNA, M212, R8).

From ROBERT MONROE HARRISON, Demerara. Encloses a letter from Charles Benjamin on the Guiana timber industry and several other documents on forests of Guiana, including a comparative statement on the prices and quality of American timber relative to Guiana hardwood. Notes that Benjamin, originally from Connecticut, is "a very respectable Merchant" in British Guiana. ALS. DNA, RG59, Cons. Disp., Demerara, vol. 1 (M-T336, R1).
    Benjamin was later (1850–1854) United States consul at Demerara.

MISCELLANEOUS LETTERS   November 19, 1827

To ENOCH LINCOLN, Portland, Maine. States: "The President being desirous to possess certain information in respect to settlements within that part of the territorial limits of Maine which is claimed by Great Britain, and especially as to the causes of the arrest and condemnation of John Baker, an American citizen, has authorized me to employ Mr. [Samuel B.] Barrell to proceed to Maine, and, if necessary, to New Brunswick, to collect the information desired." States that Barrell will communicate further with Lincoln and requests that Lincoln aid Barrell "in the execution of his commission. . . ." Copy. DNA, RG59, Dom. Letters, vol. 22, pp. 88–89 (M40, R20).

To Alexander H. Everett

No. 11.   A. H. Everett
Envoy Extraordinary and Minister Plenipotentiary to Spain.
Sir   Department of State Washington 20th. Novr 1827.
    I transmit you herewith a letter addressed to the President of the United States, and to the Secretary of State, from Stephen Hempstead Senr. and Charles S. Hempstead,[1] the former, the father, the latter, the brother of Major Thomas Hempstead, a citizen of the State of Missouri. The letter states that, in the spring of 1825, Major Hempstead went from St. Louis to New Orleans, in pursuit of a debtor of the late Missouri Fur Company, of which Major Hempstead was, at the time, the head; that he continued the pursuit of his debtor to the Bay of Honduras, where the Major engaged in some mercantile speculations,

and having shipped his property on board of a patriot vessel, he was taken and carried into the Havanna [*sic*]; and confined in Prison there, but obtained his release through the interposition of the American Consul;[2] that he then returned to New Orleans, whence he sailed in a vessel of the United States to Cadiz, where he is imprisoned on a charge of having been in the Spanish American Republican service. A letter from him dated on the 3d. of August last, states that he had then been in prison six weeks, and a part of the time in irons. This letter of the Messrs. Hempstead, has a certificate endorsed upon it by the Hon: David Barton, a Senator of the United States, stating that he knows the contents of the letter to be correct, so far as they relate to Missouri, and has no doubt of their being entirely so. The letter is accompanied by another letter, in confirmation of its statements, also herewith transmitted signed by eleven Gentlemen, and addressed to the Secretary of State. Most of them are known to me personally, or by character, as among the most eminent and respectable citizens of Missouri. I was also personally acquainted with some members of the Hempstead family, whom I knew to be respectable. I served in Congress with his brother[3] who was the first delegate from the Territory of Missouri. Assuming the facts to be true, which are contained in the letters of the Father and brother of Major Hempstead, his imprisonment is manifestly illegal and unjust, and you will therefore demand his immediate liberation, together with indemnity for the wrongs he has suffered, in consequence of his arrest and confinement. If, however, upon investigation into his case, you should find its circumstances to be different from those narrated by his connexions, and that there is legal cause for his imprisonment, you will, nevertheless, employ your good offices, officially or otherwise, as far as it may appear to you to be proper and expedient, to procure his discharge. The deep interest which is taken in his behalf, in the State of Missouri, which could only proceed from his great worth and respectability, induces the President to desire that every proper exertion should be made, to restore him again to his country and his friends. I am, with great respect, Your Obedient Servant   H. CLAY.

P.S.   Two letters from the family of Major Hempstead are also sent, herewith, to be delivered to him.   H. C.

Copy. DNA, RG59, Dip. Instr. vol. 12, pp. 41–42 (M77, R7). L draft, in DLC-HC (DNA, M212, R8).
    [1] Not found—cf. above, Hempstead to Clay, October 29, 1827.   [2] At that time, John Warner.   [3] Edward Hempstead.

To Josephus B. Stuart

My Dear Sir   Washington 20h. November 1827
    Mr. Tylever[1] delivered to me your obliging favor of the 12h. in-

stant[2] with the fine specimen of Cutlery which you had the kindness to send me, made at Auburn. It is very creditable to the artist, and affords additional evidence of the skill and capacity of our Countrymen to supply all one wants, with proper encouragement and protection. I shall retain it, with the most friendly recollections.

I shall be very glad if you can in a professional way derive any advantage from the political epidemic which you describe as prevailing in your State.[3] If we are to judge from the symptoms which the infected among you exhibit, it will surpass all your skill, great as it is, to check its progress. As for me, I have been afflicted by disease of another kind from which I hope I am recovering, 'though slowly.[4] Whether sick or well believe me always Truly your friend
Dr. J. B. Stuart.   H. CLAY

ALS. NcD.   [1] Not identified.
[2] Not found.   [3] Cf. above, Sergeant to Clay, October 24, 1827, and note.   [4] Cf. above, Clay to Johnston, October 6, 1827; Clay to Brown, October 28, 1827.

From "Amicus"

[ca. November 20, 1827]
[Reviews the charges that Clay became Secretary of State "through bargain, intrigue and management." Expresses the opinion that Clay has answered satisfactorily his critics but suggests "the propriety of demanding a committee of investigation in Congress, with full powers to procure and receive documentary and oral testimony, to sift this whole affair."]

Copy. Richmond Enquirer (Virginia), November 20, 1827. The author has not been identified.

From Francis T. Brooke

My Dear Sir   St Julien Novr 20 1827
I received a letter from our friend Southard[1] asking my opinion on the question, who is to be named as V P,   I confess to you this question has given me Some concern,   I have frequently turned in [sic] my mind without being able to come to any Satisfactory conclusion on it, and hoped that the point would be Settled at Washington by wiser heads,   it is all important that in the great race we should not be made to carry more weight than is absolutely necessary—   having never heard your name mentioned before from any Source deserving notice, I stated to Mr Southard very breifly [sic] what I thought of it—
if your friends mean to propose you[2] and none of them will be more pleased at it than myself—it ought to be done as soon as possible and with as little apparent parade as possible   if you could be named in the East at [sic] West at the Same time I see no reason to doubt that your vote here, will be fully equal to Mr Adams, but this I should

question if you are to be brought forward by your friends in Virginia on this Subject I should be glad to have your own opinion,   others were mentioned by Mr S— my friend Mr Barbour[3] among others,   if you declined it, there is no one that I would prefer to him, but if a Virginian is to be run he ought to be the Strongest man in Virginia which in these disjointed times he is not,— Mr Johnson[4] who I certainly Should not personally prefer is much the Strongest man we have,   a Strong man from N Y or Penna[5] would be very acceptable here, as many of us are fearful of Success and want aid,   you will See by the papers how we are getting on   I promise myself much from the convention at Richmond[6] but Something will depend on its address to the people of the State,   I mentioned this matter to Mr Johnson and Said he would be looked to for it,   he Seemed to think less of its importance than myself and I fear will do nothing,   on this Subject too I shall be very well pleased to have your opinion and if you have time will be glad to have at least the outlines of Such a paper,   much will depend on a proper Selection of its topics both as regards Virginia and other States— I Shall leave home for Richmd on Saturday where I shall expect to hear from you,   what would I not give for a few hours free conversation with you— Yours very Sincerely

FRANCIS BROOKE

N B   there is a Mr Semple who is at the head of the Baptist church in this State and now in George Town or Washington Superintending a Baptist college,[7]   he is an admn man and might be of great Service to us   I know him well & shall write him but if any of your friends know him they could quiken [sic] his his [sic] exertions   he can do much by writing but I wish him to take an occasion to come into the State—

I have it from pretty good authority that Mr Adams wrote a letter to Mr Jefferson on the Subject of the Panama mission and received an answer from him highly approving of it,   are there no means by which Such a letter could finds it [sic] way to the public[8]—

ALS. InU.   [1] Samuel L. Southard.
[2] Cf. above, Clay to Hammond, April 21, 1827; Rochester to Clay, October 12, November 4, 1827.   [3] James Barbour.   [4] Chapman Johnson.   [5] Cf. above, Clay to Sloane, August 28, 1827.   [6] Cf. above, Mercer to Clay, August 18, 1827, and note.
[7] Robert Baylor Semple, born in King and Queen County, Virginia, in 1769, had been ordained in 1790 and thereupon had become pastor of the Bruington Baptist Church, where he served for 40 years. In 1820 he had been elected president of the Baptist triennial convention and of the American Baptist Missionary Union, and he retained those offices until his death, in 1831. He was also financial agent and president of the board of trustees of Columbian College, Washington.   [8] Such correspondence has not been found.

From John P. Erwin

Dear Sir—   Post Office Nashville 20th. Nov. 1827.—
About twelve months since I wrote you[1] at the request of *Theo. F.*

Bradford, then about to be an applicant for the appointment of Marshal of West Tenn. under an impression that the term had then expired— I then stated the facts—vz—That Genl. Purdy[2] the Marshal had never performed, or attempted to perform any of the duties of the Office—but the acting Marshal, viz Mr. *Joel M Smith*, who was the active & efficient agent of *Duff Green*, in procuring subscribers, and super tending [*sic*] the circulation of his paper[3]— Those facts are still existing— Genl Purdy is now, & has been for some time, so much afflicted as to be unable to do any business—and his man Mr Smith is still engaged in the same way as heretofore— But all this being known, it will remain for you to consider, & determine on the expediency of removing Genl Purdy, nothwithstanding his incompetency— He is an old officer, and perhaps had his constitution impaired in the Camp— at any rate it will be so said, and believed—notwithstanding the *bottle* may have done him more injury, than the Camp— The opposition as you are aware would sound it from Maine to La. that an old & meritorious officer had been displaced, to make room for some political favorite— It seems to me questionable, whether your friends here would be acting wisely to urge such a measure on your consideration— altho it is certainly objectionable and highly improper for Genl P— to retain Smith as his deputy, when actively engaged in the service of Duff Green—

This however is for your better judgment to determine— Mr Bradford is no doubt well disposed towards you, altho he calls himself a Jackson man—   there are men in the State, and many of them too— who do not deem it necessary to disguise their aversion to J— or preference for the present Admn.— I am very Sincerely Yrs &c

J P. ERWIN

The Jacksonites talk largely about the vote of New York[4]—altho they begin to manifest some anxiety about Va.— They affect great Confidence as to Pennsylva.[5]— The Genl. himself says that State stands firm in his cause.—

ALS. DNA, RG59, A. and R. (M531, R1). Addressed to Clay, "*private*."
[1] Letter not found.   [2] Robert Purdy.   [3] Washington *United States Telegraph*.
[4] Cf. above, Sergeant to Clay, October 24, 1827, note.   [5] Cf. above, Clay to Brown, March 27, 1827, note.

From Christopher Hughes

The Hague; November; 20h. 1827.
Private; confidential! Nay! even *Tender*!

I know how exceedingly scrupulous is, His Excellency, Ze Minister of State & of foreign affairs, about the exercise of the privilege of Frank; ex. gr: he told me at dinner, at Bn. Mareuil's,[1] when I had the pleasure, (a pleasure that *stands* almost before all others, with me; seeing I am of being his *next* chair, & when, I said, that I had brought from Mount Vernon, a copy of General Lafayette's Letters to Genl. Washington, during the war of Independence; (Genl. LaF . . . [*sic*] having lost his *original* copies, & having requested Bushrod Washington, to *send him* the Copy-Book, to be made at Mt. Vernon; an affair of some 50, or 60 folio sheets!) which *said* Book of Copies, I was directed to ask Y. E. to allow to go, with the next despatches to Mr. Brown![2] Lord! I do remember what a *row* you gave me! "The Department is made a sort of common post-office; I'll not permit it; I'll reform all that &c. &c. &c."[3] My digestion was spoilt; But I sent the Book, though, for all that; Gen. La Fayette wrote me a letter of thanks; & *who lost* by this?

Another occasion, I asked Yr. E. to address a letter to my wife, at Baltimore, I being at Washington, & with you in your Room; You gave me a most kind smile & certainly said most gently, "Why Hughes, I ll do it, if you request it; but I'd rather not,"   now, as my only motive, was to tickle the vanity of my wife, by sending her a letter with your address & name. (You know we love to tickle our wives;) Why, I retired my letter from the table, & my person from the Department;— holding my head on with both hands, & glad to find it, & myself, in [sa]fety, out in the free air! Now to the point! I do implore you to pardon the liberty I take, in sending the enclosed packet to your address; I send it, in Sir C Bagot's Bag, gratis, to Liverpool; under cover to the Consul;[4] it is for one of the most amiable, accomplished & high bred gentlemen in our country, of acknowledged taste in the Beaux arts & Belles Lettres; & who has the highest opinion of and admiration for you; in some degree derived from his or rather, my conversations with him; & his knowledge of my judgement & veracity! The packet contains about 60 autographs of some of the most learned eminent & illustrious men, living & dead; & a good portion of it, is contributed from my own Correspondence. There is Byron & Dr Clarke and Campbell, & Canning, & Goodrich, & Holland & Clarence & Landsdown [*sic*] & Bonaparte—& Mirabeau & Prince deLigne, & Horace Walpole & Lady Morgan[5] & multitudes of others & more to follow;   Gilmor[6] amuses himself with this trifle & let me add that the reversion of his collection is to come back to me or, in case of my death, to my Son,[7] by virtue of an "autograph" codicil of Gilmor's, to be added to his will;   all this perhaps you dont [*sic*] care one farthing about, yet it is a harmless, & perhaps a laudable amusement, & connected with a taste for *Letters*! When ever you visit Baltimore, I do hope you will visit Gilmor's collection of pictures; the choicest in America;   I heard a Gentleman say the other day, (& he is Guardian of all the objects of the arts, belonging to his Kingdom, Mr Apostool[8] at Amsterdam;) that, if he were called on to name, *two* of the most accomplished connoisseurs, in the arts, not being professional men, he should name Sir Charles Bagot, & *Robert Gilmor*, of Baltimore; & I was proud of Baltimore; proud of

Gilmor; & proud of myself, as usual   Now, I am sure, you will have the good-ness, to send the packet after all this explanation, to my friend at Baltimore. As to Mr. Huygens,[9] he is such a twaddling; uncertain sort of youth, God knows, *when* he will start! He might have started Six weeks, or two months ago, as Bn. Verstolk told me himself; but he has been philandering and doling away his time; & now when he presents himself as ready, the States General are in Session & all the Departments have so much to do, that they have not time to think of him, or his despatches. Besides, he wants to be allowed to call himself Count.[10] & when that sort of maggot, gets into a man's brain, who can count on him? This is vile. But I'll tell you a classic one, I made this day, & that has gone to England, as capital! Lord Dudley & ward hates office, & has all the caprice of wealth & wit; (he has clear, 100,000£ St a year;) he was decoyed by his friendship for Mr. Canning to take the Dept. of State; from Mr. Cs death, he has shown great restiveness & anxiety to go back to his indolence & privacy;   they have found out an odd expedient to keep him in the Ministry;   Lady Lyndhurst, wife of the Lord Chancellor,[11] is a fine, gay & rather doubtful woman;   She is employed to keep Ward in office, & scandalous Stories are freely circulated about him & her;   The Limbs of the Law; call the wife of the Chancellor (a word without a *feminine*) "*Mrs. Chancery.*"   all this was talked over, before me, tother day, by some high Englishmen; When *I said*; mind *I said*; "Here is a *Ward in Chancery*, with a Witness." It was pronounced to be most excellent, & sent off, by post, to London;— I must send off this by Post, or I shall be too late—

Henry Clay Esqr. Washington   C. HUGHES

[Endorsed by Hughes (AE) on verso of cover, beneath an invitation to him to visit a Mr. and Mrs. Vander Fosse on the following afternoon:]

   * a very kind important man is Monsieur Vander Fosse! chief of the customs, in this Kingdom![12] I am to meet several of the Foreign Ministers chez Lui;   they really are "Excellence"! But alas! poor me! "Les absents ont tort"; says the French proverb; j'ajoute; ils sont *oubliés*. alas! alas! Helas! ! !

ALS. DLC-HC (DNA, M212, R3).
   [1] The date, not known. Hughes had been in the United States during the winter of 1825–1826 and had visited Washington several times. Cf. above, Hughes to Clay, November 23, December 1, 30, 1825; April 12, 15, 1826; Clay to Brown, April 26, 1826.
   [2] Cf. above, Washington to Clay, December 26, 1825.   [3] Cf. above, Clay to Woodward, December 12, 1825.   [4] James Maury.   [5] Dr. Charles Mansfield Clarke (1782–1857), renowned London surgeon and practitioner of midwifery; Thomas Campbell (1777–1844), Scotch poet and editor, one of the founders of London University and from 1826 to 1829 rector of Glasgow University; George Canning; Frederick John Robinson, Viscount Goderich; Henry Richard Vassel Fox, third Baron Holland; the Duke of Clarence (later, William IV); Henry Petty-Fitzmaurice, Lord Lansdowne; Napoleon Bonaparte; Honoré Gabriel Riqueti, Count de Mirabeau (1749–1791), French revolutionary leader; Karl Joseph, Prince de Ligne (1735–1814), Belgian soldier and writer and an intimate of Emperor Joseph II of Austria and Catherine the Great of Russia; probably Horace Walpole, fourth Earl of Orford (1717–1797), British litterateur and author of Gothic romances; and Sydney Owenson, Lady Morgan (1783–1859), Irish-born novelist

and writer of travel accounts.   6 Robert Gilmor (Jr.).   7 Charles John Hughes.
   8 Cornelis Apostool, born at Amsterdam in 1762, amateur painter and engraver and,
from 1808 until his death in 1844, director of the Amsterdam Museum.   9 Roger
Bangeman Huygens.   10 Cf. above, Hughes to Clay, October 5, 1827.   11 Sarah
Garay Thomas, née Brunsden, a widow, had married in 1819 John Singleton Copley, a
native of Boston and son of John Singleton Copley, the artist. The younger Copley had
been taken as a child to England, where he enjoyed a highly successful career in law and
politics. He had been named Chancellor and made Baron Lyndhurst in April, 1827.
Lady Lyndhurst was at this time about 32 years of age; she died in 1834.   12 The
Vander Fosses have not been further identified.

From Joseph M. Street

Dear Sir,   (Private)   Prairie du Chien 20th. Nov. 1827.
   I have refrained from writing you untill I have but one moment by
this opportunity. I such [sic] haste I will not venture to say any thing
politically, save what you are apprised off [sic]— some of the officers of
the army appear to against [sic] and some for the Admrs [sic] who I
have seen. Genl. Atkinson & Colo. Morgan[1] (the latter now at New
York) are Jacksonites.
   Bates[2] from Missouri is looked upon as a moderate administration
man. *Perhaps he is.* He is a smothe [sic], moderate soft spoken man,
that I think you should guardidly [sic] permit *close to you.* I merely
say this out of great caution. When there was any possibility of injury,
I would [sa]y *pranez* [sic] *garde.* I have not time to add more. This I
wish to be truly confidential, for I know not one thing against him.
But I have a foolish notion perhaps that is generally formed from the
view of the form and one examination of a mans behavior on our first
interview.—
   I presume that Commissioners will be appointed to treat with the
Winnebago Indians[3] at this place next summer. I have made an elaborate report on Indian affairs to the Secretary of War[4] by this conveyance, and have written to some members of Congress that I would be
gratified to be one of the Commissioners, and if you can give me any
aid I hope you will do so.
   Few Agents I presume, have more fully entered into an examination of Indians affairs than I have, and I flatter my self that my information communicated at this time, and viewed in relation to our intercourse with the Indians will be found strictly correct. An examination
of it will shew the Department I have not been idle since my appointment, and I hope wd. be gratifying to those *friends who were good
enough* to get me into office. You my dear sir, may rest assured that
every energy of my mind will be exerted to become eminently useful
in the Indian department. I am convinced (with a due respect for men
older in years and in Indian affairs) that our relations with the Indians
are not conducted upon the best possible ground, at the agencies at
least. There is an indefiniteness in many of our treaties that *have* [sic]
& will lead to difficulties with the Indians.

I will now say no more for the Gentleman is waiting. Devotedly your friend & servant   JOS. M. STREET.

ALS. DLC-HC (DNA, M212, R3). Addressed to Clay.
1 Henry Atkinson; Willoughby Morgan. The latter was a native of Virginia who had entered the Army as a captain of infantry from that State in 1812. He had been placed in charge of constructing Fort Crawford at Prairie du Chien in 1816 and had been raised to the rank of lieutenant colonel in 1818. After serving at various Northwestern posts between 1817 and 1822, he had returned to Prairie du Chien, where he remained in command until his death in 1832. He was breveted a colonel in November, 1828, and promoted to that rank in April, 1830.   2 Edward Bates.   3 Cf. above, Street to Clay, October 16, 1827, and note.   4 James Barbour. The report was not published.

Agreement with John Rodgers

[November 20, 1827]
—An agreement between John Rodgers and H. Clay.—

The said Rodgers being the proprietor of a Jack called Ulysses, and a Jenny called Calypso[1] lately imported from the Island of Malta for himself and his representatives, covenants with the said Clay that he, or his legal representatives upon his decease, shall retain the possession of them for the term of five years, if they should so long live. They are to be sent by the said Clay at his own expense to the state of Kentucky, and the parties are to be equally interested in the produce of the Jenny during the above term, and the amount which the Jack may earn by being put to mares or Jennies. The said Clay or his representatives are to be at the expense of keeping the above animals during the aforesaid term. The produce of the Jenny is to be sold by the mutual consent of the parties. The price at which the Jack is to be let to Jennies is to be not less than fifty dollars the season, and to mares ten dollars the season, or fifteen for insurance, or more if the said Clay shall deem it expedient. If the said Rodgers should choose to have returned to him the animals at Washington City or Maryland upon the termination of the contract, the said Clay is to be at the expense of their return.—

—Witness the hands & seals of the parties this 20h. day of November 1827—in duplicate[2]   JN RODGERS LS
                                                                H. CLAY LS

DS. Josephine Simpson Collection, Lexington, Kentucky.
1 This was the first significant importation of jack stock into the United States. "Ulysses," at this time about two years old, was sold by Clay in the fall of 1832 to Parker E. Todhunter, a son of Jacob Todhunter, of Jessamine County, Kentucky. "Calypso," described as "the largest jenny probably" in Kentucky, remained at "Ashland" and produced for Clay seven foals in seven years. Lexington, Kentucky, *Observer and Reporter*, September 6, 1832; W. S. Anderson and J. J. Hooper, *American Jack Stock and Mule Production* (Kentucky Agricultural Experiment Station, *Bulletin* no. 212 [1917]), p. 243.
2 Duplicate, DS, in DLC-Rodgers Family Papers.

INSTRUCTIONS AND DISPATCHES   November 20, 1827

To THOMAS M. RODNEY, Havana. Transmits copies of the letter (of this date) to (Alexander H.) Everett and its enclosures; instructs Rodney to "ascertain the fact whether "Major Thomas Hempstead is in Havana and, if he is confined there, to strive "to obtain his discharge"; transmits also a letter from Hempstead's family to be delivered to the Major if he is in Cuba (cf. above, Charles Hempstead to Clay, October 29, 1827). Copy. DNA, RG59, Cons. Instr., vol. 2, p. 450 (M78, R2).

From C[HARLES] D. COXE, Tripoli, "Duplicate." Reports that he was well received in his first audience with the Pasha of Tripoli (Yusuf Karamanli), who remarked that "it was so long since an American Consul had resided near him he was at length fearful The President had forgotten him. . . ." Notes that he "found the Consulate in a wretched State of ruin in the care of Mr. J. Morillo, a young Spaniard, acting under the orders of Mr. [Thomas D.] Anderson who had taken up his residence at Leghorn." States that "The Great Kahia, (brother in law to the Pacha) the proprietor of the Consular house, demanded . . . four years and eight months arrearages of rent due"; but that he refused the request, pleading lack of instruction on the question; that Morillo was arrested and his effects seized; and that Morillo, "after several vain attempts to throw this expence on the United States, at length" paid the debt. Adds that "His Highness and his Ministers" claimed they had received no presents "since the one given by Consul [Richard B.] Jones. . . , and that they expected" that fact to be considered when he made his gifts, but he refused to "encourage such pretensions" and "remarked that our Consuls in Tripoly had been exchanged or transfer'd at short intervals, and that our Government would, very likely, consider a handsome present once made, enough for two Consuls. . . ." Observes that the Pasha accepted the presents in good grace. Reviews the anxieties of the foreign community over the threat of reprisals in the wake of "the news of the battle of Navarino" (cf. above, Ombrosi to Clay, November 6, 1827) and concludes: "It is . . . clearly the interest of the Pacha of Tripoly and the Bey of Tunis [Hassein] to abstain from suffering violence to the Christians residing in their dominions" lest they incur the "vengeance" of "the English and French." LS. DNA, RG59, Cons. Disp., Tripoli, vol. 4 (M-T40, R-T5). Received July 19, 1828.

The "Kahia," the principal judicial officer over the Moors, has not been further identified.

From W[ILLIAM] TUDOR, Lima, no. 79, "Confidential." Refers to his letter of November 7, in which he "said something on the subject of an intervention by the U. S. & England to prevent the war with which Peru is threatened by Bolivar" and states that, since the present communication, being "forwarded under cover to Mr [Joel R.] Poinsett," may arrive earlier, he "will recapitulate what has occurred on the subject." Summarizes the earlier letter and expresses awareness that he has "here taken steps of considerable delicacy, but they must be considered as the acts of a private individual." ALS. DNA, RG59, Dip. Disp., Brazil, vol. 6 (M121, R8). Published in Manning (arr.), Diplomatic Correspondence . . . Latin-American Nations, III, 1840–43. Received March 10, 1828.

During a conference with the President on March 22, 1828, Clay "mentioned an imprudent movement of Tudor's to procure an application from the Peruvian Government to Great Britain and the United States for a joint mediation to protect Peru from the oppressive and usurping designs of Bolivar." Adams "disapproved this project" as "both unnecessary and impracticable. . . ." Adams, Memoirs, VII, 483–84.

From HENRY WHEATON, Copenhagen, "Private." States that he will "only write officially when" he has "something of a positive character to communicate. . . ." Reports that he has "as yet written only one official note to Count Schimmelmann, & that a very short one relating exclusively to the claim represented by Mr. [John]

Connell" (cf. above, Connell to Clay, May 24, 1827; Clay to Wheaton, May 31, 1827); that he believes an informal approach, "making, in a friendly manner & spirit, a lively impression of our resolution to insist upon the general Claims" will be more productive than "a written correspondence," in which the Minister might commit himself to "a particular line of argument"; and that the Danish plea "of *poverty*" is made with reason. Notes the causes of the impoverished condition of the country and suggests compromise as the only hope for accomplishing anything relative to the claims. Cites his assertion to Schimmelmann, concerning the case pressed by Connell: "that my Government considered the justice of the claim so absolutely clear as not to admit of any compromise without the consent of the claimants themselves. . . ." Expresses a belief that an offer will be made to Connell and that the case of the claimants may not be "so free from all doubt as we have felt our duty to represent." Observes that he is making a study of Danish commercial regulations, that Denmark refuses to adhere to the terms of British legislation concerning colonial trade, and that he expects the government "*to follow Russia* in their measures respecting" the South American Republics. Comments on the composition of the diplomatic corps in Copenhagen. ALS. DNA, RG59, Dip. Disp., Denmark, vol. 1B (M41, R3). Received March 28, 1828.

MISCELLANEOUS LETTERS   November 20, 1827

To CHARLES S. HEMPSTEAD. Acknowledges receipt of his letter of October 29, with enclosures; states that instructions are being sent to (Alexander H.) Everett (above, this date) and "our Consul at the Havana" (Thomas M. Rodney, above, this date) "to demand the discharge of" Hempstead's brother (Thomas W. Hempstead) and that "The letters from his family . . . will also be forwarded. . . ." Adds: ". . . if . . . there should appear to be legal cause for your brother's imprisonment, Mr. Everett has, nevertheless, been instructed to employ his good offices to procure his discharge." Expresses regret that, "for the want of legal authority," he cannot comply with the request to direct monetary assistance to the brother. Copy. DNA, RG59, Dom. Letters, vol. 22, pp. 89–90 (M40, R20).

On December 20, 1827, Hempstead acknowledged receipt of this letter. ALS, in DNA, RG59, Misc. Letters (M179, R65).

From Simón Bolívar

To His Excellency Henry Clay
Secretary for the Department of Foreign Relations & & &
Sir,   Bogota 21st. November 1827.
   I cannot defer availing myself of the opportunity at the departure of Mr. Watts Chargé d'Affaires of the United States of America, to express the great respect which I have for your Excellency.
   For a considerable time I have been animated with this desire, with the object to impart to Your Excellency my admiration for your brilliant talents, and your affectionate love of liberty. All America, Colombia and myself, owe to your Excellency the most perfect gratitude for the incomparable, and distinguished services which you have rendered in sustaining our Cause with the most sublime enthusiasm.— Receive then this sincere and cordial testimony which I have hastened to pay

your Excellency, and to the Government of the United States, which has contributed so much to the emancipation of her brothers in the South.

Mr. Watts by his conduct in Colombia has merited our high esteem and consideration: He has won the estimation of the government of the Republic. For my own part I must declare that the manner in which he has conducted himself in this country has been very satisfactory to its most illustrious citizens.

I have the Honor to offer to your Excellency, the distinguished consideration with which I am Your Excellency's most obedient attentive Servant.— BOLIVAR

Trans., in Beaufort T. Watts' hand. DNA, RG59, Dip. Disp., Colombia, vol. 4 (M-T33, R4). A variant translation, not significantly different in content, was published in *Niles' Weekly Register*, XXXVIII (April 24, 1830), 172–73, reprinted from Washington *Daily National Journal*, April 17, 1830. The original Spanish document has not been found. Received February 11, 1828.

DIPLOMATIC NOTES   November 21, 1827

From CHARLES R. VAUGHAN, Washington. Acknowledges receipt of Clay's note (of November 17). States that ". . . the Territory in which the proceedings have occurred lately, and which form [*sic*] the subject of Mr. Clay's note, is still in dispute" and that, consequently, "The Sovereignty and jurisdiction over that Territory has . . . remained with Great Britain, having been in the occupation & possession of the Crown previously to the conclusion of the Treaty of 1783." Expresses his conviction, "that Mr. Clay will agree with him, that there cannot be any grounds for complaint of an undue and illegal evercise of jurisdiction, whatever motive there may be, for remonstrance against the severity, with which, the Laws may have been executed."

Reports having received a letter from the Lieutenant Governor of New Brunswick, Sir Howard Douglas, dated September 11, informing him "that an alien of the name of [John] Baker, residing in a British Settlement on the Madawaska, had on the 18th July last, interrupted the passage of the mail from New Brunswick to Canada by the long established road, through that Settlement"; that Douglas, "feeling that it was his duty as Lt. Governor not to abandon any right of practical Sovereignty, which had been exercised in the disputed Territory, which has been held, occupied, & located as British Settlements for any period within the last Century, or even later, he considered, that the report which had been made to him of the conduct of Baker, was fit matter for the cognizance of the Law Officers of the Crown; and His Excellency accordingly directed the Attorney General [Thomas Wetmore] to take such measures as he might deem necessary to enforce the Municipal laws of the Province, and to repress and punish the disorders which had been committed." Transmits documents sent by Douglas at the time of the arrest, and reports not having received any information about subsequent proceedings.

Comments that Clay "will observe in the enclosed depositions, that Baker and others asserted, that in the measures which they took, they would be supported by the Government of the United States." Assures Clay that the Governor of New Brunswick "is convinced, that the Government of the United States, was not in any shape aware of the intentions of Baker and his associates," but adds that "the offensive conduct of Baker was not confined to stopping the Mail, . . .

that he had hoisted the Flag of the United States, in defiance of British Claims, and had sought to engage a Party, in an Ancient British Settlement, to transfer the possession to the United States."

Concludes by noting the resolution of Douglas "to maintain the disputed Territory in the same state in which His Excellency received it, after the conclusion of the Treaty of Ghent"; states his own conviction "that a mutual spirit of forbearance animates the General Government of the United States"; and comments that "too much vigilance cannot be exerted by the Authorities on both sides, to remove that apprehension [caused by the territorial dispute], and controul all misconduct arising out of it." LS. DNA, RG59, Notes from British Legation, vol. 14 (M50, R15). Published with enclosures in *American State Papers, Foreign Relations*, VI, 633–36.

Wetmore, a native of New York, had moved as a youth, in 1783, to New Brunswick, studied law, and entered the bar in 1788. He had been elected to the Provincial legislature in 1809 and the same year had been appointed attorney general. He retained that office until his death in 1828.

INSTRUCTIONS AND DISPATCHES   November 21, 1827

From BEAUFORT T. WATTS, Bogotá, no. 40. Reports that he has notified (Joseph R.) Revenga of his intention to take a leave of absence, because of ill health (cf. above, Watts to Clay, December 27 (2), 1826; June 27, 1827; Clay to Watts, March 8, 1827). Discusses the inadequacy of his salary and the high cost of living in this post as partial justification for his "taking temporary leave. . . ." States that he will probably remain in Cartagena until he hears from his government. Observes that Bolívar "is anxious to" remove the capital (of Colombia) to a site near Cartagena, a step "objected to upon grounds of economy and the conveniences already offered in Bogota, of its having public offices at the disposition of government—a recent and ruinous Earthquake in this city has driven away this pretext by rendering uninhabitable the greater part of the buildings. . . ."

Encloses his accounts, which he has not forwarded because of his expectation of returning to the United States, and warns that he may "be compelled . . . to draw for a quarters salary in advance." Encloses, also, other documents, including a translation of a letter, "the original of which . . . [he] will deliver in person," from (Simón) Bolívar to Clay (above, this date), and the copy of a note he has sent the Minister of Foreign Affairs (Revenga) concerning the case of the *Josephine* (cf. above, Anderson to Clay, March 18, 1825, note; Clay to Anderson, September 16, 1825; Clay to Watts, March 8, 1827). ALS. DNA, RG59, Dip. Disp., Colombia, vol. 4 (M-T33, R4). Received February 10, 1828.

MISCELLANEOUS LETTERS   November 21, 1827

To N[INIAN] EDWARDS, Belleville, Illinois. Acknowledges receipt of Edwards' letter of November 1, with its enclosures. States: "Although the letter of Govr. [Francisco Dionisio] Vives is of a confidential nature, I think we may safely rely upon the fidelity of the Mail for its regular conveyance, with any other papers left by Mr. [Daniel P.] Cook, which, it is natural, we should obtain— I should be glad, therefore, if they could be all put under secure cover, and transmitted by the first Mail.—" Closes by expressing "lively regret . . . on account of the death of Mr. Cook; and tendering to his afflicted family . . . sincere condolence." Copy. DNA, RG59, Unofficial Letter-Book of H. Clay, 10.

From RICHARD BACHE, Philadelphia. Requests, for use in his trial, "on Monday next," on a charge of assaulting John Binns, "a certified copy, under Seal, of the commission or appointment of Mr. Binns as Printer of the Laws of the United States." ALS. DNA, RG59, Misc. Letters (M179, R65). Endorsed at top of letter: "The Commonwealth of Penna vs. Richard Bache} Supreme Court of Penna. Indictment for an Assault upon John Binns Esqr, Alderman of the City of Philadelphia whilst in the execution of the duties of his office." Cf. above, Green to Clay, July 21, 1827, note.

From WILSON P. HUNT, St. Louis. Recommends John Perry and Company to supply "shot and other Castings" for the Army and Navy. Asserts that Perry is "one of those enterprizing men who has [*sic*] gone as far as any individual in the State in developing its resources, and now is one of the proprietors of Infant Iron Works located in the vicinity of inexhaustable beds of the finest Iron-Ores. . . ."
Concludes: "Well knowing the feelings you have always manifested towards Missouri (and I beg you to believe that they are here duly appreciated) and not being otherwise known to either the Secretary of the Navy [Samuel L. Southard] or War Department [James Barbour], I hope I run no risk in offering you this statement." ALS. DNA, RG45, Misc. Letters Recd., 1827, vol. 7. Endorsed on cover in Clay's hand: "Referred to the Secy of the Navy. H C." Cf. below, Southard to Clay, January 5, 1828.

From CHARLES TURELL, "Portsmouth, N. H." Solicits appointment of the (Portsmouth) *Commercial Advertiser* to publish the laws of the United States. Asserts: "It is a fact, perhaps of which you are not aware, that the [Portsmouth] *New Hampshire Gazette*, which now holds the appointment, and which has enjoyed that privilege many years is one of the most bitter of all in the country, against the administration. It is edited by [Levi] *Woodbury*, whose character as a Senator of the United States is too well known to need explanation." Notes that he was himself "very early" urged to take up the "course of the *Opposition*," but rejected it, and that the *New Hampshire Gazette*, "which had advocated the Republican cause for thirty years, and which had been recently in favor of this Administration," then appeared "in favor of Jackson." Transmits a petition (Sheafe and others to Clay, November 12, 1827) in behalf of the *Commercial Advertiser*. ALS. DNA, RG59, P. and D. of L.
The Portsmouth *New Hampshire Gazette*, founded as early as 1756, was nominally edited by Abner Greenleaf, the first mayor of Portsmouth, at this time and for many years postmaster of that city, and a close associate of Woodbury. The *New Hampshire Gazette* retained the printing patronage throughout the Adams administration.

Testimonial for John Brannan and Uriah Brown

RECOMMENDATIONS.   [*ca.* November 22, 1827]
After an attentive examination of the Prospectus to which this is subjoined, at the request of J. Brannan and U. Brown, I express with much satisfaction the opinion which I have formed, that the publication which they propose will be very useful. Similar works are published in France & England,[1] & have there been found advantageous. The Patent Office is a valuable repository, the contents of which, though accessible to all, are known to but few. By placing them within

the convenient reach of every one, the patentee, the man of inventive
genius, (to whom it is important to possess accurate knowledge of
abortive as well as successful essays,) and [t]he community at large may
be benefitted.   H CLAY.

Washington *Daily National Journal*, November 23, 1827. Cf. above, Bartow and Brannan to Clay, August 6, 1827, and note.
1 Probably a reference to Diderot and others, *Encyclopédie, ou Dictionnaire Raisonné
des Sciences, des Arts et Métiers* (cf. above, Clay to Brown, June 24, 1826; Brown to Clay,
August 12, 1826); and *The Repertory of Arts and Manufactures; Consisting of Original
Communications, Specifications of Patent Inventions, and Selections of Useful Practical
Papers. . .* , published originally in 16 volumes, London, 1794–1802; as a second series,
46 volumes, London, 1802–1825; and updated through 1862. The latter work had been
cited in an editorial in Washington *Daily National Journal*, November 19, 1827.

From Susan Wheeler (Mrs. Stephen) Decatur

My dear Mr Clay,   [*ca.* November 22, 1827]
    I hope you believe that I have too much regard for you, to wish to
incommode you even for my own gratification; but if you cou'd honor
me with your company on Monday Evening Next, to meet some of my
Diplomatic friends, you wou'd greatly oblige me; and still more so if
you cou'd prevail upon Mrs Clay to favor me with her company—
    Most of the European *Corps* who have come to this Country since
I have been out of society, have brought letters of introduction to me;
and I am afraid they may be led to conclude, from seeing that the
Secretary of State holds no communication with me, that it proceeds
from some want of respectability on my part— That the Government,
or rather the late president, has excluded me from the society of
Washington, is most true! not for any fault of mine, but by reinstating
and honoring those whose greatest merit is that of having taken my
belov'd husband's valuable life![1]— persons with whom, cost what it
may, I never can, nor never will associate!—But I beg you to

AL, fragment. DLC-HC (DNA, M212, R3). See below, Clay to Decatur, November 25,
1827.
1 Cf. below, Decatur to Clay, November 25, 1827.

From Peter B. Porter

Dear Sir,   Black Rock Nov: 22d. 1827
    Your favour of the 2d. inst.,[1] addressed to me at New York, was re-
ceived, several days ago, through the post office in this place, in accordance with instructions left with the Post Master in N. York,[2] to
forward my letters by mail. I have been thus particular in noticing this
circumstance because, in a letter I received this morning from Judge
Rochester,[3] he informs me that you were apprehensive that your letter

had not been received, and that, on an application at the post office in New York, he could get no information respecting it.

I am pleased to learn that no objection will be made to the proposed delay in the settlement of my accounts. In addition to the reasons which I assigned for the postponement, I had another inducement which I could not with propriety mention at that time. I had just heard of my nomination for the assembly, and if elected (as has turned out to be the case)[4] a journey to Washington in the winter would interfere with my legislative duties. I wish you, however, to understand that I shall consider my official duties as commissioner, & of course my salary, as terminating at the time appointed by Mr. Barclay[5] & myself for the exchange of our separate reports, which will be on the 24th. of December.

You are apprised of the extraordinary result of our late elections.[6] It has been produced, *in the country*, by strategem & party discipline on the part of the Jacksonians, and by apathy a [*sic*] want of concert among the friends of the administration. By a recent understanding & agency among the friends of Van Buren & Clinton, in a large proportion of the interior counties, our nominating conventions (composed generally of a few active partizans) have been induced to take up candidates devoted to their views—New presidential predilections having been carefully kept out of sight untill it was too late to correct the error.[7] The efficacy of their regular nominations was strikingly exhibited in the election of Mr Tracy (brother of Albert H.) to congress in place of Evans resigned.[8] The district comprises the large county of Genesee (where there is more Jacksonian strength than in any other of our western counties) and the small county of Orleans. Tracy was regularly nominated without reference to, & probably without any knowledge of his opinions in regard to the presidential candidates. Having been forced to avow his sentiments which proved to be favourable to the Administration, the Jacksonians of the district called another convention & nominated a Jackson candidate; at the same time denouncing Tracy as an Adams Man—and yet Tracy was elected by an unprecedented majority of 4000. votes in these two counties. At the same election three members of assembly who had been regularly nominated, were chosen, almost by default in Genesee, two of whom are claimed by the opposition papers as Jacksonians.[9]

On the whole, I do not consider the election as affording any fair test of the sentiments of the people of this state, a decided majority of whom, I am still satisfied, are with the administration.

Mr. Adams' ultimate success, however, in this state will, I think, depend much on the progress & fate of the Tariff question. If he is, as we understand him to be, really friendly to the American System, it would seem to me that he ought to give some decided & unequivocal expression of his views on that subject in his coming message.[10] It is so much the favourite policy & prominent topic of the politicians of the North that the friends of Genl. Jackson do not hesitate to place his superior claims to the presidency on the ground of his having publicly advocated & voted for the tariff, while Mr Adams has maintained a profound silence on the subject.[11] I think too that no eff[ort] should be spared to bring the tariff question early and distinctly before both houses of Congress, in such a manner as to shew who are its *real* friends.

I intended to have written you on the subject of the vice presidency. For the present, however, I will only say that my views accord entirely with those of Judge Rochester & Judge Thompson,[12] & that I will write you more fully on the subject on my arrival at Albany, if not sooner. Mr Taylor or Marvin[13] can give you more satisfactory information in regard to the characters & opinions of our members than I can. I was elected to the Assembly by a very large majority, & probably should have obtained nearly all the votes of this county, but for a partial division in four or five towns occasioned by the *Morgan mania.*[14]

The western counties of the State have very uniformly returned (as I predicted they would) Admn. members to the Legislature.   very respectfully & truly yrs   P. B. PORTER
Hon. H. Clay

ALS. DLC-HC (DNA, M212, R3). Endorsed on cover: *"Private."*   [1] Not found.
[2] Theodorus Bailey.   [3] William B. Rochester.   [4] Cf. above, Porter to Clay, November 6, 1827.   [5] Anthony Barclay.   [6] Cf. above, Sergeant to Clay, October 24, 1827, note.   [7] Cf. above, Strong to Clay, November 12, 1827.   [8] Phineas L. Tracy, a Batavia lawyer, filled the vacancy created by the resignation of David E. Evans. Connecticut-born Tracy, who had been graduated from Yale College in 1806, served in Congress until 1833. He was a Whig presidential elector in 1840 and presiding judge of the Genesee County court from 1841 until 1846.   [9] Republicans of Genesee County friendly to Jackson's presidential candidacy had met at LeRoy on October 24 and designated Judge William H. (incorrectly transcribed as "U," above, Evans and others to Clay, June 25, 1825) Tisdale to oppose Tracy. The latter received 5,481 votes to Tisdale's 1615. *Albany Argus,* October 31, November 22, 1827. The same meeting had approved the regular nominations of Porter for the State Senate and of Trumbull Cary, John B. Skinner, and Dennis Blakeslee as Assemblymen. Cary had settled in Batavia before the War of 1812 and shortly thereafter had become postmaster. He held that office for nearly 20 years and was a merchant and banker. Following his term in the Assembly he entered the State Senate and served for several years during the early 1830's. Skinner was already representing Genesee County in the Assembly and continued in that seat at least through 1828 and 1829. Blakeslee has been found only in the Assembly of 1828. All, as well as both Tracy and Tisdale, were publicly categorized as "anti-masonic"; but other than Tisdale, they have not been identified in relation to their views on Jackson.
[10] Adams made no reference to tariff policy in his third annual message, on December 4, 1827. He noted in his diary on November 30 that (Henry C.) Martindale had urged that the annual message include "an earnest recommendation of protection to domestic manufactures" and had emphasized the importance of the issue in western New York. Adams had replied "that the friends of the Administration in the South were equally urgent that nothing should be said upon the subject, and, on full deliberation, . . . [he] had concluded that would be the safest course—particularly as to take side prematurely would appear to interfere improperly for the purpose of exercising an influence over the House." He did promise to approve the report of the Secretary of the Treasury in recommending tariff increases. Adams, *Memoirs,* VII, 365. Secretary Richard Rush's report, transmitted on December 8, 1827, called for increased duties on woolen goods and foreign wool, fine cottons, bar iron, and hemp. *House Docs.,* 20 Cong., 1 Sess., no. 4, pp. 15–27.
[11] Cf. above, Porter to Clay, August 19, 1827, note; also, Remini, *Election of Andrew*

Jackson, 74–75. As a member of the United States Senate Jackson had voted for the tariff of 1824. U. S. Sen., *Journal*, 18 Cong., 1 Sess., p. 401.   12 William B. Rochester; Smith Thompson—cf. above, Rochester to Clay, October 12, November 4, 1827.   13 John W. Taylor; Dudley Marvin.   14 William Morgan—cf. above, Webster to Clay, November 5, 1827, note.

From William Sample

Washington, Pa Nov 22d. 1827—

Dear Sir   I received yours of the 5th. inst.[1] and would have answered it forthwith, but was desirous of seeing Mr Edward MGlaughlin [*sic*],[2] and delayed until I could ascertain whether he was at home before I would visit his residence. I have been told that he is not yet got home. Soon after I last seen you I paid him a visit: he was then absent. I waited some time expecting to see him in town, in this my expectations were not realized. On further inquiry I understood that he had went on a journey to Indiana and is still absent. As soon as he returns to this county I will loose no time in seeing him. This is the only apology for my not performing my promise. I have not forgot the obligation— Should you think proper to make use of the statement, in the mean time, I have no objections. It is in these words: On general Jacksons return home from the city of Washington, in the spring of 1825, in the house of John Chambers, in West Alexandria [*sic*],[3] Pa. Edward MGlaughlin, of Washington County, was introduced to the gen. Jackson,   after the usual salutations, Mr MGlaughlin remarked "well general we done all we could for you here, but the rascals at Washington City Cheated you out of it!" Indeed, replied Gen. Jackson, "my old friend there was cheatery [*sic*], and bribery too, the editors of the National Intelligencer,[4] were bribed to suppress the publication of honest George Kremer's letter."[5]

The above was the result of the interview between MGlaughlin and general Jackson, at the time and place and which, I expect to get Mr McGlaughlin to give a certificate of as soon as I can see him.[6] I would have got the statement from him ere this had it been possible.

My eldest son, David Sample, is desirous of applying for a warrant for admission, into the military academy at West Point.[7] He has got his papers, &c. ready to be forwarded by the hon. Mr. Lawrence,[8] who leaves home in a few days for Washington City. He is in his 17th year, and almost 6 feet high. Shall I ask your interest in his behalf? Should you feel at liberty to give him your interest in his application, I will consider it as a special favor conferred upon your Most obedient humble servant   WM SAMPLE

Hon. Henry Clay Washington City

LS. DLC-HC (DNA, M212, R3).   1 Not found.
2 Not identified.   3 Chambers, not further identified, had been a leader of dissident Republicans in Washington County as early as 1820. Cf. Russell J. Ferguson, *Early Western Pennsylvania Politics* ([Pittsburgh], 1938), 263.   West Alexander was a small borough

on the National Road, 16 miles east of Wheeling.   4 Joseph Gales, Jr., and William
W. Seaton.   5 Cf. above, Bard to Clay, March 15, 1825, note. For a statement con-
cerning its rejection of Kremer's letter to his constituents, see Washington *Daily National
Intelligencer*, February 28, 1825.   6 Sample's version of the McLaughlin-Jackson
conversation, as here reported, was published in Clay's *Supplement to the Address . . .
to the Public*, 5 (cf. below, June 10, 1828).   7 Young Sample was not admitted to the
United States Military Academy and has not been further identified.   8 Joseph
Lawrence.

INSTRUCTIONS AND DISPATCHES   November 22, 1827

From W[ILLIAM] B[EACH] LAWRENCE, London, no. 9. Notes that since his dispatch
of November 4, "no further news has reached London either from the fleet or
from Constantinople." States that "The order in Council, respecting the depredations of Greek Privateers," published in "the [London] 'Times' of yesterday, one
of the journals now forwarded," was adopted in response to "forcible complaints"
by London merchants. Reports that "It is now understood" that Parliament will
not meet until February and explains that "the Ministry are anxious to put the
Portuguese and Turkish affairs in a more settled state" before it assembles. Observes that the death of (George) Canning has "disarmed" much of the opposition
to the Ministry; discusses English politics, party leaders, and the power of the
King (George IV), who on "Two or three occasions . . . has seemed almost ommip-
otent. . ."; and concludes that "The opposition is not so much directed against
the members who belonged to Lord Liverpool [*sic*] government [cf. above, Gallatin
to Clay, February 22, 1827] or indeed even to Lord Dudley, as it is to the Marquis
of Lansdown and some of those who fill subordinate offices and have been known
as leading Whigs." ALS. DNA, RG59, Dip. Disp., Great Britain, vol. 35 (M30,
R31).

   The London *Times* of November 21, 1827, had reprinted from the *London Gazette* of November 20, an Order in Council dated November 16, 1827, which, after
alluding to the increase in "depredations which have for some time been committed upon the commerce of His Majesty's subjects in the Mediterranean seas by
armed vessels, piratically cruising under the Greek flag," decreed that "British
naval forces in the Mediterranean" should seize and send into some British port
"every armed vessel which they shall meet with . . . under the Greek flag," excepting military vessels acting under orders of the Greek Government.

To Joseph Nourse

Dept. of State, Washington Nov. 23, 1827.
[Transmits statement of estimated expenses of the Department for
the year 1828.]

   Copy. DNA, RG59, Dom. Letters, vol. 22, pp. 172–73 (M40, R20).
   Entries in the enclosure are the same as those on the estimate for 1827 (above, Clay to
Nourse, November 16, 1826), with the following exceptions: to the compensation for
clerks is added, under the Act of March 2, 1827 (cf. above, Clay to McLane, January 14,
1826, note), the sum of $4,400; the expenditure for printing the laws relates to the acts
passed by the First Session of the Twentieth Congress; the expenditure for "Distribution
of the Acts of Congress" is reduced to $3,000; no salary is provided for a Minister to
Chile (cf. above, Allen to Clay, November 4, 1825; Clay to Allen, November 1, 1826); the
total sum for salaries for the six remaining Ministers is $54,000; salaries provided for
nine Chargés d'Affaires, including one in Chile (Samuel Larned—cf. above, Clay to
Larned, November 4, 1826), amount to a total of $40,500; earlier entries for outfits are not
repeated; provision is made for an "Outfit of a Minister at London [cf. below, Clay to

Henry, December 27, 1827, note] 9,000" and "Outfit of Chargé d'Affaires at Chile and Brazil [William Tudor], and to cover an outfit to the present Chargé d'Affaires at Colombia [Beaufort T. Watts] 13,500"; "Salaries of the Secretaries of Legation" are diminished to $12,000; from the running total of expenses for foreign posts, a deduction of $100,000 is made "for unexpended balance of former Appropriations, remaining in the Treasury, applicable to this object," leaving a balance of $49,000; and the item covering expenses under "the 6th. & 7th. Articles of the Treaty of Ghent" is not repeated (cf. above, Porter to Clay, October 26, 30, 1827). "Salaries of the Commissioners and clerk for adjusting & distributing claims to indemnification, under the first Article of the Treaty of Ghent from the expiration of the appropriation to the end of the next session of Congress [cf. above, Clay to McLane, January 15, 1827, note]—Relief and protection of distressed American Seamen in Foreign Countries" require the sum of $25,000, "From which deduct for unexpended balances of former appropriations remaining in the Treasury applicable to this object—16,000." Under the headings, "Expenses of intercourse with the Barbary powers—Contingent Expenses of Foreign Intercourse," it is noted that the "balance of former appropriations for the two last objects being sufficient—Nothing is required to be appropriated therefor, for the year 1828.—" The total appropriation required is $118,000.

From Francis T. Brooke

My Dear Sir   Novr 23 1827
    I have this moment Seen The Whig[1] of wednesday,   by it you will See what is going on at Richmd,   Sidney who is B W Leigh[2] I have no doubt, has a new project—   he is pleased to Say, I have not entire confidence in the qualifications of the President and his Cabinet, but I have in their personal integrity and fair intentions towards the country—,   what ground of opposition then has he left for Mr Clinton[3] his qualifications are in Some degree upon trust, and his integrity very doubtful—   what will Mr Johnson[4] Say to this, these two gentlemen with very good intentions I have no doubt are playing a Safe game for Genl Jackson   it is not to be expected that his friends will give him up on this new ground, and as little can it be expected that the friends of the admn will give it up to elect a man never popular in Virginia, I fear these divisions will ruin a cause growing more promising every day—   I would certainly prefer Mr Clinton to Genl Jackson—but what prospect is there that the east and the west will come into the project, I am just Setting out to Richmd   Your friend   FRANCIS BROOKE

ALS. InU. Addressed to Clay.
1 Richmond *Constitutional Whig*, November 21, 1827.   2 Cf. above, Clay to Brooke, May 25, 1827, note.   3 DeWitt Clinton. "Sidney" had commented that Jackson had no qualifications for office and himself suggested Clinton as an alternative to either Adams or Jackson.   4 Chapman Johnson. The remarks had been written for the guidance of the upcoming Richmond Convention (cf. above, Mercer to Clay, August 18, 1827, note), addressed through Johnson as a delegate.

From Franklin Litchfield

Honble. Henry Clay Washington City D. Colombia [*sic*]
Dear sir,   Private   Puerto Cabello Nov. 23d 1827
    Your very esteemed and valued private Letter of the 12th. September[1] was duly received in answer to mine of the 30th July last, as pre-

sented you by my friend Mr Royal Phelps which was accompanied with a Bust of the Liberator President Bolivar.

It affords me much satisfaction to learn that said present was acceptable to you, and I flatter myself that the most favourable prognostics relative to the public measures and administration of that immortal Patriot and individual will on all occasions and at all times correspond to the best wishes of the devout friends of Colombian Independence and Liberty, as well as the personal Glory and reputation of the great and exalted standing of this distinguished Warrior and Statesman; and permit me here to insert what I have communicated to one of my friends and distinguished Member of the House of Representatives in allusion to this celebrated character that "he who has acquired such imperishable honours in the brilliant Career of Glory, the Liberator Bolivar will never eclipse his fame by adopting coercive Measures in opposition to the public Weal, for I am perfectly convinced that he will be the Champion of Liberty wherever he goes." This opinion I am rejoiced to state has been confirmed by the August Act of having taken the oath as prescribed in the existing Constitution of Colombia on his entrance into the Capital of this Republic as communicated to you in my Letter of the 20th. October last. I have suggested to my worthy friend the Honble. Edward Everett of Boston, and have taken the liberty to state the same now to you, my views on the propriety of the appointment of a special Agent under the Title of Consul General for Colombia, or the four Departments of Venezuela, Marturin [sic], Orinoco & Tulia to reside at Caracas the Capital of the aforesaid four Departments.

I have given details to Mr. Everett on this particular which I trust will meet with your approbation, as it is probable he will mention to you my ideas on said subject, as well as the propriety and necessity of allowing a Competent Salary to our Consuls in foreign Countries, in order that they may devote the whole of their time and services to the advancement of our National Welfare, and not be involved, as they now are in the bustle of Mercantile pursuits in order to procure an uncertain subsistence in their Consulates.[2] Nothing, permit me to observe, would contribute so much to the dignity and respectability of our beloved Country abroad as to allow an ample Salary to our Consuls as well as a certain sum of Money to be appropriated by them and all other public Agents of the U States, particularly in this Country for the Celebration of the 22d of February and especially the 4th. of July annually—the former in grateful remembrance of the August day which gave birth to the immortal Washington, the political Father of our Country, and the latter in commemoration of the glorious Anniversary of the Independence and Sovereignty of our great and rising Republic.

It will at all times be a source of much pleasure to me if I can render my Country any services in this Republic, where I have resided 14 years, provided they may be deemed useful and acceptable, especially if limited to the aforesaid Departments with a residence in Caracas, as my health has been considerably deteriorated in this place.

Your private advices on this subject would be a great desideratum with me.

I anticipate, Dear Sir, with pleasure the no distant period when our Presidential Chair may be filled by the distinguished and able Statesman & orater of Kentucky, whose Eloquence in the Common Councils of our native Country has been the admiration of his auditors, and his political Tenets and firmness of Character have given stability to our republican Institutions, and his transcendent Talents new honors to the well merited fame of American Diplomatists; and although the Laurels of the Hero of New Orleans are still verdant on the brow of every American, yet the Machinations of private intrigues and public declamation can never frustrate, the noble designs or retard the majestic march of the unsophisticated Patriotism, and exalted preeminence of our illustrious chief Magistrate, nor prevent the approaching reelection of him who stands firm on the broad basis of our national will, and our Nation's felicity, nor even effect the accession of another to the first Office in the Gift of the Citizens of our Union, when my present statesman shall have terminated his second term of Office. I am with the most profound respect Your very Obedient Servant

FRANKLIN LITCHFIELD

DLC-HC (DNA, M212, R3).   1 Not found.
2 No action was taken on Litchfield's proposals. By act of 1856 (11 *U. S. Stat.*, 52–65) United States consuls were finally given a fixed compensation in lieu of fees and those compensated more than $1500 annually were forbidden to engage in mercantile business.

INSTRUCTIONS AND DISPATCHES   November 23, 1827

To WILLIAM B[EACH] LAWRENCE, "Appointed Chargé d'Affaires to London," no. 1. Instructs him, by direction of the President, to take charge of American affairs at the British court "until a successor of Mr. Gallatin shall be appointed, and enter upon the duties of the mission, or until otherwise directed."

Informs him of the theft "of a very large sum" from the Petersburg office of the Bank of Virginia, by the teller, Nathaniel Snelson; of the flight of the thief to Quebec, where he boarded a vessel for Liverpool; of the bank's sending an agent, William B. Wood, to England in pursuit of him; and of a letter (not found—cf. below, Clay to Brockenbrough, November 26, 1827) to the Department of State, soliciting "the interposition of the Government of the United States with that of Great Britain, to have the person of Snelson delivered up to be returned to the U. S." Instructs him to make "application accordingly," to communicate to the British Government the enclosed documents, and to consult Wood for further information on the matter. Warns that the British Government is "under no obligation, by any existing treaty or by the public law, to surrender this fugitive" and directs him, "By way of strengthening the application," to remind that Government "of one . . . made to the Government of the United States" in the case of Michael Neilson (above, Vaughan to Clay, November 3, 1825; cf. also, above, Clay to Vaughan, November 10, December 29, 1825; Clay to Clinton, November 10, 1825; Clinton to Clay, December 19, 1825). Mentions "Another recent instance" in which a fugitive bank robber from Scotland was apprehended "without hinderance [sic]," in Savannah, Georgia, by an agent of the bank "and carried . . . back to the country from which he escaped.—" Copy. DNA, RG59, Dip. Instr., vol. 12, pp. 44–46 (M77, R7). ALI draft, in DLC-HC (DNA, M212, R8); extract published in House Docs., 21 Cong., 1 Sess., no. 66, pp. 4–5.

Snelson, "alias Maxwell," about age 50, has not been further identified. He had reportedly stolen some $40,000. Niles' Weekly Register, XXXIII (November 3, 1827), 146. On the outcome of the matter, see below, Lawrence to Clay, December 29, 1827, note.

Wood, apparently not the Canadian born actor and theater owner prominent at this time in Philadelphia, has not been further identified.

From JOHN C. GIBBES, "Saint Bartholomew." Reports that Robert M. Harrison has appointed him "Vice Consul, from the United States of America, to this Island" (cf. above, Harrison to Clay, July 14, 1827); encloses copies of his correspondence with local governing officials; notes that he cannot act "without the Document referred to by authorities here"; and suggests that Clay may wish to communicate with the American Chargé at Stockholm (John J. Appleton) in an effort to speed transmittal of that document (cf. above, Appleton to Clay, July 31, 1827). ALS. DNA, RG59, Cons. Disp., St. Bartholomew, vol. 1 (M72, R1). Received December 28.

The enclosures include Gibbes' request to local authorities for recognition of his appointment and their reply that, as they had already informed Harrison, "the Government of this Island Cannot recognize a Consul. . . , until his Diploma, with the Exequatur granted by His Majesty [Charles XIV] be presented. . . ."

Gibbes has not been further identified.

From CHRISTOPHER HUGHES, The Hague. Reports conversations with "A Mr. Richard Ward, of New York," who "requested to be permitted to explain . . . the object of his presence in Holland," where he has just arrived "at the express invitation of the Dutch Government. . . ." Calls attention to enclosures which "explain the nature, and objects, and terms, of Mr. Ward's visit to this Country" and adds that "Mr. [Cornelis Theodorus] Elout, Minister of the Marine," has named a commission to confer with Ward on the subject "of his Marine arm, (as he calls his invention!). . . ." Notes Ward's assertions "that he is rejected by his country"; that, after ten years of futile efforts to interest "the Navy Department and Navy Board, and corps of Engineers," in "his plan of Port defence and protection, . . . he had, at last, offered the benefit of his discoveries to a Third-rate Naval Power; a Power not merely friendly to his own Country, but the least likely to be in hostility with the United States"; and that "a specification and description" of his invention was "lodged several years ago . . . in the Patent Office. . . ." States his own favorable impression of Ward. ALS. DNA, RG59, Dip. Disp., Netherlands, vol. 8 (M42, R12). Received February 7, 1828.

Ward had patented in 1826 a "Railway marine," described as "preferable to the dry dock," in facilitating "careenage and repairs" of steam batteries for harbor and sea coast defence. House Docs., 21 Cong., 2 Sess., no. 50, p. 229; The Franklin Journal, and American Mechanics' Magazine. . . , III (January–June, 1827), 83.

Elout (1767–1841) had been commissioner general in colonial administration (1816–1819) and was now Minister of Marine and of Colonies (1824–1830).

To Henry B. Bascom

WASHINGTON, November 24, 1827.
My Dear Sir,—I duly received your letter of the 10th inst.,[1] in which you are pleased to ask my opinion of the utility of an agricultural professorship, which is proposed to be established in your college.[2] I think such a professorship, properly filled, and its duties performed with zeal and industry, would be productive of much benefit; and it could be no where better situated than in the fertile regions beyond the mountains. It would be a leading object with the professor, to teach the practical application of the sciences (chemistry especially) to agriculture; and also to bring into view the most approved implements of husbandry in use in different parts of the Union, and in other countries, as well as improvements which may be made from time to time.

With my best wishes for the success of your college in all its departments, I am, truly, your friend and obedient servant,

H. CLAY.

The Rev. Mr. BASCOM.

M[oses] M. Henkle, *The Life of Henry Bidleman Bascom* . . . (Nashville, 1891), 195.
[1] Not found.   [2] Madison College, Uniontown, Pennsylvania.

To Francis T. Brooke

My Dear Sir   (Confidential)   Washington 24 Nov 1827
I duly recd your favor of 20th inst. and most truly do I participate in the wish which it expressed that it was practible [*sic*] for us to have a personal interview.

On the affair of the V.P. it was understood at the last session, that at the one now near at hand the friends of the administration should bring together and compare the public opinion prevailing in the respective quarters of the country, as to the proper individual to be selected, and that measures should then be adopted to give effect to it,   As for myself I have no wish one way or the other about it so far as I am personally concerned,   One predominant desire prevails in my mind, and that is that the country shall be preserved from the calamity of the election of Genl. And. Jackson. To accomplish that object I am willing to renounce forever public life, and to resign this hour the station which I hold. I have also said, that if my name should contribute more than that of any other to his defeat, by being used for the office of V.P. I would acquiesce in its being so used. But I confess, I doubt myself whether my name would have, for the inferior office much effect on the issue of the contest for the superior One. And I am also inclined to believe that other names would answer as well as mine. I think however that it is better that the matter should remain as it dose [sic], until the meeting of Congress. Early in the Session (time enough I presume to communicate with our Virginia friends) the members will make the proposed comparison, and then the co-operation may be more effective.

On the other subject touched in your letter, the propriety of an address from the Convention about to assemble at Richmond,[1] I concur with you entirely as to its expediency. The occasion calls for it. It will be expected from the enlightened men there assembled. And the public will be disappointed if it be not able, patriotic and striking. There are so many members of the convention more competent than I am to suggest what should be its character and its contents that I will barly [sic] take the liberty of hinting, That it should make a powerful appeal to the uniform devotion of Virginia to the cause of human liberty, and to the providing of all possible guirantees [sic], of its presevation [sic].

That it should warn the people against the infatuation which has so often fatally attended Military renown.

That it should point to striking examples in other countries and times.

That it should dwell on those scenes which are passing around us—scenes which belong rather to a military campaign, (presenting as they do a succession of demonstrations) than to a peaceful civil election.

That they [sic] should hold up especially the resort which has been made to elections in numerous corps of the militia,[2] which is the first step, as the next and last is similar elections by the Pretorian [sic] Band,

That the people of Virginia, devoted as they always have been to the constitution, should be reminded, that they should not put the whole instrument at iminent peril, because some parts of it have been interpreted contrary to their judgement.

That the instrument is safe with Mr. Adams, from the formidable opposition that watches and scrutinizes all his acts, if not from his own disposition. Where as with his competition, with a drum sounding in evey [sic] village, and colors every where displayed, sustained by the whole martial spirit of the nation, the whole would be at hazard, especially where experience has shown that its most sacred provisions have been repeatedly disregarded by the idol of the opposition

Then I should think, you might awaken the magnanimity of Virginia. She has had four Presidents, the North but two.

Is it not her true interest to evince, that she is not actuated by selfish ambition?

The influence of Virginia can only be preserved in this Union by numbers or by moral power. The first she has not. The last she has; and what augmentation of it would she not produce, by making the present generation feel, and posterity own that she has thrown herself into the military crevasse which is letting in a fatal current threatening to sweep all before it!

Should the electors [*sic*] of Mr. Adams be secured by the aid of Virginia, to her weight distinctly would it [*sic*] be attributed.

She would then be the primary power, especially if both Penns. and N.York should unite on Gen J.

Whereas if all three of those states concur in supporting him, Virginia would be a mere satellite.

These hints are respectively [*sic*] suggested. They might be much extended; but I have neither time to enlarge them, or to throw them into the form of a regular composition.   I am acquainted with Mr Semple.[3] He is ardent in the cause, but thinks that he can aid more effectually by indirect than direct exertion. I am truly & cordially Your friend   H. Clay.

The Hon T. F. [*sic*] Brooke.

Copy. DLC-TJC (DNA, M212, R13).   [1] Cf. above, Mercer to Clay, August 18, 1827, note.   [2] See, *e.g.*, Washington *United States Telegraph*, October 20, 1827, reprinting from the Cincinnati *National Republican* a letter to the *Newark Advocate* on the polling of a Danville company muster. Cf. also Washington *Daily National Journal*, November 7, 1827.   [3] Robert B. Semple.

DIPLOMATIC NOTES   November 24, 1827

From Francisco Tacón, Philadelphia. Acknowledges receipt of Clay's note of October 31. States that the "Corvette Kensington . . . is not a merchant vessel"; that it "is a ship of war, built, and fitted out for the Government of Mexico, which may, as soon as delivered into its hands by those who, at present, style themselves her owners, make use of her against Spain. . ."; that the King of Spain (Ferdinand VII) "only asks that his enemies may not be assisted by these means, which the Public Law designates as contraband of war, because used immediately and exclusively in waging war."

Argues that the case cited by Clay in which Russia sold vessels to Spain is not analogous, since Russia does not consider Spain a belligerent, but "a Power at peace with the whole world," attempting to suppress an internal revolt. LS, in Spanish with trans. in State Dept. file. DNA, RG59, Notes from Spanish Legation, vol. 9 (M59, R-T12).

From Charles R. Vaughan, Washington. Transmits a copy of a letter just received from (Anthony St. John) Baker, "His Majesty's Consul General for the United States." Cites a New York law that empowers the State's Public Administrator "to take Possession of the Effects of British Mariners, who may die intestate, either on Board British Vessels or on Shore within the Limits of his Jurisdiction and to Administer to their Effects if, after a Notice of 30 days the next of kin does not appear." Points out that "It is next to impossible that a next of kin residing in England should appear within" the specified time and suggests that "the Government of the United States . . . recommend it to the Legislature of the State of New York, to modify the Law in question so as to exempt the Property of British Sailors" from its application. LS. DNA, RG59, Notes from British Legation, vol. 14 (M50, R15).

To Susan Wheeler (Mrs. Stephen) Decatur

My dear Madam.   Washington 25h. Nov. 1827.

I regret to have given you the concern which you have felt by adverting to the fact of the incomplete state in which I received your
first note.[1] It was only an omission, which all of us some times make,
to envelope the whole of a letter.

As the reason you assign in your note of yesterday[2] for withdrawing
yourself from society applies only to cases in which you apprehend you
may meet a description of persons,[3] whose presence will be disagreeable to you, ought we not to hope that you would favor us with your
company, when there is not the remotest danger of such an encounter?
It is, in the indulgence of such a hope, that Mrs. Clay and myself now
send you an invitation to a *diplomatic* dinner on friday next, at which
I am perfectly persuaded there will not be one person whom you will
not be willing to meet.

How can you think that my Republicanism is abating? Equality is
its very essence; and if we feel reluctantly compelled to deny ourselves
the gratification of visiting you, it is because of the want of that equality in the conditions of our mutual intercourse. You know that when
our respective circumstances were such as to admit of my waiting upon
you, without any obligation on your part to return the visit, that is
when Mrs. Clay was not with me, I never hesitated to pay you my
respects.

I really think, my dear Madam, you would promote greatly the happiness of your friends, and I should hope your own, by occasionally
mixing in our circles. Adequate security against the presence of unacceptable persons could always be provided. At present indeed I do
not know that any of the persons to whom you allude are in this City.

Whatever may be your determination, believe me most truly Your
friend & ob. Servt.   H. CLAY
Mrs. S. Decatur.

ALS. ViU.   [1] Above, *ca.* November 22, 1827; Clay's reply has not been found.
[2] Not found.   [3] Cf. below, Decatur to Clay, this date.

From Terence Cooney

Sir   Paris Tennessee, Nov. 25th 1827

Possibly you will recollect me as several years ago a resident of
Lexington—then of Frankfort, and subsequently as editing the "Green
River Correspondent" at Bowling green:[1] But whether I can claim to
be recognized as an acquaintance or not, I certainly have claims upon
your attention on two grounds— 1st. you was formerly my representative in Congress & 2ndly. You are the agent of the whole american
people, of whom I claim to be one— The object of this address is to

say, that I am informed by Mr. G W Terrell, the editor of the "West Tennesseean"[2] printed at this place, that the publishers of the acts of Congress &c. are to be selected during the approaching Session of Congress— The publishers of the Laws in this State have been very properly selected—one in East Tennessee—one in the middle section of the State,[3] & one in this District— The paper now enjoying the appointment in this District is the "Jackson Gazette" at Jackson— It was selected at the time when there was no other paper published in the district— The "West Tennessean" [sic] & the "Memphis Advocate"[4] have been established since— Mr. Terrell has determined to solicit the appointment when it is next made, & I have no hesitation in recommending him as more worthy of it than the present incumbent— Both papers have perhaps about an equal circulation— this place is rising rapidly into consequence while Jackson is on a stand—if not declining:—as to personal & professional merits—the highest intellectual effort that I have ever witnessed in the Jackson Gazette, was some wretched paragraph chiming in with the almost universal yell of the papers of this state, of "Bargain, barter & corruption"   It has been & is persevering, as foul & contemptible in its denunciations—as any other of the whole pack— Whilst Mr Terrill [sic] had the candor to say—on the appearance of Buchanans statement,[5] that it was downright absurdity to contend that it sustained Genl Jacksons charges—& that, unless the hero produced other & better testimony, he should be compelled to view his accusations as proceeding from the delusions of passion, & the administration as persecuted by interested calumniators:— The Jackson Gazette, on the other hand, could see no material disagreement between the Hero's accusations & Mr Buchanans statements! !

It may be well to state, that the Representative from this district (Mr Crockett)[6] is a man with whom neither Mr Terrell or myself can hold any sort of Communication— I therefore trouble you with this direct application— I believe the change[7] would at least be gratifying to all the friends of the administration— and they are numerous & respectable—in this Section

with great respect for your character as a man—& admiration of your public conduct I am &c.   TERENCE COONEY
Honl H Clay

ALS. DNA, RG59, P. and D. of L.

1 The only copies found are dated 1824, when Cooney was editor. He had also published the *Louisville Gazette* from October, 1825, until the following spring.

2 George Whitfield Terrell, born in Nelson County, Kentucky, in 1803, had moved to Tennessee as a youth and had been admitted to the bar in 1827. The following year he was named district attorney and from 1829 to 1836 attorney general. He moved to Mississippi in 1836 and to Texas in 1837. He held both legal and judicial appointments in the Texas Republic and in 1844–1845 served as its Chargé to France, Great Britain, and Spain. The Paris *West Tennesseean* had been founded in 1827.   3 *Knoxville Register; Nashville Banner and Whig.*   4 The Memphis *Advocate and Western District Intelligencer* ran from 1827 to 1833.   5 Cf. above, Ingersoll to Clay, August 11, 1827,

and note.   6 David Crockett.   7 No change was made during the remainder of
the Adams administration.

From Susan Wheeler (Mrs. Stephen) Decatur

My dear Mr Clay   George Town Nov. 25th 1827—
     I can with truth assure you that it wou'd afford me real pleasure to
accept your kind invitation for Tuesday [sic];¹ and I have no doubt
that I might do so with perfect safety, not only on that, but on many
other occasions; and yet in the course of a few years some of my best
friends might forget the peculiar circumstances of my dreadful calamity,² and I might perchance some day or other find myself in the
society of persons whom it is my strongest inclination, and my most
sacred duty forever to avoid!—and to effect this object, I never go into
the Street— I never go to any public place— I never travel in any public
conveyance and when I move from hence to Mr Carroll's,³ I rest at
some miserable hovel, the wretch'd appearance of which wou'd deter
any other traveller from approaching it— this is the course I have
pursu'd for nearly eight years— and this is the course I mean to pursue
so long as I and the authors of my calamity continue to inhabit the
same planet!—
     To such friends as may have the kindness occasionally to cheer my
desolation, I do, and shall continue to feel truly grateful; but I wou'd
rather live an *outlaw* from the whole human race, than to put it in the
power of accident to place me in the presence of persons, who so wan-
tonly, and wickedly, snatch'd from me one⁴ who, I can truly say, was
without spot or blemish!—one who for fourteen years, strew'd my daily
path with flowers! and never caus'd me a moment's pain save that
which sprung from my unbounded affection and anxiety for his preservation!— I consider the man⁵ who dealt the blow, by far the most
innocent of the three!—for he was goaded on by the envy and jealousy
of the others, who hated "the excellence they cou'd not reach"   a[s]
to Commodore Bainbridge,⁶ he and my husband had not been upon
speaking terms for four years; in consequence of his having made a
peace with Algiers before Commodore Bainbridge cou'd arrive there
with his Squadron; and I have reason to believe that he sought a reconciliation at the moment he did so, for the hope of being imploy'd [sic]
in the way he was imploy'd; and to gain the chance of ridding himself
of his rival, by the hand of another; and which he finally accomplish'd!—   My husband placed his life in the hands of Commodore
Bainbridge—he told him he did not think himself bound to meet
Commodore Barron, but that some of the officers had said he ought to
do so, and he did not think he had a right to act in any way that might
lessen their respect for him; and added, "under these circumstances I
wish you to do the best you can for me— I have no desire to lose my

own life, and nothing shall induce me to take his—" and with this knowledge, Commodore Bainbridge propos'd such such [sic] terms as render'd destruction to one or both inevitable—and knowing also that my husband was not a boy fighting for reputation—and yet he plac'd them close together, and made them take deliberate aim at each other. And Commodore Barron, seeing that the seconds were anxious to push things to extremities, said Commodore Decatur I hope we shall be better friends in another world than we have been in this!— My husband replied, "Sir I have never been your personal enemy—" and when Commodore Barron was about to offer his hand, Captain Elliott[7] order'd silence! and Commodore Bainbridge order'd them to "take aim"— Now if this was not cold blooded murder, I know not what it is! Associate with such Monsters? No-Never! I wou'd rather take my position in a State prison, and live in fellowship with avow'd cut-throats and robbers! for I believe them to be better men!— These are dreadful charges, but I have documents to prove them!

Commodore Bainbridge after having refus'd for three or four years to speak to my husband in consequence of the Treaty with Algiers,[8] made his overture towards a reconciliation in these words, "Decatur I have behav'd like a fool! but it is really vexatious that you always contrive to build reputation upon my bad luck! you began with the philadelphia[9] and you have wound up with Algiers ["]— Commodore Bainbridge commanded the Philadelphia when she was taken by the Tripolitans— and he was appointed to command the Squadron against Algiers but refus'd to sail until a seventy four cou'd be prepar'd for him— My husband went off in a frigate[10] and dictated a Treaty of peace!—

Commodore Bainbridge has always been remarkable for great prudence and caution wherever his own personal safety was concern'd; and it is therefore the more extraordinary that he shou'd have broken out in such a desperate manner the moment my husband's valuable life was plac'd in his hands! He dictated the desperate terms of the meeting with Commodore Barron—   I have his letters to prove it— and my husban[d X]

I had no intention, when I began this Note, to plague you with this horrid detail—   I therefore pray you to forgive me   Yours sincere[ly]
                                                              S. DECATUR

X thought that after having authoris'd him to prepare whatever terms he pleas'd, he w[as] bound in honor to abide by them— This he told a friend the night before his death— X   ]

ALS. DLC-HC (DNA, M212, R3). Some margins obscured in binding.
1 Cf. above, Clay to Decatur, this date.   2 Cf. above, II, 815n; III, 107n.
3 Probably Charles Carroll.   4 Stephen Decatur.   5 James Barron.
6 William Bainbridge.   7 Jesse D. Elliott.   8 Cf. above, II, 80n, 149, 158n.
9 The Philadelphia, a frigate of 36 guns, had been commissioned in 1800 and, at the request of the citizens of Philadelphia, who had financed her construction, she had been

first placed under the command of Decatur's father, Captain Stephen Decatur. The elder Decatur, who had privateered during the American Revolution and, under commission of the United States Navy in 1798, had captured the first prize of the naval war with France, had taken five additional prizes with the *Philadelphia* by March, 1801, when the conflict ended and he retired from service.   Under command of Captain Bainbridge in 1803 the *Philadelphia* had run aground off Tripoli, where she had been captured and her officers and men carried into bondage. In February, 1804, young Decatur, at the time a lieutenant, had led a boarding party which burned the frigate to forestall her use as a floating battery in harbor defense.   10 Decatur and Bainbridge had each been placed in command of squadrons in 1815 to compel Algiers to honor her treaty commitments with the United States. Decatur had been the first to complete preparations and set sail—with three frigates, one sloop, four brigs, and two schooners. His flagship was the *Guerriere*, commissioned in 1814, rated as a 44-gun frigate but mounted with 53.   By August 7, 71 days after sailing from New York, Decatur's force had effected the treaty with Algiers and settlement of claims for ship seizures by both Tunis and Tripoli. Bainbridge had not arrived at Gibraltar until September 29. There he had assembled the *Independence*, a ship-of-the-line; four frigates; two sloops of war; eight brigs; and three schooners. He had expected to reinforce Decatur but found the mission already completed. Irvin Anthony, *Decatur* (New York, 1931), 237–59 *passim*.

INSTRUCTIONS AND DISPATCHES   November 25, 1827

From W[ILLIAM] H. D. C. WRIGHT, Rio de Janeiro. Transmits copies of correspondence with "the Minister of Foreign Affairs [the Marquis of Queluz], in relation to the revisal of the decisions upon the Captured Vessels, by a 'Junta Consultiva'. . . ." ALS. DNA, RG59, Cons. Disp., Rio de Janeiro, vol. 3 (M-T172, R4). Received January 29, 1828.
    Among the enclosures are a letter signed by Queluz, October 24, 1827, and Wright's reply. In the latter Wright wrote: "To your Excellency's request that I would designate the cases, whose revising may be desired, I have to reply, that as none of those Captures are justified by the principles of blockade admitted by my Government, I can discover no ground upon which to base a distinction in the Cases, but conceive that they have equal claims to reconsideration.—" He then added: "Even in those cases in which the vessels have been restored, no damages having been awarded, for their (acknowledged) illegal detention, it is not to be presumed that the decisions have been satisfactory to my Government."

MISCELLANEOUS LETTERS   November 25, 1827

From THEODORE HUNT, St. Louis. Recommends John Perry and Company to supply "shot or shells for the Army & Navy or either of them." Notes that this "Iron establishment in Washington County in this State [Missouri]" is the "first and only one in operation." Concludes: "Had the contract been given *here*, the fact of Mess Jno Perry & Co. being friendly to the present administration would not I fear, in some instances, give them an equal chance with *others* if we can judge by what has already taken place—" ALS. DNA, RG45, Misc. Letters Recd., 1827, vol. 7. Cf. below, Southard to Clay, January 5, 1828.

Full Power to Negotiate with the Hanseatic Cities

[November 26, 1827]
[John Quincy Adams grants to Henry Clay "full power and authority, and also general and special Command to meet and confer

with the Minister Plenipotentiary of the Republics and free Hanseatic Cities of Lübec, Bremen and Hamburg, in the United States.[1] …"]

Copy. DNA, RG59, Ceremonial Communications, vol. 2, p. 71.   [1] Vincent Rumpff.

INSTRUCTIONS AND DISPATCHES   November 26, 1827

From A[LEXANDER] H. EVERETT, Madrid, no. 92. Encloses "translations of the late decree on the subject of purifications" and other documents, including "the duplicate of . . . [his] letter to the Count de Beaurepaire respecting the quarantine business . . ." (cf. above, Everett to Clay, November 8, 1826) and a copy of his note to (Manuel Gonzales) Salmón (dated November 21), transmitting the letter. Notes that "accounts from Catalonia continue favorable, and the insurrection may be considered as fairly crushed"; that "The Mission of the Viscount de Saint Priest" has been successful; and that French troops have been withdrawn from Barcelona. Reports having been assured by Salmón that, with reference to the quarantine, "the Duke de San Carlos will continue to sustain our application to the French Government" (cf. above, Everett to Clay, October 6, 1827). Observes that "The removal of the troops from Barcelona has . . . relieved our Commerce from the embarrassments in question at one of the two points where they were felt" but that he expects no change at Cádiz until troops are also withdrawn from that city. Comments on the importance of the allied victory at Navarino (cf. above, Ombrosi to Clay, November 6, 1827); interprets political developments in France (cf. above, Lafayette to Clay, October 10, 1827; Brown to Clay, November 12, 1827) as evidence of weakness of the Ministry; and expresses the opinion that in England "the hands of Govt. will be for immediate purposes strengthened rather than enfeebled by the effect of Mr. [George] Canning's death." Adds that Dom Miguel "will be accompanied from England by Mr. [Frederick James] Lamb . . . recently promoted to the place of Ambassador to Portugal." LS. DNA, RG59, Dip. Disp., Spain, vol. 28 (M31, R29). Received February 21, 1828.

From JOHN MULLOWNY, Tangier, no. 53. Reports that "the United States Ship Java under the command of Commodore W. M. Crane," on a brief visit to the port, failed to fire the customary salute; that the Bashaw (Mohamet Omemon) was displeased; but that the incident has been smoothed over. Incorporates in the dispatch copies of his correspondence with Crane and his communication to the Bashaw. ALS. DNA, RG59, Cons. Disp., Tangier, vol. 4 (M-T61, R4). Received February 23, 1828.

From DAVID OFFLEY, Smyrna. Reports that in "June last at the request of several American Merchants . . . [he] applied to the Govt. at Constantinople to know, wither [sic] American Merchant ships would be received in a friendly manner at that place & wither the rates of duties on their Cargoes would be regulated by the Tarif [sic] agreed on with . . . [him] for this place [Smyrna]"; that an answer was promised, twice; and that "On the 11th. Inst." he received an invitation "to visit Constle. as the moment was favorable for the termination of a Commercial treaty between the Porte and Govt. of the united States."
Discusses the case of "the Brig Cherub of Boston": the vessel, abandoned by her crew and the Greek privateers that had captured her, had been found by another Greek privateer and brought into port for salvage; "the U S. S. Warren arrived in search of the Cherub and took possession of her Capt. [Lawrence] Kearney giving to the Capt. of the privateer [George Leftery, not further identi-

fied] a declaration that she should be delivered to her Consignees here on Condition that they should pay such salvage as reason and justice demands"; the consignees refused to pay the sum demanded for salvage; Leftery applied to Offley to decide the issue by "Consular Tribunal"; Offley responded that the vessel "would proceed to Boston" and referred Leftery "to the Tribunals of that Country"; and Leftery is expected to "proceed to the United States for the prosecution of his claim."

Notes that there are "now four American Commercial establishments in this place who are ameanable [sic] to no other laws than those of the United States" and explains his method of settling disputes in which they become involved.

States that "The Ministers of Denmark (Baron de Hubsch-Grofsthal) and Naples (the Chevalier Romano) have obtained . . . the passage for their flags into the Black Sea"; that he understands "enquiries have been made . . . wither any person in this Country was authorized on the part of our Govt. to negociate a treaty with the Porte"; and that removal of the embargo at Constantinople "and other pacific measures lead to the expectation that the existing differences between the Allied Powers and the Porte will be amicably settled" (cf. above, Brown to Clay, July 12, November 13, 1827; Ombrosi to Clay, November 6, 1827). ALS. DNA, RG59, Cons. Disp., Smyrna, vol. 1 (M-T238, R-T1). Received March 8, 1828.

In 1815 Offley, after "personal application to the Government" at Constantinople, had obtained the establishment of tariff regulations for United States traders independent from consignment through English merchants and at duties "calculated on the European Tarifs to which an addition should be made of 15 P Cent—" His complaint at the persisting discrimination had met the reply "that if every concession was made to . . . [him] nothing would remain to be made to a minister or Agent . . . from the United States." Offley to John Quincy Adams, January 24, 1824, in ibid.

The Warren was a sloop of war commissioned at Boston in 1826 and assigned to the Mediterranean Squadron through 1830. Kearney, born in New Jersey, had entered the Navy in 1807 and had been raised to a lieutenant in 1813. Although given command of the Warren, he did not hold the rank of captain until 1832.

Baron de Hubsch-Grofsthal and the Chevalier Romano have not been further identified.

From WILLIAM TAYLOR, Veracruz. Reports "that the whole of the Mexican Naval forces are now in this port" and that he expects trouble "on account of the American Seamen who have entered on board of these vessels. . . ." Explains that, the terms of service for many of them having expired, these men "are now clamorous for their discharge and pay"; that, as "there is no money to pay them with," they will "claim the protection of this Consulate"; and that he will feel it his "duty to send them home as destitute an[d] distressed American Seamen." States that (David) Porter has commissioned one privateer and advertises that he is authorized to commission others to bring in for trial "neutral vessels found with ennemy's [sic] property on board." Adds that "The excitement against the Spaniards increases" so rapidly "that nothing short of their final expulsion will suffice" (cf. above, Taylor to Clay, November 2, 1827, note). ALS. DNA, RG59, Cons. Disp., Veracruz, vol. 1 (M183, R1). Received December 30.

MISCELLANEOUS LETTERS   November 26, 1827

To JOHN BROCKENBROUGH, "President of the Bank of Virginia." Acknowledges receipt of his "letter . . . of the 19th. instant [not found], soliciting the interposition of the Government of the United States with that of Great Britain for the purpose of obtaining the surrender of Nathaniel Snelson, charged with a robbery of the Bank of Virginia, and who has fled within the British dominions." Informs him that "the proper instructions" and his letter have been sent to William B. Lawrence (above, November 23, 1827). Copy. DNA, RG59, Dom. Letters, vol. 22, pp. 97–98 (M40, R20).

On December 1, Brockenbrough replied to Clay and conveyed his "thanks and those of the Directors of the Bank, for the prompt & kind interposition of the President & . . . [Clay] in this affair." ALS, in DNA, RG59, Misc. Letters (M179, R65).

To Enoch Lincoln

His Excellency Enoch Lincoln Portland Mne.
Sir,   Department of State Washington 27 Novr. 1827.

I have to acknowledge the receipt of the letter your Excellency did me the honor to address to me on the 16th. instant with its accompaniments, all of which have been laid before the President. He sees, with great regret, the expression of the sentiment of your Excellency that "Maine has not been treated as she has endeavored to deserve." Without engaging at this time in a discussion of the whole subject of our dispute with Great Britain about the North Eastern boundary of the United States, in which the State of Maine is so deeply interested, which would be altogether unprofitable, I am sure I shall obtain your Excellency's indulgence for one or two general observations which seemed called for by the above sentiment.

By the Treaty of Ghent, in the contingency which unhappily occurred, of a nonconcurrence between the British and American Commissioners in fixing that boundary, they were directed respectively to report to their Governments, and the difference thus left unadjusted, was to be referred to a Sovereign Arbitrator.[1] Your Excellency, in the course of the correspondence which has passed between you and this Department has protested against this reference, and your objections to it have received the most respectful consideration.[2] The fulfilment of solemn obligations imposed upon the United States by the faith of treaties, and the duty with which the President is charged by the Constitution, of taking care that the laws (of which our treaties with foreign powers form part) be faithfully executed, did not appear to leave him at liberty to decline the stipulated reference. If any other practical mode of settling the difference had occurred, or been suggested [sic] by your Excellency, to the President, it would have received friendly and deliberate consideration—

It is certainly most desirable that Nations should arrange all differences between them, by direct negotiation, rather than through the friendly agency of third powers. This has been attempted and has failed. The Government of the United States is fully convinced that the right to the territory in dispute is with us, and not with G. Britain. The convictions of Maine are not stronger, in respect to the validity of our title, than those which are entertained by the President. But Great Britain professes to believe the contrary. The parties cannot come to the same conclusion. In this State of things what ought to be done? National disputes can be settled only amicably, or by an appeal to the sword. All will agree that, before resorting to the latter dreadful alternative, every friendly and peaceful measure should be tried and have failed. It is a happy expedient, where Nations cannot themselves adjust their differences, to avail themselves of the umpirage[3] of a friendly and impartial power. It multiplies the chances of avoiding the greatest of human calamities.[4] It is true that it is a mode not free from all objection, and Mr. Gallatin[5] has adverted to one in the extract which you give from one of his despatches. But objectionable as it may be, it is better, and not more uncertain than the events of war. Your Excellency seems to think that the clearness of our right should prevent the submission of the Controversy to an Arbitrator.[6] But the other party professes to be equally convinced of the indisputable nature of his claim; and if that consideration were to operate on the one side it would equally influence the other. The consequence will be, at once, perceived. Besides this clearness of our title will attend it before the arbitrator, and, if we are not deceived in it, his favourable decision is inevitable—

The President regrets, therefore, that, in conducting the negotiation with Great Britain, he could not conform to the views of your Excellency, by refusing to carry into effect a treaty, to the execution of which the good faith of the Nation stood pledged, and which was, moreover, enjoined by the express terms of the Constitution.

But, if he could have brought himself to disregard this double obligation, under which he was placed, how would the interests of Maine been [sic] advanced? She is not in possession of the disputed territory, or, at most, but a small part.[7] Both parties stand pledged to each other to practise forbearance, and to abstain from further acts of Sovereignty on the unoccupied waste, until the question of right is settled. If that question cannot be settled by the parties themselves, and may not be settled by Arbitration, how is it to be determined? The remaining alternative has been suggested. Whether the time has arrived for the use of that does not belong to the President, but to another branch of the Government to decide.

I cannot but hope that your Excellency upon a review of the whole subject, in a spirit of candor,[8] will be disposed to think, that the Executive of the U. States has been endeavoring, with the utmost zeal, in regard to our North Eastern boundary to promote the true interests of the U. States and of the State of Maine, and that this respectable

State has been treated with neither neglect nor injustice. I am with
great respect &c &c.   HENRY CLAY.

Copy. DNA, RG59, Dom. Letters, vol. 22, pp. 99–101 (M40, R20). A draft of this letter
which had been copied into the letterbook of the State Department on November 19
(*ibid.*, 86–88) was apparently the version which Clay "took back" from President Adams
on November 26 and which the latter had "advised him to modify, so as to avoid all
the expressions which might be personally offensive." Adams (ed.), *Memoirs*, VII, 361.
The changes between versions are noted below.
    [1] Cf. above, Clay to Addington, March 27, 1825, and note.   [2] The remainder of
this paragraph was earlier written as follows: "Your Excellency, in other words, has
protested against the fulfilment of solemn obligations imposed upon the United States
by the faith of treaties; and, against the execution of the duty with which the President
is charged by the Constitution, of taking care that the laws (of which our treaties with
foreign powers form a part) be faithfully executed. And your Excellency has done this
without proposing any other practical mode of settling the difference which unfortunately exists between the Governments of the United States and Great Britain."
    [3] In the draft version the last five words were phrased as "appeal to the decision."
    [4] In the draft version this sentence follows the two succeeding ones.   [5] Albert Gal-
latin.   [6] The word "umpire" was used here in the draft.   [7] The draft version,
following the conjunction, "or," was written as follows: "at least of but a small part.
Great Britain is in actual possession of a much larger part."   [8] After the preposition
"in," the draft version was written as follows: "that spirit of candor which public functionaries especially should exercise towards each other, . . ."

From Christopher Hughes

Hague 27, November, 1827.
Extract.   Rolls[1] (London) November, Friday, 23. 1827
    "There are strong suspicions the present Ministry will break up,
before the meeting of Parliament.[2] The affair at Navarino is far from
being popular.[3] Sir John Gore is gone out to supercede [*sic*] Codrington.[4] Many persons seem to apprehend a general war, but I cannot
believe the benefit of past experience is yet wholly lost to the nations
of Europe.
    "I dined yesterday at Pollen's with Leach, Sir George Hampsen[5]
and many others &.&.&.

SIGNED—

N.B.   Leach is Master of the Rolls; Pollen Secretary idem. Sir G.
Hampsen is Brother in Law of Lords Melville and Westmoreland;[6]
but is intimate with all sides, a Toad Eater of those in power; but
withal a most clever, learned and reserved man; & no one better informed.

My Dear Sir,
    I have just seen a letter, and been permitted to make the above ex-
tract, received by an Englishman of rank, Brother to the writer;[7] the
Writer is the intimate favourite & confidential friend of Sir John
Leach ex Vice Chancellor & now master of the Rolls; Sir John gave
the best things his present office had, to the writer; a sine-cure chief

secretaryship in the Rolls, worth some 1500 £ a year; there are few men in England better informed, or more versed in ministerial and political matters, & more competent to judge of hints and phrases, than is the writer; He had just passed the day with several of the ministry; & though he dont say that the extract contains their opinion, yet I have very little doubt of the fact.

I have a letter dated "Brighton 14th." from a very clever and well informed woman of high.Life, (as they call it) and I think it contains a very accurate view of the general opinions on the Greco-Turco-Egyptian matters & the Navarin affair; so I'll give you another Extract, and from my Female sources, or resources. viz

"We have various opinions here, respecting the destruction of the Turkish Fleet, and we are very anxious about the Xtians at Constantinople.[8] The Germans here, (all the German travelling nobles in England repair to *Brighton:*) say, the allies have broken the armistice; & the Frondeurs[9] express the same opinion. I think the Greeks are a nest of Pirates & Robbers, with no idea of keeping faith with any nation; and certainly not worth the chance that now exists of war in Europe, besides which I do not comprehend why the Great Powers are to interfere between the Turks & their subjects; it is very chivalrous, and very unjust; & the English would think it very hard, if the Russians & French were to interfere in their policy in India; as they thought when the French assisted the americans in your war of independence; But the Turks are not Christians; & the Greeks in former ages, were high minded republicans who wrote beautiful verses and carved and built, as none have sculptured since their time. I am very sorry for the beginning of war; and we are all in great anxiety for Mr. & Mrs. S. Canning, who are friends of ours, & who may be in the VII Towers."[10]— Poor things may be they are! But Codrington "smote the Egyptian (othello)[11]," all in pure accident, and in absence of any notion of doing him harm; & so, if poor Mr. & Mrs. Stratford Canning are cooped up in *Jail*; why they must stay there 'til they are regularly *Bailed out*— But the VII headed Monster we are told, had not opened its jaws; & the very christian Ambassadors are employed in persuading the G. Seigneur,[12] that he had better be satisfied with one accident (done on purpose;) than provoke more.

Everybody here (excepting Meternichs [*sic*] Legation Count Mier;[13]) rejoices or affects to rejoice, at the Navarin Victory; a christian Triumph must always be a subject of rejoicing; But no one knows what to look to, as the probable result. The general impression is, that the Turks will bluster, finish by negotiating; and, at least, that *time* will be attempted to be gained; the very idea of a war, terrifies, it seems to me, all hands; no body wants it; no body is rich enough for it; & the Cabinets are all afraid of their own subjects. The unexampled and

unlooked for election disappointments in France, and the later ministerial powerlessness[14] (if I may say so) over the *nation*, have led to the
deepest & most *anxious* forbodings. I have lived, surrounded by some
of the best informed political men in Europe, the last month; some of
them old *Prefects* of Napoleon; & having France, its politics, its ar-
rondissements, its electoral colleges, & *candidates*, at their finger ends.
I will mention one man, Count de Celles, Ambassador hence to Rome,
& the Maker of the Concordat;[15] He acknowledged to me that so complete has been his disappointment in the French Elections, that he
confesses, that he *knows nothing* of France *now*. nor how things may
go. The whole affair is thus solved; viz a rooted & incurable hatred, of
the nation to the Bourbons. Yrs. truly   C. HUGHES
To Henry Clay Esquire Washington

ALS. DLC-HC (DNA, M212, R3). Copy, OHi.   [1] Chancery Office.
[2] Cf. above, Gallatin to Clay, February 22, 1827, note.   [3] Cf. above, Ombrosi to Clay,
November 6, 1827; Brown to Clay, November 12, 1827; Lawrence to Clay, November 14,
1827.   [4] Gore, who had entered the British Navy in 1781, as a boy of nine, had
become a lieutenant in 1789, had assumed his first command in 1794, and had been
knighted in 1805. He had been named a vice admiral in 1825, and from 1831 to 1835 was
commander-in-chief of the East Indies.   Although his report on Codrington's actions at
Navarino was favorable (John Knox Laughton, in *Dictionary of National Biography*,
VIII, 239), the latter was recalled in June, 1828, and spent the next several years defending his conduct. In this connection he edited *Documents Relating to the Recall . . .*
(London, 1830); *Papers Relating to the Claim Made . . . on Behalf of Himself, the Officers, Seamen and Marines, Engaged in the Battle of Navarin* (London, [1832]); *Com-
pressed Narrative of the Proceedings . . . during His Command . . . on the Mediterranean
Station . . .* (London, 1832).   [5] Sir John Leach; Sir George Hampson. Pollen has not
been identified.   Leach, born in Bedford in 1760, was educated at law, had served in
Parliament from 1806 to 1816, and had held a variety of judicial appointments. In 1817
he had been named to the Privy Council and the following year had been knighted. He
was master of the rolls, that is, chief judge of the chancery division, from May, 1827,
until his death, in 1834. Hampson, born in 1789 and also a distinguished barrister, had
inherited his title in 1820.   [6] John Fane, 10th Earl of Westmorland, born in 1759
and educated at Cambridge University, had become a member of the Privy Council in
1789 and had been lord-lieutenant of Ireland from 1788 to 1795 and lord privy seal from
1798 to 1827 (excepting 1806–1807).   [7] Neither the writer nor the recipient of the
letter has been identified.   [8] Cf. above, Dodge to Clay, November 17, 1827.
[9] Faultfinders.   [10] A Turkish prison, located in the southwest wall of Constantinople, used especially for the detention of foreign ambassadors and high Ottoman officials. It was sometimes called the "Seven Castles Tower" because of the conical shapes
on its top. Mehmet Zeki Pakalin, *Dictionary of Ottoman Historical Expressions and
Terms* (2nd. edn., 3 vols.; Istanbul, 1971), III, 614.   [11] Shakespeare (Furness [ed.],
A New Variorum Edition . . .), *Othello* (11th edn.), Act V, sc. ii, line 430.   [12] Mahmud
II. Cf. above, Hughes to Clay, September 16, 1827; Brown to Clay, October 28, 1827.
[13] Cf. above, Hughes to Clay, July 16, 1826.   [14] Cf. above, Lafayette to Clay, Oc-
tober 10, 1827, note; Everett to Clay, November 26, 1827.   [15] Cf. above, Hughes to
Clay, October 5, 1827.

From Charles W. Webber

The Hon. H. Clay
Sir   Columbia Ten: November 27th. 1827.
[Declines appointment as consul at Chihuahua[1] for "many reasons
which it would be idle to detail"; states: "If however at any time here-

after his Excellency shall think me worthy of any other appointment, the duties of which should (be) more concentrated, and not diffused over a boundless extent of territory, as is the ca(se) with the appointment he has done me the honor to tender me—with pleasure would I undertake a discharge of its duties. . . ."]

Permit me for your gratification to present you, a hasty view of the state of the politics, in this country. There is a considerable abatement of that hostility [t]hat lately existed toward the administration, in the great body of the Community; Several [c]auses may be ascribed for this, but the most efficient have bein [sic] your Lexington dinner speech,[2]—and Mr Buchannans [sic] letter;[3] in truth the administration has gained much strength with the intelligent and [r]eflecting part of the community, and there still continues to be a gradual increase, but I do not flatter myself enough can be effected, to produce any change in the electoral Vote of this State! Our Legislature lately districted the State for [e]lectors[4]—there are three districts in which probably candidates favourable to the [a]dministration may be run— In the Knoxville district it is highly probable succe[ss] may attend, an administration Candidate— In this District we could make a respectable stand,   I lately solicited Col. Andrew Erwin to become a candidate, but whether he will o[r] not is yet uncertain; I believe by using some little activity he could be elected! But it would require much management and gre[at] secrecy. In the Western District there are a few counties possessing majorities, friendly to the administration, but being small of themselves, they would be overpowered by those counted with them. Our Legislature during this session have manifested a vindictive and persecuting Spirit toward Mr. Adams and his cabinet   You, no doubt, have seen Mr. Browns resolution[s] and remarks—as also the resolution of Mr. Roge[rs] which was calculated only to elicit the free Spir[it] with which the legislature had acted upon and voted the resolutions and remarks of Mr. Brown, and to exhibit in a ludicrous wa[y] the pusalaminity [sic] of the whole body.[5] Whi[ch] last effect has been accomplished in an eminent degree. Even the Jackson party themselves, now regard the introduction of those resolutions, as an unfortunate circumstance, calculated to do much injury to their cause, by too openly displaying the rancarous [sic] and vindictive spirit with which they are actuated. They are becoming tremblingly alive to the late favourable expression of public opinion in Virginia and Pennsylvania;[6] they regard a withdrawal of those two great States from the cause of Genl. Jackson as tantamount to his defeat. However, great efforts, will be made by the delegation in Congress from this state, during this session, to completely identify the interest of Genl. Jackson with that of Pennsylvania and Virginia, a conciliatory spirit, with a hearty co operation on every measure calculated to promote the interest of either of those States, will be the policy of the Tennessee delegation, and will be observed most tenacious[ly] by them all.

In this State their [*sic*] is a universal proscription of every one favourable to the administrati[on]   the legislature have gone so far as to refuse the confir[ma]tion of several appointments made by Govr. Carro[ll] upon the ground of the incumbents being friendly to the reelection of Mr Adams; this has happened in cases where there existed, a decided superiority o[f] talents over the Jackson competition. As for myself[,] I do not expect, or even court political advancement, from the ruling powers here, and have never made any secret of my predilections for the present administration of the Unite[d] States government.

I must close this commun[ica]tion by apologizing not only for its length, but its tenor, my only apology is, that, having been raised and educated in your Old Congressional District,[7] from my infancy I have been taught to admire your Splend[id] talents, and to regard you as one of the first men of the age; consequently I feel much solicitude for your prosperity, and & [*sic*] every thing connected with your hopes, or [c]haracter, possesses with me no little interest, and must f[r]om Necessity be of much more [co]nsequence to you; I therefore deemed the [p]receding view of the political faction in [t]his State whose sole object is your prostration, [a]nd that of the executive of the U States a matter [o]f sufficient interest to justify me in present[in]g it. The motive, I feel assured, will obtain for it a grateful reception, and that [*sic*] it will [n]ot be deemed altogether obtrusive and imper[ti]nent. I am Sir with Sentimen[ts of] high admiration, Your Very obt. & humble Servt.   CHARLES W. WEBBER

ALS. DNA, RG59, Cons. Disp., Chihuahua (M-T167, R1). Margins obscured.
[1] See above, Clay to Allen, April 9, 1827, note.   [2] Above, July 12, 1827.   [3] Cf. above, Ingersoll to Clay, August 11, 1827, and note.   [4] The measure had passed a second reading on October 29. *Nashville Banner and Whig*, November 3, 1827; cf. *ibid.*, December 8, 1827.   [5] Aaron V. Brown; John A. Rogers. Cf. above, Hammond to Clay, November 5, 1827, and note.   Virginia born, Brown had been graduated from the University of North Carolina in 1814, had moved in 1815 to Nashville, where he had been admitted to the bar two years later, and in 1818 had settled in Giles County. He had served in the Tennessee Senate from 1821 to 1825 and during the Extra Session of 1826–27 and subsequently sat in the State House of Representatives from 1831 to 1833 and in Congress from 1839 to 1845. He was Governor from 1845 to 1847, a delegate to the Democratic National Convention in 1852, and Postmaster General from 1857 until 1859.
[6] Cf. above, Mercer to Clay, August 22, 1827, and note; Sergeant to Clay, October 30, 1827, and note.   [7] Probably in Jessamine County, Kentucky, where Charles Webber, possibly the father of Charles W., had been deputy clerk in 1816.

DIPLOMATIC NOTES   November 27, 1827

From JOSÉ MARÍA SALAZAR, Philadelphia. Requests that Clay present "to the consideration of the President" the subject of prize-money, amounting to $6,300, now in the hands of (Benjamin F.) Hunt, who maintains that he will pay it only to the captors of the schooner *Intrepid* or their attorneys and refuses to turn it over to Alexander Vélez, Colombian consul general. Expresses the belief "that a simple order from him [the President] addressed to the proper authority, will be sufficient, in this case, to give effect to the prerogative of the Consul General of Colombia." LS, in Spanish with trans. in State Dept. file. DNA, RG59, Notes from Colombian Legation, vol. 1, pt. 2 (M51, R2).

A letter from Vélez to Salazar, quoted in the note, and two enclosures explain that the *Intrepid*, found by a Colombian court to be a Dutch merchant vessel carrying a Spanish cargo, had been captured in 1819 by a Colombian privateer and taken into the port of Savannah (Georgia). Though from that point the documents do not agree, it appears that a United States naval vessel had taken the *Intrepid* to Charleston, where the cargo had been sold and, after a hearing by a United States Court, the proceeds of the sale had been deposited with Hunt, as agent of the Colombian crew.

Hunt, born in Watertown, Massachusetts, had become a prominent lawyer of Charleston, South Carolina, a colonel of State militia, and in 1818 a member of the South Carolina House of Representatives. For Clay's response to Salazar's proposal, see below, Clay to Salazar, December 22, 1827.

MISCELLANEOUS LETTERS   November 27, 1827

To HENRY WILSON, Pensacola. Informs him that "a commission appointing" him "Marshal of the United States for the Territory of West Florida has just been forwarded from this office to Mr. [Benjamin D.] Wright, Attorney of the United States for said territory. . . ." Copy, DNA, RG59, Dom. Letters, vol. 22, pp. 98–99 (M40, R20).

On the same day Clay wrote Wright, enclosing the commission and requesting that Wright deliver it after Wilson "shall have given the official Bond. . . , and complied with the usual forms. . . ." Copy, in *ibid.*, 99.

On February 1, 1828, Wilson acknowledged receipt of Clay's letter and transmitted assurance of his determination "to fulfill the duties of . . . [the] Office." ALS, in DNA, RG59, Acceptances and Orders for Comns. (M-T645, R2).

On February 2 Wright responded from Pensacola acknowledging receipt of Clay's letter. He observed that under the 27th section of the act of Congress of September 24, 1789 (1 *U. S. Stat.*, 87), the taking of a marshal's bond seemed "to have been confided exclusively to the Judge" but that he had, nevertheless, taken Wilson's bond and had the oath administered to him, in accordance with Clay's instructions. ALS, in *ibid.* Clay endorsed this document on the cover (AEI): "Mr. B[rent]. will see if the Bond has been properly approved. H. C."

From EDGAR MACON, Tallahassee. Reports that the "type and press" of the Tallahassee *Florida Advocate* "have been sold and transferred to Joseph D. Davenport Esqr. who now continues and conducts the said paper as heretofore." ALS. DNA, RG59, P. and D. of L. Published in Carter (ed.), *Territorial Papers*, XXIII, 937–38.

In February, 1827, Macon had taken over the Tallahassee *Florida Intelligencer*, founded in 1825, which had held the contract for publication of the laws during both Sessions of the Nineteenth Congress. Renamed by Macon as the *Florida Advocate*, the newspaper continued to hold the contract through the Twentieth Congress under Davenport's proprietorship.

Davenport retained ownership of the journal only until August, 1829, when it was merged with the Tallahassee *Floridian* (established in 1828). After a brief period as part owner of the latter paper, Davenport disappeared and has not been further identified. McMurtrie, "Beginnings of Printing. . . ," *Florida Historical Quarterly*, XXIII (October, 1944), 82–83.

From John J. Crittenden

Dear Sir, Frankfort Novr: 28th. 1827

In place of my former letter I send you the inclosed,[1] which is substantially a transcript of the first, & retains its date for the sake of consistency with the date of Davidson's letter[2] obtained upon the suggestion contained in my letter to you—

While every thing was brightening around us in the West, the intelligence of New York elections comes over us like a dark cloud[3]— I very much fear its effects upon Congress,[4] & the country at large. How has it happened? Is that State, contrary to all former expectation, really against the Administration?[5] Yr. Friend J J CRITTENDEN
Hon: H Clay Secty: of State

ALS. NcD. [1] Cf. above, Crittenden to Clay, September 3, 1827, and notes. [2] Above, Davidson to Clay, October 20, 1827 (2). [3] Cf. above, Sergeant to Clay, October 24, 1827, and note. [4] Cf. above, Clay to Taylor, September 7, 1827, and note. [5] Cf. above, Clay to Brown, March 27, 1827, and note.

INSTRUCTIONS AND DISPATCHES November 28, 1827

From JAMES BROWN, Paris, "Private." Reports that, although the returns are incomplete, the elections (cf. above, Lafayette to Clay, October 10, 1827, and note; Brown to Clay, October 28, 1827) show that all parties miscalculated the state of public opinion and that, if the friends of the Ministry retain a majority in the next chamber, it "must be so small as to render their tenure of office . . . uncomfortable and precarious . . ." (cf. above, Lafayette to Clay, October 10, 1827). Notes that "public rumor attributes to them the intention of endeavoring to press themselves on one or the other of the two oppositions" but that Villèle has "rendered himself obnoxious to" leaders of the Ultra Royalists, who "may prefer to continue united with" the liberal party "and insist upon the formation of a new ministry under their influence, comprehending some of the most moderate liberals." Observes that "An union of these two parties in the ministry will have to contend with much difficulty" and that "Whatever may be the fate of the President of the Council, it is generally thought that several of the present ministers will be compelled to leave room for a new selection." States that "The elections at Paris produced some commotions on the nights of the 19th and 20th November," which resulted in "the killing or wounding" of "fifty men and women" by police and soldiers, and that the affair is now the subject of "A judicial enquiry." Cites recent dispatches from the French Ambassador in Constantinople (the Count de Guilleminot) as the source of information that arrival there of news of the destruction of the Turkish fleet (cf. above, Ombrosi to Clay, November 6, 1827) "had occasioned no outrages on the persons or property of the christians [*sic*]; that negotiations had continued but that "the Turkish Government obstinately persisted in rejecting the proffered mediation"; and that "the Austrian ambassador

[Baron Ottenfels-Gschwind] had united heartily in advising the Porte to comply with the terms proposed by the ambassadors of the three allied powers" (Guilleminot, Stratford Canning, and Alexandre Ribeaupierre—cf. above, Hughes to Clay, September 16, 1827). Refers to the expected appearance in Paris of Miguel and adds: "On his arrival at Lisbon, the British troops will evacuate Portugal [cf. above, Brown to Clay, November 12, 1827]. The French garrison at Barcelona has been ordered home [cf. above, Everett to Clay, November 8, 26, 1827]. . . . Cadiz will be held by the French until spring, at which time it is believed the garrison will be withdrawn." ALS. DNA, RG59, Dip. Disp., France, vol. 23 (M34, R26). Received February 7, 1828.

Baron Ottenfels-Gschwind, formerly Austria's Ambassador to Russia, had been transferred in 1826 to Constantinople, where he remained at least through 1828.

From CHRISTOPHER HUGHES, The Hague. Refers to his dispatch (above, October 21, 1827) relative to the refusal of "the Netherlands Government . . . to make any modification of the Rule concerning the 10 pr. Ct. returns on the cargoes of their national vessels; nor . . . to conform to our just claims to a perfect equalization of imposts and charges, between our and their vessels. . . ." Points out that "the actual comparative state of the Trade between the two countries, happens to be so enormously in our favour; and this Government seems to be so well aware of it; that we are left to decide the question, . . . whether we will be satisfied with our present undeniable advantages, or *hazard* their deterioration, by an effort to make them better." Reports that merchants interested in the American trade "are *satisfied* with the actual state of things" and "look, *with deep anxiety*, to any measure of our Government, that may provoke reprisals, on the part of the Government of the Netherlands." Repeats, with reference to "the great and liberal system of Reciprocity, that we have tendered to the commercial World," his "*firm conviction*, that if we attempt a rigid enforcement of these principles, in our trade with this country, we shall forfeit the great advantages we now enjoy, and certainly get the worst of the game." Notes that "The same point of controversial diplomacy exists between this Government and Prussia," although "the comparison, and the balance of commercial interests, in their trade with Prussia is [*sic*] the *very reverse*, to what they are, in their trade with the United States." Adds that the Netherlands has refused to modify "its 10 pr. Ct. Law" despite a declaration by Prussia "that unless such modification were made, . . . *before* the 1st. January, 1827, the advantages and equality enjoyed by Dutch Ships, should cease. . . ." Encloses a "copy of Baron Verstolk's answer [dated December 25, 1826] to the Note" informing him of the Prussian declaration. ALS. DNA, RG59, Dip. Disp., Netherlands, vol. 8 (M42, R12). Received February 7, 1828.

MISCELLANEOUS LETTERS   November 28, 1827

From EBEN[EZER] ELMER, H[UGH] R. MERSEILLES, and others, Bridgeton, New Jersey. Report that the editor of the Bridgeton *Washington Whig* (John I. McChesney—cf. above, Southard to Clay, November 6, 1826, and note), which had published the laws of the United State until last year, "made a Sale of his establishment to certain persons. . . , and those persons about eighteen months ago made a Sale and transfer of the Same establishment to Robert Johnston Editor of the Bridgeton Observer. . . , who changed the name of his paper at that time to the Washington Whig and Bridgeton Observer & Cumberland & Cape May Advertiser." Note that the State Department, "being under the impression from the above facts, that the Washington Whig News paper had become extinct, did appoint the Said Robert Johnston Editor of the Whig and Observer to print the Laws of the United States." State that "the Washington Whig News Paper Subscription and concern was Sold and transfered [sic] by John I. Mc. Chesney the late Editor to Mr. Franklin Furguson [i.e., Ferguson] the President Editor, and that it has been continued and published by the present Editor for more than a year past, that the paper has been conducted by Mr. Furguson in a very able and Satisfactory manner & highly creditable to the Editor, that it is a paper much devoted to the cause of the present Administration and General Government, While the paper called the Whig and Observer edited by Mr. Robert Johnston, is decidedly opposed to the present Administration, and has taken a very decided and active part in promoting the Election of Andrew Jackson to Presidential Chair." Recommend that Ferguson be appointed publisher of the laws. DS, signed also by two others. DNA, RG59, P. and D. of L. Cf. above, Southard to Clay, November 6, 1826 (2); Ferguson to Clay, November 7, 1826, note.

Ebenezer Elmer, the father of Lucius Q. C. Elmer, had been born in Cumberland County, New Jersey, had served as a surgeon in the American Revolution, and had been one of the founders of the Society of the Cincinnati. After the war he had settled at Bridgeton and opened medical practice. He had served in the New Jersey Assembly from 1789 to 1795 and again in 1817 and 1819 and had been a member of Congress from 1801 to 1807. Collector of customs at Bridgeton from 1808 to 1817, he had been re-appointed to that office in 1822 and retained it until he retired from public life in 1832.

To Francis T. Brooke

My Dear Sir   Washn. 29th. Novr. 1827

I have to thank you for Mr Giles's Book,[1] and him for writing it. I care not how widely he diffuses my Tariff Speech.[2] I believe its principles will stand the test of the severest scrutiny. I hope however that Genl. Taylor will now publish his speech.[3] I understood from him that he had come under some promise to do so.

The two parties are beginning to assemble in great numbers, and we shall doubtless have a full house on the election of a speaker. The contest will be close, and if luck did not seem to be running somewhat against me,[4] at this particular period, I should say Mr. Taylor will be chosen.[5]

The rumor of the day is that Chilton is elected in K. by 27 votes.[6]
Ever Truly Your Friend   H. CLAY.
The Hon Mr Brooke.

Copy. DLC-TJC (DNA, M212, R13).
[1] William Branch Giles had published at Richmond in 1827, *Mr. Clay's Speech upon the Tariff: or the "American System," so called: or the Anglican System, in Fact, Introduced Here; and Perverted in Its Most Material Bearing upon Society, by the Omission of a System of Corn Laws, for the Protection of Agriculture, [and] Mr. Giles' Speech upon the Resolutions of Inquiry in the House of Delegates of Virginia, in Reply to Mr. Clay's Speech: also His Speech in Reply to Gen. Taylor's; Accompanied with Sundry Other Interesting Subjects. . . ,* a pamphlet of 188 pages.   [2] Cf. above, III, 683–730.
[3] Robert Barrand Taylor—cf. above, Brooke to Clay, January 31, 1827, and note. No

pamphlet copy of the speech has been found.   4 Colton, who presumably saw the
original letter, transcribes this word as "us." *Private Correspondence*. . . , 185.   5 Cf.
above, Clay to Taylor, September 7, 1827, note.   6 Thomas Chilton—see above,
Johnson to Clay, April 29, 1827, note.

From James Brown

My dear Sir   29 Novr. 1827
We have just received news from Constantinople by the way of the
Augsburg Gazettes which has rather alarmed those who had been
tranquilized by the despatches of the French Ambassador[1] to which I
had alluded in my letter.[2] These accounts which are dated two days
later mention that the Porte had manifested the deepest resentments
on hearing of the destruction of his fleet and told the Ambassadors that
he regretted he had ever listened to them, and that he was perfectly
willing they should leave his Court. It is added that he had resolved
in the course of a few days to hoist the standard of the prophet and
order all good Musselmen to arm in defense of his cause.[3] It is said
that great consternation was visible among the *franks*[4] and that the
Russian Ambassador[5] had already left Constantinople. I saw Mr. de
Villele and the Baron de Damas yesterday who stated that the accounts
from Augsburg were exaggerated and that on the 7th. things remained
on as quiet a footing as *could be expected*— The stocks rose yesterday.
It is hoped that Austria will have sufficient influence to persuade the
Porte to accede to the demands of the Allies   Should he refuse to do
so the case is one of the most embarrassing that can be imagined. If
they destroy the Ottoman Empire the difficulty will be to divide the
spoil. Russia and Austria might possibly make a division satisfactory
to them and England might content herself with the Islands but where
is France to receive her portion? It is evident that the affair has taken
a turn which was not in the contemplation of any of the parties.
     The Ministry is much mortified at the result of the elections which
will not give them, even should they obtain all the votes which are
yet uncertain, a sufficient majority to support their measures. The
weight of publick displeasure is to fall on Mr de Villele who seems to
have become more obnoxious to the opposition than any of his Colleagues. By the next opportunity you may expect to know whether we
shall have a new Ministry.[6] You know enough to enable you to say
whether or not we shall have cause to regret it. Mr de Villele has been
the most strenuous opponent of our Claims.
     I am very anxious to discover how the next Congressional campaign
will open. Sergeants Election[7] proves a change in Philadelphia. New
York I fear will be carried away by the combined efforts of Van Buren
and Clinton.[8] Louisiana will vote for Mr Adams,[9] at least I am told so
by some I have seen from that State—

It gives me pleasure to say that Mrs. Browns health about which I felt some alarm improves daily. She is however now confined as she has been for two months to the House but hopes in a few weeks to dress and go out. We have had much agreeable sociable company at home. She is much beloved by the Ladies of the Diplomatic Corps who call every day to see her.

Our old friend Genl. Smith[10] must be greatly disappointed in the Maryland elections.[11] He seemed to think they would all be for Jackson—

Give my best salutations to Mrs Clay. & believe me Dear Sir Your friend   J B.

Hon Henry Clay.

ALI. DLC-HC (DNA, M212, R3).   [1] The Count de Guilleminot.
[2] Above, November 28, 1827.   [3] Cf. below, Lawrence to Clay, December 6, 1827, note.   [4] That is, the Western Europeans.   [5] Alexandre Ribeaupierre.   [6] Cf. below, Brown to Clay, December 29, 1827, and note.   [7] On John Sergeant's election, see above, Sergeant to Clay, September 28, 1826, note; October 14, 1827, note.   [8] Cf. above, Brooke to Clay, September 21, 1827, note; Rochester to Clay, November 4, 1827; Porter to Clay, November 6, 22, 1827; Clay to Hammond, November 16, 1827.   [9] Cf. above, Clay to Brown, March 27, 1827, note.   [10] Samuel Smith.   [11] Cf. above, Clay to Blunt, September 11, 1827, note.

From Thomas Smith

Dr. Sir.   Lexn. Novr. 29. 1827.

If any thing be published during the winter at Washn. on your subject, the enclosed certificate, or the substance of it, may be useful.[1] Mr. B. is a son of Jno. Bell, Mrs. Allen's brother—a very intelligent, respectable young man—a trader to the South.[2] He gave the certificate to a friend of mine, but expressed some reluctance to its publication, on account of the abuse it might bring upon him.

The big black cloud in the direction of N. York,[3] has overshadowed every thing in this quarter. It will but increase our efforts. The Addresses generally are of good tone, and shew determination of purpose.[4] Yours truly,   THO. SMITH

ALS. DLC-TJC (DNA, M212, R13). Addressed to Clay.
[1] The statement addressed from Fayette County, November 10, 1827, by J(ohn) H(enderson) Bell to Smith (ALS, in DLC-HC [DNA, M212, R3]), was not included in the supplementary material to Clay's *Address . . . to the Public*, December 29, 1827. It asserted that Bell had heard Clay say, in Lexington, *before he was elected to Congress the last time . . .* That he (the said Clay) could not vote for Genl. Jackson to be President under any circumstances whatever; and that in his opinion there were hundreds of persons in the U. States better qualified for that office than he {the said Jackson}."   [2] The younger Bell (1798–1837) was a successful businessman, following in the steps of his father (1758–1835), who operated the farm "Stoneleigh," near Lexington, and traded hogs and cattle in the South. John Bell, born in Augusta County, Virginia, had settled in Fayette County, Kentucky, around 1790. His sister, Susannah, had married Captain William Allen.
[3] See above, Sergeant to Clay, October 24, 1827, note.   [4] Throughout November

and December the Lexington *Kentucky Reporter* had carried reports of meetings of administration supporters in various Kentucky counties and their addresses to the public.

INSTRUCTIONS AND DISPATCHES   November 29, 1827

From THOMAS L. L. BRENT, Lisbon. Encloses a "translation . . . of an article, taken from . . . the gazette of this place," showing "another amicable step on the part of Spain in regard to her relations with" Portugal. Transmits also a copy of a letter received from (Frederico) Torlade (de Azambuja), who states "that he will leave this in February next for the United States" and who comments "respecting the regulations of the salt trade at St. Ubes. . . ." ALS. DNA, RG59, Dip. Disp., Portugal, vol. 7 (M43, R6). Received February 26, 1827.

The first enclosure is a translation of an excerpt from a dispatch sent by Jose Guilherme Lima (cited by Brent as the Portuguese Chargé d'Affaires, not further identified) from Madrid, who reported that he had been assured of measures to prevent disturbance of "the tranquillity of Portugal" by the Portuguese emigrants in Spain and told that the expected arrival of Miguel "should be published. . . , and the intentions with which he goes possessed with the object of preventing their being any longer deluded by their chiefs." Torlade's letter included the statement that he had received no reply from St. Ubes to his inquiry concerning the salt trade there.

From W[ILLIAM] B. LAWRENCE, London, no. 10. Notes that fears "for the personal safety of the Ambassadors and . . . other Franks [at Constantinople], have been set at rest, but . . . the decision of the Divan as to its future course continues doubtful." Observes that Russia, meanwhile, "is pursuing those measures which must ultimately secure for her an ascendancy over the Ottoman Empire" and cites "the taking of Erivan from the Persians," overlooked amid the speculation "respecting the consequences . . . of the battle of Navarino" (cf. above, Ombrosi to Clay, November 6, 1827), as an event of great importance in future relations between Russia and Turkey. Reports that "The intended return . . . of the British troops from Portugal has been publicly announced" and that "Don Miguel is expected to arrive in London" on December 10. ALS. DNA, RG59, Dip. Disp., Great Britain, vol. 35 (M30, R31). Received February 21, 1828.

The fall on October 19, 1827, of Erivan, which had been under siege by Russian forces since the previous April, was the prelude to disintegration of the Persian defense and culminated in the Treaty of Turkmanchai of February, 1828 (see above, Middleton to Clay, September 17, 1826, note). On the battle, see *Annual Register, 1827*, pp. 291–95; *1828*, pp. 217–18.

From HENRY MIDDLETON, St. Petersburg, no. 74, "Duplicate." Suggests that the battle of Navarino (cf. above, Ombrosi to Clay, November 6, 1827) "seems likely to decide the question of Grecian Independence affirmatively, although it may be doubted whether any of the allies [France, Great Britain, and Russia—cf. above, Brown to Clay, July 12, 1827, note] were cordially disposed to promote its establishment." Encloses "a *circular* to all its Ministers abroad," which the Russian "Cabinet, aware of the alarm subsisting throughout Europe upon the Subject of the extension of the Russian Territory, has thought it necessary to issue on this occasion. . . ." Notes that "Contrary to anticipation *Erivan* has fallen" (cf. above, Lawrence to Clay, this date) and the Emperor (Nicholas I) indicates "his settled purpose of retaining his Conquest." ALS. DNA, RG59, Dip. Disp., Russia, vol. 11 (M35, R11). Dated November 17/29, 1827; received July 20, 1828. The enclosure states the determination of the Emperor to adhere to the provisions of the Treaty of London of July 6.

INSTRUCTIONS AND DISPATCHES   November 30, 1827

From THOMAS L. L. BRENT, Lisbon, no. 46. Describes measures taken by Spain to promote friendlier relations with Portugal; notes that "when it was known that the Emperor [Peter I] had appointed his brother Dom Miguel to the Regency the exultation of the ultraroyalist party [in Spain] was without bounds; and . . . they already anticipated the downfall of the Constitution in Portugal. . . , and an unrelenting persecution of the liberals." Quotes assurances given by Miguel to his sister (Isabel Maria) of "his determination to support the institutions legally granted by his brother" and his request that she "make publick this declaration and his intention of repressing factions that . . . might attempt to disturb the publick tranquillity of Portugal. . . ." Adds that Miguel also requested that "a Frigate and Sloop of war "be sent to meet him at Falmouth "and carry him to Portugal." Discusses the significance of Miguel's approach to Portugal through England rather than through Spain. States that "the liberals," disappointed "at the Emperor's not immediately visiting Portugal," have been consoled by "the return the beginning of this month of Pracas the aid [*sic*] de camp [not further identified] of General Saldanha who had been sent to the Emperor with an account of all that was passing here militating against the interests of Dom Pedro and constitutional principles." Summarizes the supposed contents of letters, not yet officially made public, brought from the Emperor by this messenger. Comments on the increased attentiveness accorded to the Queen (Carlota Joaquina) since the appointment of Miguel and the imminent departure of Sir William A'Court for Russia and the expected arrival of his successor, (Frederick James) Lamb, with Miguel. LS. DNA, RG59, Dip. Disp., Portugal, vol. 7 (M43, R6). Dated "Novembr. 31st. 1827." Received January 19, 1828.

From ALBERT GALLATIN, New York, no. 127. Reports his arrival "last night after a passage of 52 days." Notes that he "omitted to state in . . . [his] despatch No 115 [above, September 14, 1827], that Mr. [William] Huskisson complained that the laws of the United States, imposing restrictions on the Colonial Intercourse, applied exclusively to Great Britain," to which he "replied that Great Britain was the only Power that imposed in that Intercourse restrictions on American vessels." Summarizes the remainder of the conversation, during which Huskisson remarked "that Cuba, though nominally a Spanish possession, was in reality a Colony of the United States" and made clear that "it may be considered as a settled point with him, not to make the laws regulating . . . Intercourse [with the British West Indies] to depend directly or indirectly on any agreement or understanding whatever." Concludes: "If it [this trade] is again opened, it will be on such conditions as may be prescribed by Act of Parliament and to be accepted or rejected but not modified by the United States." Adds that he will later make "some further explanations . . . respecting the Maps" sent with his "despatch No. 124 [above, October 2, 1827] and the evidence to be collected or applied for under the Convention relative to the North Eastern Boundary" (cf. above, Gallatin to Clay, September 30, 1827). ALS. DNA, RG59, Dip. Disp., Great Britain, vol. 34 (M30, R30). Copy, in NHi-Gallatin Papers, vol. 15, pp. 149–50 (MR21); published in Adams (ed.), *Writings of Albert Gallatin*, II, 394.

From VINCENT GRAY, Havana, "Confidential." Warns against the appointment of George Byron Shields as "Commercial Agent of the United States at Sisal. . . ."

Describes Shields as "a Scotchman never . . . in the U States . . . but once," and charges: "It is his partners, who . . . have set afloat the recommendation [of him] in order they [sic] may the better cover" their illicit practices in trade with Sisal, New Orleans, and Havana. ALS. DNA, RG59, Cons. Disp., Havana, vol. 5 (M-T20, R5). Received January 5, 1828.

From T[HOMAS] M. RODNEY, Havana. Reports his arrival, "yesterday" (cf. above, Gray to Clay, June 13, 1827), and that he found the city healthy and trade "uncommonly [b]risk for the season." States that "The Spanish squadron under Admiral [Angel] Laborde . . . are to sail . . . for Porto Rico," where "they will be joined" by additional vessels, including "two Frigates from Cadiz and proceed [to] the [Spanish] Main. . . ." Adds that "General [Miguel] de la Torre, former Governor of [P]orto Rico, . . . is to embark in the fleet"; that "the Government here have supplied Laborde with 200.000 dollars in doubloons [t]o carry down with him"; that two Battallions [sic] have em[b]arked on board the fleet here, and they will be joined [b]y a considerable body of land forces at Porto Rico"; and that "From these premises . . . [Clay] will be able to draw the inferences" (cf. above, Gray to Clay, November 14, 1827). LS. DNA, RG59, Cons. Disp., Havana, vol. 5 (M-T20, R5). Received December 16. Margin obscured.

From W[ILLIAM] H. D. C. WRIGHT, Rio de Janeiro (1). Transmits "a most extraordinary letter," which he has received from (José Silvestre) Rebello. Also encloses a copy of his own reply, in order to show that he has "made it personal; forbearing to introduce . . . [Rebello's] Government, in a Correspondence he has forced upon" Wright. States that his only previous correspondence with Rebello occurred "some months since," when the Brazilian "requested that his Correspondence should pass through this Consulate" and Wright "assented in the most polite terms. . . ." ALS. DNA, RG59, Cons. Disp., Rio de Janeiro, vol. 3 (M-T172, R4). Received January 29, 1828. Endorsed by Clay on verso: "To be submitted to the President."

In the first enclosure Rebello, writing from Washington, August 14, 1827, thanked Wright for his "courteous atentions [sic]" and continued: "Your Government has appointed Mr. W. Tudor Chargé d'Affaires [sic] for Rio; it is to be expected, that he will try every thing in his power to accomodate [sic] matters with that country, and politness [sic] allways [sic] useful; and that has been more than once forgotten [sic] by the U. Sts. Agents there, declaring themselves servants of Governments foreigners to them, and treading under feet the laws of neutrality; I must declare to you, now that peace is made [cf. above, Wright to Clay, August 10, 22, 1827; Lawrence to Clay, October 22, 1827; Forbes to Clay, June 29, October 30, 1827], that if the state of war had continued probably more than one of the U. Sts. Agents near H. I. B. Majesty [Peter I] would have had to evacuate the Country."

In reply, November 30, 1827, Wright said, in part, ". . . I have to observe, that the deportment of United States' Agents, is a subject for the judgment of their Government, that your remarks upon those in Brazil, are presumptuous, and unfounded, and certainly not dictated by that courtesy and politeness, you so strongly recommend.—

"Your lessons upon politeness to Mr. Tudor you will please convey through some other Medium, and not make a private correspondence with me, a vehicle for impertinent remarks—"

From W[ILLIAM] H. D. C. WRIGHT, Rio de Janeiro (2). Reports that "The Brig Ruth . . . has been restored to the American Owners" (cf. above, Wright to Clay, October 27, 1827; Forbes to Clay, October 30, 1827; below, Wright to Clay, December 19, 1827); that he has sent (John M.) Forbes a document containing evidence relating to the case of the *Patrick Henry* (cf. above, Wright to Clay, October 27, 1827); that, "With regard to the War," a recent "entire change of Ministers [in Brazil] . . . may lead to a change of Measures"; that Commodore (James) Biddle has informed him of peace negotiations "through the British mediation"; and that "The Brig President Adams [cf. above, Bond to Clay, August 1, 1827] has been released." Encloses a copy of his letter to the Brazilian Government protesting the sinking of the brig *Brutus* by the squadron that attacked shipping in the River La Plata on October 3 last. Points out that, in the same letter, he remonstrated against "the practice lately originated at Montevideo, of endorsing the documents of Neutral Vessels." Transmits a document concerning the prize cases and, also, a list of the new Ministers. ALS. DNA, RG59, Cons. Disp., Rio de Janeiro, vol. 3 (M-T172, R4). Received January 29, 1828.

The enclosed list indicates that the Marquis de Aracaty has succeeded the Marquis de Queluz as Minister of Foreign Affairs.

The brig *Brutus*, of New York, a vessel of 212 tons burthen, had sailed from the Brazilian port of Santos on September 14, with a cargo of sugar, tobacco, and miscellaneous articles bound for the Pacific. Under a claimed necessity to put into port for supplies, the vessel on September 28 had entered the River La Plata and on October 2 run aground upon the Spit of Ensenada. There the Brazilean Squadron had captured her for violation of blockade. The Buenos Aires fortress, in turn, had opened fire upon the Brazilian boarding party, and the vessel had been sunk. Some $38,654 was awarded in compensation under the Brazilian convention of 1849 with the United States. *House Docs.*, 20 Cong., 1 Sess; no. 281, p. 178; *Senate Docs.*, 35 Cong., 2 Sess., no. 18, p. 116.

MISCELLANEOUS LETTERS   November 30, 1827

From S[AMUEL]. L. S[OUTHARD]., Navy Department. Transmits a report (not found) "in relation to a Mr. Robertson [*i.e.*, Philip Robinson], who is said to have been officiating at the Island of Curacoa [*sic*] as Consul of the United States." Copy. DNA, RG45, Exec. Letterbook, vol. 1821–31, p. 278.

INSTRUCTIONS AND DISPATCHES   December 1, 1827

From THOMAS L. L. BRENT, Lisbon, no. 47. Transmits a "copy of a letter from the Minister of Foreign Affairs [Candido José Xavier] respecting the sailors that committed the murders on board the American schooner Napoleon. . . , shewing that . . . the Judges having determined that it was within their competency to judge the process. . . , the delinquents have not been delivered up to the government of the United States." Reports having been informed by I(srael) P. Hutchinson that the claim in the case of the *Osprey's* cargo is "in a favorable train" and that Brent's assistance will not be needed. Refers to his "despatch No. 42" (above, July 25, 1827) and states that he has received no answer from (Samuel) Hodges (Jr.) but has "obtained the deposition of Captain [William] Prince copy of which is" enclosed. Requests further "instructions in the prosecution of this business. . . ." Encloses the reply to his letter, a copy of which accompanied his "despatch No. 44 [above, August 26, 1827] . . . respecting the salt trade at St. Ubes," and notes that the Minister of Foreign Affairs informed him "that as the measures proposed were legislative; and as the chambers were not assembled the government could not treat respecting them." LS. DNA, RG59, Dip. Disp., Portugal, vol. 7 (M43, R6). Received January 19, 1828.

From S[AMUEL] B. BARRELL, Portland, Maine. Reports having arrived in Portland on November 29 and having received from Governor (Enoch) Lincoln a promise of "all the aid which it may be in his power to render. . . ." Adds that Lincoln said he would not have appointed a State agent to investigate the boundary disturbances had he been "aware of the intention of the President to appoint an agent on behalf of the General Government; but he thinks that the appointment of Mr. Davis [*i.e.*, Charles S. Daveis] can in no event do harm and may be productive of much good. . . ."

Expresses fear that it will be "utterly impracticable" to conceal his (Barrell's) official identity when he visits the settlements on the Madawaska and Aroostook, because "at this season of the year" it is necessary to travel through Fredericton, where public opinion is highly excited. Adds that Lincoln believes Barrell can obtain the desired information only in his official capacity. States that he will, however, travel incognito if possible. Expresses intention to leave for Eastport "tomorrow morning." ALS. DNA, RG76, Northeastern Boundary, entry 87 (MR frames 647–50).

Governor Lincoln had appointed Daveis on November 5 and instructed him to go to Fredericton to inquire into the arrest and imprisonment of John Baker (cf. above, Lincoln to Clay, November 16, 1827, and note).

From Francis T. Brooke

My Dear Sir   Richmd Decemr 2d 1827
   I can very well Suppose that now you have not a moments leisure, and I shall address you as Seldom as possible— I See nothing in Virginia as yet that is very discouraging,   however that may be, it does not belong to me ever to despair in a good cause, and feeble as I know my efforts to be I shall not cease to make them, until there is nothing left for hope,   It is very desirable that the committee here Should open a correspondence with Some of the leading citizens of the other States who are embarked in the Same bottom, especially of Penna and NY—   now that Congress is assembled[1] it may be effected by a communication from Some of its members from those States to the committee pointing out to whom it Should address itself for correct information,   this might pass through me to the committee if desired—   besides information from other States it will have an affiliating effect on those engaged in the Same holy cause,   as the convention at Harrisburg will meet on the 4h of Jany and ours on the 8h[2] it may be of Some importance here to get the most correct an [*sic*] early information of its proceedings for which the papers cannot with Safety be relied on—   there will be a long and political message from Giles[3] to the assembly and I promise myself more good than injury from it, You Say nothing on the Subject of the letter of Mr Jefferson on the Panama mission to which I alluded in one of mine[4]   I have some expectation that I shall get the fact or at least Some evidence of it from another quarter   Your friend   FRANCIS, BROOKE

ALS. InU. Addressed to Clay.
1 The First Session of the Twentieth Congress began December 3, 1827.   2 Cf.
above, Sergeant to Clay, September 18, 1827, and note; Mercer to Clay, August 18, 1827,
and note.   3 William B. Giles.   4 Above, November 20, 1827.

INSTRUCTIONS, DISPATCHES   December 2, 1827

From W[ILLIAM] B. LAWRENCE, London, no. 11. Reports on, and transmits, documents relating to the case of William Kelly, who represented himself as a native
of Connecticut in an attempt to avoid being sentenced to service in the Royal
Navy after having been "detected at Liverpool in smuggling tobacco." States that,
during the course of Lawrence's investigation of the matter, Kelly confessed "himself a native of Ireland. . . ." ALS. DNA, RG59, Dip. Disp., Great Britain, vol. 35
(M30, R31). Received February 7, 1828.
    Kelly has not been further identified.

From Solomon Southwick

Dear sir,   Albany, Dec. 3, 1827.
    I do most clearly foresee in the election of Gen. Jackson, should it
take place, a fatal blow to our republican Institutions. Your ideas of a
Military President are justified by all history. Now, then, for your ear—
private ear—*but profit by it*—the most effectual way to check his chance
in this State, is to convict him of *Free Masonry*— I am told he is a zealous *mason*[1]— If so, let it be made to appear in fine southern print— It
will not do for me to bring it out first, because I am known for the implacable foe of the *Order*.[2] So help me God, I would as soon see my
country (almost) extinct, as to see the Order triumph in our present
conflict in Morgan's case[3]— nor is this enthusiasm a fanaticism. But be
this as it may—mark my words—before the Presidential Election it will
be in no man's power, he is known to be a zealous mason, to be elected
by the people in any part of this state north & west of New York. Superficial men may think the excitement will die away—they are greatly
deceived— Morgan's ghost will grow in Stature, & swell in size, till
with one foot in the Aleghany [*sic*] it will swing the other across the
whole Union! Yours truly,   S. SOUTHWICK

    ALS. DLC-HC (DNA, M212, R3). Addressed to Clay as: "*Private* . . . Strictly Confi-
dential."
    1 For a discussion of the effect of Jackson's identification with Free Masonry in the
1828 election, see Remini, *Election of Andrew Jackson*, 138–41.   2 Cf. above, Southwick to Clay, *ca.* June 1, 1826, note.   3 William Morgan—cf. above, Webster to Clay,
November 5, 1827, note.

INSTRUCTIONS AND DISPATCHES   December 3, 1827

From W[ILLIAM] TUDOR, Lima, no. 80. Acknowledges receipt of the "duplicate of
the despatch from the department signed by Mr. [Daniel] Brent, &, inclosing . . .
a commission as Chargé d'Affaires at Rio Janeiro [*sic*]" (cf. above, Clay to Tudor,
October 23, 1827, note). Accepts the appointment and states his intention of leav-

ing for Rio at "the first opportunity." Encloses a letter (not found) addressed to (John) Sergeant and requests Clay "to open it, as it contains some additional light on subjects connected with the Congress of Tacubaya." ALS. DNA, RG59, Dip. Disp., Brazil, vol. 6 (M121, R8). Published in *House Docs.*, 25 Cong., 1 Sess., no. 32, p. 29. Received March 10, 1828.

MISCELLANEOUS LETTERS   December 3, 1827

From JOHN McLEAN, "Post Office Department." Requests that instructions to the postmaster at Liverpool be obtained "through the British Minister near this Government [Charles R. Vaughan], of the same tenor as those which have been given to the post master at New York," and explains that the latter "has been instructed to make up a mail for England as often as the regular packets sail from that port, and that it be secured, in a portmanteau provided for the purpose, by the lock used for the mail of the United States." Argues that the arrangement will speed the mails by avoiding "the delays to which the correspondence is often liable in this Country, by passing through the Customs House" and that "It will also give security to letters on the voyage, which are now liable to be examined by the passengers, and if not violated, may be mislaid or lost." Notes that a similar arrangement with the French Post Office has proved to be satisfactory. LS. DNA, RG59, Misc. Letters (M179, R65).

DIPLOMATIC NOTES   December 4, 1827

From CHARLES R. VAUGHAN, Washington (1). Encloses documents relating to Indians in Lower Canada. States: "As the Indians in the village of St. Regis are part of them British Subjects, and part of them Subjects of the United States, a petty warfare has existed between them; the American Indians being the most numerous, and the most powerful.— Since, however, the Commissioners of Boundary under the Treaty of Ghent, have fixed the Line on the 45th. Parallel of Latitude North, the whole of the village of St. Regis has become British Territory, & the American Indians must be considered as Intruders. The remedy, suggested by the Governor General of Canada [George Ramsay, Earl of Dalhousie], is, that a flag staff or stone shall be placed upon the Line of Boundary, and, that the American Indians shall be required to withdraw beyond it.— In order, however, to carry this suggestion into effect, the Undersigned is desired to invite the assent and co-operation of the Government of the United States." LS. DNA, RG59, Notes from British Legation, vol. 14 (M50, R15). Published with enclosures in Manning (arr.) *Diplomatic Correspondence . . . Canadian Relations*, II, 662–63.

From CHARLES R. VAUGHAN, Washington (2). Encloses correspondence between himself and Sir James Kempt, Lieutenant Governor of Nova Scotia, in relation to the appointment of (Henry M.) Morfit as " 'Consular Commercial Agent' at Halifax"; states that the British Government has no objection "to the principle of the Appointment of a consular Agent at Halifax, for special commercial purposes," and that it is willing to recognize his "proposed Functions, provided that they are confined to the unofficial Character of a commercial agent, and that it is clearly understood, that a compliance with any future application of a similar nature, will depend upon the special circumstances which may be referred to, as making such an Appointment necessary" (cf. above, Clay to Morfit, June 4, 1827, note). LS. DNA, RG59, Notes from British Legation, vol. 14 (M50, R15).

INSTRUCTIONS AND DISPATCHES   December 4, 1827

From W[ILLIAM] B[EACH] LAWRENCE, London, no. 12. Transmits "copies of the correspondence, which passed between this Legation and Lord Dudley, in relation to the return of certain duties paid under peculiar circumstances, by the parties interested in the wreck of the American Ship 'Byron' " (see above, Howland and Company to Clay, March 1, 1827). Notes that (Albert) Gallatin's efforts in the case, "in conformity with . . . [Clay's] instructions" (above, March 29, 1827), have "been attended with the desired result." LS. DNA, RG59, Dip. Disp., Great Britain, vol. 35 (M30, R31). Received February 7, 1828.

   In one of the enclosures, Dudley informed Lawrence, on November 28, 1827, "that the Lords of the Treasury . . . have authorized the Commissioners of Customs to return to the parties the amount of the duties paid by them upon the materials saved from the wreck of the 'Byron' and exported to America."

MISCELLANEOUS LETTERS   December 4, 1827

From JON[ATHAN] H. LAURENCE, "Office of the Pacific Insurance Co   New York." States that, having learned "through Mr. [Condy] Raguet that a Gentleman [William Tudor] has recently been sent by this Government to Brazil, charged with a redress of the grievances suffered by the merchants of this Country by unjust seizures, detentions, and condemnations in Brazil," he wishes to know whether any action on the part of his company will be necessary to place its claim in the case of the *Spermo* "before the *Charge des Affaires* through an agent at Rio de Janeiro. . . ." ALS. DNA, RG76, Misc. Claims, Brazil (MR1). Endorsed by Clay on cover: "Inform him that Mr. Tudor has been instructed on the case of the Spermo [above, October 23, 1827], and that the papers relating to it in this department have been forwarded. If there be additional documents they had better be sent to the agent to be handed to Mr. Tudor. H. C." No reply to Laurence's letter has been found.

MISCELLANEOUS LETTERS   December 5, 1827

From DAVID DICKSON, New Orleans. Resigns as consul for San Antonio; recommends as his "successor Colonel Frost Thorn late of N. York but now a merchant at Nacogdoches in Texas—and that the residence of the Consul should be changed and fixed at *Nacogdoches*; and explains that "The Mexican Government have reserved from settlement all the lands on the sea board," and the few American settlers there have been removed, "hence the Commerce of the Country is *inland*, and Nacogdoches is the key to that inland trade." ALS. DNA, RG59, A. and R. (M531, R8).

   Born in New York in 1793, Thorn had early been involved in trade with Texas and in 1825 had obtained a contract as a colonizer. He was a member of the Legislature of the State of Texas-Coahuila and was later active in the Texas Revolution. He acquired great wealth from activities as a land developer, merchant, lumber dealer, banker, and operator of large farms in Louisiana and Texas.

   The Mexican colonization act of August 18, 1824, barred the States, without the consent of the Federal government, from permitting settlement by foreigners within 10 leagues of the coast or 20 leagues of the international boundary. The land colonization act of the State of Texas-Coahuila, adopted in March, 1825,

followed these terms. Bancroft, *History of the North Mexican States and Texas*
(2 vols.; San Francisco, 1889), II, in *Works*, XVI, 70, 72n; Rupert N. Richardson,
Ernest Wallace, and Adrian N. Anderson, *Texas, the Lone Star State* (3d. edn;
Englewood Cliffs, N.J.: Prentice-Hall, Inc., 1970), 51.

To Thomas Hart Benton

[December 6, 1827]

I have received a paper published on the 20th ultimo, at Lemington
[*sic*], in Virginia, in which is contained an article stating that you had,
to a gentleman of that place, expressed your disbelief of a charge injurious to me, touching the late presidential election, and that I had
communicated to you unequivocally, before the 15th of December,
1824, my determination to vote for Mr. Adams and not for General
Jackson.[1] Presuming that the publication was with your authority, I
cannot deny the expression of proper acknowledgments for the sense
of justice which has prompted you to render this voluntary and faithful
testimony.

Benton, *Thirty Years View* (2 vols.; New York, 1859–60), I, 48.

[1] Benton explains, in publishing Clay's letter (*ibid.*), that he had made the statement
to his father-in-law, Colonel James McDowell, of Rockbridge County, Virginia, on the
basis of conversation with Clay before Benton left Washington on December 15. In a
letter dated December 7, 1827, to an unidentified correspondent, concerning an item in
the Lexington *Virginia Intelligencer* of November 19, Benton asserted that the statement
was "substantially, not verbally, correct. . . ." Reprinted in *Niles' Weekly Register*,
XXXIII (February 2, 1828), 376; Clay, *Supplement to the Address*, 14–15 (cf. below, June
10, 1828).

McDowell, a native of Rockbridge County and a veteran of the War of 1812, owned
the estate known as "Cherry Grove." His younger daughter, Elizabeth, had married
Benton.

To Francis T. Brooke

My dear Sir   Washn. 6h. Decr. 1827.

I recd. your favor of the 2d. inst. Mr. Sergeant[1] informed me that he
would, in answer to a letter from Mr. Call,[2] put your Committee in
correspondence with the contemplated Convention at Harrisburg[3] &c.
Genl. P. B. Porter, who is a member of the Legislature, will be at Albany from the first of next month to some time in April, and will be a
very suitable person to correspond with. I will obtain some other
names hereafter.

We were beaten in the Speaker's election. The truth is that Mr.
Taylor[4] was heavy to carry, and the burthen could not be well thrown
off. Had some person been run on our side free from the objections
applicable to him, the difference would not have been greater than
two or three votes, but would still perhaps have been against us. Now
that the Opposition have obtained the Speaker, I suspect that both

he and they are greatly embarrassed as to the use which ought to be made of their triumph. If an Opposition complexion is given to the Committees, they assume all the responsibility of public measures. If another character is stampt upon them, it will be a virtual admission that no change of measures is desirable.

If any allusion is made in the public prints to Mr Jefferson's favorable opinion of the Panama mission, I hope the fact will be put on incontestable ground.[5] Ever truly Your friend   H CLAY
The Honble Mr. Brooke

ALS. DLC-HC (DNA, M212, R3).   [1] John Sergeant.
[2] Probably Daniel Call.   [3] Cf. above, Sergeant to Clay, September 18, 1827, and note.
[4] John W. Taylor—cf. above, Clay to Taylor, September 7, 1827, and note.   [5] Cf. above, Brooke to Clay, November 20, 1827.

DIPLOMATIC NOTES   December 6, 1827

To C[HARLES] R. VAUGHAN. Transmits "a copy of a letter from the Postmaster General" (above, McLean to Clay, December 3, 1827); requests him to "give such a direction to the proposal as will obtain the decision of the proper Department of . . . Government"; and states that "The plan seems to be recommended both by its intrinsic merit, and the experience which has been obtained in the operation of a similar arrangement with . . . France. . . ." Copy. DNA, RG59, Notes to Foreign Legations, vol. 3, pp. 405–406 (M38, R3). ALI draft, in CSmH.

INSTRUCTIONS AND DISPATCHES   December 6, 1827

From W[ILLIAM] B[EACH] LAWRENCE, London, no. 13. Reports that "no accounts . . . [have] been received . . . of the Allied Ambassadors having left Constantinople [cf. above, Brown to Clay, November 29, 1827; Lawrence to Clay, November 29, 1827], but . . . little doubt was entertained that their departure had ere this taken place." Notes that "the final decision of the Sultan [Mahmud II] is believed to be warlike" and that "In case of hostilities, the advance of the Russian army now near the Pruth . . . is considered as an event of course." States that he "had understood that peace was about to be concluded between Persia and Russia, founded on a cession of territory from the former," but he has learned that his information "was premature"; cites a belief among persons who "understand the state of things in that part of the world . . . that the arrangement . . . will not be long delayed" (see above, Lawrence to Clay, November 29, 1827, note). Acknowledges receipt of a letter from the State Department, "dated October 30th, and addressed to Mr. [Albert] Gallatin" (see above, Kershaw to Clay, October 12, 1827, note), and states that he has taken steps to obtain "the information desired." ALS. DNA, RG59, Dip. Disp., Great Britain, vol. 35 (M30, R31). Received February 7, 1828.

The Pruth River was at this time the boundary between Russia and the Ottoman Empire. Tensions arising from the intervention of the allies in the Greco-Turkish conflict and Turkish dissatisfaction with the Treaty of Ackerman (see above, Moore to Clay, November 18, 1826, and note) led the Sultan to rally his people for war. The Russians, incensed by Turkish support of the Persians in their conflict with Russia, responded by a formal declaration of war on Turkey, on April 26, 1828. On May 7 the Russian Army crossed the Pruth. *Annual Register, 1828*, pp. 219–31.

From JAMES MAURY, Liverpool. Reports that "of late the post office laws are so strictly enforced that the Masters of our Vessels frequently *cannot* comply with the orders they receive from the Collectors *not to send to the post office* the packets and dispatches sent them from Washington to forward." Explains: "All Vessells [*sic*] are now boarded in the offing by an authorised officer who takes out all their letter bags and sends them direct to the post office." Recommends "that, in future, all packets and dispatches from the Department of State be sent in a *sealed* bag to the Collector with directions to deliver it to the Master of the Vessell with instructions *not to put this bag* into any one of the Ships bags; but to keep it in his possession until he can deliver it" and, further, "that one end of all packets containing merely newspapers or pamphlets be sufficiently open to show the contents; because, in such ca[se] they would be subject to little or no expense." LS. DNA, RG59, Cons. Disp., Liverpool, vol. 4 (M141, R4). Received February 25, 1828. One margin partially obscured.

From J[OEL] R. POINSETT, Mexico, no. 108. Transmits "an order published by Commodore [David] Porter, by direction of this [Mexican] government, which has an important bearing upon the commerce of the United States with the Island of Cuba." Explains that the presence of Mexican cruisers "on the coast of Cuba" has compelled "the merchants of that Island . . . to employ foreign shipping altogether" and the Cuban Government "to permit the entrance of Spanish goods in neutral bottoms . . . on the same terms . . . as . . . Spanish vessels, so that a good many" American vessels are engaged "in that trade and, will be exposed to capture . . . under that order." States that "If the government can raise the necessary funds, the Mexican squadron will soon be at sea again"; that its intended destination will be Cartagena, where "the Commodore" will endeavor "to induce the Colombian government to carry into effect the secret convention concluded . . . about a twelvemonth ago"; but that, instead of attacking Cuba, "the combined forces, if the junction be effected," will "proceed to the coast of Spain." Comments, in a postscript: "From the manner in which I have obtained this information of the future movements of the Mexican Squadron it would be unfair to make them public." LS, postscript in Poinsett's hand. DNA, RG59, Dip. Disp., Mexico, vol. 3 (M97, R4).

Porter's order, dated November 16, proclaimed that "every vessel" carrying enemy goods or "contraband goods intended for the service of an enemy" was subject to capture.

In his dispatch no. 60, above, October 21, 1826, Poinsett had reiterated his information that "the secret Treaty of Panama . . . [contained] no direct provisions respecting Cuba" (cf. above, Poinsett to Clay, September 23, 1826), but in the later dispatch he had noted his understanding "that its [the Treaty's] ratification will, by combining the two squadrons of Mexico and Colombia, enable this government to undertake the long projected expedition against that Island."

MISCELLANEOUS LETTERS   December 6, 1827

From JOHN BROCKENBROUGH, "Bank of Virginia," Richmond. Reports having learned that (Nathaniel) Snelson has been jailed in Quebec and requests that Clay cause him to be detained there until the bank can send an officer "to obtain possession of his person & his booty." LS. DNA, RG59, Misc. Letters (M179, R65). Cf. above, Clay to Lawrence, November 23, 1827, and note.

From Thomas Washington

Sir,   Nashville, Decr. 7th 1827.—
[Though he has already recommended (Robert) Purdy for reappointment as United States marshal for the District of West Tennessee,[1] he has agreed also to write in favor of "Col. Theoderick Bradford." Discusses the qualifications of each.] As for their party politics, if that should form any consideration, Purdy belongs to the military dynasty, of course; but is one of those superannuated veterans, to whom the privilege of saying whatever he thinks, is conceded, without its being regarded—is too frank to conceal any thing—has too little penetration or design to have any momentous secrets confided to him—and in reality, aspires to nothing beyond his present station. Bradford is as much opposed to the existing order of things here, as, it seems a Tennessean dare be. He is quite a prominent member of the legislature, and were it not for the tyranny of opinion which prevails here at home, and which has stifled all the talents of the state, he would be much more extensively known than he is.—

About twelve months since, Mr. Erwin[2] put into my hands, certain papers relative to a piece of business then in agitation between you and Mr. Grundy;[3] with instructions, to await the issue of a correspondence then going on between you on the subject.[4] I have never been advised of the result, nor have I done any thing in the matter.—Yrs respectfully   Thos. Washington
The Honbl. Henry Clay.—

LS. DNA, RG59, A. and R. (M531, R1).
[1] Balch and others to Clay, November 17, 1827. For the length of Purdy's tenure, see above, Power of Attorney, June 6, 1825, note.   [2] James Erwin.   [3] Felix Grundy.
[4] Cf. above, Erwin to Clay, January 15, 1827.

INSTRUCTIONS AND DISPATCHES   December 7, 1827

To Charles Barnet, Antwerp. States, in reply to Barnet's letter of July 20, 1827, that the reference to repeal of the act of Congress concerning Mediterranean passports "probably refers to an Act of Congress, approved 1st. June 1796, entitled 'An Act providing passports for the Ships and Vessels of the United States [1 *U. S. Stat.*, 489–90],'" which has not been repealed; adds, in reply to Barnet's request for "some explanation" of the act of July 20, 1790, that "some Masters of Vessels" misinterpret the law, "But although under this Law, the absence of a seaman from the vessel for more than forty-eight hours is not supposed to forfeit his right to be received again in the vessel, the duty of the Master to receive such seamen does not relieve the Consuls and Commercial Agents of the United States from their obligation of providing subsistence and passages for the mariners and seamen of the United States who may be found destitute within their districts." Copy. DNA, RG59, Cons. Instr., vol. 2, pp. 454–55 (M78, R2).

From J[oel] R. Poinsett, Mexico, no. 109. Transmits a letter (not found) from (William) Tudor to (John) Sergeant, containing details of "several interviews" between Tudor and the Peruvian President, General (José de) Lamar; notes that "It would appear that" Peru will not ratify the treaties signed at Panama and will "take no further part in the deliberations of the American Congress." Encloses also a letter (not found) from (James) Cooley to Sergeant, "on the same subject and to the same effect. . . ." LS. DNA, RG59, Dip. Disp., Mexico, vol. 3 (M97, R4). Received January 14, 1828. Cf. above, Cooley to Clay, September 19, November 7, 1827.

From WILLIAM TUDOR, Lima, no. 81. Encloses a "despatch [above, Mariategui to Clay, November 16, 1827] from the government of Peru"; notes that similar documents have been sent to England; and explains that by this means Peru is appealing for mediation on the part of "the U. S. & . . . England" to prevent a war threatened by (Simón) Bolívar. Adds that (José de) Lamar has named a representative to go to Bogotá in the interest of peace. Expresses a belief that Bolívar will, unless faced with "insuperable obstacles in Colombia" or by "the mediation of the U. S. & England," never "desist from his purpose of enslaving South America, to which the conquest of Peru" would be the prelude. ALS. DNA, RG59, Dip. Disp., Brazil, vol. 6 (M121, R8). Received May 1, 1828. Cf. above, Tudor to Clay, August 9, September 19, November 7, 1827.

MISCELLANEOUS LETTERS   December 7, 1827

From W[ILLIAM] B. GILES, "Executive Department Richmond" (Virginia). Encloses a letter addressed to himself by "Mr [Thomas W.] White, Contractor for printing certain Journals," listing "several more of the Senate Journals missing," and asks Clay "to cause to be transmitted . . . such of . . . [them] as may be found in the Public Library." LS. DNA, RG59, Misc. Letters (M179, R65). Cf. above, Giles to Clay, October 17, 29, 1827; Clay to Giles, October 20, November 1, 1827.

From BENJAMIN D. WRIGHT, Pensacola. Acknowledges receipt of Clay's letter of November 14; reports that he has communicated the President's wish to (Charles) Mifflin, who "promptly notified Mr. [John] Inerarity of his willingness to deliver" (John Home) Purves' papers, "free of expenses"; encloses a copy of his opinion on the controversy, requested by both Mifflin and Inerarity but not acted on by the latter; and assures Clay that the sheriff (Mifflin) took custody of Purves' effects by authority of territorial legislation "relative to gran[t]ing Letters of Administration. . . ." ALS. DNA, RG59, Misc. Letters (M179, R65).

From Dominique Bouligny

Dear Sir   Washington December 8th. 1827

In answer to your esteemed favor of the 7th inst.[1] requesting me to State any recollection that I may have of a conversation which took place at your Lodgings concerning the election of President of the United States, I can say, I distinctly recollect that on the 20th. December 1824, which was the day of my arrival here from the State of Louisiana to take my seat in the Senate of the United States, I called on you the same evening and in the course of a conversation in which, I informed you that you had lost the votes of Louisiana, I desired to know who you intended to vote for as President; you then told me

without any hesitation that you would vote for Mr. Adams in preference to Gl Jackson. With great respect Yours respectfully

D BOULIGNY

ALS. DLC-HC (DNA, M212, R3). Published as supplementary material, "Appendix,"
54–55, with Clay's *Address . . . to the Public*, below, December 29, 1827. Addressed to
Clay.
[1] Not found.

INSTRUCTIONS AND DISPATCHES December 8, 1827

From CHARLES W. DABNEY, Fayal. Encloses documents "relative to the ship London Trader of New York, which disclose a nefarious transaction in which are
implicated the Judge & others of the Island of St. Mary & the Corregidor [Autos
Coelho] of the District of St. Michael & St. Mary—" Explains that the *London
Trader*, en route from New York to Gibralter, "sprang a dangerous leak" and
was stranded on a beach of St. Mary; that the crew "proceeded to dismantle the
ship & discargo the Cargo"; that "A conspiracy was formed to deprive the agent
of the Vice Consul [Thomas Hickling] (who was absent at the time) of his powers,
which were transferred to a creature of the Judges, & the consignment of this
valuable property made over to him"; that the conspirators then sold the property
and the proceeds were "paid into the public deposit," over which the Judge has
"unlimited controul"; that upon learning of these facts, Dabney addressed the
Governor General, who issued orders to correct the situation; but that the orders
were thwarted by the Corregidor, who had been charged with implementing them.
ALS. DNA, RG59, Cons. Disp., vol. 1 (M-T203, R-T1).
Coelho and the other Azores officials have not been further identified.

From J[OEL] R. POINSETT, Mexico, no. 110. States that "The movements so long
anticipated [cf. above, Poinsett to Clay, October 6, 1827; Taylor to Clay, November
26, 1827] have taken place both in the States of Puebla and of Vera Cruz, where
the legislatures were hostile to the public sentiment"; explains that, "In the latter
State," a "meeting of the people" induced the legislature to enact a law expelling
Spaniards, while in Puebla the same issue brought an outbreak of violence before
"The general government . . . by promises and caresses . . . succeeded in most
instances in dispersing" the insurgents. Reports having learned that "the leading
members of the York party [the 'Yorkinos']" have organized a secret society, popularly known as the Guadalupes (not further identified) and patterned after the
Italian Carbonari, which has spread throughout the country and has been responsible for "the insurrectionary movements in the States where the legislatures
were hostile to the views of the dominant party"; characterizes the organization
as "certainly a most dangerous instrument of political power," fortunately "wielded
by the friends of the existing institutions"; and predicts that "This machinery will
. . . be put in motion to secure the election of General [Vicente] Guerrero to the
Presidency." Encloses a translation of the bill, "for the expulsion of the Spanish
inhabitants of Mexico," now before the House of Representatives (cf. above,
Poinsett to Clay, November 10, 1827), and comments that it "will most probably
pass into a law. . . ." Adverts to the financial difficulties of the Mexican Government and notes the resignation of (Francisco) García (Salinas) from the Treasury.
Discusses an interview with President (Guadalupe) Victoria, who apologized "for
the delay in re-commencing our negociations," which he attributed "to the continued indisposition of Mr. [Sebastian] Camacho, the Secretary of Foreign Re-

lations" (cf. above, Poinsett to Clay, March 18, April 30, 1826; October 6, 1827); promised "an invitation to resume the negociations in the course of the next week"; and asked Poinsett "to assure the President of the United States of his earnest desire to conclude the pending treaties" (cf. above, Poinsett to Clay, August 10, 1827). Expresses pleasure that (José Ignacio) Esteva will resume the office of Secretary of the Treasury. LS. DNA, RG59, Dip. Disp., Mexico, vol. 3 (M97, R4).

MISCELLANEOUS LETTERS   December 9, 1827

From S[AMUEL] B. BARRELL, Eastport, Maine. Reviews his journey from Portland to Eastport, where he arrived December 7. Reports that he has "seen no evidence of the *excitement* which has been supposed to exist in relation to the arrest of [John] Baker"; that he is "inclined to believe that the information given to the Government has been much exagerrated [*sic*], if not altogether unfounded"; and that "The people of New Brunswick . . . are very sensitive upon the subject of Mr Davis' [Charles S. Daveis'] appointment and threaten him with serious consequences if he attempts to proceed to the settlements upon the disputed territory without permission from the Governor [Sir Howard Douglas]." States that, consequently, he intends to disclose his own agency upon arriving at Fredericton, as he does not believe he can proceed "in any other character than that of a public agent." Adds in relation to the right of Maine or Massachusetts to exercise jurisdiction over the disputed settlements: "Governor [Enoch] Lincoln informs me, that as to the Matawascah [*sic*] settlement, as it existed previously to the Treaty of Ghent, it is not known that any direct and immediate acts of jurisdiction have been exercised over it by Massachusetts. That the recent conveyances by Maine & Massachusetts were, as it is believed, intended as evidence of claim and occupancy, and that all the antecedent action of those States was in the view that their right was perfect over the whole disputed territory. That they had no occasion for displaying their sovereignty or that of either of them over every particular spot; but that by occupying and governing, from the earliest period, different parts, have shewn their sense of their rights, and have done everything which, constructively, was important against the pretensions, resulting from any circumstances, which may be exhibited as to actual possession and a forced and arbitrary application of power by New Brunswick."

Notes that Lincoln has indicated to him that "the whole constitutional power of Maine . . . would, under the control of the Legislature, be employed to prevent such aggressions as those have been understood to be, which have been recently suffered from New Brunswick," and that, although military force might be resorted to "for self preservation," it would be used "only in such manner and under such restrictions" as calculated to earn the approval of the Federal government. ALS. DNA, RG76, Northeastern Boundary, entry 87 (MR frames 651–56). Extract published in Manning (arr.), *Diplomatic Correspondence . . . Canadian Relations*, II, 664–65.

DIPLOMATIC NOTES   December 10, 1827

To C[HARLES] R. VAUGHAN, Washington. Summarizes the case of Nathaniel Snelson and requests Vaughan's aid with the Canadian authorities in obtaining Snelson's detention and delivery to the agent of the Bank (of Virginia). Adds: "In support of this application, which is not founded, I am aware, upon any obligation, imposed either by the public Law or by treaty, reliance is placed upon the interest which is common to all Governments to detect and punish similar offences; and upon the prompt attention which was shewn to a Similar application made by you on the 3d. November 1825. . . ." Copy. DNA, RG59, Notes to Foreign Legations, vol. 3, pp. 406–407 (M38, R3). ALI draft, in CSmH.

On December 11 Clay wrote to John Brockenbrough, president of the Bank of Virginia, acknowledging receipt of the latter's letter of December 6 and transmitting a copy of this note. Copy, in DNA, RG59, Dom. Letters, vol. 22, p. 105 (M40, R20).

From CHARLES R. VAUGHAN, Washington (1). Acknowledges receipt of Clay's note (above, December 6, 1827) and states that he "will seize the first opportunity of submitting the proposal . . . to His Majesty's Government, and he has no doubt, but that every facility will be afforded for carrying into effect, the intentions of the Government of the United States." LS. DNA, RG59, Notes from British Legation, vol. 14 (M50, R15).

On the same date Clay informed John McLean of Vaughan's reply. Copy, in DNA, RG59, Dom. Letters, vol. 22 (M40, R20).

From CHARLES R. VAUGHAN, Washington (2). Reports that he has received instructions from his Government to inquire about "the fate of Mr. Thomas Sullivan," who, according to the latter's sister, was born "in Tralee, in the County of Kerry in Ireland, . . . was by trade a Carpenter," and was probably ship's carpenter on the United States frigate *Boston* in 1813. States that Sullivan's family wishes to know whether or not "the person in question is still in existence" and requests any information "which may be derived from the Department of the Navy. . . ." LS. DNA, Notes from British Legation, vol. 14 (M50, R15).

On the same date Clay transmitted this note to the Secretary of the Navy (Samuel L. Southard) and requested the desired information. Copy, in DNA, RG59, Dom. Letters, vol. 22, p. 105 (M40, R20).

Sullivan has not been further identified. Cf. below, Southard to Clay, December 12, 1827.

The United States frigate *Boston*, 28 guns, had been built at Boston in 1798 and launched the following spring. She had been laid up in 1812, as unfit for repair, and burned at Washington two years later.

INSTRUCTIONS AND DISPATCHES   December 10, 1827

From A[LEXANDER] H. EVERETT, Madrid, no. 93. Transmits a translation of "a note from Mr [Manuel Gonzáles] Salmon on the subject of the restitution of the Columbian [*sic*] Privateer Zulmé" (cf. above, Clay to Everett, March 20, 1827; Everett to Clay, July 4, 28, 1827), of which "The purport . . . is that the Government consider the demand inadmissible, because the capture was not made within cannon shot distance from our coast. . . ." Declares that this statement does not answer "the averment" upon which the claim was based— that the vessel "was taken when lying at anchor in a narrow strait wholly comprehended within our territory. . . ." Notes that he has mentioned this fact in his reply, a copy of which is enclosed and in which he has pointed out an error in Salmón's interpretation of "the 18th article of the Treaty of 1795" (Pinckney's Treaty) and has noticed "in terms of disapprobation the unwarrantable principle, introduced into the Privateering Regulations quoted by him, which makes the obligation of one belligerent power to respect the rights of neutrals dependant upon their being respected by the other." Reports that, with regard to "the indemnity question" (cf. above, Everett to Clay, April 19, June 4, 22, 1827), Salmón informed him "A few days ago . . . that he had at last obtained from the Council of State a report upon this business, which . . . was unfavorable to the conclusion of any arrangement of the kind . . . [Everett] had proposed" (cf. above, Everett to Clay, February 13, March 31, 1827). Encloses also "two other notes, received since" his last dispatches. LS. DNA, RG59, Dip. Disp., Spain, vol. 28 (M31, R29). Received March 11, 1828.

Article 18 of Pinckney's Treaty states that when a warship or privateer of either signatory belligerent shall meet a merchant vessel of the other "sailing along the Coasts on the high Seas . . . the said Ship of war or Privateer for the avoiding of any disorder shall remain out of cannon shot and may send their boats aboard the merchant Ship . . . and may enter her to number of two or three men only to whom the master . . . shall exhibit his passports concerning the property of the ship. . . ." Parry (ed.), *Consolidated Treaty Series*, vol. 53, p. 27.

One of the enclosures last mentioned by Everett contains regulations applicable to steamboats arriving in Spanish ports; the other informs Everett of actions taken upon receipt of his note of November 21 (cf. above, Everett to Clay, November 26, 1827).

From J[OHN] M. FORBES, Montevideo. Transmits his "Despatches, Nos. 53 and 54" (above, August 28, October 30, 1827) with enclosures. Announces his arrival in Montevideo where he has come, "impelled by the strongest motives of health, and having no hope left but in a change of scene and climate," and where he expects to remain "only a fortnight." LS. DNA, RG59, Dip. Disp., Argentina, vol. 3 (M69, R4). Published in Espil (comp.), *Once Años en Buenos Aires*, 483–84.

To William B. Giles

His Excellency W. B. Giles   Departmt. of State,
Sir,   Washington 11th. Decr. 1827.
    [Acknowledges receipt of Giles' letter of December 7, with enclosure.] I immediately sent the list of the missing Journals, contained in Mr. White's note, to the Librarian,[1] who, I regret to say, after careful examination, cannot find that any of them are in the Library.[2] He thinks that the Book, heretofore transmitted to your Excellency, contains the Journals of the May and October Sessions of the respective years of 1779, 1780, 1781 & 1784, which are among those enumerated by Mr. White as missing.—

    I beg your Excellency to be persuaded, that it would have given me particular satisfaction to have been instrumental in supplying you with the Journals requested, as it will, be at all times, to render you any service in my power.— I am with great Respect, Your Excellency's obedt. Servant,   H. CLAY.

Copy. DNA, RG59, Dom. Letters, vol. 22, p. 106 (M40, R20).
[1] George Watterston.   [2] The Library of Congress.

From Jabez D. Hammond

Dear Sir,   Albany Dec. 11. 1827
    I have ascertained with deep regret that the Presidents message does not contain any recommendation in relation to an improvement of the

Tariff[1]— Much excitement has for some time past prevailed here on that subject and notwithstanding what may be said and believed of the result of the late election here,[2] those of us who have viewed attentively the ebbings & flowings of the tide of popular opinion have entertained no doubt that if the President in his Message had identified himself with the American System (and we presumed he would do so) Electors in a large majority of the Districts might have been carried triumphantly for him— We meant to have charged the Jackson party with hypocrisy in pretending friendship for the American System while at the same time they supported a party in the nation hostile to it— Why should the President omit giving an opinion on so important a Measure?—

It is said Mr. Matthew Myers, who has recently been nominated for Collector of the Customs at Ogdensburgh in this state will not be appointed— In this event David C. Judson of Ogdensburgh ought to be appointed[3]— I am very respectfully Your obedt Servt

The Hon. H. Clay   JABEZ D. HAMMOND

ALS. DLC-HC (DNA, M212, R3).   [1] Cf. above, Porter to Clay, November 22, 1827, note.   [2] Cf. above, Sergeant to Clay, October 24, 1827, and note.   [3] Myers, of Ogdensburg, who had held the collectorship on an interim appointment since August, was confirmed for regular appointment on December 31, 1827. He was removed by President Jackson, in January, 1830. Judson had represented St. Lawrence County in the New York Legislature in 1818 and had been sheriff from 1818 to 1821 and a member of the State Senate in 1821. He was a county judge from 1829 to 1840 and collector at Oswegatchie from 1840 until 1849.

DIPLOMATIC NOTES   December 11, 1827

From CHARLES R. VAUGHAN, Washington. States "that he will immediately communicate to His Excellency the Governor of Canada [the Earl of Dalhousie], the request of the Government of the United States [above, Clay to Vaughan, December 10, 1827], that Nathaniel Snelson . . . may be detained, in order to his being delivered up hereafter to an Agent of the Bank [of Virginia], who is to be authorized to take charge of him." Reminds Clay that, in the case alluded to in his note, "the surrender of [Michael] Neilson was refused by the Governor of the State of New York" (DeWitt Clinton—cf. above, Clinton to Clay, December 19, 1825; Clay to Vaughan, December 29, 1825). Expresses "his wish, that the utmost facility should be given to the arrest of malefactors of the description above mentioned, whenever an application shall be made, by either of the Governments. . . ."
LS. DNA, RG59, Notes from British Legation, vol. 14 (M50, R15).

MISCELLANEOUS LETTERS   December 11, 1827

From ALBERT GALLATIN, New York. Reports receipt of Clay's "despatch No. 36" (above, September 17, 1827), forwarded by (William Beach) Lawrence (cf. above, Lawrence to Clay, October 29, 1827). Cites the decision to exchange, at London, ratifications of the Convention of November, 1826 (cf. above, Gallatin to Clay, November 11, 13, 1826); notes an "understanding between the Plenipotentiaries" that ratifications of "the three last Conventions" (cf. above, Gallatin to Clay, August 6 [101 and 102], 7, September 30, 1827) should also be exchanged there; and adds: "but there was no special agreement to that effect; and the term of nine months may leave sufficient time for" a different arrangement. States that he has been "so much indisposed" that he has been unable "to prepare the additional explanations respecting the evidence in relation to the North Eastern boundary" (cf. above, Gallatin to Clay, November 30, 1827). ALS. DNA, RG59, Dip. Disp., Great Britain, vol. 34 (M30, R30). Copy, NHi-Gallatin Papers, Letterbook vol. 15, p. 155 (MR21).

Tax Receipt from James Hall

TREASURER'S OFFICE, VANDALIA, Dec. 12, 1827.
Received of Henry Clay Nine *Dollars and* One *Cents, being the amount of the tax due to the State of Illinois, on the following described Land for the year set forth:*

District.	Acres.	Description.			Years.	Tax.
Vincennes	160	Se	6.	14n. 10w	1827	0 92
	598	Sec.	7.	14n. 10w	"	4 73
	160	Sec	8.	14n. 10w	"	0 92
	281	W1⁄2	18.	14n. 10w	"	1 52
	160	Se	12.	14n. 11w	"	0 92
						9 01.

Countersigned.   {*Signed Duplicates.*}   JAMES HALL
E. C. Berry Auditor.   *Treasurer.*

DS, partially printed. DLC-TJC (DNA, M212, R16). Cf. above, III, 134–35, 291; Tax Receipt, June 29, 1825; Clay to Cook, June 20, 1826.

INSTRUCTIONS AND DISPATCHES   December 12, 1827

From J[AMES] COOLEY, Lima, no. 10. Describes an insurrection of the Indians "in some of the Provinces in the Department of Ayacucho" and the successful efforts of the government to quell it. States that Peru has appointed a Minister, (José de) Villa, to Colombia for the purpose of attempting to adjust the differences between the two countries; that (Juan Manuel) Yturregui (Iturregui), a wealthy young man already in England, has at his own solicitation been appointed Chargé d'Affaires, without compensation, to that country; and that "The Congress are still engaged principally in the discussion of the project of a Constitution," with little prospect of early success. Refers to the effort to obtain the mediation of the United States and England (between Peru and Colombia—cf. above, Mariategui to Clay, November 16, 1827; Tudor to Clay, December 7, 1827) and warns against "such an interference" by the United States. Notes that General (Antonio José de) Sucre (y de Alcalá) has recalled the Bolivian Minister, (Francisco Javier) Serrano (Gomez), from Lima. Reports that he (Cooley) has appointed Stanhope Prevost as acting consul at Lima and expresses a wish for his permanent appointment. ALS. DNA, RG59, Dip. Disp., Peru, vol. 1 (M-T52, R1). Extract published in Manning (arr.), *Diplomatic Correspondence . . . Latin-American Nations*, III, 1843. Received May 1, 1828.

Born in 1798, Villa had been chief clerk in the Marine Department in 1823 and secretary to the Minister of War (Juan de Berindoaga) in 1824 and 1825. Critical of Bolívar, Villa failed in his mission to Colombia. During the next five years he was in and out of favor with a succession of Peruvian governments. He served as Minister of the Hacienda in 1833 and intermittently of the Departments of War and Marine, but in 1835 he was forced into exile.

Yturregui, born in 1795, had entered business as a young man, merchandising arms, and had become active in the movement for Peruvian independence. He had been accredited by José de la Riva Agüero in 1823 as Minister Plenipotentiary to Chile, where he had sought the aid of San Martín in support of Peru. With the fall of Riva Agüero and Berindoaga from favor, during Bolívar's ascendancy (see above, Tudor to Clay, February 28, 1826, note; Larned to Clay, July 28, 1826, note), Yturregui had gone to Europe and remained there until 1832. He was subsequently Minister of Hacienda (1849) and a Senator, from 1849 to 1853 and from 1868 to 1870. In 1854 he was accorded the rank of brigadier general.

From A[LEXANDER] H. EVERETT, Madrid, "No. 3. Confidential." States that he has "intended ever since . . . [he] received the information respecting the British intrigue for revolutionising [sic] the island of Cuba and the Canaries [see above, Everett to Clay, June 9, August 17, 1827], to communicate with this [Spanish] Govt. upon the subject at the earliest favorable opportunity" and would "probably have adjourned the matter untill [sic] after the King's [Ferdinand VII's] return [cf. above, Everett to Clay, September 20, 1827], . . . about the middle of January, had not the Govt. recently shown a disposition to terminate at once the negotiation respecting Indemnities" (cf. above, Everett to Clay, December 10, 1827). Adds: "It struck me that a free communication with the Minister [Manuel Gonzáles Salmón] upon the subject alluded to would naturally produce a more friendly & confidential feeling towards the U. S. which might possibly have a favorable effect upon the decision of this question." Reports that he told Salmón "that the Govt. of the U. S. had reason to suppose that the British Govt. had organised a plan for revolutionising the islands; and . . . enquired . . . whether this Govt. had any knowledge of the proceedings"; that "Mr. Salmon seemed a little surprised" but admitted having received some information concerning possible British designs on Cuba, though he believed "every thing was tranquil & secure"; that he further told Salmón that "The object of the plan was to place the island [Cuba] under the protection of G. Britain; but . . . the form of a declaration of Independence was to be adopted in order to avoid awakening the jealousy of the U. S."; that the United States, not deceived, "could not view with indifference these movements of the British Govt. considering it . . . as a settled principle that the island must in no event pass into the possession or under the protection of any European power other than Spain" (cf. above, Clay to Everett, April 27, 1825); that the United States wished no territorial "or other direct advantage from the part which they might be compelled to take in the affairs of Cuba" but desired "to employ their influence, should it be necessary, in the manner most agreeable to the wishes and the interests of H. M." Notes that he suggested to Salmón that the time had come "for a more full & free communication of intentions & opinions respecting . . . the American Colonies in general" and, further, that a better understanding between the two countries would result "if H. M's. Govt. would consent to arrange immediately to the satisfaction of the U. S. the several questions now under negotiation." Encloses a copy of "a short confidential memorandum upon the subject," which, at Salmón's request, he has prepared for that Minister. Indicates that he is not hopeful of the result. Summarizes at length a conversation, held, after writing his "last confidential letter" (above, October 19, 1827), with (Louis Bronier de) Cluet, who denied being involved "in the troubles of Catalonia," expressed "the strongest wish that, the island of Cuba might form a part of our Confederacy," and offered his help in "delivering it up to the U. S. . . . ."

Informs Clay that he has "been for some months past in communication with" a Colombian agent, Dr. Thomas Quintero (not further identified), at whose request he has written to Salmón a note (copy enclosed) proposing an exchange of prisoners between Spain and Colombia. LS. DNA, RG59, Dip. Disp., Spain, vol. 28 (M31, R29). Extracts published in Manning (arr.), *Diplomatic Correspondence . . . Latin-American Nations*, III, 2149–52. Received March 11, 1828.

President Adams noted (*Memoirs*, VII, 473) that this dispatch gave Clay "some uneasiness."

From ALBERT GALLATIN, New York, no. 129. Begins his communication, of over 24 manuscript pages, by writing: "I will now proceed to state the additional evidence which appears to me necessary to be procured in support of the right of the United States to the contested territory along the North Eastern Boundary" (cf. above, Gallatin to Clay, November 30, December 11, 1827). Appraises this evidence in relation to British contentions and to arguments in support of the position of the United States, all of which is to be laid before the Arbiter. Continues, on December 17, by stating: "I have abstained from touching the main argument, and have alluded to others, so far only as was necessary to render intelligible what I had to say respecting new evidence; which was the object of this letter." Offers "to give any further explanation" that "may be deemed useful." Notes "some inofficial conversation," which proved fruitless, with "the British Plenipotentiaries . . . on the propriety of a temporary agreement that might prevent collision, in the contested territory, until a decision was obtained. . . ." Adds in conclusion: ". . . I may have omitted some observations concerning old evidence. . . ; and . . . it may be useful, that I should (as soon as I can have access to all my papers,) prepare and transmit to you as complete a list of all the evidence, old or new, as lies in my power." ALS. DNA, RG76, Northeastern Boundary, entry 82 (MR frames 20–32). Copy, NHi-Gallatin Papers, Letterbook vol. 15, pp. 157–79 (MR21); published in Manning (arr.), *Diplomatic Correspondence . . . Canadian Relations*, II, 666–79.

From W[ILLIAM] R. HIGINBOTHAM, Bermuda. Cites recent instances of American merchant vessels either sunk off the coast of Bermuda or entering port in distress. States that he has, "in compliance with . . . instructions" received earlier in the year "from the 5th. Auditor of the Treasury Dept. [Stephen Pleasonton]," demanded payment (for discharged seamen) conformable to the act of February 28, 1803 (cf. above, Pleasonton to Clay, April 19, 1825; Clay to Quarrier, May 12, 1825), with the result that he had anticipated and about which he has already written (above, Higinbotham to Clay, June 1, 1826), that is, "that the Masters would not comply with the same—in most cases they have not the means of making the advance or of paying their own expences [*sic*], and the Seamen finding no means of support from their own Country through the Public Agents of the United States in foreign ports would naturally seek the protection of some foreign power"; asserts that "such has been the case of the Crews of these Vessels who for want of support have shipped on board of British Vessels"; and predicts that over "100 Seamen from this port alone will be lost to the United States during the winter and employed in the British Service (perhaps their Ships of War) if some efficient measures [are] not adopted for their protection and authority given to the Public Agents [to] enforce the compliance of whatever order may be issued from the Dept of [State] under severe penalties for disobedience thereof—" Notes the "mortification" he has suffered when summoned by the Governor (Tomkyns Hilgrove Turner), who remarked "that several American Seamen had sought relief from him w[hich] from motives of humanity he gave observing that H. M. Government cou[ld] not support the distressed of every nation and why he asked does not their [own] Government provide for them—" Reports that, when he replied that he was "not authorized t[o] afford any assistance at the expence of the U. S." but "Individually" would do what he could, the Governor said, "in that case . . . they must be handed over to the Parish Officers and sent from the Island as soon as possible—this was done and they ship[ped] on board of British Vessels—" Complains that his "Accounts for the relie[f] [of] Distressed American Seamen" have not been paid in full and that his "Drafts drawn on the Secretary of State for such advances have [been] dishonoured and returned [cf. above, Babson to Clay, March 29, 1826; Quarrier to Clay, November 6, 1826; May 2, November 3, 1827; Clay to Higinbotham, April 3, June 23, 1826; November 16, 1827] . . . attended with heavy expences. . . ." LS. DNA, RG59, Cons. Disp., Bermuda, vol. 1 (M-T232, R1). Received January 11, 1828. Margin obscured in binding.

Governor Turner, born about 1766, had served in the British Army with distinction through the conflicts with the French on the Continent in 1793 and 1794 and in Egypt in 1801. He had risen to the rank of lieutenant general in 1813 and had then been knighted. His duties in later life had been largely ceremonial and administrative. He had been lieutenant governor of Jersey from 1814 to 1816 and governor of the Bermuda Islands since 1825. Remaining in the latter position until 1831, he was promoted to general in 1830.

From J[OEL] R. POINSETT, Mexico, no. 111. Transmits "copies of the Treaty between Mexico and Great Britain, signed in London on the 26th. of December, 1826" (cf. above, Gallatin to Clay, December 16, 1826; Poinsett to Clay, March 17, 1827). LS. DNA, RG59, Dip. Disp., Mexico, vol. 3 (M97, R4). Received February 10, 1828.

From J[OHN] G. A. WILLIAMSON, LaGuaira. States that he has "reason to believe that . . . communications may have been addressed to" Clay concerning his encounter with E. W. Robinson (cf. above, Williamson to Clay, September 19, 1827); expresses hope that it will not be thought that he would do anything discreditable to his office and country; and requests "that due allowance should be given to the manner and the *source* from which" such reports emanate. ALS. DNA, RG59, Cons. Disp., LaGuaira, vol. 1 (M84, R1). Received January 7, 1828.

MISCELLANEOUS LETTERS   December 12, 1827

From S[AMUEL] L. S[OUTHARD], Navy Department. Acknowledges receipt of Clay's communication of December 10, 1827 (see above, Vaughan to Clay, December 10, 1827, note). States that a search of the records of the Navy Department and the Fourth Auditor's office has failed to find a Thomas Sullivan who "ever held in our service a situation as Petty Officer"; that Sullivan could not have served on the *Boston* "at the time mentioned" because "that Ship was placed in Ordinary at the Navy Yard, Washington, in the year 1802 [*sic*], and never afterwards put in Commission." Adds that, if Vaughan can provide further information, the search "will be renewed with cheerfulness. . . ." LS. DNA, RG45, Misc. Letters (M179, R65).

Check to Robert P. Letcher

13h. Decr. 1827

No.   OFFICE OF DISCOUN[T & DEPO]SIT, [WASHING]TON,
    PAY to Robert P Letcher or order Five hundred Dollars, /100
$500 DOLLARS, /100   H. CLAY

ADS, partially printed. DLC-TJC (DNA, M212, R16). MS. torn. Endorsed on verso by Letcher.

From Francis T. Brooke

My Dear Sir   Richmd Decemr 13 1827
Our Court now sits until 4 OClock and I have a few minutes to say a word or two, I have seen a letter from Mr Sergeant[1] which is a little embarrassing—we are not authorised to say that either Mr Madison or Mr Monroe will consent to act as Electors if put on our ticket, Some of us mean to place them at the head of it, but it is not yet certain that the convention here will assent to it[2]— Mr Call[3] has been a little premature on that subject, we know that they are with us and we think when approached by the convention they will not refuse— on the subject of the v Presidency I refer you to my letter to Doctor Watkins[4] since writing it, I have conversed with Mr Johnson[5] who declines the nomination of himself, as unfitted for the office and the office for him,— if Penna can be influenced by having it, the usage of taking a citizen from a nonslavery holding State ought to be no obstacle,— if it is it is questionable whether N Carolina had not better be looked to as I fear we shall get no aid from any Virginian Johnson having declined it, our spirits are reviving here, there will be a caucus of the legislature to night, to arrange matters and time of the electoral Caucus— I see that the responsibility is now on the opposition and we must make the best use of it, Your friend   FRANCIS BROOKE

ALS. InU. Addressed to Clay.   [1] John Sergeant.
[2] For the convention, cf. above, Mercer to Clay, August 18, 1827, note. James Madison and James Monroe, in that order, headed the list of presidential electors designated by the friends of the administration in Virginia. Washington *Daily National Journal,* January 15, 1828. On the response of the ex-Presidents to this action, see below, Brooke to Clay, February 28, 1828.   [3] Daniel Call—cf. above, Clay to Brooke, December 6, 1827.
[4] Tobias Watkins.   [5] Chapman Johnson—cf. above, Brooke to Clay, November 20, 1827.

From James Brown (1)

My dear Sir,   Paris Decr. 13, 1827
I have received your letter of the 28th. of Oct which came by the New York Packet of the 15 Novr. It has removed a great deal of the anxiety we had felt on account of your health, an anxiety increased by finding that so soon after your return to Washington you had left it for the Virginia Springs.[1] I am glad to find that you are able to attend to the arduous and perplexing duties of your office and that you have made up your mind not to repine at the abuse which the Presses are throwing on you and indeed on every man of character or standing in the nation. I am sorry that Mrs. Clays health is impaired but hope the winter will restore it. Mrs. Brown has made no visits for the last three months and I have felt the most dreadful apprehensions on her account. She is now visibly improved and will I hope in a few weeks be

again restored to the gay world of which she is so fond and where she is a general favorite.

You will perceive by my dispatch of this date and by the newspapers that we have great reason to expect a change of Ministry. The people have pronounced loudly a sentence of banishment on those now in power and although I esteem some of them and particularly the one with whom I have the most to do as respectable individuals and have every reason *personally* to be grateful for the politeness with which they have conducted themselves in their relations with me yet I am not sure that my country will have any reason to regret any change which can happen. Since Mr de Villele has been in place our claims have had in him an active opponent and I have no reason to hope that his opinions in relation to them are likely to undergo a favorable change. I thank you for the hints you gave me as to the manner of executing my instructions and shall follow them. It was never my intention to have closed the negociation here before I had obtained a written answer. You may judge by the delay which has taken place in obtaining answers even on comparatively unimportant subjects how long it may be before I finish this matter with this Government. When Mr de Mareuil applied to you to refund the duties on the vessels coming from St Pierres you returned a favorable answer in three days.[2] On the 1st Septr.[3] I made a similar application to the Baron de Damas, and although I have urged him as well in conversation as by letters to give me an answer I have not yet been able to extract any thing more from him than promises that I shall soon hear from him. This is vexatious and it requires all the efforts I can command to keep me from expressing myself perhaps too strongly on the subject.

You must have been greatly disappointed at the result of the elections in New York. It is to be hoped that the western counties will be more favorable to Mr Adams. Still I presume that the general ticket system will be resorted to and that the State will give its entire vote to General Jackson.[4] I have already informed you that General Lafayette had sent on the certificate you asked.[5] I saw him last night and he assured me it had been sent. I hope it will be satisfactory. Virginia and Pennsylvania seem to change but have I apprehend delayed their efforts too long to leave a hope of giving Mr Adams a majority.[6] When I think of the active spirits at work in the State of Kentucky I greatly doubt whether Jackson will not have the majority in that State also.[7] Great changes however may take place every where in the course of twelve months—

I delayed my letter to the last moment in the hope that we might receive dispatches from Constantinople. The question of peace or war is very doubtful. Sovereigns who meant to frighten but not to fight the the [sic] Turks have in turn been frightened at finding themselves unexpectedly in an actual war whilst engaging in negociation.[8] You will find in the papers various reports such as that the Ambassadors have left Constantinople, that the Russians have crossed the Pruth &c.[9] none of which can be relied on. We must wait a few days longer and all doubts will vanish.

Ferdinand is as usual playing the fool or the madman at Barcelona into which place he made triumphal entry a few days ago amidst a silent and disatisfied [sic] population. Some hundreds, it is rumored of the malcontents have been hanged exiled or shot. It is thought another insurrection will be got up in the course of a few months.[10] Don Miguel has not yet arrived.[11] Great preparations are making for his amusement as well here as in England.

I send with this a letter for Colo. Drayton[12] on business of importance to one of his constituents which I wish him to receive immediately. My love to Mrs. Clay   Your friend & Obedt Serv

JAMES BROWN

ALS. DLC-HC (DNA, M212, R3).
[1] Cf. above, Clay to Erwin, August 4, 1827; Clay to Adams, September 24, 29, 1827; Clay to Johnston, October 6, 1827.   [2] Cf. above, Mareuil to Clay, March 13, 1827; Clay to Mareuil, March 14, 20, 1827; Clay to Rush, March 14, 1827; Rush to Clay, March 17, 1827; Clay to Brown, March 21, 1827.   [3] That is, August 1. Cf. above, Brown to Clay, August 13, 30, 1827; September 27, 1827.   [4] Cf. above, Sergeant to Clay, October 24, 1827, note.   [5] See above, Brown to Clay, November 13, 1827; Lafayette to Clay, October 10, 1827.   [6] Cf. above, Caldwell to Clay, August 8, 1827, note; Sergeant to Clay, September 23, 26, October 14, 30, 31, 1827; Mifflin to Clay, October 21, 1827; Strong to Clay, November 12, 1827; Clay to Brown, March 27, 1827, note.   [7] Cf. above, Clay to Brown, March 27, 1827, note.   [8] Cf. above, Ombrosi to Clay, November 6, 1827; Hughes to Clay, September 16, 1827; Middleton to Clay, September 29, 1827; Brown to Clay, September 29, October 12 (1), 28, November 12, 13, 28, 29, 1827; Lawrence to Clay, October 13 (2), November 14, 29, 1827; Dodge to Clay, November 17, 1827.
[9] Cf. above, Lawrence to Clay, December 6, 1827.   [10] Cf. above, Brown to Clay, September 29, 1827; Everett to Clay, November 8, 26, 1827. Ferdinand was to have been joined at Barcelona by the royal family "towards the end of October." Washington Daily National Journal, December 4, 1827. He remained there until August (1828), "till he had sated himself with the infliction of punishment, and believed that the last seeds of revolt had been destroyed." In the month of January, transports had taken 37 "ecclesiastics, secular or regular," and 256 citizens under banishment to North Africa for their part in the rebellion. Annual Register, 1828, 206. Rumors of continuing unrest recurred during the year, but the only disturbance was at Saragossa, where, without apparent political connection, a controversy developed from the efforts of churchmen to collect the tithe from market gardeners.   [11] Cf. above, Brown to Clay, September 29, October 12 (1), November 12, 1827; Lawrence to Clay, October 13, November 29, 1827; Everett to Clay, November 26, 1827; below, Brent to Clay, January 9, 1828; Lawrence to Clay, January 14, 1828.   [12] William Drayton. The enclosure has not been found.

INSTRUCTIONS AND DISPATCHES   December 13, 1827

From JAMES BROWN, Paris (2), "Private." States that election "returns from all the departments" (cf. above, Lafayette to Clay, October 10, 1827, note) have given "the combined opposition . . . a majority of from twenty to thirty members" and "will necessarily produce a change of ministry. . . ." Notes that "It is . . . now believed that Mr. de Villèle will with his colleagues remain until the commencement of the session, and employ the interval in attempting to gain sufficient support from the ranks of one or the other, or indeed both of the oppositions, to enable him to carry his measures"; that "it is not very probable that he can succeed"; and that "This victory . . . by the constitutional party, will in all probability secure the liberty of the press, and retard the progress of the congregations and jesuits, which has been so rapid and alarming since the return of the Bourbons" (cf. above, Brown to Clay, August 12, 23 [1], 1826). Reports the arrival of a courier from Constantinople, on December 2, "with dispatches which seemed to destroy all hope of an accommodation of the affairs in the east, without an appeal to arms." Terms "It . . . somewhat extraordinary" that no further information from that area has arrived. ALS. DNA, RG59, Dip. Disp., France, vol. 23 (M34, R26). Received February 23, 1828.

To Maria Gist Gratz

My Dear Madam   Washington 14h. December 1827

I received this morning your obliging letter of the 3d. instant[1] on the subject of that which I had addressed to Mr. Gratz.[2] I have a distinct recollection of the occasion, at your house, on which the conversation stated by you took place; and I am perfectly sure that your narrative of it is entirely accurate. I know not how to express, with sufficient warmth and gratitude, my very great obligations for your kindness in writing the letter and your generous permission to use it in my defence. Although I feel sensible that it would be of much benefit to me, and I should feel proud and honored by the exhibition of the name of a fair witness, among the other respectable persons who have testified to the same point, I cannot *allow* myself to use the privilege which you have given so kindly. I cannot consent to place your name in the public prints. Some rude and uncourteous Editor or Scribbler might say some thing to wound your feelings or my own on account of you.

I shall write to Mr. Blair and procure his statement,[3] which may supersede the necessity of a public use of your's, which I shall nevertheless file carefully away and preserve among my most cherished documents.

Be so kind as to tell Mr Gratz that I received his letter also this morning.[4]

After much anxious consideration of what was best to do for Henry C. Hart, his disposition &c. I concluded to put him in the Navy. He has been some weeks at Norfolk on board the Guerriere with the son of Commodore Rogers and others to receive instructions from an excellent master[6] to qualify him for his profession. I had a letter[7] from him yesterday, asking to pass the Xmas here with us, and I shall give him permission accordingly, if he can obtain a furlough. I understand he is so far well pleased. He will sail to the Mediterrenean in the course of a month or two, which is a branch of the public service admirably calculated to enable him to acquire knowledge of his duties and to attach him to his calling. I should have been glad to have had it in my power personally to consult your mother,[8] yourself and other members of your family about this arrangement; but it was necessary for me to decide quickly or lose the opportunity of his proceeding on the contemplated cruize. It will afford me much pleasure to learn that what I have done is approved.

I have nothing new to communicate to you from this place. Of politics every body is heartily tired; 'tho' we learn that the Ladies in Lexington are arrayed, under opposite standards, and take a lively interest in behalf of their respective favorites. I hope that the unusually large number of your Sex who have come here this winter with the members of Congress, their husbands and relatives, will contribute to calm the angry and excited passions, and to smooth and soften our ways.

Mrs. Clay unites with me in offering you our best respects, and I pray you to convey mine also to Mr. Gratz. Your affectionate friend
Mrs. Maria Gratz   H. CLAY

ALS. Owned by Miss Henrietta Clay, Lexington, Kentucky (now in KyLxT-Henrietta Clay Collection).
[1] Not found.   [2] Benjamin Gratz. The letter has not been found.   [3] Francis P. Blair. Cf. below, Blair to Clay, December 31, 1827, and note.   [4] Not found.
[5] John Rodgers and son, John.   [6] Joseph Smith, of Massachusetts, who had entered the Navy as a midshipman in 1809 and had been raised to the rank of lieutenant in 1813, had been named master commandant of the *Guerrière* on March 3, 1827. He attained the rank of captain in 1837 and that of rear-admiral, on the "Retired List," in 1862.   [7] Not found.   [8] Judith Cary Bell, who had married, first, Nathaniel Gist and had been widowed in 1796, had become the wife of General Charles Scott in 1807. Following the latter's death, in 1813, she lived with Maria and Benjamin Gratz in Lexington until her death, in the cholera epidemic of 1833. Henry Clay Hart was her nephew and a cousin of Maria Gist Gratz.

DIPLOMATIC NOTES   December 14, 1827

To C[HARLES] R. VAUGHAN, Washington. Transmits the report by the Secretary of the Navy (Samuel L. Southard) of this Department's search for information about Thomas Sullivan (above, Southard to Clay, December 12, 1827). Offers to cooperate further if Vaughan "should be able to suggest any mode of continuing it with a prospect of a more auspicious result." Copy. DNA, RG59, Notes to Foreign Legations, vol. 3, p. 408 (M38, R3). ALI draft, in CSmH.

INSTRUCTIONS AND DISPATCHES   December 14, 1827

From W[ILLIAM] B. LAWRENCE, London, no. 14. Reports having received, "Several weeks since," from (Alexander H.) Everett "a copy of a confidential despatch from the Spanish Minister in London [Count d'Alcudia] to his Court, giving notice of certain projects of the British Government on the islands of Cuba and the Canaries" (cf. above, Everett to Clay, August 17, 1827); adds that Everett also mentioned rumors he had heard of negotiations in London "under the mediation of the great European powers, respecting Spanish America and that he would be obliged by any information on either of these subjects"; and encloses that portion of his reply to Everett relating to the inquiries. States that "There was a rumour, last week, that Spain had actually recognized the new States" but he is convinced that there was no basis for it and, on Everett's "other point," that he considers "it entirely out of the question for England, *at this time*, to entertain views of acquiring the remaining Spanish possessions in the West Indies &c." Observes that the Count d'Alcudia's dispatch had been written before recent events in Europe. Comments on Russian victories over Persia (cf. above, Lawrence to Clay, November 29, 1827; Middleton to Clay, November 29, 1827) and, despite the necessity of preserving "Persia as a barrier between Russia and British India," the apparent lack of attention in England to these developments. Summarizes newspaper accounts of occurrences in Turkey, from which no news has been received "of a date later than the 11th. ultimo." Conjectures, "from the language of members of the opposition, that . . . much of the force of their attacks in the ensuing session of Parliament will rest" on two topics: "the Treaty [cf. above, Brown to Clay, July 12, 1827] and the late hostile occurrences" (at Navarino—cf. above, Ombrosi to Clay, November 6, 1827). Remarks that "there are many who approve of the interposition originally contemplated, who do not justify the late hostilities"; that "on this last point, the Ministry itself is said not to be unanimous"; and that "The departure of Sir John Gore for the Levant [cf. above, Hughes to Clay, November 27, 1827] . . . had for its object an enquiry into the conduct of the Commanding Admiral [Sir Edward Codrington]." Mentions decorations conferred immediately "on the officers engaged in the naval action" (at Navarino), which appear to imply approval, and explains that, as he understands, "the intention of granting the distinctions . . . originated with the King [George IV] & Duke of Clarence, . . . the proposition was sent from the Admiralty to the Home office," through error was given "to the [London] Gazette for insertion," and "Once promulgated, . . . could not be recalled. . . ." Cites a call for Parliament to meet on January 22, a date "earlier than was, some weeks since, intended, in order to enable Mr. [William] Huskisson and other Ministers, who have received appointments during the recess, to be re-elected and take their seats early in February." ALS. DNA, RG59, Dip. Disp., Great Britain, vol. 35 (M30, R31). Received February 26, 1827.

MISCELLANEOUS LETTERS   December 14, 1827

From THOMAS WHIPPLE, JR., Washington. Requests an account of the payment received by Isaac Hill to publish the laws of the United States. Continues: "This statement is necessary to undeceive the public in N. H." ALS. DNA, RG59, Misc. Letters (M179, R65).

INSTRUCTIONS AND DISPATCHES   December 15, 1827

From THOMAS L. L. BRENT, Lisbon, no. 48. Encloses translation of a letter, dated November 15, from Dom Miguel to his sister, the Regent (Isabel Maria), informing her that he will probably arrive in Portugal near the end of December, "and directing that the Peers and Deputies should be in Lisbon the 20th. in order that the Regent may the day after his arrival open the chambers for the purpose of receiving his Oath to the constitutional chart." States "that the ultraroyalist party . . . are not a little mortified" at Miguel's "earnestness to comply as soon as possible with this essential form." Reports that on December 9 "the Bank of Lisbon stopped payment" and has indirectly tried "to connect the government with the cause of their failure," to which effort "the latter have officially expressed . . . indignation. . . ." Predicts "that the Bank will finally pay all its debts" but that the reestablishment of its credit will be difficult; concludes that "this failure of the Bank has added in no slight degree to the many pressing difficulties under which all commercial transactions have laboured for some time past." LS. DNA, RG59, Dip. Disp., Portugal, vol. 7 (M43, R6). Received February 7, 1828.

Later, on the same day, Brent transmitted in an unnumbered dispatch a translation of a statement of arrangements by the bank for re-establishing credit. ALS, in *ibid.* Received February 7, 1828.

From SAMUEL LARNED, Santiago de Chile, no. 64. Reports a liberalization of regulations concerning deposits of United States naval stores; a call for "A new general and constituent Congress . . . to convene on the 12. of February next"; and the appointment, "at length," of "a Minister of Foreign Relations . . . in the person of Don Carlos Rodriguez. . . ." Notes that the appointee is "a brother of the political martyr Manuel Rodriguez" and "also a warm friend to the United States. . . ." ALS. DNA, RG59, Dip. Disp., Chile, vol. 2 (M-T2, R2). Received May 21, 1828 (ALS copy, received May 1, 1828).

Carlos Rodríguez has not been further identified. Manuel Rodríguez, born in 1785, had been educated as a lawyer but had given his life to the early movement for independence. He had been identified with the Carrera brothers, for whom he at one time served as secretary; and following their fall from power he had been arrested and, in 1818, assassinated before he was brought to trial.

From W[ILLIAM] B. LAWRENCE, London, no. 15. Reports the announcement of "two Orders in Council, dated 16th. November and issued under the 'Act to regulate the trade of the British Possessions abroad' " (cf. above, Rush to Secretary of State, March 26, 1825, note; Clay to Ogden, June 17, 1826, note). Adds: "One of these orders extends to Charlotte Town in Prince Edward's Island, the privileges of a free port . . . and the other makes considerable additions to the free warehousing ports in the British American possessions." Encloses a copy of *The London Gazette*, of December 14, 1827, in which the Orders in Council were published. ALS. DNA, RG59, Dip. Disp., Great Britain, vol. 35 (M30, R31). Published in Manning (arr.), *Diplomatic Correspondence . . . Canadian Relations*, II, 679–80. Received February 16, 1827.

The newly designated free warehousing ports were: "port of Spain, in the island of Trinidad; Nassau, in the island of New Providence; Montego Bay, in the island of Jamaica; Roseau, in the island of Dominica; and Saint Andrews, in the province of New Providence [*i.e.*, New Brunswick—see below, Lawrence to Clay, December 22, 1827]."

MISCELLANEOUS LETTERS   December 15, 1827

To HENRY M. BRACKENRIDGE, "Judge of the Superior Court of the U. S. for the D. of W. F Pensacola." Transmits "a Copy of a letter from Mr.]Benjamin D.] Wright, Attorney of the U. S. for the District of West Florida, to the President under date the 10th. of last Month, exhibiting certain charges against . . . [Brackenridge] for neglect of duty. . . ." Adds: ". . . I am now directed [by the President] to furnish you with the Copy, in order to your giving such explanations upon the subject, as, you may be of opinion will vindicate your Conduct." Copy. DNA, RG59, Dom. Letters, vol. 22, p. 108 (M40, R20). Published in Carter (ed.), *Territorial Papers*, XXIII, 951.

To John J. Crittenden

My dear Sir   Washn. 16h. Dec. 1827.

Incessant engagements have placed me in arrear to you. I have received your several letters transmitting that of mine to Mr. Blair, your statement of the conversation in which I avowed my preference for Mr. Adams over Genl. Jackson, and those of recommendation &c.[1]

My friends are some what divided about the necessity or expediency of my again addressing the public, but the major part of them concur in recommending it. I believe therefore I shall shortly present a mass of testimony which has been collected, including that of Genl La Fayette which I have recd. and which is very satisfactory.[2]

I have written to Blair and requested his statement of my having expressed the above preference in his presence.[3] As to my letter to him in Jany 1825[4] it is written in such a strain of pleasantry and friendly familiarity that I do not think it ought to be published, although properly interpreted there is nothing in it that ought to operate to my prejudice.

Although I feel grateful for your communication to the public,[5] I am inclined to think that you might have safely remained silent.

I should be extremely glad to conform to your wishes respecting the son of Mr. Marshall;[6] but the distribution of the appointments of Cadets is generally regulated by such fixed rules that a deviation from them leads to much complaint. And as it is an affair which belongs to another department, I feel restrained by considerations, which you will at once appreciate, from any positive interference in it. I have at this moment by me three or four unanswered letters from as many friends whom I would gladly serve, if in my power, soliciting my interposition in behalf of their relatives. In truth, I have found it necessary to limit myself pretty much to the office to which I am attached, or to be perpetually intermeddling in other departments. I will nevertheless bear in mind your request, and if I can with propriety second the application, it would give me real and unaffected pleasure to do so.

We are, I believe it may be fairly owned, in the minority in both houses—not as to measures, but as to the personal predilections for the Presidency. The majority is not in either large. Although it is a state of things somewhat new, I am persuaded it will do the Administration no mischief here. The responsibility of measures now rests with the Opposition. They have alleged the existence of abuses which they must, being now in the possession of power, expose and reform, or forfeit the public confidence. They cannot fail too I think to divide on such measures as the Tariff &c. And these collisions must have a good tendency on our cause.

As to N. York our friends remain confident that Mr. Adams will obtain at least 26 of the Electoral votes,[7] notwithstanding the result of the late elections.[8] That result was brought about by a secret coalition between Clinton & Van Buren, which 'though it was suspected and denounced, was nevertheless positively denied. By means of the systems of nomination, through the agency of Conventions, tickets nominally in opposition were brought out, and it was so contrived that the persons on both tickets were for Jackson in instances sufficiently numerous to ensure a Jackson majority in the Legislature. The force of habit, in voting for regular nominations, and the question of the Presidency being really agitated in only a few places, secured success to the intrigue. In many instances the Candidates were not known to have a partiality for Jackson until after the election. All agree that the Legislature will not venture on the perilous step of wresting the choice of Electors from the people and assuming it themselves. No change will probably be made in the Electoral law,[9] unless it may possibly be that of a general popular ticket, which our friends would not fear.

Mean time prospects are bright and encouraging not only in Virginia but also in North Carolina. There is a spirit now awake and in activity in both those States that justifies strong hopes of success. In Pennsa. too our friends are on the alert, and if no adverse events should arise to check the current there in our favor, we need not despair of getting its vote.[10]

In short, if things are not in all respects as we could wish them every where, there is no occasion for depression; but on the contrary enough of hope and probability to animate us to the greatest exertions.

We have heard of the equal vote for Speaker in the H. of R. in K. without having yet learnt the final issue.[11]

You see that I am obliged to write less at large than I could wish, but even in this way my letter is drawn out to an appalling length— I must therefore close it with renewed assurances of faithful friendship
Jno. J. Crittenden Esq.   H CLAY

ALS. DLC-Crittenden Papers (DNA, M212, R20).
[1] Above, September 3, November 15, 18, 19, 28 (1 and 2), 1827.   [2] See below, *Address . . . to the Public*, December 29, 1827. For Lafayette's letter, see above, October 10, 1827.   [3] Not found.   [4] Above, January 8, 1825.   [5] Cf. above, Crittenden to Clay, October 30, 1827, and note.   [6] Humphrey Marshall, son of John J. Marshall.
[7] Cf. above, Brooke to Clay, September 21, 1827, note.   [8] Cf. above, Sergeant to Clay, October 24, 1827, note.   [9] Cf. above, Clay to Brooke, December 11, 1826, note.
[10] Cf. above, Clay to Brown, March 27, 1827, note.   [11] Through seven ballots over three days, December 3–5, the Speakership count had been tied. On December 3 and 4 the candidates had been Robert J. Ward and William B. Blackburn. Late on December 5 the Jacksonites had dropped Ward and nominated John Speed Smith. Still the vote had remained tied. On December 6 Smith had been elected over Blackburn by a one-vote margin.

From Edward Ingersoll

Hon. Henry Clay
Dear Sir   Philadelphia Decr. 16. 1827
Though my natural temperament and habit of mind is sober at least if not dull and melancholic,—it so happens that whenever I allow myself the pleasure of inflicting a letter upon you I have an excitement of spirit that urges me into the peril of being pert and flippant. As this is altogether a metamorphosis effected by the pride of being privileged to engage your attention,—I lay the blame of all such sins upon you as

the moving cause—, and I beg you will exonerate me accordingly.

The only service I can do to you at present is to be brief. Therefore in a few words I will unfold the notion that now incites me to this intrusion.

You may remember that I told you I thought of asking the President to avail himself of my services as his agent at Copenhagen.[1] You and Mr. Miner,[2] to whom only, I mentioned the project, omitted to tell me of the passage of the clause which provided for such an agency, in the appropriation act, and I was saved the opportunity of being rejected as an aspirant by the President.

Well I confess I was somewhat vexed with Mr. Miner—because I wanted to take a chance, however slender, of being so recommended to the President's approbation, as to obtain from him a sort of employment which would be inexpressibly agreeable to me. I am not self-conceited—, to the best of my knowledge and belief—, I may be somewhat spoiled, and puffed up, by the notice which you have sometimes taken of me;—, but I did not, and do not now, consider myself entitled to claim anything on the score of either merit or service. As to merit I do not consider it essential; and of service I have done nothing. But as to disposition, endeavors,—and personal favor with not a very few men of political eminence—I could not help thinking unless I was greatly deceived—, and if I were the undeceiving would be useful—that compared with my old acquaintances Mesrs. Raguet, Appleton, and Brent—, or even Mr Wheaton[3]—I need not fear a scrutiny, or being put to the proof.

With such dreams—, still undispelled,—and with a particularly confident opinion that I could go through the business without very glaring blunders, no wonder that I should still think that if another opportunity is passing by, I should like to avail myself of it,—to suggest myself to the consideration of the executive as one willing to serve the nation in an inferior office connected with its foreign intercourse.

If therefore any such matter is in contemplation as the selection of a diplomatic agent of lower rank—and you can without official inpropriety apprise me of the fact,—will you extend your kindness so far as to give me the hint?[4] And in doing so, will you please to make generous allowances for any self delusion that you may possibly be inclined to ascribe to me? To propitiate which I could remind you of the entire insignificance of Mr Raguet both before and since holding a commission in your department, and with whom it implies no over weening vanity to compare myself advantageously in some respects   Most faithfully and respectfully Yours   EDWARD INGERSOLL
Hon. H. Clay.

ALS. DLC-HC (DNA, M212, R3).   1 Cf. above, Ingersoll to Clay, March 11, 1827.
2 Charles Miner.   3 Condy Raguet; John J. Appleton; Thomas L. L. Brent; Henry
Wheaton.   4 See below, Clay to Ingersoll, October 23, 1828.

Rental Agreement with Joseph Ficklin

[December 17, 1827]

It is agreed between Henry Clay and Joseph Ficklin as follows— The said Clay leases to the said Ficklin for the term of One year, commencing with the first day of January and ending with the 31st day of December 1828, the Brick House and lot[1] situate between the House and lot occupied by the Office of the Bank of the U. States and Mr. Blanchard[2] on Poplar Row in the Town of Lexington—

In consideration whereof the said Ficklin hereby obliges and binds himself to pay to the said Clay, the sum of One hundred and seventy five dollars in gold or silver coin payable quarter yearly— And to surrender to said Clay on the said 31 day of Decr. 1828, the said House and lot and premises in as good condition as they now are or may be rendered at his[3] expense natural decay and inevitable accidents only excepted.

To secure the punctual payment of the rent the said Clay reserves the right of distress for any of the rent which may remain due and of entering and taking possession of said premises—

In Testimony whereof the parties have hereto set their hands and seals this 17th. day of Decr. 1827   HENRY CLAY by Robt. Scott
                                                       JOSEPH FICKLIN

Memorandum[4]— All the locks in the house have Keys and are in good order, except the back door of the Pantry room— There are no locks to the Cellar doors nor to the Ice house or Dairy—the locks that are complete and in good order are to be returned so— The Windows are full glazed and are so to be returned—   JOSEPH FICKLIN
(his in the 13 line means Clays)

[Endorsements on verso][5]

Mr Ficklin has this day agreed to keep the within premises another year on same terms as within   ROBT SCOTT
30 December 1828

ADS, by Robert Scott for Clay, signed also by Ficklin. DLC-TJC (DNA, M212, R16).
[1] This was formerly Colonel Thomas Hart's residence.   [2] Asa Blanchard, whose residence was located on the west side of North Mill Street (Poplar Row), three doors north of Church Street.   [3] This word falls in the thirteenth line of the manuscript Agreement. Cf. below, clarification attached to the memorandum on this document.
[4] ES, in Scott's hand.   [5] The first, AES; a second, AE, a record of receipt of quarterly payments, of $43.75 each, from July 5, 1828 (apparently for the first two quarters), through January 1, 1831, omitted by the editors.

DIPLOMATIC NOTES   December 17, 1827

From J[OS]É SILVESTRE REBELLO, Washington. Notes the arrival, in the port of New York, of a privateer, the *General Brandizen*, belonging to the United Provinces of the River Plate, with a Brazilian prize; points out that the Government of the

United Provinces has been dissolved, that the privateer's letter of marque has thus become void, and that the vessel will become a pirate; and states his expectation that the United States will embargo it and its prize. ALS, in Portuguese with trans. (AL) by Rebello. DNA, RG59, Notes from Brazilian Legation, vol. 1 (M49, R1).

President Adams recorded, on December 24, 1827 (*Memoirs*, VII, 387–88), that "Mr. Clay mentioned" this note and that "The note is to be answered, and directions given to the District Attorney at New York to take the steps required by the law in the case." See below, Clay to Tillotson, December 31, 1827, and note.

MISCELLANEOUS LETTERS   December 17, 1827

From JOHN McKIM, JR., Baltimore. Reports that he has vacated his seat on the board (of directors) of the Bank (of the United States) at Philadelphia. Recommends as his successor "a Gentleman who is a large stockholder, and one the *Present Administration can place Confidence in*, Thomas Wilson," of Baltimore. ALS. DNA, RG59, Letters of Resign. and Declin. Endorsed by Clay on cover: "To be submitted to the President."

On the recommended appointment, cf. below, Clay to Trevor, January 4, 1828, and note.

From HARRY I. THORNTON, Huntsville, Alabama. Recommends (Francis W.) Armstrong for reappointment as United States marshal for the District of Alabama. States: "Majr Armstrong is the political adherent of Jackson, but by private friendship, and by constant unity of action in *State* politics, he is so identified, with the friends of the Administration in this quarter, that I feel assured, his re-appointment would be *more acceptable to them*; and from the circumstances above named, *less so*, to the clamourous friends of Jackson, than that of any other man.— I shall go down in a few days to Tuscaloosa where the session of the Legislature, & of the Supreme Court, will have convened most of the influential men of our State. I will write you from that place, or on my return" (no letter has been found). ALS. DNA, RG59, A. and R. (M531, R1). Endorsed: "Private & Confidential."

For Armstrong's re-appointment, see below, Clay to Armstrong, January 15, 1828.

Promissory Note to George Graham

[December 18, 1827]

Sixty days after date for value received, I promise to pay to George Graham or order the sum of Five hundred dollars, without defalcation. Witness my hand this 18th day of December 1827.

H CLAY

ADS. DLC-TJC (DNA, M212, R16).

From Richard Rush

My dear Mr. Clay,   10 At Night Dec 18. 1827.

Your invitation[1] and Mrs Clays to your winter evenings, got to my hands this morning, and I have passed it to my wife's.[2] She will be most happy to be with you, as often as in her power. For myself, I am a slave, a very slave, the charter of whose present existence cuts him off from all and every such indulgence, even though tendered by "Your Excellence," as Kit Hughes[3] would say. In truth, I am so galled, so whipped up, so ground down, morning noon and night, and night noon and morning, by being head overseer, and journeyman too, of the octogenarian[4] department, that I was forced to make a vow and covenant on the first day of the session, not to break bread out of my own house (and miserable brown stuff it is that I break there just now) by day or by night 'till the session is over, if it lasts 'till doomsday, and we know that it is to last almost as long. This is a hard fate to undergo, and for one who likes good cheer, and has always been accustomed to it, moderately at least; yet it is to be my fate without mitigation, unless perchance I should ever break its bonds by darkening the threshold, once in-a-while, of "our worthy little master" [5] over the way. As to our most potent sovereign lords and masters upon the hill, they would scourge me to death you know, or flay me alive, if I do not mind their business; so the only way in which I, or mortal man like me, can compass that, and mind all the other treasury business to boot, big and little which never stops, (including a daily quantum of the most horrible parts which I never should have had to mind if our said lords and masters had deigned to grant me the humble boon, I once asked of a little more clerical aid at the desks of my superannuated beaureaus [sic],) is by digging and fagging by night as well as by day. This is the long and short of the story. By leading this antisocial life—hard pennance [sic] as it is—I shall hope to flounder through the session without being impeached; and if god spares me 'till it is over, as good Christians should say, I will resume good fellowship with you and others once more I trust. But, 'till then, farewell to evening parties all, farewell to dinners; farewell to such dinners even as yours, to which when bidden I have never heretofore said nay—to all farewell. Othello's occupation's gone.[6]

I have forced an answer upon you, and a long-winded one—though the requisition is scratched out from your kind billet, being ever yours (though for this session, only from the loop-holes of my hermitage not *The* Hermitage mind)   R. RUSH

ALS. DLC-HC (DNA, M212, R3).   1 Not found.
2 Mrs. Rush was the former Catherine Elizabeth Murray, of Annapolis. The couple had married in 1809.   3 Christopher Hughes.   4 Treasury.   5 President Adams.
6 Cf. Shakespeare (Furness [ed.], *A New Variorum Edition. . .*), *Othello* (11th edn.), Act III, sc. 3, line 413.

INSTRUCTIONS AND DISPATCHES   December 18, 1827

To JAMES COOLEY, Lima. Acknowledges receipt of Cooley's dispatch no. 6, dated August 11, 1827 (above). States that (Beaufort T.) Watts' letter (to Simón Bolívar

—cf. above, Watts to Clay, June 14, 1827, note) "was written without instructions, and gave great dissatisfaction to the President." Continues: "It was a departure from that well established principle of avoiding all interference in the internal affairs of other countries, by which this Government has ever regulated its conduct; and was, moreover, objectionable as indicating a confidence in the views and purposes of Genl. Bolivar which the President regretted he was obliged not to feel. . . ."

Reports that he has been directed by the President to express the latter's satisfaction with Cooley's course in informing the Peruvian Government that he believed Watts' letter was unauthorized. Adds: "You will avail yourself of some early and fit occasion, informally, to make the Government of Peru acquainted with the substance of this despatch." Copy. DNA, RG59, Dip. Instr., vol. 12, pp. 47–48 (M77, R7). ALI draft, in DLC–HC (DNA, M212, R8).

From ALEXANDER HAMMETT, Naples. Copies his letter to Clay of June 20, 1827, and explains that the 30 percent "allowance on duties for return cargoes in Neapolitan vessels" applies not only to the East and West Indies but also to other areas, including the United States. Observes that the 10 percent advantage to others was enough to exclude United States vessels from trading at Naples, while the increase to 30 percent will be even more prejudicial. Asks whether "the American property c[on]fiscated here [cf. above, II, 505n; Clay to Appleton, May 12, 1825], [is] to be considered abandoned, u[ntil] France shall have first paid us" (cf. above, Brown to Clay, December 12, 1825; Appleton to Clay, February 14, 1826); states that in view of "these disgraceful transac[tions] . . . [he] would not longer delude" himself; and adds that, if "nothing" is "to be expected," he must seek "employment elsewhere unless the President be pleased to give . . . [him] another Situatio[n]." ALS. DNA, RG59, Cons. Disp., Naples, vol. 1 (M-T224, R-T1). Received April 26, 1828. Margin obscured in binding.

MISCELLANEOUS LETTERS   December 18, 1827

To JAMES BARBOUR. Transmits a copy of a note, with its enclosures, from the British Minister in Washington (Charles R. Vaughan), dated December 14, 1827, (i.e., December 4, 1827, above), regarding American Indians in the village of St. Regis. States: "I must, accordingly, ask the favor of you to cause the necessary enquiries to be made, by the Agents of Indian affairs, or others under the control of your Department (of War), in that quarter, and communicate the result to me, together with the opinion which may be entertained, as to the remedy suggested for preventing the recurrence of like incidents." Copy. DNA, RG59, Dom. Letters, vol. 22, pp. 108–09 (M40, R20).

MISCELLANEOUS LETTERS   December 19, 1827

From BETSEY HAWLEY, "77 Norfolk Street," New York. States that, having received no reply to her last letter (above, November 8, 1827), she sought counsel and learned that she "should proceed to get some business done at Washn. thro' the medium of a certain member of Congress" (not identified); that before taking this step, she wishes to know, because one of her counsellors believes Clay has "been induced by some misrepresentation, thus to neglect" her, what has dissuaded him "from a further attention to the subject of . . . [her] late brother's [Isaac P. Hawley's] concerns"; and that further information concerning the consul's [Franklin Litchfield's] letter to her may be obtained from "Wm. Silliman

Esq. Attorney at law No. 21 Cherry Street N. York—"   ALS. DNA, RG59, Cons.
Disp., Puerto Cabello, vol. 1 (M-T229, R1).

On December 23, Daniel Brent wrote Silliman that Clay had received Miss Hawley's letter, "full of complaints and reproaches at his not having noticed a late
communication from her. . . ." Brent added that, at Clay's direction, he had sent
her an answer (to the earlier letter—cf. above, Hawley to Clay, November 8, 1827,
note), which, apparently, she did not receive. He now enclosed a copy of that reply
and asked Silliman to get it to her, "with an assurance from this Department, that
it has received no further, or other intelligence from the Consul upon the subject
of the business in question, than is contained in that letter." Copy, in DNA, RG59,
Dom. Letters, vol. 22, p. 110 (M40, R20).

Convention of Friendship, Commerce, and Navigation with the Hanseatic Republics

[December 20, 1827]

[Henry Clay, for the United States, and Vincent Rumpff, for "the
Republic and Free Hanseatic City of Lubeck, the Republic and Free
Hanseatic City of Bremen, and the Republic and Free Hanseatic City
of Hamburg (each State for itself separately,)," agree to articles as follows: (I) each of the contracting parties guarantees to the vessels of
the other equality with its own in regard to imports from and exports
to "any foreign country"; (II) "No higher or other duties shall be imposed on" imports into either party from the other than on imports
of like articles from "any other foreign country; . . . nor shall any prohibition be imposed, on the importation or exportation of any article,
the produce or manufacture of" one party "to or from, the ports of
the" other, "which shall not equally extend to all other nations";
(III) "No priority or preference shall be given" by either party "in the
purchase of any article" produced by "their States, respectively, imported into the other, on account of . . . the character of the vessel,
whether it be of the one Party, or of the other, in which such article
was imported"; (IV) "any vessel . . . owned . . . by a Citizen, or Citizens
of" the three Hanseatic Republics, "and of which the master shall also
be a citizen, . . . and provided three fourths of the crew shall be Citizens
or Subjects of any or either of the said Republics, or of any . . . of the
States of the Confederation of Germany . . . shall . . . be . . . considered
as . . . belonging to Lubeck, Bremen, or Hamburg"; (V) any vessel belonging to a Hanseatic Republic and coming to the United States from
any of the Hanseatic ports "shall . . . be deemed to have cleared from"
its home port, "and any vessel of the United States . . . trading to the"
Hanseatic ports, "directly, or in succession, shall . . . be on the footing
of a Hanseatic vessel . . . making the same voyage"; (VI) citizens of each
party shall be free to conduct business "in all the ports and places" of
the other and are "to be treated as Citizens of the Republic in which

they reside, or at least, to be placed on a footing with Citizens or subjects of the most favored nation"; (VII) citizens of each party "shall
have power to dispose of their personal goods, within the jurisdiction
of the other, by sale, donation, testament, or otherwise"; (VIII) both
parties promise equal protection under their laws to "the Citizens of
each other"; (IX) "The Contracting Parties . . . engage mutually not
to grant any particular favor to other nations, in respect of Commerce
and navigation, which shall not immediately become common to the
other Party, who shall enjoy the same freely, if the concession was
freely made, or on allowing the same compensation, if the concession
was conditional"; (X) "The present Convention shall be in force for
. . . twelve years, . . . and further, until the end of twelve months after"
either party "shall have given notice of . . . intention to terminate" it;
(XI) "ratifications shall be exchanged at Washington, within nine
months from the date hereof, or sooner if possible."]

Miller (ed.), *Treaties. . .* , III, 387–96. The Senate gave its advice and consent, January
7, 1828. U.S. Sen., *Executive Journal*, III, 589. Ratifications were exchanged on June 2,
1828.

From Edward Colston

Dr Sir   Richmond Decr 20th. 1827

I regretted very much not having it in my power to see you on my
way down, more particularly as I was charged with a message to you
by the Revd Dr. Milnor,[1] who you may remember dined with me at
your house, and travelled up with me the next day in the stage. In the
course of conversation, he related to me the same circumstances concerning your former disagreement which you had mentioned the evening before, without the least idea of my knowing any thing about it,
until he mentioned that he really did not write the piece which gave
you offence, nor at the time you called on him did he even know the
author, but he would not make this explanation at the time, because
he thought you had no right to call upon him more than any one else,
for the authorship of such a piece, & expressed some doubt whether
you had ever known that he was not the author. I then informed him
of my impression from a conversation I had had with you, that you
continued under that belief, & received from him a commission to
make this explanation

I have been expecting with great anxiety the publication[2] you mentioned to me when we last met, & have taken the liberty of repeating
in confidence the statements you then made as to its contents. This has
excited a universal anxiety amongst your friends to see it, and I am
convinced if it does not help Mr Adams, it will at least prepare the
public mind, to receive you on a future occasion, most favorably. I

fear the thing is settled now that Jackson is to be president, but many of us cherish your character, not only from our personal friendship but from a strong political feeling that at the end of his term, you alone can save us from the Van Burens, & I am sorry to add the Clintons, & still further regret to say the Calhouns of the day[3]— For the two last I had entertained strong political partialities, & with regard to the last, a little of personal feeling was super added, but their late conduct, (not in supporting Genl: Jackson, but in their manner of doing it) has cured me of this— I rejoice to say to you, that I have taken some pains to ascertain how you stand with the friends of the administration, and find you universally preferred to any other man as the future president of the U. States. Should Genl: Jackson be elected & you return to Congress, I firmly bleive [sic] should it please God to spare you, that at the end of his term, if you should not pursue a course of unreasonable opposition to his administration, no management would be able to get the state of Virginia for either of those men, in opposition to you. You may judge then, how anxiously we all look forward to so complete an exculpation of your character.

The prospects here are not darkened much by the untoward events elsewhere, but I fear it will prevent that exertion amongst the people generally without which nothing can be done. The impression made by the confident tone of the Jackson presses with regard to New York can only be removed by demonstration   If therefore there should be a majority of friends to the administration in the legislature lately elected, & which will meet in Jany; some decisive resolution should be passed on the subject.[4] No private statements will be beleived [sic] and this has a strong tendency to damp zeal. The election of Speaker to the House,[5] & printer to the senate,[6] are unfavorable occurrences, but those we could manage if the friends of the administration were assured that New York stood firm— The late appearances in Kentucky too distress us,[7] but nothing equals the loss of the great state which had always been considered firm.

Were I to advise, I should think it would have a good effect if the president were to advise the location by law of the great Southern road[8] and its immediate commencement, leaving the selection of the particular route to Congress— I have no idea that any thing would be done in consequence, but as many proofs as possible should be accumulated, of the inimical feelings of the present party to the two great systems of Internal improvement & the tariff, and the rejection or neglect of the recommendation might have some influence in Virginia. It is very much to be desired that they should be compelled to shew what their policy is to be, as those developements [sic] would probably not aid them much in Pennsylvania: but I am under a most firm persuasion, that actuated by this fear, they will pass all the recommendations of the Harrisburg manufacturing convention[9] into law and that our Virginia representatives, however they may bluster will not defeat it. The best way to keep them to the trig. will be to throw out this insinuation, & I beleive I will contrive it.

Your friend Judge Brooke[10] has gone home to spend the holidays, was well two days since; Mr Call[11] is as zealous a man as every [sic] was & seems to prosper under the excitement— This is rather an uncomfortable tale they have on Pleasants, & which you will see his own account of in his last Whig.[12]

With the sincerest wishes for your health happiness & prosperity I am yours &c   EDWD COLSTON

ALS. DLC-HC (DNA, M212, R2). Addressed to Clay and endorsed on cover: "Private."
[1] James Milnor, born in Philadelphia in 1773, had been admitted to the bar in 1794 and had opened practice in Norristown. He had removed to Philadelphia in 1797 and subsequently had become active in politics, as a member of the city council from 1807 to 1810 and the United States House of Representatives from 1811 to 1813. Upon his return from Congress, he had trained for priesthood in the Episcopal Church. He had served briefly as an assistant minister in Philadelphia but in 1816 had become priest of St. George's Episcopal Church in New York City, where he remained until his death in 1844. Milnor had bitterly opposed the War of 1812 and during debate on the reference of petitions for suspending operation of the embargo legislation, in April and May, 1812 (cf. above, I, 641–42), had complained of the conduct of Clay as Speaker. An editorial in the Washington *Daily National Intelligencer*, May 14, 1812, had alluded to "the insinuations [of newspaper reports on the incident] in relations [sic] to Mr. CLAY . . . [as] unfounded in fact." Editor Joseph Gales, Jr., had testified "to the respectability of deportment and impartiality of conduct uniformly displayed by the Speaker . . . in the performance of the duties of his station." Reports of the debate have not been found.
[2] Probably Clay's *Address . . . to the Public*, below, December 29, 1827.   [3] Martin Van Buren; De Witt Clinton; John C. Calhoun.   [4] On the composition of the New York Legislature, cf. above, Sergeant to Clay, October 24, 1827, note. That body failed to endorse a candidate for the Presidency; but for the Republican caucus action, cf. below, Porter to Clay, January 8, 1828, note.   [5] Cf. above, Clay to Taylor, September 7, 1827, note.   [6] Cf. above, Hammond to Clay, March 28, 1827, note.   [7] Cf. above, Clay to Taylor, April 4, 1827, note.   [8] Cf. above, Speech, January 17, 1825, and note (IV, 21–22, 32n); Clay to Stuart, December 1, 1825, note.   [9] Cf. above, Clay to Crowninshield, March 18, 1827, note.   [10] Francis T. Brooke.   [11] Daniel Call.
[12] In an editorial "To the Public," dated December 18, 1827, John H. Pleasants related the circumstances as "An act of inconsiderate folly, committed many years ago, in the heat of youth and party spirit." Some time prior to the winter of 1823–1824, Pleasants, then living in Lynchburg, Virginia, had threatened to publish correspondence critical of Thomas Higginbotham, cashier of the Lynchburg Farmers' Bank (founded in 1814), unless that official lent Pleasants money. Higginbotham had not responded; and Pleasants, who professed to have acted for the amusement of himself and his friends, had "thought no more of it." Recently, however, William Radford, who had been president of the bank at the time, had made public the correspondence from Pleasants to Higginbotham, as evidence to support the Jacksonite attack upon "unprincipled men, conducting Public Presses, in the pay of the Administration." Richmond *Constitutional Whig*, December 19, 1827.

DIPLOMATIC NOTES   December 20, 1827

From FRANCISCO TACÓN, Philadelphia. States that the King (Ferdinand VII), having approved the note addressed (by Hilario de Rivas y Salmon) to Clay on May 10 and having instructed him to urge restitution to (Juan Miguel de) Losada, he wishes to know the President's decision on the matter. LS, in Spanish with trans. in State Dept. file. DNA, RG59, Notes from Spanish Legation, vol. 9 (M59, R-T12).

MISCELLANEOUS LETTERS   December 20, 1827

From JAMES BARBOUR, Department of War. Acknowledges receipt of Clay's letter of December 18, 1827, with its enclosures, and states that "The complaint, as set forth in this correspondence, is the first official notice, which has been received at this Department, of the outrage alleged to have been committed by one part of the St. Regis Indians, upon the other." Promises to "cause the necessary inquiry to be made; and such steps to be taken, as the subject complained of, may require, with a view of adjusting it, as far as practicable, and keeping the peace between the parties, for the future.—" LS. DNA, RG59, Misc. Letters (M179, R65).

DIPLOMATIC NOTES   December 21, 1827

From FRANCISCO TACÓN, Philadelphia. Reports that he has been directed by the King (Ferdinand VII) to renew the application, made by his predecessor (Hilario de Rivas y Salmon), on March 10, 1826 (above). Requests that Clay's reply to Rivas y Salmon's letter be directed to Tacón. LS, in Spanish with trans. in State Dept. file. DNA, RG59, Notes from Spanish Legation, vol. 9 (M59, R-T12).

MISCELLANEOUS LETTERS   December 21, 1827

To "the President" [JOHN QUINCY ADAMS]. Transmits documents pertaining to the " 'negotiation of the Convention of the 13th. Novr. 1826 [cf. above, Gallatin to Clay, on that date], with Great Britain, for indemnity to the claimants under the first article of the Treaty of Ghent' " as requested by a resolution of the Senate of December 14, 1827 (U. S. Sen., *Executive Journal*, III, 579). Copy. DNA, RG59, Report Books, vol. 4, p. 213. Published, with enclosures, in *American State Papers, Foreign Relations*, VI, 745–53.

To A[LBERT] GALLATIN, New York. Acknowledges receipt of Gallatin's dispatches nos. 127 to 129 inclusive (November 30, December 11 [unnumbered], 12, 1827). Comments: "The latter will be highly useful in pointing out the sources, and assisting in the collection, of evidence which it may be material to adduce before the Arbitrator provided for by the late Convention, respecting our North Eastern boundary [cf. above, Gallatin to Clay, September 30, 1827, note]." States that the Convention is currently before the Senate but that Gallatin's presence in Washington is not necessary. Expresses belief that the Senate will approve the Convention and, thereafter, "measures of preparation for the Arbitration, will be adopted. . . ." LS. NHi-Gallatin Papers (MR15). Copy, in DNA, RG59, Dip. Instr., vol. 12, pp. 48–49; ALI draft, in DLC-HC (DNA, M212, R8); published in Manning (arr.), *Diplomatic Correspondence . . . Canadian Relations*, II, 143–44.

DIPLOMATIC NOTES   December 22, 1827

To JOSÉ MARÍA SALAZAR. Acknowledges receipt of his note of November 27, 1827, and reports having submitted it to the President. Declines to determine whether the claim of (Alejandro) Vélez "is well founded or not," because "the transaction does not appear to be one in which the Government of the United States can, in the opinion of the President interfere with propriety." States that (Benjamin F.) Hunt is not an officer of the Government and, consequently, not bound by its direction; that Hunt is subject to the "control of the Court, which is competent . . .

to enforce the payment of the money to the persons or their agents entitled to receive it"; and that the case belongs "to the ordinary administration of justice. . . ." Comments that the "duties of the Consular office, are not very accurately defined," but even if they comprehended an authority to obtain the money from Hunt, "it would not follow that the Consul general has an official right to the enforcement of such a demand by any means different from those which the persons whom he represents would be obliged themselves to employ, in the event of a controversy between these and Mr. Hunt." Copy. DNA, RG59, Notes to Foreign Legations, vol. 3, pp. 408–10 (M38, R3).

INSTRUCTIONS AND DISPATCHES   December 22, 1827

From W[ILLIAM] B. LAWRENCE, London, no. 16. Summarizes, with reference to the orders in Council enclosed in his dispatch of December 15, British legislation establishing "free ports," some of which were subsequently "made warehousing ports for such goods, as may be legally imported into them respectively." Notes that the act of 6 *George IV*, chapter 114 (cf. above, Clay to Ogden, June 17, 1826, and note), "had authorized the increasing of the number of 'the Free Ports,' as well as of those which were selected for the warehousing of goods, and it was the power thus given, which was recently exercised by adding to the former class Charlotte town, and to the latter, Montego Bay in the Island of Jamaica; Roseau in the Island of Dominica; and Saint Andrews in the Province of New Brunswick, (printed erroneously in the [*London*] Gazette 'New Providence.')." Explains that "the 'free ports' are so termed, not because they are open to all nations, but from their being the only places, where foreign trade is admitted under any circumstances." Adds: "Between the warehousing system as applied to the mother country and the Colonies, there is also a most marked distinction. All goods not specifically prohibited may be imported into the United Kingdom, to be warehoused for exportation, from any place in a *British* Ship, and from any place not being a *British* Possession in a foreign ship of any Country and however navigated (vide 6 Geo. IV cap. 109. S. 21); whereas the trade of foreigners with the Colonies being considered a privilege, the right of introducing commodities even to be placed in dépôt is controlled by the acts of Parliament and the Orders in Council, by means of which the intercourse has been opened to the navigation of some powers and closed against that of others." Speculates that "The motives for the late Orders in Council will probably be found in the inconvenience already experienced by the suspension of the direct trade between the United States and the West Indies" (cf. above, Gallatin to Clay, August 19, 1826; Clay to Vaughan, March 17, 1827).

States that "during the last week" Lord Goderich offered his resignation but that, "The efforts . . . to supply the vacancy having proved unavailing," he "was induced to defer his intentions for a short period" (cf. above, Gallatin to Clay, February 22, 1827, note). Cites "a general opinion" that Goderich's "talents are not adequate to the highest employment of the State." Identifies the "three parties" now understood to exist "in the Administration: Goderich, "a moderate Tory acting with Mr. [John Charles] Herries and others of that party," "Mr [William] Huskisson, Lord Dudley and the other political friends of Mr [George] Canning," and "Lord Lansdowne and the Whigs." Predicts that "Mr. Huskisson and Lord Dudley will in any event sustain themselves" and that, "If Mr Huskisson remain in the Cabinet, the other changes, which may take place will be of little consequence."

Reports having been informed of a Convention, "concluded, on October 18 [*sic*]," between Denmark and Turkey, "by which Danish vessels were [*sic*] permitted to pass into the Black Sea, on payment of charges regulated by the Treaty."

LS. DNA, RG59, Dip. Disp., Great Britain, vol. 35 (M30, R31). Extract published in Manning (arr.), *Diplomatic Correspondence . . . Canadian Relations*, II, 680–81. Received February 23, 1828.

For the "Treaty of Commerce and Navigation between Denmark and Turkey," signed at Constantinople on October 16, 1827, see Parry (ed.), *Consolidated Treaty Series*, LXX, 449–52.

From J[OEL] R. POINSETT, Mexico, no. 112. Transmits copies of two laws, one expelling "a certain class of native Spaniards" from Mexico (cf. above, Taylor to Clay, November 2, 1827, note) and "the other establishing a new Tariff." States that the convention signed in London between Mexico and the Netherlands, the terms of which are identical to those in the treaty between Mexico and Great Britain (cf. above, Gallatin to Clay, December 16, 1826, note; Poinsett to Clay, March 17, 1827), has been ratified by the Mexican Chamber of Deputies. LS. DNA, RG59, Dip. Disp., Mexico, vol. 3 (M97, R4).

The new Mexican tariff raised the duties "on all white and brown cotton goods" to 18 cents "per vara, for vara wide, and in an equal proportion exceeding that width. . . ." Increased duties on brandy and wine were also notable. *Niles' Weekly Register*, XXXIII (November 24, 1827), 198.

For the "Treaty of Friendship, Commerce, and Navigation" between Mexico and the Netherlands, signed on June 15, 1827, see Parry (ed.), *Consolidated Treaty Series*, LXX, 245–55. Ratifications were exchanged on April 21, 1828.

From HENRY WHEATON, Copenhagen, no. 2. Acknowledges receipt of Clay's instructions of August 3 and 13. Expresses confidence in "the certainty of a satisfactory arrangement being made" in the cases of the *Fair Trader*, the *Minerva Smyth*, and the *Ariel* (cf. above, Connell to Clay, May 24, 1827; Clay to Wheaton, May 31, 1827). Describes his role in the negotiations, outlines the history of the cases, and reports a compromise agreement between (John) Connell and Count Schimmelmann by which the Danish Government is to pay the equivalent of "about 76,000 dollars . . . in full satisfaction of the claims." Notes that this sum represents from one half to three-fourths the loss sustained by the claimants. Recommends settlement of the remaining claims against Denmark (cf. above, Hughes to Clay, March 19, 1825, note; Clay to Hughes, March 24, 1825) also by compromise and, in justification of that view, points to the poor financial condition of the Kingdom, the failure of the United States "to obtain justice for similar aggressions from France & her vassal states" (cf. above, III, 154n; Brown to Clay, September 24, 27, 1825), and the belief in Denmark that the claimants are not backed by American public opinion to the extent that would induce Congress to take strong measures in their support. Adds that, although the agreement reached by Connell has not been approved by the King (Frederick VI), no difficulty is anticipated. Observes that "the diplomatic circles" believe that "the affairs of the East" (involving Turkey—cf. above, Brown to Clay, December 13, 1827) will be settled peacefully and informs Clay of the treaty "just concluded" between Denmark and Turkey (cf. above, Lawrence to Clay, this date), "under the mediation of Russia. . . ." ALS. DNA, RG59, Dip. Disp., Denmark, vol. 1B (M41, R3). Received March 18, 1828.

To Allen Trimble

My dear Sir   Washington 24h. Decr. 1827.

I recd. your favor of the 10h. inst. with a Copy of your Message[1] which I perused with much satisfaction; and I take pleasure in assuring you that I have heard it spoken of by the President and others in the most favorable terms. It is a fortunate coincidence to see the two great States of Pennsa. and Ohio coming out, so unequivocally, through their respective Chief Magistrates in favor of Internal Improvements and the Tariff.[2]

Persons well acquainted with public sentiment in N. York assert here that Mr. Adams will obtain not less than 26 votes in that State.[3] They are persons who sincerely believe what they say. I entertain myself no doubt that the late elections in N. York were brought about by secret arrangements, which were kept out of public view,[4] and that they do not afford a safe indication of the public opinion.

In Virginia and in North Carolina an encouraging spirit seems to be actively at work. In Pennsa. too it is believed that favorable changes are yet going on.

As to the fact of the opposition having secured majorities in both houses of Congress,[5] when we know that state of things is the result of a *misrespresentation* of the people and States, it ought not to alarm or depress our friends. I believe good rather than evil will grow out of it. The majorities must now approve our measures or oppose them and present their own. In the latter contingency the people will be able to judge between us. In the first, they will see that there is no cause for change. With high regard I remain Cordially Your friend
His Excellency Allen Trimble   H. CLAY

ALS. NjP.
[1] The letter and enclosure have not been found. Trimble's message, delivered to the Ohio General Assembly on December 4, had focused on the necessity for public policy in support of "our native productions." "Facilities for transportation must be created and ample protection provided against unfair foreign competition," he had stated. *Liberty Hall and Cincinnati Gazette*, December 13, 1827.   [2] John A. Shulze's message to the Pennsylvania Legislature on December 5 had stressed the same theme: "The maintenance of her [Pennsylvania's] relative rank and her ability to uphold that union, upon which our peace and happiness so much depend, is . . . *inseparably connected with internal improvement and American manufactures.*" Philadelphia *National Gazette*, December 7, 1827.   [3] Cf. above, Brooke to Clay, September 21, 1827, note.   [4] Cf. above, Sergeant to Clay, October 24, 1827, and note.   [5] Cf. above, Clay to Brown, March 27, 1827, note.

INSTRUCTIONS AND DISPATCHES   December 24, 1827

From ROBERT MONROE HARRISON, Barbados. Reports that Barbados, which he reached on December 23, and the other islands in this area are greatly in want of staves, that supplies at Martinique are nearly exhausted, and that a British warship is blocking imports "from any of the neutral Islands with that article or any other which has been taken out of an American vessel before being landed in some Port." Comments on the importance of American staves to the (British) colonies in the area and on the small direct trade between these colonies and Continental Europe. Asserts that "if the trade be unrestrained, the U States can successfully compete with any part of the world in the sale of certain articles, and might possibly find it to her advantage to take from the Colonies some portion of their produce. . . ." Cites recent information "that the Government of Martinique and

Guadelupe after the 1st January will no longer allow American Cargoes to be sold from board to board, nor landed for exportation," without payment of full duty (cf. above, Harrison to Clay, August 16, 1827). Notes that American provisions, except staves, are cheap in Barbados and "will continue so as long as the circuitous trade is allowed, and the introduction of all our *Productions into British North America; with or without the permission of the two Governments!*" States that "American vessels are to be allowed to take salt from the Salt Islands, because they are in a state of Starvation and cannot exist without us," and that, according to rumor, American vessels are to be allowed "to come in ballast to the whole of the West India Islands and take away Cargoes." Deplores the possibility that, in the latter connection, political pressure in the United States may force acceptance of this "humiliating" concession. Declares that American trade to the neutral islands continues to supply the English colonists with "as much of our productions now as they did before the interdict," that British merchants do not like this development "but . . . cannot help it," and that he does "not believe . . . it . . . possible to *frame* a *Law* that our Country men would not find means to evade or turn to their own account." Encloses lists of commercial data relating to Demerara. ALS. DNA, RG59, Cons. Disp., Barbados, vol. 1 (M-T333, R1).

By order in Council of January 26, 1828, United States ships arriving in ballast at the island of Anguilla were permitted to export salt and fruit from there, "to be carried to any Foreign Country whatever," subject to payment of the legal duties "upon such Ships, or upon the exportation of any such salt or fruit." *British and Foreign State Papers*, XV, 466–67.

From A[BRAHAM] B. NONES, Maracaibo. Comments on "the Political events of this distracted Country"; notes an expectation "that the Convention [cf. above, Watts to Clay, August 7, 1827] will Certainly meet in March" and that, in the contest between "the Executive party" and a coalition of the Liberal and Federal parties, the latter will win and "the Federal System will unquestionably be adopted. . . ." Reports having seen "a Letter from one of the Most distinguished Men of this Country. . . , in which he States that, the influence of the English Governt. is at present Great and that the operations of this Govermt. [*sic*] are greatly and in a Measure directed by her agents. . . ." States that "the Same writer . . . deplore[s] being at Such a Moment without Such aid from their brethern [*sic*] of the North, as Might be afforded from a Minister of the U.S. in Counteracting the English views &c." Observes that the suspicions regarding English "efforts to obtain the ascendancy in this Country" have grown as a result of the close association of (Simón) Bolívar with the English Minister (Alexander Cockburn). Blames the tariff and Bolívar's "decrees relating to Commerce" (cf. above, Marks to Clay, March 17, 1827; MacPherson to Clay, March 24, 1827; below, Nones to Clay, December 31, 1827) for destroying "all Confidence" and for the "Most deplorable" state of "fiscal concerns here." Notes that, having failed to obtain redress for American citizens who have suffered injustices under the decrees, he has referred "the different Cases to our Chargé d'affaires [Beaufort T. Watts]," whose only recent reply was "a Circular" stating his intention of visiting the United States (cf. above, Watts to Clay, November 21, 1827) and directing Nones, "in the event of its being Necessary," to communicate directly with the Minister of Foreign Relations (Joseph R. Revenga). LS. DNA, RG59, Cons. Disp., Maracaibo, vol. 1 (M-T62, R1).

MISCELLANEOUS LETTERS   December 24, 1827

From SAMUEL ALLINSON, Gibraltar. Expresses fear that Clay has not seen his previous letter complaining of the "bad conduct and malversation" of the United

States consul (Bernard Henry) at Gibraltar and reports that the situation has not improved. States: "Mr. Henry also has for nine months past abandoned Gibr. with all his Family, &, is living 'at home' that is in Engld.— Whether he intends resuming his Consulate is, I understand, quite doubtful— Certain it is that he has offered to sell his office—" ALS. DNA, RG59, A. and R. (M531, R4).

From S[AMUEL] B. BARRELL, Fredericton, New Brunswick. Reports his arrival on December 15 and his transmittal to Sir Howard Douglas on the following day of his "letter of introduction from Mr. [Charles R.] Vaughan" (cf. above, Clay to Vaughan, November 19, 1827, and note). States that Douglas has instructed the Attorney General (Thomas Wetmore) to co-operate fully in providing information concerning the case of (John) Baker (cf. above, Lincoln to Clay, November 16, 1827, and note; Clay to Barrell, November 19, 1827) but that this official has been too ill to attend to business. Adds that he has, "however, had free and unreserved communication with the different members of the Government" and has just "received . . . from the Attorney General . . . official copies" of documents relative to the Baker case, which has not yet come to trial. Refers to his letter of December 9 and remarks "that the case of Baker . . . turns out to be much the same as" he had thought at that time. Notes that "Mr. [Charles S.] Daveis, the Agent of the State of Maine, has not been accredited by this Government" but is still present and, with the knowledge of "this Government," proposes setting out the next morning with Barrell "to the Madawascah Settlement. . . ." ALS. DNA, RG76, Northeastern Boundary, entry 87 (MR frames 658–60). Extract published in Manning (arr.), *Diplomatic Correspondence . . . Canadian Relations*, II, 681–82. Received January 15, 1828.

From MATHEW CAREY, Philadelphia. Acknowledges receipt of Clay's (*i.e.*, Brent's) "letter covering the communication from Rome" (cf. above, Somaglia to Clay, September 22, 1827, note) and states the wish of John Wyeth, "a most respectable citizen of Harrisburg, that his son [Francis Wyeth], who publishes a paper [*Harrisburg Argus*], devoted to the support of the administration, should have the printing of the Laws." Continues: "Sound policy requires that those who support the govt. should, as far as justice & propriety warrant, have support reciprocated. To this plain truth I need not make any addition." ALS. DNA, RG59, P. and D. of L.

John Wyeth, born in Cambridge, Massachusetts, in 1770, had published the *Oracle of Dauphin County and Harrisburg Advertiser* since 1792 as a Federalist organ. His son, Francis, taking over the newspaper in November, 1827, identified it as the *Harrisburg Argus*, described as "a democratic paper, friendly to the administration." Philadelphia *United States Gazette*, November 27, 1827. It appears to have been discontinued in 1831, although another journal of the same name was published from 1843 to 1848. Francis Wyeth, who like his father had also engaged in book-selling and publishing, continued those operations until 1859.

Wyeth's journal replaced the Harrisburg *Pennsylvania Intelligencer*, of Cameron and Krause, for publication of the laws of the Twentieth Congress (cf. above, Sergeant to Clay, October 30, 1827, note).

To Henry Clay, Jr.

My dear Son   Washington 25h. Decr. 1827.

I continue to receive, through various channels, the most gratifying intelligence about your diligence, your morals and your progress. I cannot express to you how much happiness this information affords me. And if, as I hope, you should persevere in this praise worthy course, it will bring along with it honor and happiness to yourself as well as a blessing to me.

My letter you will see is dated on Xmas day, which here is not very pleasant, being wet, thawing, and extremely disagreeable under foot. We should be delighted to have you with us, and we are only consoled for your absence by the belief that you are doing well where you are— Henry C. Hart arrived today, from Norfolk. He will sail to the Mediterranean in a short time. Mr. Erwin, the father of your brother in law,[1] is also with us.

Do you find your pay sufficient to obtain for you all *allowable* comforts? If it be not, tell me frankly & you know I will supply you with any pecuniary means in my power—

All of us are proud of you, and all send you their love, and the compliments of the Season. Your affte father   H CLAY

ALS. Henry Clay Memorial Foundation, Lexington, Kentucky.
[1] Andrew Erwin; James Erwin.

From James Davidson

Frankfort 25 Decr 1827
Sir   Your letter of the 20th Ulo.[1] was not received untill it had laid in the post office a bout a week, on receipt of which I addressed Mr. G. Robertson on the subject to which your letter refered [*sic*], and enclosed I send you his answer[2] although his recolections [*sic*] are not as clear as I could have wished but suficiantly [*sic*] so. The other branch of your suggestion was attend [*sic*] to and their testimony would be entirely confirmatory of service so far as what was stated by me in the senate; but it is thought of little or no importance as almost every member in boath [*sic*] houses had no Idea that you yourself, would vote for Genl. Jackson

We have had an administration convention here on the 17th Inst which was attended by 60 or 70 counties[3] & it was composed of men of fine tallents [*sic*] and standing in society, and it would seem to be impossible to resist the conclusion, that so much moral weight & worth could be disappointed in their views   Genl T Metcalfe was recommended as a candidate for the office of Govr and Jos. R. Underwood was in like manner recommended as a candidate for the office of Lt Govr.   and they made Judicious selections for Electors[4] and I feel a strong presentiment that we will succeed.[5] I mus [*sic*] close this letter by assuring you that there will be a cordial & harty coopperation [*sic*] with us in order to save the Republic if possible. Yours Respectfully
H Clay Esqr   JAMES DAVIDSON

ALS. DLC-HC (DNA, M212, R3).   1 Not found.
2 See above, Robertson to Clay, July 5, 1827, note.   3 Cf. above, Smith to Clay, October 7, 1827, note.   4 For a listing of the electoral ticket, see Lexington *Kentucky
Gazette*, December 28, 1827.   5 Cf. above, I, 151n; Clay to Brown, March 27, 1827,
note. Underwood was defeated in his bid for the office of Lieutenant Governor.

DIPLOMATIC NOTES   December 25, 1827

To José Silvestre Rebello, Washington. Acknowledges receipt of Rebello's letter
of December 17, 1827. States that when an armed ship of a belligerent nation is
within the jurisdiction of the United States, the applicable laws "are enforced as
a matter of course, by those charged with their execution, without any special
direction from the Government in each particular case"; that to afford "a proof
of the anxious desire of the President to maintain a strict and impartial neutrality
in every respect, in the war which is at present unhappily existing, . . . the particular attention of the officers of the port of New York, has been called to their
duty of preventing any violation of our Laws with regard to the . . . Privateer
[*General Brandizen*] or her prize" (cf. below, Clay to Thompson, this date). Copy.
DNA, Notes to Foreign Legations, vol. 3, pp. 410–11 (M38, R3). L draft, in CSmH.

MISCELLANEOUS LETTERS   December 25, 1827

To Jonathan Thompson, "Collector of the Port of New York." Reports that
(José Silvestre) Rebello has notified him (above, December 17, 1827) of the arrival
at New York of an Argentine privateer (*General Brandizen*). Requests, "by direction of the President," that Thompson "guard against the violation of any of our
laws, and especially take care that there be no augmentation of the force of the
privateer, which they forbid." Copy. DNA, RG59, Dom. Letters, vol. 22, pp. 111–
12 (M40, R20).

From Betsey Hawley, New York. Requests Clay to transmit "to His Excellency
Jno. Q. Adams, President of the United States, the papers [not found] accom-
panying this note." AN. DNA, RG59, Cons. Disp., Puerto Cabello, vol. 1 (M-T229,
R1).

From Henry B. Bascom

My Dear Sir,   Madison College[1] 26 Dec 1827
    I am just informed that Mr. Wickliffe[2] intends calling on me to
prove a conversation which he alledges [*sic*] took place in my presence,
at the store of Wm. Prentiss,[3] between you & himself in 1824.[4] His object I learn is to prove, that you dissuaded him, in that conversation,
from voting for Genl. Jackson, in the event of the election coming
before congress— I recollect to have seen you at the store of Mr. Prentiss at two different times, in company with Mr Wickliffe and at one
time, I believe the conversation turned on the the [*sic*] request of the
Legislature of Ky, that the Representation of that state, should support
Genl. Jackson[5]— when, I think you observed, that in your opinion, the
request of the Legislature did not report fairly the sentiments of the
majority of the people in Ky.—   this I believe was the amount of the

conversation; and it will be out of my power to sustain the charge preferred by Mr. Wickliffe   I shall be glad to hear from you early on
this subject, and permit me to assure you, all I *know* upon this subject
will be in your favour. Truly & confidentially   H B BASCOM
Hon. H. Clay

[Postscript on verso]
4 Jany '28   my Dear Sir, after writing the within, I was suddenly
taken ill & am not yet entirely recovered. Mr. Wickliffe has not called
on me, and I presume will not. If he should it will be of no disservice
to you; but he has doubtless reflected & declined it. I have written
nothing on the subject except to *you*. Our cause is doing well in many
places— Stewart[6] writes me you are in good health & spirits, & I rejoice
to learn it— God bless you— Truly   H. B. BASCOM.
Hon. H. Clay

ALS. DLC-HC (DNA, M212, R3).   [1] Uniontown, Pennsylvania.
[2] Charles A. Wickliffe.   [3] William H. Prentiss, of Washington.   [4] Cf. above,
Smith to Clay, August 1, 1827; Johnson to Clay, September 9, 1827.   [5] Cf. above,
Kendall to Clay, December 22, 1824.   [6] Probably Andrew Stewart.

DIPLOMATIC NOTES   December 26, 1827

From CHARLES R. VAUGHAN, Washington. Transmits copies of correspondence,
between Count Münster, of Hanover, and the American Ministers in London
(Richard Rush and Rufus King) in 1824 and 1825, "relative to the establishment
of a system of reciprocity with regard to the duties levied in the Ports of the
United States and of Hanover, on the Commerce of the respective Nations" (cf.
above, King to Clay, January 12, 1826, and note). States that, since "His Britannick
Majesty [George IV] . . . as King of Hanover" has no "Minister accredited to the
Government of the United States," Vaughan has been directed to transmit the
documents and requests that Clay communicate to him "the determination of the
United States." LS. DNA, RG59, Notes from British Legation, vol. 14 (M50, R15).
    Ernst Fredrich Herbert, Count von Münster-Ledenburg (1766–1839) had been
Minister of State in Hanover in 1805. When Prussian troops occupied his home-
land the following year, he had emigrated to London and served there as Hanover's diplomatic representative.

MISCELLANEOUS LETTERS   December 26, 1827

To DEWITT CLINTON, "Governor of the State of New York." Transmits a copy of
the letter of the British Minister (Charles R. Vaughan—above, November 24, 1827),
with its enclosures, concerning a New York law. Requests that Clinton consider
"whether the time allowed to the next of kin to administer on the effects of the
deceased might not be extended, without prejudice to any interest; and, if . . . [he]
should entertain that opinion, whether it might not be expedient to invite the
attention of the Legislature of New York to the subject." Copy. DNA, RG59,
Dom. Letters, vol. 22, pp. 113–14 (M40, R20).

From H[ENRY] M. BRACKENRIDGE, Philadelphia. Defends himself at length against the "unfounded and malicious" charges brought against him by (Benjamin D.) Wright (cf. above, Clay to Brackenridge, December 15, 1827; below, White to Clay, December 29, 1827) and "most respectfully, but most earnestly," requests "the dismissal of Mr Wright, from the office of district attorney." ALS. DNA, RG59, A. and R. (M531, R1). Published in Carter (ed.), *Territorial Papers*, XXIII, 959–64.

From JOSEPH DELAFIELD, New York. Reports having received from (Peter B.) Porter "three copies of his separate report under the 7th article of the Treaty of Ghent [cf. above, II, 162, note] with accompanying documents, one copy intended for his own Government one for the British and one for the British Commissioner [Anthony Barclay]"; that the material would have arrived "in time for exchange on the 24th instant agreeably to arrangement" except for adverse weather; but that Barclay has provided only one copy of his report for exchange and 12 or 14 days will be needed to prepare a copy for Porter. Requests instructions whether to "deliver the report of the British Commissioner together with General Porters, leaving the copies of the former to be obtained hereafter from Washington" or to give Barclay's report to an engrossing clerk in New York. ALS. DNA, RG76, Northeastern Boundary, entry 142, env. 1, folder 2 (MR frames 924–26).

Clay replied, December 29, informing Delafield that there was "no such pressing urgency . . . for the report of the British Commissioner as to prevent the copy of it being made for General Porter." Copy, in DNA, RG59, Dom. Letters, vol. 22, pp. 114–15 (M40, R20).

Check to W. W. Billing

27h. Decr 1827
Pay to W. W. Billing or order thirty six dollars and 90 Cents
Cashr. of the Off. of B. U. States Washington[1]   H CLAY

ADS. DLC-TJC (DNA, M212, R16). Cf. below, Receipted Tax Bill, this date.
[1] Richard Smith.

To John F. Henry

My dear Sir   Washington 27h. Decr. 1827.
With the compliments of the Season I subjoin my hearty congratulations on an event, alluded to in your last,[1] and which will have happened before you receive this letter. I hope it will conduce to the happiness of yourself and of her who will have united her destiny with yours.[2]

I am glad to perceive that our friends in your quarter are organizing and exerting themselves in the good cause. Notwithstanding some late adverse events, I do believe that enough of hope and probability remains to justify strong anticipation of final success. Without calling to our aid any votes from Pennsa. Virginia or North Carolina (in all of which States prospects are encouraging) I do believe Mr. Adams will be re-elected, if the friendly parts of the West remain firm.[3] Whatever you see or hear from N. York rely upon it, unless I am greatly deceived, that Mr Adams will obtain from 22 to 26 votes in that State.[4] These added to the votes of N. England, N. Jersey, Maryland & Delaware[5] and the West would ensure his election. Those, therefore, who look merely to a successful issue of the contest must see enough to stimulate them. As to those, who are animated by a higher motive, that of patriotically displaying their duty, whatever may be the result, nothing need be said to urge unremitted endeavors.

The Opposition is in a most embarrassing condition in Congress. Being in the majority in both houses, it is at a great loss to know how to exercise its power. Our friends will take care and have the line clearly and distinctly drawn, and thus exhibit to the Country those who are hostile or friendly to certain great interests. When this development is made the effect cannot but prove salutary.

There will probably be no Minister appointed to England until towards the close of the Session.[6] No person is yet designated. I need not say to you that the story of my going there is idle and ridiculous, and a device of the enemy.[7]

It will be very important to circulate through your Committees of Correspondence and Vigilance[8] essays and publications communicating information to the people. I shall publish, in a short time, some testimonials[9] which have been collected to refute the Jackson and Kremer calumny. I think it will be satisfactory to my friends and I should hope that it will be extensively circulated.

With the best respects of Mrs. Clay and myself to Mrs. Henry I remain truly Your friend   H CLAY

ALS. DLC-Short Family Papers. Addressee identified by DLC.   [1] Not found.
[2] Dr. Henry and Miss Lucy E. S. Ridgely, daughter of Dr. Frederick Ridgely, were married in Lexington, Kentucky, January 1, 1828.   [3] See above, Clay to Brown, March 27, 1827, note.   [4] Cf. above, Brooke to Clay, September 21, 1827, note.   [5] Cf. above, on New England, Clay to Webster, May 28, 1827, note; on New Jersey, Clay to Brown, March 27, 1827, note; on Delaware and Maryland, Clay to Hammond, June 1, 1827.
[6] James Barbour was nominated on May 22, 1828, for the appointment and commissioned the following day.   [7] The Philadelphia *Pennsylvania Gazette* of December 12, 1827, had published such a rumour as "Amongst the *on dits* of the day. . . ." Reprinted in *Albany Argus*, December 15, 1827.   [8] Cf. above, Clay to Henry , September 27, 1827, enclosure.   [9] See below, *Address . . . to the Public*, December 29, 1827.

To Allen Trimble

My dear Sir   (Confidential)   Washn. 27h. Decr. 1827.
I hope that the Report of the Secy of the Treasury will satisfy you and other friends on account of the omission of the President's message to notice the subject of the Tariff.[1] It was a delicate topic for him to

touch. If he had mentioned it, it would have been asserted, and with some plausibility, that his object was electioneering. That he and his Cabinet are in favor of the Tariff cannot be doubted by any intelligent man. To multiply proofs of that disposition was perhaps unnecessary. There wd. have been immediately Jackson resolutions that he was insincere, and that Jackson was the only true and genuine friend of the measure. I believe that during the present Session of Congress the line will be plainly and distinctly drawn;[2] and those who are not blind will see whether the real supporters of the American System are not those who at the same time support the Administration.

Our friends ought not to be easily alarmed. I do believe that if the West does not give way Mr. Adams will be re-elected. If we are to credit well informed friends, who do not intend to deceive us, he will obtain upwards of 25 votes in N. York. That will elect him (the friendly parts of the West remaining firm) without the aid of Pennsa. or Virginia or North Carolina,[3] in all of which States the prospects are quite encouraging. Let us then not despond, but redoubling our zeal and our exertions deserve success, and we will obtain it—

We have much speculation here about a Vice President. I think our friends will agree that it is most expedient to take one from Pennsa. Virginia or Ohio.[4] Their opinions will probably be shortly reconciled. I am anxious to hear from the Conventions in K. and Ohio.

In the course of a few days I shall have published an Address[5] exhibiting a variety of testimonials (among others one from Genl. Lafayette) in refutation of Genl. Jackson's charges. I hope that it will prove satisfactory to my friends. I am with great regards Yr's faithfully
His Excellency Allen Trimble   H. CLAY

ALS. NjP.
[1] On Richard Rush's report, see above, Porter to Clay, November 22, 1827, note.
[2] Cf. above, Hammond to Clay, August 10, 1827, note.   [3] For the result of the 1828 election in Pennsylvania and North Carolina, cf. above, Clay to Brown, March 27, 1827, note; in Virginia, above, Caldwell to Clay. August 8, 1827, note.   [4] Cf. above, Mercer to Clay, August 18, 1827, note.   [5] Below, *Address . . . to the Public*, December 29, 1827.

From Francis T. Brooke

My Dear Sir,   St Julien Decemr 27 1827
I received the address of the anti Jackson meeting of Philadelphia— if it could be translated into the German language and circulated extensively in the Valley of Virginia it would have great influence,[1]   I am told that none but Jackson papers in that language from Penna are circulated in that district of the State,   this is an evil that ought to be corrected as soon as possible,   I am anxious to hear what is decided on, as to the person to be named as V P—   if Govr Shultz[2] can influence

Penna. he would have weight among our German population also, if Mr Monroe is to be named the sooner it is known the better, I can see no cause for his refusal and I think he would probably bring us the aid of Mr Madison,[3] next to these as Mr Johnson has declined it, Mr Pleasants[4] will do better than any other from Virginia, I have a letter from him and am Surprised at his objection, it is that he disagrees with the Governmt on the measures of internal improvement & the tariff, he ought to recollect that Mr Jefferson was V P when Mr Adams the elder was President, Mr P. showed me your letter[5] before I left Richmd in relation to the publication of your letter of the 4 Feb. 1825,[6] I informed him that the moment it was called for through any of the papers it Should be published, and Suggested to him that Ritchie[7] might be tempted to call for it, by an anonymous note to him, as there was no authority on the face of the letter of the 28 of January[8] to publish it, he might be induced to infer the authority in some after letter & call for it, I shall be entirely guided by your wishes on this matter, I have exerted myself to have an able address from our convention prepared[9]— on the tariff I have been so fortunate as to get Mr Madisons very lucid Views with a copy of his Seven resolutions of 1794 copied from a draft of them in Mr Jefferson's handwriting— these elucidated the question of the Colonial trade very Satisfactorily[10]— between ourselves Mr Johnson with my notes is preparing the address, but I yet hope to get one from Washington that he may make the best one possible from all that may be produced at the convention— Genl. Taylor[11] is also engaged in the Same work but this is not to Slacken the exertions of my friends at Washington   Send me a draft in due time, my notes included full vindication of the election of the Presidt and of the measures of the governmt but I have some apprehension that there will be Some dificulty [sic] on that Subject and therefore the more want the draft from Washington   Your friend

FRANCIS BROOKE

ALS. DLC-HC (DNA, M212, R3). Addressed to Clay.
1 Brooke probably referred to the address cited above, Ingersoll to Clay, October 6, 1827, note. A subsequent meeting of the Democratic Ward Committee of Philadelphia, opposed to Jackson, on November 16, had adopted resolutions expressing confidence in the administration, but apparently no address had been then presented. Philadelphia *Democratic Press*, November 17, 1827.   2 John A. Shulze.   3 James Monroe; James Madison. Both John Taliaferro and Samuel L. Southard had written to Monroe, on December 15 and 16, respectively, urging that he accept nomination for the Vice-Presidency. He declined. Harry Ammon, *James Monroe: the Quest for National Identity* (New York, 1971), 559.   4 Chapman Johnson; James Pleasants.   5 Probably addressed to John H. Pleasants, the letter has not been found.   6 Above, Clay to Brooke.   7 Thomas Ritchie.   8 Above, Clay to Brooke, January 28, 1825.
9 Cf. above, Mercer to Clay, August 18, 1827, note.   10 Offered in the House of Representatives on January 3, 1794, the resolutions had supported a general statement "That the interest of the United States would be promoted by further restrictions and higher duties, in certain cases, on the manufactures and navigation of foreign nations employed in the commerce of the United States. . . ." *Annals of Congress*, 3 Cong., 1 Sess., 155.   11 Robert Barrand Taylor.

Receipted Tax Bill

[*ca.* December 27, 1827]

Hon Henry Clay   To Washington Corporation, Dr.

To Tax on Real and Personal Property for the year 1827 $29 " 00

Deduct for prompt payment,   3 " 10

Squ. 253 lot 3 value $1479[1]   ⎫ $25 " 90

Imps   700   ⎬ Tax on 2 female

Personal   3000   ⎬ Slaves & 1 Coachee[2]   11 " 00

$ 5179   ⎭ $36 " 90

Tax on lot 9 in Square 221 in the name of the ⎫ 5 " 56[3]
Bank of United States   ⎭ ─────────
                                                  42 " 46

Received payment   W. W. BILLING *Coll. of 1st & 2d Wards.*

DS, partly printed. DLC-TJC (DNA, M212, R16). Cf. above, Receipted Tax Bill, December 23, 1826.
[1] Cf. above, Check to Dermott, November 14, 1826, and note.   [2] Probably Charlotte, Mary Anne, and Aaron Dupuy.   [3] The reasons for this item's appearance on the tax bill and for Clay's failure to include the sum in his check to Billing, above, this date, are not known.

DIPLOMATIC NOTES   December 27, 1827

From JOSÉ SILVESTRE REBELLO, Washington. Acknowledges receipt of Clay's note of December 25 (above) and expresses gratitude to Clay and to the President for calling the attention of the officers of the port of New York to the matter; reports that an Argentine corsair is anchored at Baltimore and asks that the port authorities there be alerted; requests that the United States Government, "exercising the right inherent in every Government of preventing piracies," detain the corsairs to prevent the "Roberies [*sic*], and piracies, that probably they will commit." LS, in Portuguese with trans. in State Dept. file. DNA, RG59, Notes from Brazilian Legation, vol. 1 (M49, R1).

INSTRUCTIONS AND DISPATCHES   December 27, 1827

From J[OHN] M. Forbes, Montevideo, no. 55. Reports that the Emperor of Brazil (Peter I), after two years of "the most impotent blockade" of the Argentine coast, has decreed that "all vessels which unfortunately fall into his power whether in the course of ordinary commerce or" for other reasons, must post bond guaranteeing not to sail to Buenos Aires or other Argentine ports; protests this measure as "offensive and iniquitous"; and adds that "the Government of Buenos Ayres" seems "to have established a rivality [*sic*] with the Emperor in his oppressions on our commerce." ALS. DNA, RG59, Dip. Disp., Argentina, vol. 3 (M69, R4). Published in Espil (comp.), *Once Años en Buenos Aires,* 484–86. Received March 6, 1828.

From CHRISTOPHER HUGHES, Brussels. Reports having been informed by (C. T.) Elout, Minister of Marine, "that every *possible means should be afforded* to Mr [Richard] Ward to demonstrate the merits & efficacy of his '*Marine arm*' . . ." (cf.

above, Hughes to Clay, November 23, 1827). Transmits "Nos. 1. 2. & 3; correspondence with Mr. Ward,—on his *private* affairs. . . ." ALS. DNA, RG59, Dip. Disp., Netherlands, vol. 8 (M42, R-T12). Received March 6, 1828.

MISCELLANEOUS LETTERS   December 27, 1827

From WILLIAM LEE D. EWING, Vandalia, Illinois. Recommends Daniel Hay, who "has just now finished a senatorial term" in the Illinois Legislature, for appointment as United States marshal for Illinois. Comments: "In relation to his politics, I feel it my duty to apprise you that he is your devoted friend—that he was primitively so, and that he will so continue to be, I do not hesitate to avouch. His opponent [Henry Conner] has no claim to this merit. He is, to be sure, a supporter and friend of the Administration, but it is not on account of the place you occupy in the Cabinet—being originally a supporter of Mr Adams but a bitter enemy of yours." ALS. DNA, RG 59, A. and R. (M531, R4). On the recommended appointment, cf. above, Kane to Clay, March 7, 1827, note.

Born at Paris, Kentucky, in 1795, Ewing had begun the practice of law in Shawneetown, Illinois. He served as receiver of public moneys at Vandalia from 1820 to 1830, when he was removed by President Jackson. He was also clerk of the Illinois House of Representatives from 1826 to 1828 and again in 1842; a member of the State House of Representatives in 1830, 1838, and 1840, and of the State Senate from 1832 to 1834; Governor, briefly, in 1834; a member of the United States Senate from 1835 to 1837; and auditor of public accounts from 1843 until his death in 1846.

From WILLIAM B. ROCHESTER, New York, "unofficial." Reports his intention of leaving on December 31 for "Norfolk by means of Steam-boats & Stages," to join the *Falmouth* at that port. ALS. DNA, RG59, Dip. Disp., Central America, vol. 1 (M219, R2).

The *Falmouth*, an 18-gun sloop-of-war, built at Boston in 1827, was assigned to the United States naval squadron in the West Indies.

To John McLean

28h. Decr. 1827.

Mr Clay's respects to Mr. McLean, and in reply to his note of yesterday,[1] regrets to be obliged to inform him that there is no prospect of Mr. McLean's obtaining any indemnity for the advance made by him for Mr. Cook, through the Department of State, there being nothing due to him from that department.

Mr. Clay returns inclosed the letter of Govr. Edwards.

AN. DLC-John McLean Papers (DNA, M212, R20). Letters from the Postmaster General to Ninian Edwards and the latter's reply, dated June 13 and July 1, 1828, respectively, appear to relate to Clay's note and indicate that McLean continued to seek reimbursement through settlement of Daniel Pope Cook's account for State Department services. For McLean's letter to Edwards, see Washburne (ed.), *Edwards Papers*, 340–41; for the latter's reply, see DLC-John McLean Papers. President Adams on April 26, 1828, "mentioned to Mr. [Edward] Everett the amount of money paid to Mr. Cook, and that there was probably a small balance due to his estate." Adams, *Memoirs*, VII, 520. Clay, however, below, June 3, 1828, sent to Adams a report of the contingency account, which stated that Cook had been paid $1500 for his "confidential service rendered the United States in relation to the Island of Cuba." In the spring of 1827, prior to his Cuban mission,

Cook had visited in McLean's home, "where he was kindly nursed and recruited so as to be able to travel." Edwards to Duff Green, May 6, 1827, in Washburne, *op. cit.*, 280.
1 Not found.

To Thomas Deye Owings

Dear Sir: Washington, Dec. 28, 1827.

I received your letter of the 7th instant,[1] from Frankfort, accompanied by one to the Secretary of War,[2] which I have sent to him. In these times of treachery and hypocrisy it gave me particular satisfaction to peruse your letter, and to learn from yourself, that a friendly attachment between us, which commenced thirty years ago, continues in full force. I assure you most sincerely that it would afford me much pleasure, to render evidence of my friendly feelings towards you by promoting your wishes in respect to the obtainment of an appointment. In the State of Kentucky itself you are aware that there are but few situations, and they are all filled. To appoint a citizen of one State to an office in another would be very invidious. You see, then, that prospects are pretty much confined to territorial appointments. Colonel Johnson[3] informed me that you would have accepted the office of marshal in Florida, which was lately vacant. Had I known it, I would have taken pleasure in presenting your name to the President for consideration. But before I conversed with Col. Johnson on the subject, indeed before the commencement of the Session, the office had been filled.[4] I will continue to bear in mind your wishes, and I sincerely hope that circumstances may be such as to admit of their fulfilment.[5] Whatever they may be I beg you to be assured of the sincere esteem and regard of Your obedient servant,   H. CLAY
Colonel Thomas D. Owings

LS. Owned by Mrs. Sue Bascom Steele, Lexington, Kentucky.   1 Not found.
2 James Barbour.   3 Probably Richard M. Johnson.   4 See above, Clay to Wilson, November 27, 1827.   5 Owings received no appointment.

From Christopher Hughes (1)

My dear Sir,   Private   Brussels; 28th. December, 1827.

The enclosed letter will give you the most correct, & best detailed account, of the bloody & un-christian affair of Navarine,[1] that I have yet seen. The writer is a Boy of 14 years of age; Son of a very respectable English Family,[2] living here; and, with which we are on agreeable visiting terms. He went to the same school with my Son;[3] & though 4 years older than my Boy yet they were intimate Friends; Young Sympson left school about a year since, and went aboard the Asia, Admiral Codrington[4] as a midshipman. His letter is addressed to his Mother; and it is the work of one who may still be called a child, but the story is clearly told; it gives particulars, not officially published; and places beyond all doubt who were the agressers [sic] & what were the views, intentions & expectations of the marine triumverrate [sic],[5] in invading the Port of Navarino.

There was also a list of killed & wounded on all sides; the published accounts are generally accurate; the loss of the Turks & Egyptians was computed at about 6,000.

It is very kind in young Sympson's father to give me a copy of his son's letter, made by his daughter; but it must be used with discretion; I should like the President to see it; it may not add much to the information already had; but I believe it is interesting, as the unvarnished & unreserved account of a Boy (just escaped from the nursery) of the sanguinary scene; in which he was called on, at so young an age to take an active part!

No one can yet say what will be the consequences of the Battle of Navarine [sic]; all is doubt and "guessing", & I guess the British regret the event. It is perfectly certain that the British Cabinet never anticipated such an event, or desired such a victory; it has thrown confusion among them, and great alarm for the future; the John Bull feeling of glory in the bravery and success of their admiral, will not permit the Ministry to throw any blame on Codrington; nor will their engagements and perplexing entanglement with their allies allow of it; nor will the fact of their having left a wide and confiding discretion to their admiral (which he has used with more bravery than finesse to the confusion of Downing Street;) warrant any thing like censure or such censure must recoil on his employers.[6] Upon the whole, they, to use an elegant term of my Lord Coke,[7] are completely disinfungled.

You see, that my prediction to you, in my dispatches & letters of 23d. November, of the split in the B. Ministry, is verified;[8] the Navarin [sic] affair, & the additional doubt thrown into the political aspect of Europe, has had some effect, in scaring Lord Goodrich [sic] from the helm,[9] but there are other camps; you may depend upon the following in part! Lord Goodrich is nervous, or wants nerve; (let Logicians reconcile this last phrase:) his family is hysterical & sensitive. One of his uncles shot himself on account of some ministerial discontents & confusion, in the last reign; in a great difficulty & contest between Geo. III & the Cabinet, & on the organization of a New Ministry, the King sent for this Uncle, (a Hardwicke)[10] & made it a personal request that he should take office; he yielded to the entreaties of his Sovereign; the scene, & the terms, were known to his formr political friends, & to his family; he called, that Evening at his Brother's[11] house, & was told, by the servant, that he had received orders, to refuse him the door, in case he should call; he was so offended that he returned home & shot himself; Frederick Robinson (Lord Goodrich) has inherited this morbid sensitiveness; he has been known to weep & almost faint, in the

house of commons when allusions to suicide were made; and especially at Castlereagh's death;[12] madness is in his family; his relation, the present Earl of Hardwicke, (whom I know, by correspondence) was notoriously mad, when Lord Lieutenant of Ireland; the Earl is an able & amiable man, withal;[13] and so is Lord Goodrich; but if vapours are a bad obsession in women, what are they in men called on to guide the politics of a great Country? Lord Goodrich, who began his career as a Peer with the gallant & spirited reply to Lord Londonderry (on Londonderry's coarse & stupid assault upon Mr. Canning; in which Lord Goodrich asked but, "a clear field & fair play";[14] (by the way, he & I went together in 1823, at the Warwick races, to see Crib [sic] & Spring,[15] the Boxing champions, Spar)   He is already driven from "the field," by downright want of heart, to undertake the management of public affairs; & by the influence of two women acting, to be sure, in different categories & circumstances; towit, the Marchioness of Conyngham[16] has more influence with the King, than the Premier, & carries every thing before her; this mortifies Lord Goodrich, & vexes his Wife; who is a tormenting, worrying & very pretty woman; & has always ruled the Roost in her household & bullies his Lordship into her will & way; I know her as Lady Sarah Robinson;[17] & though she is a very nice woman, she is capricious & Sovereigns over her Lord; the *two* women together (acting on different principles) & the imbecility of George IV, who is almost as mad as ever was Geo III, have driven, or will soon drive, Lord G. from the helm of affairs! But He is a Peer, & his wife a Peeress! "An occasion offers for England"[18] & I finish this letter very abruptly. I go to the Hague tomorrow. Ever & devotedly—
To Henry Clay Esq Washington U. S. A.   C. Hughes.

ALS. DLC-HC (DNA, M212, R3). Endorsed by Clay: "C Hughes Esq   The only letter enclosed was one to Chevalier [C. D. E. J. Bangeman] Huygens." Cf. below, Hughes to Clay, this date.
    [1] Cf. above, Ombrosi to Clay, November 6, 1827.   [2] Edward Sympson and his family have not been further identified.   [3] Charles John Hughes.   [4] Sir Edward Codrington. The *Asia*, his flagship, was a ship-of-the-line of 84 guns.   [5] France, Great Britain, and Russia.   [6] Cf. above, Hughes to Clay, November 27, 1827.   [7] Sir Edward Coke.   [8] See the private letter of that date; the dispatch contains no reference to this matter.   [9] Frederick John Robinson, Viscount Goderich. Cf. above, Lawrence to Clay, December 22, 1827.   [10] Charles Yorke (1722–1770), the second son of Philip Yorke (1690–1764), the first Earl of Hardwicke, had died three days after accepting the post of Lord Chancellor in the Ministry of the Duke of Grafton, a supporter of William Pitt, the first Earl of Chatham. Yorke had long hoped for advancement with Pitt but, overlooked when the latter returned to power in 1766, Yorke had resigned his place in the government. He had subsequently given assurances to the opposition leadership that he would not accept the appointment of Lord Chancellor under Grafton but weakened under pressure from George III. His death, of fever "complicated by colic and the rupture of a blood-vessel," has been attributed in large part to "the extreme nervous tension and mental suffering which he had undergone." Contemporary rumor, however, "widely believed," asserted that he had committed suicide. James McMullen Rigg, in *Dictionary of National Biography*, XXI, 1254–55.   [11] Philip Yorke (1720–1790), the second Earl of Hardwicke, who had entered the House of Lords in 1764 and was active in opposition to Pitt. This Yorke was the father of Goderich's mother, Mary Jemima Yorke Robinson.
    [12] Castlereagh, Lord Londonderry, while still Foreign Minister, had "cut his throat with a penknife. . . , and died almost immediately" in August, 1822. John Andrew

Hamilton in *Dictionary of National Biography*, XVIII, 1244.   [13] Philip Yorke (1757–1837), the third Earl of Hardwicke, was the eldest son of Charles Yorke. He had been Lord Lieutenant of Ireland from 1801 to 1806.   [14] For Goderich's defense on May 2 and 4, 1827, of his participation in George Canning's reorganization of the Cabinet (cf. above, Gallatin to Clay, February 22, 1827, note), see Hansard, *Parliamentary Debates. . .* , New Series, XVII, 472–79; 550–51 (the quotation from last column). The Marquis of Londonderry was Charles William Stewart (Vane), the third of that title, a half-brother of Lord Castlereagh. After a military career, he had been named Minister to Berlin in 1813 and to Vienna in 1814 and had represented Great Britain at the Congresses of Troppau and Laybach in 1820 and 1821 and, with Wellington, at Verona in 1822. He was a staunch Tory and vigorously opposed reform measures.   [15] Tom Cribb and Thomas Winter, the latter boxing under the name "Tom Spring." Born in Gloucestershire in 1781 Cribb had moved to London as a boy and had worked on the wharves and as a seaman. He had begun professional boxing in 1805 and had attained the pinnacle of his career by 1811. Thereafter he had become an innkeeper and sparred only for exhibition. He had been unchallenged as champion for a decade when he retired in 1821. Winter, born in Herefordshire, in 1795, had begun professional fighting in 1814 and three years later had taken his talents to London. With his reputation established by 1819, he had toured western England, sparring with his friend Cribb. Upon the latter's retirement, Winter claimed the championship. He had challenged all comers for some months in the spring of 1821, retired briefly, and then returned to the ring in the spring of 1823. He had retired by the summer of that year and spent the remainder of his life as a tavern-keeper.   [16] Elizabeth Denison, of Denbies, Surrey, the daughter of Joseph Denison, a wealthy merchant, had acquired her title by marriage to Henry, the third Baron and first Marquis Conyngham, in 1794. In 1821 she had become the mistress of George IV and the Conynghams enjoyed generous perquisites of royal favor until the King's death in 1830.   [17] Sarah Albinia Louisa Hobart, the only daughter of Robert Hobart, fourth Earl of Buckinghamshire, had married Frederick John Robinson in 1814.   [18] Quotation has not been found.

From Christopher Hughes (2)

My dear Sir,   Brussels 28th. December; 1827.

I have preferred sending the copy of Young Sympson's (British Midshipman:) account of the Battle of Navarino, by a route different from that, by which I send my letter, referring to his account, and to the circumstances of my acquaintance with his family.[1]

I am, with our sincerest good wishes to Mrs. Clay & compliments of the season ever most faithfully your Friend

Henry Clay Esq Washington   CHRISTOPHER HUGHES

ALS. DLC-HC (DNA, M212, R3). Addressed to Clay.
[1] Above, this date. Hughes' copy of the seven and a half page excerpt from Edward Sympson's letter, written at Malta, was dated from Brussels on December 27 and is here omitted by the editors.

INSTRUCTIONS AND DISPATCHES   December 28, 1827

From JAMES BROWN, Paris, no. 77. Reports that the Minister of Foreign Affairs (Baron de Damas) is still not disposed to accede to the proposal "that the question arising under the 8th article of the Louisiana Treaty, should be decided by arbitration" (cf. above, Brown to Clay, September 8, 1827; Clay to Brown, October 28, 1827). Adds: "I told him that I would send him a note containing a renewal of it, to which I should expect a written answer." Encloses a copy of that note, dated December 19. LS. DNA, RG59, Dip. Disp., France, vol. 23 (M34, R26). Published, with the copy of the note, in *House Docs.*, 22 Cong., 2 Sess., no. 147, pp. 53–62. Received March 1, 1828.

From CHRISTOPHER HUGHES, Brussels (3). Transmits tables confirming his earlier occasional notes concerning "the comparative, superior commercial prosperity of the Belgian part of this United Kingdom, and the rapid falling off, in the trade and activity, of the Ports in Holland" (cf. above, Hughes to Clay, April 14, 15, 1827). Refers particularly to "the astonishing growth of the Trade of Antwerp," not only "through the *American* branch," but in general. ALS. DNA, RG59, Dip. Disp., Netherlands, vol. 8 (M42, R12). Received February 28, 1828.

MISCELLANEOUS LETTERS   December 28, 1827

From BETSEY HAWLEY, New York. Acknowledges receipt of "a few lines from the Department of State" (cf. above, Hawley to Clay, December 19, 1827, note); professes to be pleased with Clay's action; states that, relying on compliance by the consul (Franklin Litchfield) with Clay's request, she planned "to visit Porto Cabello this winter" and is disappointed at having to await official information; rails against Litchfield and (Caleb) Brintnall; charges that "a certain clan of dastards" has conspired to defraud her; and intimates that Litchfield may have accepted a bribe. Disclaims "wishing to insinuate that" she believes "the Secretary [Clay] would wink at such a procedure" but adds that she thinks "the Consul has great confidence in his lenity." Declares that her "lacerated feelings will not . . . permit . . . [her] to defer another year, any benefit of wh[ich] . . . [she] can avail . . . [herself] by the present Session of Congress. . . ." ALS. DNA, RG59, Cons. Disp., Puerto Cabello, vol. 1 (M-T229, R1).
  Endorsed by Clay on cover: "Mr. [Daniel] Brent will have a Copy made of this Lady's correspondence with this office & sent to Mr. Litchfield with direction that he furnish such information as it calls for. H. C."
  On January 21, 1828, Brent wrote to Litchfield about Miss Hawley's complaints against both the consul and the State Department "for indifference and innatention [*sic*] to her repeated applications for information concerning the circumstances connected with the death and Estate of her Brother. . . ." By Clay's direction Brent transmitted "transcripts of a good deal of the correspondence" and urged Litchfield "to execute . . . [Miss Hawley's commission] immediately by giving her all the information she requires, and doing every thing else which may be necessary to satisfy her enquiries and remove the unfounded impressions which she seems to be under, that her case has been neglected." Copy, in DNA, RG59, Cons. Instr., vol. 2, p. 457 (M78, R2).

From GEORGE SULLIVAN, New York. Introduces the bearer, William Porter, "formerly of Boston now a merchant" in New York City, who will soon embark for Buenos Aires and "will perhaps visit other parts of South America." Adds: ". . .presuming . . . on your continued interest in the free governments of that region, so much the offspring of your own enthusiasm in their cause–, I have offered him this letter . . . with the hope that you may give him such a letter of recommendation to our ministers & agents there, as will enable him to be useful to yourself & his country while abroad–" ALS. DNA, RG59, A. and R. (M531, R6).

From LEVI WOODBURY. Requests, by direction of the Senate Commerce Committee, information which may have come to the State Department since December, 1825, "which would affect the expediency of abolishing all discriminating duties on foreign vessels and any merchandize imported therein—as to nations, who adopt a similar rule concerning the United States." AN. DNA, RG59, Misc. Letters (M179, R65).

By legislation of May 24, 1828, the reciprocity act of January 7, 1824 (see above, Lorich to Clay, March 16, 1825, note) was amended to cover indirect as well as direct trade. 4 *U. S. Stat.*, 308–309.

Address to the Public

[December 29, 1827]

[In 61 pages, including a supplemental 31-page "Appendix," Clay quotes extensively from testimonial correspondence to refute the charge of bargain implicating himself and his friends. The survey includes statements from all but two of the Congressional representatives from the West who voted for Adams.[1] Clay notes that a letter from (David) White (Jr.) has not yet been received but that the Congressman has "repeatedly, within his district after his return to Kentucky, borne unqualified testimony to the falsehood of all charges of corruption in the election." Clay expresses confidence that White will "whenever called upon repeat the same testimony" (p. 11).[2] The death of (Daniel P.) Cook, of Illinois, has prevented submission of the other statement.

[Clay then reviews the evidence of numerous occasions when, prior to coming to Washington in the fall of 1824 and consistently thereafter until the casting of his vote, he indicated his preference for Adams over Jackson for the Presidency.[3] He traces the record that Jackson had originated his charges of corruption as early as the spring of 1825[4] and contends that (George) Kremer was merely an "agent" in this attack.[5] He recounts the history of his personal relations with Jackson antecedent to the election[6] and rejects the implication that his reported invitation for Jackson to accompany him to Washington had some "object connected with the presidential election" (p. 28). He specifically denies the statements of the "widely circulated" letter of Harrison Munday,[7] "published at a period chosen to affect the Kentucky election": "I never had such a conversation with him as that letter describes, respecting Mr. Adams, who, at the time when it is alleged to have happened, was abroad, and of whom at that early period, there had been certainly no general conversation in regard to his election to the Presidency" (pp. 28–29).

[Finally, Clay explains that (Philip) Markley was appointed to office "in consequence of the very strong recommendations of him, principally for a more important office,[8] from numerous highly respectable persons of all parties, in various parts of Pennsylvania, from some of the Pennsylvania delegation, among whom Mr. (James) Buchanan took a warm and zealous interest in his behalf, and from the support given to him by the Secretary of the Treasury (Richard Rush), to which department the appointment belonged" (p. 29).

[Clay concludes as follows;] Finding me immovable by flattery or fear, the last resort has been to crush me by steady and unprecedented calumny. Whether this final aim shall be crowned with success or not, depends upon the intelligence of the American people. I make no appeal to their sympathy. I invoke only stern justice.

If truth has not lost its force, reason its sway, and the fountains of justice their purity, the decision must be auspicious. With a firm reliance upon the enlightened judgment of the public, and conscious of the zeal and uprightness with which I have executed every trust committed to my care, I await the event without alarm or apprehension. Whatever it may be, my anxious hopes will continue for the success of the great cause of human liberty, and of those high interests of national policy, to the promotion of which the best exertions of my life have been faithfully dedicated. And my humble, but earnest, prayers will be unremitted that all danger may be averted from our common country; and, especially, that our union, our liberty, and our institutions, may long survive, a cheering exception from the operation of that fatal decree, which the voice of all history has hitherto uniformly proclaimed.   H. CLAY.

WASHINGTON, *December*, 1827.

An Address of Henry Clay to the Public, Containing Certain Testimony in Refutation of the Charges against Him, Made by Gen. Andrew Jackson, Touching the Last Presidential Election (Washington, 1827). DS draft, mostly in Clay's hand, in DLC-TJC (DNA, M212, R10); published also in *Niles' Weekly Register*, XXXIII (January 5, 12, 1828), 296–315, and in numerous contemporary newspapers. For dating of the publication, see Adams, *Memoirs*, VII, 392. Textual differences between the pamphlet and the draft are minor and exist mainly in punctuation, capitalization, expansion of abbreviated words, and, in a few instances, spelling. Changes of wording within the draft appear to have been made, for the most part, in the interest of improving clarity and felicity of expression. On December 15, 1827, Clay had left the draft with John Quincy Adams, who, after reading it, returned it two days later. Of their conversation on the latter date, Adams wrote: "I advised him to change entirely the concluding paragraph, which presented the idea of his retiring from public life and being sacrificed as a victim to calumny. He asked if my objection was that it had an appearance of despondency. I said yes; but that was not all. I thought it highly probable that the base and profligate combination against him and me would succeed in their main object of bringing in General Jackson at the next Presidential election, and that one of their principal means of success will be the infamous slander which he had already more than once branded with falsehood, and upon which he would again stamp the lie by this address and its appendix. The conspiracy would, nevertheless, in all probability succeed. When suspicion has been kindled into popular delusion, truth and reason and justice spoke as to the ears of an adder—the sacrifice must be consummated before they can be heard. General Jackson will therefore be elected. But it is impossible that his Administration should give satisfaction to the people of this Union." Adams then elaborated his view upon the discord which he believed Jackson's election would occasion and concluded: "Then, too, will come the recoil of public opinion in favor of Mr. Clay, and it will be irresistible. If human nature has not changed its character, Kentucky and the Union will then do justice to him and to his slanderers. In the event of General Jackson's election, *he* would of course retire (he said he should resign, and not give the General the opportunity to remove him); he would return to his home in Kentucky, and there wait the course of events. But I thought it would be better not to allude to it in this publication, and particularly not to countenance the idea of his intending it as a final retirement. He said this re-action of public opinion he thought very probable, but that it would be so long in com-ing that it might go beyond his term of active life. I said it might be very sudden and rapid, and reminded him of the instantaneous effect in favor of DeWitt Clinton of the removal of him by the Legislature as a Canal Commissioner [see above, III, 776n; Porter to Clay, January 14, 1825, note]. I concluded, however, by remarking that I had only made the suggestion relating to the closing paragraph of his address, and he said it had already occurred to him that it might be liable to such an objection." Adams, *Memoirs*, VII, 382–83. The concluding paragraph as presented in the published version is the same as that in the draft from Clay's file, but it is complete on a separate page and was probably rewritten. No earlier draft has been found.

1 Letters, all addressed to Tobias Watkins, from Ohio by Duncan McArthur, May 18, 1827; Joseph Vance, July 12, 1827, Philemon Beecher, May 21, 1827; John Sloane, May 9, 1827; John C. Wright, May 6, 1827; Samuel F. Vinton, May 27, 1827; William McLean, May 18, 1827; Elisha Whittlesey, May 12, 1827; Mordecai Bartley, May 24, 1827; and John Patterson, May 9, 1827; from Kentucky by David Trimble, August 12, 1827; Francis Johnson, May 23 and June 12, 1827; Thomas Metcalfe, June 12, 1827; Robert P. Letcher, June 26, 1827; Richard A. Buckner, May 26, 1827; and Philip Thompson, June 19, 1827; from Missouri by John Scott, August 2, 1827; from Louisiana by Henry H. Gurley, July 17, 1827, and William L. Brent, June 4, 1827—all published in "Appendix," 31–50.

2 Cf. above, Crittenden to Clay, October 30, 1827, and note.   3 Cf. above, McClure to Clay, October 22, 1827, note (Daniel Drake's statement, which Clay intended to in-clude, was omitted); and see above, Davidson to Clay, October 20, 1827 (2); Crittenden to Clay, September 3, 1827; Johnston to Clay, November 17, 1827; Bouligny to Clay, December 8, 1827; Barbour to [Clay], August 14, 1827; Lafayette to Clay, October 10, 1827. See, also, Robert Trimble to David Trimble, August 12, 1827, published in "Ap-pendix," 42–44.   4 See Daniel Large to Samuel Wetherill, October 2, 1827, with en-dorsement by William Crowsdill, October 5, 1827—in "Appendix," 58; Andrew Wylie to Thomas McGiffin, February 15, 1828; Isaac Bennett to R. McKee and Alexander Caldwell, February 28, 1828; John Keel to Francis Johnson, February 23, 1828—in Clay's *Supplement to the Address. . .* (below, June 10, 1828), 5–7; Sample to Clay, above, November 22, 1827, and below, January 2, 1828, enclosure; and Washington *United States Telegraph*, April 28, 1827. Cf. also above, Clay to Hammond, October 30, 1827.   5 See statements by Joseph Kent, May 15, 1827; Peter S. Little, n.d.; William [L.] Brent, February 25, 1825; and William D. Digges, March 1, 1825, in "Appendix," 59–61; and cf. above, *Address*, March 26, 1825; Eaton to Clay, March 28, 31, April 2, 1825; Clay to Eaton, March 30, April 1, 1825.   6 See above, Clay to Hammond, October 30, 1827; Clay to Johnston, October 6, 1827.   7 See above, Munday to Clay, July 24, 1827.   8 Cf. above, Sutherland to Clay, February 13, 1826; Smith to Clay, April 19, 1826; Randall to Clay, April 25, 1826; Peters to Clay, October 24, 1826, note; Ingersoll to Clay, March 11, 1827.

To James Barbour

Sir   Washn. 29h. Decr. 1827.

The young man that I intended to mention to you today as an ap-plicant for a Cadet's appointment at West Point is Oswald Burton of Campbell County in Virginia.[1] He is recommended to me so strongly by Mr. Pleasants[2] that I should be very glad if he could obtain the appointment.

The other that I spoke to you about is the son of Mr. John J. Mar-shall,[3] whose name is on your Register. I will add nothing to what I said to you in his behalf. Yr's faithfy & respectfy   H. CLAY
The Honble Mr. Barbour.

ALS. DNA, RG94, Military Academy, Cadet Applications, 1827/176.
1 Robert O. Burton, of Virginia (not further identified), entered the United States Military Academy in 1828 but was not graduated.   2 Probably John H. Pleasants.
3 Humphrey Marshall. Cf. above, Crittenden to Clay, November 19, 1827; Clay to Crit-tenden, December 16, 1827.

To Levi Woodbury

Hon: Levi Woodbury &c &c

Sir   Department of State. Washington 29th. Decr 1827.

I have received a note, which, by direction of the Committee of commerce of the Senate, you did me the honor, on the 28th. instant, to address to me, requesting information whether any facts have occurred in the Department of State since December 1825, which would affect the expediency of abolishing all discriminating duties on foreign vessels and any merchandise imported therein, as to nations which adopt a similar rule concerning the United States; and I have the honor now to state, in reply, that the Government of France has, on several occasions, at Washington, and at Paris, manifested dissatisfaction with the operation of the Convention of Navigation and Commerce, of 1822,[1] although we have just arrived at the equality which is its basis. That informal intimations have been given that unless France can find in some commercial arrangements, a compensation for the disadvantage to her navigation which she attributes to the Convention, she must avail herself of one of its stipulations to put an end to it.

That during the late negotiations with England the British Government displayed an indifference, as to the renewal of the Commercial Convention of 1815, which, there is much reason to believe, was the result of a conviction that British navigation cannot sustain a competition with that of the United States, on the equal conditions which are provided for by that Convention.[2] This opinion of the cause of that indifference, derives additional strength from the rejection of the American proposal of the broad principle of the Guatemala Treaty.[3] Had that proposal been acceeded [sic] to, the equality in the terms of the competition between American and British Navigation, which is now limited to the United States and the European possessions of His Britannic Majesty, would have been extended throughout the commercial world.

That it may be fairly inferred, from correspondence which has passed between the Government of the United States, and that of the Kingdom of the Netherlands, that the latter is not very well satisfied with the effect on its navigation of the mutual abolition of all discriminating duties, in the intercourse between the two countries. That it would be difficult, otherwise, to account for some immunities yet retained by the Dutch navigation, which would appear to be contrary to the arrangement which has been made between the United States and the Netherlands. Against these immunities to the repeated remonstrances that have been made, we have been again and again reminded of the small number of Dutch, and the large number of American vessels employed in the trade between the two countries.[4]

That the other Powers with which the United States have agreed mutually to abolish all discriminating duties of tonnage and impost, are believed to be satisfied with the arrangement— No complaint, from any one of them, is recollected.

That a proposal has lately been received, from the Kingdom of Hanover, to abolish all discriminating duties on both sides.[5]

As I understand your note to limit the enquiry to *facts* affecting the expediency of abolishing all discriminating duties on tonnage and imposts, I have not supposed any opinions or views which may be entertained at this Department, to be called for, either on that subject, or on the more comprehensive principle which has been adopted in late treaties. I have the honor &c   H. CLAY.

ALS. DNA, RG59, Report Book, vol. 4, pp. 213–14. L draft, with two minor changes in Clay's hand, in DLC-HC (DNA, M212, R3).
[1] Cf. above, Mareuil to Clay, December 24, 1825; May 16, June 27, 1827; Brown to Clay, September 13, 27, 1827.   [2] See above, Gallatin to Clay, May 29, June 20, 27, August 6 (no. 102), 1827; Clay to Adams, August 16, 1827.   [3] Cf. above, Convention, December 5, 1825.   [4] Cf. above, Hughes to Clay, June 12, 1827.   [5] Above, Vaughan to Clay, December 26, 1827.

From James Brown

My dear Sir   (private)   Paris Decr. 29. 1827

In my despatch of this day[1] you will perceive that I have pursued the course you indicated in your last.[2] I found the Baron de Damas fixed in his opposition to any measure which could lead to an adjustment of our claims. It is now almost certain that we shall have a change of Ministry but you need not from that infer any change of measures so far as we are concerned. These people have other uses for their money than that of paying any claims which they can shuffle off by denying, and besides they think that they have already made indemnities enough without paying us. They say that we have upon the whole been gainers by that trade during the time of the depredations of which we complained that the claims are principally owned by insurance companies who having increased the premium with the risk had done a profitable business all the time and had little to complain of. In a word no party here seems disposed to feel for us or to advocate our claims. If they are ever obtained it must be when such a state of things shall arrive as will make our friendship of more value than the amount of the indemnity.

We hear that Admiral de Rigny has destroyed the Greek fleet at Scio. The pretext was that having accepted the mediation the Greeks were continuing to act in a hostile manner against the Turks.[3] By some it is believed that this act has been committed with the design of propitiating the Porte and preventing war. I do not think it will have that effect. Our accounts from Constantinople are to the 2nd. Inst. It was expected the Ambassadors would leave it on the following day.[4] The Russians are said to be ready to cross the Pruth.[5] No one seems to know what may follow. It is my belief that neither France England nor Austria will make war to prevent the Russians from attacking Constantinople.

Your New York election[6] has disappointed us here. Will not that State pass a law for voting by a general ticket and will not her vote decide the fate of the election? It is hardly probable that Jackson will loose [sic] Virginia and Pennsylvania although some changes appear to be going on in both.[7]

Mrs. Brown's health still gives me some concern. She has been prevented from going into large parties for nearly two months. If she was not more attached to France than myself I should ask leave to return next summer. It is an irksome affair to advocate hopeless claims, and I dislike being useless.

Our Osages have gone to Brusselles [sic] where Hughes has given them a *grand* reception. You will see a printed account of the *ceremony* with his and their speeches.[8] I wish he may get rid of them without having to advance their expences to their own country. I was glad to see them leave Paris. It was a wretched speculation and will involve those who have embarked in it.

Who will be sent to England?[9] Our affairs there surely require some one to take charge of them. I am afraid they are becoming more difficult and complicated.

Why is it that we have no treaty with Brazil? The Prussians have concluded one.[10] I hope Poinset [sic] has got over his trouble at Mexico.[11] It is now several months since the date of my last letter from him

The Infant Don Miguel after remaining a few days in Paris proceeded on Wednesday last to London. He is a handsome Prince and resembles the family of Bonapart [sic].

I think we have nearly silenced the slanders which which [sic] were circulated respecting your vote at the last Presidential election. The certificate sent you by General Lafayette[12] must have reached you long ago. He read me a copy of it which appeared to be all you could wish to establish the fact that you had long before the election expressed your determination not to vote for General Jackson.

It is rumoured that all the Ministers have tendered their resignations to the King[13] who is deliberating whether he will accept them, or insist on some of them particularly M de Villele remaining in place. If this last determination is adopted the next Session will probably be about as stormy as the one you are now holding at Washington. The Ministry is not very much at its ease in England.[14] It is thought by many persons here that it will not last long after the meeting of Parliament.   Make my respects to Mrs. Clay and receive assurances of my affection & esteem   JAMES BROWN
Hon. Henry Clay

ALS. DLC-HC (DNA, M212, R3).   1 That is, December 28, 1827.
2 Above, October 28, 1827.   3 On the Greek acceptance of the mediation of the
European allies, cf. above, Lafayette to Clay, October 10, 1827, note. The news that the
French Admiral had burned the Greek fleet at Scio had been sent from Constantinople
on December 1. London *Times*, December 29, 1827. His action culminated nearly a month
of skirmishing between the Greeks and Turks in violation of the armistice arrangements.
The London *Times* of December 31, 1827, noting widespread excitement over the incident, termed it "great nonsense to call a few transports by so pompous a title" as fleet
and upheld Rigny's measures as an attempt to stop the Greeks from plundering the
commerce of "their mediating protectors." Cf. above, Lawrence to Clay, November 22,
1827.   4 Cf. above, Brown to Clay, October 12, 1827 (1); Dodge to Clay, November
17, 1827; Hughes to Clay, November 27, 1827. The Ambassadors—Stratford Canning,
Alexandre Ribeaupierre, and the Count de Guilleminot—finally left Constantinople on
December 8. *Annual Register, 1827*, p. [321].   5 Cf. above, Lawrence to Clay, December 6, 1827.   6 Cf. above, Sergeant to Clay, October 24, 1827, note.   7 Cf.
above, Clay to Brown, March 27, 1827, notes; Caldwell to Clay, August 8, 1827, note.
     8 Cf. above, Brown to Clay, August 30, November 13, 1827. The London *Times*, Janu-
ary 2, 1828, noted the presence of the Osages at the Hague, but no reference has been
found to Christopher Hughes' activities in their behalf.   9 Cf. above, Clay to Henry,
December 27, 1827, note.   10 A Treaty of Amity, Navigation, and Commerce between
Brazil and Prussia had been signed July 9, 1827. See Parry (ed.), *Consolidated Treaty
Series*, LXXVII, 317–22. For the treaty between the United States and Brazil, see below,
Tudor to Clay, December 12, 1828.   11 Cf. above, Poinsett to Clay, July 8, 1827;
Taylor to Clay, July 10, 1827; Sergeant to Clay, August 1, 1827; Adams to Clay, October
1, 1827; Clay to Poinsett, November 19, 1827.   12 Above, October 10, 1827.
     13 Charles X. The Count de Villèle resigned on January 3, 1828. Lucas-Dubréton,
The Restoration and the July Monarchy, 119.   14 Cf. above, Lawrence to Clay, De-
cember 22, 1827; Hughes to Clay, December 28, 1827.

INSTRUCTIONS AND DISPATCHES   December 29, 1827

From W[ILLIAM] B. LAWRENCE, London, no. 17. Acknowledges receipt of Clay's
"despatch No. 1" (above, November 23, 1827) and reports that, before its arrival,
Nathaniel Snelson had been apprehended, had "made restitution of the embez-
zeled property," and had "consented to return to the United States with the police
officer sent in pursuit of him. . . ." States that no late news has been received from
the East and that "nothing even now can be affirmed with certainty respecting
the issue of the Turkish business." Notes his understanding that, though "dis-
sensions exist in the [British] Cabinet," none "of its present members, Mr. [John
Charles] Herries perhaps excepted, are favourable to the return to power of those
individuals, who last spring seceded from the Ministry" (cf. above, Gallatin to
Clay, April 14, 1827, no. 69). Encloses copies of correspondence with (John)
Backhouse relative to "[Daniel] Brent's letter to Mr. [Albert] Gallatin of 30th
October last" (see above, Kershaw to Clay, October 12, 1827, note) and remarks
that he has "been . . . given to understand, that . . . there would be no objection
to supply . . . entire copies" of the cited documents. LS. DNA, RG59, Dip. Disp.,
Great Britain, vol. 35 (M30, R31). Received February 17, 1828.
     Snelson was brought to trial on May 3, 1828, found guilty but with a recom-
mendation for leniency, and sentenced to three years' imprisonment. *Niles' Weekly Register*, XXXIV (June 7, 1828), 235.

From W[ILLIAM] H. D. C. WRIGHT, Rio de Janeiro. Encloses copies of replies from
the Minister of Foreign Affairs (Marquis of Aracaty) to a note "addressed to him,"
relative to the burning of the American Brig Brutus" (cf. above, Wright to Clay,
November 30, 1827 [2]), and to another "requesting the usual instructions" to the
customs officers "in relation to landing stores for the United States' Squadron
exempt from duties." Transmits also a copy of a third note from the same source,

stating "that after the expiration of six months, duties will be exacted upon the Stores remitted to this Empire for the use of Our Squadron. . . ." Remarks that "The Stores for the English and French Squadrons on this Station, are sent in National Transports, which have No communication with the Custom House," and states that he has replied to the Minister's last-mentioned note, requesting "information, as to the formalities observed by those Nations in remitting supplies for their Squadrons. . . ." Reports that his "information with regard to the restoration of the Brig Ruth [above, to Clay, November 30, 1827 (2)] was incorrect" and that "She is still in the possession of the Buenos Ayreans." ALS. DNA, RG59, Cons. Disp., Rio de Janeiro, vol. 3 (M-T172, R4). Received March 10, 1828.

João Carlos Augusto Oyenhausen, first Marquis of Aracaty, born in 1778, had enlisted in the Portuguese Royal Navy in 1793. After holding several subordinate administrative appointments in provincial government, he had been captain-general of São Paulo, Brazil, from 1819 to 1821 and had entered the Brazilian Cabinet as Minister of Foreign Relations and Marine in 1827. He again served in the Cabinet in 1831 but resigned in April of that year and spent the remainder of his career in the service of Portugal outside Brazil.

MISCELLANEOUS LETTERS December 29, 1827

To JAMES H. McCULLOCH, "Collector of the Port of Baltimore." Informs him of the communication from (José Silvestre) Rebello (above, December 27, 1827) and makes the same request as that to Jonathan Thompson, above, December 25, 1827. Copy. DNA, RG59, Dom. Letters, vol. 22, p. 114 (M40, R20).

From JOSEPH M. WHITE, Washington. States, by request of "Judge [Henry M.] Brackenride [sic] of Florida . . . for the information of the President," what he knows of Brackenridge's "private deportment in society, & his public conduct as an officer of the United States" (cf. above, Clay to Brackenridge, December 15, 1827). Praises him in both categories; explains that "During the last Spring . . . there was a suspencion [sic] of all the Courts [in his district] in consequence of the non publication of the Laws"; adds: "What inconvenience has resulted from a failure to hold the Court this fall, or whether a Court Can be held legally, when the Marshal [William Sebree] . . . is dead, before another appointment [cf. above, White to Clay, September 27, 1827] is a question, I do not presume to decide"; and urges as his "opinion & that of the District, that no prejudice may be excited unjustly against him to prevent his reappointment, which would be deplored in the Country as a public Calamity—" ALS. DNA, RG59, A. and R. (M531, R1). Cited, under date of December 22, in Carter (ed.), *Territorial Papers*, XXIII, 964n. The second digit of the date is not clear but is followed by the letters "th."

Brackenridge retained the judicial appointment in Florida until 1832, when he was removed by President Jackson.

From John Sergeant

Dear Sir, (Private) Philada. Decr. 30. 1827.

I came here from Harrisburg on Wednesday, and should have started for Baltimore on Friday but for a sudden attack of sore throat on Thursday night which made it impossible for me to leave the house. I am now nearly recovered and hope to be able to set out to morrow.

At Baltimore I may be detained one day to be examined as a witness, unless my arrival should be too late for that purpose, in which case I shall proceed direct to Washington. My detention at Harrisburg was longer than was expected, but it was unavoidable.

Hitherto, in Pennsa., there has been too much apathy. Just now, there is some despondency. They are both owing to the "non committal" system, which, by the way, has only been on one side. Men who are uncommitted, are in truth men whose inclinations are with us, but waiting to see what our strength will be. Being looked upon as friends, they have a power which never fails to be felt when any thing sinister happens, and they have a very natural desire when they feel alarmed themselves, to induce others to believe that there is real ground for alarm—that is, to make the cause desperate, in order to justify themselves in yielding to despair. We have too many such people— In a few days, however, the line will be better drawn, and I hope new energy infused, by the convention.[1] The election in Lancaster County, where (contrary to the confident calculation of the Jacksonites) the administration candidate has succeeded, is a favorable incident, and a fortunate omen. Judge Rogers[2] (Mr. Buchanan's friend) spoke with entire confidence of a majority of three thousand for the Jackson candidate. They will say, of course, that their vote was divided among several, but we have got the victory, and that is better than any thing they can say.[3]

The most material point for us, however, and which was the chief motive for troubling you with this letter, is to announce, seriously and firmly, that at the elections in October next, we will neither nominate, support or vote for any man who is not cordially and openly with us. This course, when the elections approach, will be mere matter of necessity, for if we are beaten at the general elections in October, no matter by what means, we shall be beaten at the electoral election in November. It is just and it is politic to declare it at once. The example of our adversary will afford us a full justification. The advantage he derives from it, shews its expediency. The timid, either profess Jacksonism or remain silent, because they do not fear opposition on that ground from the friends of the administration. It is time that we, too, should appeal to the fears of those who cannot be more worthily appealed to. For example—in Mr. Buchanan's district (this illustration must be entirely confidential) I believe there is a majority for the Administration. Yet, we have a Jackson member.

I feel anxious that this should be somehow proclaimed by our Convention, and have so said and written to our delegates. If you have the means, either through Mr. Marks and Mr. Stewart,[4] or otherwise, I wish you would have it enforced upon other members of the Convention, provided you think well of it. To me it seems quite plain.

I am not discouraged about Pennsylvania. There are parts of the State where the truth has not yet penetrated, and where prejudice yet prevails. But there is time, and I hope there will be exertion. With these, and a good cause, we shall conquer.[5] Very respectfully and truly yrs.   JOHN SERGEANT

ALS. DLC-HC (DNA, M212, R3).
[1] Cf. above, Sergeant to Clay, September 18, October 14, 1827, notes.   [2] Molton C. Rogers, born in Delaware, graduated from Princeton College, and trained for law at Litchfield, Connecticut, had opened practice at Lancaster, Pennsylvania, in 1811. He had been elected to the State Senate in 1819, had become Secretary of the Commonwealth in 1823, and from 1826 to 1851 sat on the State Supreme Court. Formerly a Federalist, he had become a Democrat shortly before the War of 1812. From the early 1820's he and Buchanan had been closely associated in both State and national politics. Klein, *Pennsylvania Politics*, 215–16.   [3] The death of the member-elect from Lancaster County to the State House of Representatives had required the holding of a special election. The administration candidate had defeated two Jacksonians by a vote of 1,693 to 1,494 and 948. *Niles' Weekly Register*, XXXIII (January 12, 1828), 315.   [4] William Marks; Andrew Stewart.   [5] Cf. above, Clay to Brown, March 27, 1827, note.

MISCELLANEOUS LETTERS   December 30, 1827

From S[AMUEL] B. BARRELL, "Houlton Plantation." Reports his arrival, "on Thursday last" (December 27), at this place, where he "fortunately found . . . several settlers from the Aroostook River, from whom" he has obtained "all the information" he could have expected "from a visit to that settlement." States that "This *ancient* settlement upon the Aroostook, if the statement of those of the settlers whom . . . [he has] seen can be relied upon, turns out to be one of about six years standing." Reports that "intelligence of recent domestic difficulties . . . will compel" (Charles S.) Daveis to "return to Portland"; that he, himself, will continue his journey alone; and that he hopes "to reach the Matawascah settlement on Wednesday or Thursday next." Acknowledges, in a postscript, "receipt of the Documents transmitted . . . from the Department on the 23d. ulto." ALS. DNA, RG76, Northeastern Boundary, entry 87, env. 3 (MR frames 662–63).

The documents here referred to, copies of those transmitted to Clay by Vaughan, November 21, 1827, had been sent by Daniel Brent. DNA, RG59, Dom. Letters, vol. 22, p. 95 (M40, R20).

From Francis P. Blair

Dear Sir: Frankfort Decr. 31. 1827.

Your letter of the 15.[1] was received yesterday— You are right in supposing that I copied your letter incorrectly.[2] You say that three of the four Crawford States preferred Mr Adams & that Va. was one of them. The mistake of the date is in the original—

You seem to have misinterpreted the matter of my reference to that letter from the first to the last. The only object that I had in returning to it & the intelligence I received from Mr Crittenden[3] as coming from a member of Congress inducing the belief on my part, that your interests were to be subserved by obtaining the vote of Kentucky for

Mr. A., was to apprize you of the facts on which I felt my self warranted in the declaration made by me at the time to Kendall[4] & others with regard to the appointment of secretary of State— I was neither willing you should suspect, that the fact relied, on by Mr K. was coined for the occasion with my connivance, nor that you should suppose I had hazarded such a Statement, even to accomplish your wishes, without having grounds for believing it my self— I trust there is nothing in either of my late letters[5] manifesting the least inclination to give publicity to any part of your correspondence with me, or in the remotest manner evidencing a wish that you should relinquish the right, which you certainly have to controul me in the use of it. On the contrary I think I have expressed to you the opinion in every letter that I have written, not only that your communications should be with held, but that Mr Kendall's interrogatories[6] should go unanswered. When spoken to by Mr Crittenden I gave him the same opinion,—at my instance he once withdrew his manuscript which he had communicated to the press & I endeavored to impress upon him the propriety of resisting every attempt to pry into private intercourse by public interrogatory— These facts I think I communicated to you & ought to have been sufficient to show that I wished no precedent, for presenting my self to the public & that I have fixed no disposition to be exonerated by you from any obligations imposed by the friendly & confidential nature of our correspondence— Where then was there any necessity for your telling me that while you would assume no right to *control* me in the use of the letter in question, you would nevertheless with hold your assent to its publication?[7] Certainly I have not asked for permission to make it public— It would have given me pain if you had ordered its publication—

I am gratified that you recognize the possibility of a determined political opposition, existing in conjunction with feelings of the utmost kindness & esteem for the object of it. When you felt yourself called on by your principles to wish the overthrow of the new court[8] (that usurping tribunal as it was called) I never for a moment supposed that you entertained any other than the best feelings towards "the Secretary"[9] of the tribunal who was indeed as deep in the treason as those who held the power— You must not suppose that I am less capable of separating my political hostilities from my personal attachments than you were on that occasion— Although therefore I may make war on the administration & may be willing to see the Federal power loosened,[10] yet I assure you nothing could give me more pain than to see your reputation as a man sullied, in order to defeat the views of a party whose principles I deem dangerous to the public welfare.

I cannot recal [*sic*] to my recollection, the conversation to which reference is made by your correspondent as occurring in my presence at Mr Gratz'[11] table in Lexington, wherein you expressed a preference for Mr Adams over Genl Jackson for the presidency— Yet from my knowledge of the person who made the communication to you, I cannot doubt its truth— The conversation to which Mr Crittenden alludes as remembered by me took place in Frankfort, I think on your last visit previously to your Setting out for the Congress of 1824 & 25. At your request I state that you then declared your intention of voting for Mr Adams in preference to Genl Jackson for the presidency, if you should find it necessary to decide between them as a representative in Congress— Yr mo ob se   F. P. BLAIR

P.S.   The last paragraph of my letter with my name attached you can publish, if you wish so to use it— The conversation to which I refer happened in the pavement between where I then lived & Harvie's[12]— We paused as we walked along & you entered fully into the motives[13] of your preference—in which questions of policy as regarded your own personal interests & our local State interests as well as considerations of a national & general character entered— I have thought it best to give only the particular point to which your enquiry is directed omitting to make any effort to recapitulate the substance of the whole conversation which I could do but imperfectly— in haste   your ob se.
                                                  F. P. BLAIR

ALS. DLC-HC (DNA, M212, R3).
[1] Not found. Cf. above, Clay to Gratz, December 14, 1827.   [2] Cf. above, Clay to Blair, January 8, 1825, and note; Crittenden to Clay, November 15, 1827, and note.
[3] John J. Crittenden—cf. above, Blair to Clay, November 14, 1827.   [4] Amos Kendall.
[5] See Blair to Clay, October 3, November 14, 1827.   [6] Above, Kendall to Clay, September 26, October 10, 1827.   [7] Cf. above, Clay to Blair, October 11, 1827.
[8] Cf. above, III, 902n.   [9] See above, Blair to Clay, February 11, 1825.   [10] Word uncertain.   [11] Benjamin Gratz.   [12] John Harvie. No contemporary publication of the Blair statement has been found.   [13] Word uncertain.

DIPLOMATIC NOTES   December 31, 1827

To [JOSÉ SILVESTRE] REBELLO. Acknowledges receipt of his "note of the 29th [*i.e.,* 27th] instant" and assures him that "the particular attention of the Collector of the Port of Baltimore" has been called "to the prompt execution of the Laws" in the case (see above, Clay to McCulloch, December 29, 1827). Copy. DNA, RG59, Notes to Foreign Legations, vol. 3, pp. 411–12 (M38, R3). L draft, in CSmH.

From J[os]É SILVESTRE REBELLO, Washington. Reports having learned that the privateer and her prize at New York (cf. above, Rebello to Clay, December 17, 1827), having lost five men from illness and desertion, have replaced them with Americans and that the Collector of Customs (Jonathan Thompson) refused to intervene on the ground that the vessels have the same number of men as when they entered the port. Protests "against this violation of the laws of Neutrality"; states that he "will apply to H. M. the Emperor [Peter I] for orders to demand adequate satisfaction"; and blames "the political intolerance" of Federal officers in New York for "such a criminal connivance. . . ." LS, in Portuguese with trans. in State Dept. file. DNA, RG59, Notes from Brazilian Legation, vol. 1 (M49, R1).

INSTRUCTIONS AND DISPATCHES   December 31, 1827

From JOSEPH MARTI Y NIN, Tenerife. Reports that Payton Gay, consul at Tenerife, has left the islands and has empowered him to act as vice consul; that he has "often" written Gay but has received no reply, not "even the least account of his existence"; and that he has had difficulty in enforcing the law because of the questionable nature of his commission. Requests that he be made an American citizen and that he be confirmed as vice consul. ALS. DNA, RG59, Cons. Disp., Tenerife (M-T690, R1).

Endorsed by Clay: "Mr. [Philip R.] F[endall]. prepare a letter recognizing the authority of V. Consul until otherwise ordered. H. C." Cf. below, Clay to Marti y Nin, April 14, 1828. Marti has not been further identified.

From A[BRAHAM] B. NONES, Maracaibo. Transmits a report on American "Commerce to this port, for the entire year" and notes that "it shews a lamentable decrease of trade," which, he thinks, "will still continue to grow worse, under the System established by the Decrees of the Libertador [Simón Bolívar] of the 8th. & 9th. March last. . . ." Describes the "disastrous State of Affairs" in the country; reports the failure of "the Electoral College of this Department," owing to the lack of a quorum at the appointed time, to choose "Deputies for the Grand Convention (cf. above, Watts to Clay, August 7, 1827; Nones to Clay, December 24, 1827); and states that "considerable sensation has been excited within the last few days, on account of a rumor of a treaty with Spain, said to be negociating through the mediation of England, for the purpose of obtaining a recognition of the Independence of the S. A. States, on the payment of an Annual Sum of Money for a certain Number of Years, and a perpetual tribute" (cf. above, Lawrence to Clay, December 14, 1827). Predicts that proposal of such a settlement will bring on "Civil War on an extended Scale. . . ." ALS. DNA, RG59, Cons. Disp., Maracaibo, vol. 1 (M-T62, R1).

The decrees of March 8 and 9, 1827, established new duties. Colombia, *Codificación Nacional de Todas las Leyes . . . desde el Año de 1821, Hecha Conforme a la Ley 13 de 1912, por la Sala de Negocios Generales del Consejo de Estado* (Bogotá, 1925), III, 19–154. Cf. also, above, Marks to Clay, March 17, 1827; MacPherson to Clay, March 24, 1827.

MISCELLANEOUS LETTERS   December 31, 1827

To ROBERT TILLOTSON, "Attorney of the U. S. for the S. District of N. York—" Transmits "a Copy of a translation (made by himself) of a Note from Mr. [José Silvestre] Rebello," complaining "of the augmentation of the force of a Buenos Ayrean privateer [*General Brandizen*] now in the Port of New York" (above, this date); requests his "immediate attention" to the matter and the adoption of "such measures as may be proper to enforce our Laws, and preserve the neutrality of the United States"; and asks that he "report . . . without unnecessary delay, the circumstances incident to the transaction to which he [Rebello] refers." Copy. DNA, RG59, Dom. Letters, vol. 22, p. 115 (M40, R20). Cf. below, Tillotson to Clay, January 4, 1828, and note.

INDEX

Republican Party (cont.):
9, 1131n, 1197, 1219n, 1229,
1261, 1278, 1301, 1373n. See
also Administration party;
Democratic Republican
Party; National Republican Party
——— (Mass.), 108, 584-5,
820n, 947-8
——— (N.H.), 566, 603-4n
——— (N.Y.), 245, 528,
1090n, 1228
——— (Pa.), 284n, 494
Republican Party (Mex.), 753,
1250
Restrepo, José Manuel, 250,
560, 684, 1012, 1057n, 1124,
1268
Revanche (vessel, Fr.), 305,
374
Revenga, Joseph R.: from,
1069; named, 1087, 1124,
1196, 1243, 1300, 1378
Reynolds, James B.: from, 15-
6, 43-5; named, 23n-4n,
114n, 893, 1170-1n
Reynolds, John, 455-6n
Ribeaupierre, ——— (Mme.
Alexandre), 1092
Ribeaupierre, Alexandre,
Count, 491, 564, 1043n-4n,
1092, 1095n-7, 1138, 1140n,
1220, 1330, 1332-4, 1343,
1358, 1398, 1400n
Rice, James, 990
Rich, Obadiah, 194, 464, 878
Richards, George H.: from,
21
Richards, Richard H., 13
Richardson, Thomas G.:
from, 720-1; to, 719-20
Richardson, William H.:
from, 730-1; named, 2, 292,
791n
Richelieu, Armand Emmanuel du Plessis, Duke de, 598
Richmond (Va.) Constitutional Whig, 185-6n, 637n,
1066n, 1187-8n, 1233-5n,
1243-4n, 1307, 1373
Richmond Convention (State;
Admin.), 924, 926n, 1058,
1065, 1077, 1225, 1291,
1307n, 1312-3, 1338, 1356,
1386
Richmond Convention (State;
Jacksonian), 1338
Richmond Enquirer (Va.),
174n, 185-6n, 199, 227-8n,
402n, 591n, 611, 637, 771,
778n, 797n, 926n, 974n,
1005n, 1036n, 1058-9n, 1065-
6n, 1150n, 1158n, 1200,
1225n, 1233n
Richmond (Va.) Jackson
Republican, 199

Richmond (Va.) Junto, 34n,
186, 291
Richmond (Va.) Turnpike
Road, 1150n
Richmond (Va.) Whig, 1201n
Ridgely, Charles Goodwin,
660n, 856, 969
Ridgely, Frederick, 1384n
Ridgely, Greenberry W.:
from, 660-2
Ridgely, Henry M., 362n, 370,
373n-4n, 1011n-3n
Ridgely, Nicholas Greenberry: from, 564-5; named,
662n
Rigg, Alexander, 936-7n
Rigg, Jonathan, 937n
Rigny, Henri Gauthier,
Count de, 1132, 1134n-5n,
1398, 1400n
Rijks Museum, 1295n
Riker, Richard: to, 328;
named, 606-7n
Rincon, José Antonio, 832,
889-90, 1224
Rincon, Manuel, 217-8n, 271,
1250
Ringgold, Tench: from, 143n,
172; to, 143; named, 207
Rios, ———, Chevalier de
los, 979, 981n
Rios, Manuel del, 582
Ripley, Henry J., 461-2n
Ripley, James W., 1085, 1156-
7n
Ripon, Frederick John Robinson, Viscount Goderich
and 1st Earl of, 224-5n,
632, 784-5n, 851, 867, 902-
3n, 943, 959n, 983n, 1045-
6n, 1068, 1293-4n, 1375,
1390-2n
Ripon, Sarah Albinia Louisa
Hobart (Mrs. Frederick
John) Robinson, Countess,
1391-2n
Ritchie, Thomas, 185-6, 199-
200n, 227-8, 550n, 637, 782n,
925-6n, 1058-9n, 1065-6n,
1386
Ritner, Joseph, 304, 340, 1023-
4n
Riva Agüero, José de la,
1353n
Rivadavia, Bernardino, 441n,
578n, 590, 732, 800-2n, 880,
938, 1214
Rivas y Salmon, Hilario de:
from, 313, 542, 628-9, 677;
to, 480, 656-60; named,
911n, 1108, 1216, 1255,
1288, 1373-4
Rives, John C., 813-4
Rives, William Cabell, 294n,
862
Roane, Samuel C., 244

Roane, Spencer, 591n
Robards, Lewis, 228-9n, 699n
Robb, Joseph: from, 730-1;
named, 778n
Robbins, Asher: from, 896-7,
945; named, 965-6n, 1016
Robbins, Nathaniel, 995n,
1005, 1155-6n
Roberdeau, Isaac, 537-8n,
884n
Robert Fulton (steamboat),
332n
Robert Porter and Son: to,
496
Roberts, Charles, 455-6n
Roberts, Hensley: from, 40-1
Roberts, John: from, 40, 360
Roberts, Jonathan, 1023
Roberts, Matthew: from, 690-
1; to, 694
Roberts, Owen Mansits, 480
Roberts, Studson, 963n
Roberts, William J., 872n
Robertson, Felix, 78n
Robertson, George: from, 747-
9; to, 751; named, 40, 65,
928, 1073, 1076n, 1121,
1123n, 1172-3, 1380
Robertson, James, 15-6, 78n
Robertson, John, 804n
Robertson, Thomas Bolling:
to, 178n, 195n; named, 178,
195, 804n
Robertson, Wyndham: from,
803-4
Robertson Family, 16
Robins, Nathaniel, 995n,
1005, 1155-6n
Robinson, ———, 792, 795n
Robinson, Edward W., 1055,
1355
Robinson, Frederick John.
See Ripon
Robinson, James Fisher:
from, 28
Robinson, Joseph, 681
Robinson, Joshua V., 849n
Robinson, Mary Jemima
Yorke, 1391n
Robinson, Philip: from, 678;
to, 416n; named, 128, 1337
Robinson, Robert Emmet,
168
Rocafuerte, Vicente, 218
Rochester, Amanda Hopkins
(Mrs. William B.), 967,
969n
Rochester, Harriet Louisa,
967, 969n
Rochester, James Hervey, 967,
969n
Rochester, Nathaniel: from,
140-1; named, 121n, 548n,
969
Rochester, Thomas H., 548,
643